P9-ARB-514

Student's
Life Application® Bible

# Student's Life Application® BIBLE

Tyndale House Publishers, Inc.
Wheaton, Illinois

Visit Tyndale's exciting Web site at www.tyndale.com

The publisher gratefully acknowledges the role of Youth for Christ/USA in preparing the Life Application Notes and Bible Helps.

The Bible text used in this edition of the *Student's Life Application Bible* is the *Holy Bible,* New Living Translation.



Cover design by Paetzold Associates.



---

**Library of Congress Cataloging-in-Publication Data**

Bible. English. New Living Translation. 1997.
Student's life application Bible : New Living Translation.
p. cm.
Includes indexes.
Summary: Includes the text of the Bible as well as notes which discuss moral dilemmas and ultimate issues, charts, maps, and personality profiles.
1. Students—Religious life. 2. Teenagers—Religious life. 3. Christian life—Biblical teaching. [1. Christian life.] I. Tyndale House Publishers. II. Title.
BS195.N394 1997a
220.5'20834—dc21 97-2960

---

ISBN 0-8423-5227-9 Hardcover
ISBN 0-8423-5226-0 Softcover
ISBN 0-8423-5228-7 Burgundy Bonded
ISBN 0-8423-5223-6 Burgundy Bonded, indexed
ISBN 0-8423-5224-4 Navy Bonded
ISBN 0-8423-5225-2 Navy Bonded, indexed

Printed in the United States of America

07 06 05 04 03 02
10 9 8 7 6 5 4 3 2

## CONTRIBUTORS

*Design Team*
Dr. Bruce B. Barton
Ron Beers
Dr. James Galvin
LaVonne Neff
David R. Veerman

*Senior Editor*
David R. Veerman

*Associate Editor*
Karen Ball

*Assistant Editors*
Kathryn S. Olson
Linda Taylor
Karen Voke

*Graphic Design*
Timothy R. Botts
Brian K. Eterno

*Production Team*
Julee Schwarzburg
Gwen Elliott
Linda Walz

WRITERS

Dr. Richard R. Dunn
Chairman, Department of Christian Education
Trinity Evangelical Divinity School
Deerfield, Illinois

Terry Prisk
Youth Communicator/Consultant
Executive Director of Contemporary Communication
Detroit, Michigan

Kent Keller
Pastor, Redeemer Presbyterian Church
Miami, Florida

Jared Reed
Pator, Faith Presbyterian Church
Miami, Florida

Len Woods
Former Editor of *Youthwalk*
Minister to Students, Christ Community Church
Ruston, Louisiana

Greg Johnson
Former Editor of *Breakaway*
Alive Communications
Colorado Springs, Colorado

Byron Emmert
Speaker and seminar leader
Youth for Christ
Mt. Lake, Minnesota

Diane Eble
Associate Editor, *Campus Life* magazine
Wheaton, Illinois

Neil Wilson
Pastor, Eureka United Methodist Church
Omro, Wisconsin

Bill Sanders
Author and speaker
Kalamazoo, Michigan

David R. Veerman
Veteran youth worker and author
The Livingstone Corporation
Carol Stream, Illinois

Thank you to the young people from the following youth groups for their invaluable assistance with this project:
*Southern Gables Church,* Denver, Colorado
*Spring Hill Camps*, Evart, Michigan
*Pekin Bible Church*, Pekin, Illinois
*Ward Presbyterian Church,* Livonia, Michigan
*First Baptist Church*, Holdrege, Nebraska
*Naperville Presbyterian Church*, Naperville, Illinois

NOTES AND FEATURES

*Book Introductions*
Jared Reed
Len Woods
David R. Veerman

*Personality Profiles*
Neil Wilson

*Moral Dilemma Notes*
Len Woods

*"I Wonder" Notes*
Greg Johnson

*"Here's What I Did" Notes*
Terry Prisk
Diane Eble

*Megathemes and Discussion Questions*
Dr. Richard R. Dunn
Dr. Bruce B. Barton

*Ultimate Issues*
Kent Keller

*Life-Changer Index*
Bill Sanders
Linda Taylor

*Maps*
Adapted from the *Life Application Bible*

*Charts*
Adapted from the *Life Application Bible*
Brian Eterno

*Memory Verses*
Brian K. Eterno

*Bible Reading Plan*
Neil Wilson

*Follow-Up/Appointments with God*
Byron Emmert

*Life Application Notes*
Adapted from the *Life Application Bible*
David R. Veerman

# CONTENTS



## OLD TESTAMENT

## NEW TESTAMENT

# A NOTE TO READERS

With 40 million copies in print, *The Living Bible* has been meeting a great need in people's hearts for more than thirty years. But even good things can be improved, so ninety evangelical scholars from various theological backgrounds and denominations were commissioned in 1989 to begin revising *The Living Bible.* The end result of this seven-year process is the *Holy Bible,* New Living Translation—a general-purpose translation that is accurate, easy to read, and excellent for study.

The goal of any Bible translation is to convey the meaning of the ancient Hebrew and Greek texts as accurately as possible to the modern reader. The New Living Translation is based on the most recent scholarship in the theory of translation. The challenge for the translators was to create a text that would make the same impact in the life of modern readers that the original text had for the original readers. In the New Living Translation, this is accomplished by translating entire thoughts (rather than just words) into natural, everyday English. The end result is a translation that is easy to read and understand and that accurately communicates the meaning of the original text.

We believe that this new translation, which combines the latest in scholarship with the best in translation style, will speak to your heart. We present the New Living Translation with the prayer that God will use it to speak his timeless truth to the church and to the world in a fresh, new way.

*The Publishers*
*July 1996*

# INTRODUCTION to the *New Living Translation*

*Translation Philosophy and Methodology*

There are two general theories or methods of Bible translation. The first has been called "formal equivalence." According to this theory, the translator attempts to render each word of the original language into the receptor language and seeks to preserve the original word order and sentence structure as much as possible. The second has been called "dynamic equivalence" or "functional equivalence." The goal of this translation theory is to produce in the receptor language the closest natural equivalent of the message expressed by the original-language text—both in meaning and in style. Such a translation attempts to have the same impact on modern readers as the original had on its own audience.

A dynamic-equivalence translation can also be called a thought-for-thought translation, as contrasted with a formal-equivalence or word-for-word translation. Of course, to translate the thought of the original language requires that the text be interpreted accurately and then be rendered in understandable idiom. So the goal of any thought-for-thought translation is to be both reliable and eminently readable. Thus, as a thought-for-thought translation, the New Living Translation seeks to be both exegetically accurate and idiomatically powerful.

In making a thought-for-thought translation, the translators must do their best to enter into the thought patterns of the ancient authors and to present the same ideas, connotations, and effects in the receptor language. In order to guard against personal biases and to ensure the accuracy of the message, a thought-for-thought translation should be created by a group of scholars who employ the best exegetical tools and who also understand the receptor language very well. With these concerns in mind, the Bible Translation Committee assigned each book of the Bible to three different scholars. Each scholar made a thorough review of the assigned book and submitted suggested revisions to the appropriate general reviewer. The general reviewer reviewed and summarized these suggestions and then proposed a first-draft revision of the text. This draft served as the basis for several additional phases of exegetical and stylistic committee review. Then the Bible Translation Committee jointly reviewed and approved every verse in the final translation.

A thought-for-thought translation prepared by a group of capable scholars has the potential to represent the intended meaning of the original text even more accurately than a word-for-word translation. This is illustrated by the various renderings of the Hebrew word *hesed.* This term cannot be adequately translated by any single English word because it can connote love, mercy, grace, kindness, faithfulness, and loyalty. The context—not the lexicon—must determine which English term is selected for translation.

The value of a thought-for-thought translation can be illustrated by comparing 1 Kings 2:10 in the King James Version, the New International Version, and the New Living Translation. "So David slept with his fathers, and was buried in the city of David" (KJV). "Then David rested with his fathers and was buried in the City of David" (NIV). "Then David died and was buried in the City of David" (NLT). Only the New Living Translation clearly translates the real meaning of the Hebrew idiom "slept with his fathers" into contemporary English.

*Written to Be Read Aloud*

It is evident in Scripture that the biblical documents were written to be read aloud, often in public worship (see Nehemiah 8; Luke 4:16-20; 1 Timothy 4:13; Revelation 1:3). It is still the case today that more people will hear the Bible read aloud in church than are likely to read it for themselves. Therefore, a new translation must communicate with clarity and power when it is read aloud. For this reason, the New Living Translation is recommended as a Bible to be used for public reading. Its living language is not only easy to understand, but it also has an emotive quality that will make an impact on the listener.

*The Texts behind the New Living Translation*

The translators of the Old Testament used the Masoretic Text of the Hebrew Bible as their standard text. They used the edition known as *Biblia Hebraica Stuttgartensia* (1977) with its up-to-date textual apparatus, a revision of Rudolf Kittel's *Biblia Hebraica* (Stuttgart, 1937). The translators also compared the Dead Sea Scrolls, the Septuagint and other Greek manuscripts, the Samaritan Pentateuch, the Syriac Peshitta, the Latin Vulgate, and any other versions or manuscripts that shed light on textual problems.

The translators of the New Testament used the two standard editions of the Greek New Testament: the *Greek New Testament,* published by the United Bible Societies (fourth revised edition, 1993), and *Novum Testamentum Graece,* edited by Nestle and Aland (twenty-seventh edition, 1993). These two editions, which have the same text but differ in punctuation and textual notes, represent the best in modern textual scholarship.

*Translation Issues*

The translators have made a conscious effort to provide a text that can be easily understood by the average reader of modern English. To this end, we have used the vocabulary and language structures commonly used by the average person. The result is a translation of the Scriptures written generally at the reading level of a junior high school student. We have avoided using language that is likely to become quickly dated or that reflects a narrow subdialect of English, with the goal of making the New Living Translation as broadly useful as possible.

But our concern for readability goes beyond the concerns of vocabulary and sentence structure. We are also concerned about historical and cultural barriers to understanding the Bible, and we have sought to translate terms shrouded in history or culture in ways that can be immediately understood by the contemporary reader. Thus, our goal of easy readability expresses itself in a number of other ways:

- Rather than translating ancient weights and measures literally, which communicates little to the modern reader, we have expressed them by means of recognizable contemporary equivalents. We have converted ancient weights and measures to modern English (American) equivalents, and we have rendered the literal Hebrew or Greek measures, along with metric equivalents, in textual footnotes.
- Instead of translating ancient currency values literally, we have generally expressed them in terms of weights in precious metals. In some cases we have used other common terms to communicate the message effectively. For example, "three shekels of silver" might become "three silver coins" or "three pieces of silver" to convey the intended message. Again, a rendering of the literal Hebrew or Greek is given in textual footnotes.
- Since the Hebrew lunar calendar fluctuates from year to year in relation to the solar calendar used today, we have translated Hebrew dates in a way that communicates with our modern readership. It was clear that we could not use the names of the Hebrew months, such as *Abib,* which are meaningless to the modern reader. Nor could we use a simple designation such as "first month," because the months of the Hebrew lunar calendar do not correspond with the months of our calendar. Thus, we have often used seasonal references to communicate the time of year when something happened. For example, "the first month" (which occurs in March and April) might be translated "early spring." Where it is possible to define a specific ancient date in terms of our modern calendar, we use modern dates in the text. Textual footnotes then give the literal Hebrew date and state the rationale for our rendering. For example, Ezra 7:9 pinpoints the date when Ezra arrived in Jerusalem: "the first day of the fifth month." This was during the seventh year of King Artaxerxes' reign (Ezra 7:7). We translate that lunar date as August 4, with a footnote giving the Hebrew and identifying the year as 458 B.C.
- Since ancient references to the time of day differ from our modern methods of denoting time, we used renderings that are instantly understandable to the modern reader. Accordingly, we have rendered specific times of day by using

approximate equivalents in terms of our common "o'clock" system. On occasion, translations such as "at dawn the next morning" or "as the sun began to set" have been used when the biblical reference is general.

- Many words in the original texts made sense to the original audience but communicate something quite different to the modern reader. In such cases, some liberty must be allowed in translation to communicate what was intended. Places identified by the term normally translated "city," for example, are often better identified as "towns" or "villages." Similarly, the term normally translated "mountain" is often better rendered "hill."
- Many words and phrases carry a great deal of cultural meaning that was obvious to the original readers but needs explanation in our own culture. For example, the phrase "they beat their breasts" (Luke 23:48) in ancient times meant that people were very upset. In our translation we chose to translate this phrase dynamically: "They went home *in deep sorrow.*" In some cases, however, we have simply illuminated the existing expression to make it immediately understandable. For example, we might have expanded the literal phrase to read "they beat their breasts *in sorrow.*"
- Metaphorical language is often difficult for contemporary readers to understand, so at times we have chosen to translate or illuminate the metaphor. For example, the ancient poet writes, "Your eyes are doves" (Song of Songs 1:15). To help the modern reader, who might be confused or distracted by a literal visualization of this image, we converted the metaphor to a simile to make the meaning immediately clear: "Your eyes are soft *like* doves." Here we also added the modifier "soft" to help the modern reader catch the significance of the metaphoric expression. A few chapters later, the poet writes, "Your neck is like the tower of David" (Song of Songs 4:4). We rendered it "Your neck is *as stately as* the tower of David" to clarify the intended positive meaning of the metaphor.
- We did not feel obligated to display all Hebrew poetry in English poetic form. Only the book of Psalms is set entirely in poetic lines. Other books, though poetic in nature, are set in prose for the sake of easier reading. Nonetheless, these prose renderings reflect the poetic language of the original Hebrew. Where a portion of text is explicitly said to be a poem or song, however, it has usually been set as such.
- One challenge we faced was in determining how to translate accurately the ancient biblical text that was originally written in a context where male-oriented terms were used to refer to humanity generally. We needed to respect the nature of the ancient context while also trying to make the translation clear to a modern audience that tends to read male-oriented language as applying only to males. Often the original text, though using masculine nouns and pronouns, clearly intends that the message be applied to both men and women. One example is found in the New Testament epistles, where the believers are called "brothers" *(adelphoi)*. Yet it is clear that these epistles were addressed to all the believers—male and female. Thus, we have usually translated this Greek word "brothers and sisters" in order to represent the historical situation more accurately.
- We have also been sensitive to passages where the text applies generally to human beings or to the human condition. In many instances we have used plural pronouns (they, them) in place of the masculine singular (he, him). For example, a traditional rendering of Proverbs 22:6 is: "Train up a child in the way he should go, and when he is old he will not turn from it." We have rendered it: "Teach your children to choose the right path, and when they are older, they will remain upon it." At times, we have also replaced third person pronouns with the second person to ensure clarity. A traditional rendering of Proverbs 26:27 is: "He who digs a pit will fall into it, and he who rolls a stone, it will come back on him." We have rendered it: "If you set a trap for others, you will get caught in it yourself. If you roll a boulder down on others, it will roll back on you." All such decisions were driven by the concern to reflect accurately the intended meaning of the original texts of Scripture.

We should emphasize, however, that all masculine nouns and pronouns used to represent God (for example, "Father") have been maintained without exception. We believe that essential traits of God's revealed character can only be conveyed through the masculine language expressed in the original texts of Scripture.

*Lexical Consistency in Terminology*

For the sake of clarity, we have maintained lexical consistency in areas such as divine names, synoptic passages, rhetorical structures, and nontheological technical terms (i.e., liturgical, cultic, zoological, botanical, cultural, and legal terms). For theological terms, we have allowed a greater semantic range of acceptable English words or phrases for a single Hebrew or Greek word. We avoided weighty theological terms that do not readily communicate to many modern readers. For example, we avoided using words such as "justification," "sanctification," and "regeneration." In place of these words (which are carryovers from Latin), we provided renderings such as "we are made right with God," "we are made holy," and "we are born anew."

*The Spelling of Proper Names*

Many individuals in the Bible, especially the Old Testament, are known by more than one name or by a number of variant names (e.g., Uzziah/Azariah). For the sake of clarity, we have tried to use a single spelling for any one individual, footnoting the literal spelling whenever we differ from it. This is especially helpful in delineating the kings of Israel and Judah. King Joash/Jehoash of Israel has been consistently called Jehoash, while King Joash/Jehoash of Judah is called Joash. A similar distinction has been used to distinguish between Joram/Jehoram of Israel and Joram/Jehoram of Judah. All such decisions were made with the goal of clarifying the text for the reader. When the ancient biblical writers clearly had a theological purpose in their choice of a variant name (e.g., Eshbaal/Ishbosheth), the different names have been maintained with an explanatory footnote.

*The Rendering of Divine Names*

All appearances of *'el*, *'elohim*, or *'eloah* have been translated "God," except where the context demands the translation "god(s)." We have rendered the tetragrammaton *(YHWH)* consistently as "the LORD," utilizing a form with small capitals that is common among English translations. This will distinguish it from the name *'adonai*, which we render "Lord." When *'adonai* and *YHWH* appear in conjunction, we have rendered it "Sovereign LORD." This also distinguishes *'adonai YHWH* from cases where *YHWH* appears with *'elohim*, which is rendered "LORD God." When *YH* (the short form of *YHWH*) and *YHWH* appear together, we have rendered it "LORD GOD." The Hebrew word *'adon* is rendered "lord," or "master," or sometimes "sir."

In the New Testament, the Greek word *Christos* has been translated as "Messiah" when the context assumes a Jewish audience. When a Gentile audience can be assumed, *Christos* has been translated as "Christ." The Greek word *kurios* is consistently translated "Lord," except in four quotations of Psalm 110:1, where it is translated "LORD."

*Textual Footnotes*

The New Living Translation provides several kinds of textual footnotes:

- All Old Testament passages that are clearly quoted in the New Testament are identified in a textual footnote in the New Testament.
- Some textual footnotes provide cultural and historical information on places, things, and people in the Bible that are probably obscure to modern readers. Such notes should aid the reader in understanding the message of the text. For example, in Acts 12:1, "King Herod" is named in this translation as "King Herod Agrippa" and is identified in a footnote as being "the nephew of Herod Antipas and a grandson of Herod the Great."
- When various ancient manuscripts contain different readings, these differences are often documented in footnotes. For instance, textual variants are footnoted when the variant reading is very familiar (usually through the King James Version). We have used footnotes when we have selected variant readings that differ from the Hebrew and Greek editions normally followed.

- When the meaning of a proper name (or a wordplay inherent in a proper name) is relevant to the meaning of the text, it is illuminated with a textual footnote. For example, the footnote at Genesis 3:20 reads: "*Eve* sounds like a Hebrew term that means 'to give life.' " This wordplay in the Hebrew illuminates the meaning of the text, which goes on to say that Eve "would be the mother of all people everywhere." If the meaning of the name is more certain, it is stated more simply. For example, the footnote at Genesis 16:11 reads: "*Ishmael* means 'God hears.' " In this case, Hagar named her son Ishmael after realizing that God had heard her cry for help.
- When we translate the meaning of a place-name that is often simply transliterated from the Hebrew or Greek, we provide a textual footnote showing the transliteration that appears in many English translations. For example, the name usually transliterated "Havvoth-jair" in Judges 10:4 has been translated "the Towns of Jair," with a footnote that gives the traditional transliteration: "Hebrew *Havvoth-jair.*"
- Textual footnotes are also used to show alternative renderings. These are prefaced with the word "Or." On occasion, we also provide notes on words or phrases that represent a translation that departs from long-standing tradition. These notes are prefaced with the words "traditionally rendered." For example, a footnote to the translation "contagious skin disease" at Leviticus 13:2 says, "Traditionally rendered *leprosy.*"

AS WE SUBMIT this translation of the Bible for publication, we recognize that any translation of the Scriptures is subject to limitations and imperfections. Anyone who has attempted to communicate the richness of God's Word into another language will realize it is impossible to make a perfect translation. Recognizing these limitations, we sought God's guidance and wisdom throughout this project. Now we pray that he will accept our efforts and use this translation for the benefit of the Church and of all people.

We pray that the New Living Translation will overcome some of the barriers of history, culture, and language that have kept people from reading and understanding God's Word. We hope that readers unfamiliar with the Bible will find the words clear and easy to understand, and that readers well versed in the Scriptures will gain a fresh perspective. We pray that readers will gain insight and wisdom for living, but most of all that they will meet the God of the Bible and be forever changed by knowing him.

*The Bible Translation Committee*
*July 1996*

# HOLY BIBLE, *New Living Translation*
# BIBLE TRANSLATION TEAM

PENTATEUCH
Daniel I. Block, General Reviewer
*The Southern Baptist Theological Seminary*

GENESIS
Allan Ross, *Trinity Episcopal Seminary*
John Sailhamer, *Northwestern College*
Gordon Wenham, *The Cheltenham and Gloucester College of Higher Education*

EXODUS
Robert Bergen, *Hannibal-LaGrange College*
Daniel I. Block, *The Southern Baptist Theological Seminary*
Eugene Carpenter, *Bethel College, Mishawaka, Indiana*

LEVITICUS
David Baker, *Ashland Theological Seminary*
Victor Hamilton, *Asbury College*
Kenneth Mathews, *Beeson Divinity School, Samford University*

NUMBERS
Dale A. Brueggemann, *Assemblies of God Division of Foreign Missions*
Roland K. Harrison (deceased), *Wycliffe College*
Gerald L. Mattingly, *Johnson Bible College*

DEUTERONOMY
J. Gordon McConville, *The Cheltenham and Gloucester College of Higher Education*
Eugene H. Merrill, *Dallas Theological Seminary*
John A. Thompson, *University of Melbourne*

HISTORICAL BOOKS
Barry J. Beitzel, General Reviewer
*Trinity Evangelical Divinity School*

JOSHUA/JUDGES
Carl E. Armerding, *Schloss Mittersill Study Centre*
Barry J. Beitzel, *Trinity Evangelical Divinity School*
Lawson Stone, *Asbury Theological Seminary*

1 & 2 SAMUEL
Barry J. Beitzel, *Trinity Evangelical Divinity School*
V. Philips Long, *Covenant Theological Seminary*
J. Robert Vannoy, *Biblical Theological Seminary*

1 & 2 KINGS
Bill T. Arnold, *Asbury Theological Seminary*
William H. Barnes, *Southeastern College of the Assemblies of God*
Frederic W. Bush, *Fuller Theological Seminary*

1 & 2 CHRONICLES
Raymond B. Dillard (deceased), *Westminster Theological Seminary*
David A. Dorsey, *Evangelical School of Theology*
Terry Eves, *Calvin College*

EZRA/NEHEMIAH/ESTHER/RUTH
William C. Williams, *Southern California College*
Hugh G. M. Williamson, *Oxford University*

POETRY
Tremper Longman III, General Reviewer
*Westminster Theological Seminary*

JOB
August Konkel, *Providence Theological Seminary*
Tremper Longman III, *Westminster Theological Seminary*
Al Wolters, *Redeemer College*

PSALMS 1–75
Mark D. Futato, *Westminster Theological Seminary in California*
Douglas Green, *Westminster Theological Seminary*
Richard Pratt, *Reformed Theological Seminary*

PSALMS 76–150
David M. Howard Jr., *Trinity Evangelical Divinity School*
Raymond C. Ortlund Jr., *Trinity Evangelical Divinity School*
Willem VanGemeren, *Trinity Evangelical Divinity School*

PROVERBS
Ted Hildebrandt, *Grace College*
Richard Schultz, *Wheaton College*
Raymond C. Van Leeuwen, *Eastern College*

ECCLESIASTES/SONG OF SONGS
Daniel C. Fredericks, *Belhaven College*
David Hubbard (deceased), *Fuller Theological Seminary*
Tremper Longman III, *Westminster Theological Seminary*

PROPHETS
John N. Oswalt, General Reviewer
*Asbury Theological Seminary*

ISAIAH
John N. Oswalt, *Asbury Theological Seminary*
Gary Smith, *Bethel Theological Seminary*
John Walton, *Moody Bible Institute*

JEREMIAH/LAMENTATIONS
G. Herbert Livingston, *Asbury Theological Seminary*
Elmer A. Martens, *Mennonite Brethren Biblical Seminary*

EZEKIEL
Daniel I. Block, *The Southern Baptist Theological Seminary*
David H. Engelhard, *Calvin Theological Seminary*
David Thompson, *Asbury Theological Seminary*

DANIEL/HAGGAI/ZECHARIAH/MALACHI
Joyce Baldwin Caine (deceased), *Trinity College, Bristol*
Douglas Gropp, *Catholic University of America*
Roy Hayden, *Oral Roberts School of Theology*

HOSEA–ZEPHANIAH
Joseph Coleson, *Nazarene Theological Seminary*
Andrew Hill, *Wheaton College*
Richard Patterson, *Professor Emeritus, Liberty University*

## GOSPELS AND ACTS

Grant R. Osborne, General Reviewer
*Trinity Evangelical Divinity School*

MATTHEW
Craig Blomberg, *Denver Conservative Baptist Seminary*
Donald A. Hagner, *Fuller Theological Seminary*
David Turner, *Grand Rapids Baptist Seminary*

MARK
Robert Guelich (deceased), *Fuller Theological Seminary*
Grant R. Osborne, *Trinity Evangelical Divinity School*

LUKE
Darrell Bock, *Dallas Theological Seminary*
Scot McKnight, *North Park College*
Robert Stein, *Bethel Theological Seminary*

JOHN
Gary M. Burge, *Wheaton College*
Philip W. Comfort, *Wheaton College*
Marianne Meye Thompson, *Fuller Theological Seminary*

ACTS
D. A. Carson, *Trinity Evangelical Divinity School*
William J. Larkin, *Columbia Biblical Seminary*
Roger Mohrlang, *Whitworth College*

## LETTERS AND REVELATION

Norman R. Ericson, General Reviewer
*Wheaton College*

ROMANS/GALATIANS
Gerald Borchert, *The Southern Baptist Theological Seminary*
Douglas J. Moo, *Trinity Evangelical Divinity School*
Thomas R. Schreiner, *Bethel Theological Seminary*

1 & 2 CORINTHIANS
Joseph Alexanian, *Trinity International University*
Linda Belleville, *North Park Theological Seminary*
Douglas A. Oss, *Central Bible College*
Robert Sloan, *Baylor University*

EPHESIANS–PHILEMON
Harold W. Hoehner, *Dallas Theological Seminary*
Moises Silva, *Gordon-Conwell Theological Seminary*
Klyne Snodgrass, *North Park Theological Seminary*

HEBREWS/JAMES/1 & 2 PETER/JUDE
Peter Davids, *Canadian Theological Seminary*
Norman R. Ericson, *Wheaton College*
William Lane (deceased), *Seattle Pacific University*
J. Ramsey Michaels, *S.W. Missouri State University*

1–3 JOHN/REVELATION
Greg Beale, *Gordon-Conwell Theological Seminary*
Robert Mounce, *Whitworth College*
M. Robert Mulholland Jr., *Asbury Theological Seminary*

## SPECIAL REVIEWERS

F. F. Bruce (deceased), *University of Manchester*
Kenneth N. Taylor, *Tyndale House Publishers*

## COORDINATING TEAM

Mark R. Norton, *Managing Editor and O.T. Coordinating Editor*
Philip W. Comfort, *N.T. Coordinating Editor*
Ronald A. Beers, *Executive Director and Stylist*
Mark D. Taylor, *Director and Chief Stylist*
Daniel W. Taylor, *Consultant*

# USER'S GUIDE

Welcome to the *Student's Life Application Bible.* God gave us his Word to tell us about himself and his plan for our life. When we read the Bible, we see God's love in action and we learn about what he wants us to do. "All Scripture is inspired by God and is useful to teach us what is true and to make us realize what is wrong in our lives. It straightens us out and teaches us to do what is right. It is God's way of preparing us in every way, fully equipped for every good thing God wants us to do" (2 Timothy 3:16-17).

You can see that reading the Bible is very important. In addition to reading, however, we should be studying the Bible. Then we can discover what God wants us to do and do it. That's what the word *application* means—putting into practice, obeying, *doing* biblical principles.

That's why the *Student's Life Application Bible* was written—to help you understand and apply God's Word. It is easy to use and packed with helpful notes and other features. You will find the notes within the text, at the beginnings and endings of books, and at the back of the Bible. These special features *are not* God's Word—only the Bible text itself speaks with God's authority. The notes and other features *are* a valuable help in understanding God's truth and seeing how the biblical principles apply to life, your life, today.

At the back of the Bible you will discover . . .

**BIBLE-READING PLAN** By following this simple plan, you will read all the major biblical themes and stories in a year.

**FOLLOW-UP FOR NEW CHRISTIANS/14 APPOINTMENTS WITH GOD** This course takes new believers through the basics of the Christian faith. Use it yourself or share it with a friend.

**LIFE-CHANGER INDEX** More than 100 topics are listed in this index. Each topic has a selection of relevant Bible passages and notes that relate. (The Scripture references listed for the notes in this section are given only to help you find the note. It may or may not actually relate to the Scripture listed.)

**INDEXES FOR MORAL DILEMMAS, "I WONDER," ULTIMATE ISSUES, CHARTS, PERSONALITY PROFILES, MAPS, AND "HERE'S WHAT I DID"** Again, Scripture references listed for these notes are to help you locate the notes easily. The notes may or may not actually relate to the Scripture listed.

**"WHERE TO FIND IT" INDEX** More than 70 of the best-known Bible stories are listed in this index, along with Jesus' parables and miracles. Use either the Scripture references or the page numbers to quickly and easily find the story, parable, or miracle you want.

It's all here. Just about everything you will need to help you understand and apply God's Word. The next step—actually taking time to read and study the Bible—is yours. *GO FOR IT!*

The following spread is a quick look at each of the special features:

Creation

Noah (undated)

2166 B.C.
Abram born

2091
Abram enters Canaan

2066
Isaac born

2006
Jacob & Esau born

**H**ave you ever turned on a TV program a few minutes late? Chances are you'll turn it off before the show is over because you can't figure out what's going on. To understand a TV program, you have to see the beginning. Now think of the Bible. If you want to find out what's going on in this big book—to get the whole picture—it helps to start with Genesis. Why? Because Genesis is the book of beginnings. It explains how just about everything got started. If you don't understand how things in this world began, it will be harder to figure out why and how God is going to end things. ■ In Genesis we marvel at the awesome creation of the entire universe by the spoken word of God. And we get our first glimpse into God's character. We see that though everything else has a definite beginning, God is eternal. He always has been and always will be. We notice God's creativeness and power, we see his hatred and judgment of sin, and we view his incredible love for his people even when they constantly disobey him. ■ Genesis is the book of beginnings: the beginning of the universe, of people, of sin, of salvation, and of an understanding of God. Take time to read Genesis. You will be amazed at how fascinating it is, and at how often other books in the Bible refer to something first mentioned in Genesis—the book of beginnings.

# Genesis

Genesis Genesis Genesis Genesis

**STATS**

PURPOSE: To record God's creation of the world and his desire to have a people set apart to worship him
AUTHOR: Moses
TO WHOM WRITTEN: The people of Israel
DATE WRITTEN: 1450–1410 B.C.
SETTING: The region presently known as the Middle East
KEY PEOPLE: Adam, Eve, Noah, Abraham, Sarah, Isaac, Rebekah, Jacob, Joseph

## BOOK INTRODUCTIONS

To get an overview of a specific Bible book, read the introduction material containing interesting summaries, timelines, and stats (the who, what, where, and when of the book).

CHAPTER **1** **THE ACCOUNT OF CREATION.** In the beginning God created* the heavens and the earth. [2]The earth was empty, a formless mass cloaked in darkness. And the Spirit of God was hovering over its surface. [3]Then God said, "Let there be light," and there was light. [4]And God saw that it was good. Then

[14]And God said, "Let bright lights appear in the sky to separate the day from the night. They will be signs to mark off the seasons, the days, and the years. [15]Let their light shine down upon the earth." And so it was. [16]For God made two great lights, the

## LIFE APPLICATION notes

On just about every page you'll find these concise mini-lessons. Each note helps explain a specific Bible passage and then tells ways you can put it into practice.

**SELF-WORTH ● ● • • ·**

**1:1-26 God created everything there is; the heavens, earth, plants, and animals were all made by God at the beginning of history. When God finished creating the earth, he then chose to make people in his image. The phrase "Let *us* make people in *our* image" in verse 26 does not mean that God created us exactly like himself, especially in a physical sense. Instead, we are reflections of God's glory. We will never be totally like God, because he is our supreme Creator. Our best hope is to reflect his character in our love, patience, forgiveness, kindness, and faithfulness.**

**We are made like God and therefore share many of his characteristics. Our worth is not defined by possessions, achievements, physical attractiveness, or popularity. Self-worth is knowing that God created us in his likeness. Criticizing or downgrading ourselves is criticizing what God has made. Because we are like God, we can feel positive about ourselves and our abilities. Knowing that you are a person of infinite worth gives you the freedom to love God, know him personally, and make a valuable contribution to the lives of those around you.**

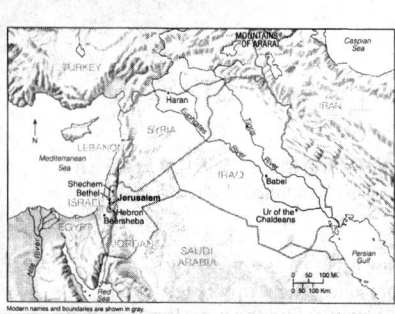

**KEY PLACES IN GENESIS**



Modern names and boundaries are shown in gray.

God created the universe and the earth. Then he made man and woman, giving them a home in a beautiful garden. Unfortunately, Adam and Eve disobeyed God and were expelled from the garden (3:24).
**Mountains of Ararat** Adam and Eve's sin brought sin into the human race. Years later, sin had run rampant and God decided to destroy the earth with a great flood. All except for Noah, his family, and two of each animal who were all safe in a huge boat. When the floods receded, the boat rested on the mountains of Ararat (8:4).
**Babel** People never learn. Again sin abounded and the pride of the people led them to build a huge tower as a monument to their own greatness—obviously they had no thought of God. As punishment, God scattered the people by giving them different languages (11:8-9).
**Ur of the Chaldeans** Abram, a descendant of Shem, was born in this great city (11:27-28).
**Haran** Terah, Lot, Abram, and Sarai left Ur and, following the fertile crescent of the Euphrates River, headed toward the land of Canaan. Along the way, they settled in the city of Haran for a while (11:31).
**Shechem** God urged Abram to leave Haran and go to a place where he would become the father of a great nation (12:1-2). So Abram, Lot, and Sarai traveled to the land of Canaan and settled near a city called Shechem (12:5-6).
**Hebron** Abraham moved on to Hebron, to "the oak grove owned by Mamre," where he put down his deepest roots (13:18). Abraham, Isaac, and Jacob all lived and were buried there.
**Beersheba** After a dispute over ownership of the well here, Abraham made a covenant with Abimelech (21:31). Years later, as Isaac was moving from place to place, God appeared to him here and passed on to him the covenant he had made with his father, Abraham (26:23-25).
**Bethel** After deceiving his brother out of both his birthright and his blessing, Jacob left Beersheba and fled to Haran. Along the way God revealed himself to Jacob in a dream and again passed on the covenant he had made with Abraham and Isaac (28:10-22). Jacob lived in Haran, worked for Laban, and married Leah and Rachel (29:15-28). After a tense meeting with his brother, Esau, Jacob returned to Bethel (35:1).
**Egypt** Jacob had 12 sons, including Joseph, Jacob's favorite. The other brothers grew jealous, until one day, out in the fields, ... Eventually, Joseph rose from Egyptian slave to

**DAYS OF CREATION**

| | DAY 2 | DAY 3 | DAY 4 | DAY 5 | DAY 6 | DAY 7 |
|---|---|---|---|---|---|---|
| LIGHT so there was light | SKY AND WATER waters separated | SEA AND LAND waters gathered | SUN, MOON, AND STARS to preside over day and night, to mark off seasons, days, and years | FISH AND BIRDS to fill the waters and the sky | ANIMALS to fill the earth MAN AND WOMAN to care for the earth and commune with God | GOD RESTED AND WAS PLEASED |

## CHARTS

These compare, contrast, and list important information to help you visualize difficult concepts or pull together related Bible facts.

## MAPS

Located in the text, the maps help you find Bible locations quickly and easily.

...ss. And God saw that it was good. [19]This ...ed on the fourth day.
...od said, "Let the waters swarm with fish ... life. Let the skies be filled with birds of ..." [21]So God created great sea creatures and ...of fish and every kind of bird. And God

Is **ANYTHING** *too hard*

LORD
?

## HIGHLIGHTED MEMORY VERSES

Key verses are artistically highlighted to help impress them in your mind.

**ADAM & EVE** were the only two humans who never experienced being young. Depending on how you feel, they may or may not have missed a lot! But try to imagine starting out life as an adult—no memories, no mistakes, no past little lessons to help you make adult decisions. . . . Most of us don't realize how much we learn or fail to learn during our growing years until it's too late.

For instance, we have many opportunities to learn as children that while there are some trustworthy people in our lives, not everyone can be trusted. We learn not to immediately trust new advice. We discover it is often helpful to compare it to wisdom we already have, or even to ask someone who has been trustworthy to evaluate the new advice. Eve got some new information: "The fruit is great. . . God's being selfish. . . you will be like him." She trusted new advice even though it went against what had been trustworthy. She ate the fruit. She failed to trust the one who had never failed her. Adam made the same mistake. New advice, no questions, no checking . . . he ate the fruit. Both of them disobeyed God. The result was death!

Like Adam and Eve, we often have to live with the painful consequences of accepting bad advice. But consequences are reminders of hard lessons. They

**UPS:**
- The first male and female, husband and wife, human beings
- First to be made in the image of God
- First caretakers of creation
- First to know God personally

**DOWNS:**
- Both tended to handle mistakes and sin by excuses or blaming others
- Acted without considering consequences
- Together they brought sin into the cre...

**STATS:**
- Where: Garden...
- Occupation: H... and wife, care... Eden
- Relatives: Son... Abel, Seth. Nu... other children.

## PERSONALITY PROFILES

These are character sketches of key Bible people—both heroes and villains—highlighting their strengths, weaknesses, successes, failures, and life lessons.

## VIOLENCE

On Friday nights at seven o'clock you're practically guaranteed to find Derek and Steve in one of two places. Check first at Derek's. If they're not there, munching pizza and watching horror movies on video, try the mall. They probably will be standing in line at the movie theater, anxiously waiting for the chance to purchase tickets for the newest cinematic tale of gore.

In the last couple of years, these guys have seen hundreds of violent movies. It doesn't matter what the plot is–deranged killers on the loose, murderous monsters on the rampage, savage mutants from outer space–as long as there are some gruesome torture scenes, lots of mutilated bodies, and gallons of blood and guts, Derek and Steve are satisfied.

"That one scene was so weak," Steve complains as he ejects a video one Friday.

"Which one?" Derek responds.

"You know, the one where he shoved the girl into that giant meat grinder. . . . I mean, the blood didn't even look real."

"Tell me about it!" Derek agrees. "Every scene in the whole movie was just ripped off

"Want to watch

"Sure. But let m

See how God fe
of violence–Genes

**MORAL DILEMMA notes**
These are real-life case studies, situations where kids like you had to make important decisions. In each of these notes, you will be told where to find a Bible passage that will help you understand what God has to say about the situations you face.

## "Here's what I did..."

Whenever I get discouraged because I can't persuade a friend of the truth of the gospel, I remind myself that we are never going to convince those who don't want to be convinced. This has been a tough thing for me to accept; there are some people I want so badly to become Christians. But
f Moses and Pharaoh. Nothing would convince
sented the one true God—not plagues, not
th of Egypt's firstborn. If calamities of this
Pharaoh to repent, I am no longer surprised that
l Christians fails to make a dent in the hearts of

d that the best tactic is the slow, steady work
led with prayer and our attempts to live the
to place the rest in God's hands.

Richard

AGE 18

**"HERE'S WHAT I DID" notes** After interviewing tons of kids, we took some of their stories and included them here. These notes tell how other young people used the principles of God's Word in specific situations in their life.

**When I read about creation and miracles in the Bible, I get confused. How do science and the Bible relate?**

The Bible and science debate has raged for many years. Conflicts arise when we look for spiritual answers from science or for scientific answers in the Bible.

A former Vietnam POW told of the time he was allowed to send a cassette tape home to his family. Realizing that it might be the last communication he would ever have with those he loved, he took extensive notes on what he would cover before he began to make the tape. His goal was to communicate the most important things that his family should know. To his wife, he talked of insurance, mortgages, child rearing, an
each mess
tions they
up without
how much

This is ex
put 66 boo
most impo
in certain s
of his love

For some
fusion, and
ies). Instea
real strugg
of whom co
they realize
be against
those who
consequen

Most of th
about living
society thar

Your mind matters to God—he wants you to think. Never be afraid to ask tough questions about the Bible or the Christian faith. But also consider the appropriateness of each question. Is this the kind of question the Bible should answer? And do the same with science, asking the right questions.

Creation and the resurrection of Jesus Christ are two of the most important tenets of the Christian faith. Although neither can be duplicated in a laboratory, they also cannot be proven to be false by science.

If God can create life from nothing, as well as raise a man from the dead, he can lead us through this life and the next. We can trust him.

**"I WONDER" notes**
If you've ever wondered about what the Bible has to say about something, or about some aspect of the Christian life, you'll probably find your questions repeated in these notes. And you'll also find interesting and thoughtful answers.

## Ultimate Issues

THE ORIGIN OF HUMANITY "It is now commonly accepted in scientific circles that human beings have become what they are today as a result of millions of years of EVOLUTION. Beginning as a one-celled animal. . . ." So reads the textbook used in biology classes in many public high schools today. "In the beginning God created the heavens and the earth. The earth was empty, a formless mass. . . ." So begins the book of Genesis. The Christian student faces a conflict: Whom to believe? Probably no other issue has drawn a sharper dividing line between religious and nonreligious thought in our society than that of the origin of the human race. Were we, as Genesis 1 and 2 state, placed here by SPECIAL DIVINE CREATION? Or did we, as many contemporary educators, philosophers, and others tell us, evolve from nothing into one-celled animals and on up the zoological chain into *Homo sapiens?* Or perhaps a third option—God created people, using the process of evolution as his "laboratory." Many young people feel the **UNEASY TENSION** that exists between these views. Their spiritual authorities—the Bible, the church, the pastor or youth minister—stand firmly in the creationist camp, while the public educational system, their biology teachers, and probably the majority of their peers lean heavily toward the evolutionist viewpoint.
ll out in precise detail how human beings came to
st and foremost, human beings, like all the rest
es that fact in the clearest of terms—God is
k 31 times in Genesis 1 alone. The idea that we
nd scientific impossibility. The FIRST LAW OF
r be created nor destroyed by natural causes. For the
ble dilemma. If only natural causes are involved, how
that something become something personal—with
y chance? Impossible. Absolutely, scientifically.
ian, then, turns to the supernatural: ***God did it.***
ginning God created the heavens and the earth . . . ,"
lity of some kind of God-directed evolution; neither
tionists will admit that their beliefs involve as much
sts'. Nobel Prize winner Ernst Chain said in 1970:
he fittest is entirely a consequence of chance
evidence and entirely irreconcilable with the facts. . . . It amazes me that [classical evolutionary theories] are swallowed so uncritically and readily, and for such a long time, by so many scientists without a murmur of protest." So the Bible, and Genesis in particular, gives us **ONE BEDROCK FACT** about the origin of humanity: God created us in his own image. Exactly how he did that remains a matter of faith, open to investigation by scientific inquiry. But the creationist position is as intellectually respectable as any of the alternatives. Every Christian can draw strength and confidence—and awe for his or her Creator—from knowing that.

**ULTIMATE ISSUE notes**
An "ultimate issue" is a tough question about life or God. These full-page notes bring up difficult questions and then give clear and helpful answers.



## MEGA themes

**BEGINNINGS** Genesis introduces God as Creator of all that exists: the universe, water, and all of life, including people, who were created in God's
ting, he
ood." When
od began his
perfection.
ify God.
ility to bring
in God's
good relation-
k to God for a

1. What have you learned about the character of God from reading Genesis 1–3?
2. What does it mean to be created in the image of the God who is Lord of all?
3. How do you feel about yourself when you think about being created in God's image?
4. How should the fact that each person is truly created in God's image affect the way you act toward people who appear to be different from you (i.e., skin color, physical disability, unusual habits)?
5. As a person who is created in God's image, how can you glorify God in your relationships with others? With nature? With God?

**MEGATHEMES**
At the end of each Bible book the main themes are presented. With each theme there is a set of questions that can be used for individual or group study.

# The OLD Testament

Creation

Noah (undated)

2166 B.C.
Abram born

2091
Abram enters Canaan

2066
Isaac born

2006
Jacob & Esau born

1929
Jacob flees to Haran

1915
Joseph born

1898
Joseph sold into slavery

1885
Joseph rules Egypt

1805
Joseph dies

Have you ever turned on a TV program a few minutes late? Chances are you'll turn it off before the show is over because you can't figure out what's going on. To understand a TV program, you have to see the beginning. Now think of the Bible. If you want to find out what's going on in this big book—to get the whole picture—it helps to start with Genesis. Why? Because Genesis is the book of beginnings. It explains how just about everything got started. If you don't understand how things in this world began, it will be harder to figure out why and how God is going to end things. ■ In Genesis we marvel at the awesome creation of the entire universe by the spoken word of God. And we get our first glimpse into God's character. We see that though everything else has a definite beginning, God is eternal. He always has been and always will be. We notice God's creativeness and power, we see his hatred and judgment of sin, and we view his incredible love for his people even when they constantly disobey him. ■ Genesis is the book of beginnings: the beginning of the universe, of people, of sin, of salvation, and of an understanding of God. Take time to read Genesis. You will be amazed at how fascinating it is, and at how often other books in the Bible refer to something first mentioned in Genesis—the book of beginnings.

## STATS

PURPOSE: To record God's creation of the world and his desire to have a people set apart to worship him

AUTHOR: Moses

TO WHOM WRITTEN: The people of Israel

DATE WRITTEN: 1450–1410 B.C.

SETTING: The region presently known as the Middle East

KEY PEOPLE: Adam, Eve, Noah, Abraham, Sarah, Isaac, Rebekah, Jacob, Joseph

CHAPTER 1 **THE ACCOUNT OF CREATION.** In the beginning God created* the heavens and the earth. 2The
earth was empty, a formless mass cloaked in darkness. And the Spirit of God was hovering over its
surface. 3Then God said, "Let there be light," and
there was light. 4And God saw that it was good. Then
he separated the light from the darkness. 5God called
the light "day" and the darkness "night." Together
these made up one day.

6And God said, "Let there be space between the
waters, to separate water from water." 7And so it was.
God made this space to separate the waters above
from the waters below. 8And God called the space
"sky." This happened on the second day.

9And God said, "Let the waters beneath the sky be
gathered into one place so dry ground may appear."
And so it was. 10God named the dry ground "land" and
the water "seas." And God saw that it was good. 11Then
God said, "Let the land burst forth with every sort of
grass and seed-bearing plant. And let there be trees that
grow seed-bearing fruit. The seeds will then produce
the kinds of plants and trees from which they came."
And so it was. 12The land was filled with seed-bearing
plants and trees, and their seeds produced plants and
trees of like kind. And God saw that it was good. 13This
all happened on the third day.

1:1 Or *In the beginning when God created,* or *When God began to create.*

14And God said, "Let bright lights appear in the
sky to separate the day from the night. They will be
signs to mark off the seasons, the days, and the
years. 15Let their light shine down upon the earth."
And so it was. 16For God made two great lights, the

## SELF-WORTH ● ● • • •

1:1-26 **God created everything there is; the heavens, earth, plants, and animals were all made by God at the beginning of history. When God finished creating the earth, he then chose to make people in his image. The phrase "Let *us* make people in *our* image" in verse 26 does not mean that God created us exactly like himself, especially in a physical sense. Instead, we are reflections of God's glory. We will never be totally like God, because he is our supreme Creator. Our best hope is to reflect his character in our love, patience, forgiveness, kindness, and faithfulness.**

**We are made like God and therefore share many of his characteristics. Our worth is not defined by possessions, achievements, physical attractiveness, or popularity. Self-worth is knowing that God created us in his likeness. Criticizing or downgrading ourselves is criticizing what God has made. Because we are like God, we can feel positive about ourselves and our abilities. Knowing that you are a person of infinite worth gives you the freedom to love God, know him personally, and make a valuable contribution to the lives of those around you.**

# KEY PLACES IN GENESIS

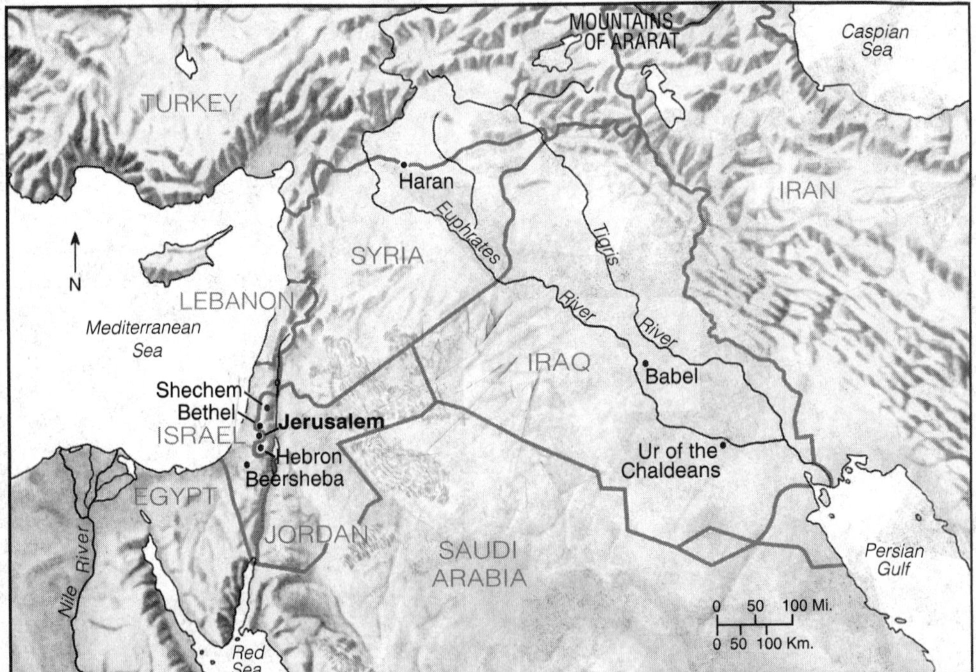


Modern names and boundaries are shown in gray.

God created the universe and the earth. Then he made man and woman, giving them a home in a beautiful garden. Unfortunately, Adam and Eve disobeyed God and were expelled from the garden (3:24).

**Mountains of Ararat** Adam and Eve's sin brought sin into the human race. Years later, sin had run rampant and God decided to destroy the earth with a great flood. All except for Noah, his family, and two of each animal who were all safe in a huge boat. When the floods receded, the boat rested on the mountains of Ararat (8:4).

**Babel** People never learn. Again sin abounded and the pride of the people led them to build a huge tower as a monument to their own greatness–obviously they had no thought of God. As punishment, God scattered the people by giving them different languages (11:8-9).

**Ur of the Chaldeans** Abram, a descendant of Shem, was born in this great city (11:27-28).

**Haran** Terah, Lot, Abram, and Sarai left Ur and, following the fertile crescent of the Euphrates River, headed toward the land of Canaan. Along the way, they settled in the city of Haran for a while (11:31).

**Shechem** God urged Abram to leave Haran and go to a place where he would become the father of a great nation (12:1-2). So Abram, Lot, and Sarai traveled to the land of Canaan and settled near a city called Shechem (12:5-6).

**Hebron** Abraham moved on to Hebron, to "the oak grove owned by Mamre," where he put down his deepest roots (13:18). Abraham, Isaac, and Jacob all lived and were buried there.

**Beersheba** After a dispute over ownership of the well here, Abraham made a covenant with Abimelech (21:31). Years later, as Isaac was moving from place to place, God appeared to him here and passed on to him the covenant he had made with his father, Abraham (26:23-25).

**Bethel** After deceiving his brother out of both his birthright and his blessing, Jacob left Beersheba and fled to Haran. Along the way God revealed himself to Jacob in a dream and again passed on the covenant he had made with Abraham and Isaac (28:10-22). Jacob lived in Haran, worked for Laban, and married Leah and Rachel (29:15-28). After a tense meeting with his brother, Esau, Jacob returned to Bethel (35:1).

**Egypt** Jacob had 12 sons, including Joseph, Jacob's favorite. The other brothers grew jealous, until one day, out in the fields, the brothers sold him to Ishmaelite traders who were going to Egypt. Eventually, Joseph rose from Egyptian slave to Pharaoh's "right hand man," saving Egypt and the surrounding country from famine. His entire family moved from Canaan to Egypt and settled there during the severe famine (46:3-4).

---

sun and the moon, to shine down upon the earth.
The greater one, the sun, presides during the day;
the lesser one, the moon, presides through the
night. He also made the stars. 17 God set these lights
in the heavens to light the earth, 18 to govern the
day and the night, and to separate the light from
the darkness. And God saw that it was good. 19 This
all happened on the fourth day.
20 And God said, "Let the waters swarm with fish
and other life. Let the skies be filled with birds of
every kind." 21 So God created great sea creatures and
every sort of fish and every kind of bird. And God

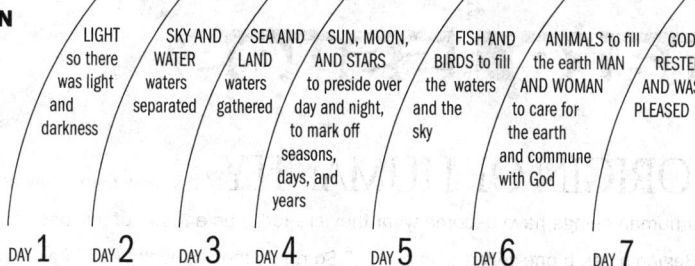

**DAYS OF CREATION**

- DAY 1: LIGHT so there was light and darkness
- DAY 2: SKY AND WATER waters separated
- DAY 3: SEA AND LAND waters gathered
- DAY 4: SUN, MOON, AND STARS to preside over day and night, to mark off seasons, days, and years
- DAY 5: FISH AND BIRDS to fill the waters and the sky
- DAY 6: ANIMALS to fill the earth MAN AND WOMAN to care for the earth and commune with God
- DAY 7: GOD RESTED AND WAS PLEASED

saw that it was good. [22]Then God blessed them, saying, "Let the fish multiply and fill the oceans. Let the birds increase and fill the earth." [23]This all happened on the fifth day.

[24]And God said, "Let the earth bring forth every kind of animal—livestock, small animals, and wildlife." And so it was. [25]God made all sorts of wild animals, livestock, and small animals, each able to reproduce more of its own kind. And God saw that it was good.

[26]Then God said, "Let us make people* in our image, to be like ourselves. They will be masters over all life—the fish in the sea, the birds in the sky, and all the livestock, wild animals,* and small animals."

[27] So God created people in his own image;
God patterned them after himself;
male and female he created them.

[28]God blessed them and told them, "Multiply and fill the earth and subdue it. Be masters over the fish and birds and all the animals." [29]And God said, "Look! I have given you the seed-bearing plants throughout the earth and all the fruit trees for your food. [30]And I have given all the grasses and other green plants to the animals and birds for their food." And so it was. [31]Then God looked over all he had made, and he saw that it was excellent in every way. This all happened on the sixth day.

## CHAPTER 2 **GOD MAKES ADAM AND EVE.**

So the creation of the heavens and the earth and everything in them was completed. [2]On the seventh day, having finished his task, God rested from all his work. [3]And God blessed the seventh day and declared it holy, because it was the day when he rested from his work of creation.

[4]This is the account of the creation of the heavens and the earth.

When the LORD God made the heavens and the earth, [5]there were no plants or grain growing on the earth, for the LORD God had not sent any rain. And no one was there to cultivate the soil. [6]But water came up out of the ground and watered all the land. [7]And the LORD God formed a man's body from the dust of the ground and breathed into it the breath of life. And the man became a living person.

[8]Then the LORD God planted a garden in Eden, in the east, and there he placed the man he had created. [9]And the LORD God planted all sorts of trees in the garden—beautiful trees that produced delicious fruit. At the center of the garden he placed the tree of life and the tree of the knowledge of good and evil.

[10]A river flowed from the land of Eden, watering the garden and then dividing into four branches. [11]One of these branches is the Pishon, which flows around the entire land of Havilah, where gold is found. [12]The gold of that land is exceptionally pure; aromatic resin and onyx stone are also found there. [13]The second branch is the Gihon, which flows around the entire land of Cush. [14]The third branch is the Tigris, which flows to the east of Asshur. The fourth branch is the Euphrates.

[15]The LORD God placed the man in the Garden of Eden to tend and care for it. [16]But the LORD God gave him this warning: "You may freely eat any fruit in the garden [17]except fruit from the tree of the knowledge of good and evil. If you eat of its fruit, you will surely die."

[18]And the LORD God said, "It is not good for the man to be alone. I will make a companion who will help him." [19]So the LORD God formed from the soil every kind of animal and bird. He brought them to Adam* to see what he would call them, and Adam chose a name for each one. [20]He gave names to all the livestock, birds, and wild animals. But still there was no companion suitable for him. [21]So the LORD God caused Adam to fall into a deep sleep. He took one of Adam's ribs* and closed up the place from which he had taken it. [22]Then the LORD God made a woman from the rib and brought her to Adam.

[23]"At last!" Adam exclaimed. "She is part of my own flesh and bone! She will be called 'woman,' because she was taken out of a man." [24]This explains why a man leaves his father and mother and is joined to his wife, and the two are united into one. [25]Now, although Adam and his wife were both naked, neither of them felt any shame.

### MARRIAGE ● ● ● • •

2:18-24 **God's creative work was not complete until he made woman. He could have made her from the dust of the ground, as he made man. God chose, however, to make her from the man's flesh and bone. In so doing, he illustrated that in marriage man and woman symbolically become one flesh. This is a mystical union of the couple's hearts and lives. Throughout the Bible, God treats this special partnership seriously. If you are planning to be married, are you willing to keep the commitment that makes the two of you one? The goal in marriage should be more than friendship; it should be oneness.**

**1:26a** Hebrew *man;* also in 1:27. **1:26b** As in Syriac version; Hebrew reads *all the earth.* **2:19** Hebrew *the man,* and so throughout this chapter. **2:21** Or *took a part of Adam's side.*

# Ultimate Issues

## THE ORIGIN OF HUMANITY

"It is now commonly accepted in scientific circles that human beings have become what they are today as a result of millions of years of EVOLUTION. Beginning as a one-celled animal. . . ." So reads the textbook used in biology classes in many public high schools today. "In the beginning God created the heavens and the earth. The earth was empty, a formless mass. . . ." So begins the book of Genesis. The Christian student faces a conflict: Whom to believe? Probably no other issue has drawn a sharper dividing line between religious and nonreligious thought in our society than that of the origin of the human race. Were we, as Genesis 1 and 2 state, placed here by SPECIAL DIVINE CREATION? Or did we, as many contemporary educators, philosophers, and others tell us, evolve from nothing into one-celled animals and on up the zoological chain into *Homo sapiens?* Or perhaps a third option—God created people, using the process of evolution as his "laboratory." Many young people feel the **UNEASY TENSION** that exists between these views. Their spiritual authorities—the Bible, the church, the pastor or youth minister—stand firmly in the creationist camp, while the public educational system, their biology teachers, and probably the majority of their peers lean heavily toward the evolutionist viewpoint. **Who's right?** Unfortunately, the Bible doesn't spell out in precise detail how human beings came to be. It does, however, give us some basic truths. First and foremost, human beings, like all the rest of the universe, are creations of God. The Bible states that fact in the clearest of terms—God is mentioned performing some part of his creative work 31 times in Genesis 1 alone. The idea that we simply materialized out of nothingness is a logical and scientific impossibility. The FIRST LAW OF THERMODYNAMICS tells us matter can neither be created nor destroyed by natural causes. For the strict naturalist/evolutionist, this is an insurmountable dilemma. If only natural causes are involved, how did nothing turn into something? And then, how did that something become something personal—with intelligence, morality, personality, and spirituality? By chance? Impossible. Absolutely, scientifically, intellectually, and **logically impossible.** The Christian, then, turns to the supernatural: ***God did it.*** It is a simple but utterly profound rationale. "In the beginning God created the heavens and the earth . . . ," and that sums it up. It does not rule out the possibility of some kind of God-directed evolution; neither does it give it any support. And frankly, honest evolutionists will admit that their beliefs involve as much faith and speculation—if not more—as the creationists'. Nobel Prize winner Ernst Chain said in 1970: "To postulate that the development and survival of the fittest is entirely a consequence of chance mutations seems to me a hypothesis based on no evidence and entirely irreconcilable with the facts. . . . It amazes me that [classical evolutionary theories] are swallowed so uncritically and readily, and for such a long time, by so many scientists without a murmur of protest." So the Bible, and Genesis in particular, gives us **ONE BEDROCK FACT** about the origin of humanity: God created us in his own image. Exactly how he did that remains a matter of faith, open to investigation by scientific inquiry. But the creationist position is as intellectually respectable as any of the alternatives. Every Christian can draw strength and confidence—and awe for his or her Creator—from knowing that.

CHAPTER **3** **THE MAN AND WOMAN SIN.** Now the serpent was the shrewdest of all the creatures the LORD
God had made. "Really?" he asked the woman. "Did
God really say you must not eat any of the fruit in the
garden?"
2"Of course we may eat it," the woman told him.
3"It's only the fruit from the tree at the center of the
garden that we are not allowed to eat. God says we
must not eat it or even touch it, or we will die."
4"You won't die!" the serpent hissed. 5"God
knows that your eyes will be opened when you eat it.
You will become just like God, knowing everything,
both good and evil."
6The woman was convinced. The fruit looked so
fresh and delicious, and it would make her so wise!
So she ate some of the fruit. She also gave some to
her husband, who was with her. Then he ate it, too.
7At that moment, their eyes were opened, and they
suddenly felt shame at their nakedness. So they
strung fig leaves together around their hips to cover
themselves.
8Toward evening they heard the LORD God walking about in the garden, so they hid themselves
among the trees. 9The LORD God called to Adam,*
"Where are you?"
10He replied, "I heard you, so I hid. I was afraid
because I was naked."
11"Who told you that you were naked?" the LORD
God asked. "Have you eaten the fruit I commanded
you not to eat?"
12"Yes," Adam admitted, "but it was the woman
you gave me who brought me the fruit, and I ate it."
13Then the LORD God asked the woman, "How
could you do such a thing?"
"The serpent tricked me," she replied. "That's
why I ate it."
14So the LORD God said to the serpent, "Because
you have done this, you will be punished. You are
singled out from all the domestic and wild animals
of the whole earth to be cursed. You will grovel in the
dust as long as you live, crawling along on your belly.
15From now on, you and the woman will be enemies,
and your offspring and her offspring will be enemies. He will crush your head, and you will strike his
heel."
16Then he said to the woman, "You will bear
children with intense pain and suffering. And
though your desire will be for your husband,* he
will be your master."
17And to Adam he said, "Because you listened to
your wife and ate the fruit I told you not to eat, I have
placed a curse on the ground. All your life you will
struggle to scratch a living from it. 18It will grow
thorns and thistles for you, though you will eat of its
grains. 19All your life you will sweat to produce food,
until your dying day. Then you will return to the
ground from which you came. For you were made
from dust, and to the dust you will return."
20Then Adam named his wife Eve,* because she
would be the mother of all people everywhere. 21And
the LORD God made clothing from animal skins for
Adam and his wife.
22Then the LORD God said, "The people have become as we are, knowing everything, both good and

**When I read about creation and miracles in the Bible, I get confused. How do science and the Bible relate?**

The Bible and science debate has raged for many years. Conflicts arise when we look for spiritual answers from science or for scientific answers in the Bible.

A former Vietnam POW told of the time he was allowed to send a cassette tape home to his family. Realizing that it might be the last communication he would ever have with those he loved, he took extensive notes on what he would cover before he began to make the tape. His goal was to communicate the most important things that his family should know. To his wife, he talked of insurance, mortgages, child rearing, and relatives. To the kids, he personalized each message so that he touched on unique situations they would face the next few years as they grew up without him. To all of them he was careful to say how much he loved them.

This is exactly the purpose behind the Bible. God put 66 books together to let his creation know the most important things about life, about what to do in certain situations, and especially about the extent of his love for them.

For some reason he chose to leave out dinosaurs, fusion, and gravity (among other significant discoveries). Instead he included stories of real people with real struggles who faced hardship and trials, many of whom conquered fears and circumstances because they realized that if God was for them, no one could be against them! Many other stories are included of those who rejected God and then experienced tragic consequences.

Most of these biblical examples tell us much more about living, surviving, and prospering in a complicated society than science could ever hope to promise.

Your mind matters to God—he wants you to think. Never be afraid to ask tough questions about the Bible or the Christian faith. But also consider the appropriateness of each question. Is this the kind of question the Bible should answer? And do the same with science, asking the right questions.

Creation and the resurrection of Jesus Christ are two of the most important tenets of the Christian faith. Although neither can be duplicated in a laboratory, they also cannot be proven to be false by science.

If God can create life from nothing, as well as raise a man from the dead, he can lead us through this life and the next. We can trust him.

**3:9** Hebrew *the man,* and so throughout this chapter. **3:16** Or *And though you may desire to control your husband.* **3:20** *Eve* sounds like a Hebrew term that means "to give life."

evil. What if they eat the fruit of the tree of life? Then they will live forever!" 23So the LORD God banished Adam and his wife from the Garden of Eden, and he sent Adam out to cultivate the ground from which he had been made. 24After banishing them from the garden, the LORD God stationed mighty angelic beings* to the east of Eden. And a flaming sword flashed back and forth, guarding the way to the tree of life.

CHAPTER **4** **CAIN, ABEL, AND SETH.** Now Adam* slept with his wife, Eve, and she became pregnant. When the time came, she gave birth to Cain,* and she said, "With the LORD's help, I have brought forth* a man!" 2Later she gave birth to a second son and named him Abel.

When they grew up, Abel became a shepherd, while Cain was a farmer. 3At harvesttime Cain brought to the LORD a gift of his farm produce, 4while Abel brought several choice lambs from the best of his flock. The LORD accepted Abel and his offering, 5but he did not accept Cain and his offering. This made Cain very angry and dejected.

6"Why are you so angry?" the LORD asked him. "Why do you look so dejected? 7You will be accepted if you respond in the right way. But if you refuse to respond correctly, then watch out! Sin is waiting to attack and destroy you, and you must subdue it."

8Later Cain suggested to his brother, Abel, "Let's go out into the fields."* And while they were there, Cain attacked and killed his brother.

9Afterward the LORD asked Cain, "Where is your brother? Where is Abel?"

"I don't know!" Cain retorted. "Am I supposed to keep track of him wherever he goes?"

## BAD APPLE ● ● • • •

**4:8-10 Adam and Eve's disobedience brought sin into the human race. They may have thought their sin (eating a "harmless" piece of fruit) wasn't very bad, but notice how quickly their sinful nature developed in the lives of their children. Simple disobedience degenerated into outright murder. Adam and Eve acted only against God, but Cain acted against both God and man. A small sin has a way of growing out of control. Let God help you with your little sins before they turn into tragedies.**

10But the LORD said, "What have you done? Listen—your brother's blood cries out to me from the ground! 11You are hereby banished from the ground you have defiled with your brother's blood. 12No longer will it yield abundant crops for you, no matter how hard you work! From now on you will be a homeless fugitive on the earth, constantly wandering from place to place."

13Cain replied to the LORD, "My punishment* is too great for me to bear! 14You have banished me from my land and from your presence; you have made me a wandering fugitive. All who see me will try to kill me!"

15The LORD replied, "They will not kill you, for I will give seven times your punishment to anyone who does." Then the LORD put a mark on Cain to warn anyone who might try to kill him. 16So Cain left the LORD's presence and settled in the land of Nod,* east of Eden.

17Then Cain's wife became pregnant and gave birth to a son, and they named him Enoch. When Cain founded a city, he named it Enoch after his son.

18 Enoch was the father of* Irad.
Irad was the father of Mehujael.
Mehujael was the father of Methushael.
Methushael was the father of Lamech.

19Lamech married two women—Adah and Zillah. 20Adah gave birth to a baby named Jabal. He became the first of the herdsmen who live in tents. 21His brother's name was Jubal, the first musician—the inventor of the harp and flute. 22To Lamech's other wife, Zillah, was born Tubal-cain. He was the first to work with metal, forging instruments of bronze and iron. Tubal-cain had a sister named Naamah.

23One day Lamech said to Adah and Zillah, "Listen to me, my wives. I have killed a youth who attacked and wounded me. 24If anyone who kills Cain is to be punished seven times, anyone who takes revenge against me will be punished seventy-seven times!"

25Adam slept with his wife again, and she gave birth to another son. She named him Seth,* for she said, "God has granted me another son in place of Abel, the one Cain killed." 26When Seth grew up, he had a son and named him Enosh. It was during his lifetime that people first began to worship the LORD.

## SATAN'S PLAN

| | |
|---|---|
| Doubt | Makes you question God's Word and his goodness |
| Discouragement | Makes you look at your problems rather than at God |
| Diversion | Makes the wrong things seem attractive so you want them more than the right things |
| Defeat | Makes you feel like a failure, so you don't even try |
| Delay | Makes you put off doing something, so it never gets done |

3:24 Hebrew *cherubim.* 4:1a Hebrew *the man.* 4:1b *Cain* sounds like a Hebrew term that can mean "bring forth" or "acquire." 4:1c Or *I have acquired.* 4:13 Or *My sin.* 4:16 *Nod* means "wandering." 4:8 As in Samaritan Pentateuch, Greek and Syriac versions, Latin Vulgate; Masoretic Text lacks *"Let's go out into the fields."* 4:18 Or *the ancestor of,* and so throughout the verse. 4:25 *Seth* probably means "granted"; the name may also mean "appointed."

CHAPTER 5 **FROM ADAM TO NOAH.** This is the history
of the descendants of Adam. When God created
people,* he made them in the likeness of God. 2He
created them male and female, and he blessed them
and called them "human."*
3When Adam was 130 years old, his son Seth was
born,* and Seth was the very image of his
father.* 4After the birth of Seth,* Adam lived
another 800 years, and he had other sons and
daughters. 5He died at the age of 930.
6When Seth was 105 years
old, his son Enosh was
born. 7After the birth
of Enosh, Seth lived
another 807 years, and
he had other sons and
daughters. 8He died at
the age of 912.
9When Enosh was 90 years
old, his son Kenan was
born. 10After the birth
of Kenan, Enosh lived
another 815 years, and
he had other sons and
daughters. 11He died at
the age of 905.
12When Kenan was 70 years
old, his son Mahalalel
was born. 13After the
birth of Mahalalel,
Kenan lived another 840
years, and he had other
sons and daughters. 14He
died at the age of 910.
15When Mahalalel was 65
years old, his son Jared
was born. 16After the
birth of Jared, Mahalalel
lived 830 years, and he
had other sons and
daughters. 17He died at
the age of 895.
18When Jared was 162 years
old, his son Enoch was
born. 19After the birth
of Enoch, Jared lived
another 800 years, and
he had other sons and
daughters. 20He died at
the age of 962.
21When Enoch was 65 years
old, his son Methuselah
was born. 22After the
birth of Methuselah,
Enoch lived another 300
years in close fellowship
with God, and he had
other sons and
daughters. 23Enoch lived 365 years in all. 24He
enjoyed a close relationship with God throughout his life. Then suddenly, he disappeared
because God took him.
25When Methuselah was 187 years old, his son
Lamech was born. 26After the birth of Lamech,
Methuselah lived another 782 years, and he had
other sons and daughters. 27He died at the age
of 969.
28When Lamech was 182 years old, his son Noah

## ADAM & EVE

**ADAM & EVE** were the only two humans who never experienced being young. Depending on how you feel, they may or may not have missed a lot! But try to imagine starting out life as an adult—no memories, no mistakes, no past little lessons to help you make adult decisions. . . . Most of us don't realize how much we learn or fail to learn during our growing years until it's too late.

For instance, we have many opportunities to learn as children that while there are some trustworthy people in our lives, not everyone can be trusted. We learn not to immediately trust new advice. We discover it is often helpful to compare it to wisdom we already have, or even to ask someone who has been trustworthy to evaluate the new advice. Eve got some new information: "The fruit is great. . . God's being selfish. . . you will be like him." She trusted new advice even though it went against what had been trustworthy. She ate the fruit. She failed to trust the one who had never failed her. Adam made the same mistake. New advice, no questions, no checking . . . he ate the fruit. Both of them disobeyed God. The result was death!

Like Adam and Eve, we often have to live with the painful consequences of accepting bad advice. But consequences are reminders of hard lessons. They are not excuses to give up or to repeat the same mistakes.

How do you evaluate new advice? Are your past mistakes and successes helping you make better decisions? How often do you seriously consider the source as well as the advice?

**UPS:**
- The first male and female, husband and wife, human beings
- First to be made in the image of God
- First caretakers of creation
- First to know God personally

**DOWNS:**
- Both tended to handle mistakes and sin by excuses or blaming others
- Acted without considering consequences
- Together they brought sin into the creation

**STATS:**
- Where: Garden of Eden
- Occupation: Husband and wife, caretakers of Eden
- Relatives: Sons: Cain, Abel, Seth. Numerous other children.

LESSONS: As Adam and Eve's descendants, we all reflect to some degree the image of God

The basic tendency to sin goes back to the beginning of the human race

God wants people who are free to sin to choose instead to trust and love him

God's design for marriage was part of Creation

KEY VERSE: "So God created people in his own image; God patterned them after himself; male and female he created them" (Genesis 1:27).

Adam and Eve's story is told in Genesis 1:26–4:26. They are also mentioned in 1 Chronicles 1:1; Job 31:33; Luke 3:38; Romans 5:14; 1 Corinthians 15:22,45; 1 Timothy 2:13-14.

5:1 Hebrew *man.* 5:2 Hebrew *man.* 5:3a Or *his son, the ancestor of Seth, was born;* similarly in 5:6, 9, 12, 15, 18, 21, 25. 5:3b Hebrew *was in his own likeness, after his image.* 5:4 Or *After the birth of this ancestor of Seth;* similarly in 5:7, 10, 13, 16, 19, 22, 26.

was born. [29]Lamech named his son Noah,* for
he said, "He will bring us relief from the painful
labor of farming this ground that the LORD has
cursed." [30]After the birth of Noah, Lamech lived
595 years, and he had other sons and daughters.
[31]He died at the age of 777.
[32]By the time Noah was 500 years old, he had three
sons: Shem, Ham, and Japheth.

CHAPTER **6** **NOAH AND THE FLOOD.** When the human population began to grow rapidly on the earth,
[2]the sons of God saw the beautiful women of the
human race and took any they wanted as their wives.
[3]Then the LORD said, "My Spirit will not put up with
humans for such a long time, for they are only
mortal flesh. In the future, they will live no more
than 120 years."
[4]In those days, and even afterward, giants* lived
on the earth, for whenever the sons of God had
intercourse with human women, they gave birth to
children who became the heroes mentioned in leg-
ends of old.

## VIOLENCE

On Friday nights at seven o'clock you're practically guaranteed to find Derek and Steve in one of two places. Check first at Derek's. If they're not there, munching pizza and watching horror movies on video, try the mall. They probably will be standing in line at the movie theater, anxiously waiting for the chance to purchase tickets for the newest cinematic tale of gore.

In the last couple of years, these guys have seen hundreds of violent movies. It doesn't matter what the plot is–deranged killers on the loose, murderous monsters on the rampage, savage mutants from outer space–as long as there are some gruesome torture scenes, lots of mutilated bodies, and gallons of blood and guts, Derek and Steve are satisfied.

"That one scene was so weak," Steve complains as he ejects a video one Friday.

"Which one?" Derek responds.

"You know, the one where he shoved the girl into that giant meat grinder. . . . I mean, the blood didn't even look real."

"Tell me about it!" Derek agrees. "Every scene in the whole movie was just ripped off from another movie."

"Want to watch *Babies with Rabies* now?"

"Sure. But let me go get some more cherry soda first."

See how God feels about individuals and societies that are tolerant of violence–Genesis 6:11-13.

[5]Now the LORD observed the extent of the
people's wickedness, and he saw that all their
thoughts were consistently and totally evil. [6]So the
LORD was sorry he had ever made them. It broke
his heart. [7]And the LORD said, "I will completely
wipe out this human race that I have created. Yes,
and I will destroy all the animals and birds, too. I

## WORRYWART ● ● ● • •

7:15-16 **Many have wondered how this animal kingdom roundup happened. Did Noah and his sons spend years collecting them? In reality the creation, along with Noah, was doing just as God had commanded. There seemed to be no problem gathering the animals–God took care of the details of that job while Noah was doing his part by building the boat. Often we do just the opposite of Noah. We worry about details in our lives over which we have no control, while neglecting specific areas (such as attitudes, relationships, responsibilities) that *are* under our control. Like Noah, concentrate on what God has given you to do, and leave the rest to him.**

am sorry I ever made them." [8]But Noah found
favor with the LORD.
[9]This is the history of Noah and his family.
Noah was a righteous man, the only blameless
man living on earth at the time. He consistently
followed God's will and enjoyed a close relationship with him. [10]Noah had three sons: Shem, Ham,
and Japheth.
[11]Now the earth had become corrupt in God's
sight, and it was filled with violence. [12]God observed all this corruption in the world, and he saw
violence and depravity everywhere. [13]So God said
to Noah, "I have decided to destroy all living creatures, for the earth is filled with violence because
of them. Yes, I will wipe them all from the face of
the earth!
[14]"Make a boat* from resinous wood and seal it
with tar, inside and out. Then construct decks and
stalls throughout its interior. [15]Make it 450 feet
long, 75 feet wide, and 45 feet high.* [16]Construct
an opening all the way around the boat, 18 inches*
below the roof. Then put three decks inside the
boat—bottom, middle, and upper—and put a
door in the side.
[17]"Look! I am about to cover the earth with a
flood that will destroy every living thing. Everything
on earth will die! [18]But I solemnly swear to keep you
safe in the boat, with your wife and your sons and
their wives. [19]Bring a pair of every kind of animal—a
male and a female—into the boat with you to keep
them alive during the flood. [20]Pairs of each kind of
bird and each kind of animal, large and small alike,
will come to you to be kept alive. [21]And remember,
take enough food for your family and for all the
animals."
[22]So Noah did everything exactly as God had commanded him.

CHAPTER **7** **GOD SENDS THE GREAT FLOOD.** Finally,
the day came when the LORD said to Noah, "Go into
the boat with all your family, for among all the
people of the earth, I consider you alone to be righteous. [2]Take along seven pairs of each animal that I
have approved for eating and for sacrifice, and take
one pair of each of the others. [3]Then select seven
pairs of every kind of bird. There must be a male and
a female in each pair to ensure that every kind of

5:29 *Noah* sounds like a Hebrew term that can mean "relief" or "comfort." 6:4 Hebrew *Nephilim.* 6:14 Traditionally rendered *an ark.*
6:15 Hebrew *300 cubits* [135 meters] *long, 50 cubits* [22.5 meters] *wide, and 30 cubits* [13.5 meters] *high.* 6:16 Hebrew *1 cubit* [45 centimeters].

living creature will survive the flood. 4One week
from today I will begin forty days and forty nights of
rain. And I will wipe from the earth all the living
things I have created."
5So Noah did exactly as the LORD had commanded him. 6He was 600 years old when the
flood came, 7and he went aboard the boat to escape—he and his wife and his sons and their
wives. 8With them were all the various kinds of
animals—those approved for eating and sacrifice
and those that were not—along with all the birds
and other small animals. 9They came into the boat
in pairs, male and female, just as God had commanded Noah. 10One week later, the flood came
and covered the earth.
11When Noah was 600 years old, on the seventeenth
day of the second month, the underground waters
burst forth on the earth, and
the rain fell in mighty torrents from the sky. 12The
rain continued to fall for
forty days and forty nights.
13But Noah had gone into
the boat that very day with
his wife and his sons—Shem,
Ham, and Japheth—and
their wives. 14With them in
the boat were pairs of every
kind of breathing animal—
domestic and wild, large and
small—along with birds and
flying insects of every kind.
15Two by two they came into
the boat, 16male and female,
just as God had commanded.
Then the LORD shut them in.
17For forty days the
floods prevailed, covering
the ground and lifting the
boat high above the earth.
18As the waters rose higher
and higher above the
ground, the boat floated
safely on the surface. 19Fi-
nally, the water covered
even the highest mountains
on the earth, 20standing
more than twenty-two feet*
above the highest peaks.
21All the living things on
earth died—birds, domes-
tic animals, wild animals,
all kinds of small animals,
and all the people. 22Every-
thing died that breathed
and lived on dry land.
23Every living thing on the
earth was wiped out—
people, animals both large
and small, and birds. They were all destroyed, and
only Noah was left alive, along with those who
were with him in the boat. 24And the water covered
the earth for 150 days.

CHAPTER **8** **THE FLOOD RECEDES.** But God remembered Noah and all the animals in the boat.
He sent a wind to blow across the waters, and the
floods began to disappear. 2The underground water sources ceased thushing, and the torrential
rains stopped. 3So the flood gradually began to
recede. After 150 days, 4exactly five months from
the time the flood began,* the boat came to rest
on the mountains of Ararat. 5Two and a half
months later,* as the waters continued to go
down, other mountain peaks began to appear.
6After another forty days, Noah opened the

**UPS:**
- First member of the Hall of Faith in Hebrews 11:4
- First shepherd
- First martyr for truth (Matthew 23:35)

**STATS:**
- Where: Just outside of Eden
- Occupation: Shepherd
- Relatives: Parents: Adam and Eve. Brother: Cain.

## ABEL

No matter what parents do, their kids don't always get along. In most cases, all the squabbling and fighting that goes on eventually creates a strong bond between brothers and sisters. We love them even when we hate them. Sometimes, though, we find it's easier to hurt than to help. The death of Adam and Eve's son Abel shows us how bad this can get.

Abel was the second child born into the world, but the first one to obey God. He worshiped in a way that pleased God. That really bothered his brother Cain. We don't know how Abel felt, but he must have known Cain was angry at him. Brothers and sisters know things like that about each other. Yet Abel trusted his brother even when Cain suggested they go out to the field together. Abel was the kind of brother worth having. Once in a while we need to let our brothers and sisters know we think they're worth having and trusting.

The Bible doesn't tell us why God liked Abel's gift and disliked Cain's, but both brothers knew what God expected. Only Abel obeyed. He is remembered for his obedience and faith (Hebrews 11:4), and he is called "righteous" (Matthew 23:35). When we know what God wants, we need to obey like Abel, no matter what the cost, and trust God to make things work out right.

LESSONS: God hears those who come to him with a right heart

God recognizes the innocent person, and sooner or later he judges the guilty

KEY VERSE: "It was by faith that Abel brought a more acceptable offering to God than Cain did. God accepted Abel's offering to show that he was a righteous man. And although Abel is long dead, he still speaks to us because of his faith" (Hebrews 11:4).

Abel's story is told in Genesis 4:1-8. He is also mentioned in Matthew 23:35; Luke 11:51; Hebrews 11:4; 12:24.

7:20 Hebrew *15 cubits* [6.8 meters]. 8:4 Hebrew *on the seventeenth day of the seventh month;* see 7:11. 8:5 Hebrew *On the first day of the tenth month;* see 7:11 and note on 8:4.

window he had made in the boat [7]and released a raven that flew back and forth until the earth was dry. [8]Then he sent out a dove to see if it could find dry ground. [9]But the dove found no place to land because the water was still too high. So it returned to the boat, and Noah held out his hand and drew the dove back inside. [10]Seven days later, Noah released the dove again. [11]This time, toward evening, the bird returned to him with a fresh olive leaf in its beak. Noah now knew that the water was almost gone. [12]A week later, he released the dove again, and this time it did not come back.

[13]Finally, when Noah was 601 years old, ten and a half months after the flood began,* Noah lifted back the cover to look. The water was drying up. [14]Two more months went by,* and at last the earth was dry! [15]Then God said to Noah, [16]"Leave the boat, all of you. [17]Release all the animals and birds so they can breed and reproduce in great numbers." [18]So Noah, his wife, and his sons and their wives left the boat. [19]And all the various kinds of animals and birds came out, pair by pair.

[20]Then Noah built an altar to the LORD and sacrificed on it the animals and birds that had been approved for that purpose. [21]And the LORD was pleased with the sacrifice and said to himself, "I will never again curse the earth, destroying all living things, even though people's thoughts and actions are bent toward evil from childhood. [22]As long as the earth remains, there will be springtime and harvest, cold and heat, winter and summer, day and night."

## MURDERERS ● ● • • •

**9:5-6 Here God explains why murder is so wrong: to kill a person is to kill one made like God. Because human beings are made in God's image, all people possess the qualities that distinguish us from animals: morality, reason, creativity, and self-worth. When we interact with others, we are interacting with beings made by God, beings to whom God offers eternal life. God wants us to recognize these special qualities in all people.**

## CHAPTER 9 **GOD'S COVENANT WITH NOAH.**

God blessed Noah and his sons and told them, "Multiply and fill the earth. [2]All the wild animals, large and small, and all the birds and fish will be afraid of you. I have placed them in your power. [3]I have given them to you for food, just as I have given you grain and vegetables. [4]But you must never eat animals that still have their lifeblood in them. [5]And murder is forbidden. Animals that kill people must die, and any person who murders must be killed. [6]Yes, you must execute anyone who murders another person, for to kill a person is to kill a living being made in God's image. [7]Now you must have many children and repopulate the earth. Yes, multiply and fill the earth!"

[8]Then God told Noah and his sons, [9]"I am making a covenant with you and your descendants, [10]and with the animals you brought with you—all these birds and livestock and wild animals. [11]I solemnly promise never to send another flood to kill all living creatures and destroy the earth." [12]And God said, "I am giving you a sign as evidence of my eternal covenant with you and all living creatures. [13]I have placed my rainbow in the clouds. It is the sign of my permanent promise to you and to all the earth. [14]When I send clouds over the earth, the rainbow will be seen in the clouds, [15]and I will remember my covenant with you and with everything that lives. Never again will there be a flood that will destroy all life. [16]When I see the rainbow in the clouds, I will remember the eternal covenant between God and every living creature on earth." [17]Then God said to Noah, "Yes, this is the sign of my covenant with all the creatures of the earth."

[18]Shem, Ham, and Japheth, the three sons of Noah, survived the Flood with their father. (Ham is the ancestor of the Canaanites.) [19]From these three sons of Noah came all the people now scattered across the earth.

[20]After the Flood, Noah became a farmer and planted a vineyard. [21]One day he became drunk on some wine he had made and lay naked in his tent. [22]Ham, the father of Canaan, saw that his father was naked and went outside and told his brothers. [23]Shem and Japheth took a robe, held it over their shoulders, walked backward into the tent, and covered their father's naked body. As they did this, they looked the other way so they wouldn't see him naked. [24]When Noah woke up from his drunken stupor, he learned what Ham, his youngest son, had done. [25]Then he cursed the descendants of Canaan, the son of Ham:

"A curse on the Canaanites!
May they be the lowest of servants
  to the descendants of Shem and Japheth."

[26]Then Noah said,

"May Shem be blessed by the LORD my God;
  and may Canaan be his servant.
[27]May God enlarge the territory of Japheth,
  and may he share the prosperity of Shem;*
  and let Canaan be his servant."

[28]Noah lived another 350 years after the Flood. [29]He was 950 years old when he died.

## CHAPTER 10

This is the history of the families of Shem, Ham, and Japheth, the three sons of Noah. Many children were born to them after the Flood.

[2]The descendants of Japheth were Gomer, Magog,
  Madai, Javan, Tubal, Meshech, and Tiras.
[3]The descendants of Gomer were Ashkenaz,
  Riphath, and Togarmah.

8:13 Hebrew *on the first day of the first month;* see 7:11. 8:14 Hebrew *The twenty-seventh day of the second month arrived;* see note on 8:13.
9:27 Hebrew *may he live in the tents of Shem.*

[4]The descendants of Javan were Elishah, Tarshish,
Kittim, and Rodanim.* [5]Their descendants
became the seafaring peoples in various lands,
each tribe with its own language.

[6]The descendants of Ham were Cush, Mizraim,*
Put, and Canaan.
[7]The descendants of Cush were Seba, Havilah,
Sabtah, Raamah, and Sabteca. The descendants
of Raamah were Sheba and Dedan.

[8]One of Cush's descendants was Nimrod, who
became a heroic warrior. [9]He was a mighty hunter
in the LORD's sight.* His name became proverbial,
and people would speak of someone as being
"like Nimrod, a mighty hunter in the LORD's
sight." [10]He built the foundation for his empire in
the land of Babylonia,* with the cities of Babel,
Erech, Akkad, and Calneh. [11]From there he
extended his reign to Assyria, where he built
Nineveh, Rehoboth-ir,
Calah, [12]and Resen—the
main city of the empire,
located between Nineveh
and Calah.
[13]Mizraim was the ancestor
of the Ludites, Anamites,
Lehabites, Naphtuhites,
[14]Pathrusites, Casluhites,
and the Caphtorites, from
whom the Philistines
came.*
[15]Canaan's oldest son was
Sidon, the ancestor of
the Sidonians. Canaan
was also the ancestor of
the Hittites, [16]Jebusites,
Amorites, Girgashites,
[17]Hivites, Arkites, Sinites,
[18]Arvadites, Zemarites,
and Hamathites.
[19]Eventually the territory
of Canaan spread from
Sidon to Gerar, near
Gaza, and to Sodom,
Gomorrah, Admah, and
Zeboiim, near Lasha.

[20]These were the descendants of Ham, identified according to their tribes, languages, territories, and nations.

[21]Sons were also born to
Shem, the older brother
of Japheth.* Shem was
the ancestor of all the
descendants of Eber. [22]The
descendants of Shem
were Elam, Asshur, Arphaxad, Lud, and Aram.
[23]The descendants of Aram were Uz, Hul, Gether,
and Mash.
[24]Arphaxad was the father of Shelah,* and Shelah
was the father of Eber. [25]Eber had two sons.
The first was named Peleg—"division"—for
during his lifetime the people of the world were
divided into different language groups and
dispersed. His brother's name was Joktan.
[26]Joktan was the ancestor of Almodad, Sheleph,
Hazarmaveth, Jerah, [27]Hadoram, Uzal, Diklah,
[28]Obal, Abimael, Sheba, [29]Ophir, Havilah, and
Jobab. [30]The descendants of Joktan lived in the
area extending from Mesha toward the eastern
hills of Sephar.

[31]These were the descendants of Shem, identified according to their tribes, languages, territories, and nations.

**UPS:**
- Only follower of God left in his generation
- Second father of the human race
- Man of patience, consistency, and obedience
- First major shipbuilder in history

**STATS:**
- Where: We're not told how far from the Garden of Eden people had settled
- Occupation: Farmer, shipbuilder, preacher
- Relatives: Grandfather: Methuselah. Father: Lamech. Sons: Ham, Shem, and Japheth.

**NOAH** The story of Noah's life involved not one, but two great and tragic floods. The first was a flood of evil. The world had become so bad that there was only one person left who remembered the God of creation, perfection, and love. Noah was the last of God's people.

God's response to this flood of evil was a 120-year-long last chance. During those years, he had Noah build a large advertisement of what God was going to do. Nothing like a huge boat built on dry land to make a point! Of course, everyone thought Noah was crazy. Despite the jeers of his friends and neighbors, Noah continued to build. When the flood came, no one could say they hadn't been warned. For Noah, obedience to God meant a long-term courageous commitment to a project.

Many of us have trouble sticking to any project, whether or not it is directed by God. Or we back off when opposition occurs. Noah obeyed God and worked on one project longer than we even expect to live. The only project we have that is like Noah's is our life. Maybe this is the biggest lesson and challenge Noah's life can give us: we should live an entire lifetime of obedience, depending on God's help.

LESSONS: God is faithful to those who obey him
God does not always protect us from trouble, but cares for us in spite of trouble
Obedience is a long-term commitment
A man may be faithful, but his sinful nature always travels with him

KEY VERSE: "So Noah did everything exactly as God had commanded him" (Genesis 6:22).

Noah's story is told in Genesis 5:29–10:32. He is also mentioned in 1 Chronicles 1:4; Isaiah 54:9; Ezekiel 14:14,20; Matthew 24:37-38; Luke 3:36; 17:26-27; Hebrews 11:7; 1 Peter 3:20; 2 Peter 2:5.

10:4 As in some Hebrew manuscripts and Greek version (see also 1 Chr 1:7); most Hebrew manuscripts read *Dodanim.* 10:6 Or *Egypt;* also in 10:13. 10:9 Hebrew *a mighty hunter before the LORD;* also in 10:9b. 10:10 Hebrew *Shinar.* 10:14 Hebrew *Casluhites, from whom the Philistines came, Caphtorites.* Compare Jer 47:4; Amos 9:7. 10:21 Or *Shem, whose older brother was Japheth.* 10:24 Greek version reads *Arphaxad was the father of Cainan, Cainan was the father of Shelah.*

[32]These are the families that came from Noah's sons, listed nation by nation according to their lines of descent. The earth was populated with the people of these nations after the Flood.

CHAPTER **11** **THE TOWER OF BABEL.** At one time the whole world spoke a single language and used the same words. [2]As the people migrated eastward, they found a plain in the land of Babylonia* and settled there. [3]They began to talk about construction projects. "Come," they said, "let's make great piles of burnt brick and collect natural asphalt to use as mortar. [4]Let's build a great city with a tower that reaches to the skies—a monument to our greatness! This will bring us together and keep us from scattering all over the world."

## TOWERING PRIDE ● ● • • •

11:4 **The tower of Babel was a great human achievement, a wonder of the world. But it was a monument to the people themselves rather than to God. We often build monuments to ourselves (expensive clothes, big house, fancy car, important job) to call attention to our achievements. These may not be wrong in themselves, but when we use them to give us identity and self-worth, they take God's place in our lives. We are free to develop in many areas, but we are not free to think we have replaced God. What "monuments" are in your life?**

[5]But the LORD came down to see the city and the tower the people were building. [6]"Look!" he said. "If they can accomplish this when they have just begun to take advantage of their common language and political unity, just think of what they will do later. Nothing will be impossible for them! [7]Come, let's go down and give them different languages. Then they won't be able to understand each other."

[8]In that way, the LORD scattered them all over the earth; and that ended the building of the city. [9]That is why the city was called Babel,* because it was there that the LORD confused the people by giving them many languages, thus scattering them across the earth.

[10]This is the history of Shem's family.

When Shem was 100 years old, his son Arphaxad was born. This happened two years after the Flood. [11]After the birth of Arphaxad, Shem lived another 500 years and had other sons and daughters.

[12]When Arphaxad was 35 years old, his son Shelah was born.* [13]After the birth of Shelah, Arphaxad lived another 403 years and had other sons and daughters.*

[14]When Shelah was 30 years old, his son Eber was born. [15]After the birth of Eber, Shelah lived another 403 years and had other sons and daughters.

[16]When Eber was 34 years old, his son Peleg was born. [17]After the birth of Peleg, Eber lived another 430 years and had other sons and daughters.

[18]When Peleg was 30 years old, his son Reu was born. [19]After the birth of Reu, Peleg lived another 209 years and had other sons and daughters.

[20]When Reu was 32 years old, his son Serug was born. [21]After the birth of Serug, Reu lived another 207 years and had other sons and daughters.

[22]When Serug was 30 years old, his son Nahor was born. [23]After the birth of Nahor, Serug lived another 200 years and had other sons and daughters.

[24]When Nahor was 29 years old, his son Terah was born. [25]After the birth of Terah, Nahor lived another 119 years and had other sons and daughters.

[26]When Terah was 70 years old, he became the father of Abram, Nahor, and Haran.

[27]This is the history of Terah's family. Terah was the father of Abram, Nahor, and Haran; and Haran had a son named Lot. [28]But while Haran was still young, he died in Ur of the Chaldeans, the place of his birth. He was survived by Terah, his father. [29]Meanwhile, Abram married Sarai, and his brother Nahor married Milcah, the daughter of their brother Haran. (Milcah had a sister named Iscah.) [30]Now Sarai was not able to have any children.

[31]Terah took his son Abram, his daughter-in-law Sarai, and his grandson Lot (his son Haran's child) and left Ur of the Chaldeans to go to the land of Canaan. But they stopped instead at the village of Haran and settled there. [32]Terah lived for 205 years* and died while still at Haran.

CHAPTER **12** **THE CALL OF ABRAM.** Then the LORD told Abram, "Leave your country, your relatives, and your father's house, and go to the land that I will show you. [2]I will cause you to become the father of a great nation. I will bless you and make you famous, and I

## DON'T MISS OUT ● ● • • •

12:2 **God promised to bless Abram and make him famous, but there was one condition. Abram had to do what God wanted him to do. This meant leaving his home and friends and traveling to a new land where God promised to build a great nation from Abram's family. Abram obeyed, leaving his home for God's promise of even greater blessings in the future. God may be trying to lead you to a place of greater service and usefulness for him. Don't let the comfort and security of your present position make you miss God's plan for you.**

11:2 Hebrew *Shinar.* 11:9 *Babel* sounds like a Hebrew term that means "confusion." 11:12 Or *his son, the ancestor of Shelah, was born;* similarly in 11:14, 16, 18, 20, 22, 24. 11:12-13 Greek version reads *[12]When Arphaxad was 135 years old, his son Cainan was born. [13]After the birth of Cainan, Arphaxad lived another 430 years and had other sons and daughters, and then he died. When Cainan was 130 years old, his son Shelah was born. After the birth of Shelah, Cainan lived another 330 years and had other sons and daughters, and then he died.* 11:32 Some ancient versions read *145 years;* compare 11:26; 12:4.

will make you a blessing to others. 3I will bless those who bless you and curse those who curse you. All the families of the earth will be blessed through you."

4So Abram departed as the LORD had instructed him, and Lot went with him. Abram was seventy-five years old when he left Haran. 5He took his wife, Sarai, his nephew Lot, and all his wealth—his livestock and all the people who had joined his household at Haran—and finally arrived in Canaan. 6Traveling through Canaan, they came to a place near Shechem and set up camp beside the oak at Moreh. At that time, the area was inhabited by Canaanites.

7Then the LORD appeared to Abram and said, "I am going to give this land to your offspring.*" And Abram built an altar there to commemorate the LORD's visit. 8After that, Abram traveled southward and set up camp in the hill country between Bethel on the west and Ai on the east. There he built an altar and worshiped the LORD. 9Then Abram traveled south by stages toward the Negev.

10At that time there was a severe famine in the land, so Abram went down to Egypt to wait it out. 11As he was approaching the borders of Egypt, Abram said to Sarai, "You are a very beautiful woman. 12When the Egyptians see you, they will say, 'This is his wife. Let's kill him; then we can have her!' 13But if you say you are my sister, then the Egyptians will treat me well because of their interest in you, and they will spare my life."

14And sure enough, when they arrived in Egypt, everyone spoke of her beauty. 15When the palace officials saw her, they sang her praises to their king, the pharaoh, and she was taken into his harem. 16Then Pharaoh gave Abram many gifts because of her—sheep, cattle, donkeys, male and female servants, and camels.

17But the LORD sent a terrible plague upon Pharaoh's household because of Sarai, Abram's wife. 18So Pharaoh called for Abram and accused him sharply. "What is this you have done to me?" he demanded. "Why didn't you tell me she was your wife? 19Why were you willing to let me marry her, saying she was your sister? Here is your wife! Take her and be gone!" 20Pharaoh then sent them out of the country under armed escort—Abram and his wife, with all their household and belongings.

## CHAPTER 13

**ABRAM AND LOT SEPARATE.** So they left Egypt and traveled north into the Negev—Abram with his wife and Lot and all that they owned, 2for Abram was very rich in livestock, silver, and gold. 3Then they continued traveling by stages toward Bethel, to the place between Bethel and Ai where they had camped before. 4This was the place where Abram had built the altar, and there he again worshiped the LORD.

5Now Lot, who was traveling with Abram, was also very wealthy with sheep, cattle, and many tents. 6But the land could not support both Abram and Lot with all their flocks and herds living so close together. There were too many animals for the available pastureland. 7So an argument broke out between the herdsmen of

12:7 Hebrew *seed.*

### ABRAHAM

As you read about Abraham's life, you will probably ask: "What on earth made God like this man so much?" Abraham made a lot of mistakes, and some of his mistakes had long-range consequences.

Yet what you will find if you read carefully is that in spite of his mistakes, Abraham trusted God with his life. This is the main fact the Bible tells us about him in both the Old and New Testaments (Genesis 15:6; Romans 4:3).

Early in life, Abraham had to make an important decision. God asked him to choose between staying at home or following God's leading. It was a choice between doing what Abraham wanted to do or doing what God wanted Abraham to do.

Of course Abraham couldn't see how much of future history was resting on his decision, but God used Abraham's obedience to affect millions of people. It was through Abraham that the Jewish nation developed and eventually Jesus Christ came into the world.

God gives us exactly the same choice he gave Abraham. Once Abraham gave his life to God, he never tried to take it back. He may have taken some wrong turns on the journey . . . but he never turned around. What have you decided about the choice God has given you? Is your basic desire to trust God and live his way, or is your goal to live life your way?

LESSONS: God desires dependence, trust, and faith in him—not faith in our ability to please him

God's plan from the beginning has been to make himself known to all people

KEY VERSE: "And Abram believed the LORD, and the LORD declared him righteous because of his faith" (Genesis 15:6).

Abraham's story is told in Genesis 11–25. He is also mentioned in Exodus 2:24; Acts 7:2-8; Romans 4; Galatians 3; Hebrews 6–7;11.

**UPS:**
- His faith pleased God
- Became the founder of the Jewish nation
- Was a successful and wealthy rancher
- Usually avoided conflicts, but when they happened he let his opponent set the rules for settling the disputes

**DOWNS:**
- Had a lifelong tendency to lie when under pressure

**STATS:**
- Where: Born in Ur of the Chaldeans; spent most of his life in the land of Canaan
- Occupation: Wealthy livestock owner
- Relatives: Brothers: Nahor and Haran. Father: Terah. Wife: Sarah. Nephew: Lot. Sons: Ishmael and Isaac.
- Contemporaries: Abimelech, Melchizedek

## FAMILY FEUD ● ● • • •

**13:5-9 Facing a potential conflict with his nephew Lot, Abram took the initiative in settling the dispute. He gave Lot first choice and showed a willingness to risk being cheated. Abram's example shows us how to respond to difficult family situations: (1) take the initiative in resolving conflicts; (2) let others have first choice, even if that means not getting what we want; (3) put family peace above personal desires.**

Abram and Lot. At that time Canaanites and Perizzites
were also living in the land.
8Then Abram talked it over with Lot. "This arguing between our herdsmen has got to stop," he
said. "After all, we are close relatives! 9I'll tell you
what we'll do. Take your choice of any section of
the land you want, and we will separate. If you
want that area over there, then I'll stay here. If you
want to stay in this area, then I'll move on to
another place."
10Lot took a long look at the fertile plains of the
Jordan Valley in the direction of Zoar. The whole
area was well watered everywhere, like the garden of
the LORD or the beautiful land of Egypt. (This was
before the LORD had destroyed Sodom and Gomorrah.) 11Lot chose that land for himself—the Jordan
Valley to the east of them. He went there with his
flocks and servants and parted company with his
uncle Abram. 12So while Abram stayed in the land of
Canaan, Lot moved his tents to a place near Sodom,
among the cities of the plain. 13The people of this
area were unusually wicked and sinned greatly
against the LORD.
14After Lot was gone, the LORD said to Abram,
"Look as far as you can see in every direction. 15I am
going to give all this land to you and your offspring*
as a permanent possession. 16And I am going to give
you so many descendants that, like dust, they cannot
be counted! 17Take a walk in every direction and
explore the new possessions I am giving you."
18Then Abram moved his camp to the oak grove
owned by Mamre, which is at Hebron. There he built
an altar to the LORD.

## CHAPTER 14

**ABRAM RESCUES LOT.** About this
time war broke out in the region. King Amraphel
of Babylonia,* King Arioch of Ellasar, King
Kedorlaomer of Elam, and King Tidal of Goiim
2fought against King Bera of Sodom, King Birsha of
Gomorrah, King Shinab of Admah, King Shemeber
of Zeboiim, and the king of Bela (now called
Zoar).
3The kings of Sodom, Gomorrah, Admah, Zeboiim, and Bela formed an alliance and mobilized
their armies in Siddim Valley (that is, the valley of
the Dead Sea*). 4For twelve years they had all been
subject to King Kedorlaomer, but now in the thirteenth year they rebelled.
5One year later, Kedorlaomer and his allies arrived. They conquered the Rephaites in Ashteroth-
karnaim, the Zuzites in Ham, the Emites in the
plain of Kiriathaim, 6and the Horites in Mount
Seir, as far as El-paran at the edge of the wilderness.
7Then they swung around to En-mishpat (now
called Kadesh) and destroyed the Amalekites, and
also the Amorites living in Hazazon-tamar.
8But now the army of the kings of Sodom, Gomorrah, Admah, Zeboiim, and Bela (now called
Zoar) prepared for battle in the valley of the Dead
Sea* 9against King Kedorlaomer of Elam and the
kings of Goiim, Babylonia, and Ellasar—four
kings against five. 10As it happened, the valley was
filled with tar pits. And as the army of the kings of
Sodom and Gomorrah fled, some slipped into the
tar pits, while the rest escaped into the mountains.
11The victorious invaders then plundered Sodom
and Gomorrah and began their long journey
home, taking all the wealth and food with them.
12They also captured Lot—Abram's nephew who
lived in Sodom—and took everything he owned.
13One of the men who escaped came and told
Abram the Hebrew, who was camped at the oak
grove belonging to Mamre the Amorite. Mamre
and his relatives, Eshcol and Aner, were Abram's
allies.
14When Abram learned that Lot had been captured, he called together the men born into his
household, 318 of them in all. He chased after
Kedorlaomer's army until he caught up with them
in Dan. 15There he divided his men and attacked
during the night from several directions.
Kedorlaomer's army fled, but Abram chased them
to Hobah, north of Damascus. 16Abram and his
allies recovered everything—the goods that had
been taken, Abram's nephew Lot with his possessions, and all the women and other captives.
17As Abram returned from his victory over
Kedorlaomer and his allies, the king of Sodom came
out to meet him in the valley of Shaveh (that is, the
King's Valley). 18Then Melchizedek, the king of Salem and a priest of God Most High, brought him
bread and wine. 19Melchizedek blessed Abram with
this blessing:

"Blessed be Abram by God Most High,
    Creator of heaven and earth.
20And blessed be God Most High,
    who has helped you conquer your enemies."

Then Abram gave Melchizedek a tenth of all the
goods he had recovered.

## GETTING IT RIGHT ● ● • • •

**15:6 Although Abram had been demonstrating his faith through his actions, it was simply believing the Lord that made Abram right with God (Romans 4:1-5). We too can have a right relationship with God by trusting him with our lives. Our outward actions—church attendance, prayer, good deeds—will not by themselves make us right with God. A right relationship is based on faith—the heartfelt inner confidence that God is who he says he is and does what he says he will do. Right actions follow naturally as by-products.**

13:15 Hebrew *seed.* 14:1 Hebrew *Shinar;* also in 14:9. 14:3 Hebrew *Salt Sea.* 14:8 Hebrew *in Siddim Valley;* see 14:3.

21 The king of Sodom told him, "Give back my people who were captured. But you may keep for yourself all the goods you have recovered."

22 Abram replied, "I have solemnly promised the LORD, God Most High, Creator of heaven and earth, 23 that I will not take so much as a single thread or sandal thong from you. Otherwise you might say, 'I am the one who made Abram rich!' 24 All I'll accept is what these young men of mine have already eaten. But give a share of the goods to my allies—Aner, Eshcol, and Mamre."

CHAPTER **15** **GOD'S COVENANT WITH ABRAM.** Afterward the LORD spoke to Abram in a vision and said to him, "Do not be afraid, Abram, for I will protect you, and your reward will be great."

2 But Abram replied, "O Sovereign LORD, what good are all your blessings when I don't even have a son? Since I don't have a son, Eliezer of Damascus, a servant in my household, will inherit all my wealth. 3 You have given me no children, so one of my servants will have to be my heir."

4 Then the LORD said to him, "No, your servant will not be your heir, for you will have a son of your own to inherit everything I am giving you." 5 Then the LORD brought Abram outside beneath the night sky and told him, "Look up into the heavens and count the stars if you can. Your descendants will be like that—too many to count!" 6 And Abram believed the LORD, and the LORD declared him righteous because of his faith. 7 Then the LORD told him, "I am the LORD who brought you out of Ur of the Chaldeans to give you this land."

8 But Abram replied, "O Sovereign LORD, how can I be sure that you will give it to me?"

9 Then the LORD told him, "Bring me a three-year-old heifer, a three-year-old female goat, a three-year-old ram, a turtledove, and a young pigeon." 10 Abram took all these and killed them. He cut each one down the middle and laid the halves side by side. He did not, however, divide the birds in half. 11 Some vultures came down to eat the carcasses, but Abram chased them away. 12 That evening, as the sun was going down, Abram fell into a deep sleep. He saw a terrifying vision of darkness and horror.

13 Then the LORD told Abram, "You can be sure that your descendants will be strangers in a foreign land, and they will be oppressed as slaves for four hundred years. 14 But I will punish the nation that enslaves them, and in the end they will come away with great wealth. 15 (But you will die in peace, at a ripe old age.) 16 After four generations your descendants will return here to this land, when the sin of the Amorites has run its course."

17 As the sun went down and it became dark, Abram saw a smoking firepot and a flaming torch pass between the halves of the carcasses. 18 So the LORD made a covenant with Abram that day and said, "I have given this land to your descendants, all the way from the border of Egypt* to the great Euphrates River—19 the

**UPS:**
- He was a successful businessman
- Peter calls him a righteous man (2 Peter 2:7-8)

**DOWNS:**
- When faced with decisions, he tended to put off deciding, then chose the easiest course of action
- When given a choice, his first reaction was to think of himself

**STATS:**
- Where: Lived first in Ur of the Chaldeans, then moved to Canaan with Abram
- Occupation: Wealthy sheep and cattle rancher, city official
- Relatives: Father: Haran. Adopted by Abram when his father died. The name of his wife, who turned into a pillar of salt, is not mentioned.

## LOT

Some people simply drift through life. They don't really make choices; they just take the easiest way. Usually, that choice turns out to be the wrong way. Lot, Abram's nephew, was a person like this. His life can help keep us from being drifters.

While still young, Lot lost his father. This must have been a difficult time for him, but he was loved and cared for by his grandfather Terah and his uncle Abram. Though they were good examples, Lot's life was full of unwise decisions. Despite Abram's attention and God's help, Lot went his own way.

By the time Lot drifted out of the picture, his life had taken an ugly turn. He had become so blended into the culture of his day that he did not want to leave it. His wife was killed during Lot's narrow escape, and his daughters committed incest with him. His drifting finally led him to destruction.

God gives us hope by showing us how he can bring good out of even failure and evil. The New Testament describes Lot as a righteous man (2 Peter 2:7-8). Even though he didn't do much about the evil surrounding him, it still bothered him deeply. And Ruth—a descendant of Moab, the child born from the incest between Lot and one of his daughters—was an ancestor of Jesus Christ.

What is the direction of your life? Are you headed toward God or away from him? If you find it easy to drift, the choice to live for God may seem difficult, but it is the one choice that makes life fit together.

LESSON: God wants us to do more than drift through life; he wants people to be an influence for him

KEY VERSE: "When Lot still hesitated, the angels seized his hand and the hands of his wife and two daughters and rushed them to safety outside the city, for the LORD was merciful" (Genesis 19:16).

Lot's story is told in Genesis 11–14; 19. He is also mentioned in Deuteronomy 2:9; Luke 17:28-32; 2 Peter 2:7-8.

15:18 Hebrew *the river of Egypt,* referring either to an eastern branch of the Nile River or to the brook of Egypt in the Sinai (see Num 34:5).

land of the Kenites, Kenizzites, Kadmonites, [20]Hittites, Perizzites, Rephaites, [21]Amorites, Canaanites, Girgashites, and Jebusites."

## CHAPTER 16 THE BIRTH OF ISHMAEL.

But Sarai, Abram's wife, had no children. So Sarai took her servant, an Egyptian woman named Hagar, [2]and gave her to Abram so she could bear his children. "The LORD has kept me from having any children," Sarai said to Abram. "Go and sleep with my servant. Perhaps I can have children through her." And Abram agreed. [3]So Sarai, Abram's wife, took Hagar the Egyptian servant and gave her to Abram as a wife. (This happened ten years after Abram first arrived in the land of Canaan.)

[4]So Abram slept with Hagar, and she became pregnant. When Hagar knew she was pregnant, she began to treat her mistress Sarai with contempt. [5]Then Sarai said to Abram, "It's all your fault! Now this servant of mine is pregnant, and she despises me, though I myself gave her the privilege of sleeping with you. The LORD will make you pay for doing this to me!*"

[6]Abram replied, "Since she is your servant, you may deal with her as you see fit." So Sarai treated her harshly, and Hagar ran away.

[7]The angel of the LORD found Hagar beside a desert spring along the road to Shur. [8]The angel said to her, "Hagar, Sarai's servant, where have you come from, and where are you going?"

### RUNAWAY ● ● • • •

**16:8 As Hagar was running away from her mistress and her problem, the Angel of the Lord gave her this advice: (1) return and face Sarai, the cause of her problem, and (2) submit to Sarai's authority. Hagar needed to work on her attitude toward Sarai, no matter how justified it may have been. Running away from our problems rarely solves them. It is wise to face our problems squarely, accept God's promise of help, correct our attitude, and act as we should.**

"I am running away from my mistress," she replied.

[9]Then the angel of the LORD said, "Return to your mistress and submit to her authority." [10]The angel added, "I will give you more descendants than you can count." [11]And the angel also said, "You are now pregnant and will give birth to a son. You are to name him Ishmael,* for the LORD has heard about your misery. [12]This son of yours will be a wild one—free and untamed as a wild donkey! He will be against everyone, and everyone will be against him. Yes, he will live at odds with the rest of his brothers."

[13]Thereafter, Hagar referred to the LORD, who had spoken to her, as "the God who sees me,"* for she said, "I have seen the One who sees me!" [14]Later that well was named Beer-lahairoi,* and it can still be found between Kadesh and Bered.

### REASON ENOUGH ● ● • • •

**17:1 The Lord told Abram, "I am God Almighty; serve me faithfully and live a blameless life." God has the same message for us today. We are to obey him because he is God—that is reason enough. If you don't think the benefits are worth it, consider who God is—the only one with the power and ability to meet your every need.**

[15]So Hagar gave Abram a son, and Abram named him Ishmael. [16]Abram was eighty-six years old at that time.

## CHAPTER 17 GOD'S COVENANT WITH ABRAM.

When Abram was ninety-nine years old, the LORD appeared to him and said, "I am God Almighty; serve me faithfully and live a blameless life. [2]I will make a covenant with you, by which I will guarantee to make you into a mighty nation." [3]At this, Abram fell face down in the dust. Then God said to him, [4]"This is my covenant with you: I will make you the father of not just one nation, but a multitude of nations! [5]What's more, I am changing your name. It will no longer be Abram; now you will be known as Abraham,* for you will be the father of many nations. [6]I will give you millions of descendants who will represent many nations. Kings will be among them!

[7]"I will continue this everlasting covenant between us, generation after generation. It will continue between me and your offspring* forever. And I will always be your God and the God of your descendants after you. [8]Yes, I will give all this land of Canaan to you and to your offspring forever. And I will be their God.

[9]"Your part of the agreement," God told Abraham, "is to obey the terms of the covenant. You and all your descendants have this continual responsibility. [10]This is the covenant that you and your descendants must keep: Each male among you must be circumcised; [11]the flesh of his foreskin must be cut off. This will be a sign that you and they have accepted this covenant. [12]Every male child must be circumcised on the eighth day after his birth. This applies not only to members of your family, but also to the servants born in your household and the foreign-born servants whom you have purchased. [13]All must be circumcised. Your bodies will thus bear the mark of my everlasting covenant. [14]Anyone who refuses to be circumcised will be cut off from the covenant family for violating the covenant."

[15]Then God added, "Regarding Sarai, your wife—her name will no longer be Sarai; from now on you will call her Sarah.* [16]And I will bless her and give you a son from her! Yes, I will bless her richly, and she will become the mother of many nations. Kings will be among her descendants!"

[17]Then Abraham bowed down to the ground, but he laughed to himself in disbelief. "How could I become a father at the age of one hundred?" he wondered. "Besides, Sarah is ninety; how could she

16:5 Hebrew *Let the LORD judge between you and me.* 16:11 *Ishmael* means "God hears." 16:13 Hebrew *El-roi.* 16:14 *Beer-lahairoi* means "well of the Living One who sees me." 17:5 *Abram* means "exalted father"; *Abraham* means "father of many." 17:7 Hebrew *seed;* also in 17:8. 17:15 *Sarah* means "princess."

have a baby?" 18And Abraham said to God, "Yes, may
Ishmael enjoy your special blessing!"
19But God replied, "Sarah, your wife, will bear you a
son. You will name him Isaac,* and I will confirm my
everlasting covenant with him and his descendants.
20As for Ishmael, I will bless him also, just as you have
asked. I will cause him to multiply and become a great
nation. Twelve princes will be among his descendants
21But my covenant is with Isaac, who will be born to
you and Sarah about this time next year."
22That ended the conversation, and God left Abraham. 23On that very day Abraham took his son Ishmael and every other male in his household and
circumcised them, cutting off their foreskins, exactly as
God had told him. 24Abraham was ninety-nine years
old at that time, 25and Ishmael his son was thirteen.
26Both were circumcised the same day, 27along with all
the other men and boys of the household, whether
they were born there or bought as servants.

CHAPTER **18** **ANGELS VISIT ABRAHAM.** The LORD
appeared again to Abraham while he was camped
near the oak grove belonging to Mamre. One day
about noon, as Abraham was sitting at the entrance
to his tent, 2he suddenly noticed three men standing
nearby. He got up and ran to meet them, welcoming
them by bowing low to the ground. 3"My lord," he
said, "if it pleases you, stop here for a while. 4Rest in
the shade of this tree while my servants get some
water to wash your feet. 5Let me prepare some food
to refresh you. Please stay awhile before continuing
on your journey."
"All right," they said. "Do as you have said."
6So Abraham ran back to the tent and said to Sarah,
"Quick! Get three measures* of your best flour, and
bake some bread." 7Then Abraham ran out to the herd
and chose a fat calf and told a servant to hurry and
butcher it. 8When the food was ready, he took some
cheese curds and milk and the roasted meat, and he
served it to the men. As they ate, Abraham waited on
them there beneath the trees.
9"Where is Sarah, your wife?" they asked him.
"In the tent," Abraham replied.
10Then one of them said, "About this time next
year I will return, and your wife Sarah will have a
son."
Now Sarah was listening to this conversation from
the tent nearby. 11And since Abraham and Sarah were
both very old, and Sarah was long past the age of
having children, 12she laughed silently to herself.
"How could a worn-out woman like me have a
baby?" she thought. "And when my master—my
husband—is also so old?"
13Then the LORD said to Abraham, "Why did
Sarah laugh? Why did she say, 'Can an old woman
like me have a baby?' 14Is anything too hard for the
LORD? About a year from now, just as I told you, I
will return, and Sarah will have a son." 15Sarah was
afraid, so she denied that she had laughed. But he
said, "That is not true. You did laugh."

Is ANYTHING too hard for the LORD

GENESIS 18:14

16Then the men got up from their meal and
started on toward Sodom. Abraham went with them
part of the way.
17"Should I hide my plan from Abraham?" the
LORD asked. 18"For Abraham will become a great and
mighty nation, and all the nations of the earth will
be blessed through him. 19I have singled him out so
that he will direct his sons and their families to keep
the way of the LORD and do what is right and just.
Then I will do for him all that I have promised." 20So
the LORD told Abraham, "I have heard that the
people of Sodom and Gomorrah are extremely evil,
and that everything they do is wicked. 21I am going
down to see whether or not these reports are true.
Then I will know."
22The two other men went on toward Sodom, but
the LORD remained with Abraham for a while.
23Abraham approached him and said, "Will you destroy both innocent and guilty alike? 24Suppose you
find fifty innocent people there within the city—will
you still destroy it, and not spare it for their sakes?
25Surely you wouldn't do such a thing, destroying the
innocent with the guilty. Why, you would be treating
the innocent and the guilty exactly the same! Surely
you wouldn't do that! Should not the Judge of all the
earth do what is right?"
26And the LORD replied, "If I find fifty innocent
people in Sodom, I will spare the entire city for their
sake."

**LYING ● ● • • .**

18:15 **Sarah lied because she was afraid of being discovered. Fear is the most common motive for lying. We are afraid that our inner thoughts and emotions will be exposed or our wrongdoings discovered. But lying causes greater complications than telling the truth and brings even more problems. If God can't be trusted with our innermost thoughts and fears, we are in greater trouble than we first imagined.**

17:19 *Isaac* means "he laughs." 18:6 Hebrew 3 *seahs,* about 15 quarts or 18 liters.

27Then Abraham spoke again. "Since I have begun, let me go on and speak further to my Lord, even though I am but dust and ashes. 28Suppose there are only forty-five? Will you destroy the city for lack of five?"

And the LORD said, "I will not destroy it if I find forty-five."

29Then Abraham pressed his request further. "Suppose there are only forty?"

And the LORD replied, "I will not destroy it if there are forty."

30"Please don't be angry, my Lord," Abraham pleaded. "Let me speak—suppose only thirty are found?"

And the LORD replied, "I will not destroy it if there are thirty."

31Then Abraham said, "Since I have dared to speak to the Lord, let me continue—suppose there are only twenty?"

And the LORD said, "Then I will not destroy it for the sake of the twenty."

32Finally, Abraham said, "Lord, please do not get angry; I will speak but once more! Suppose only ten are found there?"

And the LORD said, "Then, for the sake of the ten, I will not destroy it."

33The LORD went on his way when he had finished his conversation with Abraham, and Abraham returned to his tent.

## CHAPTER 19

**GOD DESTROYS SODOM.** That evening the two angels came to the entrance of the city of Sodom, and Lot was sitting there as they arrived. When he saw them, he stood up to meet them. Then he welcomed them and bowed low to the ground. 2"My lords," he said, "come to my home to wash your feet, and be my guests for the night. You may then get up in the morning as early as you like and be on your way again."

"Oh no," they said, "we'll just spend the night out here in the city square."

3But Lot insisted, so at last they went home with him. He set a great feast before them, complete with fresh bread made without yeast. After the meal, 4as they were preparing to retire for the night, all the men of Sodom, young and old, came from all over the city and surrounded the house. 5They shouted to Lot, "Where are the men who came to spend the night with you? Bring them out so we can have sex with them."

6Lot stepped outside to talk to them, shutting the door behind him. 7"Please, my brothers," he begged, "don't do such a wicked thing. 8Look—I have two virgin daughters. Do with them as you wish, but leave these men alone, for they are under my protection."

9"Stand back!" they shouted. "Who do you think you are? We let you settle among us, and now you are trying to tell us what to do! We'll treat you far worse than those other men!" And they lunged at Lot and began breaking down the door. 10But the two angels reached out and pulled Lot in and bolted the door. 11Then they blinded the men of Sodom so they couldn't find the doorway.

12"Do you have any other relatives here in the city?" the angels asked. "Get them out of this place—sons-in-law, sons, daughters, or anyone else. 13For we will destroy the city completely. The stench of the place has reached the LORD, and he has sent us to destroy it."

14So Lot rushed out to tell his daughters' fiancés, "Quick, get out of the city! The LORD is going to destroy it." But the young men thought he was only joking.

15At dawn the next morning the angels became insistent. "Hurry," they said to Lot. "Take your wife and your two daughters who are here. Get out of here right now, or you will be caught in the destruction of the city."

16When Lot still hesitated, the angels seized his hand and the hands of his wife and two daughters and rushed them to safety outside the city, for the LORD was merciful. 17"Run for your lives!" the angels warned. "Do not stop anywhere in the valley. And don't look back! Escape to the mountains, or you will die."

18"Oh no, my lords, please," Lot begged. 19"You have been so kind to me and saved my life, and you have granted me such mercy. But I cannot go to the mountains. Disaster would catch up to me there, and I would soon die. 20See, there is a small village nearby. Please let me go there instead; don't you see how small it is? Then my life will be saved."

21"All right," the angel said, "I will grant your request. I will not destroy that little village. 22But hurry! For I can do nothing until you are there." From that time on, that village was known as Zoar.*

23The sun was rising as Lot reached the village. 24Then the LORD rained down fire and burning sulfur from the heavens on Sodom and Gomorrah. 25He utterly destroyed them, along with the other cities and villages of the plain, eliminating all life—people, plants, and animals alike. 26But Lot's wife looked back as she was following along behind him, and she became a pillar of salt.

27The next morning Abraham was up early and hurried out to the place where he had stood in the LORD's presence. 28He looked out across the plain to Sodom and Gomorrah and saw columns of smoke

### CHAMELEON ● ● ● • •

19:14 **Lot had lived so long, and was so content, among ungodly people that he was no longer a believable witness for God. He had allowed his environment to shape him, rather than shaping his environment. Do those who know you see you as a witness for God, or are you just one of the crowd, blending in unnoticed? Lot had compromised to the point that he was almost useless to God. When he finally made a stand, nobody listened. Have you also become useless to God because you are too much like your environment? To make a difference, you must first decide to be different in what you believe and how you act.**

19:22 *Zoar* means "little."

and fumes, as from a furnace, rising from the cities
there. [29]But God had listened to Abraham's request
and kept Lot safe, removing him from the disaster
that engulfed the cities on the plain.

[30]Afterward Lot left Zoar because he was afraid of
the people there, and he went to live in a cave in the
mountains with his two daughters. [31]One day the
older daughter said to her sister, "There isn't a man
anywhere in this entire area for us to marry. And our
father will soon be too old to have children. [32]Come,
let's get him drunk with wine, and then we will sleep
with him. That way we will preserve our family line
through our father." [33]So that night they got him
drunk, and the older daughter went in and slept with
her father. He was unaware of her lying down or
getting up again.

[34]The next morning the older daughter said to her
younger sister, "I slept with our father last night. Let's
get him drunk with wine again tonight, and you go in
and sleep with him. That way our family line will be
preserved." [35]So that night they got him drunk again,
and the younger daughter
went in and slept with him.
As before, he was unaware of
her lying down or getting up
again. [36]So both of Lot's
daughters became pregnant
by their father.

[37]When the older daugh-
ter gave birth to a son, she
named him Moab.* He be-
came the ancestor of the nation now known as the
Moabites. [38]When the younger daughter gave birth to a
son, she named him Ben-
ammi.* He became the an-
cestor of the nation now
known as the Ammonites.

CHAPTER **20** **ABRAHAM TRICKS THE KING.** Now Abraham
moved south to the Negev
and settled for a while between Kadesh and Shur at a
place called Gerar. [2]Abraham
told people there that his
wife, Sarah, was his sister. So
King Abimelech sent for her
and had her brought to him
at his palace.

[3]But one night God came
to Abimelech in a dream and
told him, "You are a dead
man, for that woman you
took is married."

[4]But Abimelech had not
slept with her yet, so he said,
"Lord, will you kill an innocent man? [5]Abraham told
me, 'She is my sister,' and she herself said, 'Yes, he is
my brother.' I acted in complete innocence!"

[6]"Yes, I know you are innocent," God replied.
"That is why I kept you from sinning against me; I
did not let you touch her. [7]Now return her to her
husband, and he will pray for you, for he is a
prophet. Then you will live. But if you don't return
her to him, you can be sure that you and your entire
household will die."

[8]Abimelech got up early the next morning and
hastily called a meeting of all his servants. When he
told them what had happened, great fear swept
through the crowd. [9]Then Abimelech called for
Abraham. "What is this you have done to us?" he
demanded. "What have I done to you that deserves
treatment like this, making me and my kingdom
guilty of this great sin? This kind of thing should not
be done! [10]Why have you done this to us?"

[11]"Well," Abraham said, "I figured this to be a
godless place. I thought, 'They will want my wife and
will kill me to get her.' [12]Besides, she is my sister—we

**SARAH** Sadly, some women who really want to be mothers are not able to have children. Sometimes doctors can't figure out what's wrong, and the waiting can be terrible. Usually, a woman begins to feel hopeless and desperate. That's how Abraham's wife, Sarah, was feeling.

Then Sarah was told she was going to have a baby. She burst out laughing. She was 90 years old. Have you ever laughed out loud because you thought something was funny, only to discover that what you heard wasn't supposed to be funny? Then you know how Sarah felt. God had to gently teach her how to laugh at the right things. Maybe God is trying to teach you the same lesson.

God also got the last laugh. Sarah laughed because she thought God's plan to make a 90-year-old mother was impossible. So God had her name the baby *Isaac,* which means "laughter." God likes to do the impossible! Sarah discovered that it's much more fun to laugh with God than at him.

LESSONS: God responds to faith even in the midst of failures

God is not bound by what usually happens. He can stretch the limits and cause unheard-of events to occur.

KEY VERSE: "It was by faith that Sarah together with Abraham was able to have a child, even though they were too old and Sarah was barren" (Hebrews 11:11).

Sarah's story is told in Genesis 11–25. She is also mentioned in Isaiah 51:1; Romans 4:19; 9:9; Hebrews 11:11; 1 Peter 3:6.

**UPS:**
- Was intensely loyal to her own child
- Became the mother of a nation and an ancestor of Jesus
- Was a woman of faith. She is the first woman listed in the Hall of Faith in Hebrews 11.

**DOWNS:**
- Had trouble believing God's promises to her
- Attempted to work problems out on her own, without consulting God
- Tried to cover her own faults by blaming others

**STATS:**
- Where: Married Abram in Ur of the Chaldeans, then moved with him to Canaan
- Occupation: Wife, mother, household manager
- Relatives: Father: Terah. Husband: Abraham. Brothers: Nahor and Haran. Nephew: Lot. Son: Isaac.

19:37 *Moab* sounds like a Hebrew term that means "from father." 19:38 *Ben-ammi* means "son of my people."

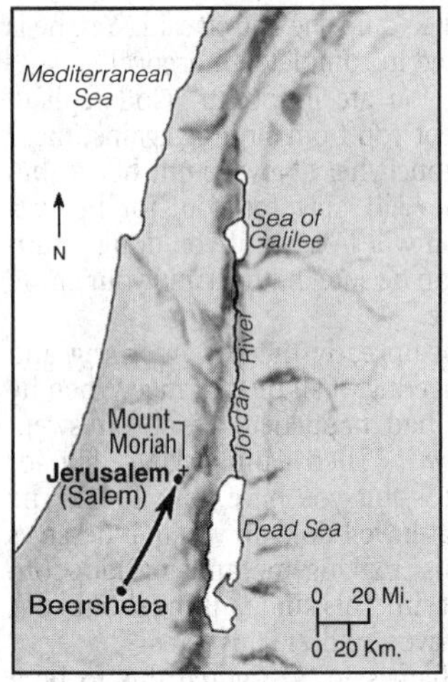


**ABRAHAM'S TRIP TO MOUNT MORIAH** Abraham and Isaac traveled the 50 or 60 miles from Beersheba to Mount Moriah in about three days. This was a very difficult three days for Abraham, who was on his way to sacrifice his beloved son, Isaac.

both have the same father, though different mothers—and I married her. [13]When God sent me to travel far from my father's home, I told her, 'Wherever we go, have the kindness to say that you are my sister.'"

[14]Then Abimelech took sheep and oxen and servants—both men and women—and gave them to Abraham, and he returned his wife, Sarah, to him. [15]"Look over my kingdom, and choose a place where you would like to live," Abimelech told him. [16]Then he turned to Sarah. "Look," he said, "I am giving your 'brother' a thousand pieces of silver* to compensate for any embarrassment I may have caused you. This will settle any claim against me in this matter."

[17]Then Abraham prayed to God, and God healed Abimelech, his wife, and the other women of the household, so they could have children. [18]For the LORD had stricken all the women with infertility as a warning to Abimelech for having taken Abraham's wife.

## CHAPTER 21

**ISAAC IS BORN.** Then the LORD did exactly what he had promised. [2]Sarah became pregnant, and she gave a son to Abraham in his old age. It all happened at the time God had said it would. [3]And Abraham named his son Isaac.* [4]Eight days after Isaac was born, Abraham circumcised him as God had commanded. [5]Abraham was one hundred years old at the time.

[6]And Sarah declared, "God has brought me laughter! All who hear about this will laugh with me. [7]For who would have dreamed that I would ever have a baby? Yet I have given Abraham a son in his old age!"

[8]As time went by and Isaac grew and was weaned, Abraham gave a big party to celebrate the happy occasion. [9]But Sarah saw Ishmael—the son of Abraham and her Egyptian servant Hagar—making fun of Isaac. [10]So she turned to Abraham and demanded, "Get rid of that servant and her son. He is not going to share the family inheritance with my son, Isaac. I won't have it!"

[11]This upset Abraham very much because Ishmael was his son. [12]But God told Abraham, "Do not be upset over the boy and your servant wife. Do just as Sarah says, for Isaac is the son through whom your descendants will be counted. [13]But I will make a nation of the descendants of Hagar's son because he also is your son."

[14]So Abraham got up early the next morning, prepared food for the journey, and strapped a container of water to Hagar's shoulders. He sent her away with their son, and she walked out into the wilderness of Beersheba, wandering aimlessly. [15]When the water was gone, she left the boy in the shade of a bush. [16]Then she went and sat down by herself about a hundred yards* away. "I don't want to watch the boy die," she said, as she burst into tears.

[17]Then God heard the boy's cries, and the angel of God called to Hagar from the sky, "Hagar, what's wrong? Do not be afraid! God has heard the boy's cries from the place where you laid him. [18]Go to him and comfort him, for I will make a great nation from his descendants."

[19]Then God opened Hagar's eyes, and she saw a well. She immediately filled her water container and gave the boy a drink. [20]And God was with the boy as he grew up in the wilderness of Paran. He became an expert archer, [21]and his mother arranged a marriage for him with a young woman from Egypt.

[22]About this time, Abimelech came with Phicol, his army commander, to visit Abraham. "It is clear that God helps you in everything you do," Abimelech said. [23]"Swear to me in God's name that you won't deceive me, my children, or my grandchildren. I have been loyal to you, so now swear that you will be loyal to me and to this country in which you are living."

[24]Abraham replied, "All right, I swear to it!" [25]Then Abraham complained to Abimelech about a well that Abimelech's servants had taken violently from Abraham's servants.

[26]"This is the first I've heard of it," Abimelech said. "And I have no idea who is responsible. Why

### PERFECT TIMING ● ● ● • •

22:7-8 **Why did God ask Abraham to perform human sacrifice? Heathen nations practiced human sacrifice, but God condemned this as a terrible sin (Leviticus 20:1-5). God did not want Isaac to die, but he wanted Abraham to prove that he loved God more than he loved his promised and long-awaited son. God was testing Abraham. The purpose of testing is to strengthen our character and deepen our commitment to God and his perfect timing. Through this difficult experience, Abraham strengthened his commitment to obey God. He also learned about God's ability to provide.**



20:16 Hebrew *1,000 shekels of silver,* about 25 pounds or 11.4 kilograms in weight. 21:3 *Isaac* means "he laughs." 21:16 Hebrew *a bowshot.*

didn't you say something about this before?" [27]Then Abraham gave sheep and oxen to Abimelech, and they made a treaty. [28]But when Abraham took seven additional ewe lambs and set them off by themselves, [29]Abimelech asked, "Why are you doing that?"

[30]Abraham replied, "They are my gift to you as a public confirmation that I dug this well." [31]So ever since, that place has been known as Beersheba—"well of the oath"—because that was where they had sworn an oath. [32]After making their covenant, Abimelech left with Phicol, the commander of his army, and they returned home to the land of the Philistines. [33]Then Abraham planted a tamarisk tree at Beersheba, and he worshiped the LORD, the Eternal God, at that place. [34]And Abraham lived in Philistine country for a long time.

## CHAPTER 22 ABRAHAM OFFERS ISAAC.

Later on God tested Abraham's faith and obedience. "Abraham!" God called.

"Yes," he replied. "Here I am."

[2]"Take your son, your only son—yes, Isaac, whom you love so much—and go to the land of Moriah. Sacrifice him there as a burnt offering on one of the mountains, which I will point out to you."

[3]The next morning Abraham got up early. He saddled his donkey and took two of his servants with him, along with his son Isaac. Then he chopped wood to build a fire for a burnt offering and set out for the place where God had told him to go. [4]On the third day of the journey, Abraham saw the place in the distance. [5]"Stay here with the donkey," Abraham told the young men. "The boy and I will travel a little farther. We will worship there, and then we will come right back."

[6]Abraham placed the wood for the burnt offering on Isaac's shoulders, while he himself carried the knife and the fire. As the two of them went on together, [7]Isaac said, "Father?"

"Yes, my son," Abraham replied.

"We have the wood and the fire," said the boy, "but where is the lamb for the sacrifice?"

[8]"God will provide a lamb, my son," Abraham answered. And they both went on together.

[9]When they arrived at the place where God had told Abraham to go, he built an altar and placed the wood on it. Then he tied Isaac up and laid him on the altar over the wood. [10]And Abraham took the knife and lifted it up to kill his son as a sacrifice to the LORD. [11]At that moment the angel of the LORD shouted to him from heaven, "Abraham! Abraham!"

"Yes," he answered. "I'm listening."

---

## ISAAC

Like it or not, your name is powerful. It sets you apart. It triggers memories of you in other people's minds. When you hear your name said you almost have to look. When people heard Isaac's name, they almost had to laugh!

Isaac's name means "laughter." As with many Bible characters, there were several reasons Isaac got his name. Isaac's name reminded his parents of their first reaction of shocked laughter when God told them they would have a son though they were quite old. At other times, his name must have reminded them of the great joy they had when Isaac was born. His name was also a reminder of God's presence, for God had told Isaac's parents to give their child that name.

In a family of active leaders, Isaac was the quiet, "mind-my-own-business" type unless he had to be involved. He was the protected only child until Abraham arranged his marriage to Rebekah. Then Isaac allowed his wife to run their family. He rarely stood his ground and found it easier to compromise or lie than to face a confrontation.

In spite of these problems, Isaac was part of God's plan. Isaac learned the importance of faith in the one true God from his father. God's promise to Abraham to create a great nation through which he would bless the world was passed on to Isaac and to his twin sons.

From time to time you may feel like Isaac—like you just go along or find it hard to stand on your own in a crowd. But remember, God works through people in spite of their shortcomings. Tell God you're available to him, weaknesses and all. You will discover that his willingness to use you is even greater than your desire to be used.

LESSONS: Patience often brings rewards

Both God's plans and his promises are larger than people

God keeps his promises! He remains faithful though we are often faithless

KEY VERSE: "Sarah, your wife, will bear you a son. You will name him Isaac, and I will confirm my everlasting covenant with him and his descendants" (Genesis 17:19).

Isaac's story is told in Genesis 17:15–35:29. He is also mentioned in Romans 9:7-8; Hebrews 11:17-20; James 2:21-24.

**UPS:**
- Was the miracle child born to 90-year-old Sarah and 100-year-old Abraham
- The first descendant in fulfillment of God's promise to Abraham
- Seems to have been a caring and consistent husband, at least until his sons were born
- Demonstrated great patience

**DOWNS:**
- Under pressure he tended to imitate his father and lie
- In conflict he tried to avoid confrontation by bargaining
- He played favorites between his sons and alienated his wife

**STATS:**
- Where: The area called the Negev, in the southern part of Palestine, between Kadesh and Shur (Genesis 20:1)
- Occupation: Wealthy livestock owner
- Relatives: Parents: Abraham and Sarah. Half brother: Ishmael. Wife: Rebekah. Twin sons: Esau and Jacob.

## GETTING MARRIED ● ● • • •

**24:4 Abraham wanted Isaac to marry a relative. This was a common and acceptable practice that had the added advantage of avoiding intermarriage with heathen neighbors. A son's wife was usually chosen by the parents. It was common for a woman to be married in her early teens, although Rebekah was probably older.**

12"Lay down the knife," the angel said. "Do not hurt the boy in any way, for now I know that you truly fear God. You have not withheld even your beloved son from me."

13Then Abraham looked up and saw a ram caught by its horns in a bush. So he took the ram and sacrificed it as a burnt offering on the altar in place of his son. 14Abraham named the place "The LORD Will Provide."* This name has now become a proverb: "On the mountain of the LORD it will be provided."

15Then the angel of the LORD called again to Abraham from heaven, 16"This is what the LORD says: Because you have obeyed me and have not withheld even your beloved son, I swear by my own self that 17I will bless you richly. I will multiply your descendants into countless millions, like the stars of the sky and the sand on the seashore. They will conquer their enemies, 18and through your descendants,* all the nations of the earth will be blessed—all because you have obeyed me." 19Then they returned to Abraham's young men and traveled home again to Beersheba, where Abraham lived for quite some time.

20Soon after this, Abraham heard that Milcah, his brother Nahor's wife, had borne Nahor eight sons. 21The oldest was named Uz, the next oldest was Buz, followed by Kemuel (the father of Aram), 22Kesed, Hazo, Pildash, Jidlaph, and Bethuel. 23Bethuel became the father of Rebekah. 24In addition to his eight sons from Milcah, Nahor had four other children from his concubine Reumah. Their names were Tebah, Gaham, Tahash, and Maacah.

CHAPTER **23** **SARAH DIES.** When Sarah was 127 years old, 2she died at Kiriath-arba (now called Hebron) in the land of Canaan. There Abraham mourned and wept for her. 3Then, leaving her body, he went to the Hittite elders and said, 4"Here I am, a stranger in a foreign land, with no place to bury my wife. Please let me have a piece of land for a burial plot."

5The Hittites replied to Abraham, 6"Certainly, for you are an honored prince among us. It will be a privilege to have you choose the finest of our tombs so you can bury her there."

7Then Abraham bowed low before them and said, 8"Since this is how you feel, be so kind as to ask Ephron son of Zohar 9to let me have the cave of Machpelah, down at the end of his field. I want to pay the full price, of course, whatever is publicly agreed upon, so I may have a permanent burial place for my family."

10Ephron was sitting there among the others, and he answered Abraham as the others listened, speaking publicly before all the elders of the town. 11"No, sir," he said to Abraham, "please listen to me. I will give you the cave and the field. Here in the presence of my people, I give it to you. Go and bury your dead."

12Abraham bowed again to the people of the land, 13and he replied to Ephron as everyone listened. "No, listen to me," he insisted. "I will buy it from you. Let me pay the full price for the field so I can bury my dead there."

14"Well," Ephron answered, 15"the land is worth four hundred pieces* of silver, but what is that between friends? Go ahead and bury your dead."

16So Abraham paid Ephron the amount he had suggested, four hundred pieces of silver, as was publicly agreed. 17He bought the plot of land belonging to Ephron at Machpelah, near Mamre. This included the field, the cave that was in it, and all the trees nearby. 18They became Abraham's permanent possession by the agreement made in the presence of the Hittite elders at the city gate. 19So Abraham buried Sarah there in Canaan, in the cave of Machpelah, near Mamre, which is at Hebron. 20The field and the cave were sold to Abraham by the Hittites as a permanent burial place.

## BEAUTY ● ● • • •

**24:15-16 Rebekah had physical beauty, but the servant was looking for a sign of inner beauty. Our appearance is important to us, and we spend time and money improving it. But how do we develop our inner beauty? Patience, kindness, and joy are the beauty treatments that help us become truly lovely—on the inside.**

CHAPTER **24** **ISAAC MARRIES REBEKAH.** Abraham was now a very old man, and the LORD had blessed him in every way. 2One day Abraham said to the man in charge of his household, who was his oldest servant, 3"Swear* by the LORD, the God of heaven and earth, that you will not let my son marry one of these local Canaanite women. 4Go instead to my homeland, to my relatives, and find a wife there for my son Isaac."

5The servant asked, "But suppose I can't find a young woman who will travel so far from home? May I then take Isaac there to live among your relatives?"

6"No!" Abraham warned. "Be careful never to take my son there. 7For the LORD, the God of heaven, who took me from my father's house and my native land, solemnly promised to give this land to my offspring.* He will send his angel ahead of you, and he will see to it that you find a young woman there to be my son's wife. 8If she is unwilling to come back with you, then you are free from this oath. But under no circumstances are you to take my son there."

9So the servant took a solemn oath* that he

22:14 Hebrew *Yahweh Yir'eh.* 22:18 Hebrew *seed.* 23:15 Hebrew *400 shekels,* about 10 pounds or 4.6 kilograms in weight; also in 23:16. 24:3 Hebrew *Put your hand under my thigh, and I will make you swear.* 24:7 Hebrew *seed.* 24:9 Hebrew *put his hand under the thigh of Abraham his master and swore an oath.*

would follow Abraham's instructions. 10He loaded
ten of Abraham's camels with gifts and set out,
taking with him the best of everything his master
owned. He traveled to Aram-naharaim* and went
to the village where Abraham's brother Nahor had
settled. 11There the servant made the camels kneel
down beside a well just outside the village. It was
evening, and the women were coming out to draw
water.
12"O LORD, God of my master," he prayed. "Give
me success and show kindness to my master, Abraham. Help me to accomplish the purpose of my
journey. 13See, here I am, standing beside this
spring, and the young women of the village are
coming out to draw water. 14This is my request. I
will ask one of them for a drink. If she says, 'Yes,
certainly, and I will water your camels, too!'—let
her be the one you have appointed as Isaac's wife.
By this I will know that you have shown kindness
to my master."
15As he was still praying, a young woman named
Rebekah arrived with a water jug on her shoulder.
Her father was Bethuel, who was the son of Abraham's brother Nahor and his wife, Milcah. 16Now
Rebekah was very beautiful, and she was a virgin; no
man had ever slept with her. She went down to the
spring, filled her jug, and came up again. 17Running
over to her, the servant asked, "Please give me a
drink."
18"Certainly, sir," she said, and she quickly lowered the jug for him to drink. 19When he had finished, she said, "I'll draw water for your camels, too,
until they have had enough!" 20So she quickly emptied the jug into the watering trough and ran down
to the well again. She kept carrying water to the
camels until they had finished drinking. 21The servant watched her in silence, wondering whether or
not she was the one the LORD intended him to meet.
22Then at last, when the camels had finished drinking, he gave her a gold ring for her nose and two large
gold bracelets* for her wrists.
23"Whose daughter are you?" he asked. "Would
your father have any room to put us up for the
night?"
24"My father is Bethuel," she replied. "My grandparents are Nahor and Milcah. 25Yes, we have plenty
of straw and food for the camels, and we have a
room for guests."
26The man fell down to the ground and worshiped
the LORD. 27"Praise be to the LORD, the God of my
master, Abraham," he said. "The LORD has been so
kind and faithful to Abraham, for he has led me
straight to my master's relatives."
28The young woman ran home to tell her family
about all that had happened. 29Now Rebekah had
a brother named Laban. 30When he saw the nose-
ring and the bracelets on his sister's wrists, and
when he heard her story, he rushed out to the
spring, where the man was still standing beside his
camels. Laban said to him, 31"Come and stay with
us, you who are blessed by the LORD. Why do you
stand here outside the village when we have a
room all ready for you and a place prepared for the
camels!"
32So the man went home with Laban, and Laban

**What does God really expect from me? I hear so much from so many people that I almost feel overwhelmed. I feel like I have to give up a lot in order to make God happy.**

One essential quality about God is that he is very personal with each individual Christian. Although he chooses not to treat everyone alike, he does have expectations of his kids.

Some Christians may tell you about God's expectations based on where they are in their walk with him. If too many people are giving you advice, it could seem as though God expects way too much. This does not mean that you should quit listening to sincere Christians who want to help. It does mean, however, that if you are feeling overwhelmed, you are probably listening too much to others and not enough to God.

So what do you do? How do you please God?

The example from the story of Cain and Abel (see Genesis 4) gives a significant piece to the puzzle. Both of these men brought something to God, but only Abel's sacrifice pleased God. One reason was because Cain's heart was not really in it. He tried to please God out of obligation instead of love.

The first key to pleasing God is found in our heart or our motivation. Do we really want to make God happy, or are we going through the motions because someone told us we should?

The second key to pleasing God is obedience: "Those who obey my commandments are the ones who love me. And because they love me, my Father will love them, and I will love them. And I will reveal myself to each one of them" (John 14:21).

Good parents want their children to obey them in the essentials of how to live, how to avoid situations that will lead to pain or scars, and how to treat other people. God is no different. But he is the perfect Father. He does not overload us with too many rules, because he knows we would get discouraged.

Obedience to God is loving him enough to listen to what he says, then following through on what we know he is telling us.

This is why reading the Bible every day is so important. We cannot obey what we do not know. All that God wants us to know is written very plainly in his Word.

Through the Holy Spirit, God speaks to us as we come to him with willing hearts. He gently shows us areas in our lives that we need to examine and change according to his timetable, not someone else's.

**24:10** *Aram-naharaim* means "Aram of the two rivers," thought to have been located between the Euphrates and Balih Rivers in northwestern Mesopotamia. **24:22** Hebrew *a gold nose-ring weighing a half shekel* [0.2 ounces or 6 grams] *and two gold bracelets weighing 10 shekels* [4 ounces or 114 grams].

**WHAT THE BIBLE SAYS ABOUT MARRIAGE**

| | |
|---|---|
| Genesis 2:18-24 | Marriage is God's idea |
| Genesis 24:58-60 | Commitment is essential to a successful marriage |
| Genesis 29:10-11 | Romance is important |
| Jeremiah 33:10-11 | Marriage holds times of great joy |
| Malachi 2:14-15 | Marriage creates the best environment for raising children |
| Matthew 5:32 | Unfaithfulness breaks the bond of trust, the foundation of all relationships |
| Matthew 19:6 | Marriage is permanent |
| Romans 7:2-3 | Ideally, only death should dissolve marriage |
| Ephesians 5:21-33 | Marriage is based on the principled practice of love, not on feelings |
| Ephesians 5:23, 32 | Marriage is a living symbol of Christ and the church |
| Hebrews 13:4 | Marriage is good and honorable |

unloaded the camels, gave him straw to bed them down, fed them, and provided water for the camel drivers to wash their feet. [33]Then supper was served. But Abraham's servant said, "I don't want to eat until I have told you why I have come."

"All right," Laban said, "tell us your mission."

[34]"I am Abraham's servant," he explained. [35]"And the LORD has blessed my master richly; he has become a great man. The LORD has given him flocks of sheep and herds of cattle, a fortune in silver and gold, and many servants and camels and donkeys. [36]When Sarah, my master's wife, was very old, she gave birth to my master's son, and my master has given him everything he owns. [37]And my master made me swear that I would not let Isaac marry one of the local Canaanite women. [38]Instead, I was to come to his relatives here in this far-off land, to his father's home. I was told to bring back a young woman from here to marry his son.

[39]"'But suppose I can't find a young woman willing to come back with me?' I asked him. [40]'You will,' he told me, 'for the LORD, in whose presence I have walked, will send his angel with you and will make your mission successful. Yes, you must get a wife for my son from among my relatives, from my father's family. [41]But if you go to my relatives and they refuse to let her come, you will be free from your oath.'

[42]"So this afternoon when I came to the spring I prayed this prayer: 'O LORD, the God of my master, Abraham, if you are planning to make my mission a success, please guide me in a special way. [43]Here I am, standing beside this spring. I will say to some young woman who comes to draw water, "Please give me a drink of water!" [44]And she will reply, "Certainly! And I'll water your camels, too!" LORD, let her be the one you have selected to be the wife of my master's son.'

[45]"Before I had finished praying these words, I saw Rebekah coming along with her water jug on her shoulder. She went down to the spring and drew water and filled the jug. So I said to her, 'Please give me a drink.' [46]She quickly lowered the jug from her shoulder so I could drink, and she said, 'Certainly, sir, and I will water your camels, too!' And she did. [47]When I asked her whose daughter she was, she told me, 'My father is Bethuel, the son of Nahor and his wife, Milcah.' So I gave her the ring and the bracelets.

[48]"Then I bowed my head and worshiped the LORD. I praised the LORD, the God of my master, Abraham, because he had led me along the right path to find a wife from the family of my master's relatives. [49]So tell me—will you or won't you show true kindness to my master? When you tell me, then I'll know what my next step should be, whether to move this way or that."

[50]Then Laban and Bethuel replied, "The LORD has obviously brought you here, so what can we say? [51]Here is Rebekah; take her and go. Yes, let her be the wife of your master's son, as the LORD has directed."

[52]At this reply, Abraham's servant bowed to the ground and worshiped the LORD. [53]Then he brought out silver and gold jewelry and lovely clothing for Rebekah. He also gave valuable presents to her mother and brother. [54]Then they had supper, and the servant and the men with him stayed there overnight. But early the next morning, he said, "Send me back to my master."

[55]"But we want Rebekah to stay at least ten days," her brother and mother said. "Then she can go."

[56]But he said, "Don't hinder my return. The LORD has made my mission successful, and I want to report back to my master."

[57]"Well," they said, "we'll call Rebekah and ask her what she thinks." [58]So they called Rebekah. "Are you willing to go with this man?" they asked her.

And she replied, "Yes, I will go."

[59]So they said good-bye to Rebekah and sent her away with Abraham's servant and his men. The woman who had been Rebekah's childhood nurse went along with her. [60]They blessed her with this blessing as she parted:

"Our sister, may you become
 the mother of many millions!
May your descendants overcome
 all their enemies."

[61]Then Rebekah and her servants mounted the camels and left with Abraham's servant.

[62]Meanwhile, Isaac, whose home was in the Negev, had returned from Beer-lahairoi. [63]One evening as he was taking a walk out in the fields, meditating, he looked up and saw the camels coming.

64When Rebekah looked up and saw Isaac, she
quickly dismounted. 65"Who is that man walking
through the fields to meet us?" she asked the servant.
And he replied, "It is my master." So Rebekah
covered her face with her veil. 66Then the servant told
Isaac the whole story.
67And Isaac brought Rebekah into his mother's
tent, and she became his wife. He loved her very
much, and she was a special comfort to him after the
death of his mother.

CHAPTER **25** **ABRAHAM DIES.** Now Abraham
married again. Keturah was his new wife, 2and she
bore him Zimran, Jokshan, Medan, Midian, Ishbak,
and Shuah. 3Jokshan's two sons were Sheba and
Dedan. Dedan's descendants were the Asshurites,
Letushites, and Leummites. 4Midian's sons were
Ephah, Epher, Hanoch,
Abida, and Eldaah. These
were all descendants of
Abraham through Keturah.
5Abraham left everything
he owned to his son Isaac.
6But before he died, he gave
gifts to the sons of his concubines and sent them off to
the east, away from Isaac.
7Abraham lived for 175
years, 8and he died at a ripe
old age, joining his ancestors
in death. 9His sons Isaac and
Ishmael buried him in the
cave of Machpelah, near
Mamre, in the field of Ephron son of Zohar the Hittite.
10This was the field Abraham
had purchased from the Hittites, where he had buried
his wife Sarah. 11After Abraham's death, God poured
out rich blessings on Isaac,
who settled near Beer-lahairoi in the Negev.
12This is the history of the
descendants of Ishmael, the
son of Abraham through
Hagar, Sarah's Egyptian servant. 13Here is a list, by their
names and clans, of Ishmael's descendants: The oldest
was Nebaioth, followed by
Kedar, Adbeel, Mibsam,
14Mishma, Dumah, Massa,
15Hadad, Tema, Jetur, Na-
phish, and Kedemah.
16These twelve sons of Ishmael became the founders
of twelve tribes that bore
their names, listed according
to the places they settled and camped. 17Ishmael
finally died at the age of 137 and joined his ancestors in death. 18Ishmael's descendants were scattered
across the country from Havilah to Shur, which is
east of Egypt in the direction of Asshur. The clans
descended from Ishmael camped close to one another.*
19This is the history of the family of Isaac, the
son of Abraham. 20When Isaac was forty years old,
he married Rebekah, the daughter of Bethuel the
Aramean from Paddan-aram and the sister of Laban. 21Isaac pleaded with the LORD to give Rebekah
a child because she was childless. So the LORD
answered Isaac's prayer, and his wife became pregnant with twins. 22But the two children struggled
with each other in her womb. So she went to ask

## REBEKAH

Some people know how to get things started. They're initiators. Like Rebekah, they naturally make the first moves. When she saw something that needed to be done, she took action—even though her actions weren't always right.

Look at what she did at the well near her home. She gave a drink to Eliezer, Abraham's servant who was looking for a wife for Isaac. That was kind. Then she offered to give a drink to his 10 thirsty camels. That really caught his attention! Often, a person's helpfulness makes a deeper impression than his or her appearance.

Other times, though, Rebekah acted without such good results. She had a favorite between her two boys—Jacob. She found ways to help him do better than his brother, Esau. But since Esau was the oldest, Rebekah's husband, Isaac, gave him more attention. This created a situation in which Rebekah ended up deceiving her husband into giving to Jacob a special blessing that was meant for Esau. She tried to accomplish God's plan *her* way—and made a mess.

Most of the time we try to think of good reasons for the things we choose to do. Often we even want to add God's approval to our actions. While it is true that our actions will not spoil God's plan, it is also true that we are responsible for what we do. Before we take action we need to be truthful about our real motives. Asking this question can help: "Am I sure God wants me to do this, or do I just want his approval on what I've decided to do anyway?" Your actions will bring great results when they are controlled by God's wisdom.

**UPS**:
- When confronted with a need she took immediate action
- She was persistent in her plans

**DOWNS**:
- Her initiative was not always balanced by wisdom
- She favored one of her sons
- She deceived her husband

**STATS:**
- Where: Haran, Canaan
- Occupation: Wife, mother, household manager
- Relatives: Parents: Bethuel and Milcah. Husband: Isaac. Brother: Laban. Twin sons: Esau and Jacob.

LESSONS: Our actions must be guided by God's Word
God even makes use of our mistakes in his plan
Parental favoritism hurts a family

KEY VERSE: "And Isaac brought Rebekah into his mother's tent, and she became his wife. He loved her very much, and she was a special comfort to him after the death of his mother" (Genesis 24:67).

Rebekah's story is told in Genesis 24–27. She is also mentioned in Romans 9:10.

**25:18** The meaning of the Hebrew is uncertain.

the LORD about it. "Why is this happening to me?" she asked.

23And the LORD told her, "The sons in your womb will become two rival nations. One nation will be stronger than the other; the descendants of your older son will serve the descendants of your younger son."

24And when the time came, the twins were born. 25The first was very red at birth. He was covered with so much hair that one would think he was wearing a piece of clothing. So they called him Esau.* 26Then the other twin was born with his hand grasping Esau's heel. So they called him Jacob.* Isaac was sixty years old when the twins were born.

27As the boys grew up, Esau became a skillful hunter, a man of the open fields, while Jacob was the kind of person who liked to stay at home. 28Isaac loved Esau in particular because of the wild game he brought home, but Rebekah favored Jacob.

29One day when Jacob was cooking some stew, Esau arrived home exhausted and hungry from a hunt. 30Esau said to Jacob, "I'm starved! Give me some of that red stew you've made." (This was how Esau got his other name, Edom—"Red.")

31Jacob replied, "All right, but trade me your birthright for it."

32"Look, I'm dying of starvation!" said Esau. "What good is my birthright to me now?"

33So Jacob insisted, "Well then, swear to me right now that it is mine." So Esau swore an oath, thereby selling all his rights as the firstborn to his younger brother. 34Then Jacob gave Esau some bread and lentil stew. Esau ate and drank and went on about his business, indifferent to the fact that he had given up his birthright.

## IMPULSE BUYING ● ● • • •

25:32-33 **Esau traded the lasting benefits of his birthright for the immediate pleasure of food. We can fall into the same trap. When we see something we want, our first impulse is to get it. But immediate pleasure often loses sight of the future.**

**Esau exaggerated his hunger. "I'm dying of starvation!" he said. This thought made his choice much easier, because if he was dying, what good was an inheritance anyway? The pressure of the moment distorted his perspective and made his decision seem urgent. We sometimes feel such great pressure in one area that nothing else seems to matter, and we lose our perspective. We can avoid making Esau's mistake by comparing the short-term satisfaction with its long-range consequences before we act.**

CHAPTER **26** **ISAAC TRICKS THE KING.** Now a severe famine struck the land, as had happened before in Abraham's time. So Isaac moved to Gerar, where Abimelech, king of the Philistines, lived.

2The LORD appeared to him there and said, "Do not go to Egypt. 3Do as I say, and stay here in this land. If you do, I will be with you and bless you. I will give all this land to you and your descendants,

## JEALOUSY ● ● • • •

26:12-16 **God kept his promise to bless Isaac. The neighboring Philistines grew jealous because everything Isaac did seemed to go right. So they filled up his wells and tried to get rid of him. Jealousy is a dividing force strong enough to tear apart the mightiest of nations or the closest of friends. When you find yourself becoming jealous of others, try thanking God for their good fortune. Before striking out in anger, consider what you could lose.**

just as I solemnly promised Abraham, your father. 4I will cause your descendants to become as numerous as the stars, and I will give them all these lands. And through your descendants* all the nations of the earth will be blessed. 5I will do this because Abraham listened to me and obeyed all my requirements, commands, regulations, and laws."

6So Isaac stayed in Gerar. 7And when the men there asked him about Rebekah, he said, "She is my sister." He was afraid to admit that she was his wife. He thought they would kill him to get her, because she was very beautiful. 8But some time later, Abimelech, king of the Philistines, looked out a window and saw Isaac fondling Rebekah.

9Abimelech called for Isaac and exclaimed, "She is obviously your wife! Why did you say she was your sister?"

"Because I was afraid someone would kill me to get her from me," Isaac replied.

10"How could you treat us this way!" Abimelech exclaimed. "Someone might have taken your wife and slept with her, and you would have made us guilty of great sin." 11Then Abimelech made a public proclamation: "Anyone who harms this man or his wife will die!"

12That year Isaac's crops were tremendous! He harvested a hundred times more grain than he planted, for the LORD blessed him. 13He became a rich man, and his wealth only continued to grow. 14He acquired large flocks of sheep and goats, great herds of cattle, and many servants. Soon the Philistines became jealous of him, 15and they filled up all of Isaac's wells with earth. These were the wells that had been dug by the servants of his father, Abraham.

16And Abimelech asked Isaac to leave the country. "Go somewhere else," he said, "for you have become too rich and powerful for us."

17So Isaac moved to the Gerar Valley and lived there instead. 18He reopened the wells his father had dug, which the Philistines had filled in after Abraham's death. Isaac renamed them, using the names Abraham had given them. 19His shepherds also dug in the Gerar Valley and found a gushing spring.

20But then the local shepherds came and claimed the spring. "This is our water," they said, and they argued over it with Isaac's herdsmen. So Isaac named the well "Argument,"* because they had argued about it with him. 21Isaac's men then dug another well, but again there was a fight over it. So Isaac named it "Opposition."* 22Abandoning that one, he

25:25 *Esau* sounds like a Hebrew term that means "hair." 25:26 *Jacob* means "he grasps the heel"; this can also figuratively mean "he deceives." 26:4 Hebrew *seed.* 26:20 Hebrew *Esek.* 26:21 Hebrew *Sitnah.*

dug another well, and the local people finally left
him alone. So Isaac called it "Room Enough,"* for
he said, "At last the LORD has made room for us, and
we will be able to thrive."
23From there Isaac moved to Beersheba, 24where
the LORD appeared to him on the night of his arrival.
"I am the God of your father, Abraham," he said.
"Do not be afraid, for I am with you and will bless
you. I will give you many descendants, and they will
become a great nation. I will do this because of my
promise to Abraham, my servant." 25Then Isaac built
an altar there and worshiped the LORD. He set up his
camp at that place, and his servants dug a well.
26One day Isaac had visitors from Gerar. King
Abimelech arrived with his adviser, Ahuzzath, and
also Phicol, his army commander. 27"Why have you
come?" Isaac asked them.
"This is obviously no
friendly visit, since you sent
me from your land in a most
unfriendly way."
28They replied, "We can
plainly see that the LORD is
with you. So we decided we
should have a treaty, a covenant between us. 29Swear
that you will not harm us,
just as we did not harm you.
We have always treated you
well, and we sent you away
from us in peace. And now
look how the LORD has
blessed you!"
30So Isaac prepared a great
feast for them, and they ate
and drank in preparation for
the treaty ceremony. 31Early
the next morning, they each
took a solemn oath of nonag-
gression. Then Isaac sent
them home again in peace.
32That very day Isaac's servants came and told him
about a well they had dug.
"We've found water!" they
said. 33So Isaac named the well
"Oath,"* and from that time
to this, the town that grew
up there has been called
Beersheba—"well of the
oath."
34At the age of forty, Esau
married a young woman
named Judith, the daughter
of Beeri the Hittite. He also
married Basemath, the
daughter of Elon the Hittite.
35But Esau's wives made life
miserable for Isaac and
Rebekah.

**PARENTS ● ● • • •**

26:34-35 **Esau married heathen women, and this really upset his parents. Most parents have a wealth of good advice because they have a lifetime of insight into their children's character. You may not agree with everything your parents say, but at least talk with them and listen carefully. This will help avoid the hard feelings Esau experienced.**

CHAPTER **27** **JACOB DECEIVES ISAAC.** When Isaac
was old and almost blind, he called for Esau, his
older son, and said, "My son?"
"Yes, Father?" Esau replied.
2"I am an old man now," Isaac said, "and I expect
every day to be my last. 3Take your bow and a quiver
full of arrows out into the open country, and hunt

**UPS:**
- Ancestor of the Edomites
- Known for his archery skill
- Able to forgive after explosive anger

**DOWNS:**
- When faced with important decisions, tended to choose according to the immediate need rather than the long-range effect
- Angered his parents by poor marriage choices

**STATS:**
- Where: Canaan
- Occupation: Skillful hunter
- Relatives: Parents: Isaac and Rebekah. Brother: Jacob. Wives: Judith, Basemath, and Mahalath.

**ESAU** You probably have had people tell you to use common sense. Have they ever explained what they meant? "Using common sense" means refusing to do something that you know will bring results you won't like. Esau had a real problem with common sense. He made many wrong decisions because he didn't stop to think about what would happen. He wanted things right away without figuring out what he would have to pay later. Trading his birthright for a bowl of stew was one example of this problem. He also chose wives in direct opposition to his parents' wishes.

What are you willing to trade for the things you want? Do you find yourself willing at times to give anything—even your family, friendships, reputation, body, or soul—to get what you feel you need *now?* Maybe, like Esau, you haven't been using common sense.

If so, your first response, also like Esau, may be to get angry. That isn't necessarily wrong, as long as you direct the energy of that anger toward finding a solution and not toward punishing yourself or others. Your greatest need probably is to find a new way to measure how important things are to you. Up until now, your only measurement may have been to ask, "Do I need this now?" But the best measurement of value comes from God and his Word. In other words, you should ask: "Is this what God wants?" A relationship with him will not only give an ultimate purpose to your life, but will also be a daily guideline for real commonsense living.

LESSONS: God allows certain events in our lives to accomplish his overall purposes, but we are still responsible for our actions

Consequences are important to consider

It is possible to have great anger and yet not sin

KEY VERSE: "And afterward, when [Esau] wanted his father's blessing, he was rejected. It was too late for repentance, even though he wept bitter tears" (Hebrews 12:17).

Esau's story is told in Genesis 25–36. He is also mentioned in Malachi 1:2; Romans 9:13; Hebrews 12:16-17.

26:22 Hebrew *Rehoboth.* 26:33 Hebrew *Shibah,* which can mean "oath" or "seven."

some wild game for me. [4]Prepare it just the way I like it so it's savory and good, and bring it here for me to eat. Then I will pronounce the blessing that belongs to you, my firstborn son, before I die."

[5]But Rebekah overheard the conversation. So when Esau left to hunt for the wild game, [6]she said to her son Jacob, "I overheard your father asking Esau [7]to prepare him a delicious meal of wild game. He wants to bless Esau in the LORD's presence before he dies. [8]Now, my son, do exactly as I tell you. [9]Go out to the flocks and bring me two fine young goats. I'll prepare your father's favorite dish from them. [10]Take the food to your father; then he can eat it and bless you instead of Esau before he dies."

## GOOD GOALS ● ● • • •

27:5-10 **When Rebekah learned that Isaac was preparing to bless Esau, she quickly devised a plan to trick him into blessing Jacob instead. Although God had already told her that Jacob would become the family leader (25:23-26), Rebekah took matters into her own hands. She resorted to doing something wrong to try to bring about what God had already said would happen. For Rebekah, the end justified the means. No matter how good we think our goals are, we should not attempt to achieve them by doing what is wrong.**

[11]"But Mother!" Jacob replied. "He won't be fooled that easily. Think how hairy Esau is and how smooth my skin is! [12]What if my father touches me? He'll see that I'm trying to trick him, and then he'll curse me instead of blessing me."

[13]"Let the curse fall on me, dear son," said Rebekah. "Just do what I tell you. Go out and get the goats."

[14]So Jacob followed his mother's instructions, bringing her the two goats. She took them and cooked a delicious meat dish, just the way Isaac liked it. [15]Then she took Esau's best clothes, which were there in the house, and dressed Jacob with them. [16]She made him a pair of gloves from the hairy skin of the young goats, and she fastened a strip of the goat's skin around his neck. [17]Then she gave him the meat dish, with its rich aroma, and some freshly baked bread. [18]Jacob carried the platter of food to his father and said, "My father?"

"Yes, my son," he answered. "Who is it—Esau or Jacob?"

[19]Jacob replied, "It's Esau, your older son. I've done as you told me. Here is the wild game, cooked the way you like it. Sit up and eat it so you can give me your blessing."

[20]Isaac asked, "How were you able to find it so quickly, my son?"

"Because the LORD your God put it in my path!" Jacob replied.

[21]Then Isaac said to Jacob, "Come over here. I want to touch you to make sure you really are Esau." [22]So Jacob went over to his father, and Isaac touched him. "The voice is Jacob's, but the hands are Esau's," Isaac said to himself. [23]But he did not recognize Jacob because Jacob's hands felt hairy just like Esau's. So Isaac pronounced his blessing on Jacob. [24]"Are you really my son Esau?" he asked.

"Yes, of course," Jacob replied.

[25]Then Isaac said, "Now, my son, bring me the meat. I will eat it, and then I will give you my blessing." So Jacob took the food over to his father, and Isaac ate it. He also drank the wine that Jacob served him. Then Isaac said, [26]"Come here and kiss me, my son."

[27]So Jacob went over and kissed him. And when Isaac caught the smell of his clothes, he was finally convinced, and he blessed his son. He said, "The smell of my son is the good smell of the open fields that the LORD has blessed. [28]May God always give you plenty of dew for healthy crops and good harvests of grain and wine. [29]May many nations become your servants. May you be the master of your brothers. May all your mother's sons bow low before you. All who curse you are cursed, and all who bless you are blessed."

[30]As soon as Isaac had blessed Jacob, and almost before Jacob had left his father, Esau returned from his hunting trip. [31]Esau prepared his father's favorite meat dish and brought it to him. Then he said, "I'm back, Father, and I have the wild game. Sit up and eat it so you can give me your blessing."

[32]But Isaac asked him, "Who are you?"

"Why, it's me, of course!" he replied. "It's Esau, your older son."

[33]Isaac began to tremble uncontrollably and said, "Then who was it that just served me wild game? I have already eaten it, and I blessed him with an irrevocable blessing before you came."

[34]When Esau understood, he let out a loud and bitter cry. "O my father, bless me, too!" he begged.

[35]But Isaac said, "Your brother was here, and he tricked me. He has carried away your blessing."

[36]Esau said bitterly, "No wonder his name is Jacob,* for he has deceived me twice, first taking my birthright and now stealing my blessing. Oh, haven't you saved even one blessing for me?"

[37]Isaac said to Esau, "I have made Jacob your master and have declared that all his brothers will be his servants. I have guaranteed him an abundance of grain and wine—what is there left to give?"

[38]Esau pleaded, "Not one blessing left for me?

## WARNING! ● ● • • •

27:11-12 **How we react to a moral dilemma often exposes our real motives. Frequently we are more worried about getting caught than about doing what is right. Jacob did not seem concerned about the deceitfulness of his mother's plan; instead he was afraid of getting in trouble while carrying it out. If you are worried about getting caught, you are probably in a position that is less than honest. Let your fear of getting caught be a warning to do right. Jacob paid a huge price for carrying out this dishonest plan.**

27:36 *Jacob* means "he grasps the heel"; this can also figuratively mean "he deceives."

O my father, bless me, too!" Then Esau broke down
and wept.
39 His father, Isaac, said to him, "You will live off
the land and what it yields, 40 and you will live by
your sword. You will serve your brother for a time,
but then you will shake loose from him and be
free."
41 Esau hated Jacob because he had stolen his
blessing, and he said to himself, "My father will
soon be dead and gone. Then I will kill Jacob."
42 But someone got wind
of what Esau was planning
and reported it to Rebekah.
She sent for Jacob and told
him, "Esau is threatening to
kill you. 43 This is what you
should do. Flee to your uncle Laban in Haran. 44 Stay
there with him until your
brother's fury is spent.
45 When he forgets what you
have done, I will send for
you. Why should I lose both
of you in one day?"
46 Then Rebekah said to
Isaac, "I'm sick and tired of
these local Hittite women.
I'd rather die than see Jacob
marry one of them."

CHAPTER **28** **JACOB IS SENT TO FIND A WIFE.** So Isaac
called for Jacob, blessed
him, and said, "Do not
marry any of these Canaanite women. 2 Instead, go at
once to Paddan-aram, to the
house of your grandfather
Bethuel, and marry one of
your uncle Laban's daugh-
ters. 3 May God Almighty
bless you and give you many
children. And may your descendants become a great
assembly of nations! 4 May
God pass on to you and
your descendants the blessings he promised to Abra-
ham. May you own this land
where we now are foreign-
ers, for God gave it to Abraham."
5 So Isaac sent Jacob away,
and he went to Paddan-
aram to stay with his uncle
Laban, his mother's brother,
the son of Bethuel the Aramean.
6 Esau heard that his
father had blessed Jacob and
sent him to Paddan-aram to
find a wife, and that he had warned Jacob not to
marry a Canaanite woman. 7 He also knew that Jacob
had obeyed his parents and gone to Paddan-aram.
8 It was now very clear to Esau that his father despised
the local Canaanite women. 9 So he visited his uncle
Ishmael's family and married one of Ishmael's
daughters, in addition to the wives he already had.
His new wife's name was Mahalath. She was the
sister of Nebaioth and the daughter of Ishmael,
Abraham's son.

---

**UPS:**
- Father of the 12 tribes of Israel
- Third in the Abrahamic line of God's plan
- Determined; willing to work long and hard for what he wanted
- Successful livestock owner

**DOWNS:**
- When faced with conflict, he relied on his own resources rather than going to God for help
- Wanted to fill his life with things

**STATS:**
- Where: Canaan
- Occupation: Shepherd, livestock owner
- Relatives: Parents: Isaac and Rebekah. Brother: Esau. Father-in-law: Laban. Wives: Rachel and Leah. Twelve sons and one daughter are named in the Bible.

**JACOB** was the third person in God's plan to start the nation of Israel from Abraham's family. But sometimes Jacob just seemed to get in the way of the plan. God used his life anyway. God works in the same way, regardless of our actions. He is willing to use people like us even though we don't cooperate perfectly.

Jacob's name means "Usurper," or "Grabber," and he certainly lived up to it. He got the name by grabbing his twin brother Esau's heel while they were being born. Later, when he grabbed his brother's birthright and blessing, he had to run for his life.

While Jacob was running away from home, God appeared to him. God let Jacob know he was real and that he planned to work through Jacob's life. Shortly after this, Jacob had to live with his uncle Laban who was just as big a grabber! Jacob got 20 years' worth of patience lessons with his uncle, but he realized he was where God wanted him to be. When Jacob did leave Laban, he had become a different kind of grabber. This time, by the Jordan River, he grabbed on to God and wouldn't let go. He realized now that everything he had grabbed in life could be taken away except for God's presence and blessing. God had changed Jacob, so he also changed his name—to Israel. Jacob had learned the lesson that no one or nothing can take God's place in our lives. By the time Jacob (Israel) was an old man, he wasn't so much a *grabber* as someone who had been *grabbed* by God. He no longer made plans without including God.

At what times and places has God made himself known to you? Are you more like the young Jacob, forcing God to track you down in the wilderness of your own plans and mistakes? Or are you more like the Jacob who placed his desires and plans before God for his approval before taking any action?

LESSONS: Security doesn't come from filling your life with things

All human intentions and actions—for good or for evil—are woven by God into his ongoing plan

KEY VERSE: "I will be with you, and I will protect you wherever you go. I will someday bring you safely back to this land. I will be with you constantly until I have finished giving you everything I have promised" (Genesis 28:15).

Jacob's story is told in Genesis 25–50. He is also mentioned in Hosea 12:2-5; Matthew 1:2; 22:32; Acts 3:13; 7:46; Romans 9:11-13; Hebrews 11:9, 20-21.

---

## PERSONALIZED FAITH ● ● • • •

**28:10-15 God's covenant promise to Abraham and Isaac was offered to Jacob as well. But it was not enough to be Abraham's grandson; Jacob had to establish his own personal relationship with God. God has no grandchildren; each of us must have a personal relationship with him. It is not enough to hear wonderful stories about Christians in your family. You need to become part of the story yourself (see Galatians 3:6-7).**

[10]Meanwhile, Jacob left Beersheba and traveled toward Haran. [11]At sundown he arrived at a good place to set up camp and stopped there for the night. Jacob found a stone for a pillow and lay down to sleep. [12]As he slept, he dreamed of a stairway that reached from earth to heaven. And he saw the angels of God going up and down on it.

[13]At the top of the stairway stood the LORD, and he said, "I am the LORD, the God of your grandfather Abraham and the God of your father, Isaac. The ground you are lying on belongs to you. I will give it to you and your descendants. [14]Your descendants will be as numerous as the dust of the earth! They will cover the land from east to west and from north to south. All the families of the earth will be blessed through you and your descendants.* [15]What's more, I will be with you, and I will protect you wherever you go. I will someday bring you safely back to this land. I will be with you constantly until I have finished giving you everything I have promised."

[16]Then Jacob woke up and said, "Surely the LORD is in this place, and I wasn't even aware of it." [17]He was afraid and said, "What an awesome place this is! It is none other than the house of God—the gateway to heaven!" [18]The next morning he got up very early. He took the stone he had used as a pillow and set it upright as a memorial pillar. Then he poured olive oil over it. [19]He named the place Bethel—"house of God"—though the name of the nearby village was Luz.

[20]Then Jacob made this vow: "If God will be with me and protect me on this journey and give me food and clothing, [21]and if he will bring me back safely to my father, then I will make the LORD my God. [22]This memorial pillar will become a place for worshiping God, and I will give God a tenth of everything he gives me."

## CHAPTER 29

**JACOB MEETS RACHEL.** Jacob hurried on, finally arriving in the land of the east. [2]He saw in the distance three flocks of sheep lying in an open field beside a well, waiting to be watered. But a heavy stone covered the mouth of the well. [3]It was the custom there to wait for all the flocks to arrive before removing the stone. After watering them, the stone would be rolled back over the mouth of the well. [4]Jacob went over to the shepherds and asked them, "Where do you live?"

"At Haran," they said.

[5]"Do you know a man there named Laban, the grandson of Nahor?"

"Yes, we do," they replied.

[6]"How is he?" Jacob asked.

"He's well and prosperous. Look, here comes his daughter Rachel with the sheep."

[7]"Why don't you water the flocks so they can get back to grazing?" Jacob asked. "They'll be hungry if you stop so early in the day."

[8]"We don't roll away the stone and begin the watering until all the flocks and shepherds are here," they replied.

[9]As this conversation was going on, Rachel arrived with her father's sheep, for she was a shepherd. [10]And because she was his cousin, the daughter of his mother's brother, and because the sheep were his uncle's, Jacob went over to the well and rolled away the stone and watered his uncle's flock. [11]Then Jacob kissed Rachel, and tears came to his eyes. [12]He explained that he was her cousin on her father's side, her aunt Rebekah's son. So Rachel quickly ran and told her father, Laban.

[13]As soon as Laban heard about Jacob's arrival, he rushed out to meet him and greeted him warmly. Laban then brought him home, and Jacob told him his story. [14]"Just think, my very own flesh and blood!" Laban exclaimed.

After Jacob had been there about a month, [15]Laban said to him, "You shouldn't work for me without pay just because we are relatives. How much do you want?"

[16]Now Laban had two daughters: Leah, who was the oldest, and her younger sister, Rachel. [17]Leah had pretty eyes,* but Rachel was beautiful in every way, with a lovely face and shapely figure. [18]Since Jacob was in love with Rachel, he told her father, "I'll work for you seven years if you'll give me Rachel, your younger daughter, as my wife."

[19]"Agreed!" Laban replied. "I'd rather give her to you than to someone outside the family."

[20]So Jacob spent the next seven years working to pay for Rachel. But his love for her was so strong that it seemed to him but a few days. [21]Finally, the time came for him to marry her. "I have fulfilled my contract," Jacob said to Laban. "Now give me my wife so we can be married."

[22]So Laban invited everyone in the neighborhood to celebrate with Jacob at a wedding feast. [23]That

## WORTH THE WAIT ● ● • • •

**29:20-28 People often wonder if waiting a long time for something they want is worth it. Jacob waited seven years to marry Rachel. After being tricked, he agreed to work seven more years for her! The most important goals and desires are worth working and waiting for. Movies and television have created the illusion that people have to wait only about an hour to solve their problems or get what they want. Don't be trapped into thinking the same is true in real life. Patience is hardest when we need it the most, but it is the key to achieving our goals.**

**28:14** Hebrew *seed.* **29:17** Or *dull eyes.* The meaning of the Hebrew is uncertain.

night, when it was dark, Laban took Leah to Jacob, and he slept with her. [24]And Laban gave Leah a servant, Zilpah, to be her maid.

[25]But when Jacob woke up in the morning—it was Leah! "What sort of trick is this?" Jacob raged at Laban. "I worked seven years for Rachel. What do you mean by this trickery?"

[26]"It's not our custom to marry off a younger daughter ahead of the firstborn," Laban replied. [27]"Wait until the bridal week is over, and you can have Rachel, too—that is, if you promise to work another seven years for me."

[28]So Jacob agreed to work seven more years. A week after Jacob had married Leah, Laban gave him Rachel, too. [29]And Laban gave Rachel a servant, Bilhah, to be her maid. [30]So Jacob slept with Rachel, too, and he loved her more than Leah. He then stayed and worked the additional seven years.

[31]But because Leah was unloved, the LORD let her have a child, while Rachel was childless. [32]So Leah became pregnant and had a son. She named him Reuben,* for she said, "The LORD has noticed my misery, and now my husband will love me." [33]She soon became pregnant again and had another son. She named him Simeon,* for she said, "The LORD heard that I was unloved and has given me another son." [34]Again she became pregnant and had a son. She named him Levi,* for she said, "Surely now my husband will feel affection for me, since I have given him three sons!" [35]Once again she became pregnant and had a son. She named him Judah,* for she said, "Now I will praise the LORD!" And then she stopped having children.

CHAPTER **30** When Rachel saw that she wasn't having any children, she became jealous of her sister. "Give me children, or I'll die!" she exclaimed to Jacob.

[2]Jacob flew into a rage. "Am I God?" he asked. "He is the only one able to give you children!"

[3]Then Rachel told him, "Sleep with my servant, Bilhah, and she will bear children for me." [4]So

## BABY CONTEST ● ● • • •

**30:4-12 Rachel and Leah were locked in a cruel contest. In their race to have more children, they both gave their servant girls to Jacob as concubines. Jacob would have been wise to refuse, even though this was an accepted custom of the day. The fact that a custom is socially acceptable does not mean it is wise or right. You will be spared much heartbreak if you look at the potential consequences—to you or others—of your actions. Are you doing anything now that might cause future problems?**

## RACHEL

For Rachel's family, the town well at Haran was an important place. Someone had to go there for water every day. Some great things happened at the well. There Rebekah met Eliezer, Abraham's servant, who had come to find a wife for Isaac. Some 40 years later, Rebekah's son Jacob met his cousin Rachel at the same well. The relationship that quickly grew between them not only reminds us that romance is not a modern invention, but also teaches us a few lessons about real love.

Jacob's love for Rachel was both patient and practical. Jacob had the patience to wait seven years for her, but he kept busy in the meantime. His faithfulness to Rachel created a strong loyalty to him in her. But Rachel was also frustrated. At first, she couldn't have children. She felt she was competing with her sister, Leah, for Jacob's affection. But she missed the point: Jacob had already freely given her his devoted love.

Sometimes we make the same mistake, thinking we can "earn" love and friendship. We even think we can somehow earn God's love. But we can't earn what God has already given us. He loves us! His love has no beginning and is incredibly patient. All we need to do is respond to God's love, which he has offered freely to us.

God's Word says in many ways, "I do love you. I have demonstrated my love by all I've done for you. I have even sacrificed my Son, Jesus, to pay the price for your sins. Now live because of my love. Respond to me; love me with your whole being; give yourself to me in thanks, not as payment. Live life fully, in the freedom of knowing you are loved."

LESSONS: Loyalty must be controlled by what is true and right

Love is accepted, not earned

KEY VERSE: "So Jacob spent the next seven years working to pay for Rachel. But his love for her was so strong that it seemed to him but a few days" (Genesis 29:20).

Rachel's story is told in Genesis 29:6–35:20. She is also mentioned in Ruth 4:11.

**UPS:**
- Showed great loyalty to her family
- Mothered Joseph and Benjamin after being barren for many years

**DOWNS:**
- Her envy and competitiveness marred her relationship with her sister, Leah
- Was capable of dishonesty by taking her loyalty too far
- Failed to recognize that Jacob's devotion was not dependent on her ability to have children

**STATS:**
- Where: Haran
- Occupation: Shepherdess, homemaker
- Relatives: Father: Laban. Aunt: Rebekah. Sister: Leah. Husband: Jacob. Sons: Joseph and Benjamin.

29:32 *Reuben* means "Look, a son!" It also sounds like the Hebrew for "He has seen my misery." 29:33 *Simeon* probably means "one who hears." 29:34 *Levi* sounds like a Hebrew term that means "being attached" or "feeling affection for." 29:35 *Judah* sounds like the Hebrew term for "praise."

Rachel gave him Bilhah to be his wife, and Jacob slept with her. [5]Bilhah became pregnant and presented him with a son. [6]Rachel named him Dan,* for she said, "God has vindicated me! He has heard my request and given me a son." [7]Then Bilhah became pregnant again and gave Jacob a second son. [8]Rachel named him Naphtali,* for she said, "I have had an intense struggle with my sister, and I am winning!"

[9]Meanwhile, Leah realized that she wasn't getting pregnant anymore, so she gave her servant, Zilpah, to Jacob to be his wife. [10]Soon Zilpah presented him with another son. [11]Leah named him Gad,* for she said, "How fortunate I am!" [12]Then Zilpah produced a second son, [13]and Leah named him Asher,* for she said, "What joy is mine! The other women will consider me happy indeed!"

[14]One day during the wheat harvest, Reuben found some mandrakes growing in a field and brought the roots to his mother, Leah. Rachel begged Leah to give some of them to her. [15]But Leah angrily replied, "Wasn't it enough that you stole my husband? Now will you steal my son's mandrake roots, too?"

Rachel said, "I will let him sleep with you tonight in exchange for the mandrake roots."

[16]So that evening, as Jacob was coming home from the fields, Leah went out to meet him. "You must sleep with me tonight!" she said. "I have paid for you with some mandrake roots my son has found." So Jacob slept with her. [17]And God answered her prayers. She became pregnant again and gave birth to her fifth son. [18]She named him Issachar,* for she said, "God has rewarded me for giving my servant to my husband as a wife." [19]Then she became pregnant again and had a sixth son. [20]She named him Zebulun,* for she said, "God has given me good gifts for my husband. Now he will honor me, for I have given him six sons." [21]Later she gave birth to a daughter and named her Dinah.

[22]Then God remembered Rachel's plight and answered her prayers by giving her a child. [23]She became pregnant and gave birth to a son. "God has removed my shame," she said. [24]And she named him Joseph,* for she said, "May the LORD give me yet another son."

[25]Soon after Joseph was born to Rachel, Jacob said to Laban, "I want to go back home. [26]Let me take my wives and children, for I have earned them from you, and let me be on my way. You know I have fully paid for them with my service to you."

[27]"Please don't leave me," Laban replied, "for I have learned by divination that the LORD has blessed me because you are here. [28]How much do I owe you? Whatever it is, I'll pay it."

[29]Jacob replied, "You know how faithfully I've served you through these many years, and how your flocks and herds have grown. [30]You had little indeed before I came, and your wealth has increased enormously. The LORD has blessed you from everything I do! But now, what about me? When should I provide for my own family?"

[31]"What wages do you want?" Laban asked again.

Jacob replied, "Don't give me anything at all. Just do one thing, and I'll go back to work for you. [32]Let me go out among your flocks today and remove all the sheep and goats that are speckled or spotted, along with all the dark-colored sheep. Give them to me as my wages. [33]This will make it easy for you to see whether or not I have been honest. If you find in my flock any white sheep or goats that are not speckled, you will know that I have stolen them from you."

[34]"All right," Laban replied. "It will be as you have said." [35]But that very day Laban went out and removed all the male goats that were speckled and spotted, the females that were speckled and spotted with any white patches, and all the dark-colored sheep. He placed them in the care of his sons, [36]and they took them three days' distance from where Jacob was. Meanwhile, Jacob stayed and cared for Laban's flock.

[37]Now Jacob took fresh shoots from poplar, almond, and plane trees and peeled off strips of the bark to make white streaks on them. [38]Then he set up these peeled branches beside the watering troughs so Laban's flocks would see them as they came to drink, for that was when they mated. [39]So when the flocks mated in front of the white-streaked branches, all of their offspring were streaked, speckled, and spotted. [40]Jacob added them to his own flock, thus separating the lambs from Laban's flock. Then at mating time, he turned the flocks toward the streaked and dark-colored rams in Laban's flock. This is how he built his flock from Laban's. [41]Whenever the stronger females were ready to mate, Jacob set up the peeled branches in front of them. [42]But he didn't do this with the weaker ones, so the weaker lambs belonged to Laban, and the stronger ones were Jacob's. [43]As a result, Jacob's flocks increased rapidly, and he became very wealthy, with many servants, camels, and donkeys.

## WAIT FOR GOD ● ● • • •

30:22-24 **Eventually God answered Rachel's prayers and gave her a child of her own. In the meantime, however, she had given her servant girl to Jacob. Trusting God when nothing seems to happen is difficult. But it is harder still to live with the consequences of taking matters into our own hands. Resist the temptation to think God has forgotten you. Have patience and courage to wait for God to act.**

## CHAPTER 31

**JACOB FLEES FROM LABAN.** But Jacob soon learned that Laban's sons were beginning to grumble. "Jacob has robbed our father!" they said. "All his wealth has been gained at our father's expense." [2]And Jacob began to notice a considerable cooling in Laban's attitude toward him.

[3]Then the LORD said to Jacob, "Return to the land

30:6 *Dan* is a play on the Hebrew term meaning "to vindicate" or "to judge." 30:8 *Naphtali* means "my struggle." 30:11 *Gad* means "good fortune." 30:13 *Asher* means "happy." 30:18 *Issachar* sounds like a Hebrew term that means "reward." 30:20 *Zebulun* probably means "honor." 30:24 *Joseph* means "may he add."

of your father and grandfather and to your relatives
there, and I will be with you."
[4]Jacob called Rachel and Leah out to the field
where he was watching the flocks, [5]so he could talk
things over with them. "Your father has turned
against me and is not treating me like he used to,"
he told them. "But the God of my father has been
with me. [6]You know how hard I have worked for
your father, [7]but he has tricked me, breaking his
wage agreement with me again and again. But God
has not allowed him to do me any harm. [8]For if he
said the speckled animals were mine, the whole
flock began to produce speckled lambs. And when
he changed his mind and said I could have the
streaked ones, then all the lambs were born
streaked. [9]In this way, God has made me wealthy at
your father's expense. [10]During the mating season,
I had a dream and saw that the male goats mating
with the flock were streaked, speckled, and spotted. [11]Then in my dream, the angel of God said to
me, 'Jacob!' And I replied, 'Yes, I'm listening!'
[12]The angel said, 'Look, and you will see that only
the streaked, speckled, and spotted males are mating with the females of your flock. For I have seen
all that Laban has done to you. [13]I am the God you
met at Bethel, the place where you anointed the
pillar of stone and made a
vow to serve me. Now leave
this country and return to
the land you came from.'"
[14]Rachel and Leah said,
"That's fine with us! There's
nothing for us here—none
of our father's wealth will
come to us anyway. [15]He has
reduced our rights to those
of foreign women. He sold
us, and what he received for
us has disappeared. [16]The
riches God has given you
from our father are legally
ours and our children's to
begin with. So go ahead
and do whatever God has
told you."
[17]So Jacob put his wives
and children on camels.
[18]He drove the flocks in
front of him—all the livestock he had acquired at
Paddan-aram—and set out
on his journey to the land
of Canaan, where his father,
Isaac, lived. [19]At the time
they left, Laban was some
distance away, shearing his
sheep. Rachel stole her
father's household gods
and took them with her.
[20]They set out secretly and
never told Laban they were
leaving. [21]Jacob took all his possessions with him
and crossed the Euphrates River, heading for the
territory of Gilead.
[22]Laban didn't learn of their flight for three days.
[23]But when he did, he gathered a group of his relatives and set out in hot pursuit. He caught up with
them seven days later in the hill country of Gilead.
[24]But the previous night God had appeared to Laban
in a dream. "Be careful about what you say to
Jacob!" he was told.
[25]So when Laban caught up with Jacob as he was
camped in the hill country of Gilead, he set up his
camp not far from Jacob's. [26]"What do you mean by
sneaking off like this?" Laban demanded. "Are my
daughters prisoners, the plunder of war, that you
have stolen them away like this? [27]Why did you slip
away secretly? I would have given you a farewell
party, with joyful singing accompanied by tambourines and harps. [28]Why didn't you let me kiss my
daughters and grandchildren and tell them good-
bye? You have acted very foolishly! [29]I could destroy
you, but the God of your father appeared to me last
night and told me, 'Be careful about what you say to
Jacob!' [30]I know you feel you must go, and you long
intensely for your childhood home, but why have
you stolen my household gods?"

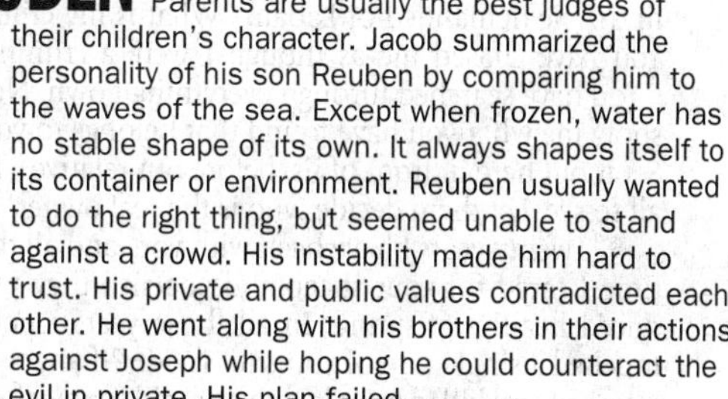

## REUBEN

Parents are usually the best judges of their children's character. Jacob summarized the personality of his son Reuben by comparing him to the waves of the sea. Except when frozen, water has no stable shape of its own. It always shapes itself to its container or environment. Reuben usually wanted to do the right thing, but seemed unable to stand against a crowd. His instability made him hard to trust. His private and public values contradicted each other. He went along with his brothers in their actions against Joseph while hoping he could counteract the evil in private. His plan failed.

Compromise has a way of destroying convictions. Without convictions, there is no direction. And lack of direction will destroy life. In Reuben's case, his early mistakes led to a real mess later on in life.

Are you the same person on the inside that you are on the outside? We may want to keep our private and public lives separate, but we can't deny that they affect each other. What convictions are present in your life at all times? How often does Jacob's description of his son, "unruly as the waves of the sea," fit your life?

LESSONS: Public and private lives must show the same integrity, or one will destroy the other

Punishment for sin may not be immediate, but it is certain

KEY VERSE: "You are as unruly as the waves of the sea, and you will be first no longer. For you slept with one of my wives; you dishonored me in my own bed." (Genesis 49:4).

Reuben's story is told in Genesis 29–50.

**UPS:**
- Saved Joseph's life by talking the other brothers out of murder
- Showed intense love for his father by offering his own sons as a guarantee that Benjamin's life would be safe

**DOWNS:**
- Gave in quickly to group pressure
- Did not directly protect Joseph from his brothers, although as eldest son he had the authority to do so
- Slept with his father's concubine

**STATS:**
- Where: Canaan, Egypt
- Occupation: Shepherd
- Relatives: Parents: Jacob and Leah. Eleven brothers, one sister.

## THE PAYOFF ● ● • • •

**31:38-42 Jacob made it a habit to do more than was expected of him. When his flocks were attacked, he took the losses rather than splitting them with Laban. He worked hard even after several pay cuts. His diligence eventually paid off; his flocks began to multiply. Making a habit of doing more than is expected can pay off. It (1) pleases God, (2) earns recognition and advancement, (3) enhances your reputation, (4) builds others' confidence in you, (5) gives you more experience and knowledge, and (6) develops your spiritual maturity.**

31 "I rushed away because I was afraid," Jacob answered. "I said to myself, 'He'll take his daughters from me by force.' 32 But as for your household gods, let the person who has taken them die! If you find anything that belongs to you, I swear before all these relatives of ours, I will give it back without question." But Jacob didn't know that Rachel had taken them.

33 Laban went first into Jacob's tent to search there, then into Leah's, and then he searched the tents of the two concubines, but he didn't find the gods. Finally, he went into Rachel's tent. 34 Rachel had taken the household gods and had stuffed them into her camel saddle, and now she was sitting on them. So although Laban searched all the tents, he couldn't find them. 35 "Forgive my not getting up, Father," Rachel explained. "I'm having my monthly period." So despite his thorough search, Laban didn't find them.

36 Then Jacob became very angry. "What did you find?" he demanded of Laban. "What is my crime? You have chased me as though I were a criminal. 37 You have searched through everything I own. Now show me what you have found that belongs to you! Set it out here in front of us, before our relatives, for all to see. Let them decide who is the real owner!

38 "Twenty years I have been with you, and all that time I cared for your sheep and goats so they produced healthy offspring. In all those years I never touched a single ram of yours for food. 39 If any were attacked and killed by wild animals, did I show them to you and ask you to reduce the count of your flock? No, I took the loss! You made me pay for every animal stolen from the flocks, whether the loss was my fault or not. 40 I worked for you through the scorching heat of the day and through cold and sleepless nights. 41 Yes, twenty years—fourteen of them earning your two daughters, and six years to get the flock. And you have reduced my wages ten times! 42 In fact, except for the grace of God—the God of my grandfather Abraham, the awe-inspiring God of my father, Isaac—you would have sent me off without a penny to my name. But God has seen your cruelty and my hard work. That is why he appeared to you last night and vindicated me."

43 Then Laban replied to Jacob, "These women are my daughters, and these children are my grandchildren, and these flocks and all that you have—all are mine. But what can I do now to my own daughters and grandchildren? 44 Come now, and we will make a peace treaty, you and I, and we will live by its terms."

45 So Jacob took a stone and set it up as a monument. 46 He also told his men to gather stones and pile them up in a heap. Jacob and Laban then sat down beside the pile of stones to share a meal. 47 They named it "Witness Pile," which is Jegar-sahadutha in Laban's language and Galeed* in Jacob's.

48 "This pile of stones will stand as a witness to remind us of our agreement," Laban said. 49 This place was also called Mizpah,* for Laban said, "May the LORD keep watch between us to make sure that we keep this treaty when we are out of each other's sight. 50 I won't know about it if you are harsh to my daughters or if you take other wives, but God will see it. 51 This heap of stones and this pillar 52 stand between us as a witness of our vows. I will not cross this line to harm you, and you will not cross it to harm me. 53 I call on the God of our ancestors—the God of your grandfather Abraham and the God of my grandfather Nahor—to punish either one of us who harms the other."

So Jacob took an oath before the awesome God of his father, Isaac, to respect the boundary line. 54 Then Jacob presented a sacrifice to God and invited everyone to a feast. Afterward they spent the night there in the hills. 55 Laban got up early the next morning, and he kissed his daughters and grandchildren and blessed them. Then he returned home.

## CHAPTER 32

**JACOB MEETS ESAU.** As Jacob and his household started on their way again, angels of God came to meet him. 2 When Jacob saw them, he exclaimed, "This is God's camp!" So he named the place Mahanaim.*

3 Jacob now sent messengers to his brother, Esau, in Edom, the land of Seir. 4 He told them, "Give this message to my master Esau: 'Humble greetings from your servant Jacob! I have been living with Uncle Laban until recently, 5 and now I own oxen, donkeys, sheep, goats, and many servants, both men and women. I have sent these messengers to inform you of my coming, hoping that you will be friendly to us.'"

6 The messengers returned with the news that Esau was on his way to meet Jacob—with an army of four hundred men! 7 Jacob was terrified at the news. He

## FRANTIC WITH FEAR ● ● • • •

**32:9-12 How would you feel knowing you were about to meet the person you had cheated out of his most precious possession? Jacob had taken Esau's birthright (25:33) and his blessings (27:27-40). Now he was about to meet this brother for the first time in 20 years, and he was frantic with fear. He collected his thoughts, however, and decided to pray. When we face a difficult conflict, we can run about frantically or we can pause to pray. Which approach will be more effective?**

31:47 *Jegar-sahadutha* means "witness pile" in Aramaic; *Galeed* means "witness pile" in Hebrew. 31:49 *Mizpah* means "watchtower."
32:2 *Mahanaim* means "two camps."

divided his household, along with the flocks and
herds and camels, into two camps. [8]He thought, "If
Esau attacks one group, perhaps the other can escape."
[9]Then Jacob prayed, "O God of my grandfather
Abraham and my father, Isaac—O LORD, you told
me to return to my land and to my relatives, and you
promised to treat me kindly. [10]I am not worthy of all
the faithfulness and unfailing love you have shown
to me, your servant. When I left home, I owned
nothing except a walking stick, and now my household fills two camps! [11]O LORD, please rescue me
from my brother, Esau. I am afraid that he is coming
to kill me, along with my wives and children. [12]But
you promised to treat me kindly and to multiply my
descendants until they become as numerous as the
sands along the seashore—too many to count."

[13]Jacob stayed where he
was for the night and prepared a present for Esau:
[14]two hundred female goats,
twenty male goats, two hundred ewes, twenty rams,
[15]thirty female camels with
their young, forty cows, ten
bulls, twenty female donkeys,
and ten male donkeys. [16]He
told his servants to lead them
on ahead, each group of animals by itself, separated by a
distance in between.

[17]He gave these instructions to the men leading the
first group: "When you meet
Esau, he will ask, 'Where are
you going? Whose servants
are you? Whose animals are
these?' [18]You should reply,
'These belong to your servant Jacob. They are a present for his master Esau! He
is coming right behind us.'"
[19]Jacob gave the same instructions to each of the
herdsmen and told them,
"You are all to say the same
thing to Esau when you see
him. [20]And be sure to say,
'Your servant Jacob is right
behind us.'" Jacob's plan
was to appease Esau with
the presents before meeting
him face to face. "Perhaps,"
Jacob hoped, "he will be
friendly to us." [21]So the presents were sent on ahead, and
Jacob spent that night in the
camp.

[22]But during the night
Jacob got up and sent his two
wives, two concubines, and eleven sons across the
Jabbok River. [23]After they were on the other side, he
sent over all his possessions. [24]This left Jacob all alone
in the camp, and a man came and wrestled with him
until dawn. [25]When the man saw that he couldn't win
the match, he struck Jacob's hip and knocked it out of
joint at the socket. [26]Then the man said, "Let me go,
for it is dawn."

But Jacob panted, "I will not let you go unless you
bless me."

[27]"What is your name?" the man asked.

He replied, "Jacob."

[28]"Your name will no longer be Jacob," the man
told him. "It is now Israel,* because you have struggled with both God and men and have won."

[29]"What is your name?" Jacob asked him.

## JUDAH

People who are leaders stand out at the right time. They don't necessarily act or look a certain way until the need for action comes along. Among their skills are the abilities to speak up, make decisions, take action, or take control. Leaders can use their skills for great good or great evil.

Jacob's fourth son, Judah, was a natural leader. His life included many opportunities to exercise his skills. Unfortunately, Judah's decisions were often shaped more by the pressures of the moment than by a desire to cooperate with God's plan. But when he did recognize his mistakes, he was willing to admit them. His experience with Tamar and the final confrontation with Joseph are both examples of Judah's willingness to take responsibility for his sins when confronted. That quality was a strength Judah passed on to his descendant David.

Whether or not we have natural leadership qualities like Judah, we do have just as hard a time as he did seeing our own sins. When we do discover we've done something wrong, we usually are not eager to admit it. From Judah we can learn that it is not wise to wait until our sins force us to admit we've done wrong. It is better to openly admit our mistakes, shoulder the blame, and seek forgiveness.

**UPS:**
- Was a natural leader—outspoken and decisive
- Thought clearly and took action in pressure situations
- Was willing to stand by his word and put himself on the line when necessary
- Was the fourth son of 12, and the one through whom God would eventually bring King David and Jesus, the Messiah

**DOWNS:**
- Suggested to his brothers they sell Joseph into slavery
- Failed to keep his promise to his daughter-in-law, Tamar

**STATS:**
- Where: Canaan, Egypt
- Occupation: Shepherd
- Relatives: Parents: Jacob and Leah. Wife: the daughter of Shua (1 Chronicles 2:3). Daughter-in-law: Tamar. Eleven brothers, one sister, and at least five sons (Genesis 29:31–30:24; 38:3-5, 27-30).

LESSONS: God is in control far beyond the immediate situation

Procrastination often brings about a worse result

Judah's offer to substitute his life for Benjamin's is a picture of what his descendant Jesus would do for all men

KEY VERSES: "Judah, your brothers will praise you. You will defeat your enemies. All your relatives will bow before you. Judah is a young lion that has finished eating its prey. Like a lion he crouches and lies down; like a lioness—who will dare to rouse him?" (Genesis 49:8-9).

Judah's story is told in Genesis 29:35–50:26. He is also mentioned in 1 Chronicles 2:4.

32:28 *Israel* means "God struggles" or "one who struggles with God."

"Why do you ask?" the man replied. Then he blessed Jacob there.

[30]Jacob named the place Peniel—"face of God"—for he said, "I have seen God face to face, yet my life has been spared." [31]The sun rose as he left Peniel,* and he was limping because of his hip. [32]That is why even today the people of Israel don't eat meat from near the hip, in memory of what happened that night.

## CHAPTER 33

Then, in the distance, Jacob saw Esau coming with his four hundred men. [2]Jacob now arranged his family into a column, with his two concubines and their children at the front, Leah and her children next, and Rachel and Joseph last. [3]Then Jacob went on ahead. As he approached his brother, he bowed low seven times before him. [4]Then Esau ran to meet him and embraced him affectionately and kissed him. Both of them were in tears.

[5]Then Esau looked at the women and children and asked, "Who are these people with you?"

"These are the children God has graciously given to me," Jacob replied. [6]Then the concubines came forward with their children and bowed low before him. [7]Next Leah came with her children, and they bowed down. Finally, Rachel and Joseph came and made their bows.

[8]"And what were all the flocks and herds I met as I came?" Esau asked.

Jacob replied, "They are gifts, my lord, to ensure your goodwill."

[9]"Brother, I have plenty," Esau answered. "Keep what you have."

### BITTERNESS ● ● • • ·

**33:1-11 It is refreshing to see Esau's change of heart when the two brothers meet again. The bitterness over losing his birthright and blessing (25:29-34) seems gone. Instead Esau is content with what he has. Jacob even exclaims how great it is to see his brother's friendly smile (33:10). Life can deal us some bad situations. We can feel cheated, as Esau did, but we don't have to remain bitter. We can remove bitterness from our lives by honestly expressing our feelings to God, forgiving those who have wronged us, and being content with what we have.**

[10]"No, please accept them," Jacob said, "for what a relief it is to see your friendly smile. It is like seeing the smile of God! [11]Please take my gifts, for God has been very generous to me. I have more than enough." Jacob continued to insist, so Esau finally accepted them.

[12]"Well, let's be going," Esau said. "I will stay with you and lead the way."

[13]But Jacob replied, "You can see, my lord, that some of the children are very young, and the flocks and herds have their young, too. If they are driven too hard, they may die. [14]So go on ahead of us. We will follow at our own pace and meet you at Seir."

[15]"Well," Esau said, "at least let me leave some of my men to guide and protect you."

### PASSION ● ● • • ·

**34:1-4 Shechem may have been a victim of "love at first sight," but his actions were impulsive and evil. Not only did he sin against Dinah; he sinned against the entire family (34:6-7). The consequences of his deed were severe both for his family and for Jacob's (34:25-31). Even Shechem's declared love for Dinah could not excuse the evil he did by raping her. Don't allow sexual passion to boil over into evil actions. Passion must be controlled.**

"There is no reason for you to be so kind to me," Jacob insisted.

[16]So Esau started back to Seir that same day. [17]Meanwhile, Jacob and his household traveled on to Succoth. There he built himself a house and made shelters for his flocks and herds. That is why the place was named Succoth.* [18]Then they arrived safely at Shechem, in Canaan, and they set up camp just outside the town. [19]Jacob bought the land he camped on from the family of Hamor, Shechem's father, for a hundred pieces of silver.* [20]And there he built an altar and called it El-Elohe-Israel.*

## CHAPTER 34

**JACOB'S SONS TAKE REVENGE.** One day Dinah, Leah's daughter, went to visit some of the young women who lived in the area. [2]But when the local prince, Shechem son of Hamor the Hivite, saw her, he took her and raped her. [3]But Shechem's love for Dinah was strong, and he tried to win her affection. [4]He even spoke to his father about it. "Get this girl for me," he demanded. "I want to marry her."

[5]Word soon reached Jacob that his daughter had been defiled, but his sons were out in the fields herding cattle so he did nothing until they returned. [6]Meanwhile, Hamor, Shechem's father, came out to discuss the matter with Jacob. [7]He arrived just as Jacob's sons were coming in from the fields. They were shocked and furious that their sister had been raped. Shechem had done a disgraceful thing against Jacob's family,* a thing that should never have been done.

[8]Hamor told Jacob and his sons, "My son Shechem is truly in love with your daughter, and he longs for her to be his wife. Please let him marry her. [9]We invite you to let your daughters marry our sons, and we will give our daughters as wives for your young men. [10]And you may live among us; the land is open to you! Settle here and trade with us. You are free to acquire property among us."

[11]Then Shechem addressed Dinah's father and brothers. "Please be kind to me, and let me have her as my wife," he begged. "I will give whatever you require. [12]No matter what dowry or gift you demand, I will pay it—only give me the girl as my wife."

[13]But Dinah's brothers deceived Shechem and Hamor because of what Shechem had done to their sister. [14]They said to them, "We couldn't possibly allow this, because you aren't circumcised. It would be a disgrace for her to marry a man like you! [15]But here is a solution. If every man among you will be

32:31 Hebrew *Penuel,* a variant name for Peniel. 33:17 *Succoth* means "shelters." 33:19 Hebrew *100 kesitahs;* the value or weight of the kesitah is no longer known. 33:20 *El-Elohe-Israel* means "God, the God of Israel." 34:7 Hebrew *in Israel.*

circumcised like we are, [16]we will intermarry with you and live here and unite with you to become one people. [17]Otherwise we will take her and be on our way."

[18]Hamor and Shechem gladly agreed, [19]and Shechem lost no time in acting on this request, for he wanted Dinah desperately. Shechem was a highly respected member of his family, [20]and he appeared with his father before the town leaders to present this proposal. [21]"Those men are our friends," they said. "Let's invite them to live here among us and ply their trade. For the land is large enough to hold them, and we can intermarry with them. [22]But they will consider staying here only on one condition. Every one of us men must be circumcised, just as they are. [23]But if we do this, all their flocks and possessions will become ours. Come, let's agree to this so they will settle here among us."

[24]So all the men agreed and were circumcised. [25]But three days later, when their wounds were still sore, two of Dinah's brothers, Simeon and Levi, took their swords, entered the town without opposition, and slaughtered every man there, [26]including Hamor and Shechem. They rescued Dinah from Shechem's house and returned to their camp. [27]Then all of Jacob's sons plundered the town because their sister had been defiled there. [28]They seized all the flocks and herds and donkeys—everything they could lay their hands on, both inside the town and outside in the fields. [29]They also took all the women and children and wealth of every kind.

[30]Afterward Jacob said to Levi and Simeon, "You have made me stink among all the people of this land—among all the Canaanites and Perizzites. We are so few that they will come and crush us. We will all be killed!"

[31]"Should he treat our sister like a prostitute?" they retorted angrily.

## CHAPTER 35

**JACOB'S RETURN TO BETHEL.** God said to Jacob, "Now move on to Bethel and settle there. Build an altar there to worship me—the God who appeared to you when you fled from your brother, Esau."

[2]So Jacob told everyone in his household, "Destroy your idols, wash yourselves, and put on clean clothing. [3]We are now going to Bethel, where I will build an altar to the God who answered my prayers when I was in distress. He has stayed with me wherever I have gone."

[4]So they gave Jacob all their idols and their earrings, and he buried them beneath the tree near Shechem. [5]When they set out again, terror from God came over the people in all the towns of that area, and no one attacked them. [6]Finally, they arrived at Luz (now called Bethel) in Canaan. [7]Jacob built an altar there and named it El-bethel,* because God had appeared to him there at Bethel when he was fleeing from Esau.

[8]Soon after this, Rebekah's old nurse, Deborah, died. She was buried beneath the oak tree in the valley below Bethel. Ever since, the tree has been called the "Oak of Weeping."*

[9]God appeared to Jacob once again when he arrived at Bethel after traveling from Paddan-aram. God blessed him [10]and said, "Your name is no longer Jacob; you will now be called Israel."* [11]Then God said, "I am God Almighty. Multiply and fill the earth! Become a great nation, even many nations. Kings will be among your descendants! [12]And I will pass on to you the land I gave to Abraham and Isaac. Yes, I will give it to you and your descendants." [13]Then God went up from the place where he had spoken to Jacob.

[14]Jacob set up a stone pillar to mark the place where God had spoken to him. He then poured wine over it as an offering to God and anointed the pillar with olive oil. [15]Jacob called the place Bethel—"house of God"—because God had spoken to him there.

[16]Leaving Bethel, they traveled on toward Ephrath (that is, Bethlehem). But Rachel's pains of childbirth began while they were still some distance away. [17]After a very hard delivery, the midwife finally exclaimed, "Don't be afraid—you have another son!" [18]Rachel was about to die, but with her last breath she named him Ben-oni; the baby's father, however, called him Benjamin.* [19]So Rachel died and was buried on the way to Ephrath (that is, Bethlehem). [20]Jacob set up a stone monument over her grave, and it can be seen there to this day.

[21]Jacob* then traveled on and camped beyond the tower of Eder. [22]While he was there, Reuben slept with Bilhah, his father's concubine, and someone told Jacob about it.

These are the names of the twelve sons of Jacob:

[23]The sons of Leah were Reuben (Jacob's oldest son), Simeon, Levi, Judah, Issachar, and Zebulun.

[24]The sons of Rachel were Joseph and Benjamin.

### INHERITANCE ● ● ● • •

35:22 **Reuben's sin was costly, although not right away. As the oldest son, he stood to receive a double portion of the family inheritance and a place of leadership among his people. Reuben may have thought he got away with his sin. No more is mentioned of it until Jacob, on his deathbed, assembled his family for the final blessing. Suddenly Jacob took away Reuben's double portion and gave it to someone else (49:4).**

**Sin's consequences can plague us long after the sin is committed. When we do something wrong we may think we can escape unnoticed, only to discover later that the sin has been quietly breeding serious consequences.**

35:7 *El-bethel* means "the God of Bethel." 35:8 Hebrew *Allon-bacuth.* 35:10 *Jacob* means "he grasps the heel"; this can also figuratively mean "he deceives"; *Israel* means "God struggles" or "one who struggles with God." 35:18 *Ben-oni* means "son of my sorrow"; *Benjamin* means "son of my right hand." 35:21 Hebrew *Israel;* also in 35:22a.

[25]The sons of Bilhah, Rachel's servant, were Dan and Naphtali.
[26]The sons of Zilpah, Leah's servant, were Gad and Asher.

These were the sons born to Jacob at Paddan-aram.

[27]So Jacob came home to his father Isaac in
Mamre, which is near Kiriath-arba (now called
Hebron), where Abraham had also lived. [28]Isaac
lived for 180 years, [29]and he died at a ripe old age,
joining his ancestors in death. Then his sons, Esau
and Jacob, buried him.

## CHAPTER 36 DESCENDANTS OF ESAU.

This is the
history of the descendants of Esau (also known as
Edom). [2]Esau married two young women from Canaan:
Adah, the daughter of Elon the Hittite; and
Oholibamah, the daughter of Anah and granddaughter
of Zibeon the Hivite. [3]He also married his
cousin Basemath, who was the daughter of Ishmael
and the sister of Nebaioth. [4]Esau and Adah had a
son named Eliphaz. Esau and Basemath had a son
named Reuel. [5]Esau and Oholibamah had sons
named Jeush, Jalam, and Korah. All these sons were
born to Esau in the land of Canaan.

[6]Then Esau took his wives, children, household
servants, cattle, and flocks—all the wealth he had
gained in the land of Canaan—and moved away
from his brother, Jacob. [7]There was not enough land
to support them both because of all their cattle and
livestock. [8]So Esau (also known as Edom) settled in
the hill country of Seir.

[9]This is a list of Esau's descendants, the Edomites,
who lived in the hill country of Seir.

[10]Among Esau's sons were Eliphaz, the son of Esau's wife Adah; and Reuel, the son of Esau's wife Basemath.
[11]The sons of Eliphaz were Teman, Omar, Zepho, Gatam, and Kenaz.
[12]Eliphaz had another son named Amalek, born to Timna, his concubine. These were all grandchildren of Esau's wife Adah.
[13]The sons of Reuel were Nahath, Zerah, Shammah, and Mizzah. These were all grandchildren of Esau's wife Basemath.
[14]Esau also had sons through Oholibamah, the daughter of Anah and granddaughter of Zibeon. Their names were Jeush, Jalam, and Korah.

[15]Esau's children and grandchildren became the
leaders of different clans.

The sons of Esau's oldest son, Eliphaz, became the leaders of the clans of Teman, Omar, Zepho, Kenaz,
[16]Korah, Gatam, and Amalek. These clans in the land of Edom were descended from Eliphaz, the son of Esau and Adah.
[17]The sons of Esau's son Reuel became the leaders of the clans of Nahath, Zerah, Shammah, and Mizzah. These clans in the land of Edom were descended from Reuel, the son of Esau and Basemath.
[18]The sons of Esau and his wife Oholibamah became the leaders of the clans of Jeush, Jalam, and Korah. These are the clans descended from Esau's wife Oholibamah, the daughter of Anah.

[19]These are all the clans descended from Esau (also
known as Edom).

[20]These are the names of the tribes that descended
from Seir the Horite, one of the families native to the
land of Seir: Lotan, Shobal, Zibeon, Anah, [21]Dishon,
Ezer, and Dishan. These were the Horite clans, the
descendants of Seir, who lived in the land of Edom.

[22]The sons of Lotan were Hori and Heman. Lotan's sister was named Timna.
[23]The sons of Shobal were Alvan, Manahath, Ebal, Shepho, and Onam.
[24]The sons of Zibeon were Aiah and Anah. This is the Anah who discovered the hot springs in the wilderness while he was grazing his father's donkeys.
[25]The son of Anah was Dishon, and Oholibamah was his daughter.
[26]The sons of Dishon* were Hemdan, Eshban, Ithran, and Keran.
[27]The sons of Ezer were Bilhan, Zaavan, and Akan.
[28]The sons of Dishan were Uz and Aran.

[29]So the leaders of the Horite clans were Lotan, Shobal,
Zibeon, Anah, [30]Dishon, Ezer, and Dishan. The
Horite clans are named after their clan leaders, who
lived in the land of Seir.

[31]These are the kings who ruled in Edom before
there were kings in Israel*:

[32]Bela son of Beor, who ruled from his city of Dinhabah.
[33]When Bela died, Jobab son of Zerah from Bozrah became king.
[34]When Jobab died, Husham from the land of the Temanites became king.
[35]When Husham died, Hadad son of Bedad became king and ruled from the city of Avith. He was the one who destroyed the Midianite army in the land of Moab.
[36]When Hadad died, Samlah from the city of Masrekah became king.

### BRAGGING ● ● • • ·

**37:6-11 Joseph's brothers were already angry over the possibility of being ruled by their little brother. Joseph then fueled the fire with his immature attitude and boastful manner. No one enjoys a braggart. Joseph learned his lesson the hard way. His angry brothers sold him into slavery to get rid of him. After several years of hardship, Joseph learned an important lesson: because our talents and knowledge come from God, it is more appropriate to thank him for them than to brag about them. Later, Joseph gives God the credit (41:16).**

36:26 Hebrew *Dishan,* a variant name for Dishon; compare 36:21, 28. 36:31 Or *before an Israelite king ruled over them.*

37 When Samlah died, Shaul from the city of
Rehoboth on the Euphrates River* became king.
38 When Shaul died, Baal-hanan son of Acbor
became king.
39 When Baal-hanan died, Hadad* became king
and ruled from the city of Pau. Hadad's wife
was Mehetabel, the daughter of Matred and
granddaughter of Me-zahab.

40 These are the leaders of the clans of Esau, who
lived in the places named for them: Timna, Alvah,
Jetheth, 41 Oholibamah, Elah, Pinon, 42 Kenaz, Teman,
Mibzar, 43 Magdiel, and Iram. These are the names
of the clans of Esau, the ancestor of the Edomites,
each clan giving its name to the area it occupied.

## CHAPTER 37

**JOSEPH'S STRANGE DREAMS.** So Jacob
settled again in the land of Canaan, where his father
had lived.

2 This is the history of Jacob's family. When Joseph
was seventeen years old, he often tended his father's
flocks with his half brothers, the sons of his father's
wives Bilhah and Zilpah. But Joseph reported to his
father some of the bad things his brothers were
doing. 3 Now Jacob* loved Joseph more than any of
his other children because Joseph had been born to
him in his old age. So one day he gave Joseph a
special gift—a beautiful robe.* 4 But his brothers
hated Joseph because of their father's partiality. They
couldn't say a kind word to him.

5 One night Joseph had a dream and promptly reported the details to his brothers, causing them to hate
him even more. 6 "Listen to this dream," he announced. 7 "We were out in the field tying up bundles
of grain. My bundle stood up, and then your bundles
all gathered around and bowed low before it!"

8 "So you are going to be our king, are you?" his
brothers taunted. And they hated him all the more
for his dream and what he had said.

9 Then Joseph had another dream and told his
brothers about it. "Listen to this dream," he said. "The
sun, moon, and eleven stars bowed low before me!"

10 This time he told his father as well as his brothers,
and his father rebuked him. "What do you mean?" his
father asked. "Will your mother, your brothers, and I
actually come and bow before you?" 11 But while his
brothers were jealous of Joseph, his father gave it some
thought and wondered what it all meant.

12 Soon after this, Joseph's brothers went to pasture
their father's flocks at Shechem. 13 When they had
been gone for some time, Jacob said to Joseph, "Your
brothers are over at Shechem with the flocks. I'm
going to send you to them."

"I'm ready to go," Joseph replied.

14 "Go and see how your brothers and the flocks
are getting along," Jacob said. "Then come back and
bring me word." So Jacob sent him on his way, and
Joseph traveled to Shechem from his home in the
valley of Hebron.

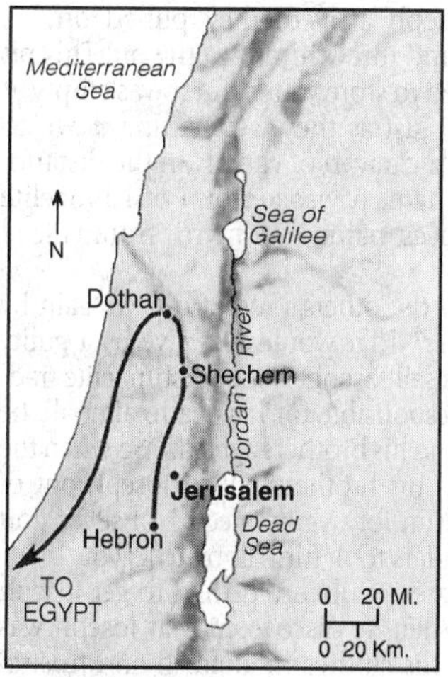

**JOSEPH GOES TO MEET HIS BROTHERS** Jacob asked Joseph to go find his brothers, who were grazing their flocks near Shechem. When Joseph arrived, he learned that his brothers had gone on to Dothan, which lay along a major trade route to Egypt. There the jealous brothers sold Joseph as a slave to a group of Ishmaelite traders who were on their way to Egypt.

15 When he arrived there, a man noticed him wandering around the countryside. "What are you looking for?" he asked.

16 "For my brothers and their flocks," Joseph replied. "Have you seen them?"

17 "Yes," the man told him, "but they are no longer
here. I heard your brothers say they were going to
Dothan." So Joseph followed his brothers to Dothan
and found them there.

18 When Joseph's brothers saw him coming, they
recognized him in the distance and made plans to
kill him. 19 "Here comes that dreamer!" they exclaimed. 20 "Come on, let's kill him and throw him
into a deep pit. We can tell our father that a wild
animal has eaten him. Then we'll see what becomes
of all his dreams!"

21 But Reuben came to Joseph's rescue. "Let's not
kill him," he said. 22 "Why should we shed his blood?
Let's just throw him alive into this pit here. That way
he will die without our having to touch him." Reuben was secretly planning to help Joseph escape, and
then he would bring him back to his father.

### UGLY RAGE ● ● • • •

37:19-20 **Could jealousy ever make you feel like killing someone? Before saying, "No way!" look at what happened in this story. Ten men were willing to kill their youngest brother over a robe and a few reported dreams. Their deep jealousy had grown into ugly rage, blinding them completely to what was right. Jealousy can be hard to recognize, because our reasons for it seem to make sense. But left unchecked, jealousy grows quickly and leads to serious sins. The longer you cultivate jealous feelings, the harder it is to uproot them. The time to deal with jealousy is when you notice yourself keeping score of what others have.**

**36:37** Hebrew *the river.* **36:39** As in some Hebrew manuscripts, Samaritan Pentateuch, and Syriac version (see also 1 Chr 1:50); most Hebrew manuscripts read *Hadar.* **37:3a** Hebrew *Israel;* also in 37:13. **37:3b** Traditionally rendered *a coat of many colors.* The exact meaning of the Hebrew is uncertain.

[23]So when Joseph arrived, they pulled off his beautiful robe [24]and threw him into the pit. This pit was normally used to store water, but it was empty at the time. [25]Then, just as they were sitting down to eat, they noticed a caravan of camels in the distance coming toward them. It was a group of Ishmaelite traders taking spices, balm, and myrrh from Gilead to Egypt.

[26]Judah said to the others, "What can we gain by killing our brother? That would just give us a guilty conscience. [27]Let's sell Joseph to those Ishmaelite traders. Let's not be responsible for his death; after all, he is our brother!" And his brothers agreed. [28]So when the traders* came by, his brothers pulled Joseph out of the pit and sold him for twenty pieces* of silver, and the Ishmaelite traders took him along to Egypt.

[29]Some time later, Reuben returned to get Joseph out of the pit. When he discovered that Joseph was missing, he tore his clothes in anguish and frustration. [30]Then he went back to his brothers and lamented, "The boy is gone! What can I do now?"

## ME FIRST ● ● ● ● •

**37:30 Reuben returned to the pit to find Joseph, but his little brother was gone. His first response, in effect, was "What is going to happen to me?" rather than "What is going to happen to Joseph?" In a tough situation, are you always concerned first about yourself? Consider the person most affected by the problem, and you are more likely to find a solution for it.**

[31]Then Joseph's brothers killed a goat and dipped the robe in its blood. [32]They took the beautiful robe to their father and asked him to identify it. "We found this in the field," they told him. "It's Joseph's robe, isn't it?"

[33]Their father recognized it at once. "Yes," he said, "it is my son's robe. A wild animal has attacked and eaten him. Surely Joseph has been torn in pieces!" [34]Then Jacob tore his clothes and put on sackcloth. He mourned deeply for his son for many days. [35]His family all tried to comfort him, but it was no use. "I will die in mourning for my son," he would say, and then begin to weep.

[36]Meanwhile, in Egypt, the traders sold Joseph to Potiphar, an officer of Pharaoh, the king of Egypt. Potiphar was captain of the palace guard.

CHAPTER **38** **JUDAH AND TAMAR.** About this time, Judah left home and moved to Adullam, where he visited a man named Hirah. [2]There he met a Canaanite woman, the daughter of Shua, and he married her. [3]She became pregnant and had a son, and Judah named the boy Er. [4]Then Judah's wife had another son, and she named him Onan. [5]And when she had a third son, she named him Shelah. At the time of Shelah's birth, they were living at Kezib.

[6]When his oldest son, Er, grew up, Judah arranged his marriage to a young woman named Tamar. [7]But Er was a wicked man in the LORD's sight, so the LORD took his life. [8]Then Judah said to Er's brother Onan, "You must marry Tamar, as our law requires of the brother of a man who has died. Her first son from you will be your brother's heir."

[9]But Onan was not willing to have a child who would not be his own heir. So whenever he had intercourse with Tamar, he spilled the semen on the ground to keep her from having a baby who would belong to his brother. [10]But the LORD considered it a wicked thing for Onan to deny a child to his dead brother. So the LORD took Onan's life, too.

[11]Then Judah told Tamar, his daughter-in-law, not to marry again at that time but to return to her parents' home. She was to remain a widow until his youngest son, Shelah, was old enough to marry her. (But Judah didn't really intend to do this because he was afraid Shelah would also die, like his two brothers.) So Tamar went home to her parents.

[12]In the course of time Judah's wife died. After the time of mourning was over, Judah and his friend Hirah the Adullamite went to Timnah to supervise the shearing of his sheep. [13]Someone told Tamar that her father-in-law had left for the sheep-shearing at Timnah. [14]Tamar was aware that Shelah had grown up, but they had not called her to come and marry him. So she changed out of her widow's clothing and covered herself with a veil to disguise herself. Then she sat beside the road at the entrance to the village of Enaim, which is on the way to Timnah. [15]Judah noticed her as he went by

## WOMEN IN JESUS' FAMILY TREE

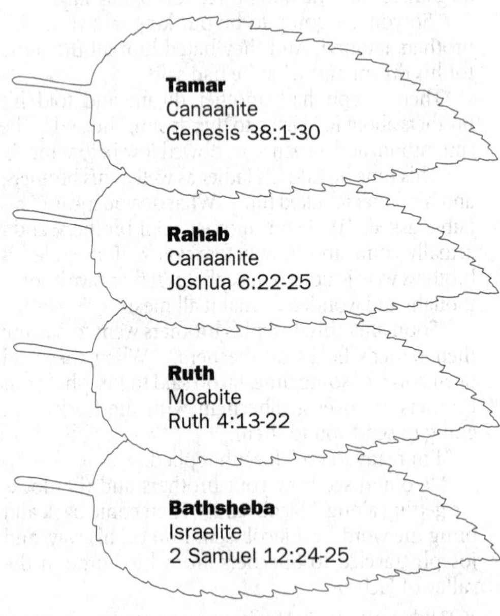


37:28a Hebrew *Midianites;* also in 37:36. 37:28b Hebrew *20 shekels,* about 8 ounces or 228 grams in weight.

and thought she was a prostitute, since her face was veiled. 16So he stopped and propositioned her to sleep with him, not realizing that she was his own daughter-in-law.

"How much will you pay me?" Tamar asked.

17"I'll send you a young goat from my flock," Judah promised.

"What pledge will you give me so I can be sure you will send it?" she asked.

18"Well, what do you want?" he inquired.

She replied, "I want your identification seal, your cord, and the walking stick you are carrying." So Judah gave these items to her. She then let him sleep with her, and she became pregnant. 19Afterward she went home, took off her veil, and put on her widow's clothing as usual.

20Judah asked his friend Hirah the Adullamite to take the young goat back to her and to pick up the pledges he had given her, but Hirah couldn't find her. 21So he asked the men who lived there, "Where can I find the prostitute* who was sitting beside the road at the entrance to the village?"

"We've never had a prostitute here," they replied. 22So Hirah returned to Judah and told him that he couldn't find her anywhere and that the men of the village had claimed they didn't have a prostitute there.

23"Then let her keep the pledges!" Judah exclaimed. "We tried our best to send her the goat. We'd be the laughingstock of the village if we went back again."

24About three months later, word reached Judah that Tamar, his daughter-in-law, was pregnant as a result of prostitution. "Bring her out and burn her!" Judah shouted.

25But as they were taking her out to kill her, she sent this message to her father-in-law: "The man who owns this identification seal and walking stick is the father of my child. Do you recognize them?"

26Judah admitted that they were his and said, "She is more in the right than I am, because I didn't keep my promise to let her marry my son Shelah." But Judah never slept with Tamar again.

27In due season the time of Tamar's delivery arrived, and she had twin sons. 28As they were being born, one of them reached out his hand, and the midwife tied a scarlet thread around the wrist of the child who appeared first, saying, "This one came out first." 29But then he drew back his hand, and the other baby was actually the first to be born. "What!" the midwife exclaimed. "How did you break out first?" And ever after, he was called Perez.* 30Then the baby with the scarlet thread on his wrist was born, and he was named Zerah.*

## CHAPTER 39 **POTIPHAR BUYS JOSEPH.**

Now when Joseph arrived in Egypt with the Ishmaelite traders, he was purchased by Potiphar, a member of the personal staff of Pharaoh, the king of Egypt. Potiphar was the captain of the palace guard.

2The LORD was with Joseph and blessed him greatly as he served in the home of his Egyptian master. 3Potiphar noticed this and realized that the LORD was with Joseph, giving him success in everything he did. 4So Joseph naturally became quite a favorite with him. Potiphar soon put Joseph in charge of his entire household and entrusted him with all his business dealings. 5From the day Joseph was put in charge, the LORD began to bless Potiphar for Joseph's sake. All his household affairs began to run smoothly, and his crops and livestock flourished. 6So Potiphar gave Joseph complete administrative responsibility over everything he owned. With Joseph there, he didn't have a worry in the world, except to decide what he wanted to eat!

Now Joseph was a very handsome and well-built young man. 7And about this time, Potiphar's wife began to desire him and invited him to sleep with her. 8But Joseph refused. "Look," he told her, "my master trusts me with everything in his entire household. 9No one here has more authority than I do! He has held back nothing from me except you, because you are his wife. How could I ever do such a wicked thing? It would be a great sin against God."

### SEDUCTION ● ● • • •

**39:9 Potiphar's wife failed to seduce Joseph, who resisted this temptation by saying it would be a sin against God. Joseph didn't say, "I'd be hurting you," or "I'd be sinning against Potiphar," or "I'd be sinning against myself." Under pressure, such excuses are easily rationalized away. Remember that sexual sin is not just between two consenting adults. It is an act of disobedience to God.**

### TURN AND RUN ● ● • • •

**39:10-15 Joseph avoided Potiphar's wife as much as possible. He refused her advances and finally *ran* from her. Sometimes merely trying to avoid temptation is not enough. We must turn and run, especially when the temptations seem very strong, as is often the case with sexual temptations.**

10She kept putting pressure on him day after day, but he refused to sleep with her, and he kept out of her way as much as possible. 11One day, however, no one else was around when he was doing his work inside the house. 12She came and grabbed him by his shirt, demanding, "Sleep with me!" Joseph tore himself away, but as he did, his shirt came off. She was left holding it as he ran from the house.

13When she saw that she had his shirt and that he had fled, 14she began screaming. Soon all the men around the place came running. "My husband has brought this Hebrew slave here to insult us!" she sobbed. "He tried to rape me, but I screamed. 15When he heard my loud cries, he ran and left his shirt behind with me."

16She kept the shirt with her, and when her husband came home that night, 17she told him her story. "That Hebrew slave you've had around here tried to make a fool of me," she said. 18"I was saved

**38:21** Hebrew *shrine prostitute;* also in 38:21b, 22. **38:29** *Perez* means "breaking out." **38:30** *Zerah* means "scarlet" or "brightness."

## POSITIVE ATTITUDE ● ● • • •

39:21-23 **As a prisoner and slave, Joseph could have seen his situation as hopeless. Instead, he did his best with each small task given him. His diligence and positive attitude were soon noticed by the chief jailer, who promoted him to prison administrator. Are you in the midst of a seemingly hopeless predicament? At work, at home, or at school, follow Joseph's example by taking each small task and doing your best. Remember how God turned Joseph's situation around. He will see your efforts and can reverse even overwhelming odds.**

only by my screams. He ran out, leaving his shirt behind!"

19After hearing his wife's story, Potiphar was furious! 20He took Joseph and threw him into the prison where the king's prisoners were held. 21But the LORD was with Joseph there, too, and he granted Joseph favor with the chief jailer. 22Before long, the jailer put Joseph in charge of all the other prisoners and over everything that happened in the prison. 23The chief jailer had no more worries after that, because Joseph took care of everything. The LORD was with him, making everything run smoothly and successfully.

CHAPTER **40** **JOSEPH EXPLAINS TWO DREAMS.** Some time later, Pharaoh's chief cup-bearer and chief baker offended him. 2Pharaoh became very angry with these officials, 3and he put them in the prison where Joseph was, in the palace of Potiphar, the captain of the guard. 4They remained in prison for quite some time, and Potiphar assigned Joseph to take care of them.

5One night the cup-bearer and the baker each had a dream, and each dream had its own meaning. 6The

## OPPORTUNITY ● ● • • •

40:8 **When the subject of dreams came up, Joseph focused everyone's attention on God. Rather than using the situation to make himself look good, he turned it into a powerful witness for the Lord. One secret of effective witnessing is to recognize opportunities to relate God to the other person's experience. When the opportunity arises, we must have the courage to speak, as Joseph did.**

next morning Joseph noticed the dejected look on their faces. 7"Why do you look so worried today?" he asked.

8And they replied, "We both had dreams last night, but there is no one here to tell us what they mean."

"Interpreting dreams is God's business," Joseph replied. "Tell me what you saw."

9The cup-bearer told his dream first. "In my dream," he said, "I saw a vine in front of me. 10It had three branches that began to bud and blossom, and soon there were clusters of ripe grapes. 11I was holding Pharaoh's wine cup in my hand, so I took the grapes and squeezed the juice into it. Then I placed the cup in Pharaoh's hand."

12"I know what the dream means," Joseph said. "The three branches mean three days. 13Within three days Pharaoh will take you out of prison and return you to your position as his chief cup-bearer. 14And please have some pity on me when you are back in his favor. Mention me to Pharaoh, and ask him to let me out of here. 15For I was kidnapped from my homeland, the land of the Hebrews, and now I'm here in jail, but I did nothing to deserve it."

16When the chief baker saw that the first dream had such a good meaning, he told his dream to Joseph, too. "In my dream," he said, "there were three baskets of pastries on my head. 17In the top basket were all kinds of bakery goods for Pharaoh, but the birds came and ate them."

18"I'll tell you what it means," Joseph told him. "The three baskets mean three days. 19Three days from now Pharaoh will cut off your head and impale your body on a pole. Then birds will come and peck away at your flesh."

20Pharaoh's birthday came three days later, and he gave a banquet for all his officials and household staff. He sent for his chief cup-bearer and chief baker, and they were brought to him from the prison. 21He then restored the chief cup-bearer to his former position, 22but he sentenced the chief baker to be impaled on a pole, just as Joseph had predicted. 23Pharaoh's cup-bearer, however, promptly forgot all about Joseph, never giving him another thought.

CHAPTER **41** **JOSEPH BECOMES THE RULER.** Two years later, Pharaoh dreamed that he was standing on the bank of the Nile River. 2In his dream, seven fat, healthy-looking cows suddenly came up out of the river and began grazing along its bank. 3Then seven other cows came up from the river, but these were very ugly and gaunt. These cows went over and stood beside the fat cows. 4Then the thin, ugly cows ate the fat ones! At this point in the dream, Pharaoh woke up.

5Soon he fell asleep again and had a second dream. This time he saw seven heads of grain on one stalk, with every kernel well formed and plump. 6Then suddenly, seven more heads appeared on the stalk, but these were shriveled and withered by the east wind. 7And these thin heads swallowed up the seven plump, well-formed heads! Then Pharaoh woke up again and realized it was a dream.

8The next morning, as he thought about it, Pharaoh became very concerned as to what the dreams might mean. So he called for all the magicians and wise men of Egypt and told them about his dreams, but not one of them could suggest what they meant. 9Then the king's cup-bearer spoke up. "Today I have been reminded of my failure," he said. 10"Some time ago, you were angry with the chief baker and me, and you imprisoned us in the palace of the captain of the guard. 11One night the chief baker and I each had a dream, and each dream had a meaning. 12We told the dreams to a young Hebrew man who was a servant of the captain of the guard. He told us what each of our dreams meant, 13and everything happened just as he said it would. I was restored to my position as cup-bearer, and the chief baker was executed and impaled on a pole."

[14]Pharaoh sent for Joseph at once, and he was brought hastily from the dungeon. After a quick shave and change of clothes, he went in and stood in Pharaoh's presence. [15]"I had a dream last night," Pharaoh told him, "and none of these men can tell me what it means. But I have heard that you can interpret dreams, and that is why I have called for you."

[16]"It is beyond my power to do this," Joseph replied. "But God will tell you what it means and will set you at ease."

[17]So Pharaoh told him the dream. "I was standing on the bank of the Nile River," he said. [18]"Suddenly, seven fat, healthy-looking cows came up out of the river and began grazing along its bank. [19]But then seven other cows came up from the river. They were very thin and gaunt—in fact, I've never seen such ugly animals in all the land of Egypt. [20]These thin, ugly cows ate up the seven fat ones that had come out of the river first, [21]but afterward they were still as ugly and gaunt as before! Then I woke up.

[22]"A little later I had another dream. This time there were seven heads of grain on one stalk, and all seven heads were plump and full. [23]Then out of the same stalk came seven withered heads, shriveled by the east wind. [24]And the withered heads swallowed up the plump ones! I told these dreams to my magicians, but not one of them could tell me what they mean."

[25]"Both dreams mean the same thing," Joseph told Pharaoh. "God was telling you what he is about to do. [26]The seven fat cows and the seven plump heads of grain both represent seven years of prosperity. [27]The seven thin, ugly cows and the seven withered heads of grain represent seven years of famine. [28]This will happen just as I have described it, for God has shown you what he is about to do. [29]The next seven years will be a period of great prosperity throughout the land of Egypt. [30]But afterward there will be seven years of famine so great that all the prosperity will be forgotten and wiped out. Famine will destroy the land. [31]This famine will be so terrible that even the memory of the good years will be erased. [32]As for having the dream twice, it means that the matter has been decreed by God and that he will make these events happen soon.

[33]"My suggestion is that you find the wisest man in Egypt and put him in charge of a nationwide program. [34]Let Pharaoh appoint officials over the land, and let them collect one-fifth of all the crops during the seven good years. [35]Have them gather all the food and grain of these good years into the royal storehouses, and store it away so there will be food in the cities. [36]That way there will be enough to eat when the seven years of famine come. Otherwise disaster will surely strike the land, and all the people will die."

[37]Joseph's suggestions were well received by Pharaoh and his advisers. [38]As they discussed who should be appointed for the job, Pharaoh said, "Who could do it better than Joseph? For he is a man who is obviously filled with the spirit of God." [39]Turning to Joseph, Pharaoh said, "Since God has revealed the meaning of the dreams to you, you are the wisest man in the land! [40]I hereby appoint you to direct this project. You will manage my household and organize all my people. Only I will have a rank higher than yours."

[41]And Pharaoh said to Joseph, "I hereby put you in charge of the entire land of Egypt." [42]Then Pharaoh placed his own signet ring on Joseph's finger as a symbol of his authority. He dressed him in beautiful clothing and placed the royal gold chain about his neck. [43]Pharaoh also gave Joseph the chariot of his second-in-command, and wherever he went the command was shouted, "Kneel down!" So Joseph was put in charge of all Egypt. [44]And Pharaoh said to Joseph, "I am the king, but no one will move a hand or a foot in the entire land of Egypt without your approval."

[45]Pharaoh renamed him Zaphenath-paneah* and gave him a wife—a young woman named Asenath, the daughter of Potiphera, priest of Heliopolis.* So Joseph took charge of the entire land of Egypt. [46]He was thirty years old when he entered the service of Pharaoh, the king of Egypt. And when Joseph left Pharaoh's presence, he made a tour of inspection throughout the land.

[47]And sure enough, for the next seven years there were bumper crops everywhere. [48]During those years, Joseph took a portion of all the crops grown in Egypt and stored them for the government in nearby cities. [49]After seven years, the granaries were filled to overflowing. There was so much grain, like sand on the seashore, that the people could not keep track of the amount.

[50]During this time, before the arrival of the first of the famine years, two sons were born to Joseph and his wife, Asenath, the daughter of Potiphera, priest of Heliopolis. [51]Joseph named his older son Manasseh,* for he said, "God has made me forget all my troubles and the family of my father." [52]Joseph named his second son Ephraim,* for he said, "God has made me fruitful in this land of my suffering."

[53]At last the seven years of plenty came to an end. [54]Then the seven years of famine began, just as

## PREPARATION ● ● • • •

41:14 **Our most important opportunities may come when we least expect them. Joseph was brought hastily from the dungeon and pushed before Pharaoh. Did he have time to prepare? Yes and no. He had no warning that he suddenly would be pulled from prison and questioned by the king. Yet Joseph was ready for almost anything because of his right relationship with God. It was not Joseph's knowledge of dreams that helped him interpret their meaning. It was his knowledge of God. Be ready for opportunities by getting to know more about God. Then you will be ready to take on almost anything that comes your way.**

**41:45a** *Zaphenath-paneah* probably means "God speaks and lives." **41:45b** Hebrew *of On;* also in 41:50. **41:51** *Manasseh* sounds like a Hebrew term that means "causing to forget." **41:52** *Ephraim* sounds like a Hebrew term that means "fruitful."

Joseph had predicted. There were crop failures in all the surrounding countries, too, but in Egypt there was plenty of grain in the storehouses. [55]Throughout the land of Egypt the people began to starve. They pleaded with Pharaoh for food, and he told them, "Go to Joseph and do whatever he tells you." [56]So with severe famine everywhere in the land, Joseph opened up the storehouses and sold grain to the Egyptians. [57]And people from surrounding lands also came to Egypt to buy grain from Joseph because the famine was severe throughout the world.

## CHAPTER 42

**JOSEPH'S BROTHERS BUY GRAIN.** When Jacob heard that there was grain available in Egypt, he said to his sons, "Why are you standing around looking at one another? [2]I have heard there is grain in Egypt. Go down and buy some for us before we all starve to death." [3]So Joseph's ten older brothers went down to Egypt to buy grain. [4]Jacob wouldn't let Joseph's younger brother, Benjamin, go with them, however, for fear some harm might come to him. [5]So Jacob's* sons arrived in Egypt along with others to buy food, for the famine had reached Canaan as well.

[6]Since Joseph was governor of all Egypt and in charge of the sale of the grain, it was to him that his brothers came. They bowed low before him, with their faces to the ground. [7]Joseph recognized them instantly, but he pretended to be a stranger. "Where are you from?" he demanded roughly.

### BAD MEMORIES ● ● • • •

**42:7 Joseph could have revealed his identity to his brothers at once. But Joseph's last memory of them was of staring in horror at their faces as slave traders carried him away. Were his brothers still evil and treacherous, or had they changed over the years? Joseph decided to put them through a few tests to find out.**

"From the land of Canaan," they replied. "We have come to buy grain."

[8]Joseph's brothers didn't recognize him, but Joseph recognized them. [9]And he remembered the dreams he had had many years before. He said to them, "You are spies! You have come to see how vulnerable our land has become."

[10]"No, my lord!" they exclaimed. "We have come to buy food. [11]We are all brothers and honest men, sir! We are not spies!"

[12]"Yes, you are!" he insisted. "You have come to discover how vulnerable the famine has made us."

[13]"Sir," they said, "there are twelve of us brothers, and our father is in the land of Canaan. Our youngest brother is there with our father, and one of our brothers is no longer with us."

[14]But Joseph insisted, "As I said, you are spies! [15]This is how I will test your story. I swear by the life of Pharaoh that you will not leave Egypt unless your youngest brother comes here. [16]One of you go and

### FULL RESPONSIBILITY ● ● • • •

**43:9 Judah accepted full responsibility for Benjamin's safety. He did not know what that might mean for him, but he was determined to carry it out. In the end it was Judah's stirring words that caused Joseph to break down and reveal himself to his brothers (44:18-34). Accepting and fulfilling responsibilities is difficult, but it builds character and confidence, earns others' respect, and motivates us to complete our work. When you have been given an assignment to complete or a responsibility to fulfill, commit yourself to seeing it through.**

get your brother! I'll keep the rest of you here, bound in prison. Then we'll find out whether or not your story is true. If it turns out that you don't have a younger brother, then I'll know you are spies."

[17]So he put them all in prison for three days. [18]On the third day Joseph said to them, "I am a God-fearing man. If you do as I say, you will live. [19]We'll see how honorable you really are. Only one of you will remain in the prison. The rest of you may go on home with grain for your families. [20]But bring your youngest brother back to me. In this way, I will know whether or not you are telling me the truth. If you are, I will spare you." To this they agreed.

[21]Speaking among themselves, they said, "This has all happened because of what we did to Joseph long ago. We saw his terror and anguish and heard his pleadings, but we wouldn't listen. That's why this trouble has come upon us."

[22]"Didn't I tell you not to do it?" Reuben asked. "But you wouldn't listen. And now we are going to die because we murdered him."

[23]Of course, they didn't know that Joseph understood them as he was standing there, for he had been speaking to them through an interpreter. [24]Now he left the room and found a place where he could weep. Returning, he talked some more with them. He then chose Simeon from among them and had him tied up right before their eyes.

[25]Joseph then ordered his servants to fill the men's sacks with grain, but he also gave secret instructions to return each brother's payment at the top of his sack. He also gave them provisions for their journey. [26]So they loaded up their donkeys with the grain and started for home.

[27]But when they stopped for the night and one of them opened his sack to get some grain to feed the donkeys, he found his money in the sack. [28]"Look!" he exclaimed to his brothers. "My money is here in my sack!" They were filled with terror and said to each other, "What has God done to us?" [29]So they came to their father, Jacob, in the land of Canaan and told him all that had happened.

[30]"The man who is ruler over the land spoke very roughly to us," they told him. "He took us for spies. [31]But we said, 'We are honest men, not spies. [32]We are twelve brothers, sons of one father; one brother has disappeared, and the youngest is with our father in the land of Canaan.' [33]Then the man, the ruler of the land, told us, 'This is the way I will

42:5 Hebrew *Israel's.*

find out if you are honest men. Leave one of your brothers here with me, and take grain for your families and go on home. 34 But bring your youngest brother back to me. Then I will know that you are honest men and not spies. If you prove to be what you say, then I will give you back your brother, and you may come as often as you like to buy grain.'"

35 As they emptied out the sacks, there at the top of each one was the bag of money paid for the grain. Terror gripped them, as it did their father. 36 Jacob exclaimed, "You have deprived me of my children! Joseph has disappeared, Simeon is gone, and now you want to take Benjamin, too. Everything is going against me!"

37 Then Reuben said to his father, "You may kill my two sons if I don't bring Benjamin back to you. I'll be responsible for him."

38 But Jacob replied, "My son will not go down with you, for his brother Joseph is dead, and he alone is left of his mother's children. If anything should happen to him, you would bring my gray head down to the grave in deep sorrow."

## CHAPTER 43 JOSEPH'S BROTHERS RETURN.

But there was no relief from the terrible famine throughout the land. 2 When the grain they had brought from Egypt was almost gone, Jacob said to his sons, "Go again and buy us a little food."

3 But Judah said, "The man wasn't joking when he warned that we couldn't see him again unless Benjamin came along. 4 If you let him come with us, we will go down and buy some food. 5 But if you don't let Benjamin go, we may as well stay at home. Remember that the man said, 'You won't be allowed to come and see me unless your brother is with you.'"

6 "Why did you ever tell him you had another brother?" Jacob* moaned. "Why did you have to treat me with such cruelty?"

7 "But the man specifically asked us about our family," they replied. "He wanted to know whether our father was still living, and he asked us if we had another brother so we told him. How could we have known he would say, 'Bring me your brother'?"

8 Judah said to his father, "Send the boy with me, and we will be on our way. Otherwise we will all die of starvation—and not only we, but you and our little ones. 9 I personally guarantee his safety. If I don't bring him back to you, then let me bear the blame forever. 10 For we could have gone and returned twice by this time if you had let him come without delay."

11 So their father, Jacob, finally said to them, "If it can't be avoided, then at least do this. Fill your bags with the best products of the land. Take them to the man as gifts—balm, honey, spices, myrrh, pistachio nuts, and almonds. 12 Take double the money that

---

### JOSEPH

Some people think they can be or do anything! That was Joseph. He was naturally self-confident. He was also Jacob's favorite son. God had given Joseph a strong sense that there were great plans for his life. Sometimes, though, he wasn't very sensitive of others' feelings. All this made Joseph's brothers jealous and angry. Eventually they tried to get rid of him.

As he grew, Joseph learned. His self-confidence was changed by the painful experiences in his life into a quiet but powerful confidence in God. He was able to survive and do well where most people would have failed. He added practical wisdom to his confidence and won the hearts of almost everyone who got to know him—Potiphar, the jailer, other prisoners, the king, and after many years even those 10 older brothers.

Perhaps you can identify with one or more of these hardships Joseph experienced—he was betrayed and deserted by his family, exposed to sexual temptation, punished for doing the right thing, imprisoned for a long time, and forgotten by those he helped. As you read his story, note what Joseph did in each case. His positive response transformed each setback into a step forward. He didn't spend much time asking why. His approach was, what shall I do now? Those who watched his life were aware that wherever Joseph went and whatever he did, God was with him. The next time things go wrong, try the Joseph approach. Start by reminding yourself God is with you. There is nothing like knowing he is there to help you work things out.

**UPS:**
- Rose in power from slave to ruler of Egypt
- Was known for his personal integrity
- Was a man of spiritual sensitivity
- Prepared a nation to survive a famine

**DOWNS:**
- His youthful pride caused friction with his brothers

**STATS:**
- Where: Canaan, Egypt
- Occupation: Shepherd, slave, convict, ruler
- Relatives: Parents: Jacob and Rachel. Eleven brothers, one sister. Wife: Asenath. Sons: Manasseh and Ephraim.

LESSONS: What matters is not so much the events or circumstances of life, but our responses to them

With God's help, any situation can be used for good, even when others intend it for evil

KEY VERSE: "Pharaoh said, 'Who could do it better than Joseph? For he is a man who is obviously filled with the spirit of God.'" (Genesis 41:38).

Joseph's story is told in Genesis 37–50. He is also mentioned in Hebrews 11:22.

---

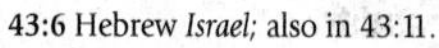

43:6 Hebrew *Israel;* also in 43:11.

you found in your sacks, as it was probably someone's mistake. 13Then take your brother and go back to the man. 14May God Almighty give you mercy as you go before the man, that he might release Simeon and return Benjamin. And if I must bear the anguish of their deaths, then so be it."

15So they took Benjamin and the gifts and double the money and hurried to Egypt, where they presented themselves to Joseph. 16When Joseph saw that Benjamin was with them, he said to the manager of his household, "These men will eat with me this noon. Take them inside and prepare a big feast." 17So the man did as he was told and took them to Joseph's palace.

18They were badly frightened when they saw where they were being taken. "It's because of the money returned to us in our sacks," they said. "He plans to pretend that we stole it. Then he will seize us as slaves and take our donkeys."

19As the brothers arrived at the entrance to the palace, they went over to the man in charge of Joseph's household. 20They said to him, "Sir, after our first trip to Egypt to buy food, 21as we were returning home, we stopped for the night and opened our sacks. The money we had used to pay for the grain was there in our sacks. Here it is; we have brought it back again. 22We also have additional money to buy more grain. We have no idea how the money got into our sacks."

23"Relax. Don't worry about it," the household manager told them. "Your God, the God of your ancestors, must have put it there. We collected your money all right." Then he released Simeon and brought him out to them.

24The brothers were then led into the palace and given water to wash their feet and food for their donkeys. 25They were told they would be eating there, so they prepared their gifts for Joseph's arrival at noon.

26When Joseph came, they gave him their gifts and bowed low before him. 27He asked them how they had been getting along, and then he said, "How is your father—the old man you spoke about? Is he still alive?"

28"Yes," they replied. "He is alive and well." Then they bowed again before him.

29Looking at his brother Benjamin, Joseph asked, "Is this your youngest brother, the one you told me about? May God be gracious to you, my son." 30Then Joseph made a hasty exit because he was overcome with emotion for his brother and wanted to cry. Going into his private room, he wept there. 31Then he washed his face and came out, keeping himself under control. "Bring on the food!" he ordered.

32Joseph ate by himself, and his brothers were served at a separate table. The Egyptians sat at their own table because Egyptians despise Hebrews and refuse to eat with them. 33Joseph told each of his brothers where to sit, and to their amazement, he seated them in the order of their ages, from oldest to youngest. 34Their food was served to them from Joseph's own table. He gave the largest serving to Benjamin—five times as much as to any of the others. So they all feasted and drank freely with him.

CHAPTER **44** **JOSEPH TESTS HIS BROTHERS.** When his brothers were ready to leave, Joseph gave these instructions to the man in charge of his household: "Fill each of their sacks with as much grain as they can carry, and put each man's money back into his sack. 2Then put my personal silver cup at the top of the youngest brother's sack, along with his grain money." So the household manager did as he was told.

3The brothers were up at dawn and set out on their journey with their loaded donkeys. 4But when they were barely out of the city, Joseph said to his household manager, "Chase after them and stop them. Ask them, 'Why have you repaid an act of kindness with such evil? 5What do you mean by stealing my master's personal silver drinking cup, which he uses to predict the future? What a wicked thing you have done!'"

6So the man caught up with them and spoke to them in the way he had been instructed. 7"What are you talking about?" the brothers responded. "What kind of people do you think we are, that you accuse us of such a terrible thing? 8Didn't we bring back the money we found in our sacks? Why would we steal silver or gold from your master's house? 9If you find his cup with any one of us, let that one die. And all the rest of us will be your master's slaves forever."

10"Fair enough," the man replied, "except that only the one who stole it will be a slave. The rest of you may go free."

11They quickly took their sacks from the backs of their donkeys and opened them. 12Joseph's servant began searching the oldest brother's sack, going on down the line to the youngest. The cup was found in Benjamin's sack! 13At this, they tore their clothing in despair, loaded the donkeys again, and returned to the city. 14Joseph was still at home when Judah and his brothers arrived, and they fell to the ground before him.

15"What were you trying to do?" Joseph demanded. "Didn't you know that a man such as I would know who stole it?"

16And Judah said, "Oh, my lord, what can we say to you? How can we plead? How can we prove our

## CHANGED LIFE ● ● • • •

44:16-34 **When Judah was younger, he showed no regard for his brother Joseph or his father, Jacob. First he convinced his brothers to sell Joseph as a slave (37:27); then he joined his brothers in lying to his father about Joseph's fate (37:32). But what a change had taken place in Judah! The man who sold one favored little brother into slavery now offered to become a slave himself to save another favored little brother. He was so concerned for his father and younger brother that he was willing to die for them. When you are ready to give up hope on yourself or others, remember that God can change even the most selfish personality.**

## INTENTIONS ● ● ● • •

45:4-8 **Although Joseph's brothers had wanted to get rid of him, God used even their evil actions to fulfill his ultimate plan. He sent Joseph ahead to preserve their lives, save Egypt, and prepare the way for the beginning of the nation of Israel. God is in control. His plans are not dictated by human actions. When others intend evil toward you, remember that they are only God's tools. As Joseph said to his brothers, "As far as I am concerned, God turned into good what you meant for evil. He brought me to the high position I have today so I could save the lives of many people" (50:20).**

innocence? God is punishing us for our sins. My lord, we have all returned to be your slaves—we and our brother who had your cup in his sack."

17 "No," Joseph said. "Only the man who stole the cup will be my slave. The rest of you may go home to your father."

18 Then Judah stepped forward and said, "My lord, let me say just this one word to you. Be patient with me for a moment, for I know you could have me killed in an instant, as though you were Pharaoh himself.

19 "You asked us, my lord, if we had a father or a brother. 20 We said, 'Yes, we have a father, an old man, and a child of his old age, his youngest son. His brother is dead, and he alone is left of his mother's children, and his father loves him very much.' 21 And you said to us, 'Bring him here so I can see him.' 22 But we said to you, 'My lord, the boy cannot leave his father, for his father would die.' 23 But you told us, 'You may not see me again unless your youngest brother is with you.' 24 So we returned to our father and told him what you had said. 25 And when he said, 'Go back again and buy us a little food,' 26 we replied, 'We can't unless you let our youngest brother go with us. We won't be allowed to see the man in charge of the grain unless our youngest brother is with us.' 27 Then my father said to us, 'You know that my wife had two sons, 28 and that one of them went away and never returned—doubtless torn to pieces by some wild animal. I have never seen him since. 29 If you take away his brother from me, too, and any harm comes to him, you would bring my gray head down to the grave in deep sorrow.'

30 "And now, my lord, I cannot go back to my father without the boy. Our father's life is bound up in the boy's life. 31 When he sees that the boy is not with us, our father will die. We will be responsible for bringing his gray head down to the grave in sorrow. 32 My lord, I made a pledge to my father that I would take care of the boy. I told him, 'If I don't bring him back to you, I will bear the blame forever.' 33 Please, my lord, let me stay here as a slave instead of the boy, and let the boy return with his brothers. 34 For how can I return to my father if the boy is not with me? I cannot bear to see what this would do to him."

CHAPTER **45** **JOSEPH FORGIVES HIS BROTHERS.** Joseph could stand it no longer. "Out, all of you!" he cried out to his attendants. He wanted to be alone with his brothers when he told them who he was. 2 Then he broke down and wept aloud. His sobs could be heard throughout the palace, and the news was quickly carried to Pharaoh's palace.

3 "I am Joseph!" he said to his brothers. "Is my father still alive?" But his brothers were speechless! They were stunned to realize that Joseph was standing there in front of them. 4 "Come over here," he said. So they came closer. And he said again, "I am Joseph, your brother whom you sold into Egypt. 5 But don't be angry with yourselves that you did this to me, for God did it. He sent me here ahead of you to preserve your lives. 6 These two years of famine will grow to seven, during which there will be neither plowing nor harvest. 7 God has sent me here to keep you and your families alive so that you will become a great nation. 8 Yes, it was God who sent me here, not you! And he has made me a counselor to Pharaoh—manager of his entire household and ruler over all Egypt.

9 "Hurry, return to my father and tell him, 'This is what your son Joseph says: God has made me master over all the land of Egypt. Come down to me right away! 10 You will live in the land of Goshen so you can be near me with all your children and grandchildren, your flocks and herds, and all that you have. 11 I will take care of you there, for there are still five years of famine ahead of us. Otherwise you and your household will come to utter poverty.'"

12 Then Joseph said, "You can see for yourselves, and so can my brother Benjamin, that I really am Joseph! 13 Tell my father how I am honored here in Egypt. Tell him about everything you have seen, and bring him to me quickly." 14 Weeping with joy, he embraced Benjamin, and Benjamin also began to weep. 15 Then Joseph kissed each of his brothers and wept over them, and then they began talking freely with him.

16 The news soon reached Pharaoh: "Joseph's brothers have come!" Pharaoh was very happy to hear this and so were his officials.

17 Pharaoh said to Joseph, "Tell your brothers to load their pack animals and return quickly to their homes in Canaan. 18 Tell them to bring your father and all of their families, and to come here to Egypt to live. Tell them, 'Pharaoh will assign to you the very best territory in the land of Egypt. You will live off the fat of the land!' 19 And tell your brothers to take wagons from Egypt to carry their wives and little ones and to bring your father here. 20 Don't worry about your belongings, for the best of all the land of Egypt is yours."

21 So the sons of Jacob* did as they were told. Joseph gave them wagons, as Pharaoh had commanded, and he supplied them with provisions for the journey. 22 And he gave each of them new clothes—but to Benjamin he gave five changes of clothes and three hundred pieces* of silver! 23 He sent his father ten donkeys loaded with the good

**45:21** Hebrew *Israel;* also in 45:28. **45:22** Hebrew *300 shekels,* about 7.5 pounds or 3.4 kilograms in weight.

things of Egypt, and ten donkeys loaded with grain and all kinds of other food to be eaten on his journey. 24So he sent his brothers off, and as they left, he called after them, "Don't quarrel along the way!" 25And they left Egypt and returned to their father, Jacob, in the land of Canaan.

26"Joseph is still alive!" they told him. "And he is ruler over all the land of Egypt!" Jacob was stunned at the news—he couldn't believe it. 27But when they had given him Joseph's messages, and when he saw the wagons loaded with the food sent by Joseph, his spirit revived.

28Then Jacob said, "It must be true! My son Joseph is alive! I will go and see him before I die."

## STRANGE PLACES ● ● • • •

46:3-4 **God told Jacob to leave his home and travel to a strange and faraway land. But God reassured him by promising to go with him and take care of him. When new situations or surroundings frighten or worry you, recognize that experiencing fear is normal. To be paralyzed by fear, however, is an indication that you question God's ability to take care of you.**

CHAPTER **46** **JACOB MOVES TO EGYPT.** So Jacob* set out for Egypt with all his possessions. And when he came to Beersheba, he offered sacrifices to the God of his father, Isaac. 2During the night God spoke to him in a vision. "Jacob! Jacob!" he called.

"Here I am," Jacob replied.

3"I am God," the voice said, "the God of your father. Do not be afraid to go down to Egypt, for I will see to it that you become a great nation there. 4I will go with you down to Egypt, and I will bring your descendants back again. But you will die in Egypt with Joseph at your side."

5So Jacob left Beersheba, and his sons brought him to Egypt. They carried their little ones and wives in the wagons Pharaoh had provided for them. 6They brought their livestock, too, and all the belongings they had acquired in the land of Canaan. Jacob and his entire family arrived in Egypt—7sons and daughters, grandsons and granddaughters—all his descendants.

8These are the names of the Israelites, the descendants of Jacob, who went with him to Egypt:

Reuben was Jacob's oldest son. 9The sons of Reuben were Hanoch, Pallu, Hezron, and Carmi.

10The sons of Simeon were Jemuel, Jamin, Ohad, Jakin, Zohar, and Shaul. (Shaul's mother was a Canaanite woman.)

11The sons of Levi were Gershon, Kohath, and Merari.

12The sons of Judah were Er, Onan, Shelah, Perez, and Zerah. (But Er and Onan had died in the land of Canaan.) The sons of Perez were Hezron and Hamul.

13The sons of Issachar were Tola, Puah,* Jashub,* and Shimron.

14The sons of Zebulun were Sered, Elon, and Jahleel.

15These are the sons of Jacob who were born to Leah in Paddan-aram, along with their sister, Dinah. In all, Jacob's descendants through Leah numbered thirty-three.

16The sons of Gad were Zephon,* Haggi, Shuni, Ezbon, Eri, Arodi, and Areli.

17The sons of Asher were Imnah, Ishvah, Ishvi, and Beriah. Their sister was named Serah. Beriah's sons were Heber and Malkiel.

18These sixteen were descendants of Jacob through Zilpah, the servant given to Leah by her father, Laban.

19The sons of Jacob's wife Rachel were Joseph and Benjamin.

20Joseph's sons, born in the land of Egypt, were Manasseh and Ephraim. Their mother was Asenath, daughter of Potiphera, priest of Heliopolis.*

21Benjamin's sons were Bela, Beker, Ashbel, Gera, Naaman, Ehi, Rosh, Muppim, Huppim, and Ard.

22These fourteen were the descendants of Jacob and his wife Rachel.

23The son of Dan was Hushim.

24The sons of Naphtali were Jahzeel, Guni, Jezer, and Shillem.

25These seven were the descendants of Jacob through Bilhah, the servant given to Rachel by her father, Laban.

26So the total number of Jacob's direct descendants who went with him to Egypt, not counting his sons' wives, was sixty-six. 27Joseph also had two sons* who had been born in Egypt. So altogether, there were seventy* members of Jacob's family in the land of Egypt.

28Jacob sent Judah on ahead to meet Joseph and get directions to the land of Goshen. And when they all arrived there, 29Joseph prepared his chariot and traveled to Goshen to meet his father. As soon as Joseph arrived, he embraced his father and wept on his shoulder for a long time. 30Then Jacob said to Joseph, "Now let me die, for I have seen you with my own eyes and know you are still alive."

31And Joseph said to his brothers and to all their households, "I'll go and tell Pharaoh that you have all come from the land of Canaan to join me. 32And I will tell him, 'These men are shepherds and livestock breeders. They have brought with them their

**46:1** Hebrew *Israel;* also in 46:30. **46:13a** As in Syriac version and Samaritan Pentateuch (see also 1 Chr 7:1); Hebrew reads *Puvah.* **46:13b** As in some Greek manuscripts and Samaritan Pentateuch (see also Num 26:24; 1 Chr 7:1); Hebrew reads *Iob.* **46:16** As in Greek version and Samaritan Pentateuch (see also Num 26:15); Hebrew reads *Ziphion.* **46:20** Hebrew *of On.* **46:27a** Greek version reads *nine sons,* probably including Joseph's grandsons through Ephraim and Manasseh (see 1 Chr 7:14-20). **46:27b** Greek version reads *seventy-five;* see note on Exod 1:5.

flocks and herds and everything they own.' [33]So
when Pharaoh calls for you and asks you about your
occupation, [34]tell him, 'We have been livestock
breeders from our youth, as our ancestors have been
for many generations.' When you tell him this, he
will let you live here in the land of Goshen, for
shepherds are despised in the land of Egypt."

CHAPTER **47** **JACOB BLESSES PHARAOH.** So Joseph
went to see Pharaoh and said, "My father and my
brothers are here from Canaan. They came with all
their flocks and herds and possessions, and they are
now in the land of Goshen."

[2]Joseph took five of his brothers with him and
presented them to Pharaoh. [3]Pharaoh asked them,
"What is your occupation?"

And they replied, "We are shepherds like our
ancestors. [4]We have come to live here in Egypt, for
there is no pasture for our flocks in Canaan. The
famine is very severe there. We request permission to
live in the land of Goshen."

[5]And Pharaoh said to Joseph, "Now that your
family has joined you here, [6]choose any place you
like for them to live. Give them the best land of
Egypt—the land of Goshen will be fine. And if any
of them have special skills, put them in charge of my
livestock, too."

[7]Then Joseph brought his father, Jacob, and presented him to Pharaoh, and Jacob blessed Pharaoh.
[8]"How old are you?" Pharaoh asked him.

[9]Jacob replied, "I have lived for 130 hard years,
but I am still not nearly as old as many of my
ancestors." [10]Then Jacob blessed Pharaoh again before he left.

[11]So Joseph assigned the best land of Egypt—the
land of Rameses—to his father and brothers, just as
Pharaoh had commanded. [12]And Joseph furnished
food to his father and brothers in amounts appropriate to the number of their dependents.

[13]Meanwhile, the famine became worse and
worse, and the crops continued to fail throughout
Egypt and Canaan. [14]Joseph collected all the money
in Egypt and Canaan in exchange for grain, and he
brought the money to Pharaoh's treasure-house.
[15]When the people of Egypt and Canaan ran out of
money, they came to Joseph crying again for food.
"Our money is gone," they said, "but give us bread.
Why should we die?"

[16]"Well, then," Joseph replied, "since your money
is gone, give me your livestock. I will give you food
in exchange." [17]So they gave their livestock to Joseph
in exchange for food. Soon all the horses, flocks,
herds, and donkeys of Egypt were in Pharaoh's possession. But at least they were able to purchase food
for that year.

[18]The next year they came again and said, "Our
money is gone, and our livestock are yours. We have
nothing left but our bodies and land. [19]Why should
we die before your very eyes? Buy us and our land in
exchange for food; we will then become servants to
Pharaoh. Just give us grain so that our lives may be
saved and so the land will not become empty and
desolate."

[20]So Joseph bought all the land of Egypt for Pharaoh. All the Egyptians sold him their fields because
the famine was so severe, and their land then belonged to Pharaoh. [21]Thus, all the people of Egypt
became servants to Pharaoh.* [22]The only land he
didn't buy was that belonging to the priests, for they
were assigned food from Pharaoh and didn't need to
sell their land.

[23]Then Joseph said to the people, "See, I have
bought you and your land for Pharaoh. I will provide you with seed, so you can plant the fields.
[24]Then when you harvest it, a fifth of your crop will
belong to Pharaoh. Keep four-fifths for yourselves,
and use it to plant the next year's crop and to feed
yourselves, your households, and your little ones."

[25]"You have saved our lives!" they exclaimed.
"May it please you, sir, to let us be Pharaoh's
servants." [26]Joseph then made it a law throughout
the land of Egypt—and it is still the law—that
Pharaoh should receive one-fifth of all the crops
grown on his land. But since Pharaoh had not
taken over the priests' land, they were exempt from
this payment.

## KEEP THE FAITH ● ● • • •

**47:1-6 The faithfulness of Joseph affected his entire family. When he was in prison, Joseph must have wondered about his future. Instead of despairing, he faithfully obeyed God and did what was right. Here we see one of the exciting results. We may not always see the effects of our faith, but we can be sure that God will honor faithfulness.**

## KEEPING YOUR WORD ● ● • • •

**47:29-31 Jacob had Joseph promise to bury him in his homeland. Few things were written in this culture, so a person's word then carried as much force as a written contract today. People today seem to find it easy to say, "I didn't mean what I said." God's people, however, are to speak the truth and live the truth. Let your words be as binding as a written contract.**

[27]So the people of Israel settled in the land of
Goshen in Egypt. And before long, they began to
prosper there, and their population grew rapidly.
[28]Jacob lived for seventeen years after his arrival in
Egypt, so he was 147 years old when he died. [29]As the
time of his death drew near, he called for his son
Joseph and said to him, "If you are pleased with me,
swear most solemnly that you will honor this, my
last request: Do not bury me in Egypt. [30]When I am
dead, take me out of Egypt and bury me beside my
ancestors." So Joseph promised that he would.
[31]"Swear that you will do it," Jacob insisted. So
Joseph gave his oath, and Jacob* bowed in worship
as he leaned on his staff.*

47:21 As in Greek version and Samaritan Pentateuch; Hebrew reads *He moved the people into the towns throughout the land of Egypt.* 47:31a Hebrew *Israel.* 47:31b As in Greek version; Hebrew reads *bowed in worship at the head of his bed.*

## CHAPTER 48 JACOB BLESSES JOSEPH'S SONS.

One day not long after this, word came to Joseph that his father was failing rapidly. So Joseph went to visit him, and he took with him his two sons, Manasseh and Ephraim. 2When Jacob heard that Joseph had arrived, he gathered his strength and sat up in bed to greet him.

3Jacob said to Joseph, "God Almighty appeared to me at Luz in the land of Canaan and blessed me. 4He said to me, 'I will make you a multitude of nations, and I will give this land of Canaan to you and your descendants as an everlasting possession.' 5Now I am adopting as my own sons these two boys of yours, Ephraim and Manasseh, who were born here in the land of Egypt before I arrived. They will inherit from me just as Reuben and Simeon will. 6But the children born to you in the future will be your own. The land they inherit will be within the territories of Ephraim and Manasseh. 7As I was returning from Paddan, Rachel died in the land of Canaan. We were still on the way, just a short distance from Ephrath (that is, Bethlehem). So with great sorrow I buried her there beside the road to Ephrath."

8Then Jacob* looked over at the two boys. "Are these your sons?" he asked.

9"Yes," Joseph told him, "these are the sons God has given me here in Egypt."

And Jacob said, "Bring them over to me, and I will bless them."

10Now Jacob was half blind because of his age and could hardly see. So Joseph brought the boys close to him, and Jacob kissed and embraced them. 11Then Jacob said to Joseph, "I never thought I would see you again, but now God has let me see your children, too."

### NEVER SO BAD • • • • •

**48:11 When Joseph became a slave, Jacob thought he was dead and wept in despair (37:34). But eventually God's plan allowed Jacob to regain not only his son, but his grandchildren as well. Circumstances are never so bad that they are beyond God's help. Jacob regained his son. Job got a new family (Job 42:10-17). Mary regained her brother Lazarus (John 11:1-44). Because we belong to a loving God, we need never despair. We never know what good he will bring out of a seemingly hopeless situation.**

12Joseph took the boys from their grandfather's knees, and he bowed low to him. 13Then he positioned the boys so Ephraim was at Jacob's left hand and Manasseh was at his right hand. 14But Jacob crossed his arms as he reached out to lay his hands on the boys' heads. So his right hand was on the head of Ephraim, the younger boy, and his left hand was on the head of Manasseh, the older.

15Then he blessed Joseph and said, "May God, the God before whom my grandfather Abraham and my father, Isaac, walked, the God who has been my shepherd all my life, 16and the angel who has kept me from all harm—may he bless these boys. May they preserve my name and the names of my grandfather Abraham and my father, Isaac. And may they become a mighty nation."

17But Joseph was upset when he saw that his father had laid his right hand on Ephraim's head. So he lifted it to place it on Manasseh's head instead. 18"No, Father," he said, "this one over here is older. Put your right hand on his head."

19But his father refused. "I know what I'm doing, my son," he said. "Manasseh, too, will become a great people, but his younger brother will become even greater. His descendants will become a multitude of nations!" 20So Jacob blessed the boys that day with this blessing: "The people of Israel will use your names to bless each other. They will say, 'May God make you as prosperous as Ephraim and Manasseh.'" In this way, Jacob put Ephraim ahead of Manasseh.

21Then Jacob said to Joseph, "I am about to die, but God will be with you and will bring you again to Canaan, the land of your ancestors. 22And I give you an extra portion* beyond what I have given your brothers—the portion that I took from the Amorites with my sword and bow."

## CHAPTER 49 JACOB BLESSES HIS SONS.

Then Jacob called together all his sons and said, "Gather around me, and I will tell you what is going to happen to you in the days to come.

2 "Come and listen, O sons of Jacob;
 listen to Israel, your father.

3 "Reuben, you are my oldest son,
 the child of my vigorous youth.
 You are first on the list in rank and honor.
4 But you are as unruly as the waves of the sea,
 and you will be first no longer.
For you slept with one of my wives;
 you dishonored me in my own bed.

5 "Simeon and Levi are two of a kind—
 men of violence.
6 O my soul, stay away from them.
 May I never be a party to their wicked plans.
For in their anger they murdered men,
 and they crippled oxen just for sport.
7 Cursed be their anger, for it is fierce;
 cursed be their wrath, for it is cruel.
Therefore, I will scatter their descendants
 throughout the nation of Israel.

### FUTURE CHOICE • • • • •

**49:3-28 Jacob blessed each of his sons and then made a prediction about each one's future. The way the men had lived played an important part in Jacob's blessing and prophecy. Our past affects our present and future. By sunrise tomorrow, our actions of today will have become part of the past. Yet they will already have begun to shape the future. What actions can you choose or avoid in order to positively shape your future?**

48:8 Hebrew *Israel;* also in 48:10, 11, 13, 14, 21. 48:22 Or *give you the ridge of land.* The meaning of the Hebrew is uncertain.

[8] "Judah, your brothers will praise you.
You will defeat your enemies.
All your relatives will bow before you.
[9] Judah is a young lion
that has finished eating its prey.
Like a lion he crouches and lies down;
like a lioness—who will dare to rouse him?
[10] The scepter will not depart from Judah,
nor the ruler's staff from his descendants,
until the coming of the one to whom it belongs,*
the one whom all nations will obey.
[11] He ties his foal to a grapevine,
the colt of his donkey to a choice vine.
He washes his clothes in wine
because his harvest is so plentiful.
[12] His eyes are darker than wine,
and his teeth are whiter than milk.

[13] "Zebulun will settle on the shores of the sea
and will be a harbor for ships;
his borders will extend to Sidon.

[14] "Issachar is a strong beast of burden,
resting among the sheepfolds.*
[15] When he sees how good the countryside is,
how pleasant the land,
he will bend his shoulder to the task
and submit to forced labor.

[16] "Dan will govern his people
like any other tribe in Israel.
[17] He will be a snake beside the road,
a poisonous viper along the path,
that bites the horse's heels
so the rider is thrown off.
[18] I trust in you for salvation, O LORD!

[19] "Gad will be plundered by marauding bands,
but he will turn and plunder them.

[20] "Asher will produce rich foods,
food fit for kings.

[21] "Naphtali is a deer let loose,
producing magnificent fawns.

[22] "Joseph is a fruitful tree,
a fruitful tree beside a fountain.
His branches reach over the wall.
[23] He has been attacked by archers,
who shot at him and harassed him.
[24] But his bow remained strong,
and his arms were strengthened
by the Mighty One of Jacob,
the Shepherd, the Rock of Israel.
[25] May the God of your ancestors help you;
may the Almighty bless you
with the blessings of the heavens above,
blessings of the earth beneath,
and blessings of the breasts and womb.
[26] May the blessings of your ancestors
be greater than the blessings of the eternal
mountains,
reaching to the utmost bounds of the
everlasting hills.
These blessings will fall on the head of Joseph,
who is a prince among his brothers.
[27] "Benjamin is a wolf that prowls.
He devours his enemies in the morning,
and in the evening he divides the plunder."

[28] These are the twelve tribes of Israel, and these are
the blessings with which Jacob* blessed his twelve
sons. Each received a blessing that was appropriate
to him.
[29] Then Jacob told them, "Soon I will die. Bury me
with my father and grandfather in the cave in Ephron's
field. [30] This is the cave in the field of Machpelah, near
Mamre in Canaan, which Abraham bought from Ephron the Hittite for a permanent burial place. [31] There
Abraham and his wife Sarah are buried. There Isaac
and his wife, Rebekah, are buried. And there I buried
Leah. [32] It is the cave that my grandfather Abraham
bought from the Hittites." [33] Then when Jacob had
finished this charge to his sons, he lay back in the bed,
breathed his last, and died.

### GOOD GRIEF ● ● • • •

**50:1-11 When Jacob died at the age of 147, Joseph wept and mourned for months. When someone close to us dies, we need a long period of time to work through our grief. Crying and sharing our feelings with others helps us recover and go on with life. Allow yourself and others the freedom to grieve over the loss of a loved one, and give yourself time enough to complete your grieving process.**

CHAPTER **50** **JACOB DIES AND IS BURIED.** Joseph
threw himself on his father and wept over him and
kissed him. [2] Then Joseph told his morticians to
embalm the body. [3] The embalming process took
forty days, and there was a period of national
mourning for seventy days. [4] When the period of
mourning was over, Joseph approached Pharaoh's
advisers and asked them to speak to Pharaoh on his
behalf. [5] He told them, "Tell Pharaoh that my father
made me swear an oath. He said to me, 'I am about
to die; take my body back to the land of Canaan, and
bury me in our family's burial cave.' Now I need to
go and bury my father. After his burial is complete, I
will return without delay."
[6] Pharaoh agreed to Joseph's request. "Go and
bury your father, as you promised," he said. [7] So
Joseph went, with a great number of Pharaoh's
counselors and advisers—all the senior officers of
Egypt. [8] Joseph also took his brothers and the entire
household of Jacob. But they left their little children
and flocks and herds in the land of Goshen. [9] So a
great number of chariots, cavalry, and people accompanied Joseph.
[10] When they arrived at the threshing floor of Atad,
near the Jordan River, they held a very great and

49:10 Or *until tribute is brought to him and the peoples obey;* traditionally rendered *until Shiloh comes.* 49:14 Or *saddlebags,* or *hearths.* 49:28 Hebrew *Israel.*

**RELIABLE ● ● • • ·**

50:5-6 **Joseph had proven himself trustworthy as Pharaoh's adviser. Because of his good record, Pharaoh was sure that he would return to Egypt as promised after burying his father in Canaan. Privileges and freedom often result when we have demonstrated our trustworthiness. Because trust must be built gradually over time, take every opportunity to prove your reliability even in minor matters.**

solemn funeral, with a seven-day period of mourning for Joseph's father. [11]The local residents, the Canaanites, renamed the place Abel-mizraim,* for they said, "This is a place of very deep mourning for these Egyptians." [12]So Jacob's sons did as he had commanded them. [13]They carried his body to the land of Canaan and buried it there in the cave of Machpelah. This is the cave that Abraham had bought for a permanent burial place in the field of Ephron the Hittite, near Mamre.

[14]Then Joseph returned to Egypt with his brothers and all who had accompanied him to his father's funeral. [15]But now that their father was dead, Joseph's brothers became afraid. "Now Joseph will pay us back for all the evil we did to him," they said. [16]So they sent this message to Joseph: "Before your father died, he instructed us [17]to say to you: 'Forgive your brothers for the great evil they did to you.' So we, the servants of the God of your father, beg you to forgive us." When Joseph received the message, he broke down and wept. [18]Then his brothers came and bowed low before him. "We are your slaves," they said.

[19]But Joseph told them, "Don't be afraid of me. Am I God, to judge and punish you? [20]As far as I am concerned, God turned into good what you meant for evil. He brought me to the high position I have today so I could save the lives of many people. [21]No, don't be afraid. Indeed, I myself will take care of you and your families." And he spoke very kindly to them, reassuring them.

[22]So Joseph and his brothers and their families continued to live in Egypt. Joseph was 110 years old when he died. [23]He lived to see three generations of descendants of his son Ephraim and the children of Manasseh's son Makir, who were treated as if they were his own.

[24]"Soon I will die," Joseph told his brothers, "but God will surely come for you, to lead you out of this land of Egypt. He will bring you back to the land he vowed to give to the descendants of Abraham, Isaac, and Jacob."

[25]Then Joseph made the sons of Israel swear an oath, and he said, "When God comes to lead us back to Canaan, you must take my body back with you." [26]So Joseph died at the age of 110. They embalmed him, and his body was placed in a coffin in Egypt.

50:11 *Abel-mizraim* means "mourning of the Egyptians."

**MUSCLE BUILDING ● ● • • ·**

50:24 **Joseph was ready to die. He had no doubts that God would keep his promise and one day bring the Israelites back to their homeland. What a tremendous example! The secret of that kind of faith is a lifetime of trusting God. Your faith is like a muscle—it grows with exercise, gaining strength over time. After a lifetime of exercising trust, your faith can be as strong as Joseph's. Then at your death, you can be confident that God will fulfill all his promises to you and to all those faithful to him who may live after you.**

# MEGA themes

**BEGINNINGS** Genesis introduces God as Creator of all that exists: the universe, water, and all of life, including people, who were created in God's own image. When God finished creating, he described all of creation as being "good." When sin entered this flawless creation, God began his plan of salvation to restore the lost perfection.

All of creation was created to glorify God. Human beings are unique in their ability to bring God glory because they are created in God's image. Because sin broke people's good relationship with God, each person must look to God for a restoration of that lost fellowship.

1. What have you learned about the character of God from reading Genesis 1–3?
2. What does it mean to be created in the image of the God who is Lord of all?
3. How do you feel about yourself when you think about being created in God's image?
4. How should the fact that each person is truly created in God's image affect the way you act toward people who appear to be different from you (i.e., skin color, physical disability, unusual habits)?
5. As a person who is created in God's image, how can you glorify God in your relationships with others? With nature? With God?

**SIN AND DISOBEDIENCE** Sin is destructive. It destroys the goodness of God's creation, ruining the life God intended. Sin results from human beings choosing to go their own way rather than obeying God. Only God can reverse the consequences of sinful choices.

No person escapes the effects of sin. Without God providing salvation, we would all be condemned to death because of sin. God offers life that is good and glorifying to himself. When a person chooses not to obey God, he or she misses out on the goodness and glory of God.

1. What are some of the changes that happened because of Adam and Eve's sin?
2. How did sinful choices affect the people in Genesis (i.e., builders of the tower of Babel, Lot and his family, Joseph's brothers)?
3. Does a person ever "get away with" sin? Explain.
4. What are some of the reasons that people who know God still choose to sin?
5. What are some reasons that you would choose to do God's will even when you felt like being disobedient?

**PROMISES** God promised to protect and provide for his people. He specifically made promises in the form of what is known as a "covenant," or a binding agreement. God made a covenant with his people as a guarantee of what they could expect from him.

God is a God of Truth; he can be trusted to keep his promises. He has not left us in the dark about who he is and what his plans are. While we may not always know all of the details of what God will do, we can be confident that he will do what he has promised.

1. What was God's covenant with Noah following the flood?
2. What was God's covenant with Abraham?
3. What do you learn about God from reading these covenants?
4. What are some of God's promises that you know from other passages of Scripture? Write out these promises in this form: "Because God has said so, I know that he _________."

**OBEDIENCE AND PROSPERITY** Choosing to obey God results in enjoying his goodness and glory. Everyone who makes the choice to obey will prosper. A person who prospers does not necessarily have the nicest possessions money can buy or become accepted in the most popular social group. Rather, true prosperity is living life as God created it to be lived—in the fullness of his blessings.

If a person truly wants to "choose life," that person must put his or her faith in God. To put one's faith in God means obeying him and trusting that he will provide for all of life's needs. God is not boring, nor is he a spoiler of fun. He created life to be enjoyed and really *lived!* Successful living, therefore, requires living in God's will.

1. In what ways was Joseph a truly successful person? What are some of the choices Joseph made that resulted in his success?
2. Joseph had to choose what to do with his hurt and bitterness from being rejected by his brothers. Based on Genesis 45:1-8, how do you think he dealt with these feelings?
3. If you were elderly, what would you want to be able to say about the life you had lived? What do you think would be a sign that your life was successful?
4. What difference will it make in your life whether or not you obey God in your youth?
5. Describe a successful teenager.

1526 B.C.
**Moses born**

1446
**Exodus from Egypt**

1445
**Ten Commandments given**

1406
**Israel enters Canaan**

1375
**Judges begin to rule**

**I** promise!" she exclaimed. But soon her words were forgotten in the rush and excitement of school. ■ Remember when you promised to do something for a friend, but then forgot? Or what about when someone made an important promise to you and then didn't come through? Promises are part of life—from innocent childhood pledges to earnest, romantic commitments. We promise to do something, be somewhere, or give something. And when others make promises to us, we expect them to keep their word. If not, we become angry, disappointed, and even heartbroken. ■ The book of Exodus is all about promises: God's promises to his people. We too are God's people. Just as God was faithful to Israel in keeping promises he made to them, he will keep every promise he has made to us: promises to love us no matter what, to care for and protect us, to help with temptation we can't handle, to comfort and teach us, and to bring us to heaven someday. ■ Do you know the promises of God? Do you realize the things God has said he will do for you and to you? If you do, you understand how incredible those promises are. If you don't, you may have no idea of the many ways God has promised to be there for you. Each and every promise God makes, he keeps. To the Israelites and to you.

## STATS

PURPOSE: To record the events of Israel's deliverance from Egypt and development as a nation

AUTHOR: Moses

DATE WRITTEN: 1450–1410 B.C., approximately the same as Genesis

WHERE WRITTEN: In the wilderness during Israel's wanderings, somewhere in the Sinai Peninsula

SETTING: Egypt. God's people, once highly favored in the land, are now slaves. A God of great miracles is about to set them free.

KEY PEOPLE: Moses, Miriam, Pharaoh, Pharaoh's daughter, Jethro, Aaron, Joshua, Bezalel

KEY PLACES: Egypt, Goshen, Nile River, Land of Midian, Red Sea, Sinai Peninsula, Mount Sinai

SPECIAL FEATURES: Exodus relates more miracles than any other Old Testament book and is noted for containing the Ten Commandments

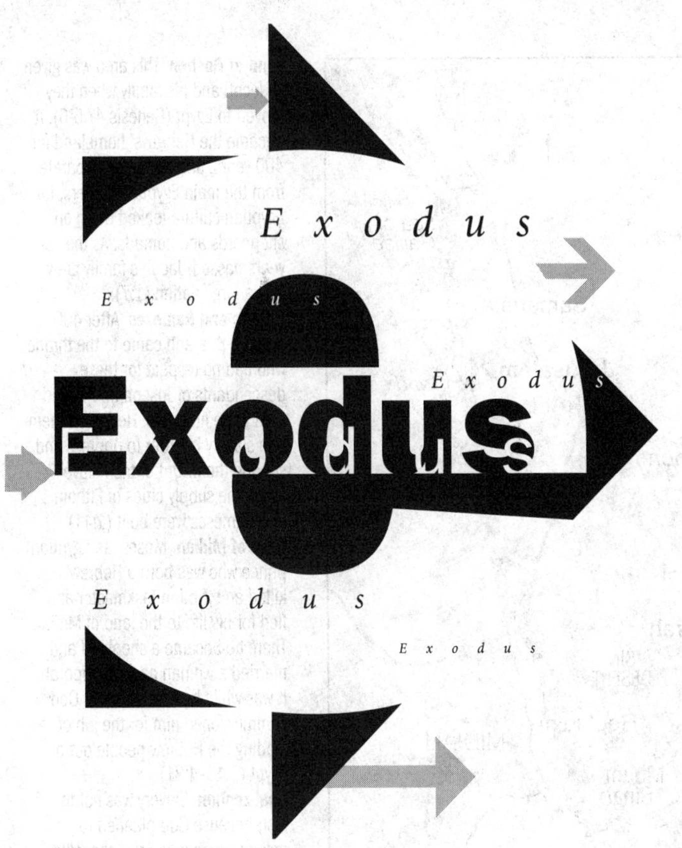


CHAPTER 1 **THE HEBREWS BECOME SLAVES.** These are
the sons of Jacob* who went with their father to
Egypt, each with his family: [2]Reuben, Simeon, Levi,
Judah, [3]Issachar, Zebulun, Benjamin, [4]Dan, Naphtali, Gad, and Asher. [5]Joseph was already down in
Egypt. In all, Jacob had seventy* direct descendants.
[6]In time, Joseph and each of his brothers died,
ending that generation. [7]But their descendants had
many children and grandchildren. In fact, they multiplied so quickly that they soon filled the land. [8]Then a
new king came to the throne of Egypt who knew
nothing about Joseph or what he had done. [9]He told
his people, "These Israelites are becoming a threat to
us because there are so many of them. [10]We must find
a way to put an end to this. If we don't and if war
breaks out, they will join our enemies and fight against
us. Then they will escape from the country."
[11]So the Egyptians made the Israelites their slaves
and put brutal slave drivers over them, hoping to
wear them down under heavy burdens. They forced
them to build the cities of Pithom and Rameses as
supply centers for the king. [12]But the more the Egyptians oppressed them, the more quickly the Israelites
multiplied! The Egyptians soon became alarmed
[13]and decided to make their slavery more bitter still.
[14]They were ruthless with the Israelites, forcing them
to make bricks and mortar and to work long hours
in the fields.
[15]Then Pharaoh, the king of Egypt, gave this order
to the Hebrew midwives, Shiphrah and Puah:
[16]"When you help the Hebrew women give birth, kill
all the boys as soon as they are born. Allow only the
baby girls to live." [17]But because the midwives feared
God, they refused to obey the king and allowed the
boys to live, too.
[18]Then the king called for the midwives. "Why
have you done this?" he demanded. "Why have you
allowed the boys to live?"
[19]"Sir," they told him, "the Hebrew women are

**FOREIGNERS ● ● • • •**

1:1 **Jacob's family had moved to Egypt at the invitation of Joseph, one of Jacob's sons, who had become a great ruler under Pharaoh. Jacob's family grew into a large nation. But, as foreigners and newcomers, their lives were quite different from the lives of the Egyptians. The Hebrews worshiped one God; the Egyptians worshiped many gods. The Hebrews were wanderers; the Egyptians had a deeply rooted culture. The Hebrews were shepherds; the Egyptians were builders. The Hebrews were also physically separated from the rest of the Egyptians: they lived in Goshen, north of the great Egyptian cultural centers.**

1:1 Hebrew *Israel.* 1:5 Dead Sea Scrolls and Greek version read *seventy-five;* see notes on Gen 46:27.

## KEY PLACES IN EXODUS

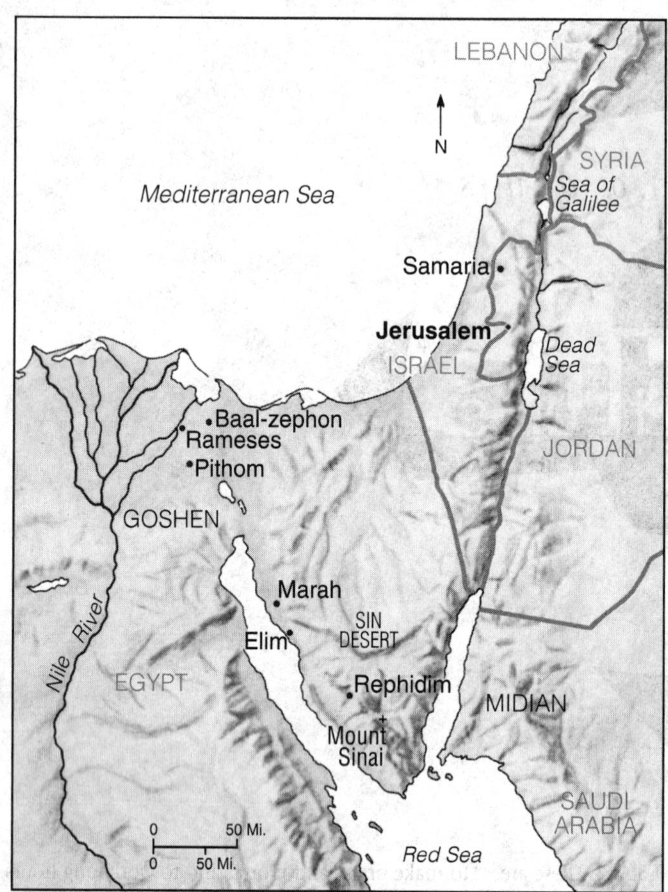

Modern names and boundaries are shown in gray.

**Land of Goshen** This area was given to Jacob and his family when they moved to Egypt (Genesis 47:5-6). It became the Hebrews' homeland for 400 years, and remained separate from the main Egyptian centers, for Egyptian culture looked down on shepherds and nomads. As the years passed, Jacob's family grew into a large nation (1:7).

**Pithom and Rameses** After 400 years, a pharaoh came to the throne who had no respect for these descendants of Joseph and feared their large numbers. He forced them into slavery in order to oppress and subdue them. Out of their slave labor, the supply cities of Pithom and Rameses were built (1:11).

**Land of Midian** Moses, an Egyptian prince who was born a Hebrew, killed an Egyptian taskmaster and fled for his life to the land of Midian. There he became a shepherd and married a woman named Zipporah. It was while he was here that God commissioned him for the job of leading the Hebrew people out of Egypt (2:15–4:31).

**Baal-zephon** Slavery was not to last, because God planned to deliver his people. After choosing Moses and Aaron to be his spokesmen to Pharaoh, God worked a series of dramatic miracles in the land of Egypt to convince Pharaoh to let the Hebrews go (5:1–12:33). When finally freed, the entire nation set out with the riches of Egypt (12:34-36). One of their first stops was at Baal-zephon (14:2), where Pharaoh, who had changed his mind, chased the Hebrews and trapped them against the Red Sea. But God parted the waters and led the people through the sea on dry land. When Pharaoh's army tried to pursue, the waters collapsed around them, and they were drowned (14:5-31).

**Marah** Moses now led the people southward. The long trek across the desert brought hot tempers and parched throats for this mass of people. At Marah, the water they found was bitter, but God sweetened it (15:22-25).

**Elim** As they continued their journey, the Hebrews (now called Israelites) came to Elim, an oasis with twelve springs (15:27).

**Sin Desert** Leaving Elim, the people headed into the Sin Desert. Here the people became hungry, so God provided them with manna that came from heaven and covered the ground each morning (16:1, 13-15). The people ate this manna until they entered the Promised Land.

**Rephidim** Moses led the people to Rephidim, where they found no water. But God miraculously provided water from a rock (17:1, 5-6). Here the Israelites encountered their first test in battle: the Amalekites attacked and were defeated (17:9-13). Moses' father-in-law, Jethro, then arrived on the scene with some sound advice on delegating responsibilities (18).

**Mount Sinai** God had previously appeared to Moses on this mountain and commissioned him to lead Israel (3:1-2). Now Moses returned with the people God had asked him to lead. For almost a year the people camped at the foot of Mount Sinai. During this time God gave them his Ten Commandments as well as other laws for right living. He also provided the blueprint for building the Tabernacle (19–40). God was forging a holy nation that was prepared to live for and serve him alone.

very strong. They have their babies so quickly that we
cannot get there in time! They are not slow in giving
birth like Egyptian women."
20So God blessed the midwives, and the Israelites
continued to multiply, growing more and more
powerful. 21And because the midwives feared God,
he gave them families of their own.
22Then Pharaoh gave this order to all his people:
"Throw all the newborn Israelite boys into the Nile
River. But you may spare the baby girls."

CHAPTER **2** **MOSES IS BORN.** During this time, a man and woman from the tribe of Levi got married. [2]The woman became pregnant and gave birth to a son. She saw what a beautiful baby he was and kept him hidden for three months. [3]But when she could no longer hide him, she got a little basket made of papyrus reeds and waterproofed it with tar and pitch. She put the baby in the basket and laid it among the reeds along the edge of the Nile River. [4]The baby's sister then stood at a distance, watching to see what would happen to him.

[5]Soon after this, one of Pharaoh's daughters came down to bathe in the river, and her servant girls walked along the riverbank. When the princess saw the little basket among the reeds, she told one of her servant girls to get it for her. [6]As the princess opened it, she found the baby boy. His helpless cries touched her heart. "He must be one of the Hebrew children," she said.

[7]Then the baby's sister approached the princess. "Should I go and find one of the Hebrew women to nurse the baby for you?" she asked.

[8]"Yes, do!" the princess replied. So the girl rushed home and called the baby's mother.

[9]"Take this child home and nurse him for me," the princess told her. "I will pay you for your help." So the baby's mother took her baby home and nursed him.

[10]Later, when he was older, the child's mother brought him back to the princess, who adopted him as her son. The princess named him Moses,* for she said, "I drew him out of the water."

[11]Many years later, when Moses had grown up, he went out to visit his people, the Israelites, and he saw how hard they were forced to work. During his visit, he saw an Egyptian beating one of the Hebrew slaves. [12]After looking around to make sure no one was watching, Moses killed the Egyptian and buried him in the sand.

[13]The next day, as Moses was out visiting his people again, he saw two Hebrew men fighting. "What are you doing, hitting your neighbor like that?" Moses said to the one in the wrong.

[14]"Who do you think you are?" the man replied. "Who appointed you to be our prince and judge? Do you plan to kill me as you killed that Egyptian yesterday?"

Moses was badly frightened because he realized that everyone knew what he had done. [15]And sure enough, when Pharaoh heard about it, he gave orders to have Moses arrested and killed. But Moses fled from Pharaoh and escaped to the land of Midian.

When Moses arrived in Midian, he sat down beside a well. [16]Now it happened that the priest of Midian had seven daughters who came regularly to this well to draw water and fill the water troughs for their father's flocks. [17]But other shepherds would often come and chase the girls and their flocks away. This time, however, Moses came to their aid, rescuing the girls from the shepherds. Then he helped them draw water for their flocks.

[18]When the girls returned to Reuel, their father, he asked, "How did you get the flocks watered so quickly today?"

[19]"An Egyptian rescued us from the shepherds," they told him. "And then he drew water for us and watered our flocks."

[20]"Well, where is he then?" their father asked. "Did you just leave him there? Go and invite him home for a meal!"

[21]Moses was happy to accept the invitation, and he settled down to live with them. In time, Reuel gave Moses one of his daughters, Zipporah, to be his wife. [22]Later they had a baby boy, and Moses named him Gershom,* for he said, "I have been a stranger in a foreign land."

[23]Years passed, and the king of Egypt died. But the Israelites still groaned beneath their burden of slavery. They cried out for help, and their pleas for deliverance rose up to God. [24]God heard their cries and remembered his covenant promise to Abraham, Isaac, and Jacob. [25]He looked down on the Israelites and felt deep concern for their welfare.

CHAPTER **3** **THE BURNING BUSH.** One day Moses was tending the flock of his father-in-law, Jethro,* the priest of Midian, and he went deep into the wilderness near Sinai,* the mountain of God. [2]Suddenly, the angel of the LORD appeared to him as a blazing fire in a bush. Moses was amazed because the bush was engulfed in flames, but it didn't burn up. [3]"Amazing!" Moses said to himself. "Why isn't that bush burning up? I must go over to see this."

[4]When the LORD saw that he had caught Moses' attention, God called to him from the bush, "Moses! Moses!"

### LYING ● ● ● • •

1:19-21 **Did God bless the Hebrew midwives for lying to Pharaoh? God blessed them not because they lied, but because they saved the lives of innocent children. This doesn't mean that a lie was necessarily the best way to answer Pharaoh. The midwives were blessed, however, for not violating the higher law of God that forbids the senseless slaughter of innocent lives.**

### FIGHT EVIL ● ● ● • •

2:3 **Moses' mother knew how wrong it would be to destroy her child. But there was little she could do to change Pharaoh's new law. Her only alternative was to hide the child and later place him in a tiny basket on the river. God used her courageous act to place her son, the Hebrew of his choice, in the house of Pharaoh. Do you sometimes feel surrounded by evil and frustrated by how little you can do about it? When faced with evil, look for ways to act against it. Then trust God to use your effort, however small it seems, in his war against evil.**

**2:10** *Moses* sounds like a Hebrew term that means "to draw out." **2:22** *Gershom* sounds like a Hebrew term that means "a stranger there."
**3:1a** Moses' father-in-law went by two names, Jethro and Reuel. **3:1b** Hebrew *Horeb,* another name for Sinai.

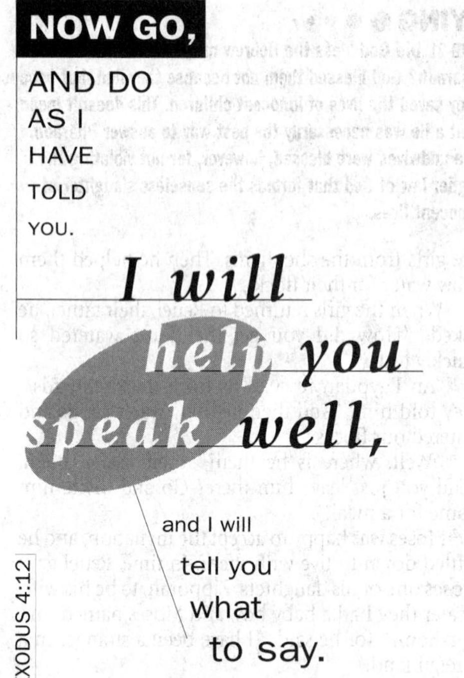
NOW GO,
AND DO AS I HAVE TOLD YOU.
I will help you speak well,
and I will tell you what to say.
EXODUS 4:12

"Here I am!" Moses replied.

5 "Do not come any closer," God told him. "Take off your sandals, for you are standing on holy ground." 6 Then he said, "I am the God of your ancestors—the God of Abraham, the God of Isaac, and the God of Jacob." When Moses heard this, he hid his face in his hands because he was afraid to look at God.

7 Then the LORD told him, "You can be sure I have seen the misery of my people in Egypt. I have heard their cries for deliverance from their harsh slave drivers. Yes, I am aware of their suffering. 8 So I have come to rescue them from the Egyptians and lead them out of Egypt into their own good and spacious land. It is a land flowing with milk and honey—the land where the Canaanites, Hittites, Amorites, Perizzites, Hivites, and Jebusites live. 9 The cries of the people of Israel have reached me, and I have seen how the Egyptians have oppressed them with heavy tasks. 10 Now go, for I am sending you to Pharaoh. You will lead my people, the Israelites, out of Egypt."

11 "But who am I to appear before Pharaoh?" Moses asked God. "How can you expect me to lead the Israelites out of Egypt?"

12 Then God told him, "I will be with you. And this will serve as proof that I have sent you: When you have brought the Israelites out of Egypt, you will return here to worship God at this very mountain."

13 But Moses protested, "If I go to the people of Israel and tell them, 'The God of your ancestors has sent me to you,' they won't believe me. They will ask, 'Which god are you talking about? What is his name?' Then what should I tell them?"

14 God replied, "I AM THE ONE WHO ALWAYS IS.* Just tell them, 'I AM has sent me to you.'" 15 God also said, "Tell them, 'The LORD,* the God of your ancestors—the God of Abraham, the God of Isaac, and the God of Jacob—has sent me to you.' This will be my name forever; it has always been my name, and it will be used throughout all generations.

16 "Now go and call together all the leaders of Israel. Tell them, 'The LORD, the God of your ancestors—the God of Abraham, Isaac, and Jacob—appeared to me in a burning bush. He said, "You can be sure that I am watching over you and have seen what is happening to you in Egypt. 17 I promise to rescue you from the oppression of the Egyptians. I will lead you to the land now occupied by the Canaanites, Hittites, Amorites, Perizzites, Hivites, and Jebusites—a land flowing with milk and honey."'

18 "The leaders of the people of Israel will accept your message. Then all of you must go straight to the king of Egypt and tell him, 'The LORD, the God of the Hebrews, has met with us. Let us go on a three-day journey into the wilderness to offer sacrifices to the LORD our God.'

19 "But I know that the king of Egypt will not let you go except under heavy pressure. 20 So I will reach out and strike at the heart of Egypt with all kinds of miracles. Then at last he will let you go. 21 And I will see to it that the Egyptians treat you well. They will load you down with gifts so you will not leave empty-handed. 22 The Israelite women will ask for silver and gold jewelry and fine clothing from their Egyptian neighbors and their neighbors' guests. With this clothing, you will dress your sons and daughters. In this way, you will plunder the Egyptians!"

## CHAPTER 4 **SIGNS OF GOD'S POWER.**

But Moses protested again, "Look, they won't believe me! They won't do what I tell them. They'll just say, 'The LORD never appeared to you.'"

2 Then the LORD asked him, "What do you have there in your hand?"

"A shepherd's staff," Moses replied.

### EXTRAORDINARY ● ● • • •

4:2-4 **A shepherd's staff was commonly a three- to six-foot wooden rod with a curved hook at the top. The shepherd used it for walking, guiding his sheep, killing snakes, and many other tasks. Still, it was just a stick. But God used the simple shepherd's staff Moses carried to teach him an important lesson. God sometimes takes joy in using ordinary things for extraordinary purposes. What are the ordinary things in your life—your voice, a pen, a hammer, a broom, a musical instrument? It is easy to assume that God can use only special skills, but he can also use your everyday contributions. Little did Moses imagine the power his simple staff would wield when it became the staff of God.**

3:14 Or *I AM WHO I AM,* or *I WILL BE WHAT I WILL BE.* 3:15 Hebrew *Yahweh;* traditionally rendered *Jehovah.*

3"Throw it down on the ground," the LORD told
him. So Moses threw it down, and it became a snake!
Moses was terrified, so he turned and ran away.
4Then the LORD told him, "Take hold of its tail."
So Moses reached out and grabbed it, and it became
a shepherd's staff again.
5"Perform this sign, and they will believe you,"
the LORD told him. "Then they will realize that the
LORD, the God of their ancestors—the God of Abraham, the God of Isaac, and the God of Jacob—really
has appeared to you."
6Then the LORD said to Moses, "Put your hand
inside your robe." Moses did so, and when he took
it out again, his hand was white as snow with leprosy.* 7"Now put your hand back into your robe
again," the LORD said. Moses did, and when he took
it out this time, it was as healthy as the rest of his
body.
8"If they do not believe the first miraculous sign,
they will believe the second," the LORD said. 9"And if
they do not believe you even after these two signs,
then take some water from the Nile River and pour
it out on the dry ground. When you do, it will turn
into blood."
10But Moses pleaded with the LORD, "O Lord,
I'm just not a good speaker. I never have been, and
I'm not now, even after you have spoken to me. I'm
clumsy with words."
11"Who makes mouths?" the LORD asked him.
"Who makes people so they can speak or not speak,
hear or not hear, see or not see? Is it not I, the LORD?
12Now go, and do as I have told you. I will help you
speak well, and I will tell you what to say."
13But Moses again pleaded, "Lord, please! Send
someone else."
14Then the LORD became angry with Moses. "All
right," he said. "What about your brother, Aaron the
Levite? He is a good speaker. And look! He is on his
way to meet you now. And when he sees you, he will
be very glad. 15You will talk to him, giving him the
words to say. I will help both of you to speak clearly,
and I will tell you what to do. 16Aaron will be your
spokesman to the people, and you will be as God to
him, telling him what to say. 17And be sure to take
your shepherd's staff along so you can perform the
miraculous signs I have shown you."
18Then Moses went back home and talked it over
with Jethro, his father-in-law. "With your permission," Moses said, "I would like to go back to Egypt
to visit my family. I don't even know whether they
are still alive."
"Go with my blessing," Jethro replied.
19Before Moses left Midian, the LORD said to him,
"Do not be afraid to return to Egypt, for all those
who wanted to kill you are dead."
20So Moses took his wife and sons, put them on a
donkey, and headed back to the land of Egypt. In his
hand he carried the staff of God.
21Then the LORD reminded him, "When you arrive
back in Egypt, go to Pharaoh and perform the
miracles I have empowered you to do. But I will
make him stubborn so he will not let the people go.
22Then you will tell him, 'This is what the LORD says:
Israel is my firstborn son. 23I commanded you to let
him go, so he could worship me. But since you have
refused, be warned! I will kill your firstborn son!'"
24On the journey, when Moses and his family had
stopped for the night, the LORD confronted Moses*
and was about to kill him. 25But Zipporah, his wife,
took a flint knife and circumcised her son. She threw

**I am having trouble letting other people know I am a Christian. I'm afraid they will laugh at me or ask a question I can't answer.**

The Bible is filled with examples of people who faced the choice of either being courageous or letting their fears tell them how to act. Learning about the courage of people in the Bible is one good reason to read it every day. The examples we find in the Bible can give us the strength to step out in faith and do things that may at first seem very frightening.

In Exodus 3, God had just finished speaking with Moses through a burning bush. Although this was an incredible miracle, Exodus 4 relates how Moses was afraid people wouldn't believe that God had actually spoken to him! He had to choose between giving in to his fears or facing them head on. Eventually, Moses chose to draw courage from God and completed the task God had given him.

Character and skill are developed by repeating an action until you can do it well enough to enjoy it. This is true with everything from skiing to skateboarding—and it is true in telling your best friends on earth about your Friend in heaven.

God does not expect you to know all the answers. When the apostle Peter was confronted by the hostile religious leaders of the day who told him to stop talking about Jesus, he answered, "We cannot stop telling about the wonderful things we have seen and heard" (Acts 4:20). He had learned the joy of sharing his faith in Christ so much that he couldn't help but share what he knew!

You have the privilege and the responsibility of sharing what you have learned and what God has done in your life. If you don't know the answer, you can always say, "That's a good question. Can I find out the answer and get back with you tomorrow?"

The key to Moses' decision to obey God's command to be his spokesman for the Israelites was remembering when God first spoke to him. The burning bush experience and God's continuing miracles gave Moses the courage to face incredible obstacles.

Rely on what God has done for you and daily lean on your growing relationship with Christ to strengthen you.

4:6 Or *with a contagious skin disease.* The Hebrew word used here can describe various skin diseases. 4:24 Or *confronted Moses' son;* Hebrew reads *confronted him.*

the foreskin at Moses' feet and said, "What a blood-smeared bridegroom you are to me!" 26(When she called Moses a "blood-smeared bridegroom," she was referring to the circumcision.) After that, the LORD left him alone.

27Now the LORD had said to Aaron, "Go out into the wilderness to meet Moses." So Aaron traveled to the mountain of God, where he found Moses and greeted him warmly. 28Moses then told Aaron everything the LORD had commanded them to do and say. And he told him about the miraculous signs they were to perform.

29So Moses and Aaron returned to Egypt and called the leaders of Israel to a meeting. 30Aaron told them everything the LORD had told Moses, and Moses performed the miraculous signs as they watched. 31The leaders were soon convinced that the LORD had sent Moses and Aaron. And when they realized that the LORD had seen their misery and was deeply concerned for them, they all bowed their heads and worshiped.

CHAPTER **5** **MAKING BRICKS WITHOUT STRAW.** After this presentation to Israel's leaders, Moses and Aaron went to see Pharaoh. They told him, "This is what the LORD, the God of Israel, says: 'Let my people go, for they must go out into the wilderness to hold a religious festival in my honor.'"

2"Is that so?" retorted Pharaoh. "And who is the LORD that I should listen to him and let Israel go? I don't know the LORD, and I will not let Israel go."

**REJECTION ● ● • • •**

**5:3 Pharaoh would not listen to Moses and Aaron because he did not know or respect God. People who do not know God may not listen to his word or his messengers. Like Moses and Aaron, we need to persist. When others reject you or your faith, don't be surprised or discouraged. Continue to tell them about God, trusting him to open closed minds and soften stubborn hearts.**

3But Aaron and Moses persisted. "The God of the Hebrews has met with us," they declared. "Let us take a three-day trip into the wilderness so we can offer sacrifices to the LORD our God. If we don't, we will surely die by disease or the sword."

4"Who do you think you are," Pharaoh shouted, "distracting the people from their tasks? Get back to work! 5Look, there are many people here in Egypt, and you are stopping them from doing their work."

6That same day Pharaoh sent this order to the slave drivers and foremen he had set over the people of Israel: 7"Do not supply the people with any more straw for making bricks. Let them get it themselves! 8But don't reduce their production quotas by a single brick. They obviously don't have enough to do. If they did, they wouldn't be talking about going into the wilderness to offer sacrifices to their God. 9Load them down with more work. Make them sweat! That will teach them to listen to these liars!"

10So the slave drivers and foremen informed the people: "Pharaoh has ordered us not to provide straw for you. 11Go and get it yourselves. Find it wherever you can. But you must produce just as many bricks as before!" 12So the people scattered throughout the land in search of straw.

13The slave drivers were brutal. "Meet your daily quota of bricks, just as you did before!" they demanded. 14Then they whipped the Israelite foremen in charge of the work crews. "Why haven't you met your quotas either yesterday or today?" they demanded.

15So the Israelite foremen went to Pharaoh and pleaded with him. "Please don't treat us like this," they begged. 16"We are given no straw, but we are still told to make as many bricks as before. We are beaten for something that isn't our fault! It is the fault of your slave drivers for making such unreasonable demands."

17But Pharaoh replied, "You're just lazy! You obviously don't have enough to do. If you did, you wouldn't be saying, 'Let us go, so we can offer sacrifices to the LORD.' 18Now, get back to work! No straw will be given to you, but you must still deliver the regular quota of bricks."

19Since Pharaoh would not let up on his demands, the Israelite foremen could see that they were in serious trouble. 20As they left Pharaoh's court, they met Moses and Aaron, who were waiting outside for them. 21The foremen said to them, "May the LORD judge you for getting us into this terrible situation with Pharaoh* and his officials. You have given them an excuse to kill us!"

22So Moses went back to the LORD and protested, "Why have you mistreated your own people like this, Lord? Why did you send me? 23Since I gave Pharaoh your message, he has been even more brutal to your people. You have not even begun to rescue them!"

CHAPTER **6** **THE HEBREWS WON'T LISTEN.** "Now you will see what I will do to Pharaoh," the LORD told Moses. "When he feels my powerful hand upon him, he will let the people go. In fact, he will be so anxious to get rid of them that he will force them to leave his land!"

2And God continued, "I am the LORD. 3I appeared to Abraham, to Isaac, and to Jacob as God Almighty,* though I did not reveal my name, the LORD,* to them. 4And I entered into a solemn covenant with them. Under its terms, I swore to give them the land of Canaan, where they were living. 5You can be sure that I have heard the groans of the people of Israel, who are now slaves to the Egyptians. I have remembered my covenant with them.

6"Therefore, say to the Israelites: 'I am the LORD,

5:21 Hebrew *for making us a stench in the nostrils of Pharaoh.* 6:3a Hebrew *El Shaddai.* 6:3b Hebrew *Yahweh;* traditionally rendered *Jehovah.*

and I will free you from your slavery in Egypt. I will redeem you with mighty power and great acts of judgment. 7I will make you my own special people, and I will be your God. And you will know that I am the LORD your God who has rescued you from your slavery in Egypt. 8I will bring you into the land I swore to give to Abraham, Isaac, and Jacob. It will be your very own property. I am the LORD!'"

9So Moses told the people what the LORD had said, but they wouldn't listen anymore. They had become too discouraged by the increasing burden of their slavery.

10Then the LORD said to Moses, 11"Go back to Pharaoh, and tell him to let the people of Israel leave Egypt."

12"But LORD!" Moses objected. "My own people won't listen to me anymore. How can I expect Pharaoh to listen? I'm no orator!"

13But the LORD ordered Moses and Aaron to return to Pharaoh, king of Egypt, and to demand that he let the people of Israel leave Egypt.

14These are the ancestors of clans from some of Israel's tribes:

The descendants of Reuben, Israel's oldest son, included Hanoch, Pallu, Hezron, and Carmi. Their descendants became the clans of Reuben.

15The descendants of Simeon included Jemuel, Jamin, Ohad, Jakin, Zohar, and Shaul (whose mother was a Canaanite). Their descendants became the clans of Simeon.

16These are the descendants of Levi, listed according to their family groups. In the first generation were Gershon, Kohath, and Merari. (Levi, their father, lived to be 137 years old.)

17 The descendants of Gershon included Libni and Shimei, each of whom is the ancestor of a clan.

18 The descendants of Kohath included Amram, Izhar, Hebron, and Uzziel. (Kohath lived to be 133 years old.)

19 The descendants of Merari included Mahli and Mushi.

These are the clans of the Levites, listed according to their genealogies.

20Amram married his father's sister Jochebed, and she bore him Aaron and Moses. (Amram lived to be 137 years old.)

21The descendants of Izhar included Korah, Nepheg, and Zicri.

22The descendants of Uzziel included Mishael, Elzaphan, and Sithri.

23Aaron married Elisheba, the daughter of Amminadab and sister of Nahshon, and she bore him Nadab, Abihu, Eleazar, and Ithamar.

24The descendants of Korah included Assir, Elkanah, and Abiasaph. Their descendants became the clans of Korah.

25Eleazar son of Aaron married one of the daughters of Putiel, and she bore him Phinehas.

These are the ancestors of the Levite clans, listed according to their family groups.

26The Aaron and Moses named in this list are the same Aaron and Moses to whom the LORD said,

## MOSES

Some people can't stay out of trouble. Moses was that kind of person. He wasn't a troublemaker; he was usually trying to do the right thing. When he saw something wrong, he tried to make it right—and he often ended up in trouble. But doing the right thing is worth it, even if we do get in trouble.

Moses was a reactor. When there was action, he reacted. Whether checking out a burning bush that didn't burn, or defending a Hebrew slave, or trying to stop a fight, Moses reacted to the world around him. God changed Moses—he helped Moses learn to react correctly. When God changes us, he works with the good qualities he gave us at the start—and he forgives and straightens us out.

Moses became a great leader because he learned to react the right way. He wasn't perfect—he even made a mistake that kept him out of the Promised Land—but God shaped and used his life anyway. God didn't change *who* or *what* Moses was; he worked on *how* Moses used what he'd been given. God wants to change us in the same way. He will make the best version of us there could ever be, if we ask him and let him.

LESSONS: God prepares, then he uses—his timetable is life-sized

God does his greatest work through frail people

KEY VERSES: "It was by faith that Moses, when he grew up, refused to be treated as the son of Pharaoh's daughter. He chose to share the oppression of God's people instead of enjoying the fleeting pleasures of sin" (Hebrews 11:24-25).

Moses' story is told in the books of Exodus through Deuteronomy. He is also mentioned in Acts 7:20-41; Hebrews 11:23-29.

**UPS:**
- Egyptian education; wilderness training
- Greatest Jewish leader; set the Exodus in motion
- Prophet and lawgiver; recorder of the Ten Commandments

**DOWNS:**
- Failed to enter the Promised Land because of disobedience to God
- Did not always recognize and use the talents of others

**STATS:**
- Where: Egypt, Midian, Wilderness of Sinai
- Occupation: Prince, shepherd, leader of the Israelites
- Relatives: Sister: Miriam. Brother: Aaron. Wife: Zipporah. Sons: Gershom and Eliezer.

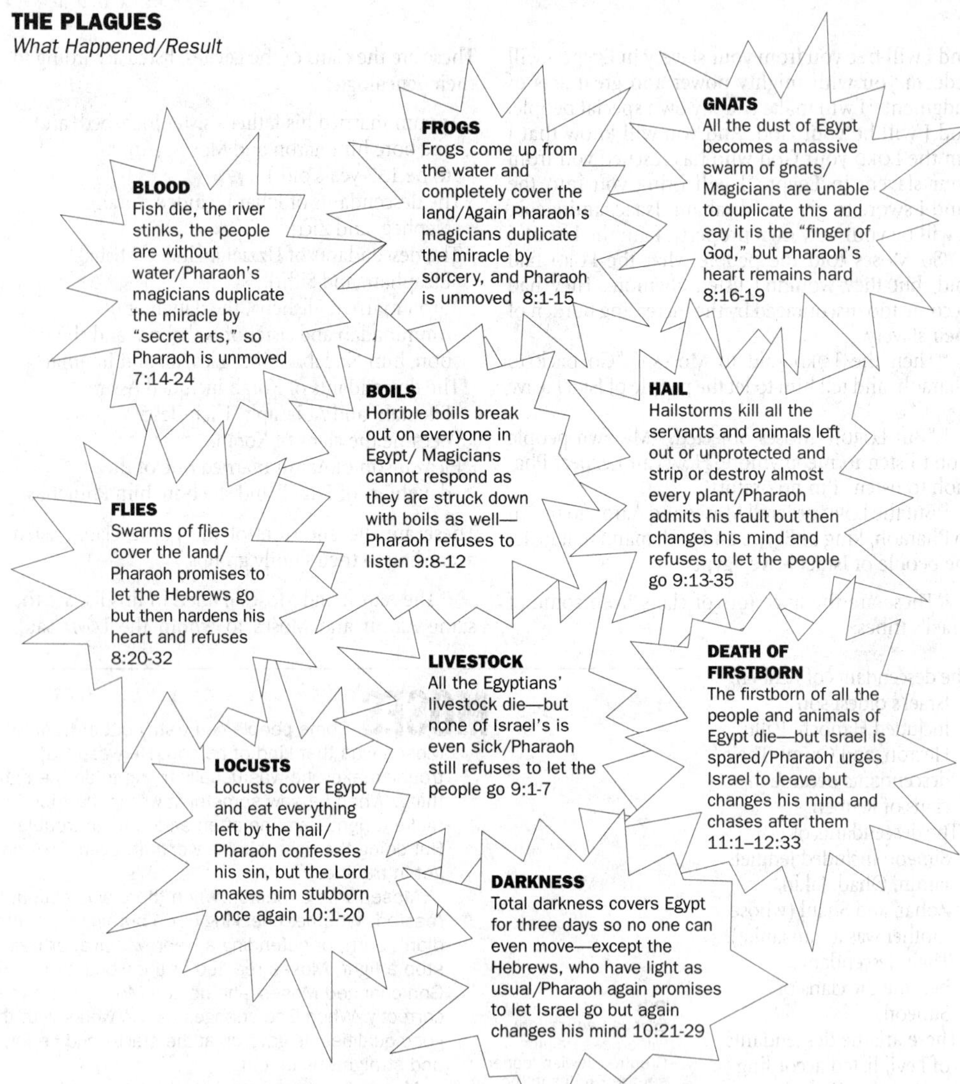

THE PLAGUES
What Happened/Result
BLOOD
Fish die, the river stinks, the people are without water/Pharaoh's magicians duplicate the miracle by "secret arts," so Pharaoh is unmoved 7:14-24
FROGS
Frogs come up from the water and completely cover the land/Again Pharaoh's magicians duplicate the miracle by sorcery, and Pharaoh is unmoved 8:1-15
GNATS
All the dust of Egypt becomes a massive swarm of gnats/ Magicians are unable to duplicate this and say it is the "finger of God," but Pharaoh's heart remains hard 8:16-19
FLIES
Swarms of flies cover the land/ Pharaoh promises to let the Hebrews go but then hardens his heart and refuses 8:20-32
LIVESTOCK
All the Egyptians' livestock die—but none of Israel's is even sick/Pharaoh still refuses to let the people go 9:1-7
BOILS
Horrible boils break out on everyone in Egypt/ Magicians cannot respond as they are struck down with boils as well—Pharaoh refuses to listen 9:8-12
HAIL
Hailstorms kill all the servants and animals left out or unprotected and strip or destroy almost every plant/Pharaoh admits his fault but then changes his mind and refuses to let the people go 9:13-35
LOCUSTS
Locusts cover Egypt and eat everything left by the hail/ Pharaoh confesses his sin, but the Lord makes him stubborn once again 10:1-20
DARKNESS
Total darkness covers Egypt for three days so no one can even move—except the Hebrews, who have light as usual/Pharaoh again promises to let Israel go but again changes his mind 10:21-29
DEATH OF FIRSTBORN
The firstborn of all the people and animals of Egypt die—but Israel is spared/Pharaoh urges Israel to leave but changes his mind and chases after them 11:1–12:33


"Lead all the people of Israel out of the land of Egypt, division by division." 27They are the ones who went to Pharaoh to ask permission to lead the people from the land of Egypt.

28At that time, the LORD had said to them, 29"I am the LORD! Give Pharaoh the message I have given you." 30This is the same Moses who had argued with the LORD, saying, "I can't do it! I'm no orator. Why should Pharaoh listen to me?"

## CHAPTER 7 **A STAFF BECOMES A SNAKE.**

Then the LORD said to Moses, "Pay close attention to this. I will make you seem like God to Pharaoh. Your brother, Aaron, will be your prophet; he will speak for you. 2Tell Aaron everything I say to you and have him announce it to Pharaoh. He will demand that the people of Israel be allowed to leave Egypt. 3But I will cause Pharaoh to be stubborn so I can multiply my miraculous signs and wonders in the land of Egypt. 4Even then Pharaoh will refuse to listen to you. So I will crush Egypt with a series of disasters, after which I will lead the forces of Israel out with

## AMBASSADOR ● ● ● ● ●

**7:1 God made Moses his representative; he was "like God to Pharaoh." We are each God's representatives–showing the world that Christians are a different people with a different lifestyle. Much of the world knows nothing about God except what it sees in the lives of God's people. What kind of God would they think you represent? Taking note of how you come across to others gives you a good indication of how well you are representing God.**

great acts of judgment. 5When I show the Egyptians my power and force them to let the Israelites go, they will realize that I am the LORD."

6So Moses and Aaron did just as the LORD had commanded them. 7Moses was eighty years old, and Aaron was eighty-three at the time they made their demands to Pharaoh.

8Then the LORD said to Moses and Aaron, 9"Pharaoh will demand that you show him a miracle to prove that God has sent you. When he makes this demand, say to Aaron, 'Throw down your shepherd's staff,' and it will become a snake."

10So Moses and Aaron went to see Pharaoh, and they performed the miracle just as the LORD had told them. Aaron threw down his staff before Pharaoh and his court, and it became a snake. 11Then Pharaoh called in his wise men and magicians, and they did the same thing with their secret arts. 12Their staffs became snakes, too! But then Aaron's snake swallowed up their snakes. 13Pharaoh's heart, however, remained hard and stubborn. He still refused to listen, just as the LORD had predicted.

14Then the LORD said to Moses, "Pharaoh is very stubborn, and he continues to refuse to let the people go. 15So go to Pharaoh in the morning as he goes down to the river. Stand on the riverbank and meet him there. Be sure to take along the shepherd's staff that turned into a snake. 16Say to him, 'The LORD, the God of the Hebrews, has sent me to say, "Let my people go, so they can worship me in the wilderness." Until now, you have refused to listen to him. 17Now the LORD says, "You are going to find out that I am the LORD." Look! I will hit the water of the Nile with this staff, and the river will turn to blood. 18The fish in it will die, and the river will stink. The Egyptians will not be able to drink any water from the Nile.'"

19Then the LORD said to Moses: "Tell Aaron to point his staff toward the waters of Egypt—all its rivers, canals, marshes, and reservoirs. Everywhere in Egypt the water will turn into blood, even the water stored in wooden bowls and stone pots in the people's homes."

20So Moses and Aaron did just as the LORD had commanded them. As Pharaoh and all of his officials watched, Moses raised his staff and hit the water of the Nile. Suddenly, the whole river turned to blood! 21The fish in the river died, and the water became so foul that the Egyptians couldn't drink it. There was blood everywhere throughout the land of Egypt. 22But again the magicians of Egypt used their secret arts, and they, too, turned water into blood. So Pharaoh's heart remained hard and stubborn. He refused to listen to Moses and Aaron, just as the LORD had predicted. 23Pharaoh returned to his palace and put the whole thing out of his mind. 24Then the Egyptians dug wells along the riverbank to get drinking water, for they couldn't drink from the river. 25An entire week passed from the time the LORD turned the water of the Nile to blood.

**TRICKERY ● ● • • •**

7:11 **How were these wise men and magicians able to duplicate Moses' miracles? Some of their feats involved trickery or illusion. But some may have used satanic power, since worshiping gods of the underworld was part of the Egyptians' religion. Ironically, whenever the magicians duplicated one of Moses' plagues, it only made matters worse. If the magicians had been as powerful as God, they would have reversed the plagues, not added to them!**

CHAPTER **8** **PHAROAH SEES GOD'S POWER.** Then the LORD said to Moses, "Go to Pharaoh once again and tell him, 'This is what the LORD says: Let my people go, so they can worship me. 2If you refuse, then listen carefully to this: I will send vast hordes of frogs across your entire land from one border to the other. 3The Nile River will swarm with them. They will come up out of the river and into your houses, even into your bedrooms and onto your beds! Every home in Egypt will be filled with them. They will fill even your ovens and your kneading bowls. 4You and your people will be overwhelmed by frogs!'"

5Then the LORD said to Moses, "Tell Aaron to point his shepherd's staff toward all the rivers, canals, and marshes of Egypt so there will be frogs in every corner of the land." 6Aaron did so, and frogs

**"Here's what I did..."**

Whenever I get discouraged because I can't persuade a friend of the truth of the gospel, I remind myself that we are never going to convince those who don't want to be convinced. This has been a tough thing for me to accept; there are some people I want so badly to become Christians. But I find solace in the story of Moses and Pharaoh. Nothing would convince Pharaoh that Moses represented the one true God—not plagues, not miracles, not even the death of Egypt's firstborn. If calamities of this magnitude couldn't move Pharaoh to repent, I am no longer surprised that the daily witness of faithful Christians fails to make a dent in the hearts of many people in our society.

However, I am convinced that the best tactic is the slow, steady work of Christ in our lives, coupled with prayer and our attempts to live the Christian life. I'm learning to place the rest in God's hands.

*Richard*

AGE 18

covered the whole land of Egypt! 7But the magicians were able to do the same thing with their secret arts. They, too, caused frogs to come up on the land.

8Then Pharaoh summoned Moses and Aaron and begged, "Plead with the LORD to take the frogs away from me and my people. I will let the people go, so they can offer sacrifices to the LORD."

9"You set the time!" Moses replied. "Tell me when you want me to pray for you, your officials, and your people. I will pray that you and your houses will be rid of the frogs. Then only the frogs in the Nile River will remain alive."

10"Do it tomorrow," Pharaoh said.

"All right," Moses replied, "it will be as you have said. Then you will know that no one is as powerful as the LORD our God. 11All the frogs will be destroyed, except those in the river."

12So Moses and Aaron left Pharaoh, and Moses pleaded with the LORD about the frogs he had sent. 13And the LORD did as Moses had promised. The frogs in the houses, the courtyards, and the fields all died. 14They were piled into great heaps, and a terrible stench filled the land. 15But when Pharaoh saw that the frogs were gone, he hardened his heart. He refused to listen to Moses and Aaron, just as the LORD had predicted.

16So the LORD said to Moses, "Tell Aaron to strike the dust with his staff. The dust will turn into swarms of gnats throughout the land of Egypt." 17So Moses and Aaron did just as the LORD had commanded them. Suddenly, gnats infested the entire land, covering the Egyptians and their animals. All the dust in the land of Egypt turned into gnats. 18Pharaoh's magicians tried to do the same thing with their secret arts, but this time they failed. And the gnats covered all the people and animals.

### STUBBORN ● ● • • •

**8:19 Some people think, *If only I could see a miracle, I would believe in God.* God gave Pharaoh just such an opportunity. When gnats infested Egypt, even the magicians agreed that this was God's work ("the finger of God") –but still Pharaoh refused to believe. He was stubborn, and stubbornness can blind a person to the truth. When you rid yourself of stubbornness, you may be surprised to discover abundant evidence of God's hand in your life.**

19"This is the finger of God!" the magicians exclaimed to Pharaoh. But Pharaoh's heart remained hard and stubborn. He wouldn't listen to them, just as the LORD had predicted.

20Next the LORD told Moses, "Get up early in the morning and meet Pharaoh as he goes down to the river. Say to him, 'This is what the LORD says: Let my people go, so they can worship me. 21If you refuse, I will send swarms of flies throughout Egypt. Your homes will be filled with them, and the ground will be covered with them. 22But it will be very different in the land of Goshen, where the Israelites live. No flies will be found there. Then you will know that I am the LORD and that I have power even in the heart of your land. 23I will make a clear distinction between your people and my people. This miraculous sign will happen tomorrow.'"

24And the LORD did just as he had said. There were terrible swarms of flies in Pharaoh's palace and in every home in Egypt. The whole country was thrown into chaos by the flies.

25Pharaoh hastily called for Moses and Aaron. "All right! Go ahead and offer sacrifices to your God," he said. "But do it here in this land. Don't go out into the wilderness."

26But Moses replied, "That won't do! The Egyptians would detest the sacrifices that we offer to the LORD our God. If we offer them here where they can see us, they will be sure to stone us. 27We must take a three-day trip into the wilderness to offer sacrifices to the LORD our God, just as he has commanded us."

28"All right, go ahead," Pharaoh replied. "I will let you go to offer sacrifices to the LORD your God in the wilderness. But don't go too far away. Now hurry, and pray for me."

29"As soon as I go," Moses said, "I will ask the LORD to cause the swarms of flies to disappear from you and all your people. But I am warning you, don't change your mind again and refuse to let the people go to sacrifice to the LORD."

30So Moses left Pharaoh and asked the LORD to remove all the flies. 31And the LORD did as Moses asked and caused the swarms to disappear. Not a single fly remained in the land! 32But Pharaoh hardened his heart again and refused to let the people go.

## CHAPTER 9

"Go back to Pharaoh," the LORD commanded Moses. "Tell him, 'This is what the LORD, the God of the Hebrews, says: Let my people go, so they can worship me. 2If you continue to oppress them and refuse to let them go, 3the LORD will send a deadly plague to destroy your horses, donkeys, camels, cattle, and sheep. 4But the LORD will again make a distinction between the property of the Israelites and that of the Egyptians. Not a single one of Israel's livestock will die!'"

5The LORD announced that he would send the plague the very next day, 6and he did it, just as he had said. The next morning all the livestock of the Egyptians began to die, but the Israelites didn't lose a single animal from their flocks and herds. 7Pharaoh sent officials to see whether it was true that none of the Israelites' animals were dead. But even after he found it to be true, his heart remained stubborn. He still refused to let the people go.

8Then the LORD said to Moses and Aaron, "Take soot from a furnace, and have Moses toss it into the sky while Pharaoh watches. 9It will spread like fine dust over the whole land of Egypt, causing boils to break out on people and animals alike."

10So they gathered soot from a furnace and went to see Pharaoh. As Pharaoh watched, Moses tossed the soot into the air, and terrible boils broke out on the people and animals throughout Egypt. 11Even the magicians were unable to stand before Moses, be-

cause the boils had broken out on them, too. 12But
the LORD made Pharaoh even more stubborn, and he
refused to listen, just as the LORD had predicted.
13Then the LORD said to Moses, "Get up early in
the morning. Go to Pharaoh and tell him, 'The
LORD, the God of the Hebrews, says: Let my people
go, so they can worship me. 14If you don't, I will send
a plague that will really speak to you and your officials and all the Egyptian people. I will prove to you
that there is no other God like me in all the earth. 15I
could have killed you all by now. I could have attacked you with a plague that would have wiped you
from the face of the earth. 16But I have let you live for
this reason—that you might see my power and that
my fame might spread throughout the earth. 17But
you are still lording it over my people, and you refuse
to let them go. 18So tomorrow at this time I will send
a hailstorm worse than any in all of Egypt's history.
19Quick! Order your livestock and servants to come
in from the fields. Every person or animal left outside will die beneath the hail.'"
20Some of Pharaoh's officials believed what the
LORD said. They immediately brought their livestock
and servants in from the fields. 21But those who had
no respect for the word of the LORD left them out in
the open.
22Then the LORD said to Moses, "Lift your hand
toward the sky, and cause the hail to fall throughout
Egypt, on the people, the animals, and the crops."
23So Moses lifted his staff toward the sky, and the
LORD sent thunder and hail, and lightning struck the
earth. The LORD sent a tremendous hailstorm against
all the land of Egypt. 24Never in all the history of
Egypt had there been a storm like that, with such
severe hail and continuous lightning. 25It left all of
Egypt in ruins. Everything left in the fields was destroyed—people, animals, and crops alike. Even all
the trees were destroyed. 26The only spot in all Egypt
without hail that day was the land of Goshen, where
the people of Israel lived.
27Then Pharaoh urgently sent for Moses and
Aaron. "I finally admit my fault," he confessed. "The
LORD is right, and my people and I are wrong.
28Please beg the LORD to end this terrifying thunder
and hail. I will let you go at once."
29"All right," Moses replied. "As soon as I leave the
city, I will lift my hands and pray to the LORD. Then
the thunder and hail will stop. This will prove to you
that the earth belongs to the LORD. 30But as for you
and your officials, I know that you still do not fear
the LORD God as you should."
31All the flax and barley were destroyed because
the barley was ripe and the flax was in bloom. 32But
the wheat and the spelt were not destroyed because
they had not yet sprouted from the ground.
33So Moses left Pharaoh and went out of the city.
As he lifted his hands to the LORD, all at once the
thunder and hail stopped, and the downpour
ceased. 34When Pharaoh saw this, he and his officials
sinned yet again by stubbornly refusing to do as they

**PERSISTENT ● ● • • •**

9:1 **This was the fifth time God sent Moses back to Pharaoh with the demand to let his people go! Moses may have been tired and discouraged by this time, but he continued to obey. Is there a difficult conflict you must face again and again? Don't give up when you know what is right to do. As Moses discovered, persistence is rewarded.**

had promised. 35Pharaoh refused to let the people
leave, just as the LORD had predicted.

CHAPTER **10** **THE LONGEST NIGHT.** Then the LORD
said to Moses, "Return to Pharaoh and again make
your demands. I have made him and his officials
stubborn so I can continue to display my power by
performing miraculous signs among them. 2You will
be able to tell wonderful stories to your children and
grandchildren about the marvelous things I am doing among the Egyptians to prove that I am the
LORD."
3So Moses and Aaron went to Pharaoh and said,
"This is what the LORD, the God of the Hebrews,
says: How long will you refuse to submit to me? Let
my people go, so they can worship me. 4If you refuse,
watch out! For tomorrow I will cover the whole
country with locusts. 5There will be so many that you
won't be able to see the ground. They will devour
everything that escaped the hailstorm, including all
the trees in the fields. 6They will overrun your palaces and the homes of your officials and all the
houses of Egypt. Never in the history of Egypt has
there been a plague like this one!" And with that,
Moses turned and walked out.
7The court officials now came to Pharaoh and
appealed to him. "How long will you let these disasters go on? Please let the Israelites go to serve the
LORD their God! Don't you realize that Egypt lies in
ruins?"
8So Moses and Aaron were brought back to Pharaoh. "All right, go and serve the LORD your God," he
said. "But tell me, just whom do you want to take
along?"
9"Young and old, all of us will go," Moses replied.
"We will take our sons and daughters and our flocks
and herds. We must all join together in a festival to
the LORD."
10Pharaoh retorted, "The LORD will certainly need
to be with you if you try to take your little ones
along! I can see through your wicked intentions.
11Never! Only the men may go and serve the LORD,
for that is what you requested." And Pharaoh threw
them out of the palace.
12Then the LORD said to Moses, "Raise your hand
over the land of Egypt to bring on the locusts. Let
them cover the land and eat all the crops still left
after the hailstorm."
13So Moses raised his staff, and the LORD caused an
east wind to blow all that day and through the night.
When morning arrived, the east wind had brought
the locusts. 14And the locusts swarmed over the land

of Egypt from border to border. It was the worst locust plague in Egyptian history, and there has never again been one like it. [15]For the locusts covered the surface of the whole country, making the ground look black. They ate all the plants and all the fruit on the trees that had survived the hailstorm. Not one green thing remained, neither tree nor plant, throughout the land of Egypt.

[16]Pharaoh quickly sent for Moses and Aaron. "I confess my sin against the LORD your God and against you," he said to them. [17]"Forgive my sin only this once, and plead with the LORD your God to take away this terrible plague."

[18]So Moses left Pharaoh and pleaded with the LORD. [19]The LORD responded by sending a strong west wind that blew the locusts out into the Red Sea.* Not a single locust remained in all the land of Egypt. [20]But the LORD made Pharaoh stubborn once again, and he did not let the people go.

[21]Then the LORD said to Moses, "Lift your hand toward heaven, and a deep and terrifying darkness will descend on the land of Egypt." [22]So Moses lifted his hand toward heaven, and there was deep darkness over the entire land for three days. [23]During all that time the people scarcely moved, for they could not see. But there was light as usual where the people of Israel lived.

[24]Then Pharaoh called for Moses. "Go and worship the LORD," he said. "But let your flocks and herds stay here. You can even take your children with you."

[25]"No," Moses said, "we must take our flocks and herds for sacrifices and burnt offerings to the LORD our God. [26]All our property must go with us; not a hoof can be left behind. We will have to choose our sacrifices for the LORD our God from among these animals. And we won't know which sacrifices he will require until we get there."

[27]So the LORD hardened Pharaoh's heart once more, and he would not let them go. [28]"Get out of here!" Pharaoh shouted at Moses. "Don't ever let me see you again! The day you do, you will die!"

[29]"Very well," Moses replied. "I will never see you again."

## CHAPTER 11 **EGYPT'S FIRSTBORN WILL DIE.**

Then the LORD said to Moses, "I will send just one more disaster on Pharaoh and the land of Egypt. After that, Pharaoh will let you go. In fact, he will be so anxious to get rid of you that he will practically force you to leave the country. [2]Tell all the Israelite men and women to ask their Egyptian neighbors for articles of silver and gold."

[3](Now the LORD had caused the Egyptians to look favorably on the people of Israel, and Moses was considered a very great man in the land of Egypt. He was respected by Pharaoh's officials and the Egyptian people alike.)

[4]So Moses announced to Pharaoh, "This is what the LORD says: About midnight I will pass through Egypt. [5]All the firstborn sons will die in every family in Egypt, from the oldest son of Pharaoh, who sits on the throne, to the oldest son of his lowliest slave. Even the firstborn of the animals will die. [6]Then a loud wail will be heard throughout the land of Egypt; there has never been such wailing before, and there never will be again. [7]But among the Israelites it will be so peaceful that not even a dog will bark. Then you will know that the LORD makes a distinction between the Egyptians and the Israelites. [8]All the officials of Egypt will come running to me, bowing low. 'Please leave!' they will beg. 'Hurry! And take all your followers with you.' Only then will I go!" Then, burning with anger, Moses left Pharaoh's presence.

[9]Now the LORD had told Moses, "Pharaoh will not listen to you. But this will give me the opportunity to do even more mighty miracles in the land of Egypt." [10]Although Moses and Aaron did these miracles in Pharaoh's presence, the LORD hardened his heart so he wouldn't let the Israelites leave the country.

### HARD-HEARTED ● ● • • •

11:10 **Did God really harden Pharaoh's heart and force him to do wrong? Before the 10 plagues began, Moses and Aaron announced what God would do if Pharaoh didn't let the people go. But their message only made Pharaoh stubborn—he was hardening his own heart. In so doing, he defied both God and his messengers. Through the first six plagues, Pharaoh's heart grew even more stubborn. After the sixth plague, God passed judgment. Sooner or later, evil people will be punished for their sins. When it became evident he wouldn't change, God confirmed Pharaoh's prideful decision and set the painful consequences of his actions in motion. God didn't force Pharaoh to reject him; rather, he gave him every opportunity to change his mind. In Ezekiel 33:11, God says, "I take no pleasure in the death of wicked people."**

## CHAPTER 12 **THE FIRST PASSOVER.**

Now the LORD gave the following instructions to Moses and Aaron while they were still in the land of Egypt: [2]"From now on, this month will be the first month of the year for you. [3]Announce to the whole community that on the tenth day of this month each family must choose a lamb or a young goat for a sacrifice. [4]If a family is too small to eat an entire lamb, let them share the lamb with another family in the neighborhood. Whether or not they share in this way depends on the size of each family and how much they can eat. [5]This animal must be a one-year-old male, either a sheep or a goat, with no physical defects.

[6]"Take special care of these lambs until the evening of the fourteenth day of this first month. Then each family in the community must slaughter its lamb. [7]They are to take some of the lamb's blood and smear it on the top and sides of the doorframe of the house where the lamb will be eaten. [8]That evening everyone must eat roast lamb with bitter herbs and bread made without yeast. [9]The meat must never be eaten raw or boiled; roast it all, including the head, legs, and internal organs. [10]Do not

10:19 Hebrew *sea of reeds.*

leave any of it until the next day. Whatever is not eaten that night must be burned before morning.

11 "Wear your traveling clothes as you eat this meal, as though prepared for a long journey. Wear your sandals, and carry your walking sticks in your hands. Eat the food quickly, for this is the LORD's Passover. 12 On that night I will pass through the land of Egypt and kill all the firstborn sons and firstborn male animals in the land of Egypt. I will execute judgment against all the gods of Egypt, for I am the LORD! 13 The blood you have smeared on your doorposts will serve as a sign. When I see the blood, I will pass over you. This plague of death will not touch you when I strike the land of Egypt.

14 "You must remember this day forever. Each year you will celebrate it as a special festival to the LORD. 15 For seven days, you may eat only bread made without yeast. On the very first day you must remove every trace of yeast from your homes. Anyone who eats bread made with yeast at any time during the seven days of the festival will be cut off from the community of Israel. 16 On the first day of the festival, and again on the seventh day, all the people must gather for a time of special worship. No work of any kind may be done on these days except in the preparation of food.

17 "Celebrate this Festival of Unleavened Bread, for it will remind you that I brought your forces out of the land of Egypt on this very day. This festival will be a permanent regulation for you, to be kept from generation to generation. 18 Only bread without yeast may be eaten from the evening of the fourteenth day of the month until the evening of the twenty-first day of the month. 19 During those seven days, there must be no trace of yeast in your homes. Anyone who eats anything made with yeast during this week will be cut off from the community of Israel. These same regulations apply to the foreigners living with you, as if they had been born among you. 20 I repeat, during those days you must not eat anything made with yeast. Wherever you live, eat only bread that has no yeast in it."

21 Then Moses called for the leaders of Israel and said, "Tell each of your families to slaughter the lamb they have set apart for the Passover. 22 Drain each lamb's blood into a basin. Then take a cluster of hyssop branches and dip it into the lamb's blood. Strike the hyssop against the top and sides of the doorframe, staining it with the blood. And remember, no one is allowed to leave the house until morning. 23 For the LORD will pass through the land and strike down the Egyptians. But when he sees the blood on the top and sides of the doorframe, the LORD will pass over your home. He will not permit the Destroyer to enter and strike down your firstborn.

24 "Remember, these instructions are permanent and must be observed by you and your descendants forever. 25 When you arrive in the land the LORD has promised to give you, you will continue to celebrate this festival. 26 Then your children will ask, 'What does all this mean? What is this ceremony about?' 27 And you will reply, 'It is the celebration of the LORD's Passover, for he passed over the homes of the Israelites in Egypt. And though he killed the Egyptians, he spared our families and did not destroy us.'" Then all the people bowed their heads and worshiped.

28 So the people of Israel did just as the LORD had commanded through Moses and Aaron. 29 And at midnight the LORD killed all the firstborn sons in the land of Egypt, from the firstborn son of Pharaoh, who sat on the throne, to the firstborn son of the captive in the dungeon. Even the firstborn of their livestock were killed. 30 Pharaoh and his officials and all the people of Egypt woke up during the night, and loud wailing was heard throughout the land of Egypt. There was not a single house where someone had not died.

31 Pharaoh sent for Moses and Aaron during the night. "Leave us!" he cried. "Go away, all of you! Go and serve the LORD as you have requested. 32 Take your flocks and herds, and be gone. Go, but give me a blessing as you leave." 33 All the Egyptians urged the people of Israel to get out of the land as quickly as possible, for they thought, "We will all die!"

34 The Israelites took with them their bread dough made without yeast. They wrapped their kneading bowls in their spare clothing and carried them on their shoulders. 35 And the people of Israel did as Moses had instructed and asked the Egyptians for clothing and articles of silver and gold. 36 The LORD caused the Egyptians to look favorably on the Israelites, and they gave the Israelites whatever they asked for. So, like a victorious army, they plundered the Egyptians!

37 That night the people of Israel left Rameses and started for Succoth. There were about 600,000 men, plus all the women and children. And they were all traveling on foot. 38 Many people who were not Israelites went with them, along with the many flocks and herds. 39 Whenever they stopped to eat, they baked bread from the yeastless dough they had brought from Egypt. It was made without yeast because the people were rushed out of Egypt and had no time to wait for bread to rise.

40 The people of Israel had lived in Egypt for 430 years. 41 In fact, it was on the last day of the 430th

## SUBSTITUTE ● ● • • •

12:23 **Every firstborn child of the Egyptians died, but the Israelite children were spared because the blood of the lamb had been placed on their doorposts. So begins the story of redemption, the central theme of the Bible.**

***Redemption*** **means "to buy back." We must recognize that if we want to be freed from the deadly consequences of our sins, a tremendous price must be paid. But we don't have to pay it. Jesus Christ, our substitute, has already redeemed us by his death on the cross. Our part is to trust him and accept his gift of eternal life (Titus 2:14; Hebrews 9:13-15, 23-26).**

## THE HEBREW CALENDAR

A Hebrew month begins in the middle of a month on our calendar today. Crops are planted in November and December and harvested in March and April.

| *Month* | *Today's Calendar* | *Bible Reference* | *Israel's Holidays* |
|---|---|---|---|
| 1 Nisan (Abib) | March–April | Exodus 13:4; 23:15; 34:18; Deuteronomy 16:1; Esther 3:7 | Passover (Leviticus 23:5); Unleavened Bread (Leviticus 23:6); Firstfruits (Leviticus 23:10) |
| 2 Iyyar (Ziv) | April–May | 1 Kings 6:1-37 | |
| 3 Sivan | May–June | Esther 8:9 | Harvest (Pentecost) (Leviticus 23:15) |
| 4 Tammuz | June–July | | |
| 5 Ab | July–August | | |
| 6 Elul | August–September | Nehemiah 6:15 | |
| 7 Tishri (Ethanim) | September–October | 1 Kings 8:2 | Trumpets (Leviticus 23:24; Numbers 29:1); Day of Atonement (Leviticus 23:27); Shelters (Tabernacles) (Leviticus 23:34) |
| 8 Marchesvan (Bul) | October–November | 1 Kings 6:38 | |
| 9 Chislev (Kislev) | November–December | Nehemiah 1:1 | Hanukkah (John 10:22) |
| 10 Tebeth | December–January | Esther 2:16 | |
| 11 Shebat | January–February | Zechariah 1:7 | |
| 12 Adar | February–March | Esther 3:7 | Purim (Esther 9:24-32) |

year that all the LORD's forces left the land. 42 This night had been reserved by the LORD to bring his people out from the land of Egypt, so this same night now belongs to him. It must be celebrated every year, from generation to generation, to remember the LORD's deliverance.

43 Then the LORD said to Moses and Aaron, "These are the regulations for the festival of Passover. No foreigners are allowed to eat the Passover lamb. 44 But any slave who has been purchased may eat it if he has been circumcised. 45 Hired servants and visiting foreigners may not eat it. 46 All who eat the lamb must eat it together in one house. You must not carry any of its meat outside, and you may not break any of its bones. 47 The whole community of Israel must celebrate this festival at the same time.

48 "If there are foreigners living among you who want to celebrate the LORD's Passover, let all the males be circumcised. Then they may come and celebrate the Passover with you. They will be treated just as if they had been born among you. But an uncircumcised male may never eat of the Passover lamb. 49 This law applies to everyone, whether a native-born Israelite or a foreigner who has settled among you."

50 So the people of Israel followed all the LORD's instructions to Moses and Aaron. 51 And that very day the LORD began to lead the people of Israel out of Egypt, division by division.

CHAPTER **13** **FIRSTBORN DEDICATED TO GOD.** Then the LORD said to Moses, 2 "Dedicate to me all the firstborn sons of Israel and every firstborn male animal. They are mine."

3 So Moses said to the people, "This is a day to remember forever—the day you left Egypt, the place of your slavery. For the LORD has brought you out by his mighty power. (Remember, you are not

**BRANDED ● ● • • •**

**13:9 The Festival of Unleavened Bread marked the Hebrews as a unique people—as though they were branded on their hands and foreheads. What do you do that marks you as a follower of God? Think about the way you act at school, demonstrate love for others, show concern for the social outcast, and treat your family—what you do in these areas will leave visible marks for all to see. While certain nationalities are marked by customs and traditions, Christians are marked by loving one another (John 13:34-35).**

to use any yeast.) 4This day in early spring* will be the anniversary of your exodus. 5You must celebrate this day when the LORD brings you into the land of the Canaanites, Hittites, Amorites, Hivites, and Jebusites. This is the land he swore to give your ancestors—a land flowing with milk and honey. 6For seven days you will eat only bread without yeast. Then on the seventh day, you will celebrate a great feast to the LORD. 7Eat only bread without yeast during those seven days. In fact, there must be no yeast in your homes or anywhere within the borders of your land during this time.

8"During these festival days each year, you must explain to your children why you are celebrating. Say to them, 'This is a celebration of what the LORD did for us when we left Egypt.' 9This annual festival will be a visible reminder to you, like a mark branded on your hands or your forehead. Let it remind you always to keep the LORD's instructions in your minds and on your lips. After all, it was the LORD who rescued you from Egypt with great power.

10"So celebrate this festival at the appointed time each year. 11And remember these instructions when the LORD brings you into the land he swore to give your ancestors long ago, the land where the Canaanites are now living. 12All firstborn sons and firstborn male animals must be presented to the LORD. 13A firstborn male donkey may be redeemed from the LORD by presenting a lamb in its place. But if you decide not to make the exchange, the donkey must be killed by breaking its neck. However, you must redeem every firstborn son.

14"And in the future, your children will ask you, 'What does all this mean?' Then you will tell them, 'With mighty power the LORD brought us out of Egypt from our slavery. 15Pharaoh refused to let us go, so the LORD killed all the firstborn males throughout the land of Egypt, both people and animals. That is why we now offer all the firstborn males to the LORD—except that the firstborn sons are always redeemed.' 16Again I say, this ceremony will be like a mark branded on your hands or your forehead. It is a visible reminder that it was the LORD who brought you out of Egypt with great power."

17When Pharaoh finally let the people go, God did not lead them on the road that runs through Philistine territory, even though that was the shortest way from Egypt to the Promised Land. God said, "If the people are faced with a battle, they might change their minds and return to Egypt." 18So God led them along a route through the wilderness toward the Red Sea,* and the Israelites left Egypt like a marching army.

19Moses took the bones of Joseph with him, for Joseph had made the sons of Israel swear that they would take his bones with them when God led them out of Egypt—as he was sure God would.

**OBSTACLES ● ● ● • •**

13:17-18 **God doesn't always work in the way that seems best to us. Instead of guiding the Israelites along the direct route from Egypt to the Promised Land, he took them by a longer route so they could avoid fighting with the Philistines. If God does not lead you along the shortest path to your goal, don't complain or resist. Follow him willingly and trust him to lead you safely around unseen obstacles. He can see the end of your journey from the beginning, and he knows the safest and best route.**

20Leaving Succoth, they camped at Etham on the edge of the wilderness. 21The LORD guided them by a pillar of cloud during the day and a pillar of fire at night. That way they could travel whether it was day or night. 22And the LORD did not remove the pillar of cloud or pillar of fire from their sight.

CHAPTER **14** **CROSSING THE RED SEA.** Then the LORD gave these instructions to Moses: 2"Tell the people to march toward Pi-hahiroth between Migdol and the sea. Camp there along the shore, opposite Baal-zephon. 3Then Pharaoh will think, 'Those Israelites are confused. They are trapped between the wilderness and the sea!' 4And once again I will harden Pharaoh's heart, and he will chase after you. I have planned this so I will receive great glory at the expense of Pharaoh and his armies. After this, the Egyptians will know that I am the LORD!" So the Israelites camped there as they were told.

5When word reached the king of Egypt that the Israelites were not planning to return to Egypt after three days, Pharaoh and his officials changed their minds. "What have we done, letting all these slaves get away?" they asked. 6So Pharaoh called out his troops and led the chase in his chariot. 7He took with him six hundred of Egypt's best chariots, along with the rest of the chariots of Egypt, each with a commander. 8The LORD continued to strengthen Pharaoh's resolve, and he chased after the people of Israel who had escaped so defiantly. 9All the forces in Pharaoh's army—all his horses, chariots, and charioteers—were used in the chase. The Egyptians caught up with the people of Israel as they were camped beside the shore near Pi-hahiroth, across from Baal-zephon.

10As Pharaoh and his army approached, the people of Israel could see them in the distance, marching toward them. The people began to panic, and they cried out to the LORD for help.

11Then they turned against Moses and complained, "Why did you bring us out here to die in the wilderness? Weren't there enough graves for us in Egypt? Why did you make us leave? 12Didn't we tell you to leave us alone while we were still in Egypt? Our Egyptian slavery was far better than dying out here in the wilderness!"

13But Moses told the people, "Don't be afraid.

**13:4** Hebrew *in the month of Abib.* This month of the Hebrew lunar calendar usually occurs in March and April. **13:18** Hebrew *sea of reeds.*

Don't be afraid.
Just
stand
where

you

are

and watch

the LORD

rescue you.

EXODUS 14:13

Just stand where you are and watch the LORD rescue you. The Egyptians that you see today will never be seen again. 14 The LORD himself will fight for you. You won't have to lift a finger in your defense!"

15 Then the LORD said to Moses, "Why are you crying out to me? Tell the people to get moving! 16 Use your shepherd's staff—hold it out over the water, and a path will open up before you through the sea. Then all the people of Israel will walk through on dry ground. 17 Yet I will harden the hearts of the Egyptians, and they will follow the Israelites into the sea. Then I will receive great glory at the expense of Pharaoh and his armies, chariots, and charioteers. 18 When I am finished with Pharaoh and his army, all Egypt will know that I am the LORD!"

19 Then the angel of God, who had been leading the people of Israel, moved to a position behind them, and the pillar of cloud also moved around behind them. 20 The cloud settled between the Israelite and Egyptian camps. As night came, the pillar of cloud turned into a pillar of fire, lighting the Israelite camp. But the cloud became darkness to the Egyptians, and they couldn't find the Israelites.

21 Then Moses raised his hand over the sea, and the LORD opened up a path through the water with a strong east wind. The wind blew all that night, turning the seabed into dry land. 22 So the people of Israel walked through the sea on dry ground, with walls of water on each side! 23 Then the Egyptians—all of Pharaoh's horses, chariots, and charioteers—followed them across the bottom of the sea. 24 But early in the morning, the LORD looked down on the Egyptian army from the pillar of fire and cloud, and he threw them into confusion. 25 Their chariot wheels began to come off, making their chariots impossible to drive. "Let's get out of here!" the Egyptians shouted. "The LORD is fighting for Israel against us!"

26 When all the Israelites were on the other side, the LORD said to Moses, "Raise your hand over the sea again. Then the waters will rush back over the Egyptian chariots and charioteers." 27 So as the sun began to rise, Moses raised his hand over the sea. The water roared back into its usual place, and the LORD swept the terrified Egyptians into the surging currents. 28 The waters covered all the chariots and charioteers—the entire army of Pharaoh. Of all the Egyptians who had chased the Israelites into the sea, not a single one survived.

29 The people of Israel had walked through the middle of the sea on dry land, as the water stood up like a wall on both sides. 30 This was how the LORD rescued Israel from the Egyptians that day. And the Israelites could see the bodies of the Egyptians washed up on the shore. 31 When the people of Israel saw the mighty power that the LORD had displayed against the Egyptians, they feared the LORD and put their faith in him and his servant Moses.

## CHAPTER 15 SONGS TO THE LORD.

Then Moses and the people of Israel sang this song to the LORD:

"I will sing to the LORD, for he has triumphed
gloriously;
he has thrown both horse and rider into the
sea.
2 The LORD is my strength and my song;
he has become my victory.
He is my God, and I will praise him;
he is my father's God, and I will exalt him!
3 The LORD is a warrior;
yes, the LORD is his name!
4 Pharaoh's chariots and armies,
he has thrown into the sea.
The very best of Pharaoh's officers
have been drowned in the Red Sea.*

### GET MOVING! ● ● ● ● ●

**14:15 God told Moses to stop praying and get moving! Prayer deserves a vital place in our life, but there is also a place for action. Sometimes we know what to do, but we pray for more guidance as an excuse to postpone doing it. If you know what you should do, then it is time to get moving.**

15:4 Hebrew *sea of reeds;* also in 15:22.

the LORD himself will FIGHT for you.

EXODUS 14:14

[5]The deep waters have covered them;
they sank to the bottom like a stone.
[6]"Your right hand, O LORD,
is glorious in power.
Your right hand, O LORD,
dashes the enemy to pieces.
[7]In the greatness of your majesty,
you overthrew those
who rose against
you.
Your anger flashed forth;
it consumed them as
fire burns straw.
[8]At the blast of your
breath, the waters
piled up!
The surging waters
stood straight like
a wall;
in the middle of the
sea the waters
became hard.
[9]"The enemy said, 'I will
chase them,
catch up with them,
and destroy
them.
I will divide the plunder,
avenging myself
against them.
I will unsheath my sword;
my power will destroy
them.'
[10]But with a blast of your
breath,
the sea covered them.
They sank like lead
in the mighty waters.
[11]"Who else among the
gods is like you,
O LORD?
Who is glorious in
holiness like you—
so awesome in splendor,
performing such wonders?
[12]You raised up your hand,
and the earth swallowed our enemies.
[13]"With unfailing love you will lead
this people whom you have ransomed.
You will guide them in your strength
to the place where your holiness dwells.
[14]The nations will hear and tremble;
anguish will grip the people of Philistia.
[15]The leaders of Edom will be terrified;
the nobles of Moab will tremble.
All the people of Canaan will melt with fear;
[16]terror and dread will overcome them.
Because of your great power,
they will be silent like a stone,
until your people pass by, O LORD,
until the people whom you purchased
pass by.
[17]You will bring them in and plant them on your
own mountain—
the place you have made as your home,
O LORD,

## MIRIAM

Ask older brothers or sisters what their greatest test in life is and they will often answer, "My younger brother (or sister)!" This is especially true when the younger one seems more successful than the older. At such times, the bonds of family loyalty can be stretched to the breaking point.

When we first meet Miriam, she is involved in one of history's most unusual baby-sitting jobs: She is watching her infant brother float down the Nile River in a waterproof cradle. When the baby is found, Miriam's quick thinking saves her brother and even allows him to be raised by his own mother. But it isn't long before the little brother she had protected grows into a great man—and their relationship changes. Moses had needed her; now, she needed him. The change wasn't easy for Miriam.

Instead of appreciating what God was doing in her brother's life, Miriam chose to criticize. Sound familiar? God had to teach Miriam and her other brother Aaron that each had a unique part in his plans. Being jealous of one another was wrong. The same lesson applies to our families, too.

What difference would it make in your family if every criticism was changed into an encouraging or loving statement? Does God want you to start the new trend?

**UPS:**
- Quick thinker under pressure
- Able leader
- Songwriter
- Prophetess

**DOWNS:**
- Was jealous of Moses' authority
- Openly criticized Moses' leadership

**STATS:**
- Where: Egypt, Sinai Peninsula
- Relatives: Brothers: Aaron and Moses

LESSON: The motives behind criticism are often more important to deal with than the criticism itself

KEY VERSE: "And Miriam sang this song: 'I will sing to the LORD, for he has triumphed gloriously; he has thrown both horse and rider into the sea.'" (Exodus 15:21).

Miriam's story is told in Exodus 2 and 15; Numbers 12 and 20:1. She is also mentioned in Deuteronomy 24:9; 1 Chronicles 6:3; Micah 6:4.

## FAMOUS SONGS IN THE BIBLE

| *Where* | *Purpose of Song* |
|---|---|
| Exodus 15:1-21 | Moses' song of victory and praise after God led Israel out of Egypt and saved them by parting the Red Sea; Miriam joined in the singing, too |
| Numbers 21:17-18 | Israel's song of praise to God for giving them water in the wilderness |
| Deuteronomy 32:1-43 | Moses' song of Israel's history with thanksgiving and praise as the Hebrews were about to enter the Promised Land |
| Judges 5:2-31 | Deborah and Barak's song of praise thanking God for Israel's victory over King Jabin's army at Mount Tabor |
| 2 Samuel 22:1-51 | David's song of thanks and praise to God for rescuing him from Saul and his other enemies |
| Song of Songs | Solomon's song of love celebrating the union of husband and wife |
| Isaiah 26:1 | Isaiah's prophetic song about how the redeemed will sing in the new Jerusalem |
| Ezra 3:11 | Israel's song of praise at the completion of the Temple's foundation |
| Luke 1:46-55 | Mary's song of praise to God for the conception of Jesus |
| Luke 1:68-79 | Zechariah's song of praise for the promise of a son |
| Acts 16:25 | Paul and Silas sang hymns in prison |
| Revelation 5:9-10 | The "new song" of the 24 elders acclaiming Christ as worthy to break the seven seals of God's scroll |
| Revelation 14:3 | The song of the 144,000 redeemed from the earth |
| Revelation 15:3-4 | The song of all the redeemed in praise of the Lamb who redeemed them |

the sanctuary, O Lord, that your hands have
made.
[18]The LORD will reign forever and ever!"

[19]When Pharaoh's horses, chariots, and charioteers rushed into the sea, the LORD brought the water crashing down on them. But the people of Israel had walked through on dry land!
[20]Then Miriam the prophet, Aaron's sister, took a tambourine and led all the women in rhythm and dance.
[21]And Miriam sang this song:

"I will sing to the LORD, for he has triumphed
gloriously;
he has thrown both horse and rider into the
sea."

[22]Then Moses led the people of Israel away from the Red Sea, and they moved out into the Shur Desert. They traveled in this desert for three days without water.
[23]When they came to Marah, they finally found water. But the people couldn't drink it because it was bitter. (That is why the place was called Marah, which means "bitter.")
[24]Then the people turned against Moses. "What are we going to drink?" they demanded.
[25]So Moses cried out to the LORD for help, and the LORD showed him a branch. Moses took the branch and threw it into the water. This made the water good to drink.

It was there at Marah that the LORD laid before them the following conditions to test their faithfulness to him:
[26]"If you will listen carefully to the voice of the LORD your God and do what is right in his sight, obeying his commands and laws, then I will not make you suffer the diseases I sent on the Egyptians; for I am the LORD who heals you."
[27]After leaving Marah, they came to Elim, where

### DISEASES ● ● • • •

15:26 **God promised that if the people obeyed him they would be free from the diseases that plagued the Egyptians. Little did they know that following the moral laws he later gave them would help keep them free from sickness. For example, following God's law against prostitution would keep them free of venereal disease. God's laws for us often keep us from harm. Men and women are complex beings. Our physical, emotional, and spiritual lives are intertwined. Modern medicine is now acknowledging what these laws assumed. If we want God to care for us, we need to submit to his directions for living.**

there were twelve springs and seventy palm trees.
They camped there beside the springs.

CHAPTER **16** **GOD SENDS MANNA AND QUAIL.** Then
they left Elim and journeyed into the Sin* Desert,
between Elim and Mount Sinai. They arrived there a
month after leaving Egypt.* 2There, too, the whole
community of Israel spoke bitterly against Moses
and Aaron.

3"Oh, that we were back in Egypt," they moaned.
"It would have been better if the LORD had killed us
there! At least there we had plenty to eat. But now
you have brought us into this desert to starve us to
death."

4Then the LORD said to Moses, "Look, I'm going
to rain down food from heaven for you. The people
can go out each day and pick up as much food as
they need for that day. I will test them in this to see
whether they will follow my instructions. 5Tell them
to pick up twice as much as usual on the sixth day of
each week."

6Then Moses and Aaron called a meeting of all the
people of Israel and told them, "In the evening you
will realize that it was the LORD who brought you out
of the land of Egypt. 7In the morning you will see the
glorious presence of the LORD. He has heard your
complaints, which are against the LORD and not
against us. 8The LORD will give you meat to eat in the
evening and bread in the morning, for he has heard
all your complaints against him. Yes, your complaints are against the LORD, not against us."

9Then Moses said to Aaron, "Say this to the entire
community of Israel: 'Come into the LORD's presence, and hear his reply to your complaints.'" 10And
as Aaron spoke to the people, they looked out toward the desert. Within the guiding cloud, they
could see the awesome glory of the LORD.

11And the LORD said to Moses, 12"I have heard the
people's complaints. Now tell them, 'In the evening
you will have meat to eat, and in the morning you
will be filled with bread. Then you will know that I
am the LORD your God.'"

13That evening vast numbers of quail arrived and
covered the camp. The next morning the desert all
around the camp was wet with dew. 14When the dew
disappeared later in the morning, thin flakes, white
like frost, covered the ground. 15The Israelites were
puzzled when they saw it. "What is it?" they asked.

And Moses told them, "It is the food the LORD has
given you. 16The LORD says that each household
should gather as much as it needs. Pick up two
quarts* for each person."

17So the people of Israel went out and gathered
this food—some getting more, and some getting
less. 18By gathering two quarts for each person, everyone had just enough. Those who gathered a lot had
nothing left over, and those who gathered only a
little had enough. Each family had just what it
needed.

## STRESSED OUT ● ● • • •

**16:2-3 It happened again. As the Israelites encountered danger, shortages, and inconvenience, they complained bitterly and longed to be back in Egypt. But as always, God provided for their needs. Difficult circumstances often lead to stress, and complaining is a natural response. The Israelites didn't really want to be back in Egypt; they just wanted life to get a little easier. In the pressure of the moment, they could not focus on the cause of their stress (in this case, lack of trust in God); they could only think about the quickest way of escape. When pressure comes your way, resist the temptation to make a quick escape. Instead, focus on God's power and wisdom to help you deal with the cause of your stress.**

19Then Moses told them, "Do not keep any of it
overnight." 20But, of course, some of them didn't
listen and kept some of it until morning. By then it
was full of maggots and had a terrible smell. And
Moses was very angry with them.

21The people gathered the food morning by morning, each family according to its need. And as the sun
became hot, the food they had not picked up melted
and disappeared. 22On the sixth day, there was twice
as much as usual on the ground—four quarts* for
each person instead of two. The leaders of the people
came and asked Moses why this had happened. 23He
replied, "The LORD has appointed tomorrow as a day
of rest, a holy Sabbath to the LORD. On this day we
will rest from our normal daily tasks. So bake or boil
as much as you want today, and set aside what is left
for tomorrow."

24The next morning the leftover food was wholesome and good, without maggots or odor. 25Moses
said, "This is your food for today, for today is a
Sabbath to the LORD. There will be no food on the
ground today. 26Gather the food for six days, but the
seventh day is a Sabbath. There will be no food on
the ground for you on that day."

27Some of the people went out anyway to gather
food, even though it was the Sabbath day. But there
was none to be found. 28"How long will these
people refuse to obey my commands and instructions?" the LORD asked Moses. 29"Do they not realize that I have given them the seventh day, the
Sabbath, as a day of rest? That is why I give you
twice as much food on the sixth day, so there will
be enough for two days. On the Sabbath day you
must stay in your places. Do not pick up food from
the ground on that day." 30So the people rested on
the seventh day.

## SCHEDULING ● ● • • •

**16:23 The Israelites were not supposed to work on the Sabbath—not even to cook food. Why? God knew that the busy routine of daily living could distract people from worshiping him. It is so easy to let school, friends, and other activities crowd our schedules so tightly that we don't spend regular time with God. Carefully guard your time with God.**

**16:1a** Not to be confused with the English word *sin.* **16:1b** Hebrew *on the fifteenth day of the second month.* The Exodus had occurred on the fourteenth day of the first month (see 12:6). **16:16** Hebrew *1 omer* [2 liters]; also in 16:18, 32, 33. **16:22** Hebrew *2 omers* [4 liters].

31 In time, the food became known as manna.* It was white like coriander seed, and it tasted like honey cakes.

32 Then Moses gave them this command from the LORD: "Take two quarts of manna and keep it forever as a treasured memorial of the LORD's provision. By doing this, later generations will be able to see the bread that the LORD provided in the wilderness when he brought you out of Egypt."

33 Moses said to Aaron, "Get a container and put two quarts of manna into it. Then store it in a sacred place* as a reminder for all future generations." 34 Aaron did this, just as the LORD had commanded Moses. He eventually placed it for safekeeping in the Ark of the Covenant.* 35 So the people of Israel ate manna for forty years until they arrived in the land of Canaan, where there were crops to eat.

36 (The container used to measure the manna was an omer, which held about two quarts.)*

## CHAPTER 17 WATER FROM THE ROCK.

At the LORD's command, the people of Israel left the Sin* Desert and moved from place to place. Eventually they came to Rephidim, but there was no water to be found there. 2 So once more the people grumbled and complained to Moses. "Give us water to drink!" they demanded.

"Quiet!" Moses replied. "Why are you arguing with me? And why are you testing the LORD?"

3 But tormented by thirst, they continued to complain, "Why did you ever take us out of Egypt? Why did you bring us here? We, our children, and our livestock will all die!"

4 Then Moses pleaded with the LORD, "What should I do with these people? They are about to stone me!"

5 The LORD said to Moses, "Take your shepherd's staff, the one you used when you struck the water of the Nile. Then call some of the leaders of Israel and walk on ahead of the people. 6 I will meet you by the rock at Mount Sinai.* Strike the rock, and water will come pouring out. Then the people will be able to drink." Moses did just as he was told; and as the leaders looked on, water gushed out.

7 Moses named the place Massah—"the place of testing"—and Meribah—"the place of arguing"—because the people of Israel argued with Moses and tested the LORD by saying, "Is the LORD going to take care of us or not?"

8 While the people of Israel were still at Rephidim, the warriors of Amalek came to fight against them. 9 Moses commanded Joshua, "Call the Israelites to arms, and fight the army of Amalek. Tomorrow, I will stand at the top of the hill with the staff of God in my hand."

10 So Joshua did what Moses had commanded. He led his men out to fight the army of Amalek. Meanwhile Moses, Aaron, and Hur went to the top of a nearby hill. 11 As long as Moses held up the staff with his hands, the Israelites had the advantage. But whenever he lowered his hands, the Amalekites gained the upper hand. 12 Moses' arms finally became too tired to hold up the staff any longer. So Aaron and Hur found a stone for him to sit on. Then they stood on each side, holding up his hands until sunset. 13 As a result, Joshua and his troops were able to crush the army of Amalek.

14 Then the LORD instructed Moses, "Write this down as a permanent record, and announce it to Joshua: I will blot out every trace of Amalek from under heaven." 15 Moses built an altar there and called it "The LORD Is My Banner."* 16 He said, "They have dared to raise their fist against the LORD's throne, so now* the LORD will be at war with Amalek generation after generation."

## CHAPTER 18 JETHRO VISITS MOSES.

Word soon reached Jethro, the priest of Midian and Moses' father-in-law, about all the wonderful things God had done for Moses and his people, the Israelites. He had heard about how the LORD had brought them safely out of Egypt.

2 Some time before this, Moses had sent his wife, Zipporah, and his two sons to live with Jethro, his father-in-law. 3 The name of Moses' first son was Gershom,* for Moses had said when the boy was born, "I have been a stranger in a foreign land." 4 The name of his second son was Eliezer,* for Moses had said at his birth, "The God of my fathers was my helper; he delivered me from the sword of Pharaoh." 5 Jethro now came to visit Moses, and he brought Moses' wife and two sons with him. They arrived while Moses and the people were camped near the mountain of God. 6 Moses was told, "Jethro, your father-in-law, has come to visit you. Your wife and your two sons are with him."

7 So Moses went out to meet his father-in-law. He bowed to him respectfully and greeted him warmly. They asked about each other's health and then went to Moses' tent to talk further. 8 Moses told his father-in-law about everything the LORD had done to rescue Israel from Pharaoh and the Egyptians. He also told him about the problems they had faced along the way and how the LORD had delivered his people from all their troubles. 9 Jethro was delighted when he heard about all that the LORD had done for Israel as he brought them out of Egypt.

### RELATIVES ●●•••

**18:8-11 Moses told his father-in-law all that God had done, convincing him that the Lord was greater than any other god. Our relatives are often the hardest people to tell about God. Yet we should look for opportunities to tell them what God is doing in our life, because we can have an important influence on them.**

16:31 *Manna* means "What is it?" See 16:15. 16:33 Hebrew *before the LORD.* 16:34 Hebrew *in front of the Testimony.* 16:36 Hebrew *An omer is one tenth of an ephah.* 17:1 Not to be confused with the English word *sin.* 17:6 Hebrew *Horeb,* another name for Sinai. 17:15 Hebrew *Yahweh Nissi.* 17:16 Or *Hands have been lifted up to the LORD's throne, and now.* 18:3 *Gershom* sounds like a Hebrew term that means "a stranger there." 18:4 *Eliezer* means "God is my helper."

10"Praise be to the LORD," Jethro said, "for he has saved you from the Egyptians and from Pharaoh. He has rescued Israel from the power of Egypt! 11I know now that the LORD is greater than all other gods, because his people have escaped from the proud and cruel Egyptians."

12Then Jethro presented a burnt offering and gave sacrifices to God. As Jethro was doing this, Aaron and the leaders of Israel came out to meet him. They all joined him in a sacrificial meal in God's presence.

13The next day, Moses sat as usual to hear the people's complaints against each other. They were lined up in front of him from morning till evening.

14When Moses' father-in-law saw all that Moses was doing for the people, he said, "Why are you trying to do all this alone? The people have been standing here all day to get your help."

15Moses replied, "Well, the people come to me to seek God's guidance. 16When an argument arises, I am the one who settles the case. I inform the people of God's decisions and teach them his laws and instructions."

17"This is not good!" his father-in-law exclaimed. 18"You're going to wear yourself out—and the people, too. This job is too heavy a burden for you to handle all by yourself. 19Now let me give you a word of advice, and may God be with you. You should continue to be the people's representative before God, bringing him their questions to be decided. 20You should tell them God's decisions, teach them God's laws and instructions, and show them how to conduct their lives. 21But find some capable, honest men who fear God and hate bribes. Appoint them as judges over groups of one thousand, one hundred, fifty, and ten. 22These men can serve the people, resolving all the ordinary cases. Anything that is too important or too complicated can be brought to you. But they can take care of the smaller matters themselves. They will help you carry the load, making the task easier for you. 23If you follow this advice, and if God directs you to do so, then you will be able to endure the pressures, and all these people will go home in peace."

24Moses listened to his father-in-law's advice and followed his suggestions. 25He chose capable men from all over Israel and made them judges over the people. They were put in charge of groups of one thousand, one hundred, fifty, and ten. 26These men were constantly available to administer justice. They brought the hard cases to Moses, but they judged the smaller matters themselves.

27Soon after this, Moses said good-bye to his father-in-law, who returned to his own land.

## CHAPTER 19

**GOD TALKS TO MOSES.** The Israelites arrived in the wilderness of Sinai exactly two months after they left Egypt.* 2After breaking camp at Rephidim, they came to the base of Mount Sinai and set up camp there.

3Then Moses climbed the mountain to appear before God. The LORD called out to him from the mountain and said, "Give these instructions to the descendants of Jacob, the people of Israel: 4'You have seen what I did to the Egyptians. You know how I brought you to myself and carried you on eagle's wings. 5Now if you will obey me and keep my covenant, you will be my own special treasure from among all the nations of the earth; for all the earth belongs to me. 6And you will be to me a kingdom of priests, my holy nation.' Give this message to the Israelites."

7Moses returned from the mountain and called together the leaders of the people and told them what the LORD had said. 8They all responded together, "We will certainly do everything the LORD asks of us." So Moses brought the people's answer back to the LORD.

9Then the LORD said to Moses, "I am going to come to you in a thick cloud so the people themselves can hear me as I speak to you. Then they will always have confidence in you."

Moses told the LORD what the people had said. 10Then the LORD told Moses, "Go down and prepare the people for my visit. Purify them today and tomorrow, and have them wash their clothing. 11Be sure they are ready on the third day, for I will come down upon Mount Sinai as all the people watch. 12Set boundary lines that the people may not pass. Warn them, 'Be careful! Do not go up on the mountain or even touch its boundaries. Those who do will certainly die! 13Any people or animals that cross the boundary must be stoned to death or shot with arrows. They must not be touched by human hands.' The people must stay away from the mountain until they hear one long blast from the ram's horn. Then they must gather at the foot of the mountain."

14So Moses went down to the people. He purified them for worship and had them wash their clothing. 15He told them, "Get ready for an important event two days from now. And until then, abstain from having sexual intercourse."

16On the morning of the third day, there was a powerful thunder and lightning storm, and a dense cloud came down upon the mountain. There was a long, loud blast from a ram's horn, and all the people trembled. 17Moses led them out from the camp to meet with God, and they stood at the foot of the mountain. 18All Mount Sinai was covered with smoke because the LORD had descended on it in the form of fire. The smoke billowed into the sky like smoke from a furnace, and the whole mountain shook with a violent earthquake. 19As the horn blast grew louder and louder, Moses spoke, and God thundered his reply for all to hear. 20The LORD came down on the top of Mount Sinai and called Moses to the top of the mountain. So Moses climbed the mountain.

21Then the LORD told Moses, "Go back down and

19:1 Hebrew *in the third month . . . on the very day,* i.e., two lunar months to the day after leaving Egypt. This day of the Hebrew lunar calendar occurs in late May or early June; compare note on 13:4.

warn the people not to cross the boundaries. They must not come up here to see the LORD, for those who do will die. [22]Even the priests who regularly come near to the LORD must purify themselves, or I will destroy them."

[23]"But, LORD, the people cannot come up on the mountain!" Moses protested. "You already told them not to. You told me to set boundaries around the mountain and to declare it off limits."

[24]But the LORD said, "Go down anyway and bring Aaron back with you. In the meantime, do not let the priests or the people cross the boundaries to come up here. If they do, I will punish them."

[25]So Moses went down to the people and told them what the LORD had said.

## CHAPTER 20 THE TEN COMMANDMENTS.

Then God instructed the people as follows:

[2]"I am the LORD your God, who rescued you from slavery in Egypt.

[3]"Do not worship any other gods besides me.

[4]"Do not make idols of any kind, whether in the shape of birds or animals or fish. [5]You must never worship or bow down to them, for I, the LORD your God, am a jealous God who will not share your affection with any other god! I do not leave unpunished the sins of those who hate me, but I punish the children for the sins of their parents to the third and fourth generations. [6]But I lavish my love on those who love me and obey my commands, even for a thousand generations.

[7]"Do not misuse the name of the LORD your God. The LORD will not let you go unpunished if you misuse his name.

### GOD'S NAME ● ● • • •

**20:7 God's name is special because it carries his personal identity. Using it frivolously or in a curse is so common today that we may fail to realize how serious it is. The way we use God's name conveys how we really feel about him. We should respect his name and use it appropriately, speaking it in praise or worship rather than in curse or jest.**

[8]"Remember to observe the Sabbath day by keeping it holy. [9]Six days a week are set apart for your daily duties and regular work, [10]but the seventh day is a day of rest dedicated to the LORD your God. On that day no one in your household may do any kind of work. This includes you, your sons and daughters, your male and female servants, your livestock, and any foreigners living among you. [11]For in six days the LORD made the heavens, the earth, the sea, and everything in them; then he rested on the seventh day. That is why the LORD blessed the Sabbath day and set it apart as holy.

[12]"Honor your father and mother. Then you will live a long, full life in the land the LORD your God will give you.

[13]"Do not murder.

[14]"Do not commit adultery.

[15]"Do not steal.

[16]"Do not testify falsely against your neighbor.

[17]"Do not covet your neighbor's house. Do not covet your neighbor's wife, male or female servant, ox or donkey, or anything else your neighbor owns."

[18]When the people heard the thunder and the loud blast of the horn, and when they saw the lightning and the smoke billowing from the mountain, they stood at a distance, trembling with fear.

[19]And they said to Moses, "You tell us what God says, and we will listen. But don't let God speak directly to us. If he does, we will die!"

[20]"Don't be afraid," Moses said, "for God has come in this way to show you his awesome power. From now on, let your fear of him keep you from sinning!"

[21]As the people stood in the distance, Moses entered into the deep darkness where God was.

[22]And the LORD said to Moses, "Say this to the people of Israel: You are witnesses that I have spoken to you from heaven. [23]Remember, you must not make or worship idols of silver or gold.

[24]"The altars you make for me must be simple altars of earth. Offer on such altars your sacrifices to me—your burnt offerings and peace offerings, your sheep and goats and your cattle. Build altars in the places where I remind you who I am, and I will come and bless you there. [25]If you build altars from stone, use only uncut stones. Do not chip or shape the stones with a tool, for that would make them unfit for holy use. [26]And you may not approach my altar by steps. If you do, someone might look up under the skirts of your clothing and see your nakedness.

## CHAPTER 21 LAWS ABOUT PEOPLE.

"Here are some other instructions you must present to Israel:

[2]"If you buy a Hebrew slave, he is to serve for only six years. Set him free in the seventh year, and he will owe you nothing for his freedom. [3]If he was single when he became your slave and then married afterward, only he will go free in the seventh year. But if he was married before he became a slave, then his wife will be freed with him.

[4]"If his master gave him a wife while he was a slave, and they had sons or daughters, then the man will be free in the seventh year, but his wife and children will still belong to his master. [5]But the slave

### PARENTS' PLACE ● ● • • •

**20:12 This is the first commandment with a promise attached. To live in peace for generations in the Promised Land, the Israelites would need to respect authority and build strong families. But what does it mean to "honor" parents? Partly, it means speaking well of them and politely to them. It also means acting in a way that shows them courtesy and respect (but not to obey them if this means disobedience to God). It means following their teaching and their example of putting God first. Parents have a special place in God's sight. Even those who find it difficult to get along with their parents are still commanded to honor them.**

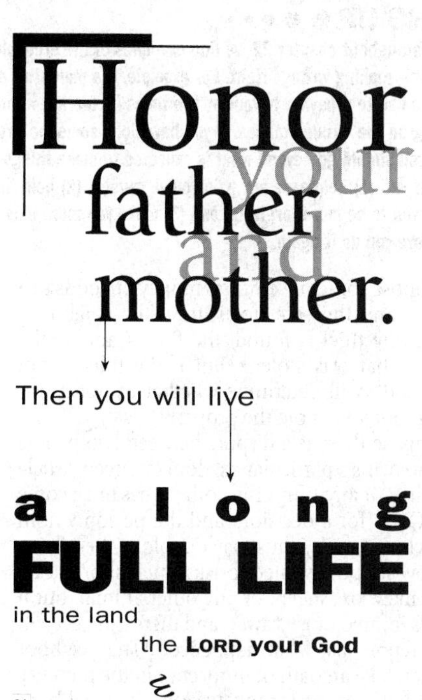
Honor
your
father
and
mother.
Then you will live
a long
FULL LIFE
in the land
the LORD your God
will give YOU.
EXODUS 20:12

may plainly declare, 'I love my master, my wife, and my children. I would rather not go free.' 6If he does this, his master must present him before God.* Then his master must take him to the door and publicly pierce his ear with an awl. After that, the slave will belong to his master forever.

7"When a man sells his daughter as a slave, she will not be freed at the end of six years as the men are. 8If she does not please the man who bought her, he may allow her to be bought back again. But he is not allowed to sell her to foreigners, since he is the one who broke the contract with her. 9And if the slave girl's owner arranges for her to marry his son, he may no longer treat her as a slave girl, but he must treat her as his daughter. 10If he himself marries her and then takes another wife, he may not reduce her food or clothing or fail to sleep with her as his wife. 11If he fails in any of these three ways, she may leave as a free woman without making any payment.

12"Anyone who hits a person hard enough to cause death must be put to death. 13But if it is an accident and God allows it to happen, I will appoint a place where the slayer can run for safety. 14However, if someone deliberately attacks and kills another person, then the slayer must be dragged even from my altar and put to death.

15"Anyone who strikes father or mother must be put to death.

16"Kidnappers must be killed, whether they are caught in possession of their victims or have already sold them as slaves.

17"Anyone who curses father or mother must be put to death.

18"Now suppose two people quarrel, and one hits the other with a stone or fist, causing injury but not death. 19If the injured person is later able to walk again, even with a crutch, the assailant will be innocent. Nonetheless, the assailant must pay for time lost because of the injury and must pay for the medical expenses.

20"If a male or female slave is beaten and dies, the owner must be punished. 21If the slave recovers after a couple of days, however, then the owner should not be punished, since the slave is the owner's property.

22"Now suppose two people are fighting, and in the process, they hurt a pregnant woman so her child is born prematurely. If no further harm results, then the person responsible must pay damages in the amount the woman's husband demands and the judges approve. 23But if any harm results, then the offender must be punished according to the injury. If the result is death, the offender must be executed. 24If an eye is injured, injure the eye of the person who did it. If a tooth gets knocked out, knock out the tooth of the person who did it. Similarly, the payment must be hand for hand, foot for foot, 25burn for burn, wound for wound, bruise for bruise.

26"If an owner hits a male or female slave in the eye and the eye is blinded, then the slave may go free because of the eye. 27And if an owner knocks out the tooth of a male or female slave, the slave should be released in payment for the tooth.

28"If a bull gores a man or woman to death, the bull must be stoned, and its flesh may not be eaten. In such a case, however, the owner will not be held liable. 29Suppose, on the other hand, that the owner knew the bull had gored people in the past, yet the bull was not kept under control. If this is true and if the bull kills someone, it must be stoned, and the owner must also be killed. 30However, the dead person's relatives may accept payment from the owner of the bull to compensate for the loss of life. The owner will have to pay whatever is demanded.

31"The same principle applies if the bull gores a boy or a girl. 32But if the bull gores a slave, either male or female, the slave's owner is to be given thirty silver coins* in payment, and the bull must be stoned.

33"Suppose someone digs or uncovers a well and fails to cover it, and then an ox or a donkey falls into it. 34The owner of the well must pay in full for the dead animal but then gets to keep it.

35"If someone's bull injures a neighbor's bull and the injured bull dies, then the two owners must sell

**21:6** Or *before the judges.* **21:32** Hebrew *30 shekels of silver,* about 12 ounces or 342 grams in weight.

the live bull and divide the money between them.
Each will also own half of the dead bull. 36 But if the
bull was known from past experience to gore, yet its
owner failed to keep it under control, the money will
not be divided. The owner of the living bull must pay
in full for the dead bull but then gets to keep it.

CHAPTER **22** **LAWS ABOUT PROPERTY.** "A fine
must be paid by anyone who steals an ox or sheep
and then kills or sells it. For oxen the fine is five
oxen for each one stolen. For sheep the fine is four
sheep for each one stolen.
2 "If a thief is caught in the act of breaking into a
house and is killed in the process, the person who
killed the thief is not guilty. 3 But if it happens in
daylight, the one who killed the thief is guilty of
murder.

## EER PRESSURE

Mike and Kenny stare in horror at the wrecked family room—stacks of greasy pizza boxes, mud and beer stains on the carpet, a broken lamp. In the downstairs bathroom, Mike is sickened by the sight and smell of vomit. The toilet is clogged and overflowing.

Upstairs, it's even worse: a leaking waterbed, liquor spilled everywhere, a framed print knocked down and broken, a trashed bathroom.

"I'm history," Mike groans. "My parents will be back tomorrow."

"Don't panic. We can clean all night. Your folks will never know we had a party."

Mike gives his friend a you-must-be-brain-dead look. "Come on, Kenny! It would take five maids and a construction crew a week to fix this mess."

How did this disaster happen? Kenny and some friends talked Mike into throwing a "Party for Profit" while his parents were away. They could get a couple of kegs, invite about 50 friends, and charge them each $10. It was a guaranteed success!

Mike refused at first, but soon he gave in. "OK," he finally said. "But only a few people!" Well, the "few" turned into more than 100, and the low-key party quickly turned into a wild nightmare.

Suppose Mike had listened to the advice of Exodus 23:2 instead of the counsel of his friends?

"A thief who is caught must pay in full for everything that was stolen. If payment is not made, the
thief must be sold as a slave to pay the debt. 4 If
someone steals an ox or a donkey or a sheep and it
is recovered alive, then the thief must pay double the
value.
5 "If an animal is grazing in a field or vineyard and
the owner lets it stray into someone else's field to
graze, then the animal's owner must pay damages in
the form of high-quality grain or grapes.
6 "If a fire gets out of control and goes into another
person's field, destroying the sheaves or the standing
grain, then the one who started the fire must pay for
the lost crops.

## PAYING UP ● ● • • ·

22:1-15 **Throughout chapter 22 we find examples of the principle of restitution– making wrongs right. For example, if a man stole an animal, he had to repay up to four or five times its market value depending on the circumstances. If you have done someone wrong, perhaps you should go beyond what is expected to make things right. This will (1) help ease any pain you've caused, (2) help the other person to be more forgiving, and (3) make you more likely to think before you do it again.**

7 "Suppose someone entrusts money or goods to a
neighbor, and they are stolen from the neighbor's
house. If the thief is found, the fine is double the
value of what was stolen. 8 But if the thief is not
found, God* will determine whether or not it was
the neighbor who stole the property.
9 "Suppose there is a dispute between two people
as to who owns a particular ox, donkey, sheep, article
of clothing, or anything else. Both parties must come
before God* for a decision, and the person whom
God declares* guilty must pay double to the other.
10 "Now suppose someone asks a neighbor to care
for a donkey, ox, sheep, or any other animal, but it
dies or is injured or gets away, and there is no eyewitness to report just what happened. 11 The neighbor
must then take an oath of innocence in the presence
of the LORD. The owner must accept the neighbor's
word, and no payment will be required. 12 But if the
animal or property was stolen, payment must be
made to the owner. 13 If it was attacked by a wild
animal, the carcass must be shown as evidence, and
no payment will be required.
14 "If someone borrows an animal from a neighbor and it is injured or killed, and if the owner was
not there at the time, the person who borrowed it
must pay for it. 15 But if the owner is there, no payment is required. And no payment is required if the
animal was rented because this loss was covered by
the rental fee.
16 "If a man seduces a virgin who is not engaged to
anyone and sleeps with her, he must pay the customary dowry and accept her as his wife. 17 But if her
father refuses to let her marry him, the man must
still pay the money for her dowry.
18 "A sorceress must not be allowed to live.
19 "Anyone who has sexual relations with an animal must be executed.
20 "Anyone who sacrifices to any god other than
the LORD must be destroyed.
21 "Do not oppress foreigners in any way. Remember, you yourselves were once foreigners in the land
of Egypt.
22 "Do not exploit widows or orphans. 23 If you do

## STRANGERS ● ● • • ·

22:21 **God warned the Israelites not to treat foreigners unfairly, because they themselves were once foreigners in Egypt. It is not easy coming to a new environment where you feel alone and out of place. Are there foreigners in your corner of the world? New arrivals at school? Immigrants from another country? Be sensitive to their struggles, and express God's love by your kindness and generosity.**

**22:8** Or *the judges.* **22:9a** Or *before the judges.* **22:9b** Or *whom the judges declare.*

and they cry out to me, then I will surely help them. 24 My anger will blaze forth against you, and I will kill you with the sword. Your wives will become widows, and your children will become fatherless.

25 "If you lend money to a fellow Hebrew in need, do not be like a money lender, charging interest. 26 If you take your neighbor's cloak as a pledge of repayment, you must return it by nightfall. 27 Your neighbor will need it to stay warm during the night. If you do not return it and your neighbor cries out to me for help, then I will hear, for I am very merciful.

28 "Do not blaspheme God* or curse anyone who rules over you.

29 "Do not hold anything back when you give me the tithe of your crops and your wine.

"You must make the necessary payment for redemption of your firstborn sons.

30 "You must also give me the firstborn of your cattle and sheep. Leave the newborn animal with its mother for seven days; then give it to me on the eighth day.

31 "You are my own holy people. Therefore, do not eat any animal that has been attacked and killed by a wild animal. Throw its carcass out for the dogs to eat.

## CHAPTER 23

"Do not pass along false reports. Do not cooperate with evil people by telling lies on the witness stand.

2 "Do not join a crowd that intends to do evil. When you are on the witness stand, do not be swayed in your testimony by the opinion of the majority. 3 And do not slant your testimony in favor of a person just because that person is poor.

4 "If you come upon your enemy's ox or donkey that has strayed away, take it back to its owner. 5 If you see the donkey of someone who hates you struggling beneath a heavy load, do not walk by. Instead, stop and offer to help.

6 "Do not twist justice against people simply because they are poor.

7 "Keep far away from falsely charging anyone with evil. Never put an innocent or honest person to death. I will not allow anyone guilty of this to go free.

8 "Take no bribes, for a bribe makes you ignore something that you clearly see. A bribe always hurts the cause of the person who is in the right.

9 "Do not oppress the foreigners living among you. You know what it is like to be a foreigner. Remember your own experience in the land of Egypt.

10 "Plant and harvest your crops for six years, 11 but let the land rest and lie fallow during the seventh year. Then let the poor among you harvest any volunteer crop that may come up. Leave the rest for the animals to eat. The same applies to your vineyards and olive groves.

12 "Work for six days, and rest on the seventh. This will give your ox and your donkey a chance to rest. It will also allow the people of your household, including your slaves and visitors, to be refreshed.

13 "Be sure to obey all my instructions. And remember, never pray to or swear by any other gods. Do not even mention their names.

14 "Each year you must celebrate three festivals in my honor. 15 The first is the Festival of Unleavened Bread. For seven days you are to eat bread made without yeast, just as I commanded you before. This festival will be an annual event at the appointed time in early spring,* for that is the anniversary of your exodus from Egypt. Everyone must bring me a sacrifice at that time. 16 You must also celebrate the Festival of Harvest,* when you bring me the first crops of your harvest. Finally, you are to celebrate the Festival of the Final Harvest* at the end of the harvest season. 17 At these three times each year, every man in Israel must appear before the Sovereign LORD.

18 "Sacrificial blood must never be offered together with bread that has yeast in it. And no sacrificial fat may be left unoffered until the next morning.

19 "As you harvest each of your crops, bring me a choice sample of the first day's harvest. It must be offered to the LORD your God.

"You must not cook a young goat in its mother's milk.

20 "See, I am sending my angel before you to lead you safely to the land I have prepared for you. 21 Pay attention to him, and obey all of his instructions. Do not rebel against him, for he will not forgive your sins. He is my representative—he bears my name. 22 But if you are careful to obey him, following all my instructions, then I will be an enemy to your enemies, and I will oppose those who oppose you. 23 For my angel will go before you and bring you into the land of the Amorites, Hittites, Perizzites, Canaanites, Hivites, and Jebusites, so you may live there. And I will destroy them. 24 Do not worship the gods of these other nations or serve them in any way, and never follow their evil example. Instead, you must utterly conquer them and break down their shameful idols.

### GOSSIP ● ● • • •

**23:1 Making up or passing along false reports was strictly forbidden by God. Gossip, slander, and false witnessing undermine families, strain neighborhood cooperation, and make chaos of the justice system. Even if you do not initiate a lie, you become responsible if you pass it along. Don't circulate rumors; squelch them.**

25 "You must serve only the LORD your God. If you do, I will bless you with food and water, and I will keep you healthy. 26 There will be no miscarriages or infertility among your people, and I will give you long, full lives.

27 "I will send my terror upon all the people whose lands you invade, and they will panic before you. 28 I will send hornets ahead of you to drive out the Hivites, Canaanites, and Hittites. 29 But I will not do this all in one year because the land would become

**22:28** Or *Do not revile your judges.* **23:15** Hebrew *in the month of Abib.* This month of the Hebrew lunar calendar usually occurs in March and April. **23:16a** Or *Festival of Weeks.* **23:16b** This was later called the Festival of Shelters; see Lev 23:33-36.

# THE ARK

You may remember the scene from *Raiders of the Lost Ark*—the Nazis have captured the Ark of the Covenant and are marching off to a remote site to open it and reveal its mysteries. Our hero, Indiana Jones, having made approximately his 436th **DEATH-DEFYING** escape, now stands poised on a ridge above the column of soldiers. He aims a bazooka at the Ark, telling them to let his girlfriend go or he'll blow it up. Dr. Belloq, the evil leader of the Nazi procession, asks what will happen if they don't let her go. "Then," replies the steely-eyed hero, "your führer has no prize." "OK, Jones," Belloq calls, stepping away from the Ark. "You win. Blow it up. . . . Yes, blow it back to God. . . . We are simply passing through history. This . . . ," he pauses and points to the Ark, "this *is* history." Knowing what his adversary will do, Belloq says, "Do as you will."

As every American movie-goer knows—having seen *Raiders* at least five or six times—Indiana Jones does not blow up the Ark. He and his girl are taken captive (again) and the Ark is left to defend itself, which of course it does in *dramatic* fashion. What is there about the ancient Hebrew Ark of the Covenant that still fascinates us, thousands of years after its disappearance? The Ark was the center of WORSHIP for the people of Israel. It was, as Exodus 25 tells us, the place where God met with his people. First Chronicles 28:2 calls it a place where God could live— literally, "a footstool." It was *the* place among the people of Israel that represented the *presence* of God Almighty. The Ark of the Covenant also played a prominent role in their life as a nation. When the armies of Israel marched off to war, they carried the Ark in front, symbolizing that God was a strong warrior for his people. Opposing armies were utterly wiped out by the power of God working through it. But when Israel tried to rely on the Ark in a magical way—trusting in the Ark to do their fighting for them, regardless of their wickedness—they found that God was quite willing to let them suffer the consequences of their sin. (See 1 Samuel 4 for an example.)

The Israelites learned that they were to treat the Ark with RESPECT AND REVERENCE. Both 1 Samuel 6 and 2 Samuel 6 contain stories of men who died as a result of their disrespectful handling of the Ark. Thoughtless actions toward the Ark were considered thoughtless actions toward God himself, and God would not tolerate it. Yet the Ark was not God. It was not an idol made of gold and acacia wood that the people were supposed to worship. Many other pagan nations had "magic boxes" to worship. But the Ark was strictly a symbol of God's abiding presence with his people. That helps us understand another important truth: We don't have an Ark today because we don't need one. While the Ark was a powerful symbol of God's involvement with his children, we have witnessed something much more awesome: God himself has come and walked in the world. In Jesus, we have a living reminder of God's love and concern. John 1:14 tells us, "So the Word became human and lived here on earth among us. He was full of unfailing love and faithfulness. And we have seen his glory, the glory of the only Son of the Father." Those of us who follow Christ today have the Holy Spirit living in us. *We* are the DWELLING PLACE of the God of Israel, the one true living God of the universe! What an honor!

So what happened to the Ark of the Covenant? No, it's not in a warehouse in Washington, D.C. One legend says that the prophet Jeremiah, knowing through God's revelation that Jerusalem would be destroyed along with the Temple, took the Ark and hid it on Mount Nebo. But the best answer is that we simply don't know. What we do know is that when we receive Christ, he comes to live within us. We no longer need "outside help" from a strange object: **We have God himself in our lives.**

a wilderness, and the wild animals would become too many to control. [30]I will drive them out a little at a time until your population has increased enough to fill the land. [31]And I will fix your boundaries from the Red Sea to the Mediterranean Sea,* and from the southern deserts to the Euphrates River.* I will help you defeat the people now living in the land, and you will drive them out ahead of you.

[32]"Make no treaties with them and have nothing to do with their gods. [33]Do not even let them live among you! If you do, they will infect you with their sin of idol worship, and that would be disastrous for you."

CHAPTER **24** **THE PEOPLE PROMISE TO OBEY.** Then the LORD instructed Moses: "Come up here to me, and bring along Aaron, Nadab, Abihu, and seventy of Israel's leaders. All of them must worship at a distance. [2]You alone, Moses, are allowed to come near to the LORD. The others must not come too close. And remember, none of the other people are allowed to climb on the mountain at all."

[3]When Moses had announced to the people all the teachings and regulations the LORD had given him, they answered in unison, "We will do everything the LORD has told us to do."

[4]Then Moses carefully wrote down all the LORD's instructions. Early the next morning he built an altar at the foot of the mountain. He also set up twelve pillars around the altar, one for each of the twelve tribes of Israel. [5]Then he sent some of the young men to sacrifice young bulls as burnt offerings and peace offerings to the LORD. [6]Moses took half the blood from these animals and drew it off into basins. The other half he splashed against the altar.

[7]Then he took the Book of the Covenant and read it to the people. They all responded again, "We will do everything the LORD has commanded. We will obey."

[8]Then Moses sprinkled the blood from the basins over the people and said, "This blood confirms the covenant the LORD has made with you in giving you these laws."

[9]Then Moses, Aaron, Nadab, Abihu, and seventy of the leaders of Israel went up the mountain. [10]There they saw the God of Israel. Under his feet there seemed to be a pavement of brilliant sapphire, as clear as the heavens. [11]And though Israel's leaders saw God, he did not destroy them. In fact, they shared a meal together in God's presence!

[12]And the LORD said to Moses, "Come up to me on the mountain. Stay there while I give you the tablets of stone that I have inscribed with my instructions and commands. Then you will teach the people from them." [13]So Moses and his assistant Joshua climbed up the mountain of God.

[14]Moses told the other leaders, "Stay here and wait for us until we come back. If there are any problems while I am gone, consult with Aaron and Hur, who are here with you."

[15]Then Moses went up the mountain, and the cloud covered it. [16]And the glorious presence of the LORD rested upon Mount Sinai, and the cloud covered it for six days. On the seventh day the LORD called to Moses from the cloud. [17]The Israelites at the foot of the mountain saw an awesome sight. The awesome glory of the LORD on the mountaintop looked like a devouring fire. [18]Then Moses disappeared into the cloud as he climbed higher up the mountain. He stayed on the mountain forty days and forty nights.

CHAPTER **25** **HOW TO BUILD THE TABERNACLE.** The LORD said to Moses, [2]"Tell the people of Israel that everyone who wants to may bring me an offering. [3]Here is a list of items you may accept on my behalf: gold, silver, and bronze; [4]blue, purple, and scarlet yarn; fine linen; goat hair for cloth; [5]tanned ram skins and fine goatskin leather; acacia wood; [6]olive oil for the lamps; spices for the anointing oil and the fragrant incense; [7]onyx stones, and other stones to be set in the ephod and the chestpiece.

[8]"I want the people of Israel to build me a sacred residence where I can live among them. [9]You must make this Tabernacle and its furnishings exactly according to the plans I will show you.

[10]"Make an Ark of acacia wood—a sacred chest 3¾ feet long, 2¼ feet wide, and 2¼ feet high.* [11]Overlay it inside and outside with pure gold, and put a molding of gold all around it. [12]Cast four rings of gold for it, and attach them to its four feet, two rings on each side. [13]Make poles from acacia wood, and overlay them with gold. [14]Fit the poles into the rings at the sides of the Ark to carry it. [15]These carrying poles must never be taken from the rings; they are to be left there permanently. [16]When the Ark is finished, place inside it the stone tablets inscribed with the terms of the covenant,* which I will give to you.

[17]"Then make the Ark's cover—the place of atonement—out of pure gold. It must be 3¾ feet long and 2¼ feet wide. [18]Then use hammered gold to make two cherubim, and place them at the two ends of the atonement cover. [19]Attach the cherubim to each end of the atonement cover, making it all one piece. [20]The cherubim will face each other, looking down on the atonement cover with their wings spread out above it. [21]Place inside the Ark the stone tablets inscribed with the terms of the covenant, which I will give to you. Then put the atonement cover on top of the Ark. [22]I will meet with you there and talk to you from above the atonement cover between the gold cherubim that hover over the Ark of the Covenant.* From there I will give you my commands for the people of Israel.

[23]"Then make a table of acacia wood, 3 feet long, 1½ feet wide, and 2¼ feet high. [24]Overlay it with pure gold and run a molding of gold around it. [25]Put a rim

**23:31a** Hebrew *from the sea of reeds to the sea of the Philistines.* **23:31b** Hebrew *the river.* **25:10** Hebrew *2½ cubits* [1.1 meters] *long, 1½ cubits* [0.7 meters] *wide, and 1½ cubits high.* In this chapter, the distance measures are calculated from the Hebrew cubit at a ratio of 18 inches or 45 centimeters per cubit. **25:16** Hebrew *place inside it the Testimony;* also in 25:21. **25:22** Or *Ark of the Testimony.*

about three inches* wide around the top edge, and put a gold molding all around the rim. [26]Make four gold rings, and put the rings at the four corners by the four legs, [27]close to the rim around the top. These rings will support the poles used to carry the table. [28]Make these poles from acacia wood and overlay them with gold. [29]And make gold plates and dishes, as well as pitchers and bowls to be used in pouring out drink offerings. [30]You must always keep the special Bread of the Presence on the table before me.

[31]"Make a lampstand of pure, hammered gold. The entire lampstand and its decorations will be one piece—the base, center stem, lamp cups, buds, and blossoms. [32]It will have six branches, three branches going out from each side of the center stem. [33]Each of the six branches will hold a cup shaped like an almond blossom, complete with buds and petals. [34]The center stem of the lampstand will be decorated with four almond blossoms, complete with buds and petals. [35]One blossom will be set beneath each pair of branches where they extend from the center stem. [36]The decorations and branches must all be one piece with the stem, and they must be hammered from pure gold. [37]Then make the seven lamps for the lampstand, and set them so they reflect their light forward. [38]The lamp snuffers and trays must also be made of pure gold. [39]You will need seventy-five pounds* of pure gold for the lampstand and its accessories.

[40]"Be sure that you make everything according to the pattern I have shown you here on the mountain.

## CHAPTER 26

"Make the Tabernacle from ten sheets of fine linen. These sheets are to be decorated with blue, purple, and scarlet yarn, with figures of cherubim skillfully embroidered into them. [2]Each sheet must be forty-two feet long and six feet wide.* All ten sheets must be exactly the same size. [3]Join five of these sheets together into one set; then join the other five sheets into a second set. [4]Put loops of blue yarn along the edge of the last sheet in each set. [5]The fifty loops along the edge of one set are to match the fifty loops along the edge of the other. [6]Then make fifty gold clasps to fasten the loops of the two sets of sheets together, making the Tabernacle a single unit.

[7]"Make heavy sheets of cloth from goat hair to cover the Tabernacle. There must be eleven of these sheets, [8]each forty-five feet long and six feet wide. All eleven of these sheets must be exactly the same size. [9]Join five of these together into one set, and join the other six into a second set. The sixth sheet of the second set is to be doubled over at the entrance of the sacred tent. [10]Put fifty loops along the edge of the last sheet in each set, [11]and fasten them together with fifty bronze clasps. In this way, the two sets will become a single unit. [12]An extra half sheet of this roof covering will be left to hang over the back of the Tabernacle, [13]and the covering will hang down an extra eighteen inches on each side. [14]On top of these coverings place a layer of tanned ram skins, and over them put a layer of fine goatskin leather. This will complete the roof covering.

[15]"The framework of the Tabernacle will consist of frames made of acacia wood. [16]Each frame must be 15 feet high and 2¼ feet wide. [17]There will be two pegs on each frame so they can be joined to the next frame. All the frames must be made this way. [18]Twenty of these frames will support the south side of the Tabernacle. [19]They will fit into forty silver bases—two bases under each frame. [20]On the north side there will also be twenty of these frames, [21]with their forty silver bases, two bases for each frame. [22]On the west side there will be six frames, [23]along with an extra frame at each corner. [24]These corner frames will be connected at the bottom and firmly attached at the top with a single ring, forming a single unit. Both of these corner frames will be made the same way. [25]So there will be eight frames on that end of the Tabernacle, supported by sixteen silver bases—two bases under each frame.

[26]"Make crossbars of acacia wood to run across the frames, five crossbars for the north side of the Tabernacle [27]and five for the south side. Also make five crossbars for the rear of the Tabernacle, which will face westward. [28]The middle crossbar, halfway up the frames, will run all the way from one end of the Tabernacle to the other. [29]Overlay the frames with gold and make gold rings to support the crossbars. Overlay the crossbars with gold as well.

[30]"Set up this Tabernacle according to the design you were shown on the mountain.

[31]"Across the inside of the Tabernacle hang a special curtain made of fine linen, with cherubim skillfully embroidered into the cloth using blue, purple, and scarlet yarn. [32]Hang this inner curtain on gold hooks set into four posts made from acacia wood and overlaid with gold. The posts will fit into silver bases. [33]When the inner curtain is in place, put the Ark of the Covenant* behind it. This curtain will separate the Holy Place from the Most Holy Place.

### EASY ACCESS ●●•••

26:31 **This curtain separated the two sacred rooms in the Tabernacle—the Holy Place and the Most Holy Place. The priest entered the Holy Place each day to commune with God and tend to the altar of incense, the lampstand, and the table of the Bread of the Presence. The Most Holy Place was where God himself dwelt, his presence resting on the Ark of the Covenant. Only the high priest could enter the Most Holy Place. Even he could do so only once a year (on the Day of Atonement) to make atonement for the sins of the nation as a whole. When Jesus Christ died on the cross, the curtain in the Temple (which had replaced the Tabernacle) tore from top to bottom (Mark 15:38), symbolizing our free access to God because of Jesus' death. No longer do people have to approach God through priests and sacrifices.**

25:25 Hebrew *a handbreadth* [8 centimeters]. 25:39 Hebrew *1 talent* [34 kilograms]. 26:2 Hebrew *28 cubits* [12.6 meters] *long and 4 cubits* [1.8 meters] *wide.* In this chapter, the distance measures are calculated from the Hebrew cubit at a ratio of 18 inches or 45 centimeters per cubit.
26:33 Or *Ark of the Testimony;* also in 26:34.

34"Then put the Ark's cover—the place of atonement—on top of the Ark of the Covenant inside the Most Holy Place. 35Place the table and lampstand across the room from each other outside the inner curtain. The lampstand must be placed on the south side, and the table must be set toward the north.

36"Make another curtain from fine linen for the entrance of the sacred tent, and embroider exquisite designs into it, using blue, purple, and scarlet yarn. 37Hang this curtain on gold hooks set into five posts made from acacia wood and overlaid with gold. The posts will fit into five bronze bases.

## CHAPTER 27

**THE ALTAR.** "Using acacia wood, make a square altar 7½ feet wide, 7½ feet long, and 4½ feet high.* 2Make a horn at each of the four corners of the altar so the horns and altar are all one piece. Overlay the altar and its horns with bronze. 3The ash buckets, shovels, basins, meat hooks, and firepans will all be made of bronze. 4Make a bronze grating, with a metal ring at each corner. 5Fit the grating halfway down into the firebox, resting it on the ledge built there. 6For moving the altar, make poles from acacia wood, and overlay them with bronze. 7To carry it, put the poles into the rings at two sides of the altar. 8The altar must be hollow, made from planks. Be careful to build it just as you were shown on the mountain.

9"Then make a courtyard for the Tabernacle, enclosed with curtains made from fine linen. On the south side the curtains will stretch for 150 feet. 10They will be held up by twenty bronze posts that fit into twenty bronze bases. The curtains will be held up with silver hooks attached to the silver rods that are attached to the posts. 11It will be the same on the north side of the courtyard—150 feet of curtains held up by twenty posts fitted into bronze bases, with silver hooks and rods. 12The curtains on the west end of the courtyard will be 75 feet long, supported by ten posts set into ten bases. 13The east end will also be 75 feet long. 14The courtyard entrance will be on the east end, flanked by two curtains. The curtain on the right side will be 22½ feet long, supported by three posts set into three bases. 15The curtain on the left side will also be 22½ feet long, supported by three posts set into three bases.

16"For the entrance to the courtyard, make a curtain that is 30 feet long. Fashion it from fine linen, and decorate it with beautiful embroidery in blue, purple, and scarlet yarn. It will be attached to four posts that fit into four bases. 17All the posts around the courtyard must be connected by silver rods, using silver hooks. The posts are to be set in solid bronze bases. 18So the entire courtyard will be 150 feet long and 75 feet wide, with curtain walls 7½ feet high, made from fine linen. The bases supporting its walls will be made of bronze.

19"All the articles used in the work of the Tabernacle, including all the tent pegs used to support the Tabernacle and the courtyard curtains, must be made of bronze.

20"Tell the people of Israel to bring you pure olive oil for the lampstand, so it can be kept burning continually. 21The lampstand will be placed outside the inner curtain of the Most Holy Place in the Tabernacle.* Aaron and his sons will keep the lamps burning in the LORD's presence day and night. This is a permanent law for the people of Israel, and it must be kept by all future generations.

## CHAPTER 28

**CLOTHES FOR THE PRIESTS.** "Your brother, Aaron, and his sons, Nadab, Abihu, Eleazar, and Ithamar, will be set apart from the common people. They will be my priests and will minister to me. 2Make special clothing for Aaron to show his separation to God—beautiful garments that will lend dignity to his work. 3Instruct all those who have special skills as tailors to make the garments that will set Aaron apart from everyone else, so he may serve me as a priest. 4They are to make a chestpiece, an ephod, a robe, an embroidered tunic, a turban, and a sash. They will also make special garments for Aaron's sons to wear when they serve as priests before me. 5These items must be made of fine linen cloth and embroidered with gold thread and blue, purple, and scarlet yarn.

6"The ephod must be made of fine linen cloth and skillfully embroidered with gold thread and blue, purple, and scarlet yarn. 7It will consist of two pieces, front and back, joined at the shoulders with two shoulder-pieces. 8And the sash will be made of the same materials: fine linen cloth embroidered with gold thread and blue, purple, and scarlet yarn. 9Take two onyx stones and engrave on them the names of the tribes of Israel. 10Six names will be on each stone, naming all the tribes in the order of their ancestors' births. 11Engrave these names in the same way a gemcutter engraves a seal. Mount the stones in gold settings. 12Fasten the two stones on the shoulder-pieces of the ephod as memorial stones for the people of Israel. Aaron will carry these names before the LORD as a constant reminder. 13The settings are to be made of gold filigree, 14and two cords made of pure gold will be attached to the settings on the shoulders of the ephod.

15"Then, with the most careful workmanship, make a chestpiece that will be used to determine God's will. Use the same materials as you did for the ephod: fine linen cloth embroidered with gold thread and blue, purple, and scarlet yarn. 16This chestpiece will be made of two folds of cloth, forming a pouch nine inches* square. 17Four rows of gemstones* will be attached to it. The first row will contain a red carnelian, a chrysolite, and an emerald. 18The second row will contain a turquoise, a sapphire, and a white moonstone. 19The

**27:1** Hebrew *5 cubits* [2.3 meters] *wide, 5 cubits long, and 3 cubits* [1.4 meters] *high.* In this chapter, the distance measures are calculated from the Hebrew cubit at a ratio of 18 inches or 45 centimeters per cubit. **27:21** Hebrew *in the Tent of Meeting, outside of the inner curtain, in front of the Testimony.* **28:16** Hebrew *1 span* [23 centimeters]. **28:17** The identification of some of these gemstones is uncertain.

third row will contain a jacinth, an agate, and an amethyst. [20]The fourth row will contain a beryl, an onyx, and a jasper. All these stones will be set in gold. [21]Each stone will represent one of the tribes of Israel, and the name of that tribe will be engraved on it as though it were a seal.

[22]"To attach the chestpiece to the ephod, make braided cords of pure gold. [23]Then make two gold rings and attach them to the top corners of the chestpiece. [24]The two gold cords will go through the rings on the chestpiece, [25]and the ends of the cords will be tied to the gold settings on the shoulder-pieces of the ephod. [26]Then make two more gold rings, and attach them to the two lower inside corners of the chestpiece next to the ephod. [27]And make two more gold rings and attach them to the ephod near the sash. [28]Then attach the bottom rings of the chestpiece to the rings on the ephod with blue cords. This will hold the chestpiece securely to the ephod above the beautiful sash. [29]In this way, Aaron will carry the names of the tribes of Israel on the chestpiece over his heart when he goes into the presence of the LORD in the Holy Place. Thus, the LORD will be reminded of his people continually. [30]Insert into the pocket of the chestpiece the Urim and Thummim, to be carried over Aaron's heart when he goes into the LORD's presence. Thus, Aaron will always carry the objects used to determine the LORD's will for his people whenever he goes in before the LORD.

[31]"Make the robe of the ephod entirely of blue cloth, [32]with an opening for Aaron's head in the middle of it. The opening will be reinforced by a woven collar* so it will not tear. [33]Make pomegranates out of blue, purple, and scarlet yarn, and attach them to the hem of the robe, with gold bells between them. [34]The gold bells and pomegranates are to alternate all the way around the hem. [35]Aaron will wear this robe whenever he enters the Holy Place to minister to the LORD, and the bells will tinkle as he goes in and out of the LORD's presence. If he wears it, he will not die.

[36]"Next make a medallion of pure gold. Using the techniques of an engraver, inscribe it with these words: SET APART AS HOLY TO THE LORD. [37]This medallion will be attached to the front of Aaron's turban by means of a blue cord. [38]Aaron will wear it on his forehead, thus bearing the guilt connected with any errors regarding the sacred offerings of the people of Israel. He must always wear it so the LORD will accept the people.

[39]"Weave Aaron's patterned tunic from fine linen cloth. Fashion the turban out of this linen as well. Also make him an embroidered sash.

[40]"Then for Aaron's sons, make tunics, sashes, and headdresses to give them dignity and respect. [41]Clothe Aaron and his sons with these garments, and then anoint and ordain them. Set them apart as holy so they can serve as my priests. [42]Also make linen underclothes for them, to be worn next to their bodies, reaching from waist to thigh. [43]These must be worn whenever Aaron and his sons enter the Tabernacle* or approach the altar in the Holy Place to perform their duties. Thus they will not incur guilt and die. This law is permanent for Aaron and his descendants.

## CHAPTER 29

**HOW TO DEDICATE THE PRIESTS.** "This is the ceremony for the dedication of Aaron and his sons as priests: Take a young bull and two rams with no physical defects. [2]Then using fine wheat flour and no yeast, make loaves of bread, thin cakes mixed with olive oil, and wafers with oil poured over them. [3]Place these various kinds of bread in a single basket, and present them at the entrance of the Tabernacle, along with the young bull and the two rams.

[4]"Present Aaron and his sons at the entrance of the Tabernacle,* and wash them with water. [5]Then put Aaron's tunic on him, along with the embroidered robe of the ephod, the ephod itself, the chestpiece, and the sash. [6]And place on his head the turban with the gold medallion. [7]Then take the anointing oil and pour it over his head. [8]Next present his sons, and dress them in their tunics [9]with their woven sashes and their headdresses. They will then be priests forever. In this way, you will ordain Aaron and his sons.

### GET SERIOUS! ● ● • • •

29:10-41 **Why the detailed rituals surrounding these sacrifices? Partly, it was for "quality control"—a centralized, standardized form of worship prevented problems from arising because of individuals worshiping on their own. Also, it differentiated the Hebrews from the heathen Canaanites they would meet in the Promised Land. These heathens performed sacrifices to their gods wherever, however, and whenever they wanted to. Finally, the Hebrew form of worship showed Israel that they should be as serious about their relationship with God as he was about his relationship with them. How about you? Are you serious about your relationship with the Lord?**

[10]"Then bring the young bull to the entrance of the Tabernacle, and Aaron and his sons will lay their hands on its head. [11]You will then slaughter it in the LORD's presence at the entrance of the Tabernacle. [12]Smear some of its blood on the horns of the altar with your finger, and pour out the rest at the base of the altar. [13]Take all the fat that covers the internal organs, also the long lobe of the liver and the two kidneys with their fat, and burn them on the altar. [14]Then take the carcass (including the skin and the dung) outside the camp, and burn it as a sin offering.

[15]"Next Aaron and his sons must lay their hands on the head of one of the rams [16]as it is slaughtered. Its blood will be collected and sprinkled on the sides of the altar. [17]Cut up the ram and wash off the internal organs and the legs. Set them alongside the head and the other pieces of the body, [18]and burn them all on the altar. This is a burnt offering to the LORD, which is very pleasing to him.

**28:32** The meaning of the Hebrew is uncertain. **28:43** Hebrew *Tent of Meeting.* **29:4** Hebrew *Tent of Meeting;* also in 29:10, 11, 30, 32, 42, 44.

19 “Now take the other ram and have Aaron and his sons lay their hands on its head 20 as it is slaughtered. Collect the blood and place some of it on the tip of the right earlobes of Aaron and his sons. Also put it on their right thumbs and the big toes of their right feet. Sprinkle the rest of the blood on the sides of the altar. 21 Then take some of the blood from the altar and mix it with some of the anointing oil. Sprinkle it on Aaron and his sons and on their clothes. In this way, they and their clothing will be set apart as holy to the LORD.

22 “Since this is the ram for the ordination of Aaron and his sons, take the fat of the ram, including the fat tail and the fat that covers the internal organs. Also, take the long lobe of the liver, the two kidneys with their fat, and the right thigh. 23 Then take one loaf of bread, one cake mixed with olive oil, and one wafer from the basket of yeastless bread that was placed before the LORD. 24 Put all these in the hands of Aaron and his sons to be lifted up as a special gift to the LORD. 25 Afterward take the bread from their hands, and burn it on the altar as a burnt offering that will be pleasing to the LORD. 26 Then take the breast of Aaron’s ordination ram, and lift it up in the LORD’s presence as a special gift to him. Afterward keep it for yourself.

27 “Set aside as holy the parts of the ordination ram that belong to Aaron and his sons. This includes the breast and the thigh that were lifted up before the LORD in the ordination ceremony. 28 In the future, whenever the people of Israel offer up peace offerings or thanksgiving offerings to the LORD, these parts will be the regular share of Aaron and his descendants.

29 “Aaron’s sacred garments must be preserved for his descendants who will succeed him, so they can be anointed and ordained in them. 30 Whoever is the next high priest after Aaron will wear these clothes for seven days before beginning to minister in the Tabernacle and the Holy Place.

31 “Take the ram used in the ordination ceremony, and boil its meat in a sacred place. 32 Aaron and his sons are to eat this meat, along with the bread in the basket, at the Tabernacle entrance. 33 They alone may eat the meat and bread used for their atonement in the ordination ceremony. The ordinary people may not eat them, for these things are set apart and holy. 34 If any of the ordination meat or bread remains until the morning, it must be burned. It may not be eaten, for it is holy.

35 “This is how you will ordain Aaron and his sons to their offices. The ordination ceremony will go on for seven days. 36 Each day you must sacrifice a young bull as an offering for the atonement of sin. Afterward make an offering to cleanse the altar. Purify the altar by making atonement for it; make it holy by anointing it with oil. 37 Make atonement for the altar every day for seven days. After that, the altar will be exceedingly holy, and whatever touches it will become holy.

38 “This is what you are to offer on the altar. Offer two one-year-old lambs each day, 39 one in the morning and the other in the evening. 40 With one of them, offer two quarts of fine flour mixed with one quart of olive oil; also, offer one quart of wine* as a drink offering. 41 Offer the other lamb in the evening, along with the same offerings of flour and wine as in the morning. It will be a fragrant offering to the LORD, an offering made by fire.

42 “This is to be a daily burnt offering given from generation to generation. Offer it in the LORD’s presence at the Tabernacle entrance, where I will meet you and speak with you. 43 I will meet the people of Israel there, and the Tabernacle will be sanctified by my glorious presence. 44 Yes, I will make the Tabernacle and the altar most holy, and I will set apart Aaron and his sons as holy, that they may be my priests. 45 I will live among the people of Israel and be their God, 46 and they will know that I am the LORD their God. I am the one who brought them out of Egypt so that I could live among them. I am the LORD their God.

## CHAPTER 30 PREPARATIONS FOR WORSHIP.

“Then make a small altar out of acacia wood for burning incense. 2 It must be eighteen inches square and three feet high,* with horns at the corners carved from the same piece of wood as the altar. 3 Overlay the top, sides, and horns of the altar with pure gold, and run a gold molding around the entire altar. 4 Beneath the molding, on opposite sides of the altar, attach two gold rings to support the carrying poles. 5 The poles are to be made of acacia wood and overlaid with gold. 6 Place the incense altar just outside the inner curtain, opposite the Ark’s cover—the place of atonement—that rests on the Ark of the Covenant.* I will meet with you there.

7 “Every morning when Aaron trims the lamps, he must burn fragrant incense on the altar. 8 And each evening when he tends to the lamps, he must again burn incense in the LORD’s presence. This must be done from generation to generation. 9 Do not offer any unholy incense on this altar, or any burnt offerings, grain offerings, or drink offerings.

10 “Once a year Aaron must purify the altar by placing on its horns the blood from the offering made for the atonement of sin. This will be a regular, annual event from generation to generation, for this is the LORD’s supremely holy altar.”

11 And the LORD said to Moses, 12 “Whenever you take a census of the people of Israel, each man who is counted must pay a ransom for himself to the LORD. Then there will be no plagues among the people as you count them. 13 His payment to the LORD will be one-fifth of an ounce* of silver. 14 All who have reached their twentieth birthday must give this offering to the

29:40 Hebrew *1/10 of an ephah* [2 liters] *of fine flour . . . 1/4 of a hin* [1 liter] *of olive oil . . . 1/4 of a hin of wine.* 30:2 Hebrew *1 cubit* [45 centimeters] *square and 2 cubits* [90 centimeters] *high.* 30:6 Or *Ark of the Testimony;* also in 30:26, 36. 30:13 Hebrew *half a shekel* [6 grams], *according to the sanctuary shekel, 20 gerahs to each shekel.*

LORD. [15]When this offering is given to the LORD to make atonement for yourselves, the rich must not give more, and the poor must not give less. [16]Use this money for the care of the Tabernacle.* It will bring you, the Israelites, to the LORD's attention, and it will make atonement for your lives."

## BUY OFF GOD? ● ● • • •

30:11-16 **The atonement money was like a census tax. It continued the principle that all the people belonged to God and therefore needed to be redeemed by a sacrifice. Whenever a census took place, everyone, both rich and poor, was required to pay a ransom. God does not discriminate between people (see Acts 10:34; Galatians 3:28). All of us need mercy and forgiveness because of our sinful thoughts and actions. There is no way the rich person can buy off God, and no way the poor can avoid paying. God's demand is that all of us come humbly before him to be forgiven and brought into his family.**

[17]And the LORD said to Moses, [18]"Make a large bronze washbasin with a bronze pedestal. Put it between the Tabernacle and the altar, and fill it with water. [19]Aaron and his sons will wash their hands and feet there [20]before they go into the Tabernacle to appear before the LORD and before they approach the altar to burn offerings to the LORD. They must always wash before ministering in these ways, or they will die. [21]This is a permanent law for Aaron and his descendants, to be kept from generation to generation."

[22]Then the LORD said to Moses, [23]"Collect choice spices—12½ pounds of pure myrrh, 6¼ pounds* each of cinnamon and of sweet cane, [24]12½ pounds of cassia, and one gallon* of olive oil. [25]Blend these ingredients into a holy anointing oil. [26]Use this scented oil to anoint the Tabernacle, the Ark of the Covenant, [27]the table and all its utensils, the lampstand and all its accessories, the incense altar, [28]the altar of burnt offering with all its utensils, and the large washbasin with its pedestal. [29]Sanctify them to make them entirely holy. After this, whatever touches them will become holy. [30]Use this oil also to anoint Aaron and his sons, sanctifying them so they can minister before me as priests. [31]And say to the people of Israel, 'This will always be my holy anointing oil. [32]It must never be poured on the body of an ordinary person, and you must never make any of it for yourselves. It is holy, and you must treat it as holy. [33]Anyone who blends scented oil like it or puts any of it on someone who is not a priest will be cut off from the community.'"

[34]These were the LORD's instructions to Moses concerning the incense: "Gather sweet spices—resin droplets, mollusk scent, galbanum, and pure frankincense—weighing out the same amounts of each. [35]Using the usual techniques of the incense maker, refine it to produce a pure and holy incense. [36]Beat some of it very fine and put some of it in front of the Ark of the Covenant, where I will meet with you in the Tabernacle. This incense is most holy. [37]Never make this incense for yourselves. It is reserved for the LORD, and you must treat it as holy. [38]Those who make it for their own enjoyment will be cut off from the community."

CHAPTER **31** **WORKMEN GIVEN SPECIAL SKILL.** The LORD also said to Moses, [2]"Look, I have chosen Bezalel son of Uri, grandson of Hur, of the tribe of Judah. [3]I have filled him with the Spirit of God, giving him great wisdom, intelligence, and skill in all kinds of crafts. [4]He is able to create beautiful objects from gold, silver, and bronze. [5]He is skilled in cutting and setting gemstones and in carving wood. Yes, he is a master at every craft!

[6]"And I have appointed Oholiab son of Ahisamach, of the tribe of Dan, to be his assistant. Moreover, I have given special skill to all the naturally talented craftsmen so they can make all the things I have instructed you to make: [7]the Tabernacle itself; the Ark of the Covenant;* the Ark's cover—the place of atonement; all the furnishings of the Tabernacle; [8]the table and all its utensils; the gold lampstand with all its accessories; the incense altar; [9]the altar of burnt offering with all its utensils; the washbasin and its pedestal; [10]the beautifully stitched, holy garments for Aaron the priest, and the garments for his sons to wear as they minister as priests; [11]the anointing oil; and the special incense for the Holy Place. They must follow exactly all the instructions I have given you."

[12]The LORD then gave these further instructions to Moses: [13]"Tell the people of Israel to keep my Sabbath day, for the Sabbath is a sign of the covenant between me and you forever. It helps you to remember that I am the LORD, who makes you holy. [14]Yes, keep the Sabbath day, for it is holy. Anyone who desecrates it must die; anyone who works on that day will be cut off from the community. [15]Work six days only, but the seventh day must be a day of total rest. I repeat: Because the LORD considers it a holy day, anyone who works on the Sabbath must be put to death. [16]The people of Israel must keep the Sabbath day forever. [17]It is a permanent sign of my covenant with them. For in six days the LORD made heaven and earth, but he rested on the seventh day and was refreshed."

## IDOLS ● ● • • •

32:1-10 **Idols again! Even though Israel had seen the invisible God in action, they still wanted the familiar gods they could see and shape into whatever image they desired. How like them we are! Our great temptation is still to shape God to our liking, to make him convenient to obey or ignore. God responds in great anger when his mercy is trampled on. The gods we create blind us to the love God wants to shower on us. God cannot work in us when we elevate anyone or anything above him. What idols do you have in your life?**

30:16 Hebrew *Tent of Meeting;* also in 30:18, 20, 26, 36. 30:23 Hebrew *500 shekels* [5.7 kilograms] *of pure myrrh, 250 shekels* [2.9 kilograms]. 30:24 Hebrew *500 shekels* [5.7 kilograms] *of cassia, according to the sanctuary shekel, and 1 hin* [3.8 liters]. 31:7 Hebrew *the Tent of Meeting; the Ark of the Testimony.*

[18]Then as the LORD finished speaking with Moses
on Mount Sinai, he gave him the two stone tablets
inscribed with the terms of the covenant,* written by
the finger of God.

CHAPTER **32** **THE GOLDEN CALF.** When Moses
failed to come back down the mountain right away,
the people went to Aaron. "Look," they said, "make
us some gods who can lead us. This man Moses, who
brought us here from Egypt, has disappeared. We
don't know what has happened to him."
[2]So Aaron said, "Tell your wives and sons and
daughters to take off their gold earrings, and then
bring them to me."
[3]All the people obeyed Aaron and brought him
their gold earrings. [4]Then Aaron took the gold,
melted it down, and molded and tooled it into the
shape of a calf. The people exclaimed, "O Israel,
these are the gods who brought you out of Egypt!"
[5]When Aaron saw how excited the people were
about it, he built an altar in front of the calf and
announced, "Tomorrow there will be a festival to the
LORD!"
[6]So the people got up early the next morning to
sacrifice burnt offerings and peace offerings. After
this, they celebrated with feasting and drinking, and
indulged themselves in pagan revelry.
[7]Then the LORD told Moses, "Quick! Go down the
mountain! The people you
brought from Egypt have defiled
themselves. [8]They have already
turned from the way I commanded them to live. They have
made an idol shaped like a calf,
and they have worshiped and
sacrificed to it. They are saying,
'These are your gods, O Israel,
who brought you out of Egypt.'"
[9]Then the LORD said, "I have
seen how stubborn and rebellious these people are. [10]Now
leave me alone so my anger can
blaze against them and destroy
them all. Then I will make you,
Moses, into a great nation instead of them."
[11]But Moses pleaded with the
LORD his God not to do it.
"O LORD!" he exclaimed. "Why
are you so angry with your own
people whom you brought from
the land of Egypt with such great
power and mighty acts? [12]The
Egyptians will say, 'God tricked
them into coming to the mountains so he could kill them and
wipe them from the face of the
earth.' Turn away from your fierce
anger. Change your mind about
this terrible disaster you are planning against your people! [13]Remember your covenant
with your servants—Abraham, Isaac, and Jacob.* You
swore by your own self, 'I will make your descendants
as numerous as the stars of heaven. Yes, I will give them
all of this land that I have promised to your descendants, and they will possess it forever.'"
[14]So the LORD withdrew his threat and didn't bring
against his people the disaster he had threatened.
[15]Then Moses turned and went down the mountain. He held in his hands the two stone tablets
inscribed with the terms of the covenant.* They were
inscribed on both sides, front and back. [16]These
stone tablets were God's work; the words on them
were written by God himself.
[17]When Joshua heard the noise of the people
shouting below them, he exclaimed to Moses, "It
sounds as if there is a war in the camp!"
[18]But Moses replied, "No, it's neither a cry of victory
nor a cry of defeat. It is the sound of a celebration."

## PRAYER POWER ● ● • • •

**32:9-14** **God was ready to destroy the whole nation because of the people's sin. But Moses pleaded for mercy, and God spared them. This is one of the countless examples in Scripture of how prayer can make a difference. Don't neglect prayer because a situation seems irreversible. Make a daily prayer list and spend time praying for others. Prayer can change things.**

## "Here's what I did..."

I loved ballet. I learned how to dance when I was 5 years old and had been doing it ever since. I practiced every day, took lessons at least once a week. I dreamed of someday joining the American Ballet Company. By the time I got to high school, ballet had become my life. Everything revolved around my dancing—even my social life. If I had a recital, I dropped out of every other activity in order to practice. And I was obsessed with my weight, unwilling to gain even a few extra ounces that might jeopardize my figure.

When I became a Christian, I never dreamed it would affect my ballet. But one day in church the sermon was on the first commandment. The pastor talked about how certain things can become gods to us if we let them become more important than God. I thought about the amount of time I spent practicing my ballet compared to the amount of time I spent reading the Bible and praying. Had ballet become my idol?

I began to pray about it, and God showed me that I had let ballet become more important than him. I decided to spend no more time practicing than I did reading the Bible and praying. I cut down on my dancing lessons and got involved in our church's youth group. It's been difficult to let up on dancing, but now it's OK that dancing is my second love. Because my first love is Jesus.

*Kristy*
AGE 16

31:18 Hebrew *the Testimony.* 32:13 Hebrew *Israel.* 32:15 Hebrew *the Testimony.*

[19]When they came near the camp, Moses saw the calf and the dancing. In terrible anger, he threw the stone tablets to the ground, smashing them at the foot of the mountain. [20]He took the calf they had made and melted it in the fire. And when the metal had cooled, he ground it into powder and mixed it with water. Then he made the people drink it.

[21]After that, he turned to Aaron. "What did the people do to you?" he demanded. "How did they ever make you bring such terrible sin upon them?"

[22]"Don't get upset, sir," Aaron replied. "You yourself know these people and what a wicked bunch they are. [23]They said to me, 'Make us some gods to lead us, for something has happened to this man Moses, who led us out of Egypt.' [24]So I told them, 'Bring me your gold earrings.' When they brought them to me, I threw them into the fire—and out came this calf!"

[25]When Moses saw that Aaron had let the people get completely out of control—and much to the amusement of their enemies—[26]he stood at the entrance to the camp and shouted, "All of you who are on the LORD's side, come over here and join me." And all the Levites came.

[27]He told them, "This is what the LORD, the God of Israel, says: Strap on your swords! Go back and forth from one end of the camp to the other, killing even your brothers, friends, and neighbors." [28]The Levites obeyed Moses, and about three thousand people died that day.

[29]Then Moses told the Levites, "Today you have been ordained for the service of the LORD, for you obeyed him even though it meant killing your own sons and brothers. Because of this, he will now give you a great blessing."

[30]The next day Moses said to the people, "You have committed a terrible sin, but I will return to the LORD on the mountain. Perhaps I will be able to obtain forgiveness for you."

[31]So Moses returned to the LORD and said, "Alas, these people have committed a terrible sin. They have made gods of gold for themselves. [32]But now, please forgive their sin—and if not, then blot me out of the record you are keeping."

[33]The LORD replied to Moses, "I will blot out whoever has sinned against me. [34]Now go, lead the people to the place I told you about. Look! My angel will lead the way before you! But when I call the people to account, I will certainly punish them for their sins."

[35]And the LORD sent a great plague upon the people because they had worshiped the calf Aaron had made.

## CHAPTER 33

**THE PEOPLE ARE SORRY.** The LORD said to Moses, "Now that you have brought these people out of Egypt, lead them to the land I solemnly promised Abraham, Isaac, and Jacob. I told them long ago that I would give this land to their descendants. [2]And I will send an angel before you to drive out the Canaanites, Amorites, Hittites, Perizzites, Hivites, and Jebusites. [3]Theirs is a land flowing with milk and honey. But I will not travel along with you, for you are a stubborn, unruly people. If I did, I would be tempted to destroy you along the way."

[4]When the people heard these stern words, they went into mourning and refused to wear their jewelry and ornaments. [5]For the LORD had told Moses to tell them, "You are an unruly, stubborn people. If I were there among you for even a moment, I would destroy you. Remove your jewelry and ornaments until I decide what to do with you." [6]So from the time they left Mount Sinai,* the Israelites wore no more jewelry.

[7]It was Moses' custom to set up the tent known as the Tent of Meeting far outside the camp. Everyone who wanted to consult with the LORD would go there.

[8]Whenever Moses went out to the Tent of Meeting, all the people would get up and stand in their tent entrances. They would all watch Moses until he disappeared inside. [9]As he went into the tent, the pillar of cloud would come down and hover at the entrance while the LORD spoke with Moses. [10]Then all the people would stand and bow low at their tent entrances. [11]Inside the Tent of Meeting, the LORD would speak to Moses face to face, as a man speaks to his friend. Afterward Moses would return to the camp, but the young man who assisted him, Joshua son of Nun, stayed behind in the Tent of Meeting.

### FRIENDS ● ● • • •

33:11 **God and Moses talked like two friends. Friends trust each other, talk to each other, and have common interests. No one can drive wedges between them. Moses never knew where he was going with God, and it didn't matter. He knew with whom he was going, and that was all that mattered.**

[12]Moses said to the LORD, "You have been telling me, 'Take these people up to the Promised Land.' But you haven't told me whom you will send with me. You call me by name and tell me I have found favor with you. [13]Please, if this is really so, show me your intentions so I will understand you more fully and do exactly what you want me to do. Besides, don't forget that this nation is your very own people."

[14]And the LORD replied, "I will personally go with you, Moses. I will give you rest—everything will be fine for you."

[15]Then Moses said, "If you don't go with us personally, don't let us move a step from this place. [16]If you don't go with us, how will anyone ever know that your people and I have found favor with you? How else will they know we are special and distinct from all other people on the earth?"

[17]And the LORD replied to Moses, "I will indeed do what you have asked, for you have found favor with me, and you are my friend."

33:6 Hebrew *Horeb,* another name for Sinai.

18 Then Moses had one more request. "Please let me see your glorious presence," he said.

19 The LORD replied, "I will make all my goodness pass before you, and I will call out my name, 'the LORD,' to you. I will show kindness to anyone I choose, and I will show mercy to anyone I choose. 20 But you may not look directly at my face, for no one may see me and live." 21 The LORD continued, "Stand here on this rock beside me. 22 As my glorious presence passes by, I will put you in the cleft of the rock and cover you with my hand until I have passed. 23 Then I will remove my hand, and you will see me from behind. But my face will not be seen."

## CHAPTER 34 MOSES TALKS WITH GOD.

The LORD told Moses, "Prepare two stone tablets like the first ones. I will write on them the same words that were on the tablets you smashed. 2 Be ready in the morning to come up Mount Sinai and present yourself to me there on the top of the mountain. 3 No one else may come with you. In fact, no one is allowed anywhere on the mountain. Do not even let the flocks or herds graze near the mountain."

4 So Moses cut two tablets of stone like the first ones. Early in the morning he climbed Mount Sinai as the LORD had told him, carrying the two stone tablets in his hands.

5 Then the LORD came down in a pillar of cloud and called out his own name, "the LORD," as Moses stood there in his presence. 6 He passed in front of Moses and said, "I am the LORD, I am the LORD, the merciful and gracious God. I am slow to anger and rich in unfailing love and faithfulness. 7 I show this unfailing love to many thousands by forgiving every kind of sin and rebellion. Even so I do not leave sin unpunished, but I punish the children for the sins of their parents to the third and fourth generations."

8 Moses immediately fell to the ground and worshiped. 9 And he said, "If it is true that I have found favor in your sight, O Lord, then please go with us. Yes, this is an unruly and stubborn people, but please pardon our iniquity and our sins. Accept us as your own special possession."

10 The LORD replied, "All right. This is the covenant I am going to make with you. I will perform wonders that have never been done before anywhere in all the earth or in any nation. And all the people around you will see the power of the LORD—the awesome power I will display through you. 11 Your responsibility is to obey all the commands I am giving you today. Then I will surely drive out all those who stand in your way—the Amorites, Canaanites, Hittites, Perizzites, Hivites, and Jebusites.

12 "Be very careful never to make treaties with the people in the land where you are going. If you do, you soon will be following their evil ways. 13 Instead, you must break down their pagan altars, smash the sacred pillars they worship, and cut down their carved images. 14 You must worship no other gods, but only the LORD, for he is a God who is passionate about his relationship with you.

15 "Do not make treaties of any kind with the people living in the land. They are spiritual prostitutes, committing adultery against me by sacrificing to their gods. If you make peace with them, they will invite you to go with them to worship their gods, and you are likely to do it. 16 And you will accept their daughters, who worship other gods, as wives for your sons. Then they will cause your sons to commit adultery against me by worshiping other gods. 17 You must make no gods for yourselves at all.

18 "Be sure to celebrate the Festival of Unleavened Bread for seven days, just as I instructed you, at the appointed time each year in early spring,* for that was when you left Egypt.

19 "Every firstborn male belongs to me—of both cattle and sheep. 20 A firstborn male donkey may be redeemed from the LORD by presenting a lamb in its place. But if you decide not to make the exchange, you must kill the donkey by breaking its neck. However, you must redeem every firstborn son. No one is allowed to appear before me without a gift.

21 "Six days are set aside for work, but on the Sabbath day you must rest, even during the seasons of plowing and harvest. 22 And you must remember to celebrate the Festival of Harvest* with the first crop of the wheat harvest, and celebrate the Festival of the Final Harvest* at the end of the harvest season. 23 Three times each year all the men of Israel must appear before the Sovereign LORD, the God of Israel. 24 No one will attack and conquer your land when you go to appear before the LORD your God those three times each year. I will drive out the nations that stand in your way and will enlarge your boundaries.

25 "You must not offer bread made with yeast as a sacrifice to me. And none of the meat of the Passover lamb may be kept over until the following morning. 26 You must bring the best of the first of each year's crop to the house of the LORD your God.

"You must not cook a young goat in its mother's milk."

27 And the LORD said to Moses, "Write down all these instructions, for they represent the terms of my covenant with you and with Israel."

28 Moses was up on the mountain with the LORD forty days and forty nights. In all that time he neither

### WONDERFUL MERCY ● ● ● • •

34:6-7 **Moses had asked to see God's glorious presence (33:18), and this was God's response. What is God's glory? It is his character, his nature, his way of relating to his creatures. Notice that God did not give Moses a vision of his power and majesty, but rather of his love. God's glory is revealed in his mercy, grace, compassion, faithfulness, forgiveness, and justice. God's love and mercy are truly wonderful, and we benefit from them. We can respond and give glory to God when our character resembles his.**

**34:18** Hebrew *in the month of Abib.* This month of the Hebrew lunar calendar usually occurs in March and April. **34:22a** Or *Festival of Weeks.* **34:22b** This was later called the Festival of Shelters; see Lev 23:33-36.

ate nor drank. At that time he wrote the terms of the covenant—the Ten Commandments—on the stone tablets.

[29]When Moses came down the mountain carrying the stone tablets inscribed with the terms of the covenant,* he wasn't aware that his face glowed because he had spoken to the LORD face to face. [30]And when Aaron and the people of Israel saw the radiance of Moses' face, they were afraid to come near him.

[31]But Moses called to them and asked Aaron and the community leaders to come over and talk with him. [32]Then all the people came, and Moses gave them the instructions the LORD had given him on Mount Sinai. [33]When Moses had finished speaking with them, he put a veil over his face. [34]But whenever he went into the Tent of Meeting to speak with the LORD, he removed the veil until he came out again. Then he would give the people whatever instructions the LORD had given him, [35]and the people would see his face aglow. Afterward he would put the veil on again until he returned to speak with the LORD.

CHAPTER **35** **GIFTS FOR THE TABERNACLE.** Now Moses called a meeting of all the people and told them, "You must obey these instructions from the LORD. [2]Each week, work for six days only. The seventh day is a day of total rest, a holy day that belongs to the LORD. Anyone who works on that day will die. [3]Do not even light fires in your homes on that day."

[4]Then Moses said to all the people, "This is what the LORD has commanded. [5]Everyone is invited to bring these offerings to the LORD: gold, silver, and bronze; [6]blue, purple, and scarlet yarn; fine linen; goat hair for cloth; [7]tanned ram skins and fine goatskin leather; acacia wood; [8]olive oil for the lamps; spices for the anointing oil and the fragrant incense; [9]onyx stones, and other stones to be set in the ephod and the chestpiece.

[10]"Come, all of you who are gifted craftsmen. Construct everything that the LORD has commanded: [11]the entire Tabernacle, including the sacred tent and its coverings, the clasps, frames, crossbars, posts, and bases; [12]the Ark and its poles; the Ark's cover—the place of atonement; the inner curtain to enclose the Ark in the Most Holy Place; [13]the table, its carrying poles, and all of its utensils; the Bread of the Presence; [14]the lampstand and its accessories; the lamp cups and the oil for lighting; [15]the incense altar and its carrying poles; the anointing oil and fragrant incense; the curtain for the entrance of the Tabernacle; [16]the altar of burnt offering; the bronze grating of the altar and its carrying poles and utensils; the large washbasin with its pedestal; [17]the curtains for the walls of the courtyard; the posts and their bases; the curtain for the entrance to the courtyard; [18]the tent pegs of the Tabernacle and courtyard and their cords; [19]the beautifully stitched clothing for the priests to wear while ministering in the Holy Place; the sacred

**POCKETBOOKS ● ● • • •**

35:21 **Those whose hearts were stirred by God gave cheerfully to the Tabernacle. They gave with great enthusiasm because they knew how important their giving was to the completion of God's house. Airline pilots and computer operators can push test buttons to see if their equipment is functioning properly. God has a quick test button he can push to see the level of our commitment—our pocketbook. Generous people aren't necessarily faithful to God. But faithful people are always generous.**

garments for Aaron and his sons to wear while officiating as priests."

[20]So all the people left Moses and went to their tents to prepare their gifts. [21]If their hearts were stirred and they desired to do so, they brought to the LORD their offerings of materials for the Tabernacle* and its furnishings and for the holy garments. [22]Both men and women came, all whose hearts were willing. Some brought to the LORD their offerings of gold—medallions, earrings, rings from their fingers, and necklaces. They presented gold objects of every kind to the LORD. [23]Others brought blue, purple, and scarlet yarn, fine linen, or goat hair for cloth. Some gave tanned ram skins or fine goatskin leather. [24]Others brought silver and bronze objects as their offering to the LORD. And those who had acacia wood brought it.

[25]All the women who were skilled in sewing and spinning prepared blue, purple, and scarlet yarn, and fine linen cloth, and they brought them in. [26]All the women who were willing used their skills to spin and weave the goat hair into cloth. [27]The leaders brought onyx stones and the other gemstones to be used for the ephod and the chestpiece. [28]They also brought spices and olive oil for the light, the anointing oil, and the fragrant incense. [29]So the people of Israel—every man and woman who wanted to help in the work the LORD had given them through Moses—brought their offerings to the LORD.

[30]And Moses told them, "The LORD has chosen Bezalel son of Uri, grandson of Hur, of the tribe of Judah. [31]The LORD has filled Bezalel with the Spirit of God, giving him great wisdom, intelligence, and skill in all kinds of crafts. [32]He is able to create beautiful objects from gold, silver, and bronze. [33]He is skilled in cutting and setting gemstones and in carving wood. In fact, he has every necessary skill. [34]And the LORD has given both him and Oholiab son of Ahisamach, of the tribe of Dan, the ability to teach their skills to others. [35]The LORD has given them special skills as jewelers, designers, weavers, and embroiderers in blue, purple, and scarlet yarn on fine linen cloth. They excel in all the crafts needed for the work.

CHAPTER **36** **BUILDING THE TABERNACLE.** "Bezalel, Oholiab, and the other craftsmen whom the LORD has gifted with wisdom, skill, and intelligence will construct and furnish the Tabernacle, just as the LORD has commanded."

[2]So Moses told Bezalel and Oholiab to begin the

34:29 Hebrew *the Testimony.* 35:21 Hebrew *Tent of Meeting.*

work, along with all those who were specially gifted by the LORD. [3]Moses gave them the materials donated by the people for the completion of the sanctuary. Additional gifts were brought each morning. [4]But finally the craftsmen left their work to meet with Moses. [5]"We have more than enough materials on hand now to complete the job the LORD has given us to do!" they exclaimed.

[6]So Moses gave the command, and this message was sent throughout the camp: "Bring no more materials! You have already given more than enough." So the people stopped bringing their offerings. [7]Their contributions were more than enough to complete the whole project.

[8]The skilled weavers first made ten sheets from fine linen. One of the craftsmen then embroidered blue, purple, and scarlet cherubim into them. [9]Each sheet was exactly the same size—forty-two feet long and six feet wide.* [10]Five of these sheets were joined together to make one set, and a second set was made of the other five. [11]Fifty blue loops were placed along the edge of the last sheet in each set. [12]The fifty loops along the edge of the first set of sheets matched the loops along the edge of the second set. [13]Then fifty gold clasps were made to connect the loops on the edge of each set. Thus the Tabernacle was joined together in one piece.

[14]Above the Tabernacle, a roof covering was made from eleven sheets of cloth made from goat hair. [15]Each sheet was exactly the same size—forty-five feet long and six feet wide. [16]The craftsmen joined five of these sheets together to make one set, and the six remaining sheets were joined to make a second set. [17]Then they made fifty loops along the edge of the last sheet in each set. [18]They also made fifty small bronze clasps to couple the loops, so the two sets of sheets were firmly attached to each other. In this way, the roof covering was joined together in one piece. [19]Then they made two more layers for the roof covering. The first was made of tanned ram skins, and the second was made of fine goatskin leather.

[20]For the framework of the Tabernacle, they made frames of acacia wood standing on end. [21]Each frame was 15 feet high and 2¼ feet wide. [22]There were two pegs on each frame so they could be joined to the next frame. All the frames were made this way. [23]They made twenty frames to support the south side, [24]along with forty silver bases, two for each frame. [25]They also made twenty frames for the north side of the Tabernacle, [26]along with forty silver bases, two for each frame. [27]The west side of the Tabernacle, which was its rear, was made from six frames, [28]plus an extra frame at each corner. [29]These corner frames were connected at the bottom and firmly attached at the top with a single ring, forming a single unit from top to bottom. They made two of these, one for each rear corner. [30]So for the west side they made a total of eight frames, along with sixteen silver bases, two for each frame.

[31]Then they made five crossbars from acacia wood to tie the frames on the south side together. [32]They made another five for the north side and five for the west side. [33]The middle crossbar of the five was halfway up the frames, along each side, running from one end to the other. [34]The frames and crossbars were all overlaid with gold. The rings used to hold the crossbars were made of pure gold.

[35]The inner curtain was made of fine linen cloth, and cherubim were skillfully embroidered into it with blue, purple, and scarlet yarn. [36]This curtain was then attached to four gold hooks set into four posts of acacia wood. The posts were overlaid with gold and set into four silver bases.

[37]Then they made another curtain for the entrance to the sacred tent. It was made of fine linen cloth and embroidered with blue, purple, and scarlet yarn. [38]This curtain was connected by five hooks to five posts. The posts with their decorated tops and bands were overlaid with gold. The five bases were molded from bronze.

## TEAMWORK ● ● • • •

**36:8-9 Making cloth (spinning and weaving) took a great deal of time in Moses' day. To own more than two or three changes of clothing was a sign of wealth! As you can imagine, the effort involved in making enough cloth for a building like the Tabernacle was staggering. It demonstrated a tremendous community effort. Churches and neighborhoods today often require this same kind of community teamwork. Without it, many essential services just wouldn't get done. What part can you play in your church or community "team"?**

CHAPTER **37** **BUILDING THE ARK.** Next Bezalel made the Ark out of acacia wood. It was 3¾ feet long, 2¼ feet wide, and 2¼ feet high.* [2]It was overlaid with pure gold inside and out, and it had a molding of gold all the way around. [3]Four gold rings were fastened to its four feet, two rings at each side. [4]Then he made poles from acacia wood and overlaid them with gold. [5]He put the poles into the rings at the sides of the Ark to carry it.

[6]Then, from pure gold, he made the Ark's cover—the place of atonement. It was 3¾ feet long and 2¼ feet wide. [7]He made two figures of cherubim out of hammered gold and placed them at the two ends of the atonement cover. [8]They were made so they were actually a part of the atonement cover—it was all one piece. [9]The cherubim faced each other as they looked down on the atonement cover, and their wings were stretched out above the atonement cover to protect it.

[10]Then he made a table out of acacia wood, 3 feet

36:9 Hebrew *28 cubits* [12.6 meters] *long and 4 cubits* [1.8 meters] *wide.* In this chapter, the distance measures are calculated from the Hebrew cubit at a ratio of 18 inches or 45 centimeters per cubit. **37:1** Hebrew *2½ cubits* [1.1 meters] *long, 1½ cubits* [0.7 meters] *wide, and 1½ cubits high.* In this chapter, the distance measures are calculated from the Hebrew cubit at a ratio of 18 inches or 45 centimeters per cubit.

long, 1½ feet wide, and 2¼ feet high. [11]It was overlaid with pure gold, with a gold molding all around the edge. [12]A rim about 3 inches* wide was attached along the edges of the table, and a gold molding ran around the rim. [13]Then he cast four rings of gold and attached them to the four table legs [14]next to the rim. These were made to hold the carrying poles in place. [15]He made the carrying poles of acacia wood and overlaid them with gold. [16]Next, using pure gold, he made the plates, dishes, bowls, and pitchers to be placed on the table. These utensils were to be used in pouring out drink offerings.

[17]Then he made the lampstand, again using pure, hammered gold. Its base, center stem, lamp cups, blossoms, and buds were all of one piece. [18]The lampstand had six branches, three going out from each side of the center stem. [19]Each of the six branches held a cup shaped like an almond blossom, complete with buds and petals. [20]The center stem of the lampstand was also decorated with four almond blossoms. [21]One blossom was set beneath each pair of branches, where they extended from the center stem. [22]The decorations and branches were all one piece with the stem, and they were hammered from pure gold. [23]He also made the seven lamps, the lamp snuffers, and the trays, all of pure gold. [24]The entire lampstand, along with its accessories, was made from seventy-five pounds* of pure gold.

[25]The incense altar was made of acacia wood. It was eighteen inches square and three feet high, with its corner horns made from the same piece of wood as the altar itself. [26]He overlaid the top, sides, and horns of the altar with pure gold and ran a gold molding around the edge. [27]Two gold rings were placed on opposite sides, beneath the molding, to hold the carrying poles. [28]The carrying poles were made of acacia wood and were overlaid with gold.

[29]Then he made the sacred oil, for anointing the priests, and the fragrant incense, using the techniques of the most skilled incense maker.

CHAPTER **38** **BUILDING THE ALTAR.** The altar for burning animal sacrifices also was constructed of acacia wood. It was 7½ feet square at the top and 4½ feet high.* [2]There were four horns, one at each of the four corners, all of one piece with the rest. This altar was overlaid with bronze. [3]Then he made all the bronze utensils to be used with the altar—the ash buckets, shovels, basins, meat hooks, and firepans. [4]Next he made a bronze grating that rested on a ledge about halfway down into the firebox. [5]Four rings were cast for each side of the grating to support the carrying poles. [6]The carrying poles themselves were made of acacia wood and were overlaid with bronze. [7]These poles were inserted into the rings at the side of the altar. The altar was hollow and was made from planks.

[8]The bronze washbasin and its bronze pedestal were cast from bronze mirrors donated by the women who served at the entrance of the Tabernacle.*

[9]Then he constructed the courtyard. The south wall was 150 feet long. It consisted of curtains made of fine linen. [10]There were twenty posts, each with its own bronze base, and there were silver hooks and rods to hold up the curtains. [11]The north wall was also 150 feet long, with twenty bronze posts and bases and with silver hooks and rods. [12]The west end was 75 feet wide. The walls were made from curtains supported by ten posts and bases and with silver hooks and rods. [13]The east end was also 75 feet wide.

[14]The courtyard entrance was on the east side, flanked by two curtains. The curtain on the right side was 22½ feet long and was supported by three posts set into three bases. [15]The curtain on the left side was also 22½ feet long and was supported by three posts set into three bases. [16]All the curtains used in the courtyard walls were made of fine linen. [17]Each post had a bronze base, and all the hooks and rods were silver. The tops of the posts were overlaid with silver, and the rods to hold up the curtains were solid silver.

[18]The curtain that covered the entrance to the courtyard was made of fine linen cloth and embroidered with blue, purple, and scarlet yarn. It was 30 feet long and 7½ feet high, just like the curtains of the courtyard walls. [19]It was supported by four posts set into four bronze bases. The tops of the posts were overlaid with silver, and the hooks and rods were also made of silver.

[20]All the tent pegs used in the Tabernacle and courtyard were made of bronze.

[21]Here is an inventory of the materials used in building the Tabernacle of the Covenant.* Moses directed the Levites to compile the figures, and Ithamar son of Aaron the priest served as recorder. [22]Bezalel son of Uri, grandson of Hur, of the tribe of Judah, was in charge of the whole project, just as the LORD had commanded Moses. [23]He was assisted by Oholiab son of Ahisamach, of the tribe of Dan, a craftsman expert at engraving, designing, and embroidering blue, purple, and scarlet yarn on fine linen cloth.

[24]The people brought gifts of gold totaling about 2,200 pounds,* all of which was used throughout the Tabernacle.

[25]The amount of silver that was given was about 7,545 pounds.* [26]It came from the tax of one-fifth of an ounce of silver* collected from each of those registered in the census. This included all the men who were twenty years old or older, 603,550 in all.

**37:12** Hebrew *a handbreadth* [8 centimeters]. **37:24** Hebrew *1 talent* [34 kilograms]. **38:1** Hebrew *5 cubits* [2.3 meters] *square at the top, and 3 cubits* [1.4 meters] *high.* In this chapter, the distance measures are calculated from the Hebrew cubit at a ratio of 18 inches or 45 centimeters per cubit. **38:8** Hebrew *Tent of Meeting;* also in 38:30. **38:21** Hebrew *the Tabernacle, the Tabernacle of the Testimony.* **38:24** Hebrew *29 talents* [2,175 pounds or 986 kilograms] *and 730 shekels* [18.3 pounds or 8.3 kilograms], *according to the sanctuary shekel.* **38:25** Hebrew *100 talents* [7,500 pounds or 3,400 kilograms] *and 1,775 shekels* [44.4 pounds or 20.2 kilograms], *according to the sanctuary shekel.* **38:26** Hebrew *1 beka* [6 grams] *per person, that is, half a shekel, according to the sanctuary shekel.*

27 The 100 bases for the frames of the sanctuary walls and for the posts supporting the inner curtain required 7,500 pounds of silver, about 75 pounds for each base.* 28 The rest of the silver, about 45 pounds,* was used to make the rods and hooks and to overlay the tops of the posts.

29 The people also brought 5,310 pounds* of bronze, 30 which was used for casting the bases for the posts at the entrance to the Tabernacle, and for the bronze altar with its bronze grating and altar utensils. 31 Bronze was also used to make the bases for the posts that supported the curtains around the courtyard, the bases for the curtain at the entrance of the courtyard, and all the tent pegs used to hold the curtains of the courtyard in place.

## CHAPTER 39 **MAKING THE PRIESTS' CLOTHING.**

For the priests, the craftsmen made beautiful garments of blue, purple, and scarlet cloth—clothing to be worn while ministering in the Holy Place. This same cloth was used for Aaron's sacred garments, just as the LORD had commanded Moses.

2 The ephod was made from fine linen cloth and embroidered with gold thread and blue, purple, and scarlet yarn. 3 A skilled craftsman made gold thread by beating gold into thin sheets and cutting it into fine strips. He then embroidered it into the linen with the blue, purple, and scarlet yarn.

4 They made two shoulder-pieces for the ephod, which were attached to its corners so it could be tied down. 5 They also made an elaborate woven sash of the same materials: fine linen cloth; blue, purple, and scarlet yarn; and gold thread, just as the LORD had commanded Moses. 6 The two onyx stones, attached to the shoulder-pieces of the ephod, were set in gold filigree. The stones were engraved with the names of the tribes of Israel, just as initials are engraved on a seal. 7 These stones served as reminders to the LORD concerning the people of Israel. All this was done just as the LORD had commanded Moses.

8 The chestpiece was made in the same style as the ephod, crafted from fine linen cloth and embroidered with gold thread and blue, purple, and scarlet yarn. 9 It was doubled over to form a pouch, nine inches* square. 10 Four rows of gemstones* were set across it. In the first row were a red carnelian, a chrysolite, and an emerald. 11 In the second row were a turquoise, a sapphire, and a white moonstone. 12 In the third row were a jacinth, an agate, and an amethyst. 13 In the fourth row were a beryl, an onyx, and a jasper. Each of these gemstones was set in gold. 14 The stones were engraved like a seal, each with the name of one of the twelve tribes of Israel.

15 To attach the chestpiece to the ephod, they made braided cords of pure gold. 16 They also made two gold rings and attached them to the top corners of the chestpiece. 17 The two gold cords were put through the gold rings on the chestpiece, 18 and the ends of the cords were tied to the gold settings on the shoulder-pieces of the ephod. 19 Two more gold rings were attached to the lower inside corners of the chestpiece next to the ephod. 20 Then two gold rings were attached to the ephod near the sash. 21 Blue cords were used to attach the bottom rings of the chestpiece to the rings on the ephod. In this way, the chestpiece was held securely to the ephod above the beautiful sash. All this was done just as the LORD had commanded Moses.

22 The robe of the ephod was woven entirely of blue yarn, 23 with an opening for Aaron's head in the middle of it. The edge of this opening was reinforced with a woven collar,* so it would not tear. 24 Pomegranates were attached to the bottom edge of the robe. These were finely crafted of blue, purple, and scarlet yarn. 25 Bells of pure gold were placed between the pomegranates along the hem of the robe, 26 with bells and pomegranates alternating all around the hem. This robe was to be worn when Aaron ministered to the LORD, just as the LORD had commanded Moses.

27 Tunics were then made for Aaron and his sons from fine linen cloth. 28 The turban, the headdresses, and the underclothes were all made of this fine linen. 29 The sashes were made of fine linen cloth and embroidered with blue, purple, and scarlet yarn, just as the LORD had commanded Moses. 30 Finally, they made the sacred medallion of pure gold to be worn on the front of the turban. Using the techniques of an engraver, they inscribed it with these words: SET APART AS HOLY TO THE LORD. 31 This medallion was tied to the turban with a blue cord, just as the LORD had commanded Moses.

### DETAILS ● ● ● • •

**39:32 The Tabernacle was finally complete to the last detail. God was keenly interested in every minute part. The Creator of the universe is concerned about even the little things. Matthew 10:30 says that God knows the number of hairs on our head. This shows that God is greatly interested in you. Don't be afraid to talk with him about any of your concerns—no matter how small or unimportant they might seem.**

32 And so at last the Tabernacle* was finished. The Israelites had done everything just as the LORD had commanded Moses. 33 And they brought the entire Tabernacle to Moses: the sacred tent with all its furnishings, the clasps, frames, crossbars, posts, and bases; 34 the layers of tanned ram skins and fine goatskin leather; the inner curtain that enclosed the Most Holy Place; 35 the Ark of the Covenant* and its carrying poles; the Ark's cover—the place of atonement; 36 the table and all its utensils; the Bread of the Presence; 37 the gold lampstand and its accessories; the lamp cups and the oil for lighting;

38:27 Hebrew *100 talents* [3,400 kilograms] *of silver, 1 talent* [34 kilograms] *for each base.* 38:28 Hebrew *1,775 shekels* [20.2 kilograms]. 38:29 Hebrew *70 talents* [5,250 pounds or 2,380 kilograms] *and 2,400 shekels* [60 pounds or 27.4 kilograms]. 39:9 Hebrew *1 span* [23 centimeters]. 39:10 The identification of some of these gemstones is uncertain. 39:23 The meaning of the Hebrew is uncertain. 39:32 Hebrew *the Tabernacle, the Tent of Meeting;* also in 39:40. 39:35 Or *Ark of the Testimony.*

38 the gold altar; the anointing oil; the fragrant incense; the curtain for the entrance of the sacred tent; 39 the bronze altar; the bronze grating; its poles and utensils; the large washbasin and its pedestal; 40 the curtains for the walls of the courtyard and the posts and bases holding them up; the curtain at the courtyard entrance; the cords and tent pegs; all the articles used in the operation of the Tabernacle; 41 the beautifully crafted garments to be worn while ministering in the Holy Place—the holy garments for Aaron the priest and for his sons to wear while on duty.

42 So the people of Israel followed all of the LORD's instructions to Moses. 43 Moses inspected all their work and blessed them because it had been done as the LORD had commanded him.

## CHAPTER 40 **THE TABERNACLE IS BUILT.**

The LORD now said to Moses, 2 "Set up the Tabernacle* on the first day of the new year.* 3 Place the Ark of the Covenant* inside, and install the inner curtain to enclose the Ark within the Most Holy Place. 4 Then bring in the table, and arrange the utensils on it. And bring in the lampstand, and set up the lamps.

5 "Place the incense altar just outside the inner curtain, opposite the Ark of the Covenant. Set up the curtain made for the entrance of the Tabernacle. 6 Place the altar of burnt offering in front of the Tabernacle entrance. 7 Set the large washbasin between the Tabernacle* and the altar and fill it with water. 8 Then set up the courtyard around the outside of the tent, and hang the curtain for the courtyard entrance.

9 "Take the anointing oil and sprinkle it on the Tabernacle and on all its furnishings to make them holy. 10 Sprinkle the anointing oil on the altar of burnt offering and its utensils, sanctifying them. Then the altar will become most holy. 11 Next anoint the large washbasin and its pedestal to make them holy.

12 "Bring Aaron and his sons to the entrance of the Tabernacle, and wash them with water. 13 Clothe Aaron with the holy garments and anoint him, setting him apart to serve me as a priest. 14 Then bring his sons and dress them in their tunics. 15 Anoint them as you did their father, so they may serve me as priests. With this anointing, Aaron's descendants are set apart for the priesthood forever, from generation to generation."

16 Moses proceeded to do everything as the LORD had commanded him. 17 So the Tabernacle was set up on the first day of the new year.* 18 Moses put it together by setting its frames into their bases and attaching the crossbars and raising the posts. 19 Then he spread the coverings over the Tabernacle framework and put on the roof layers, just as the LORD had commanded him.

20 He placed inside the Ark the stone tablets inscribed with the terms of the covenant,* and then he attached the Ark's carrying poles. He also set the Ark's cover—the place of atonement—on top of it. 21 Then he brought the Ark of the Covenant into the Tabernacle and set up the inner curtain to shield it from view, just as the LORD had commanded.

22 Next he placed the table in the Tabernacle, along the north side of the Holy Place, just outside the inner curtain. 23 And he arranged the Bread of the Presence on the table that stands before the LORD, just as the LORD had commanded.

24 He set the lampstand in the Tabernacle across from the table on the south side of the Holy Place. 25 Then he set up the lamps in the LORD's presence, just as the LORD had commanded. 26 He also placed the incense altar in the Tabernacle, in the Holy Place in front of the inner curtain. 27 On it he burned the fragrant incense made from sweet spices, just as the LORD had commanded.

28 He attached the curtain at the entrance of the Tabernacle, 29 and he placed the altar of burnt offering near the Tabernacle entrance. On it he offered a burnt offering and a grain offering, just as the LORD had commanded.

30 Next he placed the large washbasin between the Tabernacle and the altar. He filled it with water so the priests could use it to wash themselves. 31 Moses and Aaron and Aaron's sons washed their hands and feet in the basin. 32 Whenever they walked past the altar to enter the Tabernacle, they were to stop and wash, just as the LORD had commanded Moses.

33 Then he hung the curtains forming the courtyard around the Tabernacle and the altar. And he set up the curtain at the entrance of the courtyard. So at last Moses finished the work.

34 Then the cloud covered the Tabernacle, and the glorious presence of the LORD filled it. 35 Moses was no longer able to enter the Tabernacle because the cloud had settled down over it, and the Tabernacle was filled with the awesome glory of the LORD.

36 Now whenever the cloud lifted from the Tabernacle and moved, the people of Israel would set out on their journey, following it. 37 But if the cloud stayed, they would stay until it moved again. 38 The cloud of the LORD rested on the Tabernacle during the day, and at night there was fire in the cloud so all the people of Israel could see it. This continued throughout all their journeys.

### BIG CHANGES ● ● • • •

40:38 **The Israelites were once Egyptian slaves making bricks without straw. Here they were following the cloud of the Lord, carrying the Tabernacle they had built for God. Exodus begins in gloom and ends in glory. This parallels our progress through the Christian life. We begin as slaves to sin, are redeemed by God, and end our pilgrimage living with God forever. The lessons the Israelites learned along the way are lessons we too need to learn.**

40:2a Hebrew *the Tabernacle, the Tent of Meeting;* also in 40:6, 29. 40:2b Hebrew *the first day of the first month.* This day of the Hebrew lunar calendar occurs in March or early April. 40:3 Or *Ark of the Testimony;* also in 40:5, 21. 40:7 Hebrew *Tent of Meeting;* also in 40:12, 22, 24, 26, 30, 32, 34, 35. 40:17 Hebrew *the first day of the first month, in the second year.* See note on 40:2b. 40:20 Hebrew *the Testimony.*

# MEGA themes

**SLAVERY** The Israelites were slaves for 400 years. Pharaoh, the king of Egypt, mistreated them cruelly.

Physical slavery is like slavery to sin. The longer you are a slave, the more difficult it becomes to break free. Gaining freedom from sin requires God's power and the guidance of godly leaders.

1. How did the Hebrews feel about being enslaved to the Egyptians?
2. What are some examples of how people become enslaved to specific sins in their lives?
3. When you look at your own life, what types of things have the potential to become your master?
4. How does God's power enable you to live in freedom?
5. What can you do to avoid becoming a slave to sin?

**RESCUE/REDEMPTION** God rescued Israel through the leader Moses and through mighty miracles. The Passover celebration was given by God as an annual reminder of their escape from slavery.

All of us need to experience the deliverance from sin that God provides. Jesus Christ celebrated the Passover with his disciples at the Last Supper and then completed God's plan for our redemption by dying in our place.

1. Describe the characteristics that were required for a Passover lamb.
2. Why was the lamb important?
3. In what way can Jesus be described as our Passover Lamb? (Check John 1:29.)
4. If someone were to ask you, "Why did Jesus have to die?" how would you respond?
5. From what has God rescued you through the sacrifice of Jesus?
6. In what ways has being redeemed by Christ affected the way you live? How do you plan to allow this truth to affect your future?

**GUIDANCE** God guided Israel out of slavery by using the plagues, Moses' heroic courage, the miracle of the Red Sea, and the Ten Commandments.

God demonstrates his power in our life through the guidance of wise leaders and the group effort of Christian friends working together. He can be trusted to give us the guidance we need to follow his will.

1. At first, Moses had difficulty following God's guidance. What questions did Moses have for God when he was spoken to through the burning bush? What were God's responses?
2. Think about a time when you, like Moses, felt inadequate or unwilling to obey God's will in your life. What decisions did you make? If God had spoken to you in that situation, what do you think he would have said?
3. What resources has God provided to help you learn how to follow his will for you?
4. What decisions are you facing now or in the near future that will require you to rely on these resources in order to obey him?
5. What are some specific ways that you can seek God's guidance as you get ready to make the right decisions?

**TEN COMMANDMENTS** God's law system had three interwoven parts. The Ten Commandments were the first part, containing the absolutes of spiritual and moral life. The civil law was the second part, giving the people rules to manage their lives. The ceremonial law was the third part, showing them patterns for building the Tabernacle and for regular worship.

God was teaching Israel the importance of choice and responsibility. When they obeyed the conditions of the law, he blessed them; if they forgot or disobeyed, he punished them or allowed disasters to come upon them. God's moral laws, as given in Exodus, have been reflected in the legal systems of many great countries, past and present.

1. The law was given to Israel to show them their sin and their need for redemption. How does the law point us to Christ?
2. There were some very severe and immediate consequences for those who disobeyed the law. What are some of the long-term consequences facing young people who go against God's moral law (the Ten Commandments)?
3. Why does God want you to obey his moral law?

**THE NATION** God established the nation of Israel to be the source of truth and salvation to all the world. His relationship to his people was loving, yet firm. God was their direct leader in government, social concerns, and worship.

Israel's newly formed nation models for us the need to depend upon God. Whether we are rebellious or obedient, God remains our only source of absolute, eternal truth and life.

1. Describe the qualities you find in God's leadership of the Israelites.
2. Which of these qualities are most important to you in your relationship with God at this time in your life?
3. In what specific areas do you need to depend on God in your relationships at home? At school? With close friends?
4. Based on God's relationship to Israel in Exodus, how can you know that God can be trusted in these important areas?

1446 B.C.
**Exodus from Egypt**

1445
**Ten Commandments given**

1444
**Israel camps at Mt. Sinai**

1406
**Moses dies, Canaan entered**

1375
**Judges begin to rule**

1050
**United kingdom under Saul**

Jason was the coach's kid. At practice he tried hard to pay attention, but one day he knew he was doomed. Patti, the cutest girl on the cheerleading squad, stopped by. Soon she sat next to Jason on the grass, and they began to whisper together—until Jason's dad looked their way. Jason paid attention for a few minutes, but soon they were whispering again. ■ The rest of the world faded away. It was just the two of them . . . until Jason's father intruded. "Jason!" he demanded. "You are the coach's son, and I expect you to pay attention!" Jason understood. He remained attentive for the rest of the practice. ■ The coach expected Jason to listen during practice. Not because he was better than the other players, but because Jason was his son. He felt Jason's actions were a reflection on his father, so Jason should pay attention—even if no one else did. ■ The Israelites were in a similar situation. God demanded they "pay attention" because they were his chosen people, his children. God told them, "You must be holy, because I, the LORD your God, am holy" (19:2). *Holy* means set apart, good, and different. That's why God gave them the book of Leviticus. It contains laws of holiness, things they needed to do to remain holy. God also gave them the Day of Atonement so they could be forgiven. ■ The book of Leviticus is important to us, too. Our day of atonement is the day Jesus died. Because of him we can be "holy" before God even though we disobey him. Jesus' death covers everything we do wrong. ■ As you read Leviticus, consider your relationship with God. And, where it's needed, ask Christ for forgiveness.

## STATS

PURPOSE: A handbook for the Levites outlining their priestly duties in worship, and a guidebook of holy living for the Hebrews

AUTHOR: Moses

DATE OF EVENTS: 1445–1444 B.C.

SETTING: At the foot of Mount Sinai. God teaches the Israelites how to live as holy people.

KEY PEOPLE: Moses, Aaron, Nadab, Abihu, Eleazar, Ithamar

SPECIAL FEATURE: Holiness is mentioned more often (152 times) than in any other book of the Bible

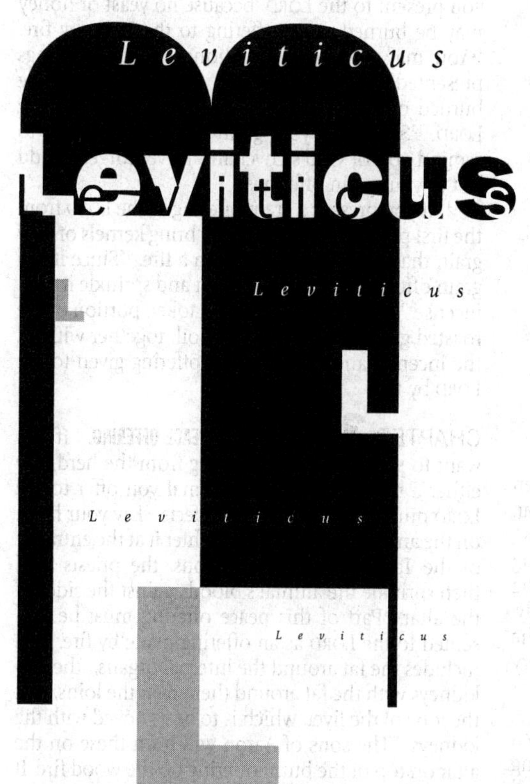


CHAPTER **1** **HOW TO GIVE A BURNT OFFERING.** The
LORD called to Moses from the Tabernacle* and said
to him, [2]"Give the following instructions to the Israelites: Whenever you present offerings to the LORD,
you must bring animals from your flocks and herds.
[3]"If your sacrifice for a whole burnt offering is
from the herd, bring a bull with no physical defects
to the entrance of the Tabernacle so it will be accepted by the LORD. [4]Lay your hand on its head so
the LORD will accept it as your substitute, thus making atonement for you. [5]Then slaughter the animal
in the LORD's presence, and Aaron's sons, the priests,
will present the blood by sprinkling it against the
sides of the altar that stands in front of the Tabernacle. [6]When the animal has been skinned and cut into
pieces, [7]the sons of Aaron the priest will build a
wood fire on the altar. [8]Aaron's sons will then put the
pieces of the animal, including its head and fat, on
the wood fire. [9]But the internal organs and legs must
first be washed with water. Then the priests will burn
the entire sacrifice on the altar. It is a whole burnt
offering made by fire, very pleasing to the LORD.
[10]"If your sacrifice for a whole burnt offering is
from the flock, bring a male sheep or goat with no
physical defects. [11]Slaughter the animal on the north
side of the altar in the LORD's presence. Aaron's sons,
the priests, will sprinkle its blood against the sides of
the altar. [12]Then you must cut the animal in pieces,
and the priests will lay the pieces of the sacrifice,
including the head and fat, on top of the wood fire
on the altar. [13]The internal organs and legs must first
be washed with water. Then the priests will burn the
entire sacrifice on the altar. It is a whole burnt offering made by fire, very pleasing to the LORD.
[14]"If you bring a bird as a burnt offering to the
LORD, choose either a turtledove or a young pigeon.
[15]The priest will take the bird to the altar, twist off its

1:1 Hebrew *Tent of Meeting;* also in 1:3, 5.

## THE COST OF SIN ● ● • • •

**1:1 Animal sacrifices were practiced in many cultures in the Middle East. God used the form of sacrifice to teach his people about faith. Sin needed to be taken seriously. When people saw the sacrificial animals being killed, they were sensitized to the importance of their sin and guilt. Our culture's casual attitude toward doing wrong ignores the cost of sin and the need for repentance and restoration. Although many of the rituals of Leviticus were fitted to the culture of the day, their purpose was to reveal a high and holy God who should be loved, obeyed, and worshiped. God's laws and sacrifices were intended to bring out true devotion of the heart. The ceremonies and rituals were the best way for the Israelites to focus their hearts on God.**

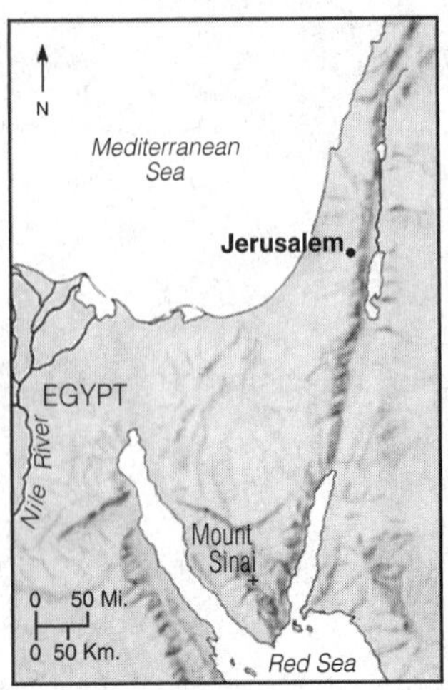


**THE ISRAELITES AT MOUNT SINAI** Throughout the book of Leviticus, the Israelites were camped at the foot of Mount Sinai. It was time to regroup as a nation and learn the importance of following God as they prepared to march toward the Promised Land.

head, and burn the head on the altar. He must then let its blood drain out against the sides of the altar. 16The priest must remove the crop and the feathers* and throw them to the east side of the altar among the ashes. 17Then, grasping the bird by its wings, the priest will tear the bird apart, though not completely. Then he will burn it on top of the wood fire on the altar. It is a whole burnt offering made by fire, very pleasing to the LORD.

## CHAPTER 2 HOW TO GIVE A GRAIN OFFERING.

"When you bring a grain offering to the LORD, the offering must consist of choice flour. You are to pour olive oil on it and sprinkle it with incense. 2Bring this offering to one of Aaron's sons, and he will take a handful of the flour mixed with olive oil, together with all the incense, and burn this token portion on the altar fire. It is an offering made by fire, very pleasing to the LORD. 3The rest of the flour will be given to Aaron and his sons. It will be considered a most holy part of the offerings given to the LORD by fire.

4"When you present some kind of baked bread as a grain offering, it must be made of choice flour mixed with olive oil but without any yeast. It may be presented in the form of cakes mixed with olive oil or wafers spread with olive oil. 5If your grain offering is cooked on a griddle, it must be made of choice flour and olive oil, and it must contain no yeast. 6Break it into pieces and pour oil on it; it is a kind of grain offering. 7If your offering is prepared in a pan, it also must be made of choice flour and olive oil.

8"No matter how a grain offering has been prepared before being offered to the LORD, bring it to the priests who will present it at the altar. 9The priests will take a token portion of the grain offering and burn it on the altar as an offering made by fire, and it will be very pleasing to the LORD. 10The rest of the grain offering will be given to Aaron and his sons as their food. It will be considered a most holy part of the offerings given to the LORD by fire.

11"Do not use yeast in any of the grain offerings you present to the LORD, because no yeast or honey may be burned as an offering to the LORD by fire. 12You may add yeast and honey to the offerings presented at harvesttime, but these must never be burned on the altar as an offering pleasing to the LORD. 13Season all your grain offerings with salt, to remind you of God's covenant. Never forget to add salt to your grain offerings.

14"If you present a grain offering to the LORD from the first portion of your harvest, bring kernels of new grain that have been roasted on a fire. 15Since it is a grain offering, put olive oil on it and sprinkle it with incense. 16The priests will take a token portion of the roasted grain mixed with olive oil, together with all the incense, and burn it as an offering given to the LORD by fire.

## CHAPTER 3 HOW TO GIVE A PEACE OFFERING.

"If you want to present a peace offering from the herd, use either a bull or a cow. The animal you offer to the LORD must have no physical defects. 2Lay your hand on the animal's head, and slaughter it at the entrance of the Tabernacle.* Aaron's sons, the priests, will then sprinkle the animal's blood against the sides of the altar. 3Part of this peace offering must be presented to the LORD as an offering made by fire. This includes the fat around the internal organs, 4the two kidneys with the fat around them near the loins, and the lobe of the liver, which is to be removed with the kidneys. 5The sons of Aaron will burn these on the altar on top of the burnt offering on the wood fire. It is an offering made by fire, very pleasing to the LORD.

6"If you present a peace offering to the LORD from the flock, you may bring either a goat or a sheep. It may be either male or female, and it must have no physical defects. 7If you bring a sheep as your gift, present it to the LORD 8by laying your hand on its head and slaughtering it at the entrance of the Tabernacle. The sons of Aaron will then sprinkle the sheep's blood against the sides of the altar. 9Part of this peace offering must be presented to the LORD as an offering made by fire. This includes the fat of the entire tail cut off near the backbone, the fat around the internal organs, 10the two kidneys with the fat around them near the loins, and the lobe of the liver, which is to be removed with the kidneys. 11The priest will burn them on the altar as food, an offering given to the LORD by fire.

12"If you bring a goat as your offering to the

**SALT ● ● • • •**

2:13 **The offerings were seasoned with salt as a reminder of the people's covenant (contract) with God. Salt is a good symbol of God's activity in a person's life, because it penetrates, preserves, and aids in healing. God wants to be active in your life. Let him become part of you, penetrating every aspect of your life, preserving you from the evil all around, and healing you of your sins and shortcomings.**

1:16 Or *the crop and its contents.* The meaning of the Hebrew is uncertain. 3:2 Hebrew *Tent of Meeting;* also in 3:8, 13.

| Offering | Burnt Offering (Lev. 1—voluntary) | Grain Offering (Lev. 2—voluntary) | Peace Offering (Lev. 3—voluntary) | Sin Offering (Lev. 4—required) | Guilt Offering (Lev. 5—required) |
|---|---|---|---|---|---|
| Purpose | To make payment for sins in general | To show honor and respect to God in worship | To express gratitude to God | To make payment for unintentional sins of uncleanness, neglect, or thoughtlessness | To make payment for sins against God and others. A sacrifice was made to God and the injured person repaid or compensated. |
| Significance | Showed a person's devotion to God | Acknowledged that everything we have belongs to God | Symbolized peace and fellowship with God | Restored the sinner to fellowship with God; showed seriousness of sin | Provided compensation for injured parties |
| Christ, the Perfect Offering | Christ's death was the perfect offering | Christ was the perfect man, who gave all of himself to God and others | Christ is the only way to fellowship with God | Christ's death restores our fellowship with God | Christ's death takes away the deadly consequences of sin |

**THE OFFERINGS**

Listed here are the five key offerings the Israelites made to God. The Jews made these offerings in order to have their sins forgiven and to restore their fellowship with God. The death of Jesus Christ made these sacrifices unnecessary. Because of Jesus' death our sins are completely forgiven and fellowship with God has been restored.

LORD, 13 lay your hand on its head, and slaughter it
at the entrance of the Tabernacle. Then the sons of
Aaron will sprinkle the goat's blood against the
sides of the altar. 14 Part of this offering must be
presented to the LORD as an offering made by fire.
This part includes the fat around the internal organs,
15 the two kidneys with the fat around them
near the loins, and the lobe of the liver, which is to
be removed with the kidneys. 16 The priest will burn
them on the altar as food, an offering made by fire;
these will be very pleasing to the LORD. Remember,
all the fat belongs to the LORD.
17 "You must never eat any fat or blood. This is a
permanent law for you and all your descendants,
wherever they may live."

CHAPTER 4 **HOW TO GIVE A SIN OFFERING.** Then the
LORD said to Moses, 2 "Give the Israelites the following
instructions for dealing with those who sin unintentionally
by doing anything forbidden by the
LORD's commands.
3 "If the high priest sins, bringing guilt upon the
entire community, he must bring to the LORD a
young bull with no physical defects. 4 He must present
the bull to the LORD at the entrance of the
Tabernacle,* lay his hand on the bull's head, and

4:4 Hebrew *Tent of Meeting;* also in 4:5, 7, 14, 16, 18.

## UNINTENDED ● ● • • •

4-5 **Have you ever done something wrong without realizing it until later? Although your sin was unintentional, it was still sin. One of the purposes of God's law was to make the Israelites aware of their unintentional sins so they would not repeat them and so they could be forgiven for them. Leviticus 4 and 5 mention some of these unintentional sins and the way the Israelites could be forgiven for them. As you read more of God's laws, keep in mind that they were meant to teach and guide the people. Let them help you become more aware of sin in your life.**

slaughter it there in the LORD's presence. [5]The priest on duty will then take some of the animal's blood into the Tabernacle, [6]dip his finger into the blood, and sprinkle it seven times before the LORD in front of the inner curtain of the Most Holy Place. [7]The priest will put some of the blood on the horns of the incense altar that stands in the LORD's presence in the Tabernacle. The rest of the bull's blood must be poured out at the base of the altar of burnt offerings at the entrance of the Tabernacle. [8]The priest must remove all the fat around the bull's internal organs, [9]the two kidneys with the fat around them near the loins, and the lobe of the liver. [10]Then he must burn them on the altar of burnt offerings, just as is done with the bull or cow sacrificed as a peace offering. [11]But the rest of the bull—its hide, meat, head, legs, internal organs, and dung—[12]must be carried away to a ceremonially clean place outside the camp, the place where the ashes are thrown. He will burn it all on a wood fire in the ash heap.

[13]"If the entire Israelite community does something forbidden by the LORD and the matter escapes the community's notice, all the people will be guilty. [14]When they discover their sin, the leaders of the community must bring a young bull for a sin offering and present it at the entrance of the Tabernacle. [15]The leaders must then lay their hands on the bull's head and slaughter it there before the LORD. [16]The priest will bring some of its blood into the Tabernacle, [17]dip his finger into the blood, and sprinkle it seven times before the LORD in front of the inner curtain. [18]He will then put some of the blood on the horns of the incense altar that stands in the LORD's presence in the Tabernacle. The rest of the blood must then be poured out at the base of the altar of burnt offerings at the entrance of the Tabernacle. [19]The priest must remove all the animal's fat and burn it on the altar, [20]following the same procedure as with the sin offering for the priest. In this way, the priest will make atonement for the people, and they will be forgiven. [21]The priest must then take what is left of the bull outside the camp and burn it there, just as is done with the sin offering for the high priest. This is a sin offering for the entire community of Israel.

[22]"If one of Israel's leaders does something forbidden by the LORD his God, he will be guilty even if he sinned unintentionally. [23]When he becomes aware of his sin, he must bring as his offering a male goat with no physical defects. [24]He is to lay his hand on the goat's head and slaughter it before the LORD at the place where burnt offerings are slaughtered. This will be his sin offering. [25]Then the priest will dip his finger into the blood of the sin offering, put it on the horns of the altar of burnt offerings, and pour out the rest of the blood at the base of the altar. [26]He must burn all the goat's fat on the altar, just as is done with the peace offering. In this way, the priest will make atonement for the leader's sin, and he will be forgiven.

[27]"If any of the citizens of Israel* do something forbidden by the LORD, they will be guilty even if they sinned unintentionally. [28]When they become aware of their sin, they must bring as their offering a female goat with no physical defects. It will be offered for their sin. [29]They are to lay a hand on the head of the sin offering and slaughter it at the place where burnt offerings are slaughtered. [30]The priest will then dip his finger into the blood, put the blood on the horns of the altar of burnt offerings, and pour out the rest of the blood at the base of the altar. [31]Those who are guilty must remove all the goat's fat, just as is done with the peace offering. Then the priest will burn the fat on the altar, and it will be very pleasing to the LORD. In this way, the priest will make atonement for them, and they will be forgiven.

[32]"If any of the people bring a sheep as their sin offering, it must be a female with no physical defects. [33]They are to lay a hand on the head of the sin offering and slaughter it at the place where the burnt offerings are slaughtered. [34]The priest will then dip his finger into the blood, put it on the horns of the altar of burnt offerings, and pour out the rest of the blood at the base of the altar. [35]Those who are guilty must remove all the sheep's fat, just as is done with a sheep presented as a peace offering. Then the priest will burn the fat on the altar on top of the offerings given to the LORD by fire. In this way, the priest will make atonement for them, and they will be forgiven.

CHAPTER **5** **WHAT TO GIVE IF ONE IS POOR.** "If any of the people are called to testify about something they have witnessed, but they refuse to testify, they will be held responsible and be subject to punishment.

[2]"Or if they touch something that is ceremonially unclean, such as the dead body of an animal that is ceremonially unclean—whether a wild animal, a domesticated animal, or an animal that scurries along the ground—they will be considered ceremo-

4:27 Hebrew *people of the land.*

## SELF-CONTROL ● ● • • •

5:4 **Have you ever sworn to do or not do something and then realized what a foolish thing you had done? God's people are called to keep their word, even if they make promises that are tough to keep. Our word should be enough. To feel we need to strengthen a promise with a vow shows that something is wrong. The only promises we ought not to keep are promises that lead to sin. A wise and self-controlled person avoids making rash vows.**

nially unclean and guilty, even if they are unaware of their defilement.

[3]"Or if they come into contact with any source of human defilement, even if they don't realize they have been defiled, they will be considered guilty as soon as they become aware of it.

[4]"Or if they make a rash vow of any kind, whether its purpose is for good or bad, they will be considered guilty even if they were not fully aware of what they were doing at the time.

[5]"When any of the people become aware of their guilt in any of these ways, they must confess their sin [6]and bring to the LORD as their penalty a female from the flock, either a sheep or a goat. This will be a sin offering to remove their sin, and the priest will make atonement for them.

[7]"If any of them cannot afford to bring a sheep, they must bring to the LORD two young turtledoves or two young pigeons as the penalty for their sin. One of the birds will be a sin offering, and the other will be a burnt offering. [8]They must bring them to the priest, who will offer one of the birds as the sin offering. The priest will wring its neck but without severing its head from the body. [9]Then he will sprinkle some of the blood of the sin offering against the sides of the altar, and the rest will be drained out at the base of the altar. [10]The priest will offer the second bird as a whole burnt offering, following all the procedures that have been prescribed. In this way, the priest will make atonement for those who are guilty, and they will be forgiven.

[11]"If any of the people cannot afford to bring young turtledoves or pigeons, they must bring two quarts* of choice flour for their sin offering. Since it is a sin offering, they must not mix it with olive oil or put any incense on it. [12]They must take the flour to the priest, who will scoop out a handful as a token portion. He will burn this flour on the altar just like any other offering given to the LORD by fire. This will be their sin offering. [13]In this way, the priest will make atonement for those who are guilty, and they will be forgiven. The rest of the flour will belong to the priest, just as with the grain offering."

[14]Then the LORD said to Moses, [15]"If any of the people sin by unintentionally defiling the LORD's sacred property, they must bring to the LORD a ram from the flock as their guilt offering. The animal must have no physical defects, and it must be of the proper value in silver as measured by the standard sanctuary shekel.* [16]They must then make restitution for whatever holy things they have defiled by paying for the loss, plus an added penalty of 20 percent. When they give their payments to the priest, he will make atonement for them with the ram sacrificed as a guilt offering, and they will be forgiven.

[17]"If any of them sin by doing something forbidden by the LORD, even if it is done unintentionally, they will be held responsible. When they become aware of their guilt, [18]they must bring to the priest a ram from the flock as a guilt offering. The animal must have no physical defects, and it must be of the proper value. In this way, the priest will make atonement for those who are guilty, and they will be forgiven. [19]This is a guilt offering, for they have been guilty of an offense against the LORD."

## STEALING ● ● • • •

6:1-7 **Here we discover that stealing involves more than just taking from someone. Finding something and not returning it, or refusing to return something borrowed are other forms of stealing. These are sins against God and not just your neighbor, a stranger, or a business. If you have gotten something deceitfully, then confess your sin to God, apologize to the owner, and return the stolen items.**

CHAPTER **6** **BURNT AND GRAIN OFFERINGS.** And the LORD said to Moses, [2]"Suppose some of the people sin against the LORD by falsely telling their neighbor that an item entrusted to their safekeeping has been lost or stolen. Or suppose they have been dishonest with regard to a security deposit, or they have taken something by theft or extortion. [3]Or suppose they find a lost item and lie about it, or they deny something while under oath, or they commit any other similar sin. [4]If they have sinned in any of these ways and are guilty, they must give back whatever they have taken by theft or extortion, whether a security deposit, or property entrusted to them, or a lost object that they claimed as their own, [5]or anything gained by swearing falsely. When they realize their guilt, they must restore the principal amount plus a penalty of 20 percent to the person they have harmed. [6]They must then bring a guilt offering to the priest, who will present it before the LORD. This offering must be a ram with no physical defects or the animal's equivalent value in silver.* [7]The priest will then make atonement for them before the LORD, and they will be forgiven."

[8]Then the LORD said to Moses, [9]"Give Aaron and his sons the following instructions regarding the whole burnt offering. The burnt offering must be left on the altar until the next morning, and the altar fire must be kept burning all night. [10]The next morning, after dressing in his special linen clothing and undergarments, the priest on duty must clean out the ashes of the burnt offering and put them beside the altar. [11]Then he must change back into his normal clothing and carry the ashes outside the camp to a place that is ceremonially clean. [12]Meanwhile, the fire on the altar must be kept burning; it must never go out. Each morning the priest will add fresh wood to the fire and arrange the daily whole burnt offering on it. He must then burn the fat of the peace offerings on top of this daily whole burnt offering. [13]Remember, the fire must be kept burning on the altar at all times. It must never go out.

[14]"These are the instructions regarding the grain

5:11 Hebrew *1/10 of an ephah* [2 liters]. 5:15 Each sanctuary shekel was about 0.4 ounces or 11 grams in weight. 6:6 Or *and the animal must be of the proper value;* Hebrew lacks *in silver;* compare 5:15.

offering. Aaron's sons must present this offering to the LORD in front of the altar. 15The priest on duty will take a handful of the choice flour that has been mixed with olive oil and sprinkled with incense. He will burn this token portion on the altar, and it will be very pleasing to the LORD. 16After burning this handful, the rest of the flour will belong to Aaron and his sons for their food. It must, however, be baked without yeast and eaten in a sacred place within the courtyard of the Tabernacle.* 17Remember, this flour may never be prepared with yeast. I have given it to the priests as their share of the offerings presented to me by fire. Like the sin offering and the guilt offering, it is most holy. 18Any of Aaron's male descendants, from generation to generation, may eat of the grain offering, because it is their regular share of the offerings given to the LORD by fire. Anyone or anything that touches this food will become holy."

19And the LORD said to Moses, 20"On the day Aaron and his sons are anointed, they must bring to the LORD a grain offering of two quarts* of choice flour, half to be offered in the morning and half to be offered in the evening. 21It must be cooked on a griddle with olive oil, and it must be well mixed and broken* into pieces. You must present this grain offering, and it will be very pleasing to the LORD. 22As the sons of the priests replace their fathers, they will be inducted into office by offering this same sacrifice on the day they are anointed. It is the LORD's regular share, and it must be completely burned up. 23All such grain offerings of the priests must be entirely burned up. None of the flour may be eaten."

24Then the LORD said to Moses, 25"Give Aaron and his sons these further instructions regarding the sin offering. The animal given as a sin offering is most holy and must be slaughtered in the LORD's presence at the place where the burnt offerings are slaughtered. 26The priest who offers the sacrifice may eat his portion in a sacred place within the courtyard of the Tabernacle. 27Anything or anyone who touches the sacrificial meat will become holy, and if the sacrificial blood splatters anyone's clothing, it must be washed off in a sacred place. 28If a clay pot is used to boil the sacrificial meat, it must be broken. If a bronze kettle is used, it must be scoured and rinsed thoroughly with water. 29Only males from a priest's family may eat of this offering, for it is most holy. 30If, however, the blood of a sin offering has been taken into the Tabernacle to make atonement in the Holy Place for the people's sins, none of that animal's meat may be eaten. It must be completely burned up.

CHAPTER **7** **GUILT AND PEACE OFFERINGS.** "These are the instructions for the guilt offering, which is most holy. 2The animal sacrificed as a guilt offering must be slaughtered where the burnt offerings are slaughtered, and its blood sprinkled against the sides of the altar. 3The priest will then offer all its fat on the altar, including the fat from the tail, the fat around the internal organs, 4the two kidneys with the fat around them near the loins, and the lobe of the liver, which is to be removed with the kidneys. 5The priests will burn these parts on the altar as an offering to the LORD made by fire. It is a guilt offering. 6All males from a priest's family may eat the meat, and it must be eaten in a sacred place, for it is most holy.

7"For both the sin offering and the guilt offering, the meat of the sacrificed animal belongs to the priest in charge of the atonement ceremony. 8In the case of the whole burnt offering, the hide of the sacrificed animal also belongs to the priest. 9Any grain offering that has been baked in an oven, prepared in a pan, or cooked on a griddle belongs to the priest who presents it. 10All other grain offerings, whether flour mixed with olive oil or dry flour, are to be shared among all the priests and their sons.

**THANKS ●●●••**

7:29 **God told the people of Israel to bring their peace offerings personally, with their own hands. They were to take time and effort to express thanks to God. You are the only person who can express your gratitude to God and to others. Take time to express thanks both to God and to others who have helped and blessed you.**

11"These are the instructions regarding the different kinds of peace offerings that may be presented to the LORD. 12If you present your peace offering as a thanksgiving offering, the usual animal sacrifice must be accompanied by various kinds of bread—loaves, wafers, and cakes—all made without yeast and soaked with olive oil. 13This peace offering of thanksgiving must also be accompanied by loaves of yeast bread. 14One of each kind of bread must be presented as a gift to the LORD. This bread will then belong to the priest who sprinkles the altar with blood from the sacrificed animal. 15The animal's meat must be eaten on the same day it is offered. None of it may be saved for the next morning.

16"However, if you bring an offering to fulfill a vow or as a freewill offering, the meat may be eaten on that same day, and whatever is left over may be eaten on the second day. 17But anything left over until the third day must be completely burned up. 18If any of the meat from this peace offering is eaten on the third day, it will not be accepted by the LORD. It will have no value as a sacrifice, and you will receive no credit for bringing it as an offering. By then, the meat will be contaminated; if you eat it, you will have to answer for your sin.

19"Meat that touches anything ceremonially unclean may not be eaten; it must be completely burned up. And as for meat that may be eaten, it may only be eaten by people who are ceremonially clean. 20Anyone who is ceremonially unclean but eats meat from a peace offering that was presented to the LORD must be cut off from the community. 21If anyone touches anything that is unclean, whether it is human defilement or an unclean animal, and then eats meat from the LORD's sacrifices, that person must be cut off from the community."

6:16 Hebrew *Tent of Meeting;* also in 6:26, 30. 6:20 Hebrew *1/10 of an ephah* [2 liters]. 6:21 The meaning of this Hebrew term is uncertain.

22Then the LORD said to Moses, 23"Give the Israelites these instructions: You must never eat fat, whether from oxen or sheep or goats. 24The fat of an animal found dead or killed by a wild animal may never be eaten, though it may be used for any other purpose. 25Anyone who eats fat from an offering given to the LORD by fire must be cut off from the community. 26Even in your homes, you must never eat the blood of any bird or animal. 27Anyone who eats blood must be cut off from the community."

28Then the LORD said to Moses, 29"Give these further instructions to the Israelites: When you present a peace offering to the LORD, bring part of it as a special gift to the LORD. 30Present it to him with your own hands as an offering given to the LORD by fire. Bring the fat of the animal, together with the breast, and present it to the LORD by lifting it up before him. 31Then the priest will burn the fat on the altar, but the breast will belong to Aaron and his sons. 32You are to give the right thigh of your peace offering to the priest as a gift. 33The right thigh must always be given to the priest who sprinkles the blood and offers the fat of the peace offering. 34For I have designated the breast and the right thigh for the priests. It is their regular share of the peace offerings brought by the Israelites. 35This is their share. It has been set apart for Aaron and his descendants from the offerings given to the LORD by fire from the time they were appointed to serve the LORD as priests. 36The LORD commanded that the Israelites were to give these portions to the priests as their regular share from the time of the priests' anointing. This regulation applies throughout the generations to come."

37These are the instructions for the whole burnt offering, the grain offering, the sin offering, the guilt offering, the ordination offering, and the peace offering. 38The LORD gave these instructions to Moses on Mount Sinai when he commanded the Israelites to bring their offerings to the LORD in the wilderness of Sinai.

## CHAPTER 8

**AARON AND HIS SONS.** The LORD said to Moses, 2"Now bring Aaron and his sons, along with their special clothing, the anointing oil, the bull for the sin offering, the two rams, and the basket of unleavened bread 3to the entrance of the Tabernacle.* Then call the entire community of Israel to meet you there."

4So Moses followed the LORD's instructions, and all the people assembled at the Tabernacle entrance. 5Moses announced to them, "The LORD has commanded what I am now going to do!" 6Then he presented Aaron and his sons and washed them with water. 7He clothed Aaron with the embroidered tunic and tied the sash around his waist. He dressed him in the robe of the ephod, along with the ephod itself, and attached the ephod with its decorative sash. 8Then Moses placed the chestpiece on Aaron and put the Urim and the Thummim inside it. 9He placed on Aaron's head the turban with the gold medallion at its front, just as the LORD had commanded him.

10Then Moses took the anointing oil and anointed the Tabernacle and everything in it, thus making them holy. 11He sprinkled the altar seven times, anointing it and all its utensils and the washbasin and its pedestal, making them holy. 12Then he poured some of the anointing oil on Aaron's head, thus anointing him and making him holy for his work. 13Next Moses presented Aaron's sons and clothed them in their embroidered tunics, their sashes, and their turbans, just as the LORD had commanded him.

14Then Moses brought in the bull for the sin offering, and Aaron and his sons laid their hands on its head 15as Moses slaughtered it. Moses took some of the blood, and with his finger he put it on the four horns of the altar to purify it. He poured out the rest of the blood at the base of the altar. In this way, he set the altar apart as holy and made atonement for it.* 16He took all the fat around the internal organs, the lobe of the liver, and the two kidneys and their fat, and he burned them all on the altar. 17The rest of the bull, including its hide, meat, and dung, was burned outside the camp, just as the LORD had commanded Moses.

18Then Moses presented the ram to the LORD for the whole burnt offering, and Aaron and his sons laid their hands on its head 19as Moses slaughtered it. Then Moses took the ram's blood and sprinkled it against the sides of the altar. 20Next he cut the ram into pieces and burned the head, some of its pieces, and the fat on the altar. 21After washing the internal organs and the legs with water, Moses burned the entire ram on the altar as a whole burnt offering. It was an offering given to the LORD by fire, very pleasing to the LORD. All this was done just as the LORD had commanded Moses.

22Next Moses presented the second ram, which was the ram of ordination. Aaron and his sons laid their hands on its head 23as Moses slaughtered it. Then Moses took some of its blood and put it on the lobe of Aaron's right ear, the thumb of his right hand, and the big toe of his right foot. 24Next he presented Aaron's sons and put some of the blood on the lobe of their right ears, the thumb of their right hands, and the big toe of their right feet. He then sprinkled the rest of the blood against the sides of the altar.

25Next he took the fat, including the fat from the tail, the fat around the internal organs, the lobe of the liver,

### WORSHIP ● ● • • .

**7:38 God gave his people many rituals and instructions to follow. All the rituals in Leviticus were meant to teach the people valuable lessons. But over time, the people became indifferent to the meanings of these rituals and they began to lose touch with God. When your church appears to be conducting dry, meaningless rituals, try rediscovering the original meaning and purpose behind each, and your worship will come alive.**

8:3 Hebrew *Tent of Meeting;* also in 8:4, 31, 33, 35. 8:15 Or *that atonement may be made on it.*

and the two kidneys with their fat, along with the right thigh. [26]On top of these he placed a loaf of unleavened bread, a cake of unleavened bread soaked with olive oil, and a thin wafer spread with olive oil. All these were taken from the basket of bread made without yeast that was placed in the LORD's presence. [27]He gave all of these to Aaron and his sons, and he presented the portions by lifting them up before the LORD. [28]Moses then took all the offerings back and burned them on the altar on top of the burnt offering as an ordination offering. It was an offering given to the LORD by fire, very pleasing to the LORD. [29]Then Moses took the breast and lifted it up in the LORD's presence. This was Moses' share of the ram of ordination, just as the LORD had commanded him.

[30]Next Moses took some of the anointing oil and some of the blood that was on the altar, and he sprinkled them on Aaron and his clothing and on his sons and their clothing. In this way, he made Aaron and his sons and their clothing holy.

[31]Then Moses said to Aaron and his sons, "Boil the rest of the meat at the Tabernacle entrance, and eat it along with the bread that is in the basket of ordination offerings, just as I commanded you. [32]Any meat or bread that is left over must then be burned up. [33]Do not leave the Tabernacle entrance for seven days, for that is the time it will take to complete the ordination ceremony. [34]What has been done today was commanded by the LORD in order to make atonement for you. [35]Remember, you must stay at the entrance of the Tabernacle day and night for seven days, doing everything the LORD requires. If you fail in this, you will die. This is what the LORD has said." [36]So Aaron and his sons did everything the LORD had commanded through Moses.

## TOTALLY HOLY ● ● • • •

8:36 **Aaron and his sons did all that the Lord told them to do. Considering the many detailed lists of Leviticus, that was a remarkable feat. They knew what God wanted, how he wanted it done, and with what attitude it was to be carried out. This shows how carefully we ought to obey God. God wants us to be thoroughly holy people, not a rough approximation of the way his followers should be.**

CHAPTER **9** **THE PRIESTS BEGIN THEIR WORK.** After the ordination ceremony, on the eighth day, Moses called together Aaron and his sons and the leaders of Israel. [2]He said to Aaron, "Take a young bull for a sin offering and a ram for a whole burnt offering, both with no physical defects, and present them to the LORD. [3]Then tell the Israelites to take a male goat for a sin offering for themselves and a year-old calf and a year-old lamb for a whole burnt offering, each with no physical defects. [4]Also tell them to take a bull* and a ram for a peace offering and flour mixed with olive oil for a grain offering. Tell them to present all these offerings to the LORD because the LORD will appear to them today."

[5]So the people brought all of these things to the entrance of the Tabernacle,* just as Moses had commanded, and the whole community came and stood there in the LORD's presence. [6]Then Moses told them, "When you have followed these instructions from the LORD, the glorious presence of the LORD will appear to you."

[7]Then Moses said to Aaron, "Approach the altar and present your sin offering and your whole burnt offering to make atonement for yourself. Then present the offerings to make atonement for the people, just as the LORD has commanded."

[8]So Aaron went to the altar and slaughtered the calf as a sin offering for himself. [9]His sons brought him the blood, and he dipped his finger into it and put it on the horns of the altar. He poured out the rest of the blood at the base of the altar. [10]Then he burned on the altar the fat, the kidneys, and the lobe of the liver from the sin offering, just as the LORD had commanded Moses. [11]The meat and the hide, however, he burned outside the camp.

[12]Next Aaron slaughtered the animal for the whole burnt offering. His sons brought him the blood, and he sprinkled it against the sides of the altar. [13]They handed the animal to him piece by piece, including the head, and he burned each part on the altar. [14]Then he washed the internal organs and the legs and also burned them on the altar as a whole burnt offering.

[15]Next Aaron presented the sacrifices for the people. He slaughtered the people's goat and presented it as their sin offering, just as he had done previously for himself. [16]Then he brought the whole burnt offering and presented it in the prescribed way. [17]He also brought the grain offering, burning a handful of the flour on the altar, in addition to the regular morning burnt offering.

[18]Then Aaron slaughtered the bull and the ram for the people's peace offering. His sons brought him the blood, and he sprinkled it against the sides of the altar. [19]Then he took the fat of the bull and the ram—the fat from the tail and from around the internal organs—along with the kidneys and the lobe of the liver. [20]He placed these fat parts on top of the breasts of these animals and then burned them on the altar. [21]Aaron then lifted up the breasts and right thighs as an offering to the LORD, just as Moses had commanded.

[22]After that, Aaron raised his hands toward the people and blessed them. Then, after presenting the sin offering, the whole burnt offering, and the peace offering, he stepped down from the altar. [23]Next Moses and Aaron went into the Tabernacle, and when they came back out, they blessed the people again, and the glorious presence of the LORD appeared to the whole community. [24]Fire blazed forth from the LORD's presence and consumed the burnt offering and the fat on the altar. When the people saw all this, they shouted with joy and fell face down on the ground.

9:4 Or *cow;* also in 9:18, 19. 9:5 Hebrew *Tent of Meeting;* also in 9:23.

**CHAPTER 10** **THE SIN OF NADAB AND ABIHU.** Aaron's sons Nadab and Abihu put coals of fire in their incense burners and sprinkled incense over it. In this way, they disobeyed the LORD by burning before him a different kind of fire than he had commanded. 2So fire blazed forth from the LORD's presence and burned them up, and they died there before the LORD.

3Then Moses said to Aaron, "This is what the LORD meant when he said,

'I will show myself holy
    among those who are near me.
I will be glorified
    before all the people.'"

And Aaron was silent.

4Then Moses called for Mishael and Elzaphan, Aaron's cousins, the sons of Aaron's uncle Uzziel. He said to them, "Come and carry the bodies of your relatives away from the sanctuary to a place outside the camp." 5So they came forward and carried them out of the camp by their tunics as Moses had commanded.

6Then Moses said to Aaron and his sons Eleazar and Ithamar, "Do not mourn by letting your hair hang loose* or by tearing your clothes. If you do, you will die, and the LORD will be angry with the whole community of Israel. However, the rest of the Israelites, your relatives, may mourn for Nadab and Abihu, whom the LORD has destroyed by fire. 7But you are not to leave the entrance of the Tabernacle,* under penalty of death, for the anointing oil of the LORD is upon you." So they did as Moses commanded.

8Then the LORD said to Aaron, 9"You and your descendants must never drink wine or any other alcoholic drink before going into the Tabernacle. If you do, you will die. This is a permanent law for you, and it must be kept by all future generations. 10You are to distinguish between what is holy and what is ordinary, what is ceremonially unclean and what is clean. 11And you must teach the Israelites all the laws that the LORD has given through Moses."

12Then Moses said to Aaron and his remaining sons, Eleazar and Ithamar, "Take what is left of the grain offering after the handful has been presented to the LORD by fire. Make sure there is no yeast in it, and eat it beside the altar, for it is most holy. 13It must be eaten in a sacred place, for it has been given to you and your descendants as your regular share of the offerings given to the LORD by fire. These are the commands I have been given. 14But the breast and thigh that were lifted up may be eaten in any place that is ceremonially clean. These parts have been given to you and to your sons and daughters as your regular share of the peace offerings presented by the people of Israel. 15The thigh and breast that are lifted up must be lifted up to the LORD along with the fat of the offerings given by fire. Then they will belong to you and your descendants forever, just as the LORD has commanded."

16When Moses demanded to know what had happened to the goat of the sin offering, he discovered that it had been burned up. As a result, he became very angry with Eleazar and Ithamar, Aaron's remaining sons. 17"Why didn't you eat the sin offering in the sanctuary area?" he demanded. "It is a holy offering! It was given to you for removing the guilt of the community and for making atonement for the people before the LORD. 18Since the animal's blood was not taken into the Holy Place, you should have eaten the meat in the sanctuary area as I ordered you."

19Then Aaron answered Moses on behalf of his sons. "Today my sons presented both their sin offering and their burnt offering to the LORD," he said. "This kind of thing has also happened to me. Would the LORD have approved if I had eaten the sin offering today?" 20And when Moses heard this, he approved.

### BLASTED ● ● • • •

**10:2 Aaron's sons were careless about following the laws for sacrifices. In response, God destroyed them with a blast of fire. Performing the sacrifices was an act of obedience. Doing them correctly showed respect for God. It is easy for us to grow careless about obeying God, to live our way instead of his. But if one way were just as good as another, God would not command us to live his way. He always has good reasons for his commands, and we always place ourselves in danger when we consciously or carelessly disobey them.**

**CHAPTER 11** **CLEAN AND UNCLEAN ANIMALS.** Then the LORD said to Moses and Aaron, 2"Give the following instructions to the Israelites: The animals you may use for food 3include those that have completely divided hooves and chew the cud. 4You may not, however, eat the animals named here* because they either have split hooves or chew the cud, but not both. The camel may not be eaten, for though it chews the cud, it does not have split hooves. 5The same is true of the rock badger* 6and the hare, so they also may never be eaten. 7And the pig may not be eaten, for though it has split hooves, it does not chew the cud. 8You may not eat the meat of these animals or touch their dead bodies. They are ceremonially unclean for you.

9"As for marine animals, you may eat whatever has both fins and scales, whether taken from fresh

### RATIONALIZING ● ● • • •

**11:8 God had strictly forbidden eating the meat of certain animals; to make sure, he forbade even touching them. He wanted the people to be totally separated from those things he had forbidden. Often we flirt with temptation, rationalizing that at least we are technically keeping the commandment not to commit the sin. But God wants us to separate ourselves completely from all sin and tempting situations.**

10:6 Or *by uncovering your heads.* 10:7 Hebrew *Tent of Meeting;* also in 10:9. 11:4 The identification of some of the animals, birds, and insects in this chapter is uncertain. 11:5 Or *coney,* or *hyrax.*

## PREPARED ● ● • • •

11:24-47 **To worship, people need to be prepared. Certain things could ceremonially defile a person, thus disqualifying him from worship. This chapter describes the things that made people "unclean" until they were "cleansed" or straightened out. Similarly, we cannot live any way we want during the week and then rush into God's presence on Sunday. Our relationship with him must be one of constant repentance and cleansing so that we are prepared to worship him and his holiness.**

water or salt water. 10You may not, however, eat marine animals that do not have both fins and scales. You are to detest them, 11and they will always be forbidden to you. You must never eat their meat or even touch their dead bodies. 12I repeat, any marine animal that does not have both fins and scales is strictly forbidden to you.

13"These are the birds you must never eat because they are detestable for you: the eagle, the vulture, the osprey, 14the buzzard, kites of all kinds, 15ravens of all kinds, 16the ostrich, the nighthawk, the seagull, hawks of all kinds, 17the little owl, the cormorant, the great owl, 18the white owl, the pelican, the carrion vulture, 19the stork, herons of all kinds, the hoopoe, and the bat.

20"You are to consider detestable all swarming insects that walk along the ground. 21However, there are some exceptions that you may eat. These include insects that jump with their hind legs: 22locusts of all varieties, crickets, bald locusts, and grasshoppers. All these may be eaten. 23But you are to consider detestable all other swarming insects that walk or crawl.

24"The following creatures make you ceremonially unclean. If you touch any of their dead bodies, you will be defiled until evening. 25If you move the dead body of an unclean animal, you must immediately wash your clothes, and you will remain defiled until evening.

26"Any animal that has divided but unsplit hooves or that does not chew the cud is unclean for you. If you touch the dead body of such an animal, you will be defiled until evening. 27Of the animals that walk on all fours, those that have paws are unclean for you. If you touch the dead body of such an animal, you will be defiled until evening. 28If you pick up and move its carcass, you must immediately wash your clothes, and you will remain defiled until evening.

29"Of the small animals that scurry or creep on the ground, these are unclean for you: the mole, the mouse, the great lizard of all varieties, 30the gecko, the monitor lizard, the common lizard, the sand lizard, and the chameleon. 31All these small animals are unclean for you. If you touch the dead body of such an animal, you will be defiled until evening. 32If such an animal dies and falls on something, that object, whatever its use, will be unclean. This is true whether the object is made of wood, cloth, leather, or sackcloth. It must be put into water, and it will remain defiled until evening. After that, it will be ceremonially clean and may be used again.

33"If such an animal dies and falls into a clay pot, everything in the pot will be defiled, and the pot must be smashed. 34If the water used to cleanse an unclean object touches any food, all of that food will be defiled. And any beverage that is in such an unclean container will be defiled. 35Any object on which the dead body of such an animal falls will be defiled. If it is a clay oven or cooking pot, it must be smashed to pieces. It has become defiled, and it will remain that way.

36"However, if the dead body of such an animal falls into a spring or a cistern, the water will still be clean. But anyone who removes the dead body will be defiled. 37If the dead body falls on seed grain to be planted in the field, the seed will still be considered clean. 38But if the seed is wet when the dead body falls on it, the seed will be defiled.

39"If an animal that is permitted for eating dies and you touch its carcass, you will be defiled until evening. 40If you eat any of its meat or carry away its carcass, you must wash your clothes. Then you will remain defiled until evening.

41"Consider detestable any animal that scurries along the ground; such animals may never be eaten. 42This includes all animals that slither along on their bellies, as well as those with four legs and those with many feet. All such animals are to be considered detestable. 43Never defile yourselves by touching such animals. 44After all, I, the LORD, am your God. You must be holy because I am holy. So do not defile yourselves by touching any of these animals that scurry along the ground. 45I, the LORD, am the one who brought you up from the land of Egypt to be your God. You must therefore be holy because I am holy.

46"These are the instructions regarding the land animals, the birds, and all the living things that move through the water or swarm over the earth, 47so you can distinguish between what is unclean and may not be eaten and what is clean and may be eaten."

## HOLY DESIGN ● ● • • •

11:44-45 **There is more to this chapter than eating right. These verses provide a key to understanding all the laws and regulations in Leviticus. God wanted his people to be *holy* (set apart, different, unique), just as he is holy. He knew they had only two options: to be separate and holy, or to compromise with their heathen neighbors and become corrupt. That is why he called them out of idolatrous Egypt and set them apart as a unique nation, dedicated to worshiping him alone and leading moral lives. That is also why he designed laws and restrictions to help them remain separate—both socially and spiritually—from the wicked heathen nations they would encounter in Canaan.**

**Christians also are called to be holy (1 Peter 1:15). Like the Israelites, we are to remain spiritually separate from the world's wickedness, even though, unlike them, we rub shoulders with unbelievers every day. It is no easy task to be holy in an unholy world, but God doesn't ask you to accomplish this on your own. Through the death of his Son, he will present you holy and blameless before him (Colossians 1:22).**

CHAPTER **12** **MOTHERS AND CHILDBIRTH.** The LORD said to Moses, "Give these instructions to the Israelites: [2]When a woman becomes pregnant and gives birth to a son, she will be ceremonially unclean for seven days, just as she is defiled during her menstrual period. [3]On the eighth day, the boy must be circumcised. [4]Then the woman must wait for thirty-three days until the time of her purification from the blood of childbirth is completed. During this time of purification, she must not touch anything that is holy. And she must not go to the sanctuary until her time of purification is over. [5]If a woman gives birth to a daughter, she will be ceremonially defiled for two weeks, just as she is defiled during her menstrual period. She must then wait another sixty-six days to be purified from the blood of childbirth.

[6]"When the time of purification is completed for either a son or a daughter, the woman must bring a year-old lamb for a whole burnt offering and a young pigeon or turtledove for a purification offering. She must take her offerings to the priest at the entrance of the Tabernacle.* [7]The priest will then present them to the LORD and make atonement for her. Then she will be ceremonially clean again after her bleeding at childbirth. These are the instructions to be followed after the birth of a son or a daughter.

[8]"If a woman cannot afford to bring a sheep, she must bring two turtledoves or two young pigeons. One will be for the whole burnt offering and the other for the purification offering. The priest will sacrifice them, thus making atonement for her, and she will be ceremonially clean."

CHAPTER **13** **CONTAGIOUS SKIN DISEASES.** The LORD said to Moses and Aaron, [2]"If some of the people notice a swelling or a rash or a shiny patch on their skin that develops into a contagious skin disease,* they must be brought to Aaron the priest or to one of his sons. [3]The priest will then examine the affected area of a person's skin. If the hair in the affected area has turned white and appears to be more than skin-deep, then it is a contagious skin disease, and the priest must pronounce the person ceremonially unclean.

[4]"But if the affected area of the skin is white but does not appear to be more than skin-deep, and if the hair in the spot has not turned white, the priest will put the infected person in quarantine for seven days. [5]On the seventh day the priest will make another examination. If the affected area has not changed or spread on the skin, then the priest will put the person in quarantine for seven more days. [6]The priest will examine the skin again on the seventh day. If the affected area has faded and not spread, the priest will pronounce the person ceremonially clean. It was only a temporary rash. So after washing the clothes, the person will be considered free of disease. [7]But if the rash continues to spread after this examination and pronouncement by the priest, the infected person must return to be examined again. [8]If the priest notices that the rash has spread, then he must pronounce this person ceremonially unclean, for it is a contagious skin disease.

[9]"Anyone who develops a contagious skin disease must go to the priest for an examination. [10]If the priest sees that some hair has turned white and an open sore appears in the affected area, [11]it is clearly a contagious skin disease, and the priest must pronounce that person ceremonially unclean. In such cases, the person need not be quarantined for further observation because it is clear that the skin is defiled by the disease.

## RIGHT RITES ● ● • • •

**12:1-4 *Unclean* did not mean "sinful," implying that sex or childbirth is dirty. Instead, it meant "not appropriate to make sacrifice." In Canaan, prostitution and fertility rites were part of worship. By contrast, in Israel, anything related to sex was avoided when worshiping God. Again, this doesn't mean that sex is unclean. It just means that there are appropriate (and inappropriate) times and places for everything.**

[12]"Now suppose the priest discovers after his examination that a rash has broken out all over someone's skin, covering the body from head to foot. [13]In such cases, the priest must examine the infected person to see if the disease covers the entire body. If it does, he will pronounce the person ceremonially clean because the skin has turned completely white. [14]But if any open sores appear, the infected person will be pronounced ceremonially unclean. [15]The priest must make this pronouncement as soon as he sees an open sore because open sores indicate the presence of a contagious skin disease. [16]However, if the open sores heal and turn white like the rest of the skin, the person must return to the priest. [17]If, after another examination, the affected areas have indeed turned completely white, then the priest will pronounce the person ceremonially clean.

[18]"If anyone has had a boil on the skin that has started to heal, [19]but a white swelling or a reddish white spot remains in its place, that person must go to the priest to be examined. [20]If the priest finds the disease to be more than skin-deep, and if the hair in the affected area has turned white, then the priest must pronounce that person ceremonially unclean. It is a contagious skin disease that has broken out in the boil. [21]But if the priest sees that there is no white hair in the affected area, and if it doesn't appear to be more than skin-deep and has faded, then the priest is to put the person in quarantine for seven days. [22]If during that time the affected area spreads on the skin, the priest must pronounce the person ceremonially unclean, because it is a contagious skin disease. [23]But if the area grows no larger and does not spread, it is merely the scar from the boil, and the priest will pronounce that person ceremonially clean.

12:6 Hebrew *Tent of Meeting.* 13:2 Traditionally rendered *leprosy.* The Hebrew word used throughout this passage is used to describe various skin diseases.

24 "If anyone has suffered a burn on the skin and the burned area changes color, becoming either a shiny reddish white or white, 25 then the priest must examine it. If the hair in the affected area turns white and the problem appears to be more than skin-deep, a contagious skin disease has broken out in the burn. The priest must then pronounce that person ceremonially unclean, for it is clearly a contagious skin disease. 26 But if the priest discovers that there is no white hair in the affected area and the problem appears to be no more than skin-deep and has faded, then the priest is to put the infected person in quarantine for seven days. 27 If at the end of that time the affected area has spread on the skin, the priest must pronounce that person ceremonially unclean, for it is clearly a contagious skin disease. 28 But if the affected area has not moved or spread on the skin and has faded, it is simply a scar from the burn. The priest must then pronounce the person ceremonially clean.

29 "If anyone, whether a man or woman, has an open sore on the head or chin, 30 the priest must examine the infection. If it appears to be more than skin-deep and fine yellow hair is found in the affected area, the priest must pronounce the infected person ceremonially unclean. The infection is a contagious skin disease of the head or chin. 31 However, if the priest's examination reveals that the infection is only skin-deep and there is no black hair in the affected area, then he must put the person in quarantine for seven days. 32 If at the end of that time the affected area has not spread and no yellow hair has appeared, and if the infection does not appear to be more than skin-deep, 33 the infected person must shave off all hair except the hair on the affected area. Then the priest must put the person in quarantine for another seven days, 34 and he will examine the infection again on the seventh day. If it has not spread and appears to be no more than skin-deep, the priest must pronounce that person ceremonially clean. After washing clothes, that person will be clean. 35 But if the infection begins to spread after the person is pronounced clean, 36 the priest must do another examination. If the infection has spread, he must pronounce the infected person ceremonially unclean, even without checking for yellow hair. 37 But if it appears that the infection has stopped spreading and black hair has grown in the affected area, then the infection has healed. The priest will then pronounce the infected person ceremonially clean.

38 "If anyone, whether a man or woman, has shiny white patches on the skin, 39 the priest must examine the affected area. If the patch is only a pale white, this is a harmless skin rash, and the person is ceremonially clean.

40 "If a man loses his hair and his head becomes bald, he is still ceremonially clean. 41 And if he loses hair on his forehead, he simply has a bald forehead; he is still clean. 42 However, if a reddish white infection appears on the front or the back of his head, this is a contagious skin disease. 43 The priest must examine him, and if he finds swelling around the reddish white sore, 44 the man is infected with a contagious skin disease and is unclean. The priest must pronounce him ceremonially unclean because of the infection.

45 "Those who suffer from any contagious skin disease must tear their clothing and allow their hair to hang loose.* Then, as they go from place to place, they must cover their mouth and call out, 'Unclean! Unclean!' 46 As long as the disease lasts, they will be ceremonially unclean and must live in isolation outside the camp.

47 "Now suppose an infectious mildew* contaminates some woolen or linen clothing, 48 some woolen or linen fabric, the hide of an animal, or anything made of leather. 49 If the affected area in the clothing, the animal hide, the fabric, or the leather has turned bright green or a reddish color, it is contaminated with an infectious mildew and must be taken to the priest to be examined. 50 After examining the affected spot, the priest will put it away for seven days. 51 On the seventh day the priest must inspect it again. If the affected area has spread, the material is clearly contaminated by an infectious mildew and is unclean. 52 The priest must burn the linen or wool clothing or the piece of leather because it has been contaminated by an infectious mildew. It must be completely destroyed by fire.

53 "But if the priest examines it again and the affected spot has not spread in the clothing, the fabric, or the leather, 54 the priest will order the contaminated object to be washed and then isolated for seven more days. 55 Then the priest must inspect the object again. If he sees that the affected area has not changed appearance after being washed, even if it did not spread, the object is defiled. It must be completely burned up, whether it is contaminated on the inside or outside. 56 But if the priest sees that the affected area has faded after being washed, he is to cut the spot from the clothing, the fabric, or the leather. 57 If the spot reappears at a later time, however, the mildew is clearly spreading, and the contaminated object must be burned up. 58 But if the spot disappears after the object is washed, it must be washed again; then it will be ceremonially clean.

59 "These are the instructions for dealing with infectious mildew in woolen or linen clothing or fabric, or in anything made of leather. This is how the priest will determine whether these things are ceremonially clean or unclean."

## CHAPTER 14

And the LORD said to Moses, 2 "The following instructions must be followed by those seeking purification from a contagious skin disease.* Those who have been healed must be brought to the priest, 3 who will examine them at a place outside the camp. If the priest finds that some-

13:45 Or *and uncover their heads.* 13:47 Traditionally rendered *leprosy.* The Hebrew term used throughout this passage is the same term used for the various skin diseases described in 13:1-46. 14:2 Traditionally rendered *leprosy.* See note at 13:2.

one has been healed of the skin disease, 4he will perform a purification ceremony, using two wild birds of a kind permitted for food, along with some cedarwood, a scarlet cloth, and a hyssop branch. 5The priest will order one of the birds to be slaughtered over a clay pot that is filled with fresh springwater. 6He will then dip the living bird, along with the cedarwood, the scarlet cloth, and the hyssop branch, into the blood of the slaughtered bird. 7The priest will also sprinkle the dead bird's blood seven times over the person being purified, and the priest will pronounce that person to be ceremonially clean. At the end of the ceremony, the priest will set the living bird free so it can fly away into the open fields.

8"The people being purified must complete the cleansing ceremony by washing their clothes, shaving off all their hair, and bathing themselves in water. Then they will be ceremonially clean and may return to live inside the camp. However, they must still remain outside their tents for seven days. 9On the seventh day, they must again shave off all their hair, including the hair of the beard and eyebrows, and wash their clothes and bathe themselves in water. Then they will be pronounced ceremonially clean.

10"On the next day, the eighth day, each person cured of the skin disease must bring two male lambs and one female year-old lamb with no physical defects, along with five quarts* of choice flour mixed with olive oil and three-fifths of a pint* of olive oil. 11Then the officiating priest will present that person for cleansing, along with the offerings, before the LORD at the entrance of the Tabernacle.* 12The priest will take one of the lambs and the olive oil and offer them as a guilt offering by lifting them up before the LORD. 13He will then slaughter the lamb there in the sacred area at the place where sin offerings and burnt offerings are slaughtered. As with the sin offering, the guilt offering will be given to the priest. It is a most holy offering. 14The priest will then take some of the blood from the guilt offering and put it on the tip of the healed person's right ear, on the thumb of the right hand, and on the big toe of the right foot.

15"Then the priest will pour some of the olive oil into the palm of his own left hand. 16He will dip his right finger into the oil and sprinkle it seven times before the LORD. 17The priest will then put some of the oil remaining in his left hand on the tip of the healed person's right ear, on the thumb of the right hand, and on the big toe of the right foot, in addition to the blood of the guilt offering. 18The oil remaining in the priest's hand will then be poured over the healed person's head. In this way, the priest will make atonement before the LORD for the person being cleansed.

19"Then the priest must offer the sin offering and again perform the atonement ceremony for the person cured of the skin disease. After that, the priest will slaughter the whole burnt offering 20and offer it on the altar along with the grain offering. In this way, the priest will make atonement for the person being cleansed, and the healed person will be ceremonially clean.

21"But anyone who cannot afford two lambs must bring one male lamb for a guilt offering, along with two quarts* of choice flour mixed with olive oil as a grain offering and three-fifths of a pint of olive oil. The guilt offering will be presented by lifting it up, thus making atonement for the person being cleansed. 22The person being cleansed must also bring two turtledoves or two young pigeons, whichever the person can afford. One of the pair must be used for a sin offering and the other for a whole burnt offering. 23On the eighth day, the person being cleansed must bring the offerings to the priest for the cleansing ceremony to be performed in the LORD's presence at the Tabernacle entrance. 24The priest will take the lamb for the guilt offering, along with the olive oil, and lift them up before the LORD as an offering to him. 25Then the priest will slaughter the lamb for the guilt offering and put some of its blood on the tip of the person's right ear, on the thumb of the right hand, and on the big toe of the right foot.

26"The priest will also pour some of the olive oil into the palm of his own left hand. 27He will dip his right finger into the oil and sprinkle some of it seven times before the LORD. 28The priest will then put some of the olive oil from his hand on the lobe of the person's right ear, on the thumb of the right hand, and on the big toe of the right foot, in addition to the blood of the guilt offering. 29The oil that is still in the priest's hand will then be poured over the person's head. In this way, the priest will make atonement for the person being cleansed.

30"Then the priest will offer the two turtledoves or the two young pigeons, whichever the person was able to afford. 31One of them is for a sin offering and the other for a whole burnt offering, to be presented along with the grain offering. In this way, the priest will make atonement before the LORD for the person being cleansed. 32These are the instructions for cleansing those who have recovered from a contagious skin disease but who cannot afford to bring the sacrifices normally required for the ceremony of cleansing."

33Then the LORD said to Moses and Aaron, 34"When you arrive in Canaan, the land I am giving you as an inheritance, I may contaminate some of your houses with an infectious mildew.* 35The

**FUNGUS ● ● • • •**

14:33-53 **Here are instructions concerning "infectious mildew" on clothing or house walls—probably a mold, fungus, or bacteria. Like mildew, this fungus could spread rapidly and promote disease. It was therefore important to check its spread as soon as possible. Is there anything in your life—an activity or relationship—that has a similar, destructive effect on you or your faith?**

**14:10a** Hebrew *3/10 of an ephah* [5.4 liters]. **14:10b** Hebrew *1 log* [0.3 liters]; also in 14:21. **14:11** Hebrew *Tent of Meeting;* also in 14:23. **14:21** Hebrew *1/10 of an ephah* [2 liters]. **14:34** Traditionally rendered *leprosy.* See note at 13:47.

owner of such a house must then go to the priest and say, 'It looks like my house has some kind of disease.' [36]Before the priest examines the house, he must have the house emptied so everything inside will not be pronounced unclean. Then the priest will go in and inspect the house. [37]If he finds bright green or reddish streaks on the walls of the house and the contamination appears to go deeper than the wall's surface, [38]he will leave the house and lock it up for seven days. [39]On the seventh day the priest must return for another inspection. If the mildew on the walls of the house has spread, [40]the priest must order that the stones from those areas be removed. The contaminated material will then be thrown into an area outside the town designated as ceremonially unclean. [41]Next the inside walls of the entire house must be scraped thoroughly and the scrapings dumped in the unclean place outside the town. [42]Other stones will be brought in to replace the ones that were removed, and the walls will be replastered.

[43]"But if the mildew reappears after all these things have been done, [44]the priest must return and inspect the house again. If he sees that the affected areas have spread, the walls are clearly contaminated with an infectious mildew, and the house is defiled. [45]It must be torn down, and all its stones, timbers, and plaster must be carried out of town to the place designated as ceremonially unclean. [46]Anyone who enters the house while it is closed will be considered ceremonially unclean until evening. [47]All who sleep or eat in the house must wash their clothing.

[48]"But if the priest returns for his inspection and finds that the affected areas have not reappeared after the fresh plastering, then he will pronounce the house clean because the infectious mildew is clearly gone. [49]To purify the house the priest will need two birds, some cedarwood, a scarlet cloth, and a hyssop branch. [50]He will slaughter one of the birds over a clay pot that is filled with fresh springwater. [51]Then he will dip the cedarwood, the hyssop branch, the scarlet cloth, and the living bird into the blood of the slaughtered bird, and he will sprinkle the house seven times. [52]After he has purified the house in this way, [53]he will release the living bird in the open fields outside the town. In this way, the priest will make atonement for the house, and it will be ceremonially clean.

[54]"These are the instructions for dealing with the various kinds of contagious skin disease* and infectious mildew,* [55]whether in clothing, in a house, [56]in a swollen area of skin, in a skin rash, or in a shiny patch of skin. [57]These instructions must be followed when dealing with any contagious skin disease or infectious mildew, to determine when something is ceremonially clean or unclean."

## CHAPTER 15

**RULES OF HEALTH.** The LORD said to Moses and Aaron, [2]"Give these further instructions to the Israelites: Any man who has a genital discharge* is ceremonially unclean because of it. [3]This defilement applies whether the discharge continues or is stopped up. In either case the man is unclean. [4]Any bedding on which he lies and anything on which he sits will be defiled.

[5]"So if you touch the man's bedding, you will be required to wash your clothes and bathe in water, and you will remain ceremonially defiled until evening. [6]If you sit where the man with the discharge has sat, you will be required to wash your clothes and bathe in water. You will then remain defiled until evening. [7]The same instructions apply if you touch the man who has the unclean discharge. [8]And if he spits on you, you must undergo the same procedure. [9]Any blanket on which the man rides will be defiled. [10]If you touch or carry anything that was under him, you will be required to wash your clothes and bathe in water, and you will remain defiled until evening. [11]If the man touches you without first rinsing his hands, then you will be required to wash your clothes and bathe in water, and you will remain defiled until evening. [12]Any clay pot touched by the man with the discharge must be broken, and every wooden utensil he touches must be rinsed with water.

[13]"When the man's discharge heals, he must count off a period of seven days. During that time, he must wash his clothes and bathe in fresh springwater. Then he will be ceremonially clean. [14]On the eighth day he must bring two turtledoves or two young pigeons and present himself to the LORD at the entrance of the Tabernacle* and give his offerings to the priest. [15]The priest will present the offerings there, one for a sin offering and the other for a whole burnt offering. In this way, the priest will make atonement for the man before the LORD for his discharge.

[16]"Whenever a man has an emission of semen, he must wash his entire body, and he will remain ceremonially defiled until evening. [17]Any clothing or leather that comes in contact with the semen must be washed, and it will remain defiled until evening. [18]After having sexual intercourse, both the man and the woman must bathe, and they will remain defiled until evening.

[19]"Whenever a woman has her menstrual period, she will be ceremonially unclean for seven days. If you touch her during that time, you will be defiled until evening. [20]Anything on which she lies or sits during that time will be defiled. [21]If you touch her

**SEX ● ● • • ·**

**15:18 This verse is not implying that sex is dirty or disgusting. God created sex, both for the enjoyment of married couples and for continuing the race and the covenant. Everything must be seen and done with a view toward God's love and control. Sex is not separate from spirituality and God's care. God is concerned about our sexual habits. We tend to separate our physical and spiritual lives, but there is an inseparable intertwining. God must be Lord over our whole self—including our private life.**

14:54 Traditionally rendered *leprosy.* See notes at 13:2 and 13:47. 15:2 Hebrew *a discharge from his flesh;* also in 15:32. 15:14 Hebrew *Tent of Meeting;* also in 15:29.

**OLD/NEW SYSTEM OF SACRIFICE**

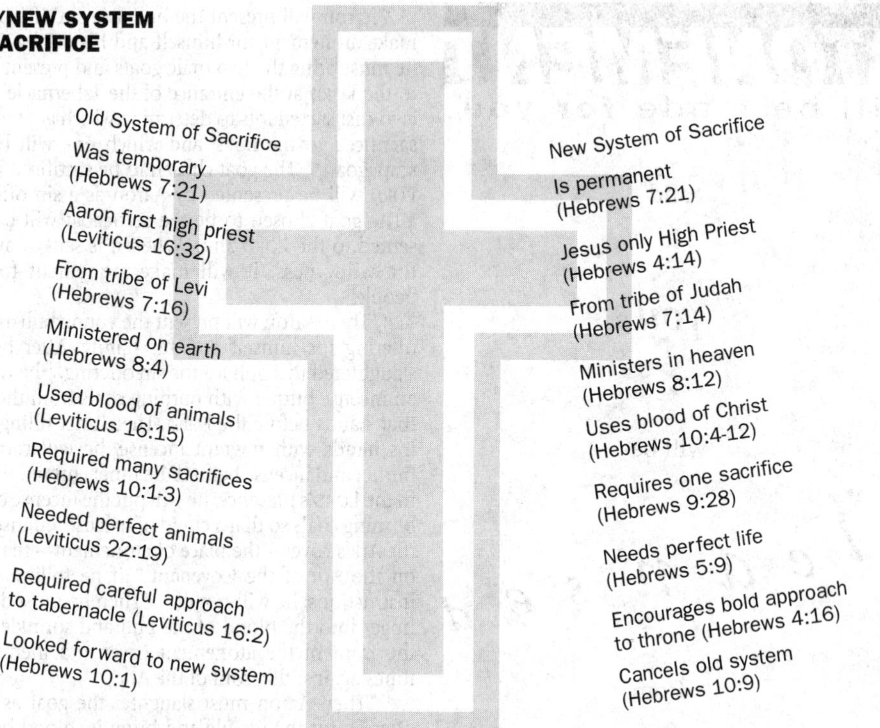
Old System of Sacrifice
Was temporary (Hebrews 7:21)
Aaron first high priest (Leviticus 16:32)
From tribe of Levi (Hebrews 7:16)
Ministered on earth (Hebrews 8:4)
Used blood of animals (Leviticus 16:15)
Required many sacrifices (Hebrews 10:1-3)
Needed perfect animals (Leviticus 22:19)
Required careful approach to tabernacle (Leviticus 16:2)
Looked forward to new system (Hebrews 10:1)
New System of Sacrifice
Is permanent (Hebrews 7:21)
Jesus only High Priest (Hebrews 4:14)
From tribe of Judah (Hebrews 7:14)
Ministers in heaven (Hebrews 8:12)
Uses blood of Christ (Hebrews 10:4-12)
Requires one sacrifice (Hebrews 9:28)
Needs perfect life (Hebrews 5:9)
Encourages bold approach to throne (Hebrews 4:16)
Cancels old system (Hebrews 10:9)

bed, you must wash your clothes and bathe in water,
and you will remain defiled until evening. 22The
same applies if you touch an object on which she
sits, 23whether it is her bedding or any piece of furni-
ture. 24If a man has sexual intercourse with her during this time, her menstrual impurity will be
transmitted to him. He will remain defiled for seven
days, and any bed on which he lies will be defiled.
25"If the menstrual flow of blood continues for
many days beyond the normal period, or if she
discharges blood unrelated to her menstruation,
the woman will be ceremonially unclean as long as
the discharge continues. 26Anything on which she
lies or sits during that time will be defiled, just as
it would be during her normal menstrual period.
27If you touch her bed or anything on which she
sits, you will be defiled. You will be required to
wash your clothes and bathe in water, and you will
remain defiled until evening.
28"When the woman's menstrual discharge stops,
she must count off a period of seven days. After that,
she will be ceremonially clean. 29On the eighth day,
she must bring two turtledoves or two young pigeons
and present them to the priest at the entrance of the
Tabernacle. 30The priest will offer one for a sin offering and the other for a whole burnt offering. In this
way, the priest will make atonement for her before
the LORD for her menstrual discharge.
31"In this way, you will keep the people of Israel
separate from things that will defile them, so they
will not die as a result of defiling my Tabernacle that
is right there among them. 32These are the instructions for dealing with a man who has been defiled
by a genital discharge or an emission of semen; 33for
dealing with a woman during her monthly menstrual period; for dealing with anyone, man or
woman, who has had a bodily discharge of any kind;
and for dealing with a man who has had intercourse
with a woman during her period."

## CHAPTER 16

**THE DAY OF ATONEMENT.** The LORD
spoke to Moses after the death of Aaron's two sons,
who died when they burned a different kind of fire
than the LORD had commanded.* 2The LORD said to
Moses, "Warn your brother Aaron not to enter the
Most Holy Place behind the inner curtain whenever he chooses; the penalty for intrusion is death.
For the Ark's cover—the place of atonement—is

16:1 Hebrew *when they approached the LORD's presence;* compare 10:1.

**GET READY ● ● • • •**

16:1-25 **Aaron had to spend hours preparing himself to meet God. But we can approach God anytime (Hebrews 4:16). What a privilege! We are offered easier access to God than the high priests of Old Testament times! Still, we must never forget that God is holy or let this privilege cause us to approach God carelessly. The way to God has been opened to us by Christ. But easy access to God does not eliminate our need to prepare our hearts as we draw near in prayer.**

ON THIS DAY
**ATONEMENT**
will be made **for you,**

and

*you*

will be

*c l e a n s e d*

from

*all*

your sins

IN THE LORD'S
**PRESENCE**

LEVITICUS 16:30

there, and I myself am present in the cloud over the atonement cover.

[3]"When Aaron enters the sanctuary area, he must follow these instructions fully. He must first bring a young bull for a sin offering and a ram for a whole burnt offering. [4]Then he must wash his entire body and put on his linen tunic and the undergarments worn next to his body. He must tie the linen sash around his waist and put the linen turban on his head. These are his sacred garments. [5]The people of Israel must then bring him two male goats for a sin offering and a ram for a whole burnt offering.

[6]"Aaron will present the bull as a sin offering, to make atonement for himself and his family. [7]Then he must bring the two male goats and present them to the LORD at the entrance of the Tabernacle.* [8]He is to cast sacred lots to determine which goat will be sacrificed to the LORD and which one will be the scapegoat.* [9]The goat chosen to be sacrificed to the LORD will be presented by Aaron as a sin offering. [10]The goat chosen to be the scapegoat will be presented to the LORD alive. When it is sent away into the wilderness, it will make atonement for the people.

[11]"Then Aaron will present the young bull as a sin offering for himself and his family. After he has slaughtered this bull for the sin offering, [12]he will fill an incense burner with burning coals from the altar that stands before the LORD. Then, after filling both his hands with fragrant incense, he will carry the burner and incense behind the inner curtain. [13]There in the LORD's presence, he will put the incense on the burning coals so that a cloud of incense will rise over the Ark's cover—the place of atonement—that rests on the Ark of the Covenant.* If he follows these instructions, he will not die. [14]Then he must dip his finger into the blood of the bull and sprinkle it on the front of the atonement cover and then seven times against the front of the Ark.

[15]"Then Aaron must slaughter the goat as a sin offering for the people and bring its blood behind the inner curtain. There he will sprinkle the blood on the atonement cover and against the front of the Ark, just as he did with the bull's blood. [16]In this way, he will make atonement for the Most Holy Place, and he will do the same for the entire Tabernacle, because of the defiling sin and rebellion of the Israelites. [17]No one else is allowed inside the Tabernacle while Aaron goes in to make atonement for the Most Holy Place. No one may enter until he comes out again after making atonement for himself, his family, and all the Israelites.

[18]"Then Aaron will go out to make atonement for the altar that stands before the LORD by smearing some of the blood from the bull and the goat on each of the altar's horns. [19]Then he must dip his finger into the blood and sprinkle it seven times over the altar. In this way, he will cleanse it from Israel's defilement and return it to its former holiness.

[20]"When Aaron has finished making atonement for the Most Holy Place, the Tabernacle, and the altar, he must bring the living goat forward. [21]He is to lay both of his hands on the goat's head and confess over it all the sins and rebellion of the Israelites. In this way, he will lay the people's sins on the head of the goat; then he will send it out into the wilderness, led by a man chosen for this task. [22]After the man sets it free in the wilderness, the goat will carry all the people's sins upon itself into a desolate land.

[23]"As Aaron enters the Tabernacle, he must take off the linen garments he wore when he entered the

16:7 Hebrew *Tent of Meeting;* also in 16:16, 17, 20, 23, 33. 16:8 Hebrew *azazel,* which in this context means "the goat of removal"; also in 16:10, 26. 16:13 Hebrew *on the Testimony,* referring to the terms of God's covenant with Israel, which were kept in the Ark.

Most Holy Place, and he must leave the garments there. [24]Then he must bathe his entire body with water in a sacred place, put on his garments, and go out to sacrifice his own whole burnt offering and the whole burnt offering for the people. In this way, he will make atonement for himself and for the people. [25]He must also burn all the fat of the sin offering on the altar.

[26]"The man chosen to send the goat out into the wilderness as a scapegoat must wash his clothes and bathe in water. Then he may return to the camp.

[27]"The bull and goat given as sin offerings, whose blood Aaron brought into the Most Holy Place to make atonement for Israel, will be carried outside the camp to be burned. This includes the animals' hides, the internal organs, and the dung. [28]The man who does the burning must wash his clothes and bathe himself in water before returning to the camp.

[29]"On the appointed day in early autumn,* you must spend the day fasting and not do any work. This is a permanent law for you, and it applies to those who are Israelites by birth, as well as to the foreigners living among you. [30]On this day, atonement will be made for you, and you will be cleansed from all your sins in the LORD's presence. [31]It will be a Sabbath day of total rest, and you will spend the day in fasting. This is a permanent law for you. [32]In future generations, the atonement ceremony will be performed by the anointed high priest who serves in place of his ancestor Aaron. He will put on the holy linen garments [33]and make atonement for the Most Holy Place, the Tabernacle, the altar, the priests, and the entire community. [34]This is a permanent law for you, to make atonement for the Israelites once each year."

Moses followed all these instructions that the LORD had given to him.

## CHAPTER 17 WARNING AGAINST SACRIFICING WRONGLY.

Then the LORD said to Moses, [2]"Give Aaron and his sons and all the Israelites these commands from the LORD: [3]If any Israelite sacrifices a bull* or a lamb or a goat anywhere inside or outside the camp [4]and does not bring it to the entrance of the Tabernacle* to present it as an offering to the LORD, that person will be guilty of a capital offense.* Such a person has shed blood and must be cut off from the community. [5]This rule will stop the Israelites from sacrificing animals in the open fields. It will cause them to bring their sacrifices to the priest at the entrance of the Tabernacle, so he can present them to the LORD as peace offerings. [6]That way the priest will be able to sprinkle the blood and burn the fat on the LORD's altar at the entrance of the Tabernacle, and it will be very pleasing to the LORD. [7]The people must no longer be unfaithful to the LORD by offering sacrifices to evil spirits* out in the fields. This is a permanent law for them, to be kept generation after generation.

[8]"Give them this command as well, which applies both to Israelites and to the foreigners living among you. If you offer a whole burnt offering or a sacrifice [9]and do not bring it to the entrance of the Tabernacle to offer it to the LORD, you will be cut off from the community.

[10]"And I will turn against anyone, whether an Israelite or a foreigner living among you, who eats or drinks blood in any form. I will cut off such a person from the community, [11]for the life of any creature is in its blood. I have given you the blood so you can make atonement for your sins. It is the blood, representing life, that brings you atonement. [12]That is why I said to the Israelites: 'You and the foreigners who live among you must never eat or drink blood.'

[13]"And this command applies both to Israelites and to the foreigners living among you. If you go hunting and kill an animal or bird that is approved for eating, you must drain out the blood and cover it with earth. [14]The life of every creature is in the blood. That is why I have told the people of Israel never to eat or drink it, for the life of any bird or animal is in the blood. So whoever eats or drinks blood must be cut off.

[15]"And this command also applies both to Israelites and the foreigners living among you. If you eat from the carcass of an animal that died a natural death or was killed by a wild animal, you must wash your clothes and bathe yourselves in water. Then you will remain ceremonially unclean until evening; after that, you will be considered clean. [16]But if you do not wash your clothes and bathe, you will be held responsible."

## CHAPTER 18 WRONG SEXUAL RELATIONSHIPS.

Then the LORD said to Moses, [2]"Say this to your people, the Israelites: I, the LORD, am your God. [3]So do not act like the people in Egypt, where you used to live, or like the people of Canaan, where I am taking you. You must not imitate their way of life. [4]You must obey all my regulations and be careful to keep my laws, for I, the LORD, am your God. [5]If you obey my

### CULTURE ● ● • • •

18:3 **The Israelites moved from one idol-infested country to another. As God helped them form a new culture, he warned them to leave all aspects of their heathen background behind. He also warned them how easy it would be to slip into the heathen culture of Canaan, where they were going. Canaan's society and religions appealed to carnal desires, especially sexual immorality and drunkenness. The Israelites were to keep themselves pure and set apart for God. God did not want his people absorbed into the surrounding culture and environment. Society may pressure us to conform to its way of life and thought, but yielding to that pressure will (1) create confusion as to which side we should be on, and (2) eliminate our effectiveness in serving God. Follow God, and don't let the culture around you mold your thoughts and actions.**

**16:29** Hebrew *On the tenth day of the seventh month.* This day of the Hebrew lunar calendar occurs in September or early October. **17:3** Or *cow.* **17:4a** Hebrew *Tent of Meeting;* also in 17:5, 6, 9. **17:4b** Hebrew *blood guilt.* **17:7** Or *goat idols.*

# THE LAW

It's universal: You see a sign that says Wet Paint; you want to touch it. Walk by a sign in a pet shop window that says, Do Not Tap on Glass! and what do you do? Tap on the glass. It's a law of human nature: Rules are made to be broken. Something inside makes us wonder, "What happens if I cross the line?" God's people are not immune to this temptation. The Old Testament seems like a series of stories about God giving Israel **RULES**—obedience meant blessing; disobedience meant punishment. So what is the role of the law for Christians today? Are we, like the people of Moses' time, obligated to obey the law or are we free of it? There are several different views on this. First, the law can be divided into three branches: ceremonial, judicial, and moral. Ceremonial laws related to sacrifices, cleansing rituals, festivals, etc. Judicial laws dealt with the government—what kind of king Israel needed, criminal codes, etc. The moral law concerned how people interacted with each other and with God. (The TEN COMMANDMENTS are the best-known section of the moral law.) There is some sharp disagreement as to how we are to view each branch, but the "majority opinion" of Christians has been that the ceremonial laws were fulfilled in Christ; the judicial laws applied to the nation of Israel alone (although these principles are the foundation for laws in the United States and other Western nations); and the moral laws are true for all people, everywhere, at all times. Now, what does the law do? It acts as: • A mirror: If you had a three-year-old draw a line on a chalkboard, you'd probably get a ***crooked*** line. If you drew a line next to it and compared them, you might think, *My line really is straight, especially compared to little Sally's.* But if someone else drew a line next to yours using a straightedge, you'd see all the imperfections in your line. It wasn't straight at all; it only looked good next to a crooked one. That's what the law does for us. It's tempting to look at bad people (by human standards) and think, *I'm a pretty good dude/dudette.* But when compared to God's perfect standard—the law—we see our sins. We see what we look like from God's point of view; and frankly, it's **not a pretty sight.** • An instructor: Though nobody likes instructors, we all need them. Paul wrote, "The law was our guardian and teacher to lead us until Christ came. So now, through faith in Christ, we are made right with God" (Galatians 3:24). The law taught the Israelites how to live before a holy God who set high standards and expected his people to live up to them: "You must be holy, because I, the LORD your God, am holy" (Leviticus 19:2). God's law also set Israel apart from pagan nations. Those other nations might worship idols; practice child sacrifice; wink at sexual immorality, divorce, dishonesty, etc. But not Israel. They were held to a HIGHER STANDARD. With God's law as instructor, there was no "grading on the curve." • An encourager: The law gave Abraham's descendants guidelines for living in a manner worthy of God. Think of the law as **training wheels.** When you first try to ride a bike, you wobble and then fall over unless you have something to keep you straight—like training wheels. They help you stay upright until you "get the hang of it." The law does that, too—it shows you how to walk uprightly before a holy God. When you read about God's laws, don't just see pointless rules and regulations designed to make our lives rough. The law shows us who we are—sinners in need of a Savior. It shows us how to live before a holy, righteous God, and how to please that awesome God—by obeying his commandments. Most important, the law pointed the people of the Old Testament toward a coming Savior, who would fulfill the law and set his people free. We don't need a law to guide us until he comes—he has come already and written his law on our hearts.

laws and regulations, you will find life through
them. I am the LORD.
6“You must never have sexual intercourse with a
close relative, for I am the LORD. 7Do not violate your
father by having sexual intercourse with your
mother. She is your mother; you must never have
intercourse with her. 8Do not have sexual intercourse
with any of your father’s wives, for this would violate
your father.
9“Do not have sexual intercourse with your sister
or half sister, whether she is your father’s daughter or
your mother’s daughter, whether she was brought up
in the same family or somewhere else.
10“Do not have sexual intercourse with your
granddaughter, whether your son’s daughter or your
daughter’s daughter; that would violate you. 11Do
not have sexual intercourse with the daughter of any
of your father’s wives; she is your half sister. 12Do not
have intercourse with your aunt, your father’s sister,
because she is your father’s close relative. 13Do not
have sexual intercourse with your aunt, your
mother’s sister, because she is your mother’s close
relative. 14And do not violate your uncle, your
father’s brother, by having sexual intercourse with
his wife; she also is your aunt. 15Do not have sexual
intercourse with your daughter-in-law; she is your
son’s wife. 16Do not have intercourse with your
brother’s wife; this would violate your brother.
17“Do not have sexual intercourse with both a
woman and her daughter or marry both a woman
and her granddaughter, whether her son’s daughter
or her daughter’s daughter. They are close relatives,
and to do this would be a horrible wickedness.
18“Do not marry a woman and her sister because
they will be rivals. But if your wife dies, then it is all
right to marry her sister.
19“Do not violate a woman by having sexual intercourse with her during her period of menstrual impurity.
20“Do not defile yourself by having sexual intercourse with your neighbor’s wife.
21“Do not give any of your children as a sacrifice
to Molech, for you must not profane the name of
your God. I am the LORD.
22“Do not practice homosexuality; it is a detestable sin.
23“A man must never defile himself by having
sexual intercourse with an animal, and a woman
must never present herself to a male animal in order
to have intercourse with it; this is a terrible perversion.
24“Do not defile yourselves in any of these ways,
because this is how the people I am expelling from
the Promised Land have defiled themselves. 25As a
result, the entire land has become defiled. That is
why I am punishing the people who live there, and
the land will soon vomit them out. 26You must
strictly obey all of my laws and regulations, and you
must not do any of these detestable things. This
applies both to you who are Israelites by birth and to
the foreigners living among you.
27“All these detestable activities are practiced by
the people of the land where I am taking you, and
the land has become defiled. 28Do not give the land
a reason to vomit you out for defiling it, as it will
vomit out the people who live there now. 29Whoever
does any of these detestable things will be cut off
from the community of Israel. 30So be careful to obey
my laws, and do not practice any of these detestable
activities. Do not defile yourselves by doing any of
them, for I, the LORD, am your God.”

CHAPTER **19** **HOLINESS IN DAILY LIFE.** The LORD
also said to Moses, 2“Say this to the entire community of Israel: You must be holy because I, the LORD
your God, am holy. 3Each of you must show respect
for your mother and father, and you must always
observe my Sabbath days of rest, for I, the LORD, am
your God. 4Do not put your trust in idols or make
gods of metal for yourselves. I, the LORD, am your
God.
5“When you sacrifice a peace offering to the LORD,
offer it properly so it will be accepted on your behalf.
6You must eat it on the same day you offer it or on
the next day at the latest. Any leftovers that remain
until the third day must be burned. 7If any of the
offering is eaten on the third day, it will be contaminated, and I will not accept it. 8If you eat it on the
third day, you will answer for the sin of profaning
what is holy to the LORD and must be cut off from
the community.
9“When you harvest your crops, do not harvest the
grain along the edges of your fields, and do not pick
up what the harvesters drop. 10It is the same with
your grape crop—do not strip every last bunch of
grapes from the vines, and do not pick up the grapes
that fall to the ground. Leave them for the poor and
the foreigners who live among you, for I, the LORD,
am your God.
11“Do not steal.
“Do not cheat one another.
“Do not lie.
12“Do not use my name to swear a falsehood and
so profane the name of your God. I am the LORD.
13“Do not cheat or rob anyone.
“Always pay your hired workers promptly.
14“Show your fear of God by treating the deaf with
respect and by not taking advantage of the blind. I
am the LORD.
15“Always judge your neighbors fairly, neither fa-
voring the poor nor showing deference to the rich.
16“Do not spread slanderous gossip among your
people.*
“Do not try to get ahead at the cost of your
neighbor’s life, for I am the LORD.
17“Do not nurse hatred in your heart for any of
your relatives.
“Confront your neighbors directly so you will not
be held guilty for their crimes.

19:16 Hebrew *Do not act as a merchant toward your own people.*

[18]"Never seek revenge or bear a grudge against anyone, but love your neighbor as yourself. I am the LORD.

[19]"You must obey all my laws.

"Do not breed your cattle with other kinds of animals. Do not plant your field with two kinds of seed. Do not wear clothing woven from two different kinds of fabric.

[20]"If a man has sexual intercourse with a slave girl who is committed to become someone else's wife, compensation must be paid. But since she had not been freed at the time, the couple will not be put to death. [21]The man, however, must bring a ram as a guilt offering and present it to the LORD at the entrance of the Tabernacle.* [22]The priest will then make atonement for him before the LORD with the sacrificial ram of the guilt offering, and the man will be forgiven.

**TEALING**

Kelli and Sandra work together at Quackers, the newest fast-food restaurant in town. It's not such a bad job. The hours are good, the uniforms—surprise!—don't look like circus costumes, and the pay is more than minimum wage. Besides, the girls have great fun (and a lot of laughs) checking out the tons of cute guys from a rival high school who frequent the place on weekends.

Today, however, when the girls come to work, there is a terse note from the boss: "I want to talk to both of you. It's very important!"

Kelli's heart drops to her shoes, and Sandra's stomach does a cartwheel. What could it mean? A raise? A promotion? Not likely. In fact, the girls are expecting the worst. See, they've been giving away free food and Quackers T-shirts to certain male customers. And Sandra took a whole box of burgers from the freezer late last Friday night to use at her Saturday pool party.

"We're dead!" Kelli moans. "We've done everything but actually take money out of the cash register!"

"No—I even did that one night."

"Sandra! You didn't! How much did you take?"

"Ten bucks."

"Oh no! What are we gonna say?"

See how Kelli and Sandra could have avoided this whole horrible headache—Leviticus 19:11.

[23]"When you enter the land and plant fruit trees, leave the fruit unharvested for the first three years and consider it forbidden.* [24]In the fourth year the entire crop will be devoted to the LORD as an outburst of praise. [25]Finally, in the fifth year you may eat the fruit. In this way, its yield will be increased. I, the LORD, am your God.

[26]"Never eat meat that has not been drained of its blood.

"Do not practice fortune-telling or witchcraft.

[27]"Do not trim off the hair on your temples or clip the edges of your beards.

**DON'T ● ● • • •**

19:18 **Don't, don't, don't. Some people think the Bible is nothing but a book of don'ts. But here we find a foundational *positive* command—one Jesus even quoted to summarize all these rules. He said to love God with all your heart, and your neighbor as yourself. He called these the greatest commandments (or rules) of all (Matthew 22:34-40). By carrying out Jesus' simple commands, we find ourselves following all of God's other laws as well.**

[28]"Never cut your bodies in mourning for the dead or mark your skin with tattoos, for I am the LORD.

[29]"Do not defile your daughter by making her a prostitute, or the land will be filled with promiscuity and detestable wickedness.

[30]"Keep my Sabbath days of rest and show reverence toward my sanctuary, for I am the LORD.

[31]"Do not rely on mediums and psychics, for you will be defiled by them. I, the LORD, am your God.

[32]"Show your fear of God by standing up in the presence of elderly people and showing respect for the aged. I am the LORD.

[33]"Do not exploit the foreigners who live in your land. [34]They should be treated like everyone else, and you must love them as you love yourself. Remember that you were once foreigners in the land of Egypt. I, the LORD, am your God.

[35]"Do not use dishonest standards when measuring length, weight, or volume. [36]Your scales and weights must be accurate. Your containers for measuring dry goods or liquids must be accurate.* I, the LORD, am your God, who brought you out of the land of Egypt. [37]You must be careful to obey all of my laws and regulations, for I am the LORD."

## CHAPTER 20

**PUNISHMENTS FOR SIN.** The LORD said to Moses, [2]"Give the Israelites these instructions, which apply to those who are Israelites by birth as well as to the foreigners living among you. If any among them devote their children as burnt offerings to Molech, they must be stoned to death by people of the community. [3]I myself will turn against them and cut them off from the community, because they have defiled my sanctuary and profaned my holy name by giving their children to Molech. [4]And if the people of the community ignore this offering of children to Molech and refuse to execute the guilty parents, [5]then I myself will turn against them and cut them off from the community, along with all those who commit prostitution by worshiping Molech.

[6]"If any among the people are unfaithful by consulting and following mediums or psychics, I will turn against them and cut them off from the community. [7]So set yourselves apart to be holy, for I, the LORD, am your God. [8]Keep all my laws and obey them, for I am the LORD, who makes you holy.

[9]"All who curse their father or mother must be put to death. They are guilty of a capital offense.

19:21 Hebrew *Tent of Meeting.* 19:23 Hebrew *consider it uncircumcised.* 19:36 Hebrew *Use an honest ephah* [a dry measure] *and an honest hin* [a liquid measure].

10 "If a man commits adultery with another man's wife, both the man and the woman must be put to death. 11 If a man has intercourse with his father's wife, both the man and the woman must die, for they are guilty of a capital offense. 12 If a man has intercourse with his daughter-in-law, both must be put to death. They have acted contrary to nature and are guilty of a capital offense.

13 "The penalty for homosexual acts is death to both parties. They have committed a detestable act and are guilty of a capital offense. 14 If a man has intercourse with both a woman and her mother, such an act is terribly wicked. All three of them must be burned to death to wipe out such wickedness from among you.

15 "If a man has sexual intercourse with an animal, he must be put to death, and the animal must be killed. 16 If a woman approaches a male animal to have intercourse with it, she and the animal must both be put to death. Both must die, for they are guilty of a capital offense.

17 "If a man has sexual intercourse with his sister, the daughter of either his father or his mother, it is a terrible disgrace. Both of them must be publicly cut off from the community. Since the man has had intercourse with his sister, he will suffer the consequences of his guilt. 18 If a man has intercourse with a woman suffering from a hemorrhage,* both of them must be cut off from the community, because he exposed the source of her flow, and she allowed him to do it.

19 "If a man has sexual intercourse with his aunt, whether his mother's sister or his father's sister, he has violated a close relative. Both parties are guilty of a capital offense. 20 If a man has intercourse with his uncle's wife, he has violated his uncle. Both the man and woman involved are guilty of a capital offense and will die childless. 21 If a man marries his brother's wife, it is an act of impurity. He has violated his brother, and the guilty couple will remain childless.

22 "You must carefully obey all my laws and regulations; otherwise the land to which I am bringing you will vomit you out. 23 Do not live by the customs of the people whom I will expel before you. It is because they do these terrible things that I detest them so much. 24 But I have promised that you will inherit their land, a land flowing with milk and honey. I, the LORD, am your God, who has set you apart from all other people.

25 "You must therefore make a distinction between ceremonially clean and unclean animals, and between clean and unclean birds. You must not defile yourselves by eating any animal or bird or creeping creature that I have forbidden. 26 You must be holy because I, the LORD, am holy. I have set you apart from all other people to be my very own.

27 "Men and women among you who act as mediums or psychics must be put to death by stoning. They are guilty of a capital offense."

## OCCULT ● ● • • •

20:6 **Everyone is interested in what the future holds, and we often look to others for guidance. But God warned about looking to the occult for advice. Mediums and psychics were outlawed because God was not the source of their information. At best, occult practitioners are fakes whose predictions cannot be trusted. At worst, they are in contact with evil spirits and are thus extremely dangerous. We don't need to look to the occult for information about the future. God has given us the Bible so that we may obtain all the information we need—and the Bible's teaching is trustworthy.**

## CHAPTER 21 RULES FOR THE PRIESTS.

The LORD said to Moses, "Tell the priests to avoid making themselves ceremonially unclean by touching a dead relative 2 unless it is a close relative—mother or father, son or daughter, brother 3 or virgin sister who was dependent because she had no husband. 4 As a husband among his relatives,* he must not defile himself.

5 "The priests must never shave their heads, trim the edges of their beards, or cut their bodies. 6 They must be set apart to God as holy and must never dishonor his name. After all, they are the ones who present the offerings to the LORD by fire, providing God with his food, and they must remain holy.

7 "The priests must not marry women defiled by prostitution or women who have been divorced, for the priests must be set apart to God as holy. 8 You must treat them as holy because they offer up food to your God. You must consider them holy because I, the LORD, am holy, and I make you holy. 9 If a priest's daughter becomes a prostitute, defiling her father's holiness as well as herself, she must be burned to death.

10 "The high priest, who has had the anointing oil poured on his head and has been ordained to wear the special priestly garments, must never let his hair hang loose* or tear his clothing. 11 He must never defile himself by going near a dead person, even if it is his father or mother. 12 He must not desecrate the sanctuary of his God by leaving it to attend his parents' funeral, because he has been made holy by the anointing oil of his God. I am the LORD.

## SELF-DESTRUCTING ● ● • • •

20:22-23 **God gave many rules to his people—but not without reason. He did not withhold good from them; he only prohibited those acts that would bring them to ruin. All of us understand God's physical laws of nature. For example, jumping off a 10-story building means death because of the law of gravity. But some of us don't understand how God's spiritual laws work. God forbids us to do certain things because he wants to keep us from self-destruction. Next time you feel like doing something that you know is wrong, remember that the consequences might be suffering and separation from the God who is trying to help you.**

**20:18** Or *a woman who is menstruating.* **21:4** The meaning of the Hebrew is uncertain. **21:10** Or *uncover his head.*

[13] "The high priest must marry a virgin. [14] He must not marry a widow, a divorced woman, or a woman defiled by prostitution. She must be a virgin from his own clan, [15] that he may not dishonor his descendants among the members of his clan, because I, the LORD, have made him holy."

[16] Then the LORD said to Moses, [17] "Tell Aaron that in all future generations, his descendants who have physical defects will not qualify to offer food to their God. [18] No one who has a defect may come near to me, whether he is blind or lame, stunted or deformed, [19] or has a broken foot or hand, [20] or has a humped back or is a dwarf, or has a defective eye, or has oozing sores or scabs on his skin, or has damaged testicles. [21] Even though he is a descendant of Aaron, his physical defects disqualify him from presenting offerings to the LORD by fire. Since he has a blemish, he may not offer food to his God. [22] However, he may eat from the food offered to God, including the holy offerings and the most holy offerings. [23] Yet because of his physical defect, he must never go behind the inner curtain or come near the altar, for this would desecrate my holy places. I am the LORD who makes them holy."

[24] So Moses gave these instructions to Aaron and his sons and to all the Israelites.

CHAPTER **22** The LORD said to Moses, [2] "Tell Aaron and his sons to treat the sacred gifts that the Israelites set apart for me with great care, so they do not profane my holy name. I am the LORD. [3] Remind them that if any of their descendants are ceremonially unclean when they approach the sacred food presented by the Israelites, they must be cut off from my presence. I am the LORD!

[4] "If any of the priests have a contagious skin disease* or any kind of discharge that makes them ceremonially unclean, they may not eat the sacred offerings until they have been pronounced clean. If any of the priests become unclean by touching a corpse, or are defiled by an emission of semen, [5] or by touching a creeping creature that is unclean, or by touching someone who is ceremonially unclean for any reason, [6] they will remain defiled until evening. They must not eat any of the sacred offerings until they have purified their bodies with water. [7] When the sun goes down, they will be clean again and may eat the sacred offerings. After all, this food has been set aside for them. [8] The priests may never eat an animal that has died a natural death or has been torn apart by wild animals, for this would defile them. I am the LORD. [9] Warn all the priests to follow these instructions carefully; otherwise they will be subject to punishment and die for violating them. I am the LORD who makes them holy.

[10] "No one outside a priest's family may ever eat the sacred offerings, even if the person lives in a priest's home or is one of his hired servants. [11] However, if the priest buys slaves with his own money, they may eat of his food. And if his slaves have

22:4 Traditionally rendered *leprosy.* See note at 13:2.

**I the LORD, AM HOLY, and I make you HOLY**

LEVITICUS 21:8

children, they also may share his food. [12] If a priest's daughter marries someone outside the priestly family, she may no longer eat the sacred offerings. [13] But if she becomes a widow or is divorced and has no children to support her, and she returns to live in her father's home, she may eat her father's food again. But other than these exceptions, only members of the priests' families are allowed to eat the sacred offerings.

[14] "Anyone who eats the sacred offerings without realizing it must pay the priest for the amount eaten, plus an added penalty of 20 percent. [15] No one may defile the sacred offerings brought to the LORD by the Israelites [16] by allowing unauthorized people to eat them. The negligent priest would bring guilt upon the people and require them to pay compensation. I am the LORD, who makes them holy."

[17] And the LORD said to Moses, [18] "Give Aaron and his sons and all the Israelites these instructions, which apply to those who are Israelites by birth as well as to the foreigners living among you. If you

**ONLY THE BEST** ● ● • • •

22:19-25 **Animals with defects were not acceptable as sacrifices because they did not represent God's holy nature. Furthermore, the animal had to be without blemish to symbolize the perfect, sinless life of Jesus Christ. When we give our best time, talent, and treasure to God, rather than giving him something tarnished or common, we show the true meaning of worship and testify to God's supreme worth.**

offer a whole burnt offering to the LORD, whether
to fulfill a vow or as a freewill offering, [19]it will be
accepted only if it is a male animal with no physical defects. It may be either a bull, a ram, or a male
goat. [20]Do not bring an animal with physical defects, because it won't be accepted on your behalf.
[21]"If you bring a peace offering to the LORD from
the herd or flock, whether to fulfill a vow or as a
freewill offering, you must offer an animal that has
no physical defects of any kind. [22]An animal that is
blind, injured, mutilated, or that has a growth, an
open sore, or a scab must never be offered to the
LORD by fire on the altar. [23]If the bull* or lamb is
deformed or stunted, it may still be offered as a
freewill offering, but it may not be offered to fulfill a
vow. [24]If an animal has damaged testicles or is cas-
trated, it may never be offered to the LORD. [25]You
must never accept mutilated or defective animals
from foreigners to be offered as a sacrifice to your
God. Such animals will not be accepted on your
behalf because they are defective."
[26]And the LORD said to Moses, [27]"When a bull or
a ram or a male goat is born, it must be left with its
mother for seven days. From the eighth day on, it
will be acceptable as an offering given to the LORD
by fire. [28]But you must never slaughter a mother
animal and her offspring on the same day, whether
from the herd or the flock. [29]When you bring a
thanksgiving offering to the LORD, it must be sacrificed properly so it will be accepted on your behalf.
[30]Eat the entire sacrificial animal on the day it is
presented. Don't leave any of it until the second
day. I am the LORD.
[31]"You must faithfully keep all my commands by
obeying them, for I am the LORD. [32]Do not treat my
holy name as common and ordinary. I must be
treated as holy by the people of Israel. It is I, the
LORD, who makes you holy. [33]It was I who rescued
you from Egypt, that I might be your very own God.
I am the LORD."

CHAPTER **23** **SPECIAL DAYS.** The LORD said to
Moses, [2]"Give the Israelites instructions regarding
the LORD's appointed festivals, the days when all of
you will be summoned to worship me. [3]You may
work for six days each week, but on the seventh day
all work must come to a complete stop. It is the
LORD's Sabbath day of complete rest, a holy day to
assemble for worship. It must be observed wherever
you live. [4]In addition to the Sabbath, the LORD has

22:23 Or *cow;* also in 22:27.

## THE FESTIVALS

Besides enjoying one Sabbath day of rest each week, the Israelites also enjoyed 19 days when national holidays were celebrated.

| *Festival* | *What It Celebrated* | *Its Importance* |
|---|---|---|
| **Passover**<br>One day<br>(Lev. 23:5) | When God spared the lives of Israel's firstborn children in Egypt and freed the Hebrews from slavery | Reminded the people of God's deliverance |
| **Unleavened Bread**<br>Seven days<br>(Lev. 23:6-8) | The Exodus from Egypt | Reminded the people they were leaving the old life behind and entering a new way of living |
| **Firstfruits**<br>One day<br>(Lev. 23:9-14) | The first crops of the barley harvest | Reminded the people how God provided for them |
| **Harvest (Pentecost)**<br>One day<br>(Lev. 23:15-22) | The end of the barley harvest and beginning of the wheat harvest | Showed joy and thanksgiving over the bountiful harvest |
| **Trumpets**<br>One day<br>(Lev. 23:23-25) | The beginning of the seventh month (civil new year) | Expressed joy and thanksgiving to God |
| **Day of Atonement**<br>One day<br>(Lev. 23:26-32) | The removal of sin from the people and the nation | Restored fellowship with God |
| **Shelters (Tabernacles)**<br>Seven days<br>(Lev. 23:33-43) | God's protection and guidance in the wilderness | Renewed Israel's commitment to God and trust in his guidance and protection |

## TRADITIONS ● ● • • •

23:1-4 **God established several national holidays each year for celebration, fellowship, and worship. Much can be learned about people by observing the holidays they celebrate and the way they celebrate them. What do your holiday traditions say about your values?**

established festivals, the holy occasions to be observed at the proper time each year.

5 "First comes the LORD's Passover, which begins at twilight on its appointed day in early spring.* 6 Then the day after the Passover celebration,* the Festival of Unleavened Bread begins. This festival to the LORD continues for seven days, and during that time all the bread you eat must be made without yeast. 7 On the first day of the festival, all the people must stop their regular work and gather for a sacred assembly. 8 On each of the next seven days, the people must present an offering to the LORD by fire. On the seventh day, the people must again stop all their regular work to hold a sacred assembly."

9 Then the LORD told Moses 10 to give these instructions to the Israelites: "When you arrive in the land I am giving you and you harvest your first crops, bring the priest some grain from the first portion of your grain harvest. 11 On the day after the Sabbath, the priest will lift it up before the LORD so it may be accepted on your behalf. 12 That same day you must sacrifice a year-old male lamb with no physical defects as a whole burnt offering to the LORD. 13 A grain offering must accompany it consisting of three quarts* of choice flour mixed with olive oil. It will be an offering given to the LORD by fire, and it will be very pleasing to him. Along with this sacrifice, you must also offer one quart* of wine as a drink offering. 14 Do not eat any bread or roasted grain or fresh kernels on that day until after you have brought this offering to your God. This is a permanent law for you, and it must be observed wherever you live.

15 "From the day after the Sabbath, the day the bundle of grain was lifted up as an offering, count off seven weeks. 16 Keep counting until the day after the seventh Sabbath, fifty days later, and bring an offering of new grain to the LORD. 17 From wherever you live, bring two loaves of bread to be lifted up before the LORD as an offering. These loaves must be baked from three quarts of choice flour that contains yeast. They will be an offering to the LORD from the first of your crops. 18 Along with this bread, present seven one-year-old lambs with no physical defects, one bull, and two rams as burnt offerings to the LORD. These whole burnt offerings, together with the accompanying grain offerings and drink offerings, will be given to the LORD by fire and will be pleasing to him. 19 Then you must offer one male goat as a sin offering and two one-year-old male lambs as a peace offering.

20 "The priest will lift up these offerings before the LORD, together with the loaves representing the first of your later crops. These offerings are holy to the LORD and will belong to the priests. 21 That same day, you must stop all your regular work and gather for a sacred assembly. This is a permanent law for you, and it must be observed wherever you live.

22 "When you harvest the crops of your land, do not harvest the grain along the edges of your fields, and do not pick up what the harvesters drop. Leave it for the poor and the foreigners living among you. I, the LORD, am your God."

23 The LORD told Moses 24 to give these instructions to the Israelites: "On the appointed day in early autumn,* you are to celebrate a day of complete rest. All your work must stop on that day. You will call the people to a sacred assembly—the Festival of Trumpets—with loud blasts from a trumpet. 25 You must do no regular work on that day. Instead, you are to present offerings to the LORD by fire."

26 Then the LORD said to Moses, 27 "Remember that the Day of Atonement is to be celebrated on the ninth day after the Festival of Trumpets.* On that day you must humble yourselves, gather for a sacred assembly, and present offerings to the LORD by fire. 28 Do no work during that entire day because it is the Day of Atonement, when atonement will be made for you before the LORD your God, and payment will be made for your sins. 29 Anyone who does not spend that day in humility will be cut off from the community. 30 And I will destroy anyone among you who does any kind of work on that day. 31 You must do no work at all! This is a permanent law for you, and it must be observed wherever you live. 32 This will be a Sabbath day of total rest for you, and on that day you must humble yourselves. This time of rest and fasting will begin the evening before the Day of Atonement* and extend until evening of that day."

33 And the LORD said to Moses, 34 "Tell the Israelites to begin the Festival of Shelters on the fifth day after the Day of Atonement.* This festival to the LORD will last for seven days. 35 It will begin with a sacred assembly on the first day, and all your regular work must stop. 36 On each of the seven festival days, you must present offerings to the LORD by fire. On the eighth day, you must gather again for a sacred assembly and present another offering to the LORD by fire. This will be a solemn closing assembly, and no regular work may be done that day.

37 "These are the LORD's appointed annual festivals. Celebrate them by gathering in sacred assemblies to present all the various offerings to the LORD by fire—whole burnt offerings and grain offerings, sacrificial meals and drink offerings—each on its proper day. 38 These festivals must be observed in addition to the LORD's regular Sabbath days. And these offerings must be given in addition to your personal gifts, the offerings you make to accompany

**23:5** Hebrew *on the fourteenth day of the first month.* This day of the Hebrew lunar calendar occurs in late March or early April. **23:6** Hebrew *On the fifteenth day of the same month.* **23:13a** Hebrew *2/10 of an ephah* [3.6 liters]; also in 23:17. **23:13b** Hebrew *1/4 of a hin* [1 liter]. **23:24** Hebrew *On the first day of the seventh month.* This day of the Hebrew lunar calendar occurs in September or early October. **23:27** Hebrew *on the tenth day of the seventh month;* see 23:24 and the note there. **23:32** Hebrew *the evening of the ninth day of the month;* see 23:24, 27 and the notes there. **23:34** Hebrew *on the fifteenth day of the seventh month;* see 23:24, 27 and the notes there.

your vows, and any freewill offerings that you present to the LORD.

[39]"Now, on the first day of the Festival of Shelters,* after you have harvested all the produce of the land, you will begin to celebrate this seven-day festival to the LORD. Remember that the first day and closing eighth day of the festival will be days of total rest. [40]On the first day, gather fruit from citrus trees,* and collect palm fronds and other leafy branches and willows that grow by the streams. Then rejoice before the LORD your God for seven days. [41]You must observe this seven-day festival to the LORD every year. This is a permanent law for you, and it must be kept by all future generations. [42]During the seven festival days, all of you who are Israelites by birth must live in shelters. [43]This will remind each new generation of Israelites that their ancestors had to live in shelters when I rescued them from the land of Egypt. I, the LORD, am your God."

[44]So Moses gave these instructions regarding the annual festivals of the LORD to the Israelites.

## CHAPTER 24 **THE MEMORIAL OFFERING.**

The LORD said to Moses, [2]"Command the people of Israel to provide you with pure olive oil for the lampstand, so it can be kept burning continually. [3]Aaron will set it up outside the inner curtain of the Most Holy Place in the Tabernacle* and must arrange to have the lamps tended continually, from evening until morning, before the LORD. This is a permanent law for you, and it must be kept by all future generations. [4]The lamps on the pure gold lampstand must be tended continually in the LORD's presence.

[5]"You must bake twelve loaves of bread from choice flour, using three quarts* of flour for each loaf. [6]Place the bread in the LORD's presence on the pure gold table, and arrange the loaves in two rows, with six in each row. [7]Sprinkle some pure frankincense near each row. It will serve as a token offering, to be burned in place of the bread as an offering given to the LORD by fire. [8]Every Sabbath day this bread must be laid out before the LORD on behalf of the Israelites as a continual part of the covenant. [9]The loaves of bread belong to Aaron and his male descendants, who must eat them in a sacred place, for they represent a most holy portion of the offerings given to the LORD by fire."

[10]One day a man who had an Israelite mother and an Egyptian father got into a fight with one of the Israelite men. [11]During the fight, this son of an Israelite woman blasphemed the LORD's name. So the man was brought to Moses for judgment. His mother's name was Shelomith. She was the daughter of Dibri of the tribe of Dan. [12]They put the man in custody until the LORD's will in the matter should become clear.

[13]Then the LORD said to Moses, [14]"Take the blasphemer outside the camp, and tell all those who heard him to lay their hands on his head. Then let the entire community stone him to death. [15]Say to the people of Israel: Those who blaspheme God will suffer the consequences of their guilt and be punished. [16]Anyone who blasphemes the LORD's name must be stoned to death by the whole community of Israel. Any Israelite or foreigner among you who blasphemes the LORD's name will surely die.

[17]"Anyone who takes another person's life must be put to death.

[18]"Anyone who kills another person's animal must pay it back in full—a live animal for the animal that was killed.

[19]"Anyone who injures another person must be dealt with according to the injury inflicted—[20]fracture for fracture, eye for eye, tooth for tooth. Whatever anyone does to hurt another person must be paid back in kind.

[21]"Whoever kills an animal must make full restitution, but whoever kills another person must be put to death.

[22]"These same regulations apply to Israelites by birth and foreigners who live among you. I, the LORD, am your God."

[23]After Moses gave all these instructions to the Israelites, they led the blasphemer outside the camp and stoned him to death, just as the LORD had commanded Moses.

## CHAPTER 25 **REST FOR THE LAND.**

While Moses was on Mount Sinai, the LORD said to him, [2]"Give these instructions to the Israelites: When you have entered the land I am giving you as an inheritance, the land itself must observe a Sabbath to the LORD every seventh year. [3]For six years you may plant your fields and prune your vineyards and harvest your crops, [4]but during the seventh year the land will enjoy a Sabbath year of rest to the LORD. Do not plant your crops or prune your vineyards during that entire year. [5]And don't store away the crops that grow naturally or process the grapes that grow on your unpruned vines. The land is to have a year of total rest. [6]But you, your male and female slaves, your hired servants, and any foreigners who live with you may eat the produce that grows naturally during the Sabbath year. [7]And your livestock and the wild animals will also be allowed to eat of the land's bounty.

[8]"In addition, you must count off seven Sabbath years, seven years times seven, adding up to forty-nine years in all. [9]Then on the Day of Atonement of the fiftieth year,* blow the trumpets loud and long throughout the land. [10]This year will be set apart as holy, a time to proclaim release for all who live there. It will be a jubilee year for you, when each of you returns to the lands that belonged to your ancestors and rejoins your clan. [11]Yes, the fiftieth year will be a jubilee for you. During that year, do not plant any

23:39 Hebrew *on the fifteenth day of the seventh month;* see 23:24 and the note there. 23:40 Or *fruit from majestic trees.* 24:3 Hebrew *the curtain of the Testimony in the Tent of Meeting.* 24:5 Hebrew *2/10 of an ephah* [3.6 liters]. 25:9 Hebrew *on the tenth day of the seventh month, on the Day of Atonement;* see 23:27 and the note there.

seeds or store away any of the crops that grow naturally, and do not process the grapes that grow on your unpruned vines. [12]It will be a jubilee year for you, and you must observe it as a special and holy time. You may, however, eat the produce that grows naturally in the fields that year. [13]In the Year of Jubilee each of you must return to the lands that belonged to your ancestors.

[14]"When you make an agreement with a neighbor to buy or sell property, you must never take advantage of each other. [15]When you buy land from your neighbor, the price of the land should be based on the number of years since the last jubilee. The seller will charge you only for the crop years left until the next Year of Jubilee. [16]The more the years, the higher the price; the fewer the years, the lower the price. After all, the person selling the land is actually selling you a certain number of harvests. [17]Show your fear of God by not taking advantage of each other. I, the LORD, am your God.

[18]"If you want to live securely in the land, keep my laws and obey my regulations. [19]Then the land will yield bumper crops, and you will eat your fill and live securely in it. [20]But you might ask, 'What will we eat during the seventh year, since we are not allowed to plant or harvest crops that year?' [21]The answer is, 'I will order my blessing for you in the sixth year, so the land will produce a bumper crop, enough to support you for three years. [22]As you plant the seed in the eighth year, you will still be eating the produce of the previous year. In fact, you will eat from the old crop until the new harvest comes in the ninth year.' [23]And remember, the land must never be sold on a permanent basis because it really belongs to me. You are only foreigners and tenants living with me.

[24]"With every sale of land there must be a stipulation that the land can be redeemed at any time. [25]If any of your Israelite relatives go bankrupt and are forced to sell some inherited land, then a close relative, a kinsman redeemer, may buy it back for them. [26]If there is no one to redeem the land but the person who sold it manages to get enough money to buy it back, [27]then that person has the right to redeem it from the one who bought it. The price of the land will be based on the number of years until the next Year of Jubilee. After buying it back, the original owner may then return to the land. [28]But if the original owner cannot afford to redeem it, then it will belong to the new owner until the next Year of Jubilee. In the jubilee year, the land will be returned to the original owner.

[29]"Anyone who sells a house inside a walled city has the right to redeem it for a full year after its sale. During that time, the seller retains the right to buy it back. [30]But if it is not redeemed within a year, then the house within the walled city will become the permanent property of the buyer. It will not be returned to the original owner in the Year of Jubilee. [31]But a house in a village—a settlement without fortified walls—will be treated like property in the

## WARNINGS ● ● • • •

26:1 **The people of the Old Testament were warned over and over against worshiping idols. We wonder how they could deceive themselves with these objects of wood and stone. Yet God could give us the same warning, because we often put idols before him. Idolatry is making anything more important than God, and our lives are full of that temptation. Money, looks, success, reputation, security, popularity—these are today's idols. As you look at these false gods that promise everything you want but nothing you need, does idolatry seem so far removed from your experience?**

open fields. Such a house may be redeemed at any time and must be returned to the original owner in the Year of Jubilee.

[32]"The Levites always have the right to redeem any house they have sold within the cities belonging to them. [33]And any property that can be redeemed by the Levites—all houses within the Levitical cities—must be returned in the Year of Jubilee. After all, the cities reserved for the Levites are the only property they own in all Israel. [34]The strip of pastureland around each of the Levitical cities may never be sold. It is their permanent ancestral property.

[35]"If any of your Israelite relatives fall into poverty and cannot support themselves, support them as you would a resident foreigner and allow them to live with you. [36]Do not demand an advance or charge interest on the money you lend them. Instead, show your fear of God by letting them live with you as your relatives. [37]Remember, do not charge your relatives interest on anything you lend them, whether money or food. [38]I, the LORD, am your God, who brought you out of Egypt to give you the land of Canaan and to be your God.

[39]"If any of your Israelite relatives go bankrupt and sell themselves to you, do not treat them as slaves. [40]Treat them instead as hired servants or as resident foreigners who live with you, and they will serve you only until the Year of Jubilee. [41]At that time they and their children will no longer be obligated to you, and they will return to their clan and ancestral property. [42]The people of Israel are my servants, whom I brought out of the land of Egypt, so they must never be sold as slaves. [43]Show your fear of God by treating them well; never exercise your power over them in a ruthless way.

[44]"However, you may purchase male or female slaves from among the foreigners who live among you. [45]You may also purchase the children of such resident foreigners, including those who have been born in your land. You may treat them as your property, [46]passing them on to your children as a permanent inheritance. You may treat your slaves like this, but the people of Israel, your relatives, must never be treated this way.

[47]"If a resident foreigner becomes rich, and if some of your Israelite relatives go bankrupt and sell themselves to such a foreigner, [48]they still retain the right of redemption. They may be bought back by a close relative—[49]an uncle, a nephew, or anyone else who is closely related. They may also redeem themselves if they can get the money. [50]The price of their

freedom will be based on the number of years left
until the next Year of Jubilee—whatever it would
cost to hire a servant for that number of years. 51 If
many years still remain, they will repay most of what
they received when they sold themselves. 52 If only a
few years remain until the Year of Jubilee, then they
will repay a relatively small amount for their redemption. 53 The foreigner must treat them as servants hired on a yearly basis. You must not allow a
resident foreigner to treat any of your Israelite relatives ruthlessly. 54 If any Israelites have not been redeemed by the time the Year of Jubilee arrives, then
they and their children must be set free at that time.
55 For the people of Israel are my servants, whom I
brought out of the land of Egypt. I, the LORD, am
your God.

CHAPTER **26** **REWARDS FOR OBEDIENCE.** "Do not
make idols or set up carved images, sacred pillars, or
shaped stones to be worshiped in your land. I, the
LORD, am your God. 2 You must keep my Sabbath
days of rest and show reverence for my sanctuary. I
am the LORD.

3 "If you keep my laws and are careful to obey my
commands, 4 I will send the seasonal rains. The land
will then yield its crops, and the trees will produce
their fruit. 5 Your threshing season will extend until
the grape harvest, and your grape harvest will extend
until it is time to plant grain again. You will eat your
fill and live securely in your land.

6 "I will give you peace in the land, and you will be
able to sleep without fear. I will remove the wild
animals from your land and protect you from your
enemies. 7 In fact, you will chase down all your enemies and slaughter them with
your swords. 8 Five of you will
chase a hundred, and a hundred
of you will chase ten thousand!
All your enemies will fall beneath
the blows of your weapons.

9 "I will look favorably upon you
and multiply your people and fulfill my covenant with you. 10 You
will have such a surplus of crops
that you will need to get rid of the
leftovers from the previous year to
make room for each new harvest.
11 I will live among you, and I will
not despise you. 12 I will walk
among you; I will be your God,
and you will be my people. 13 I, the
LORD, am your God, who brought
you from the land of Egypt so you
would no longer be slaves. I have
lifted the yoke of slavery from your
neck so you can walk free with your
heads held high.

14 "However, if you do not
listen to me or obey my commands, 15 and if you break my
covenant by rejecting my laws
and treating my regulations with contempt, 16 I will
punish you. You will suffer from sudden terrors,
with wasting diseases, and with burning fevers,
causing your eyes to fail and your life to ebb away.
You will plant your crops in vain because your
enemies will eat them. 17 I will turn against you,
and you will be defeated by all your enemies. They
will rule over you, and you will run even when no
one is chasing you!

18 "And if, in spite of this, you still disobey me, I
will punish you for your sins seven times over. 19 I will
break down your arrogant spirit by making the skies
above as unyielding as iron and the earth beneath as
hard as bronze. 20 All your work will be for nothing,
for your land will yield no crops, and your trees will
bear no fruit.

21 "If even then you remain hostile toward me and
refuse to obey, I will inflict you with seven more
disasters for your sins. 22 I will release wild animals
that will kill your children and destroy your cattle, so
your numbers will dwindle and your roads will be
deserted.

23 "And if you fail to learn a lesson from this and
continue your hostility toward me, 24 then I myself
will be hostile toward you, and I will personally
strike you seven times over for your sins. 25 I will send
armies against you to carry out these covenant
threats. If you flee to your cities, I will send a plague
to destroy you there, and you will be conquered by
your enemies. 26 I will completely destroy your food
supply, so the bread from one oven will have to be
stretched to feed ten families. They will ration your
food by weight, and even if you have food to eat, you
will not be satisfied.

## "Here's what I did..."

I know that most people, especially kids, don't usually read Leviticus for devotions, and I won't pretend that that's what I was doing. But I was involved in a read-through-the-Bible-in-a-year program, and so I had to read every word of this book. What hit me most as I read all this stuff about laws and sacrifices was how seriously God takes the way his people obey or disobey him. And he stated it so clearly for the Israelites. For example, in chapter 26 God says that obedience will bring prosperity in the Promised Land, but disobedience will bring nothing but trouble. *How could the people be so stupid*, I thought as I read. *Why would they ever disobey?* But then I thought of how I have even more evidence of God's love than those people had and *all* of his Word; and yet, I take God for granted and even disobey him on purpose at times. Then I thought of what I knew God wanted me to do that day (for one thing, I needed to apologize to my mom for something I had said). So I asked God to forgive me and went to talk with Mom. God takes obedience seriously, and so should I.

Kara

AGE 15

27 "If after this you still refuse to listen and still remain hostile toward me, 28 then I will give full vent to my hostility. I will punish you seven times over for your sins. 29 You will eat the flesh of your own sons and daughters. 30 I will destroy your pagan shrines and cut down your incense altars. I will leave your corpses piled up beside your lifeless idols, and I will despise you. 31 I will make your cities desolate and destroy your places of worship, and I will take no pleasure in your offerings of incense. 32 Yes, I myself will devastate your land. Your enemies who come to occupy it will be utterly shocked at the destruction they see. 33 I will scatter you among the nations and attack you with my own weapons. Your land will become desolate, and your cities will lie in ruins. 34 Then at last the land will make up for its missed Sabbath years as it lies desolate during your years of exile in the land of your enemies. Then the land will finally rest and enjoy its Sabbaths. 35 As the land lies in ruins, it will take the rest you never allowed it to take every seventh year while you lived in it.

36 "And for those of you who survive, I will demoralize you in the land of your enemies far away. You will live there in such constant fear that the sound of a leaf driven by the wind will send you fleeing. You will run as though chased by a warrior with a sword, and you will fall even when no one is pursuing you. 37 Yes, though no one is chasing you, you will stumble over each other in flight, as though fleeing in battle. You will have no power to stand before your enemies. 38 You will die among the foreign nations and be devoured in the land of your enemies. 39 Those still left alive will rot away in enemy lands because of their sins and the sins of their ancestors.

**GROWTH ● ● • • ·**

26:40-45 **These verses show what God meant when he said he is merciful and gracious, rich in unfailing love and faithfulness (Exodus 34:6). Even if the Israelites chose to disobey and were scattered among the heathen, God would still give them the opportunity to repent and return to him. His purpose was not to destroy them, but to help them grow. Our day-to-day experiences and hardships are sometimes overwhelming; unless we can see that God's purpose is to bring about continual growth in us, we may give up. To retain hope while we suffer shows we understand God's merciful ways of relating to his people. (See Jeremiah 29:11 too.)**

40 "But at last my people will confess their sins and the sins of their ancestors for betraying me and being hostile toward me. 41 Finally, when I have given full expression to my hostility and have brought them to the land of their enemies, then at last their disobedient hearts will be humbled, and they will pay for their sins. 42 Then I will remember my covenant with Jacob, with Isaac, and with Abraham, and I will remember the land. 43 And the land will enjoy its years of Sabbath rest as it lies deserted. At last the people will receive the due punishment for their sins, for they rejected my regulations and despised my laws.

44 "But despite all this, I will not utterly reject or despise them while they are in exile in the land of their enemies. I will not cancel my covenant with them by wiping them out. I, the LORD, am their God. 45 I will remember my ancient covenant with their ancestors, whom I brought out of Egypt while all the nations watched. I, the LORD, am their God."

46 These are the laws, regulations, and instructions that the LORD gave to the Israelites through Moses on Mount Sinai.

## CHAPTER 27

**PAYMENTS TO THE LORD.** The LORD said to Moses, 2 "Give the following instructions to the Israelites: If you make a special vow to dedicate someone to the LORD by paying the value of that person, 3 here is the scale of values to be used. A man between the ages of twenty and sixty is valued at fifty pieces of silver*; 4 a woman of that age is valued at thirty pieces of silver. 5 A boy between five and twenty is valued at twenty pieces of silver; a girl of that age is valued at ten pieces of silver. 6 A boy between the ages of one month and five years is valued at five pieces of silver; a girl of that age is valued at three pieces of silver. 7 A man older than sixty is valued at fifteen pieces of silver; a woman older than sixty is valued at ten pieces of silver. 8 If you desire to make such a vow but cannot afford to pay the prescribed amount, go to the priest and he will evaluate your ability to pay. You will then pay the amount decided by the priest.

9 "If your vow involves giving a clean animal—one that is acceptable as an offering to the LORD—then your gift to the LORD will be considered holy. 10 The animal should never be exchanged or substituted for another—neither a good animal for a bad one nor a bad animal for a good one. But if such an exchange is in fact made, then both the original animal and the substitute will be considered holy. 11 But if your vow involves an unclean animal—one that is not acceptable as an offering to the LORD—then you must bring the animal to the priest. 12 He will assess its value, and his assessment will be final. 13 If you want to redeem the animal, you must pay the value set by the priest, plus 20 percent.

14 "If you dedicate a house to the LORD, the priest must come to assess its value. The priest's assessment will be final. 15 If you wish to redeem the house, you must pay the value set by the priest, plus 20 percent. Then the house will again belong to you.

16 "If you dedicate to the LORD a piece of your ancestral property, its value will be assessed by the

27:3 Hebrew *50 shekels of silver, according to the standard sanctuary shekel,* each about 0.4 ounces or 11 grams in weight. The term *shekels* also appears in 27:4, 5, 6, 7, 16.

amount of seed required to plant it—fifty pieces of
silver for an area that produces* five bushels* of
barley seed. [17]If the field is dedicated to the LORD
in the Year of Jubilee, then the entire assessment
will apply. [18]But if the field is dedicated after the
Year of Jubilee, the priest must assess the land's
value in proportion to the years left until the next
Year of Jubilee. [19]If you decide to redeem the dedicated field, you must pay the land's value as
assessed by the priest, plus 20 percent. Then the
field will again belong to you. [20]But if you decide
not to redeem the field, or if the field is sold to
someone else by the priests, it can never be redeemed. [21]When the field is released in the Year of
Jubilee, it will be holy, a field specially set apart*
for the LORD. It will become the property of the
priests.

[22]"If you dedicate to the LORD a field that you
have purchased but which is not part of your ancestral property, [23]the priest must assess its value
based on the years until the next Year of Jubilee.
You must then give the assessed value of the land
as a sacred donation to the LORD. [24]In the Year of
Jubilee the field will be released to the original
owner from whom you purchased it. [25]All the value
assessments must be measured in terms of the
standard sanctuary shekel.*

[26]"You may not dedicate to the LORD the firstborn of your cattle or sheep because the firstborn
of these animals already belong to him. [27]However,
if it is the firstborn of a ceremonially unclean animal, you may redeem it by paying the priest's
assessment of its worth, plus 20 percent. If you do
not redeem it, the priest may sell it to someone else
for its assessed value.

## TODAY AND FOREVER ● ● • • •

27:34 **The book of Leviticus is filled with the commands God gave his people at the foot of Mount Sinai. From these commands we can learn much about God's nature and character. At first glance, Leviticus seems irrelevant to our high-tech world. But digging a little deeper, we realize that the book still speaks to us today, because God has not changed and his principles are for all times. As people and society change, we need constantly to search for ways to apply the principles of God's law to our present circumstances. God was the same in Leviticus as he is today and will be forever (Hebrews 13:8).**

[28]"However, anything specially set apart by the
LORD—whether a person, an animal, or an inherited field—must never be sold or redeemed. Anything devoted in this way has been set apart for the
LORD as holy. [29]A person specially set apart by the
LORD for destruction cannot be redeemed. Such a
person must be put to death.

[30]"A tenth of the produce of the land, whether
grain or fruit, belongs to the LORD and must be set
apart to him as holy. [31]If you want to redeem the
LORD's tenth of the fruit or grain, you must pay
its value, plus 20 percent. [32]The LORD also owns
every tenth animal counted off from your herds
and flocks. They are set apart to him as holy.
[33]The tenth animal must not be selected on the
basis of whether it is good or bad, and no substitu-
tions will be allowed. If any exchange is in fact
made, then both the original animal and the substituted one will be considered holy and cannot be
redeemed."

[34]These are the commands that the LORD gave to
the Israelites through Moses on Mount Sinai.

**27:16a** Or *requires.* **27:16b** Hebrew *1 homer* [182 liters]. **27:21** The Hebrew term used here refers to the complete consecration of things or people to the LORD, either by destroying them or by giving them as an offering; also in 27:28, 29. **27:25** Hebrew *measured according to the sanctuary shekel, 20 gerahs to each shekel.* Each sanctuary shekel was about 0.4 ounces or 11 grams in weight.

# MEGA themes

**SACRIFICE/OFFERING** There are five kinds of offerings that fulfill two main purposes. One purpose is to show praise, thankfulness, and devotion. The other purpose is atonement, the covering and removal of sin.

Sacrifices (offerings) fulfilled two functions: worship and forgiveness of sins. Through them we learn that sin has a great cost. Because men and women cannot remove their own sins, God requires that a life be given for the cleansing of each person. Until Christ, this cleansing (atonement) was accomplished through the sacrifice of an animal. Jesus' death, however, did away with this temporary system by permanently paying the penalty for our sin.

1. What differences are there between the sacrifices found in the book of Leviticus and the sacrifice provided by Jesus? (Check the book of Hebrews in the New Testament for a detailed study of the contrast between the old and new provisions of God.)
2. The worship offerings focused on praise, thankfulness, and devotion. In what ways can you bring offerings of worship to God?
3. What are some of the aspects of God that you feel are worthy of worship?
4. How does Christ's sacrifice help you worship God freely?
5. What will you do this week to bring God an offering of worship?

**HEALTH** God gave civil rules for handling food, disease, and sex. God called Israel to obey him and to be different from the surrounding nations. Through these rules, God preserved them from disease and genetic problems as well as teaching them spiritual principles.

We still are to be different morally and spiritually from the unbelievers around us. Principles for healthy living are as important today as in the day of Moses. God is concerned not just about our inner spirit but also about our outer body because it, too, was made to glorify him.

1. What are some ways that people you know abuse their body?
2. Based on what you have learned about God's view of our body, why is he against such abuse?
3. What are some of the biblical principles for taking care of your body?
4. How would following these principles improve your health?
5. Do you agree or disagree with this statement: "Taking care of your body's health is an important part of Christian discipleship"? Explain your answer.
6. Based on your answer to question 5, what changes do you need to make in how you take care of your body?

**HOLINESS** *Holy* means "separated" or "devoted." God removed his people from Egypt; then he had to remove Egypt from his people. God called his people to be committed to his ways, leaving behind the old lifestyle they had lived in Egypt.

God calls us to devote every area of our life to him. This requires learning to live in obedience to him daily so that we reflect his holiness in the world. While we may not be required to worship as the Israelites did, we are to be committed to leaving behind those things that belong to "Egypt" in our lifestyle.

1. How do you think most of your friends at school would describe a "holy" person?
2. What in their ideas is similar to and what is different from the definition of holiness that you are learning in the Scriptures?
3. What would it mean to live a holy life in your school?
4. What areas of your life still belong to "Egypt" and keep you from personal holiness? What are some specific ways to increase your devotion to God and become a clearer reflection of his holiness?

**LEVITES** The Levites and priests taught the people how to worship. They were ministers who regulated the moral, civil, and ceremonial laws of the people and supervised the health, justice, and welfare of the nation.

The Levites were servants who showed Israel the way to God. Understanding their role enables us to comprehend more of Jesus as our High Priest and our own rules through the priesthood of all believers.

1. What type of attitude would you expect the people to have toward the Levites?
2. The high priest was the one who brought the community of God's people into God's presence. In what ways does Jesus fulfill our need for a high priest?
3. Based on your responses to the first two questions, what do we learn about Jesus who, although holding a position of reverence, chose to be our servant?
4. In what ways do you need Jesus in your life today? What do you need from him as your minister, servant, and Lord?
5. How can you spend some time with the Lord today so that he can meet you right where you are?

1805 B.C.
Joseph dies

SLAVERY IN EGYPT

1446
Exodus from Egypt

1445
Ten Commandments given

1444
First census

1443
First spy mission

WILDERNESS WANDERINGS

1407
Second census;
Balaam prophesies

1406
Joshua appointed;
Canaan entered

1375
Judges begin to rule

1050
United kingdom under Saul

At noon, two weary travelers who had been walking all day wanted to get out of the heat and rest. They noticed a huge tree with branches that formed a canopy of shade. They stumbled to the shade of the tree, threw down their packs, spread their blankets, and were soon blissfully asleep. When they awoke, one of the travelers, feeling refreshed and a little arrogant, gazed into the tree and complained: "What a useless tree. There's no fruit!" He had forgotten about the tree's wonderful shade. That traveler was a lot like Israel. ■ The Israelites seemed to be sitting in God's "shade." The future looked great. God himself was leading them and they were about to enter the Promised Land. Then the people began to complain about everything. They decided they would rather be back in Egypt as slaves than where they were. Finally God got fed up and banished them to the wilderness, refusing to let them enter the Promised Land. Though God still considered these complainers his people, he was no longer ready to give them all he had promised. ■ Are we much different from the complaining Israelites? God has done, is doing, and will do so much for us. Yet we complain. "God, what are you doing?" "God, you don't care!" "God, I hate you!" We don't trust him although he has proven himself trustworthy. Do you trust God, or do you complain? You are sitting under the "shade" of God's love. Don't complain. God was leading the Israelites even when they thought he wasn't, and he is leading you.

## STATS

PURPOSE: To tell the story of how Israel prepared to enter the Promised Land, how they sinned and were punished, and how they prepared to try again

AUTHOR: Moses

TO WHOM WRITTEN: The people of Israel

DATE WRITTEN: 1450–1410 B.C.

SETTING: The vast wilderness of the Sinai region, as well as lands just south and east of Canaan

KEY PEOPLE: Moses, Aaron, Miriam, Joshua, Caleb, Eleazar, Korah, Balaam

KEY PLACES: Mount Sinai, Promised Land (Canaan), Kadesh, Mount Hor, plains of Moab

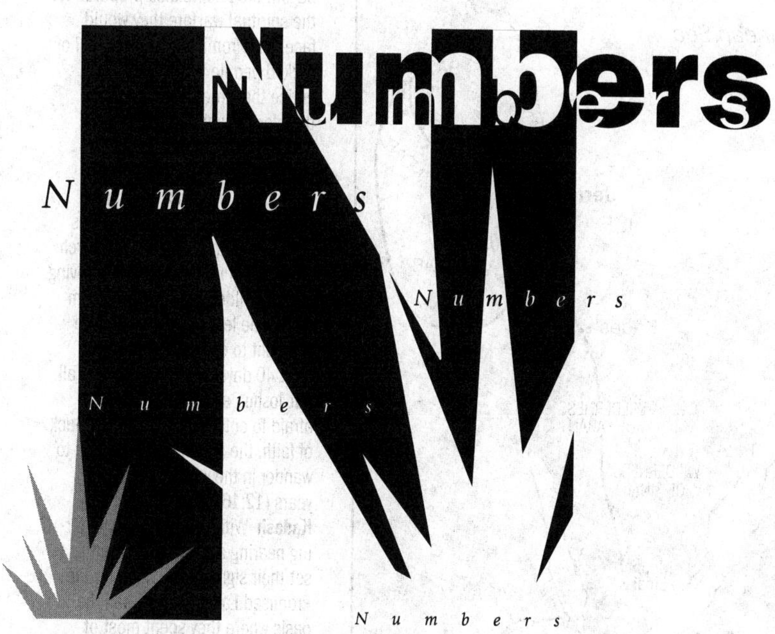


CHAPTER **1** **ISRAEL'S FIRST CENSUS.** One day in midspring,* during the second year after Israel's departure from Egypt, the LORD spoke to Moses in the
Tabernacle* in the wilderness of Sinai. He said,
[2]"Take a census of the whole community of Israel by
their clans and families. List the names of all the men
[3]twenty years old or older who are able to go to war.
You and Aaron are to direct the project, [4]assisted by
one family leader from each tribe."

[5]These are the tribes and the names of the leaders
chosen for the task:

| | *Tribe* | *Leader* |
|---|---|---|
| | Reuben | Elizur son of Shedeur |
| 6 | Simeon | Shelumiel son of Zurishaddai |
| 7 | Judah | Nahshon son of Amminadab |
| 8 | Issachar | Nethanel son of Zuar |
| 9 | Zebulun | Eliab son of Helon |
| 10 | Ephraim son of Joseph | Elishama son of Ammihud |
| | Manasseh son of Joseph | Gamaliel son of Pedahzur |
| 11 | Benjamin | Abidan son of Gideoni |
| 12 | Dan | Ahiezer son of Ammishaddai |
| 13 | Asher | Pagiel son of Ocran |
| 14 | Gad | Eliasaph son of Deuel |
| 15 | Naphtali | Ahira son of Enan |

[16]These tribal leaders, heads of their own families,
were chosen from among all the people.

[17]Now Moses and Aaron and the chosen leaders
[18]called together the whole community of Israel on
that very day.* All the people were registered according to their ancestry by their clans and families. The
men of Israel twenty years old or older were registered, one by one, [19]just as the LORD had commanded Moses. So Moses counted the people there
in the wilderness of Sinai.

[20-21]This is the number of men twenty years old or
older who were able to go to war, each listed according to his own clan and family*:

| | *Tribe* | *Number* |
|---|---|---|
| | Reuben (Jacob's* oldest son) | 46,500 |
| 22-23 | Simeon | 59,300 |
| 24-25 | Gad | 45,650 |
| 26-27 | Judah | 74,600 |
| 28-29 | Issachar | 54,400 |
| 30-31 | Zebulun | 57,400 |
| 32-33 | Ephraim son of Joseph | 40,500 |
| 34-35 | Manasseh son of Joseph | 32,200 |
| 36-37 | Benjamin | 35,400 |
| 38-39 | Dan | 62,700 |
| 40-41 | Asher | 41,500 |
| 42-43 | Naphtali | 53,400 |

[44]These were the men counted by Moses and Aaron
and the twelve leaders of Israel, all listed according

**1:1a** Hebrew *On the first day of the second month.* This day of the Hebrew lunar calendar occurs in April or early May. **1:1b** Hebrew *Tent of Meeting.* **1:18** Hebrew *on the first day of the second month;* see 1:1. **1:20-21a** In the Hebrew text, *number of men . . . family* is repeated in 1:22, 24, 26, 28, 30, 32, 34, 36, 38, 40, 42. **1:20-21b** Hebrew *Israel's.*

# KEY PLACES IN NUMBERS

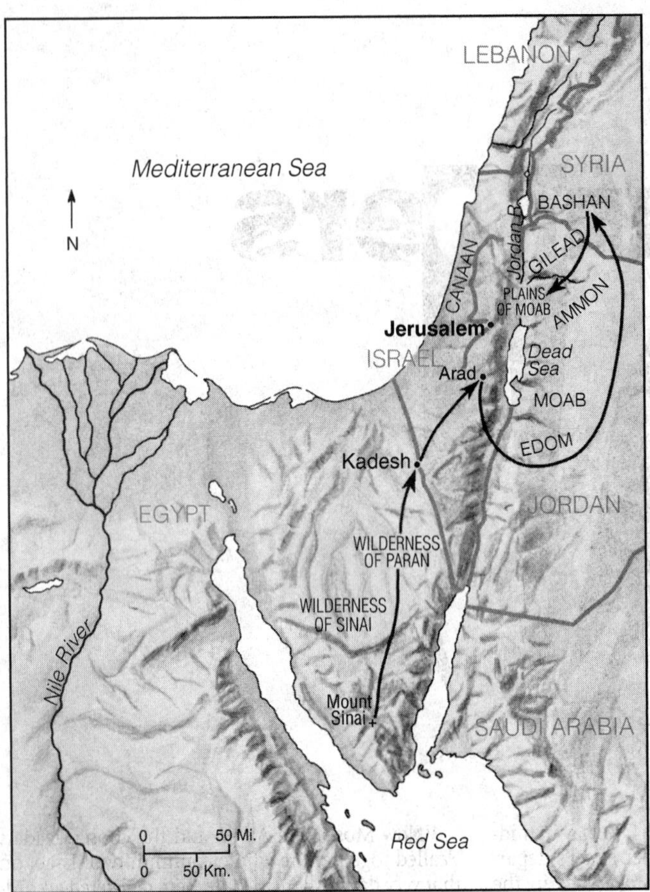

Modern names and boundaries are shown in gray.

**Mount Sinai** Numbers begins at Mount Sinai with Moses taking a census of the men eligible for battle. As the battle preparations began, the people also prepared for the spiritual warfare they would face. The Promised Land was full of wicked people who would try to entice the Israelites to sin. God, therefore, taught Moses and the Israelites how to live rightly (1:1–12:15).

**Wilderness of Paran** After a full year at Mount Sinai, the Israelites broke camp and began their march toward the Promised Land by moving into the wilderness of Paran. From there, one leader from each tribe was sent to explore the new land. After 40 days they returned, and all but Joshua and Caleb were too afraid to enter. Because of their lack of faith, the Israelites were made to wander in the wilderness for 40 years (12:16–19:22).

**Kadesh** With the years of wandering nearing an end, the Israelites set their sights once again on the Promised Land. Kadesh was the oasis where they spent most of their wilderness years. Miriam died here. And it was here that Moses angrily struck the rock, which kept him from entering the Promised Land (20).

**Arad** When the king of Arad heard that Israel was on the move, he attacked, but he was soundly defeated. Moses then led the people southward and eastward around the Dead Sea (21:1-3).

**Edom** The Israelites wanted to travel through Edom, but the king of Edom refused them passage (20:14-22). So they traveled around Edom and became very discouraged. The people complained, and God sent poisonous snakes to punish them. Only by looking at a bronze snake on a pole could those bitten be healed (21:4-9).

**Ammon** Next, King Sihon of the Amorites refused Israel passage. When he attacked, Israel defeated them (21:21-32).

**Bashan** After capturing the Amorite country, the Israelites moved up to Bashan. King Og attacked, but he was also defeated (21:33-35).

**Plains of Moab** The people camped on the plains of Moab, east of the Jordan River opposite Jericho. They were on the verge of entering the Promised Land (22:1).

**Moab** King Balak of Moab, terrified of the Israelites, called upon Balaam, a famous sorcerer, to curse Israel from the mountains above where the Israelites camped. But the Lord caused Balaam to bless them instead (22:2–24:25).

**Gilead** The tribes of Reuben and Gad decided to settle in the fertile country of Gilead east of the Jordan River because it was a good land for their sheep. But first they promised to help the other tribes conquer the land west of the Jordan River (32).

---

to their ancestral descent. 45They were counted by
families—all the men of Israel who were twenty
years old or older and able to go to war. 46The total
number was 603,550.

47But this total did not include the Levites. 48For
the LORD had said to Moses, 49"Exempt the tribe of
Levi from the census; do not include them when you
count the rest of the Israelites. 50You must put the
Levites in charge of the Tabernacle of the Covenant,*
along with its furnishings and equipment. They
must carry the Tabernacle and its equipment as you
travel, and they must care for it and camp around it.
51Whenever the Tabernacle is moved, the Levites will
take it down and set it up again. Anyone else who
goes too near the Tabernacle will be executed. 52Each
tribe of Israel will have a designated camping area
with its own family banner. 53But the Levites will
camp around the Tabernacle of the Covenant to offer

1:50 Or *Tabernacle of the Testimony;* also in 1:53.

the people of Israel protection from the LORD's fierce
anger. The Levites are responsible to stand guard
around the Tabernacle."
[54]So the Israelites did everything just as the LORD
had commanded Moses.

CHAPTER **2** **WHERE THE TRIBES CAMPED.** Then the
LORD gave these instructions to Moses and Aaron:
[2]"Each tribe will be assigned its own area in the
camp, and the various groups will camp beneath
their family banners. The Tabernacle* will be located
at the center of these tribal compounds.
[3-4]"The divisions of Judah, Issachar, and Zebulun
are to camp toward the sunrise on the east side of the
Tabernacle, beneath their family banners. These are
the names of the tribes, their leaders, and the number of their available troops:

| | *Tribe* | *Leader* | *Number* |
|---|---|---|---|
| | Judah | Nahshon son of Amminadab | 74,600 |
| 5-6 | Issachar | Nethanel son of Zuar | 54,400 |
| 7-8 | Zebulun | Eliab son of Helon | 57,400 |

[9]So the total of all the troops on Judah's side of the
camp is 186,400. These three tribes are to lead the
way whenever the Israelites travel to a new campsite.
[10-11]"The divisions of Reuben, Simeon, and Gad
are to camp on the south side of the Tabernacle,
beneath their family banners. These are the names of
the tribes, their leaders, and the number of their
available troops:

| | *Tribe* | *Leader* | *Number* |
|---|---|---|---|
| | Reuben | Elizur son of Shedeur | 46,500 |
| 12-13 | Simeon | Shelumiel son of Zurishaddai | 59,300 |
| 14-15 | Gad | Eliasaph son of Deuel* | 45,650 |

[16]So the total of all the troops on Reuben's side of the
camp is 151,450. These three tribes will be second in
line whenever the Israelites travel.
[17]"Then the Levites will set out from the middle of
the camp with the Tabernacle. All the tribes are to
travel in the same order that they camp, each in
position under the appropriate family banner.
[18-19]"The divisions of Ephraim, Manasseh, and
Benjamin are to camp on the west side of the Tabernacle, beneath their family banners. These are the
names of the tribes, their leaders, and the number of
their available troops:

| | *Tribe* | *Leader* | *Number* |
|---|---|---|---|
| | Ephraim | Elishama son of Ammihud | 40,500 |
| 20-21 | Manasseh | Gamaliel son of Pedahzur | 32,200 |
| 22-23 | Benjamin | Abidan son of Gideoni | 35,400 |

[24]So the total of all the troops on Ephraim's side of
the camp is 108,100, and they will follow the Levites
in the line of march.
[25-26]"The divisions of Dan, Asher, and Naphtali are
to camp on the north side of the Tabernacle, beneath
their family banners. These are the names of the
tribes, their leaders, and the number of their available troops:

| | *Tribe* | *Leader* | *Number* |
|---|---|---|---|
| | Dan | Ahiezer son of Ammishaddai | 62,700 |
| 27-28 | Asher | Pagiel son of Ocran | 41,500 |
| 29-30 | Naphtali | Ahira son of Enan | 53,400 |

[31]So the total of all the troops on Dan's side of the
camp is 157,600. They are to bring up the rear
whenever the Israelites move to a new campsite."
[32]In summary, the troops of Israel listed by their
families totaled 603,550. [33]The Levites were exempted from this census by the LORD's command to
Moses. [34]So the people of Israel did everything just as
the LORD had commanded Moses. Each clan and
family set up camp and marched under their banners exactly as the LORD had instructed them.

**CONTRAST ● ● • • ·**

2:34 **This must have been one of the biggest campsites the world has ever seen! It would have taken about 12 square miles to set up tents for just the 600,000 fighting men—not to mention the women and children. Moses must have had a difficult time managing such a group. In the early stages of the journey and at Mount Sinai, the people were generally obedient to both God and Moses. But when the people left Mount Sinai and traveled across the rugged wilderness, they began to complain, grumble, and disobey. Soon problems erupted, and Moses could no longer effectively manage the Israelites. The books of Exodus, Leviticus, and Numbers present a striking contrast between how much we can accomplish when we obey God, and how little we can accomplish when we don't.**

CHAPTER **3** **WHAT THE LEVITES DID.** This is the family
line of Aaron and Moses as it was recorded when the
LORD spoke to Moses on Mount Sinai: [2]Aaron's sons
were Nadab (the firstborn), Abihu, Eleazar, and Ithamar. [3]They were anointed and set apart to minister
as priests. [4]But Nadab and Abihu died in the LORD's
presence in the wilderness of Sinai when they
burned before the LORD a different kind of fire than
he had commanded. Since they had no sons, this left
only Eleazar and Ithamar to serve as priests with
their father, Aaron.
[5]Then the LORD said to Moses, [6]"Call forward the
tribe of Levi and present them to Aaron the priest as
his assistants. [7]They will serve Aaron and the whole
community, performing their sacred duties in and
around the Tabernacle.* [8]They will also maintain all
the furnishings of the sacred tent,* serving in the
Tabernacle on behalf of all the Israelites. [9]Assign the
Levites to Aaron and his sons as their assistants.
[10]Appoint Aaron and his sons to carry out the duties
of the priesthood. Anyone else who comes too near
the sanctuary must be executed!"
[11]And the LORD said to Moses, [12]"I have chosen the
Levites from among the Israelites as substitutes for

2:2 Hebrew *Tent of Meeting;* also in 2:17. 2:14-15 As in many Hebrew manuscripts, Samaritan Pentateuch, and Latin Vulgate (see also 1:14); most Hebrew manuscripts read *son of Reuel.* 3:7 Hebrew *around the Tent of Meeting, doing service at the Tabernacle.* 3:8 Hebrew *Tent of Meeting.*

all the firstborn sons of the people of Israel. The Levites are mine [13]because all the firstborn sons are mine. From the day I killed all the firstborn sons of the Egyptians, I set apart for myself all the firstborn in Israel of both men and animals. They are mine; I am the LORD."

[14]The LORD spoke again to Moses, there in the wilderness of Sinai. He said, [15]"Take a census of the tribe of Levi by its families and clans. Count every male who is one month old or older." [16]So Moses counted them, just as the LORD had commanded.

[17]Levi had three sons, who were named Gershon, Kohath, and Merari.
[18]The clans descended from Gershon were named for two of his descendants, Libni and Shimei.
[19]The clans descended from Kohath were named for four of his descendants, Amram, Izhar, Hebron, and Uzziel.
[20]The clans descended from Merari were named for two of his descendants, Mahli and Mushi.

These were the Levite clans, listed according to their family groups.

[21]The descendants of Gershon were composed of the clans descended from Libni and Shimei. [22]There were 7,500 males one month old or older among these Gershonite clans. [23]They were assigned the area to the west of the Tabernacle for their camp. [24]The leader of the Gershonite clans was Eliasaph son of Lael. [25]These two clans were responsible to care for the tent of the Tabernacle with its layers of coverings, its entry curtains, [26]the curtains of the courtyard that surrounded the Tabernacle and altar, the curtain at the courtyard entrance, the cords, and all the equipment related to their use.

[27]The descendants of Kohath were composed of the clans descended from Amram, Izhar, Hebron, and Uzziel. [28]There were 8,600* males one month old or older among these Kohathite clans. They were responsible for the care of the sanctuary. [29]They were assigned the area south of the Tabernacle for their camp. [30]The leader of the Kohathite clans was Elizaphan son of Uzziel. [31]These four clans were responsible for the care of the Ark, the table, the lampstand, the altars, the various utensils used in the sanctuary, the inner curtain, and all the equipment related to their use. [32]Eleazar the priest, Aaron's son, was the chief administrator over all the Levites, with special responsibility for the oversight of the sanctuary.

[33]The descendants of Merari were composed of the clans descended from Mahli and Mushi. [34]There were 6,200 males one month old or older among these Merarite clans. [35]They were assigned the area north of the Tabernacle for their camp. The leader of the Merarite clans was Zuriel son of Abihail. [36]These two clans were responsible for the care of the frames supporting the Tabernacle, the crossbars, the pillars, the bases, and all the equipment related to their use. [37]They were also responsible for the posts of the courtyard and all their bases, pegs, and cords.

[38]The area in front of the Tabernacle in the east toward the sunrise* was reserved for the tents of Moses and of Aaron and his sons, who had the final responsibility for the sanctuary on behalf of the people of Israel. Anyone other than a priest or Levite who came too near the sanctuary was to be executed.

[39]So among the Levite clans counted by Moses and Aaron at the LORD's command, there were 22,000 males one month old or older.

[40]Then the LORD said to Moses, "Now count all the firstborn sons in Israel who are one month old or older, and register each name. [41]The Levites will be reserved for me as substitutes for the firstborn sons of Israel; I am the LORD. And the Levites' livestock are mine as substitutes for the firstborn livestock of the whole nation of Israel."

[42]So Moses counted the firstborn sons of the people of Israel, just as the LORD had commanded. [43]The total number of firstborn sons who were one month old or older was 22,273.

[44]Now the LORD said to Moses, [45]"Take the Levites in place of the firstborn sons of the people of Israel. And take the livestock of the Levites as substitutes for the firstborn livestock of the people of Israel. The Levites will be mine; I am the LORD. [46]To redeem the 273 firstborn sons of Israel who are in excess of the number of Levites, [47]collect five pieces of silver for each person, each piece weighing the same as the standard sanctuary shekel.* [48]Give the silver to Aaron and his sons as the redemption price for the extra firstborn sons."

[49]So Moses collected redemption money for the firstborn sons of Israel who exceeded the number of Levites. [50]The silver collected on behalf of these firstborn sons of Israel came to about thirty-four pounds in weight.* [51]And Moses gave the redemption money to Aaron and his sons as the LORD had commanded.

CHAPTER **4** **JOBS FOR THE KOHATHITE CLAN.** Then the LORD said to Moses and Aaron, [2]"Take a census of the clans and families of the Kohathite division of the Levite tribe. [3]Count all the men between the ages of thirty and fifty who qualify to work in the Tabernacle.*

[4]"The duties of the Kohathites at the Tabernacle will relate to the most sacred objects. [5]When the camp moves, Aaron and his sons must enter the Tabernacle first to take down the inner curtain and cover the Ark of the Covenant* with it. [6]Then they must cover the inner curtain with fine goatskin leather, and the goatskin leather with a dark blue cloth. Finally, they must put the carrying poles of the Ark in place.

[7]"Next they must spread a blue cloth over the table, where the Bread of the Presence is displayed, and place the dishes, spoons, bowls, cups, and the

3:28 Some Greek manuscripts read *8,300;* see total in 3:39. 3:38 Hebrew *toward the sunrise, in front of the Tent of Meeting.* 3:47 Hebrew *5 shekels* [2 ounces or 57 grams] *apiece, according to the sanctuary shekel, 20 gerahs to each shekel.* 3:50 Hebrew *1,365 shekels* [15.5 kilograms], *according to the sanctuary shekel.* 4:3 Hebrew *Tent of Meeting;* also in 4:4, 15, 23, 25, 28, 30, 31, 33, 35, 37, 39, 41, 43, 47. 4:5 Or *Ark of the Testimony.*

special bread on the cloth. 8They must spread a
scarlet cloth over that, and finally a covering of fine
goatskin leather on top of the scarlet cloth. Then
they must insert the carrying poles into the table.
9"Next they must cover the lampstand with a dark
blue cloth, along with its lamps, lamp snuffers, trays,
and special jars of olive oil. 10The lampstand with its
utensils must then be covered with fine goatskin
leather, and the bundle must be placed on a carrying
frame.
11"Aaron and his sons must also spread a dark blue
cloth over the gold altar and cover this cloth with a
covering of fine goatskin leather. Then they are to
attach the carrying poles to the altar. 12All the remaining utensils of the sanctuary must be wrapped
in a dark blue cloth, covered with fine goatskin
leather, and placed on the carrying frame.
13"The ashes must be removed from the altar, and
the altar must then be covered with a purple cloth.
14All the altar utensils—the firepans, hooks, shovels,
basins, and all the containers—are to be placed on
the cloth, and a covering of fine goatskin leather
must be spread over them. Finally, the carrying poles
must be put in place. 15When Aaron and his sons
have finished covering the sanctuary and all the
sacred utensils, the Kohathites will come and carry
these things to the next destination. But they must
not touch the sacred objects, or they will die. So
these are the objects of the Tabernacle that the Kohathites must carry.
16"Eleazar son of Aaron the priest will be responsible for the oil of the lampstand, the fragrant incense, the daily grain offering, and the anointing oil.
In fact, the supervision of the entire Tabernacle and
everything in it will be Eleazar's responsibility."
17Then the LORD said to Moses and Aaron,
18"Don't let the Kohathite clans be destroyed from
among the Levites! 19This is what you must do so
they will live and not die when they approach the
most sacred objects. Aaron and his sons must always
go in with them and assign a specific duty or load to
each person. 20Otherwise they must not approach
the sanctuary and look at the sacred objects for even
a moment, or they will die."
21And the LORD said to Moses, 22"Take a census of
the clans and families of the Gershonite division of
the tribe of Levi. 23Count all the men between the
ages of thirty and fifty who are eligible to serve in the
Tabernacle.
24"The duties of the Gershonites will be in the
areas of general service and carrying loads. 25They
must carry the curtains of the Tabernacle, the Tabernacle itself with its coverings, the outer covering of
fine goatskin leather, and the curtain for the Tabernacle entrance. 26They are also to carry the curtains
for the courtyard walls that surround the Tabernacle
and altar, the curtain across the courtyard entrance,
the necessary cords, and all the altar's accessories.
The Gershonites are responsible for transporting all
these items. 27Aaron and his sons will direct the
Gershonites regarding their duties, whether it involves moving or doing other work. They must assign the Gershonites the loads they are to carry. 28So
these are the duties assigned to the Gershonites at
the Tabernacle. They will be directly responsible to
Ithamar son of Aaron the priest.
29"Now take a census of the clans and families of
the Merarite division of the Levite tribe. 30Count all
the men between the ages of thirty and fifty who are
eligible to serve in the Tabernacle.
31"Their duties at the Tabernacle will consist of carrying loads. They will be required to carry the frames
of the Tabernacle, the crossbars, the pillars with their
bases, 32the posts for the courtyard walls with their
bases, pegs, cords, accessories, and everything else related to their use. You must assign the various loads to
each man by name. 33So these are the duties of the
Merarites at the Tabernacle. They are directly responsible to Ithamar son of Aaron the priest."
34So Moses, Aaron, and the other leaders of the
community counted the Kohathite division by its
clans and families. 35The count included all the men
between thirty and fifty years of age who were eligible
for service in the Tabernacle, 36and the total number
came to 2,750. 37So this was the total of all those from
the Kohathite clans who were eligible to serve at the
Tabernacle. Moses and Aaron counted them, just as the
LORD had commanded through Moses.
38The Gershonite division was also counted by its
clans and families. 39The count included all the men
between thirty and fifty years of age who were eligible for service in the Tabernacle, 40and the total
number came to 2,630. 41So this was the total of all
those from the Gershonite clans who were eligible to
serve at the Tabernacle. Moses and Aaron counted
them, just as the LORD had commanded.
42The Merarite division was also counted by its
clans and families. 43The count included all the men
between thirty and fifty years of age who were eligible for service in the Tabernacle, 44and the total
number came to 3,200. 45So this was the total of all
those from the Merarite clans who were eligible for
service. Moses and Aaron counted them, just as the
LORD had commanded through Moses.
46So Moses, Aaron, and the leaders of Israel
counted all the Levites by their clans and families.
47All the men between thirty and fifty years of age
who were eligible for service in the Tabernacle and
for its transportation 48numbered 8,580. 49Each man
was assigned his task and told what to carry, just as
the LORD had commanded through Moses.
And so the census was completed, just as the LORD
had commanded Moses.

CHAPTER **5** **PURITY IN THE CAMP.** The LORD gave
these instructions to Moses: 2"Command the people
of Israel to remove anyone from the camp who has
a contagious skin disease* or a discharge, or who has

5:2 Traditionally rendered *leprosy.* The Hebrew word used here describes various skin diseases.

been defiled by touching a dead person. [3]This applies to men and women alike. Remove them so they will not defile the camp, where I live among you." [4]So the Israelites did just as the LORD had commanded Moses and removed such people from the camp.

[5]Then the LORD said to Moses, [6]"Give these instructions to the people of Israel: If any of the people—men or women—betray the LORD by doing wrong to another person, they are guilty. [7]They must confess their sin and make full restitution for what they have done, adding a penalty of 20 percent and returning it to the person who was wronged. [8]But if the person who was wronged is dead, and there are no near relatives to whom restitution can be made, it belongs to the LORD and must be given to the priest, along with a ram for atonement. [9]All the sacred gifts that the Israelites bring to a priest will belong to him. [10]Each priest may keep the sacred donations that he receives."

## SET THINGS RIGHT ● ● • •

**5:5-8 God included restitution, a unique concept for that day, as part of his law for Israel. When someone was robbed, the guilty person was required to restore to the victim what had been taken and pay an additional interest penalty. When we have wronged someone, we should look for ways to set things right and, if possible, leave the victim even better off than before we harmed him or her. When we have been wronged, we should seek restoration rather than striking out in revenge.**

[11]And the LORD said to Moses, [12]"Say to the people of Israel: 'Suppose a man's wife goes astray and is unfaithful to her husband. [13]Suppose she sleeps with another man, but there is no witness since she was not caught in the act. [14]If her husband becomes jealous and suspicious of his wife, even if she has not defiled herself, [15]the husband must bring his wife to the priest with an offering of two quarts* of barley flour to be presented on her behalf. Do not mix it with olive oil or frankincense, for it is a jealousy offering—an offering of inquiry to find out if she is guilty.

[16]"'The priest must then present her before the LORD. [17]He must take some holy water in a clay jar and mix it with dust from the Tabernacle floor. [18]When he has presented her before the LORD, he must unbind her hair and place the offering of inquiry—the jealousy offering—in her hands to determine whether or not her husband's suspicions are justified. The priest will stand before her, holding the jar of bitter water that brings a curse to those who are guilty. [19]The priest will put the woman under oath and say to her, "If no other man has slept with you, and you have not defiled yourself by being unfaithful, may you be immune from the effects of this bitter water that causes the curse. [20]But if you have gone astray while under your husband's authority and defiled yourself by sleeping with another man"—[21]at this point the priest must put the woman under this oath—"then may the people see that the LORD's curse is upon you when he makes you infertile.* [22]Now may this water that brings the curse enter your body and make you infertile.*" And the woman will be required to say, "Yes, let it be so." [23]Then the priest will write these curses on a piece of leather and wash them off into the bitter water. [24]He will then make the woman drink the bitter water, so it may bring on the curse and cause bitter suffering in cases of guilt.

[25]"'Then the priest will take the jealousy offering from the woman's hand, lift it up before the LORD, and carry it to the altar. [26]He will take a handful as a token portion and burn it on the altar. Then he will require the woman to drink the water. [27]If she has defiled herself by being unfaithful to her husband, the water that brings the curse will cause bitter suffering. She will become infertile,* and her name will become a curse word among her people. [28]But if she has not defiled herself and is pure, she will be unharmed and will still be able to have children.

[29]"'This is the ritual law for dealing with jealousy. If a woman defiles herself by being unfaithful to her husband, [30]or if a man is overcome with jealousy and suspicion that his wife has been unfaithful, the husband must present his wife before the LORD, and the priest will apply this entire ritual law to her. [31]The husband will be innocent of any guilt in this matter, but his wife will be held accountable for her sin.'"

CHAPTER **6** **NAZIRITE LAWS.** Then the LORD said to Moses, "Speak to the people of Israel and give them these instructions: [2]If some of the people, either men or women, take the special vow of a Nazirite, setting themselves apart to the LORD in a special way, [3]they must give up wine and other alcoholic drinks. They must not use vinegar made from wine, they must not drink other fermented drinks or fresh grape juice, and they must not eat grapes or raisins. [4]As long as they are bound by their Nazirite vow, they are not allowed to eat or drink anything that comes from a grapevine, not even the grape seeds or skins.

[5]"They must never cut their hair throughout the time of their vow, for they are holy and set apart to the LORD. That is why they must let their hair grow long. [6]And they may not go near a dead body during the entire period of their vow to the LORD, [7]even if their own father, mother, brother, or sister has died. They must not defile the hair on their head, because it is the symbol of their separation to God. [8]This applies as long as they are set apart to the LORD.

[9]"If their hair is defiled because someone suddenly falls dead beside them, they must wait for seven days and then shave their heads. Then they will be cleansed from their defilement. [10]On the eighth

5:15 Hebrew *1/10 of an ephah* [2 liters]. 5:21 Hebrew *when he causes your thigh to waste away and your abdomen to swell.* 5:22 Hebrew *enter your body so that your abdomen swells and your thigh wastes away.* 5:27 Hebrew *Her body will swell and her thigh will waste away.*

day they must bring two turtledoves or two young
pigeons to the priest at the entrance of the Tabernacle.* 11The priest will offer one of the birds for a sin
offering and the other for a burnt offering. In this
way, he will make atonement for the guilt they in-
curred from the dead body. Then they must renew
their vow that day and let their hair begin to grow
again. 12The days of their vow that were completed
before their defilement no longer count. They must
rededicate themselves to the LORD for the full term
of their vow, and each must bring a one-year-old
male lamb for a guilt offering.

13"This is the ritual law of the Nazirites. At the
conclusion of their time of separation as Nazirites,
they must each go to the entrance of the Tabernacle
14and offer these sacrifices to the LORD: a one-year-
old male lamb without defect for a burnt offering, a
one-year-old female lamb without defect for a sin
offering, a ram without defect for a peace offering,
15a basket of bread made without yeast—cakes of
choice flour mixed with olive oil and wafers spread
with olive oil—along with their prescribed grain
offerings and drink offerings. 16The priest will present these offerings before the LORD: first the sin
offering and the burnt offering; 17then the ram for a
peace offering, along with the basket of bread made
without yeast. The priest must also make the prescribed grain offering and drink offering.

18"Then the Nazirites will shave their hair at the
entrance of the Tabernacle and put it on the fire
beneath the peace-offering sacrifice. 19After each
Nazirite's head has been shaved, the priest will take
for each of them the boiled shoulder of the ram, one
cake made without yeast, and one wafer made without yeast, and put them all into the Nazirite's hands.
20The priest will then lift the gifts up before the LORD
in a gesture of offering. These are holy portions for
the priest, along with the breast and thigh pieces that
were lifted up before the LORD. After this ceremony
the Nazirites may again drink wine.

21"This is the ritual law of the Nazirites. If any
Nazirites have vowed to give the LORD anything else
beyond what is required by their normal Nazirite
vow, they must fulfill their special vow exactly as they
have promised."

22Then the LORD said to Moses, 23"Instruct Aaron
and his sons to bless the people of Israel with this
special blessing:

24'May the LORD bless you
and protect you.
25May the LORD smile on you
and be gracious to you.
26May the LORD show you his favor
and give you his peace.'

27This is how Aaron and his sons will designate the
Israelites as my people,* and I myself will bless
them."

CHAPTER 7 **OFFERINGS OF DEDICATION.** On the day
Moses set up the Tabernacle, he anointed it and set
it apart as holy, along with all its furnishings and
the altar with its utensils. 2Then the leaders of
Israel—the tribal leaders who had organized the
census—came and brought their offerings. 3To-
gether they brought six carts and twelve oxen.
There was a cart for every two leaders and an ox for
each leader. They presented these to the LORD in
front of the Tabernacle.

4Then the LORD said to Moses, 5"Receive their gifts
and use these oxen and carts for the work of the
Tabernacle.* Distribute them among the Levites according to the work they have to do." 6So Moses
presented the carts and oxen to the Levites. 7He gave
two carts and four oxen to the Gershonite division
for their work, 8and four carts and eight oxen to the
Merarite division for their work. All their work was
done under the leadership of Ithamar son of Aaron
the priest. 9But he gave none of the carts or oxen to
the Kohathite division, since they were required to
carry the sacred objects of the Tabernacle on their
shoulders.

10The leaders also presented dedication gifts for
the altar at the time it was anointed. They each
placed their gifts before the altar. 11The LORD said to
Moses, "Let each leader bring his gift on a different
day for the dedication of the altar."

12On the first day Nahshon son of Amminadab,
leader of the tribe of Judah, presented his offering.
13The offering consisted of a silver platter weighing about 3¼ pounds and a silver basin of about
1¾ pounds.* These were both filled with grain
offerings of choice flour mixed with olive oil.
14He also brought a gold container weighing
about four ounces,* which was filled with
incense. 15He brought a young bull, a ram, and
a one-year-old male lamb as a burnt offering;
16a male goat for a sin offering; 17and two oxen,
five rams, five male goats, and five one-year-old
male lambs for a peace offering. This was the
offering brought by Nahshon son of
Amminadab.

18On the second day Nethanel son of Zuar, leader of
the tribe of Issachar, presented his offering.
19The offering consisted of a silver platter weighing about 3¼ pounds and a silver basin of about
1¾ pounds. These were both filled with grain
offerings of choice flour mixed with olive oil.
20He also brought a gold container weighing
about four ounces, which was filled with
incense. 21He brought a young bull, a ram, and
a one-year-old male lamb as a burnt offering;
22a male goat for a sin offering; 23and two oxen,
five rams, five male goats, and five one-year-old
male lambs for a peace offering. This was the
offering brought by Nethanel son of Zuar.

**6:10** Hebrew *Tent of Meeting;* also in 6:13, 18. **6:27** Hebrew *will put my name on the people of Israel.* **7:5** Hebrew *Tent of Meeting;* also in 7:89. **7:13** Hebrew *silver platter weighing 130 shekels* [1.5 kilograms] *and a silver basin weighing 70 shekels* [0.8 kilograms], *according to the sanctuary shekel;* also in 7:19, 25, 31, 37, 43, 49, 55, 61, 67, 73, 79, 85. **7:14** Hebrew *10 shekels* [114 grams]; also in 7:20, 26, 32, 38, 44, 50, 56, 62, 68, 74, 80, 86.

24 On the third day Eliab son of Helon, leader of the
tribe of Zebulun, presented his offering.
25 The offering consisted of a silver platter weighing about 3¼ pounds and a silver basin of about
1¾ pounds. These were both filled with grain
offerings of choice flour mixed with olive oil.
26 He also brought a gold container weighing
about four ounces, which was filled with
incense. 27 He brought a young bull, a ram, and
a one-year-old male lamb as a burnt offering;
28 a male goat for a sin offering; 29 and two oxen,
five rams, five male goats, and five one-year-old
male lambs for a peace offering. This was the
offering brought by Eliab son of Helon.

30 On the fourth day Elizur son of Shedeur, leader of
the tribe of Reuben, presented his offering.
31 The offering consisted of a silver platter weighing about 3¼ pounds and a silver basin of about
1¾ pounds. These were both filled with grain
offerings of choice flour mixed with olive oil.
32 He also brought a gold container weighing
about four ounces, which was filled with
incense. 33 He brought a young bull, a ram, and
a one-year-old male lamb as a burnt offering;
34 a male goat for a sin offering; 35 and two oxen,
five rams, five male goats, and five one-year-old
male lambs for a peace offering. This was the
offering brought by Elizur son of Shedeur.

36 On the fifth day Shelumiel son of Zurishaddai,
leader of the tribe of Simeon, presented his offering.
37 The offering consisted of a silver platter weighing about 3¼ pounds and a silver basin of about
1¾ pounds. These were both filled with grain
offerings of choice flour mixed with olive oil.
38 He also brought a gold container weighing about
four ounces, which was filled with incense. 39 He
brought a young bull, a ram, and a one-year-old
male lamb as a burnt offering; 40 a male goat for
a sin offering; 41 and two oxen, five rams, five
male goats, and five one-year-old male lambs
for a peace offering. This was the offering
brought by Shelumiel son of Zurishaddai.

42 On the sixth day Eliasaph son of Deuel, leader of
the tribe of Gad, presented his offering.
43 The offering consisted of a silver platter weighing about 3¼ pounds and a silver basin of about
1¾ pounds. These were both filled with grain
offerings of choice flour mixed with olive oil.
44 He also brought a gold container weighing
about four ounces, which was filled with
incense. 45 He brought a young bull, a ram, and
a one-year-old male lamb as a burnt offering;
46 a male goat for a sin offering; 47 and two oxen,
five rams, five male goats, and five one-year-old
male lambs for a peace offering. This was the
offering brought by Eliasaph son of Deuel.

48 On the seventh day Elishama son of Ammihud,
leader of the tribe of Ephraim, presented his offering.
49 The offering consisted of a silver platter weighing about 3¼ pounds and a silver basin of about
1¾ pounds. These were both filled with grain
offerings of choice flour mixed with olive oil.
50 He also brought a gold container weighing
about four ounces, which was filled with
incense. 51 He brought a young bull, a ram, and
a one-year-old male lamb as a burnt offering;
52 a male goat for a sin offering; 53 and two oxen,
five rams, five male goats, and five one-year-old
male lambs for a peace offering. This was the
offering brought by Elishama son of Ammihud.

54 On the eighth day Gamaliel son of Pedahzur,
leader of the tribe of Manasseh, presented his offering.
55 The offering consisted of a silver platter weighing about 3¼ pounds and a silver basin of about
1¾ pounds. These were both filled with grain
offerings of choice flour mixed with olive oil.
56 He also brought a gold container weighing
about four ounces, which was filled with
incense. 57 He brought a young bull, a ram, and
a one-year-old male lamb as a burnt offering; 58 a
male goat for a sin offering; 59 and two oxen, five
rams, five male goats, and five one-year-old
male lambs for a peace offering. This was the
offering brought by Gamaliel son of Pedahzur.

60 On the ninth day Abidan son of Gideoni, leader of
the tribe of Benjamin, presented his offering.
61 The offering consisted of a silver platter weighing about 3¼ pounds and a silver basin of about
1¾ pounds. These were both filled with grain
offerings of choice flour mixed with olive oil.
62 He also brought a gold container weighing
about four ounces, which was filled with
incense. 63 He brought a young bull, a ram, and
a one-year-old male lamb as a burnt offering;
64 a male goat for a sin offering; 65 and two oxen,
five rams, five male goats, and five one-year-old
male lambs for a peace offering. This was the
offering brought by Abidan son of Gideoni.

66 On the tenth day Ahiezer son of Ammishaddai,
leader of the tribe of Dan, presented his offering.
67 The offering consisted of a silver platter weighing about 3¼ pounds and a silver basin of about
1¾ pounds. These were both filled with grain
offerings of choice flour mixed with olive oil.
68 He also brought a gold container weighing
about four ounces, which was filled with
incense. 69 He brought a young bull, a ram, and
a one-year-old male lamb as a burnt offering;
70 a male goat for a sin offering; 71 and two oxen,
five rams, five male goats, and five one-year-old
male lambs for a peace offering. This was the
offering brought by Ahiezer son of
Ammishaddai.

72 On the eleventh day Pagiel son of Ocran, leader of
the tribe of Asher, presented his offering.

73 The offering consisted of a silver platter weighing about 3¼ pounds and a silver basin of about
1¾ pounds. These were both filled with grain
offerings of choice flour mixed with olive oil.
74 He also brought a gold container weighing
about four ounces, which was filled with
incense. 75 He brought a young bull, a ram, and
a one-year-old male lamb as a burnt offering;
76 a male goat for a sin offering; 77 and two oxen,
five rams, five male goats, and five one-year-old
male lambs for a peace offering. This was the
offering brought by Pagiel son of Ocran.

78 On the twelfth day Ahira son of Enan, leader of the
tribe of Naphtali, presented his offering.
79 The offering consisted of a silver platter weighing about 3¼ pounds and a silver basin of about
1¾ pounds. These were both filled with grain
offerings of choice flour mixed with olive oil.
80 He also brought a gold container weighing
about four ounces, which was filled with
incense. 81 He brought a young bull, a ram, and
a one-year-old male lamb as a burnt offering;
82 a male goat for a sin offering; 83 and two oxen,
five rams, five male goats, and five one-year-old
male lambs for a peace offering. This was the
offering brought by Ahira son of Enan.

84 So this was the dedication offering for the altar,
brought by the leaders of Israel at the time it was
anointed: twelve silver platters, twelve silver basins,
and twelve gold incense containers. 85 In all, the silver
objects weighed about 60 pounds,* about 3¼
pounds for each platter and 1¾ pounds for each
basin. 86 The weight of the donated gold came to
about three pounds,* about four ounces for each of
the gold containers that were filled with incense.
87 Twelve bulls, twelve rams, and twelve one-year-old
male lambs were donated for the burnt offerings,
along with their prescribed grain offerings. Twelve
male goats were brought for the sin offerings.
88 Twenty-four young bulls, sixty rams, sixty male
goats, and sixty one-year-old male lambs were donated for the peace offerings. This was the dedication
offering for the altar after it was anointed.
89 Whenever Moses went into the Tabernacle to
speak with the LORD, he heard the voice speaking to
him from between the two cherubim above the Ark's
cover—the place of atonement—that rests on the
Ark of the Covenant.* The LORD spoke to him from
there.

CHAPTER **8** **PREPARING THE LAMPS.** The LORD said
to Moses, 2 "Tell Aaron that when he sets up the seven
lamps in the lampstand, he is to place them so their
light shines forward." 3 So Aaron did this. He set up
the seven lamps so they reflected their light forward,
just as the LORD had commanded Moses. 4 The entire
lampstand, from its base to its decorative blossoms,
was made of beaten gold. It was built according to
the exact design the LORD had shown Moses.
5 Then the LORD said to Moses, 6 "Now set the
Levites apart from the rest of the people of Israel and
make them ceremonially clean. 7 Do this by sprinkling them with the water of purification. And have
them shave their entire body and wash their clothing. Then they will be ceremonially clean. 8 Have
them bring a young bull and a grain offering of
choice flour mixed with olive oil, along with a second young bull for a sin offering. 9 Then assemble
the whole community of Israel and present the Levites at the entrance of the Tabernacle.* 10 When you
bring the Levites before the LORD, the people of
Israel must lay their hands on them. 11 Aaron must
present the Levites to the LORD as a special offering
from the people of Israel, thus dedicating them to
the LORD's service.
12 "Next the Levites will lay their hands on the
heads of the young bulls and present them to the
LORD. One will be for a sin offering and the other for
a burnt offering, to make atonement for the Levites.
13 Then have the Levites stand in front of Aaron and
his sons, and present them as a special offering to the
LORD. 14 In this way, you will set the Levites apart
from the rest of the people of Israel, and the Levites
will belong to me. 15 After this, they may go in and
out of the Tabernacle to do their work, because you
have purified them and presented them as a special
offering.

**AWESOME ● ● • • •**

7:89 **Imagine hearing the very voice of God! Moses must have trembled at the sound. Yet we have God's words recorded for us in the Bible, and we should have no less reverence and awe for them. God sometimes spoke directly to his people to tell them the proper way to live. The Bible records these conversations to give us insights into God's character. How tragic when we take these very words of God lightly.**

16 "Of all the people of Israel, the Levites are reserved for me. I have claimed them for myself in
place of all the firstborn sons of the Israelites; I have
taken the Levites as their substitutes. 17 For all the
firstborn males among the people of Israel are mine,
both people and animals. I set them apart for myself
on the night I killed all the firstborn sons of the
Egyptians. 18 Yes, I claim the Levites in place of all the
firstborn sons of Israel. 19 And of all the Israelites, I
have assigned the Levites to Aaron and his sons. They
will serve in the Tabernacle on behalf of the Israelites
and make atonement for them so no plague will
strike them when they approach the sanctuary."
20 So Moses, Aaron, and the whole community of
Israel dedicated the Levites, carefully following all
the LORD's instructions to Moses. 21 The Levites purified themselves and washed their clothes, and Aaron
presented them to the LORD as a special offering. He

7:85 Hebrew *2,400 shekels* [27.4 kilograms]. 7:86 Hebrew *120 shekels* [1.4 kilograms]. 7:89 Or *Ark of the Testimony.* 8:9 Hebrew *Tent of Meeting;* also in 8:15, 19, 22, 24, 26.

then performed the rite of atonement over them to purify them. 22From then on the Levites went into the Tabernacle to perform their duties, helping Aaron and his sons. So they carried out all the commands that the LORD gave Moses concerning the Levites.

23The LORD also instructed Moses, 24"This is the rule the Levites must follow: They must begin serving in the Tabernacle at the age of twenty-five, 25and they must retire at the age of fifty. 26After retirement they may assist their fellow Levites by performing guard duty at the Tabernacle, but they may not officiate in the service. This is how you will assign duties to the Levites."

## CHAPTER 9

**THE SECOND PASSOVER.** The LORD gave these instructions to Moses in early spring,* during the second year after Israel's departure from Egypt, while he and the rest of the Israelites were in the wilderness of Sinai: 2"Tell the Israelites to celebrate the Passover at the proper time, 3at twilight on the appointed day in early spring.* Be sure to follow all my laws and regulations concerning this celebration."

4So Moses told the people to celebrate the Passover 5in the wilderness of Sinai as twilight fell on the appointed day.* And they celebrated the festival there, just as the LORD had commanded Moses. 6But some of the men had been ceremonially defiled by touching a dead person, so they could not offer their Passover lambs that day. So they came to Moses and Aaron that day 7and said, "We have become ceremonially unclean by touching a dead person. But why should we be excluded from presenting the LORD's offering at the proper time with the rest of the Israelites?"

### EVERYONE ● ● ● • •

**9:14 Sometimes we are tempted to excuse non-Christians from following God's guidelines for living. Christmas and Easter, for example, often have other meanings for them. We would not expect them to understand Lent. Yet foreigners at this time were expected to follow the same laws and ordinances as the Israelites. God did not have a separate set of standards for unbelievers, and he still does not today. God's statement that "the same laws apply both to you and to the foreigners" emphasizes that non-Israelites were also subject to God's commands and promises. God singled out Israel for a special purpose–to be an example of how one nation could, and should, follow him. His aim, however, was to have all people obey and worship him.**

8Moses answered, "Wait here until I have received instructions for you from the LORD."

9This was the LORD's reply: 10"Say to the Israelites: 'If any of the people now or in future generations are ceremonially unclean at Passover time because of

### WHERE YOU ARE ● ● ● • •

**9:23 The Hebrews traveled and camped as God guided. When you follow God's guidance, you know you are where God wants you, whether you're moving or staying in one place. You are physically somewhere right now. Instead of praying, "God, what do you want me to do next?" ask, "God, what do you want me to do while I'm right here?" Direction from God is not just for your next big move. He has a purpose in placing you where you are right now. Begin to understand God's purpose for your life by discovering what he wants you to do now!**

touching a dead body, or if they are on a journey and cannot be present at the ceremony, they may still celebrate the LORD's Passover. 11They must offer the Passover sacrifice one month later,* at twilight on the appointed day. They must eat the lamb at that time with bitter herbs and bread made without yeast. 12They must not leave any of the lamb until the next morning, and they must not break any of its bones. They must follow all the normal regulations concerning the Passover.

13"'But those who are ceremonially clean and not away on a trip, yet still refuse to celebrate the Passover at the regular time, will be cut off from the community of Israel for failing to present the LORD's offering at the proper time. They will suffer the consequences of their guilt. 14And if foreigners living among you want to celebrate the Passover to the LORD, they must follow these same laws and regulations. The same laws apply both to you and to the foreigners living among you.'"

15The Tabernacle was set up, and on that day the cloud covered it.* Then from evening until morning the cloud over the Tabernacle appeared to be a pillar of fire. 16This was the regular pattern—at night the cloud changed to the appearance of fire. 17When the cloud lifted from over the sacred tent, the people of Israel followed it. And wherever the cloud settled, the people of Israel camped. 18In this way, they traveled at the LORD's command and stopped wherever he told them to. Then they remained where they were as long as the cloud stayed over the Tabernacle. 19If the cloud remained over the Tabernacle for a long time, the Israelites stayed for a long time, just as the LORD commanded. 20Sometimes the cloud would stay over the Tabernacle for only a few days, so the people would stay for only a few days. Then at the LORD's command they would break camp. 21Sometimes the cloud stayed only overnight and moved on the next morning. But day or night, when the cloud lifted, the people broke camp and followed. 22Whether the cloud stayed above the Tabernacle for two days, a month, or a year, the people of Israel stayed in camp and did not move on. But as soon as it lifted, they broke camp and moved on. 23So they camped or traveled at the LORD's command, and they did whatever the LORD told them through Moses.

9:1 Hebrew *in the first month.* This month of the Hebrew lunar calendar usually occurs in March and April. 9:3 Hebrew *on the fourteenth day of the first month.* This day of the Hebrew lunar calendar occurs in late March or early April. 9:5 Hebrew *on the fourteenth day of the first month;* see note on 9:3. 9:11 Hebrew *on the fourteenth day of the second month.* This day of the Hebrew lunar calendar occurs in late April or early May. 9:15 Hebrew *covered the Tabernacle, the Tent of the Testimony.*

## CHAPTER 10 THE SILVER TRUMPETS.

Now the LORD said to Moses, 2"Make two trumpets of beaten silver to be used for summoning the people to assemble and for signaling the breaking of camp. 3When both trumpets are blown, the people will know that they are to gather before you at the entrance of the Tabernacle.* 4But if only one is blown, then only the leaders of the tribes of Israel will come to you.

5"When you sound the signal to move on, the tribes on the east side of the Tabernacle will break camp and move forward. 6When you sound the signal a second time, the tribes on the south will follow. You must sound short blasts to signal moving on. 7But when you call the people to an assembly, blow the trumpets using a different signal. 8Only the priests, Aaron's descendants, are allowed to blow the trumpets. This is a permanent law to be followed from generation to generation.

9"When you arrive in your own land and go to war against your enemies, you must sound the alarm with these trumpets so the LORD your God will remember you and rescue you from your enemies. 10Blow the trumpets in times of gladness, too, sounding them at your annual festivals and at the beginning of each month to rejoice over your burnt offerings and peace offerings. The trumpets will remind the LORD your God of his covenant with you. I am the LORD your God."

11One day in midspring,* during the second year after Israel's departure from Egypt, the cloud lifted from the Tabernacle of the Covenant.* 12So the Israelites set out from the wilderness of Sinai and traveled on in stages until the cloud stopped in the wilderness of Paran.

13When the time to move arrived, the LORD gave the order through Moses. 14The tribes that camped with Judah headed the march with their banner, under the leadership of Nahshon son of Amminadab. 15The tribe of Issachar was led by Nethanel son of Zuar. 16The tribe of Zebulun was led by Eliab son of Helon.

17Then the Tabernacle was taken down, and the Gershonite and Merarite divisions of the Levites were next in the line of march, carrying the Tabernacle with them. 18Then the tribes that camped with Reuben set out with their banner, under the leadership of Elizur son of Shedeur. 19The tribe of Simeon was led by Shelumiel son of Zurishaddai. 20The tribe of Gad was led by Eliasaph son of Deuel.

21Next came the Kohathite division of the Levites, carrying the sacred objects from the Tabernacle. When they arrived at the next camp, the Tabernacle would already be set up at its new location. 22Then the tribes that camped with Ephraim set out with their banner, under the leadership of Elishama son of Ammihud. 23The tribe of Manasseh was led by Gamaliel son of Pedahzur. 24The tribe of Benjamin was led by Abidan son of Gideoni.

25Last of all, the tribes that camped with Dan set out under their banner. They served as the rear guard for all the tribal camps. The tribe of Dan headed this group, under the leadership of Ahiezer son of Ammishaddai. 26The tribe of Asher was led by Pagiel son of Ocran. 27The tribe of Naphtali was led by Ahira son of Enan.

28This was the order in which the tribes marched, division by division.

29One day Moses said to his brother-in-law, Hobab son of Reuel the Midianite, "We are on our way to the Promised Land. Come with us and we will treat you well, for the LORD has given wonderful promises to Israel!"

30But Hobab replied, "No, I will not go. I must return to my own land and family."

31"Please don't leave us," Moses pleaded. "You know the places in the wilderness where we should camp. 32Come, be our guide and we will share with you all the good things that the LORD does for us."

33They marched for three days after leaving the mountain of the LORD, with the Ark of the LORD's covenant moving ahead of them to show them where to stop and rest. 34As they moved on each day, the cloud of the LORD hovered over them. 35And whenever the Ark set out, Moses would cry, "Arise, O LORD, and let your enemies be scattered! Let them flee before you!" 36And when the Ark was set down, he would say, "Return, O LORD, to the countless thousands of Israel!"

### COMPLIMENTS ● ● • • •

**10:29-32 By complimenting Hobab's wilderness skills, Moses let him know he was needed. People cannot know you appreciate them if you do not tell them they are important to you. Complimenting those who deserve it builds lasting relationships and helps people know they are valued. Think about those who have helped you this month. What can you do to let them know how much you need and appreciate them?**

## CHAPTER 11 SOMEONE TO HELP MOSES.

The people soon began to complain to the LORD about their hardships; and when the LORD heard them, his anger blazed against them. Fire from the LORD raged among them and destroyed the outskirts of the camp. 2The people screamed to Moses for help; and when he prayed to the LORD, the fire stopped. 3After that, the area was known as Taberah—"the place of burning"—because fire from the LORD had burned among them there.

4Then the foreign rabble who were traveling with the Israelites began to crave the good things of Egypt, and the people of Israel also began to complain. "Oh, for some meat!" they exclaimed. 5"We remember all the fish we used to eat for free in Egypt. And we had all the cucumbers, melons, leeks, onions, and garlic that we wanted. 6But now our appetites are

**10:3** Hebrew *Tent of Meeting.* **10:11a** Hebrew *On the twentieth day of the second month.* This day of the Hebrew lunar calendar occurs in late April or early May. **10:11b** Or *Tabernacle of the Testimony.*

## GRATITUDE ● ● • • •

**11:4-6 Dissatisfaction comes when our attention shifts from what we have to what we don't have. The people of Israel didn't seem to notice what God was doing for them—setting them free, making them a nation, giving them a new land—because they were so wrapped up in what God wasn't doing for them. They could think of nothing but the delicious Egyptian food they had left behind. Somehow they forgot that the brutal whip of Egyptian slavery was the cost of eating that food. Before we judge the Israelites too harshly, it's helpful to think about what occupies our attention most of the time. Are we grateful for what God has given us, or are we always thinking about what we would like to have? We should not allow our unfulfilled desires to cause us to forget God's gifts of life, food, health, work, and friends.**

gone, and day after day we have nothing to eat but this manna!"

[7]The manna looked like small coriander seeds, pale yellow in color.* [8]The people gathered it from the ground and made flour by grinding it with hand mills or pounding it in mortars. Then they boiled it in a pot and made it into flat cakes. These cakes tasted like they had been cooked in olive oil. [9]The manna came down on the camp with the dew during the night.

[10]Moses heard all the families standing in front of their tents weeping, and the LORD became extremely angry. Moses was also very aggravated. [11]And Moses said to the LORD, "Why are you treating me, your servant, so miserably? What did I do to deserve the burden of a people like this? [12]Are they my children? Am I their father? Is that why you have told me to carry them in my arms—like a nurse carries a baby—to the land you swore to give their ancestors? [13]Where am I supposed to get meat for all these people? They keep complaining and saying, 'Give us meat!' [14]I can't carry all these people by myself! The load is far too heavy! [15]I'd rather you killed me than treat me like this. Please spare me this misery!"

[16]Then the LORD said to Moses, "Summon before me seventy of the leaders of Israel. Bring them to the Tabernacle* to stand there with you. [17]I will come down and talk to you there. I will take some of the Spirit that is upon you, and I will put the Spirit upon them also. They will bear the burden of the people along with you, so you will not have to carry it alone.

[18]"And tell the people to purify themselves, for tomorrow they will have meat to eat. Tell them, 'The LORD has heard your whining and complaints: "If only we had meat to eat! Surely we were better off in Egypt!" Now the LORD will give you meat, and you will have to eat it. [19]And it won't be for just a day or two, or for five or ten or even twenty. [20]You will eat it for a whole month until you gag and are sick of it. For you have rejected the LORD, who is here among you, and you have complained to him, "Why did we ever leave Egypt?"'"

[21]But Moses said, "There are 600,000 foot soldiers here with me, and yet you promise them meat for a whole month! [22]Even if we butchered all our flocks and herds, would that satisfy them? Even if we caught all the fish in the sea, would that be enough?"

[23]Then the LORD said to Moses, "Is there any limit to my power? Now you will see whether or not my word comes true!"

[24]So Moses went out and reported the LORD's words to the people. Then he gathered the seventy leaders and stationed them around the Tabernacle.* [25]And the LORD came down in the cloud and spoke to Moses. He took some of the Spirit that was upon Moses and put it upon the seventy leaders. They prophesied as the Spirit rested upon them, but that was the only time this happened.

[26]Two men, Eldad and Medad, were still in the camp when the Spirit rested upon them. They were listed among the leaders but had not gone out to the Tabernacle, so they prophesied there in the camp. [27]A young man ran and reported to Moses, "Eldad and Medad are prophesying in the camp!" [28]Joshua son of Nun, who had been Moses' personal assistant since his youth, protested, "Moses, my master, make them stop!"

[29]But Moses replied, "Are you jealous for my sake? I wish that all the LORD's people were prophets, and that the LORD would put his Spirit upon them all!" [30]Then Moses returned to the camp with the leaders of Israel.

[31]Now the LORD sent a wind that brought quail from the sea and let them fall into the camp and all around it! For many miles in every direction from the camp there were quail flying about three feet above the ground.* [32]So the people went out and caught quail all that day and throughout the night and all the next day, too. No one gathered less than fifty bushels*! They spread the quail out all over the camp. [33]But while they were still eating the meat, the anger of the LORD blazed against the people, and he caused a severe plague to break out among them. [34]So that place was called Kibroth-hattaavah—"the graves of craving"—because they buried the people there who had craved meat from Egypt. [35]From there the Israelites traveled to Hazeroth, where they stayed for some time.

## CHAPTER 12 **MIRIAM GETS LEPROSY.**

While they were at Hazeroth, Miriam and Aaron criticized Moses because he had married a Cushite woman. [2]They said, "Has the LORD spoken only through Moses? Hasn't he spoken through us, too?" But the LORD heard them.

[3]Now Moses was more humble than any other person on earth. [4]So immediately the LORD called to Moses, Aaron, and Miriam and said, "Go out to the Tabernacle,* all three of you!" And the three of them went out. [5]Then the LORD descended in the pillar of cloud and stood at the entrance of the Tabernacle.* "Aaron and Miriam!" he called, and they stepped forward. [6]And the LORD said to them, "Now listen to

**11:7** Hebrew *the color of gum resin.* **11:16** Hebrew *Tent of Meeting.* **11:24** Hebrew *the tent;* also in 11:26. **11:31** Or *there were quail 3 feet* [2 cubits or 90 centimeters] *deep on the ground.* **11:32** Hebrew *10 homers* [1.8 kiloliters]. **12:4** Hebrew *Tent of Meeting.* **12:5** Hebrew *the tent;* also in 12:10.

me! Even with prophets, I the LORD communicate by
visions and dreams. [7]But that is not how I communicate with my servant Moses. He is entrusted with
my entire house. [8]I speak to him face to face, directly
and not in riddles! He sees the LORD as he is. Should
you not be afraid to criticize him?"

[9]The LORD was furious with them, and he departed. [10]As the cloud moved from above the Tabernacle, Miriam suddenly became white as snow with
leprosy.* When Aaron saw what had happened, [11]he
cried out to Moses, "Oh, my lord! Please don't punish us for this sin we have so foolishly committed.
[12]Don't let her be like a stillborn baby, already decayed at birth."

[13]So Moses cried out to the LORD, "Heal her,
O God, I beg you!"

[14]And the LORD said to Moses, "If her father had
spit in her face, wouldn't she have been defiled for
seven days? Banish her from the camp for seven days,
and after that she may return."

[15]So Miriam was excluded from the camp for
seven days, and the people waited until she was
brought back before they traveled again. [16]Then they
left Hazeroth and camped in the wilderness of Paran.

## CHAPTER 13

**THE TWELVE SCOUTS.** The LORD now
said to Moses, [2]"Send men to explore the land of
Canaan, the land I am giving to Israel. Send one
leader from each of the twelve ancestral tribes." [3]So
Moses did as the LORD commanded him. He sent out
twelve men, all tribal leaders of Israel, from their
camp in the wilderness of Paran. [4]These were the
tribes and the names of the leaders:

| *Tribe* | *Leader* |
|---|---|
| Reuben | Shammua son of Zaccur |
| [5]Simeon | Shaphat son of Hori |
| [6]Judah | Caleb son of Jephunneh |
| [7]Issachar | Igal son of Joseph |
| [8]Ephraim | Hoshea son of Nun |
| [9]Benjamin | Palti son of Raphu |
| [10]Zebulun | Gaddiel son of Sodi |
| [11]Manasseh son of Joseph | Gaddi son of Susi |
| [12]Dan | Ammiel son of Gemalli |
| [13]Asher | Sethur son of Michael |
| [14]Naphtali | Nahbi son of Vophsi |
| [15]Gad | Geuel son of Maki |

[16]These are the names of the men Moses sent to
explore the land. By this time Moses had changed
Hoshea's name to Joshua.*

[17]Moses gave the men these instructions as he sent
them out to explore the land: "Go northward
through the Negev into the hill country. [18]See what
the land is like and find out whether the people
living there are strong or weak, few or many. [19]What
kind of land do they live in? Is it good or bad? Do
their towns have walls or are they unprotected?
[20]How is the soil? Is it fertile or poor? Are there many
trees? Enter the land boldly, and bring back samples
of the crops you see." (It happened to be the season
for harvesting the first ripe grapes.)

[21]So they went up and explored the land from the
wilderness of Zin as far as Rehob, near Lebo-hamath.
[22]Going northward, they passed first through the
Negev and arrived at Hebron, where Ahiman, Sheshai, and Talmai—all descendants of Anak—lived.
(The ancient town of Hebron was founded seven
years before the Egyptian city of Zoan.) [23]When they
came to what is now known as the valley of Eshcol,
they cut down a cluster of grapes so large that it took
two of them to carry it on a pole between them! They
also took samples of the pomegranates and figs. [24]At
that time the Israelites renamed the valley Eshcol—
"cluster"—because of the cluster of grapes they had
cut there.

### POSITIVES ● ● • • ·

13:25-29 **God told the Israelites that the rich and plentiful Promised Land would be theirs. When the scouting party reported back to Moses, they couldn't stop focusing on their fear, and so forgot God's promise to help. When facing tough decisions, don't let fear of potential difficulties blind you to God's power to help and his promise to guide.**

[25]After exploring the land for forty days, the men
returned [26]to Moses, Aaron, and the people of Israel
at Kadesh in the wilderness of Paran. They reported
to the whole community what they had seen and
showed them the fruit they had taken from the land.
[27]This was their report to Moses: "We arrived in the
land you sent us to see, and it is indeed a magnificent
country—a land flowing with milk and honey. Here
is some of its fruit as proof. [28]But the people living
there are powerful, and their cities and towns are
fortified and very large. We also saw the descendants
of Anak who are living there! [29]The Amalekites live
in the Negev, and the Hittites, Jebusites, and Amorites live in the hill country. The Canaanites live
along the coast of the Mediterranean Sea* and along
the Jordan Valley."

[30]But Caleb tried to encourage the people as they
stood before Moses. "Let's go at once to take the
land," he said. "We can certainly conquer it!"

[31]But the other men who had explored the land
with him answered, "We can't go up against them!
They are stronger than we are!" [32]So they spread

### STAND FOR TRUTH ● ● • • ·

13:31-32 **The Israelites didn't trust God—and in their self-doubt, their decision made sense. But they forgot that a promise from God is a sure thing, no matter how unlikely it seems. God's truth is set apart from feelings, situations, or majority opinions. Caleb stood for the truth—he knew God's promises could be depended on. Are you willing to stand against the pressure of popular opinion to do what God's Word says?**

**12:10** Or *with a contagious skin disease.* The Hebrew word used here can describe various skin diseases. **13:16** *Hoshea* (see 13:8) means "salvation"; *Joshua* means "The LORD is salvation." **13:29** Hebrew *the sea.*

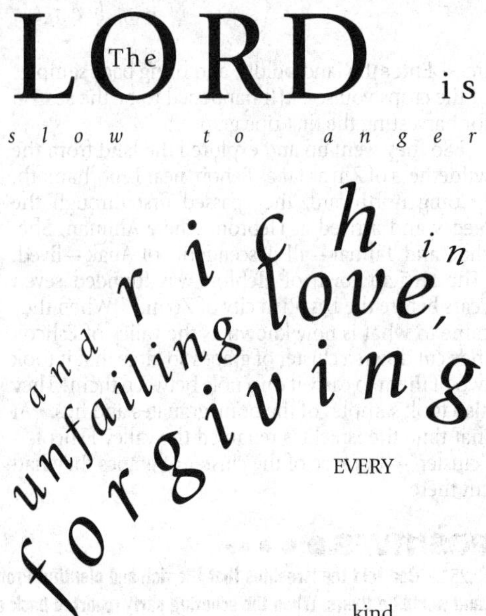
The LORD is
slow to anger
and rich in
unfailing love,
forgiving

EVERY

kind

of

sin and rebellion.

NUMBERS 14:18

discouraging reports about the land among the Israelites: "The land we explored will swallow up any who go to live there. All the people we saw were huge. 33We even saw giants* there, the descendants of Anak. We felt like grasshoppers next to them, and that's what we looked like to them!"

**CHAPTER 14** **THE PEOPLE REBEL.** Then all the people began weeping aloud, and they cried all night. 2Their voices rose in a great chorus of complaint against Moses and Aaron. "We wish we had died in Egypt, or even here in the wilderness!" they wailed. 3"Why is the LORD taking us to this country only to have us die in battle? Our wives and little ones will be carried off as slaves! Let's get out of here and return to Egypt!" 4Then they plotted among themselves, "Let's choose a leader and go back to Egypt!"

5Then Moses and Aaron fell face down on the ground before the people of Israel. 6Two of the men who had explored the land, Joshua son of Nun and Caleb son of Jephunneh, tore their clothing. 7They said to the community of Israel, "The land we explored is a wonderful land! 8And if the LORD is pleased with us, he will bring us safely into that land and give it to us. It is a rich land flowing with milk and honey, and he will give it to us! 9Do not rebel against the LORD, and don't be afraid of the people of the land. They are only helpless prey to us! They have no protection, but the LORD is with us! Don't be afraid of them!"

10But the whole community began to talk about stoning Joshua and Caleb. Then the glorious presence of the LORD appeared to all the Israelites from above the Tabernacle.* 11And the LORD said to Moses, "How long will these people reject me? Will they never believe me, even after all the miraculous signs I have done among them? 12I will disown them and destroy them with a plague. Then I will make you into a nation far greater and mightier than they are!"

13"But what will the Egyptians think when they hear about it?" Moses pleaded with the LORD. "They know full well the power you displayed in rescuing these people from Egypt. 14They will tell this to the inhabitants of this land, who are well aware that you are with this people. They know, LORD, that you have appeared in full view of your people in the pillar of cloud that hovers over them. They know that you go before them in the pillar of cloud by day and the pillar of fire by night. 15Now if you slaughter all these people, the nations that have heard of your fame will say, 16'The LORD was not able to bring them into the land he swore to give them, so he killed them in the wilderness.'

17"Please, Lord, prove that your power is as great as you have claimed it to be. For you said, 18'The LORD is slow to anger and rich in unfailing love, forgiving every kind of sin and rebellion. Even so he does not leave sin unpunished, but he punishes the children for the sins of their parents to the third and fourth generations.' 19Please pardon the sins of this people because of your magnificent, unfailing love, just as you have forgiven them ever since they left Egypt."

20Then the LORD said, "I will pardon them as you have requested. 21But as surely as I live, and as surely as the earth is filled with the LORD's glory, 22not one of these people will ever enter that land. They have seen my glorious presence and the miraculous signs I performed both in Egypt and in the wilderness, but again and again they tested me by refusing to listen. 23They will never even see the land I swore to give their ancestors. None of those who have treated me with contempt will enter it. 24But my servant Caleb is different from the others. He has remained loyal to me, and I will bring him into the land he explored. His descendants will receive their full share of that land. 25Now turn around and don't go on toward the land where the Amalekites and Canaanites live. Tomorrow you must set out for the wilderness in the direction of the Red Sea.*"

## ADVICE ● ● • • .

**14:6-10 Two wise men, Joshua and Caleb, encouraged the people to act on God's promise. The people rejected their advice and even talked of killing them. Don't be too quick to reject advice you don't like. Evaluate it carefully; weigh it against God's Word. What you are hearing may be God's message.**

13:33 Hebrew *nephilim.* 14:10 Hebrew *Tent of Meeting.* 14:25 Hebrew *sea of reeds.*

**ISRAEL'S COMPLAINING**

| Complaint | Sin | Result |
|---|---|---|
| 11:1 About their hardships | Complained about their problems instead of praying to God | Thousands of people were destroyed when God sent fire to punish them |
| 11:4 About the lack of meat | Lusted after things they didn't have | God sent quail, but as the people began to eat, God struck them with a plague that killed many |
| 14:1-4 About being stuck in the wilderness, facing the giants of the Promised Land, and wishing to return to Egypt | Openly rebelled against God's leaders and failed to trust in his promises | All who complained were not allowed to enter the Promised Land; they were doomed to wander in the wilderness until they died |
| 16:3 About Moses' and Aaron's authority and leadership | Were greedy for more power and authority | The families, friends, and possessions of Korah, Dathan, and Abiram were swallowed up by the earth. Fire then burned up the 250 other men who rebelled |
| 16:41 That Moses and Aaron caused the deaths of Korah and his conspirators | Blamed others for their own troubles | God began to destroy Israel with a plague. Moses and Aaron made atonement for the people, but 14,700 of them were killed |
| 20:2-3 About the lack of water | Refused to believe that God would provide as he had promised | Moses sinned along with the people. For this he was barred from entering the Promised Land |
| 21:5 That God and Moses brought them into the wilderness | Failed to recognize that their problems were brought on by their own disobedience | God sent poisonous snakes that killed many people and seriously injured many others |

26Then the LORD said to Moses and Aaron,
27"How long will this wicked nation complain
about me? I have heard everything the Israelites
have been saying. 28Now tell them this: 'As surely
as I live, I will do to you the very things I heard you
say. I, the LORD, have spoken! 29You will all die here
in this wilderness! Because you complained
against me, none of you who are twenty years old
or older and were counted in the census 30will enter
the land I swore to give you. The only exceptions
will be Caleb son of Jephunneh and Joshua son of
Nun.

31"'You said your children would be taken captive.
Well, I will bring them safely into the land, and they
will enjoy what you have despised. 32But as for you,
your dead bodies will fall in this wilderness. 33And
your children will be like shepherds, wandering in
the wilderness forty years. In this way, they will pay
for your faithlessness, until the last of you lies dead
in the wilderness.

34"'Because the men who explored the land were
there for forty days, you must wander in the wilderness for forty years—a year for each day, suffering the
consequences of your sins. You will discover what it
is like to have me for an enemy.' 35I, the LORD, have
spoken! I will do these things to every member of the
community who has conspired against me. They will
all die here in this wilderness!"

36Then the ten scouts who had incited the rebellion against the LORD by spreading discouraging reports about the land 37were struck dead with a plague
before the LORD. 38Of the twelve who had explored
the land, only Joshua and Caleb remained alive.

39When Moses reported the LORD's words to the
Israelites, there was much sorrow among the
people. 40So they got up early the next morning
and set out for the hill country of Canaan. "Let's
go," they said. "We realize that we have sinned, but
now we are ready to enter the land the LORD has
promised us."

41But Moses said, "Why are you now disobeying
the LORD's orders to return to the wilderness? It
won't work. 42Do not go into the land now. You will
only be crushed by your enemies because the LORD
is not with you. 43When you face the Amalekites and
Canaanites in battle, you will be slaughtered. The
LORD will abandon you because you have abandoned the LORD."

44But the people pushed ahead toward the hill
country of Canaan, despite the fact that neither
Moses nor the Ark of the LORD's covenant left the
camp. 45Then the Amalekites and the Canaanites
who lived in those hills came down and attacked
them and chased them as far as Hormah.

## CHAPTER 15 MORE RULES ABOUT OFFERINGS.
The
LORD told Moses to give these instructions to the
people of Israel: 2"When you finally settle in the land
I am going to give you, 3and you want to please the
LORD with a burnt offering or any other offering

given by fire, the sacrifice must be an animal from your flocks of sheep and goats or from your herds of cattle. When it is an ordinary burnt offering, a sacrifice to fulfill a vow, a freewill offering, or a special sacrifice at any of the annual festivals, 4whoever brings it must also give to the LORD a grain offering of two quarts* of choice flour mixed with one quart* of olive oil. 5For each lamb offered as a whole burnt offering, you must also present one quart of wine for a drink offering.

6"If the sacrifice is a ram, give three quarts* of choice flour mixed with two and a half pints* of olive oil, 7and give two and a half pints of wine for a drink offering. This sacrifice will be very pleasing to the LORD.

8"When you present a young bull as a burnt offering or a sacrifice in fulfillment of a special vow or as a peace offering to the LORD, 9then the grain offering accompanying it must include five quarts* of choice flour mixed with two quarts* of olive oil, 10plus two quarts of wine for the drink offering. This will be an offering made by fire, very pleasing to the LORD.

11"These are the instructions for what is to accompany each sacrificial bull, ram, lamb, or young goat. 12Each of you must do this with each offering you present. 13If you native Israelites want to present an offering by fire that is pleasing to the LORD, you must follow all these instructions. 14And if any foreigners living among you want to present an offering by fire, pleasing to the LORD, they must follow the same procedures. 15Native Israelites and foreigners are the same before the LORD and are subject to the same laws. This is a permanent law for you. 16The same instructions and regulations will apply both to you and to the foreigners living among you."

17The LORD also said to Moses at this time, 18"Give the people of Israel the following instructions: When you arrive in the land where I am taking you, 19you will eat from the crops that grow there. But you must set some aside as a gift to the LORD. 20Present a cake from the first of the flour you grind and set it aside as a gift, as you do with the first grain from the threshing floor. 21Throughout the generations to come, you are to present this offering to the LORD each year from the first of your ground flour.

22"But suppose some of you unintentionally fail to carry out all these commands that the LORD has given you through Moses. 23And suppose some of your descendants in the future fail to do everything the LORD has commanded through Moses. 24If the mistake was done unintentionally, and the community was unaware of it, the whole community must present a young bull for a burnt offering. It will be pleasing to the LORD, and it must be offered along with the prescribed grain offering and drink offering and with one male goat for a sin offering. 25With it the priest will make atonement for the whole community of Israel, and they will be forgiven. For it was an unintentional sin, and they have corrected it with their offering given to the LORD by fire and by their sin offering. 26The whole community of Israel will be forgiven, including the foreigners living among you, for the entire population was involved in the sin.

27"If the unintentional sin is committed by an individual, the guilty person must bring a one-year-old female goat for a sin offering. 28The priest will make atonement for the guilty person before the LORD, and that person will be forgiven. 29This same law applies both to native Israelites and the foreigners living among you.

30"But those who brazenly violate the LORD's will, whether native Israelites or foreigners, blaspheme the LORD, and they must be cut off from the community. 31Since they have treated the LORD's word with contempt and deliberately disobeyed his commands, they must be completely cut off and suffer the consequences of their guilt."

32One day while the people of Israel were in the wilderness, they caught a man gathering wood on the Sabbath day. 33He was apprehended and taken before Moses, Aaron, and the rest of the community. 34They held him in custody because they did not know what to do with him. 35Then the LORD said to Moses, "The man must be put to death! The whole community must stone him outside the camp." 36So the whole community took the man outside the camp and stoned him to death, just as the LORD had commanded Moses.

37And the LORD said to Moses, 38"Say to the people of Israel: 'Throughout the generations to come you must make tassels for the hems of your clothing and attach the tassels at each corner with a blue cord. 39The tassels will remind you of the commands of the LORD, and that you are to obey his commands instead of following your own desires and going your own ways, as you are prone to do. 40The tassels will help you remember that you must obey all my commands and be holy to your God. 41I am the LORD your God who brought you out of the land of Egypt that I might be your God. I am the LORD your God!'"

## GET FOCUSED ● ● • • •

15:39 **Instead of following our own desires and going our own way, God wants us to focus on him and on obeying his commands. Believers are to be selfless rather than self-centered.**

CHAPTER **16** **KORAH REBELS.** One day Korah son of Izhar, a descendant of Kohath son of Levi, conspired with Dathan and Abiram, the sons of Eliab, and On son of Peleth, from the tribe of Reuben. 2They incited a rebellion against Moses, involving 250 other prominent leaders, all members of the assembly. 3They went to Moses and Aaron and said, "You have gone too far! Everyone in Israel has been set apart by the LORD, and he is with all of us. What right do you have to act as though you are greater

**15:4a** Hebrew *1/10 of an ephah* [2 liters]. **15:4b** Hebrew *1/4 of a hin* [1 liter]; also in 15:5. **15:6a** Hebrew *2/10 of an ephah* [3.6 liters]. **15:6b** Hebrew *1/3 of a hin* [1.3 liters]; also in 15:7. **15:9a** Hebrew *3/10 of an ephah* [5.4 liters]. **15:9b** Hebrew *1/2 of a hin* [2 liters]; also in 15:10.

than anyone else among all these people of the LORD?"

4When Moses heard what they were saying, he threw himself down with his face to the ground. 5Then he said to Korah and his followers, "Tomorrow morning the LORD will show us who belongs to him and who is holy. The LORD will allow those who are chosen to enter his holy presence. 6You, Korah, and all your followers must do this: Take incense burners, 7and burn incense in them tomorrow before the LORD. Then we will see whom the LORD chooses as his holy one. You Levites are the ones who have gone too far!"

8Then Moses spoke again to Korah: "Now listen, you Levites! 9Does it seem a small thing to you that the God of Israel has chosen you from among all the people of Israel to be near him as you serve in the LORD's Tabernacle and to stand before the people to minister to them? 10He has given this special ministry only to you and your fellow Levites, but now you are demanding the priesthood as well! 11The one you are really revolting against is the LORD! And who is Aaron that you are complaining about him?"

12Then Moses summoned Dathan and Abiram, the sons of Eliab, but they replied, "We refuse to come! 13Isn't it enough that you brought us out of Egypt, a land flowing with milk and honey, to kill us here in this wilderness, and that you now treat us like your subjects? 14What's more, you haven't brought us into the land flowing with milk and honey or given us an inheritance of fields and vineyards. Are you trying to fool us? We will not come."

15Then Moses became very angry and said to the LORD, "Do not accept their offerings! I have not taken so much as a donkey from them, and I have never hurt a single one of them." 16And Moses said to Korah, "Come here tomorrow and present yourself before the LORD with all your followers. Aaron will also be here. 17Be sure that each of your 250 followers brings an incense burner with incense on it, so you can present them before the LORD. Aaron will also bring his incense burner."

18So these men came with their incense burners, placed burning coals and incense on them, and stood at the entrance of the Tabernacle* with Moses and Aaron. 19Meanwhile, Korah had stirred up the entire community against Moses and Aaron, and they all assembled at the Tabernacle entrance. Then the glorious presence of the LORD appeared to the whole community, 20and the LORD said to Moses and Aaron, 21"Get away from these people so that I may instantly destroy them!"

22But Moses and Aaron fell face down on the ground. "O God, the God and source of all life," they pleaded. "Must you be angry with all the people when only one man sins?"

23And the LORD said to Moses, 24"Then tell all the people to get away from the tents of Korah, Dathan, and Abiram."

25So Moses got up and rushed over to the tents of Dathan and Abiram, followed closely by the Israelite leaders. 26"Quick!" he told the people. "Get away from the tents of these wicked men, and don't touch anything that belongs to them. If you do, you will be destroyed for their sins." 27So all the people stood back from the tents of Korah, Dathan, and Abiram. Then Dathan and Abiram came out and stood at the entrances of their tents with their wives and children and little ones.

28And Moses said, "By this you will know that the LORD has sent me to do all these things that I have done—for I have not done them on my own. 29If these men die a natural death, then the LORD has not sent me. 30But if the LORD performs a miracle and the ground opens up and swallows them and all their belongings, and they go down alive into the grave, then you will know that these men have despised the LORD."

31He had hardly finished speaking the words when the ground suddenly split open beneath them. 32The earth opened up and swallowed the men, along with their households and the followers who were standing with them, and everything they owned. 33So they went down alive into the grave, along with their belongings. The earth closed over them, and they all vanished. 34All of the people of Israel fled as they heard their screams, fearing that the earth would swallow them, too. 35Then fire blazed forth from the LORD and burned up the 250 men who were offering incense.

36And the LORD said to Moses, 37"Tell Eleazar son of Aaron the priest to pull all the incense burners from the fire, for they are holy. Also tell him to scatter the burning incense 38from the burners of these men who have sinned at the cost of their lives. He must then hammer the metal of the incense burners into a sheet as a covering for the altar, for these burners have become holy because they were used in the LORD's presence. The altar covering will then serve as a warning to the people of Israel."

39So Eleazar the priest collected the 250 bronze incense burners that had been used by the men who died in the fire, and they were hammered out into a sheet of metal to cover the altar. 40This would warn the Israelites that no unauthorized man—no one

16:18 Hebrew *Tent of Meeting;* also in 16:19, 42, 43, 50.

## MOTIVATION ● ● • • •

16:8-10 **Korah wanted the special qualities God had given others, even though he had his own significant, worthwhile abilities and responsibilities. In the end, his ambition caused him to lose everything. Inappropriate ambition is greed in disguise.**

## REVENGE ● ● • • •

16:22-27 **Moses and Aaron prayed for those with whom they were most angry and frustrated. Do you pray for those who hurt you? Or do you seek revenge? Only those who have a deep relationship with God can understand that he will settle the score with those who rebel. It is not our job to seek revenge against those who wrong us. God will make certain that, in the end, justice is done.**

who was not a descendant of Aaron—should ever enter the LORD's presence to burn incense. If anyone did, the same thing would happen to him as happened to Korah and his followers. Thus, the LORD's instructions to Moses were carried out.

[41]But the very next morning the whole community began muttering again against Moses and Aaron, saying, "You two have killed the LORD's people!" [42]As the people gathered to protest to Moses and Aaron, they turned toward the Tabernacle and saw that the cloud had covered it, and the glorious presence of the LORD appeared.

[43]Moses and Aaron came and stood at the entrance of the Tabernacle, [44]and the LORD said to Moses, [45]"Get away from these people so that I can instantly destroy them!" But Moses and Aaron fell face down on the ground.

[46]And Moses said to Aaron, "Quick, take an incense burner and place burning coals on it from the altar. Lay incense on it and carry it quickly among the people to make atonement for them. The LORD's anger is blazing among them—the plague has already begun."

[47]Aaron did as Moses told him and ran out among the people. The plague indeed had already begun, but Aaron burned the incense and made atonement for them. [48]He stood between the living and the dead until the plague was stopped. [49]But 14,700 people died in that plague, in addition to those who had died in the incident involving Korah. [50]Then because the plague had stopped, Aaron returned to Moses at the entrance of the Tabernacle.

**REBELLION ● ● • • •**

17:5, 10 **After witnessing spectacular miracles, seeing the Egyptians punished by the plagues, and experiencing the actual presence of God, the Israelites still complained and rebelled. We wonder how they could be so blind and ignorant, and yet we often repeat this same pattern. We have centuries of evidence, the Bible in many translations, and the convincing results of archaeological and historical studies to show us God is who he says he is. But people today continue to disobey God and go their own way. We can escape this pattern only by paying attention to all the signs of God's presence that we have been given. Has God guided and protected you? Has he answered your prayers? Do you know Bible stories about the way God has led his people? Focus your thoughts on these things, and rebellion will become unthinkable.**

CHAPTER **17** **A ROD LIKE A FRUIT TREE.** Then the LORD said to Moses, [2]"Take twelve wooden staffs, one from each of Israel's ancestral tribes, and inscribe each tribal leader's name on his staff. [3]Inscribe Aaron's name on the staff of the tribe of Levi, for there must be one staff for the leader of each ancestral tribe. [4]Put these staffs in the Tabernacle in front of the Ark of the Covenant,* where I meet with you. [5]Buds will sprout on the staff belonging to the man I choose. Then I will finally put an end to this murmuring and complaining against you."

[6]So Moses gave the instructions to the people of Israel, and each of the twelve tribal leaders, including Aaron, brought Moses a staff. [7]Moses put the staffs in the LORD's presence in the Tabernacle of the Covenant.* [8]When he went into the Tabernacle of the Covenant the next day, he found that Aaron's staff, representing the tribe of Levi, had sprouted, blossomed, and produced almonds!

[9]When Moses brought all the staffs out from the LORD's presence, he showed them to the people. Each man claimed his own staff. [10]And the LORD said to Moses: "Place Aaron's staff permanently before the Ark of the Covenant* as a warning to rebels. This should put an end to their complaints against me and prevent any further deaths." [11]So Moses did as the LORD commanded him.

[12]Then the people of Israel said to Moses, "We are as good as dead! We are ruined! [13]Everyone who even comes close to the Tabernacle of the LORD dies. We are all doomed!"

CHAPTER **18** **DUTIES OF PRIESTS AND LEVITES.** The LORD now said to Aaron: "You, your sons, and your relatives from the tribe of Levi will be held responsible for any offenses related to the sanctuary. But you and your sons alone will be held liable for violations connected with the priesthood.

[2]"Bring your relatives of the tribe of Levi to assist you and your sons as you perform the sacred duties in front of the Tabernacle of the Covenant.* [3]But as the Levites go about their duties under your supervision, they must be careful not to touch any of the sacred objects or the altar. If they do, both you and they will die. [4]The Levites must join with you to fulfill their responsibilities for the care and maintenance of the Tabernacle,* but no one who is not a Levite may officiate with you.

[5]"You yourselves must perform the sacred duties within the sanctuary and at the altar. If you follow these instructions, the LORD's anger will never again blaze against the people of Israel. [6]I myself have chosen your fellow Levites from among the Israelites to be your special assistants. They are dedicated to the LORD for service in the Tabernacle. [7]But you and your sons, the priests, must personally handle all the sacred service associated with the altar and everything within the inner curtain. I am giving you the priesthood as your special gift of service. Any other person who comes too near the sanctuary will be put to death."

[8]The LORD gave these further instructions to Aaron: "I have put the priests in charge of all the holy gifts that are brought to me by the people of Israel. I have given these offerings to you and your sons as your regular share. [9]You are allotted the portion of the most holy offerings that is kept from the fire. From all the most holy offerings—including

17:4 Hebrew *in the Tent of Meeting before the Testimony.* 17:7 Or *Tabernacle of the Testimony;* also in 17:8. 17:10 Hebrew *before the Testimony.* 18:2 Or *Tabernacle of the Testimony.* 18:4 Hebrew *Tent of Meeting;* also in 18:6, 21, 22, 23, 31.

the grain offerings, sin offerings, and guilt offerings—that portion belongs to you and your sons. 10You must eat it as a most holy offering. All the males may eat of it, and you must treat it as most holy.

11"All the other offerings presented to me by the Israelites by lifting them up before the altar also belong to you as your regular share. Any member of your family who is ceremonially clean, male and female alike, may eat of these offerings.

12"I also give you the harvest gifts brought by the people as offerings to the LORD—the best of the olive oil, wine, and grain. 13All the firstfruits of the land that the people present to the LORD belong to you. Any member of your family who is ceremonially clean may eat this food.

14"Whatever is specially set apart for the LORD* also belongs to you.

15"The firstborn of every mother, whether human or animal, that is offered to the LORD will be yours. But you must always redeem your firstborn sons and the firstborn males of ritually unclean animals. 16Redeem them when they are one month old. The redemption price is five pieces of silver, each piece weighing the same as the standard sanctuary shekel.*

17"However, you may not redeem the firstborn of cattle, sheep, or goats. They are holy and have been set apart for the LORD. Sprinkle their blood on the altar, and burn their fat as an offering given by fire, very pleasing to the LORD. 18The meat of these animals will be yours, just like the breast and right thigh that are presented by lifting them up before the altar. 19Yes, I am giving you all these holy offerings that the people of Israel bring to the LORD. They are for you and your sons and daughters, to be eaten as your regular share. This is an unbreakable covenant* between the LORD and you and your descendants."

20And the LORD said to Aaron, "You priests will receive no inheritance of land or share of property among the people of Israel. I am your inheritance and your share. 21As for the tribe of Levi, your relatives, I will pay them for their service in the Tabernacle with the tithes from the entire land of Israel.

22"From now on, Israelites other than the priests and Levites are to stay away from the Tabernacle. If they come too near, they will be judged guilty and die. 23The Levites must serve at the Tabernacle, and they will be held responsible for any offenses against it. This is a permanent law among you. But the Levites will receive no inheritance of land among the Israelites, 24because I have given them the Israelites' tithes, which have been set apart as offerings to the LORD. This will be the Levites' share. That is why I said they would receive no inheritance of land among the Israelites."

25The LORD also told Moses, 26"Say this to the Levites: 'When you receive the tithes from the Israelites, give a tenth of the tithes you receive—a tithe of the tithe—to the LORD as a gift. 27The LORD will consider this to be your harvest offering, as though it were the first grain from your own threshing floor or wine from your own winepress. 28You must present one-tenth of the tithe received from the Israelites as a gift to the LORD. From this you must present the LORD's portion to Aaron the priest. 29Be sure to set aside the best portions of the gifts given to you as your gifts to the LORD.'

## MEAL TICKET ● ● • • •

**18:25-26 Even the Levites, who were ministers, had to tithe to support the work of the Tabernacle. No one was exempt from returning to God a portion of what was received from him. Though the Levites owned no land and operated no great enterprises, they were to treat their income the same as everyone else by giving a portion to care for the needs of the other Levites and of the Tabernacle. The tithing principle is still relevant today. God expects all his followers to supply the material needs of those who devote themselves to meeting the spiritual needs of the community of faith.**

30"Also say to the Levites: 'When you present the best part, it will be considered as though it came from your own threshing floor or winepress. 31You Levites and your families may eat this food anywhere you wish, for it is your compensation for serving in the Tabernacle. 32You will not be considered guilty for accepting the LORD's tithes if you give the best portion to the priests. But be careful not to treat the holy gifts of the people of Israel as though they were common. If you do, you will die.'"

## CHAPTER 19

**WHAT TO DO WHEN DEFILED.** The LORD said to Moses and Aaron, 2"Here is another ritual law required by the LORD: Tell the people of Israel to bring you a red heifer that has no physical defects and has never been yoked to a plow. 3Give it to Eleazar the priest, and it will be taken outside the camp and slaughtered in his presence. 4Eleazar will take some of its blood on his finger and sprinkle it seven times toward the front of the Tabernacle.* 5As Eleazar watches, the heifer must be burned—its hide, meat, blood, and dung. 6Eleazar the priest must then take cedarwood, a hyssop branch, and scarlet thread and throw them into the fire where the heifer is burning.

7"Then the priest must wash his clothes and bathe himself in water. Afterward he may return to the camp, though he will remain ceremonially unclean until evening. 8The man who burns the animal must also wash his clothes and bathe in water, and he, too, will remain unclean until evening. 9Then someone who is ceremonially clean will gather up the ashes of the heifer and place them in a purified place outside the camp. They will be kept there for the people of Israel to use in the water for the purification

18:14 The Hebrew term used here refers to the complete consecration of things or people to the LORD, either by destroying them or by giving them as an offering. 18:16 Hebrew *5 shekels* [about 2 ounces or 57 grams] *of silver, according to the sanctuary shekel, 20 gerahs to each shekel.* 18:19 Hebrew *a covenant of salt.* 19:4 Hebrew *Tent of Meeting.*

ceremony. This ceremony is performed for the removal of sin. [10]The man who gathers up the ashes of the heifer must also wash his clothes, and he will remain ceremonially unclean until evening. This is a permanent law for the people of Israel and any foreigners who live among them.

[11]"All those who touch a dead human body will be ceremonially unclean for seven days. [12]They must purify themselves on the third and seventh days with the water of purification; then they will be purified. But if they do not do this on the third and seventh days, they will continue to be unclean even after the seventh day. [13]All those who touch a dead body and do not purify themselves in the proper way defile the LORD's Tabernacle and will be cut off from the community of Israel. Since the water of purification was not sprinkled on them, their defilement continues.

## ANGER

Chad B.'s father always cautions him about his temper: "Son, someday your temper will get you into big trouble. Learn to express yourself without getting so mad. Go read Galatians 5:22-23 and pray about your attitude, OK?"

Each time Chad nods and apologizes. But the talks don't seem to accomplish much. Chad still blows up. And he ends up in at least one fistfight per month. Then, last night, Mr. B.'s prediction finally came true.

At a postgame party, some guys from a rival school showed up and started smarting off. Words were exchanged. Tempers flared. Someone got shoved. A punch was thrown. Suddenly, the friendly get-together became a small-scale riot!

As Chad squared off with one fellow, another guy came after him with a two-by-four. Chad turned into a wild man! Wrestling the board away from his surprised attacker, Chad chased both guys to their pickup truck. Before they could pull away, Chad smashed the truck's rear window and headlight, and put some major dents in the driver's door!

Minutes ago, the police came to Chad's house. In his state of semi-shock, Chad is hearing words like *assault, lawyer,* and *arrest.*

Learn a lesson from Chad, and from Moses in Numbers 20:1-12: A few minutes of unbridled anger can produce serious heartache!

[14]"This is the ritual law that applies when someone dies in a tent: Those who enter that tent, and those who were inside when the death occurred, will be ceremonially unclean for seven days. [15]Any container in the tent that was not covered with a lid is also defiled. [16]And if someone outdoors touches the corpse of someone who was killed with a sword or who died a natural death, or if someone touches a human bone or a grave, that person will be unclean for seven days.

[17]"To remove the defilement, put some of the ashes from the burnt purification offering in a jar and pour fresh water over them. [18]Then someone who is ceremonially clean must take a hyssop branch and dip it into the water. That person must sprinkle the water on the tent, on all the furnishings in the tent, and on anyone who was in the tent, or anyone who has touched a human bone, or has touched a person who was killed or who died naturally, or has touched a grave. [19]On the third and seventh days the ceremonially clean person must sprinkle the water on those who are unclean. Then on the seventh day the people being cleansed must wash their clothes and bathe themselves, and that evening they will be cleansed of their defilement.

[20]"But those who become defiled and do not purify themselves will be cut off from the community, for they have defiled the sanctuary of the LORD. Since the water of purification has not been sprinkled on them, they remain defiled. [21]This is a permanent law. Those who sprinkle the water of purification must afterward wash their clothes, and anyone who touches the water of purification will remain defiled until evening. [22]Anything and anyone that a defiled person touches will be ceremonially defiled until evening."

## CHAPTER 20

**MOSES STRIKES THE ROCK.** In early spring* the people of Israel arrived in the wilderness of Zin and camped at Kadesh. While they were there, Miriam died and was buried.

[2]There was no water for the people to drink at that place, so they rebelled against Moses and Aaron. [3]The people blamed Moses and said, "We wish we had died in the LORD's presence with our brothers! [4]Did you bring the LORD's people into this wilderness to die, along with all our livestock? [5]Why did you make us leave Egypt and bring us here to this terrible place? This land has no grain, figs, grapes, or pomegranates. And there is no water to drink!"

[6]Moses and Aaron turned away from the people and went to the entrance of the Tabernacle,* where they fell face down on the ground. Then the glorious presence of the LORD appeared to them, [7]and the LORD said to Moses, [8]"You and Aaron must take the staff and assemble the entire community. As the people watch, command the rock over there to pour out its water. You will get enough water from the rock to satisfy all the people and their livestock."

[9]So Moses did as he was told. He took the staff from the place where it was kept before the LORD. [10]Then he and Aaron summoned the people to come and gather at the rock. "Listen, you rebels!" he shouted. "Must we bring you water from this rock?" [11]Then Moses raised his hand and struck the rock twice with the staff, and water gushed out. So all the people and their livestock drank their fill.

[12]But the LORD said to Moses and Aaron, "Because you did not trust me enough to demonstrate my holiness to the people of Israel, you will not lead them into the land I am giving them!" [13]This place was known as the waters of Meribah,* because it was where the people of Israel argued with the LORD, and where he demonstrated his holiness among them.

**20:1** Hebrew *In the first month.* This month of the Hebrew lunar calendar usually occurs in March and April. **20:6** Hebrew *Tent of Meeting.* **20:13** *Meribah* means "arguing."

[14]While Moses was at Kadesh, he sent ambassadors to the king of Edom with this message:

"This message is from your relatives, the people of Israel: You know all the hardships we have been through, [15]and that our ancestors went down to Egypt. We lived there a long time and suffered as slaves to the Egyptians. [16]But when we cried out to the LORD, he heard us and sent an angel who brought us out of Egypt. Now we are camped at Kadesh, a town on the border of your land. [17]Please let us pass through your country. We will be careful not to go through your fields and vineyards. We won't even drink water from your wells. We will stay on the king's road and never leave it until we have crossed the opposite border."

[18]But the king of Edom said, "Stay out of my land or I will meet you with an army!"

[19]The Israelites answered, "We will stay on the main road. If any of our livestock drinks your water, we will pay for it. We only want to pass through your country and nothing else."

[20]But the king of Edom replied, "Stay out! You may not pass through our land." With that he mobilized his army and marched out to meet them with an imposing force. [21]Because Edom refused to allow Israel to pass through their country, Israel was forced to turn around.

[22]The whole community of Israel left Kadesh as a group and arrived at Mount Hor. [23]Then the LORD said to Moses and Aaron at Mount Hor on the border of the land of Edom, [24]"The time has come for Aaron to join his ancestors in death. He will not enter the land I am giving the people of Israel, because the two of you rebelled against my instructions concerning the waters of Meribah. [25]Now take Aaron and his son Eleazar up Mount Hor. [26]There you will remove Aaron's priestly garments and put them on Eleazar, his son. Aaron will die there and join his ancestors."

[27]So Moses did as the LORD commanded. The three of them went up Mount Hor together as the whole community watched. [28]At the summit, Moses removed the priestly garments from Aaron and put them on Eleazar, Aaron's son. Then Aaron died there on top of the mountain, and Moses and Eleazar went back down. [29]When the people realized that Aaron had died, all Israel mourned for him thirty days.

## CHAPTER 21

**VICTORY OVER ARAD.** The Canaanite king of Arad, who lived in the Negev, heard that the Israelites were approaching on the road to Atharim. So he attacked the Israelites and took some of them as prisoners. [2]Then the people of Israel made this vow to the LORD: "If you will help us conquer these people, we will completely destroy* all their towns." [3]The LORD heard their request and gave them victory over the Canaanites. The Israelites completely destroyed them and their towns, and the place has been called Hormah* ever since.

[4]Then the people of Israel set out from Mount Hor, taking the road to the Red Sea* to go around the land of Edom. But the people grew impatient along the way, [5]and they began to murmur against God and Moses. "Why have you brought us out of Egypt to die here in the wilderness?" they complained. "There is nothing to eat here and nothing to drink. And we hate this wretched manna!"

[6]So the LORD sent poisonous snakes among them, and many of them were bitten and died. [7]Then the people came to Moses and cried out, "We have sinned by speaking against the LORD and against you. Pray that the LORD will take away the snakes." So Moses prayed for the people.

[8]Then the LORD told him, "Make a replica of a poisonous snake and attach it to the top of a pole. Those who are bitten will live if they simply look at it!" [9]So Moses made a snake out of bronze and attached it to the top of a pole. Whenever those who were bitten looked at the bronze snake, they recovered!

[10]The Israelites traveled next to Oboth and camped there. [11]Then they went on to Iye-abarim, in the wilderness on the eastern border of Moab. [12]From there they traveled to the valley of Zered Brook and set up camp. [13]Then they moved to the far side of the Arnon River, in the wilderness adjacent to the territory of the Amorites. The Arnon is the boundary line between the Moabites and the Amorites. [14]For this reason *The Book of the Wars of the LORD* speaks of "the town of Waheb in the area of Suphah, and the ravines; and the Arnon River [15]and its ravines, which extend as far as the settlement of Ar on the border of Moab."

[16]From there the Israelites traveled to Beer,* which

### CONFLICT • • • • •

20:21 **Moses negotiated and reasoned with the Edomite king. When nothing worked, he was left with two choices—force a conflict or avoid it. Moses knew there would be enough barriers in the days and months ahead. There was no point in adding another one unnecessarily. Sometimes conflict is unavoidable. Sometimes, however, it isn't worth the consequences. Open warfare may seem heroic, courageous, and even righteous, but it is not always the best choice. When we can find another way to solve our problems, even if it is harder for us to do, we should consider Moses' example.**

### COMPLAINTS • • • • •

21:5 **In Psalm 78, we learn the sources of Israel's complaining: (1) they forgot the miracles God did for them, (2) they demanded more than what God had given them, (3) their repentance was insincere, and (4) they were ungrateful for what God had done for them. Our complaining often has its roots in one of these thoughtless actions and attitudes. If we can cut off the source of complaining, it will not take hold and grow in our life.**

**21:2** The Hebrew term used here refers to the complete consecration of things or people to the LORD, either by destroying them or by giving them as an offering; also in 21:3. **21:3** *Hormah* means "destruction." **21:4** Hebrew *sea of reeds.* **21:16** *Beer* means "well."

is the well where the LORD said to Moses, "Assemble
the people, and I will give them water." [17]There the
Israelites sang this song:

"Spring up, O well!
　Yes, sing about it!
[18]Sing of this well,
　which princes dug,
which great leaders hollowed out
　with their scepters and staffs."

Then the Israelites left the wilderness and proceeded on through Mattanah, [19]Nahaliel, and Ba-
moth. [20]Then they went to the valley in Moab where
Pisgah Peak overlooks the wasteland.*

[21]The Israelites now sent ambassadors to King
Sihon of the Amorites with this message:

[22]"Let us travel through your land. We will stay
on the king's road until we have crossed your
territory. We will not trample your fields or
touch your vineyards or drink your well water."

[23]But King Sihon refused to let them cross his
land. Instead, he mobilized his entire army and
attacked Israel in the wilderness, engaging them in
battle at Jahaz. [24]But the Israelites slaughtered them
and occupied their land from the Arnon River to the
Jabbok River. They went only as far as the Ammonite
border because the boundary of the Ammonites was
fortified.*

[25]So Israel captured all the towns of the Amorites
and settled in them, including the city of Heshbon
and its surrounding villages. [26]Heshbon had been
the capital of King Sihon of the Amorites. He had
conquered a former Moabite king and seized all his
land as far as the Arnon River. [27]For this reason the
ancient poets wrote this about him:

"Come to Heshbon, city of Sihon!
　May it be restored and rebuilt.
[28]A fire flamed forth from Heshbon,
　a blaze from the city of Sihon.
It burned the city of Ar in Moab;
　it destroyed the rulers of the Arnon heights.
[29]Your destruction is certain, O people of Moab!
　You are finished, O worshipers of Chemosh!
Chemosh has left his sons as refugees,
　and his daughters as captives of Sihon, the
　　Amorite king.
[30]We have utterly destroyed them,
　all the way from Heshbon to Dibon.
We have completely wiped them out
　as far away as Nophah and Medeba.*"

[31]So the people of Israel occupied the territory of
the Amorites. [32]After Moses sent men to explore the
Jazer area, they captured all the towns in the region
and drove out the Amorites who lived there. [33]Then
they turned and marched toward Bashan, but King
Og of Bashan and all his people attacked them at
Edrei. [34]The LORD said to Moses, "Do not be afraid
of him, for I have given you victory over Og and his
entire army, giving you all his land. You will do the
same to him as you did to King Sihon of the Amorites, who ruled in Heshbon." [35]And Israel was victorious and killed King Og, his sons, and his subjects;
not a single survivor remained. Then Israel occupied
their land.

## VICTORY ● ● • • ·

21:34 **God assured Moses that Israel's enemy was conquered even before the battle began! God wants to give us victory over our enemies—which usually are the problems related to sin, rather than armed soldiers. First we must believe that he can help us. Second, we must trust him to help us. Third, we must take the steps he shows us.**

CHAPTER **22** **BALAK SENDS FOR BALAAM.** Then the
people of Israel traveled to the plains of Moab and
camped east of the Jordan River, across from Jericho.
[2]Balak son of Zippor, the Moabite king, knew what
the Israelites had done to the Amorites. [3]And when
they saw how many Israelites there were, he and his
people were terrified. [4]The king of Moab said to the
leaders of Midian, "This mob will devour everything
in sight, like an ox devours grass!"

So Balak, king of Moab, [5]sent messengers to Balaam son of Beor, who was living in his native land
of Pethor* near the Euphrates River.* He sent this
message to request that Balaam come to help him:

"A vast horde of people has arrived from Egypt.
They cover the face of the earth and are
threatening me. [6]Please come and curse them
for me because they are so numerous. Then
perhaps I will be able to conquer them and
drive them from the land. I know that blessings
fall on the people you bless. I also know that the
people you curse are doomed."

[7]Balak's messengers, officials of both Moab and
Midian, set out and took money with them to pay
Balaam to curse Israel. They went to Balaam and
urgently explained to him what Balak wanted. [8]"Stay
here overnight," Balaam said. "In the morning I will
tell you whatever the LORD directs me to say." So the
officials from Moab stayed there with Balaam.

[9]That night God came to Balaam and asked him,
"Who are these men with you?"

[10]So Balaam said to God, "Balak son of Zippor,
king of Moab, has sent me this message: [11]'A vast
horde of people has come from Egypt and has
spread out over the whole land. Come at once to
curse them. Perhaps then I will be able to conquer
them and drive them from the land.'"

[12]"Do not go with them," God told Balaam. "You
are not to curse these people, for I have blessed
them!"

**21:20** Or *overlooks Jeshimon.* **21:24** Or *because the terrain of the Ammonite frontier was rugged;* Hebrew *because the boundary of the Ammonites was strong.* **21:30** Or *until fire spread to Medeba.* The meaning of the Hebrew is uncertain. **22:5a** Or *who was at Pethor in the land of the Amavites.* **22:5b** Hebrew *the river.*

[13]The next morning Balaam got up and told Balak's officials, "Go on home! The LORD will not let me go with you."

[14]So the Moabite officials returned to King Balak and reported, "Balaam refused to come with us." [15]Then Balak tried again. This time he sent a larger number of even more distinguished officials than those he had sent the first time. [16]They went to Balaam and gave him this message:

"This is what Balak son of Zippor says: Please don't let anything stop you from coming. [17]I will pay you well and do anything you ask of me. Just come and curse these people for me!"

[18]But Balaam answered them, "Even if Balak were to give me a palace filled with silver and gold, I would be powerless to do anything against the will of the LORD my God. [19]But stay here one more night to see if the LORD has anything else to say to me."

[20]That night God came to Balaam and told him, "Since these men have come for you, get up and go with them. But be sure to do only what I tell you to do."

[21]So the next morning Balaam saddled his donkey and started off with the Moabite officials. [22]But God was furious that Balaam was going, so he sent the angel of the LORD to stand in the road to block his way. As Balaam and two servants were riding along, [23]Balaam's donkey suddenly saw the angel of the LORD standing in the road with a drawn sword in his hand. The donkey bolted off the road into a field, but Balaam beat it and turned it back onto the road. [24]Then the angel of the LORD stood at a place where the road narrowed between two vineyard walls. [25]When the donkey saw the angel of the LORD standing there, it tried to squeeze by and crushed Balaam's foot against the wall. So Balaam beat the donkey again. [26]Then the angel of the LORD moved farther down the road and stood in a place so narrow that the donkey could not get by at all. [27]This time when the donkey saw the angel, it lay down under Balaam. In a fit of rage Balaam beat it again with his staff.

[28]Then the LORD caused the donkey to speak. "What have I done to you that deserves your beating me these three times?" it asked Balaam.

[29]"Because you have made me look like a fool!" Balaam shouted. "If I had a sword with me, I would kill you!"

[30]"But I am the same donkey you always ride on," the donkey answered. "Have I ever done anything like this before?"

"No," he admitted.

[31]Then the LORD opened Balaam's eyes, and he saw the angel of the LORD standing in the roadway with a drawn sword in his hand. Balaam fell face down on the ground before him.

[32]"Why did you beat your donkey those three times?" the angel of the LORD demanded. "I have come to block your way because you are stubbornly resisting me. [33]Three times the donkey saw me and shied away; otherwise, I would certainly have killed you by now and spared the donkey."

[34]Then Balaam confessed to the angel of the LORD, "I have sinned. I did not realize you were standing in the road to block my way. I will go back home if you are against my going."

[35]But the angel of the LORD told him, "Go with these men, but you may say only what I tell you to say." So Balaam went on with Balak's officials. [36]When King Balak heard that Balaam was on the way, he went out to meet him at a Moabite town on the Arnon River at the border of his land.

[37]"Did I not send you an urgent invitation? Why didn't you come right away?" Balak asked Balaam. "Didn't you believe me when I said I would reward you richly?"

[38]Balaam replied, "I have come, but I have no power to say just anything. I will speak only the messages that God gives me." [39]Then Balaam accompanied Balak to Kiriath-huzoth, [40]where the king sacrificed cattle and sheep. He sent portions of the meat to Balaam and the officials who were with him. [41]The next morning Balak took Balaam up to Bamoth-baal. From there he could see the people of Israel spread out below him.

## BLIND GREED ● ● • • •

**22:20-23 God let Balaam go with Balak's messengers, but he was angry about Balaam's greedy attitude. Balaam claimed that he would not go against God just for money, but his resolve was beginning to slip. His greed for the wealth offered by the king blinded him so that he could not see how God was trying to stop him. Though we may know what God wants us to do, we can become blinded by our greedy desire for money, possessions, or prestige. We can avoid Balaam's mistake by looking past the allure of fame or fortune to the long-range benefits of following God.**

CHAPTER **23** **BALAAM BLESSES ISRAEL.** Balaam said to King Balak, "Build me seven altars here, and prepare seven young bulls and seven rams for a sacrifice." [2]Balak followed his instructions, and the two of them sacrificed a young bull and a ram on each altar.

[3]Then Balaam said to Balak, "Stand here by your burnt offerings, and I will go to see if the LORD will respond to me. Then I will tell you whatever he reveals to me." So Balaam went alone to the top of a hill, [4]and God met him there. Balaam said to him, "I have prepared seven altars and have sacrificed a young bull and a ram on each altar."

[5]Then the LORD gave Balaam a message for King Balak and said, "Go back to Balak and tell him what I told you."

[6]When Balaam returned, the king was standing beside his burnt offerings with all the officials of Moab. [7]This was the prophecy Balaam delivered:

"Balak summoned me to come from Aram;
the king of Moab brought me from the
eastern hills.

'Come,' he said, 'curse Jacob for me!
Come and announce Israel's doom.'
8 But how can I curse
those whom God has not cursed?
How can I condemn
those whom the LORD has not condemned?
9 I see them from the cliff tops;
I watch them from the hills.
I see a people who live by themselves,
set apart from other nations.
10 Who can count Jacob's descendants, as
numerous as dust?
Who can count even a fourth of Israel's
people?
Let me die like the righteous;
let my life end like theirs."

11 Then King Balak demanded of Balaam, "What
have you done to me? I brought you to curse my
enemies. Instead, you have blessed them!"
12 But Balaam replied, "Can I say anything except
what the LORD tells me?"
13 Then King Balak told him, "Come with me to
another place. There you will see only a portion of
the nation of Israel. Curse at least that many!" 14 So
Balak took Balaam to the plateau of Zophim on
Pisgah Peak. He built seven altars there and offered
a young bull and a ram on each altar.
15 Then Balaam said to the king, "Stand here by
your burnt offering while I go to meet the LORD."
16 So the LORD met Balaam and gave him a message. Then he said, "Go back to Balak and give him
this message."
17 So Balaam returned to the place where the king
and the officials of Moab were standing beside
Balak's burnt offerings. "What did the LORD say?"
Balak asked eagerly.
18 This was the prophecy Balaam delivered:

"Rise up, Balak, and listen!
Hear me, son of Zippor.
19 God is not a man, that he should lie.
He is not a human, that he should change his
mind.
Has he ever spoken and failed to act?
Has he ever promised and not carried it
through?
20 I received a command to bless;
he has blessed, and I cannot reverse it!
21 No misfortune is in sight for Jacob;
no trouble is in store for Israel.
For the LORD their God is with them;
he has been proclaimed their king.
22 God has brought them out of Egypt;
he is like a strong ox for them.
23 No curse can touch Jacob;
no sorcery has any power against Israel.
For now it will be said of Jacob,
'What wonders God has done for Israel!'
24 These people rise up like a lioness;
like a majestic lion they stand.

23:28 Or *overlooking Jeshimon.*



## NEW VIEW ● ● ● • •

23:27 **King Balak took Balaam to several places to entice him to curse the Israelites. He thought a change of scenery might help change Balaam's mind. But changing locations won't change God's will. We must learn to face the source of our problems, especially when it is within ourselves. To make a change in geography or a change in jobs may only cloud the need for a change in heart.**

They refuse to rest
until they have feasted on prey,
drinking the blood of the slaughtered!"

25 Then Balak said to Balaam, "If you aren't going
to curse them, at least don't bless them!"
26 But Balaam replied, "Didn't I tell you that I must
do whatever the LORD tells me?"
27 Then King Balak said to Balaam, "Come, I will
take you to yet another place. Perhaps it will please
God to let you curse them from there."
28 So Balak took Balaam to the top of Mount Peor,
overlooking the wasteland.* 29 Balaam again told Balak, "Build me seven altars and prepare me seven
young bulls and seven rams for a sacrifice." 30 So
Balak did as Balaam ordered and offered a young
bull and a ram on each altar.

## CHAPTER 24

By now Balaam realized that
the LORD intended to bless Israel, so he did not resort
to divination as he often did. Instead, he turned and
looked out toward the wilderness, 2 where he saw the
people of Israel camped, tribe by tribe. Then the
Spirit of God came upon him, 3 and this is the prophecy he delivered:

"This is the prophecy of Balaam son of Beor,
the prophecy of the man whose eyes see
clearly,
4 who hears the words of God,
who sees a vision from the Almighty,
who falls down with eyes wide open:
5 How beautiful are your tents, O Jacob;
how lovely are your homes, O Israel!
6 They spread before me like groves of palms,
like fruitful gardens by the riverside.
They are like aloes planted by the LORD,
like cedars beside the waters.
7 Water will gush out in buckets;
their offspring are supplied with all they need.
Their king will be greater than Agag;
their kingdom will be exalted.
8 God brought them up from Egypt,
drawing them along like a wild ox.
He devours all the nations that oppose him,
breaking their bones in pieces,
shooting them with arrows.
9 Like a lion, Israel crouches and lies down;
like a lioness, who dares to arouse her?
Blessed is everyone who blesses you, O Israel,
and cursed is everyone who curses you."

10 King Balak flew into a rage against Balaam. He
angrily clapped his hands and shouted, "I called you

to curse my enemies! Instead, you have blessed them
three times. 11Now get out of here! Go back home! I
had planned to reward you richly, but the LORD has
kept you from your reward."
12Balaam told Balak, "Don't you remember what
I told your messengers? I said, 13'Even if Balak were
to give me a palace filled with silver and gold, I am
powerless to do anything against the will of the
LORD.' I told you that I could say only what the LORD
says! 14Now I am returning to my own people. But
first let me tell you what the Israelites will do to your
people in the future."

15This is the prophecy Balaam delivered:

"This is the message of Balaam son of Beor,
the prophecy of the man whose eyes see
clearly,
16 who hears the words of God,
who has knowledge from the Most High,
who sees a vision from the Almighty,
who falls down with eyes wide open:
17 I see him, but not in the present time.
I perceive him, but far in the distant future.
A star will rise from Jacob;
a scepter will emerge from Israel.
It will crush the foreheads of Moab's people,
cracking the skulls of the people of Sheth.
18 Edom will be taken over,
and Seir, its enemy, will be conquered,
while Israel continues on in triumph.
19 A ruler will rise in Jacob
who will destroy the survivors of Ir."

20Then Balaam looked over at the people of Amalek and delivered this prophecy:

"Amalek was the greatest of nations,
but its destiny is destruction!"

21 Then he looked over at the Kenites and prophesied:

"You are strongly situated;
your nest is set in the rocks.
22 But the Kenites will be destroyed
when Assyria* takes you captive."

23Balaam concluded his prophecies by saying:

"Alas, who can survive when God does this?
24 Ships will come from the coasts of Cyprus*;
they will oppress both Assyria and Eber,
but they, too, will be utterly destroyed."

25Then Balaam and Balak returned to their homes.

## CHAPTER 25

**MOAB SEDUCES ISRAEL.** While the Israelites were camped at Acacia,* some of the men
defiled themselves by sleeping with the local Moabite women. 2These women invited them to attend
sacrifices to their gods, and soon the Israelites were
feasting with them and worshiping the gods of
Moab. 3Before long Israel was joining in the worship
of Baal of Peor, causing the LORD's anger to blaze
against his people.
4The LORD issued the following command to
Moses: "Seize all the ringleaders and execute them
before the LORD in broad daylight, so his fierce anger
will turn away from the people of Israel." 5So Moses
ordered Israel's judges to execute everyone who had
joined in worshiping Baal of Peor.
6Just then one of the Israelite men brought a
Midianite woman into the camp, right before the
eyes of Moses and all the people, as they were
weeping at the entrance of the Tabernacle.* 7When
Phinehas son of Eleazar and grandson of Aaron the
priest saw this, he jumped up and left the assembly.
Then he took a spear 8and rushed after the man
into his tent. Phinehas thrust the spear all the way
through the man's body and into the woman's
stomach. So the plague against the Israelites was
stopped, 9but not before 24,000 people had died.
10Then the LORD said to Moses, 11"Phinehas son
of Eleazar and grandson of Aaron the priest has
turned my anger away from the Israelites by displaying passionate zeal among them on my behalf.
So I have stopped destroying all Israel as I had
intended to do in my anger. 12So tell him that I am
making my special covenant of peace with him.
13In this covenant, he and his descendants will be
priests for all time, because he was zealous for his
God and made atonement for the people of Israel."

### RIGHTEOUS ANGER ● ● • • •

25:10-11 **It is clear from Phinehas's story that some anger is proper and justified. But how can we know when our anger is appropriate and when it should be restrained? Ask these questions when you become angry: (1) Why am I angry? (2) Whose rights are being violated (mine or another's)? (3) Is the truth (a principle of God) being violated? If only your rights are at stake, it may be wiser to keep angry feelings under control. But if the truth is at stake, anger is often justified, although violence and retaliation are usually the wrong way to express it (Phinehas's case was unique). If we are becoming more and more like God, we should be angered by sin.**

14The Israelite man killed with the Midianite
woman was named Zimri son of Salu, the leader of
a family from the tribe of Simeon. 15The woman's
name was Cozbi; she was the daughter of Zur, the
leader of a Midianite clan.
16Then the LORD said to Moses, 17"Attack the Midianites and destroy them, 18because they assaulted
you with deceit by tricking you into worshiping Baal
of Peor, and because of Cozbi, the daughter of a
Midianite leader, who was killed on the day of the
plague at Peor."

## CHAPTER 26

**ISRAEL'S SECOND CENSUS.** After the
plague had ended, the LORD said to Moses and to
Eleazar son of Aaron, the priest, 2"Take a census of
all the men of Israel who are twenty years old or
older, to find out how many of each family are of

**24:22** Hebrew *Asshur;* also in 24:24. **24:24** Hebrew *Kittim.* **25:1** Hebrew *Shittim.* **25:6** Hebrew *Tent of Meeting.*

military age." [3]At that time the entire nation of Israel was camped on the plains of Moab beside the Jordan River, across from Jericho.

So Moses and Eleazar the priest issued these census instructions to the leaders of Israel: [4]"Count all the men of Israel twenty years old and older, just as the LORD commanded Moses." This is the census record of all the descendants of Israel who came out of Egypt.

[5]These were the clans descended from Reuben, Jacob's* oldest son:

The Hanochite clan, named after its ancestor Hanoch.
The Palluite clan, named after its ancestor Pallu.
[6] The Hezronite clan, named after its ancestor Hezron.
The Carmite clan, named after its ancestor Carmi.

[7]The men from all the clans of Reuben numbered 43,730.

[8]Pallu was the ancestor of Eliab, [9]and Eliab was the father of Nemuel, Dathan, and Abiram. This Dathan and Abiram are the same community leaders who conspired with Korah against Moses and Aaron, defying the LORD. [10]But the earth opened up and swallowed them with Korah, and 250 of their followers were destroyed that day by fire from the LORD. This served as a warning to the entire nation of Israel. [11]However, the sons of Korah did not die that day.

[12]These were the clans descended from the sons of Simeon:

The Nemuelite clan, named after its ancestor Nemuel.
The Jaminite clan, named after its ancestor Jamin.
The Jakinite clan, named after its ancestor Jakin.
[13]The Zerahite clan, named after its ancestor Zerah.
The Shaulite clan, named after its ancestor Shaul.

[14]The men from all the clans of Simeon numbered 22,200.

[15]These were the clans descended from the sons of Gad:

The Zephonite clan, named after its ancestor Zephon.
The Haggite clan, named after its ancestor Haggi.
The Shunite clan, named after its ancestor Shuni.
[16]The Oznite clan, named after its ancestor Ozni.
The Erite clan, named after its ancestor Eri.
[17]The Arodite clan, named after its ancestor Arodi.*
The Arelite clan, named after its ancestor Areli.

[18]The men from all the clans of Gad numbered 40,500.

[19]Judah had two sons, Er and Onan, who had died in the land of Canaan. [20]But the following clans descended from Judah's surviving sons:

The Shelanite clan, named after its ancestor Shelah.
The Perezite clan, named after its ancestor Perez.
The Zerahite clan, named after its ancestor Zerah.

[21]These were the subclans descended from the Perezites:

The Hezronites, named after their ancestor Hezron.
The Hamulites, named after their ancestor Hamul.

[22]The men from all the clans of Judah numbered 76,500.

[23]These were the clans descended from the sons of Issachar:

The Tolaite clan, named after its ancestor Tola.
The Puite clan, named after its ancestor Puah.*
[24]The Jashubite clan, named after its ancestor Jashub.
The Shimronite clan, named after its ancestor Shimron.

[25]The men from all the clans of Issachar numbered 64,300.

[26]These were the clans descended from the sons of Zebulun:

The Seredite clan, named after its ancestor Sered.
The Elonite clan, named after its ancestor Elon.
The Jahleelite clan, named after its ancestor Jahleel.

[27]The men from all the clans of Zebulun numbered 60,500.

[28]Two clans were descended from Joseph through Manasseh and Ephraim.

[29]These were the clans descended from Manasseh:
The Makirite clan, named after its ancestor Makir.
The Gileadite clan, named after its ancestor Gilead, Makir's son.

[30]These were the subclans descended from the Gileadites:

The Iezerites, named after their ancestor Iezer.
The Helekites, named after their ancestor Helek.
[31] The Asrielites, named after their ancestor Asriel.
The Shechemites, named after their ancestor Shechem.
[32]The Shemidaites, named after their ancestor Shemida.
The Hepherites, named after their ancestor Hepher.
[33] Hepher's son, Zelophehad, had no sons, but his daughters' names were Mahlah, Noah, Hoglah, Milcah, and Tirzah.

**26:5** Hebrew *Israel's.* **26:17** As in Samaritan Pentateuch and Syriac version (see also Gen 46:16); Hebrew reads *Arod.* **26:23** As in Samaritan Pentateuch, Greek and Syriac versions, and Latin Vulgate (see also 1 Chr 7:1); Hebrew reads *The Punite clan, named after its ancestor Puvah.*

34 The men from all the clans of Manasseh numbered 52,700.

35 These were the clans descended from the sons of Ephraim:

The Shuthelahite clan, named after its ancestor Shuthelah.
The Bekerite clan, named after its ancestor Beker.
The Tahanite clan, named after its ancestor Tahan.

36 This was the subclan descended from the Shuthelahites:

The Eranites, named after their ancestor Eran.

37 The men from all the clans of Ephraim numbered 32,500.

These clans of Manasseh and Ephraim were all descendants of Joseph.

38 These were the clans descended from the sons of Benjamin:

The Belaite clan, named after its ancestor Bela.
The Ashbelite clan, named after its ancestor Ashbel.
The Ahiramite clan, named after its ancestor Ahiram.
39 The Shuphamite clan, named after its ancestor Shupham.*
The Huphamite clan, named after its ancestor Hupham.

40 These were the subclans descended from the Belaites:

The Ardites, named after their ancestor Ard.*
The Naamites, named after their ancestor Naaman.

41 The men from all the clans of Benjamin numbered 45,600.

42 These were the clans descended from the sons of Dan:

The Shuhamite clan, named after its ancestor Shuham.

43 All the clans of Dan were Shuhamite clans, and the men from these clans numbered 64,400.

44 These were the clans descended from the sons of Asher:

The Imnite clan, named after its ancestor Imnah.
The Ishvite clan, named after its ancestor Ishvi.
The Beriite clan, named after its ancestor Beriah.

45 These were the subclans descended from the Beriites:

The Heberites, named after their ancestor Heber.
The Malkielites, named after their ancestor Malkiel.

46 Asher also had a daughter named Serah.

47 The men from all the clans of Asher numbered 53,400.

48 These were the clans descended from the sons of Naphtali:

The Jahzeelite clan, named after its ancestor Jahzeel.
The Gunite clan, named after its ancestor Guni.
49 The Jezerite clan, named after its ancestor Jezer.
The Shillemite clan, named after its ancestor Shillem.

50 The men from all the clans of Naphtali numbered 45,400.

51 So the total number of Israelite men counted in
the census numbered 601,730.
52 Then the LORD said to Moses, 53 "Divide the land
among the tribes in proportion to their populations,
as indicated by the census. 54 Give the larger tribes
more land and the smaller tribes less land, each
group's inheritance reflecting the size of its population. 55 Make sure you assign the land by lot, and
define the inheritance of each ancestral tribe by
means of the census listings. 56 Each inheritance must
be assigned by lot among the larger and smaller
tribal groups."

57 This is the census record for the Levites who were counted according to their clans:

The Gershonite clan, named after its ancestor Gershon.
The Kohathite clan, named after its ancestor Kohath.
The Merarite clan, named after its ancestor Merari.

58 The Libnites, the Hebronites, the Mahlites, the
Mushites, and the Korahites were all subclans of the
Levites.
Now Kohath was the ancestor of Amram, 59 and
Amram's wife was named Jochebed. She also was a
descendant of Levi, born among the Levites in the
land of Egypt. Amram and Jochebed became the
parents of Aaron, Moses, and their sister, Miriam.
60 To Aaron were born Nadab, Abihu, Eleazar, and
Ithamar. 61 But Nadab and Abihu died when they
burned before the LORD a different kind of fire than
he had commanded.
62 The men from the Levite clans who were one
month old or older numbered 23,000. But the Levites were not included in the total census figure of
the people of Israel because they were not given an
inheritance of land when it was divided among the
Israelites.
63 So these are the census figures of the people of
Israel as prepared by Moses and Eleazar the priest on
the plains of Moab beside the Jordan River, across
from Jericho. 64 Not one person that was counted in
this census had been among those counted in the
previous census taken by Moses and Aaron in the

26:39 As in some Hebrew manuscripts, Samaritan Pentateuch, Greek and Syriac versions, and Latin Vulgate; most Hebrew manuscripts read *Shephupham.* 26:40 As in Samaritan Pentateuch, some Greek manuscripts, and Latin Vulgate; Hebrew lacks *named after their ancestor Ard.*

## QUIET WORK ● ● • • •

**26:64 A new census for a new generation. Thirty-eight years had elapsed since the first great census in chapter one of Numbers. During that time, every Israelite man and woman over 20 years of age—except Caleb, Joshua, and Moses—had died, and yet God's laws and the spiritual character of the nation were still intact. Numbers records some dramatic miracles. This is a quiet but powerful miracle often overlooked: A whole nation moves from one land to another, loses its entire adult population, yet manages to maintain its spiritual direction. Sometimes we wonder why God isn't working dramatic miracles in our life. The fact is that God often works in quiet ways to bring about his long-range purposes.**

wilderness of Sinai. [65]For the LORD had said of them, "They will all die in the wilderness." The only exceptions were Caleb son of Jephunneh and Joshua son of Nun.

CHAPTER **27** **ZELOPHEHAD'S DAUGHTERS.** One day a petition was presented by the daughters of Zelophehad—Mahlah, Noah, Hoglah, Milcah, and Tirzah. Their father, Zelophehad, was the son of Hepher, son of Gilead, son of Makir, son of Manasseh, son of Joseph. [2]These women went and stood before Moses, Eleazar the priest, the tribal leaders, and the entire community at the entrance of the Tabernacle.* [3]"Our father died in the wilderness without leaving any sons," they said. "But he was not among Korah's followers, who rebelled against the LORD. He died because of his own sin. [4]Why should the name of our father disappear just because he had no sons? Give us property along with the rest of our relatives."

[5]So Moses brought their case before the LORD. [6]And the LORD replied to Moses, [7]"The daughters of Zelophehad are right. You must give them an inheritance of land along with their father's relatives. Assign them the property that would have been given to their father. [8]Moreover announce this to the people of Israel: 'If a man dies and has no sons, then give his inheritance to his daughters. [9]And if he has no daughters, turn his inheritance over to his brothers. [10]If he has no brothers, give his inheritance to his father's brothers. [11]But if his father has no brothers, pass on his inheritance to the nearest relative in his clan. The Israelites must observe this as a general legal requirement, just as the LORD commanded Moses.'"

[12]One day the LORD said to Moses, "Climb to the top of the mountains east of the river,* and look out over the land I have given the people of Israel. [13]After you have seen it, you will die as Aaron your brother did, [14]for you both rebelled against my instructions in the wilderness of Zin. When the people of Israel rebelled, you failed to demonstrate my holiness to them at the waters." (These are the waters of Meribah at Kadesh* in the wilderness of Zin.)

[15]Then Moses said to the LORD, [16]"O LORD, the God of the spirits of all living things, please appoint a new leader for the community. [17]Give them someone who will lead them into battle, so the people of the LORD will not be like sheep without a shepherd."

[18]The LORD replied, "Take Joshua son of Nun, who has the Spirit in him, and lay your hands on him. [19]Present him to Eleazar the priest before the whole community, and publicly commission him with the responsibility of leading the people. [20]Transfer your authority to him so the whole community of Israel will obey him. [21]When direction from the LORD is needed, Joshua will stand before Eleazar the priest, who will determine the LORD's will by means of sacred lots.* This is how Joshua and the rest of the community of Israel will discover what they should do."

[22]So Moses did as the LORD commanded and presented Joshua to Eleazar the priest and the whole community. [23]Moses laid his hands on him and commissioned him to his responsibilities, just as the LORD had commanded through Moses.

CHAPTER **28** **DAILY OFFERINGS.** The LORD said to Moses, [2]"Give these instructions to the people of Israel: The offerings you present to me by fire on the altar are my food, and they are very pleasing to me. See to it that they are brought at the appointed times and offered according to my instructions.

[3]"Say to them: When you present your daily whole burnt offerings to the LORD, you must offer two one-year-old male lambs with no physical defects. [4]One lamb will be sacrificed in the morning and the other in the evening. [5]With each lamb you must offer a grain offering of two quarts* of choice flour mixed with one quart* of olive oil. [6]This is the regular burnt offering ordained at Mount Sinai, an offering made by fire, very pleasing to the LORD. [7]Along with it you must present the proper drink offering, consisting of one quart of fermented drink with each lamb, poured out in the Holy Place as an offering to the LORD. [8]Offer the second lamb in the evening with the same grain offering and drink offering. It, too, is an offering made by fire, very pleasing to the LORD.

[9]"On the Sabbath day, sacrifice two one-year-old male lambs with no physical defects. They must be accompanied by a grain offering of three quarts* of choice flour mixed with olive oil, and a drink offering. [10]This is the whole burnt offering to be pre-

## GET READY ● ● • • •

**28:1-2 Offerings had to be brought regularly and carried out a certain way under the supervision of the priests. The people had to undergo a period of preparation to be sure their hearts were ready for worship. By spending this much time and preparation in worshiping God, they gave idolatry little time to influence their lives. God is pleased today when we allow nothing to come between him and us. He also is delighted by hearts that are prepared to receive his guidance.**

**27:2** Hebrew *Tent of Meeting.* **27:12** Hebrew *the mountains of Abarim.* **27:14** Hebrew *waters of Meribath-kadesh.* **27:21** Hebrew *of the Urim.*
**28:5a** Hebrew *1/10 of an ephah* [2 liters]; also in 28:13, 21, 29. **28:5b** Hebrew *1/4 of a hin* [1 liter]; also in 28:7.

sented each Sabbath day, in addition to the regular daily burnt offering and its accompanying drink offering.

11“On the first day of each month, present an extra burnt offering to the LORD of two young bulls, one ram, and seven one-year-old male lambs, all with no physical defects. 12These will be accompanied by grain offerings of choice flour mixed with olive oil—five quarts* with each bull, three quarts with the ram, 13and two quarts with each lamb. This burnt offering must be presented by fire, and it will be very pleasing to the LORD. 14You must also give a drink offering with each sacrifice: two quarts* of wine with each bull, two and a half pints* for the ram, and one quart* for each lamb. Present this monthly burnt offering on the first day of each month throughout the year.

15“Also, on the first day of each month you must offer one male goat for a sin offering to the LORD. This is in addition to the regular daily burnt offering and its accompanying drink offering.

16“On the appointed day in early spring,* you must celebrate the LORD's Passover. 17On the following day a joyous, seven-day festival will begin, but no bread made with yeast may be eaten. 18On the first day of the festival you must call a sacred assembly of the people. None of your regular work may be done on that day. 19You must present as a burnt offering to the LORD two young bulls, one ram, and seven one-year-old male lambs, all with no physical defects. 20These will be accompanied by grain offerings of choice flour mixed with olive oil—five quarts with each bull, three quarts with the ram, 21and two quarts with each of the seven lambs. 22You must also offer a male goat as a sin offering, to make atonement for yourselves. 23You will present these offerings in addition to your regular morning sacrifices. 24On each of the seven days of the festival, this is how you will prepare the food offerings to be presented by fire, very pleasing to the LORD. These will be offered in addition to the regular whole burnt offerings and drink offerings. 25On the seventh day of the festival you must call another holy assembly of the people. None of your regular work may be done on that day.

26“On the first day of the Festival of Harvest,* when you present the first of your new grain to the LORD, you must call a holy assembly of the people. None of your regular work may be done on that day. 27A special whole burnt offering will be offered that day, very pleasing to the LORD. It will consist of two young bulls, one ram, and seven one-year-old male lambs. 28These will be accompanied by grain offerings of choice flour mixed with olive oil—five quarts with each bull, three quarts with the ram, 29and two quarts with each of the seven lambs. 30Also, offer one male goat to make atonement for yourselves. 31These special burnt offerings, along with their drink offerings, are in addition to the regular daily burnt offering and its accompanying grain offering. Be sure that all the animals you sacrifice have no physical defects.

## CHAPTER 29

**FESTIVAL OF TRUMPETS.** “The Festival of Trumpets will be celebrated on the appointed day in early autumn* each year. You must call a solemn assembly of all the people on that day, and

### WORSHIP TODAY

**29:1-2 The Festival of Trumpets demonstrated three important principles that we should follow in our worship today: (1) The people gathered together to celebrate and worship. There is something special about worshiping with other believers. (2) The normal daily routine was suspended and no hard work was done. It takes time to worship, and setting aside the time allows us to prepare our heart before and reflect afterward. (3) The people sacrificed animals as burnt offerings to God. We show our commitment to God when we give something of value to him. The best gift, of course, is ourself.**

no regular work may be done. 2On that day you must present a burnt offering, very pleasing to the LORD. It will consist of one young bull, one ram, and seven one-year-old male lambs, all with no physical defects. 3These must be accompanied by grain offerings of choice flour mixed with olive oil—five quarts* with the bull, three quarts* with the ram, 4and two quarts* with each of the seven lambs. 5In addition, you must sacrifice a male goat as a sin offering, to make atonement for yourselves. 6These special sacrifices are in addition to your regular monthly and daily burnt offerings, and they must be given with their prescribed grain offerings and drink offerings. These offerings are given to the LORD by fire and are very pleasing to him.

7“Ten days later,* you must call another holy assembly of all the people. On that day, the Day of Atonement, the people must go without food, and no regular work may be done. 8You must present a burnt offering, very pleasing to the LORD. It will consist of one young bull, one ram, and seven one-year-old male lambs, all with no physical defects. 9These offerings must be accompanied by the prescribed grain offerings of choice flour mixed with olive oil—five quarts of choice flour with the bull, three quarts of choice flour with the ram, 10and two quarts of choice flour with each of the seven lambs. 11You must also sacrifice one male goat for a sin offering. This is in addition to the sin offering of atonement and the regular daily burnt offering with its grain offering, and their accompanying drink offerings.

12“Five days later,* you must call yet another

**28:9** Hebrew *2/10 of an ephah* [3.6 liters]; also in 28:12, 20, 28. **28:12** Hebrew *3/10 of an ephah* [5.4 liters]; also in 28:20, 28. **28:14a** Hebrew *1/2 of a hin* [2 liters]. **28:14b** Hebrew *1/3 of a hin* [1.3 liters]. **28:14c** Hebrew *1/4 of a hin* [1 liter]. **28:16** Hebrew *On the fourteenth day of the first month.* This day of the Hebrew lunar calendar occurs in late March or early April. **28:26** Or *Festival of Weeks.* **29:1** Hebrew *on the first day of the seventh month.* This day of the Hebrew lunar calendar occurs in September or early October. **29:3a** Hebrew *3/10 of an ephah* [5.4 liters]; also in 29:9, 14. **29:3b** Hebrew *2/10 of an ephah* [3.6 liters]; also in 29:9, 14. **29:4** Hebrew *1/10 of an ephah* [2 liters]; also in 29:10, 15. **29:7** Hebrew *On the tenth day of the seventh month;* see 29:1 and the note there. **29:12** Hebrew *On the fifteenth day of the seventh month;* see 29:1, 7 and the notes there.

holy assembly of all the people, and on that day no regular work may be done. It is the beginning of the Festival of Shelters, a seven-day festival to the LORD. [13]That day you must present a special whole burnt offering by fire, very pleasing to the LORD. It will consist of thirteen young bulls, two rams, and fourteen one-year-old male lambs, all with no physical defects. [14]Each of these offerings must be accompanied by a grain offering of choice flour mixed with olive oil—five quarts for each of the thirteen bulls, three quarts for each of the two rams, [15]and two quarts for each of the fourteen lambs. [16]You must also sacrifice a male goat as a sin offering, in addition to the regular daily burnt offering with its accompanying grain offering and drink offering.

[17]"On the second day of this seven-day festival, sacrifice twelve young bulls, two rams, and fourteen one-year-old male lambs, all with no physical defects. [18]Each of these offerings of bulls, rams, and lambs must be accompanied by the prescribed grain offering and drink offering. [19]You must also sacrifice a male goat as a sin offering, in addition to the regular daily burnt offering with its accompanying grain offering and drink offering.

[20]"On the third day of the festival, sacrifice eleven young bulls, two rams, and fourteen one-year-old male lambs, all with no physical defects. [21]Each of these offerings of bulls, rams, and lambs must be accompanied by the prescribed grain offering and drink offering. [22]You must also sacrifice a male goat as a sin offering, in addition to the regular daily burnt offering with its accompanying grain offering and drink offering.

[23]"On the fourth day of the festival, sacrifice ten young bulls, two rams, and fourteen one-year-old male lambs, all with no physical defects. [24]Each of these offerings of bulls, rams, and lambs must be accompanied by the prescribed grain offering and drink offering. [25]You must also sacrifice a male goat as a sin offering, in addition to the regular daily burnt offering with its accompanying grain offering and drink offering.

[26]"On the fifth day of the festival, sacrifice nine young bulls, two rams, and fourteen one-year-old male lambs, all with no physical defects. [27]Each of these offerings of bulls, rams, and lambs must be accompanied by the prescribed grain offering and drink offering. [28]You must also sacrifice a male goat as a sin offering, in addition to the regular daily burnt offering with its accompanying grain offering and drink offering.

[29]"On the sixth day of the festival, sacrifice eight young bulls, two rams, and fourteen one-year-old male lambs, all with no physical defects. [30]Each of these offerings of bulls, rams, and lambs must be accompanied by the prescribed grain offering and drink offering. [31]You must also sacrifice a male goat as a sin offering, in addition to the regular daily burnt offering with its accompanying grain offering and drink offering.



## PROMISES ● ● • • •

**30:1-2 Moses reminded the people that their promises to God and others must be kept. In ancient times, people did not sign written contracts. A person's word was as binding as a signature. To make a vow even more binding, an offering was given along with it. No one was forced by law to make a vow; but once made, vows had to be fulfilled. Breaking a vow meant a broken trust and a broken relationship. Trust is still the basis of our relationships with God and others. Thus a broken promise today is just as harmful as it was in Moses' day.**

[32]"On the seventh day of the festival, sacrifice seven young bulls, two rams, and fourteen one-year-old male lambs, all with no physical defects. [33]Each of these offerings of bulls, rams, and lambs must be accompanied by the prescribed grain offering and drink offering. [34]You must also sacrifice one male goat as a sin offering, in addition to the regular daily burnt offering with its accompanying grain offering and drink offering.

[35]"On the eighth day of the festival, call all the people to another holy assembly. You must do no regular work on that day. [36]You must present a burnt offering, very pleasing to the LORD. It will consist of one young bull, one ram, and seven one-year-old male lambs, all with no physical defects. [37]Each of these offerings must be accompanied by the prescribed grain offering and drink offering. [38]You must also sacrifice one male goat as a sin offering, in addition to the regular daily burnt offering with its accompanying grain offering and drink offering.

[39]"You must present these offerings to the LORD at your annual festivals. These are in addition to the sacrifices and offerings you present in connection with vows, or as freewill offerings, burnt offerings, grain offerings, drink offerings, or peace offerings."

[40]So Moses gave all of these instructions to the people of Israel, just as the LORD had commanded him.

## CHAPTER 30 LAWS CONCERNING VOWS.

Now Moses summoned the leaders of the tribes of Israel and told them, "This is what the LORD has commanded: [2]A man who makes a vow to the LORD or makes a pledge under oath must never break it. He must do exactly what he said he would do.

[3]"If a young woman makes a vow to the LORD or a pledge under oath while she is still living at her father's home, [4]and her father hears of the vow or pledge but says nothing, then all her vows and pledges will stand. [5]But if her father refuses to let her fulfill the vow or pledge on the day he hears of it, then all her vows and pledges will become invalid. The LORD will forgive her because her father would not let her fulfill them.

[6]"Now suppose a young woman takes a vow or makes an impulsive pledge and later marries. [7]If her husband learns of her vow or pledge and raises no objections on the day he hears of it, her vows and pledges will stand. [8]But if her husband refuses to accept her vow or impulsive pledge on the day he

hears of it, he nullifies her commitments, and the
LORD will forgive her. 9If, however, a woman is a
widow or is divorced, she must fulfill all her vows
and pledges no matter what.
10"Suppose a woman is married and living in her
husband's home when she makes a vow or pledge.
11If her husband hears of it and does nothing to stop
her, her vow or pledge will stand. 12But if her husband refuses to accept it on the day he hears of it, her
vow or pledge will be nullified, and the LORD will
forgive her. 13So her husband may either confirm or
nullify any vows or pledges she makes to deny herself. 14But if he says nothing on the day he hears of
it, then he is agreeing to it. 15If he waits more than a
day and then tries to nullify a vow or pledge, he will
suffer the consequences of her guilt."
16These are the regulations the LORD gave Moses
concerning relationships between a man and his
wife, and between a father and a young daughter
who still lives at home.

## CHAPTER 31

**THE WAR AGAINST MIDIAN.** Then the
LORD said to Moses, 2"Take vengeance on the Midianites for leading the Israelites into idolatry. After
that, you will die and join your ancestors."
3So Moses said to the people, "Choose some men
to fight the LORD's war of vengeance against Midian.
4From each tribe of Israel, send one thousand men
into battle." 5So they chose one thousand men from
each tribe of Israel, a total of twelve thousand men
armed for battle. 6Then Moses sent them out, a
thousand men from each tribe, and Phinehas son of
Eleazar the priest led them into battle. They carried
along the holy objects of the sanctuary and the
trumpets for sounding the charge. 7They attacked
Midian just as the LORD had commanded Moses,
and they killed all the men. 8All five of the Midianite
kings—Evi, Rekem, Zur, Hur, and Reba—died in the
battle. They also killed Balaam son of Beor with the
sword.
9Then the Israelite army captured the Midianite
women and children and seized their cattle and
flocks and all their wealth as plunder. 10They burned
all the towns and villages where the Midianites had
lived. 11After they had gathered the plunder and captives, both people and animals, 12they brought them
all to Moses and Eleazar the priest, and to the whole
community of Israel, which was camped on the
plains of Moab beside the Jordan River, across from
Jericho. 13Moses, Eleazar the priest, and all the leaders of the people went to meet them outside the
camp. 14But Moses was furious with all the military
commanders* who had returned from the battle.
15"Why have you let all the women live?" he demanded. 16"These are the very ones who followed
Balaam's advice and caused the people of Israel to
rebel against the LORD at Mount Peor. They are the
ones who caused the plague to strike the LORD's
people. 17Now kill all the boys and all the women
who have slept with a man. 18Only the young girls
who are virgins may live; you may keep them for
yourselves. 19And all of you who have killed anyone
or touched a dead body must stay outside the camp
for seven days. You must purify yourselves and your
captives on the third and seventh days. 20Also, purify
all your clothing and everything made of leather,
goat hair, or wood."
21Then Eleazar the priest said to the men who were
in the battle, "The LORD has given Moses this requirement of the law: 22Anything made of gold, silver, bronze, iron, tin, or lead—23that is, metals that
do not burn—must be passed through fire in order
to be made ceremonially pure. These metal objects
must then be further purified with the water of purification. But everything that burns must be purified
by the water alone. 24On the seventh day you must
wash your clothes and be purified. Then you may
return to the camp."
25And the LORD said to Moses, 26"You and Eleazar
the priest and the family leaders of each tribe are to
make a list of all the plunder taken in the battle,
including the people and animals. 27Then divide the
plunder into two parts, and give half to the men who
fought the battle and half to the rest of the people.
28But first give the LORD his share of the captives, cattle,
donkeys, sheep, and goats that belong to the army. Set
apart one out of every five hundred as the LORD's share.
29Give this share of their half to Eleazar the priest as an
offering to the LORD. 30Also take one of every fifty of the
captives, cattle, donkeys, sheep, and goats in the half
that belongs to the people of Israel. Give this share to
the Levites in charge of maintaining the LORD's Tabernacle." 31So Moses and Eleazar the priest did as the
LORD commanded Moses.
32The plunder remaining from the spoils that the
fighting men had taken totaled 675,000 sheep,
3372,000 cattle, 3461,000 donkeys, 35and 32,000
young girls.

### PARENTS ● ● ● • •

**30:3-8 Under Israelite law, parents could overrule their children's vows. This helped young people avoid making foolish promises or costly commitments. From this law comes an important principle for both parents and children. Young people still living at home should seek their parents' help when they make decisions. A parent's experience could save a child from a serious mistake. Parents, however, should exercise their authority with caution and grace. They should let children learn from their mistakes while protecting them from disaster.**

### GENEROSITY ● ● ● • •

**31:25-30 Moses told the Israelites to give a portion of the plunder to God. Another portion was to go to the people who remained behind. Similarly, the money we earn is not ours alone. Everything we possess comes directly or indirectly from God and ultimately belongs to him. We should return a portion to him and also share a portion with those in need.**

31:14 Hebrew *the commanders of thousands, and the commanders of hundreds;* also in 31:48, 52, 54.

# Ultimate Issues

## HOLY WAR?

"Some say that God has approved of their mob,/Esteeming their purposes alone—/Choosing sides with definite pride,/And taking their cause for his own,/Everybody loves a holy war./Draw the line and claim Divine assistance,/Slay the ones who show the most resistance—/Everybody loves a holy war"(from "Everybody Loves a Holy War" by Mark Heard). **S**hould a Christian ever go to war? Or should Christians be pacifists, refusing to take up arms no matter what the cause? **T**his is a tough issue for believers today. It wasn't much simpler for our forefathers. Though warfare has changed dramatically—from swords and spears to nuclear warheads and **STEALTH BOMBERS**—the core issue remains the same: When, if ever, is it right for God's people to go into *physical* battle? **L**et's examine God's orders for his chosen nation of Israel in the Old Testament. In Numbers 31, God tells his people to go to war with the Midianites and to utterly destroy them. After crushing the Midianite army, the Israelites took all the Midianite women and children as captives along with their possessions. God wasn't satisfied with that—through Moses, his appointed leader, God commanded the soldiers to kill all the women who had ever had sex with a man, and to kill all the boys. Only young female virgins were to be spared. Why did God require such terrible punishment for Israel's enemies? ***Aren't Christians supposed to be loving and kind peacemakers?*** **T**o answer this, we have to understand some basic differences between the Old Testament nation of Israel and God's people today. In the Old Testament, God was leading his nation to a physical Promised Land—Canaan. Along the way, for obvious reasons—who would voluntarily give up his or her home?—they were opposed by numerous other nations, like the Midianites. The problem wasn't simply that these other people were in the way. They also were guilty of practicing detestable idol worship. Among other things, these pagan nations held worship rituals involving sexual immorality, devotion to false gods, and even **child sacrifice.** No wonder God's anger burned against them, and he told Israel to cleanse Canaan of them. He didn't want their profane ways infecting his people. **F**or Christians today, however, the situation is different in some key aspects. We are being led to our Promised Land, but ours is in heaven rather than on earth. There are no pagan nations to be terminated; OUR WAR IS A SPIRITUAL ONE. **"F**or we are not fighting against people made of flesh and blood, but against the evil rulers and authorities of the unseen world, against those mighty powers of darkness who rule this world, and against wicked spirits in the heavenly realms" (Ephesians 6:12). God's people today are not determined by *nationality,* but by *spirituality.* Whereas God's blessings and promises before belonged to Abraham's physical descendants, they now belong to those who are spiritually **"grafted"** into Abraham's line (Romans 11:17). Therefore, when any nation goes to war today, its cause may be just, but it cannot be considered holy in the way Israel's wars were. Israel had God himself fighting battles for them, and he often gave Israel miraculous assistance and assurance of victory. No modern nation can make that claim—not the United States, Iran, England, Afghanistan, or even Israel. **S**o, should a Christian go to war? Unfortunately, you won't find the final answer here. We see in God's Word that God has, at times, told his people to go to war with other people; therefore, those who believe war is never right should reconsider. Still, not all wars are fought for the cause of righteousness—some would say almost none of them are. So many wars can't even be considered justified, much less holy.

36 So the half of the plunder given to the fighting
men totaled 337,500 sheep, 37 of which 675 were
the LORD's share; 38 36,000 cattle, of which 72 were
the LORD's share; 39 30,500 donkeys, of which
61 were the LORD's share; 40 16,000 young girls, of
whom 32 were the LORD's share. 41 Moses gave all
the LORD's share to Eleazar the priest, just as the
LORD had directed him.
42 The half of the plunder belonging to the
people of Israel, which Moses had separated from
the half belonging to the fighting men,
43 amounted to 337,500 sheep, 44 36,000 cattle,
45 30,500 donkeys, 46 and 16,000 young girls.
47 From the half-share given to the people, Moses
took one of every fifty prisoners and animals and
gave them to the Levites who maintained the
LORD's Tabernacle. All this was done just as the
LORD had commanded Moses.
48 Then all the military commanders came to
Moses 49 and said, "Sir, we have accounted for all
the men who went out to battle under our command; not one of us is missing! 50 So we are presenting the items of gold we captured as an
offering to the LORD from our share of the plunder—armbands, bracelets, rings, earrings, and
necklaces. This will make atonement for our lives
before the LORD."
51 So Moses and Eleazar the priest received the gold
from all the military commanders, all kinds of jewelry and crafted objects. 52 In all, the gold that the
commanders presented as a gift to the LORD weighed
about 420 pounds.* 53 All the fighting men had taken
some of the plunder for themselves. 54 So Moses and
Eleazar the priest accepted the gifts from the military
commanders and brought the gold to the Tabernacle* as a reminder to the LORD that the people of
Israel belong to him.

## CHAPTER 32 **SOME TRIBES GET THEIR LAND.**

1 Now
the tribes of Reuben and Gad owned vast numbers
of livestock. So when they saw that the lands of
Jazer and Gilead were ideally suited for their flocks
and herds, 2 they came to Moses, Eleazar the priest,
and the other leaders of the people. They said,
3 "Ataroth, Dibon, Jazer, Nimrah, Heshbon, Elealeh, Sebam, Nebo, and Beon—4 the LORD has conquered this whole area for the people of Israel. It is
ideally suited for all our flocks and herds. 5 If we
have found favor with you, please let us have this
land as our property instead of giving us land
across the Jordan River."
6 "Do you mean you want to stay back here while
your brothers go across and do all the fighting?"
Moses asked the Reubenites and Gadites. 7 "Are you
trying to discourage the rest of the people of Israel
from going across to the land the LORD has given
them? 8 This is what your ancestors did when I sent
them from Kadesh-barnea to explore the land. 9 After
they went up to the valley of Eshcol and scouted the
land, they discouraged the people of Israel from
entering the land the LORD was giving them. 10 Then
the LORD was furious with them, and he vowed, 11 'Of
all those I rescued from Egypt, no one who is twenty
years old or older will ever see the land I solemnly
promised to Abraham, Isaac, and Jacob, for they
have not obeyed me completely. 12 The only exceptions are Caleb son of Jephunneh the Kenizzite and
Joshua son of Nun, for they have wholeheartedly
followed the LORD.'
13 "The LORD was furious with Israel and made
them wander in the wilderness for forty years until
the whole generation that sinned against him had
died. 14 But here you are, a brood of sinners, doing
exactly the same thing! You are making the LORD
even angrier with Israel. 15 If you turn away from
him like this and he abandons them again in the

31:52 Hebrew *16,750 shekels* [191 kilograms]. 31:54 Hebrew *Tent of Meeting.*

**YOU** may be sure that **YOUR SIN** will find you out.

NUMBERS 32:23

### ASSUMING

32:1-19 **Three tribes (Reuben, Gad, and the half-tribe of Manasseh) wanted to live east of the Jordan River on land they had already conquered. Moses immediately assumed they had selfish motives and were trying to avoid helping the others fight for the land across the river. But Moses jumped to the wrong conclusion. In dealing with people, we must find out all the facts before making up our mind. We shouldn't automatically assume that their motives are wrong, even if their plans sound suspicious.**

wilderness, you will be responsible for destroying this entire nation!"

[16]But they responded to Moses, "We simply want to build sheepfolds for our flocks and fortified cities for our wives and children. [17]Then we will arm ourselves and lead our fellow Israelites into battle until we have brought them safely to their inheritance. Meanwhile, our families will stay in the fortified cities we build here, so they will be safe from any attacks by the local people. [18]We will not return to our homes until all the people of Israel have received their inheritance of land. [19]But we do not want any of the land on the other side of the Jordan. We would rather live here on the east side where we have received our inheritance."

[20]Then Moses said, "If you keep your word and arm yourselves for the LORD's battles, [21]and if your troops cross the Jordan until the LORD has driven out his enemies, [22]then you may return when the land is finally subdued before the LORD. You will have discharged your duty to the LORD and to the rest of the people of Israel. And the land on the east side of the Jordan will be your inheritance from the LORD. [23]But if you fail to keep your word, then you will have sinned against the LORD, and you may be sure that your sin will find you out. [24]Go ahead and build towns for your families and sheepfolds for your flocks, but do everything you have said."

[25]Then the people of Gad and Reuben replied, "We are your servants and will follow your instructions exactly. [26]Our children, wives, flocks, and cattle will stay here in the towns of Gilead. [27]But, sir, all who are able to bear arms will cross over to fight for the LORD, just as you have said."

[28]So Moses gave orders to Eleazar, Joshua, and the tribal leaders of Israel. [29]He said, "If all the men of Gad and Reuben who are able to fight the LORD's battles cross the Jordan with you, then when the land is conquered, you must give them the land of Gilead as their property. [30]But if they refuse to cross over and march ahead of you, then they must accept land with the rest of you in the land of Canaan."

[31]The tribes of Gad and Reuben said again, "Sir, we will do as the LORD has commanded! [32]We will cross the Jordan into Canaan fully armed to fight for the LORD, but our inheritance of land will be here on this side of the Jordan."

[33]So Moses assigned to the tribes of Gad, Reuben, and half the tribe of Manasseh son of Joseph the territory of King Sihon of the Amorites and the land of King Og of Bashan—the whole land with its towns and surrounding lands.

[34]The people of Gad built the towns of Dibon, Ataroth, Aroer, [35]Atroth-shophan, Jazer, Jogbehah, [36]Beth-nimrah, and Beth-haran. These were all fortified cities with sheepfolds for their flocks.

[37]The people of Reuben built the towns of Heshbon, Elealeh, Kiriathaim, [38]Nebo, Baal-meon, and Sibmah. They changed the names of some of the towns they conquered and rebuilt.

[39]Then the descendants of Makir of the tribe of Manasseh went to Gilead and conquered it, and they drove out the Amorites, who were living there. [40]So Moses gave Gilead to the Makirites, descendants of Manasseh, and they lived there. [41]The people of Jair, another clan of the tribe of Manasseh, captured many of the towns in Gilead and changed the name of that region to the Towns of Jair.* [42]Meanwhile, a man named Nobah captured the town of Kenath and its surrounding villages, and he renamed that area Nobah after himself.

## CHAPTER 33

**THE PROMISED LAND.** This is the itinerary the Israelites followed as they marched out of Egypt under the leadership of Moses and Aaron. [2]At the LORD's direction, Moses kept a written record of their progress. These are the stages of their march, identified by the different places they stopped along the way.

### RECORD ● ● • • •

**33:2 Moses recorded the Israelites' journeys as God instructed him, providing a written record of their spiritual as well as geographic progress. Have you made spiritual progress lately? Recording your thoughts about God and lessons you have learned over a period of time can be a valuable aid to spiritual growth. A record of your spiritual pilgrimage will let you check up on your progress and avoid repeating past mistakes.**

[3]They set out from the city of Rameses on the morning after the first Passover celebration in early spring.* The people of Israel left defiantly, in full view of all the Egyptians. [4]Meanwhile, the Egyptians were burying all their firstborn sons, whom the LORD had killed the night before. The LORD had defeated the gods of Egypt that night with great acts of judgment!

[5]After leaving Rameses, the Israelites set up camp at Succoth.

[6]Then they left Succoth and camped at Etham on the edge of the wilderness.

[7]They left Etham and turned back toward Pi-hahiroth, opposite Baal-zephon, and camped near Migdol.

[8]They left Pi-hahiroth and crossed the Red Sea* into the wilderness beyond. Then they traveled for three days into the Etham wilderness and camped at Marah.

[9]They left Marah and camped at Elim, where there are twelve springs of water and seventy palm trees.

[10]They left Elim and camped beside the Red Sea.*

[11]They left the Red Sea and camped in the Sin* Desert.

32:41 Hebrew *Havvoth-jair.* 33:3 Hebrew *on the fifteenth day of the first month.* This day of the Hebrew lunar calendar occurs in late March or early April. 33:8 Hebrew *the sea.* 33:10 Hebrew *sea of reeds;* also in 33:11. 33:11 Not to be confused with the English word *sin.*

12 They left the Sin Desert and camped at
Dophkah.
13 They left Dophkah and camped at Alush.
14 They left Alush and camped at Rephidim,
where there was no water for the people to
drink.
15 They left Rephidim and camped in the
wilderness of Sinai.
16 They left the wilderness of Sinai and
camped at Kibroth-hattaavah.
17 They left Kibroth-hattaavah and camped at
Hazeroth.
18 They left Hazeroth and camped at Rithmah.
19 They left Rithmah and camped at
Rimmon-perez.
20 They left Rimmon-perez and camped at
Libnah.
21 They left Libnah and camped at Rissah.
22 They left Rissah and camped at Kehelathah.
23 They left Kehelathah and camped at Mount
Shepher.
24 They left Mount Shepher and camped at
Haradah.
25 They left Haradah and camped at
Makheloth.
26 They left Makheloth and camped at Tahath.
27 They left Tahath and camped at Terah.
28 They left Terah and camped at Mithcah.
29 They left Mithcah and camped at
Hashmonah.
30 They left Hashmonah and camped at
Moseroth.
31 They left Moseroth and camped at
Bene-jaakan.
32 They left Bene-jaakan and camped at
Hor-haggidgad.
33 They left Hor-haggidgad and camped at
Jotbathah.
34 They left Jotbathah and camped at Abronah.
35 They left Abronah and camped at
Ezion-geber.
36 They left Ezion-geber and camped at Kadesh
in the wilderness of Zin.
37 They left Kadesh and camped at Mount Hor,
at the border of Edom. 38 While they were at the
foot of Mount Hor, Aaron the priest was
directed by the LORD to go up the mountain,
and there he died. This happened on a day in
midsummer,* during the fortieth year after
Israel's departure from Egypt. 39 Aaron was 123
years old when he died there on Mount Hor.
40 It was then that the Canaanite king of Arad,
who lived in the Negev in the land of Canaan,
heard that the people of Israel were approaching
his land.
41 Meanwhile, the Israelites left Mount Hor
and camped at Zalmonah.
42 Then they left Zalmonah and camped at
Punon.
43 They left Punon and camped at Oboth.
44 They left Oboth and camped at Iye-abarim
on the border of Moab.
45 They left Iye-abarim* and camped at
Dibon-gad.
46 They left Dibon-gad and camped at
Almon-diblathaim.
47 They left Almon-diblathaim and camped in
the mountains east of the river,* near Mount
Nebo.
48 They left the mountains east of the river and
camped on the plains of Moab beside the
Jordan River, across from Jericho. 49 Along the
Jordan River they camped from Beth-jeshimoth
as far as Abel-shittim on the plains of Moab.

50 While they were camped near the Jordan River
on the plains of Moab opposite Jericho, the LORD
said to Moses, 51 "Speak to the Israelites and tell
them: 'When you cross the Jordan River into the
land of Canaan, 52 you must drive out all the people
living there. You must destroy all their carved and
molten images and demolish all their pagan shrines.
53 Take possession of the land and settle in it, because
I have given it to you to occupy. 54 You must distribute
the land among the clans by sacred lot and in proportion to their size. A larger inheritance of land will
be allotted to each of the larger clans, and a smaller
inheritance will be allotted to each of the smaller
clans. The decision of the sacred lot is final. In this
way, the land will be divided among your ancestral
tribes. 55 But if you fail to drive out the people who
live in the land, those who remain will be like splin-
ters in your eyes and thorns in your sides. They will
harass you in the land where you live. 56 And I will do
to you what I had planned to do to them.'"

CHAPTER **34** **BOUNDARIES OF THE LAND.** Then the
LORD said to Moses, 2 "Give these instructions to the
Israelites: When you come into the land of Canaan,
which I am giving you as your special possession,
these will be the boundaries. 3 The southern portion
of your country will extend from the wilderness of
Zin, along the edge of Edom. The southern boundary will begin on the east at the Dead Sea.* 4 It will
then run south past Scorpion Pass* in the direction
of Zin. Its southernmost point will be Kadesh-
barnea, from which it will go to Hazar-addar, and on
to Azmon. 5 From Azmon the boundary will turn
toward the brook of Egypt and end at the Mediterranean Sea.*

6 "Your western boundary will be the coastline of
the Mediterranean Sea.

7 "Your northern boundary will begin at the
Mediterranean Sea and run eastward to Mount
Hor, 8 then to Lebo-hamath, and on through Zedad

33:38 Hebrew *on the first day of the fifth month.* This day of the Hebrew lunar calendar occurs in July or early August. 33:45 As in 33:44; Hebrew reads *Iyim,* another name for Iye-abarim. 33:47 Hebrew *the mountains of Abarim;* also in 33:48. 34:3 Hebrew *Salt Sea;* also in 34:12. 34:4 Hebrew *the ascent of Akrabbim.* 34:5 Hebrew *the sea;* also in 34:6, 7.

[9]and Ziphron to Hazar-enan. This will be your northern boundary.

[10]"The eastern boundary will start at Hazar-enan and run south to Shepham, [11]then down to Riblah on the east side of Ain. From there the boundary will run down along the eastern edge of the Sea of Galilee,* [12]and then along the Jordan River to the Dead Sea. These are the boundaries of your land."

[13]Then Moses told the Israelites, "This is the territory you are to divide among yourselves by sacred lot. The LORD commands that the land be divided up among the nine and a half remaining tribes. [14]The families of the tribes of Reuben, Gad, and half the tribe of Manasseh have already received their inheritance of land [15]on the east side of the Jordan River, across from Jericho."

[16]And the LORD said to Moses, [17]"These are the men who are to divide the land among the people: Eleazar the priest and Joshua son of Nun. [18]Also enlist one leader from each tribe to help them with the task. [19]These are the tribes and the names of the leaders:

| *Tribe* | *Leader* |
|---|---|
| Judah | Caleb son of Jephunneh |
| [20] Simeon | Shemuel son of Ammihud |
| [21] Benjamin | Elidad son of Kislon |
| [22] Dan | Bukki son of Jogli |
| [23] Manasseh son of Joseph | Hanniel son of Ephod |
| [24] Ephraim son of Joseph | Kemuel son of Shiphtan |
| [25] Zebulun | Elizaphan son of Parnach |
| [26] Issachar | Paltiel son of Azzan |
| [27] Asher | Ahihud son of Shelomi |
| [28] Naphtali | Pedahel son of Ammihud |

[29]These are the men the LORD has appointed to oversee the dividing of the land of Canaan among the Israelites."

## DO YOUR JOB ● ● • • •

34:16-29 **In God's plan for settling the land, he (1) explained what to do, (2) communicated this clearly to Moses, and (3) assigned specific people to oversee the apportionment of the land. No plan is complete until each job is assigned and everyone understands his or her responsibilities. When you have a job to do, determine what must be done, give clear instructions, and put specific people in charge of each part.**

CHAPTER **35** **TOWNS FOR THE LEVITES.** While Israel was camped beside the Jordan on the plains of Moab, across from Jericho, the LORD said to Moses, [2]"Instruct the people of Israel to give to the Levites from their property certain towns to live in, along with the surrounding pasturelands. [3]These towns will be their homes, and the surrounding lands will provide pasture for their cattle, flocks, and other livestock. [4]The pastureland assigned to the Levites around these towns will extend 1,500 feet* from the town walls in every direction. [5]Measure off 3,000 feet* outside the

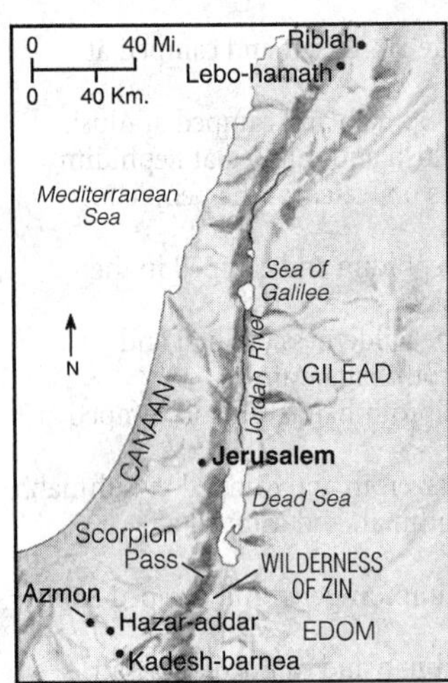


**THE BORDERS OF THE PROMISED LAND**
The borders of the Promised Land stretched from the wilderness of Zin and Kadesh-barnea in the south to Lebo-hamath and Riblah in the north, and from the Mediterranean seacoast on the west to the Jordan River on the east. The land of Gilead was also included.

town walls in every direction—east, south, west, north—with the town at the center. This area will serve as the larger pastureland for the towns.

[6]"You must give the Levites six cities of refuge, where a person who has accidentally killed someone can flee for safety. In addition, give them forty-two other towns. [7]In all, forty-eight towns with the surrounding pastureland will be given to the Levites. [8]These towns will come from the property of the people of Israel. The larger tribes will give more towns to the Levites, while the smaller tribes will give fewer. Each tribe will give in proportion to its inheritance."

[9]And the LORD said to Moses, [10]"Say this to the people of Israel: 'When you cross the Jordan into the land of Canaan, [11]designate cities of refuge for people to flee to if they have killed someone accidentally. [12]These cities will be places of protection from a dead person's relatives who want to avenge the death. The slayer must not be killed before being tried by the community. [13]Designate six cities of refuge for yourselves, [14]three on the east side of the Jordan River and three on the west in the land of Canaan. [15]These cities are for the protection of Israelites, resident foreigners, and traveling merchants. Anyone who accidentally kills someone may flee there for safety.

[16]"'But if someone strikes and kills another per-

## JUSTICE ● ● • • •

35:9-28 **If anyone died because of violence, murder was assumed, but the murder suspect was not automatically considered guilty. The people were to be intolerant of the sin, yet impartial to the accused so that he or she could have a fair trial. The cities of refuge represented God's concern for justice in a culture that did not always protect the innocent. It is unjust both to overlook wrongdoing and to jump to conclusions about guilt. When someone is accused of wrongdoing, stand up for justice, protect those not yet proven guilty, and listen carefully to all sides of the story.**

34:11 Hebrew *sea of Kinnereth.* 35:4 Hebrew *1,000 cubits* [450 meters]. 35:5 Hebrew *2,000 cubits* [900 meters].

son with a piece of iron, it must be presumed to be murder, and the murderer must be executed. 17Or if someone strikes and kills another person with a large stone, it is murder, and the murderer must be executed. 18The same is true if someone strikes and kills another person with a wooden weapon. It must be presumed to be murder, and the murderer must be executed. 19The victim's nearest relative is responsible for putting the murderer to death. When they meet, the avenger must execute the murderer. 20So if in premeditated hostility someone pushes another person or throws a dangerous object and the person dies, it is murder. 21Or if someone angrily hits another person with a fist and the person dies, it is murder. In such cases, the victim's nearest relative must execute the murderer when they meet.

22"'But suppose someone pushes another person without premeditated hostility, or throws something that unintentionally hits another person, 23or accidentally drops a stone on someone, though they were not enemies, and the person dies. 24If this should happen, the assembly must follow these regulations in making a judgment between the slayer and the avenger, the victim's nearest relative. 25They must protect the slayer from the avenger, and they must send the slayer back to live in a city of refuge until the death of the high priest.

26"'But if the slayer leaves the city of refuge, 27and the victim's nearest relative finds him outside the city limits and kills him, it will not be considered murder. 28The slayer should have stayed inside the city of refuge until the death of the high priest. But after the death of the high priest, the slayer may return to his own property. 29These are permanent laws for you to observe from generation to generation, wherever you may live.

30"'All murderers must be executed, but only if there is more than one witness. No one may be put to death on the testimony of only one witness. 31Also, you must never accept a ransom payment for the life of someone judged guilty of murder and subject to execution; murderers must always be put to death. 32And never accept a ransom payment from someone who has fled to a city of refuge, allowing the slayer to return to his property before the death of the high priest. 33This will ensure that the land where you live will not be polluted, for murder pollutes the land. And no atonement can be made for murder except by the execution of the murderer. 34You must not defile the land where you are going to live, for I live there myself. I am the LORD, who lives among the people of Israel.'"

### BITTERNESS ● ● • • •

35:33 **Murderers were to be executed because they corrupted the land. But Jesus startles us by saying that even being angry at someone can be a sin like murder (Matthew 5:21-22). Murder and anger stem from the same root. While one seems a lesser sin, it will often lead to more sin. Unchecked bitterness and anger will ultimately destroy us. We need to deal with these strong emotions in an appropriate way, before they fester and corrupt our life.**

## CHAPTER 36 EACH TRIBE'S LAND TO REMAIN SECURE.

Then the heads of the clan of Gilead—descendants of Makir, son of Manasseh, son of Joseph—came to Moses and the family leaders of Israel with a petition. 2They said, "Sir, the LORD instructed you to divide the land by sacred lot among the people of Israel. You were told by the LORD to give the inheritance of our brother Zelophehad to his daughters. 3But if any of them marries a man from another tribe, their inheritance of land will go with them to the tribe into which they marry. In this way, the total area of our tribal land will be reduced. 4Then when the Year of Jubilee comes, their inheritance of land will be added to that of the new tribe, causing it to be lost forever to our ancestral tribe."

5So Moses gave the Israelites this command from the LORD: "The men of the tribe of Joseph are right. 6This is what the LORD commands concerning the daughters of Zelophehad: Let them marry anyone they like, as long as it is within their own ancestral tribe. 7None of the inherited land may pass from tribe to tribe, for the inheritance of every tribe must remain fixed as it was first allotted. 8The daughters throughout the tribes of Israel who are in line to inherit property must marry within their tribe, so that all the Israelites will keep their ancestral property. 9No inheritance may pass from one tribe to another; each tribe of Israel must hold on to its allotted inheritance of land."

10The daughters of Zelophehad did as the LORD commanded Moses. 11Mahlah, Tirzah, Hoglah, Milcah, and Noah all married cousins on their father's side. 12They married into the clans of Manasseh son of Joseph. Thus, their inheritance of land remained within their ancestral tribe.

13These are the commands and regulations that the LORD gave to the people of Israel through Moses while they were camped on the plains of Moab beside the Jordan River, across from Jericho.

# MEGA themes

**CENSUS** Moses counted the Israelites twice. The first census organized the people into marching units for better defense. The second census prepared them to conquer the country east of the Jordan.

People have to be organized, trained, and led to be effective in making a difference in their world. Before beginning great tasks, it is always wise to count the cost that lies ahead. Preparation for being effective for God in this world also includes removing any barriers in our relationships with others so that we can work with his people to accomplish his will.

1. Musical groups are examples of how people work together to produce something greater than they could do as individuals. What other things require teamwork in order for people to reach their goals or produce the desired results?
2. In what ways is a church an example of teamwork?
3. Think of your church or perhaps your youth group. Consider these questions:
   - What can you accomplish with God through working together that could not be done if you did not have teamwork?
   - What actions or attitudes cause this group of people to fail to be a team?
   - What are some of the actions or attitudes that contribute to this group of people being successful as a team?
   - What are some specific ways you can contribute to the success of this group?
   - Finish this sentence: I am important to this group because__________.

**REBELLION** At Kadesh 12 spies were sent out into the land of Canaan to see what the fortifications of the enemies looked like. When the spies returned, 10 said that they should give up and go back to Egypt. As a result, the people refused to go into the land. Thus, the people rebelled against the will of God. The decision to rebel was not a sudden change of attitude. It came after a long period of complaining about Moses and God.

Rebellion against God is always serious. It is not something to take lightly because God's punishment for sin is often very severe. Usually, rebellion is not an abrupt, radical departure from God as much as it is a result of a long-term drifting, often characterized by griping and criticizing.

1. What do your parents most often criticize or gripe about?
2. What do your friends most often criticize or gripe about?
3. When did you complain to God about something or someone? How did you feel before you complained? Afterwards?
4. Describe a time in your life when you felt unhappy with how life was going for you and wondered if God really was taking care of you. How did you work through your feelings?
5. What is an appropriate response when you are feeling frustrated or angry because you do not understand why God is allowing your life to be the way it is? Why is it important to avoid griping or criticizing God? How can you share your feelings without becoming rebellious?

**WANDERING** Because they rebelled, the Israelites wandered 40 years in the wilderness. This shows how strongly God feels about sinful rebellion. During this time, God trained a new generation to follow him while those who still had wrong attitudes died.

God judges sin not just because he does not like it, but because he is holy and cannot tolerate sinfulness. The Israelites serve as a negative example of how God punishes sin, and a positive example of how he raises up a younger generation of people who will obey him.

1. What happens in the lives of Christians who drift away from God?
2. If you saw a friend rebelling against God, what would you tell him or her as a warning about the consequences of rebellion? What if that friend replied, "It's OK. God will forgive me"?
3. What type of people do you think God is looking for in your generation? How can you prepare yourself to avoid drifting and, instead, become one of God's leaders?

**CANAAN** Canaan was the Promised Land. It was the land God promised to Abraham, Isaac, and Jacob—the land of the covenant. Canaan was to be the dwelling place of God's people, those set apart for true spiritual worship.

Because he is holy, God punishes sin severely. However, because he is Lord, God offers grace for forgiveness of sins. Just as God's holy law and loving grace led Israel into the Promised Land, God wants to lead us into his purpose and destiny for our life.

1. List some of the things you learned about God as you read about him leading his people into Canaan.
2. Based on this knowledge, describe the kind of relationship he wants to have with you as you live out your life.
3. What are some of your dreams for the future? How should God be a part of those dreams?
4. How would you complete these thoughts for your own life: (a) God's purpose in my life is ________. (b) I can trust God with this purpose because ________.

**1805 B.C.**
**Joseph dies**

**SLAVERY IN EGYPT**

**1446**
**Exodus from Egypt**

**1445**
**Ten Commandments given**

**WILDERNESS WANDERINGS**

**1406**
**Moses' death;**
**Israelites enter Canaan**

**1375**
**Judges begin to rule**

**1050**
**United kingdom under Saul**

Do you have a "memories" drawer, a place where you keep various reminders from your past? Maybe you have a wall, or even a box filled with mementos of happy occasions. Some people save the petals off prom flowers. Others keep ticket stubs from movies, ball games, or concerts. Some store especially meaningful letters or old pictures. ■ If you are like most people, these treasures become even more meaningful to you when you are going through tough times: when you're sad or lonely or scared about the future. There is something comforting in remembering the good times you've had. Your keepsakes help you believe that everything is going to be OK. ■ The book of Deuteronomy is a book of "memories." God had made a covenant, or promise, with the slaves who first came out of Egypt, pledging to take them into the Promised Land. But the Israelites refused to obey or trust God. So he left them to wander in the wilderness until they died. ■ But a new generation had grown up, so God, through Moses, reminded them of the covenant. Moses recounted to the people the mighty acts God had done for Israel. Then he let them know that, based on the past, they must trust, obey, and love God as they advanced on their new homeland. Only such an attitude would enable them to conquer the Promised Land. ■ As you read Deuteronomy, let God remind you of the ways he has helped you in the past. Then, when you are fearful, you will trust yourself to him.

## STATS

PURPOSE: To remind the people of what God has done and encourage them to rededicate their lives to him

AUTHOR: Moses (except for the final summary which was probably written after Moses' death by Joshua)

TO WHOM WRITTEN: Israel (the new generation entering the Promised Land)

DATE WRITTEN: About 1407/6 B.C.

SETTING: The east side of the Jordan River, in view of the Promised Land

KEY PEOPLE: Moses, Joshua

KEY PLACE: The valley of Arabah in Moab, east of the Jordan River

CHAPTER **1** **MOSES TALKS TO THE PEOPLE.** This book records the words that Moses spoke to all the people of Israel while they were in the wilderness east of the Jordan River. They were camped in the Jordan Valley* near Suph, between Paran on one side and Tophel, Laban, Hazeroth, and Di-zahab on the other. [2]Normally it takes only eleven days to travel from Mount Sinai* to Kadesh-barnea, going by way of Mount Seir. [3]But forty years after the Israelites left Mount Sinai, on a day in midwinter,* Moses gave these speeches to the Israelites, telling them everything the LORD had commanded him to say. [4]This was after he had defeated King Sihon of the Amorites, who had ruled in Heshbon, and King Og of Bashan, who had ruled in Ashtaroth and Edrei.

[5]So Moses addressed the people of Israel while they were in the land of Moab east of the Jordan River. He began to explain the law as follows: [6]"When we were at Mount Sinai, the LORD our God said to us, 'You have stayed at this mountain long enough. [7]It is time to break camp and move on. Go to the hill country of the Amorites and to all the neighboring regions—the Jordan Valley, the hill country, the western foothills,* the Negev, and the coastal plain. Go to the land of the Canaanites and to Lebanon, and all the way to the great Euphrates River. [8]I am giving all this land to you! Go in and occupy it, for it is the land the LORD swore to give to your ancestors Abraham, Isaac, and Jacob, and to all their descendants.'

[9]"At that time I told you, 'You are too great a burden for me to carry all by myself. [10]The LORD your God has made you as numerous as the stars! [11]And may the LORD, the God of your ancestors, multiply you a thousand times more and bless you as he promised! [12]But how can I settle all your quarrels and problems by myself? [13]Choose some men from each tribe who have wisdom, understanding, and a good reputation, and I will appoint them as your leaders.'

## LEADERSHIP ● ● ● • ·

1:13-18 **Moses identified some of the inner qualities of good leaders: (1) wisdom, (2) understanding, (3) impartiality, and (4) the ability to recognize their limitations. These characteristics differ greatly from the ones that often help elect leaders today: good looks, wealth, popularity, willingness to do anything to get to the top. The qualities Moses identified should be evident in our life as we lead, and we should look for them in the lives of those we elect to positions of leadership.**

1:1 Hebrew *the Arabah;* also in 1:7. 1:2 Hebrew *Horeb,* another name for Sinai; also in 1:6, 19. 1:3 Hebrew *on the first day of the eleventh month.* This day of the Hebrew lunar calendar occurs in January or early February. 1:7 Hebrew *the Shephelah.*

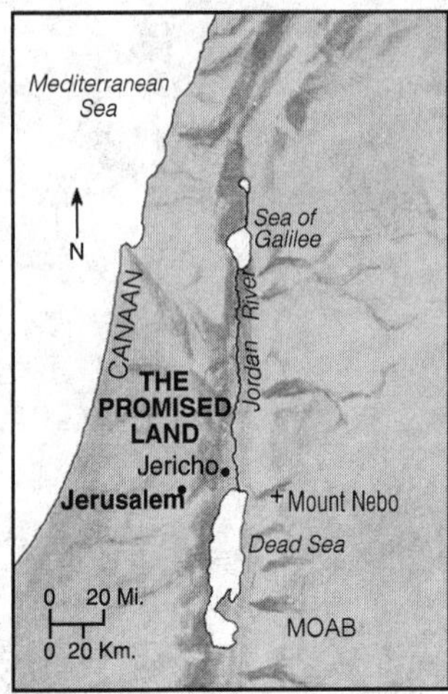


**EVENTS IN DEUTERONOMY**
The book of Deuteronomy opens with Israel camped east of the Jordan River in the Jordan Valley in the land of Moab. Just before the people crossed the river into the Promised Land, Moses delivered an inspirational speech indicating how they were to live.

14"You agreed that my plan was a good one. 15So I took the wise and respected men you had selected from your tribes and appointed them to serve as judges and officials over you. Some were responsible for a thousand people, some for a hundred, some for fifty, and some for ten. 16I instructed the judges, 'You must be perfectly fair at all times, not only to fellow Israelites, but also to the foreigners living among you. 17When you make decisions, never favor those who are rich; be fair to lowly and great alike. Don't be afraid of how they will react, for you are judging in the place of God. Bring me any cases that are too difficult for you, and I will handle them.' 18And at that time I gave you instructions about everything you were to do.

19"Then, just as the LORD our God directed us, we left Mount Sinai and traveled through the great and terrifying wilderness, which you yourselves saw, and headed toward the hill country of the Amorites. When we arrived at Kadesh-barnea, 20I said to you, 'You have now reached the land that the LORD our God is giving us. 21Look! He has placed it in front of you. Go and occupy it as the LORD, the God of your ancestors, has promised you. Don't be afraid! Don't be discouraged!'

22"But you responded, 'First, let's send out scouts to explore the land for us. They will advise us on the best route to take and decide which towns we should capture.' 23This seemed like a good idea to me, so I chose twelve scouts, one from each of your tribes. 24They crossed into the hills and came to the valley of Eshcol and explored it. 25They picked some of its fruit and brought it back to us. And they reported that the land the LORD our God had given us was indeed a good land.

26"But you rebelled against the command of the LORD your God and refused to go in. 27You murmured and complained in your tents and said, 'The LORD must hate us, bringing us here from Egypt to be slaughtered by these Amorites. 28How can we go on? Our scouts have demoralized us with their report. They say that the people of the land are taller and more powerful than we are, and that the walls of their towns rise high into the sky! They have even seen giants there—the descendants of Anak!'

29"But I said to you, 'Don't be afraid! 30The LORD your God is going before you. He will fight for you, just as you saw him do in Egypt. 31And you saw how the LORD your God cared for you again and again here in the wilderness, just as a father cares for his child. Now he has brought you to this place.' 32But even after all he did, you refused to trust the LORD your God, 33who goes before you looking for the best places to camp, guiding you by a pillar of fire at night and a pillar of cloud by day.

34"When the LORD heard your complaining, he became very angry. So he solemnly swore, 35'Not one of you from this entire wicked generation will live to see the good land I swore to give your ancestors, 36except Caleb son of Jephunneh. He will see this land because he has followed the LORD completely. I will give to him and his descendants some of the land he walked over during his scouting mission.'

37"And the LORD was also angry with me because of you. He said to me, 'You will never enter the Promised Land! 38Instead, your assistant, Joshua son of Nun, will lead the people into the land. Encourage him as he prepares to enter it. 39I will give the land to your innocent children. You were afraid they would be captured, but they will be the ones who occupy it. 40As for you, turn around now and go on back through the wilderness toward the Red Sea.*'

41"Then you confessed, 'We have sinned against the LORD! We will go into the land and fight for it, as the LORD our God has told us.' So your men strapped on their weapons, thinking it would be easy to conquer the hill country.

42"But the LORD said to me, 'Tell them not to attack, for I will not go with them. If they do, they will be crushed by their enemies.' 43This is what I told you, but you would not listen. Instead, you again rebelled against the LORD's command and arrogantly went into the hill country to fight. 44But the Amorites who lived there came out against you like a swarm of bees. They chased and battered you all the way from Seir to Hormah. 45Then you returned and wept before the LORD, but he refused to listen. 46So you stayed there at Kadesh for a long time.

## OBSTACLES ● ● • • •

**3:1-3 The Israelites faced a big problem: the well-trained army of Og, king of Bashan. The Israelites hardly stood a chance. But they won because God fought for them. God can help his people regardless of the problems they face. No matter how insurmountable the obstacles may seem, remember that God is in control, and he will keep his promises.**

1:40 Hebrew *sea of reeds.*

CHAPTER **2** **STUCK IN THE WILDERNESS.** "Then we turned around and set out across the wilderness toward the Red Sea,* just as the LORD had instructed me, and we wandered around Mount Seir for a long time. [2]Then at last the LORD said to me, [3]'You have been wandering around in this hill country long enough; turn northward. [4]Give these orders to the people: "You will be passing through the country belonging to your relatives the Edomites, the descendants of Esau, who live in Seir. The Edomites will feel threatened, so be careful. [5]Don't bother them, for I have given them all the hill country around Mount Seir as their property, and I will not give you any of their land. [6]Pay them for whatever food or water you use. [7]The LORD your God has blessed everything you have done and has watched your every step through this great wilderness. During these forty years, the LORD your God has been with you and provided for your every need so that you lacked nothing."' [8]So we went past our relatives, the descendants of Esau, who live in Seir, and avoided the road through the Arabah Valley that comes up from Elath and Ezion-geber.

"Then as we traveled northward along the desert route through Moab, [9]the LORD warned us, 'Do not bother the Moabites, the descendants of Lot, or start a war with them. I have given them Ar as their property, and I will not give you any of their land.'"

[10](A numerous and powerful race of giants called the Emites had once lived in the area of Ar. They were as tall as the Anakites, another race of giants. [11]Both the Emites and the Anakites are often referred to as the Rephaites, but the Moabites called them Emites. [12]In earlier times the Horites had lived at Mount Seir, but they were driven out and displaced by the descendants of Esau. In a similar way the peoples in Canaan were driven from the land that the LORD had assigned to Israel.)

[13]Moses continued, "Then the LORD told us to cross Zered Brook, and we did. [14]So thirty-eight years passed from the time we first arrived at Kadesh-barnea until we finally crossed Zered Brook! For the LORD had vowed that this could not happen until all the men old enough to fight in battle had died in the wilderness. [15]The LORD had lifted his hand against them until all of them had finally died.

[16]"When all the men of fighting age had died, [17]the LORD said to me, [18]'Today you will cross the border of Moab at Ar [19]and enter the land of Ammon. But do not bother the Ammonites, the descendants of Lot, or start a war with them. I have given the land of Ammon to them as their property, and I will not give you any of their land.'"

[20](That area, too, was once considered the land of the Rephaites, though the Ammonites referred to them as Zamzummites. [21]They were a numerous and powerful race, as tall as the Anakites. But the LORD destroyed them so the Ammonites could occupy their land. [22]He had similarly helped the descendants of Esau at Mount Seir, for he destroyed the Horites so they could settle there in their place. The descendants of Esau live there to this day. [23]A similar thing happened when the Caphtorites from Crete* invaded and destroyed the Avvites, who had lived in villages in the area of Gaza.)

[24]Moses continued, "Then the LORD said, 'Now cross the Arnon Gorge! Look, I will help you defeat Sihon the Amorite, king of Heshbon, and I will give you his land. Attack him and begin to occupy the land. [25]Beginning today I will make all people throughout the earth terrified of you. When they hear reports about you, they will tremble with dread and fear.'

[26]"Then from the wilderness of Kedemoth I sent ambassadors to King Sihon of Heshbon with this proposal of peace: [27]'Let us pass through your land. We will stay on the main road and won't turn off into the fields on either side. [28]We will pay for every bite of food we eat and all the water we drink. All we want is permission to pass through your land. [29]The descendants of Esau at Mount Seir allowed us to go through their country, and so did the Moabites, who live in Ar. Let us pass through until we cross the Jordan into the land the LORD our God has given us.' [30]But King Sihon refused to allow you to pass through, because the LORD your God made Sihon stubborn and defiant so he could help you defeat them, as he has now done.

[31]"Then the LORD said to me, 'Look, I have begun to hand King Sihon and his land over to you. Begin now to conquer and occupy his land.' [32]Then King Sihon declared war on us and mobilized his forces at Jahaz. [33]But the LORD our God handed him over to us, and we crushed him, his sons, and all his people. [34]We conquered all his towns and completely destroyed* everyone—men, women, and children. Not a single person was spared. [35]We took all the livestock as plunder for ourselves, along with anything of value from the towns we ransacked.

[36]"The LORD our God helped us conquer Aroer on the edge of the Arnon Gorge, the town in the gorge, and the whole area as far as Gilead. No town had walls too strong for us. [37]However, we stayed away from the Ammonites along the Jabbok River and the towns in the hill country—all the places the LORD our God had commanded us to leave alone.

CHAPTER **3** **DIVIDING THE LAND.** "Next we headed for the land of Bashan, where King Og and his army attacked us at Edrei. [2]But the LORD told me, 'Do not be afraid of him, for I have given you victory over Og and his army, giving you his entire land. Treat him just as you treated King Sihon of the Amorites, who ruled in Heshbon.' [3]So the LORD our God handed King Og and all his people over to us, and we killed them all. [4]We conquered all sixty of his towns, the entire Argob region in his kingdom of Bashan. [5]These were all fortified cities with high walls and barred gates. We also took many unwalled villages at

**2:1** Hebrew *sea of reeds.* **2:23** Hebrew *from Caphtor.* **2:34** The Hebrew term used here refers to the complete consecration of things or people to the LORD, either by destroying them or by giving them as an offering.

the same time. [6]We completely destroyed* the kingdom of Bashan, just as we had destroyed King Sihon
of Heshbon. We destroyed* all the people in every
town we conquered—men, women, and children
alike. [7]But we kept all the livestock for ourselves and
took plunder from all the towns.
[8]"We now possessed all the land of the two Amorite kings east of the Jordan River—from the Arnon
Gorge to Mount Hermon. [9](Mount Hermon is called
Sirion by the Sidonians; the Amorites call it Senir.)
[10]We had now conquered all the cities on the plateau, and all Gilead and Bashan as far as the towns
of Salecah and Edrei, which were part of Og's kingdom in Bashan. [11](Incidentally, King Og of Bashan
was the last of the giant Rephaites. His iron bed was
more than thirteen feet long and six feet wide.* It
can still be seen in the Ammonite city of Rabbah.)

## ASTROLOGY

"What's that?" Kevin asks, pointing to a book in Kim's locker.

"Oh, that," Kim responds, picking up the skinny paperback. "That's a new book on astrology I got at the drugstore yesterday."

"Astrology?!" Kevin half screams. "Don't tell me you believe all that junk!"

"Laugh if you want," Kim responds matter-of-factly. "But I've seen it come true in my life so many times it's scary! Besides, lots of people in this country believe in astrology. So really, Kevin, if you don't read your horoscope, you're the one who's out of it."

Rhonda (the noisiest girl at school) walks up. "What are you guys looking at? Oh, I have that book. It's so good! What sign are you, Kevin? . . . Or aren't you into astrology?"

"Well, it's not like I don't ever read my horoscope. I'm a Leo. Sometimes it's pretty accurate, I guess."

Kim smiles. "Well, you're welcome to borrow my copy. My mom has another one at home."

Kevin coughs nervously, "I don't know—I, uh . . ."

"Kevin, it's completely harmless!" Rhonda urges. "Astrology is interesting . . . and a lot of fun. Take the book!"

Kim stands there offering the book. Kevin reluctantly takes it as the bell rings.

Is looking to the stars for guidance just an innocent diversion? See Deuteronomy 4:19 and 17:2-5.

[12]"When we took possession of this land, I gave
the territory beyond Aroer along the Arnon Gorge,
plus half of the hill country of Gilead with its towns,
to the tribes of Reuben and Gad. [13]Then I gave the
rest of Gilead and all of Bashan—Og's former kingdom—to the half-tribe of Manasseh. (The Argob
region of Bashan used to be known as the land of the
Rephaites. [14]Jair, a leader from the tribe of Manasseh,
acquired the whole Argob region in Bashan all the
way to the borders of the Geshurites and Maaca-

## BATTLES ● ● ● • •

**3:21-22 "The LORD your God will fight for you." What encouraging news for Joshua, who was to lead his men against the persistent forces of evil in the Promised Land! Since God promised to help him win every battle, he had nothing to fear. Our battles may not be against godless armies, but they are just as real as Joshua's. Whether we are resisting temptation or battling fear, God has promised to fight with and for us as we obey him.**

thites. Jair renamed this region after himself, calling
it the Towns of Jair,* as it is still known today.) [15]I
gave Gilead to the clan of Makir. [16]And to the tribes
of Reuben and Gad I gave the area extending from
Gilead to the middle of the Arnon Gorge, all the way
to the Jabbok River on the Ammonite frontier.
[17]They also received the Jordan Valley, including the
Jordan River and its eastern banks, all the way from
the Sea of Galilee down to the Dead Sea,* with the
slopes of Pisgah on the east.
[18]"At that time I gave this command to the tribes
that will live east of the Jordan: 'Although the LORD
your God has given you this land as your property,
all your fighting men must cross the Jordan, armed
and ready to protect your Israelite relatives. [19]Your
wives, children, and numerous livestock, however,
may stay behind in the towns I have given you.
[20]When the LORD has given security to the rest of the
Israelites, as he has to you, and when they occupy
the land the LORD your God is giving them across the
Jordan River, then you may return here to the land I
have given you.'
[21]"At that time I said to Joshua, 'You have seen all
that the LORD your God has done to these two kings.
He will do the same to all the kingdoms on the west
side of the Jordan. [22]Do not be afraid of the nations
there, for the LORD your God will fight for you.'
[23]"At that time I pleaded with the LORD and said,
[24]'O Sovereign LORD, I am your servant. You have
only begun to show me your greatness and power. Is
there any god in heaven or on earth who can perform such great deeds as yours? [25]Please let me cross
the Jordan to see the wonderful land on the other
side, the beautiful hill country and the Lebanon
mountains.'
[26]"But the LORD was angry with me because of
you, and he would not listen to me. 'That's enough!'
he ordered. 'Speak of it no more. [27]You can go to
Pisgah Peak and view the land in every direction, but
you may not cross the Jordan River. [28]But commission Joshua and encourage him, for he will lead the
people across the Jordan. He will give them the land
you now see before you.' [29]So we stayed in the valley
near Beth-peor.

CHAPTER **4** **OBEY GOD.** "And now, Israel, listen
carefully to these laws and regulations that I am
about to teach you. Obey them so that you may live,
so you may enter and occupy the land the LORD, the
God of your ancestors, is giving you. [2]Do not add to

3:6 The Hebrew term used here refers to the complete consecration of things or people to the LORD, either by destroying them or by giving them as an offering. 3:11 Hebrew *9 cubits* [4.1 meters] *long and 4 cubits* [1.8 meters] *wide.* 3:14 Hebrew *Havvoth-jair.* 3:17 Hebrew *from Kinnereth to the sea of the Arabah, the Salt Sea.*

or subtract from these commands I am giving you from the LORD your God. Just obey them. 3 You saw what the LORD did to you at Baal-peor, where the LORD your God destroyed everyone who had worshiped the god Baal of Peor. 4 But all of you who were faithful to the LORD your God are still alive today.

5 "You must obey these laws and regulations when you arrive in the land you are about to enter and occupy. The LORD my God gave them to me and commanded me to pass them on to you. 6 If you obey them carefully, you will display your wisdom and intelligence to the surrounding nations. When they hear about these laws, they will exclaim, 'What other nation is as wise and prudent as this!' 7 For what great nation has a god as near to them as the LORD our God is near to us whenever we call on him? 8 And what great nation has laws and regulations as fair as this body of laws that I am giving you today?

9 "But watch out! Be very careful never to forget what you have seen the LORD do for you. Do not let these things escape from your mind as long as you live! And be sure to pass them on to your children and grandchildren. 10 Tell them especially about the day when you stood before the LORD your God at Mount Sinai,* where he told me, 'Summon the people before me, and I will instruct them. That way, they will learn to fear me as long as they live, and they will be able to teach my laws to their children.' 11 You came near and stood at the foot of the mountain, while the mountain was burning with fire. Flames shot into the sky, shrouded in black clouds and deep darkness. 12 And the LORD spoke to you from the fire. You heard his words but didn't see his form; there was only a voice. 13 He proclaimed his covenant, which he commanded you to keep—the Ten Commandments—and wrote them on two stone tablets. 14 It was at that time that the LORD commanded me to issue the laws and regulations you must obey in the land you are about to enter and occupy.

15 "But be careful! You did not see the LORD's form on the day he spoke to you from the fire at Mount Sinai. 16 So do not corrupt yourselves by making a physical image in any form—whether of a man or a woman, 17 an animal or a bird, 18 a creeping creature or a fish. 19 And when you look up into the sky and see the sun, moon, and stars—all the forces of heaven—don't be seduced by them and worship them. The LORD your God designated these heavenly bodies for all the peoples of the earth. 20 Remember that the LORD rescued you from the burning furnace of Egypt to become his own people and special possession; that is what you are today.

21 "But the LORD was very angry with me because of you. He vowed that I would never cross the Jordan River into the good land the LORD your God is giving you as your special possession. 22 Though you will cross the Jordan to occupy the land, I will die here on this side of the river. 23 So be careful not to break the covenant the LORD your God has made with you. You will break it if you make idols of any shape or form, for the LORD your God has absolutely forbidden this. 24 The LORD your God is a devouring fire, a jealous God.

25 "In the future, when you have children and grandchildren and have lived in the land a long time, do not corrupt yourselves by making idols of any kind. This is evil in the sight of the LORD your God and will arouse his anger.

26 "Today I call heaven and earth as witnesses against you. If you disobey me, you will quickly disappear from the land you are crossing the Jordan to occupy. You will live there only a short time; then you will be utterly destroyed. 27 For the LORD will scatter you among the nations, where only a few of you will survive. 28 There, in a foreign land, you will worship idols made from wood and stone, gods that neither see nor hear nor eat nor smell. 29 From there you will search again for the LORD your God. And if you search for him with all your heart and soul, you will find him.

30 "When those bitter days have come upon you far in the future, you will finally return to the LORD your God and listen to what he tells you. 31 For the LORD your God is merciful—he will not abandon you or destroy you or forget the solemn covenant he made with your ancestors.

32 "Search all of history, from the time God created people on the earth until now. Then search from one end of the heavens to the other. See if anything as great as this has ever happened before. 33 Has any nation ever heard the voice of God* speaking from fire—as you did—and survived? 34 Has any other god taken one nation for himself by rescuing it from another by means of trials, miraculous signs, wonders, war, awesome power, and terrifying acts? Yet that is what the LORD your God did for you in Egypt, right before your very eyes.

35 "He showed you these things so you would realize that the LORD is God and that there is no other god. 36 He let you hear his voice from heaven so he could instruct you. He let you see his great fire here on earth so he could speak to you from it. 37 Because he loved your ancestors, he chose to bless their descendants and personally brought you out of Egypt with a great display of power. 38 He drove out nations far greater than you, so he could bring you in and give you their land as a special possession, as it is today. 39 So remember this and keep it firmly in

**REMEMBER ● ● ● • •**

4:9 **Moses wanted to make sure that the people did not forget all they had seen God do, so he urged parents to tell their children about God's great miracles. This helped parents remember God's faithfulness, and it provided the way for passing on from one generation to the next the stories of God's great acts. It is easy to forget the wonderful ways God has worked in the lives of his people. But you can remember God's great acts of faithfulness by telling your friends what you have seen him do.**

**4:10** Hebrew *Horeb,* another name for Sinai; also in 4:15. **4:33** Or *voice of a god.*

mind: The LORD is God both in heaven and on earth, and there is no other god! [40]If you obey all the laws and commands that I will give you today, all will be well with you and your children. Then you will enjoy a long life in the land the LORD your God is giving you for all time."

[41]Then Moses set apart three cities of refuge east of the Jordan River, [42]where anyone who had accidentally killed someone without having any previous hostility could flee for safety. [43]These were the cities: Bezer on the wilderness plateau for the tribe of Reuben; Ramoth in Gilead for the tribe of Gad; Golan in Bashan for the tribe of Manasseh.

[44]This is the law that Moses handed down to the Israelites. [45]These are the stipulations, laws, and regulations that Moses gave to the people of Israel when they left Egypt, [46]and as they camped in the valley near Beth-peor east of the Jordan River. (This land was formerly occupied by the Amorites under King Sihon of Heshbon. He and his people had been destroyed by Moses and the Israelites as they came up from Egypt. [47]Israel conquered his land and that of King Og of Bashan—the two Amorite kings east of the Jordan. [48]So Israel conquered all the area from Aroer at the edge of the Arnon Gorge to Mount Sirion,* also called Mount Hermon. [49]And they took the eastern bank of the Jordan Valley as far south as the Dead Sea,* below the slopes of Pisgah.)

## CHAPTER 5 **THE TEN COMMANDMENTS.**

Moses called all the people of Israel together and said, "Listen carefully to all the laws and regulations I am giving you today. Learn them and be sure to obey them!

### COVENANT ● • • • •

**5:1 The people had entered into a covenant with God, and Moses commanded them to listen, learn, and obey his laws and regulations. Christians also have entered into a covenant with God (through Jesus Christ) and should be sensitive to what God expects. Moses' threefold command to the Israelites is excellent advice for all God's followers. *Listening* is absorbing and accepting information about God. *Learning* is understanding its meaning and implications. *Obeying* is putting into action all we have learned and understood. All three parts are essential to a growing relationship with God.**

[2]"While we were at Mount Sinai,* the LORD our God made a covenant with us. [3]The LORD did not make this covenant long ago with our ancestors, but with all of us who are alive today. [4]The LORD spoke to you face to face from the heart of the fire on the mountain. [5]I stood as an intermediary between you and the LORD, for you were afraid of the fire and did not climb the mountain. He spoke to me, and I passed his words on to you. This is what he said:

[6]"'I am the LORD your God, who rescued you from slavery in Egypt.

[7]"'Do not worship any other gods besides me.

[8]"'Do not make idols of any kind, whether in the shape of birds or animals or fish. [9]You must never worship or bow down to them, for I, the LORD your God, am a jealous God who will not share your affection with any other god! I do not leave unpunished the sins of those who hate me, but I punish the children for the sins of their parents to the third and fourth generations. [10]But I lavish my love on those who love me and obey my commands, even for a thousand generations.

[11]"'Do not misuse the name of the LORD your God. The LORD will not let you go unpunished if you misuse his name.

[12]"'Observe the Sabbath day by keeping it holy, as the LORD your God has commanded you. [13]Six days a week are set apart for your daily duties and regular work, [14]but the seventh day is a day of rest dedicated to the LORD your God. On that day no one in your household may do any kind of work. This includes you, your sons and daughters, your male and female servants, your oxen and donkeys and other livestock, and any foreigners living among you. All your male and female servants must rest as you do. [15]Remember that you were once slaves in Egypt and that the LORD your God brought you out with amazing power and mighty deeds. That is why the LORD your God has commanded you to observe the Sabbath day.

[16]"'Honor your father and mother, as the LORD your God commanded you. Then you will live a long, full life in the land the LORD your God will give you.

[17]"'Do not murder.

[18]"'Do not commit adultery.

[19]"'Do not steal.

[20]"'Do not testify falsely against your neighbor.

[21]"'Do not covet your neighbor's wife. Do not covet your neighbor's house or land, male or female servant, ox or donkey, or anything else your neighbor owns.'

[22]"The LORD spoke these words with a loud voice to all of you from the heart of the fire, surrounded by clouds and deep darkness. This was all he said at that time, and he wrote his words on two stone tablets and gave them to me. [23]But when you heard the voice from the darkness, while the mountain was blazing with fire, all your tribal leaders came to me. [24]They said, 'The LORD our God has shown us his glory and greatness, and we have heard his voice from the heart of the fire. Today we have seen God speaking to humans, and yet we live! [25]But now, why should we die? If the LORD our God speaks to us again, we will certainly die and be consumed by this awesome fire. [26]Can any living thing hear the voice of the living God from the heart of the fire and yet survive? [27]You go and listen to what the LORD our God says. Then come and tell us everything he tells you, and we will listen and obey.'

4:48 As in Syriac version (see also 3:9); Hebrew reads *Mount Sion.* **4:49** Hebrew *took the Arabah on the east side of the Jordan as far as the sea of the Arabah.* **5:2** Hebrew *Horeb,* another name for Sinai.

28"The LORD heard your request and said to me, 'I have heard what the people have said to you, and they are right. 29Oh, that they would always have hearts like this, that they might fear me and obey all my commands! If they did, they and their descendants would prosper forever. 30Go and tell them to return to their tents. 31But you stay here with me so I can give you all my commands, laws, and regulations. You will teach them to the people so they can obey them in the land I am giving to them as their inheritance.'"

32So Moses told the people, "You must obey all the commands of the LORD your God, following his instructions in every detail. 33Stay on the path that the LORD your God has commanded you to follow. Then you will live long and prosperous lives in the land you are about to enter and occupy.

CHAPTER **6** **LOVE GOD AND OBEY HIM.** "These are all the commands, laws, and regulations that the LORD your God told me to teach you so you may obey them in the land you are about to enter and occupy, 2and so you and your children and grandchildren might fear the LORD your God as long as you live. If you obey all his laws and commands, you will enjoy a long life. 3Listen closely, Israel, to everything I say. Be careful to obey. Then all will go well with you, and you will have many children in the land flowing with milk and honey, just as the LORD, the God of your ancestors, promised you.

4"Hear, O Israel! The LORD is our God, the LORD alone.* 5And you must love the LORD your God with all your heart, all your soul, and all your strength. 6And you must commit yourselves wholeheartedly to these commands I am giving you today. 7Repeat them again and again to your children. Talk about them when you are at home and when you are away on a journey, when you are lying down and when you are getting up again. 8Tie them to your hands as a reminder, and wear them on your forehead. 9Write them on the doorposts of your house and on your gates.

10"The LORD your God will soon bring you into the land he swore to give your ancestors Abraham, Isaac, and Jacob. It is a land filled with large, prosperous cities that you did not build. 11The houses will be richly stocked with goods you did not produce. You will draw water from cisterns you did not dig, and you will eat from vineyards and olive trees you did not plant. When you have eaten your fill in this land, 12be careful not to forget the LORD, who rescued you from slavery in the land of Egypt. 13You must fear the LORD your God and serve him. When you take an oath, you must use only his name.

14"You must not worship any of the gods of neighboring nations, 15for the LORD your God, who lives among you, is a jealous God. His anger will flare up against you and wipe you from the face of the earth. 16Do not test the LORD your God as you did when you complained at Massah. 17You must diligently obey the commands of the LORD your God—all the stipulations and laws he has given you. 18Do what is right and good in the LORD's sight, so all will go well with you. Then you will enter and occupy the good land that the LORD solemnly promised to give your ancestors. 19You will drive out all the enemies living in your land, just as the LORD said you would.

20"In the future your children will ask you, 'What is the meaning of these stipulations, laws, and

## HOME SCHOOLS ● ● • • •

6:4-9 **This passage is often said to be the central theme of Deuteronomy. It sets a pattern that helps us relate the Word of God to our daily life. We are to love God, think constantly about his commandments, teach his commandments to our children, and live our daily life by the guidelines in his Word. God emphasized the importance of parents' teaching the Bible to their children. The church and Christian schools must not be used to escape from this responsibility. The Bible provides so many opportunities for object lessons and practical teaching that it would be a shame to study it only one day a week. Eternal truths are most effectively learned in the loving environment of a God-fearing home.**

## "Here's what I did..."

My parents are Christians, and even though they are stricter than I'd like, I have to admit they're good parents. One day while reading the Bible, I came across the fifth commandment, the one about honoring your parents. The note in the margin pointed out that there is a promise attached to this commandment: If you follow it, you will lead a long and happy life.

What struck me is that my parents are always saying things like, "We're only saying this for your own good. We want you to be happy." It seemed like God was saying, "Your parents love you, they are trying to help you lead a happy life, so if you listen to them, your life will go better." It all made sense. For a while I felt guilty that I didn't listen to them as much as I should, but I determined to consult them more.

A few nights later I decided to talk to them about a relationship I was having trouble with. I was surprised to find that they really understood, and my mom even had some helpful advice about what she had done in a similar situation. I hadn't realized before how much wisdom my parents really have to give me.

*Amy*

AGE 15

6:4 Or *The LORD our God is one LORD,* or *The LORD our God, the LORD is one,* or *The LORD is our God, the LORD is one.*

**The LORD your God** *is* **the faithful God who keeps his covenant** *for a thousand* GENERATIONS GENERATIONS GENERATIONS GENERATIONS NERATION

DEUTERONOMY 7:9

regulations that the LORD our God has given us?' [21]Then you must tell them, 'We were Pharaoh's slaves in Egypt, but the LORD brought us out of Egypt with amazing power. [22]Before our eyes the LORD did miraculous signs and wonders, dealing terrifying blows against Egypt and Pharaoh and all his people. [23]He brought us out of Egypt so he could give us this land he had solemnly promised to give our ancestors. [24]And the LORD our God commanded us to obey all these laws and to fear him for our own prosperity and well-being, as is now the case. [25]For we are righteous when we obey all the commands the LORD our God has given us.'

CHAPTER **7** **DEFEAT THE ENEMY NATIONS.** "When the LORD your God brings you into the land you are about to enter and occupy, he will clear away many nations ahead of you: the Hittites, Girgashites, Amorites, Canaanites, Perizzites, Hivites, and Jebusites. These seven nations are all more powerful than you. [2]When the LORD your God hands these nations over to you and you conquer them, you must completely destroy* them. Make no treaties with them and show them no mercy. [3]Do not intermarry with them, and don't let your daughters and sons marry their sons and daughters. [4]They will lead your young people away from me to worship other gods. Then the anger of the LORD will burn against you, and he will destroy you. [5]Instead, you must break down their pagan altars and shatter their sacred pillars. Cut down their Asherah poles and burn their idols. [6]For you are a holy people, who belong to the LORD your God. Of all the people on earth, the LORD your God has chosen you to be his own special treasure.

[7]"The LORD did not choose you and lavish his love on you because you were larger or greater than other nations, for you were the smallest of all nations! [8]It was simply because the LORD loves you, and because he was keeping the oath he had sworn to your ancestors. That is why the LORD rescued you with such amazing power from your slavery under Pharaoh in Egypt. [9]Understand, therefore, that the LORD your God is indeed God. He is the faithful God who keeps his covenant for a thousand generations and constantly loves those who love him and obey his commands. [10]But he does not hesitate to punish and destroy those who hate him. [11]Therefore, obey all these commands, laws, and regulations I am giving you today.

[12]"If you listen to these regulations and obey them faithfully, the LORD your God will keep his covenant of unfailing love with you, as he solemnly promised your ancestors. [13]He will love you and bless you and make you into a great nation. He will give you many children and give fertility to your land and your animals. When you arrive in the land he swore to give your ancestors, you will have large crops of grain, grapes, and olives, and great herds of cattle, sheep, and goats. [14]You will be blessed above all the nations of the earth. None of your men or women will be childless, and all your livestock will bear young. [15]And the LORD will protect you from all sickness. He will not let you suffer from the terrible diseases you knew in Egypt, but he will bring them all on your enemies!

[16]"You must destroy all the nations the LORD your God hands over to you. Show them no mercy and do not worship their gods. If you do, they will trap you. [17]Perhaps you will think to yourselves, 'How can we ever conquer these nations that are so much more powerful than we are?' [18]But don't be afraid of them! Just remember what the LORD your God did to Pharaoh and to all the land of Egypt. [19]Remember the great terrors the LORD your God sent against them. You saw it all with your own eyes! And remember the miraculous signs and wonders, and the amazing power he used when he brought you out of Egypt. The LORD your God will use this same power against

**STEP-BY-STEP ● ● • • •**

7:21-24 **Moses told the Israelites that God would destroy Israel's enemies, but not all at once. God had the power to destroy those nations instantly, but he chose to do it in stages. In the same way and with the same power, God could miraculously and instantaneously change your life. Usually, however, he chooses to help you gradually, teaching you one lesson at a time. Rather than expect instant spiritual maturity and solutions to all your problems, slow down and work one step at a time, trusting God to make up the difference between where you should be and where you are now. You'll soon look back and see that a miraculous transformation has occurred.**

7:2 The Hebrew term used here refers to the complete consecration of things or people to the LORD, either by destroying them or by giving them as an offering; also in 7:26.

the people you fear. 20And then the LORD your God
will send hornets* to drive out the few survivors still
hiding from you!
21"No, do not be afraid of those nations, for the
LORD your God is among you, and he is a great and
awesome God. 22The LORD your God will drive those
nations out ahead of you little by little. You will not
clear them away all at once, for if you did, the wild
animals would multiply too quickly for you. 23But
the LORD your God will hand them over to you. He
will throw them into complete confusion until they
are destroyed. 24He will put their kings in your power,
and you will erase their names from the face of the
earth. No one will be able to stand against you, and
you will destroy them all.
25"You must burn their idols in fire, and do not
desire the silver or gold with which they are made.
Do not take it or it will become a snare to you, for it
is detestable to the LORD your God. 26Do not bring
any detestable objects into your home, for then you
will be set apart for destruction just like them. You
must utterly detest such things, for they are set apart
for destruction.

## CHAPTER 8

**DO NOT FORGET GOD.** "Be careful to obey
all the commands I am giving you today. Then you will
live and multiply, and you will enter and occupy the
land the LORD swore to give your ancestors. 2Remem-
ber how the LORD your God led you through the
wilderness for forty years, humbling you and testing
you to prove your character, and to find out whether
or not you would really obey his commands. 3Yes, he
humbled you by letting you go hungry and then feeding you with manna, a food previously unknown to
you and your ancestors. He did it to teach you that
people need more than bread for their life; real life
comes by feeding on every word of the LORD. 4For all
these forty years your clothes didn't wear out, and your
feet didn't blister or swell. 5So you should realize that
just as a parent disciplines a child, the LORD your God
disciplines you to help you.
6"So obey the commands of the LORD your God
by walking in his ways and fearing him. 7For the
LORD your God is bringing you into a good land of
flowing streams and pools of water, with springs
that gush forth in the valleys and hills. 8It is a land
of wheat and barley, of grapevines, fig trees, pomegranates, olives, and honey. 9It is a land where food
is plentiful and nothing is lacking. It is a land
where iron is as common as stone, and copper is
abundant in the hills. 10When you have eaten your
fill, praise the LORD your God for the good land he
has given you.
11"But that is the time to be careful! Beware that in
your plenty you do not forget the LORD your God
and disobey his commands, regulations, and laws.
12For when you have become full and prosperous
and have built fine homes to live in, 13and when your
flocks and herds have become very large and your
silver and gold have multiplied along with everything else, 14that is the time to be careful. Do not
become proud at that time and forget the LORD your
God, who rescued you from slavery in the land of
Egypt. 15Do not forget that he led you through the
great and terrifying wilderness with poisonous
snakes and scorpions, where it was so hot and dry.
He gave you water from the rock! 16He fed you with
manna in the wilderness, a food unknown to your
ancestors. He did this to humble you and test you for
your own good. 17He did it so you would never think
that it was your own strength and energy that made
you wealthy. 18Always remember that it is the LORD
your God who gives you power to become rich, and
he does it to fulfill the covenant he made with your
ancestors.
19"But I assure you of this: If you ever forget the
LORD your God and follow other gods, worshiping
and bowing down to them, you will certainly be
destroyed. 20Just as the LORD has destroyed other
nations in your path, you also will be destroyed for
not obeying the LORD your God.

### OBEDIENCE

Deuteronomy 8:1 tells us to obey God's commands. We do this by obeying God with . . .

| | |
|---|---|
| OUR HEART | By loving him more than any relationship, activity, achievement, or possession |
| OUR WILL | By committing ourselves completely to him |
| OUR MIND | By seeking to know him and his Word, so his principles and values form the foundation of all we think and do |
| OUR BODY | By recognizing that our strengths, talents, and sexuality are given to us by God to be used for pleasure and fulfillment according to his rules, not ours |
| OUR FINANCES | By deciding that all of the resources we have ultimately come from God, and that we are to be managers of them and not owners |
| OUR FUTURE | By deciding to make service to God and people the main purpose of our life's work |

7:20 Or *will spread panic,* or *will send a plague.* The meaning of the Hebrew is uncertain.

# COVENANTS

You've seen it in the movies or maybe on the news—leaders of two warring countries decide to end the fighting and sign a peace treaty. The representative of the losing side agrees to terms of surrender, perhaps giving up contested land or paying back some money as a war debt. The winning country's spokesman agrees that his military forces will pull out, so long as the losing side keeps up its end of the agreement. Should they ever break their word and resume the hostilities, the conquering armies will come back full force. **W**hat we call a *PEACE TREATY* was called a *covenant* in Old Testament times. It was used in situations where one kingdom defeated another in battle, or when a weaker empire wanted to avoid going to war with a more powerful one. (In case you want to impress your pastor or your Sunday school teacher, these were called "Suzerain-vassal treaties.") In short, a covenant is an agreement between two parties that binds them to do certain things for each other. For example, the stronger party agrees not to destroy the weaker one; in return, the weaker one agrees to pay **TAXES OR TRIBUTE.** Also, the covenant agreement included sections explaining what would happen if the rules were kept and if they were broken. These sections were called "blessings" and "curses." **Y**ou've already read about one such covenant (or promise) between God and Noah in Genesis 9. Then comes the story of God's covenant with Abram. God promised to give Abram many descendants and a wonderful land for their home. At first, Abram was skeptical—he was old and had no children. But God showed Abram the ***stars splashed*** across the nighttime sky, telling him his children would be that numerous. Abram asked for another sign that he would inherit Canaan for those countless descendants. In response, God showed him a vision. **A**fter God told Abram to bring before him several animals and cut them in half, Abram fell into a deep and terrified sleep. He was terrified because he thought he would have to walk between the pieces of carcass, signifying that if he disobeyed God, God would rip him in half. Instead, God did something that undoubtedly astonished Abram—he showed him **a smoking oven and a burning torch** passing between the pieces, symbolizing that God was taking the curse on himself if he should ever break his part of the agreement. In other words, God was saying to Abram, "How can you be sure you'll get this land? I swear by my own destruction that you will." Imagine Abram's surprise and relief! **Y**ou might be thinking, *That's a fascinating bit of historical trivia—but what does it have to do with me?* Just this: in the New Testament book of Romans, Paul tells us that as Christians we are in line to inherit the blessings promised to Abram (Abraham). Romans 11:17 says, "But some of these branches from Abraham's tree, some of the Jews, have been broken off. And you Gentiles, who were branches from a WILD OLIVE tree, were grafted in. So now you also receive the blessing God has promised Abraham and his children, sharing in God's rich nourishment of his special olive tree." In other words, you, as a Christian, are adopted into Abraham's family and are in line to receive the blessings God promised to him! **N**o, that doesn't mean you can pick up and head to the Holy Land to stake out some **PRIME REAL ESTATE.** Our Promised Land is in another place—a new heaven and a new earth. But as you read about God's covenant with Abram and with the nation of Israel, know with absolute certainty that God will keep his promises to you—all of them—just as he did with Israel. Your part is to enter into an agreement with him about your sin and his forgiveness through Jesus, the author of the new covenant.

CHAPTER **9** **DO NOT FORGET GOD'S MERCY.** "Hear, O Israel! Today you are about to cross the Jordan River to occupy the land belonging to nations much greater and more powerful than you. They live in cities with walls that reach to the sky! 2They are strong and tall—descendants of the famous Anakite giants. You've heard the saying, 'Who can stand up to the Anakites?' 3But the LORD your God will cross over ahead of you like a devouring fire to destroy them. He will subdue them so that you will quickly conquer them and drive them out, just as the LORD has promised.

4"After the LORD your God has done this for you, don't say to yourselves, 'The LORD has given us this land because we are so righteous!' No, it is because of the wickedness of the other nations that he is doing it. 5It is not at all because you are such righteous, upright people that you are about to occupy their land. The LORD your God will drive these nations out ahead of you only because of their wickedness, and to fulfill the oath he had sworn to your ancestors Abraham, Isaac, and Jacob. 6I will say it again: The LORD your God is not giving you this good land because you are righteous, for you are not—you are a stubborn people.

7"Remember how angry you made the LORD your God out in the wilderness. From the day you left Egypt until now, you have constantly rebelled against him. 8Remember how angry you made the LORD at Mount Sinai,* where he was ready to destroy you. 9That was when I was on the mountain receiving the tablets of stone inscribed with the covenant that the LORD had made with you. I was there for forty days and forty nights, and all that time I ate nothing and drank no water. 10The LORD gave me the covenant, the tablets on which God himself had written all the words he had spoken to you from the fire on the mountain.

11"At the end of the forty days and nights, the LORD handed me the two stone tablets with the covenant inscribed on them. 12Then the LORD said to me, 'Go down immediately because the people you led out of Egypt have become corrupt. They have already turned from the way I commanded them to live and have cast an idol for themselves from gold.'

13"The LORD said to me, 'I have been watching this people, and they are extremely stubborn. 14Leave me alone so I may destroy them and erase their name from under heaven. Then I will make a mighty nation of your descendants, a nation larger and more powerful than they are.'

15"So I came down from the fiery mountain, holding in my hands the two stone tablets of the covenant. 16There below me I could see the gold calf you had made in your terrible sin against the LORD your God. How quickly you had turned from the path the LORD had commanded you to follow! 17So I raised the stone tablets and dashed them to the ground. I smashed them before your very eyes. 18Then for forty days and nights I lay prostrate before the LORD, neither eating bread nor drinking water. I did this because you had sinned by doing what the LORD hated, thus making him very angry. 19How I feared for you, for the LORD was ready to destroy you. But again he listened to me. 20The LORD was so angry with Aaron that he wanted to destroy him. But I prayed for Aaron, and the LORD spared him. 21I took your sin—the calf you had made—and I melted it in the fire and ground it into fine dust. I threw the dust into the stream that cascades down the mountain.

22"You also made the LORD angry at Taberah,* Massah,* and Kibroth-hattaavah.* 23And at Kadesh-barnea the LORD sent you out with this command: 'Go up and take the land I have given you.' But you rebelled against the command of the LORD your God and refused to trust him or obey him. 24Yes, you have been rebelling against the LORD as long as I have known you.

**MERCY ● ● ● • •**

9:5-6 **If the Israelites were unrighteous and stubborn, why did God make such wonderful promises to them? There are two good reasons: (1) A bargain is a bargain. God and Israel had made a covenant (Genesis 15; 17; Exodus 19–20). God promised to be faithful to them and they promised to obey him. The agreement was irrevocable and eternal. Even though the Israelites rarely upheld their end of the bargain, God would always be faithful to his part. (Although he punished them several times, he always remained faithful.) (2) God's mercy is unconditional. No matter how many times the people turned from God, he was always there to restore them. It is comforting to know that despite our inconsistencies and sins, God loves us unconditionally. Eternal life is not achieved on the merit system, but on the mercy system. God loves us no matter who we are or what we have done.**

25"That is why I fell down and lay before the LORD for forty days and nights when he was ready to destroy you. 26I prayed to the LORD and said, 'O Sovereign LORD, do not destroy your own people. They are your special possession, redeemed from Egypt by your mighty power and glorious strength. 27Overlook the stubbornness and sin of these people, but remember instead your servants Abraham, Isaac, and Jacob. 28If you destroy these people, the Egyptians will say, "The LORD destroyed them because he wasn't able to bring them to the land he had sworn to give them." Or they might say, "He destroyed them because he hated them; he brought them into the wilderness to slaughter them." 29But they are your people and your special possession, whom you brought from Egypt by your mighty power and glorious strength.'

CHAPTER **10** **NEW TABLETS OF STONE.** "At that time the LORD said to me, 'Prepare two stone tablets like the first ones, and make a sacred chest of wood to keep them in. Return to me on the mountain, 2and I

9:8 Hebrew *Horeb,* another name for Sinai. 9:22a *Taberah* means "place of burning." See Num 11:1-3. 9:22b *Massah* means "place of testing." See Exod 17:1-7. 9:22c *Kibroth-hattaavah* means "graves of craving." See Num 11:31-34.

will write on the tablets the same words that were on the ones you smashed. Then place the tablets in the sacred chest—the Ark of the Covenant.'

3"So I made a chest of acacia wood and cut two stone tablets like the first two, and I took the tablets up the mountain. 4The LORD again wrote the terms of the covenant—the Ten Commandments—on them and gave them to me. They were the same words the LORD had spoken to you from the heart of the fire on the mountain as you were assembled below. 5Then I came down and placed the tablets in the Ark of the Covenant, which I had made, just as the LORD commanded me. And the tablets are still there in the Ark.

6"The people of Israel set out from the wells of the people of Jaakan* and traveled to Moserah, where Aaron died and was buried. His son Eleazar became the high priest in his place. 7Then they journeyed to Gudgodah, and from there to Jotbathah, a land with brooks of water. 8At that time the LORD set apart the tribe of Levi to carry the Ark of the LORD's covenant, to minister before the LORD, and to pronounce blessings in his name. These are still their duties. 9That is why the Levites have no share or inheritance reserved for them among the other Israelite tribes. The LORD himself is their inheritance, as the LORD your God told them.

10"As I said before, I stayed on the mountain in the LORD's presence for forty days and nights, as I had done the first time. And once again the LORD yielded to my pleas and didn't destroy you. 11But the LORD said to me, 'Get up and lead the people into the land I swore to give their ancestors, so they may take possession of it.'

## GREAT EXPECTATIONS ● ● • • •

10:12-13 **Often we ask, "What does God expect of me?" Here Moses gives a summary that is simple in form and easy to remember. Here are the essentials: (1) Fear God (have reverence for him). (2) Live according to his will. (3) Love him. (4) Worship him with all your heart and soul. (5) Obey his commands. How often we complicate faith with man-made rules, regulations, and requirements. Are you frustrated and burned out from trying hard to please God? Concentrate on his real requirements—to respect, follow, love, worship, and obey him—and find peace.**

12"And now, Israel, what does the LORD your God require of you? He requires you to fear him, to live according to his will, to love and worship him with all your heart and soul, 13and to obey the LORD's commands and laws that I am giving you today for your own good. 14The highest heavens and the earth and everything in it all belong to the LORD your God. 15Yet the LORD chose your ancestors as the objects of his love. And he chose you, their descendants, above every other nation, as is evident today. 16Therefore, cleanse your sinful hearts and stop being stubborn.

17"The LORD your God is the God of gods and Lord of lords. He is the great God, mighty and awesome, who shows no partiality and takes no bribes. 18He gives justice to orphans and widows. He shows love to the foreigners living among you and gives them food and clothing. 19You, too, must show love to foreigners, for you yourselves were once foreigners in the land of Egypt. 20You must fear the LORD your God and worship him and cling to him. Your oaths must be in his name alone. 21He is your God, the one who is worthy of your praise, the one who has done mighty miracles that you yourselves have seen. 22When your ancestors went down into Egypt, there were only seventy of them. But now the LORD your God has made you as numerous as the stars in the sky!

CHAPTER **11** "You must love the LORD your God and obey all his requirements, laws, regulations, and commands. 2Listen! I am not talking now to your children, who have never experienced the discipline of the LORD your God or seen his greatness and awesome power. 3They weren't there to see the miraculous signs and wonders he performed in Egypt against Pharaoh and all his land. 4They didn't see what the LORD did to the armies of Egypt and to their horses and chariots—how he drowned them in the Red Sea* as they were chasing you, and how he has kept them devastated to this very day! 5They didn't see how the LORD cared for you in the wilderness until you arrived here. 6They weren't there to see what he did to Dathan and Abiram (the sons of Eliab, a descendant of Reuben) when the earth opened up and swallowed them, along with their households and tents and every living thing that belonged to them. 7But you have seen all the LORD's mighty deeds with your own eyes!

8"Therefore, be careful to obey every command I am giving you today, so you may have strength to go in and occupy the land you are about to enter. 9If you obey, you will enjoy a long life in the land the LORD swore to give to your ancestors and to you, their descendants—a land flowing with milk and honey! 10For the land you are about to enter and occupy is not like the land of Egypt from which you came, where you planted your seed and dug out irrigation ditches with your foot as in a vegetable garden. 11It is a land of hills and valleys with plenty of rain—12a land that the LORD your God cares for. He watches over it day after day throughout the year!

13"If you carefully obey all the commands I am giving you today, and if you love the LORD your God with all your heart and soul, and if you worship him, 14then he will send the rains in their proper seasons so you can harvest crops of grain, grapes for wine, and olives for oil. 15He will give you lush pastureland for your cattle to graze in, and you yourselves will have plenty to eat.

16"But do not let your heart turn away from the LORD to worship other gods. 17If you do, the LORD's anger will burn against you. He will shut up the sky

**10:6** Or *set out from Beeroth of Bene-jaakan.* **11:4** Hebrew *sea of reeds.*

and hold back the rain, and your harvests will fail. Then you will quickly die in that good land the LORD is now giving you. 18So commit yourselves completely to these words of mine. Tie them to your hands as a reminder, and wear them on your forehead. 19Teach them to your children. Talk about them when you are at home and when you are away on a journey, when you are lying down and when you are getting up again. 20Write them on the doorposts of your house and on your gates, 21so that as long as the sky remains above the earth, you and your children may flourish in the land the LORD swore to give your ancestors.

22"Be careful to obey all the commands I give you; show love to the LORD your God by walking in his ways and clinging to him. 23Then the LORD will drive out all the nations in your land, though they are much greater and stronger than you. 24Wherever you set your feet, the land will be yours. Your frontiers will stretch from the wilderness in the south to Lebanon in the north, and from the Euphrates River in the east to the Mediterranean Sea in the west.* 25No one will be able to stand against you, for the LORD your God will send fear and dread ahead of you, as he promised you, wherever you go in the whole land.

26"Today I am giving you the choice between a blessing and a curse! 27You will be blessed if you obey the commands of the LORD your God that I am giving you today. 28You will receive a curse if you reject the commands of the LORD your God and turn from his way by worshiping foreign gods.

29"When the LORD your God brings you into the land to possess it, you must pronounce a blessing from Mount Gerizim and a curse from Mount Ebal. 30(These two mountains are west of the Jordan River in the land of the Canaanites who live in the Jordan Valley,* near the town of Gilgal. They are located toward the west, not far from the oaks of Moreh.) 31For you are about to cross the Jordan to occupy the land the LORD your God is giving you. When you are living in that land, 32you must be careful to obey all the laws and regulations I am giving you today.

## CHAPTER 12 ONLY ONE ALTAR FOR SACRIFICES.

"These are the laws and regulations you must obey as long as you live in the land the LORD, the God of your ancestors, is giving you.

2"When you drive out the nations that live there, you must destroy all the places where they worship their gods—high on the mountains, up on the hills, and under every green tree. 3Break down their altars and smash their sacred pillars. Burn their Asherah poles and cut down their carved idols. Erase the names of their gods from those places!

4"Do not worship the LORD your God in the way these pagan peoples worship their gods. 5Rather, you must seek the LORD your God at the place he himself will choose from among all the tribes for his name to be honored. 6There you will bring to the LORD your burnt offerings, your sacrifices, your tithes, your special gifts, your offerings to fulfill a vow, your freewill offerings, and your offerings of the firstborn animals of your flocks and herds. 7There you and your families will feast in the presence of the LORD your God, and you will rejoice in all you have accomplished because the LORD your God has blessed you.

8"Today you are doing whatever you please, but

11:24 Hebrew *to the western sea.* 11:30 Hebrew *the Arabah.*

**The Old Testament is long and sometimes boring. Why did God put it in the Bible?**

Have you ever asked one of your grandparents to tell you their whole life story? You would probably receive an all-day talk, full of wonderful stories. Though it would be fun for your grandparent, you would likely be bored because you would hear too many facts that would not relate to your life!

If, however, you asked him to relate the top ten experiences that shaped his personality and helped him make it through life, it would only take an hour, it would be fascinating, and you would learn a lot.

The Old Testament is not a detailed day-by-day account of history. Instead it is the story of the Jewish people. Their history points to Jesus Christ. Through this story, we see God's plan of sending his Son, Jesus, to die on the cross to pay the penalty for our sin.

Living at the dawn of the twenty-first century limits our appreciation of the fact that for 3000 years, the Old Testament has guided people from every walk of life. It was not just written for young people today, but also for people who needed to hear from God in A.D. 320 Rome or A.D. 1540 Germany. What this means is that not every story will affect you the way it has others through the years. But as you read through the Old Testament, you will be surprised at how many stories do relate to today. God's command to Moses and the Israelites to go into the Promised Land and possess it is the fulfillment of a promise to Abraham that God made long before Moses was even born. It shows that God has a plan for history and that he keeps his promises.

It is essential for you as a Christian to realize that your heavenly Father keeps his promises! We are able to give him control of our life because for centuries he has proven himself trustworthy. (See Hebrews 11 for a brief recap of God's faithfulness.)

The Old Testament tells us about the real-life struggles people experienced when faced with the choice of trusting God or doing things their own way.

Instead of giving us all of history to read, God has condensed his story into one book. He has even pointed out the most important lessons we need to pay attention to in order to live life to the fullest as his children.

that is not how it will be 9when you arrive in the place of rest the LORD your God is giving you. 10You will soon cross the Jordan River and live in the land the LORD your God is giving you as a special possession. When he gives you rest and security from all your enemies, 11you must bring everything I command you—your burnt offerings, your sacrifices, your tithes, your special gifts, and your offerings to fulfill a vow—to the place the LORD your God will choose for his name to be honored. 12You must celebrate there with your sons and daughters and all your servants in the presence of the LORD your God. And remember the Levites who live in your towns, for they will have no inheritance of land as their own. 13Be careful not to sacrifice your burnt offerings just anywhere. 14You may do so only at the place the LORD will choose within one of your tribal territories. There you must offer your burnt offerings and do everything I command you.

## TOGETHERNESS ● ● • • •

12:12, 18 **The Hebrews placed great emphasis on family worship. Whether offering a sacrifice or attending a great feast, the family was often together. This gave the children a healthy attitude toward worship, and it put extra meaning into it for the adults. Watching a family member confess his or her sin was just as important as celebrating a great holiday together. Although there are appropriate times to separate people by ages, some of the most meaningful worship can be experienced only when shared by old and young.**

15"But you may butcher animals for meat in any town, wherever you want, just as you do now with gazelle and deer. You may eat as many animals as the LORD your God gives you. All of you, whether ceremonially clean or unclean, may eat that meat. 16The only restriction is that you are not to eat the blood. You must pour it out on the ground like water.

17"But your offerings must not be eaten at home—neither the tithe of your grain and new wine and olive oil, nor the firstborn of your flocks and herds, nor an offering to fulfill a vow, nor your freewill offerings, nor your special gifts. 18You must eat these in the presence of the LORD your God at the place he will choose. Eat them there with your children, your servants, and the Levites who live in your towns, celebrating in the presence of the LORD your God in all you do. 19Be very careful never to forget the Levites as long as you live in your land.

20"When the LORD your God enlarges your territory as he has promised, you may eat meat whenever you want. 21It might happen that the place the LORD your God chooses for his name to be honored is a long way from your home. If so, you may butcher any of the cattle or sheep the LORD has given you, and you may eat the meat at your home as I have commanded you. 22Anyone, whether ceremonially clean or unclean, may eat that meat, just as you do now with gazelle and deer. 23The only restriction is never to eat the blood, for the blood is the life, and you must not eat the life with the meat. 24Instead, pour out the blood on the ground like water. 25Do not eat the blood; then all will go well with you and your children, because you will be doing what pleases the LORD. 26Take your sacred gifts and your offerings given to fulfill a vow to the place the LORD chooses to dwell. 27You must offer the meat and blood of your burnt offerings on the altar of the LORD your God. The blood of your other sacrifices must be poured out beside the altar of the LORD your God, but you may eat the meat. 28Be careful to obey all my commands so that all will go well with you and your children, because you will be doing what pleases the LORD your God.

29"When the LORD your God destroys the nations and you drive them out and occupy their land, 30do not be trapped into following their example in worshiping their gods. Do not say, 'How do these nations worship their gods? I want to follow their example.' 31You must not do this to the LORD your God. These nations have committed many detestable acts that the LORD hates, all in the name of their gods. They have even burned their sons and daughters as sacrifices to their gods. 32Carefully obey all the commands I give you. Do not add to them or subtract from them.

## CHAPTER 13 DON'T LISTEN TO FALSE PROPHETS.

"Suppose there are prophets among you, or those who have dreams about the future, and they promise you signs or miracles, 2and the predicted signs or miracles take place. If the prophets then say, 'Come, let us worship the gods of foreign nations,' 3do not listen to them. The LORD your God is testing you to see if you love him with all your heart and soul. 4Serve only the LORD your God and fear him alone. Obey his commands, listen to his voice, and cling to him. 5The false prophets or dreamers who try to lead you astray must be put to death, for they encourage rebellion against the LORD your God, who brought you out of slavery in the land of Egypt. Since they try to keep you from following the LORD your God, you must execute them to remove the evil from among you.

6"Suppose your brother, son, daughter, beloved wife, or closest friend comes to you secretly and says, 'Let us go worship other gods'—gods that neither you nor your ancestors have known. 7They might suggest that you worship the gods of peoples who live nearby or who come from the ends of the

## WHISPERS ● ● • • •

13:2-11 **The Israelites were warned not to listen to false prophets or to anyone else who tried to get them to worship other gods—even if this person was a close friend or family member. The temptation to abandon God's commands often sneaks up on us. It may come not with a loud shout, but in a whispering doubt. Whispers can be very persuasive, especially if they come from loved ones. But love for relatives should not take precedence over devotion to God. We can overcome whispered temptations by pouring out our feelings to God in prayer and by studying his Word.**

earth. 8If they do this, do not give in or listen, and have no pity. Do not spare or protect them. 9You must put them to death! You must be the one to initiate the execution; then all the people must join in. 10Stone the guilty ones to death because they have tried to draw you away from the LORD your God, who rescued you from the land of Egypt, the place of slavery. 11Then all Israel will hear about it and be afraid, and such wickedness will never again be done among you.

12"Suppose you hear in one of the towns the LORD your God is giving you 13that some worthless rabble among you have led their fellow citizens astray by encouraging them to worship foreign gods. 14In such cases, you must examine the facts carefully. If you find it is true and can prove that such a detestable act has occurred among you, 15you must attack that town and completely destroy* all its inhabitants, as well as all the livestock. 16Then you must pile all the plunder in the middle of the street and burn it. Put the entire town to the torch as a burnt offering to the LORD your God. That town must remain a ruin forever; it may never be rebuilt. 17Keep none of the plunder that has been set apart for destruction. Then the LORD will turn from his fierce anger and be merciful to you. He will have compassion on you and make you a great nation, just as he solemnly promised your ancestors.

18"The LORD your God will be merciful only if you obey him and keep all the commands I am giving you today, doing what is pleasing to him.

CHAPTER **14** **WHAT TO EAT AND NOT EAT.** "Since you are the people of the LORD your God, never cut yourselves or shave the hair above your foreheads for the sake of the dead. 2You have been set apart as holy to the LORD your God, and he has chosen you to be his own special treasure from all the nations of the earth.

3"You must not eat animals that are ceremonially unclean. 4These are the animals* you may eat: the ox, the sheep, the goat, 5the deer, the gazelle, the roebuck, the wild goat, the ibex, the antelope, and the mountain sheep.

6"Any animal that has split hooves and chews the cud may be eaten, 7but if the animal doesn't have both, it may not be eaten. So you may not eat the camel, the hare, or the rock badger.* They chew the cud but do not have split hooves. 8And the pig may not be eaten, for though it has split hooves, it does not chew the cud. All these animals are ceremonially unclean for you. You may not eat or even touch the dead bodies of such animals.

9"As for marine animals, you may eat whatever has both fins and scales. 10You may not, however, eat marine animals that do not have both fins and scales. They are ceremonially unclean for you.

11"You may eat any bird that is ceremonially clean. 12These are the birds you may not eat: the eagle, the vulture, the osprey, 13the buzzard, kites of all kinds, 14ravens of all kinds, 15the ostrich, the nighthawk, the seagull, hawks of all kinds, 16the little owl, the great owl, the white owl, 17the pelican, the carrion vulture, the cormorant, 18the stork, herons of all kinds, the hoopoe, and the bat.

19"All flying insects are ceremonially unclean for you and may not be eaten. 20But you may eat any winged creature that is ceremonially clean.

21"Do not eat anything that has died a natural death. You may give it to a foreigner living among you, or you may sell it to a foreigner. But do not eat it yourselves, for you are set apart as holy to the LORD your God.

"Do not boil a young goat in its mother's milk.

22"You must set aside a tithe of your crops—one-tenth of all the crops you harvest each year. 23Bring this tithe to the place the LORD your God chooses for his name to be honored, and eat it there in his presence. This applies to your tithes of grain, new wine, olive oil, and the firstborn males of your flocks and herds. The purpose of tithing is to teach you always to fear the LORD your God. 24Now the place the LORD your God chooses for his name to be honored might be a long way from your home. 25If so, you may sell the tithe portion of your crops and herds and take the money to the place the LORD your God chooses. 26When you arrive, use the money to buy anything you want—an ox, a sheep, some wine, or beer. Then feast there in the presence of the LORD your God and celebrate with your household. 27And do not forget the Levites in your community, for they have no inheritance as you do.

28"At the end of every third year bring the tithe of all your crops and store it in the nearest town. 29Give it to the Levites, who have no inheritance among you, as well as to the foreigners living among you, the orphans, and the widows in your towns, so they can eat and be satisfied. Then the LORD your God will bless you in all your work.

CHAPTER **15** **LENDING MONEY.** "At the end of every seventh year you must cancel your debts. 2This is how it must be done. Creditors must cancel the loans they have made to their fellow Israelites. They must not demand payment from their neighbors or relatives, for the LORD's time of release has arrived. 3This release from debt, however, applies only to your fellow Israelites—not to the foreigners living among you. 4There should be no poor among you, for the LORD your God will greatly bless you in the land he is giving you as a special possession. 5You will receive this blessing if you carefully obey the commands of the LORD your God that I am giving you today. 6The LORD your God will bless you as he has promised. You will lend money to many nations but will never need to borrow! You will rule many nations, but they will not rule over you!

7"But if there are any poor people in your towns

13:15 The Hebrew term used here refers to the complete consecration of things or people to the LORD, either by destroying them or by giving them as an offering; also in 13:17. 14:4 The identification of some of the animals and birds listed in this chapter is uncertain. 14:7 Or *coney,* or *hyrax.*

when you arrive in the land the LORD your God is giving you, do not be hard-hearted or tightfisted toward them. [8]Instead, be generous and lend them whatever they need. [9]Do not be mean-spirited and refuse someone a loan because the year of release is close at hand. If you refuse to make the loan and the needy person cries out to the LORD, you will be considered guilty of sin. [10]Give freely without begrudging it, and the LORD your God will bless you in everything you do. [11]There will always be some among you who are poor. That is why I am commanding you to share your resources freely with the poor and with other Israelites in need.

## POVERTY ● ● • • •

15:7-11 **God told the Israelites to help the poor among them when they arrived in the Promised Land. This was an important part of possessing the land. Many people conclude that people are poor through some fault of their own. This kind of reasoning makes it easy to close our hearts and hands against them. But we are not to invent reasons for ignoring the care of the poor. We are to respond to their needs no matter who or what was responsible for their condition. Who are the poor in your community? How could you help them?**

[12]"If an Israelite man or woman voluntarily becomes your servant and serves you for six years, in the seventh year you must set that servant free.

[13]"When you release a male servant, do not send him away empty-handed. [14]Give him a generous farewell gift from your flock, your threshing floor, and your winepress. Share with him some of the bounty with which the LORD your God has blessed you. [15]Remember that you were slaves in the land of Egypt and the LORD your God redeemed you! That is why I am giving you this command. [16]But suppose your servant says, 'I will not leave you,' because he loves you and your family, and he is well off with you. [17]In that case, take an awl and push it through his earlobe into the door. After that, he will be your servant for life.

"You must do the same for your female servants.

[18]"Do not consider it a hardship when you release your servants. Remember that for six years they have given you the services worth double the wages of hired workers, and the LORD your God will bless you in all you do.

[19]"You must set aside for the LORD your God all the firstborn males from your flocks and herds. Do not use the firstborn of your herds to work your fields, and do not shear the firstborn of your flocks. [20]Instead, you and your family must eat these animals in the presence of the LORD your God each year at the place he chooses. [21]But if this firstborn animal has any defect, such as being lame or blind, or if anything else is wrong with it, you must not sacrifice it to the LORD your God. [22]Instead, use it for food for your family at home. Anyone may eat it, whether ceremonially clean or unclean, just as anyone may eat a gazelle or deer. [23]But do not eat the blood. You must pour it out on the ground like water.

CHAPTER **16** **SPECIAL FESTIVALS.** "In honor of the LORD your God, always celebrate the Passover at the proper time in early spring,* for that was when the LORD your God brought you out of Egypt by night. [2]Your Passover sacrifice may be from either the flock or the herd, and it must be sacrificed to the LORD your God at the place he chooses for his name to be honored. [3]Eat it with bread made without yeast. For seven days eat only bread made without yeast, as you did when you escaped from Egypt in such a hurry. Eat this bread—the bread of suffering—so that you will remember the day you departed from Egypt as long as you live. [4]Let no yeast be found in any house throughout your land for seven days. And do not let any of the meat of the Passover lamb remain until the next morning.

[5]"The Passover must not be eaten in the towns that the LORD your God is giving you. [6]It must be offered at the place the LORD your God will choose for his name to be honored. Sacrifice it there as the sun goes down on the anniversary of your exodus from Egypt. [7]Roast the lamb and eat it in the place the LORD your God chooses. Then go back to your tents the next morning. [8]For the next six days you may not eat bread made with yeast. On the seventh day the people must assemble before the LORD your God, and no work may be done on that day.

[9]"Count off seven weeks from the beginning of your grain harvest. [10]Then you must celebrate the Festival of Harvest* to honor the LORD your God. Bring him a freewill offering in proportion to the blessings you have received from him. [11]It is a time to celebrate before the LORD your God at the place he chooses for his name to be honored. Celebrate with your whole family, all your servants, the Levites from your towns, and the foreigners, orphans, and widows who live among you. [12]Remember that you were slaves in Egypt, so be careful to obey all these laws.

[13]"Another celebration, the Festival of Shelters, must be observed for seven days at the end of the harvest season, after the grain has been threshed and the grapes have been pressed. [14]This festival will be a happy time of rejoicing with your family,

## PAY BACK ● ● • • •

16:16-17 **Three times a year every male was to make a journey to the sanctuary located in the city designated as the religious capital of Israel. At these feasts, each participant was encouraged to give what he could in proportion to what God had given him. God does not expect us to give more than we can, but we are blessed when we are able to give cheerfully. For some of us, 10 percent may be a burden. For most of us, it is far too little. Look around at what you have, then give in proportion to what you have been given.**

16:1 Hebrew *in the month of Abib.* This month of the Hebrew lunar calendar usually occurs in March and April. 16:10 Or *Festival of Weeks;* also in 16:16.

your servants, and with the Levites, foreigners, orphans, and widows from your towns. 15 For seven days celebrate this festival to honor the LORD your God at the place he chooses, for it is the LORD your God who gives you bountiful harvests and blesses all your work. This festival will be a time of great joy for all.

16 "Each year every man in Israel must celebrate these three festivals: the Festival of Unleavened Bread, the Festival of Harvest, and the Festival of Shelters. They must appear before the LORD your God at the place he chooses on each of these occasions, and they must bring a gift to the LORD. 17 All must give as they are able, according to the blessings given to them by the LORD your God.

18 "Appoint judges and officials for each of your tribes in all the towns the LORD your God is giving you. They will judge the people fairly throughout the land. 19 You must never twist justice or show partiality. Never accept a bribe, for bribes blind the eyes of the wise and corrupt the decisions of the godly. 20 Let true justice prevail, so you may live and occupy the land that the LORD your God is giving you.

21 "You must never set up an Asherah pole beside the altar of the LORD your God. 22 And never set up sacred pillars for worship, for the LORD your God hates them.

## CHAPTER 17

"Never sacrifice a sick or defective ox or sheep to the LORD your God, for he detests such gifts.

2 "Suppose a man or woman among you, in one of your towns that the LORD your God is giving you, has done evil in the sight of the LORD your God and has violated the covenant 3 by serving other gods or by worshiping the sun, the moon, or any of the forces of heaven, which I have strictly forbidden. 4 When you hear about it, investigate the matter thoroughly. If it is true that this detestable thing has been done in Israel, 5 then that man or woman must be taken to the gates of the town and stoned to death. 6 But never put a person to death on the testimony of only one witness. There must always be at least two or three witnesses. 7 The witnesses must throw the first stones, and then all the people will join in. In this way, you will purge all evil from among you.

8 "Suppose a case arises in a local court that is too hard for you to decide—for instance, whether someone is guilty of murder or only of manslaughter, or a difficult lawsuit, or a case involving different kinds of assault. Take such cases to the place the LORD your God will choose, 9 where the Levitical priests and the judge on duty will hear the case and decide what to do. 10 The decision they make at the place the LORD chooses will always stand. You must do exactly what they say. 11 After they have interpreted the law and reached a verdict, the sentence they impose must be fully executed; do not modify it in any way. 12 Anyone arrogant enough to

### WITNESSES ● ● • • •

**17:6-7 A person was not put to death on the testimony of only one witness. On the witness of two or three, a person could be condemned and then sentenced to death by stoning. The condemned person was taken outside the city gates, and the witnesses were the first to throw heavy stones down on him or her. Bystanders would then pelt the dying person with stones. This system would "purge" the evil by putting the idolater to death. At the same time, it protected the rights of accused persons two ways. First, by requiring several witnesses, it prevented any angry individual from giving false testimony. Second, by requiring the accusers to throw the first stones, it made them think twice about accusing unjustly. They were responsible to finish what they had started.**

reject the verdict of the judge or of the priest who represents the LORD your God must be put to death. Such evil must be purged from Israel. 13 Then everyone will hear about it and be afraid to act so arrogantly.

14 "You will soon arrive in the land the LORD your God is giving you, and you will conquer it and settle there. Then you may begin to think, 'We ought to have a king like the other nations around us.' 15 If this happens, be sure that you select as king the man the LORD your God chooses. You must appoint a fellow Israelite, not a foreigner. 16 The king must not build up a large stable of horses for himself, and he must never send his people to Egypt to buy horses there, for the LORD has told you, 'You must never return to Egypt.' 17 The king must not take many wives for himself, because they will lead him away from the LORD. And he must not accumulate vast amounts of wealth in silver and gold for himself.

18 "When he sits on the throne as king, he must copy these laws on a scroll for himself in the presence of the Levitical priests. 19 He must always keep this copy of the law with him and read it daily as long as he lives. That way he will learn to fear the LORD his God by obeying all the terms of this law. 20 This regular reading will prevent him from becoming proud and acting as if he is above his fellow citizens. It will also prevent him from turning away from these commands in the smallest way. This will ensure that he and his descendants will reign for many generations in Israel.

## CHAPTER 18

**GIVING TO PRIESTS AND LEVITES.** "Remember that the Levitical priests and the rest of the tribe of Levi will not be given an inheritance of land like the other tribes in Israel. Instead, the priests and Levites will eat from the offerings given to the LORD by fire, for that is their inheritance. 2 They will have no inheritance of their own among the Israelites. The LORD himself is their inheritance, just as he promised them.

3 "These are the parts the priests may claim as their share from the oxen and sheep that the people bring as offerings: the shoulder, the cheeks, and the stomach. 4 You must also give to the priests

## FAULTY CULTS ● ● ● • •

18:10-13 **Just as most of us are naturally curious about a magician's trick, the Israelites were curious about the occult practices of the Canaanite religions. But Satan is behind the occult, and God flatly forbade Israel to have anything to do with it. People today are still fascinated by horoscopes, fortune-telling, witchcraft, and bizarre cults. Often their interest comes from a desire to know and control the future. But Satan is no less dangerous today than he was in Moses' time. In the Bible, God tells us all we need to know about what is going to happen. The information Satan offers is likely to be distorted or completely false. With the trustworthy guidance of the Holy Spirit through the Scriptures and the church, we don't need to turn to occult sources for information— especially since the information from such sources is faulty.**

the first share of the grain, the new wine, the olive oil, and the wool at shearing time. 5For the LORD your God chose the tribe of Levi out of all your tribes to minister in the LORD's name forever.

6"Any Levite who so desires may come from any town in Israel, from wherever he is living, to the place the LORD chooses. 7He may minister there in the name of the LORD his God, just like his fellow Levites who are serving the LORD there. 8He may eat his share of the sacrifices and offerings, even if he has a private source of income.

9"When you arrive in the land the LORD your God is giving you, be very careful not to imitate the detestable customs of the nations living there. 10For example, never sacrifice your son or daughter as a burnt offering.* And do not let your people practice fortune-telling or sorcery, or allow them to interpret omens, or engage in witchcraft, 11or cast spells, or function as mediums or psychics, or call forth the spirits of the dead. 12Anyone who does these things is an object of horror and disgust to the LORD. It is because the other nations have done these things that the LORD your God will drive them out ahead of you. 13You must be blameless before the LORD your God. 14The people you are about to displace consult with sorcerers and fortune-tellers, but the LORD your God forbids you to do such things.

15"The LORD your God will raise up for you a prophet like me from among your fellow Israelites, and you must listen to that prophet. 16For this is what you yourselves requested of the LORD your God when you were assembled at Mount Sinai.* You begged that you might never again have to listen to the voice of the LORD your God or see this blazing fire for fear you would die.

17"Then the LORD said to me, 'Fine, I will do as they have requested. 18I will raise up a prophet like you from among their fellow Israelites. I will tell that prophet what to say, and he will tell the people everything I command him. 19I will personally deal with anyone who will not listen to the messages the prophet proclaims on my behalf. 20But any prophet who claims to give a message from another god or who falsely claims to speak for me must die.' 21You may wonder, 'How will we know whether the prophecy is from the LORD or not?' 22If the prophet predicts something in the LORD's name and it does not happen, the LORD did not give the message. That prophet has spoken on his own and need not be feared.

## CHAPTER 19 **CITIES OF REFUGE.** 

"The LORD your God will soon destroy the nations whose land he is giving you, and you will displace them and settle in their towns and homes. 2Then you must set apart three cities of refuge in the land the LORD your God is giving you to occupy. 3Divide the land the LORD your God is giving you into three districts, with one of these cities in each district. Keep the roads to these cities in good repair so that anyone who has killed someone can flee there for safety.

4"If someone accidentally kills a neighbor without harboring any previous hatred, the slayer may flee to any of these cities and be safe. 5For example, suppose someone goes into the forest with a neighbor to cut wood. And suppose one of them swings an ax and the ax head flies off the handle, killing the other person. In such cases, the slayer could flee to one of the cities of refuge and be safe. 6If the distance to the nearest city of refuge was too far, an enraged avenger might be able to chase down and kill the person who caused the death. The slayer would die, even though there was no death sentence and the first death had been an accident. 7That is why I am commanding you to set aside three cities of refuge.

8"If the LORD your God enlarges your territory, as he solemnly promised your ancestors, and gives you all the land he promised them, 9you must designate three additional cities of refuge. (He will give you this land if you obey all the commands I have given you—if you always love the LORD your God and walk in his ways.) 10That way you will prevent the death of innocent people in the land the LORD your God is giving you as a special possession, and you will not be held responsible for murder.

11"But suppose someone hates a neighbor and deliberately ambushes and murders that neighbor and then escapes to one of the cities of refuge. 12In that case, the leaders of the murderer's hometown must have the murderer brought back from the city of refuge and handed over to the dead person's avenger to be killed. 13Do not feel sorry for that murderer! Purge the guilt of murder from Israel so all may go well with you.

14"When you arrive in the land the LORD your God is giving you as a special possession, never steal someone's land by moving the boundary markers your ancestors set up to mark their property.

15"Never convict anyone of a crime on the testimony of just one witness. The facts of the case must be established by the testimony of two or three witnesses. 16If a malicious witness comes forward and accuses someone of a crime, 17then both the accuser and accused must appear before the priests

**18:10** Or *never make your son or daughter pass through the fire.* **18:16** Hebrew *Horeb,* another name for Sinai.

and judges who are on duty before the LORD. [18]They must be closely questioned, and if the accuser is found to be lying, [19]the accuser will receive the punishment intended for the accused. In this way, you will cleanse such evil from among you. [20]Those who hear about it will be afraid to do such an evil thing again. [21]You must never show pity! Your rule should be life for life, eye for eye, tooth for tooth, hand for hand, foot for foot.

## CHAPTER 20 RULES ABOUT WAR.

"When you go out to fight your enemies and you face horses and chariots and an army greater than your own, do not be afraid. The LORD your God, who brought you safely out of Egypt, is with you! [2]Before you go into battle, the priest will come forward to speak with the troops. [3]He will say, 'Listen to me, all you men of Israel! Do not be afraid as you go out to fight today! Do not lose heart or panic. [4]For the LORD your God is going with you! He will fight for you against your enemies, and he will give you victory!'

[5]"Then the officers of the army will address the troops and say, 'Has anyone just built a new house but not yet dedicated it? If so, go home! You might be killed in the battle, and someone else would dedicate your house! [6]Has anyone just planted a vineyard but not yet eaten any of its fruit? If so, go home! You might die in battle, and someone else would eat from it! [7]Has anyone just become engaged? Well, go home and get married! You might die in the battle, and someone else would marry your fiancée.' [8]Then the officers will also say, 'Is anyone terrified? If you are, go home before you frighten anyone else.' [9]When the officers have finished saying this to their troops, they will announce the names of the unit commanders.

[10]"As you approach a town to attack it, first offer its people terms for peace. [11]If they accept your terms and open the gates to you, then all the people inside will serve you in forced labor. [12]But if they refuse to make peace and prepare to fight, you must attack the town. [13]When the LORD your God hands it over to you, kill every man in the town. [14]But you may keep for yourselves all the women, children, livestock, and other plunder. You may enjoy the spoils of your enemies that the LORD your God has given you. [15]But these instructions apply only to distant towns, not to the towns of nations nearby.

[16]"As for the towns of the nations the LORD your God is giving you as a special possession, destroy every living thing in them. [17]You must completely destroy* the Hittites, Amorites, Canaanites, Perizzites, Hivites, and Jebusites, just as the LORD your God has commanded you. [18]This will keep the people of the land from teaching you their detestable customs in the worship of their gods, which would cause you to sin deeply against the LORD your God.

[19]"When you are besieging a town and the war drags on, do not destroy the trees. Eat the fruit, but do not cut down the trees. They are not enemies that need to be attacked! [20]But you may cut down trees that you know are not valuable for food. Use them to make the equipment you need to besiege the town until it falls.

### OUTNUMBERED ● ● • • •

20:1 **Just like the Israelites, we sometimes face overwhelming opposition. Whether at school, at work, or even at home, we can feel outnumbered and helpless. God bolstered the Israelites' confidence by reminding them that he was always with them and that he had already saved them from the potential danger. We, too, can feel secure when we consider that God is able to overcome even the most difficult odds.**

### "Here's what I did..."

It was strange how this one passage of Scripture—Ephesians 6:10-18, about putting on the whole armor of God—kept coming up again and again in one week. First it came up in my quiet time. Then we studied the same passage in the youth Bible study. Finally, my pastor preached a sermon on spiritual warfare.

Later that week my friend asked me if I would play the Ouija board with her. I felt uneasy about it, but it seemed like just a game, so I said yes. Some weird things happened; the piece that you put your fingers on really seemed to move of its own accord, and it spelled out some weird answers. I had a very creepy feeling that this was not of God. I told my friend I wanted to quit right now, that I didn't think God wanted us to do this. That night I called my youth pastor and told him about it. He pointed out that Deuteronomy 18:9-14 warns us against trying to seek the future from means other than God. He reminded me that Satan is always trying to find a way to sneak into our lives. And he reminded me of Ephesians 6 and the armor God gives us to fight the devil. I realized that God had been trying to prepare me for the temptation to use the Ouija board, but I wasn't paying close enough attention at the time.

I learned from my mistake. I will never touch or mess with a Ouija board or horoscopes or anything like that again.

*Carolyn*

AGE 16

20:17 The Hebrew term used here refers to the complete consecration of things or people to the LORD, either by destroying them or by giving them as an offering.

CHAPTER **21** **AN UNSOLVED MURDER.** "Suppose someone is found murdered in a field in the land the LORD your God is giving you, and you don't know who committed the murder. 2In such cases, your leaders and judges must determine which town is nearest the body. 3Then the leaders of that town must select a young cow that has never been trained or yoked to a plow. 4They must lead it to a valley that is neither plowed nor planted with a stream running through it. There they must break the cow's neck. 5The Levitical priests must go there also, for the LORD your God has chosen them to minister before him and to pronounce blessings in the LORD's name. And they are to decide all lawsuits and punishments.

6"The leaders of the town nearest the body must wash their hands over the young cow whose neck was broken. 7Then they must say, 'Our hands did not shed this blood, nor did we see it happen. 8O LORD, forgive your people Israel whom you have redeemed. Do not charge your people Israel with the guilt of murdering an innocent person.' Then they will be absolved of the guilt of this person's blood. 9By following these instructions and doing what is right in the LORD's sight, you will cleanse the guilt of murder from your community.

10"Suppose you go to war against your enemies and the LORD your God hands them over to you and you take captives. 11And suppose you see among the captives a beautiful woman, and you are attracted to her and want to marry her. 12If this happens, you may take her to your home, where she must shave her head, cut her fingernails, 13and change all her clothes. Then she must remain in your home for a full month, mourning for her father and mother. After that you may marry her. 14But if you marry her and then decide you do not like her, you must let her go free. You may not sell her or treat her as a slave, for you have humiliated her.

15"Suppose a man has two wives, but he loves one and not the other, and both have given him sons. And suppose the firstborn son is the son of the wife he does not love. 16When the man divides the inheritance, he may not give the larger inheritance to his younger son, the son of the wife he loves. 17He must give the customary double portion to his oldest son, who represents the strength of his father's manhood and who owns the rights of the firstborn son, even though he is the son of the wife his father does not love.

18"Suppose a man has a stubborn, rebellious son who will not obey his father or mother, even though they discipline him. 19In such cases, the father and mother must take the son before the leaders of the town. 20They must declare: 'This son of ours is stubborn and rebellious and refuses to obey. He is a worthless drunkard.' 21Then all the men of the town must stone him to death. In this way, you will cleanse this evil from among you, and all Israel will hear about it and be afraid.

22"If someone has committed a crime worthy of death and is executed and then hanged on a tree,

**RETURNS ● ● ● • •**

22:1-4 **The Hebrews were to care for and return lost animals or possessions to their rightful owners. The way of the world, by contrast, is "Finders keepers, losers weepers." To go beyond the finders-keepers rule by protecting and returning the property of others keeps us from being envious and greedy.**

23the body must never remain on the tree overnight. You must bury the body that same day, for anyone hanging on a tree is cursed of God. Do not defile the land the LORD your God is giving you as a special possession.

CHAPTER **22** **HELPING NEIGHBORS.** "If you see your neighbor's ox or sheep wandering away, don't pretend not to see it. Take it back to its owner. 2If it does not belong to someone nearby or you don't know who the owner is, keep it until the owner comes looking for it; then return it. 3Do the same if you find your neighbor's donkey, clothing, or anything else your neighbor loses. Don't pretend you did not see it.

4"If you see your neighbor's ox or donkey lying on the road, do not look the other way. Go and help your neighbor get it to its feet!

5"A woman must not wear men's clothing, and a man must not wear women's clothing. The LORD your God detests people who do this.

6"If you find a bird's nest on the ground or in a tree and there are young ones or eggs in it with the mother sitting in the nest, do not take the mother with the young. 7You may take the young, but let the mother go, so you may prosper and enjoy a long life.

8"Every new house you build must have a barrier around the edge of its flat rooftop. That way you will not bring the guilt of bloodshed on your household if someone falls from the roof.

9"Do not plant any other crop between the rows of your vineyard. If you do, you are forbidden to use either the grapes from the vineyard or the produce of the other crop.

10"Do not plow with an ox and a donkey harnessed together.

11"Do not wear clothing made of wool and linen woven together.

12"You must put tassels on the four corners of your cloaks.

13"Suppose a man marries a woman and, after sleeping with her, changes his mind about her 14and falsely accuses her of having slept with another man. He might say, 'I discovered she was not a virgin when I married her.' 15If the man does this, the woman's

**ROLES ● ● ● • •**

22:5 **This verse commands men and women not to reverse their sexual roles. It is not a statement about clothing styles. Today role rejections are common—there are men who want to become women and women who want to become men. It's not the clothing style that offends God, but using the style to act out a different sex role. God had a purpose in making us uniquely male and female.**

father and mother must bring the proof of her virginity to the leaders of the town. 16Her father must tell them, 'I gave my daughter to this man to be his wife, and now he has turned against her. 17He has accused her of shameful things, claiming that she was not a virgin when he married her. But here is the proof of my daughter's virginity.' Then they must spread the cloth before the judges. 18The judges must then punish the man. 19They will fine him one hundred pieces of silver,* for he falsely accused a virgin of Israel. The payment will be made to the woman's father. The woman will then remain the man's wife, and he may never divorce her.

20"But suppose the man's accusations are true, and her virginity could not be proved. 21In such cases, the judges must take the girl to the door of her father's home, and the men of the town will stone her to death. She has committed a disgraceful crime in Israel by being promiscuous while living in her parents' home. Such evil must be cleansed from among you.

22"If a man is discovered committing adultery, both he and the other man's wife must be killed. In this way, the evil will be cleansed from Israel.

23"Suppose a man meets a young woman, a virgin who is engaged to be married, and he has sexual intercourse with her. If this happens within a town, 24you must take both of them to the gates of the town and stone them to death. The woman is guilty because she did not scream for help. The man must die because he violated another man's wife. In this way, you will cleanse the land of evil.

25"But if the man meets the engaged woman out in the country, and he rapes her, then only the man should die. 26Do nothing to the young woman; she has committed no crime worthy of death. This case is similar to that of someone who attacks and murders a neighbor. 27Since the man raped her out in the country, it must be assumed that she screamed, but there was no one to rescue her.

28"If a man is caught in the act of raping a young woman who is not engaged, 29he must pay fifty pieces of silver* to her father. Then he must marry the young woman because he violated her, and he will never be allowed to divorce her.

30"A man must not have intercourse with his father's wife, for this would violate his father.

## CHAPTER 23 RULES ABOUT THE ASSEMBLY.

"If a man's testicles are crushed or his penis is cut off, he may not be included in the assembly of the LORD.

2"Those of illegitimate birth and their descendants for ten generations may not be included in the assembly of the LORD.

3"No Ammonites or Moabites, or any of their descendants for ten generations, may be included in the assembly of the LORD. 4These nations did not welcome you with food and water when you came out of Egypt. Instead, they tried to hire Balaam son of Beor from Pethor in Aram-naharaim* to curse you. 5(But the LORD your God would not listen to Balaam. He turned the intended curse into a blessing because the LORD your God loves you.) 6You must never, as long as you live, try to help the Ammonites or the Moabites in any way.

7"Do not detest the Edomites or the Egyptians, because the Edomites are your relatives, and you lived as foreigners among the Egyptians. 8The third generation of Egyptians who came with you from Egypt may enter the assembly of the LORD.

9"When you go to war against your enemies, stay away from everything impure.

10"Any man who becomes ceremonially defiled because of a nocturnal emission must leave the camp and stay away all day. 11Toward evening he must bathe himself, and at sunset he may return to the camp.

12"Mark off an area outside the camp for a latrine. 13Each of you must have a spade as part of your equipment. Whenever you relieve yourself, you must dig a hole with the spade and cover the excrement. 14The camp must be holy, for the LORD your God moves around in your camp to protect you and to defeat your enemies. He must not see any shameful thing among you, or he might turn away from you.

15"If slaves should escape from their masters and take refuge with you, do not force them to return. 16Let them live among you in whatever town they choose, and do not oppress them.

### SEX ●●●••

**23:17-18 Prostitution was strictly forbidden. To forbid this practice may seem obvious to us, but it may not have been so obvious to the Israelites. Almost every other religion known to them included prostitution as an important part of its worship services. Prostitution makes a mockery of God's original idea for sex. It treats sex as an isolated physical act rather than an act of commitment to another person. Outside of marriage, sex destroys relationships. Within marriage, if approached with the right attitude, it is a relationship builder. God frequently had to warn the people against the practice of extramarital sex. Today we still need to hear his warnings: Single people need to be reminded about premarital sex, and husbands and wives need to be reminded about sexual fidelity.**

17"No Israelite man or woman may ever become a temple prostitute. 18Do not bring to the house of the LORD your God any offering from the earnings of a prostitute, whether a man or a woman, for both are detestable to the LORD your God.

19"Do not charge interest on the loans you make to a fellow Israelite, whether it is money, food, or anything else that may be loaned with interest. 20You may charge interest to foreigners, but not to Israelites, so the LORD your God may bless you in everything you do in the land you are about to enter and occupy.

**22:19** Hebrew *100 shekels of silver,* about 2.5 pounds or 1.1 kilograms in weight. **22:29** Hebrew *50 shekels of silver,* about 1.25 pounds or 570 grams in weight. **23:4** *Aram-naharaim* means "Aram of the two rivers," thought to have been located between the Euphrates and Balih Rivers in northwestern Mesopotamia.

21"When you make a vow to the LORD your God, be prompt in doing whatever you promised him. For the LORD your God demands that you promptly fulfill all your vows. If you don't, you will be guilty of sin. 22However, it is not a sin to refrain from making a vow. 23But once you have voluntarily made a vow, be careful to do as you have said, for you have made a vow to the LORD your God.

24"You may eat your fill of grapes from your neighbor's vineyard, but do not take any away in a basket. 25And you may pluck a few heads of your neighbor's grain by hand, but you may not harvest it with a sickle.

## CHAPTER 24

"Suppose a man marries a woman but later discovers something about her that is shameful. So he writes her a letter of divorce, gives it to her, and sends her away. 2If she then leaves and marries another man 3and the second husband also divorces her or dies, 4the former husband may not marry her again, for she has been defiled. That would be detestable to the LORD. You must not bring guilt upon the land the LORD your God is giving you as a special possession.

5"A newly married man must not be drafted into the army or given any other special responsibilities. He must be free to be at home for one year, bringing happiness to the wife he has married.

6"It is wrong to take a pair of millstones, or even just the upper millstone, as a pledge, for the owner uses it to make a living.

7"If anyone kidnaps a fellow Israelite and treats him as a slave or sells him, the kidnapper must die. You must cleanse the evil from among you.

8"Watch all contagious skin diseases* carefully and follow the instructions of the Levitical priests; obey the commands I have given them. 9Remember what the LORD your God did to Miriam as you were coming from Egypt.

10"If you lend anything to your neighbor, do not enter your neighbor's house to claim the security. 11Stand outside and the owner will bring it out to you. 12If your neighbor is poor and has only a cloak to give as security, do not keep the cloak overnight. 13Return the cloak to its owner by sunset so your neighbor can sleep in it and bless you. And the LORD your God will count it as a righteous act.

14"Never take advantage of poor laborers, whether fellow Israelites or foreigners living in your towns. 15Pay them their wages each day before sunset because they are poor and are counting on it. Otherwise they might cry out to the LORD against you, and it would be counted against you as sin.

16"Parents must not be put to death for the sins of their children, nor the children for the sins of their parents. Those worthy of death must be executed for their own crimes.

17"True justice must be given to foreigners living among you and to orphans, and you must never accept a widow's garment in pledge of her debt.

### JUSTICE ● ● ● • •

**24:10-22 God told his people to treat the poor with justice. The powerless and poverty-stricken are often looked upon as incompetent or lazy when, in fact, they may be victims of oppression and circumstance. God says we must do all we can to help these needy ones. His justice did not permit the Israelites to insist on profits or quick payment from those who were less fortunate. Instead, his laws gave the poor every opportunity to better their situation, while providing humane options for those who couldn't. We are called to treat the poor fairly and to see that their needs are met.**

18Always remember that you were slaves in Egypt and that the LORD your God redeemed you. That is why I have given you this command.

19"When you are harvesting your crops and forget to bring in a bundle of grain from your field, don't go back to get it. Leave it for the foreigners, orphans, and widows. Then the LORD your God will bless you in all you do. 20When you beat the olives from your olive trees, don't go over the boughs twice. Leave some of the olives for the foreigners, orphans, and widows. 21This also applies to the grapes in your vineyard. Do not glean the vines after they are picked, but leave any remaining grapes for the foreigners, orphans, and widows. 22Remember that you were slaves in the land of Egypt. That is why I am giving you this command.

## CHAPTER 25

"Suppose two people take a dispute to court, and the judges declare that one is right and the other is wrong. 2If the person in the wrong is sentenced to be flogged, the judge will command him to lie down and be beaten in his presence with the number of lashes appropriate to the crime. 3No more than forty lashes may ever be given; more than forty lashes would publicly humiliate your neighbor.

4"Do not keep an ox from eating as it treads out the grain.

5"If two brothers are living together on the same property and one of them dies without a son, his widow must not marry outside the family. Instead, her husband's brother must marry her and fulfill the duties of a brother-in-law. 6The first son she bears to him will be counted as the son of the dead brother, so that his name will not be forgotten in Israel. 7But if the dead man's brother refuses to marry the widow, she must go to the town gate and say to the leaders there, 'My husband's brother refuses to preserve his brother's name in Israel—he refuses to marry me.' 8The leaders of the town will then summon him and try to reason with him. If he still insists that he doesn't want to marry her, 9the widow must walk over to him in the presence of the leaders, pull his sandal from his foot, and spit in his face. She will then say, 'This is what happens to a man who refuses to raise up a son for his brother.' 10Ever afterward his family will be referred to as 'the family of the man whose sandal was pulled off'!

11"If two Israelite men are fighting and the wife of one tries to rescue her husband by grabbing the

24:8 Traditonally rendered *leprosy.* The Hebrew word used here can describe various skin diseases.

testicles of the other man, [12]her hand must be cut off without pity.

[13]"You must use accurate scales when you weigh out merchandise, [14]and you must use full and honest measures. [15]Yes, use honest weights and measures, so that you will enjoy a long life in the land the LORD your God is giving you. [16]Those who cheat with dishonest weights and measures are detestable to the LORD your God.

[17]"Never forget what the Amalekites did to you as you came from Egypt. [18]They attacked you when you were exhausted and weary, and they struck down those who were lagging behind. They had no fear of God. [19]Therefore, when the LORD your God has given you rest from all your enemies in the land he is giving you as a special possession, you are to destroy the Amalekites and erase their memory from under heaven. Never forget this!

## CHAPTER 26 **GIVING GOD THE FIRST AND BEST.**

"When you arrive in the land the LORD your God is giving you as a special possession and you have conquered it and settled there, [2]put some of the first produce from each harvest into a basket and bring it to the place the LORD your God chooses for his name to be honored. [3]Go to the priest in charge at that time and say to him, 'With this gift I acknowledge that the LORD your God has brought me into the land he swore to give our ancestors.' [4]The priest will then take the basket from your hand and set it before the altar of the LORD your God. [5]You must then say in the presence of the LORD your God, 'My ancestor Jacob was a wandering Aramean who went to live in Egypt. His family was few in number, but in Egypt they became a mighty and numerous nation. [6]When the Egyptians mistreated and humiliated us by making us their slaves, [7]we cried out to the LORD, the God of our ancestors. He heard us and saw our hardship, toil, and oppression. [8]So the LORD brought us out of Egypt with amazing power, overwhelming terror, and miraculous signs and wonders. [9]He brought us to this place and gave us this land flowing with milk and honey! [10]And now, O LORD, I have brought you a token of the first crops you have given me from the ground.' Then place the produce before the LORD your God and worship him. [11]Afterward go and celebrate because of all the good things the LORD your God has given to you and your household. Remember to include the Levites and the foreigners living among you in the celebration.

[12]"Every third year you must offer a special tithe of your crops. You must give these tithes to the Levites, foreigners, orphans, and widows so that they will have enough to eat in your towns. [13]Then you must declare in the presence of the LORD your God, 'I have taken the sacred gift from my house and have given it to the Levites, foreigners, orphans, and widows, just as you commanded me. I have not violated or forgotten any of your commands. [14]I have not eaten any of it while in mourning; I have not touched it while I was ceremonially unclean; and I have not offered any of it to the dead. I have obeyed the LORD my God and have done everything you commanded me. [15]Look down from your holy dwelling place in heaven and bless your people Israel and the land you have given us—a land flowing with milk and honey—just as you solemnly promised our ancestors.'

[16]"Today the LORD your God has commanded you to obey all these laws and regulations. You must commit yourself to them without reservation. [17]You have declared today that the LORD is your God. You have promised to obey his laws, commands, and regulations by walking in his ways and doing everything he tells you. [18]The LORD has declared today that you are his people, his own special treasure, just as he promised, and that you must obey all his commands. [19]And if you do, he will make you greater than any other nation. Then you will receive praise, honor, and renown. You will be a nation that is holy to the LORD your God, just as he promised."

## CHAPTER 27 **THE ALTAR ON MOUNT EBAL.**

Then Moses and the leaders of Israel charged the people as follows: "Keep all these commands that I am giving you today. [2]When you cross the Jordan River and enter the land the LORD your God is giving you, set up some large stones and coat them with plaster. [3]Then write all the terms of this law on them. I repeat, you will soon cross the river to enter the land the LORD your God is giving you, a land flowing with milk and honey, just as the LORD, the God of your ancestors, promised you. [4]When you cross the Jordan, set up these stones at Mount Ebal and coat them with plaster, as I am commanding you today. [5]Then build an altar there to the LORD your God, using natural stones. [6]Do not shape the stones with an iron tool. On the altar you must offer burnt offerings to the LORD your God. [7]Sacrifice peace offerings on it also, and feast there with great joy before the LORD your God. [8]On the stones coated with plaster, you must clearly write all the terms of this law."

### JOURNEY ● ● • • •

**26:5-10 In Israelite tradition, each person was required to recite the history of God's dealings with his people. What is the history of your relationship with God? Can you put into clear and concise words what God has done for you? Find a friend with whom you can share your spiritual journey. Take turns telling your stories. This will help you clearly understand your personal spiritual history, as well as encourage and inspire you both.**

[9]Then Moses and the Levitical priests addressed all Israel as follows: "O Israel, be quiet and listen! Today you have become the people of the LORD your God. [10]So obey the LORD your God by keeping all these commands and laws that I am giving you today."

[11]That same day Moses gave this charge to the people: [12]"When you cross the Jordan River, the tribes of Simeon, Levi, Judah, Issachar, Joseph, and

## PLAIN FACTS ● ● • • •

27:15-26 **These curses were a series of oaths, spoken by the priests and affirmed by the people, by which the people promised to stay away from wrong actions. By saying *Amen*, "So be it," the people took responsibility for their actions. Sometimes looking at a list of curses like this gives us the idea that God has a bad temper and is out to crush anyone who steps out of line. But we need to see these restrictions not as threats, but as loving warnings about the plain facts of life. Just as we warn children to stay away from hot stoves and busy streets, God warns us to stay away from dangerous actions. But God does not leave us with only curses or consequences. Immediately following these curses, we discover the great blessings (positive consequences) that come from living for God (28:1-14). These give us extra incentive to obey God's laws. While all these blessings may not come in our lifetime on earth, those who obey God will experience the fullness of his blessing when he establishes the new heaven and the new earth.**

Benjamin must stand on Mount Gerizim to proclaim a blessing over the people. 13And the tribes of
Reuben, Gad, Asher, Zebulun, Dan, and Naphtali
must stand on Mount Ebal to proclaim a curse.
14Then the Levites must shout to all the people of
Israel:

15'Cursed is anyone who carves or casts idols and secretly sets them up. These idols, the work of craftsmen, are detestable to the LORD.'
And all the people will reply, 'Amen.'

16'Cursed is anyone who despises father or mother.'
And all the people will reply, 'Amen.'

17'Cursed is anyone who steals property from a neighbor by moving a boundary marker.'
And all the people will reply, 'Amen.'

18'Cursed is anyone who leads a blind person astray on the road.'
And all the people will reply, 'Amen.'

19'Cursed is anyone who is unjust to foreigners, orphans, and widows.'
And all the people will reply, 'Amen.'

20'Cursed is anyone who has sexual intercourse with his father's wife, for he has violated his father.'
And all the people will reply, 'Amen.'

21'Cursed is anyone who has sexual intercourse with an animal.'
And all the people will reply, 'Amen.'

22'Cursed is anyone who has sexual intercourse with his sister, whether she is the daughter of his father or his mother.'
And all the people will reply, 'Amen.'

23'Cursed is anyone who has sexual intercourse with his mother-in-law.'
And all the people will reply, 'Amen.'

24'Cursed is anyone who kills another person in secret.'
And all the people will reply, 'Amen.'

25'Cursed is anyone who accepts payment to kill an innocent person.'
And all the people will reply, 'Amen.'

26'Cursed is anyone who does not affirm the terms of this law by obeying them.'
And all the people will reply, 'Amen.'

## CHAPTER 28 BLESSINGS FOR OBEDIENCE.

"If you
fully obey the LORD your God by keeping all the
commands I am giving you today, the LORD your
God will exalt you above all the nations of the world.
2You will experience all these blessings if you obey
the LORD your God:

3 You will be blessed in your towns and in the country.
4 You will be blessed with many children and productive fields.
You will be blessed with fertile herds and flocks.
5 You will be blessed with baskets overflowing with fruit, and with kneading bowls filled with bread.
6 You will be blessed wherever you go, both in coming and in going.

7"The LORD will conquer your enemies when they
attack you. They will attack you from one direction,
but they will scatter from you in seven!
8"The LORD will bless everything you do and will
fill your storehouses with grain. The LORD your God
will bless you in the land he is giving you.
9"If you obey the commands of the LORD your
God and walk in his ways, the LORD will establish
you as his holy people as he solemnly promised to
do. 10Then all the nations of the world will see that
you are a people claimed by the LORD, and they will
stand in awe of you.
11"The LORD will give you an abundance of good
things in the land he swore to give your ancestors—
many children, numerous livestock, and abundant
crops. 12The LORD will send rain at the proper time
from his rich treasury in the heavens to bless all the
work you do. You will lend to many nations, but you
will never need to borrow from them. 13If you listen
to these commands of the LORD your God and carefully obey them, the LORD will make you the head
and not the tail, and you will always have the upper
hand. 14You must not turn away from any of the
commands I am giving you today to follow after
other gods and worship them.
15"But if you refuse to listen to the LORD your God
and do not obey all the commands and laws I am
giving you today, all these curses will come and
overwhelm you:

16 You will be cursed in your towns and in the country.
17 You will be cursed with baskets empty of fruit, and with kneading bowls empty of bread.
18 You will be cursed with few children and barren fields.
You will be cursed with infertile herds and flocks.

19 You will be cursed wherever you go, both in coming and in going.

20 "The LORD himself will send against you curses, confusion, and disillusionment in everything you do, until at last you are completely destroyed for doing evil and forsaking me. 21 The LORD will send diseases among you until none of you are left in the land you are about to enter and occupy. 22 The LORD will strike you with wasting disease, fever, and inflammation, with scorching heat and drought, and with blight and mildew. These devastations will pursue you until you die. 23 The skies above will be as unyielding as bronze, and the earth beneath will be as hard as iron. 24 The LORD will turn your rain into sand and dust, and it will pour down from the sky until you are destroyed.

25 "The LORD will cause you to be defeated by your enemies. You will attack your enemies from one direction, but you will scatter from them in seven! You will be an object of horror to all the kingdoms of the earth. 26 Your dead bodies will be food for the birds and wild animals, and no one will be there to chase them away.

27 "The LORD will afflict you with the boils of Egypt and with tumors, scurvy, and the itch, from which you cannot be cured. 28 The LORD will strike you with madness, blindness, and panic. 29 You will grope around in broad daylight, just like a blind person groping in the darkness, and you will not succeed at anything you do. You will be oppressed and robbed continually, and no one will come to save you.

30 "You will be engaged to a woman, but another man will ravish her. You will build a house, but someone else will live in it. You will plant a vineyard, but you will never enjoy its fruit. 31 Your ox will be butchered before your eyes, but you won't get a single bite of the meat. Your donkey will be driven away, never to be returned. Your sheep will be given to your enemies, and no one will be there to help you. 32 You will watch as your sons and daughters are taken away as slaves. Your heart will break as you long for them, but nothing you do will help. 33 A foreign nation you have never heard about will eat the crops you worked so hard to grow. You will suffer under constant oppression and harsh treatment. 34 You will go mad because of all the tragedy around you. 35 The LORD will cover you from head to foot with incurable boils.

36 "The LORD will exile you and the king you crowned to a nation unknown to you and your ancestors. Then in exile you will worship gods of wood and stone! 37 You will become an object of horror, a proverb and a mockery among all the nations to which the LORD sends you.

38 "You will plant much but harvest little, for locusts will eat your crops. 39 You will plant vineyards and care for them, but you will not drink the wine or eat the grapes, for worms will destroy the vines. 40 You will grow olive trees throughout your land, but you will never use the olive oil, for the trees will drop the fruit before it is ripe. 41 You will have sons and daughters, but you will not keep them, for they will be led away into captivity. 42 Swarms of insects will destroy your trees and crops. 43 The foreigners living among you will become stronger and stronger, while you become weaker and weaker. 44 They will lend money to you, not you to them. They will be the head, and you will be the tail!

45 "If you refuse to listen to the LORD your God and to obey the commands and laws he has given you, all these curses will pursue and overtake you until you are destroyed. 46 These horrors will serve as a sign and warning among you and your descendants forever. 47 Because you have not served the LORD your God with joy and enthusiasm for the abundant benefits you have received, 48 you will serve your enemies whom the LORD will send against you. You will be left hungry, thirsty, naked, and lacking in everything. They will oppress you harshly until you are destroyed.

## FLIPPED OUT ● ● • • •

28:34 **One of the curses for those who rejected God was that they would go mad from seeing all the tragedy around them. Do you ever feel that you will go crazy if you hear about one more rape, kidnapping, murder, or war? Much of the world's evil is a result of people's failure to acknowledge and serve God. When you hear bad news, don't groan helplessly as do unbelievers, who have no hope for the future. Remind yourself that in spite of it all, God has ultimate control and one day will come back to make everything right.**

49 "The LORD will bring a distant nation against you from the end of the earth, and it will swoop down on you like an eagle. It is a nation whose language you do not understand, 50 a fierce and heartless nation that shows no respect for the old and no pity for the young. 51 Its armies will devour your livestock and crops, and you will starve to death. They will leave you no grain, new wine, olive oil, calves, or lambs, bringing about your destruction. 52 They will lay siege to your cities until all the fortified walls in your land—the walls you trusted to protect you—are knocked down. They will attack all the towns in the land the LORD your God has given you. 53 The siege will be so severe that you will eat the flesh of your own sons and daughters, whom the LORD your God has given you. 54 The most tenderhearted man among you will have no compassion for his own brother, his beloved wife, and his surviving children. 55 He will refuse to give them a share of the flesh he is devouring—the flesh of one of his own children—because he has nothing else to eat during the siege that your enemy will inflict on all your towns. 56 The most tender and delicate woman among you—so delicate she would not so much as touch her feet to the ground—will be cruel to the husband she loves and to her own son or daughter. 57 She will hide from them the afterbirth and the new baby she has borne, so that she herself can secretly

eat them. She will have nothing else to eat during the siege and terrible distress that your enemy will inflict on all your towns.

58"If you refuse to obey all the terms of this law that are written in this book, and if you do not fear the glorious and awesome name of the LORD your God, 59then the LORD will overwhelm both you and your children with indescribable plagues. These plagues will be intense and without relief, making you miserable and unbearably sick. 60He will bring against you all the diseases of Egypt that you feared so much, and they will claim you. 61The LORD will bring against you every sickness and plague there is, even those not mentioned in this Book of the Law, until you are destroyed. 62Though you are as numerous as the stars in the sky, few of you will be left because you would not listen to the LORD your God.

63"Just as the LORD has found great pleasure in helping you to prosper and multiply, the LORD will find pleasure in destroying you, until you disappear from the land you are about to enter and occupy. 64For the LORD will scatter you among all the nations from one end of the earth to the other. There you will worship foreign gods that neither you nor your ancestors have known, gods made of wood and stone! 65There among those nations you will find no place of security and rest. And the LORD will cause your heart to tremble, your eyesight to fail, and your soul to despair. 66Your lives will hang in doubt. You will live night and day in fear, with no reason to believe that you will see the morning light. 67In the morning you will say, 'If only it were night!' And in the evening you will say, 'If only it were morning!' You will say this because of your terror at the awesome horrors you see around you. 68Then the LORD will send you back to Egypt in ships, a journey I promised you would never again make. There you will offer to sell yourselves to your enemies as slaves, but no one will want to buy you."

CHAPTER **29** **GOD'S COVENANT REVIEWED.** These are the terms of the covenant the LORD commanded Moses to make with the Israelites while they were in the land of Moab, in addition to the covenant he had made with them at Mount Sinai.*

2Moses summoned all the Israelites and said to them, "You have seen with your own eyes everything the LORD did in Egypt to Pharaoh and all his servants and his whole country—3all the great tests of strength, the miraculous signs, and the amazing wonders. 4But to this day the LORD has not given you minds that understand, nor eyes that see, nor ears that hear! 5For forty years I led you through the wilderness, yet your clothes and sandals did not wear out. 6You had no bread or wine or other strong drink, but he gave you food so you would know that he is the LORD your God. 7When we came here, King Sihon of Heshbon and King Og of Bashan came out to fight against us, but we defeated them. 8We took their land and gave it to the tribes of Reuben and Gad and to the half-tribe of Manasseh as their inheritance.

9"Therefore, obey the terms of this covenant so that you will prosper in everything you do. 10All of you—your tribal leaders, your judges, your officers, all the men of Israel—are standing today before the LORD your God. 11With you are your little ones, your wives, and the foreigners living among you who chop your wood and carry your water. 12You are standing here today to enter into a covenant with the LORD your God. The LORD is making this covenant with you today, and he has sealed it with an oath. 13He wants to confirm you today as his people and to confirm that he is your God, just as he promised you, and as he swore to your ancestors Abraham, Isaac, and Jacob. 14But you are not the only ones with whom the LORD is making this covenant with its obligations. 15The LORD your God is making this covenant with you who stand in his presence today and also with all future generations of Israel.

16"Surely you remember how we lived in the land of Egypt and how we traveled through the lands of enemy nations as we left. 17You have seen their de-

## EVIL SEEDS ● ● ● • •

29:18 **Moses cautioned that the day the Hebrews chose to turn from God, a root would be planted that would produce bitter fruit. When we decide to do what we know is wrong, we plant an evil seed that begins to grow out of control—eventually yielding a crop of sorrow and pain. But we can prevent those seeds of sin from taking root. If you have done something wrong, confess it to God and others immediately. If the seed never finds fertile soil, its bitter fruit will never ripen.**

29:1 Hebrew *Horeb,* another name for Sinai.

testable idols made of wood, stone, silver, and gold.
18The LORD made this covenant with you so that no
man, woman, family, or tribe among you would turn
away from the LORD our God to worship these gods
of other nations, and so that no root among you
would bear bitter and poisonous fruit. 19Let none of
those who hear the warnings of this curse consider
themselves immune, thinking, 'I am safe, even
though I am walking in my own stubborn way.' This
would lead to utter ruin! 20The LORD will not pardon
such people. His anger and jealousy will burn
against them. All the curses written in this book will
come down on them, and the LORD will erase their
names from under heaven. 21The LORD will separate
them from all the tribes of Israel, to pour out on
them all the covenant curses recorded in this Book of
the Law.

22"Then the generations to come, both your own
descendants and the foreigners who come from distant lands, will see the devastation of the land and
the diseases the LORD will send against it. 23They will
find its soil turned into sulfur and salt, with nothing
planted and nothing growing, not even a blade of
grass. It will be just like Sodom and Gomorrah,
Admah and Zeboiim, which the LORD destroyed in
his anger. 24The surrounding nations will ask, 'Why
has the LORD done this to his land? Why was he so
angry?'

25"And they will be told, 'This happened because
the people of the land broke the covenant they made
with the LORD, the God of their ancestors, when he
brought them out of the land of Egypt. 26They turned
to serve and worship other gods that were foreign to
them, gods that the LORD had not designated for
them. 27That is why the LORD's anger burned against
this land, bringing down on it all the curses recorded
in this book. 28In great anger and fury the LORD
uprooted his people from their land and exiled them
to another land, where they still live today!'

29"There are secret things that belong to the LORD
our God, but the revealed things belong to us and
our descendants forever, so that we may obey these
words of the law.

CHAPTER **30** **COMING BACK TO GOD.** "Suppose all
these things happen to you—the blessings and the
curses I have listed—and you meditate on them as
you are living among the nations to which the LORD
your God has exiled you. 2If at that time you return
to the LORD your God, and you and your children
begin wholeheartedly to obey all the commands I
have given you today, 3then the LORD your God will
restore your fortunes. He will have mercy on you and
gather you back from all the nations where he has
scattered you. 4Though you are at the ends of the
earth, the LORD your God will go and find you and
bring you back again. 5He will return you to the land
that belonged to your ancestors, and you will possess
that land again. He will make you even more prosperous and numerous than your ancestors!

6"The LORD your God will cleanse your heart and
the hearts of all your descendants so that you will
love him with all your heart and soul, and so you
may live! 7The LORD your God will inflict all these
curses on your enemies and persecutors. 8Then you
will again obey the LORD and keep all the commands
I am giving you today. 9The LORD your God will
make you successful in everything you do. He will
give you many children and numerous livestock, and
your fields will produce abundant harvests, for the
LORD will delight in being good to you as he was to
your ancestors. 10The LORD your God will delight in
you if you obey his voice and keep the commands
and laws written in this Book of the Law, and if you
turn to the LORD your God with all your heart and
soul.

### FRESH START ● ● • • •

**30:1-6 Moses told the Hebrews that when they were ready to return to God, he would be ready to receive them. God's mercy is unbelievable. It goes far beyond what we can imagine. Even if the Jews deliberately walked away from him and ruined their lives, God would still take them back. God wants to forgive us, too, and bring us back to himself. Some people will not learn this until their world has crashed in around them. Then the sorrow and pain seem to open their eyes to what God has been saying all along. Are you separated from God by sin? No matter how far you have wandered, God promises a fresh start if only you will turn to him.**

11"This command I am giving you today is not too
difficult for you to understand or perform. 12It is not
up in heaven, so distant that you must ask, 'Who will
go to heaven and bring it down so we can hear and
obey it?' 13It is not beyond the sea, so far away that
you must ask, 'Who will cross the sea to bring it to
us so we can hear and obey it?' 14The message is very
close at hand; it is on your lips and in your heart so
that you can obey it.

15"Now listen! Today I am giving you a choice
between prosperity and disaster, between life and
death. 16I have commanded you today to love the
LORD your God and to keep his commands, laws,
and regulations by walking in his ways. If you do
this, you will live and become a great nation, and the
LORD your God will bless you and the land you are
about to enter and occupy. 17But if your heart turns
away and you refuse to listen, and if you are drawn
away to serve and worship other gods, 18then I warn
you now that you will certainly be destroyed. You
will not live a long, good life in the land you are
crossing the Jordan to occupy.

19"Today I have given you the choice between life
and death, between blessings and curses. I call on
heaven and earth to witness the choice you make.
Oh, that you would choose life, that you and your
descendants might live! 20Choose to love the LORD
your God and to obey him and commit yourself to
him, for he is your life. Then you will live long in the
land the LORD swore to give your ancestors Abraham,
Isaac, and Jacob."

CHAPTER **31** **JOSHUA APPOINTED LEADER.** When Moses had finished saying* these things to all the people of Israel, [2]he said, "I am now 120 years old and am no longer able to lead you. The LORD has told me that I will not cross the Jordan River. [3]But the LORD your God himself will cross over ahead of you. He will destroy the nations living there, and you will take possession of their land. Joshua is your new leader, and he will go with you, just as the LORD promised. [4]The LORD will destroy the nations living in the land, just as he destroyed Sihon and Og, the kings of the Amorites. [5]The LORD will hand over to you the people who live there, and you will deal with them as I have commanded you. [6]Be strong and courageous! Do not be afraid of them! The LORD your God will go ahead of you. He will neither fail you nor forsake you."

[7]Then Moses called for Joshua, and as all Israel watched he said to him, "Be strong and courageous! For you will lead these people into the land that the LORD swore to give their ancestors. You are the one who will deliver it to them as their inheritance. [8]Do not be afraid or discouraged, for the LORD is the one who goes before you. He will be with you; he will neither fail you nor forsake you."

[9]So Moses wrote down this law and gave it to the priests, who carried the Ark of the LORD's covenant, and to the leaders of Israel. [10]Then Moses gave them this command: "At the end of every seventh year, the Year of Release, during the Festival of Shelters, [11]you must read this law to all the people of Israel when they assemble before the LORD your God at the place he chooses. [12]Call them all together—men, women, children, and the foreigners living in your towns—so they may listen and learn to fear the LORD your God and carefully obey all the terms of this law. [13]Do this so that your children who have not known these laws will hear them and will learn to fear the LORD your God. Do this as long as you live in the land you are crossing the Jordan to occupy."

[14]Then the LORD said to Moses, "The time has come for you to die. Call Joshua and take him with you to the Tabernacle,* and I will commission him there." So Moses and Joshua went and presented themselves at the Tabernacle. [15]And the LORD appeared to them in a pillar of cloud at the entrance to the sacred tent.

[16]The LORD said to Moses, "You are about to die and join your ancestors. After you are gone, these people will begin worshiping foreign gods, the gods of the land where they are going. They will abandon me and break the covenant I have made with them. [17]Then my anger will blaze forth against them. I will abandon them, hiding my face from them, and they will be destroyed. Terrible trouble will come down on them, so that they will say, 'These disasters have come because God is no longer among us!' [18]At that time I will hide my face from them on account of all the sins they have committed by worshiping other gods.

[19]"Now write down the words of this song, and teach it to the people of Israel. Teach them to sing it, so it may serve as a witness against them. [20]For I will bring them into the land I swore to give their ancestors—a land flowing with milk and honey. There they will become prosperous; they will eat all the food they want and become well nourished. Then they will begin to worship other gods; they will despise me and break my covenant. [21]Then great disasters will come down on them, and this song will stand as evidence against them, for it will never be forgotten by their descendants. I know what these people are like, even before they have entered the land I swore to give them." [22]So that very day Moses wrote down the words of the song and taught it to the Israelites.

[23]Then the LORD commissioned Joshua son of Nun with these words: "Be strong and courageous! You must bring the people of Israel into the land I swore to give them. I will be with you."

[24]When Moses had finished writing down this entire body of law in a book, [25]he gave these instructions to the Levites who carried the Ark of the LORD's covenant: [26]"Take this Book of the Law and place it beside the Ark of the Covenant of the LORD your God, so it may serve as a witness against the people of Israel. [27]For I know how rebellious and stubborn you are. Even now, while I am still with you, you have rebelled against the LORD. How much more rebellious will you be after my death! [28]Now summon all the leaders and officials of your tribes so that I can speak to them and call heaven and earth to witness against them. [29]I know that after my death you will become utterly corrupt and will turn from the path I have commanded you to follow. In the days to come, disaster will come down on you, for you will make the LORD very angry by doing what is evil in his sight."

[30]So Moses recited this entire song to the assembly of Israel:

CHAPTER **32** **MOSES' SONG.**

1 "Listen, O heavens, and I will speak!
Hear, O earth, the words that I say!
2 My teaching will fall on you like rain;
my speech will settle like dew.
My words will fall like rain on tender grass,
like gentle showers on young plants.

## REPENTANCE ● ● • • ·

31:27-29 **Moses knew that the Israelites, in spite of all they had seen of God's work, were rebellious at heart. They deserved God's punishment, although they often received his mercy instead. We, too, are stubborn and rebellious by nature. Throughout our lives we struggle with sin. Repentance once a month or once a week is not enough. We must constantly turn from our sins to God and let his mercy save us.**

31:1 As in Dead Sea Scrolls and Greek version; Masoretic Text reads *Moses went and spoke.* 31:14 Hebrew *Tent of Meeting;* also in 31:14b.

### VARIETY IN WORSHIP

Israel's worship involved all of the senses. This reinforced the meaning of the ceremony and painted a dramatic picture that worship touches all areas of life.

**SIGHT**
The beauty and symbolism of the Tabernacle; every color and hue had a meaning

**HEARING**
The use of music; there were instructions for the use of a variety of instruments, and the Bible records many songs

**SMELL**
The sacrifices were burned, emitting a familiar aroma

**TASTE**
Israel's festivals were celebrations and memorials—much of the food had symbolic importance

**TOUCH**
At the sacrifice, they were to touch the head of the animal to symbolize the fact that it was taking their place

---

3 I will proclaim the name of the LORD;
how glorious is our God!
4 He is the Rock; his work is perfect.
Everything he does is just and fair.
He is a faithful God who does no wrong;
how just and upright he is!
5 "But they have acted corruptly toward him;
when they act like that, are they really his
children?*
They are a deceitful and twisted generation.
6 Is this the way you repay the LORD,
you foolish and senseless people?
Isn't he your Father who created you?
Has he not made you and established you?
7 Remember the days of long ago;
think about the generations past.
Ask your father and he will inform you.
Inquire of your elders, and they will tell you.
8 When the Most High assigned lands to the
nations,
when he divided up the human race,
he established the boundaries of the peoples
according to the number of angelic beings.*
9 For the people of Israel belong to the LORD;
Jacob is his special possession.
10 "He found them in a desert land,
in an empty, howling wasteland.
He surrounded them and watched over them;
he guarded them as his most precious
possession.*
11 Like an eagle that rouses her chicks
and hovers over her young,
so he spread his wings to take them in
and carried them aloft on his pinions.
12 The LORD alone guided them;
they lived without any foreign gods.
13 He made them ride over the highlands;
he let them feast on the crops of the fields.
He nourished them with honey from the cliffs,
with olive oil from the hard rock.
14 He fed them curds from the herd and milk from
the flock,
together with the fat of lambs and goats.
He gave them choice rams and goats from Bashan,
together with the choicest wheat.
You drank the finest wine,
made from the juice of grapes.
15 But Israel* soon became fat and unruly;
the people grew heavy, plump, and stuffed!
Then they abandoned the God who had made
them;
they made light of the Rock of their salvation.
16 They stirred up his jealousy by worshiping
foreign gods;
they provoked his fury with detestable acts.
17 They offered sacrifices to demons, non-gods,
to gods they had not known before,
to gods only recently arrived,
to gods their ancestors had never feared.
18 You neglected the Rock who had fathered you;
you forgot the God who had given you birth.
19 "The LORD saw this and was filled with loathing.
He was provoked to anger by his own sons
and daughters.
20 He said, 'I will abandon them;
I will see to their end!
For they are a twisted generation,
children without integrity.

**32:5** The meaning of the Hebrew is uncertain. **32:8** As in Dead Sea Scrolls, which read *of the sons of God,* and Greek version, which reads *of the angels of god;* Masoretic Text reads *of the sons of Israel.* **32:10** Hebrew *as the apple of his eye.* **32:15** Hebrew *Jeshurun,* a term of endearment for Israel.

[21] They have roused my jealousy by worshiping
non-gods;
they have provoked my fury with useless idols.
Now I will rouse their jealousy by blessing other
nations;
I will provoke their fury by blessing the
foolish Gentiles.
[22] For my anger blazes forth like fire
and burns to the depths of the grave.*
It devours the earth and all its crops
and ignites the foundations of the mountains.
[23] I will heap disasters upon them
and shoot them down with my arrows.
[24] I will send against them wasting famine,
burning fever, and deadly disease.
They will be troubled by the fangs of wild beasts,
by poisonous snakes that glide in the dust.
[25] Outside, the sword will bring death,
and inside, terror will strike
both young men and young women,
both infants and the aged.
[26] I decided to scatter them,*
so even the memory of them would disappear.
[27] But I feared the taunt of the enemy,
that their adversaries might misunderstand
and say,
"Our power has triumphed!
It was not the LORD who did this!"'

[28] "Israel is a nation that lacks sense;
the people are foolish, without understanding.
[29] Oh, that they were wise and could understand
this!
Oh, that they might know their fate!
[30] How could one person chase a thousand of them,
and two people put ten thousand to flight,
unless their Rock had sold them,
unless the LORD had given them up?
[31] But the rock of our enemies is not like our Rock,
as even they recognize.*
[32] Their vine grows from the vine of Sodom,
from the vineyards of Gomorrah.
Their grapes are poison,
and their clusters are bitter.
[33] Their wine is the venom of snakes,
the deadly poison of vipers.

[34] "'I am storing up these things,
sealing them away within my treasury.
[35] I will take vengeance; I will repay those who
deserve it.
In due time their feet will slip.
Their day of disaster will arrive,
and their destiny will overtake them.'

[36] "Indeed, the LORD will judge his people,
and he will change his mind about* his servants,
when he sees their strength is gone
and no one is left, slave or free.
[37] Then he will ask, 'Where are their gods,
the rocks they fled to for refuge?
[38] Where now are those gods,
who ate the fat of their sacrifices
and drank the wine of their offerings?
Let those gods arise and help you!
Let them provide you with shelter!
[39] Look now; I myself am he!
There is no god other than me!
I am the one who kills and gives life;
I am the one who wounds and heals;
no one delivers from my power!
[40] Now I raise my hand to heaven
and declare, "As surely as I live,
[41] when I sharpen my flashing sword
and begin to carry out justice,
I will bring vengeance on my enemies
and repay those who hate me.
[42] I will make my arrows drunk with blood,
and my sword will devour flesh—
the blood of the slaughtered and the captives,
and the heads of the enemy leaders."'

[43] "Rejoice with him, O heavens,
and let all the angels of God worship him,*
for he will avenge the blood of his servants.
He will take vengeance on his enemies
and cleanse his land and his people."

[44] So Moses came with Joshua* son of Nun and recited all the words of this song to the people. [45] When
Moses had finished reciting these words to Israel, [46] he
added: "Take to heart all the words I have given you
today. Pass them on as a command to your children so
they will obey every word of this law. [47] These instructions are not mere words—they are your life! By
obeying them you will enjoy a long life in the land
you are crossing the Jordan River to occupy."

[48] That same day the LORD said to Moses, [49] "Go to
Moab, to the mountains east of the river,* and climb
Mount Nebo, which is across from Jericho. Look out
across the land of Canaan, the land I am giving to
the people of Israel as their own possession. [50] Then
you must die there on the mountain and join your
ancestors, just as Aaron, your brother, died on
Mount Hor and joined his ancestors. [51] For both of
you broke faith with me among the Israelites at the
waters of Meribah at Kadesh* in the wilderness of
Zin. You failed to demonstrate my holiness to the
people of Israel there. [52] So you will see the land from
a distance, but you may not enter the land I am
giving to the people of Israel."

## CHAPTER 33 **MOSES BLESSES THE PEOPLE.** This is
the blessing that Moses, the man of God, gave to the
people of Israel before his death:

[2] "The LORD came from Mount Sinai
and dawned upon us* from Mount Seir;

32:22 Hebrew *of Sheol.* 32:26 As in Greek version; the meaning of the Hebrew is uncertain. 32:31 The meaning of the Hebrew is uncertain. Greek version reads *our enemies are fools.* 32:36 Or *will take revenge for.* 32:43 As in Dead Sea Scrolls and Greek version; Masoretic Text reads *Rejoice with his people, O nations.* 32:44 Hebrew *Hoshea,* a variant name for Joshua. 32:49 Hebrew *the mountains of Abarim.* 32:51 Hebrew *waters of Meribath-kadesh.* 33:2a As in Greek and Syriac versions; Hebrew reads *upon them.*

he shone forth from Mount Paran
and came from Meribah-kadesh
with flaming fire at his right hand.*
3 Indeed, you love the people;
all your holy ones are in your hands.
They follow in your steps
and accept your instruction.
4 Moses charged us with the law,
the special possession of the assembly of Israel.*
5 The LORD became king in Israel*—
when the leaders of the people assembled,
when the tribes of Israel gathered."

6 Moses said this about the tribe of Reuben:*

"Let the tribe of Reuben live and not die out,
even though their tribe is small."

7 Moses said this about the tribe of Judah:

"O LORD, hear the cry of Judah
and bring them again to their people.
Give them strength to defend their cause;
help them against their enemies!"

8 Moses said this about the tribe of Levi:

"O LORD, you have given the sacred lots*
to your faithful servants the Levites.
You put them to the test at Massah
and contended with them at the waters of Meribah.
9 The Levites obeyed your word
and guarded your covenant.
They were more loyal to you
than to their parents, relatives, and children.
10 Now let them teach your regulations to Jacob;
let them give your instructions to Israel.
They will present incense before you
and offer whole burnt offerings on the altar.
11 Bless the Levites, O LORD,
and accept all their work.
Crush the loins of their enemies;
strike down their foes so they never rise again."

12 Moses said this about the tribe of Benjamin:

"The people of Benjamin are loved by the LORD
and live in safety beside him.
He surrounds them continuously
and preserves them from every harm."

13 Moses said this about the tribes of Joseph:

"May their land be blessed by the LORD
with the choice gift of rain from the heavens,
and water from beneath the earth;
14 with the riches that grow in the sun,
and the bounty produced each month;
15 with the finest crops of the ancient mountains,
and the abundance from the everlasting hills;
16 with the best gifts of the earth and its fullness,

## TALENTS ● ● • • •

33:6-25 **Note the difference in blessings God gave each tribe. To one he gave the best land, to another strength, to another safety. Too often we see someone with a particular blessing and think that God must love that person more than he loves us. Think rather that God draws out in all people their unique talents. All these gifts are needed to complete his plan. Don't be envious of the gifts others have. Instead, look for the gifts God has given you, and do the tasks he has uniquely qualified you to do.**

and the favor of the one who appeared in the burning bush.
May these blessings rest on Joseph's head,
crowning the brow of the prince among his brothers.
17 Joseph has the strength and majesty of a young bull;
his power is like the horns of a wild ox.
He will gore distant nations,
driving them to the ends of the earth.
This is my blessing for the multitudes of Ephraim
and the thousands of Manasseh."

18 Moses said this about the tribes of Zebulun and Issachar*:

"May the people of Zebulun prosper in their expeditions abroad.
May the people of Issachar prosper at home in their tents.
19 They summon the people to the mountain
to offer proper sacrifices there.
They benefit from the riches of the sea
and the hidden treasures of the sand."

20 Moses said this about the tribe of Gad:

"Blessed is the one who enlarges Gad's territory!
Gad is poised there like a lion
to tear off an arm or a head.
21 The people of Gad took the best land for themselves;
a leader's share was assigned to them.
When the leaders of the people were assembled,
they carried out the LORD's justice
and obeyed his regulations for Israel."

22 Moses said this about the tribe of Dan:

"Dan is a lion's cub,
leaping out from Bashan."

23 Moses said this about the tribe of Naphtali:

"O Naphtali, you are rich in favor
and full of the LORD's blessings;
may you possess the west and the south."

24 Moses said this about the tribe of Asher:

"May Asher be blessed above other sons;
may he be esteemed by his brothers;
may he bathe his feet in olive oil.

**33:2b** Or *came from myriads of holy ones, from the south, from his mountain slopes.* The meaning of the Hebrew is uncertain. **33:4** Hebrew *of Jacob.* **33:5** Hebrew *in Jeshurun,* a term of endearment for Israel. **33:6** Hebrew lacks *Moses said this about the tribe of Reuben.* **33:8** Hebrew *given your Thummim and Urim.* See Exod 28:30. **33:18** Hebrew lacks *and Issachar.*

## SUCCESS ● ● • • •

**34:10-12 Moses, the man who did not want to be sent to Egypt because he was "clumsy with words" (Exodus 4:10), delivered the three addresses to Israel that make up the book of Deuteronomy. God gave him the power to develop from a stuttering shepherd into a national leader and powerful orator. His courage, humility, and wisdom molded the Hebrew slaves into a nation. But Moses was one person who did not let success go to his head. In the end, God was still Moses' best friend. His love, respect, and awe for God had grown daily throughout his life. Moses knew that it was not any greatness in himself that made him successful; it was the greatness of the all-powerful God in whom he trusted.**

[25] May the bolts of your gates be of iron and bronze;
may your strength match the length of your days!"

[26] "There is no one like the God of Israel.*
He rides across the heavens to help you,
across the skies in majestic splendor.
[27] The eternal God is your refuge,
and his everlasting arms are under you.
He thrusts out the enemy before you;
it is he who cries, 'Destroy them!'
[28] So Israel will live in safety,
prosperous Jacob in security,
in a land of grain and wine,
while the heavens drop down dew.
[29] How blessed you are, O Israel!
Who else is like you, a people saved by the LORD?
He is your protecting shield
and your triumphant sword!
Your enemies will bow low before you,
and you will trample on their backs!"

CHAPTER **34** **MOSES DIES.** Then Moses went to
Mount Nebo from the plains of Moab and climbed
Pisgah Peak, which is across from Jericho. And the
LORD showed him the whole land, from Gilead as far
as Dan; [2]all the land of Naphtali; the land of
Ephraim and Manasseh; all the land of Judah, extending to the Mediterranean Sea*; [3]the Negev; the
Jordan Valley with Jericho—the city of palms—as far
as Zoar. [4]Then the LORD said to Moses, "This is the
land I promised on oath to Abraham, Isaac, and
Jacob, and I told them I would give it to their descendants. I have now allowed you to see it, but you will
not enter the land."
[5]So Moses, the servant of the LORD, died there in
the land of Moab, just as the LORD had said. [6]He was
buried* in a valley near Beth-peor in Moab, but to
this day no one knows the exact place. [7]Moses was
120 years old when he died, yet his eyesight was
clear, and he was as strong as ever. [8]The people of
Israel mourned thirty days for Moses on the plains of
Moab, until the customary period of mourning was
over.
[9]Now Joshua son of Nun was full of the spirit of
wisdom, for Moses had laid his hands on him. So
the people of Israel obeyed him and did everything
just as the LORD had commanded Moses.
[10]There has never been another prophet like
Moses, whom the LORD knew face to face. [11]The LORD
sent Moses to perform all the miraculous signs and
wonders in the land of Egypt against Pharaoh, all his
servants, and his entire land. [12]And it was through
Moses that the LORD demonstrated his mighty power
and terrifying acts in the sight of all Israel.

33:26 Hebrew *of Jeshurun,* a term of endearment for Israel. 34:2 Hebrew *the western sea.* 34:6 Hebrew *He buried him,* that is, "The LORD buried him." Samaritan Pentateuch and some Greek manuscripts read *They buried him.*

# MEGA themes

**HISTORY** Moses reviews the mighty acts of God through which he set Israel free from slavery in Egypt.

By reviewing God's promises and mighty acts, we can learn about his character. We come to know God more intimately through understanding how he has acted in the past. We can learn to do his will and to avoid Israel's mistakes.

1. What do you learn about God from Moses' review of history?
2. How would this review prepare the people to live for God in the Promised Land?
3. Review your personal history with God. What have been the high points? The low points?
4. What do you learn about God from a review of your personal history?
5. How should this prepare you to live in the present and future for him?

**LAWS** God reviews his laws with the people. The legal contract between God and his people had to be renewed for the new generation entering the Promised Land.

Commitment to God and his truth cannot be taken for granted. Each generation and each person must respond anew to God's call.

1. What was God's purpose for giving his people the law? (Check the book of Exodus as well.)
2. Why did Moses review the law for the people?
3. Why is it important to read, study, and be reminded of God's commands in your life?
4. What difference does it seem to make in your life that you have the Bible available to you for making decisions about God's will?

**LOVE** God's faithful and patient love is portrayed more often than his punishment. God reveals his love in keeping his promises to people, even when they are disobedient. God seeks the love of his people displayed in their wholehearted devotion to his will, not just by a strict, legalistic following of the law.

God's love forms the foundation for our trust in him. We can be confident that the one who loves us perfectly can be trusted with our life. Therefore, we can trust that the commands he gives us are good and are designed to help us live fully in our relationships with him and others.

1. What are some of the words that best describe God's love (e.g., *constant, merciful* . . .)?
2. What are some specific ways this love from God has made you the person you are today?
3. Can you think of some friends who need to know more of God's love? What qualities of God's love do they most need to experience? (Check your responses to question 1.)
4. What if one of those friends replied, "But I have sinned too much for God to still love me." Based on your study of God's love for the Israelites, how would you respond to such a statement? Based on how God's love has made a difference in your life, how would you respond?
5. Think of one or two friends from the list you made for question 3. What are some specific ways you could show them God's love?

**CHOICES** God reminded his people that in order to enjoy the blessings of his will for them, they would have to continue in obedience. Personal choices to obey could bring benefits to their lives; rebellion would bring disaster.

Our choices make a difference. Choosing to follow God produces good results in our lives and in our relationships with others. Choosing to abandon God's ways brings harmful results to us and to others.

1. Respond to the following statement: You always have a choice. It always makes a difference.
2. How do you feel when a friend makes a choice that leads to bad consequences in his or her life?
3. How do you feel when a friend makes a choice that is a bad one according to God's will, but it seems like he or she is not experiencing any negative consequences?
4. Is it possible for a person to make a choice against God's will and get away with it? Explain.
5. What are some of the choices facing you in the present or in the near future? Complete this statement: I will choose to obey what I believe to be God's way in my life because ________.

**TEACHING** God commanded the Israelites to teach their children his ways. They were to use ritual, instruction, and memorization to make sure that their children understood God's principles and passed them on to the next generation.

God's truth must be passed on to future generations. It is not, however, just the traditions or commands that are to be passed on. Rather, we are to teach each new generation to know and love God personally.

1. Who are some of the people from the older generation who have passed on God's truth to you?
2. How were those from the previous generation able to teach you about knowing and loving God?
3. What are some of the most important things you have learned from older Christians?
4. How would you take these things that you have learned and teach them to the children in your family? Your neighborhood? Your church?
5. Develop a plan of action for becoming an important older Christian in the life of someone younger than you (e.g., volunteer as a leader for Bible school, or become a Sunday school teacher for children, or spend time with a child in your community who needs a big brother or big sister). Now, follow your plan!

1446 **B.C.**
**Exodus from Egypt**

**1406**
**Israelites enter Canaan**

**1375**
**Judges begin to rule**

**1050**
**United kingdom under Saul**

**1010**
**David becomes king**

What characteristics are important in a leader? If you were chosen captain of the football team, head cheerleader, or student body president, what would you need to be like? Strong? Smart? Clever? Good with people? Good-looking? Enthusiastic? Devoted? ■ God called Joshua to be the leader of Israel as they were about to enter the Promised Land. Joshua was unsure about his own leadership capabilities. But God told him: "No one will be able to stand their ground against you as long as you live. For I will be with you as I was with Moses. I will not fail you or abandon you." (1:5). Then God explained the qualities Joshua needed in order to be a good leader for his people. ■ The first quality was obedience to God's law: "Be strong and very courageous. Obey all the laws Moses gave you. Do not turn away from them, and you will be successful in everything you do" (1:7). ■ The second was total dependence on God for the victory. God had taken care of Israel in the past. Joshua continued to depend on him. ■ Listen to the wisdom of this book. God does not demand that you be strong, clever, efficient, or even good-looking to be an effective leader. Instead, God wants you to obey his Word and depend on his power. Then, if God has called you, he will use you.

## STATS

PURPOSE: To give the history of Israel's conquest of the Promised Land

AUTHOR: Joshua, except for the ending, which may have been written by the high priest Phinehas, an eyewitness to the events recounted there

SETTING: Canaan, also called the Promised Land, which occupied the same general geographical territory of modern-day Israel

KEY PEOPLE: Joshua, Rahab, Achan, Phinehas, Eleazar

KEY PLACES: Jericho, Ai, Mount Ebal, Mount Gerizim, Gibeon, Gilgal, Shiloh, Shechem

SPECIAL FEATURE: Out of over a million people who left Egypt, Joshua and Caleb were the only two who lived to enter the Promised Land

CHAPTER 1 **"BE BRAVE, JOSHUA!"** After the death of
Moses the LORD's servant, the LORD spoke to Joshua
son of Nun, Moses' assistant. He said, 2"Now that
my servant Moses is dead, you must lead my people
across the Jordan River into the land I am giving
them. 3I promise you what I promised Moses: 'Everywhere you go, you will be on land I have given
you—4from the Negev Desert in the south to the
Lebanon mountains in the north, from the Euphrates River on the east to the Mediterranean Sea* on
the west, and all the land of the Hittites.' 5No one
will be able to stand their ground against you as long
as you live. For I will be with you as I was with Moses.
I will not fail you or abandon you.

6"Be strong and courageous, for you will lead my
people to possess all the land I swore to give their
ancestors. 7Be strong and very courageous. Obey all
the laws Moses gave you. Do not turn away from
them, and you will be successful in everything you
do. 8Study this Book of the Law continually. Meditate on it day and night so you may be sure to obey
all that is written in it. Only then will you succeed. 9I
command you—be strong and courageous! Do not
be afraid or discouraged. For the LORD your God is
with you wherever you go."

10Joshua then commanded the leaders of Israel,
11"Go through the camp and tell the people to get
their provisions ready. In three days you will cross
the Jordan River and take possession of the land the
LORD your God has given you."

12Then Joshua called together the tribes of Reuben, Gad, and the half-tribe of Manasseh. He told
them, 13"Remember what Moses, the servant of the
LORD, commanded you: 'The LORD your God is giving you rest and has given you this land.' 14Your
wives, children, and cattle may remain here on the
east side of the Jordan River, but your warriors, fully
armed, must lead the other tribes across the Jordan
to help them conquer their territory. Stay with them

1:4 Hebrew *the Great Sea.*

## CHALLENGE ● ● • • •

**1:5 Joshua's new job consisted of leading more than two million people into a strange new land and conquering it. What a challenge—even for a man of Joshua's caliber! Every new job is a challenge. Without God it can be frightening. With God it can be a great adventure. Just as God assured Joshua he would be with him, so he is with us as we face our new challenges. We may not conquer nations, but every day we face tough situations, difficult people, and temptations. However, God promises that he will never abandon us or fail to help us, regardless of how we feel. By asking God to direct us we can conquer many of life's challenges.**

# KEY PLACES IN JOSHUA

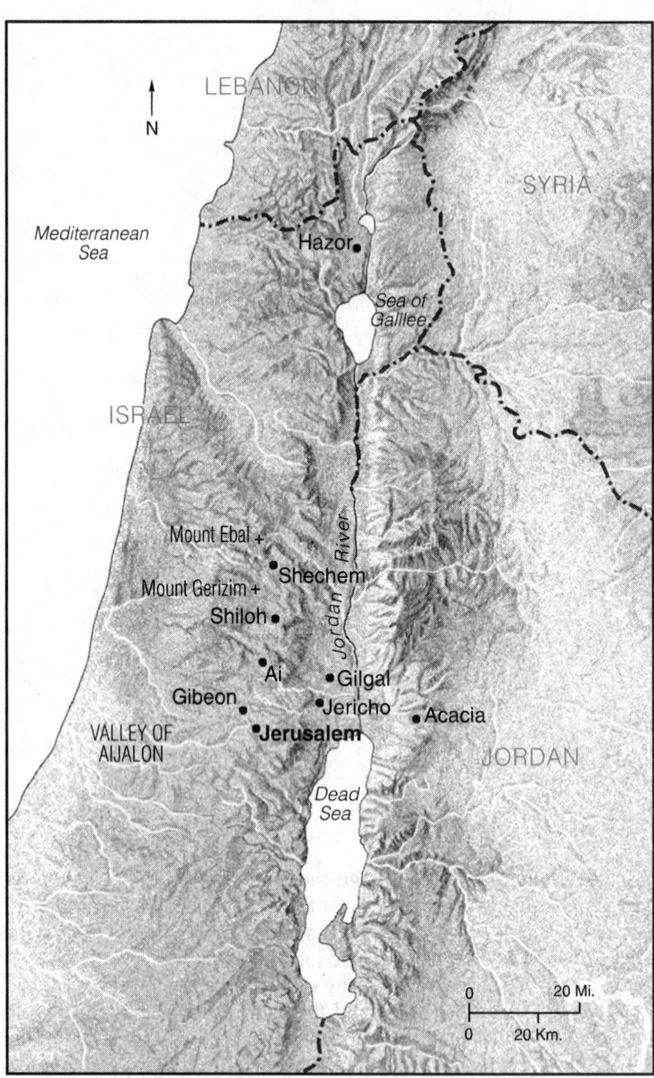


The broken lines (—·—·) indicate modern boundaries.

**Acacia** The story of Joshua begins with the Israelites camping at Acacia. The Israelites under Joshua were ready to enter and conquer Canaan. But before the nation moved out, Joshua received instructions from God (1:1-18).

**Jordan River** The entire nation prepared to cross this river, which was swollen from spring rains. After the scouts returned from Jericho with a positive report, Joshua prepared the priests and people for a miracle. As the priests carried the Ark into the Jordan River, the water stopped flowing and the entire nation crossed on dry ground into the Promised Land (2:1–4:24).

**Gilgal** After crossing the Jordan River, the Israelites camped at Gilgal, where they renewed their commitment to God and celebrated the Passover, the feast commemorating their deliverance from Egypt (see Exodus). As Joshua made plans for the attack on Jericho, an Angel appeared to him (5:1-15).

**Jericho** The walled city of Jericho seemed a formidable enemy. But when Joshua followed God's plans, the great walls were no obstacle. The city was conquered with only the obedient marching of the people (6:1-27).

**Ai** Victory could not continue without obedience to God. That is why the disobedience of one man, Achan, brought defeat to the entire nation in the first battle against Ai. But once the sin was recognized and punished, God told Joshua to take heart and go against Ai once again. This time the city was taken (7:1–8:29).

**The Mountains of Ebal and Gerizim** After the defeat of Ai, Joshua built an altar at Mount Ebal. Then the people divided themselves, half at the foot of Mount Ebal and half at the foot of Mount Gerizim. The priests stood between the mountains holding the ark of the covenant as Joshua read God's laws to all the people (8:30-35).

**Gibeon** It was just after the Israelites reaffirmed their convenant with God that their leaders made a major mistake in judgment: they were tricked into making a peace treaty with the city of Gibeon. Pretending that they had traveled a long distance, the Gibeonites asked the Israelites for a treaty. The leaders made the agreement without consulting God. The trick was soon discovered, but because the treaty had been made, Israel could not go back on its word. As a result, the Gibeonites saved their own lives, but they were forced to become Israel's slaves (9:1-27).

**Valley of Aijalon** The king of Jerusalem was very angry at the Gibeonites for making a peace treaty with Israel. He gathered armies from four other cities to attack Gibeon. Gibeon summoned Joshua for help, and Joshua took immediate action. Leaving Gilgal, he attacked the coalition by surprise. As the battle raged on and moved into the valley of Aijalon, Joshua prayed for the sun to stand still until the enemy could be destroyed (10:1-43).

**Hazor** Up north in Hazor, King Jabin mobilized the kings of the surrounding cities to unite and crush Israel. But God gave Joshua and Israel victory. Joshua conquered the entire federation (11:1-23).

**Shiloh** After the armies of Canaan were conquered, Israel gathered at Shiloh to set up the Tabernacle. This movable building had been the nation's center of worship during their years of wandering. The seven tribes who had not received their land were given their allotments (18:1–19:51).

**Shechem** Before Joshua died, he called the entire nation together at Shechem to remind them that it was God who had given them their land and that only with God's help could they keep it. The people vowed to follow God. As long as Joshua was alive, the land was at rest from war and trouble (24:1-33).

[15]until the LORD gives rest to them as he has given rest to you, and until they, too, possess the land the LORD your God is giving them. Only then may you settle here on the east side of the Jordan River in the land that Moses, the servant of the LORD, gave you."

[16]They answered Joshua, "We will do whatever you command us, and we will go wherever you send us. [17]We will obey you just as we obeyed Moses. And may the LORD your God be with you as he was with Moses. [18]Anyone who rebels against your word and does not obey your every command will be put to death. So be strong and courageous!"

## CHAPTER 2

**SPIES VISIT JERICHO.** Then Joshua secretly sent out two spies from the Israelite camp at Acacia.* He instructed them, "Spy out the land on the other side of the Jordan River, especially around Jericho." So the two men set out and came to the house of a prostitute named Rahab and stayed there that night.

[2]But someone told the king of Jericho, "Some Israelites have come here tonight to spy out the land." [3]So the king of Jericho sent orders to Rahab: "Bring out the men who have come into your house. They are spies sent here to discover the best way to attack us."

[4]Rahab, who had hidden the two men, replied, "The men were here earlier, but I didn't know where they were from. [5]They left the city at dusk, as the city gates were about to close, and I don't know where they went. If you hurry, you can probably catch up with them." [6](But she had taken them up to the roof and hidden them beneath piles of flax.) [7]So the king's men went looking for the spies along the road leading to the shallow crossing places of the Jordan River. And as soon as the king's men had left, the city gate was shut.

[8]Before the spies went to sleep that night, Rahab went up on the roof to talk with them. [9]"I know the LORD has given you this land," she told them. "We are all afraid of you. Everyone is living in terror. [10]For we have heard how the LORD made a dry path for you through the Red Sea* when you left Egypt. And we know what you did to Sihon and Og, the two Amorite kings east of the Jordan River, whose people you completely destroyed.* [11]No wonder our hearts have melted in fear! No one has the courage to fight after hearing such things. For the LORD your God is the supreme God of the heavens above and the earth below. [12]Now swear to me by the LORD that you will be kind to me and my family since I have helped you. Give me some guarantee that [13]when Jericho is conquered, you will let me live, along with my father and mother, my brothers and sisters, and all their families."

[14]"We offer our own lives as a guarantee for your safety," the men agreed. "If you don't betray us, we will keep our promise when the LORD gives us the land."

[15]Then, since Rahab's house was built into the city wall, she let them down by a rope through the window. [16]"Escape to the hill country," she told them. "Hide there for three days until the men who are searching for you have returned; then go on your way."

[17]Before they left, the men told her, "We can guarantee your safety [18]only if you leave this scarlet rope hanging from the window. And all your family members—your father, mother, brothers, and all your relatives—must be here inside the house. [19]If they go out into the street, they will be killed, and we cannot be held to our oath. But we swear that no one inside this house will be killed—not a hand will be laid on

### THE PAST ● ● ● • •

2:1 **Why would the spies stop at the house of Rahab the prostitute? Several reasons: (1) It was a good place to gather information and have no questions asked in return; (2) Rahab's house was in an ideal location for a quick escape because it was built into the city wall; (3) God directed the spies to Rahab's house because he knew her heart was open to him and that she would be instrumental in the Israelite victory over Jericho. God often uses people with simple faith to accomplish his great purposes, no matter what kind of past they have had or how insignificant they seem to be. Rahab didn't allow her past to keep her from the new role God had for her.**

### "Here's what I did..."

When I was in first grade, I memorized Joshua 1:9: "I command you—be strong and courageous! Do not be afraid or discouraged. For the Lord your God is with you wherever you go."

Recently I took part in a school play. I developed a bad case of stage fright before the performance. I didn't think I was going to make it through. I prayed, asking God to help me feel more comfortable with my part, and the verse came to mind again. I was concentrating on this encouragement, straight from God's Word, and it dispelled my fear. I remembered my lines and even did pretty well in the play, according to several people.

There have been many other times when I've recalled this verse and gained courage from it. Whenever I feel scared and alone, I remember this verse. It always comforts me.

Steve

AGE 15

---

2:1 Hebrew *Shittim.* 2:10a Hebrew *sea of reeds.* 2:10b The Hebrew term used here refers to the complete consecration of things or people to the LORD, either by destroying them or by giving them as an offering.

any of them. 20If you betray us, however, we are not bound by this oath in any way."

21"I accept your terms," she replied. And she sent them on their way, leaving the scarlet rope hanging from the window.

22The spies went up into the hill country and stayed there three days. The men who were chasing them had searched everywhere along the road, but they finally returned to the city without success. 23Then the two spies came down from the hill country, crossed the Jordan River, and reported to Joshua all that had happened to them. 24"The LORD will certainly give us the whole land," they said, "for all the people in the land are terrified of us."

## RESPONSIBILITY

Marcy, a 16-year-old junior at Jefferson High, is popular and always smiling. She seems to have it all together . . . but appearances really can be deceiving. Let's listen as she describes her inner turmoil to a friend.

"Gwen, what am I going to do? Chris asked me to be the girls' ministry leader this year."

"What does that mean?"

"Well, I'd have to be involved in all the things going on on campus. You know—Bible studies, morning prayer group, outreaches—all that stuff. Ministry leaders are expected to talk a lot about their faith. . . . That's what's so weird—I mean, out of all the people Chris could have asked, he came to me! I've only been a Christian for three years."

"Sounds like an honor—"

"Yeah, I guess so."

"—and a lot of responsibility."

"That's what has me so scared and stressed out: having to plan everything and give everybody direction. I mean, I'd kind of like to do it, but what if I can't handle it? What if I do something stupid or let Chris down? What if I turn out to be a horrible leader and they fire me or something?"

"Oh, Marcy! You'll do great and you know it."

"I don't know. . . ."

Read Joshua 1:5-9. How can that passage provide comfort and encouragement to Marcy, or to anyone who is facing big responsibilities?

CHAPTER **3** **CROSSING THE JORDAN RIVER.** Early the next morning Joshua and all the Israelites left Acacia* and arrived at the banks of the Jordan River, where they camped before crossing. 2Three days later, the Israelite leaders went through the camp 3giving these instructions to the people: "When you see the Levitical priests carrying the Ark of the Covenant of the LORD your God, follow them. 4Since you have never traveled this way before, they will guide you. Stay about a half mile* behind them, keeping a clear distance between you and the Ark. Make sure you don't come any closer."

5Then Joshua told the people, "Purify yourselves, for tomorrow the LORD will do great wonders among you."

6In the morning Joshua said to the priests, "Lift up the Ark of the Covenant and lead the people across the river." And so they started out.

7The LORD told Joshua, "Today I will begin to make you great in the eyes of all the Israelites. Now they will know that I am with you, just as I was with Moses. 8Give these instructions to the priests who are carrying the Ark of the Covenant: 'When you reach the banks of the Jordan River, take a few steps into the river and stop.'"

9So Joshua told the Israelites, "Come and listen to what the LORD your God says. 10Today you will know that the living God is among you. He will surely drive out the Canaanites, Hittites, Hivites, Perizzites, Girgashites, Amorites, and Jebusites. 11Think of it! The Ark of the Covenant, which belongs to the Lord of the whole earth, will lead you across the Jordan River! 12Now choose twelve men, one from each tribe. 13The priests will be carrying the Ark of the LORD, the Lord of all the earth. When their feet touch the water, the flow of water will be cut off upstream, and the river will pile up there in one heap."

14When the people set out to cross the Jordan, the priests who were carrying the Ark of the Covenant went ahead of them. 15Now it was the harvest season, and the Jordan was overflowing its banks. But as soon as the feet of the priests who were carrying the Ark touched the water at the river's edge, 16the water began piling up at a town upstream called Adam, which is near Zarethan. And the water below that point flowed on to the Dead Sea* until the riverbed was dry. Then all the people crossed over near the city of Jericho. 17Meanwhile, the priests who were carrying the Ark of the LORD's covenant stood on dry ground in the middle of the riverbed as the people passed by them. They waited there until everyone had crossed the Jordan on dry ground.

CHAPTER **4** When all the people were safely across the river, the LORD said to Joshua, 2"Now choose twelve men, one from each tribe. 3Tell the men to take twelve stones from where the priests are standing in the middle of the Jordan and pile them up at the place where you camp tonight."

4So Joshua called together the twelve men 5and told them, "Go into the middle of the Jordan, in front of the Ark of the LORD your God. Each of you must pick up one stone and carry it out on your shoulder—twelve stones in all, one for each of the twelve tribes. 6We will use these stones to build a memorial. In the future, your children will ask, 'What do these stones mean to you?' 7Then you can tell them, 'They remind us that the Jordan River stopped flowing when the Ark of the LORD's covenant went across.' These stones will stand as a permanent memorial among the people of Israel."

8So the men did as Joshua told them. They took

3:1 Hebrew *Shittim.* 3:4 Hebrew *about 2,000 cubits* [900 meters]. 3:16 Hebrew *the sea of the Arabah, the Salt Sea.*

twelve stones from the middle of the Jordan River,
one for each tribe, just as the LORD had commanded
Joshua. They carried them to the place where they
camped for the night and constructed the memorial
there.
9 Joshua also built another memorial of twelve
stones in the middle of the Jordan, at the place
where the priests who carried the Ark of the Covenant were standing. The memorial remains there to
this day.
10 The priests who were carrying the Ark stood in
the middle of the river until all of the LORD's instructions, which Moses had given to Joshua, were
carried out. Meanwhile, the people hurried across
the riverbed. 11 And when everyone was on the
other side, the priests crossed over with the Ark of
the LORD. 12 The armed warriors from the tribes of
Reuben, Gad, and the half-tribe of Manasseh led
the Israelites across the Jordan, just as Moses had
directed. 13 These warriors—about forty thousand
strong—were ready for battle, and they crossed
over to the plains of Jericho
in the LORD's presence.
14 That day the LORD made
Joshua great in the eyes of all
the Israelites, and for the rest
of his life they revered him
as much as they had revered
Moses.
15 The LORD had said to
Joshua, 16 "Command the
priests carrying the Ark of
the Covenant* to come up
out of the riverbed." 17 So
Joshua gave the command.
18 And as soon as the priests
carrying the Ark of the
LORD's covenant came up
out of the riverbed, the Jordan River flooded its banks
as before.
19 The people crossed the
Jordan on the tenth day of
the first month—the
month that marked their
exodus from Egypt.* They
camped at Gilgal, east of
Jericho. 20 It was there at Gilgal that Joshua piled up the
twelve stones taken from
the Jordan River. 21 Then
Joshua said to the Israelites,
"In the future, your children will ask, 'What do
these stones mean?' 22 Then
you can tell them, 'This is
where the Israelites crossed
the Jordan on dry ground.'
23 For the LORD your God
dried up the river right before your eyes, and he
kept it dry until you were all across, just as he did
at the Red Sea* when he dried it up until we had
all crossed over. 24 He did this so that all the nations
of the earth might know the power of the LORD,
and that you might fear the LORD your God forever."

CHAPTER **5** **JOSHUA CIRCUMCISES THE MEN.** When all
the Amorite kings west of the Jordan and all the
Canaanite kings who lived along the Mediterranean
coast* heard how the LORD had dried up the Jordan
River so the people of Israel could cross, they lost
heart and were paralyzed with fear.
2 At that time the LORD told Joshua, "Use knives of
flint to make the Israelites a circumcised people
again." 3 So Joshua made flint knives and circumcised the entire male population of Israel at Gibeath-
haaraloth.*
4 Joshua had to circumcise them because all the
men who were old enough to bear arms when they

## RAHAB

**UPS:**
- Relative of Boaz, and thus an ancestor of David and Jesus
- One of only two women listed in the Hall of Faith in Hebrews 11
- Resourceful, willing to help others at great cost to herself

**DOWNS:**
- She was a prostitute

**STATS:**
- Where: Jericho
- Occupation: Prostitute, innkeeper; later became a wife and mother
- Relatives: Ancestor of David and Jesus (Matthew 1:5)
- Contemporaries: Joshua

Rahab was a surprise. She was one of those people we wouldn't expect God to use. But God looks at people differently than we do.

As a prostitute in the city of Jericho, Rahab lived on the edge of society. She was used in private, rejected in public. Her house, built right into the city wall, was a natural place for the Israelite spies to hide, since they would be mistaken for Rahab's customers.

Rumors about the coming Israelite invasion were all over the city, but having spies in her home convinced Rahab there would be war. Living on the city wall, Rahab felt especially vulnerable. She was as afraid as everyone, but she alone turned to the Lord for her salvation. Her faith gave her the courage to hide the spies and lie to the authorities. All she knew of God was that the Israelites trusted and served him, but it was a start—and we all have to start knowing God someplace and sometime.

God works through people—like Rahab—whom we might reject. God remembers her because of her faith, not her profession! She was a sinner, but she didn't stay in her sin. And God rewarded her: she became one of God's people—in fact, she became a part of the lineage of Christ! If at times you feel like a failure, remember that Rahab overcame failure through her trust in God. You can do the same!

LESSON: She did not let fear affect her faith in God's ability to deliver

KEY VERSE: "It was by faith that Rahab the prostitute did not die with all the others in her city who refused to obey God. For she had given a friendly welcome to the spies" (Hebrews 11:31).

Rahab's story is told in Joshua 2 and 6. She is also mentioned in Matthew 1:5; Hebrews 11:31; and James 2:25.

4:16 Hebrew *Ark of the Testimony.* 4:19 Hebrew *the tenth day of the first month.* This day of the Hebrew lunar calendar occurs in late March or early April. 4:23 Hebrew *sea of reeds.* 5:1 Hebrew *along the sea.* 5:3 *Gibeath-haaraloth* means "hill of foreskins."

## WHY THE JEWS?

As you read the Old Testament, you may wonder, *Why the Jews? Why did God single them out for such favoritism?* That's a good question, and one that's not necessarily easy to answer. Hopefully, this will help you get some kind of handle on it. First, for reasons that are not entirely clear, God **singled out** a man named Abram from the ancient city of Ur and promised to bless him and his descendants (Genesis 12:1-3). As the chapters following that account reveal, there was a condition attached: Abram had to obey God faithfully. Even though he had numerous lapses, Abram did remain faithful to the One who had called him out from his home to a new land, Canaan. And God was true to his word, making Abram's descendants into the nation of Israel. This, then, is the primary reason God favored the Jews: He was keeping a promise made to his servant, Abram (who later became Abraham). Second, God was SETTING THE STAGE for his Son, the Messiah, to be ushered into the world many centuries later. Because God chose to have his Son born of a woman, he needed to provide an appropriate backdrop for the woman and her ancestry. This backdrop was the people of Israel, the descendants of Abraham. Guiding them throughout their history, God made sure that the scene was right for Mary, a virgin engaged to be married, to be available to be the mother of the child Jesus. At the right time, when God was ready to enter **HUMAN SPACE AND TIME,** he brought Mary and Joseph, descendants of Abraham, together to the stable in Bethlehem. His Son would be born a Jew. Third, it has been suggested that if God wanted to find an appropriate display case for his mercy and patient love, he could find no better one than the people of Israel—stubborn, rebellious, unfaithful—just like many believers today. As you continue reading the Old Testament, you will be impressed by God's protection and compassion for his people—and by how quickly they forgot him time after time. No one would have blamed God for giving up on them and starting over with a new nation. But God kept his word to Abraham and never abandoned Abraham's descendants. He punished them, rebuked them, sent them into exile—but he never forgot them or his promise. Many people today see the existence of the Jews as a powerful argument for THE EXISTENCE OF GOD. In spite of overwhelming opposition throughout history, they are still here, while most of their enemies (at least from Old Testament times) are long gone. How else could they have survived, except for the protection of a powerful, loving God who refused to give up on them? In the final analysis, we must remember that God does as he pleases. His reasons do not always make sense to us. While we cannot know with certainty why he chose to make the Jews his special people, we know that he did. Now, all those who follow Christ are members of his chosen nation. They don't become Jews, but they become God's covenant people—Christ's church. As you continue to read **the unfolding drama** we call the Old Testament, watch for ways God shows his love for his people, and thank God for his kindness to them—and to you.

---

left Egypt had died in the wilderness. [5]Those who left Egypt had all been circumcised, but none of those born after the Exodus, during the years in the wilderness, had been circumcised. [6]The Israelites wandered in the wilderness for forty years until all the men who were old enough to bear arms when they left Egypt had died. For they had disobeyed the LORD, and the LORD vowed he would not let them enter the land he had sworn to give us—a land flowing with milk and honey. [7]So Joshua circumcised their sons who had not been circumcised on the way to the Promised Land—those who had grown up to take their fathers' places. [8]After all the males had been circumcised, they rested in the camp until they were healed.

[9]Then the LORD said to Joshua, "Today I have

rolled away the shame of your slavery in Egypt." So that place has been called Gilgal* to this day.

10While the Israelites were camped at Gilgal on the plains of Jericho, they celebrated Passover on the evening of the fourteenth day of the first month—the month that marked their exodus from Egypt.* 11The very next day they began to eat unleavened bread and roasted grain harvested from the land. 12No manna appeared that day, and it was never seen again. So from that time on the Israelites ate from the crops of Canaan.

13As Joshua approached the city of Jericho, he looked up and saw a man facing him with sword in hand. Joshua went up to him and asked, "Are you friend or foe?"

14"Neither one," he replied. "I am commander of the LORD's army."

At this, Joshua fell with his face to the ground in reverence. "I am at your command," Joshua said. "What do you want your servant to do?"

15The commander of the LORD's army replied, "Take off your sandals, for this is holy ground." And Joshua did as he was told.

## CHAPTER 6 **THE FALL OF JERICHO.**

Now the gates of Jericho were tightly shut because the people were afraid of the Israelites. No one was allowed to go in or out. 2But the LORD said to Joshua, "I have given you Jericho, its king, and all its mighty warriors. 3Your entire army is to march around the city once a day for six days. 4Seven priests will walk ahead of the Ark, each carrying a ram's horn. On the seventh day you are to march around the city seven times, with the priests blowing the horns. 5When you hear the priests give one long blast on the horns, have all the people give a mighty shout. Then the walls of the city will collapse, and the people can charge straight into the city."

6So Joshua called together the priests and said, "Take up the Ark of the Covenant, and assign seven priests to walk in front of it, each carrying a ram's horn." 7Then he gave orders to the people: "March around the city, and the armed men will lead the way in front of the Ark of the LORD."

8After Joshua spoke to the people, the seven priests with the rams' horns started marching in the presence of the LORD, blowing the horns as they marched. And the priests carrying the Ark of the LORD's covenant followed behind them. 9Armed guards marched both in front of the priests and behind the Ark, with the priests continually blowing the horns. 10"Do not shout; do not even talk," Joshua commanded. "Not a single word from any of you until I tell you to shout. Then shout!" 11So the Ark of the LORD was carried around the city once that day, and then everyone returned to spend the night in the camp.

12Joshua got up early the next morning, and the priests again carried the Ark of the LORD. 13The seven priests with the rams' horns marched in front of the Ark of the LORD, blowing their horns. Armed guards marched both in front of the priests with the horns and behind the Ark of the LORD. All this time the priests were sounding their horns. 14On the second day they marched around the city once and returned to the camp. They followed this pattern for six days.

15On the seventh day the Israelites got up at dawn and marched around the city as they had done before. But this time they went around the city seven times. 16The seventh time around, as the priests sounded the long blast on their horns, Joshua commanded the people, "Shout! For the LORD has given you the city! 17The city and everything in it must be completely destroyed* as an offering to the LORD. Only Rahab the prostitute and the others in her house will be spared, for she protected our spies. 18Do not take any of the things set apart for destruction, or you yourselves will be completely destroyed, and you will bring trouble on all Israel. 19Everything made from silver, gold, bronze, or iron is sacred to the LORD and must be brought into his treasury."

20When the people heard the sound of the horns, they shouted as loud as they could. Suddenly, the walls of Jericho collapsed, and the Israelites charged straight into the city from every side and captured it. 21They completely destroyed everything in it—men and women, young and old, cattle, sheep, donkeys—everything.

22Then Joshua said to the two spies, "Keep your promise. Go to the prostitute's house and bring her out, along with all her family."

23The young men went in and brought out Rahab, her father, mother, brothers, and all the other relatives who were with her. They moved her whole family to a safe place near the camp of Israel.

24Then the Israelites burned the city and everything in it. Only the things made from silver, gold, bronze, or iron were kept for the treasury of the LORD's house. 25So Joshua spared Rahab the prostitute and her relatives who were with her in the house, because she had hidden the spies Joshua sent to Jericho. And she lives among the Israelites to this day.

26At that time Joshua invoked this curse:

"May the curse of the LORD fall on anyone
who tries to rebuild the city of Jericho.

### ALREADY WON ● ● • • •

6:2-5 **God told Joshua that the enemy was already defeated! What confidence Joshua must have had as he went into battle! Christians also fight against a defeated enemy. Our enemy, Satan, has been defeated by Christ (Romans 8:37-39; Hebrews 2:14-15; 1 John 3:8). Although we still fight battles every day and sin runs rampant in the world, we have the assurance that the war has already been won. We do not have to be paralyzed by the power of a defeated enemy; we can overcome temptation through Christ's power.**

5:9 *Gilgal* sounds like the Hebrew word *galal,* meaning "to roll." 5:10 Hebrew *the fourteenth day of the first month.* This day of the Hebrew lunar calendar occurs in late March or early April. 6:17 The Hebrew term used here refers to the complete consecration of things or people to the LORD, either by destroying them or by giving them as an offering; also in 6:18, 21.

## LESSONS ● ● • • •

7:7 **When Joshua first went against Ai (7:3), he did not consult God but relied on the strength of his army to defeat the small city. Only after Israel was defeated did they turn to God and ask, "What happened?" Too often we rely on our own skills and strength, especially when the task before us seems easy. We go to God only when the obstacles seem too great. However, only God knows what lies ahead. Consulting him, even when we are on a winning streak, may save us from grave mistakes or misjudgments. God may want us to learn lessons, remove pride, or consult others before he will work through us.**

At the cost of his firstborn son,
he will lay its foundation.
At the cost of his youngest son,
he will set up its gates."

27So the LORD was with Joshua, and his name became famous throughout the land.

## CHAPTER 7 ACHAN DISOBEYS GOD.

But Israel was unfaithful concerning the things set apart for the LORD.* A man named Achan had stolen some of these things, so the LORD was very angry with the Israelites. Achan was the son of Carmi, of the family of Zimri,* of the clan of Zerah, and of the tribe of Judah.

2Joshua sent some of his men from Jericho to spy out the city of Ai, east of Bethel, near Beth-aven.
3When they returned, they told Joshua, "It's a small town, and it won't take more than two or three thousand of us to destroy it. There's no need for all of us to go there."

4So approximately three thousand warriors were sent, but they were soundly defeated. The men of Ai
5chased the Israelites from the city gate as far as the quarries,* and they killed about thirty-six who were retreating down the slope. The Israelites were paralyzed with fear at this turn of events, and their courage melted away.

6Joshua and the leaders of Israel tore their clothing in dismay, threw dust on their heads, and bowed down facing the Ark of the LORD until evening. 7Then Joshua cried out, "Sovereign LORD, why did you bring us across the Jordan River if you are going to let the Amorites kill us? If only we had been content to stay on the other side! 8Lord, what am I to say, now that Israel has fled from its enemies? 9For when the Canaanites and all the other people living in the land hear about it, they will surround us and wipe us off the face of the earth. And then what will happen to the honor of your great name?"

10But the LORD said to Joshua, "Get up! Why are you lying on your face like this? 11Israel has sinned and broken my covenant! They have stolen the things that I commanded to be set apart for me. And they have not only stolen them; they have also lied about it and hidden the things among their belongings. 12That is why the Israelites are running from their enemies in defeat. For now Israel has been set apart for destruction. I will not remain with you any longer unless you destroy the things among you that were set apart for destruction.

13"Get up! Command the people to purify themselves in preparation for tomorrow. For this is what the LORD, the God of Israel, says: Hidden among you, O Israel, are things set apart for the LORD. You will never defeat your enemies until you remove these things. 14In the morning you must present yourselves by tribes, and the LORD will point out the tribe to which the guilty man belongs. That tribe must come forward with its clans, and the LORD will point out the guilty clan. That clan will then come forward, and the LORD will point out the guilty family. Finally, each member of the guilty family must come one by one. 15The one who has stolen what was set apart for destruction will himself be burned with fire, along with everything he has, for he has broken the covenant of the LORD and has done a horrible thing in Israel."

16Early the next morning Joshua brought the tribes of Israel before the LORD, and the tribe of Judah was singled out. 17Then the clans of Judah came forward, and the clan of Zerah was singled out. Then the families of Zerah came before the LORD, and the family of Zimri was singled out.
18Every member of Zimri's family was brought forward person by person, and Achan was singled out.

19Then Joshua said to Achan, "My son, give glory to the LORD, the God of Israel, by telling the truth. Make your confession and tell me what you have done. Don't hide it from me."

20Achan replied, "I have sinned against the LORD, the God of Israel. 21For I saw a beautiful robe imported from Babylon,* two hundred silver coins,* and a bar of gold weighing more than a pound.* I wanted them so much that I took them. They are hidden in the ground beneath my tent, with the silver buried deeper than the rest."

22So Joshua sent some men to make a search. They ran to the tent and found the stolen goods hidden there, just as Achan had said, with the silver buried beneath the rest. 23They took the things from the tent and brought them to Joshua and all the Israelites. Then they laid them on the ground in the presence of the LORD.

## NO SMALL THING ● ● • • •

7:24-25 **Achan underestimated God and didn't take his commands seriously (6:18). It may have seemed a small thing to Achan, but the effects of his sin were felt by the entire nation, especially his family. Our actions, like Achan's, affect more people than just ourselves. Beware of the temptation to rationalize your sins by saying they are too small or too personal to hurt anyone but you.**

7:1a The Hebrew term used here refers to the complete consecration of things or people to the LORD, either by destroying them or by giving them as an offering; also in 7:11, 12, 13, 15. 7:1b As in Greek version (see also 1 Chr 2:6); Hebrew reads *Zabdi.* Also in 7:17, 18. 7:5 Or *as far as Shebarim.* 7:21a Hebrew *Shinar.* 7:21b Hebrew *200 shekels of silver,* about 5 pounds or 2.3 kilograms in weight. 7:21c Hebrew *50 shekels,* about 20 ounces or 570 grams in weight.

[24]Then Joshua and all the Israelites took Achan,
the silver, the robe, the bar of gold, his sons,
daughters, cattle, donkeys, sheep, tent, and everything he had, and they brought them to the valley
of Achor. [25]Then Joshua said to Achan, "Why have
you brought trouble on us? The LORD will now
bring trouble on you." And all the Israelites stoned
Achan and his family and burned their bodies.
[26]They piled a great heap of stones over Achan,
which remains to this day. That is why the place
has been called the Valley
of Trouble* ever since. So
the LORD was no longer
angry.

CHAPTER **8** **THE ISRAEL-
ITES DEFEAT AI.** Then the LORD
said to Joshua, "Do not be
afraid or discouraged. Take
the entire army and attack
Ai, for I have given to you
the king of Ai, his people,
his city, and his land. [2]You
will destroy them as you destroyed Jericho and its king.
But this time you may keep
the captured goods and the
cattle for yourselves. Set an
ambush behind the city."

[3]So Joshua and the army
of Israel set out to attack Ai.
Joshua chose thirty thou-
sand fighting men and sent
them out at night [4]with
these orders: "Hide in ambush close behind the city
and be ready for action.
[5]When our main army at-
tacks, the men of Ai will
come out to fight as they
did before, and we will run
away from them. [6]We will
let them chase us until they
have all left the city. For
they will say, 'The Israelites
are running away from us
as they did before.' [7]Then
you will jump up from
your ambush and take
possession of the city, for
the LORD your God will give
it to you. [8]Set the city on
fire, as the LORD has commanded. You have your
orders."

[9]So they left that night
and lay in ambush between
Bethel and the west side of
Ai. But Joshua remained
among the people in the
camp that night. [10]Early the next morning Joshua
roused his men and started toward Ai, accompanied
by the leaders of Israel. [11]They camped on the north
side of Ai, with a valley between them and the city.
[12]That night Joshua sent five thousand men to lie in
ambush between Bethel and Ai, on the west side of
the city. [13]So they stationed the main army north of
the city and the ambush west of the city. Joshua
himself spent that night in the valley.

[14]When the king of Ai saw the Israelites across the

7:26 Hebrew *valley of Achor.*

## JOSHUA

Being a good leader means more than being in charge. The best leaders are those who help others learn to lead. This is true for two reasons: (1) Sometimes the job is too big for one person to do alone, so leadership has to be shared; and (2) some jobs take so long that they don't get done unless the first leader trains others to take over after he's gone. Joshua helped Moses with the huge job of leading the people of Israel. At the same time he was being trained as the new leader.

Moses made an excellent decision when he chose Joshua as his assistant. Later, God told Moses that Joshua would be the leader after he was gone. Joshua was an important part of the Exodus story. He led the army, and he was the only person allowed to go with Moses partway up the mountain when Moses received the Ten Commandments. When 12 men were sent as scouts into the Promised Land, only Joshua and Caleb were willing to tell the people that God could help them conquer the land. Joshua was always with Moses, like a shadow. His "basic training" was living with Moses, learning by watching everything his leader did and said.

Who is your Moses? Who is your Joshua? You are part of the unbroken chain of God's work in the world. Are you watching the lives of those who love God, learning from them? Can those who are watching you see how important God is in your life? Ask God to lead you to a Moses worth following. Ask him also to make you a good Joshua.

LESSONS: Effective leadership is often the product of good preparation and encouragement

The person after whom we pattern ourselves will have a definite effect on us

A person committed to God provides the best model for us

KEY VERSES: "So Moses did as the LORD commanded and presented Joshua to Eleazar the priest and the whole community. Moses laid his hands on him and commissioned him to his responsibilities, just as the LORD had commanded through Moses" (Numbers 27:22-23).

Joshua is also mentioned in Exodus 17; 24; 32–33; Numbers 11:28; 13–14; 26:65; 27:18-22; 32:12, 28; 34:17; Deuteronomy 1:38; 3:21, 28; 31:3, 14, 23; 34:9; Joshua; Judges 2; 1 Kings 16:34; and Hebrews 4:8.

**UPS:**
- Moses' assistant and successor
- One of only two adults who experienced Egyptian slavery and lived to enter the Promised Land
- Led the Israelites into their God-given homeland
- Brilliant military strategist
- Faithful to ask God's direction in the challenges he faced

**DOWNS:**
- He was unable to complete the task of possessing all the land

**STATS:**
- Where: Joshua lived in Egypt, the wilderness of Sinai, and Canaan (the Promised Land)
- Occupation: Special assistant to Moses; warrior, leader
- Relatives: Father: Nun
- Contemporaries: Moses, Caleb, Miriam, Aaron

valley, he and all his army hurriedly went out early
the next morning and attacked the Israelites at a
place overlooking the Jordan Valley.* But he didn't
realize there was an ambush behind the city.
[15]Joshua and the Israelite army fled toward the wilderness as though they were badly beaten, [16]and all
the men in the city were called out to chase after
them. In this way, they were lured away from the city.
[17]There was not a man left in Ai or Bethel* who did
not chase after the Israelites, and the city was left
wide open.

[18]Then the LORD said to Joshua, "Point your spear
toward Ai, for I will give you the city." Joshua did as
he was commanded. [19]As soon as Joshua gave the
signal, the men in ambush jumped up and poured
into the city. They quickly captured it and set it on
fire.

[20]When the men of Ai looked behind them,
smoke from the city was filling the sky, and they had
nowhere to go. For the Israelites who had fled in the
direction of the wilderness now turned on their pur-
suers. [21]When Joshua and the other Israelites saw
that the ambush had succeeded and that smoke was
rising from the city, they turned and attacked the
men of Ai. [22]Then the Israelites who were inside the
city came out and started killing the enemy from the
rear. So the men of Ai were caught in a trap, and all
of them died. Not a single person survived or escaped. [23]Only the king of Ai was taken alive and
brought to Joshua.

[24]When the Israelite army finished killing all the
men outside the city, they went back and finished off
everyone inside. [25]So the entire population of Ai was
wiped out that day—twelve thousand in all. [26]For
Joshua kept holding out his spear until everyone
who had lived in Ai was completely destroyed.*
[27]Only the cattle and the treasures of the city were
not destroyed, for the Israelites kept these for themselves, as the LORD had commanded Joshua. [28]So Ai*
became a permanent mound of ruins, desolate to
this very day.

[29]Joshua hung the king of Ai on a tree and left him
there until evening. At sunset the Israelites took
down the body and threw it in front of the city gate.
They piled a great heap of stones over him that can
still be seen today.

[30]Then Joshua built an altar to the LORD, the God
of Israel, on Mount Ebal. [31]He followed the instructions that Moses the LORD's servant had written in
the Book of the Law: "Make me an altar from stones
that are uncut and have not been shaped with iron
tools." Then on the altar they presented burnt offerings and peace offerings to the LORD. [32]And as the
Israelites watched, Joshua copied the law of Moses
onto the stones of the altar.*

[33]Then all the Israelites—foreigners and citizens
alike—along with the leaders, officers, and judges,
were divided into two groups. One group stood at

## REFRESHER COURSE ● ● • • •

8:33, 35 **After Israel's military victory, Joshua obeyed God's command by gathering the people together and reminding them of God's laws (1:8). God knows how easily we forget. We, like the Israelites, constantly need to review what God says. We should not read the Bible as we do most other books—once through quickly. We should read it daily as a constant reminder of who God is and what we can become.**

the foot of Mount Gerizim, the other at the foot of
Mount Ebal. Each group faced the other, and be-
tween them stood the Levitical priests carrying the
Ark of the LORD's covenant. This was all done accord-
ing to the instructions Moses, the servant of the
LORD, had given for blessing the people of Israel.

[34]Joshua then read to them all the blessings and
curses Moses had written in the Book of the Law.
[35]Every command Moses had ever given was read to
the entire assembly, including the women and children and the foreigners who lived among the Israelites.

CHAPTER **9** **GIBEONITES TRICK JOSHUA.** Now all the
kings west of the Jordan heard about what had happened. (These were the kings of the Hittites, Amorites, Canaanites, Perizzites, Hivites, and Jebusites,
who lived in the hill country, in the western foothills,* and along the coast of the Mediterranean
Sea* as far north as the Lebanon mountains.) [2]These
kings quickly combined their armies to fight against
Joshua and the Israelites.

[3]But when the people of Gibeon heard what had
happened to Jericho and Ai, [4]they resorted to deception to save themselves. They sent ambassadors to
Joshua, loading their donkeys with weathered saddlebags and old patched wineskins. [5]They put on
ragged clothes and worn-out, patched sandals. And
they took along dry, moldy bread for provisions.
[6]When they arrived at the camp of Israel at Gilgal,
they told Joshua and the men of Israel, "We have
come from a distant land to ask you to make a peace
treaty with us."

[7]The Israelites replied to these Hivites, "How do
we know you don't live nearby? For if you do, we
cannot make a treaty with you."

[8]They replied, "We will be your servants."

"But who are you?" Joshua demanded. "Where
do you come from?"

[9]They answered, "We are from a very distant
country. We have heard of the might of the LORD
your God and of all he did in Egypt. [10]We have also
heard what he did to the two Amorite kings east of
the Jordan River—King Sihon of Heshbon and King
Og of Bashan (who lived in Ashtaroth). [11]So our
leaders and our people instructed us, 'Prepare for a
long journey. Go meet with the people of Israel and
declare our people to be their servants, and ask for
peace.'

[12]"This bread was hot from the ovens when we

8:14 Hebrew *the Arabah.* 8:17 Some manuscripts lack *or Bethel.* 8:26 The Hebrew term used here refers to the complete consecration of things or people to the LORD, either by destroying them or by giving them as an offering. 8:28 *Ai* means "ruin." 8:32 Or *onto stones.* 9:1a Hebrew *the Shephelah.* 9:1b Hebrew *the Great Sea.*

left. But now, as you can see, it is dry and moldy. 13These wineskins were new when we filled them, but now they are old and cracked. And our clothing and sandals are worn out from our long, hard trip."

14So the Israelite leaders examined their bread, but they did not consult the LORD. 15Then Joshua went ahead and signed a peace treaty with them, and the leaders of Israel ratified their agreement with a binding oath.

16Three days later, the facts came out—these people of Gibeon lived nearby! 17The Israelites set out at once to investigate and reached their towns in three days. The names of these towns were Gibeon, Kephirah, Beeroth, and Kiriath-jearim. 18But the Israelites did not attack the towns, for their leaders had made a vow to the LORD, the God of Israel.

The people of Israel grumbled against their leaders because of the treaty. 19But the leaders replied, "We have sworn an oath in the presence of the LORD, the God of Israel. We cannot touch them. 20We must let them live, for God would be angry with us if we broke our oath. 21Let them live. But we will make them chop the wood and carry the water for the entire community."

So the Israelites kept their promise to the Gibeonites. 22But Joshua called together the Gibeonite leaders and said, "Why did you lie to us? Why did you say that you live in a distant land when you live right here among us? 23May you be cursed! From now on you will chop wood and carry water for the house of my God."

24They replied, "We did it because we were told that the LORD your God instructed his servant Moses to conquer this entire land and destroy all the people living in it. So we feared for our lives because of you. That is why we have done it. 25Now we are at your mercy—do whatever you think is right."

26Joshua did not allow the people of Israel to kill them. 27But that day he made the Gibeonites the woodchoppers and water carriers for the people of Israel and for the altar of the LORD—wherever the LORD would choose to build it. That arrangement continues to this day.

CHAPTER **10** **THE SUN AND MOON STAND STILL.** Now Adoni-zedek, king of Jerusalem, heard that Joshua had captured and completely destroyed* Ai and killed its king, just as he had destroyed the city of Jericho and killed its king. He also learned that the Gibeonites had made peace with Israel and were now their allies. 2He and his people became very afraid when they heard all this because Gibeon was a large city—as large as the royal cities and larger than Ai. And the Gibeonite men were mighty warriors. 3So King Adoni-zedek of Jerusalem sent messengers to several other kings: Hoham of Hebron, Piram of Jarmuth, Japhia of Lachish, and Debir of Eglon. 4"Come and help me destroy Gibeon," he urged them, "for they have made peace with Joshua and the people of Israel." 5So these five Amorite kings combined their armies for a united attack. They moved all their troops into place and attacked Gibeon.

6The men of Gibeon quickly sent messengers to Joshua at Gilgal, "Don't abandon your servants now!" they pleaded. "Come quickly and save us! For all the Amorite kings who live in the hill country have come out against us with their armies."

7So Joshua and the entire Israelite army left Gilgal and set out to rescue Gibeon. 8"Do not be afraid of them," the LORD said to Joshua, "for I will give you victory over them. Not a single one of them will be able to stand up to you."

9Joshua traveled all night from Gilgal and took the Amorite armies by surprise. 10The LORD threw them into a panic, and the Israelites slaughtered them in great numbers at Gibeon. Then the Israelites chased the enemy along the road to Beth-horon and attacked them at Azekah and Makkedah, killing them along the way. 11As the Amorites retreated down the road from Beth-horon, the LORD destroyed them with a terrible hailstorm that continued until they reached Azekah. The hail killed more of the enemy than the Israelites killed with the sword.

12On the day the LORD gave the Israelites victory over the Amorites, Joshua prayed to the LORD in front of all the people of Israel. He said,

"Let the sun stand still over Gibeon,
and the moon over the valley of Aijalon."

13So the sun and moon stood still until the Israelites had defeated their enemies.

Is this event not recorded in *The Book of Jashar**? The sun stopped in the middle of the sky, and it did not set as on a normal day. 14The LORD fought for Israel that day. Never before or since has there been a day like that one, when the LORD answered such a request from a human being.

15Then Joshua and the Israelite army returned to their camp at Gilgal.

16During the battle, the five kings escaped and hid in a cave at Makkedah. 17When Joshua heard that they had been found, 18he issued this command: "Cover the opening of the cave with large rocks and place guards at the entrance to keep the kings inside. 19The rest of you continue chasing the enemy and cut them down from the rear. Don't let them get back to their cities, for the LORD your God has given you victory over them."

20So Joshua and the Israelite army continued the slaughter and wiped out the five armies except for a tiny remnant that managed to reach their fortified cities. 21Then the Israelites returned safely to their camp at Makkedah. After that, no one dared to speak a word against Israel.

22Then Joshua said, "Remove the rocks covering the opening of the cave and bring the five kings to me." 23So they brought the five kings out of the

**10:1** The Hebrew term used here refers to the complete consecration of things or people to the LORD, either by destroying them or by giving them as an offering; also in 10:28, 35, 37, 39, 40. **10:13** Or *The Book of the Upright.*

cave—the kings of Jerusalem, Hebron, Jarmuth, Lachish, and Eglon. 24Joshua told the captains of his army, "Come and put your feet on the kings' necks." And they did as they were told.

25"Don't ever be afraid or discouraged," Joshua told his men. "Be strong and courageous, for the LORD is going to do this to all of your enemies." 26Then Joshua killed each of the five kings and hung them on five trees until evening.

27As the sun was going down, Joshua gave instructions for the bodies of the kings to be taken down from the trees and thrown into the cave where they had been hiding. Then they covered the opening of the cave with a large pile of stones, which remains to this very day.

## HOPE ● ● • • •

10:25 **With God's help, Israel won the battle against five armies. Such a triumph was part of God's daily business as he worked with his people for victory. Joshua told his men never to be afraid, because God would give them similar victories over all their enemies. God has often protected us and won victories in our lives. The same God who empowered Joshua and who has led us in the past will help us with our present and future needs. Reminding ourselves of his help in the past will give us hope for the struggles that lie ahead.**

28That same day Joshua completely destroyed the city of Makkedah, killing everyone in it, including the king. Not one person in the city was left alive. He killed the king of Makkedah as he had killed the king of Jericho. 29Then Joshua and the Israelites went to Libnah and attacked it. 30There, too, the LORD gave them the city and its king. They slaughtered everyone in the city and left no survivors. Then Joshua killed the king of Libnah just as he had killed the king of Jericho.

31From Libnah, Joshua and the Israelites went to Lachish and attacked it. 32And the LORD gave it to them on the second day. Here, too, the entire population was slaughtered, just as at Libnah. 33During the attack on Lachish, King Horam of Gezer had arrived with his army to help defend the city. But Joshua's men killed him and destroyed his entire army.

34Then Joshua and the Israelite army went to Eglon and attacked it. 35They captured it in one day, and as at Lachish, they completely destroyed everyone in the city. 36After leaving Eglon, they attacked Hebron, 37capturing it and all of its surrounding towns. And just as they had done at Eglon, they completely destroyed the entire population. Not one person was left alive. 38Then they turned back and attacked Debir. 39They captured the city, its king, and all of its surrounding villages. And they killed everyone in it, leaving no survivors. They completely destroyed Debir just as they had destroyed Libnah and Hebron.

40So Joshua conquered the whole region—the

## RUTHLESS ● ● • • •

10:40-43 **God had commanded Joshua to take the leadership in ridding the land of sin so God's people could occupy it. Joshua did his part thoroughly—leading the united army to weaken the inhabitants. When God orders us to eliminate sin from our life, we must not pause to debate, consider the options, negotiate a compromise, or rationalize. Instead, like Joshua, our response must be swift and complete. We must be ruthless in removing sin from our life.**

kings and people of the hill country, the Negev, the western foothills,* and the mountain slopes. He completely destroyed everyone in the land, leaving no survivors, just as the LORD, the God of Israel, had commanded. 41Joshua slaughtered them from Kadesh-barnea to Gaza and from Goshen to Gibeon. 42In a single campaign Joshua conquered all these kings and their land, for the LORD, the God of Israel, was fighting for his people. 43Then Joshua and the Israelite army returned to their camp at Gilgal.

CHAPTER **11** **THE SURPRISE ATTACK.** When King Jabin of Hazor heard what had happened, he sent urgent messages to the following kings: King Jobab of Madon; the king of Shimron; the king of Acshaph; 2all the kings of the northern hill country; the kings in the Jordan Valley* south of Galilee*; the kings in the western foothills*; the kings of Naphoth-dor on the west; 3the kings of Canaan, both east and west; the kings of the Amorites; the kings of the Hittites; the kings of the Perizzites; the kings in the Jebusite hill country; and the Hivites in the towns on the slopes of Mount Hermon, in the land of Mizpah.

4All these kings responded by mobilizing their warriors and uniting to fight against Israel. Their combined armies, along with a vast array of horses and chariots, covered the landscape like the sand on the seashore. 5They established their camp around the water near Merom to fight against Israel.

6Then the LORD said to Joshua, "Do not be afraid of them. By this time tomorrow they will all be dead. Cripple their horses and burn their chariots."

7So Joshua and his warriors traveled to the water near Merom and attacked suddenly. 8And the LORD gave them victory over their enemies. The Israelites chased them as far as Great Sidon and Misrephoth-maim, and eastward into the valley of Mizpah, until not one enemy warrior was left alive. 9Then Joshua crippled the horses and burned all the chariots, as the LORD had instructed.

10Joshua then turned back and captured Hazor and killed its king. (Hazor had at one time been the capital of the federation of all these kingdoms.) 11The Israelites completely destroyed* every living thing in the city. Not a single person was spared. And then Joshua burned the city.

12Joshua slaughtered all the other kings and their people, completely destroying them, just as Moses, the servant of the LORD, had commanded. 13However,

**10:40** Hebrew *the Shephelah.* **11:2a** Hebrew *the Arabah;* also in 11:16. **11:2b** Hebrew *of Kinnereth.* **11:2c** Hebrew *the Shephelah;* also in 11:16.
**11:11** The Hebrew term used here refers to the complete consecration of things or people to the LORD, either by destroying them or by giving them as an offering; also in 11:12, 20, 21.

Joshua did not burn any of the cities built on mounds except Hazor. 14And the Israelites took all the captured goods and cattle of the ravaged cities for themselves, but they killed all the people. 15As the LORD had commanded his servant Moses, so Moses commanded Joshua. And Joshua did as he was told, carefully obeying all of the LORD's instructions to Moses.

16So Joshua conquered the entire region—the hill country, the Negev, the land of Goshen, the western foothills, the Jordan Valley, and the mountains and lowlands of Israel. 17The Israelite territory now extended all the way from Mount Halak, which leads up to Seir, to Baal-gad at the foot of Mount Hermon in the valley of Lebanon. Joshua killed all the kings of those territories, 18waging war for a long time to accomplish this. 19No one in this region made peace with the Israelites except the Hivites of Gibeon. All the others were defeated. 20For the LORD hardened their hearts and caused them to fight the Israelites instead of asking for peace. So they were completely and mercilessly destroyed, as the LORD had commanded Moses.

21During this period, Joshua destroyed all the descendants of Anak, who lived in the hill country of Hebron, Debir, Anab, and the entire hill country of Judah and Israel. He killed them all and completely destroyed their towns. 22Not one was left in all the land of Israel, though some still remained in Gaza, Gath, and Ashdod.

23So Joshua took control of the entire land, just as the LORD had instructed Moses. He gave it to the people of Israel as their special possession, dividing the land among the tribes. So the land finally had rest from war.

## CHAPTER 12 A LIST OF CONQUERED KINGS.

These are the kings east of the Jordan River who had been killed and whose land was taken. Their territory extended from the Arnon Gorge to Mount Hermon and included all the land east of the Jordan Valley.*

2King Sihon of the Amorites, who lived in Heshbon, was defeated. His kingdom included Aroer, on the edge of the Arnon Gorge, and extended from the middle of the Arnon Gorge to the Jabbok River, which serves as a boundary for the Ammonites. This territory included half of the present area of Gilead, which lies north of the Jabbok River. 3Sihon also controlled the Jordan Valley as far north as the western shores of the Sea of Galilee* and as far south as the Dead Sea,* from Beth-jeshimoth to the slopes of Pisgah.

4King Og of Bashan, the last of the Rephaites, lived at Ashtaroth and Edrei. 5He ruled a territory stretching from Mount Hermon to Salecah in the north and to all of Bashan in the east, and westward to the boundaries of the kingdoms of Geshur and Maacah. His kingdom included the northern half of Gilead, the other portion of which was in the territory of King Sihon of Heshbon. 6Moses, the servant of the LORD, and the Israelites had destroyed the people of King Sihon and King Og. And Moses gave their land to the tribes of Reuben, Gad, and the half-tribe of Manasseh.

7The following is a list of the kings Joshua and the Israelite armies defeated on the west side of the Jordan, from Baal-gad in the valley of Lebanon to Mount Halak, which leads up to Seir. (Joshua allotted this land to the tribes of Israel as their inheritance, 8including the hill country, the western foothills,* the Jordan Valley, the mountain slopes, the Judean wilderness, and the Negev. The people who lived in this region were the Hittites, the Amorites, the Canaanites, the Perizzites, the Hivites, and the Jebusites.) These are the kings Israel defeated:

9 The king of Jericho
The king of Ai, near Bethel
10 The king of Jerusalem
The king of Hebron
11 The king of Jarmuth
The king of Lachish
12 The king of Eglon
The king of Gezer
13 The king of Debir
The king of Geder
14 The king of Hormah
The king of Arad
15 The king of Libnah
The king of Adullam
16 The king of Makkedah
The king of Bethel
17 The king of Tappuah
The king of Hepher
18 The king of Aphek
The king of Lasharon
19 The king of Madon
The king of Hazor
20 The king of Shimron-meron
The king of Acshaph
21 The king of Taanach
The king of Megiddo
22 The king of Kedesh
The king of Jokneam in Carmel
23 The king of Dor in the city of Naphoth-dor*
The king of Goyim in Gilgal*
24 The king of Tirzah.

In all, thirty-one kings and their cities were destroyed.

**PROGRESS ● ● • • •**

11:18 **The conquest of much of the land of Canaan seems to have happened quickly (we can read about it in one sitting), but it actually took seven years. We often expect quick changes in our lives and quick victories over sin. But our journey with God is a lifelong process, and the changes and victories may take time. It is easy to grow impatient with God and feel like giving up hope because things are moving too slowly. When we are close to a situation, it is difficult to see progress. But when we look back, we can see that God never stops working.**

**12:1** Hebrew *the Arabah;* also in 12:3, 8. **12:3a** Hebrew *sea of Kinnereth.* **12:3b** Hebrew *the sea of the Arabah, the Salt Sea.* **12:8** Hebrew *the Shephelah.* **12:23a** Hebrew *Naphath-dor,* a variant name for Naphoth-dor. **12:23b** Greek version reads *Goyim in Galilee.*

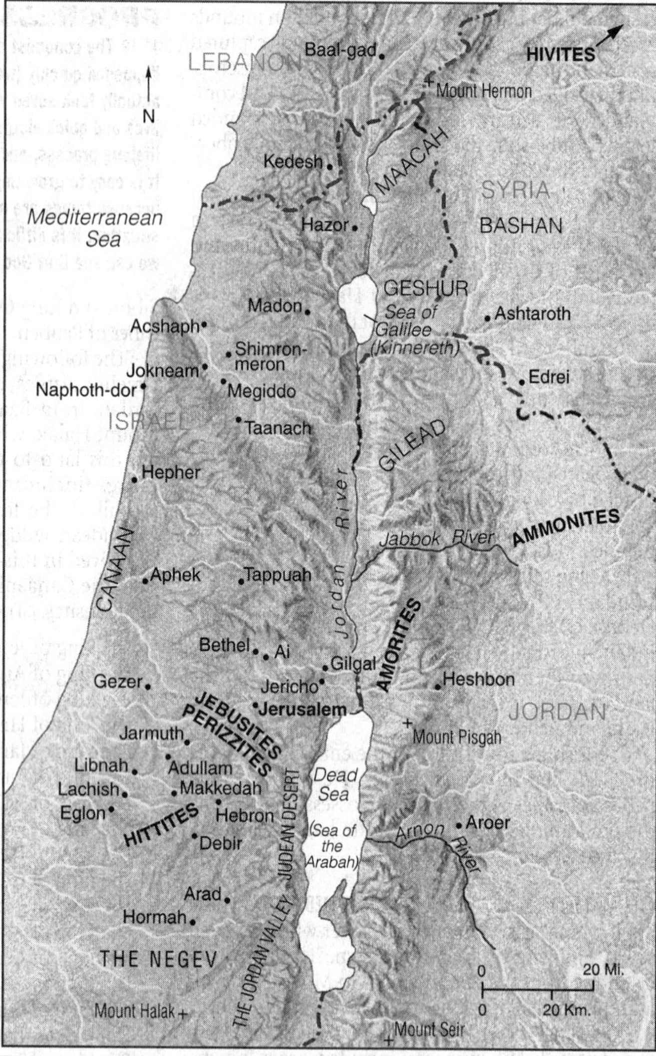

The broken lines (—·—) indicate modern boundaries.

**THE CONQUERED LAND**
Joshua displayed brilliant military strategy in the way he went about conquering the land of Canaan. He first captured the well-fortified Jericho to gain a foothold in Canaan and to demonstrate the awesome might of the God of Israel. Then he gained the hill country around Bethel. From there he subdued towns in the lowlands. Then his army conquered important cities in the north, such as Hazor. In all, Israel conquered land both east (12:1-6) and west (12:7-24) of the Jordan River, from Mount Hermon in the north to beyond the Negev to Mount Halak in the south. Thirty-one kings and their cities had been defeated. The Israelites had overpowered the Hittites, the Amorites, the Canaanites, the Perizzites, the Hivites, and the Jebusites. Other people living in Canaan were yet to be conquered.

# CHAPTER 13

**JOSHUA DIVIDES UP THE LAND.** When
Joshua was an old man, the LORD said to him, "You are
growing old, and much land remains to be conquered.
2The people still need to occupy the land of the Philistines and the Geshurites—3territory that belongs to
the Canaanites. This land extends from the stream of
Shihor, which is on the boundary of Egypt, northward
to the boundary of Ekron, 4and includes the five Philistine cities of Gaza, Ashdod, Ashkelon, Gath, and
Ekron. The land of the Avvites in the south also remains to be conquered. In the north, this area has not
yet been conquered: all the land of the Canaanites,
including Mearah (which belongs to the Sidonians),
stretching northward to Aphek on the border of the
Amorites; 5the land of the Gebalites and all of the
Lebanon mountain area to the east, from Baal-gad
beneath Mount Hermon to Lebo-hamath; 6and all the
hill country from Lebanon to Misrephoth-maim, including all the land of the Sidonians.
"I will drive these people out of the land for the
Israelites. So be sure to give this land to Israel as a
special possession, just as I have commanded you.
7Include all this territory as Israel's inheritance when
you divide the land among the nine tribes and the
half-tribe of Manasseh."

## EXPERIENCE ● ● • • •

13:1 **Joshua was getting old—he was between 85 and 100 years of age at this time. God, however, still had work for him to do. Our culture often glorifies the young and strong and sets aside those who are older. Yet older people are filled with the wisdom that comes with experience. They are capable of serving if given the chance and should be encouraged to do so. How do you treat older people?**

8Half the tribe of Manasseh and the tribes of Reuben and Gad had already received their inheritance on the east side of the Jordan, for Moses, the servant of the LORD, had previously assigned this land to them.

9Their territory extended from Aroer on the edge of the Arnon Gorge (including the town in the middle of the gorge) to the plain beyond Medeba, as far as Dibon. 10It also included all the towns of King Sihon of the Amorites, who reigned in Heshbon, and extended as far as the borders of Ammon. 11It included Gilead, the territory of the kingdoms of Geshur and Maacah, all of Mount Hermon, all of Bashan as far as Salecah, 12and all the territory of King Og of Bashan, who had reigned in Ashtaroth and Edrei. King Og was the last of the Rephaites, for Moses had attacked them and driven them out. 13But the Israelites failed to drive out the people of Geshur and Maacah, so they continue to live among the Israelites to this day.

14Moses did not assign any land to the tribe of Levi. Instead, as the LORD had promised them, their inheritance came from the offerings burned on the altar to the LORD, the God of Israel.

15Moses had assigned the following area to the families of the tribe of Reuben.

16Their territory extended from Aroer on the edge of the Arnon Gorge (including the town in the middle of the gorge) to the plain beyond Medeba. 17It included Heshbon and the other towns on the plain—Dibon, Bamoth-baal, Beth-baal-meon, 18Jahaz, Kedemoth, Mephaath, 19Kiriathaim, Sibmah, Zereth-shahar on the hill above the valley, 20Beth-peor, the slopes of Pisgah, and Beth-jeshimoth.

21The land of Reuben also included all the towns of the plain and the entire kingdom of Sihon. Sihon was the Amorite king who had reigned in Heshbon and was killed by Moses along with the chiefs of Midian—Evi, Rekem, Zur, Hur, and Reba—princes living in the region who were allied with Sihon. 22The Israelites also killed Balaam the magician, the son of Beor. 23The Jordan River marked the western boundary for the tribe of Reuben. The towns and villages in this area were given as an inheritance to the families of the tribe of Reuben.

24Moses had assigned the following area to the families of the tribe of Gad.

25Their territory included Jazer, all the towns of Gilead, and half of the land of Ammon, as far as the town of Aroer just west of Rabbah. 26It extended from Heshbon to Ramath-mizpeh and Betonim, and from Mahanaim to Lo-debar.* 27In the valley were Beth-haram, Beth-nimrah, Succoth, Zaphon, and the rest of the kingdom of King Sihon of Heshbon. The Jordan River was the western border, extending as far north as the Sea of Galilee.* 28The towns and villages in this area were given as an inheritance to the families of the tribe of Gad.

29Moses had assigned the following area to the families of the half-tribe of Manasseh.

30Their territory extended from Mahanaim, including all of Bashan, all the former kingdom of King Og, and the sixty towns of Jair in Bashan. 31It also included half of Gilead and King Og's royal cities of Ashtaroth and Edrei. All this was given to the descendants of Makir, who was Manasseh's son.

32These are the allotments Moses had made while he was on the plains of Moab, across the Jordan River, east of Jericho. 33But Moses gave no land to the tribe of Levi, for the LORD, the God of Israel, had promised to be their inheritance.

## CHAPTER 14

**WEST OF THE JORDAN RIVER.** The remaining tribes of Israel inherited land in Canaan as allotted by Eleazar the priest, Joshua son of Nun, and the tribal leaders. 2These nine and a half tribes received their inheritance by means of sacred lots, in accordance with the LORD's command through Moses. 3Moses had already given an inheritance of land to the two and a half tribes on the east side of the Jordan River. 4The tribe of Joseph had become two separate tribes—Manasseh and Ephraim. And the Levites were given no land at all, only towns to live in and the surrounding pasturelands for their flocks and herds. 5So the distribution of the land was in strict accordance with the LORD's instructions to Moses.

### PRECISELY ● ● ● • •

**14:5 The land was divided exactly as God had instructed Moses years before. Joshua did not change a word. He followed God's commands precisely. Often we believe that "almost" is close enough, and this idea can carry over into our spiritual lives. For example, we may follow God's Word as long as we agree with it, but ignore it when the demands seem difficult. But God is looking for leaders who follow instructions thoroughly.**

6A delegation from the tribe of Judah, led by Caleb son of Jephunneh the Kenizzite, came to Joshua at Gilgal. Caleb said to Joshua, "Remember what the LORD said to Moses, the man of God, about you and me when we were at Kadesh-barnea. 7I was forty years old when Moses, the servant of the LORD, sent me from Kadesh-barnea to explore the land of Canaan. I returned and gave from my heart a good report, 8but my brothers who went with me frightened the people and discouraged them from entering the Promised Land. For my part, I followed the LORD my God completely. 9So that day Moses

13:26 Or *to the territory of Debir.* 13:27 Hebrew *sea of Kinnereth.*

## INTEGRITY ● ● • • •

**14:6-12 When Joshua gave Caleb his land, he fulfilled a promise God had made to Caleb 45 years earlier. How about you? Is your word this reliable? Would you honor a 45-year-old promise? God would—and does. Even today he is honoring promises he made *thousands* of years ago. In fact, some of his greatest promises are yet to be fulfilled. This gives us much to look forward to. Let your faith grow as you realize how God keeps his word.**

promised me, 'The land of Canaan on which you were just walking will be your special possession and that of your descendants forever, because you wholeheartedly followed the LORD my God.'

10 "Now, as you can see, the LORD has kept me alive and well as he promised for all these forty-five years since Moses made this promise—even while Israel wandered in the wilderness. Today I am eighty-five years old. 11 I am as strong now as I was when Moses sent me on that journey, and I can still travel and fight as well as I could then. 12 So I'm asking you to give me the hill country that the LORD promised me. You will remember that as scouts we found the Anakites living there in great, walled cities. But if the LORD is with me, I will drive them out of the land, just as the LORD said."

13 So Joshua blessed Caleb son of Jephunneh and gave Hebron to him as an inheritance. 14 Hebron still belongs to the descendants of Caleb son of Jephunneh the Kenizzite because he wholeheartedly followed the LORD, the God of Israel. 15 (Previously Hebron had been called Kiriath-arba. It had been named after Arba, a great hero of the Anakites.)

And the land had rest from war.

## CHAPTER 15

**LAND FOR JUDAH.** The land assigned to the families of the tribe of Judah reached southward to the border of Edom, with the wilderness of Zin being its southernmost point.

2 The southern boundary began at the south bay of the Dead Sea,* 3 ran south of Scorpion Pass* into the wilderness of Zin and went south of Kadesh-barnea to Hezron. Then it went up to Addar, where it turned toward Karka. 4 From there it passed to Azmon, until it finally reached the brook of Egypt, which it followed to the Mediterranean Sea.* This was their* southern boundary.

5 The eastern boundary extended along the Dead Sea to the mouth of the Jordan River.

The northern boundary began at the bay where the Jordan River empties into the Dead Sea, 6 crossed to Beth-hoglah, then proceeded north of Beth-arabah to the stone of Bohan. (Bohan was Reuben's son.) 7 From that point it went through the valley of Achor to Debir, turning north toward Gilgal, which is across from the slopes of Adummim on the south side of the valley. From there the border extended to the springs at En-shemesh and on to En-rogel. 8 The boundary then passed through the valley of the son of Hinnom, along the southern slopes of the Jebusites, where the city of Jerusalem is located. Then it went west to the top of the mountain above the valley of Hinnom, and on up to the northern end of the valley of Rephaim. 9 From there the border extended from the top of the mountain to the spring at the waters of Nephtoah,* and from there to the towns on Mount Ephron. Then it turned toward Baalah (that is, Kiriath-jearim). 10 The border circled west of Baalah to Mount Seir, passed along to the town of Kesalon on the northern slope of Mount Jearim, and went down to Beth-shemesh and on to Timnah. 11 The boundary line then proceeded to the slope of the hill north of Ekron, where it turned toward Shikkeron and Mount Baalah. It passed Jabneel and ended at the Mediterranean Sea.

12 The western boundary was the shoreline of the Mediterranean Sea.*

These are the boundaries for the families of the tribe of Judah.

13 The LORD instructed Joshua to assign some of Judah's territory to Caleb son of Jephunneh. So Caleb was given the city of Arba (that is, Hebron), which had been named after Anak's ancestor. 14 Caleb drove out the three Anakites—Sheshai, Ahiman, and Talmai—descendants of Anak.

15 Then he fought against the people living in the town of Debir (formerly called Kiriath-sepher). 16 Caleb said, "I will give my daughter Acsah in marriage to the one who attacks and captures Kiriath-sepher." 17 Othniel, the son of Caleb's brother Kenaz, was the one who conquered it, so Acsah became Othniel's wife.

18 When Acsah married Othniel, she urged him* to ask her father for an additional field. As she got down off her donkey, Caleb asked her, "What is it? What can I do for you?"

19 She said, "Give me a further blessing. You have been kind enough to give me land in the Negev; please give me springs as well." So Caleb gave her the upper and lower springs.

20 This was the inheritance given to the families of the tribe of Judah.

21 The towns of Judah situated along the borders of Edom in the extreme south are Kabzeel, Eder, Jagur, 22 Kinah, Dimonah, Adadah, 23 Kedesh, Hazor, Ithnan, 24 Ziph, Telem, Bealoth, 25 Hazor-hadattah, Kerioth-hezron (that is, Hazor), 26 Amam, Shema, Moladah, 27 Hazar-gaddah, Heshmon, Beth-pelet, 28 Hazar-shual, Beersheba, Biziothiah, 29 Baalah, Iim, Ezem, 30 Eltolad, Kesil, Hormah, 31 Ziklag, Madmannah, Sansannah, 32 Lebaoth, Shilhim, Ain, and Rimmon. In all, there were twenty-nine of these towns with their surrounding villages.

33 The following towns situated in the western

15:2 Hebrew *the Salt Sea;* also in 15:5. **15:3** Hebrew *Akrabbim.* **15:4a** Hebrew *the sea;* also in 15:11. **15:4b** Hebrew *your.* **15:9** Or *the spring at Me-nephtoah.* **15:12** Hebrew *the Great Sea;* also in 15:47. **15:18** Some Greek manuscripts read *Othniel urged her.*

foothills* were also given to Judah: Eshtaol,
Zorah, Ashnah, [34]Zanoah, En-gannim, Tappuah,
Enam, [35]Jarmuth, Adullam, Socoh, Azekah,
[36]Shaaraim, Adithaim, Gederah, and Gederothaim. In all, there were fourteen towns with
their surrounding villages.

[37]Also included were Zenan, Hadashah, Migdalgad,
[38]Dilean, Mizpeh, Joktheel, [39]Lachish,
Bozkath, Eglon, [40]Cabbon, Lahmam, Kitlish,
[41]Gederoth, Beth-dagon, Naamah, and Makkedah—sixteen towns with their surround- ing villages.
[42]Besides these, there were Libnah, Ether, Ashan,
[43]Iphtah, Ashnah, Nezib, [44]Keilah, Aczib, and
Mareshah—nine towns with their surrounding villages.

[45]The territory of the tribe of Judah also
included all the towns and villages of Ekron.
[46]From Ekron the boundary extended west and
included the towns near Ashdod with their
surrounding villages. [47]It also included Ashdod
with its towns and villages and Gaza with its
towns and villages, as far as the brook of Egypt
and along the coast of the Mediterranean Sea.

[48]Judah also received the following towns in the
hill country: Shamir, Jattir, Socoh, [49]Dannah,
Kiriath-sannah (that is, Debir), [50]Anab, Eshtemoh,
Anim, [51]Goshen, Holon, and Giloh—eleven
towns with their surrounding villages.

[52]Also included were the towns of Arab,
Dumah, Eshan, [53]Janim, Beth-tappuah, Aphekah,
[54]Humtah, Kiriath-arba (that is, Hebron), and
Zior—nine towns with their surrounding villages.

[55]Besides these, there were Maon, Carmel,
Ziph, Juttah, [56]Jezreel, Jokdeam, Zanoah, [57]Kain,
Gibeah, and Timnah—ten towns with their
surrounding villages.

[58]In addition, there were Halhul, Beth-zur,
Gedor, [59]Maarath, Beth-anoth, and Eltekon—six
towns with their surrounding villages. [60]There
were also Kiriath-baal (that is, Kiriath-jearim)
and Rabbah—two towns with their surrounding villages.

[61]In the wilderness there were the towns of
Beth-arabah, Middin, Secacah, [62]Nibshan, the
City of Salt, and En-gedi—six towns with their
surrounding villages.

[63]But the tribe of Judah could not drive out the
Jebusites, who lived in the city of Jerusalem, so the
Jebusites live there among the people of Judah to
this day.

## CHAPTER 16 LAND FOR EPHRAIM.

The allotment to the descendants of Joseph
extended from the Jordan River near Jericho,
east of the waters of Jericho, through the
wilderness and into the hill country of Bethel.
[2]From Bethel (that is, Luz)* it ran over to
Ataroth in the territory of the Arkites. [3]Then it
descended westward to the territory of the
Japhletites as far as Lower Beth-horon, then to
Gezer and on over to the Mediterranean Sea.*

[4]The families of Joseph's sons, Manasseh and
Ephraim, received their inheritance.
[5]The following territory was given to the families
of the tribe of Ephraim as their inheritance.

The eastern boundary of their inheritance began
at Ataroth-addar. From there it ran to Upper
Beth-horon, [6]then on to the Mediterranean Sea.
The northern boundary began at the Mediterranean, ran east past Micmethath, then curved
eastward past Taanath-shiloh to the east of Janoah.
[7]From Janoah it turned southward to Ataroth
and Naarah, touched Jericho, and ended at the
Jordan River. [8]From Tappuah the border
extended westward, following the Kanah Ravine
to the Mediterranean Sea. This is the inheritance
given to the families of the tribe of Ephraim.

[9]Ephraim was also given some towns with
surrounding villages in the territory of the
half-tribe of Manasseh. [10]They did not drive the
Canaanites out of Gezer, however, so the people
of Gezer live as slaves among the people of
Ephraim to this day.

## CHAPTER 17 LAND FOR MANASSEH.

The next allotment of land was given to the half-tribe of Manasseh,
the descendants of Joseph's older son. Gilead and
Bashan on the east side of the Jordan had already
been given to the family of Makir because he was a
great warrior. (Makir was Manasseh's oldest son and
was the father of Gilead.) [2]Land on the west side of
the Jordan was allotted to the remaining families
within the tribe of Manasseh: Abiezer, Helek, Asriel,
Shechem, Hepher, and Shemida.

[3]However, Zelophehad son of Hepher, who was

**DOUBLE ● ● ● • •**

**16:1 Though Joseph was one of Jacob's 12 sons, he did not have a tribe named after him. This was because Joseph, as the oldest son of Jacob's wife Rachel, received a double portion of the inheritance. This double portion was given to Joseph's two sons, Ephraim and Manasseh, whom Jacob considered as his own (Genesis 48:5). The largest territory and the greatest influence in the northern half of Israel belonged to the tribes of Ephraim and Manasseh.**

**TRADITION ● ● ● • •**

**17:3-4 Although women did not traditionally receive property as inheritance in Israelite society, Moses put justice ahead of tradition and gave these five women the land they deserved (see Numbers 27:1-11). In fact, God told Moses to add a law that would help other women in similar circumstances inherit property as well. Joshua was now carrying out this law. It is easy to refuse to honor a reasonable request because "things have never been done that way before." But it is best for us, like Moses and Joshua, to look carefully at the purpose of the law and the merits of each case before deciding, rather than basing our decision solely on tradition.**

15:33 Hebrew *the Shephelah.* 16:2 As in Greek version (also see 18:13); Hebrew reads *From Bethel to Luz.* 16:3 Hebrew *the sea;* also in 16:6, 8.

a descendant of Manasseh, Makir, and Gilead, had no sons. Instead, he had five daughters. Their names were Mahlah, Noah, Hoglah, Milcah, and Tirzah. [4]These women came to Eleazar the priest, Joshua son of Nun, and the Israelite leaders and said, "The LORD commanded Moses to give us an inheritance along with the men of our tribe."

So Joshua gave them an inheritance along with their uncles, as the LORD had commanded. [5]As a result, Manasseh's inheritance came to ten parcels of land, in addition to the land of Gilead and Bashan across the Jordan River, [6]because the female descendants of Manasseh received an inheritance along with the male descendants. (The land of Gilead was given to the rest of the male descendants of Manasseh.)

[7]The boundary of the tribe of Manasseh extended from the border of Asher to Micmethath, which is east of Shechem. Then the boundary went south from Micmethath to the people living near the spring of Tappuah. [8](The land surrounding Tappuah belonged to Manasseh, but the town of Tappuah, on the border of Manasseh's territory, belonged to the tribe of Ephraim.) [9]From the spring of Tappuah, the border of Manasseh followed the northern side of the Kanah Ravine to the Mediterranean Sea.* (Several towns in Manasseh's territory belonged to the tribe of Ephraim.) [10]The land south of the ravine belonged to Ephraim, and the land north of the ravine belonged to Manasseh, with the Mediterranean Sea forming Manasseh's western border. North of Manasseh was the territory of Asher, and to the east was the territory of Issachar.

[11]The following towns within the territory of Issachar and Asher were given to Manasseh: Beth-shan,* Ibleam, Dor (that is, Naphoth-dor),* Endor, Taanach, and Megiddo, with their respective villages. [12]But the descendants of Manasseh were unable to occupy these towns. They could not drive out the Canaanites who continued to live there. [13]Later on, however, when the Israelites became strong enough, they forced the Canaanites to work as slaves. But they did not drive them out of the land.

[14]The descendants of Joseph came to Joshua and asked, "Why have you given us only one portion of land when the LORD has given us so many people?"

[15]Joshua replied, "If the hill country of Ephraim is not large enough for you, clear out land for yourselves in the forest where the Perizzites and Rephaites live."

[16]They said, "The hill country is not enough for us, and the Canaanites in the lowlands around Beth-shan and the valley of Jezreel have iron chariots—they are too strong for us."

[17]Then Joshua said to the tribes of Ephraim and Manasseh, the descendants of Joseph, "Since you are so large and strong, you will be given more than one portion. [18]The forests of the hill country will be yours as well. Clear as much of the land as you wish and live there. And I am sure you can drive out the Canaanites from the valleys, too, even though they are strong and have iron chariots."

## CHAPTER 18

**JOSHUA ASSIGNS THE REST.** Now that the land was under Israelite control, the entire Israelite assembly gathered at Shiloh and set up the Tabernacle.* [2]But there remained seven tribes who had not yet been allotted their inheritance.

[3]Then Joshua asked them, "How long are you going to wait before taking possession of the remaining land the LORD, the God of your ancestors, has given to you? [4]Select three men from each tribe, and I will send them out to survey the unconquered territory. They will return to me with a written report of their proposed divisions of the inheritance. [5]The scouts will map the land into seven sections, excluding Judah's territory in the south and Joseph's territory in the north. [6]Then I will cast sacred lots in the presence of the LORD our God to decide which section will be assigned to each tribe. [7]However, the Levites will not receive any land. Their role as priests of the LORD is their inheritance. And the tribes of Gad, Reuben, and the half-tribe of Manasseh won't receive any more land, for they have already received their inheritance, which Moses, the servant of the LORD, gave them on the east side of the Jordan River."

### PUTTING OFF ● ● • • •

18:3-6 **Joshua asked why some of the tribes were putting off the job of possessing the land. Often we delay doing jobs that seem large, difficult, boring, or disagreeable. But to continue putting them off shows lack of discipline, poor stewardship of time, and—in some cases—disobedience to God. Jobs we don't enjoy require concentration, teamwork, twice as much time, lots of encouragement, and accountability. Remember this when you are tempted to procrastinate.**

[8]As the men who were mapping out the land started on their way, Joshua commanded them, "Go and survey the land. Then return to me with your written report, and I will assign the land to the tribes by casting sacred lots in the presence of the LORD here at Shiloh." [9]The men did as they were told and mapped the entire territory into seven sections, listing the towns in each section. Then they returned to Joshua in the camp at Shiloh. [10]There at Shiloh, Joshua cast sacred lots in the presence of the LORD to determine which tribe should have each section.

[11]The first allotment of land went to the families of the tribe of Benjamin. It lay between the territory previously assigned to the tribes of Judah and Joseph.

**17:9** Hebrew *the sea;* also in 17:10. **17:11a** Hebrew *Beth-shean,* a variant name for Beth-shan; also in 17:16. **17:11b** The meaning of the Hebrew here is uncertain. **18:1** Hebrew *Tent of Meeting.*

12The northern boundary began at the Jordan
River, went north of the slope of Jericho, then
west through the hill country and the wilderness
of Beth-aven. 13From there the boundary went
south to Luz (that is, Bethel) and proceeded
down to Ataroth-addar to the top of the hill
south of Lower Beth-horon.
14The boundary then ran south along the
western edge of the hill facing Beth-horon, ending
at the village of Kiriath-baal (that is, Kiriath-
jearim), one of the towns belonging to the tribe
of Judah. This was the western boundary.
15The southern boundary began at the outskirts
of Kiriath-jearim. From there it ran westward*
to the spring at the waters of Nephtoah,* 16and
down to the base of the mountain beside the
valley of the son of Hinnom, at the northern end
of the valley of Rephaim. From there it went
down the valley of Hinnom, crossing south of the
slope where the Jebusites lived, and continued
down to En-rogel. 17From En-rogel the boundary
proceeded northeast to En-shemesh and on to
Geliloth (which is across from the slopes of
Adummim). Then it went down to the stone of
Bohan. (Bohan was Reuben's son.) 18From there it
passed along the north side of the slope overlooking the Jordan Valley.* The border then went
down into the valley, 19ran past the north slope of
Beth-hoglah, and ended at the north bay of the
Dead Sea,* which is the southern end of the
Jordan River.
20The eastern boundary was the Jordan River.

This was the inheritance for the families of the tribe
of Benjamin.

21These were the towns given to the families of the
tribe of Benjamin.

Jericho, Beth-hoglah, Emek-keziz, 22Beth-arabah,
Zemaraim, Bethel, 23Avvim, Parah, Ophrah,
24Kephar-ammoni, Ophni, and Geba—twelve
towns with their villages. 25Also Gibeon, Ramah,
Beeroth, 26Mizpeh, Kephirah, Mozah, 27Rekem,
Irpeel, Taralah, 28Zela, Haeleph, Jebus (that is,
Jerusalem), Gibeah, and Kiriath-jearim*—
fourteen towns with their villages.

This was the inheritance given to the families of the
tribe of Benjamin.

## CHAPTER 19

**LAND FOR SIMEON.** The second allot-
ment of land went to the families of the tribe of
Simeon. Their inheritance was surrounded by
Judah's territory.

2Simeon's inheritance included Beersheba, Sheba,
Moladah, 3Hazar-shual, Balah, Ezem, 4Eltolad,
Bethul, Hormah, 5Ziklag, Beth-marcaboth,
Hazar-susah, 6Beth-lebaoth, and Sharuhen—
thirteen towns with their villages. 7It also
included Ain, Rimmon, Ether, and Ashan—four
towns with their villages, 8including all the
villages as far south as Baalath-beer (also known
as Ramah of the Negev).

This was the inheritance of the families of the tribe
of Simeon. 9Their inheritance came from part of
what had been given to Judah because Judah's
territory was too large for them. So the tribe of
Simeon received an inheritance within the territory
of Judah.

10The third allotment of land went to the families
of the tribe of Zebulun.

The boundary of Zebulun's inheritance started
at Sarid. 11From there it went west, going past
Maralah, touching Dabbesheth, and proceeding
to the brook east of Jokneam. 12In the other
direction, the boundary line went east from
Sarid to the border of Kisloth-tabor, and from
there to Daberath and up to Japhia. 13Then it
continued east to Gath-hepher, Eth-kazin, and
Rimmon and turned toward Neah. 14The
northern boundary of Zebulun passed Hanna-
thon and ended at the valley of Iphtah-el. 15The
towns in these areas included Kattath, Nahalal,
Shimron, Idalah, and Bethlehem—twelve towns
with their surrounding villages.

16This was the inheritance of the families of the tribe
of Zebulun.

17The fourth allotment of land went to the families of the tribe of Issachar.

18Its boundaries included the following towns:
Jezreel, Kesulloth, Shunem, 19Hapharaim,
Shion, Anaharath, 20Rabbith, Kishion, Ebez,
21Remeth, En-gannim, En-haddah, and Beth-
pazzez. 22The boundary also touched Tabor,
Shahazumah, and Beth-shemesh, ending at
the Jordan River—sixteen towns with their
surrounding villages.

23This was the inheritance of the families of the tribe
of Issachar.

24The fifth allotment of land went to the families
of the tribe of Asher.

25Its boundaries included these towns: Helkath,
Hali, Beten, Acshaph, 26Allammelech, Amad,
and Mishal. The boundary on the west went
from Carmel to Shihor-libnath, 27turned east
toward Beth-dagon, and ran as far as Zebulun
in the valley of Iphtah-el, running north to Beth-
emek and Neiel. It then continued north to
Cabul, 28Abdon,* Rehob, Hammon, Kanah, and
as far as Greater Sidon. 29Then the boundary
turned toward Ramah and the fortified city of
Tyre and came to the Mediterranean Sea* at
Hosah. The territory also included Mehebel,

**18:15a** Or *it went to Ephron, and.* The meaning of the Hebrew is uncertain. **18:15b** Or *the spring at Me-nephtoah.* **18:18** Hebrew *the Arabah.* **18:19** Hebrew *Salt Sea.* **18:28** As in Greek version; Hebrew reads *Kiriath.* **19:28** As in some Hebrew manuscripts (see also 21:30); most Hebrew manuscripts read *Ebron.* **19:29** Hebrew *the sea.*

## WEAK FAITH ● ● ● • •

19:47-48 **The tribe of Dan thought that some of their land looked difficult to conquer, so they chose to migrate to Laish where they knew victory would be easier. Anyone can trust God when the going is easy. It is when everything looks impossible that our faith and courage are put to the test. Have faith that God is great enough to tackle your most difficult situations.**

Aczib, 30Ummah, Aphek, and Rehob—twenty-
two towns with their surrounding villages.

31This was the inheritance of the families of the tribe of Asher.

32The sixth allotment of land went to the families of the tribe of Naphtali.

33Its boundary ran from Heleph, from the oak
at Zaanannim, and extended across to Adami-
nekeb, Jabneel, and as far as Lakkum, ending
at the Jordan River. 34The western boundary ran
past Aznoth-tabor, then to Hukkok, and touched
the boundary of Zebulun in the south, the
boundary of Asher on the west, and the Jordan
River* on the east. 35The fortified cities included
in this territory were Ziddim, Zer, Hammath,
Rakkath, Kinnereth, 36Adamah, Ramah, Hazor,
37Kedesh, Edrei, En-hazor, 38Yiron, Migdal-el,
Horem, Beth-anath, and Beth-shemesh—
nineteen cities with their surrounding villages.

39This was the inheritance of the families of the tribe of Naphtali.

40The seventh and last allotment of land went to the families of the tribe of Dan.

41The towns within Dan's inheritance included
Zorah, Eshtaol, Ir-shemesh, 42Shaalabbin,
Aijalon, Ithlah, 43Elon, Timnah, Ekron, 44Eltekeh,
Gibbethon, Baalath, 45Jehud, Bene-berak,
Gath-rimmon, 46and Me-jarkon, also Rakkon
along with the territory across from Joppa.
47But the tribe of Dan had trouble taking
possession of their land, so they fought against
the town of Laish.* They captured it, slaughtered
its people, and settled there. They renamed the
city Dan after their ancestor.

48This was the inheritance of the families of the tribe of Dan—these towns with their villages.

49After all the land was divided among the tribes, the Israelites gave a special piece of land to Joshua as his inheritance. 50For the LORD had said he could have any town he wanted. He chose Timnath-serah in the hill country of Ephraim. He rebuilt the town and lived there.

51These are the territories that Eleazar the priest, Joshua son of Nun, and the tribal leaders gave as an inheritance to the tribes of Israel by casting sacred lots in the presence of the LORD at the entrance of the Tabernacle* at Shiloh. So the division of the land was completed.

## CHAPTER 20 **CITIES OF REFUGE.**

The LORD said to Joshua, 2"Now tell the Israelites to designate the cities of refuge, as I instructed Moses. 3Anyone who kills another person unintentionally can run to one of these cities and be protected from the relatives of the one who was killed, for the relatives may seek to avenge the killing.

4"Upon reaching one of these cities, the one who caused the accidental death will appear before the leaders at the city gate and explain what happened. They must allow the accused to enter the city and live there among them. 5If the relatives of the victim come to avenge the killing, the leaders must not release the accused to them, for the death was accidental. 6But the person who caused the death must stay in that city and be tried by the community and found innocent. Then the one declared innocent because the death was accidental must continue to live in that city until the death of the high priest who was in office at the time of the accident. After that, the one found innocent is free to return home."

7The following cities were designated as cities of refuge: Kedesh of Galilee, in the hill country of Naphtali; Shechem, in the hill country of Ephraim; and Kiriath-arba (that is, Hebron), in the hill country of Judah. 8On the east side of the Jordan River, across from Jericho, the following cities were designated as cities of refuge: Bezer, in the wilderness plain of the tribe of Reuben; Ramoth in Gilead, in the territory of the tribe of Gad; and Golan in Bashan, in the land of the tribe of Manasseh. 9These cities were set apart for Israelites as well as the foreigners living among them. Anyone who accidentally killed another person could take refuge in one of these cities. In this way, they could escape being killed in revenge prior to standing trial before the community.

## CHAPTER 21 **TOWNS FOR THE LEVITES.**

Then the leaders of the tribe of Levi came to consult with Eleazar the priest, Joshua son of Nun, and the leaders of the other tribes of Israel. 2They spoke to them at Shiloh in the land of Canaan, saying, "The LORD instructed Moses to give us towns to live in and pasturelands for our cattle." 3So by the command of the LORD the Levites were given as their inheritance the following towns with their pasturelands.

4The descendants of Aaron, who were members of the Kohathite clan within the tribe of Levi, were given thirteen towns that were originally assigned to the tribes of Judah, Simeon, and Benjamin. 5The other families of the Kohathite clan were allotted ten towns from the territories of Ephraim, Dan, and the half-tribe of Manasseh.

6The clan of Gershon received thirteen towns from the tribes of Issachar, Asher, Naphtali, and the half-tribe of Manasseh in Bashan.

7The clan of Merari received twelve cities from the tribes of Reuben, Gad, and Zebulun.

8So the Israelites obeyed the LORD's command to

19:34 Hebrew *and Judah at the Jordan River.* 19:47 Hebrew *Leshem,* another name for Laish. 19:51 Hebrew *Tent of Meeting.*

Moses and assigned these towns and pasturelands to the Levites by casting sacred lots.

9The Israelites gave the following towns from the tribes of Judah and Simeon 10to the descendants of Aaron, who were members of the Kohathite clan within the tribe of Levi, since the sacred lot fell to them first: 11Kiriath-arba (that is, Hebron), in the hill country of Judah, along with its surrounding pasturelands. (Arba was an ancestor of Anak.) 12But the fields beyond the city and the surrounding villages were given to Caleb son of Jephunneh.

13The following towns with their pasturelands were given to the descendants of Aaron the priest: Hebron (a city of refuge for those who accidentally killed someone), Libnah, 14Jattir, Eshtemoa, 15Holon, Debir, 16Ain, Juttah, and Beth-shemesh—nine towns from these two tribes.

17From the tribe of Benjamin the priests were given the following towns with their surrounding pasturelands: Gibeon, Geba, 18Anathoth, and Almon—four towns. 19So thirteen towns were given to the priests, the descendants of Aaron.

20The rest of the Kohathite clan from the tribe of Levi was allotted these towns and pasturelands from the tribe of Ephraim: 21Shechem (a city of refuge for those who accidentally killed someone), Gezer, 22Kibzaim, and Beth-horon—four towns.

23The following towns and pasturelands were allotted to the priests from the tribe of Dan: Eltekeh, Gibbethon, 24Aijalon, and Gath-rimmon—four towns.

25The half-tribe of Manasseh allotted the following towns with their pasturelands to the priests: Taanach and Gath-rimmon—two towns. 26So ten towns with their pasturelands were given to the rest of the Kohathite clan.

27The descendants of Gershon, another clan within the tribe of Levi, received two towns with their pasturelands from the half-tribe of Manasseh: Golan in Bashan (a city of refuge) and Be-eshterah.

28From the tribe of Issachar they received Kishion, Daberath, 29Jarmuth, and En-gannim—four towns with their pasturelands.

30From the tribe of Asher they received Mishal, Abdon, 31Helkath, and Rehob—four towns and their pasturelands.

32From the tribe of Naphtali they received Kedesh in Galilee (a city of refuge), Hammoth-dor, and Kartan—three towns with their pasturelands.

33So thirteen towns and their pasturelands were allotted to the clan of Gershon.

34The rest of the Levites—the Merari clan—were given the following towns from the tribe of Zebulun: Jokneam, Kartah, 35Dimnah, and Nahalal—four towns with their pasturelands.

36From the tribe of Reuben they received Bezer, Jahaz,* 37Kedemoth, and Mephaath—four towns with their pasturelands.

38From the tribe of Gad they received Ramoth in Gilead (a city of refuge), Mahanaim, 39Heshbon, and Jazer—four towns with their pasturelands. 40So twelve towns were allotted to the clan of Merari.

41The total number of towns and pasturelands within Israelite territory given to the Levites came to forty-eight. 42Every one of these towns had pasturelands surrounding it.

43So the LORD gave to Israel all the land he had sworn to give their ancestors, and they conquered it and settled there. 44And the LORD gave them rest on every side, just as he had solemnly promised their ancestors. None of their enemies could stand against them, for the LORD helped them conquer all their enemies. 45All of the good promises that the LORD had given Israel came true.

## CHAPTER 22 THE EASTERN TRIBES RETURN HOME.

Then Joshua called together the tribes of Reuben, Gad, and the half-tribe of Manasseh. 2He told them, "You have done as Moses, the servant of the LORD, commanded you, and you have obeyed every order I have given you. 3You have not deserted the other tribes, even though the campaign has lasted for such a long time. You have been careful to obey the commands of the LORD your God up to the present day. 4And now the LORD your God has given the other tribes rest, as he promised them. So go home now to the land Moses, the servant of the LORD, gave you on the east side of the Jordan River. 5But be very careful to obey all the commands and the law that Moses gave to you. Love the LORD your God, walk in all his ways, obey his commands, be faithful to him, and serve him with all your heart and all your soul."

6So Joshua blessed them and sent them home. 7Now Moses had given the land of Bashan to the half-tribe of Manasseh east of the Jordan. The other half of the tribe was given land west of the Jordan. As Joshua sent them away, he blessed them 8and said, "Share with your relatives back home the great wealth you have taken from your enemies. Share with them your large herds of cattle, your silver and gold, your bronze and iron, and your clothing."

9So the men of Reuben, Gad, and the half-tribe of Manasseh left the rest of Israel at Shiloh in the land of Canaan. They started the journey back to their own land of Gilead, the territory that belonged to them according to the LORD's command through Moses.

### FINISH THE JOB ● ● • • •

**22:2-4 Before the conquest had begun, these tribes were given land on the east side of the Jordan River. But before they could settle down they first had to promise to help the other tribes conquer the land on the west side (Numbers 32:20-22). They had patiently and diligently carried out their promised duties. Joshua now commended them for doing just that. At last they are permitted to return to their families and build their cities. Follow-through is vital in God's work. Beware of the temptation to quit early and leave God's work undone.**

**21:36** Hebrew *Jahzah,* a variant name for Jahaz.

10But while they were still in Canaan, before they crossed the Jordan River, Reuben, Gad, and the half-tribe of Manasseh built a very large altar near the Jordan River at a place called Geliloth.

11When the rest of Israel heard they had built the altar at Geliloth west of the Jordan River, in the land of Canaan, 12the whole assembly gathered at Shiloh and prepared to go to war against their brother tribes. 13First, however, they sent a delegation led by Phinehas son of Eleazar, the priest. They crossed the river to talk with the tribes of Reuben, Gad, and the half-tribe of Manasseh. 14In this delegation were ten high officials of Israel, one from each of the ten tribes, and each a leader within the family divisions of Israel.

## REACTIONS ● ● • • •

22:11-34 **When the tribes of Reuben and Gad and the half-tribe of Manasseh built an altar at the Jordan River, the rest of Israel feared that these tribes were starting their own religion and rebelling against God. But before beginning an all-out war, Phinehas led a delegation to learn the truth. He was prepared to negotiate rather than fight if a battle was not necessary. When he learned that the altar was for a memorial rather than for heathen sacrifice, war was averted and unity restored.**

**We would benefit from a similar approach to resolving conflicts. Assuming the worst about the intentions of others only brings trouble. Israel averted the threat of civil war by asking before assaulting. Beware of reacting before you hear the whole story.**

15When they arrived in the land of Gilead, they said to the tribes of Reuben, Gad, and the half-tribe of Manasseh, 16"The whole community of the LORD demands to know why you are betraying the God of Israel. How could you turn away from the LORD and build an altar in rebellion against him? 17Was our sin at Peor not enough? We are not yet fully cleansed of it, even after the plague that struck the entire assembly of the LORD. 18And yet today you are turning away from following the LORD. If you rebel against the LORD today, he will be angry with all of us tomorrow. 19If you need the altar because your land is defiled, then join us on our side of the river, where the LORD lives among us in his Tabernacle, and we will share our land with you. But do not rebel against the LORD or draw us into your rebellion by building another altar for yourselves. There is only one true altar of the LORD our God. 20Didn't God punish all the people of Israel when Achan, a member of the clan of Zerah, sinned by stealing the things set apart for the LORD*? He was not the only one who died because of that sin."

21Then the people of Reuben, Gad, and the half-tribe of Manasseh answered these high officials: 22"The LORD alone is God! The LORD alone is God! We have not built the altar in rebellion against the LORD. If we have done so, do not spare our lives this day. But the LORD knows, and let all Israel know, too, 23that we have not built an altar for ourselves to turn away from the LORD. Nor will we use it for our burnt offerings or grain offerings or peace offerings. If we have built it for this purpose, may the LORD himself punish us.

24"We have built this altar because we fear that in the future your descendants will say to ours, 'What right do you have to worship the LORD, the God of Israel? 25The LORD has placed the Jordan River as a barrier between our people and your people. You have no claim to the LORD.' And your descendants may make our descendants stop worshiping the LORD. 26So we decided to build the altar, not for burnt sacrifices, 27but as a memorial. It will remind our descendants and your descendants that we, too, have the right to worship the LORD at his sanctuary with our burnt offerings, sacrifices, and peace offerings. Then your descendants will not be able to say to ours, 'You have no claim to the LORD.' 28If they say this, our descendants can reply, 'Look at this copy of the LORD's altar that our ancestors made. It is not for burnt offerings or sacrifices; it is a reminder of the relationship both of us have with the LORD.' 29Far be it from us to rebel against the LORD or turn away from him by building our own altar for burnt offerings, grain offerings, or sacrifices. Only the altar of the LORD our God that stands in front of the Tabernacle may be used for that purpose."

30When Phinehas the priest and the high officials heard this from the tribes of Reuben, Gad, and the half-tribe of Manasseh, they were satisfied. 31Phinehas son of Eleazar, the priest, replied to them, "Today we know the LORD is among us because you have not sinned against the LORD as we thought. Instead, you have rescued Israel from being destroyed by the LORD."

32Then Phinehas son of Eleazar, the priest, and the ten high officials left the tribes of Reuben and Gad in Gilead and returned to the land of Canaan to tell the Israelites what had happened. 33And all the Israelites were satisfied and praised God and spoke no more of war against Reuben and Gad. 34The people of Reuben and Gad named the altar "Witness,"* for they said, "It is a witness between us and them that the LORD is our God, too."

## CHAPTER 23 JOSHUA'S FINAL ORDERS.

The years passed, and the LORD had given the people of Israel rest from all their enemies. Joshua, who was now very old, 2called together all the elders, leaders,

## REALITY ● ● • • •

23:12-16 **This chilling prediction about the consequences of intermarriage with the Canaanite nations eventually became a reality. Numerous stories in the book of Judges show what Israel had to suffer because of failure to follow God wholeheartedly. God was supremely loving and patient with Israel, just as he is today with us. But we must not confuse his patience with approval. Beware of demanding your own way, because eventually you may get it—along with all its painful consequences.**

22:20 The Hebrew term used here refers to the complete consecration of things or people to the LORD, either by destroying them or by giving them as an offering. 22:34 Hebrew *edh*. Some manuscripts lack this word.

judges, and officers of Israel. He said to them, "I
am an old man now. 3You have seen everything the
LORD your God has done for you during my lifetime. The LORD your God has fought for you
against your enemies. 4I have allotted to you as an
inheritance all the land of the nations yet unconquered, as well as the land of those we have already
conquered—from the Jordan River to the Mediterranean Sea* in the west. 5This land will be yours,
for the LORD your God will drive out all the people
living there now. You will live there instead of
them, just as the LORD your God promised you.
6"So be strong! Be very careful to follow all the
instructions written in the Book of the Law of Moses.
Do not deviate from them in any way. 7Make sure
you do not associate with the other people still
remaining in the land. Do not even mention the
names of their gods, much less swear by them or
worship them. 8But be faithful to the LORD your God
as you have done until now.
9"For the LORD has driven out great and powerful
nations for you, and no one has yet been able to
defeat you. 10Each one of you will put to flight a
thousand of the enemy, for the LORD your God fights
for you, just as he has promised. 11So be very careful
to love the LORD your God.
12"But if you turn away from him and intermarry
with the survivors of these nations remaining among
you, 13then know for certain that the LORD your God
will no longer drive them out from your land. Instead, they will be a snare and a trap to you, a pain
in your side and a thorn in your eyes, and you will
be wiped out from this good land the LORD your God
has given you.
14"Soon I will die, going the way of all the earth.
Deep in your hearts you know that every promise of
the LORD your God has come true. Not a single one
has failed! 15But as surely as the LORD your God has
given you the good things he promised, he will also
bring disaster on you if you disobey him. He will
completely wipe you out from this good land he has
given you. 16If you break the covenant of the LORD
your God by worshiping and serving other gods, his
anger will burn against you, and you will quickly be
wiped out from the good land he has given you."

## CHAPTER 24 JOSHUA'S GOOD-BYE SPEECH.

Then
Joshua summoned all the people of Israel to Shechem, along with their elders, leaders, judges, and
officers. So they came and presented themselves to
God.
2Joshua said to the people, "This is what the LORD,
the God of Israel, says: Your ancestors, including
Terah, the father of Abraham and Nahor, lived beyond the Euphrates River,* and they worshiped
other gods. 3But I took your ancestor Abraham from
the land beyond the Euphrates and led him into the
land of Canaan. I gave him many descendants
through his son Isaac. 4To Isaac I gave Jacob and
Esau. To Esau I gave the hill country of Seir, while
Jacob and his children went down into Egypt.
5"Then I sent Moses and Aaron, and I brought
terrible plagues on Egypt; and afterward I brought
you out as a free people. 6But when your ancestors
arrived at the Red Sea,* the Egyptians chased after
you with chariots and horses. 7When you cried out
to the LORD, I put darkness between you and the
Egyptians. I brought the sea crashing down on the
Egyptians, drowning them. With your very own eyes
you saw what I did. Then you lived in the wilderness
for many years.
8"Finally, I brought you into the land of the Amorites on the east side of the Jordan. They fought

**If Christ controls my life, where does my freedom of choice fit in?**

One way that God demonstrated his love for us was by giving us the freedom of choice.

Someone once said, "There is a door to your heart that can only be opened from the inside."

You make the choice to open the door of your heart to Jesus Christ when you receive him as Savior and Lord. Although his Spirit is at work prompting you to respond to his love, the choice is yours.

Picture your life like a house. Jesus Christ knocks on the front door and you decide to let him in (Revelation 3:20). Where do you invite him next? Some Christians live their whole life with Christ still standing in the entryway! Obviously this is not a very good way to treat an invited guest.

During your entire life as a Christian, you use your God-given freedom of choice to invite him into the rest of your house (your life) or to leave him at the front door.

Although your life is much more complicated than a house, let's take the illustration one step further.

In your house you probably have rooms that need repair. The living room, for example, could represent your relationships at home. How does the room look? When problems occur in this room the solution is to ask the Master Carpenter, Jesus, for some renovation. Through his Word, other people, and the prodding of the Holy Spirit, God gently tells us how to make things right.

This passage in Joshua (24:14) tells of his challenge to the nation of Israel: "Put away forever the idols your ancestors worshiped when they lived beyond the Euphrates River and in Egypt. Serve the Lord alone." The Israelites were faced with a choice of who they were going to serve. On this day, they chose to serve the living God instead of idols made by human hands.

Every day you will be faced with the choice of serving God or something else. God loves you too much to take that choice away from you.

He has given to you the privilege of having him come into every area of your life.

23:4 Hebrew *the Great Sea.* 24:2 Hebrew *the river;* also in 24:3, 14, 15. 24:6 Hebrew *sea of reeds.*

against you, but I gave you victory over them, and you took possession of their land. [9]Then Balak son of Zippor, king of Moab, started a war against Israel. He asked Balaam son of Beor to curse you, [10]but I would not listen to him. Instead, I made Balaam bless you, and so I rescued you from Balak.

[11]"When you crossed the Jordan River and came to Jericho, the men of Jericho fought against you. There were also many others who fought you, including the Amorites, the Perizzites, the Canaanites, the Hittites, the Girgashites, the Hivites, and the Jebusites. But I gave you victory over them. [12]And I sent hornets ahead of you to drive out the two kings of the Amorites. It was not your swords or bows that brought you victory. [13]I gave you land you had not worked for, and I gave you cities you did not build—the cities in which you are now living. I gave you vineyards and olive groves for food, though you did not plant them.

[14]"So honor the LORD and serve him wholeheartedly. Put away forever the idols your ancestors worshiped when they lived beyond the Euphrates River and in Egypt. Serve the LORD alone. [15]But if you are unwilling to serve the LORD, then choose today whom you will serve. Would you prefer the gods your ancestors served beyond the Euphrates? Or will it be the gods of the Amorites in whose land you now live? But as for me and my family, we will serve the LORD."

[16]The people replied, "We would never forsake the LORD and worship other gods. [17]For the LORD our God is the one who rescued us and our ancestors from slavery in the land of Egypt. He performed mighty miracles before our very eyes. As we traveled through the wilderness among our enemies, he preserved us. [18]It was the LORD who drove out the Amorites and the other nations living here in the land. So we, too, will serve the LORD, for he alone is our God."

[19]Then Joshua said to the people, "You are not able to serve the LORD, for he is a holy and jealous God. He will not forgive your rebellion and sins. [20]If you forsake the LORD and serve other gods, he will turn against you and destroy you, even though he has been so good to you."

[21]But the people answered Joshua, saying, "No, we are determined to serve the LORD!"

## YOUR CHOICE ● ● • • •

24:15 **The people had to decide whether they would obey the Lord, who had proven his trustworthiness, or obey the local gods, which were only man-made idols. It's easy to slip into a quiet rebellion—going about life in your own way. But the time comes when you have to choose who or what will control you. The choice is yours. Will it be God, or your own limited personality, or another imperfect substitute? Once you have chosen to be controlled by God's Spirit, reaffirm your choice every day.**

[22]"You are accountable for this decision," Joshua said. "You have chosen to serve the LORD."

"Yes," they replied, "we are accountable."

[23]"All right then," Joshua said, "destroy the idols among you, and turn your hearts to the LORD, the God of Israel."

[24]The people said to Joshua, "We will serve the LORD our God. We will obey him alone."

[25]So Joshua made a covenant with the people that day at Shechem, committing them to a permanent and binding contract between themselves and the LORD. [26]Joshua recorded these things in the Book of the Law of God. As a reminder of their agreement, he took a huge stone and rolled it beneath the oak tree beside the Tabernacle of the LORD.

[27]Joshua said to all the people, "This stone has heard everything the LORD said to us. It will be a witness to testify against you if you go back on your word to God."

[28]Then Joshua sent the people away, each to his own inheritance.

[29]Soon after this, Joshua son of Nun, the servant of the LORD, died at the age of 110. [30]They buried him in the land he had inherited, at Timnath-serah in the hill country of Ephraim, north of Mount Gaash.

[31]Israel served the LORD throughout the lifetime of Joshua and of the leaders who outlived him—those who had personally experienced all that the LORD had done for Israel.

[32]The bones of Joseph, which the Israelites had brought along with them when they left Egypt, were buried at Shechem, in the parcel of ground Jacob had bought from the sons of Hamor for one hundred pieces of silver.* This land was located in the territory allotted to the tribes of Ephraim and Manasseh, the descendants of Joseph.

[33]Eleazar son of Aaron also died. He was buried in the hill country of Ephraim, in the town of Gibeah, which had been given to his son Phinehas.

**24:32** Hebrew *100 kesitahs;* the value or weight of the kesitah is no longer known.

# MEGA themes

**SUCCESS** God gave success to the Israelites when they obeyed his master plan, not when they followed their own desires. Victory came when they trusted in him rather than in their military power, money, muscle, or mental capacity.

God's work done in God's way will bring success. The standard for success, however, is not to be set by the society around us but by God's Word. We must adjust our mind to God's way of thinking in order to see his standard for success.

1. Think of an adult whom your parent(s) view as successful. What is it about that person that makes him or her a success in your parent's mind?
2. What type of people are considered successful in your school?
3. Based upon the majority of commercials you see on television or in magazines, what is the media's image of a successful person?
4. What seems to be God's definition of success for Joshua? (See chapter 1.)
5. In what ways was Joshua a success according to God's point of view? What qualities in Joshua's life most contributed to this success?
6. Write a list of what you think God wants for your life in terms of being successful. What can you do to develop some of the qualities that Joshua had so that you will indeed become successful?

**FAITH** The Israelites demonstrated their faith by trusting God daily to save and guide them. By noticing how God fulfilled his promises in the past, they developed strong confidence that he would be faithful in the future.

Our strength to do God's work comes from trusting him. His promises reassure us of his love. We can be confident that God will be there to guide us in the decisions and struggles we face.

1. What factors helped the Israelites' faith grow?
2. What is happening in your life now that is contributing to the growth of your faith?
3. What else needs to happen to help your faith grow? What does God want you to do to increase your faith?

**GUIDANCE** God gave instructions to Israel for every aspect of their lives. His law guided their daily living and his specific marching orders gave them victory in battle.

Guidance from God for daily living can be found in his Word. By staying in touch with God, we will have the wisdom needed to meet life's great challenges.

1. Describe a time in your life when you felt you needed God's guidance. (It may be right now!)
2. How did you seek God's guidance during that time? What were the results?
3. What makes it difficult at times for us to know God's will for specific areas of our lives?
4. The more you know of God, the more you will know of his will. What resources has God given you for knowing more about him and his will for you?
5. At times, all Christians need God's guidance. How can you specifically prepare for those times before they occur? What can you do to seek God's guidance when they do occur?

**LEADERSHIP** Joshua was an example of an excellent leader. He was confident in God's strength, courageous in the face of opposition, and willing to seek God's advice.

To be a strong leader like Joshua, we must be ready to listen and to move quickly when God speaks. Once we have his instructions, we must carry them out. Strong leaders are characterized by their commitment to follow God first.

1. What were Joshua's strengths as a leader?
2. What types of challenges did Joshua face as a leader of the people?
3. All Christians have opportunities to be leaders for Christ. You do not have to hold an office or title in order to be a leader. What type of challenges are facing you as you try to lead friends closer to Christ in your church? School? Neighborhood?
4. What are your strengths as God's leader? What qualities do you need to develop as you are becoming an adult so that, like Joshua, you will spend your life leading others closer to God?

**CONQUEST** God commanded his people to conquer the Canaanites and take all their land. Completing this mission would have fulfilled God's promise to Abraham and brought judgment on the evil people living there. Unfortunately, Israel never finished the job.

Israel was faithful in accomplishing the mission at first, but their commitment faltered. To love God means more than being enthusiastic about him. Discipleship is more than "spiritual highs." We must complete all the work he gives us and apply his instructions to every part of our lives.

1. What was the difference in the lives of the Israelites when they were being successful and victorious as opposed to when they failed?
2. What can you learn from the Israelites' examples of success and failure?
3. Christians should look at a life of faith as a long-term process in which the goal is to finish stronger than we were when we began. Based on this study of Joshua and the Israelites' entry into the Promised Land, how can you insure yourself of victory over the obstacles that lie ahead in your life?

**1446 B.C.**
**Exodus from Egypt**

**1406**
**Israelites enter Canaan**

**1375**
**Period of the Judges begins**

**1367–1327**
**Othniel**

**1209–1169**
**Deborah**

**1162–1122**
**Gideon**

**1105**
**Samuel born**

**1075–1055**
**Samson**

**1050**
**Saul anointed**

**1010**
**David becomes king**

**S**uperman, Batman, Wonder Woman, Spiderman. Superheroes. The world longs for them. Always arriving in the nick of time to ward off evil, beat up bad guys, prevent corruption, and promote truth and justice and goodness. Unfortunately, there are no superheroes. And, eventually, every human being will let us down. ■The book of Judges is about heroes—12 people God used to deliver Israel from its enemies. No way were they superheroes. Some didn't want the job. One was even a murderer. But God used them to rescue Israel. ■Judges talks about the horrible results of sin, but also about God's mercy. The people of Israel had become evil. Judges describes them this way: "In those days Israel had no king, so the people did whatever seemed right in their own eyes" (17:6). They intermarried with wicked people and worshiped strange gods. When the stench of their actions became unbearable to God, he would raise up a neighboring nation to conquer them. Then the people would repent and turn back to God . . . and he would send a "judge" to rescue them. ■Let the book of Judges remind you that God uses normal people to do his work; let it remind you of the effects of sin; and let it remind you that, above all, God is merciful to sinful people when they ask for forgiveness.

## STATS

PURPOSE: To show that God's judgment against sin is certain, and his forgiveness of sin and restoration of fellowship is just as certain for those who repent

AUTHOR: Probably Samuel

SETTING: The land of Canaan, later called Israel. God had helped the Israelites conquer Canaan, which had been inhabited by a host of wicked nations. But they were in danger of losing this Promised Land because they compromised their convictions and disobeyed God.

KEY PEOPLE: Othniel, Ehud, Deborah, Gideon, Abimelech, Jephthah, Samson, Delilah

SPECIAL FEATURE: Records Israel's first civil war

CHAPTER **1** **GOD GIVES VICTORY.** After Joshua died, the Israelites asked the LORD, "Which tribe should attack the Canaanites first?"

2The LORD answered, "Judah, for I have given them victory over the land."

3The leaders of Judah said to their relatives from the tribe of Simeon, "Join with us to fight against the Canaanites living in the territory allotted to us. Then we will help you conquer your territory." So the men of Simeon went with Judah.

4When the men of Judah attacked, the LORD gave them victory over the Canaanites and Perizzites, and they killed ten thousand enemy warriors at the town of Bezek. 5While at Bezek they encountered King Adoni-bezek and fought against him, and the Canaanites and Perizzites were defeated. 6Adoni-bezek escaped, but the Israelites soon captured him and cut off his thumbs and big toes. 7Adoni-bezek said, "I once had seventy kings with thumbs and big toes cut off, eating scraps from under my table. Now God has paid me back for what I did to them." They took him to Jerusalem, and he died there.

8The men of Judah attacked Jerusalem and captured it, killing all its people and setting the city on fire. 9Then they turned south to fight the Canaanites living in the hill country, the Negev, and the western foothills.* 10Judah marched against the Canaanites in Hebron (formerly called Kiriath-arba), defeating the forces of Sheshai, Ahiman, and Talmai. 11From there they marched against the people living in the town of Debir (formerly called Kiriath-sepher).

12Then Caleb said, "I will give my daughter Acsah in marriage to the one who attacks and captures Kiriath-sepher." 13Othniel, the son of Caleb's younger brother Kenaz, was the one who conquered it, so Acsah became Othniel's wife.

14When Acsah married Othniel, she urged him* to ask her father for an additional field. As she got

1:9 Hebrew *the Shephelah.* 1:14 Greek version and Latin Vulgate read *he urged her.*

## COEXISTENCE ● ● ● • •

1:1 **The Canaanites were all the people who lived in Canaan (the Promised Land). They lived in city-states where each city had its own government, army, and laws. One reason Canaan was so difficult to conquer was that each city had to be defeated individually. There was no single king who could surrender the entire country into the hands of the Israelites.**

**However, Canaan's greatest threat to Israel was not its military, but its religion. Canaanite religion idealized evil traits: cruelty in war, sexual immorality, selfish greed, and materialism. It was a "me first, anything goes" society. Obviously, the religions of Israel and Canaan could not coexist.**

# KEY PLACES IN JUDGES

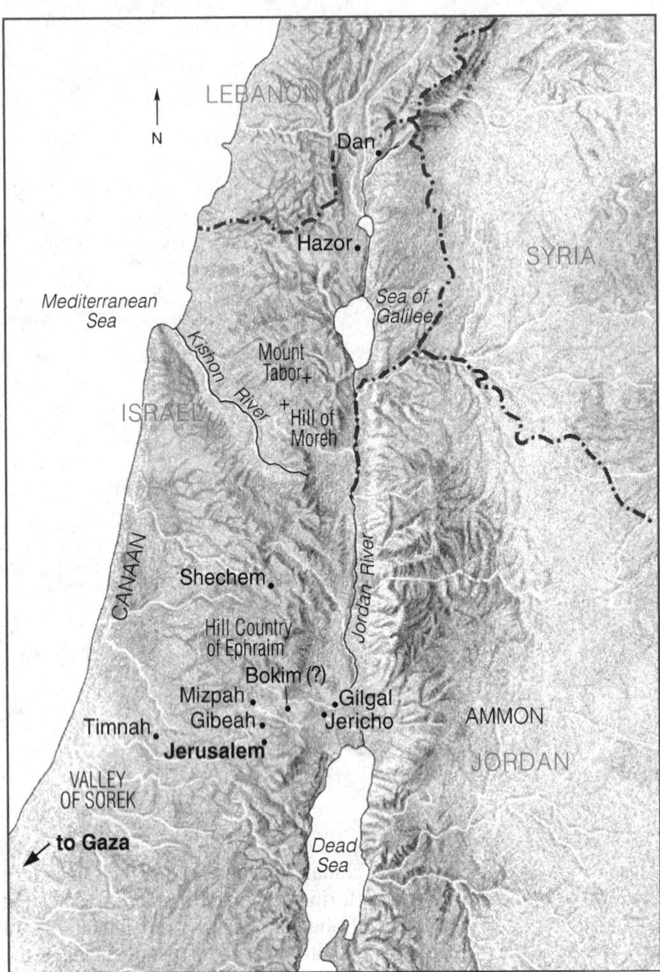


**Bokim** The Angel of the Lord appeared at Bokim, informing the Israelites that their sin and disobedience had broken their agreement with God. Their punishment would be oppression (1:1–3:11).

**Jericho** King Eglon of Moab, one of Israel's first oppressors, conquered much of Israel—including Jericho. Ehud, who was supposed to deliver tax money to King Eglon, killed the Moabite king, escaped, then returned with an army that defeated the Moabites and freed Israel (3:12-31).

**Hazor** After Ehud's death, King Jabin of Hazor conquered Israel, oppressing them for 20 years. Then Deborah became Israel's leader (4:1–5:31).

**Hill of Moreh** After 40 years of peace, the Midianites began harassing the Israelites. God chose Gideon, a humble farmer, to be Israel's deliverer. Gideon attacked the Midianite army camped near the hill of Moreh and sent the enemy running away in confusion (6:1–7:25).

**Shechem** From Gideon's relations with a concubine in Shechem came a son named Abimelech, who was treacherous and power hungry. Because he wanted to be king, he killed 69 of his 70 half brothers. Though men of Shechem rebelled against Abimelech, he gathered an army and defeated them. His lust for power led him to ransack two other cities. A woman finally killed him by dropping a millstone on his head (8:28–9:57).

**Land of Ammon** Again Israel turned from God; so God turned from them. But when the Ammonite army got ready to attack, Israel threw away her idols and called upon God. Jephthah, a prostitute's son who had been run out of Israel, was asked to return and lead Israel's army. After defeating the Ammonites, Jephthah became involved in a war with the tribe of Ephraim (10:1–12:15).

**Timnah** Samson, a miracle child promised by God to a barren couple, was to begin to free Israel from the Philistines. God commanded that Samson was to be a Nazirite—one who took a vow to be set apart for special service to God. Samson's hair could never be cut. But when Samson grew up, he did not take his responsibility to God seriously. He even wanted to marry a Philistine girl in Timnah (13:1–14:20).

**Valley of Sorek** Samson killed thousands of Philistines. The nation's leaders got their chance to stop him when Delilah, a Philistine woman from the valley of Sorek, stole Samson's heart. (15:1–16:20).

**Gaza** The Philistines held a great festival in Gaza to celebrate Samson's imprisonment and to humiliate him before the crowds. When he was brought out as the entertainment, he pushed on the main pillars of the building, collapsing it and killing thousands of Philistines. The prophecy that he would begin to free Israel from the Philistines had come true (16:21-31).

**Hill Country of Ephraim** Here lived a man named Micah, who hired his own priest to perform priestly duties in the shrine that housed his collection of idols. Micah assumed that God's opinions of what was right would agree with his (17:1-13).

**Dan** The tribe of Dan migrated north to find new territory. They sent warriors to scout out the land. They came upon the city of Laish and slaughtered the unarmed and innocent citizens, renaming the conquered city Dan (18:1-31).

**Gibeah** A man and his concubine stopped in Gibeah, thinking they would be safe. But some perverts gathered and demanded that the man have sex with them. Instead, the man and his host pushed the concubine out the door. She was raped and abused all night. When the man found her body the next morning, he cut it into 12 pieces and sent the parts to each tribe of Israel, demonstrating that the nation had sunk to its lowest spiritual level (19:1-30).

**Mizpah** The leaders of Israel came to Mizpah to decide how to punish Gibeah. But the city leaders refused to turn the criminals over, so Israel took vengeance upon the whole tribe of Benjamin. When the battle ended, the entire tribe had been destroyed except for a few men. Israel was now ready for spiritual renewal (20:1–21:25).

down off her donkey, Caleb asked her, "What is it? What can I do for you?"

15She said, "Give me a further blessing. You have been kind enough to give me land in the Negev; please give me springs as well." So Caleb gave her the upper and lower springs.

16When the tribe of Judah left Jericho,* the Kenites, who were descendants of Moses' father-in-law, traveled with them into the wilderness of Judah. They settled among the people there, near the town of Arad in the Negev.

17Then Judah joined with Simeon to fight against the Canaanites living in Zephath, and they completely destroyed* the town. So the town was named Hormah.* 18In addition, Judah captured the cities of Gaza, Ashkelon, and Ekron, along with their surrounding territories.

19The LORD was with the people of Judah, and they took possession of the hill country. But they failed to drive out the people living in the plains because the people there had iron chariots. 20The city of Hebron was given to Caleb as Moses had promised. And Caleb drove out the people living there, who were descendants of the three sons of Anak. 21The tribe of Benjamin, however, failed to drive out the Jebusites, who were living in Jerusalem. So to this day the Jebusites live in Jerusalem among the people of Benjamin.

22The descendants of Joseph attacked the town of Bethel, and the LORD was with them. 23They sent spies to Bethel (formerly known as Luz), 24who confronted a man coming out of the city. They said to him, "Show us a way into the city, and we will have mercy on you." 25So he showed them a way in, and they killed everyone in the city except for this man and his family. 26Later the man moved to the land of the Hittites, where he built a city. He named the city Luz, and it is known by that name to this day.

27The tribe of Manasseh failed to drive out the people living in Beth-shan,* Taanach, Dor, Ibleam, Megiddo, and their surrounding villages, because the Canaanites were determined to stay in that region. 28When the Israelites grew stronger, they forced the Canaanites to work as slaves, but they never did drive them out of the land.

29The tribe of Ephraim also failed to drive out the Canaanites living in Gezer, and so the Canaanites continued to live there among them.

30The tribe of Zebulun also failed to drive out the Canaanites living in Kitron and Nahalol, who continued to live among them. But they forced them to work as slaves.

31The tribe of Asher also failed to drive out the residents of Acco, Sidon, Ahlab, Aczib, Helbah, Aphik, and Rehob. 32In fact, because they did not drive them out, the Canaanites dominated the land where the people of Asher lived.

33The tribe of Naphtali also failed to drive out the residents of Beth-shemesh and Beth-anath. Instead, the Canaanites dominated the land where they lived. Nevertheless, the people of Beth-shemesh and Beth-anath were sometimes forced to work as slaves for the people of Naphtali.

34As for the tribe of Dan, the Amorites forced them into the hill country and would not let them come down into the plains. 35The Amorites were determined to stay in Mount Heres, Aijalon, and Shaalbim, but when the descendants of Joseph became stronger, they forced the Amorites to work as slaves. 36The boundary of the Amorites ran from Scorpion Pass* to Sela and continued upward from there.

CHAPTER **2** **THE COVENANT IS BROKEN.** The angel of the LORD went up from Gilgal to Bokim with a message for the Israelites. He told them, "I brought you out of Egypt into this land that I swore to give your ancestors, and I said I would never break my covenant with you. 2For your part, you were not to make any covenants with the people living in this land; instead, you were to destroy their altars. Why, then, have you disobeyed my command? 3Since you have done this, I will no longer drive out the people living in your land. They will be thorns in your sides, and their gods will be a constant temptation to you." 4When the angel of the LORD finished speaking, the Israelites wept loudly. 5So they called the place "Weeping,"* and they offered sacrifices to the LORD.

6After Joshua sent the people away, each of the tribes left to take possession of the land allotted to them. 7And the Israelites served the LORD throughout the lifetime of Joshua and the leaders who outlived him—those who had seen all the great things the LORD had done for Israel.

8Then Joshua son of Nun, the servant of the LORD, died at the age of 110. 9They buried him in the land he had inherited, at Timnath-serah* in the hill country of Ephraim, north of Mount Gaash.

10After that generation died, another generation grew up who did not acknowledge the LORD or remember the mighty things he had done for Israel. 11Then the Israelites did what was evil in the LORD's

**PERSEVERE ● ● ● • •**

1:19-36 **Why didn't God's people follow through and completely obey his command to destroy the evil Canaanites? (1) They had been fighting for a long time and were tired. (2) They were afraid the enemy was too strong. (3) Since Joshua's death, the tribes were no longer unified in purpose. (4) They thought they could handle the temptation and be more prosperous by doing business with the Canaanites. We, too, often fail to drive sin from our life. Often we know what to do but just don't follow through. This results in a gradual deterioration of our relationship with God. In our battles, we may grow tired and want rest, but we need to remember that victory comes only from obeying God and living according to his purpose.**

1:16 Hebrew *the city of palms.* 1:17a The Hebrew term used here refers to the complete consecration of things or people to the LORD, either by destroying them or by giving them as an offering. 1:17b *Hormah* means "destruction." 1:27 Hebrew *Beth-shean,* a variant name for Beth-shan. 1:36 Hebrew *Akrabbim.* 2:5 Hebrew *Bokim.* 2:9 Hebrew *Timnath-heres,* a variant name for Timnath-serah.

# Ultimate Issues

## OTHER RELIGIONS

If you've been paying attention as you've read so far, you have noticed that God takes a dim view (to put it mildly) of other religions. In the Ten Commandments he told the Israelites to have no other gods. And whenever they encountered foreigners who worshiped ***strange and different*** idols, God was quite brutal in his instructions on how to deal with them. As you read passages like Joshua 10–12, where Joshua and the people of Israel conquered city after city, putting all the inhabitants to death, you may wonder, "Why is God so intolerant? Why is he so rough on LIFELESS IDOLS and the people who believe in them?" **A**dmittedly, such harsh measures seem strange to us, unaccustomed as we are to idol worship and the rituals involved. But God had good reason for his absolute hatred and destruction of these pagan religions. First, many of them, such as the followers of Molech, practiced detestable rituals—even child sacrifice—as part of their **disgusting** worship ceremonies (see Deuteronomy 12:31). Obviously, a holy God could not possibly allow such abominations. He had to put them to a drastic, but justified, end. He did. **S**econd, God knew what prolonged contact with these pagan religions would do to his chosen people. Just like being exposed to a FATAL VIRUS, the Jews ran the risk of being infected. Pagan religions too often were the spiritual equivalents of cancer. Because of God's concern for his people—he didn't want them destroyed by these false religions—he told them to eliminate the source of the disease as **RADICALLY** as a surgeon removing a malignant tumor. Though painful and costly, it was necessary for survival. If they failed to remove the cancer—as they often did—it would grow back and threaten to destroy them. Then it would be up to God to do the "surgery" himself, which he did in the form of persecution and exile. It was far better for Israel to do it right in the first place. **A**ll Christians struggle with the temptation to worship idols. Our idols today—money, sex, status, alcohol, boyfriends or girlfriends—don't look much like the idols the Israelites encountered. But they are just as ***real and rampant***—and just as dangerous—as those others. When you're tempted to put one of them in the place of God, learn a lesson from the Old Testament. As one person said, summing up the insight he gained from reading these accounts, "Don't mess with this God." **T**hen he added, "Thank God for his mercy."

---

sight and worshiped the images of Baal. 12 They abandoned the LORD, the God of their ancestors, who had
brought them out of Egypt. They chased after other
gods, worshiping the gods of the people around them.
And they angered the LORD. 13 They abandoned the
LORD to serve Baal and the images of Ashtoreth. 14 This
made the LORD burn with anger against Israel, so he
handed them over to marauders who stole their possessions. He sold them to their enemies all around,
and they were no longer able to resist them. 15 Every
time Israel went out to battle, the LORD fought against
them, bringing them defeat, just as he promised. And
the people were very distressed.

16 Then the LORD raised up judges to rescue the
Israelites from their enemies. 17 Yet Israel did not
listen to the judges but prostituted themselves to
other gods, bowing down to them. How quickly they
turned away from the path of their ancestors, who
had walked in obedience to the LORD's commands.
18 Whenever the LORD placed a judge over Israel, he
was with that judge and rescued the people from
their enemies throughout the judge's lifetime. For
the LORD took pity on his people, who were burdened by oppression and suffering. 19 But when the
judge died, the people returned to their corrupt ways,
behaving worse than those who had lived before
them. They followed other gods, worshiping and
bowing down to them. And they refused to give up
their evil practices and stubborn ways.

### PEER PRESSURE ● ● • • •

2:11-15 **This generation of Israelites abandoned the faith of their parents and began worshiping the gods of their neighbors. Many things can tempt us to abandon what we know is right. The desire to be accepted by others can lead us into behavior that is unacceptable to God. Don't be pressured into disobedience.**

[20]So the LORD burned with anger against Israel. He said, "Because these people have violated the covenant I made with their ancestors and have ignored my commands, [21]I will no longer drive out the nations that Joshua left unconquered when he died. [22]I did this to test Israel—to see whether or not they would obey the LORD as their ancestors did." [23]That is why the LORD did not quickly drive the nations out or allow Joshua to conquer them all.

CHAPTER **3** **CANAANITES LEFT IN THE LAND.** The LORD left certain nations in the land to test those Israelites who had not participated in the wars of Canaan. [2]He did this to teach warfare to generations of Israelites who had no experience in battle. [3]These were the nations: the Philistines (those living under the five Philistine rulers), all the Canaanites, the Sidonians, and the Hivites living in the hill country of Lebanon from Mount Baal-hermon to Lebo-hamath. [4]These people were left to test the Israelites—to see whether they would obey the commands the LORD had given to their ancestors through Moses.

[5]So Israel lived among the Canaanites, Hittites, Amorites, Perizzites, Hivites, and Jebusites, [6]and they intermarried with them. Israelite sons married their daughters, and Israelite daughters were given in marriage to their sons. And the Israelites worshiped their gods.

[7]The Israelites did what was evil in the LORD's sight. They forgot about the LORD their God, and they worshiped the images of Baal and the Asherah poles. [8]Then the LORD burned with anger against Israel, and he handed them over to King Cushan-rishathaim of Aram-naharaim.* And the Israelites were subject to Cushan-rishathaim for eight years.

[9]But when Israel cried out to the LORD for help, the LORD raised up a man to rescue them. His name was Othniel, the son of Caleb's younger brother, Kenaz. [10]The Spirit of the LORD came upon him, and he became Israel's judge. He went to war against King Cushan-rishathaim of Aram, and the LORD gave Othniel victory over him. [11]So there was peace in the land for forty years. Then Othniel son of Kenaz died.

[12]Once again the Israelites did what was evil in the LORD's sight, so the LORD gave King Eglon of Moab control over Israel. [13]Together with the Ammonites and Amalekites, Eglon attacked Israel and took possession of Jericho.* [14]And the Israelites were subject to Eglon of Moab for eighteen years.

[15]But when Israel cried out to the LORD for help, the LORD raised up a man to rescue them. His name was Ehud son of Gera, of the tribe of Benjamin, who was left-handed. The Israelites sent Ehud to deliver their tax money to King Eglon of Moab. [16]So Ehud made himself a double-edged dagger that was eighteen inches* long, and he strapped it to his right thigh, keeping it hidden under his clothing. [17]He brought the tax money to Eglon, who was very fat.

The LORD
took pity on his people
who were
BURDENED
by
oppression
and
suffering
JUDGES 2:18

[18]After delivering the payment, Ehud sent home those who had carried the tax money.

[19]But when Ehud reached the stone carvings near Gilgal, he turned back. He came to Eglon and said, "I have a secret message for you." So the king commanded his servants to be silent and sent them all out of the room. [20]Ehud walked over to Eglon as he was sitting alone in a cool upstairs room and said, "I have a message for you from God!" As King Eglon rose from his seat, [21]Ehud reached with his left hand, pulled out the dagger strapped to his right thigh, and plunged it into the king's belly. [22]The dagger went so deep that the handle disappeared beneath the king's fat. So Ehud left the dagger in, and the king's bowels emptied. [23]Then Ehud closed and locked the doors and climbed down the latrine and escaped through the sewage access.

[24]After Ehud was gone, the king's servants returned and found the doors to the upstairs room locked. They thought he might be using the latrine, [25]so they

3:8 *Aram-naharaim* means "Aram of the two rivers," thought to have been located between the Euphrates and Balih Rivers in northwestern Mesopotamia. 3:13 Hebrew *the city of palms.* 3:16 Hebrew *1 cubit* [45 centimeters].

waited. But when the king didn't come out after a long delay, they became concerned and got a key. And when they opened the door, they found their master dead on the floor.

[26]While the servants were waiting, Ehud escaped, passing the idols on his way to Seirah. [27]When he arrived in the hill country of Ephraim, Ehud sounded a call to arms. Then he led a band of Israelites down from the hills. [28]"Follow me," he said, "for the LORD has given you victory over Moab your enemy." So they followed him. And the Israelites took control of the shallows of the Jordan River across from Moab, preventing anyone from crossing. [29]They attacked the Moabites and killed about ten thousand of their strongest and bravest warriors. Not one of them escaped. [30]So Moab was conquered by Israel that day, and the land was at peace for eighty years.

[31]After Ehud, Shamgar son of Anath rescued Israel. He killed six hundred Philistines with an ox goad.

## SIN ● ● • • •

4:1 **Israel's sin was also against the Lord. Our sins harm both ourselves and others, but all sin is ultimately against God because it disregards his commands and his authority over our lives. When confessing his sin, David prayed, "Against you, and you alone, have I sinned; I have done what is evil in your sight" (Psalm 51:4). Recognizing the seriousness of sin is the first step toward removing it from our lives.**

CHAPTER **4** **DEBORAH AND BARAK.** After Ehud's death, the Israelites again did what was evil in the LORD's sight. [2]So the LORD handed them over to King Jabin of Hazor, a Canaanite king. The commander of his army was Sisera, who lived in Harosheth-haggoyim. [3]Sisera, who had nine hundred iron chariots, ruthlessly oppressed the Israelites for twenty years. Then the Israelites cried out to the LORD for help.

[4]Deborah, the wife of Lappidoth, was a prophet who had become a judge in Israel. [5]She would hold court under the Palm of Deborah, which stood between Ramah and Bethel in the hill country of Ephraim, and the Israelites came to her to settle their disputes. [6]One day she sent for Barak son of Abinoam, who lived in Kedesh in the land of Naphtali. She said to him, "This is what the LORD, the God of Israel, commands you: Assemble ten thousand warriors from the tribes of Naphtali and Zebulun at Mount Tabor. [7]I will lure Sisera, commander of Jabin's army, along with his chariots and warriors, to the Kishon River. There I will give you victory over him."

[8]Barak told her, "I will go, but only if you go with me!"

[9]"Very well," she replied, "I will go with you. But since you have made this choice, you will receive no honor. For the LORD's victory over Sisera will be at

## A TRUE LEADER ● ● • • •

4:9 **How did Deborah command such respect? She was responsible for leading the people into battle. But more than that, she influenced them to live for God after the battle was over. Her personality drew people together and commanded the respect of even Barak, a military general. She was also a prophetess, whose main role was to encourage the people to obey God. Those who lead must not forget about the spiritual condition of those being led. A true leader is concerned for people, not just success.**

the hands of a woman." So Deborah went with Barak to Kedesh. [10]At Kedesh, Barak called together the tribes of Zebulun and Naphtali, and ten thousand warriors marched up with him. Deborah also marched with them.

[11]Now Heber the Kenite, a descendant of Moses' brother-in-law* Hobab, had moved away from the other members of his tribe and pitched his tent by the Oak of Zaanannim, near Kedesh.

[12]When Sisera was told that Barak son of Abinoam had gone up to Mount Tabor, [13]he called for all nine hundred of his iron chariots and all of his warriors, and they marched from Harosheth-haggoyim to the Kishon River.

[14]Then Deborah said to Barak, "Get ready! Today the LORD will give you victory over Sisera, for the LORD is marching ahead of you." So Barak led his ten thousand warriors down the slopes of Mount Tabor into battle. [15]When Barak attacked, the LORD threw Sisera and all his charioteers and warriors into a panic. Then Sisera leaped down from his chariot and escaped on foot. [16]Barak chased the enemy and their chariots all the way to Harosheth-haggoyim, killing all of Sisera's warriors. Not a single one was left alive.

[17]Meanwhile, Sisera ran to the tent of Jael, the wife of Heber the Kenite, because Heber's family was on friendly terms with King Jabin of Hazor. [18]Jael went out to meet Sisera and said to him, "Come into my tent, sir. Come in. Don't be afraid." So he went into her tent, and she covered him with a blanket.

[19]"Please give me some water," he said. "I'm thirsty." So she gave him some milk to drink and covered him again.

[20]"Stand at the door of the tent," he told her. "If anybody comes and asks you if there is anyone here, say no."

[21]But when Sisera fell asleep from exhaustion, Jael quietly crept up to him with a hammer and tent peg. Then she drove the tent peg through his temple and into the ground, and so he died.

[22]When Barak came looking for Sisera, Jael went out to meet him. She said, "Come, and I will show you the man you are looking for." So he followed her into the tent and found Sisera lying there dead, with the tent peg through his temple.

[23]So on that day Israel saw God subdue Jabin, the Canaanite king. [24]And from that time on Israel became stronger and stronger against King Jabin, until they finally destroyed him.

4:11 Or *father-in-law.*

CHAPTER **5** **THE SONG OF DEBORAH.** On that day
Deborah and Barak son of Abinoam sang this song:

2 "When Israel's leaders take charge,
and the people gladly follow—
bless the LORD!

3 "Listen, you kings!
Pay attention, you mighty rulers!
For I will sing to the LORD.
I will lift up my song to the LORD, the God of Israel.

4 "LORD, when you set out from Seir
and marched across the fields of Edom,
the earth trembled
and the cloudy skies poured down rain.
5 The mountains quaked at the coming of the LORD.
Even Mount Sinai shook in the presence of the LORD, the God of Israel.

6 "In the days of Shamgar son of Anath, and in the days of Jael,
people avoided the main roads,
and travelers stayed on crooked side paths.
7 There were few people left in the villages of Israel—
until Deborah arose as a mother for Israel.
8 When Israel chose new gods,
war erupted at the city gates.
Yet not a shield or spear could be seen
among forty thousand warriors in Israel!
9 My heart goes out to Israel's leaders,
and to those who gladly followed.
Bless the LORD!

10 "You who ride on fine donkeys
and sit on fancy saddle blankets, listen!
And you who must walk along the road, listen!
11 Listen to the village musicians* gathered at the watering holes.
They recount the righteous victories of the LORD,
and the victories of his villagers in Israel.
Then the people of the LORD
marched down to the city gates.

12 "Wake up, Deborah, wake up!
Wake up, wake up, and sing a song!
Arise, Barak!
Lead your captives away, son of Abinoam!

13 "Down from Tabor marched the remnant against the mighty.
The people of the LORD marched down
against mighty warriors.
14 They came down from Ephraim—a land that once belonged to the Amalekites,
and Benjamin also followed you.
From Makir the commanders marched down;
from Zebulun came those who carry the rod of authority.

5:11 The meaning of the Hebrew is uncertain.

15 The princes of Issachar were with Deborah and Barak.
They followed Barak, rushing into the valley.
But in the tribe of Reuben
there was great indecision.
16 Why did you sit at home among the sheepfolds—
to hear the shepherds whistle for their flocks?
In the tribe of Reuben
there was great indecision.
17 Gilead remained east of the Jordan.
And Dan, why did he stay home?
Asher sat unmoved at the seashore,
remaining in his harbors.
18 But Zebulun risked his life,
as did Naphtali, on the battlefield.

19 "The kings of Canaan fought at Taanach near Megiddo's springs,
but they carried off no treasures of battle.
20 The stars fought from heaven.
The stars in their orbits fought against Sisera.
21 The Kishon River swept them away—
that ancient river, the Kishon.
March on, my soul, with courage!
22 Then the horses' hooves hammered the ground,
the galloping, galloping of Sisera's mighty steeds.
23 'Let the people of Meroz be cursed,' said the angel of the LORD.
'Let them be utterly cursed
because they did not come to help the LORD,
to help the LORD against the mighty warriors.'

24 "Most blessed is Jael,
the wife of Heber the Kenite.
May she be blessed above all women who live in tents.
25 Sisera asked for water,
and Jael gave him milk.
In a bowl fit for kings,
she brought him yogurt.
26 Then with her left hand she reached for a tent peg,
and with her right hand she reached for the workman's hammer.
She hit Sisera, crushing his head.
She pounded the tent peg through his head,
piercing his temples.
27 He sank, he fell,
he lay dead at her feet.

28 "From the window Sisera's mother looked out.
Through the window she watched for his return, saying,

**SONGS ● ● • • .**

5:1-31 **In victory, Barak and Deborah sang praises to God. Songs of praise focus our attention on God, give us an outlet for spiritual celebration, and remind us of God's faithfulness and character. Whether you are in the middle of a great victory or a difficult problem, singing praises to God can have a positive effect on your attitude.**

'Why is his chariot so long in coming?
Why don't we hear the sound of chariot wheels?'
29 A reply comes from her wise women,
and she repeats these words to herself:
30 'They are dividing the captured goods they found—
a woman or two for every man.
There are gorgeous robes for Sisera,
and colorful, beautifully embroidered robes for me.'

31 "LORD, may all your enemies die as Sisera did!
But may those who love you rise like the sun at full strength!"

Then there was peace in the land for forty years.

CHAPTER **6** **GIDEON BECOMES ISRAEL'S JUDGE.** Again
the Israelites did what was evil in the LORD's sight. So
the LORD handed them over to the Midianites for
seven years. 2The Midianites were so cruel that the
Israelites fled to the mountains, where they made
hiding places for themselves in caves and dens.
3Whenever the Israelites planted their crops, marauders from Midian, Amalek, and the people of the
east would attack Israel, 4camping in the land and
destroying crops as far away as Gaza. They left the
Israelites with nothing to eat, taking all the sheep,
oxen, and donkeys. 5These enemy hordes, coming
with their cattle and tents as thick as locusts, arrived
on droves of camels too numerous to count. And
they stayed until the land was stripped bare. 6So
Israel was reduced to starvation by the Midianites.
Then the Israelites cried out to the LORD for help.
7When they cried out to the LORD because of
Midian, 8the LORD sent a prophet to the Israelites. He
said, "This is what the LORD, the God of Israel, says:
I brought you up out of slavery in Egypt 9and rescued
you from the Egyptians and from all who oppressed
you. I drove out your enemies and gave you their
land. 10I told you, 'I am the LORD your God. You must
not worship the gods of the Amorites, in whose land
you now live.' But you have not listened to me."
11Then the angel of the LORD came and sat beneath the oak tree at Ophrah, which belonged to
Joash of the clan of Abiezer. Gideon son of Joash had
been threshing wheat at the bottom of a winepress
to hide the grain from the Midianites. 12The angel of
the LORD appeared to him and said, "Mighty hero,
the LORD is with you!"
13"Sir," Gideon replied, "if the LORD is with us,
why has all this happened to us? And where are all
the miracles our ancestors told us about? Didn't they
say, 'The LORD brought us up out of Egypt'? But now
the LORD has abandoned us and handed us over to
the Midianites."
14Then the LORD turned to him and said, "Go with
the strength you have and rescue Israel from the
Midianites. I am sending you!"
15"But Lord," Gideon replied, "how can I rescue

## LAME EXCUSES ● ● • • •

6:14-16 **God promised to give Gideon the strength he needed to overcome the opposition. In spite of this clear promise for strength, Gideon made excuses. He saw only his limitations and weaknesses. He failed to see how God could work through him.**

**Like Gideon, we are called to serve God in specific ways. Although God promises us the tools and strength we need, we often make excuses, too. Reminding God of our limitations only implies that he does not know all about us or that he has made a mistake in evaluating our character. Don't spend time making excuses. Instead spend it doing what God wants.**

Israel? My clan is the weakest in the whole tribe of
Manasseh, and I am the least in my entire family!"
16The LORD said to him, "I will be with you. And
you will destroy the Midianites as if you were fighting against one man."
17Gideon replied, "If you are truly going to help
me, show me a sign to prove that it is really the LORD
speaking to me. 18Don't go away until I come back
and bring my offering to you."
The LORD answered, "I will stay here until you
return."
19Gideon hurried home. He cooked a young goat,
and with half a bushel* of flour he baked some
bread without yeast. Then, carrying the meat in a
basket and the broth in a pot, he brought them out
and presented them to the angel, who was under the
oak tree.
20The angel of God said to him, "Place the meat
and the unleavened bread on this rock, and pour the
broth over it." And Gideon did as he was told. 21Then
the angel of the LORD touched the meat and bread
with the staff in his hand, and fire flamed up from
the rock and consumed all he had brought. And the
angel of the LORD disappeared.
22When Gideon realized that it was the angel of
the LORD, he cried out, "Sovereign LORD, I have seen
the angel of the LORD face to face!"
23"It is all right," the LORD replied. "Do not be
afraid. You will not die." 24And Gideon built an altar

## GET GOING ● ● • • •

6:37 **Was Gideon really testing God or was he simply asking God for more encouragement? In either case, though his motive was right (to obey God and defeat the enemy), his method was less than ideal. Gideon seems to have known that his requests might displease God (6:39), and yet he demanded two miracles (6:37, 39) even after witnessing the miraculous fire from the rock (6:21). It is true that to make good decisions we need facts. Gideon had all the facts, but still he hesitated. He delayed his obedience because he wanted even more proof.**

**Demanding extra signs was an indication of Gideon's unbelief. Fear often makes us wait for more confirmation when we should be taking action. Visible signs are unnecessary if they only confirm what we already know to be true. Today the greatest means of God's guidance is his Word. Unlike Gideon, we have God's complete, revealed Word. If you want to have more of God's guidance, don't ask for signs; study God's Word (2 Timothy 3:16-17).**

6:19 Hebrew *1 ephah* [18 liters].

to the LORD there and named it "The LORD Is
Peace."* The altar remains in Ophrah in the land of
the clan of Abiezer to this day.
[25]That night the LORD said to Gideon, "Take the
second best bull from your father's herd, the one that
is seven years old. Pull down your father's altar to
Baal, and cut down the Asherah pole standing beside
it. [26]Then build an altar to the LORD your God here
on this hill, laying the stones carefully. Sacrifice the
bull as a burnt offering on the altar, using as fuel the
wood of the Asherah pole
you cut down." [27]So Gideon
took ten of his servants and
did as the LORD had commanded.
But he did it at
night because he was afraid
of the other members of his
father's household and the
people of the town. He knew
what would happen if they
found out who had done it.
[28]Early the next morning,
as the people of the town
began to stir, someone discovered
that the altar of Baal
had been knocked down
and that the Asherah pole
beside it was gone. In their
place a new altar had been
built, and it had the remains
of a sacrifice on it. [29]The
people said to each other,
"Who did this?" And after
asking around and making a
careful search, they learned
that it was Gideon, the son
of Joash.
[30]"Bring out your son,"
they shouted to Joash. "He
must die for destroying the
altar of Baal and for cutting
down the Asherah pole."
[31]But Joash shouted to the
mob, "Why are you defending
Baal? Will you argue his
case? Whoever pleads his
case will be put to death by
morning! If Baal truly is a
god, let him defend himself
and destroy the one who
knocked down his altar!"
[32]From then on Gideon was
called Jerubbaal, which
means "Let Baal defend
himself," because he
knocked down Baal's altar.
[33]Soon afterward the armies
of Midian, Amalek,
and the people of the east
formed an alliance against
Israel and crossed the Jordan, camping in the valley
of Jezreel. [34]Then the Spirit of the LORD took possession
of Gideon. He blew a ram's horn as a call to
arms, and the men of the clan of Abiezer came to
him. [35]He also sent messengers throughout Manasseh,
Asher, Zebulun, and Naphtali, summoning
their warriors, and all of them responded.
[36]Then Gideon said to God, "If you are truly going
to use me to rescue Israel as you promised, [37]prove it
to me in this way. I will put some wool on the

## GIDEON

Most of us want to know God's plan for our lives, but we're not always sure how to find it. It is easy to think that God's guidance is something hidden and that we might miss it if we are not watching. But if we're always looking around for God's next assignment, we will probably not do a very good job on what he has us doing now. If all you think about is tomorrow's test, you may miss the answers that are given in today's class. Fortunately, the Bible gives us a better way to understand God's guidance. In the Bible's descriptions of how God guided people, we can see that God usually showed them what he wanted next while they were completely involved in obeying him right where they were. A good example of this kind of guidance is seen in Gideon's life.

Times were hard. Gideon's job was to get food for his family. The Midianite invaders were determined to stop him. Read about Gideon's plan to accomplish his mission. He was busy doing his duty when God's messenger arrived. If God's messenger showed up in your life today, would he find you doing what you are supposed to be doing?

Gideon was surprised by God's orders. He found out God wanted to use him to help defeat the Midianites—but he had a few doubts. He still felt responsible for his family. He wasn't sure this was really God's command or if he was the right person for the task. Sometimes we ask questions about God's Word because we want to be sure. But sometimes we ask questions because we really don't want to obey. God was patient with Gideon's questions and doubts—he knew Gideon wanted to obey. Gideon made mistakes, but he was still God's servant. You can be sure that God will guide you as long as your desire is to serve and obey him wherever you are.

LESSONS: God expands and uses the abilities he has already built into us

God uses us in spite of our limitations and failures

Even those who make great spiritual progress can easily fall into sin if they don't consistently follow God

KEY VERSES: "'But Lord,' Gideon replied, 'how can I rescue Israel? My clan is the weakest in the whole tribe of Manasseh, and I am the least in my entire family!' The LORD said to him, 'I will be with you. And you will destroy the Midianites as if you were fighting against one man'" (Judges 6:15-16).

His story is told in Judges 6–8. He is also mentioned in Hebrews 11:32.

**UPS:**
- Israel's fifth judge
- A military strategist who was expert at surprise
- A member of the Hall of Faith in Hebrews
- Defeated the Midianite army
- Was offered the title of king by the people of Israel
- Though slow to be convinced, acted on his convictions

**DOWNS:**
- Feared that his own limitations would prevent God from working
- Collected Midianite gold and made a symbol which became an object of worship
- Through a sexual relationship outside marriage, fathered a son who would bring great grief and tragedy to both Gideon's family and the nation of Israel
- Failed to establish the nation in God's ways; after he died they all went back to idol worship

**STATS:**
- Where: Ophrah, valley of Jezreel, well of Harod
- Occupation: Farmer, warrior, and judge
- Relatives: Father: Joash. Son: Abimelech.
- Contemporaries: King Zebah, King Zalmunna

**6:24** Hebrew *Yahweh Shalom.*

OTHNIEL (40 years)
He captured a powerful Canaanite city
*Judges 3:7-11*

EHUD (80 years)
He killed Eglon and defeated the Moabites
*Judges 3:12-30*

SHAMGAR
He killed 600 Philistines with an ox goad
*Judges 3:31*

DEBORAH (40 years)
She defeated General Sisera and the Canaanites and later sang a victory song with Barak
*Judges 4–5*

GIDEON (40 years)
He used a fleece to determine God's will and defeated 135,000 Midianites with 300 men
*Judges 6–8*

TOLA (23 years)
*Judges 10:1-2*

JAIR (22 years)
He had 30 sons
*Judges 10:3-5*

JEPHTHAH (6 years)
He made a rash vow, defeated the Ammonites, and later battled Ephraim
*Judges 10:6–12:7*

IBZAN (7 years)
He had 30 sons and 30 daughters
*Judges 12:8-10*

ELON (10 years)
*Judges 12:11-12*

ABDON (8 years)
He had 40 sons and 30 grandsons, each of whom had his own donkey
*Judges 12:13-15*

SAMSON (20 years)
He was betrayed by Delilah but destroyed thousands of Philistines
*Judges 13–16*

---

threshing floor tonight. If the fleece is wet with dew
in the morning but the ground is dry, then I will
know that you are going to help me rescue Israel as
you promised." 38And it happened just that way.
When Gideon got up the next morning, he squeezed
the fleece and wrung out a whole bowlful of water.
39Then Gideon said to God, "Please don't be
angry with me, but let me make one more request.
This time let the fleece remain dry while the ground
around it is wet with dew." 40So that night God did
as Gideon asked. The fleece was dry in the morning,
but the ground was covered with dew.

CHAPTER **7** **GIDEON'S ARMY OF 300.** So Jerubbaal
(that is, Gideon) and his army got up early and went
as far as the spring of Harod. The armies of Midian
were camped north of them in the valley near the hill
of Moreh. 2The LORD said to Gideon, "You have too
many warriors with you. If I let all of you fight the
Midianites, the Israelites will boast to me that they
saved themselves by their own strength. 3Therefore, tell
the people, 'Whoever is timid or afraid may leave* and
go home.'" Twenty-two thousand of them went home,
leaving only ten thousand who were willing to fight.
4But the LORD told Gideon, "There are still too
many! Bring them down to the spring, and I will sort
out who will go with you and who will not." 5When
Gideon took his warriors down to the water, the
LORD told him, "Divide the men into two groups. In
one group put all those who cup water in their hands
and lap it up with their tongues like dogs. In the
other group put all those who kneel down and drink
with their mouths in the stream." 6Only three hundred of the men drank from their hands. All the
others got down on their knees and drank with their
mouths in the stream. 7The LORD told Gideon,
"With these three hundred men I will rescue you and
give you victory over the Midianites. Send all the
others home." 8So Gideon collected the provisions
and rams' horns of the other warriors and sent them
home. But he kept the three hundred men with him.
Now the Midianite camp was in the valley just
below Gideon. 9During the night, the LORD said,
"Get up! Go down into the Midianite camp, for I
have given you victory over them! 10But if you are

**THANK GOD ● ● • • ·**

7:15 **Gideon stood just outside the enemy camp and thanked God. Rituals, motions, or loud praise would have announced his presence to the enemy, so Gideon's thanksgiving must have been a silent attitude of joy, worship, and praise to God. Similarly, we can thank God silently and constantly even in the middle of difficult situations.**

7:3 Hebrew *leave Mount Gilead.* The identity of Mount Gilead is uncertain in this context. It is perhaps used here as another name for Mount Gilboa.

afraid to attack, go down to the camp with your
servant Purah. 11Listen to what the Midianites are
saying, and you will be greatly encouraged. Then you
will be eager to attack."
So Gideon took Purah and went down to the
outposts of the enemy camp. 12The armies of Midian, Amalek, and the people of the east had settled
in the valley like a swarm of locusts. Their camels
were like grains of sand on the seashore—too many
to count! 13Gideon crept up just as a man was telling
his friend about a dream. The man said, "I had this
dream, and in my dream a loaf of barley bread came
tumbling down into the Midianite camp. It hit a
tent, turned it over, and knocked it flat!"
14His friend said, "Your dream can mean only one
thing—God has given Gideon son of Joash, the Israelite, victory over all the armies united with Midian!"
15When Gideon heard the dream and its interpretation, he thanked God. Then he returned to the Israelite
camp and shouted, "Get up! For the LORD has given
you victory over the Midianites!" 16He divided the
three hundred men into three groups and gave each
man a ram's horn and a clay jar with a torch in it.
17Then he said to them, "Keep your eyes on me. When
I come to the edge of the camp, do just as I do. 18As
soon as my group blows the rams' horns, those of you
on the other sides of the camp blow your horns and
shout, 'For the LORD and for Gideon!'"
19It was just after midnight, after the changing of
the guard, when Gideon and the one hundred men
with him reached the outer edge of the Midianite
camp. Suddenly, they blew the horns and broke their
clay jars. 20Then all three groups blew their horns
and broke their jars. They held the blazing torches in
their left hands and the horns in their right hands
and shouted, "A sword for the LORD and for Gideon!" 21Each man stood at his position around the
camp and watched as all the Midianites rushed
around in a panic, shouting as they ran. 22When the
three hundred Israelites blew their horns, the LORD
caused the warriors in the camp to fight against each
other with their swords. Those who were not killed
fled to places as far away as Beth-shittah near Zererah
and to the border of Abel-meholah near Tabbath.
23Then Gideon sent for the warriors of Naphtali,
Asher, and Manasseh, who joined in the chase after
the fleeing army of Midian. 24Gideon also sent messengers throughout the hill country of Ephraim, saying, "Come down to attack the Midianites. Cut them
off at the shallows of the Jordan River at Beth-
barah." And the men of Ephraim did as they were
told. 25They captured Oreb and Zeeb, the two Midianite generals, killing Oreb at the rock of Oreb, and
Zeeb at the winepress of Zeeb. And they continued
to chase the Midianites. Afterward the Israelites
brought the heads of Oreb and Zeeb to Gideon, who
was by the Jordan.

CHAPTER **8** **GIDEON'S WISE ANSWER.** Then the
people of Ephraim asked Gideon, "Why have you
treated us this way? Why didn't you send for us when
you first went out to fight the Midianites?" And they
argued heatedly with Gideon.
2But Gideon replied, "What have I done compared to you? Aren't the last grapes of Ephraim's
harvest better than the entire crop of my little clan of

**A friend says that my new faith in Christ is too narrow. He doesn't think Christ is the only way to God. Why can't God allow different ideas by other religions?**

Suppose your history teacher told you that Columbus discovered America in 1492. Just then, four other people raised their hands and said, "I think he discovered America in 1454 [or 1678 or 1543 or 1733]. What makes you the authority on history anyway? We are going to believe what we think is right."

Do these kids have the freedom to believe what they think is right? Of course they do.

A wise teacher would respond, "You may believe any date you choose to believe, but there is only one right answer and I have told you what it is. If you put a different answer on the test at the end of the term, it will be checked wrong."

God has given people the freedom to choose what they want to believe about who he is and what his plan is for human beings. But when the test scores are graded at the end of the age, there will be only one right answer.

During this period in Jewish history they had no leader, so it says that "the people did whatever seemed right in their own eyes" (Judges 17:6). What this means is that not only did people choose to disobey God as their leader, but their actions were evil as well! Throughout history people have behaved according to what they believe about God.

If people believe that God does not exist or that God does not care how we live and treat each other, they will likely act accordingly. Usually, this means that they treat themselves or others like there will be no final exam when they pass on to the next life!

Jesus said, "I am the way, the truth, and the life. No one can come to the Father except through me" (John 14:6). This means that God grades on a pass/fail basis depending on what we have done with his Son, Jesus.

Many people would like to believe that God grades on a curve. In other words, if you do good things or go to church more than others or give more money than 60 percent of the rest of the world, you will get into heaven. Jesus makes it clear, however, that there is only one way to heaven.

God has given people the freedom to believe any religion they want. But the final authority is not their own beliefs. There is only one right answer. God's standard is faith in Jesus Christ, his death on the cross—so that our sin would not eternally separate us from God—and his resurrection.

Abiezer? 3God gave you victory over Oreb and Zeeb, the generals of the Midianite army. What have I done compared to that?" When the men of Ephraim heard Gideon's answer, they were no longer angry.

4Gideon then crossed the Jordan River with his three hundred men, and though they were exhausted, they continued to chase the enemy. 5When they reached Succoth, Gideon asked the leaders of the town, "Will you please give my warriors some food? They are very tired. I am chasing Zebah and Zalmunna, the kings of Midian."

6But the leaders of Succoth replied, "You haven't caught Zebah and Zalmunna yet. Catch them first, and then we will feed your warriors."

7So Gideon said, "After the LORD gives me victory over Zebah and Zalmunna, I will return and tear your flesh with the thorns and briers of the wilderness."

8From there Gideon went up to Peniel* and asked for food, but he got the same answer. 9So he said to the people of Peniel, "After I return in victory, I will tear down this tower."

10By this time Zebah and Zalmunna were in Karkor with a remnant of 15,000 warriors—all that remained of the allied armies of the east—for 120,000 had already been killed. 11Gideon circled around by the caravan route east of Nobah and Jogbehah, taking the Midianite army by surprise. 12Zebah and Zalmunna, the two Midianite kings, fled, but Gideon chased them down and captured all their warriors.

13After this, Gideon returned by way of Heres Pass. 14There he captured a young man from Succoth and demanded that he write down the names of all the seventy-seven rulers and leaders in the town. 15Gideon then returned to Succoth and said to the leaders, "Here are Zebah and Zalmunna. When we were here before, you taunted me, saying, 'You haven't caught Zebah and Zalmunna yet. Catch them first, and then we will feed your exhausted warriors.'" 16Then Gideon took the leaders of the town and taught them a lesson, punishing them with thorns and briers from the wilderness. 17He also knocked down the tower of Peniel and killed all the men in the town.

18Then Gideon asked Zebah and Zalmunna, "The men you killed at Tabor—what were they like?"

"Like you," they replied. "They all had the look of a king's son."

19"They were my brothers!" Gideon exclaimed. "As surely as the LORD lives, I wouldn't kill you if you hadn't killed them."

20Turning to Jether, his oldest son, he said, "Kill them!" But Jether did not draw his sword, for he was only a boy and was afraid.

21Then Zebah and Zalmunna said to Gideon, "Don't ask a boy to do a man's job! Do it yourself!" So Gideon killed them both and took the royal ornaments from the necks of their camels.

22Then the Israelites said to Gideon, "Be our ruler! You and your son and your grandson will be our rulers, for you have rescued us from Midian."

23But Gideon replied, "I will not rule over you, nor will my son. The LORD will rule over you! 24However, I have one request. Each of you can give me an earring out of the treasures you collected from your fallen enemies." (The enemies, being Ishmaelites, all wore gold earrings.)

25"Gladly!" they replied. They spread out a cloak, and each one threw in a gold earring he had gathered. 26The weight of the gold earrings was forty-three pounds,* not including the crescents and pendants, the royal clothing of the kings, or the chains around the necks of their camels. 27Gideon made a sacred ephod from the gold and put it in Ophrah, his hometown. But soon all the Israelites prostituted themselves by worshiping it, and it became a trap for Gideon and his family.

28That is the story of how Israel subdued Midian, which never recovered. Throughout the rest of Gideon's lifetime—about forty years—the land was at peace.

29Then Gideon* son of Joash returned home. 30He had seventy sons, for he had many wives. 31He also had a concubine in Shechem, who bore him a son named Abimelech. 32Gideon died when he was very old, and he was buried in the grave of his father, Joash, at Ophrah in the land of the clan of Abiezer.

33As soon as Gideon was dead, the Israelites prostituted themselves by worshiping the images of Baal, making Baal-berith their god. 34They forgot the LORD their God, who had rescued them from all their enemies surrounding them. 35Nor did they show any loyalty to the family of Jerubbaal (that is, Gideon), despite all the good he had done for Israel.

## TEMPTATION ● ● • • •

8:31 **This relationship between Gideon and a concubine produced a son who tore apart Gideon's family and caused tragedy for the nation. Gideon's story illustrates the fact that heroes in battle are not always heroes in daily life. Gideon led the nation, but could not lead his family. No matter who you are, moral laxness will cause problems. Just because you have won a single battle with temptation does not mean you will automatically win the next. We need to be constantly watchful against temptation. Sometimes Satan's strongest attacks come after a victory.**

## CHAPTER 9 **ABIMELECH TRIES TO BECOME KING.**

One day Gideon's* son Abimelech went to Shechem to visit his mother's brothers. He said to them and to the rest of his mother's family, 2"Ask the people of Shechem whether they want to be ruled by all seventy of Gideon's sons or by one man. And remember, I am your own flesh and blood!"

3So Abimelech's uncles spoke to all the people of Shechem on his behalf. And after listening to their proposal, they decided in favor of Abimelech be-

**8:8** Hebrew *Penuel*, a variant name for Peniel; also in 8:9, 17. **8:26** Hebrew *1,700 shekels* [19.4 kilograms]. **8:29** Hebrew *Jerubbaal*; see 6:32. **9:1** Hebrew *Jerubbaal's* (see 6:32); also in 9:2, 24.

**PRIORITIES ● ● ● • •**

**9:16 Jotham told the story about the trees in order to help the people set good priorities. He did not want them to appoint a leader of low character. As we serve in leadership positions, we should examine our motives. Do we just want praise, prestige, or power? In the parable, the good trees chose to be productive and to provide benefits to people. Make sure these are your priorities if you want to be a leader.**

cause he was their relative. 4They gave him seventy silver coins from the temple of Baal-berith, which he used to hire some soldiers who agreed to follow him. 5He took the soldiers to his father's home at Ophrah, and there, on one stone, they killed all seventy of his half brothers. But the youngest brother, Jotham, escaped and hid. 6Then the people of Shechem and Beth-millo called a meeting under the oak beside the pillar* at Shechem and made Abimelech their king.

7When Jotham heard about this, he climbed to the top of Mount Gerizim and shouted, "Listen to me, people of Shechem! Listen to me if you want God to listen to you! 8Once upon a time the trees decided to elect a king. First they said to the olive tree, 'Be our king!' 9But it refused, saying, 'Should I quit producing the olive oil that blesses both God and people, just to wave back and forth over the trees?'

10"Then they said to the fig tree, 'You be our king!' 11But the fig tree also refused, saying, 'Should I quit producing my sweet fruit just to wave back and forth over the trees?'

12"Then they said to the grapevine, 'You be our king!' 13But the grapevine replied, 'Should I quit producing the wine that cheers both God and people, just to wave back and forth over the trees?'

14"Then all the trees finally turned to the thornbush and said, 'Come, you be our king!' 15And the thornbush replied, 'If you truly want to make me your king, come and take shelter in my shade. If not, let fire come out from me and devour the cedars of Lebanon.'

16"Now make sure you have acted honorably and in good faith by making Abimelech your king, and that you have done right by Gideon* and all of his descendants. Have you treated my father with the honor he deserves? 17For he fought for you and risked his life when he rescued you from the Midianites. 18But now you have revolted against my father and his descendants, killing his seventy sons on one stone. And you have chosen his slave woman's son, Abimelech, to be your king just because he is your relative. 19If you have acted honorably and in good faith toward Gideon and his descendants, then may you find joy in Abimelech, and may he find joy in you. 20But if you have not acted in good faith, then may fire come out from Abimelech and devour the people of Shechem and Beth-millo; and may fire come out from the people of Shechem and Beth-millo and devour Abimelech!" 21Then Jotham escaped and lived in Beer because he was afraid of his brother Abimelech.

22After Abimelech had ruled over Israel for three years, 23God stirred up trouble* between Abimelech and the people of Shechem, and they revolted. 24In the events that followed, God punished Abimelech and the men of Shechem for murdering Gideon's seventy sons. 25The people of Shechem set an ambush for Abimelech on the hilltops and robbed everyone who passed that way. But someone warned Abimelech about their plot.

26At that time Gaal son of Ebed moved to Shechem with his brothers and gained the confidence of the people of Shechem. 27During the annual harvest festival at Shechem, held in the temple of the local god, the wine flowed freely, and everyone began cursing Abimelech. 28"Who is Abimelech?" Gaal shouted. "He's not a true descendant of Shechem!* Why should we be Abimelech's servants? He's merely the son of Gideon, and Zebul is his administrator. Serve the men of Hamor, who are Shechem's true descendants. Why should we serve Abimelech? 29If I were in charge, I would get rid of Abimelech. I would say* to him, 'Get some more soldiers, and come out and fight!'"

30But when Zebul, the leader of the city, heard what Gaal was saying, he was furious. 31He sent messengers to Abimelech in Arumah,* telling him, "Gaal son of Ebed and his brothers have come to live in Shechem, and now they are inciting the city to rebel against you. 32Come by night with an army and hide out in the fields. 33In the morning, as soon as it is daylight, storm the city. When Gaal and those who are with him come out against you, you can do with them as you wish."

34So Abimelech and his men went by night and split into four groups, stationing themselves around Shechem. 35Gaal was standing at the city gates when Abimelech and his army came out of hiding. 36When Gaal saw them, he said to Zebul, "Look, there are people coming down from the hilltops!"

Zebul replied, "It's just the shadows of the hills that look like men."

37But again Gaal said, "No, people are coming down from the hills.* And another group is coming down the road past the Diviners' Oak.*"

38Then Zebul turned on him triumphantly. "Now where is that big mouth of yours?" he demanded. "Wasn't it you that said, 'Who is Abimelech, and why should we be his servants?' The men you mocked are right outside the city! Go out and fight them!"

39Gaal then led the men of Shechem into battle against Abimelech, 40but he was defeated and ran away. Many of Shechem's warriors were killed, and the ground was covered with dead bodies all the way

**9:6** The meaning of the Hebrew is uncertain. **9:16** Hebrew *Jerubbaal* (see 6:32); also in 9:19, 28, 57. **9:23** Hebrew *sent a disturbing spirit.* **9:28** Hebrew *Who is Shechem?* **9:29** As in Greek version; Hebrew reads *And he said.* **9:31** Hebrew *Tormah;* see 9:41. **9:37a** Or *the center of the land.* **9:37b** Hebrew *Elon-meonenim.*

## NOTEWORTHY ● ● • • •

**10:1-5 In five verses we read about two men who judged Israel for a total of 45 years. Yet all we know about them besides the length of their rules is that one had 30 sons who rode around on 30 donkeys. What are you doing for God that is worth noting? When your life is over, will people remember more than just what was in your bank account or the number of years you lived?**

to the city gate. [41]Abimelech stayed in Arumah, and Zebul drove Gaal and his brothers out of Shechem.

[42]The next day the people of Shechem went out into the fields to battle. When Abimelech heard about it, [43]he divided his men into three groups and set an ambush in the fields. When Abimelech saw the people coming out of the city, he and his men jumped up from their hiding places and attacked them. [44]Abimelech and his group stormed the city gate to keep the men of Shechem from getting back in, while Abimelech's other two groups cut them down in the fields. [45]The battle went on all day before Abimelech finally captured the city. He killed the people, leveled the city, and scattered salt all over the ground.

[46]When the people who lived in the tower of Shechem heard what had happened, they took refuge within the walls of the temple of Baal-berith.* [47]Someone reported to Abimelech that the people were gathered together in the temple, [48]so he led his forces to Mount Zalmon. He took an ax and chopped some branches from a tree, and he put them on his shoulder. "Quick, do as I have done!" he told his men. [49]So each of them cut down some branches, following Abimelech's example. They piled the branches against the walls of the temple and set them on fire. So all the people who had lived in the tower of Shechem died, about a thousand men and women.

[50]Then Abimelech attacked the city of Thebez and captured it. [51]But there was a strong tower inside the city, and the entire population fled to it. They barricaded themselves in and climbed up to the roof of the tower. [52]Abimelech followed them to attack the tower. But as he prepared to set fire to the entrance, [53]a woman on the roof threw down a millstone that landed on Abimelech's head and crushed his skull. [54]He said to his young armor bearer, "Draw your sword and kill me! Don't let it be said that a woman killed Abimelech!" So the young man stabbed him with his sword, and he died. [55]When Abimelech's men saw that he was dead, they disbanded and returned to their homes.

[56]Thus, God punished Abimelech for the evil he had done against his father by murdering his seventy brothers. [57]God also punished the men of Shechem for all their evil. So the curse of Jotham son of Gideon came true.

CHAPTER **10** **TOLA AND JAIR.** After Abimelech's death, Tola, the son of Puah and descendant of Dodo, came to rescue Israel. He was from the tribe of Issachar but lived in the town of Shamir in the hill country of Ephraim. [2]He was Israel's judge for twenty-three years. When he died, he was buried in Shamir.

[3]After Tola died, a man from Gilead named Jair judged Israel for twenty-two years. [4]His thirty sons rode around on thirty donkeys, and they owned thirty towns in the land of Gilead, which are still called the Towns of Jair.* [5]When Jair died, he was buried in Kamon.

[6]Again the Israelites did evil in the LORD's sight. They worshiped images of Baal and Ashtoreth, and the gods of Aram, Sidon, Moab, Ammon, and Philistia. Not only this, but they abandoned the LORD and no longer served him at all. [7]So the LORD burned with anger against Israel, and he handed them over to the Philistines and the Ammonites, [8]who began to oppress them that year. For eighteen years they oppressed all the Israelites east of the Jordan River in the land of the Amorites (that is, in Gilead). [9]The Ammonites also crossed to the west side of the Jordan and attacked Judah, Benjamin, and Ephraim. The Israelites were in great distress. [10]Finally, they cried out to the LORD, saying, "We have sinned against you because we have abandoned you as our God and have served the images of Baal."

## PUNISHMENT ● ● • • •

**10:7-10 God permitted the heathen nations to oppress the Israelites because of their sin (2:1-3). Because God is just, he will punish sin (Leviticus 26). God allows problems and pressures to enter our life in order to lovingly draw us back into relationship with him. When problems arise, before you ask, "Why me?" ask, "Is God trying to say something to me through this?"**

[11]The LORD replied, "Did I not rescue you from the Egyptians, the Amorites, the Ammonites, the Philistines, [12]the Sidonians, the Amalekites, and the Maonites? When they oppressed you, you cried out to me, and I rescued you. [13]Yet you have abandoned me and served other gods. So I will not rescue you anymore. [14]Go and cry out to the gods you have chosen! Let them rescue you in your hour of distress!"

[15]But the Israelites pleaded with the LORD and said, "We have sinned. Punish us as you see fit, only rescue us today from our enemies." [16]Then the Israelites put aside their foreign gods and served the LORD. And he was grieved by their misery.

[17]At that time the armies of Ammon had gathered for war and were camped in Gilead, preparing to attack Israel's army at Mizpah. [18]The leaders of Gilead said to each other, "Whoever attacks the Ammonites first will become ruler over all the people of Gilead."

CHAPTER **11** **JEPHTHAH'S FOOLISH VOW.** Now Jephthah of Gilead was a great warrior. He was the son of Gilead, but his mother was a prostitute. [2]Gilead's wife

**9:46** Hebrew *El-berith,* another name for Baal-berith; compare 9:4. **10:4** Hebrew *Havvoth-jair.*

| Person | Known as | Task | Reference |
|---|---|---|---|
| JACOB | A liar | To "father" the Israelite nation | Genesis 27 |
| JOSEPH | A slave | To save his family | Genesis 39–47 |
| MOSES | A shepherd in exile (and a murderer) | To lead Israel out of bondage into the Promised Land | Exodus 3 |
| GIDEON | A farmer | To deliver Israel from Midian | Judges 6:11 |
| JEPHTHAH | The son of a prostitute | To deliver Israel from the Ammonites | Judges 11:1 |
| HANNAH | A housewife | To be the mother of Samuel | 1 Samuel 1 |
| DAVID | A shepherd boy and youngest of the family | To be Israel's greatest king | 1 Samuel 16 |
| EZRA | A scribe | To lead the return to Judah and to write some of the Bible | Ezra, Nehemiah |
| ESTHER | An orphan | To save her people from massacre | Esther |
| MARY | A peasant girl | To be the mother of Christ | Luke 1:27–38 |
| MATTHEW | A tax collector | To be an apostle and Gospel writer | Matthew 9:9 |
| LUKE | A Greek physician | To be a companion of Paul and a Gospel writer | Colossians 4:14 |
| PETER | A fisherman | To be an apostle, a leader of the early church, and a writer of two New Testament letters | Matthew 4:18–20 |

**GOD USES COMMON PEOPLE**
God uses all sorts of people to do his work—people like you and me!

also had several sons, and when these half brothers
grew up, they chased Jephthah off the land. "You
will not get any of our father's inheritance," they said,
"for you are the son of a prostitute." 3So Jephthah
fled from his brothers and lived in the land of Tob.
Soon he had a large band of rebels following him.
4At about this time, the Ammonites began their
war against Israel. 5When the Ammonites attacked,
the leaders of Gilead sent for Jephthah in the land of
Tob. They said, 6"Come and be our commander!
Help us fight the Ammonites!"
7But Jephthah said to them, "Aren't you the ones
who hated me and drove me from my father's
house? Why do you come to me now when you're in
trouble?"
8"Because we need you," they replied. "If you will
lead us in battle against the Ammonites, we will
make you ruler over all the people of Gilead."
9Jephthah said, "If I come with you and if the
LORD gives me victory over the Ammonites, will you
really make me ruler over all the people?"
10"The LORD is our witness," the leaders replied.
"We promise to do whatever you say."
11So Jephthah went with the leaders of Gilead,
and he became their ruler and commander of
the army. At Mizpah, in the presence of the
LORD, Jephthah repeated what he had said to the
leaders.
12Then Jephthah sent messengers to the king of
Ammon, demanding to know why Israel was being
attacked. 13The king of Ammon answered Jephthah's messengers, "When the Israelites came out
of Egypt, they stole my land from the Arnon River
to the Jabbok River and all the way to the Jordan.
Now then, give back the land peaceably."
14Jephthah sent this message back to the Ammonite king:

**REJECTION ● ● ● • •**

**11:1-2 Jephthah, an illegitimate son of Gilead, was chased out of the country by his half brothers. He suffered as a result of another person's decision and not for any wrong he had done. Yet in spite of his brothers' rejection, God used him. If you are suffering from unfair rejection, don't blame others and become discouraged. Remember how God used Jephthah despite his unjust circumstances, and realize that God is able to use you even if you feel rejected by people.**

15"This is what Jephthah says: Israel did not steal any land from Moab or Ammon. 16When the people of Israel arrived at Kadesh on their journey from Egypt after crossing the Red Sea,* 17they sent messengers to the king of Edom asking for permission to pass through his land. But their request was denied. Then they asked the king of Moab for similar permission, but he wouldn't let them pass through either. So the people of Israel stayed in Kadesh.

18"Finally, they went around Edom and Moab through the wilderness. They traveled along Moab's eastern border and camped on the other side of the Arnon River. But they never once crossed the Arnon River into Moab.

19"Then Israel sent messengers to King Sihon of the Amorites, who ruled from Heshbon, asking for permission to cross through his land to get to their destination. 20But King Sihon didn't trust Israel to pass through his land. Instead, he mobilized his army at Jahaz and attacked them. 21But the LORD, the God of Israel, gave his people victory over King Sihon. So Israel took control of all the land of the Amorites, who lived in that region, 22from the Arnon River to the Jabbok River, and from the wilderness to the Jordan.

23"So you see, it was the LORD, the God of Israel, who took away the land from the Amorites and gave it to Israel. Why, then, should we give it to you? 24You keep whatever your god Chemosh gives you, and we will keep whatever the LORD our God gives us. 25Are you any better than Balak son of Zippor, king of Moab? Did he try to make a case against Israel for disputed land? Did he go to war? No, of course not. 26But now after three hundred years you make an issue of this! Israel has been living here all this time, spread across the land from Heshbon to Aroer and in all the towns along the Arnon River. Why have you made no effort to recover it before now? 27I have not sinned against you. Rather, you have wronged me by attacking me. Let the LORD, who is judge, decide today which of us is right—Israel or Ammon."

28But the king of Ammon paid no attention to Jephthah's message.

29At that time the Spirit of the LORD came upon Jephthah, and he went throughout the land of Gilead and Manasseh, including Mizpah in Gilead, and led an army against the Ammonites. 30And Jephthah made a vow to the LORD. He said, "If you give me victory over the Ammonites, 31I will give to the LORD the first thing coming out of my house to greet me when I return in triumph. I will sacrifice it as a burnt offering."

32So Jephthah led his army against the Ammonites, and the LORD gave him victory. 33He thoroughly defeated the Ammonites from Aroer to an area near Minnith—twenty towns—and as far away as Abel-keramim. Thus Israel subdued the Ammonites.

34When Jephthah returned home to Mizpah, his daughter—his only child—ran out to meet him, playing on a tambourine and dancing for joy. 35When he saw her, he tore his clothes in anguish. "My daughter!" he cried out. "My heart is breaking! What a tragedy that you came out to greet me. For I have made a vow to the LORD and cannot take it back."

36And she said, "Father, you have made a promise to the LORD. You must do to me what you have promised, for the LORD has given you a great victory over your enemies, the Ammonites. 37But first let me go up and roam in the hills and weep with my friends for two months, because I will die a virgin."

38"You may go," Jephthah said. And he let her go away for two months. She and her friends went into the hills and wept because she would never have children. 39When she returned home, her father kept his vow, and she died a virgin. So it has become a custom in Israel 40for young Israelite women to go away for four days each year to lament the fate of Jephthah's daughter.

## NO DEALS ● ● • • •

11:34-35 **Jephthah's rash vow brought him unspeakable grief. In the heat of emotion or personal turmoil it is easy to make foolish promises to God. These promises might sound very spiritual when we make them, but they often produce only guilt and frustration when we are forced to fulfill them. Making spiritual "deals" only brings disappointment. God does not want promises for the future, but obedience for today.**

CHAPTER **12** **JEPHTHAH ATTACKS EPHRAIM.** Then the tribe of Ephraim mobilized its army and crossed over to Zaphon. They sent this message to Jephthah: "Why didn't you call for us to help you fight against Ammon? We are going to burn down your house with you in it!"

2"I summoned you at the beginning of the dispute, but you refused to come!" Jephthah said. "You failed to help us in our struggle against Ammon. 3So I risked my life and went to battle without you, and the LORD gave me victory over the Ammonites. So why have you come to fight me?"

4The leaders of Ephraim responded, "The men of Gilead are nothing more than rejects from Ephraim and Manasseh." So Jephthah called out his army and attacked the men of Ephraim and defeated them.

5Jephthah captured the shallows of the Jordan, and whenever a fugitive from Ephraim tried to go back across, the men of Gilead would challenge him. "Are you a member of the tribe of Ephraim?" they would ask. If the man said, "No, I'm not," 6they would tell him to say "Shibboleth." If he was from Ephraim, he would say "Sibboleth," because people from Ephraim cannot pronounce the word correctly. Then they would take him and kill him at the shallows of the Jordan River. So forty-two thousand Ephraimites were killed at that time.

11:16 Hebrew *sea of reeds.*

[7]Jephthah was Israel's judge for six years. When he died, he was buried in one of the towns of Gilead.

[8]After Jephthah, Ibzan became Israel's judge. He lived in Bethlehem, [9]and he had thirty sons and thirty daughters. He married his daughters to men outside his clan and brought in thirty young women from outside his clan to marry his sons. Ibzan judged Israel for seven years. [10]When he died, he was buried at Bethlehem.

[11]After him, Elon from Zebulun became Israel's judge. He judged Israel for ten years. [12]When he died, he was buried at Aijalon in Zebulun.

[13]After Elon died, Abdon son of Hillel, from Pirathon, became Israel's judge. [14]He had forty sons and thirty grandsons, who rode on seventy donkeys. He was Israel's judge for eight years. [15]Then he died and was buried at Pirathon in Ephraim, in the hill country of the Amalekites.

CHAPTER **13** **THE BIRTH OF SAMSON.** Again the Israelites did what was evil in the LORD's sight, so the LORD handed them over to the Philistines, who kept them in subjection for forty years.

[2]In those days, a man named Manoah from the tribe of Dan lived in the town of Zorah. His wife was unable to become pregnant, and they had no children. [3]The angel of the LORD appeared to Manoah's wife and said, "Even though you have been unable to have children, you will soon become pregnant and give birth to a son. [4]You must not drink wine or any other alcoholic drink or eat any forbidden food. [5]You will become pregnant and give birth to a son, and his hair must never be cut. For he will be dedicated to God as a Nazirite from birth. He will rescue Israel from the Philistines."

[6]The woman ran and told her husband, "A man of God appeared to me! He was like one of God's angels, terrifying to look at. I didn't ask where he was from, and he didn't tell me his name. [7]But he told me, 'You will become pregnant and give birth to a son. You must not drink wine or any other alcoholic drink or eat any forbidden food. For your son will be dedicated to God as a Nazirite from the moment of his birth until the day of his death.'"

[8]Then Manoah prayed to the LORD. He said, "Lord, please let the man of God come back to us again and give us more instructions about this son who is to be born."

[9]God answered his prayer, and the angel of God appeared once again to his wife as she was sitting in the field. But her husband, Manoah, was not with

## A JOB TO DO ● ● • • •

13:5 **Manoah's wife was told that her son would rescue the Israelites from Philistine oppression, but it wasn't until David's day that the Philistine opposition was completely crushed (2 Samuel 8:1). Samson's part in subduing the Philistines was just the beginning, but it was important nonetheless. It was the task God had given Samson to do. Be faithful in following God even if you don't see instant results, because you might be beginning an important job that others will finish.**

## SAMSON

If it hasn't already happened, sooner or later someone is going to talk to you about your potential. "Potential" is what you could become compared to what you are right now. Samson had incredible potential! He had the potential to be a great servant of God. God planned to use him to lead the Israelites. To help him, God gave Samson enormous physical strength. (The special strength God has given you may not be physical, but he has built into you the potential to be a great servant of his.) Unfortunately, Samson became an example of what happens when we don't live up to God's plan for our life.

Samson's life included many opportunities to help his people. He wasted most of his chances. Yet, in spite of all his mistakes, God still used him. The last thing Samson did before he died was an act that started the work God had planned for him all along. Even if it is the last thing you do, you can start being obedient to God.

The New Testament does not mention Samson's failures or his great feats of strength. In Hebrews 11:32-33, he is simply called one who "by faith . . . received what God had promised." In the end, Samson recognized his dependence on God, and God turned his failures and defeats into victory. Samson's story teaches us that it is never too late to start over. However badly we may have failed in the past, today is not too late for us to put our complete trust in God.

**UPS:**
- Dedicated to God from birth as a Nazirite
- Known for his feats of strength
- Listed in the Hall of Faith in Hebrews
- Began to free Israel from Philistine oppression

**DOWNS:**
- Violated his vow and God's laws on many occasions
- Was controlled by sensuality
- Confided in the wrong people
- Used his gifts and abilities unwisely

**STATS:**
- Where: Zorah, Timnah, Ashkelon, Gaza, Valley of Sorek
- Occupation: Judge
- Relatives: Father: Manoah
- Contemporaries: Delilah, Samuel (who might have been born while Samson was a judge)

LESSONS: Great strength in one area of life does not make up for weaknesses in other areas

God's presence does not overwhelm a person's will

God can use people of faith in spite of their mistakes

KEY VERSE: "You will become pregnant and give birth to a son, and his hair must never be cut. For he will be dedicated to God as a Nazirite from birth. He will rescue Israel from the Philistines" (Judges 13:5).

His story is told in Judges 13–16. He is also mentioned in Hebrews 11:32.

her. 10So she quickly ran and told her husband, "The man who appeared to me the other day is here again!"

11Manoah ran back with his wife and asked, "Are you the man who talked to my wife the other day?"

"Yes," he replied, "I am."

12So Manoah asked him, "When your words come true, what kind of rules should govern the boy's life and work?"

13The angel of the LORD replied, "Be sure your wife follows the instructions I gave her. 14She must not eat grapes or raisins, drink wine or any other alcoholic drink, or eat any forbidden food."

15Then Manoah said to the angel of the LORD, "Please stay here until we can prepare a young goat for you to eat."

16"I will stay," the angel of the LORD replied, "but I will not eat anything. However, you may prepare a burnt offering as a sacrifice to the LORD." (Manoah didn't realize it was the angel of the LORD.)

17Then Manoah asked the angel of the LORD, "What is your name? For when all this comes true, we want to honor you."

18"Why do you ask my name?" the angel of the LORD replied. "You wouldn't understand if I told you."

19Then Manoah took a young goat and a grain offering and offered it on a rock as a sacrifice to the LORD. And as Manoah and his wife watched, the LORD did an amazing thing. 20As the flames from the altar shot up toward the sky, the angel of the LORD ascended in the fire. When Manoah and his wife saw this, they fell with their faces to the ground.

21The angel did not appear again to Manoah and his wife. Manoah finally realized it was the angel of the LORD, 22and he said to his wife, "We will die, for we have seen God!"

23But his wife said, "If the LORD were going to kill us, he wouldn't have accepted our burnt offering and grain offering. He wouldn't have appeared to us and told us this wonderful thing and done these miracles."

24When her son was born, they named him Samson. And the LORD blessed him as he grew up. 25And in Mahaneh-dan, which is located between the towns of Zorah and Eshtaol, the Spirit of the LORD began to take hold of him.

CHAPTER **14** **SAMSON GETS MARRIED.** One day when Samson was in Timnah, he noticed a certain Philistine woman. 2When he returned home, he told his father and mother, "I want to marry a young Philistine woman I saw in Timnah."

3His father and mother objected strenuously, "Isn't there one woman in our tribe or among all the Israelites you could marry? Why must you go to the pagan Philistines to find a wife?"

But Samson told his father, "Get her for me. She is the one I want." 4His father and mother didn't realize the LORD was at work in this, creating an opportunity to disrupt the Philistines, who ruled over Israel at that time.

5As Samson and his parents were going down to Timnah, a young lion attacked Samson near the vineyards of Timnah. 6At that moment the Spirit of the LORD powerfully took control of him, and he ripped the lion's jaws apart with his bare hands. He did it as easily as if it were a young goat. But he didn't tell his father or mother about it. 7When Samson arrived in Timnah, he talked with the woman and was very pleased with her.

8Later, when he returned to Timnah for the wedding, he turned off the path to look at the carcass of the lion. And he found that a swarm of bees had made some honey in the carcass. 9He scooped some of the honey into his hands and ate it along the way. He also gave some to his father and mother, and they ate it. But he didn't tell them he had taken the honey from the carcass of the lion.

10As his father was making final arrangements for the marriage, Samson threw a party at Timnah, as was the custom of the day. 11Thirty young men from the town were invited to be his companions. 12Samson said to them, "Let me tell you a riddle. If you solve my riddle during these seven days of the celebration, I will give you thirty plain linen robes and thirty fancy robes. 13But if you can't solve it, then you must give me thirty linen robes and thirty fancy robes."

"All right," they agreed, "let's hear your riddle."

14So he said:

"From the one who eats came something to eat;
out of the strong came something sweet."

Three days later they were still trying to figure it out. 15On the fourth* day they said to Samson's wife, "Get the answer to the riddle from your husband, or we will burn down your father's house with you in it. Did you invite us to this party just to make us poor?"

16So Samson's wife came to him in tears and said, "You don't love me; you hate me! You have given my people a riddle, but you haven't told me the answer."

"I haven't even given the answer to my father or mother," he replied. "Why should I tell you?" 17So she cried whenever she was with him and kept it up for the rest of the celebration. At last, on the seventh day, he told her the answer because of her persistent nagging. Then she gave the answer to the young men.

18So before sunset of the seventh day, the men of the town came to Samson with their answer:

"What is sweeter than honey?
What is stronger than a lion?"

Samson replied, "If you hadn't plowed with my heifer, you wouldn't have found the answer to my riddle!" 19Then the Spirit of the LORD powerfully took control of him. He went down to the town of

14:15 As in Greek version; Hebrew reads *seventh*.

Ashkelon, killed thirty men, took their belongings, and gave their clothing to the men who had answered his riddle. But Samson was furious about what had happened, and he went back home to live with his father and mother. [20]So his wife was given in marriage to the man who had been Samson's best man at the wedding.

CHAPTER **15** **SAMSON KILLS MANY ENEMIES.** Later on, during the wheat harvest, Samson took a young goat as a present to his wife. He intended to sleep with her, but her father wouldn't let him in. [2]"I really thought you hated her," her father explained, "so I gave her in marriage to your best man. But look, her sister is more beautiful than she is. Marry her instead."

[3]Samson said, "This time I cannot be blamed for everything I am going to do to you Philistines." [4]Then he went out and caught three hundred foxes. He tied their tails together in pairs, and he fastened a torch to each pair of tails. [5]Then he lit the torches and let the foxes run through the fields of the Philistines. He burned all their grain to the ground, including the grain still in piles and all that had been bundled. He also destroyed their grapevines and olive trees.

[6]"Who did this?" the Philistines demanded.

"Samson," was the reply, "because his father-in-law from Timnah gave Samson's wife to be married to his best man." So the Philistines went and got the woman and her father and burned them to death.

[7]"Because you did this," Samson vowed, "I will take my revenge on you, and I won't stop until I'm satisfied!" [8]So he attacked the Philistines with great fury and killed many of them. Then he went to live in a cave in the rock of Etam.

[9]The Philistines retaliated by setting up camp in Judah and raiding the town of Lehi. [10]The men of Judah asked the Philistines, "Why have you attacked us?"

The Philistines replied, "We've come to capture Samson. We have come to pay him back for what he did to us."

[11]So three thousand men of Judah went down to get Samson at the cave in the rock of Etam. They said to Samson, "Don't you realize the Philistines rule over us? What are you doing to us?"

But Samson replied, "I only paid them back for what they did to me."

[12]But the men of Judah told him, "We have come to tie you up and hand you over to the Philistines."

"All right," Samson said. "But promise that you won't kill me yourselves."

[13]"We will tie you up and hand you over to the Philistines," they replied. "We won't kill you." So they tied him up with two new ropes and led him away from the rock.

[14]As Samson arrived at Lehi, the Philistines came shouting in triumph. But the Spirit of the LORD powerfully took control of Samson, and he snapped the ropes on his arms as if they were burnt strands of flax, and they fell from his wrists. [15]Then he picked up a donkey's jawbone that was lying on the ground and killed a thousand Philistines with it. [16]And Samson said,

"With the jawbone of a donkey,
I've made heaps on heaps!
With the jawbone of a donkey,
I've killed a thousand men!"

[17]When he finished speaking, he threw away the jawbone; and the place was named Jawbone Hill.*

[18]Now Samson was very thirsty, and he cried out to the LORD, "You have accomplished this great victory by the strength of your servant. Must I now die of thirst and fall into the hands of these pagan people?" [19]So God caused water to gush out of a hollow in the ground at Lehi, and Samson was revived as he drank. Then he named that place "The Spring of the One Who Cried Out,"* and it is still in Lehi to this day.

[20]Samson was Israel's judge for twenty years, while the Philistines ruled the land.

CHAPTER **16** **SAMSON'S FOOLISH CHOICES.** One day Samson went to the Philistine city of Gaza and spent the night with a prostitute. [2]Word soon spread that Samson was there, so the men of Gaza gathered together and waited all night at the city gates. They kept quiet during the night, saying to themselves, "When the light of morning comes, we will kill him."

[3]But Samson stayed in bed only until midnight. Then he got up, took hold of the city gates with its two posts, and lifted them, bar and all, right out of the ground. He put them on his shoulders and carried them all the way to the top of the hill across from Hebron.

[4]Later Samson fell in love with a woman named

15:17 Hebrew *Ramath-lehi.* 15:19 Hebrew *En-hakkore.*

## BOOMERANG ● ● • • •

15:1-20 **Samson's reply in 15:11 tells the story of this chapter: "I only paid them back for what they did to me." Revenge is an uncontrollable monster. Each act of retaliation brings another. It is a boomerang that cannot be thrown without cost to the thrower. The revenge cycle can be halted only by forgiveness.**

## EXHAUSTION ● ● • • •

15:18 **Samson was physically and emotionally exhausted. After a great personal victory, his attitude declined quickly into self-pity—"Must I now die of thirst?" Emotionally, we are most vulnerable after a great effort or when faced with real physical needs. Depression often follows great achievements, so don't be surprised if you feel drained after a personal victory.**

**During these times of vulnerability, avoid the temptation to think that God owes you for your efforts. It was *his* strength that gave you victory. Concentrate on keeping your attitudes, actions, and words focused on God instead of yourself.**

Delilah, who lived in the valley of Sorek. [5]The leaders of the Philistines went to her and said, "Find out from Samson what makes him so strong and how he can be overpowered and tied up securely. Then each of us will give you eleven hundred pieces* of silver."

[6]So Delilah said to Samson, "Please tell me what makes you so strong and what it would take to tie you up securely."

[7]Samson replied, "If I am tied up with seven new bowstrings that have not yet been dried, I will be as weak as anyone else."

## ENSUALITY

It seems that Carrie and her boyfriend Dale have everything going for them:

- They are believers in Christ.
- They come from solid Christian homes.
- Friends constantly tease them by saying, "You guys are so good together. . . . You're just like an old married couple!"
- They are seniors at one of the best Christian schools in the country.
- They both have been accepted to a prestigious Christian college in the Midwest.
- They plan to marry in three years.
- They want to go to South America as missionaries.

Amazing, isn't it? The relationship seems perfect. Proud parents, teachers, and church leaders agree that Carrie and Dale each have been specially gifted by God, and so they predict great things. Says Coach Acker, "Those two will be mightily used by the Lord."

Well, if the scenario seems almost too good to be true, it is. In just about two weeks, this perfect couple will see their dream world collapse right before their eyes.

See, Carrie and Dale have let their physical relationship get out of hand. And now Carrie is pregnant.

Read another sad story about a young man with tremendous spiritual potential who let sexual passion ruin his life—Judges 16.

[8]So the Philistine leaders brought Delilah seven new bowstrings, and she tied Samson up with them. [9]She had hidden some men in one of the rooms of her house, and she cried out, "Samson! The Philistines have come to capture you!" But Samson snapped the bowstrings as if they were string that had been burned in a fire. So the secret of his strength was not discovered.

[10]Afterward Delilah said to him, "You made fun of me and told me a lie! Now please tell me how you can be tied up securely."

[11]Samson replied, "If I am tied up with brand-new ropes that have never been used, I will be as weak as anyone else."

[12]So Delilah took new ropes and tied him up with them. The men were hiding in the room as before, and again Delilah cried out, "Samson! The Philistines have come to capture you!" But Samson snapped the ropes from his arms as if they were thread.

[13]Then Delilah said, "You have been making fun of me and telling me lies! Won't you please tell me how you can be tied up securely?"

Samson replied, "If you weave the seven braids of my hair into the fabric on your loom and tighten it with the loom shuttle,* I will be as weak as anyone else."

So while he slept, Delilah wove the seven braids of his hair into the fabric [14]and tightened it with the loom shuttle. Again she cried out, "Samson! The Philistines have come to capture you!" But Samson woke up, pulled back the loom shuttle, and yanked his hair away from the loom and the fabric.

[15]Then Delilah pouted, "How can you say you love me when you don't confide in me? You've made fun of me three times now, and you still haven't told me what makes you so strong!" [16]So day after day she nagged him until he couldn't stand it any longer.

[17]Finally, Samson told her his secret. "My hair has never been cut," he confessed, "for I was dedicated to God as a Nazirite from birth. If my head were shaved, my strength would leave me, and I would become as weak as anyone else."

[18]Delilah realized he had finally told her the truth, so she sent for the Philistine leaders. "Come back one more time," she said, "for he has told me everything." So the Philistine leaders returned and brought the money with them. [19]Delilah lulled Samson to sleep with his head in her lap, and she called in a man to shave off his hair, making his capture certain. And his strength left him. [20]Then she cried out, "Samson! The Philistines have come to capture you!"

When he woke up, he thought, "I will do as before and shake myself free." But he didn't realize the LORD had left him.

[21]So the Philistines captured him and gouged out his eyes. They took him to Gaza, where he was bound with bronze chains and made to grind grain in the prison. [22]But before long his hair began to grow back.

## LOVE FOOL ● ● • • •

16:15 **Samson was deceived because he wanted to believe Delilah's lies. How can you keep your desire for love from deceiving you? (1) Decide what type of person you will love before passion takes over. (2) Make sure that you find your companion's personality, temperament, and commitment to solve problems as gratifying as his or her kisses. (3) Be patient. The second look often reveals what is beneath the pleasant appearance and attentive touch.**

## NAGGING ● ● • • •

16:16-17 **Delilah kept asking Samson for the secret of his strength until he finally grew tired of hearing her nagging and gave in. What a pitiful excuse for disobedience. Don't allow anyone, no matter how attractive or persuasive, to talk you into doing wrong.**

16:5 Hebrew *1,100 shekels,* about 28 pounds or 12.5 kilograms in weight. 16:13 As in Greek version; Hebrew lacks *on your loom and tighten it with the loom shuttle.*

[23]The Philistine leaders held a great festival, offering sacrifices and praising their god, Dagon. They
said, "Our god has given us victory over our enemy
Samson!"
[24]When the people saw him, they praised their
god, saying, "Our god has delivered our enemy to
us! The one who killed so many of us is now in our
power!"
[25]Half drunk by now, the people demanded,
"Bring out Samson so he can perform for us!" So he
was brought from the prison and made to stand at
the center of the temple, between the two pillars
supporting the roof.
[26]Samson said to the servant who was leading him
by the hand, "Place my hands against the two pillars.
I want to rest against them." [27]The temple was completely filled with people. All the Philistine leaders
were there, and there were about three thousand on
the roof who were watching Samson and making fun
of him.
[28]Then Samson prayed to the LORD, "Sovereign
LORD, remember me again. O God, please
strengthen me one more time so that I may pay back
the Philistines for the loss of my eyes." [29]Then Samson put his hands on the center pillars of the temple
and pushed against them with all his might. [30]"Let
me die with the Philistines," he prayed. And the
temple crashed down on the Philistine leaders and
all the people. So he killed more people when he
died than he had during his entire lifetime.
[31]Later his brothers and other relatives went down to
get his body. They took him back home and buried
him between Zorah and Eshtaol, where his father, Manoah, was buried. Samson had been Israel's judge for twenty years.

CHAPTER **17** **MICAH'S IDOLS.** A man named Micah
lived in the hill country of
Ephraim. [2]One day he said
to his mother, "I heard you
curse the thief who stole
eleven hundred pieces* of
silver from you. Well, here
they are. I was the one who
took them."
"The LORD bless you for
admitting it," his mother
replied. [3]He returned the
money to her, and she said,
"I now dedicate these silver
coins to the LORD. In honor
of my son, I will have an
image carved and an idol
cast." [4]So his mother took
two hundred of the silver
coins to a silversmith, who
made them into an image and an idol. And these
were placed in Micah's house.
[5]Micah set up a shrine, and he made a sacred
ephod and some household idols. Then he installed
one of his sons as the priest. [6]In those days Israel had
no king, so the people did whatever seemed right in
their own eyes.
[7]One day a young Levite from Bethlehem in Judah
[8]arrived in that area of Ephraim, looking for a good
place to live. He happened to stop at Micah's house
as he was traveling through. [9]"Where are you from?"
Micah asked him.
And he replied, "I am a Levite from Bethlehem in
Judah, and I am looking for a place to live."
[10]"Stay here with me," Micah said, "and you can be
a father and priest to me. I will give you ten pieces* of

## SALVAGED ● ● ● • •

**16:28-30 In spite of Samson's past, God still answered his prayer and destroyed the heathen temple and worshipers. God still loved Samson. He was willing to hear Samson's prayer of confession and repentance and use him this final time.**

**One of the effects of sin in our life is that it keeps us from feeling like praying. But perfect moral behavior is not a condition for prayer. Don't let guilt feelings over sin keep you apart from God. No matter how long you have been away from God, he is ready to hear from you and restore you to a right relationship. Every situation can be salvaged if you are willing to turn again to him. If God could still work in Samson's situation, he can certainly make something worthwhile out of yours.**

## DELILAH

There are two very different ways to get a reputation. One way is to help others do great things. Another is to keep others from doing great things. Delilah was only one person in Samson's life, but she almost completely ruined him. She persuaded him to go against what God wanted him to do. Because of what she thought she could get, Delilah used her persistence to wear Samson down. Others couldn't defeat his strength, but Delilah deceived him by pretending to love him, and he finally told her the secret of his strength. He found out too late that he couldn't trust her.

Delilah is never mentioned again in the Bible. But she is frequently remembered as an example of someone who betrayed a friend. That one relationship earned her a permanent reputation of the worst kind.

Are people helped by knowing you? Do they find that your friendship makes them want to be the best they can be? Even more important, does knowing you help their relationship with God?

**UPS:**
- Persistent when faced with obstacles

**DOWNS:**
- Valued money more than relationships
- Betrayed the man who trusted her

**STATS:**
- Where: Valley of Sorek
- Contemporary: Samson

LESSON: We need to be people who can be trusted

KEY VERSES: "So day after day she nagged him until he couldn't stand it any longer. Finally, Samson told her his secret" (Judges 16:16-17).

Her story is told in Judges 16.

17:2 Hebrew *1,100 shekels,* about 28 pounds or 12.5 kilograms in weight. 17:10 Hebrew *10 shekels,* about 4 ounces or 114 grams in weight.

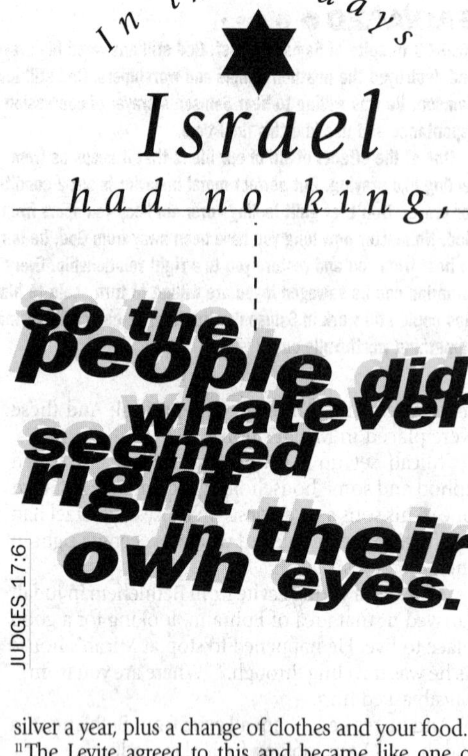


silver a year, plus a change of clothes and your food." 11The Levite agreed to this and became like one of Micah's sons. 12So Micah ordained the Levite as his personal priest, and he lived in Micah's house. 13"I know the LORD will bless me now," Micah said, "because I have a Levite serving as my priest."

## CHAPTER 18 THE DANITES STEAL MICAH'S IDOLS.

Now in those days Israel had no king. And the tribe of Dan was trying to find a place to settle, for they had not yet driven out the people who lived in the land assigned to them. 2So the men of Dan chose five warriors from among their clans, who lived in the towns of Zorah and Eshtaol, to scout out a land for them to settle in.

When these warriors arrived in the hill country of Ephraim, they came to Micah's home and spent the night there. 3Noticing the young Levite's accent, they took him aside and asked him, "Who brought you here, and what are you doing? Why are you here?" 4He told them about his agreement with Micah and that he was Micah's personal priest.

5Then they said, "Ask God whether or not our journey will be successful."

6"Go in peace," the priest replied. "For the LORD will go ahead of you on your journey."

7So the five men went on to the town of Laish, where they noticed the people living carefree lives, like the Sidonians; they were peaceful and secure. The people were also wealthy because their land was very fertile. And they lived a great distance from Sidon and had no allies nearby.

8When the men returned to Zorah and Eshtaol, their relatives asked them, "What did you find?"

9The men replied, "Let's attack! We have seen the land, and it is very good. You should not hesitate to go and take possession of it. 10When you get there, you will find the people living carefree lives. God has given us a spacious and fertile land, lacking in nothing!"

11So six hundred warriors from the tribe of Dan set out from Zorah and Eshtaol. 12They camped at a place west of Kiriath-jearim in Judah, which is called Mahaneh-dan* to this day. 13Then they went up into the hill country of Ephraim and came to the house of Micah.

14The five men who had scouted out the land around Laish said to the others, "There is a shrine here with a sacred ephod, some household idols, a carved image, and a cast idol. It's obvious what we ought to do." 15So the five men went over to Micah's house, where the young Levite lived, and greeted him kindly. 16As the six hundred warriors from the tribe of Dan stood just outside the gate, 17the five spies entered the shrine and took the carved image, the sacred ephod, the household idols, and the cast idol.

18When the priest saw the men carrying all the sacred objects out of Micah's shrine, he said, "What are you doing?"

19"Be quiet and come with us," they said. "Be a father and priest to all of us. Isn't it better to be a priest for an entire tribe of Israel than just for the household of one man?" 20The young priest was quite happy to go with them, so he took along the sacred ephod, the household idols, and the carved image. 21They started on their way again, placing their children, livestock, and possessions in front of them.

### MOTIVES • • • • •

18:1-6 **Through this entire incident, no one desired to worship God; instead they wanted to use God for selfish gain. Today some people go to church to feel better, be accepted, relieve guilt, and gain friends. Beware of following God for selfish gains rather than selfless service.**

22When the people from the tribe of Dan were quite a distance from Micah's home, Micah and some of his neighbors came chasing after them. 23They were shouting as they caught up with them. The men of Dan turned around and said, "What do you want? Why have you called these men together and chased after us like this?"

24"What do you mean, What do I want?" Micah replied. "You've taken away all my gods and my priest, and I have nothing left!"

25The men of Dan said, "Watch what you say! Some of us are short-tempered, and they might get angry and kill you and your family." 26So the men of Dan went on their way. When Micah saw that there were too many of them for him to attack, he turned around and went home.

18:12 *Mahaneh-dan* means "the camp of Dan."

[27]Then, with Micah's idols and his priest, the men of Dan came to the town of Laish, whose people were peaceful and secure. They attacked and killed all the people and burned the town to the ground. [28]There was no one to rescue the residents of the town, for they lived a great distance from Sidon and had no allies nearby. This happened in the valley near Beth-rehob.

Then the people of the tribe of Dan rebuilt the town and lived there. [29]They renamed the town Dan after their ancestor, Israel's son, but it had originally been called Laish.

[30]Then they set up the carved image, and they appointed Jonathan son of Gershom, a descendant of Moses,* as their priest. This family continued as priests for the tribe of Dan until the Exile. [31]So Micah's carved image was worshiped by the tribe of Dan as long as the Tabernacle of God remained at Shiloh.

## CHAPTER 19

**A HORRIBLE CRIME.** Now in those days Israel had no king. There was a man from the tribe of Levi living in a remote area of the hill country of Ephraim. One day he brought home a woman from Bethlehem in Judah to be his concubine. [2]But she was unfaithful to him and returned to her father's home in Bethlehem. After about four months, [3]her husband took a servant and an extra donkey to Bethlehem to persuade her to come back. When he arrived at her father's house, she took him inside, and her father welcomed him. [4]Her father urged him to stay awhile, so he stayed three days, eating, drinking, and sleeping there.

[5]On the fourth day the man was up early, ready to leave, but the woman's father said, "Have something to eat before you go." [6]So the two of them sat down together and had something to eat and drink. Then the woman's father said, "Please stay the night and enjoy yourself." [7]The man got up to leave, but his father-in-law kept urging him to stay, so he finally gave in and stayed the night. [8]On the morning of the fifth day he was up early again, ready to leave, and again the woman's father said, "Have something to eat; then you can leave some time this afternoon." So they had another day of feasting.

[9]That afternoon, as he and his concubine and servant were preparing to leave, his father-in-law said, "Look, it's getting late. Stay the night and enjoy yourself. Tomorrow you can get up early and be on your way."

[10]But this time the man was determined to leave. So he took his two saddled donkeys and his concubine and headed in the direction of Jebus (that is, Jerusalem). [11]It was late in the day when they reached Jebus, and the man's servant said to him, "It's getting too late to travel; let's stay in this Jebusite city tonight."

[12]"No," his master said, "we can't stay in this foreign city where there are no Israelites. We will go on to Gibeah. [13]We will find a place to spend the night in either Gibeah or Ramah." [14]So they went on. The sun was setting as they came to Gibeah, a town in the land of Benjamin, [15]so they stopped there to spend the night. They rested in the town square, but no one took them in for the night.

[16]That evening an old man came home from his work in the fields. He was from the hill country of Ephraim, but he was living in Gibeah in the territory of Benjamin. [17]When he saw the travelers sitting in the town square, he asked them where they were from and where they were going.

[18]"We have been in Bethlehem in Judah," the man replied. "We are on our way home to a remote area in the hill country of Ephraim, and we're going to the Tabernacle of the LORD. But no one has taken us in for the night, [19]even though we have everything we need. We have straw and fodder for our donkeys and plenty of bread and wine for ourselves."

[20]"You are welcome to stay with me," the old man said. "I will give you anything you might need. But whatever you do, don't spend the night in the square." [21]So he took them home with him and fed their donkeys. After they washed their feet, they had supper together.

[22]While they were enjoying themselves, some of the wicked men in the town surrounded the house. They began beating at the door and shouting to the old man, "Bring out the man who is staying with you so we can have sex with him."

[23]The old man stepped outside to talk to them. "No, my brothers, don't do such an evil thing. For this man is my guest, and such a thing would be shameful. [24]Here, take my virgin daughter and this man's concubine. I will bring them out to you, and you can do whatever you like to them. But don't do such a shameful thing to this man."

[25]But they wouldn't listen to him. Then the Levite took his concubine and pushed her out the door. The men of the town abused her all night, taking turns raping her until morning. Finally, at dawn, they let her go. [26]At daybreak the woman returned to the house where her husband was staying. She collapsed at the door of the house and lay there until it was light.

### CONCUBINES ● ● • • •

**19:1-26 Having concubines was an accepted part of Israelite society, though this is not what God intended (Genesis 2:24). A concubine had the duties, but not the privileges, of being a wife. Her primary purposes were to give the man sexual pleasure, to bear additional children, and to contribute more help to the household or estate.**

**This man clearly did not love his concubine the way God wants a husband to love his wife: being willing to give his own life for her (Ephesians 5:25). This awful story illustrates the fact that unthinkable sin can result when we choose to fulfill our own desires rather than following God's design. God's plan is for one husband and one wife to be committed to each other with a sacrificial, life-long love.**

**18:30** As in an ancient Hebrew tradition, some Greek manuscripts, and Latin Vulgate; Masoretic Text reads *of Manasseh.*

27When her husband opened the door to leave, he found her there. She was lying face down, with her hands on the threshold. 28He said, "Get up! Let's go!" But there was no answer.* So he put her body on his donkey and took her home.

29When he got home, he took a knife and cut his concubine's body into twelve pieces. Then he sent one piece to each tribe of Israel. 30Everyone who saw it said, "Such a horrible crime has not been committed since Israel left Egypt. Shouldn't we speak up and do something about this?"

CHAPTER **20** **ISRAEL ATTACKS BENJAMIN.** Then all the Israelites, from Dan to Beersheba and from the land of Gilead, came together in one large assembly and stood in the presence of the LORD at Mizpah. 2The leaders of all the people and all the tribes of Israel—400,000 warriors armed with swords—took their positions in the assembly of the people of God. 3(Word soon reached the land of Benjamin that the other tribes had gone up to Mizpah.) The Israelites then asked how this terrible crime had happened.

## GOVERNMENT ● ● • • •

19:30 **The horrible crime described in this chapter wasn't Israel's worst offense. Even worse was the nation's failure to establish a government based upon God's moral principles, where the law of God was the law of the land. As a result, laws were usually unenforced and crime was ignored. Sexual perversion and lawlessness were a by-product of Israel's disobedience to God. The Israelites weren't willing to speak up until events had gone too far.**

**Whenever we get away from God and his Word, all sorts of evil can follow. Our drifting away from God may be slow and almost imperceptible, with the ultimate results affecting a future generation. We must continually call our nation back to God and tell people about Christ.**

4The Levite, the husband of the woman who had been murdered, said, "My concubine and I came to Gibeah, a town in the land of Benjamin, to spend the night. 5That night some of the leaders of Gibeah surrounded the house, planning to kill me, and they raped my concubine until she was dead. 6So I cut her body into twelve pieces and sent the pieces throughout the land of Israel, for these men have committed this terrible and shameful crime. 7Now then, the entire community of Israel must decide what should be done about this!"

8And all the people stood up together and replied, "Not one of us will return home. 9Instead, we will draw lots to decide who will attack Gibeah. 10One tenth of the men from each tribe will be chosen to supply the warriors with food, and the rest of us will take revenge on Gibeah* for this shameful thing they have done in Israel." 11So all the Israelites were united, and they gathered together to attack the town.

12The Israelites sent messengers to the tribe of Benjamin, saying, "What a terrible thing has been done among you! 13Give up these evil men from Gibeah so we can execute them and purge Israel of this evil."

But the people of Benjamin would not listen. 14Instead, they came from their towns and gathered at Gibeah to fight the Israelites. 15Twenty-six thousand of their warriors armed with swords arrived in Gibeah to join the seven hundred warriors who lived there. 16Seven hundred of Benjamin's warriors were left-handed, each of whom could sling a rock and hit a target within a hairsbreadth, without missing. 17Israel had 400,000 warriors armed with swords, not counting Benjamin's warriors.

18Before the battle the Israelites went to Bethel and asked God, "Which tribe should lead the attack against the people of Benjamin?"

The LORD answered, "Judah is to go first."

19So the Israelites left early the next morning and camped near Gibeah. 20Then they advanced toward Gibeah to attack the men of Benjamin. 21But Benjamin's warriors, who were defending the town, came out and killed twenty-two thousand Israelites in the field that day.

22But the Israelites took courage and assembled at the same place they had fought the previous day. 23(For they had gone up to Bethel and wept in the presence of the LORD until evening. Then they asked the LORD, "Should we fight against our relatives from Benjamin again?" And the LORD said, "Go out and fight against them.")

24So they went out to fight against the warriors of Benjamin, 25but the men of Benjamin killed another eighteen thousand Israelites, all of whom were experienced with a sword.

26Then all the Israelites went up to Bethel and wept in the presence of the LORD and fasted until evening. They also brought burnt offerings and peace offerings to the LORD. 27And the Israelites went up seeking direction from the LORD. (In those days the Ark of the Covenant of God was in Bethel, 28and Phinehas son of Eleazar and grandson of Aaron was the priest.) The Israelites asked the LORD, "Should we fight against our relatives from Benjamin again or should we stop?"

The LORD said, "Go! Tomorrow I will give you victory over them."

29So the Israelites set an ambush all around Gibeah. 30They went out on the third day and assembled at the same place as before. 31When the warriors of Benjamin came out to attack, they were drawn away from the town. And as they had done before, they began to kill the Israelites. About thirty Israelites died in the open fields and along the roads leading to Bethel and Gibeah.

32Then the warriors of Benjamin shouted, "We're defeating them as we did in the first battle!" But the Israelites had agreed in advance to run away so that the men of Benjamin would chase them along the roads and be drawn away from the town.

19:28 Greek version adds *for she was dead.* 20:10 Hebrew *Geba,* in this case, a variant for Gibeah; also in 20:33.

[33]When the main group of Israelite warriors reached Baal-tamar, they turned and prepared to attack. Then the Israelites hiding in ambush west of Gibeah jumped up from where they were [34]and advanced against Benjamin from behind. The fighting was so heavy that Benjamin didn't realize the impending disaster. [35]So the LORD helped Israel defeat Benjamin, and that day the Israelites killed 25,100 of Benjamin's warriors, all of whom were experienced with a sword. [36]Then the men of Benjamin saw that they were beaten.

The Israelites had retreated from Benjamin's warriors in order to give those hiding in ambush more room to maneuver. [37]Then those who were in hiding rushed in from all sides and killed everyone in the town. [38]They sent up a large cloud of smoke from the town, [39]which was the signal for the Israelites to turn and attack Benjamin's warriors.

By that time Benjamin's warriors had killed about thirty Israelites, and they shouted, "We're defeating them as we did in the first battle!" [40]But when the warriors of Benjamin looked behind them and saw the smoke rising into the sky from every part of the town, [41]the Israelites turned and attacked. At this point Benjamin's warriors realized disaster was near and became terrified. [42]So they ran toward the wilderness, but the Israelites chased after them and killed them. [43]The Israelites surrounded the men of Benjamin and were relentless in chasing them down, finally overtaking them east of Gibeah. [44]Eighteen thousand of Benjamin's greatest warriors died in that day's battle. [45]The survivors fled into the wilderness toward the rock of Rimmon, but Israel killed five thousand of them along the road. They continued the chase until they had killed another two thousand near Gidom.

[46]So the tribe of Benjamin lost twenty-five thousand brave warriors that day, [47]leaving only six hundred men who escaped to the rock of Rimmon, where they lived for four months. [48]Then the Israelites returned and slaughtered every living thing in all the towns—the people, the cattle—everything. They also burned down every town they came to.

## CHAPTER 21

**WIVES FOR THE MEN OF BENJAMIN.** The Israelites had vowed at Mizpah never to give their daughters in marriage to a man from the tribe of Benjamin. [2]And the people went to Bethel and sat in the presence of God until evening, raising their voices and weeping bitterly. [3]"O LORD, God of Israel," they cried out, "why has this happened? Now one of our tribes is missing!"

[4]Early the next morning the people built an altar and presented their burnt offerings and peace offerings on it. [5]Then they said, "Was any tribe of Israel not represented when we held our council in the presence of the LORD at Mizpah?" At that time they had taken a solemn oath in the LORD's presence, vowing that anyone who refused to come must die.

[6]The Israelites felt deep sadness for Benjamin and said, "Today we have lost one of the tribes from our family; it is nearly wiped out. [7]How can we find wives for the few who remain, since we have sworn by the LORD not to give them our daughters in marriage?"

[8]So they asked, "Was anyone absent when we presented ourselves to the LORD at Mizpah?" And they discovered that no one from Jabesh-gilead had attended. [9]For after they counted all the people, no one from Jabesh-gilead was present. [10]So they sent twelve thousand warriors to Jabesh-gilead with orders to kill everyone there, including women and children. [11]"This is what you are to do," they said. "Completely destroy* all the males and every woman who is not a virgin." [12]Among the residents of Jabesh-gilead they found four hundred young virgins who had never slept with a man, and they brought them to the camp at Shiloh in the land of Canaan.

[13]The Israelite assembly sent a peace delegation to the little remnant of Benjamin who were living at the rock of Rimmon. [14]Then the men of Benjamin returned to their homes, and the four hundred women of Jabesh-gilead who were spared were given to them as wives. But there were not enough women for all of them.

[15]The people felt sorry for Benjamin because the LORD had left this gap in the tribes of Israel. [16]So the Israelite leaders asked, "How can we find wives for the few who remain, since all the women of the tribe of Benjamin are dead? [17]There must be heirs for the survivors so that an entire tribe of Israel will not be lost forever. [18]But we cannot give them our own daughters in marriage because we have sworn with a solemn oath that anyone who does this will fall under God's curse."

[19]Then they thought of the annual festival of the LORD held in Shiloh, between Lebonah and Bethel, along the east side of the road that goes from Bethel to Shechem. [20]They told the men of Benjamin who still needed wives, "Go and hide in the vineyards. [21]When the women of Shiloh come out for their dances, rush out from the vineyards, and each of you can take one of them home to be your

### QUICK ACTION ● ● • • •

20:46-48 **The effects of the horrible rape and murder should never have been felt outside the community where the crime happened. The local people should have brought the criminals to justice and corrected the laxness that originally permitted this crime. Instead, first the town and then the entire tribe defended this wickedness, even going to war over it. To prevent unresolved problems from turning into major conflicts, firm action must be taken quickly, wisely, and forcefully *before* the situation gets out of hand.**

21:11 The Hebrew term used here refers to the complete consecration of things or people to the LORD, either by destroying them or by giving them as an offering.

## HEROES ● ● ● • •

21:25 **During the time of the judges, the people of Israel experienced trouble because they became their own authority and acted on their own opinions of right and wrong. This produced horrendous results. Our world is similar. Individuals, groups, and societies have made themselves the final authorities without reference to God. When people selfishly try to satisfy their personal desires at all costs, everyone pays the price.**

**It is the ultimate heroic act to submit all our plans, desires, and motives to God. Men like Gideon, Jephthah, and Samson are known for their heroism in battle. But their personal lives were far from heroic.**

**To be truly heroic, we must go into battle each day in our home, school, church, and society to make God's kingdom a reality. Our weapons are the standards, morals, truths, and convictions we receive from God's Word. We will lose the battle if we gather the spoils of earthly treasures rather than seeking the treasures of heaven.**

wife! 22And when their fathers and brothers come
to us in protest, we will tell them, 'Please be understanding. Let them have your daughters, for we
didn't find enough wives for them when we destroyed Jabesh-gilead. And you are not guilty of
breaking the vow since you did not give your
daughters in marriage to them.'"
23So the men of Benjamin did as they were told.
They kidnapped the women who took part in the
celebration and carried them off to the land of their
own inheritance. Then they rebuilt their towns and
lived in them. 24So the assembly of Israel departed by
tribes and families, and they returned to their own
homes.
25In those days Israel had no king, so the people
did whatever seemed right in their own eyes.

# MEGA themes

**DECLINE/COMPROMISE** The people faced decline and failure because they compromised their high spiritual purpose in many ways. They abandoned their mission to drive all the people out of the land, and they adopted the customs of the people living around them.

Society offers many rewards to those who compromise their faith: wealth, acceptance, recognition, power, and influence. But when God gives us a mission, it must not be polluted by a desire for approval from social groups.

1. List some of the ways you have seen people compromise their faith and values for wealth, pleasure, power, acceptance, etc.
2. Can you think of a time when you compromised your faith and/or values? At the time, how were you feeling? Why did you make the choice you made? How did you feel after you realized the price you had paid?
3. The Israelites began living entirely different life-styles following a few major compromises. Why does it get easier and easier to compromise after you have done it for a while?
4. Why does it get easier not to compromise if you continually make decisions based on your faith and values?
5. Consider the temptations that you face in school, at work, or with friends. Given the many opportunities you have to make choices that would compromise your faith and values, it takes a serious commitment not to compromise. Fill in the following statement of faith with some specific areas where you must choose not to compromise: I will not compromise my faith and values in the area of ________ because of my commitment to trust God with my life.

**DECAY/APOSTASY** Israel's moral downfall had its roots in the fierce independence that each tribe cherished. It led to the people doing whatever seemed right in their own eyes. There was no unity in government or in worship. Law and order broke down. Finally idol worship and man-made religion led to the complete abandoning of faith in God.

We can expect things to fall apart when we value anything more highly than God. If we value our own independence more than God, we are putting an idol in our heart, and soon our life will become a temple to the god of self. We must constantly keep God first in our life and in all our desires.

1. The Israelites had difficulty giving up their idols. What are the idols in our contemporary society? How do people worship these idols?
2. List the top three "idols" that you find among those your age. What is it about these "idols" that attracts people to them?

3. All idols are false representations of God's truth. How does knowing and obeying God's truth keep you from idols?
4. What is there in your life that you are tempted to put in God's place? What do you know about God that causes you to believe that you should have him first in your life? How can this be accomplished?

**DEFEAT/OPPRESSION** God used evil oppressors to punish the Israelites for their sin, to bring them to the point of repentance, and to test their allegiance to him.

Rebelling against God leads to disaster. God may use oppression to bring wandering hearts back to him. At times God's love is tough.

1. Why did God allow the Israelites' enemies to defeat them?
2. How did these defeats affect the people?
3. Why does it often take painful experiences to turn people from their rebellion against God? What does this teach you about human nature?
4. In what ways are you currently expressing your commitment to Christ? In what areas are you expressing rebellion? Besides the fact that this may result in painful experiences, why should you turn away from rebellion and turn toward God?

**REPENTANCE** Decline, decay, and defeat caused the people to cry out for help. They vowed to turn from idolatry and to turn to God for mercy and deliverance.

Idolatry gains a foothold in our heart when we make anything more important than God. We must identify modern idols in our heart, renounce them, and turn to God for his love and mercy.

1. Describe the feelings of the people when they repented of their sin and rebellion. What led to those feelings?
2. Is repentance an emotion or an action? Explain your response.
3. To *repent* means literally "turning from," that is, changing direction. Describe a time in your life when you turned from a sin or sinful attitude and redirected your life toward God. What did you do? What was the evidence of your repentance?
4. Looking back at question 4 under DEFEAT/OPPRESSION, perhaps you see the need to repent today. What are some new directions you can take that will lead you back toward the Lord who lovingly draws you?

**DELIVERANCE/HEROES** Because Israel repented, God raised up heroes to deliver his people from their path of sin and the oppression it brought. He used many kinds of people to accomplish this purpose.

God's love and mercy are available to all people. Anyone who is dedicated to God can be used for his service. Real heroes recognize the futility of human effort without God's leading.

1. What qualities did the judges possess that enabled them to make a difference for God?
2. What seem to be the differences between the superstars that our society idolizes and the people God uses as heroes?
3. What people have made the biggest positive impact in your life? In what ways could they be described as God's heroes?
4. What qualities would God's hero need in your school? At your church? In your community?
5. God wants to make a difference in you. He wants you to be a hero for his plan in the world. What qualities do you possess that he could use to make an impact in others' lives?
6. To make a difference in our world, we must begin by seeking a difference in our life. In what areas do you need to grow so that you will be better prepared to be God's hero?

**M**om, that food looks awful!" "Dad, you always make me take out the garbage." "She's the worst teacher ever!" "My allowance isn't enough." "I hate the way I look." Sound familiar? Everyone likes to complain. When things don't go exactly as we think they should, we are quick to let others know we feel cheated and angry. ■ In the book of Ruth, we read of Naomi's complaints. Her husband and two sons had recently died, and she decided to blame God. She figured that since God had caused her loved ones' deaths, he deserved her anger. ■ But God didn't deserve her anger. And Naomi learned that God wasn't to be blamed for her family members' deaths; he was to be thanked for his kindness. ■ We tend to complain against God. If something in life is wrong, we conclude that it must be his fault. The book of Ruth reminds us strongly and clearly that this is not the case. God is not to be blamed for our problems, but praised for his goodness. ■ Read the book of Ruth—a story of relationships, rescue, and romance—and thank God for his goodness in your life.

## STATS

PURPOSE: To show how three people remained strong in character and true to God even when the society around them was collapsing

AUTHOR: Unknown. Some think it was Samuel, but internal evidence suggests that it was written after his death.

DATE WRITTEN: Sometime after the period of the judges (1375–1050 B.C.)

SETTING: A dark time in Israel's history when people lived to please themselves, not God (Judges 17:6)

KEY PEOPLE: Ruth, Naomi, Boaz

KEY PLACES: Moab, Bethlehem

CHAPTER 1 **RUTH GOES HOME WITH NAOMI.** In the
days when the judges ruled in Israel, a man from
Bethlehem in Judah left the country because of a
severe famine. He took his wife and two sons and
went to live in the country of Moab. 2The man's
name was Elimelech, and his wife was Naomi. Their
two sons were Mahlon and Kilion. They were Eph-
rathites from Bethlehem in the land of Judah. During their stay in Moab, 3Elimelech died and Naomi
was left with her two sons. 4The two sons married
Moabite women. One married a woman named Orpah, and the other a woman named Ruth. But about
ten years later, 5both Mahlon and Kilion died. This
left Naomi alone, without her husband or sons.
6Then Naomi heard in Moab that the LORD had
blessed his people in Judah by giving them good
crops again. So Naomi and her daughters-in-law got
ready to leave Moab to return to her homeland.
7With her two daughters-in-law she set out from the
place where she had been living, and they took the
road that would lead them back to Judah.
8But on the way, Naomi said to her two daughters-
in-law, "Go back to your mothers' homes instead of
coming with me. And may the LORD reward you for
your kindness to your husbands and to me. 9May the
LORD bless you with the security of another marriage." Then she kissed them good-bye, and they all
broke down and wept.

10"No," they said. "We want to go with you to
your people."
11But Naomi replied, "Why should you go on
with me? Can I still give birth to other sons who
could grow up to be your husbands? 12No, my
daughters, return to your parents' homes, for I am
too old to marry again. And even if it were possible,
and I were to get married tonight and bear sons,

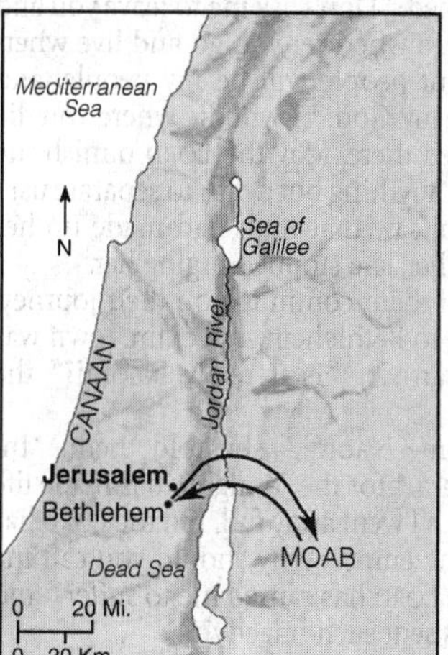


**SETTING FOR THE STORY**
Elimelech, Naomi, and their sons traveled from Bethlehem to the land of Moab because of a famine. After her husband and sons died, Naomi returned to Bethlehem with her daughter-in-law Ruth.

then what? [13]Would you wait for them to grow up and refuse to marry someone else? No, of course not, my daughters! Things are far more bitter for me than for you, because the LORD himself has caused me to suffer."

[14]And again they wept together, and Orpah kissed her mother-in-law good-bye. But Ruth insisted on staying with Naomi. [15]"See," Naomi said to her, "your sister-in-law has gone back to her people and to her gods. You should do the same."

**OMMITMENT**

Wendy and Susan have been friends ever since the third grade. Girl Scouts, softball, Sunday school—they've done it all together.

As they've grown older, however, the girls have developed vastly different interests. In fact, now, as teenagers, they couldn't be more opposite.

Wendy is short and round. Extremely outgoing, she makes good grades and keeps everyone in the band in stitches. She's also very involved in the drama club. Susan is tall, pretty, and extremely shy. An average student, Susan dates quite a bit and works at an expensive dress shop in the mall.

Since the two girls have such contrasting personalities, nobody can quite understand why they're still friends. But they are. They're best friends.

Just how close are they? Well, get this: last week, Wendy and Susan made Saturday plans to go shopping. The very next day, Susan got a call from the cutest guy at school (a guy she's secretly liked all year). The call went like this:

"Susan? Hi, this is Brett. Listen, I was just wondering if you'd like to go horseback riding this Saturday?"

"This weekend?" Susan paused. "Um, Brett, I'd really like to, but I kind of already made plans. Can we do it some other time?"

Would you have been that loyal to a friend? Read about another woman who understood the meaning of commitment—Ruth 1:1-18.

[16]But Ruth replied, "Don't ask me to leave you and turn back. I will go wherever you go and live wherever you live. Your people will be my people, and your God will be my God. [17]I will die where you die and will be buried there. May the LORD punish me severely if I allow anything but death to separate us!" [18]So when Naomi saw that Ruth had made up her mind to go with her, she stopped urging her.

[19]So the two of them continued on their journey. When they came to Bethlehem, the entire town was stirred by their arrival. "Is it really Naomi?" the women asked.

[20]"Don't call me Naomi," she told them. "Instead, call me Mara,* for the Almighty has made life very bitter for me. [21]I went away full, but the LORD has brought me home empty. Why should you call me Naomi when the LORD has caused me to suffer* and the Almighty has sent such tragedy?"

[22]So Naomi returned from Moab, accompanied by her daughter-in-law Ruth, the young Moabite woman. They arrived in Bethlehem at the beginning of the barley harvest.

## CHAPTER 2

**RUTH GLEANS IN THE FIELDS.** Now there was a wealthy and influential man in Bethlehem named Boaz, who was a relative of Naomi's husband, Elimelech.

[2]One day Ruth said to Naomi, "Let me go out into the fields to gather leftover grain behind anyone who will let me do it."

And Naomi said, "All right, my daughter, go ahead." [3]So Ruth went out to gather grain behind the harvesters. And as it happened, she found herself working in a field that belonged to Boaz, the relative of her father-in-law, Elimelech.

[4]While she was there, Boaz arrived from Bethlehem and greeted the harvesters. "The LORD be with you!" he said.

"The LORD bless you!" the harvesters replied.

[5]Then Boaz asked his foreman, "Who is that girl over there?"

[6]And the foreman replied, "She is the young woman from Moab who came back with Naomi. [7]She asked me this morning if she could gather grain behind the harvesters. She has been hard at work ever since, except for a few minutes' rest over there in the shelter."

[8]Boaz went over and said to Ruth, "Listen, my daughter. Stay right here with us when you gather grain; don't go to any other fields. Stay right behind the women working in my field. [9]See which part of the field they are harvesting, and then follow them. I have warned the young men not to bother you. And when you are thirsty, help yourself to the water they have drawn from the well."

[10]Ruth fell at his feet and thanked him warmly. "Why are you being so kind to me?" she asked. "I am only a foreigner."

[11]"Yes, I know," Boaz replied. "But I also know about the love and kindness you have shown your mother-in-law since the death of your husband. I have heard how you left your father and mother and your own land to live here among complete strangers. [12]May the LORD, the God of Israel, under whose wings you have come to take refuge, reward you fully."

[13]"I hope I continue to please you, sir," she replied. "You have comforted me by speaking so

**ADVICE ● ● • • •**

3:5 **As a foreigner, Ruth may have thought that Naomi's advice was odd. But Ruth followed the advice because she knew Naomi was kind, trustworthy, and filled with moral integrity. Each of us knows a parent, older friend, or relative who is always looking out for our best interests. The experience and knowledge of such a person can be invaluable. Imagine what Ruth's life would have been like had she ignored her mother-in-law.**

1:20 *Naomi* means "pleasant"; *Mara* means "bitter." 1:21 Or *has testified against me.*

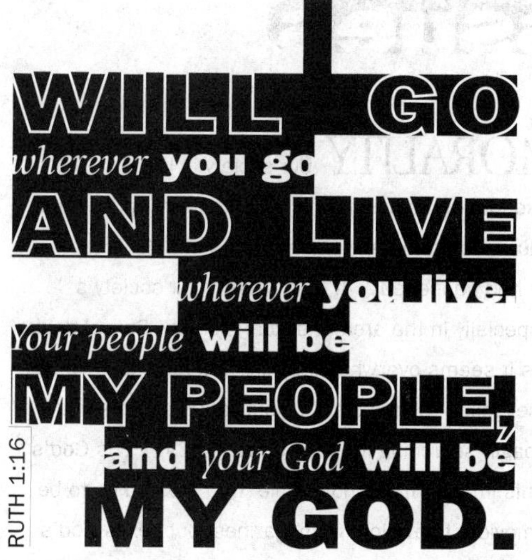
WILL GO
wherever you go
AND LIVE
wherever you live.
Your people will be
MY PEOPLE,
and your God will be
MY GOD.
RUTH 1:16

kindly to me, even though I am not as worthy as your
workers."
14At lunchtime Boaz called to her, "Come over
here and help yourself to some of our food. You can
dip your bread in the wine if you like." So she sat
with his harvesters, and Boaz gave her food—more
than she could eat.
15When Ruth went back to work again, Boaz ordered his young men, "Let her gather grain right
among the sheaves without stopping her. 16And pull
out some heads of barley from the bundles and drop
them on purpose for her. Let her pick them up, and
don't give her a hard time!"
17So Ruth gathered barley there all day, and when
she beat out the grain that evening, it came to about
half a bushel.* 18She carried it back into town and
showed it to her mother-in-law. Ruth also gave her
the food that was left over from her lunch.
19"So much!" Naomi exclaimed. "Where did you
gather all this grain today? Where did you work? May
the LORD bless the one who helped you!"
So Ruth told her mother-in-law about the man in
whose field she had worked. And she said, "The man
I worked with today is named Boaz."
20"May the LORD bless him!" Naomi told her
daughter-in-law. "He is showing his kindness to us as
well as to your dead husband.* That man is one of our
closest relatives, one of our family redeemers."
21Then Ruth said, "What's more, Boaz even told
me to come back and stay with his harvesters until
the entire harvest is completed."
22"This is wonderful!" Naomi exclaimed. "Do as
he said. Stay with his workers right through the
whole harvest. You will be safe there, unlike in other
fields."
23So Ruth worked alongside the women in Boaz's
fields and gathered grain with them until the end of
the barley harvest. Then she worked with them
through the wheat harvest, too. But all the while she
lived with her mother-in-law.

CHAPTER 3 **RUTH MARRIES BOAZ.** One day Naomi
said to Ruth, "My daughter, it's time that I found a
permanent home for you, so that you will be provided for. 2Boaz is a close relative of ours, and he's
been very kind by letting you gather grain with his
workers. Tonight he will be winnowing barley at the
threshing floor. 3Now do as I tell you—take a bath
and put on perfume and dress in your nicest clothes.
Then go to the threshing floor, but don't let Boaz see
you until he has finished his meal. 4Be sure to notice
where he lies down; then go and uncover his feet and
lie down there. He will tell you what to do."
5"I will do everything you say," Ruth replied. 6So
she went down to the threshing floor that night and
followed the instructions of her mother-in-law.
7After Boaz had finished his meal and was in good
spirits, he lay down beside the heap of grain and
went to sleep. Then Ruth came quietly, uncovered his
feet, and lay down. 8Around midnight, Boaz suddenly woke up and turned over. He was surprised to

i wonder...

**Who wrote the Bible, and how do I know if it really came from God?**

God gave the words that are in the Bible by working in the minds of his chosen writers. Then these men wrote down what he wanted.

The Bible contains 66 books written by 40 authors at various points in history. Many of the "books" are actually letters.

If you know a mathematician, ask him or her the probability of 66 separate documents, written over a period of 1,500 years by 40 different authors, not having any contradictions. He'd have to conclude what you've described is mathematically impossible. Yet that is what God did as he wrote and arranged the Bible.

The theme, the history, the way the Bible reveals God's character, and, especially, the way it describes God's way of bringing salvation to people, are consistent throughout.

More important than how we got the Bible is why. God gave the Bible to us to prepare us for anything, to help us do good to everyone.

God's Word also serves as our offensive weapon against all the problems we encounter. "For the word of God is full of living power. It is sharper than the sharpest knife, cutting deep into our innermost thoughts and desires. It exposes us for what we really are" (Hebrews 4:12).

God is in the business of molding our character and strengthening us for future use. He's given us all of the resources for strength we'll ever need, in the Bible.

2:17 Hebrew *about an ephah* [18 liters]. 2:20 Hebrew *to the living and to the dead.*

## SEXUAL MORALITY

Our society is like a department-store window that a mischievous boy broke into so he could switch all the items' price tags. The next day, people unknowingly paid the wrong amounts for items and walked out; some got great deals, some got ripped off—all were unaware of what had happened. It's no secret: Our society's moral values are seriously **OUT OF ORDER**—especially in the area of sexual morality. Sexual desire has always created major moral problems. Sometimes it seems overwhelming, like you have to have sex with someone or explode. How can we deal with our sexuality—and society's glorification of sex—in a way that is acceptable to a holy God? The place to begin searching for SEXUAL SANITY is God's Word. Genesis 1:26-27 tells us that God made us in his image, male and female. God created us to be sexual beings! We often think sex is the invention of movies, television, or magazines, but sex is God's idea. What the media and the non-Christian world have done is exploit and cheapen God's good gift. Unfortunately, the world has learned to shout louder and package messages better than the church. Some Christian college students put it this way: "The church isn't talking about sex, and the media lies." The world's lie is this: If it feels good, do it. There's nothing new about this philosophy. The ancient Greeks called it **"hedonism."** What *is* new, though, is the widespread devastation it is producing in countless lives: • the U.S. has the highest teenage pregnancy rate among Western "developed" countries; • one in eight female college students is a victim of date rape or attempted rape; • over 50 percent of American teenagers are sexually active by age 18; • a study by the Rhode Island Rape Crisis Center showed that 65 percent of the boys and 47 percent of the girls in seventh to ninth grade say it's OK for a man to force a woman to have sex if they've been dating over six months; • a study of persons with AIDS in New York City indicates that 29 percent of those infected contracted the disease as teenagers. Horrifying? Yes. Surprising? Hardly. What would you expect from our ***pursuit-of-pleasure*** morality? If ever there was a time to lift up the biblical standard of sexual morality, it's now. And the Bible has some straightforward words about sexual behavior. Hebrews 13:4 says, "Give honor to marriage, and remain faithful to one another in marriage. God will surely judge people who are immoral and those who commit adultery." Paul writes in 1 Corinthians 6:13, 18-20: "Our bodies were not made for sexual immorality. They were made for the Lord, and the Lord cares about our bodies. . . . Run away from sexual sin! No other sin so clearly affects the body as this one does. For sexual immorality is a sin against your own body. Or don't you know that your body is the temple of the Holy Spirit, who lives in you and was given to you by God? You do not belong to yourself, for God bought you with a high price. So you must honor God with your body." The principle is clear: God made sex to be part of the bond between a husband and wife. Anything else is sin. Though the Bible isn't specific about dating activities, the main biblical instruction is plain: Sex outside of marriage is sin, and our bodies were never meant for this kind of sin. Of course, this leaves a sizable GRAY AREA of what is and isn't acceptable in God's eyes. Go to an older Christian for counsel in these matters, remembering that the issue isn't "How much can I do before I'm sinning?" If you want to please God, the question is, "What would God have me do in my opposite-sex relationships? How can I best honor him and the other person?" Navigating the waters of sexual morality is difficult, but with the Bible, prayer, and other Christians' input as your compass, you can do it without **crashing on the rocks** of sexual sin.

find a woman lying at his feet! [9]"Who are you?" he demanded.

"I am your servant Ruth," she replied. "Spread the corner of your covering over me, for you are my family redeemer."

[10]"The LORD bless you, my daughter!" Boaz exclaimed. "You are showing more family loyalty now than ever by not running after a younger man, whether rich or poor. [11]Now don't worry about a thing, my daughter. I will do what is necessary, for everyone in town knows you are an honorable woman. [12]But there is one problem. While it is true that I am one of your family redeemers, there is another man who is more closely related to you than I am. [13]Stay here tonight, and in the morning I will talk to him. If he is willing to redeem you, then let him marry you. But if he is not willing, then as surely as the LORD lives, I will marry you! Now lie down here until morning."

[14]So Ruth lay at Boaz's feet until the morning, but she got up before it was light enough for people to recognize each other. For Boaz said, "No one must know that a woman was here at the threshing floor." [15]Boaz also said to her, "Bring your cloak and spread it out." He measured out six scoops* of barley into the cloak and helped her put it on her back. Then Boaz* returned to the town.

[16]When Ruth went back to her mother-in-law, Naomi asked, "What happened, my daughter?"

Ruth told Naomi everything Boaz had done for her, [17]and she added, "He gave me these six scoops of barley and said, 'Don't go back to your mother-in-law empty-handed.'"

[18]Then Naomi said to her, "Just be patient, my daughter, until we hear what happens. The man won't rest until he has followed through on this. He will settle it today."

CHAPTER **4** So Boaz went to the town gate and took a seat there. When the family redeemer he had mentioned came by, Boaz called out to him, "Come over here, friend. I want to talk to you." So they sat down together. [2]Then Boaz called ten leaders from the town and asked them to sit as witnesses. [3]And Boaz said to the family redeemer, "You know Naomi, who came back from Moab. She is selling the land that belonged to our relative Elimelech. [4]I felt that I should speak to you about it so that you can redeem it if you wish. If you want the land, then buy it here in the presence of these witnesses. But if you don't want it, let me know right away, because I am next in line to redeem it after you."

The man replied, "All right, I'll redeem it."

[5]Then Boaz told him, "Of course, your purchase of the land from Naomi also requires that you marry Ruth, the Moabite widow. That way, she can have children who will carry on her husband's name and keep the land in the family."

[6]"Then I can't redeem it," the family redeemer

## RUTH & NAOMI

Real friends enjoy each other's company. Friendship weaves lives together. One of the greatest friendships described in the Bible was between Ruth and Naomi. In fact, we know more about their friendship than we know about them as individuals. In our world today we sometimes try too hard to make it on our own. Ruth and Naomi teach us how wonderful a good friendship can be.

Naomi and Ruth did not share many of the typical things that bring people together. They came from different cultures, families, and places. Naomi was older than Ruth. Ruth had been married to Naomi's son. But both women had lost their husbands. They were left with almost nothing but each other.

Yet there was real freedom in their friendship. Often in relationships people try to hold each other too tightly. Friendship can fade when there is no room to breathe. Naomi was willing to let Ruth return to her family. Ruth was willing to leave her homeland to go to Israel. Naomi even helped arrange Ruth's marriage to Boaz although she knew it would change their relationship.

God was always part of Naomi and Ruth's friendship. Ruth met God through Naomi as the older woman allowed Ruth to see, hear, and feel all the joy and sorrow of her relationship with God. How often do you feel that your thoughts, feelings, and questions about God should be kept from your best friends? If you are really getting to know God, he wants to be part of all your friendships.

LESSON: God's living presence in a relationship overcomes differences that might otherwise create division and disharmony

KEY VERSE: "But Ruth replied, 'Don't ask me to leave you and turn back. I will go wherever you go and live wherever you live. Your people will be my people, and your God will be my God'" (Ruth 1:16).

Their story is told in the book of Ruth. Ruth is also mentioned in Matthew 1:5.

**UPS:**
- A relationship where the greatest bond was their faith in God
- A relationship of strong mutual commitment
- A relationship in which each person tried to do what was best for the other

**STATS:**
- Where: Moab, Bethlehem
- Occupation: Wives, widows, gleaners
- Relatives: Elimelech, Mahlon, Chilion, Orpah, Boaz

3:15a Hebrew *six measures,* an unknown quantity. 3:15b Most Hebrew manuscripts read *he;* many Hebrew manuscripts, Syriac version, and Latin Vulgate read *she.*

replied, "because this might endanger my own
estate. You redeem the land; I cannot do it."
[7]In those days it was the custom in Israel for
anyone transferring a right of purchase to remove his
sandal and hand it to the other party. This publicly
validated the transaction. [8]So the other family redeemer drew off his sandal as he said to Boaz, "You
buy the land."
[9]Then Boaz said to the leaders and to the crowd
standing around, "You are witnesses that today I
have bought from Naomi all the property of Elimelech, Kilion, and Mahlon. [10]And with the land I have
acquired Ruth, the Moabite widow of Mahlon, to be
my wife. This way she can have a son to carry on the
family name of her dead husband and to inherit the
family property here in his hometown. You are all
witnesses today."
[11]Then the leaders and all the people standing there
replied, "We are witnesses! May the LORD make the
woman who is now coming into your home like
Rachel and Leah, from whom all the nation of Israel
descended! May you be great in Ephrathah and famous in Bethlehem. [12]And may the LORD give you
descendants by this young woman who will be like
those of our ancestor Perez, the son of Tamar and
Judah."
[13]So Boaz married Ruth and took her home to live
with him. When he slept with her, the LORD enabled
her to become pregnant, and she gave birth to a son.
[14]And the women of the town said to Naomi, "Praise
the LORD who has given you a family redeemer today!

## TOUGH TIMES • • • • •

4:15 **God brought great blessings out of Naomi's tragedy, even greater blessings than "seven sons" (indicating the great blessing of an abundance of heirs). Throughout her tough times, Naomi continued to trust God. And God, in his time, blessed her greatly. Even in our sorrow and calamity, God can bring great blessings. Be like Naomi, and don't turn your back on God when tragedy strikes. Don't ask, "How can God allow this to happen to me?" Instead, trust him. He will be with you even in the hard times.**

May he be famous in Israel. [15]May this child restore
your youth and care for you in your old age. For he is
the son of your daughter-in-law who loves you so
much and who has been better to you than seven
sons!"
[16]Naomi took care of the baby and cared for him
as if he were her own. [17]The neighbor women said,
"Now at last Naomi has a son again!" And they
named him Obed. He became the father of Jesse and
the grandfather of David.
[18]This is their family line beginning with their
ancestor Perez:

Perez was the father of Hezron.
19 Hezron was the father of Ram.
Ram was the father of Amminadab.
20 Amminadab was the father of Nahshon.
Nahshon was the father of Salmon.
21 Salmon was the father of Boaz.
Boaz was the father of Obed.
22 Obed was the father of Jesse.
Jesse was the father of David.

# MEGA themes

**FAITHFULNESS** Ruth's faithfulness to Naomi as a daughter-in-law and friend is a great example of love and loyalty. Ruth, Naomi, and Boaz were also faithful to God and his laws. Throughout the story we see how God is faithful in return.

Ruth's life was guided by faithfulness toward God, and that was exhibited in her loyalty to the people she knew. We should also imitate God's faithfulness by being loyal and loving in our relationships.

1. Describe the type of relationship Ruth had with Naomi.
2. How did this relationship reflect Ruth's relationship with God?
3. What have you learned through other people about God's love? When and how did you learn these things?
4. How does growing in your relationship with God enable you to have deeper relationships with the important people in your life?
5. Who are your important friends? What are some specific ways you could show them more of God's love?

**KINDNESS** Ruth showed great kindness to Naomi. And Boaz showed kindness to Ruth—a despised Moabite woman with no money. God showed his kindness to Ruth, Naomi, and Boaz by bringing them together for his purposes.

Just as Boaz showed his kindness by buying back land to guarantee Ruth and Naomi's inheritance, so Christ showed his kindness by purchasing us to guarantee our eternal life. God's kindness in providing a redeemer for our lives should motivate us to love and honor him.

1. What makes kindness such an important quality?
2. What do you learn about the kindness of God from the life of Ruth? from the life of Jesus?
3. What could a person learn about God's kindness from seeing your relationships with your friends? your family?
4. In what ways could you display more of this kindness in your important relationships?

**INTEGRITY** Ruth showed high moral character by being loyal to Naomi, by her clean break from her former land and customs, and by her hard work in the field. Boaz showed integrity in his moral standards, his honesty, and by following through on his commitments.

When we have experienced God's faithfulness and kindness, we should respond by living a godly life. Just as Ruth's and Boaz's values contrasted with those of the culture portrayed in Judges, so should our life stand out from the world around us.

1. Give examples of people you know or know about who have integrity.
2. Give examples of people you know or know about who lack integrity.
3. What is the connection between being a witness for Jesus Christ and being a person of integrity?
4. List several specific areas where Christians might be tempted to compromise their integrity as followers of Christ.
5. What can you do to help maintain your integrity?

**PROTECTION** We see God's care and protection of Naomi and Ruth. His supreme control over circumstances brings them safety and security. God guides the minds and activities of people to fulfill his purpose.

No matter how devastating our present situation may be, we can hope in God. His resources are infinite. We must believe that he can work in any person's life, whether that person is a king or a stranger in a foreign land.

1. Think of a time when, as a child, you were frightened and an adult comforted you. What was it about that person that calmed your fears? How did you feel toward that person?
2. Every person has fears. What are some of the things that cause you to feel afraid or insecure?
3. What qualities do you find in God that tend to calm your fears and bring you a sense of security?
4. What fears do you have about the present? About the future?
5. To whom can you go to be reminded of God's secure love?
6. Do you know someone who is in a very difficult, possibly scary, time in his or her life? Based on your understanding of God and the way he uses us to communicate his protection, how can you help this person?

**PROSPERITY/BLESSING** Ruth and Naomi came to Bethlehem as poor widows, but they soon became prosperous through Ruth's marriage to Boaz. Ruth became a mother (and eventually the great-grandmother of King David). Yet the greatest blessing was not the money, the marriage, or the children; it was the quality of love and respect between Ruth, Boaz, and Naomi.

We tend to think of blessings in terms of prosperity rather than the high-quality relationships that God makes possible for us. No matter what our economic situation, we can love and respect the people God has brought into our life. In so doing, we give and receive blessings.

1. Define what the word *rich* means to you.
2. What is dangerous about always comparing what you have with what others have?
3. What should be your attitude about gaining riches?
4. Some Christians have large amounts of possessions, and others have very little. Is the person with more possessions more blessed by God? Explain.
5. Summarize what you think is God's will for you concerning gaining possessions and becoming rich.
6. What does it mean for you to be blessed by God?

1105 B.C.
Samuel born

1080
Saul born

1050
Saul becomes king

1040
David born

1025
David anointed; Goliath slain

1010
David becomes king of Judah

1003
David becomes king of Israel

970
Solomon becomes king

930
The kingdom is divided

**S**usan, is that you?" Susan had just answered her phone, expecting it to be Jill, her best friend. Instead, the voice was unfamiliar. ■ "Yeah," she replied. "Who is this?" ■ "Oh, my name is Eric. You don't know me, but I see you at school a lot." ■ Susan was popular—she had been voted class princess and had been dating the captain of the basketball team, Allen. ■ "Why did you call me?" she asked. ■ Eric said that he just wanted to talk. So they did, for an hour that night, and for several hours over the next few weeks—about everything they could think of. ■ Susan started looking forward to Eric's calls. She wanted to meet him, but he always refused. She wondered what he looked like. So far, she'd only dated popular guys: a football player, the class president, a guy with a new Porsche, and now Allen—about the cutest guy in school. ■ Soon, though, Susan realized Eric's popularity didn't really matter. He had become a good friend. She started to understand that though we often judge people by what we see on the outside, what really matters is what's on the inside. ■ First Samuel shows how looks can be deceiving. It tells about the first two kings of Israel: Saul and David. Saul was tall, handsome, and brave. He looked like a king. David, on the other hand, didn't look like a leader, much less a king. He was young and small. ■ Yet Saul, who looked like a king, proved he wasn't worthy to be one, while David, who wasn't so impressive, became a great king. ■ As you read 1 Samuel, watch the rise and fall of Saul and the rise of David. Remember that while people judge by outward appearances, God looks at thoughts and intentions (1 Samuel 16:7).

## STATS

PURPOSE: To record the life of Samuel, Israel's last judge; the reign and decline of Saul, Israel's first king; and the choice and preparation of David, Israel's greatest king

AUTHOR: Probably Samuel, but also includes writings from the prophets Nathan and Gad (1 Chronicles 29:29)

SETTING: The book begins in the days of the judges and describes Israel's transition from a theocracy (being led by God) to a monarchy (being led by a king)

KEY PEOPLE: Eli, Hannah, Samuel, Saul, Jonathan, David

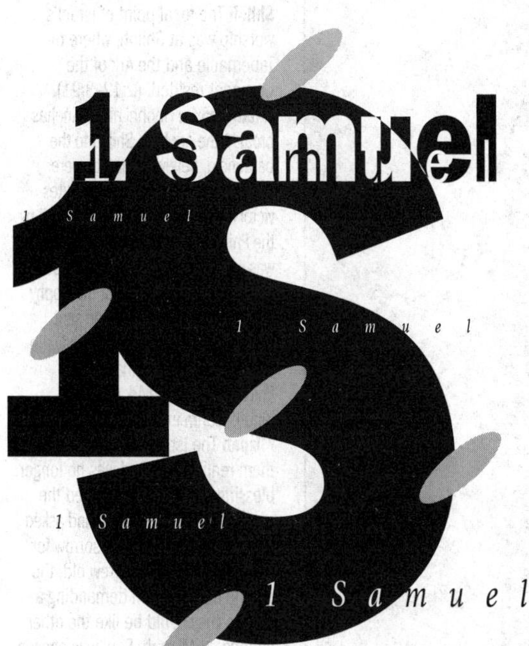


CHAPTER **1** **SAMUEL IS BORN.** There was a man named Elkanah who lived in Ramah* in the hill country of Ephraim. He was the son of Jeroham and grandson of Elihu, from the family of Tohu and the clan of Zuph. 2Elkanah had two wives, Hannah and Peninnah. Peninnah had children, while Hannah did not.

3Each year Elkanah and his family would travel to Shiloh to worship and sacrifice to the LORD Almighty at the Tabernacle. The priests of the LORD at that time were the two sons of Eli—Hophni and Phinehas. 4On the day Elkanah presented his sacrifice, he would give portions of the sacrifice to Peninnah and each of her children. 5But he gave Hannah a special portion* because he loved her very much, even though the LORD had given her no children. 6But Peninnah made fun of Hannah because the LORD had closed her womb. 7Year after year it was the same—Peninnah would taunt Hannah as they went to the Tabernacle.* Hannah would finally be reduced to tears and would not even eat.

8"What's the matter, Hannah?" Elkanah would ask. "Why aren't you eating? Why be so sad just because you have no children? You have me—isn't that better than having ten sons?"

9Once when they were at Shiloh, Hannah went over to the Tabernacle* after supper to pray to the LORD. Eli the priest was sitting at his customary place beside the entrance. 10Hannah was in deep anguish, crying bitterly as she prayed to the LORD. 11And she made this vow: "O LORD Almighty, if you will look down upon my sorrow and answer my prayer and give me a son, then I will give him back to you. He will be yours for his entire lifetime, and as a sign that he has been dedicated to the LORD, his hair will never be cut."*

12As she was praying to the LORD, Eli watched her. 13Seeing her lips moving but hearing no sound, he thought she had been drinking. 14"Must you come here drunk?" he demanded. "Throw away your wine!"

15"Oh no, sir!" she replied, "I'm not drunk! But I am very sad, and I was pouring out my heart to

### GOD'S PLAN ● ● • • •

**1:7 Part of God's plan for Hannah involved postponing her years of childbearing. While Peninnah and Elkanah looked at Hannah's circumstances, God was moving ahead with his plan. Can you thin of others who are struggling with the way God is working in their lives and who need your support? By supporting those who are struggling, you may help them stay obedient to God and confiden in his plan for their lives.**

1:1 Hebrew *Ramathaim-zophim;* compare 1:19. 1:5 Or *a double portion.* The meaning of the Hebrew is uncertain. 1:7 Hebrew *the house of the LORD;* also in 1:24. 1:9 Hebrew *the Temple of the LORD.* 1:11 Some manuscripts add *He will drink neither wine nor intoxicants.*

# KEY PLACES IN 1 SAMUEL

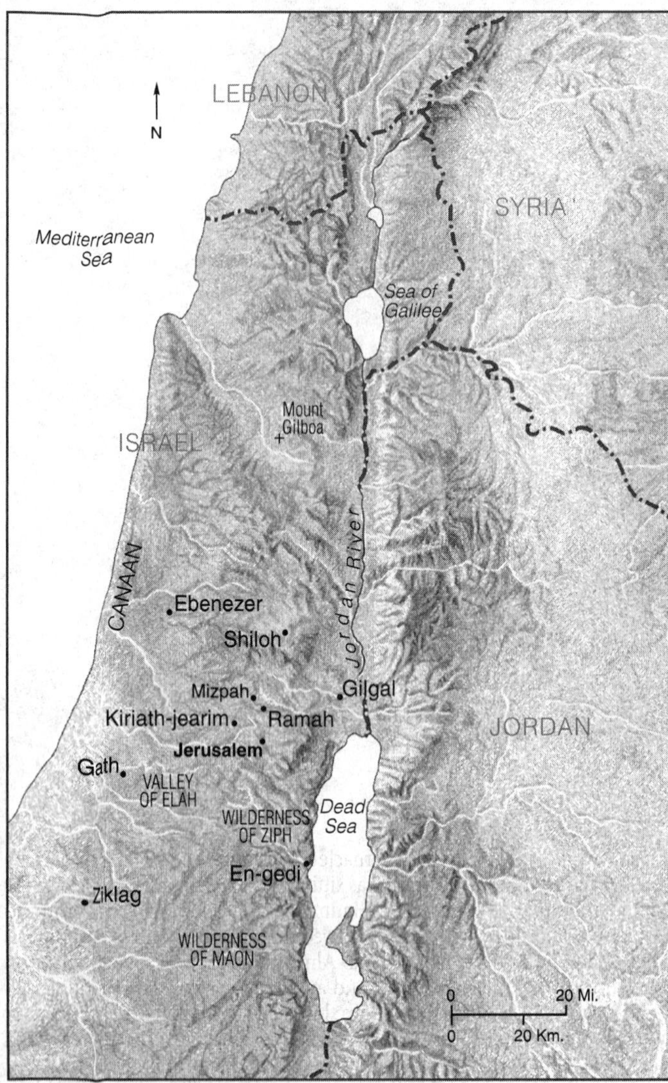


The broken lines (—·—·) indicate modern boundaries.

**Ramah** Samuel was born in Ramah. Before his birth, Samuel's mother, Hannah, made a promise to God that she would dedicate her son to serve God (1:1–2:11).

**Shiloh** The focal point of Israel's worship was at Shiloh, where the Tabernacle and the Ark of the Covenant resided. (2:12–3:21).

**Kiriath-jearim** Hophni and Phinehas brought the Ark from Shiloh to the battlefield, believing that its mere presence would bring the Israelites victory. The Israelites were defeated by the Philistines at Ebenezer, and the Ark was captured. However, the Philistines found that the Ark was not the trophy they expected, because God sent plagues upon every Philistine city the Ark was brought to. Finally, the Philistines sent the Ark back to Kiriath-jearim in Israel (4:1–7:1).

**Mizpah** The Israelites' defeat made them realize that God was no longer blessing them. Samuel called the people together at Mizpah and asked them to fast and pray in sorrow for their sins. As Samuel grew old, the people came to him demanding a king so they could be like the other nations. At Mizpah, Saul was chosen by sacred lot to be Israel's first king with the blessing, but not the approval, of God and Samuel (7:2–10:27).

**Gilgal** A battle with the Ammonites proved Saul's leadership abilities. He protected the people of Jabesh-gilead and scattered the Ammonite army. Samuel and the people crowned Saul as king of Israel at Gilgal (11:1-15).

**Valley of Elah** Saul won many other battles, but over time he proved to be arrogant, sinful, and rebellious until God finally rejected him as king. Unknown to Saul, a young man named David was anointed to be Israel's next king. But it would be many years before David would sit upon the throne. In one particular battle in the valley of Elah, David killed Goliath, the Philistines' mightiest soldier. The Israelites praised David more than Saul, causing Saul to plot to kill David (12:1–22:23).

**The Wilderness** Even anointed kings face troubles. David ran for his life from Saul, hiding in the wildernesses of Ziph, Maon, and En-gedi. Though he had opportunities to kill Saul, David refused to do so because Saul was God's anointed king (23:1–26:25).

**Gath** David moved his men and family to Gath, the Philistine city where King Achish lived. Saul then stopped chasing him. The Philistines seemed to welcome this famous fugitive from Israel (27:1-4).

**Ziklag** In return for his pretended loyalty to King Achish, David asked for a city for his men and family. Achish gave him Ziklag. From there David conducted raids against the Geshurites, Girzites, and the Amalekites, making sure no one escaped to tell the tale (27:5-12). Later David conquered the Amalekites after they raided Ziklag (30:1-31).

**Mount Gilboa** War with the Philistines broke out again in the north, near Mount Gilboa. Saul, who no longer relied on God, consulted a witch (a "medium") in a desperate attempt to contact Samuel for help. In the meantime, David was sent back to Ziklag because the Philistine commanders did not trust his loyalty in battle against Israel. The Philistines slaughtered the Israelites on Mount Gilboa, killing King Saul and his three sons, including David's loyal friend Jonathan. Without God, Saul had led a bitter and misguided life. His sinful actions affected him and hurt his family and nation (28:1–31:13).

the LORD. 16Please don't think I am a wicked
woman! For I have been praying out of great anguish and sorrow."
17"In that case," Eli said, "cheer up! May the God
of Israel grant the request you have asked of him."
18"Oh, thank you, sir!" she exclaimed. Then she
went back and began to eat again, and she was no
longer sad.
19The entire family got up early the next morning and went to worship the LORD once more. Then
they returned home to Ramah. When Elkanah
slept with Hannah, the LORD remembered her request, 20and in due time she gave birth to a son. She
named him Samuel,* for she said, "I asked the
LORD for him."
21The next year Elkanah, Peninnah, and their children went on their annual trip to offer a sacrifice to
the LORD. 22But Hannah did not go. She told her
husband, "Wait until the baby is weaned. Then I will
take him to the Tabernacle and leave him there with
the LORD permanently."*
23"Whatever you think is best," Elkanah agreed.
"Stay here for now, and may the LORD help you keep
your promise." So she stayed home and nursed the
baby.
24When the child was weaned, Hannah took
him to the Tabernacle in Shiloh. They brought
along a three-year-old bull* for the sacrifice and
half a bushel* of flour and some wine. 25After
sacrificing the bull, they took the child to Eli.
26"Sir, do you remember me?" Hannah asked. "I
am the woman who stood here several years ago
praying to the LORD. 27I asked the LORD to give me
this child, and he has given me my request. 28Now
I am giving him to the LORD, and he will belong to
the LORD his whole life." And they* worshiped the
LORD there.

CHAPTER **2** **HANNAH'S PRAYER OF PRAISE.** Then Hannah prayed:

"My heart rejoices in the LORD!
  Oh, how the LORD has blessed me!
Now I have an answer for my enemies,
  as I delight in your deliverance.
2 No one is holy like the LORD!
  There is no one besides you;
  there is no Rock like our God.

3 "Stop acting so proud and haughty!
  Don't speak with such arrogance!
The LORD is a God who knows your deeds;
  and he will judge you for what you have done.
4 Those who were mighty are mighty no more;
  and those who were weak are now strong.
5 Those who were well fed are now starving;
  and those who were starving are now full.
The barren woman now has seven children;
  but the woman with many children will have
    no more.

## DISCOURAGED ● ● • • •

1:18 **The change in Hannah's attitude may be attributed to three factors: (1) her honest prayer to God (1:11), (2) her resolve to leave the problem with God (1:18), and (3) the encouragement she received from Eli. This is the antidote for discouragement: tell God how you really feel and leave your problems with him.**

6 The LORD brings both death and life;
  he brings some down to the grave but raises
    others up.
7 The LORD makes one poor and another rich;
  he brings one down and lifts another up.
8 He lifts the poor from the dust—
  yes, from a pile of ashes!
He treats them like princes,
  placing them in seats of honor.
"For all the earth is the LORD's,
  and he has set the world in order.
9 He will protect his godly ones,
  but the wicked will perish in darkness.
No one will succeed by strength alone.
10 Those who fight against the LORD will be
    broken.
He thunders against them from heaven;
  the LORD judges throughout the earth.
He gives mighty strength to his king;
  he increases the might of his anointed one."

11Then Elkanah and Hannah returned home to
Ramah without Samuel. And the boy became the
LORD's helper, for he assisted Eli the priest.
12Now the sons of Eli were scoundrels who had no
respect for the LORD 13or for their duties as priests.
Whenever anyone offered a sacrifice, Eli's sons
would send over a servant with a three-pronged fork.
While the meat of the sacrificed animal was still
boiling, 14the servant would stick the fork into the
pot and demand that whatever it brought up be
given to Eli's sons. All the Israelites who came to
worship at Shiloh were treated this way. 15Sometimes
the servant would come even before the animal's fat
had been burned on the altar. He would demand raw
meat before it had been boiled so that it could be
used for roasting.
16The man offering the sacrifice might reply, "Take
as much as you want, but the fat must first be burned."
Then the servant would demand, "No, give it to me
now, or I'll take it by force." 17So the sin of these young

## HELP! ● ● • • •

2:2 **Hannah praised God for being a "rock"—firm, strong, and unchanging. In our fast-paced world, friends come and go and circumstances change. It's difficult to find a solid foundation that will not change. Those who devote their lives to people, causes, possessions, or other finite things are trusting things that will all pass away. But God is always present and ready to help, even when everything else seems to be falling apart.**

1:20 *Samuel* sounds like the Hebrew term for "asked of God" or "heard by God." 1:22 Some manuscripts add *I will offer him as a Nazirite for all time.* 1:24a As in Dead Sea Scrolls, Greek and Syriac versions; Masoretic Text reads *3 bulls.* 1:24b Hebrew *and an ephah* [18 liters]. 1:28 Or *he.*

## LISTENING ● ● • • •

**3:1-5 Although this was the era when God still gave direct and audible messages to his people, such messages became rare in the days of Eli. Why? Look at the attitude of Eli's sons. They either refused to listen to God or allowed greed to get in the way of any communication with him.**

**Listening and responding are vital in a relationship with God. Although God may not use the sound of a human voice, he speaks just as clearly today through his Word. To receive his messages, we must be ready to listen and to act upon what he tells us. Like Samuel, be ready to say "Yes, your servant is listening" (3:10) when God calls you to action.**

men was very serious in the LORD's sight, for they treated the LORD's offerings with contempt.

[18]Now Samuel, though only a boy, was the LORD's helper. He wore a linen tunic just like that of a priest.* [19]Each year his mother made a small coat for him and brought it to him when she came with her husband for the sacrifice. [20]Before they returned home, Eli would bless Elkanah and his wife and say, "May the LORD give you other children to take the place of this one she gave to the LORD.*" [21]And the LORD gave Hannah three sons and two daughters. Meanwhile, Samuel grew up in the presence of the LORD.

[22]Now Eli was very old, but he was aware of what his sons were doing to the people of Israel. He knew, for instance, that his sons were seducing the young women who assisted at the entrance of the Tabernacle.* [23]Eli said to them, "I have been hearing reports from the people about the wicked things you are doing. Why do you keep sinning? [24]You must stop, my sons! The reports I hear among the LORD's people are not good. [25]If someone sins against another person, God* can mediate for the guilty party. But if someone sins against the LORD, who can intercede?" But Eli's sons wouldn't listen to their father, for the LORD was already planning to put them to death.

[26]Meanwhile, as young Samuel grew taller, he also continued to gain favor with the LORD and with the people.

[27]One day a prophet came to Eli and gave him this message from the LORD: "Didn't I reveal myself to your ancestors when the people of Israel were slaves in Egypt? [28]I chose your ancestor Aaron* from among all his relatives to be my priest, to offer sacrifices on my altar, to burn incense, and to wear the priestly garments* as he served me. And I assigned the sacrificial offerings to you priests. [29]So why do you scorn my sacrifices and offerings? Why do you honor your sons more than me—for you and they have become fat from the best offerings of my people!

[30]"Therefore, the LORD, the God of Israel, says: The terrible things you are doing cannot continue! I had promised that your branch of the tribe of Levi* would always be my priests. But I will honor only those who honor me, and I will despise those who despise me. [31]I will put an end to your family, so it will no longer serve as my priests. All the members of your family will die before their time. None will live to a ripe old age. [32]You will watch with envy as I pour out prosperity on the people of Israel. But no members of your family will ever live out their days. [33]Those who are left alive will live in sadness and grief, and their children will die a violent death.* [34]And to prove that what I have said will come true, I will cause your two sons, Hophni and Phinehas, to die on the same day!

[35]"Then I will raise up a faithful priest who will serve me and do what I tell him to do. I will bless his descendants, and his family will be priests to my anointed kings forever. [36]Then all of your descendants will bow before his descendants, begging for money and food. 'Please,' they will say, 'give us jobs among the priests so we will have enough to eat.'"

CHAPTER **3** **GOD SPEAKS TO SAMUEL.** Meanwhile, the boy Samuel was serving the LORD by assisting Eli. Now in those days messages from the LORD were very rare, and visions were quite uncommon.

[2]One night Eli, who was almost blind by now, had just gone to bed. [3]The lamp of God had not yet gone out, and Samuel was sleeping in the Tabernacle* near the Ark of God. [4]Suddenly, the LORD called out, "Samuel! Samuel!"

"Yes?" Samuel replied. "What is it?" [5]He jumped up and ran to Eli. "Here I am. What do you need?"

"I didn't call you," Eli replied. "Go on back to bed." So he did.

[6]Then the LORD called out again, "Samuel!"

Again Samuel jumped up and ran to Eli. "Here I am," he said. "What do you need?"

"I didn't call you, my son," Eli said. "Go on back to bed."

[7]Samuel did not yet know the LORD because he had never had a message from the LORD before. [8]So now the LORD called a third time, and once more Samuel jumped up and ran to Eli. "Here I am," he said. "What do you need?"

Then Eli realized it was the LORD who was calling the boy. [9]So he said to Samuel, "Go and lie down

## NEW AND FRESH ● ● • • •

**4:5-8 The Philistines were frightened by stories of how God intervened for Israel when they left Egypt. But Israel had turned away from God and now clung only to a form of godliness.**

**People, churches, and organizations often try to live on the memories of God's blessings. Israel wrongly assumed that because God had given them victory in the past he would do it again, even though they had strayed far from him. Today, spiritual victories come by continually renewing our relationship with God. Don't live off the past. Keep your relationship with God new and fresh.**

2:18 Hebrew *He wore a linen ephod.* 2:20 As in Greek version; Hebrew reads *this one she requested of the LORD in prayer.* 2:22 Hebrew *Tent of Meeting.* Some manuscripts lack this entire sentence. 2:25 Or *the judges.* 2:28a Hebrew *your father.* 2:28b Hebrew *an ephod.* 2:30 Hebrew *that your house and your father's house.* 2:33 As in Dead Sea Scrolls, which read *die by the sword;* Masoretic Text reads *die like mortals.* 3:3 Hebrew *the Temple of the LORD.*

again, and if someone calls again, say, 'Yes, LORD, your
servant is listening.'" So Samuel went back to bed.
[10]And the LORD came and called as before, "Samuel! Samuel!"
And Samuel replied, "Yes, your servant is listening."
[11]Then the LORD said to Samuel, "I am about to do
a shocking thing in Israel. [12]I am going to carry out
all my threats against Eli and his family. [13]I have
warned him continually that judgment is coming for
his family, because his sons are blaspheming God*
and he hasn't disciplined them. [14]So I have vowed
that the sins of Eli and his sons will never be forgiven
by sacrifices or offerings."
[15]Samuel stayed in bed until morning, then got up
and opened the doors of the Tabernacle* as usual.
He was afraid to tell Eli what the LORD had said to
him. [16]But Eli called out to
him, "Samuel, my son."
"Here I am," Samuel re-
plied.
[17]"What did the LORD say
to you? Tell me everything.
And may God punish you if
you hide anything from me!"
[18]So Samuel told Eli everything; he didn't hold anything back. "It is the LORD's
will," Eli replied. "Let him do
what he thinks best."
[19]As Samuel grew up, the
LORD was with him, and
everything Samuel said was
wise and helpful. [20]All the
people of Israel from one
end of the land to the other
knew that Samuel was con-
firmed as a prophet of the
LORD. [21]The LORD continued
to appear at Shiloh and gave
messages to Samuel there at
the Tabernacle. [1]And Samuel's words went out to all
the people of Israel.

## CHAPTER 4 **THE ARK IS STOLEN.**

At that time Israel
was at war with the Philistines. The Israelite army was
camped near Ebenezer, and
the Philistines were at Aphek.
[2]The Philistines attacked and
defeated the army of Israel,
killing four thousand men.
[3]After the battle was over, the
army of Israel retreated to
their camp, and their leaders
asked, "Why did the LORD allow us to be defeated by the
Philistines?" Then they said, "Let's bring the Ark of the
Covenant of the LORD from Shiloh. If we carry it into
battle with us, it* will save us from our enemies."
[4]So they sent men to Shiloh to bring back the Ark
of the Covenant of the LORD Almighty, who is enthroned between the cherubim. Hophni and Phinehas, the sons of Eli, helped carry the Ark of God to
where the battle was being fought. [5]When the Israelites saw the Ark of the Covenant of the LORD coming
into the camp, their shout of joy was so loud that it
made the ground shake!
[6]"What's going on?" the Philistines asked.
"What's all the shouting about in the Hebrew
camp?" When they were told it was because the Ark
of the LORD had arrived, [7]they panicked. "The gods
have* come into their camp!" they cried. "This is a
disaster! We have never had to face anything like this

## SAMUEL

We often wonder about the childhood of great people. We have little information about the early years of most of the people mentioned in the Bible. One delightful exception is Samuel, who was born as a result of God's answer to Hannah's prayer for a child. (In fact, the name "Samuel" comes from the Hebrew expression, "asked of God.") God had plans for Samuel from the start. He used Samuel in many different and important ways. The reason God was able to use Samuel so much is because Samuel was willing to be one thing—God's servant. What would it take for God to use our lives as much?

Samuel's life teaches us that those who are faithful to God in small things will be trusted with greater things. Little jobs like helping the high priest may not have seemed very important, but God was using those jobs to train Samuel for bigger responsibilities. We can't tell what parts of today are preparations for tomorrow. But God knows!

Samuel moved ahead because he was listening to God's directions. Too often we ask God to control our life without being willing to give up the goals we've chosen. We ask God to help us get where *we* want to go. The first step in correcting this tendency is to turn over both the control and destination of our life to him. The second step is to be obedient to what we already know God wants us to do. The third step is to watch for further direction from his Word—God's map for life.

**UPS:**
- Used by God to assist Israel's transition from a loosely governed tribal people to a monarchy
- Anointed the first two kings of Israel
- The last and most effective of Israel's judges
- Listed in the Hall of Faith in Hebrews 11

**DOWNS:**
- Unable to instill in his sons the same relationship he had with God

**STATS:**
- Where: Ephraim
- Occupation: Judge, prophet, priest
- Relatives: Mother: Hannah. Father: Elkanah. Sons: Joel and Abijah.
- Contemporaries: Eli, Saul, David

LESSONS: The significance of what people accomplish in life is directly related to their relationship with God

The kind of person we are is more important than anything we might do

KEY VERSES: "As Samuel grew up, the LORD was with him, and everything Samuel said was wise and helpful. All the people of Israel from one end of the land to the other knew that Samuel was confirmed as a prophet of the LORD" (1 Samuel 3:19-20).

His story is told in 1 Samuel 1–28. He is also mentioned in Psalm 99:6; Jeremiah 15:1; Acts 3:24; 13:20; Hebrews 11:32.

3:13 As in Greek version; Hebrew reads *his sons have made themselves contemptible.* 3:15 Hebrew *the house of the LORD.* 4:3 Or *he.* 4:7 Or *A god has.*

before! [8]Who can save us from these mighty gods of Israel? They are the same gods who destroyed the Egyptians with plagues when Israel was in the wilderness. [9]Fight as you never have before, Philistines! If you don't, we will become the Hebrews' slaves just as they have been ours!"

[10]So the Philistines fought desperately, and Israel was defeated again. The slaughter was great; thirty thousand Israelite men died that day. The survivors turned and fled to their tents. [11]The Ark of God was captured, and Hophni and Phinehas, the two sons of Eli, were killed.

[12]A man from the tribe of Benjamin ran from the battlefront and arrived at Shiloh later that same day. He had torn his clothes and put dust on his head to show his grief. [13]Eli was waiting beside the road to hear the news of the battle, for his heart trembled for the safety of the Ark of God. When the messenger arrived and told what had happened, an outcry resounded throughout the town. [14]"What is all the noise about?" Eli asked.

The messenger rushed over to Eli, [15]who was ninety-eight years old and blind. [16]He said to Eli, "I have just come from the battlefront—I was there this very day."

"What happened?" Eli demanded.

[17]"Israel has been defeated," the messenger replied. "Thousands of Israelite troops are dead on the battlefield. Your two sons, Hophni and Phinehas, were killed, too. And the Ark of God has been captured."

[18]When the messenger mentioned what had happened to the Ark, Eli fell backward from his seat beside the gate. He broke his neck and died, for he was old and very fat. He had led Israel for forty years.

[19]Eli's daughter-in-law, the wife of Phinehas, was pregnant and near her time of delivery. When she heard that the Ark of God had been captured and that her husband and father-in-law were dead, her labor pains suddenly began. [20]She died in childbirth, but before she passed away the midwives tried to encourage her. "Don't be afraid," they said. "You have a baby boy!" But she did not answer or respond in any way.

[21]She named the child Ichabod—"Where is the glory?"—murmuring, "Israel's glory is gone." She named him this because the Ark of God had been captured and because her husband and her father-in-law were dead. [22]Then she said, "The glory has departed from Israel, for the Ark of God has been captured."

CHAPTER **5** **PHILISTINES ARE PUNISHED.** After the Philistines captured the Ark of God, they took it from the battleground at Ebenezer to the city of Ashdod. [2]They carried the Ark of God into the temple of Dagon and placed it beside the idol of Dagon. [3]But when the citizens of Ashdod went to see it the next morning, Dagon had fallen with his face to the ground in front of the Ark of the LORD! So they set the idol up again. [4]But the next morning the same thing happened—the idol had fallen face down before the Ark of the LORD again. This time his head and hands had broken off and were lying in the doorway. Only the trunk of his body was left intact. [5]That is why to this day neither the priests of Dagon nor anyone who enters the temple of Dagon will step on its threshold.

[6]Then the LORD began to afflict the people of Ashdod and the nearby villages with a plague of tumors.* [7]When the people realized what was happening, they cried out, "We can't keep the Ark of the God of Israel here any longer! He is against us! We will all be destroyed along with our god Dagon." [8]So they called together the rulers of the five Philistine cities and asked, "What should we do with the Ark of the God of Israel?"

### PAIN ● ● • • •

5:6-7 **Although the Philistines had just witnessed a great victory by Israel's God over their idol, Dagon, they didn't act upon that insight until they were personally afflicted with tumors (probably boils). Similarly, many people don't respond to biblical truth until they experience personal pain and suddenly feel they have no place else to turn. Are you willing to listen to God for truth's sake, or do you turn to him only when you are afflicted?**

The rulers discussed it and replied, "Move it to the city of Gath." So they moved the Ark of the God of Israel to Gath. [9]But when the Ark arrived at Gath, the LORD began afflicting its people, young and old, with a plague of tumors, and there was a great panic.

[10]So they sent the Ark of God to the city of Ekron, but when the people of Ekron saw it coming they cried out, "They are bringing the Ark of the God of Israel here to kill us, too!" [11]So the people summoned the rulers again and begged them, "Please send the Ark of the God of Israel back to its own country, or it* will kill us all." For the plague from God had already begun, and great fear was sweeping across the city. [12]Those who didn't die were afflicted with tumors; and there was weeping everywhere.

CHAPTER **6** **THE ARK COMES BACK.** The Ark of the LORD remained in Philistine territory seven months in all. [2]Then the Philistines called in their priests and diviners and asked them, "What should we do about the Ark of the LORD? Tell us how to return it to its own land."

[3]"Send the Ark of the God of Israel back, along with a gift," they were told. "Send a guilt offering so the plague will stop. Then, if the plague doesn't stop, you will know that God didn't send the plague after all."

[4]"What sort of guilt offering should we send?" they asked.

And they were told, "Since the plague has struck both you and your five rulers, make five gold tumors

5:6 Greek version and Latin Vulgate read *tumors. And rats appeared in their land, and death and destruction were throughout the city.* 5:11 Or *he.*

and five gold rats, just like those that have ravaged your land. 5 Make these things to show honor to the God of Israel. Perhaps then he will stop afflicting you, your gods, and your land. 6 Don't be stubborn and rebellious as Pharaoh and the Egyptians were. They wouldn't let Israel go until God had ravaged them with dreadful plagues. 7 Now build a new cart, and find two cows that have just had calves. Make sure the cows have never been yoked to a cart. Hitch the cows to the cart, but shut their calves away from them in a pen. 8 Put the Ark of the LORD on the cart, and beside it place a chest containing the gold rats and gold tumors. Then let the cows go wherever they want. 9 If they cross the border of our land and go to Beth-shemesh, we will know it was the LORD who brought this great disaster upon us. If they don't, we will know that the plague was simply a coincidence and was not sent by the LORD at all."

10 So these instructions were carried out. Two cows with newborn calves were hitched to the cart, and their calves were shut up in a pen. 11 Then the Ark of the LORD and the chest containing the gold rats and gold tumors were placed on the cart. 12 And sure enough, the cows went straight along the road toward Beth-shemesh, lowing as they went. The Philistine rulers followed them as far as the border of Beth-shemesh.

13 The people of Beth-shemesh were harvesting wheat in the valley, and when they saw the Ark, they were overjoyed! 14 The cart came into the field of a man named Joshua and stopped beside a large rock. So the people broke up the wood of the cart for a fire and killed the cows and sacrificed them to the LORD as a burnt offering. 15 Several men of the tribe of Levi lifted the Ark of the LORD and the chest containing the gold rats and gold tumors from the cart and placed them on the large rock. Many burnt offerings and sacrifices were offered to the LORD that day by the people of Beth-shemesh. 16 The five Philistine rulers watched all this and then returned to Ekron that same day.

17 The five gold tumors that were sent by the Philistines as a guilt offering to the LORD were gifts from the rulers of Ashdod, Gaza, Ashkelon, Gath, and Ekron. 18 The five gold rats represented the five Philistine cities and their surrounding villages, which were controlled by the five rulers. The large rock at Beth-shemesh, where they set the Ark of the LORD, still stands in the field of Joshua as a reminder of what happened there.

19 But the LORD killed seventy men* from Beth-shemesh because they looked into the Ark of the LORD. And the people mourned greatly because of what the LORD had done. 20 "Who is able to stand in the presence of the LORD, this holy God?" they cried out. "Where can we send the Ark from here?" 21 So they sent messengers to the people at Kiriath-jearim and told them, "The Philistines have returned the Ark of the LORD. Please come here and get it!"

## INGREDIENT ● ● • • •

**6:9 The Philistines acknowledged the existence of the Hebrew God, but only as one of many "gods" whose favor they sought. Thinking of God in this way made it easy for them to ignore God's demand that people worship him alone. Many people "worship" God this way. They see him as just one ingredient in a successful life. But God is not an ingredient—he is the source of life itself. Are you a "Philistine," seeing God's favor as just one ingredient in the good life?**

## CHAPTER 7

**GOD SENDS THUNDER.** So the men of Kiriath-jearim came to get the Ark of the LORD. They took it to the hillside home of Abinadab and ordained Eleazar, his son, to be in charge of it. 2 The Ark remained in Kiriath-jearim for a long time—twenty years in all. During that time, all Israel mourned because it seemed that the LORD had abandoned them.

3 Then Samuel said to all the people of Israel, "If you are really serious about wanting to return to the LORD, get rid of your foreign gods and your images of Ashtoreth. Determine to obey only the LORD; then he will rescue you from the Philistines." 4 So the Israelites destroyed their images of Baal and Ashtoreth and worshiped only the LORD.

5 Then Samuel told them, "Come to Mizpah, all of you. I will pray to the LORD for you." 6 So they gathered there and, in a great ceremony, drew water from a well and poured it out before the LORD. They also went without food all day and confessed that they had sinned against the LORD. So it was at Mizpah that Samuel became Israel's judge.

7 When the Philistine rulers heard that all Israel had gathered at Mizpah, they mobilized their army and advanced. The Israelites were badly frightened when they learned that the Philistines were approaching. 8 "Plead with the LORD our God to save us from the Philistines!" they begged Samuel. 9 So Samuel took a young lamb and offered it to the LORD as a whole burnt offering. He pleaded with the LORD to help Israel, and the LORD answered.

10 Just as Samuel was sacrificing the burnt

## ON THE SHELF ● ● • • •

**7:2-3 Sorrow gripped Israel for 20 years. The Ark was put away like an unwanted box in an attic, and it seemed as if the Lord had abandoned his people. Samuel, now a grown man, roused them to action by saying that if they were truly sorry, they should do something about it. How easy it is for us to complain about our problems, even to God, while we refuse to act, to change, and to do what he requires. We don't even take the advice he has already given us. Do you ever feel as if God has abandoned you? Check to see if there is anything he has already told you to do. You may not be able to receive new guidance until you have acted on his previous directions.**

6:19 As in a few Hebrew manuscripts; most Hebrew manuscripts and Greek version read *50,070 men.* Perhaps the text should be understood to read *the LORD killed 70 men and 50 oxen.*

# Ultimate Issues

## WORSHIP

Imagine a married couple arguing over how seldom he expresses his affections for her. "You never tell me you love me," she complains. "I said I loved you when we got married," he replies. "Until I say otherwise, assume that's still true." Few wives would be satisfied by this husband's answer. ***People in love*** want and need to be told—more than once—that they are loved. God is like that, too. He's not insecure, but like any good father, he likes to hear his children express their love directly to him. This is the essence of what we call *worship.* Israel had a lengthy list of instructions concerning the Sabbath (see Exodus 35). A lot of those instructions sound strange to us—lampstands, altars, sacrifices, priestly garments, etc. But we can draw principles from these instructions to help us worship the God who is the same yesterday, today, and forever. Here are some of these principles, listed according to the *who, what, when, where,* and *why* of worship. **Who:** Easy, right? We worship *God.* But many churches tend to shift the focus of worship from God to human beings. We don't necessarily "worship" ourselves, but too often we **ZERO IN** on *what God does for us.* It's OK to praise God for his goodness. But there's a danger in thinking of God primarily in terms of how he can bless us, protect us, make us happy, etc. If we're not careful, we'll start to think that he exists for our benefit, not the other way around. Remember: we worship God, *not* what he does for us. **What:** Worship is giving God the glory and obedience he deserves. In a sense, all of life should be "worship"—obedience given out of love and respect to our great God. But there is also the need for specified times of focused attention to praise, prayer, the teaching of God's Word, etc. Our "whole-life" worship is like a shotgun—unfocused. Special times of worship, especially on Sundays, are LIKE A LASER—much more intense and specific. **When:** While any time is acceptable to honor God with praise and adoration, the Scriptures teach us to set aside certain regular times to gather for worship. The early church began to meet on the first day of the week, as opposed to the Jewish custom of meeting on the last. Churches today often meet Sunday mornings, Sunday nights, and Wednesday nights. It is important that we meet together regularly (Hebrews 10:23-25). **Where:** There are almost as many different places where Christians worship as there are Christians: church buildings, houses, schools, stores, shelters, tents, prisons, hospitals, ships, and on and on. The first Christians often gathered in SECRET PLACES, like caves and catacombs. Jesus clearly taught it's not the place that's important, but the person (John 4:1-42). You can worship God anywhere. **Why:** The *why* of worship is simple and twofold: First, we worship because God wants us to. This brings out an extremely vital truth that is too often misunderstood. Worship is not primarily for us; it's for God. The important thing is not whether *we* enjoyed the sermon, music, etc. It's whether or not *God* is pleased with our offering of ourselves to him. **S**econd, we worship because we need to. When we bow before God and acknowledge his greatness, majesty, patience, and love toward us, he is pleased, and we are placed in the proper relationship to him. When we worship, we are reminded that he is God, and we are not; and that "we are his people, the sheep of his pasture" (Psalm 100:3). **T**here is much more to say about worship, such as the elements of worship: music, preaching, prayer, communion, etc. Those issues are beyond our scope here. The crucial point is that we worship. **Our Father is waiting to hear from us.**

**S**ee Exodus 35 for more about worship.

offering, the Philistines arrived for battle. But the LORD spoke with a mighty voice of thunder from heaven, and the Philistines were thrown into such confusion that the Israelites defeated them. 11The men of Israel chased them from Mizpah to Beth-car, slaughtering them all along the way.

12Samuel then took a large stone and placed it between the towns of Mizpah and Jeshanah.* He named it Ebenezer—"the stone of help"—for he said, "Up to this point the LORD has helped us!" 13So the Philistines were subdued and didn't invade Israel again for a long time. And throughout Samuel's lifetime, the LORD's powerful hand was raised against the Philistines. 14The Israelite towns near Ekron and Gath that the Philistines had captured were restored to Israel, along with the rest of the territory that the Philistines had taken. And there was also peace between Israel and the Amorites in those days.

15Samuel continued as Israel's judge for the rest of his life. 16Each year he traveled around, setting up his court first at Bethel, then at Gilgal, and then at Mizpah. He judged the people of Israel at each of these places. 17Then he would return to his home at Ramah, and he would hear cases there, too. And Samuel built an altar to the LORD at Ramah.

CHAPTER **8** **ISRAEL DEMANDS A KING.** As Samuel grew old, he appointed his sons to be judges over Israel. 2Joel and Abijah, his oldest sons, held court in Beersheba. 3But they were not like their father, for they were greedy for money. They accepted bribes and perverted justice.

4Finally, the leaders of Israel met at Ramah to discuss the matter with Samuel. 5"Look," they told him, "you are now old, and your sons are not like you. Give us a king like all the other nations have."

6Samuel was very upset with their request and went to the LORD for advice. 7"Do as they say," the LORD replied, "for it is me they are rejecting, not you. They don't want me to be their king any longer. 8Ever since I brought them from Egypt they have continually forsaken me and followed other gods. And now they are giving you the same treatment. 9Do as they ask, but solemnly warn them about how a king will treat them."

10So Samuel passed on the LORD's warning to the people. 11"This is how a king will treat you," Samuel said. "The king will draft your sons into his army and make them run before his chariots. 12Some will be commanders of his troops, while others will be slave laborers. Some will be forced to plow in his fields and harvest his crops, while others will make his weapons and chariot equipment. 13The king will take your daughters from you and force them to cook and bake and make perfumes for him. 14He will take away the best of your fields and vineyards and olive groves and give them to his own servants. 15He will take a tenth of your harvest and distribute it among his officers and attendants. 16He will want your male and female slaves and demand the finest of your cattle* and donkeys for his own use. 17He will demand a tenth of your flocks, and you will be his slaves. 18When that day comes, you will beg for relief from this king you are demanding, but the LORD will not help you."

19But the people refused to listen to Samuel's warning. "Even so, we still want a king," they said. 20"We want to be like the nations around us. Our king will govern us and lead us into battle."

21So Samuel told the LORD what the people had said, 22and the LORD replied, "Do as they say, and give them a king." Then Samuel agreed and sent the people home.

---

**So many things try to crowd God out of my life. How much of me does God want?**

He wants all of you. God does not want to be just another addition to your life—he wants everything you do to revolve around him!

Bike tires are only as strong as the hub of the wheel. If a tire was made up only of rim and spokes, the wheel would soon collapse under the constant pounding and pressure.

The spokes in our life are those things that are important to us: family, friends, school, sports, entertainment, etc. If our life revolves around any one of these "spokes," eventually the constant pounding and pressures of our world will wear us down and possibly cause us to collapse!

God knows this and has provided the strong center that will hold us together. By ignoring God and trying to run our own life, we will be living as though we believe the spokes are strong enough to carry us.

For centuries the Jewish people complained to God and asked him for a king to rule over them. What they were actually saying was, "God, since we can't see you, we can't trust you to take care of us. Give us someone we can see who will rule over us." Eventually God gave in to their request. (See 1 Samuel 8:7.) The results, however, were devastating. Because they put their focus on what a person could do for them (a weak "spoke"!), their enemies soon overpowered the entire nation until all of the people of Israel were forced to live away from the Promised Land.

The Old Testament graphically describes what happened when God's people rejected him as their leader (the hub).

Jesus Christ should be the hub of our life. This means that we should consult him and his Word first.

When things begin to crowd out your relationship with God, try writing down all of your priorities. Ask a trusted Christian friend if he or she thinks any one of these "spokes" is taking the place of God in your life.

---

**7:12** As in Greek version; Hebrew reads *Shen.* **8:16** As in Greek version; Hebrew reads *young men.*

CHAPTER **9** **SAUL BECOMES KING.** Kish was a rich, influential man from the tribe of Benjamin. He was the son of Abiel and grandson of Zeror, from the family of Becorath and the clan of Aphiah. 2His son Saul was the most handsome man in Israel—head and shoulders taller than anyone else in the land.

3One day Kish's donkeys strayed away, and he told Saul, "Take a servant with you, and go look for them." 4So Saul took one of his servants and traveled all through the hill country of Ephraim, the land of Shalishah, the Shaalim area, and the entire land of Benjamin, but they couldn't find the donkeys anywhere. 5Finally, they entered the region of Zuph, and Saul said to his servant, "Let's go home. By now my father will be more worried about us than about the donkeys!"

## BY DESIGN ● ● • • •

9:3-10:16 **Often we think that events just happen to us, but as we learn from this story about Saul, God often uses common occurrences to lead us where he wants. It is important to evaluate all situations as potential "divine appointments" designed to shape our life. Think of all the good and bad circumstances that have affected you lately. Can you see God's purpose in them? Perhaps he is building a certain quality in your life or leading you to serve him in a new area.**

6But the servant said, "I've just thought of something! There is a man of God who lives here in this town. He is held in high honor by all the people because everything he says comes true. Let's go find him. Perhaps he can tell us which way to go."

7"But we don't have anything to offer him," Saul replied. "Even our food is gone, and we don't have a thing to give him."

8"Well," the servant said, "I have one small silver piece.* We can at least offer it to him and see what happens!" 9(In those days if people wanted a message from God, they would say, "Let's go and ask the seer," for prophets used to be called seers.)

10"All right," Saul agreed, "let's try it!" So they started into the town where the man of God was.

11As they were climbing a hill toward the town, they met some young women coming out to draw water. So Saul and his servant asked, "Is the seer here today?"

12"Yes," they replied. "Stay right on this road. He is at the town gates. He has just arrived to take part in a public sacrifice up on the hill. 13Hurry and catch him before he goes up the hill to eat. The guests won't start until he arrives to bless the food."

14So they entered the town, and as they passed through the gates, Samuel was coming out toward them to climb the hill. 15Now the LORD had told Samuel the previous day, 16"About this time tomorrow I will send you a man from the land of Benjamin. Anoint him to be the leader of my people, Israel. He will rescue them from the Philistines, for I

## HIDING ● ● • • •

10:22 **When the king was to be chosen, Saul already knew that he was the one (10:1). Instead of coming forward, however, he hid. Often we hide from important responsibilities because we are afraid of failure, afraid of what others will think, or perhaps unsure about how to proceed. Don't run from your responsibilities.**

have looked down on my people in mercy and have heard their cry."

17When Samuel noticed Saul, the LORD said, "That's the man I told you about! He will rule my people."

18Just then Saul approached Samuel at the gateway and asked, "Can you please tell me where the seer's house is?"

19"I am the seer!" Samuel replied. "Go on up the hill ahead of me to the place of sacrifice, and we'll eat there together. In the morning I will tell you what you want to know and send you on your way. 20And don't worry about those donkeys that were lost three days ago, for they have been found. And I am here to tell you that you and your family are the focus of all Israel's hopes."

21Saul replied, "But I'm only from Benjamin, the smallest tribe in Israel, and my family is the least important of all the families of that tribe! Why are you talking like this to me?"

22Then Samuel brought Saul and his servant into the great hall and placed them at the head of the table, honoring them above the thirty special guests. 23Samuel then instructed the cook to bring Saul the finest cut of meat, the piece that had been set aside for the guest of honor. 24So the cook brought it in and placed it before Saul. "Go ahead and eat it," Samuel said. "I was saving it for you even before I invited these others!" So Saul ate with Samuel.

25After the feast, when they had returned to the town, Samuel took Saul up to the roof of the house and prepared a bed for him there.* 26At daybreak the next morning, Samuel called up to Saul, "Get up! It's time you were on your way." So Saul got ready, and he and Samuel left the house together. 27When they reached the edge of town, Samuel told Saul to send his servant on ahead. After the servant was gone, Samuel said, "Stay here, for I have received a special message for you from God."

CHAPTER **10** Then Samuel took a flask of olive oil and poured it over Saul's head. He kissed Saul on the cheek and said, "I am doing this because the LORD has appointed you to be the leader of his people Israel.* 2When you leave me today, you will see two men beside Rachel's tomb at Zelzah, on the border of Benjamin. They will tell you that the donkeys have been found and that your father is worried about you and is asking, 'Have you seen my son?'

3"When you get to the oak of Tabor, you will see three men coming toward you who are on their way to worship God at Bethel. One will be bringing three young goats, another will have three loaves of bread,

9:8 Hebrew 1/4 *shekel of silver,* about 0.1 ounces or 3 grams in weight. 9:25 As in Greek version; Hebrew reads *and talked with him there.* 10:1 Greek version reads *Israel. And you will rule over the LORD's people and save them from their enemies around them. This will be the sign to you that the LORD has appointed you to be leader over his inheritance.*

and the third will be carrying a skin of wine. [4]They
will greet you and offer you two of the loaves, which
you are to accept.
[5]"When you arrive at Gibeah of God,* where the
garrison of the Philistines is located, you will meet a
band of prophets coming down from the altar on the
hill. They will be playing a harp, a tambourine, a flute,
and a lyre, and they will be prophesying. [6]At that time
the Spirit of the LORD will come upon you with power,
and you will prophesy with them. You will be changed
into a different person. [7]After these signs take place, do
whatever you think is best, for God will be with you.
[8]Then go down to Gilgal ahead of me and wait for me
there seven days. I will join you there to sacrifice burnt
offerings and peace offerings.
When I arrive, I will give you
further instructions."
[9]As Saul turned and started
to leave, God changed his
heart, and all Samuel's signs
were fulfilled that day.
[10]When Saul and his servant
arrived at Gibeah, they saw
the prophets coming toward
them. Then the Spirit of God
came upon Saul, and he, too,
began to prophesy. [11]When
his friends heard about it,
they exclaimed, "What? Is
Saul a prophet? How did the
son of Kish become a
prophet?" [12]But one of the
neighbors responded, "It
doesn't matter who his father
is; anyone can become a
prophet."* So that is the origin of the saying "Is Saul a
prophet?"
[13]When Saul had finished
prophesying, he climbed the
hill to the altar. [14]"Where in
the world have you been?"
Saul's uncle asked him.
"We went to look for the
donkeys," Saul replied, "but
we couldn't find them. So we
went to the prophet Samuel
to ask him where they were."
[15]"Oh? And what did he
say?" his uncle asked.
[16]"He said the donkeys
had been found," Saul re-
plied. But Saul didn't tell his
uncle that Samuel had
anointed him to be king.
[17]Later Samuel called all
the people of Israel to meet
before the LORD at Mizpah.
[18]And he gave them this message from the LORD, the God
of Israel: "I brought you from Egypt and rescued you
from the Egyptians and from all of the nations that
were oppressing you. [19]But though I have done so
much for you, you have rejected me and said, 'We want
a king instead!' Now, therefore, present yourselves
before the LORD by tribes and clans."
[20]So Samuel called the tribal leaders together before the LORD, and the tribe of Benjamin was chosen.* [21]Then he brought each family of the tribe of
Benjamin before the LORD, and the family of the
Matrites was chosen. And finally Saul son of Kish
was chosen from among them. But when they
looked for him, he had disappeared! [22]So they asked
the LORD, "Where is he?"

**SAUL** First impressions don't always turn out to be right. Sometimes a person who has a great image looks very different when we discover his or her abilities or qualities. Saul was one of those people. He looked like a king, but he lacked the traits that would have helped him be a good one. He often forgot or disobeyed God's directions. He was God's chosen leader, but God's choice did not mean that Saul was capable of being king on his own. He needed God's help. We do, too.

During his reign, Saul had his greatest successes when he obeyed God. His greatest failures resulted from acting on his own. Saul had the raw materials to be a good leader— appearance, courage, and action. Even his weaknesses could have been used by God if Saul had recognized them and left them in God's control. His own choices cut him off from God and eventually alienated him from his own people.

From Saul we learn that while our strengths and abilities make us useful, it is our weaknesses that make us usable. Our skills and talents make us tools, but our failures and shortcomings remind us that we need a craftsman in control of our life. Whatever we accomplish on our own is only a hint of what God could do through our life. Does he control your life?

LESSONS: God wants obedience from the heart, not mere acts of religious ritual

Obedience always involves sacrifice, but sacrifice is not always obedience

God wants to make use of our strengths and weaknesses

Our weaknesses should help us remember our need for God's guidance and help

KEY VERSES: "But Samuel replied, 'What is more pleasing to the LORD: your burnt offerings and sacrifices or your obedience to his voice? Obedience is far better than sacrifice. Listening to him is much better than offering the fat of rams. Rebellion is as bad as the sin of witchcraft, and stubbornness is as bad as worshiping idols. So because you have rejected the word of the LORD, he has rejected you from being king'" (1 Samuel 15:22-23).

His story is told in 1 Samuel 9–31. He is also mentioned in Acts 13:21.

**UPS:**
- First God-appointed king of Israel
- Known for his personal courage and generosity
- Stood tall, with a striking appearance

**DOWNS:**
- Leadership abilities did not match the expectations created by his appearance
- Impulsive by nature, he tended to overstep his bounds
- Jealous of David, he tried to kill him
- Deliberately disobeyed God on several occasions

**STATS:**
- Where: The land of Benjamin
- Occupation: King of Israel
- Relatives: Father: Kish. Sons: Jonathan, Ishbosheth, Abinadab, and Malchishua. Wife: Ahinoam. Daughters: Merab and Michal.

10:5 Hebrew *Gibeath-elohim.* 10:12 Hebrew *responded, "Who is their father?"* 10:20 Hebrew *chosen by lot;* also in 10:21.

And the LORD replied, "He is hiding among the baggage." [23]So they found him and brought him out, and he stood head and shoulders above anyone else.

[24]Then Samuel said to all the people, "This is the man the LORD has chosen as your king. No one in all Israel is his equal!"

And all the people shouted, "Long live the king!"

[25]Then Samuel told the people what the rights and duties of a king were. He wrote them down on a scroll and placed it before the LORD. Then Samuel sent the people home again.

[26]When Saul returned to his home at Gibeah, a band of men whose hearts God had touched became his constant companions. [27]But there were some wicked men who complained, "How can this man save us?" And they despised him and refused to bring him gifts. But Saul ignored them.*

## CHAPTER 11

**A SURPRISE ATTACK.** About a month later,* King Nahash of Ammon led his army against the Israelite city of Jabesh-gilead. But the citizens of Jabesh asked for peace. "Make a treaty with us, and we will be your servants," they pleaded.

[2]"All right," Nahash said, "but only on one condition. I will gouge out the right eye of every one of you as a disgrace to all Israel!"

[3]"Give us seven days to send messengers throughout Israel!" replied the leaders of Jabesh. "If none of our relatives will come to save us, we will agree to your terms."

[4]When the messengers came to Gibeah, Saul's hometown, and told the people about their plight, everyone broke into tears. [5]Saul was plowing in the field, and when he returned to town, he asked, "What's the matter? Why is everyone crying?" So they told him about the message from Jabesh.

### ANGER ● • • • •

**11:6 Anger is a powerful emotion. Often it is used wrongly to hurt others with words or physical violence. But anger directed at sin and the mistreatment of others is not wrong. Saul was angered by the Ammonites' threat to humiliate and mistreat his fellow Israelites. God used Saul's anger to bring justice and freedom. When injustice or sin makes you angry, ask God how you can channel that anger in constructive ways to help bring about a positive change.**

[6]Then the Spirit of God came mightily upon Saul, and he became very angry. [7]He took two oxen and cut them into pieces and sent the messengers to carry them throughout Israel with this message: "This is what will happen to the oxen of anyone who refuses to follow Saul and Samuel into battle!" And the LORD made the people afraid of Saul's anger, and all of them came out together as one. [8]When Saul mobilized them at Bezek, he found that there were 300,000 men of Israel, in addition to 30,000* from Judah.

[9]So Saul sent the messengers back to Jabesh-gilead to say, "We will rescue you by noontime tomorrow!" What joy there was throughout the city when that message arrived!

[10]The men of Jabesh then told their enemies, "Tomorrow we will come out to you, and you can do to us as you wish." [11]But before dawn the next morning, Saul arrived, having divided his army into three detachments. He launched a surprise attack against the Ammonites and slaughtered them the whole morning. The remnant of their army was so badly scattered that no two of them were left together.

[12]Then the people exclaimed to Samuel, "Now where are those men who said Saul shouldn't rule over us? Bring them here, and we will kill them!"

[13]But Saul replied, "No one will be executed today, for today the LORD has rescued Israel!"

[14]Then Samuel said to the people, "Come, let us all go to Gilgal to reaffirm Saul's kingship." [15]So they went to Gilgal, and in a solemn ceremony before the LORD they crowned him king. Then they offered peace offerings to the LORD, and Saul and all the Israelites were very happy.

## CHAPTER 12

**SAMUEL'S FAREWELL ADDRESS.** Then Samuel addressed the people again: "I have done as you asked and given you a king. [2]I have selected him ahead of my own sons, and I stand here, an old, gray-haired man. I have served as your leader since I was a boy. [3]Now tell me as I stand before the LORD and before his anointed one—whose ox or donkey have I stolen? Have I ever cheated any of you? Have I ever oppressed you? Have I ever taken a bribe? Tell me and I will make right whatever I have done wrong."

[4]"No," they replied, "you have never cheated or oppressed us in any way, and you have never taken even a single bribe."

[5]"The LORD and his anointed one are my witnesses," Samuel declared, "that you can never accuse me of robbing you."

"Yes, it is true," they replied.

[6]"It was the LORD who appointed Moses and Aaron," Samuel continued. "He brought your ancestors out of the land of Egypt. [7]Now stand here quietly before the LORD as I remind you of all the great things the LORD has done for you and your ancestors.

[8]"When the Israelites were* in Egypt and cried out to the LORD, he sent Moses and Aaron to rescue them from Egypt and to bring them into this land. [9]But the people soon forgot about the LORD their God, so he let them be conquered by Sisera, the general of Hazor's army, and by the Philistines and the king of Moab.

[10]"Then they cried to the LORD again and con-

10:27 Dead Sea Scroll 4QSam$^{a}$ continues: *Nahash, king of the Ammonites, had been grievously oppressing the Gadites and Reubenites who lived east of the Jordan River. He gouged out the right eye of each of the Israelites living there, and he didn't allow anyone to come and rescue them. In fact, of all the Israelites east of the Jordan, there wasn't a single one whose right eye Nahash had not gouged out. But there were seven thousand men who had escaped from the Ammonites, and they had settled in Jabesh-gilead.* 11:1 As in Greek version; Hebrew lacks *About a month later.* 11:8 Dead Sea Scrolls and Greek version read *70,000.* 12:8 Hebrew *When Jacob was.*

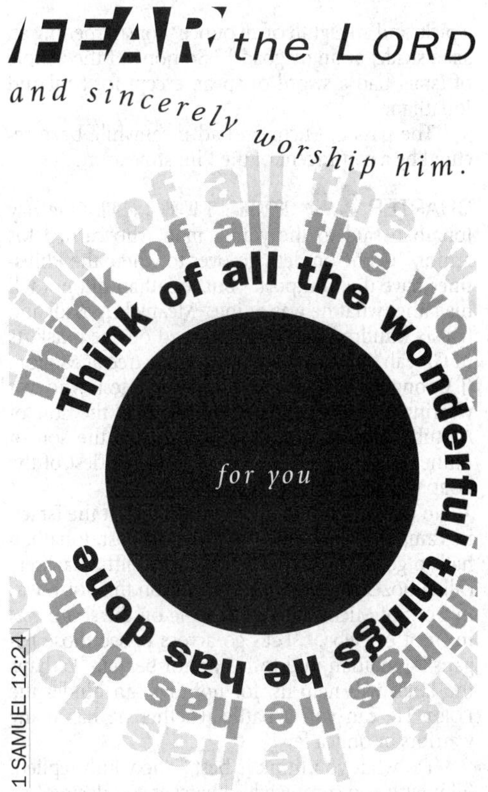
FEAR the LORD
and sincerely worship him.
Think of all the wonderful things he has done
for you
1 SAMUEL 12:24

fessed, 'We have sinned by turning away from the
LORD and worshiping the images of Baal and Ashtoreth. But we will worship you and you alone if you
will rescue us from our enemies.' 11Then the LORD
sent Gideon,* Barak,* Jephthah, and Samuel* to
save you, and you lived in safety.
12"But when you were afraid of Nahash, the king
of Ammon, you came to me and said that you
wanted a king to reign over you, even though the
LORD your God was already your king. 13All right,
here is the king you have chosen. Look him over. You
asked for him, and the LORD has granted your request.
14"Now if you will fear and worship the LORD and
listen to his voice, and if you do not rebel against the
LORD's commands, and if you and your king follow
the LORD your God, then all will be well. 15But if you
rebel against the LORD's commands and refuse to
listen to him, then his hand will be as heavy upon
you as it was upon your ancestors.
16"Now stand here and see the great thing the
LORD is about to do. 17You know that it does not rain
at this time of the year during the wheat harvest. I
will ask the LORD to send thunder and rain today.
Then you will realize how wicked you have been in
asking the LORD for a king!"
18So Samuel called to the LORD, and the LORD sent
thunder and rain. And all the people were terrified
of the LORD and of Samuel. 19"Pray to the LORD your
God for us, or we will die!" they cried out to Samuel.
"For now we have added to our sins by asking for a
king."
20"Don't be afraid," Samuel reassured them. "You
have certainly done wrong, but make sure now that
you worship the LORD with all your heart and that
you don't turn your back on him in any way. 21Don't
go back to worshiping worthless idols that cannot
help or rescue you—they really are useless! 22The
LORD will not abandon his chosen people, for that
would dishonor his great name. He made you a
special nation for himself.
23"As for me, I will certainly not sin against the
LORD by ending my prayers for you. And I will continue to teach you what is good and right. 24But be
sure to fear the LORD and sincerely worship him.
Think of all the wonderful things he has done for
you. 25But if you continue to sin, you and your king
will be destroyed."

## CHAPTER 13

**SAUL'S MISTAKE.** Saul was thirty*
years old when he became king, and he reigned for
forty-two years.*
2Saul selected three thousand special troops from
the army of Israel and sent the rest of the men home.
He took two thousand of the chosen men with him
to Micmash and the hill country of Bethel. The other
thousand went with Saul's son Jonathan to Gibeah
in the land of Benjamin.
3Soon after this, Jonathan attacked and defeated
the garrison of Philistines at Geba. The news spread
quickly among the Philistines that Israel was in revolt, so Saul sounded the call to arms throughout
Israel. 4He announced that the Philistine garrison at
Geba had been destroyed, and he warned the people
that the Philistines now hated the Israelites more
than ever. So the entire Israelite army mobilized
again and met Saul at Gilgal.
5The Philistines mustered a mighty army of three
thousand* chariots, six thousand horsemen, and as
many warriors as the grains of sand along the seashore! They camped at Micmash east of Beth-aven.
6When the men of Israel saw the vast number of
enemy troops, they lost their nerve entirely and tried
to hide in caves, holes, rocks, tombs, and cisterns.
7Some of them crossed the Jordan River and escaped
into the land of Gad and Gilead.
Meanwhile, Saul stayed at Gilgal, and his men

### SELF DESTRUCTING ● ● • • •

12:25 **If we continue sinning, we will not enjoy fellowship with God and we will end up destroying ourselves. Persisting in unhealthy habits, immoral thoughts, or harbored resentments and failing to heed God's Word are examples of destructive behavior.**

12:11a Hebrew *Jerubbaal,* another name for Gideon; see Judg 7:1. 12:11b As in Greek and Syriac versions; Hebrew reads *Bedan.* 12:11c Greek and Syriac versions read *Samson.* 13:1a As in a few Greek manuscripts; the number is missing in the Hebrew. 13:1b Hebrew *reigned . . . and two;* the number is incomplete in the Hebrew. Compare Acts 13:21. 13:5 As in Greek and Syriac versions; Hebrew reads *30,000.*

were trembling with fear. [8]Saul waited there seven days for Samuel, as Samuel had instructed him earlier, but Samuel still didn't come. Saul realized that his troops were rapidly slipping away. [9]So he demanded, "Bring me the burnt offering and the peace offerings!" And Saul sacrificed the burnt offering himself. [10]Just as Saul was finishing with the burnt offering, Samuel arrived. Saul went out to meet and welcome him, [11]but Samuel said, "What is this you have done?"

Saul replied, "I saw my men scattering from me, and you didn't arrive when you said you would, and the Philistines are at Micmash ready for battle. [12]So I said, 'The Philistines are ready to march against us, and I haven't even asked for the LORD's help!' So I felt obliged to offer the burnt offering myself before you came."

### EXCUSES ● ● • • •

**13:12-13 Saul had plenty of excuses for his disobedience. But Samuel zeroed in on the real issue: "You have disobeyed the command of the LORD your God." Like Saul, we often gloss over our mistakes and sins, trying to justify and spiritualize our actions because of our "special" circumstances. Our excuses, however, are nothing more than disobedience. God knows our true motives. He forgives, restores, and blesses only when we are honest about our sins. By trying to hide his sins behind excuses, Saul lost his kingship (13:14).**

[13]"How foolish!" Samuel exclaimed. "You have disobeyed the command of the LORD your God. Had you obeyed, the LORD would have established your kingdom over Israel forever. [14]But now your dynasty must end, for the LORD has sought out a man after his own heart. The LORD has already chosen him to be king over his people, for you have not obeyed the LORD's command."

[15]Samuel then left Gilgal and went on his way, but the rest of the troops went with Saul to meet the army. They went up from Gilgal to Gibeah in the land of Benjamin.* When Saul counted the men who were still with him, he found only six hundred left! [16]Saul and Jonathan and the troops with them were staying at Geba, near Gibeah, in the land of Benjamin. The Philistines set up their camp at Micmash. [17]Three raiding parties soon left the camp of the Philistines. One went north toward Ophrah in the land of Shual, [18]another went west to Beth-horon, and the third moved toward the border above the valley of Zeboim near the wilderness.

[19]There were no blacksmiths in the land of Israel in those days. The Philistines wouldn't allow them for fear they would make swords and spears for the Hebrews. [20]So whenever the Israelites needed to sharpen their plowshares, picks, axes, or sickles,* they had to take them to a Philistine blacksmith. [21](The schedule of charges was as follows: a quarter of an ounce of silver* for sharpening a plowshare or a pick, and an eighth of an ounce* for sharpening an ax, a sickle, or an ox goad.) [22]So none of the people of Israel had a sword or spear, except for Saul and Jonathan.

[23]The pass at Micmash had meanwhile been secured by a contingent of the Philistine army.

## CHAPTER 14

**JONATHAN'S DARING PLAN.** One day Jonathan said to the young man who carried his armor, "Come on, let's go over to where the Philistines have their outpost." But Jonathan did not tell his father what he was doing. [2]Meanwhile, Saul and his six hundred men were camped on the outskirts of Gibeah, around the pomegranate tree at Migron. [3](Among Saul's men was Ahijah the priest, who was wearing the linen ephod. Ahijah was the son of Ahitub, Ichabod's brother. Ahitub was the son of Phinehas and the grandson of Eli, the priest of the LORD who had served at Shiloh.)

No one realized that Jonathan had left the Israelite camp. [4]To reach the Philistine outpost, Jonathan had to go down between two rocky cliffs that were called Bozez and Seneh. [5]The cliff on the north was in front of Micmash, and the one on the south was in front of Geba. [6]"Let's go across to see those pagans," Jonathan said to his armor bearer. "Perhaps the LORD will help us, for nothing can hinder the LORD. He can win a battle whether he has many warriors or only a few!"

[7]"Do what you think is best," the youth replied. "I'm with you completely, whatever you decide."

[8]"All right then," Jonathan told him. "We will cross over and let them see us. [9]If they say to us, 'Stay where you are or we'll kill you,' then we will stop and not go up to them. [10]But if they say, 'Come on up and fight,' then we will go up. That will be the LORD's sign that he will help us defeat them."

[11]When the Philistines saw them coming, they shouted, "Look! The Hebrews are crawling out of their holes!" [12]Then they shouted to Jonathan, "Come on up here, and we'll teach you a lesson!"

"Come on, climb right behind me," Jonathan said to his armor bearer, "for the LORD will help us defeat them!" [13]So they climbed up using both hands and feet, and the Philistines fell back as

### SURROUNDED ● ● • • •

**14:6 Jonathan and his armor bearer weren't much of a force to attack the huge Philistine army. But while everyone else was afraid, these men trusted God, knowing that the size of the enemy army had no relationship to God's ability to help them. God honored the faith and brave action of these two men with a tremendous victory.**

**Have you ever felt surrounded by the "enemy" or faced overwhelming odds? God is never intimidated by the size of the enemy or the complexity of a problem. With him, there are always enough resources to resist the pressures and win your battles. If God has called you to action, then bravely commit what few resources you have to God and rely upon him to give you the victory.**

13:15 As in Greek version; Hebrew reads *Samuel left Gilgal and went to Gibeah in the land of Benjamin.* 13:20 As in Greek version; Hebrew reads *or plowshares.* 13:21a Hebrew *1 pim* [8 grams]. 13:21b Hebrew *1/3 of a shekel* [4 grams].

Jonathan and his armor bearer killed them right and left. [14]They killed about twenty men in all, and their bodies were scattered over about half an acre.* [15]Suddenly, panic broke out in the Philistine army, both in the camp and in the field, including even the outposts and raiding parties. And just then an earthquake struck, and everyone was terrified.

[16]Saul's lookouts in Gibeah saw a strange sight—the vast army of Philistines began to melt away in every direction. [17]"Find out who isn't here," Saul ordered. And when they checked, they found that Jonathan and his armor bearer were gone. [18]Then Saul shouted to Ahijah, "Bring the ephod here!" For at that time Ahijah was wearing the ephod in front of the Israelites.* [19]But while Saul was talking to the priest, the shouting and confusion in the Philistine camp grew louder and louder. So Saul said to Ahijah, "Never mind; let's get going!"*

[20]Then Saul and his six hundred men rushed out to the battle and found the Philistines killing each other. There was terrible confusion everywhere. [21]Even the Hebrews who had gone over to the Philistine army revolted and joined in with Saul, Jonathan, and the rest of the Israelites. [22]Likewise, the men who were hiding in the hills joined the chase when they saw the Philistines running away. [23]So the LORD saved Israel that day, and the battle continued to rage even out beyond Beth-aven.

[24]Now the men of Israel were worn out that day, because Saul had made them take an oath, saying, "Let a curse fall on anyone who eats before evening—before I have full revenge on my enemies." So no one ate a thing all day, [25]even though they found honeycomb on the ground in the forest. [26]They didn't even touch the honey because they all feared the oath they had taken.

[27]But Jonathan had not heard his father's command, and he dipped a stick into a piece of honeycomb and ate the honey. After he had eaten it, he felt much better. [28]But one of the men saw him and said, "Your father made the army take a strict oath that anyone who eats food today will be cursed. That is why everyone is weary and faint."

[29]"My father has made trouble for us all!" Jonathan exclaimed. "A command like that only hurts us. See how much better I feel now that I have eaten this little bit of honey. [30]If the men had been allowed to eat freely from the food they found among our enemies, think how many more we could have killed!"

[31]But hungry as they were, they chased and killed the Philistines all day from Micmash to Aijalon, growing more and more faint. [32]That evening they flew upon the battle plunder and butchered the sheep, cattle, and calves, but they ate them without draining the blood. [33]Someone reported to Saul, "Look, the men are sinning against the LORD by eating meat that still has blood in it."

"That is very wrong," Saul said. "Find a large stone and roll it over here. [34]Then go out among the troops and tell them, 'Bring the cattle and sheep here to kill them and drain the blood. Do not sin against the LORD by eating meat with the blood still in it.'" So that night all the troops brought their animals and slaughtered them there. [35]And Saul built an altar to the LORD, the first one he had ever built.

[36]Then Saul said, "Let's chase the Philistines all night and destroy every last one of them."

His men replied, "We'll do whatever you think is best."

But the priest said, "Let's ask God first."

[37]So Saul asked God, "Should we go after the Philistines? Will you help us defeat them?" But God made no reply that day.

[38]Then Saul said to the leaders, "Something's wrong! I want all my army commanders to come here. We must find out what sin was committed today. [39]I vow by the name of the LORD who rescued Israel that the sinner will surely die, even if it is my own son Jonathan!" But no one would tell him what the trouble was. [40]Then Saul said, "Jonathan and I will stand over here, and all of you stand over there." And the people agreed.

[41]Then Saul prayed, "O LORD, God of Israel, please show us who is guilty and who is innocent. Are Jonathan and I guilty, or is the sin among the others?"* And Jonathan and Saul were chosen* as the guilty ones, and the people were declared innocent.

[42]Then Saul said, "Now choose* between me and Jonathan." And Jonathan was shown to be the guilty one.

[43]"Tell me what you have done," Saul demanded of Jonathan.

"I tasted a little honey," Jonathan admitted. "It was only a little bit on the end of a stick. Does that deserve death?"

[44]"Yes, Jonathan," Saul said, "you must die! May God strike me dead if you are not executed for this."

## VOWS ● ● • • •

**14:24-25 Saul made an oath without thinking through the implications. The results? (1) Saul's men were too tired to fight; (2) they were so hungry they ate raw meat that still contained blood, which was against God's law; (3) Saul almost killed his own son (14:42-44).**

**Saul's impulsive vow sounded heroic, but its disastrous side effects made it little more than "shooting off at the mouth." If you are in the middle of a conflict, guard against impulsive statements that you may be forced to honor.**

14:14 Hebrew *half a yoke;* a "yoke" was the amount of land plowed by a pair of yoked oxen in one day. 14:18 As in some Greek manuscripts; Hebrew reads *"Bring the Ark of God." For at that time the Ark of God was with the Israelites.* 14:19 Hebrew *Withdraw your hand.* 14:41a Greek version adds *If the fault is with me or my son Jonathan, respond with Urim; but if the men of Israel are at fault, respond with Thummim.* 14:41b Hebrew *chosen by lot.* 14:42 Hebrew *draw lots.*

45But the people broke in and said to Saul, "Should Jonathan, who saved Israel today, die? Far from it! As surely as the LORD lives, not one hair on his head will be touched, for he has been used of God to do a mighty miracle today." So the people rescued Jonathan, and he was not put to death. 46Then Saul called back the army from chasing the Philistines, and the Philistines returned home.

47Now when Saul had secured his grasp on Israel's throne, he fought against his enemies in every direction—against Moab, Ammon, Edom, the kings of Zobah, and the Philistines. And wherever he turned, he was victorious. 48He did great deeds and conquered the Amalekites, saving Israel from all those who had plundered them.

## LYING

On her way out the door for a company party, Mrs. Richards addresses her sophomore daughter, whom she has just grounded. "Janel, remember– no visitors, and under no circumstances may you leave the house."

"Yes, ma'am," mumbles the hacked-off teen.

After her mom leaves, Janel grabs the phone. "Katherine, everything's cool." Ten minutes later Katherine is there.

"How 'bout checking the mall to see if Greg's there?" Janel suggests.

"What if your mom calls?"

"Oh, I'll just tell her I was taking a bath."

The girls go to the mall. They eat ice cream and return home. Janel slides into bed, thinking, "My mom is so out of it . . . I could have stayed out till midnight."

The next morning, Mrs. Richards, obviously ticked, summons Janel into the living room.

"Care to tell me about last night?"

"Huh?" Janel asks.

"Where did you go?"

"What are you talking about?" (It's an Oscar-caliber performance.)

"Look, Janel," Mrs. Richards states, "I know what you did. On my way to the party, I got a run in my hose. I stopped at the mall to get another pair, and guess who I saw there?"

Janel sees her life flash before her eyes!

For a reminder of the high cost of dishonesty and disobedience, read 1 Samuel 15:1-23.

49Saul's sons included Jonathan, Ishbosheth,* and Malkishua. He also had two daughters: Merab, who was older, and Michal. 50Saul's wife was Ahinoam, the daughter of Ahimaaz. The commander of Saul's army was his cousin Abner, his uncle Ner's son. 51Abner's father, Ner, and Saul's father, Kish, were brothers; both were sons of Abiel.

52The Israelites fought constantly with the Philistines throughout Saul's lifetime. So whenever Saul saw a young man who was brave and strong, he drafted him into his army.

CHAPTER **15** **SAUL FAILS TO OBEY.** One day Samuel said to Saul, "I anointed you king of Israel because the LORD told me to. Now listen to this message from the LORD! 2This is what the LORD Almighty says: 'I have decided to settle accounts with the nation of Amalek for opposing Israel when they came from Egypt. 3Now go and completely destroy* the entire Amalekite nation—men, women, children, babies, cattle, sheep, camels, and donkeys.'"

4So Saul mobilized his army at Telaim. There were 200,000 troops in addition to 10,000 men from Judah. 5Then Saul went to the city of Amalek and lay in wait in the valley. 6Saul sent this message to the Kenites: "Move away from where the Amalekites live or else you will die with them. For you were kind to the people of Israel when they came up from Egypt." So the Kenites packed up and left.

7Then Saul slaughtered the Amalekites from Havilah all the way to Shur, east of Egypt. 8He captured Agag, the Amalekite king, but completely destroyed everyone else. 9Saul and his men spared Agag's life and kept the best of the sheep and cattle, the fat calves and lambs—everything, in fact, that appealed to them. They destroyed only what was worthless or of poor quality.

10Then the LORD said to Samuel, 11"I am sorry that I ever made Saul king, for he has not been loyal to me and has again refused to obey me." Samuel was so deeply moved when he heard this that he cried out to the LORD all night.

12Early the next morning Samuel went to find Saul. Someone told him, "Saul went to Carmel to set up a monument to himself; then he went on to Gilgal."

13When Samuel finally found him, Saul greeted him cheerfully. "May the LORD bless you," he said. "I have carried out the LORD's command!"

14"Then what is all the bleating of sheep and lowing of cattle I hear?" Samuel demanded.

15"It's true that the army spared the best of the sheep and cattle," Saul admitted. "But they are going to sacrifice them to the LORD your God. We have destroyed everything else."

16Then Samuel said to Saul, "Stop! Listen to what the LORD told me last night!"

"What was it?" Saul asked.

17And Samuel told him, "Although you may think

## FAILURE ● ● • • •

15:13-14 **Saul thought he had won a great victory over the Amalekites, but God saw it as a great failure because Saul had disobeyed him and then had lied to Samuel about the results of the battle. Saul may have thought his lie wouldn't be detected, or that what he did was not wrong. Saul was mistaken.**

**Dishonest people soon begin to believe the lies they construct around themselves. Then they lose the ability to tell the difference between telling the truth and lying. By believing your own lies, you will move away from God. That is why honesty is so important in our relationships, both with God and with others.**

14:49 Hebrew *Ishvi,* a variant name for Ishbosheth; also known as Eshbaal. 15:3 The Hebrew term used here refers to the complete consecration of things or people to the LORD, either by destroying them or by giving them as an offering; also in 15:8, 9, 15, 18, 20, 21.

little of yourself, are you not the leader of the tribes
of Israel? The LORD has anointed you king of Israel.
[18]And the LORD sent you on a mission and told you,
'Go and completely destroy the sinners, the Amalekites, until they are all dead.' [19]Why haven't you
obeyed the LORD? Why did you rush for the plunder
and do exactly what the LORD said not to do?"
[20]"But I did obey the LORD," Saul insisted. "I carried
out the mission he gave me. I brought back King Agag,
but I destroyed everyone else. [21]Then my troops
brought in the best of the sheep and cattle and plunder
to sacrifice to the LORD your
God in Gilgal."
[22]But Samuel replied,
"What is more pleasing to
the LORD: your burnt offerings and sacrifices or your
obedience to his voice? Obedience is far better than sacrifice. Listening to him is much
better than offering the fat of
rams. [23]Rebellion is as bad as
the sin of witchcraft, and
stubbornness is as bad as
worshiping idols. So because
you have rejected the word of
the LORD, he has rejected you
from being king."
[24]Then Saul finally ad-
mitted, "Yes, I have sinned.
I have disobeyed your in-
structions and the LORD's
command, for I was afraid
of the people and did what
they demanded. [25]Oh,
please, forgive my sin now
and go with me to worship
the LORD."
[26]But Samuel replied, "I
will not return with you!
Since you have rejected the
LORD's command, he has rejected you from being the
king of Israel."
[27]As Samuel turned to go,
Saul grabbed at him to try to
hold him back and tore his
robe. [28]And Samuel said to
him, "See? The LORD has
torn the kingdom of Israel
from you today and has
given it to someone else—
one who is better than you.
[29]And he who is the Glory of
Israel will not lie, nor will he
change his mind, for he is
not human that he should
change his mind!"
[30]Then Saul pleaded
again, "I know I have sinned.
But please, at least honor me before the leaders and
before my people by going with me to worship the
LORD your God." [31]So Samuel finally agreed and went
with him, and Saul worshiped the LORD.
[32]Then Samuel said, "Bring King Agag to me."
Agag arrived full of smiles, for he thought, "Surely
the worst is over, and I have been spared!"* [33]But
Samuel said, "As your sword has killed the sons of
many mothers, now your mother will be childless."
And Samuel cut Agag to pieces before the LORD at
Gilgal. [34]Then Samuel went home to Ramah, and

## DAVID

When we think of David, we think of a shepherd, poet, giant-killer, king, ancestor of Jesus—in short, we think of one of the greatest heroes in the Old Testament. But other words could also be used to describe David: betrayer, liar, adulterer, murderer. The first list includes qualities we all might like to have; the second, qualities that might be true of any one of us. What five or six words would summarize your life?

The Bible makes no effort to hide David's failures. Yet he is remembered and respected as a godly hero. Knowing how much more we are like David in his failures than in his successes, we should be curious to find out what made God refer to David as a man after God's heart.

David believed as deeply as he could that God was loving and forgiving. He was a man who lived with great energy and joy. He sinned many times, but he was quick to confess his sins. His confessions were from the heart and his repentance was real. David never took God's forgiveness lightly or his blessing for granted. In return, God never held back from David either his forgiveness or the consequences of his actions. David experienced the joy of forgiveness even when he had to suffer the consequences of his sins.

One big example David gives to us is that while he sinned greatly, he did not sin repeatedly. He didn't make the same mistakes over and over. Rather, he learned from his mistakes because he accepted the suffering they brought. Often we don't seem to learn from our mistakes or the consequences that come from those mistakes. The next time you make a mistake, think how you could be more like David.

**UPS:**
- Greatest king of Israel
- Ancestor of Jesus Christ
- Listed in the Hall of Faith in Hebrews 11
- Described by God as "a man after his own heart" (1 Samuel 13:14)

**DOWNS:**
- Committed adultery with Bathsheba
- Arranged the murder of Uriah, Bathsheba's husband
- Directly disobeyed God in taking a census of the people

**STATS:**
- Where: Bethlehem, Jerusalem
- Occupation: Shepherd, musician, poet, soldier, king
- Relatives: Father: Jesse. Wives included Michal, Ahinoam, Bathsheba, Abigail. Sons: Absalom, Amnon, Solomon, Adonijah. Daughter: Tamar. Seven brothers.
- Contemporaries: Saul, Jonathan, Samuel, Nathan

LESSONS: Willingness to honestly admit our mistakes is the first step in dealing with them

Forgiveness does not remove the consequences of sin

God greatly desires our complete trust and worship

KEY VERSES: "For you are God, O Sovereign LORD. Your words are truth, and you have promised these good things to me, your servant. And now, may it please you to bless me and my family so that our dynasty may continue forever before you. For when you grant a blessing to your servant, O Sovereign LORD, it is an eternal blessing!" (2 Samuel 7:28-29).

His story is told in 1 Samuel 16—1 Kings 2. He is also mentioned in Amos 6:5; Matthew 1:1, 6; 22:43-45; Luke 1:32; Romans 1:3; Hebrews 11:32.

15:32 Dead Sea Scrolls and Greek version read *Agag arrived hesitantly, for he thought, "Surely this is the bitterness of death."*

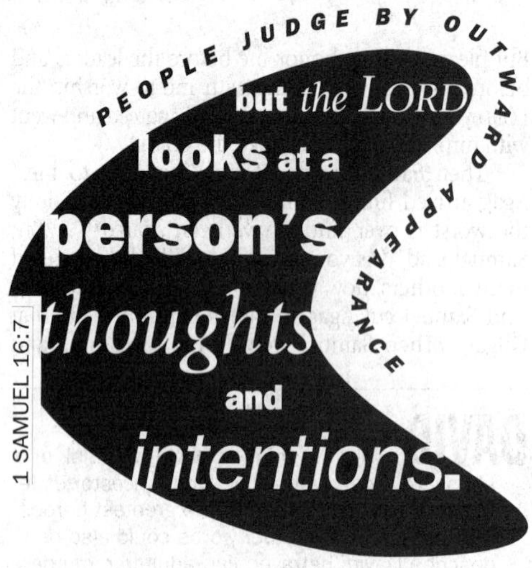
PEOPLE JUDGE BY OUTWARD APPEARANCE
but the LORD
looks at a
person's
thoughts
and
intentions.
1 SAMUEL 16:7

Saul returned to his house at Gibeah. 35Samuel never went to meet with Saul again, but he mourned constantly for him. And the LORD was sorry he had ever made Saul king of Israel.

CHAPTER **16** **SAMUEL ANOINTS DAVID.** Finally, the LORD said to Samuel, "You have mourned long enough for Saul. I have rejected him as king of Israel. Now fill your horn with olive oil and go to Bethlehem. Find a man named Jesse who lives there, for I have selected one of his sons to be my new king."

2But Samuel asked, "How can I do that? If Saul hears about it, he will kill me."

"Take a heifer with you," the LORD replied, "and say that you have come to make a sacrifice to the LORD. 3Invite Jesse to the sacrifice, and I will show you which of his sons to anoint for me."

4So Samuel did as the LORD instructed him. When he arrived at Bethlehem, the leaders of the town became afraid. "What's wrong?" they asked. "Do you come in peace?"

5"Yes," Samuel replied. "I have come to sacrifice to the LORD. Purify yourselves and come with me to the sacrifice." Then Samuel performed the purification rite for Jesse and his sons and invited them, too.

6When they arrived, Samuel took one look at Eliab and thought, "Surely this is the LORD's anointed!" 7But the LORD said to Samuel, "Don't judge by his appearance or height, for I have rejected him. The LORD doesn't make decisions the way you do! People judge by outward appearance, but the LORD looks at a person's thoughts and intentions."

8Then Jesse told his son Abinadab to step forward and walk in front of Samuel. But Samuel said, "This is not the one the LORD has chosen." 9Next Jesse summoned Shammah, but Samuel said, "Neither is this the one the LORD has chosen." 10In the same way all seven of Jesse's sons were presented to Samuel. But Samuel said to Jesse, "The LORD has not chosen any of these." 11Then Samuel asked, "Are these all the sons you have?"

"There is still the youngest," Jesse replied. "But he's out in the fields watching the sheep."

"Send for him at once," Samuel said. "We will not sit down to eat until he arrives."

12So Jesse sent for him. He was ruddy and handsome, with pleasant eyes. And the LORD said, "This is the one; anoint him."

13So as David stood there among his brothers, Samuel took the olive oil he had brought and poured it on David's head. And the Spirit of the LORD came mightily upon him from that day on. Then Samuel returned to Ramah.

14Now the Spirit of the LORD had left Saul, and the LORD sent a tormenting spirit that filled him with depression and fear. 15Some of Saul's servants suggested a remedy. "It is clear that a spirit from God is tormenting you," they said. 16"Let us find a good musician to play the harp for you whenever the tormenting spirit is bothering you. The harp music will quiet you, and you will soon be well again."

17"All right," Saul said. "Find me someone who plays well and bring him here."

18One of the servants said to Saul, "The son of Jesse is a talented harp player. Not only that; he is brave and strong and has good judgment. He is also a fine-looking young man, and the LORD is with him."

19So Saul sent messengers to Jesse to say, "Send me your son David, the shepherd." 20Jesse responded by sending David to Saul, along with a young goat and a donkey loaded down with food and wine. 21So David went to Saul and served him. Saul liked David very much, and David became one of Saul's armor bearers.

22Then Saul sent word to Jesse asking, "Please let David join my staff, for I am very pleased with him." 23And whenever the tormenting spirit from God troubled Saul, David would play the harp. Then Saul would feel better, and the tormenting spirit would go away.

CHAPTER **17** **DAVID FIGHTS GOLIATH.** The Philistines now mustered their army for battle and camped between Socoh in Judah and Azekah at

## GOOD LOOKS ● ● • • •

**16:7 Saul was tall and handsome; he was an impressive-looking man. Samuel may have been trying to find someone who looked like Saul to be Israel's next king, but God warned him against judging by appearance alone. When people judge by outward appearance, they may overlook quality individuals who simply lack the particular physical qualities that society currently admires. But appearance doesn't reveal what people are really like or what their true value is.**

**Fortunately, God judges by character, not appearances. And because only God can see the inside, only he can accurately judge people. While we spend hours each week maintaining our outward appearance, we should do even more to develop our inner character. While everyone can see your face, only you and God know what your heart really looks like. Which is the more attractive part of you?**

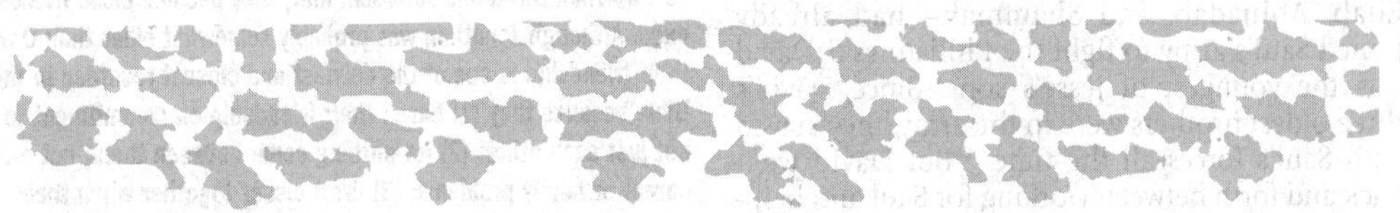

| Object | Reference | Who used it? | How was it used? |
|---|---|---|---|
| **a shepherd's staff** | Exodus 4:2-4 | Moses | To work miracles before Pharaoh |
| **a ram's horn** | Joshua 6:3-5 | Joshua | To flatten the walls of Jericho |
| **a fleece** | Judges 6:36-40 | Gideon | To confirm God's will |
| **horns, jars, and torches** | Judges 7:19-22 | Gideon | To defeat the Midianites |
| **jawbone** | Judges 15:15 | Samson | To kill 1,000 Philistines |
| **small stone** | 1 Samuel 17:40 | David | To kill Goliath |
| **oil** | 2 Kings 4:1-7 | Elisha | To demonstrate God's power to provide |
| **a river** | 2 Kings 5:9-14 | Elisha | To heal a man of leprosy |
| **linen belt** | Jeremiah 13:1-11 | Jeremiah | As an object lesson of God's wrath |
| **pottery** | Jeremiah 19:1-13 | Jeremiah | As an object lesson of God's wrath |
| **food and water** | Ezekiel 4:9-17 | Ezekiel | As an object lesson of judgment |
| **five loaves of bread and two fish** | Mark 6:30-44 | Jesus | To feed a crowd of over 5,000 people |

**SIMPLE OBJECTS** God often uses simple, ordinary objects to accomplish his tasks in the world. They only need to be dedicated to him for his use. What do you have that God can use? Anything and everything is a possible "instrument" for him.

Ephes-dammim. [2]Saul countered by gathering his
troops near the valley of Elah. [3]So the Philistines and
Israelites faced each other on opposite hills, with the
valley between them.

[4]Then Goliath, a Philistine champion from
Gath, came out of the Philistine ranks to face the
forces of Israel. He was a giant of a man, measuring
over nine feet* tall! [5]He wore a bronze helmet and
a coat of mail that weighed 125 pounds.* [6]He also
wore bronze leggings, and he slung a bronze javelin over his back. [7]The shaft of his spear was as
heavy and thick as a weaver's beam, tipped with an
iron spearhead that weighed fifteen pounds.* An
armor bearer walked ahead of him carrying a huge
shield.

[8]Goliath stood and shouted across to the Israelites, "Do you need a whole army to settle this?
Choose someone to fight for you, and I will represent the Philistines. We will settle this dispute in
single combat! [9]If your man is able to kill me, then
we will be your slaves. But if I kill him, you will be
our slaves! [10]I defy the armies of Israel! Send me a
man who will fight with me!" [11]When Saul and the
Israelites heard this, they were terrified and deeply
shaken.

[12]Now David was the son of a man named Jesse,
an Ephrathite from Bethlehem in the land of
Judah. Jesse was an old man at that time, and he
had eight sons in all. [13]Jesse's three oldest sons—

**GROWTH ● ● • • •**

**16:19-21 When Saul asked David to join his palace staff, he obviously did not know that David had been secretly anointed king (16:12). Saul's invitation presented an excellent opportunity for the young, future king to gain firsthand information about leading a nation.**

**Sometimes our plans—even the ones we think God has approved—have to be put on hold indefinitely. Like David, we can use this waiting time profitably. We can choose to learn and grow in our present circumstances, whatever they may be.**

17:4 Hebrew *6 cubits and 1 span* [which totals about 9.75 feet or 3 meters]; Greek version and Dead Sea Scrolls read *4 cubits and 1 span* [which totals about 6.75 feet or 2 meters]. 17:5 Hebrew *5,000 shekels* [57 kilograms]. 17:7 Hebrew *600 shekels* [6.8 kilograms].

Eliab, Abinadab, and Shammah—had already joined Saul's army to fight the Philistines. 14David was the youngest of Jesse's sons. Since David's three oldest brothers were in the army, they stayed with Saul's forces all the time. 15But David went back and forth between working for Saul and helping his father with the sheep in Bethlehem.

16For forty days, twice a day, morning and evening, the Philistine giant strutted in front of the Israelite army.

17One day Jesse said to David, "Take this half-bushel* of roasted grain and these ten loaves of bread to your brothers. 18And give these ten cuts of cheese to their captain. See how your brothers are getting along, and bring me back a letter from them.*"

19David's brothers were with Saul and the Israelite army at the valley of Elah, fighting against the Philistines. 20So David left the sheep with another shepherd and set out early the next morning with the gifts. He arrived at the outskirts of the camp just as the Israelite army was leaving for the battlefield with shouts and battle cries. 21Soon the Israelite and Philistine forces stood facing each other, army against army. 22David left his things with the keeper of supplies and hurried out to the ranks to greet his brothers. 23As he was talking with them, he saw Goliath, the champion from Gath, come out from the Philistine ranks, shouting his challenge to the army of Israel.

24As soon as the Israelite army saw him, they began to run away in fright. 25"Have you seen the giant?" the men were asking. "He comes out each day to challenge Israel. And have you heard about the huge reward the king has offered to anyone who kills him? The king will give him one of his daughters for a wife, and his whole family will be exempted from paying taxes!"

## OUTLOOK ● ● • • •

17:26 **What a difference outlook or perspective can make! Saul saw only a giant and a young boy. David, however, saw a mortal man defying almighty God. He knew he would not be alone when he faced Goliath; God would fight with him. He looked at his situation from God's point of view. Viewing impossible situations from God's point of view helps us put giant problems in perspective.**

26David talked to some others standing there to verify the report. "What will a man get for killing this Philistine and putting an end to his abuse of Israel?" he asked them. "Who is this pagan Philistine anyway, that he is allowed to defy the armies of the living God?" 27And David received the same reply as before: "What you have been hearing is true. That is the reward for killing the giant."

28But when David's oldest brother, Eliab, heard David talking to the men, he was angry. "What are you doing around here anyway?" he demanded.

**17:17** Hebrew *ephah* [18 liters]. **17:18** Hebrew *and take their pledge.*

## FRIENDSHIP ● ● • • •

18:1-4 **When David and Jonathan met, they became close friends at once. Although Jonathan was probably somewhat older than David, their friendship is one of the deepest and closest recorded in the Bible because they (1) based their friendship on commitment to God, not just each other; (2) let nothing come between them, not even career or family problems; (3) drew closer together when their friendship was tested; and (4) were able to remain friends to the end.**

**Jonathan, the prince of Israel, later realized that David, and not he, would be king (23:17). But that did not weaken his love for David. Jonathan would much rather lose the throne of Israel than his closest friend.**

"What about those few sheep you're supposed to be taking care of? I know about your pride and dishonesty. You just want to see the battle!"

29"What have I done now?" David replied. "I was only asking a question!" 30He walked over to some others and asked them the same thing and received the same answer. 31Then David's question was reported to King Saul, and the king sent for him.

32"Don't worry about a thing," David told Saul. "I'll go fight this Philistine!"

33"Don't be ridiculous!" Saul replied. "There is no way you can go against this Philistine. You are only a boy, and he has been in the army since he was a boy!"

34But David persisted. "I have been taking care of my father's sheep," he said. "When a lion or a bear comes to steal a lamb from the flock, 35I go after it with a club and take the lamb from its mouth. If the animal turns on me, I catch it by the jaw and club it to death. 36I have done this to both lions and bears, and I'll do it to this pagan Philistine, too, for he has defied the armies of the living God! 37The LORD who saved me from the claws of the lion and the bear will save me from this Philistine!"

Saul finally consented. "All right, go ahead," he said. "And may the LORD be with you!"

38Then Saul gave David his own armor—a bronze helmet and a coat of mail. 39David put it on, strapped the sword over it, and took a step or two to see what it was like, for he had never worn such things before. "I can't go in these," he protested. "I'm not used to them." So he took them off again. 40He picked up five smooth stones from a stream and put them in his shepherd's bag. Then, armed only with his shepherd's staff and sling, he started across to fight Goliath.

41Goliath walked out toward David with his shield bearer ahead of him, 42sneering in contempt at this ruddy-faced boy. 43"Am I a dog," he roared at David, "that you come at me with a stick?" And he cursed David by the names of his gods. 44"Come over here, and I'll give your flesh to the birds and wild animals!" Goliath yelled.

45David shouted in reply, "You come to me with sword, spear, and javelin, but I come to you in the name of the LORD Almighty—the God of the armies of Israel, whom you have defied. 46Today the LORD will conquer you, and I will kill you and cut off your head. And then I will give the dead bodies of your men to the birds and wild animals, and the whole world will know that there is a God in Israel! 47And everyone will know that the LORD does not need weapons to rescue his people. It is his battle, not ours. The LORD will give you to us!"

48As Goliath moved closer to attack, David quickly ran out to meet him. 49Reaching into his shepherd's bag and taking out a stone, he hurled it from his sling and hit the Philistine in the forehead. The stone sank in, and Goliath stumbled and fell face downward to the ground. 50So David triumphed over the Philistine giant with only a stone and sling. And since he had no sword, 51he ran over and pulled Goliath's sword from its sheath. David used it to kill the giant and cut off his head.

When the Philistines saw that their champion was dead, they turned and ran. 52Then the Israelites gave a great shout of triumph and rushed after the Philistines, chasing them as far as Gath* and the gates of Ekron. The bodies of the dead and wounded Philistines were strewn all along the road from Shaaraim, as far as Gath and Ekron. 53Then the Israelite army returned and plundered the deserted Philistine camp. 54(David took Goliath's head to Jerusalem, but he stored the Philistine's armor in his own tent.)

55As Saul watched David go out to fight Goliath, he asked Abner, the general of his army, "Abner, whose son is he?"

"I really don't know," Abner said.

56"Well, find out!" the king told him.

57After David had killed Goliath, Abner brought him to Saul with the Philistine's head still in his hand. 58"Tell me about your father, my boy," Saul said.

And David replied, "His name is Jesse, and we live in Bethlehem."

## CHAPTER 18 DAVID AND JONATHAN.

After David had finished talking with Saul, he met Jonathan, the king's son. There was an immediate bond of love between them, and they became the best of friends. 2From that day on Saul kept David with him at the palace and wouldn't let him return home. 3And Jonathan made a special vow to be David's friend, 4and he sealed the pact by giving him his robe, tunic, sword, bow, and belt.

5Whatever Saul asked David to do, David did it successfully. So Saul made him a commander in his army, an appointment that was applauded by the fighting men and officers alike. 6But something happened when the victorious Israelite army was returning home after David had killed Goliath. Women came out from all the towns along the way to celebrate and to cheer for King Saul, and they sang and danced for joy with tambourines and cymbals.* 7This was their song:

### JONATHAN

Loyalty is one of life's most costly qualities and is the most unselfish part of love. To be loyal, you cannot live only for yourself. Loyal people not only stand by their commitments, they are also willing to suffer for them. Jonathan is a shining example of loyalty. Sometimes he was forced to deal with a conflict between his loyalties to his father, Saul, and to his friend David. His solution to that conflict teaches us both how to be loyal and what must guide loyalty. In Jonathan, truth always guided loyalty.

Jonathan found the source of truth in his relationship with God. He realized that no matter what, he must be loyal to him. It was this ultimate loyalty to God that gave Jonathan the wisdom to deal effectively with the complicated situations in his life. He was loyal to Saul because Saul was his father and the king. He was loyal to David because David was his friend. But his loyalty to God helped him see the limits of each of those other relationships.

The conflicting demands of our relationships can be real challenges to us as well. If we try to settle these conflicts only at the human level, we will be constantly dealing with a sense of betrayal. No other human can claim the loyalty we can only give to God. If we communicate to our friends that our number-one loyalty is to God and his truth, many of our choices will be much clearer. The truth in his Word, the Bible, will bring wisdom to our decisions. Do those closest to you know who has your greatest loyalty?

**UPS:**
- Brave, loyal, and a natural leader
- Closest friend David ever had
- Did not put his personal well-being ahead of those he loved
- Depended on God

**STATS:**
- Occupation: Military leader
- Relatives: Father: Saul. Mother: Ahinoam. Brothers: Abinadab, Malchishua, and Ishbosheth. Sisters: Merab and Michal. Son: Mephibosheth.

LESSONS: Loyalty is one of the strongest aspects of courage

An allegiance to God puts all other relationships in perspective

Great friendships are costly

KEY VERSE: "How I weep for you, my brother Jonathan! Oh, how much I loved you! And your love for me was deep, deeper than the love of women!" (2 Samuel 1:26).

His story is told in 1 Samuel 13–31. He is also mentioned in 2 Samuel 9.

17:52 As in some Greek manuscripts; Hebrew reads *a valley.* 18:6 The type of instrument represented by the final word is uncertain.

"Saul has killed his thousands,
and David his ten thousands!"

[8]This made Saul very angry. "What's this?" he said. "They credit David with ten thousands and me with only thousands. Next they'll be making him their king!" [9]So from that time on Saul kept a jealous eye on David.

[10]The very next day, in fact, a tormenting spirit from God overwhelmed Saul, and he began to rave like a madman. David began to play the harp, as he did whenever this happened. But Saul, who had a spear in his hand, [11]suddenly hurled it at David, intending to pin him to the wall. But David jumped aside and escaped. This happened another time, too, [12]for Saul was afraid of him, and he was jealous because the LORD had left him and was now with David. [13]Finally, Saul banned him from his presence and appointed him commander over only a thousand men, but David faithfully led his troops into battle.

[14]David continued to succeed in everything he did, for the LORD was with him. [15]When Saul recognized this, he became even more afraid of him. [16]But all Israel and Judah loved David because he was so successful at leading his troops into battle.

[17]One day Saul said to David, "I am ready to give you my older daughter, Merab, as your wife. But first you must prove yourself to be a real warrior by fighting the LORD's battles." For Saul thought to himself, "I'll send him out against the Philistines and let them kill him rather than doing it myself."

## POPULARITY ● ● • • •

18:15-18 **While Saul's popularity made him proud and arrogant, David remained humble even when the entire nation praised him. Although David succeeded in almost everything he tried and became famous throughout the land, he refused to use his popular support to his advantage against Saul. Don't allow popularity to twist your perception of your own importance. It's easy to be humble when you're not on center stage, but how will you react to praise and honor?**

[18]"Who am I, and what is my family in Israel that I should be the king's son-in-law?" David exclaimed. "My father's family is nothing!" [19]So* when the time came for the wedding, Saul gave Merab in marriage to Adriel, a man from Meholah.

[20]In the meantime, Saul's daughter Michal had fallen in love with David, and Saul was delighted when he heard about it. [21]"Here's another chance to see him killed by the Philistines!" Saul said to himself. But to David he said, "I have a way for you to become my son-in-law after all!"

[22]Then Saul told his men to say confidentially to David, "The king really likes you, and so do we. Why don't you accept the king's offer and become his son-in-law?"

[23]When Saul's men said these things to David, he replied, "How can a poor man from a humble family afford the bride price for the daughter of a king?"

[24]When Saul's men reported this back to the king, [25]he told them, "Tell David that all I want for the bride price is one hundred Philistine foreskins! Vengeance on my enemies is all I really want." But what Saul had in mind was that David would be killed in the fight.

[26]David was delighted to accept the offer. So before the time limit expired, [27]he and his men went out and killed two hundred Philistines and presented all their foreskins to the king. So Saul gave Michal to David to be his wife.

[28]When the king realized how much the LORD was with David and how much Michal loved him, [29]he became even more afraid of him, and he remained David's enemy for the rest of his life. [30]Whenever the Philistine army attacked, David was more successful against them than all the rest of Saul's officers. So David's name became very famous throughout the land.

CHAPTER **19** **SAUL TRIES TO KILL DAVID.** Saul now urged his servants and his son Jonathan to assassinate David. But Jonathan, because of his close friendship with David, [2]told him what his father was planning. "Tomorrow morning," he warned him, "you must find a hiding place out in the fields. [3]I'll ask my father to go out there with me, and I'll talk to him about you. Then I'll tell you everything I can find out."

[4]The next morning Jonathan spoke with his father about David, saying many good things about him. "Please don't sin against David," Jonathan pleaded. "He's never done anything to harm you. He has always helped you in any way he could. [5]Have you forgotten about the time he risked his life to kill the Philistine giant and how the LORD brought a great victory to Israel as a result? You were certainly happy about it then. Why should you murder an innocent man like David? There is no reason for it at all!"

[6]So Saul listened to Jonathan and vowed, "As surely as the LORD lives, David will not be killed." [7]Afterward Jonathan called David and told him what had happened. Then he took David to see Saul, and everything was as it had been before.

[8]War broke out shortly after that, and David led his troops against the Philistines. He attacked them with such fury that they all ran away.

[9]But one day as Saul was sitting at home, the tormenting spirit from the LORD suddenly came upon him again. As David played his harp for the king, [10]Saul hurled his spear at David in an attempt to kill him. But David dodged out of the way and escaped into the night, leaving the spear stuck in the wall.

[11]Then Saul sent troops to watch David's house. They were told to kill David when he came out the next morning. But Michal, David's wife, warned him, "If you don't get away tonight, you will be dead

18:19 Or *But.*

by morning." 12So she helped him climb out through a window, and he escaped. 13Then she took an idol* and put it in his bed, covered it with blankets, and put a cushion of goat's hair at its head. 14When the troops came to arrest David, she told them he was sick and couldn't get out of bed.

15"Then bring him to me in his bed," Saul ordered, "so I can kill him as he lies there!" And he sent them back to David's house. 16But when they came to carry David out, they discovered that it was only an idol in the bed with a cushion of goat's hair at its head.

17"Why have you tricked me and let my enemy escape?" Saul demanded of Michal.

"I had to," Michal replied. "He threatened to kill me if I didn't help him."

18So David got away and went to Ramah to see Samuel, and he told him all that Saul had done to him. Then Samuel took David with him to live at Naioth. 19When the report reached Saul that David was at Naioth in Ramah, 20he sent troops to capture him. But when they arrived and saw Samuel and the other prophets prophesying, the Spirit of God came upon Saul's men, and they also began to prophesy. 21When Saul heard what had happened, he sent other troops, but they, too, prophesied! The same thing happened a third time! 22Finally, Saul himself went to Ramah and arrived at the great well in Secu. "Where are Samuel and David?" he demanded.

"They are at Naioth in Ramah," someone told him. 23But on the way to Naioth the Spirit of God came upon Saul, and he, too, began to prophesy! 24He tore off his clothes and lay on the ground all day and all night, prophesying in the presence of Samuel. The people who were watching exclaimed, "What? Is Saul a prophet, too?"

## CHAPTER 20

**JONATHAN WARNS DAVID.** David now fled from Naioth in Ramah and found Jonathan. "What have I done?" he exclaimed. "What is my crime? How have I offended your father that he is so determined to kill me?"

2"That's not true!" Jonathan protested. "I'm sure he's not planning any such thing, for he always tells me everything he's going to do, even the little things. I know he wouldn't hide something like this from me. It just isn't so!"

3Then David took an oath before Jonathan and said, "Your father knows perfectly well about our friendship, so he has said to himself, 'I won't tell Jonathan—why should I hurt him?' But I swear to you that I am only a step away from death! I swear it by the LORD and by your own soul!"

4"Tell me what I can do!" Jonathan exclaimed.

5David replied, "Tomorrow we celebrate the new moon festival. I've always eaten with your father on this occasion, but tomorrow I'll hide in the field and stay there until the evening of the third day. 6If your father asks where I am, tell him I asked permission to go home to Bethlehem for an annual family sacrifice. 7If he says, 'Fine!' then you will know all is well. But if he is angry and loses his temper, then you will know he was planning to kill me. 8Show me this kindness as my sworn friend—for we made a covenant together before the LORD—or kill me yourself if I have sinned against your father. But please don't betray me to him!"

9"Never!" Jonathan exclaimed. "You know that if I had the slightest notion my father was planning to kill you, I would tell you at once."

10Then David asked, "How will I know whether or not your father is angry?"

11"Come out to the field with me," Jonathan replied. And they went out there together. 12Then Jonathan told David, "I promise by the LORD, the God of Israel, that by this time tomorrow, or the next day at the latest, I will talk to my father and let you know at once how he feels about you. If he speaks favorably about you, I will let you know. 13But if he is angry and wants you killed, may the LORD kill me if I don't warn you so you can escape and live. May the LORD be with you as he used to be with my father. 14And may you treat me with the faithful love of the LORD as long as I live. But if I die, 15treat my family with this faithful love, even when the LORD destroys all your enemies."

16So Jonathan made a covenant with David,* saying, "May the LORD destroy all your enemies!" 17And Jonathan made David reaffirm his vow of friendship again, for Jonathan loved David as much as he loved himself.

18Then Jonathan said, "Tomorrow we celebrate the new moon festival. You will be missed when your place at the table is empty. 19The day after tomorrow, toward evening, go to the place where you hid before, and wait there by the stone pile.* 20I will come out and shoot three arrows to the side of the stone pile as though I were shooting at a target. 21Then I will send a boy to bring the arrows back. If you hear me tell him, 'They're on this side,' then you will know, as surely as the LORD lives, that all is well, and there is no trouble. 22But if I tell him, 'Go farther—the arrows are still ahead of you,' then it will mean that you must leave immediately, for the LORD is sending you away. 23And may the LORD make us keep our promises to each other, for he has witnessed them."

24So David hid himself in the field, and when the new moon festival began, the king sat down to eat.

**PROTECTION ● ● ● • •**

19:23 **Jonathan spoke up for David (19:4); Michal helped him escape (19:11-17); Samuel gave him a place to hide (19:18); and the Spirit of God interrupted Saul's manhunt (19:23). Each of these events protected David from harm or death. They were more than coincidence; God was at work. When you are spared from harm, recognize that God may be protecting you because he has a purpose for you.**

19:13 Hebrew *teraphim;* also in 19:16. 20:16 Hebrew *with the house of David.* 20:19 Hebrew *the stone Ezel.* The meaning of the Hebrew is uncertain.

25He sat at his usual place against the wall, with Jonathan sitting opposite him* and Abner beside him. But David's place was empty. 26Saul didn't say anything about it that day, for he said to himself, "Something must have made David ceremonially unclean. Yes, that must be why he's not here." 27But when David's place was empty again the next day, Saul asked Jonathan, "Why hasn't the son of Jesse been here for dinner either yesterday or today?"

28Jonathan replied, "David earnestly asked me if he could go to Bethlehem. 29He wanted to take part in a family sacrifice. His brother demanded that he be there, so I told him he could go. That's why he isn't here."

30Saul boiled with rage at Jonathan. "You stupid son of a whore!"* he swore at him. "Do you think I don't know that you want David to be king in your place, shaming yourself and your mother? 31As long as that son of Jesse is alive, you'll never be king. Now go and get him so I can kill him!"

32"But what has he done?" Jonathan demanded. "Why should he be put to death?" 33Then Saul hurled his spear at Jonathan, intending to kill him. So at last Jonathan realized that his father was really determined to kill David. 34Jonathan left the table in fierce anger and refused to eat all that day, for he was crushed by his father's shameful behavior toward David.

35The next morning, as agreed, Jonathan went out into the field and took a young boy with him to gather his arrows. 36"Start running," he told the boy, "so you can find the arrows as I shoot them." So the boy ran, and Jonathan shot an arrow beyond him. 37When the boy had almost reached the arrow, Jonathan shouted, "The arrow is still ahead of you. 38Hurry, hurry, don't wait." So the boy quickly gathered up the arrows and ran back to his master. 39He, of course, didn't understand what Jonathan meant; only Jonathan and David knew. 40Then Jonathan gave his bow and arrows to the boy and told him to take them back to the city.

41As soon as the boy was gone, David came out from where he had been hiding near the stone pile.* Then David bowed to Jonathan with his face to the ground. Both of them were in tears as they embraced each other and said good-bye, especially David. 42At last Jonathan said to David, "Go in peace, for we have made a pact in the LORD's name. We have entrusted each other and each other's children into the LORD's hands forever." Then David left, and Jonathan returned to the city.

## CHAPTER 21 **DAVID EATS THE HOLY BREAD.**

David went to the city of Nob to see Ahimelech the priest. Ahimelech trembled when he saw him. "Why are you alone?" he asked. "Why is no one with you?"

2"The king has sent me on a private matter," David said. "He told me not to tell anyone why I am here. I have told my men where to meet me later. 3Now, what is there to eat? Give me five loaves of bread or anything else you have."

4"We don't have any regular bread," the priest replied. "But there is the holy bread, which I guess you can have if your young men have not slept with any women recently."

5"Don't worry," David replied. "I never allow my men to be with women when they are on a campaign. And since they stay clean even on ordinary trips, how much more on this one!"

6So, since there was no other food available, the priest gave him the holy bread—the Bread of the Presence that was placed before the LORD in the Tabernacle. It had just been replaced that day with fresh bread.

7Now Doeg the Edomite, Saul's chief herdsman, was there that day for ceremonial purification.*

8David asked Ahimelech, "Do you have a spear or sword? The king's business was so urgent that I didn't even have time to grab a weapon!"

9"I only have the sword of Goliath the Philistine, whom you killed in the valley of Elah," the priest replied. "It is wrapped in a cloth behind the ephod. Take that if you want it, for there is nothing else here."

"There is nothing like it!" David replied. "Give it to me!"

10So David escaped from Saul and went to King Achish of Gath. 11But Achish's officers weren't happy about his being there. "Isn't this David, the king of the land?" they asked. "Isn't he the one the people honor with dances, singing, 'Saul has killed his thousands, and David his ten thousands'?"

12David heard these comments and was afraid of what King Achish might do to him. 13So he pretended to be insane, scratching on doors and drooling down his beard. 14Finally, King Achish said to his men, "Must you bring me a madman? 15We already have enough of them around here! Why should I let someone like this be my guest?"

## CHAPTER 22 **DAVID HIDES IN A CAVE.**

So David left Gath and escaped to the cave of Adullam. Soon his brothers and other relatives joined him there. 2Then others began coming—men who were in trouble or in debt or who were just discontented—until David was the leader of about four hundred men.

### LYING ● ● • • •

21:2 **David lied to protect himself from Saul (21:10). Some excuse this lie because a war was going on and it is the duty of a good soldier to deceive the enemy. But nowhere in Scripture is David's lie condoned. In fact, his lie led to the death of 85 priests (22:9-19). David's small lie seemed harmless enough, but it led to tragedy. The Bible makes it very clear that lying is wrong (Leviticus 19:11). Lying, like every other sin, is serious in God's sight and may lead to all sorts of harmful consequences. All sins must be avoided regardless of whether or not we can foresee their potential consequences.**

20:25 As in Greek version; Hebrew reads *with Jonathan standing.* 20:30 Hebrew *You son of a perverse and rebellious woman.* 20:41 As in Greek version; Hebrew reads *near the south edge.* 21:7 Hebrew *was detained before the LORD.*

[3]Later David went to Mizpeh in Moab, where he
asked the king, "Would you let my father and
mother live here under royal protection until I know
what God is going to do for me?" [4]The king agreed,
and David's parents stayed in Moab while David was
living in his stronghold.
[5]One day the prophet Gad told David, "Leave the
stronghold and return to the land of Judah." So
David went to the forest of Hereth. [6]The news of his
arrival in Judah soon reached Saul. At the time, the
king was sitting beneath a tamarisk tree on the hill at
Gibeah, holding his spear and surrounded by his
officers.
[7]"Listen here, you men of Benjamin!" Saul
shouted when he heard the news. "Has David promised you fields and vineyards? Has he promised to
make you commanders in his army? [8]Is that why you
have conspired against me? For not one of you has
ever told me that my own son is on David's side.
You're not even sorry for me. Think of it! My own
son—encouraging David to try and kill me!"
[9]Then Doeg the Edomite, who was standing there
with Saul's men, spoke up. "When I was at Nob," he
said, "I saw David talking to Ahimelech the priest.
[10]Ahimelech consulted the LORD to find out what
David should do. Then he gave David food and the
sword of Goliath the Philistine."
[11]King Saul immediately sent for Ahimelech and
all his family, who served as priests at Nob. [12]When
they arrived, Saul shouted at him, "Listen to me, you
son of Ahitub!"
"What is it, my king?" Ahimelech asked.
[13]"Why have you and David conspired against
me?" Saul demanded. "Why did you give him food
and a sword? Why have you inquired of God for
him? Why did you encourage him to revolt against
me and to come here and attack me?"
[14]"But sir," Ahimelech replied, "is there anyone
among all your servants who is as faithful as David,
your son-in-law? Why, he is the captain of your
bodyguard and a highly honored member of your
household! [15]This was certainly not the first time I
had consulted God for him! Please don't accuse me
and my family in this matter, for I knew nothing of
any plot against you."
[16]"You will surely die, Ahimelech, along with
your entire family!" the king shouted. [17]And he
ordered his bodyguards, "Kill these priests of the
LORD, for they are allies and conspirators with
David! They knew he was running away from me,
but they didn't tell me!" But Saul's men refused to
kill the LORD's priests.
[18]Then the king said to Doeg, "You do it." So
Doeg turned on them and killed them, eighty-five
priests in all, all still wearing their priestly tunics.
[19]Then he went to Nob, the city of the priests, and
killed the priests' families—men and women, children and babies, and all the cattle, donkeys, and
sheep.
[20]Only Abiathar, one of the sons of Ahimelech,
escaped and fled to David. [21]When he told David
that Saul had killed the priests of the LORD, [22]David
exclaimed, "I knew it! When I saw Doeg there that
day, I knew he would tell Saul. Now I have caused the
death of all your father's family. [23]Stay here with me,
and I will protect you with my own life, for the same
person wants to kill us both."

## FAITHFULNESS ● ● • • •

**22:18-19** **Why did God allow 85 innocent priests to be killed? Scripture does not give a specific answer to this question, but it gives some insight into the issue.**

**Serving God is not a ticket to guaranteed wealth, success, or health. While God does not promise that good people will never be touched by the evil in this world, we can find comfort in his promise that ultimately all evil will be abolished. Those who have remained faithful through their trials will experience untold blessings in the age to come (Matthew 5:11-12; Revelation 21:1-7; 22:1-21).**

CHAPTER **23** **DAVID PROTECTS KEILAH.** One day
news came to David that the Philistines were at
Keilah stealing grain from the threshing floors.
[2]David asked the LORD, "Should I go and attack
them?"
"Yes, go and save Keilah," the LORD told him.
[3]But David's men said, "We're afraid even here in
Judah. We certainly don't want to go to Keilah to
fight the whole Philistine army!"
[4]So David asked the LORD again, and again the
LORD replied, "Go down to Keilah, for I will help you
conquer the Philistines."
[5]So David and his men went to Keilah. They
slaughtered the Philistines and took all their livestock and rescued the people of Keilah. [6]Abiathar the
priest went to Keilah with David, taking the ephod
with him to get answers for David from the LORD.
[7]Saul soon learned that David was at Keilah.
"Good!" he exclaimed. "We've got him now! God
has handed him over to me, for he has trapped
himself in a walled city!"
[8]So Saul mobilized his entire army to march to
Keilah and attack David and his men. [9]But David
learned of Saul's plan and told Abiathar the priest
to bring the ephod and ask the LORD what he
should do. [10]And David prayed, "O LORD, God of
Israel, I have heard that Saul is planning to come
and destroy Keilah because I am here. [11]Will the

## DECISIONS ● ● • • •

**23:2 David sought the Lord's guidance *before* he took action, probably through the Urim and Thummim that Abiathar the priest had brought (23:6). He listened to God's directions and then proceeded accordingly. Rather than trying to find God's will *after* the fact or having to ask God to undo the results of our hasty decisions, we should take time to discern God's will beforehand. We can hear him speak through the counsel of others, through his Word, and through the leading of his Spirit in our heart, as well as through circumstances.**

## FRIENDS ● ● • • •

**23:16-18 This may have been the last time David and Jonathan were together. As true friends they were more than just companions who enjoyed each other's company. They encouraged each other's faith in God and trusted each other with their deepest thoughts and closest confidences. These are the marks of true friendship.**

**As Jonathan prepared to leave David, he not only promised to be David's friend to the end, but he also encouraged David to remember God's faithfulness. As a friend, remember that you have even more to offer than companionship.**

men of Keilah surrender me to him?* And will Saul actually come as I have heard? O LORD, God of Israel, please tell me."

And the LORD said, "He will come."

[12]Again David asked, "Will these men of Keilah really betray me and my men to Saul?"

And the LORD replied, "Yes, they will betray you."

[13]So David and his men—about six hundred of them now—left Keilah and began roaming the countryside. Word soon reached Saul that David had escaped, so he didn't go to Keilah after all. [14]David now stayed in the strongholds of the wilderness and in the hill country of Ziph. Saul hunted him day after day, but God didn't let him be found.

[15]One day near Horesh, David received the news that Saul was on the way to Ziph to search for him and kill him. [16]Jonathan went to find David and encouraged him to stay strong in his faith in God. [17]"Don't be afraid," Jonathan reassured him. "My father will never find you! You are going to be the king of Israel, and I will be next to you, as my father is well aware." [18]So the two of them renewed their covenant of friendship before the LORD. Then Jonathan returned home, while David stayed at Horesh.

[19]But now the men of Ziph went to Saul in Gibeah and betrayed David to him. "We know where David is hiding," they said. "He is in the strongholds of Horesh on the hill of Hakilah, which is in the southern part of Jeshimon. [20]Come down whenever you're ready, O king, and we will catch him and hand him over to you!"

[21]"The LORD bless you," Saul said. "At last someone is concerned about me! [22]Go and check again to be sure of where he is staying and who has seen him there, for I know that he is very crafty. [23]Discover his hiding places, and come back with a more definite report. Then I'll go with you. And if he is in the area at all, I'll track him down, even if I have to search every hiding place in Judah!"

[24]So the men of Ziph returned home ahead of Saul. Meanwhile, David and his men had moved into the wilderness of Maon in the Arabah Valley south of Jeshimon. [25]When David heard that Saul and his men were searching for him, he went even farther into the wilderness to the great rock, and he remained there in the wilderness of Maon. But Saul kept after him. [26]He and David were now on opposite sides of a mountain. Just as Saul and his men began to close in on David and his men, [27]an urgent message reached Saul that the Philistines were raiding Israel again. [28]So Saul quit the chase and returned to fight the Philistines. Ever since that time, the place where David was camped has been called the Rock of Escape.* [29]David then went to live in the strongholds of En-gedi.

## CHAPTER 24 **DAVID REFUSES TO GET EVEN.**

After Saul returned from fighting the Philistines, he was told that David had gone into the wilderness of En-gedi. [2]So Saul chose three thousand special troops from throughout Israel and went to search for David and his men near the rocks of the wild goats. [3]At the place where the road passes some sheepfolds, Saul went into a cave to relieve himself. But as it happened, David and his men were hiding in that very cave!

[4]"Now's your opportunity!" David's men whispered to him. "Today is the day the LORD was talking about when he said, 'I will certainly put Saul into your power, to do with as you wish.'" Then David crept forward and cut off a piece of Saul's robe.

[5]But then David's conscience began bothering him because he had cut Saul's robe. [6]"The LORD knows I shouldn't have done it," he said to his men. "It is a serious thing to attack the LORD's anointed one, for the LORD himself has chosen him." [7]So David sharply rebuked his men and did not let them kill Saul.

## RESPECT ● ● • • •

**24:5 David had great respect for Saul, even though Saul was trying to kill him. Although Saul was in a state of sin and rebellion against God, David still respected the position he held as God's anointed king. David knew he would one day be king—but he also knew it was not right to strike down the man God had placed on the throne. If David assassinated Saul, he would be setting a precedent for his own opponents to remove him some day.**

**Romans 13:1-7 teaches that God has placed the government and its leaders in power. We may not know why, but like David, we are to respect the positions and roles of those to whom God has given authority. There is one exception, however. Because God is our highest authority, we should not allow a leader to force us to violate God's law.**

After Saul had left the cave and gone on his way, [8]David came out and shouted after him, "My lord the king!" And when Saul looked around, David bowed low before him.

[9]Then he shouted to Saul, "Why do you listen to the people who say I am trying to harm you? [10]This very day you can see with your own eyes it isn't true. For the LORD placed you at my mercy back there in the cave, and some of my men told me to kill you, but I spared you. For I said, 'I will never harm him—he is the LORD's anointed one.' [11]Look, my father, at what I have in my hand. It is a piece of your robe! I cut it off, but I didn't kill you. This proves that

23:11 Some manuscripts lack the first sentence of 23:11. 23:28 Hebrew *Sela-hammahlekoth*.

I am not trying to harm you and that I have not sinned against you, even though you have been hunting for me to kill me. 12The LORD will decide between us. Perhaps the LORD will punish you for what you are trying to do to me, but I will never harm you. 13As that old proverb says, 'From evil people come evil deeds.' So you can be sure I will never harm you. 14Who is the king of Israel trying to catch anyway? Should he spend his time chasing one who is as worthless as a dead dog or a flea? 15May the LORD judge which of us is right and punish the guilty one. He is my advocate, and he will rescue me from your power!"

16Saul called back, "Is that really you, my son David?" Then he began to cry. 17And he said to David, "You are a better man than I am, for you have repaid me good for evil. 18Yes, you have been wonderfully kind to me today, for when the LORD put me in a place where you could have killed me, you didn't do it. 19Who else would let his enemy get away when he had him in his power? May the LORD reward you well for the kindness you have shown me today. 20And now I realize that you are surely going to be king, and Israel will flourish under your rule. 21Now, swear to me by the LORD that when that happens you will not kill my family and destroy my line of descendants!"

22So David promised, and Saul went home. But David and his men went back to their stronghold.

## CHAPTER 25

**ABIGAIL STOPS A FIGHT.** Now Samuel died, and all Israel gathered for his funeral. They buried him near his home at Ramah.

Then David moved down to the wilderness of Maon.* 2There was a wealthy man from Maon who owned property near the village of Carmel. He had three thousand sheep and a thousand goats, and it was sheep-shearing time. 3This man's name was Nabal, and his wife, Abigail, was a sensible and beautiful woman. But Nabal, a descendant of Caleb, was mean and dishonest in all his dealings.

4When David heard that Nabal was shearing his sheep, 5he sent ten of his young men to Carmel. He told them to deliver this message: 6"Peace and prosperity to you, your family, and everything you own! 7I am told that you are shearing your sheep and goats. While your shepherds stayed among us near Carmel, we never harmed them, and nothing was ever stolen from them. 8Ask your own servants, and they will tell you this is true. So would you please be kind to us, since we have come at a time of celebration? Please give us any provisions you might have on hand." 9David's young men gave this message to Nabal and waited for his reply.

10"Who is this fellow David?" Nabal sneered. "Who does this son of Jesse think he is? There are lots of servants these days who run away from their masters. 11Should I take my bread and water and the meat I've slaughtered for my shearers and give it to a band of outlaws who come from who knows where?" 12So David's messengers returned and told him what Nabal had said.

13"Get your swords!" was David's reply as he strapped on his own. Four hundred men started off with David, and two hundred remained behind to guard their equipment.

14Meanwhile, one of Nabal's servants went to Abigail and told her, "David sent men from the wilderness to talk to our master, and he insulted them. 15But David's men were very good to us, and we never suffered any harm from them. Nothing was stolen from us the whole time they were with us. 16In fact, day and night they were like a wall of protection to us and the sheep. 17You'd better think fast, for there is going to be trouble for our master and his whole family. He's so ill-tempered that no one can even talk to him!"

18Abigail lost no time. She quickly gathered two hundred loaves of bread, two skins of wine, five dressed sheep, nearly a bushel* of roasted grain, one hundred raisin cakes, and two hundred fig cakes. She packed them on donkeys and said to her servants, 19"Go on ahead. I will follow you shortly." But she didn't tell her husband what she was doing.

20As she was riding her donkey into a mountain ravine, she saw David and his men coming toward her. 21David had just been saying, "A lot of good it did to help this fellow. We protected his flocks in the wilderness, and nothing he owned was lost or stolen. But he has repaid me evil for good. 22May God deal with me severely if even one man of his household is still alive tomorrow morning!"

23When Abigail saw David, she quickly got off her donkey and bowed low before him. 24She fell at his feet and said, "I accept all blame in this matter, my lord. Please listen to what I have to say. 25I know Nabal is a wicked and ill-tempered man; please don't pay any attention to him. He is a fool, just as his name suggests.* But I never even saw the messengers you sent.

### LISTENING ● ● • • •

25:24 **David was in no mood to listen when he set out for Nabal's property (25:13, 22). Nevertheless, he stopped to hear what Abigail had to say. If he had ignored her, he would have been guilty of taking vengeance into his own hands. No matter how right we think we are, we must always be careful to stop and listen to what others have to say. The extra time and effort can save us much pain and trouble in the long run.**

26"Now, my lord, as surely as the LORD lives and you yourself live, since the LORD has kept you from murdering and taking vengeance into your own hands, let all your enemies be as cursed as Nabal is. 27And here is a present I have brought to you and your young men. 28Please forgive me if I have offended in any way. The LORD will surely reward you with a lasting dynasty, for you are fighting the LORD's

25:1 As in Greek version; Hebrew reads *Paran.* 25:18 Hebrew *5 seahs* [30 liters]. 25:25 The name *Nabal* means "fool."

## GOD FIRST ● ● ● ● •

**26:8-11 The strongest moral decisions are the ones we make before temptation strikes. David was determined to follow God. This carried over into his decision not to murder God's chosen king, Saul, even when David's men and the circumstances seemed to make it possible. Whom would you have been like in such a situation—David or David's men? To be like David and follow God, we must realize that we can't do wrong in order to execute justice. Even when our closest friends counsel us to do a certain action that seems right, we must always put God's commands first.**

battles. And you have not done wrong throughout
your entire life.
29"Even when you are chased by those who seek
your life, you are safe in the care of the LORD your
God, secure in his treasure pouch! But the lives of
your enemies will disappear like stones shot from a
sling! 30When the LORD has done all he promised
and has made you leader of Israel, 31don't let this be
a blemish on your record. Then you won't have to
carry on your conscience the staggering burden of
needless bloodshed and vengeance. And when the
LORD has done these great things for you, please
remember me!"
32David replied to Abigail, "Praise the LORD, the
God of Israel, who has sent you to meet me today!
33Thank God for your good sense! Bless you for
keeping me from murdering the man and carrying
out vengeance with my own hands. 34For I swear by
the LORD, the God of Israel, who has kept me from
hurting you, that if you had not hurried out to meet
me, not one of Nabal's men would be alive tomorrow morning." 35Then David accepted her gifts and
told her, "Return home in peace. We will not kill
your husband."
36When Abigail arrived home, she found that Nabal had thrown a big party and was celebrating like
a king. He was very drunk, so she didn't tell him
anything about her meeting with David until the
next morning. 37The next morning when he was
sober, she told him what had happened. As a result
he had a stroke,* and he lay on his bed paralyzed.
38About ten days later, the LORD struck him and he
died.
39When David heard that Nabal was dead, he said,
"Praise the LORD, who has paid back Nabal and kept
me from doing it myself. Nabal has received the
punishment for his sin." Then David wasted no time
in sending messengers to Abigail to ask her to become his wife.
40When the messengers arrived at Carmel, they
told Abigail, "David has sent us to ask if you will
marry him."
41She bowed low to the ground and responded,
"Yes, I am even willing to become a slave to David's
servants!" 42Quickly getting ready, she took along
five of her servant girls as attendants, mounted her
donkey, and went with David's messengers. And so
she became his wife. 43David also married Ahinoam
from Jezreel, making both of them his wives. 44Saul,
meanwhile, had given his daughter Michal, David's
wife, to a man from Gallim named Palti son of Laish.

CHAPTER **26** **DAVID SNEAKS INTO CAMP.** Now
some messengers from Ziph came back to Saul at
Gibeah to tell him, "David is hiding on the hill of
Hakilah, which overlooks Jeshimon." 2So Saul
took three thousand of his best troops and went to
hunt him down in the wilderness of Ziph. 3Saul
camped along the road beside the hill of Hakilah,
near Jeshimon, where David was hiding. But David
knew of Saul's arrival, 4so he sent out spies to
watch his movements.
5David slipped over to Saul's camp one night to
look around. Saul and his general, Abner son of Ner,
were sleeping inside a ring formed by the slumbering
warriors. 6"Will anyone volunteer to go in there with
me?" David asked Ahimelech the Hittite and Abishai
son of Zeruiah, Joab's brother.
"I'll go with you," Abishai replied. 7So David
and Abishai went right into Saul's camp and found
him asleep, with his spear stuck in the ground
beside his head. Abner and the warriors were lying
asleep around him. 8"God has surely handed your
enemy over to you this time!" Abishai whispered
to David. "Let me thrust that spear through him.
I'll pin him to the ground, and I won't need to
strike twice!"
9"No!" David said. "Don't kill him. For who can
remain innocent after attacking the LORD's anointed
one? 10Surely the LORD will strike Saul down someday, or he will die in battle or of old age. 11But the
LORD forbid that I should kill the one he has
anointed! But I'll tell you what—we'll take his spear
and his jug of water and then get out of here!"
12So David took the spear and jug of water that
were near Saul's head. Then he and Abishai got away
without anyone seeing them or even waking up,
because the LORD had put Saul's men into a deep
sleep. 13David climbed the hill opposite the camp
until he was at a safe distance. 14Then he shouted
down to Abner and Saul, "Wake up, Abner!"
"Who is it?" Abner demanded.
15"Well, Abner, you're a great man, aren't you?"
David taunted. "Where in all Israel is there anyone
as mighty? So why haven't you guarded your master
the king when someone came to kill him? 16This
isn't good at all! I swear by the LORD that you and
your men deserve to die, because you failed to protect your master, the LORD's anointed! Look around!

## CREATIVITY ● ● ● ● •

**26:15-16 David could have killed Saul and Abner and made a point, but he would have disobeyed God and set into motion unknown consequences. Instead, he took a water jug and a spear, showing that he had had the opportunity to do evil but had not done it. David made the point that he had great respect for both God and God's chosen king. When you need to make a point, look for creative, God-honoring ways to do so. It will have a more significant impact.**

25:37 Hebrew *his heart failed him.*

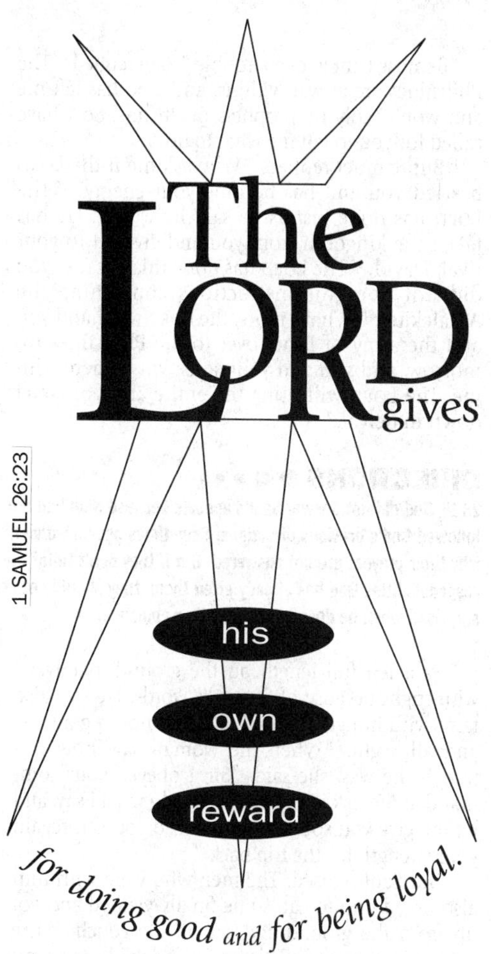
The
LORD
gives
his
own
reward
for doing good and for being loyal.
1 SAMUEL 26:23

Where are the king's spear and the jug of water that were beside his head?"

[17]Saul recognized David's voice and called out, "Is that you, my son David?"

And David replied, "Yes, my lord the king. [18]Why are you chasing me? What have I done? What is my crime? [19]But now let my lord the king listen to his servant. If the LORD has stirred you up against me, then let him accept my offering. But if this is simply a human scheme, then may those involved be cursed by the LORD. For you have driven me from my home, so I can no longer live among the LORD's people and worship as I should. [20]Must I die on foreign soil, far from the presence of the LORD? Why has the king of Israel come out to search for a single flea? Why does he hunt me down like a partridge on the mountains?"

[21]Then Saul confessed, "I have sinned. Come back home, my son, and I will no longer try to harm you, for you valued my life today. I have been a fool and very, very wrong."

[22]"Here is your spear, O king," David replied. "Let one of your young men come over and get it. [23]The LORD gives his own reward for doing good and for being loyal, and I refused to kill you even when the LORD placed you in my power, for you are the LORD's anointed one. [24]Now may the LORD value my life, even as I have valued yours today. May he rescue me from all my troubles."

[25]And Saul said to David, "Blessings on you, my son David. You will do heroic deeds and be a great conqueror." Then David went away, and Saul returned home.

CHAPTER **27** **DAVID AMONG THE PHILISTINES.** But David kept thinking to himself, "Someday Saul is going to get me. The best thing for me to do is escape to the Philistines. Then Saul will stop hunting for me, and I will finally be safe."

[2]So David took his six hundred men and their families and went to live at Gath under the protection of King Achish. [3]David brought his two wives along with him—Ahinoam of Jezreel and Abigail of Carmel, Nabal's widow. [4]Word soon reached Saul that David had fled to Gath, so he stopped hunting for him.

[5]One day David said to Achish, "If it is all right with you, we would rather live in one of the country towns instead of here in the royal city." [6]So Achish gave him the town of Ziklag (which still belongs to the kings of Judah to this day), [7]and they lived there among the Philistines for a year and four months.

[8]David and his men spent their time raiding the Geshurites, the Girzites, and the Amalekites—people who had lived near Shur, along the road to Egypt, since ancient times. [9]David didn't leave one person alive in the villages he attacked. He took the sheep, cattle, donkeys, camels, and clothing before returning home to see King Achish.

[10]"Where did you make your raid today?" Achish would ask.

And David would reply, "Against the south of Judah, the Jerahmeelites, and the Kenites."

[11]No one was left alive to come to Gath and tell where he had really been. This happened again and again while he was living among the Philistines. [12]Achish believed David and thought to himself, "By now the people of Israel must hate him bitterly. Now he will have to stay here and serve me forever!"

## PRETENSE ● ● • • •

27:10-12 **Was David wrong in falsely reporting his activities to Achish? No doubt David was lying, but he may have felt this was justified in a time of war against a heathen enemy. David knew he would one day be Israel's king. The Philistines were still his enemies, but this was an excellent place to hide from Saul. When Achish asked David to go into battle against Israel, David agreed, once again pretending loyalty to the Philistines (29:2-3). Whether he would have actually fought Saul's army we can't know, but we can be sure that his ultimate loyalty was to God and not to Achish or Saul.**

## OCCULT ● ● • • •

**28:3-8 It was Saul who had banned all mediums and psychics from Israel, but in desperation he turned to one for counsel. Although he had removed the sin of witchcraft from the land, he did not remove it from his heart. We may make a great show of denouncing sin, but if our heart does not change, the sins will return. Knowing what is right and condemning what is wrong does not take the place of *doing* what is right.**

CHAPTER **28** **SAUL VISITS A WITCH.** About that time the Philistines mustered their armies for another war with Israel. King Achish told David, "You and your men will be expected to join me in battle."

[2]"Very well!" David agreed. "Now you will see for yourself what we can do."

Then Achish told David, "I will make you my personal bodyguard for life."

[3]Meanwhile, Samuel had died, and all Israel had mourned for him. He was buried in Ramah, his hometown. And Saul had banned all mediums and psychics from the land of Israel.

[4]The Philistines set up their camp at Shunem, and Saul and the armies of Israel camped at Gilboa. [5]When Saul saw the vast Philistine army, he became frantic with fear. [6]He asked the LORD what he should do, but the LORD refused to answer him, either by dreams or by sacred lots* or by the prophets. [7]Saul then said to his advisers, "Find a woman who is a medium, so I can go and ask her what to do."

His advisers replied, "There is a medium at Endor."

[8]So Saul disguised himself by wearing ordinary clothing instead of his royal robes. Then he went to the woman's home at night, accompanied by two of his men.

"I have to talk to a man who has died," he said. "Will you call up his spirit for me?"

[9]"Are you trying to get me killed?" the woman demanded. "You know that Saul has expelled all the mediums and psychics from the land. Why are you setting a trap for me?"

[10]But Saul took an oath in the name of the LORD and promised, "As surely as the LORD lives, nothing bad will happen to you for doing this."

[11]Finally, the woman said, "Well, whose spirit do you want me to call up?"

"Call up Samuel," Saul replied.

[12]When the woman saw Samuel, she screamed, "You've deceived me! You are Saul!"

[13]"Don't be afraid!" the king told her. "What do you see?"

"I see a god* coming up out of the earth," she said.

[14]"What does he look like?" Saul asked.

"He is an old man wrapped in a robe," she replied. Saul realized that it was Samuel, and he fell to the ground before him.

[15]"Why have you disturbed me by calling me back?" Samuel asked.

"Because I am in deep trouble," Saul replied. "The Philistines are at war with us, and God has left me and won't reply by prophets or dreams. So I have called for you to tell me what to do."

[16]But Samuel replied, "Why ask me if the LORD has left you and has become your enemy? [17]The LORD has done just as he said he would. He has taken the kingdom from you and given it to your rival, David. [18]The LORD has done this because you did not obey his instructions concerning the Amalekites. [19]What's more, the LORD will hand you and the army of Israel over to the Philistines tomorrow, and you and your sons will be here with me. The LORD will bring the entire army of Israel down in defeat."

## DIRECTIONS ● ● • • •

**28:15 God did not answer Saul's appeals because Saul had not followed God's previous directions. Sometimes people wonder why their prayers are not answered. But if they don't fulfill the responsibilities God has already given them, they should not be surprised when he does not give further guidance.**

[20]Saul fell full length on the ground, paralyzed with fright because of Samuel's words. He was also faint with hunger, for he had eaten nothing all day and all night. [21]When the woman saw how distraught he was, she said, "Sir, I obeyed your command at the risk of my life. [22]Now do what I say, and let me give you something to eat so you can regain your strength for the trip back."

[23]But Saul refused. The men who were with him also urged him to eat, so he finally yielded and got up from the ground and sat on the couch. [24]The woman had been fattening a calf, so she hurried out and killed it. She kneaded dough and baked unleavened bread. [25]She brought the meal to Saul and his men, and they ate it. Then they went out into the night.

CHAPTER **29** **DAVID LEAVES THE PHILISTINES.** The entire Philistine army now mobilized at Aphek, and the Israelites camped at the spring in Jezreel. [2]As the Philistine rulers were leading out their troops in groups of one hundred and one thousand, David and his men marched at the rear with King Achish. [3]But the Philistine commanders demanded, "What are these Hebrews doing here?"

And Achish told them, "This is David, the man who ran away from King Saul of Israel. He's been with me for years, and I've never found a single fault in him since he defected to me."

[4]But the Philistine commanders were angry. "Send him back!" they demanded. "He can't go into the battle with us. What if he turns against us? Is there any better way for him to reconcile himself with his master than by turning on us in battle? [5]Isn't this the same David about whom the women

28:6 Hebrew *by Urim*. 28:13 Or *gods*.

of Israel sing in their dances, 'Saul has killed his thousands, and David his ten thousands'?"

6So Achish finally summoned David and his men. "I swear by the LORD," he told them, "you are some of the finest men I've ever met. I think you should go with us, but the other Philistine rulers won't hear of it. 7Please don't upset them, but go back quietly."

8"What have I done to deserve this treatment?" David demanded. "Why can't I fight the enemies of my lord, the king?"

9But Achish insisted, "As far as I'm concerned, you're as perfect as an angel of God. But my commanders are afraid to have you with them in the battle. 10Now get up early in the morning, and leave with your men as soon as it gets light." 11So David headed back into the land of the Philistines, while the Philistine army went on to Jezreel.

## CHAPTER 30

Three days later, when David and his men arrived home at their town of Ziklag, they found that the Amalekites had made a raid into the Negev and had burned Ziklag to the ground. 2They had carried off the women and children and everyone else but without killing anyone. 3When David and his men saw the ruins and realized what had happened to their families, 4they wept until they could weep no more. 5David's two wives, Ahinoam of Jezreel and Abigail, the widow of Nabal of Carmel, were among those captured. 6David was now in serious trouble because his men were very bitter about losing their wives and children, and they began to talk of stoning him. But David found strength in the LORD his God.

7Then he said to Abiathar the priest, "Bring me the ephod!" So Abiathar brought it. 8Then David asked the LORD, "Should I chase them? Will I catch them?"

And the LORD told him, "Yes, go after them. You will surely recover everything that was taken from you!" 9So David and his six hundred men set out, and they soon came to Besor Brook. 10But two hundred of the men were too exhausted to cross the brook, so David continued the pursuit with his four hundred remaining troops.

11Some of David's troops found an Egyptian man in a field and brought him to David. They gave him some bread to eat and some water to drink. 12They also gave him part of a fig cake and two clusters of raisins because he hadn't had anything to eat or drink for three days and nights. It wasn't long before his strength returned.

13"To whom do you belong, and where do you come from?" David asked him.

"I am an Egyptian—the slave of an Amalekite," he replied. "My master left me behind three days ago because I was sick. 14We were on our way back from raiding the Kerethites in the Negev, the territory of Judah, and the land of Caleb, and we had just burned Ziklag."

15"Will you lead me to them?" David asked.

### SCAPEGOAT ● ● • • •

30:6 **Faced with the tragedy of losing their families, David's soldiers began to turn against him and even talked about killing him. Instead of planning a rescue, they looked for someone to blame. But David began looking for a solution rather than a scapegoat. When facing problems, remember that it is useless to look for someone to blame or criticize. Instead, consider how you can help find a solution.**

The young man replied, "If you swear by God's name that you will not kill me or give me back to my master, then I will guide you to them."

16So the Egyptian led them to the Amalekite encampment. When David and his men arrived, the Amalekites were spread out across the fields, eating and drinking and dancing with joy because of the vast amount of plunder they had taken from the Philistines and the land of Judah. 17David and his men rushed in among them and slaughtered them throughout that night and the entire next day until evening. None of the Amalekites escaped except four hundred young men who fled on camels. 18David got back everything the Amalekites had taken, and he rescued his two wives. 19Nothing was missing: small or great, son or daughter, nor anything else that had been taken. David brought everything back. 20His troops rounded up all the flocks and herds and drove them on ahead. "These all belong to David as his reward!" they said.

21When they reached Besor Brook and met the two hundred men who had been too tired to go with them, David greeted them joyfully. 22But some troublemakers among David's men said, "They didn't go with us, so they can't have any of the plunder. Give them their wives and children, and tell them to be gone."

23But David said, "No, my brothers! Don't be selfish with what the LORD has given us. He has kept us safe and helped us defeat the enemy. 24Do you think anyone will listen to you when you talk like this? We share and share alike—those who go to battle and those who guard the equipment." 25From then on David made this a law for all of Israel, and it is still followed.

26When he arrived at Ziklag, David sent part of the plunder to the leaders of Judah, who were his friends. "Here is a present for you, taken from the LORD's enemies," he said. 27The gifts were sent to the leaders of the following towns where David and his men had been: Bethel, Ramoth-negev,

### KINDNESS ● ● • • •

30:11-15 **The Amalekites cruelly left this servant to die, but God used him to help David. David and his men treated the young man kindly, and he returned the kindness by leading them to the enemy, the Amalekites. Treat those you meet with respect and dignity no matter how insignificant they may seem. You never know how God might use them to help you or haunt you, depending on your response to them.**

## CHARACTER ● ● • • •

**31:3-4 Saul was tall, handsome, strong, rich, and powerful. But all of this was not enough to make him someone we should copy. He was tall physically, but he was small in God's eyes. He was handsome, but his sin made him ugly. He was strong, but his lack of faith made him weak. He was rich, but he was spiritually bankrupt. He could give orders to many, but he couldn't command their respect or allegiance. Saul looked good on the outside, but he was decaying on the inside. Godly character is much more valuable than good looks.**

Jattir, [28]Aroer, Siphmoth, Eshtemoa, [29]Racal,* the towns of the Jerahmeelites, the towns of the Kenites, [30]Hormah, Bor-ashan, Athach, [31]Hebron, and all the other places they had visited.

CHAPTER **31** **SAUL DIES IN BATTLE.** Now the Philistines attacked Israel, forcing the Israelites to flee.
Many were slaughtered on the slopes of Mount
Gilboa. [2]The Philistines closed in on Saul and his
sons, and they killed three of his sons—Jonathan,
Abinadab, and Malkishua. [3]The fighting grew very
fierce around Saul, and the Philistine archers
caught up with him and wounded him severely.
[4]Saul groaned to his armor bearer, "Take your
sword and kill me before these pagan Philistines
run me through and humiliate me." But his armor
bearer was afraid and would not do it. So Saul took
his own sword and fell on it. [5]When his armor
bearer realized that Saul was dead, he fell on his
own sword and died beside the king. [6]So Saul,
three of his sons, his armor bearer, and his troops
all died together that same day.
[7]When the Israelites on the other side of the
Jezreel Valley and beyond the Jordan saw that their
army had been routed and that Saul and his sons
were dead, they abandoned their towns and fled.
So the Philistines moved in and occupied their
towns.
[8]The next day, when the Philistines went out to
strip the dead, they found the bodies of Saul and his
three sons on Mount Gilboa. [9]So they cut off Saul's
head and stripped off his armor. Then they proclaimed the news of Saul's death in their pagan
temple and to the people throughout the land of
Philistia. [10]They placed his armor in the temple of
the Ashtoreths, and they fastened his body to the
wall of the city of Beth-shan.
[11]But when the people of Jabesh-gilead heard what
the Philistines had done to Saul, [12]their warriors
traveled all night to Beth-shan and took the bodies
of Saul and his sons down from the wall. They
brought them to Jabesh, where they burned the
bodies. [13]Then they took their remains and buried
them beneath the tamarisk tree at Jabesh, and they
fasted for seven days.

30:29 Greek version reads *Carmel.*

## OBEDIENCE ● ● • • •

**31:13 Saul's death was also the death of an ideal—Israel could no longer believe that having a king like the other nations would solve all their troubles. The real problem was not the form of government, but the sinful king. Saul tried to please God with spurts of religiosity, but real spirituality takes a lifetime of consistent obedience.**

**Heroic, spiritual lives are built by stacking days of obedience one on top of the other. Like a brick, each obedient act is small in itself, but in time the acts pile up, building a huge wall of strong character—a great defense against temptation. We should strive for consistent obedience each day.**

# MEGA themes

**KING** Because Israel had corrupt priests and judges, the people wanted a king. They wanted to be organized like the surrounding nations. Although it was against his original purpose, God answered their request and gave them Saul.

Unfortunately, establishing a monarchy did not solve Israel's problems. God wants each person to give the genuine devotion of his or her mind and heart to him—not to some "king." No government or set of laws can substitute for the rule of God.

1. List a few reasons for describing God as the King.
2. What does it mean when you say Jesus Christ is Lord in a person's life?
3. How do you feel about having God as your King? If you consider Jesus to be Lord, what difference does it make in your daily life?

**GOD'S CONTROL** Israel prospered as long as the people regarded God as their true King. When the leaders strayed from God and his law, he intervened in their lives and overruled their actions. This way, God maintained ultimate control.

God is always at work in this world, even when we can't see what he is doing. No matter what kinds of pressures we must endure or how many changes we must face, ultimately God is in control. When we grow confident of God's sovereignty, we can face the difficult situations in our life with boldness.

1. As King, God is in control of the world. Has there been a time you felt God was not in control? How did you feel? What were you thinking? How did you choose to deal with the situation?
2. God is in control, even when you do not feel like he is. How can you be sure this is true?
3. What difference does it make for you that God is in control of the world?
4. In what areas of your life do you feel the need to know that he is in control? How will you deal with those times when it seems like he is not in control? How can you prepare yourself for those times?

**LEADERSHIP** God guided his people using different forms of leadership: judges, priests, prophets, and kings. Those chosen for these different offices, such as Eli, Samuel, Saul, and David, portrayed different styles of leadership. Yet the success of each leader depended on his devotion to God.

When Eli, Samuel, Saul, and David disobeyed God, they faced tragic consequences. Sin affected what they achieved for God, as well as how they raised their children. Being a true leader means letting God guide your activities, values, and goals—including your relationships in your family.

1. Evaluate the strengths and weaknesses of the following leaders:
   a. Eli b. Samuel c. Saul d. David
2. Taking the best from each leader, what qualities characterize godly leadership?
3. Taking the worst from each leader, what qualities characterize leadership that's not godly?
4. What characteristics of godly leadership do you possess?
5. What characteristics do you see in yourself that you must always be giving over to God so that they do not trap you or lead you into sin?
6. Each of us has a chance to be a leader by leading others toward Christ. Describe the kind of leader you want to be for God.

**OBEDIENCE** To God, "obedience is far better than sacrifice" (15:22). God wanted his people to obey, serve, and follow him with a whole heart, rather than maintaining a superficial commitment based on traditions or ceremonies.

Although we don't have to perform all the Jewish sacrifices, we may still rely on outward observances to substitute for inward commitment. God wants all our work and worship to be motivated by genuine, heartfelt devotion to him.

1. Rewrite 1 Samuel 15:22 in your own words.
2. In what ways can being "religious" interfere with a person's relationship with God?
3. What is the connection in your life between loving God and obeying God? What is the connection between obedience and sacrifice?

**GOD'S FAITHFULNESS** God faithfully kept the promises he made to Israel. He responded to his people with tender mercy and swift justice. In showing mercy, he faithfully acted in the best interest of his people. In showing justice, he was faithful to his word and perfect moral nature.

God's mercy is seen in the way he withholds the punishment for our sins. Because God is faithful, he can be counted on to show us mercy. Yet God is also just and will not tolerate rebellion. His faithfulness and unselfish love should inspire us to dedicate ourselves to him completely. We must never take this precious mercy for granted.

1. What do you learn about God's mercy from his relationships with the following people?
   a. Eli b. Samuel c. Saul
   d. David e. The Hebrew nation
2. What do you learn about God's justice from those relationships?
3. How are both his loving mercy and holy justice examples of his faithfulness?
4. How should Christians respond to our faithful God? Why?
5. Complete these statements:
   a. Because God is faithful, I know:
   b. Because God is faithful, I will:

1375 B.C.
**Judges begin to rule**

1050
**Saul becomes king**

1010
**Saul dies; David is king of Judah**

1003
**David becomes king of all Israel**

997(?)
**David and Bathsheba sin**

991
**Solomon born**

980(?)
**David's census**

970
**David dies; Solomon made king**

930
**The kingdom is divided**

**G**enuine heroes are hard to find—those men and women who excel in their careers and in life. They are people we watch carefully and even copy. The problem is that whenever we put them on pedestals, they all seem to fall. Under the magnifying glass of public scrutiny, people's shortcomings and weaknesses become painfully obvious, and we become very disappointed. ■That's the way it is with any human being. All of us sin and fall . . . all the time. But somehow we expect our heroes to be bigger than life, to be perfect. ■David was the essence of a hero. Strong, brave, handsome, forceful, and committed. He had reached the top of the world. He was king, his enemies were defeated, and the people loved him. But David was human, too, and at the pinnacle of his success he fell, committing lust, adultery, and murder. ■With modern heroes, that would be the end of the story—another one bites the dust. But with David, there was more. Recognizing his sin, he turned back to God and led the nation God's way. His comeback complete, he again became a "man after [God's] own heart." ■Do you need a hero? David would be a good one. Not for his glory and accomplishments—and certainly not for his sin—but for his humble repentance and his determination to do things God's way.

## STATS

PURPOSE: (1) To record the history of David's reign; (2) to demonstrate effective leadership under God; (3) to reveal that one person *can* make a difference; (4) to show the personal qualities that please God; (5) to depict David as an ideal leader of an imperfect kingdom, and to foreshadow Christ, who will be the ideal leader of a new and perfect kingdom (chapter 7)

AUTHOR: Unknown. Some have suggested that Nathan's son Zabud may have been the author (1 Kings 4:5). The book also includes the writings of Nathan and Gad (1 Chronicles 29:29).

DATE WRITTEN: 930 B.C.; written soon after David's reign, 1010–970 B.C.

SETTING: The land of Israel under David's rule

SPECIAL FEATURE: This book was named after the prophet who anointed David and guided him in godly living

# 2 Samuel

**CHAPTER 1** After the death of Saul, David returned from his victory over the Amalekites and
spent two days in Ziklag. 2On the third day after
David's return, a man arrived from the Israelite
battlefront. He had torn his clothes and put dirt on
his head to show that he was in mourning. He fell
to the ground before David in deep respect.
3"Where have you come from?" David asked.
"I escaped from the Israelite camp," the man
replied.
4"What happened?" David demanded. "Tell me
how the battle went."
The man replied, "Our entire army fled. Many
men are dead and wounded on the battlefield, and
Saul and his son Jonathan have been killed."
5"How do you know that Saul and Jonathan are
dead?" David demanded.
6The young man answered, "I happened to be on
Mount Gilboa. I saw Saul there leaning on his spear
with the enemy chariots closing in on him. 7When he
turned and saw me, he cried out for me to come to
him. 'How can I help?' I asked him. 8And he said to
me, 'Who are you?' I replied, 'I am an Amalekite.'
9Then he begged me, 'Come over here and put me out
of my misery, for I am in terrible pain and want to die.'
10"So I killed him," the Amalekite told David,
"for I knew he couldn't live. Then I took his crown
and one of his bracelets so I could bring them to
you, my lord."
11David and his men tore their clothes in sorrow
when they heard the news. 12They mourned and
wept and fasted all day for Saul and his son Jonathan, and for the LORD's army and the nation of
Israel, because so many had died that day. 13Then
David said to the young man who had brought the
news, "Where are you from?"
And he replied, "I am a foreigner, an Amalekite,
who lives in your land."
14"Were you not afraid to kill the LORD's anointed
one?" David asked. 15Then David said to one of his
men, "Kill him!" So the man thrust his sword into
the Amalekite and killed him. 16"You die self-
condemned," David said, "for you yourself confessed
that you killed the LORD's anointed one."

**GRIEF ● ● ● • •**

1:1-12 **David and his men were visibly shaken over Saul's death: "They mourned and wept and fasted all day." This showed their genuine sorrow over the loss of their king, their friend Jonathan, and the other soldiers of Israel who died that day. They were not ashamed to grieve. Today, expressing our emotions is considered by some to be a sign of weakness. Those who wish to appear strong try to hide their grief. But mourning can help us deal with our intense sorrow when a loved one dies.**

# KEY PLACES IN 2 SAMUEL

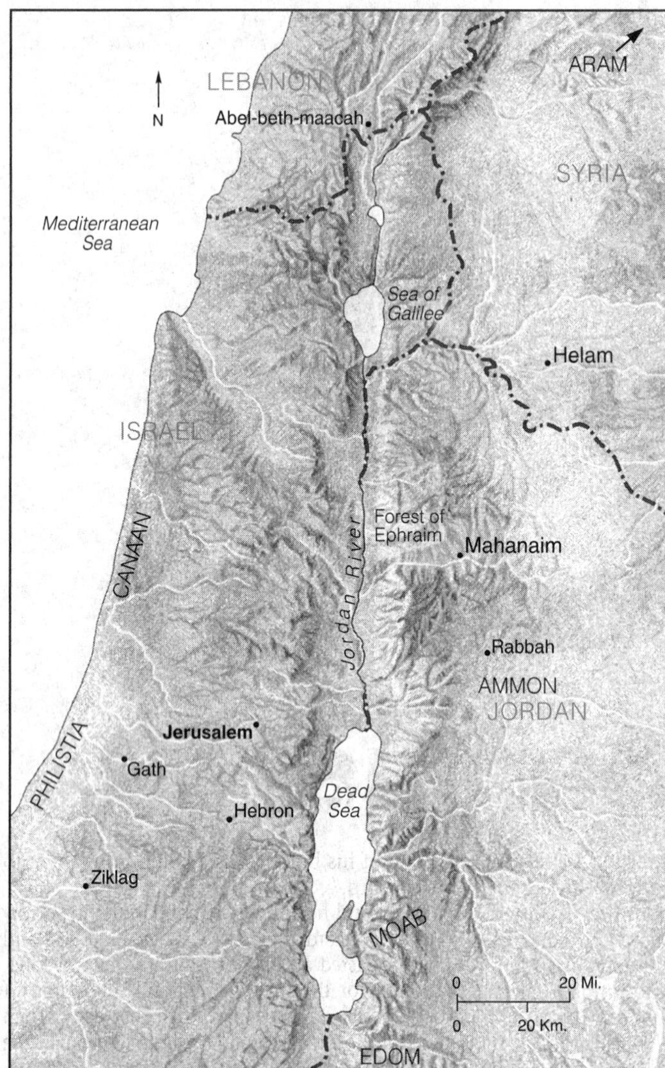

The broken lines (—·—) indicate modern boundaries.

**Hebron** After Saul's death, David moved from the Philistine city of Ziklag to Hebron, where the tribe of Judah crowned him king. But the rest of Israel's tribes backed Saul's son Ishbosheth, and crowned him king at Mahanaim. As a result, there was war between Judah and the rest of the tribes of Israel until Ishbosheth was assassinated. Then all of Israel pledged loyalty to David as their king (1:1–5:5).

**Jerusalem** One of David's first battles as king occurred at the fortress city of Jerusalem. David and his troops took the city by surprise, and it became his capital. It was here that David brought the Ark of the Covenant and made a special agreement with God (5:6–7:29).

**Gath** The Philistines were Israel's constant enemy, though they did give David sanctuary when he was hiding from Saul (1 Samuel 27). But when Saul died and David became king, the Philistines planned to defeat him. In a battle near Jerusalem, David and his troops routed the Philistines (5:17-25), but they were not completely subdued until David conquered Gath (8:1).

**Moab** During the time of the judges, Moab controlled many cities in Israel and demanded heavy taxes (Judges 3:12-30). David conquered Moab and, in turn, levied tribute from them (8:2).

**Edom** Though the Edomites and the Israelites traced their ancestry back to the same man, Isaac (Genesis 25:19-23), they were long-standing enemies. David defeated the Edomites and forced them to pay tribute (8:14).

**Rabbah** The Ammonites insulted David's ambassadors and turned a peacemaking mission into angry warfare. The Ammonites called tens of thousands of mercenaries, but David defeated this alliance first at Helam, then at Rabbah, the capital city (9:1–12:31).

**Mahanaim** David had victory in the field, but problems at home. His son, Absalom, incited a rebellion and crowned himself king at Hebron. David and his men fled to Mahanaim. Acting on bad advice, Absalom mobilized his army to fight David (13:1–17:29).

**Forest of Ephraim** The armies of Absalom and David fought in the forest of Ephraim. Absalom's hair got caught in a tree, and Joab, David's general, found and killed him. With Absalom's death, the rebellion died (18:1–19:43).

**Abel-beth-maacah** A man named Sheba also incited a rebellion against David. He fled to Abel-beth-maacah, but Joab and a small troop besieged the city. The citizens of Abel killed Sheba themselves (20:1-26). David's victories laid the foundation for the peaceful reign of his son Solomon.

---

17 Then David composed a funeral song for Saul
and Jonathan. 18 Later he commanded that it be
taught to all the people of Judah. It is known as the
Song of the Bow, and it is recorded in *The Book of
Jashar.**

19 Your pride and joy, O Israel, lies dead on the hills!
How the mighty heroes have fallen!
20 Don't announce the news in Gath,
or the Philistines will rejoice.

1:18 Or *The Book of the Upright.*

Don't proclaim it in the streets of Ashkelon,
or the pagans will laugh in triumph.

21 O mountains of Gilboa,
let there be no dew or rain upon you or your slopes.
For there the shield of the mighty was defiled;
the shield of Saul will no longer be anointed with oil.
22 Both Saul and Jonathan killed their strongest foes;
they did not return from battle empty-handed.

23 How beloved and gracious were Saul and Jonathan!
They were together in life and in death.
They were swifter than eagles;
they were stronger than lions.

24 O women of Israel, weep for Saul,
for he dressed you in fine clothing and gold ornaments.

25 How the mighty heroes have fallen in battle!
Jonathan lies dead upon the hills.
26 How I weep for you, my brother Jonathan!
Oh, how much I loved you!
And your love for me was deep,
deeper than the love of women!

27 How the mighty heroes have fallen!
Stripped of their weapons, they lie dead.

## CHAPTER 2 **JUDAH CROWNS DAVID KING.** 
After this,
David asked the LORD, "Should I move back to
Judah?"
And the LORD replied, "Yes."
Then David asked, "Which town should I go to?"
And the LORD replied, "Hebron."
2David's wives were Ahinoam from Jezreel and
Abigail, the widow of Nabal from Carmel. So David
and his wives 3and his men and their families all
moved to Judah, and they settled near the town of
Hebron. 4Then Judah's leaders came to David and
crowned him king over the tribe of Judah.
When David heard that the men of Jabesh-gilead
had buried Saul, 5he sent them this message: "May
the LORD bless you for being so loyal to your king
and giving him a decent burial. 6May the LORD be
loyal to you in return and reward you with his unfailing love! And I, too, will reward you for what you
have done. 7And now that Saul is dead, I ask you to
be my strong and loyal subjects like the people of
Judah, who have anointed me as their new king."
8But Abner son of Ner, the commander of Saul's
army, had already gone to Mahanaim with Saul's son
Ishbosheth.* 9There he proclaimed Ishbosheth king
over Gilead, Jezreel, Ephraim, Benjamin, the land of
the Ashurites, and all the rest of Israel. 10Ishbosheth
was forty years old when he became king, and he
ruled from Mahanaim for two years. Meanwhile, the
tribe of Judah remained loyal to David. 11David
made Hebron his capital, and he ruled as king of
Judah for seven and a half years.
12One day Abner led some of Ishbosheth's troops
from Mahanaim to Gibeon. 13About the same time,
Joab son of Zeruiah led David's troops from Hebron,
and they met Abner at the pool of Gibeon. The two
groups sat down there, facing each other from opposite sides of the pool. 14Then Abner suggested to
Joab, "Let's have a few of our warriors put on an
exhibition of hand-to-hand combat."
"All right," Joab agreed. 15So twelve men were chosen from each side to fight against each other. 16Each
one grabbed his opponent by the hair and thrust his
sword into the other's side so that all of them died. The
place has been known ever since as the Field of
Swords.* 17The two armies then began to fight each
other, and by the end of the day Abner and the men of
Israel had been defeated by the forces of David.
18Joab, Abishai, and Asahel, the three sons of Zeruiah, were among David's forces that day. Asahel
could run like a deer, 19and he began chasing Abner.
He was relentless and single-minded in his pursuit.
20When Abner looked back and saw him coming, he
called out, "Is that you, Asahel?"
"Yes, it is," he replied.
21"Go fight someone else!" Abner warned. "Take
on one of the younger men and strip him of his
weapons." But Asahel refused and kept right on
chasing Abner.
22Again Abner shouted to him, "Get away from
here! I will never be able to face your brother Joab if
I have to kill you!" 23But Asahel would not give up,
so Abner thrust the butt end of his spear through
Asahel's stomach, and the spear came out through
his back. He stumbled to the ground and died there.
And everyone who came by that spot stopped and
stood still when they saw Asahel lying there.
24When Joab and Abishai found out what had
happened, they set out after Abner. The sun was just
going down as they arrived at the hill of Ammah

**2:8** Also known as *Eshbaal.* **2:16** Hebrew *Helkath-hazzurim.*

### SEEING GOOD ● ● • • •

1:17-27 **Saul had caused much trouble for David, but when he died, David composed a funeral song for the king and his son. David had every reason to hate Saul, yet he chose not to. He chose to look at the good Saul had done and to forget the times when Saul had attacked him. It takes courage to lay aside hatred and hurt in order to show respect for another person—especially an enemy.**

### STUBBORN ● ● • • •

2:21-23 **Abner repeatedly warned Asahel to turn back or risk losing his life, but Asahel refused to turn from his self-imposed duty. Persistence is a good trait if it is for a worthy cause. But if the goal is only personal honor or gain, persistence may be no more than stubbornness. Asahel's stubbornness not only cost his life, but also spurred unfortunate disunity in David's army for years to come (3:26-27; 1 Kings 2:28-35). Before you decide to pursue a goal, make sure it is worthy of your devotion.**

near Giah, along the road to the wilderness of Gibeon. [25]Abner's troops from the tribe of Benjamin regrouped there at the top of the hill to take a stand. [26]Abner shouted down to Joab, "Must we always solve our differences with swords? Don't you realize the only thing we will gain is bitterness toward each other? When will you call off your men from chasing their Israelite brothers?"

[27]Then Joab said, "God only knows what would have happened if you hadn't spoken, for we would have chased you all night if necessary." [28]So Joab blew his trumpet, and his men stopped chasing the troops of Israel.

[29]All that night Abner and his men retreated through the Jordan Valley.* They crossed the Jordan River, traveling all through the morning,* and they did not stop until they arrived at Mahanaim.

[30]Meanwhile, Joab and his men also returned home. When Joab counted his casualties, he discovered that only nineteen men were missing, in addition to Asahel. [31]But three hundred and sixty of Abner's men, all from the tribe of Benjamin, had been killed. [32]Joab and his men took Asahel's body to Bethlehem and buried him there beside his father. Then they traveled all night and reached Hebron at daybreak.

### BACKBONE ● ● • • •

3:7 **Ishbosheth was right to speak out against Abner's behavior, but he didn't have the moral strength to maintain his authority (3:11). Lack of moral backbone became the root of Israel's troubles over the next four centuries. Only four of the next forty kings of Israel were called "good." It takes courage and strength to stand firm in your convictions and to confront wrongdoing in the face of opposition. When you believe something is wrong, do not let yourself be talked out of your position. Firmly attack the wrong and uphold the right.**

## CHAPTER 3

**DAVID BECOMES STRONGER.** That was the beginning of a long war between those who had been loyal to Saul and those who were loyal to David. As time passed David became stronger and stronger, while Saul's dynasty became weaker and weaker.

[2]These were the sons who were born to David in Hebron:

The oldest was Amnon, whose mother was Ahinoam of Jezreel.
[3] The second was Kileab, whose mother was Abigail, the widow of Nabal from Carmel.
The third was Absalom, whose mother was Maacah, the daughter of Talmai, king of Geshur.
[4] The fourth was Adonijah, whose mother was Haggith.
The fifth was Shephatiah, whose mother was Abital.
[5] The sixth was Ithream, whose mother was David's wife Eglah.

These sons were all born to David in Hebron.

[6]As the war went on, Abner became a powerful leader among those who were loyal to Saul's dynasty. [7]One day Ishbosheth,* Saul's son, accused Abner of sleeping with one of his father's concubines, a woman named Rizpah. [8]Abner became furious. "Am I a Judean dog to be kicked around like this?" he shouted. "After all I have done for you and your father by not betraying you to David, is this my reward—that you find fault with me about this woman? [9]May God deal harshly with me if I don't help David get all that the LORD has promised him! [10]I should just go ahead and give David the rest of Saul's kingdom. I should set him up as king over Israel as well as Judah, from Dan to Beersheba." [11]Ishbosheth didn't dare say another word because he was afraid of what Abner might do.

[12]Then Abner sent messengers to David, saying, "Let's make an agreement, and I will help turn the entire nation of Israel over to you."

[13]"All right," David replied, "but I will not negotiate with you unless you bring back my wife Michal, Saul's daughter, when you come."

[14]David then sent this message to Ishbosheth, Saul's son: "Give me back my wife Michal, for I bought her with the lives of one hundred Philistines." [15]So Ishbosheth took Michal away from her husband Palti* son of Laish. [16]Palti followed along behind her as far as Bahurim, weeping as he went. Then Abner told him, "Go back home!" So Palti returned.

[17]Meanwhile, Abner had consulted with the leaders of Israel. "For some time now," he told them, "you have wanted to make David your king. [18]Now is the time! For the LORD has said, 'I have chosen David to save my people from the Philistines and from all their other enemies.'" [19]Abner also spoke with the leaders of the tribe of Benjamin. Then he went to Hebron to tell David that all the people of Israel and Benjamin supported him.

[20]When Abner came to Hebron with his twenty men, David entertained them with a great feast. [21]Then Abner said to David, "Let me go and call all the people of Israel to your side. They will make a covenant with you to make you their king. Then you will be able to rule over everything your heart desires." So David sent Abner safely on his way.

[22]But just after Abner left, Joab and some of David's troops returned from a raid, bringing much plunder with them. [23]When Joab was told that Abner had just been there visiting the king and had been sent away in safety, [24]he rushed to see the king. "What have you done?" he demanded. "What do you mean by letting Abner get away? [25]You know perfectly well that he came to spy on you and to discover everything you are doing!"

[26]Joab then left David and sent messengers to catch up with Abner. They found him at the pool of Sirah and brought him back with them. But David knew nothing about it. [27]When Abner arrived at Hebron,

**2:29a** Hebrew *the Arabah.* **2:29b** Or *continued on through the Bithron.* The meaning of the Hebrew is uncertain. **3:7** Also known as *Eshbaal.* **3:15** As in 1 Sam 25:44; Hebrew reads *Paltiel,* a variant name for Palti.

Joab took him aside at the gateway as if to speak with
him privately. But then he drew his dagger and killed
Abner in revenge for killing his brother Asahel.
28When David heard about it, he declared, "I vow
by the LORD that I and my people are innocent of this
crime against Abner. 29Joab and his family are the
guilty ones. May his family in every generation be
cursed with a man who has open sores or leprosy*
or who walks on crutches* or who dies by the sword
or who begs for food!"
30So Joab and his brother Abishai killed Abner
because Abner had killed their brother Asahel at the
battle of Gibeon.
31Then David said to Joab and all those who were
with him, "Tear your clothes and put on sackcloth.
Go into deep mourning for Abner." And King David
himself walked behind the procession to the grave.
32They buried Abner in Hebron, and the king and all
the people wept at his graveside. 33Then the king
sang this funeral song for Abner:

"Should Abner have died as fools die?
34Your hands were not bound;
your feet were not chained.
No, you were murdered—
the victim of a wicked plot."

All the people wept again for Abner. 35David had
refused to eat anything the day of the funeral, and
now everyone begged him to eat. But David had
made a vow, saying, "May God kill me if I eat anything before sundown." 36This pleased the people
very much. In fact, everything the king did pleased
them! 37So everyone in Judah and Israel knew that
David was not responsible for Abner's death.
38Then King David said to the people, "Do you not
realize that a great leader and a great man has fallen
today in Israel? 39And even though I am the anointed
king, these two sons of Zeruiah—Joab and Abishai—
are too strong for me to control. So may the LORD
repay these wicked men for their wicked deeds."

CHAPTER **4** **KING ISHBOSHETH IS MURDERED.** When
Ishbosheth* heard about Abner's death at Hebron,
he lost all courage, and his people were paralyzed
with fear. 2Now there were two brothers, Baanah and
Recab, who were captains of Ishbosheth's raiding
parties. They were sons of Rimmon, a member of the
tribe of Benjamin who lived in Beeroth. The town of
Beeroth is now part of Benjamin's territory 3because
the original people of Beeroth fled to Gittaim, where
they still live as foreigners.
4(Saul's son Jonathan had a son named Mephibosheth,* who was crippled as a child. He was five
years old when Saul and Jonathan were killed at the
battle of Jezreel. When news of the battle reached the
capital, the child's nurse grabbed him and fled. But
she fell and dropped him as she was running, and he
became crippled as a result.)
5One day Recab and Baanah, the sons of Rimmon

## BE BOLD! ● ● ● • •

4:1 **Ishbosheth was a man who took his courage from another man (Abner) rather than from God. When Abner died, Ishbosheth was left with nothing. In crisis and under pressure, he collapsed in fear. Fear can paralyze us, but faith and trust in God can overcome fear (2 Timothy 1:6-8; Hebrews 13:6). If we trust in God, we will be free to respond boldly to the events around us.**

from Beeroth, went to Ishbosheth's home around
noon as he was taking a nap. 6The doorkeeper, who
had been sifting wheat, became drowsy and fell asleep.
So Recab and Baanah slipped past the doorkeeper,
went into Ishbosheth's bedroom, and stabbed him in
the stomach. Then they escaped. 7But before leaving,
they cut off his head as he lay there on his bed. Taking
his head with them, they fled across the Jordan Valley*
through the night. 8They arrived at Hebron and presented Ishbosheth's head to David. "Look!" they exclaimed. "Here is the head of Ishbosheth, the son of
your enemy Saul who tried to kill you. Today the LORD
has given you revenge on Saul and his entire family!"
9But David said to Recab and Baanah, "As surely
as the LORD lives, the one who saves me from my
enemies, I will tell you the truth. 10Once before,
someone told me, 'Saul is dead,' thinking he was
bringing me good news. But I seized him and killed
him at Ziklag. That's the reward I gave him for his
news! 11Now what reward should I give the wicked
men who have killed an innocent man in his own
house and on his own bed? Should I not also demand your very lives?" 12So David ordered his young
men to kill them, and they did. They cut off their
hands and feet and hung their bodies beside the
pool in Hebron. Then they took Ishbosheth's head
and buried it in Abner's tomb in Hebron.

CHAPTER **5** **DAVID BECOMES KING.** Then all the
tribes of Israel went to David at Hebron and told
him, "We are all members of your family. 2For a long
time, even while Saul was our king, you were the one
who really led Israel. And the LORD has told you,
'You will be the shepherd of my people Israel. You
will be their leader.'" 3So there at Hebron, David
made a covenant with the leaders of Israel before the
LORD. And they anointed him king of Israel.
4David was thirty years old when he began to
reign, and he reigned forty years in all. 5He had
reigned over Judah from Hebron for seven years and

## PATIENCE ● ● ● • •

5:4-5 **David did not become king of all Israel until he was 37 years old, although he had been promised the kingship many years earlier (1 Samuel 16:13). During those years, David had to wait patiently for the fulfillment of God's promise. If you feel pressured to achieve instant results and success, remember David's patience. Just as his time of waiting prepared him for his important task, a waiting period may help prepare you by strengthening your spiritual character.**

**3:29a** Or *or a contagious skin disease.* The Hebrew word used here can describe various skin diseases. **3:29b** Or *who is effeminate;* Hebrew reads *who handles a spindle.* **4:1** Also known as *Eshbaal.* **4:4** Also known as *Meribbaal.* **4:7** Hebrew *the Arabah.*

## HIGHS AND LOWS OF DAVID'S LIFE

The Bible calls David a man after God's own heart (Acts 13:22), but that didn't mean his life was free of troubles. David's life was full of highs and lows. Some of David's troubles were a result of his sins; some were a result of the sins of others. We can't always control our ups and downs, but we can trust God every day. We can be certain that he will help us through our trials, just as he helped David. In the end, he will reward us for our consistent faith.

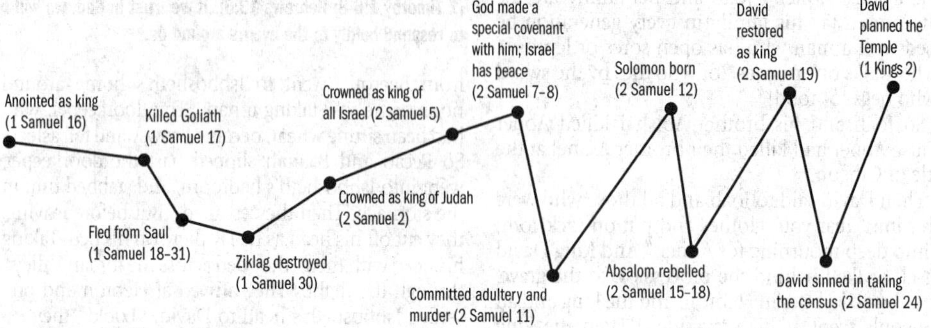

Anointed as king (1 Samuel 16)
Killed Goliath (1 Samuel 17)
Fled from Saul (1 Samuel 18–31)
Ziklag destroyed (1 Samuel 30)
Crowned as king of Judah (2 Samuel 2)
Crowned as king of all Israel (2 Samuel 5)
God made a special covenant with him; Israel has peace (2 Samuel 7–8)
Committed adultery and murder (2 Samuel 11)
Solomon born (2 Samuel 12)
Absalom rebelled (2 Samuel 15–18)
David restored as king (2 Samuel 19)
David sinned in taking the census (2 Samuel 24)
David planned the Temple (1 Kings 2)

six months, and from Jerusalem he reigned over all Israel and Judah for thirty-three years.

6 David then led his troops to Jerusalem to fight against the Jebusites. "You'll never get in here," the Jebusites taunted. "Even the blind and lame could keep you out!" For the Jebusites thought they were safe. 7 But David captured the fortress of Zion, now called the City of David.

8 When the insulting message from the defenders of the city reached David, he told his own troops, "Go up through the water tunnel into the city and destroy those 'lame' and 'blind' Jebusites. How I hate them." That is the origin of the saying, "The blind and the lame may not enter the house."* 9 So David made the fortress his home, and he called it the City of David. He built additional fortifications around the city, starting at the Millo* and working inward. 10 And David became more and more powerful, because the LORD God Almighty was with him.

## BATTLES ● ● • • •

**5:19-25 David fought his battles the way God instructed him. In each instance he (1) asked if he should fight or not; (2) followed instructions carefully; and (3) gave God the glory. We can err in our "battles" by ignoring these steps and instead (1) doing what we want without considering God's will; (2) doing things our way and ignoring advice in the Bible or from other wise people; and (3) taking the glory ourselves or giving it to someone else without acknowledging the help we received from God. All of these responses are sinful.**

11 Then King Hiram of Tyre sent messengers to David, along with carpenters and stonemasons to build him a palace. Hiram also sent many cedar logs for lumber. 12 And David realized that the LORD had made him king over Israel and had made his kingdom great for the sake of his people Israel.

13 After moving from Hebron to Jerusalem, David married more wives and concubines, and he had many sons and daughters. 14 These are the names of David's sons who were born in Jerusalem: Shimea,* Shobab, Nathan, Solomon, 15 Ibhar, Elishua, Nepheg, Japhia, 16 Elishama, Eliada, and Eliphelet.

17 When the Philistines heard that David had been anointed king of Israel, they mobilized all their forces to capture him. But David was told they were coming and went into the stronghold. 18 The Philistines arrived and spread out across the valley of Rephaim. 19 So David asked the LORD, "Should I go out to fight the Philistines? Will you hand them over to me?"

The LORD replied, "Yes, go ahead. I will certainly give you the victory."

20 So David went to Baal-perazim and defeated the Philistines there. "The LORD has done it!" David exclaimed. "He burst through my enemies like a raging flood!" So David named that place Baal-perazim (which means "the Lord who bursts through"). 21 The Philistines had abandoned their idols there, so David and his troops confiscated them.

22 But after a while the Philistines returned and again spread out across the valley of Rephaim. 23 And once again David asked the LORD what to do. "Do not attack them straight on," the LORD replied. "Instead, circle around behind them and attack them near the balsam trees. 24 When you hear a sound like marching feet in the tops of the balsam trees, attack! That will be the signal that the LORD is moving ahead of you to strike down the Philistines." 25 So David did what the LORD commanded, and he struck down the Philistines all the way from Gibeon* to Gezer.

## CHAPTER 6 **DAVID BRINGS THE ARK HOME.**

Then David mobilized thirty thousand special troops. 2 He led them to Baalah of Judah* to bring home the Ark

5:8 The meaning of this saying is uncertain. 5:9 Or *the supporting terraces.* The meaning of the Hebrew is uncertain. 5:14 As in parallel text at 1 Chr 3:5; Hebrew reads *Shammua,* a variant name for Shimea. 5:25 As in Greek version (see also 1 Chr 14:16); Hebrew reads *Geba.* 6:2 *Baalah of Judah* is another name for Kiriath-jearim; compare 1 Chr 13:6.

of God, which bears the name of the LORD Almighty,
who is enthroned between the cherubim. 3They
placed the Ark of God on a new cart and brought it
from the hillside home of Abinadab. Uzzah and
Ahio, Abinadab's sons, were guiding the cart 4with
the Ark of God on it, with Ahio walking in front.
5David and all the people of Israel were celebrating
before the LORD with all their might, singing songs*
and playing all kinds of musical instruments—lyres,
harps, tambourines, castanets, and cymbals.
6But when they arrived at
the threshing floor of Nacon,
the oxen stumbled, and Uzzah put out his hand to
steady the Ark of God. 7Then
the LORD's anger blazed out
against Uzzah for doing this,
and God struck him dead beside the Ark of God. 8David
was angry because the LORD's
anger had blazed out against
Uzzah. He named that place
Perez-uzzah (which means
"outbreak against Uzzah").
It is still called that today.
9David was now afraid of
the LORD and asked, "How
can I ever bring the Ark of
the LORD back into my
care?" 10So David decided
not to move the Ark of the
LORD into the City of David.
He took it instead to the
home of Obed-edom of
Gath. 11The Ark of the LORD
remained there with the
family of Obed-edom for
three months, and the LORD
blessed him and his entire
household.
12Then King David was
told, "The LORD has blessed
Obed-edom's home and
everything he has because of
the Ark of God." So David
went there and brought the
Ark to the City of David
with a great celebration.
13After the men who were
carrying it had gone six
steps, they stopped and
waited so David could sacrifice an ox and a fattened
calf. 14And David danced before the LORD with all his
might, wearing a priestly tunic.* 15So David and all Israel brought up the Ark of the LORD with much
shouting and blowing of trumpets.
16But as the Ark of the LORD entered the City of
David, Michal, the daughter of Saul, looked down
from her window. When she saw King David leaping
and dancing before the LORD, she was filled with
contempt for him.
17The Ark of the LORD was placed inside the

## MICHAL

Sometimes love is not enough—especially if that love is little more than the strong emotional attraction that grows between a hero and an admirer. To Michal, Saul's daughter, the courageous young David must have seemed like a dream come true. Her feelings for this hero gradually became obvious to others, and eventually her father heard about her love for David. Seeing this as an opportunity to get rid of his rival, Saul promised Michal's hand in marriage in exchange for David's success in the impossible mission of killing one hundred Philistines. But David was victorious. As a result, Saul lost a daughter, and David became even more popular with the people.

Michal's love for David did not have time to be tested by the realities of marriage. Instead, she became involved in saving his life. Her quick thinking helped him escape, but the price was Saul's anger and Michal's separation from David. Her father gave her to another man, Palti, although David eventually took her back.

Unlike her brother Jonathan, Michal did not have the kind of deep relationship with God that would have helped her come through the difficulties in her life. Instead, she became bitter. She could not share David's joyful worship of God, so she hated it. When the same faith in God is not shared by a couple, the one who could hold them together sometimes seems to come between them. Sadly, Michal never bore David any children.

Beyond feeling sorry for her, we need to see Michal as a person like us. How quickly and easily we become bitter when life takes unexpected turns. But bitterness cannot change the bad things that have happened. Often, bitterness only makes a bad situation worse. On the other hand, a willingness to turn to God gives him the opportunity to bring good out of our difficulties. That willingness has two parts: asking God for his guidance, and looking for that guidance in his Word.

LESSONS: We are not as responsible for what happens to us as we are for how we respond to our circumstances

Disobedience to God almost always harms us as well as others

KEY VERSE: "But as the Ark of the LORD entered the City of David, Michal, the daughter of Saul, looked down from her window. When she saw King David leaping and dancing before the LORD, she was filled with contempt for him" (2 Samuel 6:16).

Michal's story is told in 1 Samuel 14–2 Samuel 6. She is also mentioned in 1 Chronicles 15:29.

**UPS:**
- Loved David and became his first wife
- Saved David's life
- Could think and act quickly when it was needed

**DOWNS:**
- Lied under pressure
- Allowed herself to become bitter over her circumstances
- In her unhappiness, hated David because of his love for God

**STATS:**
- Occupation: Daughter of one king (Saul) and wife of another (David)
- Relatives: Parents: Saul and Ahinoam. Brothers: Abinadab, Jonathan, Malchishua. Sister: Merab. Husbands: David and Palti.

6:5 As in Greek version (see also 1 Chr 13:8); Hebrew reads *cypress trees.* 6:14 Hebrew *a linen ephod.*

**NO ● ● • • •**

7:8-16 **David's request was good, but God said no. This does not mean that God rejected David. In fact, God was planning to do something even greater in David's life than allowing him the prestige of building the Temple. Although God turned down David's request, he promised that David's descendants would rule the kingdom forever. David's earthly dynasty ended four centuries later, but Jesus Christ, a direct descendant of David, was the ultimate fulfillment of this promise (Acts 2:22-36). Christ will reign for eternity—first in his spiritual kingdom, and ultimately on earth in the New Jerusalem (Luke 1:30-33; Revelation 21). Have you prayed with good intentions, only to have God say no? Realize that this is not rejection, but God's way of fulfilling a greater purpose in your life.**

special tent that David had prepared for it. And David sacrificed burnt offerings and peace offerings to the LORD. [18]When he had finished, David blessed the people in the name of the LORD Almighty. [19]Then he gave a gift of food to every man and woman in Israel: a loaf of bread, a cake of dates,* and a cake of raisins. Then everyone went home.

[20]When David returned home to bless his family, Michal came out to meet him and said in disgust, "How glorious the king of Israel looked today! He exposed himself to the servant girls like any indecent person might do!"

[21]David retorted to Michal, "I was dancing before the LORD, who chose me above your father and his family! He appointed me as the leader of Israel, the people of the LORD. So I am willing to act like a fool in order to show my joy in the LORD. [22]Yes, and I am willing to look even more foolish than this, but I will be held in honor by the girls of whom you have spoken!" [23]So Michal, the daughter of Saul, remained childless throughout her life.

CHAPTER **7** When the LORD had brought peace to the land and King David was settled in his palace, [2]David summoned Nathan the prophet. "Look!" David said. "Here I am living in this beautiful cedar palace, but the Ark of God is out in a tent!"

[3]Nathan replied, "Go ahead and do what you have in mind, for the LORD is with you."

[4]But that same night the LORD said to Nathan,

[5]"Go and tell my servant David, 'This is what the LORD says: Are you the one to build me a temple to live in? [6]I have never lived in a temple, from the day I brought the Israelites out of Egypt until now. My home has always been a tent, moving from one place to another. [7]And I have never once complained to Israel's leaders, the shepherds of my people Israel. I have never asked them, "Why haven't you built me a beautiful cedar temple?"'

[8]"Now go and say to my servant David, 'This is what the LORD Almighty says: I chose you to lead my people Israel when you were just a shepherd boy, tending your sheep out in the pasture. [9]I have been with you wherever you have gone, and I have destroyed all your enemies. Now I will make your name famous throughout the earth! [10]And I have provided a permanent homeland for my people Israel, a secure place where they will never be disturbed. It will be their own land where wicked nations won't oppress them as they did in the past, [11]from the time I appointed judges to rule my people. And I will keep you safe from all your enemies.

"'And now the LORD declares that he will build a house for you—a dynasty of kings! [12]For when you die, I will raise up one of your descendants, and I will make his kingdom strong. [13]He is the one who will build a house—a temple—for my name. And I will establish the throne of his kingdom forever. [14]I will be his father, and he will be my son. If he sins, I will use other nations to punish him. [15]But my unfailing love will not be taken from him as I took it from Saul, whom I removed before you. [16]Your dynasty and your kingdom will continue for all time before me, and your throne will be secure forever.'"

[17]So Nathan went back to David and told him everything the LORD had said.

[18]Then King David went in and sat before the LORD and prayed, "Who am I, O Sovereign LORD, and what is my family, that you have brought me this far? [19]And now, Sovereign LORD, in addition to everything else, you speak of giving me a lasting dynasty! Do you deal with everyone this way,* O Sovereign LORD? [20]What more can I say? You know what I am really like, Sovereign LORD. [21]For the sake of your promise and according to your will, you have done all these great things and have shown them to me.

[22]"How great you are, O Sovereign LORD! There is no one like you—there is no other God. We have never even heard of another god like you! [23]What other nation on earth is like Israel? What other nation, O God, have you redeemed from slavery to be your own people? You made a great name for yourself when you rescued your people from Egypt. You performed awesome miracles and drove out the nations and gods that stood in their way. [24]You made Israel your people forever, and you, O LORD, became their God.

[25]"And now, O LORD God, do as you have promised concerning me and my family. Confirm it as a promise that will last forever. [26]And may your name be honored forever so that all the world will say, 'The LORD Almighty is God over Israel!' And may the dynasty of your servant David be established in your presence.

[27]"O LORD Almighty, God of Israel, I have been bold enough to pray this prayer because you have revealed that you will build a house for me—an eternal dynasty! [28]For you are God, O Sovereign LORD. Your words are truth, and you have promised

6:19 Or *a portion of meat.* The meaning of the Hebrew is uncertain. 7:19 The meaning of the Hebrew is uncertain.

these good things to me, your servant. [29]And now, may it please you to bless me and my family so that our dynasty may continue forever before you. For when you grant a blessing to your servant, O Sovereign LORD, it is an eternal blessing!"

CHAPTER **8** **DAVID STRENGTHENS HIS KINGDOM.** After this, David subdued and humbled the Philistines by conquering Gath, their largest city.* [2]David also conquered the land of Moab. He made the people lie down on the ground in a row, and he measured them off in groups with a length of rope. He measured off two groups to be executed for every one group to be spared. The Moabites who were spared became David's servants and brought him tribute money.

[3]David also destroyed the forces of Hadadezer son of Rehob, king of Zobah, when Hadadezer marched out to strengthen his control along the Euphrates River. [4]David captured seventeen hundred charioteers* and twenty thousand foot soldiers. Then he crippled all but one hundred of the chariot horses.

[5]When Arameans from Damascus arrived to help Hadadezer, David killed twenty-two thousand of them. [6]Then he placed several army garrisons in Damascus, the Aramean capital, and the Arameans became David's subjects and brought him tribute money. So the LORD gave David victory wherever he went. [7]David brought the gold shields of Hadadezer's officers to Jerusalem, [8]along with a large amount of bronze from Hadadezer's cities of Tebah* and Berothai.

[9]When King Toi of Hamath heard that David had destroyed the army of Hadadezer, [10]he sent his son Joram to congratulate David on his success. Hadadezer and Toi had long been enemies, and there had been many wars between them. Joram presented David with many gifts of silver, gold, and bronze. [11]King David dedicated all these gifts to the LORD, along with the silver and gold he had set apart from the other nations he had subdued—[12]Edom,* Moab, Ammon, Philistia, and Amalek—and from Hadadezer son of Rehob, king of Zobah.

[13]So David became very famous. After his return he destroyed eighteen thousand Edomites* in the Valley of Salt. [14]He placed army garrisons throughout Edom, and all the Edomites became David's subjects. This was another example of how the LORD made David victorious wherever he went.

[15]David reigned over all Israel and was fair to everyone. [16]Joab son of Zeruiah was commander of the army. Jehoshaphat son of Ahilud was the royal historian. [17]Zadok son of Ahitub and Ahimelech son of Abiathar were the priests. Seraiah was the court secretary. [18]Benaiah son of Jehoiada was captain of the king's bodyguard.* David's sons served as priestly leaders.*

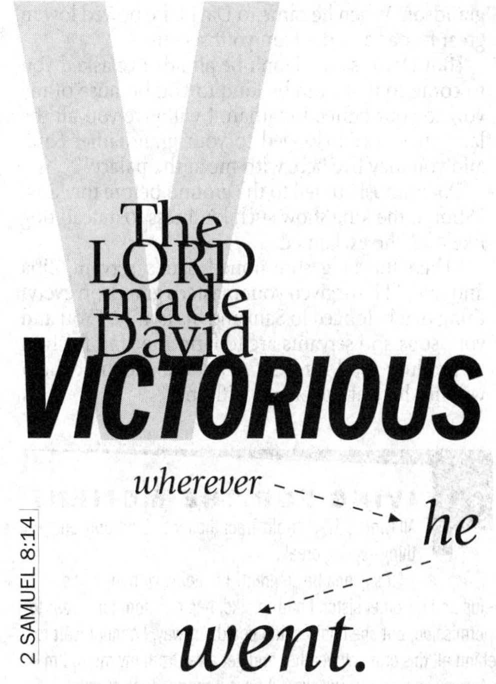
The LORD made David
VICTORIOUS
wherever he went.
2 SAMUEL 8:14

CHAPTER **9** **DAVID IS KIND TO MEPHIBOSHETH.** One day David began wondering if anyone in Saul's family was still alive, for he had promised Jonathan that he would show kindness to them. [2]He summoned a man named Ziba, who had been one of Saul's servants. "Are you Ziba?" the king asked.

"Yes sir, I am," Ziba replied.

[3]The king then asked him, "Is anyone still alive from Saul's family? If so, I want to show God's kindness to them in any way I can."

Ziba replied, "Yes, one of Jonathan's sons is still alive, but he is crippled."

[4]"Where is he?" the king asked.

"In Lo-debar," Ziba told him, "at the home of Makir son of Ammiel." [5]So David sent for him and brought him from Makir's home. [6]His name was Mephibosheth*; he was Jonathan's son and Saul's

**THE PUBLIC EYE ● ● ● • •**

8:15 **Everything David did pleased the people (3:36), not because he tried to please them, but because he tried to please God. Often those who try the hardest to become popular never make it. But the praise of people is not that important. Don't spend your time devising ways to please others so you will be accepted in the public eye. Instead, strive to do what is right—and both God and people will respect your convictions.**

8:1 Hebrew *by conquering Metheg-ammah,* a name which means "the bridle," possibly referring to the size of the city or the tribute money taken from it. Compare 1 Chr 18:1. 8:4 Greek version reads *1,000 chariots and 7,000 charioteers;* compare 1 Chr 18:4. 8:8 As in some Greek manuscripts (see also 1 Chr 18:8); Hebrew reads *Betah.* 8:12 As in a few Hebrew manuscripts and Greek and Syriac versions (see also 8:14; 1 Chr 18:11); most Hebrew manuscripts read *Aram.* 8:13 As in a few Hebrew manuscripts and Greek and Syriac versions (see also 8:14; 1 Chr 18:12); most Hebrew manuscripts read *Arameans.* 8:18a Hebrew *of the Kerethites and Pelethites.* 8:18b Hebrew *David's sons were priests;* compare parallel text at 1 Chr 18:17. 9:6 Also known as *Meribbaal.*

grandson. When he came to David, he bowed low in great fear and said, "I am your servant."

[7]But David said, "Don't be afraid! I've asked you to come so that I can be kind to you because of my vow to your father, Jonathan. I will give you all the land that once belonged to your grandfather Saul, and you may live here with me at the palace!"

[8]Mephibosheth fell to the ground before the king. "Should the king show such kindness to a dead dog like me?" he exclaimed.

[9]Then the king summoned Saul's servant Ziba and said, "I have given your master's grandson everything that belonged to Saul and his family. [10]You and your sons and servants are to farm the land for him to produce food for his family. But Mephibosheth will live here at the palace with me."

## LIVING FOR THE MOMENT

All winter, 17-year-old Traci thought about only one thing—spring break.

"It's gonna be so great! I'm going with my three best friends and my older sister. I had to, like, beg my mom for a year to get her permission, but she finally said I could. Anyway, I cannot wait to leave behind all this crummy weather and get away from my mom. I'm serious. Anyway, in just a few weeks, I'll have it made—tons of rays, millions of guys, and no nosy mother!"

That was before. Now spring break is history, and it's not so much fun to get Traci talking about her trip. In fact, it's sad. See, the minute Traci hit the beach, she forgot everything she stands for. She let herself get sucked up into the "let-it-all-hang-out, party-till-you-puke, if-it-feels-good-do-it" mentality. And that attitude has left Traci with a lot of scars.

"Why didn't I listen? My friends and my sister kept telling me to mellow out. But I just blew them off and went out by myself. The third night I met these college guys at a poolside party and started hanging out with them. The next thing I remember, I was waking up in a motel room . . . in bed with some guy I'd never seen before. I don't even know what happened."

For another look at the consequences of living for the moment, read 2 Samuel 11–12.

Ziba, who had fifteen sons and twenty servants, replied, [11]"Yes, my lord; I will do all that you have commanded." And from that time on, Mephibosheth ate regularly with David, as though he were one of his own sons. [12]Mephibosheth had a young son named Mica. And from then on, all the members of Ziba's household were Mephibosheth's servants. [13]And Mephibosheth, who was crippled in both feet, moved to Jerusalem to live at the palace.

CHAPTER **10** **A KING MOCKS DAVID'S MEN.** Some time after this, King Nahash of the Ammonites died, and his son Hanun became king. [2]David said, "I am going to show complete loyalty to Hanun because his father, Nahash, was always completely loyal to

## BALANCE ● ● • • •

10:12 **There must be a balance between our actions and our faith in God. In this verse, Joab says, "Let us fight bravely." In other words, do what you can. Plan the battle strategy, use your mind to figure out the best techniques, and use your resources. But he also says, "May the LORD's will be done." He knew that the outcome was in God's hands. In the same way, we are to use our mind and our resources to obey God, while living by faith and trusting God for the outcome.**

me." So David sent ambassadors to express sympathy to Hanun about his father's death.

But when David's ambassadors arrived in the land of Ammon, [3]Hanun's advisers said to their master, "Do you really think these men are coming here to honor your father? No! David has sent them to spy out the city so that they can come in and conquer it!" [4]So Hanun seized David's ambassadors and shaved off half of each man's beard, cut off their robes at the buttocks, and sent them back to David in shame. [5]When David heard what had happened, he sent messengers to tell the men to stay at Jericho until their beards grew out, for they were very embarrassed by their appearance.

[6]Now the people of Ammon realized how seriously they had angered David, so they hired twenty thousand Aramean mercenaries from the lands of Beth-rehob and Zobah, one thousand from the king of Maacah, and twelve thousand from the land of Tob. [7]When David heard about this, he sent Joab and the entire Israelite army to fight them. [8]The Ammonite troops drew up their battle lines at the entrance of the city gates, while the Arameans from Zobah and Rehob and the men from Tob and Maacah positioned themselves to fight in the open fields.

[9]When Joab saw that he would have to fight on two fronts, he chose the best troops in his army. He placed them under his personal command and led them out to fight the Arameans in the fields. [10]He left the rest of the army under the command of his brother Abishai, who was to attack the Ammonites. [11]"If the Arameans are too strong for me, then come over and help me," Joab told his brother. "And if the Ammonites are too strong for you, I will come and help you. [12]Be courageous! Let us fight bravely to save our people and the cities of our God. May the LORD's will be done."

[13]When Joab and his troops attacked, the Arameans began to run away. [14]And when the Ammonites saw the Arameans running, they ran from Abishai and retreated into the city. After the battle was over, Joab returned to Jerusalem.

[15]The Arameans now realized that they were no match for Israel. So when they regrouped, [16]they were joined by additional Aramean troops summoned by Hadadezer from the other side of the Euphrates River.* These troops arrived at Helam under the command of Shobach, the commander of all Hadadezer's forces. [17]When David heard what was happening, he mobilized all Israel, crossed the Jordan River, and led the army to He-

10:16 Hebrew *the river.*

lam. The Arameans positioned themselves there in battle formation and then attacked David. 18But again the Arameans fled from the Israelites. This time David's forces killed seven hundred charioteers and forty thousand horsemen,* including Shobach, the commander of their army. 19When Hadadezer and his Aramean allies realized they had been defeated by Israel, they surrendered to them and became their subjects. After that, the Arameans were afraid to help the Ammonites.

CHAPTER **11** **DAVID AND BATHSHEBA.** The following spring, the time of year when kings go to war, David sent Joab and the Israelite army to destroy the Ammonites. In the process they laid siege to the city of Rabbah. But David stayed behind in Jerusalem.

2Late one afternoon David got out of bed after taking a nap and went for a stroll on the roof of the palace. As he looked out over the city, he noticed a woman of unusual beauty taking a bath. 3He sent someone to find out who she was, and he was told, "She is Bathsheba, the daughter of Eliam and the wife of Uriah the Hittite." 4Then David sent for her; and when she came to the palace, he slept with her. (She had just completed the purification rites after having her menstrual period.) Then she returned home. 5Later, when Bathsheba discovered that she was pregnant, she sent a message to inform David.

6So David sent word to Joab: "Send me Uriah the Hittite." 7When Uriah arrived, David asked him how Joab and the army were getting along and how the war was progressing. 8Then he told Uriah, "Go on home and relax." David even sent a gift to Uriah after he had left the palace. 9But Uriah wouldn't go home. He stayed that night at the palace entrance with some of the king's other servants.

10When David heard what Uriah had done, he summoned him and asked, "What's the matter with you? Why didn't you go home last night after being away for so long?"

11Uriah replied, "The Ark and the armies of Israel and Judah are living in tents,* and Joab and his officers are camping in the open fields. How could I go home to wine and dine and sleep with my wife? I swear that I will never be guilty of acting like that."

12"Well, stay here tonight," David told him, "and tomorrow you may return to the army." So Uriah stayed in Jerusalem that day and the next. 13Then David invited him to dinner and got him drunk. But even then he couldn't get Uriah to go home to his wife. Again he slept at the palace entrance.

14So the next morning David wrote a letter to Joab and gave it to Uriah to deliver. 15The letter instructed Joab, "Station Uriah on the front lines where the battle is fiercest. Then pull back so that he will be killed." 16So Joab assigned Uriah to a spot close to the city wall where he knew the enemy's strongest men were fighting. 17And Uriah was killed along with several other Israelite soldiers.

## TEMPTATION • • • • •

11:3-4 **As David gazed from his palace roof, he saw a beautiful woman taking a bath, and lust filled his heart. He should have left the roof and fled from the temptation. Instead, he went further by asking about Bathsheba. The results of letting temptation stay in his heart were devastating.**

**To flee temptation: (1) Ask God in earnest prayer to help you stay away from people, places, and situations that offer temptation. (2) Memorize and meditate on portions of Scripture that combat your specific weaknesses. At the root of most temptation is a real need or desire that God can fill. (3) Find another believer with whom you can openly share your temptations and call this person for help when temptation strikes.**

18Then Joab sent a battle report to David. 19He told his messenger, "Report all the news of the battle to the king. 20But he might get angry and ask, 'Why did the troops go so close to the city? Didn't they know there would be shooting from the walls? 21Wasn't Gideon's son Abimelech killed* at Thebez by a woman who threw a millstone down on him?' Then tell him, 'Uriah the Hittite was killed, too.'"

22So the messenger went to Jerusalem and gave a complete report to David. 23"The enemy came out against us," he said. "And as we chased them back to the city gates, 24the archers on the wall shot arrows at us. Some of our men were killed, including Uriah the Hittite."

25"Well, tell Joab not to be discouraged," David said. "The sword kills one as well as another! Fight harder next time, and conquer the city!"

26When Bathsheba heard that her husband was dead, she mourned for him. 27When the period of mourning was over, David sent for her and brought her to the palace, and she became one of his wives. Then she gave birth to a son. But the LORD was very displeased with what David had done.

CHAPTER **12** **NATHAN SCOLDS DAVID.** So the LORD sent Nathan the prophet to tell David this story: "There were two men in a certain town. One was rich, and one was poor. 2The rich man owned many sheep and cattle. 3The poor man owned nothing but a little lamb he had worked hard to buy. He raised that little lamb, and it grew up with his children. It ate from the man's own plate and drank from his cup. He cuddled it in his arms like a baby daughter. 4One day a guest arrived at the home of the rich man. But instead of killing a lamb from his own flocks for

## CONFRONT • • • • •

12:1-12 **As a prophet, Nathan was required to confront sin, even the sin of a king. It took great courage, skill, and tact to speak to David in a way that would make him aware of his wrong actions. When you have to confront someone with unpleasant news, pray for courage, skill, and tact. How you present your message may be as important as what you say.**

**10:18** Some Greek manuscripts read *foot soldiers;* compare parallel text at 1 Chr 19:18. **11:11** Or *at Succoth.* **11:21** Hebrew *Was not Abimelech son of Jerubbesheth killed.*

## DATE RAPE

**S**tudies indicate the horrifying fact that as many as one out of every five women has been or will be raped. In America, a rape occurs EVERY SIX MINUTES. One in eight female college students will experience rape or attempted rape, usually from a date or acquaintance. Even men are not immune: 16 percent of male college students admit to having been forced into having sex. (These figures do not include incest or other family-related sexual abuse.) **M**ost experts agree that these frightening numbers may reflect only a fraction of the reality. As much as 90 percent of all rapes go UNREPORTED. We have a terrible plague on our hands—one we as Christians and churches must respond to. **W**hat should you do if you've been a rape victim? **F**irst, understand you *are* a victim. What happened was not your fault. If you said no, and a man, any man—boyfriend, stranger, father, acquaintance—forced himself on you, you were raped. The circumstances make no difference. If you said no and he ignored you, you were raped. It was not your fault. **S**econd, realize you are not alone. There are, unfortunately, countless women who share your experience, who understand your pain. Find one of those women—a counselor at a rape treatment center, a hospital staff worker, or someone you know—and **tell your story.** Talking about it helps break the power the incident(s) has over you; not talking about it will keep you a victim forever. **T**hird, understand that whatever guilt you experience—and many women experience intense guilt—is ***false guilt.*** Regardless of what your conscience—or *he*—may tell you, you did nothing to deserve this. You may have exercised poor judgment in your choice of a person, place, or activity, but that's all you're guilty of: poor judgment. Don't take responsibility for someone else's sin. **I**f you have been a rape victim, seek help. And remember, the best source of help is God himself. He alone is able to heal your damaged body, emotions, and spirit. Turn to God and let him make you whole again. He can do it. **I**f you are a guy who is trying to help a girl work through this shattering experience, consider this: never tell a rape victim she should "just get over it" or "get on with her life." Every woman who has been sexually violated wants to do just that, but it is impossible to "carry on" as though the rape never happened. Rape changes a woman's life. Not allowing her to deal with the pain, fear, and conflict encourages her to deny the problem. The **inner anguish** must be dealt with. There is no way to gauge when a woman will recover from this kind of devastation. Try to be patient, supportive, and loving. **I**f you are a guy who has committed rape, or if you consider it OK to force a girl to do anything sexually against her will, consider this: There is *no* excuse for rape or sexual abuse. **NONE.** The Bible has very harsh words for people who commit sexual immorality and for those who victimize others. Consider Galatians 6:7: "Don't be misled. Remember that you can't ignore God and get away with it. You will always reap what you sow!" Don't think you can mock God's laws and abuse his image—which is what you do when you abuse any person—and get away with it. The thought of God's wrath waiting to be poured out on those who commit such sins should be enough to stop anyone in his tracks. And don't try to justify the act by saying, "She said no, but her body said yes," or "She wouldn't have gone out with me if she didn't want it, too." If a woman says no, she means no. Ignore this and you are legally guilty of rape—and ***you can go to jail.*** **I**f you have committed this sin, cry out to God for mercy and forgiveness, and seek counseling. If you don't, not only are innocent women in danger; so is your soul. Don't test God's wrath. Confess, repent, and get help. God is waiting—and willing—to help you.

food, he took the poor man's lamb and killed it and
served it to his guest."

[5]David was furious. "As surely as the LORD lives,"
he vowed, "any man who would do such a thing
deserves to die! [6]He must repay four lambs to the
poor man for the one he stole and for having no
pity."

[7]Then Nathan said to David, "You are that man!
The LORD, the God of Israel, says, 'I anointed you
king of Israel and saved you from the power of Saul.
[8]I gave you his house and his wives and the kingdoms of Israel and Judah. And if that had not been
enough, I would have given you much, much more.
[9]Why, then, have you despised the word of the LORD
and done this horrible deed? For you have murdered
Uriah and stolen his wife. [10]From this time on, the
sword will be a constant threat to your family, because you have despised me by taking Uriah's wife to
be your own.

[11]"'Because of what you have done, I, the LORD,
will cause your own household to rebel against you.
I will give your wives to another man, and he will go
to bed with them in public view. [12]You did it secretly,
but I will do this to you openly in the sight of all
Israel.'"

[13]Then David confessed to Nathan, "I have sinned
against the LORD."

Nathan replied, "Yes, but the LORD has forgiven
you, and you won't die for this sin. [14]But you have
given the enemies of the LORD great opportunity to
despise and blaspheme him, so your child will die."

[15]After Nathan returned to his home, the LORD
made Bathsheba's baby deathly ill. [16]David begged
God to spare the child. He went without food and
lay all night on the bare ground. [17]The leaders of the
nation pleaded with him to get up and eat with
them, but he refused. [18]Then on the seventh day the
baby died. David's advisers were afraid to tell him.
"He was so broken up about the baby being sick,"
they said. "What will he do to himself when we tell
him the child is dead?"

[19]But when David saw them whispering, he realized what had happened. "Is the baby dead?" he
asked.

"Yes," they replied. [20]Then David got up from the
ground, washed himself, put on lotions, and
changed his clothes. Then he went to the Tabernacle
and worshiped the LORD. After that, he returned to
the palace and ate. [21]His advisers were amazed. "We
don't understand you," they told him. "While the
baby was still living, you wept and refused to eat. But
now that the baby is dead, you have stopped your
mourning and are eating again."

[22]David replied, "I fasted and wept while the child
was alive, for I said, 'Perhaps the LORD will be gracious to me and let the child live.' [23]But why should
I fast when he is dead? Can I bring him back again?
I will go to him one day, but he cannot return to me."

[24]Then David comforted Bathsheba, his wife, and
slept with her. She became pregnant and gave birth
to a son, and they named him Solomon. The LORD
loved the child [25]and sent word through Nathan the
prophet that his name should be Jedidiah—"beloved of the LORD"—because the LORD loved him.

[26]Meanwhile, Joab and the Israelite army were
successfully ending their siege of Rabbah, the capital
of Ammon. [27]Joab sent messengers to tell David, "I
have fought against Rabbah and captured its water
supply.* [28]Now bring the rest of the army and finish
the job, so you will get credit for the victory instead
of me."

[29]So David led the rest of his army to Rabbah and
captured it. [30]David removed the crown from the
king's head,* and it was placed on David's own
head. The crown was made of gold and set with
gems, and it weighed about seventy-five pounds.*
David took a vast amount of plunder from the city.
[31]He also made slaves of the people of Rabbah and
forced them to labor with saws, picks, and axes, and
to work in the brick kilns. That is how he dealt with
the people of all the Ammonite cities. Then David
and his army returned to Jerusalem.

CHAPTER **13** **AMNON RAPES TAMAR.** David's son
Absalom had a beautiful sister named Tamar. And
Amnon, her half brother, fell desperately in love with
her. [2]Amnon became so obsessed with Tamar that he
became ill. She was a virgin, and it seemed impossible that he could ever fulfill his love for her.

[3]Now Amnon had a very crafty friend—his
cousin Jonadab. He was the son of David's brother
Shimea.* [4]One day Jonadab said to Amnon, "What's
the trouble? Why should the son of a king look so
dejected morning after morning?"

So Amnon told him, "I am in love with Tamar,
Absalom's sister."

[5]"Well," Jonadab said, "I'll tell you what to do.
Go back to bed and pretend you are sick. When your
father comes to see you, ask him to let Tamar come
and prepare some food for you. Tell him you'll feel
better if she feeds you."

[6]So Amnon pretended to be sick. And when the
king came to see him, Amnon asked him, "Please let
Tamar come to take care of me and cook something
for me to eat." [7]So David agreed and sent Tamar to
Amnon's house to prepare some food for him.

[8]When Tamar arrived at Amnon's house, she went
to the room where he was lying down so he could
watch her mix some dough. Then she baked some
special bread for him. [9]But when she set the serving
tray before him, he refused to eat. "Everyone get out
of here," Amnon told his servants. So they all left.
[10]Then he said to Tamar, "Now bring the food into
my bedroom and feed it to me here." So Tamar took
it to him. [11]But as she was feeding him, he grabbed
her and demanded, "Come to bed with me, my
darling sister."

[12]"No, my brother!" she cried. "Don't be foolish!

**12:27** Or *captured the city of water.* **12:30a** Greek version reads *removed the crown of Milcom;* compare 1 Kgs 11:5. Milcom, also called Molech, was the god of the Ammonites. **12:30b** Hebrew *1 talent* [34 kilograms]. **13:3** Hebrew *Shimeah* (also in 13:32), a variant name for Shimea; compare 1 Chr 2:13.

Don't do this to me! You know what a serious crime
it is to do such a thing in Israel. 13 Where could I go
in my shame? And you would be called one of the
greatest fools in Israel. Please, just speak to the king
about it, and he will let you marry me."
14 But Amnon wouldn't listen to her, and since he
was stronger than she was, he raped her. 15 Then
suddenly Amnon's love turned to hate, and he hated
her even more than he had loved her. "Get out of
here!" he snarled at her.

## LOVE VS. LUST ● ● • • •

**13:14-15 Love and lust are very different. After Amnon raped his half-sister, his "love" turned to hate. Although he had claimed to be in love, he was actually overcome by lust. Love is patient; lust requires immediate sexual satisfaction. Love is kind; lust is harsh. Love does not demand its own way; lust does. You can read about the characteristics of real love in 1 Corinthians 13.**

16 "No, no!" Tamar cried. "To reject me now is a
greater wrong than what you have already done to
me."
But Amnon wouldn't listen to her. 17 He shouted
for his servant and demanded, "Throw this woman
out, and lock the door behind her!"
18 So the servant put her out. She was wearing a
long, beautiful robe,* as was the custom in those
days for the king's virgin daughters. 19 But now
Tamar tore her robe and put ashes on her head.
And then, with her face in her hands, she went
away crying.
20 Her brother Absalom saw her and asked, "Is it
true that Amnon has been with you? Well, don't be
so upset. Since he's your brother anyway, don't worry
about it." So Tamar lived as a desolate woman in
Absalom's house. 21 When King David heard what
had happened, he was very angry. 22 And though
Absalom never spoke to Amnon about it, he hated
Amnon deeply because of what he had done to his
sister.
23 Two years later, when Absalom's sheep were
being sheared at Baal-hazor near Ephraim, Absalom
invited all the king's sons to come to a feast. 24 He
went to the king and said, "My sheep-shearers are
now at work. Would the king and his servants please
come to celebrate the occasion with me?"
25 The king replied, "No, my son. If we all came, we
would be too much of a burden on you." Absalom
pressed him, but the king wouldn't come, though he
sent his thanks.
26 "Well, then," Absalom said, "if you can't come,
how about sending my brother Amnon instead?"
"Why Amnon?" the king asked. 27 But Absalom
kept on pressing the king until he finally agreed to
let all his sons attend, including Amnon.
28 Absalom told his men, "Wait until Amnon gets
drunk; then at my signal, kill him! Don't be afraid.
I'm the one who has given the command. Take
courage and do it!" 29 So at Absalom's signal they
murdered Amnon. Then the other sons of the king
jumped on their mules and fled.
30 As they were on the way back to Jerusalem, this
report reached David: "Absalom has killed all your
sons; not one is left alive!" 31 The king jumped up,
tore his robe, and fell prostrate on the ground. His
advisers also tore their clothes in horror and sorrow.
32 But just then Jonadab, the son of David's
brother Shimea, arrived and said, "No, not all your
sons have been killed! It was only Amnon! Absalom has been plotting this ever since Amnon raped
his sister Tamar. 33 No, your sons aren't all dead! It
was only Amnon." 34 Meanwhile Absalom escaped.
Then the watchman on the Jerusalem wall saw a
great crowd coming toward the city from the west.
He ran to tell the king, "I see a crowd of people
coming from the Horonaim road* along the side of
the hill."
35 "Look!" Jonadab told the king. "There they are
now! Your sons are coming, just as I said." 36 They
soon arrived, weeping and sobbing, and the king
and his officials wept bitterly with them. 37 And
David mourned many days for his son Amnon.
Absalom fled to his grandfather, Talmai son of
Ammihud, the king of Geshur. 38 He stayed there in
Geshur for three years. 39 And David, now reconciled
to Amnon's death, longed to be reunited with his
son Absalom.*

CHAPTER **14** **A WIDOW ASKS FOR HELP.** Joab realized how much the king longed to see Absalom.
2 So he sent for a woman from Tekoa who had a
reputation for great wisdom. He said to her, "Pretend you are in mourning; wear mourning clothes
and don't bathe or wear any perfume. Act like a
woman who has been in deep sorrow for a long
time. 3 Then go to the king and tell him the story I
am about to tell you." Then Joab told her what to
say.
4 When the woman approached the king, she fell
with her face down to the floor in front of him and
cried out, "O king! Help me!"
5 "What's the trouble?" the king asked.
"I am a widow," she replied. 6 "My two sons had
a fight out in the field. And since no one was there
to stop it, one of them was killed. 7 Now the rest of
the family is demanding, 'Let us have your son. We
will execute him for murdering his brother. He
doesn't deserve to inherit his family's property.'
But if I do that, I will have no one left, and my
husband's name and family will disappear from
the face of the earth."
8 "Leave it to me," the king told her. "Go home,
and I'll see to it that no one touches him."
9 "Oh, thank you, my lord," she replied. "And I'll
take the responsibility if you are criticized for helping me like this."
10 "Don't worry about that!" the king said. "If

13:18 Or *a robe with sleeves,* or *an ornamented robe.* The meaning of the Hebrew is uncertain. 13:34 As in Greek version; Hebrew reads *from the road behind him.* 13:39 Or *no longer felt a need to go out after Absalom.*

2/11/04

# Just one life and one chance

## MY ANSWER

Billy Graham

**Dear Billy Graham:** I respect people who believe in heaven, but as far as I'm concerned, I'll take my chances. After all, if there is life after death, God will give me another chance to be saved after I die, won't he? — H.F.

**Dear Reader:** Nowhere does the Bible teach that we will have a second chance after we die to turn to Christ and be saved. (Nor does it teach reincarnation — the belief that we will return to earth again and again, so we can have another chance after this life is over.)

Instead, it says that what we do with Christ right now will determine our eternal destiny — either in heaven with God, or in hell, separated from God forever. The Bible says, "man is destined to die once, and after that to face judgment" (Hebrews 9:27).

The same warning is found in one of Jesus' parables, in which a rich man who had ignored God all his life died and went to hell. There he begged to be given even a few drops of water from heaven — but it was too late. He was told by the heavenly messenger, "between us and you a great chasm has been fixed, so that those who want to go from here to you cannot, nor can anyone cross over from there to us" (Luke 16:26).

ron and Katherine; Salyers, Ron and nnifer; Von Essen, Scott and Dawn.

## . Vincent Women's Hospital

**Boys** – Dennis, Marcus and Brandi; rrell, Travis and Angelica; Lister, Patk and Amy; Marnin, Jeromy and Tifny; Mims, Sean and Andrea; Philpott, seph and Elizabeth; Sharif, Tim and istin; Wynn, Garland, and Brown, ene.

**Girls** – Housel, Robert and Amy; binson, Kenyatta, and Harris, Amber; ertz, Jeffry and Kelley.

## ishard Memorial Hospital

**Boy** – Roberts, Naomi.

**Girls** – Ballard, Dartersa; Clanton, wendolyn; Garcia, Sonia; Gonzales, ana; Valladares, Tarlanda.

# Marriage licenses

Olusegun E. Adeyemo; Sabainah L. deniyan.

James G. Bowers; Sharon A. Young.

Mario Casimiro; Lisa M. Winebrenner.

ton.

# Divorce lawsuits filed

Allen, Robert E.; Mary L. Allen.

Arnett, Marty D.; Stacey L. Arnett.

Bragg, Dennis W.; Jennifer L. Bragg.

Carter, Shontie R.; Angelic M. Carter.

Clay, Padro D.; Amanda L. Clay.

Fall, Mamadou; Cheyenne M. Silverthorne-Fall.

Gentry, James Jr.; Kimberly Thomson.

Gosar, Dilip; Monica Gosar.

Hampton, Larry Jr.; Marcellina N. Hampton.

Hunter, David L. Jr.; Cassandra Hunter.

Jackson, Emanuel; Angela Jackson.

Johnson, Bradley; Katina Johnson.

Knapp, Timothy A.; Patricia D. Knapp.

Maxie, Henry; Tracie Maxie.

Paris, Kevin D.; Debra J. Paris.

Parker, Charles L. Jr.; Donna M. Parker.

Rutherford, Jack C.; Kimberly S. Rutherford.

Wallace, Walter Lee Jr.; Tammy R. Wallace.

Wilkins, Malcolm; Tracey N. Wilkins.

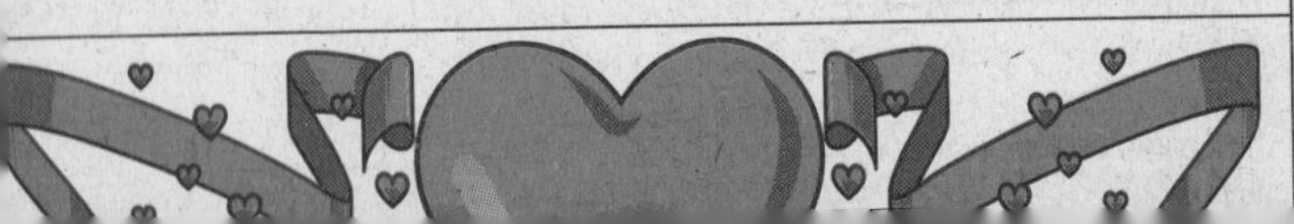

anyone objects, bring them to me. I can assure you
they will never complain again!"
11Then she said, "Please swear to me by the LORD
your God that you won't let anyone take vengeance
against my son. I want no more bloodshed."
"As surely as the LORD lives," he replied, "not a
hair on your son's head will be disturbed!"
12"Please let me ask one more thing of you!" she
said.
"Go ahead," he urged. "Speak!"
13She replied, "Why don't you do as much for all the
people of God as you have promised to do for me? You
have convicted yourself in making this decision,
because you have refused to bring home your own
banished son. 14All of us must die eventually. Our lives
are like water spilled out on the ground, which
cannot be gathered up
again. That is why God tries
to bring us back when we
have been separated from
him. He does not sweep
away the lives of those he
cares about—and neither
should you!
15"But I have come to
plead with you for my son
because my life and my
son's life have been threatened. I said to myself, 'Perhaps the king will listen to
me 16and rescue us from
those who would cut us off
from God's people. 17Yes,
the king will give us peace
of mind again.' I know that
you are like an angel of God
and can discern good from
evil. May the LORD your
God be with you."
18"I want to know one
thing," the king replied.
"Yes, my lord?" she
asked.
19"Did Joab send you
here?"
And the woman replied,
"My lord the king, how can I
deny it? Nobody can hide
anything from you. Yes, Joab
sent me and told me what to
say. 20He did it to place the
matter before you in a different light. But you are as wise
as an angel of God, and you
understand everything that
happens among us!"
21So the king sent for Joab
and told him, "All right, go
and bring back the young
man Absalom."
22Joab fell to the ground before the king and
blessed him and said, "At last I know that I have
gained your approval, for you have granted me this
request!"
23Then Joab went to Geshur and brought Absalom
back to Jerusalem. 24But the king gave this order:
"Absalom may go to his own house, but he must
never come into my presence." So Absalom did not
see the king.
25Now no one in Israel was as handsome as Absalom. From head to foot, he was the perfect specimen
of a man. 26He cut his hair only once a year, and then
only because it was too heavy to carry around. When
he weighed it out, it came to five pounds!* 27He had
three sons and one daughter. His daughter's name
was Tamar, and she was very beautiful.

## ABSALOM

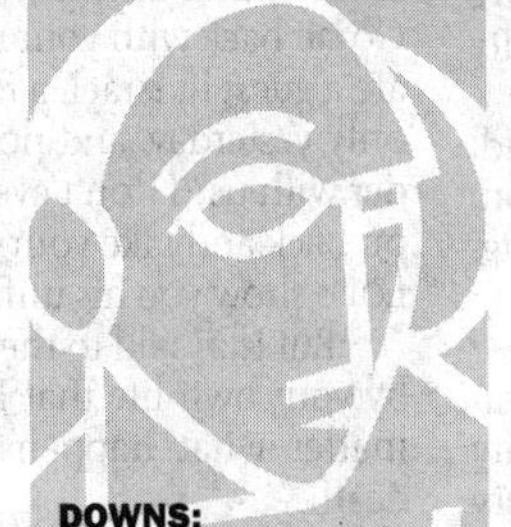

Sometimes parents make big mistakes that get passed on to their children. It's like a sad instant-replay. David saw his son Absalom make some of the same mistakes he had made. Even though God forgave David, his sins still hurt the rest of his family. Our sins sometimes also leave a lasting mark on our life, even after we've asked God to forgive us. Our sins hurt others, too.

Absalom was the kind of person who looks and talks great, but turns out to be bad on the inside. It seemed he would make the perfect king. The people loved him. But it takes a lot more than good looks to be a good leader. One of the biggest ways we disappoint others is by seeming to be one kind of person on the outside while on the inside, as people later discover, we are actually very different.

David's sins took him away from God; repentance brought him back. But Absalom sinned and kept on sinning. As you read his story you will see that he got a lot of advice from people, but he chose the wrong advice too often.

Maybe you are a lot like Absalom. You know your life is going the wrong way fast. Absalom's most basic problem was that he never admitted, "I was wrong. I need forgiveness." Forgiveness is exactly what God offers to us, but we can't experience it until we confess our sins to God. Absalom not only walked away from his father David's love, he also rejected God's love. Your life doesn't have to hold the same tragedy. God's love is waiting.

**DOWNS:**
- Avenged the rape of his sister Tamar by killing his half brother Amnon
- Plotted against his father to take away the throne
- Consistently listened to the wrong advice

**STATS:**
- Where: Hebron
- Occupation: Prince
- Relatives: Father: David. Mother: Maacah. Brothers: Amnon, Chileab, Solomon, and others. Sister: Tamar
- Contemporaries: Nathan, Jonadab, Joab, Ahithophel, Hushai

LESSONS: The sins of parents are often repeated and amplified in their children

A smart man gets a lot of advice; a wise man evaluates the advice he gets

Actions against God's plans will fail sooner or later

KEY VERSE: "But while he was there, he sent secret messengers to every part of Israel to stir up a rebellion against the king. 'As soon as you hear the trumpets,' his message read, 'you will know that Absalom has been crowned king in Hebron'" (2 Samuel 15:10).

Absalom's story is told in 2 Samuel 3:3; 13–19.

**14:26** Hebrew *200 shekels* [2.3 kilograms] *by the royal standard.*

## INDECISIVE ● ● ● • •

14:28 **David only made halfhearted efforts to raise his children. In 13:21-39, David did not punish Amnon for his sin, nor did he deal decisively with Absalom's murder of Amnon. When David finally allowed Absalom back, he did not speak to him for two years. Such indecisiveness became David's undoing. When sin is ignored, it will bring greater pain than if it is dealt with immediately.**

28Absalom lived in Jerusalem for two years without getting to see the king. 29Then Absalom sent for Joab to ask him to intercede for him, but Joab refused to come. Absalom sent for him a second time, but again Joab refused to come. 30So Absalom said to his servants, "Go and set fire to Joab's barley field, the field next to mine." So they set his field on fire, as Absalom had commanded.

31Then Joab came to Absalom and demanded, "Why did your servants set my field on fire?"

32And Absalom replied, "Because I wanted you to ask the king why he brought me back from Geshur if he didn't intend to see me. I might as well have stayed there. Let me see the king; if he finds me guilty of anything, then let him execute me."

33So Joab told the king what Absalom had said. Then at last David summoned his estranged son, and Absalom came and bowed low before the king, and David kissed him.

## CHAPTER 15

**ABSALOM REBELS.** After this, Absalom bought a chariot and horses, and he hired fifty footmen to run ahead of him. 2He got up early every morning and went out to the gate of the city. When people brought a case to the king for judgment, Absalom would ask where they were from, and they would tell him their tribe. 3Then Absalom would say, "You've really got a strong case here! It's too bad the king doesn't have anyone to hear it. 4I wish I were the judge. Then people could bring their problems to me, and I would give them justice!" 5And when people tried to bow before him, Absalom wouldn't let them. Instead, he took them by the hand and embraced them. 6So in this way, Absalom stole the hearts of all the people of Israel.

7After four years,* Absalom said to the king, "Let me go to Hebron to offer a sacrifice to the LORD in fulfillment of a vow I made to him. 8For while I was at Geshur, I promised to sacrifice to him in Hebron if he would bring me back to Jerusalem."

9"All right," the king told him. "Go and fulfill your vow."

So Absalom went to Hebron. 10But while he was there, he sent secret messengers to every part of Israel to stir up a rebellion against the king. "As soon as you hear the trumpets," his message read, "you will know that Absalom has been crowned king in Hebron." 11He took two hundred men from Jerusalem with him as guests, but they knew nothing of his intentions. 12While he was offering the sacrifices, he sent for Ahithophel, one of David's counselors who lived in Giloh. Soon many others also joined Absalom, and the conspiracy gained momentum.

13A messenger soon arrived in Jerusalem to tell King David, "All Israel has joined Absalom in a conspiracy against you!"

14"Then we must flee at once, or it will be too late!" David urged his men. "Hurry! If we get out of the city before he arrives, both we and the city of Jerusalem will be spared from disaster."

15"We are with you," his advisers replied. "Do what you think is best." 16So the king and his household set out at once. He left no one behind except ten of his concubines to keep the palace in order. 17The king and his people set out on foot, and they paused at the edge of the city 18to let David's troops move past to lead the way. There were six hundred Gittites who had come with David from Gath, along with the king's bodyguard.*

19Then the king turned to Ittai, the captain of the Gittites, and asked, "Why are you coming with us? Go on back with your men to King Absalom, for you are a guest in Israel, a foreigner in exile. 20You arrived only yesterday, and now should I force you to wander with us? I don't even know where we will go. Go on back and take your troops with you, and may the LORD show you his unfailing love and faithfulness.*"

21But Ittai said to the king, "I vow by the LORD and by your own life that I will go wherever you go, no matter what happens—whether it means life or death."

22David replied, "All right, come with us." So Ittai and his six hundred men and their families went along.

23There was deep sadness throughout the land as the king and his followers passed by. They crossed the Kidron Valley and then went out toward the wilderness.

24Abiathar and Zadok and the Levites took the Ark of the Covenant of God and set it down beside the road. Then they offered sacrifices there until everyone had passed by. 25David instructed Zadok to take the Ark of God back into the city. "If the LORD sees fit," David said, "he will bring me back to see the Ark and the Tabernacle again. 26But if he is through with me, then let him do what seems best to him."

27Then the king told Zadok the priest, "Look,* here is my plan. You and Abiathar* should return quietly to the city with your son Ahimaaz and Abiathar's son

## COURAGE ● ● ● • •

15:14 **Had David not escaped from Jerusalem, the ensuing fight might have destroyed both him and the innocent inhabitants of the city. Some fights that we think are necessary may be costly and destructive to those around us. In such cases, it may be wise to back down and save the fight for another day—even if doing so hurts our pride. It takes courage to stand and fight, but it also takes courage to back down when you must for the sake of others.**

15:7 As in Greek and Syriac versions; Hebrew reads *40 years.* **15:18** Hebrew *the Kerethites and Pelethites.* **15:20** As in Greek version; Hebrew reads *and may unfailing love and faithfulness go with you.* **15:27a** As in Greek version; Hebrew reads *Are you a seer?* or *Do you see?* **15:27b** Hebrew lacks *and Abiathar;* compare 15:29.

Jonathan. 28I will stop at the shallows of the Jordan River* and wait there for a message from you. Let me know what happens in Jerusalem before I disappear into the wilderness." 29So Zadok and Abiathar took the Ark of God back to the city and stayed there.

30David walked up the road that led to the Mount of Olives, weeping as he went. His head was covered and his feet were bare as a sign of mourning. And the people who were with him covered their heads and wept as they climbed the mountain. 31When someone told David that his adviser Ahithophel was now backing Absalom, David prayed, "O LORD, let Ahithophel give Absalom foolish advice!"

32As they reached the spot at the top of the Mount of Olives where people worshiped God, David found Hushai the Arkite waiting for him. Hushai had torn his clothing and put dirt on his head as a sign of mourning. 33But David told him, "If you go with me, you will only be a burden. 34Return to Jerusalem and tell Absalom, 'I will now be your adviser, just as I was your father's adviser in the past.' Then you can frustrate and counter Ahithophel's advice. 35Zadok and Abiathar, the priests, are there. Tell them the plans that are being made to capture me, 36and they will send their sons Ahimaaz and Jonathan to find me and tell me what is going on." 37So David's friend Hushai returned to Jerusalem, getting there just as Absalom arrived.

CHAPTER **16** **ZIBA JOINS DAVID.** David was just past the top of the hill when Ziba, the servant of Mephibosheth,* caught up with him. He was leading two donkeys loaded with two hundred loaves of bread, one hundred clusters of raisins, one hundred bunches of summer fruit, and a skin of wine. 2"What are these for?" the king asked Ziba.

And Ziba replied, "The donkeys are for your people to ride on, and the bread and summer fruit are for the young men to eat. The wine is to be taken with you into the wilderness for those who become faint."

3"And where is Mephibosheth?" the king asked him.

"He stayed in Jerusalem," Ziba replied. "He said, 'Today I will get back the kingdom of my grandfather Saul.'"

4"In that case," the king told Ziba, "I give you everything Mephibosheth owns."

"Thank you, sir," Ziba replied. "I will always do whatever you want me to do."

5As David and his party passed Bahurim, a man came out of the village cursing them. It was Shimei son of Gera, a member of Saul's family. 6He threw stones at the king and the king's officers and all the mighty warriors who surrounded them. 7"Get out of here, you murderer, you scoundrel!" he shouted at David. 8"The LORD is paying you back for murdering Saul and his family. You stole his throne, and now the LORD has given it to your son Absalom. At last you will taste some of your own medicine, you murderer!"

9"Why should this dead dog curse my lord the king?" Abishai son of Zeruiah demanded. "Let me go over and cut off his head!"

10"No!" the king said. "What am I going to do with you sons of Zeruiah! If the LORD has told him to curse me, who am I to stop him?" 11Then David said to Abishai and the other officers, "My own son is trying to kill me. Shouldn't this relative of Saul* have even more reason to do so? Leave him alone and let him curse, for the LORD has told him to do it. 12And perhaps the LORD will see that I am being wronged and will bless me because of these curses." 13So David and his men continued on, and Shimei kept pace with them

## CHECK IT OUT ● ● ● • •

16:4 **David believed Ziba's charge against Mephibosheth without checking into it. Don't be hasty to accept someone's condemnation of another person, especially when the accuser may profit from the other's downfall. David should have been skeptical of Ziba's comments until he checked them out for himself.**

**My older brother is always making fun of my new faith. How do I get him to stop?**

People ridicule what they don't understand or what they wish they had themselves. It's really tough, though, when it comes from someone in your own family! (See 2 Samuel 15.)

Your best defense is a quiet offense: Don't repay evil for evil. Don't retaliate when people say unkind things about you. Instead, pay them back with a blessing. That is what God wants you to do, and he will bless you for it (1 Peter 3:9).

When anyone makes fun of your faith, hold your tongue, pray for the person, be kind to him or her, and then wait for God's blessing. This verse ends with a promise directly from God. Though it doesn't say when or how God will bless you, it promises that he will.

Here are some steps to take when facing opposition for your faith (see 1 Peter 3:13-15):

First, check your attitude. If you understand that God is allowing you to experience this for a reason, you'll be able to thank him for it. It means that he believes in you enough to allow you to be tested!

Second, quietly trust yourself to Christ. You trusted Christ to be Lord of your life; now allow him to be Lord over your circumstances. God is trying to develop your character.

Third, be real and be ready to explain your faith when the opportunities arise. Admit your faults, and don't act like you're superior or better than the other person. This may disarm them to the point where they will see that you're not a threat. Then you may be able to share about Christ.

Even doing all of this still may not relieve the tension. But, "it is better to suffer for doing good . . . than to suffer for doing wrong!" (1 Peter 3:17).

**15:28** Hebrew *at the crossing points of the wilderness.* **16:1** Also known as *Meribbaal.* **16:11** Hebrew *this Benjaminite.*

on a nearby hillside, cursing as he went and throwing stones at David and tossing dust into the air.

[14]The king and all who were with him grew weary along the way, so they rested when they reached the Jordan River.*

[15]Meanwhile, Absalom and his men arrived at Jerusalem, accompanied by Ahithophel. [16]When David's friend Hushai the Arkite arrived, he went immediately to see Absalom. "Long live the king!" he exclaimed. "Long live the king!"

[17]"Is this the way you treat your friend David?" Absalom asked him. "Why aren't you with him?"

[18]"I'm here because I work for the man who is chosen by the LORD and by Israel," Hushai replied. [19]"And anyway, why shouldn't I serve you? I helped your father, and now I will help you!"

[20]Then Absalom turned to Ahithophel and asked him, "What should I do next?"

[21]Ahithophel told him, "Go and sleep with your father's concubines, for he has left them here to keep the house. Then all Israel will know that you have insulted him beyond hope of reconciliation, and they will give you their support." [22]So they set up a tent on the palace roof where everyone could see it, and Absalom went into the tent to sleep with his father's concubines.

[23]Absalom followed Ahithophel's advice, just as David had done. For every word Ahithophel spoke seemed as wise as though it had come directly from the mouth of God.

## CHAPTER 17 **ABSALOM FOLLOWS BAD ADVICE.**

Now Ahithophel urged Absalom, "Let me choose twelve thousand men to start out after David tonight. [2]I will catch up to him while he is weary and discouraged. He and his troops will panic, and everyone will run away. Then I will kill only the king, [3]and I will bring all the people back to you as a bride returns to her husband. After all, it is only this man's life that you seek.* Then all the people will remain unharmed and peaceful." [4]This plan seemed good to Absalom and to all the other leaders of Israel.

[5]But then Absalom said, "Bring in Hushai the Arkite. Let's see what he thinks about this." [6]When Hushai arrived, Absalom told him what Ahithophel had said. Then he asked, "What is your opinion? Should we follow Ahithophel's advice? If not, speak up."

[7]"Well," Hushai replied, "this time I think Ahithophel has made a mistake. [8]You know your father and his men; they are mighty warriors. Right now they are probably as enraged as a mother bear who has been robbed of her cubs. And remember that your father is an experienced soldier. He won't be spending the night among the troops. [9]He has probably already hidden in some pit or cave. And when he comes out and attacks and a few of your men fall, there will be panic among your troops, and everyone will start shouting that your men are being slaugh-

### VANITY ● ● ● • •

17:11 **Hushai appealed to Absalom through flattery, and Absalom was trapped by his vanity. Hushai predicted great glory for Absalom if he personally led the entire army against David. "Pride goes before destruction" (Proverbs 16:18) is an appropriate comment on Absalom's ambitions.**

tered. [10]Then even the bravest of them, though they have the heart of a lion, will be paralyzed with fear. For all Israel knows what a mighty man your father is and how courageous his warriors are.

[11]"I suggest that you mobilize the entire army of Israel, bringing them from as far away as Dan and Beersheba. That way you will have an army as numerous as the sand on the seashore. And I think that you should personally lead the troops. [12]When we find David, we can descend on him like the dew that falls to the ground, so that not one of his men is left alive. [13]And if David has escaped into some city, you will have the entire army of Israel there at your command. Then we can take ropes and drag the walls of the city into the nearest valley until every stone is torn down."

[14]Then Absalom and all the leaders of Israel said, "Hushai's advice is better than Ahithophel's." For the LORD had arranged to defeat the counsel of Ahithophel, which really was the better plan, so that he could bring disaster upon Absalom!

[15]Then Hushai reported to Zadok and Abiathar, the priests, what Ahithophel had said and what he himself had suggested instead. [16]"Quick!" he told them. "Find David and urge him not to stay at the shallows of the Jordan River* tonight. He must go across at once into the wilderness beyond. Otherwise he will die and his entire army with him."

[17]Jonathan and Ahimaaz had been staying at En-rogel so as not to be seen entering and leaving the city. Arrangements had been made for a servant girl to bring them the message they were to take to King David. [18]But a boy saw them leaving En-rogel to go to David, and he told Absalom about it. Meanwhile, they escaped to Bahurim, where a man hid them inside a well in his courtyard. [19]The man's wife put a cloth over the top of the well with grain on it to dry in the sun; so no one suspected they were there.

[20]When Absalom's men arrived, they asked her, "Have you seen Ahimaaz and Jonathan?"

She replied, "They were here, but they crossed the brook." Absalom's men looked for them without success and returned to Jerusalem.

[21]Then the two men crawled out of the well and hurried on to King David. "Quick!" they told him, "cross the Jordan tonight!" And they told him how Ahithophel had advised that he be captured and killed. [22]So David and all the people with him went across the Jordan River during the night, and they were all on the other bank before dawn.

[23]Meanwhile, Ahithophel was publicly disgraced when Absalom refused his advice. So he saddled his donkey, went to his hometown, set his affairs in

16:14 As in Greek version (see also 17:16); Hebrew reads *when they reached their destination.* 17:3 As in Greek version; Hebrew reads *like the return of all is the man whom you seek.* 17:16 Hebrew *at the crossing points of the wilderness.*

order, and hanged himself. He died there and was buried beside his father.

[24]David soon arrived at Mahanaim. By now, Absalom had mobilized the entire army of Israel and was leading his troops across the Jordan River. [25]Absalom had appointed Amasa as commander of his army, replacing Joab, who had been commander under David. (Amasa was Joab's cousin. His father was Jether,* an Ishmaelite.* His mother, Abigail daughter of Nahash, was the sister of Joab's mother, Zeruiah.) [26]Absalom and the Israelite army set up camp in the land of Gilead.

[27]When David arrived at Mahanaim, he was warmly greeted by Shobi son of Nahash of Rabbah, an Ammonite, and by Makir son of Ammiel of Lodebar, and by Barzillai of Gilead from Rogelim. [28]They brought sleeping mats, cooking pots, serving bowls, wheat and barley flour, roasted grain, beans, lentils, [29]honey, butter, sheep, and cheese for David and those who were with him. For they said, "You must all be very tired and hungry and thirsty after your long march through the wilderness."

CHAPTER **18** **ABSALOM IS DEFEATED.** David now appointed generals and captains to lead his troops. [2]One-third were placed under Joab, one-third under Joab's brother Abishai son of Zeruiah, and one-third under Ittai the Gittite. The king told his troops, "I am going out with you."

[3]But his men objected strongly. "You must not go," they urged. "If we have to turn and run—and even if half of us die—it will make no difference to Absalom's troops; they will be looking only for you. You are worth ten thousand of us, and it is better that you stay here in the city and send us help if we need it."

[4]"If you think that's the best plan, I'll do it," the king finally agreed. So he stood at the gate of the city as all the divisions of troops passed by. [5]And the king gave this command to Joab, Abishai, and Ittai: "For my sake, deal gently with young Absalom." And all the troops heard the king give this order to his commanders.

[6]So the battle began in the forest of Ephraim, [7]and the Israelite troops were beaten back by David's men. There was a great slaughter, and twenty thousand men laid down their lives that day. [8]The battle raged all across the countryside, and more men died because of the forest than were killed by the sword.

[9]During the battle, Absalom came unexpectedly upon some of David's men. He tried to escape on his mule, but as he rode beneath the thick branches of a great oak, his head got caught. His mule kept going and left him dangling in the air. [10]One of David's men saw what had happened and told Joab, "I saw Absalom dangling in a tree."

[11]"What?" Joab demanded. "You saw him there and didn't kill him? I would have rewarded you with ten pieces of silver* and a hero's belt!"

[12]"I wouldn't do it for a thousand pieces of silver,*" the man replied. "We all heard the king say to you and Abishai and Ittai, 'For my sake, please don't harm young Absalom.' [13]And if I had betrayed the king by killing his son—and the king would certainly find out who did it—you yourself would be the first to abandon me."

[14]"Enough of this nonsense," Joab said. Then he took three daggers and plunged them into Absalom's heart as he dangled from the oak still alive. [15]Ten of Joab's young armor bearers then surrounded Absalom and killed him. [16]Then Joab blew the trumpet, and his men returned from chasing the army of Israel. [17]They threw Absalom's body into a deep pit in the forest and piled a great heap of stones over it. And the army of Israel fled to their homes.

[18]During his lifetime, Absalom had built a monument to himself in the King's Valley, for he had said, "I have no son to carry on my name." He named the monument after himself, and it is known as Absalom's Monument to this day.

[19]Then Zadok's son Ahimaaz said, "Let me run to the king with the good news that the LORD has saved him from his enemy Absalom."

[20]"No," Joab told him, "it wouldn't be good news to the king that his son is dead. You can be my messenger some other time, but not today."

[21]Then Joab said to a man from Cush, "Go tell the king what you have seen." The man bowed and ran off.

[22]But Ahimaaz continued to plead with Joab, "Whatever happens, please let me go, too."

"Why should you go, my son?" Joab replied. "There will be no reward for you."

[23]"Yes, but let me go anyway," he begged.

Joab finally said, "All right, go ahead." Then Ahimaaz took a shortcut across the plain of the Jordan and got to Mahanaim ahead of the man from Cush.

[24]While David was sitting at the city gate, the watchman climbed to the roof of the gateway by the wall. As he looked, he saw a lone man running toward them. [25]He shouted the news down to David, and the king replied, "If he is alone, he has news."

As the messenger came closer, [26]the watchman saw another man running toward them. He shouted down, "Here comes another one!"

The king replied, "He also will have news."

[27]"The first man runs like Ahimaaz son of Zadok," the watchman said.

"He is a good man and comes with good news," the king replied.

[28]Then Ahimaaz cried out to the king, "All is well!" He bowed low with his face to the ground and said, "Blessed be the LORD your God, who has handed over the rebels who dared to stand against you."

[29]"What about young Absalom?" the king demanded. "Is he all right?"

Ahimaaz replied, "When Joab told me to come,

**17:25a** Hebrew *Ithra,* a variant name for Jether. **17:25b** As in some Greek manuscripts (see also 1 Chr 2:17); Hebrew reads *an Israelite.*
**18:11** Hebrew *10 shekels of silver,* about 4 ounces or 114 grams in weight. **18:12** Hebrew *1,000 shekels,* about 25 pounds or 11.4 kilograms in weight.

## UNDESERVED ● ● • • •

**18:33 Why was David so upset over the death of his rebel son? (1) David realized that he, in part, was responsible for Absalom's death. Nathan, the prophet, had said that because David had killed Uriah, his own sons would rebel against him; (2) David was angry at Joab and his officers for killing Absalom against his wishes; (3) David truly loved his son even though Absalom did nothing to deserve David's love. Just as God bestows undeserved grace upon us, David was gracious to Absalom.**

there was a lot of commotion. But I didn't know what was happening."

30"Wait here," the king told him. So Ahimaaz stepped aside.

31Then the man from Cush arrived and said, "I have good news for my lord the king. Today the LORD has rescued you from all those who rebelled against you."

32"What about young Absalom?" the king demanded. "Is he all right?"

And the Cushite replied, "May all of your enemies, both now and in the future, be as that young man is!"

33The king was overcome with emotion. He went up to his room over the gateway and burst into tears. And as he went, he cried, "O my son Absalom! My son, my son Absalom! If only I could have died instead of you! O Absalom, my son, my son."

CHAPTER **19** **DAVID RETURNS TO JERUSALEM.** Word soon reached Joab that the king was weeping and mourning for Absalom. 2As the troops heard of the king's deep grief for his son, the joy of that day's victory was turned into deep sadness. 3They crept back into the city as though they were ashamed and had been beaten in battle. 4The king covered his face with his hands and kept on weeping, "O my son Absalom! O Absalom, my son, my son!"

5Then Joab went to the king's room and said to him, "We saved your life today and the lives of your sons, your daughters, and your wives and concubines. Yet you act like this, making us feel ashamed, as though we had done something wrong. 6You seem to love those who hate you and hate those who love you. You have made it clear today that we mean nothing to you. If Absalom had lived and all of us had died, you would be pleased. 7Now go out there and congratulate the troops, for I swear by the LORD that if you don't, not a single one of them will remain here tonight. Then you will be worse off than you have ever been." 8So the king went out and sat at the city gate, and as the news spread throughout the city that he was there, everyone went to him.

Meanwhile, the Israelites who supported Absalom had fled to their homes. 9And throughout the tribes of Israel there was much discussion and argument going on. The people were saying, "The king saved us from our enemies, the Philistines, but Absalom chased him out of the country. 10Now Absalom, whom we anointed to rule over us, is dead. Let's ask David to come back and be our king again."

11Then King David sent Zadok and Abiathar, the priests, to say to the leaders of Judah, "Why are you the last ones to reinstate the king? For I have heard that all Israel is ready, and only you are holding out. 12Yet you are my relatives, my own tribe, my own flesh and blood! Why are you the last ones to welcome me back?" 13And David told them to tell Amasa, "Since you are my nephew, may God strike me dead if I do not appoint you as commander of my army in place of Joab." 14Then Amasa convinced all the leaders of Judah, and they responded unanimously. They sent word to the king, "Return to us, and bring back all those who are with you."

15So the king started back to Jerusalem. And when he arrived at the Jordan River, the people of Judah came to Gilgal to meet him and escort him across the river. 16Then Shimei son of Gera, the man from Bahurim in Benjamin, hurried across with the men of Judah to welcome King David. 17A thousand men from the tribe of Benjamin were with him, including Ziba, the servant of Saul, and Ziba's fifteen sons and twenty servants. They rushed down to the Jordan to arrive ahead of the king. 18They all crossed the ford and worked hard ferrying the king's household across the river, helping them in every way they could.

As the king was about to cross the river, Shimei fell down before him. 19"My lord the king, please forgive me," he pleaded. "Forget the terrible thing I did when you left Jerusalem. 20I know how much I sinned. That is why I have come here today, the very first person in all Israel* to greet you."

## THE CROWD ● ● • • •

**19:8-10 Just a few days before, Absalom had turned the hearts of Israel away from David. Here the people wanted David back as their king. Because crowds are known to be fickle, there must be a higher moral code to follow than the pleasure of the majority. Following the moral principles given in God's Word will help you avoid being swayed by the crowd.**

21Then Abishai son of Zeruiah said, "Shimei should die, for he cursed the LORD's anointed king!"

22"What am I going to do with you sons of Zeruiah!" David exclaimed. "This is not a day for execution but for celebration! I am once again the king of Israel!" 23Then, turning to Shimei, David vowed, "Your life will be spared."

24Now Mephibosheth,* Saul's grandson, arrived from Jerusalem to meet the king. He had not washed his feet or clothes nor trimmed his beard since the day the king left Jerusalem. 25"Why didn't you come with me, Mephibosheth?" the king asked him.

26Mephibosheth replied, "My lord the king, my servant Ziba deceived me. I told him, 'Saddle my donkey so that I can go with the king.' For as you know I am crippled. 27Ziba has slandered me by

19:20 Hebrew *the house of Joseph.* 19:24 Also known as *Meribbaal.*

saying that I refused to come. But I know that you are
like an angel of God, so do what you think is best.
28All my relatives and I could expect only death from
you, my lord, but instead you have honored me
among those who eat at your own table! So how can
I complain?"

29"All right," David replied. "My decision is that you
and Ziba will divide your land equally between you."

30"Give him all of it," Mephibosheth said. "I am
content just to have you back again, my lord!"

31Barzillai of Gilead now arrived from Rogelim to
conduct the king across the Jordan. 32He was very
old, about eighty, and very wealthy. He was the one
who had provided food for the king during his stay
in Mahanaim. 33"Come across with me and live in
Jerusalem," the king said to Barzillai. "I will take care
of you there."

34"No," he replied, "I am far too old for that. 35I
am eighty years old today, and I can no longer enjoy
anything. Food and wine are no longer tasty, and I
cannot hear the musicians as they play. I would only
be a burden to my lord the king. 36Just to go across
the river with you is all the honor I need! 37Then let
me return again to die in my own town, where my
father and mother are buried. But here is my son
Kimham. Let him go with you and receive whatever
good things you want to give him."

38"Good," the king agreed. "Kimham will go with
me, and I will do for him whatever I would have
done for you." 39So all the people crossed the Jordan
with the king. After David had blessed and embraced
him, Barzillai returned to his own home. 40The king
then went on to Gilgal, taking Kimham with him. All
the army of Judah and half the army of Israel escorted him across the river.

41But the men of Israel complained to the king
that the men of Judah had gotten to do most of the
work in helping him cross the Jordan. 42"Why not?"
the men of Judah replied. "The king is one of our
own tribe. Why should this make you angry? We
have charged him nothing. And he hasn't fed us or
even given us gifts!"

43"But there are ten tribes in Israel," the others
replied. "So we have ten times as much right to the
king as you do. Why did you treat us with such
contempt? Remember, we were the first to speak of
bringing him back to be our king again." The argument continued back and forth, and the men of
Judah were very harsh in their replies.

CHAPTER **20** **SHEBA REBELS AGAINST DAVID.** Then a
troublemaker named Sheba son of Bicri, a man from
the tribe of Benjamin, blew a trumpet and shouted,
"We have nothing to do with David. We want no
part of this son of Jesse. Come on, you men of Israel,
let's all go home!" 2So the men of Israel deserted
David and followed Sheba. But the men of Judah
stayed with their king and escorted him from the
Jordan River to Jerusalem.

3When the king arrived at his palace in Jerusalem,
he instructed that the ten concubines he had left to
keep house should be placed in seclusion. Their
needs were to be cared for, he said, but he would no
longer sleep with them. So each of them lived like a
widow until she died.

4Then the king instructed Amasa to mobilize the
army of Judah within three days and to report back at
that time. 5So Amasa went out to notify the troops, but
it took him longer than the three days he had been
given. 6Then David said to Abishai, "That troublemaker Sheba is going to hurt us more than Absalom
did. Quick, take my troops and chase after him before
he gets into a fortified city where we can't reach him."

7So Abishai and Joab set out after Sheba with an
elite guard from Joab's army and the king's own
bodyguard.* 8As they arrived at the great stone in
Gibeon, Amasa met them, coming from the opposite direction. Joab was wearing his uniform with a
dagger strapped to his belt. As he stepped forward to
greet Amasa, he secretly slipped the dagger from its
sheath. 9"How are you, my cousin?" Joab said and
took him by the beard with his right hand as though
to kiss him. 10Amasa didn't notice the dagger in his
left hand, and Joab stabbed him in the stomach with
it so that his insides gushed out onto the ground.
Joab did not need to strike again, and Amasa soon
died. Joab and his brother Abishai left him lying
there and continued after Sheba.

11One of Joab's young officers shouted to Amasa's
troops, "If you are for Joab and David, come and
follow Joab." 12But Amasa lay in his blood in the
middle of the road, and Joab's officer saw that a
crowd was gathering around to stare at him. So he
pulled him off the road into a field and threw a cloak
over him. 13With Amasa's body out of the way, everyone went on with Joab to capture Sheba.

14Meanwhile, Sheba had traveled across Israel to
mobilize his own clan of Bicri at the city of Abel-beth-maacah. 15When Joab's forces arrived, they attacked Abel-beth-maacah and built a ramp against
the city wall and began battering it down. 16But a
wise woman in the city called out to Joab, "Listen to

**JUSTICE ● ● • • ·**

20:7-10 **Once again Joab's murderous treachery went unpunished, just as it did when he killed Abner (3:26-27). Eventually, however, justice caught up with him (1 Kings 2:28-35). It may seem that sin and treachery often go unpunished, but God's justice is not limited to this life's rewards. Even if Joab had died of old age, he would have to face the day of judgment.**

**SPEAK UP ● ● • • ·**

20:16-22 **Joab's men were attacking the city, and it looked as if it would be destroyed. Though women in that society were usually quiet in public, this woman spoke out. She stopped Joab's attack, not with weapons, but with wise words and a plan of action. Sometimes the courage to speak a few sensible words can prevent great disaster.**

**20:7** Hebrew *the Kerethites and Pelethites;* also in 20:23.

me, Joab. Come over here so I can talk to you." [17]As he approached, the woman asked, "Are you Joab?"

"I am," he replied.

So she said, "Listen carefully to your servant."

"I'm listening," he said.

[18]Then she continued, "There used to be a saying, 'If you want to settle an argument, ask advice at the city of Abel.' [19]I am one who is peace loving and faithful in Israel. But you are destroying a loyal city. Why do you want to destroy what belongs to the LORD?"

[20]And Joab replied, "Believe me, I don't want to destroy your city! [21]All I want is a man named Sheba son of Bicri from the hill country of Ephraim, who has revolted against King David. If you hand him over to me, we will leave the city in peace."

"All right," the woman replied, "we will throw his head over the wall to you." [22]Then the woman went to the people with her wise advice, and they cut off Sheba's head and threw it out to Joab. So he blew the trumpet and called his troops back from the attack, and they all returned to their homes. Joab returned to the king at Jerusalem.

[23]Joab once again became the commander of David's army. Benaiah son of Jehoiada was commander of the king's bodyguard. [24]Adoniram* was in charge of the labor force. Jehoshaphat son of Ahilud was the royal historian. [25]Sheva was the court secretary. Zadok and Abiathar were the priests. [26]Ira the Jairite was David's personal priest.

## RAIN ● ● • • •

21:1 **Farmers relied heavily on spring and fall rains for their crops. If the rains stopped or came at the wrong time, or if the plants became insect-infested, drastic food shortages could occur in the coming year. Agriculture at that time was completely dependent upon natural conditions. There were no irrigation methods, fertilizers, or pesticides. Even moderate variations in rainfall or insect activity could destroy an entire harvest.**

## CHAPTER 21

**SAUL'S SONS ARE EXECUTED.** There was a famine during David's reign that lasted for three years, so David asked the LORD about it. And the LORD said, "The famine has come because Saul and his family are guilty of murdering the Gibeonites."

[2]So King David summoned the Gibeonites. They were not part of Israel but were all that was left of the nation of the Amorites. Israel had sworn not to kill them, but Saul, in his zeal, had tried to wipe them out. [3]David asked them, "What can I do for you to make amends? Tell me so that the LORD will bless his people again."

[4]"Well, money won't do it," the Gibeonites replied. "And we don't want to see the Israelites executed in revenge."

## SNOW WHITE ● ● • • •

22:22-24 **David was not saying that he had never sinned. Psalm 51 shows his tremendous anguish over his sin against Uriah and Bathsheba. But David understood God's faithfulness and was writing this hymn from God's perspective. He knew that God had made him clean again—"whiter than snow," (Psalm 51:7) with a "clean heart" (Psalm 51:10). Through the death and resurrection of Jesus Christ, we also are made clean and perfect. Our sin is replaced with his purity and forgiveness; God no longer sees our sin.**

"What can I do then?" David asked. "Just tell me and I will do it for you."

[5]Then they replied, "It was Saul who planned to destroy us, to keep us from having any place at all in Israel. [6]So let seven of Saul's sons or grandsons be handed over to us, and we will execute them before the LORD at Gibeon, on the mountain of the LORD.*"

"All right," the king said, "I will do it." [7]David spared Jonathan's son Mephibosheth,* who was Saul's grandson, because of the oath David and Jonathan had sworn before the LORD. [8]But he gave them Saul's two sons Armoni and Mephibosheth, whose mother was Rizpah daughter of Aiah. He also gave them the five sons of Saul's daughter Merab,* the wife of Adriel son of Barzillai from Meholah. [9]The men of Gibeon executed them on the mountain before the LORD. So all seven of them died together at the beginning of the barley harvest.

[10]Then Rizpah, the mother of two of the men, spread sackcloth on a rock and stayed there the entire harvest season. She prevented vultures from tearing at their bodies during the day and stopped wild animals from eating them at night. [11]When David learned what Rizpah, Saul's concubine, had done, [12]he went to the people of Jabesh-gilead and asked for the bones of Saul and his son Jonathan. (When Saul and Jonathan had died in a battle with the Philistines, it was the people of Jabesh-gilead who had retrieved their bodies from the public square of the Philistine city of Beth-shan.) [13]So David brought the bones of Saul and Jonathan, as well as the bones of the men the Gibeonites had executed. [14]He buried them all in the tomb of Kish, Saul's father, at the town of Zela in the land of Benjamin. After that, God ended the famine in the land of Israel.

[15]Once again the Philistines were at war with Israel. And when David and his men were in the thick of battle, David became weak and exhausted. [16]Ishbi-benob was a descendant of the giants*; his bronze spearhead weighed more than seven pounds,* and he was armed with a new sword. He had cornered David and was about to kill him. [17]But Abishai son of Zeruiah came to his rescue and killed the Philistine. After that, David's men declared, "You are not going out to battle again! Why should we risk snuffing out the light of Israel?"

[18]After this, there was another battle against the

**20:24** As in Greek version (see also 1 Kgs 4:6; 5:14); Hebrew reads *Adoram.* **21:6** As in Greek version (see also 21:9); Hebrew reads *at Gibeah of Saul, the chosen of the LORD.* **21:7** Also known as *Meribbaal.* **21:8** As in a few Hebrew and Greek manuscripts and Syriac version (see also 1 Sam 18:19); most Hebrew manuscripts read *Michal.* **21:16a** As in Greek version; Hebrew reads *a descendant of the Rephaites;* also in 21:18, 20, 22. **21:16b** Hebrew *300 shekels* [3.4 kilograms].

Philistines at Gob. As they fought, Sibbecai from
Hushah killed Saph, another descendant of the
giants. [19]In still another battle at Gob, Elhanan son
of Jair* from Bethlehem killed the brother of Goliath of Gath.* The handle of his spear was as thick as
a weaver's beam! [20]In another battle with the Philistines at Gath, a huge man with six fingers on each
hand and six toes on each foot—a descendant of the
giants—[21]defied and taunted Israel. But he was killed
by Jonathan, the son of David's brother Shimea.*
[22]These four Philistines were descended from the
giants of Gath, but they were killed by David and his
warriors.

## CHAPTER 22 **DAVID'S SONG OF PRAISE.**

David sang
this song to the LORD after the LORD had rescued him
from all his enemies and from Saul. [2]These are the
words he sang:

"The LORD is my rock, my fortress, and my savior;
[3] my God is my rock, in whom I find protection.
He is my shield, the strength of my salvation,
and my stronghold,
my high tower, my savior, the one who saves
me from violence.
[4] I will call on the LORD, who is worthy of praise,
for he saves me from my enemies.

[5] "The waves of death surrounded me;
the floods of destruction
swept over me.
[6] The grave* wrapped its ropes
around me;
death itself stared me in the
face.
[7] But in my distress I cried out
to the LORD;
yes, I called to my God for
help.
He heard me from his
sanctuary;
my cry reached his ears.

[8] "Then the earth quaked and
trembled;
the foundations of the
heavens shook;
they quaked because of his
anger.
[9] Smoke poured from his
nostrils;
fierce flames leaped from
his mouth;
glowing coals flamed forth
from him.
[10] He opened the heavens and
came down;
dark storm clouds were
beneath his feet.
[11] Mounted on a mighty angel,* he flew,
soaring* on the wings of the wind.
[12] He shrouded himself in darkness,
veiling his approach with dense rain clouds.
[13] A great brightness shone before him,
and bolts of lightning blazed forth.
[14] The LORD thundered from heaven;
the Most High gave a mighty shout.
[15] He shot his arrows and scattered his enemies;
his lightning flashed, and they were confused.
[16] Then at the command of the LORD,
at the blast of his breath,
the bottom of the sea could be seen,
and the foundations of the earth were laid bare.

[17] "He reached down from heaven and rescued me;
he drew me out of deep waters.
[18] He delivered me from my powerful enemies,
from those who hated me and were too strong
for me.
[19] They attacked me at a moment when I was weakest,
but the LORD upheld me.
[20] He led me to a place of safety;
he rescued me because he delights in me.
[21] The LORD rewarded me for doing right;
he compensated me because of my innocence.
[22] For I have kept the ways of the LORD;
I have not turned from my God to follow evil.

## "Here's what I did..."

I was at a summer camp in Florida. Our group wanted to go swimming in the Gulf of Mexico, but we couldn't because there was a hurricane off the coast at the time and the riptides and undertow were too strong.

After dinner I walked down to the beach to look for a hat I had lost. Another guy in my group noticed four boys about 100 feet out in the water. They started swimming in, but one couldn't make it. He kept drifting farther out. The other boy I was with ran into the water to save him. I stood on the shore for 10 seconds and then without thinking jumped in also.

When I was halfway to the boy the guy from my group passed me; he couldn't make it so he had turned back. When I finally reached the boy, he was semiconscious. I grabbed him and tried to walk back to shore, but the water was over my head. I told the boy that every time there was a wave we would kick and try to ride it. I began to pray; I didn't know whether to just try to save my own life or hang onto the guy and keep trying to swim. I remembered 2 Samuel 22:17 and 2 Samuel 22:40a. I kept on swimming. After five minutes I stopped swimming; I was able to stand up. Before long we were on the shore. I believe the only reason I made it was because God was giving me the strength. I never saw the boy again.

Mike

AGE 16

21:19a As in parallel text at 1 Chr 20:5; Hebrew reads *son of Jaare-oregim.* 21:19b As in parallel text at 1 Chr 20:5; Hebrew reads *killed Goliath of Gath.* 21:21 As in parallel text at 1 Chr 20:7; Hebrew reads *Shimei,* a variant name for Shimea. 22:6 Hebrew *Sheol.* 22:11a Hebrew *cherub.* 22:11b As in some Hebrew manuscripts (see also Ps 18:10); other Hebrew manuscripts read *appearing.*

[23] For all his laws are constantly before me;
I have never abandoned his principles.
[24] I am blameless before God;
I have kept myself from sin.
[25] The LORD rewarded me for doing right,
because of my innocence in his sight.

[26] "To the faithful you show yourself faithful;
to those with integrity you show integrity.
[27] To the pure you show yourself pure,
but to the wicked you show yourself hostile.
[28] You rescue those who are humble,
but your eyes are on the proud to humiliate them.
[29] O LORD, you are my light;
yes, LORD, you light up my darkness.
[30] In your strength I can crush an army;
with my God I can scale any wall.

[31] "As for God, his way is perfect.
All the LORD's promises prove true.
He is a shield for all who look to him for protection.
[32] For who is God except the LORD?
Who but our God is a solid rock?
[33] God is my strong fortress;
he has made my way safe.
[34] He makes me as surefooted as a deer,
leading me safely along the mountain heights.
[35] He prepares me for battle;
he strengthens me to draw a bow of bronze.
[36] You have given me the shield of your salvation;
your help* has made me great.
[37] You have made a wide path for my feet
to keep them from slipping.

[38] "I chased my enemies and destroyed them;
I did not stop until they were conquered.
[39] I consumed them; I struck them down so they could not get up;
they fell beneath my feet.
[40] You have armed me with strength for the battle;
you have subdued my enemies under my feet.
[41] You made them turn and run;
I have destroyed all who hated me.
[42] They called for help, but no one came to rescue them.
They cried to the LORD, but he refused to answer them.
[43] I ground them as fine as the dust of the earth;
I swept them into the gutter like dirt.

[44] "You gave me victory over my accusers.
You preserved me as the ruler over nations;
people I don't even know now serve me.
[45] Foreigners cringe before me;
as soon as they hear of me, they submit.
[46] They all lose their courage
and come trembling from their strongholds.

[47] "The LORD lives! Blessed be my rock!
May God, the rock of my salvation, be exalted!
[48] He is the God who pays back those who harm me;
he subdues the nations under me
[49] and rescues me from my enemies.
You hold me safe beyond the reach of my enemies;
you save me from violent opponents.
[50] For this, O LORD, I will praise you among the nations;
I will sing joyfully to your name.
[51] You give great victories to your king;
you show unfailing love to your anointed,
to David and all his descendants forever."

22:36 As in Dead Sea Scrolls; most Hebrew manuscripts read *your answering.*

## GOD'S MAN ● ● • • •

22:51 **The book of 2 Samuel describes David's reign. Since the Israelites first entered the Promised Land under Joshua, they had been struggling to unite the nation and drive out the wicked inhabitants. At this time, after more than 400 years, Israel was finally at peace. David had accomplished what no leader before him, judge or king, had done. His administration was run on the principle of dedication to God and to the well-being of the people. Yet David also sinned. Despite his sins, however, the Bible calls David a man after God's own heart (1 Samuel 13:14; Acts 13:22), because when he sinned he recognized it and confessed it before God. David committed his life to God and remained loyal to God throughout his lifetime. Reading the Psalms gives an even deeper insight into David's love for God.**

## CHAPTER 23

**DAVID'S LAST WORDS.** These are the last words of David:

"David, the son of Jesse, speaks—
David, the man to whom God gave such wonderful success,
David, the man anointed by the God of Jacob,
David, the sweet psalmist of Israel.

[2] "The Spirit of the LORD speaks through me;
his words are upon my tongue.
[3] The God of Israel spoke.
The Rock of Israel said to me:
'The person who rules righteously,
who rules in the fear of God,
[4] he is like the light of the morning,
like the sunrise bursting forth in a cloudless sky,
like the refreshing rains that bring tender grass from the earth.'

[5] "It is my family God has chosen!
Yes, he has made an everlasting covenant with me.

## POURED OUT ● ● • • •

23:16 **David poured out the water as an offering to God because he was so moved by the sacrifice it represented. When Hebrews offered sacrifices, they never consumed the blood. It represented life, and they poured it out before God. David would not drink this water, which represented the lives of his soldiers. Instead, he offered it to God.**

His agreement is eternal, final, sealed.
He will constantly look after my safety and success.
6 But the godless are like thorns to be thrown away,
for they tear the hand that touches them.
7 One must be armed to chop them down;
they will be utterly consumed with fire."

8These are the names of David's mightiest men. The first was Jashobeam the Hacmonite,* who was commander of the Three—the three greatest warriors among David's men. He once used his spear to kill eight hundred enemy warriors in a single battle.*

9Next in rank among the Three was Eleazar son of Dodai, a descendant of Ahoah. Once Eleazar and David stood together against the Philistines when the entire Israelite army had fled. 10He killed Philistines until his hand was too tired to lift his sword, and the LORD gave him a great victory that day. The rest of the army did not return until it was time to collect the plunder!

11Next in rank was Shammah son of Agee from Harar. One time the Philistines gathered at Lehi and attacked the Israelites in a field full of lentils. The Israelite army fled, 12but Shammah held his ground in the middle of the field and beat back the Philistines. So the LORD brought about a great victory.

13Once during harvesttime, when David was at the cave of Adullam, the Philistine army was camped in the valley of Rephaim. The Three (who were among the Thirty—an elite group among David's fighting men) went down to meet him there. 14David was staying in the stronghold at the time, and a Philistine detachment had occupied the town of Bethlehem. 15David remarked longingly to his men, "Oh, how I would love some of that good water from the well in Bethlehem, the one by the gate." 16So the Three broke through the Philistine lines, drew some water from the well, and brought it back to David. But he refused to drink it. Instead, he poured it out before the LORD. 17"The LORD forbid that I should drink this!" he exclaimed. "This water is as precious as the blood of these men who risked their lives to bring it to me." So David did not drink it. This is an example of the exploits of the Three.

18Abishai son of Zeruiah, the brother of Joab, was the leader of the Thirty.* He once used his spear to kill three hundred enemy warriors in a single battle. It was by such feats that he became as famous as the Three. 19Abishai was the most famous of the Thirty* and was their commander, though he was not one of the Three.

20There was also Benaiah son of Jehoiada, a valiant warrior from Kabzeel. He did many heroic deeds, which included killing two of Moab's mightiest warriors. Another time he chased a lion down into a pit. Then, despite the snow and slippery ground, he caught the lion and killed it. 21Another time, armed only with a club, he killed a great Egyptian warrior who was armed with a spear. Benaiah

## DAVID'S MIGHTY MEN

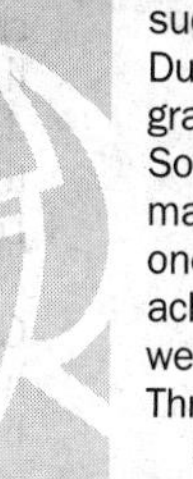

One way to understand David's success is to notice the kind of men who followed him. During the time he was being hunted by Saul, David gradually built a fighting force of several hundred men. Some were relatives, others were outcasts of society, many were in trouble with the law. They all had at least one trait in common—complete devotion to David. Their achievements made them famous. Among these men were elite military groups like "the Thirty" and "the Three." They were true heroes.

Scripture gives the impression that these men were motivated to greatness by the personal qualities of their leader. David inspired them to achieve beyond their goals and meet their true potential. Likewise, the leaders we follow and the causes to which we commit ourselves will affect our life. David's effectiveness was clearly connected with his awareness of God's leading. He was a good leader when he was following *his* Leader. Do you know whom the people you respect most are following? Your answer should help you decide whether or not they deserve your loyalty. Do you also recognize God's leading in your life? No one can lead you to excellence as your Creator can.

**UPS:**
- Able
- Shared many special skills
- Though frequently outnumbered, were consistently victorious
- Loyal to David

**STATS:**
- Where: They came from all over Israel (primarily Judah and Benjamin), and from some of the other surrounding nations as well
- Occupations: Various backgrounds—almost all were fugitives

LESSONS: Greatness is often inspired by the quality and character of leadership

Even a small force of able and loyal men can accomplish great feats

KEY VERSES: "So David left Gath and escaped to the cave of Adullam. Soon his brothers and other relatives joined him there. Then others began coming—men who were in trouble or in debt or who were just discontented—until David was the leader of about four hundred men" (1 Samuel 22:1-2).

Their stories are told in 1 Samuel 22—2 Samuel 23:39. They are also mentioned in 1 Chronicles 11–12.

23:8a As in parallel text at 1 Chr 11:11; Hebrew reads *Josheb-basshebeth the Tahkemonite.* 23:8b As in some Greek manuscripts (see also 1 Chr 11:11); the Hebrew is uncertain, though it might be rendered *the Three. It was Adino the Eznite who killed eight hundred men at one time.* 23:18 As in a few Hebrew manuscripts and Syriac version; most Hebrew manuscripts read *the Three.* 23:19 As in Syriac version; Hebrew reads *the Three.*

wrenched the spear from the Egyptian's hand and
killed him with it. 22 These are some of the deeds that
made Benaiah almost as famous as the Three. 23 He
was more honored than the other members of the
Thirty, though he was not one of the Three. And
David made him commander of his bodyguard.
24 Other members of the Thirty included:

Asahel, Joab's brother;
Elhanan son of Dodo from Bethlehem;
25 Shammah from Harod;
Elika from Harod;
26 Helez from Pelon*;
Ira son of Ikkesh from Tekoa;
27 Abiezer from Anathoth;
Sibbecai* from Hushah;
28 Zalmon from Ahoah;
Maharai from Netophah;
29 Heled* son of Baanah from Netophah;
Ithai* son of Ribai from Gibeah (from the tribe of Benjamin);
30 Benaiah from Pirathon;
Hurai* from Nahale-gaash*;
31 Abi-albon the Arbathite;
Azmaveth from Bahurim;
32 Eliahba from Shaalbon;
the sons of Jashen;
33 Jonathan son of Shagee* from Harar;
Ahiam son of Sharar from Harar;
34 Eliphelet son of Ahasbai from Maacah;
Eliam son of Ahithophel from Giloh;
35 Hezro from Carmel;
Paarai from Arba;
36 Igal son of Nathan from Zobah;
Bani from Gad;
37 Zelek from Ammon;
Naharai from Beeroth (Joab's armor bearer);
38 Ira from Jattir;
Gareb from Jattir;
39 Uriah the Hittite.

There were thirty-seven in all.

## CHAPTER 24 **DAVID TAKES A CENSUS.**

Once again
the anger of the LORD burned against Israel, and he
caused David to harm them by taking a census. "Go
and count the people of Israel and Judah," the LORD
told him.
2 So the king said to Joab, the commander of his
army, "Take a census of all the people in the land—
from Dan in the north to Beersheba in the south—
so that I may know how many people there are."
3 But Joab replied to the king, "May the LORD your
God let you live until there are a hundred times as
many people in your kingdom as there are now! But
why do you want to do this?"
4 But the king insisted that they take the census, so
Joab and his officers went out to count the people of
Israel. 5 First they crossed the Jordan and camped at
Aroer, south of the town in the valley, in the direction of Gad. Then they went on to Jazer, 6 then to
Gilead in the land of Tahtim-hodshi* and to Dan-
jaan and around to Sidon. 7 Then they came to the
stronghold of Tyre, and all the cities of the Hivites
and Canaanites. Finally, they went south to Judah as
far as Beersheba. 8 Having gone through the entire
land, they completed their task in nine months and
twenty days and then returned to Jerusalem. 9 Joab
reported the number of people to the king. There
were 800,000 men of military age in Israel and
500,000 in Judah.
10 But after he had taken the census, David's conscience began to bother him. And he said to the
LORD, "I have sinned greatly and shouldn't have
taken the census. Please forgive me, LORD, for doing
this foolish thing."
11 The next morning the word of the LORD came to
the prophet Gad, who was David's seer. This was the
message: 12 "Go and say to David, 'This is what the
LORD says: I will give you three choices. Choose one
of these punishments, and I will do it.'"
13 So Gad came to David and asked him, "Will you
choose three* years of famine throughout the land,
three months of fleeing from your enemies, or three
days of severe plague throughout your land? Think
this over and let me know what answer to give the
LORD."
14 "This is a desperate situation!" David replied to
Gad. "But let us fall into the hands of the LORD, for
his mercy is great. Do not let me fall into human
hands."
15 So the LORD sent a plague upon Israel that morning, and it lasted for three days. Seventy thousand
people died throughout the nation. 16 But as the
death angel was preparing to destroy Jerusalem, the
LORD relented and said to the angel, "Stop! That is
enough!" At that moment the angel of the LORD was
by the threshing floor of Araunah the Jebusite.
17 When David saw the angel, he said to the LORD,
"I am the one who has sinned and done wrong! But
these people are innocent—what have they done?
Let your anger fall against me and my family."
18 That day Gad came to David and said to him,
"Go and build an altar to the LORD on the threshing
floor of Araunah the Jebusite."
19 So David went to do what the LORD had commanded him. 20 When Araunah saw the king and his
men coming toward him, he came forward and
bowed before the king with his face to the ground.
21 "Why have you come, my lord?" Araunah asked.
And David replied, "I have come to buy your
threshing floor and to build an altar to the LORD
there, so that the LORD will stop the plague."

**23:26** As in parallel text at 1 Chr 11:27 (see also 1 Chr 27:10); Hebrew reads *from Palti.* **23:27** As in some Greek manuscripts (see also 1 Chr 11:29); Hebrew reads *Mebunnai.* **23:29a** As in some Hebrew manuscripts (see also 1 Chr 11:30); most Hebrew manuscripts read *Heleb.* **23:29b** As in parallel text at 1 Chr 11:31; Hebrew reads *Ittai.* **23:30a** As in some Greek manuscripts (see also 1 Chr 11:32); Hebrew reads *Hiddai.* **23:30b** Or *from the ravines of Gaash.* **23:33** As in parallel text at 1 Chr 11:34; Hebrew reads *Jonathan, Shammah;* some Greek manuscripts read *Jonathan son of Shammah.* **24:6** Greek version reads *to Gilead and to Kadesh in the land of the Hittites.* **24:13** As in Greek version (see also 1 Chr 21:12); Hebrew reads *seven.*

[22]"Take it, my lord, and use it as you wish," Araunah said to David. "Here are oxen for the burnt offering, and you can use the threshing tools and ox yokes for wood to build a fire on the altar. [23]I will give it all to you, and may the LORD your God accept your sacrifice."
[24]But the king replied to Araunah, "No, I insist on buying it, for I cannot present burnt offerings to the LORD my God that have cost me nothing." So David paid him fifty pieces of silver* for the threshing floor and the oxen. [25]David built an altar there to the LORD and offered burnt offerings and peace offerings. And the LORD answered his prayer, and the plague was stopped.

**24:24** Hebrew *50 shekels of silver,* about 20 ounces or 570 grams in weight.

# MEGA themes

**KINGDOM GROWTH** Under David's leadership, Israel grew rapidly. With the growth came many changes; from tribal independence to centralized government, from the leadership of judges to a monarchy, from decentralized worship to worship at Jerusalem.

No matter how much growth or how many changes we experience, God will meet our needs if we love him and highly regard his principles.

1. What do you think life was like in Israel during the high points of David's reign?
2. How did God supply his blessing through David?
3. What are some of the "high points" of your life? How did God bless you during those times?
4. Why do some people seem to forget God when things are going great?
5. List a couple of principles you can use to guide you when everything seems to be going great for you.

**PERSONAL GREATNESS** David's popularity and influence increased greatly. He realized that the Lord was behind his success because he wanted to pour out his kindness on Israel.

God graciously favors us because of what Christ has done. God does not regard personal greatness as something to be used selfishly, but as an instrument to carry out his work among his people. The greatness we should desire is to love others as God loves us. We should never use or take advantage of someone for our own benefit.

1. When God exalted David, how did he respond? How did others respond?
2. What attitude should we have toward those who are raised up by God to be our leaders?
3. What qualities would be seen by God as qualities of greatness?
4. What would it take for you to achieve true greatness?

**JUSTICE** King David showed justice, mercy, and fairness to Saul's family, enemies, rebels, allies, and close friends alike. His just rule was grounded in his faith and knowledge of God.

Although David was the most just of all Israel's kings, he was still imperfect. His use of justice offered hope for a heavenly, ideal kingdom. This hope will never be satisfied in the hearts of human beings until Christ, the Son of David, comes to rule in perfect justice forever.

1. How is God's justice revealed in David's life?
2. What difference does it make whether or not you live according to God's will?
3. How should you respond when another Christian indicates concern about the justice of a decision you are making?
4. As an individual Christian, what can you do to work for justice in the world?

**CONSEQUENCES OF SIN** David's sin with Bathsheba had consequences that ruined both his family and the nation. David's prosperity and ease led him from triumph to temptation—to trouble.

Temptation quite often comes when a person's life has no direction. Sometimes we may think that sinful pleasures will bring us a sense of life and adventure; but sin creates a cycle of suffering that is not worth the fleeting pleasure or "rush" it offers.

1. What led to David's choosing to sin with Bathsheba?
2. List a few of the results of that choice and other sinful choices that followed.
3. What causes Christians to choose sin even though they know what is right?
4. Suppose you sinned against God knowingly and then nothing seemed to go wrong in your life. Could it then be said that you had "gotten away with it"? Explain.
5. Based on this study of 2 Samuel, what areas of your life need to be changed in order to avoid the type of mistakes that David made?

1010 B.C.
David becomes king

970
Solomon becomes king

959
Temple completed

930
The kingdom divides

925
Shishak invades Jerusalem

910
Asa becomes king of Judah

875
Elijah begins his ministry

874
Ahab becomes king of Israel

872
Jehoshaphat becomes king of Judah

857
Ben-hadad attacks Samaria

853
Ahab dies in battle

Here's a quick quiz. What do you think of when you hear each of these names: Solomon . . . Elijah . . . Ahab . . . Jezebel . . . Nadab? ■The usual response for Solomon would be "wisdom" or "the Temple." For Elijah, you might answer, "prophet" or "defeated the Baal worshipers on the mountain." Ahab and Jezebel are most certainly associated with evil. And you may not even have heard of Nadab. ■It's amazing what people remember about other people, even after they're gone. Whether good or evil, a person's reputation often remains long after his or her death. ■First Kings tells the stories of many of the leaders of Israel. Some, like Solomon, take chapters to relate. Others, like Nadab, just take a line or two. No matter what the length, when we read these accounts we gain a snapshot of what these people were like—their character and their lives. As we read, we can learn what it takes to be someone who is remembered for good and not for evil, for following God and not self. ■What would your friends and acquaintances say if given your name in a similar quiz? What kind of a reputation are you building?

## STATS

PURPOSE: To contrast the lives of those who live for God with the lives of those who refuse to do so, using the history of the kings of Israel and Judah

AUTHOR: Unknown. Possibly Jeremiah or a group of prophets.

SETTING: The once great nation of Israel turns into a divided land, both physically and spiritually

KEY PEOPLE: David, Solomon, Rehoboam, Jeroboam, Elijah, Ahab, Jezebel

SPECIAL FEATURE: The books of 1 and 2 Kings were originally one book

CHAPTER **1** **SOLOMON BECOMES KING.** Now King
David was very old, and no matter how many blankets covered him, he could not keep warm. [2]So his
advisers told him, "We will find a young virgin who
will wait on you and be your nurse. She will lie in
your arms and keep you warm." [3]So they searched
throughout the country for a beautiful girl, and they
found Abishag from Shunem and brought her to the
king. [4]The girl was very beautiful, and she waited on
the king and took care of him. But the king had no
sexual relations with her.
[5]About that time David's son Adonijah, whose
mother was Haggith, decided to make himself king in
place of his aged father. So he provided himself with
chariots and horses* and recruited fifty men to run in
front of him. [6]Now his father, King David, had never
disciplined him at any time, even by asking, "What are
you doing?" Adonijah was a very handsome man and
had been born next after Absalom. [7]Adonijah took
Joab son of Zeruiah and Abiathar the priest into his
confidence, and they agreed to help him become king.
[8]But among those who remained loyal to David and
refused to support Adonijah were Zadok the priest,
Benaiah son of Jehoiada, Nathan the prophet, Shimei,
Rei, and David's personal bodyguard.
[9]Adonijah went to the stone of Zoheleth* near the
spring of En-rogel, where he sacrificed sheep, oxen,
and fattened calves. He invited all his brothers—the
other sons of King David—and all the royal officials
of Judah. [10]But he did not invite Nathan the prophet,
or Benaiah, or the king's bodyguard, or his brother
Solomon.
[11]Then Nathan the prophet went to Bathsheba,
Solomon's mother, and asked her, "Did you realize
that Haggith's son, Adonijah, has made himself king
and that our lord David doesn't even know about it?
[12]If you want to save your own life and the life of your
son Solomon, follow my counsel. [13]Go at once to
King David and say to him, 'My lord, didn't you
promise me that my son Solomon would be the next
king and would sit upon your throne? Then why has

**ACTION ● ● ● • •**

1:5-14 **When Nathan learned of Adonijah's conspiracy, he immediately tried to stop it. He was a man of both faith and action. Nathan knew the right course to take—that Solomon should be king—and he moved quickly when he saw someone trying to block what was right. We often know what is right, but don't act on it. Perhaps we don't want to get involved, or maybe we are lazy. Don't stop with prayer, good intentions, or angry feelings. Take the action needed to correct the situation.**

1:5 Or *and charioteers.* 1:9 Or *to the Serpent's Stone;* Greek version supports reading *Zoheleth* as a proper name.

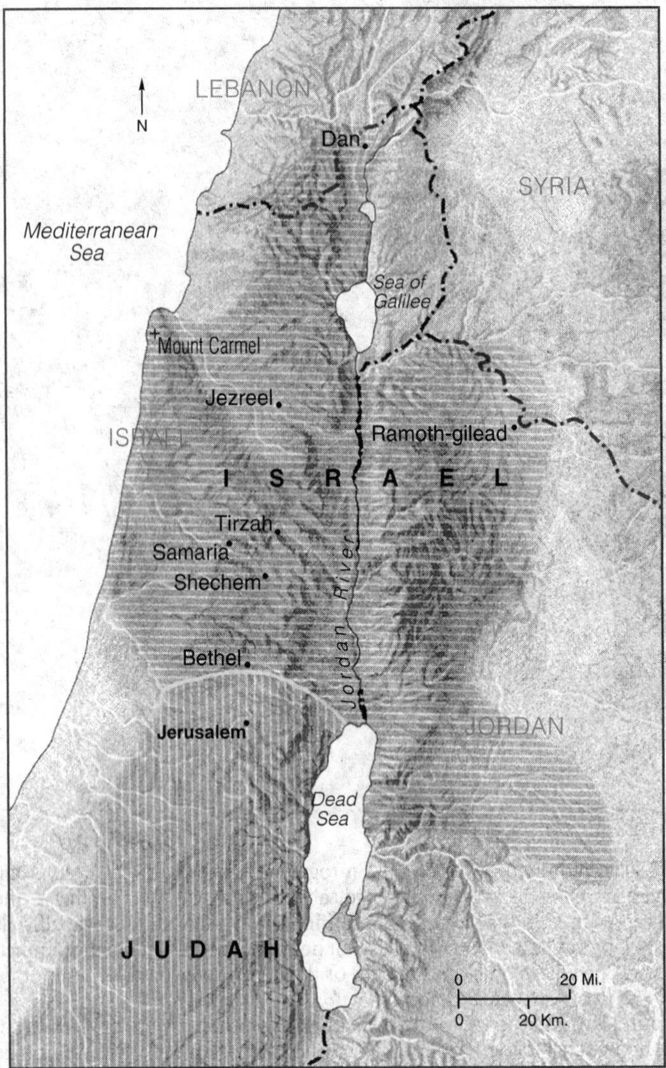


The broken lines (—·—·) indicate modern boundaries.

David's son Solomon brought Israel into its golden age. His wealth and wisdom were acclaimed worldwide. But he ignored God in his later years (1:1–11:25).

**Shechem** After Solomon's death, Israel assembled at Shechem to inaugurate his son Rehoboam. However, Rehoboam foolishly angered the people by threatening even higher taxes, which caused a revolt (11:26–12:19).

**Israel** Jeroboam, leader of the rebels, was made king of Israel, now called the northern kingdom. Jeroboam made Shechem his capital city (12:20,25).

**Judah** Only the tribes of Judah and Benjamin remained loyal to Rehoboam. These two tribes became the southern kingdom. Rehoboam returned to Judah from Shechem and prepared to force the rebels into submission, but a prophet's message halted these plans (12:21-24).

**Jerusalem** Jerusalem was the capital city of Judah. Its Temple, built by Solomon, was the focal point of Jewish worship. This worried Jeroboam. How could he keep his people loyal if they were constantly going to Rehoboam's capital to worship (12:26-27)?

**Dan** Jeroboam's solution was to set up his own worship centers. He had two calf idols made and proclaimed them to be Israel's gods. One was placed in Dan, and the people were told that they could go there instead of to Jerusalem to worship (12:28-29).

**Bethel** The other idol made at Jeroboam's command was placed in Bethel. The people of the northern kingdom had two convenient locations for worship in their own country. But their sin displeased God. Meanwhile, in Jerusalem, Rehoboam was also allowing idolatry to creep in. The two nations were constantly at war (12:29–15:26).

**Tirzah** Baasha became king of Israel after assassinating Nadab. He moved the capital from Shechem to Tirzah (15:27–16:22).

**Samaria** Israel continued to gain and lose kings through plots, assassinations, and warfare. When Omri became king, he bought a hill on which he built a new capital city, Samaria. Omri's son, Ahab, became the most wicked king of Israel. His wife, Jezebel, worshiped Baal. Ahab erected a temple to Baal in Samaria (16:23-34).

**Mount Carmel** Great evil often brings great people who oppose it. Elijah challenged the prophets of Baal and Asherah at Mount Carmel, where he would prove that they were false prophets. There Elijah humiliated these prophets and then executed them (17:1–18:46).

**Jezreel** Elijah returned to Jezreel. But Queen Jezebel, furious at the execution of her prophets, vowed to kill Elijah. He ran for his life, but God cared for and encouraged him. During his travels, he anointed the future kings of Syria and Israel, as well as his own replacement, Elisha (19:1-21).

**Ramoth-gilead** The king of Syria declared war on Israel and was defeated in two battles. But the Syrians occupied Ramoth-gilead. Ahab and Jehoshaphat joined forces to recover the city. In this battle, Ahab was killed. Later, Jehoshaphat died (20:1–22:53).

Adonijah become king?' [14]And while you are still
talking with him, I will come and confirm everything you have said."

[15]So Bathsheba went into the king's bedroom. He
was very old now, and Abishag was taking care of
him. [16]Bathsheba bowed low before him.

"What can I do for you?" he asked her.

[17]She replied, "My lord, you vowed to me by the
LORD your God that my son Solomon would be the
next king and would sit on your throne. [18]But instead,
Adonijah has become the
new king, and you do not
even know about it. [19]He has
sacrificed many oxen, fattened calves, and sheep, and
he has invited all your sons
and Abiathar the priest and
Joab, the commander of the
army. But he did not invite
your servant Solomon. [20]And
now, my lord the king, all Israel is waiting for your decision as to who will become
king after you. [21]If you do not
act, my son Solomon and I
will be treated as criminals as
soon as you are dead."

[22]While she was still
speaking with the king, Nathan the prophet arrived.
[23]The king's advisers told
him, "Nathan the prophet is
here to see you."

Nathan went in and
bowed low before the king.
[24]He asked, "My lord, have
you decided that Adonijah
will be the next king and that
he will sit on your throne?
[25]Today he has sacrificed
many oxen, fattened calves,
and sheep, and he has in-
vited your sons to attend the
celebration. He also invited
Joab, the commander of the
army,* and Abiathar the
priest. They are feasting and
drinking with him and
shouting, 'Long live King
Adonijah!' [26]But I myself,
your servant, was not invited;
neither were Zadok the
priest, Benaiah son of Jehoiada, nor Solomon. [27]Has my
lord really done this without
letting any of his servants
know who should be the
next king?"

[28]"Call Bathsheba,"
David said. So she came back in and stood before the
king. [29]And the king vowed, "As surely as the LORD
lives, who has rescued me from every danger, [30]today
I decree that your son Solomon will be the next king
and will sit on my throne, just as I swore to you
before the LORD, the God of Israel."

[31]Then Bathsheba bowed low before him again
and exclaimed, "May my lord King David live forever!"

[32]Then King David ordered, "Call Zadok the priest,

## SOLOMON

**UPS:**
- Third king of Israel, David's chosen heir
- The wisest man who ever lived
- Author of Ecclesiastes and Song of Solomon, as well as many of the proverbs and some of the psalms
- Built God's Temple in Jerusalem
- Diplomat, trader, collector, patron of the arts

**DOWNS:**
- Sealed many foreign agreements by marrying heathen women
- Allowed his wives to affect his loyalty to God
- Taxed his people excessively and drafted them into a labor force

**STATS:**
- Where: Jerusalem
- Occupation: King of Israel
- Relatives: Father: David. Mother: Bathsheba. Brothers: Absalom, Adonijah. Sister: Tamar. Son: Rehoboam.

Having wisdom doesn't help unless you use it. Early in his life, Solomon had the sense to realize his need for wisdom. But even when he asked God to give him wisdom to be a good king, he was already showing poor judgment as a man. He married a heathen woman as part of a political deal. She was the first of several hundred wives he married. In doing this, Solomon went against not only his father's last words, but also God's direct commands. His actions remind us how easy it is to know what is right and yet not do it.

God's gift of wisdom to Solomon did not mean that he couldn't make mistakes. He had been given great opportunities as the king of God's chosen people, but with those opportunities came great responsibilities. Solomon took advantage of the opportunities, building temples and palaces, but he became infamous as a king who charged high taxes and overworked his people.

Little is mentioned in the Bible about the last decade of Solomon's reign. Ecclesiastes probably records his final reflections on life. In that book, we observe a man proving through bitter experience that finding meaning in life apart from God doesn't work. Real security and contentment are only found in a personal relationship with God. The contentment we find in the opportunities and successes of this life is real, but temporary. The more we expect those feelings to last, the more quickly they are gone. Be sure to balance your pursuit of all the opportunities in life with keeping up with your responsibilities. Or, as Solomon put it, "Don't let the excitement of youth cause you to forget your Creator. Honor him in your youth before you grow old and no longer enjoy living" (Ecclesiastes 12:1).

LESSONS: Effective leadership can be nullified by an ineffective personal life

Solomon failed to obey God and did not learn the lesson of repentance until late in life

Knowing what actions are required of us means little if we don't have the will to perform those actions

KEY VERSE: "Wasn't this exactly what led King Solomon of Israel into sin? . . . There was no king from any nation who could compare to him, and God loved him and made him king over all Israel. But even he was led into sin by his foreign wives" (Nehemiah 13:26).

Solomon's story is told in 2 Samuel 12:24—1 Kings 11:43. He is also mentioned in 1 Chronicles 28–29; 2 Chronicles 1–9; Nehemiah 13:26; Psalm 72; and Matthew 6:29; 12:42.

**1:25** As in Greek version; Hebrew reads *invited the commanders of the army.*

| | POWER | PLEASURE | PASSION | PRAISE AND POPULARITY |
|---|---|---|---|---|
| **The Appeal of Idols** | The people wanted freedom from the authority of both God and the priests. They wanted their religion to fit their lifestyle, not their lifestyle to fit their religion. | Idol worship exalted sensuality without responsibility or guilt. People acted out the vicious and sensuous personalities of the gods they worshiped, thus gaining approval for their degraded lives. | Humanity was reduced to little more than animals. The people did not have to be viewed as unique individuals but could be exploited sexually, politically, and economically. | The high and holy nature of God was replaced by gods who were more a reflection of human nature, thus more culturally suitable to the people. These gods no longer required sacrifice, just a token of appeasement. |
| **Modern Parallel** | People do not want to answer to a greater authority. God wants us to have the Holy Spirit's power to help others instead of having power over others. | People deify pleasure, seeking it at the expense of everything else. God calls us to seek the kind of pleasure that leads to long-range rewards instead of seeking pleasure that leads to long-range disaster. | Like animals, people let physical drives and passions rule them. God calls us to redirect our passions to areas that build others up instead of seeking passion that exploits others. | Sacrifice is seen as a self-inflicted punishment, making no sense. Success is to be sought at all costs. God calls us to praise him and those who honor him instead of seeking praise for ourselves. |

**THE APPEAL OF IDOLS** On the surface, the lives of the kings don't make sense. How could they run to idolatry so fast when they had God's Word (at least some of it), the prophets, and the example of David? Above are some of the reasons for the enticement of idols. As societies change and evolve, they often throw out norms and values no longer considered necessary or acceptable. Believers must be careful not to follow society's example when it discards God's Word. When society does that, only godlessness and evil remain.

---

Nathan the prophet, and Benaiah son of Jehoiada."
When they came into the king's presence, 33the king
said to them, "Take Solomon and my officers down to
Gihon Spring. Solomon is to ride on my personal
mule. 34There Zadok the priest and Nathan the
prophet are to anoint him king over Israel. Then blow
the trumpets and shout, 'Long live King Solomon!'
35When you bring him back here, he will sit on my
throne. He will succeed me as king, for I have appointed him to be ruler over Israel and Judah."
36"Amen!" Benaiah son of Jehoiada replied. "May
the LORD, the God of my lord the king, decree it to
be so. 37And may the LORD be with Solomon as he
has been with you, and may he make Solomon's
reign even greater than yours!"
38So Zadok the priest, Nathan the prophet, Benaiah son of Jehoiada, and the king's bodyguard* took
Solomon down to Gihon Spring, and Solomon rode
on King David's personal mule. 39There Zadok the
priest took a flask of olive oil from the sacred tent
and poured it on Solomon's head. Then the trumpets were blown, and all the people shouted, "Long
live King Solomon!" 40And all the people returned
with Solomon to Jerusalem, playing flutes and
shouting for joy. The celebration was so joyous and
noisy that the earth shook with the sound.
41Adonijah and his guests heard the celebrating
and shouting just as they were finishing their banquet. When Joab heard the sound of trumpets, he
asked, "What's going on? Why is the city in such an
uproar?"
42And while he was still speaking, Jonathan son of
Abiathar the priest arrived. "Come in," Adonijah
said to him, "for you are a good man. You must have
good news."
43"Not at all!" Jonathan replied. "Our lord King
David has just declared Solomon king! 44The king
sent him down to Gihon Spring with Zadok the
priest, Nathan the prophet, and Benaiah son of Jehoiada, protected by the king's bodyguard. They had
him ride on the king's own mule, 45and Zadok and
Nathan have anointed him as the new king. They
have just returned, and the whole city is celebrating
and rejoicing. That's what all the noise is about.
46Moreover, Solomon is now sitting on the royal
throne as king. 47All the royal officials went to King
David and congratulated him, saying, 'May your
God make Solomon's fame even greater than your
own, and may Solomon's kingdom be even greater
than yours!' Then the king bowed his head in worship as he lay in his bed, 48and he spoke these words:

1:38 Hebrew *the Kerethites and Pelethites;* also in 1:44.

## GOD FIRST ● ● • • ·

1:49-50 **Sometimes it takes getting caught before someone is willing to give up his scheme. When Adonijah learned that his plans had been exposed, he ran in panic to the sacred altar, the highest symbol of God's mercy and forgiveness. He went there, however, *after* his plans for treason were exposed. If Adonijah had first considered what God wanted, he might have avoided trouble. Don't wait until you have made a mess of things to run to God; it's much better to seek God's guidance *before* you act.**

'Blessed be the LORD, the God of Israel, who today has chosen someone to sit on my throne while I am still alive to see it.'"

49Then all of Adonijah's guests jumped up in panic from the banquet table and quickly went their separate ways. 50Adonijah himself was afraid of Solomon, so he rushed to the sacred tent and caught hold of the horns of the altar. 51Word soon reached Solomon that Adonijah had seized the horns of the altar and that he was pleading, "Let Solomon swear today that he will not kill me!"

52Solomon replied, "If he proves himself to be loyal, he will not be harmed.* But if he does not, he will die." 53So King Solomon summoned Adonijah, and they brought him down from the altar. He came and bowed low before the king, and Solomon dismissed him, saying, "Go on home."

## CHAPTER 2 **INSTRUCTIONS FOR SOLOMON.**

As the time of King David's death approached, he gave this charge to his son Solomon: 2"I am going where everyone on earth must someday go. Take courage and be a man. 3Observe the requirements of the LORD your God and follow all his ways. Keep each of the laws, commands, regulations, and stipulations written in the law of Moses so that you will be successful in all you do and wherever you go. 4If you do this, then the LORD will keep the promise he made to me: 'If your descendants live as they should and follow me faithfully with all their heart and soul, one of them will always sit on the throne of Israel.'

5"And there is something else. You know that Joab son of Zeruiah murdered my two army commanders, Abner son of Ner and Amasa son of Jether. He pretended that it was an act of war, but it was done in a time of peace,* staining his belt and sandals with the blood of war. 6Do with him what you think best, but don't let him die in peace.

7"Be kind to the sons of Barzillai of Gilead. Make them permanent guests of the king, for they took care of me when I fled from your brother Absalom.

8"And remember Shimei son of Gera, the man from Bahurim in Benjamin. He cursed me with a terrible curse as I was fleeing to Mahanaim. When he came down to meet me at the Jordan River, I swore by the LORD that I would not kill him. 9But that oath does not make him innocent. You are a wise man, and you will know how to arrange a bloody death for him."

10Then David died and was buried in the City of David. 11He had reigned over Israel for forty years, seven of them in Hebron and thirty-three in Jerusalem. 12Solomon succeeded him as king, replacing his father, David, and he was firmly established on the throne.

13One day Adonijah, whose mother was Haggith, came to see Bathsheba, Solomon's mother. "Have you come to make trouble?" she asked him.

"No," he said, "I come in peace. 14In fact, I have a favor to ask of you."

"What is it?" she asked.

15He replied, "As you know, the kingdom was mine; everyone expected me to be the next king. But the tables were turned, and everything went to my brother instead; for that is the way the LORD wanted it. 16So now I have just one favor to ask of you. Please don't turn me down."

"What is it?" she asked.

17He replied, "Speak to King Solomon on my behalf, for I know he will do anything you request. Ask him to give me Abishag, the girl from Shunem, as my wife."

18"All right," Bathsheba replied. "I will speak to the king for you."

19So Bathsheba went to King Solomon to speak on Adonijah's behalf. The king rose from his throne to meet her, and he bowed down before her. When he sat down on his throne again, he ordered that a throne be brought for his mother, and she sat at his right hand.

20"I have one small request to make of you," she said. "I hope you won't turn me down."

"What is it, my mother?" he asked. "You know I won't refuse you."

21"Then let your brother Adonijah marry Abishag, the girl from Shunem," she replied.

### MOTIVES ● ● • • •

**2:23-24 In this plot against Solomon, all the conspirators lost. Adonijah and Joab were killed, and the priest, Abiathar, lost his job. They all thought they would gain something by their alliance: influence, position, recognition, authority. But they had a poor leader and wrong motives. Consider your motives carefully before making alliances with others.**

22"How can you possibly ask me to give Abishag to Adonijah?" Solomon demanded. "You might as well be asking me to give him the kingdom! You know that he is my older brother, and that he has Abiathar the priest and Joab son of Zeruiah on his side." 23Then King Solomon swore solemnly by the LORD: "May God strike me dead if Adonijah has not sealed his fate with this request. 24The LORD has confirmed me and placed me on the throne of my father, David; he has established my dynasty as he promised. So as surely as the LORD lives, Adonijah will die this very day!" 25So King Solomon ordered Benaiah son of Jehoiada to execute him, and Adonijah was put to death.

26Then the king said to Abiathar the priest, "Go back to your home in Anathoth. You deserve to die, but I will not kill you now, because you carried the Ark of the Sovereign LORD for my father, and you suffered right along with him through all his troubles." 27So Solomon deposed Abiathar from his

1:52 Hebrew *not a hair on his head will be touched.* 2:5 Or *He murdered them during a time of peace as revenge for deaths they had caused in time of war.*

## INROADS ● ● • • •

**3:1 Marriage between royal families was a common practice in the ancient Near East because it secured peace. Although Solomon's marital alliances built friendships with surrounding nations, they were also the beginning of his downfall. These relationships became inroads for heathen ideas and practices. Solomon's foreign wives brought their idols to Jerusalem and eventually lured him into idolatry (11:1-8).**

**It is easy to minimize religious differences in order to encourage the development of a friendship. But seemingly small differences can have an enormous impact upon a relationship. God gives us standards to follow for all our relationships, including marriage. If we follow God's will, we will not be lured away from our true focus.**

position as priest of the LORD, thereby fulfilling the decree the LORD had made at Shiloh concerning the descendants of Eli.

[28]Although he had not followed Absalom earlier, Joab had also joined Adonijah's revolt. When Joab heard about Adonijah's death, he ran to the sacred tent of the LORD and caught hold of the horns of the altar. [29]When news of this reached King Solomon, he sent Benaiah son of Jehoiada to execute him.

[30]Benaiah went into the sacred tent of the LORD and said to Joab, "The king orders you to come out!"

But Joab answered, "No, I will die here."

So Benaiah returned to the king and told him what Joab had said.

[31]"Do as he said," the king replied. "Kill him there beside the altar and bury him. This will remove the guilt of his senseless murders from me and from my father's family. [32]Then the LORD will repay him for the murders of two men who were more righteous and better than he. For my father was no party to the deaths of Abner son of Ner, commander of the army of Israel, and Amasa son of Jether, commander of the army of Judah. [33]May Joab and his descendants be forever guilty of these murders, and may the LORD grant peace to David and his descendants and to his throne forever."

[34]So Benaiah son of Jehoiada returned to the sacred tent and killed Joab, and Joab was buried at his home in the wilderness. [35]Then the king appointed Benaiah to command the army in place of Joab, and he installed Zadok the priest to take the place of Abiathar.

[36]The king then sent for Shimei and told him, "Build a house here in Jerusalem and live there. But don't step outside the city to go anywhere else. [37]On the day you cross the Kidron Valley, you will surely die; your blood will be on your own head."

[38]Shimei replied, "Your sentence is fair; I will do whatever my lord the king commands." So Shimei lived in Jerusalem for a long time.

[39]But three years later, two of Shimei's slaves escaped to King Achish of Gath. When Shimei learned where they were, [40]he saddled his donkey and went to Gath to search for them. When he had found them, he took them back to Jerusalem.

[41]Solomon heard that Shimei had left Jerusalem and had gone to Gath and returned. [42]So he sent for Shimei and demanded, "Didn't I make you swear by the LORD and warn you not to go anywhere else, or you would surely die? And you replied, 'The sentence is fair; I will do as you say.' [43]Then why haven't you kept your oath to the LORD and obeyed my command?"

[44]The king also said to Shimei, "You surely remember all the wicked things you did to my father, King David. May the LORD punish you for them. [45]But may I receive the LORD's rich blessings, and may one of David's descendants always sit on this throne." [46]Then, at the king's command, Benaiah son of Jehoiada took Shimei outside and killed him.

So the kingdom was now firmly in Solomon's grip.

CHAPTER **3** **SOLOMON ASKS FOR WISDOM.** Solomon made an alliance with Pharaoh, the king of Egypt, and married one of his daughters. He brought her to live in the City of David until he could finish building his palace and the Temple of the LORD and the wall around the city. [2]At that time the people of Israel sacrificed their offerings at local altars, for a temple honoring the name of the LORD had not yet been built.

[3]Solomon loved the LORD and followed all the instructions of his father, David, except that Solomon, too, offered sacrifices and burned incense at the local altars. [4]The most important of these altars was at Gibeon, so the king went there and sacrificed one thousand burnt offerings. [5]That night the LORD appeared to Solomon in a dream, and God said, "What do you want? Ask, and I will give it to you!"

## WISE GUY ● ● • • •

**3:6-9 When given a chance to have anything in the world, Solomon asked for wisdom so that he could lead well and make right decisions. We can ask God for this same wisdom (James 1:5). Notice that Solomon asked for wisdom to carry out his job. He did not ask God to do the job for him. We should not ask God to do *for* us what he wants to equip us to do ourselves. Instead we should ask God to give us the wisdom to know what to do and the courage to follow through on it.**

[6]Solomon replied, "You were wonderfully kind to my father, David, because he was honest and true and faithful to you. And you have continued this great kindness to him today by giving him a son to succeed him. [7]O LORD my God, now you have made me king instead of my father, David, but I am like a little child who doesn't know his way around. [8]And here I am among your own chosen people, a nation so great they are too numerous to count! [9]Give me an understanding mind so that I can govern your people well and know the difference between right and wrong. For who by himself is able to govern this great nation of yours?"

[10]The Lord was pleased with Solomon's reply and was glad that he had asked for wisdom. [11]So God replied, "Because you have asked for wisdom in governing my people and have not asked for a long

life or riches for yourself or the death of your enemies—12I will give you what you asked for! I will give you a wise and understanding mind such as no one else has ever had or ever will have! 13And I will also give you what you did not ask for—riches and honor! No other king in all the world will be compared to you for the rest of your life! 14And if you follow me and obey my commands as your father, David, did, I will give you a long life."

15Then Solomon woke up and realized it had been a dream. He returned to Jerusalem and stood before the Ark of the Lord's covenant, where he sacrificed burnt offerings and peace offerings. Then he invited all his officials to a great banquet.

16Some time later, two prostitutes came to the king to have an argument settled. 17"Please, my lord," one of them began, "this woman and I live in the same house. I gave birth to a baby while she was with me in the house. 18Three days later, she also had a baby. We were alone; there were only two of us in the house.
19But her baby died during the night when she rolled over on it. 20Then she got up in the night and took my son from beside me while I was asleep. She laid her dead child in my arms and took mine to sleep beside her. 21And in the morning when I tried to nurse my son, he was dead! But when I looked more closely in the morning light, I saw that it wasn't my son at all."

22Then the other woman interrupted, "It certainly was your son, and the living child is mine."

"No," the first woman said, "the dead one is yours, and the living one is mine." And so they argued back and forth before the king.

23Then the king said, "Let's get the facts straight. Both of you claim the living child is yours, and each says that the dead child belongs to the other. 24All right, bring me a sword." So a sword was brought to the king. 25Then he said, "Cut the living child in two and give half to each of these women!"

26Then the woman who really was the mother of the living child, and who loved him very much, cried out, "Oh no, my lord! Give her the child—please do not kill him!"

But the other woman said, "All right, he will be neither yours nor mine; divide him between us!"

27Then the king said, "Do not kill him, but give the baby to the woman who wants him to live, for she is his mother!"

28Word of the king's decision spread quickly throughout all Israel, and the people were awed as they realized the great wisdom God had given him to render decisions with justice.

## CHAPTER 4

**SOLOMON'S CABINET MEMBERS.** So Solomon was king over all Israel, 2and these were his high officials:

Azariah son of Zadok was the priest.
3 Elihoreph and Ahijah, the sons of Shisha, were court secretaries.
Jehoshaphat son of Ahilud was the royal historian.
4 Benaiah son of Jehoiada was commander of the army.
Zadok and Abiathar were the priests.
5 Azariah son of Nathan presided over the district governors.
Zabud son of Nathan, a priest, was a trusted adviser to the king.
6 Ahishar was manager of palace affairs.
Adoniram son of Abda was in charge of the labor force.

---

**With so many things out there that I want and so many things I know I need, how do I know what to pray for?**

Do you realize your mom or dad are faced with the same question every time they go to the grocery store? They know what you want to eat, but they buy what you need to eat. Their experience and wisdom keep you healthy!

God also wants you to be healthy. He knows exactly what to give you and when to give it to you. Jesus said: "You parents—if your children ask for a loaf of bread, do you give them a stone instead? Or if they ask for a fish, do you give them a snake? Of course not! If you sinful people know how to give good gifts to your children, how much more will your heavenly Father give good gifts to those who ask him" (Matthew 7:9-11).

Your mother was probably very glad the day you asked for an apple for a snack instead of ice cream (has that day come?). It shows you are becoming aware of what it will take to keep yourself healthy. Though ice cream tastes better, apples are far better for you.

Our requests to God can sometimes be very selfish, centered only on what we want and not what we need. God the Father longs for the day when we ask him for what we really need or, better yet, what others need.

Solomon had the privilege of asking for anything he wanted from God. Of all of the choices available to him, Solomon made the one that was most pleasing to God—he asked for wisdom. God responded by giving Solomon more wisdom than any other man, and God gave him riches and honor as well, so that others could benefit from the wisdom God gave him. (See 1 Kings 3:3-14.)

Although a child whines for candy an hour before dinner, a wise parent will always say no. Likewise, selfish prayers are rarely answered yes by God because he loves us too much.

The best things to pray for are those that ultimately will help other people. Good examples of the right kinds of things to pray for are character qualities (like patience, self-control, gentleness) that will help you get along better with other people and will help point others toward Christ. Another example is praying for the health of someone who is sick (James 5:14-16).

When you have needs, however, you should never be afraid to ask God to meet them. He loves to answer the prayers of his children!

7Solomon also had twelve district governors who
were over all Israel. They were responsible for providing food from the people for the king's household.
Each of them arranged provisions for one month of
the year.
8These are the names of the twelve governors:

Ben-hur, in the hill country of Ephraim.
9 Ben-deker, in Makaz, Shaalbim, Beth-shemesh, and Elon-bethhanan.
10 Ben-hesed, in Arubboth, including Socoh and all the land of Hepher.
11 Ben-abinadab, in Naphoth-dor.* (He was married to Taphath, one of Solomon's daughters.)
12 Baana son of Ahilud, in Taanach and Megiddo, all of Beth-shan* near Zarethan below Jezreel, and all the territory from Beth-shan to Abel-meholah and over to Jokmeam.
13 Ben-geber, in Ramoth-gilead, including the Towns of Jair (named for Jair son of Manasseh) in Gilead, and in the Argob region of Bashan, including sixty great fortified cities with gates barred with bronze.
14 Ahinadab son of Iddo, in Mahanaim.
15 Ahimaaz, in Naphtali. (He was married to Basemath, another of Solomon's daughters.)
16 Baana son of Hushai, in Asher and in Aloth.
17 Jehoshaphat son of Paruah, in Issachar.
18 Shimei son of Ela, in Benjamin.
19 Geber son of Uri, in the land of Gilead,* including the territories of King Sihon of the Amorites and King Og of Bashan.

And there was one governor over the land of Judah.*

## IDEAL ● ● • • •

**4:20-25 Throughout most of his reign, Solomon applied his wisdom well because he sought after God. The fruits of this wisdom were peace, security, and prosperity for the nation. Solomon's era is often looked upon as the ideal of what any nation can become when united in trust and obedience to God.**

20The people of Judah and Israel were as numerous as the sand on the seashore. They were very
contented, with plenty to eat and drink. 21King Solomon ruled all the kingdoms from the Euphrates
River* to the land of the Philistines, as far south as
the border of Egypt. The conquered peoples of those
lands sent tribute money to Solomon and continued
to serve him throughout his lifetime.
22The daily food requirements for Solomon's palace were 150 bushels of choice flour and 300 bushels
of meal,* 23ten oxen from the fattening pens, twenty
pasture-fed cattle, one hundred sheep or goats, as
well as deer, gazelles, roebucks, and choice fowl.
24Solomon's dominion extended over all the king-

## FAMILY TIME ● ● • • •

**5:13-14 Solomon drafted three times the number of workers needed for the Temple project and then arranged their schedules so they didn't have to be away from home for long periods of time. This showed his concern for the welfare of his workers and the importance he placed on family life. The strength of a nation is in direct proportion to the strength of its families. Solomon wisely recognized that family should always be a top priority. As you structure your own work or arrange the schedules of others, watch for the impact of your plans on your family.**

doms west of the Euphrates River, from Tiphsah to
Gaza. And there was peace throughout the entire
land. 25Throughout the lifetime of Solomon, all of
Judah and Israel lived in peace and safety. And from
Dan to Beersheba, each family had its own home
and garden.
26Solomon had four thousand* stalls for his chariot horses and twelve thousand horses.* 27The district governors faithfully provided food for King
Solomon and his court, each during his assigned
month. 28They also brought the necessary barley and
straw for the royal horses in the stables.
29God gave Solomon great wisdom and understanding, and knowledge too vast to be measured.
30In fact, his wisdom exceeded that of all the wise
men of the East and the wise men of Egypt. 31He was
wiser than anyone else, including Ethan the Ezrahite
and Heman, Calcol, and Darda—the sons of Mahol.
His fame spread throughout all the surrounding
nations. 32He composed some 3,000 proverbs and
wrote 1,005 songs. 33He could speak with authority
about all kinds of plants, from the great cedar of
Lebanon to the tiny hyssop that grows from cracks in
a wall. He could also speak about animals, birds,
reptiles, and fish. 34And kings from every nation sent
their ambassadors to listen to the wisdom of Solomon.

## CHAPTER 5 **SOLOMON BUILDS THE TEMPLE.**

King Hi-
ram of Tyre had always been a loyal friend of David,
so when he learned that David's son Solomon was
the new king of Israel, Hiram sent ambassadors to
congratulate him. 2Then Solomon sent this message
back to Hiram:

3"You know that my father, David, was not able
to build a Temple to honor the name of the
LORD his God because of the many wars he
waged with surrounding nations. He could not
build until the LORD gave him victory over all
his enemies. 4But now the LORD my God has
given me peace on every side, and I have no
enemies and all is well. 5So I am planning to
build a Temple to honor the name of the LORD
my God, just as he instructed my father that I
should do. For the LORD told him, 'Your son,
whom I will place on your throne, will build the
Temple to honor my name.' 6Now please

4:11 Hebrew *Naphath-dor,* a variant name for Naphoth-dor. 4:12 Hebrew *Beth-shean,* a variant name for Beth-shan; also in 4:12b. 4:19a Greek version reads *of Gad;* compare 4:13. 4:19b As in some Greek manuscripts; Hebrew lacks *of Judah.* The meaning of the Hebrew is uncertain. 4:21 Hebrew *the river;* also in 4:24. 4:22 Hebrew *30 cors* [5.5 kiloliters] *of choice flour and 60 cors* [11 kiloliters] *of meal.* 4:26a As in some Greek manuscripts (see also 2 Chr 9:25); Hebrew reads *40,000.* 4:26b Or *12,000 charioteers.*

command that cedars from Lebanon be cut for
me. Let my men work alongside yours, and I
will pay your men whatever wages you ask. As
you know, there is no one among us who can
cut timber like you Sidonians!"

7When Hiram received Solomon's message, he
was very pleased and said, "Praise the LORD for
giving David a wise son to be king of the great
nation of Israel." 8Then he sent this reply to Solomon:

"I have received your message, and I will do as
you have asked concerning the timber. I can
supply you with both cedar and cypress. 9My
servants will bring the logs from the Lebanon
mountains to the Mediterranean Sea and build
them into rafts. We will float them along the
coast to whatever place you choose. Then we
will break the rafts apart and deliver the timber
to you. You can pay me with food for my
household."

10So Hiram produced for Solomon as much cedar
and cypress timber as he desired. 11In return Solomon sent him an annual payment of 100,000 bushels* of wheat for his household and 110,000
gallons* of olive oil. 12So the LORD gave great wisdom to Solomon just as he had promised. And
Hiram and Solomon made a formal alliance of
peace.

13Then King Solomon enlisted 30,000 laborers
from all Israel. 14He sent them to Lebanon in shifts,
10,000 every month, so that each man would be one
month in Lebanon and two months at home. Adoniram was in charge of this labor force. 15Solomon
also enlisted 70,000 common laborers, 80,000
stonecutters in the hill country, 16and 3,600* foremen to supervise the work. 17At the king's command,
the stonecutters quarried and shaped costly blocks
of stone for the foundation of the Temple. 18Men
from the city of Gebal helped Solomon's and Hiram's builders prepare the timber and stone for the
Temple.

## CHAPTER 6

It was in midspring,* during the
fourth year of Solomon's reign, that he began the
construction of the Temple of the LORD. This was 480
years after the people of Israel were delivered from
their slavery in the land of Egypt.

2The Temple that King Solomon built for the
LORD was 90 feet long, 30 feet wide, and 45 feet
high.* 3The foyer at the front of the Temple was
30 feet wide, running across the entire width of the
Temple. It projected outward 15 feet from the front
of the Temple. 4Solomon also made narrow, recessed
windows throughout the Temple.

5A complex of rooms was built against the outer
walls of the Temple, all the way around the sides and
rear of the building. 6The complex was three stories
high, the bottom floor being 7½ feet wide, the second floor 9 feet wide, and the top floor 10½ feet
wide. The rooms were connected to the walls of the
Temple by beams resting on ledges built out from
the wall. So the beams were not inserted into the
walls themselves.

7The stones used in the construction of the
Temple were prefinished at the quarry, so the entire
structure was built without the sound of hammer, ax,
or any other iron tool at the building site.

8The entrance to the bottom floor* was on the
south side of the Temple. There were winding stairs
going up to the second floor, and another flight of
stairs between the second and third floors. 9After
completing the Temple structure, Solomon put in a
ceiling made of beams and planks of cedar. 10As
already stated, there was a complex of rooms on
three sides of the building, attached to the Temple
walls by cedar timbers. Each story of the complex
was 7½ feet high.

11Then the LORD gave this message to Solomon:
12"Concerning this Temple you are building, if you
keep all my laws and regulations and obey all my
commands, I will fulfill through you the promise I
made to your father, David. 13I will live among the
people of Israel and never forsake my people."

14So Solomon finished building the Temple. 15The
entire inside, from floor to ceiling, was paneled with
wood. He paneled the walls and ceilings with cedar,
and he used cypress for the floors. 16He partitioned
off an inner sanctuary—the Most Holy Place—at the
far end of the Temple. It was 30 feet deep and was
paneled with cedar from floor to ceiling. 17The main
room of the Temple, outside the Most Holy Place,
was 60 feet long. 18Cedar paneling completely covered the stone walls throughout the Temple, and the
paneling was decorated with carvings of gourds and
open flowers.

19Solomon prepared the inner sanctuary in the
rear of the Temple, where the Ark of the LORD's
covenant would be placed. 20This inner sanctuary
was 30 feet long, 30 feet wide, and 30 feet high.
Solomon overlaid its walls and ceiling with pure

### RESPECT ● ● • • •

6:7 **In honor of God, the Temple in Jerusalem was built without the sound of a hammer or any tool at the building site. This meant cutting the stone miles away at the quarry. The people's honor and respect for God extended to every aspect of constructing this building in which to worship him. This detail is recorded not to teach us how to build a church, but to show us the importance of demonstrating care, concern, honor, and respect for God and his sanctuary. How do you, in your actions and attitude, treat the place in which you worship God?**

**5:11a** Hebrew *20,000 cors* [3,640 kiloliters]. **5:11b** As in Greek version, which reads *20,000 baths* [420 kiloliters] (see also 2 Chr 2:10); Hebrew reads *20 cors,* about 800 gallons or 3.6 kiloliters in volume. **5:16** As in some Greek manuscripts (see also 2 Chr 2:2, 18); Hebrew reads *3,300.* **6:1** Hebrew *in the month of Ziv, which is the second month.* This month of the Hebrew lunar calendar usually occurs in April and May. **6:2** Hebrew *60 cubits* [27 meters] *long, 20 cubits* [9 meters] *wide, and 30 cubits* [13.5 meters] *high.* In this chapter, the distance measures are calculated from the Hebrew cubit at a ratio of 18 inches or 45 centimeters per cubit. **6:8** As in Greek version; Hebrew reads *middle floor.*

gold. He also overlaid the altar made of cedar.* 21Then he overlaid the rest of the Temple's interior with pure gold, and he made gold chains to protect the entrance to the Most Holy Place. 22So he finished overlaying the entire Temple with gold, including the altar that belonged to the Most Holy Place.

23Within the inner sanctuary Solomon placed two cherubim made of olive wood, each 15 feet tall. 24The wingspan of each of the cherubim was 15 feet, each wing being 7½ feet long. 25The two cherubim were identical in shape and size; 26each was 15 feet tall. 27Solomon placed them side by side in the inner sanctuary of the Temple. Their outspread wings reached from wall to wall, while their inner wings touched at the center of the room. 28He overlaid the two cherubim with gold.

29All the walls of the inner sanctuary and the main room were decorated with carvings of cherubim, palm trees, and open flowers. 30The floor in both rooms was overlaid with gold.

31For the entrance to the inner sanctuary, Solomon made double doors of olive wood with five-sided doorposts. 32These doors were decorated with carvings of cherubim, palm trees, and open flowers, and the doors were overlaid with gold.

33Then he made four-sided doorposts of olive wood for the entrance to the Temple. 34There were two folding doors of cypress wood, and each door was hinged to fold back upon itself. 35These doors were decorated with carvings of cherubim, palm trees, and open flowers, and the doors were overlaid with gold.

36The walls of the inner courtyard were built so that there was one layer of cedar beams after every three layers of hewn stone.

37The foundation of the LORD's Temple was laid in midspring* of the fourth year of Solomon's reign. 38The entire building was completed in every detail by midautumn* of the eleventh year of his reign. So it took seven years to build the Temple.

## CHAPTER 7 **SOLOMON BUILDS HIS PALACE.**

Solomon also built a palace for himself, and it took him thirteen years to complete the construction.

2One of Solomon's buildings was called the Palace of the Forest of Lebanon. It was 150 feet long, 75 feet wide, and 45 feet high.* The great cedar ceiling beams rested on four rows of cedar pillars. 3It had a cedar roof supported by forty-five rafters that rested on three rows of pillars, fifteen in each row. 4On each of the side walls there were three rows of windows facing each other. 5All the doorways were rectangular in frame; they were in sets of three, facing each other.

6He also built the Hall of Pillars, which was 75 feet long and 45 feet wide. There was a porch at its front, covered by a canopy that was supported by pillars.

7There was also the Hall of the Throne, also known as the Hall of Judgment, where Solomon sat to hear legal matters. It was paneled with cedar from floor to ceiling.* 8Solomon's living quarters surrounded a courtyard behind this hall; they were built the same way. He also built similar living quarters for Pharaoh's daughter, one of his wives. 9All these buildings were built entirely from huge, costly blocks of stone, cut and trimmed to exact measure on all sides. 10Some of the huge foundation stones were 15 feet long, and some were 12 feet long. 11The costly blocks of stone used in the walls were also cut to measure, and cedar beams were also used. 12The walls of the great courtyard were built so that there was one layer of cedar beams after every three layers of hewn stone, just like the walls of the inner courtyard of the LORD's Temple with its entrance foyer.

13King Solomon then asked for a man named Huram* to come from Tyre, 14for he was a craftsman skilled in bronze work. He was half Israelite, since his mother was a widow from the tribe of Naphtali, and his father had been a foundry worker from Tyre. So he came to work for King Solomon.

15Huram cast two bronze pillars, each 27 feet tall and 18 feet in circumference. 16For the tops of the pillars he made capitals of molded bronze, each 7½ feet tall. 17Each capital was decorated with seven sets of latticework and interwoven chains. 18He also made two rows of pomegranates that encircled the latticework to decorate the capitals over the pillars. 19The capitals on the columns inside the foyer were shaped like lilies, and they were 6 feet tall. 20Each capital on the two pillars had two hundred pomegranates in two rows around them, beside the rounded surface next to the latticework. 21Huram set the pillars at the entrance of the Temple, one toward the south and one toward the north. He named the one on the south Jakin, and the one on the north Boaz.* 22The capitals on the pillars were shaped like lilies. And so the work on the pillars was finished.

23Then Huram cast a large round tank, 15 feet across from rim to rim; it was called the Sea. It was 7½ feet deep and about 45 feet in circumference. 24The Sea was encircled just below its rim by two rows of decorative gourds. There were about six gourds per foot* all the way around, and they had been cast as part of the tank.

25The Sea rested on a base of twelve bronze oxen, all facing outward. Three faced north, three faced west, three faced south, and three faced east. 26The walls of the Sea were about three inches* thick, and its rim flared out like a cup and resembled

6:20 Or *overlaid the altar with cedar.* The meaning of the Hebrew is uncertain. 6:37 Hebrew *in the month of Ziv.* This month of the Hebrew lunar calendar usually occurs in April and May. 6:38 Hebrew *in the month of Bul, which is the eighth month.* This month of the Hebrew lunar calendar usually occurs in October and November. 7:2 Hebrew *100 cubits* [45 meters] *long, 50 cubits* [22.5 meters] *wide, and 30 cubits* [13.5 meters] *high.* In this chapter, the distance measures are calculated from the Hebrew cubit at a ratio of 18 inches or 45 centimeters per cubit. 7:7 As in Syriac version and Latin Vulgate; Hebrew reads *from floor to floor.* 7:13 Hebrew *Hiram* (also in 7:40, 45); compare 2 Chr 2:13. This is not the same person mentioned in 5:1. 7:21 Jakin probably means "he establishes"; Boaz probably means "in him is strength." 7:24 Or *20 gourds per meter;* Hebrew reads *10 per cubit.* 7:26a Hebrew *a handbreadth* [8 centimeters].

a lily blossom. It could hold about 11,000 gallons*
of water.
27 Huram also made ten bronze water carts, each
6 feet long, 6 feet wide, and 4½ feet tall. 28 They were
constructed with side panels braced with crossbars.
29 Both the panels and the crossbars were decorated
with carved lions, oxen, and cherubim. Above and
below the lions and oxen were wreath decorations.
30 Each of these carts had four bronze wheels and
bronze axles. At each corner of the carts were supporting posts for the bronze basins; these supports
were decorated with carvings of wreaths on each
side. 31 The top of each cart had a circular frame for
the basin. It projected 1½ feet above the cart's top
like a round pedestal, and its opening was 2¼ feet
across; it was decorated on the outside with carvings
of wreaths. The panels of the carts were square, not
round. 32 Under the panels were four wheels that
were connected to axles that had been cast as one
unit with the cart. The wheels were 2¼ feet in diam-
eter 33 and were similar to chariot wheels. The axles,
spokes, rims, and hubs were all cast from molten
bronze.
34 There were supports at each of the four corners
of the carts, and these, too, were cast as one unit with
the cart. 35 Around the top of each cart there was a rim
9 inches wide.* The supports and side panels were
cast as one unit with the cart. 36 Carvings of cherubim, lions, and palm trees decorated the panels and
supports wherever there was room, and there were
wreaths all around. 37 All ten water carts were the
same size and were made alike, for each was cast
from the same mold.
38 Huram also made ten bronze basins, one for
each cart. Each basin was 6 feet across and could
hold 220 gallons* of water. 39 He arranged five water
carts on the south side of the Temple and five on the
north side. The Sea was placed at the southeast corner of the Temple. 40 He also made the necessary pots,
shovels, and basins.

So at last Huram completed everything King Solomon had assigned him to make for the Temple of the
LORD:

41 two pillars,
two bowl-shaped capitals on top of the pillars,
two networks of chains that decorated the
capitals,
42 four hundred pomegranates that hung from
the chains on the capitals (two rows of
pomegranates for each of the chain networks
that were hung around the capitals on top of
the pillars),
43 the ten water carts holding the ten basins,
44 the Sea and the twelve oxen under it,
45 the pots, the shovels, and the basins.

All these utensils for the Temple of the LORD that
Huram made for Solomon were made of burnished

## STAINED GLASS ● ● • • •

**7:41-46 Huram's items of bronze would look strange in today's churches, but some Christians use other articles to enhance worship. Stained-glass windows, crosses, pulpits, hymn books, baptisteries, and communion tables serve as aids to worship. While the instruments of worship may change, the purpose—to give honor and praise to God—should never change.**

bronze. 46 The king had them cast in clay molds in
the Jordan Valley between Succoth and Zarethan.
47 Solomon did not weigh all the utensils because
there were so many; the weight of the bronze could
not be measured.
48 So Solomon made all the furnishings of the
Temple of the LORD:

the gold altar,
the gold table for the Bread of the Presence,
49 the gold lampstands, five on the south and five
on the north, in front of the Most Holy Place,
the flower decorations, lamps, and tongs, all of
gold,
50 the cups, lamp snuffers, basins, dishes, and
firepans, all of pure gold,
the doors for the entrances to the Most Holy
Place and the main room of the Temple, with
their fronts overlaid with gold.

51 So King Solomon finished all his work on the
Temple of the LORD. Then Solomon brought all
the gifts his father, David, had dedicated—the silver,
the gold, and the other utensils—and he stored
them in the treasuries of the LORD's Temple.

## CHAPTER 8

**THE ARK AND THE TEMPLE.** Solomon
then summoned the leaders of all the tribes and
families of Israel to assemble in Jerusalem. They
were to bring the Ark of the LORD's covenant from its
location in the City of David, also known as Zion, to
its new place in the Temple. 2 They all assembled
before the king at the annual Festival of Shelters in
early autumn.* 3 When all the leaders of Israel arrived, the priests picked up the Ark. 4 Then the priests
and Levites took the Ark of the LORD, along with the
Tabernacle* and all its sacred utensils, and carried
them up to the Temple. 5 King Solomon and the
entire community of Israel sacrificed sheep and oxen
before the Ark in such numbers that no one could
keep count!
6 Then the priests carried the Ark of the LORD's
covenant into the inner sanctuary of the Temple—
the Most Holy Place—and placed it beneath the
wings of the cherubim. 7 The cherubim spread their
wings over the Ark, forming a canopy over the Ark
and its carrying poles. 8 These poles were so long
that their ends could be seen from the front entrance of the Temple's main room—the Holy
Place—but not from outside it. They are still there

**7:26b** Hebrew *2,000 baths* [42 kiloliters]. **7:35** Hebrew *half a cubit wide* [22.5 centimeters]. **7:38** Hebrew *40 baths* [840 liters]. **8:2** Hebrew *at the festival in the month Ethanim, which is the seventh month.* The Festival of Shelters began on the fifteenth day of the seventh month on the Hebrew lunar calendar. This occurs on our calendar in late September or early October. **8:4** Hebrew *Tent of Meeting.*

to this day. 9Nothing was in the Ark except the two stone tablets that Moses had placed there at Mount Sinai,* where the LORD made a covenant with the people of Israel as they were leaving the land of Egypt.

10As the priests came out of the inner sanctuary, a cloud filled the Temple of the LORD. 11The priests could not continue their work because the glorious presence of the LORD filled the Temple.

12Then Solomon prayed, "O LORD, you have said that you would live in thick darkness. 13But I have built a glorious Temple for you, where you can live forever!"

14Then the king turned around to the entire community of Israel standing before him and gave this blessing: 15"Blessed be the LORD, the God of Israel, who has kept the promise he made to my father, David. 16For he told my father, 'From the day I brought my people Israel out of Egypt, I have never chosen a city among the tribes of Israel as the place where a temple should be built to honor my name. But now I have chosen David to be king over my people.'"

17Then Solomon said, "My father, David, wanted to build this Temple to honor the name of the LORD, the God of Israel. 18But the LORD told him, 'It is right for you to want to build the Temple to honor my name, 19but you are not the one to do it. One of your sons will build it instead.'

20"And now the LORD has done what he promised, for I have become king in my father's place. I have built this Temple to honor the name of the LORD, the God of Israel. 21And I have prepared a place there for the Ark, which contains the covenant that the LORD made with our ancestors when he brought them out of Egypt."

## GOD'S HOME ● ● • • •

**8:27 Solomon declared that even the highest heavens couldn't contain God. Isn't it amazing that, though the heavens can't contain him, he is willing to live in the hearts of those who love him? The God of the universe has taken up residence in the lives of his people—he lives in us! What are you doing to welcome him home?**

22Then Solomon stood with his hands lifted toward heaven before the altar of the LORD in front of the entire community of Israel. 23He prayed, "O LORD, God of Israel, there is no God like you in all of heaven or earth. You keep your promises and show unfailing love to all who obey you and are eager to do your will. 24You have kept your promise to your servant David, my father. You made that promise with your own mouth, and today you have fulfilled it with your own hands. 25And now, O LORD, God of Israel, carry out your further promise to your servant David, my father. For you said to him, 'If your descendants guard their behavior as you have done, they will always reign over Israel.' 26Now, O God of Israel, fulfill this promise to your servant David, my father.

27"But will God really live on earth? Why, even the highest heavens cannot contain you. How much less this Temple I have built! 28Listen to my prayer and my request, O LORD my God. Hear the cry and the prayer that your servant is making to you today. 29May you watch over this Temple both day and night, this place where you have said you would put your name. May you always hear the prayers I make toward this place. 30May you hear the humble and earnest requests from me and your people Israel when we pray toward this place. Yes, hear us from heaven where you live, and when you hear, forgive.

31"If someone wrongs another person and is required to take an oath of innocence in front of the altar at this Temple, 32then hear from heaven and judge between your servants—the accuser and the accused. Punish the guilty party and acquit the one who is innocent.

33"If your people Israel are defeated by their enemies because they have sinned against you, and if they turn to you and call on your name and pray to you here in this Temple, 34then hear from heaven and forgive their sins and return them to this land you gave their ancestors.

35"If the skies are shut up and there is no rain because your people have sinned against you, and then they pray toward this Temple and confess your name and turn from their sins because you have punished them, 36then hear from heaven and forgive the sins of your servants, your people Israel. Teach them to do what is right, and send rain on your land that you have given to your people as their special possession.

37"If there is a famine in the land, or plagues, or crop disease, or attacks of locusts or caterpillars, or if your people's enemies are in the land besieging their towns—whatever the trouble is—38and if your people offer a prayer concerning their troubles or sorrow, raising their hands toward this Temple, 39then hear from heaven where you live, and forgive. Give your people whatever they deserve, for you alone know the human heart. 40Then they will fear you and walk in your ways as long as they live in the land you gave to our ancestors.

41"And when foreigners hear of you and come from distant lands to worship your great name—42for they will hear of you and of your mighty miracles and your power—and when they pray toward this Temple, 43then hear from heaven where you live, and grant what they ask of you. Then all the people of the earth will come to know and fear you, just as your own people Israel do. They, too, will know that this Temple I have built bears your name.

44"If your people go out at your command to fight their enemies, and if they pray to the LORD toward this city that you have chosen and toward this Temple that I have built for your name, 45then hear their prayers from heaven and uphold their cause.

46"If they sin against you—and who has never sinned?—you may become angry with them and let

8:9 Hebrew *at Horeb,* another name for Sinai.

their enemies conquer them and take them captive to a foreign land far or near. [47]But in that land of exile, they may turn to you again in repentance and pray, 'We have sinned, done evil, and acted wickedly.' [48]Then if they turn to you with their whole heart and soul and pray toward the land you gave to their ancestors, toward this city you have chosen, and toward this Temple I have built to honor your name, [49]then hear their prayers from heaven where you live. Uphold their cause [50]and forgive your people who have sinned against you. Make their captors merciful to them, [51]for they are your people—your special possession—whom you brought out of the iron-smelting furnace of Egypt.

[52]"May your eyes be open to my requests and to the requests of your people Israel. Hear and answer them whenever they cry out to you. [53]For when you brought our ancestors out of Egypt, O Sovereign LORD, you told your servant Moses that you had separated Israel from among all the nations of the earth to be your own special possession."

[54]When Solomon finished making these prayers and requests to the LORD, he stood up in front of the altar of the LORD, where he had been kneeling with his hands raised toward heaven. [55]He stood there and shouted this blessing over the entire community of Israel: [56]"Praise the LORD who has given rest to his people Israel, just as he promised. Not one word has failed of all the wonderful promises he gave through his servant Moses. [57]May the LORD our God be with us as he was with our ancestors; may he never forsake us. [58]May he give us the desire to do his will in everything and to obey all the commands, laws, and regulations that he gave our ancestors. [59]And may these words that I have prayed in the presence of the LORD be before him constantly, day and night, so that the LORD our God may uphold my cause and the cause of his people Israel, fulfilling our daily needs. [60]May people all over the earth know that the LORD is God and that there is no other god. [61]And may you, his people, always be faithful to the LORD our God. May you always obey his laws and commands, just as you are doing today."

[62]Then the king and all Israel with him offered sacrifices to the LORD. [63]Solomon sacrificed peace offerings to the LORD numbering 22,000 oxen and 120,000 sheep. And so the king and all Israel dedicated the Temple of the LORD. [64]That same day the king dedicated the central area of the courtyard in front of the LORD's Temple. He offered burnt offerings, grain offerings, and the fat of peace offerings there, because the bronze altar in the LORD's presence was too small to handle so many offerings.

[65]Then Solomon and all Israel celebrated the Festival of Shelters* in the presence of the LORD their God. A large crowd had gathered from as far away as Lebo-hamath in the north to the brook of Egypt in the south. The celebration went on for fourteen days in all—seven days for the dedication of the altar and seven days for the Festival of Shelters.* [66]After the festival was over,* Solomon sent the people home. They blessed the king as they went, and they were all joyful and happy because the LORD had been good to his servant David and to his people Israel.

## CHAPTER 9

**GOD'S WARNING TO SOLOMON.** So Solomon finished building the Temple of the LORD, as well as the royal palace. He completed everything he had planned to do. [2]Then the LORD appeared to Solomon a second time, as he had done before at Gibeon. [3]The LORD said to him, "I have heard your prayer and your request. I have set apart this Temple you have built so that my name will be honored there forever. I will always watch over it and care for it. [4]As for you, if you will follow me with integrity and godliness, as David your father did, always obeying my commands and keeping my laws and regulations, [5]then I will establish the throne of your dynasty over Israel forever. For I made this promise to your father, David: 'You will never fail to have a successor on the throne of Israel.'

### PRAYER PATTERNS • • • • •

**8:56-61 Solomon blessed the people and prayed for them. His prayer can be a pattern for our prayers. He had five basic requests: (1) for God's presence (8:57); (2) for the desire to do God's will in everything (8:58); (3) for help with daily needs (8:59); (4) for the desire and ability to obey God's laws and commands (8:58,61); and (5) for the spread of God's kingdom to the entire world (8:60). These prayer requests are just as appropriate today as they were in Solomon's time.**

[6]"But if you or your descendants abandon me and disobey my commands and laws, and if you go and worship other gods, [7]then I will uproot the people of Israel from this land I have given them. I will reject this Temple that I have set apart to honor my name. I will make Israel an object of mockery and ridicule among the nations. [8]And though this Temple is impressive now, it will become an appalling sight for all who pass by. They will scoff and ask, 'Why did the LORD do such terrible things to his land and to his Temple?' [9]And the answer will be, 'Because his people forgot the LORD their God, who brought their ancestors out of Egypt, and they worshiped other gods instead. That is why the LORD has brought all these disasters upon them.'"

[10]Now at the end of the twenty years during which Solomon built the Temple of the LORD and the royal palace, [11]Solomon gave twenty towns in the land of Galilee to King Hiram of Tyre as payment for all the cedar and cypress lumber and gold he had furnished for the construction of the buildings. [12]Hiram came from Tyre to see the towns Solomon had given him, but he was not at all pleased with them. [13]"What kind of towns are these, my brother?" he asked. "These towns are worthless!" So Hiram called that area

**8:65a** Hebrew *the festival;* see note on 8:2. **8:65b** Hebrew *seven days and seven days, fourteen days;* compare parallel text at 2 Chr 7:8-10. **8:66** Hebrew *On the eighth day,* probably referring to the day following the seven-day Festival of Shelters; compare parallel text at 2 Chr 7:9-10.

Cabul—"worthless"—as it is still known today. [14]Hi-
ram had sent Solomon nine thousand pounds* of
gold.
[15]This is the account of the forced labor that Solomon conscripted to build the LORD's Temple, the royal
palace, the Millo,* the wall of Jerusalem, and the cities
of Hazor, Megiddo, and Gezer. [16](The king of Egypt
had attacked and captured Gezer, killing the Canaanite
population and burning it down. He gave the city to
his daughter as a wedding gift when she married Solomon. [17]So Solomon rebuilt the city of Gezer.) He also
built up the towns of Lower Beth-horon, [18]Baalath, and
Tamar* in the desert, within his land. [19]He built towns
as supply centers and constructed cities where his
chariots and horses* could be kept. He built to his
heart's content in Jerusalem and Lebanon and
throughout the entire realm.

## DATING

Watch what happened when Lizza, a 15-year-old Christian, started dating Matt, an older non-Christian.

February–Lizza brought Matt to some youth group meetings and activities. He said her church friends were "OK," but he wanted her to do things with his friends, too.

March–Lizza asked Matt to the spring retreat. He snapped, "Lizza! If you want to date St. Peter, go for it. But that's not for me, OK?"

April–Lizza began going to parties and heavy metal concerts with Matt and his pals.

May–Lizza's church/youth group attendance dropped drastically. She quit youth choir.

June–Lizza had her first cigarette, beer, and sexual experience.

July–Lizza and her parents fought almost all month because she wouldn't "break up with that bum!"

August–Lizza has now gone 4 1/2 months without reading her Bible (she isn't even sure where it is).

"Wait a minute!" you say. "Do Christian/non-Christian relationships always turn out bad? Haven't Christians fallen in love with non-Christians and led them to the Lord?" Yes. But that is rare. It's a sad fact that healthy Christian/non-Christian dating situations are the exception. First Kings 11:1-13 shows how you can get burned through close relationships with those who don't share your spiritual beliefs and values.

[20]There were still some people living in the land
who were not Israelites, including Amorites, Hittites,
Perizzites, Hivites, and Jebusites. [21]These were descendants of the nations that Israel had not completely destroyed.* So Solomon conscripted them
for his labor force, and they serve in the labor force
to this day. [22]But Solomon did not conscript any of
the Israelites for forced labor. Instead, he assigned
them to serve as fighting men, government officials,
officers in his army, commanders of his chariots, and

## ROYAL FAMILIES ● ● ● • •

9:16 **At this time, Israel and Egypt were the world powers in the Near East. During Solomon's reign the Egyptian king captured Gezer. To make peace, Solomon married one of Pharaoh's daughters. Intermarriage among royal families was common, but it was not endorsed by God (Deuteronomy 17:17). Because the princess's dowry included the city of Gezer, which the Egyptian king had conquered earlier, it was returned to Israel.**

charioteers. [23]He also appointed 550 of them to
supervise the various projects.
[24]After Solomon moved his wife, Pharaoh's
daughter, from the City of David to the new palace
he had built for her, he constructed the Millo.
[25]Three times each year Solomon offered burnt
offerings and peace offerings to the LORD on the altar
he had built. He also burned incense to the LORD.
And so he finished the work of building the Temple.
[26]Later King Solomon built a fleet of ships at
Ezion-geber, a port near Elath* in the land of Edom,
along the shore of the Red Sea.* [27]Hiram sent experienced crews of sailors to sail the ships with Solomon's men. [28]They sailed to Ophir and brought back
to Solomon some sixteen tons* of gold.

CHAPTER **10** **THE QUEEN OF SHEBA VISITS.** When the
queen of Sheba heard of Solomon's reputation, which
brought honor to the name of the LORD, she came to
test him with hard questions. [2]She arrived in Jerusalem
with a large group of attendants and a great caravan of
camels loaded with spices, huge quantities of gold,
and precious jewels. When she met with Solomon,
they talked about everything she had on her mind.
[3]Solomon answered all her questions; nothing was too
hard for the king to explain to her. [4]When the queen
of Sheba realized how wise Solomon was, and when
she saw the palace he had built, [5]she was breathless.
She was also amazed at the food on his tables, the
organization of his officials and their splendid clothing, the cup-bearers and their robes, and the burnt
offerings Solomon made at the Temple of the LORD.
[6]She exclaimed to the king, "Everything I heard in
my country about your achievements and wisdom is
true! [7]I didn't believe it until I arrived here and saw
it with my own eyes. Truly I had not heard the half
of it! Your wisdom and prosperity are far greater than
what I was told. [8]How happy these people must be!
What a privilege for your officials to stand here day
after day, listening to your wisdom! [9]The LORD your
God is great indeed! He delights in you and has
placed you on the throne of Israel. Because the LORD
loves Israel with an eternal love, he has made you
king so you can rule with justice and righteousness."
[10]Then she gave the king a gift of nine thousand
pounds* of gold, and great quantities of spices and
precious jewels. Never again were so many spices
brought in as those the queen of Sheba gave to
Solomon.

9:14 Hebrew *120 talents* [4 metric tons]. 9:15 Or *the supporting terraces;* also in 9:24. 9:18 The marginal *Qere* reading of the Masoretic Text reads *Tadmor.* 9:19 Or *and charioteers.* 9:21 The Hebrew term used here refers to the complete consecration of things or people to the LORD, either by destroying them or by giving them as an offering. 9:26a As in Greek version (see also 2 Kgs 14:22; 16:6); Hebrew reads *Eloth.* 9:26b Hebrew *sea of reeds.* 9:28 Hebrew *420 talents* [14 metric tons]. 10:10 Hebrew *120 talents* [4 metric tons].

11(When Hiram's ships brought gold from Ophir, they also brought rich cargoes of almug wood and precious jewels. 12The king used the almug wood to make railings for the Temple of the LORD and the royal palace, and to construct harps and lyres for the musicians. Never before or since has there been such a supply of beautiful almug wood.)

13King Solomon gave the queen of Sheba whatever she asked for, besides all the other customary gifts he had so generously given. Then she and all her attendants left and returned to their own land.

14Each year Solomon received about twenty-five tons* of gold. 15This did not include the additional revenue he received from merchants and traders, all the kings of Arabia, and the governors of the land.

16King Solomon made two hundred large shields of hammered gold, each containing over fifteen pounds* of gold. 17He also made three hundred smaller shields of hammered gold, each containing nearly four pounds* of gold. The king placed these shields in the Palace of the Forest of Lebanon.

18Then the king made a huge ivory throne and overlaid it with pure gold. 19The throne had six steps and a rounded back. On both sides of the seat were armrests, with the figure of a lion standing on each side of the throne. 20Solomon made twelve other lion figures, one standing on each end of each of the six steps. No other throne in all the world could be compared with it!

21All of King Solomon's drinking cups were solid gold, as were all the utensils in the Palace of the Forest of Lebanon. They were not made of silver because silver was considered of little value in Solomon's day!

22The king had a fleet of trading ships* that sailed with Hiram's fleet. Once every three years the ships returned, loaded down with gold, silver, ivory, apes, and peacocks.*

23So King Solomon became richer and wiser than any other king in all the earth. 24People from every nation came to visit him and to hear the wisdom God had given him. 25Year after year, everyone who came to visit brought him gifts of silver and gold, clothing, weapons, spices, horses, and mules.

26Solomon built up a huge force of chariots and horses. He had fourteen hundred chariots and twelve thousand horses.* He stationed many of them in the chariot cities, and some near him in Jerusalem. 27The king made silver as plentiful in Jerusalem as stones. And valuable cedarwood was as common as the sycamore wood that grows in the foothills of Judah.* 28Solomon's horses were imported from Egypt* and from Cilicia*; the king's traders acquired them from Cilicia at the standard price. 29At that time, Egyptian chariots delivered to Jerusalem could be purchased for 600 pieces of silver,* and horses could be bought for 150 pieces of silver.* Many of these were then resold to the kings of the Hittites and the kings of Aram.

## CHAPTER 11

**SOLOMON TURNS FROM GOD.** Now King Solomon loved many foreign women. Besides Pharaoh's daughter, he married women from Moab, Ammon, Edom, Sidon, and from among the Hittites. 2The LORD had clearly instructed his people not to intermarry with those nations, because the women they married would lead them to worship their gods. Yet Solomon insisted on loving them anyway. 3He had seven hundred wives and three hundred concubines. And sure enough, they led his heart away from the LORD. 4In Solomon's old age, they turned his heart to worship their gods instead of trusting only in the LORD his God, as his father, David, had done. 5Solomon worshiped Ashtoreth, the goddess of the Sidonians, and Molech,* the detestable god of the Ammonites. 6Thus, Solomon did what was evil in the LORD's sight; he refused to follow the LORD completely, as his father, David, had done. 7On the Mount of Olives, east of Jerusalem, he even built a shrine for Chemosh, the detestable god of Moab, and another for Molech, the detestable god of the Ammonites. 8Solomon built such shrines for all his foreign wives to use for burning incense and sacrificing to their gods.

9The LORD was very angry with Solomon, for his heart had turned away from the LORD, the God of

### OBEDIENCE ● ● • • •

**11:2 Although Solomon had clear instructions from God *not* to marry women from foreign nations, he chose to disregard God's commands. He married not one, but many heathen wives, who subsequently led him away from God. God knows our human strengths and weaknesses, and his commands are always for our good. Some people ignore God's commands, but there are inevitable negative consequences resulting from such action. It is not enough to know God's Word or even to believe it; we must follow it and apply it to life's daily activities and decisions. Take God's commands seriously. Like Solomon, the wisest man who ever lived, we are not as strong as we may think.**

### PRESSURE ● ● • • •

**11:4 Solomon handled great pressures in running the government, but he could not handle the pressures from his wives who wanted him to worship their gods. In marriage and other close friendships, it is difficult to resist pressure to compromise. Our love leads us to identify with the desires of those we care about.**

**Faced with such pressure, Solomon at first *resisted* it, maintaining pure faith. Then he *tolerated* a more widespread practice of idolatry. Finally he himself became involved in idolatrous worship; he *rationalized* away the potential danger to himself and the kingdom. It is because we naturally wish to identify with those we love that God told Solomon (and us) not to marry those who do not share our commitment to him.**

10:14 Hebrew *666 talents* [23 metric tons]. 10:16 Hebrew *600 shekels* [6.8 kilograms]. 10:17 Hebrew *3 minas* [1.8 kilograms]. 10:22a Hebrew *fleet of ships of Tarshish.* 10:22b Or *and baboons.* 10:26 Or *12,000 charioteers.* 10:27 Hebrew *the Shephelah.* 10:28a Possibly *Muzur,* a district near Cilicia; also in 10:29. 10:28b Hebrew *Kue,* probably another name for Cilicia. 10:29a Hebrew *600 shekels of silver,* about 15 pounds or 6.8 kilograms in weight. 10:29b Hebrew *150 [shekels],* about 3.8 pounds or 1.7 kilograms in weight. 11:5 Hebrew *Milcom,* a variant name for Molech; also in 11:33.

Israel, who had appeared to him twice. 10He had warned Solomon specifically about worshiping other gods, but Solomon did not listen to the LORD's command. 11So now the LORD said to him, "Since you have not kept my covenant and have disobeyed my laws, I will surely tear the kingdom away from you and give it to one of your servants. 12But for the sake of your father, David, I will not do this while you are still alive. I will take the kingdom away from your son. 13And even so, I will let him be king of one tribe, for the sake of my servant David and for the sake of Jerusalem, my chosen city."

14Then the LORD raised up Hadad the Edomite, a member of Edom's royal family, to be an enemy against Solomon. 15Years before, David had gone to Edom with Joab, his army commander, to bury some Israelites who had died in battle. While there, the Israelite army had killed nearly every male in Edom. 16Joab and the army had stayed there for six months, killing them. 17But Hadad and a few of his father's royal officials had fled. (Hadad was a very small child at the time.) 18They escaped from Midian and went to Paran, where others joined them. Then they traveled to Egypt and went to Pharaoh, who gave them a home, food, and some land. 19Pharaoh grew very fond of Hadad, and he gave him a wife—the sister of Queen Tahpenes. 20She bore him a son, Genubath, who was brought up in Pharaoh's palace among Pharaoh's own sons.

21When the news reached Hadad in Egypt that David and his commander Joab were both dead, he said to Pharaoh, "Let me return to my own country."

22"Why?" Pharaoh asked him. "What do you lack here? How have we disappointed you that you want to go home?"

"Nothing is wrong," he replied. "But even so, I must return home."

23God also raised up Rezon son of Eliada to be an enemy against Solomon. Rezon had fled from his master, King Hadadezer of Zobah, 24and had become the leader of a gang of rebels. After David conquered Hadadezer, Rezon and his men fled to Damascus, where he became king. 25Rezon was Israel's bitter enemy for the rest of Solomon's reign, and he made trouble, just as Hadad did. Rezon hated Israel intensely and continued to reign in Aram.

26Another rebel leader was Jeroboam son of Nebat, one of Solomon's own officials. He came from the city of Zeredah in Ephraim, and his mother was Zeruah, a widow. 27This is the story behind his rebellion. Solomon was rebuilding the Millo* and repairing the walls of the city of his father, David. 28Jeroboam was a very capable young man, and when Solomon saw how industrious he was, he put him in charge of the labor force from the tribes of Ephraim and Manasseh.*

29One day as Jeroboam was leaving Jerusalem, the prophet Ahijah from Shiloh met him on the road, wearing a new cloak. The two of them were alone in a field, 30and Ahijah took the new cloak he was wearing and tore it into twelve pieces. 31Then he said to Jeroboam, "Take ten of these pieces, for this is what the LORD, the God of Israel, says: 'I am about to tear the kingdom from the hand of Solomon, and I will give ten of the tribes to you! 32But I will leave him one tribe for the sake of my servant David and for the sake of Jerusalem, which I have chosen out of all the tribes of Israel. 33For Solomon has abandoned me and worshiped Ashtoreth, the goddess of the Sidonians; Chemosh, the god of Moab; and Molech, the god of the Ammonites. He has not followed my ways and done what is pleasing in my sight. He has not obeyed my laws and regulations as his father, David, did.

34"'But I will not take the entire kingdom from Solomon at this time. For the sake of my servant David, the one whom I chose and who obeyed my commands and laws, I will let Solomon reign for the rest of his life. 35But I will take the kingdom away from his son and give ten of the tribes to you. 36His son will have one tribe so that the descendants of David my servant will continue to reign* in Jerusalem, the city I have chosen to be the place for my name. 37And I will place you on the throne of Israel, and you will rule over all that your heart desires. 38If you listen to what I tell you and follow my ways and do whatever I consider to be right, and if you obey my laws and commands, as my servant David did, then I will always be with you. I will establish an enduring dynasty for you as I did for David, and I will give Israel to you. 39But I will punish the descendants of David because of Solomon's sin—though not forever.'"

40Solomon tried to kill Jeroboam, but he fled to King Shishak of Egypt and stayed there until Solomon died.

41The rest of the events in Solomon's reign, including his wisdom, are recorded in *The Book of the Acts of Solomon.* 42Solomon ruled in Jerusalem over all Israel for forty years. 43When Solomon died, he was buried in the city of his father, David. Then his son Rehoboam became the next king.

CHAPTER **12** **THE KINGDOM SPLITS IN TWO.** Rehoboam went to Shechem, where all Israel had gathered to make him king. 2When Jeroboam son of Nebat heard of Solomon's death, he returned from Egypt,* for he had fled to Egypt to escape from King

## GOOD ADVICE ● ● • • •

12:6-8 **Rehoboam asked for advice, but he didn't carefully evaluate that advice. If he had, he would have realized that the advice offered by the older men was wiser than that of his peers. To evaluate advice, ask if it is realistic, workable, and consistent with the Bible. Determine if the results of following the advice will be fair, make improvements, and give a positive solution or direction. Seek counsel from those who are more experienced and wiser. Advice is helpful only if we evaluate it with God's standards in mind.**

11:27 Or *the supporting terraces.* 11:28 Hebrew *from the house of Joseph.* 11:36 Hebrew *will continue to have a lamp.* 12:2 As in Greek version and Latin Vulgate (see also 2 Chr 10:2); Hebrew reads *he lived in Egypt.*

Solomon. 3The leaders of Israel sent for Jeroboam, and the whole assembly of Israel went to speak with Rehoboam. 4"Your father was a hard master," they said. "Lighten the harsh labor demands and heavy taxes that your father imposed on us. Then we will be your loyal subjects."

5Rehoboam replied, "Give me three days to think this over. Then come back for my answer." So the people went away.

6Then King Rehoboam went to discuss the matter with the older men who had counseled his father, Solomon. "What is your advice?" he asked. "How should I answer these people?"

7The older counselors replied, "If you are willing to serve the people today and give them a favorable answer, they will always be your loyal subjects."

8But Rehoboam rejected the advice of the elders and instead asked the opinion of the young men who had grown up with him and who were now his advisers. 9"What is your advice?" he asked them. "How should I answer these people who want me to lighten the burdens imposed by my father?"

10The young men replied, "This is what you should tell those complainers: 'My little finger is thicker than my father's waist—if you think he was hard on you, just wait and see what I'll be like! 11Yes, my father was harsh on you, but I'll be even harsher! My father used whips on you, but I'll use scorpions!'"

12Three days later, Jeroboam and all the people returned to hear Rehoboam's decision, just as the king had requested. 13But Rehoboam spoke harshly to them, for he rejected the advice of the older counselors 14and followed the counsel of his younger advisers. He told the people, "My father was harsh on you, but I'll be even harsher! My father used whips on you, but I'll use scorpions!" 15So the king paid no attention to the people's demands. This turn of events was the will of the LORD, for it fulfilled the LORD's message to Jeroboam son of Nebat through the prophet Ahijah from Shiloh.

16When all Israel realized that the king had rejected their request, they shouted, "Down with David and his dynasty! We have no share in Jesse's son! Let's go home, Israel! Look out for your own house, O David!" So the people of Israel returned home. 17But Rehoboam continued to rule over the Israelites who lived in the towns of Judah.

18King Rehoboam sent Adoniram,* who was in charge of the labor force, to restore order, but all Israel stoned him to death. When this news reached King Rehoboam, he quickly jumped into his chariot and fled to Jerusalem. 19The northern tribes of Israel have refused to be ruled by a descendant of David to this day.

20When the people of Israel learned of Jeroboam's return from Egypt, they called an assembly and made him king over all Israel. So only the tribe of Judah remained loyal to the family of David.

**DO RIGHT ● ● • • •**

12:28 **All Jewish men were required to travel to the Temple three times each year (Deuteronomy 16:16), but Jeroboam set up his own worship centers and told his people it was too much trouble to travel all the way to Jerusalem. Those who obeyed Jeroboam were disobeying God. Some ideas, although practical, may include suggestions that lead you away from God. Don't let anyone talk you out of doing what is right by telling you that your actions are not worth the effort. Do what God wants no matter what the cost in time, energy, reputation, or resources.**

21When Rehoboam arrived at Jerusalem, he mobilized the armies of Judah and Benjamin—180,000 select troops—to fight against the army of Israel and to restore the kingdom to himself. 22But God said to Shemaiah, the man of God, 23"Say to Rehoboam son of Solomon, king of Judah, and to all the people of Judah and Benjamin, 24'This is what the LORD says: Do not fight against your relatives, the Israelites. Go back home, for what has happened is my doing!'" So they obeyed the message of the LORD and went home, as the LORD had commanded.

25Jeroboam then built up the city of Shechem in the hill country of Ephraim, and it became his capital. Later he went and built up the town of Peniel.* 26Jeroboam thought to himself, "Unless I am careful, the kingdom will return to the dynasty of David. 27When they go to Jerusalem to offer sacrifices at the Temple of the LORD, they will again give their allegiance to King Rehoboam of Judah. They will kill me and make him their king instead."

28So on the advice of his counselors, the king made two gold calves. He said to the people, "It is too much trouble for you to worship in Jerusalem. O Israel, these are the gods who brought you out of Egypt!"

29He placed these calf idols at the southern and northern ends of Israel—in Bethel and in Dan. 30This became a great sin, for the people worshiped them, traveling even as far as Dan.

31Jeroboam built shrines at the pagan high places and ordained priests from the rank and file of the people—those who were not from the priestly tribe of Levi. 32Jeroboam also instituted a religious festival in Bethel, held on a day in midautumn,* similar to the annual Festival of Shelters in Judah. There at Bethel he himself offered sacrifices to the calves he had made. And it was at Bethel that he appointed priests for the pagan shrines he had made. 33So on the appointed day in midautumn, a day that he himself had designated, Jeroboam offered sacrifices on the altar at Bethel. He instituted a religious festival for Israel, and he went up to the altar to burn incense.

CHAPTER **13** **A PROPHET DENOUNCES JEROBOAM.** At the LORD's command, a man of God from Judah went to Bethel, and he arrived there just as Jeroboam was approaching the altar to offer a sacrifice. 2Then

12:18 As in some Greek manuscripts and Syriac version (see also 4:6; 5:14); Hebrew reads *Adoram.* 12:25 Hebrew *Penuel,* a variant name for Peniel. 12:32 Hebrew *on the fifteenth day of the eighth month* (also in 12:33). This day of the Hebrew lunar calendar occurs in late October or early November, exactly one month after the annual Festival of Shelters in Judah (see Lev 23:34).

at the LORD's command, he shouted, "O altar, altar! This is what the LORD says: A child named Josiah will be born into the dynasty of David. On you he will sacrifice the priests from the pagan shrines who come here to burn incense, and human bones will be burned on you." [3]That same day the man of God gave a sign to prove his message, and he said, "The LORD has promised to give this sign: This altar will split apart, and its ashes will be poured out on the ground."

[4]King Jeroboam was very angry with the man of God for speaking against the altar. So he pointed at the man and shouted, "Seize that man!" But instantly the king's hand became paralyzed in that position, and he couldn't pull it back. [5]At the same time a wide crack appeared in the altar, and the ashes poured out, just as the man of God had predicted in his message from the LORD.

[6]The king cried out to the man of God, "Please ask the LORD your God to restore my hand again!" So the man of God prayed to the LORD, and the king's hand became normal again.

[7]Then the king said to the man of God, "Come to the palace with me and have something to eat, and I will give you a gift."

**HEARSAY ● ● • • .**

13:7-32 **This prophet had been given strict orders from God not to eat or drink anything while on his mission (13:9). He died because he listened to a man who claimed to have a message from God, rather than to God himself. The prophet should have followed God's word instead of hearsay. Trust what Scripture says rather than what someone claims is true. And disregard what others claim to be messages from God if their words contradict the Bible.**

[8]But the man of God said to the king, "Even if you gave me half of everything you own, I would not go with you. I would not eat any food or drink any water in this place. [9]For the LORD gave me this command: 'You must not eat any food or drink any water while you are there, and do not return to Judah by the same way you came.'" [10]So he left Bethel and went home another way.

[11]As it happened, there was an old prophet living in Bethel, and his sons came home and told him what the man of God had done in Bethel that day. They also told him what he had said to the king. [12]The old prophet asked them, "Which way did he go?" So they told their father which road the man of God had taken. [13]"Quick, saddle the donkey," the old man said. And when they had saddled the donkey for him, [14]he rode after the man of God and found him sitting under an oak tree.

The old prophet asked him, "Are you the man of God who came from Judah?"

"Yes," he replied, "I am."

[15]Then he said to the man of God, "Come home with me and eat some food."

[16]"No, I cannot," he replied. "I am not allowed to eat any food or drink any water here in this place. [17]For the LORD gave me this command: 'You must not eat any food or drink any water while you are there, and do not return to Judah by the same way you came.'"

[18]But the old prophet answered, "I am a prophet, too, just as you are. And an angel gave me this message from the LORD: 'Bring him home with you, and give him food to eat and water to drink.'" But the old man was lying to him. [19]So they went back together, and the man of God ate some food and drank some water at the prophet's home.

[20]Then while they were sitting at the table, a message from the LORD came to the old prophet. [21]He cried out to the man of God from Judah, "This is what the LORD says: You have defied the LORD's message and have disobeyed the command the LORD your God gave you. [22]You came back to this place and ate food and drank water where he told you not to eat or drink. Because of this, your body will not be buried in the grave of your ancestors."

[23]Now after the man of God had finished eating and drinking, the prophet saddled his own donkey for him, [24]and the man of God started off again. But as he was traveling along, a lion came out and killed him. His body lay there on the road, with the donkey and the lion standing beside it. [25]People came by and saw the body lying in the road and the lion standing beside it, and they went and reported it in Bethel, where the old prophet lived.

[26]When the old prophet heard the report, he said, "It is the man of God who disobeyed the LORD's command. The LORD has fulfilled his word by causing the lion to attack and kill him."

[27]Then the prophet said to his sons, "Saddle a donkey for me." So they saddled a donkey, [28]and he went out and found the body lying in the road. The donkey and lion were still standing there beside it, for the lion had not eaten the body nor attacked the donkey. [29]So the prophet laid the body of the man of God on the donkey and took it back to the city to mourn over him and bury him. [30]He laid the body in his own grave, crying out in grief, "Oh, my brother!"

[31]Afterward the prophet said to his sons, "When I die, bury me in the grave where the man of God is buried. Lay my bones beside his bones. [32]For the message the LORD told him to proclaim against the altar in Bethel and against the pagan shrines in the towns of Samaria will surely come true."

[33]But even after this, Jeroboam did not turn from his evil ways. He continued to choose priests from the rank and file of the people. Anyone who wanted to could become a priest for the pagan shrines. [34]This became a great sin and resulted in the destruction of Jeroboam's kingdom and the death of all his family.

CHAPTER **14** **JEROBOAM'S SON DIES.** At that time Jeroboam's son Abijah became very sick. [2]So Jeroboam told his wife, "Disguise yourself so that no one will recognize you as the queen. Then go to the prophet Ahijah at Shiloh—the man who told me I would become king. [3]Take him a gift of ten loaves of bread, some cakes, and a jar of honey, and ask him what will happen to the boy."

[4]So Jeroboam's wife went to Ahijah's home at Shiloh. He was an old man now and could no longer see. [5]But the LORD had told Ahijah, "Jeroboam's wife will come here, pretending to be someone else. She will ask you about her son, for he is very sick. You must give her the answer that I give you."

[6]So when Ahijah heard her footsteps at the door, he called out, "Come in, wife of Jeroboam! Why are you pretending to be someone else?" Then he told her, "I have bad news for you. [7]Give your husband, Jeroboam, this message from the LORD, the God of Israel: 'I promoted you from the ranks of the common people and made you ruler over my people Israel. [8]I ripped the kingdom away from the family of David and gave it to you. But you have not been like my servant David, who obeyed my commands and followed me with all his heart and always did whatever I wanted him to do. [9]You have done more evil than all who lived before you. You have made other gods and have made me furious with your gold calves. And since you have turned your back on me, [10]I will bring disaster on your dynasty and kill all your sons, slave or free alike. I will burn up your royal dynasty as one burns up trash until it is all gone. [11]I, the LORD, vow that the members of your family who die in the city will be eaten by dogs, and those who die in the field will be eaten by vultures.'"

[12]Then Ahijah said to Jeroboam's wife, "Go on home, and when you enter the city, the child will die. [13]All Israel will mourn for him and bury him. He is the only member of your family who will have a proper burial, for this child is the only good thing that the LORD, the God of Israel, sees in the entire family of Jeroboam. [14]And the LORD will raise up a king over Israel who will destroy the family of Jeroboam. This will happen today, even now! [15]Then the LORD will shake Israel like a reed whipped about in a stream. He will uproot the people of Israel from this good land that he gave their ancestors and will scatter them beyond the Euphrates River,* for they have angered the LORD by worshiping Asherah poles. [16]He will abandon Israel because Jeroboam sinned and made all of Israel sin along with him."

[17]So Jeroboam's wife returned to Tirzah, and the child died just as she walked through the door of her home. [18]When the people of Israel buried him, they mourned for him, as the LORD had promised through the prophet Ahijah.

[19]The rest of the events of Jeroboam's reign, all his wars and how he ruled, are recorded in *The Book of the History of the Kings of Israel.* [20]Jeroboam reigned in Israel twenty-two years. When Jeroboam died, his son Nadab became the next king.

[21]Meanwhile, Rehoboam son of Solomon was king in Judah. He was forty-one years old when he became king, and he reigned seventeen years in Jerusalem, the city the LORD had chosen from among all the tribes of Israel as the place to honor his name. Rehoboam's mother was Naamah, an Ammonite woman. [22]During Rehoboam's reign, the people of Judah did what was evil in the LORD's sight, arousing his anger with their sin, for it was even worse than that of their ancestors. [23]They built pagan shrines and set up sacred pillars and Asherah poles on every high hill and under every green tree. [24]There were even shrine prostitutes throughout the land. The people imitated the detestable practices of the pagan nations the LORD had driven from the land ahead of the Israelites.

## RANSACKED ● ● • •

14:25 **Just five years after Solomon died, the Temple and palace were ransacked by foreign invaders. How quickly the glory, power, and money disappeared! When the people became spiritually corrupt and immoral (14:24), it was just a short time until they lost everything. Their possessions and wealth had become more important to them than God. When we remove God from our life, everything else becomes useless, no matter how valuable it seems.**

[25]In the fifth year of King Rehoboam's reign, King Shishak of Egypt came up and attacked Jerusalem. [26]He ransacked the Temple of the LORD and the royal palace and stole everything, including all the gold shields Solomon had made. [27]Afterward Rehoboam made bronze shields as substitutes, and he entrusted them to the care of the palace guard officers. [28]Whenever the king went to the Temple of the LORD, the guards would carry them along and then return them to the guardroom.

[29]The rest of the events in Rehoboam's reign and all his deeds are recorded in *The Book of the History of the Kings of Judah.* [30]There was constant war between Rehoboam and Jeroboam. [31]When Rehoboam died, he was buried among his ancestors in the City of David. His mother was Naamah, an Ammonite woman. Then his son Abijam* became the next king.

## CHAPTER 15

**ABIJAM RULES JUDAH.** Abijam* began to rule over Judah in the eighteenth year of Jeroboam's reign in Israel. [2]He reigned in Jerusalem three years. His mother was Maacah, the daughter of Absalom.* [3]He committed the same sins as his father before him, and his heart was not right with the LORD his God, as the heart of his ancestor David had been. [4]But for David's sake, the LORD his God allowed his dynasty to continue,* and he gave Abijam a son to rule after him in Jerusalem. [5]For David had done what was pleasing in the LORD's sight and had obeyed the LORD's commands throughout his life, except in the affair concerning Uriah the Hittite.

[6]There was war between Abijam and Jeroboam*

14:15 Hebrew *the river.* 14:31 Also known as *Abijah.* 15:1 Also known as *Abijah.* 15:2 Hebrew *Abishalom* (also in 15:10), a variant name for Absalom; compare 2 Chr 11:20. 15:4 Hebrew *gave him a lamp in Jerusalem.* 15:6 As in a few Hebrew manuscripts; most Hebrew manuscripts read *between Rehoboam and Jeroboam.*

throughout Abijam's reign. [7]The rest of the events in Abijam's reign and all his deeds are recorded in *The Book of the History of the Kings of Judah.* There was constant war between Abijam and Jeroboam. [8]When Abijam died, he was buried in the City of David. Then his son Asa became the next king.

[9]Asa began to rule over Judah in the twentieth year of Jeroboam's reign in Israel. [10]He reigned in Jerusalem forty-one years. His grandmother* was Maacah, the daughter of Absalom. [11]Asa did what was pleasing in the LORD's sight, as his ancestor David had done. [12]He banished the shrine prostitutes from the land and removed all the idols his ancestors had made. [13]He even deposed his grandmother Maacah from her position as queen mother because she had made an obscene Asherah pole. He cut down the pole and burned it in the Kidron Valley. [14]Although the pagan shrines were not completely removed, Asa remained faithful to the LORD throughout his life. [15]He brought into the Temple of the LORD the silver and gold and the utensils that he and his father had dedicated.

[16]There was constant war between King Asa of Judah and King Baasha of Israel. [17]King Baasha of Israel invaded Judah and fortified Ramah in order to prevent anyone from entering or leaving King Asa's territory in Judah. [18]Asa responded by taking all the silver and gold that was left in the treasuries of the LORD's Temple and the royal palace. He sent it with some of his officials to Ben-hadad son of Tabrimmon and grandson of Hezion, the king of Aram, who was ruling in Damascus, along with this message:

> [19]"Let us renew the treaty that existed between your father and my father. See, I am sending you a gift of silver and gold. Break your treaty with King Baasha of Israel so that he will leave me alone."

[20]Ben-hadad agreed to King Asa's request and sent his armies to attack Israel. They conquered the towns of Ijon, Dan, Abel-beth-maacah, and all Kinnereth, with all the land of Naphtali. [21]As soon as Baasha of Israel heard what was happening, he abandoned his project of fortifying Ramah and withdrew to Tirzah. [22]Then King Asa sent an order throughout Judah, requiring that everyone, without exception, help to carry away the building stones and timbers that Baasha had been using to fortify Ramah. Asa used these materials to fortify the town of Geba in Benjamin and the town of Mizpah.

[23]The rest of the events in Asa's reign, the extent of his power, and the names of the cities he built are recorded in *The Book of the History of the Kings of Judah.* In his old age his feet became diseased. [24]When Asa died, he was buried with his ancestors in the City of David. Then his son Jehoshaphat became the next king.

[25]Nadab son of Jeroboam began to rule over Israel in the second year of King Asa's reign in Judah. He reigned in Israel two years. [26]But he did what was evil in the LORD's sight and followed the example of his father, continuing the sins of idolatry that Jeroboam had led Israel to commit.

[27]Then Baasha son of Ahijah, from the tribe of Issachar, plotted against Nadab and assassinated him while he and the Israelite army were laying siege to the Philistine town of Gibbethon. [28]Baasha killed Nadab in the third year of King Asa's reign in Judah, and he became the next king of Israel. [29]He immediately killed all the descendants of King Jeroboam, so that not one of the royal family was left, just as the LORD had promised concerning Jeroboam by the prophet Ahijah from Shiloh. [30]This was done because Jeroboam had aroused the anger of the LORD, the God of Israel, by the sins he had committed and the sins he had led Israel to commit. [31]The rest of the events in Nadab's reign and all his deeds are recorded in *The Book of the History of the Kings of Israel.*

[32]There was constant war between Asa and King Baasha of Israel. [33]Baasha began to rule over Israel in the third year of King Asa's reign in Judah. Baasha reigned in Tirzah twenty-four years. [34]But he did what was evil in the LORD's sight and followed the example of Jeroboam, continuing the sins of idolatry that Jeroboam had led Israel to commit.

## CHAPTER 16

**BAASHA RULES ISRAEL.** This message from the LORD was delivered to King Baasha by the prophet Jehu son of Hanani: [2]"I lifted you out of the dust to make you ruler of my people Israel, but you have followed the evil example of Jeroboam. You have aroused my anger by causing my people to sin. [3]So now I will destroy you and your family, just as I destroyed the descendants of Jeroboam son of Nebat. [4]Those of your family who die in the city will be eaten by dogs, and those who die in the field will be eaten by the vultures."

[5]The rest of the events in Baasha's reign and the extent of his power are recorded in *The Book of the History of the Kings of Israel.* [6]When Baasha died, he was buried in Tirzah. Then his son Elah became the next king.

[7]This message from the LORD had been spoken against Baasha and his family through the prophet Jehu son of Hanani. It was delivered because Baasha had done what was evil in the LORD's sight, arousing him to anger by his sins, just like the family of Jeroboam, and also because Baasha had destroyed the family of Jeroboam.

### MISTAKES ● ● • • •

**16:1-7 God destroyed Jeroboam's descendants for their flagrant sins, and yet King Baasha repeated the same mistakes. He did not learn from the example of those who went before him; he did not stop to think that his sin would be punished. Make sure you learn the lessons from your own past, the lives of others, and the lives of those whose stories are told in the Bible. Don't repeat their mistakes.**

15:10 Hebrew *his mother* (also in 15:13); compare 15:2.

[8]Elah son of Baasha began to rule over Israel from
Tirzah in the twenty-sixth year of King Asa's reign in
Judah. He reigned in Israel two years. [9]Then Zimri,
who commanded half of the royal chariots, made
plans to kill him. One day in Tirzah, Elah was getting
drunk at the home of Arza, the supervisor of the
palace. [10]Zimri walked in
and struck him down and
killed him. This happened
in the twenty-seventh year
of King Asa's reign in Judah.
Then Zimri became the next
king.
[11]Zimri immediately
killed the entire royal family
of Baasha, and he did not
leave a single male child. He
even destroyed distant relatives and friends. [12]So Zimri
destroyed the dynasty of Baasha as the LORD had promised through the prophet
Jehu. [13]This happened because of the sins of Baasha
and his son Elah and because of all the sins they led
Israel to commit, arousing
the anger of the LORD, the
God of Israel, with their
idols. [14]The rest of the events
in Elah's reign and all his
deeds are recorded in *The
Book of the History of the
Kings of Israel.*
[15]Zimri began to rule over
Israel from Tirzah in the
twenty-seventh year of King
Asa's reign in Judah, but he
reigned only seven days.
When the army of Israel,
which was then engaged in
attacking the Philistine
town of Gibbethon, [16]heard
that Zimri had assassinated
the king, they chose Omri,
commander of the army, as
their new king. [17]So Omri
led the army of Israel away
from Gibbethon to attack
Tirzah, Israel's capital.
[18]When Zimri saw that the
city had been taken, he went
into the citadel of the king's
house and burned it down
over himself and died in the
flames. [19]For he, too, had
done what was evil in the
LORD's sight and followed
the example of Jeroboam,
continuing the sins of idolatry that Jeroboam had led
Israel to commit. [20]The rest of the events of Zimri's
reign and his conspiracy are recorded in *The Book of
the History of the Kings of Israel.*
[21]But now the people of Israel were divided into
two groups. Half the people tried to make Tibni son
of Ginath their king, while the other half supported

## AHAB

The kings of Israel and Judah, both good and evil, had prophets sent by God to advise, confront, and aid them. King David had a faithful friend in God's prophet Nathan; Ahab could have had an equally faithful friend in Elijah. But while David listened to Nathan and was willing to repent of his sins, Ahab saw Elijah as his enemy. Why? Because Elijah always brought bad news to Ahab, and Ahab refused to acknowledge that it was his own constant disobedience to God and persistent idol worship, not Elijah's prophecies, that brought the evil on his nation. He blamed Elijah for bringing the prophecies of judgment, rather than taking Elijah's advice and changing his evil ways.

Ahab was trapped by his own choices, and he was unwilling to take the right action. As king, he was responsible to God and his prophet Elijah, but he was married to an evil woman who led him into idol worship. He was a childish man who brooded for days if he did not get his own way. He took his evil wife's advice, listened only to the "prophets" who gave good news, and surrounded himself with people who encouraged him to do whatever he wanted. But the value of advice cannot be judged by the number of people for or against it. Ahab consistently chose to follow the majority opinion of his friends, and that led to his death.

It may seem nice to have someone encourage us to do whatever we want because advice that goes against our wishes is difficult to accept. However, our decisions must be based on the quality of the advice, not its attractiveness or what our friends think. God encourages us to get advice from wise counselors, but how can we test the advice we receive? Advice that agrees with the principles in God's Word is reliable. We must always separate advice from our own desires or whatever our friends say, and weigh it against God's commands. He will never lead us to do what he has forbidden in his Word. Unlike Ahab, we should trust godly counselors and have the courage to stand against those who want us to do otherwise.

**UPS:**
- Eighth king of Israel
- Capable leader and military strategist

**DOWNS:**
- Was the most evil king of Israel
- Married Jezebel, a heathen woman, and allowed her to promote Baal worship
- Brooded about not being able to get a piece of land, so his wife had its owner, Naboth, killed
- Was used to getting his own way, and got depressed when he didn't

**STATS:**
- Where: Northern kingdom of Israel
- Occupation: King
- Relatives: Wife: Jezebel. Father: Omri. Sons: Ahaziah, Jehoram.
- Contemporaries: Elijah, Naboth, Jehu, Ben-hadad, Jehoshaphat

LESSONS: The choice of a mate will have a significant effect on life—physically, spiritually, and emotionally
Selfishness, left unchecked, can lead to great evil

KEY VERSES: "But Ahab did what was evil in the LORD's sight, even more than any of the kings before him. And as though it were not enough to live like Jeroboam, he married Jezebel, the daughter of King Ethbaal of the Sidonians, and he began to worship Baal. First he built a temple and an altar for Baal in Samaria. Then he set up an Asherah pole. He did more to arouse the anger of the LORD, the God of Israel, than any of the other kings of Israel before him" (1 Kings 16:30-33).

Ahab's story is told in 1 Kings 16:28–22:40. He is also mentioned in 2 Chronicles 18–22 and Micah 6:16.

## THE PROPHETS

They step off the page like something out of a science fiction novel or a fantasy—wild men wearing strange clothes, seeing mind-boggling visions, hearing God's voice, and preaching a bone-chilling message: repent or you will pay. They were the prophets, the men and women God sent to the nation of Israel (and occasionally to other nations) as his spokesmen, and they were a bizarre bunch. Some, like Isaiah and Daniel, were powerful men in the life of the nation. They held important government positions or served as the king's advisers. Obadiah, on the other hand, was a farmer, called from his simple life to be God's messenger. Elijah must have been a strange sight, walking around in **black camel's hair** and preaching against Israel's idolatries. Hosea married a prostitute on God's orders. There is at least one prophetess—Huldah—whose story is in 2 Kings 22:14-20. These people all lived different lifestyles and preached to the nation of Israel under a variety of circumstances. What did they have in common? Who were they? First, these were God's appointed speakers. While the priests spoke to God for the people, the prophets spoke to the people for God. As mentioned, their messages often were not popular or well received. Often they called on the people to turn from their sins and worship of false gods before the one true God punished them. TIME AFTER TIME their messages were ignored, and Israel suffered as a result. The prophets preached primarily two kinds of messages: first, they watched the current spiritual status of Israel and called for repentance. Second, they spoke of times to come and events to happen in the future. Many people claimed to be prophets, and sometimes there was confusion over who to believe when the "prophets" disagreed. There were, however, tests used to determine who was or wasn't a true prophet.

• True prophets spoke whenever and whatever God told them to. They didn't dream up prophecies and oracles and then say they came from God. In other religions, pagan prophets constantly tried to manipulate their gods into doing what they wanted, like using *"rain-dances"* to coax the gods to send rain. Israel's prophets were different. God took the initiative in speaking to them, telling them precisely what to say and do. Then they spoke to the people, often beginning with, "The Lord says . . ."

• Any prediction given about the future had to come true or the prophet was considered false. The Old Testament is filled with amazing predictions of events, sometimes many centuries into the future. An incredible number of them, especially those concerning Israel's fate and the coming Messiah, have come true with **PHENOMENAL ACCURACY.** Others, particularly those concerning the end times, are now developing or still remain to be seen. But if ever a prophet could be shown to have made an error concerning a future event, he was considered a false prophet. There is disagreement today about whether or not we still have true prophets of God. Since there are people who see it as their mission to call the people of God to repentance for sin, it is hard to deny that there are many such prophets now among us. But it is far more undecided whether we have within the body of Christ people who can describe the future because God has given them special revelation. A great many people have made fools of themselves (and their followers) by predicting future events, especially the second coming of Christ. Their "prophecies" fell apart and crashed down around them. It would seem, then, that the wisest course regarding this kind of predictive prophesying is a good dose of GODLY SKEPTICISM.

• Above all else, the prophets pointed to the one who would come and who would be greater than all the prophets: Jesus Christ, the Messiah.

Omri. [22]But Omri's supporters defeated the supporters of Tibni son of Ginath. So Tibni was killed, and Omri became the next king.

[23]Omri began to rule over Israel in the thirty-first year of King Asa's reign in Judah. He reigned twelve years in all, six of them in Tirzah. [24]Then Omri bought the hill now known as Samaria from its owner, Shemer, for 150 pounds of silver.* He built a city on it and called the city Samaria in honor of Shemer. [25]But Omri did what was evil in the LORD's sight, even more than any of the kings before him. [26]He followed the example of Jeroboam, continuing the sins of idolatry that Jeroboam had led Israel to commit. Thus, he aroused the anger of the LORD, the God of Israel. [27]The rest of the events in Omri's reign, the extent of his power, and all his deeds are recorded in *The Book of the History of the Kings of Israel.* [28]When Omri died, he was buried in Samaria. Then his son Ahab became the next king.

[29]Ahab son of Omri began to rule over Israel in the thirty-eighth year of King Asa's reign in Judah. He reigned in Samaria twenty-two years. [30]But Ahab did what was evil in the LORD's sight, even more than any of the kings before him. [31]And as though it were not enough to live like Jeroboam, he married Jezebel, the daughter of King Ethbaal of the Sidonians, and he began to worship Baal. [32]First he built a temple and an altar for Baal in Samaria. [33]Then he set up an Asherah pole. He did more to arouse the anger of the LORD, the God of Israel, than any of the other kings of Israel before him.

[34]It was during his reign that Hiel, a man from Bethel, rebuilt Jericho. When he laid the foundations, his oldest son, Abiram, died. And when he finally completed it by setting up the gates, his youngest son, Segub, died. This all happened according to the message from the LORD concerning Jericho spoken by Joshua son of Nun.

## CHAPTER 17

**RAVENS FEED ELIJAH.** Now Elijah, who was from Tishbe in Gilead, told King Ahab, "As surely as the LORD, the God of Israel, lives—the God whom I worship and serve—there will be no dew or rain during the next few years unless I give the word!"

[2]Then the LORD said to Elijah, [3]"Go to the east and hide by Kerith Brook at a place east of where it enters the Jordan River. [4]Drink from the brook and eat what the ravens bring you, for I have commanded them to bring you food."

[5]So Elijah did as the LORD had told him and camped beside Kerith Brook. [6]The ravens brought him bread and meat each morning and evening, and he drank from the brook. [7]But after a while the brook dried up, for there was no rainfall anywhere in the land.

[8]Then the LORD said to Elijah, [9]"Go and live in the village of Zarephath, near the city of Sidon. There is a widow there who will feed you. I have given her my instructions."

[10]So he went to Zarephath. As he arrived at the gates of the village, he saw a widow gathering sticks, and he asked her, "Would you please bring me a cup of water?" [11]As she was going to get it, he called to her, "Bring me a bite of bread, too."

[12]But she said, "I swear by the LORD your God that I don't have a single piece of bread in the house. And I have only a handful of flour left in the jar and a little cooking oil in the bottom of the jug. I was just gathering a few sticks to cook this last meal, and then my son and I will die."

[13]But Elijah said to her, "Don't be afraid! Go ahead and cook that 'last meal,' but bake me a little loaf of bread first. Afterward there will still be enough food for you and your son. [14]For this is what the LORD, the God of Israel, says: There will always be plenty of flour and oil left in your containers until the time when the LORD sends rain and the crops grow again!"

[15]So she did as Elijah said, and she and Elijah and her son continued to eat from her supply of flour and oil for many days. [16]For no matter how much they used, there was always enough left in the containers, just as the LORD had promised through Elijah.

[17]Some time later, the woman's son became sick. He grew worse and worse, and finally he died. [18]She then said to Elijah, "O man of God, what have you done to me? Have you come here to punish my sins by killing my son?"

[19]But Elijah replied, "Give me your son." And he took the boy's body from her, carried him up to the upper room, where he lived, and laid the body on his bed. [20]Then Elijah cried out to the LORD, "O LORD my God, why have you brought tragedy on this widow who has opened her home to me, causing her son to die?"

[21]And he stretched himself out over the child three times and cried out to the LORD, "O LORD my God, please let this child's life return to him." [22]The LORD heard Elijah's prayer, and the life of the child returned, and he came back to life! [23]Then Elijah brought him down from the upper room and gave him to his mother. "Look, your son is alive!" he said.

16:24 Hebrew *for 2 talents* [68 kilograms] *of silver.*

### PROVIDENCE ● ● • • •

17:1-9 **In a nation that was required by law to care for its prophets, it is ironic that God turned to ravens (unclean birds) and a widow (a foreigner from Jezebel's home territory) to care for Elijah. God has help where we least expect it. He provides for us in ways that go beyond our narrow definitions or expectations. No matter how bitter our trials or how seemingly hopeless our situation, we should look for God's hand of care. We may find his providence in some strange places!**

### TRIALS ● ● • • •

17:17 **Even when God has done a miracle in our life, our troubles may not be over. The famine was a terrible experience, but the worst was yet to come. God's provision is never given in order to let us rest upon it. We are to depend on him as each new trial faces us.**

## PROPHETS—FALSE AND TRUE

The false prophets were an obstacle to bringing God's word to the people. They would bring "messages" that contradicted the words of the true prophets. They gave messages that appealed to the people's sinful nature and comforted their fears. False prophets told people what they wanted to hear; true prophets told God's truth.

| *False Prophets* | *True Prophets* |
|---|---|
| Worked for political purposes to benefit themselves | Worked for spiritual purposes to serve God and the people |
| Held positions of great wealth | Owned little or nothing |
| Gave false messages | Spoke only true messages |
| Spoke only what the people wanted to hear | Spoke only what God told them to say—no matter how unpopular |

24 Then the woman told Elijah, "Now I know for
sure that you are a man of God, and that the LORD
truly speaks through you."

CHAPTER **18** **ELIJAH DEFEATS BAAL'S PROPHETS.** After
many months passed, in the third year of the
drought, the LORD said to Elijah, "Go and present
yourself to King Ahab. Tell him that I will soon send
rain!" 2 So Elijah went to appear before Ahab.
Meanwhile, the famine had become very severe in
Samaria. 3 So Ahab summoned Obadiah, who was in
charge of the palace. (Now Obadiah was a devoted
follower of the LORD. 4 Once when Jezebel had tried
to kill all the LORD's prophets, Obadiah had hidden
one hundred of them in two caves. He had put fifty
prophets in each cave and had supplied them with
food and water.) 5 Ahab said to Obadiah, "We must
check every spring and valley to see if we can find
enough grass to save at least some of my horses and
mules." 6 So they divided the land between them.
Ahab went one way by himself, and Obadiah went
another way by himself.
7 As Obadiah was walking along, he saw Elijah
coming toward him. Obadiah recognized him at
once and fell to the ground before him. "Is it really
you, my lord Elijah?" he asked.
8 "Yes, it is," Elijah replied. "Now go and tell your
master I am here."
9 "Oh, sir," Obadiah protested, "what harm have I
done to you that you are sending me to my death at
the hands of Ahab? 10 For I swear by the LORD your
God that the king has searched every nation and
kingdom on earth from end to end to find you. And
each time when he was told, 'Elijah isn't here,' King
Ahab forced the king of that nation to swear to the
truth of his claim. 11 And now you say, 'Go and tell
your master that Elijah is here'! 12 But as soon as I
leave you, the Spirit of the LORD will carry you away
to who knows where. When Ahab comes and cannot
find you, he will kill me. Yet I have been a true
servant of the LORD all my life. 13 Has no one told you,
my lord, about the time when Jezebel was trying to
kill the LORD's prophets? I hid a hundred of them in
two caves and supplied them with food and water.
14 And now you say, 'Go and tell your master that
Elijah is here'! Sir, if I do that, I'm as good as dead!"
15 But Elijah said, "I swear by the LORD Almighty,
in whose presence I stand, that I will present myself
to Ahab today."
16 So Obadiah went to tell Ahab that Elijah had
come, and Ahab went out to meet him. 17 "So it's you,
is it—Israel's troublemaker?" Ahab asked when he
saw him.
18 "I have made no trouble for Israel," Elijah replied. "You and your family are the troublemakers,
for you have refused to obey the commands of the
LORD and have worshiped the images of Baal instead. 19 Now bring all the people of Israel to Mount
Carmel, with all 450 prophets of Baal and the 400
prophets of Asherah, who are supported by Jezebel."
20 So Ahab summoned all the people and the
prophets to Mount Carmel. 21 Then Elijah stood in
front of them and said, "How long are you going to
waver between two opinions? If the LORD is God,
follow him! But if Baal is God, then follow him!"
But the people were completely silent.
22 Then Elijah said to them, "I am the only prophet
of the LORD who is left, but Baal has 450 prophets.
23 Now bring two bulls. The prophets of Baal may
choose whichever one they wish and cut it into pieces
and lay it on the wood of their altar, but without
setting fire to it. I will prepare the other bull and lay it
on the wood on the altar, but not set fire to it. 24 Then

### STAND FIRM ● ● • • •

18:21 **Elijah challenged the people to take a stand—to follow whoever was the true God. Why did so many people waver between the two choices? Perhaps some were not sure. Many, however, knew that the Lord was God, but they enjoyed the sinful pleasures and other benefits that came with following Ahab and his idolatrous worship. It is important to take a stand for the Lord. If we just drift along with whatever is pleasant and easy, we will someday discover that we have been worshiping a false god—ourselves.**

call on the name of your god, and I will call on the
name of the LORD. The god who answers by setting fire
to the wood is the true God!" And all the people
agreed.
25Then Elijah said to the prophets of Baal, "You go
first, for there are many of you. Choose one of the
bulls and prepare it and call on the name of your
god. But do not set fire to
the wood."
26So they prepared one of
the bulls and placed it on the
altar. Then they called on the
name of Baal all morning,
shouting, "O Baal, answer
us!" But there was no reply of
any kind. Then they danced
wildly around the altar they
had made.
27About noontime Elijah
began mocking them. "You'll
have to shout louder," he
scoffed, "for surely he is a
god! Perhaps he is deep in
thought, or he is relieving
himself. Or maybe he is away
on a trip, or he is asleep and
needs to be wakened!"
28So they shouted louder,
and following their normal
custom, they cut themselves
with knives and swords until
the blood gushed out. 29They
raved all afternoon until the
time of the evening sacrifice,
but still there was no reply, no
voice, no answer.
30Then Elijah called to the
people, "Come over here!"
They all crowded around him
as he repaired the altar of the
LORD that had been torn
down. 31He took twelve
stones, one to represent each
of the tribes of Israel,* 32and
he used the stones to rebuild
the LORD's altar. Then he dug
a trench around the altar
large enough to hold about
three gallons.* 33He piled
wood on the altar, cut the
bull into pieces, and laid the
pieces on the wood. Then he
said, "Fill four large jars with
water, and pour the water
over the offering and the
wood." After they had done
this, 34he said, "Do the same
thing again!" And when they
were finished, he said, "Now
do it a third time!" So they did as he said, 35and the
water ran around the altar and even overflowed the
trench.
36At the customary time for offering the evening
sacrifice, Elijah the prophet walked up to the altar
and prayed, "O LORD, God of Abraham, Isaac, and
Jacob,* prove today that you are God in Israel and

## ELIJAH

Elijah's complete commitment to God shocks and challenges us. God made him a confronter rather than a comforter. He had to speak God's words to a king who often rejected his message. Elijah experienced real loneliness even though he was working for God.

It is interesting to read about the amazing miracles God accomplished through Elijah, but it is more helpful to think about the relationship they shared. All that happened in Elijah's life began with the step we can take—he responded to the miracle of being able to know God.

In Elijah's life we really see the thrills of victory and the agonies of defeat. God had to teach Elijah that many of his problems came from missing God's presence. He showed the depressed prophet a windstorm, an earthquake, and a fire—just the kind of awesome things we usually think prove God's power. But God told Elijah that we can know him even better in the quiet, when he comes like a whisper.

Elijah also had to learn another lesson. He was part of God's plan, and he knew about God's power and presence, but he was lonely sometimes because he didn't know that God also had other people in his plan. God had to remind Elijah there were 7,000 others in Israel who were faithful.

Even today, God speaks more often through the quiet and obvious than the spectacular and unusual. God has work for us to do even when we feel fear and failure. And God always has more plans and people than we know about. We may want to be heroes for God, but it all starts with a relationship with him. The real miracle in Elijah's life was his very personal relationship with God.

**UPS:**
- The most famous and dramatic of Israel's prophets
- Predicted the beginning and end of a three-year drought
- Used by God to restore a dead child to his mother
- God's representative in a showdown with priests of Baal and Asherah
- Appeared with Moses and Jesus in the New Testament transfiguration scene

**DOWNS:**
- Chose to work alone and paid for it through isolation
- Fled in fear from Jezebel when she threatened his life

**STATS:**
- Where: Gilead
- Occupation: Prophet
- Contemporaries: Ahab, Jezebel, Ahaziah, Obadiah, Jehu, Hazael

LESSONS: We are never as alone as we may feel; God is always there

God speaks more frequently in persistent whispers than in shouts

KEY VERSES: "At the customary time for offering the evening sacrifice, Elijah the prophet walked up to the altar and prayed, "O LORD, God of Abraham, Isaac, and Jacob, prove today that you are God in Israel and that I am your servant. Prove that I have done all this at your command." . . . Immediately the fire of the LORD flashed down from heaven and burned up the young bull, the wood, the stones, and the dust. It even licked up all the water in the ditch!" (1 Kings 18:36, 38).

Elijah's story is told in 1 Kings 17:1—2 Kings 2:11. He is also mentioned in 2 Chronicles 21:12-15; Malachi 4:5-6; Matthew 11:14; 16:14; 17:3-13; 27:47-49; Luke 1:17; 4:25-26; John 1:19-25; Romans 11:2-4; James 5:17-18.

18:31 Hebrew *each of the tribes of the sons of Jacob to whom the LORD had said, "Your name will be Israel."* 18:32 Hebrew *2 seahs* [12 liters] *of seed.*
18:36 Hebrew *and Israel.*

## WHAT IT TAKES ● ● ● • •

18:36-38 **Just as God flashed fire from heaven for Elijah, he will help us accomplish what he commands us to do. The proof may not be as dramatic in our life as in Elijah's, but God will make resources available to us in creative ways to accomplish his purposes. He will give us the wisdom to raise a family, the courage to take a stand for truth, or the means to provide help for someone in need. Like Elijah, we can have faith that, whatever God commands us to do, he will provide what we need to carry it through.**

that I am your servant. Prove that I have done all this at your command. [37]O LORD, answer me! Answer me so these people will know that you, O LORD, are God and that you have brought them back to yourself."

[38]Immediately the fire of the LORD flashed down from heaven and burned up the young bull, the wood, the stones, and the dust. It even licked up all the water in the ditch! [39]And when the people saw it, they fell on their faces and cried out, "The LORD is God! The LORD is God!"

[40]Then Elijah commanded, "Seize all the prophets of Baal. Don't let a single one escape!" So the people seized them all, and Elijah took them down to the Kishon Valley and killed them there.

[41]Then Elijah said to Ahab, "Go and enjoy a good meal! For I hear a mighty rainstorm coming!"

[42]So Ahab prepared a feast. But Elijah climbed to the top of Mount Carmel and fell to the ground and prayed. [43]Then he said to his servant, "Go and look out toward the sea."

The servant went and looked, but he returned to Elijah and said, "I didn't see anything." Seven times Elijah told him to go and look, and seven times he went. [44]Finally the seventh time, his servant told him, "I saw a little cloud about the size of a hand rising from the sea."

Then Elijah shouted, "Hurry to Ahab and tell him, 'Climb into your chariot and go back home. If you don't hurry, the rain will stop you!'"

[45]And sure enough, the sky was soon black with clouds. A heavy wind brought a terrific rainstorm, and Ahab left quickly for Jezreel. [46]Now the LORD gave special strength to Elijah. He tucked his cloak into his belt and ran ahead of Ahab's chariot all the way to the entrance of Jezreel.

## CHAPTER 19 GOD WHISPERS TO ELIJAH.

When Ahab got home, he told Jezebel what Elijah had done and that he had slaughtered the prophets of Baal. [2]So Jezebel sent this message to Elijah: "May the gods also kill me if by this time tomorrow I have failed to take your life like those whom you killed."

[3]Elijah was afraid and fled for his life. He went to Beersheba, a town in Judah, and he left his servant there. [4]Then he went on alone into the desert, traveling all day. He sat down under a solitary broom tree and prayed that he might die. "I have had enough, LORD," he said. "Take my life, for I am no better than my ancestors."

[5]Then he lay down and slept under the broom tree. But as he was sleeping, an angel touched him and told him, "Get up and eat!" [6]He looked around and saw some bread baked on hot stones and a jar of water! So he ate and drank and lay down again.

[7]Then the angel of the LORD came again and touched him and said, "Get up and eat some more, for there is a long journey ahead of you."

[8]So he got up and ate and drank, and the food gave him enough strength to travel forty days and forty nights to Mount Sinai,* the mountain of God. [9]There he came to a cave, where he spent the night.

But the LORD said to him, "What are you doing here, Elijah?"

[10]Elijah replied, "I have zealously served the LORD God Almighty. But the people of Israel have broken their covenant with you, torn down your altars, and killed every one of your prophets. I alone am left, and now they are trying to kill me, too."

[11]"Go out and stand before me on the mountain," the LORD told him. And as Elijah stood there, the LORD passed by, and a mighty windstorm hit the mountain. It was such a terrible blast that the rocks were torn loose, but the LORD was not in the wind. After the wind there was an earthquake, but the LORD was not in the earthquake. [12]And after the earthquake there was a fire, but the LORD was not in the fire. And after the fire there was the sound of a gentle whisper. [13]When Elijah heard it, he wrapped his face in his cloak and went out and stood at the entrance of the cave.

And a voice said, "What are you doing here, Elijah?"

[14]He replied again, "I have zealously served the LORD God Almighty. But the people of Israel have broken their covenant with you, torn down your altars, and killed every one of your prophets. I alone am left, and now they are trying to kill me, too."

[15]Then the LORD told him, "Go back the way you came, and travel to the wilderness of Damascus. When you arrive there, anoint Hazael to be king of Aram. [16]Then anoint Jehu son of Nimshi to be king of Israel, and anoint Elisha son of Shaphat from Abel-meholah to replace you as my prophet. [17]Anyone who escapes from Hazael will be killed by Jehu, and those who escape Jehu will be killed by Elisha!

## DEPRESSION ● ● ● • •

19:3-4 **Elijah experienced the depths of fatigue and discouragement just after his two great spiritual victories: the defeat of the prophets of Baal and the answered prayer for rain. Often discouragement sets in after great spiritual experiences, especially those requiring physical effort or producing emotional excitement. To lead him out of depression, God first let Elijah rest and eat. Then God confronted him with the need to return to his mission in life—to be God's prophet. Elijah's battles were not over; there was still work for him to do. When you feel let down after a great spiritual experience, remember that God's purpose for your life is not over yet.**

19:8 Hebrew *Horeb,* another name for Sinai.

After the
EARTHQUAKE
there was
A FIRE,
but the LORD was not in the fire.
And after the fire
there was
the sound of a gentle whisper.
1 KINGS 19:12

[18]Yet I will preserve seven thousand others in Israel who have never bowed to Baal or kissed him!"

[19]So Elijah went and found Elisha son of Shaphat plowing a field with a team of oxen. There were eleven teams of oxen ahead of him, and he was plowing with the twelfth team. Elijah went over to him and threw his cloak across his shoulders and walked away again. [20]Elisha left the oxen standing there, ran after Elijah, and said to him, "First let me go and kiss my father and mother good-bye, and then I will go with you!"

Elijah replied, "Go on back! But consider what I have done to you."

[21]Elisha then returned to his oxen, killed them, and used the wood from the plow to build a fire to roast their flesh. He passed around the meat to the other plowmen, and they all ate. Then he went with Elijah as his assistant.

CHAPTER **20** **GOD GIVES ISRAEL VICTORY.** Now King Ben-hadad of Aram mobilized his army, supported by the chariots and horses of thirty-two allied kings. They went to besiege Samaria, the Israelite capital, and launched attacks against it. [2]Ben-hadad sent messengers into the city to relay this message to King Ahab of Israel: "This is what Ben-hadad says: [3]'Your silver and gold are mine, and so are the best of your wives and children!'"

[4]"All right, my lord," Ahab replied. "All that I have is yours!"

[5]Soon Ben-hadad's messengers returned again and said, "This is what Ben-hadad says: 'I have already demanded that you give me your silver, gold, wives, and children. [6]But about this time tomorrow I will send my officials to search your palace and the homes of your people. They will take away everything you consider valuable!'"

[7]Then Ahab summoned all the leaders of the land and said to them, "Look how this man is stirring up trouble! I already agreed when he sent the message demanding that I give him my wives and children and silver and gold."

[8]"Don't give in to any more demands," the leaders and people advised.

[9]So Ahab told the messengers from Ben-hadad, "Say this to my lord the king: 'I will give you everything you asked for the first time, but this last demand of yours I simply cannot meet.'" So the messengers returned to Ben-hadad with the response.

[10]Then Ben-hadad sent this message to Ahab: "May the gods bring tragedy on me, and even worse than that, if there remains enough dust from Samaria to provide more than a handful for each of my soldiers."

[11]The king of Israel sent back this answer: "A warrior still dressing for battle should not boast like a warrior who has already won."

[12]This reply of Ahab's reached Ben-hadad and the other kings as they were drinking in their tents.* "Prepare to attack!" Ben-hadad commanded his officers. So they prepared to attack the city.

[13]Then a prophet came to see King Ahab and told him, "This is what the LORD says: Do you see all these enemy forces? Today I will hand them all over to you. Then you will know that I am the LORD."

## WHISPERS ● ● ● • •

19:11-13 **Elijah knew that the gentle whisper was God's voice. He realized that God doesn't reveal himself only in powerful, miraculous ways. To look for God only in something big (camps, churches, conferences, visible leaders) may be to miss him, because he is often found gently whispering in the quietness of a humbled heart. Are you listening for God? Step back from the noise and activity of your busy life and listen humbly and quietly for his guidance. It may come when you least expect it.**

[14]Ahab asked, "How will he do it?"

And the prophet replied, "This is what the LORD says: The troops of the provincial commanders will do it."

"Should we attack first?" Ahab asked.

"Yes," the prophet answered.

[15]So Ahab mustered the troops of the 232 provincial commanders. Then he called out the rest of his army of seven thousand men. [16]About noontime, as Ben-hadad and the thirty-two allied kings were still in their tents getting drunk, [17]the troops of the provincial commanders marched out of the city. As they approached, Ben-hadad's scouts reported to him, "Some troops are coming from Samaria."

[18]"Take them alive," Ben-hadad commanded, "whether they have come for peace or for war."

[19]But by now Ahab's provincial commanders had led the army out to fight. [20]Each Israelite soldier killed his Aramean opponent, and suddenly the entire Aramean army panicked and fled. The Israelites chased them, but King Ben-hadad and a few others escaped on horses. [21]However, the other horses and

20:12 Or *in Succoth;* also in 20:16.

chariots were destroyed, and the Arameans were killed in a great slaughter.

22 Afterward the prophet said to King Ahab, "Get ready for another attack by the king of Aram next spring."

23 After their defeat, Ben-hadad's officers said to him, "The Israelite gods are gods of the hills; that is why they won. But we can beat them easily on the plains. 24 Only this time replace the kings with field commanders! 25 Recruit another army like the one you lost. Give us the same number of horses, chariots, and men, and we will fight against them in the plains. There's not a shadow of a doubt that we will beat them." So King Ben-hadad did as they suggested. 26 The following spring he called up the Aramean army and marched out against Israel, this time at Aphek. 27 Israel then mustered its army, set up supply lines, and moved into the battle. But the Israelite army looked like two little flocks of goats in comparison to the vast Aramean forces that filled the countryside!

**BATTLE ● ● • • •**

20:23 **Since the days of Joshua, Israel's soldiers had had a reputation for being superior fighters in the hills, but ineffective in the open plains and valleys because they did not use chariots in battle. Horse-drawn chariots, useless in hilly terrain and dense forests, could easily run down great numbers of foot soldiers on the plains. What Ben-hadad's officers did not understand was that it was God who made the difference in battle, not the chariots. When faced with emotional or spiritual battles, remember that victory doesn't come from how you fight, but from having God at your side.**

28 Then the man of God went to the king of Israel and said, "This is what the LORD says: The Arameans have said that the LORD is a god of the hills and not of the plains. So I will help you defeat this vast army. Then you will know that I am the LORD."

29 The two armies camped opposite each other for seven days, and on the seventh day the battle began. The Israelites killed 100,000 Aramean foot soldiers in one day. 30 The rest fled behind the walls of Aphek, but the wall fell on them and killed another 27,000. Ben-hadad fled into the city and hid in a secret room. 31 Ben-hadad's officers said to him, "Sir, we have heard that the kings of Israel are very merciful. So let's humble ourselves by wearing sackcloth and putting ropes on our heads. Then perhaps King Ahab will let you live."

32 So they put on sackcloth and ropes and went to the king of Israel and begged, "Your servant Ben-hadad says, 'Please let me live!'"

The king of Israel responded, "Is he still alive? He is my brother!"

33 The men were quick to grasp at this straw of hope, and they replied, "Yes, your brother Ben-hadad!"

"Go and get him," the king of Israel told them. And when Ben-hadad arrived, Ahab invited him up into his chariot!

34 Ben-hadad told him, "I will give back the towns my father took from your father, and you may establish places of trade in Damascus, as my father did in Samaria."

Then Ahab said, "I will let you go under these conditions." So they made a treaty, and Ben-hadad was set free.

35 Meanwhile, the LORD instructed one of the group of prophets to say to another man, "Strike me!" But the man refused to strike the prophet. 36 Then the prophet told him, "Because you have not obeyed the voice of the LORD, a lion will kill you as soon as you leave me." And sure enough, when he had gone, a lion attacked and killed him.

37 Then the prophet turned to another man and said, "Strike me!" So he struck the prophet and wounded him.

38 The prophet waited for the king beside the road, having placed a bandage over his eyes to disguise himself. 39 As the king passed by, the prophet called out to him, "Sir, I was in the battle, and a man brought me a prisoner. He said, 'Guard this man; if for any reason he gets away, you will either die or pay a fine of seventy-five pounds* of silver!' 40 But while I was busy doing something else, the prisoner disappeared!"

"Well, it's your own fault," the king replied. "You have determined your own judgment."

41 Then the prophet pulled the bandage from his eyes, and the king of Israel recognized him as one of the prophets. 42 And the prophet told him, "This is what the LORD says: Because you have spared the man I said must be destroyed,* now you must die in his place, and your people will die instead of his people." 43 So the king of Israel went home to Samaria angry and sullen.

## CHAPTER 21

**AHAB STEALS A VINEYARD.** King Ahab had a palace in Jezreel, and near the palace was a vineyard owned by a man named Naboth. 2 One day Ahab said to Naboth, "Since your vineyard is so convenient to the palace, I would like to buy it to use as a vegetable garden. I will give you a better vineyard in exchange, or if you prefer, I will pay you for it."

3 But Naboth replied, "The LORD forbid that I should give you the inheritance that was passed down by my ancestors." 4 So Ahab went home angry and sullen because of Naboth's answer. The king went to bed with his face to the wall and refused to eat!

5 "What in the world is the matter?" his wife, Jezebel, asked him. "What has made you so upset that you are not eating?"

**BLINDNESS ● ● • • •**

21:20 **Ahab still refused to admit his sin against God. Instead he accused Elijah of being his enemy. When we are blinded by envy and hatred, it is almost impossible to see our own sin.**

20:39 Hebrew *1 talent* [34 kilograms]. 20:42 The Hebrew term used here refers to the complete consecration of things or people to the LORD, either by destroying them or by giving them as an offering.

6"I asked Naboth to sell me his vineyard or to
trade it, and he refused!" Ahab told her.
7"Are you the king of Israel or not?" Jezebel asked.
"Get up and eat and don't worry about it. I'll get you
Naboth's vineyard!"
8So she wrote letters in Ahab's name, sealed them
with his seal, and sent them to the elders and other
leaders of the city where Naboth lived. 9In her letters
she commanded: "Call the citizens together for fasting and prayer and give Naboth a place of honor.
10Find two scoundrels* who will accuse him of cursing God and the king. Then take him out and stone
him to death."
11So the elders and other leaders followed the
instructions Jezebel had written in the letters. 12They
called for a fast and put Naboth at a prominent place
before the people. 13Then two scoundrels accused
him before all the people of cursing God and the
king. So he was dragged outside the city and stoned
to death. 14The city officials then sent word to Jezebel, "Naboth has been stoned to death."
15When Jezebel heard the news, she said to Ahab,
"You know the vineyard Naboth wouldn't sell you?
Well, you can have it now! He's dead!" 16So Ahab
immediately went down to the vineyard to claim it.
17But the LORD said to Elijah, who was from
Tishbe, 18"Go down to meet King Ahab, who rules in
Samaria. He will be at Naboth's vineyard in Jezreel,
taking possession of it. 19Give him this message:
'This is what the LORD says: Isn't killing Naboth bad
enough? Must you rob him, too? Because you have
done this, dogs will lick your blood outside the city
just as they licked the blood of Naboth!'"
20"So my enemy has found me!" Ahab exclaimed
to Elijah.
"Yes," Elijah answered, "I have come because you
have sold yourself to what is evil in the LORD's sight.
21The LORD is going to bring disaster to you and
sweep you away. He will not let a single one of your
male descendants, slave or free alike, survive in Israel! 22He is going to destroy your family as he did
the family of Jeroboam son of Nebat and the family
of Baasha son of Ahijah, for you have made him very
angry and have led all of Israel into sin. 23The LORD
has also told me that the dogs of Jezreel will eat the
body of your wife, Jezebel, at the city wall. 24The
members of your family who die in the city will be
eaten by dogs, and those who die in the field will be
eaten by vultures."
25No one else so completely sold himself to what
was evil in the LORD's sight as did Ahab, for his wife,
Jezebel, influenced him. 26He was especially guilty
because he worshiped idols just as the Amorites had
done—the people whom the LORD had driven from
the land ahead of the Israelites.
27When Ahab heard this message, he tore his
clothing, dressed in sackcloth, and fasted. He even
slept in sackcloth and went about in deep mourning.
28Then another message from the LORD came to
Elijah, who was from Tishbe: 29"Do you see how
Ahab has humbled himself before me? Because he
has done this, I will not do what I promised during
his lifetime. It will happen to his sons; I will destroy
all his descendants."

### NEVER TOO LATE ● ● • • •

21:29 **Ahab was more wicked than any other king of Israel (16:30; 21:25), but when he repented in deep humility, God took notice and reduced his punishment. The same Lord who was merciful to Ahab wants to be merciful to you. No matter how bad you've acted, it is never too late to humble yourself, turn to God, and ask for forgiveness.**

## CHAPTER 22

**AHAB DIES IN BATTLE.** For three years
there was no war between Aram and Israel. 2Then
during the third year, King Jehoshaphat of Judah
went to visit King Ahab of Israel. 3During the visit,
Ahab said to his officials, "Do you realize that the
Arameans are still occupying our city of Ramoth-
gilead? And we haven't done a thing about it!"
4Then he turned to Jehoshaphat and asked, "Will
you join me in fighting against Ramoth-gilead?"
And Jehoshaphat replied to King Ahab, "Why, of
course! You and I are brothers, and my troops are
yours to command. Even my horses are at your
service." 5Then Jehoshaphat added, "But first let's
find out what the LORD says."
6So King Ahab summoned his prophets, about
four hundred of them, and asked them, "Should I go
to war against Ramoth-gilead or not?"
They all replied, "Go right ahead! The Lord will
give you a glorious victory!"
7But Jehoshaphat asked, "Isn't there a prophet of
the LORD around, too? I would like to ask him the
same question."
8King Ahab replied, "There is still one prophet of
the LORD, but I hate him. He never prophesies anything but bad news for me! His name is Micaiah son
of Imlah."
"You shouldn't talk like that," Jehoshaphat said.
"Let's hear what he has to say."
9So the king of Israel called one of his officials and
said, "Quick! Go and get Micaiah son of Imlah."
10King Ahab of Israel and King Jehoshaphat of
Judah, dressed in their royal robes, were sitting on
thrones at the threshing floor near the gate of Samaria. All of Ahab's prophets were prophesying
there in front of them. 11One of them, Zedekiah son
of Kenaanah, made some iron horns and proclaimed, "This is what the LORD says: With these
horns you will gore the Arameans to death!"
12All the other prophets agreed. "Yes," they said,
"go up to Ramoth-gilead and be victorious, for the
LORD will give you victory!"
13Meanwhile, the messenger who went to get Micaiah said to him, "Look, all the prophets are promising victory for the king. Be sure that you agree with
them and promise success."

21:10 Hebrew *two sons of Belial;* also in 21:13.

14But Micaiah replied, "As surely as the LORD lives, I will say only what the LORD tells me to say."

15When Micaiah arrived before the king, Ahab asked him, "Micaiah, should we go to war against Ramoth-gilead or not?"

And Micaiah replied, "Go right ahead! The LORD will give the king a glorious victory!"

16But the king replied sharply, "How many times must I demand that you speak only the truth when you speak for the LORD?"

17So Micaiah told him, "In a vision I saw all Israel scattered on the mountains, like sheep without a shepherd. And the LORD said, 'Their master has been killed. Send them home in peace.'"

18"Didn't I tell you?" the king of Israel said to Jehoshaphat. "He does it every time. He never prophesies anything but bad news for me."

19Then Micaiah continued, "Listen to what the LORD says! I saw the LORD sitting on his throne with all the armies of heaven around him, on his right and on his left. 20And the LORD said, 'Who can entice Ahab to go into battle against Ramoth-gilead so that he can be killed there?' There were many suggestions, 21until finally a spirit approached the LORD and said, 'I can do it!'

22"'How will you do this?' the LORD asked.

"And the spirit replied, 'I will go out and inspire all Ahab's prophets to speak lies.'

"'You will succeed,' said the LORD. 'Go ahead and do it.'

23"So you see, the LORD has put a lying spirit in the mouths of your prophets. For the LORD has determined disaster for you."

24Then Zedekiah son of Kenaanah walked up to Micaiah and slapped him across the face. "When did the Spirit of the LORD leave me to speak to you?" he demanded.

25And Micaiah replied, "You will find out soon enough when you find yourself hiding in some secret room!"

26King Ahab of Israel then ordered, "Arrest Micaiah and take him back to Amon, the governor of the city, and to my son Joash. 27Give them this order from the king: 'Put this man in prison, and feed him nothing but bread and water until I return safely from the battle!'"

28But Micaiah replied, "If you return safely, the LORD has not spoken through me!" Then he added to those standing around, "Take note of what I have said."

29So the king of Israel and King Jehoshaphat of Judah led their armies against Ramoth-gilead. 30Now King Ahab said to Jehoshaphat, "As we go into battle, I will disguise myself so no one will recognize me, but you wear your royal robes." So Ahab disguised himself, and they went into battle.

31Now the king of Aram had issued these orders to his thirty-two charioteers: "Attack only the king of Israel!" 32So when the Aramean charioteers saw Jehoshaphat in his royal robes, they went after him. "There is the king of Israel!" they shouted. But when Jehoshaphat cried out, 33the charioteers realized he was not the king of Israel, and they stopped chasing him.

34An Aramean soldier, however, randomly shot an arrow at the Israelite troops, and the arrow hit the king of Israel between the joints of his armor. "Get me out of here!" Ahab groaned to the driver of his chariot. "I have been badly wounded!" 35The battle raged all that day, and Ahab was propped up in his chariot facing the Arameans. The blood from his wound ran down to the floor of his chariot, and as evening arrived he died. 36Just as the sun was setting, the cry ran through his troops: "It's all over—return home!" 37So the king died, and his body was taken to Samaria and buried there. 38Then his chariot was washed beside the pool of Samaria, where the prostitutes bathed, and dogs came and licked the king's blood, just as the LORD had promised.

39The rest of the events in Ahab's reign and the story of the ivory palace and the cities he built are recorded in *The Book of the History of the Kings of Israel.* 40When Ahab died, he was buried among his ancestors. Then his son Ahaziah became the next king.

41Jehoshaphat son of Asa began to rule over Judah in the fourth year of King Ahab's reign in Israel. 42He was thirty-five years old when he became king, and he reigned in Jerusalem twenty-five years. His mother was Azubah, the daughter of Shilhi. 43Jehoshaphat was a good king, following the example of his father, Asa. He did what was pleasing in the LORD's sight. During his reign, however, he failed to remove all the pagan shrines, and the people still offered sacrifices and burned incense there. 44Jehoshaphat also made peace with the king of Israel.

45The rest of the events in Jehoshaphat's reign, the extent of his power, and the wars he waged are recorded in *The Book of the History of the Kings of Judah.* 46He banished from the land the rest of the shrine prostitutes, who still continued their practices from the days of his father, Asa. 47There was no king in Edom at that time, only a deputy.

48Jehoshaphat also built a fleet of trading ships* to sail to Ophir for gold. But the ships never set sail, for they were wrecked at Ezion-geber. 49At that time Ahaziah son of Ahab proposed to Jehoshaphat, "Let my men sail an expedition with your men." But Jehoshaphat refused the offer.

50When Jehoshaphat died, he was buried with his ancestors in the City of David. Then his son Jehoram became the next king.

51Ahaziah son of Ahab began to rule over Israel in the seventeenth year of King Jehoshaphat's reign in Judah. He reigned in Samaria two years. 52But he did what was evil in the LORD's sight, following the example of his father and mother and the example of Jeroboam son of Nebat, who had led Israel into the sin of idolatry. 53He served Baal and worshiped him, arousing the anger of the LORD, the God of Israel, just as his father had done.

22:48 Hebrew *fleet of ships of Tarshish.*

# MEGA themes

**THE KING** Solomon's wisdom, power, and achievements brought honor to the Israelite nation and to God. All the kings of Israel and Judah were told to obey God and to govern according to his laws. But their tendency to abandon God's Word and to worship other gods led them to change the religion and government to meet their personal desires. This neglect of God's law led to their downfall.

Wisdom, power, and achievement do not ultimately come from any human source; they are from God. No matter how we lead or govern, we won't do well if we ignore God's guidelines. Whether or not we are in a position of leadership, we can be successful by listening to and obeying God's Word.

1. What qualities were characteristic of the kings whose reigns were successful? Of those who failed?
2. Which of these characteristics were evident in the life of Solomon?
3. How did each king's relationship with God affect the people?
4. What qualities will you look for in those whom you follow as Christian teachers, pastors, and disciplers?

**THE TEMPLE** Solomon's Temple was a beautiful place of worship and prayer. It was the place of God's special presence and housed the Ark of the Covenant containing the Ten Commandments.

A beautiful house of worship doesn't always indicate that the people gathered there are truly worshiping God. God wants to live in our heart, not just meet us in a sanctuary. We need to worship God daily as individuals and once or twice a week with others.

1. Why was building the Temple so important to Solomon?
2. Solomon was successful in building the Temple, but in other ways he failed to glorify God. What do you learn about worshiping God as you read about Solomon's life and reign?
3. Many people believe that being a "good Christian" means going to church every week. Do you agree or disagree? Why?
4. List some specific ways you can "enter the Temple" to worship God, whether you are inside or outside of a church building. Commit yourself to personally worship God at least once a day during the coming week.

**OTHER GODS** Although the Israelites had God's law and had experienced his presence among them, they became attracted to other gods. When this happened, their hearts became cold to God's law, resulting in the ruin of families and government, and eventually leading to the destruction of the nation.

Through the years, the people took on the false qualities of the false gods they worshiped. They became cruel, power-hungry, and sexually perverse. We tend to become what we worship. Unless we serve the one true God, we will become slaves to whatever takes his place.

1. In what ways did the Israelites worship false gods? What were the results of this worship?
2. What are some of the false gods of our society?
3. What is the same and what is different between the results of the Israelites' false worship and the "worship" of false gods in modern culture?
4. Why do Christians still need to beware of the attraction of false gods?
5. What will you do to ensure that you never fall into the trap of false worship?

**PROPHETIC MESSAGE** The prophet's responsibility was to confront and correct any deviation from God's law. Elijah brought a bolt of judgment against Israel. His messages and miracles warned the evil and rebellious kings and people.

The Bible, sermons that teach the truth, and the wise counsel of believers are warnings to us. Anyone who points out how we may be moving away from God's Word is a blessing. Changing our life in order to obey God often takes painful discipline and hard work. We should seek people who will be honest with us about weaknesses in our life.

1. List several of the judgments that Elijah announced.
2. What do you learn about God's will for his people from these judgments?
3. In what ways do these judgments apply to contemporary churches? To Christians today?
4. What is happening in your relationship with God that you know is in his will?

**SIN/REPENTANCE** Each king had God's Word, a priest or prophet, and the lessons of the past to draw him back to God. All the people had the same resources. Whenever they turned away from their sin and returned to God, God heard their prayers and forgave them.

God hears us when we pray. We have the assurance of forgiveness if we are willing to trust him and turn from sin. When God forgives us, he provides a fresh start and a new desire to live for him.

1. How did God respond to the kings who repented?
2. Contrast those kings' lives with the lives of those who chose to continue in their rebellion. How did God respond to those rebellious kings?
3. What does this study reveal to you about how you should deal with sin when God reveals it to you?
4. Spend a few moments reflecting on your life as it compares to God's will. Write a list of sins that you need to confess to God. Once you have written the list and prayed over each item, destroy the list as a symbol of the fresh start God provides his people when they turn from their sins and to him.

**930 B.C.**
**The kingdom divides**

**848**
**Elijah's ministry transfers to Elisha**

**841**
**Jehu becomes king of Israel**

**835**
**Joash becomes king of Judah**

**793**
**Jeroboam II becomes king of Israel**

**760**
**Amos's ministry begins**

**753**
**Hosea's ministry begins**

**742**
**Micah's ministry begins**

**740**
**Isaiah's ministry begins**

**722**
**Israel (northern kingdom) falls**

**715**
**Hezekiah becomes king of Judah**

**640**
**Josiah becomes king of Judah**

**627**
**Jeremiah's ministry begins**

**605**
**First captivity of Judah–Daniel taken**

**597**
**Second captivity of Judah–Ezekiel taken**

**586**
**Judah (southern kingdom) falls**

**H**e used to be such a nice guy. But since he became president, he thinks he owns the school!" ■ "We used to be friends. But she turned into a snob about a week after making cheerleader!" ■ Maybe you've heard, thought, or even spoken lines like that. It's amazing, isn't it, how some people change when they get a little power or an important position? Suddenly they're in the spotlight, and you're not good enough or popular enough or rich enough to be seen with them. ■ Someone else put it this way: "Power corrupts." ■ Of course, it doesn't always happen that way. Now and then someone who has made it to the top will remember who he or she is and the people who put him or her there. But with so many examples on the other side (politicians, businessmen, athletes, entertainment stars, etc.), it's clear that such people are the exceptions. ■ Second Kings tells about the leaders of the two nations of Israel and Judah. These kings could have used their power to help their people and lead them God's way. But of the 12 northern kings (in Israel) and the 16 southern kings (in Judah) whose stories are recorded in 2 Kings, only two—Hezekiah and Josiah—are called "good." ■ As you read, learn from the negative examples of the kings and determine to be God's person—even if you win the race, get elected, or gain the prize.

## STATS

PURPOSE: To demonstrate the fate that awaits all who refuse to make God their true leader

AUTHOR: Unknown. Possibly Jeremiah or a group of prophets.

SETTING: The once united nation of Israel has been divided into two kingdoms, Israel and Judah, for over a century

KEY PEOPLE: Elijah, Elisha, Shunammite woman, Naaman, Jezebel, Jehu, Joash, Hezekiah, Sennacherib, Isaiah, Manasseh, Josiah, Jehoiakim, Zedekiah, Nebuchadnezzar

SPECIAL FEATURE: The 17 prophetic books at the end of the Old Testament give great insights into the time period of 2 Kings

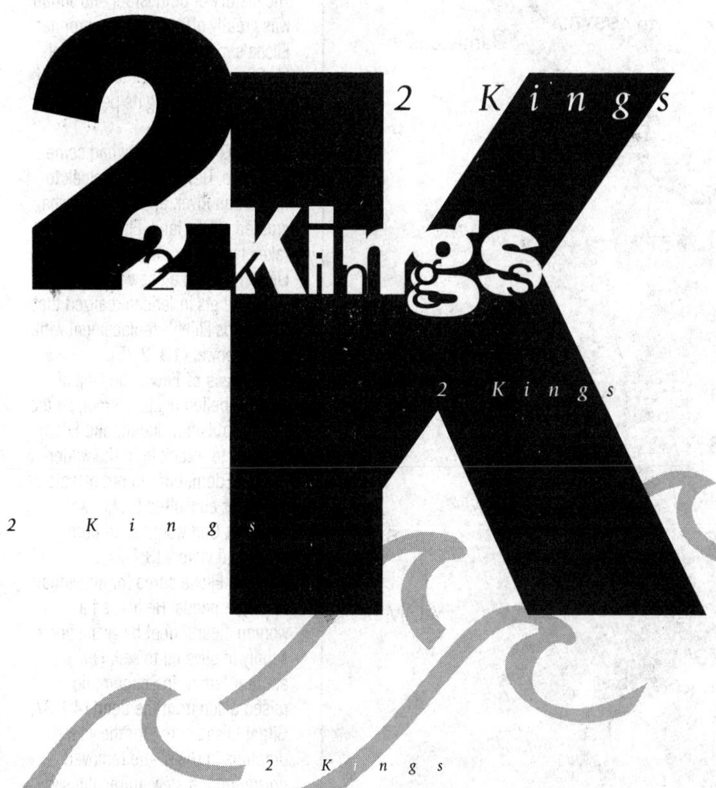


CHAPTER 1 **KING AHAZIAH DIES FOR HIS SIN.** After King
Ahab's death, the nation of Moab declared its independence from Israel.
2One day Israel's new king, Ahaziah, fell through
the latticework of an upper room at his palace in
Samaria, and he was seriously injured. So he sent
messengers to the temple of Baal-zebub, the god of
Ekron, to ask whether he would recover.
3But the angel of the LORD told Elijah, who was from
Tishbe, "Go and meet the messengers of the king of
Samaria and ask them, 'Why are you going to Baal-zebub, the god of Ekron, to ask whether the king will
get well? Is there no God in Israel? 4Now, therefore, this
is what the LORD says: You will never leave the bed on
which you are lying, but you will surely die.'" So Elijah
went to deliver the message.
5When the messengers returned to the king, he
asked them, "Why have you returned so soon?"
6They replied, "A man came up to us and said, 'Go
back to the king and give him this message from the
LORD: Why are you sending men to Baal-zebub, the
god of Ekron, to ask whether you will get well? Is there
no God in Israel? Now, since you have done this, you
will never leave the bed on which you are lying, but
you will surely die.'"
7"Who was this man?" the king demanded.
"What did he look like?"
8They replied, "He was a hairy man,* and he wore
a leather belt around his waist."
"It was Elijah from Tishbe!" the king exclaimed.
9Then he sent an army captain with fifty soldiers to
arrest him. They found him sitting on top of a hill.
The captain said to him, "Man of God, the king has
commanded you to come along with us."
10But Elijah replied to the captain, "If I am a man
of God, let fire come down from heaven and destroy
you and your fifty men!" Then fire fell from heaven
and killed them all.
11So the king sent another captain with fifty men.
The captain said to him, "Man of God, the king says
that you must come down right away."
12Elijah replied, "If I am a man of God, let fire
come down from heaven and destroy you and your
fifty men!" And again the fire of God fell from
heaven and killed them all.
13Once more the king sent a captain with fifty
men. But this time the captain fell to his knees before
Elijah. He pleaded with him, "O man of God, please
spare my life and the lives of these, your fifty servants. 14See how the fire from heaven has destroyed
the first two groups. But now please spare my life!"
15Then the angel of the LORD said to Elijah, "Don't
be afraid. Go with him." So Elijah got up and went
to the king.

**1:8** Or *He was wearing clothing made of hair.*

# KEY PLACES IN 2 KINGS

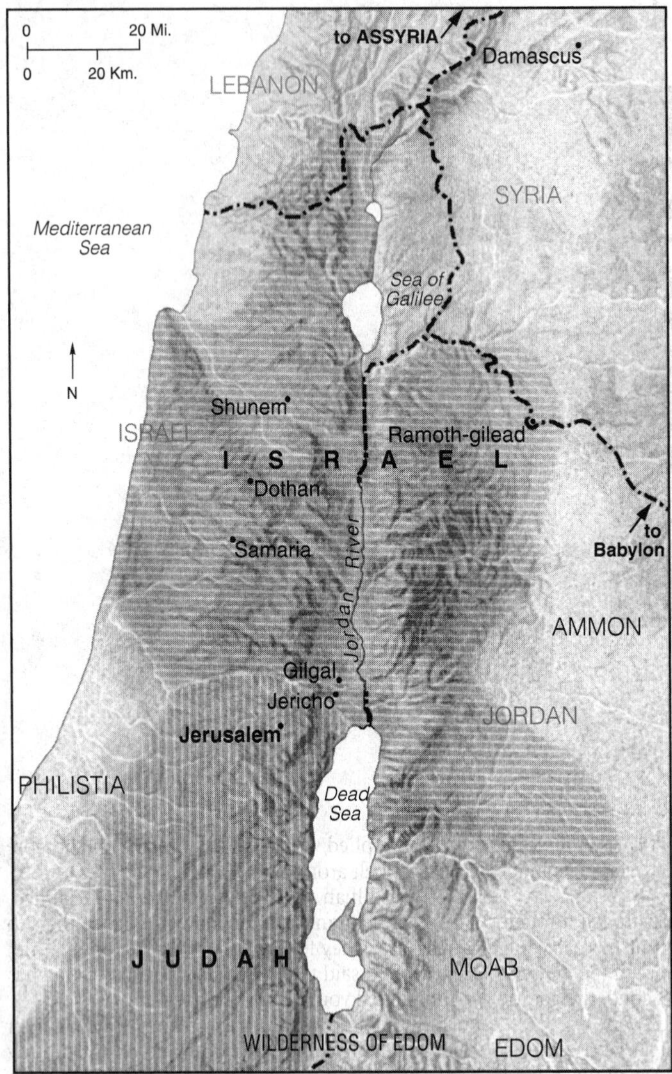


The broken lines (—·—·) indicate modern boundaries.

The history of both Israel and Judah was greatly affected by the prophet Elisha's ministry. He served Israel for 50 years, fighting the idolatry of its kings and calling its people back to God.

**Jericho** Elijah's ministry had come to an end. He touched his cloak to the Jordan River, and he and Elisha crossed on dry land. Elijah was taken by God in a whirlwind, and Elisha returned alone with the cloak. The prophets in Jericho realized that Elisha was Elijah's replacement with Elijah's power (1:1–2:25).

**Wilderness of Edom** The king of Moab rebelled against Israel, so the nations of Israel, Judah, and Edom decided to attack from the wilderness of Edom, but ran out of water. The kings consulted Elisha, who said that God would send both water and victory (3:1-27).

**Shunem** Elisha cared for individuals and their needs. He helped a woman clear a debt by giving her a supply of olive oil to sell. For another family, in Shunem, he raised a son from the dead (4:1-37).

**Gilgal** Elisha cared for the young prophets in Gilgal—he removed poison from a stew, miraculously fed everyone with a small amount of food, and even caused an ax head to float so someone could retrieve it. (4:38–6:7).

**Dothan** Although he cured an Aramean commander's leprosy, Elisha was loyal to Israel. He knew the Aramean army's battle plans and kept Israel's king informed. The Aramean king tracked Elisha down in Dothan and surrounded the city, hoping to kill him. But Elisha prayed that the Arameans would be blinded—and they were! Then he led the blinded army into Samaria, Israel's capital city (6:8-23).

**Samaria** The Arameans didn't learn their lesson. Later they besieged Samaria. Ironically, Israel's king thought it was Elisha's fault, but Elisha said food would be available in abundance the next day. True to Elisha's word, the Lord caused panic in the Aramean camp and the enemy ran, leaving their supplies to Samaria's starving people (6:24–7:20).

**Damascus** Despite Elisha's loyalty to Israel, he obeyed God and traveled to Damascus, the capital of Aram. King Ben-hadad was sick, and he sent Hazael to ask Elisha if he would recover. Elisha knew the king would die, and told this to Hazael. Hazael then murdered Ben-hadad, making himself king. Later Israel and Judah joined forces to fight this new Aramean threat (8:1-29).

**Ramoth-gilead** As Israel and Judah warred with Syria, Elisha sent a young prophet to Ramoth-gilead to anoint Jehu as Israel's next king. Jehu set out to destroy the wicked dynasties of Israel and Judah, killing Kings Joram and Ahaziah and wicked Queen Jezebel. He then destroyed King Ahab's family and all the Baal worshipers in Israel (9:1–11:1).

**Jerusalem** Power-hungry Athaliah became queen of Judah when her son Ahaziah was killed. She had all her grandsons killed except Joash, who was hidden by his aunt. Joash was crowned king at the age of seven and overthrew Athaliah. Meanwhile in Samaria, the Arameans continued to harass Israel. Israel's new king met with Elisha and was told that he would be victorious over Aram three times (11:2–13:19).

Following Elisha's death came a series of evil kings in Israel. Their idolatry and rejection of God caused their downfall. The Assyrian empire captured Samaria and took most of the Israelites into captivity (13:20–17:41). Jerusalem fell to the next world power, Babylon, and its people were taken captive (18:1–25:30).

16And Elijah said to the king, "This is what the
LORD says: Why did you send messengers to Baal-
zebub, the god of Ekron, to ask whether you will get
well? Is there no God in Israel? Now, since you have
done this, you will never leave the bed on which you
are lying, but you will surely die."
17So Ahaziah died, just as the LORD had promised
through Elijah. Since Ahaziah did not have a son to
succeed him, his brother Joram* became the next
king. This took place in the second year of the reign of
Jehoram son of Jehoshaphat, king of Judah. 18The rest
of the events in Ahaziah's reign are recorded in *The
Book of the History of the Kings of Israel.*

CHAPTER **2** **A WHIRLWIND TAKES ELIJAH AWAY.** When
the LORD was about to take Elijah up to heaven in
a whirlwind, Elijah and Elisha were traveling from
Gilgal. 2And Elijah said to Elisha, "Stay here, for
the LORD has told me to go to Bethel."
But Elisha replied, "As surely as the LORD lives and
you yourself live, I will never leave you!" So they
went on together to Bethel.
3The group of prophets from Bethel came to Elisha and asked him, "Did you know that the LORD is
going to take your master away from you today?"
"Quiet!" Elisha answered. "Of course I know it."
4Then Elijah said to Elisha, "Stay here, for the
LORD has told me to go to Jericho."
But Elisha replied again, "As surely as the LORD
lives and you yourself live, I will never leave you." So
they went on together to Jericho.
5Then the group of prophets from Jericho came to
Elisha and asked him, "Did you know that the LORD is
going to take your master away from you today?"
"Quiet!" he answered again. "Of course I know it."
6Then Elijah said to Elisha, "Stay here, for the
LORD has told me to go to the Jordan River."
But again Elisha replied, "As surely as the LORD
lives and you yourself live, I will never leave you." So
they went on together.
7Fifty men from the group of prophets also went
and watched from a distance as Elijah and Elisha
stopped beside the Jordan River. 8Then Elijah folded
his cloak together and struck the water with it. The
river divided, and the two of them went across on
dry ground!
9When they came to the other side, Elijah said to
Elisha, "What can I do for you before I am taken
away?"
And Elisha replied, "Please let me become your
rightful successor."*
10"You have asked a difficult thing," Elijah replied.
"If you see me when I am taken from you, then you
will get your request. But if not, then you won't."
11As they were walking along and talking, suddenly a chariot of fire appeared, drawn by horses of
fire. It drove between them, separating them, and
Elijah was carried by a whirlwind into heaven. 12Eli-
sha saw it and cried out, "My father! My father! The

## PURE MOTIVES ● ● • • •

2:9 **Elisha asked to become Elijah's rightful successor. In the original Hebrew, Elisha literally asks Elijah for "a double share of your spirit." This was a bold request, but God granted it. Why? Because Elisha's motives were pure. His main goal was not to be better or more powerful than Elijah, but to accomplish more for God. If our motives are pure, we don't have to be afraid to ask great things from God. When we ask God for great power or ability, we need to examine our desires and get rid of any selfishness we find.**

chariots and charioteers of Israel!" And as they disappeared from sight, Elisha tore his robe in two.
13Then Elisha picked up Elijah's cloak and returned to the bank of the Jordan River. 14He struck
the water with the cloak and cried out, "Where is the
LORD, the God of Elijah?" Then the river divided,
and Elisha went across.
15When the group of prophets from Jericho saw
what happened, they exclaimed, "Elisha has become
Elijah's successor!"* And they went to meet him and
bowed down before him. 16"Sir," they said, "just say the
word and fifty of our strongest men will search the
wilderness for your master. Perhaps the Spirit of the LORD
has left him on some mountain or in some valley."
"No," Elisha said, "don't send them." 17But they
kept urging him until he was embarrassed, and he
finally said, "All right, send them." So fifty men
searched for three days but did not find Elijah. 18Eli-
sha was still at Jericho when they returned. "Didn't I
tell you not to go?" he asked.
19Now the leaders of the town of Jericho visited
Elisha. "We have a problem, my lord," they told
him. "This town is located in beautiful natural surroundings, as you can see. But the water is bad, and
the land is unproductive."
20Elisha said, "Bring me a new bowl with salt in
it." So they brought it to him. 21Then he went out to
the spring that supplied the town with water and
threw the salt into it. And he said, "This is what the
LORD says: I have made this water wholesome. It will
no longer cause death or infertility.*" 22And sure
enough! The water has remained wholesome ever
since, just as Elisha said.
23Elisha left Jericho and went up to Bethel. As he
was walking along the road, a group of boys from the
town began mocking and making fun of him. "Go
away, you baldhead!" they chanted. "Go away, you

## VERBAL ABUSE ● ● • • •

2:23-25 **These boys made fun of God's messenger and paid for it with their lives. Making fun of religious leaders has been a popular sport through the ages. To take a stand for God is to be different from the world and vulnerable to verbal abuse. But when we are cynical and sarcastic toward religious leaders, we are in danger of mocking not just the people, but also their spiritual message. We need to pray for leaders, not laugh at them. True leaders, those who follow God, need to be heard with respect and encouraged in their ministry.**

1:17 Hebrew *Jehoram,* a variant name for Joram. 2:9 Hebrew *Let me inherit a double share of your spirit.* 2:15 Hebrew *The spirit of Elijah rests upon Elisha.* 2:21 Or *or make the land unproductive.*

# MIRACLES

"I can't believe that!" said Alice. "Can't you?" the Queen said in a pitying tone. "Try again: draw a long breath and shut your eyes." Alice laughed. "There's no use trying," she said: "One can't believe impossible things." "I daresay you haven't had much practice," said the Queen. "When I was your age, I did it for half an hour a day. Why, sometimes I've believed as many as ***six impossible things before breakfast.***" (From *Through the Looking Glass,* Lewis Carroll, [New York: Penguin Books, 1985], chapter 5.) Do you sometimes feel as if you're being asked to believe the impossible as you read the Bible? Fire from heaven . . . flaming chariots . . . little boys coming back to life . . . FLOATING AX HEADS . . . and many other incredible stories. Sometimes it seems you're looking at an issue of *Tales of the Supernatural* instead of God's Word. Is the Bible all true, or is it full of myths and fairy tales? Do miracles really happen? First we need to define what a miracle is. You hear the word a lot. Perhaps this definition will help: A miracle is any outwardly observable event that breaks the normal laws of nature. This includes miracles of nature (e.g., the parting of the Red Sea); healings (e.g., Naaman); and supernatural displays (e.g., appearances of angels or the writing on the wall in Daniel). By definition, miracles take place by God's initiative, not a human being's. They aren't predictable. And that's one of the problems. We tend to be skeptical of anything that cannot be photographed, documented, or otherwise objectively "proven." Often, our first response to accounts of something unusual is, "Right. Prove it." When no proof is offered, we are (often rightly) unconvinced. The miracles recorded in the Bible, however, are different than an ELVIS SIGHTING or an encounter with **BIGFOOT.** The miracles in the Bible often were witnessed by more than one or two people. The plagues in Egypt were experienced by thousands of people. It's hard to fake that kind of testimony. The parting of the Red Sea would have been tough to fake, too—either the water rolled back or it didn't. When that many people see and experience something miraculous, it's hard to laugh it off as the story of a couple of crazies. As someone has said in regard to the resurrection of Christ, if one person tells you a dead man got out of his grave, you lock him up. If two people say it, it's a conspiracy. If five hundred people say it, you go down to the cemetery and ***check it out.*** So it is with many of the miracles recorded in the Scriptures. There are too many eyewitnesses to discount them. Another argument to consider is the logical one. If there is a God and he created the universe and set up the laws that govern it, why would it be inconsistent or unbelievable for him to **bend or break the rules** he made in the first place? The answer is simple: it's not. It is logical that the one who made natural law can act in ways that go beyond it. Still . . . it's hard to believe something like that unless you see it for yourself. Unfortunately, most of us have never seen anything we could legitimately call a miracle. The great Christian writer C. S. Lewis puts it like this: "You are probably quite right in thinking that you will never see a miracle done. . . . They come on great occasions. . . . If we were heroic missionaries, apostles or martyrs, it would be different. But why you or I? . . . How likely is it that you or I will be present when a peace treaty is signed, when a dictator commits suicide? That we should see a miracle is even less likely" (C. S. Lewis, *Miracles* [New York: Macmillan, 1978], pp. 167–168). Just as we believe in other world-changing events without the benefit of being there, so the biblical writers ask us to believe their testimonies of God's supernatural actions in human history. These writings are just one more way God demonstrates his sovereign control and his intense personal involvement in our lives.

baldhead!" [24]Elisha turned around and looked at them, and he cursed them in the name of the LORD. Then two bears came out of the woods and mauled forty-two of them. [25]From there Elisha went to Mount Carmel and finally returned to Samaria.

CHAPTER **3** **ELISHA HELPS KING JEHOSHAPHAT.** Ahab's son Joram* began to rule over Israel in the eighteenth year of King Jehoshaphat's reign in Judah. He reigned in Samaria twelve years. [2]He did what was evil in the LORD's sight, but he was not as wicked as his father and mother. He at least tore down the sacred pillar of Baal that his father had set up. [3]Nevertheless he continued in the sins of idolatry that Jeroboam son of Nebat had led the people of Israel to commit.

[4]King Mesha of Moab and his people were sheep breeders. They used to pay the king of Israel an annual tribute of 100,000 lambs and the wool of 100,000 rams. [5]But after Ahab's death, the king of Moab rebelled against the king of Israel. [6]So King Joram mustered the army of Israel and marched from Samaria. [7]On the way, he sent this message to King Jehoshaphat of Judah: "The king of Moab has rebelled against me. Will you help me fight him?"

And Jehoshaphat replied, "Why, of course! You and I are brothers, and my troops are yours to command. Even my horses are at your service." [8]Then Jehoshaphat asked, "What route will we take?"

"We will attack from the wilderness of Edom," Joram replied. [9]The king of Edom and his troops joined them, and all three armies traveled along a roundabout route through the wilderness for seven days. But there was no water for the men or their pack animals.

[10]"What should we do?" the king of Israel cried out. "The LORD has brought the three of us here to let the king of Moab defeat us."

[11]But King Jehoshaphat of Judah asked, "Is there no prophet of the LORD with us? If there is, we can ask the LORD what to do."

One of King Joram's officers replied, "Elisha son of Shaphat is here. He used to be Elijah's personal assistant.*"

[12]Jehoshaphat said, "Then the LORD will speak through him." So the kings of Israel, Judah, and Edom went to consult with Elisha.

[13]"I want no part of you," Elisha said to the king of Israel. "Go to the pagan prophets of your father and mother!"

But King Joram said, "No! For it was the LORD who called us three kings here to be destroyed by the king of Moab!"

[14]Elisha replied, "As surely as the LORD Almighty lives, whom I serve, I would not bother with you except for my respect for King Jehoshaphat of Judah. [15]Now bring me someone who can play the harp."

While the harp was being played, the power of the LORD came upon Elisha, [16]and he said, "This is what the LORD says: This dry valley will be filled with pools of water! [17]You will see neither wind nor rain, says the LORD, but this valley will be filled with water. You will have plenty for yourselves and for your cattle and your other animals. [18]But this is only a simple thing for the LORD, for he will make you victorious over the army of Moab! [19]You will conquer the best of their cities, even the fortified ones. You will cut down all their trees, stop up all their springs, and ruin all their good land with stones."

[20]And sure enough, the next day at about the time when the morning sacrifice was offered, water suddenly appeared! It was flowing from the direction of Edom, and soon there was water everywhere.

**DOOM ●●•••**

**3:11-20 Jehoshaphat's request for a "prophet of the LORD" shows how true worship and religious experience in both Israel and Judah had declined. In David's day, both the high priest and the prophets gave the king advice. But most of the priests had left Israel, and God's prophets were seen as messengers of doom (1 Kings 22:18). This miracle predicted by Elisha affirmed God's power and authority and validated Elisha's ministry.**

[21]Meanwhile, when the people of Moab heard about the three armies marching against them, they mobilized every man who could fight, young and old, and stationed themselves along their border. [22]But when they got up the next morning, the sun was shining across the water, making it look as red as blood. [23]"It's blood!" the Moabites exclaimed. "The three armies have attacked and killed each other! Let's go and collect the plunder!"

[24]When they arrived at the Israelite camp, the army of Israel rushed out and attacked the Moabites, who turned and ran. The army of Israel chased them into the land of Moab, destroying everything as they went. [25]They destroyed the cities, covered their good land with stones, stopped up the springs, and cut down the good trees. Finally, only Kir-hareseth was left, but even that came under attack.*

[26]When the king of Moab saw that he was losing the battle, he led seven hundred of his warriors in a desperate attempt to break through the enemy lines near the king of Edom, but they failed to escape. [27]So he took his oldest son, who would have been the next king, and sacrificed him as a burnt offering on the wall. As a result, the anger against Israel was great, so they withdrew and returned to their own land.

CHAPTER **4** **ELISHA HELPS A POOR WIDOW.** One day the widow of one of Elisha's fellow prophets came to Elisha and cried out to him, "My husband who served you is dead, and you know how he feared the LORD. But now a creditor has come, threatening to take my two sons as slaves."

3:1 Hebrew *Jehoram,* a variant name for Joram; also in 3:6. 3:11 Hebrew *He used to pour water on the hands of Elijah.* 3:25 Hebrew *until only Kir-hareseth was left, with its stones, but the slingers surrounded and attacked it.*

## EMPTY JARS ● ● • • •

**4:6 The woman and her sons collected empty jars from their neighbors, and they began to pour oil into them from their one small jar. The oil stopped pouring only when they ran out of containers. The number of jars they gathered was an indication of their faith. God's provision was as large as their faith and willingness to obey. Beware of limiting God's blessings by a lack of faith and obedience.**

2"What can I do to help you?" Elisha asked. "Tell me, what do you have in the house?"

"Nothing at all, except a flask of olive oil," she replied.

3And Elisha said, "Borrow as many empty jars as you can from your friends and neighbors. 4Then go into your house with your sons and shut the door behind you. Pour olive oil from your flask into the jars, setting the jars aside as they are filled."

5So she did as she was told. Her sons brought many jars to her, and she filled one after another. 6Soon every container was full to the brim!

"Bring me another jar," she said to one of her sons.

"There aren't any more!" he told her. And then the olive oil stopped flowing.

7When she told the man of God what had happened, he said to her, "Now sell the olive oil and pay your debts, and there will be enough money left over to support you and your sons."

8One day Elisha went to the town of Shunem. A wealthy woman lived there, and she invited him to eat some food. From then on, whenever he passed that way, he would stop there to eat.

9She said to her husband, "I am sure this man who stops in from time to time is a holy man of God. 10Let's make a little room for him on the roof and furnish it with a bed, a table, a chair, and a lamp. Then he will have a place to stay whenever he comes by."

11One day Elisha returned to Shunem, and he went up to his room to rest. 12He said to his servant Gehazi, "Tell the woman I want to speak to her." When she arrived, 13Elisha said to Gehazi, "Tell her that we appreciate the kind concern she has shown us. Now ask her what we can do for her. Does she want me to put in a good word for her to the king or to the commander of the army?"

"No," she replied, "my family takes good care of me."

14Later Elisha asked Gehazi, "What do you think we can do for her?"

He suggested, "She doesn't have a son, and her husband is an old man."

15"Call her back again," Elisha told him. When the woman returned, Elisha said to her as she stood in the doorway, 16"Next year at about this time you will be holding a son in your arms!"

"No, my lord!" she protested. "Please don't lie to me like that, O man of God." 17But sure enough, the woman soon became pregnant. And at that time the following year she had a son, just as Elisha had said.

18One day when her child was older, he went out to visit his father, who was working with the harvesters. 19Suddenly he complained, "My head hurts! My head hurts!"

His father said to one of the servants, "Carry him home to his mother."

20So the servant took him home, and his mother held him on her lap. But around noontime he died. 21She carried him up to the bed of the man of God, then shut the door and left him there. 22She sent a message to her husband: "Send one of the servants and a donkey so that I can hurry to the man of God and come right back."

23"Why today?" he asked. "It is neither a new moon festival nor a Sabbath."

But she said, "It's all right." 24So she saddled the donkey and said to the servant, "Hurry! Don't slow down on my account unless I tell you to."

25As she approached the man of God at Mount Carmel, Elisha saw her in the distance. He said to Gehazi, "Look, the woman from Shunem is coming. 26Run out to meet her and ask her, 'Is everything all right with you, with your husband, and with your child?'"

"Yes," the woman told Gehazi, "everything is fine."

27But when she came to the man of God at the mountain, she fell to the ground before him and caught hold of his feet. Gehazi began to push her away, but the man of God said, "Leave her alone. Something is troubling her deeply, and the LORD has not told me what it is."

28Then she said, "It was you, my lord, who said I would have a son. And didn't I tell you not to raise my hopes?"

29Then Elisha said to Gehazi, "Get ready to travel; take my staff and go! Don't talk to anyone along the way. Go quickly and lay the staff on the child's face." 30But the boy's mother said, "As surely as the LORD lives and you yourself live, I won't go home unless you go with me." So Elisha returned with her.

31Gehazi hurried on ahead and laid the staff on the child's face, but nothing happened. There was no sign of life. He returned to meet Elisha and told him, "The child is still dead."

32When Elisha arrived, the child was indeed dead, lying there on the prophet's bed. 33He went in alone and shut the door behind him and prayed to the LORD. 34Then he lay down on the child's body, placing his mouth on the child's mouth, his eyes on the child's eyes, and his hands on the child's hands. And the child's body began to grow warm again! 35Elisha got up and walked back and forth in the room a few times. Then he stretched himself out again on the child. This time the boy sneezed seven times and opened his eyes!

## REAL CONCERN ● ● • • •

**4:32-36 Elisha's prayer and method of raising the dead boy show God's personal care for hurting people. We must express genuine concern for others as we carry God's message to them. Only then will we faithfully represent our compassionate Father in heaven.**

36Then Elisha summoned Gehazi. "Call the
child's mother!" he said. And when she came in,
Elisha said, "Here, take your son!" 37She fell at his
feet, overwhelmed with gratitude. Then she picked
up her son and carried him downstairs.
38Elisha now returned to Gilgal, but there was a
famine in the land. One day as the group of prophets
was seated before him, he said to his servant, "Put on
a large kettle and make some stew for these men."
39One of the young men went out into the field to
gather vegetables and came back with a pocketful of
wild gourds. He shredded them and put them into
the kettle without realizing they were poisonous.
40But after the men had eaten a bite or two they cried
out, "Man of God, there's
poison in this stew!" So they
would not eat it.
41Elisha said, "Bring me
some flour." Then he threw
it into the kettle and said,
"Now it's all right; go ahead
and eat." And then it did not
harm them!
42One day a man from
Baal-shalishah brought the
man of God a sack of fresh
grain and twenty loaves of
barley bread made from the
first grain of his harvest. Elisha said, "Give it to the group
of prophets* so they can eat."
43"What?" his servant exclaimed. "Feed one hundred
people with only this?"
But Elisha repeated,
"Give it to the group of
prophets so they can eat, for
the LORD says there will be
plenty for all. There will
even be some left over!"
44And sure enough, there
was plenty for all and some
left over, just as the LORD
had promised.

## CHAPTER 5 NAAMAN IS HEALED.

The king of Aram had high admiration for Naaman, the commander of his army, because through him the LORD had given Aram great victories. But though Naaman was a mighty warrior, he suffered from leprosy.*
2Now groups of Aramean
raiders had invaded the land
of Israel, and among their
captives was a young girl who
had been given to Naaman's wife as a maid. 3One day
the girl said to her mistress, "I wish my master would
go to see the prophet in Samaria. He would heal him
of his leprosy."

### LEPROSY ● ● ● • •

5:1 **Leprosy, much like AIDS today, was one of the most feared diseases of the time. It was extremely contagious and, in many cases, incurable. In its worst forms, leprosy led to death. Many lepers were forced out of the cities into quarantined camps. Since Naaman still held his post, he probably had a mild form of the disease, or perhaps it was still in the early stages. In either case, his career would be tragically shortened by his disease.**

## ELISHA

Few "replacements" in the Bible were as effective as Elisha, who was Elijah's replacement as God's prophet to Israel. But Elisha had a great example to follow in Elijah. Elisha got to know God through the old prophet. He followed, watched, and served his teacher in order to learn the knowledge and wisdom he needed for the work to which God had called him. The person you will become and the work you will do are being shaped by the people you follow today. Are they worth following?

Though Elijah and Elisha were both prophets, each had his own style and a different job to do. Because Elijah did a good job of confronting evil and idol worship, Elisha was able to be a comforter. He showed people how much God cared. The Bible records eighteen encounters between Elisha and people who needed help.

Elisha saw more *in* life than most people because he recognized that with God there was more *to* life. He knew that all we are and have comes from God. The miracles done through Elisha put people in touch with the personal and all-powerful God. Elijah would have been proud of his replacement's work.

We, too, have great examples to follow—both people in the Bible and those today who have positively influenced our life. We must resist the tendency to think about the limitations that our family background or environment creates for us. Instead, we should ask God to use us for his purpose—perhaps, like Elijah, to win great conflicts or, like Elisha, to compassionately care for the daily needs of those around us. Ask God to use you as only he can.

**UPS:**
- Elijah's successor as a prophet of God
- Had a ministry that lasted over 50 years
- Had a major impact on four nations: Israel, Judah, Moab, and Syria
- A man of integrity who did not try to enrich himself at others' expense
- Did many miracles to help those in need

**STATS:**
- Where: From the tribe of Issachar, prophesied to northern kingdom
- Occupation: Farmer, prophet
- Relatives: Father: Shaphat
- Contemporaries: Elijah, Ahab, Jezebel, Jehu

LESSONS: In God's eyes, one measure of greatness is the willingness to serve the poor as well as the powerful

An effective replacement not only learns from his master, but also builds upon his master's achievements

KEY VERSE: "When they came to the other side, Elijah said to Elisha, 'What can I do for you before I am taken away?' And Elisha replied, 'Please let me become your rightful successor'" (2 Kings 2:9).

Elisha's story is told in 1 Kings 19:16—2 Kings 13:20. He is also mentioned in Luke 4:27.

---

4:42 Hebrew *to the people;* also in 4:43. 5:1 Or *from a contagious skin disease.* The Hebrew word used here and throughout this passage can describe various skin diseases.

[4]So Naaman told the king what the young girl from Israel had said. [5]"Go and visit the prophet," the king told him. "I will send a letter of introduction for you to carry to the king of Israel." So Naaman started out, taking as gifts 750 pounds of silver, 150 pounds of gold,* and ten sets of clothing. [6]The letter to the king of Israel said: "With this letter I present my servant Naaman. I want you to heal him of his leprosy."

[7]When the king of Israel read it, he tore his clothes in dismay and said, "This man sends me a leper to heal! Am I God, that I can kill and give life? He is only trying to find an excuse to invade us again."

[8]But when Elisha, the man of God, heard about the king's reaction, he sent this message to him: "Why are you so upset? Send Naaman to me, and he will learn that there is a true prophet here in Israel."

[9]So Naaman went with his horses and chariots and waited at the door of Elisha's house. [10]But Elisha sent a messenger out to him with this message: "Go and wash yourself seven times in the Jordan River. Then your skin will be restored, and you will be healed of leprosy."

## HUMILITY ● ● • • ·

**5:9-15 Naaman, a great hero, was used to getting respect, and he was outraged when Elisha treated him like an ordinary person. To wash in a great river would be one thing, but the Jordan was small and dirty. To wash in the Jordan, Naaman thought, was beneath a man of his position. But Naaman had to humble himself and obey Elisha's commands in order to be healed.**

**Obedience to God begins with humility. We must believe that his way is better than our own. We may not always understand his ways of working, but by humbly obeying, we will receive his blessings. We must remember that (1) God's ways are best; (2) God wants our obedience more than anything else; and (3) God can use anything to accomplish his purposes.**

[11]But Naaman became angry and stalked away. "I thought he would surely come out to meet me!" he said. "I expected him to wave his hand over the leprosy and call on the name of the LORD his God and heal me! [12]Aren't the Abana River and Pharpar River of Damascus better than all the rivers of Israel put together? Why shouldn't I wash in them and be healed?" So Naaman turned and went away in a rage.

[13]But his officers tried to reason with him and said, "Sir, if the prophet had told you to do some great thing, wouldn't you have done it? So you should certainly obey him when he says simply to go and wash and be cured!" [14]So Naaman went down to the Jordan River and dipped himself seven times, as the man of God had instructed him. And his flesh became as healthy as a young child's, and he was healed!

[15]Then Naaman and his entire party went back to find the man of God. They stood before him, and

## MONEY ● ● • • ·

**5:20-27 Gehazi saw a perfect opportunity to get rich by selfishly asking for the reward Elisha had refused. Unfortunately, there were three problems with his plan: (1) he willingly accepted money for what he didn't do; (2) he wrongly implied that money could be exchanged for God's free gift of healing and mercy; and (3) he lied and tried to cover up his motives for accepting the money. Although Gehazi had been a helpful servant, personal gain had become more important to him than serving God.**

**This passage is not teaching that money is evil; instead, it is warning against obtaining it wrongly. True service is motivated by love and devotion to God and seeks no personal gain. As you serve God, check your motives—you can't serve both God and money (Matthew 6:24).**

Naaman said, "I know at last that there is no God in all the world except in Israel. Now please accept my gifts."

[16]But Elisha replied, "As surely as the LORD lives, whom I serve, I will not accept any gifts." And though Naaman urged him to take the gifts, Elisha refused.

[17]Then Naaman said, "All right, but please allow me to load two of my mules with earth from this place, and I will take it back home with me. From now on I will never again offer any burnt offerings or sacrifices to any other god except the LORD. [18]However, may the LORD pardon me in this one thing. When my master the king goes into the temple of the god Rimmon to worship there and leans on my arm, may the LORD pardon me when I bow, too."

[19]"Go in peace," Elisha said. So Naaman started home again.

[20]But Gehazi, Elisha's servant, said to himself, "My master should not have let this Aramean get away without accepting his gifts. As surely as the LORD lives, I will chase after him and get something from him." [21]So Gehazi set off after him.

When Naaman saw him running after him, he climbed down from his chariot and went to meet him. "Is everything all right?" Namaan asked.

[22]"Yes," Gehazi said, "but my master has sent me to tell you that two young prophets from the hill country of Ephraim have just arrived. He would like 75 pounds* of silver and two sets of clothing to give to them."

[23]"By all means, take 150 pounds* of silver," Naaman insisted. He gave him two sets of clothing, tied up the money in two bags, and sent two of his servants to carry the gifts for Gehazi. [24]But when they arrived at the hill, Gehazi took the gifts from the servants and sent the men back. Then he hid the gifts inside the house.

[25]When he went in to his master, Elisha asked him, "Where have you been, Gehazi?"

"I haven't been anywhere," he replied.

[26]But Elisha asked him, "Don't you realize that I was there in spirit when Naaman stepped down from his chariot to meet you? Is this the time to

5:5 Hebrew *10 talents* [340 kilograms] *of silver, 6,000 shekels* [68 kilograms] *of gold.* 5:22 Hebrew *1 talent* [34 kilograms]. 5:23 Hebrew *2 talents* [68 kilograms].

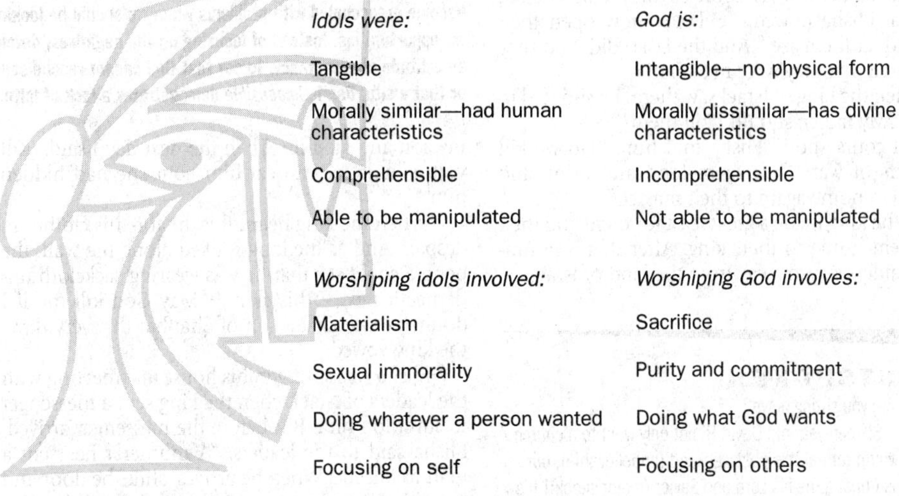

**GOD OR IDOLS**

Why did people continually turn to idols instead of to God?

| *Idols were:* | *God is:* |
|---|---|
| Tangible | Intangible—no physical form |
| Morally similar—had human characteristics | Morally dissimilar—has divine characteristics |
| Comprehensible | Incomprehensible |
| Able to be manipulated | Not able to be manipulated |

| *Worshiping idols involved:* | *Worshiping God involves:* |
|---|---|
| Materialism | Sacrifice |
| Sexual immorality | Purity and commitment |
| Doing whatever a person wanted | Doing what God wants |
| Focusing on self | Focusing on others |

receive money and clothing and olive groves and
vineyards and sheep and oxen and servants? 27Be-
cause you have done this, you and your children and
your children's children will suffer from Naaman's
leprosy forever." When Gehazi left the room, he was
leprous; his skin was as white as snow.

CHAPTER **6** **A SERVANT SEES A FIERY ARMY.** One day
the group of prophets came to Elisha and told him,
"As you can see, this place where we meet with you
is too small. 2Let's go down to the Jordan River,
where there are plenty of logs. There we can build a
new place for us to meet."

"All right," he told them, "go ahead."

3"Please come with us," someone suggested.

"I will," he said.

4When they arrived at the Jordan, they began
cutting down trees. 5But as one of them was chop-
ping, his ax head fell into the river. "Ah, my lord!" he
cried. "It was a borrowed ax!"

6"Where did it fall?" the man of God asked. When
he showed him the place, Elisha cut a stick and threw
it into the water. Then the ax head rose to the surface
and floated. 7"Grab it," Elisha said to him. And the
man reached out and grabbed it.

8When the king of Aram was at war with Israel, he
would confer with his officers and say, "We will
mobilize our forces at such and such a place."

9But immediately Elisha, the man of God, would
warn the king of Israel, "Do not go near that place,
for the Arameans are planning to mobilize their
troops there." 10So the king of Israel would send
word to the place indicated by the man of God,
warning the people there to be on their guard. This
happened several times.

11The king of Aram became very upset over this.
He called in his officers and demanded, "Which of
you is the traitor? Who has been informing the king
of Israel of my plans?"

12"It's not us, my lord," one of the officers replied.
"Elisha, the prophet in Israel, tells the king of Israel
even the words you speak in the privacy of your
bedroom!"

13The king commanded, "Go and find out where
Elisha is, and we will send troops to seize him."

And the report came back: "Elisha is at Dothan."
14So one night the king of Aram sent a great army
with many chariots and horses to surround the city.
15When the servant of the man of God got up early
the next morning and went outside, there were
troops, horses, and chariots everywhere.

"Ah, my lord, what will we do now?" he cried out
to Elisha.

16"Don't be afraid!" Elisha told him. "For there
are more on our side than on theirs!" 17Then Elisha
prayed, "O LORD, open his eyes and let him see!"
The LORD opened his servant's eyes, and when he
looked up, he saw that the hillside around Elisha was
filled with horses and chariots of fire.

18As the Aramean army advanced toward them,
Elisha prayed, "O LORD, please make them blind."
And the LORD did as Elisha asked. 19Then Elisha went
out and told them, "You have come the wrong way!

**EYES OF FAITH ● ● • • •**

6:16-17 **Elisha's servant was no longer afraid when he saw God's mighty heavenly army. Faith reveals that God is doing more for his people than we could ever realize through sight alone. When you face situations that seem insurmountable, remember that spiritual resources are there even if you can't see them. Look through the eyes of faith and let God show you his resources. If you don't see God working in your life, there may be a problem with your spiritual eyesight.**

This isn't the right city! Follow me, and I will take
you to the man you are looking for." And he led
them to Samaria. [20]As soon as they had entered
Samaria, Elisha prayed, "O LORD, now open their
eyes and let them see." And the LORD did, and they
discovered that they were in Samaria.
[21]When the king of Israel saw them, he shouted to
Elisha, "My father, should I kill them?"
[22]"Of course not!" Elisha told him. "Do we kill
prisoners of war? Give them food and drink and
send them home again to their master."
[23]So the king made a great feast for them and then
sent them home to their king. After that, the Aramean raiders stayed away from the land of Israel.

## OUTSPOKEN

Are you sitting down?

Sixteen-year-old David H. not only went to a church youth retreat this past weekend (unbelievable), but he also asked Jesus Christ to be his Lord and Savior (major shock)! It's not a joke; I was there. David was dead serious.

Remember now, this is the same guy who stayed wasted for almost his whole freshman year. We're talking about the most outspoken enemy of the Christian students at Lanier High School.

At school on Monday, word quickly got around about David's surprising decision. When David's wild partying buds approached him to find out what really happened, David brushed them off, saying, "Hey, it's kind of private. I'd rather not talk about it now."

Puzzled, David's best friend, Randy, dropped by after school.

"C'mon, Dave," he urged. "I'm curious . . . tell me the deal."

David froze. He knew he made the right decision at the retreat. He felt liberated, closer to God, and a whole lot happier inside. And yet he didn't want to be abused by his cynical, definitely non-Christian friends.

What do you think? Should he tell Randy what happened—and risk catching a lot of grief? Or should he just hope his friends find God on their own?

Can you relate to David's fear of sharing the Good News? Read 2 Kings 6:24–7:11 (and take special note of 7:9).

[24]Some time later, however, King Ben-hadad of
Aram mobilized his entire army and besieged Samaria. [25]As a result there was a great famine in the
city. After a while even a donkey's head sold for two
pounds of silver, and a cup of dove's dung cost about
two ounces* of silver.
[26]One day as the king of Israel was walking along
the wall of the city, a woman called to him, "Please
help me, my lord the king!"
[27]"If the LORD doesn't help you, what can I do?" he
retorted. "I have neither food nor wine to give you."
[28]But then the king asked, "What is the matter?"
She replied, "This woman proposed that we eat
my son one day and her son the next. [29]So we cooked

## EXPECT

**7:1-2 When Elisha prophesied God's deliverance, the king's officer said it couldn't happen. The officer's faith and hope were gone, but God's words came true anyway! (7:14-16). Sometimes we become preoccupied with problems when we should be looking for opportunities. Instead of focusing on the negatives, develop an attitude of expectancy. To say that God *cannot* rescue someone or that a situation is *impossible* demonstrates a lack of faith.**

my son and ate him. Then the next day I said, 'Kill
your son so we can eat him,' but she had hidden
him."
[30]When the king heard this, he tore his clothes in
despair. And as the king walked along the wall, the
people could see that he was wearing sackcloth underneath next to his skin. [31]"May God kill me if I
don't execute Elisha son of Shaphat this very day,"
the king vowed.
[32]Elisha was sitting in his house at a meeting with
the leaders of Israel when the king sent a messenger
to summon him. But before the messenger arrived,
Elisha said to the leaders, "A murderer has sent a
man to kill me. When he arrives, shut the door and
keep him out. His master will soon follow him."
[33]While Elisha was still saying this, the messenger
arrived. And the king* said, "It is the LORD who has
brought this trouble on us! Why should I wait any
longer for the LORD?"

CHAPTER 7 **FOUR LEPERS VISIT AN ENEMY CAMP.** Elisha
replied, "Hear this message from the LORD! This is
what the LORD says: By this time tomorrow in the
markets of Samaria, five quarts of fine flour will cost
only half an ounce of silver,* and ten quarts of barley
grain will cost only half an ounce of silver.*"
[2]The officer assisting the king said to the man of
God, "That couldn't happen even if the LORD
opened the windows of heaven!"
But Elisha replied, "You will see it happen, but
you won't be able to eat any of it!"
[3]Now there were four men with leprosy* sitting at
the entrance of the city gates. "Why should we sit
here waiting to die?" they asked each other. [4]"We
will starve if we stay here, and we will starve if we go
back into the city. So we might as well go out and
surrender to the Aramean army. If they let us live, so
much the better. But if they kill us, we would have
died anyway."

## SHARING THE NEWS

**7:3-10 The lepers discovered the deserted camp and realized their lives had been spared. At first they kept the wonderful news to themselves, forgetting their fellow citizens who were starving in the city. The Good News about Jesus Christ must be shared, too, for no news is more important. We must not forget those who are dying without it. We must not become so preoccupied with our own faith that we neglect sharing it with those around us. Our "wonderful news," like that of the lepers, will not "wait until morning."**

6:25 Hebrew *sold for 80 shekels* [0.9 kilograms] *of silver, and 1/4 of a cab* [0.3 liters] *of dove's dung cost 5 shekels* [57 grams]. *Dove's dung* may be a variety of wild vegetable. 6:33 Hebrew *he.* 7:1a Hebrew *1 seah* [6 liters] *of fine flour will cost 1 shekel* [11 grams]; also in 7:16, 18. 7:1b Hebrew *2 seahs* [12 liters] *of barley grain will cost 1 shekel* [11 grams]; also in 7:16, 18. 7:3 Or *with a contagious skin disease.* The Hebrew word used here and throughout this passage can describe various skin diseases.

5So that evening they went out to the camp of the
Arameans, but no one was there! 6For the Lord had
caused the whole army of Aram to hear the clatter of
speeding chariots and the galloping of horses and
the sounds of a great army approaching. "The king
of Israel has hired the Hittites and Egyptians* to
attack us!" they cried out. 7So they panicked and fled
into the night, abandoning their tents, horses, donkeys, and everything else, and they fled for their lives.
8When the lepers arrived at the edge of the camp,
they went into one tent after another, eating, drinking wine, and carrying out silver and gold and clothing and hiding it. 9Finally, they said to each other,
"This is not right. This is wonderful news, and we
aren't sharing it with anyone! If we wait until morning, some terrible calamity will certainly fall upon
us. Come on, let's go back and tell the people at the
palace."
10So they went back to the city and told the gatekeepers what had happened—that they had gone
out to the Aramean camp and no one was there! The
horses and donkeys were tethered and the tents were
all in order, but there was not a single person
around. 11Then the gatekeepers shouted the news to
the people in the palace.
12The king got out of bed in the middle of the
night and told his officers, "I know what has happened. The Arameans know we are starving, so they
have left their camp and have hidden in the fields.
They are expecting us to leave the city, and then they
will take us alive and capture the city."
13One of his officers replied, "We had better send
out scouts to check into this. Let them take five of the
remaining horses. If something happens to them, it
won't be a greater loss than if they stay here and die
with the rest of us."
14So two chariots with horses were prepared, and
the king sent scouts to see what had happened to the
Aramean army. 15They went all the way to the Jordan
River, following a trail of clothing and equipment
that the Arameans had thrown away in their mad
rush to escape. The scouts returned and told the king
about it. 16Then the people of Samaria rushed out
and plundered the Aramean camp. So it was true
that five quarts of fine flour were sold that day for
half an ounce of silver, and ten quarts of barley grain
were sold for half an ounce of silver, just as the LORD
had promised. 17The king appointed his officer to
control the traffic at the gate, but he was knocked
down and trampled to death as the people rushed
out.

So everything happened exactly as the man of
God had predicted when the king came to his house.
18The man of God had said to the king, "By this time
tomorrow in the markets of Samaria, five quarts of
fine flour will cost half an ounce of silver, and ten
quarts of barley grain will cost half an ounce of
silver." 19The king's officer had replied, "That
couldn't happen even if the LORD opened the windows of heaven!" And the man of God had said,
"You will see it happen, but you won't be able to eat
any of it!" 20And so it was, for the people trampled
him to death at the gate!

CHAPTER **8** **A WOMAN GETS HER LAND BACK.** Elisha
had told the woman whose son he had brought
back to life, "Take your family and move to some
other place, for the LORD has called for a famine on
Israel that will last for seven years." 2So the woman
did as the man of God instructed. She took her
family and lived in the land of the Philistines for
seven years.
3After the famine ended she returned to the land
of Israel, and she went to see the king about getting
back her house and land. 4As she came in, the king
was talking with Gehazi, the servant of the man of
God. The king had just said, "Tell me some stories
about the great things Elisha has done." 5And Gehazi
was telling the king about the time Elisha had
brought a boy back to life. At that very moment, the

7:6 Possibly *and the people of Muzur,* a district near Cilicia.

**Which is more important, living like a Christian or telling others about my new faith in Christ?**

Try to remember the best Christmas present you ever received. What did you do after your family was through opening presents? More than likely, you called your best friend to tell him or her about your present.

Forgiveness from sin is the greatest gift you will ever receive! It is impossible to keep quiet about it if you truly recognize how important this free gift really is.

Compare the four men with leprosy who discovered the empty camp (2 Kings 7:3-15) to a group of five-year-olds waking up Christmas morning with more presents than they could ever open! The joy and amazement the lepers experienced was beyond their wildest dreams. God had given them something that was simply too wonderful to keep to themselves.

Unfortunately, some people take for granted the gift of salvation through Jesus Christ. These are often the people who say little about their faith. For other Christians, having Christ as Savior is the most exciting present they have ever been given! Of course, having a present does not automatically mean that others will know about it. We must tell them.

The choice for the four men with leprosy—keeping their discovery a secret or telling others about it—probably was tough to make because their disease separated them from other people.

Our sin is like leprosy. We cannot always tell its effects, but left unchecked, the disease gets progressively worse. Having our sin cleansed when we receive the gift of forgiveness through Christ should bring the same joy a leper would have when suddenly cleansed.

Our response in thankfulness to God should cause us to tell all who will listen!

mother of the boy walked in to make her appeal to the king.

"Look, my lord!" Gehazi exclaimed. "Here is the woman now, and this is her son—the very one Elisha brought back to life!"

[6]"Is this true?" the king asked her. And she told him that it was. So he directed one of his officials to see to it that everything she had lost was restored to her, including the value of any crops that had been harvested during her absence.

[7]Now Elisha went to Damascus, the capital of Aram, where King Ben-hadad lay sick. Someone told the king that the man of God had come. [8]When the king heard the news, he said to Hazael, "Take a gift to the man of God. Then tell him to ask the LORD if I will get well again."

[9]So Hazael loaded down forty camels with the finest products of Damascus as a gift for Elisha. He went in to him and said, "Your servant Ben-hadad, the king of Aram, has sent me to ask you if he will recover."

[10]And Elisha replied, "Go and tell him, 'You will recover.' But the LORD has shown me that he will actually die!" [11]Elisha stared at Hazael* with a fixed gaze until Hazael became uneasy. Then the man of God started weeping.

[12]"What's the matter, my lord?" Hazael asked him.

## PEACE ● ● ● • •

9:18-19 **The riders met Jehu and asked if he came in peace and friendship. But Jehu responded, "What do you know about peace?" These qualities, properly understood, come from God. They are not genuine except when rooted in belief in God and love for him. Jehu knew the men represented a disobedient, wicked king. Don't seek friendship with those who are enemies of the good and the true. Lasting peace and genuine friendship can come only from knowing the God who gave these to us.**

Elisha replied, "I know the terrible things you will do to the people of Israel. You will burn their fortified cities, kill their young men, dash their children to the ground, and rip open their pregnant women!"

[13]Then Hazael replied, "How could a nobody like me* ever accomplish such a great feat?"

But Elisha answered, "The LORD has shown me that you are going to be the king of Aram."

[14]When Hazael went back, the king asked him, "What did Elisha tell you?"

And Hazael replied, "He told me that you will surely recover."

[15]But the next day Hazael took a blanket, soaked it in water, and held it over the king's face until he died. Then Hazael became the next king of Aram.

[16]Jehoram son of King Jehoshaphat of Judah began to rule over Judah in the fifth year of King Joram's reign in Israel. Joram was the son of Ahab. [17]Jehoram was thirty-two years old when he became king, and he reigned in Jerusalem eight years. [18]But Jehoram followed the example of the kings of Israel and was as wicked as King Ahab, for he had married one of Ahab's daughters. So Jehoram did what was evil in the LORD's sight. [19]But the LORD was not willing to destroy Judah, for he had made a covenant with David and promised that his descendants would continue to rule forever.*

[20]During Jehoram's reign, the Edomites revolted against Judah and crowned their own king. [21]So Jehoram* went with all his chariots to attack the town of Zair.* The Edomites surrounded him and his charioteers, but he escaped at night under cover of darkness. Jehoram's army, however, deserted him and fled. [22]Edom has been independent from Judah to this day. The town of Libnah revolted about that same time.

[23]The rest of the events in Jehoram's reign and all his deeds are recorded in *The Book of the History of the Kings of Judah.* [24]When Jehoram died, he was buried with his ancestors in the City of David. Then his son Ahaziah became the next king.

[25]Ahaziah son of Jehoram began to rule over Judah in the twelfth year of King Joram's reign in Israel. King Joram was the son of Ahab. [26]Ahaziah was twenty-two years old when he became king, and he reigned in Jerusalem one year. His mother was Athaliah, a granddaughter of King Omri of Israel. [27]Ahaziah followed the evil example of King Ahab's family, doing what was evil in the LORD's sight, because he was related by marriage to the family of Ahab.

[28]Ahaziah joined King Joram of Israel in his war against King Hazael of Aram at Ramoth-gilead. When King Joram was wounded in the battle, [29]he returned to Jezreel to recover from his wounds. While Joram was there, King Ahaziah of Judah went to visit him.

## CHAPTER 9 **JEHU WILL BE KING.**

Meanwhile, Elisha the prophet had summoned a member of the group of prophets. "Get ready to go to Ramoth-gilead," he told him. "Take this vial of olive oil with you, [2]and find Jehu son of Jehoshaphat and grandson of Nimshi. Call him into a back room away from his friends, [3]and pour the oil over his head. Say to him, 'This is what the LORD says: I anoint you to be the king over Israel.' Then open the door and run for your life!"

[4]So the young prophet did as he was told and went to Ramoth-gilead. [5]When he arrived there, he found Jehu sitting in a meeting with the other army officers. "I have a message for you, Commander," he said.

"For which one of us?" Jehu asked.

"For you, Commander," he replied.

[6]So Jehu left the others and went into the house. Then the young prophet poured the oil over Jehu's head and said, "This is what the LORD, the God of Israel, says: I anoint you king over the LORD's people, Israel. [7]You are to destroy the family of Ahab, your master. In this way, I will avenge the murder of my

**8:11** Hebrew *He stared at him.* **8:13** Hebrew *a dog.* **8:19** Hebrew *promised to give a lamp to David and his descendants forever.* **8:21a** Hebrew *Joram,* a variant name for Jehoram; also in 8:23, 24. **8:21b** Greek version reads *Seir.*

prophets and all the LORD's servants who were killed by Jezebel. [8]The entire family of Ahab must be wiped out—every male, slave and free alike, in Israel. [9]I will destroy the family of Ahab as I destroyed the families of Jeroboam son of Nebat and of Baasha son of Ahijah. [10]Dogs will eat Ahab's wife, Jezebel, at the plot of land in Jezreel, and no one will bury her." Then the young prophet opened the door and ran.

[11]Jehu went back to his fellow officers, and one of them asked him, "What did that crazy fellow want? Is everything all right?"

"You know the way such a man babbles on," Jehu replied.

[12]"You're lying," they said. "Tell us." So Jehu told them what the man had said and that at the LORD's command he had been anointed king over Israel.

[13]They quickly spread out their cloaks on the bare steps and blew a trumpet, shouting, "Jehu is king!"

[14]So Jehu son of Jehoshaphat and grandson of Nimshi formed a conspiracy against King Joram. (Now Joram had been with the army at Ramoth-gilead, defending Israel against the forces of King Hazael of Aram. [15]But Joram* had been wounded in the fighting and had returned to Jezreel to recover from his wounds.) So Jehu told the men with him, "Since you want me to be king, don't let anyone escape to Jezreel to report what we have done."

[16]Then Jehu got into a chariot and rode to Jezreel to find King Joram, who was lying there wounded. King Ahaziah of Judah was there, too, for he had gone to visit him. [17]The watchman on the tower of Jezreel saw Jehu and his company approaching, so he shouted to Joram, "I see a company of troops coming!"

"Send out a rider to find out if they are coming in peace," King Joram shouted back.

[18]So a rider went out to meet Jehu and said, "The king wants to know whether you are coming in peace."

Jehu replied, "What do you know about peace? Get behind me!"

The watchman called out to the king, "The rider has met them, but he is not returning."

[19]So the king sent out a second rider. He rode up to them and demanded, "The king wants to know whether you come in peace."

Again Jehu answered, "What do you know about peace? Get behind me!"

[20]The watchman exclaimed, "The rider has met them, but he isn't returning either! It must be Jehu son of Nimshi, for he is driving so recklessly."

[21]"Quick! Get my chariot ready!" King Joram commanded.

Then King Joram of Israel and King Ahaziah of Judah rode out in their chariots to meet Jehu. They met him at the field that had belonged to Naboth of Jezreel. [22]King Joram demanded, "Do you come in peace, Jehu?"

Jehu replied, "How can there be peace as long as the idolatry and witchcraft of your mother, Jezebel, are all around us?"

[23]Then King Joram reined the chariot horses around and fled, shouting to King Ahaziah, "Treason, Ahaziah!" [24]Then Jehu drew his bow and shot Joram between the shoulders. The arrow pierced his heart, and he sank down dead in his chariot.

[25]Jehu said to Bidkar, his officer, "Throw him into the field of Naboth of Jezreel. Do you remember when you and I were riding along behind his father, Ahab? The LORD pronounced this message against him: [26]'I solemnly swear that I will repay him here on Naboth's property, says the LORD, for the murder of Naboth and his sons that I saw yesterday.' So throw him out on Naboth's field, just as the LORD said."

## "Here's what I did..."

I had always been a leader: class president, a member of the leadership team in our youth group, vice president of the Key Club—anything I was involved in, I ended up being a leader of some sort. And I always assumed that leadership meant enjoying certain privileges: respect, being treated well, people listening to me when I made suggestions or comments, even a certain amount of special consideration when decisions were made.

Then I read 2 Kings, and saw how the different kinds of leaders affected their people. Good kings led their people in ways that pleased the Lord, and that resulted in them being blessed. Evil kings led their people into disaster and destruction. So much seemed to depend on the leaders!

One day not long after that, I read Matthew 20:25-28, and I finally realized that my idea of leadership was all wrong. I usually thought only of myself; here Jesus was saying that *real leaders must be humble servants.* After being in the habit of serving myself, it was difficult to serve, as Jesus said. Putting others first made leadership harder, not easier.

I talked about it with my youth leader. She encouraged me to look at a few other verses—Romans 5:3-4 and 8:18. These verses talk about how difficulties have a purpose: to strengthen our faith. Serving others doesn't come naturally, and sometimes it hurts to give up my own rights. But I'm finding that following Jesus' way is helping my faith to grow—and some people even think I'm a better leader!

*Amanda*

AGE 17

9:15 Hebrew *Jehoram,* a variant name for Joram; also in 9:17, 21, 22, 23, 24.

27When King Ahaziah of Judah saw what was happening, he fled along the road to Beth-haggan. Jehu rode after him, shouting, "Shoot him, too!" So they shot Ahaziah in his chariot at the Ascent of Gur, near Ibleam. He was able to go on as far as Megiddo, but he died there. 28His officials took him by chariot to Jerusalem, where they buried him with his ancestors in the City of David. 29Ahaziah's reign over Judah had begun in the eleventh year of King Joram's reign in Israel.

30When Jezebel, the queen mother, heard that Jehu had come to Jezreel, she painted her eyelids and fixed her hair and sat at a window. 31When Jehu entered the gate of the palace, she shouted at him, "Have you come in peace, you murderer? You are just like Zimri, who murdered his master!"

32Jehu looked up and saw her at the window and shouted, "Who is on my side?" And two or three eunuchs looked out at him. 33"Throw her down!" Jehu yelled. So they threw her out the window, and some of her blood spattered against the wall and on the horses. And Jehu trampled her body under his horses' hooves.

34Then Jehu went into the palace and ate and drank. Afterward he said, "Someone go and bury this cursed woman, for she is the daughter of a king." 35But when they went out to bury her, they found only her skull, her feet, and her hands.

36When they returned and told Jehu, he stated, "This fulfills the message from the LORD, which he spoke through his servant Elijah from Tishbe: 'At the plot of land in Jezreel, dogs will eat Jezebel's flesh. 37Her body will be scattered like dung on the field of Jezreel, so that no one will be able to recognize her.'"

## CHAPTER **10**

**JEHU KILLS AHAB'S FAMILY.** Now Ahab had seventy sons living in the city of Samaria. So Jehu wrote a letter and sent copies to Samaria, to the officials of the city,* to the leaders of the people, and to the guardians of King Ahab's sons. The letter said, 2"The king's sons are with you, and you have at your disposal chariots, horses, a fortified city, and weapons. As soon as you receive this letter, 3select the best qualified of King Ahab's sons to be your king, and prepare to fight for Ahab's dynasty."

4But they were paralyzed with fear and said, "Two kings couldn't stand against this man! What can we do?" 5So the palace and city administrators, together with the other leaders and the guardians of the king's sons, sent this message to Jehu: "We are your servants and will do anything you tell us. We will not make anyone king; do whatever you think is best."

6Jehu responded with a second letter: "If you are on my side and are going to obey me, bring the heads of the king's sons to me at Jezreel at about this time tomorrow."

Now the seventy sons of the king were being cared for by the leaders of Samaria, where they had been raised since childhood. 7When the letter arrived, the leaders killed all seventy of the king's sons. They placed their heads in baskets and presented them to Jehu at Jezreel. 8A messenger went to Jehu and said, "They have brought the heads of the king's sons."

So Jehu ordered, "Pile them in two heaps at the entrance of the city gate, and leave them there until morning."

9In the morning he went out and spoke to the crowd that had gathered around them. "You aren't to blame," he told them. "I am the one who conspired against my master and killed him. But who killed all these? 10You can be sure that the message of the LORD that was spoken concerning Ahab's family will not fail. The LORD declared through his servant Elijah that this would happen." 11Then Jehu killed all of Ahab's relatives living in Jezreel and all his important officials, personal friends, and priests. So Ahab was left without a single survivor.

12Then Jehu set out for Samaria. Along the way, while he was at Beth-eked of the Shepherds, 13he met some relatives of King Ahaziah of Judah. "Who are you?" he asked them.

And they replied, "We are relatives of King Ahaziah. We are going to visit the sons of King Ahab and the queen mother."

14"Take them alive!" Jehu shouted to his men. And they captured all forty-two of them and killed them at the well of Beth-eked. None of them escaped.

15When Jehu left there, he met Jehonadab son of Recab, who was coming to meet him. After they had greeted each other, Jehu said to him, "Are you as loyal to me as I am to you?"

"Yes, I am," Jehonadab replied.

"If you are," Jehu said, "then give me your hand." So Jehonadab put out his hand, and Jehu helped him into the chariot. 16Then Jehu said, "Now come with me, and see how devoted I am to the LORD." So Jehonadab rode along with him. 17When Jehu arrived in Samaria, he killed everyone who was left there from Ahab's family, just as the LORD had promised through Elijah.

18Then Jehu called a meeting of all the people of the city and said to them, "Ahab hardly worshiped Baal at all compared to the way I will worship him! 19Summon all the prophets and worshipers of Baal, and call together all his priests. See to it that every

### TOLERANCE ● ● • • •

10:23-29 **Israel was supposed to be intolerant of any religion that did not worship the true God. The religions of surrounding nations were evil and corrupt, based on sexual promiscuity, political favors, greed, and materialism. They were designed to destroy life, not uphold it. Israel was God's special nation, chosen to be an example of what was right, true, and fair. But Israel's kings, priests, and elders, contaminated by surrounding pagan beliefs, had become tolerant and apathetic. We are to be completely intolerant of sin and remove it from our life. It is one thing to be tolerant of others' views, but we should not condone actions that lead people away from God's standards of living.**

10:1 As in some Greek manuscripts and Latin Vulgate (see also 10:6); Hebrew reads *of Jezreel.*

one of them comes, for I am going to offer a great sacrifice to Baal. Any of Baal's worshipers who fail to come will be put to death." But Jehu's plan was to destroy all the worshipers of Baal.

[20]Then Jehu ordered, "Prepare a solemn assembly to worship Baal!" So they did. [21]He sent messengers throughout all Israel summoning those who worshiped Baal. They all came and filled the temple of Baal from one end to the other. [22]And Jehu instructed the keeper of the wardrobe, "Be sure that every worshiper of Baal wears one of these robes." So robes were given to them.

[23]Then Jehu went into the temple of Baal with Jehonadab son of Recab. Jehu said to the worshipers of Baal, "Make sure that only those who worship Baal are here. Don't let anyone in who worships the LORD!" [24]So they were all inside the temple to offer sacrifices and burnt offerings. Now Jehu had surrounded the building with eighty of his men and had warned them, "If you let anyone escape, you will pay for it with your own life."

[25]As soon as Jehu had finished sacrificing the burnt offering, he commanded his guards and officers, "Go in and kill all of them. Don't let a single one escape!" So they killed them all with their swords, and the guards and officers dragged their bodies outside. Then Jehu's men went into the fortress* of the temple of Baal. [26]They dragged out the sacred pillar used in the worship of Baal and destroyed it. [27]They broke down the sacred pillar of Baal and wrecked the temple of Baal, converting it into a public toilet. That is what it is used for to this day. [28]Thus, Jehu destroyed every trace of Baal worship from Israel. [29]He did not, however, destroy the gold calves at Bethel and Dan, the great sin that Jeroboam son of Nebat had led Israel to commit.

[30]Nonetheless the LORD said to Jehu, "You have done well in following my instructions to destroy the family of Ahab. Because of this I will cause your descendants to be the kings of Israel down to the fourth generation." [31]But Jehu did not obey the law of the LORD, the God of Israel, with all his heart. He refused to turn from the sins of idolatry that Jeroboam had led Israel to commit.

[32]At about that time the LORD began to reduce the size of Israel's territory. King Hazael conquered several sections of the country [33]east of the Jordan River, including all of Gilead, Gad, Reuben, and Manasseh. He conquered the area from the town of Aroer by the Arnon Gorge to as far north as Gilead and Bashan.

[34]The rest of the events in Jehu's reign and all his deeds and achievements are recorded in *The Book of the History of the Kings of Israel.* [35]When Jehu died, he was buried with his ancestors in Samaria. Then his son Jehoahaz became the next king. [36]In all, Jehu reigned over Israel from Samaria for twenty-eight years.

## LIP SERVICE • • • • •

10:30-31 **Jehu did much of what the Lord told him to, but he did not obey him with all his heart. Jehu had become God's *instrument* for carrying out justice, but he had not become God's *servant.* As a result, Jehu gave only lip service to God while he worshiped the golden calves. Check the condition of your heart toward God. We can be very active in our work for God and still not give the heartfelt obedience he desires.**

## CHAPTER 11

**JOASH BECOMES KING.** When Athaliah, the mother of King Ahaziah of Judah, learned that her son was dead, she set out to destroy the rest of the royal family. [2]But Ahaziah's sister Jehosheba, the daughter of King Jehoram,* took Ahaziah's infant son, Joash, and stole him away from among the rest of the king's children, who were about to be killed. Jehosheba put Joash and his nurse in a bedroom to hide him from Athaliah, so the child was not murdered. [3]Joash and his nurse remained hidden in the Temple of the LORD for six years while Athaliah ruled over the land.

[4]In the seventh year of Athaliah's reign, Jehoiada the priest summoned the commanders, the Carite mercenaries, and the guards to come to the Temple of the LORD. He made a pact with them and made them swear an oath of loyalty there in the LORD's Temple; then he showed them the king's son.

[5]Jehoiada told them, "This is what you must do. A third of you who are on duty on the Sabbath are to guard the royal palace itself. [6]Another third of you are to stand guard at the Sur Gate. And the final third must stand guard behind the palace guard. These three groups will all guard the palace. [7]The other two units who are off duty on the Sabbath must stand guard for the king at the LORD's Temple. [8]Form a bodyguard for the king and keep your weapons in hand. Any unauthorized person who approaches you must be killed. Stay right beside the king at all times."

[9]So the commanders did everything just as Jehoiada the priest ordered. The commanders took charge of the men reporting for duty that Sabbath, as well as those who were going off duty. They brought them all to Jehoiada the priest, [10]and he supplied them with the spears and shields that had once belonged to King David and were stored in the Temple of the LORD. [11]The guards stationed themselves around the king, with their weapons ready. They formed a line from the south side of the Temple around to the north side and all around the altar.

[12]Then Jehoiada brought out Joash, the king's son, and placed the crown on his head. He presented Joash with a copy of God's covenant and proclaimed him king. They anointed him, and all the people clapped their hands and shouted, "Long live the king!"

## PROMISES • • • • •

11:1 **This story is continued from 9:27, where Ahaziah, Athaliah's son, had been killed by Jehu. Athaliah's attempt to kill all of Ahaziah's sons was futile, because God had promised that the Messiah would be born through David's royal descendants (2 Samuel 7). God keeps his promises.**

10:25 Hebrew *city.* 11:2 Hebrew *Joram,* a variant name for Jehoram.

[13]When Athaliah heard all the noise made by the guards and the people, she hurried to the LORD's Temple to see what was happening. [14]And she saw the newly crowned king standing in his place of authority by the pillar, as was the custom at times of coronation. The officers and trumpeters were surrounding him, and people from all over the land were rejoicing and blowing trumpets. When Athaliah saw all this, she tore her clothes in despair and shouted, "Treason! Treason!"

[15]Then Jehoiada the priest ordered the commanders who were in charge of the troops, "Take her out of the Temple, and kill anyone who tries to rescue her. Do not kill her here in the Temple of the LORD." [16]So they seized her and led her out to the gate where horses enter the palace grounds, and she was killed there.

[17]Then Jehoiada made a covenant between the LORD and the king and the people that they would be the LORD's people. He also made a covenant between the king and the people. [18]And all the people of the land went over to the temple of Baal and tore it down. They demolished the altars and smashed the idols to pieces, and they killed Mattan the priest of Baal in front of the altars.

Jehoiada the priest stationed guards at the Temple of the LORD. [19]Then the commanders, the Carite mercenaries, the guards, and all the people of the land escorted the king from the Temple of the LORD. They went through the gate of the guards and into the palace, and the king took his seat on the royal throne. [20]So all the people of the land rejoiced, and the city was peaceful because Athaliah had been killed at the king's palace.

[21]Joash* was seven years old when he became king.

## INPUT ● ● • • •

12:2 **God's input yields good output. Joash had a good teacher in Jehoiada, the high priest. As long as he lived, Jehoiada's faith in God influenced Joash for good. Good intent must be fortified with good content. As long as Joash heeded Jehoiada's good instruction, he fulfilled God's plan for his life. All our plans and actions must be guided by God, and his counsel is made clear to us in his Word. Our lives will be productive if we heed God's counsel.**

## CHAPTER 12

**JOASH RULES JUDAH.** Joash* began to rule over Judah in the seventh year of King Jehu's reign in Israel. He reigned in Jerusalem forty years. His mother was Zibiah, from Beersheba. [2]All his life Joash did what was pleasing in the LORD's sight because Jehoiada the priest instructed him. [3]Yet even so, he did not destroy the pagan shrines, and the people still offered sacrifices and burned incense there.

[4]One day King Joash said to the priests, "Collect all the money brought as a sacred offering to the LORD's Temple, whether it is a regular assessment, a payment of vows, or a voluntary gift. [5]Let the priests take some of that money to pay for whatever repairs are needed at the Temple."

[6]But by the twenty-third year of Joash's reign, the priests still had not repaired the Temple. [7]So King Joash called for Jehoiada and the other priests and asked them, "Why haven't you repaired the Temple? Don't use any more gifts for your own needs. From now on, it must all be spent on getting the Temple into good condition." [8]So the priests agreed not to collect any more money from the people, and they also agreed not to undertake the repairs of the Temple themselves.

## ACTIONS ● ● • • •

12:3 **Joash didn't go far enough in removing sin from the nation, but he did much that was good and right. When we aren't sure if we've gone far enough in correcting our actions, we can ask: (1) Does the Bible expressly prohibit this action? (2) Does this action take me away from loving, worshiping, or serving God? (3) Does it make me its slave? (4) Is it bringing out the best in me, consistent with God's purpose? (5) Does it benefit other believers?**

[9]Then Jehoiada the priest bored a hole in the lid of a large chest and set it on the right-hand side of the altar at the entrance of the Temple of the LORD. The priests guarding the entrance put all of the people's contributions into the chest. [10]Whenever the chest became full, the court secretary and the high priest counted the money that had been brought to the LORD's Temple and put it into bags. [11]Then they gave the money to the construction supervisors, who used it to pay the people working on the LORD's Temple—the carpenters, the builders, [12]the masons, and the stonecutters. They also used the money to buy timber and cut stone for repairing the LORD's Temple, and they paid any other expenses related to the Temple's restoration.

[13]The money brought to the Temple was not used for making silver cups, lamp snuffers, basins, trumpets, or other articles of gold or silver for the Temple of the LORD. [14]It was paid out to the workmen, who used it for the Temple repairs. [15]No accounting was required from the construction supervisors, because they were honest and faithful workers. [16]However, the money that was contributed for guilt offerings and sin offerings was not brought into the LORD's Temple. It was given to the priests for their own use.

[17]About this time King Hazael of Aram went to war against Gath and captured it. Then he turned to attack Jerusalem. [18]King Joash collected all the sacred objects that Jehoshaphat, Jehoram, and Ahaziah, the previous kings of Judah, had dedicated, along with what he himself had dedicated. He sent them all to Hazael, along with all the gold in the treasuries of the LORD's Temple and the royal palace. So Hazael called off his attack on Jerusalem.

[19]The rest of the events in Joash's reign and all his deeds are recorded in *The Book of the History of the Kings of Judah.* [20]But his officers plotted against him and

11:21 Hebrew *Jehoash,* a variant name for Joash. 12:1 Hebrew *Jehoash,* a variant name for Joash; also in 12:2, 4, 6, 7, 18.

assassinated him at Beth-millo on the road to Silla.
21The assassins were Jozabad son of Shimeath and
Jehozabad son of Shomer—both trusted advisers. Joash was buried with his ancestors in the City of David.
Then his son Amaziah became the next king.

## CHAPTER 13 JEHOAHAZ RULES ISRAEL.

Jehoahaz
son of Jehu began to rule over Israel in the twenty-
third year of King Joash's reign in Judah. He reigned
in Samaria seventeen years. 2But he did what was evil
in the LORD's sight. He followed the example of
Jeroboam son of Nebat, continuing the sins of idolatry that Jeroboam son of Nebat had led Israel to
commit. 3So the LORD was very angry with Israel, and
he allowed King Hazael of Aram and his son Ben-
hadad to defeat them time after time.
4Then Jehoahaz prayed for the LORD's help, and
the LORD heard his prayer. The LORD could see how
terribly the king of Aram was oppressing Israel. 5So
the LORD raised up a deliverer to rescue the Israelites
from the tyranny of the Arameans. Then Israel lived
in safety again as they had in former days. 6But they
continued to sin, following the evil example of Jeroboam. They even set up an Asherah pole in Samaria.
7Finally, Jehoahaz's army was reduced to fifty
mounted troops, ten chariots, and ten thousand foot
soldiers. The king of Aram had killed the others like
they were dust under his feet.
8The rest of the events in Jehoahaz's reign and all
his deeds, including the extent of his power, are
recorded in *The Book of the History of the Kings of
Israel.* 9When Jehoahaz died, he was buried in Samaria with his ancestors. Then his son Jehoash*
became the next king.
10Jehoash son of Jehoahaz began to rule over Israel
in the thirty-seventh year of King Joash's reign in
Judah. He reigned in Samaria sixteen years. 11But he
did what was evil in the LORD's sight. He refused to
turn from the sins of idolatry that Jeroboam son of
Nebat had led Israel to commit. 12The rest of the
events in Jehoash's reign and all his deeds, including
the extent of his power and his war with King Amaziah of Judah, are recorded in *The Book of the History
of the Kings of Israel.* 13When Jehoash died, he was
buried with his ancestors in Samaria. Then his son
Jeroboam II became the next king.
14When Elisha was in his last illness, King Jehoash
of Israel visited him and wept over him. "My father!
My father! The chariots and charioteers of Israel!" he
cried.
15Elisha told him, "Get a bow and some arrows."
And the king did as he was told.
16Then Elisha told the king of Israel to put his
hand on the bow, and Elisha laid his own hands on
the king's hands. 17Then he commanded, "Open
that eastern window," and he opened it. Then he
said, "Shoot!" So he did.
Then Elisha proclaimed, "This is the LORD's arrow,
full of victory over Aram, for you will completely
conquer the Arameans at Aphek. 18Now pick up the
other arrows and strike them against the ground." So
the king picked them up and struck the ground three
times. 19But the man of God was angry with him.
"You should have struck the ground five or six
times!" he exclaimed. "Then you would have beaten
Aram until they were entirely destroyed. Now you
will be victorious only three times."
20Then Elisha died and was buried.
Groups of Moabite raiders used to invade the land
each spring. 21Once when some Israelites were burying a man, they spied a band of these raiders. So they
hastily threw the body they were burying into the
tomb of Elisha. But as soon as the body touched
Elisha's bones, the dead man revived and jumped to
his feet!
22King Hazael of Aram had oppressed Israel during the entire reign of King Jehoahaz. 23But the LORD
was gracious to the people of Israel, and they were
not totally destroyed. He pitied them because of his
covenant with Abraham, Isaac, and Jacob. And to
this day he still has not completely destroyed them
or banished them from his presence.
24King Hazael of Aram died, and his son Ben-
hadad became the next king. 25Then Jehoash son of
Jehoahaz recaptured from Ben-hadad son of Hazael
the towns that Hazael had taken from Jehoash's
father, Jehoahaz. Jehoash defeated Ben-hadad on
three occasions, and so recovered the Israelite towns.

## CHAPTER 14 AMAZIAH RULES JUDAH.

Amaziah son
of Joash began to rule over Judah in the second year
of the reign of King Jehoash* of Israel. 2Amaziah was
twenty-five years old when he became king, and he
reigned in Jerusalem twenty-nine years. His mother
was Jehoaddin, from Jerusalem. 3Amaziah did what
was pleasing in the LORD's sight, but not like his
ancestor David. Instead, he followed the example of
his father, Joash. 4Amaziah did not destroy the pagan
shrines, where the people offered sacrifices and
burned incense.

### YES! ● ● ● • •

13:4-6 **The Lord heard Jehoahaz's prayer for help. God delayed his judgment on Israel when they turned to him for help, but they did not sustain their dependence on God for long. Although there were periodic breaks in their idol worship, there was rarely evidence of genuine faith. It is not enough to say no to sin; we must also say yes to a life of commitment to God.**

### PARTIAL VICTORY ● ● ● • •

13:15-19 **When Jehoash was told to strike the ground with the arrows, he did it only halfheartedly. As a result, Elisha told him that his victory over Aram would not be complete. Receiving the full benefits of God's plan for our life requires full receptiveness of and obedience to God's commands. If we don't follow God's complete instructions, we should not be surprised if his full benefits and blessings are not present.**

**13:9** Hebrew *Joash,* a variant name for Jehoash; also in 13:10, 12, 13, 14, 25. **14:1** Hebrew *Joash,* a variant name for Jehoash; also in 14:13, 23, 27.

[5]When Amaziah was well established as king, he executed the men who had assassinated his father. [6]However, he did not kill the children of the assassins, for he obeyed the command of the LORD written in the Book of the Law of Moses: "Parents must not be put to death for the sins of their children, nor the children for the sins of their parents. Those worthy of death must be executed for their own crimes."*

**RICH ● ● ● • •**

14:28 **Jeroboam had no devotion to God, yet under his warlike policies and skillful administration Israel enjoyed power and prosperity. The prophets Amos and Hosea, however, tell us what was really happening within the kingdom (Hosea 13:4-8; Amos 6:11-13). Jeroboam's administration ignored policies of justice, so the rich became richer and the poor, poorer. The rich people grew self-centered; the poor grew discouraged. If you are experiencing prosperity, remember that God holds us accountable for how we attain success and how we use our wealth.**

[7]It was Amaziah who killed ten thousand Edomites in the Valley of Salt. He also conquered Sela and changed its name to Joktheel, as it is called to this day.

[8]One day Amaziah sent this challenge to Israel's king Jehoash, the son of Jehoahaz and grandson of Jehu: "Come and meet me in battle!"

[9]But King Jehoash of Israel replied to King Amaziah of Judah with this story: "Out in the Lebanon mountains a thistle sent a message to a mighty cedar tree: 'Give your daughter in marriage to my son.' But just then a wild animal came by and stepped on the thistle, crushing it! [10]You have indeed destroyed Edom and are very proud about it. Be content with your victory and stay at home! Why stir up trouble that will bring disaster on you and the people of Judah?"

[11]But Amaziah refused to listen, so King Jehoash of Israel mobilized his army against King Amaziah of Judah. The two armies drew up their battle lines at Beth-shemesh in Judah. [12]Judah was routed by the army of Israel, and its army scattered and fled for home. [13]King Jehoash of Israel captured King Amaziah of Judah at Beth-shemesh and marched on to Jerusalem. Then Jehoash ordered his army to demolish six hundred feet* of Jerusalem's wall, from the Ephraim Gate to the Corner Gate. [14]He carried off all the gold and silver and all the utensils from the Temple of the LORD, as well as from the palace treasury. He also took hostages and returned to Samaria.

[15]The rest of the events in Jehoash's reign, including the extent of his power and his war with King Amaziah of Judah, are recorded in *The Book of the History of the Kings of Israel.* [16]When Jehoash died, he was buried with his ancestors in Samaria. Then his son Jeroboam II became the next king.

[17]King Amaziah of Judah lived on for fifteen years after the death of King Jehoash of Israel. [18]The rest of the events in Amaziah's reign are recorded in *The Book of the History of the Kings of Judah.* [19]There was a conspiracy against Amaziah's life in Jerusalem, and he fled to Lachish. But his enemies sent assassins after him, and they killed him there. [20]They brought him back to Jerusalem on a horse, and he was buried with his ancestors in the City of David.

[21]The people of Judah then crowned Amaziah's sixteen-year-old son, Uzziah,* as their next king. [22]After his father's death, Uzziah rebuilt the town of Elath and restored it to Judah.

[23]Jeroboam II, the son of Jehoash, began to rule over Israel in the fifteenth year of King Amaziah's reign in Judah. Jeroboam reigned in Samaria forty-one years. [24]He did what was evil in the LORD's sight. He refused to turn from the sins of idolatry that Jeroboam son of Nebat had led Israel to commit. [25]Jeroboam II recovered the territories of Israel between Lebo-hamath and the Dead Sea,* just as the LORD, the God of Israel, had promised through Jonah son of Amittai, the prophet from Gath-hepher. [26]For the LORD saw the bitter suffering of everyone in Israel, and how they had absolutely no one to help them. [27]And because the LORD had not said he would blot out the name of Israel completely, he used Jeroboam II, the son of Jehoash, to save them.

[28]The rest of the events in the reign of Jeroboam II and all his deeds, including the extent of his power, his wars, and how he recovered for Israel both Damascus and Hamath, which had belonged to Judah,* are recorded in *The Book of the History of the Kings of Israel.* [29]When Jeroboam II died, he was buried with his ancestors, the kings of Israel. Then his son Zechariah became the next king.

## CHAPTER **15**

**UZZIAH RULES JUDAH.** Uzziah* son of Amaziah began to rule over Judah in the twenty-seventh year of the reign of King Jeroboam II of Israel. [2]He was sixteen years old when he became king, and he reigned in Jerusalem fifty-two years. His mother was Jecoliah, from Jerusalem. [3]He did what was pleasing in the LORD's sight, just as his father, Amaziah, had done. [4]But he did not destroy the pagan shrines, where the people offered sacrifices and burned incense. [5]The LORD struck the king with

**MODELS ● ● ● • •**

15:4 **Although Uzziah accomplished a great deal, he failed to destroy the high places in Judah where the people worshiped idols, just as his father (Amaziah) and grandfather (Joash) had failed to do. Uzziah imitated the kings he had heard stories about and watched while growing up. Although Uzziah's father and grandfather were basically good kings, they were poor models in some important areas. To rise above the influence of poor models, we must find better ones. Christ provides a perfect model. No matter how you were raised or who influenced your life, you can move beyond those limitations by taking Christ as your example and consciously trying to live as he did.**

14:6 Deut 24:16. 14:13 Hebrew *400 cubits* [180 meters]. 14:21 Hebrew *Azariah,* a variant name for Uzziah. 14:25 Hebrew *the sea of the Arabah.* 14:28 Or *to Yaudi.* 15:1 Hebrew *Azariah,* a variant name for Uzziah; also in 15:6, 7, 8, 17, 23, 27.

leprosy,* which lasted until the day of his death; he lived in a house by himself. The king's son Jotham was put in charge of the royal palace, and he governed the people of the land.

[6]The rest of the events in Uzziah's reign and all his deeds are recorded in *The Book of the History of the Kings of Judah.* [7]When Uzziah died, he was buried near his ancestors in the City of David. Then his son Jotham became the next king.

[8]Zechariah son of Jeroboam II began to rule over Israel in the thirty-eighth year of King Uzziah's reign in Judah. He reigned in Samaria six months. [9]Zechariah did what was evil in the LORD's sight, as his ancestors had done. He refused to turn from the sins of idolatry that Jeroboam son of Nebat had led Israel to commit. [10]Then Shallum son of Jabesh conspired against Zechariah, assassinated him in public,* and became the next king. [11]The rest of the events in Zechariah's reign are recorded in *The Book of the History of the Kings of Israel.* [12]So the LORD's message to Jehu came true: "Your descendants will be kings of Israel down to the fourth generation."

[13]Shallum son of Jabesh began to rule over Israel in the thirty-ninth year of King Uzziah's reign in Judah. Shallum reigned in Samaria only one month. [14]Then Menahem son of Gadi went to Samaria from Tirzah and assassinated him, and he became the next king. [15]The rest of the events in Shallum's reign, including his conspiracy, are recorded in *The Book of the History of the Kings of Israel.*

[16]At that time Menahem destroyed the town of Tappuah* and all the surrounding countryside as far as Tirzah, because its citizens refused to surrender the town. He killed the entire population and ripped open the pregnant women.

[17]Menahem son of Gadi began to rule over Israel in the thirty-ninth year of King Uzziah's reign in Judah. He reigned in Samaria ten years. [18]But Menahem did what was evil in the LORD's sight. During his entire reign, he refused to turn from the sins of idolatry that Jeroboam son of Nebat had led Israel to commit. [19]Then King Tiglath-pileser* of Assyria invaded the land. But Menahem paid him thirty-seven tons* of silver to gain his support in tightening his grip on royal power. [20]Menahem extorted the money from the rich of Israel, demanding that each of them pay twenty ounces* of silver in the form of a special tax. So the king of Assyria turned from attacking Israel and did not stay in the land. [21]The rest of the events in Menahem's reign and all his deeds are recorded in *The Book of the History of the Kings of Israel.* [22]When Menahem died, his son Pekahiah became the next king.

[23]Pekahiah son of Menahem began to rule over Israel in the fiftieth year of King Uzziah's reign in Judah. He reigned in Samaria two years. [24]But Pekahiah did what was evil in the LORD's sight. He refused to turn from the sins of idolatry that Jeroboam son of Nebat had led Israel to commit.

[25]Then Pekah son of Remaliah, the commander of Pekahiah's army, conspired against him. With fifty men from Gilead, Pekah assassinated the king, along with Argob and Arieh, in the citadel of the palace at Samaria. Pekah then became the next king of Israel. [26]The rest of the events in Pekahiah's reign and all his deeds are recorded in *The Book of the History of the Kings of Israel.*

## INFLUENCE ● ● • • •

15:8 **Zechariah was an evil king because he encouraged Israel to sin by worshiping idols. Sin in our own lives is serious, but even more terrible than sinning ourselves is encouraging others to disobey God. We are responsible for the way we influence others. Beware of double sins: ones that not only hurt us, but also hurt others by encouraging them to sin.**

[27]Pekah son of Remaliah began to rule over Israel in the fifty-second year of King Uzziah's reign in Judah. He reigned in Samaria twenty years. [28]But Pekah did what was evil in the LORD's sight. He refused to turn from the sins of idolatry that Jeroboam son of Nebat had led Israel to commit. [29]During his reign, King Tiglath-pileser of Assyria attacked Israel again, and he captured the towns of Ijon, Abel-beth-maacah, Janoah, Kedesh, and Hazor. He also conquered the regions of Gilead, Galilee, and Naphtali, and he took the people to Assyria as captives. [30]Then Hoshea son of Elah conspired against Pekah and assassinated him. He began to rule over Israel in the twentieth year of Jotham son of Uzziah. [31]The rest of the events in Pekah's reign and all his deeds are recorded in *The Book of the History of the Kings of Israel.*

[32]Jotham son of Uzziah began to rule over Judah in the second year of King Pekah's reign in Israel. [33]He was twenty-five years old when he became king, and he reigned in Jerusalem sixteen years. His mother was Jerusha, the daughter of Zadok.

[34]Jotham did what was pleasing in the LORD's sight, just as his father Uzziah had done. [35]But he did not destroy the pagan shrines, where the people offered sacrifices and burned incense. He was the one who rebuilt the upper gate of the Temple of the LORD.

## PRIORITY ● ● • • •

15:34-35 **Much good can be said of Jotham and his reign as king of Judah, but he failed in a most critical area: he didn't destroy the pagan shrines where the people worshiped idols, although leaving them clearly violated the first commandment (Exodus 20:3). Like Jotham, we may live a basically good life and yet miss doing what is most important. A lifetime of doing good is not enough if we make the crucial mistake of not following God with all our heart. A true follower of God puts him first in all areas of life.**

15:5 Or *with a contagious skin disease.* The Hebrew word used here and throughout this passage can describe various skin diseases. 15:10 Or *at Ibleam.* 15:16 As in some Greek manuscripts; Hebrew reads *Tiphsah.* 15:19a Hebrew *Pul,* another name for Tiglath-pileser. 15:19b Hebrew *1,000 talents* [34 metric tons]. 15:20 Hebrew *50 shekels* [570 grams].

[36]The rest of the events in Jotham's reign and all his deeds are recorded in *The Book of the History of the Kings of Judah.* [37]In those days the LORD began to send King Rezin of Aram and King Pekah of Israel to attack Judah. [38]When Jotham died, he was buried with his ancestors in the City of David. Then his son Ahaz became the next king.

## CHAPTER 16

**AHAZ RULES JUDAH.** Ahaz son of Jotham began to rule over Judah in the seventeenth year of King Pekah's reign in Israel. [2]Ahaz was twenty years old when he became king, and he reigned in Jerusalem sixteen years. He did not do what was pleasing in the sight of the LORD his God, as his ancestor David had done. [3]Instead, he followed the example of the kings of Israel, even sacrificing his own son in the fire.* He imitated the detestable practices of the pagan nations the LORD had driven from the land ahead of the Israelites. [4]He offered sacrifices and burned incense at the pagan shrines and on the hills and under every green tree.

[5]Then King Rezin of Aram and King Pekah of Israel declared war on Ahaz. They besieged Jerusalem but did not conquer it. [6]At that time the king of Edom* recovered the town of Elath for Edom.* He drove out the people of Judah and sent Edomites* to live there, as they do to this day.

[7]King Ahaz sent messengers to King Tiglath-pileser of Assyria with this message: "I am your servant and your vassal.* Come up and rescue me from the attacking armies of Aram and Israel." [8]Then Ahaz took the silver and gold from the Temple of the LORD and the palace treasury and sent it as a gift to the Assyrian king. [9]So the Assyrians attacked the Aramean capital of Damascus and led its population away as captives, resettling them in Kir. They also killed King Rezin.

### CALLOUS WORSHIP ● ● • • •

16:10-16 **Evil King Ahaz copied heathen religious customs, changed the Temple services, and used the Temple altar for his personal benefit. In so doing, he demonstrated a callous disregard for God's commands. We condemn Ahaz for his action, but we do the same thing if we try to mold God's message to fit our personal preferences. We must worship God for who he is, not what we would selfishly like him to be.**

[10]King Ahaz then went to Damascus to meet with King Tiglath-pileser of Assyria. While he was there, he noticed an unusual altar. So he sent a model of the altar to Uriah the priest, along with its design in full detail. [11]Uriah built an altar just like it by following the king's instructions, and it was ready for the king when he returned from Damascus. [12]When the king returned, he inspected the altar and made offerings on it. [13]The king presented a burnt offering and a grain offering, poured a drink offering over it, and sprinkled the blood of peace offerings on it.

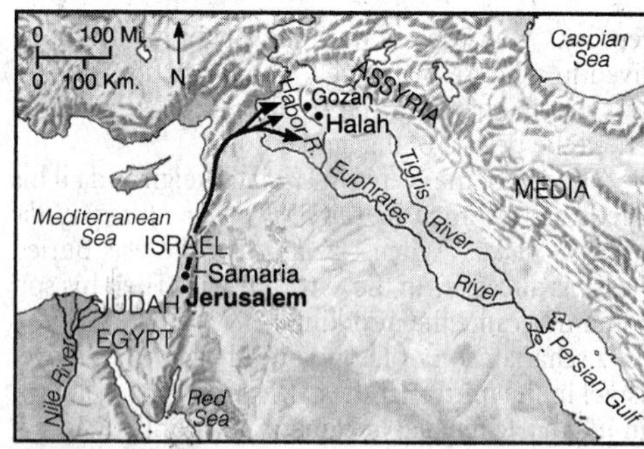


**ISRAEL TAKEN CAPTIVE**
Finally the sins of Israel's people caught up with them. God allowed Assyria to defeat and disperse the people. They were led into captivity, swallowed up by the mighty, evil Assyrian empire. Sin always brings discipline, and the consequences of that sin are sometimes irreversible.

[14]Then King Ahaz removed the old bronze altar from the front of the LORD's Temple, which had stood between the entrance and the new altar, and placed it on the north side of the new altar. [15]He said to Uriah the priest, "Use the new altar for the morning sacrifices of burnt offering, the evening grain offering, the king's burnt offering and grain offering, and the offerings of the people, including their drink offerings. The blood from the burnt offerings and sacrifices should be sprinkled over the new altar. The old bronze altar will be only for my personal use." [16]Uriah the priest did just as King Ahaz instructed him.

[17]Then the king removed the side panels and basins from the portable water carts. He also removed the Sea from the backs of the bronze oxen and placed it on the stone pavement. [18]In deference to the king of Assyria, he also removed the canopy that had been constructed inside the palace for use on the Sabbath day,* as well as the king's outer entrance to the Temple of the LORD.

[19]The rest of the events in Ahaz's reign and his deeds are recorded in *The Book of the History of the Kings of Judah.* [20]When Ahaz died, he was buried with his ancestors in the City of David. Then his son Hezekiah became the next king.

## CHAPTER 17

**ISRAEL IS TAKEN INTO CAPTIVITY.** Hoshea son of Elah began to rule over Israel in the twelfth year of King Ahaz's reign in Judah. He reigned in Samaria nine years. [2]He did what was evil in the LORD's sight, but not as much as the kings of Israel who ruled before him.

[3]King Shalmaneser of Assyria attacked and defeated King Hoshea, so Israel was forced to pay heavy annual tribute to Assyria. [4]Then Hoshea conspired against the king of Assyria by asking King So of Egypt* to help him shake free of Assyria's power and by refusing to pay the annual tribute to Assyria. When the king of Assyria

16:3 Or *even making his son pass through the fire.* **16:6a** As in Latin Vulgate; Hebrew reads *Rezin king of Aram.* **16:6b** As in Latin Vulgate; Hebrew reads *Aram.* **16:6c** As in marginal *Qere* reading of the Masoretic Text, Greek version, and Latin Vulgate; Hebrew reads *Arameans.* **16:7** Hebrew *your son.* **16:18** The meaning of the Hebrew is uncertain. **17:4** Or *by asking the king of Egypt at Sais.*

discovered this treachery, he arrested him and put him in prison for his rebellion.

[5]Then the king of Assyria invaded the entire land, and for three years he besieged Samaria. [6]Finally, in the ninth year of King Hoshea's reign, Samaria fell, and the people of Israel were exiled to Assyria. They were settled in colonies in Halah, along the banks of the Habor River in Gozan, and among the cities of the Medes.

[7]This disaster came upon the nation of Israel because the people worshiped other gods, sinning against the LORD their God, who had brought them safely out of their slavery in Egypt. [8]They had imitated the practices of the pagan nations the LORD had driven from the land before them, as well as the practices the kings of Israel had introduced. [9]The people of Israel had also secretly done many things that were not pleasing to the LORD their God. They built pagan shrines for themselves in all their towns, from the smallest outpost to the largest walled city. [10]They set up sacred pillars and Asherah poles at the top of every hill and under every green tree. [11]They burned incense at the shrines, just like the nations the LORD had driven from the land ahead of them. So the people of Israel had done many evil things, arousing the LORD's anger. [12]Yes, they worshiped idols, despite the LORD's specific and repeated warnings. [13]Again and again the LORD had sent his prophets and seers to warn both Israel and Judah: "Turn from all your evil ways. Obey my commands and laws, which are contained in the whole law that I commanded your ancestors and which I gave you through my servants the prophets."

[14]But the Israelites would not listen. They were as stubborn as their ancestors and refused to believe in the LORD their God. [15]They rejected his laws and the covenant he had made with their ancestors, and they despised all his warnings. They worshiped worthless idols and became worthless themselves. They followed the example of the nations around them, disobeying the LORD's command not to imitate them. [16]They defied all the commands of the LORD their God and made two calves from metal. They set up an Asherah pole and worshiped Baal and all the forces of heaven. [17]They even sacrificed their own sons and daughters in the fire.* They consulted fortune-tellers and used sorcery and sold themselves to evil, arousing the LORD's anger.

[18]And because the LORD was angry, he swept them from his presence. Only the tribe of Judah remained in the land. [19]But even the people of Judah refused to obey the commands of the LORD their God. They walked down the same evil paths that Israel had established. [20]So the LORD rejected all the descendants of Israel. He punished them by handing them over to their attackers until they were destroyed. [21]For when the LORD tore Israel away from the kingdom of David, they chose Jeroboam son of Nebat as their king. Then Jeroboam drew Israel away from following the LORD and made them commit a great sin. [22]And the people of Israel persisted in all the evil

## COPYING ● ● • • •

**17:7-17 The Lord judged the people of Israel because they copied the evil customs of the surrounding nations, worshiping false gods, accommodating heathen customs, and following their own desires. It is not safe to copy the world's customs, because godless people tend to live selfishly. And to live for yourself, as Israel learned, brings serious consequences from God. Sometimes it is difficult and painful to follow God, but consider the alternative. You can live for God, or die for yourself. Determine to be God's person and do what he says regardless of the cost. What God thinks of you is infinitely more important than what the world thinks. (See Romans 12:1-2; 1 John 2:15-17.)**

ways of Jeroboam. They did not turn from these sins of idolatry [23]until the LORD finally swept them away, just as all his prophets had warned would happen. So Israel was carried off to the land of Assyria, where they remain to this day.

[24]And the king of Assyria transported groups of people from Babylon, Cuthah, Avva, Hamath, and Sepharvaim and resettled them in the towns of Samaria, replacing the people of Israel. So the Assyrians took over Samaria and the other towns of Israel. [25]But since these foreign settlers did not worship the LORD when they first arrived, the LORD sent lions among them to kill some of them.

[26]So a message was sent to the king of Assyria: "The people whom you have resettled in the towns of Israel* do not know how to worship the God of the land. He has sent lions among them to destroy them because they have not worshiped him correctly."

[27]The king of Assyria then commanded, "Send one of the exiled priests from Samaria back to Israel. Let him teach the new residents the religious customs of the God of the land." [28]So one of the priests who had been exiled from Samaria returned to Bethel and taught the new residents how to worship the LORD.

[29]But these various groups of foreigners also continued to worship their own gods. In town after town where they lived, they placed their idols at the pagan shrines that the people of Israel had built. [30]Those from Babylon worshiped idols of their god Succoth-benoth. Those from Cuthah worshiped their god Nergal. And those from Hamath worshiped Ashima. [31]The Avvites worshiped their gods Nibhaz and Tartak. And the people from Sepharvaim even burned their own children as sacrifices to Adrammelech and Anammelech.

## GOOD LUCK CHARMS ● ● • • •

**17:27-29 The new settlers in Israel worshiped God without giving up their heathen customs. They worshiped God to appease him rather than to please him, treating him as a good luck charm or just another idol to add to their collection. A similar attitude is common today. Many people claim to believe in God while refusing to give up attitudes and actions that God denounces. God cannot be added to the values we already have. He must come first, and his Word must shape all our actions and attitudes.**

**17:17** Or *They even made their sons and daughters pass through the fire.* **17:26** Hebrew *of Samaria;* also in 17:29.

**Hezekiah trusted in the LORD, the God of Israel.**

2 KINGS 18:5

*There was never another king like him.*

32These new residents worshiped the LORD, but they
appointed from among themselves priests to offer
sacrifices at the pagan shrines. 33And though they worshiped the LORD, they continued to follow the religious customs of the nations from which they came.
34And this is still going on among them today. They
follow their former practices instead of truly worshiping the LORD and obeying the laws, regulations, instructions, and commands he gave the descendants of
Jacob, whose name he changed to Israel. 35For the
LORD had made a covenant with the descendants of
Jacob and commanded them: "Do not worship any
other gods or bow before them or serve them or offer
sacrifices to them. 36Worship only the LORD, who
brought you out of Egypt with such mighty miracles
and power. You must worship him and bow before
him; offer sacrifices to him alone. 37Be careful to obey
all the laws, regulations, instructions, and commands
that he wrote for you. You must not worship any other
gods. 38Do not forget the covenant I made with you,
and do not worship other gods. 39You must worship
only the LORD your God. He is the one who will rescue
you from all your enemies."

40But the people would not listen and continued
to follow their old ways. 41So while these new residents worshiped the LORD, they also worshiped their
idols. And to this day their descendants do the same.

CHAPTER **18** **HEZEKIAH RULES JUDAH.** Hezekiah
son of Ahaz began to rule over Judah in the third
year of King Hoshea's reign in Israel. 2He was
twenty-five years old when he became king, and he
reigned in Jerusalem twenty-nine years. His
mother was Abijah,* the daughter of Zechariah.
3He did what was pleasing in the LORD's sight, just
as his ancestor David had done. 4He removed the
pagan shrines, smashed the sacred pillars, and
knocked down the Asherah poles. He broke up the
bronze serpent that Moses had made, because the
people of Israel had begun to worship it by burning incense to it. The bronze serpent was called
Nehushtan.*

5Hezekiah trusted in the LORD, the God of Israel.
There was never another king like him in the land of
Judah, either before or after his time. 6He remained
faithful to the LORD in everything, and he carefully
obeyed all the commands the LORD had given
Moses. 7So the LORD was with him, and Hezekiah
was successful in everything he did. He revolted
against the king of Assyria and refused to pay him
tribute. 8He also conquered the Philistines as far
distant as Gaza and its territory, from their smallest
outpost to their largest walled city.

9During the fourth year of Hezekiah's reign,
which was the seventh year of King Hoshea's reign
in Israel, King Shalmaneser of Assyria attacked Israel and began a siege on the city of Samaria.
10Three years later, during the sixth year of King
Hezekiah's reign and the ninth year of King Hoshea's reign in Israel, Samaria fell. 11At that time the
king of Assyria deported the Israelites to Assyria
and put them in colonies in Halah, along the
banks of the Habor River in Gozan, and among the
cities of the Medes. 12For they had refused to listen
to the LORD their God. Instead, they had violated
his covenant—all the laws the LORD had given
through his servant Moses.

13In the fourteenth year of King Hezekiah's reign,
King Sennacherib of Assyria came to attack the fortified cities of Judah and conquered them. 14King Hezekiah sent this message to the king of Assyria at
Lachish: "I have done wrong. I will pay whatever
tribute money you demand if you will only go
away." The king of Assyria then demanded a settlement of more than eleven tons of silver and about
one ton of gold.* 15To gather this amount, King
Hezekiah used all the silver stored in the Temple of
the LORD and in the palace treasury. 16Hezekiah even
stripped the gold from the doors of the LORD's
Temple and from the doorposts he had overlaid with
gold, and he gave it all to the Assyrian king.

17Nevertheless the king of Assyria sent his commander in chief, his field commander, and his per-

## IDOL CURE ● ● • • •

18:4 **The bronze serpent had been made to cure the Israelites of a deadly plague (Numbers 21:4-9). It demonstrated God's presence and power and reminded the people of his mercy and forgiveness. But it had become an object of worship instead of a reminder of *whom* to worship, so Hezekiah was forced to destroy it. We must be careful that the things we use to aid our worship don't become objects of worship themselves. Most objects are not made to be idols—they become idols by the way people use them.**

18:2 As in parallel text at 2 Chr 29:1; Hebrew reads *Abi,* a variant name for Abijah. 18:4 *Nehushtan* sounds like the Hebrew terms that mean "snake," "bronze," and "unclean thing." 18:14 Hebrew *300 talents* [10 metric tons] *of silver and 30 talents* [1 metric ton] *of gold.*

sonal representative from Lachish with a huge army to confront King Hezekiah in Jerusalem. The Assyrians stopped beside the aqueduct that feeds water into the upper pool, near the road leading to the field where cloth is bleached.
18They summoned King Hezekiah, but the king sent these officials to meet with them: Eliakim son of Hilkiah, the palace administrator, Shebna the court secretary, and Joah son of Asaph, the royal historian.
19Then the Assyrian king's personal representative sent this message to King Hezekiah:

"This is what the great king of Assyria says: What are you trusting in that makes you so confident?
20Do you think that mere words can substitute for military skill and strength? Which of your allies will give you any military backing against Assyria?
21Will Egypt? If you lean on Egypt, you will find it to be a stick that breaks beneath your weight and pierces your hand. The pharaoh of Egypt is completely unreliable!
22"But perhaps you will say, 'We are trusting in the LORD our God!' But isn't he the one who was insulted by King Hezekiah? Didn't Hezekiah tear down his shrines and altars and make everyone in Judah worship only at the altar here in Jerusalem?
23"I'll tell you what! My master, the king of Assyria, will strike a bargain with you. If you can find two thousand horsemen in your entire army, he will give you two thousand horses for them to ride on!
24With your tiny army, how can you think of challenging even the weakest contingent of my master's troops, even with the help of Egypt's chariots and horsemen*?
25What's more, do you think we have invaded your land without the LORD's direction? The LORD himself told us, 'Go and destroy it!'"

18:24 Or *and charioteers.*

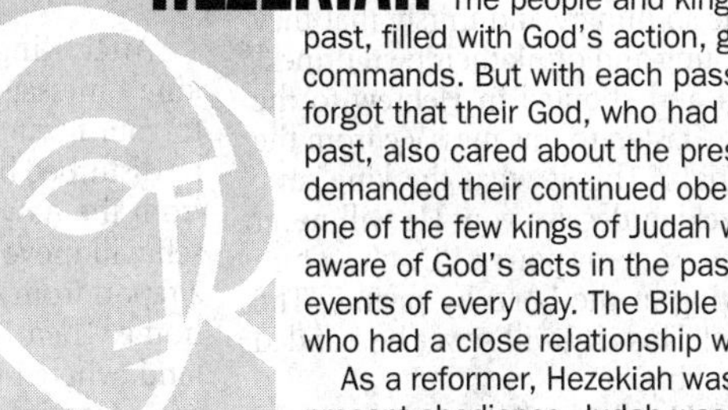

## HEZEKIAH

The people and kings of Judah had a rich past, filled with God's action, guidance, and commands. But with each passing generation, they forgot that their God, who had cared for them in the past, also cared about the present and the future—and demanded their continued obedience. Hezekiah was one of the few kings of Judah who was constantly aware of God's acts in the past and his interest in the events of every day. The Bible describes him as a king who had a close relationship with God.

As a reformer, Hezekiah was most concerned with present obedience. Judah was filled with visual reminders of the people's lack of trust in God, and Hezekiah boldly cleaned house. Altars, idols, and heathen temples were destroyed. Not even the bronze serpent Moses had made in the wilderness was spared—it had become an idol. The temple in Jerusalem, whose doors had been nailed shut by Hezekiah's own father, was cleaned and reopened. The Passover was reinstituted as a national holiday, and there was revival in Judah.

Although he had a natural inclination to respond to present problems, Hezekiah wasn't concerned for the future. He took few actions to preserve the effects of his sweeping reforms. His successful efforts made him proud. His unwise display of wealth to the Babylonian delegation got Judah included on Babylon's "Nations to Conquer" list. When Isaiah told Hezekiah of the foolishness of this, the king answered by saying he was thankful that any evil consequences would be delayed until after he died. And the lives of three kings who followed him—Manasseh, Amon, and Josiah—were deeply affected by both Hezekiah's accomplishments *and* his weaknesses.

The past affects your decisions and actions today, and these, in turn, affect the future. Remember that part of the success of your past will be measured by what you do with it now and how well you use it to prepare for the future.

**UPS:**
- Was the king of Judah who instigated civil and religious reforms
- Had a personal, growing relationship with God
- Devoted to a powerful prayer life
- Noted as the patron of several chapters in the book of Proverbs (Proverbs 25:1)

**DOWNS:**
- Showed little interest or wisdom in planning for the future and protecting for others the spiritual heritage he enjoyed
- Rashly showed all his wealth to messengers from Babylon

**STATS:**
- Where: Jerusalem
- Occupation: 13th king of Judah, the southern kingdom
- Relatives: Father: Ahaz. Mother: Abi. Son: Manasseh.
- Contemporaries: Isaiah, Hoshea, Micah, Sennacherib

LESSONS: Sweeping reforms are short-lived when little action is taken to preserve them for the future

Past obedience to God does not remove the possibility of present disobedience

Complete dependence on God brings amazing results

KEY VERSES: "Hezekiah trusted in the LORD, the God of Israel. There was never another king like him in the land of Judah, either before or after his time. He remained faithful to the LORD in everything, and he carefully obeyed all the commands the LORD had given Moses" (2 Kings 18:5-6).

Hezekiah's story is told in 2 Kings 16:20–20:21; 2 Chronicles 28:27–32:33; Isaiah 36:1–39:8. He is also mentioned in Proverbs 25:1; Isaiah 1:1; Jeremiah 15:4; 26:18-19; Hosea 1:1; Micah 1:1.

26Then Eliakim son of Hilkiah, Shebna, and Joah said to the king's representative, "Please speak to us in Aramaic, for we understand it well. Don't speak in Hebrew, for the people on the wall will hear."

27But Sennacherib's representative replied, "My master wants everyone in Jerusalem to hear this, not just you. He wants them to know that if you do not surrender, this city will be put under siege. The people will become so hungry and thirsty that they will eat their own dung and drink their own urine."

28Then he stood and shouted in Hebrew to the people on the wall, "Listen to this message from the great king of Assyria! 29This is what the king says: Don't let King Hezekiah deceive you. He will never be able to rescue you from my power. 30Don't let him fool you into trusting in the LORD by saying, 'The LORD will rescue us! This city will never be handed over to the Assyrian king.'

31"Don't listen to Hezekiah! These are the terms the king of Assyria is offering: Make peace with me—open the gates and come out. Then I will allow each of you to continue eating from your own garden and drinking from your own well. 32Then I will arrange to take you to another land like this one—a country with bountiful harvests of grain and wine, bread and vineyards, olive trees and honey—a land of plenty. Choose life instead of death!

"Don't listen to Hezekiah when he tries to mislead you by saying, 'The LORD will rescue us!' 33Have the gods of any other nations ever saved their people from the king of Assyria? 34What happened to the gods of Hamath and Arpad? And what about the gods of Sepharvaim, Hena, and Ivvah? Did they rescue Samaria from my power? 35What god of any nation has ever been able to save its people from my power? Name just one! So what makes you think that the LORD can rescue Jerusalem?"

36But the people were silent and did not answer because Hezekiah had told them not to speak. 37Then Eliakim son of Hilkiah, the palace administrator, Shebna the court secretary, and Joah son of Asaph, the royal historian, went back to Hezekiah. They tore their clothes in despair, and they went in to see the king and told him what the Assyrian representative had said.

## CHAPTER 19

**ISAIAH TELLS OF GOD'S PLAN.** When King Hezekiah heard their report, he tore his clothes and put on sackcloth and went into the Temple of the LORD to pray. 2And he sent Eliakim the palace administrator, Shebna the court secretary, and the leading priests, all dressed in sackcloth, to the prophet Isaiah son of Amoz. 3They told him, "This is what King Hezekiah says: This is a day of trouble, insult, and disgrace. It is like when a child is ready to be born, but the mother has no strength to deliver it. 4But perhaps the LORD your God has heard the Assyrian representative defying the living God and will punish him for his words. Oh, pray for those of us who are left!"

19:9 Hebrew *of Cush.*

### PRAYER ● ● • • •

**19:1 Sennacherib, whose armies had captured all the fortified cities of Judah, sent a message telling Hezekiah to surrender because resistance was futile. Realizing the situation was hopeless, Hezekiah went to the Temple and prayed. He knew that God specializes in impossible situations. God answered Hezekiah's prayer and delivered Judah by sending an army to attack the Assyrian capital, forcing Sennacherib to leave at once. Prayer should be our first response in any crisis. Our problems are God's opportunities.**

5After King Hezekiah's officials delivered the king's message to Isaiah, 6the prophet replied, "Say to your master, 'This is what the LORD says: Do not be disturbed by this blasphemous speech against me from the Assyrian king's messengers. 7Listen! I myself will move against him, and the king will receive a report from Assyria telling him that he is needed at home. Then I will make him want to return to his land, where I will have him killed with a sword.'"

8Meanwhile, the Assyrian representative left Jerusalem and went to consult his king, who had left Lachish and was attacking Libnah. 9Soon afterward King Sennacherib received word that King Tirhakah of Ethiopia* was leading an army to fight against him. Before leaving to meet the attack, he sent this message back to Hezekiah in Jerusalem:

10"This message is for King Hezekiah of Judah. Don't let this God you trust deceive you with promises that Jerusalem will not be captured by the king of Assyria. 11You know perfectly well what the kings of Assyria have done wherever they have gone. They have crushed everyone who stood in their way! Why should you be any different? 12Have the gods of other nations rescued them—such nations as Gozan, Haran, Rezeph, and the people of Eden who were in Tel-assar? The former kings of Assyria destroyed them all! 13What happened to the king of Hamath and the king of Arpad? What happened to the kings of Sepharvaim, Hena, and Ivvah?"

14After Hezekiah received the letter and read it, he went up to the LORD's Temple and spread it out before the LORD. 15And Hezekiah prayed this prayer before the LORD: "O LORD, God of Israel, you are enthroned between the mighty cherubim! You alone are God of all the kingdoms of the earth. You alone created the heavens and the earth. 16Listen to me, O LORD, and hear! Open your eyes, O LORD, and see! Listen to Sennacherib's words of defiance against the living God.

17"It is true, LORD, that the kings of Assyria have

### NO FEAR ● ● • • •

**19:15-19 Although Hezekiah came boldly to God, he did not take him for granted or approach him flippantly. Instead, he acknowledged God's sovereignty and Judah's total dependence upon him. Hezekiah's prayer provides a good model for us. We should not be afraid to approach God with our prayers, but we must come to him with respect for who he is and what he can do.**

destroyed all these nations, just as the message says.
[18]And they have thrown the gods of these nations
into the fire and burned them. But of course the
Assyrians could destroy them! They were not gods at
all—only idols of wood and stone shaped by human
hands. [19]Now, O LORD our God, rescue us from his
power; then all the kingdoms of the earth will know
that you alone, O LORD, are God."

[20]Then Isaiah son of Amoz sent this message to
Hezekiah: "This is what the LORD, the God of Israel,
says: I have heard your prayer about King Sennacherib of Assyria. [21]This is the message that the LORD
has spoken against him:

'The virgin daughter of Zion
despises you and laughs at you.
The daughter of Jerusalem
scoffs and shakes her head as you flee.

[22]'Whom do you think you have been insulting
and ridiculing?
Against whom did you raise your voice?
At whom did you look in such proud
condescension?
It was the Holy One of Israel!

[23]By your messengers you have mocked the Lord.
You have said, "With my many chariots
I have conquered the highest mountains—
yes, the remotest peaks of Lebanon.
I have cut down its tallest cedars
and its choicest cypress trees.
I have reached its farthest corners
and explored its deepest forests.

[24]I have dug wells in many a foreign land
and refreshed myself with their water.
I even stopped up the rivers of Egypt
so that my armies could go across!"

[25]'But have you not heard?
It was I, the LORD, who decided this long ago.
Long ago I planned what I am now causing to
happen,
that you should crush fortified cities into
heaps of rubble.

[26]That is why their people have so little power
and are such easy prey for you.
They are as helpless as the grass,
as easily trampled as tender green shoots.
They are like grass sprouting on a housetop,
easily scorched by the sun.

[27]'But I know you well—
your comings and goings and all you do.
I know the way you have raged against me.

[28]And because of your arrogance against me,
which I have heard for myself,
I will put my hook in your nose
and my bridle in your mouth.
I will make you return
by the road on which you came.'"

[29]Then Isaiah said to Hezekiah, "Here is the proof
that the LORD will protect this city from Assyria's
king. This year you will eat only what grows up by
itself, and next year you will eat what springs up
from that. But in the third year you will plant crops
and harvest them; you will tend vineyards and eat
their fruit. [30]And you who are left in Judah, who have
escaped the ravages of the siege, will take root again
in your own soil, and you will flourish and multiply.
[31]For a remnant of my people will spread out from
Jerusalem, a group of survivors from Mount Zion.
The passion of the LORD Almighty will make this
happen!

[32]"And this is what the LORD says about the king of
Assyria: His armies will not enter Jerusalem to shoot
their arrows. They will not march outside its gates with
their shields and build banks of earth against its walls.
[33]The king will return to his own country by the road
on which he came. He will not enter this city, says the
LORD. [34]For my own honor and for the sake of my
servant David, I will defend it."

[35]That night the angel of the LORD went out to the
Assyrian camp and killed 185,000 Assyrian troops.
When the surviving Assyrians* woke up the next
morning, they found corpses everywhere. [36]Then
King Sennacherib of Assyria broke camp and returned to his own land. He went home to his capital
of Nineveh and stayed there. [37]One day while he was
worshiping in the temple of his god Nisroch, his
sons Adrammelech and Sharezer killed him with
their swords. They then escaped to the land of Ararat,
and another son, Esarhaddon, became the next king
of Assyria.

## IN THE MINORITY ● ● • • •

**20:5-6 Over a 100-year period of Judah's history (732-640 B.C.), Hezekiah was the only faithful king; but what a difference he made! Because of Hezekiah's faith and prayer, God healed him and saved his city from the Assyrians. You can make a difference, too, even if your faith puts you in the minority. Faith and prayer, if they are sincere and directed toward the one true God, can bring about change in any situation.**

CHAPTER **20** **HEZEKIAH GETS SICK.** About that
time Hezekiah became deathly ill, and the prophet
Isaiah son of Amoz went to visit him. He gave the
king this message: "This is what the LORD says: Set
your affairs in order, for you are going to die. You will
not recover from this illness."

[2]When Hezekiah heard this, he turned his face to
the wall and prayed to the LORD, [3]"Remember,
O LORD, how I have always tried to be faithful to you
and do what is pleasing in your sight." Then he
broke down and wept bitterly.

[4]But before Isaiah had left the middle courtyard,
this message came to him from the LORD: [5]"Go back
to Hezekiah, the leader of my people. Tell him, 'This
is what the LORD, the God of your ancestor David,
says: I have heard your prayer and seen your tears. I

19:35 Hebrew *When they.*

## OCCULT ● ● ● • •

**21:6 Manasseh was an evil king, and he angered God with his sin. Listed among his sins are occult practices– soothsaying and witchcraft, and consulting spiritists and mediums. God has specific laws against the occult (Leviticus 19:31; Deuteronomy 18:9-13) because it demonstrates a lack of faith in him, involves sinful actions, and opens the door to demonic influences. Today, many books, television shows, and games emphasize fortune-telling, seances, and other occult practices. Don't let desire to know the future or the mistaken belief that superstition is harmless lead you into any occult practices. They are counterfeits of God's power and have as their root a system of beliefs totally opposed to God.**

will heal you, and three days from now you will get out of bed and go to the Temple of the LORD. 6I will add fifteen years to your life, and I will rescue you and this city from the king of Assyria. I will do this to defend my honor and for the sake of my servant David.'"

7Then Isaiah said to Hezekiah's servants, "Make an ointment from figs and spread it over the boil." They did this, and Hezekiah recovered!

8Meanwhile, Hezekiah had said to Isaiah, "What sign will the LORD give to prove that he will heal me and that I will go to the Temple of the LORD three days from now?"

9Isaiah replied, "This is the sign that the LORD will give you to prove he will do as he promised. Would you like the shadow on the sundial to go forward ten steps or backward ten steps?"

10"The shadow always moves forward," Hezekiah replied. "Make it go backward instead." 11So Isaiah asked the LORD to do this, and he caused the shadow to move ten steps backward on the sundial of Ahaz!

12Soon after this, Merodach-baladan son of Baladan, king of Babylon, sent Hezekiah his best wishes and a gift, for he had heard that Hezekiah had been very sick. 13Hezekiah welcomed the Babylonian envoys and showed them everything in his treasure-houses—the silver, the gold, the spices, and the aromatic oils. He also took them to see his armory and showed them all his other treasures—everything! There was nothing in his palace or kingdom that Hezekiah did not show them.

14Then Isaiah the prophet went to King Hezekiah and asked him, "What did those men want? Where were they from?"

Hezekiah replied, "They came from the distant land of Babylon."

15"What did they see in your palace?" Isaiah asked.

"They saw everything," Hezekiah replied. "I showed them everything I own—all my treasures."

16Then Isaiah said to Hezekiah, "Listen to this message from the LORD: 17The time is coming when everything you have—all the treasures stored up by your ancestors—will be carried off to Babylon. Nothing will be left, says the LORD. 18Some of your own descendants will be taken away into exile. They will become eunuchs who will serve in the palace of Babylon's king."

19Then Hezekiah said to Isaiah, "This message you have given me from the LORD is good." But the king was thinking, "At least there will be peace and security during my lifetime."

20The rest of the events in Hezekiah's reign, including the extent of his power and how he built a pool and dug a tunnel to bring water into the city, are recorded in *The Book of the History of the Kings of Judah.* 21When Hezekiah died, his son Manasseh became the next king.

## CHAPTER 21

**MANASSEH RULES JUDAH.** Manasseh was twelve years old when he became king, and he reigned in Jerusalem fifty-five years. His mother was Hephzibah. 2He did what was evil in the LORD's sight, imitating the detestable practices of the pagan nations whom the LORD had driven from the land ahead of the Israelites. 3He rebuilt the pagan shrines his father, Hezekiah, had destroyed. He constructed altars for Baal and set up an Asherah pole, just as King Ahab of Israel had done. He also bowed before all the forces of heaven and worshiped them. 4He even built pagan altars in the Temple of the LORD, the place where the LORD had said his name should be honored. 5He built these altars for all the forces of heaven in both courtyards of the LORD's Temple. 6Manasseh even sacrificed his own son in the fire.* He practiced sorcery and divination, and he consulted with mediums and psychics. He did much that was evil in the LORD's sight, arousing his anger.

7Manasseh even took an Asherah pole he had made and set it up in the Temple, the very place where the LORD had told David and his son Solomon: "My name will be honored here forever in this Temple and in Jerusalem—the city I have chosen from among all the other tribes of Israel. 8If the Israelites will obey my commands—the whole law that was given through my servant Moses—I will not send them into exile from this land that I gave their ancestors." 9But the people refused to listen, and Manasseh led them to do even more evil than the pagan nations whom the LORD had destroyed when the Israelites entered the land.

10Then the LORD said through his servants the prophets: 11"King Manasseh of Judah has done many detestable things. He is even more wicked than the

21:6 Or *even made his son pass through the fire.*

## FUTURE LEADERS ● ● ● • •

**22:1-2 In reading the biblical lists of kings, it is rare to find one who obeyed God completely. Josiah was such a person, and he was only eight years old when he began to reign. For 18 years he reigned obediently; then, when he was 26, he began the reforms based on God's laws. Children are the future leaders of our churches and our world. A person's major work for God may have to wait until he is an adult, but no one is ever too young to take God seriously and obey him. Josiah's early years laid the base for his later task of reforming Judah.**

Amorites, who lived in this land before Israel. He has
led the people of Judah into idolatry. [12]So this is what
the LORD, the God of Israel, says: I will bring such
disaster on Jerusalem and Judah that the ears of
those who hear about it will tingle with horror. [13]I
will judge Jerusalem by the same standard I used for
Samaria and by the same measure I used for the
family of Ahab. I will wipe away the people of Jerusalem as one wipes a dish and turns it upside down.
[14]Then I will reject even those few of my people who
are left, and I will hand them over as plunder for
their enemies. [15]For they have done great evil in my
sight and have angered me
ever since their ancestors
came out of Egypt."

[16]Manasseh also murdered
many innocent people until
Jerusalem was filled from
one end to the other with
innocent blood. This was in
addition to the sin that he
caused the people of Judah
to commit, leading them to
do evil in the LORD's sight.

[17]The rest of the events in
Manasseh's reign and all
his deeds, including the
sins he committed, are recorded in *The Book of the
History of the Kings of Judah.*
[18]When Manasseh died, he
was buried in the palace garden, the garden of Uzza.
Then his son Amon became
the next king.

[19]Amon was twenty-two
years old when he became
king, and he reigned in Jerusalem two years. His mother
was Meshullemeth, the
daughter of Haruz from Jotbah. [20]He did what was evil
in the LORD's sight, just as
his father, Manasseh, had
done. [21]He followed the example of his father, worshiping the same idols that
his father had worshiped.
[22]He abandoned the LORD,
the God of his ancestors,
and he refused to follow the
LORD's ways.

[23]Then Amon's own servants plotted against him
and assassinated him in his
palace. [24]But the people of
the land killed all those who
had conspired against King
Amon, and they made his
son Josiah the next king.

[25]The rest of the events in
Amon's reign and all his deeds are recorded in *The
Book of the History of the Kings of Judah.* [26]He was
buried in his tomb in the garden of Uzza. Then his
son Josiah became the next king.

CHAPTER **22** **JOSIAH BECOMES KING.** Josiah was
eight years old when he became king, and he reigned
in Jerusalem thirty-one years. His mother was Jedidah, the daughter of Adaiah from Bozkath. [2]He did
what was pleasing in the LORD's sight and followed
the example of his ancestor David. He did not turn
aside from doing what was right.

## JOSIAH

Most children have big dreams of what they want to be when they grow up. Few of them get the chance Josiah had to become a king at age eight! Young King Josiah was different in other ways, too. He was not at all like his father or grandfather, who had both been very evil rulers. But he reminded many of his great-grandfather Hezekiah. They both had close, personal relationships with God.

At a young age, Josiah already understood that there was spiritual sickness in his land. In a sense, Josiah began his search for God by destroying and cleaning up whatever he found that didn't belong to the worship of the true God. Along the way, God's Word, the scrolls containing God's law, was rediscovered. For Josiah, it was better than finding a hidden treasure map. His reaction makes us realize how often we take God's Word for granted.

As the scroll of God's law was read to Josiah, he was shocked, frightened, and humbled. He realized that he and the nation had a long way to go to get right with God. He tried everything he could to help his people know God. Although he changed many things, he couldn't change hearts. On the outside, the people cooperated with Josiah, but there were few changes on the inside.

How would you describe your relationship with God? Would you have to admit that you usually just "go along" with God like the people of Judah? Or are you, like Josiah, deeply humbled by God's Word and anxious to do what he wants? Humble obedience pleases God. Outside changes aren't enough. You must allow God's Word to humble you and his Spirit to change your life, both inside and out.

LESSONS: God consistently responds to those who turn from their sins and who have a humble heart

Even sweeping outward reforms are of little lasting value if there are no changes in people's lives

KEY VERSES: "'But a beautiful palace does not make a great king! Why did your father, Josiah, reign so long? Because he was just and right in all his dealings. That is why God blessed him. He made sure that justice and help were given to the poor and needy, and everything went well for him. Isn't that what it means to know me?' asks the LORD" (Jeremiah 22:15-16).

Josiah's story is told in 2 Kings 21:24–23:30; 2 Chronicles 33:25–35:26. He is also mentioned in Jeremiah 1–3; 22:11-17.

**UPS:**
- King of Judah
- Wanted to know God and obey him
- A reformer like his great-grandfather, Hezekiah
- Cleaned out the Temple and revived obedience to God's laws

**DOWN:**
- Became involved in a military conflict that he had been warned against

**STATS:**
- Where: Jerusalem
- Occupation: Eighteenth king of Judah, the southern kingdom
- Relatives: Father: Amon. Mother: Jedidah. Son: Jehoahaz.
- Contemporaries: Jeremiah, Huldah, Hilkiah, Zephaniah

## TURNAROUND ● ● • • •

**22:19 When Josiah realized how corrupt his nation had become, he tore his clothes and wept before God. Then God had mercy on him. Josiah used the customs of his day to show his repentance. When we repent today, we are unlikely to tear our clothing, but weeping, fasting, and making restitution or apologies (if our sin has involved others) are all acts of repentance that demonstrate our sincerity. The hardest part of repentance is changing the behavior that originally produced the sin.**

[3]In the eighteenth year of his reign, King Josiah sent Shaphan son of Azaliah and grandson of Meshullam, the court secretary, to the Temple of the LORD. He told him, [4]"Go up to Hilkiah the high priest and have him count the money the gatekeepers have collected from the people at the LORD's Temple. [5]Entrust this money to the men assigned to supervise the Temple's restoration. Then they can use it to pay workers to repair the Temple of the LORD. [6]They will need to hire carpenters, builders, and masons. Also have them buy the timber and the cut stone needed to repair the Temple. [7]But there will be no need for the construction supervisors to keep account of the money they receive, for they are honest people."

[8]Hilkiah the high priest said to Shaphan the court secretary, "I have found the Book of the Law in the LORD's Temple!" Then Hilkiah gave the scroll to Shaphan, and he read it.

[9]Shaphan returned to the king and reported, "Your officials have given the money collected at the Temple of the LORD to the workers and supervisors at the Temple." [10]Shaphan also said to the king, "Hilkiah the priest has given me a scroll." So Shaphan read it to the king.

[11]When the king heard what was written in the Book of the Law, he tore his clothes in despair. [12]Then he gave these orders to Hilkiah the priest, Ahikam son of Shaphan, Acbor son of Micaiah, Shaphan the court secretary, and Asaiah the king's personal adviser: [13]"Go to the Temple and speak to the LORD for me and for the people and for all Judah. Ask him about the words written in this scroll that has been found. The LORD's anger is burning against us because our ancestors have not obeyed the words in this scroll. We have not been doing what this scroll says we must do."

[14]So Hilkiah the priest, Ahikam, Acbor, Shaphan, and Asaiah went to the newer Mishneh section* of Jerusalem to consult with the prophet Huldah. She was the wife of Shallum son of Tikvah and grandson of Harhas, the keeper of the Temple wardrobe. [15]She said to them, "The LORD, the God of Israel, has spoken! Go and tell the man who sent you, [16]'This is what the LORD says: I will destroy this city and its people, just as I stated in the scroll you read. [17]For my people have abandoned me and worshiped pagan gods, and I am very angry with them for everything they have done. My anger is burning against this place, and it will not be quenched.'

**22:14** Or *the Second Quarter,* a newer section of Jerusalem.

[18]"But go to the king of Judah who sent you to seek the LORD and tell him: 'This is what the LORD, the God of Israel, says concerning the message you have just heard: [19]You were sorry and humbled yourself before the LORD when you heard what I said against this city and its people, that this land would be cursed and become desolate. You tore your clothing in despair and wept before me in repentance. So I have indeed heard you, says the LORD. [20]I will not send the promised disaster against this city until after you have died and been buried in peace. You will not see the disaster I am going to bring on this place.'" So they took her message back to the king.

CHAPTER **23** **JOSIAH OBEYS GOD'S LAW.** Then the king summoned all the leaders of Judah and Jerusalem. [2]And the king went up to the Temple of the LORD with all the people of Judah and Jerusalem, and the priests, and the prophets—all the people from the least to the greatest. There the king read to them the entire Book of the Covenant that had been found in the LORD's Temple. [3]The king took his place of authority beside the pillar and renewed the covenant in the LORD's presence. He pledged to obey the LORD by keeping all his commands, regulations, and laws with all his heart and soul. In this way, he confirmed all the terms of the covenant that were written in the scroll, and all the people pledged themselves to the covenant.

## JUST DO IT! ● ● • • •

**23:4-7 When Josiah realized the terrible state of Judah's religious life, he did something about it. It is not enough to say we believe what is right; we must respond with action, doing what faith requires. This is what James was emphasizing when he wrote, "faith that does not result in good deeds is useless" (James 2:20).**

[4]Then the king instructed Hilkiah the high priest and the leading priests and the Temple gatekeepers to remove from the LORD's Temple all the utensils that were used to worship Baal, Asherah, and all the forces of heaven. The king had all these things burned outside Jerusalem on the terraces of the Kidron Valley, and he carried the ashes away to Bethel. [5]He did away with the pagan priests, who had been appointed by the previous kings of Judah, for they had burned incense at the pagan shrines throughout Judah and even in the vicinity of Jerusalem. They had also offered incense to Baal, and to the sun, the moon, the constellations, and to all the forces of heaven. [6]The king removed the Asherah pole from the LORD's Temple and took it outside Jerusalem to the Kidron Valley, where he burned it. Then he ground the pole to dust and threw the dust in the public cemetery. [7]He also tore down the houses of the shrine prostitutes that were

inside the Temple of the LORD, where the women wove coverings for the Asherah pole.

[8]Josiah brought back to Jerusalem all the priests of the LORD, who were living in other towns of Judah. He also defiled all the pagan shrines, where they had burned incense, from Geba to Beersheba. He destroyed the shrines at the entrance to the gate of Joshua, the governor of Jerusalem. This gate was located to the left of the city gate as one enters the city. [9]The priests who had served at the pagan shrines were not allowed to serve at the LORD's altar in Jerusalem, but they were allowed to eat unleavened bread with the other priests.

[10]Then the king defiled the altar of Topheth in the valley of Ben-hinnom, so no one could ever again use it to sacrifice a son or daughter in the fire* as an offering to Molech. [11]He removed from the entrance of the LORD's Temple the horse statues that the former kings of Judah had dedicated to the sun. They were near the quarters of Nathan-melech the eunuch, an officer of the court. The king also burned the chariots dedicated to the sun.

[12]Josiah tore down the altars that the kings of Judah had built on the palace roof above the upper room of Ahaz. The king destroyed the altars that Manasseh had built in the two courtyards of the LORD's Temple. He smashed them to bits and scattered the pieces in the Kidron Valley. [13]The king also desecrated the pagan shrines east of Jerusalem and south of the Mount of Corruption, where King Solomon of Israel had built shrines for Ashtoreth, the detestable goddess of the Sidonians; and for Chemosh, the detestable god of the Moabites; and for Molech,* the detestable god of the Ammonites. [14]He smashed the sacred pillars and cut down the Asherah poles. Then he desecrated these places by scattering human bones over them.

[15]The king also tore down the altar at Bethel, the pagan shrine that Jeroboam son of Nebat had made when he led Israel into sin. Josiah crushed the stones to dust and burned the Asherah pole. [16]Then as Josiah was looking around, he noticed several tombs in the side of the hill. He ordered that the bones be brought out, and he burned them on the altar at Bethel to desecrate it. This happened just as the LORD had promised through the man of God as Jeroboam stood beside the altar at the festival. Then Josiah turned and looked up at the tomb of the man of God* who had predicted these things. [17]"What is that monument over there?" Josiah asked.

And the people of the town told him, "It is the tomb of the man of God who came from Judah and predicted the very things that you have just done to the altar at Bethel!"

[18]Josiah replied, "Leave it alone. Don't disturb his bones." So they did not burn his bones or those of the old prophet from Samaria.

[19]Then Josiah demolished all the buildings at the pagan shrines in the towns of Samaria, just as he had done at Bethel. They had been built by the various kings of Israel and had made the LORD very angry. [20]He executed the priests of the pagan shrines on their own altars, and he burned human bones on the altars to desecrate them. Finally, he returned to Jerusalem.

[21]King Josiah then issued this order to all the people: "You must celebrate the Passover to the LORD your God, as it is written in the Book of the Covenant." [22]There had not been a Passover celebration like that since the time when the judges ruled in Israel, throughout all the years of the kings of Israel and Judah. [23]This Passover was celebrated to the LORD in Jerusalem during the eighteenth year of King Josiah's reign.

[24]Josiah also exterminated the mediums and psychics, the household gods, and every other kind of idol worship, both in Jerusalem and throughout the land of Judah. He did this in obedience to all the laws written in the scroll that Hilkiah the priest had found in the LORD's Temple. [25]Never before had there been a king like Josiah, who turned to the LORD with all his heart and soul and strength, obeying all the laws of Moses. And there has never been a king like him since.

[26]Even so, the LORD's anger burned against Judah because of all the great evils of King Manasseh, and he did not hold back his fierce anger from them. [27]For the LORD had said, "I will destroy Judah just as I have destroyed Israel. I will banish the people from my presence and reject my chosen city of Jerusalem and the Temple where my name was to be honored."

[28]The rest of the events in Josiah's reign and all his deeds are recorded in *The Book of the History of the Kings of Judah.*

[29]While Josiah was king, Pharaoh Neco, king of Egypt, went to the Euphrates River to help the king of Assyria. King Josiah marched out with his army to fight him, but King Neco killed him when they met at Megiddo. [30]Josiah's officers took his body back in a chariot from Megiddo to Jerusalem and buried him in his own tomb. Then the people anointed his son Jehoahaz and made him the next king.

[31]Jehoahaz was twenty-three years old when he became king, and he reigned in Jerusalem three months. His mother was Hamutal, the daughter of Jeremiah from Libnah. [32]He did what was evil in the LORD's sight, just as his ancestors had done.

### PARTY TIME! ● ● • • •

23:21-23 **When Josiah rediscovered the Passover in the Book of the Covenant, he ordered everyone to observe the ceremonies exactly as prescribed. This Passover celebration was to have been a yearly holiday celebrated in remembrance of the entire nation's deliverance from slavery in Egypt (Exodus 12), but it had not been kept for many years. As a result, "there had not been a Passover celebration like that since the time when the judges ruled in Israel." It is a common misconception that God is against celebration, wanting to take all the fun out of life. In reality, God wants to give us life in its fullness (John 10:10), and those who love him have the most to celebrate.**

23:10 Or *to make a son or daughter pass through the fire.* 23:13 Hebrew *Milcom,* a variant name for Molech. 23:16 As in Greek version; Hebrew lacks *as Jeroboam stood beside the altar at the festival. Then Josiah turned and looked up at the tomb of the man of God.*

33Pharaoh Neco put Jehoahaz in prison at Riblah in the land of Hamath to prevent him from ruling from Jerusalem. He also demanded that Judah pay 7,500 pounds of silver and 75 pounds of gold* as tribute. 34Pharaoh Neco then installed Eliakim, another of Josiah's sons, to reign in place of his father, and he changed Eliakim's name to Jehoiakim. Jehoahaz was taken to Egypt as a prisoner, where he died.

35In order to get the silver and gold demanded as tribute by Pharaoh Neco, Jehoiakim collected a tax from the people of Judah, requiring them to pay in proportion to their wealth.

36Jehoiakim was twenty-five years old when he became king, and he reigned in Jerusalem eleven years. His mother was Zebidah, the daughter of Pedaiah from Rumah. 37He did what was evil in the LORD's sight, just as his ancestors had done.

CHAPTER **24** **JEHOIAKIM AND BABYLON.** During Jehoiakim's reign, King Nebuchadnezzar of Babylon invaded the land of Judah. Jehoiakim surrendered and paid him tribute for three years but then rebelled. 2Then the LORD sent bands of Babylonian,* Aramean, Moabite, and Ammonite raiders against Judah to destroy it, just as the LORD had promised through his prophets. 3These disasters happened to Judah according to the LORD's command. He had decided to remove Judah from his presence because of the many sins of Manasseh. 4He had filled Jerusalem with innocent blood, and the LORD would not forgive this.

5The rest of the events in Jehoiakim's reign and all his deeds are recorded in *The Book of the History of the Kings of Judah.* 6When Jehoiakim died, his son Jehoiachin became the next king. 7The king of Egypt never returned after that, for the king of Babylon occupied the entire area formerly claimed by Egypt—from the brook of Egypt to the Euphrates River.

8Jehoiachin was eighteen years old when he became king, and he reigned in Jerusalem three months. His mother was Nehushta, the daughter of Elnathan from Jerusalem. 9Jehoiachin did what was evil in the LORD's sight, just as his father had done.

10During Jehoiachin's reign, the officers of King Nebuchadnezzar of Babylon came up against Jerusalem and besieged it. 11Nebuchadnezzar himself arrived at the city during the siege. 12Then King Jehoiachin, along with his advisers, nobles, and officials, and the queen mother, surrendered to the Babylonians.

In the eighth year of Nebuchadnezzar's reign, he took Jehoiachin prisoner. 13As the LORD had said beforehand, Nebuchadnezzar carried away all the treasures from the LORD's Temple and the royal palace. They cut apart all the gold vessels that King Solomon of Israel had placed in the Temple. 14King Nebuchadnezzar took ten thousand captives from Jerusalem, including all the princes and the best of

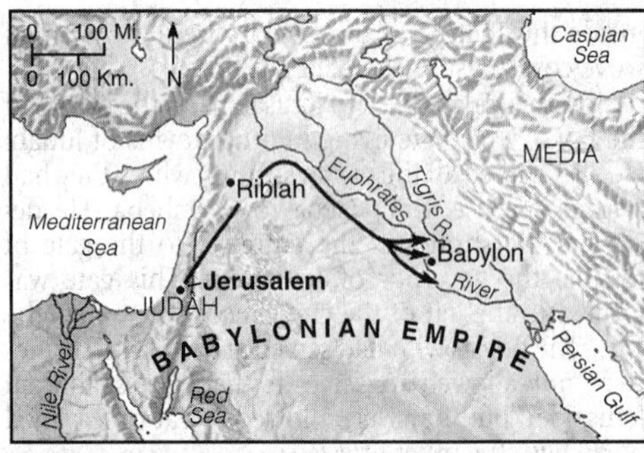


**JUDAH EXILED**
Evil permeated Judah, and God's anger flared against his rebellious people. Babylon conquered Assyria and became the new world power. The Babylonian army marched into Jerusalem, burned the Temple, tore down the city's massive walls, and carried off the people into captivity.

the soldiers, craftsmen, and smiths. So only the poorest people were left in the land.

15Nebuchadnezzar led King Jehoiachin away as a captive to Babylon, along with his wives and officials, the queen mother, and all Jerusalem's elite. 16He also took seven thousand of the best troops and one thousand craftsmen and smiths, all of whom were strong and fit for war. 17Then the king of Babylon installed Mattaniah, Jehoiachin's uncle, as the next king, and he changed Mattaniah's name to Zedekiah.

18Zedekiah was twenty-one years old when he became king, and he reigned in Jerusalem eleven years. His mother was Hamutal, the daughter of Jeremiah from Libnah. 19But Zedekiah did what was evil in the LORD's sight, just as Jehoiakim had done. 20So the LORD, in his anger, finally banished the people of Jerusalem and Judah from his presence and sent them into exile.

Then Zedekiah rebelled against the king of Babylon.

CHAPTER **25** **JERUSALEM GETS DEMOLISHED.** So on January 15,* during the ninth year of Zedekiah's reign, King Nebuchadnezzar of Babylon led his entire army against Jerusalem. They surrounded the city and built siege ramps against its walls. 2Jerusalem was kept under siege until the eleventh year of King Zedekiah's reign.

3By July 18 of Zedekiah's eleventh year,* the famine in the city had become very severe, with the last of the food entirely gone. 4Then a section of the city wall was broken down, and all the soldiers made plans to escape from the city. But since the city was surrounded by the Babylonians,* they waited for nightfall and fled through the gate between the two walls behind the king's gardens. They made a dash across the fields, in the direction of the Jordan Valley.*

**23:33** Hebrew *100 talents* [3.4 metric tons] *of silver and 1 talent* [34 kilograms] *of gold.* **24:2** Or *Chaldean.* **25:1** Hebrew *on the tenth day of the tenth month,* of the Hebrew calendar. A number of events in 2 Kings can be cross-checked with dates in surviving Babylonian records and related accurately to our modern calendar. This event occurred on January 15, 588 B.C. **25:3** Hebrew *By the ninth day,* that is, "of the fourth month of Zedekiah's eleventh year" (compare Jer 52:6 and the note there). This event of the Hebrew lunar calendar occurred on July 18, 586 B.C.; also see note on 25:1. **25:4a** Or *the Chaldeans;* also in 25:5, 13, 25, 26. **25:4b** Hebrew *the Arabah.*

5But the Babylonians chased after them and caught
the king on the plains of Jericho, for by then his men
had all abandoned him. 6They brought him to the
king of Babylon at Riblah, where sentence was passed
against him. 7The king of Babylon made Zedekiah
watch as all his sons were killed. Then they gouged out
Zedekiah's eyes, bound him in bronze chains, and led
him away to Babylon.
8On August 14 of that year,* which was the
nineteenth year of Nebuchadnezzar's reign,
Nebuzaradan, captain of the guard, an official of
the Babylonian king, arrived in Jerusalem. 9He
burned down the Temple of the LORD, the royal
palace, and all the houses of Jerusalem. He destroyed all the important buildings in the city.
10Then the captain of the guard supervised the
entire Babylonian* army as they tore down the
walls of Jerusalem. 11Nebuzaradan, captain of
the guard, then took as exiles those who remained
in the city, along with the rest of the people and the
troops who had declared their allegiance to the
king of Babylon. 12But the captain of the guard
allowed some of the poorest people to stay behind
in Judah to care for the vineyards and fields.
13The Babylonians broke up the bronze pillars,
the bronze water carts, and the bronze Sea that were
at the LORD's Temple, and they carried all the bronze
away to Babylon. 14They also took all the pots, shovels, lamp snuffers, dishes, and all the other bronze
utensils used for making sacrifices at the Temple.
15Nebuzaradan, captain of the guard, also took the
firepans and basins, and all the other utensils made
of pure gold or silver.
16The bronze from the two pillars, the water carts,
and the Sea was too great to be weighed. These things
had been made for the LORD's Temple in the days of
King Solomon. 17Each of the pillars was 27 feet* tall.
The bronze capital on top of each pillar was 7½ feet*
high and was decorated with a network of bronze
pomegranates all the way around.
18The captain of the guard took with him as
prisoners Seraiah the chief priest, his assistant
Zephaniah, and the three chief gatekeepers. 19And
of the people still hiding in the city, he took an
officer of the Judean army, five of the king's personal advisers, the army commander's chief secretary, who was in charge of recruitment, and sixty
other citizens. 20Nebuzaradan the commander
took them all to the king of Babylon at Riblah.
21And there at Riblah, in the land of Hamath, the
king of Babylon had them all put to death. So the
people of Judah were sent into exile from their
land.
22Then King Nebuchadnezzar appointed Gedaliah son of Ahikam and grandson of Shaphan as
governor over the people left in Judah. 23When all
the army commanders and their men learned that

## EARLY WARNINGS ● ● • • •

25:21 **Judah, like Israel, was unfaithful to God. So God, as he had warned, allowed Judah to be destroyed and taken away (Deuteronomy 28). The book of Lamentations records the prophet Jeremiah's sorrow at seeing Jerusalem destroyed. God will fulfill his promises, and he will carry out his warnings. When he speaks words of warning to us, through his Word or through other believers, we need to heed what we are told. To continue in our sin is to invite destruction. Have you received any warnings in your life lately? How will you respond to them?**

the king of Babylon had appointed Gedaliah as governor, they joined him at Mizpah. These included
Ishmael son of Nethaniah, Johanan son of Kareah,
Seraiah son of Tanhumeth the Netophathite, and
Jaazaniah son of the Maacathite, and all their men.
24Gedaliah vowed to them that the Babylonian officials meant them no harm. "Live in the land and serve
the king of Babylon, and all will go well for you," he
promised. 25But in midautumn of that year,* Ishmael
son of Nethaniah and grandson of Elishama, who was
of the royal family, went to Mizpah with ten men and
assassinated Gedaliah and everyone with him, both
Judeans and Babylonians.
26Then all the people of Judah, from the least to
the greatest, as well as the army commanders, fled in
panic to Egypt, for they were afraid of what the
Babylonians would do to them.
27In the thirty-seventh year of King Jehoiachin's
exile in Babylon, Evil-merodach ascended to the
Babylonian throne. He was kind to Jehoiachin and
released him from prison on April 2 of that year.*
28He spoke pleasantly to Jehoiachin and gave him
preferential treatment over all the other exiled
kings in Babylon. 29He supplied Jehoiachin with
new clothes to replace his prison garb and allowed
him to dine at the king's table for the rest of his life.
30The Babylonian king also gave him a regular
allowance to cover his living expenses until the day
of his death.

## STRAIGHTENED OUT ● ● • • •

25:30 **The book of 2 Kings opens with Elijah being carried to heaven—the destination awaiting those who follow God. But the book ends with the people of Judah being carried off to foreign lands as humiliated slaves—the result of failing to follow God.**

**Second Kings is an illustration of what happens when we make anything more important than God, when we make ruinous alliances, when our conscience becomes desensitized to right and wrong, and when we are no longer able to discern God's purpose for our life. We may fail, like the people of Judah and Israel, but God's promises do not. He is always there to help us straighten out our life and start over. And that is just what happens in the book of Ezra. When the people acknowledged their sins, God was ready and willing to help them return to their land and start again.**

**25:8** Hebrew *On the seventh day of the fifth month,* of the Hebrew calendar. This day was August 14, 586 B.C.; also see note on 25:1. **25:10** Or *Chaldean;* also in 25:24. **25:17a** Hebrew *18 cubits* [8.1 meters]. **25:17b** As in parallel texts at 1 Kgs 7:16, 2 Chr 3:15, and Jer 52:22, all of which read *5 cubits* [2.3 meters]; Hebrew reads *3 cubits,* which is 4.5 feet or 1.4 meters. **25:25** Hebrew *in the seventh month,* of the Hebrew calendar. This month occurred in October and November 586 B.C. **25:27** Hebrew *on the twenty-seventh day of the twelfth month,* of the Hebrew calendar. This day was April 2, 561 B.C.; also see note on 25:1.

# MEGA themes

**ELISHA** The purpose of Elisha's ministry was to restore respect for God and his message. Elisha stood firmly against the evil kings of Israel. By faith, with courage and prayer, he revealed not only God's judgment on sin, but also his mercy, love, and tenderness toward faithful people.

Elisha's mighty miracles showed that God controls not only great armies, but also events in everyday life. God's care is not reserved for kings and leaders, but is for all who are willing to follow him. He can perform miracles in our life.

1. If you were writing a letter of reference for Elisha, how would you describe him?
2. What evidence do you find that Elisha had a heart willing to serve God?
3. Can you think of two people you know who have displayed evidence of hearts that were willing to serve God?
4. Who are the people in your life who need to see evidence of this willing heart in you? What can you do to be an example for them? What will you do to be God's living testimony of power to them?

**IDOLATRY** Every evil king in both Israel and Judah encouraged idolatry. These false gods represented war, cruelty, power, and sex; and the people began to take on their characteristics. Although they had God's law, priests, and prophets to guide them, the evil kings sought false priests and prophets whom they could control and manipulate to their own advantage.

An idol is any idea, ability, possession, or person that we regard more highly than God. We condemn Israel and Judah for foolishly worshiping idols, but we also worship other gods—power, money, physical attractiveness, and so on. Behind this "idol" worship is the desire to control our destiny, our pleasure, and other people. Even those who believe in God must resist the lure of these attractive idols.

1. Idols led to great destruction when the kings turned to them. What could have been so attractive about worshiping these idols? What did the kings hope to gain?
2. List just a few of the things in life that can only be supplied by the one true God.
3. With this knowledge in mind, what is it that you think attracts so many young people to idolatry, to replacing the worship of God with the worship of power, pleasure, or possessions?
4. How could you specifically communicate to those around you (without just making an announcement or handing them a Bible) the truth about who God is and that he alone should be worshiped?

**EVIL KINGS/GOOD KINGS** The northern kingdom, Israel, had 19 evil kings and no good ones; the southern kingdom, Judah, had 12 evil kings and 8 good ones. Thus, only 20 percent of all the kings of both kingdoms followed God. The evil kings were shortsighted, thinking that they could control their nation's destiny by importing other religions with their idols, forming alliances with heathen nations and enriching themselves. The good kings had to spend most of their time undoing the evil done by their predecessors.

Although the evil kings led the people into sin, they were not the only ones responsible for the downfall of their nation. The priests, princes, heads of families, and military leaders all had to cooperate with the proposed evil plans and practices in order for them to be carried out. We cannot discharge our responsibility to obey God by blaming our leaders.

1. What qualities did the good kings have in common?
2. What qualities did the evil kings have in common?
3. Contrast the effect the good kings had on the people with the effect the evil kings had.
4. What leaders can you point out as ones who made or are making a good difference in the lives of their followers? What leaders made or are making an evil difference in the lives of their followers?
5. List several ways a Christian young person can choose to be a person of influence in the home, church, school, and community.
6. What choices have you decided to make that wil affect people for God's glory?

**GOD'S PATIENCE** As recorded in Deuteronomy, God told his people that if they obeyed him they would live successfully; if they disobeyed, they would be judged and destroyed. God had been patient with the people for hundreds of years. He sent many prophets, including Elisha, to guide them, and he gave ample warning of coming destruction. But even God's patience has limits.

God is patient with us. In his mercy, he gives us many opportunities to hear his message, turn from sin, and believe in him. But his patience does not mean that he is indifferent to how we live, or that we are free to ignore his warnings. His patience should make us want to come to him now.

1. What does it mean to have patience?
2. Give several examples of God's patience with the Hebrews.
3. What evidence do you see of God's patience in your life?
4. A Christian friend seems to have the attitude that since God is so patient, we do not have to be so concerned about whether or not we sin. Based on 2 Kings, how would you correct the error in this friend's thinking?
5. In view of God's patience, how will you choose to live your life?

**JUDGMENT** Both kingdoms were destroyed as punishment for their sins. After King Solomon's reign, Israel lasted only 209 years before the Assyrians destroyed it; Judah lasted 345 years before the Babylonians conquered Jerusalem. After repeated warnings to his people, God used these evil nations as instruments for his justice.

When we reject God's commands and purpose for our life, the consequences are severe. He will not ignore unbelief or rebellion. To avoid the penalty for sin, we must believe in Christ and accept his sacrificial death on our behalf, or we will be judged. Having accepted Christ, we must still remain sensitive and responsive to God's will.

1. Would you describe God's discipline of his people as gentle, mild, serious, or severe? Explain.
2. What does this judgment reveal to you about God?
3. What does the death of Jesus on the cross reveal about the love of God? What does Jesus' death reveal about the holiness of God?
4. As a Christian who has been redeemed by Christ, how should you respond to the fact that God is a God of judgment?
5. What effect does God's holiness have on your daily choices? On the relationships you have with others? On the way you approach God?

1050 B.C.
**Saul becomes king**

1010
**Saul dies; David becomes king of Judah**

1003
**David becomes king of all Israel**

1000
**David captures Jerusalem**

997(?)
**David captures Rabbah**

980(?)
**David's census**

970
**Solomon becomes king**

930
**The kingdom divides**

I promise that we will demolish them tonight!" The coach's voice booms over the PA in the packed gymnasium. With those words the student body begins to clap and yell wildly. Somewhere in the back a few people start chanting, "Beat the Raiders! Beat the Raiders!" More people join in until soon everyone is screaming in unison. ■ Pep rallies can draw a school together. And for those few moments, all differences are forgotten as the crowd focuses on the one objective—winning the big game. ■ First Chronicles can be considered a written pep rally. Writing for the Jews who had returned to their homeland, the author attempts to form a sense of national conscience and awaken a sense of national pride and unity. ■ Beginning with Adam, 1 Chronicles relates the exciting history of Israel. By recalling the past, the author hopes to spur the Israelites on to a great future. But 1 Chronicles is more than a history lesson. It is a recounting of the spiritual strength of the nation. That, the author writes, is the hope for the greatness of the new Israel. Only as the nation unites in its worship of God can it regain the importance and vitality it once had. ■ We, too, have a great spiritual heritage—built by men and women who have contributed to any spiritual vitality we see today. As you read 1 Chronicles, learn to trace your heritage, and commit yourself to doing your part to pass on God's truth to the next generation.

## STATS

PURPOSE: To unify God's people, to trace the Davidic line, and to teach that genuine worship ought to be the center of individual and national life

AUTHOR: Ezra, according to Jewish tradition

TO WHOM WRITTEN: All Israel

DATE WRITTEN: Approximately 430 B.C.; recording events which occurred about 1000–960 B.C.

SETTING: First Chronicles parallels 2 Samuel and serves as a commentary on it. Written after the exile from a priestly point of view, 1 Chronicles emphasizes the religious history of Judah and Israel.

KEY PLACES: Hebron, Jerusalem, the Temple

CHAPTER **1** **ADAM'S DESCENDANTS.** The descendants of Adam were Seth, Enosh, 2Kenan, Mahalalel,
Jared, 3Enoch, Methuselah, Lamech, 4and Noah.
The sons of Noah were* Shem, Ham, and Japheth.
5The descendants of Japheth were Gomer, Magog, Madai, Javan, Tubal, Meshech, and Tiras.
6The descendants of Gomer were Ashkenaz, Riphath,* and Togarmah.
7The descendants of Javan were Elishah, Tarshish, Kittim, and Rodanim.
8The descendants of Ham were Cush, Mizraim,* Put, and Canaan.
9The descendants of Cush were Seba, Havilah,
Sabtah, Raamah, and Sabteca. The descendants
of Raamah were Sheba and Dedan. 10Cush was
also the ancestor of Nimrod, who was known across the earth as a heroic warrior.
11Mizraim was the ancestor of the Ludites, Anamites,
Lehabites, Naphtuhites, 12Pathrusites, Casluhites,
and the Caphtorites, from whom the Philistines came.*
13Canaan's oldest son was Sidon, the ancestor of
the Sidonians. Canaan was also the ancestor of
the Hittites, 14Jebusites, Amorites, Girgashites,
15Hivites, Arkites, Sinites, 16Arvadites, Zemarites,
and Hamathites.
17The descendants of Shem were Elam, Asshur, Arphaxad, Lud, and Aram.
The descendants of Aram were* Uz, Hul, Gether, and Mash.*
18Arphaxad was the father of Shelah. Shelah was
the father of Eber. 19Eber had two sons. The first
was named Peleg—"division"—for during his lifetime the people of the world were divided into different language groups and dispersed. His brother's name was Joktan.
20Joktan was the ancestor of Almodad, Sheleph,
Hazarmaveth, Jerah, 21Hadoram, Uzal, Diklah,

**SPECIAL ● ● • • •**

1:1 **This record of names demonstrates that God is interested not only in nations, but also in individuals. Although billions of people have lived since Adam, God knows and remembers the face and name of each person. Each individual is more than a name on a list. He or she is a special person whom God knows and loves. As we recognize and accept God's love, we discover that we are unique as individuals and that we belong with the rest of his family.**

**1:4** As in Greek version (see also Gen 5:3-32); Hebrew lacks *The sons of Noah were.* **1:6** As in some Hebrew manuscripts and Greek version (see also Gen 10:3); most Hebrew manuscripts read *Diphath.* **1:8** Or *Egypt;* also in 1:11. **1:12** Hebrew *Casluhites, from whom the Philistines came, Caphtorites.* See Jer 47:4; Amos 9:7. **1:17a** As in one Hebrew manuscript and some Greek manuscripts (see also Gen 10:23); most Hebrew manuscripts lack *The descendants of Aram were.* **1:17b** As in parallel text at Gen 10:23; Hebrew reads *and Meshech.*

# KEY PLACES IN 1 CHRONICLES

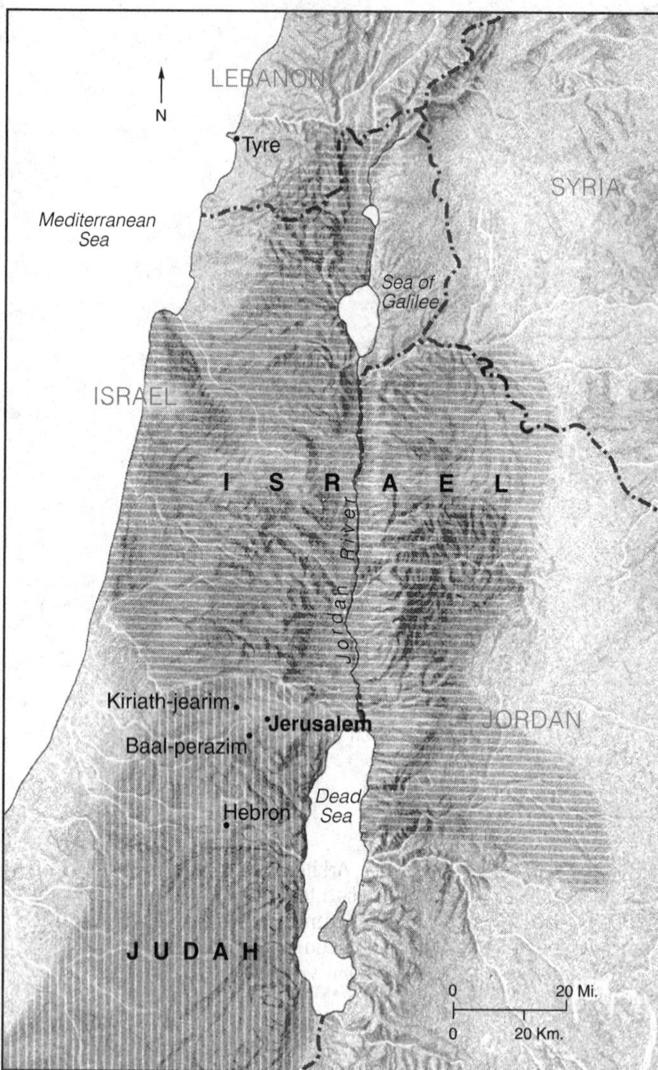


The broken lines (—·—·) indicate modern boundaries.

The genealogies of 1 Chronicles present an overview of Israel's history. The first nine chapters are filled with genealogies tracing the lineages of people from the Creation to the Exile in Babylon. Saul's death is recorded in chapter 10. Chapter 11 begins the history of David's reign over Israel.

**Hebron** Although David had been anointed king years earlier, his reign began when the leaders of Israel accepted him as king at Hebron (11:1-3).

**Jerusalem** David set out to complete the conquest of the land begun by Joshua. He attacked Jerusalem, captured it, and made it his capital (11:4–12:40).

**Kiriath-jearim** The Ark of the Covenant, which had been captured by the Philistines in battle and then returned (1 Samuel 4–6), was in safekeeping in Kiriath-jearim. David summoned all Israel to this city to join in bringing the Ark to Jerusalem. Unfortunately, it was not moved according to God's instructions, and as a result one man died. David left the Ark in the home of Obed-edom until he could discover how to transport it correctly (13:1-14).

**Tyre** David did much building in Jerusalem. King Hiram of Tyre sent workers and supplies to help build David's palace. Cedar, abundant in the mountains north of Israel, was a valuable and hardy wood for the beautiful buildings in Jerusalem (14:1–17:27).

**Baal-perazim** David was not very popular with the Philistines because he had slain Goliath, one of their greatest warriors (1 Samuel 17). When David began to rule over a united Israel, the Philistines set out to capture him. But David and his army attacked the Philistines at Baal-perazim as they approached Jerusalem. David's army defeated the mighty Philistines twice, causing all the surrounding nations to fear his power (14:11-17). After this battle, David moved the Ark to Jerusalem, this time in accordance with God's instructions for the transportation of the Ark. There was great celebration as the Ark was brought into Jerusalem (15:1–17:27). David spent the remainder of his life making preparations for the building of the Temple, a central place for the worship of God (18:1–29:30).

---

22Obal,* Abimael, Sheba, 23Ophir, Havilah, and
Jobab. All these were descendants of Joktan.

24So this is the family line descended from Shem:
Arphaxad, Shelah,* 25Eber, Peleg, Reu, 26Serug,
Nahor, Terah, 27and Abram, later known as
Abraham.

28The sons of Abraham were Isaac and Ishmael.

29The sons of Ishmael were Nebaioth (the oldest),
Kedar, Adbeel, Mibsam, 30Mishma, Dumah,
Massa, Hadad, Tema, 31Jetur, Naphish, and
Kedemah. These were the sons of Ishmael.

32The sons of Keturah, Abraham's concubine, were
Zimran, Jokshan, Medan, Midian, Ishbak, and
Shuah.

1:22 As in some Hebrew manuscripts and Syriac version (see also Gen 10:28); most Hebrew manuscripts read *Ebal.* 1:24 Some Greek manuscripts read *Arphaxad, Cainan, Shelah.* See notes on Gen 10:24; 11:12-13.

The sons of Jokshan were Sheba and Dedan.
[33]The sons of Midian were Ephah, Epher, Hanoch, Abida, and Eldaah.
All these were sons of Abraham by his concubine Keturah.
[34]Abraham was the father of Isaac. The sons of Isaac were Esau and Israel.*
[35]The sons of Esau were Eliphaz, Reuel, Jeush, Jalam, and Korah.
[36]The sons of Eliphaz were Teman, Omar, Zepho,* Gatam, Kenaz, and Amalek, who was born to Timna.*
[37]The sons of Reuel were Nahath, Zerah, Shammah, and Mizzah.
[38]The sons of Seir were Lotan, Shobal, Zibeon, Anah, Dishon, Ezer, and Dishan.
[39]The sons of Lotan were Hori and Heman.* Lotan's sister was named Timna.
[40]The sons of Shobal were Alvan,* Manahath, Ebal, Shepho,* and Onam.
The sons of Zibeon were Aiah and Anah.
[41]The son of Anah was Dishon.
The sons of Dishon were Hemdan,* Eshban, Ithran, and Keran.
[42]The sons of Ezer were Bilhan, Zaavan, and Akan.*
The sons of Dishan* were Uz and Aran.

[43]These are the kings who ruled in Edom before there were kings in Israel*:

Bela son of Beor, who ruled from his city of Dinhabah.
[44]When Bela died, Jobab son of Zerah from Bozrah became king.
[45]When Jobab died, Husham from the land of the Temanites became king.
[46]When Husham died, Hadad son of Bedad became king and ruled from the city of Avith. He was the one who destroyed the Midianite army in the land of Moab.
[47]When Hadad died, Samlah from the city of Masrekah became king.
[48]When Samlah died, Shaul from the city of Rehoboth on the Euphrates River* became king.
[49]When Shaul died, Baal-hanan son of Acbor became king.
[50]When Baal-hanan died, Hadad became king and ruled from the city of Pau.* His wife was

## ISHMAEL

Have you ever wondered whether you were born into the wrong family? That question must have haunted Ishmael at times. His life was trapped in a conflict between two jealous women. Ishmael's stepmother, Sarah, got impatient with God, so she decided to have a child through another woman. Since Hagar was a servant, she allowed herself to be used this way. But Hagar's pregnancy gave birth to strong feelings of superiority toward Sarah. Into this tense atmosphere Ishmael was born.

Much of what happened to Ishmael cannot be blamed on him. He was caught in a process much bigger than himself. But his actions showed that he chose to become part of the problem, not the solution. He chose to live in his circumstances instead of living above them.

The choice Ishmael had is one we all must make. There are circumstances over which we have no control (heredity, for instance), but there are others over which we do have control (our decisions). We all have inherited a sin-oriented nature. It can be partly controlled—but not overcome—by human effort. Ishmael's life is a picture of the mess we make when we don't try to change those things that we can change.

The God of the Bible has offered us a solution. His answer is not control, but a changed life freely given by God. To begin a changed life, trust in God to forgive your sinful past, and ask him to help you change your attitude toward him and others.

LESSON: God's plans even use people's mistakes

KEY VERSES: "Then God heard the boy's cries, and the angel of God called to Hagar from the sky, 'Hagar, what's wrong? Do not be afraid! God has heard the boy's cries from the place where you laid him. Go to him and comfort him, for I will make a great nation from his descendants'" (Genesis 21:17-18).

Ishmael's story is told in Genesis 16–17; 21; 25–28; 36. He is also mentioned in 1 Chronicles 1:28-31; Galatians 4:28-29.

**UPS:**
- One of the first to experience the physical sign of God's covenant—circumcision
- Known for his ability as an archer and hunter
- Fathered 12 sons who became leaders of warrior tribes

**DOWNS:**
- Failed to recognize the place of his half brother, Isaac, and mocked him

**STATS:**
- Where: Canaan and Egypt
- Occupation: Archer, hunter, warrior
- Relatives: Parents: Hagar and Abraham. Half brother: Isaac.

1:34 *Israel* is the name that God gave to Jacob. 1:36a As in many Hebrew manuscripts and a few Greek manuscripts (see also Gen 36:11); most Hebrew manuscripts read *Zephi.* 1:36b As in some Greek manuscripts (see also Gen 36:12); Hebrew reads *Kenaz, Timna, and Amalek.* 1:39 As in parallel text at Gen 36:22; Hebrew reads *and Homam.* 1:40a As in many Hebrew manuscripts and a few Greek manuscripts (see also Gen 36:23); most Hebrew manuscripts read *Alian.* 1:40b As in some Hebrew manuscripts (see also Gen 36:23); most Hebrew manuscripts read *Shephi.* 1:41 As in many Hebrew manuscripts and some Greek manuscripts (see also Gen 36:26); most Hebrew manuscripts read *Hamran.* 1:42a As in many Hebrew and Greek manuscripts (see also Gen 36:27); most Hebrew manuscripts read *Jaakan.* 1:42b Hebrew *Dishon;* compare 1:38 and parallel text at Gen 36:28. 1:43 Or *before an Israelite king ruled over them.* 1:48 Hebrew *the river.* 1:50 As in many Hebrew manuscripts, some Greek manuscripts, Syriac version, and Latin Vulgate (see also Gen 36:39); most Hebrew manuscripts read *Pai.*

## REPUTATION ● ● • • •

**2:3 This long genealogy not only lists names, but also gives us insights into some of the people. Here, almost as an epitaph, the genealogy states that Er "was a wicked man, so the LORD killed him." Now, centuries later, this is all we know of the man. Each of us is forging a reputation, developing personal qualities by which we will be remembered. How would God summarize your life up to now? Some defiantly claim that how they live is their own business, but Scripture teaches that the way you live today will determine how you will be remembered by others and how you will be judged by God. What you do now *does* matter.**

Mehetabel, the daughter of Matred and granddaughter of Me-zahab. [51] Then Hadad died.

The clan leaders of Edom were Timna, Alvah,*
Jetheth, [52]Oholibamah, Elah, Pinon, [53]Kenaz,
Teman, Mibzar, [54]Magdiel, and Iram. These were
the clan leaders of Edom.

CHAPTER **2** **JACOB'S DESCENDANTS.** The sons of
Israel* were Reuben, Simeon, Levi, Judah,
Issachar, Zebulun, [2]Dan, Joseph, Benjamin,
Naphtali, Gad, and Asher.

[3]Judah had three sons through Bathshua, a
Canaanite woman. Their names were Er, Onan,
and Shelah. But the oldest son, Er, was a wicked
man, so the LORD killed him. [4]Later Judah
had twin sons through Tamar, his widowed
daughter-in-law. Their names were Perez and
Zerah. So Judah had five sons in all.

[5]The sons of Perez were Hezron and Hamul.

[6]The sons of Zerah were Zimri, Ethan, Heman,
Calcol, and Darda*—five in all.

[7]Achan* son of Carmi, one of Zerah's
descendants, brought disaster on Israel by
taking plunder that had been set apart for the
LORD.*

[8]The son of Ethan was Azariah.

[9]The sons of Hezron were Jerahmeel, Ram, and
Caleb.*

[10] Ram was the father of Amminadab.
Amminadab was the father of Nahshon, a leader
of Judah.

[11] Nahshon was the father of Salmon.*
Salmon was the father of Boaz.

[12] Boaz was the father of Obed.
Obed was the father of Jesse.

[13]Jesse's first son was Eliab, his second was
Abinadab, his third was Shimea, [14]his fourth was
Nethanel, his fifth was Raddai, [15]his sixth was
Ozem, and his seventh was David.

[16]Their sisters were named Zeruiah and
Abigail. Zeruiah had three sons named Abishai,
Joab, and Asahel. [17]Abigail married a man
named Jether, an Ishmaelite, and they had a son
named Amasa.

[18]Hezron's son Caleb had two wives named
Azubah and Jerioth. Azubah's sons were named
Jesher, Shobab, and Ardon. [19]After Azubah died,
Caleb married Ephrathah,* and they had a son
named Hur. [20]Hur was the father of Uri. Uri was
the father of Bezalel.

[21]When Hezron was sixty years old, he married
Gilead's sister, the daughter of Makir. They had a
son named Segub. [22]Segub was the father of Jair,
who ruled twenty-three towns in the land of
Gilead. [23](Later Geshur and Aram captured the
Towns of Jair* and also took Kenath and its
sixty surrounding villages.) All these were
descendants of Makir, the father of Gilead.

[24]Soon after Hezron died in the town of Caleb-
ephrathah, his wife Abijah gave birth to a son
named Ashhur (the father of* Tekoa).

[25]The sons of Jerahmeel, the oldest son of Hezron,
were Ram (the oldest), Bunah, Oren, Ozem, and
Ahijah. [26]Jerahmeel had a second wife named
Atarah. She was the mother of Onam.

[27]The sons of Ram, the oldest son of Jerahmeel,
were Maaz, Jamin, and Eker.

[28]The sons of Onam were Shammai and Jada. The
sons of Shammai were Nadab and Abishur.

[29]The sons of Abishur and his wife Abihail were
Ahban and Molid.

[30]The sons of Nadab were Seled and Appaim. Seled
died without children, [31]but Appaim had a son
named Ishi. The son of Ishi was Sheshan.
Sheshan had a descendant named Ahlai.

[32]Shammai's brother, Jada, had two sons named
Jether and Jonathan. Jether died without
children, [33]but Jonathan had two sons named
Peleth and Zaza. These were all descendants of
Jerahmeel.

[34]Sheshan had no sons, though he did have
daughters. He also had an Egyptian servant
named Jarha. [35]Sheshan gave one of his
daughters to be the wife of Jarha, and they had a
son named Attai.

[36] Attai was the father of Nathan.
Nathan was the father of Zabad.

[37] Zabad was the father of Ephlal.
Ephlal was the father of Obed.

[38] Obed was the father of Jehu.
Jehu was the father of Azariah.

[39] Azariah was the father of Helez.
Helez was the father of Eleasah.

[40] Eleasah was the father of Sismai.
Sismai was the father of Shallum.

[41] Shallum was the father of Jekamiah.
Jekamiah was the father of Elishama.

[42]The oldest son of Caleb, the brother of
Jerahmeel, was Mesha, the father of Ziph.

1:51 As in parallel text at Gen 36:40; Hebrew reads *Aliah.* **2:1** *Israel* is the name that God gave to Jacob. **2:6** As in many Hebrew manuscripts, some Greek manuscripts, and Syriac version (see also 1 Kgs 4:31); Hebrew reads *Dara.* **2:7a** Hebrew *Achar;* compare Josh 7:1. *Achar* means "disaster." **2:7b** The Hebrew term used here refers to the complete consecration of things or people to the LORD, either by destroying them or by giving them as an offering. **2:9** Hebrew *Kelubai,* a variant name for Caleb; compare 2:18. **2:11** As in Greek version (see also Ruth 4:21); Hebrew reads *Salma.* **2:19** Hebrew *Ephrath,* a variant name for Ephrathah; compare 2:50 and 4:4. **2:23** Or *captured Havvoth-jair.* **2:24** Or *the founder of;* also in 2:42, 45, 49-52 and perhaps other instances where the text reads *the father of.*

Caleb's second son was Mareshah, the father of
Hebron.*
43 The sons of Hebron were Korah, Tappuah, Rekem,
and Shema. 44 Shema was the father of Raham.
Raham was the father of Jorkeam. Rekem was the
father of Shammai. 45 The son of Shammai was
Maon. Maon was the father of Beth-zur.
46 Caleb's concubine Ephah gave birth to Haran,
Moza, and Gazez. Haran was the father of
Gazez.
47 The sons of Jahdai were Regem, Jotham, Geshan,
Pelet, Ephah, and Shaaph.
48 Another of Caleb's concubines, Maacah, gave
birth to Sheber and Tirhanah. 49 She also gave
birth to Shaaph (the father of Madmannah)
and Sheva (the father of Macbenah and Gibea).
Caleb also had a daughter named Acsah. 50 These
were all descendants of Caleb.
The sons of Hur, the oldest son of Caleb's wife
Ephrathah, were Shobal (the father of Kiriath-
jearim), 51 Salma (the father of Bethlehem), and
Hareph (the father of Beth-gader).
52 The descendants of Shobal (the father of Kiriath-
jearim) were Haroeh, half the Manahathites,
53 and the families of Kiriath-jearim—the
Ithrites, Puthites, Shumathites, and Mishraites,
from whom came the people of Zorah and
Eshtaol.
54 The descendants of Salma were Bethlehem, the
Netophathites, Atroth-beth-joab, the other half of
the Manahathites, the Zorites, 55 and the families
of scribes living at Jabez—the Tirathites,
Shimeathites, and Sucathites. All these were
Kenites who descended from Hammath, the
father of the family of Recab.*

## CHAPTER 3 **DAVID'S DESCENDANTS.**

These were the
sons who were born to David in Hebron:

The oldest was Amnon, whose mother was
Ahinoam of Jezreel.
The second was Kileab,* whose mother was
Abigail from Carmel.
2 The third was Absalom, whose mother was
Maacah, the daughter of Talmai, king of
Geshur.
The fourth was Adonijah, whose mother was
Haggith.
3 The fifth was Shephatiah, whose mother was
Abital.
The sixth was Ithream, whose mother was Eglah.

4 These six sons were born to David in Hebron, where
he reigned seven and a half years.

Then David moved the capital to Jerusalem,
where he reigned another thirty-three years. 5 The
sons born to David in Jerusalem included Shimea,
Shobab, Nathan, and Solomon. Bathsheba,* the
daughter of Ammiel, was the mother of these sons.
6 David also had nine other sons: Ibhar, Elishua,*
Elpelet,* 7 Nogah, Nepheg, Japhia, 8 Elishama, Eliada, and Eliphelet.
9 These were the sons of David, not including the
sons of his concubines. David also had a daughter
named Tamar.
10 The descendants of Solomon were Rehoboam,
Abijah, Asa, Jehoshaphat, 11 Jehoram,* Ahaziah,
Joash, 12 Amaziah, Uzziah,* Jotham, 13 Ahaz,
Hezekiah, Manasseh, 14 Amon, and Josiah.

**STORIES ● • • • •**

3:10-14 **Many of King Solomon's descendants ruled the nation of Judah. For Rehoboam's story, see 2 Chronicles 10–12. For Jehoshaphat's story, see 2 Chronicles 17–20. For Uzziah's story, see 2 Chronicles 26. For Hezekiah's story, see 2 Kings 18–20. For Josiah's story, see 2 Kings 22–23.**

15 The sons of Josiah were Johanan (the oldest),
Jehoiakim (the second), Zedekiah (the third),
and Jehoahaz* (the fourth).
16 Jehoiakim was succeeded by his son Jehoiachin; he,
in turn, was succeeded by his uncle Zedekiah.*
17 The sons of Jehoiachin,* who was taken prisoner
by the Babylonians, were Shealtiel, 18 Malkiram,
Pedaiah, Shenazzar, Jekamiah, Hoshama, and
Nedabiah.
19 The sons of Pedaiah were Zerubbabel and Shimei.
The sons of Zerubbabel were Meshullam and
Hananiah. He also had a daughter named
Shelomith. 20 His five other sons were Hashubah,
Ohel, Berekiah, Hasadiah, and Jushab-hesed.
21 The sons of Hananiah were Pelatiah and Jeshaiah.
Jeshaiah's son was Rephaiah. Rephaiah's son was
Arnan. Arnan's son was Obadiah. Obadiah's son
was Shecaniah.
22 Shecaniah's descendants were Shemaiah and his
sons, Hattush, Igal, Bariah, Neariah, and
Shaphat—six in all.
23 The sons of Neariah were Elioenai, Hizkiah, and
Azrikam—three in all.
24 The sons of Elioenai were Hodaviah, Eliashib,
Pelaiah, Akkub, Johanan, Delaiah, and
Anani—seven in all.

## CHAPTER 4 **JUDAH'S DESCENDANTS.**

Some of the
descendants of Judah were Perez, Hezron,
Carmi, Hur, and Shobal.
2 Shobal's son Reaiah was the father of Jahath.
Jahath was the father of Ahumai and Lahad.
These were the families of the Zorathites.
3 The descendants of* Etam were Jezreel, Ishma,

2:42 The meaning of the Hebrew is uncertain. 2:55 Or *the founder of Beth-recab.* 3:1 As in parallel text at 2 Sam 3:3; Hebrew reads *Daniel.* 3:5 Hebrew *Bathshua,* a variant name for Bathsheba. 3:6a As in some Hebrew and Greek manuscripts (see also 14:5-7 and 2 Sam 5:15); most Hebrew manuscripts read *Elishama.* 3:6b Hebrew *Eliphelet;* compare parallel text at 14:5-7. 3:11 Hebrew *Joram,* a variant name for Jehoram. 3:12 Hebrew *Azariah,* a variant name for Uzziah. 3:15 Hebrew *Shallum,* another name for Jehoahaz. 3:16 Hebrew *The descendants of Jehoiakim were his son Jeconiah* [a variant name for Jehoiachin] *and his son Zedekiah.* 3:17 Hebrew *Jeconiah,* a variant name for Jehoiachin. 4:3 As in Greek version; Hebrew reads *father of.* The meaning of the Hebrew is uncertain.

Idbash, Hazzelelponi (his daughter), [4]Penuel (the father of* Gedor), and Ezer (the father of Hushah). These were the descendants of Hur (the firstborn of Ephrathah), the ancestor of Bethlehem.

[5]Ashhur (the father of Tekoa) had two wives, named Helah and Naarah. [6]Naarah gave birth to Ahuzzam, Hepher, Temeni, and Haahashtari. [7]Helah gave birth to Zereth, Izhar, Ethnan, [8]and Koz, who became the ancestor of Anub, Zobebah, and all the families of Aharhel son of Harum.

[9]There was a man named Jabez who was more distinguished than any of his brothers. His mother named him Jabez* because his birth had been so painful. [10]He was the one who prayed to the God of Israel, "Oh, that you would bless me and extend my lands! Please be with me in all that I do, and keep me from all trouble and pain!" And God granted him his request.

## REMEMBERED ● ● • • •

4:10 **Jabez is remembered as "the one who prayed to the God of Israel." It is significant that he is remembered for a prayer rather than a heroic act. In his prayer, he asked God to (1) bless him, (2) extend his lands, (3) be with him in all he did, and (4) keep him from trouble and pain. Jabez acknowledged God as the true center of his work. When we pray for God's blessing, we should also pray that he will take his rightful position as Lord over all areas of our life. Then we, too, may be remembered for more than just a heroic deed.**

[11]Kelub (the brother of Shuhah) was the father of Mehir. Mehir was the father of Eshton. [12]Eshton was the father of Beth-rapha, Paseah, and Tehinnah. Tehinnah was the father of Ir-nahash. These were the descendants of Recah.

[13]The sons of Kenaz were Othniel and Seraiah. Othniel's sons were Hathath and Meonothai.* [14]Meonothai was the father of Ophrah. Seraiah was the father of Joab, the founder of the Valley of Craftsmen,* so called because many craftsmen lived there.

[15]The sons of Caleb son of Jephunneh were Iru, Elah, and Naam. The son of Elah was Kenaz.

[16]The sons of Jehallelel were Ziph, Ziphah, Tiria, and Asarel.

[17]The sons of Ezrah were Jether, Mered, Epher, and Jalon. Mered married an Egyptian woman, who became the mother of Miriam, Shammai, and Ishbah (the father of Eshtemoa). [18]Mered also married a woman of Judah, who became the mother of Jered (the father of Gedor), Heber (the father of Soco), and Jekuthiel (the father of Zanoah). Mered's Egyptian wife was named Bithiah, and she was an Egyptian princess.

[19]Hodiah's wife was the sister of Naham. One of her sons was the father of Keilah the Garmite, and another was the father of Eshtemoa the Maacathite.

[20]The sons of Shimon were Amnon, Rinnah, Ben-hanan, and Tilon.

The descendants of Ishi were Zoheth and Ben-zoheth.

[21]Shelah was one of Judah's sons. The descendants of Shelah were Er (the father of Lecah), Laadah (the father of Mareshah), the families of linen workers at Beth-ashbea, [22]Jokim, the people of Cozeba, Joash, and Saraph, who ruled over Moab and Jashubi-lehem. These names all come from ancient records. [23]They were the potters who lived in Netaim and Gederah. They all worked for the king.

[24]The sons of Simeon were Nemuel, Jamin, Jarib, Zerah, and Shaul.

[25]The descendants of Shaul were Shallum, Mibsam, and Mishma.

[26]The descendants of Mishma were Hammuel, Zaccur, and Shimei.

[27]Shimei had sixteen sons and six daughters, but none of his brothers had large families. So Simeon's tribe never became as large as the tribe of Judah.

[28]They lived in Beersheba, Moladah, Hazar-shual, [29]Bilhah, Ezem, Tolad, [30]Bethuel, Hormah, Ziklag, [31]Beth-marcaboth, Hazar-susim, Beth-biri, and Shaaraim. These towns were under their control until the time of King David.

[32]Their descendants also lived in Etam, Ain, Rimmon, Token, and Ashan—five towns [33]and their surrounding villages as far away as Baalath.* This was their territory, and these names are recorded in their family genealogy.

[34]Other descendants of Simeon included Meshobab, Jamlech, Joshah son of Amaziah, [35]Joel, Jehu son of Joshibiah, son of Seraiah, son of Asiel, [36]Elioenai, Jaakobah, Jeshohaiah, Asaiah, Adiel, Jesimiel, Benaiah, [37]and Ziza son of Shiphi, son of Allon, son of Jedaiah, son of Shimri, son of Shemaiah.

[38]These were the names of some of the leaders of Simeon's wealthy clans, [39]who traveled to the region of Gedor, in the east part of the valley, seeking pastureland for their flocks. [40]They found lush pastures there, and the land was quiet and peaceful.

Some of Ham's descendants had been living in the region of Gedor. [41]But during the reign of King Hezekiah of Judah, the leaders of Simeon invaded it and completely destroyed* the homes of the descendants of Ham and of the Meunites. They killed everyone who lived there and took the land for themselves, because they wanted its good pasture-

4:4 Or *the founder of;* also in 4:12, 14, 17-18, and perhaps other instances where the text reads *the father of.* 4:9 *Jabez* sounds like a Hebrew term meaning "distress" or "pain." 4:13 As in some Greek manuscripts and Latin Vulgate; Hebrew lacks *and Meonothai.* 4:14 Or *Joab, the father of Ge-harashim.* 4:33 As in some Greek manuscripts (see also Josh 19:8); Hebrew reads *Baal.* 4:41 The Hebrew term used here refers to the complete consecration of things or people to the LORD, either by destroying them or by giving them as an offering.

land for their flocks. [42]Five hundred of these invaders from the tribe of Simeon went to Mount Seir, led by Pelatiah, Neariah, Rephaiah, and Uzziel—all sons of Ishi. [43]They destroyed the few Amalekites who had survived, and they have lived there ever since.

CHAPTER **5** **REUBEN'S DESCENDANTS.** The oldest son of Israel* was Reuben. But since he dishonored his father by sleeping with one of his father's concubines, his birthright was given to the sons of his brother Joseph. For this reason, Reuben is not listed in the genealogy as the firstborn son. [2]It was the descendants of Judah that became the most powerful tribe and provided a ruler for the nation,* but the birthright belonged to Joseph.

[3]The sons of Reuben, the oldest son of Israel, were Hanoch, Pallu, Hezron, and Carmi.
[4]The descendants of Joel were Shemaiah, Gog,
Shimei, [5]Micah, Reaiah, Baal, [6]and Beerah.
Beerah was the leader of the Reubenites when they were taken into captivity by King Tiglath-pileser* of Assyria.
[7]Beerah's relatives are listed in their genealogy by
their clans: Jeiel (the leader), Zechariah, [8]and
Bela son of Azaz, son of Shema, son of Joel.
These Reubenites lived in the area that stretches from Aroer to Nebo and Baal-meon.
[9]And since they had so many cattle in the land of Gilead, they spread eastward toward the edge of the desert that stretches to the Euphrates River.
[10]During the reign of Saul, the Reubenites defeated the Hagrites in battle. Then they moved into the Hagrite settlements all along the eastern edge of Gilead.
[11]Across from the Reubenites in the land of Bashan
lived the descendants of Gad, who were spread
as far east as Salecah. [12]Joel was the leader in the
land of Bashan, and Shapham was second-in-command, along with Janai and Shaphat.
[13]Their relatives, the leaders of seven other clans,
were Michael, Meshullam, Sheba, Jorai, Jacan,
Zia, and Eber. [14]These were all descendants of
Abihail son of Huri, son of Jaroah, son of Gilead, son of Michael, son of Jeshishai, son of Jahdo,
son of Buz. [15]Ahi son of Abdiel, son of Guni, was
the leader of their clans.

[16]The Gadites lived in the land of Gilead, in Bashan
and its villages, and throughout the Sharon Plain.
[17]All of these were listed in the genealogical records
during the days of King Jotham of Judah and King Jeroboam of Israel.

[18]There were 44,760 skilled warriors in the armies
of Reuben, Gad, and the half-tribe of Manasseh. They were all skilled in combat and armed with shields, swords, and bows. [19]They waged war against
the Hagrites, the Jeturites, the Naphishites, and the
Nodabites. [20]They cried out to God during the battle,

## CONSEQUENCES ● ● • • •

5:1 **Reuben's sin of incest was recorded for all future generations to read. The purpose of this epitaph, however, was not to smear Reuben's name, but to show that painful memories aren't the only results of sin. The real consequences of sin are ruined lives. As the oldest son, Reuben was the rightful heir to both a double portion of his father's estate and the leadership of Abraham's descendants, who had grown into a large tribe. But his sin stripped away his rights and privileges and ruined his family. Before you give in to temptation, take a close look at the disastrous consequences your sin may have in your life and the lives of others.**

and he answered their prayer because they trusted in him. So the Hagrites and all their allies were defeated. [21]The plunder taken from the Hagrites included 50,000 camels, 250,000 sheep, 2,000 donkeys, and 100,000 captives. [22]Many of the Hag-
rites were killed in the battle because God was fighting against them. So they lived in their land until they were taken away into exile.
[23]The half-tribe of Manasseh spread through the
land from Bashan to Baal-hermon, Senir, and Mount
Hermon. They were very numerous. [24]These were the
leaders of their clans: Epher, Ishi, Eliel, Azriel, Jeremiah, Hodaviah, and Jahdiel. Each of these men had
a great reputation as a warrior and leader. [25]But they
were unfaithful and violated their covenant with the God of their ancestors. They worshiped the gods of
the nations that God had destroyed. [26]So the God of
Israel caused King Pul of Assyria (also known as Tiglath-pileser) to invade the land and lead away the people of Reuben, Gad, and the half-tribe of Manasseh as captives. The Assyrians exiled them to Halah, Habor, Hara, and the Gozan River, where they remain to this day.

## WARRIORS ● ● • • •

5:24-25 **As warriors and leaders, these men had established excellent reputations for their great skill and leadership qualities. But in God's eyes they failed in the most important quality—putting God first in their lives. If you try to measure up to society's standards for fame and success, you will be in danger of neglecting your true quest—to please and obey God. In the end, God alone examines our heart and determines our standing.**

CHAPTER **6** **LEVI'S DESCENDANTS.** The sons of Levi were Gershon, Kohath, and Merari.
[2]The descendants of Kohath included Amram,
Izhar, Hebron, and Uzziel.
[3]The children of Amram were Aaron, Moses, and
Miriam.
The sons of Aaron were Nadab, Abihu, Eleazar, and Ithamar.

[4] Eleazar was the father of Phinehas.
Phinehas was the father of Abishua.

5:1 *Israel* is the name that God gave to Jacob. 5:2 Or *and from Judah came a prince.* 5:6 Hebrew *Tilgath-pilneser,* a variant name for Tiglath-pileser; also in 5:26.

5 Abishua was the father of Bukki.
Bukki was the father of Uzzi.
6 Uzzi was the father of Zerahiah.
Zerahiah was the father of Meraioth.
7 Meraioth was the father of Amariah.
Amariah was the father of Ahitub.
8 Ahitub was the father of Zadok.
Zadok was the father of Ahimaaz.
9 Ahimaaz was the father of Azariah.
Azariah was the father of Johanan.
10 Johanan was the father of Azariah, the high
priest at the Temple built by Solomon in
Jerusalem.
11 Azariah was the father of Amariah.
Amariah was the father of Ahitub.
12 Ahitub was the father of Zadok.
Zadok was the father of Shallum.
13 Shallum was the father of Hilkiah.
Hilkiah was the father of Azariah.
14 Azariah was the father of Seraiah.
Seraiah was the father of Jehozadak, 15 who went
into exile when the LORD sent the people of
Judah and Jerusalem into captivity under
Nebuchadnezzar.
16 The sons of Levi were Gershon,* Kohath, and
Merari.
17 The descendants of Gershon included Libni and
Shimei.
18 The descendants of Kohath included Amram,
Izhar, Hebron, and Uzziel.
19 The descendants of Merari included Mahli and
Mushi.

The following were the Levite clans, listed according to their ancestral descent:

20 The descendants of Gershon included Libni, Jahath,
Zimmah, 21 Joah, Iddo, Zerah, and Jeatherai.
22 The descendants of Kohath included Amminadab,
Korah, Assir, 23 Elkanah, Abiasaph,* Assir,
24 Tahath, Uriel, Uzziah, and Shaul.
25 The descendants of Elkanah included Amasai,
Ahimoth, 26 Elkanah, Zophai, Nahath, 27 Eliab,
Jeroham, Elkanah, and Samuel.*
28 The sons of Samuel were Joel* (the older) and
Abijah (the second).
29 The descendants of Merari included Mahli, Libni,
Shimei, Uzzah, 30 Shimea, Haggiah, and Asaiah.

31 David assigned the following men to lead the
music at the house of the LORD after he put the Ark
there. 32 They ministered with music there at the
Tabernacle* until Solomon built the Temple of the
LORD in Jerusalem. Then they carried on their work
there, following all the regulations handed down to
them. 33 These are the men who served, along with
their sons:

## TALENTS ● ● • • •

**6:31-32 The builders and craftsmen had completed the Temple, and the priests and the Levites had been given their responsibilities for taking care of it. Now it was time for another group of people—the musicians—to exercise their talents for God. Some of the musicians' names are recorded here, showing you don't have to be an ordained minister to serve God. Builders, craftsmen, worship assistants, choir members, and songleaders all had significant contributions to make. God has given you a unique combination of talents. Use them to serve him.**

Heman the musician was from the clan of Kohath.
His genealogy was traced back through Joel,
Samuel, 34 Elkanah, Jeroham, Eliel, Toah, 35 Zuph,
Elkanah, Mahath, Amasai, 36 Elkanah, Joel,
Azariah, Zephaniah, 37 Tahath, Assir, Abiasaph,
Korah, 38 Izhar, Kohath, Levi, and Israel.*
39 Heman's first assistant was Asaph from the clan
of Gershon.* Asaph's genealogy was traced back
through Berekiah, Shimea, 40 Michael, Baaseiah,
Malkijah, 41 Ethni, Zerah, Adaiah, 42 Ethan,
Zimmah, Shimei, 43 Jahath, Gershon, and Levi.
44 Heman's second assistant was Ethan from the
clan of Merari. Ethan's genealogy was traced
back through Kishi, Abdi, Malluch, 45 Hashabiah, Amaziah, Hilkiah, 46 Amzi, Bani, Shemer,
47 Mahli, Mushi, Merari, and Levi.

48 Their relatives, also Levites, were appointed to various other tasks in the Tabernacle, the house of God.

49 Only Aaron and his descendants served as
priests. They presented the offerings on the altar of
burnt offering and the altar of incense, and they
performed all the other duties related to the Most
Holy Place. They made atonement for Israel by following all the commands that Moses, the servant of
God, had given them.

50 The descendants of Aaron were Eleazar,
Phinehas, Abishua, 51 Bukki, Uzzi, Zerahiah,
52 Meraioth, Amariah, Ahitub, 53 Zadok, and
Ahimaaz.

54 This is a record of the towns and territory assigned by means of sacred lots to the descendants of
Aaron who were from the clan of Kohath. 55 This
included Hebron and its surrounding pasturelands
in Judah, 56 but the fields and outlying areas were
given to Caleb son of Jephunneh. 57 So the descendants of Aaron were given the following towns, each
with its surrounding pasturelands: Hebron (a city of
refuge), Libnah, Jattir, Eshtemoa, 58 Holon,* Debir,
59 Ain,* Juttah,* and Beth-shemesh. 60 And from the
territory of Benjamin they were given Gibeon,*
Geba, Alemeth, and Anathoth, each with its pasturelands. So a total of thirteen towns was given to the
descendants of Aaron. 61 The remaining descendants

**6:16** Hebrew *Gershom,* a variant name for Gershon (see 6:1); also in 6:17, 20, 43, 62, 71. **6:23** Hebrew *Ebiasaph,* a variant name for Abiasaph (also in 6:37); compare parallel text at Exod 6:24. **6:27** As in some Greek manuscripts (see also 6:33-34); Hebrew lacks *and Samuel.* **6:28** As in some Greek manuscripts and the Syriac version (see also 6:33 and 1 Sam 8:2); Hebrew lacks *Joel.* **6:32** Hebrew *the Tabernacle, the Tent of Meeting.* **6:38** *Israel* is the name that God gave to Jacob. **6:39** Hebrew lacks *from the clan of Gershon;* see 6:43. **6:58** As in parallel text at Josh 21:15; Hebrew reads *Hilen.* **6:59a** As in parallel text at Josh 21:16; Hebrew reads *Ashan.* **6:59b** As in Syriac version (see also Josh 21:16); Hebrew lacks *Juttah.* **6:60** As in parallel text at Josh 21:17; Hebrew lacks *Gibeon.*

of Kohath received ten towns from the territory of
the half-tribe of Manasseh by means of sacred lots.
62The descendants of Gershon received by sacred
lots thirteen towns from the territories of Issachar,
Asher, Naphtali, and from the Bashan area of Manasseh, east of the Jordan.
63The descendants of Merari received by sacred
lots twelve towns from the territories of Reuben,
Gad, and Zebulun.
64So the people of Israel assigned all these towns
and pasturelands to the Levites. 65The towns in the
territories of Judah, Simeon, and Benjamin, mentioned above, were also assigned by means of sacred
lots.
66The descendants of Kohath received from the
territory of Ephraim these towns, each with its surrounding pasturelands: 67Shechem (a city of refuge
in the hill country of Ephraim), Gezer, 68Jokmeam,
Beth-horon, 69Aijalon, and Gath-rimmon. 70The remaining descendants of Kohath were assigned these
towns from the territory of the half-tribe of Manasseh: Aner and Bileam, each with its pasturelands.
71The descendants of Gershon received from the
territory of the half-tribe of Manasseh the town of
Golan in Bashan with its pasturelands and Ashtaroth
with its pasturelands. 72From the territory of Issachar,
they were given Kedesh, Daberath, 73Ramoth, and
Anem, with their pasturelands. 74From the territory
of Asher, they received Mashal, Abdon, 75Hukok, and
Rehob, each with its pasturelands. 76From the territory of Naphtali, they were given Kedesh in Galilee,
Hammon, and Kiriathaim, each with its pasturelands.
77The remaining descendants of Merari received
from the territory of Zebulun the towns of Jokneam,
Kartah,* Rimmono, and Tabor, each with its pasturelands. 78From the territory of Reuben, east of the
Jordan River opposite Jericho, they received Bezer (a
desert town), Jahaz,* 79Kedemoth, and Mephaath,
each with its pasturelands. 80And from the territory
of Gad, they received Ramoth in Gilead, Mahanaim,
81Heshbon, and Jazer, each with its pasturelands.

CHAPTER **7** **ISSACHAR'S DESCENDANTS.** The four
sons of Issachar were Tola, Puah, Jashub, and
Shimron.
2The sons of Tola were Uzzi, Rephaiah, Jeriel,
Jahmai, Ibsam, and Shemuel. Each of them was
the leader of an ancestral clan. At the time of
King David, the total number of men available
for military service from these families was
22,600.
3The son of Uzzi was Izrahiah. The sons of Izrahiah
were Michael, Obadiah, Joel, and Isshiah. These
five became the leaders of clans. 4The total
number of men available for military service
among their descendants was 36,000, for all five
of them had many wives and many sons.
5The total number of men available for military
service from all the clans of the tribe of Issachar
was 87,000. All of them were listed in their tribal
genealogy.
6Three of Benjamin's sons were Bela, Beker, and
Jediael.
7The sons of Bela were Ezbon, Uzzi, Uzziel,
Jerimoth, and Iri. These five warriors were the
leaders of clans. The total number of men
available for military service among their
descendants was 22,034. All of them were listed
in their family genealogy.
8The sons of Beker were Zemirah, Joash, Eliezer,
Elioenai, Omri, Jeremoth, Abijah, Anathoth,
and Alemeth. 9According to their family
genealogy, there were 20,200 men available for
military service among their descendants, in
addition to their clan leaders.
10The son of Jediael was Bilhan. The sons of Bilhan
were Jeush, Benjamin, Ehud, Kenaanah, Zethan,
Tarshish, and Ahishahar. 11They were the leaders
of the clans of Jediael, and their descendants
included 17,200 men available for military
service.
12The sons of Ir were Shuppim and Huppim.
Hushim was the son of Aher.
13The sons of Naphtali were Jahzeel,* Guni, Jezer,
and Shillem.* They were all descendants of
Jacob's wife Bilhah.
14The sons of Manasseh, born to his Aramean
concubine, were Asriel and Makir. Makir was the
father of Gilead.
15Makir found wives for Huppim and Shuppim.
Makir's sister was named Maacah. One of his
descendants was Zelophehad, who had only
daughters.
16Makir's wife, Maacah, gave birth to a son whom
she named Peresh. His brother's name was
Sheresh. The sons of Peresh were Ulam and
Rakem. 17The son of Ulam was Bedan. All these
were considered Gileadites, descendants of
Makir son of Manasseh.
18Makir's sister Hammoleketh gave birth to Ishhod,
Abiezer, and Mahlah.
19The sons of Shemida were Ahian, Shechem,
Likhi, and Aniam.
20The descendants of Ephraim were Shuthelah,

## BY THE BOOK ● • • • •

**6:49 Aaron and his descendants strictly followed the details of worship commanded by God through Moses. They did not choose only those commands they *wanted* to obey. Note what happened to Uzzah when important details in handling the Ark of the Covenant were neglected (13:6-10). We should not obey God selectively, choosing which commands we will obey and which we will ignore. God's Word has authority over *every* aspect of our lives, not just over selected portions.**

6:77 As in Greek version (see also Josh 21:34); Hebrew lacks *Jokneam, Kartah*. 6:78 Hebrew *Jahzah*, a variant name for Jahaz. 7:13a As in parallel text at Gen 46:24; Hebrew reads *Jahziel*, a variant name for Jahzeel. 7:13b As in some Hebrew and Greek manuscripts (see also Gen 46:24; Num 26:49); most Hebrew manuscripts read *Shallum*.

Bered, Tahath, Eleadah, Tahath, [21]Zabad, and
Shuthelah.
Ephraim's sons Ezer and Elead were killed
trying to steal livestock from the local farmers
near Gath. [22]Their father, Ephraim, mourned for
them a long time, and his relatives came to
comfort him. [23]Afterward Ephraim slept with his
wife, and she became pregnant and gave birth to
a son. Ephraim named him Beriah* because of
the tragedy his family had suffered.
[24]Ephraim had a daughter named Sheerah.
She built the towns of Lower and Upper
Beth-horon and Uzzen-sheerah.
[25]Ephraim's line of descent was Rephah, Resheph,
Telah, Tahan, [26]Ladan, Ammihud, Elishama,
[27]Nun, and Joshua.

[28]The descendants of Ephraim lived in the territory that included Bethel and its surrounding towns
to the south, Naaran to the east, Gezer and its villages to the west, and Shechem and its surrounding
villages to the north as far as Ayyah and its towns.
[29]Along the border of Manasseh were the towns of
Beth-shan,* Taanach, Megiddo, Dor, and their surrounding villages. The descendants of Joseph son of
Israel* lived in these towns.
[30]The sons of Asher were Imnah, Ishvah, Ishvi, and
Beriah. They had a sister named Serah.
[31]The sons of Beriah were Heber and Malkiel (the
father of Birzaith).
[32]The sons of Heber were Japhlet, Shomer, and
Hotham. They had a sister named Shua.
[33]The sons of Japhlet were Pasach, Bimhal, and
Ashvath.
[34]The sons of Shomer were Ahi, Rohgah, Hubbah,
and Aram.
[35]The sons of his brother Helem* were Zophah,
Imna, Shelesh, and Amal.
[36]The sons of Zophah were Suah, Harnepher,
Shual, Beri, Imrah, [37]Bezer, Hod, Shamma,
Shilshah, Ithran,* and Beera.
[38]The sons of Jether were Jephunneh, Pispah,
and Ara.
[39]The sons of Ulla were Arah, Hanniel, and Rizia.

[40]Each of these descendants of Asher was the head of
an ancestral clan. They were all skilled warriors and
prominent leaders. There were 26,000 men available
for military service among the descendants listed in
their tribal genealogy.

## CHAPTER 8 BENJAMIN'S DESCENDANTS.

The sons
of Benjamin, in order of age, included Bela (the
oldest), Ashbel, Aharah, [2]Nohah, and Rapha.
[3]The sons of Bela were Addar, Gera, Abihud,*
[4]Abishua, Naaman, Ahoah, [5]Gera, Shephuphan,
and Huram.
[6]The sons of Ehud, leaders of the clans living at
Geba, were driven out and moved to Manahath.
[7]Ehud's sons were Naaman, Ahijah, and Gera.
Gera, the father of Uzza and Ahihud, led them
when they moved.
[8]After Shaharaim divorced his wives Hushim and
Baara, he had children in the land of Moab.
[9]Hodesh, his new wife, gave birth to Jobab, Zibia,
Mesha, Malcam, [10]Jeuz, Sakia, and Mirmah. These
sons all became the leaders of clans.
[11]Shaharaim's wife Hushim had already given birth
to Abitub and Elpaal. [12]The sons of Elpaal were
Eber, Misham, Shemed (who built Ono and Lod
and their villages), [13]Beriah, and Shema. They
were the leaders of the clans living in Aijalon,
and they drove out the inhabitants of Gath.

[14]Ahio, Shashak, Jeremoth, [15]Zebadiah, Arad, Eder,
[16]Michael, Ishpah, and Joha were the sons of
Beriah.
[17]Zebadiah, Meshullam, Hizki, Heber, [18]Ishmerai,
Izliah, and Jobab were the sons of Elpaal.
[19]Jakim, Zicri, Zabdi, [20]Elienai, Zillethai, Eliel,
[21]Adaiah, Beraiah, and Shimrath were the sons
of Shimei.
[22]Ishpan, Eber, Eliel, [23]Abdon, Zicri, Hanan,
[24]Hananiah, Elam, Anthothijah, [25]Iphdeiah, and
Penuel were the sons of Shashak.

### APPROVAL ● ● • • ·

8:8-10 **Divorce and polygamy are sometimes recorded in the Old Testament without critical comments. This does not mean that God takes them lightly. Malachi 2:15-16 says, "Guard yourself; remain loyal to the wife of your youth. 'For I hate divorce!' says the LORD, the God of Israel." Jesus explained that although divorce was allowed, it was not God's will: "Moses permitted divorce as a concession to your hard-hearted wickedness, but it was not what God had originally intended" (Matthew 19:8). Don't assume that God approves of something because it isn't vigorously condemned in every Scripture reference.**

[26]Shamsherai, Shehariah, Athaliah, [27]Jaareshiah,
Elijah, and Zicri were the sons of Jeroham.

[28]These were the leaders of the ancestral clans, and
they were listed in their tribal genealogy. They all
lived in Jerusalem.

[29]Jeiel* (the father of* Gibeon) lived in Gibeon.
His wife's name was Maacah, [30]and his oldest
son was named Abdon. Jeiel's other sons were
Zur, Kish, Baal, Ner,* Nadab, [31]Gedor, Ahio,
Zechariah,* [32]and Mikloth, who was the father
of Shimeam.* All these families lived near each
other in Jerusalem.
[33]Ner was the father of Kish. Kish was the father of
Saul. Saul was the father of Jonathan,
Malkishua, Abinadab, and Eshbaal.

7:23 *Beriah* sounds like a Hebrew term meaning "tragedy" or "misfortune." 7:29a Hebrew *Beth-shean,* a variant name for Beth-shan. 7:29b *Israel* is the name that God gave to Jacob. 7:35 Possibly another name for *Hotham;* compare 7:32. 7:37 Possibly another name for *Jether;* compare 7:38. 8:3 Possibly *Gera the father of Ehud;* compare 8:6. 8:29a As in some Greek manuscripts (see also 9:35); Hebrew lacks *Jeiel.* 8:29b Or *the founder of.* 8:30 As in some Greek manuscripts (see also 9:36); Hebrew lacks *Ner.* 8:31 As in parallel text at 9:37; Hebrew reads *Zeker,* a variant name for Zechariah. 8:32 As in parallel text at 9:38; Hebrew reads *Shimeah,* a variant name for Shimeam.

[34]Jonathan was the father of Meribbaal. Meribbaal was the father of Micah. [35]Micah was the father of Pithon, Melech, Tahrea,* and Ahaz.

[36] Ahaz was the father of Jadah.*
Jadah was the father of Alemeth, Azmaveth, and Zimri.
Zimri was the father of Moza.

[37] Moza was the father of Binea.
Binea was the father of Rephaiah.*
Rephaiah was the father of Eleasah.
Eleasah was the father of Azel.

[38]Azel had six sons: Azrikam, Bokeru, Ishmael, Sheariah, Obadiah, and Hanan. These were the sons of Azel.

[39]Azel's brother Eshek had three sons: Ulam (the oldest), Jeush (the second), and Eliphelet (the third). [40]The sons of Ulam were all skilled warriors and expert archers. They had many sons and grandsons—150 in all.

All these were descendants of Benjamin.

## CHAPTER 9 THE EXILED PEOPLE RETURN HOME.

All Israel was listed in the genealogical record in *The Book of the Kings of Israel.*

The people of Judah were exiled to Babylon because they were unfaithful to the LORD. [2]The first to return to their property in their former towns were common people. With them came some of the priests, Levites, and Temple assistants. [3]People from the tribes of Judah, Benjamin, Ephraim, and Manasseh came and settled in Jerusalem.

[4]One family that returned was that of Uthai son of Ammihud, son of Omri, son of Imri, son of Bani, a descendant of Perez son of Judah.

[5]Others returned from the Shilonite clan, including Asaiah (the oldest) and his sons.

[6]From the Zerahite clan, Jeuel returned with his relatives.

In all, 690 families from the tribe of Judah returned.

[7]From the tribe of Benjamin came Sallu son of Meshullam, son of Hodaviah, son of Hassenuah; [8]Ibneiah son of Jeroham; Elah son of Uzzi, son of Micri; Meshullam son of Shephatiah, son of Reuel, son of Ibnijah.

[9]These men were all leaders of clans, and they were listed in their tribal genealogy. In all, 956 families from the tribe of Benjamin returned.

[10]Among the priests who returned were Jedaiah, Jehoiarib, Jakin, [11]Azariah son of Hilkiah, son of Meshullam, son of Zadok, son of Meraioth, son of Ahitub. Azariah was the chief officer of the house of God.

[12]Other returning priests were Adaiah son of Jeroham, son of Pashhur, son of Malkijah, and Maasai son of Adiel, son of Jahzerah, son of Meshullam, son of Meshillemith, son of Immer.

### SPEAK OUT ● ● • • •

9:1 **Although every person in Judah did not worship idols, the entire nation was carried away into captivity. Everyone was affected by the sin of some. Even if we don't participate in a certain widespread wrongdoing, we will still be affected by those who do. It is not enough to say, "I don't do it." We must speak out against the sins of our society.**

[13]In all, 1,760 priests returned. They were heads of clans and very able men. They were responsible for ministering at the house of God.

[14]The Levites who returned were Shemaiah son of Hasshub, son of Azrikam, son of Hashabiah, a descendant of Merari; [15]Bakbakkar; Heresh; Galal; Mattaniah son of Mica, son of Zicri, son of Asaph; [16]Obadiah son of Shemaiah, son of Galal, son of Jeduthun; and Berekiah son of Asa, son of Elkanah, who lived in the area of Netophah.

[17]The gatekeepers who returned were Shallum, Akkub, Talmon, Ahiman, and their relatives. Shallum was the chief gatekeeper. [18]Prior to this time, they were responsible for the King's Gate on the east side. These men served as gatekeepers for the camps of the Levites.

[19]Shallum was the son of Kore, a descendant of Abiasaph,* from the clan of Korah. He and his relatives, the Korahites, were responsible for guarding the entrance to the sanctuary, just as their ancestors had guarded the Tabernacle in the camp of the LORD.

[20]Phinehas son of Eleazar had been in charge of the gatekeepers in earlier times, and the LORD had been with him. [21]And later Zechariah son of Meshelemiah had been responsible for guarding the entrance to the Tabernacle.*

[22]In all, there were 212 gatekeepers in those days, and they were listed by genealogies in their villages. David and Samuel the seer had appointed their ancestors because they were reliable men. [23]These

### BE PREPARED ● ● • • •

9:22-32 **The priests and Levites put a great deal of time and care into worship. Not only did they perform rather complicated tasks (described in Leviticus 1–9), they also took care of many pieces of equipment. Everything relating to worship was carefully prepared and maintained so both they and all the people could enter worship with their minds and hearts focused on God.**

**In our busy world, it is easy to rush into our one-hour-a-week worship service without thinking about worship beforehand. We reflect and worry about the week's problems; we pray about whatever comes into our mind; and we do not meditate on the words we are singing. But God wants our worship to be conducted "properly and in order" (1 Corinthians 14:40). Just as we would prepare to meet an important person or a guest, we should carefully prepare to meet and worship our King.**

8:35 As in parallel text at 9:41; Hebrew reads *Tarea,* a variant name for Tahrea. 8:36 As in parallel text at 9:42; Hebrew reads *Jehoaddah,* a variant name for Jadah. 8:37 As in parallel text at 9:43; Hebrew reads *Raphah,* a variant name for Rephaiah. 9:19 Hebrew *Ebiasaph,* a variant name for Abiasaph; compare Exod 6:24. 9:21 Hebrew *Tent of Meeting.*

gatekeepers and their descendants, by their divisions, were responsible for guarding the entrance to
the house of the LORD, the house that was formerly
a tent. 24The gatekeepers were stationed on all four
sides—east, west, north, and south. 25From time to
time, their relatives in the villages came to share their
duties for seven-day periods.
26The four chief gatekeepers, all Levites, were in an
office of great trust, for they were responsible for the
rooms and treasuries at the house of God. 27They
would spend the night around the house of God,
since it was their duty to guard it. It was also their job
to open the gates every morning.
28Some of the gatekeepers were assigned to care
for the various utensils used in worship. They
checked them in and out to avoid any loss. 29Others
were responsible for the furnishings, the items in the
sanctuary, and the supplies such as choice flour,
wine, olive oil, incense, and spices. 30But it was the
priests who prepared the spices and incense. 31Matti-
thiah, a Levite and the oldest son of Shallum the
Korahite, was entrusted with baking the bread used
in the offerings. 32And some members of the clan of
Kohath were in charge of preparing the bread to be
set on the table each Sabbath day.
33The musicians, all prominent Levites, lived at
the Temple. They were exempt from other responsibilities there since they were on duty at all hours.
34All these men lived in Jerusalem. They were the
heads of Levite families and were listed as prominent
leaders in their tribal genealogy.
35Jeiel (the father of* Gibeon) lived in Gibeon. His
wife's name was Maacah, 36and his oldest son was
named Abdon. Jeiel's other sons were Zur, Kish,
Baal, Ner, Nadab, 37Gedor, Ahio, Zechariah, and
Mikloth. 38Mikloth was the father of Shimeam. All
these families lived near each other in Jerusalem.
39Ner was the father of Kish. Kish was the father of
Saul. Saul was the father of Jonathan, Malkishua, Abinadab, and Eshbaal.
40Jonathan was the father of Meribbaal. Meribbaal
was the father of Micah. 41The sons of Micah
were Pithon, Melech, Tahrea, and Ahaz.*
42Ahaz was the father of Jadah.*
Jadah was the father of Alemeth, Azmaveth, and
Zimri.
Zimri was the father of Moza.
43Moza was the father of Binea.
Binea's son was Rephaiah.
Rephaiah's son was Eleasah.
Eleasah's son was Azel.
44Azel had six sons, and their names were Azrikam,
Bokeru, Ishmael, Sheariah, Obadiah, and
Hanan. These were the sons of Azel.

CHAPTER **10** **SAUL DIES; DAVID BECOMES KING.** Now
the Philistines attacked Israel, forcing the Israelites
to flee. Many were slaughtered on the slopes of

**IN PURSUIT ● ● • • •**

10:13-14 **Saul's unfaithfulness was both active and passive; he not only did wrong, he also *failed* to do right. He actively disobeyed by attempting murder, ignoring God's instructions, and seeking guidance from a witch. He passively disobeyed by neglecting to ask God for guidance as he ran the kingdom. Obedience, too, is both passive and active. It is not enough just to avoid what is wrong; we need to actively pursue what is right.**

Mount Gilboa. 2The Philistines closed in on Saul
and his sons, and they killed three of his sons—Jonathan, Abinadab, and Malkishua. 3The fighting grew
very fierce around Saul, and the Philistine archers
caught up with him and wounded him severely.
4Saul groaned to his armor bearer, "Take your sword
and run me through before these pagan Philistines
come and humiliate me." But his armor bearer was
afraid and would not do it. So Saul took his own
sword and fell on it. 5When his armor bearer realized
that Saul was dead, he fell on his own sword and
died. 6So Saul and his three sons died there together,
bringing his dynasty to an end.
7When the Israelites in the Jezreel Valley saw that
their army had been routed and that Saul and his
sons were dead, they abandoned their towns and
fled. So the Philistines moved in and occupied their
towns.
8The next day when the Philistines went out to
strip the dead, they found the bodies of Saul and his
sons on Mount Gilboa. 9So they stripped off Saul's
armor and cut off his head. Then they proclaimed
the news of Saul's death before their idols and to the
people throughout the land of Philistia. 10They
placed his armor in the temple of their gods, and
they fastened his head to the wall in the temple of
Dagon.
11But when the people of Jabesh-gilead heard what
the Philistines had done to Saul, 12their warriors
went out and brought the bodies of Saul and his
three sons back to Jabesh. Then they buried their
remains beneath the oak tree at Jabesh, and they
fasted for seven days.
13So Saul died because he was unfaithful to the
LORD. He failed to obey the LORD's command, and
he even consulted a medium 14instead of asking the
LORD for guidance. So the LORD killed him and
turned his kingdom over to David son of Jesse.

CHAPTER **11** **DAVID CONQUERS JERUSALEM.** Then all
Israel went to David at Hebron and told him, "We
are all members of your family. 2For a long time, even
while Saul was our king, you were the one who really
led Israel. And the LORD your God has told you, 'You
will be the shepherd of my people Israel. You will be
their leader.'" 3So there at Hebron David made a
covenant with the leaders of Israel before the LORD.
They anointed him king of Israel, just as the LORD
had promised through Samuel.
4Then David and all Israel went to Jerusalem (or
Jebus, as it used to be called), where the Jebusites,

**9:35** Or *the founder of.* **9:41** As in Syriac version and Latin Vulgate (see also 8:35); Hebrew lacks *and Ahaz.* **9:42** As in some Hebrew manuscripts and Greek version (see also 8:36); Hebrew reads *Jarah.*

original inhabitants of the land, lived. 5 The people
of Jebus said to David, "You will never get in here!"
But David captured the fortress of Zion, now called
the City of David.
6 David had said to his troops, "Whoever leads the
attack against the Jebusites will become the commander of my armies!" And Joab, the son of David's
sister Zeruiah, led the attack, so he became the commander of David's armies.
7 David made the fortress his home, and that is
why it is called the City of David. 8 He extended the
city from the Millo* to the surrounding area, while
Joab rebuilt the rest of Jerusalem. 9 And David became more and more powerful, because the LORD
Almighty was with him.
10 These are the leaders of David's mighty men.
Together with all Israel, they determined to make
David their king, just as the LORD had promised
concerning Israel. 11 Here is the record of David's
mightiest men:

The first was Jashobeam the Hacmonite, who was
commander of the Three—the three greatest warriors among David's men.* He once used his spear
to kill three hundred enemy warriors in a single
battle.
12 Next in rank among the Three was Eleazar son of
Dodai,* a descendant of Ahoah. 13 He was with
David in the battle against the Philistines at Pas-
dammim. The battle took place in a field full of
barley, and the Israelite army fled. 14 But Eleazar and
David held their ground in the middle of the field
and beat back the Philistines. So the LORD saved
them by giving them a great victory.
15 Once when David was at the rock near the cave
of Adullam, the Philistine army was camped in the
valley of Rephaim. The Three (who were among the
Thirty—an elite group among David's fighting men)
went down to meet him there. 16 David was staying in
the stronghold at the time, and a Philistine detachment had occupied the town of Bethlehem. 17 David
remarked longingly to his men, "Oh, how I would
love some of that good water from the well in Bethlehem, the one by the gate." 18 So the Three broke
through the Philistine lines, drew some water from
the well, and brought it back to David. But David
refused to drink it. Instead, he poured it out before
the LORD. 19 "God forbid that I should drink this!" he
exclaimed. "This water is as precious as the blood of
these men who risked their lives to bring it to me."
So David did not drink it. This is an example of the
exploits of the Three.
20 Abishai, the brother of Joab, was the leader of
the Thirty.* He once used his spear to kill three
hundred enemy warriors in a single battle. It was by
such feats that he became as famous as the Three.
21 Abishai was the most famous of the Thirty and was
their commander, though he was not one of the
Three.
22 There was also Benaiah son of Jehoiada, a valiant warrior from Kabzeel. He did many heroic
deeds, which included killing two of Moab's mightiest warriors. Another time he chased a lion down
into a pit. Then, despite the snow and slippery
ground, he caught the lion and killed it. 23 Another
time, armed with only a club, he killed an Egyptian
warrior who was seven and a half feet* tall and
whose spear was as thick as a weaver's beam. Benaiah wrenched the spear from the Egyptian's hand
and killed him with it. 24 These are some of the deeds
that made Benaiah as famous as the Three. 25 He was
more honored than the other members of the Thirty,
though he was not one of the Three. And David
made him commander of his bodyguard.
26 These were also included among David's mighty
men:

Asahel, Joab's brother;
Elhanan son of Dodo from Bethlehem;
27 Shammah from Harod;*
Helez from Pelon;
28 Ira son of Ikkesh from Tekoa;
Abiezer from Anathoth;
29 Sibbecai from Hushah;
Zalmon* from Ahoah;
30 Maharai from Netophah;
Heled son of Baanah from Netophah;
31 Ithai son of Ribai from Gibeah (from the tribe of
Benjamin);
Benaiah from Pirathon;
32 Hurai from near Nahale-gaash*;
Abi-albon* the Arbathite;
33 Azmaveth from Bahurim*;
Eliahba from Shaalbon;
34 the sons of Jashen* from Gizon;
Jonathan son of Shagee from Harar;
35 Ahiam son of Sharar* from Harar;
Eliphal son of Ur;
36 Hepher from Mekerah;
Ahijah from Pelon;
37 Hezro from Carmel;
Paarai* son of Ezbai;

**FAME ● ● • • •**

11:9 **King David's power and fame increased as a direct result of his consistent trust in God. In contrast, King Saul's power and fame decreased because he wanted all the credit for himself and ignored God (1 Samuel 15:17-26). Those who are concerned about building a name for themselves risk losing the very recognition they crave. Like David, we should be concerned for righteousness, honesty, and excellence, and leave the fame up to God.**

**11:8** Or *the supporting terraces.* The meaning of the Hebrew is uncertain. **11:11** As in some Greek manuscripts (see also 2 Sam 23:8); Hebrew *commander of the Thirty,* or *commander of the captains.* **11:12** As in parallel text at 2 Sam 23:9 (see also 1 Chr 27:4); Hebrew reads *Dodo,* a variant name for Dodai. **11:20** As in Syriac version; Hebrew reads *the Three;* also in 11:21. **11:23** Hebrew *5 cubits* [2.3 meters]. **11:27** As in parallel text at 2 Sam 23:25; Hebrew reads *Shammoth from Haror.* **11:29** As in parallel text at 2 Sam 23:28; Hebrew reads *Ilai.* **11:32a** Or *from the ravines of Gaash.* **11:32b** As in parallel text at 2 Sam 23:31; Hebrew reads *Abiel.* **11:33** As in parallel text at 2 Sam 23:31; Hebrew reads *Baharum.* **11:34** As in parallel text at 2 Sam 23:32; Hebrew reads *sons of Hashem.* **11:35** As in parallel text at 2 Sam 23:33; Hebrew reads *son of Sacar.* **11:37** As in parallel text at 2 Sam 23:35; Hebrew reads *Naarai.*

[38]Joel, the brother of Nathan;
Mibhar son of Hagri;
[39]Zelek from Ammon;
Naharai from Beeroth (Joab's armor bearer);
[40]Ira from Jattir;
Gareb from Jattir;
[41]Uriah the Hittite;
Zabad son of Ahlai;
[42]Adina son of Shiza, the Reubenite leader who had thirty men with him;
[43]Hanan son of Maacah;
Joshaphat from Mithna;
[44]Uzzia from Ashtaroth;
Shama and Jeiel, the sons of Hotham, from Aroer;
[45]Jediael son of Shimri;
Joha, his brother, from Tiz;
[46]Eliel from Mahavah;
Jeribai and Joshaviah, the sons of Elnaam;
Ithmah from Moab;
[47]Eliel and Obed;
Jaasiel from Zobah.

## CHAPTER 12

**MORE WARRIORS JOIN DAVID.** The following men joined David at Ziklag while he was
hiding from Saul son of Kish. They were among the
warriors who fought beside David in battle. [2]All of
them were expert archers, and they could shoot arrows or sling stones with their left hand as well as
their right. They were all relatives of Saul from the
tribe of Benjamin. [3]Their leader was Ahiezer son of
Shemaah from Gibeah; his brother Joash was second-in-command. These were the other warriors:

Jeziel and Pelet, sons of Azmaveth;
Beracah and Jehu from Anathoth;
[4] Ishmaiah from Gibeon, a famous warrior and leader among the Thirty;
Jeremiah, Jahaziel, Johanan, and Jozabad from Gederah;
[5] Eluzai, Jerimoth, Bealiah, Shemariah, and Shephatiah from Haruph;
[6] Elkanah, Isshiah, Azarel, Joezer, and Jashobeam, who were Korahites;
[7] Joelah and Zebadiah, sons of Jeroham from Gedor.

[8]Some brave and experienced warriors from the
tribe of Gad also defected to David while he was at
the stronghold in the wilderness. They were expert
with both shield and spear, as fierce as lions and as
swift as deer on the mountains.

[9] Ezer was their leader.
Obadiah was second.
Eliab was third.
[10]Mishmannah was fourth.
Jeremiah was fifth.
[11]Attai was sixth.
Eliel was seventh.
[12]Johanan was eighth.
Elzabad was ninth.
[13]Jeremiah was tenth.
Macbannai was eleventh.

[14]These warriors from Gad were army commanders.
The weakest among them could take on a hundred
regular troops, and the strongest could take on a
thousand! [15]They crossed the Jordan River during its
seasonal flooding at the beginning of the year and
drove out all the people living in the lowlands on
both the east and west banks.

[16]Others from Benjamin and Judah came to David
at the stronghold. [17]David went out to meet them
and said, "If you have come in peace to help me, we
are friends. But if you have come to betray me to my
enemies when I am innocent, then may the God of
our ancestors see and judge you."

[18]Then the Spirit came upon Amasai, who later
became a leader among the Thirty, and he said,

"We are yours, David!
We are on your side, son of Jesse.
Peace and prosperity be with you,
and success to all who help you,
for your God is the one who helps you."

So David let them join him, and he made them
officers over his troops.

### HOLY SPIRIT ● ● ● • •

12:18 **How did the Holy Spirit work in Old Testament times? When there was an important job to be done, God chose a person to do it, and the Spirit gave that person the needed power and ability. The Spirit gave Bezalel artistic ability (Exodus 31:1-5), Jephthah military prowess (Judges 11:29), David power to rule (1 Samuel 16:13), and Zechariah an authoritative word of prophecy (2 Chronicles 24:20). Here the Holy Spirit came upon David's warriors. The Spirit came upon individuals in order to accomplish specific goals. Beginning at Pentecost, however, the Spirit came upon all believers (Acts 2:14-21). That same Spirit is ready to equip you.**

[19]Some men from Manasseh defected from the
Israelite army and joined David when he went with
the Philistines to fight against Saul. But as it turned
out, the Philistine leaders refused to let David and
his men go with them. After much discussion, they
sent them back, for they said, "It will cost us our
lives if David switches loyalties to Saul and turns
against us."

[20]Here is a list of the men from Manasseh who
defected to David as he was returning to Ziklag:
Adnah, Jozabad, Jediael, Michael, Jozabad, Elihu,
and Zillethai. Each commanded a thousand troops
from the tribe of Manasseh. [21]They helped David
chase down bands of raiders, for they were all brave
and able warriors who became commanders in his
army. [22]Day after day more men joined David until
he had a great army, like the army of God.

[23]These are the numbers of armed warriors who
joined David at Hebron. They were all eager to see
David become king instead of Saul, just as the LORD
had promised.

24From the tribe of Judah, there were 6,800 warriors armed with shields and spears.
25From the tribe of Simeon, there were 7,100 warriors.
26From the tribe of Levi, there were 4,600 troops.
27This included Jehoiada, leader of the family of Aaron, who had 3,700 under his command.
28This also included Zadok, a young warrior, with twenty-two members of his family who were all officers.
29From the tribe of Benjamin, Saul's relatives, there were 3,000 warriors. Most of the men from Benjamin had remained loyal to Saul until this time.
30From the tribe of Ephraim, there were 20,800 warriors, each famous in his own clan.
31From the half-tribe of Manasseh west of the Jordan, 18,000 men were sent for the express purpose of helping David become king.
32From the tribe of Issachar, there were 200 leaders of the tribe with their relatives. All these men understood the temper of the times and knew the best course for Israel to take.
33From the tribe of Zebulun, there were 50,000 skilled warriors. They were fully armed and prepared for battle and completely loyal to David.
34From the tribe of Naphtali, there were 1,000 officers and 37,000 warriors armed with shields and spears.
35From the tribe of Dan, there were 28,600 warriors, all prepared for battle.
36From the tribe of Asher, there were 40,000 trained warriors, all prepared for battle.
37From the east side of the Jordan River—where the tribes of Reuben and Gad and the half-tribe of Manasseh lived—there were 120,000 troops armed with every kind of weapon.

38All these men came in battle array to Hebron
with the single purpose of making David the king of
Israel. In fact, all Israel agreed that David should be
their king. 39They feasted and drank with David for
three days, for preparations had been made by their
relatives for their arrival. 40And people from as far
away as Issachar, Zebulun, and Naphtali brought
food on donkeys, camels, mules, and oxen. Vast
supplies of flour, fig cakes, raisins, wine, olive oil,
cattle, and sheep were brought to the celebration.
There was great joy throughout the land of Israel.

## CHAPTER 13 DAVID CELEBRATES BUT UZZAH DIES.

David consulted with all his officials, including the
generals and captains of his army. 2Then he addressed the entire assembly of Israel as follows: "If
you approve and if it is the will of the LORD our
God, let us send messages to all the Israelites
throughout the land, including the priests and Levites in their towns and pasturelands. Let us invite
them to come and join us. 3It is time to bring back

### THE ARK ● ● • • ·

**13:3 The Ark of God is also called the Ark of the Covenant. It rested in the Most Holy Place in the Temple and was the most sacred artifact of the Hebrew faith. It was a large box containing the stone tablets on which God had written the Ten Commandments (Exodus 25:10-22). David had already made Jerusalem his political capital (11:4-9). At this time, he brought the Ark there in hopes of making it the nation's center for worship, too.**

the Ark of our God, for we neglected it during the
reign of Saul."
4The whole assembly agreed to this, for the
people could see it was the right thing to do. 5So
David summoned all the people of Israel, from
one end of the country to the other,* to join in
bringing the Ark of God from Kiriath-jearim.
6Then David and all Israel went to Baalah of Judah
(also called Kiriath-jearim) to bring back the Ark of
God, which bears the name of the LORD who is
enthroned between the cherubim. 7They transported the Ark of God from the house of Abinadab
on a new cart, with Uzzah and Ahio guiding it.
8David and all Israel were celebrating before God
with all their might, singing and playing all kinds
of musical instruments—lyres, harps, tambourines, cymbals, and trumpets.
9But when they arrived at the threshing floor of
Nacon,* the oxen stumbled, and Uzzah put out his
hand to steady the Ark. 10Then the LORD's anger
blazed out against Uzzah, and he struck him dead
because he had laid his hand on the Ark. So Uzzah
died there in the presence of God. 11David was angry
because the LORD's anger had blazed out against
Uzzah. He named that place Perez-uzzah (which
means "outbreak against Uzzah"). It is still called
that today.
12David was now afraid of God and asked, "How
can I ever bring the Ark of God back into my care?"
13So David decided not to move the Ark into the
City of David. He took it instead to the home of
Obed-edom of Gath. 14The Ark of God remained
there with the family of Obed-edom for three
months, and the LORD blessed him and his entire
household.

## CHAPTER 14 GOD BLESSES DAVID.

Now King Hi-
ram of Tyre sent messengers to David, along with
stonemasons and carpenters to build him a palace.
Hiram also sent many cedar logs for lumber. 2And
David realized that the LORD had made him king
over Israel and had made his kingdom very great for
the sake of his people Israel.
3Then David married more wives in Jerusalem,
and they had many sons and daughters. 4These are
the names of David's sons who were born in Jerusalem: Shimea,* Shobab, Nathan, Solomon, 5Ibhar,
Elishua, Elpelet, 6Nogah, Nepheg, Japhia, 7Elishama,
Eliada,* and Eliphelet.

**13:5** Hebrew *from the Shihor of Egypt to Lebo-hamath.* **13:9** As in parallel text at 2 Sam 6:6; Hebrew reads *Kidon.* **14:4** Hebrew *Shammua,* a variant name for Shimea; compare 3:5. **14:7** Hebrew *Beeliada,* a variant name for Eliada; compare 3:8 and parallel text at 2 Sam 5:16.

8When the Philistines heard that David had been
anointed king over all Israel, they mobilized all their
forces to capture him. But David was told they were
coming, so he and his men marched out to meet
them. 9The Philistines had arrived in the valley of
Rephaim and raided it. 10So David asked God,
"Should I go out to fight the Philistines? Will you
hand them over to me?"

The LORD replied, "Yes, go ahead. I will give you
the victory."

11So David and his troops went to Baal-perazim
and defeated the Philistines there. "God has done
it!" David exclaimed. "He used me to burst
through my enemies like a raging flood!" So that
place was named Baal-perazim (which means "the
Lord who bursts through"). 12The Philistines had
abandoned their idols* there, so David gave orders
to burn them up.

13But after a while, the Philistines returned and
raided the valley again. 14And once again David
asked God what to do. "Do not attack them straight
on," God replied. "Instead, circle around behind
them and attack them near the balsam trees. 15When

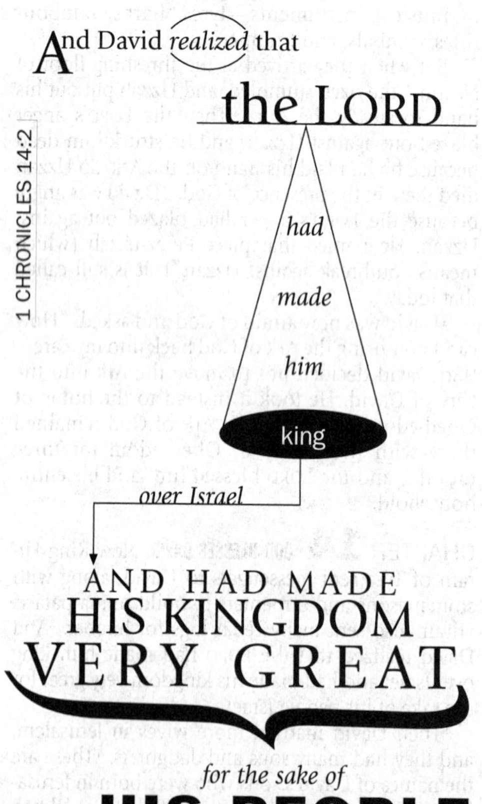

And David realized that
the LORD
had
made
him
king
over Israel
AND HAD MADE
HIS KINGDOM
VERY GREAT
for the sake of
HIS PEOPLE
1 CHRONICLES 14:2

## GOD FIRST ● ● ● • •

14:10 **Before David went to battle, he talked to God, asking for his presence and guidance. Too often we wait until we are in the middle of trouble before turning to God. By then the consequences of our actions are already unfolding. When do you ask for God's help? Only as a desperate last resort? Instead, go to God first! Like David, you may receive incredible help and avoid serious trouble.**

you hear a sound like marching feet in the tops of the
balsam trees, attack! That will be the signal that God
is moving ahead of you to strike down the Philistines." 16So David did what God commanded, and
he struck down the Philistine army all the way from
Gibeon to Gezer.

17So David's fame spread everywhere, and the
LORD caused all the nations to fear David.

CHAPTER **15** **THE ARK COMES BACK.** David now
built several buildings for himself in the City of
David. He also prepared a place for the Ark of God
and set up a special tent there to shelter it. 2Then
he issued these instructions: "When we transport
the Ark of God this time, no one except the Levites
may carry it. The LORD has chosen them to carry
the Ark of the LORD and to minister before him
forever."

3Then David summoned all the Israelites to Jerusalem to bring the Ark of the LORD to the place he
had prepared for it. 4These are the priests* and Levites who were called together:

5There were 120 from the clan of Kohath, with
Uriel as their leader.
6There were 220 from the clan of Merari, with
Asaiah as their leader.
7There were 130 from the clan of Gershon,* with
Joel as their leader.
8There were 200 descendants of Elizaphan, with
Shemaiah as their leader.
9There were 80 descendants of Hebron, with Eliel
as their leader.
10There were 112 descendants of Uzziel, with
Amminadab as their leader.

11Then David summoned the priests, Zadok and
Abiathar, and these Levite leaders: Uriel, Asaiah,
Joel, Shemaiah, Eliel, and Amminadab. 12He said
to them, "You are the leaders of the Levite families.
You must purify yourselves and all your fellow
Levites, so you can bring the Ark of the LORD, the
God of Israel, to the place I have prepared for it.
13Because you Levites did not carry the Ark the first
time, the anger of the LORD our God burst out
against us. We failed to ask God how to move it in
the proper way." 14So the priests and the Levites
purified themselves in order to bring the Ark of the
LORD, the God of Israel, to Jerusalem. 15Then the
Levites carried the Ark of God on their shoulders
with its carrying poles, just as the LORD had instructed Moses.

14:12 Hebrew *their gods;* compare parallel text at 2 Sam 5:21. 15:4 Hebrew *descendants of Aaron.* 15:7 Hebrew *Gershom,* a variant name for Gershon.

16David also ordered the Levite leaders to appoint
a choir of Levites who were singers and musicians to
sing joyful songs to the accompaniment of lyres,
harps, and cymbals. 17So the Levites appointed Heman son of Joel, Asaph son of Berekiah, and Ethan
son of Kushaiah from the clan of Merari to direct the
musicians. 18The following men were chosen as their
assistants: Zechariah, Jaaziel, Shemiramoth, Jehiel,
Unni, Eliab, Benaiah, Maaseiah, Mattithiah,
Eliphelehu, Mikneiah, and the gatekeepers, Obed-
edom and Jeiel.
19Heman, Asaph, and Ethan were chosen to sound
the bronze cymbals. 20Zechariah, Aziel, Shemiramoth, Jehiel, Unni, Eliab, Maaseiah, and Benaiah
were chosen to play the lyres.* 21Mattithiah,
Eliphelehu, Mikneiah, Obed-edom, Jeiel, and Azaziah were chosen to play the harps.* 22Kenaniah, the
head Levite, was chosen as the choir leader because
of his skill.
23Berekiah and Elkanah were chosen to guard the
Ark. 24Shebaniah, Joshaphat, Nethanel, Amasai,
Zechariah, Benaiah, and Eliezer—all of whom were
priests—were chosen to blow the trumpets as they
marched in front of the Ark of God. Obed-edom and
Jehiah were chosen to guard the Ark.
25Then David and the leaders of Israel and the
generals of the army went to the home of Obed-
edom to bring the Ark of the LORD's covenant up to
Jerusalem with a great celebration. 26And because
God was clearly helping the Levites as they carried
the Ark of the LORD's covenant, they sacrificed seven
bulls and seven lambs. 27David was dressed in a robe
of fine linen, as were the Levites who carried the Ark,
the singers, and Kenaniah the song leader. David was
also wearing a priestly tunic.* 28So all Israel brought
up the Ark of the LORD's covenant to Jerusalem with
shouts of joy, the blowing of horns and trumpets, the
crashing of cymbals, and loud playing on harps and
lyres.
29But as the Ark of the LORD's covenant entered the
City of David, Michal, the daughter of Saul, looked
down from her window. When she saw King David
dancing and leaping for joy, she was filled with
contempt for him.

## CHAPTER 16

**DAVID PRAISES GOD.** So they brought
the Ark of God into the special tent David had
prepared for it, and they sacrificed burnt offerings
and peace offerings before God. 2When he had finished, David blessed the people in the name of the
LORD. 3Then he gave a gift of food to every man and
woman in Israel: a loaf of bread, a cake of dates,*
and a cake of raisins.
4David appointed the following Levites to lead the
people in worship before the Ark of the LORD by
asking for his blessings and giving thanks and praise
to the LORD, the God of Israel. 5Asaph, the leader of
this group, sounded the cymbals. His assistants were

### EXACTLY ● ● ● • •

15:13-15 **When David's first attempt to move the Ark failed (13:8-14), he learned an important lesson: When God gives specific instructions, it is wise to follow them precisely. This time David saw to it that the Levites carried the Ark (Numbers 4:5-15). We may not fully understand the reasons behind God's instructions, but we can know that his wisdom is complete and his judgment infallible. The way to know God's instructions is to know his Word. But just as children do not understand the reasons for all their parents' instructions until they are adults, we will not understand all of God's instructions in this life. It is far better to obey God first, and then seek to know the reasons.**

Zechariah (the second), then Jeiel, Shemiramoth,
Jehiel, Mattithiah, Eliab, Benaiah, Obed-edom, and
Jeiel. They played the harps and lyres. 6The priests,
Benaiah and Jahaziel, played the trumpets regularly
before the Ark of God's covenant.
7That day David gave to Asaph and his fellow
Levites this song of thanksgiving to the LORD:

8 Give thanks to the LORD and proclaim his greatness.
Let the whole world know what he has done.
9 Sing to him; yes, sing his praises.
Tell everyone about his miracles.
10 Exult in his holy name;
O worshipers of the LORD, rejoice!
11 Search for the LORD and for his strength,
and keep on searching.
12 Think of the wonderful works he has done,
the miracles, and the judgments he handed down,
13 O children of Israel, God's servant,
O descendants of Jacob, God's chosen one.

14 He is the LORD our God.
His rule is seen throughout the land.
15 He always stands by his covenant*—
the commitment he made to a thousand generations.
16 This is the covenant he made with Abraham
and the oath he swore to Isaac.
17 He confirmed it to Jacob as a decree,
to the people of Israel as a never-ending treaty:
18 "I will give you the land of Canaan
as your special possession."

19 He said this when they were few in number,
a tiny group of strangers in Canaan.

### THANK YOU ● ● ● • •

16:7-36 **Does it ever seem that a simple "thank you" to God is not enough to express your appreciation? Four elements of true thanksgiving are found in the following song: (1) *remembering* what God has done, (2) *telling* others about it, (3) *showing* God's glory to others, and (4) *offering* gifts of self, time, and resources. Get into the habit of fully expressing your thanks to God.**

15:20 Hebrew adds *according to Alamoth,* which is probably a musical term. The meaning of the Hebrew is uncertain. 15:21 Hebrew adds *according to the Sheminith,* which is probably a musical term. The meaning of the Hebrew is uncertain. 15:27 Hebrew *a linen ephod.* 16:3 Or *a portion of meat.* The meaning of the Hebrew is uncertain. 16:15 As in some Greek manuscripts (see also Ps 105:8); Hebrew reads *Remember his covenant forever.*

## MUSIC IN BIBLE TIMES

Paul clearly puts forth the Christian's view that things are not good or bad in and of themselves (see Romans 14 and 1 Corinthians 14:7-8, 26). The point always should be to worship the Lord or help others by means of the things of this world, including music. Music was created by God and can be returned to him in praise. Does the music you play or listen to have a negative impact upon your relationship with God or a positive one?

| *Highlights of musical use in Scripture* | *References* |
|---|---|
| Jubal was the first musician | Genesis 4:21 |
| Miriam and other women sang and danced to praise God | Exodus 15:1-21 |
| The priest was to have bells on his robes | Exodus 28:34-35 |
| Jericho fell to the sound of rams' horns | Joshua 6:4-20 |
| Saul experienced the soothing effect of music | 1 Samuel 16:14-23 |
| The king's coronation was accompanied by music | 1 Kings 1:39-40 |
| David organized the use of music for worship | 1 Chronicles 16:4-7 |
| The Ark of the Covenant was accompanied by trumpeters | 1 Chronicles 16:6 |
| There were musicians for the king's court | Ecclesiastes 2:8 |
| Everything was to be used by everyone to praise the Lord | Psalm 150 |
| Jesus and the disciples sang a hymn | Matthew 26:30 |
| Paul and Silas sang in jail | Acts 16:25 |
| We are to sing to the Lord with thankful hearts | Colossians 3:16 |

In the New Testament, worship continued in the synagogues until the Christians became unwelcome there, so there was a rich musical heritage already established. The fact that music is mentioned less often in the New Testament does not mean it was less important.

---

20 They wandered back and forth between nations,
from one kingdom to another.
21 Yet he did not let anyone oppress them.
He warned kings on their behalf:
22 "Do not touch these people I have chosen,
and do not hurt my prophets."
23 Let the whole earth sing to the LORD!
Each day proclaim the good news that he saves.
24 Publish his glorious deeds among the nations.
Tell everyone about the amazing things he does.
25 Great is the LORD! He is most worthy of praise!
He is to be revered above all gods.
26 The gods of other nations are merely idols,
but the LORD made the heavens!
27 Honor and majesty surround him;
strength and beauty are in his dwelling.
28 O nations of the world, recognize the LORD,
recognize that the LORD is glorious and strong.
29 Give to the LORD the glory he deserves!
Bring your offering and come to worship him.
Worship the LORD in all his holy splendor.
30 Let all the earth tremble before him.
The world is firmly established and cannot be shaken.
31 Let the heavens be glad, and let the earth rejoice!
Tell all the nations that the LORD is king.
32 Let the sea and everything in it shout his praise!
Let the fields and their crops burst forth with joy!
33 Let the trees of the forest rustle with praise before the LORD!
For he is coming to judge the earth.
34 Give thanks to the LORD, for he is good!
His faithful love endures forever.
35 Cry out, "Save us, O God of our salvation!
Gather and rescue us from among the nations,
so we can thank your holy name
and rejoice and praise you."
36 Blessed be the LORD, the God of Israel,
from everlasting to everlasting!

And all the people shouted "Amen!" and praised the LORD.

[37]David arranged for Asaph and his fellow Levites to minister regularly before the Ark of the LORD's covenant, doing whatever needed to be done each day. [38]This group included Obed-edom (son of Jeduthun), Hosah, and sixty-eight other Levites as gatekeepers.

[39]Meanwhile, David stationed Zadok the priest and his fellow priests at the Tabernacle of the LORD on the hill of Gibeon, where they continued to minister before the LORD. [40]They sacrificed the regular burnt offerings to the LORD each morning and evening on the altar set aside for that purpose, obeying everything written in the law of the LORD, which he had given to Israel. [41]David also appointed Heman, Jeduthun, and the others chosen by name to give thanks to the LORD, "for his faithful love endures forever." [42]They used their trumpets, cymbals, and other instruments to accompany the songs of praise to God. And the sons of Jeduthun were appointed as gatekeepers.

[43]Then all the people returned to their homes, and David returned home to bless his family.

## CHAPTER 17 GOD MAKES A PROMISE TO DAVID.

Now when David was settled in his palace, he said to Nathan the prophet, "Here I am living in this beautiful cedar palace, but the Ark of the LORD's covenant is out in a tent!"

[2]Nathan replied, "Go ahead with what you have in mind, for God is with you."

[3]But that same night God said to Nathan,

[4]"Go and tell my servant David, 'This is what the LORD says: You are not the one to build me a temple to live in. [5]I have never lived in a temple, from the day I brought the Israelites out of Egypt until now. My home has always been a tent, moving from one place to another. [6]And I never once complained to Israel's leaders,* the shepherds of my people. I have never asked them, "Why haven't you built me a beautiful cedar temple?"'

[7]"Now go and say to my servant David, 'This is what the LORD Almighty says: I chose you to lead my people Israel when you were just a shepherd boy, tending your sheep out in the pasture. [8]I have been with you wherever you have gone, and I have destroyed all your enemies. Now I will make your name famous throughout the earth! [9]And I have provided a permanent homeland for my people Israel, a secure place where they will never be disturbed. It will be their own land where wicked nations won't oppress them as they did in the past, [10]from the time I appointed judges to rule my people. And I will subdue all your enemies.

"'And now I declare that the LORD will build a house for you—a dynasty of kings! [11]For when you die, I will raise up one of your sons, and I will make his kingdom strong. [12]He is the one who will build a house—a temple—for me. And I will establish his throne forever. [13]I will be his father, and he will be my son. I will not take my unfailing love from him as I took it from Saul, who ruled before you. [14]I will establish him over my dynasty and my kingdom for all time, and his throne will be secure forever.'"

[15]So Nathan went back to David and told him everything the LORD had said.

[16]Then King David went in and sat before the LORD and prayed, "Who am I, O LORD God, and what is my family, that you have brought me this far? [17]And now, O God, in addition to everything else, you speak of giving me a lasting dynasty! You speak as though I were someone very great,* O LORD God! [18]What more can I say about the way you have honored me? You know what I am really like. [19]For my sake, O LORD, and according to your will, you have done all these great things and have made them known.

[20]"O LORD, there is no one like you—there is no other God. We have never even heard of another god like you! [21]What other nation on earth is like Israel? What other nation, O God, have you redeemed from slavery to be your own people? You made a great name for yourself when you rescued your people from Egypt. You performed awesome miracles and drove out the nations that stood in their way. [22]You chose Israel to be your people forever, and you, O LORD, have become their God.

[23]"And now, O LORD, do as you have promised concerning me and my family. May it be a promise that will last forever. [24]And may your name be established and honored forever so that all the world will say, 'The LORD Almighty is God over Israel!' And may the dynasty of your servant David be established in your presence.

[25]"O my God, I have been bold enough to pray this prayer because you have revealed that you will build a house for me—an eternal dynasty! [26]For you are God, O LORD. And you have promised these good things to me, your servant. [27]And now, it has pleased you to bless me and my family so that our dynasty will continue forever before you. For when you grant a blessing, O LORD, it is an eternal blessing!"

## CHAPTER 18 DAVID CONQUERS MANY ENEMIES.

After this, David subdued and humbled the Philistines by conquering Gath and its surrounding towns. [2]David

### THE REAL KING ● ● • •

**17:16-27 David responded to God's answer and promises with deep humility, not resentment. This king who had conquered his enemies and was loved by his people said, "Who am I . . . that you have brought me this far?" David recognized that God was the *true* King. God has done just as much for us, and he plans to do even more! Like David, we should humble ourselves and give glory to God, saying, "O LORD, there is no one like you."**

17:6 As in Greek version (see also 2 Sam 7:7); Hebrew reads *judges.* 17:17 The meaning of the Hebrew is uncertain.

## GLORY ● ● • • ·

18:6, 14 **God gave David victory and David was a just ruler. Although we are not promised victory in every military battle, we see in David's glowing success a hint of what Christ's reign will be like—complete victory and just government. If David's glory was great, how much greater Christ's glory will be. Our confidence is that we can be rightly related to Jesus Christ through faith. One day we will share in his glory as we reign with him.**

also conquered the land of Moab, and the Moabites became David's subjects and brought him tribute money.

3Then David destroyed the forces of King Hadadezer of Zobah, as far as Hamath,* when Hadadezer marched out to strengthen his control along the Euphrates River. 4David captured one thousand chariots, seven thousand charioteers, and twenty thousand foot soldiers. Then he crippled all but one hundred of the chariot horses.

5When Arameans from Damascus arrived to help Hadadezer, David killed twenty-two thousand of them. 6Then he placed several army garrisons in Damascus, the Aramean capital, and the Arameans became David's subjects and brought him tribute money. So the LORD gave David victory wherever he went. 7David brought the gold shields of Hadadezer's officers to Jerusalem, 8along with a large amount of bronze from Hadadezer's cities of Tebah* and Cun. Later Solomon melted the bronze and used it for the Temple. He molded it into the bronze Sea, the pillars, and the various bronze utensils used at the Temple.

9When King Toi* of Hamath heard that David had destroyed the army of King Hadadezer of Zobah, 10he sent his son Joram* to congratulate David on his success. Hadadezer and Toi had long been enemies, and there had been many wars between them. Joram presented David with many gifts of gold, silver, and bronze. 11King David dedicated all these gifts to the LORD, along with the silver and gold he had taken from the other nations he had subdued—Edom, Moab, Ammon, Philistia, and Amalek.

12Abishai son of Zeruiah destroyed eighteen thousand Edomites in the Valley of Salt. 13He placed army garrisons throughout Edom, and all the Edomites became David's subjects. This was another example of how the LORD made David victorious wherever he went.

14David reigned over all Israel and was fair to everyone. 15Joab son of Zeruiah was commander of the army. Jehoshaphat son of Ahilud was the royal historian. 16Zadok son of Ahitub and Ahimelech* son of Abiathar were the priests. Seraiah* was the court secretary. 17Benaiah son of Jehoiada was captain of the king's bodyguard.* David's sons served as the king's chief assistants.

## CHAPTER 19 DAVID DEFENDS HIS PEOPLE.

Some time after this, King Nahash of the Ammonites died, and his son Hanun* became king. 2David said, "I am going to show complete loyalty to Hanun because his father, Nahash, was always completely loyal to me." So David sent ambassadors to express sympathy to Hanun about his father's death.

But when David's ambassadors arrived in the land of Ammon, 3Hanun's advisers said to him, "Do you really think these men are coming here to honor your father? No! David has sent them to spy out the land so that they can come in and conquer it!" 4So Hanun seized David's ambassadors and shaved their beards, cut off their robes at the buttocks, and sent them back to David in shame. 5When David heard what had happened, he sent messengers to tell the men to stay at Jericho until their beards grew out, for they were very embarrassed by their appearance.

6Now the people of Ammon realized how seriously they had angered David, so Hanun and the Ammonites sent thirty-eight tons* of silver to hire chariots and troops from Aram-naharaim, Aram-maacah, and Zobah. 7They also hired thirty-two thousand chariots and secured the support of the king of Maacah and his army. These forces camped at Medeba, where they were joined by the Ammonite troops that Hanun had recruited from his own towns. 8When David heard about this, he sent Joab and all his warriors to fight them. 9The Ammonite troops drew up their battle lines at the gate of the city, while the other kings positioned themselves to fight in the open fields.

10When Joab saw that he would have to fight on two fronts, he chose the best troops in his army. He placed them under his personal command and led them out to fight the Arameans in the fields. 11He left the rest of the army under the command of his brother Abishai, who was to attack the Ammonites. 12"If the Arameans are too strong for me, then come over and help me," Joab told his brother. "And if the Ammonites are too strong for you, I will help you. 13Be courageous! Let us fight bravely to save our people and the cities of our God. May the LORD's will be done."

14When Joab and his troops attacked, the Arameans began to run away. 15And when the Ammonites saw the Arameans running, they ran from Abishai

## SPRING INTO WAR ● ● • • ·

20:1 **Why was spring the season when wars usually began? During the winter, opposing kings plotted and planned future conquests. Then, when the fair weather permitted it, their pent-up rage and energy broke forth into war. Look for the "springs" in your life, the times when you are most sensitive to the conflicts around you. Then determine to diffuse them by confessing your fear, bitterness, and anger to God, allowing him to heal them.**

**18:3** The meaning of the Hebrew is uncertain. **18:8** Hebrew reads *Tibhath,* a variant name for Tebah; compare parallel text at 2 Sam 8:8. **18:9** As in parallel text at 2 Sam 8:9; Hebrew reads *Tou;* also in 18:10. **18:10** As in parallel text at 2 Sam 8:10; Hebrew reads *Hadoram,* a variant name for Joram. **18:16a** As in some Hebrew manuscripts, Syriac version, and Latin Vulgate (see also 2 Sam 8:17); most Hebrew manuscripts read *Abimelech.* **18:16b** As in parallel text at 2 Sam 8:17; Hebrew reads *Shavsha.* **18:17** Hebrew *of the Kerethites and Pelethites.* **19:1** Hebrew lacks *Hanun;* compare parallel text at 2 Sam 10:1. **19:6** Hebrew *1,000 talents* [34 metric tons].

and retreated into the city. Then Joab returned to Jerusalem.

[16]The Arameans now realized that they were no match for Israel, so they summoned additional Aramean troops from the other side of the Euphrates River.* These troops arrived under the command of Shobach,* the commander of all Hadadezer's forces. [17]When David heard what was happening, he mobilized all Israel, crossed the Jordan River, and positioned his troops in battle formation. Then he engaged the enemy troops in battle, and they fought against him. [18]But again the Arameans fled from the Israelites. This time David's forces killed seven thousand charioteers and forty thousand foot soldiers, including Shobach, the commander of their army. [19]When the servants of Hadadezer realized they had been defeated by Israel, they surrendered to David and became his subjects. After that, the Arameans were no longer willing to help the Ammonites.

CHAPTER **20** **DAVID DEFEATS THE AMMONITES.** The following spring, the time of year when kings go to war, Joab led the Israelite army in successful attacks against the towns and villages of the Ammonites. In the process they laid siege to the city of Rabbah and destroyed it. But David had stayed behind in Jerusalem.

[2]When David arrived at Rabbah, he removed the crown from the king's head,* and it was placed on David's own head. The crown was made of gold and set with gems, and it weighed about seventy-five pounds.* David took a vast amount of plunder from the city. [3]He also made slaves of the people of Rabbah and forced them to labor with saws, picks, and axes.* That is how he dealt with the people of all the Ammonite cities. Then David and his army returned to Jerusalem.

[4]After this, war broke out with the Philistines at Gezer. As they fought, Sibbecai from Hushah killed Saph,* a descendant of the giants,* and so the Philistines were subdued. [5]During another battle with the Philistines, Elhanan son of Jair killed Lahmi, the brother of Goliath of Gath. The handle of Lahmi's spear was as thick as a weaver's beam! [6]In another battle with the Philistines at Gath, a huge man with six fingers on each hand and six toes on each foot—a descendant of the giants—[7]defied and taunted Israel. But he was killed by Jonathan, the son of David's brother Shimea. [8]These Philistines were descendants of the giants of Gath, but they were killed by David and his warriors.

CHAPTER **21** **DAVID COUNTS THE PEOPLE.** Satan rose up against Israel and caused David to take a census of the Israelites. [2]David gave these orders to Joab and his commanders: "Take a census of all the people in the land—from Beersheba in the south to Dan in the north—and bring me the totals so I may know how many there are."

[3]But Joab replied, "May the LORD increase the number of his people a hundred times over! But why, my lord, do you want to do this? Are they not all your servants? Why must you cause Israel to sin?"

[4]But the king insisted that Joab take the census, so Joab traveled throughout Israel to count the people. Then he returned to Jerusalem [5]and reported the number of people to David. There were 1,100,000 men of military age in Israel, and 470,000 in Judah. [6]But Joab did not include the tribes of Levi and Benjamin in the census because he was so distressed at what the king had made him do.

**CONFESSION ● ● • • •**

**21:8 When David realized his sin, he took full responsibility, admitted he was wrong, and asked God to forgive him. Many people want to add God and his blessings to their life without acknowledging their personal sin and guilt. But confession and repentance must come before receiving forgiveness. Like David, we must take full responsibility for our actions and confess them to God before we can expect him to forgive us and continue his work in our life.**

[7]God was very displeased with the census, and he punished Israel for it. [8]Then David said to God, "I have sinned greatly and shouldn't have taken the census. Please forgive me for doing this foolish thing."

[9]Then the LORD spoke to Gad, David's seer. This was the message: [10]"Go and say to David, 'This is what the LORD says: I will give you three choices. Choose one of these punishments, and I will do it.'"

[11]So Gad came to David and said, "These are the choices the LORD has given you. [12]You may choose three years of famine, three months of destruction by your enemies, or three days of severe plague as the angel of the LORD brings devastation throughout the land of Israel. Think this over and let me know what answer to give the LORD."

[13]"This is a desperate situation!" David replied to Gad. "But let me fall into the hands of the LORD, for his mercy is very great. Do not let me fall into human hands."

[14]So the LORD sent a plague upon Israel, and seventy thousand people died as a result. [15]And God sent an angel to destroy Jerusalem. But just as the angel was preparing to destroy it, the LORD relented and said to the death angel, "Stop! That is enough!" At that moment the angel of the LORD was standing by the threshing floor of Araunah* the Jebusite.

[16]David looked up and saw the angel of the LORD standing between heaven and earth with his sword drawn, stretched out over Jerusalem. So David and the leaders of Israel put on sackcloth to show their distress and fell down with their faces to the ground.

**19:16a** Hebrew *the river.* **19:16b** As in parallel text at 2 Sam 10:16; Hebrew reads *Shophach;* also in 19:18. **20:2a** Greek version and Latin Vulgate read *removed the crown of Milcom;* compare 1 Kgs 11:5. Milcom, also called Molech, was the god of the Ammonites. **20:2b** Hebrew *1 talent* [34 kilograms]. **20:3** As in parallel text at 2 Sam 12:31; Hebrew reads *and saws.* **20:4a** As in parallel text at 2 Sam 21:18; Hebrew reads *Sippai.* **20:4b** Hebrew *descendant of the Rephaites;* also in 20:6, 8. **21:15** As in parallel text at 2 Sam 24:16; Hebrew reads *Ornan,* another name for Araunah; also in 21:18-28.

[17]And David said to God, "I am the one who called for the census! I am the one who has sinned and done wrong! But these people are innocent—what have they done? O LORD my God, let your anger fall against me and my family, but do not destroy your people."

[18]Then the angel of the LORD told Gad to instruct David to build an altar to the LORD at the threshing floor of Araunah the Jebusite. [19]So David obeyed the instructions the LORD had given him through Gad. [20]Araunah, who was busy threshing wheat at the time, turned and saw the angel there. His four sons, who were with him, ran away and hid. [21]When Araunah saw the king approaching, he left his threshing floor and bowed to the ground before David.

[22]David said to Araunah, "Let me buy this threshing floor from you at its full price. Then I will build an altar to the LORD there, so that he will stop the plague."

[23]"Take it, my lord, and use it as you wish," Araunah said to David. "Here are oxen for the burnt offerings, and you can use the threshing tools for wood to build a fire on the altar. And take the wheat for the grain offering. I will give it all to you."

[24]But the king replied to Araunah, "No, I insist on paying what it is worth. I cannot take what is yours and give it to the LORD. I will not offer a burnt offering that has cost me nothing!" [25]So David gave Araunah six hundred pieces of gold* in payment for the threshing floor. [26]David built an altar there to the LORD and sacrificed burnt offerings and peace offerings. And when David prayed, the LORD answered him by sending fire from heaven to burn up the offering on the altar. [27]Then the LORD spoke to the angel, who put the sword back into its sheath.

[28]When David saw that the LORD had answered his prayer, he offered sacrifices there at Araunah's threshing floor. [29]At that time, the Tabernacle of the LORD and the altar that Moses made in the wilderness were located at the hill of Gibeon. [30]But David was not able to go there to inquire of God, because he was terrified by the drawn sword of the angel of the LORD.

## CHAPTER 22

**THE TEMPLE MATERIALS.** Then David said, "This will be the location for the Temple of the LORD God and the place of the altar for Israel's burnt offerings!"

[2]So David gave orders to call together the foreigners living in Israel, and he assigned them the task of preparing blocks of stone for building the Temple of God. [3]David provided large amounts of iron for the nails that would be needed for the doors in the gates and for the clamps, and more bronze than they could ever weigh. [4]He also provided innumerable cedar logs, for the men of Tyre and Sidon had brought vast amounts of cedar to David. [5]David said, "My son Solomon is still young and inexperienced, and the Temple of the LORD must be a magnificent structure, famous and glorious throughout the world. So I will begin making preparations for it now." So David collected vast amounts of building materials before his death.

[6]Then David sent for his son Solomon and instructed him to build a Temple for the LORD, the God of Israel. [7]"I wanted to build a Temple to honor the name of the LORD my God," David told him. [8]"But the LORD said to me, 'You have killed many men in the great battles you have fought. And since you have shed so much blood before me, you will not be the one to build a Temple to honor my name. [9]But you will have a son who will experience peace and rest. I will give him peace with his enemies in all the surrounding lands. His name will be Solomon,* and I will give peace and quiet to Israel during his reign. [10]He is the one who will build a Temple to honor my name. He will be my son, and I will be his father. And I will establish the throne of his kingdom over Israel forever.'

[11]"Now, my son, may the LORD be with you and give you success as you follow his instructions in building the Temple of the LORD your God. [12]And may the LORD give you wisdom and understanding, that you may obey the law of the LORD your God as you rule over Israel. [13]For if you carefully obey the laws and regulations that the LORD gave to Israel through Moses, you will be successful. Be strong and courageous; do not be afraid or lose heart!

### WHOLEHEARTEDLY ● ● • • •

22:12-13 **David learned that it takes *total* dedication to please God—obeying with all you heart (22:19). This requires both right decisions (good judgment) and right attitudes (strength, courage, and enthusiasm). It isn't enough just to understand what God wants; your heart must be totally dedicated to him. Jesus said, "Anyone who puts a hand to the plow and then looks back is not fit for the Kingdom of God" (Luke 9:62). Remove the distractions that pull you away from God, and serve him wholeheartedly.**

[14]"I have worked hard to provide materials for building the Temple of the LORD—nearly four thousand tons of gold, nearly forty thousand tons of silver,* and so much iron and bronze that it cannot be weighed. I have also gathered lumber and stone for the walls, though you may need to add more. [15]You have many skilled stonemasons and carpenters and craftsmen of every kind available to you. [16]They are expert goldsmiths and silversmiths and workers of bronze and iron. Now begin the work, and may the LORD be with you!"

[17]Then David ordered all the leaders of Israel to assist Solomon in this project. [18]"The LORD your God is with you," he declared. "He has given you peace with the surrounding nations. He has handed them over to me, and they are now subject to the LORD and his people. [19]Now seek the LORD your God with all your heart. Build the sanctuary of the LORD God so

21:25 Hebrew *600 shekels of gold,* about 15 pounds or 6.8 kilograms in weight. 22:9 *Solomon* sounds like and is probably derived from the Hebrew word for "peace." 22:14 Hebrew *100,000 talents* [3,400 metric tons] *of gold, 1,000,000 talents* [34,000 metric tons] *of silver.*

that you can bring the Ark of the LORD's covenant and the holy vessels of God into the Temple built to honor the LORD's name."

CHAPTER **23** **DAVID GIVES THE LEVITES JOBS.** When David was an old man, he appointed his son Solomon to be king over Israel. [2]David summoned all the political leaders of Israel, together with the priests and Levites, for the coronation ceremony. [3]All the Levites who were thirty years old or older were counted, and the total came to thirty-eight thousand. [4]Then David said, "Twenty-four thousand of them will supervise the work at the Temple of the LORD. Six thousand are to serve as officials and judges. [5]Four thousand will work as gatekeepers, and another four thousand will praise the LORD with the musical instruments I have made." [6]Then David divided the Levites into divisions named after the clans descended from the three sons of Levi—Gershon, Kohath, and Merari.

[7]The Gershonite family units were defined by their lines of descent from Libni* and Shimei, the sons of Gershon. [8]Three of the descendants of Libni were Jehiel (the family leader), Zetham, and Joel. [9]These were the leaders of the family of Libni.

Three of the descendants of Shimei were Shelomoth, Haziel, and Haran. [10]Four other descendants of Shimei were Jahath, Ziza,* Jeush, and Beriah. [11]Jahath was the family leader, and Ziza was next. Jeush and Beriah were counted as a single family because neither had many sons.

[12]The descendants of Kohath included Amram, Izhar, Hebron, and Uzziel.

[13]The sons of Amram were Aaron and Moses. Aaron and his descendants were set apart to dedicate the most holy things, to offer sacrifices in the LORD's presence, to serve the LORD, and to pronounce blessings in his name forever.

[14]As for Moses, the man of God, his sons were included with the tribe of Levi. [15]The sons of Moses were Gershom and Eliezer.

[16]The descendants of Gershom included Shebuel, the family leader.

[17]Eliezer had only one son, Rehabiah, the family leader. Rehabiah had numerous descendants.

[18]The descendants of Izhar included Shelomith, the family leader.

[19]The descendants of Hebron included Jeriah (the family leader), Amariah (the second), Jahaziel (the third), and Jekameam (the fourth).

[20]The descendants of Uzziel included Micah (the family leader) and Isshiah (the second).

[21]The descendants of Merari included Mahli and Mushi.

The sons of Mahli were Eleazar and Kish. [22]Eleazar died with no sons, only daughters. His daughters married their cousins, the sons of Kish.

[23]The three sons of Mushi were Mahli, Eder, and Jerimoth.

[24]These were the descendants of Levi by clans, the leaders of their family groups, registered carefully by name. Each had to be twenty years old or older to qualify for service in the house of the LORD. [25]For David said, "The LORD, the God of Israel, has given us peace, and he will always live in Jerusalem. [26]Now the Levites will no longer need to carry the Tabernacle and its utensils from place to place." [27]It was according to David's final instructions that all the Levites twenty years old or older were registered for service.

[28]The work of the Levites was to assist the priests, the descendants of Aaron, as they served at the house of the LORD. They also took care of the courtyards and side rooms, helped perform the ceremonies of purification, and served in many other ways in the house of God. [29]They were in charge of the sacred bread that was set out on the table, the choice flour for the grain offerings, the wafers made without yeast, the cakes cooked in olive oil, and the other mixed breads. They were also responsible to check all the weights and measures. [30]And each morning and evening they stood before the LORD to sing songs of thanks and praise to him. [31]They assisted with the burnt offerings that were presented to the LORD on Sabbath days, at new moon celebrations, and at all the appointed festivals. The proper number of Levites served in the LORD's presence at all times, following all the procedures they had been given.

[32]And so, under the supervision of the priests, the Levites watched over the Tabernacle and the Temple* and faithfully carried out their duties of service at the house of the LORD.

**TOGETHER ● ● ● • •**

**23:28-32 Priests and Levites had different Temple jobs. Priests performed the sacrifices. Levites helped the priests, working as elders, deacons, custodians, assistants, musicians, and more. Both priests and Levites came from the tribe of Levi, but priests had to be descendants of Aaron, Israel's first high priest (Exodus 28:1-3). Temple worship could not have taken place without the combined efforts of the priests and Levites. Their responsibilities differed, but they were equally important to God's plan. No matter what place of service you have in the church, you are important to the healthy functioning of the congregation.**

CHAPTER **24** **DAVID DIVIDES THE PRIESTS.** This is how Aaron's descendants, the priests, were divided into groups for service. The sons of Aaron were Nadab, Abihu, Eleazar, and Ithamar. [2]But Nadab and Abihu died before their father did, and they had no sons. So only Eleazar and Ithamar were left to carry on as priests.

**23:7** Hebrew *Ladan* (also in 23:8-9), another name for Libni; compare 6:17. **23:10** As in Greek version and Latin Vulgate (see also 23:11); Hebrew reads *Zina.* **23:32** Hebrew *the Tent of Meeting and the sanctuary.*

[3]With the help of Zadok, who was a descendant of
Eleazar, and of Ahimelech, who was a descendant of
Ithamar, David divided Aaron's descendants into
groups according to their various duties. [4]Eleazar's
descendants were divided into sixteen groups and
Ithamar's into eight, for there were more family
leaders among the descendants of Eleazar.

[5]All tasks were assigned to the various groups by
means of sacred lots so that no preference would be
shown, for there were many qualified officials serving God in the sanctuary from among the descendants of both Eleazar and Ithamar. [6]Shemaiah son of
Nethanel, a Levite, acted as secretary and wrote
down the names and assignments in the presence of
the king, Zadok the priest, Ahimelech son of Abiathar, and the family leaders of the priests and Levites.
The descendants of Eleazar and Ithamar took turns
casting lots.

[7] The first lot fell to Jehoiarib.
The second lot fell to Jedaiah.
[8] The third lot fell to Harim.
The fourth lot fell to Seorim.
[9] The fifth lot fell to Malkijah.
The sixth lot fell to Mijamin.
[10] The seventh lot fell to Hakkoz.
The eighth lot fell to Abijah.
[11] The ninth lot fell to Jeshua.
The tenth lot fell to Shecaniah.
[12] The eleventh lot fell to Eliashib.
The twelfth lot fell to Jakim.
[13] The thirteenth lot fell to Huppah.
The fourteenth lot fell to Jeshebeab.
[14] The fifteenth lot fell to Bilgah.
The sixteenth lot fell to Immer.
[15] The seventeenth lot fell to Hezir.
The eighteenth lot fell to Happizzez.
[16] The nineteenth lot fell to Pethahiah.
The twentieth lot fell to Jehezkel.
[17] The twenty-first lot fell to Jakin.
The twenty-second lot fell to Gamul.
[18] The twenty-third lot fell to Delaiah.
The twenty-fourth lot fell to Maaziah.

[19]Each group carried out its duties in the house of the
LORD according to the procedures established by
their ancestor Aaron in obedience to the commands
of the LORD, the God of Israel.

[20]These were the other family leaders descended
from Levi:

From the descendants of Amram, the leader was Shebuel.*
From the descendants of Shebuel, the leader was Jehdeiah.
[21] From the descendants of Rehabiah, the leader was Isshiah.
[22] From the descendants of Izhar, the leader was Shelomith.*
From the descendants of Shelomith, the leader was Jahath.
[23] From the descendants of Hebron, Jeriah was the leader,* Amariah was second-in-command, Jahaziel was third, and Jekameam was fourth.
[24] From the descendants of Uzziel, the leader was Micah.
From the descendants of Micah, the leader was
Shamir, [25]along with Isshiah, the brother of Micah.
From the descendants of Isshiah, the leader was Zechariah.
[26] From the descendants of Merari, the leaders were Mahli and Mushi.
From the descendants of Jaaziah, the leader was Beno.
[27] From the descendants of Merari through Jaaziah, the leaders were Beno, Shoham, Zaccur, and Ibri.
[28] From the descendants of Mahli, the leader was Eleazar, though he had no sons.
[29] From the descendants of Kish, the leader was Jerahmeel.
[30] From the descendants of Mushi, the leaders were Mahli, Eder, and Jerimoth.

These were the descendants of Levi in their various families. [31]Like the descendants of Aaron, they
were assigned to their duties by means of sacred
lots, without regard to age or rank. It was done in
the presence of King David, Zadok, Ahimelech,
and the family leaders of the priests and the Levites.

CHAPTER **25** **THE MUSICIANS' DUTIES.** David and the army commanders then appointed men from the families of Asaph, Heman, and Jeduthun to proclaim God's messages to the accompaniment of harps, lyres, and cymbals. Here is a list of their names and their work:

[2]From the sons of Asaph, there were Zaccur, Joseph, Nethaniah, and Asarelah. They worked under the direction of their father, Asaph, who proclaimed God's messages by the king's orders.
[3]Jeduthun had six sons: Gedaliah, Zeri, Jeshaiah, Shimei,* Hashabiah, and Mattithiah. They worked under the direction of their father, Jeduthun, who proclaimed God's messages to

**PITCH IN ● ● • • ·**

25:1-7 **There were many ways to contribute to the worship in the Tabernacle. Some proclaimed God's messages (25:1), some led in prayer (25:3), and others played instruments and sang (25:6-7). God wants all his people to participate in worship. You may not be a master musician, a prophet, or a teacher, but God can use whatever you have to offer. Develop your special gifts to offer in service to God (Romans 12:3-8; 1 Corinthians 12:29-31).**

24:20 Hebrew *Shubael* (also in 24:20b), a variant name for Shebuel; compare 23:16 and 26:24. 24:22 Hebrew *Shelomoth* (also in 24:22b), a variant name for Shelomith; compare 23:18. 24:23 Hebrew *From the descendants of Jeriah;* compare 23:19. 25:3 As in one Hebrew manuscript and some Greek manuscripts (see also 25:17); most Hebrew manuscripts lack *Shimei.*

the accompaniment of the harp, offering thanks and praise to the LORD.

[4]Heman's sons were Bukkiah, Mattaniah, Uzziel,
Shubael,* Jerimoth, Hananiah, Hanani, Eliathah,
Geddalti, Romamti-ezer, Joshbekashah, Mallothi,
Hothir, and Mahazioth. [5]All these were the sons
of Heman, the king's seer, for God had honored
him with fourteen sons and three daughters.

[6]All these men were under the direction of their
fathers as they made music at the house of the LORD.
Their responsibilities included the playing of cymbals, lyres, and harps at the house of God. Asaph,
Jeduthun, and Heman reported directly to the king.
[7]They and their families were all trained in making
music before the LORD, and each of them—288 in
all—was an accomplished musician. [8]The musicians
were appointed to their particular term of service by
means of sacred lots, without regard to whether they
were young or old, teacher or student.

[9] The first lot fell to Joseph of the Asaph clan and twelve of his sons and relatives.*

The second lot fell to Gedaliah and twelve of his sons and relatives.

[10] The third lot fell to Zaccur and twelve of his sons and relatives.

[11] The fourth lot fell to Zeri* and twelve of his sons and relatives.

[12] The fifth lot fell to Nethaniah and twelve of his sons and relatives.

[13] The sixth lot fell to Bukkiah and twelve of his sons and relatives.

[14] The seventh lot fell to Asarelah* and twelve of his sons and relatives.

[15] The eighth lot fell to Jeshaiah and twelve of his sons and relatives.

[16] The ninth lot fell to Mattaniah and twelve of his sons and relatives.

[17] The tenth lot fell to Shimei and twelve of his sons and relatives.

[18] The eleventh lot fell to Uzziel* and twelve of his sons and relatives.

[19] The twelfth lot fell to Hashabiah and twelve of his sons and relatives.

[20] The thirteenth lot fell to Shubael and twelve of his sons and relatives.

[21] The fourteenth lot fell to Mattithiah and twelve of his sons and relatives.

[22] The fifteenth lot fell to Jerimoth* and twelve of his sons and relatives.

[23] The sixteenth lot fell to Hananiah and twelve of his sons and relatives.

[24] The seventeenth lot fell to Joshbekashah* and twelve of his sons and relatives.

[25] The eighteenth lot fell to Hanani and twelve of his sons and relatives.

[26] The nineteenth lot fell to Mallothi and twelve of his sons and relatives.

[27] The twentieth lot fell to Eliathah and twelve of his sons and relatives.

[28] The twenty-first lot fell to Hothir and twelve of his sons and relatives.

[29] The twenty-second lot fell to Geddalti* and twelve of his sons and relatives.

[30] The twenty-third lot fell to Mahazioth and twelve of his sons and relatives.

[31] The twenty-fourth lot fell to Romamti-ezer and twelve of his sons and relatives.

## CHAPTER 26 **THE GATEKEEPERS' DUTIES.** These are the divisions of the gatekeepers:

From the Korahites, there was Meshelemiah son
of Kore, of the family of Asaph. [2]The sons of
Meshelemiah were Zechariah (the oldest), Jediael
(the second), Zebadiah (the third), Jathniel (the
fourth), [3]Elam (the fifth), Jehohanan (the sixth),
and Eliehoenai (the seventh).

[4]The sons of Obed-edom, also gatekeepers, were
Shemaiah (the oldest), Jehozabad (the second),
Joah (the third), Sacar (the fourth), Nethanel
(the fifth), [5]Ammiel (the sixth), Issachar (the
seventh), and Peullethai (the eighth). God had
richly blessed Obed-edom.

[6]Obed-edom's son Shemaiah had sons with
great ability who earned positions of great
authority in the clan. [7]Their names were Othni,
Rephael, Obed, and Elzabad. Their relatives, Elihu
and Semakiah, were also very capable men.

[8]All of these descendants of Obed-edom,
including their sons and grandsons—sixty-two
of them in all—were very capable men, well
qualified for their work.

[9]Meshelemiah's eighteen sons and relatives were also very capable men.

[10]Hosah, of the Merari clan, appointed Shimri as
the leader among his sons, though he was not
the oldest. [11]His other sons included Hilkiah (the
second), Tebaliah (the third), and Zechariah (the
fourth). Hosah's sons and relatives, who served as
gatekeepers, numbered thirteen in all.

[12]These divisions of the gatekeepers were named for
their family leaders, and like the other Levites, they
served at the house of the LORD. [13]They were assigned by families for guard duty at the various gates,
without regard to age or training, for it was all decided by means of sacred lots.

[14]The responsibility for the east gate went to
Meshelemiah* and his group. The north gate was
assigned to his son Zechariah, a man of unusual wisdom. [15]The south gate went to Obed-edom, and his
sons were put in charge of the storehouses. [16]Shuppim

25:4 Hebrew *Shebuel,* a variant name for Shubael; compare 25:20. 25:9 As in Greek version; Hebrew lacks *and twelve of his sons and relatives.* 25:11 Hebrew *Izri,* a variant name for Zeri; compare 25:3. 25:14 Hebrew *Jesharelah,* a variant name for Asarelah; compare 25:2. 25:18 Hebrew *Azarel,* a variant name for Uzziel; compare 25:4. 25:22 Hebrew *Jeremoth,* a variant name for Jerimoth; compare 25:4. 25:24 Hebrew *Joshbekasha,* a variant name for Joshbekashah; compare 25:4. 25:29 Hebrew *Giddalti,* a variant name for Geddalti; compare 25:4. 26:14 Hebrew *Shelemiah,* a variant name for Meshelemiah; compare 26:2.

**PRINCIPLES TO LIVE BY**

King David gave his son Solomon principles to guide him through life (see 1 Chronicles 28:9-10). These same ideas are ones that any Christian can learn and follow.

1 Get to know God personally.

2 Learn God's commands and discover what he wants you to do.

3 Worship God with a clean heart.

4 Serve God with a willing mind.

5 Be faithful.

6 Don't become discouraged.

---

and Hosah were assigned the west gate and the gateway leading up to the Temple.* Guard duties were divided evenly. [17]Six Levites were assigned each day to the east gate, four to the north gate, four to the south gate, and two to each of the storehouses. [18]Six were assigned each day to the west gate, four to the gateway leading up to the Temple, and two to the courtyard.*

[19]These were the divisions of the gatekeepers from the clans of Korah and Merari.

[20]Other Levites, led by Ahijah, were in charge of the treasuries of the house of God and the storerooms. [21]From the family of Libni* in the clan of Gershon, Jehiel* was the leader. [22]The sons of Jehiel, Zetham and his brother Joel, were in charge of the treasuries of the house of the LORD.

**LOOT ● ● • • •**

26:27 **War spoils rightfully belonged to the victorious army. These soldiers, however, gave their portion of all the battle plunder to the Temple to express their dedication to God. Like these soldiers, we should think of what we *can* give, rather than what we are obligated to give. Is your giving a matter of rejoicing rather than duty? Give as a response of joy and love for God and others.**

[23]These are the leaders that descended from Amram, Izhar, Hebron, and Uzziel:

[24]From the clan of Amram, Shebuel was a descendant of Gershom son of Moses. He was the chief officer of the treasuries. [25]His relatives through Eliezer were Rehabiah, Jeshaiah, Joram, Zicri, and Shelomoth.

[26]Shelomoth and his relatives were in charge of the treasuries that held all the things dedicated to the LORD by King David, the family leaders, and the generals and captains and other officers of the army. [27]These men had dedicated some of the plunder they had gained in battle to maintain the house of the LORD. [28]Shelomoth and his relatives also cared for the items dedicated to the LORD by Samuel the seer, Saul son of Kish, Abner son of Ner, and Joab son of Zeruiah. All the other dedicated items were in their care, too.

[29]From the clan of Izhar came Kenaniah. He and his sons were appointed to serve as public administrators and judges throughout Israel.

[30]From the clan of Hebron came Hashabiah. He and his relatives—seventeen hundred capable men—were put in charge of the Israelite lands west of the Jordan River. They were responsible for all matters related to the things of the LORD and the service of the king in that area.

[31]Also from the clan of Hebron came Jeriah,* who was the leader of the Hebronites according to the genealogical records. (In the fortieth year of David's reign, a search was made in the records, and capable men from the clan of Hebron were found at Jazer in the land of Gilead.) [32]There were twenty-seven hundred capable men among the relatives of Jeriah. King David sent them to the east side of the Jordan River and put them in charge of the tribes of Reuben and Gad and the half-tribe of Manasseh. They were responsible for all matters related to the things of God and the service of the king.

CHAPTER **27** **THE COMMANDERS OF THE ARMY.** This is the list of Israelite generals and captains, and their officers, who served the king by supervising the army divisions that were on duty each month of the year. Each division served for one month and had twenty-four thousand troops.

[2]Jashobeam son of Zabdiel was commander of the first division, which was on duty during the first month. There were twenty-four thousand troops in his division. [3]He was a descendant of Perez and was in charge of all the army officers for the first month.

[4]Dodai, a descendant of Ahoah, was commander of the second division, which was on duty during the second month. There were twenty-four thousand troops in his division, and Mikloth was his chief officer.

[5]Benaiah son of Jehoiada the priest was commander of the third division, which was on duty during the third month. There were twenty-four

26:16 Or *the gate of Shalleketh on the upper road* (also in 26:18). The meaning of the Hebrew is uncertain. 26:18 Or *the colonnade.* The meaning of the Hebrew is uncertain. 26:21a Hebrew *Ladan,* another name for Libni; compare 6:17. 26:21b Hebrew *Jehieli* (also in 26:22), a variant name for Jehiel; compare 23:8. 26:31 Hebrew *Jerijah,* a variant name for Jeriah; compare 23:19.

thousand troops in his division. 6 This was the
Benaiah who commanded David's elite military
group known as the Thirty. His son Ammizabad
was his chief officer.
7 Asahel, the brother of Joab, was commander of
the fourth division, which was on duty during
the fourth month. There were twenty-four
thousand troops in his division. Asahel was
succeeded by his son Zebadiah.
8 Shammah* the Izrahite was commander of the
fifth division, which was on duty during the
fifth month. There were twenty-four thousand
troops in his division.
9 Ira son of Ikkesh from Tekoa was commander of
the sixth division, which was on duty during the
sixth month. There were twenty-four thousand
troops in his division.
10 Helez, a descendant of Ephraim from Pelon, was
commander of the seventh division, which was
on duty during the seventh month. There were
twenty-four thousand troops in his division.
11 Sibbecai, a descendant of Zerah from Hushah, was
commander of the eighth division, which was on
duty during the eighth month. There were twenty-
four thousand troops in his division.
12 Abiezer from Anathoth in the territory of Benjamin
was commander of the ninth division, which was
on duty during the ninth month. There were
twenty-four thousand troops in his division.
13 Maharai, a descendant of Zerah from Netophah,
was commander of the tenth division, which
was on duty during the tenth month. There were
twenty-four thousand troops in his division.
14 Benaiah from Pirathon in Ephraim was commander of the eleventh division, which was on
duty during the eleventh month. There were
twenty-four thousand troops in his division.
15 Heled,* a descendant of Othniel from Netophah,
was commander of the twelfth division, which
was on duty during the twelfth month. There were
twenty-four thousand troops in his division.

16 The following were the tribes of Israel and their
leaders:

| *Tribe* | *Leader* |
|---|---|
| Reuben | Eliezer son of Zicri |
| Simeon | Shephatiah son of Maacah |
| 17 Levi | Hashabiah son of Kemuel |
| Aaron (the priests) | Zadok |
| 18 Judah | Elihu (a brother of David) |
| Issachar | Omri son of Michael |
| 19 Zebulun | Ishmaiah son of Obadiah |
| Naphtali | Jeremoth son of Azriel |
| 20 Ephraim | Hoshea son of Azaziah |
| Manasseh (west) | Joel son of Pedaiah |
| 21 Manasseh (east*) | Iddo son of Zechariah |
| Benjamin | Jaasiel son of Abner |
| 22 Dan | Azarel son of Jeroham |

These were the leaders of the tribes of Israel.
23 When David took his census, he did not count
those who were younger than twenty years of age,
because the LORD had promised to make the Israelites as numerous as the stars in heaven. 24 Joab began
the census but never finished it because the anger of
God broke out against Israel. The final total was
never recorded in King David's official records.
25 Azmaveth son of Adiel was in charge of the
palace treasuries.
Jonathan son of Uzziah was in charge of the regional
treasuries throughout the towns, villages, and
fortresses of Israel.
26 Ezri son of Kelub was in charge of the field workers
who farmed the king's lands.
27 Shimei from Ramah was in charge of the king's
vineyards.
Zabdi from Shepham was responsible for the grapes
and the supplies of wine.

**Recently I realized that I have been living off of the faith of my parents. How do I make my faith my own?**

This may be the most significant realization of your life. Some young people never understand that God wants us to know him personally. Living off of someone else's faith is like borrowing something from a friend. No matter what you borrow—a bike, clothes, skateboard, tapes, or faith—it isn't yours and must be returned.

Solomon was challenged to "get to know the God of your ancestors" (1 Chronicles 28:9). In other words, he wasn't to settle for hearing how someone else trusted God. He needed to find out for himself.

During these years, your faith will be tested. Friends who do not believe in Christ may see nothing wrong with doing things that would cause your conscience to start screaming in protest. That's when you will have to make a choice: will you go along with your friends or will you stand on what you believe? If your faith is strong (if it is yours and not your parents' or your youth leader's), no amount of pressure from friends will be able to blow you away (Matthew 7:21-29).

Consider taking these steps to help develop your faith. First, make sure you have asked Jesus Christ to forgive your sin and come into your life. This is the first step to a personal relationship with God. Second, begin to ask questions about the Bible. God wants you to understand it as well as believe and obey it. God is not afraid of honest questions asked with good motives. Third, look for other Christians who are excited about developing their faith in God—people who do not want to settle for second best. Being around growing Christians is contagious. What you learn from them will convince you that being a Christian is worth the work and is 100 percent right for you!

27:8 Hebrew *Shamhuth,* another name for Shammah; compare 11:27 and 2 Sam 23:25. 27:15 Hebrew *Heldai,* a variant name for Heled; compare 11:30 and 2 Sam 23:29. 27:21 Hebrew *in Gilead.*

[28]Baal-hanan from Geder was in charge of the
king's olive groves and sycamore-fig trees in the
foothills of Judah.*
Joash was responsible for the supplies of olive oil.
[29]Shitrai from Sharon was in charge of the cattle on
the Sharon Plain.
Shaphat son of Adlai was responsible for the cattle
in the valleys.
[30]Obil the Ishmaelite was in charge of the camels.
Jehdeiah from Meronoth was in charge of the
donkeys.
[31]Jaziz the Hagrite was in charge of the king's sheep.
All these officials were overseers of King David's
property.

## THE BOSS

"I just wish God would leave me alone. It's like I can't get away from him."

"What do you mean, Reed?"

"Well, my parents go to church all the time and they make *me* go–to everything."

"And you don't like that?"

"I'd rather do almost anything else–even homework. But with my parents, attendance isn't open for discussion."

"Your older brother is a missionary, isn't he?"

"Yeah."

"Do you stay in touch?"

"He sends me these thick letters every month–they're like handwritten sermons telling me to make Jesus the Lord of my life. I wish he'd let me live the way I want to live."

"How is that?"

"Well, I don't want to *totally* forget God, but I think it's extreme to think and talk about him all the time. I want to live my life without having to think about God every single day."

"Reed, are you a Christian? Have you ever really trusted Christ?"

"Yeah. When I was eleven."

"But now you're saying you want to live for God on *your* terms? Whenever you feel like it?"

"I guess so."

Like Reed, a lot of Christians don't want Christ to be their Master and Boss. They want to control their own lives. They believe they can do whatever they desire and still find fulfillment.

See 1 Chronicles 28:9 for the real secret to satisfaction in life.

[32]Jonathan, David's uncle, was a wise counselor
to the king, a man of great insight, and a scribe.
Jehiel the Hacmonite was responsible to teach the
king's sons. [33]Ahithophel was the royal adviser.
Hushai the Arkite was the king's friend. [34]Ahitho-
phel was succeeded by Jehoiada son of Benaiah
and by Abiathar. Joab was commander of the Israelite army.

CHAPTER **28** **PLANS FOR THE TEMPLE.** David summoned all his officials to Jerusalem—the leaders
of the tribes, the commanders of the twelve army

## DUTY-BOUND ● ● • • •

28:8 **David told Solomon to obey every one of God's commands to ensure Israel's prosperity and the continuation of David's descendants upon the throne. It was the solemn duty of the king to study and obey God's laws. The teachings of Scripture are the keys to security, happiness, and justice, but you'll never discover them unless you search God's Word. If God's will is ignored and his teaching neglected, anything we attempt to build, even if it has God's name on it, is headed for collapse. Get to know God's commands through regular Bible study, and obey them every day.**

divisions, the other generals and captains, the overseers of the royal property and livestock, the palace
officials, the mighty men, and all the other warriors in the kingdom. [2]David rose and stood before
them and addressed them as follows: "My brothers
and my people! It was my desire to build a temple
where the Ark of the LORD's covenant, God's footstool, could rest permanently. I made the necessary
preparations for building it, [3]but God said to me,
'You must not build a temple to honor my name,
for you are a warrior and have shed much blood.'
[4]"Yet the LORD, the God of Israel, has chosen me
from among all my father's family to be king over
Israel forever. For he has chosen the tribe of Judah to
rule, and from among the families of Judah, he
chose my father's family. And from among my
father's sons, the LORD was pleased to make me king
over all Israel. [5]And from among my sons—for the
LORD has given me many children—he chose Solomon to succeed me on the throne of his kingdom of
Israel. [6]He said to me, 'Your son Solomon will build
my Temple and its courtyards, for I have chosen him
as my son, and I will be his father. [7]And if he continues to obey my commands and regulations as he
does now, I will make his kingdom last forever.' [8]So
now, with God as our witness, I give you this charge
for all Israel, the LORD's assembly: Be careful to obey
all the commands of the LORD your God, so that you
may possess this good land and leave it to your
children as a permanent inheritance.
[9]"And Solomon, my son, get to know the God of
your ancestors. Worship and serve him with your
whole heart and with a willing mind. For the LORD
sees every heart and understands and knows every
plan and thought. If you seek him, you will find
him. But if you forsake him, he will reject you
forever. [10]So take this seriously. The LORD has chosen you to build a Temple as his sanctuary. Be
strong, and do the work."
[11]Then David gave Solomon the plans for the
Temple and its surroundings, including the treasuries, the upstairs rooms, the inner rooms, and
the inner sanctuary where the Ark's cover—the
place of atonement—would be kept. [12]David also
gave Solomon all the plans he had in mind* for
the courtyards of the LORD's Temple, the outside
rooms, the treasuries of God's Temple, and the
rooms for the dedicated gifts. [13]The king also gave
Solomon the instructions concerning the work of

27:28 Hebrew *the Shephelah.* 28:12 Or *the plans of the spirit that was with him.*

IF YOU
seek
HIM
YOU WILL
find
HIM
1 CHRONICLES 28:9

the various divisions of priests and Levites in the Temple of the LORD. And he gave specifications for the items in the LORD's Temple which were to be used for worship and sacrifice.

[14]David gave instructions regarding how much gold and silver should be used to make the necessary items. [15]He told Solomon the amount of gold needed for the gold lampstands and lamps, and the amount of silver for the silver lampstands and lamps, depending on how each would be used. [16]He designated the amount of gold for the table on which the Bread of the Presence would be placed and the amount of silver for other tables.

[17]David also designated the amount of gold for the solid gold meat hooks used to handle the sacrificial meat and for the basins, pitchers, and dishes, as well as the amount of silver for every dish. [18]Finally, he designated the amount of refined gold for the altar of incense and for the gold cherubim, whose wings were stretched out over the Ark of the LORD's covenant. [19]"Every part of this plan," David told Solomon, "was given to me in writing from the hand of the LORD.*"

[20]Then David continued, "Be strong and courageous, and do the work. Don't be afraid or discouraged by the size of the task, for the LORD God, my God, is with you. He will not fail you or forsake you. He will see to it that all the work related to the Temple of the LORD is finished correctly. [21]The various divisions of priests and Levites will serve in the Temple of God. Others with skills of every kind will volunteer, and the leaders and the entire nation are at your command."

## CHAPTER 29

**THE PEOPLE BRING GIFTS.** Then King David turned to the entire assembly and said, "My son Solomon, whom God has chosen to be the next king of Israel, is still young and inexperienced. The work ahead of him is enormous, for the Temple he will build is not just another building—it is for the LORD God himself! [2]Using every resource at my command, I have gathered as much as I could for building the Temple of my God. Now there is enough gold, silver, bronze, iron, and wood, as well as great quantities of onyx, other precious stones, costly jewels, and all kinds of fine stone and marble. [3]And now because of my devotion to the Temple of my God, I am giving all of my own private treasures of gold and silver to help in the construction. This is in addition to the building materials I have already collected for his holy Temple. [4]I am donating more than 112 tons of gold* from Ophir and over 262 tons of refined silver* to be used for overlaying the walls of the buildings [5]and for the other gold and silver work to be done by the craftsmen. Now then, who will follow my example? Who is willing to give offerings to the LORD today?"

[6]Then the family leaders, the leaders of the tribes of Israel, the generals and captains of the army, and the king's administrative officers all gave willingly. [7]For the construction of the Temple of God, they gave almost 188 tons of gold,* 10,000 gold coins,* about 375 tons of silver,* about 675 tons of bronze,* and about 3,750 tons of iron.* [8]They also contributed numerous precious stones, which were deposited in the treasury of the house of the LORD under the care of Jehiel, a descendant of Gershon. [9]The people rejoiced over the offerings, for they had given freely and wholeheartedly to the LORD, and King David was filled with joy.

[10]Then David praised the LORD in the presence of the whole assembly: "O LORD, the God of our ancestor Israel,* may you be praised forever and ever! [11]Yours, O LORD, is the greatness, the power, the glory, the victory, and the majesty. Everything in the heavens and on earth is yours, O LORD, and this is your kingdom. We adore you as the one who is over all things. [12]Riches and honor come from you alone, for you rule over everything. Power and might are in your hand, and it is at your discretion that people are made great and given strength.

### ALL-KNOWING ● ● • • •

28:9 **Nothing can be hidden from God. He sees and understands everything in our heart. David found this out the hard way when God sent Nathan to expose David's sins of adultery and murder (2 Samuel 12). David told Solomon to be completely open with God and dedicated to him. It makes no sense to try to hide any thoughts or actions from an all-knowing God. This should cause you joy, not fear, because God knows even the worst things about you and loves you anyway.**

**28:19** Or *was written under the direction of the LORD.* **29:4a** Hebrew *3,000 talents* [102 metric tons] *of gold.* **29:4b** Hebrew *7,000 talents* [238 metric tons] *of silver.* **29:7a** Hebrew *5,000 talents* [170 metric tons] *of gold.* **29:7b** Hebrew *10,000 darics* [a Persian coin] *of gold,* about 185 pounds or 84 kilograms in weight. **29:7c** Hebrew *10,000 talents* [340 metric tons] *of silver.* **29:7d** Hebrew *18,000 talents* [612 metric tons] *of bronze.* **29:7e** Hebrew *100,000 talents* [3,400 metric tons] *of iron.* **29:10** *Israel* is the name that God gave to Jacob.

### GOOD HEART ● ● • • •

**29:19 A person with a loyal heart *wants* to obey God. This is what David wished for Solomon—a heart that desired, above all else, to serve God. Do you find it hard to do what God wants, or even harder to want to do it? God can give you a loyal heart that wants to do his will. If you have believed in Jesus Christ, this is already happening in you. Paul wrote, "God is working in you, giving you the desire to obey him and the power to do what pleases him" (Philippians 2:13).**

13 "O our God, we thank you and praise your glorious name! 14 But who am I, and who are my people, that we could give anything to you? Everything we have has come from you, and we give you only what you have already given us! 15 We are here for only a moment, visitors and strangers in the land as our ancestors were before us. Our days on earth are like a shadow, gone so soon without a trace.

16 "O LORD our God, even these materials that we have gathered to build a Temple to honor your holy name come from you! It all belongs to you! 17 I know, my God, that you examine our hearts and rejoice when you find integrity there. You know I have done all this with good motives, and I have watched your people offer their gifts willingly and joyously.

18 "O LORD, the God of our ancestors Abraham, Isaac, and Israel, make your people always want to obey you. See to it that their love for you never changes. 19 Give my son Solomon the wholehearted desire to obey all your commands, decrees, and principles, and to build this Temple, for which I have made all these preparations."

20 Then David said to the whole assembly, "Give praise to the LORD your God!" And the entire assembly praised the LORD, the God of their ancestors, and they bowed low and knelt before the LORD and the king.

21 The next day they brought a thousand bulls, a thousand rams, and a thousand male lambs as burnt offerings to the LORD. They also brought drink offerings and many other sacrifices on behalf of Israel. 22 They feasted and drank in the LORD's presence with great joy that day.

And again they crowned David's son Solomon as their new king. They anointed him before the LORD as their leader, and they anointed Zadok as their priest. 23 So Solomon took the throne of the LORD in place of his father, David, and he prospered greatly, and all Israel obeyed him. 24 All the royal officials, the army commanders, and the sons of King David pledged their loyalty to King Solomon. 25 And the LORD exalted Solomon so the entire nation of Israel stood in awe of him, and he gave Solomon even greater wealth and honor than his father.

26 So David son of Jesse reigned over all Israel. 27 He ruled Israel for forty years in all, seven years from Hebron and thirty-three years from Jerusalem. 28 He died at a ripe old age, having enjoyed long life, wealth, and honor. Then his son Solomon ruled in his place. 29 All the events of King David's reign, from beginning to end, are written in *The Record of Samuel the Seer, The Record of Nathan the Prophet,* and *The Record of Gad the Seer.* 30 These accounts include the mighty deeds of his reign and everything that happened to him and to Israel and to all the surrounding kingdoms.

# MEGA themes

**GOD'S PEOPLE** By retelling Israel's history in the genealogies and the stories of the kings, the writer laid the true spiritual foundation for the nation. God kept his promises, and we are reminded of them in the historical record of his people, leaders, prophets, priests, and kings.

Israel's past formed a reliable basis for rebuilding the nation after the Exile. God's promises are written in the Bible—we can know God and trust him to keep his word. Like Israel, we can have no higher goal in life than serving God. Like Israel, we will find God to be trustworthy and faithful.

1. As you review Israel's history, what qualities of God are most evident? What do you learn about the people themselves?
2. There were definite differences in the lives of the people when they were submissive to God's will, as opposed to times when they ignored and/or rebelled against God. In what ways do you see a similar pattern developing in your life?
3. Think about the next 10 years of your life. How important is "doing God's will" in your future? Explain this importance.
4. Now think about the next generation. If God blesses you with children, what spiritual heritage do you want to give to them? How can you begin in the present to prepare that future heritage?

**DAVID** The story of David's life and his relationship with God showed that he was God's appointed leader. David's devotion to God, the law, the Temple, true worship, the people, and justice sets the standard for what God's chosen king should have been.

Jesus Christ came to earth as a descendant of David. One day Christ will rule as King over all the earth. His strength and justice will fulfill God's ideal for the king. He is our hope.

1. Write out a review of David's life.
2. From looking at David's life, what do you learn about God? About living in God's will?
3. Do most people seek God's purposes in their lives or do they seem to live life based merely on what they want? Explain.
4. What do you think God wants to accomplish in your life? What can you do to see that God's purpose is accomplished in your life?

**TRUE WORSHIP** David brought the Ark of the Covenant to the Tabernacle at Jerusalem to restore true worship to the people. God chose priests and Levites to guide the people in faithful worship. This worship was to be an important, central part of the Israelites' daily lives.

When we acknowledge and focus on God as the true King, we experience worship. This worship is to be the center of our life, with the rest of our thoughts and activities organized around God's kingship. Today we are all priests in the sense that each of us, in Christ, can personally enter into worship. Thus we also can encourage one another to deeper worship.

1. Describe the ways that the Israelites worshiped God.
2. Describe how you worship God.
3. In your worship, what is the importance of the church? Other Christians? The Bible?
4. In what ways can Christians be "priests" for one another? Picture your Christian friends. What can you do to be a "priest" for one of them?

**970 B.C.**
**Solomon becomes king**

**966–959**
**Temple built**

**930**
**The kingdom divides**

**910**
**Asa becomes king of Judah**

**872**
**Jehoshaphat becomes king of Judah**

**853**
**Ahab killed in battle**

**841**
**Athaliah seizes the throne**

**792**
**Uzziah becomes king of Judah**

**722**
**Israel (northern kingdom) falls**

**715**
**Hezekiah becomes king of Judah**

**701**
**Sennacherib taunts Hezekiah**

**640**
**Josiah becomes king**

**622**
**Book of the Law found**

**586**
**Judah (southern kingdom) falls**

**538**
**Cyrus's decree**

Mom, I promise I'll never be late again! Please!" The mother desperately wanted to believe her daughter. But no matter how strong her promises to get in on time, she was always late. ■ "Honey," she began, "I'm sorry. But for the rest of the weekend you're grounded." The mother had been more than fair; now she had to mete out punishment. ■ Many times during Israel's history, God sent messengers to the country's leaders threatening punishment for their disobedience. Each time, the leaders would beg for one more chance, but they never kept their promises. Finally God allowed them to be conquered and taken into captivity. ■ Second Chronicles was written after the return of some of the Jews from that captivity. The author reminded these people of their forefathers' sin and its results. Only by truly submitting to God could Israel regain its strength as a nation. "If my people who are called by my name will humble themselves and pray and seek my face and turn from their wicked ways, I will hear from heaven and will forgive their sins and heal their land" (7:14). ■ Second Chronicles was written for you, too. God punishes those who ignore him, but he blesses those who obey. Read this book and dedicate yourself to following after God.

## STATS

PURPOSE: To unify the nation around true worship of Jehovah by showing his standard for judging kings. The righteous kings of Judah and the religious revivals under their rule are highlighted, and the sins of the evil kings are exposed.

AUTHOR: Ezra, according to Jewish tradition

TO WHOM WRITTEN: All Israel

DATE WRITTEN: Approximately 430 B.C.; recording events from the beginning of Solomon's reign (970 B.C.) to the beginning of the Babylonian captivity (586 B.C.)

SETTING: Second Chronicles parallels 1 and 2 Kings and serves as their commentary.

KEY PEOPLE: Solomon, the queen of Sheba, Rehoboam, Asa, Jehoshaphat, Jehoram, Joash, Uzziah, Ahaz, Hezekiah, Manasseh, Josiah

KEY PLACES: Jerusalem, the Temple

SPECIAL FEATURES: Includes a detailed record of the Temple's construction

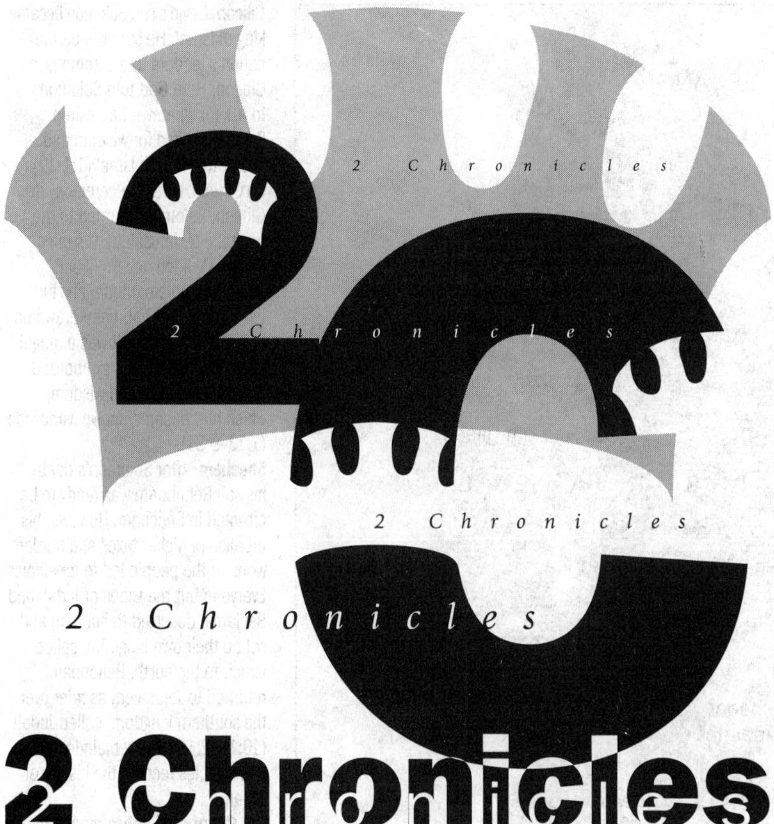


# 2 Chronicles

CHAPTER **1** **SOLOMON ASKS GOD FOR WISDOM.** Solomon, the son of King David, now took firm control
of the kingdom, for the LORD his God was with him
and made him very powerful. [2]He called together all
Israel—the generals and captains of the army, the
judges, and all the political and clan leaders. [3]Then
Solomon led the entire assembly to the hill at Gibeon where God's Tabernacle* was located. This was
the Tabernacle that Moses, the LORD's servant, had
constructed in the wilderness. [4]David had already
moved the Ark of God from Kiriath-jearim to the
special tent he had prepared for it in Jerusalem. [5]But
the bronze altar made by Bezalel son of Uri and
grandson of Hur was still at Gibeon in front of the
Tabernacle of the LORD. So Solomon and the people
gathered in front of it to consult the LORD. [6]There in
front of the Tabernacle, Solomon went up to the
bronze altar in the LORD's presence and sacrificed a
thousand burnt offerings on it.

[7]That night God appeared to Solomon in a dream
and said, "What do you want? Ask, and I will give it
to you!"

[8]Solomon replied to God, "You have been so
faithful and kind to my father, David, and now you
have made me king in his place. [9]Now, LORD God,
please keep your promise to David my father, for you
have made me king over a people as numerous as the
dust of the earth! [10]Give me wisdom and knowledge
to rule them properly, for who is able to govern this
great nation of yours?"

[11]God said to Solomon, "Because your greatest
desire is to help your people, and you did not ask for
personal wealth and honor or the death of your
enemies or even a long life, but rather you asked for
wisdom and knowledge to properly govern my
people, [12]I will certainly give you the wisdom and
knowledge you requested. And I will also give you
riches, wealth, and honor such as no other king has
ever had before you or will ever have again!" [13]Then
Solomon returned to Jerusalem from the Tabernacle
at the hill of Gibeon, and he reigned over Israel.

1:3 Hebrew *Tent of Meeting;* also in 1:6, 13.

## PRIORITIES

1:11-12 **Solomon could have had anything, but he asked for wisdom to rule the nation. God approved of the way Solomon ordered his priorities, and he gave him the wisdom he asked for *and* riches, wealth, and honor. Jesus also spoke about priorities. He said that when we put God first, everything we really need will fall into place (Matthew 6:33). This does not guarantee that we will be wealthy and famous like Solomon. It means that when we wisely put God first, the wisdom he gives us will enable us to live a rich, rewarding life.**

# KEY PLACES IN 2 CHRONICLES

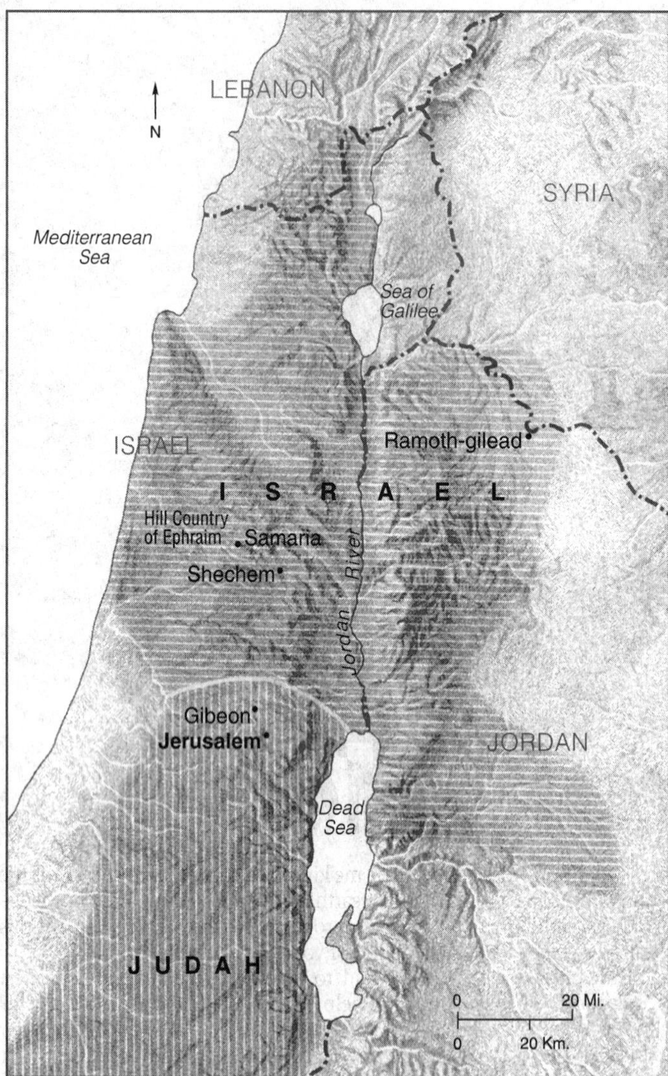

The broken lines (–·–·) indicate modern boundaries.

**Gibeon** David's son Solomon became king of Israel. He summoned the nation's leaders to a ceremony in Gibeon. Here God told Solomon to ask for whatever he desired. Solomon asked for wisdom and knowledge to rule Israel (1:1-12).

**Jerusalem** After the ceremony in Gibeon, Solomon returned to the capital city, Jerusalem. His reign began a golden age for Israel. Solomon implemented plans for the Temple that had been drawn up by his father, David. It was a magnificent construction. It symbolized Solomon's wealth and wisdom, which had become known worldwide (1:13–9:31).

**Shechem** After Solomon's death, his son Rehoboam was ready to be crowned in Shechem. However, his promise of higher taxes and harder work for the people led to rebellion. Everyone but the tribes of Judah and Benjamin deserted Rehoboam and set up their own kingdom, called Israel, to the north. Rehoboam returned to Jerusalem as ruler over the southern kingdom, called Judah (10:1–12:16). The remainder of 2 Chronicles records the history of Judah.

**Hill Country of Ephraim** Abijah became the next king of Judah, and soon war broke out between Israel and Judah. When the armies of the two nations arrived for battle in the hill country of Ephraim, Israel had twice as many troops as Judah. It looked like Judah's defeat was certain. But they cried out to God, and God gave them victory over Israel. In their history as separate nations, Judah did have a few godly kings who instituted reforms and brought the people back to God. Israel, however, had a succession of only evil kings (13:1-22).

**Aram** Asa, a godly king, removed every trace of idol worship from Judah and renewed the people's covenant with God in Jerusalem. But King Baasha of Israel built a fortress to control traffic into Judah. Instead of looking to God for guidance, Asa took the silver and gold from the Temple and sent it to the king of Aram, requesting his help against King Baasha. As a result, God became angry with Judah (14:1–16:14).

**Samaria** Although Jehoshaphat was a godly king, he allied himself with Israel's most evil king, Ahab. Ahab's capital was in Samaria. Ahab wanted help fighting for Ramoth-gilead. Jehoshaphat wanted advice, but rather than listening to God's prophet who had promised defeat, he joined Ahab in battle (17:1–18:27).

**Ramoth-gilead** The alliance with Israel against Ramoth-gilead ended in defeat and Ahab's death. Although shaken by his defeat, Jehoshaphat returned to Jerusalem and to God. But his son Jehoram was a wicked king, as was *his* son, Ahaziah. And history repeated itself. Ahaziah formed an alliance with Israel's King Jehoram (who had the same name as his brother) to do battle with the Arameans at Ramoth-gilead. This led to the death of both kings (18:28–22:9).

**Jerusalem** The rest of Judah's history recorded in 2 Chronicles centers on Jerusalem. Some kings caused Judah to sin by promoting idol worship. Others cleaned up the idol worship, reopened and restored the Temple, and, in the case of Josiah, tried to follow God's laws as they were written by Moses. In spite of the few good influences, a series of evil kings sent Judah into a downward spiral that ended with the Babylonian empire overrunning the country. The Temple was burned, the walls of the city were broken down, and the people were deported to Babylon.

14Solomon built up a huge military force, which
included fourteen hundred chariots and twelve
thousand horses.* He stationed many of them in the
chariot cities, and some near him in Jerusalem.
15During Solomon's reign, silver and gold were as
plentiful in Jerusalem as stones. And valuable cedarwood was as common as the sycamore wood that
grows in the foothills of Judah.* 16Solomon's horses
were imported from Egypt* and from Cilicia*; the
king's traders acquired them from Cilicia at the standard price. 17At that time, Egyptian chariots delivered
to Jerusalem could be purchased for 600 pieces of
silver,* and horses could be bought for 150 pieces of
silver.* Many of these were then resold to the kings
of the Hittites and the kings of Aram.

## CHAPTER 2 **SOLOMON MAKES PLANS.**

Solomon
now decided that the time had come to build a
Temple for the LORD and a royal palace for himself.
2He enlisted a force of 70,000 common laborers,
80,000 stonecutters in the hill country, and 3,600
foremen. 3Solomon also sent this message to King
Hiram* at Tyre:

"Send me cedar logs like the ones that were
supplied to my father, David, when he was
building his palace. 4I am about to build a
Temple to honor the name of the LORD my God.
It will be a place set apart to burn incense and
sweet spices before him, to display the special
sacrificial bread, and to sacrifice burnt offerings
each morning and evening, on the Sabbaths, at
new moon celebrations, and at the other
appointed festivals of the LORD our God. He has
commanded Israel to do these things forever.

5"This will be a magnificent Temple because
our God is an awesome God, greater than any
other. 6But who can really build him a worthy
home? Not even the highest heavens can
contain him! So who am I to consider building
a Temple for him, except as a place to burn
sacrifices to him?

7"So send me a master craftsman who can
work with gold, silver, bronze, and iron; someone who is expert at dyeing purple, scarlet, and
blue cloth; and a skilled engraver who can work
with the craftsmen of Judah and Jerusalem who
were selected by my father, David. 8Also send
me cedar, cypress, and almug* logs from
Lebanon, for I know that your men are without
equal at cutting timber. I will send my men to
help them. 9An immense amount of timber will
be needed, for the Temple I am going to build
will be very large and magnificent. 10I will pay
your men 100,000 bushels of crushed wheat,

**CELEBRATE ● ● • • •**

2:4 **A celebration is an occasion of joy, and remembering God's goodness to his people was certainly a reason to be joyful. God wanted Israel to celebrate certain occasions regularly because the people were so forgetful, so quick to turn to other gods. In church we use celebrations to recall God's goodness. Because we have short memories, too, Christmas, Easter, and other special occasions are designed to help us remember what God has done for us.**

100,000 bushels of barley,* 110,000 gallons of
wine, and 110,000 gallons of olive oil.*"

11King Hiram sent this letter of reply to Solomon:

"It is because the LORD loves his people that he
has made you their king! 12Blessed be the LORD,
the God of Israel, who made the heavens and the
earth! He has given David a wise son, gifted with
skill and understanding, who will build a Temple
for the LORD and a royal palace for himself.

13"I am sending you a master craftsman
named Huram-abi. He is a brilliant man, 14the
son of a woman from Dan in Israel; his father is
from Tyre. He is skillful at making things from
gold, silver, bronze, and iron. He also knows all
about stonework, carpentry, and weaving. He is
an expert in dyeing purple, blue, and scarlet
cloth and in working with linen. He is also an
engraver and can follow any design given to
him. He will work with your craftsmen and
those appointed by my lord David, your father.

15"Send along the wheat, barley, olive oil, and
wine that you mentioned. 16We will cut whatever
timber you need from the Lebanon mountains
and will float the logs in rafts down the coast of
the Mediterranean Sea to Joppa. From there you
can transport the logs up to Jerusalem."

17Solomon took a census of all foreigners in the
land of Israel, like the census his father had taken,
and he counted 153,600. 18He enlisted 70,000 of
them as common laborers, 80,000 as stonecutters in
the hill country, and 3,600 as foremen.

## CHAPTER 3 **THE CONSTRUCTION BEGINS.**

So Solomon
began to build the Temple of the LORD in Jerusalem
on Mount Moriah, where the LORD had appeared to
Solomon's father, King David. The Temple was built
on the threshing floor of Araunah* the Jebusite, the
site that David had selected. 2The construction began in midspring,* during the fourth year of Solomon's reign.

3The foundation for the Temple of God was
ninety feet long and thirty feet wide.* 4The foyer at
the front of the Temple was thirty feet wide, running

1:14 Or *12,000 charioteers.* 1:15 Hebrew *the Shephelah.* 1:16a Possibly *Muzur,* a district near Cilicia; also in 1:17. 1:16b Hebrew *Kue,* probably another name for Cilicia. 1:17a Hebrew *600 shekels of silver,* about 15 pounds or 6.8 kilograms in weight. 1:17b Hebrew *150 shekels,* about 3.8 pounds or 1.7 kilograms in weight. 2:3 Hebrew *Huram,* a variant name for Hiram; also in 2:11, 12. 2:8 Hebrew *algum,* a variant name for almug; compare 9:10-11 and parallel text at 1 Kgs 10:11-12. 2:10a Hebrew *20,000 cors* [3,640 kiloliters] *of crushed wheat, 20,000 cors of barley.* 2:10b Hebrew *20,000 baths* [420 kiloliters] *of wine, and 20,000 baths of olive oil.* 3:1 Hebrew reads *Ornan,* another name for Araunah; compare 2 Sam 24:16. 3:2 Hebrew *on the second day of the second month.* This day of the Hebrew lunar calendar occurs in April or early May. 3:3 Hebrew *60 cubits* [27 meters] *long and 20 cubits* [9 meters] *wide.* In this chapter, the distance measures are calculated from the Hebrew cubit at a ratio of 18 inches or 45 centimeters per cubit.

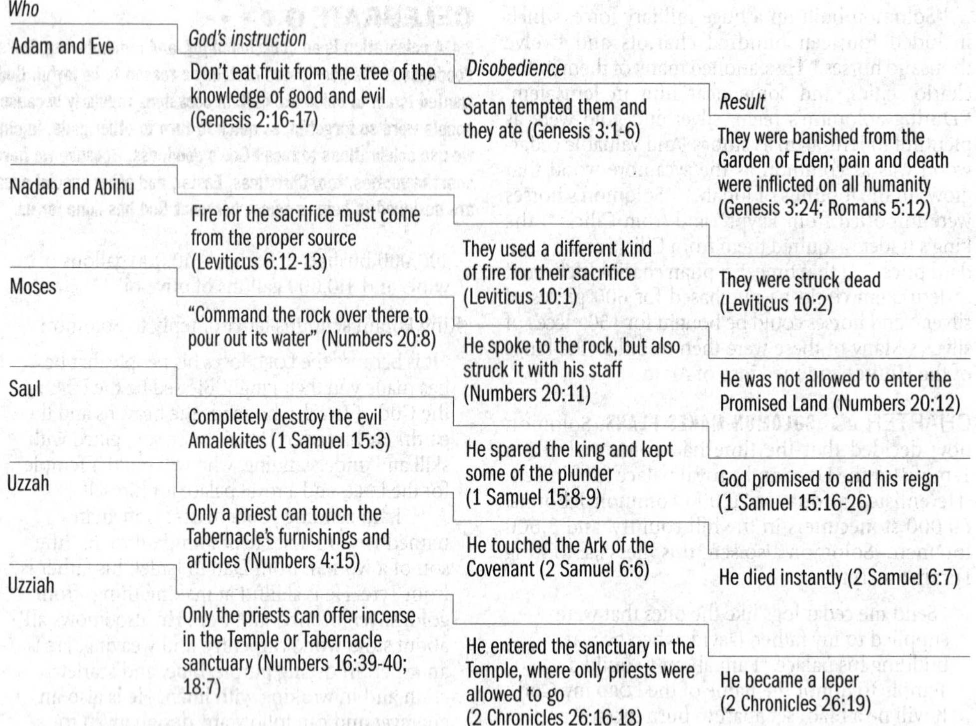

| Who | God's instruction | Disobedience | Result |
|---|---|---|---|
| Adam and Eve | Don't eat fruit from the tree of the knowledge of good and evil (Genesis 2:16-17) | Satan tempted them and they ate (Genesis 3:1-6) | They were banished from the Garden of Eden; pain and death were inflicted on all humanity (Genesis 3:24; Romans 5:12) |
| Nadab and Abihu | Fire for the sacrifice must come from the proper source (Leviticus 6:12-13) | They used a different kind of fire for their sacrifice (Leviticus 10:1) | They were struck dead (Leviticus 10:2) |
| Moses | "Command the rock over there to pour out its water" (Numbers 20:8) | He spoke to the rock, but also struck it with his staff (Numbers 20:11) | He was not allowed to enter the Promised Land (Numbers 20:12) |
| Saul | Completely destroy the evil Amalekites (1 Samuel 15:3) | He spared the king and kept some of the plunder (1 Samuel 15:8-9) | God promised to end his reign (1 Samuel 15:16-26) |
| Uzzah | Only a priest can touch the Tabernacle's furnishings and articles (Numbers 4:15) | He touched the Ark of the Covenant (2 Samuel 6:6) | He died instantly (2 Samuel 6:7) |
| Uzziah | Only the priests can offer incense in the Temple or Tabernacle sanctuary (Numbers 16:39-40; 18:7) | He entered the sanctuary in the Temple, where only priests were allowed to go (2 Chronicles 26:16-18) | He became a leper (2 Chronicles 26:19) |

**CAREFUL OBEDIENCE**

Solomon and his workers carefully followed God's instructions (4:7). As a result, the Temple work was blessed by God and completed in every detail. Here are a few examples of (1) people in the Bible who did not carefully follow one of God's instructions and (2) the resulting consequences. It is not enough to obey God halfheartedly.

across the entire width of the Temple. The inner walls of the foyer and the ceiling were overlaid with pure gold. The roof of the foyer was thirty feet* high.

5The main room of the Temple was paneled with cypress wood, overlaid with pure gold, and decorated with carvings of palm trees and chains. 6The walls of the Temple were decorated with beautiful jewels and with pure gold from the land of Parvaim. 7All the walls, beams, doors, and thresholds throughout the Temple were overlaid with gold, and figures of cherubim were carved on the walls.

8The Most Holy Place was thirty feet wide, corresponding to the width of the Temple, and it was also thirty feet deep. Its interior was overlaid with about twenty-three tons* of pure gold. 9They used gold nails that weighed about twenty ounces* each. The walls of the upper rooms were also overlaid with pure gold.

10Solomon made two figures shaped like cherubim and overlaid them with gold. These were placed in the Most Holy Place. 11The total wingspan of the two cherubim standing side by side was 30 feet. One wing of the first figure was 7½ feet long, and it touched the Temple wall. The other wing, also 7½ feet long, touched one of the wings of the second figure. 12In the same way, the second figure had one wing 7½ feet long that touched the opposite wall. The other wing, also 7½ feet long, touched the wing of the first figure. 13So the wingspan of both cherubim together was 30 feet. They both stood and faced out toward the main room of the Temple. 14Across the entrance of the Most Holy Place, Solomon hung a curtain made of fine linen and blue, purple, and scarlet yarn, with figures of cherubim embroidered on it.

15For the front of the Temple, Solomon made two pillars that were 27 feet* tall, each topped by a capital extending upward another 7½ feet. 16He made a network of interwoven chains and used them to decorate the tops of the pillars. He also made one hundred decorative pomegranates and attached them to the chains. 17Then he set up the two pillars at the entrance of the Temple, one to the south of the entrance and the other to the north. He named the one on the south Jakin, and the one on the north Boaz.*

3:4 As in some Greek and Syriac manuscripts, which read *20 cubits* [9 meters]; Hebrew reads *120 cubits,* which is 180 feet or 54 meters. 3:8 Hebrew *600 talents* [20.4 metric tons]. 3:9 Hebrew *50 shekels* [570 grams]. 3:15 As in Syriac version (see also 1 Kgs 7:15; 2 Kgs 25:17; Jer 52:21), which reads *18 cubits* [8.1 meters]; Hebrew reads *35 cubits,* which is 52.5 feet or 15.8 meters. 3:17 Jakin probably means "he establishes"; Boaz probably means "in him is strength."

CHAPTER **4** **HURAM-ABI'S SKILLFUL WORK.** Solomon
also made a bronze altar 30 feet long, 30 feet wide,
and 15 feet high.* 2Then he cast a large round tank,
15 feet across from rim to rim; it was called the Sea.
It was 7½ feet deep and about 45 feet in circumference. 3The Sea was encircled just below its rim by two
rows of figures that resembled oxen. There were
about six oxen per foot* all the way around, and
they had been cast as part of the tank.
4The Sea rested on a base of twelve bronze oxen,
all facing outward. Three faced north, three faced
west, three faced south, and three faced east. 5The
walls of the Sea were about three inches* thick, and
its rim flared out like a cup and resembled a lily
blossom. It could hold about 16,500 gallons* of
water.
6He also made ten basins for water to wash the
offerings, five to the south of the Sea and five to the
north. The priests used the Sea itself, and not the
basins, for their own washing.
7Solomon then cast ten gold lampstands according to the specifications that had been given and put
them in the Temple. Five were placed against the
south wall, and five were placed against the north
wall. 8He also built ten tables and placed them in the
Temple, five along the south wall and five along the
north wall. Then he molded one hundred gold basins.
9Solomon also built a courtyard for the priests and
the large outer courtyard. He made doors for the
courtyard entrances and overlaid them with bronze.
10The Sea was placed near the southeast corner of the
Temple.
11Huram-abi also made the necessary pots, shovels, and basins.
So at last Huram-abi completed everything King
Solomon had assigned him to make for the Temple
of God:

12 two pillars,
two bowl-shaped capitals on top of the pillars,
two networks of chains that decorated the capitals,
13 four hundred pomegranates that hung from the chains on the capitals (two rows of pomegranates for each of the chain networks that were hung around the capitals on top of the pillars),
14 the water carts holding the basins,
15 the Sea and the twelve oxen under it,
16 the pots, the shovels, the meat hooks, and all the related utensils.

Huram-abi made all these things out of burnished
bronze for the Temple of the LORD, just as King
Solomon had requested. 17The king had them cast in
clay molds in the Jordan Valley between Succoth and
Zarethan.* 18Such great quantities of bronze were
used that its weight could not be determined.
19So Solomon made all the furnishings for the
Temple of God:

the gold altar;
the tables for the Bread of the Presence;
20 the lampstands and their lamps of pure gold to burn in front of the Most Holy Place as prescribed;
21 the flower decorations, lamps, and tongs, all of pure gold;
22 the lamp snuffers, basins, dishes, and firepans, all of pure gold;
the doors for the entrances to the Most Holy Place and the main room of the Temple, overlaid with gold.

CHAPTER **5** **THE ARK AND THE TEMPLE.** When Solomon had finished all the work related to building
the Temple of the LORD, he brought in the gifts
dedicated by his father, King David, including all the
silver and gold and all the utensils. These were stored
in the treasuries of the Temple of God.
2Solomon then summoned the leaders of all the
tribes and families of Israel to assemble in Jerusalem.
They were to bring the Ark of the LORD's covenant
from its location in the City of David, also known as
Zion, to its new place in the Temple. 3They all assembled before the king at the annual Festival of Shelters
in early autumn.* 4When all the leaders of Israel
arrived, the Levites moved the Ark, 5along with the
special tent* and all its sacred utensils. The Levitical
priests carried them all up to the Temple. 6King
Solomon and the entire community of Israel sacrificed sheep and oxen before the Ark in such numbers
that no one could keep count!
7Then the priests carried the Ark of the LORD's
covenant into the inner sanctuary of the Temple—
the Most Holy Place—and placed it beneath the
wings of the cherubim. 8The cherubim spread their
wings out over the Ark, forming a canopy over the
Ark and its carrying poles. 9These poles were so long
that their ends could be seen from the front entrance
of the Temple's main room—the Holy Place—but
not from outside it. They are still there to this day.
10Nothing was in the Ark except the two stone tablets
that Moses had placed there at Mount Sinai,* when

**WORSHIP TOOLS ● • • •**

4:11-16 **Pots, shovels, and basins—these implements of worship are not familiar to us. Although the articles we use to aid our worship have changed, the purpose of worship remains the same: to give honor and praise to God. We must never confuse our worship of God with the things we use to help us worship him.**

4:1 Hebrew *20 cubits* [9 meters] *long, 20 cubits wide, and 10 cubits* [4.5 meters] *high.* In this chapter, the distance measures are calculated from the Hebrew cubit at a ratio of 18 inches or 45 centimeters per cubit. 4:3 Or *20 oxen per meter;* Hebrew reads *10 per cubit.* 4:5a Hebrew *a handbreadth* [8 centimeters]. 4:5b Hebrew *3,000 baths* [63 kiloliters]. 4:17 As in parallel text at 1 Kgs 7:46; Hebrew reads *Zeredah.* 5:3 Hebrew *at the festival that is in the seventh month.* The Festival of Shelters began on the fifteenth day of the seventh month of the Hebrew lunar calendar. This occurs on our calendar in late September or early October. 5:5 Hebrew *Tent of Meeting.* 5:10 Hebrew *Horeb,* another name for Sinai.

## LIVING WORSHIP ● ● • • •

5:13 **The first service at the Temple began with honoring God and acknowledging his presence and goodness. In the same way, our worship should begin with a recognition of God's love. Praise God first, and then you will be prepared to present your needs to him. Recalling God's love and mercy will bring daily worship to life. Psalm 107 is an example of how David recalled God's loving-kindness.**

the LORD made a covenant with the people of Israel after they left Egypt.

[11]Then the priests left the Holy Place. All the priests who were present had purified themselves, whether or not they were on duty that day. [12]And the Levites who were musicians—Asaph, Heman, Jeduthun, and all their sons and brothers—were dressed in fine linen robes and stood at the east side of the altar playing cymbals, harps, and lyres. They were joined by 120 priests who were playing trumpets. [13]The trumpeters and singers performed together in unison to praise and give thanks to the LORD. Accompanied by trumpets, cymbals, and other instruments, they raised their voices and praised the LORD with these words:

"He is so good!
His faithful love endures forever!"

At that moment a cloud filled the Temple of the LORD. [14]The priests could not continue their work because the glorious presence of the LORD filled the Temple of God.

CHAPTER **6** **SOLOMON BLESSES THE PEOPLE.** Then Solomon prayed, "O LORD, you have said that you would live in thick darkness. [2]But I have built a glorious Temple for you, where you can live forever!"

[3]Then the king turned around to the entire community of Israel standing before him and gave this blessing: [4]"Blessed be the LORD, the God of Israel, who has kept the promise he made to my father, David. For he told my father, [5]'From the day I brought my people out of Egypt, I have never chosen a city among the tribes of Israel as the place where a temple should be built to honor my name. Nor have I chosen a king to lead my people Israel. [6]But now I have chosen Jerusalem as that city, and David as that king.'"

[7]Then Solomon said, "My father, David, wanted to build this Temple to honor the name of the LORD, the God of Israel. [8]But the LORD told him, 'It is right for you to want to build the Temple to honor my name, [9]but you will not be the one to do it. One of your sons will build it instead.'

[10]"And now the LORD has done what he promised, for I have become king in my father's place. I have built this Temple to honor the name of the LORD, the God of Israel. [11]There I have placed the Ark, and in the Ark is the covenant that the LORD made with the people of Israel."

[12]Then Solomon stood with his hands spread out before the altar of the LORD in front of the entire community of Israel. [13]He had made a bronze platform 7½ feet long, 7½ feet wide, and 4½ feet high* and had placed it at the center of the Temple's outer courtyard. He stood on the platform before the entire assembly, and then he knelt down and lifted his hands toward heaven. [14]He prayed, "O LORD, God of Israel, there is no God like you in all of heaven and earth. You keep your promises and show unfailing love to all who obey you and are eager to do your will. [15]You have kept your promise to your servant David, my father. You made that promise with your own mouth, and today you have fulfilled it with your own hands. [16]And now, O LORD, God of Israel, carry out your further promise to your servant David, my father. For you said to him, 'If your descendants guard their behavior and obey my law as you have done, they will always reign over Israel.' [17]Now, O LORD, God of Israel, fulfill this promise to your servant David.

[18]"But will God really live on earth among people? Why, even the highest heavens cannot contain you. How much less this Temple I have built! [19]Listen to my prayer and my request, O LORD my God. Hear the cry and the prayer that your servant is making to you. [20]May you watch over this Temple both day and night, this place where you have said you would put your name. May you always hear the prayers I make toward this place. [21]May you hear the humble and earnest requests from me and your people Israel when we pray toward this place. Yes, hear us from heaven where you live, and when you hear, forgive.

## MARVEL ● ● • • •

6:18 **Solomon marveled that the Temple could contain the power of God and that God would be willing to live on earth among sinful people. We marvel that God, through his Son, Jesus, dwelt among us in human form to reveal his eternal purposes to us. In doing so, God was reaching out to humanity in love. God wants us to reach back in return and get to know him. Only then will we come to love him with all our heart. Don't simply marvel at God's power, take the time to get to know him.**

[22]"If someone wrongs another person and is required to take an oath of innocence in front of the altar at this Temple, [23]then hear from heaven and judge between your servants—the accuser and the accused. Punish the guilty party, and acquit the one who is innocent.

[24]"If your people Israel are defeated by their enemies because they have sinned against you, and if they turn to you and call on your name and pray to you here in this Temple, [25]then hear from heaven and forgive their sins and return them to this land you gave their ancestors.

[26]"If the skies are shut up and there is no rain because your people have sinned against you, and

6:13 Hebrew *5 cubits* [2.3 meters] *long, 5 cubits wide, and 3 cubits* [1.4 meters] *high.*

then they pray toward this Temple and confess your name and turn from their sins because you have punished them, 27then hear from heaven and forgive the sins of your servants, your people Israel. Teach them to do what is right, and send rain on your land that you have given to your people as their special possession.

28"If there is a famine in the land, or plagues, or crop disease, or attacks of locusts or caterpillars, or if your people's enemies are in the land besieging their towns—whatever the trouble is—29and if your people offer a prayer concerning their troubles or sorrow, raising their hands toward this Temple, 30then hear from heaven where you live, and forgive. Give your people whatever they deserve, for you alone know the human heart. 31Then they will fear you and walk in your ways as long as they live in the land you gave to our ancestors.

32"And when foreigners hear of you and your mighty miracles, and they come from distant lands to worship your great name and to pray toward this Temple, 33then hear from heaven where you live, and grant what they ask of you. Then all the people of the earth will come to know and fear you, just as your own people Israel do. They, too, will know that this Temple I have built bears your name.

34"If your people go out at your command to fight their enemies, and if they pray to you toward this city that you have chosen and toward this Temple that I have built for your name, 35then hear their prayers from heaven and uphold their cause.

36"If they sin against you—and who has never sinned?—you may become angry with them and let their enemies conquer them and take them captive to a foreign land far or near. 37But in that land of exile, they may turn to you again in repentance and pray, 'We have sinned, done evil, and acted wickedly.' 38Then if they turn to you with their whole heart and soul and pray toward the land you gave to their ancestors, toward this city you have chosen, and toward this Temple I have built to honor your name, 39then hear their prayers from heaven where you live. Uphold their cause and forgive your people who have sinned against you.

40"O my God, be attentive to all the prayers made to you in this place. 41And now, O LORD God, arise and enter this resting place of yours, where your magnificent Ark has been placed. May your priests, O LORD God, be clothed with salvation, and may your saints rejoice in your goodness. 42O LORD God, do not reject your anointed one. Remember your unfailing love for your servant David.*"

## CHAPTER 7 **GOD'S GLORY FILLS THE TEMPLE.**

When Solomon finished praying, fire flashed down from heaven and burned up the burnt offerings and

### FAR AWAY ● ● ● • •

6:30 **Have you ever felt far away from God—separated by personal problems and feelings of failure? In his prayer, Solomon underscores the fact that God stands ready to hear us, to forgive our sins, and to restore our relationship to him. God is waiting and listening for our confessions of guilt and our willingness to obey him. He is ready to forgive us and to restore us to fellowship with him. Don't wait to experience this loving forgiveness.**

sacrifices, and the glorious presence of the LORD filled the Temple. 2The priests could not even enter the Temple of the LORD because the glorious presence of the LORD filled it. 3When all the people of Israel saw the fire coming down and the glorious presence of the LORD filling the Temple, they fell face down on the ground and worshiped and praised the LORD, saying,

"He is so good!
His faithful love endures forever!"

4Then the king and all the people offered sacrifices to the LORD. 5King Solomon offered a sacrifice of 22,000 oxen and 120,000 sheep. And so the king and all the people dedicated the Temple of God. 6The priests took their assigned positions, and so did the Levites who were singing, "His faithful love endures forever!" They accompanied the singing with music from the instruments King David had made for praising the LORD. On the other side of the Levites, the priests blew the trumpets, while all Israel stood.

7Solomon then dedicated the central area of the courtyard in front of the LORD's Temple so they could present burnt offerings and the fat from peace offerings there. He did this because the bronze altar he had built could not handle all the burnt offerings, grain offerings, and sacrificial fat.

8For the next seven days they celebrated the Festival of Shelters* with huge crowds gathered from all the tribes of Israel. They came from as far away as Lebo-hamath in the north, to the brook of Egypt in the south. 9On the eighth day they had a closing ceremony, for they had celebrated the dedication of the altar for seven days and the Festival of Shelters for seven days. 10Then at the end of the celebration,* Solomon sent the people home. They were all joyful and happy because the LORD had been so good to David and Solomon and to his people Israel.

11So Solomon finished building the Temple of the LORD, as well as the royal palace. He completed everything he had planned to do. 12Then one night the LORD appeared to Solomon and said, "I have heard your prayer and have chosen this Temple as the place for making sacrifices. 13At times I might shut up the heavens so that no rain falls, or I might command locusts to devour your crops, or I might send plagues among you. 14Then if my

**6:42** Or *Remember the faithfulness of your servant David.* **7:8** Hebrew *the festival* (also in 7:9); see note on 5:3. **7:10** Hebrew *Then on the twenty-seventh day of the seventh month.* This day of the Hebrew lunar calendar occurs in late September or early October.

## FORGIVEN ● ● ● • •

**7:14 In chapter 6, Solomon asked God to make provisions for the people when they sinned. God answered with four conditions for forgiveness: (1) humble yourself by admitting your sins, (2) pray to God, asking for forgiveness, (3) search for God continually, and (4) turn from sinful habits. True repentance is more than talk—it is changed behavior. Whether we sin individually, as a group, or as a nation, following these steps will lead to forgiveness.**

people who are called by my name will humble themselves and pray and seek my face and turn from their wicked ways, I will hear from heaven and will forgive their sins and heal their land. [15]I will listen to every prayer made in this place, [16]for I have chosen this Temple and set it apart to be my home forever. My eyes and my heart will always be here.

[17]"As for you, if you follow me as your father, David, did and obey all my commands, laws, and regulations, [18]then I will not let anyone take away your throne. This is the same promise I gave your father, David, when I said, 'You will never fail to have a successor who rules over Israel.'

[19]"But if you abandon me and disobey the laws and commands I have given you, and if you go and worship other gods, [20]then I will uproot the people of Israel from this land of mine that I have given them. I will reject this Temple that I have set apart to honor my name. I will make it a spectacle of contempt among the nations. [21]And though this Temple is impressive now, it will become an appalling sight to all who pass by. They will ask, 'Why has the LORD done such terrible things to his land and to his Temple?' [22]And the answer will be, 'Because his people abandoned the LORD, the God of their ancestors, who brought them out of Egypt, and they worshiped other gods instead. That is why he brought all these disasters upon them.'"

CHAPTER **8** **SOLOMON'S MANY ACHIEVEMENTS.** It was now twenty years since Solomon had become king, and the great building projects of the LORD's Temple and his own royal palace were completed. [2]Solomon now turned his attention to rebuilding the towns that King Hiram* had given him, and he settled Israelites in them. [3]It was at this time, too, that Solomon fought against the city of Hamath-zobah and conquered it. [4]He rebuilt Tadmor in the desert and built towns in the region of Hamath as supply centers. [5]He fortified the cities of Upper Beth-horon and Lower Beth-horon, rebuilding their walls and installing barred gates. [6]He also rebuilt Baalath and other supply centers at this time and constructed cities where his chariots and horses* could be kept. He built to his heart's content in Jerusalem and Lebanon and throughout the entire realm.

[7]There were still some people living in the land who were not Israelites, including Hittites, Amorites, Perizzites, Hivites, and Jebusites. [8]These were descendants of the nations that Israel had not completely destroyed. So Solomon conscripted them for his labor force, and they serve in the labor force to this day. [9]But Solomon did not conscript any of the Israelites for forced labor. Instead, he assigned them to serve as fighting men, officers in his army, commanders of his chariots, and charioteers. [10]King Solomon also appointed 250 of them to supervise the various projects.

[11]Solomon moved his wife, Pharaoh's daughter, from the City of David to the new palace he had built for her. He said, "My wife must not live in King David's palace, for the Ark of the LORD has been there, and it is holy ground."

[12]Then Solomon sacrificed burnt offerings to the LORD on the altar he had built in front of the foyer of the Temple. [13]The number of sacrifices varied from day to day according to the commands Moses had given. Extra sacrifices were offered on the Sabbaths, on new moon festivals, and at the three annual festivals—the Passover celebration, the Festival of Harvest,* and the Festival of Shelters. [14]In

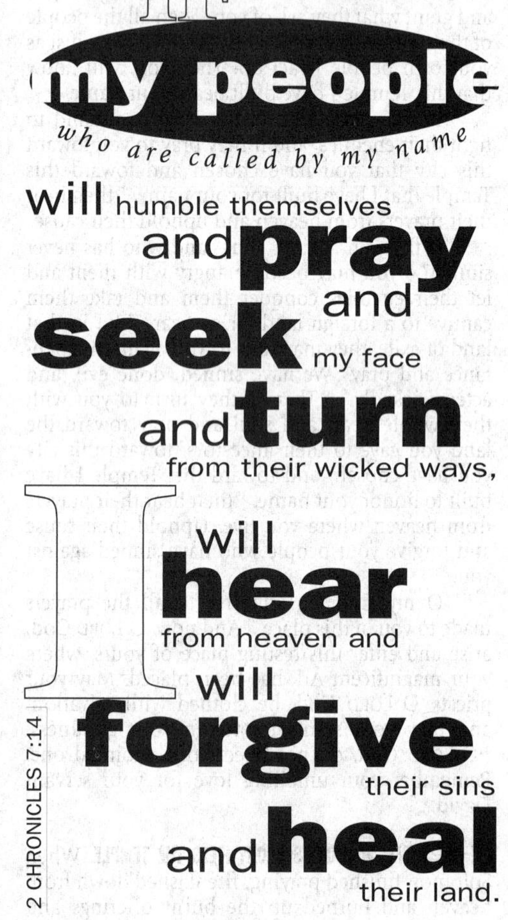

IF
my people
who are called by my name
will humble themselves
and pray
and
seek my face
and turn
from their wicked ways,
I will
hear
from heaven and
will
forgive
their sins
and heal
their land.
2 CHRONICLES 7:14

8:2 Hebrew *Huram,* a variant name for Hiram; also in 8:18. 8:6 Or *and charioteers.* 8:13 Or *Festival of Weeks.*

assigning the priests to their duties, Solomon followed the regulations of his father, David. He also
assigned the Levites to lead the people in praise
and to assist the priests in their daily duties. And
he assigned the gatekeepers to their gates by their
divisions, following the commands of David, the
man of God. 15Solomon did not deviate in any way
from David's commands concerning the priests
and Levites and the treasuries.

16So Solomon made sure that all the work related
to building the Temple of the LORD was carried out,
from the day its foundation was laid to the day of its
completion.

17Later Solomon went to Ezion-geber and Elath,*
ports in the land of Edom, along the shore of the Red
Sea.* 18Hiram sent him ships commanded by his
own officers and manned by experienced crews of
sailors. These ships sailed to the land of Ophir with
Solomon's men and brought back to Solomon almost seventeen tons* of gold.

CHAPTER **9** **THE QUEEN OF SHEBA VISITS.** When the
queen of Sheba heard of Solomon's reputation, she
came to Jerusalem to test him with hard questions.
She arrived with a large group of attendants and a
great caravan of camels loaded with spices, huge
quantities of gold, and precious jewels. 2When she
met with Solomon, they talked about everything she
had on her mind. Solomon answered all her questions; nothing was too hard for him to explain to her.
3When the queen of Sheba realized how wise Solomon was, and when she saw the palace he had built,
4she was breathless. She was also amazed at the food
on his tables, the organization of his officials and
their splendid clothing, the cup-bearers and their
robes, and the burnt offerings Solomon made at the
Temple of the LORD.

5She exclaimed to the king, "Everything I heard in
my country about your achievements and wisdom is
true! 6I didn't believe it until I arrived here and saw
it with my own eyes. Truly I had not heard the half
of it! Your wisdom is far greater than what I was told.
7How happy these people must be! What a privilege
for your officials to stand here day after day, listening
to your wisdom! 8The LORD your God is great indeed! He delights in you and has placed you on the
throne to rule for him. Because God loves Israel so
much and desires this kingdom to last forever, he has
made you king so you can rule with justice and
righteousness."

9Then she gave the king a gift of nine thousand
pounds* of gold, and great quantities of spices and
precious jewels. Never before had there been spices
as fine as those the queen of Sheba gave to Solomon.

10(When the crews of Hiram and Solomon
brought gold from Ophir, they also brought rich
cargoes of almug wood* and precious jewels. 11The
king used the almug wood to make steps* for the
Temple of the LORD and the royal palace, and to
construct harps and lyres for the musicians. Never
before had there been such beautiful instruments in
Judah.)

12King Solomon gave the queen of Sheba whatever
she asked for—gifts of greater value than the gifts
she had given him. Then she and all her attendants
left and returned to their own land.

13Each year Solomon received about 25 tons* of
gold. 14This did not include the additional revenue
he received from merchants and traders. All the
kings of Arabia and the governors of the land also
brought gold and silver to Solomon.

15King Solomon made two hundred large shields
of hammered gold, each containing over 15 pounds*
of gold. 16He also made three hundred smaller
shields of hammered gold, each containing about
7½ pounds* of gold. The king placed these shields
in the Palace of the Forest of Lebanon.

17Then the king made a huge ivory throne and
overlaid it with pure gold. 18The throne had six steps,
and there was a footstool of gold attached to it. On
both sides of the seat were armrests, with the figure
of a lion standing on each side of the throne. 19Solo-
mon made twelve other lion figures, one standing
on each end of each of the six steps. No other throne
in all the world could be compared with it!

## THE QUEEN ● ● • • •

9:1-8 **The queen of Sheba had heard about Solomon's wisdom, but she was overwhelmed when she saw for herself the fruits of that wisdom. Although Solomon had married Pharaoh's daughter, he was still sincerely trying to follow God at this stage in his life. When people get to know you and begin to ask hard questions, will your responses reflect God? Your life is your most powerful witness; let others see God at work in you.**

20All of King Solomon's drinking cups were solid
gold, as were all the utensils in the Palace of the
Forest of Lebanon. They were not made of silver
because silver was considered of little value in Solomon's day!

21The king had a fleet of trading ships* manned by
the sailors sent by Hiram.* Once every three years
the ships returned, loaded down with gold, silver,
ivory, apes, and peacocks.*

22So King Solomon became richer and wiser than
any other king in all the earth. 23Kings from every
nation came to visit him and to hear the wisdom
God had given him. 24Year after year, everyone who
came to visit brought him gifts of silver and gold,
clothing, weapons, spices, horses, and mules.

25Solomon had four thousand stalls for his chariot
horses and twelve thousand horses.* He stationed
many of them in the chariot cities, and some near him

**8:17a** As in Greek version (see also 2 Kgs 14:22; 16:6); Hebrew reads *Eloth.* **8:17b** Hebrew *the sea.* **8:18** Hebrew *450 talents* [15.3 metric tons]. **9:9** Hebrew *120 talents* [4 metric tons]. **9:10** Hebrew *algum wood* (also in 9:11); compare parallel text at 1 Kgs 10:11-12. **9:11** Or *gateways.* The meaning of the Hebrew is uncertain. **9:13** Hebrew *666 talents* [23 metric tons]. **9:15** Hebrew *600 shekels* [6.8 kilograms]. **9:16** Hebrew *300 shekels* [3.4 kilograms]. **9:21a** Hebrew *fleet of ships that could sail to Tarshish.* **9:21b** Hebrew *Huram,* a variant name for Hiram. **9:21c** Or *and baboons.* **9:25** Or *12,000 charioteers.*

in Jerusalem. [26]He ruled over all the kings from the Euphrates River* to the land of the Philistines and the border of Egypt. [27]The king made silver as plentiful in Jerusalem as stones. And valuable cedarwood was as common as the sycamore wood that grows in the foothills of Judah.* [28]Solomon's horses were imported from Egypt* and many other countries.

[29]The rest of the events of Solomon's reign, from beginning to end, are recorded in *The Record of Nathan the Prophet* and in *The Prophecy of Ahijah from Shiloh,* and also in *The Visions of Iddo the Seer,* concerning Jeroboam son of Nebat. [30]Solomon ruled in Jerusalem over all Israel for forty years. [31]When he died, he was buried in the city of his father, David. Then his son Rehoboam became the next king.

## PEERS ● ● • • ·

10:1-14 **Following bad advice can cause disaster. Rehoboam lost the chance to rule a peaceful, united kingdom because he rejected the advice of Solomon's older counselors, preferring that of his peers. Rehoboam made two errors in seeking advice: (1) he did not give extra consideration to the suggestions of those who knew the situation better than he, and (2) he did not ask God for wisdom to discern which was the better option.**

**It is easy to follow the advice of our peers because they often feel as we do. But their view may be limited. It is important to listen carefully to those who have more experience than we do, those who can see the bigger picture.**

CHAPTER **10** **REHOBOAM TAKES BAD ADVICE.** Rehoboam went to Shechem, where all Israel had gathered to make him king. [2]When Jeroboam son of Nebat heard of Solomon's death, he returned from Egypt, for he had fled to Egypt to escape from King Solomon. [3]The leaders of Israel sent for Jeroboam, and he and all Israel went together to speak with Rehoboam. [4]"Your father was a hard master," they said. "Lighten the harsh labor demands and heavy taxes that your father imposed on us. Then we will be your loyal subjects."

[5]Rehoboam replied, "Come back in three days for my answer." So the people went away.

[6]Then King Rehoboam went to discuss the matter with the older men who had counseled his father, Solomon. "What is your advice?" he asked. "How should I answer these people?"

[7]The older counselors replied, "If you are good to the people and show them kindness and do your best to please them, they will always be your loyal subjects."

[8]But Rehoboam rejected the advice of the elders and instead asked the opinion of the young men who had grown up with him and who were now his advisers. [9]"What is your advice?" he asked them. "How should I answer these people who want me to lighten the burdens imposed by my father?"

[10]The young men replied, "This is what you should tell those complainers: 'My little finger is thicker than my father's waist—if you think he was hard on you, just wait and see what I'll be like! [11]Yes, my father was harsh on you, but I'll be even harsher! My father used whips on you, but I'll use scorpions!'"

[12]Three days later, Jeroboam and all the people returned to hear Rehoboam's decision, just as the king had requested. [13]But Rehoboam spoke harshly to them, for he rejected the advice of the older counselors [14]and followed the counsel of his younger advisers. He told the people, "My father was harsh on you, but I'll be even harsher! My father used whips on you, but I'll use scorpions!" [15]So the king paid no attention to the people's demands. This turn of events was the will of God, for it fulfilled the prophecy of the LORD spoken to Jeroboam son of Nebat by the prophet Ahijah from Shiloh.

[16]When all Israel realized that the king had rejected their request, they shouted, "Down with David and his dynasty! We have no share in Jesse's son! Let's go home, Israel! Look out for your own house, O David!" So all Israel returned home. [17]But Rehoboam continued to rule over the Israelites who lived in the towns of Judah.

[18]King Rehoboam sent Adoniram,* who was in charge of the labor force, to restore order, but the Israelites stoned him to death. When this news reached King Rehoboam, he quickly jumped into his chariot and fled to Jerusalem. [19]The northern tribes of Israel have refused to be ruled by a descendant of David to this day.

## GREEDY ● ● • • ·

10:16-19 **In trying to have it all, Rehoboam lost almost everything. Motivated by greed and power, he pressed too hard and divided his kingdom. He didn't need more money or power because he had inherited the richest kingdom in the world. He didn't need more control because the land was at peace. His demands were based on selfishness rather than reason or spiritual discernment. Those who selfishly insist on having it all often wind up with little or nothing.**

CHAPTER **11** **GOD SAYS NOT TO FIGHT.** When Rehoboam arrived at Jerusalem, he mobilized the armies of Judah and Benjamin—180,000 select troops—to fight against the army of Israel and to restore the kingdom to himself. [2]But the LORD said to Shemaiah, the man of God, [3]"Say to Rehoboam son of Solomon, king of Judah, and to all the Israelites in Judah and Benjamin: [4]'This is what the LORD says: Do not fight against your relatives. Go back home, for what has happened is my doing!'" So they obeyed the message of the LORD and did not fight against Jeroboam.

[5]Rehoboam remained in Jerusalem and fortified

**9:26** Hebrew *the river.* **9:27** Hebrew *the Shephelah.* **9:28** Possibly *Muzur,* a district near Cilicia. **10:18** Hebrew *Hadoram,* a variant name for Adoniram; compare 1 Kgs 4:6; 5:14; 12:18.

various cities for the defense of Judah. 6He built up
Bethlehem, Etam, Tekoa, 7Beth-zur, Soco, Adullam,
8Gath, Mareshah, Ziph, 9Adoraim, Lachish, Azekah,
10Zorah, Aijalon, and Hebron. These became the
fortified cities of Judah and Benjamin. 11Rehoboam
strengthened their defenses and stationed commanders in them. In each of them, he stored supplies of food, olive oil, and wine. 12He also put
shields and spears in these towns as a further safety
measure. So only Judah and Benjamin remained
under his control.

13But all the priests and Levites living among the
northern tribes of Israel sided with Rehoboam. 14The
Levites even abandoned their homes and property
and moved to Judah and Jerusalem, because Jeroboam and his sons would not allow them to serve
the LORD as priests. 15Jeroboam appointed his own
priests to serve at the pagan shrines, where they
worshiped the goat and calf idols he had made.
16From all over Israel, those who sincerely wanted to
worship the LORD, the God of Israel, followed the
Levites to Jerusalem, where they could offer sacrifices
to the LORD, the God of their ancestors. 17This
strengthened the kingdom of Judah, and for three
years they supported Rehoboam son of Solomon
and earnestly sought to obey the LORD as they had
done during the reigns of David and Solomon.

18Rehoboam married his cousin Mahalath, the
daughter of David's son Jerimoth and of Abihail, the
daughter of Eliab. (Eliab was one of David's brothers, a son of Jesse.) 19Mahalath had three sons—Jeush, Shemariah, and Zaham.

20Later Rehoboam married another cousin,
Maacah, the daughter of Absalom. Maacah gave
birth to Abijah, Attai, Ziza, and Shelomith. 21Reho-
boam loved Maacah more than any of his other
wives and concubines. In all, he had eighteen wives
and sixty concubines, and they gave birth to twenty-
eight sons and sixty daughters. 22Rehoboam made
Maacah's son Abijah chief among the princes, making it clear that he would be the next king. 23Reho-
boam also wisely gave responsibilities to his other
sons and stationed them in the fortified cities
throughout the land of Judah and Benjamin. He
provided them with generous provisions and arranged for each of them to have several wives.

CHAPTER **12** **EGYPT CONQUERS JERUSALEM.** But
when Rehoboam was firmly established and strong,
he abandoned the law of the LORD, and all Israel
followed him in this sin. 2Because they were unfaithful to the LORD, King Shishak of Egypt attacked
Jerusalem in the fifth year of King Rehoboam's reign.
3He came with twelve hundred chariots, sixty thousand horsemen, and a countless army of foot soldiers, including Libyans, Sukkites, and Ethiopians.*
4Shishak conquered Judah's fortified cities and then
advanced to attack Jerusalem.

5The prophet Shemaiah then met with Rehoboam
and Judah's leaders, who had all fled to Jerusalem

**GOOD TIMES ● ●●●•**

12:1 **At the height of his popularity and power, Rehoboam abandoned the Lord. What happened? Often it is more difficult to be a believer in good times than in bad. Tough times push us toward God; but easy times can make us feel self-sufficient and self-satisfied. When everything is going right, guard your faith closely.**

because of Shishak. Shemaiah told them, "This is
what the LORD says: You have abandoned me, so I am
abandoning you to Shishak."

6The king and the leaders of Israel humbled themselves and said, "The LORD is right in doing this to us!"

7When the LORD saw their change of heart, he gave
this message to Shemaiah: "Since the people have
humbled themselves, I will not completely destroy
them and will soon give them some relief. I will not
use Shishak to pour out my anger on Jerusalem. 8But
they will become his subjects, so that they can learn
how much better it is to serve me than to serve
earthly rulers."

9So King Shishak of Egypt came to Jerusalem and
took away all the treasures of the Temple of the LORD
and of the royal palace, including all of Solomon's
gold shields. 10King Rehoboam later replaced them
with bronze shields and entrusted them to the care
of the captain of his bodyguard. 11Whenever the king
went to the Temple of the LORD, the guards would
carry them along and then return them to the guardroom. 12Because Rehoboam humbled himself, the
LORD's anger was turned aside, and he did not destroy him completely. And there was still goodness
in the land of Judah.

13King Rehoboam firmly established himself in
Jerusalem and continued to rule. He was forty-one
years old when he became king, and he reigned
seventeen years in Jerusalem, the city the LORD had
chosen from among all the tribes of Israel as the
place to honor his name. Rehoboam's mother was
Naamah, a woman from Ammon. 14But he was an
evil king, for he did not seek the LORD with all his
heart.

15The rest of the events of Rehoboam's reign, from
beginning to end, are recorded in *The Record of Shemaiah the Prophet* and in *The Record of Iddo the Seer,*
which are part of the genealogical record. Rehoboam
and Jeroboam were continually at war with each
other. 16When Rehoboam died, he was buried in the
City of David. Then his son Abijah became the next
king.

CHAPTER **13** **ABIJAH DEFEATS JEROBOAM.** Abijah
began to rule over Judah in the eighteenth year of
Jeroboam's reign in Israel. 2He reigned in Jerusalem
three years. His mother was Maacah,* a daughter of
Uriel from Gibeah.

Then war broke out between Abijah and Jeroboam. 3Judah, led by King Abijah, fielded 400,000
seasoned warriors, while Jeroboam mustered
800,000 courageous men from Israel. 4When the

12:3 Hebrew *and Cushites.* 13:2 As in most Greek manuscripts and Syriac version (see also 2 Chr 11:20-21; 1 Kgs 15:2); Hebrew reads *Micaiah.*

army of Judah arrived in the hill country of Ephraim, Abijah stood on Mount Zemaraim and shouted to Jeroboam and the Israelite army: "Listen to me! [5]Don't you realize that the LORD, the God of Israel, made an unbreakable covenant* with David, giving him and his descendants the throne of Israel forever? [6]Yet Jeroboam son of Nebat, who was a mere servant of David's son Solomon, became a traitor to his master. [7]Then a whole gang of scoundrels joined him, defying Solomon's son Rehoboam when he was young and inexperienced and could not stand up to them. [8]Do you really think you can stand against the kingdom of the LORD that is led by the descendants of David? Your army is vast indeed, but with you are those gold calves that Jeroboam made as your gods! [9]And you have chased away the priests of the LORD and the Levites and have appointed your own priests, just like the pagan nations. You let anyone become a priest these days! Whoever comes to be dedicated with a young bull and seven rams can become a priest of these so-called gods of yours!

## GOLD CALVES ● ● • • •

13:8 **Jeroboam's army was cursed because of the gold calves they carried with them. It was as though they had put sin into a physical form so they could haul it around. Consider carefully the things you cherish. If you value anything more than God, it becomes your golden calf and one day will condemn you. Let go of anything that interferes with your relationship with God.**

[10]"But as for us, the LORD is our God, and we have not abandoned him. Only the descendants of Aaron serve the LORD as priests, and the Levites alone may help them in their work. [11]They present burnt offerings and fragrant incense to the LORD every morning and evening. They place the Bread of the Presence on the holy table, and they light the gold lampstand every evening. We are following the instructions of the LORD our God, but you have abandoned him. [12]So you see, God is with us. He is our leader. His priests blow their trumpets and lead us into battle against you. O people of Israel, do not fight against the LORD, the God of your ancestors, for you will not succeed!"

[13]Meanwhile, Jeroboam had secretly sent part of his army around behind the men of Judah to ambush them. [14]When Judah realized that they were being attacked from the front and the rear, they cried out to the LORD for help. Then the priests blew the trumpets, [15]and the men of Judah began to shout. At the sound of their battle cry, God defeated Jeroboam and the Israelite army and routed them before Abijah and the army of Judah. [16]The Israelite army fled from Judah, and God handed them over to Judah in defeat. [17]Abijah and his army inflicted heavy losses on them; there were 500,000 casualties among Israel's finest troops that day. [18]So Judah defeated Israel because they trusted in the LORD, the God of their ancestors. [19]Abijah and his army pursued Jeroboam's troops and captured some of his towns, including Bethel, Jeshanah, and Ephron, along with their surrounding villages.

[20]So Jeroboam of Israel never regained his power during Abijah's lifetime, and finally the LORD struck him down and he died. [21]By contrast, Abijah of Judah grew more and more powerful. He married fourteen wives and had twenty-two sons and sixteen daughters. [22]The rest of the events of Abijah's reign, including his words and deeds, are recorded in *The Commentary of Iddo the Prophet.*

CHAPTER **14** **ASA RULES JUDAH.** When Abijah died, he was buried in the City of David. Then his son Asa became the next king. There was peace in the land for ten years, [2]for Asa did what was pleasing and good in the sight of the LORD his God. [3]He removed the pagan altars and the shrines. He smashed the sacred pillars and cut down the Asherah poles. [4]He commanded the people of Judah to seek the LORD, the God of their ancestors, and to obey his law and his commands. [5]Asa also removed the pagan shrines, as well as the incense altars from every one of Judah's towns. So Asa's kingdom enjoyed a period of peace. [6]During those peaceful years, he was able to build up the fortified cities throughout Judah. No one tried to make war against him at this time, for the LORD was giving him rest from his enemies. [7]Asa told the people of Judah, "Let us build towns and fortify them with walls, towers, gates, and bars. The land is ours because we sought the LORD our God, and he has given us rest from our enemies." So they went ahead with these projects and brought them to completion.

## BE PREPARED ● ● • • •

14:7 **Times of peace are not just for resting. They allow us to prepare for times of trouble. King Asa recognized the period of peace as the right time to build his defenses. He knew that it would be too late to prepare defenses at the moment of attack. It also is difficult to withstand spiritual attack unless defenses are prepared beforehand. Decisions about what to do when temptations arise must be made with a cool head in the peace of untroubled moments, long before the heat of temptation is upon us. Build your defenses now, before temptation strikes.**

[8]King Asa had an army of 300,000 warriors from the tribe of Judah, armed with large shields and spears. He also had an army of 280,000 warriors from the tribe of Benjamin, armed with small shields and bows. Both armies were composed of courageous fighting men.

[9]Once an Ethiopian* named Zerah attacked Judah with an army of a million men* and three hundred chariots. They advanced to the city of Mareshah, [10]so Asa deployed his armies for battle in the valley north of Mareshah.* [11]Then Asa cried out to the LORD his God, "O LORD, no one but you can help the powerless against the mighty! Help us, O LORD our God, for we

**13:5** Hebrew *a covenant of salt.* **14:9a** Hebrew *a Cushite.* **14:9b** Or *an army of thousands and thousands;* Hebrew reads *an army of a thousand thousands.* **14:10** Or *in the Zephathah Valley near Mareshah.*

trust in you alone. It is in your name that we have come against this vast horde. O LORD, you are our God; do not let mere men prevail against you!"

[12]So the LORD defeated the Ethiopians* in the presence of Asa and the army of Judah, and the enemy fled. [13]Asa and his army pursued them as far as Gerar, and so many Ethiopians fell that they were unable to rally. They were destroyed by the LORD and his army, and the army of Judah carried off vast quantities of plunder. [14]While they were at Gerar, they attacked all the towns in that area, and terror from the LORD came upon the people there. As a result, vast quantities of plunder were taken from these towns, too. [15]They also attacked the camps of herdsmen and captured many sheep and camels before finally returning to Jerusalem.

CHAPTER **15** **ASA REBUILDS THE ALTAR.** Then the Spirit of God came upon Azariah son of Oded, [2]and he went out to meet King Asa as he was returning from the battle. "Listen to me, Asa!" he shouted. "Listen, all you people of Judah and Benjamin! The LORD will stay with you as long as you stay with him! Whenever you seek him, you will find him. But if you abandon him, he will abandon you. [3]For a long time, Israel was without the true God, without a priest to teach them, and without God's law. [4]But whenever you were in distress and turned to the LORD, the God of Israel, and sought him out, you found him. [5]During those dark times, it was not safe to travel. Problems troubled the nation on every hand. [6]Nation fought against nation, and city against city, for God was troubling you with every kind of problem. [7]And now, you men of Judah, be strong and courageous, for your work will be rewarded."

[8]When Asa heard this message from Azariah the prophet,* he took courage and removed all the idols in the land of Judah and Benjamin and in the towns he had captured in the hill country of Ephraim. And he repaired the altar of the LORD, which stood in front of the foyer of the LORD's Temple.

[9]Then Asa called together all the people of Judah and Benjamin, along with the people of Ephraim, Manasseh, and Simeon who had settled among them. Many had moved to Judah during Asa's reign when they saw that the LORD his God was with him. [10]The people gathered at Jerusalem in late spring,* during the fifteenth year of Asa's reign. [11]On that day they sacrificed to the LORD some of the animals they had taken as plunder in the battle—seven hundred oxen and seven thousand sheep and goats. [12]Then they entered into a covenant to seek the LORD, the God of their ancestors, with all their heart and soul. [13]They agreed that anyone who refused to seek the LORD, the God of Israel, would be put to death—whether young or old, man or woman. [14]They shouted out their oath of loyalty to the LORD with trumpets blaring and horns sounding. [15]All were happy about this covenant, for they had entered into it with all their hearts. Eagerly they sought after God, and they found him. And the LORD gave them rest from their enemies on every side.

[16]King Asa even deposed his grandmother Maacah from her position as queen mother because she had made an obscene Asherah pole. He cut down the pole, broke it up, and burned it in the Kidron Valley. [17]Although the pagan shrines were not completely removed from Israel, Asa remained fully committed to the LORD throughout his life. [18]He brought into the Temple of God the silver and gold and the utensils that he and his father had dedicated. [19]So there was no more war until the thirty-fifth year of Asa's reign.

CHAPTER **16** **ASA FORGETS GOD.** In the thirty-sixth year of Asa's reign, King Baasha of Israel invaded Judah and fortified Ramah in order to prevent anyone from entering or leaving King Asa's territory in Judah. [2]Asa responded by taking the silver and gold from the treasuries of the LORD's Temple and from the royal palace. He sent it to King Ben-hadad of Aram, who was ruling in Damascus, along with this message:

> [3]"Let us renew the treaty that existed between your father and my father. See, I am sending you a gift of silver and gold. Break your treaty with King Baasha of Israel so that he will leave me alone."

[4]Ben-hadad agreed to King Asa's request and sent his armies to attack Israel. They conquered the towns of Ijon, Dan, Abel-beth-maacah,* and all the store cities in Naphtali. [5]As soon as Baasha of Israel heard what was happening, he abandoned his project of fortifying Ramah. [6]Then King Asa called out all the men of Judah to carry away the building stones and timbers that Baasha had been using to fortify Ramah. Asa used these materials to fortify the towns of Geba and Mizpah.

[7]At that time Hanani the seer came to King Asa and told him, "Because you have put your trust in the king of Aram instead of in the LORD your God, you missed your chance to destroy the army of the king of Aram. [8]Don't you remember what happened to the Ethiopians* and Libyans and their vast army, with all of their chariots and horsemen*? At that time you relied on the LORD, and he handed them all over to you. [9]The eyes of the LORD search the whole earth in order to strengthen those whose hearts are fully committed to him. What a fool you have been! From now on, you will be at war." [10]Asa became so

**THE TRUTH ● ● ● • •**

**16:10 Asa was angry with Hanani's message, so he threw the prophet in jail. God's truth will not always be welcomed with open arms, especially when it reveals people's sins. But we must speak and live by God's truth, regardless of the consequences.**

14:12 Hebrew *Cushites;* also in 14:13. 15:8 As in Syriac version and Latin Vulgate (see also 15:1); Hebrew reads *from Oded the prophet.* 15:10 Hebrew *in the third month.* This month of the Hebrew lunar calendar usually occurs in May and June. 16:4 As in parallel text at 1 Kgs 15:20; Hebrew reads *Abel-maim,* another name for Abel-beth-maacah. 16:8a Hebrew *Cushites.* 16:8b Or *and charioteers.*

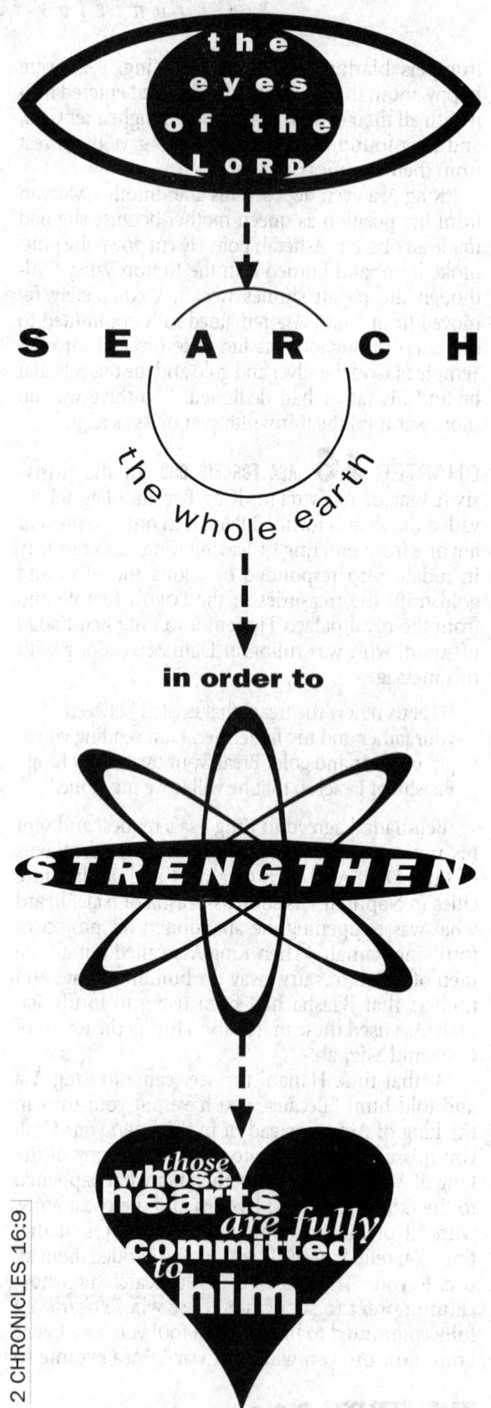
the eyes of the LORD
SEARCH
the whole earth
in order to
STRENGTHEN
those whose hearts are fully committed to him
2 CHRONICLES 16:9

angry with Hanani for saying this that he threw him into prison. At that time, Asa also began to oppress some of his people.

[11]The rest of the events of Asa's reign, from beginning to end, are recorded in *The Book of the Kings of Judah and Israel.* [12]In the thirty-ninth year of his reign, Asa developed a serious foot disease. Even when the disease became life threatening, he did not seek the LORD's help but sought help only from his physicians. [13]So he died in the forty-first year of his reign. [14]He was buried in the tomb he had carved out for himself in the City of David. He was laid on a bed perfumed with sweet spices and ointments, and at his funeral the people built a huge fire in his honor.

CHAPTER **17** **JEHOSHAPHAT RULES JUDAH.** Then Jehoshaphat, Asa's son, became the next king. He strengthened Judah to stand against any attack from Israel. [2]He stationed troops in all the fortified cities of Judah, and he assigned additional garrisons to the land of Judah and to the towns of Ephraim that his father, Asa, had conquered.

[3]The LORD was with Jehoshaphat because he followed the example of his father's early years* and did not worship the images of Baal. [4]He sought his father's God and obeyed his commands instead of following the practices of the kingdom of Israel. [5]So the LORD established Jehoshaphat's control over the kingdom of Judah. All the people of Judah brought gifts to Jehoshaphat, so he became very wealthy and highly esteemed. [6]He was committed to the ways of the LORD. He knocked down the pagan shrines and destroyed the Asherah poles.

[7]In the third year of his reign, Jehoshaphat sent out his officials to teach in all the towns of Judah. These officials included Ben-hail, Obadiah, Zechariah, Nethanel, and Micaiah. [8]He sent Levites along with them, including Shemaiah, Nethaniah, Zebadiah, Asahel, Shemiramoth, Jehonathan, Adonijah, Tobijah, and Tob-adonijah. He also sent out the priests, Elishama and Jehoram. [9]They took copies of the Book of the Law of the LORD and traveled around through all the towns of Judah, teaching the people.

[10]Then the fear of the LORD fell over all the surrounding kingdoms so that none of them declared war on Jehoshaphat. [11]Some of the Philistines brought him gifts and silver as tribute, and the Arabs brought seventy-seven hundred rams and seventy-seven hundred male goats.

[12]So Jehoshaphat became more and more powerful and built fortresses and store cities throughout Judah. [13]He stored numerous supplies in Judah's towns and stationed an army of seasoned troops at Jerusalem. [14]His army was enrolled according to ancestral clans.

From Judah, there were 300,000 troops organized
in units of one thousand, under the command
of Adnah. [15]Next in command was Jehohanan,
who commanded 280,000 troops. [16]Next was
Amasiah son of Zicri, who volunteered for the
LORD's service, with 200,000 troops under his
command.

17:3 Some Hebrew manuscripts read *the example of his father, David.*

[17]From Benjamin, there were 200,000 troops equipped with bows and shields. They were under the command of Eliada, a veteran soldier.
[18]Next in command was Jehozabad, who commanded 180,000 armed men.

[19]These were the troops stationed in Jerusalem to serve the king, besides those Jehoshaphat stationed in the fortified cities throughout Judah.

CHAPTER **18** **JEHOSHAPHAT AND AHAB.** Now Jehoshaphat enjoyed great riches and high esteem, and he arranged for his son to marry the daughter of King Ahab of Israel. [2]A few years later, he went to Samaria to visit Ahab, who prepared a great banquet for him and his officials. They butchered great numbers of sheep and oxen for the feast. Then Ahab enticed Jehoshaphat to join forces with him to attack Ramoth-gilead. [3]"Will you join me in fighting against Ramoth-gilead?" Ahab asked.

And Jehoshaphat replied, "Why, of course! You and I are brothers, and my troops are yours to command. We will certainly join you in battle." [4]Then Jehoshaphat added, "But first let's find out what the LORD says."

[5]So King Ahab summoned his prophets, four hundred of them, and asked them, "Should we go to war against Ramoth-gilead or not?"

They all replied, "Go ahead, for God will give you a great victory!"

[6]But Jehoshaphat asked, "Isn't there a prophet of the LORD around, too? I would like to ask him the same question."

[7]King Ahab replied, "There is still one prophet of the LORD, but I hate him. He never prophesies anything but bad news for me! His name is Micaiah son of Imlah."

"You shouldn't talk like that," Jehoshaphat said. "Let's hear what he has to say."

[8]So the king of Israel called one of his officials and said, "Quick! Go and get Micaiah son of Imlah."

[9]King Ahab of Israel and King Jehoshaphat of Judah, dressed in their royal robes, were sitting on thrones at the threshing floor near the gate of Samaria. All of Ahab's prophets were prophesying there in front of them. [10]One of them, Zedekiah son of Kenaanah, made some iron horns and proclaimed, "This is what the LORD says: With these horns you will gore the Arameans to death!"

[11]All the other prophets agreed. "Yes," they said, "go up to Ramoth-gilead and be victorious. The LORD will give you a glorious victory!"

[12]Meanwhile, the messenger who went to get Micaiah said to him, "Look, all the prophets are promising victory for the king. Be sure that you agree with them and promise success."

[13]But Micaiah replied, "As surely as the LORD lives, I will say only what my God tells me to say."

[14]When Micaiah arrived before the king, Ahab asked him, "Micaiah, should we go to war against Ramoth-gilead or not?"

---

## JEHOSHAPHAT

What do you think: Do children usually learn from their parents' mistakes, or just repeat them? In the lives of the people in the Bible, the examples given by parents affected their children in powerful and long-lasting ways. This is true of Jehoshaphat, the son of King Asa. For much of his life, Jehoshaphat seems to have learned from his father's mistakes. But a closer look shows that he also learned some bad habits from his father.

When the problems were big and obvious, like the need for religious education for the people or a large army coming to attack, Jehoshaphat knew he needed God's help. When in trouble, he turned to God right away. But in day-to-day plans and actions, Jehoshaphat forgot about God. He is remembered for the good things he did with God's help, but he also is remembered for the mistakes he made when he didn't depend on God.

We make the same mistake Jehoshaphat made when we only depend on God during difficult times. Then when things get out of hand, we want him to get us out of the mess we've gotten ourselves into. God wants to help us—not only with the big decisions, but also with our daily situations. It's when we think we can control our daily life without his help that we end up making big mistakes. Have you asked God to be in every part of your life today?

KEY VERSES: "Jehoshaphat was a good king, following the ways of his father, Asa. He did what was pleasing in the LORD's sight. During his reign, however, he failed to remove all the pagan shrines, and the people never fully committed themselves to following the God of their ancestors" (2 Chronicles 20:32-33).

Jehoshaphat's story is told in 1 Kings 15:24–22:50 and 2 Chronicles 17:1–21:1. He is also mentioned in 2 Kings 3:1-14 and Joel 3:2, 12.

**UPS:**
- A bold follower of God, he reminded the people of the early years with his father, Asa
- Carried out a national program of religious education
- Had many military victories
- Developed an extensive legal structure throughout the kingdom

**DOWNS:**
- Failed to recognize the long-term results of his decisions
- Did not completely destroy idolatry in the land
- Became entangled with evil King Ahab through alliances
- Became Ahaziah's business partner in an ill-fated shipping venture

**STATS:**
- Where: Jerusalem
- Occupation: King of Judah
- Relatives: Father: Asa. Mother: Azubah. Son: Jehoram. Daughter-in-law: Athaliah.
- Contemporaries: Ahab, Jezebel, Micaiah, Ahaziah, Jehu

And Micaiah replied, "Go right ahead! It will be a glorious victory!"

[15]But the king replied sharply, "How many times must I demand that you speak only the truth when you speak for the LORD?"

[16]So Micaiah told him, "In a vision I saw all Israel scattered on the mountains, like sheep without a shepherd. And the LORD said, 'Their master has been killed. Send them home in peace.'"

[17]"Didn't I tell you?" the king of Israel said to Jehoshaphat. "He does it every time. He never prophesies anything but bad news for me."

[18]Then Micaiah continued, "Listen to what the LORD says! I saw the LORD sitting on his throne with all the armies of heaven on his right and on his left.
[19]And the LORD said, 'Who can entice King Ahab of Israel to go into battle against Ramoth-gilead so that he can be killed there?' There were many suggestions, [20]until finally a spirit approached the LORD and said, 'I can do it!'

"'How will you do this?' the LORD asked.

[21]"And the spirit replied, 'I will go out and inspire all Ahab's prophets to speak lies.'

"'You will succeed,' said the LORD. 'Go ahead and do it.'

## DISGUISED ● ● • • •

18:22 **Micaiah prophesied death for King Ahab (18:16, 27), so Ahab disguised himself to fool the enemy. Apparently the disguise worked, but that didn't thwart the prophecy. A random Aramean arrow found a crack in his armor and killed him. God's will is always fulfilled despite the defenses people try to erect. God can use anything, even an error, to bring his will to pass. This is good news for God's followers because we can trust him to work his plans and keep his promises, no matter what the circumstances.**

[22]"So you see, the LORD has put a lying spirit in the mouths of your prophets. For the LORD has determined disaster for you."

[23]Then Zedekiah son of Kenaanah walked up to Micaiah and slapped him across the face. "When did the Spirit of the LORD leave me to speak to you?" he demanded.

[24]And Micaiah replied, "You will find out soon enough, when you find yourself hiding in some secret room!"

[25]King Ahab of Israel then ordered, "Arrest Micaiah and take him back to Amon, the governor of the city, and to my son Joash. [26]Give them this order from the king: 'Put this man in prison, and feed him nothing but bread and water until I return safely from the battle!'"

[27]But Micaiah replied, "If you return safely, the LORD has not spoken through me!" Then he added to those standing around, "Take note of what I have said."

[28]So the king of Israel and King Jehoshaphat of Judah led their armies against Ramoth-gilead. [29]Now
King Ahab said to Jehoshaphat, "As we go into battle, I will disguise myself so no one will recognize me, but you wear your royal robes." So Ahab disguised himself, and they went into battle.

[30]Now the king of Aram had issued these orders to his charioteers: "Attack only the king of Israel!"
[31]So when the Aramean charioteers saw Jehoshaphat in his royal robes, they went after him. "There is the king of Israel!" they shouted. But Jehoshaphat cried out to the LORD to save him, and God helped him by turning the attack away from him.
[32]As soon as the charioteers realized he was not the king of Israel, they stopped chasing him.

[33]An Aramean soldier, however, randomly shot an arrow at the Israelite troops, and the arrow hit the king of Israel between the joints of his armor. "Get me out of here!" Ahab groaned to the driver of his chariot. "I have been badly wounded!" [34]The battle raged all that day, and Ahab propped himself up in his chariot facing the Arameans until evening. Then, just as the sun was setting, he died.

## CHAPTER 19

**A MESSAGE FOR JEHOSHAPHAT.** When King Jehoshaphat of Judah arrived safely home to Jerusalem, [2]Jehu son of Hanani the seer went out to meet him. "Why should you help the wicked and love those who hate the LORD?" he asked the king. "What you have done has brought the LORD's anger against you. [3]There is some good in you, however, for you have removed the Asherah poles throughout the land, and you have committed yourself to seeking God."

[4]So Jehoshaphat lived in Jerusalem, but he went out among the people, traveling from Beersheba to the hill country of Ephraim, encouraging the people to return to the LORD, the God of their ancestors. [5]He appointed judges throughout the nation in all the fortified cities, [6]and he gave them these instructions: "Always think carefully before pronouncing judgment. Remember that you do not judge to please people but to please the LORD. He will be with you when you render the verdict in each case that comes before you. [7]Fear the LORD and judge with care, for the LORD our God does not tolerate perverted justice, partiality, or the taking of bribes."

[8]Jehoshaphat appointed some of the Levites and priests and clan leaders in Israel to serve as judges in Jerusalem for cases concerning both the law of the LORD and civil disputes. [9]These were his in-

## ACCOUNTABLE ● ● • • •

19:5-10 **Jehoshaphat delegated some of the responsibilities for ruling and judging the people, but he warned his appointees that they were accountable to God for the standards they used to judge others. Jehoshaphat's advice is helpful for all leaders: (1) allow God to help you be just (19:6); (2) be impartial (19:7); (3) be honest (19:9); (4) act out of fear of God, not men (19:9).**

structions to them: "You must always act in the fear of the LORD, with integrity and with undivided hearts. 10Whenever a case comes to you from fellow citizens in an outlying town, whether a murder case or some other violation of God's instructions, commands, laws, or regulations, you must warn them not to sin against the LORD, so that his anger will not come against you and them. Do this and you will not be guilty.

11"Amariah the high priest will have final say in all cases concerning the LORD. Zebadiah son of Ishmael, a leader from the tribe of Judah, will have final say in all civil cases. The Levites will assist you in making sure that justice is served. Take courage as you fulfill your duties, and may the LORD be with those who do what is right."

CHAPTER **20** **GOD GIVES A VICTORY.** After this, the armies of the Moabites, Ammonites, and some of the Meunites* declared war on Jehoshaphat. 2Messengers came and told Jehoshaphat, "A vast army from Edom* is marching against you from beyond the Dead Sea.* They are already at Hazazon-tamar." (This was another name for En-gedi.) 3Jehoshaphat was alarmed by this news and sought the LORD for guidance. He also gave orders that everyone throughout Judah should observe a fast. 4So people from all the towns of Judah came to Jerusalem to seek the LORD.

5Jehoshaphat stood before the people of Judah and Jerusalem in front of the new courtyard at the Temple of the LORD. 6He prayed, "O LORD, God of our ancestors, you alone are the God who is in heaven. You are ruler of all the kingdoms of the earth. You are powerful and mighty; no one can stand against you! 7O our God, did you not drive out those who lived in this land when your people arrived? And did you not give this land forever to the descendants of your friend Abraham? 8Your people settled here and built this Temple for you. 9They said, 'Whenever we are faced with any calamity such as war, disease, or famine, we can come to stand in your presence before this Temple where your name is honored. We can cry out to you to save us, and you will hear us and rescue us.'

10"And now see what the armies of Ammon, Moab, and Mount Seir are doing. You would not let our ancestors invade those nations when Israel left Egypt, so they went around them and did not destroy them. 11Now see how they reward us! For they have come to throw us out of your land, which you gave us as an inheritance. 12O our God, won't you stop them? We are powerless against this mighty army that is about to attack us. We do not know what to do, but we are looking to you for help."

13As all the men of Judah stood before the LORD with their little ones, wives, and children, 14the Spirit of the LORD came upon one of the men standing there. His name was Jahaziel son of Zechariah, son of Benaiah, son of Jeiel, son of Mattaniah, a Levite who was a descendant of Asaph. 15He said, "Listen, King Jehoshaphat!

**I like the people in my church, but sometimes the worship service seems boring and confusing. Are all of the songs, readings, and rituals necessary?**

A family decided to get a new refrigerator, and so they bought one that was the top of the line. Then they filled it with groceries. It was Friday and they had a trip out of town planned, so they left. When they returned on Sunday, they opened the refrigerator door and were overwhelmed by a terrible odor. All of the food had spoiled!

There had been no power failure and the refrigerator wasn't broken. Instead, they had forgotten to plug it in! Their brand-new appliance, stuffed with food, was useless (and smelly) without being plugged into the power.

We need to be plugged in too, and worship is one way to do this. In worship we recognize God as the one who is in control and who has the power to change our circumstances and life. (See 2 Chronicles 20:20-22.)

Jehoshaphat discovered this fact very graphically as he sent the worshipers out with his army. As the worshipers were singing, God miraculously provided a victory!

Worship takes many forms. Most of the songs and readings come right from Scripture. If you concentrate on the meaning behind what is being sung or read, you will see that the words communicate very important facts about God.

When we sing a song many times, we will memorize it more easily. You can probably sing every word of your favorite popular songs. Music helps us remember.

Another purpose of worship is to encourage us to grow in our faith. With all of the negative influences around us, we need to be filled with courage to go out to face the world. This courage can help us live the Christian life when it seems that there is a war going on around us.

Worship is also the time for us to praise God for who he is and to thank him for all he has done. Being in church with our brothers and sisters in Christ is like a family reunion—worshiping together.

Ephesians 5:19 was written during a time when Christians were put in prison for their faith. It says that believers should always "sing psalms and hymns and spiritual songs among yourselves, making music to the Lord in your hearts." By doing what this verse talks about, believers were able to encourage each other as they reminded themselves of the faithfulness, goodness, and strength of God.

**20:1** As in some Greek manuscripts (see also 26:7); Hebrew reads *Ammonites.* **20:2a** As in one Hebrew manuscript; most Hebrew manuscripts and ancient versions read *Aram.* **20:2b** Hebrew *the sea.*

## BATTLES ● ● • • •

**20:15** **As the enemy bore down on Judah, God spoke through Jahaziel: "Do not be afraid! Don't be discouraged . . . for the battle is not yours, but God's." We may not fight an enemy army, but every day we battle temptation, pressure, and "those mighty powers of darkness who rule this world" (Ephesians 6:12) who want us to rebel against God. We must remember that, as believers, we have God's Spirit in us. If we ask for God's help when we face struggles, he will fight for us. And God always triumphs.**

**How do we let God fight for us? (1) By realizing the battle is not ours, but God's; (2) by recognizing human limitations and allowing God's strength and power to work through our fears and weaknesses; (3) by making sure our battle is for God and not just our own selfish desires; and (4) by asking God for help.**

Listen, all you people of Judah and Jerusalem! This is what the LORD says: Do not be afraid! Don't be discouraged by this mighty army, for the battle is not yours, but God's. [16]Tomorrow, march out against them. You will find them coming up through the ascent of Ziz at the end of the valley that opens into the wilderness of Jeruel. [17]But you will not even need to fight. Take your positions; then stand still and watch the LORD's victory. He is with you, O people of Judah and Jerusalem. Do not be afraid or discouraged. Go out there tomorrow, for the LORD is with you!"

[18]Then King Jehoshaphat bowed down with his face to the ground. And all the people of Judah and Jerusalem did the same, worshiping the LORD. [19]Then the Levites from the clans of Kohath and Korah stood to praise the LORD, the God of Israel, with a very loud shout.

[20]Early the next morning the army of Judah went out into the wilderness of Tekoa. On the way Jehoshaphat stopped and said, "Listen to me, all you people of Judah and Jerusalem! Believe in the LORD your God, and you will be able to stand firm. Believe in his prophets, and you will succeed." [21]After consulting the leaders of the people, the king appointed singers to walk ahead of the army, singing to the LORD and praising him for his holy splendor. This is what they sang:

"Give thanks to the LORD;
his faithful love endures forever!"

[22]At the moment they began to sing and give praise, the LORD caused the armies of Ammon, Moab, and Mount Seir to start fighting among themselves. [23]The armies of Moab and Ammon turned against their allies from Mount Seir and killed every one of them. After they had finished off the army of Seir, they turned on each other.

[24]So when the army of Judah arrived at the lookout point in the wilderness, there were dead bodies lying on the ground for as far as they could see. Not a single one of the enemy had escaped. [25]King Jehoshaphat and his men went out to gather the plunder. They found vast amounts of equipment, clothing,* and other valuables—more than they could carry. There was so much plunder that it took them three days just to collect it all! [26]On the fourth day they gathered in the Valley of Blessing,* which got its name that day because the people praised and thanked the LORD there. It is still called the Valley of Blessing today.

[27]Then they returned to Jerusalem, with Jehoshaphat leading them, full of joy that the LORD had given them victory over their enemies. [28]They marched into Jerusalem to the music of harps, lyres, and trumpets and proceeded to the Temple of the LORD. [29]When the surrounding kingdoms heard that the LORD himself had fought against the enemies of Israel, the fear of God came over them. [30]So Jehoshaphat's kingdom was at peace, for his God had given him rest on every side.

[31]So Jehoshaphat ruled over the land of Judah. He was thirty-five years old when he became king, and he reigned in Jerusalem twenty-five years. His mother was Azubah, the daughter of Shilhi. [32]Jehoshaphat was a good king, following the ways of his father, Asa. He did what was pleasing in the LORD's sight. [33]During his reign, however, he failed to remove all the pagan shrines, and the people never fully committed themselves to following the God of their ancestors. [34]The rest of the events of Jehoshaphat's reign, from beginning to end, are recorded in *The Record of Jehu Son of Hanani*, which is included in *The Book of the Kings of Israel.*

[35]But near the end of his life, King Jehoshaphat of Judah made an alliance with King Ahaziah of Israel, who was a very wicked man.* [36]Together they built a fleet of trading ships* at the port of Ezion-geber. [37]Then Eliezer son of Dodavahu from Mareshah prophesied against Jehoshaphat. He said, "Because you have allied yourself with King Ahaziah, the LORD will destroy your work." So the ships met with disaster and never put out to sea.*

## CHAPTER 21 **JEHORAM DISPLEASES GOD.**

When Jehoshaphat died, he was buried with his ancestors in the City of David. Then his son Jehoram became the next king. [2]Jehoram's brothers—the other sons of Jehoshaphat—were Azariah, Jehiel, Zechariah, Azariahu, Michael, and Shephatiah. [3]Their father had given each of them valuable gifts of silver, gold, and costly items, and also the ownership of some of

## MADE RIGHT ● ● • • •

**21:8-11** **Jehoram's reign was marked by sin and cruelty. He married a woman who worshiped idols; he killed his six brothers; he allowed and even promoted idol worship. Yet he was not killed in battle or by treachery—he died by a lingering and painful disease (21:18-19). Just because punishment is not immediate or dramatic does not mean God is indifferent to our sin. We cannot ignore God's laws and think we are immune from the consequences of our sin. There can be no healing or deliverance for those who rebel against God until their relationship with God is made right.**

**20:25** As in some Hebrew manuscripts and Latin Vulgate; most Hebrew manuscripts read *corpses.* **20:26** Hebrew *valley of Beracah.* **20:35** Or *who made him do what was wrong.* **20:36** Hebrew *fleet of ships that could go to Tarshish.* **20:37** Hebrew *never set sail for Tarshish.*

Judah's fortified cities. However, Jehoram became king because he was the oldest. [4]But when Jehoram had become solidly established as king, he killed all his brothers and some of the other leaders of Israel.

[5]Jehoram was thirty-two years old when he became king, and he reigned in Jerusalem eight years. [6]But Jehoram followed the example of the kings of Israel and was as wicked as King Ahab, for he had married one of Ahab's daughters. So Jehoram did what was evil in the LORD's sight. [7]But the LORD was not willing to destroy David's dynasty, for he had made a covenant with David and promised that his descendants would continue to rule forever.*

[8]During Jehoram's reign, the Edomites revolted against Judah and crowned their own king. [9]So Jehoram went to attack Edom with his full army and all his chariots. The Edomites surrounded him and his charioteers, but he escaped at night under cover of darkness. [10]Edom has been independent from Judah to this day. The town of Libnah revolted about that same time, because Jehoram had abandoned the LORD, the God of his ancestors. [11]He had built pagan shrines in the hill country of Judah and had led the people of Jerusalem and Judah to give themselves to pagan gods.

[12]Then Elijah the prophet wrote Jehoram this letter:

> "This is what the LORD, the God of your ancestor David, says: You have not followed the good example of your father, Jehoshaphat, or your grandfather King Asa of Judah. [13]Instead, you have been as evil as the kings of Israel. You have led the people of Jerusalem and Judah to worship idols, just as King Ahab did in Israel. And you have even killed your own brothers, men who were better than you. [14]So now the LORD is about to strike you, your people, your children, your wives, and all that is yours with a heavy blow. [15]You yourself will be stricken with a severe intestinal disease until it causes your bowels to come out."

[16]Then the LORD stirred up the Philistines and the Arabs, who lived near the Ethiopians,* to attack Jehoram. [17]They marched against Judah, broke down its defenses, and carried away everything of value in the royal palace, including his sons and his wives. Only his youngest son, Ahaziah,* was spared.

[18]It was after this that the LORD struck Jehoram with the severe intestinal disease. [19]In the course of time, at the end of two years, the disease caused his bowels to come out, and he died in agony. His people did not build a great fire to honor him at his funeral as they had done for his ancestors. [20]Jehoram was thirty-two years old when he became king, and he reigned in Jerusalem eight years. No one was sorry when he died. He was buried in the City of David, but not in the royal cemetery.

## CHAPTER 22

**AHAZIAH GETS EVIL ADVICE.** Then the people of Jerusalem made Ahaziah, Jehoram's youngest son, their next king. The marauding bands of Arabs had killed all the older sons. So Ahaziah son of Jehoram reigned as king of Judah. [2]Ahaziah was twenty-two* years old when he became king, and he reigned in Jerusalem one year. His mother was Athaliah, a granddaughter of King Omri of Israel. [3]Ahaziah also followed the evil example of King Ahab's family, for his mother encouraged him in doing wrong. [4]He did what was evil in the LORD's sight, just as Ahab had done. After the death of his father, members of Ahab's family became his advisers, and they led him to ruin.

### EVALUATION ● ● • • •

22:4-5 **Although it is good to seek advice, we must also carefully weigh what is said. Ahaziah had advisers, but they were wicked and led him to ruin. When you seek advice, listen carefully and use God's Word to "test everything that is said. Hold on to what is good" (1 Thessalonians 5:21).**

[5]Following their evil advice, Ahaziah made an alliance with King Joram,* the son of King Ahab of Israel. They went out to fight King Hazael of Aram at Ramoth-gilead, and the Arameans wounded Joram in the battle. [6]Joram returned to Jezreel to recover from his wounds, and King Ahaziah* of Judah went to Jezreel to visit him. [7]But this turned out to be a fatal mistake, for God had decided to punish Ahaziah. It was during this visit that Ahaziah went out with Joram to meet Jehu son of Nimshi, whom the LORD had appointed to end the dynasty of Ahab.

[8]While Jehu was executing judgment against the family of Ahab, he happened to meet some of Judah's officials and Ahaziah's relatives* who were attending Ahaziah. So Jehu killed them all. [9]Then Jehu's men searched for Ahaziah, and they found him hiding in the city of Samaria. They brought him to Jehu, who killed him. Ahaziah was given a decent burial because the people said, "He was the grandson of Jehoshaphat—a man who sought the LORD with all his heart." None of the surviving members of Ahaziah's family was capable of ruling the kingdom.

[10]When Athaliah, the mother of King Ahaziah of Judah, learned that her son was dead, she set out to destroy the rest of Judah's royal family. [11]But Ahaziah's sister Jehosheba,* the daughter of King Jehoram, took Ahaziah's infant son, Joash, and stole him away from among the rest of the king's children, who were about to be killed. She put Joash and his nurse in a bedroom. In this way, Jehosheba, the wife

**21:7** Hebrew *promised to give a lamp to David and his descendants forever.* **21:16** Hebrew *the Cushites.* **21:17** Hebrew *Jehoahaz,* a variant name for Ahaziah; compare 22:1. **22:2** As in some Greek manuscripts and Syriac version (see also 2 Kgs 8:26); Hebrew reads *forty-two.* **22:5** Hebrew *Jehoram,* a variant name for Joram; also in 22:6, 7. **22:6** Some Hebrew manuscripts, Greek and Syriac versions, and Latin Vulgate (see also 2 Kgs 8:29); most Hebrew manuscripts read *Azariah.* **22:8** As in Greek version (see also 2 Kgs 10:13); Hebrew reads *and sons of the brothers of Ahaziah.* **22:11** As in parallel text at 2 Kgs 11:2; Hebrew reads *Jehoshabeath,* a variant name for Jehosheba.

of Jehoiada the priest, hid the child so that Athaliah could not murder him. [12]Joash remained hidden in the Temple of God for six years while Athaliah ruled over the land.

CHAPTER **23** **YOUNG JOASH BECOMES KING.** In the seventh year of Athaliah's reign, Jehoiada the priest decided to act. He got up his courage and made a pact with five army commanders: Azariah son of Jeroham, Ishmael son of Jehohanan, Azariah son of Obed, Maaseiah son of Adaiah, and Elishaphat son of Zicri. [2]These men traveled secretly throughout Judah and summoned the Levites and clan leaders in Judah's towns to come to Jerusalem. [3]They all gathered at the Temple of God, where they made a covenant with Joash, the young king.

### COURAGE ● ● • • ·

**23:1 Although it could have cost him his life, this priest gathered up his courage and did what was right, restoring the Temple worship and anointing the new king. There are times when we must correct a wrong or speak out for what is right. When such a situation arises, gather up your courage and take action.**

Jehoiada said to them, "The time has come for the king's son to reign! The LORD has promised that a descendant of David will be our king. [4]This is what you must do. When the priests and Levites come on duty on the Sabbath, a third of them will serve as gatekeepers. [5]Another third will go over to the royal palace, and the final third will be at the Foundation Gate. Everyone else should stay in the courtyards of the LORD's Temple. [6]Remember, only the priests and Levites on duty may enter the Temple of the LORD, for they are set apart as holy. The rest of the people must obey the LORD's instructions and stay outside. [7]You Levites, form a bodyguard for the king and keep your weapons in hand. Any unauthorized person who enters the Temple must be killed. Stay right beside the king at all times."

[8]So the Levites and the people did everything just as Jehoiada the priest ordered. The commanders took charge of the men reporting for duty that Sabbath, as well as those who were going off duty. Jehoiada the priest did not let anyone go home after their shift ended. [9]Then Jehoiada supplied the commanders with the spears and shields that had once belonged to King David and were stored in the Temple of God. [10]He stationed the guards around the king, with their weapons ready. They formed a line from the south side of the Temple around to the north side and all around the altar.

[11]Then Jehoiada and his sons brought out Joash, the king's son, and placed the crown on his head. They presented Joash with a copy of God's laws and proclaimed him king. Then they anointed him, and everyone shouted, "Long live the king!"

[12]When Athaliah heard the noise of the people running and the shouts of praise to the king, she hurried to the LORD's Temple to see what was happening. [13]And she saw the newly crowned king standing in his place of authority by the pillar at the Temple entrance. The officers and trumpeters were surrounding him, and people from all over the land were rejoicing and blowing trumpets. Singers with musical instruments were leading the people in a great celebration. When Athaliah saw all this, she tore her clothes in despair and shouted, "Treason! Treason!"

[14]Then Jehoiada the priest ordered the commanders who were in charge of the troops, "Take her out of the Temple, and kill anyone who tries to rescue her. Do not kill her here in the Temple of the LORD." [15]So they seized her and led her out to the gate where horses enter the palace grounds, and they killed her there.

[16]Then Jehoiada made a covenant between himself and the king and the people that they would be the LORD's people. [17]And all the people went over to the temple of Baal and tore it down. They demolished the altars and smashed the idols, and they killed Mattan the priest of Baal in front of the altars. [18]Jehoiada now put the Levitical priests in charge of the Temple of the LORD, following all the instructions given by David. He also commanded them to present burnt offerings to the LORD, as prescribed by the law of Moses, and to sing and rejoice as David had instructed. [19]He stationed gatekeepers at the gates of the LORD's Temple to keep those who were ceremonially unclean from entering.

[20]Then the commanders, nobles, rulers, and all the people escorted the king from the Temple of the LORD. They went through the Upper Gate and into the palace, and they seated the king on the royal throne. [21]So all the people of the land rejoiced, and the city was peaceful because Athaliah had been killed.

CHAPTER **24** **JOASH REPAIRS THE TEMPLE.** Joash was seven years old when he became king, and he reigned in Jerusalem forty years. His mother was Zibiah, from Beersheba. [2]Joash did what was pleasing in the LORD's sight throughout the lifetime of Jehoiada the priest. [3]Jehoiada chose two wives for Joash, and he had sons and daughters.

[4]Some time later, Joash decided to repair and restore the Temple of the LORD. [5]He summoned the priests and Levites and gave them these instructions: "Go at once to all the towns of Judah and collect the required annual offerings, so that we can repair the

### PROSPERITY ● ● • • ·

**24:17-18 If everything went so well in Judah when the people worshiped God, why did they turn away from him? Prosperity is both a blessing and a curse. While it can be a sign of God's blessing to those who follow him, it carries with it the potential for moral and spiritual decline. Rich people are tempted to become self-sufficient and proud—to take God for granted. In times of prosperity, we must not lose sight of the fact that God is the source of our blessings.**

Temple of your God. Do not delay!" But the Levites
did not act right away.
6So the king called for Jehoiada the high priest
and asked him, "Why haven't you demanded that
the Levites go out and collect the Temple taxes from
the towns of Judah and from Jerusalem? Moses, the
servant of the LORD, levied this tax on the community of Israel in order to maintain the Tabernacle of
the Covenant.*"
7Over the years, the followers of wicked Athaliah
had broken into the Temple of God, and they had
used all the dedicated things from the Temple of the
LORD to worship the images of Baal. 8So now Joash
gave instructions for a chest to be made and set
outside the gate leading to the Temple of the LORD.
9Then a proclamation was sent throughout Judah
and Jerusalem, telling the people to bring to the
LORD the tax that Moses, the
servant of God, had re-
quired of the Israelites in the
wilderness. 10This pleased
all the leaders and the
people, and they gladly
brought their money and
filled the chest with it.
11Whenever the chest be-
came full, the Levites carried
it to the king's officials. Then
the court secretary and an
officer of the high priest
counted the money and took
the chest back to the Temple
again. This went on day after
day, and a large amount of
money was collected. 12The
king and Jehoiada gave the
money to the construction
supervisors, who hired masons and carpenters to restore the Temple of the LORD.
They also hired metal-
workers, who made articles
of iron and bronze for the
LORD's Temple.
13So the men in charge of
the renovation worked
hard, and they made steady
progress. They restored the
Temple of God according to
its original design and
strengthened it. 14When all
the repairs were finished,
they brought the remaining
money to the king and Je-
hoiada. It was used to make
utensils for the Temple of
the LORD—utensils for worship services and for burnt
offerings, including ladles
and other vessels made of
gold and silver. And the burnt offerings were sacrificed continually in the Temple of the LORD during
the lifetime of Jehoiada the priest.
15Jehoiada lived to a very old age, finally dying at
130. 16He was buried among the kings in the City of
David, because he had done so much good in Israel
for God and his Temple.
17But after Jehoiada's death, the leaders of Judah
came and bowed before King Joash and persuaded
the king to listen to their advice. 18They decided to
abandon the Temple of the LORD, the God of their
ancestors, and they worshiped Asherah poles and
idols instead! Then the anger of God burned against
Judah and Jerusalem because of their sin. 19The LORD
sent prophets to bring them back to him, but the
people would not listen.
20Then the Spirit of God came upon Zechariah

## JOASH

All parents want their children to make the right decisions. But to do this, children first must learn to make *their own* decisions. The bad choices we make on our own can be our best teachers in learning to make right choices. Children don't develop the skills for wise decision making if parents decide everything for them. King Joash had this problem, in an unusual way.

Joash wasn't raised by his parents—they had been killed. An aunt and uncle protected and raised the young prince. When Joash became king at age seven, his uncle Jehoiada made most of the decisions for him. Jehoiada was a good man, but he never taught Joash what he needed to know to be a good king. After Jehoiada died, it only took Joash a short time to make a mess of his life and his kingdom. We prove how well we've learned the lessons we need to learn when we're on our own.

Even though Joash depended on Jehoiada, it seems he never learned to be dependent on Jehoiada's God. Like many children, Joash's knowledge of God was secondhand. He worshiped his uncle's God instead of having his own relationship with God. Is your relationship with God just part of your family tradition, or is there something real and important between you and him? God wants you to know him personally!

LESSONS: A good and hopeful start can be ruined by an evil end

Even the best counsel is ineffective if it doesn't help us make wise decisions

As helpful or hurtful as others may be, we are individually responsible for what we do

KEY VERSES: "But after Jehoiada's death, the leaders of Judah came and bowed before King Joash and persuaded the king to listen to their advice. They decided to abandon the Temple of the LORD, the God of their ancestors, and they worshiped Asherah poles and idols instead! Then the anger of God burned against Judah and Jerusalem because of their sin" (2 Chronicles 24:17-18).

Joash's story is told in 2 Kings 11:1–14:23 and 2 Chronicles 22:11–25:25.

**UPS:**
- Carried out extensive repairs on the Temple
- Was faithful to God as long as Jehoiada was alive

**DOWNS:**
- Allowed idolatry to continue among his people
- Used the Temple treasures to bribe King Hazael of Syria
- Killed Jehoiada's son Zechariah
- Allowed his advisers to lead the people away from God

**STATS:**
- Where: Jerusalem
- Occupation: King of Judah
- Relatives: Father: Ahaziah. Mother: Zibiah. Grandmother: Athaliah. Aunt: Jehosheba. Uncle: Jehoiada. Son: Amaziah. Cousin: Zechariah.
- Contemporaries: Jehu, Hazael

24:6 Hebrew *Tent of the Testimony.*

son of Jehoiada the priest. He stood before the people and said, "This is what God says: Why do you disobey the LORD's commands so that you cannot prosper? You have abandoned the LORD, and now he has abandoned you!"

21 Then the leaders plotted to kill Zechariah, and by order of King Joash himself, they stoned him to death in the courtyard of the LORD's Temple. 22 That was how King Joash repaid Jehoiada for his love and loyalty—by killing his son. Zechariah's last words as he died were, "May the LORD see what they are doing and hold them accountable!"

23 At the beginning of the year, the Aramean army marched against Joash. They invaded Judah and Jerusalem and killed all the leaders of the nation. Then they sent all the plunder back to their king in Damascus. 24 Although the Arameans attacked with only a small army, the LORD helped them conquer the much larger army of Judah. The people of Judah had abandoned the LORD, the God of their ancestors, so judgment was executed against Joash.

25 The Arameans withdrew, leaving Joash severely wounded. But his own officials decided to kill him for murdering the son of Jehoiada the priest. They assassinated him as he lay in bed. Then he was buried in the City of David, but not in the royal cemetery. 26 The assassins were Jozabad,* the son of an Ammonite woman named Shimeath, and Jehozabad, the son of a Moabite woman named Shomer.*

27 The complete story about the sons of Joash, the prophecies about him, and the record of his restoration of the Temple of God are written in *The Commentary on the Book of the Kings.* When Joash died, his son Amaziah became the next king.

## CHAPTER 25 **AMAZIAH DOES GOOD AND EVIL.**

Amaziah was twenty-five years old when he became king, and he reigned in Jerusalem twenty-nine years. His mother was Jehoaddin,* from Jerusalem. 2 Amaziah did what was pleasing in the LORD's sight, but not wholeheartedly.

3 When Amaziah was well established as king, he executed the men who had assassinated his father. 4 However, he did not kill the children of the assassins, for he obeyed the command of the LORD written in the Book of the Law of Moses: "Parents must not be put to death for the sins of their children, nor the children for the sins of their parents. Those worthy of death must be executed for their own crimes."*

5 Another thing Amaziah did was to organize the army, assigning leaders to each clan from Judah and Benjamin. Then he took a census and found that he had an army of 300,000 men twenty years old and older, all trained in the use of spear and shield. 6 He also paid about 7,500 pounds* of silver to hire 100,000 experienced fighting men from Israel.

7 But a man of God came to the king and said, "O king, do not hire troops from Israel, for the LORD is not with Israel. He will not help those people of Ephraim! 8 If you let them go with your troops into battle, you will be defeated no matter how well you fight. God will overthrow you, for he has the power to help or to frustrate."

9 Amaziah asked the man of God, "But what should I do about the silver I paid to hire the army of Israel?"

The man of God replied, "The LORD is able to give you much more than this!" 10 So Amaziah discharged the hired troops and sent them back to Ephraim. This made them angry with Judah, and they returned home in a great rage.

### DECISIONS ● ● • • •

25:9-10 **Amaziah made a financial agreement with wicked Israelite soldiers, offering to pay them to fight for him (25:6). But before they could go to battle, Amaziah received the prophet's warning—and so he sent the soldiers home with their pay. Although it cost him plenty, Amaziah wisely realized that the money was not worth the ruin the alliance could cause. How would you have chosen? Money must never stand in the way of making right decisions. The Lord's blessing is priceless, worth more than any amount of money.**

11 Then Amaziah summoned his courage and led his army to the Valley of Salt, where they killed ten thousand Edomite troops from Seir. 12 They captured another ten thousand and took them to the top of a cliff and threw them off, dashing them to pieces on the rocks below.

13 Meanwhile, the hired troops that Amaziah had sent home raided several of the towns of Judah between Samaria and Beth-horon, killing three thousand people and carrying off great quantities of plunder.

14 When King Amaziah returned from defeating the Edomites, he brought with him idols taken from the people of Seir. He set them up as his own gods, bowed down in front of them, and presented sacrifices to them! 15 This made the LORD very angry, and he sent a prophet to ask, "Why have you worshiped gods who could not even save their own people from you?"

16 But the king interrupted him and said, "Since when have I asked your advice? Be quiet now before I have you killed!"

So the prophet left with this warning: "I know that God has determined to destroy you because you have done this and have not accepted my counsel."

17 After consulting with his advisers, King Amaziah of Judah sent this challenge to Israel's king Jehoash,* the son of Jehoahaz and grandson of Jehu: "Come and meet me in battle!"

18 But King Jehoash of Israel replied to King Amaziah of Judah with this story: "Out in the Lebanon

24:26a As in parallel text at 2 Kgs 12:21; Hebrew reads *Zabad.* **24:26b** As in parallel text at 2 Kgs 12:21; Hebrew reads *Shimrith.* **25:1** As in parallel text at 2 Kgs 14:2; Hebrew reads *Jehoaddan,* a variant name for Jehoaddin. **25:4** Deut 24:16. **25:6** Hebrew *100 talents* [3.4 metric tons]. **25:17** Hebrew *Joash,* a variant name for Jehoash; also in 25:18, 21, 23, 25.

mountains, a thistle sent a message to a mighty cedar tree: 'Give your daughter in marriage to my son.' But just then a wild animal came by and stepped on the thistle, crushing it! [19]You may be very proud of your conquest of Edom, but my advice is to stay home. Why stir up trouble that will bring disaster on you and the people of Judah?"

[20]But Amaziah would not listen, for God was arranging to destroy him for worshiping the gods of Edom. [21]So King Jehoash of Israel mobilized his army against King Amaziah of Judah. The two armies drew up their battle lines at Beth-shemesh in Judah. [22]Judah was routed by the army of Israel, and its army scattered and fled for home. [23]King Jehoash of Israel captured King Amaziah of Judah at Beth-shemesh and brought him back to Jerusalem. Then Jehoash ordered his army to demolish six hundred feet* of Jerusalem's wall, from the Ephraim Gate to the Corner Gate. [24]He carried off all the gold and silver and all the utensils from the Temple of God that had been in the care of Obed-edom. He also seized the treasures of the royal palace, along with hostages, and then returned to Samaria.

[25]King Amaziah of Judah lived on for fifteen years after the death of King Jehoash of Israel. [26]The rest of the events of Amaziah's reign, from beginning to end, are recorded in *The Book of the Kings of Judah and Israel.* [27]After Amaziah turned away from the LORD, there was a conspiracy against his life in Jerusalem, and he fled to Lachish. But his enemies sent assassins after him, and they killed him there. [28]They brought him back to Jerusalem on a horse, and he was buried with his ancestors in the City of David.*

## CHAPTER 26 **A KING TURNS INTO A LEPER.**

The people of Judah then crowned Amaziah's sixteen-year-old son, Uzziah, as their next king. [2]After his father's death, Uzziah rebuilt the town of Elath* and restored it to Judah. [3]Uzziah was sixteen when he became king, and he reigned in Jerusalem fifty-two years. His mother was Jecoliah, from Jerusalem. [4]He did what was pleasing in the LORD's sight, just as his father, Amaziah, had done. [5]Uzziah sought God during the days of Zechariah, who instructed him in the fear of God. And as long as the king sought the LORD, God gave him success.

[6]He declared war on the Philistines and broke down the walls of Gath, Jabneh, and Ashdod. Then he built new towns in the Ashdod area and in other parts of Philistia. [7]God helped him not only with his wars against the Philistines, but also in his battles with the Arabs of Gur* and in his wars with the Meunites. [8]The Meunites* paid annual tribute to him, and his fame spread even to Egypt, for he had become very powerful.

[9]Uzziah built fortified towers in Jerusalem at the Corner Gate, at the Valley Gate, and at the angle in the wall. [10]He also constructed forts in the wilderness and dug many water cisterns, because he kept great herds of livestock in the foothills of Judah* and on the plains. He was also a man who loved the soil. He had many workers who cared for his farms and vineyards, both on the hillsides and in the fertile valleys.

[11]Uzziah had an army of well-trained warriors, ready to march into battle, unit by unit. This great army of fighting men had been mustered and organized by Jeiel, the secretary of the army, and his assistant, Maaseiah. They were under the direction of Hananiah, one of the king's officials. [12]Twenty-six hundred clan leaders commanded these regiments of seasoned warriors. [13]The army consisted of 307,500 men, all elite troops. They were prepared to assist the king against any enemy. [14]Uzziah provided the entire army with shields, spears, helmets, coats of mail, bows, and sling stones. [15]And he produced machines mounted on the walls of Jerusalem, designed by brilliant men to shoot arrows and hurl stones* from the towers and the corners of the wall. His fame spread far and wide, for the LORD helped him wonderfully until he became very powerful.

[16]But when he had become powerful, he also became proud, which led to his downfall. He sinned against the LORD his God by entering the sanctuary of the LORD's Temple and personally burning incense on the altar. [17]Azariah the high priest went in after him with eighty other priests of the LORD, all brave men. [18]They confronted King Uzziah and said, "It is not for you, Uzziah, to burn incense to the LORD. That is the work of the priests alone, the sons of Aaron who are set apart for this work. Get out of the sanctuary, for you have sinned. The LORD God will not honor you for this!"

[19]Uzziah was furious and refused to set down the incense burner he was holding. But as he was standing there with the priests before the incense altar in the LORD's Temple, leprosy* suddenly broke out on

### WATCH OUT ● ● • • •

25:14 **After the victory, Amaziah returned and burned incense to idols. We are very susceptible to sin after great victories. It is then that we feel confident. We let our defenses down, and Satan attacks with all sorts of temptations. When you win, watch out. After the mountain peaks come the valleys.**

### ATTITUDE CHECK ● ● • • •

26:16 **After God gave Uzziah great blessings and power, he became proud and corrupt. It is true that "pride goes before destruction, and haughtiness before a fall" (Proverbs 16:18). If God has given you money, influence, popularity, and power, be thankful and careful. God hates pride. Check your attitudes and remember to give God the credit for what you have. Use your gifts in ways that please him.**

**25:23** Hebrew *400 cubits* [180 meters]. **25:28** As in some Hebrew manuscripts and other ancient versions (see also 2 Kgs 14:20); most Hebrew manuscripts read *the city of Judah.* **26:2** As in Greek version (see also 2 Kgs 14:22; 16:6); Hebrew reads *Eloth.* **26:7** As in Greek version; Hebrew reads *Gur-baal.* **26:8** As in Greek version; Hebrew reads *Ammonites.* Compare 26:7. **26:10** Hebrew *the Shephelah.* **26:15** Or *designed by brilliant men to protect those who shot arrows and stones.* **26:19** Or *a contagious skin disease.* The Hebrew word used here and throughout this passage can describe various skin diseases.

# Ultimate Issues

## ABORTION

"**K**eep your laws off my body!" scream the words on one placard. A woman in an opposing group carries a sign with a picture of an aborted baby. The caption reads "Who imposed their morality on this little one?" The news programs run story after story, pro-life and pro-abortion forces hold endless debates, and courts and legislatures are all but paralyzed over this most heated social issue: Abortion. **O**bviously, this is not a simple, one-dimensional issue. Besides the central problem of whether or not it is ever right to take the life of **an unborn person,** there are the related issues of parental consent for girls under 18 who want to have an abortion; legalizing abortion up to a certain age of the fetus (e.g., three months); "harvesting" fetal tissues to help people with diseases like Parkinson's disease; and many more. While these concerns complicate the issue, there is one question that cuts across all of them: who can say what's right? **I**f a person (a judge, a doctor, or a legislator) or a human institution (THE SUPREME COURT or the Senate) makes a decision in this matter, there is always the potential for another person or institution to overturn that decision later on. It has happened countless times. What is needed, it would seem, is a judgment or a ruling from someone or something higher than human opinion. **F**or 2,000 years, Christians have turned to the Bible for just such input. Believing the Bible to be God's own words on matters such as this, Jesus' followers have historically looked to the Scriptures for answers to life's most important—and most difficult—questions. **U**nfortunately, there is no verse of Scripture that says, "Thus saith the Lord: abortion is wrong [or right]." If there was, it would be an open-and-shut case for believers. There are, however, passages that give principles that apply to this difficult topic. In Psalm 139, David praises God for overseeing his life, starting before he was born. David thanks God first for the fantastic way the human body is **DESIGNED AND CONSTRUCTED** and then for the fact that every day of his life is "scheduled" and "recorded in [God's] book." **I**f indeed God is the Creator and Designer of human (and all other forms of) life, it is a logical conclusion that no one should treat that life lightly. If we are God's workmanship, who has the right to tamper with or destroy that workmanship? (Another verse, 2 Chronicles 28:3, shows how evil one king was by saying that he even sacrificed his own children to idols.) Yet, tragically, that is what has happened in contemporary society. Abortion has become simply a means of birth control, of removing an unwanted complication. For those who take seriously THE SANCTITY OF LIFE as an expression of God's handiwork, this can be seen only as an abomination, a sin of the most serious kind. As such, we as a society desperately need to cry out to God in repentance and ask his forgiveness for what we have allowed to be done to millions of his little ones. **T**here are a number of related topics (being made in the image of God, sexual morality, etc.) and Scripture passages (e.g., Exodus 21:22-25; Leviticus 24:17-22; Jeremiah 1:4-5) that are closely related to the abortion issue. Concerned Christians should think through their stand on the rights of the unborn in relation to these other issues and in light of the whole counsel of God, not just one passage. (One principle which should always be kept in mind when considering abortion or any other moral problem is *forgiveness.*) Psalm 139 is a good place to start.

his forehead. [20]When Azariah and the other priests saw the leprosy, they rushed him out. And the king himself was eager to get out because the LORD had struck him. [21]So King Uzziah had leprosy until the day he died. He lived in isolation, excluded from the Temple of the LORD. His son Jotham was put in charge of the royal palace, and he governed the people of the land.

[22]The rest of the events of Uzziah's reign, from beginning to end, are recorded by the prophet Isaiah son of Amoz. [23]So Uzziah died, and since he had leprosy, he was buried nearby in a burial field belonging to the kings. Then his son Jotham became the next king.

## CHAPTER 27 **KING JOTHAM FOLLOWS GOD.**

Jotham was twenty-five years old when he became king, and he reigned in Jerusalem sixteen years. His mother was Jerusha, the daughter of Zadok. [2]He did what was pleasing in the LORD's sight, just as his father, Uzziah, had done. But unlike him, Jotham did not enter the Temple of the LORD. Nevertheless, the people continued in their corrupt ways.

[3]Jotham rebuilt the Upper Gate to the LORD's Temple and also did extensive rebuilding on the wall at the hill of Ophel. [4]He built towns in the hill country of Judah and constructed fortresses and towers in the wooded areas. [5]Jotham waged war against the Ammonites and conquered them. For the next three years, he received from them an annual tribute of 7,500 pounds* of silver, 50,000 bushels of wheat, and 50,000 bushels of barley.*

[6]King Jotham became powerful because he was careful to live in obedience to the LORD his God.

[7]The rest of the events of Jotham's reign, including his wars and other activities, are recorded in *The Book of the Kings of Israel and Judah.* [8]He was twenty-five years old when he became king, and he reigned in Jerusalem sixteen years. [9]When he died, he was buried in the City of David, and his son Ahaz became the next king.

## CHAPTER 28 **AHAZ ANGERS GOD.**

Ahaz was twenty years old when he became king, and he reigned in Jerusalem sixteen years. He did not do what was pleasing in the sight of the LORD, as his ancestor David had done. [2]Instead, he followed the example of the kings of Israel and cast images for the worship of Baal. [3]He offered sacrifices in the valley of the son of Hinnom, even sacrificing his own sons in the fire.* He imitated the detestable practices of the pagan nations whom the LORD had driven from the land ahead of the Israelites. [4]He offered sacrifices and burned incense at the pagan shrines and on the hills and under every green tree.

[5]That is why the LORD his God allowed the king of Aram to defeat Ahaz and to exile large numbers of his people to Damascus. The armies of Israel also defeated Ahaz and inflicted many casualties on his army. [6]In a single day Pekah son of Remaliah, Israel's king, killed 120,000 of Judah's troops because they had abandoned the LORD, the God of their ancestors. [7]Then Zicri, a warrior from Ephraim, killed Maaseiah, the king's son; Azrikam, the king's palace commander; and Elkanah, the king's second-in-command. [8]The armies of Israel captured 200,000 women and children from Judah and took tremendous amounts of plunder, which they took back to Samaria.

[9]But a prophet of the LORD named Oded was there in Samaria when the army of Israel returned home. He went out to meet them and said, "The LORD, the God of your ancestors, was angry with Judah and let you defeat them. But you have gone too far, killing them without mercy, and all heaven is disturbed. [10]And now you are planning to make slaves of these people from Judah and Jerusalem. What about your own sins against the LORD your God? [11]Listen to me and return these captives you have taken, for they are your own relatives. Watch out, because now the LORD's fierce anger has been turned against you!"

[12]Then some of the leaders of Israel*—Azariah son of Jehohanan, Berekiah son of Meshillemoth, Jehizkiah son of Shallum, and Amasa son of Hadlai—agreed with this and confronted the men returning from battle. [13]"You must not bring the prisoners here!" they declared. "We cannot afford to add to our sins and guilt. Our guilt is already great, and the LORD's fierce anger is already turned against Israel."

[14]So the warriors released the prisoners and handed over the plunder in the sight of all the leaders and people. [15]Then the four men mentioned by name came forward and distributed clothes from the plunder to the prisoners who were naked. They provided clothing and sandals to wear, gave them enough food and drink, and dressed their wounds

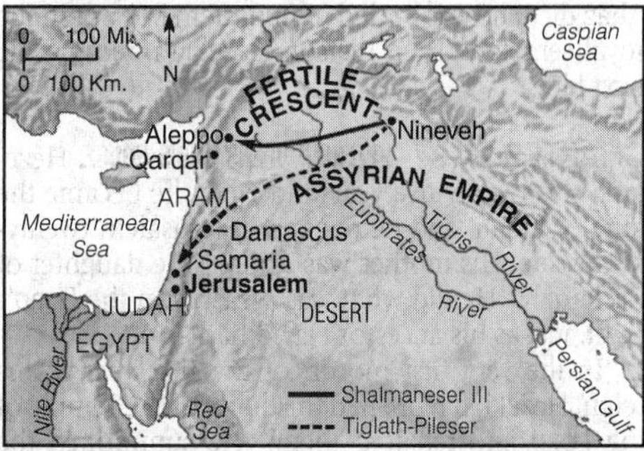


**THE ASSYRIAN EMPIRE**
The mighty Assyrian empire extended north from the Persian Gulf, across the Fertile Crescent, and south to Egypt. Shalmaneser III extended the empire toward the Mediterranean Sea by conquering cities as far west as Qarqar. Tiglath-pileser extended the empire south into Aram, Judah, and Philistia. It was Shalmaneser V who destroyed Samaria, Israel's capital.

**27:5a** Hebrew *100 talents* [3.4 metric tons]. **27:5b** Hebrew *10,000 cors* [1,820 kiloliters] *of wheat, and 10,000 cors of barley.* **28:3** Or *even making his sons pass through the fire.* **28:12** Hebrew *Ephraim,* referring to the northern kingdom of Israel.

## REACTIVATE ● ● • • •

**29:11 The Levites, chosen by God to serve in the Temple, had been kept from their duties by Ahaz's wickedness (28:24). But Hezekiah called them back into service, reminding them that the Lord had chosen them to minister.**

**We may not have to face a wicked king, but pressures or responsibilities can render us inactive and ineffective. When you have been given the responsibility to minister, don't neglect your duty. If your Christian service has been rendered inactive, whether by choice or by force, look for the opportunities (and listen to the "Hezekiahs") God will send your way to help you resume your responsibilities. Then, like the Levites, be ready for action (29:12-15).**

with olive oil. They put those who were weak on
donkeys and took all the prisoners back to their own
land—to Jericho, the city of palms. Then they returned to Samaria.

16About that time King Ahaz of Judah asked the
king of Assyria for help against his enemies. 17The
armies of Edom had again invaded Judah and taken
captives. 18And the Philistines had raided towns located in the foothills of Judah* and in the Negev.
They had already captured Beth-shemesh, Aijalon,
Gederoth, Soco with its villages, Timnah with its
villages, and Gimzo with its villages, and the Philistines had occupied these towns. 19The LORD was
humbling Judah because of King Ahaz of Judah,* for
he had encouraged his people to sin and had been
utterly unfaithful to the LORD. 20So when King
Tiglath-pileser* of Assyria arrived, he oppressed King
Ahaz instead of helping him. 21Ahaz took valuable
items from the LORD's Temple, the royal palace, and
from the homes of his officials and gave them to the
king of Assyria as tribute. But even this did not help
him.

22And when trouble came to King Ahaz, he became even more unfaithful to the LORD. 23He offered
sacrifices to the gods of Damascus who had defeated
him, for he said, "These gods helped the kings of
Aram, so they will help me, too, if I sacrifice to
them." But instead, they led to his ruin and the ruin
of all Israel. 24The king took the utensils from the
Temple of God and broke them into pieces. He shut
the doors of the LORD's Temple so that no one could
worship there and then set up altars to pagan gods
in every corner of Jerusalem. 25He made pagan
shrines in all the towns of Judah for offering sacrifices to other gods. In this way, he aroused the anger
of the LORD, the God of his ancestors.

26The rest of the events of Ahaz's reign and all his
dealings, from beginning to end, are recorded in *The
Book of the Kings of Judah and Israel.* 27When King
Ahaz died, he was buried in Jerusalem but not in the
royal cemetery. Then his son Hezekiah became the
next king.

CHAPTER **29** **HEZEKIAH OPENS GOD'S HOUSE.** Hezekiah was twenty-five years old when he became the
king of Judah, and he reigned in Jerusalem twenty-
nine years. His mother was Abijah, the daughter of
Zechariah. 2He did what was pleasing in the LORD's
sight, just as his ancestor David had done.

3In the very first month of the first year of his
reign, Hezekiah reopened the doors of the Temple of
the LORD and repaired them. 4He summoned the
priests and Levites to meet him at the courtyard east
of the Temple. 5He said to them, "Listen to me, you
Levites! Purify yourselves, and purify the Temple of
the LORD, the God of your ancestors. Remove all the
defiled things from the sanctuary. 6Our ancestors
were unfaithful and did what was evil in the sight of
the LORD our God. They abandoned the LORD and
his Temple; they turned their backs on him. 7They
also shut the doors to the Temple's foyer, and they
snuffed out the lamps. They stopped burning incense and presenting burnt offerings at the sanctuary
of the God of Israel. 8That is why the LORD's anger
has fallen upon Judah and Jerusalem. He has made
us an object of dread, horror, and ridicule, as you can
so plainly see. 9Our fathers have been killed in battle,
and our sons and daughters and wives are in captivity. 10But now I will make a covenant with the LORD,
the God of Israel, so that his fierce anger will turn
away from us. 11My dear Levites, do not neglect your
duties any longer! The LORD has chosen you to stand
in his presence, to minister to him, and to lead the
people in worship and make offerings to him."

12Then these Levites got right to work:

From the clan of Kohath: Mahath son of Amasai
and Joel son of Azariah.
From the clan of Merari: Kish son of Abdi and
Azariah son of Jehallelel.
From the clan of Gershon: Joah son of Zimmah
and Eden son of Joah.
13 From the family of Elizaphan: Shimri and Jeiel.
From the family of Asaph: Zechariah and
Mattaniah.
14 From the family of Heman: Jehiel and Shimei.
From the family of Jeduthun: Shemaiah and
Uzziel.

15These men called together their fellow Levites,
and they purified themselves. Then they began to
purify the Temple of the LORD, just as the king had
commanded. They were careful to follow all the
LORD's instructions in their work. 16The priests went
into the sanctuary of the Temple of the LORD to
cleanse it, and they took out to the Temple courtyard
all the defiled things they found. From there the
Levites carted it all out to the Kidron Valley.

17The work began on a day in early spring,* and
in eight days they had reached the foyer of the LORD's
Temple. Then they purified the Temple of the LORD
itself, which took another eight days. So the entire
task was completed in sixteen days.

18Then the Levites went to King Hezekiah and
gave him this report: "We have purified the Temple
of the LORD, the altar of burnt offering with all its

**28:18** Hebrew *the Shephelah.* **28:19** Hebrew *of Israel.* **28:20** Hebrew *Tilgath-pilneser,* a variant name for Tiglath-pileser. **29:17** Hebrew *on the first day of the first month.* This day of the Hebrew lunar calendar occurs in March or early April.

utensils, and the table of the Bread of the Presence with all its utensils. 19We have also recovered all the utensils taken by King Ahaz when he was unfaithful and closed the Temple. They are now in front of the altar of the LORD, purified and ready for use."

20Early the next morning King Hezekiah gathered the city officials and went to the Temple of the LORD. 21They brought seven bulls, seven rams, seven lambs, and seven male goats as a sin offering for the kingdom, for the Temple, and for Judah. The king commanded the priests, who were descendants of Aaron, to sacrifice the animals on the altar of the LORD. 22So they killed the bulls, and the priests took the blood and sprinkled it on the altar. Next they killed the rams and sprinkled their blood on the altar. And finally, they did the same with the lambs. 23The male goats for the sin offering were then brought before the king and the assembly of people, who laid their hands on them. 24The priests then killed the goats as a sin offering and sprinkled their blood on the altar to make atonement for the sins of all Israel. The king had specifically commanded that this burnt offering and sin offering should be made for all Israel.

25King Hezekiah then stationed the Levites at the Temple of the LORD with cymbals, harps, and lyres. He obeyed all the commands that the LORD had given to King David through Gad, the king's seer, and the prophet Nathan. 26The Levites then took their positions around the Temple with the instruments of David, and the priests took their positions with the trumpets. 27Then Hezekiah ordered that the burnt offering be placed on the altar. As the burnt offering was presented, songs of praise to the LORD were begun, accompanied by the trumpets and other instruments of David, king of Israel. 28The entire assembly worshiped the LORD as the singers sang and the trumpets blew, until all the burnt offerings were finished. 29Then the king and everyone with him bowed down in worship. 30King Hezekiah and the officials ordered the Levites to praise the LORD with the psalms of David and Asaph the seer. So they offered joyous praise and bowed down in worship.

31Then Hezekiah declared, "The dedication ceremony has come to an end. Now bring your sacrifices and thanksgiving offerings to the Temple of the LORD." So the people brought their sacrifices and thanksgiving offerings, and those whose hearts were willing brought burnt offerings, too. 32The people brought to the LORD seventy bulls, one hundred rams, and two hundred lambs for burnt offerings. 33They also brought six hundred bulls and three thousand sheep as sacrifices. 34But there were too few priests to prepare all the burnt offerings, so their relatives the Levites helped them until the work was finished and until more priests had been purified. For the Levites had been more conscientious about purifying themselves than the priests. 35There was an abundance of burnt offerings, along with the usual drink offerings, and a great deal of fat from the many peace offerings. So the Temple of the LORD was restored to service. 36And Hezekiah and all the people rejoiced greatly because of what God had done for the people, for everything had been accomplished so quickly.

## CHAPTER 30

**PASSOVER–HAPPY AGAIN.** King Hezekiah now sent word to all Israel and Judah, and he wrote letters of invitation to Ephraim and Manasseh. He asked everyone to come to the Temple of the LORD at Jerusalem to celebrate the Passover of the LORD, the God of Israel. 2The king, his officials, and all the community of Jerusalem decided to celebrate Passover a month later than usual.* 3They were unable to celebrate it at the regular time because not enough priests could be purified by then, and the people had not yet assembled at Jerusalem. 4This plan for keeping the Passover seemed right to the king and all the people. 5So they sent a proclamation throughout all Israel, from Beersheba in the south to Dan in the north, inviting everyone to come to Jerusalem to celebrate the Passover of the LORD, the God of Israel. The people had not been celebrating it in great numbers as prescribed in the law.

### FIRST PLACE ● ● ● • •

30:6-9 **Hezekiah was a king dedicated to God and to the spiritual life of the nation. He sent letters throughout Judah and Israel urging everyone to return to God. He told them not to be stubborn, but to submit themselves to the Lord. We, too, must temper our stubborn selfishness by putting God first in our life, acknowledging that he knows what is best for us, and living his way.**

6At the king's command, messengers were sent throughout Israel and Judah. They carried letters which said:

"O people of Israel, return to the LORD, the God of Abraham, Isaac, and Israel,* so that he will return to the few of us who have survived the conquest of the Assyrian kings. 7Do not be like your ancestors and relatives who abandoned the LORD, the God of their ancestors, and became an object of derision, as you yourselves can see. 8Do not be stubborn, as they were, but submit yourselves to the LORD. Come to his Temple which he has set apart as holy forever. Worship the LORD your God so that his fierce anger will turn away from you. 9For if you return to the LORD, your relatives and your children will be treated mercifully by their captors, and they will be able to return to this land. For the LORD your God is gracious and merciful. If you return to him, he will not continue to turn his face from you."

10The messengers went from town to town throughout Ephraim and Manasseh and as far as the territory of Zebulun. But most of the people just laughed at the messengers and made fun of them. 11However, some from Asher, Manasseh, and Zebulun humbled themselves and went to Jerusalem. 12At the same time, God's

**30:2** Hebrew *in the second month.* This month of the Hebrew lunar calendar usually occurs in April and May. **30:6** *Israel* is the name that God gave to Jacob.

hand was on the people in the land of Judah, giving them a strong desire to unite in obeying the orders of the king and his officials, who were following the word of the LORD. [13]And so a huge crowd assembled at Jerusalem in midspring* to celebrate Passover and the Festival of Unleavened Bread. [14]They set to work and removed the pagan altars from Jerusalem. They took away all the incense altars and threw them into the Kidron Valley.

[15]On the appointed day in midspring, one month later than usual,* the people slaughtered their Passover lambs. Then the priests and Levites became ashamed, so they purified themselves and brought burnt offerings to the Temple of the LORD. [16]They took their places at the Temple according to the regulations found in the law of Moses, the man of God. The Levites brought the sacrificial blood to the priests, who then sprinkled it on the altar.

[17]Since many of the people there had not purified themselves, the Levites had to slaughter their Passover lambs for them, to set them apart for the LORD. [18]Most of those who came from Ephraim, Manasseh, Issachar, and Zebulun had not purified themselves. But King Hezekiah prayed for them, and they were allowed to eat the Passover meal anyway, even though this was contrary to God's laws. For Hezekiah said, "May the LORD, who is good, pardon those [19]who decide to follow the LORD, the God of their ancestors, even though they are not properly cleansed for the ceremony." [20]And the LORD listened to Hezekiah's prayer and healed the people.

[21]So the people of Israel who were present in Jerusalem celebrated the Festival of Unleavened Bread for seven days with great joy. Each day the Levites and priests sang to the LORD, accompanied by loud instruments.* [22]Hezekiah encouraged the Levites for the skill they displayed as they served the LORD. So for seven days the celebration continued. Peace offerings were sacrificed, and the people confessed their sins to the LORD, the God of their ancestors.

[23]The entire assembly then decided to continue the festival another seven days, so they celebrated joyfully for another week. [24]King Hezekiah gave the people one thousand bulls and seven thousand sheep for offerings, and the officials donated one thousand bulls and ten thousand sheep. Meanwhile, many more priests purified themselves.

[25]The entire assembly of Judah rejoiced, including the priests, the Levites, all who came from the land of Israel, the foreigners who came to the festival, and all those who lived in Judah. [26]There was great joy in the city, for Jerusalem had not seen a celebration like this one since the days of Solomon, King David's son. [27]Then the Levitical priests stood and blessed the people, and God heard them from his holy dwelling in heaven.

## OFF THE TOP ● ● • • •

31:4-6 **Hezekiah reinstated the practice of tithing—giving the first portion of one's income to the priests and Levites so they could be free to serve God and minister to the people. The people responded immediately and generously with their first crops. God's work needs the support of his people. Does God receive the first portion of your income? Generosity makes our giving delightful to God (2 Corinthians 8–9). How different the church would be today if all believers consistently followed this pattern.**

CHAPTER **31** **THE PEOPLE WORSHIP AGAIN.** Now when the festival ended, the Israelites who attended went to all the towns of Judah, Benjamin, Ephraim, and Manasseh, and they smashed the sacred pillars, cut down the Asherah poles, and removed the pagan shrines and altars. After this, the Israelites returned to their own towns and homes.

[2]Hezekiah then organized the priests and Levites into divisions to offer the burnt offerings and peace offerings, and to worship and give thanks and praise to the LORD at the gates of the Temple. [3]The king also made a personal contribution of animals for the daily morning and evening burnt offerings, as well as for the weekly Sabbath festivals and monthly new moon festivals, and for the other annual festivals as required in the law of the LORD. [4]In addition, he required the people in Jerusalem to bring the prescribed portion of their income to the priests and Levites, so they could devote themselves fully to the law of the LORD.

[5]The people responded immediately and generously with the first of their crops and grain, new wine, olive oil, honey, and all the produce of their fields. They brought a tithe of all they owned. [6]The people who had moved to Judah from Israel, and the people of Judah themselves, brought in the tithes of their cattle and sheep and a tithe of the things that had been dedicated to the LORD their God, and they piled them up in great heaps. [7]The first of these tithes was brought in late spring,* and the heaps continued to grow until early autumn.* [8]When Hezekiah and his officials came and saw these huge piles, they thanked the LORD and his people Israel!

[9]"Where did all this come from?" Hezekiah asked the priests and Levites.

[10]And Azariah the high priest, from the family of Zadok, replied, "Since the people began bringing

## FRIGHTENING ● ● • • •

32:1-8 **When King Hezekiah was confronted with the frightening prospect of an Assyrian invasion, he made two important decisions. He did everything he could to deal with the situation, and he trusted God for the outcome. That is exactly what we must do when faced with difficult or frightening situations. Do everything you possibly can to solve the problem or improve the situation. As you do this, commit it to God in prayer and trust him for the solution.**

**30:13** Hebrew *in the second month.* This month of the Hebrew lunar calendar usually occurs in April and May. **30:15** Hebrew *On the fourteenth day of the second month.* This day of the Hebrew lunar calendar occurs in late April or early May. **30:21** Or *sang to the LORD with all their strength.* **31:7a** Hebrew *in the third month.* This month of the Hebrew lunar calendar usually occurs in May and June. **31:7b** Hebrew *in the seventh month.* This month of the Hebrew lunar calendar usually occurs in September and October.

their gifts to the LORD's Temple, we have had enough to eat and plenty to spare, for the LORD has blessed his people."

11Hezekiah decided to have storerooms prepared in the Temple of the LORD, and this was done. 12Then all the gifts and tithes were faithfully brought to the Temple. Conaniah the Levite was put in charge, assisted by his brother Shimei. 13The supervisors under them were Jehiel, Azaziah, Nahath, Asahel, Jerimoth, Jozabad, Eliel, Ismakiah, Mahath, and Benaiah. These appointments were made by King Hezekiah and Azariah, the chief official in the Temple of God.

14Kore son of Imnah the Levite, who was the gatekeeper at the East Gate, was put in charge of distributing the freewill offerings of God, the gifts, and the things that had been dedicated to the LORD. 15His faithful assistants were Eden, Miniamin, Jeshua, Shemaiah, Amariah, and Shecaniah. They distributed the gifts among the families of priests in their towns, by their divisions, dividing the gifts fairly among young and old alike. 16They also distributed the gifts to all males three years old or older, regardless of their place in the genealogical records, who came daily to the LORD's Temple to perform their official duties, by their divisions. 17And they distributed gifts to the priests who were listed in the genealogical records by families, and to the Levites twenty years old or older who were listed according to their jobs and their divisions. 18Food allotments were also given to all the families listed in the genealogical records, including the little babies, the wives, and the sons and daughters. For they had all been faithful in purifying themselves. 19As for the priests, the descendants of Aaron, who were living in the open villages around the towns, men were appointed to distribute portions to every male among the priests and to all the Levites listed in the genealogical records.

20In this way, King Hezekiah handled the distribution throughout all Judah, doing what was pleasing and good in the sight of the LORD his God. 21In all that he did in the service of the Temple of God and in his efforts to follow the law and the commands, Hezekiah sought his God wholeheartedly. As a result, he was very successful.

CHAPTER **32** **AN ANGEL FIGHTS FOR JUDAH.** After Hezekiah had faithfully carried out this work, King Sennacherib of Assyria invaded Judah. He laid siege to the fortified cities, giving orders for his army to break through their walls. 2When Hezekiah realized that Sennacherib also intended to attack Jerusalem, 3he consulted with his officials and military advisers, and they decided to stop the flow of the springs outside the city. 4They organized a huge work crew to stop the flow of the springs, cutting off the brook that ran through the fields. For they said, "Why should the kings of Assyria come here and find plenty of water?"

5Then Hezekiah further strengthened his defenses by repairing the wall wherever it was broken down and by adding to the fortifications and constructing a second wall outside the first. He also reinforced the Millo* in the City of David and

## MANASSEH

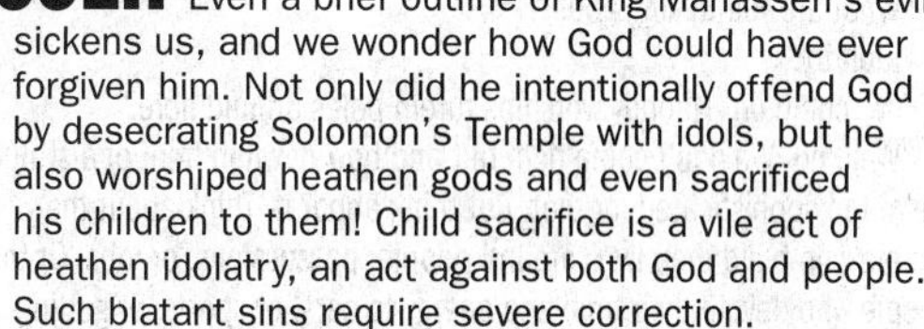

Even a brief outline of King Manasseh's evil sickens us, and we wonder how God could have ever forgiven him. Not only did he intentionally offend God by desecrating Solomon's Temple with idols, but he also worshiped heathen gods and even sacrificed his children to them! Child sacrifice is a vile act of heathen idolatry, an act against both God and people. Such blatant sins require severe correction.

God showed justice to Manasseh in warning and punishing him. He showed mercy in responding to Manasseh's heartfelt repentance by forgiving and restoring him. Given the nature of Manasseh's rebellion, we are not surprised by God's punishment—defeat and exile at the hands of the Assyrians. But Manasseh's repentance and God's forgiveness are unexpected. Manasseh's life was changed. He was given a new start.

How far has God gone to get your attention? Have you ever, like Manasseh, come to your senses and cried out to God for help? Only your repentance and a prayer for a new attitude stand between you and God's complete forgiveness.

LESSONS: God will go a long way to get someone's attention

Forgiveness is limited not by the amount of sin, but by our willingness to repent

KEY VERSES: "But while in deep distress, Manasseh sought the LORD his God and cried out humbly to the God of his ancestors. And when he prayed, the LORD listened to him and was moved by his request for help. So the LORD let Manasseh return to Jerusalem and to his kingdom. Manasseh had finally realized that the LORD alone is God!" (2 Chronicles 33:12-13).

Manasseh's story is told in 2 Kings 21:1-18 and 2 Chronicles 32:33–33:20. He is also mentioned in Jeremiah 15:4.

**UPS:**
- Despite the bitter consequences of his sins, he learned from them
- Humbly repented of his sins before God

**DOWNS:**
- Challenged God's authority and was defeated
- Reversed many of the positive effects of his father Hezekiah's rule
- Sacrificed his children to idols

**STATS**
- Occupation: King of Judah
- Relatives: Father: Hezekiah. Mother: Hephzibah. Son: Amon.

32:5 Or *the supporting terraces.*

manufactured large numbers of weapons and
shields. 6He appointed military officers over the
people and asked them to assemble before him in
the square at the city gate. Then Hezekiah encouraged them with this address: 7"Be strong and courageous! Don't be afraid of the king of Assyria or his
mighty army, for there is a power far greater on our
side! 8He may have a great army, but they are just
men. We have the LORD our God to help us and to
fight our battles for us!" These words greatly encouraged the people.

## TONE AGE

Chuck normally uses anthropology class to snooze or do algebra homework. Not today. Mr. Roper spent the hour talking about the religious beliefs of certain Stone Age tribes. The discussion of human sacrifices and strange rituals had Chuck paying extra special attention.

After school, he continued to rattle on about what he had heard. "Annie, how in the world can those people actually bow down to a piece of wood or stone? Don't you think that's weird?"

"Well, it is pretty strange. But we do almost the same thing in this country."

"What are you talking about?"

"Idolatry."

"Aw, come on! Nobody worships totem poles around here."

"Well, no. We don't come right out and bow down in front of a statue. We're too sophisticated for that. But think about it. Think about the people who build their lives around people, possessions, or jobs. Or the people who devote their time and energy to cars, or sports, or getting good grades, or–"

"Hey! What's wrong with sports?"

"Nothing! . . . unless it becomes your whole life. Chuck, anything that becomes more important than God is an idol."

Annie's right. The Bible repeatedly warns us not to let things or people replace God in our life. See the story of King Josiah in 2 Chronicles 34.

9Then King Sennacherib of Assyria, while still besieging the town of Lachish, sent officials to Jerusalem with this message for Hezekiah and all the
people in the city:

10"This is what King Sennacherib of Assyria says:
What are you trusting in that makes you think
you can survive my siege of Jerusalem?
11Hezekiah has said, 'The LORD our God will
rescue us from the king of Assyria.' Surely
Hezekiah is misleading you, sentencing you to
death by famine and thirst! 12Surely you must
realize that Hezekiah is the very person who
destroyed all the LORD's shrines and altars. He
commanded Judah and Jerusalem to worship at
only the one altar at the Temple and to make
sacrifices on it alone.

13"Surely you must realize what I and the other
kings of Assyria before me have done to all the
people of the earth! Were any of the gods of those
nations able to rescue their people from my
power? 14Name just one time when any god,
anywhere, was able to rescue his people from me!
What makes you think your God can do any
better? 15Don't let Hezekiah fool you! Don't let
him deceive you like this! I say it again—no god
of any nation has ever yet been able to rescue his
people from me or my ancestors. How much less
will your God rescue you from my power!"

16And Sennacherib's officials further mocked the
LORD God and his servant Hezekiah, heaping insult
upon insult. 17The king also sent letters scorning the
LORD, the God of Israel. He wrote, "Just as the gods
of all the other nations failed to rescue their people
from my power, so the God of Hezekiah will also
fail." 18The Assyrian officials who brought the letters
shouted this in the Hebrew language to the people
gathered on the walls of the city, trying to terrify
them so it would be easier to capture the city. 19These
officials talked about the God of Jerusalem as
though he were one of the pagan gods, made by
human hands.

20Then King Hezekiah and the prophet Isaiah son
of Amoz cried out in prayer to God in heaven. 21And
the LORD sent an angel who destroyed the Assyrian
army with all its commanders and officers. So Sennacherib returned home in disgrace to his own land.
And when he entered the temple of his god, some of
his own sons killed him there with a sword. 22That is
how the LORD rescued Hezekiah and the people of
Jerusalem from King Sennacherib of Assyria and
from all the others who threatened them. So there
was peace at last throughout the land. 23From then
on King Hezekiah became highly respected among
the surrounding nations, and many gifts for the
LORD arrived at Jerusalem, with valuable presents for
King Hezekiah, too.

24About that time, Hezekiah became deathly ill.
He prayed to the LORD, who healed him and gave
him a miraculous sign. 25But Hezekiah did not respond appropriately to the kindness shown him,
and he became proud. So the LORD's anger came
against him and against Judah and Jerusalem.
26Then Hezekiah repented of his pride, and the
people of Jerusalem humbled themselves. So the
LORD's anger did not come against them during
Hezekiah's lifetime.

27Hezekiah was very wealthy and held in high esteem. He had to build special treasury buildings for his
silver, gold, precious stones, and spices, and for his
shields and other valuable items. 28He also constructed
many storehouses for his grain, new wine, and olive
oil; and he made many stalls for his cattle and folds for
his flocks of sheep and goats. 29He built many towns
and acquired vast flocks and herds, for God had given
him great wealth. 30He blocked up the upper spring of
Gihon and brought the water down through a tunnel
to the west side of the City of David. And so he
succeeded in everything he did.

31 However, when ambassadors arrived from Babylon to ask about the remarkable events that had taken place in the land, God withdrew from Hezekiah in order to test him and to see what was really in his heart.

32 The rest of the events of Hezekiah's reign and his acts of devotion are recorded in *The Vision of the Prophet Isaiah Son of Amoz,* which is included in *The Book of the Kings of Judah and Israel.* 33 When Hezekiah died, he was buried in the upper area of the royal cemetery, and all Judah and Jerusalem honored him at his death. Then his son Manasseh became the next king.

CHAPTER **33** **MANASSEH'S HEART IS CHANGED.** Manasseh was twelve years old when he became king, and he reigned in Jerusalem fifty-five years. 2 He did what was evil in the LORD's sight, imitating the detestable practices of the pagan nations whom the LORD had driven from the land ahead of the Israelites. 3 He rebuilt the pagan shrines his father Hezekiah had destroyed. He constructed altars for the images of Baal and set up Asherah poles. He also bowed before all the stars of heaven and worshiped them. 4 He even built pagan altars in the Temple of the LORD, the place where the LORD had said his name should be honored forever. 5 He put these altars for the stars of heaven in both courtyards of the LORD's Temple. 6 Manasseh even sacrificed his own sons in the fire* in the valley of the son of Hinnom. He practiced sorcery, divination, and witchcraft, and he consulted with mediums and psychics. He did much that was evil in the LORD's sight, arousing his anger.

7 Manasseh even took a carved idol he had made and set it up in God's Temple, the very place where God had told David and his son Solomon: "My name will be honored here forever in this Temple and in Jerusalem—the city I have chosen from among all the other tribes of Israel. 8 If the Israelites will obey my commands—all the instructions, laws, and regulations given through Moses—I will not send them into exile from this land that I gave their ancestors." 9 But Manasseh led the people of Judah and Jerusalem to do even more evil than the pagan nations whom the LORD had destroyed when the Israelites entered the land.

10 The LORD spoke to Manasseh and his people, but they ignored all his warnings. 11 So the LORD sent the Assyrian armies, and they took Manasseh prisoner. They put a ring through his nose, bound him in bronze chains, and led him away to Babylon. 12 But while in deep distress, Manasseh sought the LORD his God and cried out humbly to the God of his ancestors. 13 And when he prayed, the LORD listened to him and was moved by his request for help. So the LORD let Manasseh return to Jerusalem and to his kingdom. Manasseh had finally realized that the LORD alone is God!

14 It was after this that Manasseh rebuilt the outer wall of the City of David, from west of the Gihon Spring in the Kidron Valley to the Fish Gate, and continuing around the hill of Ophel, where it was built very high. And he stationed his military officers in all of the fortified cities of Judah. 15 Manasseh also removed the foreign gods from the hills and the idol from the LORD's Temple. He tore down all the altars he had built on the hill where the Temple stood and all the altars that were in Jerusalem, and he dumped them outside the city. 16 Then he restored the altar of the LORD and sacrificed peace offerings and thanksgiving offerings on it. He also encouraged the people of Judah to worship the LORD, the God of Israel. 17 However, the people still sacrificed at the pagan shrines, but only to the LORD their God.

18 The rest of the events of Manasseh's reign, his prayer to God, and the words the seers spoke to him in the name of the LORD, the God of Israel, are recorded in *The Book of the Kings of Israel.* 19 Manasseh's prayer, the account of the way God answered him, and an account of all his sins and unfaithfulness are recorded in *The Record of the Seers.** It includes a list of the locations where he built pagan shrines and set up Asherah poles and idols before he repented. 20 When Manasseh died, he was buried at his palace. Then his son Amon became the next king.

21 Amon was twenty-two years old when he became king, and he reigned in Jerusalem two years. 22 He did what was evil in the LORD's sight, just as his father Manasseh had done. He worshiped and sacrificed to all the idols his father had made. 23 But unlike his father, he did not humble himself before the LORD. Instead, Amon sinned even more.

24 At last Amon's own officials plotted against him and assassinated him in his palace. 25 But the people of the land killed all those who had conspired against King Amon, and they made his son Josiah the next king.

**BEYOND FORGIVENESS? ● ● • • •**

33:12-13 **In a list of corrupt kings, Manasseh would rank near the top. His life is a catalog of evil deeds including idol worship, sacrificing his own children, and Temple desecration. Eventually, however, he realized his sins and cried out to God for forgiveness. And God listened. If God can forgive Manasseh, surely he can forgive anyone. Are you burdened by overpowering guilt? Do you doubt that anyone could forgive what you have done? Take heart– until death, no one is beyond God's forgiveness.**

CHAPTER **34** **THE BOOK OF THE LAW IS FOUND.** Josiah was eight years old when he became king, and he reigned in Jerusalem thirty-one years. 2 He did what was pleasing in the LORD's sight and followed the example of his ancestor David. He did not turn aside from doing what was right.

3 During the eighth year of his reign, while he was still young, Josiah began to seek the God of his ancestor David. Then in the twelfth year, he began to purify Judah and Jerusalem, destroying all the pagan shrines, the Asherah poles, and the carved idols and cast

33:6 Or *even made his sons pass through the fire.* 33:19 Or *The Record of Hozai.*

## UNREAD ● ● • • ·

34:31 **When Josiah read the book that Hilkiah discovered (34:14), he responded with repentance and humility and promised to follow God's commandments as written in the book. The Bible is God's Word to us, "full of living power" (Hebrews 4:12), but we cannot know what God wants us to do if we do not read it. And even reading God's Word is not enough; we must be willing to do what it says. There is not much difference between the book hidden in the Temple and the Bible hidden on the bookshelf. An unread Bible is just as useless as a lost one.**

images. [4]He saw to it that the altars for the images of Baal and their incense altars were torn down. He also made sure that the Asherah poles, the carved idols, and the cast images were smashed and scattered over the graves of those who had sacrificed to them. [5]Then he burned the bones of the pagan priests on their own altars, and so he purified Judah and Jerusalem.

[6]He did the same thing in the towns of Manasseh, Ephraim, and Simeon, even as far as Naphtali. [7]He destroyed the pagan altars and the Asherah poles, and he crushed the idols into dust. He cut down the incense altars throughout the land of Israel and then returned to Jerusalem.

[8]In the eighteenth year of his reign, after he had purified the land and the Temple, Josiah appointed Shaphan son of Azaliah, Maaseiah the governor of Jerusalem, and Joah son of Joahaz, the royal historian, to repair the Temple of the LORD his God. [9]They gave Hilkiah the high priest the money that had been collected by the Levites who served as gatekeepers at the Temple of God. The gifts were brought by people from Manasseh, Ephraim, and from all the remnant of Israel, as well as from all Judah, Benjamin, and the people of Jerusalem. [10]He entrusted the money to the men assigned to supervise the restoration of the LORD's Temple. Then they paid the workers who did the repairs and renovation. [11]Thus, they hired carpenters and masons and purchased cut stone for the walls and timber for the rafters and beams. They restored what earlier kings of Judah had allowed to fall into ruin.

[12]The workers served faithfully under the leadership of Jahath and Obadiah, Levites of the Merarite clan, and Zechariah and Meshullam, Levites of the Kohathite clan. Other Levites, all of whom were skilled musicians, [13]were put in charge of the laborers of the various trades. Still others assisted as secretaries, officials, and gatekeepers.

[14]As Hilkiah the high priest was recording the money collected at the LORD's Temple, he found the Book of the Law of the LORD as it had been given through Moses. [15]Hilkiah said to Shaphan the court secretary, "I have found the Book of the Law in the LORD's Temple!" Then Hilkiah gave the scroll to Shaphan.

[16]Shaphan took the scroll to the king and reported, "Your officials are doing everything they were assigned to do. [17]The money that was collected at the Temple of the LORD has been given to the supervisors and workmen." [18]Shaphan also said to the king, "Hilkiah the priest has given me a scroll." So Shaphan read it to the king.

[19]When the king heard what was written in the law, he tore his clothes in despair. [20]Then he gave these orders to Hilkiah, Ahikam son of Shaphan, Acbor son of Micaiah,* Shaphan the court secretary, and Asaiah the king's personal adviser: [21]"Go to the Temple and speak to the LORD for me and for all the remnant of Israel and Judah. Ask him about the words written in this scroll that has been found. The LORD's anger has been poured out against us because our ancestors have not obeyed the word of the LORD. We have not been doing what this scroll says we must do."

[22]So Hilkiah and the other men went to the newer Mishneh section* of Jerusalem to consult with the prophet Huldah. She was the wife of Shallum son of Tikvah and grandson of Harhas,* the keeper of the Temple wardrobe. [23]She said to them, "The LORD, the God of Israel, has spoken! Go and tell the man who sent you, [24]'This is what the LORD says: I will certainly destroy this city and its people. All the curses written in the scroll you have read will come true. [25]For the people of Judah have abandoned me and worshiped pagan gods, and I am very angry with them for everything they have done. My anger will be poured out against this place, and nothing will be able to stop it.'

[26]"But go to the king of Judah who sent you to seek the LORD and tell him: 'This is what the LORD, the God of Israel, says concerning the message you have just heard: [27]You were sorry and humbled yourself before God when you heard what I said against this city and its people. You humbled yourself and tore your clothing in despair and wept before me in repentance. So I have indeed heard you, says the LORD. [28]I will not send the promised disaster against this city and its people until after you have died and been buried in peace. You will not see the disaster I am going to bring on this place.'" So they took her message back to the king.

[29]Then the king summoned all the leaders of Judah and Jerusalem. [30]And the king went up to the Temple of the LORD with all the people of Judah and Jerusalem and the priests and the Levites—all the people from the greatest to the least. There the king read to them the entire Book of the Covenant that had been found in the LORD's Temple. [31]The king took his place of authority beside the pillar and renewed the covenant in the LORD's presence. He pledged to obey the LORD by keeping all his commands, regulations, and laws with all his heart and soul. He promised to obey all the terms of the covenant that were written in the scroll. [32]And he required everyone in Jerusalem and the people of Benjamin to make a similar pledge. As the people of Jerusalem did this, they renewed their covenant with God, the God of their ancestors.

[33]So Josiah removed all detestable idols from the entire land of Israel and required everyone to worship the LORD their God. And throughout the rest of his lifetime, they did not turn away from the LORD, the God of their ancestors.

**34:20** As in parallel text at 2 Kgs 22:12; Hebrew reads *Abdon son of Micah.* **34:22a** Or *the Second Quarter,* a newer section of Jerusalem. **34:22b** As in parallel text at 2 Kgs 22:14; Hebrew reads *son of Tokhath, son of Hasrah.*

CHAPTER **35** **JOSIAH CELEBRATES PASSOVER.** Then
Josiah announced that the Passover of the LORD would
be celebrated in Jerusalem on the appointed day in
early spring.* The Passover lambs were slaughtered at
twilight of that day. [2]Josiah also assigned the priests to
their duties and encouraged them in their work at the
Temple of the LORD. [3]He issued this order to the Levites, who had been set apart to serve the LORD and
were teachers in Israel: "Since the Ark is now in Solomon's Temple and you do not need to carry it back and
forth on your shoulders, spend your time serving the
LORD your God and his people Israel. [4]Report for duty
according to the family divisions of your ancestors,
following the written instructions of King David of
Israel and the instructions of his son Solomon. [5]Then
stand in your appointed holy places and help the
families assigned to you as they bring their offerings to
the Temple. [6]Slaughter the Passover lambs, purify yourselves, and prepare to help those who come. Follow all
the instructions that the LORD gave through Moses."

[7]Then Josiah contributed from his personal property thirty thousand lambs and young goats for the
people's Passover offerings, and three thousand bulls.
[8]The king's officials also made willing contributions to
the people, priests, and Levites. Hilkiah, Zechariah,
and Jehiel, the administrators of God's Temple, gave
the priests twenty-six hundred lambs and young goats
and three hundred bulls as Passover offerings. [9]The
Levite leaders—Conaniah and his brothers Shemaiah
and Nethanel, and Hashabiah, Jeiel, and Jozabad—
gave five thousand lambs and young goats and five
hundred bulls to the Levites for their Passover offerings.

[10]When everything was ready for the Passover celebration, the priests and the Levites took their places,
organized by their divisions, according to the king's
orders. [11]The Levites then slaughtered the Passover
lambs and presented the blood to the priests, who
sprinkled the blood on the altar while the Levites
prepared the animals. [12]They divided the burnt offerings among the people by their family groups, so they
could offer them to the LORD according to the instructions recorded in the Book of Moses. They did the
same with the bulls. [13]Then they roasted the Passover
lambs as prescribed; and they boiled the holy offerings
in pots, kettles, and pans, and brought them out
quickly so the people could eat them.

[14]Afterward the Levites prepared a meal for themselves and for the priests, because the priests had
been busy from morning till night offering the burnt
offerings and the fat portions. The Levites took responsibility for all these preparations. [15]The musicians, descendants of Asaph, were in their assigned
places, following the orders given by David, Asaph,
Heman, and Jeduthun, the king's seer. The gatekeepers guarded the gates and did not need to leave their
posts of duty, for their meals were brought to them
by their fellow Levites.

[16]The entire ceremony for the LORD's Passover was
completed that day. All the burnt offerings were sacrificed on the altar of the LORD, as King Josiah had
ordered. [17]All the Israelites present in Jerusalem celebrated Passover and the Festival of Unleavened Bread
for seven days. [18]Never since the time of the prophet
Samuel had there been such a Passover. None of the
kings of Israel had ever kept a Passover as Josiah did,
involving all the priests and Levites, all the people of
Jerusalem, and people from all over Judah and Israel.
[19]This Passover celebration took place in the eighteenth year of Josiah's reign.

[20]After Josiah had finished restoring the Temple,
King Neco of Egypt led his army up from Egypt to do
battle at Carchemish on the Euphrates River, and Josiah and his army marched out to fight him. [21]But King
Neco sent ambassadors to Josiah with this message:

"What do you want with me, king of Judah?
I have no quarrel with you today! I only want
to fight the nation with which I am at war.
And God has told me to hurry! Do not interfere
with God, who is with me, or he will destroy you."

[22]But Josiah refused to listen to Neco, to whom
God had indeed spoken, and he would not turn
back. Instead, he led his army into battle on the
plain of Megiddo. He laid aside his royal robes so the
enemy would not recognize him. [23]But the enemy
archers hit King Josiah with their arrows and
wounded him. He cried out to his men, "Take me
from the battle, for I am badly wounded!"

[24]So they lifted Josiah out of his chariot and placed
him in another chariot. Then they brought him back
to Jerusalem, where he died. He was buried there in
the royal cemetery. And all Judah and Jerusalem
mourned for him. [25]The prophet Jeremiah composed
funeral songs for Josiah, and to this day choirs still sing
these sad songs about his death. These songs of sorrow
have become a tradition and are recorded in *The Book
of Laments.* [26]The rest of the events of Josiah's reign and
his acts of devotion done according to the written law

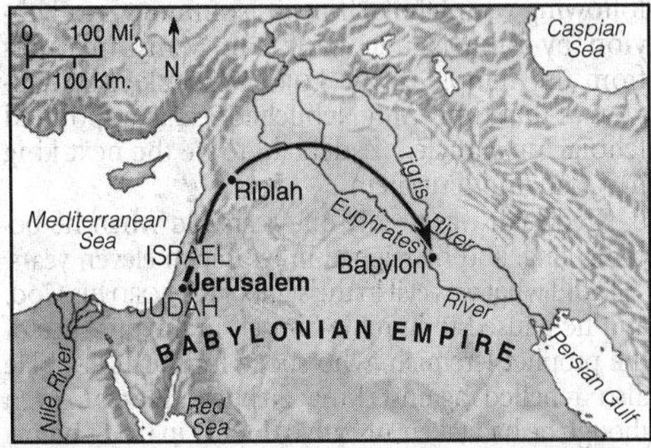


**EXILE TO BABYLON**
Despite Judah's few good kings and timely reforms, the people never truly changed. Their evil continued, and finally God used the Babylonian empire under Nebuchadnezzar to conquer Judah, destroy Jerusalem, and take the people captive to Babylon.

35:1 Hebrew *on the fourteenth day of the first month.* This day of the Hebrew lunar calendar occurs in late March or early April.

**BEYOND REMEDY ● ● • • •**

**36:16 God warned Judah about its sin and continually restored the people to his favor, only to have them turn away. Eventually the situation was beyond remedy. Beware of harboring sin in your heart. The day will come when remedy is no longer possible and God's judgment replaces his mercy. Sin often repeated, but never repented of, invites disaster. Confess and turn from your sins now.**

of the LORD, 27from beginning to end, are recorded in *The Book of the Kings of Israel and Judah.*

CHAPTER **36** **JERUSALEM IS DESTROYED.** Then the people of the land took Josiah's son Jehoahaz and made him the next king in Jerusalem. 2Jehoahaz* was twenty-three years old when he became king, but he reigned only three months. 3Then he was deposed by Neco, the king of Egypt, who demanded a tribute from Judah of 7,500 pounds of silver and 75 pounds of gold.* 4The king of Egypt appointed Eliakim, the brother of Jehoahaz, as the next king of Judah and Jerusalem, and he changed Eliakim's name to Jehoiakim. Then Neco took Jehoahaz to Egypt as a prisoner.

5Jehoiakim was twenty-five years old when he became king, and he reigned in Jerusalem eleven years. But he did what was evil in the sight of the LORD his God. 6Then King Nebuchadnezzar of Babylon came to Jerusalem and captured it, and he bound Jehoiakim in chains and led him away to Babylon. 7Nebuchadnezzar also took some of the treasures from the Temple of the LORD, and he placed them in his palace* in Babylon. 8The rest of the events of Jehoiakim's reign, including all the evil things he did and everything found against him, are recorded in *The Book of the Kings of Israel and Judah.* Then his son Jehoiachin became the next king.

9Jehoiachin was eighteen* years old when he became king, but he reigned in Jerusalem only three months and ten days. Jehoiachin did what was evil in the LORD's sight. 10In the spring of the following year, Jehoiachin was summoned to Babylon by King Nebuchadnezzar. Many treasures from the Temple of the LORD were taken to Babylon at that time. And Nebuchadnezzar appointed Jehoiachin's uncle,* Zedekiah, to be the next king in Judah and Jerusalem.

11Zedekiah was twenty-one years old when he became king, and he reigned in Jerusalem eleven years. 12He did what was evil in the sight of the LORD his God, and he refused to humble himself in the presence of the prophet Jeremiah, who spoke for the LORD. 13He also rebelled against King Nebuchadnezzar, even though he had taken an oath of loyalty in God's name. Zedekiah was a hard and stubborn man, refusing to turn to the LORD, the God of Israel.

14All the leaders of the priests and the people became more and more unfaithful. They followed the pagan practices of the surrounding nations, desecrating the Temple of the LORD in Jerusalem.

15The LORD, the God of their ancestors, repeatedly sent his prophets to warn them, for he had compassion on his people and his Temple. 16But the people mocked these messengers of God and despised their words. They scoffed at the prophets until the LORD's anger could no longer be restrained and there was no remedy.

17So the LORD brought the king of Babylon against them. The Babylonians* killed Judah's young men, even chasing after them into the Temple. They had no pity on the people, killing both young and old, men and women, healthy and sick. God handed them all over to Nebuchadnezzar. 18The king also took home to Babylon all the utensils, large and small, used in the Temple of God, and the treasures from both the LORD's Temple and the royal palace. He also took with him all the royal princes. 19Then his army set fire to the Temple of God, broke down the walls of Jerusalem, burned all the palaces, and completely destroyed everything of value.* 20The few who survived were taken away to Babylon, and they became servants to the king and his sons until the kingdom of Persia came to power. 21So the message of the LORD spoken through Jeremiah was fulfilled. The land finally enjoyed its Sabbath rest, lying desolate for seventy years, just as the prophet had said.

22In the first year of King Cyrus of Persia,* the LORD fulfilled Jeremiah's prophecy by stirring the heart of Cyrus to put this proclamation into writing and to send it throughout his kingdom:

> 23"This is what King Cyrus of Persia says: The LORD, the God of heaven, has given me all the kingdoms of the earth. He has appointed me to build him a Temple at Jerusalem in the land of Judah. All of you who are the LORD's people may return to Israel for this task. May the LORD your God be with you!"

**STRIPPED ● ● • • •**

**36:22-23 Second Chronicles focuses on the rise and fall of the worship of God as symbolized by the Jerusalem Temple. David planned the Temple; Solomon built it and then put on the greatest dedication service the world had ever seen. Worship in the Temple was superbly organized. But several evil kings defiled the Temple and degraded worship so that the people revered idols more highly than God. Finally, King Nebuchadnezzar of Babylon destroyed the Temple (36:19). The kings were gone, the Temple was destroyed, and the people were removed. The nation was stripped to its very foundation. But fortunately there was a greater foundation—God himself. When everything in life seems stripped away from us, we too still have God—his Word, his presence, and his promises.**

36:2 Hebrew *Joahaz,* a variant name for Jehoahaz; also in 36:4. 36:3 Hebrew *100 talents* [3.4 metric tons] *of silver and 1 talent* [34 kilograms] *of gold.* 36:7 Or *temple.* 36:9 As in one Hebrew manuscript, some Greek manuscripts, and Syriac version (see also 2 Kgs 24:8); most Hebrew manuscripts read *eight.* 36:10 As in parallel text at 2 Kgs 24:17; Hebrew reads *brother,* or *relative.* 36:17 Or *Chaldeans.* 36:19 Or *destroyed all the valuable Temple utensils.* 36:22 The first year of Cyrus's reign was 538 B.C.

# MEGA themes

**TEMPLE** The Temple was the symbol of God's presence and the place set aside for worship and prayer. Built by Solomon from the plans God gave to David, the Temple was the nation's spiritual center.

1. How did the people feel about the Temple? What caused them to feel this way?
2. What did the Temple provide for the nation?
3. Because Christians are the temple of God, what attitude should they have toward each other?
4. What attitudes keep the body of Christ from fulfilling its intended role as the temple?
5. Is there a Christian toward whom you have a negative attitude? How could you improve your attitude and restore that relationship?

**PEACE** Solomon and his descendants were faithful to God. They experienced victory in battle, success in government, and peace with other nations. Peace was, and is, the result of loyalty to God and his law.

Only God can bring true peace, and he is greater than any enemy, army, or national alliance. Israel's peace and survival as a nation depended on its faithfulness to God. Our obedience to God as individuals and as a nation is also vital to our individual and national peace today.

1. What causes nations to go to war? families to break apart? friends to fight?
2. What do the above causes have in common?
3. What was the source of Israel's peace?
4. What does it mean to you to "be at peace"?
5. Jesus said, "God blesses those who work for peace" (Matthew 5:9). What does it mean to work for peace?
6. What can you do to work for peace?

**PRAYER** After Solomon died, the kingdom divided. When a king led the Israelites into idolatry, the nation suffered. When the king and his people prayed to God for deliverance and they turned from their sinful ways, God delivered them.

God still answers prayer. We have God's promise that if we humble ourselves, seek him, turn from our sin, and pray, God will hear, heal, and forgive us. When we pray, we should be seeking to know and experience God's will for our lives.

1. Describe the attitudes of the king and the people as they went to God in prayer.
2. How did the people put their prayers into action?
3. What attitudes do you think are most important for you to have when you pray?
4. What are five important prayer requests in your life today? What can you expect from God when you share these with him?
5. Take ten minutes to bring your requests and your life before God. Approach your prayers not as a time to share your "shopping list" with God, but as a time to understand more of your Father's love, provision, and grace for you.

**REFORM** Although idolatry and injustice were common, some kings led the people back to God and reformed their society. This involved destroying idols, obeying the law, and restoring the priesthood.

1. Changes in the society began with people coming back to God. What caused the people to return to God? What did they do next?
2. What changes need to take place in the world? in your community? in your school?
3. Christian young people can be agents of change in the world, but to do so they must have a desire for a relationship with God and a commitment to obey him. What changes would happen if a group of committed Christian friends were to begin to work together in your school? in your community?
4. Seek God's will in your own life and in the lives of your Christian friends. Share your vision with them of how, with God's help, you could join together to create positive change.

**COLLAPSE** In 586 B.C. the Babylonians completely destroyed Solomon's beautiful Temple. The Israelites had abandoned God. Therefore God brought judgment upon his people, and they were carried off into captivity.

Although our disobedience may not be as obvious as Israel's, quite often our commitment to God is casual, or even phony. When we forget that all our power, wisdom, and wealth come from God and not from ourselves, we are in danger of suffering the same spiritual and moral collapse that Israel experienced.

1. What decisions led to the collapse of Judah?
2. What causes men and women in leadership positions, who claim to be serving God, to turn away from God and become immoral?
3. In what specific ways can you prevent such failure in your life? How can you be a person who changes your world, rather than someone who is changed by it?

**586 B.C.**
**Jerusalem destroyed; exiles to Babylon**

**539**
**Babylon overthrown by Cyrus**

**538**
**Cyrus's decree to return**

**537**
**Exiles return to Jerusalem**

**536**
**Temple construction begins**

**530**
**Temple work halted**

**522**
**Darius becomes king of Persia**

**520**
**Temple work resumed; messages of Haggai, Zechariah given**

**516**
**Temple completed**

**458**
**Ezra comes to Jerusalem**

**445**
**Nehemiah comes to Jerusalem**

When a celebrity commits suicide, we can't believe it. *After all,* we think, *he had everything: millions of fans, talent, good looks, a beautiful wife, fame, and fortune. What more could he want?* From all surface appearances, the person's life seemed perfect. Inside, though—where it really counts—it was full of loneliness, depression, and turmoil. ■ Ezra, a devoted priest and scribe, knew what was important. He was concerned for the Jews living in Jerusalem. Years earlier, under Zerubbabel's leadership, a group of Jews had been given permission to leave Babylon and return to build the Temple. Though the returnees had met with some opposition, eventually they were successful. The Temple was completed and dedicated. Everything looked good on the outside. ■ But when Ezra reached Jerusalem, he wept. The people *looked* obedient because they had rebuilt the Temple, but their personal and spiritual lives were in shambles. The inside had fallen apart. Ezra realized that if this went unchanged, the new nation of Israel would commit spiritual suicide. ■ How does your "inside life" match with your outside? Read Ezra and decide to be a person who follows God in every area.

## STATS

PURPOSE: To show God's faithfulness and the way he kept his promise to restore his people to their land

AUTHOR: Not stated, but probably Ezra

DATE WRITTEN: Around 450 B.C., recording events from about 538–450 B.C. (omitting 516–458 B.C.). Possibly begun earlier in Babylon and finished in Jerusalem.

SETTING: Ezra follows 2 Chronicles as a history of the Jews, recording their return to the Promised Land after their captivity

KEY PEOPLE: Cyrus, Zerubbabel, Haggai, Zechariah, Darius, Artaxerxes I, Ezra

KEY PLACES: Babylon, Jerusalem

SPECIAL FEATURES: Ezra and Nehemiah originally were one book in the Hebrew Bible and, with Esther, comprise the post-captivity historical books. The post-captivity prophetic books are Haggai, Zechariah, and Malachi. Haggai and Zechariah should be studied with Ezra since they prophesied during the period of the reconstruction.

CHAPTER 1 **THE ISRAELITES RETURN HOME.** In the first year of King Cyrus of Persia,* the LORD fulfilled Jeremiah's prophecy by stirring the heart of Cyrus to put this proclamation into writing and to send it throughout his kingdom:

2"This is what King Cyrus of Persia says: The LORD, the God of heaven, has given me all the kingdoms of the earth. He has appointed me to build him a Temple at Jerusalem in the land of Judah. 3All of you who are his people may return to Jerusalem in Judah to rebuild this Temple of the LORD, the God of Israel, who lives in Jerusalem. And may your God be with you! 4Those who live in any place where Jewish survivors are found should contribute toward their expenses by supplying them with silver and gold, supplies for the journey, and livestock, as well as a freewill offering for the Temple of God in Jerusalem."

5Then God stirred the hearts of the priests and Levites and the leaders of the tribes of Judah and Benjamin to return to Jerusalem to rebuild the Temple of the LORD. 6And all their neighbors assisted by giving them vessels of silver and gold, supplies for the journey, and livestock. They gave them many choice gifts in addition to all the freewill offerings.

7King Cyrus himself brought out the valuable items which King Nebuchadnezzar had taken from the LORD's Temple in Jerusalem and had placed in the temple of his own gods. 8Cyrus directed Mithredath, the treasurer of Persia, to count these items and present them to Sheshbazzar, the leader of the exiles returning to Judah.*

## CAPTIVES ● ● • • •

**1:1 The book of Ezra opens in 538 B.C., 48 years after Nebuchadnezzar destroyed Jerusalem, defeated the southern kingdom of Judah, and carried the Jews away to Babylon as captives (2 Kings 25; 2 Chronicles 36). Nebuchadnezzar died in 562, and because his successor was not strong, Babylon was overthrown by Persia in 539, just prior to the events recorded in this book. Both the Babylonians and the Persians had a relaxed policy toward their captives, allowing them to own land and homes and to take ordinary jobs. Many of the Jews, like Daniel, Mordecai, and Esther, rose to prominent positions within the nation. King Cyrus of Persia went a step further: he allowed many groups of exiles, including the Jews, to return to their homeland. By doing this, he hoped to win their loyalty and thus provide buffer zones around the borders of his empire.**

1:1 The first year of Cyrus's reign was 538 B.C. 1:8 Hebrew *Sheshbazzar, the prince of Judah.*

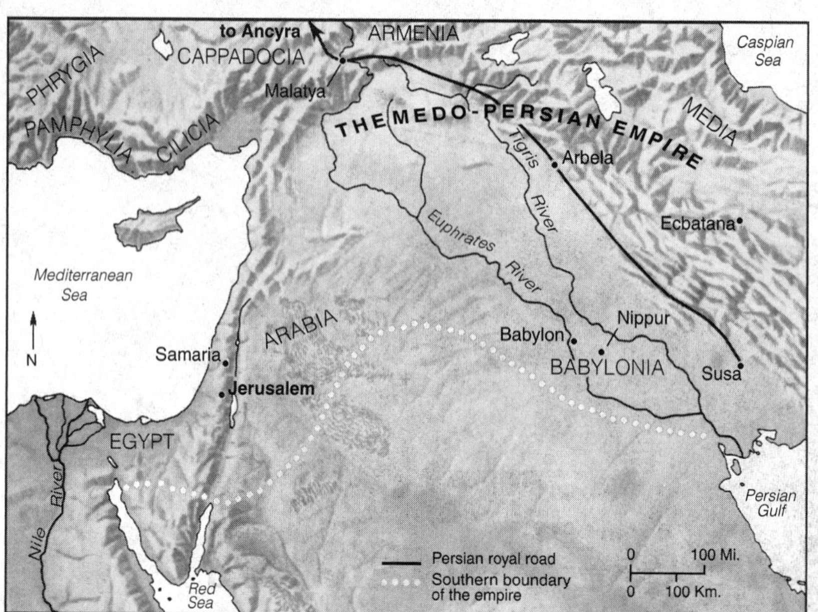


**THE MEDO-PERSIAN EMPIRE** The Medo-Persian empire included the lands of Media and Persia, much of the area shown on this map and more. The Jewish exiles were concentrated in the area around Nippur in the Babylonian province. King Cyrus's decree, which allowed the Israelites to return to their homeland and rebuild the Temple, was discovered in the palace of Achmetha (also called Ecbatana).

9 These were the items Cyrus donated:

gold trays . . . . . . . . . . 30
silver trays . . . . . . . . . . 1,000
silver censers* . . . . . . . . . . 29
10 gold bowls . . . . . . . . . . 30
silver bowls . . . . . . . . . . 410
other items . . . . . . . . . . 1,000

11 In all, 5,400 gold and silver items were turned over to Sheshbazzar to take back to Jerusalem when the exiles returned there from Babylon.

## CHAPTER 2

Here is the list of the Jewish exiles of the provinces who returned from their captivity to Jerusalem and to the other towns of Judah. They had been deported to Babylon by King Nebuchadnezzar.
2 Their leaders were Zerubbabel, Jeshua, Nehemiah, Seraiah, Reelaiah, Mordecai, Bilshan, Mispar, Bigvai, Rehum, and Baanah. This is the number of the men of Israel who returned from exile:

3 The family of Parosh . . . . . . . . . . 2,172
4 The family of Shephatiah . . . . . . . . . . 372
5 The family of Arah . . . . . . . . . . 775
6 The family of Pahath-moab (descendants of Jeshua and Joab) . . . . 2,812
7 The family of Elam . . . . . . . . . . 1,254
8 The family of Zattu . . . . . . . . . . 945
9 The family of Zaccai . . . . . . . . . . 760
10 The family of Bani . . . . . . . . . . 642
11 The family of Bebai . . . . . . . . . . 623
12 The family of Azgad . . . . . . . . . . 1,222
13 The family of Adonikam . . . . . . . . . . 666
14 The family of Bigvai . . . . . . . . . . 2,056
15 The family of Adin . . . . . . . . . . 454
16 The family of Ater (descendants of Hezekiah) . . . . . . . . . . 98
17 The family of Bezai . . . . . . . . . . 323
18 The family of Jorah . . . . . . . . . . 112
19 The family of Hashum . . . . . . . . . . 223
20 The family of Gibbar . . . . . . . . . . 95
21 The people of Bethlehem . . . . . . . . . . 123
22 The people of Netophah . . . . . . . . . . 56
23 The people of Anathoth . . . . . . . . . . 128
24 The people of Beth-azmaveth* . . . . . . . . . . 42
25 The peoples of Kiriath-jearim,* Kephirah, and Beeroth . . . . . . . . . . 743
26 The peoples of Ramah and Geba . . . . . . . . . . 621
27 The people of Micmash . . . . . . . . . . 122
28 The peoples of Bethel and Ai . . . . . . . . . . 223
29 The citizens of Nebo . . . . . . . . . . 52
30 The citizens of Magbish . . . . . . . . . . 156
31 The citizens of Elam . . . . . . . . . . 1,254
32 The citizens of Harim . . . . . . . . . . 320
33 The citizens of Lod, Hadid, and Ono . . . . . . . 725
34 The citizens of Jericho . . . . . . . . . . 345
35 The citizens of Senaah . . . . . . . . . . 3,630

36 These are the priests who returned from exile:

The family of Jedaiah (through the line of Jeshua) . . . . . . . . 973
37 The family of Immer . . . . . . . . . . 1,052
38 The family of Pashhur . . . . . . . . . . 1,247
39 The family of Harim . . . . . . . . . . 1,017

40 These are the Levites who returned from exile:

The families of Jeshua and Kadmiel (descendants of Hodaviah) . . . . . . . . . . 74

1:9 The meaning of this Hebrew word is uncertain. 2:24 As in parallel text at Neh 7:28; Hebrew reads *Azmaveth*. 2:25 As in some Hebrew manuscripts and Greek version (see also Neh 7:29); Hebrew reads *Kiriath-arim*.

41 The singers of the family of Asaph . . . . . . . . . 128
42 The gatekeepers of the families of Shallum, Ater,
Talmon, Akkub, Hatita, and Shobai . . . . 139

43 The descendants of the following Temple
servants returned from exile:
Ziha, Hasupha, Tabbaoth,
44 Keros, Siaha, Padon,
45 Lebanah, Hagabah, Akkub,
46 Hagab, Shalmai,* Hanan,
47 Giddel, Gahar, Reaiah,
48 Rezin, Nekoda, Gazzam,
49 Uzza, Paseah, Besai,
50 Asnah, Meunim, Nephusim,
51 Bakbuk, Hakupha, Harhur,
52 Bazluth, Mehida, Harsha,
53 Barkos, Sisera, Temah,
54 Neziah, and Hatipha.

55 The descendants of these servants of King
Solomon returned from exile:
Sotai, Sophereth,* Peruda,
56 Jaalah, Darkon, Giddel,
57 Shephatiah, Hattil, Pokereth-hazzebaim, and
Ami.

58 In all, the Temple servants and the descendants of
Solomon's servants numbered 392.

59 Another group returned to Jerusalem at this time
from the towns of Tel-melah, Tel-harsha, Kerub, Addan, and Immer. However, they could not prove that
they or their families were descendants of Israel.
60 This group consisted of the families of Delaiah,
Tobiah, and Nekoda—a total of 652 people.

61 Three families of priests—Hobaiah, Hakkoz,
and Barzillai—also returned to Jerusalem. (This Barzillai had married a woman who was a descendant
of Barzillai of Gilead, and he had taken her family
name.) 62 But they had lost their genealogical records,
so they were not allowed to serve as priests. 63 The
governor would not even let them eat the priests'
share of food from the sacrifices until there was a
priest who could consult the LORD about the matter
by means of sacred lots.*

64 So a total of 42,360 people returned to Judah,
65 in addition to 7,337 servants and 200 singers, both
men and women. 66 They took with them 736 horses,
245 mules, 67 435 camels, and 6,720 donkeys.

68 When they arrived at the Temple of the LORD in
Jerusalem, some of the family leaders gave generously toward the rebuilding of God's Temple on its
original site, 69 and each leader gave as much as he
could. The total of their gifts came to 61,000 gold
coins,* 6,250 pounds* of silver, and 100 robes for
the priests.

70 So the priests, the Levites, the singers, the gatekeepers, the Temple servants, and some of the common people settled in villages near Jerusalem. The
rest of the people returned to the other towns of
Judah from which they had come.

## CHAPTER 3

**THE NEW TEMPLE.** Now in early autumn,* when the Israelites had settled in their
towns, all the people assembled together as one
person in Jerusalem. 2 Then Jeshua son of Jehozadak* with his fellow priests and Zerubbabel son of
Shealtiel with his family began to rebuild the altar of
the God of Israel so they could sacrifice burnt offerings on it, as instructed in the law of Moses, the man
of God. 3 Even though the people were afraid of the
local residents, they rebuilt the altar at its old site.
Then they immediately began to sacrifice burnt offerings on the altar to the LORD. They did this each
morning and evening.

4 They celebrated the Festival of Shelters as prescribed in the law of Moses, sacrificing the burnt offerings specified for each day of the festival. 5 They also
offered the regular burnt offerings and the offerings
required for the new moon celebrations and the other
annual festivals to the LORD. Freewill offerings were
also sacrificed to the LORD by the people. 6 Fifteen days
before the Festival of Shelters began,* the priests had
begun to sacrifice burnt offerings to the LORD. This was
also before they had started to lay the foundation of
the LORD's Temple.

7 Then they hired masons and carpenters and
bought cedar logs from the people of Tyre and Sidon, paying them with food, wine, and olive oil. The
logs were brought down from the Lebanon mountains and floated along the coast of the Mediterranean Sea to Joppa, for King Cyrus had given
permission for this.

8 The construction of the Temple of God began in
midspring,* during the second year after they arrived
in Jerusalem. The work force was made up of everyone who had returned from exile, including Zerubbabel son of Shealtiel, Jeshua son of Jehozadak and
his fellow priests, and all the Levites. The Levites who
were twenty years old or older were put in charge of
rebuilding the LORD's Temple. 9 The workers at the
Temple of God were supervised by Jeshua with his
sons and relatives, and Kadmiel and his sons, all

**PREPARE ● ● • • •**

**3:8 It took from autumn (3:1) to spring just to *prepare* to build the Temple. During this time, the altar was built, materials were ordered and collected, and workers were hired. The exiles took some time to make plans because the project was important to them. Preparation may not feel heroic or spiritual, but it is vital to any project meant to be done well.**

2:46 As in the marginal *Qere* reading of the Masoretic Text (see also Neh 7:48); Hebrew text reads *Shamlai.* 2:55 As in parallel text at Neh 7:57; Hebrew reads *Hassophereth.* 2:63 Hebrew *consult the Urim and Thummim about the matter.* 2:69a Hebrew *61,000 darics of gold,* about 1,100 pounds or 500 kilograms in weight. 2:69b Hebrew *5,000 minas* [3 metric tons]. 3:1 Hebrew *in the seventh month.* The year is not specific, so it may have been during Cyrus's first year (538 B.C.) or second year (537 B.C.). The seventh month of the Hebrew lunar calendar occurred in September/October 538 B.C. and October/November 537 B.C. 3:2 Hebrew *Jozadak,* a variant name for Jehozadak; also in 3:8. 3:6 Hebrew *On the first day of the seventh month.* This day of the Hebrew lunar calendar occurs in September or October. The Festival of Shelters began on the fifteenth day of the seventh month. 3:8 Hebrew *in the second month.* This month of the Hebrew lunar calendar occurred in April and May 536 B.C.

descendants of Hodaviah.* They were helped in this task by the Levites of the family of Henadad.

[10]When the builders completed the foundation of the LORD's Temple, the priests put on their robes and took their places to blow their trumpets. And the Levites, descendants of Asaph, clashed their cymbals to praise the LORD, just as King David had prescribed. [11]With praise and thanks, they sang this song to the LORD:

"He is so good!
His faithful love for Israel endures forever!"

Then all the people gave a great shout, praising the LORD because the foundation of the LORD's Temple had been laid.

[12]Many of the older priests, Levites, and other leaders remembered the first Temple, and they wept aloud when they saw the new Temple's foundation. The others, however, were shouting for joy. [13]The joyful shouting and weeping mingled together in a loud commotion that could be heard far in the distance.

CHAPTER **4** **ENEMIES TRY TO STOP THE TEMPLE.** The enemies of Judah and Benjamin heard that the exiles were rebuilding a Temple to the LORD, the God of Israel. [2]So they approached Zerubbabel and the other leaders and said, "Let us build with you, for we worship your God just as you do. We have sacrificed to him ever since King Esarhaddon of Assyria brought us here."

**OBSTACLES ● ● • • •**

4:1-6 **Believers can expect opposition as they do God's work (2 Timothy 3:12). Unbelievers and evil spiritual forces are always working against God and his people. The opposition may involve offers of alliance (4:2), attempts to discourage and intimidate (4:4-5), or unjust accusations (4:6). If you learn to expect this opposition, you won't be halted by it. Move ahead with the work God has planned for you, and trust him to show you the way to overcome the obstacles.**

[3]But Zerubbabel, Jeshua, and the other leaders of Israel replied, "You may have no part in this work, for we have nothing in common. We alone will build the Temple for the LORD, the God of Israel, just as King Cyrus of Persia commanded us."

[4]Then the local residents tried to discourage and frighten the people of Judah to keep them from their work. [5]They bribed agents to work against them and to frustrate their aims. This went on during the entire reign of King Cyrus of Persia and lasted until King Darius of Persia took the throne.

[6]Years later when Xerxes* began his reign, the enemies of Judah wrote him a letter of accusation against the people of Judah and Jerusalem. [7]And even later, during the reign of King Artaxerxes of Persia,* the enemies of Judah, led by Bishlam, Mithredath, and Tabeel, sent a letter to Artaxerxes in the Aramaic language, and it was translated for the king. [8]Rehum* the governor and Shimshai the court secretary wrote the letter, telling King Artaxerxes about the situation in Jerusalem. [9]They greeted the king for all their colleagues—the judges and local leaders, the people of Tarpel, the Persians, the Babylonians, and the people of Erech and Susa (that is, Elam). [10]They also sent greetings from the rest of the people whom the great and noble Ashurbanipal* had deported and relocated in Samaria and throughout the neighboring lands of the province west of the Euphrates River. [11]This is a copy of the letter they sent him:

"To Artaxerxes, from your loyal subjects in the province west of the Euphrates River.

[12]"Please be informed that the Jews who came here to Jerusalem from Babylon are rebuilding this rebellious and evil city. They have already laid the foundation for its walls and will soon complete them. [13]But we wish you to know that if this city is rebuilt and its walls are completed, it will be much to your disadvantage, for the Jews will then refuse to pay their tribute, customs, and tolls to you.

[14]"Since we are loyal to you as your subjects and we do not want to see you dishonored in this way, we have sent you this information. [15]We suggest that you search your ancestors' records, where you will discover what a rebellious city this has been in the past. In fact, it was destroyed because of its long history of sedition against the kings and countries who attempted to control it. [16]We declare that if this city is rebuilt and its walls are completed, the province west of the Euphrates River will be lost to you."

[17]Then Artaxerxes made this reply:

"To Rehum the governor, Shimshai the court secretary, and their colleagues living in Samaria and throughout the province west of the Euphrates River.

[18]"Greetings. The letter you sent has been translated and read to me. [19]I have ordered a search to be made of the records and have indeed found that Jerusalem has in times past been a hotbed of insurrection against many kings. In fact, rebellion and sedition are normal there! [20]Powerful kings have ruled over Jerusalem and the entire province west of the Euphrates River and have received vast tribute, customs, and tolls. [21]Therefore, issue orders to have these people stop their work. That city must not be rebuilt except at my express command. [22]Do not delay, for we must not permit the situation to get out of control."

[23]When this letter from King Artaxerxes was read

3:9 Hebrew *sons of Judah* (i.e., *bene Yehudah*). *Bene* might also be read here as the proper name Binnui; *Yehudah* is probably another name for Hodaviah. Compare 2:40; Neh 7:43; 1 Esdras 5:58. 4:6 Hebrew *Ahasuerus,* another name for Xerxes. He reigned 486–465 B.C. 4:7 Artaxerxes reigned 465–424 B.C. 4:8 The original text of 4:8–6:18 is in Aramaic. 4:10 Aramaic *Osnappar,* another name for Ashurbanipal.

to Rehum, Shimshai, and their colleagues, they
hurried to Jerusalem and forced the Jews to stop
building.
24The work on the Temple of God in Jerusalem
had stopped, and it remained at a standstill until the
second year of the reign of King Darius of Persia.*

CHAPTER **5** **THE REBUILDING CONTINUES.** At that time
the prophets Haggai and Zechariah son of Iddo
prophesied in the name of the God of Israel to the
Jews in Judah and Jerusalem. 2Zerubbabel son of
Shealtiel and Jeshua son of Jehozadak* responded
by beginning the task of rebuilding the Temple of
God in Jerusalem. And the prophets of God were
with them and helped them.
3But Tattenai, governor of the province west of the
Euphrates, and Shethar-bozenai and their colleagues
soon arrived in Jerusalem and asked, "Who gave you
permission to rebuild this Temple and restore this
structure?" 4They also asked for a list of the names of
all the people who were working on the Temple. 5But
because their God was watching over them, the leaders of the Jews were not prevented from building
until a report was sent to Darius and he returned his
decision.
6This is the letter that Tattenai the governor, Shethar-bozenai, and the other officials of the province
west of the Euphrates River sent to King Darius:

7"Greetings to King Darius. 8We wish to inform
you that we went to the construction site of the
Temple of the great God in the province of
Judah. It is being rebuilt with specially prepared
stones, and timber is being laid in its walls. The
work is going forward with great energy and
success. 9We asked the leaders, 'Who gave you
permission to rebuild this Temple and restore
this structure?' 10And we demanded their names
so that we could tell you who the leaders were.
11"This was their answer: 'We are the servants
of the God of heaven and earth, and we are
rebuilding the Temple that was built here many
years ago by a great king of Israel. 12But because
our ancestors angered the God of heaven, he
abandoned them to King Nebuchadnezzar of
Babylon,* who destroyed this Temple and exiled
the people to Babylonia. 13However, King Cyrus
of Babylon,* during the first year of his reign,
issued a decree that the Temple of God should
be rebuilt. 14King Cyrus returned the gold and
silver utensils that Nebuchadnezzar had taken
from the Temple of God in Jerusalem and had
placed in the temple of Babylon. These items
were taken from that temple and delivered into
the safekeeping of a man named Sheshbazzar,
whom King Cyrus appointed as governor of
Judah. 15The king instructed him to return the
utensils to their place in Jerusalem and to
rebuild the Temple of God there as it had been
before. 16So this Sheshbazzar came and laid the
foundations of the Temple of God in Jerusalem.
The people have been working on it ever since,
though it is not yet completed.'
17"So now, if it pleases the king, we request
that you search in the royal archives of Babylon
to discover whether King Cyrus ever issued a
decree to rebuild God's Temple in Jerusalem.
And then let the king send us his decision in
this matter."

CHAPTER **6** **KING DARIUS APPROVES.** So King Darius
issued orders that a search be made in the Babylonian archives, where treasures were stored. 2But it
was at the fortress at Ecbatana in the province of
Media that a scroll was found. This is what it said:

3"Memorandum:
"In the first year of King Cyrus's reign, a decree
was sent out concerning the Temple of God at
Jerusalem. It must be rebuilt on the site where
Jews used to offer their sacrifices, retaining the
original foundations. Its height will be ninety
feet, and its width will be ninety feet.* 4Every
three layers of specially prepared stones will be
topped by a layer of timber. All expenses will be
paid by the royal treasury. 5And the gold and
silver utensils, which were taken to Babylon by
Nebuchadnezzar from the Temple of God in
Jerusalem, will be taken back to Jerusalem and
put into God's Temple as they were before."

6So King Darius sent this message:

"To Tattenai, governor of the province west of
the Euphrates River, to Shethar-bozenai, and to
your colleagues and other officials west of the
Euphrates:
"Stay away from there! 7Do not disturb the
construction of the Temple of God. Let it be

**BOLD ● ● • • ·**

5:11 **While rebuilding the Temple, the workers were confronted by the Persia-appointed governor demanding to know who gave permission for their construction project (5:3). This could have been intimidating, but, as we learn from the letter, they boldly replied, "We are the servants of the God of heaven and earth."**

**It is not always easy to speak up for our faith in an unbelieving world, but we must. The way to deal with pressure and intimidation is to recognize that we are workers for God. Our allegiance is to him first, people second. When we contemplate the reactions and criticisms of hostile people, we can become paralyzed with fear. If we make a policy of offending no one or pleasing everyone, our effectiveness will be stopped. God is our leader, and his rewards are most important. So don't be intimidated. Let others know by your actions and words whom you serve first.**

**4:24** The second year of Darius's reign was 520 B.C. **5:2** Aramaic *Jozadak,* a variant name for Jehozadak. **5:12** Aramaic *Nebuchadnezzar the Chaldean.* **5:13** King Cyrus of Persia is here identified as the king of Babylon because Persia had conquered the Babylonian Empire. **6:3** Aramaic *Its height will be 60 cubits* [27 meters], *and its width will be 60 cubits.* It is commonly held that this verse should be emended to read: "Its height will be 45 feet, its length will be 90 feet, and its width will be 30 feet"; compare 1 Kgs 6:2. The emendation regarding the width is supported by the Syriac version.

rebuilt on its former site, and do not hinder the governor of Judah and the leaders of the Jews in their work. [8]Moreover I hereby decree that you are to help these leaders of the Jews as they rebuild this Temple of God. You must pay the full construction costs without delay from my taxes collected in your province so that the work will not be discontinued. [9]Give the priests in Jerusalem whatever is needed in the way of young bulls, rams, and lambs for the burnt offerings presented to the God of heaven. And without fail, provide them with the wheat, salt, wine, and olive oil that they need each day. [10]Then they will be able to offer acceptable sacrifices to the God of heaven and pray for me and my sons.

## VALUES

See Sylvia, the brown-haired girl sitting on the bench in front of the gym? Watch her for a few minutes.

Though she seems pretty happy on the outside, on the inside she's seriously confused!

It all started two weeks ago when she attended an after-school debate on this resolution: "Resolved: Absolute standards for human behavior do not exist."

What Sylvia first saw as an easy opportunity for some quick extra credit in speech class has turned into a long and difficult struggle of the soul. She's not sure what she thinks about anything . . . or even *how* to think about anything.

"The team that was to argue in favor of the resolution just about had me convinced," Sylvia says, "but then the other team raised a lot of troubling questions in my mind.

"Even though the crowd ended up voting for the resolution, I'm not so sure. I mean, if there aren't any hard and fast rules about anything, then nothing makes sense. 'Right' and 'wrong' don't have meaning.

"There must be some values that hold true for everyone. But once you get beyond murder and child abuse, I'm not sure what they are."

If you are looking for some help concerning how you should live and what values to base your actions upon, take a lesson from an Old Testament scribe named Ezra. Read Ezra 7:10 to find out the best standard for right and wrong.

[11]"Those who violate this decree in any way will have a beam pulled from their house. Then they will be tied to it and flogged, and their house will be reduced to a pile of rubble.* [12]May the God who has chosen the city of Jerusalem as the place to honor his name destroy any king or nation that violates this command and destroys this Temple. I, Darius, have issued this decree. Let it be obeyed with all diligence."

[13]Tattenai, governor of the province west of the Euphrates River, and Shethar-bozenai and their colleagues complied at once with the command of King

## TIMING

**6:16-22 Feasting and celebration were in order at the great Temple dedication. But the priests and Levites were organized into groups in order to "serve at the Temple of God . . . following all the instructions recorded in the Book of Moses." There is a time to celebrate, but there also is a time to work. Both, in their time, are proper and necessary when worshiping and serving God; and God is evident in both.**

Darius. [14]So the Jewish leaders continued their work, and they were greatly encouraged by the preaching of the prophets Haggai and Zechariah son of Iddo. The Temple was finally finished, as had been commanded by the God of Israel and decreed by Cyrus, Darius, and Artaxerxes, the kings of Persia. [15]The Temple was completed on March 12,* during the sixth year of King Darius's reign.

[16]The Temple of God was then dedicated with great joy by the people of Israel, the priests, the Levites, and the rest of the people who had returned from exile. [17]During the dedication ceremony for the Temple of God, one hundred young bulls, two hundred rams, and four hundred lambs were sacrificed. And twelve male goats were presented as a sin offering for the twelve tribes of Israel. [18]Then the priests and Levites were divided into their various divisions to serve at the Temple of God in Jerusalem, following all the instructions recorded in the Book of Moses.

[19]On April 21* the returned exiles celebrated Passover. [20]The priests and Levites had purified themselves and were ceremonially clean. So they slaughtered the Passover lamb for all the returned exiles, for the other priests, and for themselves. [21]The Passover meal was eaten by the people of Israel who had returned from exile and by the others in the land who had turned from their immoral customs to worship the LORD, the God of Israel. [22]They ate the Passover meal and celebrated the Festival of Unleavened Bread for seven days. There was great joy throughout the land because the LORD had changed the attitude of the king of Assyria* toward them, so that he helped them to rebuild the Temple of God, the God of Israel.

## CHAPTER 7

**EZRA COMES TO TEACH.** Many years later, during the reign of King Artaxerxes of Persia,* there was a man named Ezra. He was the son* of Seraiah, son of Azariah, son of Hilkiah, [2]son of Shallum, son of Zadok, son of Ahitub, [3]son of Amariah, son of Azariah, son* of Meraioth, [4]son of Zerahiah, son of Uzzi, son of Bukki, [5]son of Abishua, son of Phinehas, son of Eleazar, son of Aaron the high priest. [6]This Ezra was a scribe, well versed in the law of Moses, which the LORD, the God of Israel, had given to the people of Israel. He came up to Jerusalem from Babylon, and the king gave him everything he asked for, because the gracious hand of the LORD his God was on him. [7]Some of the people of Israel, as

6:11 Aramaic *a dunghill.* 6:15 Aramaic *on the third day of the month Adar,* of the Hebrew calendar. This event occurred on March 12, 515 B.C.; also see note on 3:1. 6:19 Hebrew *On the fourteenth day of the first month,* of the Hebrew calendar. This event occurred on April 21, 515 B.C.; also see note on 3:1. 6:22 King Darius of Persia is here identified as the king of Assyria because Persia had conquered the Babylonian Empire, which included the earlier Assyrian Empire. 7:1a Artaxerxes reigned 465–424 B.C. 7:1b Or *descendant;* see 1 Chr 6:14. 7:3 Or *descendant;* see 1 Chr 6:6-10.

There was
great
joy
throughout the land.
EZRA 6:22

well as some of the priests, Levites, singers, gatekeepers, and Temple servants, traveled up to Jerusalem
with him in the seventh year of King Artaxerxes'
reign.
8Ezra arrived in Jerusalem in August* of that year.
9He had left Babylon on April 8* and came to Jerusalem on August 4,* for the gracious hand of his
God was on him. 10This was because Ezra had determined to study and obey the law of the LORD and to
teach those laws and regulations to the people of
Israel.
11King Artaxerxes had given a copy of the following
letter to Ezra, the priest and scribe who studied and
taught the commands and laws of the LORD to Israel:

12"Greetings* from Artaxerxes, the king of kings,
to Ezra the priest, the teacher of the law of the
God of heaven.

13"I decree that any of the people of Israel in my
kingdom, including the priests and Levites, may
volunteer to return to Jerusalem with you. 14I
and my Council of Seven hereby instruct you to
conduct an inquiry into the situation in Judah
and Jerusalem, based on your God's law, which
is in your hand. 15We also commission you to
take with you some silver and gold, which we
are freely presenting as an offering to the God of
Israel who lives in Jerusalem.
16"Moreover you are to take any silver and
gold which you may obtain from the province
of Babylon, as well as the freewill offerings of
the people and the priests that are presented for
the Temple of their God in Jerusalem. 17These
donations are to be used specifically for the
purchase of bulls, rams, lambs, and the
appropriate grain offerings and drink offerings,
all of which will be offered on the altar of the
Temple of your God in Jerusalem. 18Any money
that is left over may be used in whatever way
you and your colleagues feel is the will of your
God. 19But as for the utensils we are entrusting
to you for the service of the Temple of your
God, deliver them in full to the God of
Jerusalem. 20If you run short of money for
anything necessary for your God's Temple or for
any similar needs, you may requisition funds
from the royal treasury.
21"I, Artaxerxes the king, hereby send this
decree to all the treasurers in the province west
of the Euphrates River: 'You are to give Ezra
whatever he requests of you, for he is a priest
and teacher of the law of the God of heaven.
22You are to give him up to 7,500 pounds* of
silver, 500 bushels* of wheat, 550 gallons of
wine, 550 gallons of olive oil,* and an
unlimited supply of salt. 23Be careful to provide
whatever the God of heaven demands for his
Temple, for why should we risk bringing God's
anger against the realm of the king and his
sons? 24I also decree that no priest, Levite, singer,
gatekeeper, Temple servant, or other worker in
this Temple of God will be required to pay taxes
of any kind.'
25"And you, Ezra, are to use the wisdom God
has given you to appoint magistrates and judges
who know your God's laws to govern all the
people in the province west of the Euphrates
River. If the people are not familiar with those
laws, you must teach them. 26Anyone who
refuses to obey the law of your God and the law
of the king will be punished immediately by

**TAX-EXEMPT ● ● ● • •**

7:24 **Why did Artaxerxes exempt Temple workers from paying taxes? He recognized that the priests and Levites filled an important role in society as spiritual leaders, so he freed them of tax burdens. Artaxerxes, a pagan king, recognized and supported the principle of keeping worldly burdens off the shoulders of spiritual workers. Today that responsibility is given to churches.**

7:8 Hebrew *in the fifth month.* This month of the Hebrew lunar calendar occurred in August and September 458 B.C. **7:9a** Hebrew *on the first day of the first month,* of the Hebrew calendar. This event occurred on April 8, 458 B.C.; also see note on 3:1. **7:9b** Hebrew *on the first day of the fifth month,* of the Hebrew calendar. This event occurred on August 4, 458 B.C.; also see note on 3:1. **7:12** The original text of 7:12-26 is in Aramaic. **7:22a** Aramaic *100 talents* [3.4 metric tons]. **7:22b** Aramaic *100 cors* [18.2 kiloliters]. **7:22c** Aramaic *100 baths* [2.1 kiloliters] *of wine, 100 baths of olive oil.*

death, banishment, confiscation of goods, or
imprisonment."

27 Praise the LORD, the God of our ancestors, who
made the king want to beautify the Temple of the
LORD in Jerusalem! 28 And praise him for demonstrating such unfailing love to me by honoring me
before the king, his council, and all his mighty
princes! I felt encouraged because the gracious
hand of the LORD my God was on me. And I gathered some of the leaders of Israel to return with me
to Jerusalem.

CHAPTER **8** **THE EXILES WHO RETURNED.** Here is a list
of the family leaders and the genealogies of those
who came with me from Babylon during the reign of
King Artaxerxes:

2 From the family of Phinehas: Gershom.
From the family of Ithamar: Daniel.
3 From the family of David: Hattush son of
Shecaniah.
From the family of Parosh: Zechariah and 150
other men.
4 From the family of Pahath-moab: Eliehoenai son
of Zerahiah and 200 other men.
5 From the family of Zattu*: Shecaniah son of
Jahaziel and 300 other men.
6 From the family of Adin: Ebed son of Jonathan
and 50 other men.
7 From the family of Elam: Jeshaiah son of
Athaliah and 70 other men.
8 From the family of Shephatiah: Zebadiah son
of Michael and 80 other men.
9 From the family of Joab: Obadiah son of Jehiel
and 218 other men.
10 From the family of Bani*: Shelomith son of
Josiphiah and 160 other men.
11 From the family of Bebai: Zechariah son of Bebai
and 28 other men.
12 From the family of Azgad: Johanan son of
Hakkatan and 110 other men.
13 From the family of Adonikam, who came later*:
Eliphelet, Jeuel, Shemaiah, and 60 other
men.
14 From the family of Bigvai: Uthai, Zaccur, and
70 other men.

15 I assembled the exiles at the Ahava Canal, and
we camped there for three days while I went over
the lists of the people and the priests who had
arrived. I found that not one Levite had volunteered to come along. 16 So I sent for Eliezer, Ariel,
Shemaiah, Elnathan, Jarib, Elnathan, Nathan,
Zechariah, and Meshullam, who were leaders of
the people. I also sent for Joiarib and Elnathan,
who were very wise men. 17 I sent them to Iddo, the
leader of the Levites at Casiphia, to ask him and his
relatives and the Temple servants to send us ministers for the Temple of God at Jerusalem. 18 Since the
gracious hand of our God was on us, they sent us a
man named Sherebiah, along with eighteen of his
sons and brothers. He was a very astute man and a
descendant of Mahli, who was a descendant of Levi
son of Israel.* 19 They also sent Hashabiah, together with Jeshaiah from the descendants of Merari, and twenty of his sons and brothers, 20 and 220
Temple servants. The Temple servants were assistants to the Levites—a group of Temple workers
first instituted by King David. They were all listed
by name.

**JOURNEY ● ● ● • •**

**8:21 Ezra and the people traveled approximately nine hundred miles on foot. The trip took them through dangerous and difficult territory and lasted about four months. They prayed that God would protect them and give them a good journey. Our journeys today may not be as difficult and dangerous as Ezra's, but we should feel free to ask God for guidance and protection.**

21 And there by the Ahava Canal, I gave orders for
all of us to fast and humble ourselves before our
God. We prayed that he would give us a safe journey
and protect us, our children, and our goods as we
traveled. 22 For I was ashamed to ask the king for
soldiers and horsemen to accompany us and protect
us from enemies along the way. After all, we had told
the king, "Our God protects all those who worship
him, but his fierce anger rages against those who
abandon him." 23 So we fasted and earnestly prayed
that our God would take care of us, and he heard our
prayer.

24 I appointed twelve leaders of the priests—
Sherebiah, Hashabiah, and ten other priests—25 to
be in charge of transporting the silver, the gold, the
gold bowls, and the other items that the king, his
council, his leaders, and the people of Israel had
presented for the Temple of God. 26 I weighed the
treasure as I gave it to them and found the totals to
be as follows:

24 tons* of silver,
7,500 pounds* of silver utensils,
7,500 pounds* of gold,
27 20 gold bowls, equal in value to 1,000 gold
coins,*
2 fine articles of polished bronze, as precious
as gold.

28 And I said to these priests, "You and these
treasures have been set apart as holy to the LORD.
This silver and gold is a freewill offering to the
LORD, the God of our ancestors. 29 Guard these treasures well until you present them, without an
ounce lost, to the leading priests, the Levites, and
the leaders of Israel at the storerooms of the LORD's
Temple in Jerusalem." 30 So the priests and the Le-

8:5 As in some Greek manuscripts (see also 1 Esdras 8:32); Hebrew lacks *Zattu.* 8:10 As in some Greek manuscripts (see also 1 Esdras 8:36); Hebrew lacks *Bani.* 8:13 The meaning of the Hebrew for this phrase is uncertain. 8:18 *Israel* is the name that God gave to Jacob. 8:26a Hebrew *650 talents* [22 metric tons]. 8:26b Hebrew *100 talents* [3.4 metric tons]. 8:26c Hebrew *100 talents* [3.4 metric tons]. 8:27 Hebrew *1,000 darics,* about 19 pounds or 8.6 kilograms in weight.

vites accepted the task of transporting these treasures to the Temple of our God in Jerusalem.
31We broke camp at the Ahava Canal on
April 19* and started off to Jerusalem. And the
gracious hand of our God protected us and saved
us from enemies and bandits along the way. 32So at
last we arrived safely in Jerusalem, where we rested
for three days.
33On the fourth day after our arrival, the silver,
gold, and other valuables were weighed at the
Temple of our God and entrusted to Meremoth son
of Uriah the priest and to Eleazar son of Phinehas,
along with Jozabad son of Jeshua and Noadiah son
of Binnui—both of whom were Levites. 34Everything
was accounted for by number and weight, and the
total weight was officially recorded.
35Then the exiles who had returned from captivity
sacrificed burnt offerings to the God of Israel. They
presented twelve oxen for the people of Israel, as well
as ninety-six rams and seventy-seven lambs. They
also offered twelve goats as a sin offering. All this was
given as a burnt offering to the LORD. 36The king's
decrees were delivered to his lieutenants and the
governors of the province west of the Euphrates
River, who then cooperated by supporting the
people and the Temple of God.

CHAPTER **9** **EZRA CONFESSES HIS PEOPLE'S SIN.** But
then the Jewish leaders came to me and said, "Many
of the people of Israel, and even some of the priests
and Levites, have not kept themselves separate from
the other peoples living in the land. They have taken
up the detestable practices of the Canaanites, Hittites, Perizzites, Jebusites, Ammonites, Moabites,
Egyptians, and Amorites. 2For the men of Israel have
married women from these people and have taken
them as wives for their sons. So the holy race has
become polluted by these mixed marriages. To make
matters worse, the officials and leaders are some of
the worst offenders."
3When I heard this, I tore my clothing, pulled
hair from my head and beard, and sat down utterly
shocked. 4Then all who trembled at the words of
the God of Israel came and sat with me because
of this unfaithfulness of his people. And I sat there
utterly appalled until the time of the evening sacrifice.
5At the time of the sacrifice, I stood up from
where I had sat in mourning with my clothes torn.
I fell to my knees, lifted my hands to the LORD my
God. 6I prayed, "O my God, I am utterly ashamed;
I blush to lift up my face to you. For our sins are
piled higher than our heads, and our guilt has
reached to the heavens. 7Our whole history has
been one of great sin. That is why we and our kings
and our priests have been at the mercy of the pagan
kings of the land. We have been killed, captured,
robbed, and disgraced, just as we are today.
8"But now we have been given a brief moment

### MARRIAGE ● ● • • •

9:2 **Opposition to mixed marriage was not racial prejudice, because Jews and non-Jews of this area were of the same semitic backgound. The reasons were strictly spiritual. Some Israelites had married heathen spouses and had lost track of God's purpose for them. The New Testament says that believers should not marry unbelievers (2 Corinthians 6:14). Such marriages cannot have unity in the most important issue in life—commitment and obedience to God. Because marriage involves two people becoming one, faith may become an issue. One spouse may have to compromise beliefs for the sake of unity. Don't allow emotion or passion to blind you to the ultimate importance of marrying someone with whom you can truly be united.**

of grace, for the LORD our God has allowed a few of
us to survive as a remnant. He has given us security
in this holy place. Our God has brightened our
eyes and granted us some relief from our slavery.
9For we were slaves, but in his unfailing love our
God did not abandon us in our slavery. Instead, he
caused the kings of Persia to treat us favorably. He
revived us so that we were able to rebuild the
Temple of our God and repair its ruins. He has
given us a protective wall in Judah and Jerusalem.
10"And now, O our God, what can we say after all
of this? For once again we have ignored your commands! 11Your servants the prophets warned us
that the land we would possess was totally defiled
by the detestable practices of the people living
there. From one end to the other, the land is filled
with corruption. 12You told us not to let our daughters marry their sons, and not to let our sons marry
their daughters, and not to help those nations in
any way. You promised that if we avoided these
things, we would become a prosperous nation. You
promised that we would enjoy the good produce of
the land and leave this prosperity to our children
as an inheritance forever.
13"Now we are being punished because of our
wickedness and our great guilt. But we have actually been punished far less than we deserve, for
you, our God, have allowed some of us to survive
as a remnant. 14But now we are again breaking your
commands and intermarrying with people who do
these detestable things. Surely your anger will destroy us until even this little remnant no longer
survives. 15O LORD, God of Israel, you are just. We

### ON HIS KNEES ● ● • • •

9:5-15 **After learning about the sins of the people, Ezra fell to his knees in prayer. His heartfelt prayer provides a good perspective on sin. He recognized (1) that sin is serious (9:6); (2) that no one sins without affecting others (9:7); (3) that he was not sinless, although he didn't have a heathen wife (9:10); and (4) that God's love and mercy had spared the nation when they did nothing to deserve it (9:8-9,15). It is easy to view sin lightly in a world that sees it as inconsequential, but we should view sin as seriously as Ezra did.**

**8:31** Hebrew *on the twelfth day of the first month,* of the Hebrew calendar. This event occurred on April 19, 458 B.C.; see note on 7:9a.

## OBEDIENCE ●●•••

**10:3 Why were the people commanded to divorce their wives and leave their children? Ezra's strong act, though very difficult for many, was necessary to preserve Israel as a nation committed to God. The exiles of the Northern Kingdom of Israel had lost both their spiritual and physical identity through intermarriage. Their heathen spouses had caused the people to worship idols. Ezra did not want this to happen to the exiles of the Southern Kingdom of Judah.**

**But we must not conclude from this incident that God approves of divorce. Elsewhere in Scripture, God makes it clear that he hates divorce (Malachi 2:15-16; Matthew 19:8). The Israelites had disobeyed by intermarrying in the first place, and now they found themselves being forced to choose between two painful and unpleasant options: continue in these sinful marriages or divorce and send their children away. We must be very careful to obey the guidelines and commands God has given us in his Word, so that we don't find ourselves facing a no-win situation as the Israelites did here.**

stand before you in our guilt as nothing but an
escaped remnant, though in such a condition none
of us can stand in your presence."

CHAPTER **10** **THE PEOPLE CONFESS THEIR SIN.**
While Ezra prayed and made this confession,
weeping and throwing himself to the ground in
front of the Temple of God, a large crowd of people
from Israel—men, women, and children—gathered and wept bitterly with him. 2 Then Shecaniah
son of Jehiel, a descendant of Elam, said to Ezra,
"We confess that we have been unfaithful to our
God, for we have married these pagan women of
the land. But there is hope for Israel in spite of this.
3 Let us now make a covenant with our God to
divorce our pagan wives and to send them away
with their children. We will follow the advice given
by you and by the others who respect the commands of our God. We will obey the law of God.
4 Take courage, for it is your duty to tell us how to
proceed in setting things straight, and we will cooperate fully."

5 So Ezra stood up and demanded that the leaders of the priests and the Levites and all the people
of Israel swear that they would do as Shecaniah
had said. And they all swore a solemn oath. 6 Then
Ezra left the front of the Temple of God and went
to the room of Jehohanan son of Eliashib. He
spent the night* there, but he did not eat any food
or drink. He was still in mourning because of the
unfaithfulness of the returned exiles. 7 Then a proclamation was made throughout Judah and Jerusalem that all the returned exiles should come to
Jerusalem. 8 Those who failed to come within three
days would, if the leaders and elders so decided,
forfeit all their property and be expelled from the
assembly of the exiles.

9 Within three days, all the people of Judah and
Benjamin had gathered in Jerusalem. This took place
on December 19,* and all the people were sitting in
the square before the Temple of God. They were
trembling both because of the seriousness of the
matter and because it was raining. 10 Then Ezra the
priest stood and said to them: "You have sinned, for
you have married pagan women. Now we are even
more deeply under condemnation than we were
before. 11 Confess your sin to the LORD, the God of
your ancestors, and do what he demands. Separate
yourselves from the people of the land and from
these pagan women."

12 Then the whole assembly raised their voices
and answered, "Yes, you are right; we must do as
you say!" 13 Then they added, "This isn't something that can be done in a day or two, for many of
us are involved in this extremely sinful affair. This
is the rainy season, so we cannot stay out here
much longer. 14 Let our leaders act on behalf of us
all. Everyone who has a pagan wife will come at the
scheduled time with the leaders and judges of his
city, so that the fierce anger of our God may be
turned away from us concerning this affair." 15 Only
Jonathan son of Asahel and Jahzeiah son of Tikvah
opposed this course of action, and Meshullam and
Shabbethai the Levite supported them.

16 So this was the plan that they followed. Ezra
selected leaders to represent their families, designat-
ing each of the representatives by name. On December 29,* the leaders sat down to investigate the
matter. 17 By March 27 of the next year* they had
finished dealing with all the men who had married
pagan wives.

18 These are the priests who had married pagan
wives:

From the family of Jeshua son of Jehozadak* and
his brothers: Maaseiah, Eliezer, Jarib, and
Gedaliah. 19 They vowed to divorce their wives,
and they each acknowledged their guilt by
offering a ram as a guilt offering.
20 From the family of Immer: Hanani and Zebadiah.
21 From the family of Harim: Maaseiah, Elijah,
Shemaiah, Jehiel, and Uzziah.
22 From the family of Pashhur: Elioenai, Maaseiah,
Ishmael, Nethanel, Jozabad, and Elasah.

## CHANGED ●●•••

**10:3-4, 11 Following Ezra's earnest prayer, the people admitted their sin to God. Then they asked for direction in restoring their relationship with God. True repentance does not end when we speak words of confession—that would be mere lip service. It must lead to corrected behavior and changed attitudes. When you sin and are truly sorry, confess this to God, ask his forgiveness, and accept his grace and mercy. Then, as an act of thankfulness for your forgiveness, change your ways.**

10:6 As in parallel text at 1 Esdras 9:2; Hebrew reads *He went.* 10:9 Hebrew *on the twentieth day of the ninth month,* of the Hebrew calendar. This event occurred on December 19, 458 B.C.; also see note on 7:9a. 10:16 Hebrew *On the first day of the tenth month,* of the Hebrew calendar. This event occurred on December 29, 458 B.C.; also see note on 7:9a. 10:17 Hebrew *By the first day of the first month,* of the Hebrew calendar. This event occurred on March 27, 457 B.C.; also see note on 7:9a. 10:18 Hebrew *Jozadak,* a variant name for Jehozadak.

[23]These are the Levites who were guilty: Jozabad,
Shimei, Kelaiah (also called Kelita), Pethahiah,
Judah, and Eliezer.

[24]This is the singer who was guilty: Eliashib.

These are the gatekeepers who were guilty:
Shallum, Telem, and Uri.

[25]These are the other people of Israel who were
guilty:

From the family of Parosh: Ramiah, Izziah,
Malkijah, Mijamin, Eleazar, Hashabiah,* and
Benaiah.
[26]From the family of Elam: Mattaniah, Zechariah,
Jehiel, Abdi, Jeremoth, and Elijah.
[27]From the family of Zattu: Elioenai, Eliashib,
Mattaniah, Jeremoth, Zabad, and Aziza.
[28]From the family of Bebai: Jehohanan, Hananiah,
Zabbai, and Athlai.
[29]From the family of Bani: Meshullam, Malluch,
Adaiah, Jashub, Sheal, and Jeremoth.
[30]From the family of Pahath-moab: Adna, Kelal,
Benaiah, Maaseiah, Mattaniah, Bezalel, Binnui,
and Manasseh.
[31]From the family of Harim: Eliezer, Ishijah,
Malkijah, Shemaiah, Shimeon, [32]Benjamin,
Malluch, and Shemariah.

## REBUILT ● ● • • •

**10:44 The book of Ezra opens with God's Temple in ruins and the people of Judah captive in Babylon. Ezra tells of the return of God's people, the rebuilding of the Temple, and the restoration of the sacrificial worship system. Similarly, God is able to restore and rebuild the lives of people today. No one is so far away from God that he or she cannot be restored. Repentance is all that is required. No matter how far we have strayed, or how long it has been since we have worshiped God, he is able to restore our relationship to him and rebuild our life.**

[33]From the family of Hashum: Mattenai, Mattattah,
Zabad, Eliphelet, Jeremai, Manasseh, and
Shimei.
[34]From the family of Bani: Maadai, Amram, Uel,
[35]Benaiah, Bedeiah, Keluhi, [36]Vaniah,
Meremoth, Eliashib, [37]Mattaniah, Mattenai, and
Jaasu.
[38]From the family of Binnui*: Shimei, [39]Shelemiah,
Nathan, Adaiah, [40]Macnadebai, Shashai, Sharai,
[41]Azarel, Shelemiah, Shemariah, [42]Shallum,
Amariah, and Joseph.
[43]From the family of Nebo: Jeiel, Mattithiah,
Zabad, Zebina, Jaddai, Joel, and Benaiah.

[44]Each of these men had a pagan wife, and some
even had children by these wives.*

10:25 As in parallel text at 1 Esdras 9:26; Hebrew reads *Malkijah.* 10:37-38 As in Greek version; Hebrew reads *Jaasu,* [38]*Bani, Binnui.* 10:44 Or *and they sent them away with their children.* The meaning of the Hebrew is uncertain.

# MEGA themes

**JEWS RETURN** By returning to the land of Israel from Babylon, the Jews showed their faith in God's promise to restore them as his people. They returned not only to their homeland, but also to the place where their forefathers had promised to follow God.

God shows his mercy to every generation. He compassionately restores his people. No matter how difficult our present "captivity," we are never far from his love and mercy. He restores us when we return to him.

1. Imagine that you are one of those who returned to the homeland after being released from captivity. How do you feel? What are you thinking about as you return to your home?
2. Undoubtedly this generation of Jews had heard about the sins that had led their forefathers into captivity. What type of commitment to God do you think they carried with them as they returned to Jerusalem? How do you think they would use their new freedom to worship?
3. In what sense were you a slave to sin until you received Christ's forgiveness? How are you using your freedom in Christ to worship God?
4. Identify creative ways (1) to worship God in your freedom and (2) to communicate this freedom to those still enslaved by sin.

**OPPOSITION** Opposition came soon after the altar was built and the Temple foundation was laid. For more than six years, the enemies of the Jews used deceit to hinder the building. Finally, there was a decree to stop construction altogether. This opposition severely tested the Jews' wavering faith.

There always will be people who oppose God's work. The life of faith is never easy, but God can overrule all opposition. We must not falter or withdraw from our enemies; we need to stay active and patient. God is with us in every circumstance.

1. Why and how did some people try to keep the Jews from building the Temple?
2. Why do some people strongly oppose Christianity and Christians? Give some examples of how they do this.
3. When have you thought about giving up your Christian witness because you felt alone or opposed? How did you work through those feelings so that you did not give up?
4. If a Christian friend was facing tough opposition from kids at school who were making fun of him and trying to discourage his faith, what would you do to encourage him to remain true to Christ?
5. Do you know someone who needs encouragement because of obstacles and/or opposition he or she is facing? List specific ways you can encourage that person. How will you do this in the next week?
6. If you were (or are) facing opposition, to whom could you go for encouragement?

**GOD'S WORD** When the people returned to the Promised Land, they were also returning to the influence of God's Word. The prophets Haggai and Zechariah helped encourage them, while Ezra's preaching of Scripture built them up. God's Word gave them what they needed to do God's work.

We also need the encouragement and direction of God's Word. We must never waver in our commitment to hear and obey his Word and to keep the Word in our life daily.

1. What was the main message God gave through Haggai? Through Zechariah? Through Ezra?
2. What difference did it make whether or not the people obeyed the prophets' messages?
3. What are some of the most important lessons you have learned through reading and studying God's Word?
4. What difference has obeying (or not obeying) God's Word made in your life?
5. Based on this study, what would you tell a new

Christian about the importance of the Bible in the Christian life?

**FAITH/ACTION** The urging of Israel's leaders motivated the people to complete the Temple. But over the years, many of them had intermarried with idol worshipers and adopted their heathen practices. It wasn't until their faith was tested and strengthened that they removed these sins from their lives.

Faith led God's people to complete the Temple and to remove sin from their society. As we trust God with our heart and mind, we also must put our faith into action.

1. In this book, how did the Jews put their faith into action?
2. In the last year, what decisions did you make as a result of your faith in God? The last month? The last week?
3. What decisions are you facing right now that will give you the opportunity to act on your faith?
4. The people supported each other in their commitment to put their faith into action. To whom can you turn for support in the decisions you listed in question 3?

586 B.C.
Jerusalem destroyed; exiles go to Babylon

537
First exiles return to Jerusalem

516
Temple completed

486
Ahasuerus (Xerxes I) becomes king of Persia

465
Artaxerxes I becomes king of Persia

458
Ezra comes to Jerusalem

445
Nehemiah comes to Jerusalem; wall completed

433
Nehemiah returns to Babylon

432
Nehemiah goes back to Jerusalem

430(?)
Malachi begins his ministry

Are you a leader? Most people think they are leaders, but real leadership is proven in adversity, in working through tough problems and painful situations. When tough times come, many would-be leaders find they fall apart. ■ Nehemiah was a proven leader. He left a secure position in the government of Persia to return to his homeland and rebuild the walls of Jerusalem. He succeeded, too, despite incredible obstacles and opposition. The book of Nehemiah tells his story. ■ We often dream of the glory and the praise of leadership, but we tend to forget about the turmoil and difficulty leadership can carry. God uses men and women who show the same tenacity that Nehemiah had. Unfortunately, not many people are like Nehemiah. Read the book to see true leadership in action. And ask God to help you become a leader like Nehemiah.

## STATS

PURPOSE: Nehemiah is the last of the Old Testament historical books. It records the history of the third return to Jerusalem after captivity, telling how the walls were rebuilt and how the people were renewed in their faith.

AUTHOR: Much of the book is written in the first person, suggesting Nehemiah as the author. Nehemiah probably wrote the book, with Ezra serving as editor.

DATE WRITTEN: Approximately 445–432 B.C.

SETTING: Zerubbabel led the first return to Jerusalem in 537 B.C. In 458, Ezra led the second return. Finally, in 445, Nehemiah returned with the third group of exiles to rebuild the city walls.

KEY PEOPLE: Nehemiah, Ezra, Sanballat, Tobiah

KEY PLACE: Jerusalem

SPECIAL FEATURE: The book shows the fulfillment of the prophecies of Zechariah and Daniel concerning the rebuilding of Jerusalem's walls

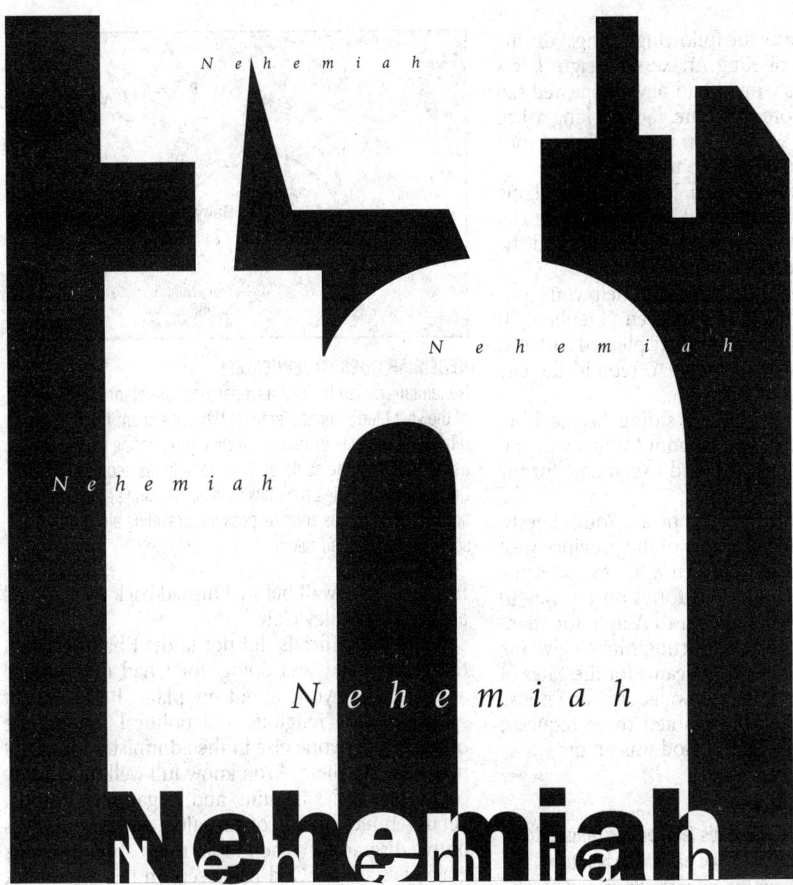


# Nehemiah

CHAPTER **1** **NEHEMIAH BEGS TO GO HOME.** These are
the memoirs of Nehemiah son of Hacaliah.
In late autumn of the twentieth year of King Artaxerxes' reign,* I was at the fortress of Susa. 2Hanani, one
of my brothers, came to visit me with some other men
who had just arrived from Judah. I asked them about
the Jews who had survived the captivity and about
how things were going in Jerusalem. 3They said to me,
"Things are not going well for those who returned to
the province of Judah. They are in great trouble and
disgrace. The wall of Jerusalem has been torn down,
and the gates have been burned."
4When I heard this, I sat down and wept. In fact, for
days I mourned, fasted, and prayed to the God of
heaven. 5Then I said, "O LORD, God of heaven, the
great and awesome God who keeps his covenant of
unfailing love with those who love him and obey his
commands, 6listen to my prayer! Look down and see
me praying night and day for your people Israel. I
confess that we have sinned against you. Yes, even my
own family and I have sinned! 7We have sinned terribly by not obeying the commands, laws, and regulations that you gave us through your servant Moses.
8"Please remember what you told your servant
Moses: 'If you sin, I will scatter you among the
nations. 9But if you return to me and obey my commands, even if you are exiled to the ends of the earth,
I will bring you back to the place I have chosen for
my name to be honored.'
10"We are your servants, the people you rescued by
your great power and might. 11O Lord, please hear
my prayer! Listen to the prayers of those of us who
delight in honoring you. Please grant me success
now as I go to ask the king* for a great favor. Put it
into his heart to be kind to me."
In those days I was the king's cup-bearer.

## TAKE ACTION ● ● • • •

1:4 **Nehemiah was deeply grieved about the condition of Jerusalem, but he didn't just brood about it. After his initial grief, he poured his heart out to God (1:5-11) and looked for ways to improve the situation. He put all his resources of knowledge, experience, and organization into determining what should be done. When tragic news comes to you, first pray. Then seek ways to move beyond grief to specific action that offers help to those who need it.**

1:1 Hebrew *In the month of Kislev of the twentieth year.* A number of dates in the book of Nehemiah can be cross-checked with dates in surviving Persian records and related accurately to our modern calendar. This month of the Hebrew lunar calendar occurred in November and December 446 B.C. The *twentieth year* probably refers to the reign of King Artaxerxes I; compare 2:1; 5:14. 1:11 Hebrew *stand before this man.*

## CHAPTER 2

Early the following spring,* during the twentieth year of King Artaxerxes' reign, I was serving the king his wine. I had never appeared sad in his presence before this time. 2So the king asked me, "Why are you so sad? You aren't sick, are you? You look like a man with deep troubles."

Then I was badly frightened, 3but I replied, "Long live the king! Why shouldn't I be sad? For the city where my ancestors are buried is in ruins, and the gates have been burned down."

4The king asked, "Well, how can I help you?"

With a prayer to the God of heaven, 5I replied, "If it please Your Majesty and if you are pleased with me, your servant, send me to Judah to rebuild the city where my ancestors are buried."

6The king, with the queen sitting beside him, asked, "How long will you be gone? When will you return?" So the king agreed, and I set a date for my departure.

7I also said to the king, "If it please Your Majesty, give me letters to the governors of the province west of the Euphrates River, instructing them to let me travel safely through their territories on my way to Judah. 8And please send a letter to Asaph, the manager of the king's forest, instructing him to give me timber. I will need it to make beams for the gates of the Temple fortress, for the city walls, and for a house for myself." And the king granted these requests, because the gracious hand of God was on me.

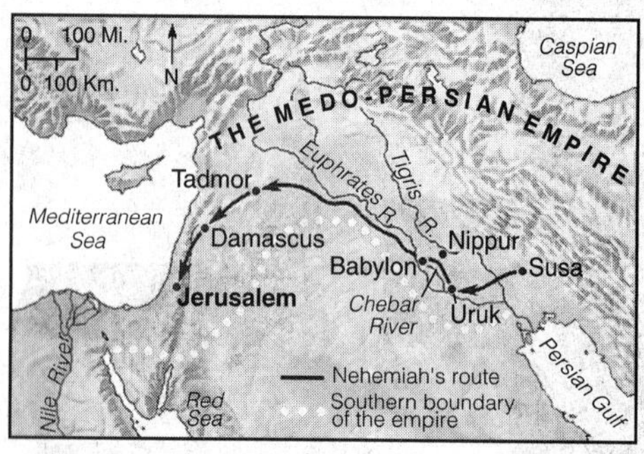


**NEHEMIAH GOES TO JERUSALEM**
Nehemiah worked in Susa as a personal assistant for the king of the vast Medo-Persian empire. When he heard that the rebuilding projects in Jerusalem were progressing slowly, he asked the king if he could go there to help his people complete the task of rebuilding their city's walls. The king agreed to let him go; so he left as soon as possible, traveling along much the same route Ezra had taken.

### HAVE NO FEAR

2:3 **Nehemiah wasn't ashamed to admit his fear, but he refused to allow fear to stop him from doing what God had called him to do. When we allow our fears to rule our life, we make them more powerful than God. Is there something God wants you to do, but fear is holding you back? God is greater than all our fears. Recognizing your fear is the first step in committing it to God. If God has called you to a task, he will help you accomplish it.**

9When I came to the governors of the province west of the Euphrates River, I delivered the king's letters to them. The king, I should add, had sent along army officers and horsemen to protect me. 10But when Sanballat the Horonite and Tobiah the Ammonite official heard of my arrival, they were very angry that someone had come who was interested in helping Israel.

11Three days after my arrival at Jerusalem, 12I slipped out during the night, taking only a few others with me. I had not told anyone about the plans God had put in my heart for Jerusalem. We took no pack animals with us, except the donkey that I myself was riding. 13I went out through the Valley Gate, past the Jackal's Well,* and over to the Dung Gate to inspect the broken walls and burned gates. 14Then I went to the Fountain Gate and to the King's Pool, but my donkey couldn't get through the rubble. 15So I went up the Kidron Valley* instead, inspecting the wall before I turned back and entered again at the Valley Gate.

16The city officials did not know I had been out there or what I was doing, for I had not yet said anything to anyone about my plans. I had not yet spoken to the religious and political leaders, the officials, or anyone else in the administration. 17But now I said to them, "You know full well the tragedy of our city. It lies in ruins, and its gates are burned. Let us rebuild the wall of Jerusalem and rid ourselves of this disgrace!" 18Then I told them about how the gracious hand of God had been on me, and about my conversation with the king.

They replied at once, "Good! Let's rebuild the wall!" So they began the good work.

19But when Sanballat, Tobiah, and Geshem the Arab heard of our plan, they scoffed contemptuously. "What are you doing, rebelling against the king like this?" they asked.

20But I replied, "The God of heaven will help us succeed. We his servants will start rebuilding this wall. But you have no stake or claim in Jerusalem."

## CHAPTER 3

**THE BUILDERS OF THE CITY WALL.** Then Eliashib the high priest and the other priests started to rebuild at the Sheep Gate. They dedicated it and set up its doors, building the wall as far as the Tower of the Hundred, which they dedicated, and the Tower of Hananel. 2People from the city of Jericho worked next to them, and beyond them was Zaccur son of Imri.

3The Fish Gate was built by the sons of Hassenaah. They did the whole thing—laid the beams, hung the doors, and put the bolts and bars in place. 4Meremoth son of Uriah and grandson of Hakkoz repaired the next section of wall. Beside him were Meshullam son of Berekiah and grandson of Meshezabel, and then Zadok son of Baana. 5Next

2:1 Hebrew *In the month of Nisan.* This month of the Hebrew lunar calendar occurred in April and May 445 B.C. 2:13 Or *Serpent's Well.* 2:15 Hebrew *the valley.*

were the people from Tekoa, though their leaders
refused to help.

[6]The Old City Gate* was repaired by Joiada son of
Paseah and Meshullam son of Besodeiah. They laid
the beams, set up the doors, and installed the bolts
and bars. [7]Next to them were Melatiah from Gibeon,
Jadon from Meronoth, and people from Gibeon and
Mizpah, the headquarters of the governor of the
province west of the Euphrates River. [8]Next was Uzziel son of Harhaiah, a goldsmith by trade, who also
worked on the wall. Beyond him was Hananiah, a
manufacturer of perfumes. They left out* a section
of Jerusalem as far as the Broad Wall.

[9]Rephaiah son of Hur, the leader of half the
district of Jerusalem, was next to them on the wall.
[10]Next Jedaiah son of Harumaph repaired the wall
beside his own house, and next to him was Hattush
son of Hashabneiah. [11]Then came Malkijah son of
Harim and Hasshub son of Pahath-moab, who
repaired the Tower of the Ovens, in addition to
another section of the wall. [12]Shallum son of Hal-
lohesh and his daughters repaired the next section.
He was the leader of the other half of the district of
Jerusalem.

[13]The people from Zanoah, led by Hanun, rebuilt
the Valley Gate, hung its doors, and installed the
bolts and bars. They also repaired the fifteen hundred feet* of wall to the Dung Gate.

[14]The Dung Gate was repaired by Malkijah son of
Recab, the leader of the Beth-hakkerem district. After
rebuilding it, he hung the doors and installed the
bolts and bars.

[15]Shallum son of Col-hozeh, the leader of the
Mizpah district, repaired the Fountain Gate. He rebuilt it, roofed it, hung its doors, and installed its
bolts and bars. Then he repaired the wall of the pool
of Siloam* near the king's garden, and he rebuilt the
wall as far as the stairs that descend from the City of
David. [16]Next to him was Nehemiah son of Azbuk,
the leader of half the district of Beth-zur. He rebuilt
the wall to a place opposite the royal cemetery as far
as the water reservoir and the House of the Warriors.

[17]Next was a group of Levites working under the
supervision of Rehum son of Bani. Then came Hashabiah, the leader of half the district of Keilah, who
supervised the building of the wall on behalf of his
own district. [18]Next down the line were his countrymen led by Binnui* son of Henadad, the leader of
the other half of the district of Keilah.

[19]Next to them, Ezer son of Jeshua, the leader of
Mizpah, repaired another section of wall opposite
the armory by the buttress. [20]Next to him was Baruch
son of Zabbai, who repaired an additional section
from the buttress to the door of the home of Eliashib
the high priest. [21]Meremoth son of Uriah and grandson of Hakkoz rebuilt another section of the wall
extending from a point opposite the door of Eliashib's house to the side of the house.

[22]Then came the priests from the surrounding
region. [23]After them, Benjamin, Hasshub, and Azariah son of Maaseiah and grandson of Ananiah repaired the sections next to their own houses. [24]Next
was Binnui son of Henadad, who rebuilt another
section of the wall from Azariah's house to the buttress and the corner. [25]Palal son of Uzai carried on
the work from a point opposite the buttress and the
corner to the upper tower that projects from the
king's house beside the court of the guard. Next to
him were Pedaiah son of Parosh [26]and the Temple
servants living on the hill of Ophel, who repaired the
wall as far as the Water Gate toward the east and the
projecting tower. [27]Then came the people of Tekoa,
who repaired another section opposite the great projecting tower and over to the wall of Ophel.

[28]The priests repaired the wall up the hill from the
Horse Gate, each one doing the section immediately
opposite his own house. [29]Next Zadok son of Immer
also rebuilt the wall next to his own house, and
beyond him was Shemaiah son of Shecaniah, the
gatekeeper of the East Gate. [30]Next Hananiah son of
Shelemiah and Hanun, the sixth son of Zalaph,
repaired another section, while Meshullam son of
Berekiah rebuilt the wall next to his own house.
[31]Malkijah, one of the goldsmiths, repaired the wall
as far as the housing for the Temple servants and
merchants, opposite the Inspection Gate. Then he
continued as far as the upper room at the corner.
[32]The other goldsmiths and merchants repaired the
wall from that corner to the Sheep Gate.

CHAPTER **4** **NEHEMIAH BUILDS THE WALLS.** Sanballat
was very angry when he learned that we were rebuilding the wall. He flew into a rage and mocked
the Jews, [2]saying in front of his friends and the
Samarian army officers, "What does this bunch of
poor, feeble Jews think they are doing? Do they think
they can build the wall in a day if they offer enough
sacrifices? Look at those charred stones they are pulling out of the rubbish and using again!"

[3]Tobiah the Ammonite, who was standing beside

## VISION ● ● • • ·

**2:17-18 Spiritual renewal often begins with one person's vision. Nehemiah had a vision, and he shared it with enthusiasm, inspiring Jerusalem's leaders to rebuild the wall.**

**We frequently underestimate people and don't challenge them with our dreams for God's work in the world. When God plants an idea in your mind to accomplish something for him, share it with others and trust the Holy Spirit to impress them with similar thoughts. Don't see yourself as the only one through whom God is working. Often God uses one person to express the vision and others to turn it into reality. When you encourage and inspire others, you put teamwork into action to accomplish God's goals.**

3:6 Or *The Mishneh Gate,* or *The Jeshanah Gate.* 3:8 Or *They restored.* 3:13 Hebrew *1,000 cubits* [450 meters]. 3:15 Hebrew *pool of Shelah,* another name for the pool of Siloam. 3:18 As in a few Hebrew manuscripts, some Greek manuscripts, and Syriac version (see also 3:24; 10:9); most Hebrew manuscripts read *Bavvai.*

him, remarked, "That stone wall would collapse if even a fox walked along the top of it!"

4Then I prayed, "Hear us, O our God, for we are being mocked. May their scoffing fall back on their own heads, and may they themselves become captives in a foreign land! 5Do not ignore their guilt. Do not blot out their sins, for they have provoked you to anger here in the presence of* the builders."

6At last the wall was completed to half its original height around the entire city, for the people had worked very hard. 7But when Sanballat and Tobiah and the Arabs, Ammonites, and Ashdodites heard that the work was going ahead and that the gaps in the wall were being repaired, they became furious. 8They all made plans to come and fight against Jerusalem and to bring about confusion there. 9But we prayed to our God and guarded the city day and night to protect ourselves.

## PPOSITION

At a church camp this summer, Billy was challenged to "try to start a Bible study at your school when classes start again in the fall."

*That's an awesome idea!* Billy thought. So he started praying about it and, in time, he became convinced that this was something God wanted him to do. Billy decided to go for it. He never dreamed such a simple plan would become such a big deal.

From the beginning, he's encountered opposition.

- The principal doesn't want to give him a room (even though Billy keeps assuring him that the Bible study will not take place during school hours).
- No faculty members will agree to sponsor the group.
- A few Christian friends are urging him to forget it.
- A lot of Billy's classmates are calling him "the Pope" and "Brother Billy."
- One big guy (who's very anti-Christian) has been trying to pick a fight during P.E. class.

With all these obstacles, Billy is wondering whether it's worth it after all. "I don't have to start a Bible study to be a good Christian. Besides, I can do without all this grief."

Is Billy right in dumping his plan? Would you like to learn how to remain calm in the face of opposition? Are you interested in discovering the secret to hanging in there when people mock your faith? Read Nehemiah 4.

10Then the people of Judah began to complain that the workers were becoming tired. There was so much rubble to be moved that we could never get it done by ourselves. 11Meanwhile, our enemies were saying, "Before they know what's happening, we will swoop down on them and kill them and end their work."

12The Jews who lived near the enemy came and told us again and again, "They will come from all directions and attack us!"* 13So I placed armed guards behind the lowest parts of the wall in the exposed areas. I stationed the people to stand guard by families, armed with swords, spears, and bows.

14Then as I looked over the situation, I called together the leaders and the people and said to them, "Don't be afraid of the enemy! Remember the Lord, who is great and glorious, and fight for your friends, your families, and your homes!"

15When our enemies heard that we knew of their plans and that God had frustrated them, we all returned to our work on the wall. 16But from then on, only half my men worked while the other half stood guard with spears, shields, bows, and coats of mail. The officers stationed themselves behind the people of Judah 17who were building the wall. The common laborers carried on their work with one hand supporting their load and one hand holding a weapon. 18All the builders had a sword belted to their side. The trumpeter stayed with me to sound the alarm.

19Then I explained to the nobles and officials and all the people, "The work is very spread out, and we are widely separated from each other along the wall. 20When you hear the blast of the trumpet, rush to wherever it is sounding. Then our God will fight for us!"

21We worked early and late, from sunrise to sunset. And half the men were always on guard. 22I also told everyone living outside the walls to move into Jerusalem. That way they and their servants could go on guard duty at night as well as work during the day. 23During this time, none of us—not I, nor my relatives, nor my servants, nor the guards who were with me—ever took off our clothes. We carried our weapons with us at all times, even when we went for water.*

CHAPTER **5** **NEHEMIAH DEFENDS THE POOR.** About this time some of the men and their wives raised a cry of protest against their fellow Jews. 2They were saying, "We have such large families. We need more money just so we can buy the food we need to survive." 3Others said, "We have mortgaged our fields, vineyards, and homes to get food during the famine." 4And others said, "We have already borrowed to the limit on our fields and vineyards to pay our taxes. 5We belong to the same family, and our children are just like theirs. Yet we must sell our children into slavery just to get enough money to live. We have already sold some of our daughters, and we are helpless to do anything about it, for our fields and vineyards are already mortgaged to others."

6When I heard their complaints, I was very angry. 7After thinking about the situation, I spoke out against these nobles and officials. I told them, "You are oppressing your own relatives by charging them interest when they borrow money!" Then I called a public meeting to deal with the problem.

4:5 Or *for they have thrown insults in the face of.* 4:12 The meaning of the Hebrew is uncertain. 4:23 Hebrew *Each his weapon the water.* The meaning of the Hebrew is uncertain.

8At the meeting I said to them, "The rest of us are
doing all we can to redeem our Jewish relatives who
have had to sell themselves to pagan foreigners, but
you are selling them back into slavery again. How
often must we redeem them?" And they had nothing
to say in their defense.
9Then I pressed further, "What you are doing is
not right! Should you not walk in the fear of our God
in order to avoid being mocked by enemy nations?
10I myself, as well as my brothers and my workers,
have been lending the people money and grain, but
now let us stop this business of loans. 11You must
restore their fields, vineyards, olive groves, and
homes to them this very day. Repay the interest you
charged on their money, grain, wine, and olive oil."
12Then they replied, "We will give back everything
and demand nothing more from the people. We will
do as you say." Then I called the priests and made the
nobles and officials formally vow to do what they
had promised.
13I shook out the fold of my robe and said, "If you
fail to keep your promise, may God shake you from
your homes and from your property!"
The whole assembly responded, "Amen," and
they praised the LORD. And the people did as they
had promised.
14I would like to mention that for the entire twelve
years that I was governor of Judah—from the twentieth until the thirty-second year of the reign of King
Artaxerxes*—neither I nor my officials drew on our
official food allowance. 15This was quite a contrast to
the former governors who had laid heavy burdens
on the people, demanding a daily ration of food and
wine, besides a pound* of silver. Even their assistants
took advantage of the people. But because of my fear
of God, I did not act that way. 16I devoted myself to
working on the wall and refused to acquire any land.
And I required all my officials to spend time working
on the wall. 17I asked for nothing, even though I
regularly fed 150 Jewish officials at my table, besides
all the visitors from other lands! 18The provisions
required at my expense for each day were one ox, six
fat sheep, and a large number of domestic fowl. And
every ten days we needed a large supply of all kinds
of wine. Yet I refused to claim the governor's food
allowance because the people were already having a
difficult time.

19Remember, O my God, all that I have done for
these people, and bless me for it.

CHAPTER **6** **NEHEMIAH FINISHES THE WALL.** When
Sanballat, Tobiah, Geshem the Arab, and the rest of
our enemies found out that I had finished rebuilding
the wall and that no gaps remained—though we had
not yet hung the doors in the gates—2Sanballat and
Geshem sent me a message asking me to meet them
at one of the villages* in the plain of Ono. But I
realized they were plotting to harm me, 3so I replied

### TIRED ● ● • • •

4:10-14 **Accomplishing any large task is tiring. There are always pressures that bring discouragement—the task seems impossible, it can never be finished, or too many things are working against you. The only cure for fatigue and discouragement is focusing on God's purposes. Nehemiah reminded the workers of their calling, of their goal, and of God's protection. If you are overwhelmed by an assignment, feeling tired and discouraged, remember God's purpose for your life and the special purpose of the project.**

by sending this message to them: "I am doing a great
work! I cannot stop to come and meet with you."
4Four times they sent the same message, and each
time I gave the same reply. 5The fifth time, Sanballat's servant came with an open letter in his hand,
6and this is what it said:

"Geshem* tells me that everywhere he goes he
hears that you and the Jews are planning to
rebel and that is why you are building the wall.
According to his reports, you plan to be their
king. 7He also reports that you have appointed
prophets to prophesy about you in Jerusalem,
saying, 'Look! There is a king in Judah!'
"You can be very sure that this report will get
back to the king, so I suggest that you come and
talk it over with me."

8My reply was, "You know you are lying. There is
no truth in any part of your story." 9They were just
trying to intimidate us, imagining that they could
break our resolve and stop the work. So I prayed for
strength to continue the work.
10Later I went to visit Shemaiah son of Delaiah
and grandson of Mehetabel, who was confined to
his home. He said, "Let us meet together inside the
Temple of God and bolt the doors shut. Your enemies are coming to kill you tonight."
11But I replied, "Should someone in my position
run away from danger? Should someone in my position enter the Temple to save his life? No, I won't do
it!" 12I realized that God had not spoken to him, but
that he had uttered this prophecy against me because
Tobiah and Sanballat had hired him. 13They were
hoping to intimidate me and make me sin by following his suggestion. Then they would be able to accuse and discredit me.

### COURAGE ● ● • • •

6:10-13 **When Nehemiah was attacked personally, he refused to give in to fear and flee to the Temple. According to God's law, it would have been wrong for Nehemiah to go into the Temple to hide because he wasn't a priest (Numbers 18:22). If he had run for his life, he would have undermined the courage he was trying to instill in the people. Leaders are targets for attacks. Make it a practice to pray for those in authority (1 Timothy 2:2). Pray that they will stand against personal attacks and temptation. They need God-given courage to overcome fear.**

5:14 That is, from 445 to 433 B.C. 5:15 Hebrew *40 shekels* [456 grams]. 6:2 As in Greek version; Hebrew reads *at Kephirim*. 6:6 Hebrew *Gashmu*, another name for Geshem.

14 Remember, O my God, all the evil things that
Tobiah and Sanballat have done. And remember
Noadiah the prophet and all the prophets like
her who have tried to intimidate me.

15 So on October 2* the wall was finally finished—
just fifty-two days after we had begun. 16 When our
enemies and the surrounding nations heard about it,
they were frightened and humiliated. They realized
that this work had been done with the help of our
God.

17 During those fifty-two days, many letters went
back and forth between Tobiah and the officials of
Judah. 18 For many in Judah had sworn allegiance to
him because his father-in-law was Shecaniah son of
Arah and because his son Jehohanan was married to
the daughter of Meshullam son of Berekiah. 19 They
kept telling me what a wonderful man Tobiah was,
and then they told him everything I said. And Tobiah
sent many threatening letters to intimidate me.

## CHAPTER 7

1 After the wall was finished and I
had hung the doors in the gates, the gatekeepers,
singers, and Levites were appointed. 2 I gave the responsibility of governing Jerusalem to my brother
Hanani, along with Hananiah, the commander of
the fortress, for he was a faithful man who feared
God more than most. 3 I said to them, "Do not leave
the gates open during the hottest part of the day.*
And while the gatekeepers are still on duty, have
them shut and bar the doors. Appoint the residents
of Jerusalem to act as guards, everyone on a regular
watch. Some will serve at their regular posts and
some in front of their own homes."

### FOLLOW-UP ● ● • • •

7:3-4 **The wall was complete, but the work was not finished. Nehemiah assigned each family the task of protecting the section of wall next to their home. It is tempting to relax our guard and rest on past accomplishments after we have completed a large task. But we must continue to serve and to take care of all that God has entrusted to us. Following through after a project is completed is as vital as doing the project itself.**

4 At that time the city was large and spacious, but the
population was small. And only a few houses were
scattered throughout the city. 5 So my God gave me the
idea to call together all the leaders of the city, along
with the ordinary citizens, for registration. I had found
the genealogical record of those who had first returned
to Judah. This is what was written there:

6 "Here is the list of the Jewish exiles of the provinces who returned from their captivity to Jerusalem
and to the other towns of Judah. They had been
deported to Babylon by King Nebuchadnezzar.
7 Their leaders were Zerubbabel, Jeshua, Nehemiah,
Seraiah,* Reelaiah,* Nahamani, Mordecai, Bilshan,
Mispar,* Bigvai, Rehum,* and Baanah. This is the
number of men of Israel who returned from exile:

8 The family of Parosh . . . . . . . . . . . . . . . . . . 2,172
9 The family of Shephatiah . . . . . . . . . . . . . . . . 372
10 The family of Arah . . . . . . . . . . . . . . . . . . . 652
11 The family of Pahath-moab
(descendants of Jeshua and Joab) . . . . 2,818
12 The family of Elam . . . . . . . . . . . . . . . . . . 1,254
13 The family of Zattu . . . . . . . . . . . . . . . . . . . 845
14 The family of Zaccai . . . . . . . . . . . . . . . . . . 760
15 The family of Bani* . . . . . . . . . . . . . . . . . . . 648
16 The family of Bebai . . . . . . . . . . . . . . . . . . . 628
17 The family of Azgad . . . . . . . . . . . . . . . . . 2,322
18 The family of Adonikam . . . . . . . . . . . . . . . . 667
19 The family of Bigvai . . . . . . . . . . . . . . . . . 2,067
20 The family of Adin . . . . . . . . . . . . . . . . . . . 655
21 The family of Ater
(descendants of Hezekiah) . . . . . . . . . . . 98
22 The family of Hashum . . . . . . . . . . . . . . . . . 328
23 The family of Bezai . . . . . . . . . . . . . . . . . . . 324
24 The family of Jorah* . . . . . . . . . . . . . . . . . . 112
25 The family of Gibbar* . . . . . . . . . . . . . . . . . . 95
26 The peoples of Bethlehem
and Netophah . . . . . . . . . . . . . . . . . . . 188
27 The people of Anathoth . . . . . . . . . . . . . . . . 128
28 The people of Beth-azmaveth . . . . . . . . . . . . . . 42
29 The peoples of Kiriath-jearim,
Kephirah, and Beeroth . . . . . . . . . . . . . . 743
30 The peoples of Ramah and Geba . . . . . . . . . . . 621
31 The people of Micmash . . . . . . . . . . . . . . . . 122
32 The peoples of Bethel and Ai . . . . . . . . . . . . . 123
33 The people of Nebo . . . . . . . . . . . . . . . . . . . . 52
34 The citizens of Elam . . . . . . . . . . . . . . . . . 1,254
35 The citizens of Harim . . . . . . . . . . . . . . . . . 320
36 The citizens of Jericho . . . . . . . . . . . . . . . . . 345
37 The citizens of Lod, Hadid, and Ono . . . . . . . 721
38 The citizens of Senaah . . . . . . . . . . . . . . . 3,930

39 "These are the priests who returned from exile:

The family of Jedaiah
(through the line of Jeshua) . . . . . . . . . 973
40 The family of Immer . . . . . . . . . . . . . . . . . 1,052
41 The family of Pashhur . . . . . . . . . . . . . . . 1,247
42 The family of Harim . . . . . . . . . . . . . . . . . 1,017

43 "These are the Levites who returned from exile:

The families of Jeshua and Kadmiel
(descendants of Hodaviah*) . . . . . . . . . . 74
44 The singers of the family of Asaph . . . . . . . . . . 148
45 The gatekeepers of the families of
Shallum, Ater, Talmon, Akkub,
Hatita, and Shobai . . . . . . . . . . . . . . . . 138

46 "The descendants of the following Temple
servants returned from exile:
Ziha, Hasupha, Tabbaoth,
47 Keros, Siaha,* Padon,

6:15 Hebrew *on the twenty-fifth day of the month Elul,* of the Hebrew calendar. This event occurred on October 2, 445 B.C.; also see note on 1:1.
7:3 Or *Keep the gates of Jerusalem closed until the sun is hot.* 7:7a As in parallel text at Ezra 2:2; Hebrew reads *Azariah.* 7:7b As in parallel text at Ezra 2:2; Hebrew reads *Raamiah.* 7:7c As in parallel text at Ezra 2:2; Hebrew reads *Mispereth.* 7:7d As in parallel text at Ezra 2:2; Hebrew reads *Nehum.*
7:15 As in parallel text at Ezra 2:10; Hebrew reads *Binnui.* 7:24 As in parallel text at Ezra 2:18; Hebrew reads *Hariph.* 7:25 As in parallel text at Ezra 2:20; Hebrew reads *Gibeon.* 7:43 As in parallel text at Ezra 2:40; Hebrew reads *Hodevah.* 7:47 As in parallel text at Ezra 2:44; Hebrew reads *Sia.*

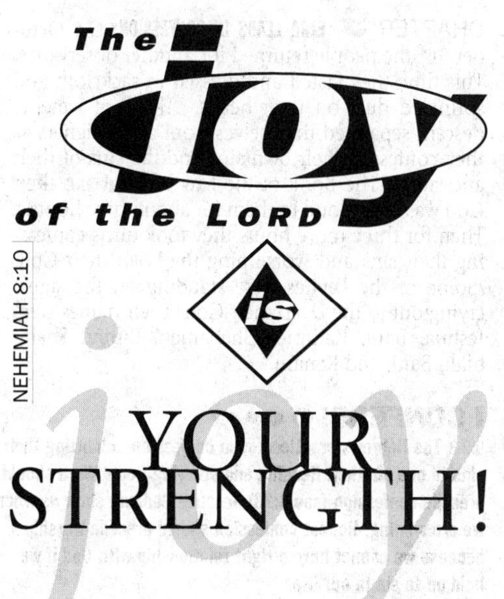
The joy of the LORD
is
YOUR STRENGTH!
NEHEMIAH 8:10

[48] Lebanah, Hagabah, Shalmai,
[49] Hanan, Giddel, Gahar,
[50] Reaiah, Rezin, Nekoda,
[51] Gazzam, Uzza, Paseah,
[52] Besai, Meunim, Nephusim,*
[53] Bakbuk, Hakupha, Harhur,
[54] Bazluth,* Mehida, Harsha,
[55] Barkos, Sisera, Temah,
[56] Neziah, and Hatipha.

[57] "The descendants of these servants of King
Solomon returned from exile:
Sotai, Sophereth, Peruda,*
[58] Jaalah,* Darkon, Giddel,
[59] Shephatiah, Hattil, Pokereth-hazzebaim, and Ami.*

[60] "In all, the Temple servants and the descendants of
Solomon's servants numbered 392.

[61] "Another group returned to Jerusalem at this
time from the towns of Tel-melah, Tel-harsha, Kerub,
Addan,* and Immer. However, they could not prove
that they or their families were descendants of Israel.
[62] This group included the families of Delaiah, Tobiah, and Nekoda—a total of 642 people.
[63] "Three families of priests—Hobaiah, Hakkoz,
and Barzillai—also returned to Jerusalem. (This Barzillai had married a woman who was a descendant
of Barzillai of Gilead, and he had taken her family
name.) [64] But they had lost their genealogical records,
so they were not allowed to serve as priests. [65] The
governor would not even let them eat the priests'
share of food from the sacrifices until there was a
priest who could consult the LORD about the matter
by means of sacred lots.*

[66] "So a total of 42,360 people returned to Judah,
[67] in addition to 7,337 servants and 245 singers, both
men and women. [68] They took with them 736 horses,
245 mules,* [69] 435 camels, and 6,720 donkeys.

[70] "Some of the family leaders gave gifts for the
work. The governor gave to the treasury 1,000 gold
coins,* 50 gold basins, and 530 robes for the priests.
[71] The other leaders gave to the treasury a total of
20,000 gold coins* and some 2,750 pounds* of
silver for the work. [72] The rest of the people gave
20,000 gold coins, about 2,500 pounds* of silver,
and 67 robes for the priests.

[73] "So the priests, the Levites, the gatekeepers, the
singers, the Temple servants, along with some of the
people—that is to say, all Israel—settled in their
own towns."

Now in midautumn,* when the Israelites had
settled in their towns, [1] all the people assembled
together as one person at the square just inside the
Water Gate. They asked Ezra the scribe to bring out
the Book of the Law of Moses, which the LORD had
given for Israel to obey.

CHAPTER **8** **EZRA READS THE LAW.** [2] So on October 8*
Ezra the priest brought the scroll of the law before the
assembly, which included the men and women and all
the children old enough to understand. [3] He faced the
square just inside the Water Gate from early morning
until noon and read aloud to everyone who could
understand. All the people paid close attention to the
Book of the Law. [4] Ezra the scribe stood on a high
wooden platform that had been made for the occasion. To his right stood Mattithiah, Shema, Anaiah,
Uriah, Hilkiah, and Maaseiah. To his left stood Pedaiah, Mishael, Malkijah, Hashum, Hashbaddanah,
Zechariah, and Meshullam. [5] Ezra stood on the platform in full view of all the people. When they saw him
open the book, they all rose to their feet.

[6] Then Ezra praised the LORD, the great God, and
all the people chanted, "Amen! Amen!" as they
lifted their hands toward heaven. Then they bowed

**APPLY IT ● ● ● ● ●**

8:1-5 **The people paid close attention to Ezra as he read God's Word, and their lives were changed. Because we hear the Bible so often, we can become dulled to its words and immune to its teachings. Instead, we should *listen* carefully to every verse and ask the Holy Spirit to help us answer the question, "How does this apply to *my* life?"**

**7:52** As in parallel text at Ezra 2:50; Hebrew reads *Nephushesim.* **7:54** As in parallel text at Ezra 2:52; Hebrew reads *Bazlith.* **7:57** As in parallel text at Ezra 2:55; Hebrew reads *Perida.* **7:58** As in parallel text at Ezra 2:56; Hebrew reads *Jaala.* **7:59** As in parallel text at Ezra 2:57; Hebrew reads *Amon.* **7:61** As in parallel text at Ezra 2:59; Hebrew reads *Addon.* **7:65** Hebrew *consult the Urim and Thummim about the matter.* **7:68** As in some Hebrew manuscripts (see also Ezra 2:66); most Hebrew manuscripts lack this verse. **7:70** Hebrew *1,000 darics of gold,* about 19 pounds or 8.6 kilograms in weight. **7:71a** Hebrew *20,000 darics of gold,* about 375 pounds or 170 kilograms in weight; also in 7:72. **7:71b** Hebrew *2,200 minas* [1.3 metric tons]. **7:72** Hebrew *2,000 minas* [1.2 metric tons]. **7:73** Hebrew *in the seventh month.* This month of the Hebrew lunar calendar occurred in October and November 445 B.C. **8:2** Hebrew *on the first day of the seventh month,* of the Hebrew calendar. This event occurred on October 8, 445 B.C.; also see note on 1:1.

## ACT ON IT! ● ● • • •

8:13-14 **After Ezra read God's laws to the people, they studied them further and then acted upon them. A careful reading of Scripture always calls for a response to these questions: "What should I *do* with this knowledge?" "How should my life change?" We must *do* something about what we have learned if it is to have real significance for our life.**

down and worshiped the LORD with their faces to the ground.

7Now the Levites—Jeshua, Bani, Sherebiah, Jamin, Akkub, Shabbethai, Hodiah, Maaseiah, Kelita, Azariah, Jozabad, Hanan, and Pelaiah—instructed the people who were standing there. 8They read from the Book of the Law of God and clearly explained the meaning of what was being read, helping the people understand each passage. 9Then Nehemiah the governor, Ezra the priest and scribe, and the Levites who were interpreting for the people said to them, "Don't weep on such a day as this! For today is a sacred day before the LORD your God." All the people had been weeping as they listened to the words of the law.

10And Nehemiah* continued, "Go and celebrate with a feast of choice foods and sweet drinks, and share gifts of food with people who have nothing prepared. This is a sacred day before our Lord. Don't be dejected and sad, for the joy of the LORD is your strength!"

11And the Levites, too, quieted the people, telling them, "Hush! Don't weep! For this is a sacred day." 12So the people went away to eat and drink at a festive meal, to share gifts of food, and to celebrate with great joy because they had heard God's words and understood them.

13On October 9* the family leaders and the priests and Levites met with Ezra to go over the law in greater detail. 14As they studied the law, they discovered that the LORD had commanded through Moses that the Israelites should live in shelters during the festival to be held that month.* 15He had said that a proclamation should be made throughout their towns and especially in Jerusalem, telling the people to go to the hills to get branches from olive, wild olive, myrtle, palm, and fig trees. They were to use these branches to make shelters in which they would live during the festival, as it was prescribed in the law.

16So the people went out and cut branches and used them to build shelters on the roofs of their houses, in their courtyards, in the courtyards of God's Temple, or in the squares just inside the Water Gate and the Ephraim Gate. 17So everyone who had returned from captivity lived in these shelters for the seven days of the festival, and everyone was filled with great joy! The Israelites had not celebrated this way since the days of Joshua son of Nun. 18Ezra read from the Book of the Law of God on each of the seven days of the festival. Then on October 15* they held a solemn assembly, as the law of Moses required.

CHAPTER **9** **EZRA LEADS IN CONFESSION.** On October 31* the people returned for another observance. This time they fasted and dressed in sackcloth and sprinkled dust on their heads. 2Those of Israelite descent separated themselves from all foreigners as they confessed their own sins and the sins of their ancestors. 3The Book of the Law of the LORD their God was read aloud to them for about three hours.* Then for three more hours they took turns confessing their sins and worshiping the LORD their God. 4Some of the Levites were standing on the stairs, crying out to the LORD their God. Their names were Jeshua, Bani, Kadmiel, Shebaniah, Bunni, Sherebiah, Bani, and Kenani.

## I CONFESS! ● ● • • •

9:2-3 **The Hebrews practiced open confession, admitting their sins to one another. Reading and studying God's Word should precede confession (see 8:18) because God can show us where we are sinning. Honest confession should precede worship because we cannot have a right relationship with God if we hold on to sin in our life.**

5Then the leaders of the Levites—Jeshua, Kadmiel, Bani, Hashabneiah, Sherebiah, Hodiah, Shebaniah, and Pethahiah—called out to the people: "Stand up and praise the LORD your God, for he lives from everlasting to everlasting!"

Then they continued, "Praise his glorious name! It is far greater than we can think or say. 6You alone are the LORD. You made the skies and the heavens and all the stars. You made the earth and the seas and everything in them. You preserve and give life to everything, and all the angels of heaven worship you.

7"You are the LORD God, who chose Abram and brought him from Ur of the Chaldeans and renamed him Abraham. 8When he had proved himself faithful, you made a covenant with him to give him and his descendants the land of the Canaanites, Hittites, Amorites, Perizzites, Jebusites, and Girgashites. And you have done what you promised, for you are always true to your word.

9"You saw the sufferings and sorrows of our ancestors in Egypt, and you heard their cries from beside the Red Sea.* 10You displayed miraculous signs and wonders against Pharaoh, his servants, and all his people, for you knew how arrogantly the Egyptians were treating them. You have a glorious reputation that has never been forgotten. 11You divided the sea for your people so they could walk through on dry land! And then you hurled their enemies into the depths of the sea. They sank like stones beneath the mighty waters. 12You led our ancestors by a pillar of cloud during the day and a pillar of fire at night so that they could find their way.

13"You came down on Mount Sinai and spoke to

**8:10** Hebrew *he.* **8:13** Hebrew *On the second day,* of the seventh month of the Hebrew calendar. This event occurred on October 9, 445 B.C.; also see notes on 1:1 and 8:2. **8:14** Hebrew *in the seventh month.* This month of the Hebrew lunar calendar usually occurs in September and October. See Lev 23:39-43. **8:18** Hebrew *on the eighth day,* of the seventh month of the Hebrew calendar. This event occurred on October 15, 445 B.C.; also see notes on 1:1 and 8:2. **9:1** Hebrew *On the twenty-fourth day of that same month,* the seventh month of the Hebrew calendar. This event occurred on October 31, 445 B.C.; also see note on 1:1. **9:3** Hebrew *for a quarter of a day.* **9:9** Hebrew *sea of reeds.*

them from heaven. You gave them regulations and instructions that were just, and laws and commands that were true. 14 You instructed them concerning the laws of your holy Sabbath. And you commanded them, through Moses your servant, to obey all your commands, laws, and instructions.

15 "You gave them bread from heaven when they were hungry and water from the rock when they were thirsty. You commanded them to go and take possession of the land you had sworn to give them. 16 But our ancestors were a proud and stubborn lot, and they refused to obey your commands.

17 "They refused to listen and did not remember the miracles you had done for them. Instead, they rebelled and appointed a leader to take them back to their slavery in Egypt! But you are a God of forgiveness, gracious and merciful, slow to become angry, and full of unfailing love and mercy. You did not abandon them, 18 even though they made an idol shaped like a calf and said, 'This is your god who brought you out of Egypt!' They sinned and committed terrible blasphemies. 19 But in your great mercy you did not abandon them to die in the wilderness. The pillar of cloud still led them forward by day, and the pillar of fire showed them the way through the night. 20 You sent your good Spirit to instruct them, and you did not stop giving them bread from heaven or water for their thirst. 21 For forty years you sustained them in the wilderness. They lacked nothing in all that time. Their clothes did not wear out, and their feet did not swell!

22 "Then you helped our ancestors conquer great kingdoms and many nations, and you placed your people in every corner of the land. They completely took over the land of King Sihon of Heshbon and the land of King Og of Bashan. 23 You made their descendants as numerous as the stars in the sky and brought them into the land you had promised to their ancestors. 24 They went in and took possession of the land. You subdued whole nations before them. Even the kings and the Canaanites, who inhabited the land, were powerless! Your people could deal with them as they pleased. 25 Our ancestors captured fortified cities and fertile land. They took over houses full of good things, with cisterns already dug and vineyards and olive groves and orchards in abundance. So they ate until they were full and grew fat and enjoyed themselves in all your blessings.

26 "But despite all this, they were disobedient and rebelled against you. They threw away your law, they killed the prophets who encouraged them to return to you, and they committed terrible blasphemies. 27 So you handed them over to their enemies. But in their time of trouble they cried to you, and you heard them from heaven. In great mercy, you sent them deliverers who rescued them from their enemies.

28 "But when all was going well, your people turned to sin again, and once more you let their enemies conquer them. Yet whenever your people cried to you again for help, you listened once more from heaven. In your wonderful mercy, you rescued them repeatedly! 29 You warned them to return to your law, but they became proud and obstinate and disobeyed your commands. They did not follow your regulations, by which people will find life if only they obey. They stubbornly turned their backs on you and refused to listen. 30 In your love, you were patient with them for many years. You sent your Spirit, who, through the prophets, warned them about their sins. But still they wouldn't listen! So once again you allowed the pagan inhabitants of the land to conquer them. 31 But in your great mercy, you did not destroy them completely or abandon them forever. What a gracious and merciful God you are!

32 "And now, our God, the great and mighty and awesome God, who keeps his covenant of unfailing love, do not let all the hardships we have suffered be as nothing to you. Great trouble has come upon us and upon our kings and princes and priests and prophets and ancestors from the days when the kings of Assyria first triumphed over us until now. 33 Every time you punished us you were being just. We have sinned greatly, and you gave us only what we deserved. 34 Our kings, princes, priests, and ancestors did not obey your law or listen to your commands and solemn warnings. 35 Even while they had their own kingdom, they did not serve you even though you showered your goodness on them. You gave them a large, fertile land, but they refused to turn from their wickedness.

36 "So now today we are slaves here in the land of plenty that you gave to our ancestors! We are slaves among all this abundance! 37 The lush produce of this land piles up in the hands of the kings whom you have set over us because of our sins. They have power over us and our cattle. We serve them at their pleasure, and we are in great misery.

38 "Yet in spite of all this,* we are making a solemn promise and putting it in writing. On this sealed document are the names of our princes and Levites and priests."

9:38 Or *Because of all this.*

## AMAZING PATIENCE ● ● • • •

9:16-21 **Seeing how God continued to be with his people shows that his patience is amazing! In spite of our repeated failings, pride, and stubbornness, he is always gracious and merciful (9:17), and his Spirit is always ready to instruct (9:20). Realizing the extent of God's forgiveness helps us forgive those who fail us, even "seventy times seven" times if necessary (Matthew 18:21-22).**

## SHOWERED ● ● • • •

9:35-36 **Sometimes the very blessings God has showered on us make us forget him. We often are tempted to rely on money for security rather than on God. As you see what happened to the Israelites, look at your own life. Do your blessings make you thankful to God and draw you closer to him, or do they make you feel independent and forgetful of God?**

CHAPTER **10** **THE PEOPLE AGREE TO OBEY.** The document was ratified and sealed with the following names:

Nehemiah the governor, the son of Hacaliah.
The priests who signed were Zedekiah, [2]Seraiah,
Azariah, Jeremiah, [3]Pashhur, Amariah, Malkijah,
[4]Hattush, Shebaniah, Malluch, [5]Harim, Meremoth, Obadiah, [6]Daniel, Ginnethon, Baruch,
[7]Meshullam, Abijah, Mijamin, [8]Maaziah, Bilgai,
and Shemaiah. These were the priests.
[9]The Levites who signed were Jeshua son of
Azaniah, Binnui from the family of Henadad,
Kadmiel, [10]and their fellow Levites: Shebaniah,
Hodiah, Kelita, Pelaiah, Hanan, [11]Mica, Rehob,
Hashabiah, [12]Zaccur, Sherebiah, Shebaniah,
[13]Hodiah, Bani, and Beninu.
[14]The leaders who signed were Parosh, Pahath-moab, Elam, Zattu, Bani, [15]Bunni, Azgad, Bebai,
[16]Adonijah, Bigvai, Adin, [17]Ater, Hezekiah, Azzur,
[18]Hodiah, Hashum, Bezai, [19]Hariph, Anathoth,
Nebai, [20]Magpiash, Meshullam, Hezir, [21]Meshezabel, Zadok, Jaddua, [22]Pelatiah, Hanan, Anaiah,
[23]Hoshea, Hananiah, Hasshub, [24]Hallohesh, Pilha,
Shobek, [25]Rehum, Hashabnah, Maaseiah, [26]Ahiah,
Hanan, Anan, [27]Malluch, Harim, and Baanah.

[28]The rest of the people—the priests, Levites, gatekeepers, singers, Temple servants, and all who had separated themselves from the pagan people of the land in order to serve God, and who were old enough to understand—[29]now all heartily bound themselves with an oath. They vowed to accept the curse of God if they failed to obey the law of God as issued by his servant Moses. They solemnly promised to carefully follow all the commands, laws, and regulations of the LORD their Lord.

## COMMITTED ● ● • • •

10:28-29 **The wall was completed, and the covenant God made with his people in the days of Moses was restored (Deuteronomy 8). This covenant includes principles that are important for us today. Our relationship with God goes far beyond church attendance and regular devotions. It should affect our relationships (10:30), our time (10:31), and our material resources (10:32-40). When you chose to follow God, you promised to serve him. The Israelites had fallen away from the original commitment they had made to follow God. We must be careful not to do the same.**

[30]"We promise not to let our daughters marry the pagan people of the land, nor to let our sons marry their daughters. [31]We further promise that if the people of the land should bring any merchandise or grain to be sold on the Sabbath or on any other holy day, we will refuse to buy it. And we promise not to do any work every seventh year and to cancel the debts owed to us by other Jews.

[32]"In addition, we promise to obey the command to pay the annual Temple tax of an eighth of an ounce of silver,* so that there will be enough money to care for the Temple of our God. [33]This will provide for the Bread of the Presence; for the regular grain offerings and burnt offerings; for the offerings on the Sabbaths, the new moon celebrations, and the annual festivals; for the holy offerings; and for the sin offerings to make atonement for Israel. It will also provide for the other items necessary for the work of the Temple of our God.

[34]"We have cast sacred lots to determine when—at regular times each year—the families of the priests, Levites, and the common people should bring wood to God's Temple to be burned on the altar of the LORD our God, as required in the law.

## GIFTS ● ● • • •

10:36 **This practice was instituted at the time of the Exodus from Egypt. The people needed to relearn the importance of dedicating the firstfruits of their yield to God. Nehemiah was simply reinstating this practice from the early days of the nation (Exodus 13:1-2; Numbers 3:40-51).**

**We, too, need to remember that everything that we have–possessions, talents, money, friends, etc.–is from God. We should dedicate all that we have to his use. Don't withhold anything from God. Instead, ask him to show you how to honor him with your time, talents, relationships, and possessions.**

[35]"We promise always to bring the first part of every harvest to the LORD's Temple—whether it be a crop from the soil or from our fruit trees. [36]We agree to give to God our oldest sons and the firstborn of all our herds and flocks, just as the law requires. We will present them to the priests who minister in the Temple of our God. [37]We will store the produce in the storerooms of the Temple of our God. We will bring the best of our flour and other grain offerings, the best of our fruit, and the best of our new wine and olive oil. And we promise to bring to the Levites a tenth of everything our land produces, for it is the Levites who collect the tithes in all our rural towns. [38]A priest—a descendant of Aaron—will be with the Levites as they receive these tithes. And a tenth of all that is collected as tithes will be delivered by the Levites to the Temple of our God and placed in the storerooms. [39]The people and the Levites must bring these offerings of grain, new wine, and olive oil to the Temple and place them in the sacred containers near the ministering priests, the gatekeepers, and the singers.

"So we promise together not to neglect the Temple of our God."

CHAPTER **11** **THE MOVE INTO THE NEW CITY.** Now the leaders of the people were living in Jerusalem, the holy city, at this time. A tenth of the people from the other towns of Judah and Benjamin were chosen by sacred lots to live there, too, while the rest stayed where they were. [2]And the people commended everyone who volunteered to resettle in Jerusalem.

10:32 Hebrew *tax of 1/3 of a shekel* [4 grams].

3Here is a list of the names of the provincial officials who came to Jerusalem. Most of the people, priests, Levites, Temple servants, and descendants of Solomon's servants continued to live in their own homes in the various towns of Judah, 4but some of the people from Judah and Benjamin resettled in Jerusalem.

From the tribe of Judah: Athaiah son of Uzziah, son of Zechariah, son of Amariah, son of Shephatiah, son of Mahalalel, of the family of Perez; 5and Maaseiah son of Baruch, son of Col-hozeh, son of Hazaiah, son of Adaiah, son of Joiarib, son of Zechariah, of the family of Shelah.* 6There were also 468 descendants of Perez who lived in Jerusalem—all outstanding men.

7From the tribe of Benjamin: Sallu son of Meshullam, son of Joed, son of Pedaiah, son of Kolaiah, son of Maaseiah, son of Ithiel, son of Jeshaiah; 8and after him there were Gabbai and Sallai, and a total of 928 relatives. 9Their chief officer was Joel son of Zicri, who was assisted by Judah son of Hassenuah, second-in-command over the city.

10From the priests: Jedaiah son of Joiarib; Jakin; 11and Seraiah son of Hilkiah, son of Meshullam, son of Zadok, son of Meraioth, son of Ahitub, the supervisor of the Temple of God; 12together with 822 of their associates, who worked at the Temple. Also, there was Adaiah son of Jeroham, son of Pelaliah, son of Amzi, son of Zechariah, son of Pashhur, son of Malkijah; 13and 242 of his associates, who were heads of their families. There were also Amashsai son of Azarel, son of Ahzai, son of Meshillemoth, son of Immer; 14and 128 of his outstanding associates. Their chief officer was Zabdiel son of Haggedolim.

15From the Levites: Shemaiah son of Hasshub, son of Azrikam, son of Hashabiah, son of Bunni; 16Shabbethai and Jozabad, who were in charge of the work outside the Temple of God; 17Mattaniah son of Mica, son of Zabdi, a descendant of Asaph, who opened the thanksgiving services with prayer; Bakbukiah, who was Mattaniah's assistant; and Abda son of Shammua, son of Galal, son of Jeduthun. 18In all, there were 284 Levites in the holy city.

19From the gatekeepers: Akkub, Talmon, and 172 of their associates, who guarded the gates.

20The other priests, Levites, and the rest of the Israelites lived wherever their family inheritance was located in any of the towns of Judah. 21However, the Temple servants, whose leaders were Ziha and Gishpa, all lived on the hill of Ophel.

22The chief officer of the Levites in Jerusalem was Uzzi son of Bani, son of Hashabiah, son of Mattaniah, son of Mica, a descendant of Asaph, whose family served as singers at God's Temple. 23They were under royal orders, which determined their daily activities.

24Pethahiah son of Meshezabel, a descendant of Zerah son of Judah, was the king's agent in all matters of public administration.

25Some of the people of Judah lived in Kiriath-arba with its villages, Dibon with its villages, and Jekabzeel with its villages. 26They also lived in Jeshua, Moladah, Beth-pelet, 27Hazar-shual, Beer-sheba with its villages, 28Ziklag, and Meconah with its villages. 29They were also in En-rimmon, Zorah, Jarmuth, 30Zanoah, and Adullam with their villages. They were also in Lachish and its nearby fields and Azekah with its surrounding villages. So the people of Judah were living all the way from Beersheba to the valley of Hinnom.

31Some of the people of Benjamin lived at Geba, Micmash, Aija, and Bethel with its surrounding villages. 32They were also in Anathoth, Nob, Ananiah, 33Hazor, Ramah, Gittaim, 34Hadid, Zeboim, Neballat, 35Lod, Ono, and the Valley of Craftsmen.* 36Some of the Levites who lived in Judah were sent to live with the tribe of Benjamin.

**VOLUNTEER ● ● ● • •**

11:1 **The exiles who returned were few in number compared to Jerusalem's population in the days of the kings. Because the walls had been rebuilt on their original foundations, the city seemed sparsely populated. Nehemiah asked one-tenth of the people from the outlying areas to move inside the city walls to keep large areas of the city from being vacant. Apparently these people did not want to move into the city. Only a few volunteered. Finally, Nehemiah cast lots to determine who among the remaining people would have to move.**

**How do you respond when God calls you into action? Do you resist or grumble about what you are being asked to do? Or are you a willing volunteer? Ask God to help you become someone who is willing to follow God's call, no matter where it may lead.**

## CHAPTER 12 THE PRIESTS AND LEVITES.

Here is the list of the priests and Levites who had returned with Zerubbabel son of Shealtiel and Jeshua the high priest:

Seraiah, Jeremiah, Ezra,
2 Amariah, Malluch, Hattush,
3 Shecaniah, Harim,* Meremoth,
4 Iddo, Ginnethon,* Abijah,
5 Miniamin, Moadiah,* Bilgah,
6 Shemaiah, Joiarib, Jedaiah,
7 Sallu, Amok, Hilkiah, and Jedaiah.

These were the leaders of the priests and their associates in the days of Jeshua.

8The Levites who had returned with them were Jeshua, Binnui, Kadmiel, Sherebiah, Judah, and Mattaniah, who with his associates was in charge of the songs of thanksgiving. 9Their associates, Bakbukiah and Unni, stood opposite them during the service.

**11:5** Hebrew *son of the Shilonite.* **11:35** Or *and Ge-harashim.* **12:3** Hebrew *Rehum;* compare 7:42; 12:15; Ezra 2:39. **12:4** As in some Hebrew manuscripts and Latin Vulgate (see also 12:16); most Hebrew manuscripts read *Ginnethoi.* **12:5** Hebrew *Mijamin, Maadiah;* compare 12:17.

## MUSIC ● ● • • ·

12:35-36 **Music was an important part of the dedication of the city wall. It still is an important part of worship today. We delight God when we sing our praises to him. What is there in your life that you can sing praises to God about? Take some time to sing your own praise song to him today. He is a willing and appreciative audience.**

10 Jeshua the high priest was the father of Joiakim.
Joiakim was the father of Eliashib.
Eliashib was the father of Joiada.
11 Joiada was the father of Johanan.*
Johanan was the father of Jaddua.

12 Now when Joiakim was high priest, the family leaders of the priests were as follows:

Meraiah was leader of the family of Seraiah.
Hananiah was leader of the family of Jeremiah.
13 Meshullam was leader of the family of Ezra.
Jehohanan was leader of the family of Amariah.
14 Jonathan was leader of the family of Malluch.*
Joseph was leader of the family of Shecaniah.*
15 Adna was leader of the family of Harim.
Helkai was leader of the family of Meremoth.*
16 Zechariah was leader of the family of Iddo.
Meshullam was leader of the family of Ginnethon.
17 Zicri was leader of the family of Abijah.
There was also a* leader of the family of Miniamin.
Piltai was leader of the family of Moadiah.
18 Shammua was leader of the family of Bilgah.
Jehonathan was leader of the family of Shemaiah.
19 Mattenai was leader of the family of Joiarib.
Uzzi was leader of the family of Jedaiah.
20 Kallai was leader of the family of Sallu.*
Eber was leader of the family of Amok.
21 Hashabiah was leader of the family of Hilkiah.
Nethanel was leader of the family of Jedaiah.

22 During the reign of Darius II of Persia,* a list was compiled of the family leaders of the Levites and the priests in the days of the following high priests: Eliashib, Joiada, Johanan, and Jaddua. 23 The heads of the Levite families were recorded in *The Book of History* down to the days of Johanan, the grandson* of Eliashib.

24 These were the family leaders of the Levites: Hashabiah, Sherebiah, Jeshua, Binnui,* Kadmiel, and other associates, who stood opposite them during the ceremonies of praise and thanksgiving, one section responding to the other, just as commanded by David, the man of God. 25 This included Mattaniah, Bakbukiah, and Obadiah.

Meshullam, Talmon, and Akkub were the gatekeepers in charge of the storerooms at the gates. 26 These all served in the days of Joiakim son of Jeshua, son of Jehozadak,* and in the days of Nehemiah the governor and of Ezra the priest and scribe.

27 During the dedication of the new wall of Jerusalem, the Levites throughout the land were asked to come to Jerusalem to assist in the ceremonies. They were to take part in the joyous occasion with their songs of thanksgiving and with the music of cymbals, lyres, and harps. 28 The singers were brought together from Jerusalem and its surrounding villages and from the villages of the Netophathites. 29 They also came from Beth-gilgal and the area of Geba and Azmaveth, for the singers had built their own villages around Jerusalem. 30 The priests and Levites first dedicated themselves, then the people, the gates, and the wall.

31 I led the leaders of Judah to the top of the wall and organized two large choirs to give thanks. One of the choirs proceeded southward* along the top of the wall to the Dung Gate. 32 Hoshaiah and half the leaders of Judah followed them, 33 along with Azariah, Ezra, Meshullam, 34 Judah, Benjamin, Shemaiah, Jeremiah, 35 and some priests who played trumpets. Then came Zechariah son of Jonathan, son of Shemaiah, son of Mattaniah, son of Micaiah, son of Zaccur, a descendant of Asaph. 36 And finally came Zechariah's colleagues Shemaiah, Azarel, Milalai, Gilalai, Maai, Nethanel, Judah, and Hanani. They used the musical instruments prescribed by David, the man of God. Ezra the scribe led this procession. 37 At the Fountain Gate they went straight up the steps on the ascent of the city wall toward the City of David. They passed the house of David and then proceeded to the Water Gate on the east.

38 The second choir went northward* around the other way to meet them. I followed them, with the other half of the people, along the top of the wall past the Tower of the Ovens to the Broad Wall, 39 then past the Ephraim Gate to the Old City Gate,* past the Fish Gate and the Tower of Hananel, and went on to the Tower of the Hundred. Then we continued on to the Sheep Gate and stopped at the Guard Gate.

40 The two choirs that were giving thanks then proceeded to the Temple of God, where they took their places. So did I, together with the group of leaders who were with me. 41 We went together with the trumpet-playing priests—Eliakim, Maaseiah,

## DEDICATION ● ● • • ·

12:44-47 **The dedication of the city wall was characterized by joy, praise, and singing (12:24, 27-29, 35-36, 40-42). Nehemiah repeatedly mentioned King David, who began the custom of using choirs in worship. In David's day, Israel was a vigorous, God-fearing nation. These exiles who had returned wanted their rebuilt Jerusalem to be the hub of a renewed nation that was strengthened by God. Therefore, they dedicated themselves and their city to God.**

**12:11** Hebrew *Jonathan;* compare 12:22. **12:14a** As in Greek version (see also 10:4; 12:2); Hebrew reads *Malluchi.* **12:14b** As in many Hebrew manuscripts, some Greek manuscripts, and Syriac version (see also 12:3); most Hebrew manuscripts read *Shebaniah.* **12:15** As in some Greek manuscripts (see also 12:3); Hebrew reads *Meraioth.* **12:17** Hebrew lacks the name of this family leader. **12:20** Hebrew *Sallai;* compare 12:7. **12:22** Hebrew *Darius the Persian.* **12:23** Hebrew *son;* compare 12:10-11. **12:24** Hebrew *son of* (i.e., *ben*), which should probably be read here as the proper name Binnui; compare Ezra 3:9 and the note there. **12:26** Hebrew *Jozadak,* a variant name for Jehozadak. **12:31** Hebrew *to the right.* **12:38** Hebrew *to the left.* **12:39** Or *the Mishneh Gate,* or *the Jeshanah Gate.*

Miniamin, Micaiah, Elioenai, Zechariah, and Hananiah—42and the singers—Maaseiah, Shemaiah, Eleazar, Uzzi, Jehohanan, Malkijah, Elam, and Ezer. They played and sang loudly and clearly under the direction of Jezrahiah the choir director.

43Many sacrifices were offered on that joyous day, for God had given the people cause for great joy. The women and children also participated in the celebration, and the joy of the people of Jerusalem could be heard far away.

44On that day men were appointed to be in charge of the storerooms for the gifts, the first part of the harvest, and the tithes. They were responsible to collect these from the fields as required by the law for the priests and Levites, for all the people of Judah valued the priests and Levites and their work. 45They performed the service of their God and the service of purification, as required by the laws of David and his son Solomon, and so did the singers and the gatekeepers. 46The custom of having choir directors to lead the choirs in hymns of praise and thanks to God began long ago in the days of David and Asaph. 47So now, in the days of Zerubbabel and of Nehemiah, the people brought a daily supply of food for the singers, the gatekeepers, and the Levites. The Levites, in turn, gave a portion of what they received to the priests, the descendants of Aaron.

## CHAPTER 13

**FOREIGNERS ARE SENT AWAY.** On that same day, as the Book of Moses was being read, the people found a statement which said that no Ammonite or Moabite should ever be permitted to enter the assembly of God. 2For they had not been friendly to the Israelites when they left Egypt. Instead, they hired Balaam to curse them, though our God turned the curse into a blessing. 3When this law was read, all those of mixed ancestry were immediately expelled from the assembly.

4Before this had happened, Eliashib the priest, who had been appointed as supervisor of the storerooms of the Temple of our God and who was also a relative of Tobiah, 5had converted a large storage room and placed it at Tobiah's disposal. The room had previously been used for storing the grain offerings, frankincense, Temple utensils, and tithes of grain, new wine, olive oil, and the special portion set aside for the priests. Moses had decreed that these offerings belonged to the Levites, the singers, and the gatekeepers.

6I was not in Jerusalem at that time, for I had returned to the king in the thirty-second year of the reign of King Artaxerxes of Babylon,* though I later received his permission to return. 7When I arrived back in Jerusalem and learned the extent of this evil deed of Eliashib—that he had provided Tobiah with a room in the courtyards of the Temple of God—8I became very upset and threw all of Tobiah's belongings from the room. 9Then I demanded that the rooms be purified, and I brought back the utensils for God's Temple, the grain offerings, and the frankincense.

10I also discovered that the Levites had not been given what was due them, so they and the singers who were to conduct the worship services had all returned to work their fields. 11I immediately confronted the leaders and demanded, "Why has the Temple of God been neglected?" Then I called all the Levites back again and restored them to their proper duties. 12And once more all the people of Judah began bringing their tithes of grain, new wine, and olive oil to the Temple storerooms.

13I put Shelemiah the priest, Zadok the scribe, and Pedaiah, one of the Levites, in charge of the storerooms. And I appointed Hanan son of Zaccur and grandson of Mattaniah as their assistant. These men had an excellent reputation, and it was their job to make honest distributions to their fellow Levites.

> 14Remember this good deed, O my God, and do not forget all that I have faithfully done for the Temple of my God.

15One Sabbath day I saw some men of Judah treading their winepresses. They were also bringing in bundles of grain and loading them on their donkeys. And on that day they were bringing their wine, grapes, figs, and all sorts of produce to Jerusalem to sell. So I rebuked them for selling their produce on the Sabbath. 16There were also some men from Tyre bringing in fish and all kinds of merchandise. They were selling it on the Sabbath to the people of Judah—and in Jerusalem at that!

17So I confronted the leaders of Judah, "Why are you profaning the Sabbath in this evil way? 18Wasn't it enough that your ancestors did this sort of thing, so that our God brought the present troubles upon us and our city? Now you are bringing even more wrath upon the people of Israel by permitting the Sabbath to be desecrated in this way!" 19So I commanded that from then on the gates of the city should be shut as darkness fell every Friday evening,* not to be opened until the Sabbath ended. I also sent some of my own servants to guard the gates so that no merchandise could be brought in on the Sabbath day. 20The merchants and tradesmen with a variety of wares camped outside Jerusalem once or twice. 21But I spoke sharply

### INFLUENCE ● ● • • •

13:3 **"Those of mixed ancestry" refers to the Moabites and Ammonites, two nations who were bitter enemies of Israel (13:1). God's law clearly stated that these two peoples should never be allowed in the Temple (Deuteronomy 23:3-5). This had nothing to do with racial prejudice, because God loves all people. Rather, it was because the relationships between Jews and the heathen led the Jews into sin. While God wants all people to come to him (2 Peter 3:9), he warns believers to stay away from those intent on evil (Proverbs 24:1). We need to be careful about the people we spend time with, because, like Israel, we may find that unbelievers are more of an influence on us than we are on them.**

**13:6** The thirty-second year of Artaxerxes was 433 B.C. **13:19** Hebrew *on the day before the Sabbath.*

to them and said, "What are you doing out here, camping around the wall? If you do this again, I will arrest you!" And that was the last time they came on the Sabbath. [22]Then I commanded the Levites to purify themselves and to guard the gates in order to preserve the holiness of the Sabbath.

Remember this good deed also, O my God!
Have compassion on me according to your great and unfailing love.

[23]About the same time I realized that some of the men of Judah had married women from Ashdod, Ammon, and Moab. [24]Even worse, half their children spoke in the language of Ashdod or some other people and could not speak the language of Judah at all. [25]So I confronted them and called down curses on them. I beat some of them and pulled out their hair. I made them swear before God that they would not let their children intermarry with the pagan people of the land.

[26]"Wasn't this exactly what led King Solomon of Israel into sin?" I demanded. "There was no king from any nation who could compare to him, and God loved him and made him king over all Israel. But even he was led into sin by his foreign wives. [27]How could you even think of committing this sinful deed and acting unfaithfully toward God by marrying foreign women?"

[28]One of the sons of Joiada* son of Eliashib the high priest had married a daughter of Sanballat the Horonite, so I banished him from my presence.

[29]Remember them, O my God, for they have defiled the priesthood and the promises and vows of the priests and Levites.

[30]So I purged out everything foreign and assigned tasks to the priests and Levites, making certain that each knew his work. [31]I also made sure that the supply of wood for the altar was brought at the proper times and that the first part of the harvest was collected for the priests.

Remember this in my favor, O my God.

13:28 Hebrew *Jehoiada*, a variant name for Joiada.

# MEGA themes

**VISION** Although the Jews completed the Temple in 516 B.C., the city walls remained in shambles for the next 70 years. The walls represented power, protection, and beauty. The walls also were needed to protect the Temple from attack. God put the desire in Nehemiah's heart to rebuild the walls, giving him a vision for the work.

Does God have a vision for us? Are there "walls" that need to be built today? God still wants his people to be united and trained to do his work. As we recognize deep needs in our world, God can give us the vision and desire to "build." Look for construction projects that you can complete for God.

1. Nehemiah's vision for doing what God wanted began with his relationship with God. Based on the first chapter, how would you describe that relationship?
2. What qualities can you find in Nehemiah that could serve as your example of what it means to be God's visionary?
3. How can you prepare yourself now to be a person who not only has a vision for God's will, but who also is used by God to fulfill that vision?
4. You may not be ready for a task as large as Nehemiah's, but what small tasks are available to you that would be "building" for God's people? How will you begin your "construction project" in the coming days?

**PRAYER** Both Nehemiah and Ezra responded to problems with prayer. When Nehemiah began his work he recognized the problem, prayed right away, and then acted on the problem.

Prayer still is God's way to solve problems. Prayer and action go hand-in-hand. Through prayer, God guides our preparation, teamwork, and efforts to carry out his will. Without prayer, we are limited to our own finite resources.

1. How did prayer enter into Nehemiah's preparation for doing God's work?
2. Describe the importance of both attitude and action in terms of Nehemiah's prayer life.
3. Complete this sentence: I can prepare myself to be God's builder by beginning with prayer that includes ________.
4. Write out a prayer to God based on the "construction project" you listed above under VISION.

**LEADERSHIP** Nehemiah was an excellent leader. He was spiritually ready to heed God's call. He used careful planning, teamwork, problem solving, and courage to get the work done. Although he had tremendous faith, he never avoided the extra work necessary for good leadership.

Being God's leader is not just getting recognition, holding a position, or being the boss. It requires planning, hard work, courage, and perseverance. And there is no substitute for doing the difficult work. In order to lead others, you need to follow God's direction in your own life.

1. What are a few specific examples of Nehemiah's excellent leadership?
2. Based upon your study of Nehemiah and your experience with leaders you have known personally, make a list of the qualities that make a strong leader.
3. Evaluate yourself based on your list from question 2. Which qualities are your strengths? Which are your weaknesses?
4. Describe ways in which you could use your strengths to influence others for Christ. Also, how can you develop those strengths and overcome your weaknesses?

**PROBLEMS** After the work began, Nehemiah faced scorn, slander, and threats from enemies, as well as fear, conflict, and discouragement from his own workers. Although these problems were difficult, they did not stop Nehemiah from finishing the work.

When difficulties come, it is easy to get discouraged. But remember, there are no triumphs without troubles. When problems arise, we must face them squarely and press on to complete God's work. We do not have to retreat—our God is a God of absolute victory.

1. How would you have felt had you been Nehemiah when he faced all of his problems? What would you have wanted to do when you were threatened and slandered?
2. Nehemiah overcame these problems. What seems to have been the key to his not giving in or giving up?
3. Choose one problem you have faced in the past or are now facing in your attempts to obey God. Based on Nehemiah's example, what will you do to be an overcomer rather than being a person who is overcome?

**REPENTANCE** Although God had enabled them to build the wall, the work wasn't complete until the people rebuilt their lives spiritually. Ezra taught the people God's Word. As they listened, they recognized the sin in their lives, admitted it, and took steps to remove it.

Recognizing and admitting sin is not enough. Being serious about God must result in a changed life, or it is merely enthusiasm. God does not want halfhearted measures. We must not only remove sin from our life, but also ask God to move into the center of all we do.

1. Based on Nehemiah, do you think the following statement is true or false: "God is not just concerned that we take care of big tasks, he wants our entire life surrendered to him." Explain your answer based only on the book of Nehemiah.
2. What are examples of "little things" in your life that are important to God, although no one else may ever notice them?
3. The people in Jerusalem responded to the new wall with a recommitment to God in all of life. After reading chapters 10 and 11, write out some statements of your own recommitment to live all of your life, from the heart, for God.

586 B.C.
**Jerusalem destroyed; exiles go to Babylon**

537
**First exiles return to Jerusalem**

516
**Temple completed**

486
**Ahasuerus (Xerxes I) becomes king of Persia**

479
**Esther becomes queen**

474
**Haman's decree to destroy the Jews**

473
**First Feast of Purim**

Overflowing with fans, the gymnasium rocks with excitement. It's the crucial moment—the one anticipated all season—but joy mixes with fear and tension. Only one point behind, the team could find its season ending abruptly. But two seconds remain in the game, and *their* player is at the free throw line. Cheers erupt as the ball swishes through the hoop. But then silence engulfs the stands as the player approaches the line for the second shot. Everything seems to be on the line—the play-offs, the dreams, the season. But the shooter's training pays off. The basket is made, the game is won, and a hero is made. He came through when it counted. ■ In Persia, Esther similarly faced a crucial moment—but the stakes were the lives of thousands. All the Jews in Persia were to be killed, and Esther, the queen and a Jew, was the only one who could save them. She could make the difference. She could have pled "not me," or looked for an easy out. But Esther knew God had placed her in an influential position "for just such a time as this" (4:14). She seized the moment and took action, regardless of the consequences (4:16). Because of Esther, lives were spared, the victory won. ■ Read Esther and commit yourself to act for God when he gives you the opportunity. Remember, he places you where you can make a difference "for just such a time as this."

## STATS

PURPOSE: To demonstrate God's sovereignty and his loving care for his people

AUTHOR: Unknown. Possibly Mordecai (9:29). Some have suggested Ezra or Nehemiah because of the similarity of the writing style.

DATE WRITTEN: Approximately 483–471 B.C. (Esther became queen in 479)

SETTING: Although Esther follows Nehemiah in the Bible, the events are about 30 years prior to those recorded in Nehemiah. The story is set in the Persian empire, and most of the action takes place in the king's palace in Susa, the Persian capital.

KEY PEOPLE: Esther, Mordecai, King Xerxes, Haman

KEY PLACE: The king's palace in Susa, Persia

SPECIAL FEATURES: Esther is one of only two books named for women (Ruth is the other). The book is unusual in that, in the original version, God's name doesn't appear in it. This caused some early church leaders to question its inclusion in the Bible. But God's presence is clear throughout the book.

CHAPTER 1 **TROUBLE IN THE PALACE.** This happened
in the days of King Xerxes,* who reigned over 127
provinces stretching from India to Ethiopia.* 2At
that time he ruled his empire from his throne at the
fortress of Susa. 3In the third year of his reign, he gave
a banquet for all his princes and officials. He invited
all the military officers of Media and Persia, as well
as the noblemen and provincial officials. 4The celebration lasted six months*—a tremendous display
of the opulent wealth and glory of his empire.

5When it was all over, the king gave a special
banquet for all the palace servants and officials—
from the greatest to the least. It lasted for seven
days and was held at Susa in the courtyard of the
palace garden. 6The courtyard was decorated with
beautifully woven white and blue linen hangings,
fastened by purple ribbons to silver rings embed-
ded in marble pillars. Gold and silver couches
stood on a mosaic pavement of porphyry, marble,
mother-of-pearl, and other costly stones. 7Drinks
were served in gold goblets of many designs, and
there was an abundance of royal wine, just as the
king had commanded. 8The only restriction on the
drinking was that no one should be compelled to
take more than he wanted. But those who wished
could have as much as they pleased, for the king
had instructed his staff to let everyone decide this
matter for himself.

9Queen Vashti gave a banquet for the women of
the palace at the same time.

10On the seventh day of the feast, when King Xerxes
was half drunk with wine, he told Mehuman, Biztha,
Harbona, Bigtha, Abagtha, Zethar, and Carcas, the
seven eunuchs who attended him, 11to bring Queen
Vashti to him with the royal crown on her head. He
wanted all the men to gaze on her beauty, for she was
a very beautiful woman. 12But when they conveyed the
king's order to Queen Vashti, she refused to come. This
made the king furious, and he burned with anger.

13He immediately consulted with his advisers,
who knew all the Persian laws and customs, for he
always asked their advice. 14The names of these men
were Carshena, Shethar, Admatha, Tarshish, Meres,
Marsena, and Memucan—seven high officials of

**DECISIONS ● ● • • •**

1:10-11 **Xerxes made a rash, half-drunk decision, based purely on feelings. His self-restraint and practical wisdom were weakened by too much wine, and he later regretted his decision (2:1). Poor decisions are made when clear thinking is not involved. Base your decisions on careful thinking, not on the spur of the moment.**

**1:1a** Hebrew *Ahasuerus,* another name for Xerxes; also throughout the book of Esther. **1:1b** Hebrew *to Cush.* **1:4** Hebrew *180 days.*

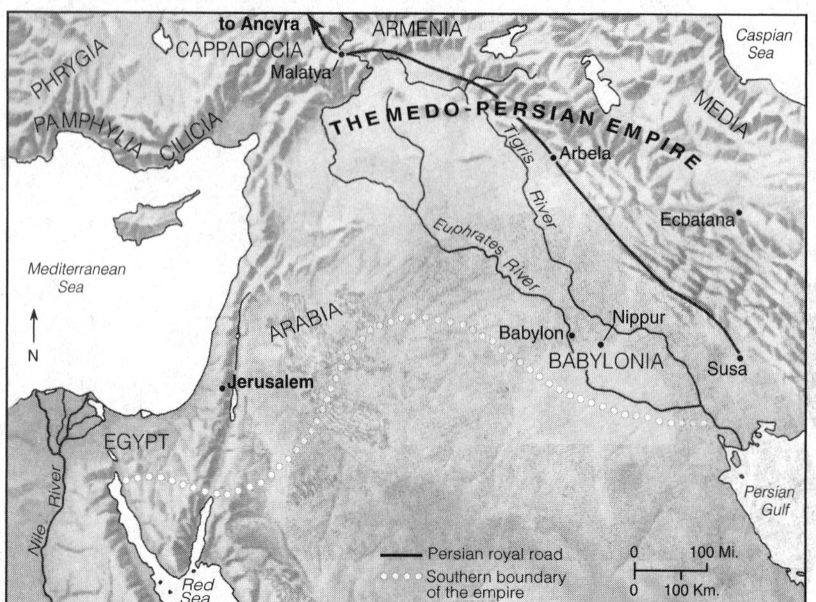


**THE WORLD OF ESTHER'S DAY**
Esther lived in the capital of the vast Medo-Persian empire, which incorporated the provinces of Media and Persia, as well as the previous empires of Assyria and Babylon. Esther, a Jewess, was chosen by King Xerxes to be his queen. The story of how she saved her people takes place in the palace in Susa.

Persia and Media. They were his closest associates
and held the highest positions in the empire.
15"What must be done to Queen Vashti?" the king
demanded. "What penalty does the law provide for
a queen who refuses to obey the king's orders, properly sent through his eunuchs?"
16Memucan answered the king and his princes,
"Queen Vashti has wronged not only the king but
also every official and citizen throughout your empire. 17Women everywhere will begin to despise their
husbands when they learn that Queen Vashti has
refused to appear before the king. 18Before this day is
out, the wife of every one of us, your officials
throughout the empire, will hear what the queen did
and will start talking to their husbands the same way.
There will be no end to the contempt and anger
throughout your realm. 19So if it please the king, we
suggest that you issue a written decree, a law of the
Persians and Medes that cannot be revoked. It
should order that Queen Vashti be forever banished
from your presence and that you choose another
queen more worthy than she. 20When this decree is
published throughout your vast empire, husbands
everywhere, whatever their rank, will receive proper
respect from their wives!"
21The king and his princes thought this made
good sense, so he followed Memucan's counsel. 22He
sent letters to all parts of the empire, to each province in its own script and language, proclaiming that
every man should be the ruler of his home.

CHAPTER **2** **ESTHER BECOMES QUEEN.** But after Xerxes' anger had cooled, he began thinking about
Vashti and what she had done and the decree he had
made. 2So his attendants suggested, "Let us search
the empire to find beautiful young virgins for the
king. 3Let the king appoint agents in each province
to bring these beautiful young women into the royal
harem at Susa. Hegai, the eunuch in charge, will see
that they are all given beauty treatments. 4After that,
the young woman who pleases you most will be
made queen instead of Vashti." This advice was very
appealing to the king, so he put the plan into effect
immediately.
5Now at the fortress of Susa there was a certain Jew
named Mordecai son of Jair. He was from the tribe
of Benjamin and was a descendant of Kish and
Shimei. 6His family* had been exiled from Jerusalem to Babylon by King Nebuchadnezzar, along with
King Jehoiachin* of Judah and many others. 7This
man had a beautiful and lovely young cousin, Ha-
dassah, who was also called Esther. When her father
and mother had died, Mordecai adopted her into his
family and raised her as his own daughter. 8As a
result of the king's decree, Esther, along with many
other young women, was brought to the king's
harem at the fortress of Susa and placed in Hegai's
care. 9Hegai was very impressed with Esther and

## RESPECT AND LOVE ● ● ● • •

**1:20-21 One way to rule is to issue edicts that force people to comply. King Xerxes and his advisers responded this way. But in Matthew 20:25-26, Jesus states that this is how people in the world act, lording it over everyone. As believers, we are to act differently. God offers his free gift of salvation to all (Titus 2:11), and he tells us to treat each other with respect and love (1 Corinthians 13).**

2:6a Hebrew *He.* 2:6b Hebrew *Jeconiah,* a variant name for Jehoiachin.

treated her kindly. He quickly ordered a special menu for her and provided her with beauty treatments. He also assigned her seven maids specially chosen from the king's palace, and he moved her and her maids into the best place in the harem.
[10]Esther had not told anyone of her nationality and family background, for Mordecai had told her
not to. [11]Every day Mordecai would take a walk near the courtyard of the harem to ask about Esther and to find out what was happening to her.
[12]Before each young woman was taken to the king's bed, she was given the prescribed twelve months of beauty treatments—six months with oil of myrrh, followed by six months with special perfumes and ointments.
[13]When the time came for her to go in to the king, she was given her choice of whatever clothing or jewelry she wanted to enhance her beauty.
[14]That evening she was taken to the king's private rooms, and the next morning she was brought to the second harem,* where the king's wives lived. There she would be under the care of Shaashgaz, another of the king's eunuchs. She would live there for the rest of her life, never going to the king again unless he had especially enjoyed her and requested her by name.
[15]When it was Esther's turn* to go to the king, she accepted the advice of Hegai, the eunuch in charge of the harem. She asked for nothing except what he suggested, and she was admired by everyone who saw her.
[16]When Esther was taken to King Xerxes at the royal palace in early winter* of the seventh year of his reign,
[17]the king loved her more than any of the other young women. He was so delighted with her that he set the royal crown on her head and declared her queen instead of
Vashti. [18]To celebrate the occasion, he gave a banquet in Esther's honor for all his princes and servants, giving generous gifts to everyone and declaring a public festival for the provinces.
[19]Even after all the young women had been transferred to the second harem* and Mordecai had become a palace official,
[20]Esther continued to keep her nationality and family background a secret. She was still following Mordecai's orders, just as she did when she was living in his home.
[21]One day as Mordecai was on duty at the palace, two of the king's eunuchs, Bigthana* and Teresh—

## ESTHER

Most of us really want to feel secure, even though we know that security in this life carries no guarantees—possessions can be destroyed or lost, beauty fades, relationships can be broken, and death is always waiting. So what we hope will bring security doesn't last. Real security has to be found in something or Someone else. Only when our security depends on God's unchanging love for us can we face the challenges that life is sure to bring our way.

In Esther's day, kings could have any and as many wives as they wished, but Esther became King Xerxes' queen. God placed her in a special position to represent her people, the Jews, who were in danger. She had to risk her own security to help others. Have you noticed how often we don't help people because we are afraid of what might happen to us?

Esther made her plans carefully. She got help. Knowing she needed God's help, too, Esther had all her people fasting and praying. Realizing God is with us is the best medicine for the feeling that we're all alone. As you read her story, you will be amazed how God and Esther worked together. God was behind the scenes, but he made things happen! The way Esther acted showed how much she depended on God for her security.

How much of your security lies in what you have, who you are, or what others think of you? God has a definite plan in placing you where you are right now. *He put you there to serve him.* As in Esther's case, this may involve risking your security. Are you willing to let God be your ultimate security?

**UPS:**
- Her beauty and character won the heart of Persia's king
- Combined courage with careful planning
- Open to advice and willing to act
- More concerned for others than for her own security

**STATS:**
- Where: Persian empire
- Occupation: Xerxes' wife, queen of Persia
- Relatives: Cousin: Mordecai. Husband: Xerxes. Father: Abihail.

LESSONS: Serving God often demands that we risk our own security

God has a purpose for the situations in which he places us

Courage, while often vital, does not replace careful planning

KEY VERSE: "Go and gather together all the Jews of Susa and fast for me. Do not eat or drink for three days, night or day. My maids and I will do the same. And then, though it is against the law, I will go in to see the king. If I must die, I am willing to die" (Esther 4:16).

Esther's story is told in the book of Esther.

**2:14** Or *to another part of the harem.* **2:15** Hebrew *the turn of Esther, the daughter of Abihail, who was Mordecai's uncle, who had adopted her.* **2:16** Hebrew *in the tenth month, the month of Tebeth.* A number of dates in the book of Esther can be cross-checked with dates in surviving Persian records and related accurately to our modern calendar. This month of the Hebrew lunar calendar occurred in December 479 B.C. and January 478 B.C. **2:19** The meaning of the Hebrew is uncertain. **2:21** Hebrew *Bigthan;* compare 6:2.

who were guards at the door of the king's private quarters—became angry at King Xerxes and plotted to assassinate him. 22 But Mordecai heard about the plot and passed the information on to Queen Esther. She then told the king about it and gave Mordecai credit for the report. 23 When an investigation was made and Mordecai's story was found to be true, the two men were hanged on a gallows.* This was all duly recorded in *The Book of the History of King Xerxes' Reign*.

CHAPTER **3** **HAMAN TRICKS THE KING.** Some time later, King Xerxes promoted Haman son of Hammedatha the Agagite to prime minister, making him the most powerful official in the empire next to the king himself. 2 All the king's officials would bow down before Haman to show him respect whenever he passed by, for so the king had commanded. But Mordecai refused to bow down or show him respect.

## TAKING A STAND

You wouldn't want to be in Ryan's shoes.

He's in the middle of a sticky situation and none of his options are very appealing.

See, in just a few minutes, Ryan and K.D. will be face to face with one of Mrs. Seal's infamous geometry exams. But K.D. just announced, "Hey, Ryan! You've got to help me out, dude. I didn't have time to study last night. I don't know any of the formulas. So look, just write big and when I tap you on the shoulder, lean to your left, OK?"

Lunch is almost over. The bell will be ringing any minute. Ryan's mind is racing:

"Do I let K.D. copy off me just this once? But what if I get accused of cheating? I probably should tell him no now—before class starts. But then he'll tell everyone I wouldn't help him out, and I'll never hear the end of it. Sheesh, what am I going to do?

"It ticks me off the way he uses people. . . . It's not my fault if he fails. He shouldn't be so lazy. Still, I don't want everybody thinking I'm a geek. Maybe I should—"

BBBBRRRIIIINNNNNGGGGG!!!

What would you do in Ryan's shoes?

Chapters 3 and 4 of the exciting book of Esther are about taking a stand for what is right, no matter what. Read about the young queen who made tough decisions when the stakes were—literally—life and death.

3 Then the palace officials at the king's gate asked Mordecai, "Why are you disobeying the king's command?" 4 They spoke to him day after day, but still he refused to comply with the order. So they spoke to Haman about this to see if he would tolerate Mordecai's conduct, since Mordecai had told them he was a Jew.

### CONVICTION ● ● ● • •

3:2 **Mordecai's faith was based on conviction. He did not first take a poll to determine the safest or most popular course of action; he had the courage to stand alone. Doing what is right is not always popular. Those who do right will often be in the minority. But to obey God is more important than to obey people (Acts 5:29).**

5 When Haman saw that Mordecai would not bow down or show him respect, he was filled with rage. 6 So he decided it was not enough to lay hands on Mordecai alone. Since he had learned that Mordecai was a Jew, he decided to destroy all the Jews throughout the entire empire of Xerxes.

7 So in the month of April,* during the twelfth year of King Xerxes' reign, lots were cast (the lots were called *purim*) to determine the best day and month to take action. And the day selected was March 7, nearly a year later.*

8 Then Haman approached King Xerxes and said, "There is a certain race of people scattered through all the provinces of your empire. Their laws are different from those of any other nation, and they refuse to obey even the laws of the king. So it is not in the king's interest to let them live. 9 If it please Your Majesty, issue a decree that they be destroyed, and I will give 375 tons* of silver to the government administrators so they can put it into the royal treasury."

10 The king agreed, confirming his decision by removing his signet ring from his finger and giving it to Haman son of Hammedatha the Agagite—the enemy of the Jews. 11 "Keep the money," the king told Haman, "but go ahead and do as you like with these people."

12 On April 17* Haman called in the king's secretaries and dictated letters to the princes, the governors of the respective provinces, and the local officials of each province in their own scripts and languages. These letters were signed in the name of King Xerxes, sealed with his ring, 13 and sent by messengers into all the provinces of the empire. The letters decreed that all Jews—young and old, including women and children—must be killed, slaughtered, and annihilated on a single day. This was scheduled to happen nearly a year later on March 7.* The property of the Jews would be given to those who killed them. 14 A copy of this decree was to be issued in every province and made known to all the people, so that they would be ready to do their duty on the appointed day. 15 At the king's command, the decree went out by the swiftest messengers, and it was proclaimed in the fortress of Susa. Then the king and Haman sat down to drink, but the city of Susa fell into confusion.

CHAPTER **4** When Mordecai learned what had been done, he tore his clothes, put on sackcloth and ashes, and went out into the city, crying

2:23 Or *on a pole.* 3:7a Hebrew *in the first month, the month of Nisan.* This month of the Hebrew lunar calendar occurred in April and May 474 B.C.; also see note on 2:16. 3:7b As in Greek version, which reads *the thirteenth day of the twelfth month, the month of Adar* (see also 3:13). Hebrew reads *in the twelfth month,* of the Hebrew calendar. The date selected was March 7, 473 B.C.; also see note on 2:16. 3:9 Hebrew *10,000 talents* [340 metric tons]. 3:12 Hebrew *On the thirteenth day of the first month,* of the Hebrew calendar. This event occurred on April 17, 474 B.C.; also see note on 2:16. 3:13 Hebrew *on the thirteenth day of the twelfth month, the month of Adar,* of the Hebrew calendar. The date selected was March 7, 473 B.C.; also see note on 2:16.

## HOW GOD WORKS IN THE WORLD

| | *God's will . . . What God wants done—He works through . . .* | | |
|---|---|---|---|
| **God's action** | ▼ *Natural order*<br>▼ God set into action through creation a normal working of his universe. He also revealed his expectations of people through his Word and people's consciences. | ▼ *Miracles*<br>▼ God breaks into the natural order to respond to the expressed needs of people. | ▼ *Providence*<br>▼ God overrules the natural order to accomplish an act that people may or may not have requested. |
| **Examples from Esther** | ▼ God gave Esther natural beauty.<br>▲ Esther planned a way to save her people. | ▼ God allowed Esther to speak to the king.<br>▲ The people prayed and fasted. | ▼ God allowed Mordecai to overhear a plot.<br>▲ Mordecai trusted God to accomplish what was impossible in human terms. |
| | *Our will . . . What we want done—We either . . .* | | |
| **Action we can take** | ▲ *Plan*<br>▲ Can make plans based on the order and dependability of God's creation. Know and obey his words. | ▲ *Pray*<br>▲ Can ask God to intervene in certain affairs while realizing that our knowledge and perspective are limited. | ▲ *Trust & Obey*<br>▲ Can trust that God is in control even when the circumstances may not seem to indicate that he is. |
| | *or . . .* | | |
| **Mistakes we can make** | ▼ *Disobey*<br>▼ Can violate the natural order, disobey God's commands. | ▼ *Demand*<br>▼ Can assume that we understand what is needed and expect God to agree and answer our prayers that way. | ▼ *Despair*<br>▼ Can assume God doesn't answer prayer or respond to our needs and live as though there is nothing but the natural order. |

with a loud and bitter wail. 2He stood outside the
gate of the palace, for no one was allowed to enter
while wearing clothes of mourning. 3And as news
of the king's decree reached all the provinces, there
was great mourning among the Jews. They fasted,
wept, and wailed, and many people lay in sackcloth and ashes.

4When Queen Esther's maids and eunuchs came
and told her about Mordecai, she was deeply distressed. She sent clothing to him to replace the
sackcloth, but he refused it. 5Then Esther sent for
Hathach, one of the king's eunuchs who had been
appointed as her attendant. She ordered him to go
to Mordecai and find out what was troubling him
and why he was in mourning. 6So Hathach went
out to Mordecai in the square in front of the palace
gate.

7Mordecai told him the whole story and told
him how much money Haman had promised to
pay into the royal treasury for the destruction of
the Jews. 8Mordecai gave Hathach a copy of the
decree issued in Susa that called for the death of all
Jews, and he asked Hathach to show it to Esther.
He also asked Hathach to explain it to her and to
urge her to go to the king to beg for mercy and
plead for her people. 9So Hathach returned to Esther with Mordecai's message.

10Then Esther told Hathach to go back and relay
this message to Mordecai: 11"The whole world
knows that anyone who appears before the king in
his inner court without being invited is doomed to
die unless the king holds out his gold scepter. And
the king has not called for me to come to him in
more than a month." 12So Hathach gave Esther's
message to Mordecai.

13Mordecai sent back this reply to Esther: "Don't
think for a moment that you will escape there in
the palace when all other Jews are killed. 14If you

## Ultimate Issues

### WOMEN OF THE BIBLE

Depending on your point of view, you may be thrilled, irritated, intrigued, or just surprised to see a book of the Bible—two, even—named for a woman. The Bible is, admittedly, a MALE-DOMINATED work. But, as the books of Ruth and Esther point out, women are very important in the story of God's redemption of humanity. Ruth is the story of a young widow who, out of loyalty, follows her mother-in-law back to Jerusalem to live. In the midst of **TOUGH TIMES** for the two of them, Ruth shows she is a hard worker and a woman of integrity and high moral character. God rewards her faithfulness by providing her a new husband, Boaz, a good man who had attained some measure of wealth and could therefore provide for both women. In addition, Ruth and Boaz become the great-grandparents of David, the king of Israel, and ancestors of Jesus, the Jewish Messiah. Ruth is an excellent role model for young believers today, female or male. Esther is the story of another faithful woman in radically different circumstances. A young Jewish girl in exile in Babylon, Esther, by virtue of her GOOD LOOKS, catches the eye of King Xerxes and is made queen. Even as queen, however, she has to watch her step, being careful not to displease her husband and risk being banished or even killed. There comes a point, though, where she must risk the king's displeasure to save her people, the Jews, from **mass destruction.** Although afraid at *first to stick her neck out,* she finally decides to risk it, saying, "Though it is against the law, I will go in to see the king. If I must die, I am willing to die" (Esther 4:16). That's gutsy, courageous faith, the kind that Christian women—and men—today would do well to imitate. Although these are the only two books named for women, there are lots of other stories of important women in Scripture; some good, some bad. If you're interested, look at the accounts of Rahab (Joshua 2; 6); Deborah (Judges 4–5); Jezebel (1 Kings 16—2 Kings 9); Mary and Martha (Luke 10); and, of course, Mary, Jesus' mother (Luke 1–2; John 19, etc.). For a number of reasons, cultural and otherwise, most of the prominent characters in the Bible are men. But women play a vital role in the unfolding drama of both the Old and New Testaments, just as they do in God's work in the world today.

---

keep quiet at a time like this, deliverance for the
Jews will arise from some other place, but you and
your relatives will die. What's more, who can say
but that you have been elevated to the palace for
just such a time as this?"
15Then Esther sent this reply to Mordecai: 16"Go
and gather together all the Jews of Susa and fast for
me. Do not eat or drink for three days, night or day.
My maids and I will do the same. And then, though
it is against the law, I will go in to see the king. If I
must die, I am willing to die." 17So Mordecai went
away and did as Esther told him.

CHAPTER **5** **QUEEN ESTHER DEFEATS HAMAN.** Three
days later, Esther put on her royal robes and entered
the inner court of the palace, just across from the
king's hall. The king was sitting on his royal throne,
facing the entrance. 2When he saw Queen Esther
standing there in the inner court, he welcomed her,
holding out the gold scepter to her. So Esther approached and touched its tip.
3Then the king asked her, "What do you want,
Queen Esther? What is your request? I will give it to
you, even if it is half the kingdom!"
4And Esther replied, "If it please Your Majesty, let
the king and Haman come today to a banquet I have
prepared for the king."
5The king turned to his attendants and said, "Tell
Haman to come quickly to a banquet, as Esther has
requested." So the king and Haman went to Esther's
banquet.
6And while they were drinking wine, the king said
to Esther, "Now tell me what you really want. What
is your request? I will give it to you, even if it is half
the kingdom!"
7Esther replied, "This is my request and deepest
wish. 8If Your Majesty is pleased with me and wants
to grant my request, please come with Haman to-

morrow to the banquet I will prepare for you. Then tomorrow I will explain what this is all about."

[9]What a happy man Haman was as he left the banquet! But when he saw Mordecai sitting at the gate, not standing up or trembling nervously before him, he was furious. [10]However, he restrained himself and went on home. Then he gathered together his friends and Zeresh, his wife, [11]and boasted to them about his great wealth and his many children. He bragged about the honors the king had given him and how he had been promoted over all the other officials and leaders.

[12]Then Haman added, "And that's not all! Queen Esther invited only me and the king himself to the banquet she prepared for us. And she has invited me to dine with her and the king again tomorrow!" [13]Then he added, "But all this is meaningless as long as I see Mordecai the Jew just sitting there at the palace gate."

[14]So Haman's wife, Zeresh, and all his friends suggested, "Set up a gallows* that stands seventy-five feet* tall, and in the morning ask the king to hang Mordecai on it. When this is done, you can go on your merry way to the banquet with the king." This pleased Haman immensely, and he ordered the gallows set up.

CHAPTER **6** That night the king had trouble sleeping, so he ordered an attendant to bring the historical records of his kingdom so they could be read to him. [2]In those records he discovered an account of how Mordecai had exposed the plot of Bigthana and Teresh, two of the eunuchs who guarded the door to the king's private quarters. They had plotted to assassinate the king. [3]"What reward or recognition did we ever give Mordecai for this?" the king asked.

His attendants replied, "Nothing has been done."

[4]"Who is that in the outer court?" the king inquired. Now, as it happened, Haman had just arrived in the outer court of the palace to ask the king to hang Mordecai from the gallows* he had prepared.

[5]So the attendants replied to the king, "Haman is out there."

"Bring him in," the king ordered. [6]So Haman came in, and the king said, "What should I do to honor a man who truly pleases me?"

Haman thought to himself, "Whom would the king wish to honor more than me?" [7]So he replied, "If the king wishes to honor someone, [8]he should bring out one of the king's own royal robes, as well as the king's own horse with a royal emblem on its head. [9]Instruct one of the king's most noble princes to dress the man in the king's robe and to lead him through the city square on the king's own horse. Have the prince shout as they go, 'This is what happens to those the king wishes to honor!'"

[10]"Excellent!" the king said to Haman. "Hurry and get the robe and my horse, and do just as you have said for Mordecai the Jew, who sits at the gate of the palace. Do not fail to carry out everything you have suggested."

[11]So Haman took the robe and put it on Mordecai, placed him on the king's own horse, and led him through the city square, shouting, "This is what happens to those the king wishes to honor!" [12]Afterward Mordecai returned to the palace gate, but Haman hurried home dejected and completely humiliated.

**BRAGGING ● ● • • •**

6:12 **Just the night before (5:9-14), Haman had bragged about his position and the honor he was about to receive. Now he was humiliated and soon to be marked for death (7:8-10). How quickly the course of life can change! Because we cannot predict what will happen, it is best to avoid bragging (James 4:13-16). God is displeased with this kind of self-confidence and self-reliance.**

[13]When Haman told his wife, Zeresh, and all his friends what had happened, they said, "Since Mordecai—this man who has humiliated you—is a Jew, you will never succeed in your plans against him. It will be fatal to continue to oppose him." [14]While they were still talking, the king's eunuchs arrived to take Haman to the banquet Esther had prepared.

CHAPTER **7** So the king and Haman went to Queen Esther's banquet. [2]And while they were drinking wine that day, the king again asked her, "Tell me what you want, Queen Esther. What is

**5:14a** Or *a pole.* **5:14b** Hebrew *50 cubits* [22.5 meters]. **6:4** Or *from the pole.*

your request? I will give it to you, even if it is half the kingdom!"

[3]And so Queen Esther replied, "If Your Majesty is pleased with me and wants to grant my request, my petition is that my life and the lives of my people will be spared. [4]For my people and I have been sold to those who would kill, slaughter, and annihilate us. If we had only been sold as slaves, I could remain quiet, for that would have been a matter too trivial to warrant disturbing the king."

[5]"Who would do such a thing?" King Xerxes demanded. "Who would dare touch you?"

[6]Esther replied, "This wicked Haman is our enemy." Haman grew pale with fright before the king and queen. [7]Then the king jumped to his feet in a rage and went out into the palace garden.

But Haman stayed behind to plead for his life with Queen Esther, for he knew that he was doomed. [8]In despair he fell on the couch where Queen Esther was reclining, just as the king returned from the palace garden. "Will he even assault the queen right here in the palace, before my very eyes?" the king roared. And as soon as the king spoke, his attendants covered Haman's face, signaling his doom.

[9]Then Harbona, one of the king's eunuchs, said, "Haman has set up a gallows* that stands seventy-five feet* tall in his own courtyard. He intended to use it to hang Mordecai, the man who saved the king from assassination."

"Then hang Haman on it!" the king ordered. [10]So they hanged Haman on the gallows he had set up for Mordecai, and the king's anger was pacified.

CHAPTER **8** **A NEW LAW TO PROTECT THE JEWS.** On that same day King Xerxes gave the estate of Haman, the enemy of the Jews, to Queen Esther. Then Mordecai was brought before the king, for Esther had told the king how they were related. [2]The king took off his signet ring—which he had taken back from Haman—and gave it to Mordecai. And Esther appointed Mordecai to be in charge of Haman's property.

[3]Now once more Esther came before the king, falling down at his feet and begging him with tears to stop Haman's evil plot against the Jews. [4]Again the king held out the gold scepter to Esther. So she rose and stood before him [5]and said, "If Your Majesty is pleased with me and if he thinks it is right, send out a decree reversing Haman's orders to destroy the Jews throughout all the provinces of the king. [6]For how can I endure to see my people and my family slaughtered and destroyed?"

[7]Then King Xerxes said to Queen Esther and Mordecai the Jew, "I have given Esther the estate of Haman, and he has been hanged on the gallows* because he tried to destroy the Jews. [8]Now go ahead and send a message to the Jews in the king's name, telling them whatever you want, and seal it with the king's signet ring. But remember that whatever is written in the king's name and sealed with his ring can never be revoked."

[9]So on June 25* the king's secretaries were summoned. As Mordecai dictated, they wrote a decree to the Jews and to the princes, governors, and local officials of all the 127 provinces stretching from India to Ethiopia.* The decree was written in the scripts and languages of all the peoples of the empire, including the Jews. [10]Mordecai wrote in the name of King Xerxes and sealed the message with the king's signet ring. He sent the letters by swift messengers, who rode horses especially bred for the king's service.

[11]The king's decree gave the Jews in every city authority to unite to defend their lives. They were allowed to kill, slaughter, and annihilate anyone of any nationality or province who might attack them or their children and wives, and to take the property of their enemies. [12]The day chosen for this event throughout all the provinces of King Xerxes was March 7 of the next year.* [13]A copy of this decree was to be recognized as law in every province and proclaimed to all the people. That way the Jews would be ready on that day to take revenge on their enemies. [14]So urged on by the king's command, the messengers rode out swiftly on horses bred for the king's service. The same decree was also issued at the fortress of Susa.

[15]Then Mordecai put on the royal robe of blue and white and the great crown of gold, and he wore an outer cloak of fine linen and purple. And the people of Susa celebrated the new decree. [16]The Jews were filled with joy and gladness and were honored everywhere. [17]In every city and province, wherever the king's decree arrived, the Jews rejoiced and had a great celebration and declared a public festival and holiday. And many of the people of the land became Jews themselves, for they feared what the Jews might do to them.

CHAPTER **9** **THE JEWS DEFEAT THEIR ENEMIES.** So on March 7* the two decrees of the king were put into effect. On that day, the enemies of the Jews had hoped to destroy them, but quite the opposite happened. [2]The Jews gathered in their cities throughout all the king's provinces to defend themselves against anyone who might try to harm them. But no one could make a stand against them, for everyone was afraid of them. [3]And all the commanders of the provinces, the princes, the governors, and the royal officials helped the Jews for fear of Mordecai. [4]For

## PAY THE PRICE ● ● • • ·

8:15-17 **Everyone wants to be a hero and receive praise, honor, and wealth. But few are willing to pay the price. Mordecai served the government faithfully for years, bore Haman's hatred and oppression, and risked his life for his people. The price to be paid by God's heroes is long-term commitment. Are you ready and willing to pay the price?**

**7:9a** Or *a pole;* also in 7:10. **7:9b** Hebrew *50 cubits* [22.5 meters]. **8:7** Or *on the pole.* **8:9a** Hebrew *on the twenty-third day of the third month, the month of Sivan,* of the Hebrew calendar. This event occurred on June 25, 474 B.C.; also see note on 2:16. **8:9b** Hebrew *to Cush.* **8:12** Hebrew *the thirteenth day of the twelfth month, the month of Adar,* of the Hebrew calendar. The date selected was March 7, 473 B.C.; also see note on 2:16. **9:1** Hebrew *on the thirteenth day of the twelfth month, the month of Adar,* of the Hebrew calendar. This event occurred on March 7, 473 B.C.; also see note on 2:16.

Mordecai had been promoted in the king's palace, and his fame spread throughout all the provinces as he became more and more powerful.

5But the Jews went ahead on the appointed day and struck down their enemies with the sword. They killed and annihilated their enemies and did as they pleased with those who hated them. 6They killed five hundred people in the fortress of Susa. 7They also killed Parshandatha, Dalphon, Aspatha, 8Poratha, Adalia, Aridatha, 9Parmashta, Arisai, Aridai, and Vaizatha—10the ten sons of Haman son of Hammedatha, the enemy of the Jews. But they did not take any plunder.

11That evening, when the king was informed of the number of people killed in the fortress of Susa, 12he called for Queen Esther and said, "The Jews have killed five hundred people in the fortress of Susa alone and also Haman's ten sons. If they have done that here, what has happened in the rest of the provinces? But now, what more do you want? It will be granted to you; tell me and I will do it."

13And Esther said, "If it please Your Majesty, give the Jews in Susa permission to do again tomorrow as they have done today, and have the bodies of Haman's ten sons hung from the gallows.*"

14So the king agreed, and the decree was announced in Susa. They also hung the bodies of Haman's ten sons from the gallows. 15Then the Jews at Susa gathered together on March 8* and killed three hundred more people, though again they took no plunder.

16Meanwhile, the other Jews throughout the king's provinces had gathered together to defend their lives. They gained relief from all their enemies, killing seventy-five thousand of those who hated them. But they did not take any plunder. 17Throughout the provinces this was done on March 7.* Then on the following day* they rested, celebrating their victory with a day of feasting and gladness. 18But the Jews at Susa continued killing their enemies on the second day also, and then rested on the third day,* making that their day of feasting and gladness. 19So to this day, rural Jews living in unwalled villages celebrate an annual festival and holiday in late winter,* when they rejoice and send gifts to each other.

20Mordecai recorded these events and sent letters to the Jews near and far, throughout all the king's provinces, 21encouraging them to celebrate an annual festival on these two days. 22He told them to celebrate these days with feasting and gladness and by giving gifts to each other and to the poor. This would commemorate a time when the Jews gained relief from their enemies, when their sorrow was turned into gladness and their mourning into joy.

23So the Jews adopted Mordecai's suggestion and began this annual custom. 24Haman son of Hammedatha the Agagite, the enemy of the Jews, had plotted to crush and destroy them on the day and month determined by casting lots (the lots were called *purim*). 25But when Esther came before the king, he issued a decree causing Haman's evil plot to backfire, and Haman and his sons were hanged on the gallows. 26(That is why this celebration is called Purim, because it is the ancient word for casting lots.) So because of Mordecai's letter and because of what they had experienced, 27the Jews throughout the realm agreed to inaugurate this tradition and to pass it on to their descendants and to all who became Jews. They declared they would never fail to celebrate these two prescribed days at the appointed time each year. 28These days would be remembered and kept from generation to generation and celebrated by every family throughout the provinces and cities of the empire. These days would never cease to be celebrated among the Jews, nor would the memory of what happened ever die out among their descendants.

29Then Queen Esther, the daughter of Abihail, along with Mordecai the Jew, wrote another letter putting the queen's full authority behind Mordecai's letter to establish the Festival of Purim. 30In addition, letters wishing peace and security were sent to the Jews throughout the 127 provinces of the empire of Xerxes. 31These letters established the Festival of Purim—an annual celebration of these days at the appointed time, decreed by both Mordecai the Jew and Queen Esther. (The people decided to observe this festival, just as they had decided for themselves and their descendants to establish the times of fasting and mourning.) 32So the command of Esther confirmed the practices of Purim, and it was all written down in the records.

## CHAPTER 10 **GOD REWARDS MORDECAI.**

King Xerxes imposed tribute throughout his empire, even to the distant coastlands. 2His great achievements and the full account of the greatness of Mordecai, whom the king had promoted, are recorded in *The Book of the History of the Kings of Media and Persia.* 3Mordecai the Jew became the prime minister, with authority next to that of King Xerxes himself. He was very great among the Jews, who held him in high esteem, because he worked for the good of his people and was a friend at the royal court for all of them.

### AVAILABLE ● ● • • •

9:29-31 **Among Jews, women were expected to be quiet, to serve in the home, and to stay on the fringe of religious and political life. But Esther was a Jewish woman who broke through the cultural norms, stepping outside her expected role to risk her life to help God's people. Whatever your place in life, God can use you. Be open, available, and ready—God may use you to do what others are afraid even to consider.**

**9:13** Or *the pole;* also in 9:14, 25. **9:15** Hebrew *the fourteenth day of the month of Adar,* of the Hebrew calendar. This event occurred on March 8, 473 B.C.; also see note on 2:16. **9:17a** Hebrew *on the thirteenth day of the month of Adar,* of the Hebrew calendar. This event occurred on March 7, 473 B.C.; also see note on 2:16. **9:17b** Hebrew *on the fourteenth day,* of the Hebrew month of Adar. **9:18** Hebrew *killing their enemies on the thirteenth day and the fourteenth day, and then rested on the fifteenth day,* of the Hebrew month of Adar. **9:19** Hebrew *on the fourteenth day of the month of Adar.* This day of the Hebrew lunar calendar usually occurs in March.

# MEGA themes

**IN CONTROL** The book of Esther tells of the circumstances that were essential for the survival of God's people in Persia. The "circumstances" were not the result of chance, but of God's grand design. God is in control of every area of life.

With God in charge, we can take courage. He can guide us through the circumstances we face in our life. We should expect God to display his power in carrying out his will.

1. Esther showed great courage in the face of frightening circumstances. How would you have felt if you were Esther, risking your life for your people?
2. How do Esther's choices reflect a trust in God's control of her life?
3. Think of a time when things worked out just the opposite of what you had wanted and expected. How did you feel toward God?
4. What choices in your life show that you believe that God is in control?
5. In what areas of your life do you want to learn to trust God's control more? How can you begin to do this today?

**RACISM** The Jews in Persia had been a minority since their deportation from Judea 100 years earlier. Haman was a descendant of King Agag, an enemy of the Jews. Lust for power and pride drove Haman to hate Mordecai, Esther's cousin. Haman convinced the king to kill all the Jews.

Racial hatred is always sinful. We must never condone it in any form. Every person on earth has intrinsic worth because God created human beings in his image. Therefore, God's people must stand against racism whenever and wherever it occurs. We must learn to see others with God's "eyes," rather than through the often cloudy lenses of our own cultural "glasses."

1. What results did racial hatred have in the book of Esther?
2. What are some results of racial hatred we have seen in history? In the present world?
3. Are there people in your school and/or community who suffer because of racial hatred? Who are they?
4. What could Christians in your school and/or community do to show how God's love overcomes racial hatred?

**DELIVERANCE** In March the Jews celebrate the Feast of Purim, which symbolizes God's deliverance. *Purim* means dice, such as those used by Haman to set the date for the extermination of all Jews from Persia. But God overruled, using Queen Esther to intercede on behalf of the Jews.

Because God is in control of history, he is never frustrated by any turn of events or by any human action. He is able to save us from the evil in this world and deliver us from sin and death. Because we trust God, we should not fear what people may do to us; instead, we should be confident in God's control.

1. Haman planned the destruction of the Jews. What did he learn about God when he tried to carry out his plan?
2. Where else in the Bible did God deliver his people?
3. What are specific instances where you know that God intervened to deliver you?
4. What does this study of deliverance teach you about placing your confidence in God? What difference can this confidence make in your life?

**ACTION** Faced with death, Esther and Mordecai set aside their own fear and took action. Mordecai took great risks to talk with Esther about the situation; Esther risked her life by asking King Xerxes to save the Jews. They were not paralyzed by fear.

When outnumbered and powerless, it is natural to feel helpless. Instead, Esther and Mordecai resisted and acted with courage. It is not enough to know that God is in control, we must courageously follow God's guidance.

1. Complete this sentence: Esther showed herself to be a woman of action when ________.
2. From what you've read in this book, describe Esther's view of God.

3. Why can you tell a person's view of God more by how he or she acts than what he or she says?
4. How would you describe your view of God based on your actions this past week? What strengths do you see? Weaknesses?

**WISDOM** The Jews were a minority in a world hostile to them. It took great wisdom for Mordecai to survive. Serving as a faithful official of the king, Mordecai took steps to understand and work with the Persian law. Yet he did not compromise his integrity.

It takes great wisdom to survive in a nonbelieving world. In a setting that is for the most part hostile to Christianity, we can demonstrate wisdom by giving respect to what is true and good and by standing against what is wrong. An important step in becoming mature is learning to distinguish good from evil. God will help us in that process through his Word, his Spirit, and the body of Christ, the church.

1. How does Mordecai provide an example of godly wisdom in an ungodly environment?
2. In what ways does God want believers to be active in non-Christian environments? What makes this difficult?
3. What situations or relationships do you face where you need godly wisdom in order to not compromise your faith?
4. What sources does God give you for getting the godly wisdom you need?
5. What specific wisdom will you seek from God through his Word, through prayer, and through godly advice in order to be a more effective witness for Christ?

**W**hy me, God?" Have you ever thought, whispered, or screamed that question? Have you ever thought that God was against you personally? At one time or another, everyone does . . . even people in the Bible. That is not surprising. What *is* surprising is God's answer to their questions. ■ Job loved God, and everything was going great in his life. He had money, land, possessions, and a large, wonderful family. But one day his world fell apart. He lost everything . . . except his life, a bitter wife, and accusing "friends." As you might imagine, Job asked why. Why him? Why now? The book of Job tells this story, and it gives God's reply. And after God spoke, Job was silent. Job is a book about success, tragedy, friends, and faith. As you read Job, allow God to begin changing your ideas about suffering. Learn to trust God even when you don't understand.

## STATS

PURPOSE: To demonstrate God's sovereignty and the meaning of true faith. It addresses the question, Why do the righteous suffer?

AUTHOR: Possibly Job. Some have suggested Moses, Solomon, or Elihu.

DATE WRITTEN: Unknown. Records events that probably occurred during the time of the patriarchs, approximately 2000–1800 B.C.

SETTING: The land of Uz, probably located northeast of Palestine, near desert land between Damascus and the Euphrates River

KEY PEOPLE: Job, Eliphaz the Temanite, Bildad the Shuhite, Zophar the Naamathite, Elihu the Buzite

SPECIAL FEATURES: Job is the first of the poetic books in the Hebrew Bible. Many believe this to be the oldest book in the Bible. The book gives us insights into the work of Satan. Ezekiel 14:14, 20 and James 5:11 mention Job as a historical character.

CHAPTER **1** **JOB LOSES EVERYTHING.** There was a man named Job who lived in the land of Uz. He was blameless, a man of complete integrity. He feared God and stayed away from evil. [2]He had seven sons and three daughters. [3]He owned seven thousand sheep, three thousand camels, five hundred teams of oxen, and five hundred female donkeys, and he employed many servants. He was, in fact, the richest person in that entire area.

[4]Every year when Job's sons had birthdays, they invited their brothers and sisters to join them for a celebration. On these occasions they would get together to eat and drink. [5]When these celebrations ended—and sometimes they lasted several days—Job would purify his children. He would get up early in the morning and offer a burnt offering for each of them. For Job said to himself, "Perhaps my children have sinned and have cursed God in their hearts." This was Job's regular practice.

[6]One day the angels* came to present themselves before the LORD, and Satan the Accuser came with them. [7]"Where have you come from?" the LORD asked Satan.

And Satan answered the LORD, "I have been going back and forth across the earth, watching everything that's going on."

[8]Then the LORD asked Satan, "Have you noticed my servant Job? He is the finest man in all the earth—a man of complete integrity. He fears God and will have nothing to do with evil."

[9]Satan replied to the LORD, "Yes, Job fears God, but not without good reason! [10]You have always protected him and his home and his property from harm. You have made him prosperous in everything he does. Look how rich he is! [11]But take away everything he has, and he will surely curse you to your face!"

[12]"All right, you may test him," the LORD said to

**WHY ME?** ●●●●●

1:1 **When reading the book of Job, we have information that the characters of the story do not. Job, the main character of the book, lost all he had through no fault of his own. As he struggled to understand why all this was happening to him, it became clear that he was not meant to know the reasons. He would have to face life with the answers and explanations held back. Only then would his faith fully develop.**

**We must experience life as Job did—one day at a time and without complete answers to all of life's questions. Will we, like Job, trust God no matter what? Or will we give in to the temptation to say that God doesn't really care?**

1:6 Hebrew *the sons of God.*

Satan. "Do whatever you want with everything he possesses, but don't harm him physically." So Satan left the LORD's presence.

[13]One day when Job's sons and daughters were dining at the oldest brother's house, [14]a messenger arrived at Job's home with this news: "Your oxen were plowing, with the donkeys feeding beside them, [15]when the Sabeans raided us. They stole all the animals and killed all the farmhands. I am the only one who escaped to tell you."

[16]While he was still speaking, another messenger arrived with this news: "The fire of God has fallen from heaven and burned up your sheep and all the shepherds. I am the only one who escaped to tell you."

[17]While he was still speaking, a third messenger arrived with this news: "Three bands of Chaldean raiders have stolen your camels and killed your servants. I am the only one who escaped to tell you."

[18]While he was still speaking, another messenger arrived with this news: "Your sons and daughters were feasting in their oldest brother's home. [19]Suddenly, a powerful wind swept in from the desert and hit the house on all sides. The house collapsed, and all your children are dead. I am the only one who escaped to tell you."

[20]Job stood up and tore his robe in grief. Then he shaved his head and fell to the ground before God. [21]He said,

"I came naked from my mother's womb,
    and I will be stripped of everything when I die.
The LORD gave me everything I had,
    and the LORD has taken it away.
Praise the name of the LORD!"

[22]In all of this, Job did not sin by blaming God.

## HEARTBREAK ● • • •

**1:20-22 Job did not hide his overwhelming grief. This emotional display did not mean he had lost his faith in God; instead, it showed that he was human and that he loved his family. God created our emotions, and it is not sinful to express them as Job did. If you have experienced deep loss, disappointment, or heartbreak, admit your feelings to yourself and others, and grieve.**

CHAPTER **2** One day the angels* came again to present themselves before the LORD, and Satan the Accuser came with them. [2]"Where have you come from?" the LORD asked Satan.

And Satan answered the LORD, "I have been going back and forth across the earth, watching everything that's going on."

[3]Then the LORD asked Satan, "Have you noticed my servant Job? He is the finest man in all the earth—a man of complete integrity. He fears God and will have nothing to do with evil. And he has maintained his integrity, even though you persuaded me to harm him without cause."

2:1 Hebrew *the sons of God.* 3:8 Hebrew *rouse Leviathan.*

## SILENT COMFORT ● • • •

2:13 **Why did Job's friends arrive and then just sit quietly? According to Jewish tradition, people who come to comfort someone in mourning are not to speak until the mourner speaks. Often the best response to another person's suffering is silence. Job's friends realized that his pain was too deep to be healed with mere words, so they said nothing. (If only they had *continued* to just sit quietly!) Often, we feel we must say something spiritual and insightful to a hurting friend. Perhaps what he or she needs most is just our presence, showing that we care. Pat answers and trite quotations say much less than caring silence and loving companionship.**

[4]Satan replied to the LORD, "Skin for skin—he blesses you only because you bless him. A man will give up everything he has to save his life. [5]But take away his health, and he will surely curse you to your face!"

[6]"All right, do with him as you please," the LORD said to Satan. "But spare his life." [7]So Satan left the LORD's presence, and he struck Job with a terrible case of boils from head to foot.

[8]Then Job scraped his skin with a piece of broken pottery as he sat among the ashes. [9]His wife said to him, "Are you still trying to maintain your integrity? Curse God and die."

[10]But Job replied, "You talk like a godless woman. Should we accept only good things from the hand of God and never anything bad?" So in all this, Job said nothing wrong.

[11]Three of Job's friends were Eliphaz the Temanite, Bildad the Shuhite, and Zophar the Naamathite. When they heard of the tragedy he had suffered, they got together and traveled from their homes to comfort and console him. [12]When they saw Job from a distance, they scarcely recognized him. Wailing loudly, they tore their robes and threw dust into the air over their heads to demonstrate their grief. [13]Then they sat on the ground with him for seven days and nights. And no one said a word, for they saw that his suffering was too great for words.

CHAPTER **3** **JOB: I WISH I HAD DIED AT BIRTH.** At last Job spoke, and he cursed the day of his birth. [2]He said:

[3]"Cursed be the day of my birth, and cursed be the night when I was conceived. [4]Let that day be turned to darkness. Let it be lost even to God on high, and let it be shrouded in darkness. [5]Yes, let the darkness and utter gloom claim it for its own. Let a black cloud overshadow it, and let the darkness terrify it. [6]Let that night be blotted off the calendar, never again to be counted among the days of the year, never again to appear among the months. [7]Let that night be barren. Let it have no joy. [8]Let those who are experts at cursing—those who are ready to rouse the sea monster*—curse that day. [9]Let its morning stars remain dark. Let it hope for light, but in vain; may it never see the morning light. [10]Curse it for its failure to shut my mother's womb, for letting me be born to all this trouble.

[11]"Why didn't I die at birth as I came from the
womb? [12]Why did my mother let me live? Why did
she nurse me at her breasts? [13]For if I had died at
birth, I would be at peace now, asleep and at rest.
[14]I would rest with the world's kings and prime
ministers, famous for their great construction projects. [15]I would rest with wealthy princes whose
palaces were filled with gold and silver. [16]Why was
I not buried like a stillborn child, like a baby who
never lives to see the light? [17]For in death the
wicked cease from troubling, and the weary are at
rest. [18]Even prisoners are at ease in death, with no
guards to curse them. [19]Rich and poor are there
alike, and the slave is free from his master.
[20]"Oh, why should light be given to the weary, and
life to those in misery?
[21]They long for death, and it
won't come. They search for
death more eagerly than for
hidden treasure. [22]It is a
blessed relief when they finally die, when they find the
grave. [23]Why is life given to
those with no future, those
destined by God to live in
distress? [24]I cannot eat for
sighing; my groans pour out
like water. [25]What I always
feared has happened to me.
What I dreaded has come to
be. [26]I have no peace, no
quietness. I have no rest; instead, only trouble comes."

## CHAPTER 4 ELIPHAZ: WORDS.

Then Eliphaz the
Temanite replied to Job:
[2]"Will you be patient and
let me say a word? For who
could keep from speaking
out?
[3]"In the past you have encouraged many a troubled
soul to trust in God; you
have supported those who
were weak. [4]Your words have
strengthened the fallen; you
steadied those who wavered.
[5]But now when trouble
strikes, you faint and are
broken. [6]Does your reverence for God give you no
confidence? Shouldn't you
believe that God will care for
those who are upright?
[7]"Stop and think! Does
the innocent person perish?
When has the upright per-
son been destroyed? [8]My ex-
perience shows that those who plant trouble and
cultivate evil will harvest the same. [9]They perish by a
breath from God. They vanish in a blast of his anger.
[10]Though they are fierce young lions, they will all be
broken and destroyed. [11]The fierce lion will starve,
and the cubs of the lioness will be scattered.
[12]"This truth was given me in secret, as though
whispered in my ear. [13]It came in a vision at night as
others slept. [14]Fear gripped me; I trembled and
shook with terror. [15]A spirit* swept past my face. Its
wind sent shivers up my spine. [16]It stopped, but I
couldn't see its shape. There was a form before my
eyes, and a hushed voice said, [17]'Can a mortal be just
and upright before God? Can a person be pure before the Creator?'

4:15 Or *wind*.

---

**JOB** The first question most children learn to ask is *why*. It doesn't take long for kids to notice that things don't just happen. There's a system. The system is called cause and effect. When kids ask why, they are trying to figure out the system.

Sometimes, though, we don't know why. We think that good things should happen to people who do good things, and that bad things should happen to people who do bad things. It often works out that way—but not always. Job was a man who did many good things and had many terrible things happen to him. His life can teach us what God wants us to do when we don't understand what is happening to us.

When the question *why* becomes important, we can use the letters of that word to remind us of Job's lessons. We need to *wait*, *hope*, and *yield*.

*Waiting* is hard. Our "instant" age has taught us to expect answers and help fast. Job wanted to know why. When God finally spoke, he didn't offer Job an answer. He showed Job that it is better to know God than to know answers.

That's why *hope* is important. When we remember that God loves us, that he has good plans for us, and that he is more powerful than any situation we might encounter, we have hope. Hope means we trust God even if we never find out why something happened.

*Yielding* means wanting to do whatever God wants. It means praying like this: "God, I'm willing to wait and hope, because you are my God." Are there some areas in your life that need this prayer?

LESSONS: Knowing God is better than knowing answers
God is not arbitrary or uncaring
Pain is not always punishment

KEY VERSES: "For examples of patience in suffering, look at the prophets who spoke in the name of the Lord. We give great honor to those who endure under suffering. Job is an example of a man who endured patiently. From his experience we see how the Lord's plan finally ended in good, for he is full of tenderness and mercy" (James 5:10-11).

Job's story is told in the book of Job. He is also referred to in Ezekiel 14:14, 20.

**UPS:**
- A man of faith, patience, and endurance
- Known as a generous and caring person
- Very wealthy

**DOWN:**
- Allowed his suffering to overwhelm him and make him question God

**STATS:**
- Where: Land of Uz
- Occupation: Wealthy land and livestock owner
- Relatives: Wife and first ten children not named. Daughters from the second set of children: Jemimah, Keziah, Keren-happuch.
- Contemporaries: Eliphaz, Bildad, Zophar, Elihu

[18]"If God cannot trust his own angels and has charged some of them with folly, [19]how much less will he trust those made of clay! Their foundation is dust, and they are crushed as easily as moths. [20]They are alive in the morning, but by evening they are dead, gone forever without a trace. [21]Their tent collapses; they die in ignorance.

CHAPTER **5** "You may cry for help, but no one listens. You may turn to the angels,* but they give you no help. [2]Surely resentment destroys the fool, and jealousy kills the simple. [3]From my experience, I know that fools who turn from God may be successful for the moment, but then comes sudden disaster. [4]Their children are abandoned far from help, with no one to defend them. [5]Their harvests are stolen, and their wealth satisfies the thirst of many others, not themselves! [6]But evil does not spring from the soil, and trouble does not sprout from the earth. [7]People are born for trouble as predictably as sparks fly upward from a fire.

[8]"My advice to you is this: Go to God and present your case to him. [9]For he does great works too marvelous to understand. He performs miracles without number. [10]He gives rain for the earth. He sends water for the fields. [11]He gives prosperity to the poor and humble, and he takes sufferers to safety. [12]He frustrates the plans of the crafty, so their efforts will not succeed. [13]He catches those who think they are wise in their own cleverness, so that their cunning schemes are thwarted. [14]They grope in the daylight as though they were blind; they see no better in the daytime than at night. [15]He rescues the poor from the cutting words of the strong. He saves them from the clutches of the powerful. [16]And so at last the poor have hope, and the fangs of the wicked are broken.

**GOOD ADVICE ● ● • • •**

**5:17 Eliphaz was correct—it is a blessing to be disciplined by God when we do wrong. His advice, however, did not apply to Job. As we know from the beginning of the book, Job's suffering was not a result of sin. We sometimes give people excellent advice only to learn that it does not apply to them and is therefore not very helpful. All those who offer counsel from God's Word should take care to thoroughly understand a person's situation *before* giving advice.**

[17]"But consider the joy of those corrected by God! Do not despise the chastening of the Almighty when you sin. [18]For though he wounds, he also bandages. He strikes, but his hands also heal. [19]He will rescue you again and again so that no evil can touch you. [20]He will save you from death in time of famine, from the power of the sword in time of war. [21]You will be safe from slander and will have no fear of destruction when it comes. [22]You will laugh at destruction and famine; wild animals will not terrify you. [23]You will be at peace with the stones of the field, and its wild animals will be at peace with you. [24]You will know that your home is kept safe. When

5:1 Hebrew *the holy ones.*

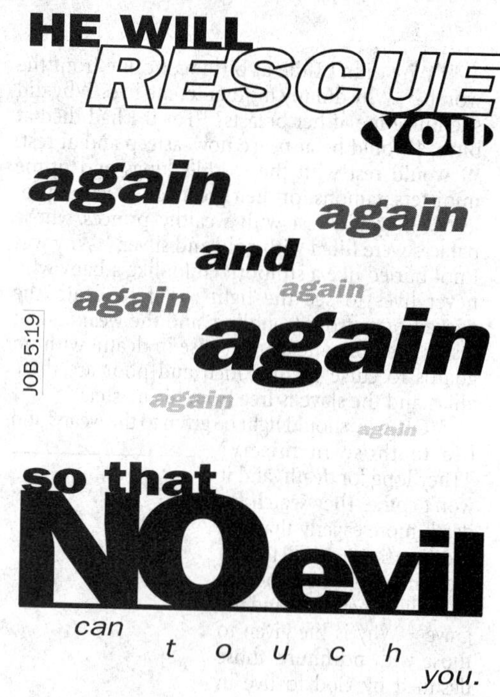
HE WILL
RESCUE
YOU
again
again
and
again
again
again
again
again
again
so that
NO evil
can
t o u c h
you.
JOB 5:19

you visit your pastures, nothing will be missing. [25]Your children will be many; your descendants will be as plentiful as grass! [26]You will live to a good old age. You will not be harvested until the proper time!

[27]"We have found from experience that all this is true. Listen to my counsel, and apply it to yourself."

CHAPTER **6** **JOB: WHY AM I SUFFERING?** Then Job spoke again:

[2]"If my sadness could be weighed and my troubles be put on the scales, [3]they would be heavier than all the sands of the sea. That is why I spoke so rashly. [4]For the Almighty has struck me down with his arrows. He has sent his poisoned arrows deep within my spirit. All God's terrors are arrayed against me. [5]Don't I have a right to complain? Wild donkeys bray when they find no green grass, and oxen low when they have no food. [6]People complain when there is no salt in their food. And how tasteless is the uncooked white of an egg! [7]My appetite disappears when I look at it; I gag at the thought of eating it!

[8]"Oh, that I might have my request, that God would grant my hope. [9]I wish he would crush me. I wish he would reach out his hand and kill me. [10]At least I can take comfort in this: Despite the pain, I have not denied the words of the Holy One. [11]But I do not have the strength to endure. I do not have a goal that encourages me to carry on. [12]Do I have strength as hard as stone? Is my body made of bronze? [13]No, I am utterly helpless, without any chance of success.

[14]"One should be kind to a fainting friend, but you have accused me without the slightest fear of the Almighty. [15]My brother, you have proved as unreliable as

a seasonal brook that overflows its banks in the spring 16when it is swollen with ice and melting snow. 17But when the hot weather arrives, the water disappears. The brook vanishes in the heat. 18The caravans turn aside to be refreshed, but there is nothing there to drink, and so they perish in the desert. 19With high hopes, the caravans from Tema and from Sheba stop for water, 20but finding none, their hopes are dashed. 21You, too, have proved to be of no help. You have seen my calamity, and you are afraid. 22But why? Have I ever asked you for a gift? Have I begged you to use any of your wealth on my behalf? 23Have I ever asked you to rescue me from my enemies? Have I asked you to save me from ruthless people?

24"All I want is a reasonable answer—then I will keep quiet. Tell me, what have I done wrong? 25Honest words are painful, but what do your criticisms amount to? 26Do you think your words are convincing when you disregard my cry of desperation? 27You would even send an orphan into slavery* or sell a friend. 28Look at me! Would I lie to your face? 29Stop assuming my guilt, for I am righteous. Don't be so unjust. 30Do you think I am lying? Don't I know the difference between right and wrong?

CHAPTER **7** "Is this not the struggle of all humanity? A person's life is long and hard, like that of a hired hand, 2like a worker who longs for the day to end, like a servant waiting to be paid. 3I, too, have been assigned months of futility, long and weary nights of misery. 4When I go to bed, I think, 'When will it be morning?' But the night drags on, and I toss till dawn. 5My skin is filled with worms and scabs. My flesh breaks open, full of pus.

6"My days are swifter than a weaver's shuttle flying back and forth. They end without hope. 7O God, remember that my life is but a breath, and I will never again experience pleasure. 8You see me now, but not for long. Your eyes will be on me, but I will be dead. 9Just as a cloud dissipates and vanishes, those who die will not come back. 10They are gone forever from their home—never to be seen again.

11"I cannot keep from speaking. I must express my anguish. I must complain in my bitterness. 12Am I a sea monster that you place a guard on me? 13If I think, 'My bed will comfort me, and I will try to forget my misery with sleep,' 14you shatter me with dreams. You terrify me with visions. 15I would rather die of strangulation than go on and on like this. 16I hate my life. I do not want to go on living. Oh, leave me alone for these few remaining days.

17"What are mere mortals, that you should make so much of us? 18For you examine us every morning and test us every moment. 19Why won't you leave me alone—even for a moment*? 20Have I sinned? What have I done to you, O watcher of all humanity? Why have you made me your target? Am I a burden to you? 21Why not just pardon my sin and take away my guilt? For soon I will lie down in the dust and die. When you look for me, I will be gone."

6:27 Hebrew *even gamble over an orphan.* 7:19 Hebrew *long enough to swallow my spittle.*

**STRUGGLES ● ● ● • •**

6:8-9 **In his grief, Job wanted to give in, to be freed from his discomfort, and to die. But God did not grant Job's request. He had a greater plan for him. Our tendency, like Job's, is to want to give up and get out when the going gets tough. To trust God in the good times is commendable, but to trust him during the difficult times tests us to our limits and exercises our faith. In your struggles, large or small, trust that God is in control (Romans 8:28).**

CHAPTER **8** **BILDAD: IF YOU WERE PURE.** Then Bildad the Shuhite replied to Job:

2"How long will you go on like this? Your words are a blustering wind. 3Does God twist justice? Does the Almighty twist what is right? 4Your children obviously sinned against him, so their punishment was well deserved. 5But if you pray to God and seek the favor of the Almighty, 6if you are pure and live with complete integrity, he will rise up and restore your happy home. 7And though you started with little, you will end with much.

8"Just ask the former generation. Pay attention to the experience of our ancestors. 9For we were born but yesterday and know so little. Our days on earth are as transient as a shadow. 10But those who came before us will teach you. They will teach you from the wisdom of former generations.

11"Can papyrus reeds grow where there is no marsh? Can bulrushes flourish where there is no water? 12While they are still flowering, not ready to be cut, they begin to wither. 13Such is the fate of all who forget God. The hope of the godless comes to nothing. 14Everything they count on will collapse. They are leaning on a spiderweb. 15They cling to their home for security, but it won't last. They try to hold it fast, but it will not endure. 16The godless seem so strong, like a lush plant growing in the sunshine, its branches spreading across the garden. 17Its roots grow down through a pile of rocks to hold it firm. 18But when it is uprooted, it isn't even missed! 19That is the end of its life, and others spring up from the earth to replace it.

20"But look! God will not reject a person of integrity, nor will he make evildoers prosper. 21He will yet fill your mouth with laughter and your lips with shouts of joy. 22Those who hate you will be clothed with shame, and the tent of the wicked will be destroyed."

**FEELING SECURE ● ● ● • •**

8:14-15 **Bildad wrongly assumed that Job was trusting in something other than God for security, so he pointed out that such supports will collapse. One of man's basic needs is security, and people will do almost anything to feel secure. Eventually, however, our money, possessions, knowledge, and relationships will fail or be gone. Only God can give lasting security. What have you trusted for your security? How lasting is it? If you have a secure foundation with God, then feelings of insecurity cannot uproot you.**

# SUFFERING AND EVIL

Sooner or later, every Christian faces this question: Why does God allow suffering and evil? Why do horrible things happen to good people? Theologians and philosophers express it like this: "If God is good, he must not be all-powerful, otherwise he wouldn't allow evil. If he *is* all-powerful, he must not be good." Does God see what's going on here? Does he care? If so, why doesn't he intervene? The book of Job addresses this question more than any portion of Scripture. For reasons unknown to Job, a series of crushing catastrophes hit him, leaving him to ask, ***"Why me, God?"*** And God responds (chapters 38–41) with his longest unbroken speech in the Bible—but he never tells Job why. He basically tells Job that as God he can do whatever he wants, and that's all the answer Job needs. Big help, right? It's like the story about the guy who goes home from work one day to find his wife gone, the kids moved out, and his house empty. Then **the dog bites him.** He lifts his hands toward heaven and cries out, "Why me, God?" From the skies there comes a rumbling voice saying: "Frankly, Sam, there's just something about you that ticks me off." The fact that God doesn't answer Job's question is somewhat disturbing. But the following perspectives may help when you are faced with suffering and evil. First, remember that though God never answered Job directly, he didn't condemn Job for asking. He just reminded Job who he was talking to. It seems that ***why*** is a question we are free to ask, but God is not bound to answer. Sometimes he will; sometimes he won't. Second, remember that we live in a broken world of sinful people. It is a **PLANET IN REBELLION** against its Creator; it should hardly surprise us that believers are caught in the **crossfire.** When you are tempted to blame God for your suffering, think of it like this. It's like giving a fragile, priceless family heirloom to a child. He looks it over and then smashes it to the floor. As he stands there in the midst of the shattered pieces of what you gave him, he shakes his clenched fist in your face and says, "Look what you've done! Look at this ***piece of junk*** you gave me!" The child is wrong; you gave him a wonderful, treasured possession and he ruined it. God gave us a perfect world; we've turned it into the chaos it is today. Third, remember that being a Christian—or a "good person"—does not exempt you from pain and suffering. Jesus even guaranteed us (in John 16:33) that we will experience trials and heartache. But we can be comforted: Jesus overcame suffering and we can, too. It's easy to serve God WHEN LIFE IS SUNNY; the test is how we respond when the storm washes over us. And if you're serious about following Jesus, brace yourself: storms will come. Fourth, contrary to what a lot of Christians believe, God does not promise his children happiness. He's much more concerned with our holiness, and that involves pain and sacrifice. Worthwhile things seldom, if ever, come without great cost. Following Jesus is no exception. Of course, God isn't a cosmic killjoy, getting his kicks out of ***watching us squirm.*** He just wants us to imitate his Son—even when it isn't all fun and games. Finally, when nothing else helps, remember this: when you or someone you love suffers, no one hurts more than God. He's a good Father, and it pains him deeply to see his children hurt. He feels with us so genuinely that he got personally involved in our struggle—he became a man and suffered and died for us. So when you hurt, remember: YOU NEVER CRY ALONE. God knows, God sees, and God cares.

CHAPTER **9** **JOB HAS MORE QUESTIONS.** Then Job spoke again:

2"Yes, I know this is all true in principle. But how can a person be declared innocent in the eyes of God? 3If someone wanted to take God to court,* would it be possible to answer him even once in a thousand times? 4For God is so wise and so mighty. Who has ever challenged him successfully?

5"Without warning, he moves the mountains, overturning them in his anger. 6He shakes the earth from its place, and its foundations tremble. 7If he commands it, the sun won't rise and the stars won't shine. 8He alone has spread out the heavens and marches on the waves of the sea. 9He made all the stars—the Bear, Orion, the Pleiades, and the constellations of the southern sky. 10His great works are too marvelous to understand. He performs miracles without number.

11"Yet when he comes near, I cannot see him. When he moves on, I do not see him go. 12If he sends death to snatch someone away, who can stop him? Who dares to ask him, 'What are you doing?' 13And God does not restrain his anger. The mightiest forces against him* are crushed beneath his feet.

14"And who am I, that I should try to answer God or even reason with him? 15Even if I were innocent, I would have no defense. I could only plead for mercy. 16And even if I summoned him and he responded, he would never listen to me. 17For he attacks me without reason,* and he multiplies my wounds without cause. 18He will not let me catch my breath, but fills me instead with bitter sorrows. 19As for strength, he has it. As for justice, who can challenge him? 20Though I am innocent, my own mouth would pronounce me guilty. Though I am blameless, it* would prove me wicked.

21"I am innocent, but it makes no difference to me—I despise my life. 22Innocent or wicked, it is all the same to him. That is why I say, 'He destroys both the blameless and the wicked.' 23He laughs when a plague suddenly kills the innocent. 24The whole earth is in the hands of the wicked, and God blinds the eyes of the judges and lets them be unfair. If not he, then who?

25"My life passes more swiftly than a runner. It flees away, filled with tragedy. 26It disappears like a swift boat, like an eagle that swoops down on its prey. 27If I decided to forget my complaints, if I decided to end my sadness and be cheerful, 28I would dread all the pain he would send. For I know you will not hold me innocent, O God. 29Whatever happens, I will be found guilty. So what's the use of trying? 30Even if I were to wash myself with soap and cleanse my hands with lye to make them absolutely clean, 31you would plunge me into a muddy ditch, and I would be so filthy my own clothing would hate me.

32"God is not a mortal like me, so I cannot argue with him or take him to trial. 33If only there were a mediator who could bring us together, but there is none. 34The mediator could make God stop beating me, and I would no longer live in terror of his punishment. 35Then I could speak to him without fear, but I cannot do that in my own strength.

CHAPTER **10** "I am disgusted with my life. Let me complain freely. I will speak in the bitterness of my soul. 2I will say to God, 'Don't simply condemn me—tell me the charge you are bringing against me. 3What do you gain by oppressing me? Why do you reject me, the work of your own hands, while sending joy and prosperity to the wicked? 4Are your eyes only those of a human? Do you see things as people see them? 5Is your lifetime merely human? Is your life so short 6that you are in a hurry to probe for my guilt, to search for my sin? 7Although you know I am not guilty, no one can rescue me from your power.

8"'You formed me with your hands; you made me, and yet you completely destroy me. 9Remember that I am made of dust—will you turn me back to dust so soon? 10You guided my conception and formed me in the womb.* 11You clothed me with skin and flesh, and you knit my bones and sinews together. 12You gave me life and showed me your unfailing love. My life was preserved by your care.

13"'Yet your real motive—I know this was your intent—14was to watch me, and if I sinned, you would not forgive my iniquity. 15If I am guilty, too bad for me. And even if I'm innocent, I am filled with shame and misery so that I can't hold my head high. 16And if I hold my head high, you hunt me like a lion and display your awesome power against me. 17Again and again you witness against me. You pour out an ever-increasing volume of anger upon me and bring fresh armies against me.

18"'Why, then, did you bring me out of my mother's womb? Why didn't you let me die at birth? 19Then I would have been spared this miserable existence. I would have gone directly from the womb to the grave. 20I have only a little time left, so leave me alone—that I may have a little moment of comfort 21before I leave for the land of darkness and utter gloom, never to return. 22It is a land as dark as midnight, a land of utter gloom where confusion reigns and the light is as dark as midnight.'"

## HOW UNFAIR! ● ● • • •

10:1 **When we face baffling affliction, a natural response is to feel sorry for ourselves. Pain pushes us toward self-pity. At this point we are only one step from self-righteousness, where we keep track of life's injustices and say, "Look what happened to me; how unfair it is!" This comes close to saying that God is unfair. Remember that life's trials, whether allowed by God or sent by God, can help us grow and mature. When facing difficult situations, ask, "What can I learn and how can I grow?" rather than "Who did this to me and how can I get out of it?"**

9:3 Or *If God wanted to take a person to court.* 9:13 Hebrew *The helpers of Rahab,* the name of a mythical sea monster that represents chaos in ancient literature. 9:17 As in Syriac version; Hebrew reads *with a storm.* 9:20 Or *he.* 10:10 Hebrew *You poured me out like milk and curdled me like cheese.*

CHAPTER **11** **ZOPHAR: SEE YOURSELF.** Then Zophar the Naamathite replied to Job:

2"Shouldn't someone answer this torrent of words? Is a person proved innocent just by talking a lot? 3Should I remain silent while you babble on? When you mock God, shouldn't someone make you ashamed? 4You claim, 'My teaching is pure,' and 'I am clean in the sight of God.' 5If only God would speak; if only he would tell you what he thinks! 6If only he would tell you the secrets of wisdom, for true wisdom is not a simple matter. Listen! God is doubtless punishing you far less than you deserve!

7"Can you solve the mysteries of God? Can you discover everything there is to know about the Almighty? 8Such knowledge is higher than the heavens—but who are you? It is deeper than the underworld*—what can you know in comparison to him? 9It is broader than the earth and wider than the sea. 10If God comes along and puts a person in prison, or if he calls the court to order, who is going to stop him? 11For he knows those who are false, and he takes note of all their sins. 12An empty-headed person won't become wise any more than a wild donkey can bear human offspring*!

## NO HIDING FROM GOD ● ● ● • •

**11:11 Zophar incorrectly assumed that Job was hiding secret faults and sins. Although his assumption was wrong, he explained quite accurately that God knows and sees everything. We are often tempted by the thought, *No one will ever know!* Perhaps we can hide some sin from others, but we can do *nothing* without God knowing about it. Our very thoughts are known to God, so of course he will notice our sins. Job understood this as well as Zophar did, but it didn't apply to his current dilemma.**

13"If only you would prepare your heart and lift up your hands to him in prayer! 14Get rid of your sins and leave all iniquity behind you. 15Then your face will brighten in innocence. You will be strong and free of fear. 16You will forget your misery. It will all be gone like water under the bridge. 17Your life will be brighter than the noonday. Any darkness will be as bright as morning. 18You will have courage because you will have hope. You will be protected and will rest in safety. 19You will lie down unafraid, and many will look to you for help. 20But the wicked will lose hope. They have no escape. Their hope becomes despair."

CHAPTER **12** **JOB: I LONG TO SPEAK TO GOD.** Then Job spoke again:

2"You really know everything, don't you? And when you die, wisdom will die with you! 3Well, I know a few things myself—and you're no better than I am. Who doesn't know these things you've been saying? 4Yet my friends laugh at me. I am a man who calls on God and receives an answer. I am a just and blameless man, yet they laugh at me. 5People who are at ease mock those in trouble. They give a

## GUIDANCE ● ● ● • •

**12:24-25 Job affirms that no leader has any real wisdom apart from God. No research or report can outweigh God's opinion. When we look for guidance for our lives, we must recognize that God's wisdom is superior to any the world has to offer.**

push to people who are stumbling. 6But even robbers are left in peace, and those who provoke God—and God has them in his power—live in safety!

7"Ask the animals, and they will teach you. Ask the birds of the sky, and they will tell you. 8Speak to the earth, and it will instruct you. Let the fish of the sea speak to you. 9They all know that the LORD has done this. 10For the life of every living thing is in his hand, and the breath of all humanity. 11Just as the mouth tastes good food, so the ear tests the words it hears. 12Wisdom belongs to the aged, and understanding to those who have lived many years.

13"But true wisdom and power are with God; counsel and understanding are his. 14What he destroys cannot be rebuilt. When he closes in on someone, there is no escape. 15If he holds back the rain, the earth becomes a desert. If he releases the waters, they flood the earth.

16"Yes, strength and wisdom are with him; deceivers and deceived are both in his power. 17He leads counselors away stripped of good judgment; he drives judges to madness. 18He removes the royal robe of kings. With ropes around their waist, they are led away. 19He leads priests away stripped of status; he overthrows the mighty. 20He silences the trusted adviser, and he removes the insight of the elders. 21He pours disgrace upon princes and confiscates weapons from the strong.

22"He floods the darkness with light; he brings light to the deepest gloom. 23He raises up nations, and he destroys them. He makes nations expand, and he abandons them. 24He takes away the understanding of kings, and he leaves them wandering in a wasteland without a path. 25They grope in the darkness without a light. He makes them stagger like drunkards.

CHAPTER **13** "Look, I have seen many instances such as you describe. I understand what you are saying. 2I know as much as you do. You are no better than I am. 3Oh, how I long to speak directly to the Almighty. I want to argue my case with God himself. 4For you are smearing me with lies. As doctors, you are worthless quacks. 5Please be quiet! That's the smartest thing you could do. 6Listen to my charge; pay attention to my arguments.

7"Are you defending God by means of lies and dishonest arguments? 8You should be impartial witnesses, but will you slant your testimony in his favor? Will you argue God's case for him? 9Be careful that he doesn't find out what you are doing! Or do you think you can fool him as easily as you fool people? 10No, you will be in serious trouble with him if even in your hearts you slant your testimony in his favor. 11Doesn't his majesty strike terror into your

11:8 Hebrew *Sheol.* 11:12 Or *bear a tame colt.*

heart? Does not your fear of him seize you? [12]Your statements have about as much value as ashes. Your defense is as fragile as a clay pot.

[13]"Be silent now and leave me alone. Let me speak—and I will face the consequences. [14]Yes, I will take my life in my hands and say what I really think. [15]God might kill me, but I cannot wait. I am going to argue my case with him. [16]But this is what will save me: that I am not godless. If I were, I would be thrown from his presence.

[17]"Listen closely to what I am about to say. Hear me out. [18]I have prepared my case; I will be proved innocent. [19]Who can argue with me over this? If you could prove me wrong, I would remain silent until I die.

[20]"O God, there are two things I beg of you, and I will be able to face you. [21]Remove your hand from me, and don't terrify me with your awesome presence. [22]Now summon me, and I will answer! Or let me speak to you, and you reply. [23]Tell me, what have I done wrong? Show me my rebellion and my sin. [24]Why do you turn away from me? Why do you consider me your enemy? [25]Would you terrify a leaf that is blown by the wind? Would you chase a dry stalk of grass?

[26]"You write bitter accusations against me and bring up all the sins of my youth. [27]You put my feet in stocks. You watch all my paths. You trace all my footprints. [28]I waste away like rotting wood, like a moth-eaten coat.

## CHAPTER 14

"How frail is humanity! How short is life, and how full of trouble! [2]Like a flower, we blossom for a moment and then wither. Like the shadow of a passing cloud, we quickly disappear. [3]Must you keep an eye on such a frail creature and demand an accounting from me? [4]Who can create purity in one born impure? No one! [5]You have decided the length of our lives. You know how many

### GUARANTEED LIFE ● ● • • •

14:14-15 **Life is brief and full of trouble, Job lamented in his closing remarks. Sickness, loneliness, disappointment, and the deaths of others caused him to say that life is not fair. Still, Job held on to the one truth that also gives hope to us: resurrection. God's solution to an unfair world is to guarantee life with him forever. No matter how unfair your present world seems, God offers the hope of being in his presence eternally.**

months we will live, and we are not given a minute longer. [6]So give us a little rest, won't you? Turn away your angry stare. We are like hired hands, so let us finish the task you have given us.

[7]"If a tree is cut down, there is hope that it will sprout again and grow new branches. [8]Though its roots have grown old in the earth and its stump decays, [9]at the scent of water it may bud and sprout again like a new seedling.

[10]"But when people die, they lose all strength. They breathe their last, and then where are they? [11]As water evaporates from a lake and as a river disappears in drought, [12]people lie down and do not rise again. Until the heavens are no more, they will not wake up nor be roused from their sleep.

[13]"I wish you would hide me with the dead and forget me there until your anger has passed. But mark your calendar to think of me again! [14]If mortals die, can they live again? This thought would give me hope, and through my struggle I would eagerly wait for release. [15]You would call and I would answer, and you would yearn for me, your handiwork. [16]For then you would count my steps, instead of watching for my sins. [17]My sins would be sealed in a pouch, and you would cover over my iniquity.

[18]"But as mountains fall and crumble and as rocks fall from a cliff, [19]as water wears away the stones and floods wash away the soil, so you destroy people's hope. [20]You always overpower them, and then they

---

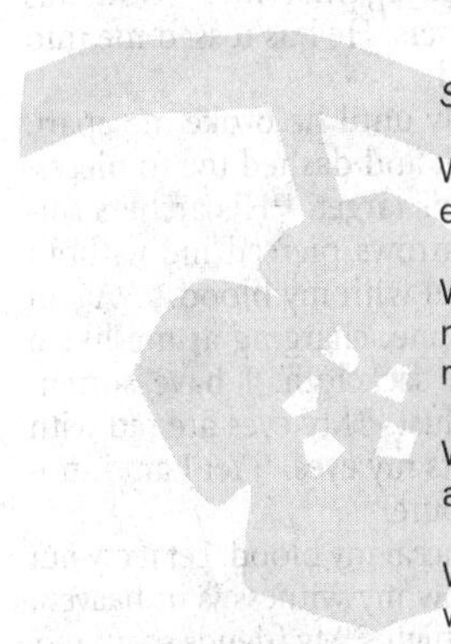

**HOW SUFFERING AFFECTS US**

| *Suffering is helpful when:* | *Suffering is harmful when:* |
|---|---|
| We turn to God for understanding, endurance, and deliverance | We become hardened and reject God |
| We ask important questions we might not take time to think about in our normal routine | We refuse to ask any questions and miss any lessons that might be good for us |
| We let it prepare us to identify with and comfort others who suffer | We allow it to make us self-centered and selfish |
| We are open to being helped by others who are obeying God | We withdraw from the help others can give |
| We realize we can identify with what Christ suffered on the cross for us | We accuse God of being unjust and perhaps lead others to reject him |
| We are sensitized to the amount of suffering in the world | We refuse to be open to any changes in our lives |

pass from the scene. You disfigure them in death and send them away. 21They never know if their sons grow up in honor or sink to insignificance. 22They are absorbed in their own pain and grief."

## CHAPTER 15 **ELIPHAZ: HAVE YOU NO FEAR?** Then Eliphaz the Temanite replied:

2"You are supposed to be a wise man, and yet you give us all this foolish talk. You are nothing but a windbag. 3It isn't right to speak so foolishly. What good do such words do? 4Have you no fear of God, no reverence for him? 5Your sins are telling your mouth what to say. Your words are based on clever deception. 6But why should I condemn you? Your own mouth does!

7"Were you the first person ever born? Were you born before the hills were made? 8Were you listening at God's secret council? Do you have a monopoly on wisdom? 9What do you know that we don't? What do you understand that we don't? 10On our side are aged, gray-haired men much older than your father!

11"Is God's comfort too little for you? Is his gentle word not enough? 12What has captured your reason? What has weakened your vision, 13that you turn against God and say all these evil things? 14Can a mortal be pure? Can a human be just? 15Why, God doesn't even trust the angels*! Even the heavens cannot be absolutely pure in his sight. 16How much less pure is a corrupt and sinful person with a thirst for wickedness!

17"If you will listen, I will answer you from my own experience. 18And it is confirmed by the experience of wise men who have heard the same thing from their fathers, 19those to whom the land was given long before any foreigners arrived.

20"Wicked people are in pain throughout their lives. 21They are surrounded by terrors, and even on good days they fear the attack of the destroyer. 22They dare not go out into the darkness for fear they will be murdered. 23They wander abroad for bread, saying, 'Where is it?'* They know their ruin is certain. 24That dark day terrifies them. They live in distress and anguish, like a king preparing for an attack. 25For they have clenched their fists against God, defying the Almighty. 26Holding their strong shields, they defiantly charge against him.

27"These wicked people are fat and rich, 28but their cities will be ruined. They will live in abandoned houses that are ready to tumble down. 29They will not continue to be rich. Their wealth will not endure, and their possessions will no longer spread across the horizon.

30"They will not escape the darkness. The flame will burn them up, and the breath of God will destroy everything they have. 31Let them no longer trust in empty riches. They are only fooling themselves, for emptiness will be their only reward. 32They will be cut down in the prime of life, and all they counted on will disappear. 33They will be like a vine whose grapes are harvested before they are ripe, like an olive tree that sheds its blossoms so the fruit cannot form. 34For the godless are barren. Their homes, enriched through bribery, will be consumed by fire. 35They conceive trouble and evil, and their hearts give birth only to deceit."

## CHAPTER 16 **JOB: YOU ARE NO HELP.** Then Job spoke again:

2"I have heard all this before. What miserable comforters you are! 3Won't you ever stop your flow of foolish words? What have I said that makes you speak so endlessly? 4I could say the same things if you were in my place. I could spout off my criticisms against you and shake my head at you. 5But that's not what I would do. I would speak in a way that helps you. I would try to take away your grief. 6But as it is, my grief remains no matter how I defend myself. And it does not help if I refuse to speak.

### PAT ANSWERS ● ● • • •

**16:1-5 Job's friends were supposed to be comforting him in his grief. Instead they condemned him for causing his own suffering. Job began his reply to Eliphaz by calling him and his friends "miserable comforters." Job's words reveal several ways to become a better comforter to those in pain: (1) don't talk just for the sake of talking; (2) don't sermonize by giving pat answers; (3) don't criticize; (4) put yourself in the other person's place; and (5) offer sincere help and encouragement. Try Job's suggestions, knowing that they are given by a person who needed great comfort. The best comforters are those who know something about personal suffering.**

7"O God, you have ground me down and devastated my family. 8You have reduced me to skin and bones—as proof, they say, of my sins. 9God hates me and tears angrily at my flesh. He gnashes his teeth at me and pierces me with his eyes. 10People jeer and laugh at me. They slap my cheek in contempt. A mob gathers against me. 11God has handed me over to sinners. He has tossed me into the hands of the wicked.

12"I was living quietly until he broke me apart. He took me by the neck and dashed me to pieces. Then he set me up as his target. 13His archers surrounded me, and his arrows pierced me without mercy. The ground is wet with my blood.* 14Again and again he smashed me, charging at me like a warrior. 15Here I sit in sackcloth. I have surrendered, and I sit in the dust. 16My eyes are red with weeping; darkness covers my eyes. 17Yet I am innocent, and my prayer is pure.

18"O earth, do not conceal my blood. Let it cry out on my behalf. 19Even now my witness is in heaven. My advocate is there on high. 20My friends scorn me, but I pour out my tears to God. 21Oh, that someone would mediate between God and me, as a person mediates between friends. 22For soon I must go down that road from which I will never return.

15:15 Hebrew *the holy ones.* 15:23 Greek version reads *He is appointed to be food for a vulture.* 16:13 Hebrew *my gall.*

CHAPTER **17** "My spirit is crushed, and I am near death. The grave is ready to receive me. [2]I am surrounded by mockers. I watch how bitterly they taunt me.

[3]"You must defend my innocence, O God, since no one else will stand up for me. [4]You have closed their minds to understanding, but do not let them triumph. [5]They denounce their companions for their own advantage, so let their children faint with hunger.

[6]"God has made a mockery of me among the people; they spit in my face. [7]My eyes are dim with weeping, and I am but a shadow of my former self. [8]The upright are astonished when they see me. The innocent are aroused against the ungodly. [9]The righteous will move onward and forward, and those with pure hearts will become stronger and stronger.

[10]"As for all of you, come back and try again! But I will not find a wise man among you. [11]My days are over. My hopes have disappeared. My heart's desires are broken. [12]They say that night is day and day is night; how they pervert the truth! [13]I might go to the grave and make my bed in darkness. [14]And I might call the grave my father, and the worm my mother and my sister. [15]But where then is my hope? Can anyone find it? [16]No, my hope will go down with me to the grave. We will rest together in the dust!"

CHAPTER **18** **BILDAD: YOU ARE WICKED.** Then Bildad the Shuhite replied:

[2]"How long before you stop talking? Speak sense if you want us to answer! [3]Do you think we are cattle? Do you think we have no intelligence? [4]You may tear your hair out in anger, but will that cause the earth to be abandoned? Will it make rocks fall from a cliff?

[5]"The truth remains that the light of the wicked will be snuffed out. The sparks of their fire will not glow. [6]The light in their tent will grow dark. The lamp hanging above them will be quenched. [7]The confident stride of the wicked will be shortened. Their own schemes will be their downfall.

[8]"The wicked walk into a net. They fall into a pit that's been dug in the path. [9]A trap grabs them by the heel. A noose tightens around them. [10]A snare lies hidden in the ground. A rope lies coiled on their path.

[11]"Terrors surround the wicked and trouble them at every step. [12]Their vigor is depleted by hunger, and calamity waits for them to stumble. [13]Disease eats their skin; death devours their limbs. [14]They are torn from the security of their tent, and they are brought down to the king of terrors. [15]The home of the wicked will disappear beneath a fiery barrage of burning sulfur. [16]Their roots will dry up, and their branches will wither. [17]All memory of their existence will perish from the earth. No one will remember them. [18]They will be thrust from light into darkness, driven from the world. [19]They will have neither children nor grandchildren, nor any survivor in their home country. [20]People in the west are appalled at their fate; people in the east are horrified. [21]They will say, 'This was the home of a wicked person, the place of one who rejected God.'"

### NEVER-ENDING HOPE ● ● • • •

17:15 **Job gave up hope of any future restoration of wealth and family, and he wrapped himself in thoughts of death and the rest from grief and pain it promised. The rewards Job's friends mentioned all were related to this present life. They were silent about the possibility of life after death. We must be careful to avoid viewing life only in terms of this present world, because God promises the faithful a never-ending future.**

CHAPTER **19** **JOB: IMPATIENT BUT TRUSTING GOD.** Then Job spoke again:

[2]"How long will you torture me? How long will you try to break me with your words? [3]Ten times now you have meant to insult me. You should be ashamed of dealing with me so harshly. [4]And even if I have sinned, that is my concern, not yours. [5]You are trying to overcome me, using my humiliation as evidence of my sin, [6]but it is God who has wronged me. I cannot defend myself, for I am like a city under siege.

[7]"I cry out for help, but no one hears me. I protest, but there is no justice. [8]God has blocked my way and plunged my path into darkness. [9]He has stripped me of my honor and removed the crown from my head. [10]He has demolished me on every side, and I am finished. He has destroyed my hope. [11]His fury burns against me; he counts me as an enemy. [12]His troops advance. They build up roads to attack me. They camp all around my tent.

[13]"My relatives stay far away, and my friends have turned against me. [14]My neighbors and my close friends are all gone. [15]The members of my household have forgotten me. The servant girls consider me a stranger. I am like a foreigner to them. [16]I call my servant, but he doesn't come; I even plead with him! [17]My breath is repulsive to my wife. I am loathsome to my own family. [18]Even young children despise me. When I stand to speak, they turn their backs on me. [19]My close friends abhor me. Those I loved have turned against me. [20]I have been reduced to skin and bones and have escaped death by the skin of my teeth.

[21]"Have mercy on me, my friends, have mercy, for the hand of God has struck me. [22]Why must you persecute me as God does? Why aren't you satisfied with my anguish?

[23]"Oh, that my words could be written. Oh, that they could be inscribed on a monument, [24]carved with an iron chisel and filled with lead, engraved forever in the rock.

[25]"But as for me, I know that my Redeemer lives, and that he will stand upon the earth at last. [26]And after my body has decayed, yet in my body I will see

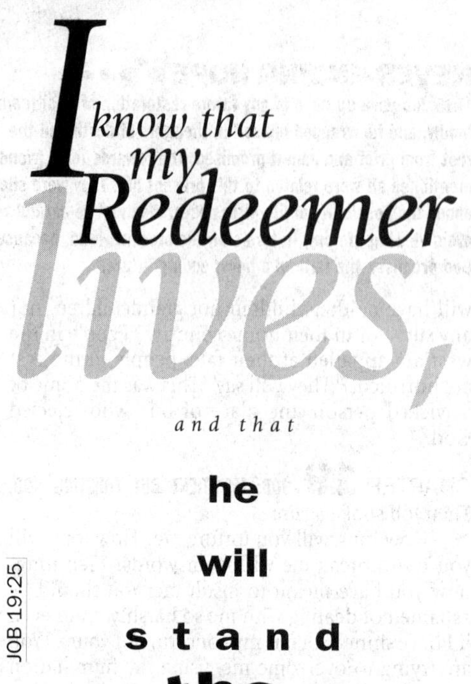
I know that my Redeemer lives,
and that
he
will
stand
upon the earth
at last.
JOB 19:25

God*! 27I will see him for myself. Yes, I will see him with my own eyes. I am overwhelmed at the thought!

28"How dare you go on persecuting me, saying, 'It's his own fault'? 29I warn you, you yourselves are in danger of punishment for your attitude. Then you will know that there is judgment."

CHAPTER **20** **ZOPHAR: I HAVE THE ANSWER.** Then Zophar the Naamathite replied:

2"I must reply because I am greatly disturbed. 3I have had to endure your insults, but now my spirit prompts me to reply.

4"Don't you realize that ever since people were first placed on the earth, 5the triumph of the wicked has been short-lived and the joy of the godless has been only temporary? 6Though the godless man's pride reaches to the heavens and though his head touches the clouds, 7yet he will perish forever, thrown away like his own dung. Those who knew him will ask, 'Where is he?' 8He will fade like a dream and not be found. He will vanish like a vision in the night. 9Neither his friends nor his family will ever see him again. 10His children will beg from the poor, for he must give back his ill-gotten wealth. 11He was just a young man, but his bones will lie in the dust.

12"He enjoyed the taste of his wickedness, letting it melt under his tongue. 13He savored it, holding it long in his mouth. 14But suddenly, the food he has eaten turns sour within him, a poisonous venom in his stomach. 15He will vomit the wealth he swallowed. God won't let him keep it down. 16He will suck the poison of snakes. The viper will kill him. 17He will never again enjoy abundant streams of olive oil or rivers of milk and honey. 18His labors will not be rewarded. His wealth will bring him no joy. 19For he oppressed the poor and left them destitute. He foreclosed on their homes. 20He was always greedy but never satisfied. Of all the things he dreamed about, nothing remains. 21Nothing is left after he finishes gorging himself; therefore, his prosperity will not endure.

22"In the midst of plenty, he will run into trouble, and disasters will destroy him. 23May God give him a bellyful of trouble. May God rain down his anger upon him. 24He will try to escape, but God's arrow will pierce him. 25The arrow is pulled from his body, and the arrowhead glistens with blood.* The terrors of death are upon him.

26"His treasures will be lost in deepest darkness. A wildfire will devour his goods, consuming all he has left. 27The heavens will reveal his guilt, and the earth will give testimony against him. 28A flood will sweep away his house. God's anger will descend on him in torrents. 29This is the fate that awaits the wicked. It is the inheritance decreed by God."

CHAPTER **21** **JOB: YOU DO NOT UNDERSTAND.** Then Job spoke again:

2"Listen closely to what I am saying. You can console me by listening to me. 3Bear with me, and let me speak. After I have spoken, you may mock me.

4"My complaint is with God, not with people. No wonder I'm so impatient. 5Look at me and be stunned. Put your hand over your mouth in shock. 6When I think about what I am saying, I shudder. My body trembles.

7"The truth is that the wicked live to a good old age. They grow old and wealthy. 8They live to see their children grow to maturity, and they enjoy their grandchildren. 9Their homes are safe from every fear, and God does not punish them. 10Their bulls never

**PAYBACK ● ● • • •**

20:6-7 **Although Zophar was wrong in directing this tirade against Job, he was correct in talking about the final end of evil people. At first, sin seems enjoyable and attractive. Lying, stealing, or oppressing others often brings temporary gain to those who practice these sins. Some even live a long time with ill-gotten gain. But in the end, God's justice will prevail. What Zophar missed is that judgment for these sins may not come in the lifetime of the sinner. Punishment may be deferred until the last judgment, when sinners will be eternally cut off from God. We should not be impressed with the success and power of evil people. God's judgment on them is certain.**

19:26 Or *without my body I will see God.* 20:25 Hebrew *with gall.*

fail to breed. Their cows bear calves without miscar-
riage. 11Their children skip about like lambs in a
flock of sheep. 12They sing with tambourine and
harp. They make merry to the sound of the flute.
13They spend their days in prosperity; then they go
down to the grave in peace. 14All this, even though
they say to God, 'Go away. We want no part of you
and your ways.15Who is the Almighty, and why
should we obey him? What good will it do us if we
pray?' 16But their prosperity is not of their own doing, so I will have nothing to do with that kind of
thinking.
17"Yet the wicked get away with it time and time
again. They rarely have trouble, and God skips them
when he distributes sorrows in his anger. 18Are they
driven before the wind like straw? Are they carried
away by the storm? Not at all!
19"'Well,' you say, 'at least God will punish their
children!' But I say that God should punish the ones
who sin, not their children! Let them feel their own
penalty. 20Let their own eyes see their destruction. Let
them drink deeply of the anger of the Almighty. 21For
when they are dead, they will not care what happens
to their family.
22"But who can teach a lesson to God, the supreme Judge? 23One person dies in prosperity and
security, 24the very picture of good health. 25Another
person dies in bitter poverty, never having tasted the
good life. 26Both alike are buried in the same dust,
both eaten by the same worms.
27"Look, I know your thoughts. I know the
schemes you plot against me. 28You will tell me of
rich and wicked people who came to disaster because of their sins. 29But I tell you to ask those who
have been around, and they can tell you the truth.
30Evil people are spared in times of calamity and are
allowed to escape. 31No one rebukes them openly.
No one repays them for what they have done.
32When they are carried to the grave, an honor guard
keeps watch at their tomb. 33A great funeral procession goes to the cemetery. Many pay their respects as
the body is laid to rest and the earth gives sweet
repose.
34"How can you comfort me? All your explanations are wrong!"

CHAPTER **22** **ELIPHAZ: YOU MUST GIVE IN.** Then Eliphaz the Temanite replied:
2"Can a person's actions be of benefit to God?
Can even a wise person be helpful to him? 3Is it any
pleasure to the Almighty if you are righteous? Would
it be any gain to him if you were perfect? 4Is it
because of your reverence for him that he accuses
and judges you? 5Not at all! It is because of your
wickedness! Your guilt has no limit!
6"For example, you must have lent money to your
friend and then kept the clothing he gave you as a
pledge. Yes, you stripped him to the bone. 7You must
have refused water for the thirsty and food for the
hungry. 8After all, you think the land belongs to the
powerful and that those who are privileged have a
right to it! 9You must have sent widows away without
helping them and crushed the strength of orphans.
10That is why you are surrounded by traps and sudden fears. 11That is why you cannot see in the darkness, and waves of water cover you.
12"God is so great—higher than the heavens,
higher than the farthest stars. 13But you reply, 'That's
why God can't see what I am doing! How can he
judge through the thick darkness? 14For thick clouds
swirl about him, and he cannot see us. He is way up
there, walking on the vault of heaven.'
15"Will you continue on the old paths where evil
people have walked? 16They were snatched away in
the prime of life, and the foundations of their lives
were washed away forever. 17For they said to God,
'Leave us alone! What can the Almighty do for us?'
18But they forgot that he had filled their homes with
good things, so I will have nothing to do with that
kind of thinking.
19"Now the righteous will be happy to see the
wicked destroyed, and the innocent will laugh them
to scorn. 20They will say, 'Surely our enemies have
been destroyed. The last of them have been consumed in the fire.'
21"Stop quarreling with God! If you agree with
him, you will have peace at last, and things will go
well for you. 22Listen to his instructions, and store
them in your heart. 23If you return to the Almighty
and clean up your life, you will be restored. 24Give
up your lust for money, and throw your precious
gold into the river. 25Then the Almighty himself
will be your treasure. He will be your precious
silver!
26"Then you will delight yourself in the Almighty
and look up to God. 27You will pray to him, and he
will hear you, and you will fulfill your vows to him.
28Whatever you decide to do will be accomplished,
and light will shine on the road ahead of you. 29If
someone is brought low and you say, 'Help him up,'
God will save the downcast. 30Then even sinners will
be rescued by your pure hands."

## SUCCESS ● ● • • •

21:7-18 **Job refuted Zophar's idea that evil people never experience wealth and happiness, pointing out that in the real world the wicked do indeed prosper. God does what he wants to individuals (21:22-25), and people should not use their circumstances to measure their own goodness or God's—prosperity and goodness are not necessarily related. To Job's friends, success was based on outward performance; to God, however, success is based on a person's heart.**

## ABOUT YOUR ATTITUDE ● ● • • •

21:22 **In the middle of Job's confusion about his suffering, he asked, "But who can teach a lesson to God, the supreme Judge?" Even if your personal struggles seem as great and difficult as Job's, your response will indicate your current attitude toward God. Rather than becoming angry with God, continue to trust him, no matter what your circumstances may be. Although it is sometimes difficult to see, God *is* in control.**

## DEEP PURPOSES ● ● ● • •

**23:14 Job wavered back and forth, first proclaiming loyalty to God and then calling God his enemy. His friends' words and his own suspicions were undermining his confidence in God. When affliction comes, it is natural to blame God and to think that our suffering must be divine punishment. But we must not assume that God is being hostile toward us. His purposes go deeper than our ability to grasp all that is really happening. While this sounds like a pat answer, it is the same answer God gave Job in chapters 38–41. We shouldn't demand to know why certain calamities hit us. Often we cannot know, or are not meant to know, until later.**

## CHAPTER 23 **JOB: I WANT TO FIND GOD.**

Then Job spoke again:

2 "My complaint today is still a bitter one, and I try hard not to groan aloud. 3 If only I knew where to find God, I would go to his throne and talk with him there. 4 I would lay out my case and present my arguments. 5 Then I would listen to his reply and understand what he says to me. 6 Would he merely argue with me in his greatness? No, he would give me a fair hearing. 7 Fair and honest people can reason with him, so I would be acquitted by my Judge.

8 "I go east, but he is not there. I go west, but I cannot find him. 9 I do not see him in the north, for he is hidden. I turn to the south, but I cannot find him. 10 But he knows where I am going. And when he has tested me like gold in a fire, he will pronounce me innocent.

11 "For I have stayed in God's paths; I have followed his ways and not turned aside. 12 I have not departed from his commands but have treasured his word in my heart. 13 Nevertheless, his mind concerning me remains unchanged, and who can turn him from his purposes? Whatever he wants to do, he does. 14 So he will do for me all he has planned. He controls my destiny. 15 No wonder I am so terrified in his presence. When I think of it, terror grips me. 16 God has made my heart faint; the Almighty has terrified me. 17 Darkness is all around me; thick, impenetrable darkness is everywhere.

## CHAPTER 24

"Why doesn't the Almighty open the court and bring judgment? Why must the godly wait for him in vain? 2 Evil people steal land by moving the boundary markers. They steal flocks of sheep, 3 and they even take donkeys from the poor and fatherless. A poor widow must surrender her valuable ox as collateral for a loan. 4 The poor are kicked aside; the needy must hide together for safety. 5 Like the wild donkeys in the desert, the poor must spend all their time just getting enough to keep body and soul together. They go into the desert to search for food for their children. 6 They harvest a field they do not own, and they glean in the vineyards of the wicked. 7 All night they lie naked in the cold, without clothing or covering. 8 They are soaked by mountain showers, and they huddle against the rocks for want of a home.

9 "The wicked snatch a widow's child from her breast; they take the baby as a pledge for a loan. 10 The poor must go about naked, without any clothing. They are forced to carry food while they themselves are starving. 11 They press out olive oil without being allowed to taste it, and they tread in the winepress as they suffer from thirst. 12 The groans of the dying rise from the city, and the wounded cry for help, yet God does not respond to their moaning.

13 "Wicked people rebel against the light. They refuse to acknowledge its ways. They will not stay in its paths. 14 The murderer rises in the early dawn to kill the poor and needy; at night he is a thief. 15 The adulterer waits for the twilight, for he says, 'No one will see me then.' He masks his face so no one will know him. 16 They break into houses at night and sleep in the daytime. They are not acquainted with the light. 17 The black night is their morning. They ally themselves with the terrors of the darkness.

18 "But they disappear from the earth as quickly as foam is swept down a river. Everything they own is cursed, so that no one enters their vineyard. 19 Death consumes sinners just as drought and heat consume snow. 20 Even the sinner's own mother will forget him. Worms will find him sweet to eat. No one will remember him. Wicked people are broken like a tree in the storm. 21 For they have taken advantage of the childless who have no protecting sons. They refuse to help the needy widows.

22 "God, in his power, drags away the rich. They may rise high, but they have no assurance in life. 23 They may be allowed to live in security, but God is always watching them. 24 And though they are great now, in a moment they will be gone like all others, withered like heads of grain.

25 "Can anyone claim otherwise? Who can prove me wrong?"

## CHAPTER 25 **BILDAD: WHO STANDS BEFORE GOD?**

Then Bildad the Shuhite replied:

2 "God is powerful and dreadful. He enforces peace in the heavens. 3 Who is able to count his heavenly army? Does his light not shine on all the earth? 4 How can a mere mortal stand before God and claim to be righteous? Who in all the earth is pure? 5 God is so glorious that even the moon and stars scarcely shine compared to him. 6 How much less are mere people, who are but worms in his sight?"

## CHAPTER 26 **JOB: I WILL NEVER AGREE.**

Then Job spoke again:

2 "How you have helped the powerless! How you have saved a person who has no strength! 3 How

## GREATER RESULTS ● ● ● • •

**26:2-4 With great sarcasm, Job attacked his friends' comments. Their theological explanations failed to bring any relief because they were unable to turn their knowledge into helpful counsel. When dealing with people, it is more important to love and understand them than to analyze them or give advice. Compassion produces greater results than criticism or blame.**

you have enlightened my stupidity! What wise things you have said! 4Where have you gotten all these wise sayings? Whose spirit speaks through you?

5"The dead tremble in their place beneath the waters. 6The underworld* is naked in God's presence. There is no cover for the place of destruction. 7God stretches the northern sky over empty space and hangs the earth on nothing. 8He wraps the rain in his thick clouds, and the clouds do not burst with the weight. 9He shrouds his throne with his clouds. 10He created the horizon when he separated the waters; he set the boundaries for day and night. 11The foundations of heaven tremble at his rebuke. 12By his power the sea grew calm. By his skill he crushed the great sea monster.* 13His Spirit made the heavens beautiful, and his power pierced the gliding serpent.

14"These are some of the minor things he does, merely a whisper of his power. Who can understand the thunder of his power?"

CHAPTER **27** **JOB: FEAR THE LORD.** Job continued speaking:

2"I make this vow by the living God, who has taken away my rights, by the Almighty who has embittered my soul. 3As long as I live, while I have breath from God, 4my lips will speak no evil, and my tongue will speak no lies. 5I will never concede that you are right; until I die, I will defend my innocence. 6I will maintain my innocence without wavering. My conscience is clear for as long as I live.

7"May my enemy be punished like the wicked, my adversary like evil men. 8For what hope do the godless have when God cuts them off and takes away their life? 9Will God listen to their cry when trouble comes upon them? 10Can they take delight in the Almighty? Can they call to God at any time?

11"I will teach you about God's power. I will not conceal anything that concerns the Almighty. 12But I don't need to, for you yourselves have seen all this; yet you are saying all these useless things to me.

13"This is what the wicked will receive from God; this is their inheritance from the Almighty. 14If they have a multitude of children, their children will die in war or starve to death. 15Those who survive will be brought down to the grave by a plague, with no one to mourn them, not even their wives.

16"Evil people may have all the money in the world, and they may store away mounds of clothing. 17But the righteous will wear that clothing, and the innocent will divide all that money. 18The houses built by the wicked are as fragile as a spiderweb, as flimsy as a shelter made of branches.

19"The wicked go to bed rich but wake up to find that all their wealth is gone. 20Terror overwhelms them, and they are blown away in the storms of the night. 21The east wind carries them away, and they are gone. It sweeps them away. 22It whirls down on them without mercy. They struggle to flee from its power. 23But everyone jeers at them and mocks them.

CHAPTER **28** "People know how to mine silver and refine gold. 2They know how to dig iron from the earth and smelt copper from stone. 3They know how to put light into darkness and explore the farthest, darkest regions of the earth as they search for ore. 4They sink a mine shaft into the earth far from where anyone lives. They descend on ropes, swinging back and forth. 5Bread comes from the earth, but below the surface the earth is melted as by fire.

## CLEAR CONSCIENCE ● ● • • •

27:6 **To all the accusations, Job was able to declare that his conscience was clear. Only right living before God can bring a clear conscience, and how important Job's record became as he was being accused! Like Job, we can't claim sinless lives, but we *can* claim forgiven lives. When we confess our sins to God, we are forgiven and can live our lives with clear consciences (1 John 1:9).**

6"People know how to find sapphires and gold dust—7treasures that no bird of prey can see, no falcon's eye observe—8for they are deep within the mines. No wild animal has ever walked upon those treasures; no lion has set his paw there. 9People know how to tear apart flinty rocks and overturn the roots of mountains. 10They cut tunnels in the rocks and uncover precious stones. 11They dam up the trickling streams and bring to light the hidden treasures.

12"But do people know where to find wisdom? Where can they find understanding? 13No one knows where to find it, for it is not found among the living. 14'It is not here,' says the ocean. 'Nor is it here,' says the sea.

15"It cannot be bought for gold or silver. 16Its value is greater than all the gold of Ophir, greater than precious onyx stone or sapphires. 17Wisdom is far more valuable than gold and crystal. It cannot be purchased with jewels mounted in fine gold. 18Coral and valuable rock crystal are worthless in trying to get it. The price of wisdom is far above pearls. 19Topaz from Ethiopia* cannot be exchanged for it. Its value is greater than the purest gold.

20"But do people know where to find wisdom?

## WISE WITHOUT GOD? ● ● • • •

28:12 **People can perform all kinds of technological wonders. They can find stars invisible to the eye, they can visit space, they can store volumes of information on a microchip. But even the greatest scientists, on their own, are at a loss to discover wisdom for their daily lives. Only God can show them where to look to find wisdom because he is the source of wisdom. True wisdom is having God's perspective on life. As the Creator of life, only he knows what is best for his creation. It is fruitless for us to try to become wise merely through our own observations and efforts because God alone sees the greater purpose for his world.**

**26:6** Hebrew *Sheol.* **26:12** Hebrew *Rahab,* the name of a mythical sea monster that represents chaos in ancient literature. **28:19** Hebrew *from Cush.*

Where can they find understanding? 21For it is hidden from the eyes of all humanity. Even the sharp-eyed birds in the sky cannot discover it. 22But Destruction and Death say, 'We have heard a rumor of where wisdom can be found.'

23"God surely knows where it can be found, 24for he looks throughout the whole earth, under all the heavens. 25He made the winds blow and determined how much rain should fall. 26He made the laws of the rain and prepared a path for the lightning. 27Then, when he had done all this, he saw wisdom and measured it. He established it and examined it thoroughly. 28And this is what he says to all humanity: 'The fear of the Lord is true wisdom; to forsake evil is real understanding.'"

## PORNOGRAPHY

Cary's problem started three years ago when he and some friends found an abandoned trailer in the woods behind their neighborhood. Cary was 12. Inside the trailer were several pornographic magazines. The guys quickly wore a path to their new hideout, and Cary made himself the guardian of the group's "erotic treasures."

One winter night, the ramshackle trailer—including the nasty pictures—mysteriously went up in smoke. The other boys moved on to other things. But Cary was hooked. He couldn't seem to see enough naked bodies. Whether it was through explicit videos, graphic novels, or trashy movies on cable, Cary was almost totally controlled by his desire to see some skin.

Not only did Cary's obsession bring him great frustration (because pornography is such a lie), but it also caused him unbelievable guilt. He couldn't even glance at a woman without mentally undressing her. And no matter how hard he tried, he couldn't get all the dirty images out of his mind. Christ's warning about lust (Matthew 5:28) haunted him.

Thank the Lord that Cary finally had enough sense to talk to Bill, his youth leader. Bill got Cary into a good Bible study, and he now prays with him and checks up on him regularly.

Cary's gonna make it.

See one of the verses Cary and Bill studied: Job 31:1. It is a great example to follow for those who struggle with lust!

## CHAPTER 29 **JOB: GOD'S CARE FOR ME.** Job continued speaking:

2"I long for the years gone by when God took care of me, 3when he lighted the way before me and I walked safely through the darkness. 4In my early years, the friendship of God was felt in my home. 5The Almighty was still with me, and my children were around me. 6In those days my cows produced milk in abundance, and my olive groves poured out streams of olive oil.

7"Those were the days when I went to the city gate and took my place among the honored leaders. 8The young stepped aside when they saw me, and even the aged rose in respect at my coming. 9The princes stood in silence and put their hands over their mouths. 10The highest officials of the city stood quietly, holding their tongues in respect.

11"All who heard of me praised me. All who saw me spoke well of me. 12For I helped the poor in their need and the orphans who had no one to help them. 13I helped those who had lost hope, and they blessed me. And I caused the widows' hearts to sing for joy. 14All I did was just and honest. Righteousness covered me like a robe, and I wore justice like a turban. 15I served as eyes for the blind and feet for the lame. 16I was a father to the poor and made sure that even strangers received a fair trial. 17I broke the jaws of godless oppressors and made them release their victims.

18"I thought, 'Surely I will die surrounded by my family after a long, good life. 19For I am like a tree whose roots reach the water, whose branches are refreshed with the dew. 20New honors are constantly bestowed on me, and my strength is continually renewed.'

21"Everyone listened to me and valued my advice. They were silent as they waited for me to speak. 22And after I spoke, they had nothing to add, for my counsel satisfied them. 23They longed for me to speak as they longed for rain. They waited eagerly, for my words were as refreshing as the spring rain. 24When they were discouraged, I smiled at them. My look of approval was precious to them. 25I told them what they should do and presided over them as their chief. I lived as a king among his troops and as one who comforts those who mourn.

## CHAPTER 30

"But now I am mocked by those who are younger than I, by young men whose fathers are not worthy to run with my sheepdogs. 2A lot of good they are to me—those worn-out wretches! 3They are gaunt with hunger and flee to the deserts and the wastelands, desolate and gloomy. 4They eat coarse leaves, and they burn the roots of shrubs for heat. 5They are driven from civilization, and people shout after them as if they were thieves. 6So now they live in frightening ravines and in caves and among the rocks. 7They sound like animals as they howl among the bushes; they huddle together for shelter beneath the nettles. 8They are nameless fools, outcasts of civilization.

9"And now their sons mock me with their vulgar song! They taunt me! 10They despise me and won't come near me, except to spit in my face. 11For God has cut the cords of my tent. He has humbled me, so they have thrown off all restraint. 12These outcasts oppose me to my face. They send me sprawling; they lay traps in my path. 13They block my road and do everything they can to hasten my calamity, knowing full well that I have no one to help me. 14They come at me from all directions. They rush upon me when I am down. 15I live in terror now. They hold me in contempt, and my prosperity has vanished as a cloud before a strong wind.

16"And now my heart is broken. Depression haunts my days. 17My weary nights are filled with pain as though something were relentlessly gnawing at my bones. 18With a strong hand, God grabs my garment. He grips me by the collar of my tunic. 19He has thrown me into the mud. I have become as dust and ashes.

20"I cry to you, O God, but you don't answer me. I stand before you, and you don't bother to look. 21You have become cruel toward me. You persecute me with your great power. 22You throw me into the whirlwind and destroy me in the storm. 23And I know that you are sending me to my death—the destination of all who live.

24"Surely no one would turn against the needy when they cry for help. 25Did I not weep for those in trouble? Was I not deeply grieved for the needy? 26So I looked for good, but evil came instead. I waited for the light, but darkness fell. 27My heart is troubled and restless. Days of affliction have come upon me. 28I walk in gloom, without sunlight. I stand in the public square and cry for help. 29But instead, I am considered a brother to jackals and a companion to ostriches. 30My skin has turned dark, and my bones burn with fever. 31My harp plays sad music, and my flute accompanies those who weep.

## CHAPTER 31

"I made a covenant with my eyes not to look with lust upon a young woman. 2What has God above chosen for us? What is our inheritance from the Almighty on high? 3It is calamity for the wicked, misfortune for those who do evil. 4He sees everything I do and every step I take.

5"Have I lied to anyone or deceived anyone? 6Let God judge me on the scales of justice, for he knows my integrity. 7If I have strayed from his pathway, or if my heart has lusted for what my eyes have seen, or if I am guilty of any other sin, 8then let someone else harvest the crops I have planted, and let all that I have planted be uprooted.

9"If my heart has been seduced by a woman, or if I have lusted for my neighbor's wife, 10then may my wife belong to another man; may other men sleep with her. 11For lust is a shameful sin, a crime that should be punished. 12It is a devastating fire that destroys to hell. It would wipe out everything I own.

13"If I have been unfair to my male or female servants, if I have refused to hear their complaints, 14how could I face God? What could I say when he questioned me about it? 15For God created both me and my servants. He created us both.

16"Have I refused to help the poor, or crushed the hopes of widows who looked to me for help? 17Have I been stingy with my food and refused to share it with hungry orphans? 18No, from childhood I have cared for orphans, and all my life I have cared for widows. 19Whenever I saw someone who was homeless and without clothes, 20did they not praise me for providing wool clothing to keep them warm? 21If my arm has abused an orphan because I thought I could get away with it, 22then let my shoulder be wrenched out of place! Let my arm be torn from its socket! 23That would be better than facing the judgment sent by God. For if the majesty of God opposes me, what hope is there?

24"Have I put my trust in money or felt secure because of my gold? 25Does my happiness depend on my wealth and all that I own? 26Have I looked at the sun shining in the skies, or the moon walking down its silver pathway, 27and been secretly enticed in my heart to worship them? 28If so, I should be punished by the judges, for it would mean I had denied the God of heaven.

### COVER-UP ● ● • • •

31:33-34 **Job declared that he did not try to hide his sin as people normally do. The fear that our sins will be discovered leads us to patterns of deception. We cover up with lies so that we will appear good to others. But we cannot hide from God. Do you try to keep people from seeing the real you? Acknowledge your sins and free yourself to receive forgiveness and a new life.**

29"Have I ever rejoiced when my enemies came to ruin or become excited when harm came their way? 30No, I have never cursed anyone or asked for revenge. 31My servants have never let others go hungry. 32I have never turned away a stranger but have opened my doors to everyone. 33Have I tried to hide my sins as people normally do, hiding my guilt in a closet? 34Have I feared the crowd and its contempt, so that I refused to acknowledge my sin and would not go outside?

35"If only I had someone who would listen to me and try to see my side! Look, I will sign my name to my defense. Let the Almighty show me that I am wrong. Let my accuser write out the charges against me. 36I would face the accusation proudly. I would treasure it like a crown. 37For I would tell him exactly what I have done. I would come before him like a prince.

38"If my land accuses me and all its furrows weep together, 39or if I have stolen its crops or murdered its owners, 40then let thistles grow on that land instead of wheat and weeds instead of barley."

Job's words are ended.

## CHAPTER 32

**ELIHU: I AM FULL OF WORDS.** Job's three friends refused to reply further to him because he kept insisting on his innocence.

2Then Elihu son of Barakel the Buzite, of the clan of Ram, became angry. He was angry because Job refused to admit that he had sinned and that God was right in punishing him. 3He was also angry with Job's three friends because they had condemned God* by their inability to answer Job's arguments. 4Elihu had waited for the others to speak because they were older than he. 5But when he saw that they had no further reply, he spoke out angrily.

6Elihu son of Barakel the Buzite said, "I am young and you are old, so I held back and did not dare to tell you what I think. 7I thought, 'Those who are

**32:3** As in ancient Hebrew scribal tradition; the Masoretic Text makes no reference to God.

## WISDOM LIVED OUT ● ● • • •

**32:8-9 It is not enough to recognize a great truth; the truth must be lived out in our lives. Elihu recognized the truth that God was the only source of real wisdom, but he did not use God's wisdom to help Job. While he recognized where wisdom came from, he did not seek to acquire it. Becoming wise is an ongoing, lifelong pursuit. Don't be content just to know about wisdom; make it part of your life.**

older should speak, for wisdom comes with age.' [8]Surely it is God's Spirit within people, the breath of the Almighty within them, that makes them intelligent. [9]But sometimes the elders are not wise. Sometimes the aged do not understand justice. [10]So listen to me and let me express my opinion.

[11]"I have waited all this time, listening very carefully to your arguments, listening to you grope for words. [12]I have listened, but not one of you has refuted Job or answered his arguments. [13]And don't tell me, 'He is too wise for us. Only God can convince him.' [14]If Job had been arguing with me, I would not answer with that kind of logic! [15]You sit there baffled, with no further response. [16]Should I continue to wait, now that you are silent? Must I also remain silent? [17]No, I will say my piece. I will speak my mind. I surely will. [18]For I am pent up and full of words, and the spirit within me urges me on. [19]I am like a wine cask without a vent. My words are ready to burst out! [20]I must speak to find relief, so let me give my answers. [21]I won't play favorites or try to flatter anyone. [22]And if I tried, my Creator would soon do away with me.

CHAPTER **33** "Listen, Job, to what I have to say. [2]Now that I have begun to speak, let me continue. [3]I speak with all sincerity; I speak the truth. [4]For the Spirit of God has made me, and the breath of the Almighty gives me life. [5]Answer me, if you can; make your case and take your stand.

[6]"Look, you and I are the same before God. I, too, was formed from clay. [7]So you don't need to be afraid of me. I am not some great person to make you nervous and afraid.

[8]"You have said it in my hearing. I have heard your very words. [9]You said, 'I am pure; I am innocent; I have not sinned. [10]God is picking a quarrel with me, and he considers me to be his enemy. [11]He puts my feet in the stocks and watches every move I make.'

[12]"In this you are not right, and I will show you why. As you yourself have said, 'God is greater than any person.' [13]So why are you bringing a charge against him? You say, 'He does not respond to people's complaints.' [14]But God speaks again and again, though people do not recognize it. [15]He speaks in dreams, in visions of the night when deep sleep falls on people as they lie in bed. [16]He whispers in their ear and terrifies them with his warning. [17]He causes them to change their minds; he keeps them from pride. [18]He keeps them from the grave, from crossing over the river of death. [19]Or God disciplines people with sickness and pain, with ceaseless aching in their bones. [20]They lose their appetite and do not care for even the most delicious food. [21]They waste away to skin and bones. [22]They are at death's door; the angels of death wait for them.

[23]"But if a special messenger from heaven is there to intercede for a person, to declare that he is upright, [24]God will be gracious and say, 'Set him free. Do not make him die, for I have found a ransom for his life.' [25]Then his body will become as healthy as a child's, firm and youthful again. [26]When he prays to God, he will be accepted. And God will receive him with joy and restore him to good standing. [27]He will declare to his friends, 'I sinned, but it was not worth it. [28]God rescued me from the grave, and now my life is filled with light.'

[29]"Yes, God often does these things for people. [30]He rescues them from the grave so they may live in the light of the living. [31]Mark this well, Job. Listen to me, and let me say more. [32]But if you have anything to say, go ahead. I want to hear it, for I am anxious to see you justified. [33]But if not, then listen to me. Keep silent and I will teach you wisdom!"

CHAPTER **34** **ELIHU: LISTEN TO ME.** Then Elihu said:

[2]"Listen to me, you wise men. Pay attention, you who have knowledge. [3]'Just as the mouth tastes good food, the ear tests the words it hears.' [4]So let us discern for ourselves what is right; let us learn together what is good. [5]For Job has said, 'I am innocent, but God has taken away my rights. [6]I am innocent, but they call me a liar. My suffering is incurable, even though I have not sinned.'

[7]"Has there ever been a man as arrogant as Job, with his thirst for irreverent talk? [8]He seeks the companionship of evil people. He spends his time with wicked men. [9]He has even said, 'Why waste time trying to please God?'

[10]"Listen to me, you who have understanding. Everyone knows that God doesn't sin! The Almighty can do no wrong. [11]He repays people according to their deeds. He treats people according to their ways. [12]There is no truer statement than this: God will not do wrong. The Almighty cannot twist justice. [13]Who put the world in his care? Who has set the whole world in place? [14]If God were to take back his spirit* and withdraw his breath, [15]all life would cease, and humanity would turn again to dust.

[16]"Listen now and try to understand. [17]Could God govern if he hated justice? Are you going to condemn the almighty Judge? [18]For he says to kings and nobles, 'You are wicked and unjust.' [19]He doesn't care how great a person may be, and he doesn't pay any more attention to the rich than to the poor. He made them all. [20]In a moment they die. At midnight they all pass away; the mighty are removed without human hand.

[21]"For God carefully watches the way people live; he sees everything they do. [22]No darkness is thick enough to hide the wicked from his eyes. [23]For it is not up to mortals to decide when to come before

**34:14** Or *his Spirit.*

God in judgment. 24He brings the mighty to ruin without asking anyone, and he sets up others in their places. 25He watches what they do, and in the night he overturns them, destroying them. 26He openly strikes them down for their wickedness. 27For they turned aside from following him. They have no respect for any of his ways. 28So they cause the poor to cry out, catching God's attention. Yes, he hears the cries of the needy. 29When he is quiet, who can make trouble? But when he hides his face, who can find him? 30He prevents the godless from ruling so they cannot be a snare to the people.

31"Why don't people say to God, 'I have sinned, but I will sin no more'? 32Or 'I don't know what evil I have done; tell me, and I will stop at once'?

33"Must God tailor his justice to your demands? But you have rejected him! The choice is yours, not mine. Go ahead, share your wisdom with us. 34After all, bright people will tell me, and wise people will hear me say, 35'Job speaks without knowledge; his words lack insight.' 36Job, you deserve the maximum penalty for the wicked way you have talked. 37For now you have added rebellion and blasphemy against God to your other sins."

## CHAPTER 35

Then Elihu said:

2"Do you think it is right for you to claim, 'I am righteous before God'? 3Yet you also ask, 'What's the use of living a righteous life? How will it benefit me?'

4"I will answer you and all your friends, too. 5Look up into the sky and see the clouds high above you. 6If you sin, what do you accomplish against him? Even if you sin again and again, what effect will it have on him? 7If you are good, is this some great gift to him? What could you possibly give him? 8No, your sins affect only people like yourself, and your good deeds affect only other people.

9"The oppressed cry out beneath the wrongs that are done to them. They groan beneath the power of the mighty. 10Yet they don't ask, 'Where is God my Creator, the one who gives songs in the night? 11Where is the one who makes us wiser than the animals and birds?'

12"And if they do cry out and God does not answer, it is because of their pride. 13But it is wrong to say God doesn't listen, to say the Almighty isn't concerned. 14And it is even more false to say he doesn't see what is going on. He will bring about justice if you will only wait. 15But do you cry out against him because he does not respond in anger? 16Job, you have protested in vain. You have spoken like a fool."

## CHAPTER 36

**ELIHU: I AM DEFENDING GOD.** Elihu continued speaking:

2"Let me go on, and I will show you the truth of what I am saying. For I have not finished defending God! 3I will give you many illustrations of the righteousness of my Creator. 4I am telling you the honest truth, for I am a man of well-rounded knowledge.

5"God is mighty, yet he does not despise anyone! He is mighty in both power and understanding. 6He does not let the wicked live but gives justice to the afflicted. 7His eyes never leave the innocent, but he establishes and exalts them with kings forever. 8If troubles come upon them and they are enslaved and afflicted, 9he takes the trouble to show them the reason. He shows them their sins, for they have behaved proudly. 10He gets their attention and says they must turn away from evil.

11"If they listen and obey God, then they will be blessed with prosperity throughout their lives. All their years will be pleasant. 12But if they refuse to listen to him, they will perish in battle and die from lack of understanding. 13For the godless are full of resentment. Even when he punishes them, they refuse to cry out to him for help. 14They die young after wasting their lives in immoral living. 15But by means of their suffering, he rescues those who suffer. For he gets their attention through adversity.

16"God has led you away from danger, giving you freedom. You have prospered in a wide and pleasant valley. 17But you are too obsessed with judgment on the godless. Don't worry, justice will be upheld. 18But watch out, or you may be seduced with wealth. Don't let yourself be bribed into sin. 19Could all your wealth and mighty efforts keep you from distress? 20Do not long for the cover of night, for that is when people will be destroyed. 21Be on guard! Turn back from evil, for it was to prevent you from getting into a life of evil that God sent this suffering.

22"Look, God is all-powerful. Who is a teacher like him? 23No one can tell him what to do. No one can say to him, 'You have done wrong.' 24Instead, glorify his mighty works, singing songs of praise. 25Everyone has seen these things, but only from a distance.

### GOD'S DIMENSIONS • • • • •

36:26 **One theme in the poetic literature of the Bible is that we cannot know God completely. This does not mean that we cannot have any knowledge about God, because the Bible is full of details about who God is, how we can know him, and how we can have an eternal relationship with him. What it means is that we can never know enough to answer all of life's questions (Ecclesiastes 3:11), to predict our own future, or to manipulate God for our own ends. Life always has more questions than answers, and we must constantly go to God for fresh insights into life's dilemmas. (See 37:19-24.)**

26"Look, God is exalted beyond what we can understand. His years are without number. 27He draws up the water vapor and then distills it into rain. 28The rain pours down from the clouds, and everyone benefits from it. 29Can anyone really understand the spreading of the clouds and the thunder that rolls forth from heaven? 30See how he spreads the lightning around him and how it lights up the depths of the sea. 31By his mighty acts he governs the people, giving them food in abundance. 32He fills his hands with lightning bolts. He hurls each at its target. [33]The thunder announces his presence; the storm announces his indignant anger.*

## CHAPTER 37

"My heart pounds as I think of this. It leaps within me. [2]Listen carefully to the thunder of God's voice as it rolls from his mouth. [3]It rolls across the heavens, and his lightning flashes out in every direction. [4]Then comes the roaring of the thunder—the tremendous voice of his majesty. He does not restrain the thunder when he speaks. [5]God's voice is glorious in the thunder. We cannot comprehend the greatness of his power.

[6]"He directs the snow to fall on the earth and tells the rain to pour down. [7]Everyone stops working at such a time so they can recognize his power. [8]The wild animals hide in the rocks or in their dens. [9]The stormy wind comes from its chamber, and the driving winds bring the cold. [10]God's breath sends the ice, freezing wide expanses of water. [11]He loads the clouds with moisture, and they flash with his lightning. [12]The clouds turn around and around under his direction. They do whatever he commands throughout the earth. [13]He causes things to happen on earth, either as a punishment or as a sign of his unfailing love.

[14]"Listen, Job; stop and consider the wonderful miracles of God! [15]Do you know how God controls the storm and causes the lightning to flash forth from his clouds? [16]Do you understand how he balances the clouds with wonderful perfection and skill? [17]When you are sweltering in your clothes and the south wind dies down and everything is still, [18]he makes the skies reflect the heat like a giant mirror. Can you do that?

### FROM A WHIRLWIND ● ● • • •

**38:1 From a whirlwind, God spoke. Surprisingly, he didn't answer any of Job's questions. They were not the heart of the issue. Instead, God used Job's ignorance of the earth's natural order to reveal his ignorance of God's moral order. If Job did not understand the workings of God's physical creation, how could he possibly understand God's mind and character? There is no standard or criterion higher than God himself by which to judge. God himself is the standard. Our only option is to submit to his authority and care.**

[19]"You think you know so much, so teach the rest of us what to say to God. We are too ignorant to make our own arguments. [20]Should God be told that I want to speak? Can we speak when we are confused? [21]We cannot look at the sun, for it shines brightly in the sky when the wind clears away the clouds. [22]Golden splendor comes from the mountain of God. He is clothed in dazzling splendor. [23]We cannot imagine the power of the Almighty, yet he is so just and merciful that he does not oppress us. [24]No wonder people everywhere fear him. People who are truly wise show him reverence."

## CHAPTER 38

**THE LORD SPEAKS TO JOB.** Then the LORD answered Job from the whirlwind:

[2]"Who is this that questions my wisdom with such ignorant words? [3]Brace yourself, because I have some questions for you, and you must answer them.

[4]"Where were you when I laid the foundations of the earth? Tell me, if you know so much. [5]Do you know how its dimensions were determined and who did the surveying? [6]What supports its foundations, and who laid its cornerstone [7]as the morning stars sang together and all the angels* shouted for joy?

[8]"Who defined the boundaries of the sea as it burst from the womb, [9]and as I clothed it with clouds and thick darkness? [10]For I locked it behind barred gates, limiting its shores. [11]I said, 'Thus far and no farther will you come. Here your proud waves must stop!'

[12]"Have you ever commanded the morning to appear and caused the dawn to rise in the east? [13]Have you ever told the daylight to spread to the ends of the earth, to bring an end to the night's wickedness? [14]For the features of the earth take shape as the light approaches, and the dawn is robed in red. [15]The light disturbs the haunts of the wicked, and it stops the arm that is raised in violence.

[16]"Have you explored the springs from which the seas come? Have you walked about and explored their depths? [17]Do you know where the gates of death are located? Have you seen the gates of utter gloom? [18]Do you realize the extent of the earth? Tell me about it if you know!

[19]"Where does the light come from, and where does the darkness go? [20]Can you take it to its home? Do you know how to get there? [21]But of course you know all this! For you were born before it was all created, and you are so very experienced!

[22]"Have you visited the treasuries of the snow? Have you seen where the hail is made and stored? [23]I have reserved it for the time of trouble, for the day of battle and war. [24]Where is the path to the origin of light? Where is the home of the east wind?

[25]"Who created a channel for the torrents of rain? Who laid out the path for the lightning? [26]Who makes the rain fall on barren land, in a desert where no one lives? [27]Who sends the rain that satisfies the parched ground and makes the tender grass spring up?

[28]"Does the rain have a father? Where does dew come from? [29]Who is the mother of the ice? Who gives birth to the frost from the heavens? [30]For the water turns to ice as hard as rock, and the surface of the water freezes.

### LIMITED KNOWLEDGE ● ● • • •

**39:1-30 God asked Job several questions about the animal kingdom in order to demonstrate how limited Job's knowledge really was. God was not seeking answers from Job. Instead, he was getting Job to recognize and submit to God's power and sovereignty. Only then would he be able to hear what God was really saying to him.**

36:33 Or *even the cattle know when a storm is coming.* The meaning of the Hebrew is uncertain. 38:7 Hebrew *sons of God.*

31“Can you hold back the movements of the stars? Are you able to restrain the Pleiades or Orion? 32Can you ensure the proper sequence of the seasons or guide the constellation of the Bear with her cubs across the heavens? 33Do you know the laws of the universe and how God rules the earth?

34“Can you shout to the clouds and make it rain? 35Can you make lightning appear and cause it to strike as you direct it? 36Who gives intuition and instinct? 37Who is wise enough to count all the clouds? Who can tilt the water jars of heaven, 38turning the dry dust to clumps of mud?

39“Can you stalk prey for a lioness and satisfy the young lions' appetites 40as they lie in their dens or crouch in the thicket? 41Who provides food for the ravens when their young cry out to God as they wander about in hunger?

## CHAPTER 39

“Do you know when the mountain goats give birth? Have you watched as the wild deer are born? 2Do you know how many months they carry their young? Are you aware of the time of their delivery? 3They crouch down to give birth to their young and deliver their offspring. 4Their young grow up in the open fields, then leave their parents and never return.

5“Who makes the wild donkey wild? 6I have placed it in the wilderness; its home is the wasteland. 7It hates the noise of the city, and it has no driver to shout at it. 8The mountains are its pastureland, where it searches for every blade of grass.

9“Will the wild ox consent to being tamed? Will it stay in your stall? 10Can you hitch a wild ox to a plow? Will it plow a field for you? 11Since it is so strong, can you trust it? Can you go away and trust the ox to do your work? 12Can you rely on it to return, bringing your grain to the threshing floor?

13“The ostrich flaps her wings grandly, but they are no match for the feathers of the stork. 14She lays her eggs on top of the earth, letting them be warmed in the dust. 15She doesn't worry that a foot might crush them or that wild animals might destroy them. 16She is harsh toward her young, as if they were not her own. She is unconcerned though they die, 17for God has deprived her of wisdom. He has given her no understanding. 18But whenever she jumps up to run, she passes the swiftest horse with its rider.

19“Have you given the horse its strength or clothed its neck with a flowing mane? 20Did you give it the ability to leap forward like a locust? Its majestic snorting is something to hear! 21It paws the earth and rejoices in its strength. When it charges to war, 22it is unafraid. It does not run from the sword. 23The arrows rattle against it, and the spear and javelin flash. 24Fiercely it paws the ground and rushes forward into battle when the trumpet blows. 25It snorts at the sound of the bugle. It senses the battle even at a distance. It quivers at the noise of battle and the shout of the captain's commands.

26“Are you the one who makes the hawk soar and spread its wings to the south? 27Is it at your command that the eagle rises to the heights to make its nest? 28It lives on the cliffs, making its home on a distant, rocky crag. 29From there it hunts its prey, keeping watch with piercing eyes. 30Its nestlings gulp down blood, for it feeds on the carcass of the slaughtered.”

## CHAPTER 40

**JOB: I AM NOTHING.** Then the LORD said to Job, 2“Do you still want to argue with the Almighty? You are God's critic, but do you have the answers?”

3Then Job replied to the LORD, 4“I am nothing—how could I ever find the answers? I will put my hand over my mouth in silence. 5I have said too much already. I have nothing more to say.”

6Then the LORD answered Job from the whirlwind:

7“Brace yourself, because I have some questions for you, and you must answer them. 8Are you going to discredit my justice and condemn me so you can say you are right? 9Are you as strong as God, and can you thunder with a voice like his? 10All right then, put on your robes of state, your majesty and splendor. 11Give vent to your anger. Let it overflow against the proud. 12Humiliate the proud with a glance; walk on the wicked where they stand. 13Bury them in the dust. Imprison them in the world of the dead. 14Then even I would praise you, for your own strength would save you.

15“Take a look at the mighty hippopotamus.* I made it, just as I made you. It eats grass like an ox. 16See its powerful loins and the muscles of its belly. 17Its tail is as straight as a cedar. The sinews of its thighs are tightly knit together. 18Its bones are tubes of bronze. Its limbs are bars of iron. 19It is a prime example of God's amazing handiwork. Only its Creator can threaten it. 20The mountains offer it their best food, where all the wild animals play. 21It lies down under the lotus plants, hidden by the reeds. 22The lotus plants give it shade among the willows beside the stream. 23It is not disturbed by raging rivers, not even when the swelling Jordan rushes down upon it. 24No one can catch it off guard or put a ring in its nose and lead it away.

## CHAPTER 41

“Can you catch a crocodile* with a hook or put a noose around its jaw? 2Can you tie it with a rope through the nose or pierce its jaw

### ARGUING WITH GOD ● ● • • ·

**40:2-5 In what ways do you argue with the Almighty? Do you demand answers when things don't go your way, when you get cut from a team, when someone close to you is ill or dies, when money is tight, when you fail, or when unexpected changes occur? The next time you are tempted to complain to God, consider how much he loves you and remember Job's reaction when he had his chance to speak. Are you worse off than Job, or more righteous? Give God a chance to reveal his greater purposes for you, but remember that they may unfold over the course of your life and not at any given moment.**

40:15 Hebrew *at behemoth.* 41:1 Hebrew *Leviathan;* also throughout the following passage.

## LOCKED INTO TIME ● ● • • •

42:1-6 **Throughout the book, Job's friends had asked him to admit his sin and ask for forgiveness, and eventually Job did indeed repent. Ironically, Job's repentance was not the kind called for by his friends. He did not ask for forgiveness for secret sins, but for questioning God's sovereignty and justice. Job repented of his attitude and acknowledged God's great power and perfect justice. We sin when we angrily ask, "If God is in control, how could he let this happen?" Since we are locked into time, unable to see beyond today, we cannot know the reasons for everything that happens. Thus we often must choose between anger and trust. Will you trust God with your unanswered questions?**

with a spike? 3Will it beg you for mercy or implore you for pity? 4Will it agree to work for you? Can you make it be your slave for life? 5Can you make it a pet like a bird, or give it to your little girls to play with? 6Will merchants try to buy it? Will they sell it in their shops? 7Will its hide be hurt by darts, or its head by a harpoon? 8If you lay a hand on it, you will never forget the battle that follows, and you will never try it again!

9"No, it is useless to try to capture it. The hunter who attempts it will be thrown down. 10And since no one dares to disturb the crocodile, who would dare to stand up to me? 11Who will confront me and remain safe*? Everything under heaven is mine.

12"I want to emphasize the tremendous strength in the crocodile's limbs and throughout its enormous frame. 13Who can strip off its hide, and who can penetrate its double layer of armor*? 14Who could pry open its jaws? For its teeth are terrible! 15The overlapping scales on its back make a shield. 16They are close together so no air can get between them. 17They lock together so nothing can penetrate them.

18"When it sneezes, it flashes light! Its eyes are like the red of dawn. 19Fire and sparks leap from its mouth. 20Smoke streams from its nostrils like steam from a boiling pot on a fire of dry rushes. 21Yes, its breath would kindle coals, for flames shoot from its mouth.

22"The tremendous strength in its neck strikes terror wherever it goes. 23Its flesh is hard and firm, not soft and fat. 24Its heart is as hard as rock, as hard as a millstone. 25When it rises, the mighty are afraid, gripped by terror. 26No sword can stop it, nor spear nor dart nor pointed shaft. 27To the crocodile, iron is nothing but straw, and bronze is rotten wood. 28Arrows cannot make it flee. Stones shot from a sling are as ineffective as straw. 29Clubs do no good, and it laughs at the swish of the javelins. 30Its belly is covered with scales as sharp as glass. They tear up the ground as it drags through the mud.

31"The crocodile makes the water boil with its commotion. It churns the depths. 32The water glistens in its wake. One would think the sea had turned white. 33There is nothing else so fearless anywhere on earth. 34Of all the creatures, it is the proudest. It is the king of beasts."

CHAPTER **42** **GOD GIVES JOB GOOD GIFTS.** Then Job replied to the LORD:

2"I know that you can do anything, and no one can stop you. 3You ask, 'Who is this that questions my wisdom with such ignorance?' It is I. And I was talking about things I did not understand, things far too wonderful for me.

4"You said, 'Listen and I will speak! I have some questions for you, and you must answer them.'

5"I had heard about you before, but now I have seen you with my own eyes. 6I take back everything I said, and I sit in dust and ashes to show my repentance."

7After the LORD had finished speaking to Job, he said to Eliphaz the Temanite: "I am angry with you and with your two friends, for you have not been right in what you said about me, as my servant Job was. 8Now take seven young bulls and seven rams and go to my servant Job and offer a burnt offering for yourselves. My servant Job will pray for you, and I will accept his prayer on your behalf. I will not treat you as you deserve, for you have not been right in what you said about me, as my servant Job was."

## FRIENDS AGAIN ● ● • • •

42:8-10 **After receiving much criticism, Job was still able to pray for his three friends. It is difficult to forgive someone who has accused you of wrongdoing, but Job did. Are you praying for those who have wronged you? Can you forgive them? Follow the actions of Job, whom God called a good man, and pray for those who wrong you.**

9So Eliphaz the Temanite, Bildad the Shuhite, and Zophar the Naamathite did as the LORD commanded them, and the LORD accepted Job's prayer.

10When Job prayed for his friends, the LORD restored his fortunes. In fact, the LORD gave him twice as much as before! 11Then all his brothers, sisters, and former friends came and feasted with him in his home. And they consoled him and comforted him because of all the trials the LORD had brought against him. And each of them brought him a gift of money* and a gold ring.

12So the LORD blessed Job in the second half of his life even more than in the beginning. For now he had fourteen thousand sheep, six thousand camels, one thousand teams of oxen, and one thousand female donkeys. 13He also gave Job seven more sons and three more daughters. 14He named his first daughter Jemimah, the second Keziah, and the third Keren-happuch. 15In all the land there were no other women as lovely as the daughters of Job. And their father put them into his will along with their brothers.

16Job lived 140 years after that, living to see four generations of his children and grandchildren. 17Then he died, an old man who had lived a long, good life.

41:11 As in Greek version; Hebrew reads *confront me that I must pay.* 41:13 As in Greek version; Hebrew reads *its bridle.* 42:11 Hebrew *a kesitah;* the value or weight of the kesitah is no longer known.

# MEGA themes

**SUFFERING** Through no fault of his own, Job lost his wealth, children, and health. Even his friends were convinced that Job had brought this suffering upon himself. For Job, the greatest trial was not the pain or loss; it was his inability to understand why God was allowing him to suffer.

Suffering can be, but is not always, a penalty for sin. In the same way, prosperity is not always a reward for being good. Those who love God are not exempt from trouble. Although we may not be able to understand fully the pain we experience, it can lead us to rediscover God. He is always present, even in suffering.

1. If you were in Job's position, what would you have been thinking about yourself? About God?
2. Describe Job's attitude toward God throughout his suffering. In light of his personal pain, what does this tell you about Job's relationship with God?
3. Have you ever known someone who maintained a strong faith in God even when he or she was suffering? If so, explain what you observed in his or her life.
4. How does Job's example give you hope as you live in a world that often includes suffering, even for God's children?

**SATAN'S ATTACKS** Satan tried to drive a wedge between Job and God by getting Job to believe that God's governing of the world was not just and good. Satan had to ask God for permission to take Job's wealth, children, and health away. Satan was limited to what God allowed.

We must learn to recognize Satan's attacks, but we should not fear them. Satan cannot exceed the limits that God sets. Don't let any experience separate you from God. Although you can't control how or when Satan may attack, you can always choose how you will respond when it happens.

1. What did you learn about Satan from the book of Job?
2. Many people think of God and Satan as opposing equals, sort of like the "force" from the Star Wars movies, which had a powerful good side and an equally powerful dark side. What do you read in Job that shows you the error of this view?
3. What does this book teach you about how Christians should respond to the reality of Satan's power?
4. What examples do you see of Satan's work in the world? How should you respond to these situations?

**TRUSTING GOD'S GOODNESS** God is all-wise and all-powerful. His will is perfect, yet he doesn't always act in ways we understand. Job's suffering didn't make sense because everyone believed that good people were supposed to prosper. When Job was at the point of despair, God spoke, revealing his great power and wisdom.

Although God is present everywhere, at times he may seem far away. This may cause us to feel alone and to doubt his care for us. We should serve God for who he is, not for what we feel. He is never insensitive to our suffering. Because God is sufficient, we must hold on to him. This fact is greater than any feeling we might have that he has abandoned us.

1. What do you think it means to trust God with your circumstances? How did Job show this trust in God?
2. How did God reveal to Job that he (God) was worthy of that trust?
3. What circumstances or problems in the world cause people to question God's goodness?
4. What can you do to build your trust in God, even when it feels like his goodness is not present (e.g., in your pain and suffering)?

**PRIDE** Job's friends were sure that they were correct in their judgment of him. God rebuked them for their pride and arrogance. Man's wisdom is always partial and temporary.

We must be careful not to judge others who are suffering, because we may be demonstrating the sin of pride. And we should be cautious in declaring how sure we are about why God treats us the way he does. When we congratulate ourselves for being right, we become proud. We should always be willing to listen and to learn.

1. How did each of Job's friends display pride?
2. Why is pride so dangerous? Give an example of how a person's pride (someone you have known or read about) led to disaster.
3. How does God view pride? Why does he see it that way?
4. Give an example of a time when you struggled with pride in your attitude toward another person. How were you feeling about the person? About yourself?
5. What specific actions can you take to keep yourself from falling into this sin in the future?

Emotions. We experience countless feelings every day, ranging from exuberant joy to deep grief. We feel pain when someone we love dies. We feel anger when things go wrong. We feel confusion when we don't understand. And we feel joy when something good happens. Emotions add spice and color to life. ■ The book of Psalms is about emotions. The pages are filled with them: anger, confusion, joy, pain, humility, bewilderment, contentment—all directed toward God. God created us with emotions, and he knows they will be part of our dealings with him. ■ Many people read the book of Psalms because of its honesty. Rather than ignoring the "negative" emotions or condemning them as sinful, the writers faced their feelings and continued to talk with God. ■ Psalms also is loved because of the clear picture of God it presents. Our emotions change constantly, but God is constant. While we fret, worry, and shout about injustice, God remains calm. When we fall on our face before him because of our awful sin, he isn't surprised—he is gentle and ready to forgive. Psalms reminds us that God is exalted, the Creator and Ruler of the world, and worthy of worship. He alone is God. ■ How are you feeling today? Angry? Afraid? Frustrated? Or are you joyful, happy, and excited? Read Psalms and express yourself honestly to God.

## STATS

PURPOSE: To provide poetry for the expression of praise, worship, and confession to God

AUTHORS: David wrote 73 psalms; Asaph wrote 12; the descendants of Korah wrote 10; Solomon wrote 2; Heman (with the descendants of Korah), Ethan, and Moses each wrote 1; and 50 psalms are anonymous, though the New Testament ascribes two of the anonymous psalms—Psalms 2 and 95—to David (See Acts 4:25; Hebrews 4:7)

DATE WRITTEN: Between the time of Moses (around 1440 B.C.) and the Babylonian captivity (586 B.C.)

SETTING: For the most part, the psalms were not intended to be narrations of historical events. However, they often parallel events in history, such as David's flight from Saul and his sin with Bathsheba.

KEY PERSON: David

KEY PLACE: God's holy Temple

SPECIAL FEATURES: Psalms has a unified plan, but each psalm can be read and understood alone. Psalms is probably the most widely read book of the Bible, because it is easy to relate to the writers' emotions.

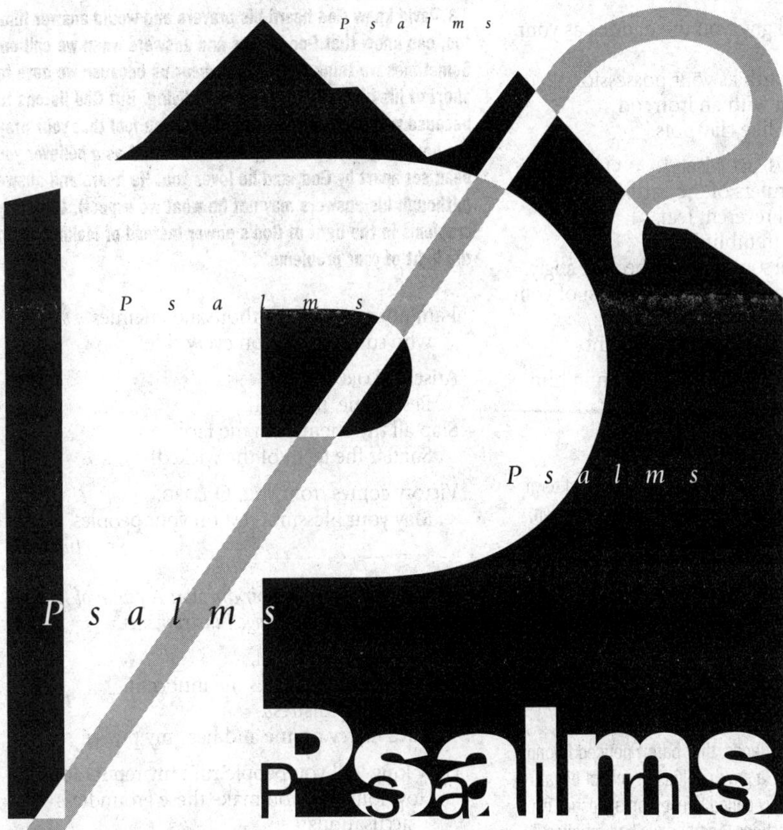


**BOOK ONE (Psalms 1–41)**

## PSALM 1

[1] Oh, the joys of those
who do not follow the advice of the wicked,
or stand around with sinners,
or join in with scoffers.
[2] But they delight in doing everything the LORD wants;
day and night they think about his law.
[3] They are like trees planted along the riverbank,
bearing fruit each season without fail.
Their leaves never wither,
and in all they do, they prosper.
[4] But this is not true of the wicked.
They are like worthless chaff, scattered by the wind.
[5] They will be condemned at the time of judgment.
Sinners will have no place among the godly.
[6] For the LORD watches over the path of the godly,
but the path of the wicked leads to destruction.

## PSALM 2

[1] Why do the nations rage?
Why do the people waste their time with futile plans?
[2] The kings of the earth prepare for battle;
the rulers plot together
against the LORD
and against his anointed one.
[3] "Let us break their chains," they cry,
"and free ourselves from this slavery."
[4] But the one who rules in heaven laughs.
The Lord scoffs at them.
[5] Then in anger he rebukes them,
terrifying them with his fierce fury.
[6] For the LORD declares, "I have placed my chosen king on the throne
in Jerusalem, my holy city.*"
[7] The king proclaims the LORD's decree:
"The LORD said to me, 'You are my son.*
Today I have become your Father.*

**FREEDOM ● ● ● • ·**

2:3 **People often think they will be free if they can get away from God. Yet we all inevitably serve somebody or something, whether a human king, the wishes of friends, or our own selfish desires. Just as a fish is not free when it leaves the water and a tree is not free when it leaves the soil, we are not free when we leave the Lord. The one sure route to freedom is wholeheartedly serving God the Creator. He can set you free to be who he created you to be.**

**2:6** Hebrew *on Zion, my holy mountain.* **2:7a** Or *Son;* also in 2:12. **2:7b** Or *Today I reveal you as my son.*

[8] Only ask, and I will give you the nations as your inheritance,
the ends of the earth as your possession.
[9] You will break them with an iron rod
and smash them like clay pots.'"

[10] Now then, you kings, act wisely!
Be warned, you rulers of the earth!
[11] Serve the LORD with reverent fear,
and rejoice with trembling.
[12] Submit to God's royal son, or he will become angry,
and you will be destroyed in the midst of your pursuits—
for his anger can flare up in an instant.

But what joy for all who find protection in him!

## FRIENDSHIP

Last year Rhonda moved from a small Midwest town to Chicago. She didn't want to leave her hometown, but her dad got a job offer he'd been wanting to get for years. Rhonda left behind close friends, a great youth group, a good school, and 14 years' worth of memories.

Chicago was a brand-new world. In Baxter everybody knew everybody else (not to mention everybody else's business). In Chicago Rhonda felt invisible. The first month, she cried almost every night.

Even when Rhonda's family found a church with a big youth group, things didn't improve. Nobody in the group really reached out. They were so into their own little circle of friends, they barely noticed Rhonda.

At about that same time, however, a group of kids at school began reaching out to "the new girl." One guy called himself an agnostic. Two of the girls claimed to have had abortions. Another guy had a police record. None of them went to church.

When Rhonda's parents expressed concern about her choice of friends, Rhonda retorted, "Well, they may be a little bit on the wild side, but at least they treat me like a person. I'd rather hang out with them than with those fakes at the church!"

What would you do in Rhonda's situation? Do friends really affect the direction of our life? Read Psalm 1, noting especially the first verse.

## PSALM 3

*A psalm of David, regarding the time David fled from his son Absalom.*

[1] O LORD, I have so many enemies;
so many are against me.
[2] So many are saying,
"God will never rescue him!" *Interlude**

[3] But you, O LORD, are a shield around me,
my glory, and the one who lifts my head high.
[4] I cried out to the LORD,
and he answered me from his holy mountain.
*Interlude*

[5] I lay down and slept.
I woke up in safety,
for the LORD was watching over me.

## OFF THE CEILING ● ● • • •

4:3 **David knew God heard his prayers and would answer him. We, too, can know that God listens and answers when we call on him. Sometimes we think God will not hear us because we have fallen short of his high standards for holy living. But God listens to us because we have been forgiven. When you feel that your prayers are bouncing off the ceiling, remember that as a believer you have been set apart by God, and he loves you. He hears and answers (although his answers may not be what we expect). Look at your problems in the light of God's power instead of looking at God in the light of your problems.**

[6] I am not afraid of ten thousand enemies
who surround me on every side.

[7] Arise, O LORD!
Rescue me, my God!
Slap all my enemies in the face!
Shatter the teeth of the wicked!

[8] Victory comes from you, O LORD.
May your blessings rest on your people.
*Interlude*

## PSALM 4

*For the choir director: A psalm of David, to be accompanied by stringed instruments.*

[1] Answer me when I call,
O God who declares me innocent.
Take away my distress.
Have mercy on me and hear my prayer.

[2] How long will you people ruin my reputation?
How long will you make these groundless accusations?
How long will you pursue lies? *Interlude*

[3] You can be sure of this:
The LORD has set apart the godly for himself.
The LORD will answer when I call to him.

[4] Don't sin by letting anger gain control over you.
Think about it overnight and remain silent.
*Interlude*

[5] Offer proper sacrifices,
and trust in the LORD.

[6] Many people say, "Who will show us better times?"
Let the smile of your face shine on us, LORD.
[7] You have given me greater joy
than those who have abundant harvests of grain and wine.

[8] I will lie down in peace and sleep,
for you alone, O LORD, will keep me safe.

## PSALM 5

*For the choir director: A psalm of David, to be accompanied by the flute.*

[1] O LORD, hear me as I pray;
pay attention to my groaning.
[2] Listen to my cry for help, my King and my God,
for I will never pray to anyone but you.

3:2 Hebrew *Selah.* The meaning of this word is uncertain, though it is probably a musical or literary term. It is rendered *Interlude* throughout the Psalms.

[3] Listen to my voice in the morning, LORD.
Each morning I bring my requests to you and wait expectantly.

[4] O God, you take no pleasure in wickedness;
you cannot tolerate the slightest sin.
[5] Therefore, the proud will not be allowed to stand in your presence,
for you hate all who do evil.
[6] You will destroy those who tell lies.
The LORD detests murderers and deceivers.

[7] Because of your unfailing love, I can enter your house;
with deepest awe I will worship at your Temple.
[8] Lead me in the right path, O LORD,
or my enemies will conquer me.
Tell me clearly what to do,
and show me which way to turn.

[9] My enemies cannot speak one truthful word.
Their deepest desire is to destroy others.
Their talk is foul, like the stench from an open grave.
Their speech is filled with flattery.
[10] O God, declare them guilty.
Let them be caught in their own traps.
Drive them away because of their many sins,
for they rebel against you.

[11] But let all who take refuge in you rejoice;
let them sing joyful praises forever.
Protect them,
so all who love your name may be filled with joy.
[12] For you bless the godly, O LORD,
surrounding them with
your shield of love.

## PSALM 6 *For the choir director: A psalm of David, to be accompanied by an eight-stringed instrument.**

[1] O LORD, do not rebuke me in your anger
or discipline me in your rage.
[2] Have compassion on me, LORD, for I am weak.
Heal me, LORD, for my body is in agony.
[3] I am sick at heart.
How long, O LORD, until you restore me?

[4] Return, O LORD, and rescue me.
Save me because of your unfailing love.
[5] For in death, who remembers you?
Who can praise you from the grave?

6:TITLE Hebrew *with stringed instruments; according to the sheminith.*

**REVENGE ● ● • • •**

7:1-6 **Have you ever been falsely accused or badly hurt and wanted revenge? David wrote this psalm in response to the slanderous accusations of those who claimed he was trying to kill King Saul and seize the throne (1 Samuel 24:9-11). Instead of seeking revenge, David cried out to God for justice. The proper response to slander is prayer, not revenge. God says, "I will take vengeance; I will repay those who deserve it" (Romans 12:19; Deuteronomy 32:35-36). Instead of striking back, ask God to take your case, bring justice, and restore your reputation.**

[6] I am worn out from sobbing.
Every night tears drench my bed;
my pillow is wet from weeping.
[7] My vision is blurred by grief;
my eyes are worn out because of all my enemies.

[8] Go away, all you who do evil,
for the LORD has heard my crying.
[9] The LORD has heard my plea;
the LORD will answer my prayer.
[10] May all my enemies be disgraced and terrified.
May they suddenly turn back in shame.

## PSALM 7 *A psalm of David, which he sang to the LORD concerning Cush of the tribe of Benjamin.*

[1] I come to you for protection, O LORD my God.
Save me from my persecutors—rescue me!
[2] If you don't, they will maul me like a lion,
tearing me to pieces with no one to rescue me.
[3] O LORD my God, if I have done wrong
or am guilty of injustice,

## "Here's what I did..."

There was a time a couple of years ago when I was really down on myself, depressed and very confused. I couldn't do anything to make myself feel better. I prayed about it and one night I opened my Bible looking for consolation. I leafed through the Psalms, remembering that a Christian friend had once told me that whenever he felt bad, it helped to read the Psalms.

What caught my eye that night was the heading for Psalm 6: "A prayer for deliverance in time of distress. God is able to deliver us." That's what I felt—distressed; and what I needed was deliverance. I read and reread that psalm. It spoke straight to my heart, and it showed me that God was there for me, as always. Do I ever love him!

Now whenever I'm in doubt about God's love and care, I turn to that psalm. It reminds me that God is always there and that he will lead me through any dark time I experience, just as he did that one night when I first read Psalm 6.

*Jenna*

AGE 17

## Ultimate Issues

### MADE IN THE IMAGE OF GOD

"Van Gogh's *Irises* sells for $53.9 million." Art sales don't usually make headlines, but occasionally you'll see a front-page story about a particular painting being sold for an ASTRONOMICAL sum. To the untrained eye, even such an extremely expensive work may seem to be only a few lines splashed across the canvas, holding no meaning or appeal. What makes such a picture worth so much? The answer is found tucked away, almost unnoticeably, in the lower right-hand corner—the artist's signature. Even if the image on the canvas seems rather ordinary or commonplace, the name VAN GOGH or GAUGUIN or REMBRANDT scrawled somewhere on it makes the piece priceless. The reason the artwork is worth so much is simple: It came from the hands of a master. The same is true of humanity. Some people think that human beings are valuable because we have somehow acquired dignity in a meaningless universe. Others think our value comes from being the most highly evolved creatures on this planet. But Psalm 8 teaches that what makes us worthwhile is the fact that we are made in the image of God. In spite of our sinfulness, in spite of the fact that we have broken God's laws and warped his creation, we still bear the image of the One who made us. It's easy to believe this of kind, attractive, thoughtful people. But it is just as true of the murderer on **death row** and the terrorist who bombs airports. We're not God's image-bearers because we're good, but because he created us. Our worth is based on his work, not on our goodness—which is a good thing because we are full of sinfulness. We're like a masterpiece that has had mud and filth splattered on it. Underneath the dirt, we still have the Master's signature on us. That should help guide how we treat each other—even the people we don't like. When you are confronted by people who seem to exist only to make your life unpleasant—the classmate who majors in being obnoxious, the parent who seems only to criticize and put down, the teacher who takes pleasure in putting red marks on your papers—remember: that person bears the signature of the Master Artist. So do you. Regardless of our sinfulness, that fact makes each of us ***the most priceless object in the universe.***

---

4 if I have betrayed a friend
  or plundered my enemy without cause,
5 then let my enemies capture me.
  Let them trample me into the ground.
  Let my honor be left in the dust. *Interlude*
6 Arise, O LORD, in anger!
  Stand up against the fury of my enemies!
  Wake up, my God, and bring justice!
7 Gather the nations before you.
  Sit on your throne high above them.
8 The LORD passes judgment on the nations.
  Declare me righteous, O LORD,
  for I am innocent, O Most High!
9 End the wickedness of the ungodly,
  but help all those who obey you.
For you look deep within the mind and heart,
  O righteous God.
10 God is my shield,
  saving those whose hearts are true and right.
11 God is a judge who is perfectly fair.
  He is angry with the wicked every day.
12 If a person does not repent,
  God* will sharpen his sword;
  he will bend and string his bow.
13 He will prepare his deadly weapons
  and ignite his flaming arrows.
14 The wicked conceive evil;
  they are pregnant with trouble
  and give birth to lies.
15 They dig a pit to trap others
  and then fall into it themselves.
16 They make trouble,
  but it backfires on them.

**NATURALLY ● ● • • •**

9:1-2 **One of the natural results of praising God is witnessing. When we know God is wonderful, we naturally want to tell others and have them praise God with us.**

7:12 Hebrew *he.*

They plan violence for others,
but it falls on their own heads.
17 I will thank the LORD because he is just;
I will sing praise to the name of the LORD
Most High.

PSALM **8** *For the choir director: A psalm of David, to be accompanied by a stringed instrument.**

1 O LORD, our Lord, the majesty of your name fills
the earth!
Your glory is higher than the heavens.

2 You have taught children and nursing infants
to give you praise.*
They silence your enemies
who were seeking revenge.
3 When I look at the night sky and see the work
of your fingers—
the moon and the stars you have set in
place—
4 what are mortals that you should think of us,
mere humans that you should care for us?*
5 For you made us only a little lower than God,*
and you crowned us with glory and honor.
6 You put us in charge of everything you made,
giving us authority over all things—
7 the sheep and the cattle
and all the wild animals,
8 the birds in the sky, the fish in the sea,
and everything that swims the ocean
currents.

9 O LORD, our Lord, the majesty of your name fills
the earth!

PSALM **9** *For the choir director: A psalm of David, to be sung to the tune "Death of the Son."*

1 I will thank you, LORD, with all my heart;
I will tell of all the marvelous things you have
done.
2 I will be filled with joy because of you.
I will sing praises to your name, O Most High.

3 My enemies turn away in retreat;
they are overthrown and destroyed before you.
4 For you have judged in my favor;
from your throne, you have judged with
fairness.

5 You have rebuked the nations and destroyed the
wicked;
you have wiped out their names forever.
6 My enemies have met their doom;
their cities are perpetual ruins.
Even the memory of their uprooted cities is
lost.

7 But the LORD reigns forever,
executing judgment from his throne.
8 He will judge the world with justice
and rule the nations with fairness.

9 The LORD is a shelter for the oppressed,
a refuge in times of trouble.
10 Those who know your name trust in you,
for you, O LORD, have never abandoned
anyone who searches for you.

11 Sing praises to the LORD who reigns in
Jerusalem.*
Tell the world about his unforgettable deeds.
12 For he who avenges murder cares for the helpless.
He does not ignore those who cry to him for
help.

13 LORD, have mercy on me.
See how I suffer at the hands of those who
hate me.
Snatch me back from the jaws of death.
14 Save me, so I can praise you publicly at
Jerusalem's gates,
so I can rejoice that you have rescued me.

**DOUBTS ● ● • • ·**

**10:1 To the psalmist, God seemed far away. "Why do you hide when I need you the most?" he asked God. But though he had honest doubts, he did not stop praying or assume that God no longer cared. He was not complaining but was asking God to hurry to his aid. It is during those times when we feel most alone or oppressed that we need to keep praying, telling God about our troubles.**

15 The nations have fallen into the pit they dug for
others.
They have been caught in their own trap.
16 The LORD is known for his justice.
The wicked have trapped themselves in their
own snares. *Quiet Interlude**

17 The wicked will go down to the grave.*
This is the fate of all the nations who ignore
God.
18 For the needy will not be forgotten forever;
the hopes of the poor will not always be
crushed.

19 Arise, O LORD!
Do not let mere mortals defy you!
Let the nations be judged in your presence!
20 Make them tremble in fear, O LORD.
Let them know they are merely human.
*Interlude*

PSALM **10**

1 O LORD, why do you stand so far away?
Why do you hide when I need you the most?
2 Proud and wicked people viciously oppress the
poor.
Let them be caught in the evil they plan for
others.

8:TITLE Hebrew *according to the gittith.* 8:2 As in Greek version; Hebrew reads *to show strength.* 8:4 Hebrew *what is man that you should think of him, the son of man that you should care for him?* 8:5 Or *a little lower than the angels;* Hebrew reads *Elohim.* 9:11 Hebrew *Zion;* also in 9:14. 9:16 Hebrew *Higgaion Selah.* The meaning of this phrase is uncertain. 9:17 Hebrew *to Sheol.*

[3] For they brag about their evil desires;
they praise the greedy and curse the LORD.
[4] These wicked people are too proud to seek God.
They seem to think that God is dead.
[5] Yet they succeed in everything they do.
They do not see your punishment awaiting them.
They pour scorn on all their enemies.
[6] They say to themselves, "Nothing bad will ever happen to us!
We will be free of trouble forever!"
[7] Their mouths are full of cursing, lies, and threats.
Trouble and evil are on the tips of their tongues.
[8] They lurk in dark alleys,
murdering the innocent who pass by.

They are always searching
for some helpless victim.
[9] Like lions they crouch silently,
waiting to pounce on the helpless.
Like hunters they capture their victims
and drag them away in nets.
[10] The helpless are overwhelmed and collapse;
they fall beneath the strength of the wicked.
[11] The wicked say to themselves, "God isn't watching!
He will never notice!"
[12] Arise, O LORD!
Punish the wicked, O God!
Do not forget the helpless!
[13] Why do the wicked get away with cursing God?
How can they think, "God will never call us to account"?

[14] But you do see the trouble and grief they cause.
You take note of it and punish them.
The helpless put their trust in you.
You are the defender of orphans.

[15] Break the arms of these wicked, evil people!
Go after them until the last one is destroyed!
[16] The LORD is king forever and ever!
Let those who worship other gods be swept from the land.

[17] LORD, you know the hopes of the helpless.
Surely you will listen to their cries and comfort them.
[18] You will bring justice to the orphans and the oppressed,
so people can no longer terrify them.

## PSALM 11 *For the choir director: A psalm of David.*

[1] I trust in the LORD for protection.
So why do you say to me,
"Fly to the mountains for safety!
[2] The wicked are stringing their bows
and setting their arrows in the bowstrings.

### LYING LIPS ● ● • • •

12:2-4 **We may be tempted to believe that lies are relatively harmless, even useful at times. But deceit, flattery, boasting, and lies are not overlooked by God. Each of these sins originates from a bad attitude that eventually is expressed in our speech. The tongue can be our greatest enemy because, though small, it can do great damage (James 3:5). Be careful how you use yours.**

They shoot from the shadows at those who do right.
[3] The foundations of law and order have collapsed.
What can the righteous do?"

[4] But the LORD is in his holy Temple;
the LORD still rules from heaven.
He watches everything closely,
examining everyone on earth.
[5] The LORD examines both the righteous and the wicked.
He hates everyone who loves violence.
[6] He rains down blazing coals on the wicked,
punishing them with burning sulfur and scorching winds.
[7] For the LORD is righteous, and he loves justice.
Those who do what is right will see his face.

## PSALM 12 *For the choir director: A psalm of David, to be accompanied by an eight-stringed instrument.**

[1] Help, O LORD, for the godly are fast disappearing!
The faithful have vanished from the earth!
[2] Neighbors lie to each other,
speaking with flattering lips and insincere hearts.
[3] May the LORD bring their flattery to an end
and silence their proud tongues.
[4] They say, "We will lie to our hearts' content.
Our lips are our own—who can stop us?"

[5] The LORD replies, "I have seen violence done to the helpless,
and I have heard the groans of the poor.
Now I will rise up to rescue them,
as they have longed for me to do."
[6] The LORD's promises are pure,
like silver refined in a furnace,
purified seven times over.

[7] Therefore, LORD, we know you will protect the oppressed,
preserving them forever from this lying generation,
[8] even though the wicked strut about,
and evil is praised throughout the land.

## PSALM 13 *For the choir director: A psalm of David.*

[1] O LORD, how long will you forget me? Forever?
How long will you look the other way?
[2] How long must I struggle with anguish in my soul,

12:TITLE Hebrew *according to the sheminith.*

with sorrow in my heart every day?
How long will my enemy have the upper hand?

3 Turn and answer me, O LORD my God!
Restore the light to my eyes, or I will die.
4 Don't let my enemies gloat, saying, "We have defeated him!"
Don't let them rejoice at my downfall.
5 But I trust in your unfailing love.
I will rejoice because you have rescued me.
6 I will sing to the LORD
because he has been so good to me.

## PSALM 14 *For the choir director: A psalm of David.*

1 Only fools say in their hearts,
"There is no God."
They are corrupt, and their actions are evil;
no one does good!

2 The LORD looks down from heaven
on the entire human race;
he looks to see if there is even one with real understanding,
one who seeks for God.
3 But no, all have turned away from God;
all have become corrupt.
No one does good,
not even one!

4 Will those who do evil never learn?
They eat up my people like bread;
they wouldn't think of praying to the LORD.
5 Terror will grip them,
for God is with those who obey him.
6 The wicked frustrate the plans of the oppressed,
but the LORD will protect his people.
7 Oh, that salvation would come from Mount Zion to rescue Israel!
For when the LORD restores his people,
Jacob will shout with joy,
and Israel will rejoice.

## PSALM 15 *A psalm of David.*

1 Who may worship in your sanctuary, LORD?
Who may enter your presence on your holy hill?

2 Those who lead blameless lives
and do what is right,
speaking the truth from sincere hearts.
3 Those who refuse to slander others
or harm their neighbors
or speak evil of their friends.
4 Those who despise persistent sinners,
and honor the faithful followers of the LORD
and keep their promises even when it hurts.
5 Those who do not charge interest on the money they lend,
and who refuse to accept bribes to testify against the innocent.

Such people will stand firm forever.

## PSALM 16 *A psalm of David.*

1 Keep me safe, O God,
for I have come to you for refuge.

2 I said to the LORD, "You are my Master!
All the good things I have are from you."
3 The godly people in the land
are my true heroes!
I take pleasure in them!
4 Those who chase after other gods will be filled with sorrow.
I will not take part in their sacrifices
or even speak the names of their gods.
5 LORD, you alone are my inheritance, my cup of blessing.
You guard all that is mine.
6 The land you have given me is a pleasant land.
What a wonderful inheritance!

7 I will bless the LORD who guides me;
even at night my heart instructs me.

## "Here's what I did..."

I couldn't get out of my mind what my friend had told me. She said that when she was eight years old, her oldest brother raped her—more than once.

I felt angry, mainly at God. I just couldn't understand it. How could God let such a terrible thing happen to such a wonderful person? Why hadn't he done anything to stop it—like have the phone ring, or someone come to the door, or someone come home? Anything!

This really bothered me for a long time. Then I was reading in the Psalms, and I came across Psalm 13. I saw that the psalmist was angry at God, too—he was actually complaining to God! That gave me freedom to spill out my heart to God. I told God all my bitter and confused thoughts concerning what happened to my friend. I cried. I even lashed out at God. And the result of telling God what was on my mind and my heart was an incredible peace. Psalm 13 showed me that God always wants to hear what's on my mind, even when I'm angry with him. In the end, I found that God is there for me—even if I don't always understand all his ways.

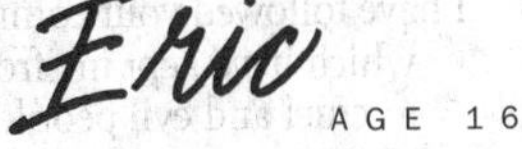


AGE 16

## REASONS TO READ PSALMS

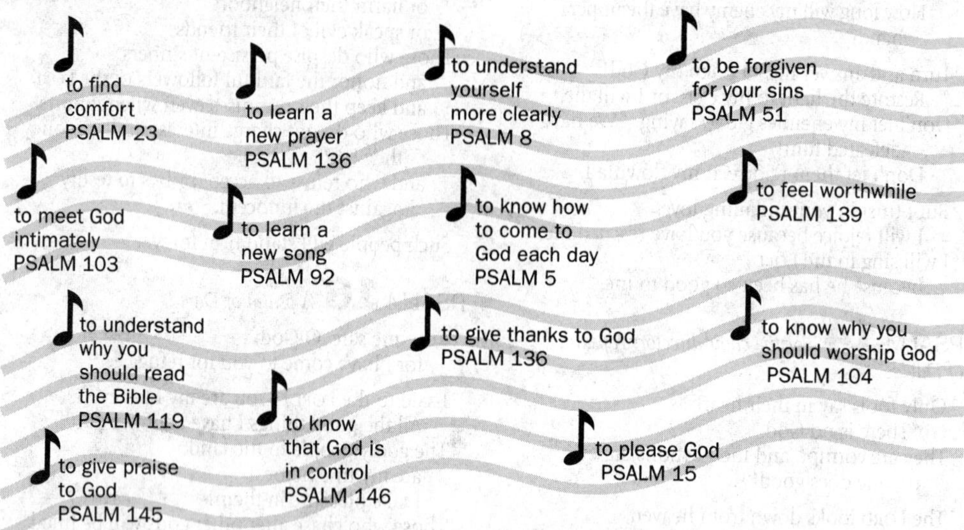


God's Word was written to be studied, understood, and applied, and the book of Psalms lends itself most directly to application. We may turn to Psalms looking for something, but sooner or later we will meet Someone. As we read and memorize the psalms, we will discover how much they are already part of us. They put our deepest hurts, longings, thoughts, and prayers into words. They gently push us toward being what God designed us to be—people who love and live for him.

---

8 I know the LORD is always with me.
I will not be shaken, for he is right beside me.
9 No wonder my heart is filled with joy,
and my mouth* shouts his praises!
My body rests in safety.
10 For you will not leave my soul among the dead*
or allow your godly one* to rot in the grave.
11 You will show me the way of life,
granting me the joy of your presence
and the pleasures of living with you forever.

## PSALM 17 *A prayer of David.*

1 O LORD, hear my plea for justice.
Listen to my cry for help.
Pay attention to my prayer,
for it comes from an honest heart.
2 Declare me innocent,
for you know those who do right.

3 You have tested my thoughts and examined my heart in the night.
You have scrutinized me and found nothing amiss,
for I am determined not to sin in what I say.
4 I have followed your commands,
which have kept me from going along with cruel and evil people.
5 My steps have stayed on your path;
I have not wavered from following you.

6 I am praying to you because I know you will answer, O God.
Bend down and listen as I pray.
7 Show me your unfailing love in wonderful ways.
You save with your strength
those who seek refuge from their enemies.
8 Guard me as the apple of your eye.
Hide me in the shadow of your wings.
9 Protect me from wicked people who attack me,
from murderous enemies who surround me.
10 They are without pity.
Listen to their boasting.
11 They track me down, surround me,
and throw me to the ground.
12 They are like hungry lions, eager to tear me apart—
like young lions in hiding, waiting for their chance.

13 Arise, O LORD!
Stand against them and bring them to their knees!
Rescue me from the wicked with your sword!
14 Save me by your mighty hand, O LORD,
from those whose only concern is earthly gain.
May they have their punishment in full.
May their children inherit more of the same,

16:9 As in Greek version; Hebrew reads *glory.* 16:10a Hebrew *in Sheol.* 16:10b Or *your Holy One.*

and may the judgment continue to their
children's children.
[15] But because I have done what is right, I will see
you.
When I awake, I will be fully satisfied,
for I will see you face to face.

## PSALM 18

*For the choir director: A psalm of David, the servant of the LORD. He sang this song to the LORD on the day the LORD rescued him from all his enemies and from Saul.*

[1] I love you, LORD; you are my strength.
[2] The LORD is my rock, my fortress, and my savior;
my God is my rock, in whom I find protection.
He is my shield, the strength of my salvation,
and my stronghold.
[3] I will call on the LORD, who is worthy of praise,
for he saves me from my enemies.

[4] The ropes of death surrounded me;
the floods of destruction swept over me.
[5] The grave* wrapped its ropes around me;
death itself stared me in the face.
[6] But in my distress I cried out to the LORD;
yes, I prayed to my God for help.
He heard me from his sanctuary;
my cry reached his ears.

[7] Then the earth quaked and trembled;
the foundations of the mountains shook;
they quaked because of his anger.
[8] Smoke poured from his nostrils;
fierce flames leaped from his mouth;
glowing coals flamed forth from him.
[9] He opened the heavens and came down;
dark storm clouds were beneath his feet.
[10] Mounted on a mighty angel,* he flew,
soaring on the wings of the wind.
[11] He shrouded himself in darkness,
veiling his approach with dense rain clouds.
[12] The brilliance of his presence broke through the
clouds,
raining down hail and burning coals.
[13] The LORD thundered from heaven;
the Most High gave a mighty shout.*
[14] He shot his arrows and scattered his enemies;
his lightning flashed, and they were greatly
confused.
[15] Then at your command, O LORD,
at the blast of your breath,
the bottom of the sea could be seen,
and the foundations of the earth were laid bare.

[16] He reached down from heaven and rescued me;
he drew me out of deep waters.
[17] He delivered me from my powerful enemies,
from those who hated me and were too strong
for me.
[18] They attacked me at a moment when I was
weakest,
but the LORD upheld me.
[19] He led me to a place of safety;
he rescued me because he delights in me.
[20] The LORD rewarded me for doing right;
he compensated me because of my innocence.
[21] For I have kept the ways of the LORD;
I have not turned from my God to follow
evil.
[22] For all his laws are constantly before me;
I have never abandoned his principles.
[23] I am blameless before God;
I have kept myself from sin.

**A friend of mine is convinced that being good will get him into heaven. I'm starting to agree with him. God won't send people who live good lives to hell, will he?**

Teachers have developed two systems for grading their students' performance. First, there is the "curve." Put simply, in a particular class 50 percent of the students will score above the average, 50 percent will score below. Often those who score below the average still have a chance to pass. That's why students seem to like this system best.

Then there is the "set" scale. With this system, a certain percentage determines your grade. If you get below a 75 percent grade, for example, you fail.

Most people would like to believe that God grades on a curve. In other words, if they're better than others, it will be all right with God. All they have to do to pass is not kill anyone or steal, mind their own business, and wait for heaven.

Unfortunately, God doesn't grade that way.

Psalm 14:1-3 is clear. There isn't anyone who is good. Not one! All of us have strayed away. This doesn't mean we're all murderers, it means our heart is stained with the sin of Adam—the desire to be god of our life and run it ourself. No one has a pure heart. (See Luke 18:18-26 for a great illustration.)

God has *one* method of salvation. In his wisdom, he gave everyone the opportunity to go to heaven by faith, not by works. All a person has to do to be saved is believe that Christ paid the penalty for sin and rose again from the dead: "God saved you by his special favor when you believed. And you can't take credit for this; it is a gift from God. Salvation is not a reward for the good things we have done, so none of us can boast about it" (Ephesians 2:8-9).

Most people say this is too simple. But that's the whole idea! God isn't trying to make it tough on us. He wants us to be with him forever!

Throughout your life you will run into people who believe that simply living a good life means heaven awaits. A good life is important to point people to a holy God, but it will not buy you a ticket to heaven. That ticket has already been paid for by Jesus Christ! And you must come to him to get it.

**18:5** Hebrew *Sheol.* **18:10** Hebrew *a cherub.* **18:13** As in Greek version (see also 2 Sam 22:14); Hebrew adds *raining down hail and burning coals.*

## SHIELD ● ● • • •

18:30 **Many say belief in God is a crutch for weak people who cannot make it on their own. God is indeed a shield to protect us when we are too weak to face certain trials by ourselves. He strengthens, protects, and guides us in order to send us back into an evil world to fight for him. David was not a coward; he was a mighty warrior who, with all his armies and weapons, knew that only God could ultimately protect and save him.**

24 The LORD rewarded me for doing right,
because of the innocence of my hands in his sight.
25 To the faithful you show yourself faithful;
to those with integrity you show integrity.
26 To the pure you show yourself pure,
but to the wicked you show yourself hostile.
27 You rescue those who are humble,
but you humiliate the proud.
28 LORD, you have brought light to my life;
my God, you light up my darkness.
29 In your strength I can crush an army;
with my God I can scale any wall.

30 As for God, his way is perfect.
All the LORD's promises prove true.
He is a shield for all who look to him for protection.
31 For who is God except the LORD?
Who but our God is a solid rock?
32 God arms me with strength;
he has made my way safe.
33 He makes me as surefooted as a deer,
leading me safely along the mountain heights.
34 He prepares me for battle;
he strengthens me to draw a bow of bronze.
35 You have given me the shield of your salvation.
Your right hand supports me;
your gentleness has made me great.
36 You have made a wide path for my feet
to keep them from slipping.

37 I chased my enemies and caught them;
I did not stop until they were conquered.
38 I struck them down so they could not get up;
they fell beneath my feet.
39 You have armed me with strength for the battle;
you have subdued my enemies under my feet.
40 You made them turn and run;
I have destroyed all who hated me.
41 They called for help, but no one came to rescue them.
They cried to the LORD, but he refused to answer them.
42 I ground them as fine as dust carried by the wind.
I swept them into the gutter like dirt.
43 You gave me victory over my accusers.
You appointed me as the ruler over nations;
people I don't even know now serve me.
44 As soon as they hear of me, they submit;
foreigners cringe before me.

19:3 Or *There is no speech or language where their voice is not heard.*

45 They all lose their courage
and come trembling from their strongholds.

46 The LORD lives! Blessed be my rock!
May the God of my salvation be exalted!
47 He is the God who pays back those who harm me;
he subdues the nations under me
48 and rescues me from my enemies.
You hold me safe beyond the reach of my enemies;
you save me from violent opponents.
49 For this, O LORD, I will praise you among the nations;
I will sing joyfully to your name.
50 You give great victories to your king;
you show unfailing love to your anointed,
to David and all his descendants forever.

## PSALM 19

*For the choir director: A psalm of David.*

1 The heavens tell of the glory of God.
The skies display his marvelous craftsmanship.
2 Day after day they continue to speak;
night after night they make him known.
3 They speak without a sound or a word;
their voice is silent in the skies;*
4 yet their message has gone out to all the earth,
and their words to all the world.

The sun lives in the heavens
where God placed it.
5 It bursts forth like a radiant bridegroom
after his wedding.
It rejoices like a great athlete
eager to run the race.
6 The sun rises at one end of the heavens
and follows its course to the other end.
Nothing can hide from its heat.

7 The law of the LORD is perfect,
reviving the soul.
The decrees of the LORD are trustworthy,
making wise the simple.
8 The commandments of the LORD are right,
bringing joy to the heart.
The commands of the LORD are clear,
giving insight to life.
9 Reverence for the LORD is pure,
lasting forever.
The laws of the LORD are true;
each one is fair.
10 They are more desirable than gold,
even the finest gold.

## GREATNESS ● ● • • •

18:35 **David offers an interesting twist to the concept of greatness, saying that God's gentleness made him great. Our society believes that greatness is attained through a combination of opportunity, talent, and aggressiveness. But true greatness comes from living according to God's laws and standards and recognizing that all we have comes from the gentleness of God's mercy.**

The Heavens The Heavens The Heavens tell of the GLORY OF GOD The skies The skies The skies display HIS MARVELOUS CRAFTSMANSHIP

PSALM 19:1

They are sweeter than honey,
even honey dripping from the comb.
11 They are a warning to those who hear them;
there is great reward for those who obey them.

12 How can I know all the sins lurking in my heart?
Cleanse me from these hidden faults.
13 Keep me from deliberate sins!
Don't let them control me.
Then I will be free of guilt
and innocent of great sin.

14 May the words of my mouth and the thoughts
of my heart
be pleasing to you,
O LORD, my rock and my redeemer.

PSALM **20** *For the choir director: A psalm of David.*

1 In times of trouble, may the LORD respond to
your cry.
May the God of Israel* keep you safe from
all harm.
2 May he send you help from his sanctuary
and strengthen you from Jerusalem.*
3 May he remember all your gifts
and look favorably on your burnt offerings.
*Interlude*

4 May he grant your heart's desire
and fulfill all your plans.
5 May we shout for joy when we hear of your
victory,
flying banners to honor our God.
May the LORD answer all your prayers.

6 Now I know that the LORD saves his anointed
king.
He will answer him from his holy heaven
and rescue him by his great power.
7 Some nations boast of their armies and
weapons,*
but we boast in the LORD our God.
8 Those nations will fall down and collapse,
but we will rise up and stand firm.

9 Give victory to our king, O LORD!
Respond to our cry for help.

PSALM **21** *For the choir director: A psalm of David.*

1 How the king rejoices in your strength,
O LORD!
He shouts with joy because of your victory.
2 For you have given him his heart's desire;
you have held back nothing that he
requested. *Interlude*

3 You welcomed him back with success and
prosperity.
You placed a crown of finest gold on his head.
4 He asked you to preserve his life,
and you have granted his request.
The days of his life stretch on forever.
5 Your victory brings him great honor,
and you have clothed him with splendor
and majesty.
6 You have endowed him with eternal blessings.
You have given him the joy of being in your
presence.

**GUILT ● ● ● • •**

19:12-13 **Many Christians are plagued by guilt. Guilt can play an important role in bringing us to Christ and in keeping us behaving properly, but it should not cripple us or make us fearful. God fully and completely forgives us—even for those sins we do unknowingly.**

20:1 Hebrew *of Jacob.* 20:2 Hebrew *Zion.* 20:7 Hebrew *chariots and horses.*

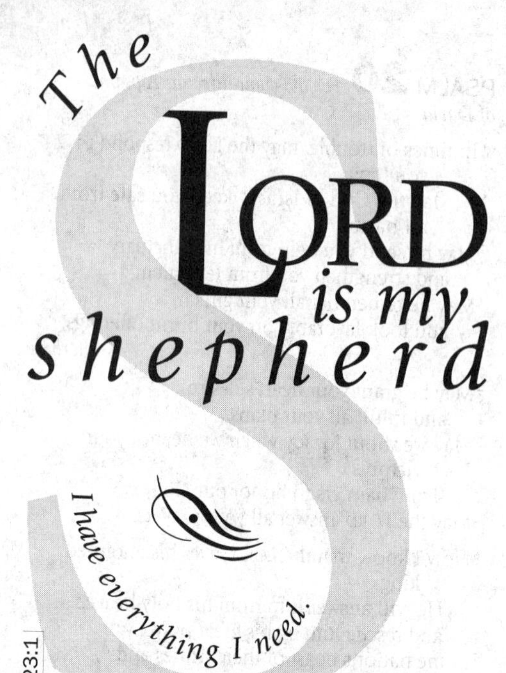
The
LORD
is my
shepherd
I have everything I need.
PSALM 23:1

7 For the king trusts in the LORD.
The unfailing love of the Most High will keep him from stumbling.
8 You will capture all your enemies.
Your strong right hand will seize all those who hate you.
9 You will destroy them as in a flaming furnace
when you appear.
The LORD will consume them in his anger;
fire will devour them.
10 You will wipe their children from the face of the earth;
they will never have descendants.
11 Although they plot against you,
their evil schemes will never succeed.
12 For they will turn and run
when they see your arrows aimed at them.
13 We praise you, LORD, for all your glorious power.
With music and singing we celebrate your mighty acts.

## PSALM **22** *For the choir director: A psalm of David, to be sung to the tune "Doe of the Dawn."*

1 My God, my God! Why have you forsaken me?
Why do you remain so distant?
Why do you ignore my cries for help?
2 Every day I call to you, my God, but you do not answer.
Every night you hear my voice, but I find no relief.
3 Yet you are holy.
The praises of Israel surround your throne.
4 Our ancestors trusted in you,
and you rescued them.
5 You heard their cries for help and saved them.
They put their trust in you and were never disappointed.

6 But I am a worm and not a man.
I am scorned and despised by all!
7 Everyone who sees me mocks me.
They sneer and shake their heads, saying,
8 "Is this the one who relies on the LORD?
Then let the LORD save him!
If the LORD loves him so much,
let the LORD rescue him!"
9 Yet you brought me safely from my mother's womb
and led me to trust you when I was a nursing infant.
10 I was thrust upon you at my birth.
You have been my God from the moment I was born.
11 Do not stay so far from me,
for trouble is near,
and no one else can help me.
12 My enemies surround me like a herd of bulls;
fierce bulls of Bashan have hemmed me in!
13 Like roaring lions attacking their prey,
they come at me with open mouths.
14 My life is poured out like water,
and all my bones are out of joint.
My heart is like wax,
melting within me.
15 My strength has dried up like sunbaked clay.
My tongue sticks to the roof of my mouth.
You have laid me in the dust and left me for dead.
16 My enemies surround me like a pack of dogs;
an evil gang closes in on me.
They have pierced my hands and feet.
17 I can count every bone in my body.
My enemies stare at me and gloat.
18 They divide my clothes among themselves
and throw dice* for my garments.
19 O LORD, do not stay away!
You are my strength; come quickly to my aid!
20 Rescue me from a violent death;
spare my precious life from these dogs.
21 Snatch me from the lions' jaws,
and from the horns of these wild oxen.
22 Then I will declare the wonder of your name to my brothers and sisters.
I will praise you among all your people.
23 Praise the LORD, all you who fear him!
Honor him, all you descendants of Jacob!

22:18 Hebrew *cast lots.*

Show him reverence, all you descendants of
Israel!
24 For he has not ignored the suffering of the
needy.
He has not turned and walked away.
He has listened to their cries for help.

25 I will praise you among all the people;
I will fulfill my vows in the presence of those
who worship you.
26 The poor will eat and be satisfied.
All who seek the LORD will praise him.
Their hearts will rejoice with everlasting
joy.
27 The whole earth will acknowledge the LORD
and return to him.
People from every nation will bow down
before him.
28 For the LORD is king!
He rules all the nations.
29 Let the rich of the earth feast and worship.
Let all mortals—those born to die—bow
down in his presence.
30 Future generations will also serve him.
Our children will hear about the wonders of
the Lord.
31 His righteous acts will be told to those yet
unborn.
They will hear about everything he has done.

## PSALM 23 *A psalm of David.*

1 The LORD is my shepherd;
I have everything I need.
2 He lets me rest in green meadows;
he leads me beside peaceful streams.
3 He renews my strength.
He guides me along right paths,
bringing honor to his name.
4 Even when I walk
through the dark valley of death,*
I will not be afraid,
for you are close beside me.
Your rod and your staff
protect and comfort me.
5 You prepare a feast for me
in the presence of my enemies.
You welcome me as a guest,
anointing my head with oil.
My cup overflows with blessings.
6 Surely your goodness and unfailing love will
pursue me
all the days of my life,
and I will live in the house of the LORD
forever.

## PSALM 24 *A psalm of David.*

1 The earth is the LORD's, and everything in it.
The world and all its people belong to him.

23:4 Or *the darkest valley.* 24:6 Hebrew *of Jacob.*

### BEST INTERESTS ●●•••

**23:2-3 When we allow God our Shepherd to guide us, we have contentment. When we choose to sin, however, we are choosing to go our own way and we cannot blame God for the environment in which we find ourself. Our Shepherd knows the "green meadows" and "peaceful streams" that will renew us. We will reach these places only by following him obediently. Rebelling against the Shepherd's leading is actually rebelling against our own best interests for the future. We must remember this the next time we are tempted to go our way rather than the Shepherd's way.**

2 For he laid the earth's foundation on the seas
and built it on the ocean depths.
3 Who may climb the mountain of the LORD?
Who may stand in his holy place?
4 Only those whose hands and hearts are pure,
who do not worship idols
and never tell lies.
5 They will receive the LORD's blessing
and have right standing with God their savior.
6 They alone may enter God's presence
and worship the God of Israel.* *Interlude*

7 Open up, ancient gates!
Open up, ancient doors,
and let the King of glory enter.
8 Who is the King of glory?
The LORD, strong and mighty,
the LORD, invincible in battle.
9 Open up, ancient gates!
Open up, ancient doors,
and let the King of glory enter.
10 Who is the King of glory?
The LORD Almighty—
he is the King of glory. *Interlude*

## PSALM 25 *A psalm of David.*

1 To you, O LORD, I lift up my soul.
2 I trust in you, my God!
Do not let me be disgraced,
or let my enemies rejoice in my defeat.
3 No one who trusts in you will ever be
disgraced,
but disgrace comes to those who try to
deceive others.

### ENEMIES ●●•••

**25:2 Seventy-two psalms—almost half the book—speak about enemies. Enemies are those who not only oppose us, but also oppose God's way of living. Enemies can also be temptations—money, success, prestige, lust. And our greatest enemy is Satan. David asked God to keep his enemies from overcoming him because they opposed what God stood for. If his enemies succeeded, David feared that many would think that living for God was futile. David did not question his own faith—he knew that God would triumph. But he didn't want his enemies' success to be an obstacle to the faith of others.**

[4] Show me the path where I should walk,
O LORD;
point out the right road for me to follow.
[5] Lead me by your truth and teach me,
for you are the God who saves me.
All day long I put my hope in you.
[6] Remember, O LORD, your unfailing love and
compassion,
which you have shown from long ages past.
[7] Forgive the rebellious sins of my youth;
look instead through the eyes of your
unfailing love,
for you are merciful, O LORD.

[8] The LORD is good and does what is right;
he shows the proper path to those who go
astray.
[9] He leads the humble in what is right,
teaching them his way.
[10] The LORD leads with unfailing love and
faithfulness
all those who keep his covenant and obey his
decrees.

[11] For the honor of your name, O LORD,
forgive my many, many sins.
[12] Who are those who fear the LORD?
He will show them the path they should
choose.
[13] They will live in prosperity,
and their children will inherit the Promised
Land.
[14] Friendship with the LORD is reserved for those
who fear him.
With them he shares the secrets of his
covenant.
[15] My eyes are always looking to the LORD for help,
for he alone can rescue me from the traps of
my enemies.

[16] Turn to me and have mercy on me,
for I am alone and in deep distress.
[17] My problems go from bad to worse.
Oh, save me from them all!
[18] Feel my pain and see my trouble.
Forgive all my sins.
[19] See how many enemies I have,
and how viciously they hate me!
[20] Protect me! Rescue my life from them!
Do not let me be disgraced, for I trust in you.
[21] May integrity and honesty protect me,
for I put my hope in you.

[22] O God, ransom Israel
from all its troubles.

## PSALM 26 *A psalm of David.*

[1] Declare me innocent, O LORD,
for I have acted with integrity;
I have trusted in the LORD without wavering.
[2] Put me on trial, LORD, and cross-examine me.
Test my motives and affections.
[3] For I am constantly aware of your unfailing love,
and I have lived according to your truth.
[4] I do not spend time with liars
or go along with hypocrites.
[5] I hate the gatherings of those who do evil,
and I refuse to join in with the wicked.

[6] I wash my hands to declare my innocence.
I come to your altar, O LORD,
[7] singing a song of thanksgiving
and telling of all your miracles.
[8] I love your sanctuary, LORD,
the place where your glory shines.

[9] Don't let me suffer the fate of sinners.
Don't condemn me along with murderers.
[10] Their hands are dirty with wicked schemes,
and they constantly take bribes.

[11] But I am not like that; I do what is right.
So in your mercy, save me.
[12] I have taken a stand,
and I will publicly praise the LORD.

## PSALM 27 *A psalm of David.*

[1] The LORD is my light and my salvation—
so why should I be afraid?
The LORD protects me from danger—
so why should I tremble?
[2] When evil people come to destroy me,
when my enemies and foes attack me,
they will stumble and fall.
[3] Though a mighty army surrounds me,
my heart will know no fear.
Even if they attack me,
I remain confident.

[4] The one thing I ask of the LORD—
the thing I seek most—
is to live in the house of the LORD all the days
of my life,
delighting in the LORD's perfections
and meditating in his Temple.
[5] For he will conceal me there when troubles
come;
he will hide me in his sanctuary.
He will place me out of reach on a high rock.
[6] Then I will hold my head high,
above my enemies who surround me.
At his Tabernacle I will offer sacrifices with
shouts of joy,
singing and praising the LORD with music.

### ANY TEST ● ● • • •

**27:5 We often run to God when we are experiencing difficulties. But David sought God's guiding presence *every day.* When troubles came his way, he was already in God's presence and prepared to handle any test. Believers can call to God for help at any time. How shortsighted it is to call on God only after trouble has come! Many of our problems could be avoided or handled far more easily by constantly relying on God's help and direction.**

[7] Listen to my pleading, O LORD.
Be merciful and answer me!
[8] My heart has heard you say, "Come and talk with me."
And my heart responds, "LORD, I am coming."
[9] Do not hide yourself from me.
Do not reject your servant in anger.
You have always been my helper.
Don't leave me now; don't abandon me,
O God of my salvation!
[10] Even if my father and mother abandon me,
the LORD will hold me close.

[11] Teach me how to live, O LORD.
Lead me along the path of honesty,
for my enemies are waiting for me to fall.
[12] Do not let me fall into their hands.
For they accuse me of things I've never done
and breathe out violence against me.
[13] Yet I am confident that I will see the LORD's goodness
while I am here in the land of the living.

[14] Wait patiently for the LORD.
Be brave and courageous.
Yes, wait patiently for the LORD.

## PSALM 28 *A psalm of David.*

[1] O LORD, you are my rock of safety.
Please help me; don't refuse to answer me.
For if you are silent,
I might as well give up and die.
[2] Listen to my prayer for mercy
as I cry out to you for help,
as I lift my hands toward your holy sanctuary.

[3] Don't drag me away with the wicked—
with those who do evil—
those who speak friendly words to their neighbors
while planning evil in their hearts.
[4] Give them the punishment they so richly deserve!
Measure it out in proportion to their wickedness.
Pay them back for all their evil deeds!
Give them a taste of what they have done to others.
[5] They care nothing for what the LORD has done
or for what his hands have made.
So he will tear them down like old buildings,
and they will never be rebuilt!

[6] Praise the LORD!
For he has heard my cry for mercy.
[7] The LORD is my strength, my shield from every danger.
I trust in him with all my heart.
He helps me, and my heart is filled with joy.
I burst out in songs of thanksgiving.

[8] The LORD protects his people
and gives victory to his anointed king.

### MASQUERADE ● ● • • •

**28:3-5 It's easy to pretend friendship. Wicked people often masquerade in goodness, pretending kindness or friendship to gain their own ends. David, in his royal position, may have met many who pretended friendship for selfish reasons. David knew God would punish them accordingly, but he prayed that their punishment would come swiftly. True believers live honest lives before God and others.**

[9] Save your people!
Bless Israel, your special possession!
Lead them like a shepherd,
and carry them forever in your arms.

## PSALM 29 *A psalm of David.*

[1] Give honor to the LORD, you angels;
give honor to the LORD for his glory and strength.
[2] Give honor to the LORD for the glory of his name.
Worship the LORD in the splendor of his holiness.

[3] The voice of the LORD echoes above the sea.
The God of glory thunders.
The LORD thunders over the mighty sea.
[4] The voice of the LORD is powerful;
the voice of the LORD is full of majesty.
[5] The voice of the LORD splits the mighty cedars;
the LORD shatters the cedars of Lebanon.
[6] He makes Lebanon's mountains skip like a calf
and Mount Hermon* to leap like a young bull.
[7] The voice of the LORD strikes with lightning bolts.
[8] The voice of the LORD makes the desert quake;
the LORD shakes the desert of Kadesh.
[9] The voice of the LORD twists mighty oaks*
and strips the forests bare.
In his Temple everyone shouts, "Glory!"
[10] The LORD rules over the floodwaters.
The LORD reigns as king forever.
[11] The LORD gives his people strength.
The LORD blesses them with peace.

## PSALM 30 *A psalm of David, sung at the dedication of the Temple.*

[1] I will praise you, LORD, for you have rescued me.
You refused to let my enemies triumph over me.
[2] O LORD my God, I cried out to you for help,
and you restored my health.
[3] You brought me up from the grave, O LORD.
You kept me from falling into the pit of death.
[4] Sing to the LORD, all you godly ones!
Praise his holy name.
[5] His anger lasts for a moment,
but his favor lasts a lifetime!
Weeping may go on all night,
but joy comes with the morning.

**29:6** Hebrew *Sirion,* another name for Mount Hermon. **29:9** Or *causes the deer to writhe in labor.*

**SECURITY ● ● • • •**

30:6-7 **Prosperity had made David feel invincible. Although he knew his riches and power had come from God, they had gone to his head, making him proud. Wealth, power, and fame have an intoxicating effect on people, making them feel self-reliant, self-secure, and independent of God. But this is a false security that is shattered easily. Don't be trapped by the false security of prosperity. Depend on God for your security and you won't be shaken when worldly possessions disappear.**

6 When I was prosperous I said,
"Nothing can stop me now!"
7 Your favor, O LORD, made me as secure as a mountain.
Then you turned away from me, and I was shattered.

8 I cried out to you, O LORD.
I begged the Lord for mercy, saying,
9 "What will you gain if I die,
if I sink down into the grave?
Can my dust praise you from the grave?
Can it tell the world of your faithfulness?
10 Hear me, LORD, and have mercy on me.
Help me, O LORD."

11 You have turned my mourning into joyful dancing.
You have taken away my clothes of mourning
and clothed me with joy,
12 that I might sing praises to you and not be silent.
O LORD my God, I will give you thanks forever!

## PSALM 31 *For the choir director: A psalm of David.*

1 O LORD, I have come to you for protection;
don't let me be put to shame.
Rescue me, for you always do what is right.
2 Bend down and listen to me;
rescue me quickly.
Be for me a great rock of safety,
a fortress where my enemies cannot reach me.

3 You are my rock and my fortress.
For the honor of your name, lead me out of this peril.
4 Pull me from the trap my enemies set for me,
for I find protection in you alone.
5 I entrust my spirit into your hand.
Rescue me, LORD, for you are a faithful God.

6 I hate those who worship worthless idols.
I trust in the LORD.
7 I am overcome with joy because of your unfailing love,
for you have seen my troubles,
and you care about the anguish of my soul.
8 You have not handed me over to my enemy
but have set me in a safe place.

9 Have mercy on me, LORD, for I am in distress.
My sight is blurred because of my tears.
My body and soul are withering away.
10 I am dying from grief;
my years are shortened by sadness.
Misery* has drained my strength;
I am wasting away from within.
11 I am scorned by all my enemies
and despised by my neighbors—
even my friends are afraid to come near me.
When they see me on the street,
they turn the other way.
12 I have been ignored as if I were dead,
as if I were a broken pot.
13 I have heard the many rumors about me,
and I am surrounded by terror.
My enemies conspire against me,
plotting to take my life.

14 But I am trusting you, O LORD,
saying, "You are my God!"
15 My future is in your hands.
Rescue me from those who hunt me down relentlessly.
16 Let your favor shine on your servant.
In your unfailing love, save me.
17 Don't let me be disgraced, O LORD,
for I call out to you for help.
Let the wicked be disgraced;
let them lie silent in the grave.
18 May their lying lips be silenced—
those proud and arrogant lips that accuse the godly.

19 Your goodness is so great!
You have stored up great blessings for those who honor you.
You have done so much for those who come to you for protection,
blessing them before the watching world.
20 You hide them in the shelter of your presence,
safe from those who conspire against them.
You shelter them in your presence,
far from accusing tongues.

21 Praise the LORD,
for he has shown me his unfailing love.
He kept me safe when my city was under attack.
22 In sudden fear I had cried out,
"I have been cut off from the LORD!"
But you heard my cry for mercy
and answered my call for help.

23 Love the LORD, all you faithful ones!
For the LORD protects those who are loyal to him,
but he harshly punishes all who are arrogant.
24 So be strong and take courage,
all you who put your hope in the LORD!

## PSALM 32 *A psalm of David.*

1 Oh, what joy for those
whose rebellion is forgiven,

31:10 Or *Sin.*

whose sin is put out of sight!
2 Yes, what joy for those
whose record the LORD has cleared of sin,
whose lives are lived in complete honesty!

3 When I refused to confess my sin,
I was weak and miserable,
and I groaned all day long.
4 Day and night your hand of discipline was heavy on me.
My strength evaporated like water in the summer heat. *Interlude*

5 Finally, I confessed all my sins to you
and stopped trying to hide them.
I said to myself, "I will confess my rebellion to the LORD."
And you forgave me! All my guilt is gone. *Interlude*

6 Therefore, let all the godly confess their rebellion to you while there is time,
that they may not drown in the floodwaters of judgment.
7 For you are my hiding place;
you protect me from trouble.
You surround me with songs of victory. *Interlude*

8 The LORD says, "I will guide you along the best pathway for your life.
I will advise you and watch over you.
9 Do not be like a senseless horse or mule
that needs a bit and bridle to keep it under control."

10 Many sorrows come to the wicked,
but unfailing love surrounds those who trust the LORD.
11 So rejoice in the LORD and be glad, all you who obey him!
Shout for joy, all you whose hearts are pure!

## PSALM 33

1 Let the godly sing with joy to the LORD,
for it is fitting to praise him.
2 Praise the LORD with melodies on the lyre;
make music for him on the ten-stringed harp.
3 Sing new songs of praise to him;
play skillfully on the harp and sing with joy.

4 For the word of the LORD holds true,
and everything he does is worthy of our trust.
5 He loves whatever is just and good,
and his unfailing love fills the earth.

6 The LORD merely spoke,
and the heavens were created.
He breathed the word,
and all the stars were born.
7 He gave the sea its boundaries
and locked the oceans in vast reservoirs.

8 Let everyone in the world fear the LORD,
and let everyone stand in awe of him.
9 For when he spoke, the world began!
It appeared at his command.

10 The LORD shatters the plans of the nations
and thwarts all their schemes.
11 But the LORD's plans stand firm forever;
his intentions can never be shaken.

12 What joy for the nation whose God is the LORD,
whose people he has chosen for his own.

13 The LORD looks down from heaven
and sees the whole human race.
14 From his throne he observes
all who live on the earth.
15 He made their hearts,
so he understands everything they do.
16 The best-equipped army cannot save a king,
nor is great strength enough to save a warrior.
17 Don't count on your warhorse to give you victory—
for all its strength, it cannot save you.

18 But the LORD watches over those who fear him,
those who rely on his unfailing love.
19 He rescues them from death
and keeps them alive in times of famine.

20 We depend on the LORD alone to save us.
Only he can help us, protecting us like a shield.
21 In him our hearts rejoice,
for we are trusting in his holy name.
22 Let your unfailing love surround us, LORD,
for our hope is in you alone.

### BELIEVING ● ● • • •

**33:4 A person's words are measured by the quality of his or her character. If your friends trust what you say, it is because they trust you. If you trust what God says, it is because you trust him to be the God he claims to be. If you doubt his words, you doubt the integrity of God himself. If you believe that God is truly God, then believe what he says!**

## PSALM 34

*A psalm of David, regarding the time he pretended to be insane in front of Abimelech, who sent him away.*

1 I will praise the LORD at all times.
I will constantly speak his praises.
2 I will boast only in the LORD;
let all who are discouraged take heart.
3 Come, let us tell of the LORD's greatness;
let us exalt his name together.

4 I prayed to the LORD, and he answered me,
freeing me from all my fears.
5 Those who look to him for help will be radiant with joy;
no shadow of shame will darken their faces.
6 I cried out to the LORD in my suffering, and he heard me.
He set me free from all my fears.

**ENOUGH ● ● ● • •**

**34:9-10 "Those who honor him will have all they need." This is not a blanket promise that all Christians will be rich. It is David's observation of God's goodness—all those who call upon God will be answered, sometimes in unexpected ways. Remember, our deepest needs are spiritual. Many Christians face unbearable poverty and hardship. David was saying that to have God is to have all that a person needs. God is enough. If you feel you don't have everything you need, ask yourself: (1) Is this really a need? (2) Is this really good for me? (3) Is this the best time for me to have what I desire? Even if you answer yes to all three questions, God may allow you to go without to help you grow more dependent on him. We may need to learn that we need *him* more than those things.**

7 For the angel of the LORD guards all who fear
him,
and he rescues them.

8 Taste and see that the LORD is good.
Oh, the joys of those who trust in him!
9 Let the LORD's people show him reverence,
for those who honor him will have all they
need.
10 Even strong young lions sometimes go hungry,
but those who trust in the LORD will never
lack any good thing.

11 Come, my children, and listen to me,
and I will teach you to fear the LORD.
12 Do any of you want to live
a life that is long and good?
13 Then watch your tongue!
Keep your lips from telling lies!
14 Turn away from evil and do good.
Work hard at living in peace with others.
15 The eyes of the LORD watch over those who
do right;
his ears are open to their cries for help.
16 But the LORD turns his face against those who
do evil;
he will erase their memory from the earth.

17 The LORD hears his people when they call to
him for help.
He rescues them from all their troubles.
18 The LORD is close to the brokenhearted;
he rescues those who are crushed in spirit.

19 The righteous face many troubles,
but the LORD rescues them from each and
every one.
20 For the LORD protects them from harm—
not one of their bones* will be broken!

21 Calamity will surely overtake the wicked,
and those who hate the righteous will be
punished.
22 But the LORD will redeem those who serve him.
Everyone who trusts in him will be freely
pardoned.

34:20 Hebrew *protects him from harm—not one of his bones.*

## PSALM 35 *A psalm of David.*

1 O LORD, oppose those who oppose me.
Declare war on those who are attacking me.
2 Put on your armor, and take up your shield.
Prepare for battle, and come to my aid.
3 Lift up your spear and javelin
and block the way of my enemies.
Let me hear you say,
"I am your salvation!"

4 Humiliate and disgrace those trying to kill me;
turn them back in confusion.
5 Blow them away like chaff in the wind—
a wind sent by the angel of the LORD.
6 Make their path dark and slippery,
with the angel of the LORD pursuing them.
7 Although I did them no wrong,
they laid a trap for me.
Although I did them no wrong,
they dug a pit for me.
8 So let sudden ruin overtake them!
Let them be caught in the snare they set for
me!
Let them fall to destruction in the pit they dug
for me.

9 Then I will rejoice in the LORD.
I will be glad because he rescues me.
10 I will praise him from the bottom of my heart:
"LORD, who can compare with you?
Who else rescues the weak and helpless from the
strong?
Who else protects the poor and needy from
those who want to rob them?"

11 Malicious witnesses testify against me.
They accuse me of things I don't even know
about.
12 They repay me with evil for the good I do.
I am sick with despair.
13 Yet when they were ill,
I grieved for them.
I even fasted and prayed for them,
but my prayers returned unanswered.
14 I was sad, as though they were my friends or
family,
as if I were grieving for my own mother.

15 But they are glad now that I am in trouble;
they gleefully join together against me.
I am attacked by people I don't even know;
they hurl slander at me continually.
16 They mock me with the worst kind of profanity,
and they snarl at me.

17 How long, O Lord, will you look on and do
nothing?
Rescue me from their fierce attacks.
Protect my life from these lions!
18 Then I will thank you in front of the entire
congregation.
I will praise you before all the people.

[19] Don't let my treacherous enemies
rejoice over my defeat.
Don't let those who hate me without cause
gloat over my sorrow.
[20] They don't talk of peace;
they plot against innocent people
who are minding their own business.
[21] They shout that they have seen me doing wrong.
"Aha," they say. "Aha!
With our own eyes we saw him do it!"
[22] O LORD, you know all about this.
Do not stay silent.
Don't abandon me now, O Lord.
[23] Wake up! Rise to my defense!
Take up my case, my God and my Lord.
[24] Declare me "not guilty," O LORD my God, for
you give justice.
Don't let my enemies laugh about me in my
troubles.
[25] Don't let them say, " Look! We have what we
wanted!
Now we will eat him alive!"
[26] May those who rejoice at my troubles
be humiliated and disgraced.
May those who triumph over me
be covered with shame and dishonor.
[27] But give great joy to those
who have stood with me in my defense.
Let them continually say, "Great is the LORD,
who enjoys helping his servant."
[28] Then I will tell everyone of your justice and
goodness,
and I will praise you all day long.

## PSALM 36 *For the choir director: A psalm of David, the servant of the LORD.*

[1] Sin whispers to the wicked,
deep within their
hearts.
They have no fear of God
to restrain them.
[2] In their blind conceit,
they cannot see how wicked
they really are.
[3] Everything they say is crooked
and deceitful.
They refuse to act wisely or
do what is good.
[4] They lie awake at night,
hatching sinful plots.
Their course of action is
never good.
They make no attempt to
turn from evil.
[5] Your unfailing love, O LORD,
is as vast as the heavens;
your faithfulness reaches
beyond the clouds.
[6] Your righteousness is like the mighty
mountains,
your justice like the ocean depths.
You care for people and animals alike, O LORD.
[7] How precious is your unfailing love, O God!
All humanity finds shelter
in the shadow of your wings.
[8] You feed them from the abundance of your own
house,
letting them drink from your rivers of
delight.
[9] For you are the fountain of life,
the light by which we see.
[10] Pour out your unfailing love on those who love
you;
give justice to those with honest hearts.
[11] Don't let the proud trample me;
don't let the wicked push me around.
[12] Look! They have fallen!
They have been thrown down, never to rise
again.

## PSALM 37 *A psalm of David.*

[1] Don't worry about the wicked.
Don't envy those who do wrong.
[2] For like grass, they soon fade away.
Like springtime flowers, they soon wither.

### TREASURE ● ● • • •

37:1 **We should never envy the popularity or wealth of the wicked. No matter how much they have, it will fade and vanish like grass that withers and dies. Those who follow God live in a different manner than the wicked. And in the end, the godly will have far greater treasures in heaven. What the unbeliever gets lasts a lifetime, if he is lucky. What you get from following God lasts an eternity.**

### "Here's what I did..."

There are two Scriptures that sustain me daily. Because I have a disease called Epstein–Barr, I am always fatigued and often in pain. Psalm 34 reminds me that I can rely on God constantly for every ounce of strength I need, and it reminds me that God does hear the cry of those who are trusting him. I rely on these verses constantly for the "now" of every day.

Jeremiah 29:11 is my source of hope for the future. It reminds me that my constant worry about college and about ever getting over my illness is totally unnecessary; everything that happens is part of God's plan for my life. His plan is for good, not disaster, and he intends to give me a future and a hope. He truly will take care of everything as I trust him.

I have memorized these passages, and I remind myself of the words whenever I need to—which is almost every day! They are a great source of comfort to me.

*Anita*

AGE 17

[3] Trust in the LORD and do good.
Then you will live safely in the land and prosper.
[4] Take delight in the LORD,
and he will give you your heart's desires.

[5] Commit everything you do to the LORD.
Trust him, and he will help you.
[6] He will make your innocence as clear as the dawn,
and the justice of your cause will shine like the noonday sun.

[7] Be still in the presence of the LORD,
and wait patiently for him to act.
Don't worry about evil people who prosper
or fret about their wicked schemes.

[8] Stop your anger!
Turn from your rage!
Do not envy others—
it only leads to harm.
[9] For the wicked will be destroyed,
but those who trust in the LORD will possess the land.

[10] In a little while, the wicked will disappear.
Though you look for them, they will be gone.
[11] Those who are gentle and lowly will possess the land;
they will live in prosperous security.

[12] The wicked plot against the godly;
they snarl at them in defiance.
[13] But the Lord just laughs,
for he sees their day of judgment coming.

[14] The wicked draw their swords
and string their bows
to kill the poor and the oppressed,
to slaughter those who do right.
[15] But they will be stabbed through the heart with their own swords,
and their bows will be broken.

[16] It is better to be godly and have little
than to be evil and possess much.
[17] For the strength of the wicked will be shattered,
but the LORD takes care of the godly.
[18] Day by day the LORD takes care of the innocent,
and they will receive a reward that lasts forever.
[19] They will survive through hard times;
even in famine they will have more than enough.
[20] But the wicked will perish.
The LORD's enemies are like flowers in a field—
they will disappear like smoke.

[21] The wicked borrow and never repay,
but the godly are generous givers.
[22] Those blessed by the LORD will inherit the land,
but those cursed by him will die.

[23] The steps of the godly are directed by the LORD.
He delights in every detail of their lives.
[24] Though they stumble, they will not fall,
for the LORD holds them by the hand.

[25] Once I was young, and now I am old.
Yet I have never seen the godly forsaken,
nor seen their children begging for bread.
[26] The godly always give generous loans to others,
and their children are a blessing.

[27] Turn from evil and do good,
and you will live in the land forever.
[28] For the LORD loves justice,
and he will never abandon the godly.

He will keep them safe forever,
but the children of the wicked will perish.
[29] The godly will inherit the land
and will live there forever.

[30] The godly offer good counsel;
they know what is right from wrong.
[31] They fill their hearts with God's law,
so they will never slip from his path.

[32] Those who are evil spy on the godly,
waiting for an excuse to kill them.
[33] But the LORD will not let the wicked succeed
or let the godly be condemned when they are brought before the judge.

[34] Don't be impatient for the LORD to act!
Travel steadily along his path.
He will honor you, giving you the land.
You will see the wicked destroyed.

[35] I myself have seen it happen—
proud and evil people thriving like mighty trees.
[36] But when I looked again, they were gone!
Though I searched for them, I could not find them!

[37] Look at those who are honest and good,
for a wonderful future lies before those who love peace.
[38] But the wicked will be destroyed;
they have no future.

[39] The LORD saves the godly;
he is their fortress in times of trouble.
[40] The LORD helps them,
rescuing them from the wicked.
He saves them,
and they find shelter in him.

## PSALM **38** *A psalm of David, to bring us to the LORD's remembrance.*

[1] O LORD, don't rebuke me in your anger!
Don't discipline me in your rage!
[2] Your arrows have struck deep,
and your blows are crushing me.

[3] Because of your anger, my whole body is sick;
my health is broken because of my sins.

[4] My guilt overwhelms me—
it is a burden too heavy to bear.
[5] My wounds fester and stink
because of my foolish sins.
[6] I am bent over and racked with pain.
My days are filled with grief.
[7] A raging fever burns within me,
and my health is broken.
[8] I am exhausted and completely crushed.
My groans come from an anguished heart.

[9] You know what I long for, Lord;
you hear my every sigh.
[10] My heart beats wildly, my strength fails,
and I am going blind.
[11] My loved ones and friends stay away, fearing my disease.
Even my own family stands at a distance.
[12] Meanwhile, my enemies lay traps for me;
they make plans to ruin me.
They think up treacherous deeds all day long.
[13] But I am deaf to all their threats.
I am silent before them as one who cannot speak.
[14] I choose to hear nothing,
and I make no reply.

[15] For I am waiting for you, O LORD.
You must answer for me, O Lord my God.
[16] I prayed, "Don't let my enemies gloat over me
or rejoice at my downfall."
[17] I am on the verge of collapse,
facing constant pain.
[18] But I confess my sins;
I am deeply sorry for what I have done.
[19] My enemies are many;
they hate me though I have done nothing against them.
[20] They repay me evil for good
and oppose me because I stand for the right.

[21] Do not abandon me, LORD.
Do not stand at a distance, my God.
[22] Come quickly to help me, O Lord my savior.

## PSALM 39 *For Jeduthun, the choir director: A psalm of David.*

[1] I said to myself, "I will watch what I do
and not sin in what I say.
I will curb my tongue
when the ungodly are around me."
[2] But as I stood there in silence—
not even speaking of good things—
the turmoil within me grew to the bursting point.
[3] My thoughts grew hot within me
and began to burn,
igniting a fire of words:
[4] "LORD, remind me how brief my time on earth will be.
Remind me that my days are numbered,
and that my life is fleeing away.

**LIFE ● ● • • •**

39:4 **Life is short no matter how long we live. If there is something important we want to do, we must not put it off for a better day. Ask yourself, "If I had only six months to live, what would I do?" Tell someone that you love him or her? Deal with an undisciplined area in your life? Tell someone about Jesus? Life is short—don't neglect what is truly important.**

[5] My life is no longer than the width of my hand.
An entire lifetime is just a moment to you;
human existence is but a breath." *Interlude*
[6] We are merely moving shadows,
and all our busy rushing ends in nothing.
We heap up wealth for someone else to spend.
[7] And so, Lord, where do I put my hope?
My only hope is in you.
[8] Rescue me from my rebellion,
for even fools mock me when I rebel.
[9] I am silent before you; I won't say a word.
For my punishment is from you.
[10] Please, don't punish me anymore!
I am exhausted by the blows from your hand.
[11] When you discipline people for their sins,
their lives can be crushed like the life of a moth.
Human existence is as frail as breath. *Interlude*

[12] Hear my prayer, O LORD!
Listen to my cries for help!
Don't ignore my tears.
For I am your guest—
a traveler passing through,
as my ancestors were before me.
[13] Spare me so I can smile again
before I am gone and exist no more.

## PSALM 40 *For the choir director: A psalm of David.*

[1] I waited patiently for the LORD to help me,
and he turned to me and heard my cry.
[2] He lifted me out of the pit of despair,
out of the mud and the mire.
He set my feet on solid ground
and steadied me as I walked along.
[3] He has given me a new song to sing,
a hymn of praise to our God.
Many will see what he has done and be astounded.
They will put their trust in the LORD.

[4] Oh, the joys of those who trust the LORD,
who have no confidence in the proud,
or in those who worship idols.
[5] O LORD my God, you have done many miracles for us.
Your plans for us are too numerous to list.
If I tried to recite all your wonderful deeds,
I would never come to the end of them.

[6] You take no delight in sacrifices or offerings.
Now that you have made me listen, I finally understand—
you don't require burnt offerings or sin offerings.
[7] Then I said, "Look, I have come.
And this has been written about me in your scroll:
[8] I take joy in doing your will, my God,
for your law is written on my heart."
[9] I have told all your people about your justice.
I have not been afraid to speak out,
as you, O LORD, well know.
[10] I have not kept this good news hidden in my heart;
I have talked about your faithfulness and saving power.
I have told everyone in the great assembly
of your unfailing love and faithfulness.

[11] LORD, don't hold back your tender mercies from me.
My only hope is in your unfailing love and faithfulness.
[12] For troubles surround me—
too many to count!
They pile up so high
I can't see my way out.
They are more numerous than the hairs on my head.
I have lost all my courage.

[13] Please, LORD, rescue me!
Come quickly, LORD, and help me.
[14] May those who try to destroy me
be humiliated and put to shame.
May those who take delight in my trouble
be turned back in disgrace.
[15] Let them be horrified by their shame,
for they said, "Aha! We've got him now!"

[16] But may all who search for you
be filled with joy and gladness.
May those who love your salvation
repeatedly shout, "The LORD is great!"

[17] As for me, I am poor and needy,
but the Lord is thinking about me right now.
You are my helper and my savior.
Do not delay, O my God.

## PSALM 41 *For the choir director: A psalm of David.*

[1] Oh, the joys of those who are kind to the poor.
The LORD rescues them in times of trouble.
[2] The LORD protects them
and keeps them alive.
He gives them prosperity
and rescues them from their enemies.
[3] The LORD nurses them when they are sick
and eases their pain and discomfort.
[4] "O LORD," I prayed, "have mercy on me.
Heal me, for I have sinned against you."
[5] But my enemies say nothing but evil about me.
"How soon will he die and be forgotten?"
they ask.
[6] They visit me as if they are my friends,
but all the while they gather gossip,
and when they leave, they spread it everywhere.
[7] All who hate me whisper about me,
imagining the worst for me.
[8] "Whatever he has, it is fatal," they say.
"He will never get out of that bed!"
[9] Even my best friend, the one I trusted completely,
the one who shared my food,
has turned against me.

[10] LORD, have mercy on me.
Make me well again, so I can pay them back!
[11] I know that you are pleased with me,
for you have not let my enemy triumph over me.
[12] You have preserved my life because I am innocent;
you have brought me into your presence forever.

[13] Bless the LORD, the God of Israel,
who lives forever from eternal ages past.
Amen and amen!

**BOOK TWO (Psalms 42–72)**

## PSALM 42 *For the choir director: A psalm of the descendants of Korah.*

[1] As the deer pants for streams of water,
so I long for you, O God.
[2] I thirst for God, the living God.
When can I come and stand before him?
[3] Day and night, I have only tears for food,
while my enemies continually taunt me, saying,
"Where is this God of yours?"

[4] My heart is breaking
as I remember how it used to be:
I walked among the crowds of worshipers,
leading a great procession to the house of God,
singing for joy and giving thanks—
it was the sound of a great celebration!

[5] Why am I discouraged?
Why so sad?

### DEPRESSION ● ● • • •

**42:1-6 Depression is one of the most common emotional ailments. One cure for depression is to meditate on the record of God's goodness to his people. This will take your mind off the present situation and give hope that it will improve. It will focus your thoughts on God's ability to help you rather than on your inability to help yourself. When you feel depressed, take advantage of this psalm's antidepressant. Read the Bible's accounts of God's goodness and meditate on them.**

I will put my hope in God!
I will praise him again—
my Savior and [6]my God!
Now I am deeply discouraged,
but I will remember your kindness—
from Mount Hermon, the source of the Jordan,
from the land of Mount Mizar.
7 I hear the tumult of the raging seas
as your waves and surging tides sweep over me.
8 Through each day the LORD pours his unfailing love upon me,
and through each night I sing his songs,
praying to God who gives me life.
9 "O God my rock," I cry,
"Why have you forsaken me?
Why must I wander in darkness,
oppressed by my enemies?"
10 Their taunts pierce me like a fatal wound.
They scoff, "Where is this God of yours?"
11 Why am I discouraged?
Why so sad?
I will put my hope in God!
I will praise him again—
my Savior and my God!

## PSALM 43

1 O God, take up my cause!
Defend me against these ungodly people.
Rescue me from these unjust liars.
2 For you are God, my only safe haven.
Why have you tossed me aside?
Why must I wander around in darkness,
oppressed by my enemies?
3 Send out your light and your truth;
let them guide me.
Let them lead me to your holy mountain,
to the place where you live.
4 There I will go to the altar of God,
to God—the source of all my joy.
I will praise you with my harp,
O God, my God!
5 Why am I discouraged?
Why so sad?
I will put my hope in God!
I will praise him again—
my Savior and my God!

## PSALM 44

*For the choir director: A psalm of the descendants of Korah.*

1 O God, we have heard it with our own ears—
our ancestors have told us
of all you did in other days,
in days long ago:
2 You drove out the pagan nations
and gave all the land to our ancestors;
you crushed their enemies,
setting our ancestors free.
3 They did not conquer the land with their swords;
it was not their own strength that gave them victory.
It was by your mighty power that they succeeded;
it was because you favored them and smiled on them.
4 You are my King and my God.
You command victories for your people.*
5 Only by your power can we push back our enemies;
only in your name can we trample our foes.
6 I do not trust my bow;
I do not count on my sword to save me.
7 It is you who gives us victory over our enemies;
it is you who humbles those who hate us.
8 O God, we give glory to you all day long
and constantly praise your name. *Interlude*
9 But now you have tossed us aside in dishonor.
You no longer lead our armies to battle.
10 You make us retreat from our enemies
and allow them to plunder our land.
11 You have treated us like sheep waiting to be slaughtered;
you have scattered us among the nations.
12 You sold us—your precious people—for a pittance.
You valued us at nothing at all.
13 You have caused all our neighbors to mock us.
We are an object of scorn and derision to the nations around us.
14 You have made us the butt of their jokes;
we are scorned by the whole world.

### DELIVERED ● ● ● ●

44:22-26 **The writer cried to God to save his people by his constant love—they "are being slaughtered like sheep." Nothing can separate us from God's love, not even death (Romans 8:36-39). When you fear for your life, ask God for deliverance and remember that even physical death cannot separate you from him.**

15 We can't escape the constant humiliation;
shame is written across our faces.
16 All we hear are the taunts of our mockers.
All we see are our vengeful enemies.
17 All this has happened despite our loyalty to you.
We have not violated your covenant.
18 Our hearts have not deserted you.
We have not strayed from your path.
19 Yet you have crushed us in the desert.
You have covered us with darkness and death.
20 If we had turned away from worshiping our God
or spread our hands in prayer to foreign gods,
21 God would surely have known it,
for he knows the secrets of every heart.
22 For your sake we are killed every day;
we are being slaughtered like sheep.

44:4 Hebrew *for Jacob.*

[23] Wake up, O Lord! Why do you sleep?
Get up! Do not reject us forever.
[24] Why do you look the other way?
Why do you ignore our suffering and oppression?
[25] We collapse in the dust,
lying face down in the dirt.
[26] Rise up! Come and help us!
Save us because of your unfailing love.

## PSALM 45 *For the choir director: A psalm of the descendants of Korah, to be sung to the tune "Lilies." A love song.*

[1] My heart overflows with a beautiful thought!
I will recite a lovely poem to the king,
for my tongue is like the pen of a skillful poet.

[2] You are the most handsome of all.
Gracious words stream from your lips.
God himself has blessed you forever.
[3] Put on your sword, O mighty warrior!
You are so glorious, so majestic!
[4] In your majesty, ride out to victory,
defending truth, humility, and justice.
Go forth to perform awe-inspiring deeds!
[5] Your arrows are sharp,
piercing your enemies' hearts.
The nations fall before you,
lying down beneath your feet.

### CONFIDENCE ● ● • • •

**46:1-3 The fear of mountains or cities suddenly crumbling into the sea by a nuclear blast haunts many people today. But the psalmist says that even if the world ends, "We will not fear." Even in the face of utter destruction, he expressed a quiet confidence in God's ability to save him. It seems impossible to face the end of the world without fear, but the Bible is clear: God is our eternal refuge, even in the face of total destruction.**

[6] Your throne, O God,* endures forever and ever.
Your royal power is expressed in justice.
[7] You love what is right and hate what is wrong.
Therefore God, your God, has anointed you,
pouring out the oil of joy on you more than on anyone else.
[8] Your robes are perfumed with myrrh, aloes, and cassia.
In palaces decorated with ivory,
you are entertained by the music of harps.
[9] Kings' daughters are among your concubines.
At your right side stands the queen,
wearing jewelry of finest gold from Ophir!

[10] Listen to me, O royal daughter; take to heart what I say.
Forget your people and your homeland far away.
[11] For your royal husband delights in your beauty;
honor him, for he is your lord.
[12] The princes of Tyre* will shower you with gifts.

### THE MAP ● ● • • •

**48:14 We often pray for God's guidance as we struggle with decisions. What we need is both guidance and a guide—a map that gives us landmarks and directions and a constant companion who has an intimate knowledge of the way and will make sure we interpret the map correctly. The Bible is just such a map, and God is our constant companion and guide. Lean upon both the map and the Guide.**

People of great wealth will entreat your favor.

[13] The bride, a princess, waits within her chamber,
dressed in a gown woven with gold.
[14] In her beautiful robes, she is led to the king,
accompanied by her bridesmaids.
[15] What a joyful, enthusiastic procession
as they enter the king's palace!

[16] Your sons will become kings like their father.
You will make them rulers over many lands.

[17] I will bring honor to your name in every generation.
Therefore, the nations will praise you forever and ever.

## PSALM 46 *For the choir director: A psalm of the descendants of Korah, to be sung by soprano voices.* A song.*

[1] God is our refuge and strength,
always ready to help in times of trouble.
[2] So we will not fear, even if earthquakes come
and the mountains crumble into the sea.
[3] Let the oceans roar and foam.
Let the mountains tremble as the waters surge! *Interlude*

[4] A river brings joy to the city of our God,
the sacred home of the Most High.
[5] God himself lives in that city; it cannot be destroyed.
God will protect it at the break of day.
[6] The nations are in an uproar,
and kingdoms crumble!
God thunders,
and the earth melts!

[7] The LORD Almighty is here among us;
the God of Israel* is our fortress. *Interlude*

[8] Come, see the glorious works of the LORD:
See how he brings destruction upon the world
[9] and causes wars to end throughout the earth.
He breaks the bow and snaps the spear in two;
he burns the shields with fire.

[10] "Be silent, and know that I am God!
I will be honored by every nation.
I will be honored throughout the world."

[11] The LORD Almighty is here among us;
the God of Israel is our fortress. *Interlude*

45:6 Or *Your divine throne.* 45:12 Hebrew *The daughter of Tyre.* 46:TITLE Hebrew *according to alamoth.* 46:7 Hebrew *of Jacob;* also in 46:11.

**PSALM 47** *For the choir director: A psalm of the descendants of Korah.*

1 Come, everyone, and clap your hands for joy!
Shout to God with joyful praise!
2 For the LORD Most High is awesome.
He is the great King of all the earth.
3 He subdues the nations before us,
putting our enemies beneath our feet.
4 He chose the Promised Land as our inheritance,
the proud possession of Jacob's descendants,
whom he loves. *Interlude*

5 God has ascended with a mighty shout.
The LORD has ascended with trumpets blaring.
6 Sing praise to God, sing praises;
sing praise to our King, sing praises!

7 For God is the King over all the earth.
Praise him with a psalm!
8 God reigns above the nations,
sitting on his holy throne.
9 The rulers of the world have gathered together.
They join us in praising the God of Abraham.
For all the kings of the earth belong to God.
He is highly honored everywhere.

**PSALM 48** *A psalm of the descendants of Korah. A song.*

1 How great is the LORD,
and how much we should praise him
in the city of our God,
which is on his holy mountain!
2 It is magnificent in elevation—
the whole earth rejoices to see it!
Mount Zion, the holy mountain,*
is the city of the great King!
3 God himself is in Jerusalem's towers.
He reveals himself as her defender.

4 The kings of the earth joined forces
and advanced against the city.
5 But when they saw it, they were stunned;
they were terrified and ran away.
6 They were gripped with terror,
like a woman writhing in the pain of childbirth
7 or like the mighty ships of Tarshish
being shattered by a powerful east wind.

8 We had heard of the city's glory,
but now we have seen it ourselves—
the city of the LORD Almighty.
It is the city of our God;
he will make it safe forever. *Interlude*
9 O God, we meditate on your unfailing love
as we worship in your Temple.
10 As your name deserves, O God,
you will be praised to the ends of the earth.
Your strong right hand is filled with victory.
11 Let the people on Mount Zion rejoice.
Let the towns of Judah be glad,
for your judgments are just.
12 Go, inspect the city of Jerusalem.*
Walk around and count the many towers.
13 Take note of the fortified walls,
and tour all the citadels,
that you may describe them
to future generations.
14 For that is what God is like.
He is our God forever and ever,
and he will be our guide until we die.

**PSALM 49** *For the choir director: A psalm of the descendants of Korah.*

1 Listen to this, all you people!
Pay attention, everyone in the world!
2 High and low,
rich and poor—listen!

## "Here's what I did..."

Everything was going wrong in my life. My parents were getting a divorce. My boyfriend broke up with me. I couldn't concentrate in school, so my grades started going down.

It began to affect my faith. I couldn't understand why God was letting all this happen to me. When I prayed, I felt like I was talking to myself. I guess I was mad at God, blaming him in my heart for the things that were happening.

I tried to read the Bible anyway, even though I was struggling spiritually. One day I read Psalm 46. Verse 10 really made me stop and think. This verse seemed to say, "Stop looking at your problems and look at me. Look at who I am." I realized God was in charge—he knew exactly what he was doing and had a purpose in mind for what I was going through. I just needed to accept it and believe he is a loving God who would never do a thing to hurt me.

That changed my perspective. Instead of blaming God, I asked him to help me through my struggles. And he has. Things are still rough sometimes, but now I know that God is for me, and he will work things out for good. As Romans 8:31 says, "If God is for us, who can ever be against us?"

*Jodi*
AGE 17

**48:2** Or *Mount Zion, in the far north;* Hebrew reads *Mount Zion, the heights of Zaphon.* **48:12** Hebrew *Zion.*

## VICTIMS ● ● • • •

**51:4 Although David sinned with Bathsheba, he said he had sinned against God. When someone steals, murders, or slanders, it is against someone else—a victim. According to the world's standards, sex between two "consenting adults" is acceptable because nobody "gets hurt." But people *do* get hurt—in David's case, a man was murdered and a baby died. All sin hurts us and others, and ultimately it offends God because sin in any form is a rebellion against his way of living. When tempted to do wrong, remember that you will be sinning against God. That may help you stay on the right track.**

[3] For my words are wise,
and my thoughts are filled with insight.
[4] I listen carefully to many proverbs
and solve riddles with inspiration from a harp.

[5] There is no need to fear when times of trouble come,
when enemies are surrounding me.
[6] They trust in their wealth
and boast of great riches.
[7] Yet they cannot redeem themselves from death*
by paying a ransom to God.
[8] Redemption does not come so easily,
for no one can ever pay enough
[9] to live forever
and never see the grave.

[10] Those who are wise must finally die,
just like the foolish and senseless,
leaving all their wealth behind.
[11] The grave is their eternal home,
where they will stay forever.
They may name their estates after themselves,
but they leave their wealth to others.
[12] They will not last long despite their riches—
they will die like the animals.
[13] This is the fate of fools,
though they will be remembered as being so wise. *Interlude*

[14] Like sheep, they are led to the grave,
where death will be their shepherd.
In the morning the godly will rule over them.
Their bodies will rot in the grave,
far from their grand estates.
[15] But as for me, God will redeem my life.
He will snatch me from the power of death. *Interlude*

[16] So don't be dismayed when the wicked grow rich,
and their homes become ever more splendid.
[17] For when they die, they carry nothing with them.
Their wealth will not follow them into the grave.
[18] In this life they consider themselves fortunate,
and the world loudly applauds their success.
[19] But they will die like all others before them
and never again see the light of day.
[20] People who boast of their wealth don't understand
that they will die like the animals.

49:7 *Or no one can redeem the life of another.*

## PSALM 50 *A psalm of Asaph.*

[1] The mighty God, the LORD, has spoken;
he has summoned all humanity from east to west!
[2] From Mount Zion, the perfection of beauty,
God shines in glorious radiance.
[3] Our God approaches with the noise of thunder.
Fire devours everything in his way,
and a great storm rages around him.
[4] Heaven and earth will be his witnesses
as he judges his people:
[5] "Bring my faithful people to me—
those who made a covenant with me by giving sacrifices."
[6] Then let the heavens proclaim his justice,
for God himself will be the judge. *Interlude*

[7] "O my people, listen as I speak.
Here are my charges against you, O Israel:
I am God, your God!
[8] I have no complaint about your sacrifices
or the burnt offerings you constantly bring to my altar.
[9] But I want no more bulls from your barns;
I want no more goats from your pens.
[10] For all the animals of the forest are mine,
and I own the cattle on a thousand hills.
[11] Every bird of the mountains
and all the animals of the field belong to me.
[12] If I were hungry, I would not mention it to you,
for all the world is mine and everything in it.
[13] I don't need the bulls you sacrifice;
I don't need the blood of goats.
[14] What I want instead is your true thanks to God;
I want you to fulfill your vows to the Most High.
[15] Trust me in your times of trouble,
and I will rescue you,
and you will give me glory."

[16] But God says to the wicked:
"Recite my laws no longer,
and don't pretend that you obey me.
[17] For you refuse my discipline
and treat my laws like trash.
[18] When you see a thief, you help him,
and you spend your time with adulterers.
[19] Your mouths are filled with wickedness,
and your tongues are full of lies.
[20] You sit around and slander a brother—
your own mother's son.
[21] While you did all this, I remained silent,
and you thought I didn't care.
But now I will rebuke you,
listing all my charges against you.
[22] Repent, all of you who ignore me,
or I will tear you apart,
and no one will help you.
[23] But giving thanks is a sacrifice that truly honors me.

If you keep to my path,
I will reveal to you the salvation of God."

## PSALM 51

*For the choir director: A psalm of David, regarding the time Nathan the prophet came to him after David had committed adultery with Bathsheba.*

1 Have mercy on me, O God,
because of your unfailing love.
Because of your great compassion,
blot out the stain of my sins.
2 Wash me clean from my guilt.
Purify me from my sin.

3 For I recognize my shameful deeds—
they haunt me day and night.
4 Against you, and you alone, have I sinned;
I have done what is evil in your sight.
You will be proved right in what you say,
and your judgment against me is just.

5 For I was born a sinner—
yes, from the moment my mother conceived me.
6 But you desire honesty from the heart,
so you can teach me to be wise in my inmost being.
7 Purify me from my sins,* and I will be clean;
wash me, and I will be whiter than snow.
8 Oh, give me back my joy again;
you have broken me—
now let me rejoice.
9 Don't keep looking at my sins.
Remove the stain of my guilt.
10 Create in me a clean heart, O God.
Renew a right spirit within me.
11 Do not banish me from your presence,
and don't take your Holy Spirit from me.
12 Restore to me again the joy of your salvation,
and make me willing to obey you.
13 Then I will teach your ways to sinners,
and they will return to you.
14 Forgive me for shedding blood, O God who saves;
then I will joyfully sing of your forgiveness.
15 Unseal my lips, O Lord,
that I may praise you.

16 You would not be pleased with sacrifices,
or I would bring them.
If I brought you a burnt offering,
you would not accept it.
17 The sacrifice you want is a broken spirit.
A broken and repentant heart, O God,
you will not despise.

18 Look with favor on Zion and help her;
rebuild the walls of Jerusalem.
19 Then you will be pleased with worthy sacrifices
and with our whole burnt offerings;
and bulls will again be sacrificed on your altar.

51:7 Hebrew *Purify me with the hyssop branch.*

## PSALM 52

*For the choir director: A psalm of David, regarding the time Doeg the Edomite told Saul that Ahimelech had given refuge to David.*

1 You call yourself a hero, do you?
Why boast about this crime of yours,
you who have disgraced God's people?
2 All day long you plot destruction.
Your tongue cuts like a sharp razor;
you're an expert at telling lies.
3 You love evil more than good
and lies more than truth. *Interlude*

4 You love to say things that harm others,
you liar!
5 But God will strike you down once and for all.
He will pull you from your home
and drag you from the land of the living. *Interlude*

---

**I heard something about a sin that God cannot forgive. What is it?**

What you are referring to is sinning against the Holy Spirit. "Every sin or blasphemy can be forgiven—except blasphemy against the Holy Spirit, which can never be forgiven. . . . Blasphemy against the Holy Spirit will never be forgiven, either in this world or in the world to come" (Matthew 12:31-32).

As you read in Psalm 51, everyone is born a sinner (verse 5). Left to ourselves we certainly would die, because our sinful nature separates us from God and from life (Romans 3:23; 6:23).

The good news is God did not leave us on our own. He sent Jesus to pay the penalty for us and to die in our place. This way he killed sin forever. All who receive Christ into their life and accept his gift of forgiveness are forgiven—period (John 1:12).

The only sin that cannot be forgiven is when someone refuses to receive Christ, ignoring or rejecting the Holy Spirit's work in his or her life.

The incident that caused King David to pray the prayer in Psalm 51 is found in 2 Samuel 12:1-23. David not only committed adultery, but he had the woman's husband murdered so he could marry her! That's pretty bad behavior for anyone, let alone a king.

When confronted with his sin a year after those events, David repented. He asked God to forgive him and to renew their relationship once again.

Though David's sins were great, God forgave him. God is always willing to forgive those who admit their mistakes and who genuinely try not to repeat them.

It has been said that the only sin God cannot forgive is the one we have not confessed.

By daily coming to God in humility, trust, and dependence, we show him that we mean business in keeping our relationship with him clean and growing.

David's prayer is the perfect example of a humble heart seeking after the only thing in life that really matters: a close relationship with God.

## FOOLS ● ● • • •

**53:1 Echoing the message of Psalm 14, David proclaimed that "only fools say in their hearts, 'There is no God.'" People may say there is no God in order to cover their sin, to have an excuse to continue in sin, and/or to ignore the Judge so they can avoid the judgment. A "fool" is not necessarily lacking intelligence; many atheists and unbelievers are highly learned. Fools are people who reject God, the only one who can save them.**

[6]The righteous will see it and be amazed.
They will laugh and say,
[7]"Look what happens to mighty warriors
who do not trust in God.
They trust their wealth instead
and grow more and more bold in their
wickedness."
[8]But I am like an olive tree,
thriving in the house of God.
I trust in God's unfailing love
forever and ever.
[9]I will praise you forever, O God,
for what you have done.
I will wait for your mercies
in the presence of your people.

## PSALM 53 *For the choir director: A meditation of David.*

[1]Only fools say in their hearts,
"There is no God."
They are corrupt, and their actions are evil;
no one does good!
[2]God looks down from heaven
on the entire human race;
he looks to see if there is even one with real
understanding,
one who seeks for God.
[3]But no, all have turned away from God;
all have become corrupt.
No one does good,
not even one!
[4]Will those who do evil never learn?
They eat up my people like bread;
they wouldn't think of praying to God.
[5]But then terror will grip them,
terror like they have never known before.
God will scatter the bones of your enemies.
You will put them to shame, for God has
rejected them.
[6]Oh, that salvation would come from Mount
Zion to rescue Israel!
For when God restores his people,
Jacob will shout with joy, and Israel will rejoice.

## PSALM 54 *For the choir director: A meditation of David, regarding the time the Ziphites came and said to Saul, "We know where David is hiding." To be accompanied by stringed instruments.*

[1]Come with great power, O God, and rescue me!
Defend me with your might.
[2]O God, listen to my prayer.
Pay attention to my plea.
[3]For strangers are attacking me;
violent men are trying to kill me.
They care nothing for God. *Interlude*
[4]But God is my helper.
The Lord is the one who keeps me alive!
[5]May my enemies' plans for evil be turned against
them.
Do as you promised and put an end to them.
[6]I will sacrifice a voluntary offering to you;
I will praise your name, O LORD,
for it is good.
[7]For you will rescue me from my troubles
and help me to triumph over my enemies.

## PSALM 55 *For the choir director: A psalm of David, to be accompanied by stringed instruments.*

[1]Listen to my prayer, O God.
Do not ignore my cry for help!
[2]Please listen and answer me,
for I am overwhelmed by my troubles.
[3]My enemies shout at me,
making loud and wicked threats.
They bring trouble on me,
hunting me down in their anger.
[4]My heart is in anguish.
The terror of death overpowers me.
[5]Fear and trembling overwhelm me.
I can't stop shaking.
[6]Oh, how I wish I had wings like a dove;
then I would fly away and rest!
[7]I would fly far away
to the quiet of the wilderness. *Interlude*
[8]How quickly I would escape—
far away from this wild storm of hatred.
[9]Destroy them, Lord, and confuse their speech,
for I see violence and strife in the city.
[10]Its walls are patrolled day and night against
invaders,
but the real danger is wickedness within the
city.
[11]Murder and robbery are everywhere there;
threats and cheating are rampant in the streets.
[12]It is not an enemy who taunts me—
I could bear that.
It is not my foes who so arrogantly insult me—
I could have hidden from them.
[13]Instead, it is you—my equal,
my companion and close friend.

## REAL FRIENDS ● ● • • •

**55:12-14 Nothing hurts as much as a wound from a "friend." Real friends, however, stick by you in times of trouble and bring healing, love, acceptance, and understanding. There will be times when friends lovingly confront us, but their motive will be to help. What kind of friend are you? Faithful or fickle? Don't betray those you love.**

[14]What good fellowship we enjoyed
as we walked together to the house of God.

[15]Let death seize my enemies by surprise;
let the grave* swallow them alive,
for evil makes its home within them.

[16]But I will call on God,
and the LORD will rescue me.
[17]Morning, noon, and night
I plead aloud in my distress,
and the LORD hears my voice.
[18]He rescues me and keeps me safe
from the battle waged against me,
even though many still oppose me.
[19]God, who is king forever,
will hear me and will humble them. *Interlude*
For my enemies refuse to change their ways;
they do not fear God.

[20]As for this friend of mine, he betrayed me;
he broke his promises.
[21]His words are as smooth as cream,
but in his heart is war.
His words are as soothing as lotion,
but underneath are daggers!
[22]Give your burdens to the LORD,
and he will take care of you.
He will not permit the
godly to slip and fall.

[23]But you, O God, will send the
wicked
down to the pit of
destruction.
Murderers and liars will die
young,
but I am trusting you to
save me.

## PSALM 56

*For the choir director: A psalm of David, regarding the time the Philistines seized him in Gath. To be sung to the tune "Dove on Distant Oaks."*

[1]O God, have mercy on me.
The enemy troops press in
on me.
My foes attack me all day
long.
[2]My slanderers hound me
constantly,
and many are boldly
attacking me.
[3]But when I am afraid,
I put my trust in you.
[4]O God, I praise your word.
I trust in God, so why
should I be afraid?
What can mere mortals
do to me?

### CHANGELESS ● ● • • •

59:10 **David was hunted by those whose love had turned to jealousy, which was driving them to want to murder him. Trusted friends had turned against him. What changeable love these people had! But David knew that God's love for him was *changeless*. God's love for everyone who trusts him is changeless. When the love of others fails or disappoints us, we can rest in God's changeless love.**

[5]They are always twisting what I say;
they spend their days plotting ways to harm me.
[6]They come together to spy on me—
watching my every step, eager to kill me.
[7]Don't let them get away with their wickedness;
in your anger, O God, throw them to the
ground.

[8]You keep track of all my sorrows.
You have collected all my tears in your bottle.
You have recorded each one in your book.

[9]On the very day I call to you for help,
my enemies will retreat.
This I know: God is on my side.*
[10]O God, I praise your word.
Yes, LORD, I praise your word.
[11]I trust in God, so why should I be afraid?
What can mere mortals do to me?

### "Here's what I did..."

I'll never forget the day my father collapsed and was rushed to the hospital. The doctor told my mother and me that he'd suffered a severe heart attack and was now teetering between life and death; it could go either way. Standing with my mother by his bed, I prayed harder than I'd ever prayed before. I thought about how my father always reached out to others for Jesus, and I couldn't believe that God would be done with him yet. It almost seemed that God was reassuring me of this, but I asked him for a promise from his Word. I didn't want to go just on feelings. The verse he brought to mind is Psalm 57:1: "Have mercy on me, O God, have mercy! I look to you for protection. I will hide beneath the shadow of your wings until this violent storm is past."

I felt God was saying through this verse that if I took refuge in him and trusted him completely to be in control of the doctors and everything involved in my father's care, he would answer my prayer and make my father well. I was not to worry and not to try to make anything happen; hands off. I was to leave everything absolutely in God's hands and trust him for the outcome.

That's what I did. And I discovered that God is so faithful: my father did recover. God has continued to use Dad in marvelous ways to bring others to trust in Christ. And I learned something invaluable about trusting God and leaving everything in his hands when I'm facing life's storms.

David
AGE 17

55:15 Hebrew *let Sheol.* 56:9 Or *By this I will know that God is on my side.*

[12] I will fulfill my vows to you, O God,
and offer a sacrifice of thanks for your help.
[13] For you have rescued me from death;
you have kept my feet from slipping.
So now I can walk in your presence, O God,
in your life-giving light.

## PSALM 57

*For the choir director: A psalm of David, regarding the time he fled from Saul and went into the cave. To be sung to the tune "Do Not Destroy!"*

[1] Have mercy on me, O God, have mercy!
I look to you for protection.
I will hide beneath the shadow of your wings
until this violent storm is past.
[2] I cry out to God Most High,
to God who will fulfill his purpose for me.
[3] He will send help from heaven to save me,
rescuing me from those who are out to get me.
*Interlude*
My God will send forth his unfailing love and faithfulness.

[4] I am surrounded by fierce lions
who greedily devour human prey—
whose teeth pierce like spears and arrows,
and whose tongues cut like swords.
[5] Be exalted, O God, above the highest heavens!
May your glory shine over all the earth.

[6] My enemies have set a trap for me.
I am weary from distress.
They have dug a deep pit in my path,
but they themselves have fallen into it.
*Interlude*

[7] My heart is confident in you, O God;
no wonder I can sing your praises!
[8] Wake up, my soul!
Wake up, O harp and lyre!
I will waken the dawn with my song.
[9] I will thank you, Lord, in front of all the people.
I will sing your praises among the nations.
[10] For your unfailing love is as high as the heavens.
Your faithfulness reaches to the clouds.

[11] Be exalted, O God, above the highest heavens.
May your glory shine over all the earth.

## PSALM 58

*For the choir director: A psalm of David, to be sung to the tune "Do Not Destroy!"*

[1] Justice—do you rulers know the meaning of the word?
Do you judge the people fairly?
[2] No, all your dealings are crooked;
you hand out violence instead of justice.
[3] These wicked people are born sinners;
even from birth they have lied and gone their own way.
[4] They spit poison like deadly snakes;
they are like cobras that refuse to listen,
[5] ignoring the tunes of the snake charmers,
no matter how skillfully they play.

[6] Break off their fangs, O God!
Smash the jaws of these lions, O LORD!
[7] May they disappear like water into thirsty ground.
Make their weapons useless in their hands.*
[8] May they be like snails that dissolve into slime,
like a stillborn child who will never see the sun.
[9] God will sweep them away, both young and old,
faster than a pot heats on an open flame.

[10] The godly will rejoice when they see injustice avenged.
They will wash their feet in the blood of the wicked.
[11] Then at last everyone will say,
"There truly is a reward for those who live for God;
surely there is a God who judges justly here on earth."

## PSALM 59

*For the choir director: A psalm of David, regarding the time Saul sent soldiers to watch David's house in order to kill him. To be sung to the tune "Do Not Destroy!"*

[1] Rescue me from my enemies, O God.
Protect me from those who have come to destroy me.
[2] Rescue me from these criminals;
save me from these murderers.

[3] They have set an ambush for me.
Fierce enemies are out there waiting,
though I have done them no wrong, O LORD.
[4] Despite my innocence, they prepare to kill me.
Rise up and help me! Look on my plight!
[5] O LORD God Almighty, the God of Israel,
rise up to punish hostile nations.
Show no mercy to wicked traitors. *Interlude*

[6] They come at night,
snarling like vicious dogs
as they prowl the streets.
[7] Listen to the filth that comes from their mouths,
the piercing swords that fly from their lips.
"Who can hurt us?" they sneer.

[8] But LORD, you laugh at them.
You scoff at all the hostile nations.
[9] You are my strength; I wait for you to rescue me,
for you, O God, are my place of safety.
[10] In his unfailing love, my God will come and help me.
He will let me look down in triumph on all my enemies.

[11] Don't kill them, for my people soon forget such lessons;
stagger them with your power, and bring them to their knees,
O Lord our shield.

58:7 Or *Let them be trodden down and wither like grass.* The meaning of the Hebrew is uncertain.

[12]Because of the sinful things they say,
because of the evil that is on their lips,
let them be captured by their pride,
their curses, and their lies.
[13]Destroy them in your anger!
Wipe them out completely!
Then the whole world will know
that God reigns in Israel.* *Interlude*

[14]My enemies come out at night,
snarling like vicious dogs
as they prowl the streets.
[15]They scavenge for food
but go to sleep unsatisfied.*

[16]But as for me, I will sing about your power.
I will shout with joy each morning because of
your unfailing love.
For you have been my refuge,
a place of safety in the day of distress.

[17]O my Strength, to you I sing praises,
for you, O God, are my refuge,
the God who shows me unfailing love.

## PSALM 60

*For the choir director: A psalm of David useful for teaching, regarding the time David fought Aram-naharaim and Aram-zobah, and Joab returned and killed twelve thousand Edomites in the Valley of Salt. To be sung to the tune "Lily of the Testimony."*

[1]You have rejected us, O God, and broken our
defenses.
You have been angry with us; now restore us
to your favor.
[2]You have shaken our land and split it open.
Seal the cracks before it completely collapses.
[3]You have been very hard on us,
making us drink wine that sent us reeling.
[4]But you have raised a banner for those who
honor you—
a rallying point in the face of attack. *Interlude*

[5]Use your strong right arm to save us,
and rescue your beloved people.
[6]God has promised this by his holiness*:
"I will divide up Shechem with joy.
I will measure out the valley of Succoth.
[7]Gilead is mine,
and Manasseh is mine.
Ephraim will produce my warriors,
and Judah will produce my kings.
[8]Moab will become my lowly servant,
and Edom will be my slave.
I will shout in triumph over the Philistines."

[9]But who will bring me into the fortified city?
Who will bring me victory over Edom?
[10]Have you rejected us, O God?
Will you no longer march with our armies?
[11]Oh, please help us against our enemies,
for all human help is useless.
[12]With God's help we will do mighty things,
for he will trample down our foes.

## PSALM 61

*For the choir director: A psalm of David, to be accompanied by stringed instruments.*

[1]O God, listen to my cry!
Hear my prayer!
[2]From the ends of the earth,
I will cry to you for help,
for my heart is overwhelmed.
Lead me to the towering rock of safety,
[3]for you are my safe refuge,
a fortress where my enemies cannot
reach me.
[4]Let me live forever in your sanctuary,
safe beneath the shelter of your wings!
*Interlude*

[5]For you have heard my vows, O God.
You have given me an inheritance reserved for
those who fear your name.

[6]Add many years to the life of the king!
May his years span the generations!
[7]May he reign under God's protection forever.
Appoint your unfailing love and faithfulness
to watch over him.

[8]Then I will always sing praises to your name
as I fulfill my vows day after day.

### EVERY DAY ● ● • • •

**61:8 David continually praised God through both the good and difficult times of his life. His commitment to praise God every day showed his reverence for God. Do you find something to praise God for each day? As you do, you will find your heart elevated from daily distractions to lasting confidence.**

## PSALM 62

*For Jeduthun, the choir director: A psalm of David.*

[1]I wait quietly before God,
for my salvation comes from him.
[2]He alone is my rock and my salvation,
my fortress where I will never be shaken.

[3]So many enemies against one man—
all of them trying to kill me.
To them I'm just a broken-down wall
or a tottering fence.
[4]They plan to topple me from my high position.
They delight in telling lies about me.
They are friendly to my face,
but they curse me in their hearts. *Interlude*

[5]I wait quietly before God,
for my hope is in him.
[6]He alone is my rock and my salvation,
my fortress where I will not be shaken.
[7]My salvation and my honor come from God
alone.

59:13 Hebrew *in Jacob.* 59:15 Or *and growl if they don't get enough.* 60:6 Or *in his sanctuary.*

He is my refuge, a rock where no enemy can reach me.
8 O my people, trust in him at all times.
Pour out your heart to him,
for God is our refuge. *Interlude*

9 From the greatest to the lowliest—
all are nothing in his sight.
If you weigh them on the scales,
they are lighter than a puff of air.
10 Don't try to get rich
by extortion or robbery.
And if your wealth increases,
don't make it the center of your life.

11 God has spoken plainly,
and I have heard it many times:
Power, O God, belongs to you;
12 unfailing love, O Lord, is yours.
Surely you judge all people
according to what they have done.

## PSALM 63

*A psalm of David, regarding a time when David was in the wilderness of Judah.*

1 O God, you are my God;
I earnestly search for you.
My soul thirsts for you;
my whole body longs for you
in this parched and weary land
where there is no water.

2 I have seen you in your sanctuary
and gazed upon your power and glory.
3 Your unfailing love is better to me than life itself;
how I praise you!
4 I will honor you as long as I live,
lifting up my hands to you in prayer.
5 You satisfy me more than the richest of foods.
I will praise you with songs of joy.

6 I lie awake thinking of you,
meditating on you through the night.
7 I think how much you have helped me;
I sing for joy in the shadow of your protecting wings.
8 I follow close behind you;
your strong right hand holds me securely.

9 But those plotting to destroy me will come to ruin.
They will go down into the depths of the earth.
10 They will die by the sword
and become the food of jackals.

11 But the king will rejoice in God.
All who trust in him will praise him,
while liars will be silenced.

## PSALM 64

*For the choir director: A psalm of David.*

1 O God, listen to my complaint.
Do not let my enemies' threats overwhelm me.

### FORGIVEN ● ● • • ·

65:3 **Although sins fill our heart, God will forgive them all if we ask sincerely. Do you feel as though God could never forgive you, that your sins are too many, or that some of them are too great? Don't worry! God can and will forgive them all. Nobody is beyond redemption, and nobody is so full of sin that he cannot be made clean.**

2 Protect me from the plots of the wicked,
from the scheming of those who do evil.
3 Sharp tongues are the swords they wield;
bitter words are the arrows they aim.
4 They shoot from ambush at the innocent,
attacking suddenly and fearlessly.
5 They encourage each other to do evil
and plan how to set their traps.
"Who will ever notice?" they ask.
6 As they plot their crimes, they say,
"We have devised the perfect plan!"
Yes, the human heart and mind are cunning.

7 But God himself will shoot them down.
Suddenly, his arrows will pierce them.
8 Their own words will be turned against them,
destroying them.
All who see it happening will shake their heads in scorn.
9 Then everyone will stand in awe,
proclaiming the mighty acts of God,
realizing all the amazing things he does.

10 The godly will rejoice in the LORD
and find shelter in him.
And those who do what is right
will praise him.

## PSALM 65

*For the choir director: A psalm of David. A song.*

1 What mighty praise, O God,
belongs to you in Zion.
We will fulfill our vows to you,
2 for you answer our prayers,
and to you all people will come.
3 Though our hearts are filled with sins,
you forgive them all.
4 What joy for those you choose to bring near,
those who live in your holy courts.
What joys await us
inside your holy Temple.

5 You faithfully answer our prayers with awesome deeds,
O God our savior.
You are the hope of everyone on earth,
even those who sail on distant seas.
6 You formed the mountains by your power
and armed yourself with mighty strength.
7 You quieted the raging oceans
with their pounding waves
and silenced the shouting of the nations.
8 Those who live at the ends of the earth
stand in awe of your wonders.

From where the sun rises to where it sets,
you inspire shouts of joy.
9 You take care of the earth and water it,
making it rich and fertile.
The rivers of God will not run dry;
they provide a bountiful harvest of grain,
for you have ordered it so.
10 You drench the plowed ground with rain,
melting the clods and leveling the ridges.
You soften the earth with showers
and bless its abundant crops.
11 You crown the year with a bountiful harvest;
even the hard pathways overflow with
abundance.
12 The wilderness becomes a lush pasture,
and the hillsides blossom with joy.
13 The meadows are clothed with flocks of sheep,
and the valleys are carpeted with grain.
They all shout and sing for joy!

## PSALM 66 *For the choir director: A psalm. A song.*

1 Shout joyful praises to God, all the earth!
2 Sing about the glory of his name!
Tell the world how glorious he is.
3 Say to God, "How awesome are your deeds!
Your enemies cringe before your mighty power.
4 Everything on earth will worship you;
they will sing your praises,
shouting your name in glorious songs."
*Interlude*

5 Come and see what our God has done,
what awesome miracles he does for his
people!
6 He made a dry path through the Red Sea,*
and his people went across on foot.
Come, let us rejoice in who he is.
7 For by his great power he rules forever.
He watches every movement of the nations;
let no rebel rise in defiance. *Interlude*

8 Let the whole world bless our God
and sing aloud his praises.
9 Our lives are in his hands,
and he keeps our feet from stumbling.
10 You have tested us, O God;
you have purified us like silver melted in a
crucible.
11 You captured us in your net
and laid the burden of slavery on our backs.
12 You sent troops to ride across our broken bodies.
We went through fire and flood.
But you brought us to a place of great
abundance.
13 Now I come to your Temple with burnt offerings
to fulfill the vows I made to you—
14 yes, the sacred vows you heard me make
when I was in deep trouble.
15 That is why I am sacrificing burnt offerings to
you—
the best of my rams as a pleasing aroma.
And I will sacrifice bulls and goats. *Interlude*

16 Come and listen, all you who fear God,
and I will tell you what he did for me.
17 For I cried out to him for help,
praising him as I spoke.
18 If I had not confessed the sin in my heart,
my Lord would not have listened.
19 But God did listen!
He paid attention to my prayer.
20 Praise God, who did not ignore my prayer
and did not withdraw his unfailing love from
me.

### PROMISES ● ● • • •

66:14-15 **People sometimes make bargains with God, saying, "If you heal me (or get me out of this mess), I'll obey you for the rest of my life." Soon after they recover, however, the vow is often forgotten and the old lifestyle resumes. This writer had made a promise to God, but he remembered the promise and paid his vow. God always keeps his promises, and he wants us to follow his example. Be careful to follow through on whatever you promise to do.**

## PSALM 67 *For the choir director: A psalm, to be accompanied by stringed instruments. A song.*

1 May God be merciful and bless us.
May his face shine with favor upon us.
*Interlude*

2 May your ways be known throughout the earth,
your saving power among people everywhere.
3 May the nations praise you, O God.
Yes, may all the nations praise you.
4 How glad the nations will be, singing for joy,
because you govern them with justice
and direct the actions of the whole world.
*Interlude*

5 May the nations praise you, O God.
Yes, may all the nations praise you.
6 Then the earth will yield its harvests,
and God, our God, will richly bless us.
7 Yes, God will bless us,
and people all over the world will fear him.

## PSALM 68 *For the choir director: A psalm of David. A song.*

1 Arise, O God, and scatter your enemies.
Let those who hate God run for their lives.
2 Drive them off like smoke blown by the wind.
Melt them like wax in fire.
Let the wicked perish in the presence of God.
3 But let the godly rejoice.
Let them be glad in God's presence.
Let them be filled with joy.

66:6 Hebrew *the sea.*

[4] Sing praises to God and to his name!
Sing loud praises to him who rides the clouds.
His name is the LORD—
rejoice in his presence!

[5] Father to the fatherless, defender of widows—
this is God, whose dwelling is holy.
[6] God places the lonely in families;
he sets the prisoners free and gives them joy.
But for rebels, there is only famine and
distress.

[7] O God, when you led your people from Egypt,
when you marched through the wilderness,
*Interlude*
[8] the earth trembled, and the heavens poured rain
before you, the God of Sinai,
before God, the God of Israel.
[9] You sent abundant rain, O God,
to refresh the weary Promised Land.
[10] There your people finally settled,
and with a bountiful harvest, O God,
you provided for your needy people.

[11] The Lord announces victory,
and throngs of women shout the happy news.
[12] Enemy kings and their armies flee,
while the women of Israel divide the plunder.
[13] Though they lived among the sheepfolds,
now they are covered with silver and gold,
as a dove is covered by its wings.
[14] The Almighty scattered the enemy kings
like a blowing snowstorm on Mount Zalmon.

[15] The majestic mountains of Bashan
stretch high into the sky.
[16] Why do you look with envy, O rugged
mountains,
at Mount Zion, where God has chosen to live,
where the LORD himself will live forever?

[17] Surrounded by unnumbered thousands of
chariots,
the Lord came from Mount Sinai into his
sanctuary.
[18] When you ascended to the heights,
you led a crowd of captives.
You received gifts from the people,
even from those who rebelled against you.
Now the LORD God will live among us here.

[19] Praise the Lord; praise God our savior!
For each day he carries us in his arms.
*Interlude*
[20] Our God is a God who saves!
The Sovereign LORD rescues us from death.

[21] But God will smash the heads of his enemies,
crushing the skulls of those who love their
guilty ways.
[22] The Lord says, "I will bring my enemies down
from Bashan;
I will bring them up from the depths of the
sea.
[23] You, my people, will wash your feet in their
blood,
and even your dogs will get their share!"

[24] Your procession has come into view, O God—
the procession of my God and King
as he goes into the sanctuary.
[25] Singers are in front, musicians are behind;
with them are young women playing
tambourines.
[26] Praise God, all you people of Israel;
praise the LORD, the source of Israel's life.
[27] Look, the little tribe of Benjamin leads the way.
Then comes a great throng of rulers from
Judah
and all the rulers of Zebulun and Naphtali.

[28] Summon your might, O God.
Display your power, O God, as you have in
the past.
[29] The kings of the earth are bringing tribute
to your Temple in Jerusalem.
[30] Rebuke these enemy nations—
these wild animals lurking in the reeds,
this herd of bulls among the weaker calves.
Humble those who demand tribute from us.*
Scatter the nations that delight in war.
[31] Let Egypt come with gifts of precious metals;
let Ethiopia* bow in submission to God.
[32] Sing to God, you kingdoms of the earth.
Sing praises to the Lord. *Interlude*

[33] Sing to the one who rides across the ancient
heavens,
his mighty voice thundering from the sky.

**BREATHLESS ● ● • • •**

**68:34-35 We should feel an overwhelming sense of awe when we come before the Lord in his sanctuary. Surrounding us are countless signs of his wonderful power; shining down upon us are countless signs of his majesty. Unlimited power and unspeakable majesty leave us breathless in his presence. When you catch your breath, praise the Lord!**

[34] Tell everyone about God's power.
His majesty shines down on Israel;
his strength is mighty in the heavens.
[35] God is awesome in his sanctuary.
The God of Israel gives power and strength to
his people.

Praise be to God!

## PSALM 69 *For the choir director: A psalm of David, to be sung to the tune "Lilies."*

[1] Save me, O God,
for the floodwaters are up to my neck.
[2] Deeper and deeper I sink into the mire;
I can't find a foothold to stand on.
I am in deep water,
and the floods overwhelm me.

**68:30** Or *Humble them until they submit, bringing pieces of silver as tribute.* **68:31** Hebrew *Cush.*

[3] I am exhausted from crying for help;
my throat is parched and dry.
My eyes are swollen with weeping,
waiting for my God to help me.

[4] Those who hate me without cause
are more numerous than the hairs on my head.
These enemies who seek to destroy me
are doing so without cause.
They attack me with lies,
demanding that I give back what I didn't steal.

[5] O God, you know how foolish I am;
my sins cannot be hidden from you.
[6] Don't let those who trust in you stumble
because of me,
O Sovereign LORD Almighty.
Don't let me cause them to be humiliated,
O God of Israel.
[7] For I am mocked and shamed for your sake;
humiliation is written all over my face.
[8] Even my own brothers pretend they don't know me;
they treat me like a stranger.
[9] Passion for your house burns within me,
so those who insult you are also insulting me.
[10] When I weep and fast before the LORD,
they scoff at me.
[11] When I dress in sackcloth to show sorrow,
they make fun of me.
[12] I am the favorite topic of town gossip,
and all the drunkards sing about me.

[13] But I keep right on praying to you, LORD,
hoping this is the time you will show me favor.
In your unfailing love, O God,
answer my prayer with your sure salvation.
[14] Pull me out of the mud;
don't let me sink any deeper!
Rescue me from those who hate me,
and pull me from these deep waters.
[15] Don't let the floods overwhelm me,
or the deep waters swallow me,
or the pit of death devour me.

[16] Answer my prayers, O LORD,
for your unfailing love is wonderful.
Turn and take care of me,
for your mercy is so plentiful.
[17] Don't hide from your servant;
answer me quickly, for I am in deep trouble!
[18] Come and rescue me;
free me from all my enemies.

[19] You know the insults I endure—
the humiliation and disgrace.
You have seen all my enemies
and know what they have said.

[20] Their insults have broken my heart,
and I am in despair.
If only one person would show some pity;
if only one would turn and comfort me.
[21] But instead, they give me poison for food;
they offer me sour wine to satisfy my thirst.

[22] Let the bountiful table set before them become a snare,
and let their security become a trap.
[23] Let their eyes go blind so they cannot see,
and let their bodies grow weaker and weaker.
[24] Pour out your fury on them;
consume them with your burning anger.
[25] May their homes become desolate
and their tents be deserted.
[26] To those you have punished, they add insult to injury;
they scoff at the pain of those you have hurt.
[27] Pile their sins up high,
and don't let them go free.
[28] Erase their names from the Book of Life;
don't let them be counted among the righteous.

[29] I am suffering and in pain.
Rescue me, O God, by your saving power.

[30] Then I will praise God's name with singing,
and I will honor him with thanksgiving.
[31] For this will please the LORD more than
sacrificing an ox
or presenting a bull with its horns and hooves.
[32] The humble will see their God at work and be glad.
Let all who seek God's help live in joy.
[33] For the LORD hears the cries of his needy ones;
he does not despise his people who are oppressed.

[34] Praise him, O heaven and earth,
the seas and all that move in them.
[35] For God will save Jerusalem*
and rebuild the towns of Judah.
His people will live there
and take possession of the land.
[36] The descendants of those who obey him will inherit the land,
and those who love him will live there in safety.

## PSALM 70

*For the choir director: A psalm of David, to bring us to the LORD's remembrance.*

[1] Please, God, rescue me!
Come quickly, LORD, and help me.
[2] May those who try to destroy me
be humiliated and put to shame.
May those who take delight in my trouble
be turned back in disgrace.
[3] Let them be horrified by their shame,
for they said, "Aha! We've got him now!"

69:35 Hebrew *Zion*.

## DOWN IN THE DUMPS

In the movie *The Accidental Tourist,* the main characters are a husband and wife named Macon and Sarah Leary. Their son Ethan has died tragically, leaving them in despair, struggling to pull their lives back together. In one particularly touching scene, Sarah says to her husband: "I should have agreed to teach summer school or something. I open my eyes in the morning and I think, *Why bother getting up? Why bother eating? Why bother breathing?"* This isn't just a scene from a movie—it's an experience common to people everywhere. Life can be terribly unfair, terribly tragic. When we're in the depths of despair, we feel like Sarah Leary: Why bother going on at all? There are those who feel that Christians are—or should be—immune to depression. "After all," they say, "what have you got to be depressed about? You have a relationship with God, a family of brothers and sisters who love you, and a guaranteed ticket to heaven." When the person carrying the weight of GLOOM hears this, he is not only depressed, he feels guilty as well because it's "unspiritual" to be down in the dumps. For those who struggle with feelings of depression, there is good news and bad news. **THE BAD NEWS** is that such feelings are a fact of life in this broken world. Humanity's fall into sin in the Garden of Eden affected every area of our existence. Look at it this way: When you inhabit a planet in open rebellion against its Creator, it's not surprising that sometimes you get caught in the cross fire. Depression is just one of the ways that we can be wounded. Now ***the good news***: You are not alone. As Psalm 73 (and many other passages) clearly shows, even God's chosen people experience anxiety, despair, and darkness in their soul. (If Psalm 73 doesn't convince you, check out the accounts of Jesus' experience in Gethsemane. Matthew 26 speaks of Jesus' soul being "crushed with grief to the point of death." Don't be surprised when you face grief.) Feeling down—really down—seems to be an occasional fact of life. Obviously, depression that is too deep or lasts too long indicates a need for counseling; but there is nothing unusual or unspiritual about "walking through the dark valley" from time to time. So when you are caught in one of those unpleasant times, don't add guilt to your load. There's nothing wrong with you. When sailing through stormy seas, expect a little motion discomfort. And know for certain that **the Captain is not asleep on the bridge.** He'll guide you safely through.

---

4 But may all who search for you
be filled with joy and gladness.
May those who love your salvation
repeatedly shout, "God is great!"
5 But I am poor and needy;
please hurry to my aid, O God.
You are my helper and my savior;
O LORD, do not delay!

## PSALM 71

1 O LORD, you are my refuge;
never let me be disgraced.
2 Rescue me! Save me from my enemies, for you
are just.
Turn your ear to listen and set me free.
3 Be to me a protecting rock of safety,
where I am always welcome.
Give the order to save me,
for you are my rock and my fortress.
4 My God, rescue me from the power of the
wicked,
from the clutches of cruel oppressors.
5 O Lord, you alone are my hope.
I've trusted you, O LORD, from childhood.
6 Yes, you have been with me from birth;
from my mother's womb you have cared for
me.
No wonder I am always praising you!
7 My life is an example to many,
because you have been my strength and
protection.
8 That is why I can never stop praising you;
I declare your glory all day long.

[9]And now, in my old age, don't set me aside.
Don't abandon me when my strength is failing.
[10]For my enemies are whispering against me.
They are plotting together to kill me.
[11]They say, "God has abandoned him.
Let's go and get him,
for there is no one to help him now."

[12]O God, don't stay away.
My God, please hurry to help me.
[13]Bring disgrace and destruction on those who accuse me.
May humiliation and shame cover
those who want to harm me.

[14]But I will keep on hoping for you to help me;
I will praise you more and more.
[15]I will tell everyone about your righteousness.
All day long I will proclaim your saving power,
for I am overwhelmed by how much you have done for me.
[16]I will praise your mighty deeds, O Sovereign LORD.
I will tell everyone that you alone are just and good.

[17]O God, you have taught me from my earliest childhood,
and I have constantly told others about the wonderful things you do.
[18]Now that I am old and gray,
do not abandon me, O God.
Let me proclaim your power to this new generation,
your mighty miracles to all who come after me.
[19]Your righteousness, O God, reaches to the highest heavens.
You have done such wonderful things.
Who can compare with you, O God?
[20]You have allowed me to suffer much hardship,
but you will restore me to life again
and lift me up from the depths of the earth.
[21]You will restore me to even greater honor
and comfort me once again.

[22]Then I will praise you with music on the harp,
because you are faithful to your promises, O God.
I will sing for you with a lyre,
O Holy One of Israel.
[23]I will shout for joy and sing your praises,
for you have redeemed me.
[24]I will tell about your righteous deeds
all day long,
for everyone who tried to hurt me
has been shamed and humiliated.

## PSALM 72 *A psalm of Solomon.*

[1]Give justice to the king, O God,
and righteousness to the king's son.

### PANIC ●●•••

70:4 **This short psalm was David's plea for God to rush to his aid. Yet even in this moment of panic, praise was not forgotten. Praise is important because it helps us remember who God is. Often our prayers are filled with requests for ourself and others; we forget to thank God for what he has done and to worship him for who he is. Don't take God for granted or treat him as a vending machine. Even in the midst of his fear, David praised God.**

[2]Help him judge your people in the right way;
let the poor always be treated fairly.
[3]May the mountains yield prosperity for all,
and may the hills be fruitful,
because the king does what is right.
[4]Help him to defend the poor,
to rescue the children of the needy,
and to crush their oppressors.
[5]May he live* as long as the sun shines,
as long as the moon continues in the skies.
Yes, forever!
[6]May his reign be as refreshing as the springtime rains—
like the showers that water the earth.
[7]May all the godly flourish during his reign.
May there be abundant prosperity until the end of time.

[8]May he reign from sea to sea,
and from the Euphrates River* to the ends of the earth.
[9]Desert nomads will bow before him;
his enemies will fall before him in the dust.
[10]The western kings of Tarshish and the islands
will bring him tribute.
The eastern kings of Sheba and Seba
will bring him gifts.
[11]All kings will bow before him,
and all nations will serve him.

[12]He will rescue the poor when they cry to him;
he will help the oppressed, who have no one to defend them.
[13]He feels pity for the weak and the needy,
and he will rescue them.
[14]He will save them from oppression and from violence,
for their lives are precious to him.

[15]Long live the king!
May the gold of Sheba be given to him.
May the people always pray for him
and bless him all day long.

### HELPLESS ●●•••

72:12-14 **God cares for the needy and the poor because they are precious to him. If God feels so strongly about the poor and loves them so deeply, how can we ignore their plight? Examine what you are doing to reach out with God's love to the poor, weak, and needy in the world. Are you ignoring them?**

72:5 As in Greek version; Hebrew reads *May they fear you.* 72:8 Hebrew *the river.*

[16]May there be abundant crops throughout the land,
flourishing even on the mountaintops.
May the fruit trees flourish as they do in Lebanon,
sprouting up like grass in a field.
[17]May the king's name endure forever;
may it continue as long as the sun shines.
May all nations be blessed through him
and bring him praise.

[18]Bless the LORD God, the God of Israel,
who alone does such wonderful things.
[19]Bless his glorious name forever!
Let the whole earth be filled with his glory.
Amen and amen!

[20](This ends the prayers of David son of Jesse.)

## INJUSTICE

"It isn't fair!" Joyce sobs. "I try really hard to live for the Lord. I go to church, read my Bible, pray every day, try to be a witness to my friends—everything! But does it do any good? No way! My life is still the worst. My family is awful, my fat body is a wreck, I never get asked out, I have only two friends, and I can't even pass geometry! You'd think God would at least reward me a little bit.

"On the other hand, Amy has it made! She's tan and beautiful. She has dates every weekend. She makes straight A's without even trying. Her family is rich—I mean, how many other kids get their own Miata convertible? She never has any problems. Her life is totally perfect . . . and here's the big rip-off: she's not even a Christian! In fact, she couldn't care less about God. She's wild!

"It doesn't make any sense. Why do I get shot down for doing what's right, and she gets rewarded for being 'Miss Party'?

"Doesn't God see what's going on? Doesn't he care? I'm serious . . . there is absolutely no justice in this world. I might as well live like a heathen for all the good it does me."

Ever feel like Joyce? Ever wonder why some non-Christians seem to have perfect lives, while so many of God's people struggle and have lives full of pain? A follower of God named Asaph once asked some of the very same questions. Psalm 73 describes the answers he found.

## BOOK THREE (Psalms 73–89)

## PSALM 73 *A psalm of Asaph.*

[1]Truly God is good to Israel,
to those whose hearts are pure.

[2]But as for me, I came so close to the edge of the cliff!
My feet were slipping, and I was almost gone.
[3]For I envied the proud
when I saw them prosper despite their wickedness.
[4]They seem to live such a painless life;
their bodies are so healthy and strong.

### HATE ●●●••

**74:8 When enemy armies defeated Israel, they sacked Jerusalem, trying to wipe out every trace of God. This has often been the response of people who hate God. Today many are trying to erase all traces of God from traditions in our society and subjects taught in our schools. Do what you can to help maintain a Christian influence, but don't become discouraged when others appear to make great strides in eliminating all traces of God. They cannot eliminate his presence in the lives of believers.**

[5]They aren't troubled like other people
or plagued with problems like everyone else.
[6]They wear pride like a jeweled necklace,
and their clothing is woven of cruelty.
[7]These fat cats have everything
their hearts could ever wish for!
[8]They scoff and speak only evil;
in their pride they seek to crush others.
[9]They boast against the very heavens,
and their words strut throughout the earth.
[10]And so the people are dismayed and confused,
drinking in all their words.
[11]"Does God realize what is going on?" they ask.
"Is the Most High even aware of what is happening?"
[12]Look at these arrogant people—
enjoying a life of ease while their riches multiply.

[13]Was it for nothing that I kept my heart pure
and kept myself from doing wrong?
[14]All I get is trouble all day long;
every morning brings me pain.
[15]If I had really spoken this way,
I would have been a traitor to your people.
[16]So I tried to understand why the wicked prosper.
But what a difficult task it is!
[17]Then one day I went into your sanctuary, O God,
and I thought about the destiny of the wicked.
[18]Truly, you put them on a slippery path
and send them sliding over the cliff to destruction.
[19]In an instant they are destroyed,
swept away by terrors.
[20]Their present life is only a dream
that is gone when they awake.
When you arise, O Lord,
you will make them vanish from this life.

[21]Then I realized how bitter I had become,
how pained I had been by all I had seen.
[22]I was so foolish and ignorant—
I must have seemed like a senseless animal to you.
[23]Yet I still belong to you;
you are holding my right hand.
[24]You will keep on guiding me with your counsel,
leading me to a glorious destiny.
[25]Whom have I in heaven but you?
I desire you more than anything on earth.

[26] My health may fail, and my spirit may grow weak,
but God remains the strength of my heart;
he is mine forever.
[27] But those who desert him will perish,
for you destroy those who abandon you.
[28] But as for me, how good it is to be near God!
I have made the Sovereign LORD my shelter,
and I will tell everyone about the wonderful
things you do.

## PSALM 74 *A psalm of Asaph.*

[1] O God, why have you rejected us forever?
Why is your anger so intense against the sheep
of your own pasture?
[2] Remember that we are the people you chose in
ancient times,
the tribe you redeemed as your own special
possession!
And remember Jerusalem,* your home here
on earth.
[3] Walk through the awful ruins of the city;
see how the enemy has destroyed your
sanctuary.
[4] There your enemies shouted their victorious
battle cries;
there they set up their battle standards.
[5] They chopped down the entrance
like woodcutters in a forest.
[6] With axes and picks,
they smashed the carved paneling.
[7] They set the sanctuary on fire, burning it to the
ground.
They utterly defiled the place that bears your
holy name.
[8] Then they thought, "Let's destroy everything!"
So they burned down all the places where
God was worshiped.
[9] We see no miraculous signs
as evidence that you will save us.
All the prophets are gone;
no one can tell us when it will end.
[10] How long, O God, will you allow our enemies to
mock you?
Will you let them dishonor your name forever?
[11] Why do you hold back your strong right hand?
Unleash your powerful fist and deliver a
deathblow.
[12] You, O God, are my king from ages past,
bringing salvation to the earth.
[13] You split the sea by your strength
and smashed the sea monster's heads.
[14] You crushed the heads of Leviathan
and let the desert animals eat him.
[15] You caused the springs and streams to gush forth,
and you dried up rivers that never run dry.
[16] Both day and night belong to you;
you made the starlight* and the sun.
[17] You set the boundaries of the earth,
and you make both summer and winter.
[18] See how these enemies scoff at you, LORD.
A foolish nation has dishonored your name.
[19] Don't let these wild beasts destroy your doves.
Don't forget your afflicted people forever.
[20] Remember your covenant promises,
for the land is full of darkness and violence!
[21] Don't let the downtrodden be constantly
disgraced!
Instead, let these poor and needy ones give
praise to your name.
[22] Arise, O God, and defend your cause.
Remember how these fools insult you all day
long.
[23] Don't overlook these things your enemies have
said.
Their uproar of rebellion grows ever louder.

## PSALM 75 *For the choir director: A psalm of Asaph, to be sung to the tune "Do Not Destroy!" A song.*

[1] We thank you, O God!
We give thanks because you are near.
People everywhere tell of your mighty
miracles.

**TIMING ● ● • • ·**

75:2 **Children have difficulty grasping the concept of time. "It's not time yet" is not a reason they easily understand. They only comprehend the present. As limited human beings, we can't comprehend God's perspective on time. We want everything now, not recognizing that God's timing is better for us. When God is ready, he will do what needs to be done, not what we would like him to do. We may be impatient as children, but it is clear that God's timing is perfect, so we should accept it.**

[2] God says, "At the time I have planned,
I will bring justice against the wicked.
[3] When the earth quakes and its people live in
turmoil,
I am the one who keeps its foundations firm.
*Interlude*
[4] "I warned the proud, 'Stop your boasting!'
I told the wicked, 'Don't raise your fists!
[5] Don't lift your fists in defiance at the heavens
or speak with rebellious arrogance.'"
[6] For no one on earth—from east or west,
or even from the wilderness—
can raise another person up.
[7] It is God alone who judges;
he decides who will rise and who will fall.
[8] For the LORD holds a cup in his hand;
it is full of foaming wine mixed with spices.
He pours the wine out in judgment,
and all the wicked must drink it,
draining it to the dregs.

**74:2** Hebrew *Mount Zion.* **74:16** Or *moon;* Hebrew reads *light.*

[9] But as for me, I will always proclaim what God has done;
I will sing praises to the God of Israel.*
[10] For God says, "I will cut off the strength of the wicked,
but I will increase the power of the godly."

## PSALM 76 *For the choir director: A psalm of Asaph, to be accompanied by stringed instruments. A song.*

[1] God is well known in Judah;
his name is great in Israel.
[2] Jerusalem* is where he lives;
Mount Zion is his home.
[3] There he breaks the arrows of the enemy,
the shields and swords and weapons of his foes. *Interlude*

[4] You are glorious and more majestic
than the everlasting mountains.*
[5] The mightiest of our enemies have been plundered.
They lie before us in the sleep of death.
No warrior could lift a hand against us.
[6] When you rebuked them, O God of Jacob,
their horses and chariots stood still.

[7] No wonder you are greatly feared!
Who can stand before you when your anger explodes?
[8] From heaven you sentenced your enemies;
the earth trembled and stood silent before you.
[9] You stand up to judge those who do evil, O God,
and to rescue the oppressed of the earth. *Interlude*

[10] Human opposition only enhances your glory,
for you use it as a sword of judgment.*

[11] Make vows to the LORD your God, and fulfill them.
Let everyone bring tribute to the Awesome One.
[12] For he breaks the spirit of princes
and is feared by the kings of the earth.

## PSALM 77 *For Jeduthun, the choir director: A psalm of Asaph.*

[1] I cry out to God without holding back.
Oh, that God would listen to me!
[2] When I was in deep trouble,
I searched for the Lord.
All night long I pray, with hands lifted toward heaven, pleading.
There can be no joy for me until he acts.
[3] I think of God, and I moan,
overwhelmed with longing for his help. *Interlude*

[4] You don't let me sleep.
I am too distressed even to pray!
[5] I think of the good old days, long since ended,
[6] when my nights were filled with joyful songs.
I search my soul and think about the difference now.
[7] Has the Lord rejected me forever?
Will he never again show me favor?
[8] Is his unfailing love gone forever?
Have his promises permanently failed?
[9] Has God forgotten to be kind?
Has he slammed the door on his compassion? *Interlude*

[10] And I said, "This is my fate,
that the blessings of the Most High have changed to hatred."
[11] I recall all you have done, O LORD;
I remember your wonderful deeds of long ago.
[12] They are constantly in my thoughts.
I cannot stop thinking about them.

[13] O God, your ways are holy.
Is there any god as mighty as you?
[14] You are the God of miracles and wonders!
You demonstrate your awesome power among the nations.
[15] You have redeemed your people by your strength,
the descendants of Jacob and of Joseph by your might. *Interlude*

[16] When the Red Sea* saw you, O God,
its waters looked and trembled!
The sea quaked to its very depths.
[17] The clouds poured down their rain;
the thunder rolled and crackled in the sky.
Your arrows of lightning flashed.
[18] Your thunder roared from the whirlwind;
the lightning lit up the world!
The earth trembled and shook.
[19] Your road led through the sea,
your pathway through the mighty waters—
a pathway no one knew was there!
[20] You led your people along that road like a flock of sheep,
with Moses and Aaron as their shepherds.

## PSALM 78 *A psalm of Asaph.*

[1] O my people, listen to my teaching.
Open your ears to what I am saying,
[2] for I will speak to you in a parable.
I will teach you hidden lessons from our past—
[3] stories we have heard and know,
stories our ancestors handed down to us.
[4] We will not hide these truths from our children
but will tell the next generation about the glorious deeds of the LORD.
We will tell of his power and the mighty miracles he did.

75:9 Hebrew *of Jacob.* 76:2 Hebrew *Salem,* another name for Jerusalem. 76:4 As in Greek version; Hebrew reads *than mountains filled with beasts of prey.* 76:10 The meaning of the Hebrew is uncertain. 77:16 Hebrew *the waters.*

5 For he issued his decree to Jacob;
he gave his law to Israel.
He commanded our ancestors
to teach them to their children,
6 so the next generation might know them—
even the children not yet born—
that they in turn might teach their children.
7 So each generation can set its hope anew on
God,
remembering his glorious miracles
and obeying his commands.
8 Then they will not be like their ancestors—
stubborn, rebellious, and unfaithful,
refusing to give their hearts to God.

9 The warriors of Ephraim, though fully armed,
turned their backs and fled when the day of
battle came.
10 They did not keep God's covenant,
and they refused to live by his law.
11 They forgot what he had done—
the wonderful miracles he had shown them,
12 the miracles he did for their ancestors in
Egypt, on the plain of Zoan.
13 For he divided the sea before them and led them
through!
The water stood up like walls beside them!
14 In the daytime he led them by a cloud,
and at night by a pillar of fire.
15 He split open the rocks in the wilderness
to give them plenty of water, as from a
gushing spring.
16 He made streams pour from the rock,
making the waters flow down like a river!

17 Yet they kept on with their sin,
rebelling against the Most High in the desert.
18 They willfully tested God in their hearts,
demanding the foods they craved.
19 They even spoke against God himself, saying,
"God can't give us food in the desert.
20 Yes, he can strike a rock so water gushes out,
but he can't give his people bread and meat."
21 When the LORD heard them, he was angry.
The fire of his wrath burned against Jacob.
Yes, his anger rose against Israel,
22 for they did not believe God
or trust him to care for them.
23 But he commanded the skies to open—
he opened the doors of heaven—
24 and rained down manna for them to eat.
He gave them bread from heaven.
25 They ate the food of angels!
God gave them all they could hold.
26 He released the east wind in the heavens
and guided the south wind by his mighty
power.
27 He rained down meat as thick as dust—
birds as plentiful as the sands along the
seashore!
28 He caused the birds to fall within their camp
and all around their tents.
29 The people ate their fill.
He gave them what they wanted.
30 But before they finished eating this food they
had craved,
while the meat was yet in their mouths,
31 the anger of God rose against them,
and he killed their strongest men;
he struck down the finest of Israel's young
men.
32 But in spite of this, the people kept on sinning.
They refused to believe in his miracles.
33 So he ended their lives in failure
and gave them years of terror.

34 When God killed some of them, the rest finally
sought him.
They repented and turned to God.
35 Then they remembered that God was their rock,
that their redeemer was the Most High.
36 But they followed him only with their words;
they lied to him with their tongues.
37 Their hearts were not loyal to him.
They did not keep his covenant.
38 Yet he was merciful and forgave their sins
and didn't destroy them all.
Many a time he held back his anger
and did not unleash his fury!
39 For he remembered that they were merely mortal,
gone in a moment like a breath of wind,
never to return.

40 Oh, how often they rebelled against him in the
desert
and grieved his heart in the wilderness.
41 Again and again they tested God's patience
and frustrated the Holy One of Israel.
42 They forgot about his power
and how he rescued them from their enemies.
43 They forgot his miraculous signs in Egypt,
his wonders on the plain of Zoan.
44 For he turned their rivers into blood,
so no one could drink from the streams.
45 He sent vast swarms of flies to consume them
and hordes of frogs to ruin them.
46 He gave their crops to caterpillars;
their harvest was consumed by locusts.
47 He destroyed their grapevines with hail
and shattered their sycamores with sleet.
48 He abandoned their cattle to the hail,
their livestock to bolts of lightning.
49 He loosed on them his fierce anger—
all his fury, rage, and hostility.
He dispatched against them
a band of destroying angels.

## ALL TALK

78:36-37 **Over and over the children of Israel said they would follow God, but then they turned away from him. The problem was that they followed God with words and not with their hearts, thus their repentance was empty. Talk is cheap. God wants our life to back up our spiritual claims and promises—he wants us to be true believers.**

## BASIC TRAINING ● ● • • •

78:71-72 **Although David had been on the throne when this psalm was written, he is called a shepherd and not a king. Shepherding, a common profession in biblical times, was a highly responsible job. The flocks were completely dependent upon shepherds for guidance, provision, and protection. David had spent his early years as a shepherd (1 Samuel 16:10-11). This was a training ground for the future responsibilities God had in store for him. When he was ready, God took him from caring for sheep to caring for Israel, God's people. Don't treat your present situation lightly or irresponsibly; it may be God's training ground for your future.**

50 He turned his anger against them;
he did not spare the Egyptians' lives
but handed them over to the plague.
51 He killed the oldest son in each Egyptian family,
the flower of youth throughout the land of Egypt.*
52 But he led his own people like a flock of sheep,
guiding them safely through the wilderness.
53 He kept them safe so they were not afraid;
but the sea closed in upon their enemies.
54 He brought them to the border of his holy land,
to this land of hills he had won for them.
55 He drove out the nations before them;
he gave them their inheritance by lot.
He settled the tribes of Israel into their homes.
56 Yet though he did all this for them,
they continued to test his patience.
They rebelled against the Most High
and refused to follow his decrees.
57 They turned back and were as faithless as their parents had been.
They were as useless as a crooked bow.
58 They made God angry by building altars to other gods;
they made him jealous with their idols.
59 When God heard them, he was very angry,
and he rejected Israel completely.
60 Then he abandoned his dwelling at Shiloh,
the Tabernacle where he had lived among the people.
61 He allowed the Ark of his might to be captured;
he surrendered his glory into enemy hands.
62 He gave his people over to be butchered by the sword,
because he was so angry with his own people—his special possession.
63 Their young men were killed by fire;
their young women died before singing their wedding songs.
64 Their priests were slaughtered,
and their widows could not mourn their deaths.
65 Then the Lord rose up as though waking from sleep,
like a mighty man aroused from a drunken stupor.
66 He routed his enemies
and sent them to eternal shame.
67 But he rejected Joseph's descendants;
he did not choose the tribe of Ephraim.
68 He chose instead the tribe of Judah,
Mount Zion, which he loved.
69 There he built his towering sanctuary,
as solid and enduring as the earth itself.
70 He chose his servant David,
calling him from the sheep pens.
71 He took David from tending the ewes and lambs
and made him the shepherd of Jacob's descendants—
God's own people, Israel.
72 He cared for them with a true heart
and led them with skillful hands.

## PSALM 79 *A psalm of Asaph.*

1 O God, pagan nations have conquered your land, your special possession.
They have defiled your holy Temple
and made Jerusalem a heap of ruins.
2 They have left the bodies of your servants
as food for the birds of heaven.
The flesh of your godly ones
has become food for the wild animals.
3 Blood has flowed like water all around Jerusalem;
no one is left to bury the dead.
4 We are mocked by our neighbors,
an object of scorn and derision to those around us.

5 O LORD, how long will you be angry with us? Forever?
How long will your jealousy burn like fire?
6 Pour out your wrath on the nations that refuse to recognize you—
on kingdoms that do not call upon your name.
7 For they have devoured your people Israel,*
making the land a desolate wilderness.
8 Oh, do not hold us guilty for our former sins!
Let your tenderhearted mercies quickly meet our needs,
for we are brought low to the dust.
9 Help us, O God of our salvation!
Help us for the honor of your name.
Oh, save us and forgive our sins
for the sake of your name.
10 Why should pagan nations be allowed to scoff,
asking, "Where is their God?"

## BE PREPARED ● ● • • •

79:10 **Can we expect God to care for us so others won't scoff at our beliefs? In the end, God will bring himself glory (76:10), but in the meantime, we must endure suffering with patience and allow God to purify us through it. For reasons that we do not know, the heathen are allowed to scoff at believers. We should be prepared for criticism, jokes, and unkind remarks because God does not place us beyond the attacks of scoffers.**

78:51 Hebrew *in the tents of Ham.* 79:7 Hebrew *Jacob.*

Show us your vengeance against the nations,
for they have spilled the blood of your servants.
11 Listen to the moaning of the prisoners.
Demonstrate your great power by saving those condemned to die.
12 O Lord, take sevenfold vengeance on our neighbors
for the scorn they have hurled at you.
13 Then we your people, the sheep of your pasture,
will thank you forever and ever,
praising your greatness from generation to generation.

## PSALM 80 *For the choir director: A psalm of Asaph, to be sung to the tune "Lilies of the Covenant."*

1 Please listen, O Shepherd of Israel,
you who lead Israel* like a flock.
O God, enthroned above the cherubim,
display your radiant glory
2 to Ephraim, Benjamin, and Manasseh.
Show us your mighty power.
Come to rescue us!

3 Turn us again to yourself, O God.
Make your face shine down upon us.
Only then will we be saved.

4 O LORD God Almighty,
how long will you be angry and reject our prayers?
5 You have fed us with sorrow
and made us drink tears by the bucketful.
6 You have made us the scorn of neighboring nations.
Our enemies treat us as a joke.

7 Turn us again to yourself, O God Almighty.
Make your face shine down upon us.
Only then will we be saved.
8 You brought us from Egypt as though we were a tender vine;
you drove away the pagan nations and transplanted us into your land.
9 You cleared the ground for us,
and we took root and filled the land.
10 The mountains were covered with our shade;
the mighty cedars were covered with our branches.
11 We spread our branches west to the Mediterranean Sea,
our limbs east to the Euphrates River.*
12 But now, why have you broken down our walls
so that all who pass may steal our fruit?
13 The boar from the forest devours us,
and the wild animals feed on us.
14 Come back, we beg you, O God Almighty.
Look down from heaven and see our plight.
Watch over and care for this vine
15 that you yourself have planted,
this son you have raised for yourself.
16 For we are chopped up and burned by our enemies.
May they perish at the sight of your frown.
17 Strengthen the man you love,
the son of your choice.
18 Then we will never forsake you again.
Revive us so we can call on your name once more.

19 Turn us again to yourself, O LORD God Almighty.
Make your face shine down upon us.
Only then will we be saved.

## PSALM 81 *For the choir director: A psalm of Asaph, to be accompanied by a stringed instrument.**

1 Sing praises to God, our strength.
Sing to the God of Israel.*
2 Sing! Beat the tambourine.
Play the sweet lyre and the harp.
3 Sound the trumpet for a sacred feast
when the moon is new,
when the moon is full.

### HOLIDAYS ●●●••

**81:3-5 Israel's sacred feasts reminded the nation of God's great miracles. They were times of rejoicing and times to renew one's strength for life's daily struggles. At Christmas, do most of your thoughts revolve around presents? Is Easter only a warm anticipation of spring, and Thanksgiving only a good meal? Remember the spiritual origins of these special days, and use them as opportunities to worship God for his goodness to you, your family, and your nation.**

4 For this is required by the laws of Israel;
it is a law of the God of Jacob.
5 He made it a decree for Israel*
when he attacked Egypt to set us free.

I heard an unknown voice that said,
6 "Now I will relieve your shoulder of its burden;
I will free your hands from their heavy tasks.
7 You cried to me in trouble, and I saved you;
I answered out of the thundercloud.
I tested your faith at Meribah,
when you complained that there was no water.
*Interlude*

8 "Listen to me, O my people, while I give you stern warnings.
O Israel, if you would only listen!
9 You must never have a foreign god;
you must not bow down before a false god.
10 For it was I, the LORD your God,
who rescued you from the land of Egypt.
Open your mouth wide, and I will fill it with good things.

11 "But no, my people wouldn't listen.
Israel did not want me around.

80:1 Hebrew *Joseph.* 80:11 Hebrew *west to the sea, . . . east to the river.* 81:TITLE Hebrew *according to the gittith.* 81:1 Hebrew *of Jacob.* 81:5 Hebrew *for Joseph.*

[12] So I let them follow their blind and stubborn way,
living according to their own desires.
[13] But oh, that my people would listen to me!
Oh, that Israel would follow me, walking in my paths!
[14] How quickly I would then subdue their enemies!
How soon my hands would be upon their foes!
[15] Those who hate the LORD would cringe before him;
their desolation would last forever.
[16] But I would feed you with the best of foods.
I would satisfy you with wild honey from the rock."

## PSALM 82 *A psalm of Asaph.*

[1] God presides over heaven's court;
he pronounces judgment on the judges:
[2] "How long will you judges hand down unjust decisions?
How long will you shower special favors on the wicked? *Interlude*
[3] "Give fair judgment to the poor and the orphan;
uphold the rights of the oppressed and the destitute.
[4] Rescue the poor and helpless;
deliver them from the grasp of evil people.
[5] But these oppressors know nothing;
they are so ignorant!
And because they are in darkness,
the whole world is shaken to the core.
[6] I say, 'You are gods
and children of the Most High.
[7] But in death you are mere men.
You will fall as any prince,
for all must die.'"
[8] Rise up, O God, and judge the earth,
for all the nations belong to you.

## PSALM 83 *A psalm of Asaph. A song.*

[1] O God, don't sit idly by,
silent and inactive!
[2] Don't you hear the tumult of your enemies?
Don't you see what your arrogant enemies are doing?
[3] They devise crafty schemes against your people,
laying plans against your precious ones.
[4] "Come," they say, "let us wipe out Israel as a nation.
We will destroy the very memory of its existence."
5 This was their unanimous decision.
They signed a treaty as allies against you—
6 these Edomites and Ishmaelites,
Moabites and Hagrites,
7 Gebalites, Ammonites, and Amalekites,
and people from Philistia and Tyre.

84:TITLE Hebrew *according to the gittith.*



### BLOWN AWAY ● ● • • •

**83:13-18 The rulers of the nations exercise great power, changing the course of history and its peoples. Surrounding Judah were heathen nations that sought its downfall. Asaph prayed that God would blow these nations away like chaff before the wind until, in their defeat, they recognized that the Lord is above all rulers of the earth. Sometimes we must be dragged in the dust before we will look up and see the Lord; we must be defeated before we can have the ultimate victory. Wouldn't it be better to seek the Lord in times of prosperity than to wait until his judgment is upon us?**

[8] Assyria has joined them, too,
and is allied with the descendants of Lot. *Interlude*
[9] Do to them as you did to the Midianites
or as you did to Sisera and Jabin at the Kishon River.
[10] They were destroyed at Endor,
and their decaying corpses fertilized the soil.
[11] Let their mighty nobles die as Oreb and Zeeb did.
Let all their princes die like Zebah and Zalmunna,
[12] for they said, "Let us seize for our own use
these pasturelands of God!"
[13] O my God, blow them away like whirling dust,
like chaff before the wind!
[14] As a fire roars through a forest
and as a flame sets mountains ablaze,
[15] chase them with your fierce storms;
terrify them with your tempests.
[16] Utterly disgrace them
until they submit to your name, O LORD.
[17] Let them be ashamed and terrified forever.
Make them failures in everything they do,
[18] until they learn that you alone are called the LORD,
that you alone are the Most High, supreme over all the earth.

## PSALM 84 *For the choir director: A psalm of the descendants of Korah, to be accompanied by a stringed instrument.**

[1] How lovely is your dwelling place,
O LORD Almighty.
[2] I long, yes, I faint with longing
to enter the courts of the LORD.
With my whole being, body and soul,
I will shout joyfully to the living God.
[3] Even the sparrow finds a home there,
and the swallow builds her nest
and raises her young—
at a place near your altar,
O LORD Almighty, my King and my God!
[4] How happy are those who can live in your house,
always singing your praises. *Interlude*
[5] Happy are those who are strong in the LORD,
who set their minds on a pilgrimage to Jerusalem.

6 When they walk through the Valley of Weeping,*
it will become a place of refreshing springs,
where pools of blessing collect after the rains!
7 They will continue to grow stronger,
and each of them will appear before God in
Jerusalem.*
8 O LORD God Almighty, hear my prayer.
Listen, O God of Israel.* *Interlude*
9 O God, look with favor upon the king, our
protector!
Have mercy on the one you have anointed.

10 A single day in your courts
is better than a thousand anywhere else!
I would rather be a gatekeeper in the house of
my God
than live the good life in the homes of the
wicked.
11 For the LORD God is our light and protector.
He gives us grace and glory.
No good thing will the LORD withhold
from those who do what is right.
12 O LORD Almighty,
happy are those who trust in you.

## PSALM 85 *For the choir director: A psalm of the descendants of Korah.*

1 LORD, you have poured out amazing blessings on
your land!
You have restored the fortunes of Israel.*
2 You have forgiven the guilt of your people—
yes, you have covered all their sins. *Interlude*
3 You have withdrawn your fury.
You have ended your blazing anger.
4 Now turn to us again, O God of our salvation.
Put aside your anger against us.
5 Will you be angry with us always?
Will you prolong your wrath to distant
generations?
6 Won't you revive us again,
so your people can rejoice in you?
7 Show us your unfailing love, O LORD,
and grant us your salvation.
8 I listen carefully to what God the LORD is saying,
for he speaks peace to his people, his faithful
ones.
But let them not return to their foolish ways.
9 Surely his salvation is near to those who honor
him;
our land will be filled with his glory.

10 Unfailing love and truth have met together.
Righteousness and peace have kissed!
11 Truth springs up from the earth,
and righteousness smiles down from heaven.
12 Yes, the LORD pours down his blessings.
Our land will yield its bountiful crops.
13 Righteousness goes as a herald before him,
preparing the way for his steps.

## PSALM 86 *A prayer of David.*

1 Bend down, O LORD, and hear my prayer;
answer me, for I need your help.
2 Protect me, for I am devoted to you.
Save me, for I serve you and trust you.
You are my God.
3 Be merciful, O Lord,
for I am calling on you constantly.
4 Give me happiness, O Lord,
for my life depends on you.
5 O Lord, you are so good, so ready to forgive,
so full of unfailing love for all who ask your
aid.
6 Listen closely to my prayer, O LORD;
hear my urgent cry.
7 I will call to you whenever trouble strikes,
and you will answer me.
8 Nowhere among the pagan gods is there a god
like you, O Lord.
There are no other miracles like yours.
9 All the nations—and you made each one—
will come and bow before you, Lord;
they will praise your great and holy name.
10 For you are great and perform great miracles.
You alone are God.
11 Teach me your ways, O LORD,
that I may live according to your truth!
Grant me purity of heart,
that I may honor you.
12 With all my heart I will praise you, O Lord my
God.
I will give glory to your name forever,

### WHOLEHEARTED ● ● • • •

86:11-12 **Praising God with all our heart means appreciating him and honoring him in all areas of life. We need to show our loyalty to him in every part of our life, not just in going to church. If we praise God with all our heart, then our work, relationships, use of money, and desires will be in keeping with his will.**

13 for your love for me is very great.
You have rescued me from the depths of
death*!
14 O God, insolent people rise up against me;
violent people are trying to kill me.
And you mean nothing to them.
15 But you, O Lord, are a merciful and gracious
God,
slow to get angry,
full of unfailing love and truth.
16 Look down and have mercy on me.
Give strength to your servant;
yes, save me, for I am your servant.
17 Send me a sign of your favor.
Then those who hate me will be put to
shame,
for you, O LORD, help and comfort me.

84:6 Hebrew *valley of Baca.* 84:7 Hebrew *Zion.* 84:8 Hebrew *of Jacob.* 85:1 Hebrew *of Jacob.* 86:13 Hebrew *of Sheol.*

PSALM **87** *A psalm of the descendants of Korah. A song.*

[1] On the holy mountain stands the city founded
by the LORD.
[2] He loves the city of Jerusalem
more than any other city in Israel.*
[3] O city of God,
what glorious things are said of you! *Interlude*
[4] I will record Egypt* and Babylon among those
who know me—
also Philistia and Tyre, and even distant
Ethiopia.*
They have all become citizens of Jerusalem!
[5] And it will be said of Jerusalem,*
"Everyone has become a citizen here."
And the Most High will personally bless this city.
[6] When the LORD registers the nations,
he will say, "This one has become a citizen
of Jerusalem." *Interlude*
[7] At all the festivals, the people will sing,
"The source of my life is in Jerusalem!"

PSALM **88** *For the choir director: A psalm of the descendants of Korah, to be sung to the tune "The Suffering of Affliction." A psalm of Heman the Ezrahite. A song.*

[1] O LORD, God of my salvation,
I have cried out to you day and night.
[2] Now hear my prayer;
listen to my cry.
[3] For my life is full of troubles,
and death draws near.
[4] I have been dismissed as one who is dead,
like a strong man with no strength left.
[5] They have abandoned me to death,
and I am as good as dead.
I am forgotten,
cut off from your care.
[6] You have thrust me down to the lowest pit,
into the darkest depths.
[7] Your anger lies heavy on me;
wave after wave engulfs me. *Interlude*
[8] You have caused my friends to loathe me;
you have sent them all away.
I am in a trap with no way of escape.
[9] My eyes are blinded by my tears.
Each day I beg for your help, O LORD;
I lift my pleading hands to you for mercy.
[10] Of what use to the dead are your miracles?
Do the dead get up and praise you? *Interlude*
[11] Can those in the grave declare your unfailing love?
In the place of destruction, can they proclaim
your faithfulness?
[12] Can the darkness speak of your miracles?
Can anyone in the land of forgetfulness talk
about your righteousness?
[13] O LORD, I cry out to you.
I will keep on pleading day by day.
[14] O LORD, why do you reject me?
Why do you turn your face away from me?
[15] I have been sickly and close to death since my
youth.
I stand helpless and desperate before your
terrors.
[16] Your fierce anger has overwhelmed me.
Your terrors have cut me off.
[17] They swirl around me like floodwaters all day
long.
They have encircled me completely.
[18] You have taken away my companions and loved
ones;
only darkness remains.

PSALM **89** *A psalm of Ethan the Ezrahite.*

[1] I will sing of the tender mercies of the LORD
forever!
Young and old will hear of your faithfulness.
[2] Your unfailing love will last forever.
Your faithfulness is as enduring as the heavens.
[3] The LORD said, "I have made a solemn
agreement with David, my chosen servant.
I have sworn this oath to him:
[4] 'I will establish your descendants as kings
forever;
they will sit on your throne from now until
eternity.'" *Interlude*
[5] All heaven will praise your miracles, LORD;
myriads of angels will praise you for your
faithfulness.
[6] For who in all of heaven can compare with the
LORD?
What mightiest angel is anything like the
LORD?
[7] The highest angelic powers stand in awe of God.
He is far more awesome than those who
surround his throne.
[8] O LORD God Almighty!
Where is there anyone as mighty as you,
LORD?
Faithfulness is your very character.
[9] You are the one who rules the oceans.
When their waves rise in fearful storms, you
subdue them.

**AMBASSADOR ● ● • • •**

89:14-15 **God's throne is pictured with a foundation of righteousness and justice, and he is attended by mercy and truth. These describe fundamental aspects of the way God deals with people. As God's ambassadors, we should deal with people similarly. Make sure your actions flow out of righteousness, justice, love, and truth because any unfair, unloving, or dishonest action cannot come from God.**

87:2 Hebrew *He loves the gates of Zion more than all the dwellings of Jacob.* 87:4a Hebrew *Rahab,* the name of a mythical sea monster that represents chaos in ancient literature. The name is used here as a poetic name for Egypt. 87:4b Hebrew *Cush.* 87:5 Hebrew *Zion.*

[10] You are the one who crushed the great sea
monster.*
You scattered your enemies with your mighty
arm.
[11] The heavens are yours, and the earth is yours;
everything in the world is yours—you created
it all.
[12] You created north and south.
Mount Tabor and Mount Hermon praise your
name.
[13] Powerful is your arm!
Strong is your hand!
Your right hand is lifted high in glorious
strength.
[14] Your throne is founded on two strong
pillars—righteousness and justice.
Unfailing love and truth walk before you as
attendants.
[15] Happy are those who hear the joyful call to
worship,
for they will walk in the light of your presence,
LORD.
[16] They rejoice all day long in your wonderful
reputation.
They exult in your righteousness.
[17] You are their glorious strength.
Our power is based on your favor.
[18] Yes, our protection comes from the LORD,
and he, the Holy One of Israel, has given us
our king.

[19] You once spoke in a vision to your prophet and
said,
"I have given help to a warrior.
I have selected him from the common people
to be king.
[20] I have found my servant David.
I have anointed him with my holy oil.
[21] I will steady him,
and I will make him strong.
[22] His enemies will not get the best of him,
nor will the wicked overpower him.
[23] I will beat down his adversaries before him
and destroy those who hate him.
[24] My faithfulness and unfailing love will be with
him,
and he will rise to power because of me.
[25] I will extend his rule from the Mediterranean Sea
in the west
to the Tigris and Euphrates rivers in the east.*
[26] And he will say to me, 'You are my Father,
my God, and the Rock of my salvation.'
[27] I will make him my firstborn son,
the mightiest king on earth.
[28] I will love him and be kind to him forever;
my covenant with him will never end.
[29] I will preserve an heir for him;
his throne will be as endless as the days of
heaven.
[30] But if his sons forsake my law
and fail to walk in my ways,
[31] if they do not obey my decrees
and fail to keep my commands,
[32] then I will punish their sin with the rod,
and their disobedience with beating.

**Does God get tired of hearing about our troubles? I get frustrated when I struggle with the same problems over and over.**

Do you know someone who complains a lot? Perhaps you have a little brother or sister, a friend, or an acquaintance at school who is always complaining. Complainers aren't much fun to be around.

Complaining means that we aren't happy with what is going on around us and we think that by telling others we want something to change, it will happen. It also means we want attention. Complaining shines the spotlight on us for a while, and people give us attention. Sometimes, that's all we really wanted in the first place!

If you have been reading through Psalms, you can see that the psalmist seems to complain a lot! He is always in some sort of trouble, and he always wants God to get him out of it (see Psalm 88, for example). Sound familiar?

The motivation behind our complaining is the key issue. When surrounded by enemies, David cried to God for protection. He had nowhere else to turn. Although this may seem like complaining, it actually is a very honest way to pray. God never gets tired of hearing us and coming to our rescue if we need his help.

But sometimes we complain or ask God for help because we have made wrong choices that have gotten us into trouble. Our natural response is to ask God to get us out of it. Although God always listens to us, he knows that the solution is not found in his coming to the rescue.

Instead, we must ask for forgiveness and then change the behavior that caused the problem in the first place. Some troubles are best solved by being humble and admitting we are wrong.

But if trouble comes from people or situations that are beyond our control, God is not only quick to hear, but also quick to answer. Either he will provide the internal resources necessary to handle the problem ("God's peace, which is far more wonderful than the human mind can understand" [Philippians 4:7]) or he will provide the way of escape. "Remember that the temptations that come into your life are no different from what others experience. And God is faithful. He will keep the temptation from becoming so strong that you can't stand up against it. When you are tempted, he will show you a way out so that you will not give in to it" (1 Corinthians 10:13).

**89:10** Hebrew *Rahab,* the name of a mythical sea monster that represents chaos in ancient literature. **89:25** Hebrew *I will set his hand on the sea, his right hand on the rivers.*

[33] But I will never stop loving him,
nor let my promise to him fail.
[34] No, I will not break my covenant;
I will not take back a single word I said.
[35] I have sworn an oath to David,
and in my holiness I cannot lie:
[36] His dynasty will go on forever;
his throne is as secure as the sun,
[37] as eternal as the moon,
my faithful witness in the sky!" *Interlude*
[38] But now you have rejected him.
Why are you so angry with the one you chose as king?
[39] You have renounced your covenant with him,
for you have thrown his crown in the dust.
[40] You have broken down the walls protecting him
and laid in ruins every fort defending him.
[41] Everyone who comes along has robbed him
while his neighbors mock.
[42] You have strengthened his enemies against him
and made them all rejoice.
[43] You have made his sword useless
and have refused to help him in battle.
[44] You have ended his splendor
and overturned his throne.
[45] You have made him old before his time
and publicly disgraced him. *Interlude*
[46] O LORD, how long will this go on?
Will you hide yourself forever?
How long will your anger burn like fire?
[47] Remember how short my life is,
how empty and futile this human existence!
[48] No one can live forever; all will die.
No one can escape the power of the grave. *Interlude*
[49] Lord, where is your unfailing love?
You promised it to David with a faithful pledge.
[50] Consider, Lord, how your servants are disgraced!
I carry in my heart the insults of so many people.
[51] Your enemies have mocked me, O LORD;
they mock the one you anointed as king.
[52] Blessed be the LORD forever!
Amen and amen!

## Book Four (Psalms 90–106)

## PSALM 90

*A prayer of Moses, the man of God.*

[1] Lord, through all the generations
you have been our home!
[2] Before the mountains were created,
before you made the earth and the world,
you are God, without beginning or end.

[3] You turn people back to dust, saying,
"Return to dust!"
[4] For you, a thousand years are as yesterday!
They are like a few hours!
[5] You sweep people away like dreams that disappear
or like grass that springs up in the morning.
[6] In the morning it blooms and flourishes,
but by evening it is dry and withered.
[7] We wither beneath your anger;
we are overwhelmed by your fury.
[8] You spread out our sins before you—
our secret sins—and you see them all.
[9] We live our lives beneath your wrath.
We end our lives with a groan.

[10] Seventy years are given to us!
Some may even reach eighty.
But even the best of these years are filled with pain and trouble;
soon they disappear, and we are gone.
[11] Who can comprehend the power of your anger?
Your wrath is as awesome as the fear you deserve.
[12] Teach us to make the most of our time,
so that we may grow in wisdom.

[13] O LORD, come back to us!
How long will you delay?
Take pity on your servants!
[14] Satisfy us in the morning with your unfailing love,
so we may sing for joy to the end of our lives.
[15] Give us gladness in proportion to our former misery!
Replace the evil years with good.
[16] Let us see your miracles again;
let our children see your glory at work.
[17] And may the Lord our God show us his approval
and make our efforts successful.
Yes, make our efforts successful!

### THE PROTECTOR ● ● • • •

**91:5-6 God is a refuge, a shelter when we are afraid. The writer's faith in God as Protector would carry him through all the dangers and fears of life. This should be a picture of our trust—trading all our fears for faith in him, no matter what kind of fear it may be.**

## PSALM 91

[1] Those who live in the shelter of the Most High
will find rest in the shadow of the Almighty.
[2] This I declare of the LORD:
He alone is my refuge, my place of safety;
he is my God, and I am trusting him.
[3] For he will rescue you from every trap
and protect you from the fatal plague.
[4] He will shield you with his wings.
He will shelter you with his feathers.
His faithful promises are your armor and protection.
[5] Do not be afraid of the terrors of the night,
nor fear the dangers of the day,
[6] nor dread the plague that stalks in darkness,
nor the disaster that strikes at midday.

[7]Though a thousand fall at your side,
though ten thousand are dying around you,
these evils will not touch you.
[8]But you will see it with your eyes;
you will see how the wicked are punished.
[9]If you make the LORD your refuge,
if you make the Most High your shelter,
[10]no evil will conquer you;
no plague will come near your dwelling.
[11]For he orders his angels
to protect you wherever you go.
[12]They will hold you with their hands
to keep you from striking your foot on a stone.
[13]You will trample down lions and poisonous snakes;
you will crush fierce lions and serpents under your feet!
[14]The LORD says, "I will rescue those who love me.
I will protect those who trust in my name.
[15]When they call on me, I will answer;
I will be with them in trouble.
I will rescue them and honor them.
[16]I will satisfy them with a long life
and give them my salvation."

## PSALM 92 *A psalm to be sung on the LORD's Day. A song.*

[1]It is good to give thanks to the LORD,
to sing praises to the Most High.
[2]It is good to proclaim your unfailing love in the morning,
your faithfulness in the evening,
[3]accompanied by the harp and lute
and the harmony of the lyre.
[4]You thrill me, LORD, with all you have done for me!
I sing for joy because of what you have done.
[5]O LORD, what great miracles you do!
And how deep are your thoughts.
[6]Only an ignorant person would not know this!
Only a fool would not understand it.
[7]Although the wicked flourish like weeds,
and evildoers blossom with success,
there is only eternal destruction ahead of them.
[8]But you are exalted in the heavens.
You, O LORD, continue forever.
[9]Your enemies, LORD, will surely perish;
all evildoers will be scattered.

[10]But you have made me as strong as a wild bull.
How refreshed I am by your power!
[11]With my own eyes I have seen the downfall of my enemies;
with my own ears I have heard the defeat of my wicked opponents.
[12]But the godly will flourish like palm trees
and grow strong like the cedars of Lebanon.

**ELDERLY ● ● ● • •**

92:14 **Honoring God is not limited to young people who are still blessed with physical strength and vitality. Even in old age, devoted believers can produce spiritual fruit. There are many faithful older people who have much to share and teach from a lifetime of living with God. Seek out an elderly friend or relative to tell you about life experiences with the Lord and challenge you to new heights of spiritual living.**

[13]For they are transplanted into the LORD's own house.
They flourish in the courts of our God.
[14]Even in old age they will still produce fruit;
they will remain vital and green.
[15]They will declare, "The LORD is just!
He is my rock!
There is nothing but goodness in him!"

## PSALM 93

[1]The LORD is king! He is robed in majesty.
Indeed, the LORD is robed in majesty and armed with strength.
The world is firmly established;
it cannot be shaken.

[2]Your throne, O LORD, has been established from time immemorial.
You yourself are from the everlasting past.
[3]The mighty oceans have roared, O LORD.
The mighty oceans roar like thunder;
the mighty oceans roar as they pound the shore.
[4]But mightier than the violent raging of the seas,
mightier than the breakers on the shore—
the LORD above is mightier than these!
[5]Your royal decrees cannot be changed.
The nature of your reign, O LORD, is holiness forever.

## PSALM 94

[1]O LORD, the God to whom vengeance belongs,
O God of vengeance, let your glorious justice be seen!
[2]Arise, O judge of the earth.
Sentence the proud to the penalties they deserve.
[3]How long, O LORD?
How long will the wicked be allowed to gloat?
[4]Hear their arrogance!
How these evildoers boast!
[5]They oppress your people, LORD,
hurting those you love.
[6]They kill widows and foreigners
and murder orphans.
[7]"The LORD isn't looking," they say,
"and besides, the God of Israel* doesn't care."
[8]Think again, you fools!
When will you finally catch on?

94:7 Hebrew *of Jacob.*

## HATE EVIL ● ● • • •

**97:10 A sincere desire to please God will result in an alignment of your desires with God's desires. You will love what God loves and hate what God hates. If you do not despise the actions of people who take advantage of others, if you admire people who look out only for themselves, or if you envy those who get ahead using any means to accomplish their ends, then your primary desire in life is not to please God. Learn to love God's ways and hate evil in every form—not only the obvious sins, but the socially acceptable ones as well.**

9 Is the one who made your ears deaf?
Is the one who formed your eyes blind?
10 He punishes the nations—won't he also
punish you?
He knows everything—doesn't he also know
what you are doing?
11 The LORD knows people's thoughts,
that they are worthless!

12 Happy are those whom you discipline, LORD,
and those whom you teach from your law.
13 You give them relief from troubled times
until a pit is dug for the wicked.
14 The LORD will not reject his people;
he will not abandon his own special
possession.
15 Judgment will come again for the righteous,
and those who are upright will have a
reward.

16 Who will protect me from the wicked?
Who will stand up for me against evildoers?
17 Unless the LORD had helped me,
I would soon have died.
18 I cried out, "I'm slipping!"
and your unfailing love, O LORD, supported
me.
19 When doubts filled my mind,
your comfort gave me renewed hope and
cheer.

20 Can unjust leaders claim that God is on their
side—
leaders who permit injustice by their laws?
21 They attack the righteous
and condemn the innocent to death.
22 But the LORD is my fortress;
my God is a mighty rock where I can hide.
23 God will make the sins of evil people fall back
upon them.
He will destroy them for their sins.
The LORD our God will destroy them.

## PSALM 95

1 Come, let us sing to the LORD!
Let us give a joyous shout to the rock of our
salvation!
2 Let us come before him with thanksgiving.
Let us sing him psalms of praise.
3 For the LORD is a great God,
the great King above all gods.
4 He owns the depths of the earth,
and even the mightiest mountains are his.
5 The sea belongs to him, for he made it.
His hands formed the dry land, too.

6 Come, let us worship and bow down.
Let us kneel before the LORD our maker,
7 for he is our God.
We are the people he watches over,
the sheep under his care.

Oh, that you would listen to his voice today!
8 The LORD says, "Don't harden your hearts as
Israel did at Meribah,
as they did at Massah in the wilderness.
9 For there your ancestors tried my patience;
they courted my wrath though they had seen
my many miracles.
10 For forty years I was angry with them, and
I said,
'They are a people whose hearts turn away
from me.
They refuse to do what I tell them.'
11 So in my anger I made a vow:
'They will never enter my place of rest.'"

## PSALM 96

1 Sing a new song to the LORD!
Let the whole earth sing to the LORD!
2 Sing to the LORD; bless his name.
Each day proclaim the good news that he
saves.
3 Publish his glorious deeds among the nations.
Tell everyone about the amazing things he
does.
4 Great is the LORD! He is most worthy of praise!
He is to be revered above all the gods.
5 The gods of other nations are merely idols,
but the LORD made the heavens!
6 Honor and majesty surround him;
strength and beauty are in his sanctuary.

7 O nations of the world, recognize the LORD;
recognize that the LORD is glorious and
strong.
8 Give to the LORD the glory he deserves!
Bring your offering and come to worship
him.
9 Worship the LORD in all his holy splendor.
Let all the earth tremble before him.
10 Tell all the nations that the LORD is king.
The world is firmly established and cannot
be shaken.
He will judge all peoples fairly.

11 Let the heavens be glad, and let the earth rejoice!
Let the sea and everything in it shout his
praise!
12 Let the fields and their crops burst forth with
joy!
Let the trees of the forest rustle with praise
13 before the LORD!

For the LORD is coming!
He is coming to judge the earth.
He will judge the world with righteousness
and all the nations with his truth.

## PSALM 97

1 The LORD is king! Let the earth rejoice!
Let the farthest islands be glad.
2 Clouds and darkness surround him.
Righteousness and justice are the foundation of his throne.
3 Fire goes forth before him
and burns up all his foes.
4 His lightning flashes out across the world.
The earth sees and trembles.
5 The mountains melt like wax before the LORD,
before the Lord of all the earth.
6 The heavens declare his righteousness;
every nation sees his glory.
7 Those who worship idols are disgraced—
all who brag about their worthless gods—
for every god must bow to him.
8 Jerusalem* has heard and rejoiced,
and all the cities of Judah are glad
because of your justice, LORD!
9 For you, O LORD, are most high over all the earth;
you are exalted far above all gods.

10 You who love the LORD, hate evil!
He protects the lives of his godly people
and rescues them from the power of the wicked.
11 Light shines on the godly,
and joy on those who do right.
12 May all who are godly be happy in the LORD
and praise his holy name!

## PSALM 98 *A psalm.*

1 Sing a new song to the LORD,
for he has done wonderful deeds.
He has won a mighty victory
by his power and holiness.
2 The LORD has announced his victory
and has revealed his righteousness to every nation!
3 He has remembered his promise to love and be faithful to Israel.
The whole earth has seen the salvation of our God.

4 Shout to the LORD, all the earth;
break out in praise and sing for joy!
5 Sing your praise to the LORD with the harp,
with the harp and melodious song,
6 with trumpets and the sound of the ram's horn.
Make a joyful symphony before the LORD, the King!
7 Let the sea and everything in it shout his praise!
Let the earth and all living things join in.
8 Let the rivers clap their hands in glee!
Let the hills sing out their songs of joy
9 before the LORD.

For the LORD is coming to judge the earth.
He will judge the world with justice,
and the nations with fairness.

## PSALM 99

1 The LORD is king!
Let the nations tremble!
He sits on his throne between the cherubim.
Let the whole earth quake!
2 The LORD sits in majesty in Jerusalem,*
supreme above all the nations.
3 Let them praise your great and awesome name.
Your name is holy!
4 Mighty king, lover of justice,
you have established fairness.
You have acted with justice
and righteousness throughout Israel.*
5 Exalt the LORD our God!
Bow low before his feet, for he is holy!

6 Moses and Aaron were among his priests;
Samuel also called on his name.
They cried to the LORD for help,
and he answered them.
7 He spoke to them from the pillar of cloud,
and they followed the decrees and principles he gave them.
8 O LORD our God, you answered them.
You were a forgiving God,
but you punished them when they went wrong.
9 Exalt the LORD our God
and worship at his holy mountain in Jerusalem,
for the LORD our God is holy!

### FAMILY NAME • • • • •

**99:3 Everyone, even kings and rulers, should praise God's great and holy name because his name symbolizes his nature, his personage, and his reputation. But the name of God is used so often in vulgar conversation that we have lost sight of its holiness. How easy it is to treat God lightly in everyday life! If you claim him as your Father, live in a way that is worthy of the family name. Honor God's name by both your *words* and your *life*.**

## PSALM 100 *A psalm of thanksgiving.*

1 Shout with joy to the LORD, O earth!
2 Worship the LORD with gladness.
Come before him, singing with joy.
3 Acknowledge that the LORD is God!
He made us, and we are his.
We are his people, the sheep of his pasture.

97:8 Hebrew *Zion.* 99:2 Hebrew *Zion.* 99:4 Hebrew *Jacob.*

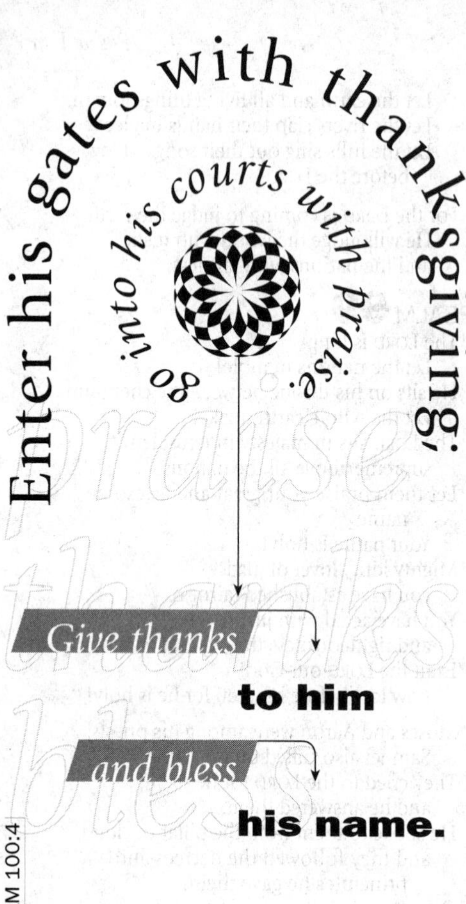
Enter his gates with thanksgiving;
go into his courts with praise.
Give thanks
to him
and bless
his name.
PSALM 100:4

[4] Enter his gates with thanksgiving;
go into his courts with praise.
Give thanks to him and bless his name.
[5] For the LORD is good.
His unfailing love continues forever,
and his faithfulness continues to each generation.

## PSALM 101 *A psalm of David.*

[1] I will sing of your love and justice.
I will praise you, LORD, with songs.
[2] I will be careful to live a blameless life—
when will you come to my aid?
I will lead a life of integrity
in my own home.
[3] I will refuse to look at
anything vile and vulgar.
I hate all crooked dealings;
I will have nothing to do with them.
[4] I will reject perverse ideas
and stay away from every evil.
[5] I will not tolerate people who slander their neighbors.
I will not endure conceit and pride.
[6] I will keep a protective eye on the godly,
so they may dwell with me in safety.
Only those who are above reproach
will be allowed to serve me.
[7] I will not allow deceivers to serve me,
and liars will not be allowed to enter my presence.
[8] My daily task will be to ferret out criminals
and free the city of the LORD from their grip.

## PSALM 102 *A prayer of one overwhelmed with trouble, pouring out problems before the LORD.*

[1] LORD, hear my prayer!
Listen to my plea!
[2] Don't turn away from me
in my time of distress.
Bend down your ear
and answer me quickly when I call to you,
[3] for my days disappear like smoke,
and my bones burn like red-hot coals.
[4] My heart is sick, withered like grass,
and I have lost my appetite.
[5] Because of my groaning,
I am reduced to skin and bones.
[6] I am like an owl in the desert,
like a lonely owl in a far-off wilderness.
[7] I lie awake,
lonely as a solitary bird on the roof.
[8] My enemies taunt me day after day.
They mock and curse me.
[9] I eat ashes instead of my food.
My tears run down into my drink
[10] because of your anger and wrath.
For you have picked me up and thrown me out.
[11] My life passes as swiftly as the evening shadows.
I am withering like grass.
[12] But you, O LORD, will rule forever.
Your fame will endure to every generation.
[13] You will arise and have mercy on Jerusalem*—
and now is the time to pity her,
now is the time you promised to help.
[14] For your people love every stone in her walls
and show favor even to the dust in her streets.
[15] And the nations will tremble before the LORD.
The kings of the earth will tremble before his glory.
[16] For the LORD will rebuild Jerusalem.
He will appear in his glory.
[17] He will listen to the prayers of the destitute.
He will not reject their pleas.
[18] Let this be recorded for future generations,
so that a nation yet to be created will praise the LORD.
[19] Tell them the LORD looked down
from his heavenly sanctuary.
He looked to the earth from heaven

**102:13** Hebrew *Zion;* also in 102:16.

20 to hear the groans of the prisoners,
to release those condemned to die.
21 And so the LORD's fame will be celebrated in Zion,
his praises in Jerusalem,
22 when multitudes gather together
and kingdoms come to worship the LORD.

23 He has cut me down in midlife,
shortening my days.
24 But I cried to him, "My God, who lives forever,
don't take my life while I am still so young!
25 In ages past you laid the foundation of the earth,
and the heavens are the work of your hands.
26 Even they will perish, but you remain forever;
they will wear out like old clothing.
You will change them like a garment,
and they will fade away.
27 But you are always the same;
your years never end.
28 The children of your people
will live in security.
Their children's children
will thrive in your presence."

## PSALM 103 *A psalm of David.*

1 Praise the LORD, I tell myself;
with my whole heart, I will praise his holy name.
2 Praise the LORD, I tell myself,
and never forget the good things he does for me.
3 He forgives all my sins
and heals all my diseases.
4 He ransoms me from death
and surrounds me with love and tender mercies.
5 He fills my life with good things.
My youth is renewed like the eagle's!
6 The LORD gives righteousness
and justice to all who are treated unfairly.
7 He revealed his character to Moses
and his deeds to the people of Israel.
8 The LORD is merciful and gracious;
he is slow to get angry and full of unfailing love.
9 He will not constantly accuse us,
nor remain angry forever.
10 He has not punished us for all our sins,
nor does he deal with us as we deserve.
11 For his unfailing love toward those who fear him
is as great as the height of the heavens above the earth.
12 He has removed our rebellious acts
as far away from us as the east is from the west.
13 The LORD is like a father to his children,
tender and compassionate to those who fear him.
14 For he understands how weak we are;
he knows we are only dust.
15 Our days on earth are like grass;
like wildflowers, we bloom and die.
16 The wind blows, and we are gone—
as though we had never been here.
17 But the love of the LORD remains forever
with those who fear him.
His salvation extends to the children's children
18 of those who are faithful to his covenant,
of those who obey his commandments!

19 The LORD has made the heavens his throne;
from there he rules over everything.
20 Praise the LORD, you angels of his,
you mighty creatures who carry out his plans,
listening for each of his commands.
21 Yes, praise the LORD, you armies of angels
who serve him and do his will!
22 Praise the LORD, everything he has created,
everywhere in his kingdom.
As for me—I, too, will praise the LORD.

### PLENTY ● ● • • •

**103:3-18 David's praise focused on God's glorious acts. It is easy to complain about life, but David's list gives us plenty for which to praise God—his love, forgiveness, salvation, kindness, mercy, justice, patience, tenderness—we receive all of these without deserving any of them. No matter how difficult your life's journey, you can always count your blessings—past, present, and future. When you feel as though you have nothing for which to praise God, read David's list.**

## PSALM 104

1 Praise the LORD, I tell myself;
O LORD my God, how great you are!
You are robed with honor and with majesty;
2 you are dressed in a robe of light.
You stretch out the starry curtain of the heavens;
3 you lay out the rafters of your home in the rain clouds.
You make the clouds your chariots;
you ride upon the wings of the wind.
4 The winds are your messengers;
flames of fire are your servants.
5 You placed the world on its foundation
so it would never be moved.
6 You clothed the earth with floods of water,
water that covered even the mountains.
7 At the sound of your rebuke, the water fled;
at the sound of your thunder, it fled away.
8 Mountains rose and valleys sank
to the levels you decreed.
9 Then you set a firm boundary for the seas,
so they would never again cover the earth.

10 You make the springs pour water into ravines,
so streams gush down from the mountains.
11 They provide water for all the animals,
and the wild donkeys quench their thirst.

[12]The birds nest beside the streams
and sing among the branches of the trees.
[13]You send rain on the mountains from your heavenly home,
and you fill the earth with the fruit of your labor.
[14]You cause grass to grow for the cattle.
You cause plants to grow for people to use.
You allow them to produce food from the earth—
[15] wine to make them glad,
olive oil as lotion for their skin,
and bread to give them strength.
[16]The trees of the LORD are well cared for—
the cedars of Lebanon that he planted.
[17]There the birds make their nests,
and the storks make their homes in the firs.
[18]High in the mountains are pastures for the wild goats,
and the rocks form a refuge for rock badgers.*
[19]You made the moon to mark the seasons
and the sun that knows when to set.
[20]You send the darkness, and it becomes night,
when all the forest animals prowl about.
[21]Then the young lions roar for their food,
but they are dependent on God.
[22]At dawn they slink back
into their dens to rest.
[23]Then people go off to their work;
they labor until the evening shadows fall again.

## CREATION ● ● • • •

**104:24 Creation is filled with stunning variety, revealing the rich creativity, goodness, and wisdom of our loving God. As you observe your natural surroundings, thank God for his creativity. Take a fresh look at people, seeing each one as his unique creation, each with his or her own special talents, abilities, and gifts.**

[24]O LORD, what a variety of things you have made!
In wisdom you have made them all.
The earth is full of your creatures.
[25]Here is the ocean, vast and wide,
teeming with life of every kind,
both great and small.
[26]See the ships sailing along,
and Leviathan, which you made to play in the sea.
[27]Every one of these depends on you
to give them their food as they need it.
[28]When you supply it, they gather it.
You open your hand to feed them, and they are satisfied.
[29]But if you turn away from them, they panic.
When you take away their breath, they die
and turn again to dust.
[30]When you send your Spirit, new life is born
to replenish all the living of the earth.
[31]May the glory of the LORD last forever!
The LORD rejoices in all he has made!
[32]The earth trembles at his glance;
the mountains burst into flame at his touch.
[33]I will sing to the LORD as long as I live.
I will praise my God to my last breath!
[34]May he be pleased by all these thoughts about him,
for I rejoice in the LORD.
[35]Let all sinners vanish from the face of the earth;
let the wicked disappear forever.
As for me—I will praise the LORD!

Praise the LORD!

## PSALM 105

[1]Give thanks to the LORD and proclaim his greatness.
Let the whole world know what he has done.
[2]Sing to him; yes, sing his praises.
Tell everyone about his miracles.
[3]Exult in his holy name;
O worshipers of the LORD, rejoice!
[4]Search for the LORD and for his strength,
and keep on searching.
[5]Think of the wonderful works he has done,
the miracles and the judgments he handed down,
[6]O children of Abraham, God's servant,
O descendants of Jacob, God's chosen one.
[7]He is the LORD our God.
His rule is seen throughout the land.
[8]He always stands by his covenant—
the commitment he made to a thousand generations.
[9]This is the covenant he made with Abraham
and the oath he swore to Isaac.
[10]He confirmed it to Jacob as a decree,
to the people of Israel as a never-ending treaty:
[11]"I will give you the land of Canaan
as your special possession."
[12]He said this when they were few in number,
a tiny group of strangers in Canaan.
[13]They wandered back and forth between nations,
from one kingdom to another.
[14]Yet he did not let anyone oppress them.
He warned kings on their behalf:
[15]"Do not touch these people I have chosen,
and do not hurt my prophets."
[16]He called for a famine on the land of Canaan,
cutting off its food supply.
[17]Then he sent someone to Egypt ahead of them—
Joseph, who was sold as a slave.
[18]There in prison, they bruised his feet with fetters
and placed his neck in an iron collar.
[19]Until the time came to fulfill his word,
the LORD tested Joseph's character.
[20]Then Pharaoh sent for him and set him free;
the ruler of the nation opened his prison door.
[21]Joseph was put in charge of all the king's household;
he became ruler over all the king's possessions.

104:18 Or *coneys,* or *hyraxes.*

[22] He could instruct the king's aides as he pleased
and teach the king's advisers.
[23] Then Israel arrived in Egypt;
Jacob lived as a foreigner in the land of Ham.
[24] And the LORD multiplied the people of Israel
until they became too mighty for their enemies.
[25] Then he turned the Egyptians against the Israelites,
and they plotted against the LORD's servants.

[26] But the LORD sent Moses his servant,
along with Aaron, whom he had chosen.
[27] They performed miraculous signs among the Egyptians,
and miracles in the land of Ham.
[28] The LORD blanketed Egypt in darkness,
for they had defied his commands to let his people go.
[29] He turned the nation's water into blood,
poisoning all the fish.
[30] Then frogs overran the land;
they were found even in the king's private rooms.
[31] When he spoke, flies descended on the Egyptians,
and gnats swarmed across Egypt.
[32] Instead of rain, he sent murderous hail,
and flashes of lightning overwhelmed the land.
[33] He ruined their grapevines and fig trees
and shattered all the trees.
[34] He spoke, and hordes of locusts came—
locusts beyond number.
[35] They ate up everything green in the land,
destroying all the crops.
[36] Then he killed the oldest child in each Egyptian home,
the pride and joy of each family.

[37] But he brought his people safely out of Egypt,
loaded with silver and gold;
there were no sick or feeble people among them.
[38] Egypt was glad when they were gone,
for the dread of them was great.
[39] The LORD spread out a cloud above them as a covering
and gave them a great fire to light the darkness.
[40] They asked for meat, and he sent them quail;
he gave them manna—bread from heaven.
[41] He opened up a rock, and water gushed out
to form a river through the dry and barren land.
[42] For he remembered his sacred promise
to Abraham his servant.
[43] So he brought his people out of Egypt with joy,
his chosen ones with rejoicing.
[44] He gave his people the lands of pagan nations,
and they harvested crops that others had planted.

### HE IS THERE ● ● ● • •

**105:4 If God seems far away, keep searching for him. God rewards those who sincerely look for him (Hebrews 11:6). Jesus promised, "keep on looking, and you will find" (Matthew 7:7). David suggested a valuable way to search out God—become familiar with the way he has helped his people in the past. The Bible records the history of God's people. In searching its pages we will discover a loving God who is waiting for us to find him.**

[45] All this happened so they would follow his principles
and obey his laws.

Praise the LORD!

## PSALM 106

[1] Praise the LORD!

Give thanks to the LORD, for he is good!
His faithful love endures forever.
[2] Who can list the glorious miracles of the LORD?
Who can ever praise him half enough?
[3] Happy are those who deal justly with others
and always do what is right.

[4] Remember me, too, LORD, when you show favor to your people;
come to me with your salvation.
[5] Let me share in the prosperity of your chosen ones.
Let me rejoice in the joy of your people;
let me praise you with those who are your heritage.

[6] Both we and our ancestors have sinned.
We have done wrong! We have acted wickedly!
[7] Our ancestors in Egypt
were not impressed by the LORD's miracles.
They soon forgot his many acts of kindness to them.
Instead, they rebelled against him at the Red Sea.*
[8] Even so, he saved them—
to defend the honor of his name
and to demonstrate his mighty power.
[9] He commanded the Red Sea* to divide, and a dry path appeared.
He led Israel across the sea bottom that was as dry as a desert.
[10] So he rescued them from their enemies
and redeemed them from their foes.
[11] Then the water returned and covered their enemies;
not one of them survived.
[12] Then at last his people believed his promises.
Then they finally sang his praise.

[13] Yet how quickly they forgot what he had done!
They wouldn't wait for his counsel!
[14] In the wilderness, their desires ran wild,
testing God's patience in that dry land.

**106:7** Hebrew *at the sea, the sea of reeds.* **106:9** Hebrew *sea of reeds;* also in 106:22.

[15] So he gave them what they asked for,
but he sent a plague along with it.
[16] The people in the camp were jealous of Moses
and envious of Aaron, the LORD's holy priest.
[17] Because of this, the earth opened up;
it swallowed Dathan
and buried Abiram and the other rebels.
[18] Fire fell upon their followers;
a flame consumed the wicked.

[19] The people made a calf at Mount Sinai*;
they bowed before an image made of gold.
[20] They traded their glorious God
for a statue of a grass-eating ox!
[21] They forgot God, their savior,
who had done such great things in Egypt—
[22] such wonderful things in that land,
such awesome deeds at the Red Sea.
[23] So he declared he would destroy them.
But Moses, his chosen one, stepped between
the LORD and the people.
He begged him to turn from his anger and not
destroy them.

[24] The people refused to enter the pleasant land,
for they wouldn't believe his promise to care
for them.
[25] Instead, they grumbled in their tents
and refused to obey the LORD.
[26] Therefore, he swore
that he would kill them in the wilderness,
[27] that he would scatter their descendants among
the nations,
exiling them to distant lands.

[28] Then our ancestors joined in the worship of Baal
at Peor;
they even ate sacrifices offered to the dead!
[29] They angered the LORD with all these things,
so a plague broke out among them.
[30] But Phinehas had the courage to step in,
and the plague was stopped.
[31] So he has been regarded as a righteous man
ever since that time.

[32] At Meribah, too, they angered the LORD,
causing Moses serious trouble.
[33] They made Moses angry,*
and he spoke foolishly.

[34] Israel failed to destroy the nations in the land,
as the LORD had told them to.
[35] Instead, they mingled among the pagans
and adopted their evil customs.
[36] They worshiped their idols,
and this led to their downfall.
[37] They even sacrificed their sons
and their daughters to the demons.
[38] They shed innocent blood,
the blood of their sons and daughters.
By sacrificing them to the idols of Canaan,
they polluted the land with murder.

106:19 Hebrew *at Horeb,* another name for Sinai. 106:33 Hebrew *They embittered his spirit.*

## TROUBLES ● ● • • •

106:40-42 **God allowed trouble to come to the Israelites to help them. Our troubles can be helpful because they (1) humble us, (2) pull us from the allurements of the world and drive us back to God, (3) quicken our prayers, (4) allow us to experience more of God's faithfulness, (5) make us more dependent upon God, (6) encourage us to submit to God's purpose for our life, and (7) make us more compassionate to others in trouble.**

[39] They defiled themselves by their evil deeds,
and their love of idols was adultery in the
LORD's sight.

[40] That is why the LORD's anger burned against his
people,
and he abhorred his own special possession.
[41] He handed them over to pagan nations,
and those who hated them ruled over them.
[42] Their enemies crushed them
and brought them under their cruel power.
[43] Again and again he delivered them,
but they continued to rebel against him,
and they were finally destroyed by their sin.
[44] Even so, he pitied them in their distress
and listened to their cries.
[45] He remembered his covenant with them
and relented because of his unfailing love.
[46] He even caused their captors
to treat them with kindness.
[47] O LORD our God, save us!
Gather us back from among the nations,
so we can thank your holy name
and rejoice and praise you.

[48] Blessed be the LORD, the God of Israel,
from everlasting to everlasting!
Let all the people say, "Amen!"
Praise the LORD!

### BOOK FIVE (Psalms 107–150)

## PSALM 107

[1] Give thanks to the LORD, for he is good!
His faithful love endures forever.
[2] Has the LORD redeemed you? Then speak out!
Tell others he has saved you from your
enemies.
[3] For he has gathered the exiles from many
lands,
from east and west, from north and south.

[4] Some wandered in the desert,
lost and homeless.
[5] Hungry and thirsty,
they nearly died.
[6] "LORD, help!" they cried in their trouble,
and he rescued them from their distress.
[7] He led them straight to safety,
to a city where they could live.
[8] Let them praise the LORD for his great love
and for all his wonderful deeds to them.

[9] For he satisfies the thirsty
and fills the hungry with good things.
[10] Some sat in darkness and deepest gloom,
miserable prisoners in chains.
[11] They rebelled against the words of God,
scorning the counsel of the Most High.
[12] That is why he broke them with hard labor;
they fell, and no one helped them rise again.
[13] "LORD, help!" they cried in their trouble,
and he saved them from their distress.
[14] He led them from the darkness and deepest
gloom;
he snapped their chains.
[15] Let them praise the LORD for his great love
and for all his wonderful deeds to them.
[16] For he broke down their prison gates of bronze;
he cut apart their bars of iron.

[17] Some were fools in their rebellion;
they suffered for their sins.
[18] Their appetites were gone,
and death was near.
[19] "LORD, help!" they cried in their trouble,
and he saved them from their distress.
[20] He spoke, and they were healed—
snatched from the door of death.
[21] Let them praise the LORD for his great love
and for all his wonderful deeds to them.
[22] Let them offer sacrifices of thanksgiving
and sing joyfully about his glorious acts.

[23] Some went off in ships,
plying the trade routes of the world.
[24] They, too, observed the LORD's power in action,
his impressive works on the deepest seas.
[25] He spoke, and the winds rose,
stirring up the waves.
[26] Their ships were tossed to the heavens
and sank again to the depths;
the sailors cringed in terror.
[27] They reeled and staggered like drunkards
and were at their wits' end.
[28] "LORD, help!" they cried in their trouble,
and he saved them from their distress.
[29] He calmed the storm to a whisper
and stilled the waves.
[30] What a blessing was that stillness
as he brought them safely into harbor!
[31] Let them praise the LORD for his great love
and for all his wonderful deeds to them.
[32] Let them exalt him publicly before the
congregation
and before the leaders of the nation.

[33] He changes rivers into deserts,
and springs of water into dry land.
[34] He turns the fruitful land into salty wastelands,
because of the wickedness of those who live
there.
[35] But he also turns deserts into pools of water,
the dry land into flowing springs.
[36] He brings the hungry to settle there
and build their cities.
[37] They sow their fields, plant their vineyards,
and harvest their bumper crops.
[38] How he blesses them!
They raise large families there,
and their herds of cattle increase.

[39] When they decrease in number and become
impoverished
through oppression, trouble, and sorrow,
[40] the LORD pours contempt on their princes,
causing them to wander in trackless
wastelands.
[41] But he rescues the poor from their distress
and increases their families like vast flocks of
sheep.
[42] The godly will see these things and be glad,
while the wicked are stricken silent.
[43] Those who are wise will take all this to heart;
they will see in our history the faithful love
of the LORD.

**STRENGTH ● ● • • •**

107:28-32 **Sometimes we feel as though all is hopeless. But trouble can lead us to depend on God as we cry to him for help. When he saves us, we will praise him for the good he has done. Then we understand that God can bring good out of troubles because our afflictions strengthen our faith.**

## PSALM 108 *A psalm of David. A song.*

[1] My heart is confident in you, O God;
no wonder I can sing your praises!
Wake up, my soul!
[2] Wake up, O harp and lyre!
I will waken the dawn with my song.
[3] I will thank you, LORD, in front of all the people.
I will sing your praises among the nations.
[4] For your unfailing love is higher than the
heavens.
Your faithfulness reaches to the clouds.
[5] Be exalted, O God, above the highest heavens.
May your glory shine over all the earth.

[6] Use your strong right arm to save me,
and rescue your beloved people.
[7] God has promised this by his holiness*:
"I will divide up Shechem with joy.
I will measure out the valley of Succoth.
[8] Gilead is mine,
and Manasseh is mine.
Ephraim will produce my warriors,
and Judah will produce my kings.
[9] Moab will become my lowly servant,
and Edom will be my slave.
I will shout in triumph over the Philistines."
[10] But who will bring me into the fortified city?
Who will bring me victory over Edom?

**108:7** Or *in his sanctuary.*

[11] Have you rejected us, O God?
Will you no longer march with our armies?
[12] Oh, please help us against our enemies,
for all human help is useless.
[13] With God's help we will do mighty things,
for he will trample down our foes.

## STAKE A CLAIM ● ● ● • •

**108:13** **Do our prayers end with requests just to make it through stressful situations? David prayed not just for rescue, but for victory. With God's help we can claim more than just survival, we can claim victory! Look for ways God can use your distress as an opportunity to show his mighty power.**

## PSALM 109 *For the choir director: A psalm of David.*

[1] O God, whom I praise,
don't stand silent and aloof
[2] while the wicked slander me
and tell lies about me.
[3] They are all around me with their hateful words,
and they fight against me for no reason.
[4] I love them, but they try to destroy me—
even as I am praying for them!
[5] They return evil for good,
and hatred for my love.

[6] Arrange for an evil person to turn on him.
Send an accuser to bring him to trial.
[7] When his case is called for judgment,
let him be pronounced guilty.
Count his prayers as sins.
[8] Let his years be few;
let his position be given to someone else.
[9] May his children become fatherless,
and may his wife become a widow.
[10] May his children wander as beggars;
may they be evicted from their ruined homes.
[11] May creditors seize his entire estate,
and strangers take all he has earned.
[12] Let no one be kind to him;
let no one pity his fatherless children.
[13] May all his offspring die.
May his family name be blotted out in a single generation.
[14] May the LORD never forget the sins of his ancestors;
may his mother's sins never be erased from the record.
[15] May these sins always remain before the LORD,
but may his name be cut off from human memory.
[16] For he refused all kindness to others;
he persecuted the poor and needy,
and he hounded the brokenhearted to death.
[17] He loved to curse others;
now you curse him.
He never blessed others;
now don't you bless him.
[18] Cursing is as much a part of him as his clothing,
or as the water he drinks,
or the rich food he eats.
[19] Now may his curses return and cling to him like clothing;
may they be tied around him like a belt.
[20] May those curses become the LORD's punishment for my accusers
who are plotting against my life.
[21] But deal well with me, O Sovereign LORD,
for the sake of your own reputation!
Rescue me because you are so faithful and good.
[22] For I am poor and needy,
and my heart is full of pain.
[23] I am fading like a shadow at dusk;
I am falling like a grasshopper that is brushed aside.
[24] My knees are weak from fasting,
and I am skin and bones.
[25] I am an object of mockery to people everywhere;
when they see me, they shake their heads.

[26] Help me, O LORD my God!
Save me because of your unfailing love.
[27] Let them see that this is your doing,
that you yourself have done it, LORD.
[28] Then let them curse me if they like,
but you will bless me!
When they attack me, they will be disgraced!
But I, your servant, will go right on rejoicing!
[29] Make their humiliation obvious to all;
clothe my accusers with disgrace.
[30] But I will give repeated thanks to the LORD,
praising him to everyone.
[31] For he stands beside the needy,
ready to save them from those who condemn them.

## PSALM 110 *A psalm of David.*

[1] The LORD said to my Lord,
"Sit in honor at my right hand
until I humble your enemies,
making them a footstool under your feet."
[2] The LORD will extend your powerful dominion from Jerusalem*;
you will rule over your enemies.

110:2 Hebrew *Zion.*

## ON THE FENCE? ● ● ● • •

**110:1-7** **Many people have a vague belief in God, but refuse to accept Jesus as anything more than a great human teacher. But the Bible does not allow that option. Both the Old and New Testaments proclaim the deity of the One who came to save and to reign. This psalm shows God's promise of sending the Messiah. The New Testament clearly shows that Jesus is God's Son, the Messiah. You can't straddle the fence, calling Jesus "just a good teacher," because the Bible clearly calls him the Messiah.**

3 In that day of battle,
your people will serve you willingly.
Arrayed in holy garments,
your vigor will be renewed each day like the morning dew.
4 The LORD has taken an oath and will not break his vow:
"You are a priest forever in the line of Melchizedek."
5 The Lord stands at your right hand to protect you.
He will strike down many kings in the day of his anger.
6 He will punish the nations
and fill them with their dead;
he will shatter heads
over the whole earth.
7 But he himself will be refreshed from brooks along the way.
He will be victorious.

## PSALM 111

1 Praise the LORD!

I will thank the LORD with all my heart
as I meet with his godly people.
2 How amazing are the deeds of the LORD!
All who delight in him should ponder them.
3 Everything he does reveals his glory and majesty.
His righteousness never fails.
4 Who can forget the wonders he performs?
How gracious and merciful is our LORD!
5 He gives food to those who trust him;
he always remembers his covenant.
6 He has shown his great power to his people
by giving them the lands of other nations.
7 All he does is just and good,
and all his commandments are trustworthy.
8 They are forever true,
to be obeyed faithfully and with integrity.
9 He has paid a full ransom for his people.
He has guaranteed his covenant with them forever.
What a holy, awe-inspiring name he has!
10 Reverence for the LORD is the foundation of true wisdom.
The rewards of wisdom come to all who obey him.

Praise his name forever!

## PSALM 112

1 Praise the LORD!

Happy are those who fear the LORD.
Yes, happy are those who delight in doing what he commands.
2 Their children will be successful everywhere;
an entire generation of godly people will be blessed.
3 They themselves will be wealthy,
and their good deeds will never be forgotten.
4 When darkness overtakes the godly, light will come bursting in.
They are* generous, compassionate, and righteous.
5 All goes well for those who are generous,
who lend freely and conduct their business fairly.
6 Such people will not be overcome by evil circumstances.
Those who are righteous will be long remembered.
7 They do not fear bad news;
they confidently trust the LORD to care for them.
8 They are confident and fearless
and can face their foes triumphantly.
9 They give generously to those in need.
Their good deeds will never be forgotten.
They will have influence and honor.
10 The wicked will be infuriated when they see this.
They will grind their teeth in anger;
they will slink away, their hopes thwarted.

### FEARLESS ● ● • • •

112:1, 7-8 **We all want to live without fear; our heroes are fearless people who face dangers and overcome them. The psalmist teaches us that *fear* of God can lead to a *fearless* life. To fear God means to respect and reverence him as the almighty Lord. When we trust God completely to take care of us, we will find that our other fears—even of death itself—will subside.**

## PSALM 113

1 Praise the LORD!

Yes, give praise, O servants of the LORD.
Praise the name of the LORD!
2 Blessed be the name of the LORD
forever and ever.
3 Everywhere—from east to west—
praise the name of the LORD.
4 For the LORD is high above the nations;
his glory is far greater than the heavens.

5 Who can be compared with the LORD our God,
who is enthroned on high?
6 Far below him are the heavens and the earth.
He stoops to look,
7 and he lifts the poor from the dirt
and the needy from the garbage dump.
8 He sets them among princes,
even the princes of his own people!
9 He gives the barren woman a home,
so that she becomes a happy mother.

Praise the LORD!

## PSALM 114

1 When the Israelites escaped from Egypt—
when the family of Jacob left that foreign land—

112:4 Greek version reads *The LORD is.*

[2]the land of Judah became God's sanctuary,
and Israel became his kingdom.

[3]The Red Sea* saw them coming and hurried out of their way!
The water of the Jordan River turned away.
[4]The mountains skipped like rams,
the little hills like lambs!
[5]What's wrong, Red Sea, that made you hurry out of their way?
What happened, Jordan River, that you turned away?
[6]Why, mountains, did you skip like rams?
Why, little hills, like lambs?

[7]Tremble, O earth, at the presence of the Lord,
at the presence of the God of Israel.*
[8]He turned the rock into pools of water;
yes, springs of water came from solid rock.

## PSALM 115

[1]Not to us, O LORD, but to you goes all the glory
for your unfailing love and faithfulness.
[2]Why let the nations say,
"Where is their God?"
[3]For our God is in the heavens,
and he does as he wishes.
[4]Their idols are merely things of silver and gold,
shaped by human hands.
[5]They cannot talk, though they have mouths,
or see, though they have eyes!
[6]They cannot hear with their ears,
or smell with their noses,
[7] or feel with their hands,
or walk with their feet,
or utter sounds with their throats!
[8]And those who make them are just like them,
as are all who trust in them.

[9]O Israel, trust the LORD!
He is your helper; he is your shield.
[10]O priests of Aaron, trust the LORD!
He is your helper; he is your shield.
[11]All you who fear the LORD, trust the LORD!
He is your helper; he is your shield.

[12]The LORD remembers us,
and he will surely bless us.
He will bless the people of Israel
and the family of Aaron, the priests.
[13]He will bless those who fear the LORD,
both great and small.

[14]May the LORD richly bless
both you and your children.
[15]May you be blessed by the LORD,
who made heaven and earth.
[16]The heavens belong to the LORD,
but he has given the earth to all humanity.

### THINKING OF YOU ● ● • • •

**115:12 "The LORD remembers us" says the psalm writer. What a fantastic truth! There are many times when we feel isolated, alone, and abandoned, even by God. In reality, he sees, understands, and is thinking about us. When depressed or struggling, be encouraged that God keeps you in his thoughts. If he thinks about you, surely his help is near.**

[17]The dead cannot sing praises to the LORD,
for they have gone into the silence of the grave.
[18]But we can praise the LORD
both now and forever!

Praise the LORD!

## PSALM 116

[1]I love the LORD because he hears
and answers my prayers.
[2]Because he bends down and listens,
I will pray as long as I have breath!
[3]Death had its hands around my throat;
the terrors of the grave* overtook me.
I saw only trouble and sorrow.
[4]Then I called on the name of the LORD:
"Please, LORD, save me!"
[5]How kind the LORD is! How good he is!
So merciful, this God of ours!
[6]The LORD protects those of childlike faith;
I was facing death, and then he saved me.
[7]Now I can rest again,
for the LORD has been so good to me.
[8]He has saved me from death,
my eyes from tears,
my feet from stumbling.
[9]And so I walk in the LORD's presence
as I live here on earth!
[10]I believed in you, so I prayed,
"I am deeply troubled, LORD."
[11]In my anxiety I cried out to you,
"These people are all liars!"
[12]What can I offer the LORD
for all he has done for me?
[13]I will lift up a cup symbolizing his salvation;
I will praise the LORD's name for saving me.
[14]I will keep my promises to the LORD
in the presence of all his people.

[15]The LORD's loved ones are precious to him;
it grieves him when they die.
[16]O LORD, I am your servant;
yes, I am your servant, the son of your handmaid,
and you have freed me from my bonds!
[17]I will offer you a sacrifice of thanksgiving
and call on the name of the LORD.
[18]I will keep my promises to the LORD
in the presence of all his people,
[19]in the house of the LORD,
in the heart of Jerusalem.

Praise the LORD!

**114:3** Hebrew *the sea;* also in 114:5. **114:7** Hebrew *of Jacob.* **116:3** Hebrew *of Sheol.*

## PSALM 117

[1] Praise the LORD, all you nations.
Praise him, all you people of the earth.
[2] For he loves us with unfailing love;
the faithfulness of the LORD endures forever.

Praise the LORD!

## PSALM 118

[1] Give thanks to the LORD, for he is good!
His faithful love endures forever.

[2] Let the congregation of Israel repeat:
"His faithful love endures forever."
[3] Let Aaron's descendants, the priests, repeat:
"His faithful love endures forever."
[4] Let all who fear the LORD repeat:
"His faithful love endures forever."

[5] In my distress I prayed to the LORD,
and the LORD answered me and rescued me.
[6] The LORD is for me, so I will not be afraid.
What can mere mortals do to me?
[7] Yes, the LORD is for me; he will help me.
I will look in triumph at those who hate me.
[8] It is better to trust the LORD
than to put confidence in people.
[9] It is better to trust the LORD
than to put confidence in princes.

[10] Though hostile nations surrounded me,
I destroyed them all in the name of the LORD.
[11] Yes, they surrounded and attacked me,
but I destroyed them all in the name of the
LORD.
[12] They swarmed around me like bees;
they blazed against me like a roaring flame.
But I destroyed them all in the name of the
LORD.
[13] You did your best to kill me, O my enemy,
but the LORD helped me.
[14] The LORD is my strength and my song;
he has become my victory.
[15] Songs of joy and victory are sung in the camp of
the godly.
The strong right arm of the LORD has done
glorious things!
[16] The strong right arm of the LORD is raised in
triumph.
The strong right arm of the LORD has done
glorious things!
[17] I will not die, but I will live
to tell what the LORD has done.
[18] The LORD has punished me severely,
but he has not handed me over to death.

[19] Open for me the gates where the righteous enter,
and I will go in and thank the LORD.
[20] Those gates lead to the presence of the LORD,
and the godly enter there.
[21] I thank you for answering my prayer
and saving me!

[22] The stone rejected by the builders
has now become the cornerstone.
[23] This is the LORD's doing,
and it is marvelous to see.
[24] This is the day the LORD has made.
We will rejoice and be glad in it.
[25] Please, LORD, please save us.
Please, LORD, please give us success.
[26] Bless the one who comes in the name of the
LORD.
We bless you from the house of the LORD.
[27] The LORD is God, shining upon us.
Bring forward the sacrifice and put it on the
altar.
[28] You are my God, and I will praise you!
You are my God, and I will exalt you!

[29] Give thanks to the LORD, for he is good!
His faithful love endures forever.

## PSALM 119

[1] Happy are people of integrity,
who follow the law of the LORD.
[2] Happy are those who obey his decrees
and search for him with all their hearts.
[3] They do not compromise with evil,
and they walk only in his paths.
[4] You have charged us
to keep your commandments carefully.
[5] Oh, that my actions would consistently
reflect your principles!
[6] Then I will not be disgraced
when I compare my life with your
commands.
[7] When I learn your righteous laws,
I will thank you by living as I should!
[8] I will obey your principles.
Please don't give up on me!

[9] How can a young person stay pure?
By obeying your word and following its rules.
[10] I have tried my best to find you—
don't let me wander from your commands.
[11] I have hidden your word in my heart,
that I might not sin against you.
[12] Blessed are you, O LORD;
teach me your principles.
[13] I have recited aloud
all the laws you have given us.
[14] I have rejoiced in your decrees
as much as in riches.
[15] I will study your commandments
and reflect on your ways.

### DETERRENT ● ● • • •

119:11 **Hiding God's Word in our heart and mind is a deterrent to sin. This alone should inspire us to want to memorize Scripture. But memorization alone will not keep us from sin; we must also put God's Word to work in our life, making it a vital guide to everything we do.**

**119** This psalm is a Hebrew acrostic poem; there are 22 stanzas, one for each letter of the Hebrew alphabet. The 8 verses within each stanza begin with the Hebrew letter of its section.

**RULES ● ● ● • •**

119:12-18 **Most of us don't like rules because we think they keep us from doing what we want. So it may seem strange to hear the psalmist talk of rejoicing in God's laws as much as in riches (119:14). But God's laws were given to free us to be all he wants us to be. They restrict us from doing those things that will cripple us and keep us from being our best. God's laws are guidelines to help us follow in his path and not wander onto paths that would lead to destruction.**

[16] I will delight in your principles
and not forget your word.

[17] Be good to your servant,
that I may live and obey your word.
[18] Open my eyes to see
the wonderful truths in your law.
[19] I am but a foreigner here on earth;
I need the guidance of your commands.
Don't hide them from me!
[20] I am overwhelmed continually
with a desire for your laws.
[21] You rebuke those cursed proud ones
who wander from your commands.
[22] Don't let them scorn and insult me,
for I have obeyed your decrees.
[23] Even princes sit and speak against me,
but I will meditate on your principles.
[24] Your decrees please me;
they give me wise advice.

[25] I lie in the dust, completely discouraged;
revive me by your word.
[26] I told you my plans, and you answered.
Now teach me your principles.
[27] Help me understand the meaning of your
commandments,
and I will meditate on your wonderful
miracles.
[28] I weep with grief;
encourage me by your word.
[29] Keep me from lying to myself;
give me the privilege of knowing your law.
[30] I have chosen to be faithful;
I have determined to live by your laws.
[31] I cling to your decrees.
LORD, don't let me be put to shame!
[32] If you will help me,
I will run to follow your commands.

[33] Teach me, O LORD,
to follow every one of your principles.
[34] Give me understanding and I will obey your law;
I will put it into practice with all my heart.
[35] Make me walk along the path of your commands,
for that is where my happiness is found.
[36] Give me an eagerness for your decrees;
do not inflict me with love for money!
[37] Turn my eyes from worthless things,
and give me life through your word.*
[38] Reassure me of your promise,
which is for those who honor you.
[39] Help me abandon my shameful ways;
your laws are all I want in life.
[40] I long to obey your commandments!
Renew my life with your goodness.

[41] LORD, give to me your unfailing love,
the salvation that you promised me.
[42] Then I will have an answer for those who taunt
me,
for I trust in your word.
[43] Do not snatch your word of truth from me,
for my only hope is in your laws.
[44] I will keep on obeying your law
forever and forever.
[45] I will walk in freedom,
for I have devoted myself to your
commandments.
[46] I will speak to kings about your decrees,
and I will not be ashamed.
[47] How I delight in your commands!
How I love them!
[48] I honor and love your commands.
I meditate on your principles.

[49] Remember your promise to me,
for it is my only hope.
[50] Your promise revives me;
it comforts me in all my troubles.
[51] The proud hold me in utter contempt,
but I do not turn away from your law.
[52] I meditate on your age-old laws;
O LORD, they comfort me.
[53] I am furious with the wicked,
those who reject your law.
[54] Your principles have been the music of my life
throughout the years of my pilgrimage.
[55] I reflect at night on who you are, O LORD,
and I obey your law because of this.
[56] This is my happy way of life:
obeying your commandments.

[57] LORD, you are mine!
I promise to obey your words!
[58] With all my heart I want your blessings.
Be merciful just as you promised.
[59] I pondered the direction of my life,
and I turned to follow your statutes.
[60] I will hurry, without lingering,
to obey your commands.
[61] Evil people try to drag me into sin,
but I am firmly anchored to your law.
[62] At midnight I rise to thank you
for your just laws.
[63] Anyone who fears you is my friend—
anyone who obeys your commandments.
[64] O LORD, the earth is full of your unfailing love;
teach me your principles.

[65] You have done many good things for me, LORD,
just as you promised.
[66] I believe in your commands;
now teach me good judgment and knowledge.

119:37 Some manuscripts read *in your ways.*

[67] I used to wander off until you disciplined me;
but now I closely follow your word.
[68] You are good and do only good;
teach me your principles.
[69] Arrogant people have made up lies about me,
but in truth I obey your commandments with all my heart.
[70] Their hearts are dull and stupid,
but I delight in your law.
[71] The suffering you sent was good for me,
for it taught me to pay attention to your principles.
[72] Your law is more valuable to me
than millions in gold and silver!

[73] You made me; you created me.
Now give me the sense to follow your commands.
[74] May all who fear you find in me a cause for joy,
for I have put my hope in your word.
[75] I know, O LORD, that your decisions are fair;
you disciplined me because I needed it.
[76] Now let your unfailing love comfort me,
just as you promised me, your servant.
[77] Surround me with your tender mercies so I may live,
for your law is my delight.
[78] Bring disgrace upon the arrogant people who lied about me;
meanwhile, I will concentrate on your commandments.
[79] Let me be reconciled
with all who fear you and know your decrees.
[80] May I be blameless in keeping your principles;
then I will never have to be ashamed.

[81] I faint with longing for your salvation;
but I have put my hope in your word.
[82] My eyes are straining to see your promises come true.
When will you comfort me?
[83] I am shriveled like a wineskin in the smoke,
exhausted with waiting.
But I cling to your principles and obey them.
[84] How long must I wait?
When will you punish those who persecute me?
[85] These arrogant people who hate your law
have dug deep pits for me to fall into.
[86] All your commands are trustworthy.
Protect me from those who hunt me down without cause.
[87] They almost finished me off,
but I refused to abandon your commandments.
[88] In your unfailing love, spare my life;
then I can continue to obey your decrees.

[89] Forever, O LORD,
your word stands firm in heaven.
[90] Your faithfulness extends to every generation,
as enduring as the earth you created.
[91] Your laws remain true today,
for everything serves your plans.
[92] If your law hadn't sustained me with joy,
I would have died in my misery.
[93] I will never forget your commandments,
for you have used them to restore my joy and health.
[94] I am yours; save me!
For I have applied myself to obey your commandments.
[95] Though the wicked hide along the way to kill me,
I will quietly keep my mind on your decrees.
[96] Even perfection has its limits,
but your commands have no limit.

[97] Oh, how I love your law!
I think about it all day long.
[98] Your commands make me wiser than my enemies,
for your commands are my constant guide.
[99] Yes, I have more insight than my teachers,
for I am always thinking of your decrees.
[100] I am even wiser than my elders,
for I have kept your commandments.
[101] I have refused to walk on any path of evil,
that I may remain obedient to your word.
[102] I haven't turned away from your laws,
for you have taught me well.
[103] How sweet are your words to my taste;
they are sweeter than honey.

## WISER ●●●••

119:97-104 **God's Word makes us wise—wiser than our enemies, wiser than any teachers who ignore it. True wisdom is not amassing knowledge, but *applying* knowledge in a life-changing way. Intelligent or experienced people are not necessarily wise. Wisdom comes from allowing what God teaches to make a difference in our life.**

[104] Your commandments give me understanding;
no wonder I hate every false way of life.

[105] Your word is a lamp for my feet
and a light for my path.
[106] I've promised it once, and I'll promise again:
I will obey your wonderful laws.
[107] I have suffered much, O LORD;
restore my life again, just as you promised.
[108] LORD, accept my grateful thanks
and teach me your laws.
[109] My life constantly hangs in the balance,
but I will not stop obeying your law.
[110] The wicked have set their traps for me along your path,
but I will not turn from your commandments.
[111] Your decrees are my treasure;
they are truly my heart's delight.
[112] I am determined to keep your principles,
even forever, to the very end.

[113] I hate those who are undecided about you,
but my choice is clear—I love your law.

[114] You are my refuge and my shield;
your word is my only source of hope.
[115] Get out of my life, you evil-minded people,
for I intend to obey the commands of my God.
[116] LORD, sustain me as you promised, that I may live!
Do not let my hope be crushed.
[117] Sustain me, and I will be saved;
then I will meditate on your principles continually.
[118] But you have rejected all who stray from your principles.
They are only fooling themselves.
[119] All the wicked of the earth are the scum you skim off;
no wonder I love to obey your decrees!
[120] I tremble in fear of you;
I fear your judgments.

[121] Don't leave me to the mercy of my enemies,
for I have done what is just and right.
[122] Please guarantee a blessing for me.
Don't let those who are arrogant oppress me!
[123] My eyes strain to see your deliverance,
to see the truth of your promise fulfilled.
[124] I am your servant;
deal with me in unfailing love,
and teach me your principles.

## MEDICINE ● ● • • •

**119:125 Faith comes alive at the points where we apply Scripture to our life. Like the psalmist, we need the common sense and the desire to apply Scripture where we need help. The Bible is similar to medicine—it goes to work only when you put it on the infected areas. As you read the Bible, be on the alert for lessons, commands, or examples that you can apply to situations in your life.**

[125] Give discernment to me, your servant;
then I will understand your decrees.
[126] LORD, it is time for you to act,
for these evil people have broken your law.
[127] Truly, I love your commands
more than gold, even the finest gold.
[128] Truly, each of your commandments is right.
That is why I hate every false way.

[129] Your decrees are wonderful.
No wonder I obey them!
[130] As your words are taught, they give light;
even the simple can understand them.
[131] I open my mouth, panting expectantly,
longing for your commands.
[132] Come and show me your mercy,
as you do for all who love your name.
[133] Guide my steps by your word,
so I will not be overcome by any evil.
[134] Rescue me from the oppression of evil people;
then I can obey your commandments.
[135] Look down on me with love;
teach me all your principles.
[136] Rivers of tears gush from my eyes
because people disobey your law.

[137] O LORD, you are righteous,
and your decisions are fair.
[138] Your decrees are perfect;
they are entirely worthy of our trust.
[139] I am overwhelmed with rage,
for my enemies have disregarded your words.
[140] Your promises have been thoroughly tested;
that is why I love them so much.
[141] I am insignificant and despised,
but I don't forget your commandments.
[142] Your justice is eternal,
and your law is perfectly true.
[143] As pressure and stress bear down on me,
I find joy in your commands.
[144] Your decrees are always fair;
help me to understand them, that I may live.

[145] I pray with all my heart; answer me, LORD!
I will obey your principles.
[146] I cry out to you; save me,
that I may obey your decrees.
[147] I rise early, before the sun is up;
I cry out for help and put my hope in your words.
[148] I stay awake through the night,
thinking about your promise.
[149] In your faithful love, O LORD, hear my cry;
in your justice, save my life.
[150] Those lawless people are coming near to attack me;
they live far from your law.
[151] But you are near, O LORD,
and all your commands are true.
[152] I have known from my earliest days
that your decrees never change.

[153] Look down upon my sorrows and rescue me,
for I have not forgotten your law.
[154] Argue my case; take my side!
Protect my life as you promised.
[155] The wicked are far from salvation,
for they do not bother with your principles.
[156] LORD, how great is your mercy;
in your justice, give me back my life.
[157] Many persecute and trouble me,
yet I have not swerved from your decrees.
[158] I hate these traitors
because they care nothing for your word.
[159] See how I love your commandments, LORD.
Give back my life because of your unfailing love.

## PEACEMAKER ● ● • • •

**120:7 Peacemaking is not very popular because it is more human to fight for what is right. The glory of battle is the hope of winning, but someone must be a loser. The glory of peacemaking is that it may actually produce two winners. Peacemaking is God's way, so we should carefully and prayerfully attempt to be peacemakers.**

He will not let you stumble and fall;
the one who watches over you will not sleep.
PSALM 121:3

[160] All your words are true;
all your just laws will stand forever.
[161] Powerful people harass me without cause,
but my heart trembles only at your word.
[162] I rejoice in your word
like one who finds a great treasure.
[163] I hate and abhor all falsehood,
but I love your law.
[164] I will praise you seven times a day
because all your laws are just.
[165] Those who love your law have great peace
and do not stumble.
[166] I long for your salvation, LORD,
so I have obeyed your commands.
[167] I have obeyed your decrees,
and I love them very much.
[168] Yes, I obey your commandments and decrees,
because you know everything I do.

[169] O LORD, listen to my cry;
give me the discerning mind you promised.
[170] Listen to my prayer;
rescue me as you promised.
[171] Let my lips burst forth with praise,
for you have taught me your principles.
[172] Let my tongue sing about your word,
for all your commands are right.
[173] Stand ready to help me,
for I have chosen to follow your commandments.
[174] O LORD, I have longed for your salvation,
and your law is my delight.
[175] Let me live so I can praise you,
and may your laws sustain me.
[176] I have wandered away like a lost sheep;
come and find me,
for I have not forgotten your commands.

## PSALM 120 *A song for the ascent to Jerusalem.*

[1] I took my troubles to the LORD;
I cried out to him, and he answered my prayer.
[2] Rescue me, O LORD, from liars
and from all deceitful people.
[3] O deceptive tongue, what will God do to you?
How will he increase your punishment?
[4] You will be pierced with sharp arrows
and burned with glowing coals.

[5] How I suffer among these scoundrels of Meshech!
It pains me to live with these people from Kedar!
[6] I am tired of living here
among people who hate peace.
[7] As for me, I am for peace;
but when I speak, they are for war!

## PSALM 121 *A song for the ascent to Jerusalem.*

[1] I look up to the mountains—
does my help come from there?
[2] My help comes from the LORD,
who made the heavens and the earth!

[3] He will not let you stumble and fall;
the one who watches over you will not sleep.
[4] Indeed, he who watches over Israel
never tires and never sleeps.

[5] The LORD himself watches over you!
The LORD stands beside you as your protective shade.
[6] The sun will not hurt you by day,
nor the moon at night.
[7] The LORD keeps you from all evil
and preserves your life.
[8] The LORD keeps watch over you as you come and go,
both now and forever.

## PSALM 122 *A song for the ascent to Jerusalem. A psalm of David.*

[1] I was glad when they said to me,
"Let us go to the house of the LORD."
[2] And now we are standing here
inside your gates, O Jerusalem.
[3] Jerusalem is a well-built city,
knit together as a single unit.
[4] All the people of Israel—the LORD's people—
make their pilgrimage here.

**FOR OTHERS ● ● • • •**

122:6-9 **The psalmist was not praying for his own peace and prosperity, but for his fellow citizens of Jerusalem. This is intercessory prayer, prayer on the behalf of others. Such prayer is unselfish. Too often we pray for our own needs and desires when we should be interceding for others. Will you pray for someone in need today?**

They come to give thanks to the name of the
LORD
as the law requires.
5 Here stand the thrones where judgment is given,
the thrones of the dynasty of David.

6 Pray for the peace of Jerusalem.
May all who love this city prosper.
7 O Jerusalem, may there be peace within your
walls
and prosperity in your palaces.
8 For the sake of my family and friends, I will say,
"Peace be with you."
9 For the sake of the house of the LORD our God,
I will seek what is best for you, O Jerusalem.

## PSALM **123** *A song for the ascent to Jerusalem.*

1 I lift my eyes to you,
O God, enthroned in heaven.
2 We look to the LORD our God for his mercy,
just as servants keep their eyes on their master,
as a slave girl watches her mistress for the
slightest signal.

3 Have mercy on us, LORD, have mercy,
for we have had our fill of contempt.
4 We have had our fill of the scoffing of the proud
and the contempt of the arrogant.

## PSALM **124** *A song for the ascent to Jerusalem. A psalm of David.*

1 If the LORD had not been on our side—
let Israel now say—
2 if the LORD had not been on our side
when people rose up against us,
3 they would have swallowed us alive
because of their burning anger against us.
4 The waters would have engulfed us;
a torrent would have overwhelmed us.
5 Yes, the raging waters of their fury
would have overwhelmed our very lives.

6 Blessed be the LORD,
who did not let their teeth tear us apart!
7 We escaped like a bird from a hunter's trap.
The trap is broken, and we are free!
8 Our help is from the LORD,
who made the heavens and the earth.

## PSALM **125** *A song for the ascent to Jerusalem.*

1 Those who trust in the LORD are as secure as
Mount Zion;
they will not be defeated but will endure
forever.
2 Just as the mountains surround and protect
Jerusalem,
so the LORD surrounds and protects his
people, both now and forever.
3 The wicked will not rule the godly,
for then the godly might be forced to do
wrong.
4 O LORD, do good to those who are good,
whose hearts are in tune with you.
5 But banish those who turn to crooked ways,
O LORD.
Take them away with those who do evil.
And let Israel have quietness and peace.

## PSALM **126** *A song for the ascent to Jerusalem.*

1 When the LORD restored his exiles to Jerusalem,*
it was like a dream!
2 We were filled with laughter,
and we sang for joy.
And the other nations said,
"What amazing things the LORD has done for
them."
3 Yes, the LORD has done amazing things for us!
What joy!

4 Restore our fortunes, LORD,
as streams renew the desert.
5 Those who plant in tears
will harvest with shouts of joy.
6 They weep as they go to plant their seed,
but they sing as they return with the harvest.

## PSALM **127** *A song for the ascent to Jerusalem. A psalm of Solomon.*

1 Unless the LORD builds a house,
the work of the builders is useless.
Unless the LORD protects a city,
guarding it with sentries will do no good.
2 It is useless for you to work so hard
from early morning until late at night,
anxiously working for food to eat;
for God gives rest to his loved ones.

3 Children are a gift from the LORD;
they are a reward from him.
4 Children born to a young man
are like sharp arrows in a warrior's hands.
5 How happy is the man whose quiver is full of
them!
He will not be put to shame when he
confronts his accusers at the city gates.

## PSALM **128** *A song for the ascent to Jerusalem.*

1 How happy are those who fear the LORD—
all who follow his ways!
2 You will enjoy the fruit of your labor.
How happy you will be! How rich your life!

126:1 Hebrew *Zion.*

[3]Your wife will be like a fruitful vine,
flourishing within your home.
And look at all those children!
There they sit around your table
as vigorous and healthy as young olive trees.
[4]That is the LORD's reward
for those who fear him.

[5]May the LORD continually bless you from Zion.
May you see Jerusalem prosper as long as you live.
[6]May you live to enjoy your grandchildren.
And may Israel have quietness and peace.

## PSALM 129 *A song for the ascent to Jerusalem.*

[1]From my earliest youth my enemies have persecuted me—
let Israel now say—
[2]from my earliest youth my enemies have persecuted me,
but they have never been able to finish me off.
[3]My back is covered with cuts,
as if a farmer had plowed long furrows.
[4]But the LORD is good;
he has cut the cords used by the ungodly to bind me.

[5]May all who hate Jerusalem*
be turned back in shameful defeat.
[6]May they be as useless as grass on a rooftop,
turning yellow when only half grown,
[7]ignored by the harvester,
despised by the binder.
[8]And may those who pass by refuse to give them this blessing:
"The LORD's blessings be upon you;
we bless you in the LORD's name."

## PSALM 130 *A song for the ascent to Jerusalem.*

[1]From the depths of despair, O LORD,
I call for your help.
[2]Hear my cry, O Lord.
Pay attention to my prayer.

[3]LORD, if you kept a record of our sins,
who, O Lord, could ever survive?
[4]But you offer forgiveness,
that we might learn to fear you.

[5]I am counting on the LORD;
yes, I am counting on him.
I have put my hope in his word.
[6]I long for the Lord
more than sentries long for the dawn,
yes, more than sentries long for the dawn.

[7]O Israel, hope in the LORD;
for with the LORD there is unfailing love
and an overflowing supply of salvation.
[8]He himself will free Israel
from every kind of sin.

## PSALM 131 *A song for the ascent to Jerusalem. A psalm of David.*

[1]LORD, my heart is not proud;
my eyes are not haughty.
I don't concern myself with matters too great
or awesome for me.
[2]But I have stilled and quieted myself,
just as a small child is quiet with its mother.
Yes, like a small child is my soul within me.
[3]O Israel, put your hope in the LORD—
now and always.

### NUMBER ONE ● ● • • •

127:1 **Families establish homes and sentries guard cities, but both of these activities are futile unless God is with them. A family without God can never experience the spiritual bond God brings to relationships. A city without God will crumble from evil and corruption on the inside. Don't make the mistake of leaving God out of your life—if you do, it will be lived in vain. Make God your highest priority and let him do the building.**

## PSALM 132 *A song for the ascent to Jerusalem.*

[1]LORD, remember David
and all that he suffered.
[2]He took an oath before the LORD.
He vowed to the Mighty One of Israel,*
[3]"I will not go home;
I will not let myself rest.
[4]I will not let my eyes sleep
nor close my eyelids in slumber
[5]until I find a place to build a house for the LORD,
a sanctuary for the Mighty One of Israel."
[6]We heard that the Ark was in Ephrathah;
then we found it in the distant countryside of Jaar.
[7]Let us go to the dwelling place of the LORD;
let us bow low before him.
[8]Arise, O LORD, and enter your sanctuary,
along with the Ark, the symbol of your power.
[9]Your priests will be agents of salvation;
may your loyal servants sing for joy.
[10]For the sake of your servant David,
do not reject the king you chose for your people.
[11]The LORD swore to David
a promise he will never take back:
"I will place one of your descendants on your throne.
[12]If your descendants obey the terms of my covenant
and follow the decrees that I teach them,
then your royal line will never end."
[13]For the LORD has chosen Jerusalem*;
he has desired it as his home.
[14]"This is my home where I will live forever," he said.

129:5 Hebrew *Zion.* 132:2 Hebrew *of Jacob;* also in 132:5. 132:13 Hebrew *Zion.*

"I will live here, for this is the place I desired.
[15] I will make this city prosperous
and satisfy its poor with food.
[16] I will make its priests the agents of salvation;
its godly people will sing for joy.
[17] Here I will increase the power of David;
my anointed one will be a light for my people.
[18] I will clothe his enemies with shame,
but he will be a glorious king."

## PSALM 133 *A song for the ascent to Jerusalem. A psalm of David.*

[1] How wonderful it is, how pleasant,
when brothers live together in harmony!
[2] For harmony is as precious as the fragrant anointing oil
that was poured over Aaron's head,
that ran down his beard
and onto the border of his robe.
[3] Harmony is as refreshing as the dew from Mount Hermon
that falls on the mountains of Zion.
And the LORD has pronounced his blessing,
even life forevermore.

## PSALM 134 *A song for the ascent to Jerusalem.*

[1] Oh, bless the LORD, all you servants of the LORD,
you who serve as night watchmen in the house of the LORD.
[2] Lift your hands in holiness,
and bless the LORD.
[3] May the LORD, who made heaven and earth,
bless you from Jerusalem.*

## PSALM 135

[1] Praise the LORD!

Praise the name of the LORD!
Praise him, you who serve the LORD,
[2] you who serve in the house of the LORD,
in the courts of the house of our God.
[3] Praise the LORD, for the LORD is good;
celebrate his wonderful name with music.
[4] For the LORD has chosen Jacob for himself,
Israel for his own special treasure.

[5] I know the greatness of the LORD—
that our Lord is greater than any other god.
[6] The LORD does whatever pleases him
throughout all heaven and earth,
and on the seas and in their depths.
[7] He causes the clouds to rise over the earth.
He sends the lightning with the rain
and releases the wind from his storehouses.
[8] He destroyed the firstborn in each Egyptian home,
both people and animals.
[9] He performed miraculous signs and wonders in Egypt;
Pharaoh and all his people watched.
[10] He struck down great nations
and slaughtered mighty kings—
[11] Sihon king of the Amorites,
Og king of Bashan,
and all the kings of Canaan.
[12] He gave their land as an inheritance,
a special possession to his people Israel.
[13] Your name, O LORD, endures forever;
your fame, O LORD, is known to every generation.
[14] For the LORD will vindicate his people
and have compassion on his servants.

[15] Their idols are merely things of silver and gold,
shaped by human hands.
[16] They cannot talk, though they have mouths,
or see, though they have eyes!
[17] They cannot hear with their ears
or smell with their noses.
[18] And those who make them are just like them,
as are all who trust in them.

[19] O Israel, praise the LORD!
O priests of Aaron, praise the LORD!
[20] O Levites, praise the LORD!
All you who fear the LORD, praise the LORD!
[21] The LORD be praised from Zion,
for he lives here in Jerusalem.

Praise the LORD!

### WORSHIP ● ● • • •

**135:18 In subtle, imperceptible ways we become like the "gods" we worship. So if the true God is your God, you will become more like him as you worship him. What are your gods? What takes priority in your life? Choose carefully, because you will take on the characteristics of whatever you worship.**

## PSALM 136

[1] Give thanks to the LORD, for he is good!
*His faithful love endures forever.*
[2] Give thanks to the God of gods.
*His faithful love endures forever.*
[3] Give thanks to the Lord of lords.
*His faithful love endures forever.*

[4] Give thanks to him who alone does mighty miracles.
*His faithful love endures forever.*
[5] Give thanks to him who made the heavens so skillfully.
*His faithful love endures forever.*
[6] Give thanks to him who placed the earth on the water.
*His faithful love endures forever.*
[7] Give thanks to him who made the heavenly lights—
*His faithful love endures forever.*

134:3 Hebrew *Zion.*

8 the sun to rule the day,
*His faithful love endures forever.*
9 and the moon and stars to rule the night.
*His faithful love endures forever.*

10 Give thanks to him who killed the firstborn of Egypt.
*His faithful love endures forever.*
11 He brought Israel out of Egypt.
*His faithful love endures forever.*
12 He acted with a strong hand and powerful arm.
*His faithful love endures forever.*
13 Give thanks to him who parted the Red Sea.*
*His faithful love endures forever.*
14 He led Israel safely through,
*His faithful love endures forever.*
15 but he hurled Pharaoh and his army into the sea.
*His faithful love endures forever.*
16 Give thanks to him who led his people through the wilderness.
*His faithful love endures forever.*

17 Give thanks to him who struck down mighty kings.
*His faithful love endures forever.*
18 He killed powerful kings—
*His faithful love endures forever.*
19 Sihon king of the Amorites,
*His faithful love endures forever.*
20 and Og king of Bashan.
*His faithful love endures forever.*
21 God gave the land of these kings as an inheritance—
*His faithful love endures forever.*
22 a special possession to his servant Israel.
*His faithful love endures forever.*

23 He remembered our utter weakness.
*His faithful love endures forever.*
24 He saved us from our enemies.
*His faithful love endures forever.*
25 He gives food to every living thing.
*His faithful love endures forever.*

26 Give thanks to the God of heaven.
*His faithful love endures forever.*

## PSALM 137

1 Beside the rivers of Babylon, we sat and wept
as we thought of Jerusalem.*
2 We put away our lyres,
hanging them on the branches of the willow trees.
3 For there our captors demanded a song of us.
Our tormentors requested a joyful hymn:
"Sing us one of those songs of Jerusalem!"
4 But how can we sing the songs of the LORD
while in a foreign land?

5 If I forget you, O Jerusalem,
let my right hand forget its skill upon the harp.
6 May my tongue stick to the roof of my mouth
if I fail to remember you,
if I don't make Jerusalem my highest joy.

7 O LORD, remember what the Edomites did
on the day the armies of Babylon captured Jerusalem.
"Destroy it!" they yelled.
"Level it to the ground!"
8 O Babylon, you will be destroyed.
Happy is the one who pays you back
for what you have done to us.
9 Happy is the one who takes your babies
and smashes them against the rocks!

**PLANS ● • • • •**

**138:8 Each of us makes plans for our future. We work hard to see those dreams come true. But to truly make the most of life, we must include God's plans in our plans. He alone knows what is best for us. As you make plans and dream dreams, talk with God about them.**

## PSALM 138 *A psalm of David.*

1 I give you thanks, O LORD, with all my heart;
I will sing your praises before the gods.
2 I bow before your holy Temple as I worship.
I will give thanks to your name
for your unfailing love and faithfulness,
because your promises are backed
by all the honor of your name.
3 When I pray, you answer me;
you encourage me by giving me the strength I need.

4 Every king in all the earth will give you thanks, O LORD,
for all of them will hear your words.
5 Yes, they will sing about the LORD's ways,
for the glory of the LORD is very great.
6 Though the LORD is great, he cares for the humble,
but he keeps his distance from the proud.

7 Though I am surrounded by troubles,
you will preserve me against the anger of my enemies.
You will clench your fist against my angry enemies!
Your power will save me.
8 The LORD will work out his plans for my life—
for your faithful love, O LORD, endures forever.
Don't abandon me, for you made me.

## PSALM 139 *For the choir director: A psalm of David.*

1 O LORD, you have examined my heart
and know everything about me.
2 You know when I sit down or stand up.
You know my every thought when far away.

136:13 Hebrew *sea of reeds;* also in 136:15. 137:1 Hebrew *Zion;* also in 137:3.

# Ultimate Issues

## ABORTION

"Keep your laws off my body!" scream the words on one placard. A woman in an opposing group carries a sign with a picture of an aborted baby. The caption reads "Who imposed their morality on this little one?" The news programs run story after story, pro-life and pro-abortion forces hold endless debates, and courts and legislatures are all but paralyzed over this most heated social issue: Abortion. **O**bviously, this is not a simple, one-dimensional issue. Besides the central problem of whether or not it is ever right to take the life of an unborn person, there are the related issues of parental consent for girls under 18 who want to have an abortion; legalizing abortion up to a certain age of the fetus (e.g., three months); "harvesting" fetal tissues to help people with diseases like Parkinson's disease; and many more. While these concerns complicate the issue, there is one question that cuts across all of them: ***Who can say what's right?*** **I**f a person (a judge, a doctor, or a legislator) or a human institution (the Supreme Court or the Senate) makes a decision in this matter, there is always the potential for another person or institution to overturn that decision later on. It has happened countless times. What is needed, it would seem, is a judgment or a ruling from someone or something higher than human opinion. **F**or 2,000 YEARS, Christians have turned to the Bible for just such input. Believing the Bible to be God's own words on matters such as this, Jesus' followers have historically looked to the Scriptures for answers to life's most important—and most difficult—questions. **U**nfortunately, there is no verse of Scripture that says, "Thus saith the Lord: abortion is wrong [or right]." If there was, it would be an OPEN-AND-SHUT case for believers. There are, however, passages that give principles that apply to this difficult topic. In Psalm 139, David praises God for overseeing his life, starting before he was born. David thanks God first for the fantastic way the human body is designed and constructed and then for the fact that every day of his life is "laid out" and "recorded in [God's] book." **I**f indeed God is the Creator and Designer of human (and all other forms of) life, it is a logical conclusion that no one should treat that life lightly. If we are God's workmanship, who has **THE RIGHT TO TAMPER** with or destroy that workmanship? (Another verse, 2 Chronicles 28:3, shows how evil one king was by saying that he even sacrificed his own children to idols.) Yet, tragically, that is what has happened in contemporary society. Abortion has become simply a means of birth control, of removing an unwanted complication. For those who take seriously the sanctity of life as an expression of God's handiwork, this can be seen only as an abomination, a sin of the most serious kind. As such, we as a society desperately need to cry out to God in repentance and ask his forgiveness for what we have allowed to be done to **millions of his little ones.** **T**here are a number of related topics (being made in the image of God, sexual morality, etc.) and Scripture passages (e.g., Exodus 21:22-25; Leviticus 24:17-22; Jeremiah 1:4-5) that are closely related to the abortion issue. Concerned Christians should think through their stand on the rights of the unborn in relation to these other issues and in light of the whole counsel of God, not just one passage. (One principle which should always be kept in mind when considering abortion or any other moral problem is forgiveness.) Psalm 139 is a good place to start.

[3] You chart the path ahead of me
and tell me where to stop and rest.
Every moment you know where I am.
[4] You know what I am going to say
even before I say it, LORD.
[5] You both precede and follow me.
You place your hand of blessing on my
head.
[6] Such knowledge is too wonderful for me,
too great for me to know!

[7] I can never escape from your spirit!
I can never get away from your presence!
[8] If I go up to heaven, you are there;
if I go down to the place of the dead,* you
are there.
[9] If I ride the wings of the morning,
if I dwell by the farthest oceans,
[10] even there your hand will guide me,
and your strength will support me.
[11] I could ask the darkness to hide me
and the light around me to become night—
[12] but even in darkness I cannot hide from
you.
To you the night shines as bright as day.
Darkness and light are both alike to you.

[13] You made all the delicate, inner parts of my
body
and knit me together in my mother's womb.
[14] Thank you for making me so wonderfully
complex!
Your workmanship is
marvelous—and how
well I know it.
[15] You watched me as I was
being formed in utter
seclusion,
as I was woven together in
the dark of the womb.
[16] You saw me before I was born.
Every day of my life was
recorded in your book.
Every moment was laid out
before a single day had
passed.

[17] How precious are your
thoughts about me,*
O God!
They are innumerable!
[18] I can't even count them;
they outnumber the grains
of sand!
And when I wake up in the
morning,
you are still with me!

[19] O God, if only you would
destroy the wicked!
Get out of my life, you
murderers!

139:8 Hebrew *to Sheol.* 139:17 Or *How precious to me are your thoughts.*

**RESPECT ● ● ● • •**

139:13-15 **God's character goes into the creation of every person. When you feel worthless or even begin to hate yourself, remember that God's Spirit is ready and willing to work within you to make your character all God meant it to be. God thinks of you constantly (139:17-18). We should have as much respect for ourselves as our Maker has for us.**

[20] They blaspheme you;
your enemies take your name in vain.
[21] O LORD, shouldn't I hate those who hate you?
Shouldn't I despise those who resist you?
[22] Yes, I hate them with complete hatred,
for your enemies are my enemies.
[23] Search me, O God, and know my heart;
test me and know my thoughts.
[24] Point out anything in me that offends you,
and lead me along the path of everlasting
life.

## PSALM 140 *For the choir director: A psalm of David.*

[1] O LORD, rescue me from evil people.
Preserve me from those who are violent,
[2] those who plot evil in their hearts
and stir up trouble all day long.
[3] Their tongues sting like a snake;
the poison of a viper drips from their lips.
*Interlude*

## "Here's what I did..."

I had an unusual, frightening experience at the beginning of tenth grade: I ate an apple that some disturbed person had tampered with. It wasn't poisonous—not like it would have killed me—but it did make me pretty sick. Most of all, the experience scared me. For about a year and a half, I wouldn't eat anything unless I shared it with someone, or someone else tried a bite first and was OK.

Finally the fear got to me. I talked to my youth worker about it. She encouraged me to read Psalm 140, and to realize that God was there to help and protect me—no matter what! Then she pointed out that God didn't want me to give in to a spirit of fear, and she showed me 2 Timothy 1:7. That verse became very meaningful to me. I memorized it and reminded myself of it over and over, until eventually I began to believe that most people could be trusted, that most people weren't out to hurt me. I have been learning that "God has not given us a spirit of fear and timidity, but of power, love, and self-discipline." I'm very thankful for this verse; God is using it to deliver me from my fear.

*Melinda*

AGE 18

[4] O LORD, keep me out of the hands of the wicked.
Preserve me from those who are violent,
for they are plotting against me.
[5] The proud have set a trap to catch me;
they have stretched out a net;
they have placed traps all along the way.
*Interlude*

[6] I said to the LORD, "You are my God!"
Listen, O LORD, to my cries for mercy!
[7] O Sovereign LORD, my strong savior,
you protected me on the day of battle.
[8] LORD, do not give in to their evil desires.
Do not let their evil schemes succeed,
O God.
*Interlude*

## ABORTION

"Maybe you made a mistake—or maybe the test is wrong."

"I don't think so. . . . Oh, Kris, what am I gonna do?" The tears begin to roll down Sarah's face. "I'm pregnant!"

Kris hugs her friend. "Look, don't panic. Everything's gonna work out. My sister will help us. She knows about this clinic. The doctors are good, and nobody else has to find out."

Sarah is shocked. "You mean an abortion?"

"Well, do you have any better ideas? C'mon, Sarah, you're only 17. What are you gonna do with a kid? And what would you tell your mom?"

"I don't know . . . I'm so confused." Sarah sighs, wiping her eyes on her sleeve. "What would you do? I mean, could you kill your own baby?"

"What do you mean, 'kill'? It's just a bunch of cells! It's not a person yet. If you were six or seven months pregnant, I'd tell you not to do it. But you're probably only about five weeks along. I don't see what else you can do."

"You really think it's right?"

"Well, let's just say I don't think it's wrong."

Sarah is obviously in deep thought. "Well, how soon can you call your sister?"

Kris picks up the phone. "I bet she's at her dorm right now."

Is Sarah making the right decision? Is Kris right about when life begins? See Psalm 139:13-18.

[9] Let my enemies be destroyed
by the very evil they have planned for me.
[10] Let burning coals fall down on their heads,
or throw them into the fire,
or into deep pits from which they can't escape.
[11] Don't let liars prosper here in our land.
Cause disaster to fall with great force on the violent.
[12] But I know the LORD will surely help those they persecute;
he will maintain the rights of the poor.
[13] Surely the godly are praising your name,
for they will live in your presence.

## PSALM 141 *A psalm of David.*

[1] O LORD, I am calling to you. Please hurry!
Listen when I cry to you for help!
[2] Accept my prayer as incense offered to you,
and my upraised hands as an evening offering.
[3] Take control of what I say, O LORD,
and keep my lips sealed.
[4] Don't let me lust for evil things;
don't let me participate in acts of wickedness.
Don't let me share in the delicacies
of those who do evil.

[5] Let the godly strike me!
It will be a kindness!
If they reprove me, it is soothing medicine.
Don't let me refuse it.

But I am in constant prayer
against the wicked and their deeds.
[6] When their leaders are thrown down from a cliff,
they will listen to my words and find them pleasing.
[7] Even as a farmer breaks up the soil and brings up rocks,
so the bones of the wicked will be scattered
without a decent burial.
[8] I look to you for help, O Sovereign LORD.
You are my refuge; don't let them kill me.
[9] Keep me out of the traps they have set for me,
out of the snares of those who do evil.
[10] Let the wicked fall into their own snares,
but let me escape.

## PSALM 142 *A psalm of David, regarding his experience in the cave. A prayer.*

[1] I cry out to the LORD;
I plead for the LORD's mercy.
[2] I pour out my complaints before him
and tell him all my troubles.
[3] For I am overwhelmed,
and you alone know the way I should turn.
Wherever I go,
my enemies have set traps for me.
[4] I look for someone to come and help me,
but no one gives me a passing thought!
No one will help me;
no one cares a bit what happens to me.
[5] Then I pray to you, O LORD.
I say, "You are my place of refuge.
You are all I really want in life.
[6] Hear my cry,
for I am very low.
Rescue me from my persecutors,
for they are too strong for me.
[7] Bring me out of prison
so I can thank you.
The godly will crowd around me,
for you treat me kindly."

## PSALM 143 *A psalm of David.*

1 Hear my prayer, O LORD;
listen to my plea!
Answer me because you are faithful and righteous.
2 Don't bring your servant to trial!
Compared to you, no one is perfect.
3 My enemy has chased me.
He has knocked me to the ground.
He forces me to live in darkness like those in the grave.
4 I am losing all hope;
I am paralyzed with fear.
5 I remember the days of old.
I ponder all your great works.
I think about what you have done.
6 I reach out for you.
I thirst for you as parched land thirsts for rain.
*Interlude*

7 Come quickly, LORD, and answer me,
for my depression deepens.
Don't turn away from me,
or I will die.
8 Let me hear of your unfailing love to me in the morning,
for I am trusting you.
Show me where to walk,
for I have come to you in prayer.
9 Save me from my enemies, LORD;
I run to you to hide me.
10 Teach me to do your will,
for you are my God.
May your gracious Spirit lead me forward
on a firm footing.
11 For the glory of your name, O LORD, save me.
In your righteousness, bring me out of this distress.
12 In your unfailing love, cut off all my enemies
and destroy all my foes,
for I am your servant.

## PSALM 144 *A psalm of David.*

1 Bless the LORD, who is my rock.
He gives me strength for war
and skill for battle.
2 He is my loving ally and my fortress,
my tower of safety, my deliverer.
He stands before me as a shield, and I take refuge in him.
He subdues the nations* under me.

3 O LORD, what are mortals that you should notice us,
mere humans that you should care for us?
4 For we are like a breath of air;
our days are like a passing shadow.

5 Bend down the heavens, LORD, and come down.
Touch the mountains so they billow smoke.

### THE TONGUE ● ● • • •

**141:3 James wrote that "the tongue is a small thing, but what enormous damage it can do" (James 3:5). On the average, a person opens his mouth approximately 700 times a day to speak. David wisely asked God to help him keep his mouth shut—sometimes even as he underwent persecution. Jesus himself was silent before his accusers (Matthew 26:63). Knowing the power of the tongue, we would do well to ask God to guard what we say so that our words will bring honor to his name.**

6 Release your lightning bolts and scatter your enemies!
Release your arrows and confuse them!
7 Reach down from heaven and rescue me;
deliver me from deep waters,
from the power of my enemies.
8 Their mouths are full of lies;
they swear to tell the truth, but they lie.

9 I will sing a new song to you, O God!
I will sing your praises with a ten-stringed harp.
10 For you grant victory to kings!
You are the one who rescued your servant David.
11 Save me from the fatal sword!
Rescue me from the power of my enemies.
Their mouths are full of lies;
they swear to tell the truth, but they lie.

12 May our sons flourish in their youth
like well-nurtured plants.
May our daughters be like graceful pillars,
carved to beautify a palace.
13 May our farms be filled
with crops of every kind.
May the flocks in our fields multiply by the thousands,
even tens of thousands,
14 and may our oxen be loaded down with produce.
May there be no breached walls, no forced exile,
no cries of distress in our squares.
15 Yes, happy are those who have it like this!
Happy indeed are those whose God is the LORD.

## PSALM 145 *A psalm of praise of David.*

1 I will praise you, my God and King,
and bless your name forever and ever.
2 I will bless you every day,
and I will praise you forever.
3 Great is the LORD! He is most worthy of praise!
His greatness is beyond discovery!

4 Let each generation tell its children
of your mighty acts.
5 I will meditate* on your majestic, glorious splendor
and your wonderful miracles.

144:2 Some manuscripts read *my people.* 145:5 Some manuscripts read *They will speak.*

## WHERE TO GET HELP IN THE BOOK OF PSALMS

*When you feel . . .*

Afraid 3, 4, 27, 46, 49, 56, 91, 118
Alone 9, 10, 12, 13, 27, 40, 43
"Burned Out" 6, 63
Cheated 41
Confused 10, 12, 73
Depressed 27, 34, 42, 43, 88, 143
Distressed 13, 25, 31, 40, 107
Elated 19, 96
Guilty 19, 32, 38, 51
Hateful 11
Impatient 13, 27, 37, 40
Insecure 3, 5, 12, 91
Insulted 41, 70
Jealous 37
Like Quitting 29, 43, 145
Lost 23, 139
Overwhelmed 25, 69, 142
Penitent/Sorry 32, 51, 66
Proud 14, 30, 49
Purposeless 14, 25, 39, 49, 90
Sad 13
Self-confident 24
Tense 4
Thankful 118, 136, 138
Threatened 3, 11, 17
Tired/Weak 6, 13, 18, 28, 29, 40, 86
Trapped 7, 17, 42, 88, 142
Unimportant 8, 90, 139
Vengeful 3, 7, 109
Worried 37
Worshipful 8, 19, 27, 29, 150

*When you're facing . . .*

Atheists 10, 14, 19, 52, 53, 115
Competition 133
Criticism 35, 56, 120
Danger 11
Death 6, 71, 90
Decisions 1, 119
Discrimination 54
Doubts 34, 37, 94
Evil people 10, 35, 36, 49, 52, 109, 140
Enemies 3, 25, 35, 41, 56, 59
Handicap/Illness 6, 139
Heresy 14
Hypocrisy 26, 28, 40, 50
Lies 5, 12, 120
Old Age 71, 92
Persecution 1, 3, 7, 56
Poverty 9, 10, 12
Punishment 6, 38, 39
Slander/Insults 7, 15, 35, 43, 120
Slaughter 6, 46, 83
Sorrow 23, 34
Success 18, 112, 127, 128
Temptation 38, 141
Troubles 34, 55, 86, 102, 142, 145
Verbal Cruelty 35, 120

*When you want . . .*

Acceptance 139
Answers 4, 17
Confidence 46, 71
Courage 11, 42
Fellowship with God 5, 16, 25, 27, 37, 133
Forgiveness 32, 38, 40, 51, 69, 86, 103, 130
Friendship 16
Godliness 15, 25
Guidance 1, 5, 15, 19, 25, 32, 48
Healing 6, 41
Hope 16, 17, 18, 23, 27
Humility 19, 147
Illumination 19
Integrity 24, 25
Joy 9, 16, 28, 126
Justice 2, 7, 14, 26, 37, 49, 58, 82
Knowledge 2, 8, 18, 19, 25, 29, 97, 103
Leadership 72
Miracles 60, 111
Money 15, 16, 17, 49
Peace 3, 4
Perspective 2, 11
Prayer 5, 17, 27, 61
Protection 3, 4, 7, 16, 17, 18, 23, 27, 31, 91, 121, 125
Provision 23
Rest 23, 27
Salvation 26, 37, 49, 126
Stability 11, 33, 46
Vindication 9, 14, 28, 35, 109
Wisdom 1, 16, 19, 64, 111

---

6 Your awe-inspiring deeds will be on every tongue;
I will proclaim your greatness.
7 Everyone will share the story of your wonderful goodness;
they will sing with joy of your righteousness.

8 The LORD is kind and merciful,
slow to get angry, full of unfailing love.
9 The LORD is good to everyone.
He showers compassion on all his creation.
10 All of your works will thank you, LORD,
and your faithful followers will bless you.
11 They will talk together about the glory of your kingdom;
they will celebrate examples of your power.
12 They will tell about your mighty deeds
and about the majesty and glory of your reign.
13 For your kingdom is an everlasting kingdom.
You rule generation after generation.

The LORD is faithful in all he says;
he is gracious in all he does.*
14 The LORD helps the fallen
and lifts up those bent beneath their loads.
15 All eyes look to you for help;
you give them their food as they need it.
16 When you open your hand,
you satisfy the hunger and thirst of every living thing.

17 The LORD is righteous in everything he does;
he is filled with kindness.
18 The LORD is close to all who call on him,
yes, to all who call on him sincerely.
19 He fulfills the desires of those who fear him;
he hears their cries for help and rescues them.
20 The LORD protects all those who love him,
but he destroys the wicked.

145:13 The last two lines of 145:13 are not found in many of the ancient manuscripts.

[21] I will praise the LORD,
and everyone on earth will bless his holy name
forever and forever.

## PSALM 146

[1] Praise the LORD!

Praise the LORD, I tell myself.
[2] I will praise the LORD as long as I live.
I will sing praises to my God even with my
dying breath.

[3] Don't put your confidence in powerful people;
there is no help for you there.
[4] When their breathing stops, they return to the
earth,
and in a moment all their plans come to an
end.
[5] But happy are those who have the God of Israel*
as their helper,
whose hope is in the LORD their God.
[6] He is the one who made heaven and earth,
the sea, and everything in them.
He is the one who keeps every promise forever,
[7] who gives justice to the oppressed
and food to the hungry.
The LORD frees the prisoners.
[8] The LORD opens the eyes of the blind.
The LORD lifts the burdens of those bent beneath
their loads.
The LORD loves the righteous.
[9] The LORD protects the foreigners among us.
He cares for the orphans and widows,
but he frustrates the plans of the wicked.

[10] The LORD will reign forever.
O Jerusalem,* your God is King in every
generation!

Praise the LORD!

## PSALM 147

[1] Praise the LORD!

How good it is to sing praises to our God!
How delightful and how right!
[2] The LORD is rebuilding Jerusalem
and bringing the exiles back to Israel.
[3] He heals the brokenhearted,
binding up their wounds.
[4] He counts the stars
and calls them all by name.
[5] How great is our Lord! His power is absolute!
His understanding is beyond comprehension!
[6] The LORD supports the humble,
but he brings the wicked down into the dust.

[7] Sing out your thanks to the LORD;
sing praises to our God, accompanied by
harps.
[8] He covers the heavens with clouds,
provides rain for the earth,
and makes the green grass grow in mountain
pastures.
[9] He feeds the wild animals,
and the young ravens cry to him for food.
[10] The strength of a horse does not impress him;
how puny in his sight is the strength of a man.
[11] Rather, the LORD's delight is in those who honor
him,
those who put their hope in his unfailing love.

[12] Praise the LORD, O Jerusalem!
Praise your God, O Zion!
[13] For he has fortified the bars of your gates
and blessed your children within you.
[14] He sends peace across your nation
and satisfies you with plenty of the finest
wheat.
[15] He sends his orders to the world—
how swiftly his word flies!
[16] He sends the snow like white wool;
he scatters frost upon the ground like ashes.
[17] He hurls the hail like stones.
Who can stand against his freezing cold?
[18] Then, at his command, it all melts.
He sends his winds, and the ice thaws.

[19] He has revealed his words to Jacob,
his principles and laws to Israel.
[20] He has not done this with any other nation;
they do not know his laws.

Praise the LORD!

## PSALM 148

[1] Praise the LORD!

Praise the LORD from the heavens!
Praise him from the skies!
[2] Praise him, all his angels!
Praise him, all the armies of heaven!
[3] Praise him, sun and moon!
Praise him, all you twinkling stars!
[4] Praise him, skies above!
Praise him, vapors high above the clouds!
[5] Let every created thing give praise to the LORD,
for he issued his command, and they came
into being.
[6] He established them forever and forever.
His orders will never be revoked.

[7] Praise the LORD from the earth,
you creatures of the ocean depths,

**UNLIMITED ● ● • • •**

**147:5 Sometimes we feel as though we don't understand ourself—what we want, how we feel, what's wrong with us, or what we should do about it. But God's understanding is unlimited and therefore he understands us fully. If you feel troubled and don't understand yourself, remember that God understands you perfectly. Take your mind off yourself and focus it on God. Strive to become more and more like him. The more you learn about God and his ways, the better you will understand yourself.**

146:5 Hebrew *of Jacob.* 146:10 Hebrew *Zion.*

## YOUR MUSIC ● ● • • •

149:3-5 **Although the Bible invites us to praise God, we often aren't sure how to go about it. Here, several ways are suggested—with your voice, in music, in your actions. God enjoys his people. We should enjoy praising him as well.**

[8] fire and hail, snow and storm,
wind and weather that obey him,
[9] mountains and all hills,
fruit trees and all cedars,
[10] wild animals and all livestock,
reptiles and birds,
[11] kings of the earth and all people,
rulers and judges of the earth,
[12] young men and maidens,
old men and children.
[13] Let them all praise the name of the LORD.
For his name is very great;
his glory towers over the earth and heaven!
[14] He has made his people strong,
honoring his godly ones—
the people of Israel who are close to him.

Praise the LORD!

## PSALM 149

[1] Praise the LORD!

Sing to the LORD a new song.
Sing his praises in the assembly of the faithful.
[2] O Israel, rejoice in your Maker.
O people of Jerusalem,* exult in your King.
[3] Praise his name with dancing,
accompanied by tambourine and harp.

149:2 Hebrew *Zion*.

[4] For the LORD delights in his people;
he crowns the humble with salvation.
[5] Let the faithful rejoice in this honor.
Let them sing for joy as they lie on their beds.
[6] Let the praises of God be in their mouths,
and a sharp sword in their hands—
[7] to execute vengeance on the nations
and punishment on the peoples,
[8] to bind their kings with shackles
and their leaders with iron chains,
[9] to execute the judgment written against them.
This is the glory of his faithful ones.

Praise the LORD!

## PSALM 150

[1] Praise the LORD!

Praise God in his heavenly dwelling;
praise him in his mighty heaven!
[2] Praise him for his mighty works;
praise his unequaled greatness!
[3] Praise him with a blast of the trumpet;
praise him with the lyre and harp!
[4] Praise him with the tambourine and dancing;
praise him with stringed instruments and flutes!
[5] Praise him with a clash of cymbals;
praise him with loud clanging cymbals.
[6] Let everything that lives sing praises to the LORD!

Praise the LORD!

# MEGA themes

**PRAISE** Psalms are songs of praise to God as our Creator, Sustainer, and Redeemer. Praise is recognizing, appreciating, and expressing God's greatness.

When we think about God, we want to praise him. The more we know of him, the more we will appreciate what he has done. We should focus on his specific, unique attributes as we worship him.

1. Read Psalm 145. How do you think the psalmist was feeling toward God when he wrote these verses? How do you feel when you read them?
2. What specific characteristics of God are praised?
3. Does praise always begin with feeling positive toward God? Explain your response.
4. How can praising God lead to a change of attitude, thoughts, and feelings?
5. List the ways you can live a life of praise to God. In other words, how can you become a living psalm?

**GOD'S POWER** God is all-powerful, and he always acts at the right time. He is in control of every situation. God's power is shown as he reveals himself in creation, history, and the Bible.

When we feel powerless, God can help us. His strength can overcome the despair of any pain or trial. We can always pray that he will deliver, protect, and sustain. And he will answer.

1. How is God's power revealed in the following psalms: 19; 21; 78?
2. How have you seen God's power in your life?
3. In what ways do you need God's power at the present time? How do you think you may need him in the future?
4. What do you learn from Psalms about relying on God's power during these times of need?

**FORGIVENESS** Many psalms are intense prayers asking God for forgiveness. God forgives us when we confess our sin and turn from it.

Because God forgives us, we can pray to him honestly and directly. When we receive God's forgiveness, we move from being separated from him to being close to him, from feeling guilty to feeling loved.

1. Psalm 51 is David's prayer after his sin with Bathsheba. Read this prayer with the following questions in mind: How was David feeling about himself? How was David feeling toward God?
2. What are David's specific prayer requests?
3. When you are facing a sin that you need to confess and repent of, how do you feel about yourself? About God?
4. Take a few moments to seek God's forgiveness in areas in which you have sinned.

**THANKFULNESS** We should be grateful to God for his personal concern, help, and mercy. He protects, guides, and forgives us, and he provides everything we need.

When we realize how much we benefit from knowing God, we can fully express our thanks to him. By thanking him often, we will develop spontaneity in our prayer life.

1. Read Psalms 100 and 136.
2. Make your own "Thanksgiving" list using the following statements:
   I thank God that he is ________.
   I thank God for showing me his love by ______.
   I thank God for the people I love, including ________.
   I thank God for providing me with ________.
   I thank God for helping me ________.
   I thank God that I am ________.
3. Write a prayer of thanksgiving to help you remember that God is your source of all that is good and eternal.

**TRUST** God is faithful and just. When we put our trust in him, he calms our heart. Because he has been faithful throughout history, we can trust him now.

People can be unfair and friends may desert us, but we can trust in God. Knowing God intimately drives away doubt, fear, and loneliness. We should remember that he is God, even when our feelings seem to be saying something else.

1. Psalm 23 is a psalm of trust in God. Complete this sentence: Psalm 23 shows that David trusts God because God ________.
2. Psalm 91 also expresses trust in God. Describe the psalmist's relationship with God.
3. What is the basis of your trust in God?
4. In what area of your life do you find it the most difficult to trust God? What truth do you find in Psalms that can build your trust in God?

**T**homas has a problem. He worked all summer to earn the money he now holds in his hands. It isn't a lot, a few hundred dollars, but it represents two months of long hours doing odd jobs. Thomas wonders what he should do with the money. Mom and Dad want him to put it into the bank. But his friends urge him to spend it. ("After all," they say, "it's *his* money.") Thomas isn't sure what to do. He wishes he were wiser about such things. ■There are lots of areas where most of us would like to have more wisdom, the ability to make good (wise) decisions. Lots of people are smart (book knowledge), but only a few are wise. ■Proverbs was written by Solomon, the wisest man who ever lived. In this book he shares his wisdom on such varied topics as money, marriage, family life, discipline, friends, laziness, speech, relationships, temptation, and leadership. Solomon's purpose was "to teach people wisdom and discipline, and to help them understand wise sayings." ■Proverbs is a book of answers—answers to our questions about everyday life. As you read, ask God to make the wisdom of Solomon your wisdom too. And ask God to help you begin your steps toward wisdom by trusting him.

## STATS

PURPOSE: To teach people how to be understanding, just, and fair in everything they do; to make the simple-minded wise; to warn young men about some problems they will face; and to help the wise become good leaders (see 1:2-6). In short, to help people apply divine wisdom to daily life and to provide them with moral instruction.

AUTHOR: Solomon wrote most of this book; Agur and Lemuel contributed some of the later sections

DATE WRITTEN: Solomon wrote and compiled most of these proverbs early in his reign

SETTING: This is a book of wise sayings, a textbook for teaching people how to live a godly life through the repetition of wise thought

SPECIAL FEATURES: The book uses varied *literary forms:* poems, brief parables, pointed questions, and couplets. Other *literary devices* include antithesis, comparison, and personification.

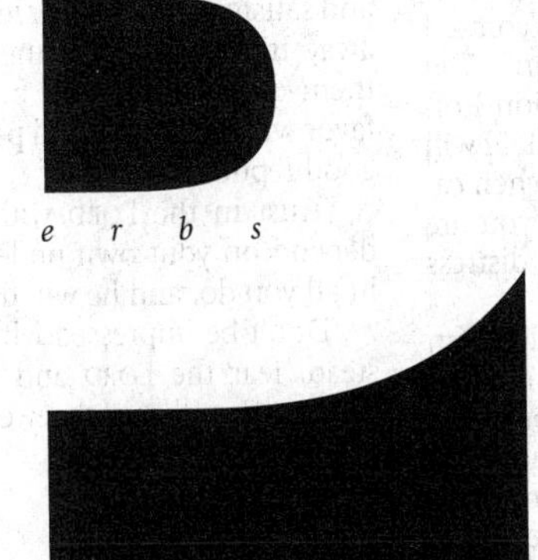

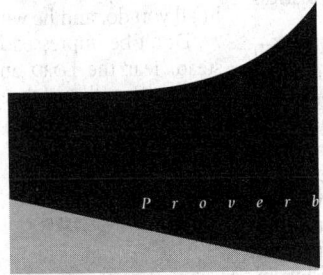

CHAPTER **1** **THE REASON FOR PROVERBS.** These are
the proverbs of Solomon, David's son, king of Israel.
[2]The purpose of these proverbs is to teach people
wisdom and discipline, and to help them understand wise sayings. [3]Through these proverbs, people
will receive instruction in discipline, good conduct,
and doing what is right, just, and fair. [4]These proverbs will make the simpleminded clever. They will
give knowledge and purpose to young people.
[5]Let those who are wise listen to these proverbs
and become even wiser. And let those who understand receive guidance [6]by exploring the depth of
meaning in these proverbs, parables, wise sayings,
and riddles.
[7]Fear of the LORD is the beginning of knowledge.
Only fools despise wisdom and discipline.
[8]Listen, my child,* to what your father teaches
you. Don't neglect your mother's teaching. [9]What
you learn from them will crown you with grace and
clothe you with honor.
[10]My child, if sinners entice you, turn your back on
them! [11]They may say, "Come and join us. Let's hide
and kill someone! Let's ambush the innocent! [12]Let's
swallow them alive as the grave swallows its victims.
Though they are in the prime of life, they will go
down into the pit of death. [13]And the loot we'll get!
We'll fill our houses with all kinds of things! [14]Come
on, throw in your lot with us; we'll split our loot with
you."
[15]Don't go along with them, my child! Stay far
away from their paths. [16]They rush to commit
crimes. They hurry to commit murder. [17]When a bird
sees a trap being set, it stays away. [18]But not these
people! They set an ambush for themselves; they
booby-trap their own lives! [19]Such is the fate of all
who are greedy for gain. It ends up robbing them of
life.
[20]Wisdom shouts in the streets. She cries out in the
public square. [21]She calls out to the crowds along the

1:8 Hebrew *my son;* also in 1:10, 15.

## TURN AND RUN ● ● • • •

1:10-19 **Sin is attractive because it offers a quick route to prosperity and makes us feel like "one of the crowd." When we go along with others and refuse to listen to the truth, our own appetites become our masters. We'll do anything to satisfy them. But sin is deadly. We must learn to make choices not on the basis of flashy appeal or short-range pleasure, but in view of the long-range effects. Sometimes this means steering clear of people who want to draw us into activities we know are wrong. We can't be friendly with sin and expect our life to remain unaffected. Turn and run—this is not cowardly; it is both brave and smart.**

**CHOICES ● ● ● ● ●**

**2:9-10 Wisdom comes through a constant process of growth. First, we must trust and honor God. Second, we must realize that the Bible reveals God's wisdom to us. Third, we must learn to make right choices. Fourth, when we make sinful or mistaken choices, we must learn from our errors. People don't develop all aspects of wisdom at once. For example, some people have more insight than discretion; others have more knowledge than common sense. But we can pray for all the aspects of wisdom and seek to develop them in our life.**

main street, and to those in front of city hall. 22"You
simpletons!" she cries. "How long will you go on
being simpleminded? How long will you mockers
relish your mocking? How long will you fools fight
the facts? 23Come here and listen to me! I'll pour out
the spirit of wisdom upon you and make you wise.
24"I called you so often, but you didn't come. I
reached out to you, but you paid no attention. 25You
ignored my advice and rejected the correction I offered. 26So I will laugh when you are in trouble! I will
mock you when disaster overtakes you—27when calamity overcomes you like a storm, when you are
engulfed by trouble, and when anguish and distress
overwhelm you.
28"I will not answer when they cry for help. Even
though they anxiously search for me, they will not find
me. 29For they hated knowledge and chose not to fear
the LORD. 30They rejected my advice and paid no attention when I corrected them. 31That is why they must eat
the bitter fruit of living their own way. They must
experience the full terror of the path they have chosen.
32For they are simpletons who turn away from me—to
death. They are fools, and their own complacency will
destroy them. 33But all who listen to me will live in
peace and safety, unafraid of harm."

CHAPTER **2** **WISDOM COMES FROM GOD.** My child,*
listen to me and treasure my instructions. 2Tune your
ears to wisdom, and concentrate on understanding.
3Cry out for insight and understanding. 4Search for
them as you would for lost money or hidden treasure.
5Then you will understand what it means to fear the
LORD, and you will gain knowledge of God. 6For the
LORD grants wisdom! From his mouth come knowledge and understanding. 7He grants a treasure of good
sense to the godly. He is their shield, protecting those
who walk with integrity. 8He guards the paths of justice
and protects those who are faithful to him.
9Then you will understand what is right, just, and
fair, and you will know how to find the right course
of action every time. 10For wisdom will enter your
heart, and knowledge will fill you with joy. 11Wise
planning will watch over you. Understanding will
keep you safe.
12Wisdom will save you from evil people, from
those whose speech is corrupt. 13These people turn
from right ways to walk down dark and evil paths.
14They rejoice in doing wrong, and they enjoy evil as
it turns things upside down. 15What they do is
crooked, and their ways are wrong.
16Wisdom will save you from the immoral woman,
from the flattery of the adulterous woman. 17She has
abandoned her husband and ignores the covenant she
made before God. 18Entering her house leads to death;
it is the road to hell.* 19The man who visits her is
doomed. He will never reach the paths of life.
20Follow the steps of good men instead, and stay
on the paths of the righteous. 21For only the upright
will live in the land, and those who have integrity
will remain in it. 22But the wicked will be removed
from the land, and the treacherous will be destroyed.

CHAPTER **3** **WISDOM IS PRICELESS.** My child,* never
forget the things I have taught you. Store my commands in your heart, 2for they will give you a long
and satisfying life. 3Never let loyalty and kindness get
away from you! Wear them like a necklace; write
them deep within your heart. 4Then you will find
favor with both God and people, and you will gain a
good reputation.
5Trust in the LORD with all your heart; do not
depend on your own understanding. 6Seek his will
in all you do, and he will direct your paths.
7Don't be impressed with your own wisdom. Instead, fear the LORD and turn your back on evil.
8Then you will gain renewed health and vitality.

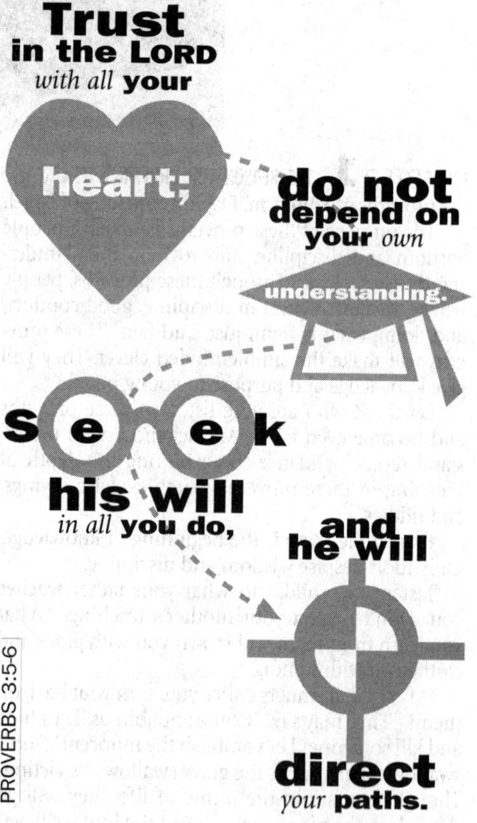

Trust
in the LORD
with all your
heart;
do not
depend on
your own
understanding.
Seek
his will
in all you do,
and
he will
direct
your paths.
PROVERBS 3:5-6

2:1 Hebrew *My son.* 2:18 Hebrew *to the spirits of the dead.* 3:1 Hebrew *My son;* also in 3:11, 21.

9Honor the LORD with your wealth and with the
best part of everything your land produces. 10Then he
will fill your barns with grain, and your vats will
overflow with the finest wine.
11My child, don't ignore it when the LORD disciplines you, and don't be discouraged when he corrects you. 12For the LORD corrects those he loves, just
as a father corrects a child* in whom he delights.
13Happy is the person who finds wisdom and gains
understanding. 14For the profit of wisdom is better
than silver, and her wages are better than gold. 15Wis-
dom is more precious than rubies; nothing you desire
can compare with her. 16She offers you life in her right
hand, and riches and honor in her left. 17She will guide
you down delightful paths; all her ways are satisfying.
18Wisdom is a tree of life to those who embrace her;
happy are those who hold her tightly.
19By wisdom the LORD founded the earth; by understanding he established the heavens. 20By his
knowledge the deep fountains of the earth burst
forth, and the clouds poured down rain.
21My child, don't lose sight of good planning and
insight. Hang on to them, 22for they fill you with life
and bring you honor and respect. 23They keep you
safe on your way and keep your feet from stumbling.
24You can lie down without fear and enjoy pleasant
dreams. 25You need not be afraid of disaster or the
destruction that comes upon the wicked, 26for the
LORD is your security. He will keep your foot from
being caught in a trap.
27Do not withhold good from those who deserve
it when it's in your power to help them. 28If you can
help your neighbor now, don't say, "Come back
tomorrow, and then I'll help you."
29Do not plot against your neighbors, for they
trust you. 30Don't make accusations against someone who hasn't wronged you.
31Do not envy violent people; don't copy their
ways. 32Such wicked people are an abomination to
the LORD, but he offers his friendship to the godly.
33The curse of the LORD is on the house of the
wicked, but his blessing is on the home of the upright.
34The LORD mocks at mockers, but he shows favor
to the humble.
35The wise inherit honor, but fools are put to
shame!

## CHAPTER 4 **YOU CAN LEARN WISDOM.** My children,*
listen to me. Listen to your father's instruction. Pay
attention and grow wise, 2for I am giving you good
guidance. Don't turn away from my teaching. 3For I,
too, was once my father's son, tenderly loved by my
mother as an only child.
4My father told me, "Take my words to heart.
Follow my instructions and you will live. 5Learn to be
wise, and develop good judgment. Don't forget or
turn away from my words. 6Don't turn your back on
wisdom, for she will protect you. Love her, and she
will guard you. 7Getting wisdom is the most important thing you can do! And whatever else you do, get
good judgment. 8If you prize wisdom, she will exalt
you. Embrace her and she will honor you. 9She will
place a lovely wreath on your head; she will present
you with a beautiful crown."
10My child,* listen to me and do as I say, and you
will have a long, good life. 11I will teach you wisdom's ways and lead you in straight paths. 12If you
live a life guided by wisdom, you won't limp or
stumble as you run. 13Carry out my instructions;
don't forsake them. Guard them, for they will lead
you to a fulfilled life.

**I'm always giving in to my friends. Lots of times this goes against what I think a Christian should do. How do I withstand the pressure?**

If every young person had a dollar for every time friends asked him or her to "come along," most could pay for four years of college!

Being included feels great, and everyone needs friends. But friends don't always have our welfare at heart. In fact, sometimes they only want us to join them so they can feel better about doing whatever it is they want to do.

But is this really pressure?

When someone invites you to go along with a questionable (or bad) situation and you give in, you haven't succumbed to peer pressure. You have chosen to do something wrong and have concealed your true identity.

Too often we hide our real character, hoping to be liked by a group or person. We want to be accepted. Unfortunately, this often works. If it didn't, people wouldn't do it!

Everyone is tempted to bend their rules or beliefs in order for someone to like them. During the teenage years, this kind of pressure can be intense, and it can generate a hungry urge to do what others are doing in order to fit in.

But God wants to provide the inner muscle you'll need to combat the outer pressure you feel. Ask him to give you the courage and strength to say no.

He also wants to teach you what to do. Remember when Mom or Dad taught you to do something like bake cookies or start a lawnmower? They didn't just tell you to do it, they showed you how.

God shows us how to act through the teachings and stories in the Bible.

Commands like "Don't copy the behavior and customs of this world, but let God transform you into a new person by changing the way you think" (Romans 12:2) need to be read to understand God's heart. But examples from throughout the Bible can help.

Consider these: Joseph ran from temptation (Genesis 39:12), and Daniel prayed his way through it (Daniel 6:10). And like the counsel in Proverbs 1:10, sometimes we just have to realize that the consequences are not worth the risk.

3:12 Hebrew *a son.* 4:1 Hebrew *My sons.* 4:10 Hebrew *My son;* also in 4:20.

[14]Do not do as the wicked do or follow the path of evildoers. [15]Avoid their haunts. Turn away and go somewhere else, [16]for evil people cannot sleep until they have done their evil deed for the day. They cannot rest unless they have caused someone to stumble. [17]They eat wickedness and drink violence!

[18]The way of the righteous is like the first gleam of dawn, which shines ever brighter until the full light of day. [19]But the way of the wicked is like complete darkness. Those who follow it have no idea what they are stumbling over.

[20]Pay attention, my child, to what I say. Listen carefully. [21]Don't lose sight of my words. Let them penetrate deep within your heart, [22]for they bring life and radiant health to anyone who discovers their meaning.

[23]Above all else, guard your heart, for it affects everything you do.*

[24]Avoid all perverse talk; stay far from corrupt speech.

[25]Look straight ahead, and fix your eyes on what lies before you. [26]Mark out a straight path for your feet; then stick to the path and stay safe. [27]Don't get sidetracked; keep your feet from following evil.

## AFFECTIONS ● ● • • •

4:23-27 **Our heart—our feelings of love and desire—dictates to a great extent how we live because we always find time to do what we enjoy. Solomon tells us to guard our heart, making sure we concentrate on those desires that will keep us on the right path. Make sure your affections are pushing you in the right direction. Put boundaries on your desires; don't go after everything you see. Look straight ahead, keeping your eyes fixed on your goal. Don't get sidetracked; watch out for detours that lead to temptation.**

CHAPTER **5** **RUN FROM SIN.** My son, pay attention to my wisdom; listen carefully to my wise counsel. [2]Then you will learn to be discreet and will store up knowledge.

[3]The lips of an immoral woman are as sweet as honey, and her mouth is smoother than oil. [4]But the result is as bitter as poison, sharp as a double-edged sword. [5]Her feet go down to death; her steps lead straight to the grave.* [6]For she does not care about the path to life. She staggers down a crooked trail and doesn't even realize where it leads.

[7]So now, my sons, listen to me. Never stray from what I am about to say: [8]Run from her! Don't go near the door of her house! [9]If you do, you will lose your honor and hand over to merciless people everything you have achieved in life. [10]Strangers will obtain your wealth, and someone else will enjoy the fruit of your labor. [11]Afterward you will groan in anguish when disease consumes your body, [12]and you will say, "How I hated discipline! If only I had not demanded my own way! [13]Oh, why didn't I listen to my teachers? Why didn't I pay attention to those who gave me instruction? [14]I have come to the brink of utter ruin, and now I must face public disgrace."

[15]Drink water from your own well—share your love only with your wife.* [16]Why spill the water of your springs in public, having sex with just anyone?* [17]You should reserve it for yourselves. Don't share it with strangers.

[18]Let your wife be a fountain of blessing for you. Rejoice in the wife of your youth. [19]She is a loving doe, a graceful deer. Let her breasts satisfy you always. May you always be captivated by her love. [20]Why be captivated, my son, with an immoral woman, or embrace the breasts of an adulterous woman?

[21]For the LORD sees clearly what a man does, examining every path he takes. [22]An evil man is held captive by his own sins; they are ropes that catch and hold him. [23]He will die for lack of self-control; he will be lost because of his incredible folly.

CHAPTER **6** **RUN FROM FOOLISHNESS.** My child,* if you co-sign a loan for a friend or guarantee the debt of someone you hardly know—[2]if you have trapped yourself by your agreement and are caught by what you said—[3]quick, get out of it if you possibly can! You have placed yourself at your friend's mercy. Now swallow your pride; go and beg to have your name erased. [4]Don't put it off. Do it now! Don't rest until you do. [5]Save yourself like a deer escaping from a hunter, like a bird fleeing from a net.

[6]Take a lesson from the ants, you lazybones. Learn from their ways and be wise! [7]Even though they have no prince, governor, or ruler to make them work, [8]they labor hard all summer, gathering food for the winter. [9]But you, lazybones, how long will you sleep? When will you wake up? I want you to learn this lesson: [10]A little extra sleep, a little more slumber, a little folding of the hands to rest—[11]and poverty will pounce on you like a bandit; scarcity will attack you like an armed robber.

[12]Here is a description of worthless and wicked people: They are constant liars, [13]signaling their true intentions to their friends by making signs with their eyes and feet and fingers. [14]Their perverted hearts plot evil. They stir up trouble constantly. [15]But they will be destroyed suddenly, broken beyond all hope of healing.

## EXPERIENCE ● ● • • •

6:20-24 **It is natural and good for children as they grow toward adulthood to strive to become independent of their parents. Young adults, however, should take care not to turn a deaf ear to their parents—to reject their advice just when they may need it most. If you are struggling with a decision or looking for insight, check with your parents or other older adults who know you well. Their extra years of experience may have given them the wisdom you seek.**

4:23 Hebrew *for from it flow the springs of life.* 5:5 Hebrew *to Sheol.* 5:15 Hebrew *Drink water from your own cistern, flowing water from your own well.* 5:16 Hebrew *Why spill your springs in public, your streams in the streets?* 6:1 Hebrew *My son.*

[16]There are six things the LORD hates—no, seven things he detests:

17 haughty eyes,
a lying tongue,
hands that kill the innocent,
18 a heart that plots evil,
feet that race to do wrong,
19 a false witness who pours out lies,
a person who sows discord among brothers.

[20]My son, obey your father's commands, and don't neglect your mother's teaching. [21]Keep their words always in your heart. Tie them around your neck. [22]Wherever you walk, their counsel can lead you. When you sleep, they will protect you. When you wake up in the morning, they will advise you. [23]For these commands and this teaching are a lamp to light the way ahead of you. The correction of discipline is the way to life.

[24]These commands and this teaching will keep you from the immoral woman, from the smooth tongue of an adulterous woman. [25]Don't lust for her beauty. Don't let her coyness seduce you. [26]For a prostitute will bring you to poverty, and sleeping with another man's wife may cost you your very life. [27]Can a man scoop fire into his lap and not be burned? [28]Can he walk on hot coals and not blister his feet? [29]So it is with the man who sleeps with another man's wife. He who embraces her will not go unpunished.

[30]Excuses might be found for a thief who steals because he is starving. [31]But if he is caught, he will be fined seven times as much as he stole, even if it means selling everything in his house to pay it back.

[32]But the man who commits adultery is an utter fool, for he destroys his own soul. [33]Wounds and constant disgrace are his lot. His shame will never be erased. [34]For the woman's husband will be furious in his jealousy, and he will have no mercy in his day of vengeance. [35]There is no compensation or bribe that will satisfy him.

CHAPTER **7** **KEEP YOURSELF PURE.** Follow my advice, my son; always treasure my commands. [2]Obey them and live! Guard my teachings as your most precious possession.* [3]Tie them on your fingers as a reminder. Write them deep within your heart.

[4]Love wisdom like a sister; make insight a beloved member of your family. [5]Let them hold you back from an affair with an immoral woman, from listening to the flattery of an adulterous woman.

[6]I was looking out the window of my house one day [7]and saw a simpleminded young man who lacked common sense. [8]He was crossing the street near the house of an immoral woman. He was strolling down the path by her house [9]at twilight, as the day was fading, as the dark of night set in. [10]The woman approached him, dressed seductively and sly of heart. [11]She was the brash, rebellious type who never stays at home. [12]She is often seen in the streets and markets, soliciting at every corner.

[13]She threw her arms around him and kissed him, and with a brazen look she said, [14]"I've offered my sacrifices and just finished my vows. [15]It's you I was looking for! I came out to find you, and here you are! [16]My bed is spread with colored sheets of finest linen imported from Egypt. [17]I've perfumed my bed with myrrh, aloes, and cinnamon. [18]Come, let's drink our fill of love until morning. Let's enjoy each other's caresses, [19]for my husband is not home. He's away on a long trip. [20]He has taken a wallet full of money with him, and he won't return until later in the month."

[21]So she seduced him with her pretty speech. With her flattery she enticed him. [22]He followed her at once, like an ox going to the slaughter or like a trapped stag, [23]awaiting the arrow that would pierce its heart. He was like a bird flying into a snare, little knowing it would cost him his life.

[24]Listen to me, my sons, and pay attention to my words. [25]Don't let your hearts stray away toward her. Don't wander down her wayward path. [26]For she has been the ruin of many; numerous men have been her victims. [27]Her house is the road to the grave.* Her bedroom is the den of death.

CHAPTER **8** **WISDOM GIVES GOOD ADVICE.** Listen as wisdom calls out! Hear as understanding raises her voice! [2]She stands on the hilltop and at the crossroads. [3]At the entrance to the city, at the city gates, she cries aloud, [4]"I call to you, to all of you! I am

## "Here's what I did..."

Sometimes reading Scripture is like getting a good swift kick in the pants! That's what happened to me, anyway.

I've had this problem with procrastination and laziness. Basically I just don't make an effort with things that bore me (like school or chores my parents want me to do). One day I was reading along in Proverbs 6:6-11, which describes what a lazy person is like—and I knew that it was talking about me! Those verses taught me that putting things off isn't just a bad habit, it's a sin that can lead to some pretty bad consequences. This passage helped motivate me to quit sitting around, to take some action even if I don't feel like it.

John

AGE 14

7:2 Hebrew *as the apple of your eye.* 7:27 Hebrew *to Sheol.*

raising my voice to all people. [5]How naive you are!
Let me give you common sense. O foolish ones, let
me give you understanding. [6]Listen to me! For I have
excellent things to tell you. Everything I say is right,
[7]for I speak the truth and hate every kind of deception. [8]My advice is wholesome and good. There is
nothing crooked or twisted in it. [9]My words are plain
to anyone with understanding, clear to those who
want to learn.

[10]"Choose my instruction rather than silver, and
knowledge over pure gold. [11]For wisdom is far more
valuable than rubies. Nothing you desire can be
compared with it.

[12]"I, Wisdom, live together with good judgment. I
know where to discover knowledge and discernment.
[13]All who fear the LORD will hate evil. That is why I hate
pride, arrogance, corruption, and perverted speech.
[14]Good advice and success belong to me. Insight and
strength are mine. [15]Because of me, kings reign, and
rulers make just laws. [16]Rulers lead with my help,
and nobles make righteous judgments.

**HEATING**

If Tucker spent half as much time actually studying as he does trying to invent new ways to avoid doing his schoolwork, he probably could make straight A's. Just look at some of his schemes:

- He knows of a company that sells term papers. For a few bucks and an hour's worth of editing, he can turn in a top-notch report on almost any subject.
- He gets his friends to divide the daily algebra assignments. In study hall they each spend about 15 minutes doing a part of the homework (instead of an hour or more doing the whole thing by themselves). Tucker takes the pages to his dad's office on the way home from school, makes photocopies for everyone, and passes them out first thing in the morning.
- Tucker has never read an assigned literary work for English class. Between videos and Cliffs Notes, he can always fake it.
- Two of his teachers use the exact same tests from last year. Tucker bought old copies from two college freshmen.
- He has a programmable watch that can store up to 100 facts and dates. On exam days, the watch gets a mean workout!

Tucker laughs at how stupid his teachers are and at how many people get away with cheating.

See Proverbs 11:1 for a look at how God views Tucker's lifestyle.

[17]"I love all who love me. Those who search for me
will surely find me. [18]Unending riches, honor,
wealth, and justice are mine to distribute. [19]My gifts
are better than the purest gold, my wages better than
sterling silver! [20]I walk in righteousness, in paths of
justice. [21]Those who love me inherit wealth, for I fill
their treasuries.

[22]"The LORD formed me from the beginning, before he created anything else. [23]I was appointed in

## HYPNOTIZED ● ● ● • •

9:17 **There is something hypnotic and intoxicating about wickedness. One sin leads us to want more; sinful behavior seems more exciting than the "boring" Christian life. That is why many people put aside all thought of wisdom's sumptuous banquet (9:1-6) in order to eat the stolen food of foolishness, the harlot. Don't be deceived—sin is dangerous. Before reaching for forbidden fruit, take a long look at what happens to those who eat it.**

ages past, at the very first, before the earth began. [24]I
was born before the oceans were created, before the
springs bubbled forth their waters. [25]Before the
mountains and the hills were formed, I was born—
[26]before he had made the earth and fields and the
first handfuls of soil.

[27]"I was there when he established the heavens,
when he drew the horizon on the oceans. [28]I was
there when he set the clouds above, when he established the deep fountains of the earth. [29]I was there
when he set the limits of the seas, so they would not
spread beyond their boundaries. And when he
marked off the earth's foundations, [30]I was the archi-
tect at his side. I was his constant delight, rejoicing
always in his presence. [31]And how happy I was with
what he created—his wide world and all the human
family!

[32]"And so, my children,* listen to me, for happy
are all who follow my ways. [33]Listen to my counsel
and be wise. Don't ignore it.

[34]"Happy are those who listen to me, watching for
me daily at my gates, waiting for me outside my
home! [35]For whoever finds me finds life and wins
approval from the LORD. [36]But those who miss me
have injured themselves. All who hate me love
death."

CHAPTER **9** **KNOWING GOD RESULTS IN WISDOM.** Wisdom has built her spacious house with seven pillars.
[2]She has prepared a great banquet, mixed the wines,
and set the table. [3]She has sent her servants to invite
everyone to come. She calls out from the heights
overlooking the city. [4]"Come home with me," she
urges the simple. To those without good judgment,
she says, [5]"Come, eat my food, and drink the wine I
have mixed. [6]Leave your foolish ways behind, and
begin to live; learn how to be wise."

[7]Anyone who rebukes a mocker will get a smart
retort. Anyone who rebukes the wicked will get hurt.
[8]So don't bother rebuking mockers; they will only
hate you. But the wise, when rebuked, will love you
all the more. [9]Teach the wise, and they will be wiser.
Teach the righteous, and they will learn more.

[10]Fear of the LORD is the beginning of wisdom.
Knowledge of the Holy One results in understanding.

[11]Wisdom will multiply your days and add years to
your life. [12]If you become wise, you will be the one
to benefit. If you scorn wisdom, you will be the one
to suffer.

[13]The woman named Folly is loud and brash. She
is ignorant and doesn't even know it. [14]She sits in her

8:32 Hebrew *my sons.*

doorway on the heights overlooking the city. [15]She calls out to men going by who are minding their own business. [16]"Come home with me," she urges the simple. To those without good judgment, she says, [17]"Stolen water is refreshing; food eaten in secret tastes the best!" [18]But the men don't realize that her former guests are now in the grave.*

## CHAPTER 10 GOD'S WISDOM IS FOR EVERYONE.

The proverbs of Solomon:

A wise child* brings joy to a father; a foolish child brings grief to a mother.

[2]Ill-gotten gain has no lasting value, but right living can save your life.

[3]The LORD will not let the godly starve to death, but he refuses to satisfy the craving of the wicked.

[4]Lazy people are soon poor; hard workers get rich.

[5]A wise youth works hard all summer; a youth who sleeps away the hour of opportunity brings shame.

[6]The godly are showered with blessings; evil people cover up their harmful intentions.

[7]We all have happy memories of the godly, but the name of a wicked person rots away.

[8]The wise are glad to be instructed, but babbling fools fall flat on their faces.

[9]People with integrity have firm footing, but those who follow crooked paths will slip and fall.

[10]People who wink at wrong cause trouble, but a bold reproof promotes peace.*

[11]The words of the godly lead to life; evil people cover up their harmful intentions.

[12]Hatred stirs up quarrels, but love covers all offenses.

[13]Wise words come from the lips of people with understanding, but fools will be punished with a rod.

[14]Wise people treasure knowledge, but the babbling of a fool invites trouble.

[15]The wealth of the rich is their fortress; the poverty of the poor is their calamity.

[16]The earnings of the godly enhance their lives, but evil people squander their money on sin.

[17]People who accept correction are on the pathway to life, but those who ignore it will lead others astray.

[18]To hide hatred is to be a liar; to slander is to be a fool.

[19]Don't talk too much, for it fosters sin. Be sensible and turn off the flow!

[20]The words of the godly are like sterling silver; the heart of a fool is worthless.

[21]The godly give good advice, but fools are destroyed by their lack of common sense.

[22]The blessing of the LORD makes a person rich, and he adds no sorrow with it.

[23]Doing wrong is fun for a fool, while wise conduct is a pleasure to the wise.

[24]The fears of the wicked will all come true; so will the hopes of the godly.

[25]Disaster strikes like a cyclone, whirling the wicked away, but the godly have a lasting foundation.

[26]Lazy people are a pain to their employer. They are like smoke in the eyes or vinegar that sets the teeth on edge.

[27]Fear of the LORD lengthens one's life, but the years of the wicked are cut short.

[28]The hopes of the godly result in happiness, but the expectations of the wicked are all in vain.

[29]The LORD protects the upright but destroys the wicked.

[30]The godly will never be disturbed, but the wicked will be removed from the land.

[31]The godly person gives wise advice, but the tongue that deceives will be cut off.

[32]The godly speak words that are helpful, but the wicked speak only what is corrupt.

### WASTED TIME ● ● • • •

10:4-5 **Every day has 24 hours filled with opportunities to grow, serve, and be productive. It is so easy to waste time, letting life slip from our grasp. Instead, refuse to be a lazy person, sleeping or squandering the hours meant for productive work. See time as God's gift, and seize the opportunities to live for him.**

## CHAPTER 11 GOD HATES CHEATING.

The LORD hates cheating, but he delights in honesty.

[2]Pride leads to disgrace, but with humility comes wisdom.

[3]Good people are guided by their honesty; treacherous people are destroyed by their dishonesty.

[4]Riches won't help on the day of judgment, but right living is a safeguard against death.

[5]The godly are directed by their honesty; the wicked fall beneath their load of sin.

[6]The godliness of good people rescues them; the ambition of treacherous people traps them.

[7]When the wicked die, their hopes all perish, for they rely on their own feeble strength.

[8]God rescues the godly from danger, but he lets the wicked fall into trouble.

[9]Evil words destroy one's friends; wise discernment rescues the godly.

[10]The whole city celebrates when the godly succeed; they shout for joy when the godless die.

[11]Upright citizens bless a city and make it prosper, but the talk of the wicked tears it apart.

[12]It is foolish to belittle a neighbor; a person with good sense remains silent.

[13]A gossip goes around revealing secrets, but those who are trustworthy can keep a confidence.

[14]Without wise leadership, a nation falls; with many counselors, there is safety.

[15]Guaranteeing a loan for a stranger is dangerous; it is better to refuse than to suffer later.

[16]Beautiful women obtain wealth, and violent men get rich.

**9:18** Hebrew *in Sheol.* **10:1** Hebrew *son;* also in 10:1b. **10:10** As in Greek version; Hebrew reads *but babbling fools fall flat on their faces.*

## CAUGHT ● ● ● • •

11:31 **Contrary to popular opinion, no one sins and gets away with it. Ultimately, the faithful are rewarded for their faith and the wicked are punished for their sins. Don't think for a moment that "it won't matter" or "nobody will know" or "we won't get caught." (See also 1 Peter 4:18.)**

17Your own soul is nourished when you are kind, but you destroy yourself when you are cruel.
18Evil people get rich for the moment, but the reward of the godly will last.
19Godly people find life; evil people find death.
20The LORD hates people with twisted hearts, but he delights in those who have integrity.
21You can be sure that evil people will be punished, but the children of the godly will go free.
22A woman who is beautiful but lacks discretion is like a gold ring in a pig's snout.
23The godly can look forward to happiness, while the wicked can expect only wrath.
24It is possible to give freely and become more wealthy, but those who are stingy will lose everything.
25The generous prosper and are satisfied; those who refresh others will themselves be refreshed.
26People curse those who hold their grain for higher prices, but they bless the one who sells to them in their time of need.
27If you search for good, you will find favor; but if you search for evil, it will find you!
28Trust in your money and down you go! But the godly flourish like leaves in spring.
29Those who bring trouble on their families inherit only the wind. The fool will be a servant to the wise.
30The godly are like trees that bear life-giving fruit, and those who save lives are wise.
31If the righteous are rewarded here on earth, how much more true that the wicked and the sinner will get what they deserve!

CHAPTER **12** **GAIN WISDOM: AVOID MISTAKES.** To learn, you must love discipline; it is stupid to hate correction.
2The LORD approves of those who are good, but he condemns those who plan wickedness.
3Wickedness never brings stability; only the godly have deep roots.
4A worthy wife is her husband's joy and crown; a shameful wife saps his strength.
5The plans of the godly are just; the advice of the wicked is treacherous.
6The words of the wicked are like a murderous ambush, but the words of the godly save lives.
7The wicked perish and are gone, but the children of the godly stand firm.
8Everyone admires a person with good sense, but a warped mind is despised.
9It is better to be a nobody with a servant than to be self-important but have no food.
10The godly are concerned for the welfare of their animals, but even the kindness of the wicked is cruel.
11Hard work means prosperity; only fools idle away their time.
12Thieves are jealous of each other's loot, while the godly bear their own fruit.
13The wicked are trapped by their own words, but the godly escape such trouble.
14People can get many good things by the words they say; the work of their hands also gives them many benefits.
15Fools think they need no advice, but the wise listen to others.
16A fool is quick-tempered, but a wise person stays calm when insulted.
17An honest witness tells the truth; a false witness tells lies.

## COOL ● ● ● • •

12:16 **When someone insults you, it is natural to insult in return. But this solves nothing and only encourages trouble. Instead, "keep your cool" and answer slowly and quietly. Your positive response will achieve positive results.**

18Some people make cutting remarks, but the words of the wise bring healing.
19Truth stands the test of time; lies are soon exposed.
20Deceit fills hearts that are plotting evil; joy fills hearts that are planning peace!
21No real harm befalls the godly, but the wicked have their fill of trouble.
22The LORD hates those who don't keep their word, but he delights in those who do.
23Wise people don't make a show of their knowledge, but fools broadcast their folly.
24Work hard and become a leader; be lazy and become a slave.
25Worry weighs a person down; an encouraging word cheers a person up.
26The godly give good advice to their friends;* the wicked lead them astray.
27Lazy people don't even cook the game they catch, but the diligent make use of everything they find.
28The way of the godly leads to life; their path does not lead to death.

CHAPTER **13** **THE WAY TO SUCCESS.** A wise child* accepts a parent's discipline; a young mocker refuses to listen.
2Good people enjoy the positive results of their words, but those who are treacherous crave violence.
3Those who control their tongue will have a long life; a quick retort can ruin everything.
4Lazy people want much but get little, but those who work hard will prosper and be satisfied.

12:26 Or *The godly are cautious in friendship,* or *the godly are freed from evil.* The meaning of the Hebrew is uncertain. 13:1 Hebrew *son.*

5 Those who are godly hate lies; the wicked come to shame and disgrace.

6 Godliness helps people all through life, while the evil are destroyed by their wickedness.

7 Some who are poor pretend to be rich; others who are rich pretend to be poor.

8 The rich can pay a ransom, but the poor won't even get threatened.

9 The life of the godly is full of light and joy, but the sinner's light is snuffed out.

10 Pride leads to arguments; those who take advice are wise.

11 Wealth from get-rich-quick schemes quickly disappears; wealth from hard work grows.

12 Hope deferred makes the heart sick, but when dreams come true, there is life and joy.

13 People who despise advice will find themselves in trouble; those who respect it will succeed.

14 The advice of the wise is like a life-giving fountain; those who accept it avoid the snares of death.

15 A person with good sense is respected; a treacherous person walks a rocky road.

16 Wise people think before they act; fools don't and even brag about it!

17 An unreliable messenger stumbles into trouble, but a reliable messenger brings healing.

18 If you ignore criticism, you will end in poverty and disgrace; if you accept criticism, you will be honored.

19 It is pleasant to see dreams come true, but fools will not turn from evil to attain them.

20 Whoever walks with the wise will become wise; whoever walks with fools will suffer harm.

21 Trouble chases sinners, while blessings chase the righteous!

22 Good people leave an inheritance to their grandchildren, but the sinner's wealth passes to the godly.

23 A poor person's farm may produce much food, but injustice sweeps it all away.

24 If you refuse to discipline your children, it proves you don't love them; if you love your children, you will be prompt to discipline them.

25 The godly eat to their hearts' content, but the belly of the wicked goes hungry.

## CHAPTER 14

**ANGER CAUSES MISTAKES.** A wise woman builds her house; a foolish woman tears hers down with her own hands.

2 Those who follow the right path fear the LORD; those who take the wrong path despise him.

3 The talk of fools is a rod for their backs,* but the words of the wise keep them out of trouble.

4 An empty stable stays clean, but no income comes from an empty stable.

5 A truthful witness does not lie; a false witness breathes lies.

6 A mocker seeks wisdom and never finds it, but knowledge comes easily to those with understanding.

7 Stay away from fools, for you won't find knowledge there.

8 The wise look ahead to see what is coming, but fools deceive themselves.

9 Fools make fun of guilt, but the godly acknowledge it and seek reconciliation.

10 Each heart knows its own bitterness, and no one else can fully share its joy.

11 The house of the wicked will perish, but the tent of the godly will flourish.

12 There is a path before each person that seems right, but it ends in death.

13 Laughter can conceal a heavy heart; when the laughter ends, the grief remains.

14 Backsliders get what they deserve; good people receive their reward.

15 Only simpletons believe everything they are told! The prudent carefully consider their steps.

16 The wise are cautious* and avoid danger; fools plunge ahead with great confidence.

17 Those who are short-tempered do foolish things, and schemers are hated.

18 The simpleton is clothed with folly, but the wise person is crowned with knowledge.

19 Evil people will bow before good people; the wicked will bow at the gates of the godly.

20 The poor are despised even by their neighbors, while the rich have many "friends."

21 It is sin to despise one's neighbors; blessed are those who help the poor.

22 If you plot evil, you will be lost; but if you plan good, you will be granted unfailing love and faithfulness.

23 Work brings profit, but mere talk leads to poverty!

24 Wealth is a crown for the wise; the effort of fools yields only folly.

25 A truthful witness saves lives, but a false witness is a traitor.

26 Those who fear the LORD are secure; he will be a place of refuge for their children.

27 Fear of the LORD is a life-giving fountain; it offers escape from the snares of death.

28 A growing population is a king's glory; a dwindling nation is his doom.

29 Those who control their anger have great understanding; those with a hasty temper will make mistakes.

30 A relaxed attitude lengthens life; jealousy rots it away.

### RECONCILE ● ● ● • •

**14:9 How rarely we find reconciliation around us today! Siblings argue. Husbands and wives part ways. People continue to hold on to past bitterness. But the common bond of God's people should be hearts that seek after reconciliation. When you know you have wronged someone, own up to it and ask yourself, "How can I make things right with this person?"**

14:3 Hebrew *a rod of pride.* 14:16 Hebrew *The wise fear.*

[31]Those who oppress the poor insult their Maker, but those who help the poor honor him.
[32]The wicked are crushed by their sins, but the godly have a refuge when they die.
[33]Wisdom is enshrined in an understanding heart; wisdom is not* found among fools.
[34]Godliness exalts a nation, but sin is a disgrace to any people.
[35]A king rejoices in servants who know what they are doing; he is angry with those who cause trouble.

CHAPTER **15** **GOD DELIGHTS IN OUR PRAYERS.** A gentle answer turns away wrath, but harsh words stir up anger.
[2]The wise person makes learning a joy; fools spout only foolishness.
[3]The LORD is watching everywhere, keeping his eye on both the evil and the good.
[4]Gentle words bring life and health; a deceitful tongue crushes the spirit.

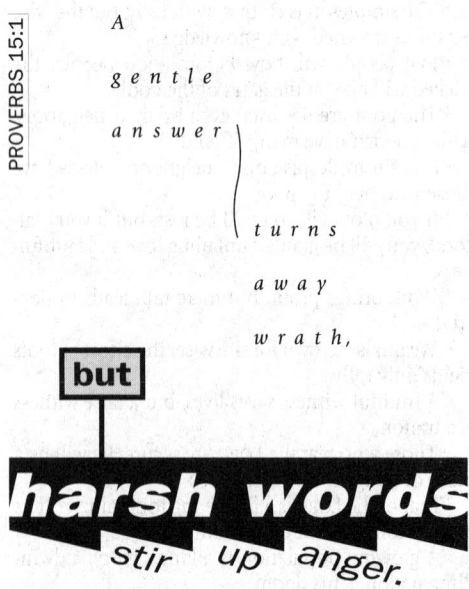

PROVERBS 15:1

*A gentle answer turns away wrath,*

**but**

**harsh words**

stir up anger.

[5]Only a fool despises a parent's discipline; whoever learns from correction is wise.
[6]There is treasure in the house of the godly, but the earnings of the wicked bring trouble.
[7]Only the wise can give good advice; fools cannot do so.
[8]The LORD hates the sacrifice of the wicked, but he delights in the prayers of the upright.
[9]The LORD despises the way of the wicked, but he loves those who pursue godliness.
[10]Whoever abandons the right path will be severely punished; whoever hates correction will die.

## QUIET ● ● ● • •

15:1 **Have you ever tried to argue in a whisper? It is hard to argue with someone who insists on answering softly. On the other hand, a rising voice almost always triggers an angry response. If the most important goal is to win the argument, then you had better warm up your vocal cords. But if your goal is to seek peace, then a consistently quiet response is your best choice.**

[11]Even the depths of Death and Destruction* are known by the LORD. How much more does he know the human heart!
[12]Mockers don't love those who rebuke them, so they stay away from the wise.
[13]A glad heart makes a happy face; a broken heart crushes the spirit.
[14]A wise person is hungry for truth, while the fool feeds on trash.
[15]For the poor, every day brings trouble; for the happy heart, life is a continual feast.
[16]It is better to have little with fear for the LORD than to have great treasure with turmoil.
[17]A bowl of soup with someone you love is better than steak with someone you hate.
[18]A hothead starts fights; a cool-tempered person tries to stop them.
[19]A lazy person has trouble all through life; the path of the upright is easy!
[20]Sensible children bring joy to their father; foolish children despise their mother.
[21]Foolishness brings joy to those who have no sense; a sensible person stays on the right path.
[22]Plans go wrong for lack of advice; many counselors bring success.
[23]Everyone enjoys a fitting reply; it is wonderful to say the right thing at the right time!
[24]The path of the wise leads to life above; they leave the grave* behind.
[25]The LORD destroys the house of the proud, but he protects the property of widows.
[26]The LORD despises the thoughts of the wicked, but he delights in pure words.
[27]Dishonest money brings grief to the whole family, but those who hate bribes will live.
[28]The godly think before speaking; the wicked spout evil words.
[29]The LORD is far from the wicked, but he hears the prayers of the righteous.
[30]A cheerful look brings joy to the heart; good news makes for good health.
[31]If you listen to constructive criticism, you will be at home among the wise.
[32]If you reject criticism, you only harm yourself; but if you listen to correction, you grow in understanding.
[33]Fear of the LORD teaches a person to be wise; humility precedes honor.

CHAPTER **16** **PRIDE LEADS TO TROUBLE.** We can gather our thoughts, but the LORD gives the right answer.

14:33 As in Greek version; Hebrew lacks *not.* 15:11 Hebrew *Sheol and Abaddon.* 15:24 Hebrew *Sheol.*

2 People may be pure in their own eyes, but the LORD examines their motives.

3 Commit your work to the LORD, and then your plans will succeed.

4 The LORD has made everything for his own purposes, even the wicked for punishment.

5 The LORD despises pride; be assured that the proud will be punished.

6 Unfailing love and faithfulness cover sin; evil is avoided by fear of the LORD.

7 When the ways of people please the LORD, he makes even their enemies live at peace with them.

8 It is better to be poor and godly than rich and dishonest.

9 We can make our plans, but the LORD determines our steps.

10 The king speaks with divine wisdom; he must never judge unfairly.

11 The LORD demands fairness in every business deal; he sets the standard.

12 A king despises wrongdoing, for his rule depends on his justice.

13 The king is pleased with righteous lips; he loves those who speak honestly.

14 The anger of the king is a deadly threat; the wise do what they can to appease it.

15 When the king smiles, there is life; his favor refreshes like a gentle rain.

16 How much better to get wisdom than gold, and understanding than silver!

17 The path of the upright leads away from evil; whoever follows that path is safe.

18 Pride goes before destruction, and haughtiness before a fall.

19 It is better to live humbly with the poor than to share plunder with the proud.

20 Those who listen to instruction will prosper; those who trust the LORD will be happy.

21 The wise are known for their understanding, and instruction is appreciated if it's well presented.

22 Discretion is a life-giving fountain to those who possess it, but discipline is wasted on fools.

23 From a wise mind comes wise speech; the words of the wise are persuasive.

24 Kind words are like honey—sweet to the soul and healthy for the body.

25 There is a path before each person that seems right, but it ends in death.

26 It is good for workers to have an appetite; an empty stomach drives them on.

27 Scoundrels hunt for scandal; their words are a destructive blaze.

28 A troublemaker plants seeds of strife; gossip separates the best of friends.

29 Violent people deceive their companions, leading them down a harmful path.

30 With narrowed eyes, they plot evil; without a word, they plan their mischief.

31 Gray hair is a crown of glory; it is gained by living a godly life.

32 It is better to be patient than powerful; it is better to have self-control than to conquer a city.

33 We may throw the dice, but the LORD determines how they fall.

**I hear Christians talk a lot about God's will. Has God planned out everything I'll ever do?**

Follow these instructions: Put your right hand straight up in the air. Next place your index finger in your left ear (come on, your left ear). Now clap your hands.

Who controlled your hand and fingers?

Tough question. Especially if you were silly enough to do what we asked. But we know from experience that when people give us instructions, *we* choose whether or not we obey.

The question, however, is who has ultimate control— you or God. This question has been debated for centuries, and the discussion can get quite complicated. For now, let's keep it as simple as possible.

We each have a will, a part within our brains that is the "chooser." Because we are human, the things we do sometimes don't match up with what God wants us to do. It isn't God's will for us to sin.

Of course, God is strong enough to force his will on us. But because he loves us, he allows us to have choices. What loving, earthly father would force his child to say, "I love you, Daddy"? There would be no satisfaction at all in forced expressions of love.

God does not force us to follow him. And it is obvious that many use their will to reject Christ. In essence, they choose to go to hell!

Putting all of these facts together points to the conclusion that God has allowed us to use our will to sometimes go against his will. One of the highest acts of love you can give someone is the opportunity to reject you. This is exactly what God has done.

So what *is* God's will for us? First, it is to know him.

Second, it is to help others. "For we are God's masterpiece. He has created us anew in Christ Jesus, so that we can do the good things he planned for us long ago" (Ephesians 2:10).

Third, it is to be filled with the Holy Spirit. "So be careful how you live, not as fools but as those who are wise. Make the most of every opportunity for doing good in these evil days. Don't act thoughtlessly, but try to understand what the Lord wants you to do. Don't be drunk with wine, because that will ruin your life. Instead, let the Holy Spirit fill and control you" (Ephesians 5:15-18).

By allowing God to fill you, you are really saying, "God, take my will and help me do what you want." You are following the good advice of Proverbs 16:9.

CHAPTER **17** **TRUE FRIENDS ARE LOYAL.** A dry crust eaten in peace is better than a great feast with strife.

[2]A wise slave will rule over the master's shameful sons and will share their inheritance.

[3]Fire tests the purity of silver and gold, but the LORD tests the heart.

[4]Wrongdoers listen to wicked talk; liars pay attention to destructive words.

[5]Those who mock the poor insult their Maker; those who rejoice at the misfortune of others will be punished.

**MOCKING ● ● • • •**

17:5 **Few acts are as cruel as making fun of those who are less fortunate, but many people do it because it makes them feel good to be better off or more successful than someone else. Mocking the poor is mocking the God who made them. We also mock God when we mock the weak, or those who are different, or anyone who is an easy target. When you catch yourself putting down others just for fun, stop. If you don't, you will drag yourself down and anger God.**

[6]Grandchildren are the crowning glory of the aged; parents are the pride of their children.

[7]Eloquent speech is not fitting for a fool; even less are lies fitting for a ruler.

[8]A bribe seems to work like magic for those who give it; they succeed in all they do.

[9]Disregarding another person's faults preserves love; telling about them separates close friends.

[10]A single rebuke does more for a person of understanding than a hundred lashes on the back of a fool.

[11]Evil people seek rebellion, but they will be severely punished.

[12]It is safer to meet a bear robbed of her cubs than to confront a fool caught in folly.

[13]If you repay evil for good, evil will never leave your house.

[14]Beginning a quarrel is like opening a floodgate, so drop the matter before a dispute breaks out.

[15]The LORD despises those who acquit the guilty and condemn the innocent.

[16]It is senseless to pay tuition to educate a fool who has no heart for wisdom.

[17]A friend is always loyal, and a brother is born to help in time of need.

[18]It is poor judgment to co-sign a friend's note, to become responsible for a neighbor's debts.

[19]Anyone who loves to quarrel loves sin; anyone who speaks boastfully* invites disaster.

[20]The crooked heart will not prosper; the twisted tongue tumbles into trouble.

[21]It is painful to be the parent of a fool; there is no joy for the father of a rebel.

[22]A cheerful heart is good medicine, but a broken spirit saps a person's strength.

[23]The wicked accept secret bribes to pervert justice.

[24]Sensible people keep their eyes glued on wisdom, but a fool's eyes wander to the ends of the earth.

[25]A foolish child* brings grief to a father and bitterness to a mother.

[26]It is wrong to fine the godly for being good or to punish nobles for being honest!

[27]A truly wise person uses few words; a person with understanding is even-tempered.

[28]Even fools are thought to be wise when they keep silent; when they keep their mouths shut, they seem intelligent.

CHAPTER **18** **GET THE FACTS BEFORE DECIDING.** A recluse is self-indulgent, snarling at every sound principle of conduct.

[2]Fools have no interest in understanding; they only want to air their own opinions.

[3]When the wicked arrive, contempt, shame, and disgrace are sure to follow.

[4]A person's words can be life-giving water; words of true wisdom are as refreshing as a bubbling brook.

[5]It is wrong for a judge to favor the guilty or condemn the innocent.

[6]Fools get into constant quarrels; they are asking for a beating.

**There are "friends" who destroy each other, but a *real* friend sticks closer than a brother.**

PROVERBS 18:24

17:19 Or *who builds up defenses;* Hebrew reads *who makes a high gate.* 17:25 Hebrew *son.*

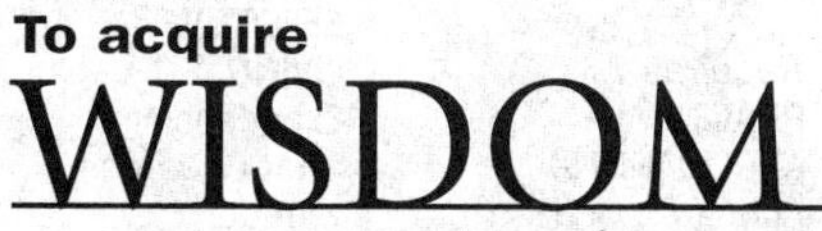

To acquire
WISDOM
is to love
oneself;
people who
cherish
UNDERSTANDING
will prosper
prosper
prosper
prosper.

PROVERBS 19:8

⁷The mouths of fools are their ruin; their lips get them into trouble.
⁸What dainty morsels rumors are—but they sink deep into one's heart.
⁹A lazy person is as bad as someone who destroys things.
¹⁰The name of the LORD is a strong fortress; the godly run to him and are safe.
¹¹The rich think of their wealth as an impregnable defense; they imagine it is a high wall of safety.
¹²Haughtiness goes before destruction; humility precedes honor.
¹³What a shame, what folly, to give advice before listening to the facts!
¹⁴The human spirit can endure a sick body, but who can bear it if the spirit is crushed?
¹⁵Intelligent people are always open to new ideas. In fact, they look for them.
¹⁶Giving a gift works wonders; it may bring you before important people!
¹⁷Any story sounds true until someone sets the record straight.
¹⁸Casting lots can end arguments and settle disputes between powerful opponents.
¹⁹It's harder to make amends with an offended friend than to capture a fortified city. Arguments separate friends like a gate locked with iron bars.
²⁰Words satisfy the soul as food satisfies the stomach; the right words on a person's lips bring satisfaction.
²¹Those who love to talk will experience the consequences, for the tongue can kill or nourish life.
²²The man who finds a wife finds a treasure and receives favor from the LORD.
²³The poor plead for mercy; the rich answer with insults.
²⁴There are "friends" who destroy each other, but a real friend sticks closer than a brother.

## CHAPTER 19 A LAZY MAN GOES HUNGRY.

It is better to be poor and honest than to be a fool and dishonest.
²Zeal without knowledge is not good; a person who moves too quickly may go the wrong way.
³People ruin their lives by their own foolishness and then are angry at the LORD.
⁴Wealth makes many "friends"; poverty drives them away.
⁵A false witness will not go unpunished, nor will a liar escape.
⁶Many beg favors from a prince; everyone is the friend of a person who gives gifts!
⁷If the relatives of the poor despise them, how much more will their friends avoid them. The poor call after them, but they are gone.
⁸To acquire wisdom is to love oneself; people who cherish understanding will prosper.
⁹A false witness will not go unpunished, and a liar will be destroyed.
¹⁰It isn't right for a fool to live in luxury or for a slave to rule over princes!
¹¹People with good sense restrain their anger; they earn esteem by overlooking wrongs.
¹²The king's anger is like a lion's roar, but his favor is like dew on the grass.
¹³A foolish child* is a calamity to a father; a nagging wife annoys like a constant dripping.
¹⁴Parents can provide their sons with an inheritance of houses and wealth, but only the LORD can give an understanding wife.
¹⁵A lazy person sleeps soundly—and goes hungry.
¹⁶Keep the commandments and keep your life; despising them leads to death.
¹⁷If you help the poor, you are lending to the LORD—and he will repay you!
¹⁸Discipline your children while there is hope. If you don't, you will ruin their lives.
¹⁹Short-tempered people must pay their own penalty. If you rescue them once, you will have to do it again.
²⁰Get all the advice and instruction you can, and be wise the rest of your life.

### TRUE FRIEND ● ● • • •

**18:24 Many people today feel cut off and alienated from others. Being in a crowd just makes people more aware of their isolation. Lonely people don't need to hear "Have a nice day." They need friends who will stick close, listen, care, and offer help when it is needed–in good and bad times. It is better to have one such friend than dozens of superficial acquaintances. Instead of wishing you could find a true friend, seek to become one yourself. There are people who need your friendship. Ask God to reveal them to you, and then take on the challenge of being a true friend.**

19:13 Hebrew *son;* also in 19:27.

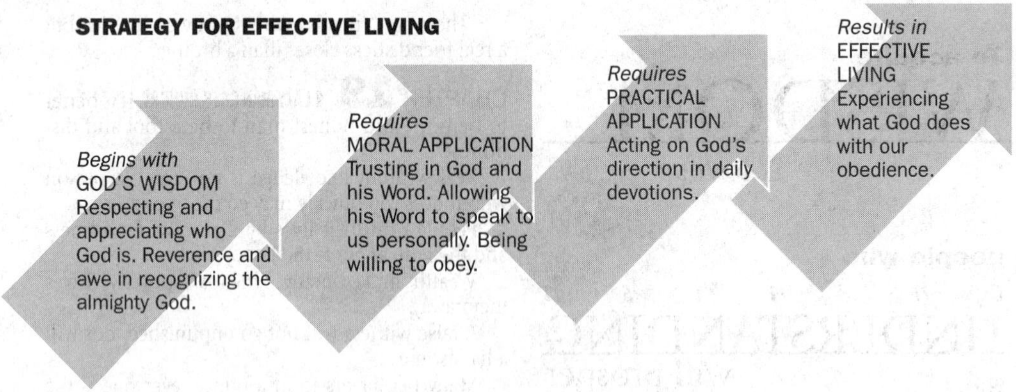

**STRATEGY FOR EFFECTIVE LIVING**

*Begins with*
GOD'S WISDOM
Respecting and appreciating who God is. Reverence and awe in recognizing the almighty God.

*Requires*
MORAL APPLICATION
Trusting in God and his Word. Allowing his Word to speak to us personally. Being willing to obey.

*Requires*
PRACTICAL APPLICATION
Acting on God's direction in daily devotions.

*Results in*
EFFECTIVE LIVING
Experiencing what God does with our obedience.

21You can make many plans, but the LORD's purpose will prevail.
22Loyalty makes a person attractive. And it is better
to be poor than dishonest.
23Fear of the LORD gives life, security, and protection from harm.
24Some people are so lazy that they won't even lift
a finger to feed themselves.
25If you punish a mocker, the simpleminded will
learn a lesson; if you reprove the wise, they will be
all the wiser.
26Children who mistreat their father or chase away
their mother are a public disgrace and an embarrassment.
27If you stop listening to instruction, my child, you
have turned your back on knowledge.
28A corrupt witness makes a mockery of justice;
the mouth of the wicked gulps down evil.
29Mockers will be punished, and the backs of fools
will be beaten.

CHAPTER **20** **YOUR ACTIONS TELL ABOUT YOU.** Wine
produces mockers; liquor leads to brawls. Whoever
is led astray by drink cannot be wise.
2The king's fury is like a lion's roar; to rouse his
anger is to risk your life.
3Avoiding a fight is a mark of honor; only fools
insist on quarreling.
4If you are too lazy to plow in the right season, you
will have no food at the harvest.
5Though good advice lies deep within a person's
heart, the wise will draw it out.
6Many will say they are loyal friends, but who can
find one who is really faithful?
7The godly walk with integrity; blessed are their
children after them.
8When a king judges, he carefully weighs all the
evidence, distinguishing the bad from the good.
9Who can say, "I have cleansed my heart; I am
pure and free from sin"?
10The LORD despises double standards of every
kind.
11Even children are known by the way they act,
whether their conduct is pure and right.
12Ears to hear and eyes to see—both are gifts from
the LORD.
13If you love sleep, you will end in poverty. Keep
your eyes open, and there will be plenty to eat!
14The buyer haggles over the price, saying, "It's
worthless," then brags about getting a bargain!
15Wise speech is rarer and more valuable than
gold and rubies.
16Be sure to get collateral from anyone who guarantees the debt of a stranger. Get a deposit if someone guarantees the debt of a foreigner.*
17Stolen bread tastes sweet, but it turns to gravel in
the mouth.
18Plans succeed through good counsel; don't go to
war without the advice of others.
19A gossip tells secrets, so don't hang around with
someone who talks too much.
20If you curse your father or mother, the lamp of
your life will be snuffed out.
21An inheritance obtained early in life is not a
blessing in the end.
22Don't say, "I will get even for this wrong." Wait
for the LORD to handle the matter.
23The LORD despises double standards; he is not
pleased by dishonest scales.
24How can we understand the road we travel? It is
the LORD who directs our steps.
25It is dangerous to make a rash promise to God
before counting the cost.
26A wise king finds the wicked, lays them out like
wheat, then runs the crushing wheel over them.
27The LORD's searchlight penetrates the human
spirit,* exposing every hidden motive.

**LOOKS ● ● • • •**

19:22 **You can't do much about the body with which you were born. However, you can do a lot about what is on the inside. Inwardly, you can be as attractive as you want to be. You can have kindness, for example, in any amount you choose. You can control your most important asset: the attractiveness of your character.**

20:16 An alternate reading in the Hebrew text is *the debt of an adulterous woman;* compare 27:13. 20:27 Or *The human spirit is the LORD's searchlight.*

28Unfailing love and faithfulness protect the king;
his throne is made secure through love.
29The glory of the young is their strength; the gray
hair of experience is the splendor of the old.
30Physical punishment cleanses away evil;* such
discipline purifies the heart.

CHAPTER **21** **LEARN BY LISTENING.** The king's
heart is like a stream of water directed by the LORD;
he turns it wherever he pleases.
2People may think they are doing what is right,
but the LORD examines the heart.
3The LORD is more pleased when we do what is
just and right than when we give him sacrifices.
4Haughty eyes, a proud heart, and evil actions are
all sin.
5Good planning and hard work lead to prosperity,
but hasty shortcuts lead to poverty.
6Wealth created by lying is a vanishing mist and a
deadly trap.*
7Because the wicked refuse to do what is just, their
violence boomerangs and destroys them.
8The guilty walk a crooked path; the innocent
travel a straight road.
9It is better to live alone in the corner of an attic
than with a contentious wife in a lovely home.
10Evil people love to harm others; their neighbors
get no mercy from them.
11A simpleton can learn only by seeing mockers
punished; a wise person learns from instruction.
12The Righteous One* knows what is going on in
the homes of the wicked; he will bring the wicked to
disaster.
13Those who shut their ears to the cries of the poor
will be ignored in their own time of need.
14A secret gift calms anger; a secret bribe pacifies
fury.
15Justice is a joy to the godly, but it causes dismay
among evildoers.
16The person who strays from common sense will
end up in the company of the dead.
17Those who love pleasure become poor; wine
and luxury are not the way to riches.
18Sometimes the wicked are punished to save the
godly, and the treacherous for the upright.
19It is better to live alone in the desert than with a
crabby, complaining wife.
20The wise have wealth and luxury, but fools
spend whatever they get.
21Whoever pursues godliness and unfailing love
will find life, godliness, and honor.
22The wise conquer the city of the strong and level
the fortress in which they trust.
23If you keep your mouth shut, you will stay out of
trouble.
24Mockers are proud and haughty; they act with
boundless arrogance.
25The desires of lazy people will be their ruin, for

**MOTIVES ● ● ● • •**

21:2 **People can find an excuse for doing almost anything, but God looks behind the excuse to the motives. We often have to make difficult choices in areas of life where the right action is hard to discern. We can help ourself make such decisions by trying to identify our motives first, and then asking, "Would God be pleased with my real reasons for doing this?" God is not pleased when we do good deeds only to receive something back.**

their hands refuse to work. 26They are always greedy
for more, while the godly love to give!
27God loathes the sacrifice of an evil person, especially when it is brought with ulterior motives.
28A false witness will be cut off, but an attentive
witness will be allowed to speak.
29The wicked put up a bold front, but the upright
proceed with care.
30Human plans, no matter how wise or well advised, cannot stand against the LORD.
31The horses are prepared for battle, but the victory belongs to the LORD.

CHAPTER **22** **GIVING CAN MAKE YOU HAPPY.** Choose
a good reputation over great riches, for being held in
high esteem is better than having silver or gold.
2The rich and the poor have this in common: The
LORD made them both.
3A prudent person foresees the danger ahead and
takes precautions; the simpleton goes blindly on and
suffers the consequences.
4True humility and fear of the LORD lead to riches,
honor, and long life.
5The deceitful walk a thorny, treacherous road;
whoever values life will stay away.
➤ 6Teach your children to choose the right path, and
when they are older, they will remain upon it.
7Just as the rich rule the poor, so the borrower is
servant to the lender.
8Those who plant seeds of injustice will harvest
disaster, and their reign of terror will end.
9Blessed are those who are generous, because they
feed the poor.
10Throw out the mocker, and fighting, quarrels,
and insults will disappear.
11Anyone who loves a pure heart and gracious
speech is the king's friend.
12The LORD preserves knowledge, but he ruins the
plans of the deceitful.
13The lazy person is full of excuses, saying, "If I go
outside, I might meet a lion in the street and be
killed!"
14The mouth of an immoral woman is a deep pit;
those living under the LORD's displeasure will fall
into it.
➤ 15A youngster's heart is filled with foolishness, but
discipline will drive it away.
16A person who gets ahead by oppressing the poor
or by showering gifts on the rich will end in poverty.

**20:30** The meaning of the Hebrew is uncertain. **21:6** As in Greek version; Hebrew reads *mist for those who seek death.* **21:12** Or *The righteous man.*

[17]Listen to the words of the wise; apply your heart to my instruction. [18]For it is good to keep these sayings deep within yourself, always ready on your lips. [19]I am teaching you today—yes, you—so you will trust in the LORD. [20]I have written thirty sayings for you, filled with advice and knowledge. [21]In this way, you may know the truth and bring an accurate report to those who sent you.

[22]Do not rob the poor because they are poor or exploit the needy in court. [23]For the LORD is their defender. He will injure anyone who injures them.

[24]Keep away from angry, short-tempered people, [25]or you will learn to be like them and endanger your soul.

[26]Do not co-sign another person's note or put up a guarantee for someone else's loan. [27]If you can't pay it, even your bed will be snatched from under you.

## DRINKING

The first time 13-year-old Paul drank with his friends, Mario and Cleve, it was kind of exciting. With the help of a college student, the three guys managed to get a six-pack—two beers each. It wasn't enough to get smashed, but it was enough to get a slight buzz. Sipping slowly as they sat around a campfire, the boys laughed for several hours. The next day Mario suggested, "We should do this more often!"

So each weekend they played the game, always coming up with a new scheme to acquire alcohol. Once they stumbled upon a block party where there were three "unguarded" kegs just sitting there. Another time they swiped a bottle of vodka from a neighbor's liquor cabinet. Another time a high school senior bought them some tequila and showed them how to shoot it.

Every now and then one of the guys would overdo it and end up with a mean hangover. But they never got caught. It didn't affect their grades at school since they only did it on weekends. Everything was cool . . . until Paul went on a church retreat one weekend.

Now Paul won't go with Mario and Cleve anymore. He thinks they're headed for trouble. And they think he's turned into a religious fanatic.

See one of the passages that changed Paul's mind about drinking. Read Proverbs 23:29-35.

[28]Do not steal your neighbor's property by moving the ancient boundary markers set up by your ancestors.

[29]Do you see any truly competent workers? They will serve kings rather than ordinary people.

CHAPTER **23** **CRITICISM CAN HELP YOU.** When dining with a ruler, pay attention to what is put before you. [2]If you are a big eater, put a knife to your throat, [3]and don't desire all the delicacies—deception may be involved.

[4]Don't weary yourself trying to get rich. Why waste

### COMPANIONS ● ● • • •

22:24-25 **People tend to become like those around them. Even the negative characteristics sometimes rub off. The Bible exhorts us to be cautious in our choice of companions. Choose companions who have the characteristics you would like to develop in your own life.**

your time? [5]For riches can disappear as though they had the wings of a bird!

[6]Don't eat with people who are stingy; don't desire their delicacies. [7]"Eat and drink," they say, but they don't mean it. They are always thinking about how much it costs. [8]You will vomit up the delicious food they serve, and you will have to take back your words of appreciation for their "kindness."

[9]Don't waste your breath on fools, for they will despise the wisest advice.

[10]Don't steal the land of defenseless orphans by moving the ancient boundary markers, [11]for their Redeemer is strong. He himself will bring their charges against you.

[12]Commit yourself to instruction; attune your ears to hear words of knowledge.

[13]Don't fail to correct your children. They won't die if you spank them. [14]Physical discipline may well save them from death.*

[15]My child,* how I will rejoice if you become wise. [16]Yes, my heart will thrill when you speak what is right and just.

[17]Don't envy sinners, but always continue to fear the LORD. [18]For surely you have a future ahead of you; your hope will not be disappointed.

[19]My child, listen and be wise. Keep your heart on the right course. [20]Do not carouse with drunkards and gluttons, [21]for they are on their way to poverty. Too much sleep clothes a person with rags.

[22]Listen to your father, who gave you life, and don't despise your mother's experience when she is old. [23]Get the truth and don't ever sell it; also get wisdom, discipline, and discernment. [24]The father of godly children has cause for joy. What a pleasure it is to have wise children.* [25]So give your parents joy! May she who gave you birth be happy.

[26]O my son, give me your heart. May your eyes delight in my ways of wisdom. [27]A prostitute is a deep pit; an adulterous woman is treacherous.* [28]She hides and waits like a robber, looking for another victim who will be unfaithful to his wife.

[29]Who has anguish? Who has sorrow? Who is always fighting? Who is always complaining? Who has unnecessary bruises? Who has bloodshot eyes? [30]It is the one who spends long hours in the taverns, trying out new drinks. [31]Don't let the sparkle and smooth taste of wine deceive you. [32]For in the end it bites like a poisonous serpent; it stings like a viper. [33]You will see hallucinations, and you will say crazy things. [34]You will stagger like a sailor tossed at sea, clinging to a swaying mast. [35]And you will say, "They hit me, but I didn't feel it. I didn't even know it when they beat me up. When will I wake up so I can have another drink?"

23:14 Hebrew *from Sheol.* 23:15 Hebrew *My son;* also in 23:19. 23:24 Hebrew *a wise son.* 23:27 Hebrew *is a narrow well.*

CHAPTER **24** **PLANS ARE AS BAD AS ACTIONS.** Don't envy evil people; don't desire their company. 2For they spend their days plotting violence, and their words are always stirring up trouble.

3A house is built by wisdom and becomes strong through good sense. 4Through knowledge its rooms are filled with all sorts of precious riches and valuables.

5A wise man is mightier than a strong man,* and a man of knowledge is more powerful than a strong man. 6So don't go to war without wise guidance; victory depends on having many counselors.

7Wisdom is too much for a fool. When the leaders gather, the fool has nothing to say.

8A person who plans evil will get a reputation as a troublemaker. 9The schemes of a fool are sinful; everyone despises a mocker.

10If you fail under pressure, your strength is not very great.

11Rescue those who are unjustly sentenced to death; don't stand back and let them die. 12Don't try to avoid responsibility by saying you didn't know about it. For God knows all hearts, and he sees you. He keeps watch over your soul, and he knows you knew! And he will judge all people according to what they have done.

13My child,* eat honey, for it is good, and the honeycomb is sweet to the taste. 14In the same way, wisdom is sweet to your soul. If you find it, you will have a bright future, and your hopes will not be cut short.

15Do not lie in wait like an outlaw at the home of the godly. And don't raid the house where the godly live. 16They may trip seven times, but each time they will rise again. But one calamity is enough to lay the wicked low.

17Do not rejoice when your enemies fall into trouble. Don't be happy when they stumble. 18For the LORD will be displeased with you and will turn his anger away from them.

19Do not fret because of evildoers; don't envy the wicked. 20For the evil have no future; their light will be snuffed out.

21My child, fear the LORD and the king, and don't associate with rebels. 22For you will go down with them to sudden disaster. Who knows where the punishment from the LORD and the king will end?

23Here are some further sayings of the wise:

It is wrong to show favoritism when passing judgment. 24A judge who says to the wicked, "You are innocent," will be cursed by many people and denounced by the nations. 25But blessings are showered on those who convict the guilty.

26It is an honor to receive an honest reply.

27Develop your business first before building your house.

28Do not testify spitefully against innocent neighbors; don't lie about them. 29And don't say, "Now I can pay them back for all their meanness to me! I'll get even!"

**ALCOHOL ● ● • • •**

23:29-30 **The soothing comfort of alcohol is only temporary. Real relief comes from dealing with the cause of anguish and sorrow, and turning to God for peace. Don't lose yourself in alcohol; find yourself in God.**

30I walked by the field of a lazy person, the vineyard of one lacking sense. 31I saw that it was overgrown with thorns. It was covered with weeds, and its walls were broken down. 32Then, as I looked and thought about it, I learned this lesson: 33A little extra sleep, a little more slumber, a little folding of the hands to rest—34and poverty will pounce on you like a bandit; scarcity will attack you like an armed robber.

CHAPTER **25** **KEEP YOUR PROMISES.** These are more proverbs of Solomon, collected by the advisers of King Hezekiah of Judah.

2It is God's privilege to conceal things and the king's privilege to discover them.

3No one can discover the height of heaven, the depth of the earth, or all that goes on in the king's mind!

4Remove the dross from silver, and the sterling will be ready for the silversmith. 5Remove the wicked from the king's court, and his reign will be made secure by justice.

6Don't demand an audience with the king or push for a place among the great. 7It is better to wait for an invitation than to be sent to the end of the line, publicly disgraced!

Just because you see something, 8don't be in a hurry to go to court. You might go down before your neighbors in shameful defeat. 9So discuss the matter with them privately. Don't tell anyone else, 10or others may accuse you of gossip. Then you will never regain your good reputation.

11Timely advice is as lovely as golden apples in a silver basket.

12Valid criticism is as treasured by the one who heeds it as jewelry made from finest gold.

13Faithful messengers are as refreshing as snow in the heat of summer. They revive the spirit of their employer.

14A person who doesn't give a promised gift is like clouds and wind that don't bring rain.

15Patience can persuade a prince, and soft speech can crush strong opposition.

16Do you like honey? Don't eat too much of it, or it will make you sick!

17Don't visit your neighbors too often, or you will wear out your welcome.

18Telling lies about others is as harmful as hitting

**LYING ● ● • • •**

25:18 **Lying is vicious. Its effects can be as permanent as those of a stab wound. The next time you are tempted to pass on a bit of gossip, imagine yourself striking the victim of your remarks with a sword. This image may shock you into silence.**

**24:5** As in Greek version; Hebrew reads *A wise man is strength.* **24:13** Hebrew *My son;* also in 24:21.

them with an ax, wounding them with a sword, or shooting them with a sharp arrow.

[19]Putting confidence in an unreliable person is like chewing with a toothache or walking on a broken foot.

[20]Singing cheerful songs to a person whose heart is heavy is as bad as stealing someone's jacket in cold weather or rubbing salt in a wound.

[21]If your enemies are hungry, give them food to eat. If they are thirsty, give them water to drink. [22]You will heap burning coals on their heads, and the LORD will reward you.

[23]As surely as a wind from the north brings rain, so a gossiping tongue causes anger!

[24]It is better to live alone in the corner of an attic than with a contentious wife in a lovely home.

[25]Good news from far away is like cold water to the thirsty.

[26]If the godly compromise with the wicked, it is like polluting a fountain or muddying a spring.

[27]Just as it is not good to eat too much honey, it is not good for people to think about all the honors they deserve.

[28]A person without self-control is as defenseless as a city with broken-down walls.

## LAZINESS ● ● • • •

26:13-16 **If a person is not willing to work, he can find endless excuses to avoid it. But laziness is more dangerous than a fierce lion. The less you do, the less you want to do, and the more useless you become. To overcome laziness, take a few small steps toward change. Set a concrete, realistic goal. Figure out the steps needed to reach it. Pray for strength and persistence. And follow those steps. To keep your excuses from making you useless, stop making useless excuses.**

CHAPTER **26** **REBELS ARE IMPOSSIBLE.** Honor doesn't go with fools any more than snow with summer or rain with harvest.

[2]Like a fluttering sparrow or a darting swallow, an unfair curse will not land on its intended victim.

[3]Guide a horse with a whip, a donkey with a bridle, and a fool with a rod to his back!

[4]When arguing with fools, don't answer their foolish arguments, or you will become as foolish as they are.

[5]When arguing with fools, be sure to answer their foolish arguments, or they will become wise in their own estimation.

[6]Trusting a fool to convey a message is as foolish as cutting off one's feet or drinking poison!

[7]In the mouth of a fool, a proverb becomes as limp as a paralyzed leg.

[8]Honoring a fool is as foolish as tying a stone to a slingshot.

[9]A proverb in a fool's mouth is as dangerous as a thornbush brandished by a drunkard.

[10]An employer who hires a fool or a bystander is like an archer who shoots recklessly.

[11]As a dog returns to its vomit, so a fool repeats his folly.

[12]There is more hope for fools than for people who think they are wise.

[13]The lazy person is full of excuses, saying, "I can't go outside because there might be a lion on the road! Yes, I'm sure there's a lion out there!"

[14]As a door turns back and forth on its hinges, so the lazy person turns over in bed.

[15]Some people are so lazy that they won't lift a finger to feed themselves.

[16]Lazy people consider themselves smarter than seven wise counselors.

[17]Yanking a dog's ears is as foolish as interfering in someone else's argument.

[18]Just as damaging as a mad man shooting a lethal weapon [19]is someone who lies to a friend and then says, "I was only joking."

[20]Fire goes out for lack of fuel, and quarrels disappear when gossip stops.

[21]A quarrelsome person starts fights as easily as hot embers light charcoal or fire lights wood.

[22]What dainty morsels rumors are—but they sink deep into one's heart.

[23]Smooth* words may hide a wicked heart, just as a pretty glaze covers a common clay pot.

[24]People with hate in their hearts may sound pleasant enough, but don't believe them. [25]Though they pretend to be kind, their hearts are full of all kinds of evil. [26]While their hatred may be concealed by trickery, it will finally come to light for all to see.

[27]If you set a trap for others, you will get caught in it yourself. If you roll a boulder down on others, it will roll back and crush you.

[28]A lying tongue hates its victims, and flattery causes ruin.

CHAPTER **27** **JEALOUSY IS DANGEROUS.** Don't brag about tomorrow, since you don't know what the day will bring.

[2]Don't praise yourself; let others do it!

[3]A stone is heavy and sand is weighty, but the resentment caused by a fool is heavier than both.

[4]Anger is cruel, and wrath is like a flood, but who can survive the destructiveness of jealousy?

## NAGGING ● ● • • •

27:15-16 **Nagging, a steady stream of unwanted advice, is a form of torture. People nag because they think they're not getting through, but nagging hinders communication more than it helps. When tempted to engage in this destructive habit, stop and examine your motives. Are you more concerned about yourself– about getting your way or being right–than about the person you are pretending to help? If you truly are concerned about other people, is there a more effective way to get through to them? Surprise them with words of love and patience, and see what happens.**

**26:23** As in Greek version; Hebrew reads *Burning.*

5 An open rebuke is better than hidden love!

6 Wounds from a friend are better than many kisses from an enemy.

7 Honey seems tasteless to a person who is full, but even bitter food tastes sweet to the hungry.

8 A person who strays from home is like a bird that strays from its nest.

9 The heartfelt counsel of a friend is as sweet as perfume and incense.

10 Never abandon a friend—either yours or your father's. Then in your time of need, you won't have to ask your relatives for assistance. It is better to go to a neighbor than to a relative who lives far away.

11 My child,* how happy I will be if you turn out to be wise! Then I will be able to answer my critics.

12 A prudent person foresees the danger ahead and takes precautions. The simpleton goes blindly on and suffers the consequences.

13 Be sure to get collateral from anyone who guarantees the debt of a stranger. Get a deposit if someone guarantees the debt of an adulterous woman.

14 If you shout a pleasant greeting to your neighbor too early in the morning, it will be counted as a curse!

15 A nagging wife is as annoying as the constant dripping on a rainy day. 16 Trying to stop her complaints is like trying to stop the wind or hold something with greased hands.

17 As iron sharpens iron, a friend sharpens a friend.

18 Workers who tend a fig tree are allowed to eat its fruit. In the same way, workers who protect their employer's interests will be rewarded.

19 As a face is reflected in water, so the heart reflects the person.

20 Just as Death and Destruction* are never satisfied, so human desire is never satisfied.

21 Fire tests the purity of silver and gold, but a person is tested by being praised.

22 You cannot separate fools from their foolishness, even though you grind them like grain with mortar and pestle.

23 Know the state of your flocks, and put your heart into caring for your herds, 24 for riches don't last forever, and the crown might not be secure for the next generation. 25 After the hay is harvested, the new crop appears, and the mountain grasses are gathered in, 26 your sheep will provide wool for clothing, and your goats will be sold for the price of a field. 27 And you will have enough goats' milk for you, your family, and your servants.

## CHAPTER 28

**ADMIT YOUR MISTAKES.** The wicked run away when no one is chasing them, but the godly are as bold as lions.

2 When there is moral rot within a nation, its government topples easily. But with wise and knowledgeable leaders, there is stability.

3 A poor person who oppresses the poor is like a pounding rain that destroys the crops.

### INTENTIONS ● ● • • •

**28:9 God does not listen to our prayers if we intend to go back to our sin as soon as we get off our knees. If we want to forsake our sin and follow him, however, he willingly listens—no matter how bad our sin has been. What closes his ears is not the depth of our sin, but the shallowness of our "repentance."**

4 To reject the law is to praise the wicked; to obey the law is to fight them.

5 Evil people don't understand justice, but those who follow the LORD understand completely.

6 It is better to be poor and honest than rich and crooked.

7 Young people who obey the law are wise; those who seek out worthless companions bring shame to their parents.

8 A person who makes money by charging interest will lose it. It will end up in the hands of someone who is kind to the poor.

9 The prayers of a person who ignores the law are despised.

10 Those who lead the upright into sin will fall into their own trap, but the honest will inherit good things.

11 Rich people picture themselves as wise, but their real poverty is evident to the poor.

12 When the godly succeed, everyone is glad. When the wicked take charge, people go into hiding.

13 People who cover over their sins will not prosper. But if they confess and forsake them, they will receive mercy.

14 Blessed are those who have a tender conscience,* but the stubborn are headed for serious trouble.

15 A wicked ruler is as dangerous to the poor as a lion or bear attacking them.

16 Only a stupid prince will oppress his people, but a king will have a long reign if he hates dishonesty and bribes.

17 A murderer's tormented conscience will drive him into the grave. Don't protect him!

18 The honest will be rescued from harm, but those who are crooked will be destroyed.

19 Hard workers have plenty of food; playing around brings poverty.

20 The trustworthy will get a rich reward. But the person who wants to get rich quick will only get into trouble.

21 Showing partiality is never good, yet some will do wrong for something as small as a piece of bread.

22 A greedy person tries to get rich quick, but it only leads to poverty.

23 In the end, people appreciate frankness more than flattery.

> 24 Robbing your parents and then saying, "What's wrong with that?" is as serious as committing murder.

25 Greed causes fighting; trusting the LORD leads to prosperity.

27:11 Hebrew *My son.* 27:20 Hebrew *Sheol and Abaddon.* 28:14 Hebrew *those who fear.*

# Ultimate Issues

## LOOKING FOR A PERFECT 10

**W**ANTED: LIFE PARTNER. Must have a body that can stop traffic, money to last two lifetimes (mine and yours), hair that looks like it belongs in a ***shampoo commercial,*** great sense of humor, high IQ (just below mine), well-paying job, your own (hot) car. Must love my kind of music (loud), sports, and everything about me. Send resume and photo to: Is That Too Much to Ask? Inc. P.O. Box 101010 FantasyLand, U.S.A. 12345.

**S**ound familiar? Everybody seems to have an image of the perfect guy or girl. Perfect looks, perfect personality, perfect relationship . . . But think about it. What *really* makes someone a perfect 10? Looks: Thanks to *Playboy,* MTV, *Seventeen,* and a million other influences today, we are bombarded by images of unbelievably attractive men and women. The message is **as subtle as a sledgehammer:** Use our product and you will not only look as good as our models do, but you will find yourself surrounded by other beautiful people. You will be happy, popular, and adored.

**L**ooks *are* important. Anyone who says otherwise is kidding him or herself. There's nothing wrong with wanting to look your best, or with being attracted to good-looking people. But when looking good becomes an obsession—when you have to wear certain clothes, spend hours getting ready for school or a date, throw down a small fortune on cosmetics, colognes, hair products, etc.—you've bought into the MADISON AVENUE lie. You are more than your looks. You're *beautiful,* not because of your physical appearance, but because you were made in the image of God!

**P**ersonality: Everybody knows the joke. You've been set up for a blind date, you ask what he (or she) looks like and they say, "He (or she) has a *great* personality." Which tells you one thing: you're going to the movies with either Godzilla or Frankenstein's Bride.

**B**ut there's another side: an attractive guy or girl who has the personality of a **DEAD SQUID.** If you've encountered this, you know personality *is* important. You can only spend so much time looking at each other. Looks may draw attention, but personality keeps it. Or kills it.

**S**pirituality: *Hmmm,* you may be thinking. *Looks and personality, OK. But what is "spirituality"?* Everyone has a spiritual nature. That's what makes you more than a mass of oxygen-absorbing molecules, glands, and hormones. If you belong to Christ, you are spiritually alive. If not, you're spiritually dead. (For more on this, see Romans 3; Galatians 5:16-26; Ephesians 2:1-10.) When you're thinking about spending the rest of your life with someone, you need to look for more than looks and personality. You need to be spiritually compatible, too.

**P**roverbs 31:10-31 gives a vivid, lively picture of what a truly spiritual woman is like. And she's no PLASTIC SAINT, sitting home reading the Bible till her husband shows up. She's strong, intelligent, industrious, compassionate, wise: "She is clothed with strength and dignity (v. 25)." (When you get right down to it, that's a good description of a godly man, too.)

**S**ure, good looks are great. But everyone—*everyone*—grows old, gets wrinkles, and adds a few pounds. A relationship based on looks or personality is doomed to failure. Don't believe it? Try to find a successful, faithful marriage in Hollywood, ***Body Beautiful*** capital of the world.

**T**he only cement that can bond two people together for life is mutual commitment to God and to each other. When you're ready to find a partner for life, make the spiritual dimension your primary requirement. There's nothing wrong with looking for a perfect 10. Just remember, it takes more than beauty or a pleasant temperament to add up to someone whose love will last. So take a look at Proverbs 31. It's a great snapshot image of a person who has that something more. (For more on the subject of marriage itself, see the Ultimate Issue on marriage in Ephesians.)

[26]Trusting oneself is foolish, but those who walk in wisdom are safe.

[27]Whoever gives to the poor will lack nothing. But a curse will come upon those who close their eyes to poverty.

[28]When the wicked take charge, people hide. When the wicked meet disaster, the godly multiply.

CHAPTER **29** **GOD REWARDS FAIRNESS.** Whoever stubbornly refuses to accept criticism will suddenly be broken beyond repair.

[2]When the godly are in authority, the people rejoice. But when the wicked are in power, they groan.

[3]The man who loves wisdom brings joy to his father, but if he hangs around with prostitutes, his wealth is wasted.

[4]A just king gives stability to his nation, but one who demands bribes destroys it.

[5]To flatter people is to lay a trap for their feet.

[6]Evil people are trapped by sin, but the righteous escape, shouting for joy.

[7]The godly know the rights of the poor; the wicked don't care to know.

[8]Mockers can get a whole town agitated, but those who are wise will calm anger.

[9]If a wise person takes a fool to court, there will be ranting and ridicule but no satisfaction.

[10]The bloodthirsty hate the honest, but the upright seek out the honest.

[11]A fool gives full vent to anger, but a wise person quietly holds it back.

[12]If a ruler honors liars, all his advisers will be wicked.

[13]The poor and the oppressor have this in common—the LORD gives light to the eyes of both.

[14]A king who is fair to the poor will have a long reign.

[15]To discipline and reprimand a child produces wisdom, but a mother is disgraced by an undisciplined child.

[16]When the wicked are in authority, sin increases. But the godly will live to see the tyrant's downfall.

[17]Discipline your children, and they will give you happiness and peace of mind.

[18]When people do not accept divine guidance, they run wild. But whoever obeys the law is happy.

[19]For a servant, mere words are not enough—discipline is needed. For the words may be understood, but they are not heeded.

[20]There is more hope for a fool than for someone who speaks without thinking.

[21]A servant who is pampered from childhood will later become a rebel.

[22]A hot-tempered person starts fights and gets into all kinds of sin.

[23]Pride ends in humiliation, while humility brings honor.

[24]If you assist a thief, you are only hurting yourself. You will be punished if you report the crime, but you will be cursed if you don't.

[25]Fearing people is a dangerous trap, but to trust the LORD means safety.

[26]Many seek the ruler's favor, but justice comes from the LORD.

[27]The godly despise the wicked; the wicked despise the godly.

CHAPTER **30** **WONDERFUL THINGS.** The message of
Agur son of Jakeh. An oracle.*
I am weary, O God; I am weary and worn out,
O God.* [2]I am too ignorant to be human, and I lack
common sense. [3]I have not mastered human wis-
dom, nor do I know the Holy One.

[4]Who but God goes up to heaven and comes back down? Who holds the wind in his fists? Who wraps up the oceans in his cloak? Who has created the whole wide world? What is his name—and his son's name? Tell me if you know!

[5]Every word of God proves true. He defends all
who come to him for protection. [6]Do not add to
his words, or he may rebuke you, and you will be

## "Here's what I did..."

I went to England with a missions group to do street evangelism right after I graduated from high school. Once I got out on the street, supposedly ready to talk to someone, I froze. I was struck with fear and couldn't say a word.

It really bothered me. That evening I looked up "fear" in a concordance, and read through several Scriptures. The verse that helped me most was Proverbs 29:25: "Fearing people is a dangerous trap, but to trust the LORD means safety." I realized that I had fallen into Satan's trap because I was afraid of people—what they would think of me, even what they might do to me, if I tried to share the gospel. I vowed that I would trust in God.

The next day I was still nervous, but I asked God to keep me from falling into the trap of fear and to help me know what to say. Things went much better. As I trusted God to help and protect me during that missions trip, I grew more and more bold in sharing my faith. I actually came to enjoy it! But I might have stayed stuck in fear if I hadn't found that verse and really applied it to my situation.

Kristen

AGE 19

**30:1a** Or *son of Jakeh from Massa.* **30:1b** The Hebrew can also be translated *The man declares this to Ithiel, to Ithiel and to Ucal.*

**HOW GOD IS DESCRIBED IN PROVERBS**

Proverbs is a book about wise living. It often focuses on a person's response and attitude toward God, who is the source of wisdom. And a number of proverbs point out aspects of God's character. Knowing God helps us on the way to wisdom.

GOD . . .
is aware of all that happens—15:3
knows all people—15:11; 16:2; 21:2
is the maker of all things—16:4
controls all things—16:33; 21:30
is a strong fortress—18:10
rescues good people from danger—11:8, 21
rewards the godly—11:31
blesses good people, condemns the wicked—12:2
delights in our prayers—15:8, 29
loves those who obey him—11:27; 15:9-10; 16:20; 22:12
cares for poor, sick, and widows—15:25; 22:22-23
purifies hearts—17:3
hates evil—17:5; 21:27; 28:9

OUR RESPONSE SHOULD BE . . .
to reverence God—10:27; 14:26-27; 15:16; 16:6; 19:23; 28:14
to obey God's Word—13:13; 19:16
to please God—16:7; 20:12; 21:3
to trust God—22:17-19; 29:25

---

found a liar. [7]O God, I beg two favors from you
before I die. [8]First, help me never to tell a lie.
Second, give me neither poverty nor riches! Give
me just enough to satisfy my needs. [9]For if I grow
rich, I may deny you and say, "Who is the LORD?"
And if I am too poor, I may steal and thus insult
God's holy name.

[10]Never slander a person to his employer. If
you do, the person will curse you, and you will pay
for it.

[11]Some people curse their father and do not thank
their mother. [12]They feel pure, but they are filthy and
unwashed. [13]They are proud beyond description and
disdainful. [14]They devour the poor with teeth as
sharp as swords or knives. They destroy the needy
from the face of the earth.

[15]The leech has two suckers that cry out, "More,
more!"* There are three other things—no, four!—
that are never satisfied:
[16] the grave,
the barren womb,
the thirsty desert,
the blazing fire.

[17]The eye that mocks a father and despises a
mother will be plucked out by ravens of the valley
and eaten by vultures.

[18]There are three things that amaze me—no, four
things I do not understand:
[19] how an eagle glides through the sky,
how a snake slithers on a rock,
how a ship navigates the ocean,
how a man loves a woman.
[20]Equally amazing is how an adulterous woman can
satisfy her sexual appetite, shrug her shoulders, and
then say, "What's wrong with that?"

[21]There are three things that make the earth tremble—no, four it cannot endure:
[22] a slave who becomes a king,
an overbearing fool who prospers,
[23] a bitter woman who finally gets a husband,
a servant girl who supplants her mistress.

[24]There are four things on earth that are small but
unusually wise:
[25] Ants—they aren't strong,
but they store up food for the winter.
[26] Rock badgers*—they aren't powerful,
but they make their homes among the rocky cliffs.
[27] Locusts—they have no king,
but they march like an army in ranks.
[28] Lizards—they are easy to catch,
but they are found even in kings' palaces.

[29]There are three stately monarchs on the earth—
no, four:
[30] the lion, king of animals, who won't turn aside
for anything,
[31] the strutting rooster,
the male goat,
a king as he leads his army.

[32]If you have been a fool by being proud or plotting evil, don't brag about it—cover your mouth
with your hand in shame.

30:15 Hebrew *two daughters who cry out, "Give, give!"* 30:26 Or *coneys*, or *hyraxes*.

## IDEAL WOMAN ● ● ● • •

31:10-31 **Proverbs has a lot to say about women. How fitting that the book ends with a picture of a woman of strong character, great wisdom, many skills, and great compassion.**

**Some people have the mistaken idea that the ideal woman in the Bible is retiring, servile, and entirely domestic. Not so! This woman is an excellent wife and mother. She also is a manufacturer, importer, manager, realtor, farmer, seamstress, upholsterer, and merchant. Her strength and dignity do not come from her amazing achievements, however. They are a result of her reverence for God. In our society where physical appearance counts for so much, it may surprise us to realize that her appearance is never mentioned. Her attractiveness comes entirely from her character.**

**The woman described in this chapter has outstanding abilities. Her family's social position is high. In fact, she may not be one woman at all—she may be a composite portrait of ideal womanhood. Do not see her as a model to imitate in every detail; your days are not long enough to do everything she does! See her instead as an inspiration to be all you can be. We can't be just like her, but we can learn from her industry, integrity, and resourcefulness.**

[33]As the beating of cream yields butter, and a blow
to the nose causes bleeding, so anger causes quarrels.

CHAPTER **31** These are the sayings of King
Lemuel, an oracle* that his mother taught him.
[2]O my son, O son of my womb, O son of my
promises, [3]do not spend your strength on women,
on those who ruin kings.
[4]And it is not for kings, O Lemuel, to guzzle wine.
Rulers should not crave liquor. [5]For if they drink,
they may forget their duties and be unable to give
justice to those who are oppressed. [6]Liquor is for the
dying, and wine for those in deep depression. [7]Let
them drink to forget their poverty and remember
their troubles no more.
[8]Speak up for those who cannot speak for themselves; ensure justice for those who are perishing.
[9]Yes, speak up for the poor and helpless, and see that
they get justice.
[10]Who can find a virtuous and capable wife? She
is worth more than precious rubies. [11]Her husband
can trust her, and she will greatly enrich his life. [12]She
will not hinder him but help him all her life.
[13]She finds wool and flax and busily spins it.
[14]She is like a merchant's ship; she brings her food
from afar. [15]She gets up before dawn to prepare
breakfast for her household and plan the day's
work for her servant girls. [16]She goes out to inspect
a field and buys it; with her earnings she plants a
vineyard.
[17]She is energetic and strong, a hard worker. [18]She
watches for bargains; her lights burn late into the
night. [19]Her hands are busy spinning thread, her
fingers twisting fiber.
[20]She extends a helping hand to the poor and
opens her arms to the needy.
[21]She has no fear of winter for her household
because all of them have warm* clothes. [22]She quilts
her own bedspreads. She dresses like royalty in
gowns of finest cloth.
[23]Her husband is well known, for he sits in the
council meeting with the other civic leaders.
[24]She makes belted linen garments and sashes to
sell to the merchants.
[25]She is clothed with strength and dignity, and she
laughs with no fear of the future. [26]When she speaks,
her words are wise, and kindness is the rule when she
gives instructions. [27]She carefully watches all that
goes on in her household and does not have to bear
the consequences of laziness.
[28]Her children stand and bless her. Her husband
praises her: [29]"There are many virtuous and capable
women in the world, but you surpass them all!"
[30]Charm is deceptive, and beauty does not last;
but a woman who fears the LORD will be greatly
praised. [31]Reward her for all she has done. Let her
deeds publicly declare her praise.

31:1 Or *of Lemuel, king of Massa.* 31:21 As in Greek version; Hebrew *scarlet.*

# MEGA themes

**WISDOM** God wants his people to be wise. Two kinds of people portray two contrasting paths of life: The fool is the wicked, stubborn person who hates or ignores God; the wise person seeks to know and love God.

When we choose God's way, he grants us wisdom. His Word, the Bible, leads us to live right, have right relationships, and make right decisions.

1. Read 1:7 and 9:10. What did Solomon teach was the key to being wise?
2. What will be the results of wisdom in a person's life? (Check 3:13-26.)
3. How has knowing God and learning about his Word increased your personal wisdom?
4. In what areas of your life would you like to have more wisdom? Based on your study of Proverbs, how will you find that wisdom?

**RELATIONSHIPS** Proverbs gives us advice for developing our personal relationships with others, including friends, family members, and coworkers. In every relationship, we must show love, dedication, and high moral standards.

To relate to people, we need consistency, sensitivity, and discipline to use the wisdom God gives us. If we don't treat others according to the wisdom God gives, our relationships will suffer.

1. What type of relationships does Proverbs encourage? Discourage?
2. Why does the writer devote so much attention to avoiding sexual immorality? What wisdom is given regarding sex outside of marriage?
3. What seem to be the qualities that make relationships, including friendships and marriages, deeper and stronger? What ruins such relationships?
4. List three important relationships in your life. From what you've read in Proverbs, what should you change in those relationships?

**SPEECH** What we say shows our real attitude toward others. How we talk reveals what we're really like. Our speech is a test of how wise we've become.

To be wise in our speech we need to use self-control. Our words should be honest and well chosen. We need to remember that what we say affects others.

1. When is it hardest to control what you say?
2. What circumstances can cause you to lose control of your words? How do you feel after you blow it? How does this usually affect others?
3. Proverbs encourages speaking honestly, but with self-control. When have you been hurt by someone who did not speak with wisdom? How did it affect your relationship with that person?
4. List some specific actions you could take to develop honesty and self-control in your speech.

**WORK** God controls the final outcome of all we do. However, we must carry out our work with diligence and discipline, not laziness.

Because God evaluates how we live, we should work purposefully. We must never be lazy or self-satisfied. We don't always have to be the best in comparison to others, but we should always do our best with what God has given us.

1. What does Proverbs teach about the person who is lazy and unwilling to work?
2. What does Proverbs teach about the person who is diligent and self-disciplined?
3. How does being disciplined help you as a student?
4. How does being disciplined help you in your Christian life?
5. What is one area where you need to develop this discipline? Write out a specific plan for this development. (Be diligent in carrying it out!)

**SUCCESS** Although people work very hard for money and fame, God considers a good reputation, moral character, and spiritual devotion to obey him to be the true measures of success.

A successful relationship with God counts for eternity. Everything else is only temporary. All our resources, time, and talents come from God. We should do our best to use them wisely.

1. According to Proverbs, what is the value of riches? How important is wealth to most people who want to be successful?
2. How do your friends measure success? How do you think they will measure success when they are adults?
3. Do you agree or disagree with your friends' values? Explain.
4. How do you think God measures success?

**P**arty hearty! Do what feels good. Don't worry about tomorrow because we're all going to die soon anyway." You've probably heard expressions like that, or even know people who live that way. It's a very popular philosophy—but it's not a new one. In fact, essentially the same message appears in the Bible. Centuries ago, King Solomon wrote "People should eat and drink and enjoy the fruits of their labor, for these are gifts from God" (Ecclesiastes 3:13). Solomon knew what he was talking about. As a very intelligent and wealthy king, he had spent a lifetime experiencing and analyzing everything the world had to offer. Wine, women, song . . . Solomon had done it all. His conclusion? Life is short, boring, and empty, so enjoy pleasure while you can! ■ "Wait a minute," you might interrupt. "You mean one of the Bible writers says that life is meaningless, so we should live it up?" ■ That's right. But there's a punch line. Solomon's last word is that to really enjoy life, we need to keep God right at the center of everything. Without God, people merely exist, moving quickly from the excitement of youth to the bitterness of old age. But with God, we can enjoy each moment, relationship, and experience along the way. ■ Read Ecclesiastes, Solomon's analysis of life, . . . and then have a real party!

## STATS

PURPOSE: To spare future generations the bitterness of learning through their own experience that life is meaningless apart from God

AUTHOR: Solomon, although no passages mention him by name

TO WHOM WRITTEN: Solomon's subjects in particular, and all people in general

DATE WRITTEN: Probably around 935 B.C., late in Solomon's life

SETTING: Solomon looks back on his life, much of which was lived apart from God

CHAPTER **1** **IS LIFE WORTH LIVING?** These are the words of the Teacher,* King David's son, who ruled in Jerusalem.

2"Everything is meaningless," says the Teacher, "utterly meaningless!"

3What do people get for all their hard work? 4Gen-
erations come and go, but nothing really changes.
5The sun rises and sets and hurries around to rise
again. 6The wind blows south and north, here and
there, twisting back and forth, getting nowhere. 7The
rivers run into the sea, but the sea is never full. Then the water returns again to the rivers and flows again
to the sea. 8Everything is so weary and tiresome! No matter how much we see, we are never satisfied. No matter how much we hear, we are not content.

9History merely repeats itself. It has all been done
before. Nothing under the sun is truly new. 10What
can you point to that is new? How do you know it
didn't already exist long ago? 11We don't remember
what happened in those former times. And in future generations, no one will remember what we are doing now.

12I, the Teacher, was king of Israel, and I lived in
Jerusalem. 13I devoted myself to search for understanding and to explore by wisdom everything being done in the world. I soon discovered that God has
dealt a tragic existence to the human race. 14Every-
thing under the sun is meaningless, like chasing the
wind. 15What is wrong cannot be righted. What is missing cannot be recovered.

16I said to myself, "Look, I am wiser than any of the kings who ruled in Jerusalem before me. I have greater wisdom and knowledge than any of them."
17So I worked hard to distinguish wisdom from foolishness. But now I realize that even this was like
chasing the wind. 18For the greater my wisdom, the
greater my grief. To increase knowledge only increases sorrow.

1:1 Hebrew *Koheleth;* this term is rendered "the Teacher" throughout this book.

## MEANING ●●•••

1:8-11 **Many people feel restless and dissatisfied. They wonder, (1) "If I am in God's will, why am I so dissatisfied?" (2) "What is the meaning of life?" (3) "When I look back on it all, will I be happy with my accomplishments?" (4) "Why do I feel burned out, disillusioned, dry?" (5) "What will become of me?" In this book, Solomon tests our faith, challenging us to find true and lasting meaning in God alone. If you take a hard look at your life, as Solomon did his, you will see how important serving God is over all other options. Perhaps God is asking you to rethink your purpose and direction in life.**

# Ultimate Issues

## IS THERE MEANING TO LIFE?

**W**HITEFISH, MONTANA: Police today reported finding the bodies of 16-year-old "John Doe" and a 10-year-old friend. Doe apparently shot the younger boy to death and then turned the gun on himself. He left behind a note saying he was "bored with life" (AP News Service). **S**ixteen years old . . . and "bored with life." *Literally* bored to death. What a statement about our world! Unfortunately, it's not an isolated statement. The sad fact is that **suicide** is the second leading cause of death among American teenagers today. Many people, including young people, struggle to find meaning and purpose in life. If you are struggling with this, the book of Ecclesiastes was written for you. **T**he message of Ecclesiastes is brutally straightforward. The writer, Solomon, tells us that he has tried everything life has to offer—wine, women, and song (the ancient equivalent of ***sex, drugs, and rock 'n' roll***). His conclusion is this: "Fear God and keep his commands, for this is the duty of every person" (12:13). **I**n other words, the book of Ecclesiastes tells us (and it needs to be read as a whole if we are to understand it properly): God gives meaning to our lives. No God, no meaning. **T**hink of it this way: without God, you are just A BUNCH OF MOLECULES THROWN TOGETHER BY CHANCE. If there is no God, you came from—and are headed toward—impersonal nothingness. Any attempt at finding purpose is utterly ridiculous, doomed to failure. You might just as well be a lizard, or a rock, or *nothing at all* . . . if there is no God. **S**ounds pretty bleak, doesn't it? It *is* bleak, if we subtract God from the equation. This belief that there is no God and therefore no meaning is what has driven many, including some of the greatest minds in history, to despair, alcoholism, and even suicide. The noted historian Will Durant put it this way: "The greatest question of our time is not communism versus individualism, not Europe versus America, not even the East versus the West; it is whether men can live without God." **T**rina Paulus examines this question from another, wonderfully creative angle in her book *Hope for the Flowers.* The book tells the story of **a caterpillar named Stripe** and his quest for meaning. One day Stripe sees a giant column made of caterpillars standing on top of other caterpillars. All of them are trying to climb over the others to get to the top. So Stripe begins to climb, too, until he gets near the top—where he finds he can go no higher. Then someone says that to get any farther, they'd have to get rid of some of the other caterpillars. The column begins to shake, and Stripe sees caterpillars fall and hears them scream. **T**hen—SILENCE. **F**rustration surges through Stripe at the thought that this was the only way up. Then he hears a tiny whisper from the top: "There's nothing here at all!" It's answered by another: "Quiet, fool! They'll hear you down the pillar. We're where *they* want to get. That's what's here!" **S**tripe feels frozen. The top isn't so high after all! It only looks good from the bottom. There's another whisper: "Look over there—another pillar—and there, too—everywhere!" Angry and frustrated, Stripe moans, "My pillar, only one of thousands. Millions of caterpillars climbing nowhere! Something is really wrong but . . . what else *is* there?" **T**he good news is: there *is* something more. We don't have to run pointlessly after illusions like a slightly more sophisticated version of ***a hamster on a treadmill.*** There is a personal God who created you, knows you by name, loves you, and wants you to know him intimately. He gives purpose and meaning to life as he calls us to follow him in HIS GRAND ADVENTURE. **I**f you're searching for meaning, follow the writer of Ecclesiastes to its source: a lifelong personal encounter with God.

CHAPTER **2** **A GOOD TIME ISN'T EVERYTHING.** I said to myself, "Come now, let's give pleasure a try. Let's look for the 'good things' in life." But I found that this, too, was meaningless. [2]"It is silly to be laughing all the time," I said. "What good does it do to seek only pleasure?" [3]After much thought, I decided to cheer myself with wine. While still seeking wisdom, I clutched at foolishness. In this way, I hoped to experience the only happiness most people find during their brief life in this world.

[4]I also tried to find meaning by building huge homes for myself and by planting beautiful vineyards. [5]I made gardens and parks, filling them with all kinds of fruit trees. [6]I built reservoirs to collect the water to irrigate my many flourishing groves. [7]I bought slaves, both men and women, and others were born into my household. I also owned great herds and flocks, more than any of the kings who lived in Jerusalem before me. [8]I collected great sums of silver and gold, the treasure of many kings and provinces. I hired wonderful singers, both men and women, and had many beautiful concubines. I had everything a man could desire!

[9]So I became greater than any of the kings who ruled in Jerusalem before me. And with it all, I remained clear-eyed so that I could evaluate all these things. [10]Anything I wanted, I took. I did not restrain myself from any joy. I even found great pleasure in hard work, an additional reward for all my labors. [11]But as I looked at everything I had worked so hard to accomplish, it was all so meaningless. It was like chasing the wind. There was nothing really worthwhile anywhere.

[12]So I decided to compare wisdom and folly, and anyone else would come to the same conclusions I did. [13]Wisdom is of more value than foolishness, just as light is better than darkness. [14]For the wise person sees, while the fool is blind. Yet I saw that wise and foolish people share the same fate. [15]Both of them die. Just as the fool will die, so will I. So of what value is all my wisdom? Then I said to myself, "This is all so meaningless!" [16]For the wise person and the fool both die, and in the days to come, both will be forgotten.

[17]So now I hate life because everything done here under the sun is so irrational. Everything is meaningless, like chasing the wind. [18]I am disgusted that I must leave the fruits of my hard work to others. [19]And who can tell whether my successors will be wise or foolish? And yet they will control everything I have gained by my skill and hard work. How meaningless!

[20]So I turned in despair from hard work. It was not the answer to my search for satisfaction in this life. [21]For though I do my work with wisdom, knowledge, and skill, I must leave everything I gain to people who haven't worked to earn it. This is not only foolish but highly unfair. [22]So what do people get for all their hard work? [23]Their days of labor are filled with pain and grief; even at night they cannot rest. It is all utterly meaningless.

[24]So I decided there is nothing better than to enjoy food and drink and to find satisfaction in work. Then I realized that this pleasure is from the hand of God. [25]For who can eat or enjoy anything apart from him? [26]God gives wisdom, knowledge, and joy to

**PARTY ● ● ● • •**

2:24-26 **Is Solomon recommending we make life a big, wild party? No, he is encouraging us to take pleasure in what we're doing now and to enjoy life because it comes from God's hand. True enjoyment in life comes only as we follow God's guidelines for living. Those who really know how to enjoy life are the ones who take life each day as a gift from God, thanking him for it and serving him in it.**

## "Here's what I did..."

When I graduated from junior high school, I was popular and successful academically. I had everything going for me. During the summer before senior high school, though, I realized things would be different. Most of the friends I knew wouldn't be going to the same high school with me. I'd have to start over.

That summer I decided to live it up. I went to party after party with my friends and had a lot of fun. But in between these times I felt depressed. I was living for the moment, and somehow that felt lonely.

One day I was flipping through the Bible, and I decided to read the book of Ecclesiastes. The whole book really spoke to me. Here was a guy I could identify with. He too seemed to be living for the moment, and he found it just as empty as I did! One verse especially expressed my feelings: "But as I looked at everything I had worked so hard to accomplish, it was all so meaningless. It was like chasing the wind" (2:11). My whole summer to that point had been consumed with chasing pleasure—grasping for the wind. That verse may sound depressing, but it actually made me feel better. Here was someone who knew how I was feeling, and expressed it perfectly.

After reading Ecclesiastes, I realized how futile it is to strive after material possessions, money, fame, and even popularity. They are all fleeting. Once they've gone, so has happiness. But if you follow God's ways, there's nothing to take your happiness away.

Rick

AGE 16

those who please him. But if a sinner becomes wealthy, God takes the wealth away and gives it to those who please him. Even this, however, is meaningless, like chasing the wind.

## CHAPTER 3 **THERE'S A RIGHT TIME FOR EVERYTHING.**

1 There is a time for everything,
a season for every activity under heaven.
2 A time to be born and a time to die.
A time to plant and a time to harvest.
3 A time to kill and a time to heal.
A time to tear down and a time to rebuild.
4 A time to cry and a time to laugh.
A time to grieve and a time to dance.
5 A time to scatter stones and a time to gather stones.
A time to embrace and a time to turn away.
6 A time to search and a time to lose.
A time to keep and a time to throw away.
7 A time to tear and a time to mend.
A time to be quiet and a time to speak up.
8 A time to love and a time to hate.
A time for war and a time for peace.

### LEASURE

At a youth rally, the speaker is pleading with the students—begging them not to make the mistakes he made.

"Please hear what I'm saying. When I was your age, I was empty inside. I came from a broken home. I hated myself and everybody else. I tried everything to fill the hole inside: drugs, alcohol, sleeping around, partying.

"I tried to convince myself I was having a good time. And those things did feel good . . . for a while. But the feeling was only temporary. No matter what I did, I couldn't shake that inner loneliness and hurt.

"Everything I did to try to ease my pain only made my hurt increase. Listen to me: You will never find what you're really looking for until you accept the love of Jesus Christ. Coming to know him—the Lord of life—will bring you the peace you so desperately need. There is life nowhere else."

As the speaker concludes, Lorraine thinks, "Yeah, he says all this after he's had all his fun. Maybe I'll just have a good time now . . . and get serious about God later."

The book of Ecclesiastes describes King Solomon's frantic search for satisfaction. Chapters 1 and 2 relate all the different ways he tried to find fulfillment apart from God. His conclusion is in 12:13-14.

Will you listen to the voices of experience and save yourself a lot of heartache? Or will you be stubborn and learn the hard way?

9 What do people really get for all their hard
work? 10 I have thought about this in connection
with the various kinds of work God has given
people to do. 11 God has made everything beautiful
for its own time. He has planted eternity in the
human heart, but even so, people cannot see the
whole scope of God's work from beginning to end.
12 So I concluded that there is nothing better for
people than to be happy and to enjoy themselves
as long as they can. 13 And people should eat and
drink and enjoy the fruits of their labor, for these
are gifts from God.
14 And I know that whatever God does is final.
Nothing can be added to it or taken from it. God's
purpose in this is that people should fear him.
15 Whatever exists today and whatever will exist in the
future has already existed in the past. For God calls
each event back in its turn.*
16 I also noticed that throughout the world there is
evil in the courtroom. Yes, even the courts of law are
corrupt! 17 I said to myself, "In due season God will
judge everyone, both good and bad, for all their
deeds."
18 Then I realized that God allows people to continue in their sinful ways so he can test them. That
way, they can see for themselves that they are no
better than animals. 19 For humans and animals
both breathe the same air,* and both die. So
people have no real advantage over the animals.
How meaningless! 20 Both go to the same place—
the dust from which they came and to which they
must return. 21 For who can prove that the human
spirit goes upward and the spirit of animals goes
downward into the earth? 22 So I saw that there is
nothing better for people than to be happy in their
work. That is why they are here! No one will bring
them back from death to enjoy life in the future.

## CHAPTER 4 **I WOULD RATHER BE DEAD.**

Again I observed all the oppression that takes place in our
world. I saw the tears of the oppressed, with no one
to comfort them. The oppressors have great power,
and the victims are helpless. 2 So I concluded that the
dead are better off than the living. 3 And most fortunate of all are those who were never born. For they
have never seen all the evil that is done in our world.
4 Then I observed that most people are motivated
to success by their envy of their neighbors. But this,
too, is meaningless, like chasing the wind.
5 Foolish people refuse to work and almost starve.
6 They feel it is better to be lazy and barely survive
than to work hard, especially when in the long run
everything is so futile.
7 I observed yet another example of meaninglessness in our world. 8 This is the case of a man who is
all alone, without a child or a brother, yet who works
hard to gain as much wealth as he can. But then he
asks himself, "Who am I working for? Why am I
giving up so much pleasure now?" It is all so meaningless and depressing.
9 Two people can accomplish more than twice as
much as one; they get a better return for their
labor. 10 If one person falls, the other can reach out
and help. But people who are alone when they fall
are in real trouble. 11 And on a cold night, two under

3:15 Hebrew *For God calls the past to account.* 3:19 Or *both have the same spirit.*

the same blanket can gain warmth from each other. But how can one be warm alone? [12]A person standing alone can be attacked and defeated, but two can stand back-to-back and conquer. Three are even better, for a triple-braided cord is not easily broken.

[13]It is better to be a poor but wise youth than to be an old and foolish king who refuses all advice. [14]Such a youth could come from prison and succeed. He might even become king, though he was born in poverty. [15]Everyone is eager to help such a youth, even to help him take the throne. [16]He might become the leader of millions and be very popular. But then the next generation grows up and rejects him! So again, it is all meaningless, like chasing the wind.

CHAPTER **5** **HAVE RESPECT FOR GOD.** As you enter the house of God, keep your ears open and your mouth shut! Don't be a fool who doesn't realize that mindless offerings to God are evil. [2]And don't make rash promises to God, for he is in heaven, and you are only here on earth. So let your words be few.

[3]Just as being too busy gives you nightmares, being a fool makes you a blabbermouth.

[4]So when you make a promise to God, don't delay in following through, for God takes no pleasure in fools. Keep all the promises you make to him. [5]It is better to say nothing than to promise something that you don't follow through on. [6]In such cases, your mouth is making you sin. And don't defend yourself by telling the Temple messenger that the promise you made was a mistake. That would make God angry, and he might wipe out everything you have achieved.

[7]Dreaming all the time instead of working is foolishness. And there is ruin in a flood of empty words. Fear God instead.

[8]If you see a poor person being oppressed by the powerful and justice being miscarried throughout the land, don't be surprised! For every official is under orders from higher up, and matters of justice only get lost in red tape and bureaucracy. [9]Even the king milks the land for his own profit!*

[10]Those who love money will never have enough. How absurd to think that wealth brings true happiness! [11]The more you have, the more people come to help you spend it. So what is the advantage of wealth—except perhaps to watch it run through your fingers!

[12]People who work hard sleep well, whether they eat little or much. But the rich are always worrying and seldom get a good night's sleep.

[13]There is another serious problem I have seen in the world. Riches are sometimes hoarded to the harm of the saver, [14]or they are put into risky investments that turn sour, and everything is lost. In the end, there is nothing left to pass on to one's children. [15]People who live only for wealth come to the end of their lives as naked and empty-handed as on the day they were born.

[16]And this, too, is a very serious problem. As people come into this world, so they depart. All their hard work is for nothing. They have been working for the wind, and everything will be swept away. [17]Throughout their lives, they live under a cloud—frustrated, discouraged, and angry.

[18]Even so, I have noticed one thing, at least, that is good. It is good for people to eat well, drink a good glass of wine, and enjoy their work—whatever they do under the sun—for however long God lets them live. [19]And it is a good thing to receive wealth from God and the good health to enjoy it. To enjoy your work and accept your lot in life—that is indeed a gift from God. [20]People who do this rarely look with sorrow on the past, for God has given them reasons for joy.

CHAPTER **6** **IS LIFE REALLY WORTH LIVING?** There is another serious tragedy I have seen in our world. [2]God gives great wealth and honor to some people and gives them everything they could ever want, but then he

5:9 The meaning of the Hebrew is uncertain.

## "Here's what I did..."

I really wanted to grow in my walk with God, so I vowed that I would have a quiet time every night. For a while everything went very well. I felt I understood what I read, and as I tried to apply the Bible to my daily life, I began to see changes in myself. That excited me.

But then I went through a period of time when I didn't seem to be getting anything out of the Bible. For some reason, one night I started reading Ecclesiastes. I felt stressed, in a rush to get to my homework so I could get to bed at a decent hour. When I came across the passage in chapter 5, verses 1-7, I suddenly woke up! I remembered that I had vowed to spend time with God every day and that it was *God* I was treating so rudely by rushing through my time with him. My attitude was all wrong. Having a quiet time wasn't like some chore I had to do; it was a privilege to meet with the awesome God of the universe! I asked God to forgive me for my attitude and thanked him for speaking to me through his Word.

AGE 16

doesn't give them the health to enjoy it. They die, and others get it all! This is meaningless—a sickening tragedy.

3A man might have a hundred children and live to be very old. But if he finds no satisfaction in life and in the end does not even get a decent burial, I say he would have been better off born dead. 4I realize that his birth would have been meaningless and ended in darkness. He wouldn't even have had a name, 5and he would never have seen the sun or known of its existence. Yet he would have had more peace than he has in growing up to be an unhappy man. 6He might live a thousand years twice over but not find contentment. And since he must die like everyone else—well, what's the use?

## FLATTERY ● ● ● • •

**7:5-6 Have you ever been paid a compliment when you knew it was inappropriate or merely an attempt to flatter you? Some people would rather feel good than know the truth. Too often, pleasant compliments are valued above helpful information (Proverbs 27:6). Solomon reminds us that it is far better to face honest criticism than to wallow in the compliments of fools.**

7All people spend their lives scratching for food, but they never seem to have enough. 8Considering this, do wise people really have any advantage over fools? Do poor people gain anything by being wise and knowing how to act in front of others?

9Enjoy what you have rather than desiring what you don't have. Just dreaming about nice things is meaningless; it is like chasing the wind.

10Everything has already been decided. It was known long ago what each person would be. So there's no use arguing with God about your destiny.

11The more words you speak, the less they mean. So why overdo it?

12In the few days of our empty lives, who knows how our days can best be spent? And who can tell what will happen in the future after we are gone?

CHAPTER **7** **SOME TIPS FOR A MEANINGFUL LIFE.** A good reputation is more valuable than the most expensive perfume. In the same way, the day you die is better than the day you are born.

2It is better to spend your time at funerals than at festivals. For you are going to die, and you should think about it while there is still time.

3Sorrow is better than laughter, for sadness has a refining influence on us.

4A wise person thinks much about death, while the fool thinks only about having a good time now.

5It is better to be criticized by a wise person than to be praised by a fool! 6Indeed, a fool's laughter is quickly gone, like thorns crackling in a fire. This also is meaningless.

7Extortion turns wise people into fools, and bribes corrupt the heart.

8Finishing is better than starting. Patience is better than pride.

9Don't be quick-tempered, for anger is the friend of fools.

10Don't long for "the good old days," for you don't know whether they were any better than today.

11Being wise is as good as being rich; in fact, it is better. 12Wisdom or money can get you almost anything, but it's important to know that only wisdom can save your life.

13Notice the way God does things; then fall into line. Don't fight the ways of God, for who can straighten out what he has made crooked?

14Enjoy prosperity while you can. But when hard times strike, realize that both come from God. That way you will realize that nothing is certain in this life.

15In this meaningless life, I have seen everything, including the fact that some good people die young and some wicked people live on and on. 16So don't be too good or too wise! Why destroy yourself? 17On the other hand, don't be too wicked either—don't be a fool! Why should you die before your time? 18So try to walk a middle course—but those who fear God will succeed either way.

19A wise person is stronger than the ten leading citizens of a town!

20There is not a single person in all the earth who is always good and never sins.

21Don't eavesdrop on others—you may hear your servant laughing at you. 22For you know how often you yourself have laughed at others.

23All along I have tried my best to let wisdom guide my thoughts and actions. I said to myself, "I am determined to be wise." But it didn't really work. 24Wisdom is always distant and very difficult to find. 25I searched everywhere, determined to find wisdom and to understand the reason for things. I was determined to prove to myself that wickedness is stupid and that foolishness is madness.

26I discovered that a seductive woman is more bitter than death. Her passion is a trap, and her soft hands will bind you. Those who please God will escape from her, but sinners will be caught in her snare.

27"This is my conclusion," says the Teacher. "I came to this result after looking into the matter from every possible angle. 28Just one out of every thousand men I interviewed can be said to be upright, but not one woman! 29I discovered that God created people to be upright, but they have each turned to follow their own downward path."

## CONSEQUENCES ● ● ● • •

**8:11 We should never assume that God doesn't care if we have sinned, or that sin has no consequences, simply because he hasn't punished us immediately. Unfortunately, it is easier to sin when we don't feel immediate consequences. When a young child does something wrong without being discovered, it will be much easier for him to do the wrong again. But God knows every wrong we commit, and one day we *will* have to answer for everything we have done (12:14).**

CHAPTER **8** **OBEY THE LAW.** How wonderful to be
wise, to be able to analyze and interpret things. Wisdom lights up a person's face, softening its hardness.
2Obey the king because you have vowed before
God to do this. 3Don't try to avoid doing your duty,
and don't take a stand with those who plot evil. For
the king will punish those who disobey him. 4The
king's command is backed by great power. No one
can resist or question it. 5Those who obey him will
not be punished. Those who are wise will find a time
and a way to do what is right. 6Yes, there is a time and
a way for everything, even as people's troubles lie
heavily upon them.
7Indeed, how can people avoid what they don't
know is going to happen? 8None of us can hold back
our spirit from departing. None of us has the power
to prevent the day of our death. There is no escaping
that obligation, that dark battle. And in the face of
death, wickedness will certainly not rescue those
who practice it.
9I have thought deeply about all that goes on here
in the world, where people have the power to hurt each
other. 10I have seen wicked people buried with honor.
How strange that they were the very ones who fre-
quented the Temple and are praised* in the very city
where they committed their crimes! 11When a crime is
not punished, people feel it is safe to do wrong. 12But
even though a person sins a hundred times and still
lives a long time, I know that those who fear God will
be better off. 13The wicked will
never live long, good lives, for
they do not fear God. Their days
will never grow long like the evening shadows.
14And this is not all that is
meaningless in our world. In this
life, good people are often
treated as though they were
wicked, and wicked people are
often treated as though they were
good. This is so meaningless!
15So I recommend having fun,
because there is nothing better
for people to do in this world
than to eat, drink, and enjoy life.
That way they will experience
some happiness along with all
the hard work God gives them.
16In my search for wisdom, I
tried to observe everything that
goes on all across the earth. I discovered that there is ceaseless activity, day and night. 17This
reminded me that no one can discover everything God has created
in our world, no matter how hard
they work at it. Not even the wisest people know everything, even
if they say they do.

CHAPTER **9** **LIFE IS WORTH LIVING: DO IT WELL.** This,
too, I carefully explored: Even though the actions of
godly and wise people are in God's hands, no one
knows whether or not God will show them favor in
this life. 2The same destiny ultimately awaits everyone, whether they are righteous or wicked, good or
bad,* ceremonially clean or unclean, religious or
irreligious. Good people receive the same treatment
as sinners, and people who take oaths are treated like
people who don't.
3It seems so tragic that one fate comes to all.
That is why people are not more careful to be good.
Instead, they choose their own mad course, for
they have no hope. There is nothing ahead but
death anyway. 4There is hope only for the living.
For as they say, "It is better to be a live dog than a
dead lion!"
5The living at least know they will die, but the
dead know nothing. They have no further reward,
nor are they remembered. 6Whatever they did in
their lifetime—loving, hating, envying—is all long
gone. They no longer have a part in anything here
on earth. 7So go ahead. Eat your food and drink
your wine with a happy heart, for God approves of
this! 8Wear fine clothes, with a dash of cologne!
9Live happily with the woman you love through
all the meaningless days of life that God has
given you in this world. The wife God gives you is
your reward for all your earthly toil. 10Whatever

## "Here's what I did..."

My best friend and I weren't speaking. We had had an argument, and I still stewed over some of the things she had said to me. I wasn't going to let her get away with treating me like she did!

Then I came across two verses: Ecclesiastes 10:12, "It is pleasant to listen to wise words, but the speech of fools brings them to ruin," and 1 Peter 4:8, "Most important of all, continue to show deep love for each other, for love covers a multitude of sins." As I read these verses over and over, whatever we had argued about became less and less important, and maintaining a friendship with someone who also knew God's love became very important. I also realized that there were some faults in *me* that needed her forgiveness.

I didn't waste any time. I called my friend on the phone, read her the passages, and told her I was sorry for letting something petty come between us. She cried a little and said she was so glad I had called, and that she didn't feel right either about us fighting.

These verses clearly showed me how precious Christian friendship is; it's something to be guarded and treasured. I thank God for not letting me throw away the gift he had given me in my friend and for helping me to work things out with my friend.

*Amy*

AGE 17

8:10 As in some Hebrew manuscripts and Greek version; many Hebrew manuscripts read *and are forgotten.* 9:2 As in Greek and Syriac versions, and Latin Vulgate; Hebrew lacks *or bad.*

*Here is my final conclusion:*

# Fear GOD and obey HIS commands,

*for this is the duty of every person.*

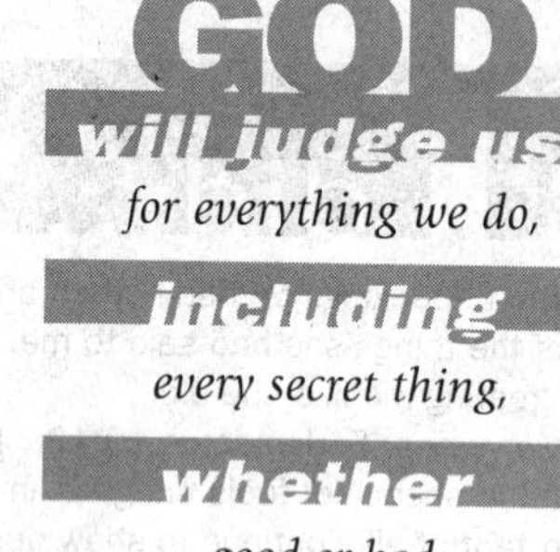

GOD
will judge us
for everything we do,
including
every secret thing,
whether

*good or bad.*

ECCLESIASTES 12:13-14

you do, do well. For when you go to the grave, there will be no work or planning or knowledge or wisdom.

11 I have observed something else in this world of ours. The fastest runner doesn't always win the race, and the strongest warrior doesn't always win the battle. The wise are often poor, and the skillful are not necessarily wealthy. And those who are educated don't always lead successful lives. It is all decided by chance, by being at the right place at the right time.

12 People can never predict when hard times might come. Like fish in a net or birds in a snare, people are often caught by sudden tragedy.

13 Here is another bit of wisdom that has impressed me as I have watched the way our world works. 14 There was a small town with only a few people living in it, and a great king came with his army and besieged it. 15 There was a poor, wise man living there who knew how to save the town, and so it was rescued. But afterward no one thought any more about him. 16 Then I realized that though wisdom is better than strength, those who are wise will be despised if they are poor. What they say will not be appreciated for long. 17 But even so, the quiet words of a wise person are better than the shouts of a foolish king. 18 A wise person can overcome weapons of war, but one sinner can destroy much that is good.

CHAPTER **10** **BEHAVE WISELY.** Dead flies will cause even a bottle of perfume to stink! Yes, an ounce of foolishness can outweigh a pound of wisdom and honor.

2 The hearts of the wise lead them to do right, and the hearts of the foolish lead them to do evil. 3 You can identify fools just by the way they walk down the street!

4 If your boss is angry with you, don't quit! A quiet spirit can overcome even great mistakes.

5 There is another evil I have seen as I have watched the world go by. Kings and rulers make a grave mistake 6 if they give foolish people great authority, and if they fail to give people of proven worth their rightful place of dignity. 7 I have even seen servants riding like princes—and princes walking like servants.

8 When you dig a well, you may fall in. When you demolish an old wall, you could be bitten by a snake. 9 When you work in a quarry, stones might fall and crush you! When you chop wood, there is danger with each stroke of your ax! Such are the risks of life.

10 Since a dull ax requires great strength, sharpen the blade. That's the value of wisdom; it helps you succeed.

11 It does no good to charm a snake after it has bitten you.

12 It is pleasant to listen to wise words, but the speech of fools brings them to ruin.

13 Since fools base their thoughts on foolish premises, their conclusions will be wicked madness.

**MONEY ● ● • • •**

10:19 **Government leaders, businesses, families, and even churches get trapped into thinking money is the answer to every problem. But just as the effects of liquor are only temporary, the soothing effect of the last purchase soon wears off, and we have to buy more. Scripture recognizes that money is necessary for survival, but it warns against the love of money (see Matthew 6:24; 1 Timothy 6:10; Hebrews 13:5). Money can be dangerous; we use it to deceive ourselves, thinking that wealth is the easiest way to get everything we want. The love of money is sinful because we trust it, rather than God, to solve our problems. Those who pursue money's empty promises will discover one day that they have nothing because they are spiritually bankrupt.**

14Foolish people claim to know all about the future and tell everyone the details! But who can really know what is going to happen?

15Fools are so exhausted by a little work that they have no strength for even the simplest tasks.

16Destruction is certain for the land whose king is a child* and whose leaders feast in the morning. 17Happy is the land whose king is a nobleman and whose leaders feast only to gain strength for their work, not to get drunk.

18Laziness lets the roof leak, and soon the rafters begin to rot.

19A party gives laughter, and wine gives happiness, and money gives everything!

20Never make light of the king, even in your thoughts. And don't make fun of a rich man, either. A little bird may tell them what you have said.

CHAPTER **11** **KEEP IT UP: GOD WILL HONOR YOU.** Give generously, for your gifts will return to you later.* 2Divide your gifts among many, for you do not know what risks might lie ahead.

3When the clouds are heavy, the rains come down. When a tree falls, whether south or north, there it lies.

4If you wait for perfect conditions, you will never get anything done.

5God's ways are as hard to discern as the pathways of the wind, and as mysterious as a tiny baby being formed in a mother's womb.

6Be sure to stay busy and plant a variety of crops, for you never know which will grow—perhaps they all will.

7Light is sweet; it's wonderful to see the sun! 8When people live to be very old, let them rejoice in every day of life. But let them also remember that the dark days will be many. Everything still to come is meaningless.

9Young man, it's wonderful to be young! Enjoy every minute of it. Do everything you want to do; take it all in. But remember that you must give an account to God for everything you do. 10So banish grief and pain, but remember that youth, with a whole life before it, still faces the threat of meaninglessness.

CHAPTER **12** **HONOR GOD.** Don't let the excitement of youth cause you to forget your Creator. Honor him in your youth before you grow old and no longer enjoy living. 2It will be too late then to remember him, when the light of the sun and moon and stars is dim to your old eyes, and there is no silver lining left among the clouds. 3Your limbs will tremble with age, and your strong legs will grow weak. Your teeth will be too few to do their work, and you will be blind, too. 4And when your teeth are gone, keep your lips tightly closed when you eat! Even the chirping of birds will wake you up. But you yourself will be deaf and tuneless, with a quavering voice. 5You will be afraid of heights and of falling, white-haired and withered, dragging along without any sexual desire. You will be standing at death's door. And as you near your everlasting home, the mourners will walk along the streets.

**CHOICES ● ● • • •**

11:10 **Often people say, "It doesn't matter." But many of our choices will be irreversible—they will stay with us for a lifetime. What you do when you're young *does* matter. Enjoy life now, but don't do anything—physically, morally, or spiritually—that will prevent you from enjoying life when you are old.**

**I recently became a Christian, but I'm having second thoughts. I'm afraid I'll miss out on a lot of fun during my teenage years. Can't I wait until later to live for Christ?**

A speaker once related a dream he'd had. The location was hell, and the demons were trying to think of ways to stop people from accepting Christ.

Each demon brought an idea to Satan and was told to try it. The ideas included the typical ones people think are responsible for turning others away: drugs, sexual temptations, intellectualism, money, fame, status, etc.

All of these strategies were tried, but they weren't very effective.

Finally, one demon suggested a plan that surprised everyone. "Let's tell people that believing the Bible and following Christ are the right things to do; and tell them that being a committed believer is the only way to live life. But," he concluded, "tell them to do it—*tomorrow!*"

That has become Satan's strategy—and for many people tomorrow never comes!

This delaying tactic works like Novocain. It numbs people and keeps them from turning to the truth when they hear it.

We are creatures of habit. We've learned almost everything—reading, writing, math, speech—by doing the same thing over and over. Our thoughts about God are the same way. Believing we can play now and get committed later fulfills Satan's strategy.

Thought patterns become habits; habits become beliefs; beliefs become actions; and actions determine our eternity!

You may be afraid you'll miss out on the fun, but those "good times" don't last. Most of what the world pursues is shallow and meaningless (though sometimes "fun" for a while).

Ecclesiastes 11:9–12:8 makes it clear that to live life to the fullest, we must follow God—not in fear that he wants to take away our fun, but in faith that he wants to make our life into something wonderful.

Life begins the moment we realize that the world doesn't revolve around us, but around God who made the world and all that is in it.

**10:16** Or *whose king is a servant.* **11:1** Hebrew *Throw your bread on the waters, for after many days you will find it again.*

## CURES • • • • •

12:13-14 **Solomon presents his antidotes for the two main ailments presented in this book: those who lack purpose and direction in life should respect God and follow his principles for living; those who think life is unfair should remember that God will review every person's life to determine how he or she has responded to him. Have you committed your life to him, both present and future? Does your life measure up to his standards?**

[6]Yes, remember your Creator now while you are
young, before the silver cord of life snaps and the
golden bowl is broken. Don't wait until the water jar
is smashed at the spring and the pulley is broken at
the well. [7]For then the dust will return to the earth,
and the spirit will return to God who gave it.
[8]"All is meaningless," says the Teacher, "utterly
meaningless."

12:12 Hebrew *my son.*

[9]Because the Teacher was wise, he taught the
people everything he knew. He collected proverbs and classified them. [10]Indeed, the Teacher
taught the plain truth, and he did so in an interesting way.
[11]A wise teacher's words spur students to action
and emphasize important truths. The collected
sayings of the wise are like guidance from a shepherd.
[12]But, my child,* be warned: There is no end of
opinions ready to be expressed. Studying them can
go on forever and become very exhausting!
[13]Here is my final conclusion: Fear God and obey
his commands, for this is the duty of every person.
[14]God will judge us for everything we do, including
every secret thing, whether good or bad.

# MEGA themes

**SEARCHING** Solomon searched for satisfaction almost as though it were a scientific experiment. In his search he discovered that life without God was meaningless. True happiness does not come from accumulating or attaining honors—we always want more than we can have, and there are circumstances beyond our control that can snatch away all our possessions and achievements.

People are still searching for meaning, enjoyment, fulfillment, and satisfaction. Yet the more they try to get, the more they realize how little they really have. No lasting pleasure or happiness is possible without God. Above all else, we should strive to know and love God, trusting him for true joy in life.

1. List all the ways in which Solomon searched for happiness and satisfaction.
2. In what ways do people today search for happiness and satisfaction?
3. How do most of your peers at school hope to find satisfaction in the present? In the future, as adults?
4. If you were to give a personal testimony of the satisfaction found in Christ, what would you say? To whom would you want to say this?
5. How can you share this testimony by example and word with those in your school, and/or with your friends at church, who are searching in the wrong places for satisfaction and happiness?

**EMPTINESS** Solomon shows how empty it is to pursue life's pleasures in place of a relationship with the eternal God. The search for pleasure, wealth, and success ultimately is disappointing. Nothing in the world can satisfy our longing, restless heart.

The cure for emptiness is to focus on God. Develop a fear or reverence for God throughout your life, and fill your life with serving God and others rather than selfishly chasing after pleasures.

1. Perhaps you have heard someone say, "He had everything, but he was empty inside." What do you think it means to be "empty" inside?
2. Who are some stars, athletes, or prominent people who seem to have all they could want, yet live seemingly empty lives (filled with drugs, broken relationships, sexual immorality, etc.)?
3. According to the book of Ecclesiastes, the answer to the emptiness of life is ________. How does this answer fill the emptiness?
4. What choices are you making now that will ensure that your life will continue to increase in fulfillment rather than becoming an empty shell? What difference does it make whether you do this when you are young?

**WORK** Solomon tried to shake people's confidence in their own efforts, abilities, and wisdom. He did this to direct them to faith in God as the only sound basis for living. Without God, there is no lasting reward or benefit in hard work.

Work done with the wrong attitude leaves us empty. Work accepted as an assignment from God can be seen as a gift. Examine what you expect from your efforts at school and/or on the job. God gives you abilities and opportunities to work and to make a contribution with your life.

1. What seems to be the attitude most people have toward working?
2. How do you feel about the work you have to do, including school work and responsibilities at home? Describe your attitude.
3. What does the book of Ecclesiastes present as the proper attitude toward work?
4. Describe the attitude that will be most effective in enabling people to do their work for God. How can you develop this attitude, beginning with the work you have to do this week?

**DEATH** The certainty of death makes all human achievements futile. God has a plan for human destiny that goes beyond life and death. The reality of aging and dying reminds us of the end to come, when God will judge each person's life.

Life does not seem to be short when a person is young, yet the years pass all too quickly. Because life is so short, we need wisdom greater than this world can offer. We need the words of God. If we listen to him, his wisdom will spare us the bitterness of ending life without having fulfilled a worthwhile purpose.

1. To a person who does not know God through Christ, death could be described as ________.
2. To a person who is a Christian, death could be described as ________.
3. How do you feel about your own death?
4. Explain how your faith in Christ affects your thoughts and feelings regarding your death.
5. How does the knowledge of life after death influence the way you live life before death?

**WISDOM** Human wisdom doesn't have all the answers. Knowledge and education have their limits. To understand life, we need the wisdom that can be found only in God's Word to us—the Bible.

When we realize that God will evaluate all we do, we should learn to live wisely, remembering that God is with us at each moment. We can have God's wisdom only when we obey him.

1. What limits of human wisdom frustrated Solomon?
2. How can you tap into God's wisdom when your human knowledge and understanding fail you?
3. Since God has revealed himself, what can you do to get beyond the limits of human reasoning?

Check out the words to the top 40 songs, and you'll probably find a sensuous mix of I-got-to-have-you-now lyrics. Check out the supermarket tabloids, and you'll find stories of adultery, divorce, and affairs by an assortment of entertainment figures. The message comes through loud and clear: lust is in, love is out; independence is in, marriage is out. In fact, it seems that commitment has become a dirty word. ■ That's not what God had in mind when he created sex and love, or when he began marriage. Sex is meant to be an exciting, fulfilling physical union of a man and a woman who are protected by the commitment of marriage—not an act of self-gratification. Love is meant to be a self-giving action, not a self-centered emotion. ■ Nowhere are the true meanings of love and sex more beautifully portrayed than in the Song of Songs. Here we get an intimate glimpse into the personal relationship between the king (Solomon) and his bride. Love, sex, and marriage are celebrated in the context of living the way God designed us to live. ■ Don't fall for cultural lies and myths about love. Read Song of Songs and commit yourself to living God's way. Believe me, the payoff is terrific!

## STATS

PURPOSE: To tell of the love between a bridegroom (King Solomon) and his bride, to affirm the sanctity of marriage, and to picture God's love for his people

AUTHOR: Solomon

DATE WRITTEN: Probably early in Solomon's reign

SETTING: Israel—the Shulamite woman's garden and the king's palace

KEY PEOPLE: King Solomon, the Shulamite woman, and the daughters of Jerusalem

CHAPTER **1** **THE WEDDING DAY.** This is Solomon's song of songs, more wonderful than any other.

*Young Woman:** [2]"Kiss me again and again, for your love is sweeter than wine. [3]How fragrant your cologne, and how pleasing your name! No wonder all the young women love you! [4]Take me with you. Come, let's run! Bring me into your bedroom, O my king.*"

*Young Women of Jerusalem:* "How happy we are for him! We praise his love even more than wine."

*Young Woman:* "How right that the young women love you!

[5]"I am dark and beautiful, O women of Jerusalem, tanned as the dark tents of Kedar. Yes, even as the tents of Solomon!

[6]"Don't look down on me, you fair city girls, just because my complexion is so dark. The sun has burned my skin. My brothers were angry with me and sent me out to tend the vineyards in the hot sun. Now see what it has done to me!*

[7]"Tell me, O my love, where are you leading your flock today? Where will you rest your sheep at noon? For why should I wander like a prostitute* among the flocks of your companions?"

*Young Man:* [8]"If you don't know, O most beautiful woman, follow the trail of my flock to the shepherds' tents, and there feed your young goats. [9]What a lovely filly you are, my beloved one!* [10]How lovely are your cheeks, with your earrings setting them afire! How stately is your neck, accented with a long string of jewels. [11]We will make earrings of gold for you and beads of silver."

*Young Woman:* [12]"The king is lying on his couch, enchanted by the fragrance of my perfume. [13]My lover is like a sachet of myrrh lying between my breasts. [14]He is like a bouquet of flowers in the gardens of En-gedi."

*Young Man:* [15]"How beautiful you are, my beloved, how beautiful! Your eyes are soft like doves."

*Young Woman:* [16]"What a lovely, pleasant sight you are, my love, as we lie here on the grass, [17]shaded by cedar trees and spreading firs."

## A TREAT ● ● ● ● ●

1:1-4 **This vivid description of a love relationship begins with a picture of love itself. Love is "sweeter than wine." We can enjoy love. God created it as a gift to us and a treat for all our senses.**

1:1 The headings identifying the speakers are not in the original text, though the Hebrew usually gives clues by means of the gender of the person speaking. 1:4 Or *The king has brought me into his bedroom.* 1:6 Hebrew *My own vineyard I have neglected.* 1:7 Hebrew *like a veiled woman.* 1:9 Hebrew *I compare you, my beloved, to a mare among Pharaoh's chariots.*

## CHAPTER 2 MEMORIES OF COURTSHIP.

*Young Woman:* "I am the rose of Sharon, the lily of the valley."

*Young Man:* [2]"Yes, compared to other women, my beloved is like a lily among thorns."

*Young Woman:* [3]"And compared to other youths, my lover is like the finest apple tree in the orchard. I am seated in his delightful shade, and his fruit is delicious to eat. [4]He brings me to the banquet hall, so everyone can see how much he loves me. [5]Oh, feed me with your love—your 'raisins' and your 'apples'—for I am utterly lovesick! [6]His left hand is under my head, and his right hand embraces me.

[7]"Promise me, O women of Jerusalem, by the swift gazelles and the deer of the wild, not to awaken love until the time is right.*

[8]"Ah, I hear him—my lover! Here he comes, leaping on the mountains and bounding over the hills. [9]My lover is like a swift gazelle or a young deer. Look, there he is behind the wall! Now he is looking in through the window, gazing into the room.

### VIRGINITY

Cassie's 16th birthday tomorrow promises to be awesome. She'll finally get her driver's license, and she finally can officially date!

She and her boyfriend, Paul, will be able to leave . . . in a car . . . by themselves . . . for a whole evening! No more brothers barging into the living room. No more being dropped off at parties. Privacy at last!

Today Cassie got a package from her older sister Beth, who got married last month. Enclosed was a long letter–one of those that you keep forever. It said a lot of things, but maybe the best part was this advice: "Cass, I know how much you love Paul, and I know it will be hard for you two to stay pure now that you're officially dating. Take it from someone who waited: Sex is best when you save it for marriage! I promise you–virgins get the last (and the loudest and longest) laugh.

"Most of my friends–even my Christian friends–didn't wait. They traded short-term pleasure for long-term pain. Don't make that mistake! Make the commitment to God that you won't let your physical relationship get out of control!

"Give Paul a hug from me. And know that Mike and I pray for you two every single day. I love you, Cass.

"Beth"

What a great letter! Read another beautiful description of a virgin bride on her wedding night in Song of Songs 4. Note especially verse 12.

[10]"My lover said to me, 'Rise up, my beloved, my fair one, and come away. [11]For the winter is past, and the rain is over and gone. [12]The flowers are springing up, and the time of singing birds has come, even the cooing of turtledoves. [13]The fig trees are budding, and the grapevines are in blossom. How delicious they smell! Yes, spring is here! Arise, my beloved, my fair one, and come away.'"

### OVERPOWERED ● ● ● • •

**2:7 Feelings of love can create intimacy that overpowers reason. Young people too often are in a hurry to develop an intimate relationship based on their strong feelings. But feelings aren't enough to support a lasting relationship. This verse encourages us not to force romance lest the feelings of love grow faster than the commitment needed to make love last. Patiently wait for feelings of love and commitment to develop together.**

*Young Man:* [14]"My dove is hiding behind some rocks, behind an outcrop on the cliff. Let me see you; let me hear your voice. For your voice is pleasant, and you are lovely."

*Young Women of Jerusalem:* [15]"Quick! Catch all the little foxes before they ruin the vineyard of your love, for the grapevines are all in blossom."

*Young Woman:* [16]"My lover is mine, and I am his. He feeds among the lilies! [17]Before the dawn comes and the shadows flee away, come back to me, my love. Run like a gazelle or a young stag on the rugged mountains.*"

## CHAPTER 3 MEMORIES OF ENGAGEMENT.

*Young Woman:* "One night as I lay in bed, I yearned deeply for my lover, but he did not come. [2]So I said to myself, 'I will get up now and roam the city, searching for him in all its streets and squares.' But my search was in vain. [3]The watchmen stopped me as they made their rounds, and I said to them, 'Have you seen him anywhere, this one I love so much?' [4]A little while later I found him and held him. I didn't let him go until I had brought him to my childhood home, into my mother's bedroom, where I had been conceived.

[5]"Promise me, O women of Jerusalem, by the swift gazelles and the deer of the wild, not to awaken love until the time is right.*"

*Young Women of Jerusalem:* [6]"Who is this sweeping in from the deserts like a cloud of smoke along the ground? Who is it that smells of myrrh and frankincense and every other spice? [7]Look, it is Solomon's carriage, with sixty of Israel's mightiest men surrounding it. [8]They are all skilled swordsmen and experienced warriors. Each one wears a sword on his thigh, ready to defend the king against an attack during the night.

[9]"King Solomon has built a carriage for himself from wood imported from Lebanon's forests. [10]Its posts are of silver, its canopy is gold, and its seat is upholstered in purple cloth. Its interior was a gift of love from the young women of Jerusalem."

*Young Woman:* [11]"Go out to look upon King Solomon, O young women of Jerusalem.* See the crown with which his mother crowned him on his wedding day, the day of his gladness."

2:7 Or *not to awaken love until it is ready.* 2:17 Or *on the hills of Bether.* 3:5 Or *not to awaken love until it is ready.* 3:11 Hebrew *Zion.*

## CHAPTER 4

*Young Man:* "How beautiful you are, my beloved, how beautiful! Your eyes behind your veil are like doves. Your hair falls in waves, like a flock of goats frisking down the slopes of Gilead. 2Your teeth are as white as sheep, newly shorn and washed. They are perfectly matched; not one is missing. 3Your lips are like a ribbon of scarlet. Oh, how beautiful your mouth! Your cheeks behind your veil are like pomegranate halves—lovely and delicious. 4Your neck is as stately as the tower of David, jeweled with the shields of a thousand heroes. 5Your breasts are like twin fawns of a gazelle, feeding among the lilies. 6Before the dawn comes and the shadows flee away, I will go to the mountain of myrrh and to the hill of frankincense. 7You are so beautiful, my beloved, so perfect in every part.

8"Come with me from Lebanon, my bride. Come down* from the top of Mount Amana, from Mount Senir and Mount Hermon, where lions have their dens and panthers prowl. 9You have ravished my heart, my treasure, my bride. I am overcome by one glance of your eyes, by a single bead of your necklace. 10How sweet is your love, my treasure, my bride! How much better it is than wine! Your perfume is more fragrant than the richest of spices. 11Your lips, my bride, are as sweet as honey. Yes, honey and cream are under your tongue. The scent of your clothing is like that of the mountains and the cedars of Lebanon.

12"You are like a private garden, my treasure, my bride! You are like a spring that no one else can drink from, a fountain of my own. 13You are like a lovely orchard bearing precious fruit, with the rarest of perfumes: 14nard and saffron, calamus and cinnamon, myrrh and aloes, perfume from every incense tree, and every other lovely spice. 15You are a garden fountain, a well of living water, as refreshing as the streams from the Lebanon mountains."

*Young Woman:* 16"Awake, north wind! Come, south wind! Blow on my garden and waft its lovely perfume to my lover. Let him come into his garden and eat its choicest fruits."

## CHAPTER 5 A DISTURBING DREAM.

*Young Man:* "I am here in my garden, my treasure, my bride! I gather my myrrh with my spices and eat my honeycomb with my honey. I drink my wine with my milk."

*Young Women of Jerusalem:* "Oh, lover and beloved, eat and drink! Yes, drink deeply of this love!"

*Young Woman:* 2"One night as I was sleeping, my heart awakened in a dream. I heard the voice of my lover. He was knocking at my bedroom door. 'Open to me, my darling, my treasure, my lovely dove,' he said, 'for I have been out in the night. My head is soaked with dew, my hair with the wetness of the night.'

3"But I said, 'I have taken off my robe. Should I get dressed again? I have washed my feet. Should I get them soiled?'

4"My lover tried to unlatch the door, and my heart thrilled within me. 5I jumped up to open it. My hands dripped with perfume, my fingers with lovely myrrh, as I pulled back the bolt. 6I opened to my lover, but he was gone. I yearned for even his voice! I searched for him, but I couldn't find him anywhere. I called to him, but there was no reply. 7The watchmen found me as they were making their rounds; they struck and wounded me. The watchman on the wall tore off my veil.

8"Make this promise to me, O women of Jerusalem! If you find my beloved one, tell him that I am sick with love."

*Young Women of Jerusalem:* 9"O woman of rare beauty, what is it about your loved one that brings you to tell us this?"

### WHY WAIT? ● ● • • •

4:12 **In comparing his bride to a private garden, Solomon was praising her virginity. Virginity, considered old-fashioned by many people today, has always been God's plan for unmarried people—and with good reason. Sex without marriage is cheap. It cannot compare with the joy of giving yourself completely to the one who is totally committed to you.**

*Young Woman:* 10"My lover is dark and dazzling, better than ten thousand others! 11His head is the finest gold, and his hair is wavy and black. 12His eyes are like doves beside brooks of water; they are set like jewels. 13His cheeks are like sweetly scented beds of spices. His lips are like perfumed lilies. His breath is like myrrh. 14His arms are like round bars of gold, set with chrysolite. His body is like bright ivory, aglow with sapphires. 15His legs are like pillars of marble set in sockets of the finest gold, strong as the cedars of Lebanon. None can rival him. 16His mouth is altogether sweet; he is lovely in every way. Such, O women of Jerusalem, is my lover, my friend."

## CHAPTER 6 WOW! WHAT A BEAUTIFUL BRIDE.

*Young Women of Jerusalem:* "O rarest of beautiful women, where has your lover gone? We will help you find him."

*Young Woman:* 2"He has gone down to his garden, to his spice beds, to graze and to gather the lilies. 3I am my lover's, and my lover is mine. He grazes among the lilies!"

*Young Man:* 4"O my beloved, you are as beautiful as the lovely town of Tirzah. Yes, as beautiful as Jerusalem! You are as majestic as an army with banners! 5Look away, for your eyes overcome me!

4:8 Or *Look down.*

# Ultimate Issues

## SEX—WHY IS GOD SO NARROW-MINDED?

"Your rounded thighs are like jewels . . . Your navel is as delicious as a goblet filled with wine. . . . You are tall and slim like a palm tree, and your breasts are like its clusters of dates. I said, 'I will climb up into the palm tree and take hold of its branches.' Now may your breasts be like grape clusters, and THE SCENT OF YOUR BREATH like apples. May your kisses be as exciting as the best wine, smooth and sweet, flowing gently over lips and teeth" (Song of Songs 7:1-9). Wow! What is writing like this doing in the Bible? We expect to find sexual messages in movies, music, and magazines—but in the Bible? No wonder the Song of Songs has caused so much confusion, controversy, and even embarrassment. The Song of Songs is not the only place where the Bible talks about sex (for example, see 1 Corinthians 6; Galatians 5:16-25; Ephesians 5:1-3; Hebrews 13:4). But it is here that the Scriptures reach their highest, most beautiful and poetic affirmation of the goodness of sex as God's gift to men and women. Believe it: Sex *is* God's invention—not Hollywood's or MTV's—which leads to several important observations: **• Sex is *good*.** God's people haven't done a very good job in communicating this fact. We've treated this aspect of God's creation as if it were shameful or to be avoided. But God created sex, and he created us as sexual creatures; therefore, sex is good. Regardless of the dangers and trouble surrounding sex, this fact remains: Sex is part of God's creative plan for men and women. **• Sex is *powerful*.** Of all the ways people have of expressing themselves to one another, sex is the most powerful. It involves a person's total being. When sex is kept in its proper context—marriage—it is a powerful vehicle for good, for bringing a husband and wife together as one. Unfortunately, when sex is expressed before or outside of marriage, it can be powerfully destructive. Think of it like this: Say you give a six-year-old the keys to a hot new Ferrari and send him out to drive it in the Grand Prix. You know what will happen. A six-year-old isn't physically, mentally, or emotionally prepared to handle the car or the course. He'll crash and burn and get hurt badly. It's the same with people who are young and not married—they are not prepared mentally, emotionally, or spiritually for the experience of sex. They may think they're ready, but sex is powerful, and it requires a strong structure to support and contain it. Which leads to our final observation: **• Sex is *made for marriage*.** Period. Sex is such an explosive force between two people that it must be expressed in an environment of love, support, and commitment. Especially commitment. That's what is missing in sex outside of marriage—commitment. Sex is **100 PERCENT PHYSICAL COMMITMENT.** Unless there is 100 percent emotional, financial, social, and spiritual commitment, the relationship will be unbalanced and will probably collapse, leading to pain, anger, shame, and much more. Those who decide to become sexually involved in spite of God's instructions shouldn't be surprised when, like our young Ferrari driver, they **crash and burn.** Sex, as the Song of Songs says so beautifully, is God's idea. If you follow his leading—including waiting until marriage to have sex—you'll experience one of God's greatest gifts in a way that is fulfilling to you and pleasing to him.

---

Your hair falls in waves, like a flock of goats
frisking down the slopes of Gilead. 6Your teeth
are as white as newly washed sheep. They are
perfectly matched; not one missing. 7Your cheeks
behind your veil are like pomegranate halves—
lovely and delicious. 8There may be sixty wives, all
queens, and eighty concubines and unnumbered
virgins available to me. 9But I would still choose
my dove, my perfect one, the only beloved
daughter of her mother! The young women are

delighted when they see her; even queens and concubines sing her praises! [10]'Who is this,' they ask, 'arising like the dawn, as fair as the moon, as bright as the sun, as majestic as an army with banners?'

[11]"I went down into the grove of nut trees and out to the valley to see the new growth brought on by spring. I wanted to see whether the grapevines were budding yet, or whether the pomegranates were blossoming. [12]Before I realized it, I found myself in my princely bed with my beloved one.*"

*Young Women of Jerusalem:* [13]"Return, return to us, O maid of Shulam. Come back, come back, that we may see you once again."

*Young Man:* "Why do you gaze so intently at this young woman of Shulam, as she moves so gracefully between two lines of dancers?*"

## CHAPTER 7 THE BRIDE TELLS OF HER LOVE.

*Young Man:* "How beautiful are your sandaled feet, O queenly maiden. Your rounded thighs are like jewels, the work of a skilled craftsman. [2]Your navel is as delicious as a goblet filled with wine. Your belly is lovely, like a heap of wheat set about with lilies. [3]Your breasts are like twin fawns of a gazelle. [4]Your neck is as stately as an ivory tower. Your eyes are like the sparkling pools in Heshbon by the gate of Bath-rabbim. Your nose is as fine as the tower of Lebanon overlooking Damascus. [5]Your head is as majestic as Mount Carmel, and the sheen of your hair radiates royalty. A king is held captive in your queenly tresses.

[6]"Oh, how delightful you are, my beloved; how pleasant for utter delight! [7]You are tall and slim like a palm tree, and your breasts are like its clusters of dates. [8]I said, 'I will climb up into the palm tree and take hold of its branches.' Now may your breasts be like grape clusters, and the scent of your breath like apples. [9]May your kisses be as exciting as the best wine, smooth and sweet, flowing gently over lips and teeth.*"

*Young Woman:* [10]"I am my lover's, the one he desires. [11]Come, my love, let us go out into the fields and spend the night among the wildflowers.* [12]Let us get up early and go out to the vineyards. Let us see whether the vines have budded, whether the blossoms have opened, and whether the pomegranates are in flower. And there I will give you my love. [13]There the mandrakes give forth their fragrance, and the rarest fruits are at our doors, the new as well as old, for I have stored them up for you, my lover."

### MORE LOVE

**7:1-13** **As a marriage matures, there should be more love and freedom between marriage partners. It is good and healthy for a married couple to enjoy and appreciate each other's body. When marriage partners are secure in their love and relationship, they find the freedom to initiate and enjoy acts of love. As you grow in your relationships to the opposite sex, remember that God knows what he is doing where love and sex are concerned. Don't accept anything less than the kind of love he wants for you: the secure, freeing, wonderful love that you will find only in marriage.**

## CHAPTER 8 THE POWER OF LOVE.

*Young Woman:* "Oh, if only you were my brother, who nursed at my mother's breast. Then I could kiss you no matter who was watching, and no one would criticize me. [2]I would bring you to my childhood home, and there you would teach me. I would give you spiced wine to drink, my sweet pomegranate wine. [3]Your left hand would be under my head and your right hand would embrace me.

[4]"I want you to promise, O women of Jerusalem, not to awaken love until the time is right.*"

*Young Women of Jerusalem:* [5]"Who is this coming up from the desert, leaning on her lover?"

*Young Woman:* "I aroused you under the apple tree, where your mother gave you birth, where in great pain she delivered you. [6]Place me like a seal over your heart, or like a seal on your arm. For love is as strong as death, and its jealousy is as enduring as the grave. Love flashes like fire, the brightest kind of flame. [7]Many waters cannot quench love; neither can rivers drown it. If a man tried to buy love with everything he owned, his offer would be utterly despised."

*The Young Woman's Brothers:* [8]"We have a little sister too young for breasts. What will we do if someone asks to marry her? [9]If she is chaste, we will strengthen and encourage her. But if she is promiscuous, we will shut her off from men.*"

*Young Woman:* [10]"I am chaste, and I am now full breasted. And my lover is content with me.

[11]"Solomon has a vineyard at Baal-hamon, which he rents to some farmers there. Each of them pays one thousand pieces of silver* for its

### PRICELESS

**8:6-7** **In this final description of their love, the girl includes some of its significant characteristics (see also 1 Corinthians 13). Love is as strong as death; it cannot be killed by time or disaster; and it cannot be bought for any price because it is freely given. Love is priceless, and even the richest king cannot buy it. It must be accepted as a gift from God and then shared within the guidelines God provides.**

6:12 Or *among the royal chariots of my people,* or *among the chariots of Amminadab.* The meaning of the Hebrew is uncertain. 6:13 Or *as you would at the movements of two armies?* or *as you would at the dance of Mahanaim?* The meaning of the Hebrew is uncertain. 7:9 As in Greek and Syriac versions and Latin Vulgate; Hebrew reads *over lips of sleepers.* 7:11 Or *in the villages.* 8:4 Or *not to awaken love until it is ready.* 8:9 Hebrew *If she is a wall, we will build battlements of silver on her; but if she is a door, we will surround her with panels of cedar.* 8:11 Hebrew *1,000 shekels of silver,* about 25 pounds or 11.4 kilograms in weight; also in 8:12.

use. 12But as for my own vineyard, O Solomon, you can take my thousand pieces of silver. And I will give two hundred pieces of silver* to those who care for its vines."

*Young Man:* 13"O my beloved, lingering in the gardens, how wonderful that your companions can listen to your voice. Let me hear it, too!"

*Young Woman:* 14"Come quickly, my love! Move like a swift gazelle or a young deer on the mountains of spices."

**8:12** Hebrew *200 [shekels]*, about 5 pounds or 2.3 kilograms in weight.

# MEGA themes

**LOVE** As the beauty and wonder of romance unfolded between Solomon and his bride, the intense power of love affected the two lovers' hearts, minds, and bodies.

Love is a powerful expression of feeling and commitment between two people; it is not to be regarded casually. We should not try to manipulate others into loving us, and love should not be pushed in a relationship.

1. The love in Song of Songs is a very intense human love. List several words that could be used to describe this love.
2. When you think of marriage, what qualities do you want to be present in the love you will share with your spouse? Describe the qualities you want your spouse to have as an individual.
3. Explain God's role in the love between a man and a woman.
4. What implications does this study have for dating?
5. What impact does this study have on the way you view marriage? How could you apply this in the future?

**SEX** Sex is God's gift to his creatures. God endorses sex, but because sex is given as an ultimate gift for life, God says its expression should be limited to those who are committed to each other in marriage.

God wants sex to be motivated by love and commitment, not lust. God is glorified by sex within a godly marriage—sex that is for mutual pleasure, not selfish enjoyment.

1. What is different about Song of Song's description of sex and sexual desire and the way sex is presented on TV and in the movies?
2. How does Solomon feel about his bride? How does she feel about him?
3. Is the primary attraction between the couple in this book a physical attraction? Explain.
4. What do you learn about God's design of sexuality for you in reading the Song of Songs? List several principles that can serve as your guidelines for sexual decision making.

**COMMITMENT** The power of love requires more than feelings to protect it. Sexual expression is such an integral part of our selfhood that we need the boundary of marriage to safeguard our love. Marriage is the celebration of daily commitment to each other.

Romance keeps a marriage interesting, and commitment keeps romance from dwindling away. The decision to commit yourself to your spouse alone *begins* at the marriage altar. It must be maintained day by day. In a world filled with divorce and brokenness, God calls us to learn to live according to commitment.

1. What words in Song of Songs represent commitment?
2. Would this commitment best be described as a one-time commitment, a daily commitment, neither, or a combination of both? Explain.
3. What impact does a marriage with strong commitment have on the children in that family? What impact does weak commitment have on them?
4. List the things that strengthen commitment in a marriage. List the things that weaken commitment.
5. How can you make choices now, in friendship and dating, that will prepare you for a future

marriage with a strong commitment? What role does God play in that preparation?

**BEAUTY** The two lovers praise the beauty they see in each other. The language they use shows the spontaneity and mystery of love. Our praise should not be limited to physical beauty. Beautiful personality and moral purity also should be praised.

The love one feels for a husband or wife reveals that person's inner beauty, and those inner qualities keep love alive. Don't look for just physical attractiveness in a spouse. Look for the qualities that don't fade with time—spiritual commitment, integrity, sensitivity, and sincerity. Character lasts much longer than good looks.

1. When you think of beauty, what comes to your mind first?
2. Describe the difference between a person's physical beauty and a person's inner beauty.
3. Give an example of a person you know who has true inner beauty. What makes this person so beautiful?
4. If you were looking for a husband or wife, what inner qualities would you most want him or her to have? Why are these important to you?
5. What inner qualities do you want to bring to a marriage someday? In what ways can you deepen those qualities in your present relationships?

**PROBLEMS** Over time, feelings of loneliness, indifference, and isolation came between Solomon and his bride. During those times, love grew cold and barriers arose.

Through careful communication, lovers can be reconciled, commitment can be renewed, and romance can be refreshed. Don't let walls come between you two. Take care of problems while they are still small.

1. Why do all human relationships include conflict?
2. What principles do you find in Song of Songs that can be applied to working through difficult problems in relationships?
3. Where are your areas of interpersonal conflict? What are you doing in response to the problems you are facing now?
4. What can you do to apply the principles of Song of Songs to the conflicts you are facing in relationships now?

760 B.C.
Amos becomes a prophet

753
Hosea becomes a prophet

742
Micah becomes a prophet

740
Isaiah becomes a prophet

735
Ahaz becomes king of Judah

732
Hoshea becomes king of Israel

722
Israel falls to the Assyrians

715
Hezekiah becomes king of Judah

701
Sennacherib surrounds Jerusalem

697
Manasseh becomes king of Judah

681
Isaiah's ministry ends

640
Josiah becomes king of Judah

Slowly, on shaky legs, Matt walked to the front of the room, the fluttering in his stomach growing with every step. As he turned to face the class he was sure everyone could hear the relentless pounding of his heart. Wiping his sweat-moistened palms on his pants, he pulled out his note cards and began to speak. ■ Stage fright. We know it all too well. According to many studies, the greatest fear most people have is doing what Matt did . . . giving a speech. You're in front of everyone, exposed and vulnerable—and the pressure can be incredible. ■ Now, if you think that's tough, imagine being a prophet. Not only would you have to speak in public, but usually the messages you would have to give would *not* be what people want to hear. As a prophet, you would have to speak of sin, judgment, and changes that had to be made. And often you would have to confront kings, men who could pronounce the death sentence on a whim. Sometimes, to really make a point, you would have to act out your messages. That wouldn't be too much fun either, but true prophets spoke out for God, regardless of how they felt. ■ Isaiah was one of the greatest prophets who ever lived, and the book of Isaiah contains his messages. In this book, you'll see Isaiah in action as he stays close to God and speaks to the people. That takes courage! As you read, listen to God's word for you, and determine to be a person of courage, too, faithfully taking God's message wherever he sends you.

## STATS

PURPOSE: To call the nation of Judah back to God and to tell of God's salvation through the Messiah

AUTHOR: The prophet Isaiah, son of Amoz

DATE WRITTEN: The events of chapters 1–39 occurred during Isaiah's ministry, so they were probably written about 700 B.C. Chapters 40–66, however, may have been written near the end of his life, about 681 B.C.

SETTING: Isaiah is speaking and writing mainly in Jerusalem

KEY PEOPLE: Isaiah, his two sons Shear-Jashub and Maher-Shalal-Hash-Baz

SPECIAL FEATURES: The book of Isaiah contains both prose and poetry and uses personification (attributing personal qualities to divine beings or inanimate objects). Also, many of the prophecies in Isaiah contain predictions that foretell both a soon-to-occur event and a distant, future event at the same time.

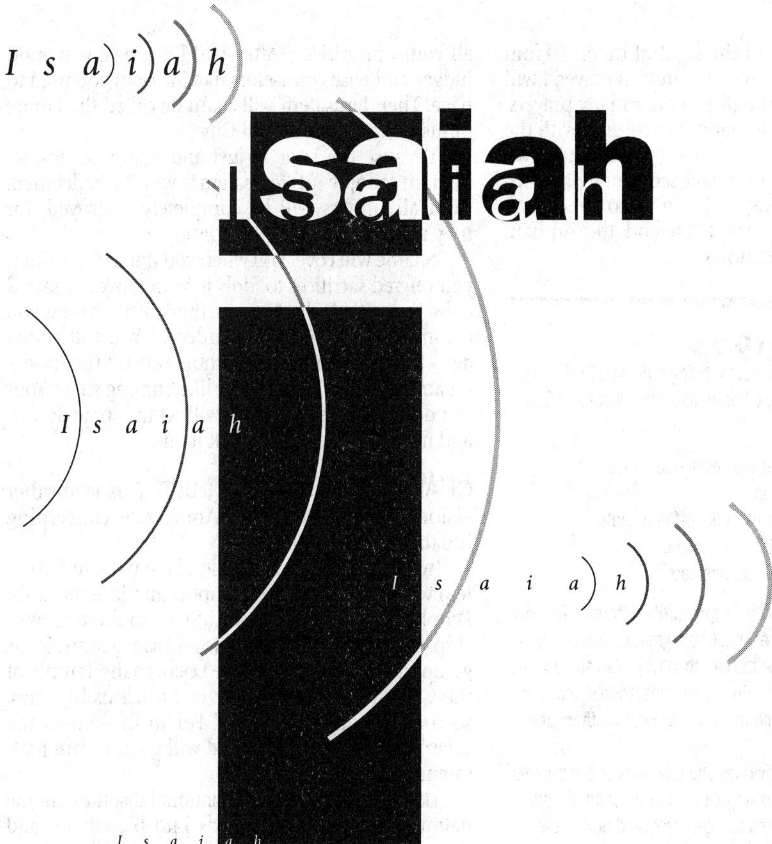


CHAPTER 1 **GOD'S MESSAGE TO HIS PEOPLE.** These visions concerning Judah and Jerusalem came to Isaiah son of Amoz during the reigns of Uzziah, Jotham, Ahaz, and Hezekiah—all kings of Judah.

[2]Hear, O heavens! Listen, O earth! This is what the LORD says: "The children I raised and cared for have turned against me. [3]Even the animals—the donkey and the ox—know their owner and appreciate his care, but not my people Israel. No matter what I do for them, they still do not understand."

[4]Oh, what a sinful nation they are! They are loaded down with a burden of guilt. They are evil and corrupt children who have turned away from the LORD. They have despised the Holy One of Israel, cutting themselves off from his help.

[5]Why do you continue to invite punishment? Must you rebel forever? Your head is injured, and your heart is sick. [6]You are sick from head to foot—covered with bruises, welts, and infected wounds—without any ointments or bandages. [7]Your country lies in ruins, and your cities are burned. As you watch, foreigners plunder your fields and destroy everything they see. [8]Jerusalem* stands abandoned like a watchman's shelter in a vineyard or field after the harvest is over. It is as helpless as a city under siege. [9]If the LORD Almighty had not spared a few of us, we would have been wiped out as completely as Sodom and Gomorrah.

[10]Listen to the LORD, you leaders of Israel! Listen to the law of our God, people of Israel. You act just like the rulers and people of Sodom and Gomorrah. [11]"I am sick of your sacrifices," says the LORD. "Don't bring me any more burnt offerings! I don't want the fat from your rams or other animals. I don't want to see the blood from your offerings of bulls and rams and goats. [12]Why do you keep parading through my courts with your worthless sacrifices? [13]The incense you bring me is a stench in my nostrils! Your celebrations of the new moon and the Sabbath day, and your special days for fasting—even your most pious meetings—are all sinful and false. I want nothing more to do with them. [14]I hate all your festivals and

1:8 Hebrew *The daughter of Zion.*

## CUT OFF ● ● ● • •

**1:4-9 As long as the people of Judah continued to sin, they cut themselves off from God's help. Has sin ever made you feel lonely and separated from God? Remember, God does not abandon you—it is your sin that cuts you off from him. The only sure cure for this kind of loneliness is to restore a meaningful relationship with God by confessing your sin, obeying his instructions, and communicating regularly with him (see Psalm 140:13; Isaiah 1:16-19; 1 John 1:9).**

sacrifices. I cannot stand the sight of them! 15From now on, when you lift up your hands in prayer, I will refuse to look. Even though you offer many prayers, I will not listen. For your hands are covered with the blood of your innocent victims. 16Wash yourselves and be clean! Let me no longer see your evil deeds. Give up your wicked ways. 17Learn to do good. Seek justice. Help the oppressed. Defend the orphan. Fight for the rights of widows.

## O RELIGIOUS

If there were a contest for being religious, Terri probably would take home first prize. Just look: She

- rarely misses church.
- sings in the choir. (And sometimes even does solos!)
- is an officer in her youth group.
- puts 10 percent of all she earns in the offering plate.
- reads two chapters in her Bible every night.
- says a blessing before every meal she eats.

Yes, you would assume that Terri is a deeply spiritual person. Anyone involved in all those religious activities must be a great Christian, right?

Well, look again. If Terri is so close to God, then why does she use the language she uses? And why does she rip her classmates to shreds the way she does? And how come she's so mean to her little brothers and to her grandmother?

If Terri's so together spiritually, why does she talk back to her parents almost every day? If she is such an example of a mature child of God, why does she go to some of the parties she goes to? (And how in the world does she justify doing what she does at those parties?)

"Religious" people can brag about their religious activities all they want—God isn't impressed. In fact, he says that when our life is full of sin, our religious activities aren't worth a hill of beans. To please him, our life must be consistent in every way. See Isaiah 1:10-17.

18"Come now, let us argue this out," says the LORD. "No matter how deep the stain of your sins, I can remove it. I can make you as clean as freshly fallen snow. Even if you are stained as red as crimson, I can make you as white as wool. 19If you will only obey me and let me help you, then you will have plenty to eat. 20But if you keep turning away and refusing to listen, you will be destroyed by your enemies. I, the LORD, have spoken!"

21See how Jerusalem, once so faithful, has become a prostitute. Once the home of justice and righteousness, she is now filled with murderers. 22Once like pure silver, you have become like worthless slag. Once so pure, you are now like watered-down wine. 23Your leaders are rebels, the companions of thieves. All of them take bribes and refuse to defend the orphans and the widows.

24Therefore, the Lord, the LORD Almighty, the Mighty One of Israel, says, "I will pour out my fury on you, my enemies! 25I will turn against you. I will melt you down and skim off your slag. I will remove all your impurities. 26Afterward I will give you good judges and wise counselors like the ones you used to have. Then Jerusalem will again be called the Home of Justice and the Faithful City."

27Because the LORD is just and righteous, the repentant people of Jerusalem* will be redeemed. 28But all sinners will be completely destroyed, for they refuse to come to the LORD.

29Shame will cover you when you think of the times you offered sacrifices to idols in your groves of sacred oaks. You will blush when you think of all the sins you committed in your sacred gardens. 30You will wither away like an oak or garden without water. 31The strongest among you will disappear like burning straw. Your evil deeds are the spark that will set the straw on fire, and no one will be able to put it out.

CHAPTER **2** **WALK IN GOD'S LIGHT.** This is another vision that Isaiah son of Amoz saw concerning Judah and Jerusalem:

2In the last days, the Temple of the LORD in Jerusalem will become the most important place on earth. People from all over the world will go there to worship. 3Many nations will come and say, "Come, let us go up to the mountain of the LORD, to the Temple of the God of Israel.* There he will teach us his ways, so that we may obey him." For in those days the LORD's teaching and his word will go out from Jerusalem.

4The LORD will settle international disputes. All the nations will beat their swords into plowshares and their spears into pruning hooks. All wars will stop, and military training will come to an end. 5Come, people of Israel, let us walk in the light of the LORD!

6The LORD has rejected the people of Israel because they have made alliances with foreigners from the East who practice magic and divination, just like the Philistines. 7Israel has vast treasures of silver and gold and many horses and chariots. 8The land is filled with idols. The people bow down and worship these things they have made. 9So now everyone will be humbled and brought low. The LORD cannot simply ignore their sins!

10Crawl into caves in the rocks. Hide from the terror of the LORD and the glory of his majesty. 11The day is coming when your pride will be brought low and the LORD alone will be exalted. 12In that day the LORD Almighty will punish the proud, bringing them down to the dust. 13He will cut down the tall cedars of Lebanon and the mighty oaks of Bashan. 14He will level the high mountains and hills. 15He

## STAINS ● ● • • •

**1:18 A deep stain is virtually impossible to remove from clothing; the stain of sin seems equally permanent. But God can remove the stain of sin from our lives just as he promised to do for the Israelites. We don't have to go through life permanently soiled. Through prayer we can be assured that Christ has forgiven our worst sins and removed our most indelible stains (Psalm 51:1-7).**

1:27 Hebrew *Zion*. 2:3 Hebrew *of Jacob;* also in 2:5, 6.

will break down every high tower and wall. 16He will destroy the great trading ships* and all the small boats in the harbor. 17The arrogance of all people will be brought low. Their pride will lie in the dust. The LORD alone will be exalted! 18Idols will be utterly abolished and destroyed.

19When the LORD rises to shake the earth, his enemies will crawl with fear into holes in the ground. They will hide in caves in the rocks from the terror of the LORD and the glory of his majesty. 20They will abandon their gold and silver idols to the moles and bats. 21They will crawl into caverns and hide among the jagged rocks at the tops of cliffs. In this way, they will try to escape the terror of the LORD and the glory of his majesty as he rises to shake the earth.

22Stop putting your trust in mere humans. They are as frail as breath. How can they be of help to anyone?

## CHAPTER 3 **A WELL-EARNED PUNISHMENT.**

The Lord, the LORD Almighty, will cut off the supplies of food and water from Jerusalem and Judah. 2He will destroy all the nation's leaders—the heroes, soldiers, judges, prophets, diviners, elders, 3army officers, honorable citizens, advisers, skilled magicians, and expert enchanters. 4Then he will appoint children to rule over them, and anarchy will prevail. 5People will take advantage of each other—man against man, neighbor fighting neighbor. Young people will revolt against authority, and nobodies will sneer at honorable people.

6In those days a man will say to his brother, "Since you have a cloak, you be our leader! Take charge of this heap of ruins!"

7"No!" he will reply. "I can't help. I don't have any extra food or clothes. Don't ask me to get involved!"

8Judah and Jerusalem will lie in ruins because they speak out against the LORD and refuse to obey him. They have offended his glorious presence among them. 9The very look on their faces gives them away and displays their guilt. They sin openly like the people of Sodom. They are not one bit ashamed. How terrible it will be for them! They have brought about their own destruction.

10But all will be well for those who are godly. Tell them, "You will receive a wonderful reward!" 11But say to the wicked, "Your destruction is sure. You, too, will get what you deserve. Your well-earned punishment is on the way."

12Children oppress my people, and women rule over them. O my people, can't you see what fools your rulers are? They are leading you down a pretty garden path to destruction.

13The LORD takes his place in court. He is the great prosecuting attorney, presenting his case against his people! 14The leaders and the princes will be the first to feel the LORD's judgment. "You have ruined Israel, which is my vineyard. You have taken advantage of the poor, filling your barns with grain extorted from

### RELIABLE ● ● • • •

2:22 **People are "nothing" compared to God. They are undependable, sinful, and mortal. Often we trust human beings with our life and our future instead of trusting the all-knowing God. Beware of people who want you to trust them instead of God. Remember that only God is completely reliable, because only God loves us with an eternal love (Psalm 100:5).**

helpless people. 15How dare you grind my people into the dust like that!" demands the Lord, the LORD Almighty.

16Next the LORD will judge the women of Jerusalem,* who walk around with their noses in the air, with tinkling ornaments on their ankles. Their eyes rove among the crowds, flirting with the men. 17The Lord will send a plague of scabs to ornament their heads. Yes, the LORD will make them bald for all to see!

18The Lord will strip away their artful beauty—their ornaments, headbands, and crescent necklaces; 19their earrings, bracelets, and veils of shimmering gauze. 20Gone will be their scarves, ankle chains, sashes, perfumes, and charms; 21their rings, jewels, 22party clothes, gowns, capes, and purses; 23their mirrors, linen garments, head ornaments, and shawls. 24Instead of smelling of sweet perfume, they will stink. They will wear ropes for sashes, and their well-set hair will fall out. They will wear rough sackcloth instead of rich robes. Their beauty will be gone. Only shame will be left to them.

25The men of the city will die in battle. 26The gates of Jerusalem* will weep and mourn. The city will be like a ravaged woman, huddled on the ground.

## CHAPTER 4 **GOD'S HOLY PEOPLE.**

In that day few men will be left alive. Seven women will fight over each of them and say, "Let us all marry you! We will provide our own food and clothing. Only let us be called by your name so we won't be mocked as old maids."

2But in the future, Israel—the branch of the LORD—will be lush and beautiful, and the fruit of the land will be the pride of its people. 3All those whose names are written down, who have survived the destruction of Jerusalem, will be a holy people. 4The Lord will wash the moral filth from the women of Jerusalem.* He will cleanse Jerusalem of its bloodstains by a spirit of judgment that burns like fire. 5Then the LORD will provide shade for

### FASHION ● ● • • •

3:16-26 **The women of Judah had placed their emphasis on clothing and jewelry rather than on God. They dressed to be noticed, to gain approval, and to be fashionable. Instead of being concerned about the oppression around them (3:14-15), they were self-serving and self-centered. Those who misuse their possessions will end up with nothing. These verses are not an indictment against clothing and jewelry, but a judgment on those who use them lavishly while blind to the needs of others. When God blesses you, don't flaunt your wealth. Use what you have to help others.**

**2:16** Hebrew *every ship of Tarshish.* **3:16** Hebrew *the daughters of Zion.* **3:26** Hebrew *Zion.* **4:4** Hebrew *from the daughters of Zion.*

# Ultimate Issues

**WHO IS GOD?** The Eastern person says, "God is within you," or "God is illusion." The New Ager says, "I am God. You are God. Everyone is a part of God, and God is a part of everyone." The philosopher says, "God is the ultimate concept." The atheist says, "There is no God." The Christian says, "There is a God, and he is not you or me. God is different and separate from his creation. We are made in his image, and we can know him." So who's right? Who is God? "In the year King Uzziah died, I saw the Lord. He was sitting on a lofty throne, and THE TRAIN OF HIS ROBE filled the Temple." So writes the prophet Isaiah in the sixth chapter of the book named for him. Isaiah also wondered what God was like. Isaiah had received messages from God for Israel, and he had delivered them faithfully. But around the time of King Uzziah's death (approximately 740 B.C.), Isaiah not only heard a message, he got a glimpse of God! Understandably, Isaiah was overwhelmed. What does the Bible say about what Isaiah saw? Any study of what God is like should begin with a look at the names given for him in Scripture. Each name—Elohim, Adonai, El Shaddai, Yahweh (or Jehovah), Abba—holds meaning about God's nature and character. The Bible puts God's characteristics into basically two categories: the "incommunicable" ones, those he does not share with his creation; and the "communicable" ones, those he does share with us. The incommunicable attributes include: EXISTENCE—before anything else existed, God was. The idea that something or some*one* exists outside of time is mind-boggling. Still, it is a logical necessity that something had to come first, and that first something had to always exist. The Bible's answer to this mystery is straightforward: "Before the mountains were created, before you made the earth . . . You are God, without beginning or end" (Psalm 90:2). IMMUTABILITY—which means God never changes; he is the same yesterday, today, and forever (Malachi 3:6). You never have to worry about God's actions from one day to the next—he is forever consistent. Unlike the "gods" of other religions—moody, fickle, often cruel, and all-too-human—the One True God is eternally the same. In a constantly changing world, it is comforting to know there is always one source of stability. INFINITY—God is beyond all boundaries. He is limitless. This infinity is expressed in different ways. In regard to *time,* God is eternal; he always was, is, and will be. In regard to *space,* he is omnipresent, or everywhere at once. No corner of the universe lacks his presence. In regard to *power,* he is omnipotent, or all-powerful. God can do anything that is consistent with his character. (There are ***some things God cannot do***—he cannot lie, break a promise, be less than God, etc.) God alone is the power of creation: he spoke, and the universe was created. God will someday speak another kind of word and bring the curtain down. In regard to *knowledge,* he is omniscient, or all-knowing. There is nothing and no one that God does not know completely. He knows everything about you. We can comprehend God's communicable attributes because he shares them with us to some degree. These include the abilities to think, to love, to make moral judgments, to communicate, to work, and so on. Though God's ability in these areas is LIGHT-YEARS beyond ours, he has given us some capacity to resemble him in certain areas. Remember, we are made in the image of God. There are many different ideas and belief systems centered around the question, Who is God? Christianity is based on the confident assertion that the real God, the God of Isaiah and of the Bible, has revealed himself to us, and we can know him.

Jerusalem* and all who assemble there. There will be a canopy of smoke and cloud throughout the day and clouds of fire at night, covering the glorious land. [6]It will be a shelter from daytime heat and a hiding place from storms and rain.

## CHAPTER 5 **SOUR GRAPES IN GOD'S GARDEN.**

Now I will sing a song for the one I love about his vineyard:

My beloved has a vineyard
 on a rich and fertile hill.
2 He plowed the land, cleared its stones,
 and planted it with choice vines.
In the middle he built a watchtower
 and carved a winepress in the nearby rocks.
Then he waited for a harvest of sweet grapes,
 but the grapes that grew were wild and sour.
3 "Now, you people of Jerusalem and Judah,
 you have heard the case; you be the judges.
4 What more could I have done
 to cultivate a rich harvest?
Why did my vineyard give me wild grapes
 when I expected sweet ones?
5 Now this is what I am going to do to my
 vineyard:
I will tear down its fences
 and let it be destroyed.
I will break down its walls
 and let the animals trample it.
6 I will make it a wild place.
 I will not prune the vines or hoe the ground.
 I will let it be overgrown with briers and thorns.
I will command the clouds
 to drop no more rain on it."

7 This is the story of the LORD's people.
 They are the vineyard of the LORD Almighty.
 Israel and Judah are his pleasant garden.
He expected them to yield a crop of justice,
 but instead he found bloodshed.
He expected to find righteousness,
 but instead he heard cries of oppression.

[8]Destruction is certain for you who buy up property so others have no place to live. Your homes are built on great estates so you can be alone in the land. [9]But the LORD Almighty has sealed your awful fate. With my own ears I heard him say, "Many beautiful homes will stand deserted, the owners dead or gone. [10]Ten acres* of vineyard will not produce even six gallons* of wine. Ten measures of seed will yield only one measure* of grain."

[11]Destruction is certain for you who get up early to begin long drinking bouts that last late into the night. [12]You furnish lovely music and wine at your grand parties; the harps, lyres, tambourines, and flutes are superb! But you never think about the LORD or notice what he is doing. [13]So I will send my people into exile far away because they do not know me. The great and honored among them will starve, and the common people will die of thirst.

[14]The grave* is licking its chops in anticipation of Jerusalem, this delicious morsel. Her great and lowly will be swallowed up, with all her drunken crowds. [15]In that day the arrogant will be brought down to the dust; the proud will be humbled. [16]But the LORD Almighty is exalted by his justice. The holiness of God is displayed by his righteousness. [17]In those days flocks will feed among the ruins; lambs and kids* will pasture there.

[18]Destruction is certain for those who drag their sins behind them, tied with cords of falsehood. [19]They even mock the Holy One of Israel and say, "Hurry up and do something! Quick, show us what you can do. We want to see what you have planned."

[20]Destruction is certain for those who say that evil is good and good is evil; that dark is light and light is dark; that bitter is sweet and sweet is bitter.

[21]Destruction is certain for those who think they are wise and consider themselves to be clever.

[22]Destruction is certain for those who are heroes when it comes to drinking, who boast about all the liquor they can hold. [23]They take bribes to pervert justice. They let the wicked go free while punishing the innocent.

[24]Therefore, they will all disappear like burning straw. Their roots will rot and their flowers wither, for they have rejected the law of the LORD Almighty. They have despised the word of the Holy One of Israel. [25]That is why the anger of the LORD burns against his people. That is why he has raised his fist to crush them. The hills tremble, and the rotting bodies of his people are thrown as garbage into the streets. But even then the LORD's anger will not be satisfied. His fist is still poised to strike!

### HEROES ● ● ● • •

**5:13 The nation's heroes—the great and honored among them—would suffer the same humiliation as the common people. Why? Because they lived by their own values rather than God's. Many of today's heroes in TV, movies, and books are idolized because of their ability to live as they please. Are your heroes those who defy God, or those who defy the world in order to serve God?**

[26]He will send a signal to the nations far away. He will whistle to those at the ends of the earth, and they will come racing toward Jerusalem. [27]They will not get tired or stumble. They will run without stopping for rest or sleep. Not a belt will be loose, not a sandal thong broken. [28]Their arrows will be sharp and their bows ready for battle. Sparks will fly from their horses' hooves as the wheels of their chariots spin like the wind. [29]Roaring like lions, they will pounce on their prey. They will seize my people and carry them off into captivity, and no one will be there to rescue them. [30]The enemy nations will growl over

4:5 Hebrew *Mount Zion.* 5:10a Hebrew *A ten yoke,* that is, the area of land plowed by ten teams of oxen in one day. 5:10b Hebrew *a bath* [21 liters]. 5:10c Hebrew *A homer* [5 bushels or 182 liters] *of seed will yield only an ephah* [0.5 bushels or 18.2 liters]. 5:14 Hebrew *Sheol.* 5:17 As in Greek version; Hebrew reads *strangers.*

**GREATNESS ● ● • • •**

6:1-7 **Isaiah's lofty view of God in 6:1-4 gives us a sense of God's greatness, mystery, and power. Isaiah's recognition of his sinfulness before God encourages us to confess our sin. His picture of forgiveness reminds us that we, too, are forgiven. When we recognize how great our God is, how sinful we are, and the extent of his forgiveness, we will be energized to do his work. How does your concept of the greatness of God measure up to Isaiah's?**

their victims like the roaring of the sea. A cloud of darkness and sorrow will hover over Israel. The clouds will blot out the light.

CHAPTER **6** **GOD CALLS ISAIAH.** In the year King Uzziah died, I saw the Lord. He was sitting on a lofty throne, and the train of his robe filled the Temple. [2]Hovering around him were mighty seraphim, each with six wings. With two wings they covered their faces, with two they covered their feet, and with the remaining two they flew. [3]In a great chorus they sang, "Holy, holy, holy is the LORD Almighty! The whole earth is filled with his glory!" [4]The glorious singing shook the Temple to its foundations, and the entire sanctuary was filled with smoke.

[5]Then I said, "My destruction is sealed, for I am a sinful man and a member of a sinful race. Yet I have seen the King, the LORD Almighty!"

[6]Then one of the seraphim flew over to the altar, and he picked up a burning coal with a pair of tongs. [7]He touched my lips with it and said, "See, this coal has touched your lips. Now your guilt is removed, and your sins are forgiven."

[8]Then I heard the Lord asking, "Whom should I send as a messenger to my people? Who will go for us?"

And I said, "Lord, I'll go! Send me."

[9]And he said, "Yes, go. But tell my people this: 'You will hear my words, but you will not understand. You will see what I do, but you will not perceive its meaning.' [10]Harden the hearts of these people. Close their ears, and shut their eyes. That way, they will not see with their eyes, hear with their ears, understand with their hearts, and turn to me for healing."

[11]Then I said, "Lord, how long must I do this?"

And he replied, "Until their cities are destroyed, with no one left in them. Until their houses are deserted and the whole country is an utter wasteland. [12]Do not stop until the LORD has sent everyone away to distant lands and the entire land of Israel lies deserted. [13]Even if only a tenth—a remnant—survive, it will be invaded again and burned. Israel will remain a stump, like a tree that is cut down, but the stump will be a holy seed that will grow again."

CHAPTER **7** **IMMANUEL—GOD IS WITH US.** During the reign of Ahaz son of Jotham and grandson of Uzziah, Jerusalem was attacked by King Rezin of Aram and King Pekah of Israel, the son of Remaliah. The city withstood the attack, however, and was not taken.

[2]The news had come to the royal court: "Aram is allied with Israel* against us!" So the hearts of the king and his people trembled with fear, just as trees shake in a storm.

[3]Then the LORD said to Isaiah, "Go out to meet King Ahaz, you and your son Shear-jashub.* You will find the king at the end of the aqueduct that feeds water into the upper pool, near the road leading to the field where cloth is bleached. [4]Tell him to stop worrying. Tell him he doesn't need to fear the fierce anger of those two burned-out embers, King Rezin of Aram and Pekah son of Remaliah.

[5]"Yes, the kings of Aram and Israel are coming against you. They are saying, [6]'We will invade Judah and throw its people into panic. Then we will fight our way into Jerusalem and install the son of Tabeel as Judah's king.'

[7]"But this is what the Sovereign LORD says: This invasion will never happen, [8]because Aram is no stronger than its capital, Damascus. And Damascus is no stronger than its king, Rezin. As for Israel, within sixty-five years it will be crushed and completely destroyed. [9]Israel is no stronger than its capital, Samaria. And Samaria is no stronger than its king, Pekah son of Remaliah. You do not believe me? If you want me to protect you, learn to believe what I say."

[10]Not long after this, the LORD sent this message to King Ahaz: [11]"Ask me for a sign, Ahaz, to prove that I will crush your enemies as I have promised. Ask for anything you like, and make it as difficult as you want."

[12]But the king refused. "No," he said, "I wouldn't test the LORD like that."

[13]Then Isaiah said, "Listen well, you royal family of David! You aren't satisfied to exhaust my patience. You exhaust the patience of God as well! [14]All right then, the Lord himself will choose the sign. Look! The virgin* will conceive a child! She will give birth to a son and will call him Immanuel—'God is with us.' [15]By the time this child is old enough to eat curds and honey, he will know enough to choose what is right and reject what is wrong. [16]But before he knows right from wrong, the two kings you fear so much—the kings of Israel and Aram—will both be dead.

[17]"The LORD will bring a terrible curse on you, your nation, and your family. You will soon experi-

**CHOICES ● ● • • •**

8:6, 14-15 **Because the people of Judah rejected God's gentle care, choosing instead to seek help from other nations, God would punish them. Here we see two distinct attributes of God—his love and his wrath. Ignoring God's love and guidance results in sin and invites his wrath. We must recognize the consequences of our choices. God seeks to protect us from bad choices, but he still gives us the freedom to make them.**

7:2 Hebrew *Ephraim,* referring to the northern kingdom of Israel; also in 7:5, 8, 9, 17. 7:3 *Shear-jashub* means "A remnant will return." 7:14 Or *young woman.*

ence greater terror than has been known in all the
years since Solomon's empire was divided into Israel
and Judah. The mighty king of Assyria will come
with his great army!"
18 In that day the LORD will whistle for the army of
Upper Egypt and for the army of Assyria. They will
swarm around you like flies. Like bees, they will sting
and kill. 19 They will come in vast hordes, spreading
across the whole land. They will settle in the fertile
areas and also in the desolate valleys, caves, and
thorny places. 20 In that day the Lord will take this
"razor"—these Assyrians you have hired to protect
you—and use it to shave off everything: your land,
your crops, and your people.*
21 When they finally stop plundering, a farmer will
be fortunate to have a cow and two sheep left. 22 The
few people still left in the land
will live on curds and wild honey
because that is all the land will
produce. 23 In that day the lush
vineyards, now worth as much as
a thousand pieces of silver,* will
become patches of briers and
thorns. 24 The entire land will be
one vast brier patch, a hunting
ground overrun by wildlife. 25 No
one will go to the fertile hillsides
where the gardens once grew, for
briers and thorns will cover
them. Cattle, sheep, and goats
will graze there.

CHAPTER **8** **ISAIAH PREDICTS AN
INVASION.** Again the LORD said to
me, "Make a large signboard and
clearly write this name on it:
Maher-shalal-hash-baz.*" 2 I
asked Uriah the priest and Zechariah son of Jeberekiah, both
known as honest men, to testify
that I had written it before the
child was conceived.
3 Then I slept with my wife, and
she became pregnant and had a
son. And the LORD said, "Call
him Maher-shalal-hash-baz.
4 This name prophesies that
within a couple of years, before
this child is old enough to say
'Papa' or 'Mama,' the king of Assyria will invade both Damascus
and Samaria and carry away their
riches."
5 Then the LORD spoke to me
again and said, 6 "The people of
Judah have rejected my gentle
care* and are rejoicing over what
will happen to King Rezin and
King Pekah. 7 Therefore, the LORD will overwhelm
them with a mighty flood from the Euphrates
River*—the king of Assyria and all his mighty armies. 8 This flood will overflow all its channels and
sweep into Judah. It will submerge Immanuel's land
from one end to the other.
9 "The Assyrians will cry, 'Do your best to defend
yourselves, but you will be shattered! Listen all you
nations. Prepare for battle—and die! Yes, die! 10 Call
your councils of war, develop your strategies, prepare
your plans of attack—and then die! For God is with
us!*'"
11 The LORD has said to me in the strongest terms:
"Do not think like everyone else does. 12 Do not be
afraid that some plan conceived behind closed doors
will be the end of you. 13 Do not fear anything except

## "Here's what I did..."

I always had trouble with peer pressure. I became a Christian in seventh grade, but had trouble really living like one. I was good at wisecracks and putting people down, for one thing. And I swore a lot. But probably the biggest weakness I had was partying. When someone asked me to go to a party, it was like I couldn't say no. Then when I got there, if there was drinking, I couldn't resist. I tried a couple of times, but people would ask why I wasn't having a beer. Once I even tried to tell them it was because I was a Christian. I shouldn't have said that. They joked about my being too "holy" for them, and I felt so bad I gave in and even drank too much that night. After that, I was afraid to say anything about my faith because I thought it would be worse if I said something and then didn't act at all like a Christian.

Still, I read my Bible. And I started going to youth group in our church. That helped me change some, but I continued to feel like a hypocrite.

One day I was reading in Isaiah, and for some reason Isaiah 7:9 leaped out at me. It said, "If you want me to protect you, learn to believe what I say." I had been praying that God would make me a stronger Christian. This verse seemed to be saying to me that I hadn't really believed that God could change me, or that he could help me do what's right rather than give in to pressure.

Reading that verse was a turning point for me. I decided that I had to learn more about my faith and God's promises, and more about how God's Holy Spirit worked in my life. I spent more time with my church friends and less with my school friends. At first that was difficult, but it turned out to be easier than I thought. The youth group often had things planned for the weekend, so when someone invited me to a party, I could honestly say I had other plans. I'm still struggling with peer pressure, but it's less of a struggle now. The more I learn about God, the more I see how he works in me through his Holy Spirit, and the more I believe God, the more he really does protect me.

*Jason*

AGE 16

7:20 Hebrew *shave off the head, the hair of the legs, and the beard.* 7:23 Hebrew *1,000 shekels of silver,* about 25 pounds or 11.4 kilograms in weight. 8:1 *Maher-shalal-hash-baz* means "Swift to plunder and quick to spoil." 8:6 Hebrew *rejected the gently flowing waters of Shiloah.* 8:7 Hebrew *the river.* 8:10 Hebrew *Immanuel!*

**NAMES FOR MESSIAH**

Isaiah uses five names to describe the Messiah (9:6). These names have special meaning to us.

| WONDERFUL | COUNSELOR | MIGHTY GOD | EVERLASTING FATHER | PRINCE OF PEACE |
|---|---|---|---|---|
| He is exceptional, distinguished, and without peers. | He gives the right advice. | He is God himself. | He is timeless; he is God our Father. | His government is one of justice and peace. |

the LORD Almighty. He alone is the Holy One. If you fear him, you need fear nothing else. [14]He will keep you safe. But to Israel and Judah he will be a stone that causes people to stumble and a rock that makes them fall. And for the people of Jerusalem he will be a trap that entangles them. [15]Many of them will stumble and fall, never to rise again. Many will be captured."

[16]I will write down all these things as a testimony of what the LORD will do. I will entrust it to my disciples, who will pass it down to future generations. [17]I will wait for the LORD to help us, though he has turned away from the people of Israel.* My only hope is in him. [18]I and the children the LORD has given me have names* that reveal the plans the LORD Almighty has for his people. [19]So why are you trying to find out the future by consulting mediums and psychics? Do not listen to their whisperings and mutterings. Can the living find out the future from the dead? Why not ask your God?

[20]"Check their predictions against my testimony," says the LORD. "If their predictions are different from mine, it is because there is no light or truth in them. [21]My people will be led away as captives, weary and hungry. And because they are hungry, they will rage and shake their fists at heaven and curse their king and their God. [22]Wherever they look, there will be trouble and anguish and dark despair. They will be thrown out into the darkness."

**BLAME ● ● • • •**

8:21 **After rejecting God's plan for their lives, the people of Judah blamed God for their trials. People continually blame God for their self-induced problems. How do you respond to the unpleasant results of your sin? Where do you fix the blame? Instead of blaming God, look for ways to grow through your failures.**

CHAPTER **9** **THE COMING MESSIAH.** Nevertheless, that time of darkness and despair will not go on forever. The land of Zebulun and Naphtali will soon be humbled, but there will be a time in the future when Galilee of the Gentiles, which lies along the road that runs between the Jordan and the sea, will be filled with glory. [2]The people who walk in darkness will see a great light—a light that will shine on all who live in the land where death casts its shadow. [3]Israel will again be great, and its people will rejoice as people rejoice at harvesttime. They will shout with joy like warriors dividing the plunder. [4]For God will break the chains that bind his people and the whip that scourges them, just as he did when he destroyed the army of Midian with Gideon's little band. [5]In that day of peace, battle gear will no longer be issued. Never again will uniforms be bloodstained by war. All such equipment will be burned.

[6]For a child is born to us, a son is given to us. And the government will rest on his shoulders. These will be his royal titles: Wonderful Counselor,* Mighty God, Everlasting Father, Prince of Peace. [7]His ever expanding, peaceful government will never end. He will rule forever with fairness and justice from the throne of his ancestor David. The passionate commitment of the LORD Almighty will guarantee this!

[8]The Lord has spoken out against that braggart Israel, [9]and the people of Israel* and Samaria will soon discover it. In their pride and arrogance they say, [10]"Our land lies in ruins now, but we will rebuild it better than before. We will replace the broken bricks with cut stone, the fallen sycamore trees with cedars." [11]The LORD will reply to their bragging by bringing Rezin's enemies, the Assyrians, against them—[12]along with Arameans from the east and Philistines from the west. With bared fangs, they will devour Israel. But even then the LORD's anger will not be satisfied. His fist is still poised to strike. [13]For after all this punishment, the people will still not repent and turn to the LORD Almighty.

[14]Therefore, in a single day, the LORD will destroy both the head and the tail, the palm branch and the reed. [15]The leaders of Israel are the head, and the lying prophets are the tail. [16]For the leaders of the people have led them down the path of destruction. [17]That is why the Lord has no joy in the young men and no mercy on even the widows and orphans. For they are all hypocrites, speaking wickedness with lies. But even then the LORD's anger will not be satisfied. His fist is still poised to strike.

[18]This wickedness is like a brushfire. It burns not only briers and thorns but the forests, too. Its burning sends up vast clouds of smoke. [19]The land is blackened by the fury of the LORD Almighty. The people are fuel for the fire, and no one spares anyone else. [20]They fight against their own neighbors to steal food, but they will still be hungry. In the end they

8:17 Hebrew *the house of Jacob.* 8:18 *Isaiah* means "The LORD will save"; *Shear-jashub* means "A remnant will return"; and *Maher-shalal-hash-baz* means "Swift to plunder and quick to spoil." 9:6 Or *Wonderful, Counselor.* 9:9 Hebrew *of Ephraim,* referring to the northern kingdom of Israel.

will even eat their own children.* [21]Manasseh will feed on Ephraim, Ephraim will feed on Manasseh, and both will devour Judah. But even then the LORD's anger will not be satisfied. His fist is still poised to strike.

## CHAPTER 10 GOD WILL PROTECT HIS PEOPLE.

Destruction is certain for the unjust judges, for those who issue unfair laws. [2]They deprive the poor, the widows, and the orphans of justice. Yes, they rob widows and fatherless children! [3]What will you do when I send desolation upon you from a distant land? To whom will you turn for help? Where will your treasures be safe? [4]I will not help you. You will stumble along as prisoners or lie among the dead. But even then the LORD's anger will not be satisfied. His fist is still poised to strike.

[5]"Destruction is certain for Assyria, the whip of my anger. Its military power is a club in my hand. [6]Assyria will enslave my people, who are a godless nation. It will plunder them, trampling them like dirt beneath its feet. [7]But the king of Assyria will not know that it is I who sent him. He will merely think he is attacking my people as part of his plan to conquer the world. [8]He will say, 'Each of my princes will soon be a king, ruling a conquered land. [9]We will destroy Calno just as we did Carchemish. Hamath will fall before us as Arpad did. And we will destroy Samaria just as we did Damascus. [10]Yes, we have finished off many a kingdom whose gods were far greater than those in Jerusalem and Samaria. [11]So when we have defeated Samaria and her gods, we will destroy Jerusalem with hers.' "

[12]After the Lord has used the king of Assyria to accomplish his purposes in Jerusalem, he will turn against the king of Assyria and punish him—for he is proud and arrogant. [13]He boasts, "By my own power and wisdom I have won these wars. By my own strength I have captured many lands, destroyed their kings, and carried off their treasures. [14]By my greatness I have robbed their nests of riches and gathered up kingdoms as a farmer gathers eggs. No one can even flap a wing against me or utter a peep of protest."

[15]Can the ax boast greater power than the person who uses it? Is the saw greater than the person who saws? Can a whip strike unless a hand is moving it? Can a cane walk by itself?

[16]Listen now, king of Assyria! Because of all your evil boasting, the Lord, the LORD Almighty, will send a plague among your proud troops, and a flaming fire will ignite your glory. [17]The LORD, the Light of Israel and the Holy One, will be a flaming fire that will destroy them. In a single night he will burn those thorns and briers, the Assyrians. [18]Assyria's vast army is like a glorious forest, yet it will be destroyed. The LORD will completely destroy Assyria's warriors, and they will waste away like sick people in a plague.

### ARROGANCE ● ● • • •

9:8-10 **Israel was called proud and arrogant for saying, in essence, "We've faced a temporary setback, but by our own strength we will rebuild our city." Though God made Israel a nation and gave them the land they occupied, the people put their trust in themselves rather than in him. Too often we take pride in our accomplishments, forgetting that God has given us every ability we have. We even become proud of our unique status as Christians. God is not pleased with *any* pride or trust in ourselves because it cuts off our contact with him.**

[19]Only a few from all that mighty army will survive—so few that a child could count them!

[20]Then at last those left in Israel and Judah* will trust the LORD, the Holy One of Israel. They will no longer depend on the Assyrians, who would destroy them. [21]A remnant of them will return* to the Mighty God. [22]But though the people of Israel are as numerous as the sand on the seashore, only a few of them will return at that time. The LORD has rightly decided to destroy his people. [23]Yes, the Lord, the LORD Almighty, has already decided to consume them.

[24]So this is what the Lord, the LORD Almighty, says: "My people in Jerusalem,* do not be afraid of the Assyrians when they oppress you just as the Egyptians did long ago. [25]It will not last very long. In a little while my anger against you will end, and then my anger will rise up to destroy them."

[26]The LORD Almighty will beat them with his whip, as he did when Gideon triumphed over the Midianites at the rock of Oreb, or when the LORD's staff was raised to drown the Egyptian army in the sea. [27]In that day the LORD will end the bondage of his people. He will break the yoke of slavery and lift it from their shoulders.*

[28]Look, the mighty armies of Assyria are coming! They are now at Aiath, now at Migron. They are storing some of their equipment at Micmash. [29]They are crossing the pass and are staying overnight at Geba. Fear strikes the city of Ramah. All the people of Gibeah—the city of Saul—are running for their lives. [30]Well may you scream in terror, you people of Gallim! Shout out a warning to Laishah, for the mighty army comes. Poor Anathoth, what a fate is yours! [31]There go the people of Madmenah, all fleeing. And the citizens of Gebim are preparing to run.

### THE REMNANT ● ● • • •

10:20-21 **Those who remained faithful to God despite the horrors of the invasion were called the remnant. The key to being a part of the remnant was *faith.* Being a descendant of Abraham, living in the Promised Land, having trusted God at one time—none of these characteristics were good enough. Are you relying on your Christian heritage, the rituals of worship, or past experiences to put you in a right relationship with God? The key to being set apart by God is faith in him.**

**9:20** Or *eat their own arms.* **10:20** Hebrew *and the house of Jacob.* **10:21** Hebrew *Shear-jashub;* see 7:3; 8:18. **10:24** Hebrew *Zion.* **10:27** As in Greek version; Hebrew reads *The yoke will be broken, for you have grown so fat.*

32But the enemy stops at Nob for the rest of that day. He shakes his fist at Mount Zion in Jerusalem.

33But look! The Lord, the LORD Almighty, will chop down the mighty tree! He will destroy all that vast army of Assyria—officers and high officials alike. 34The Mighty One will cut down the enemy as an ax cuts down the forest trees in Lebanon.

## CHAPTER 11 **GOD PROMISES A PERFECT LEADER.**

Out of the stump of David's family* will grow a shoot—yes, a new Branch bearing fruit from the old root. 2And the Spirit of the LORD will rest on him—the Spirit of wisdom and understanding, the Spirit of counsel and might, the Spirit of knowledge and the fear of the LORD. 3He will delight in obeying the LORD. He will never judge by appearance, false evidence, or hearsay. 4He will defend the poor and the exploited. He will rule against the wicked and destroy them with the breath of his mouth. 5He will be clothed with fairness and truth.

### FAIR TREATMENT ● ● ● • •

**11:3-5 We all long for fair treatment from others, but do we give it? We hate those who base their judgments on appearance, false evidence, or hearsay. But we can be quick to judge others using those same criteria. Only Christ can be the perfectly fair judge. And only as Christ governs our heart can we learn to be as fair in our treatment of others as we expect them to be with us.**

6In that day the wolf and the lamb will live together; the leopard and the goat will be at peace. Calves and yearlings will be safe among lions, and a little child will lead them all. 7The cattle will graze among bears. Cubs and calves will lie down together. And lions will eat grass as the livestock do. 8Babies will crawl safely among poisonous snakes. Yes, a little child will put its hand in a nest of deadly snakes and pull it out unharmed. 9Nothing will hurt or destroy in all my holy mountain. And as the waters fill the sea, so the earth will be filled with people who know the LORD.

10In that day the heir to David's throne* will be a banner of salvation to all the world. The nations will rally to him, for the land where he lives will be a glorious place. 11In that day the Lord will bring back a remnant of his people for the second time, returning them to the land of Israel from Assyria, Lower Egypt, Upper Egypt, Ethiopia,* Elam, Babylonia,* Hamath, and all the distant coastlands.

12He will raise a flag among the nations for Israel to rally around. He will gather the scattered people of Judah from the ends of the earth. 13Then at last the jealousy between Israel* and Judah will end. They will not fight against each other anymore. 14They will join forces to swoop down on Philistia to the west. Together they will attack and plunder the nations to the east. They will occupy all the lands of Edom, Moab, and Ammon.

15The LORD will make a dry path through the Red Sea.* He will wave his hand over the Euphrates River,* sending a mighty wind to divide it into seven streams that can easily be crossed. 16He will make a highway from Assyria for the remnant there, just as he did for Israel long ago when they returned from Egypt.

## CHAPTER 12 **SINGING GOD'S PRAISE.**

In that day you will sing:

"Praise the LORD!
He was angry with me,
but now he comforts me.
2 See, God has come to save me.
I will trust in him and not be afraid.
The LORD GOD is my strength and my song;
he has become my salvation."

3With joy you will drink deeply from the fountain of salvation! 4In that wonderful day you will sing:

"Thank the LORD!
Praise his name!
Tell the world what he has done.
Oh, how mighty he is!
5 Sing to the LORD,
for he has done wonderful things.
Make known his praise around the world.
6 Let all the people of Jerusalem* shout his praise
with joy!
For great is the Holy One of Israel who lives
among you."

## CHAPTER 13 **BABYLON WILL BE DESTROYED.**

Isaiah son of Amoz received this message concerning the destruction of Babylon:

2"See the flags waving as the enemy attacks. Cheer them on, O Israel! Wave to them as they march against Babylon to destroy the palaces of the high and mighty. 3I, the LORD, have assigned this task to these armies, and they will rejoice when I am exalted. I have called them to satisfy my anger."

4Hear the noise on the mountains! Listen, as the armies march! It is the noise and the shout of many nations. The LORD Almighty has brought them here to form an army. 5They came from countries far away. They are the LORD's weapons; they carry his anger with them and will destroy the whole land. 6Scream in terror, for the LORD's time has arrived—the time for the Almighty to destroy. 7Every arm is paralyzed with fear. Even the strongest hearts melt 8and are afraid. Fear grips them with terrible pangs, like those of a woman about to give birth. They look helplessly at one another as the flames of the burning city reflect on their faces. 9For see, the day of the LORD is coming—the terrible day of his fury and fierce anger. The land will be destroyed and all the sinners with it. 10The heavens will be black above them. No light will shine from stars or sun or moon.

**11:1** Hebrew *the line of Jesse.* Jesse was King David's father. **11:10** Hebrew *the root of Jesse.* **11:11a** Hebrew *Pathros, Cush.* **11:11b** Hebrew *Shinar.* **11:13** Hebrew *Ephraim,* referring to the northern kingdom of Israel. **11:15a** Hebrew *sea of Egypt.* **11:15b** Hebrew *the river.* **12:6** Hebrew *Zion.*

[11]"I, the LORD, will punish the world for its evil and the wicked for their sin. I will crush the arrogance of the proud and the haughtiness of the mighty. [12]Few will be left alive when I have finished my work. People will be as scarce as gold—more rare than the gold of Ophir. [13]For I will shake the heavens, and the earth will move from its place. I, the LORD Almighty, will show my fury and fierce anger."

[14]Everyone will run until exhausted, rushing back to their own lands like hunted deer, wandering like sheep without a shepherd. [15]Anyone who is captured will be run through with a sword. [16]Their little children will be dashed to death right before their eyes. Their homes will be sacked and their wives raped by the attacking hordes. [17]For I will stir up the Medes against Babylon, and no amount of silver or gold will buy them off. [18]The attacking armies will shoot down the young people with arrows. They will have no mercy on helpless babies and will show no compassion for the children.

[19]Babylon, the most glorious of kingdoms, the flower of Chaldean culture, will be devastated like Sodom and Gomorrah when God destroyed them. [20]Babylon will never rise again. Generation after generation will come and go, but the land will never again be lived in. Nomads will refuse to camp there, and shepherds will not allow their sheep to stay overnight. [21]Wild animals of the desert will move into the ruined city. The houses will be haunted by howling creatures. Ostriches will live among the ruins, and wild goats will come there to dance. [22]Hyenas will howl in its fortresses, and jackals will make their dens in its palaces. Babylon's days are numbered; its time of destruction will soon arrive.

## CHAPTER 14

**GOD PROMISES TO LOVE HIS PEOPLE.** But the LORD will have mercy on the descendants of Jacob. Israel will be his special people once again. He will bring them back to settle once again in their own land. And people from many different nations will come and join them there and become a part of the people of Israel.* [2]The nations of the world will help the LORD's people to return, and those who come to live in their land will serve them. Those who captured Israel will be captured, and Israel will rule over its enemies.

[3]In that wonderful day when the LORD gives his people rest from sorrow and fear, from slavery and chains, [4]you will taunt the king of Babylon. You will say, "The mighty man has been destroyed. Yes, your insolence is ended. [5]For the LORD has crushed your wicked power and broken your evil rule. [6]You persecuted the people with unceasing blows of rage and held the nations in your angry grip. Your tyranny was unrestrained. [7]But at last the land is at rest and is quiet. Finally it can sing again! [8]Even the trees of the forest—the cypress trees and the cedars of Lebanon—sing out this joyous song: 'Your power is broken! No one will come to cut us down now!'

[9]"In the place of the dead* there is excitement over your arrival. World leaders and mighty kings long dead are there to see you. [10]With one voice they all cry out, 'Now you are as weak as we are! [11]Your might and power are gone; they were buried with you. All the pleasant music in your palace has ceased. Now maggots are your sheet and worms your blanket.'

[12]"How you are fallen from heaven, O shining star, son of the morning! You have been thrown down to the earth, you who destroyed the nations of the world. [13]For you said to yourself, 'I will ascend to heaven and set my throne above God's stars. I will preside on the mountain of the gods far away in the north. [14]I will climb to the highest heavens and be like the Most High.' [15]But instead, you will be brought down to the place of the dead, down to its lowest depths. [16]Everyone there will stare at you and ask, 'Can this be the one who shook the earth and the kingdoms of the world? [17]Is this the one who destroyed the world and made it into a wilderness? Is this the king who demolished the world's greatest cities and had no mercy on his prisoners?'

[18]"The kings of the nations lie in stately glory in their tombs, [19]but you will be thrown out of your grave like a worthless branch. Like a corpse trampled underfoot, you will be dumped into a mass grave with those killed in battle. You will descend to the pit. [20]You will not be given a proper burial, for you have destroyed your nation and slaughtered your people. Your son will not succeed you as king. [21]Kill the children of this sinner! Do not let them rise and conquer the land or rebuild the cities of the world."

### UTTER RUIN ● ● • • •

13:20 **Even before Babylon became a world power, Isaiah prophesied that its destruction would be so complete that it would never rise again. The city was conquered in 539 B.C. by Cyrus. The details of Isaiah's prophecy may not be fulfilled until the end times.**

### POWER FAILURE ● ● • • •

14:5-6 **Power is temporary. God permitted Babylon to have power for a purpose—to chastise his wayward people. When the purpose ended, so did the power. Beware of placing confidence in human power—one day it will fade, no matter how secure it appears.**

[22]This is what the LORD Almighty says: "I, myself, have risen against him! I will destroy his children and his children's children, so they will never sit on his throne. [23]I will make Babylon into a desolate land, a place of porcupines, filled with swamps and marshes. I will sweep the land with the broom of destruction. I, the LORD Almighty, have spoken!"

[24]The LORD Almighty has sworn this oath: "It will all happen as I have planned. It will come about according to my purposes. [25]I will break the Assyrians when they are in Israel; I will trample them on my mountains. My people will no longer be their slaves. [26]I have a plan for the whole earth, for my mighty power reaches throughout the world. [27]The

14:1 Hebrew *the house of Jacob.* 14:9 Hebrew *Sheol;* also in 14:15.

LORD Almighty has spoken—who can change his plans? When his hand moves, who can stop him?"

[28]This message came to me the year King Ahaz died: [29]Do not rejoice, you Philistines, that the king who attacked you is dead. For even though that whip is broken, his son will be worse than his father ever was. From that snake a poisonous snake will be born, a fiery serpent to destroy you! [30]I will feed the poor in my pasture; the needy will lie down in peace. But as for you, I will wipe you out with famine. I will destroy the few who remain.

[31]Weep, you Philistine cities, for you are doomed! Melt in fear, for everyone will be destroyed. A powerful army is coming out of the north. Each soldier rushes forward ready to fight. [32]What should we tell the enemy messengers? Tell them that the LORD has built Jerusalem,* and that the poor of his people will find refuge in its walls.

CHAPTER **15** **WHAT GOD WILL DO TO MOAB.** This message came to me concerning Moab:

In one night your cities of Ar and Kir will be destroyed. [2]Your people in Dibon will mourn at their temples and shrines, weeping for the fate of Nebo and Medeba. They will shave their heads in sorrow and cut off their beards. [3]They will wear sackcloth as they wander the streets. From every home will come the sound of weeping. [4]The cries from the cities of Heshbon and Elealeh will be heard far away, even in Jahaz! The bravest warriors of Moab will cry out in utter terror.

**THE ENEMY ● ● • • •**

**15:1 Moab was east of the Dead Sea. The Moabites were descendants of Lot through his incestuous relationship with his older daughter (Genesis 19:31-38). Moab had always been Israel's enemy. They oppressed Israel and invaded their land (Judges 3:12-14), fought against Saul (1 Samuel 14:47), and fought against David (2 Samuel 8:2, 11-12). Moab would be punished for its harsh treatment of Israel.**

[5]My heart weeps for Moab. Its people flee to Zoar and Eglath-shelishiyah. Weeping, they climb the road to Luhith. Their crying can be heard all along the road to Horonaim. [6]Even the waters of Nimrim are dried up! The grassy banks are scorched, and the tender plants are gone. [7]The desperate refugees take only the possessions they can carry and flee across the Ravine of Willows. [8]The whole land of Moab is a land of weeping from one end to the other—from Eglaim to Beer-elim. [9]The stream near Dibon* runs red with blood, but I am still not finished with Dibon! Lions will hunt down the survivors, both those who try to run and those who remain behind.

CHAPTER **16** Moab's refugees at Sela send lambs to Jerusalem* as a token of alliance with the king of Judah. [2]The women of Moab are left like homeless birds at the shallow crossings of the Arnon River. [3]"Help us," they cry. "Defend us against our enemies. Protect us from their relentless attack. Do not betray us. [4]Let our outcasts stay among you. Hide them from our enemies until the terror is past."

When oppression and destruction have ceased and enemy raiders have disappeared, [5]then David's throne will be established by love. From that throne a faithful king will reign, one who always does what is just and right.

[6]Is this Moab, the proud land we have heard so much about? Its pride and insolence are all gone now! [7]The entire land of Moab weeps. Yes, you people of Moab, mourn for the delicacies of Kir-hareseth. [8]Weep for the abandoned farms of Heshbon and the vineyards at Sibmah. The wine from those vineyards used to make the rulers of the nations drunk. Moab was once like a spreading grapevine. Her tendrils spread out as far as Jazer and trailed out into the desert. Her shoots once reached as far as the Dead Sea.* [9]But now the enemy has completely destroyed that vine. So I wail and lament for Jazer and the vineyards of Sibmah. My tears will flow for Heshbon and Elealeh, for their summer fruits and harvests have all been destroyed.

[10]Gone now is the gladness; gone is the joy of harvest. The happy singing in the vineyards will be heard no more. The treading out of grapes in the winepresses has ceased forever. I have ended all their harvest joys. [11]I will weep for Moab. My sorrow for Kir-hareseth* will be very great. [12]On the hilltops the people of Moab will pray in anguish to their idols, but it will do them no good. They will cry to the gods in their temples, but no one will come to save them.

[13]The LORD has already said this about Moab in the past. [14]But now the LORD says, "Within three years, without fail, the glory of Moab will be ended, and few of its people will be left alive."

CHAPTER **17** **WHAT GOD WILL DO TO ARAM.** This message came to me concerning Damascus:

"Look, Damascus will disappear! It will become a heap of ruins. [2]The cities of Aroer will be deserted. Sheep will graze in the streets and lie down unafraid. There will be no one to chase them away. [3]The fortified cities of Israel* will also be destroyed, and the power of Damascus will end. The few left in Aram will share the fate of Israel's departed glory," says the LORD Almighty.

[4]"In that day the glory of Israel* will be very dim, for poverty will stalk the land. [5]Israel will be abandoned like the grainfields in the valley of Rephaim after the harvest. [6]Only a few of its people will be left, like the stray olives left on the tree after the harvest. Only two or three remain in the highest branches, four or five out on the tips of the limbs. Yes, Israel will be stripped bare of people," says the LORD, the God of Israel.

14:32 Hebrew *Zion.* 15:9 As in Dead Sea Scrolls, some Greek manuscripts, and Latin Vulgate; Masoretic Text reads *Dimon;* also in 15:9b. 16:1 Hebrew *to the daughter of Zion.* 16:8 Hebrew *the sea.* 16:11 Hebrew *Kir-heres,* a variant name for Kir-hareseth. 17:3 Hebrew *of Ephraim,* referring to the northern kingdom of Israel. 17:4 Hebrew *of Jacob.*

**ISAIAH**
served as a prophet
to Judah from 740 B.C.
to 681 B.C.

| | |
|---|---|
| *Climate of the times* | Society was in a great upheavel. Under King Ahaz and King Manasseh the people reverted to idolatry, and there was even child sacrifice. |
| *Main message* | Although judgment from other nations was inevitable, the people could still have a special relationship with God. |
| *Importance of message* | Sometimes we must suffer judgment and discipline before we are restored to God. |
| *Contemporary prophets* | Hosea (753–715)<br>Micah (742–687) |

7Then at last the people will think of their Creator
and have respect for the Holy One of Israel. 8They
will no longer ask their idols for help or worship
what their own hands have made. They will never
again bow down to their Asherah poles or burn
incense on the altars they built.
9Their largest cities will be as deserted as overgrown thickets. They will become like the cities the
Amorites abandoned when the Israelites came here
so long ago. 10Why? Because you have turned from
the God who can save you—the Rock who can hide
you. You may plant the finest imported grapevines,
11and they may grow so well that they blossom on
the very morning you plant them, but you will never
pick any grapes from them. Your only harvest will be
a load of grief and incurable pain.
12Look! The armies rush forward like waves thundering toward the shore. 13But though they roar like
breakers on a beach, God will silence them. They
will flee like chaff scattered by the wind or like dust
whirling before a storm. 14In the evening Israel waits
in terror, but by dawn its enemies are dead. This is
the just reward of those who plunder and destroy the
people of God.

CHAPTER **18** **WHAT GOD WILL DO TO ETHIOPIA.** Destruction is certain for the land of Ethiopia,* which
lies at the headwaters of the Nile. Its winged sail-
boats glide along the river, 2and ambassadors are
sent in fast boats down the Nile. Go home, swift
messengers! Take a message to your land divided by
rivers, to your tall, smooth-skinned people, who are
feared far and wide for their conquests and destruction.
3When I raise my battle flag on the mountain, let
all the world take notice. When I blow the trumpet,
listen! 4For the LORD has told me this: "I will watch
quietly from my dwelling place—as quietly as the
heat rises on a summer day, or as the dew forms on
an autumn morning during the harvest."
5Even before you begin your attack, while your
plans are ripening like grapes, the LORD will cut you
off as though with pruning shears. He will snip your
spreading branches. 6Your mighty army will be left
dead in the fields for the mountain birds and wild
animals to eat. The vultures will tear at corpses all
summer. The wild animals will gnaw at bones all
winter.
7But the time will come when the LORD Almighty
will receive gifts from this land divided by rivers,
from this tall, smooth-skinned people, who are
feared far and wide for their conquests and destruction. They will bring the gifts to the LORD Almighty
in Jerusalem,* the place where his name dwells.

CHAPTER **19** **WHAT GOD WILL DO TO EGYPT.** This
message came to me concerning Egypt:
Look! The LORD is advancing against Egypt, riding
on a swift cloud. The idols of Egypt tremble. The
hearts of the Egyptians melt with fear.
2"I will make the Egyptians fight against each
other—brother against brother, neighbor against
neighbor, city against city, province against province.
3The Egyptians will lose heart, and I will confuse
their plans. They will plead with their idols for wisdom. They will call on spirits, mediums, and psychics to show them which way to turn. 4I will hand
Egypt over to a hard, cruel master, to a fierce king,"
says the Lord, the LORD Almighty.
5The waters of the Nile will fail to rise and flood
the fields. The riverbed will be parched and dry.
6The canals of the Nile will dry up, and the streams

18:1 Hebrew *Cush.* 18:7 Hebrew *on Mount Zion.*

**DEPENDENCE ● ● • • •**

17:7-11 **God's message to Damascus is one of complete destruction. The Assyrians had turned from the God who could save them and depended instead on their idols and their own strength. No matter how successful they were, God's judgment was sure. Often we depend on the trappings of success (e.g., expensive cars, clothes, homes) to give us fulfillment. But God says we will reap grief and pain if we depend on things of this world to give us security. If we don't want the same treatment Damascus received, we must turn from these false allurements and trust in God.**

**UNITY ● ● ● • •**

**19:23-25 In Jesus Christ, former enemies may unite in love. In Christ, people and nations who are poles apart politically will bow at his feet as brothers and sisters; Christ breaks down every barrier that threatens relationships.**

of Egypt will become foul with rotting reeds and rushes. [7]All the greenery along the riverbank will wither and blow away. All the crops will dry up, and everything will die. [8]The fishermen will weep for lack of work. Those who fish with hooks and those who use nets will all be unemployed. [9]The weavers will have no flax or cotton, for the crops will fail. [10]The weavers and all the workers will be sick at heart.

[11]What fools are the counselors of Zoan! Their best counsel to the king of Egypt is stupid and wrong. Will they still boast of their wisdom? Will they dare tell Pharaoh about their long line of wise ancestors? [12]What has happened to your wise counselors, Pharaoh? If they are so wise, let them tell you what the LORD Almighty is going to do to Egypt. [13]The wise men from Zoan are fools, and those from Memphis* are deluded. The leaders of Egypt have ruined the land with their foolish counsel. [14]The LORD has sent a spirit of foolishness on them, so all their suggestions are wrong. They cause the land of Egypt to stagger like a sick drunkard. [15]Nobody in Egypt, whether rich or poor, important or unknown, can offer any help.

[16]In that day the Egyptians will be as weak as women. They will cower in fear beneath the upraised fist of the LORD Almighty. [17]Just to speak the name of Israel will strike deep terror in their hearts, for the LORD Almighty has laid out his plans against them.

[18]In that day five of Egypt's cities will follow the LORD Almighty. They will even begin to speak the Hebrew language.* One of these will be Heliopolis, the City of the Sun. [19]In that day there will be an altar to the LORD in the heart of Egypt, and there will be a monument to the LORD at its border. [20]It will be a sign and a witness to the LORD Almighty in the land of Egypt. When the people cry to the LORD for help against those who oppress them, he will send them a savior who will rescue them.

[21]In that day the LORD will make himself known to the Egyptians. Yes, they will know the LORD and will give their sacrifices and offerings to him. They will make promises to the LORD and keep them. [22]The LORD will strike Egypt in a way that will bring healing. For the Egyptians will turn to the LORD, and he will listen to their pleas and heal them.

[23]In that day Egypt and Assyria will be connected by a highway. The Egyptians and Assyrians will move freely between their lands, and they will worship the same God. [24]And Israel will be their ally. The three will be together, and Israel will be a blessing to them. [25]For the LORD Almighty will say, "Blessed be Egypt, my people. Blessed be Assyria, the land I have made. Blessed be Israel, my special possession!"

## CHAPTER 20 **ISAIAH GOES BAREFOOT.**

In the year when King Sargon of Assyria captured the Philistine city of Ashdod, [2]the LORD told Isaiah son of Amoz, "Take off all your clothes, including your sandals." Isaiah did as he was told and walked around naked and barefoot.

[3]Then the LORD said, "My servant Isaiah has been walking around naked and barefoot for the last three years. This is a sign—a symbol of the terrible troubles I will bring upon Egypt and Ethiopia.* [4]For the king of Assyria will take away the Egyptians and Ethiopians* as prisoners. He will make them walk naked and barefoot, both young and old, their buttocks uncovered, to the shame of Egypt. [5]How dismayed will be the Philistines, who counted on the power of Ethiopia and boasted of their allies in Egypt! [6]They will say, 'If this can happen to Egypt, what chance do we have? For we counted on Egypt to protect us from the king of Assyria.'"

## CHAPTER 21 **WHAT GOD WILL DO TO BABYLON.**

This message came to me concerning the land of Babylonia*:

Disaster is roaring down on you from the desert, like a whirlwind sweeping in from the Negev. [2]I see an awesome vision: I see you plundered and destroyed. Go ahead, you Elamites and Medes, take part in the siege. Babylon will fall, and the groaning of all the nations she enslaved will end. [3]My stomach aches and burns with pain. Sharp pangs of horror are upon me, like the pangs of a woman giving birth. I grow faint when I hear what God is planning; I am blinded with dismay. [4]My mind reels; my heart races. The sleep I once enjoyed at night is now a faint memory. I lie awake, trembling.

[5]Look! They are preparing a great feast. They are spreading rugs for people to sit on. Everyone is eating and drinking. Quick! Grab your shields and prepare for battle! You are being attacked!

[6]Meanwhile, the Lord said to me, "Put a watchman on the city wall to shout out what he sees. [7]Tell him to sound the alert when he sees chariots drawn by horses and warriors mounted on donkeys and camels."

[8]Then the watchman* called out, "Day after day I have stood on the watchtower, my lord. Night after night I have remained at my post. [9]Now at last—look! Here come the chariots and warriors!" Then the watchman said, "Babylon is fallen! All the idols of Babylon lie broken on the ground!"

[10]O my people, threshed and winnowed, I have

**THE NEWS ● ● ● • •**

**21:11-12 Everyone wants to hear the good news that all troubles are over and prosperity lies ahead. The watchman tells how to get that good news—turn to God, and seek him with all your heart. Without God, the news of world events and the world's future is anything but good. Without God, our personal future is bad news.**

19:13 Hebrew *Noph.* 19:18 Hebrew *the language of Canaan.* 20:3 Hebrew *Cush;* also in 20:5. 20:4 Hebrew *Cushites.* 21:1 Hebrew *the desert of the sea.* 21:8 As in Dead Sea Scrolls and Syriac version; Masoretic Text reads *a lion.*

told you everything the LORD Almighty, the God of
Israel, has said.

11This message came to me concerning Edom*:
Someone from Edom* keeps calling to me,
"Watchman, how much longer until morning?
When will the night be over?"
12The watchman replies, "Morning is coming, but
night will soon follow. If you wish to ask again, then
come back and ask."

13This message came to me concerning Arabia:
O caravans from Dedan, hide in the deserts of
Arabia. 14O people of Tema, bring food and water to
these weary refugees. 15They have fled from drawn
swords and sharp arrows and the terrors of war.
16"But within a year,"* says the Lord, "all the glory of
Kedar will come to an end. 17Only a few of its courageous archers will survive. I, the LORD, the God of
Israel, have spoken!"

CHAPTER **22** **WHAT GOD WILL DO TO JERUSALEM.** This
message came to me concerning Jerusalem*:
What is happening? Why is everyone running to
the rooftops? 2The whole city is in a terrible uproar.
What do I see in this reveling city? Bodies are lying
everywhere, killed by famine and disease.* 3All your
leaders flee. They surrender without resistance. The
people try to slip away, but they are captured, too.
4Leave me alone to weep; do not try to comfort me.
Let me cry for my people as I watch them being
destroyed.
5Oh, what a day of crushing trouble! What a day
of confusion and terror the Lord, the LORD Almighty,
has brought upon the Valley of Vision! The walls of
Jerusalem have been broken, and cries of death echo
from the mountainsides. 6Elamites are the archers;
Arameans drive the chariots. The men of Kir hold up
the shields. 7They fill your beautiful valleys and
crowd against your gates. 8Judah's defenses have
been stripped away. You run to the armory for your
weapons. 9You inspect the walls of Jerusalem* to see
what needs to be repaired. You store up water in the
lower pool. 10You check the houses and tear some
down to get stone to fix the walls. 11Between the city
walls, you build a reservoir for water from the old
pool. But all your feverish plans are to no avail
because you never ask God for help. He is the one
who planned this long ago.
12The Lord, the LORD Almighty, called you to weep
and mourn. He told you to shave your heads in
sorrow for your sins and to wear clothes of sackcloth
to show your remorse. 13But instead, you dance and
play; you slaughter sacrificial animals, feast on meat,
and drink wine. "Let's eat, drink, and be merry," you
say. "What's the difference, for tomorrow we die."
14The LORD Almighty has revealed to me that this sin
will never be forgiven you until the day you die. That
is the judgment of the Lord, the LORD Almighty.

**CONSEQUENCES ● ● • • •**

22:4 **Isaiah had warned his people, but they did not repent—so they experienced God's judgment. Because Isaiah cared for the people, he was hurt by their punishment and he mourned deeply for them. Sometimes people we care for ignore our attempts to help them, and then they suffer the consequences of actions we tried to stop. We grieve at those times because of our concern. God expects us to be involved with others—this may cause us to suffer with them.**

15Furthermore, the Lord, the LORD Almighty,
told me to confront Shebna, the palace administrator, and to give him this message: 16"Who do you
think you are, building a beautiful tomb for yourself in the rock? 17For the LORD is about to seize you
and hurl you away. He is going to send you into
captivity, you strong man! 18He will crumple you
up into a ball and toss you away into a distant,
barren land. There you will die, and there your
glorious chariots will remain, broken and useless.
You are a disgrace to your master.
19"Yes, I will drive you out of office," says the
LORD. "I will pull you down from your high position. 20And then I will call my servant Eliakim son of
Hilkiah to replace you. 21He will have your royal
robes, your title, and your authority. And he will be
a father to the people of Jerusalem and Judah. 22I will
give him the key to the house of David—the highest
position in the royal court. He will open doors, and
no one will be able to shut them; he will close doors,
and no one will be able to open them. 23He will
bring honor to his family name, for I will drive him
firmly in place like a tent stake. 24He will be loaded
down with responsibility, and he will bring honor to
even the lowliest members of his family."
25The LORD Almighty says: "When that time
comes, I will pull out the stake that seemed so firm.
It will come out and fall to the ground. Everything it
supports will fall with it. I, the LORD, have spoken!"

**HOPE ● ● • • •**

22:13-14 **The people said, "Let's eat, drink, and be merry" because they had given up hope. Today, we see people giving up hope as well. There are two common responses to hopelessness: despair and self-indulgence. But this life is not all there is, so we should not act as if we have no hope. The proper response is to turn to God and trust in his promise of a perfect and just future in the new world he will create.**

CHAPTER **23** **WHAT GOD WILL DO TO TYRE.** This message came to me concerning Tyre:
Weep, O ships of Tarshish, returning home from
distant lands! Weep for your harbor at Tyre because
it is gone! The rumors you heard in Cyprus* are all
true. 2Mourn in silence, you people of the coast and
you merchants of Sidon. Your traders crossed the sea,
3sailing over deep waters. They brought you grain

21:11a Hebrew *Dumah,* which means "silence" or "stillness." It is a wordplay on the word *Edom.* 21:11b Hebrew *Seir,* another name for Edom. 21:16 Hebrew *Within a year, like the years of a hired hand.* Some ancient manuscripts read *Within three years,* as in 16:14. 22:1 Hebrew *concerning the Valley of Vision.* 22:2 Hebrew *killed, but not by sword and not in battle.* 22:9 Hebrew *the city of David.* 23:1 Hebrew *Kittim;* also in 23:12.

from Egypt* and harvests from along the Nile. You were the merchandise mart of the world.

4But now you are put to shame, city of Sidon, fortress on the sea. For the sea says, "Now I am childless; I have no sons or daughters." 5When Egypt hears the news about Tyre, there will be great sorrow. 6Flee now to Tarshish! Wail, you people who live by the sea! 7How can this silent ruin be all that is left of your once joyous city? What a history was yours! Think of all the colonists you sent to distant lands.

8Who has brought this disaster on Tyre, empire builder and chief trader of the world? 9The LORD Almighty has done it to destroy your pride and show his contempt for all human greatness. 10Come, Tarshish, sweep over your mother Tyre like the flooding Nile, for the city is defenseless. 11The LORD holds out his hand over the seas. He shakes the kingdoms of the earth. He has spoken out against Phoenicia* and depleted its strength. 12He says, "Never again will you rejoice, O daughter of Sidon. Once you were a lovely city, but you will never again be strong. Even if you flee to Cyprus, you will find no rest."

## STOP SIN ● ● • • •

24:4-5 **Not only the people suffered from their sins; even the land suffered with bad crops and crime. Today we see the results of sin in our own land–pollution, crime, poverty, and more. Sin affects every aspect of society so extensively that even those faithful to God suffer. We cannot blame God for these conditions because human sin has brought them about. The more we who are believers renounce sin and share God's Word with others, the more we slow our society's deterioration. We must not give up: sin is rampant, but we can make a difference.**

13Look at the land of Babylonia*—the people of that land are gone! The Assyrians have handed Babylon over to the wild beasts. They have built siege ramps against its walls, torn down its palaces, and turned it into a heap of rubble.

14Wail, O ships of Tarshish, for your home port is destroyed! 15For seventy years, the length of a king's life, Tyre will be forgotten. But then the city will come back to life and sing sweet songs like a prostitute. 16Long absent from her lovers, she will take a harp, walk the streets, and sing her songs, so that she will again be remembered. 17Yes, after seventy years the LORD will revive Tyre. But she will be no different than she was before. She will return again to all her evil ways around the world. 18But in the end her businesses will give their profits to the LORD. Her wealth will not be hoarded but will be used to provide good food and fine clothing for the LORD's priests.

## CHAPTER 24 **TROUBLE IS COMING!**

Look! The LORD is about to destroy the earth and make it a vast wasteland. See how he is scattering the people over the face of the earth. 2Priests and laypeople, servants and masters, maids and mistresses, buyers and sellers, lenders and borrowers, bankers and debtors—none will be spared. 3The earth will be completely emptied and looted. The LORD has spoken!

4The earth dries up, the crops wither, the skies refuse to rain. 5The earth suffers for the sins of its people, for they have twisted the instructions of God, violated his laws, and broken his everlasting covenant. 6Therefore, a curse consumes the earth and its people. They are left desolate, destroyed by fire. Few will be left alive.

7All the joys of life will be gone. The grape harvest will fail, and there will be no wine. The merrymakers will sigh and mourn. 8The clash of tambourines will be stilled; the happy cries of celebration will be heard no more. The melodious chords of the harp will be silent. 9Gone are the joys of wine and song; strong drink now turns bitter in the mouth.

10The city writhes in chaos; every home is locked to keep out looters. 11Mobs gather in the streets, crying out for wine. Joy has reached its lowest ebb. Gladness has been banished from the land. 12The city is left in ruins, with its gates battered down. 13Throughout the earth the story is the same—like the stray olives left on the tree or the few grapes left on the vine after harvest, only a remnant is left.

14But all who are left will shout and sing for joy. Those in the west will praise the LORD's majesty. 15In eastern lands, give glory to the LORD. In the coastlands of the sea, praise the name of the LORD, the God of Israel. 16Listen to them as they sing to the LORD from the ends of the earth. Hear them singing praises to the Righteous One!

But my heart is heavy with grief. I am discouraged, for evil still prevails, and treachery is everywhere. 17Terror and traps and snares will be your lot, you people of the earth. 18Those who flee in terror will fall into a trap, and those who escape the trap will step into a snare.

Destruction falls on you from the heavens. The world is shaken beneath you. 19The earth has broken down and has utterly collapsed. Everything is lost, abandoned, and confused. 20The earth staggers like a drunkard. It trembles like a tent in a storm. It falls and will not rise again, for its sins are very great.

21In that day the LORD will punish the fallen angels in the heavens and the proud rulers of the nations on earth. 22They will be rounded up and put in prison until they are tried and condemned. 23Then the LORD Almighty will mount his throne on Mount Zion. He will rule gloriously in Jerusalem, in the sight of all the leaders of his people. There will be such glory that the brightness of the sun and moon will seem to fade away.

## CHAPTER 25 **A DAY OF REJOICING.**

O LORD, I will honor and praise your name, for you are my God. You do such wonderful things! You planned them long ago, and now you have accomplished them. 2You turn mighty cities into heaps of ruins. Cities with strong walls are turned to rubble. Beautiful palaces in distant lands disappear and will never be

23:3 Hebrew *from Shihor,* a branch of the Nile River. 23:11 Hebrew *Canaan.* 23:13 Or *Chaldea.*

rebuilt. 3Therefore, strong nations will declare your
glory; ruthless nations will revere you.
4But to the poor, O LORD, you are a refuge from
the storm. To the needy in distress, you are a shelter
from the rain and the heat. For the oppressive acts of
ruthless people are like a storm beating against a
wall, 5or like the relentless heat of the desert. But you
silence the roar of foreign nations. You cool the land
with the shade of a cloud. So the boastful songs of
ruthless people are stilled.
6In Jerusalem,* the LORD Almighty will spread a
wonderful feast for everyone around the world. It
will be a delicious feast of good food, with clear,
well-aged wine and choice beef. 7In that day he will
remove the cloud of gloom, the shadow of death
that hangs over the earth. 8He will swallow up death
forever! The Sovereign LORD will wipe away all tears.
He will remove forever all insults and mockery
against his land and people. The LORD has spoken!
9In that day the people will proclaim, "This is our
God. We trusted in him, and he saved us. This is the
LORD, in whom we trusted. Let us rejoice in the
salvation he brings!" 10For the LORD's good hand will
rest on Jerusalem.
Moab will be crushed like trampled straw and left
to rot. 11God will push down Moab's people as a
swimmer pushes down water with his hands. He will
end their pride and all their evil works. 12The high
walls of Moab will be demolished and ground to dust.

## CHAPTER 26 **THE PEOPLE SING.** In that day, everyone in the land of Judah will sing this song:

Our city is now strong!
We are surrounded by the walls of God's salvation.
2 Open the gates to all who are righteous;
allow the faithful to enter.
3 You will keep in perfect peace all who trust in you,
whose thoughts are fixed on you!
4 Trust in the LORD always,
for the LORD GOD is the eternal Rock.
5 He humbles the proud
and brings the arrogant city to the dust.
Its walls come crashing down!
6 The poor and oppressed trample it underfoot.

7 But for those who are righteous,
the path is not steep and rough.
You are a God of justice,
and you smooth out the road ahead of them.
8 LORD, we love to obey your laws;
our heart's desire is to glorify your name.
9 All night long I search for you;
earnestly I seek for God.
For only when you come to judge the earth
will people turn from wickedness and do what is right.
10 Your kindness to the wicked does not make them do good.

25:6 Hebrew *On this mountain;* also in 25:10.

> YOU WILL KEEP IN *perfect* PEACE *all* who *trust in you,* *whose thoughts* *thoughts* *thoughts* *thoughts* *are* fixed *on you!*
>
> ISAIAH 26:3

They keep doing wrong and take no notice of the LORD's majesty.
11 O LORD, they do not listen when you threaten.
They do not see your upraised fist.
Show them your eagerness to defend your people.
Perhaps then they will be ashamed.
Let your fire consume your enemies.

12 LORD, you will grant us peace,
for all we have accomplished is really from you.
13 O LORD our God, others have ruled us,
but we worship you alone.
14 Those we served before are dead and gone.
Never again will they return!
You attacked them and destroyed them,
and they are long forgotten.
15 We praise you, LORD!
You have made our nation great;
you have extended our borders!

16 LORD, in distress we searched for you.
We were bowed beneath the burden of your discipline.
17 We were like a woman about to give birth,
writhing and crying out in pain.
When we are in your presence, LORD,
18 we, too, writhe in agony,
but nothing comes of our suffering.
We have done nothing to rescue the world;
no one has been born to populate the earth.
19 Yet we have this assurance:
Those who belong to God will live;
their bodies will rise again!

Those who sleep in the earth
will rise up and sing for joy!
For God's light of life will fall like dew
on his people in the place of the dead!

[20]Go home, my people, and lock your doors! Hide until the LORD's anger against your enemies has passed. [21]Look! The LORD is coming from heaven to punish the people of the earth for their sins. The earth will no longer hide those who have been murdered. They will be brought out for all to see.

### SECRET PLOTS ● ● • • •

**26:21 When God comes to judge the earth, the guilty will find no place to hide. Jesus said that secret plots will become public information because his truth, like a light shining in a dark corner, will reveal them (Matthew 10:26). Instead of trying to hide your shameful thoughts and actions from God, confess them to him and receive his forgiveness.**

## CHAPTER 27

**GOD STOPS FEELING ANGRY.** In that day the LORD will take his terrible, swift sword and punish Leviathan, the swiftly moving serpent, the coiling, writhing serpent, the dragon of the sea.

[2]"In that day we will sing of the pleasant vineyard. [3]I, the LORD, will watch over it and tend its fruitful vines. Each day I will water them; day and night I will watch to keep enemies away. [4]My anger against Israel will be gone. If I find briers and thorns bothering her, I will burn them up. [5]These enemies will be spared only if they surrender and beg for peace and protection."

[6]The time is coming when my people will take root. Israel will bud and blossom and fill the whole earth with her fruit! [7]Has the LORD punished Israel in the same way he has punished her enemies? No, for he devastated her enemies, [8]but he has punished Israel only a little. He has exiled her from her land as though blown away in a storm from the east. [9]The LORD did this to purge away Israel's* sin. When he has finished, all the pagan altars will be crushed to dust. There won't be an Asherah pole or incense altar left standing. [10]Israel's fortified cities will be silent and empty, the houses abandoned, the streets covered with grass. Cattle will graze there, chewing on twigs and branches.

[11]The people are like the dead branches of a tree, broken off and used for kindling beneath the cooking pots. Israel is a foolish and stupid nation, for its people have turned away from God. Therefore, the one who made them will show them no pity or mercy. [12]Yet the time will come when the LORD will gather them together one by one like handpicked grain. He will bring them to his great threshing floor—from the Euphrates River* in the east to the brook of Egypt in the west. [13]In that day the great trumpet will sound. Many who were dying in exile in Assyria and Egypt will return to Jerusalem to worship the LORD on his holy mountain.

## CHAPTER 28

**A WONDERFUL TEACHER.** Destruction is certain for the city of Samaria—the pride and joy of the drunkards of Israel*! It sits in a rich valley, but its glorious beauty will suddenly disappear. Destruction is certain for that city—the pride of a people brought low by wine. [2]For the Lord will send the mighty Assyrian army against it. Like a mighty hailstorm and a torrential rain, they will burst upon it and dash it to the ground. [3]The proud city of Samaria—the pride and joy of the drunkards of Israel—will be trampled beneath its enemies' feet. [4]It sits in a fertile valley, but its glorious beauty will suddenly disappear. It will be greedily snatched up, as an early fig is hungrily picked and eaten.

[5]Then at last the LORD Almighty will himself be Israel's crowning glory. He will be the pride and joy of the remnant of his people. [6]He will give a longing for justice to their judges. He will give great courage to their warriors who stand at the gates.

[7]Now, however, Israel is being led by drunks! The priests and prophets reel and stagger from beer and wine. They make stupid mistakes as they carry out their responsibilities. [8]Their tables are covered with vomit; filth is everywhere. [9]They say, "Who does the LORD think we are? Why does he speak to us like this? Are we little children, barely old enough to talk? [10]He tells us everything over and over again, a line at a time, in very simple words!*"

### SIMPLICITY ● ● • • •

**28:13 God used repetition and simple words to get his messages through to the people. Do you find that God has to teach you the same lessons over and over? The simplicity of God's message can be a stumbling block for some (28:9-10), leading them to think it must have little value. We must not be too proud to heed God's simple message.**

[11]Since they refuse to listen, God will speak to them through foreign oppressors who speak an unknown language! [12]God's people could have rest in their own land if they would only obey him, but they will not listen. [13]So the LORD will spell out his message for them again, repeating it over and over, a line at a time, in very simple words. Yet they will stumble over this simple, straightforward message. They will be injured, trapped, and captured.

[14]Therefore, listen to this message from the LORD, you scoffing rulers in Jerusalem. [15]You boast that you have struck a bargain to avoid death and have made a deal to dodge the grave.* You say, "The Assyrians can never touch us, for we have built a strong refuge made of lies and deception." [16]Therefore, this is what the Sovereign LORD says: "Look! I am placing a foundation stone in Jerusalem.* It is firm, a tested

27:9 Hebrew *Jacob's.* 27:12 Hebrew *the river.* 28:1 Hebrew *of Ephraim,* referring to the northern kingdom of Israel; also in 28:3. 28:10 The Hebrew text for this verse may simply be childish sounds that have no meaning, or perhaps a childish mimicking of the prophet's words. Also in 28:13. 28:15 Hebrew *Sheol;* also in 28:18. 28:16a Hebrew *in Zion.*

and precious cornerstone that is safe to build on.
Whoever believes need never run away again.*
17"I will take the measuring line of justice and the
plumb line of righteousness to check the foundation
wall you have built. Your refuge looks strong, but
since it is made of lies, a hailstorm will knock it
down. Since it is made of deception, the enemy will
come like a flood to sweep it away. 18I will cancel the
bargain you made to avoid death, and I will overturn
your deal to dodge the grave. When the terrible
enemy floods in, you will be trampled into the
ground. 19Again and again that flood will come,
morning after morning, day and night, until you are
carried away."
This message will bring terror to your people. 20For
you have no place of refuge—the bed you have made
is too short to lie on. The blankets are too narrow to
cover you. 21The LORD will come suddenly and in
anger, as he did against the Philistines at Mount
Perazim and against the Amorites at Gibeon. He will
come to do a strange, unusual thing: He will destroy
his own people! 22So scoff no more, or your punishment will be even greater. For the Lord, the LORD
Almighty, has plainly told me that he is determined
to crush you.
23Listen to me; listen as I plead! 24Does a farmer
always plow and never sow? Is he forever cultivating
the soil and never planting it? 25Does he not finally
plant his seeds for dill, cummin, wheat, barley, and
spelt, each in its own section of his land? 26The
farmer knows just what to do, for God has given him
understanding. 27He doesn't thresh all his crops the
same way. A heavy sledge is never used on dill; rather,
it is beaten with a light stick. A threshing wheel is
never rolled on cummin; instead, it is beaten softly
with a flail. 28Bread grain is easily crushed, so he
doesn't keep on pounding it. He threshes it under
the wheels of a cart, but he doesn't pulverize it. 29The
LORD Almighty is a wonderful teacher, and he gives
the farmer great wisdom.

CHAPTER **29** **NO ONE CAN HIDE FROM GOD.** "Destruction is certain for Ariel,* the City of David. Year
after year you offer your many sacrifices. 2Yet I will
bring disaster upon you, and there will be much
weeping and sorrow. For Jerusalem will become as
her name Ariel means—an altar covered with blood.
3I will be your enemy, surrounding Jerusalem and
attacking its walls. I will build siege towers around it
and will destroy it. 4Your voice will whisper like a
ghost from the earth where you will lie buried.
5"But suddenly, your ruthless enemies will be
driven away like chaff before the wind. 6In an instant, I, the LORD Almighty, will come against them
with thunder and earthquake and great noise, with
whirlwind and storm and consuming fire. 7All the
nations fighting against Jerusalem* will vanish like
a dream! Those who are attacking her walls will
vanish like a vision in the night. 8A hungry person
dreams of eating but is still hungry. A thirsty person
dreams of drinking but is still faint from thirst when
morning comes. In the same way, your enemies will
dream of a victorious conquest over Jerusalem,* but
all to no avail."
9Are you amazed and incredulous? Do you not
believe it? Then go ahead and be blind if you must.
You are stupid, but not from wine! You stagger, but
not from beer! 10For the LORD has poured out on you
a spirit of deep sleep. He has closed the eyes of your

**It seems like every other month my dad is complaining about hearing of another TV preacher getting into trouble or a local pastor who molested someone. What do I say to people who point to the hypocrites in this world as their reason for giving God the cold shoulder?**

Unfortunately, even some of God's children act shamefully. In fact, there probably is not a Christian alive who, at one time or another, hasn't betrayed God by his or her actions.

The word "hypocrite" means "playact," to claim to be a certain type of person while acting like someone else. God is pretty upset at hypocrites, those who claim to be his followers but really aren't.

Jesus said, "Beware of the yeast of the Pharisees—beware of their hypocrisy. The time is coming when everything will be revealed; all that is secret will be made public. Whatever you have said in the dark will be heard in the light, and what you have whispered behind closed doors will be shouted from the housetops for all to hear!" (Luke 12:1-3).

When our world's final act draws to a close, some of the first to receive God's wrath will be those who have been playacting with God (see Isaiah 29:13-14). He is not amused or impressed; they will be judged.

Unfortunately, there is nothing you can do to prevent strangers from misrepresenting Christ. The only person you can prevent being a hypocrite is you. Here are some ways to keep from becoming a hypocrite:

First, watch your own actions closely. Though God reads your heart, other people see your actions first (see 2 Corinthians 13:5). If what you say doesn't match what you say you believe, get ready to be called a hypocrite.

Second, don't come down on other people too hard. Remember, the only difference between you and those who aren't Christians is that you've received the gift of forgiveness.

Third, be quick to admit when you make a mistake. True humility is rare in our culture. For some reason, people are drawn to those who can readily admit their mistakes. It's called being genuine.

**28:16b** Greek version reads *Anyone who believes in him will not be disappointed.* **29:1** *Ariel* sounds like a Hebrew term that means "hearth" or "altar." **29:7** Hebrew *Ariel.* **29:8** Hebrew *Mount Zion.*

**ALLIANCES TODAY**
Isaiah warned Judah not to ally with Egypt (30:1-7; 31:1-3). He knew that trust in any nation or military might was futile. Judah's only hope was to trust in God. Although we don't consciously put our hope for deliverance in political alliances in quite the same way, we often put our hope in other forces.

GOVERNMENT
We rely on government legislation to protect the moral decisions we want made, but legislation cannot change people's hearts.

SCIENCE
We enjoy the benefits of science and technology. We look to scientific predictions and analysis before we look to the Bible.

MEDICAL CARE
We regard medicine as the way to prolong life and preserve its quality—quite apart from faith and moral living.

EDUCATION
We act as though education and degrees can guarantee our future and success without considering what God plans for our future.

FINANCIAL SYSTEMS
We place our faith in financial "security," making as much money as we can for ourselves and forgetting that, while being wise with our money, we must trust God for our needs.

prophets and visionaries. 11All these future events are
a sealed book to them. When you give it to those
who can read, they will say, "We can't read it because
it is sealed." 12When you give it to those who cannot
read, they will say, "Sorry, we don't know how to
read."

13And so the Lord says, "These people say they are
mine. They honor me with their lips, but their hearts
are far away. And their worship of me amounts to
nothing more than human laws learned by rote.*
14Because of this, I will do wonders among these
hypocrites. I will show that human wisdom is foolish and even the most brilliant people lack understanding."

15Destruction is certain for those who try to hide
their plans from the LORD, who try to keep him in
the dark concerning what they do! "The LORD can't
see us," you say to yourselves. "He doesn't know
what is going on!" 16How stupid can you be? He is
the Potter, and he is certainly greater than you. You
are only the jars he makes! Should the thing that was
created say to the one who made it, "He didn't make
us"? Does a jar ever say, "The potter who made me
is stupid"?

17Soon—and it will not be very long—the wilderness of Lebanon will be a fertile field once again.
And the fertile fields will become a lush and fertile
forest. 18In that day deaf people will hear words read
from a book, and blind people will see through the
gloom and darkness. 19The humble will be filled
with fresh joy from the LORD. Those who are poor
will rejoice in the Holy One of Israel. 20Those who
intimidate and harass will be gone, and all those
who plot evil will be killed. 21Those who make the
innocent guilty by their false testimony will disappear. And those who use trickery to pervert justice
and tell lies to tear down the innocent will be no
more.

22That is why the LORD, who redeemed Abraham,

**HYPOCRISY ● ● • • •**

29:13-14 **The people claimed to belong to God, but because they were disobedient and merely went through the motions, God punished them. Religion had become routine instead of real. Isaiah condemned the people for being hypocrites. Jesus quoted this verse (Matthew 15:8; Mark 7:6-7) when he spoke to the Pharisees, the religious leaders of his day. We all are capable of hypocrisy. Often we slip into routine forms of worship that mean nothing to us. If we want to be called God's people, we must be obedient and worship him honestly and sincerely.**

29:13 Greek version reads *Their worship is a farce, for they merely teach human commands and teachings.*

says to the people of Israel,* "My people will no
longer pale with fear or be ashamed. 23For when they
see their many children and material blessings, they
will recognize the holiness of the Holy One of Israel.
They will stand in awe of the God of Israel. 24Those
in error will then believe the truth, and those who
constantly complain will accept instruction.

CHAPTER **30** **GOD IS WAITING.** "Destruction is
certain for my rebellious children," says the LORD.
"You make plans that are contrary to my will. You
weave a web of plans that are not from my Spirit,
thus piling up your sins. 2For without consulting me,
you have gone down to Egypt to find help. You have
put your trust in Pharaoh for his protection. 3But in
trusting Pharaoh, you will be humiliated and disgraced. 4For though his power extends to Zoan and
Hanes, 5it will all turn out to your shame. He will not
help you even one little bit."

6Look at the animals moving slowly across the
terrible desert to Egypt—donkeys and camels loaded
with treasure to pay for Egypt's aid. On through the
wilderness they go, where lions and poisonous
snakes live. All this, and Egypt will give you nothing
in return. 7Egypt's promises are worthless! I call her
the Harmless Dragon.*

8Now go and write down these words concerning
Egypt. They will then stand until the end of time as
a witness to Israel's unbelief. 9For these people are
stubborn rebels who refuse to pay any attention to
the LORD's instructions.

10They tell the prophets, "Shut up! We don't want
any more of your reports." They say, "Don't tell us
the truth. Tell us nice things. Tell us lies. 11Forget all
this gloom. We have heard more than enough about
your 'Holy One of Israel.' We are tired of listening to
what he has to say."

12This is the reply of the Holy One of Israel:
"Because you despise what I tell you and trust instead in oppression and lies, 13calamity will come
upon you suddenly. It will be like a bulging wall that
bursts and falls. In an instant it will collapse and
come crashing down. 14You will be smashed like a
piece of pottery—shattered so completely that there
won't be a piece left that is big enough to carry coals
from a fireplace or a little water from the well."

15The Sovereign LORD, the Holy One of Israel,
says, "Only in returning to me and waiting for me
will you be saved. In quietness and confidence is
your strength. But you would have none of it. 16You
said, 'No, we will get our help from Egypt. They will
give us swift horses for riding into battle.' But the
only swiftness you are going to see is the swiftness of
your enemies chasing you! 17One of them will chase
a thousand of you. Five of them will make all of you
flee. You will be left like a lonely flagpole on a distant
mountaintop."

18But the LORD still waits for you to come to him
so he can show you his love and compassion. For the
LORD is a faithful God. Blessed are those who wait for
him to help them.

19O people of Zion, who live in Jerusalem, you
will weep no more. He will be gracious if you ask for
help. He will respond instantly to the sound of your
cries. 20Though the Lord gave you adversity for food
and affliction for drink, he will still be with you to
teach you. You will see your teacher with your own
eyes, 21and you will hear a voice say, "This is the way;
turn around and walk here." 22Then you will destroy
all your silver idols and gold images. You will throw
them out like filthy rags. "Ugh!" you will say to
them. "Begone!"

23Then the LORD will bless you with rain at planting time. There will be wonderful harvests and
plenty of pastureland for your cattle. 24The oxen and
donkeys that till the ground will eat good grain, its
chaff having been blown away by the wind. 25In that
day, when your enemies are slaughtered, there will
be streams of water flowing down every mountain
and hill. 26The moon will be as bright as the sun, and
the sun will be seven times brighter—like the light
of seven days! So it will be when the LORD begins to
heal his people and cure the wounds he gave them.

## HIDING ● ● • • •

**29:15-16 The people of Jerusalem tried to hide their plans from God. They thought God couldn't see them and didn't know what was happening. It's strange that so many people think they can hide from God. In Psalm 139 we learn that God has examined us and knows everything about us. Would you be embarrassed if your best friends knew your personal thoughts? Remember that God knows all of them.**

27Look! The LORD is coming from far away, burning with anger, surrounded by a thick, rising smoke.
His lips are filled with fury; his words consume like
fire. 28His anger pours out like a flood on his enemies, sweeping them all away. He will sift out the
proud nations. He will bridle them and lead them
off to their destruction.

29But the people of God will sing a song of joy, like
the songs at the holy festivals. You will be filled with
joy, as when a flutist leads a group of pilgrims to
Jerusalem—the mountain of the LORD—to the Rock
of Israel. 30And the LORD will make his majestic voice
heard. With angry indignation he will bring down
his mighty arm on his enemies. It will descend with
devouring flames, with cloudbursts, thunderstorms,
and huge hailstones, bringing their destruction. 31At
the LORD's command, the Assyrians will be shattered. He will strike them down with his rod. 32And
as the LORD strikes them, his people will keep time
with the music of tambourines and harps. 33To-
pheth—the place of burning—has long been ready
for the Assyrian king; it has been piled high with
wood. The breath of the LORD, like fire from a vol-
cano, will set it ablaze.

29:22 Hebrew *of Jacob;* also in 29:23. 30:7 Hebrew *Rahab who sits still.* Rahab is the name of a mythical sea monster that represents chaos in ancient literature. The name is used here as a poetic name for Egypt.

## IDOLS ● ● ● • •

**31:7 Someday these people would throw their idols away, recognizing that the idols were nothing but wood or stone. Idols such as money, fame, or success are seductive. Instead of contributing to our spiritual development, they rob us of our thoughts, time, energy, and devotion to God. At first they seem exciting and promise to take us places, but in the end we will find that we have become their slaves. We need to recognize their worthlessness now, before they rob us of our freedom.**

## CHAPTER 31 **THE SWORD OF GOD.**

Destruction is certain for those who look to Egypt for help, trusting their cavalry and chariots instead of looking to the LORD, the Holy One of Israel. 2In his wisdom, the LORD will send great disaster; he will not change his mind. He will rise against those who are wicked, and he will crush their allies, too. 3For these Egyptians are mere humans, not God! Their horses are puny flesh, not mighty spirits! When the LORD clenches his fist against them, they will stumble and fall among those they are trying to help. They will all fall down and die together.

4But the LORD has told me this: "When a lion, even a young one, kills a sheep, it pays no attention to the shepherd's shouts and noise. It just goes right on eating. In the same way, the LORD Almighty will come and fight on Mount Zion. He will not be frightened away! 5The LORD Almighty will hover over Jerusalem as a bird hovers around its nest. He will defend and save the city; he will pass over it and rescue it."

6Therefore, my people, though you are such wicked rebels, come and return to the LORD. 7I know the glorious day will come when every one of you will throw away the gold idols and silver images that your sinful hands have made.

8"The Assyrians will be destroyed, but not by the swords of men. The sword of God will strike them, and they will panic and flee. The strong young Assyrians will be taken away as captives. 9Even their generals will quake with terror and flee when they see the battle flags," says the LORD, whose flame burns brightly in Jerusalem.

## CHAPTER 32 **A PROMISE OF PEACE.**

Look, a righteous king is coming! And honest princes will rule under him. 2He will shelter Israel from the storm and the wind. He will refresh her as a river in the desert and as the cool shadow of a large rock in a hot and weary land. 3Then everyone who can see will be looking for God, and those who can hear will listen to his voice. 4Even the hotheads among them will be full of sense and understanding. Those who stammer in uncertainty will speak out plainly.

5In that day ungodly fools will not be heroes. Wealthy cheaters will not be respected as outstanding citizens. 6Everyone will recognize ungodly fools for what they are. They spread lies about the LORD; they deprive the hungry of food and give no water to the thirsty. 7The smooth tricks of evil people will be exposed, including all the lies they use to oppress the poor in the courts. 8But good people will be generous to others and will be blessed for all they do.

9Listen, you women who lie around in lazy ease. Listen to me, and I will tell you of your reward. 10In a short time—in just a little more than a year—you careless ones will suddenly begin to care. For your fruit crop will fail, and the harvest will never take place. 11Tremble, you women of ease; throw off your unconcern. Strip off your pretty clothes, and wear sackcloth in your grief. 12Beat your breasts in sorrow for your bountiful farms that will soon be gone, and for those fruitful vines of other years. 13For your land will be overgrown with thorns and briers. Your joyful homes and happy cities will be gone. 14The palace and the city will be deserted, and busy towns will be empty. Herds of donkeys and goats will graze on the hills where the watchtowers are, 15until at last the Spirit is poured down upon us from heaven. Then the wilderness will become a fertile field, and the fertile field will become a lush and fertile forest. 16Justice will rule in the wilderness and righteousness in the fertile field. 17And this righteousness will bring peace. Quietness and confidence will fill the land forever.

## AT EASE ● ● ● • •

**32:9-13 The people turned their backs on God and concentrated on their own best interests. This warning is not just to the women of Israel, but to all who lie around in lazy ease enjoying crops, clothes, land, and cities while an enemy approaches. Wealth and luxury bring false security, lulling us into thinking all is well when disaster is around the corner. By abandoning God's purpose for our life, we also abandon his help.**

18My people will live in safety, quietly at home. They will be at rest. 19Even though the forest will be destroyed and the city torn down, 20God will greatly bless his people. Wherever they plant seed, bountiful crops will spring up. Their flocks and herds will graze in green pastures.

## CHAPTER 33 **GOD'S GREAT FORGIVENESS.**

Destruction is certain for you Assyrians,* who have destroyed everything around you but have never felt destruction yourselves. You expect others to respect their promises to you, while you betray your promises to them. Now you, too, will be betrayed and destroyed!

2But LORD, be merciful to us, for we have waited for you. Be our strength each day and our salvation in times of trouble. 3The enemy runs at the sound of your voice. When you stand up, the nations flee! 4Just as locusts strip the fields and vines, so Jerusalem will strip the fallen army of Assyria!

5Though the LORD is very great and lives in heaven, he will make Jerusalem* his home of justice and righteousness. 6In that day he will be your sure

33:1 Hebrew *for you, O destroyer . . . O betrayer.* The Hebrew text does not specifically name Assyria as the object of this prophecy. 33:5 Hebrew *Zion.*

foundation, providing a rich store of salvation, wisdom, and knowledge. The fear of the LORD is the key to this treasure.

7But now your ambassadors weep in bitter disappointment, for Assyria has refused their petition for peace. 8Your roads are deserted; no one travels them anymore. The Assyrians have broken their peace pact and care nothing for the promises they made before witnesses.* They have no respect for anyone. 9All the land of Israel is in trouble. Lebanon has been destroyed. The plain of Sharon is now a wilderness. Bashan and Carmel have been plundered.

10But the LORD says: "I will stand up and show my power and might. 11You Assyrians will gain nothing by all your efforts. Your own breath will turn to fire and kill you. 12Your people will be burned up completely, like thorns cut down and tossed in a fire. 13Listen to what I have done, you nations far away! And you that are near, acknowledge my might!"

14The sinners in Jerusalem* shake with fear. "Which one of us," they cry, "can live here in the presence of this all-consuming fire?" 15The ones who can live here are those who are honest and fair, who reject making a profit by fraud, who stay far away from bribes, who refuse to listen to those who plot murder, who shut their eyes to all enticement to do wrong. 16These are the ones who will dwell on high. The rocks of the mountains will be their fortress of safety. Food will be supplied to them, and they will have water in abundance.

17Your eyes will see the king in all his splendor, and you will see a land that stretches into the distance. 18You will think back to this time of terror when the Assyrian officers outside your walls counted your towers and estimated how much plunder they would get from your fallen city. 19But soon they will all be gone. These fierce, violent people with a strange, unknown language will disappear.

20Instead, you will see Zion as a place of worship and celebration. You will see Jerusalem, a city quiet and secure. 21The LORD will be our Mighty One. He will be like a wide river of protection that no enemy can cross. 22For the LORD is our judge, our lawgiver, and our king. He will care for us and save us. 23The enemies' sails hang loose on broken masts with useless tackle. Their treasure will be divided by the people of God. Even the lame will win their share! 24The people of Israel will no longer say, "We are sick and helpless," for the LORD will forgive their sins.

## CHAPTER 34

**COME AND LISTEN.** Come here and listen, O nations of the earth. Let the world and everything in it hear my words. 2For the LORD is enraged against the nations. His fury is against all their armies. He will completely destroy* them, bringing about their slaughter. 3Their dead will be left unburied, and the stench of rotting bodies will fill the land. The mountains will flow with their blood. 4The heavens above will melt away and disappear like a rolled-up scroll. The stars will fall from the sky, just as withered leaves and fruit fall from a tree.

5And when my sword has finished its work in the heavens, then watch. It will fall upon Edom, the nation I have completely destroyed. 6The sword of the LORD is drenched with blood. It is covered with fat as though it had been used for killing lambs and goats and rams for a sacrifice. Yes, the LORD will offer a great sacrifice in the rich city of Bozrah. He will make a mighty slaughter in Edom. 7The strongest will die—veterans and young men, too. The land will be soaked with blood and the soil enriched with fat. 8For it is the day of the LORD's vengeance, the year when Edom will be paid back for all it did to Israel.* 9The streams of Edom will be filled with burning pitch, and the ground will be covered with fire.

10This judgment on Edom will never end; the smoke of its burning will rise forever. The land will lie deserted from generation to generation. No one will live there anymore. 11It will be haunted by the horned owl, the hawk, the screech owl, and the raven.* For God will bring chaos and destruction to that land. 12It will be called the Land of Nothing, and its princes soon will all be gone. 13Thorns will overrun its palaces; nettles will grow in its forts. The ruins will become a haunt for jackals and a home for ostriches. 14Wild animals of the desert will mingle there with hyenas, their howls filling the night. Wild goats will bleat at one another among the ruins, and night creatures will come there to rest. 15There the owl will make her nest and lay her eggs. She will hatch her young and cover them with her wings. And the vultures will come, each one with its mate.

16Search the book of the LORD, and see what he will do. He will not miss a single detail. Not one of these birds and animals will be missing, and none will lack a mate, for the LORD has promised this. His Spirit will make it all come true. 17He has surveyed and divided the land and deeded it over to those creatures. They will possess it forever, from generation to generation.

### PROMISES • • • • •

33:1 **The Assyrians continually broke their promises but demanded that others keep theirs. It is easy to put ourselves in the same selfish position, demanding our rights while violating the rights of others. Broken promises shatter trust and destroy relationships. Determine to make no promises you can't keep; and, equally important, ask forgiveness for past promises you have broken. Exercise the same fairness with others that you demand for yourself.**

33:8 As in Dead Sea Scrolls; Masoretic Text reads *care nothing for the cities.* 33:14 Hebrew *in Zion.* 34:2 The Hebrew term used here refers to the complete consecration of things or people to the LORD, either by destroying them or by giving them as an offering; also in 34:5. 34:8 Hebrew *to Zion.* 34:11 The identification of some of these birds is uncertain.

CHAPTER **35** **STREAMS IN THE DESERT.** Even the wilderness will rejoice in those days. The desert will blossom with flowers. [2]Yes, there will be an abundance of flowers and singing and joy! The deserts will become as green as the mountains of Lebanon, as lovely as Mount Carmel's pastures and the plain of Sharon. There the LORD will display his glory, the splendor of our God.

[3]With this news, strengthen those who have tired hands, and encourage those who have weak knees. [4]Say to those who are afraid, "Be strong, and do not fear, for your God is coming to destroy your enemies. He is coming to save you." [5]And when he comes, he will open the eyes of the blind and unstop the ears of the deaf. [6]The lame will leap like a deer, and those who cannot speak will shout and sing! Springs will gush forth in the wilderness, and streams will water the desert. [7]The parched ground will become a pool, and springs of water will satisfy the thirsty land. Marsh grass and reeds and rushes will flourish where desert jackals once lived.

[8]And a main road will go through that once deserted land. It will be named the Highway of Holiness. Evil-hearted people will never travel on it. It will be only for those who walk in God's ways; fools will never walk there. [9]Lions will not lurk along its course, and there will be no other dangers. Only the redeemed will follow it. [10]Those who have been ransomed by the LORD will return to Jerusalem,* singing songs of everlasting joy. Sorrow and mourning will disappear, and they will be overcome with joy and gladness.

## VISIONS ● ● ● • •

35:1-10 **In chapters 1–34, Isaiah delivered a message of judgment on all nations, including Israel and Judah, for rejecting God. Although there were glimpses of relief and restoration for the remnant of faithful believers, the climate of wrath, fury, judgment, and destruction prevailed. Now Isaiah breaks through with a vision of beauty and encouragement. God is just as complete in his mercy as he is severe in his judgment. God's complete moral perfection is revealed by his hatred of all sin, and this leads to judgment. This same moral perfection is revealed in his love for all he has created. This leads to mercy for those who have been less than perfect but who have sincerely loved and obeyed him.**

CHAPTER **36** **AN ANGEL DESTROYS AN ARMY.** In the fourteenth year of King Hezekiah's reign, King Sennacherib of Assyria came to attack the fortified cities of Judah and conquered them. [2]Then the king of Assyria sent his personal representative with a huge army from Lachish to confront King Hezekiah in Jerusalem. The Assyrians stopped beside the aqueduct that feeds water into the upper pool, near the road leading to the field where cloth is bleached.

[3]These are the officials who went out to meet with them: Eliakim son of Hilkiah, the palace administrator, Shebna the court secretary, and Joah son of Asaph, the royal historian. [4]Then the Assyrian king's personal representative sent this message to King Hezekiah:

"This is what the great king of Assyria says: What are you trusting in that makes you so confident? [5]Do you think that mere words can substitute for military skill and strength? Which of your allies will give you any military backing against Assyria? [6]Will Egypt? If you lean on Egypt, you will find it to be a stick that breaks beneath your weight and pierces your hand. The Pharaoh of Egypt is completely unreliable!

[7]"But perhaps you will say, 'We are trusting in the LORD our God!' But isn't he the one who was insulted by King Hezekiah? Didn't Hezekiah tear down his shrines and altars and make everyone in Judah worship only at the altar here in Jerusalem?

[8]"I'll tell you what! My master, the king of Assyria, will strike a bargain with you. If you can find two thousand horsemen in your entire army, he will give you two thousand horses for them to ride on! [9]With your tiny army, how can you think of challenging even the weakest contingent of my master's troops, even with the help of Egypt's chariots and horsemen*? [10]What's more, do you think we have invaded your land without the LORD's direction? The LORD himself told us, 'Go and destroy it!'"

[11]Then Eliakim, Shebna, and Joah said to the king's representative, "Please speak to us in Aramaic, for we understand it well. Don't speak in Hebrew, for the people on the wall will hear."

[12]But Sennacherib's representative replied, "My master wants everyone in Jerusalem to hear this, not just you. He wants them to know that if you do not surrender, this city will be put under siege. The people will become so hungry and thirsty that they will eat their own dung and drink their own urine."

[13]Then he stood and shouted in Hebrew to the people on the wall, "Listen to this message from the great king of Assyria! [14]This is what the king says: Don't let King Hezekiah deceive you. He will never be able to rescue you. [15]Don't let him fool you into

## DECEIT ● ● ● • •

36:7 **The field commander (Rabshakeh) from Assyria claimed that Hezekiah insulted God by tearing down his altars in the hills and making the people worship in Jerusalem. But Hezekiah's reform sought to eliminate idol worship (which occurred mainly in the hills) so that the people worshiped only the true God. Either the Assyrians didn't know about the religion of the true God, or they wanted to deceive the people into thinking they had angered a powerful god. In the same way, Satan tries to confuse or deceive us. People don't necessarily need to be sinful to be ineffective for God; they need only be confused about what God wants. To avoid Satan's deceit, study God's Word carefully and regularly. When you know what God says, you will not fall for Satan's lies.**

35:10 Hebrew *Zion.* 36:9 Or *and charioteers.*

trusting in the LORD by saying, 'The LORD will rescue us! This city will never be handed over to the Assyrian king.'

16 "Don't listen to Hezekiah! These are the terms the king of Assyria is offering: Make peace with me—open the gates and come out. Then I will allow each of you to continue eating from your own garden and drinking from your own well. 17 Then I will arrange to take you to another land like this one—a country with bountiful harvests of grain and wine, bread and vineyards—a land of plenty.

18 "Don't let Hezekiah mislead you by saying, 'The LORD will rescue us!' Have the gods of any other nations ever saved their people from the king of Assyria? 19 What happened to the gods of Hamath and Arpad? And what about the gods of Sepharvaim? Did they rescue Samaria from my power? 20 What god of any nation has ever been able to save its people from my power? Name just one! So what makes you think that the LORD can rescue Jerusalem?"

21 But the people were silent and did not answer because Hezekiah had told them not to speak. 22 Then Eliakim son of Hilkiah, the palace administrator, Shebna the court secretary, and Joah son of Asaph, the royal historian, went back to Hezekiah. They tore their clothes in despair, and they went in to see the king and told him what the Assyrian representative had said.

## CHAPTER 37

When King Hezekiah heard their report, he tore his clothes and put on sackcloth and went into the Temple of the LORD to pray. 2 And he sent Eliakim the palace administrator, Shebna the court secretary, and the leading priests, all dressed in sackcloth, to the prophet Isaiah son of Amoz. 3 They told him, "This is what King Hezekiah says: This is a day of trouble, insult, and disgrace. It is like when a child is ready to be born, but the mother has no strength to deliver it. 4 But perhaps the LORD your God has heard the Assyrian representative defying the living God and will punish him for his words. Oh, pray for those of us who are left!"

5 After King Hezekiah's officials delivered the king's message to Isaiah, 6 the prophet replied, "Say to your master, 'This is what the LORD says: Do not be disturbed by this blasphemous speech against me from the Assyrian king's messengers. 7 Listen! I myself will make sure that the king will receive a report from Assyria telling him that he is needed at home. Then I will make him want to return to his land, where I will have him killed with a sword.'"

8 Meanwhile, the Assyrian representative left Jerusalem and went to consult his king, who had left Lachish and was attacking Libnah. 9 Soon afterward King Sennacherib received word that King Tirhakah of Ethiopia* was leading an army to fight against him. Before leaving to meet the attack, he sent this message back to Hezekiah in Jerusalem:

> 10 "This message is for King Hezekiah of Judah. Don't let this God you trust deceive you with promises that Jerusalem will not be captured by the king of Assyria. 11 You know perfectly well what the kings of Assyria have done wherever they have gone. They have crushed everyone who stood in their way! Why should you be any different? 12 Have the gods of other nations rescued them—such nations as Gozan, Haran, Rezeph, and the people of Eden who were in Tel-assar? The former kings of Assyria destroyed them all! 13 What happened to the king of Hamath and the king of Arpad? What happened to the kings of Sepharvaim, Hena, and Ivvah?"

14 After Hezekiah received the letter and read it, he went up to the LORD's Temple and spread it out before the LORD. 15 And Hezekiah prayed this prayer before the LORD: 16 "O LORD Almighty, God of Israel, you are enthroned between the mighty cherubim! You alone are God of all the kingdoms of the earth. You alone created the heavens and the earth. 17 Listen to me, O LORD, and hear! Open your eyes, O LORD, and see! Listen to Sennacherib's words of defiance against the living God.

18 "It is true, LORD, that the kings of Assyria have destroyed all these nations, just as the message says. 19 And they have thrown the gods of these nations into the fire and burned them. But of course the Assyrians could destroy them! They were not gods at all—only idols of wood and stone shaped by human hands. 20 Now, O LORD our God, rescue us from his power; then all the kingdoms of the earth will know that you alone, O LORD, are God."

21 Then Isaiah son of Amoz sent this message to Hezekiah: "This is what the LORD, the God of Israel, says: This is my answer to your prayer concerning King Sennacherib of Assyria. 22 This is the message that the LORD has spoken against him:

'The virgin daughter of Zion
  despises you and laughs at you.
The daughter of Jerusalem
  scoffs and shakes her head as you flee.

23 'Whom do you think you have been insulting
    and ridiculing?
  Against whom did you raise your voice?
At whom did you look in such proud
    condescension?
  It was the Holy One of Israel!

### THE ANSWER ● ● ● • •

**37:8-10 Although the answer to Hezekiah's prayer was already in motion because Tirhakah was poised to attack, Hezekiah did not know it. He persisted in prayer and faith even though he could not see the answer coming. When we pray, we must have faith that God has already prepared the best answer. Our task is to ask in faith and wait.**

37:9 Hebrew *of Cush*.

## RADICAL CHANGE ● ● ● • •

38:1-5 **When Isaiah told Hezekiah of his impending death, Hezekiah immediately turned to God. God responded to Hezekiah's prayer, allowing him to live another 15 years. In response to fervent prayer, God may change the course of our life, too. Never hesitate to ask God for radical changes if you will honor him with those changes.**

24 By your messengers you have mocked the Lord.
  You have said, "With my many chariots
I have conquered the highest mountains—
  yes, the remotest peaks of Lebanon.
I have cut down its tallest cedars
  and its choicest cypress trees.
I have reached its farthest corners
  and explored its deepest forests.
25 I have dug wells in many a foreign land
  and refreshed myself with their water.
I even stopped up the rivers of Egypt
  so that my armies could go across!"
26 'But have you not heard?
  It was I, the LORD, who decided this long ago.
Long ago I planned what I am now causing to
    happen,
  that you should crush fortified cities into
    heaps of rubble.
27 That is why their people have so little power
  and are such easy prey for you.
They are as helpless as the grass,
  as easily trampled as tender green shoots.
They are like grass sprouting on a housetop,
  easily scorched by the sun.
28 'But I know you well—
  your comings and goings and all you do.
  I know the way you have raged against me.
29 And because of your arrogance against me,
  which I have heard for myself,
I will put my hook in your nose
  and my bridle in your mouth.
I will make you return
  by the road on which you came.'"

30Then Isaiah said to Hezekiah, "Here is the proof
that the LORD will protect this city from Assyria's
king. This year you will eat only what grows up by
itself, and next year you will eat what springs up
from that. But in the third year you will plant crops
and harvest them; you will tend vineyards and eat
their fruit. 31And you who are left in Judah, who have
escaped the ravages of the siege, will take root again
in your own soil, and you will flourish and multiply.
32For a remnant of my people will spread out from
Jerusalem, a group of survivors from Mount Zion.
The passion of the LORD Almighty will make this
happen!

33"And this is what the LORD says about the
king of Assyria: His armies will not enter Jerusalem to shoot their arrows. They will not march
outside its gates with their shields and build banks
of earth against its walls. 34The king will return to
his own country by the road on which he came. He
will not enter this city, says the LORD. 35For my own
honor and for the sake of my servant David, I will
defend it."

36That night the angel of the LORD went out to the
Assyrian camp and killed 185,000 Assyrian troops.
When the surviving Assyrians* woke up the next
morning, they found corpses everywhere. 37Then King
Sennacherib of Assyria broke camp and returned to his
own land. He went home to his capital of Nineveh and
stayed there. 38One day while he was worshiping in the
temple of his god Nisroch, his sons Adrammelech and
Sharezer killed him with their swords. They then escaped to the land of Ararat, and another son, Esarhaddon, became the next king of Assyria.

## CHAPTER 38 **A KING ASKS FOR A MIRACLE.**

About
that time Hezekiah became deathly ill, and the
prophet Isaiah son of Amoz went to visit him. He
gave the king this message: "This is what the LORD
says: Set your affairs in order, for you are going to die.
You will not recover from this illness."

2When Hezekiah heard this, he turned his face to
the wall and prayed to the LORD, 3"Remember,
O LORD, how I have always tried to be faithful to you
and do what is pleasing in your sight." Then he
broke down and wept bitterly.

4Then this message came to Isaiah from the LORD:
5"Go back to Hezekiah and tell him, 'This is what
the LORD, the God of your ancestor David, says: I
have heard your prayer and seen your tears. I will add
fifteen years to your life, 6and I will rescue you and
this city from the king of Assyria. Yes, I will defend
this city.

7"'And this is the sign that the LORD will give you
to prove he will do as he promised: 8I will cause the
sun's shadow to move ten steps backward on the
sundial of Ahaz!'" So the shadow on the sundial
moved backward ten steps.

9When King Hezekiah was well again, he wrote
this poem about his experience:

10 I said, "In the prime of my life,
  must I now enter the place of the dead?
  Am I to be robbed of my normal years?"
11 I said, "Never again will I see the LORD GOD
  while still in the land of the living.
Never again will I see my friends
  or laugh with those who live in this world.

## UNDERCURRENT ● ● ● • •

39:8 **Hezekiah, one of Judah's most faithful kings, worked hard throughout his reign to stamp out idol worship and to purify the worship of the true God at the Jerusalem Temple. Nevertheless, he knew his kingdom was not pure. Powerful undercurrents of evil invited destruction, and only God's miraculous interventions preserved Judah from its enemies. Here Hezekiah expressed gratefulness that God was preserving peace during his reign. As soon as Hezekiah died, evil burst forth under the leadership of Manasseh, Hezekiah's son, who actually rebuilt the centers of idolatry his father had destroyed.**

37:36 Hebrew *When they.*

[12] My life has been blown away
like a shepherd's tent in a storm.
It has been cut short,
as when a weaver cuts cloth from a loom.
Suddenly, my life was over.
[13] I waited patiently all night,
but I was torn apart as though by lions.
Suddenly, my life was over.
[14] Delirious, I chattered like a swallow or a crane,
and then I moaned like a mourning dove.
My eyes grew tired of looking to heaven for help.
I am in trouble, Lord. Help me!"
[15] But what could I say?
For he himself had sent this sickness.
Now I will walk humbly throughout my years
because of this anguish I have felt.
[16] Lord, your discipline is good,
for it leads to life and health.
You have restored my health
and have allowed me to live!
[17] Yes, it was good for me to suffer this anguish,
for you have rescued me from death
and have forgiven all my sins.
[18] For the dead cannot praise you;
they cannot raise their voices in praise.
Those who go down to destruction
can no longer hope in your faithfulness.
[19] Only the living can praise you as I do today.
Each generation can make known your
faithfulness to the next.
[20] Think of it—the LORD has healed me!
I will sing his praises with instruments
every day of my life
in the Temple of the LORD.

[21] Isaiah had said to Hezekiah's servants, "Make an
ointment from figs and spread it over the boil, and
Hezekiah will recover."
[22] And Hezekiah had asked, "What sign will prove
that I will go to the Temple of the LORD three days
from now?"

CHAPTER **39** **MESSENGERS FROM BABYLON.** Soon
after this, Merodach-baladan son of Baladan, king of
Babylon, sent Hezekiah his best wishes and a gift. He
had heard that Hezekiah had been very sick and that
he had recovered. [2] Hezekiah welcomed the Babylonian envoys and showed them everything in his
treasure-houses—the silver, the gold, the spices, and
the aromatic oils. He also took them to see his
armory and showed them all his other treasures—
everything! There was nothing in his palace or kingdom that Hezekiah did not show them.
[3] Then Isaiah the prophet went to King Hezekiah
and asked him, "What did those men want? Where
were they from?"
Hezekiah replied, "They came from the distant
land of Babylon."
[4] "What did they see in your palace?" asked Isaiah.
"They saw everything," Hezekiah replied. "I
showed them everything I own—all my treasures."
[5] Then Isaiah said to Hezekiah, "Listen to this
message from the LORD Almighty: [6] The time is coming when everything you have—all the treasures
stored up by your ancestors—will be carried off to
Babylon. Nothing will be left, says the LORD. [7] Some
of your own descendants will be taken away into
exile. They will become eunuchs who will serve in
the palace of Babylon's king."
[8] Then Hezekiah said to Isaiah, "This message you
have given me from the LORD is good." But the king
was thinking, "At least there will be peace and security during my lifetime."

**COMFORT ● ● • • ·**

**40:1 God's people still had 100 years of trouble before Jerusalem would fall, then 70 years of exile. So God told Isaiah to speak tenderly and to comfort Jerusalem. When your life seems to be falling apart, ask God to comfort you. You may not escape hard times, but you can find God's comfort during them. Sometimes, however, the only comfort we have is in the knowledge that someday we will be with God. Appreciate the comfort and encouragement found in God's Word, his presence, and his people.**

CHAPTER **40** **GOD WILL FEED HIS FLOCK.** "Comfort,
comfort my people," says your God. [2] "Speak tenderly to Jerusalem. Tell her that her sad days are gone
and that her sins are pardoned. Yes, the LORD has
punished her in full for all her sins."
[3] Listen! I hear the voice of someone shouting,
"Make a highway for the LORD through the wilderness. Make a straight, smooth road through the desert for our God. [4] Fill the valleys and level the hills.
Straighten out the curves and smooth off the rough
spots. [5] Then the glory of the LORD will be revealed,
and all people will see it together. The LORD has
spoken!"
[6] A voice said, "Shout!"
I asked, "What should I shout?"
"Shout that people are like the grass that dies
away. Their beauty fades as quickly as the beauty of
flowers in a field. [7] The grass withers, and the flowers
fade beneath the breath of the LORD. And so it is with
people. [8] The grass withers, and the flowers fade, but
the word of our God stands forever."
[9] Messenger of good news, shout to Zion from the
mountaintops! Shout louder to Jerusalem—do not
be afraid. Tell the towns of Judah, "Your God is
coming!" [10] Yes, the Sovereign LORD is coming in all
his glorious power. He will rule with awesome
strength. See, he brings his reward with him as he
comes. [11] He will feed his flock like a shepherd. He
will carry the lambs in his arms, holding them close
to his heart. He will gently lead the mother sheep
with their young.
[12] Who else has held the oceans in his hand?
Who has measured off the heavens with his fingers? Who else knows the weight of the earth or has
weighed out the mountains and the hills? [13] Who

is able to advise the Spirit of the LORD? Who knows enough to be his teacher or counselor? 14Has the LORD ever needed anyone's advice? Does he need instruction about what is good or what is best? 15No, for all the nations of the world are nothing in comparison with him. They are but a drop in the bucket, dust on the scales. He picks up the islands as though they had no weight at all. 16All Lebanon's forests do not contain sufficient fuel to consume a sacrifice large enough to honor him. All Lebanon's sacrificial animals would not make an offering worthy of our God. 17The nations of the world are as nothing to him. In his eyes they are less than nothing—mere emptiness and froth.

18To whom, then, can we compare God? What image might we find to resemble him? 19Can he be compared to an idol formed in a mold, overlaid with gold, and decorated with silver chains? 20Or is a poor person's wooden idol better? Can God be compared to an idol that must be placed on a stand so it won't fall down?

21Have you never heard or understood? Are you deaf to the words of God—the words he gave before the world began? Are you so ignorant? 22It is God who sits above the circle of the earth. The people below must seem to him like grasshoppers! He is the one who spreads out the heavens like a curtain and makes his tent from them. 23He judges the great people of the world and brings them all to nothing. 24They hardly get started, barely taking root, when he blows on them and their work withers. The wind carries them off like straw.

25"To whom will you compare me? Who is my equal?" asks the Holy One.

26Look up into the heavens. Who created all the stars? He brings them out one after another, calling each by its name. And he counts them to see that none are lost or have strayed away.

## STRENGTH ● ● • • •

**40:29-31 Even the strongest people get tired at times, but God's power and strength never diminish. He is never too tired or too busy to help and listen. His strength is our source of strength. When you feel all of life crushing you and you cannot go another step, remember that you can ask God to renew your strength.**

27O Israel, how can you say the LORD does not see your troubles? How can you say God refuses to hear your case? 28Have you never heard or understood? Don't you know that the LORD is the everlasting God, the Creator of all the earth? He never grows faint or weary. No one can measure the depths of his understanding. 29He gives power to those who are tired and worn out; he offers strength to the weak. 30Even youths will become exhausted, and young men will give up. 31But those who wait on the LORD will find new strength. They will fly high on wings like eagles. They will run and not grow weary. They will walk and not faint.

## THE FUTURE ● ● • • •

**41:4 Each generation gets caught up in its own problems, but God's plan embraces all generations. When your great-grandparents lived, God worked personally in the lives of his people. When your great-grandchildren live, God will still work personally in the lives of his people. He is the only One who sees as clearly a hundred years from now as he saw a hundred years ago. When you are concerned about the future, talk with God—he knows the generations of the future as well as he knows the generations of the past.**

## CHAPTER 41 DON'T BE AFRAID, ISRAEL!

"Listen in silence before me, you lands beyond the sea. Bring your strongest arguments. Come now and speak. The court is ready for your case.

2"Who has stirred up this king from the east, who meets victory at every step? Who, indeed, but the LORD? He gives him victory over many nations and permits him to trample their kings underfoot. He puts entire armies to the sword. He scatters them in the wind with his bow. 3He chases them away and goes on safely, though he is walking over unfamiliar ground. 4Who has done such mighty deeds, directing the affairs of the human race as each new generation marches by? It is I, the LORD, the First and the Last. I alone am he."

5The lands beyond the sea watch in fear. Remote lands tremble and mobilize for war. 6They encourage one another with the words, "Be strong!" 7The craftsmen rush to make new idols. The carver hurries the goldsmith, and the molder helps at the anvil. "Good," they say. "It's coming along fine." Carefully they join the parts together, then fasten the thing in place so it won't fall over.

8"But as for you, Israel my servant, Jacob my chosen one, descended from my friend Abraham, 9I have called you back from the ends of the earth so you can serve me. For I have chosen you and will not throw you away. 10Don't be afraid, for I am with you. Do not be dismayed, for I am your God. I will strengthen you. I will help you. I will uphold you with my victorious right hand.

11"See, all your angry enemies lie there, confused and ashamed. Anyone who opposes you will die. 12You will look for them in vain. They will all be gone! 13I am holding you by your right hand—I, the LORD your God. And I say to you, 'Do not be afraid. I am here to help you. 14Despised though you are, O Israel, don't be afraid, for I will help you. I am the LORD, your Redeemer. I am the Holy One of Israel.' 15You will be a new threshing instrument with many sharp teeth. You will tear all your enemies apart, making chaff of mountains. 16You will toss them in the air, and the wind will blow them all away; a whirlwind will scatter them. And the joy of the LORD will fill you to overflowing. You will glory in the Holy One of Israel.

17"When the poor and needy search for water and there is none, and their tongues are parched from thirst, then I, the LORD, will answer them. I, the God of Israel, will never forsake them. 18I will open up

rivers for them on high plateaus. I will give them
fountains of water in the valleys. In the deserts they
will find pools of water. Rivers fed by springs will
flow across the dry, parched ground. 19I will plant
trees—cedar, acacia, myrtle, olive, cypress, fir, and
pine—on barren land. 20Everyone will see this
miracle and understand that it is the LORD, the Holy
One of Israel, who did it.
21"Can your idols make such claims as these? Let
them come and show what they can do!" says the
LORD, the King of Israel.* 22"Let them try to tell us
what happened long ago or what the future holds.
23Yes, that's it! If you are gods, tell what will occur in
the days ahead. Or perform a mighty miracle that
will fill us with amazement and fear. Do something,
whether good or bad! 24But no! You are less than
nothing and can do nothing at all. Anyone who
chooses you becomes filthy, just like you!
25"But I have stirred up a leader from the north
and east. He will come against the nations and call
on my name, and I will give him victory over kings
and princes. He will trample them as a potter treads
on clay.
26"Who but I have told you this would happen?
Who else predicted this, making you admit that he
was right? No one else said a word! 27I was the first
to tell Jerusalem, 'Look! Help is on the way!' 28Not
one of your idols told you this. Not one gave any
answer when I asked. 29See, they are all foolish,
worthless things. Your idols are all as empty as the
wind.

CHAPTER **42** **GOD'S CHOSEN ONE.** "Look at my
servant, whom I strengthen. He is my chosen one,
and I am pleased with him. I have put my Spirit
upon him. He will reveal justice to the nations. 2He
will be gentle—he will not shout or raise his voice in
public. 3He will not crush those who are weak or
quench the smallest hope. He will bring full justice
to all who have been wronged.
4He will not stop until truth and
righteousness prevail throughout
the earth. Even distant lands beyond the sea will wait for his instruction."
5God, the LORD, created the
heavens and stretched them out.
He created the earth and everything in it. He gives breath and
life to everyone in all the world.
And it is he who says, 6"I, the
LORD, have called you to demonstrate my righteousness. I will
guard and support you, for I
have given you to my people as
the personal confirmation of my
covenant with them. And you
will be a light to guide all nations to me. 7You will open the
eyes of the blind and free the
captives from prison. You will release those who sit
in dark dungeons.
8"I am the LORD; that is my name! I will not give
my glory to anyone else. I will not share my praise
with carved idols. 9Everything I prophesied has come
true, and now I will prophesy again. I will tell you the
future before it happens."

10 Sing a new song to the LORD!
Sing his praises from the ends of the earth!
Sing, all you who sail the seas,
all you who live in distant coastlands.
11 Join in the chorus, you desert towns;
let the villages of Kedar rejoice!
Let the people of Sela sing for joy;
shout praises from the mountaintops!
12 Let the coastlands glorify the LORD;
let them sing his praise.
13 The LORD will march forth like a mighty man;
he will come out like a warrior, full of fury.
He will shout his thundering battle cry,
and he will crush all his enemies.
14 He will say, "I have long been silent;
yes, I have restrained myself.
But now I will give full vent to my fury;
I will gasp and pant like a woman giving birth.
15 I will level the mountains and hills
and bring a blight on all their greenery.
I will turn the rivers into dry land
and will dry up all the pools.
16 I will lead blind Israel down a new path,
guiding them along an unfamiliar way.
I will make the darkness bright before them
and smooth out the road ahead of them.
Yes, I will indeed do these things;
I will not forsake them.
17 But those who trust in idols,
calling them their gods—
they will be turned away in shame.

## "Here's what I did..."

I recently switched schools. In my old school, I knew everyone. In this new, much larger school, I knew no one. The situation forced me to depend on God. I knew that I really needed God's help and guidance to make it through those first few months.

During this time, I memorized Isaiah 41:10 and Philippians 4:13. Whenever I felt unnoticed or afraid to talk to someone, I would repeat these verses to myself. I remembered that God was with me, he will strengthen me, and that he has already won the victory for me. These two verses became a lifeline to me. They helped me make the adjustments so that now I do have friends and I feel pretty comfortable at my new school.

Amy
AGE 15

41:21 Hebrew *the King of Jacob.*

[18]"Oh, how deaf and blind you are toward me! Why won't you listen? Why do you refuse to see? [19]Who in all the world is as blind as my own people, my servant? Who is as deaf as my messengers? Who is as blind as my chosen people, the servant of the LORD? [20]You see and understand what is right but refuse to act on it. You hear, but you don't really listen."

[21]The LORD has magnified his law and made it truly glorious. Through it he had planned to show the world that he is righteous. [22]But what a sight his people are, for they have been robbed, enslaved, imprisoned, and trapped. They are fair game for all and have no one to protect them. [23]Will not even one of you apply these lessons from the past and see the ruin that awaits you? [24]Who allowed Israel to be robbed and hurt? Was it not the LORD? It was the LORD whom we sinned against, for the people would not go where he sent them, nor would they obey his law. [25]That is why he poured out such fury on them and destroyed them in battle. They were set on fire and burned, but they still refused to understand.

## CHAPTER 43

**NO OTHER SAVIOR.** But now, O Israel, the LORD who created you says: "Do not be afraid, for I have ransomed you. I have called you by name; you are mine. [2]When you go through deep waters and great trouble, I will be with you. When you go through rivers of difficulty, you will not drown! When you walk through the fire of oppression, you will not be burned up; the flames will not consume you. [3]For I am the LORD, your God, the Holy One of Israel, your Savior. I gave Egypt, Ethiopia,* and Seba as a ransom for your freedom. [4]Others died that you might live. I traded their lives for yours because you are precious to me. You are honored, and I love you.

[5]"Do not be afraid, for I am with you. I will gather you and your children from east and west [6]and from north and south. I will bring my sons and daughters back to Israel from the distant corners of the earth. [7]All who claim me as their God will come, for I have made them for my glory. It was I who created them."

[8]Bring out the people who have eyes but are blind, who have ears but are deaf. [9]Gather the nations together! Which of their idols has ever foretold such things? Can any of them predict something even a single day in advance? Where are the witnesses of such predictions? Who can verify that they spoke the truth?

[10]"But you are my witnesses, O Israel!" says the LORD. "And you are my servant. You have been chosen to know me, believe in me, and understand that I alone am God. There is no other God; there never has been and never will be. [11]I am the LORD, and there is no other Savior. [12]First I predicted your deliverance; I declared what I would do, and then I did it—I saved you. No foreign god has ever done this before. You are witnesses that I am the only God," says the LORD. [13]"From eternity to eternity I am God. No one can oppose what I do. No one can reverse my actions."

[14]The LORD your Redeemer, the Holy One of Israel, says: "For your sakes I will send an invading army against Babylon. And the Babylonians* will be forced to flee in those ships they are so proud of. [15]I am the LORD, your Holy One, Israel's Creator and King. [16]I am the LORD, who opened a way through the waters, making a dry path through the sea. [17]I called forth the mighty army of Egypt with all its chariots and horses. I drew them beneath the waves, and they drowned, their lives snuffed out like a smoldering candlewick.

[18]"But forget all that—it is nothing compared to what I am going to do. [19]For I am about to do a brand-new thing. See, I have already begun! Do you not see it? I will make a pathway through the wilderness for my people to come home. I will create rivers for them in the desert! [20]The wild animals in the fields will thank me, the jackals and ostriches, too, for giving them water in the wilderness. Yes, I will make springs in the desert, so that my chosen people can be refreshed. [21]I have made Israel for myself, and they will someday honor me before the whole world.

[22]"But, my dear people, you refuse to ask for my help. You have grown tired of me! [23]You have not brought me lambs for burnt offerings. You have not honored me with sacrifices, though I have not burdened and wearied you with my requests for grain offerings and incense. [24]You have not brought me fragrant incense or pleased me with the fat from sacrifices. Instead, you have burdened me with your sins and wearied me with your faults.

[25]"I—yes, I alone—am the one who blots out your sins for my own sake and will never think of them again. [26]Let us review the situation together, and you can present your case if you have one. [27]From the very beginning, your ancestors sinned against me—all your leaders broke my laws. [28]That is why I have disgraced your priests and assigned Israel a future of complete destruction* and shame.

## CHAPTER 44

**IDOLS ARE FALSE GODS.** "But now, listen to me, Jacob my servant, Israel my chosen one. [2]The LORD who made you and helps you says: O Jacob, my servant, do not be afraid. O Israel,* my chosen one, do not fear. [3]For I will give you abundant water to quench your thirst and to moisten your parched fields. And I will pour out my Spirit and my blessings on your children. [4]They will thrive like

**WITNESS ● ● • • •**

43:10-11 **Israel's task was to be a witness, telling the world who God is and what he has done. Believers today share the responsibility of being God's witnesses. Do people know what God is like through your words and example? They cannot see God directly, but they can see him reflected in you.**

43:3 Hebrew *Cush.* 43:14 Or *Chaldeans.* 43:28 The Hebrew term used here refers to the complete consecration of things or people to the LORD, either by destroying them or by giving them as an offering. 44:2 Hebrew *Jeshurun,* a term of endearment for Israel.

**TODAY'S IDOLATRY**
God asks, "Who but a fool would make his own god—an idol that cannot help him one bit!" (44:10). We think of idols as statues of wood or stone, but in reality an idol is anything natural that is given sacred value and power. If your answer to any of the following questions is anyone other than God, you need to check out who you are ultimately worshiping.

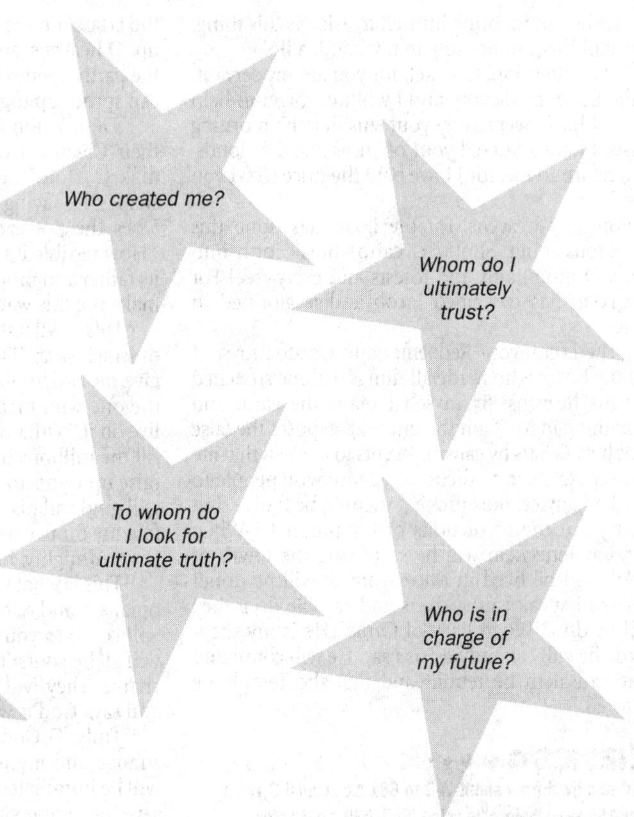
Who created me?
Whom do I ultimately trust?
To whom do I look for ultimate truth?
To whom do I look for security and happiness?
Who is in charge of my future?

watered grass, like willows on a riverbank. 5Some
will proudly claim, 'I belong to the LORD.' Others
will say, 'I am a descendant of Jacob.' Some will write
the LORD's name on their hands and will take the
honored name of Israel as their own.
6"This is what the LORD, Israel's King and Redeemer,
the LORD Almighty, says: I am the First and
the Last; there is no other God. 7Who else can tell
you what is going to happen in the days ahead? Let
them tell you if they can and thus prove their power.
Let them do as I have done since ancient times. 8Do
not tremble; do not be afraid. Have I not proclaimed
from ages past what my purposes are for you? You
are my witnesses—is there any other God? No!
There is no other Rock—not one!"
9How foolish are those who manufacture idols to
be their gods. These highly valued objects are really
worthless. They themselves are witnesses that this is
so, for their idols neither see nor know. No wonder
those who worship them are put to shame. 10Who
but a fool would make his own god—an idol that
cannot help him one bit! 11All who worship idols
will stand before the LORD in shame, along with all
these craftsmen—mere humans—who claim they
can make a god. Together they will stand in terror
and shame.
12The blacksmith stands at his forge to make a
sharp tool, pounding and shaping it with all his
might. His work makes him hungry and thirsty, weak
and faint. 13Then the wood-carver measures and
marks out a block of wood, takes the tool, and carves
the figure of a man. Now he has a wonderful idol
that cannot even move from where it is placed! 14He
cuts down cedars; he selects the cypress and the oak;
he plants the cedar in the forest to be nourished by
the rain. 15And after his care, he uses part of the wood
to make a fire to warm himself and bake his bread.
Then—yes, it's true—he takes the rest of it and
makes himself a god for people to worship! He
makes an idol and bows down and praises it! 16He
burns part of the tree to roast his meat and to keep
himself warm. 17Then he takes what's left and makes
his god: a carved idol! He falls down in front of it,
worshiping and praying to it. "Rescue me!" he says.
"You are my god!"
18Such stupidity and ignorance! Their eyes are
closed, and they cannot see. Their minds are shut,
and they cannot think. 19The person who made the
idol never stops to reflect, "Why, it's just a block of
wood! I burned half of it for heat and used it to bake
my bread and roast my meat. How can the rest of it
be a god? Should I bow down to worship a chunk of
wood?" 20The poor, deluded fool feeds on ashes. He
is trusting something that can give him no help at

all. Yet he cannot bring himself to ask, "Is this thing, this idol that I'm holding in my hand, a lie?"

21"Pay attention, O Israel, for you are my servant. I, the LORD, made you, and I will not forget to help you. 22I have swept away your sins like the morning mists. I have scattered your offenses like the clouds. Oh, return to me, for I have paid the price to set you free."

23Sing, O heavens, for the LORD has done this wondrous thing. Shout, O earth! Break forth into song, O mountains and forests and every tree! For the LORD has redeemed Jacob and is glorified in Israel.

24The LORD, your Redeemer and Creator, says: "I am the LORD, who made all things. I alone stretched out the heavens. By myself I made the earth and everything in it. 25I am the one who exposes the false prophets as liars by causing events to happen that are contrary to their predictions. I cause wise people to give bad advice, thus proving them to be fools. 26But I carry out the predictions of my prophets! When they say Jerusalem will be saved and the towns of Judah will be lived in once again, it will be done! 27When I speak to the rivers and say, 'Be dry!' they will be dry. 28When I say of Cyrus, 'He is my shepherd,' he will certainly do as I say. He will command that Jerusalem be rebuilt and that the Temple be restored."

**PROPHECIES ● ● • • •**

**44:28 Isaiah, who lived from about 740 to 681 B.C., called Cyrus by name almost 150 years before he ruled (559–530 B.C.)! Later historians said that Cyrus read this prophecy and was so moved that he carried it out. Isaiah also had predicted the fall of Jerusalem more than 100 years before it happened (586 B.C.), and the rebuilding of the Temple about 200 years before it happened. Obviously these prophecies came from a God who knows the future.**

## CHAPTER 45

**THE ONE, TRUE GOD.** This is what the LORD says to Cyrus, his anointed one, whose right hand he will empower. Before him, mighty kings will be paralyzed with fear. Their fortress gates will be opened, never again to shut against him. 2This is what the LORD says: "I will go before you, Cyrus, and level the mountains.* I will smash down gates of bronze and cut through bars of iron. 3And I will give you treasures hidden in the darkness—secret riches. I will do this so you may know that I am the LORD, the God of Israel, the one who calls you by name.

4"And why have I called you for this work? It is for the sake of Jacob my servant, Israel my chosen one. I called you by name when you did not know me. 5I am the LORD; there is no other God. I have prepared you, even though you do not know me, 6so all the world from east to west will know there is no other God. I am the LORD, and there is no other. 7I am the one who creates the light and makes the darkness. I am the one who sends good times and bad times. I, the LORD, am the one who does these things. 8Open up, O heavens, and pour out your righteousness. Let the earth open wide so salvation and righteousness can sprout up together. I, the LORD, created them.

9"Destruction is certain for those who argue with their Creator. Does a clay pot ever argue with its maker? Does the clay dispute with the one who shapes it, saying, 'Stop, you are doing it wrong!' Does the pot exclaim, 'How clumsy can you be!' 10How terrible it would be if a newborn baby said to its father and mother, 'Why was I born? Why did you make me this way?'"

11This is what the LORD, the Creator and Holy One of Israel, says: "Do you question what I do? Do you give me orders about the work of my hands? 12I am the one who made the earth and created people to live on it. With my hands I stretched out the heavens. All the millions of stars are at my command. 13I will raise up Cyrus to fulfill my righteous purpose, and I will guide all his actions. He will restore my city and free my captive people—and not for a reward! I, the LORD Almighty, have spoken!"

14This is what the LORD says: "The Egyptians, Ethiopians,* and Sabeans will be subject to you. They will come to you with all their merchandise, and it will all be yours. They will follow you as prisoners in chains. They will fall to their knees in front of you and say, 'God is with you, and he is the only God.'"

15Truly, O God of Israel, our Savior, you work in strange and mysterious ways. 16All who make idols will be humiliated and disgraced. 17But the LORD will save the people of Israel with eternal salvation. They will never again be humiliated and disgraced throughout everlasting ages. 18For the LORD is God, and he created the heavens and earth and put everything in place. He made the world to be lived in, not to be a place of empty chaos.

"I am the LORD," he says, "and there is no other. 19I publicly proclaim bold promises. I do not whisper obscurities in some dark corner so no one can understand what I mean. And I did not tell the people of Israel* to ask me for something I did not plan to give. I, the LORD, speak only what is true and right.

20"Gather together and come, you fugitives from surrounding nations. What fools they are who carry around their wooden idols and pray to gods that cannot save! 21Consult together, argue your case, and state your proofs that idol worship pays. Who made these things known long ago? What idol ever told you they would happen? Was it not

**BAD TIMES ● ● • • •**

**45:7 God tells us that he sends the good times and the bad. Our life is sprinkled with both types of experiences, and both are needed for us to grow spiritually. When good times come, thank God and use your prosperity for him. When bad times come, don't resent them, but ask what you can learn from this refining experience to make you a better servant of God.**

45:2 As in Dead Sea Scrolls and Greek version; Masoretic Text reads *the swellings.* 45:14 Hebrew *Cushites.* 45:19 Hebrew *of Jacob.*

I, the LORD? For there is no other God but me—a
just God and a Savior—no, not one! [22]Let all the
world look to me for salvation! For I am God; there
is no other. [23]I have sworn by my own name, and I
will never go back on my word: Every knee will
bow to me, and every tongue will confess allegiance to my name."

[24]The people will declare, "The LORD is the source
of all my righteousness and strength." And all who
were angry with him will come to him and be
ashamed. [25]In the LORD all the generations of Israel
will be justified, and in him they will boast.

## CHAPTER 46 WHO CAN COMPARE TO GOD?

The idols
of Babylon, Bel and Nebo, are being hauled away on
ox carts. But look! The beasts are staggering under
the weight! [2]Both the idols and the ones carrying
them are bowed down. The gods cannot protect the
people, and the people cannot protect the gods. They
go off into captivity together.

[3]"Listen to me, all you who are left in Israel. I
created you and have cared for you since before you
were born. [4]I will be your God throughout your
lifetime—until your hair is white with age. I made
you, and I will care for you. I will carry you along and
save you.

[5]"To whom will you compare me? Who is my
equal? [6]Some people pour out their silver and gold
and hire a craftsman to make a god from it. Then
they bow down and worship it! [7]They carry it around
on their shoulders, and when they set it down, it
stays there. It cannot even move! And when someone prays to it, there is no answer. It has no power to
get anyone out of trouble.

[8]"Do not forget this, you guilty ones. [9]And do not
forget the things I have done
throughout history. For I am
God—I alone! I am God, and
there is no one else like me. [10]Only
I can tell you what is going to happen even before it happens. Everything I plan will come to pass, for
I do whatever I wish. [11]I will call a
swift bird of prey from the east—a
leader from a distant land who
will come and do my bidding. I
have said I would do it, and I will.
[12]Listen to me, you stubborn, evil
people! [13]For I am ready to set
things right, not in the distant future, but right now! I am ready to
save Jerusalem* and give my glory
to Israel.

## CHAPTER 47 GOD'S REVENGE.

"Come, Babylon, unconquered
one, sit in the dust. For your days
of glory, pomp, and honor have
ended. O daughter of Babylonia,* never again will you be the
lovely princess, tender and delicate. [2]Take heavy
millstones and grind the corn. Remove your veil and
strip off your robe. Expose yourself to public view.
[3]You will be naked and burdened with shame. I will
take vengeance against you and will not negotiate."

[4]Our Redeemer, whose name is the LORD Almighty, is the Holy One of Israel.

[5]"O daughter of Babylonia, sit now in darkness
and silence. Never again will you be known as the
queen of kingdoms. [6]For I was angry with my chosen
people and began their punishment by letting them
fall into your hands. But you, Babylon, showed them
no mercy. You have forced even the elderly to carry
heavy burdens. [7]You thought, 'I will reign forever as
queen of the world!' You did not care at all about my
people or think about the consequences of your
actions.

[8]"You are a pleasure-crazy kingdom, living at ease
and feeling secure, bragging as if you were the greatest in the world! You say, 'I'm self-sufficient and not
accountable to anyone! I will never be a widow or
lose my children.' [9]Well, those two things will come
upon you in a moment: widowhood and the loss of

### POWER ● ● • • •

47:8-9 **Caught up in the pursuit of power and pleasure, Babylon believed in its own greatness and claimed to be the *only* power on earth. Babylon felt completely secure. Nebuchadnezzar, its king, called himself "god," but the true God taught him a powerful lesson by taking everything away from him (Daniel 4:27-37). Our society is addicted to pleasure and power, but these can pass away quickly. Look at your own life and ask yourself how you can be more responsible with the talents and possessions God has given you. How can you use your life to honor God rather than yourself?**

### "Here's what I did..."

When my family moved from Mexico to the United States, everything familiar to me was gone. I had to learn a new language, adjust to totally different ways of doing things, and make friends with people who seemed to have grown up on a different planet rather than in a different country. I was very, very lonely for a long time.

I turned often to the Bible. So many verses were meaningful to me. But Isaiah 46:4 especially helped because it spoke of God's tender care and how he would be with me always, even when I'm old. I would imagine God right there with me in this strange school, and I'd talk to him in my heart, telling him how I felt. It was a great comfort to know that he was right there with me and that he cared. I knew he heard my prayers and understood—and I could speak to him in Spanish! This experience has brought me closer to God as I depend on him every day for the understanding and help I need to make this adjustment.

Julio

AGE 16

46:13 Hebrew *Zion.* 47:1 Or *Chaldea;* also in 47:5.

your children. Yes, these calamities will come upon you, despite all your witchcraft and magic.

10"You felt secure in all your wickedness. 'No one sees me,' you said. Your 'wisdom' and 'knowledge' have caused you to turn away from me and claim, 'I am self-sufficient and not accountable to anyone!' 11So disaster will overtake you suddenly, and you won't be able to charm it away. Calamity will fall upon you, and you won't be able to buy your way out. A catastrophe will arise so fast that you won't know what hit you.

12"Call out the demon hordes you have worshiped all these years. Ask them to help you strike terror into the hearts of people once again. 13You have more than enough advisers, astrologers, and stargazers. Let them stand up and save you from what the future holds. 14But they are as useless as dried grass burning in a fire. They cannot even save themselves! You will get no help from them at all. Their hearth is not a place to sit for warmth. 15And all your friends, those with whom you have done business since childhood, will slip away and disappear, unable to help.

**PLAIN ● • • •**

48:16 **God's message has been told plainly and clearly, not in secret. We have a tendency to complicate God's message. When God talks through his messenger, whomever he has chosen, our job is to listen. The closer we come to God, the better we can listen to what he says.**

## CHAPTER 48 **NO PEACE FOR THE WICKED.**

"Listen to me, O family of Jacob, who are called by the name of Israel and born into the family of Judah. Listen, you who take oaths in the name of the LORD and call on the God of Israel. You don't follow through on any of your promises, 2even though you call yourself the holy city and talk about depending on the God of Israel, whose name is the LORD Almighty. 3Time and again I warned you about what was going to happen in the future. Then suddenly I took action, and all my predictions came true.

4"I know how stubborn and obstinate you are. Your necks are as unbending as iron. You are as hardheaded as bronze. 5That is why I told you ahead of time what I was going to do. That way, you could never say, 'My idols did it. My wooden image and metal god commanded it to happen!' 6You have heard my predictions and seen them fulfilled, but you refuse to admit it. Now I will tell you new things I have not mentioned before, secrets you have not yet heard. 7They are brand new, not things from the past. So you cannot say, 'We knew that all the time!'

8"Yes, I will tell you of things that are entirely new, for I know so well what traitors you are. You have been rebels from your earliest childhood, rotten through and through. 9Yet for my own sake and for the honor of my name, I will hold back my anger and not wipe you out. 10I have refined you but not in

**DESERTED ● ● • • •**

49:14-15 **The people of Israel felt that God had deserted them in Babylon, but Isaiah points out that God would never leave them, as a mother would not leave her little child. When we feel that God has deserted us, we must ask if we have deserted God.**

the way silver is refined. Rather, I have refined you in the furnace of suffering. 11I will rescue you for my sake—yes, for my own sake! That way, the pagan nations will not be able to claim that their gods have conquered me. I will not let them have my glory!

12"Listen to me, O family of Jacob, Israel my chosen one! I alone am God, the First and the Last. 13It was my hand that laid the foundations of the earth. The palm of my right hand spread out the heavens above. I spoke, and they came into being.

14"Have any of your idols ever told you this? Come, all of you, and listen: 'The LORD has chosen Cyrus as his ally. He will use him to put an end to the empire of Babylon, destroying the Babylonian* armies.' 15I have said it: I am calling Cyrus! I will send him on this errand and will help him succeed. 16Come closer and listen. I have always told you plainly what would happen so you would have no trouble understanding."

And now the Sovereign LORD and his Spirit have sent me with this message: 17"The LORD, your Redeemer, the Holy One of Israel, says: I am the LORD your God, who teaches you what is good and leads you along the paths you should follow. 18Oh, that you had listened to my commands! Then you would have had peace flowing like a gentle river and righteousness rolling like waves. 19Then you would have become as numerous as the sands along the seashore—too many to count! There would have been no need for your destruction."

20Yet even now, be free from your captivity! Leave Babylon and the Babylonians,* singing as you go! Shout to the ends of the earth that the LORD has redeemed his servants, the people of Israel.* 21They were not thirsty when he led them through the desert. He divided the rock, and water gushed out for them to drink.

22"But there is no peace for the wicked," says the LORD.

## CHAPTER 49 **A LIGHT FOR THE WORLD.**

Listen to me, all of you in far-off lands! The LORD called me before my birth; from within the womb he called me by name. 2He made my words of judgment as sharp as a sword. He has hidden me in the shadow of his hand. I am like a sharp arrow in his quiver.

3He said to me, "You are my servant, Israel, and you will bring me glory."

4I replied, "But my work all seems so useless! I have spent my strength for nothing and to no purpose at all. Yet I leave it all in the LORD's hand; I will trust God for my reward."

5And now the LORD speaks—he who formed me in my mother's womb to be his servant, who commissioned me to bring his people of Israel back to

48:14 Or *Chaldean.* 48:20a Or *the Chaldeans.* 48:20b Hebrew *his servant, Jacob.*

him. The LORD has honored me, and my God has given me strength. 6He says, "You will do more than restore the people of Israel to me. I will make you a light to the Gentiles, and you will bring my salvation to the ends of the earth."

7The LORD, the Redeemer and Holy One of Israel, says to the one who is despised and rejected by a nation, to the one who is the servant of rulers: "Kings will stand at attention when you pass by. Princes will bow low because the LORD has chosen you. He, the faithful LORD, the Holy One of Israel, chooses you."

8This is what the LORD says: "At just the right time, I will respond to you. On the day of salvation, I will help you. I will give you as a token and pledge to Israel. This will prove that I will reestablish the land of Israel and reassign it to its own people again. 9Through you I am saying to the prisoners of darkness, 'Come out! I am giving you your freedom!' They will be my sheep, grazing in green pastures and on hills that were previously bare. 10They will neither hunger nor thirst. The searing sun and scorching desert winds will not reach them anymore. For the LORD in his mercy will lead them beside cool waters. 11And I will make my mountains into level paths for them. The highways will be raised above the valleys. 12See, my people will return from far away, from lands to the north and west, and from as far south as Egypt.*"

13Sing for joy, O heavens! Rejoice, O earth! Burst into song, O mountains! For the LORD has comforted his people and will have compassion on them in their sorrow.

14Yet Jerusalem* says, "The LORD has deserted us; the Lord has forgotten us."

15"Never! Can a mother forget her nursing child? Can she feel no love for a child she has borne? But even if that were possible, I would not forget you! 16See, I have written your name on my hand. Ever before me is a picture of Jerusalem's walls in ruins. 17Soon your descendants will come back, and all who are trying to destroy you will go away. 18Look and see, for all your children will come back to you. As surely as I live," says the LORD, "they will be like jewels or bridal ornaments for you to display.

19"Even the most desolate parts of your abandoned land will soon be crowded with your people. Your enemies who enslaved you will be far away. 20The generations born in exile will return and say, 'We need more room! It's crowded here!' 21Then you will think to yourself, 'Who has given me all these descendants? For most of my children were killed, and the rest were carried away into exile. I was left here all alone. Who bore these children? Who raised them for me?'"

22This is what the Sovereign LORD says: "See, I will give a signal to the godless nations. They will carry your little sons back to you in their arms; they will bring your daughters on their shoulders. 23Kings and queens will serve you. They will care for all your needs. They will bow to the earth before you and lick the dust from your feet. Then you will know that I am the LORD. Those who wait for me will never be put to shame."

24Who can snatch the plunder of war from the hands of a warrior? Who can demand that a tyrant* let his captives go? 25But the LORD says, "The captives of warriors will be released, and the plunder of tyrants will be retrieved. For I will fight those who fight you, and I will save your children. 26I will feed your enemies with their own flesh. They will be drunk with rivers of their own blood. All the world will know that I, the LORD, am your Savior and Redeemer, the Mighty One of Israel.*"

**I used to look up my horoscope every day in the paper before a friend told me it was satanic. Do Christians believe in astrology?**

There are many "windows" that may lead people into satanic influence.

When Saul was king of Israel and in trouble, he consulted a medium (a witch) to gain knowledge of the future (see 1 Samuel 28). Isaiah 47:12-15 shows how effective such foretellers of the future really are. Many other passages deal with astrology, divination, wizards, sorcery, and soothsayers (see Deuteronomy 18:10-11; 2 Chronicles 33:6; Daniel 2:1-2; Acts 8:9-11; 16:16).

If Satan can get people to take in evil small doses at a time, eventually they may become desensitized and not recognize that they are being fed something that will dull their interest in God.

It's like the boy who tried to boil a frog. He filled up a beaker with water, put it on the Bunsen burner until it was boiling, and then put the frog in. Immediately the frog jumped out of the water. Had the boy put the frog in cold water and then slowly turned up the heat, the frog would have gotten used to its surroundings and put up with the increasing heat, unaware it was boiling to death.

Satan would never get anyone to follow him if he revealed all his evil. Instead, he slowly gives us small doses of evil until we're so desensitized to it that it seems a normal part of life.

This is the strategy: to capture our mind through one small compromise into darkness after another.

Our best defense is to know the truth of the Word of God, so we can discern when we are being tempted by evil. God knows it is real. And Jesus came to destroy the works of the devil. Remember, "the Spirit who lives in you is greater than the spirit who lives in the world" (1 John 4:4).

49:12 As in Dead Sea Scrolls, which read *from the region of Aswan,* which is in southern Egypt. Masoretic Text reads *from the region of Sinim.*
49:14 Hebrew *Zion.* 49:24 As in Dead Sea Scrolls, Syriac version, and Latin Vulgate (also see 49:25); Masoretic Text reads *a righteous person.*
49:26 Hebrew *of Jacob.*

## CHAPTER 50 GOD'S SERVANT OBEYS.

The LORD asks, "Did I sell you as slaves to my creditors? Is that why you are not here? Is your mother gone because I divorced her and sent her away? No, you went away as captives because of your sins. And your mother, too, was taken because of your sins. 2Was I too weak to save you? Is that why the house is silent and empty when I come home? Is it because I have no power to rescue? No, that is not the reason! For I can speak to the sea and make it dry! I can turn rivers into deserts covered with dying fish. 3I am the one who sends darkness out across the skies, bringing it to a state of mourning."

4The Sovereign LORD has given me his words of wisdom, so that I know what to say to all these weary ones. Morning by morning he wakens me and opens my understanding to his will. 5The Sovereign LORD has spoken to me, and I have listened. I do not rebel or turn away. 6I give my back to those who beat me and my cheeks to those who pull out my beard. I do not hide from shame, for they mock me and spit in my face.

7Because the Sovereign LORD helps me, I will not be dismayed. Therefore, I have set my face like a stone, determined to do his will. And I know that I will triumph. 8He who gives me justice is near. Who will dare to oppose me now? Where are my enemies? Let them appear! 9See, the Sovereign LORD is on my side! Who will declare me guilty? All my enemies will be destroyed like old clothes that have been eaten by moths!

10Who among you fears the LORD and obeys his servant? If you are walking in darkness, without a ray of light, trust in the LORD and rely on your God. 11But watch out, you who live in your own light and warm yourselves by your own fires. This is the reward you will receive from me: You will soon lie down in great torment.

### RIDICULE ● ● • • •

**51:7 Isaiah encouraged those who served God to discern right from wrong and to follow God's laws. He also gave them hope when they faced people's scorn or slander because of their faith. We need not fear when people ridicule us for our faith because God is with us and truth will prevail. If people make fun of you or dislike you because you believe in God, remember that they are not against you personally, but against God. He will deal with them; you should concentrate on loving and obeying him.**

## CHAPTER 51 THE PEOPLE MUST FEAR GOD.

"Listen to me, all who hope for deliverance—all who seek the LORD! Consider the quarry from which you were mined, the rock from which you were cut! 2Yes, think about your ancestors Abraham and Sarah, from whom you came. Abraham was alone when I called him. But when I blessed him, he became a great nation."

3The LORD will comfort Israel* again and make her deserts blossom. Her barren wilderness will become as beautiful as Eden—the garden of the LORD. Joy and gladness will be found there. Lovely songs of thanksgiving will fill the air.

4"Listen to me, my people. Hear me, Israel, for my law will be proclaimed, and my justice will become a light to the nations. 5My mercy and justice are coming soon. Your salvation is on the way. I will rule the nations. They will wait for me and long for my power. 6Look up to the skies above, and gaze down on the earth beneath. For the skies will disappear like smoke, and the earth will wear out like a piece of clothing. The people of the earth will die like flies, but my salvation lasts forever. My righteous rule will never end!

7"Listen to me, you who know right from wrong and cherish my law in your hearts. Do not be afraid of people's scorn or their slanderous talk. 8For the moth will destroy them as it destroys clothing. The worm will eat away at them as it eats wool. But my righteousness will last forever. My salvation will continue from generation to generation."

9Wake up, LORD! Robe yourself with strength! Rouse yourself as in the days of old when you slew Egypt, the dragon of the Nile.* 10Are you not the same today, the one who dried up the sea, making a path of escape when you saved your people? 11Those who have been ransomed by the LORD will return to Jerusalem,* singing songs of everlasting joy. Sorrow and mourning will disappear, and they will be overcome with joy and gladness.

12"I, even I, am the one who comforts you. So why are you afraid of mere humans, who wither like the grass and disappear? 13Yet you have forgotten the LORD, your Creator, the one who put the stars in the sky and established the earth. Will you remain in constant dread of human oppression? Will you continue to fear the anger of your enemies from morning till night? 14Soon all you captives will be released! Imprisonment, starvation, and death will not be your fate! 15For I am the LORD your God, who stirs up the sea, causing its waves to roar. My name is the LORD Almighty. 16And I have put my words in your mouth and hidden you safely within my hand. I set all the stars in space and established the earth. I am the one who says to Israel, 'You are mine!'"

17Wake up, wake up, O Jerusalem! You have drunk enough from the cup of the LORD's fury. You have drunk the cup of terror, tipping out its last drops. 18Not one of your children is left alive to help you or tell you what to do. 19These two things have been your lot: desolation and destruction, famine and war. And who is left to sympathize? Who is left to comfort you? 20For your children have fainted and lie in the streets, helpless as antelopes caught in a net. The LORD has poured out his fury; God has rebuked them.

21But now listen to this, you afflicted ones, who sit

51:3 Hebrew *Zion;* also in 51:16. 51:9 Hebrew *slew Rahab the dragon.* Rahab is the name of a mythical sea monster that represents chaos in ancient literature. The name is used here as a poetic name for Egypt. 51:11 Hebrew *Zion.*

in a drunken stupor, though not from drinking wine.
[22]This is what the Sovereign LORD, your God and
Defender, says: "See, I am taking the terrible cup
from your hands. You will drink no more of my fury.
It is gone at last! [23]But I will put that cup into the
hands of those who tormented you. I will give it to
those who trampled you into the dust and walked on
your backs."

CHAPTER **52** **GOD BRINGS HIS PEOPLE HOME.** Wake
up, wake up, O Zion! Clothe yourselves with strength.
Put on your beautiful clothes, O holy city of Jerusalem,
for unclean and godless people will no longer enter
your gates. [2]Rise from the dust, O Jerusalem. Remove
the slave bands from your neck, O captive daughter of
Zion. [3]For this is what the LORD says: "When I sold you
into exile, I received no payment. Now I can redeem
you without paying for you."

[4]This is what the Sovereign LORD says: "Long ago
my people went to live as resident foreigners in
Egypt. Now they have been oppressed without cause
by Assyria. [5]And now, what is this?" asks the LORD.
"Why are my people enslaved again? Those who rule
them shout in exultation. My name is being blasphemed all day long. [6]But I will reveal my name to
my people, and they will come to know its power.
Then at last they will recognize that it is I who speaks
to them."

[7]How beautiful on the mountains are the feet of
those who bring good news of peace and salvation, the
news that the God of Israel* reigns! [8]The watchmen
shout and sing with joy, for before their very eyes they
see the LORD bringing his people home to Jerusalem.*
[9]Let the ruins of Jerusalem break into joyful song, for
the LORD has comforted his people. He has redeemed
Jerusalem. [10]The LORD will demonstrate his holy
power before the eyes of all the nations. The ends of
the earth will see the salvation of our God.

[11]Go now, leave your bonds and slavery. Put Babylon behind you, with everything it represents, for it
is unclean to you. You are the LORD's holy people.
Purify yourselves, you who carry home the vessels of
the LORD. [12]You will not leave in a hurry, running for
your lives. For the LORD will go ahead of you, and the
God of Israel will protect you from behind.

[13]See, my servant will prosper; he will be highly
exalted. [14]Many were amazed when they saw him*—
beaten and bloodied, so disfigured one would
scarcely know he was a person. [15]And he will again
startle* many nations. Kings will stand speechless in
his presence. For they will see what they had not
previously been told about; they will understand
what they had not heard about.

CHAPTER **53** Who has believed our message?
To whom will the LORD reveal his saving power? [2]My
servant grew up in the LORD's presence like a tender
green shoot, sprouting from a root in dry and sterile
ground. There was nothing beautiful or majestic

**MESSIAH ● ● • • •**

52:13 **The servant, as the term is used here, is the Messiah, our Lord Jesus. He would be highly exalted because of his sacrifice, described in chapter 53.**

about his appearance, nothing to attract us to him.
[3]He was despised and rejected—a man of sorrows,
acquainted with bitterest grief. We turned our backs
on him and looked the other way when he went by.
He was despised, and we did not care.

[4]Yet it was our weaknesses he carried; it was our
sorrows* that weighed him down. And we thought
his troubles were a punishment from God for his
own sins! [5]But he was wounded and crushed for our
sins. He was beaten that we might have peace. He
was whipped, and we were healed! [6]All of us have
strayed away like sheep. We have left God's paths to
follow our own. Yet the LORD laid on him the guilt
and sins of us all.

[7]He was oppressed and treated harshly, yet he never
said a word. He was led as a lamb to the slaughter. And
as a sheep is silent before the shearers, he did not open
his mouth. [8]From prison and trial they led him away
to his death. But who among the people realized that
he was dying for their sins—that he was suffering their
punishment? [9]He had done no wrong, and he never
deceived anyone. But he was buried like a criminal; he
was put in a rich man's grave.

[10]But it was the LORD's good plan to crush him and
fill him with grief. Yet when his life is made an
offering for sin, he will have a multitude of children,
many heirs. He will enjoy a long life, and the LORD's
plan will prosper in his hands. [11]When he sees all
that is accomplished by his anguish, he will be satisfied. And because of what he has experienced, my
righteous servant will make it possible for many to
be counted righteous, for he will bear all their sins.
[12]I will give him the honors of one who is mighty
and great, because he exposed himself to death. He
was counted among those who were sinners. He
bore the sins of many and interceded for sinners.

CHAPTER **54** **EVERLASTING LOVE.** "Sing, O childless woman! Break forth into loud and joyful song,
O Jerusalem, even though you never gave birth to a
child. For the woman who could bear no children
now has more than all the other women," says the
LORD. [2]"Enlarge your house; build an addition;
spread out your home! [3]For you will soon be bursting at the seams. Your descendants will take over
other nations and live in their cities.

[4]"Fear not; you will no longer live in shame. The
shame of your youth and the sorrows of widowhood
will be remembered no more, [5]for your Creator will
be your husband. The LORD Almighty is his name!
He is your Redeemer, the Holy One of Israel, the God
of all the earth. [6]For the LORD has called you back
from your grief—as though you were a young wife

52:7 Hebrew *of Zion.* 52:8 Hebrew *to Zion.* 52:14 As in Syriac version; Hebrew reads *you.* 52:15 Or *cleanse.* 53:4 Or *Yet it was our sicknesses he carried; it was our diseases.*

He
was
WOUNDED
and
CRUSHED
for
OUR SINS.
He
was
beaten
that we might have
PEACE.
He
was
whipped,
and we were
HEALED!

ISAIAH 53:5

abandoned by her husband," says your God. [7]"For a brief moment I abandoned you, but with great compassion I will take you back. [8]In a moment of anger I turned my face away for a little while. But with everlasting love I will have compassion on you," says the LORD, your Redeemer.

[9]"Just as I swore in the time of Noah that I would never again let a flood cover the earth and destroy its life, so now I swear that I will never again pour out my anger on you. [10]For the mountains may depart and the hills disappear, but even then I will remain loyal to you. My covenant of blessing will never be broken," says the LORD, who has mercy on you.

[11]"O storm-battered city, troubled and desolate! I will rebuild you on a foundation of sapphires and make the walls of your houses from precious jewels. [12]I will make your towers of sparkling rubies and your gates and walls of shining gems. [13]I will teach all your citizens, and their prosperity will be great. [14]You will live under a government that is just and fair. Your enemies will stay far away; you will live in peace. Terror will not come near. [15]If any nation comes to fight you, it will not be because I sent them to punish you. Your enemies will always be defeated because I am on your side. [16]I have created the blacksmith who fans the coals beneath the forge and makes the weapons of destruction. And I have created the armies that destroy. [17]But in that coming day, no weapon turned against you will succeed. And everyone who tells lies in court will be brought to justice. These benefits are enjoyed by the servants of the LORD; their vindication will come from me. I, the LORD, have spoken!

CHAPTER **55** **A PROMISE OF JOY AND PEACE.** "Is anyone thirsty? Come and drink—even if you have no money! Come, take your choice of wine or milk—it's all free! [2]Why spend your money on food that does not give you strength? Why pay for food that does you no good? Listen, and I will tell you where to get food that is good for the soul!

[3]"Come to me with your ears wide open. Listen, for the life of your soul is at stake. I am ready to make an everlasting covenant with you. I will give you all the mercies and unfailing love that I promised to David. [4]He displayed my power by being my witness and a leader among the nations. [5]You also will command the nations, and they will come running to obey, because I, the LORD your God, the Holy One of Israel, have made you glorious."

[6]Seek the LORD while you can find him. Call on him now while he is near. [7]Let the people turn from their wicked deeds. Let them banish from their minds the very thought of doing wrong! Let them turn to the LORD that he may have mercy on them. Yes, turn to our God, for he will abundantly pardon.

[8]"My thoughts are completely different from yours," says the LORD. "And my ways are far beyond anything you could imagine. [9]For just as the heavens

**REUNION ● • • • •**

**54:6-8 God says that he has abandoned Israel for a brief time, so she is like a young wife abandoned by her husband. But he still calls Israel his own. The God we serve is holy, and he cannot tolerate sin. When Israel blatantly sinned, God in his anger chose to punish her. Sin separates us from God and brings us pain and suffering. But if we confess our sin and repent, God forgives us. Have you ever been separated from a loved one and then experienced joy when that person returned? You can experience the same joy when you repent and return to God.**

are higher than the earth, so are my ways higher than your ways and my thoughts higher than your thoughts.

10"The rain and snow come down from the heavens and stay on the ground to water the earth. They cause the grain to grow, producing seed for the farmer and bread for the hungry. 11It is the same with my word. I send it out, and it always produces fruit. It will accomplish all I want it to, and it will prosper everywhere I send it. 12You will live in joy and peace. The mountains and hills will burst into song, and the trees of the field will clap their hands! 13Where once there were thorns, cypress trees will grow. Where briers grew, myrtles will sprout up. This miracle will bring great honor to the LORD's name; it will be an everlasting sign of his power and love.

CHAPTER **56** **GOD WILL COME TO THE RESCUE.** "Be just and fair to all," says the LORD. "Do what is right and good, for I am coming soon to rescue you. 2Blessed are those who are careful to do this. Blessed are those who honor my Sabbath days of rest by refusing to work. And blessed are those who keep themselves from doing wrong.

3"And my blessings are for Gentiles, too, when they commit themselves to the LORD. Do not let them think that I consider them second-class citizens. And my blessings are also for the eunuchs. They are as much mine as anyone else. 4For I say this to the eunuchs who keep my Sabbath days holy, who choose to do what pleases me and commit their lives to me: 5I will give them—in my house, within my walls—a memorial and a name far greater than the honor they would have received by having sons and daughters. For the name I give them is an everlasting one. It will never disappear!

6"I will also bless the Gentiles who commit themselves to the LORD and serve him and love his name, who worship him and do not desecrate the Sabbath day of rest, and who have accepted his covenant. 7I will bring them also to my holy mountain of Jerusalem and will fill them with joy in my house of prayer. I will accept their burnt offerings and sacrifices, because my Temple will be called a house of prayer for all nations. 8For the Sovereign LORD, who brings back the outcasts of Israel, says: I will bring others, too, besides my people Israel."

9Come, wild animals of the field! Come, wild animals of the forest! Come and devour my people! 10For the leaders of my people—the LORD's watchmen, his shepherds—are blind to every danger. They are like silent watchdogs that give no warning when danger comes. They love to lie around, sleeping and dreaming. 11And they are as greedy as dogs, never satisfied. They are stupid shepherds, all following their own path, all of them intent on personal gain.

12"Come," they say. "We will get some wine and have a party. Let's all get drunk. Let this go on and on, and tomorrow will be even better."

**CALL NOW ● ● • • •**

55:6 **Isaiah tells us to call upon the Lord while he is near. God is not planning to move away from us, but we often move far from God or erect a barrier between ourself and him. Don't wait until you have drifted away from God to seek him. Turning to God may be far more difficult later in life. Or God may come to judge the earth before you decide to seek him. Do it now while you can, before it is too late.**

CHAPTER **57** **A REWARD FOR LOVING GOD.** The righteous pass away; the godly often die before their time. And no one seems to care or wonder why. No one seems to understand that God is protecting them from the evil to come. 2For the godly who die will rest in peace.

3"But you—come here, you witches' children, you offspring of adulterers and prostitutes! 4Whom do you mock, making faces and sticking out your tongues? You children of sinners and liars! 5You worship your idols with great passion beneath every green tree. You slaughter your children as human sacrifices down in the valleys, under overhanging rocks. 6Your gods are the smooth stones in the valleys. You worship them with drink offerings and grain offerings. They, not I, are your inheritance. Does all this make me happy? 7You have committed adultery on the mountaintops by worshiping idols there, and so you have been unfaithful to me. 8Behind closed doors, you have set up your idols and worship them instead of me. This is adultery, for you are loving these idols instead of loving me. You have climbed right into bed with these detestable gods. 9You have given olive oil and perfume to Molech* as your gift. You have traveled far, even into the world of the dead,* to find new gods to love. 10You grew weary in your search, but you never gave up. You strengthened yourself and went on. 11Why were you more afraid of them than of me? How is it that you don't even remember me or think about me? Is it because I have not corrected you that you have no fear of me?

12"Now I will expose your so-called good deeds that you consider so righteous. None of them will benefit or save you. 13Let's see if your idols can do anything for you when you cry to them for help. They are so helpless that a breath of wind can knock them down! But whoever trusts in me will possess the land and inherit my holy mountain. 14I will say, 'Rebuild the road! Clear away the rocks and stones so my people can return from captivity.'"

15The high and lofty one who inhabits eternity, the Holy One, says this: "I live in that high and holy

**GOOD DEEDS ● ● • • •**

57:12 **Isaiah warned these people that their righteousness and good deeds would not save them any more than their weak, worthless idols. We cannot gain our salvation through good deeds because our best deeds are not good enough to outweigh our sins. Salvation is a gift from God.**

**57:9a** Or *to the king.* **57:9b** Hebrew *into Sheol.*

## TRUE WORSHIP ● ● • • •

58:1-7 **True worship was more than religious ritual, going to the Temple every day, and listening to Scripture readings. These people missed the point of a living, vital relationship with God. He doesn't want us fasting or acting pious when we have unforgiven sin in our heart and perform sinful practices with our hands. Even more important than correct worship and doctrine is genuine compassion for the poor, the helpless, and the oppressed.**

place with those whose spirits are contrite and humble. I refresh the humble and give new courage to those with repentant hearts. [16]For I will not fight against you forever; I will not always show my anger. If I did, all people would pass away—all the souls I have made. [17]I was angry and punished these greedy people. I withdrew myself from them, but they went right on sinning. [18]I have seen what they do, but I will heal them anyway! I will lead them and comfort those who mourn. [19]Then words of praise will be on their lips. May they have peace, both near and far, for I will heal them all," says the LORD. [20]"But those who still reject me are like the restless sea. It is never still but continually churns up mire and dirt. [21]There is no peace for the wicked," says my God.

## CHAPTER 58 **GOD TELLS THE PEOPLE TO SHARE.**

"Shout with the voice of a trumpet blast. Tell my people Israel* of their sins! [2]Yet they act so pious! They come to the Temple every day and seem delighted to hear my laws. You would almost think this was a righteous nation that would never abandon its God. They love to make a show of coming to me and asking me to take action on their behalf. [3]'We have fasted before you!' they say. 'Why aren't you impressed? We have done much penance, and you don't even notice it!'

"I will tell you why! It's because you are living for yourselves even while you are fasting. You keep right on oppressing your workers. [4]What good is fasting when you keep on fighting and quarreling? This kind of fasting will never get you anywhere with me. [5]You humble yourselves by going through the motions of penance, bowing your heads like a blade of grass in the wind. You dress in sackcloth and cover yourselves with ashes. Is this what you call fasting? Do you really think this will please the LORD?

[6]"No, the kind of fasting I want calls you to free those who are wrongly imprisoned and to stop oppressing those who work for you. Treat them fairly and give them what they earn. [7]I want you to share your food with the hungry and to welcome poor wanderers into your homes. Give clothes to those who need them, and do not hide from relatives who need your help.

[8]"If you do these things, your salvation will come like the dawn. Yes, your healing will come quickly. Your godliness will lead you forward, and the glory of the LORD will protect you from behind. [9]Then when you call, the LORD will answer. 'Yes, I am here,' he will quickly reply.

"Stop oppressing the helpless and stop making false accusations and spreading vicious rumors! [10]Feed the hungry and help those in trouble. Then your light will shine out from the darkness, and the darkness around you will be as bright as day. [11]The LORD will guide you continually, watering your life when you are dry and keeping you healthy, too. You will be like a well-watered garden, like an ever-flowing spring. [12]Your children will rebuild the deserted ruins of your cities. Then you will be known as the people who rebuild their walls and cities.

[13]"Keep the Sabbath day holy. Don't pursue your own interests on that day, but enjoy the Sabbath and speak of it with delight as the LORD's holy day. Honor the LORD in everything you do, and don't follow your own desires or talk idly. If you do this, [14]the LORD will be your delight. I will give you great honor and give you your full share of the inheritance I promised to Jacob, your ancestor. I, the LORD, have spoken!"

## CHAPTER 59 **GOD TELLS HIS PEOPLE TO OBEY.**

Listen! The LORD is not too weak to save you, and he is not becoming deaf. He can hear you when you call. [2]But there is a problem—your sins have cut you off from God. Because of your sin, he has turned away and will not listen anymore. [3]Your hands are the hands of murderers, and your fingers are filthy with sin. Your mouth is full of lies, and your lips are tainted with corruption.

[4]No one cares about being fair and honest. Their lawsuits are based on lies. They spend their time plotting evil deeds and then doing them. [5]They spend their time and energy spinning evil plans that end up in deadly actions. [6]They cheat and shortchange everyone. Nothing they do is productive; all their activity is filled with sin. Violence is their trademark. [7]Their feet run to do evil, and they rush to commit murder. They think only about sinning. Wherever they go, misery and destruction follow them. [8]They do not know what true peace is or what it means to be just and good. They continually do wrong, and those who follow them cannot experience a moment's peace.

[9]It is because of all this evil that deliverance is far from us. That is why God doesn't punish those who injure us. No wonder we are in darkness when we expected light. No wonder we are walking in the gloom. [10]No wonder we grope like blind people and stumble along. Even at brightest noontime, we fall down as though it were dark. No wonder we are like

## WALL ● ● • • •

59:1-12 **Sin offends our holy God. Because God is holy, he cannot ignore, excuse, or tolerate sin as though it doesn't matter. Sin cuts people off from him, forming a wall to isolate God from the people he loves. No wonder this long list of sins makes God angry and forces him to look the other way. People who die with their sin unforgiven separate themselves eternally from God. God wants them to live with him forever, but he cannot take them into his holy presence unless their sin is removed.**

58:1 Hebrew *Jacob.*

corpses when compared to vigorous young men! 11We growl like hungry bears; we moan like mournful doves. We look for justice, but it is nowhere to be found. We look to be rescued, but it is far away from us. 12For our sins are piled up before God and testify against us. Yes, we know what sinners we are. 13We know that we have rebelled against the LORD. We have turned our backs on God. We know how unfair and oppressive we have been, carefully planning our deceitful lies. 14Our courts oppose people who are righteous, and justice is nowhere to be found. Truth falls dead in the streets, and fairness has been outlawed. 15Yes, truth is gone, and anyone who tries to live a godly life is soon attacked.

The LORD looked and was displeased to find that there was no justice. 16He was amazed to see that no one intervened to help the oppressed. So he himself stepped in to save them with his mighty power and justice. 17He put on righteousness as his body armor and placed the helmet of salvation on his head. He clothed himself with the robes of vengeance and godly fury. 18He will repay his enemies for their evil deeds. His fury will fall on his foes in distant lands. 19Then at last they will respect and glorify the name of the LORD throughout the world. For he will come like a flood tide driven by the breath of the LORD.

20"The Redeemer will come to Jerusalem,*" says the LORD, "to buy back those in Israel* who have turned from their sins. 21And this is my covenant with them," says the LORD. "My Spirit will not leave them, and neither will these words I have given you. They will be on your lips and on the lips of your children and your children's children forever. I, the LORD, have spoken!

## CHAPTER 60 THE GLORY OF THE LORD.

"Arise, Jerusalem! Let your light shine for all the nations to see! For the glory of the LORD is shining upon you. 2Darkness as black as night will cover all the nations of the earth, but the glory of the LORD will shine over you. 3All nations will come to your light. Mighty kings will come to see your radiance.

4"Look and see, for everyone is coming home! Your sons are coming from distant lands; your little daughters will be carried home. 5Your eyes will shine, and your hearts will thrill with joy, for merchants from around the world will come to you. They will bring you the wealth of many lands. 6Vast caravans of camels will converge on you, the camels of Midian and Ephah. From Sheba they will bring gold and incense for the worship of the LORD. 7The flocks of Kedar will be given to you, and the rams of Nebaioth will be brought for my altars. In that day I will make my Temple glorious.

8"And what do I see flying like clouds to Israel, like doves to their nests? 9They are the ships of Tarshish, reserved to bring the people of Israel home. They will bring their wealth with them, and it will bring great

**PATIENCE ● ● ● • •**

60:1-22 **As we read these promises, we long for their fulfillment. But we must patiently wait for God's timing. God is in control of history, and he weaves all our lives together into his plan.**

honor to the LORD your God, the Holy One of Israel, for he will fill you with splendor.

10"Foreigners will come to rebuild your cities. Kings and rulers will send you aid. For though I have destroyed you in my anger, I will have mercy on you through my grace. 11Your gates will stay open around the clock to receive the wealth of many lands. The kings of the world will be led as captives in a victory procession. 12For the nations that refuse to be your allies will be destroyed. 13The glory of Lebanon will be yours—the forests of cypress, fir, and pine—to beautify my sanctuary. My Temple will be glorious!

14"The children of your tormentors will come and bow before you. Those who despised you will kiss your feet. They will call you the City of the LORD, and Zion of the Holy One of Israel.

15"Though you were once despised and hated and rebuffed by all, you will be beautiful forever. You will be a joy to all generations, for I will make you so. 16Powerful kings and mighty nations will bring the best of their goods to satisfy your every need. You will know at last that I, the LORD, am your Savior and Redeemer, the Mighty One of Israel.* 17I will exchange your bronze for gold, your iron for silver, your wood for bronze, and your stones for iron. Peace and righteousness will be your leaders! 18Violence will disappear from your land; the desolation and destruction of war will end. Salvation will surround you like city walls, and praise will be on the lips of all who enter there.

19"No longer will you need the sun or moon to give you light, for the LORD your God will be your everlasting light, and he will be your glory. 20The sun will never set; the moon will not go down. For the LORD will be your everlasting light. Your days of mourning will come to an end. 21All your people will be righteous. They will possess their land forever, for I will plant them there with my own hands in order to bring myself glory. 22The smallest family will multiply into a large clan. The tiniest group will become a mighty nation. I, the LORD, will bring it all to pass at the right time."

## CHAPTER 61 GOOD NEWS.

The Spirit of the Sovereign LORD is upon me, because the LORD has appointed me to bring good news to the poor. He has sent me to comfort the brokenhearted and to announce that captives will be released and prisoners will be freed.* 2He has sent me to tell those who mourn that the time of the LORD's favor has come,* and with it, the day of God's anger against their enemies. 3To all who mourn in Israel,* he will give beauty for ashes, joy instead of mourning, praise

59:20a Hebrew *to Zion.* 59:20b Hebrew *in Jacob.* 60:16 Hebrew *of Jacob.* 61:1 Greek version reads *and the blind will see.* 61:2 Or *to proclaim the acceptable year of the LORD.* 61:3 Hebrew *in Zion.*

instead of despair. For the LORD has planted them like strong and graceful oaks for his own glory.

4They will rebuild the ancient ruins, repairing cities long ago destroyed. They will revive them, though they have been empty for many generations. 5Foreigners will be your servants. They will feed your flocks and plow your fields and tend your vineyards. 6You will be called priests of the LORD, ministers of our God. You will be fed with the treasures of the nations and will boast in their riches. 7Instead of shame and dishonor, you will inherit a double portion of prosperity and everlasting joy.

8"For I, the LORD, love justice. I hate robbery and wrongdoing. I will faithfully reward my people for their suffering and make an everlasting covenant with them. 9Their descendants will be known and honored among the nations. Everyone will realize that they are a people the LORD has blessed."

10I am overwhelmed with joy in the LORD my God! For he has dressed me with the clothing of salvation and draped me in a robe of righteousness. I am like a bridegroom in his wedding suit or a bride with her jewels. 11The Sovereign LORD will show his justice to the nations of the world. Everyone will praise him! His righteousness will be like a garden in early spring, filled with young plants springing up everywhere.

**INJUSTICE ● ● • • •**

**61:8 We suffer for many reasons—our own mistakes, someone else's mistakes, injustice. When we suffer for our own mistakes, we get what we deserve. When we suffer because of others or injustice, God is angry. God in his mercy says that his people have suffered enough. God will reward those who suffer because of injustice. He will settle all accounts.**

## CHAPTER 62 **ISAIAH'S PRAYER.**

Because I love Zion, because my heart yearns for Jerusalem, I cannot remain silent. I will not stop praying for her until her righteousness shines like the dawn, and her salvation blazes like a burning torch.

2The nations will see your righteousness. Kings will be blinded by your glory. And the LORD will give you a new name. 3The LORD will hold you in his hands for all to see—a splendid crown in the hands of God. 4Never again will you be called the Godforsaken City* or the Desolate Land.* Your new name will be the City of God's Delight* and the Bride of God,* for the LORD delights in you and will claim you as his own. 5Your children will care for you with joy, O Jerusalem, just as a young man cares for his bride. Then God will rejoice over you as a bridegroom rejoices over his bride.

6O Jerusalem, I have posted watchmen on your walls; they will pray to the LORD day and night for the fulfillment of his promises. Take no rest, all you who pray. 7Give the LORD no rest until he makes Jerusalem the object of praise throughout the earth.

8The LORD has sworn to Jerusalem by his own strength: "I will never again hand you over to your enemies. Never again will foreign warriors come and take away your grain and wine. 9You raised it, and you will keep it, praising the LORD. Within the courtyards of the Temple, you yourselves will drink the wine that you have pressed."

10Go out! Prepare the highway for my people to return! Smooth out the road; pull out the boulders; raise a flag for all the nations to see. 11The LORD has sent this message to every land: "Tell the people of Israel,* 'Look, your Savior is coming. See, he brings his reward with him as he comes.'" 12They will be called the Holy People and the People Redeemed by the LORD. And Jerusalem will be known as the Desirable Place and the City No Longer Forsaken.

## CHAPTER 63 **GOD IS LOVING AND KIND.**

Who is this who comes from Edom, from the city of Bozrah, with his clothing stained red? Who is this in royal robes, marching in the greatness of his strength?

"It is I, the LORD, announcing your salvation! It is I, the LORD, who is mighty to save!"

2Why are your clothes so red, as if you have been treading out grapes?

3"I have trodden the winepress alone; no one was there to help me. In my anger I have trampled my enemies as if they were grapes. In my fury I have trampled my foes. It is their blood that has stained my clothes. 4For the time has come for me to avenge my people, to ransom them from their oppressors. 5I looked, but no one came to help my people. I was amazed and appalled at what I saw. So I executed vengeance alone; unaided, I passed down judgment. 6I crushed the nations in my anger and made them stagger and fall to the ground."

7I will tell of the LORD's unfailing love. I will praise the LORD for all he has done. I will rejoice in his great goodness to Israel, which he has granted according to his mercy and love. 8He said, "They are my very own people. Surely they will not be false again." And he became their Savior. 9In all their suffering he also suffered, and he personally rescued them. In his love and mercy he redeemed them. He lifted them up and carried them through all the years.

10But they rebelled against him and grieved his Holy Spirit. That is why he became their enemy and fought against them. 11Then they remembered those days of old when Moses led his people out of Egypt. They cried out, "Where is the one who brought Israel through the sea, with Moses as their shepherd? Where is the one who sent his Holy Spirit to be among his people? 12Where is the one whose power divided the sea before them, when Moses lifted up his hand, establishing his reputation forever? 13Where is the one who led them through the bottom of the sea? They were like fine stallions racing through the desert, never stumbling. 14As with cattle going down into a peaceful valley, the Spirit of the

**62:4a** Hebrew *Azubah,* which means "forsaken." **62:4b** Hebrew *Shemamah,* which means "desolate." **62:4c** Hebrew *Hephzibah,* which means "my delight is in her." **62:4d** Hebrew *Beulah,* which means "married." **62:11** Hebrew *Tell the daughter of Zion.*

LORD gave them rest. You led your people, LORD, and gained a magnificent reputation."

[15]LORD, look down from heaven and see us from your holy, glorious home. Where is the passion and the might you used to show on our behalf? Where are your mercy and compassion now? [16]Surely you are still our Father! Even if Abraham and Jacob* would disown us, LORD, you would still be our Father. You are our Redeemer from ages past. [17]LORD, why have you allowed us to turn from your path? Why have you given us stubborn hearts so we no longer fear you? Return and help us, for we are your servants and your special possession. [18]How briefly your holy people possessed the holy place, and now our enemies have destroyed it. [19]LORD, why do you treat us as though we never belonged to you? Why do you act as though we had never been known as your people?

## CHAPTER 64 GOD IS LIKE A POTTER.

Oh, that you would burst from the heavens and come down! How the mountains would quake in your presence! [2]As fire causes wood to burn and water to boil, your coming would make the nations tremble. Then your enemies would learn the reason for your fame! [3]When you came down long ago, you did awesome things beyond our highest expectations. And oh, how the mountains quaked! [4]For since the world began, no ear has heard, and no eye has seen a God like you, who works for those who wait for him! [5]You welcome those who cheerfully do good, who follow godly ways.

But we are not godly. We are constant sinners, so your anger is heavy on us. How can people like us be saved? [6]We are all infected and impure with sin. When we proudly display our righteous deeds, we find they are but filthy rags. Like autumn leaves, we wither and fall. And our sins, like the wind, sweep us away. [7]Yet no one calls on your name or pleads with you for mercy. Therefore, you have turned away from us and turned us over to our sins.

[8]And yet, LORD, you are our Father. We are the clay, and you are the potter. We are all formed by your hand. [9]Oh, don't be so angry with us, LORD. Please don't remember our sins forever. Look at us, we pray, and see that we are all your people.

[10]Your holy cities are destroyed; even Jerusalem is a desolate wilderness. [11]The holy, beautiful Temple where our ancestors praised you has been burned down, and all the things of beauty are destroyed. [12]After all this, LORD, must you still refuse to help us? Will you continue to be silent and punish us?

## CHAPTER 65 NEW HEAVENS AND NEW EARTH.

The LORD says, "People who never before inquired about me are now asking about me. I am being found by people who were not looking for me. To them I have said, 'I am here!'

[2]"I opened my arms to my own people all day long, but they have rebelled. They follow their own evil paths and thoughts. [3]All day long they insult me to my face by worshiping idols in their sacred gardens. They burn incense on the rooftops of their homes. [4]At night they go out among the graves and secret places to worship evil spirits. They also eat pork and other forbidden foods. [5]Yet they say to each other, 'Don't come too close or you will defile me! I am holier than you!' They are a stench in my nostrils, an acrid smell that never goes away.

[6]"Look, my decree is written out in front of me: I will not stand silent; I will repay them in full! Yes, I will repay them—[7]both for their own sins and for those of their ancestors," says the LORD. "For they also burned incense on the mountains and insulted me on the hills. I will pay them back in full!

[8]"But I will not destroy them all," says the LORD. "For just as good grapes are found among a cluster of bad ones (and someone will say, 'Don't throw them all away—there are some good grapes there!'), so I will not destroy all Israel. For I still have true servants there. [9]I will preserve a remnant of the people of Israel* and of Judah to possess my land. Those I choose will inherit it and serve me there. [10]For my people who have searched for me, the plain of Sharon will again be filled with flocks, and the valley of Achor will be a place to pasture herds.

[11]"But because the rest of you have forsaken the LORD and his Temple and worship the gods of Fate and Destiny, [12]I will 'destine' you to the sword. All of you will bow before the executioner, for when I called, you did not answer. When I spoke, you did not listen. You deliberately sinned—before my very eyes—and chose to do what you know I despise."

[13]Therefore, this is what the Sovereign LORD says: "You will starve, but my servants will eat. You will be thirsty, but they will drink. You will be sad and ashamed, but they will rejoice. [14]You will cry in sorrow and despair, while my servants sing for joy. [15]Your name will be a curse word among my people, for the Sovereign LORD will destroy you and call his true servants by another name. [16]All who invoke a blessing or take an oath will do so by the God of truth. For I will put aside my anger and forget the evil of earlier days.

[17]"Look! I am creating new heavens and a new earth—so wonderful that no one will even think about the old ones anymore. [18]Be glad; rejoice forever in my creation! And look! I will create Jerusalem as a place of happiness. Her people will be a source of joy. [19]I will rejoice in Jerusalem and delight in my people. And the sound of weeping and crying will be heard no more.

**DETERMINATION ● ● • • •**

62:1-7 **Isaiah's zeal for his country and his desire to see the work of salvation completed caused him to pray continually, hoping that Israel would be saved. We should have Isaiah's determination to see God's will done. This is what we mean when we pray, "May your kingdom come soon. May your will be done here on earth, just as it is in heaven" (Matthew 6:10). It is good to keep praying for others.**

63:16 Hebrew *Israel.* 65:9 Hebrew *remnant of Jacob.*

**DRAMA ● ● • • •**

66:22-24 **Isaiah brings his book to a close with great drama. For the faithless, there is a sobering portrayal of judgment. For the faithful, there is a glorious picture of rich reward—"As surely as my new heavens and earth will remain, so will you always be my people, with a name that will never disappear." The contrast is so striking that it would seem that everyone would want to follow God. But often we are just as foolish and reluctant to change as the Israelites. We are just as negligent in feeding the poor, working for justice, and obeying God's Word. Make sure you are among those who will be richly blessed.**

20"No longer will babies die when only a few days old. No longer will adults die before they have lived a full life. No longer will people be considered old at one hundred! Only sinners will die that young! 21In those days, people will live in the houses they build and eat the fruit of their own vineyards. 22It will not be like the past, when invaders took the houses and confiscated the vineyards. For my people will live as long as trees and will have time to enjoy their hard-won gains. 23They will not work in vain, and their children will not be doomed to misfortune. For they are people blessed by the LORD, and their children, too, will be blessed. 24I will answer them before they even call to me. While they are still talking to me about their needs, I will go ahead and answer their prayers! 25The wolf and lamb will feed together. The lion will eat straw like the ox. Poisonous snakes will strike no more. In those days, no one will be hurt or destroyed on my holy mountain. I, the LORD, have spoken!"

## CHAPTER 66

This is what the LORD says: "Heaven is my throne, and the earth is my footstool. Could you ever build me a temple as good as that? Could you build a dwelling place for me? 2My hands have made both heaven and earth, and they are mine. I, the LORD, have spoken!

"I will bless those who have humble and contrite hearts, who tremble at my word. 3But those who choose their own ways, delighting in their sins, are cursed. Their offerings will not be accepted. When such people sacrifice an ox, it is no more acceptable than a human sacrifice. When they sacrifice a lamb or bring an offering of grain, it is as bad as putting a dog or the blood of a pig on the altar! When they burn incense, it is as if they had blessed an idol. 4I will send great troubles against them—all the things they feared. For when I called, they did not answer. When I spoke, they did not listen. They deliberately sinned—before my very eyes—and chose to do what they know I despise."

5Hear this message from the LORD, and tremble at his words: "Your close relatives hate you and throw you out for being loyal to my name. 'Let the LORD be honored!' they scoff. 'Be joyful in him!' But they will be put to shame. 6What is all the commotion in the city? What is that terrible noise from the Temple? It is the voice of the LORD taking vengeance against his enemies.

7"Before the birth pains even begin, Jerusalem gives birth to a son. 8Who has ever seen or heard of anything as strange as this? Has a nation ever been born in a single day? Has a country ever come forth in a mere moment? But by the time Jerusalem's* birth pains begin, the baby will be born; the nation will come forth. 9Would I ever bring this nation to the point of birth and then not deliver it?" asks the LORD. "No! I would never keep this nation from being born," says your God.

10"Rejoice with Jerusalem! Be glad with her, all you who love her and mourn for her. 11Delight in Jerusalem! Drink deeply of her glory even as an infant drinks at its mother's generous breasts. 12Peace and prosperity will overflow Jerusalem like a river," says the LORD. "The wealth of the nations will flow to her. Her children will be nursed at her breasts, carried in her arms, and treated with love. 13I will comfort you there as a child is comforted by its mother."

14When you see these things, your heart will rejoice. Vigorous health will be yours! Everyone will see the good hand of the LORD on his people—and his anger against his enemies. 15See, the LORD is coming with fire, and his swift chariots of destruction roar like a whirlwind. He will bring punishment with the fury of his anger and the flaming fire of his hot rebuke. 16The LORD will punish the world by fire and by his sword, and many will be killed by the LORD.

17"Those who 'purify' themselves in a sacred garden, feasting on pork and rats and other forbidden meats, will come to a terrible end," says the LORD. 18"I can see what they are doing, and I know what they are thinking. So I will gather all nations and peoples together, and they will see my glory. 19I will perform a sign among them. And I will send those who survive to be messengers to the nations—to Tarshish, to the Libyans* and Lydians* (who are famous as archers), to Tubal and Greece,* and to all the lands beyond the sea that have not heard of my fame or seen my glory. There they will declare my glory to the nations. 20They will bring the remnant of your people back from every nation. They will bring them to my holy mountain in Jerusalem as an offering to the LORD. They will ride on horses, in chariots and wagons, and on mules and camels," says the LORD. 21"And I will appoint some of those who return to be my priests and Levites. I, the LORD, have spoken!

22"As surely as my new heavens and earth will remain, so will you always be my people, with a name that will never disappear," says the LORD. 23"All humanity will come to worship me from week to week and from month to month. 24And as they go out, they will see the dead bodies of those who have rebelled against me. For the worms that devour them will never die, and the fire that burns them will never go out. All who pass by will view them with utter horror."

66:8 Hebrew *Zion's.* 66:19a As in some Greek manuscripts, which read *Put* [Libya]; Hebrew reads *Pul.* 66:19b Hebrew *Lud.* 66:19c Hebrew *Javan.*

# MEGA themes

**HOLINESS** God is highly exalted above all his creatures. His moral perfection stands in contrast to evil people and nations. God is perfect and sinless, so he is in perfect control of his power, judgment, love, and mercy. His holy nature is our yardstick for morality.

Because God alone is without sin, he alone can help us with our sin. It is only right that we regard him as supreme in power and moral perfection. We must never treat God as common or ordinary. He—and only he—deserves our devotion.

1. God's holiness reveals how much he is beyond human beings. How do you feel when you consider his holiness?
2. How did Isaiah respond to God's holiness in 6:1-8?
3. What did God do for Isaiah because of his reaction?
4. What do you learn about God when you consider both his holiness and his personal love for you? How do you feel? How will you respond? (Check how Isaiah responded.)

**PUNISHMENT** Because God is holy, he requires his people to treat others justly. He promised to punish Israel, Judah, and other nations for faithless immorality and idolatry. Their true faith had degenerated into national pride and empty religious rituals.

We must trust in God alone and obey his commands. We cannot ignore his call to justice nor give in to selfishness. If we harden our heart against his message, we surely will be punished.

1. Whom does God punish?
2. If God forgives us, can we avoid all the consequences of our sins? Explain your answer, giving biblical support.
3. If a Christian friend were to say, "What difference does it make whether or not I sin?" how would you respond?
4. God does not want you to obey him just to avoid punishment. What is the heart motivation God wants you to have as you obey his will? Give yourself a heart check-up. How are you doing?

**SALVATION/MESSIAH** God promised to send a Savior—he knew that without one we would all stand condemned by his judgment. Christ's perfect sacrifice, his servant life, and his coming kingdom all are foretold by Isaiah. Through Christ, the promise of redemption and restoration are fulfilled.

Christ died to save us from sin. Salvation is in him alone. Trust Christ fully and experience the forgiveness and the wholeness he brings as your Prince of Peace.

1. Read Isaiah 9:6 and chapter 53. These describe Christ, our Savior and Messiah. What do these two contrasting descriptions reveal about Christ?
2. The Messiah was sent by God to save those who trusted him for their deliverance. Describe how you came to know and trust Christ. (If you have never trusted him, prayerfully seek him through his Word, through talking with people you trust who are Christians, and in prayer.)
3. What difference do you think it makes in your daily life that Christ is your Savior?
4. What areas of your life need recommitting to Christ? Open yourself up to him in trust. Christ came to deliver you and will not reject you if you seek him as Lord.

**HOPE** God promises comfort, deliverance, and restoration in his future kingdom. The Messiah will rule over his faithful followers in the age to come. Hope is possible because Christ is coming.

We can be hopeful because God has compassion for those who repent. No matter how bleak our current situation, or how evil the world becomes, we must continue to be God's faithful people who hope for his return.

1. In the latter part of the book, Isaiah begins to focus on the future when Christ will reign in his full glory. What seems to be Isaiah's attitude about this future? How did it affect his present?
2. Has there been a time when you had almost lost hope? How did you feel? What enabled you not to give up?
3. What can we expect God to provide in the future? How does this help you keep going, even when everything feels hopeless?
4. How would you live differently if there were no hope?

640 B.C.
**Zephaniah becomes a prophet**

627
**Jeremiah becomes a prophet**

612
**Habakkuk becomes a prophet**

609
**King Josiah killed in battle**

605
**Daniel taken captive**

597
**Ezekiel taken captive**

593
**Ezekiel begins to prophesy in Babylon**

586
**Judah falls; Jerusalem destroyed; Jeremiah's ministry ends**

537
**First exiles return to Judah**

"You big crybaby. Stop your blubbering!" ■ Tears can seem embarrassing and awkward—even a sign of weakness. When we were young, tears came easily over a broken toy, a skinned knee, and other assorted real or imagined hurts. As we grew older, we learned to hide our feelings, especially our sadness. We tried to look tough or put on a happy face. That's a shame, really, because tears are important. In fact, tears can tell us a lot about people, letting us see what affects them deeply, what they care about . . . what breaks their heart. ■ Jeremiah is called the weeping prophet. In his books (Jeremiah and Lamentations), it seems as though all he does is cry. But Jeremiah's tears did not stem from immaturity, self-centeredness, or weakness. Jeremiah wept because he loved deeply, and because he knew the truth: that his beloved nation was in trouble and that God would punish them. He tried to tell the people, but they wouldn't listen. So he cried. ■ What brings tears to your eyes? What do you cry about? Most of us need to be more like Jeremiah, filled with compassion and concern. We need to cry out to God and minister to others with a broken and loving heart.

## STATS

PURPOSE: To urge God's people to turn from their sins and to turn back to God

AUTHOR: Jeremiah

TO WHOM WRITTEN: Judah (the southern kingdom) and its capital city, Jerusalem

DATE WRITTEN: During Jeremiah's ministry, approximately 627–586 B.C.

SETTING: Jeremiah ministered during the reigns of Judah's last five kings—Josiah, Jehoahaz, Jehoiakim, Jehoiachin (Coniah), and Zedekiah. The nation was sliding quickly toward destruction and was eventually conquered by Babylon in 586 B.C. (see 2 Kings 21–25). The prophet Zephaniah preceded Jeremiah; Habakkuk was his contemporary.

KEY PEOPLE: Judah's kings (listed above), Baruch, Ebed-Melech, King Nebuchadnezzar, the Rechabites

KEY PLACES: Anathoth, Jerusalem, Ramah, Egypt

SPECIAL FEATURES: The book of Jeremiah is a combination of history, poetry, and biography. Jeremiah often used symbolism to communicate his message.

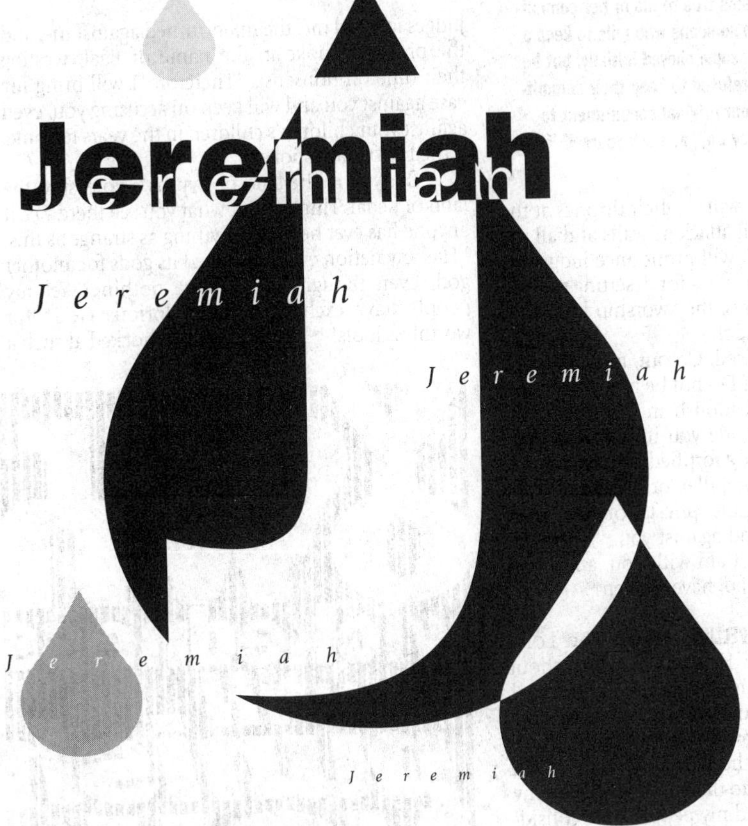


CHAPTER **1** **GOD CALLS JEREMIAH.** These are the
words of Jeremiah son of Hilkiah, one of the priests
from Anathoth, a town in the land of Benjamin.
2The LORD first gave messages to Jeremiah during the
thirteenth year of King Josiah's reign in Judah.* 3He
continued to give messages throughout the reign of
Josiah's son, King Jehoiakim, until the eleventh year
of King Zedekiah's reign in Judah. In August of that
year,* the people of Jerusalem were taken away as
captives.

4The LORD gave me a message. He said, 5"I knew
you before I formed you in your mother's womb.
Before you were born I set you apart and appointed
you as my spokesman to the world."

6"O Sovereign LORD," I said, "I can't speak for
you! I'm too young!"

7"Don't say that," the LORD replied, "for you must
go wherever I send you and say whatever I tell you.
8And don't be afraid of the people, for I will be with
you and take care of you. I, the LORD, have spoken!"

9Then the LORD touched my mouth and said,
"See, I have put my words in your mouth! 10Today I
appoint you to stand up against nations and kingdoms. You are to uproot some and tear them down,
to destroy and overthrow them. You are to build
others up and plant them."

11Then the LORD said to me, "Look, Jeremiah!
What do you see?"

And I replied, "I see a branch from an almond
tree."

12And the LORD said, "That's right, and it means
that I am watching,* and I will surely carry out my
threats of punishment."

13Then the LORD spoke to me again and asked,
"What do you see now?"

And I replied, "I see a pot of boiling water, tipping
from the north."

14"Yes," the LORD said, "for terror from the north
will boil out on the people of this land. 15Listen! I am
calling the armies of the kingdoms of the north to

**TODAY ● ● • • •**

**1:2-3 God spoke many times to Jeremiah over many years, but Jeremiah's job was to determine what God wanted him to do each day. So it is with us. God has given us his Word, with many messages. But as we search the Scriptures, we must keep asking, "What do you want me to do for you *today*?"**

1:2 The thirteenth year of Josiah's reign was 627 B.C. 1:3 Hebrew *In the fifth month,* of the Hebrew calendar. A number of events in Jeremiah can be cross-checked with dates in surviving Babylonian records and related accurately to our modern calendar. This month in the eleventh year of Zedekiah's reign occurred in August and September 586 B.C. Also see 52:12 and the note there. 1:12 The Hebrew word for "watching" sounds like the word for "almond tree."

**STAY TRUE ● ● ● • •**

2:2 **We appreciate a friend who remains true to his or her commitments, and we are disappointed with someone who fails to keep a promise. God was pleased when his people obeyed initially, but he became angry with them when they refused to keep their commitment. Temptations distract us from our original commitment to God. Think about your promise to obey God, and ask yourself if you are remaining true.**

come to Jerusalem. They will set their thrones at the
gates of the city. They will attack its walls and all the
other towns of Judah. 16 I will pronounce judgment
on my people for all their evil—for deserting me and
worshiping other gods. Yes, they worship idols that
they themselves have made!
17 "Get up and get dressed. Go out, and tell them
whatever I tell you to say. Do not be afraid of them,
or I will make you look foolish in front of them.
18 For see, today I have made you immune to their
attacks. You are strong like a fortified city that cannot
be captured, like an iron pillar or a bronze wall.
None of the kings, officials, priests, or people of
Judah will be able to stand against you. 19 They will
try, but they will fail. For I am with you, and I will
take care of you. I, the LORD, have spoken!"

CHAPTER **2** **GOD'S REBELLIOUS PEOPLE.** The LORD
gave me another message. He said, 2 "Go and shout
in Jerusalem's streets: 'This is what the LORD says: I
remember how eager you were to please me as a
young bride long ago, how you loved me and followed me even through the barren wilderness. 3 In
those days Israel was holy to the LORD, the first of my
children.* All who harmed my people were considered guilty, and disaster fell upon them. I, the LORD,
have spoken!'"

**SPARKLING WATER ● ● ● • •**

2:13 **Who would set aside a sparkling fountain of water for a cistern, a pit that collected rain water? God told the Israelites that that was what they were doing when they turned from him, the fountain of living water, to idols. Not only that, the cisterns they chose were cracked and empty. The people had built religious systems to store truth in, but they were worthless. Why should we cling to the broken promises of unstable "cisterns" (money, power, religious systems, or whatever) when God promises to constantly refresh us with himself, the living water (John 4:10)?**

4 Listen to the word of the LORD, people of Jacob—
all you families of Israel! 5 This is what the LORD says:
"What sin did your ancestors find in me that led
them to stray so far? They worshiped foolish idols,
only to become foolish themselves. 6 They did not
ask, 'Where is the LORD who brought us safely out of
Egypt and led us through the barren wilderness—a
land of deserts and pits, of drought and death, where
no one lives or even travels?'
7 "And when I brought you into a fruitful land to
enjoy its bounty and goodness, you defiled my land
and corrupted the inheritance I had promised you.
8 The priests did not ask, 'Where is the LORD?' The
judges ignored me, the rulers turned against me, and
the prophets spoke in the name of Baal, wasting
their time on nonsense. 9 Therefore, I will bring my
case against you and will keep on accusing you, even
against your children's children in the years to come.
I, the LORD, have spoken!
10 "Go west to the land of Cyprus*; go east to the
land of Kedar. Think about what you see there. See if
anyone has ever heard of anything as strange as this.
11 Has any nation ever exchanged its gods for another
god, even though its gods are nothing? Yet my
people have exchanged their glorious God* for
worthless idols! 12 The heavens are shocked at such a

**YOUR OWN wickedness will punish YOU!**

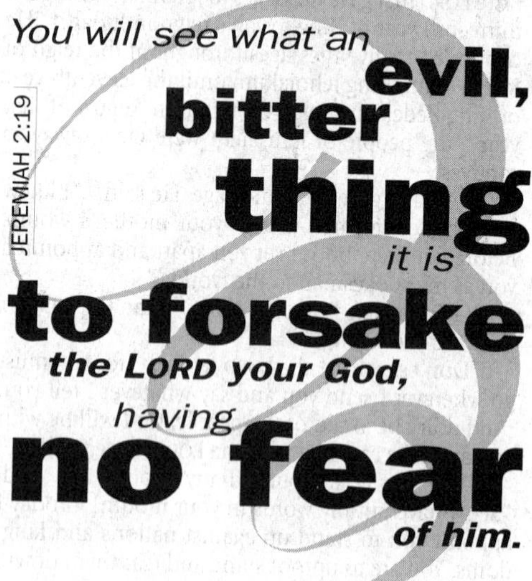

You will see what an
evil,
bitter
thing
it is
to forsake
the LORD your God,
having
no fear
of him.
JEREMIAH 2:19

2:3 Hebrew *the firstfruits of his harvest.* 2:10 Hebrew *Kittim.* 2:11 Hebrew *their Glory.*

thing and shrink back in horror and dismay, says the
LORD. [13]For my people have done two evil things:
They have forsaken me—the fountain of living water. And they have dug for themselves cracked cisterns that can hold no water at all!
[14]"Why has Israel become a nation of slaves? Why
has she been carried away as plunder? [15]Lions have
roared against her. The land has been destroyed, and
the cities are now in ruins. No one lives in them
anymore. [16]Egyptians, marching from their cities of
Memphis* and Tahpanhes, have utterly destroyed Israel's glory and power. [17]And you have brought this on
yourselves by rebelling against the LORD your God
when he wanted to lead you and show you the way!
[18]"What have you gained by your alliances with
Egypt and Assyria? What good to
you are the waters of the Nile* and
the Euphrates*? [19]Your own wickedness will punish you. You will
see what an evil, bitter thing it is to
forsake the LORD your God, having
no fear of him. I, the Lord, the
LORD Almighty, have spoken!
[20]Long ago I broke your yoke and
tore away the chains of your slavery, but still you would not obey
me. On every hill and under every
green tree, you have prostituted
yourselves by bowing down to
idols.
[21]"How could this happen?
When I planted you, I chose a
vine of the purest stock—the very
best. How did you grow into this
corrupt wild vine? [22]No amount
of soap or lye can make you
clean. You are stained with guilt
that cannot be washed away. I,
the Sovereign LORD, have spoken!
[23]"You say, 'That's not true! We
haven't worshiped the images of
Baal!' But how can you say that?
Go and look in any valley in the
land! Face the awful sins you
have done. You are like a restless
female camel, desperate for a
male! [24]You are like a wild donkey, sniffing the wind at mating
time. Who can restrain your lust?
Those who desire you do not
even need to search, for you
come running to them! [25]Why do
you refuse to turn from all this
running after other gods? But you
say, 'Don't waste your breath. I
have fallen in love with these foreign gods, and I can't stop loving
them now!'
[26]"Like a thief, Israel feels
shame only when she gets caught. Kings, officials,
priests, and prophets—all are alike in this. [27]To an
image carved from a piece of wood they say, 'You are
my father.' To an idol chiseled out of stone they say,
'You are my mother.' They turn their backs on me, but
in times of trouble they cry out for me to save them!
[28]Why don't you call on these gods you have made?
When danger comes, let them save you if they can! For
you have as many gods as there are cities and towns in
Judah. [29]Why do you accuse me of doing wrong? You
are the ones who have rebelled, says the LORD. [30]I have
punished your children, but it did them no good. They
still refuse to obey. You yourselves have killed your
prophets as a lion kills its prey.
[31]"O my people, listen to the words of the LORD!

## "Here's what I did..."

The topic of abortion comes up often in school, among friends and elsewhere. I had thought through my position in theory, but when my best friend told me she was pregnant and was going to get an abortion, it wasn't theoretical anymore.

When Lee called me on the phone one night and asked me to come talk, I knew something was wrong. As soon as we were alone, she blurted out: "I'm pregnant. And I have an appointment at an abortion clinic tomorrow."

I couldn't believe my ears. Lee was a Christian. We had discussed abortion often and had agreed on our stance: It was wrong. Now Lee was telling me she was going to have one tomorrow!

Trying to keep calm, I told her I realized it was her decision. Then I said, "You know I don't believe in abortion. You always said you didn't, either. It doesn't make it any more right now that you're pregnant. It's still a baby we're talking about.

"This is your decision. But as your friend, I want to make sure you've thought this through. Can we read a few passages of Scripture and pray together? Then I promise, I'll stick by you, whatever you decide."

We read Jeremiah 1:4-5 and Psalm 139. I told her, "Whenever I read these passages, they say to me that God knows us from the very beginning, and that he has a plan for each person. That's why I think you should have this baby, Lee. God will take care of your baby because he already loves the baby. And he'll take care of you, too."

We cried together, but I really believed what I said. I asked Lee if I could pray for the baby. She nodded, crying. So I prayed that God would give Lee the courage to make the right choice, and that he would take care of her baby.

Lee didn't promise she wouldn't have the abortion. I prayed hard all the next day. That evening, she called and said she hadn't gone through with it. I told her I was very happy and thought she made the right choice.

Lee will tell you that she believes she made the right choice, too. She had a beautiful girl that she placed for adoption with a loving Christian couple. It hurts her to think about the baby, but she knows she did the right thing.

Lori

AGE 17

2:16 Hebrew *Noph.* 2:18a Hebrew *of Shihor,* a branch of the Nile River. 2:18b Hebrew *the river.*

Have I been like a desert to Israel? Have I been to them a land of darkness? Why then do my people say, 'At last we are free from God! We won't have anything to do with him anymore!' [32]Does a young woman forget her jewelry? Does a bride hide her wedding dress? No! Yet for years on end my people have forgotten me.

[33]"How you plot and scheme to win your lovers. The most experienced prostitute could learn from you! [34]Your clothing is stained with the blood of the innocent and the poor. You killed them even though they didn't break into your houses! [35]And yet you say, 'I haven't done anything wrong. Surely he isn't angry with me!' Now I will punish you severely because you claim you have not sinned.

[36]"First here, then there—you flit from one ally to another asking for help. But your new friends in Egypt will let you down, just as Assyria did before. [37]In despair, you will be led into exile with your hands on your heads, for the LORD has rejected the nations you trust. You will not succeed despite their help.

## FORGETTING ● ● • • •

2:31-32 **Forgetting can be dangerous, whether it is intentional or an oversight. Israel forgot God by focusing its affections on the allurements of the world. The more we focus on the world's pleasures, the easier it becomes to forget God's care, love, dependability, guidance, and most of all, God himself. What pleases you most? Have you been forgetting God lately?**

## MINIMIZED ● ● • • •

3:4-5 **Notice how the people of Israel tried to make their sin seem small. When we know we've done something wrong, we want to downplay the error by saying "It wasn't that bad!" thereby relieving some of the guilt we feel. As we minimize our sinfulness, we naturally shy away from making changes, and so we keep on sinning. But if we view every wrong attitude and action as a serious offense to God, we will begin to understand what living for God is all about. Is there sin in your life that you've written off as too small to worry about? God says we must confess every sin, and in confessing it, turn from it.**

## CHAPTER 3 **THE PEOPLE GIVE UP GOD FOR IDOLS.**

"If a man divorces a woman and she marries someone else, he is not to take her back again, for that would surely corrupt the land. But you have prostituted yourself with many lovers, says the LORD. Yet I am still calling you to come back to me.

[2]"Look all around you. Is there anywhere in the entire land where you have not been defiled by your adulteries? You sit like a prostitute beside the road waiting for a client. You sit alone like a nomad in the desert. You have polluted the land with your prostitution and wickedness. [3]That is why even the spring rains have failed. For you are a prostitute and are completely unashamed. [4]Yet you say to me, 'Father, you have been my guide since the days of my youth. [5]Surely you won't be angry about such a little thing! Surely you can forget it!' So you talk, and keep right on doing all the evil you can."

[6]During the reign of King Josiah, the LORD said to me, "Have you seen what fickle Israel does? Like a wife who commits adultery, Israel has worshiped other gods on every hill and under every green tree. [7]I thought that after she had done all this she would return to me. But she did not come back. And though her faithless sister Judah saw this, [8]she paid no attention. She saw that I had divorced faithless Israel and sent her away. But now Judah, too, has left me and given herself to prostitution. [9]Israel treated it all so lightly—she thought nothing of committing adultery by worshiping idols made of wood and stone. So now the land has been greatly defiled. [10]But in spite of all this, her faithless sister Judah has never sincerely returned to me. She has only pretended to be sorry," says the LORD.

[11]Then the LORD said to me, "Even faithless Israel is less guilty than treacherous Judah! [12]Therefore, go and say these words to Israel,* 'This is what the LORD says: O Israel, my faithless people, come home to me again, for I am merciful. I will not be angry with you forever. [13]Only acknowledge your guilt. Admit that you rebelled against the LORD your God and committed adultery against him by worshiping idols under every green tree. Confess that you refused to follow me. I, the LORD, have spoken!'"

[14]"Return home, you wayward children," says the LORD, "for I am your husband. I will bring you again to the land of Israel*—one from here and two from there, from wherever you are scattered. [15]And I will give you leaders after my own heart, who will guide you with knowledge and understanding.

[16]"And when your land is once more filled with people," says the LORD, "you will no longer wish for 'the good old days' when you possessed the Ark of the LORD's covenant. Those days will not be missed or even thought about, and there will be no need to rebuild the Ark. [17]In that day Jerusalem will be known as The Throne of the LORD. All nations will come there to honor the LORD. They will no longer stubbornly follow their own evil desires. [18]In those days the people of Judah and Israel will return together from exile in the north. They will return to the land I gave their ancestors as an inheritance forever.

[19]"I thought to myself, 'I would love to treat you as my own children!' I wanted nothing more than to give you this beautiful land—the finest inheritance in the world. I looked forward to your calling me 'Father,' and I thought you would never turn away from me again. [20]But you have betrayed me, you people of Israel! You have been like a faithless wife who leaves her husband," says the LORD.

[21]Voices are heard high on the windswept mountains, the weeping and pleading of Israel's people. For they have forgotten the LORD their God and wandered far from his ways.

3:12 Hebrew *toward the north.* 3:14 Hebrew *to Zion.*

22"My wayward children," says the LORD, "come
back to me, and I will heal your wayward hearts."
"Yes, we will come," the people reply, "for you are
the LORD our God. 23Our worship of idols and our
religious orgies on the hills and mountains are completely false. Only in the LORD our God will Israel
ever find salvation. 24From childhood we have
watched as everything our ancestors worked for—
their flocks and herds, their sons and daughters—
was squandered on a delusion. 25Let us now lie down
in shame and dishonor, for we and our ancestors
have always sinned against the LORD our God. We
have never obeyed him."

CHAPTER **4** **GOD ASKS HIS PEOPLE TO OBEY.** "O Israel,
come back to me," says the LORD. "If you will throw
away your detestable idols and go astray no more,
2and if you will swear by my name alone, and begin
to live good, honest lives and uphold justice, then
you will be a blessing to the nations of the world,
and all people will come and praise my name."
3This is what the LORD says to the people of Judah
and Jerusalem: "Plow up the hard ground of your
hearts! Do not waste your good seed among thorns.
4Cleanse your minds and hearts before the LORD, or
my anger will burn like an unquenchable fire because of all your sins.
5"Shout to Jerusalem and to all Judah! Tell them
to sound the alarm throughout the land: 'Run for
your lives! Flee to the fortified cities!' 6Send a signal
toward Jerusalem*: 'Flee now! Do not delay!' For I
am bringing terrible destruction upon you from the
north."
7A lion stalks from its den, a destroyer of nations.
And it is headed for your land! Your towns will lie in
ruins, empty of people. 8So put on clothes of mourning and weep with broken hearts, for the fierce anger
of the LORD is still upon us.
9"In that day," says the LORD, "the king and the
officials will tremble in fear. The priests and the
prophets will be struck with horror."
10Then I said, "O Sovereign LORD, the people have
been deceived by what you said, for you promised
peace for Jerusalem. Yet the sword is even now
poised to strike them dead!"
11The time is coming when the LORD will say to the
people of Jerusalem, "A burning wind is blowing in
from the desert. It is not a gentle breeze useful for
winnowing grain. 12It is a roaring blast sent by me!
Now I will pronounce your destruction!"
13Our enemy rushes down on us like a storm
wind! His chariots are like whirlwinds; his horses are
swifter than eagles. How terrible it will be! Our
destruction is sure! 14O Jerusalem, cleanse your
hearts that you may be saved. How long will you
harbor your evil thoughts? 15From Dan and the hill
country of Ephraim, your destruction has been announced.
16"Warn the surrounding nations and announce
to Jerusalem: 'The enemy is coming from a distant
land, raising a battle cry against the towns of Judah.
17They surround Jerusalem like watchmen surrounding a field, for my people have rebelled against me,'"
says the LORD. 18"Your own actions have brought this
upon you. This punishment is a bitter dose of your
own medicine. It has pierced you to the heart!"
19My heart, my heart—I writhe in pain! My heart

**My mom used to go to church a lot, but she doesn't anymore. What can I do to get her to give God more attention?**

Going from a close relationship with Christ to total neglect is like going from a two-wheel bike to one with training wheels. It seems safer, but it's not half the fun.

You may see many people who start out strong in their walk with God, but for some reason they begin to fade and eventually drop off.

Remember, the Christian life is not a sprint—it's a long-distance race, a marathon! How you start is not nearly as important as how you finish.

In a long race, many people get weary of waiting for the prize and decide to drop out. Your mother may be an example of that. She seems to have turned her attention elsewhere, forgetting about the race altogether.

As Jeremiah 2:13 says, when people reject God, they need other things to hold life together. But those other things are just "cracked cisterns" that don't hold anything of value.

And like the person who goes back to the bike with training wheels because it's safer, some people allow distractions to push God aside.

Some people believe that the Christian life means having their problems solved immediately, always being treated right by people, never having doubts about the future, always having prayers answered right away, and always feeling good about church. Those people are pursuing the wrong goals! They will be disappointed, grow tired, and tend to drop out.

Our goal should be to get to know the God who created us and loved us enough to die on a cross to save us from sin—then we'll never get tired of the faith. There's always something new to discover about the richness and depth of God's love for us. If we work to let God change our selfish characters into selfless characters, the race will never seem too long.

Don't try to change your mom. She'll likely not appreciate it, no matter how good your motives are. Instead, give God permission to change you! Focus on how well *you* are doing, and let God take care of your mom.

Become more diligent in doing your chores and homework. Begin to treat your brothers and sisters better than you have. Pray for your mom to see these changes. Then give God time to work. Remember, he wants her to have a right relationship with him even more than you do!

4:6 Hebrew *Zion.*

**FAITHFUL ● ● ● • •**

4:27 **God warned that destruction was certain, but he promised that a remnant would remain faithful to him and would be spared, even though the nation would be wiped out. God is committed to preserving those who are faithful to him.**

pounds within me! I cannot be still. For I have heard the blast of enemy trumpets and the roar of their battle cries. [20]Waves of destruction roll over the land, until it lies in complete desolation. Suddenly, every tent is destroyed; in a moment, every shelter is crushed. [21]How long must this go on? How long must I be surrounded by war and death?

[22]"My people are foolish and do not know me," says the LORD. "They are senseless children who have no understanding. They are clever enough at doing wrong, but they have no talent at all for doing right!"

[23]I looked at the earth, and it was empty and formless. I looked at the heavens, and there was no light. [24]I looked at the mountains and hills, and they trembled and shook. [25]I looked, and all the people were gone. All the birds of the sky had flown away. [26]I looked, and the fertile fields had become a wilderness. The cities lay in ruins, crushed by the LORD's fierce anger.

[27]This is what the LORD says: "The whole land will be ruined, but I will not destroy it completely. [28]The earth will mourn, the heavens will be draped in black, because of my decree against my people. I have made up my mind and will not change it."

[29]At the noise of marching armies, the people flee in terror from the cities. They hide in the bushes and run for the mountains. All the cities have been abandoned—not a person remains! [30]What are you doing, you who have been plundered? Why do you dress up in your most beautiful clothing and jewelry? Why do you brighten your eyes with mascara? It will do you no good! Your allies despise you and will kill you.

[31]I hear a great cry, like that of a woman giving birth to her first child. It is the cry of Jerusalem's people* gasping for breath, pleading for help, prostrate before their murderers.

CHAPTER **5** **NO RESPECT FOR GOD.** "Run up and down every street in Jerusalem," says the LORD. "Look high and low; search throughout the city! If you can find even one person who is just and honest, I will not destroy the city. [2]Even when they are under oath, saying, 'As surely as the LORD lives,' they all tell lies!"

[3]LORD, you are searching for honesty. You struck your people, but they paid no attention. You crushed them, but they refused to turn from sin. They are determined, with faces set like stone; they have refused to repent.

[4]Then I said, "But what can we expect from the poor and ignorant? They don't know the ways of the LORD. They don't understand what God expects of them. [5]I will go and speak to their leaders. Surely they will know the LORD's ways and what God requires of them." But the leaders, too, had utterly rejected their God. [6]So now a lion from the forest will attack them; a wolf from the desert will pounce on them. A leopard will lurk near their towns, tearing apart any who dare to venture out. For their rebellion is great, and their sins are many.

[7]"How can I pardon you? For even your children have turned from me. They have sworn by gods that are not gods at all! I fed my people until they were fully satisfied. But they thanked me by committing adultery and lining up at the city's brothels. [8]They are well-fed, lusty stallions, each neighing for his neighbor's wife. [9]Should I not punish them for this?" asks the LORD. "Should I not avenge myself against a nation such as this?

[10]"Go down the rows of the vineyards and destroy them, but leave a scattered few alive. Strip the branches from the vine, for they do not belong to the LORD. [11]The people of Israel and Judah are full of treachery against me," says the LORD. [12]"They have lied about the LORD and have said, 'He won't bother us! No disasters will come upon us! There will be no war or famine! [13]God's prophets are windbags full of words with no divine authority. Their predictions of disaster will fall on themselves!'"

[14]Therefore, this is what the LORD God Almighty

**STRIPPED ● ● • •**

5:22-24 **What is your attitude when you come into God's presence? We should come with fear and trembling (awe and respect), for God sets the boundaries of the roaring seas and establishes the rains and harvests. God had to strip away all the things that Israel had grown to respect more than him. Without them, the people could once again reverence God. Don't wait until God removes the objects of your reverence and respect before you think of him as you should.**

says: "Because the people are talking like this, I will give you messages that will burn them up as if they were kindling wood. [15]O Israel, I will bring a distant nation against you," says the LORD. "It is a mighty nation, an ancient nation, a people whose language you do not know, whose speech you cannot understand. [16]Their weapons are deadly; their warriors are mighty. [17]They will eat your harvests and your children's bread, your flocks of sheep and your herds of cattle. Yes, they will eat your grapes and figs. And they will destroy your fortified cities, which you think are so safe.

[18]"Yet even in those days I will not blot you out completely," says the LORD. [19]"And when your people ask, 'Why is the LORD our God doing this to us?' you must reply, 'You rejected him and gave yourselves to foreign gods in your own land. Now you will serve foreigners in a land that is not your own.'

[20]"Make this announcement to Israel* and to Judah: [21]Listen, you foolish and senseless people—who have eyes but do not see, who have ears but do not hear. [22]Do you have no respect for me? Why do

4:31 Hebrew *the daughter of Zion.* 5:20 Hebrew *to the house of Jacob.*

| **JEREMIAH** served as a prophet to Judah from 627 B.C. until the Exile in 586 B.C. | *Climate of the times* | Society was deteriorating economically, politically, spiritually. Wars and captivity threatened the people. God's Word was outlawed. |
|---|---|---|
| | *Main message* | Repentance from sin would postpone Judah's coming judgment at the hands of Babylon. |
| | *Importance of message* | Repentance is one of the greatest needs in our immoral world. God's promises to the faithful shine brightly by bringing hope for tomorrow and strength for today. |
| | *Contemporary prophets* | Habakkuk (612–589)<br>Zephaniah (640–621) |

you not tremble in my presence? I, the LORD, am the one who defines the ocean's sandy shoreline, an everlasting boundary that the waters cannot cross. The waves may toss and roar, but they can never pass the bounds I set.

23"But my people have stubborn and rebellious hearts. They have turned against me and have chosen to practice idolatry.
24They do not say from the heart, 'Let us live in awe of the LORD our God, for he gives us rain each spring and fall, assuring us of plentiful harvests.'
25Your wickedness has deprived you of these wonderful blessings. Your sin has robbed you of all these good things.

26"Among my people are wicked men who lie in wait for victims like a hunter hiding in a blind. They are continually setting traps for other people.
27Like a cage filled with birds, their homes are filled with evil plots. And the result? Now they are great and rich.
28They are well fed and well groomed, and there is no limit to their wicked deeds. They refuse justice to orphans and deny the rights of the poor.
29Should I not punish them for this?" asks the LORD. "Should I not avenge myself against a nation such as this?

30"A horrible and shocking thing has happened in this land—
31the prophets give false prophecies, and the priests rule with an iron hand. And worse yet, my people like it that way! But what will you do when the end comes?

CHAPTER **6** **ONE LAST WARNING.** "Run for your lives, you people of Benjamin! Flee from Jerusalem! Sound the alarm in Tekoa! Send up a signal at Beth-hakkerem! Warn everyone that a powerful army is coming from the north to destroy this nation.
2O Jerusalem,* you are my beautiful and delicate daughter—but I will destroy you!
3Enemy shepherds will surround you. They will set up camp around the city and divide your pastures for their flocks.
4They shout, 'Prepare for battle and attack at noon! But now the day is fading, and the evening shadows are falling.
5So let us attack by night and destroy her palaces!'"

6This is what the LORD Almighty says: "Cut down the trees for battering rams. Build ramps against the walls of Jerusalem. This is the city to be punished, for she is wicked through and through.
7She spouts evil like a fountain! Her streets echo with the sounds of violence and destruction. Her sickness and sores are ever before me.
8This is your last warning, Jerusalem! If you do not listen, I will empty the land."

9This is what the LORD Almighty says: "Disaster will fall upon you. Even the few who remain in Israel will be gleaned again, as when a harvester checks each vine a second time to pick the grapes that were missed."

10To whom can I give warning? Who will listen when I speak? Their ears are closed, and they cannot hear. They scorn the word of the LORD. They don't want to listen at all.
11So now I am filled with the LORD's fury. Yes, I am weary of holding it in!

"I will pour out my fury over Jerusalem, even on children playing in the streets, on gatherings of young men, and on husbands and wives and grandparents.
12Their homes will be turned over to their enemies, and so will their fields and their wives. For I will punish the people of this land," says the LORD.

13"From the least to the greatest, they trick others to get what does not belong to them. Yes, even my prophets and priests are like that!
14They offer superficial treatments for my people's mortal wound. They give assurances of peace when all is war.
15Are they ashamed when they do these disgusting things? No, not at all—they don't even blush! Therefore, they will lie among the slaughtered. They will be humbled beneath my punishing anger," says the LORD.

6:2 Hebrew *Zion.*

## OUR RESPONSIBILITY • • • •

**6:10 The people became angry and wanted no part of God's commands. Living for God did not appear very exciting. There are people today, too, who dislike God's demand for disciplined living. As unsettling as people's responses might be, we must continue to share God's Word. Our responsibility is to present God's Word—their responsibility is to accept it. We must not let what people want to hear determine what we say.**

16So now the LORD says, "Stop right where you are! Look for the old, godly way, and walk in it. Travel its path, and you will find rest for your souls. But you reply, 'No, that's not the road we want!' 17I set watchmen over you who said, 'Listen for the sound of the trumpet!' But you replied, 'No! We won't pay attention!'

18"Therefore, listen to this, all you nations. Take note of my people's condition. 19Listen, all the earth! I will bring disaster upon my people. It is the fruit of their own sin because they refuse to listen to me. They have rejected all my instructions. 20There is no use now in offering me sweet incense from Sheba. Keep your expensive perfumes! I cannot accept your burnt offerings. Your sacrifices have no sweet fragrance for me."

21Therefore, this is what the LORD says: "I will put obstacles in my people's path. Fathers and sons will both fall over them. Neighbors and friends will collapse together."

22This is what the LORD says: "See a great army marching from the north! A great nation is rising against you from far-off lands. 23They are fully armed for slaughter. They are cruel and show no mercy. As they ride forward, the noise of their army is like a roaring sea. They are marching in battle formation to destroy you, Jerusalem.*"

24We have heard reports about the enemy, and we are weak with fright. Fear and pain have gripped us, like that of a woman about to give birth. 25Don't go out to the fields! Don't travel the roads! The enemy is everywhere, and they are ready to kill. We are terrorized at every turn! 26Now my people, dress yourselves in sackcloth, and sit among the ashes. Mourn and weep bitterly, as for the loss of an only son. For suddenly, the destroying armies will be upon you!

## RITUALS ● ● • • •

**7:8 The people followed a worship ritual but maintained a sinful lifestyle. It was religion without personal commitment to God. We can fall easily into this trap. Attending church, taking communion, teaching Sunday school, singing in the choir—all are empty exercises unless we are doing them for God.**

27"Jeremiah, I have made you a tester of metals, that you may determine the quality of my people. 28Are they not the worst of rebels, full of slander? They are as insolent as bronze, as hard and cruel as iron. All of them lead others into corruption. 29The bellows blow fiercely. The refining fire grows hotter. But it will never purify and cleanse them because there is no purity in them to refine. 30I will label them 'Rejected Silver' because I, the LORD, am discarding them."

CHAPTER **7** **FALSE WORSHIP.** The LORD gave another message to Jeremiah. He said, 2"Go to the entrance of the LORD's Temple, and give this message to the people: 'O Judah, listen to this message from the LORD! Listen to it, all of you who worship here! 3The LORD Almighty, the God of Israel, says: Even now, if you quit your evil ways, I will let you stay in your own land. 4But do not be fooled by those who repeatedly promise your safety because the Temple of the LORD is here. 5I will be merciful only if you stop your wicked thoughts and deeds and are fair to others; 6and if you stop exploiting foreigners, orphans, and widows; and if you stop your murdering; and if you stop worshiping idols as you now do to your own harm. 7Then I will let you stay in this land that I gave to your ancestors to keep forever.

8"'Do you think that because the Temple is here you will never suffer? Don't fool yourselves! 9Do you really think you can steal, murder, commit adultery, lie, and worship Baal and all those other new gods of yours, 10and then come here and stand before me in my Temple and chant, "We are safe!"—only to go right back to all those evils again? 11Do you think this Temple, which honors my name, is a den of thieves? I see all the evil going on there, says the LORD.

## HURT ● ● • • •

**7:19 This verse answers the question, "Who gets hurt when we turn away from God?" We do! Separating oneself from God is like keeping a green plant away from sunlight or water, or cutting off its food supply. God is our only source of spiritual strength. Cut yourself off from that source, and you cut off life itself.**

12"'Go to the place at Shiloh where I once put the Tabernacle to honor my name. See what I did there because of all the wickedness of my people, the Israelites. 13While you were doing these wicked things, says the LORD, I spoke to you about it repeatedly, but you would not listen. I called out to you, but you refused to answer. 14So just as I destroyed Shiloh, I will now destroy this Temple that was built to honor my name, this Temple that you trust for help, this place that I gave to you and your ancestors. 15And I will send you into exile, just as I did your relatives, the people of Israel.*'

16"Pray no more for these people, Jeremiah. Do not weep or pray for them, and don't beg me to help them, for I will not listen to you. 17Do you not see what they are doing throughout the towns of Judah and in the streets of Jerusalem? 18No wonder I am so angry! Watch how the children gather wood and the fathers build sacrificial fires. See how the women knead dough and make cakes to offer to the Queen of Heaven. And they give drink offerings to their other idol gods! 19Am I the one they are hurting?" asks the LORD. "Most of all, they hurt themselves, to their own shame."

20So the Sovereign LORD says: "I will pour out my terrible fury on this place. Its people, animals, trees, and crops will be consumed by the unquenchable fire of my anger."

21This is what the LORD Almighty, the God of Israel, says: "Away with your burnt offerings and sacrifices! Eat them yourselves! 22When I led your ancestors out

6:23 Hebrew *daughter of Zion.* 7:15 Hebrew *of Ephraim,* referring to the northern kingdom of Israel.

of Egypt, it was not burnt offerings and sacrifices I wanted from them. [23]This is what I told them: 'Obey me, and I will be your God, and you will be my people. Only do as I say, and all will be well!'

[24]"But my people would not listen to me. They kept on doing whatever they wanted, following the stubborn desires of their evil hearts. They went backward instead of forward. [25]From the day your ancestors left Egypt until now, I have continued to send my prophets—day in and day out. [26]But my people have not listened to me or even tried to hear. They have been stubborn and sinful—even worse than their ancestors.

[27]"Tell them all this, but do not expect them to listen. Shout out your warnings, but do not expect them to respond. [28]Say to them, 'This is the nation whose people will not obey the LORD their God and who refuse to be taught. Truth has vanished from among them; it is no longer heard on their lips. [29]O Jerusalem, shave your head in mourning, and weep alone on the mountains. For the LORD has rejected and forsaken this generation that has provoked his fury.'

[30]"The people of Judah have sinned before my very eyes," says the LORD. "They have set up their abominable idols right in my own Temple, defiling it. [31]They have built the pagan shrines of Topheth in the valley of the son of Hinnom, where they sacrifice their little sons and daughters in the fire. I have never commanded such a horrible deed; it never even crossed my mind to command such a thing! [32]So beware, for the time is coming," says the LORD, "when that place will no longer be called Topheth or the valley of the son of Hinnom, but the Valley of Slaughter. They will bury so many bodies in Topheth that there won't be room for all the graves. [33]The corpses of my people will be food for the vultures and wild animals, and no one will be left to scare them away. [34]I will put an end to the happy singing and laughter in the streets of Jerusalem. The joyful voices of bridegrooms and brides will no longer be heard in the towns of Judah. The land will lie in complete desolation.

## CHAPTER 8

"In that day," says the LORD, "the enemy will break open the graves of the kings and officials of Judah, and the graves of the priests, prophets, and common people. [2]They will dig out their bones and spread them out on the ground before the sun, moon, and stars—the gods my people have loved, served, and worshiped. Their bones will not be gathered up again or buried but will be scattered on the ground like dung. [3]And the people of this evil nation who survive will wish to die rather than live where I will send them. I, the LORD Almighty, have spoken!

[4]"Jeremiah, say to the people, 'This is what the LORD says: When people fall down, don't they get up again? When they start down the wrong road and discover their mistake, don't they turn back? [5]Then why do these people keep going along their self-destructive path, refusing to turn back, even though I have warned them? [6]I listen to their conversations, and what do I hear? Is anyone sorry for sin? Does anyone say, "What a terrible thing I have done"? No! All are running down the path of sin as swiftly as a horse rushing into battle! [7]The stork knows the time of her migration, as do the turtledove, the swallow, and the crane.* They all return at the proper time each year. But not my people! They do not know what the LORD requires of them.

[8]"'How can you say, "We are wise because we have the law of the LORD," when your teachers have twisted it so badly? [9]These wise teachers will be shamed by exile for their sin, for they have rejected the word of the LORD. Are they so wise after all? [10]I will give their wives and their farms to others. From the least to the greatest, they trick others to get what does not belong to them. Yes, even my prophets and priests are like that. [11]They offer superficial treatments for my people's mortal wound. They give assurances of peace when all is war. [12]Are they ashamed when they do these disgusting things? No, not at all—they don't even blush! Therefore, they will lie among the slaughtered. They will be humbled when they are punished, says the LORD. [13]I will take away their rich harvests of figs and grapes. Their fruit trees will all die. All the good things I prepared for them will soon be gone. I, the LORD, have spoken!'

### BEWARE ● ● • • •

**8:11 The prophets and priests were giving false assurances rather than correction. How can we correct a fault or turn from a sin if our leaders tell us all is well? Beware of people who are always agreeable. At best, they give you no help; at worst, they may be trying to manipulate you.**

[14]"Then the people will say, 'Why should we wait here to die? Come, let's go to the fortified cities to die there. For the LORD our God has decreed our destruction and has given us a cup of poison to drink because we sinned against the LORD. [15]We hoped for peace, but no peace came. We hoped for a time of healing, but found only terror. [16]The snorting of the enemies' warhorses can be heard all the way from the land of Dan in the north! The whole land trembles at the approach of the terrible army, for it is coming to devour the land and everything in it—cities and people alike.'

[17]"I will send these enemy troops among you like poisonous snakes you cannot charm," says the LORD. "No matter what you do, they will bite you, and you will die."

[18]My grief is beyond healing; my heart is broken. [19]Listen to the weeping of my people; it can be heard all across the land.

"Has the LORD abandoned Jerusalem*?" the people ask. "Is her King no longer there?"

8:7 The identification of some of these birds is uncertain. 8:19 Hebrew *Zion*.

"Oh, why have they angered me with their carved
idols and worthless gods?" asks the LORD.
20"The harvest is finished, and the summer is
gone," the people cry, "yet we are not saved!"
21I weep for the hurt of my people. I am stunned
and silent, mute with grief. 22Is there no medicine in
Gilead? Is there no physician there? Why is there no
healing for the wounds of my people?

## CHAPTER 9

**JEREMIAH CRIES.** Oh, that my eyes
were a fountain of tears; I would weep forever! I
would sob day and night for all my people who have
been slaughtered. 2Oh, that I could go away and
forget them and live in a shack in the desert, for they
are all adulterous and treacherous.
3"My people bend their tongues like bows to
shoot lies. They refuse to stand up for the truth. And
they only go from bad to worse! They care nothing
for me," says the LORD.

### PRIORITIES

In August, some guys from Adams High are sitting around discussing their summers:

Brandon: "Get this—my Dad is paying me $8 an hour to make deliveries! Counting that and my afternoon lawn business, I'm gonna clear $3,000 easy!"

Jim: "That's great, but money ain't gonna help you block on the football field. I've been in the gym every day. So far, I've increased my bench press from 200 to 250 pounds! I'll be all-district this year."

Glenn: "Too bad you didn't work out your brain muscle! I've had the best of all possible summers. I'm in shape, I earned a little money, I had a great social life, and I just got back from computer camp—"

All (laughing): "Computer camp?! You're kidding!"

Glenn: "Hey, laugh all you want. We'll see who's laughing next spring when I get a scholarship to Princeton or Harvard, and you guys are dinking around at some junior college."

Jim: "What about you, Rick? Didn't you just go on some church trip?"

Rick's kind of embarrassed. He did just return from a mission trip to Mexico. It was incredible, but compared to making tons of money, turning into Arnold Schwarzenegger, or getting a scholarship, it doesn't seem like much.

Can you relate to Rick's feelings? What does this scene show us about priorities? See Jeremiah 9:23-24 for a clear look at what really matters.

4"Beware of your neighbor! Beware of your
brother! They all take advantage of one another and
spread their slanderous lies. 5They all fool and de-
fraud each other; no one tells the truth. With practiced tongues they tell lies; they wear themselves out
with all their sinning. 6They pile lie upon lie and
utterly refuse to come to me," says the LORD.
7Therefore, the LORD Almighty says, "See, I will
melt them in a crucible and test them like metal.
What else can I do with them? 8For their tongues aim
lies like poisoned arrows. They promise peace to

### BROKEN

8:20-22 **These verses provide a vivid picture of Jeremiah's emotions as he watched his people reject God. He responded with anguish to a world dying in sin. We watch that same world still dying in sin, still rejecting God. But how often is our heart broken for our lost friends and neighbors, our lost world? Only when we have Jeremiah's kind of concern will we be moved to help. We must begin by asking God to break our heart for the world he loves.**

their neighbors while planning to kill them. 9Should
I not punish them for this?" asks the LORD. "Should
I not avenge myself against a nation such as this?"
10I will weep for the mountains and wail for the
desert pastures. For they are desolate and empty of
life; the lowing of cattle is heard no more; the birds
and wild animals all have fled.
11"I will make Jerusalem into a heap of ruins," says
the LORD. "It will be a place haunted by jackals. The
towns of Judah will be ghost towns, with no one
living in them."
12Who is wise enough to understand all this? Who
has been instructed by the LORD and can explain it to
others? Why has the land been ruined so completely
that no one even dares to travel through it?
13The LORD replies, "This has happened because my
people have abandoned the instructions I gave them;
they have refused to obey my law. 14Instead, they have
stubbornly followed their own desires and worshiped
the images of Baal, as their ancestors taught them. 15So
now, listen to what the LORD Almighty, the God of
Israel, says: Look! I will feed them with bitterness and
give them poison to drink. 16I will scatter them around
the world, and they will be strangers in distant lands.
Their enemies will chase them with the sword until I
have destroyed them completely."
17This is what the LORD Almighty says: "Think
about what is going on! Call for the mourners to
come. 18Quick! Begin your weeping! Let the tears
flow from your eyes. 19Hear the people of Jerusalem*
crying in despair, 'We are ruined! Disaster has come
upon us! We must leave our land, because our
homes have been torn down.'"
20Listen, you women, to the words of the LORD;
open your ears to what he has to say. Teach your
daughters to wail; teach one another how to lament.
21For death has crept in through our windows and
has entered our mansions. It has killed off the flower
of our youth: Children no longer play in the streets,
and young men no longer gather in the squares.
22And the LORD says, "Bodies will be scattered across
the fields like dung, or like bundles of grain after the
harvest. No one will be left to bury them."
23This is what the LORD says: "Let not the wise
man gloat in his wisdom, or the mighty man in his
might, or the rich man in his riches. 24Let them boast
in this alone: that they truly know me and understand that I am the LORD who is just and righteous,
whose love is unfailing, and that I delight in these
things. I, the LORD, have spoken!
25"A time is coming," says the LORD, "when I will
punish all those who are circumcised in body but

9:19 Hebrew *Zion*.

not in spirit—26the Egyptians, Edomites, Ammonites, Moabites, the people who live in distant
places,* and yes, even the people of Judah. Like all
these pagan nations, the people of Israel also have
uncircumcised hearts."

CHAPTER **10** **THE GOD OF CREATION.** Hear the
word of the LORD, O Israel! 2This is what the LORD
says: "Do not act like other nations who try to read
their future in the stars. Do not be afraid of their
predictions, even though other nations are terrified
by them. 3Their ways are futile and foolish. They cut
down a tree and carve an idol. 4They decorate it with
gold and silver and then fasten it securely with hammer and nails so it won't fall over. 5There stands their
god like a helpless scarecrow in a garden! It cannot
speak, and it needs to be carried because it cannot
walk. Do not be afraid of such gods, for they can
neither harm you nor do you any good."

6LORD, there is no one like you! For you are great,
and your name is full of power. 7Who would not fear
you, O King of nations? That title belongs to you
alone! Among all the wise people of the earth and in
all the kingdoms of the world, there is no one like you.

8The wisest of people who worship idols are stupid and foolish. The things they worship are made
of wood! 9They bring beaten sheets of silver from
Tarshish and gold from Uphaz, and they give these
materials to skillful craftsmen who make their idols.
Then they dress these gods in royal purple robes
made by expert tailors. 10But the LORD is the only true
God, the living God. He is the everlasting King! The
whole earth trembles at his anger. The nations hide
before his wrath.

11Say this to those who worship other gods: "Your
so-called gods, who did not make the heavens and
earth, will vanish from the earth."*

12 But God made the earth by his power,
and he preserves it by his wisdom.
He has stretched out the heavens
by his understanding.
13 When he speaks, there is thunder in the heavens.
He causes the clouds to rise over the earth.
He sends the lightning with the rain
and releases the wind from his storehouses.
14 Compared to him, all people are foolish
and have no knowledge at all!
They make idols, but the idols will disgrace their
makers,
for they are frauds.
They have no life or power in them.
15 Idols are worthless; they are lies!
The time is coming when they will all be
destroyed.
16 But the God of Israel* is no idol!
He is the Creator of everything that exists,
including Israel, his own special possession.
The LORD Almighty is his name!

17"Pack your bag and prepare to leave; the siege is
about to begin," 18says the LORD. "For suddenly, I
will fling you from this land and pour great troubles
upon you. At last you will feel my anger."

19My wound is desperate, and my grief is great. My
sickness is incurable, but I must bear it. 20My home
is gone, and no one is left to help me rebuild it. My
children have been taken away, and I will never see
them again. 21The shepherds of my people have lost
their senses. They no longer follow the LORD or ask
what he wants of them. Therefore, they fail completely, and their flocks are scattered. 22Listen! Hear
the terrifying roar of great armies as they roll down
from the north. The towns of Judah will be destroyed
and will become a haunt for jackals.

**STAR CHARTS ● ● • • •**

10:2-3 **Everyone would like to know the future. Decisions would be easier, failures avoided, and success assured. The people of Judah wanted to know the future, too, and they tried to discern by reading signs in the sky (like horoscopes). Jeremiah's response applies today: God made the stars that people consult. No one will discover the future in made-up charts of God's stars. God, who promises to guide you, knows your future and will be with you all the way. He may not reveal your future to you, but he will walk with you as the future unfolds. Don't trust the stars; trust the One who made the stars.**

23I know, LORD, that a person's life is not his own.
No one is able to plan his own course. 24So correct
me, LORD, but please be gentle. Do not correct me in
anger, for I would die. 25Pour out your wrath on the
nations that refuse to recognize you—on nations
that do not call upon your name. For they have
utterly devoured your people Israel,* making the
land a desolate wilderness.

CHAPTER **11** **REMEMBER GOD'S PROMISE.** The LORD
gave another message to Jeremiah. He said, 2"Remind the people of Judah and Jerusalem about the
terms of their covenant with me. 3Say to them, 'This
is what the LORD, the God of Israel, says: Cursed is
anyone who does not obey the terms of my covenant! 4For I said to your ancestors when I brought
them out of slavery in Egypt, "If you obey me and do
whatever I command you, then you will be my
people, and I will be your God." 5I said this so I
could keep my promise to your ancestors to give you
a land flowing with milk and honey—the land you
live in today.'"

Then I replied, "So be it,* LORD!"

6Then the LORD said, "Broadcast this message in
the streets of Jerusalem. Go from town to town
throughout the land and say, 'Remember the covenant your ancestors made, and do everything they
promised. 7For I solemnly warned your ancestors
when I brought them out of Egypt, repeating over
and over again to this day: "Obey me!" 8But your

**9:26** Or *the people who clip the corners of their hair.* **10:11** The original text of this verse is in Aramaic. **10:16** Hebrew *the Portion of Jacob.* **10:25** Hebrew *Jacob.* **11:5** Hebrew *Amen.*

# Ultimate Issues

## IDOLATRY

A drunken orgy around a golden calf . . . the latest sports car . . . offering sacrifices to Baal . . . teenagers screaming approval at a rock 'n' roll concert . . . What do these scenes have in common? They all represent forms of idol worship. *"Wait a minute,"* you say. "The golden calf and Baal worship, OK; but what in the world does this have to do with fast cars and rock 'n' roll?" Just this: an idol doesn't have to be a "religious" object. An idol is *anything* we desire above God and his will for our lives. Ouch! We can see the evil in what Israel did, and we're sure we would never commit that sin. But for us, idolatry comes in more subtle forms. Instead of a golden calf, we're enticed by A "GOLDEN" CREDIT CARD. Instead of Baal, we "worship" ball players, imitating them from their hairstyles to their shoes. Instead of Temple prostitutes, we're seduced by the glossy covers of skin magazines peering from behind magazine racks and the explicit sex **CABLE TV** brings into our homes. So are credit cards, sports, or sex wrong? Of course not. All those things may have a place in the lives of God's people. The problem comes in using them the wrong way, or in loving things (or people) more than we love God. That's when it becomes idolatry. Why is idolatry so bad? Why does God hate it so much? First, worshiping a false god (anything that comes before the *real* God is a *false* god) degrades us. It makes us less than what we are intended to be. We are made in the image of God, with the opportunity through Christ to know him and, in some ways, to be like him. When we worship an idol—a lesser god—we aim much lower and, all too often, hit our target. We become like the phony instead of **THE GENUINE ARTICLE.** Psalm 115:8 says, "Those who make [idols] are just like them." In other words, you come to resemble what you worship. We should think seriously before giving our undying allegiance to someone. Is the person you admire a worthy role model? Is he or she a Christian? Does his or her lifestyle reflect Christlike values? Too often, our "heroes" are a photographic negative of Christ—blasphemous, obscene, self-centered heathens. Be careful—***you become like what you worship.*** Second, idolatry often is subtle and hard to detect. Think about a boyfriend or girlfriend you have or used to have. (OK—one you wish you had.) Usually, the relationship starts out fine: physically, you're under control; emotionally, you make each other feel more positive; spiritually, you build each other up. But as time passes, it gets more and more difficult to keep your sexual relationship in check . . . you begin to depend on each other to an unhealthy degree . . . and your spiritual growth slows to ZERO MILES PER HOUR. Why? While there can be lots of reasons, often the problem is that you have (maybe unintentionally) committed idolatry together. You put each other before God, which is disastrous for your relationship with each other and with him. Confession and repentance can make it right; but often the relationship is so warped that you have to end it. Idolatry has a way of creeping in and destroying parts of your life, just as cancer destroys parts of your body. We must guard against idolatry's **creeping poison.** Finally, idol worship steals from God. Nobody with functional brain cells would knowingly do that. When we love someone or something else more than God, we rob him of the worship and loyalty that rightly belong only to him. In Exodus 20:4-5, God says: "Do not make idols of any kind . . . for I, the LORD your God, am a jealous God." He alone is worthy of our love and trust. History is crowded with people who would be gods, but there's only one God who would be man. Don't commit idolatry. Give your devotion to the God who loved you enough to die for you; worship only him.

ancestors did not pay any attention; they would not even listen. Instead, they stubbornly followed their own evil desires. And because they refused to obey, I brought upon them all the curses described in our covenant.'"

9Again the LORD spoke to me and said, "I have discovered a conspiracy against me among the people of Judah and Jerusalem. 10They have returned to the sins of their forefathers. They have refused to listen to me and are worshiping idols. Israel and Judah have both broken the covenant I made with their ancestors. 11Therefore, says the LORD, I am going to bring calamity upon them, and they will not escape. Though they beg for mercy, I will not listen to their cries. 12Then the people of Judah and Jerusalem will pray to their idols and offer incense before them. But the idols will not save them when disaster strikes! 13Look now, people of Judah, you have as many gods as there are cities and towns. Your altars of shame—altars for burning incense to your god Baal—are along every street in Jerusalem.

14"Pray no more for these people, Jeremiah. Do not weep or pray for them, for I will not listen to them when they cry out to me in distress. 15What right do my beloved people have to come to my Temple, where they have done so many immoral things? Can their sacrifices avert their destruction? They actually rejoice in doing evil!

16"I, the LORD, once called them a thriving olive tree, beautiful to see and full of good fruit. But now I have sent the fury of their enemies to burn them with fire, leaving them charred and broken. 17I, the LORD Almighty, who planted this olive tree, have ordered it destroyed. For the people of Israel and Judah have done evil, provoking my anger by offering incense to Baal."

18Then the LORD told me about the plots my enemies were making against me. 19I had been as unaware as a lamb on the way to its slaughter. I had no idea that they were planning to kill me! "Let's destroy this man and all his words," they said. "Let's kill him, so his name will be forgotten forever."

20O LORD Almighty, you are just, and you examine the deepest thoughts of hearts and minds. Let me see your vengeance against them, for I have committed my cause to you.

21The men of Anathoth wanted me dead. They said they would kill me if I did not stop speaking in the LORD's name. 22So this is what the LORD Almighty says about them: "I will punish them! Their young men will die in battle, and their little boys and girls will starve. 23Not one of these plotters from Anathoth will survive, for I will bring disaster upon them when their time of punishment comes."

## CHAPTER 12

**JEREMIAH COMPLAINS TO GOD.** LORD, you always give me justice when I bring a case before you. Now let me bring you this complaint: Why are the wicked so prosperous? Why are evil people so happy? 2You have planted them, and they have taken root and prospered. Your name is on their lips, but in their hearts they give you no credit at all. 3But as for me, LORD, you know my heart. You see me and test my thoughts. Drag these people away like helpless sheep to be butchered! Set them aside to be slaughtered!

4How long must this land weep? Even the grass in the fields has withered. The wild animals and birds have disappeared because of the evil in the land. Yet the people say, "The LORD won't do anything!"

5Then the LORD replied to me, "If racing against mere men makes you tired, how will you race against horses? If you stumble and fall on open ground, what will you do in the thickets near the Jordan? 6Even your own brothers, members of your own family, have turned on you. They have plotted, raising a cry against you. Do not trust them, no matter how pleasantly they speak.

### TOUGH TIMES ● ● ● • •

12:5-6 **Life was difficult for Jeremiah despite his love for and obedience to God. When he asked God for relief, God's reply in effect was, "If you think this is bad, how are you going to cope when it gets really tough?" Not all of God's answers to prayer are nice or easy to accept. Any Christian who has experienced war, grief, or a serious illness knows this. But we are to be committed to God even when the going gets tough, and when he doesn't answer our prayers with immediate relief.**

7"I have abandoned my people, my special possession. I have surrendered my dearest ones to their enemies. 8My chosen people have roared at me like a lion of the forest, so I have treated them as though I hated them. 9My chosen people have become as disgusting to me as a vulture. And indeed, they are surrounded by vultures. Bring on the wild beasts to pick their corpses clean!

10"Many rulers have ravaged my vineyard, trampling down the vines and turning all its beauty into a barren wilderness. 11They have made it an empty wasteland; I hear its mournful cry. The whole land is desolate, and no one even cares. 12Destroying armies plunder the land. The sword of the LORD kills people from one end of the nation to the other. No one will escape! 13My people have planted wheat but are harvesting thorns. They have worked hard, but it has done them no good. They will harvest a crop of shame, for the fierce anger of the LORD is upon them."

14Now this is what the LORD says: "As for all the evil nations reaching out for the inheritance I gave my people Israel, I will uproot them from their lands just as Judah will be uprooted from hers. 15But afterward I will return and have compassion on all of them. I will bring them home to their own lands again, each nation to its own inheritance. 16And if these nations quickly learn the ways of my people, and if they learn to swear by my name, saying, 'As surely as the LORD lives' (just as they taught my people to swear by the name of Baal), then they will be given a place among my people. 17But any nation who refuses to obey me will be uprooted and destroyed. I, the LORD, have spoken!"

## CHAPTER 13 GOOD FOR NOTHING.

This is what the LORD said to me: "Go and buy a linen belt and put it around your waist, but do not wash it." 2So I bought the belt as the LORD directed me and put it around my waist. 3Then the LORD gave me another message: 4"Take the linen belt you are wearing, and go to the Euphrates River.* Hide it there in a hole in the rocks." 5So I went and hid it at the Euphrates as the LORD had instructed me.

6A long time afterward, the LORD said to me, "Go back to the Euphrates and get the linen belt that I told you to hide there." 7So I went to the Euphrates and dug it out of the hole where I had hidden it. But now it was mildewed and falling apart. The belt was useless.

8Then I received this message from the LORD: 9"The LORD says: This illustrates how I will rot away the pride of Judah and Jerusalem. 10These wicked people refuse to listen to me. They stubbornly follow their own desires and worship idols. Therefore, they will become like this linen belt—good for nothing! 11As a belt clings to a person's waist, so I created Judah and Israel to cling to me," says the LORD. "They were to be my people, my pride, my glory—an honor to my name. But they would not listen to me.

### USELESS ● ● • • •

13:1-11 **Actions speak louder than words. Jeremiah often used vivid object lessons to arouse the people's curiosity and get his point across. This lesson of the linen belt illustrated Judah's destiny. Although the people had once been close to God, their pride had made them useless. A proud person may look important, but God says his pride makes him good for nothing. Pride rots our heart until we lose our usefulness to God.**

12"So tell them, 'The LORD, the God of Israel, says: All your wineskins will be full of wine.' And they will reply, 'Of course, you don't need to tell us how prosperous we will be!' 13Then tell them, 'No, this is what the LORD means: I will make everyone in this land so confused that they will seem drunk—from the king sitting on David's throne and from the priests and the prophets, right on down to the common people. 14I will smash them one against the other, even parents against children, says the LORD. I will not let my pity or mercy or compassion keep me from destroying them.'"

15Listen! Do not be proud, for the LORD has spoken. 16Give glory to the LORD your God before it is too late. Acknowledge him before he brings darkness upon you, causing you to stumble and fall on the dark mountains. For then, when you look for light, you will find only terrible darkness. 17And if you still refuse to listen, I will weep alone because of your pride. My eyes will overflow with tears because the LORD's flock will be led away into exile.

18Say to the king and his mother, "Come down

### DANGER ● ● • • •

13:15 **While it is good to respect our country and our church, our loyalties always carry a hidden danger—pride. When is pride harmful? When it causes us (1) to look down on others; (2) to be selfish with our resources; (3) to force our solutions on others' problems; (4) to think God is blessing us because of our own merits; (5) to be content with our plans rather than seeking God's plans.**

from your thrones and sit in the dust, for your glorious crowns will soon be snatched from your heads." 19The towns of the Negev will close their gates, and no one will be able to open them. The people of Judah will be taken away as captives. They will all be carried into exile.

20See the armies marching down from the north! Where is your flock—your beautiful flock—that he gave you to care for? 21How will you feel when the LORD sets your foreign allies over you as rulers? You will writhe in pain like a woman giving birth! 22You may ask yourself, "Why is all this happening to me?" It is because of your many sins! That is why you have been raped and destroyed by invading armies. 23Can an Ethiopian* change the color of his skin? Can a leopard take away its spots? Neither can you start doing good, for you always do evil.

24"I will scatter you, just as chaff is scattered by the winds blowing in from the desert. 25This is your allotment, that which is due you," says the LORD. "I have measured it out especially for you, because you have forgotten me and put your trust in false gods. 26I myself will expose you to shame. 27I am keenly aware of your adultery and lust, and your abominable idol worship out in the fields and on the hills. Your destruction is sure, Jerusalem! How long will it be before you are pure?"

## CHAPTER 14 GOD LOSES HIS PATIENCE.

This message came to Jeremiah from the LORD, explaining why he was holding back the rain: 2"Judah wilts; her businesses have ground to a halt. All the people sit on the ground in mourning, and a great cry rises from Jerusalem. 3The nobles send servants to get water, but all the wells are dry. The servants return with empty pitchers, confused and desperate, covering their heads in grief. 4The ground is parched and cracked for lack of rain. The farmers are afraid; they, too, cover their heads. 5The deer abandons her newborn fawn because there is no grass. 6The wild donkeys stand on the bare hills panting like thirsty jackals. They strain their eyes looking for grass to eat, but there is none to be found."

7The people say, "LORD, our wickedness has caught up with us. We have sinned against you. So please, help us for the sake of your own reputation. 8O Hope of Israel, our Savior in times of trouble! Why are you like a stranger to us? Why are you like someone passing through the land, stopping only for the night? 9Are you also confused? Are you helpless to save us? You are right here among us, LORD. We are known as your people. Please don't abandon us now!"

13:4 Hebrew *Perath;* also in 13:5, 6, 7. 13:23 Hebrew *a Cushite.*

10 So the LORD replies to his people, "You love to
wander far from me and do not follow in my paths.
Now I will no longer accept you as my people. I will
remember all your wickedness and will punish you
for your sins."
11 Then the LORD said to me, "Do not pray for these
people anymore. 12 When they fast in my presence, I
will pay no attention. When they present their burnt
offerings and grain offerings to me, I will not accept
them. In return, I will give them only war, famine,
and disease."
13 Then I said, "O Sovereign LORD, their prophets
are telling them, 'All is well—no war or famine will
come. The LORD will surely send you peace.'"
14 Then the LORD said, "These prophets are telling
lies in my name. I did not send them or tell them to
speak. I did not give them any messages. They prophesy of visions and revelations they have never seen or
heard. They speak foolishness made up in their own
lying hearts. 15 Therefore, says the LORD, I will punish
these lying prophets, for they have spoken in my name
even though I never sent them. They say that no war or
famine will come, but they themselves will die by war
and famine! 16 As for the people to whom they prophesy—their bodies will be thrown out into the streets of
Jerusalem, victims of famine and war. There will be no
one left to bury them. Husbands, wives, sons, and
daughters—all will be gone. For I will pour out their
own wickedness on them.
17 "Now, Jeremiah, say this to them: 'Night and day
my eyes overflow with tears. I cannot stop weeping,
for my virgin daughter—my precious people—has
been run through with a sword and lies mortally
wounded on the ground. 18 If I go out into the fields,
I see the bodies of people slaughtered by the enemy.
If I walk the city streets, there I see people who have
died of starvation. The prophets and priests continue
with their work, but they do not know what they are
doing.'"
19 LORD, have you completely rejected Judah? Do
you really hate Jerusalem*? Why have you wounded
us past all hope of healing? We hoped for peace, but
no peace came. We hoped for a time of healing but
found only terror.
20 LORD, we confess our wickedness and that of our
ancestors, too. We all have sinned against you. 21 For
the sake of your own name, LORD, do not abandon
us. Do not disgrace yourself and the throne of your
glory. Do not break your covenant with us. Please
don't forget us!
22 Can any of the foreign gods send us rain? Does
it fall from the sky by itself? No, it comes from you,
the LORD our God! Only you can do such things. So
we will wait for you to help us.

CHAPTER **15** **JERUSALEM, A CITY IN TROUBLE.** Then
the LORD said to me, "Even if Moses and Samuel
stood before me pleading for these people, I
wouldn't help them. Away with them! Get them out
of my sight! 2 And if they say to you, 'But where can
we go?' tell them, 'This is what the LORD says: Those
who are destined for death, to death; those who are
destined for war, to war; those who are destined for
famine, to famine; those who are destined for captivity, to captivity.'
3 "I will send four kinds of destroyers against
them," says the LORD. "I will send the sword to kill,
the dogs to drag away, the vultures to devour, and the
wild animals to finish up what is left. 4 Because of the
wicked things Manasseh son of Hezekiah, king of
Judah, did in Jerusalem, I will make my people an
object of horror to all the kingdoms of the earth.
5 "Who will feel sorry for you, Jerusalem? Who will
weep for you? Who will even bother to ask how you
are? 6 You have forsaken me and turned your back on
me," says the LORD. "Therefore, I will raise my
clenched fists to destroy you. I am tired of always
giving you another chance. 7 I will winnow you like
grain at the gates of your cities and take away everything you hold dear. I will destroy my own people,
because they refuse to turn back to me from all their
evil ways.
8 "There will be more widows than the grains of
sand along the seashore. At noontime I will bring a
destroyer against the mothers of young men. I will
cause anguish and terror to come upon them suddenly. 9 The mother of seven grows faint and gasps
for breath; her sun has gone down while it is yet day.
She sits childless now, disgraced and humiliated.
And those who are left, I will hand over to the enemy
to be killed," says the LORD.
10 Then I said, "What sadness is mine, my mother.
Oh, that I had died at birth! I am hated everywhere
I go. I am neither a lender who has threatened to
foreclose nor a borrower who refuses to pay—yet
they all curse me."
11 The LORD replied, "All will be well with you,
Jeremiah. Your enemies will ask you to plead on
their behalf in times of trouble and distress. 12 Can a
man break a bar of iron from the north, or a bar of
bronze? 13 Because of all my people's sins against me,
I will hand over their wealth and treasures as plunder
to the enemy. 14 I will tell their enemies to take them
as captives to a foreign land. For my anger blazes
forth like fire, and it will consume them."
15 Then I said, "LORD, you know I am suffering for
your sake. Punish my persecutors! Don't let them
kill me! Be merciful to me and give them what they
deserve! 16 Your words are what sustain me. They

14:19 Hebrew *Zion.*

**TOO LATE ● ● • • •**

14:11-12 **The people of Judah had stretched God's patience. Their false repentance and empty rituals had continued long enough, and so God turned deaf ears to their cries. For a third time, God told Jeremiah not to pray for the people. Why should people pray to God, when he was less important to them than handmade idols of wood or stone? Why not let the idols answer their prayers? If you are putting something ahead of God when all is going well, will you be content to trust in this false god when you are in trouble?**

## INFLUENCE ● ● • • •

**15:17-21 Jeremiah accused God of not helping him when he really needed it. Jeremiah had taken his eyes off God's purposes and was feeling sorry for himself. He was angry, hurt, and afraid. In response, God didn't get angry at Jeremiah; he answered by reminding Jeremiah of his promise—"You will be my spokesman." There are three important lessons in this passage: (1) in prayer we can reveal our deepest thoughts to God; (2) God expects us to trust no matter what; and (3) we are here to influence others for God.**

bring me great joy and are my heart's delight, for I bear your name, O LORD God Almighty. [17]I never joined the people in their merry feasts. I sat alone because your hand was on me. I burst with indignation at their sins. [18]Why then does my suffering continue? Why is my wound so incurable? Your help seems as uncertain as a seasonal brook. It is like a spring that has gone dry."

[19]The LORD replied, "If you return to me, I will restore you so you can continue to serve me. If you speak words that are worthy, you will be my spokesman. You are to influence them; do not let them influence you! [20]They will fight against you like an attacking army, but I will make you as secure as a fortified wall. They will not conquer you, for I will protect and deliver you. I, the LORD, have spoken! [21]Yes, I will certainly keep you safe from these wicked men. I will rescue you from their cruel hands."

## CHAPTER 16 A PEOPLE WHO TRY TO RUN FROM GOD.

The LORD gave me another message. He said, [2]"Do not marry or have children in this place. [3]For this is what the LORD says about the children born here in this city and about their mothers and fathers: [4]They will die from terrible diseases. No one will mourn for them or bury them, and they will lie scattered on the ground like dung. They will die from war and famine, and their bodies will be food for the vultures and wild animals.

[5]"Do not go to their funerals to mourn and show sympathy for them," says the LORD, "for I have removed my protection and peace from them. I have taken away my unfailing love and my mercy. [6]Both the great and the lowly will die in this land. No one will bury them or mourn for them. Their friends will not cut themselves or shave their heads in sadness. [7]No one will offer a meal to comfort those who mourn for the dead—not even for the death of a mother or a father. No one will send a cup of wine to console them.

[8]"And do not go to their feasts and parties. Do not eat and drink with them at all. [9]For the LORD Almighty, the God of Israel, says: In your own lifetime, before your very eyes, I will put an end to the happy singing and laughter in this land. The joyful voices of bridegrooms and brides will no longer be heard.

[10]"When you tell the people all these things, they will ask, 'Why has the LORD decreed such terrible things against us? What have we done to deserve such treatment? What is our sin against the LORD our God?' [11]Tell them that this is the LORD's reply: It is because your ancestors were unfaithful to me. They worshiped other gods and served them. They abandoned me. They did not keep my law. [12]And you are even worse than your ancestors! You stubbornly follow your own evil desires and refuse to listen to me. [13]So I will throw you out of this land and send you into a foreign land where you and your ancestors have never been. There you can worship idols all you like—and I will grant you no favors!

[14]"But the time is coming," says the LORD, "when people who are taking an oath will no longer say, 'As surely as the LORD lives, who rescued the people of Israel from the land of Egypt.' [15]Instead, they will say, 'As surely as the LORD lives, who brought the people of Israel back to their own land from the land of the north and from all the countries to which he had exiled them.' For I will bring them back to this land that I gave their ancestors.

[16]"But now I am sending for many fishermen who will catch them," says the LORD. "I am sending for hunters who will search for them in the forests and caves. [17]I am watching them closely, and I see every sin. They cannot hope to hide from me. [18]I will punish them doubly for all their sins, because they have defiled my land with lifeless images of their detestable gods and filled my inheritance with their evil deeds."

[19]LORD, you are my strength and fortress, my refuge in the day of trouble! Nations from around the world will come to you and say, "Our ancestors were foolish, for they worshiped worthless idols. [20]Can people make their own god? The gods they make are not real gods at all!"

[21]"So now I will show them my power and might," says the LORD. "At last they will know that I am the LORD."

## HE KNOWS ● ● • • •

**16:17 Small children think that if they can't see you, then you can't see them. The people may have wished that hiding from God was as simple as closing their eyes. Although they closed their eyes to their sinful ways, their sins certainly weren't hidden from God. He who sees all cannot be deceived. Do you have a sinful attitude or action that you hope God won't notice? He knows about it. The first step to repentance is to acknowledge that God knows about our sins.**

## CHAPTER 17 A GREEN AND GROWING TREE.

The LORD says, "My people act as though their evil ways are laws to be obeyed, inscribed with a diamond point on their stony hearts, or with an iron chisel on the corners of their altars. [2]Even their children go to worship at their sacred altars and Asherah poles, beneath every green tree and on every high hill. [3]So I will give all your wealth and treasures—together with your pagan shrines—as plunder to your enemies, for sin runs rampant in your land. [4]The wonderful inheritance I have reserved for you will slip out of your hands, and I will send you away as captives to a foreign land. For you have kindled my anger into a roaring fire that will burn forever."

[5]This is what the LORD says: "Cursed are those

who put their trust in mere humans and turn their hearts away from the LORD. 6They are like stunted shrubs in the desert, with no hope for the future. They will live in the barren wilderness, on the salty flats where no one lives.

7"But blessed are those who trust in the LORD and have made the LORD their hope and confidence. 8They are like trees planted along a riverbank, with roots that reach deep into the water. Such trees are not bothered by the heat or worried by long months of drought. Their leaves stay green, and they go right on producing delicious fruit.

9"The human heart is most deceitful and desperately wicked. Who really knows how bad it is? 10But I know! I, the LORD, search all hearts and examine secret motives. I give all people their due rewards, according to what their actions deserve."

11Like a bird that hatches eggs she has not laid, so are those who get their wealth by unjust means. Sooner or later they will lose their riches and, at the end of their lives, will become poor old fools.

12But we worship at your throne—eternal, high, and glorious! 13O LORD, the hope of Israel, all who turn away from you will be disgraced and shamed. They will be buried in a dry and dusty grave, for they have forsaken the LORD, the fountain of living water.

14O LORD, you alone can heal me; you alone can save. My praises are for you alone! 15People scoff at me and say, "What is this 'message from the LORD' you keep talking about? Why don't your predictions come true?"

16LORD, I have not abandoned my job as a shepherd for your people. I have not urged you to send disaster. It is your message I have given them, not my own. 17LORD, do not desert me now! You alone are my hope in the day of disaster. 18Bring shame and terror on all who persecute me, but give me peace. Yes, bring double destruction upon them!

19Then the LORD said to me, "Go and stand in the gates of Jerusalem, first at the gate where the king goes out, and then at each of the other gates. 20Say to all the people, 'Listen to this message from the LORD, you kings of Judah and all you people of Judah and everyone living in Jerusalem. 21This is what the LORD says: Listen to my warning and live! Stop carrying on your trade at Jerusalem's gates on the Sabbath day. 22Do not do your work on the Sabbath, but make it a holy day. I gave this command to your ancestors, 23but they did not listen or obey. They stubbornly refused to pay attention and would not respond to discipline.

24"'But if you obey me, says the LORD, and do not carry on your trade or work on the Sabbath day, and if you keep it holy, 25then this nation will continue forever. There will always be a descendant of David sitting on the throne here in Jerusalem. Kings and their officials will always ride among the people of Judah in chariots and on horses, and this city will remain forever. 26And from all around Jerusalem, from the towns of Judah and Benjamin, from the western foothills* and the hill country and the Negev, the people will come with their burnt offerings and sacrifices. They will bring their grain offerings, incense, and thanksgiving offerings to the LORD's Temple.

27"'But if you do not listen to me and refuse to keep the Sabbath holy, and if on the Sabbath day you bring loads of merchandise through the gates of Jerusalem just as on other days, then I will set fire to these gates. The fire will spread to the palaces, and no one will be able to put out the roaring flames.'"

**I have done some pretty awful things in my life—things that other kids never even think about doing. How could God forgive me for what I've done?**

Recognizing that you've done wrong is 90 percent of the battle.

Usually people who build up years of wrong actions also have built a shell around their hearts. This shell protects them from feeling guilty about the wrong they have done. As the shell gets harder and thicker, they continue a downward spiral, doing more and more things that are wrong.

Jeremiah, a prophet of God, looked at the human tendency to sin and came to this conclusion: "The human heart is most deceitful and desperately wicked. Who really knows how bad it is? But I know! I, the LORD, search all hearts and examine secret motives. I give all people their due rewards, according to what their actions deserve" (Jeremiah 17:9-10).

As you'll notice, this verse doesn't say that some people's hearts are more wicked than others. All of us have the potential for actions that destroy ourselves and others.

Thankfully, God has chosen not to leave us this way. We all would be without hope if it weren't for God's grace. God says in Isaiah 43:25, "I—yes, I alone—am the one who blots out your sins for my own sake and will never think of them again."

Whatever you have done, God is not surprised and will forgive you if you let him. Your own recognition of wrong is the first step. God has opened up your heart so you can take a look at its ugliness. Now you must decide whether you want to leave it that way, or allow him to come in and clean it up.

"'Come now, let us argue this out,' says the LORD. 'No matter how deep the stain of your sins, I can remove it. I can make you as clean as freshly fallen snow. Even if you are stained as red as crimson, I can make you as white as wool'" (Isaiah 1:18).

Don't give up—give in . . . to God. Ask him to forgive you and help you start over.

17:26 Hebrew *the Shephelah.*

## SUICIDE

"I curse the day I was born! . . . Why was I ever born? My entire life has been filled with trouble, sorrow, and shame." This doesn't sound like one of God's greatest prophets. Yet it is! It's Jeremiah, pouring his heart out to God, wishing he'd never been born. Everyone has felt that way at one time or another. Most of us have wished we could just **check out** of this life. For some, though, that desire gets so intense that they act on it. Suicide is the third leading cause of death among American teenagers. Everyone occasionally faces despair, but why does one person struggle through while another ends his life? The critical factor is loss of hope. A suicidal person looks at his or her problems and says, **"IT'S DARK OUTSIDE,** and I am powerless to change things. What's more, I have no hope that things will get better." What does God think about suicide? Unfortunately, the Bible does not give a simple here's-what-God-says-about-the-issue answer. But it does give us some helpful principles. First, we aren't the author of life, God is. There are no "self-made" men or women. You're here because God made you in his image; because he loves you, he wants to know you, and he wants you to know him. When someone commits suicide, he or she is saying, "Look, God, you goofed when you let me slip into this world. So I'm going to correct your mistake." But life—and death—are GOD'S TERRITORY. To trespass on that holy ground means you've decided to play God. God does not look on it lightly. However, suicide is not an unforgivable sin. Jesus said there is only one of those, and it isn't suicide. This doesn't mean suicide is OK. Actually, suicide is one of the most selfish, cowardly, and hateful acts anyone can commit. Those who have ever had to deal with someone's suicide know: the EMOTIONAL DEVASTATION for those left behind is unbelievable. Suicide doesn't solve problems. It dumps them on someone else, multiplied many times over. Don't believe the lie that "everyone will be better off without me." They won't. You'll just cause overwhelming pain and heartbreak. So what do you do when you—or someone you care about—decide you simply want to end it all? First, remember you're not alone. Everyone has felt that way. If others can deal with it, you can, too. Second, don't lose hope. Things can get better. Sometimes all you need is time. Mitch Anthony, founder of the National Suicide Help Center, puts it like this: "Suicide is a permanent solution to a temporary problem. It's like cutting off your leg because your little toe hurts." Third, know the **DANGER SIGNALS** that indicate someone might be considering suicide: going through a family crisis; being the victim of abuse or neglect; drug abuse (yours or a family member's); death of a friend or family member; approaching the anniversary date of a significant loss or death; previous suicide attempts; family history of suicide; preoccupation with death and/or talk of suicide. If you or a friend are experiencing one or more of these signals, talk to someone you can trust—someone trained to help you with your problems. Counseling is extremely important. Finally, remember, even if it seems no one else cares about you and your pain, God cares. He cares deeply. Pour your troubles out to him. He understands because he, too, has experienced the depths of human experience. When you are tempted to give up, to take the coward's way out and end it all, remember what Winston Churchill once said: "Success is never final; failure is never fatal; *it is courage that counts.*" And Jesus says, "Take heart, because I have overcome the world" (John 16:33).

CHAPTER **18** **NO ONE LISTENS TO JEREMIAH.** The LORD gave another message to Jeremiah. He said, 2“Go down to the shop where clay pots and jars are made. I will speak to you while you are there.” 3So I did as he told me and found the potter working at his wheel. 4But the jar he was making did not turn out as he had hoped, so the potter squashed the jar into a lump of clay and started again.

5Then the LORD gave me this message: 6“O Israel, can I not do to you as this potter has done to his clay? As the clay is in the potter’s hand, so are you in my hand. 7If I announce that a certain nation or kingdom is to be uprooted, torn down, and destroyed, 8but then that nation renounces its evil ways, I will not destroy it as I had planned. 9And if I announce that I will build up and plant a certain nation or kingdom, making it strong and great, 10but then that nation turns to evil and refuses to obey me, I will not bless that nation as I had said I would.

11“Therefore, Jeremiah, go and warn all Judah and Jerusalem. Say to them, ‘This is what the LORD says: I am planning disaster against you instead of good. So turn from your evil ways, each of you, and do what is right.’ ”

12But they replied, “Don’t waste your breath. We will continue to live as we want to, following our own evil desires.”

13Then the LORD said, “Has anyone ever heard of such a thing, even among the pagan nations? My virgin Israel has done something too terrible to understand! 14Does the snow ever melt high up in the mountains of Lebanon? Do the cold, flowing streams from the crags of Mount Hermon ever run dry? 15These can be counted on, but not my people! For they have deserted me and turned to worthless idols. They have stumbled off the ancient highways of good, and they walk the muddy paths of sin. 16Therefore, their land will become desolate, a monument to their stupidity. All who pass by will be astonished and shake their heads in amazement at its utter desolation. 17I will scatter my people before their enemies as the east wind scatters dust. And in all their trouble I will turn my back on them and refuse to notice their distress.”

18Then the people said, “Come on, let’s find a way to stop Jeremiah. We have our own priests and wise men and prophets. We don’t need him to teach the law and give us advice and prophecies. Let’s spread rumors about him and ignore what he says.”

19LORD, help me! Listen to what they are planning to do to me! 20Should they repay evil for good? They have set a trap to kill me, though I pleaded for them and tried to protect them from your anger. 21So let their children starve! Let the sword pour out their blood! Let their wives become widows without any children! Let their old men die in a plague, and let their young men be killed in battle! 22Let screaming be heard from their homes as warriors come suddenly upon them. For they have dug a pit for me, and they have hidden traps along my path.

23LORD, you know all about their murderous plots

**NOT AFRAID ● ● • • •**

18:18 **Jeremiah’s words and actions challenged the people’s social and moral behavior. He wasn’t afraid to give unpopular criticism. The people could either obey Jeremiah or silence him. They chose the latter. They did not think they needed Jeremiah; their false prophets told them what they wanted to hear.**

against me. Don’t forgive their crimes and blot out their sins. Let them die before you. Deal with them in your anger.

CHAPTER **19** **JERUSALEM WILL BE DESTROYED.** The LORD said to me, “Go and buy a clay jar. Then ask some of the leaders of the people and of the priests to follow you. 2Go out into the valley of the son of Hinnom by the entrance to the Potsherd Gate, and repeat to them the words that I give you. 3Say to them, ‘Listen to this message from the LORD, you kings of Judah and citizens of Jerusalem! This is what the LORD Almighty, the God of Israel, says: I will bring such a terrible disaster on this place that the ears of those who hear about it will ring!

4“ ‘For Israel has forsaken me and turned this valley into a place of wickedness. The people burn incense to foreign gods—idols never before worshiped by this generation, by their ancestors, or by the kings of Judah. And they have filled this place with the blood of innocent children. 5They have built pagan shrines to Baal, and there they burn their sons as sacrifices to Baal. I have never commanded such a horrible deed; it never even crossed my mind to command such a thing! 6So beware, for the time is coming, says the LORD, when this place will no longer be called Topheth or the valley of the son of Hinnom, but the Valley of Slaughter. 7For I will upset the battle plans of Judah and Jerusalem and let invading armies slaughter them. The enemy will leave the dead bodies as food for the vultures and wild animals. 8I will wipe Jerusalem from the face of the earth, making it a monument to their stupidity. All who pass by will be appalled and will gasp at the destruction they see there. 9I will see to it that your enemies lay siege to the city until all the food is gone. Then those trapped inside will have to eat their own sons and daughters and friends. They will be driven to utter despair.’

10“As these men watch, Jeremiah, smash the jar you brought with you. 11Then say to them, ‘This is what the LORD Almighty says: As this jar lies shattered, so I will shatter the people of Judah and Jerusalem beyond all hope of repair. They will bury the bodies in Topheth until there is no more room. 12This is what I will do to this place and its people, says the LORD. I will cause this city to become defiled like Topheth. 13Yes, all the houses in Jerusalem,

**GARBAGE ● ● • • •**

19:1-6 **This valley was the garbage dump of Jerusalem and the place where children were sacrificed to the god Molech. It is also mentioned in 7:31-32.**

including the palace of Judah's kings, will become like Topheth—all the houses where you burned incense on the rooftops to your star gods, and where drink offerings were poured out to your idols.'"

[14]Then Jeremiah returned from Topheth where he had delivered this message, and he stopped in front of the Temple of the LORD. He said to the people there, [15]"This is what the LORD Almighty, the God of Israel, says: I will bring disaster upon this city and its surrounding towns just as I promised, because you have stubbornly refused to listen to me."

## CHAPTER 20 JEREMIAH IS ARRESTED.

Now Pashhur son of Immer, the priest in charge of the Temple of the LORD, heard what Jeremiah was saying. [2]So he arrested Jeremiah the prophet and had him whipped and put in stocks at the Benjamin Gate of the LORD's Temple.

### STUNG! ● ● • • •

20:1-3 **Pashhur heard Jeremiah's words and, because of his guilt, locked Jeremiah up instead of taking his message to heart and acting on it. The truth sometimes stings, but our reaction to the truth shows what we are made of. We can deny the changes and destroy the evidence of our misdeeds, or we can take the truth humbly to heart and let it change us. Pashhur may have thought he was a strong leader, but he was really a coward.**

[3]The next day, when Pashhur finally released him, Jeremiah said, "Pashhur, the LORD has changed your name. From now on you are to be called 'The Man Who Lives in Terror.'* [4]For this is what the LORD says: I will send terror upon you and all your friends, and you will watch as they are slaughtered by the swords of the enemy. I will hand the people of Judah over to the king of Babylon. He will take them captive to Babylon or run them through with the sword. [5]And I will let your enemies plunder Jerusalem. All the famed treasures of the city—the precious jewels and gold and silver of your kings—will be carried off to Babylon. [6]As for you, Pashhur, you and all your household will go as captives to Babylon. There you will die and be buried, you and all your friends to whom you promised that everything would be all right."

[7]O LORD, you persuaded me, and I allowed myself to be persuaded. You are stronger than I am, and you overpowered me. Now I am mocked by everyone in the city. [8]Whenever I speak, the words come out in a violent outburst. "Violence and destruction!" I shout. So these messages from the LORD have made me a household joke. [9]And I can't stop! If I say I'll never mention the LORD or speak in his name, his word burns in my heart like a fire. It's like a fire in my bones! I am weary of holding it in!

[10]I have heard the many rumors about me. They call me "The Man Who Lives in Terror." And they say, "If you say anything, we will report it." Even my old friends are watching me, waiting for a fatal slip. "He will trap himself," they say, "and then we will get our revenge on him."

[11]But the LORD stands beside me like a great warrior. Before him they will stumble. They cannot defeat me. They will be shamed and thoroughly humiliated. Their dishonor will never be forgotten. [12]O LORD Almighty! You know those who are righteous, and you examine the deepest thoughts of hearts and minds. Let me see your vengeance against them, for I have committed my cause to you. [13]Now I will sing out my thanks to the LORD! Praise the LORD! For though I was poor and needy, he delivered me from my oppressors.

[14]Yet I curse the day I was born! May the day of my birth not be blessed. [15]I curse the messenger who told my father, "Good news—you have a son!" [16]Let him be destroyed like the cities of old that the LORD overthrew without mercy. Terrify him all day long with battle shouts, [17]for he did not kill me at birth. Oh, that I had died in my mother's womb, that her body had been my grave! [18]Why was I ever born? My entire life has been filled with trouble, sorrow, and shame.

## CHAPTER 21 GOD'S ANSWER TO THE KING IS NO.

The LORD spoke through Jeremiah when King Zedekiah sent Pashhur son of Malkijah and Zephaniah son of Maaseiah, the priest, to speak with him. They begged Jeremiah, [2]"Please ask the LORD to help us. King Nebuchadnezzar* of Babylon has begun his attack on Judah. Perhaps the LORD will be gracious and do a mighty miracle as he has done in the past. Perhaps he will force Nebuchadnezzar to withdraw his armies."

[3]Jeremiah replied, "Go back to King Zedekiah and tell him, [4]'This is what the LORD, the God of Israel, says: I will make your weapons useless against the king of Babylon and the Babylonians* who are attacking you. Yes, I will bring your enemies right into the heart of this city. [5]I myself will fight against you with great power, for I am very angry. You have made me furious! [6]I will send a terrible plague upon this city, and both people and animals will die. [7]And then, says the LORD, even after King Zedekiah, his officials, and everyone else in the city have survived war, famine, and disease, I will hand them over to King Nebuchadnezzar of Babylon. He will slaughter them all without mercy, pity, or compassion.'

[8]"Tell all the people, 'This is what the LORD says: Take your choice of life or death! [9]Everyone who stays in Jerusalem will die from war, famine, or disease, but those who go out and surrender to the Babylonians will live. [10]For I have decided to bring disaster and not good upon this city, says the LORD. It will be captured by the king of Babylon, and he will reduce it to ashes.'

[11]"Say to the royal family of Judah, 'Listen to this message from the LORD! [12]This is what the LORD says

20:3 Hebrew *Magor-missabib,* which means "surrounded by terror"; also in 20:10. 21:2 Hebrew *Nebuchadrezzar,* a variant name for Nebuchadnezzar; also in 21:7. 21:4 Or *Chaldeans;* also in 21:9.

to the dynasty of David: Give justice to the people you judge! Help those who have been robbed; rescue them from their oppressors. Do what is right, or my anger will burn like an unquenchable fire because of all your sins. 13I will fight against this city of Jerusalem that boasts, "We are safe on our mountain! No one can touch us here." 14And I myself will punish you for your sinfulness, says the LORD. I will light a fire in your forests that will burn up everything around you.'"

## CHAPTER 22

**EVIL KINGS WILL BE JUDGED.** Then the LORD said to me, "Go over and speak directly to the king of Judah. Say to him, 2'Listen to this message from the LORD, you king of Judah, sitting on David's throne. Let your officials and your people listen, too. 3This is what the LORD says: Be fair-minded and just. Do what is right! Help those who have been robbed; rescue them from their oppressors. Quit your evil deeds! Do not mistreat foreigners, orphans, and widows. Stop murdering the innocent! 4If you obey me, there will always be a descendant of David sitting on the throne here in Jerusalem. The king will ride through the palace gates in chariots and on horses, with his parade of officials and subjects. 5But if you refuse to pay attention to this warning, I swear by my own name, says the LORD, that this palace will become a pile of rubble.'"

6Now this is what the LORD says concerning the royal palace: "You are as beloved to me as fruitful Gilead and the green forests of Lebanon. But I will destroy you and leave you deserted, with no one living within your walls. 7I will call for wreckers, who will bring out their tools to dismantle you. They will tear out all your fine cedar beams and throw them on the fire. 8People from many nations will pass by the ruins of this city and say to one another, 'Why did the LORD destroy such a great city?' 9And the answer will be, 'Because they violated their covenant with the LORD their God by worshiping other gods.'"

10Do not weep for the dead king or mourn his loss. Instead, weep for the captive king being led away! For he will never return to see his native land again. 11For this is what the LORD says about Jehoahaz,* who succeeded his father, King Josiah, and was taken away as a captive: "He will never return. 12He will die in a distant land and never again see his own country."

13And the LORD says, "Destruction is certain for Jehoiakim,* who builds his palace with forced labor.* By not paying wages, he builds injustice into its walls and oppression into its doorframes and ceilings. 14He says, 'I will build a magnificent palace with huge rooms and many windows, paneled throughout with fragrant cedar and painted a lovely red.'

15"But a beautiful palace does not make a great king! Why did your father, Josiah, reign so long? Because he was just and right in all his dealings. That is why God blessed him. 16He made sure that justice and help were given to the poor and needy, and everything went well for him. Isn't that what it means to know me?" asks the LORD. 17"But you! You are full of selfish greed and dishonesty! You murder the innocent, oppress the poor, and reign ruthlessly."

18Therefore, this is the LORD's decree of punishment against King Jehoiakim, who succeeded his father, Josiah, on the throne: "His family will not weep for him when he dies. His subjects will not even care that he is dead. 19He will be buried like a dead donkey—dragged out of Jerusalem and dumped outside the gate! 20Weep, for your allies are all gone. Search for them in Lebanon. Shout for them at Bashan. Search for them in the regions east of the river.* See, they are all destroyed. Not one is left to help you.

21"When you were prosperous, I warned you, but you replied, 'Don't bother me.' Since childhood you have been that way—you simply will not listen! 22And now your allies have all disappeared with a puff of wind. All your friends have been taken away as captives. Surely at last you will see your wickedness and be ashamed. 23It may be nice to live in a beautiful palace lined with lumber from the cedars of Lebanon, but soon you will cry and groan in anguish—anguish like that of a woman about to give birth.

24"And as surely as I live," says the LORD, "I will abandon you, Jehoiachin* son of Jehoiakim, king of Judah. Even if you were the signet ring on my right hand, I would pull you off. 25I will hand you over to those who seek to kill you, of whom you are so desperately afraid—to King Nebuchadnezzar* of Babylon and the mighty Babylonian* army. 26I will expel you and your mother from this land, and you will die in a foreign country. 27You will never again return to the land of your desire.

28"Why is this man Jehoiachin like a discarded, broken dish? Why are he and his children to be exiled to distant lands? 29O earth, earth, earth! Listen to this message from the LORD! 30This is what the LORD says: Let the record show that this man Jehoiachin was childless, for none of his children will ever sit on the throne of David to rule in Judah. His life will amount to nothing."

### INHERITED ● ● ● • •

22:15-16 **God passed judgment on King Jehoiakim. His father, Josiah, had been one of Judah's great kings, but Jehoiakim was evil. Josiah had been faithful with his responsibility to teach his son and to model right living, but Jehoiakim had been unfaithful with his responsibility to imitate his father. God's judgment was on unfaithful Jehoiakim. He could not claim his father's blessings when he had not followed his father's God. We may inherit our parents' money, but we cannot inherit their faith or blessings. A great heritage, a good education, or a beautiful home doesn't guarantee a strong character. We must choose and build our own relationship with God.**

**22:11** Hebrew *Shallum,* another name for Jehoahaz. **22:13a** The brother and successor of the exiled Jehoahaz. **22:13b** Hebrew *by unrighteousness.* **22:20** Hebrew *in Abarim.* **22:24** Hebrew *Coniah,* a variant name for Jehoiachin; also in 22:28, 30. **22:25a** Hebrew *Nebuchadrezzar,* a variant name for Nebuchadnezzar. **22:25b** Or *Chaldean.*

## CORRUPTION ● ● • • •

**23:9-14 How did the nation become so corrupt? A major factor was false prophecy. The false prophets had a large, enthusiastic audience and were very popular because they made the people believe that all was well. By contrast, Jeremiah's message from God was unpopular because it showed the people how bad they were. There are four warning signs of false prophets– characteristics we need to watch for even today: (1) They may appear to live according to religious principles, but they do not speak God's message; (2) They water down God's message to make it more acceptable; (3) They encourage their listeners, often subtly, to disobey God; (4) They tend to be arrogant and self-serving, appealing to the desires of their audience instead of being true to God's Word.**

## CHAPTER 23 A PERFECT KING WILL COME.

"I will
send disaster upon the leaders of my people—the
shepherds of my sheep—for they have destroyed
and scattered the very ones they were expected to
care for," says the LORD.
2This is what the LORD, the God of Israel, says
to these shepherds: "Instead of leading my flock to
safety, you have deserted them and driven them to
destruction. Now I will pour out judgment on you
for the evil you have done to them. 3But I will
gather together the remnant of my flock from
wherever I have driven them. I will bring them
back into their own fold, and they will be fruitful
and increase in number. 4Then I will appoint responsible shepherds to care for them, and they will
never be afraid again. Not a single one of them will
be lost or missing," says the LORD.
5"For the time is coming," says the LORD, "when I
will place a righteous Branch on King David's
throne. He will be a King who rules with wisdom. He
will do what is just and right throughout the land.
6And this is his name: 'The LORD Is Our Righteousness.'* In that day Judah will be saved, and Israel will
live in safety.
7"In that day," says the LORD, "when people are
taking an oath, they will no longer say, 'As surely as
the LORD lives, who rescued the people of Israel from
the land of Egypt.' 8Instead, they will say, 'As surely
as the LORD lives, who brought the people of Israel
back to their own land from the land of the north
and from all the countries to which he had exiled
them.' Then they will live in their own land."
9My heart is broken because of the false prophets,
and I tremble uncontrollably. I stagger like a drunkard, like someone overcome by wine, because of the
holy words the LORD has spoken against them. 10For
the land is full of adultery, and it lies under a curse.
The land itself is in mourning—its pastures are dried
up. For the prophets do evil and abuse their power.
11"The priests are like the prophets, all ungodly,
wicked men. I have seen their despicable acts right
here in my own Temple," says the LORD. 12"Therefore, their paths will be dark and slippery. They will
be chased down dark and treacherous trails, where
they will fall. For I will bring disaster upon them
when their time of punishment comes. I, the LORD,
have spoken!
13"I saw that the prophets of Samaria were terribly
evil, for they prophesied by Baal and led my people
of Israel into sin. 14But now I see that the prophets of
Jerusalem are even worse! They commit adultery,
and they love dishonesty. They encourage those who
are doing evil instead of turning them away from
their sins. These prophets are as wicked as the people
of Sodom and Gomorrah once were."
15Therefore, this is what the LORD Almighty says
concerning the prophets: "I will feed them with
bitterness and give them poison to drink. For it is
because of Jerusalem's prophets that wickedness fills
this land. 16This is my warning to my people," says
the LORD Almighty. "Do not listen to these prophets
when they prophesy to you, filling you with futile
hopes. They are making up everything they say. They
do not speak for the LORD! 17They keep saying to
these rebels who despise my word, 'Don't worry! The
LORD says you will have peace!' And to those who
stubbornly follow their own evil desires, they say,
'No harm will come your way!'
18"But can you name even one of these prophets
who knows the LORD well enough to hear what he is
saying? Has even one of them cared enough to
listen? 19Look! The LORD's anger bursts out like a
storm, a whirlwind that swirls down on the heads of
the wicked. 20The anger of the LORD will not diminish until it has finished all his plans. In the days to
come, you will understand all this very clearly.

## LIVE IT! ● ● • • •

**23:28 True prophets and false prophets are as different as chaff and wheat. Worthless chaff blows away with the wind, while wheat remains to nourish many. To share God's Word is a great responsibility because the way we present it and live it will encourage people either to accept it or reject it. Whether we speak from a pulpit, teach in a class, or share with friends, our responsibility is to accurately communicate and live out God's Word. As you share God's Word with friends and neighbors, they will look for its effectiveness in your life. Unless it has changed you, why should they let it change them? If you don't live it, don't preach it!**

21"I have not sent these prophets, yet they claim to
speak for me. I have given them no message, yet they
prophesy. 22If they had listened to me, they would
have spoken my words and turned my people from
their evil ways. 23Am I a God who is only in one
place?" asks the LORD. "Do they think I cannot see
what they are doing? 24Can anyone hide from me?
Am I not everywhere in all the heavens and earth?"
asks the LORD.
25"I have heard these prophets say, 'Listen to the
dream I had from God last night.' And then they
proceed to tell lies in my name. 26How long will this
go on? If they are prophets, they are prophets of
deceit, inventing everything they say. 27By telling
these false dreams, they are trying to get my people

23:6 Hebrew *Yahweh Tsidqenu.*

to forget me, just as their ancestors did by worshiping the idols of Baal. 28Let these false prophets tell their dreams, but let my true messengers faithfully proclaim my every word. There is a difference between chaff and wheat! 29Does not my word burn like fire?" asks the LORD. "Is it not like a mighty hammer that smashes rock to pieces?

30"Therefore," says the LORD, "I stand against these prophets who get their messages from each other—31these smooth-tongued prophets who say, 'This prophecy is from the LORD!' 32Their imaginary dreams are flagrant lies that lead my people into sin. I did not send or appoint them, and they have no message at all for my people," says the LORD.

33"Suppose one of the people or one of the prophets or priests asks you, 'What prophecy has the LORD burdened you with now?' You must reply, 'You are the burden!* The LORD says he will abandon you!' 34If any prophet, priest, or anyone else says, 'I have a prophecy from the LORD,' I will punish that person along with his entire family. 35You should keep asking each other, 'What is the LORD's answer?' or 'What is the LORD saying?' 36But stop using this phrase, 'prophecy from the LORD.' For people are using it to give authority to their own ideas, turning upside down the words of our God, the living God, the LORD Almighty.

37"This is what you should say to the prophets: 'What is the LORD's answer?' or 'What is the LORD saying?' 38But suppose they respond, 'This is a prophecy from the LORD!' Then you should say, 'This is what the LORD says: Because you have used this phrase, "prophecy from the LORD," even though I warned you not to use it, 39I will forget you completely. I will expel you from my presence, along with this city that I gave to you and your ancestors. 40And I will make you an object of ridicule, and your name will be infamous throughout the ages.'"

## CHAPTER 24 GOOD AND BAD FIGS.

After King Nebuchadnezzar* of Babylon exiled Jehoiachin* son of Jehoiakim, king of Judah, to Babylon along with the princes of Judah and all the skilled craftsmen, the LORD gave me this vision. I saw two baskets of figs placed in front of the LORD's Temple in Jerusalem. 2One basket was filled with fresh, ripe figs, while the other was filled with figs that were spoiled and could not be eaten.

3Then the LORD said to me, "What do you see, Jeremiah?"

I replied, "Figs, some very good and some very bad."

4Then the LORD gave me this message: 5"This is what the LORD, the God of Israel, says: The good figs represent the exiles I sent from Judah to the land of the Babylonians.* 6I have sent them into captivity for their own good. I will see that they are well treated,

### FIGS ● ● • • •

24:2-10 **The good figs represented the exiles to Babylon—not because they were good, but because their hearts would respond to God. So he would preserve them and bring them back to the land. The bad figs represented those who remained in Judah or ran away to Egypt. The people believed they would be blessed if they remained in the land, but the opposite was true because God would use the captivity to refine the exiles. We may believe we are blessed when life goes well and cursed when it does not. But trouble is a blessing when it makes us stronger, and prosperity is a curse if it entices us away from God. If you are facing trouble, ask God to help you grow stronger for him. If things are going your way, ask God to help you use your prosperity faithfully for him.**

and I will bring them back here again. I will build them up and not tear them down. I will plant them and not uproot them. 7I will give them hearts that will recognize me as the LORD. They will be my people, and I will be their God, for they will return to me wholeheartedly.

8"But the rotten figs," the LORD said, "represent King Zedekiah of Judah, his officials, all the people left in Jerusalem, and those who live in Egypt. I will treat them like spoiled figs, too rotten to eat. 9I will make them an object of horror and evil to every nation on earth. They will be disgraced and mocked, taunted and cursed, wherever I send them. 10I will send war, famine, and disease until they have vanished from the land of Israel, which I gave to them and their ancestors."

## CHAPTER 25 DISASTER AHEAD.

This message for all the people of Judah came to Jeremiah from the LORD during the fourth year of Jehoiakim's reign* over Judah. This was the year when King Nebuchadnezzar* of Babylon began his reign.

2Jeremiah the prophet said to the people in Judah and Jerusalem, 3"For the past twenty-three years—from the thirteenth year of Josiah son of Amon,* king of Judah, until now—the LORD has been giving me his messages. I have faithfully passed them on to you, but you have not listened.

4"Again and again, the LORD has sent you his

### DON'T QUIT! ● ● • • •

25:2-6 **Imagine preaching the same message for 23 years and continually being rejected! Jeremiah faced this, but because he had committed his life to God he continued to proclaim the message "Turn from the evil road you are traveling and from the evil things you are doing." Regardless of the people's response, Jeremiah did not give up. God never stops loving us, even when we reject him. We can thank God that he won't give up on us, and, like Jeremiah, we can commit ourselves to never giving God up. No matter how people respond when you tell them about God, remain faithful to his high call and continue to witness for him.**

**23:33** As in Greek version and Latin Vulgate; Hebrew reads *What burden?* **24:1a** Hebrew *Nebuchadrezzar,* a variant name for Nebuchadnezzar. **24:1b** Hebrew *Jeconiah,* a variant name for Jehoiachin. **24:5** Or *Chaldeans.* **25:1a** The fourth year of Jehoiakim's reign and the accession year of Nebuchadnezzar's reign was 605 B.C. **25:1b** Hebrew *Nebuchadrezzar,* a variant name for Nebuchadnezzar; also in 25:9. **25:3** The thirteenth year of Josiah's reign was 627 B.C.

**WITH US ● ● • • •**

26:16-17, 24 **Jeremiah's life was in serious danger, but God used officials and wise men to protect him. God spared Jeremiah because his work was not done. Believers, even some of God's prophets, sometimes die painful deaths. God does not promise to keep every follower from suffering. But he promises to be with us in the middle of trials.**

prophets, but you have not listened or even tried to hear. [5]Each time the message was this: 'Turn from the evil road you are traveling and from the evil things you are doing. Only then will I let you live in this land that the LORD gave to you and your ancestors forever. [6]Do not make me angry by worshiping the idols you have made. Then I will not harm you.'

[7]"But you would not listen to me," says the LORD. "You made me furious by worshiping your idols, bringing on yourselves all the disasters you now suffer. [8]And now the LORD Almighty says: Because you have not listened to me, [9]I will gather together all the armies of the north under King Nebuchadnezzar of Babylon, whom I have appointed as my deputy. I will bring them all against this land and its people and against the other nations near you. I will completely destroy* you and make you an object of horror and contempt and a ruin forever. [10]I will take away your happy singing and laughter. The joyful voices of bridegrooms and brides will no longer be heard. Your businesses will fail, and all your homes will stand silent and dark. [11]This entire land will become a desolate wasteland. Israel and her neighboring lands will serve the king of Babylon for seventy years.

[12]"Then, after the seventy years of captivity are over, I will punish the king of Babylon and his people for their sins, says the LORD. I will make the country of the Babylonians* an everlasting wasteland. [13]I will bring upon them all the terrors I have promised in this book—all the penalties announced by Jeremiah against the nations. [14]Many nations and great kings will enslave the Babylonians, just as they enslaved my people. I will punish them in proportion to the suffering they cause my people."

[15]Then the LORD, the God of Israel, said to me, "Take from my hand this cup filled to the brim with my anger, and make all the nations to whom I send you drink from it. [16]When they drink from it, they will stagger, crazed by the warfare I will send against them."

[17]So I took the cup of anger from the LORD and made all the nations drink from it—every nation the LORD sent me to. [18]I went to Jerusalem and the other towns of Judah, and their kings and officials drank from the cup. From that day until this, they have been a desolate ruin, an object of horror, contempt, and cursing. [19]I went to Egypt and spoke to Pharaoh, his officials, his princes, and his people. They, too, drank from that terrible cup, [20]along with all the foreigners living in that land. So did all the kings of the land of Uz and the kings of the Philistine cities of Ashkelon, Gaza, Ekron, and what remains of Ashdod. [21]Then I went to the nations of Edom, Moab, and Ammon, [22]and the kings of Tyre and Sidon, and the kings of the regions across the sea. [23]I went to Dedan, Tema, and Buz, and to the people who live in distant places.* [24]I went to the kings of Arabia, the kings of the nomadic tribes of the desert, [25]and to the kings of Zimri, Elam, and Media. [26]And I went to the kings of the northern countries, far and near, one after the other—all the kingdoms of the world. And finally, the king of Babylon* himself drank from the cup of the LORD's anger.

[27]Then the LORD said to me, "Now tell them, 'The LORD Almighty, the God of Israel, says: Drink from this cup of my anger. Get drunk and vomit, and you will fall to rise no more, for I am sending terrible wars against you.' [28]And if they refuse to accept the cup, tell them, 'The LORD Almighty says: You must drink from it. You cannot escape! [29]I have begun to punish Jerusalem, the city where my own name is honored. Now should I let you go unpunished? No, you will not escape disaster. I will call for war against all the nations of the earth. I, the LORD Almighty, have spoken!'

[30]"Now prophesy all these things, and say to them, 'The LORD will roar loudly against his own land from his holy dwelling in heaven. He will shout against everyone on the earth, like the harvesters do as they crush juice from the grapes. [31]His cry of judgment will reach the ends of the earth, for the LORD will bring his case against all the nations. He will judge all the people of the earth, slaughtering the wicked with his sword. The LORD has spoken!'"

[32]This is what the LORD Almighty says: "Look! Disaster will fall upon nation after nation! A great whirlwind of fury is rising from the most distant corners of the earth!"

[33]In that day those the LORD has slaughtered will fill the earth from one end to the other. No one will mourn for them or gather up their bodies to bury them. They will be scattered like dung on the ground.

[34]Weep and moan, you evil shepherds! Roll in the dust, you leaders of the flock! The time of your slaughter has arrived; you will fall and shatter like fragile pottery. [35]You will find no place to hide; there will be no way to escape.

[36]Listen to the frantic cries of the shepherds, to the leaders of the flock shouting in despair, for the LORD is spoiling their pastures. [37]Peaceful meadows will be turned into a wasteland by the LORD's fierce anger. [38]He has left his den like a lion seeking its prey, and their land will be made desolate by the sword of the enemy and the LORD's fierce anger.

## CHAPTER 26 JEREMIAH ALMOST DIES.

This message came to Jeremiah from the LORD early in the reign of Jehoiakim son of Josiah,* king of Judah.

25:9 The Hebrew term used here refers to the complete consecration of things or people to the LORD, either by destroying them or by giving them as an offering. 25:12 Or *Chaldeans.* 25:23 Or *who clip the corners of their hair.* 25:26 Hebrew *of Sheshach,* a code name for Babylon. 26:1 The first year of Jehoiakim's reign was 608 B.C.

2The LORD said, "Stand out in front of the Temple of the LORD, and make an announcement to the people who have come there to worship from all over Judah. Give them my entire message; include every word. 3Perhaps they will listen and turn from their evil ways. Then I will be able to withhold the disaster I am ready to pour out on them because of their sins.

4"Say to them, 'This is what the LORD says: If you will not listen to me and obey the law I have given you, 5and if you will not listen to my servants, the prophets—for I sent them again and again to warn you, but you would not listen to them—6then I will destroy this Temple as I destroyed Shiloh, the place where the Tabernacle was located. And I will make Jerusalem an object of cursing in every nation on earth.'"

7The priests, the prophets, and all the people listened to Jeremiah as he spoke in front of the LORD's Temple. 8But when Jeremiah had finished his message, saying everything the LORD had told him to say, the priests and prophets and all the people at the Temple mobbed him. "Kill him!" they shouted. 9"What right do you have to prophesy in the LORD's name that this Temple will be destroyed like Shiloh? What do you mean, saying that Jerusalem will be destroyed?" And all the people threatened him as he stood in front of the Temple.

10When the officials of Judah heard what was happening, they rushed over from the palace and sat down at the New Gate of the Temple to hold court. 11The priests and prophets presented their accusations to the officials and the people. "This man should die!" they said. "You have heard with your own ears what a traitor he is, for he has prophesied against this city."

12Then Jeremiah spoke in his own defense. "The LORD sent me to prophesy against this Temple and this city," he said. "The LORD gave me every word that I have spoken. 13But if you stop your sinning and begin to obey the LORD your God, he will cancel this disaster that he has announced against you. 14As for me, I am helpless and in your power—do with me as you think best. 15But if you kill me, rest assured that you will be killing an innocent man! The responsibility for such a deed will lie on you, on this city, and on every person living in it. For it is absolutely true that the LORD sent me to speak every word you have heard."

16Then the officials and the people said to the priests and prophets, "This man does not deserve the death sentence, for he has spoken to us in the name of the LORD our God."

17Then some of the wise old men stood and spoke to the people there. 18They said, "Think back to the days when Micah of Moresheth prophesied during the reign of King Hezekiah of Judah. He told the people of Judah, 'This is what the LORD Almighty says: Mount Zion will be plowed like an open field; Jerusalem will be reduced to rubble! A great forest will grow on the hilltop, where the Temple now stands.'* 19But did King Hezekiah and the people kill him for saying this? No, they turned from their sins and worshiped the LORD. They begged him to have mercy on them. Then the LORD held back the terrible disaster he had pronounced against them. If we kill Jeremiah, who knows what will happen to us?"

20(At this time, Uriah son of Shemaiah from Kiriath-jearim was also prophesying for the LORD. And he predicted the same terrible disaster against the city and nation as Jeremiah did. 21When King Jehoiakim and the army officers and officials heard what he was saying, the king sent someone to kill him. But Uriah heard about the plot and escaped to Egypt. 22Then King Jehoiakim sent Elnathan son of Acbor to Egypt along with several other men to capture Uriah. 23They took him prisoner and brought him back to King Jehoiakim. The king then killed Uriah with a sword and had him buried in an unmarked grave.)

24Ahikam son of Shaphan also stood with Jeremiah and persuaded the court not to turn him over to the mob to be killed.

## CHAPTER 27 **THE PEOPLE WILL BE SLAVES.**

This message came to Jeremiah from the LORD early in the reign of Zedekiah* son of Josiah, king of Judah.

2The LORD said to me, "Make a yoke, and fasten it on your neck with leather thongs. 3Then send messages to the kings of Edom, Moab, Ammon, Tyre, and Sidon through their ambassadors to King Zedekiah in Jerusalem. 4Give them this message for their masters: 'This is what the LORD Almighty, the God of Israel, says: 5By my great power I have made the earth and all its people and every animal. I can give these things of mine to anyone I choose. 6Now I will give your countries to King Nebuchadnezzar of Babylon, who is my servant. I have put everything, even the wild animals, under his control. 7All the nations will serve him and his son and his grandson until his time is up. But then many nations and great kings will conquer and rule over Babylon. 8So you must submit to Babylon's king and serve him; put your neck under Babylon's yoke! I will punish any nation that refuses to be his slave, says the LORD. I will send war, famine, and disease upon that nation until Babylon has conquered it.

9"'Do not listen to your false prophets, fortune-tellers, interpreters of dreams, mediums, and sorcerers who say, "The king of Babylon will not conquer you." 10They are all liars, and I will drive you from

### TRUE FRIEND ● ● • • •

27:9-11 **The false prophets told the people what they wanted to hear, even though these "prophets" knew the message was not true. The people in Jeremiah's day needed a true friend like Jeremiah, who brought God's painful, corrective word. A true friend speaks the truth no matter how much it hurts to hear. Seek friends who speak truthfully, even though their correction is painful. Someone who flatters you by telling you lies is not a true friend.**

**26:18** Mic 3:12. **27:1** As in some Hebrew manuscripts and Syriac version (see also 27:3, 12); most Hebrew manuscripts read *Jehoiakim.*

"For

# I

*know the plans*

*I have for you,"*

*says the LORD.*

"They are plans
for good
and not for disaster,
to give you
a future
and
a hope."
JEREMIAH 29:11

your land and send you far away to die. 11But the people of any nation that submits to the king of Babylon will be allowed to stay in their own country to farm the land as usual. I, the LORD, have spoken!'"

12Then I repeated this same message to King Zedekiah of Judah. "If you want to live, submit to the king of Babylon and his people," I said. 13"Why do you insist on dying—you and your people? Why should you choose war, famine, and disease, which the LORD will bring against every nation that refuses to submit to Babylon's king? 14Do not listen to the false prophets who keep telling you, 'The king of Babylon will not conquer you.' They are liars. 15This is what the LORD says: I have not sent these prophets! They are telling you lies in my name, so I will drive you from this land. You will all die—you and all these prophets, too."

16Then I spoke to the priests and the people and said, "This is what the LORD says: Do not listen to your prophets who claim that soon the gold utensils taken from my Temple will be returned from Babylon. It is all a lie! 17Do not listen to them. Surrender to the king of Babylon, and you will live. Why should this whole city be destroyed? 18If they really are the LORD's prophets, let them pray to the LORD Almighty about the gold utensils that are still left in the LORD's Temple and in the king's palace and in the palaces of Jerusalem. Let them pray that these remaining articles will not be carried away with you to Babylon!

19"For this is what the LORD Almighty says about the bronze pillars in front of the Temple, the bronze Sea in the Temple courtyard, the bronze water carts, and all the other ceremonial articles. 20King Nebuchadnezzar of Babylon left them here when he exiled Jehoiachin* son of Jehoiakim, king of Judah, to Babylon, along with all the other important people of Judah and Jerusalem. 21Yes, this is what the LORD Almighty, the God of Israel, says about the precious things kept in the Temple and in the palace of Judah's king: 22They will all be carried away to Babylon and will stay there until I send for them, says the LORD. But someday I will bring them back to Jerusalem again."

## CHAPTER 28

**A FALSE PROPHET.** One day in late summer* of that same year—the fourth year of the reign of Zedekiah, king of Judah—Hananiah son of Azzur, a prophet from Gibeon, addressed me publicly in the Temple while all the priests and people listened. He said, 2"The LORD Almighty, the God of Israel, says: I will remove the yoke of the king of Babylon from your necks. 3Within two years, I will bring back all the Temple treasures that King Nebuchadnezzar carried off to Babylon. 4And I will bring back Jehoiachin* son of Jehoiakim, king of Judah, and all the other captives that were taken to Babylon. I will surely break the yoke that the king of Babylon has put on your necks. I, the LORD, have spoken!"

5Jeremiah responded to Hananiah as they stood in front of all the priests and people at the Temple. 6He said, "Amen! May your prophecies come true! I hope the LORD does everything you say. I hope he does bring back from Babylon the treasures of this Temple and all our loved ones. 7But listen now to the solemn words I speak to you in the presence of all these people. 8The ancient prophets who preceded you and me spoke against many nations, always warning of war, famine, and disease. 9So a prophet who predicts peace must carry the burden of proof.

### THE TRUTH HURTS ● ● • • ·

**28:8-17 Jeremiah spoke the truth, but it was unpopular; Hananiah spoke lies, but his deceitful words brought false hope and comfort to the people. God had already outlined the marks of a true prophet: a true prophet's predictions always come true and his words never contradict previous revelation (Deuteronomy 13; 18:9-22). Jeremiah's predictions were already coming true, from Hananiah's death to the Babylonian invasions. But the people still preferred to listen to comforting lies rather than painful truth. Do your best to be open to God's words to you, even if you don't particularly like what he has to say. As painful as it may sometimes be, the truth is always best.**

27:20 Hebrew *Jeconiah,* a variant name for Jehoiachin. 28:1 Hebrew *In the fifth month,* of the Hebrew calendar. This month in the fourth year of Zedekiah's reign occurred in August and September 593 B.C. Also see note on 1:3. 28:4 Hebrew *Jeconiah,* a variant name for Jehoiachin.

Only when his predictions come true can it be
known that he is really from the LORD."
10Then Hananiah the prophet took the yoke off
Jeremiah's neck and broke it. 11And Hananiah said
again to the crowd that had gathered, "The LORD has
promised that within two years he will break the
yoke of oppression from all the nations now subject
to King Nebuchadnezzar of Babylon." At that, Jeremiah left the Temple area.
12Soon afterward the LORD gave this message to
Jeremiah: 13"Go and tell Hananiah, 'This is what the
LORD says: You have broken a wooden yoke, but you
have replaced it with a yoke of iron. 14The LORD
Almighty, the God of Israel, says: I have put a yoke of
iron on the necks of all these nations, forcing them
into slavery under King Nebuchadnezzar of Babylon. I have put everything, even the wild animals,
under his control.'"
15Then Jeremiah the prophet said to Hananiah,
"Listen, Hananiah! The LORD has not sent you, but
the people believe your lies. 16Therefore, the LORD
says you must die. Your life will end this very year
because you have rebelled against the LORD."
17Two months later,* Hananiah died.

## CHAPTER 29

**MORE WARNINGS.** Jeremiah wrote a
letter from Jerusalem to the elders, priests, prophets,
and all the people who had been exiled to Babylon
by King Nebuchadnezzar. 2This was after King Jehoiachin,* the queen mother, the court officials, the
leaders of Judah, and all the craftsmen had been
deported from Jerusalem. 3He sent the letter with
Elasah son of Shaphan and Gemariah son of Hilkiah, when they went to Babylon as King Zedekiah's
ambassadors to Nebuchadnezzar. This is what Jeremiah's letter said:

4The LORD Almighty, the God of Israel, sends
this message to all the captives he has exiled to
Babylon from Jerusalem: 5"Build homes, and
plan to stay. Plant gardens, and eat the food you
produce. 6Marry, and have children. Then find
spouses for them, and have many grandchildren.
Multiply! Do not dwindle away! 7And work for
the peace and prosperity of Babylon. Pray to the
LORD for that city where you are held captive, for
if Babylon has peace, so will you."
8The LORD Almighty, the God of Israel, says,
"Do not let the prophets and mediums who are
there in Babylon trick you. Do not listen to their
dreams 9because they prophesy lies in my name.
I have not sent them," says the LORD. 10"The
truth is that you will be in Babylon for seventy
years. But then I will come and do for you all
the good things I have promised, and I will
bring you home again. 11For I know the plans I
have for you," says the LORD. "They are plans
for good and not for disaster, to give you a
future and a hope. 12In those days when you
pray, I will listen. 13If you look for me in earnest,
you will find me when you seek me. 14I will be
found by you," says the LORD. "I will end your
captivity and restore your fortunes. I will gather
you out of the nations where I sent you and
bring you home again to your own land."
15You may claim that the LORD has raised up
prophets for you in Babylon. 16But this is what the

**I'm afraid to give my whole life to God. I'm afraid he's going to ask me to do things later on, like be a missionary in another country. I really don't want to do that. What happens if I hold back part of my life from God?**

Imagine going out for basketball and telling the coach that you only want to practice, not play in the games. Or that you only want to play in the first half of each game. How would your coach react? What would your teammates say?

Undoubtedly they would be a little put off by your selfish attitude. After all, if you're going to be on the team, you should play in the games. And if you play, you shouldn't avoid the last half when your team might need you the most. Playing the game is a lot better than practice, and the second half is when the game is on the line!

Unfortunately, many Christians, by their attitudes and their actions, tell the Coach (God) two things: they don't really want the benefits and the fun of playing on the team (except heaven, of course); and they don't want to contribute during the times when other people might need them the most!

God wants your whole life, so he can make something extraordinary out of it. Jesus told his followers, "The thief's purpose is to steal and kill and destroy. My purpose is to give life in all its fullness" (John 10:10). That's a level of trust you haven't reached yet.

The Christian life was never meant to be done halfway. You're either sold out to God or sold out to the world. For God to give you "abundant life," you must give your life in full to God. Jesus said, "If you cling to your life, you will lose it; but if you give it up for me, you will find it" (Matthew 10:39).

And don't worry about what God will ask of you. If he asks you to be a missionary, in effect he is saying; "I know you better than anyone else does. I made you, and I love you more than you'll ever know. Because I put you together, I know what it will take to make you the happiest and most fulfilled in life. If you choose any other direction, you'll be settling for second best. Please don't."

God's goal isn't to make his kids miserable. Just take a look at Jeremiah 29:11-13. You'll see that God wants to lead us in a direction that will cause us to say, "The game wasn't easy, God, especially the last quarter. But thanks for believing in me enough to put me in—I really had fun."

**28:17** Hebrew *In the seventh month of that same year.* See 28:1 and the note there. **29:2** Hebrew *Jeconiah,* a variant name for Jehoiachin.

LORD says about the king who sits on David's throne and all those still living here in Jerusalem—your relatives who were not exiled to Babylon. [17]This is what the LORD Almighty says: "I will send war, famine, and disease upon them and make them like rotting figs—too bad to eat. [18]Yes, I will pursue them with war, famine, and disease, and I will scatter them around the world. In every nation where I send them, I will make them an object of damnation, horror, contempt, and mockery. [19]For they refuse to listen to me, though I have spoken to them repeatedly through my prophets. And you who are in exile have not listened either," says the LORD.

[20]Therefore, listen to this message from the LORD, all you captives there in Babylon. [21]This is what the LORD Almighty, the God of Israel, says about your prophets—Ahab son of Kolaiah and Zedekiah son of Maaseiah—who are telling you lies in my name: "I will turn them over to Nebuchadnezzar* for a public execution. [22]Their terrible fate will become proverbial, so that whenever the Judean exiles want to curse someone they will say, 'May the LORD make you like Zedekiah and Ahab, whom the king of Babylon burned alive!' [23]For these men have done terrible things among my people. They have committed adultery with their neighbors' wives and have lied in my name. I am a witness to this," says the LORD.

## SCANDALOUS ● ● ● ● ●

**30:15 Judah protested its punishment, even though the sin that caused it was scandalous. But punishment is an opportunity for growth, because it makes us aware of sin's consequences. The people should have asked how they could profit from their mistakes. Remember this the next time you are corrected.**

[24]The LORD sent this message to Shemaiah the Nehelamite in Babylon: [25]"This is what the LORD Almighty, the God of Israel, says: You wrote a letter on your own authority to Zephaniah son of Maaseiah, the priest, and you sent copies to the other priests and people in Jerusalem. You said to Zephaniah, [26]'The LORD has appointed you to replace Jehoiada as the priest in charge of the house of the LORD. You are responsible to put anyone who claims to be a prophet in the stocks and neck irons. [27]So why have you done nothing to stop Jeremiah from Anathoth, who pretends to be a prophet among you? [28]Jeremiah sent a letter here to Babylon, predicting that our captivity will be a long one. He said we should build homes and plan to stay for many years. He said we should plant fruit trees, because we will be here to eat the fruit for many years to come.'"

[29]But when Zephaniah the priest received Shemaiah's letter, he took it to Jeremiah and read it to him. [30]Then the LORD gave this message to Jeremiah: [31]"Send an open letter to all the exiles in Babylon.

## MAGNIFICENT LOVE ● ● ● ● ●

**31:3 God reaches toward his people with kindness motivated by deep and everlasting love. God is eager to do the best for his people if they will only let him. After many words of warning about sin, this reminder of God's magnificent love is refreshing. We may often think of God with dread or fear; but if we look carefully, we can see him lovingly drawing us toward himself.**

Tell them, 'This is what the LORD says concerning Shemaiah the Nehelamite: Since he has prophesied to you when I did not send him and has tricked you into believing his lies, [32]I will punish him and his family. None of his descendants will see the good things I will do for my people, for he has taught you to rebel against me. I, the LORD, have spoken!'"

## CHAPTER 30 **BRINGING BACK THE PEOPLE.**

The LORD gave another message to Jeremiah. He said, [2]"This is what the LORD, the God of Israel, says: Write down for the record everything I have said to you, Jeremiah. [3]For the time is coming when I will restore the fortunes of my people of Israel and Judah. I will bring them home to this land that I gave to their ancestors, and they will possess it and live here again. I, the LORD, have spoken!"

[4]This is the message the LORD gave concerning Israel and Judah: [5]"This is what the LORD says: I have heard the people crying; there is only fear and trembling. [6]Now let me ask you a question: Do men give birth to babies? Then why do they stand there, ashen-faced, hands pressed against their sides like women about to give birth? [7]In all history there has never been such a time of terror. It will be a time of trouble for my people Israel.* Yet in the end, they will be saved!

[8]"For in that day, says the LORD Almighty, I will break the yoke from their necks and snap their chains. Foreigners will no longer be their masters. [9]For my people will serve the LORD their God and David their king, whom I will raise up for them.

[10]"So do not be afraid, Jacob, my servant; do not be dismayed, Israel, says the LORD. For I will bring you home again from distant lands, and your children will return from their exile. Israel will return and will have peace and quiet in their own land, and no one will make them afraid. [11]For I am with you and will save you, says the LORD. I will completely destroy the nations where I have scattered you, but I will not destroy you. But I must discipline you; I cannot let you go unpunished.

[12]"This is what the LORD says: Yours is an incurable bruise, a terrible wound. [13]There is no one to help you or bind up your injury. You are beyond the help of any medicine. [14]All your allies have left you and do not care about you anymore. I have wounded you cruelly, as though I were your enemy. For your sins are many, and your guilt is great. [15]Why do you protest your punishment—this wound that has no cure? I have had to punish you because your sins are many and your guilt is great.

[16]"But in that coming day, all who destroy you will

**29:21** Hebrew *Nebuchadrezzar,* a variant name for Nebuchadnezzar. **30:7** Hebrew *Jacob;* also in 30:10b.

be destroyed, and all your enemies will be sent into exile. Those who plunder you will be plundered, and those who attack you will be attacked. [17]I will give you back your health and heal your wounds, says the LORD.

"Now you are called an outcast—'Jerusalem* for whom nobody cares.' [18]But the LORD says this: When I bring you home again from your captivity and restore your fortunes, Jerusalem will be rebuilt on her ruins. The palace will be reconstructed as it was before. [19]There will be joy and songs of thanksgiving, and I will multiply my people and make of them a great and honored nation. [20]Their children will prosper as they did long ago. I will establish them as a nation before me, and I will punish anyone who hurts them. [21]They will have their own ruler again, and he will not be a foreigner. I will invite him to approach me, says the LORD, for who would dare to come unless invited? [22]You will be my people, and I will be your God."

[23]Look! The LORD's anger bursts out like a storm, a driving wind that swirls down on the heads of the wicked. [24]The fierce anger of the LORD will not diminish until it has finished all his plans. In the days to come, you will understand all this.

CHAPTER **31** **GOD STILL LOVES THE PEOPLE.** "In that day," says the LORD, "I will be the God of all the families of Israel, and they will be my people. [2]I will care for the survivors as they travel through the wilderness. I will again come to give rest to the people of Israel."

[3]Long ago the LORD said to Israel: "I have loved you, my people, with an everlasting love. With unfailing love I have drawn you to myself. [4]I will rebuild you, my virgin Israel. You will again be happy and dance merrily with tambourines. [5]Again you will plant your vineyards on the mountains of Samaria and eat from your own gardens there. [6]The day will come when watchmen will shout from the hill country of Ephraim, 'Come, let us go up to Jerusalem* to worship the LORD our God.'"

[7]Now this is what the LORD says: "Sing with joy for Israel*! Shout for the greatest of nations! Shout out with praise and joy: 'Save your people, O LORD, the remnant of Israel!' [8]For I will bring them from the north and from the distant corners of the earth. I will not forget the blind and lame, the expectant mothers and women about to give birth. A great company will return! [9]Tears of joy will stream down their faces, and I will lead them home with great care. They will walk beside quiet streams and not stumble. For I am Israel's father, and Ephraim is my oldest child.

[10]"Listen to this message from the LORD, you nations of the world; proclaim it in distant coastlands: The LORD, who scattered his people, will gather them together and watch over them as a shepherd does his flock. [11]For the LORD has redeemed Israel from those too strong for them. [12]They will come home and sing songs of joy on the heights of Jerusalem. They will be radiant because of the many gifts the LORD has given them—the good crops of wheat, wine, and oil, and the healthy flocks and herds. Their life will be like a watered garden, and all their sorrows will be gone. [13]The young women will dance for joy, and the men—old and young—will join in the celebration. I will turn their mourning into joy. I will comfort them and exchange their sorrow for rejoicing. [14]I will supply the priests with an abundance of offerings. I will satisfy my people with my bounty. I, the LORD, have spoken!"

[15]This is what the LORD says: "A cry of anguish is heard in Ramah—mourning and weeping unrestrained. Rachel weeps for her children, refusing to be comforted—for her children are dead."

[16]But now the LORD says, "Do not weep any longer, for I will reward you. Your children will come back to you from the distant land of the enemy. [17]There is hope for your future," says the LORD. "Your children will come again to their own land. [18]I have heard Israel* saying, 'You disciplined me severely, but I deserved it. I was like a calf that needed to be trained for the yoke and plow. Turn me again to you and restore me, for you alone are the LORD my God. [19]I turned away from God, but then I was sorry. I kicked myself for my stupidity! I was thoroughly ashamed of all I did in my younger days.'

[20]"Is not Israel still my son, my darling child?" asks the LORD. "I had to punish him, but I still love him. I long for him and surely will have mercy on him.

[21]"Set up road signs; put up guideposts. Mark well the path by which you came. Come back again, my virgin Israel; return to your cities here. [22]How long will you wander, my wayward daughter? For the LORD will cause something new and different to happen—Israel will embrace her God.*"

[23]This is what the LORD Almighty, the God of Israel, says: "When I bring them back again, the people of Judah and its cities will again say, 'The LORD bless you—O righteous home, O holy mountain!' [24]And city dwellers and farmers and shepherds alike will live together in peace and happiness. [25]For I have given rest to the weary and joy to the sorrowing."

[26]At this, I woke up and looked around. My sleep had been very sweet.

[27]"The time will come," says the LORD, "when I

**RETURN ● ● • • •**

31:18-20 **These verses describe grief and mourning. Ephraim was one of the major tribes of the northern kingdom (Israel). Although the northern kingdom had sunk into the most degrading sins, God still loved the people. A remnant would turn to God, repenting of their sins, and God would forgive. God still loves you, despite what you have done. He will forgive you if you will return to him.**

**30:17** Hebrew *Zion.* **31:6** Hebrew *Zion;* also in 31:12. **31:7** Hebrew *Jacob;* also in 31:11. **31:18** Hebrew *Ephraim,* referring to the northern kingdom of Israel; also in 31:20. **31:22** Hebrew *a woman will court a suitor.*

## REVOLUTION ● ● • • •

31:33 **The old covenant, broken by the people, would be replaced by a new covenant. The foundation of this new covenant is Christ (Hebrews 8:6). It is revolutionary, involving not only Israel and Judah, but also the Gentiles. It offers a unique personal relationship with God himself, with his laws inscribed on heart instead of on stone. Jeremiah looked forward to the day when Jesus would come to establish this covenant. For us today, this covenant is here. We have the wonderful opportunity to make a fresh start and establish a permanent, personal relationship with God.**

will greatly increase the population and multiply the number of cattle here in Israel and Judah. 28 In the past I uprooted and tore down this nation. I overthrew it, destroyed it, and brought disaster upon it. But in the future I will plant it and build it up," says the LORD.

29 "The people will no longer quote this proverb: 'The parents eat sour grapes, but their children's mouths pucker at the taste.' 30 All people will die for their own sins—those who eat the sour grapes will be the ones whose mouths will pucker.

31 "The day will come," says the LORD, "when I will make a new covenant with the people of Israel and Judah. 32 This covenant will not be like the one I made with their ancestors when I took them by the hand and brought them out of the land of Egypt. They broke that covenant, though I loved them as a husband loves his wife," says the LORD.

33 "But this is the new covenant I will make with the people of Israel on that day," says the LORD. "I will put my laws in their minds, and I will write them on their hearts. I will be their God, and they will be my people. 34 And they will not need to teach their neighbors, nor will they need to teach their family, saying, 'You should know the LORD.' For everyone, from the least to the greatest, will already know me," says the LORD. "And I will forgive their wickedness and will never again remember their sins."

35 It is the LORD who provides the sun to light the day and the moon and stars to light the night. It is he who stirs the sea into roaring waves. His name is the LORD Almighty, and this is what he says: 36 "I am as likely to reject my people Israel as I am to do away with the laws of nature! 37 Just as the heavens cannot be measured and the foundation of the earth cannot be explored, so I will not consider casting them away forever for their sins. I, the LORD, have spoken!

38 "The time is coming," says the LORD, "when all Jerusalem will be rebuilt for me, from the Tower of Hananel to the Corner Gate. 39 A measuring line will be stretched out over the hill of Gareb and across to Goah. 40 And the entire area—including the graveyard and ash dump in the valley, and all the fields out to the Kidron Valley on the east as far as the Horse Gate—will be holy to the LORD. The city will never again be captured or destroyed."

CHAPTER **32** **JEREMIAH BUYS A FIELD.** The following message came to Jeremiah from the LORD in the tenth year of the reign of Zedekiah,* king of Judah. This was also the eighteenth year of the reign of King Nebuchadnezzar.* 2 Jerusalem was under siege from the Babylonian army, and Jeremiah was imprisoned in the courtyard of the guard in the royal palace. 3 King Zedekiah had put him there because he continued to give this prophecy: "This is what the LORD says: I am about to hand this city over to the king of Babylon. 4 King Zedekiah will be captured by the Babylonians* and taken to the king of Babylon to be judged and sentenced. 5 I will take Zedekiah to Babylon and will deal with him there. If you fight against the Babylonians, you will never succeed."

6 At that time the LORD sent me a message. He said, 7 "Your cousin Hanamel son of Shallum will come and say to you, 'Buy my field at Anathoth. By law you have the right to buy it before it is offered to anyone else.'"

8 Then, just as the LORD had said he would, Hanamel came and visited me in the prison. He said, "Buy my field at Anathoth in the land of Benjamin. By law you have the right to buy it before it is offered to anyone else, so buy it for yourself." Then I knew for sure that the message I had heard was from the LORD.

9 So I bought the field at Anathoth, paying Hanamel seventeen pieces* of silver for it. 10 I signed and sealed the deed of purchase before witnesses, weighed out the silver, and paid him. 11 Then I took the sealed deed and an unsealed copy of the deed, which contained the terms and conditions of the purchase, 12 and I handed them to Baruch son of Neriah and grandson of Mahseiah. I did all this in the presence of my cousin Hanamel, the witnesses who had signed the deed, and all the men of Judah who were there.

13 Then I said to Baruch as they all listened, 14 "The LORD Almighty, the God of Israel, says: Take both this sealed deed and the unsealed copy, and put them into a pottery jar to preserve them for a long time. 15 For the LORD Almighty, the God of Israel, says: Someday people will again own property here in this land and will buy and sell houses and vineyards and fields."

16 Then after I had given the papers to Baruch, I prayed to the LORD: 17 "O Sovereign LORD! You have made the heavens and earth by your great power. Nothing is too hard for you! 18 You are loving and kind to thousands, though children suffer for their parents' sins. You are the great and powerful God, the LORD Almighty. 19 You have all wisdom and do great and mighty miracles. You are very aware of the conduct of all people, and you reward them according to their deeds. 20 You performed miraculous signs and wonders in the land of Egypt—things still remembered to this day! And you have continued to

**32:1a** The tenth year of Zedekiah's reign and the eighteenth year of Nebuchadnezzar's reign was 587 B.C. **32:1b** Hebrew *Nebuchadrezzar,* a variant name for Nebuchadnezzar; also in 32:28. **32:4** Or *Chaldeans;* also in 32:5, 24, 25, 28, 29, 43. **32:9** Hebrew *17 shekels,* about 7 ounces or 194 grams in weight.

do great miracles in Israel and all around the world.
You have made your name very great, as it is today.
21"You brought Israel out of Egypt with mighty
signs and wonders, with great power and overwhelming terror. 22You gave the people of Israel this
land that you had promised their ancestors long
before—a land flowing with milk and honey. 23Our
ancestors came and conquered it and lived in it, but
they refused to obey you or follow your law. They
have hardly done one thing you told them to! That
is why you have sent this terrible disaster upon them.
24"See how the siege ramps have been built
against the city walls! Because of war, famine, and
disease, the city has been handed over to the Babylonians, who will conquer it. Everything has happened
just as you said it would. 25And yet, O Sovereign
LORD, you have told me to buy the field—paying
good money for it before these witnesses—even
though the city will soon belong to the Babylonians."
26Then this message came to Jeremiah from the
LORD: 27"I am the LORD, the God of all the peoples of
the world. Is anything too hard for me? 28I will hand
this city over to the Babylonians and to Nebuchadnezzar, king of Babylon, and he will capture it. 29The
Babylonians outside the walls will come in and set
fire to the city. They will burn down all these houses,
where the people caused my fury to rise by offering
incense to Baal on the rooftops and by pouring out
drink offerings to other gods. 30Israel and Judah have
done nothing but wrong since their earliest days.
They have infuriated me with all their evil deeds,"
says the LORD. 31"From the time this city was built
until now, it has done nothing but anger me, so I am
determined to get rid of it.
32"The sins of Israel and Judah—the sins of the
people of Jerusalem, the kings, the officials, the
priests, and the prophets—stir up my anger. 33My
people have turned their backs on me and have
refused to return. Day after day, year after year, I
taught them right from wrong, but they would not
listen or obey. 34They have set up their abominable
idols right in my own Temple, defiling it. 35They have
built pagan shrines to Baal in the valley of the son of
Hinnom, and there they sacrifice their sons and
daughters to Molech. I have never commanded such
a horrible deed; it never even crossed my mind to
command such a thing. What an incredible evil,
causing Judah to sin so greatly!
36"Now I want to say something more about this
city. You have been saying, 'It will fall to the king of
Babylon through war, famine, and disease.' But this
is what the LORD, the God of Israel, says: 37I will
surely bring my people back again from all the countries where I will scatter them in my fury. I will bring
them back to this very city and let them live in peace
and safety. 38They will be my people, and I will be
their God. 39And I will give them one heart and mind
to worship me forever, for their own good and for
the good of all their descendants.
40"And I will make an everlasting covenant with
them, promising not to stop doing good for them. I
will put a desire in their hearts to worship me, and
they will never leave me. 41I will rejoice in doing
good to them and will faithfully and wholeheartedly
replant them in this land. 42Just as I have sent all
these calamities upon them, so I will do all the good
I have promised them. I, the LORD, have spoken!
43"Fields will again be bought and sold in this
land about which you now say, 'It has been ravaged
by the Babylonians, a land where people and animals have all disappeared.' 44Yes, fields will once
again be bought and sold—deeds signed and sealed
and witnessed—in the land of Benjamin and here in
Jerusalem, in the towns of Judah and in the hill
country, in the foothills of Judah* and in the Negev,
too. For someday I will restore prosperity to them. I,
the LORD, have spoken!"

**TRUST ● ● • • •**

32:6-12 **Trust doesn't come easy. It wasn't easy for Jeremiah to publicly buy land already captured by the enemy. But he trusted God. It wasn't easy for David to think that he would become king, even after he was anointed. But he trusted God (1 Samuel 16–31). It wasn't easy for Moses to believe that he and his people would escape Egypt, even after God spoke to him from a burning bush. But he trusted God (Exodus 3:1–4:20). It isn't easy for us to believe that God can transform our life when we see the mess we've made. But we must trust God. He who worked in the lives of biblical heroes is the same God who offers to work in our life, if we will let him.**

CHAPTER **33** **A WONDERFUL PROMISE.** While Jeremiah was still confined in the courtyard of the guard,
the LORD gave him this second message: 2"The LORD,
the Maker of the heavens and earth—the LORD is his
name—says this: 3Ask me and I will tell you some
remarkable secrets about what is going to happen
here. 4For this is what the LORD, the God of Israel,
says: Though you have torn down the houses of this
city and even the king's palace to get materials to
strengthen the walls against the siege weapons of the
enemy, 5the Babylonians* will still enter. The men of
this city are already as good as dead, for I have
determined to destroy them in my terrible anger. I
have abandoned them because of all their wickedness.
6"Nevertheless, the time will come when I will
heal Jerusalem's damage and give her prosperity and
peace. 7I will restore the fortunes of Judah and Israel
and rebuild their cities. 8I will cleanse away their sins
against me, and I will forgive all their sins of rebellion. 9Then this city will bring me joy, glory, and
honor before all the nations of the earth! The people
of the world will see the good I do for my people and
will tremble with awe!
10"This is what the LORD says: You say, 'This land
has been ravaged, and the people and animals have

32:44 Hebrew *the Shephelah.* 33:5 Or *Chaldeans.*

all disappeared.' Yet in the empty streets of Jerusalem and Judah's other towns, there will be heard once more [11]the sounds of joy and laughter. The joyful voices of bridegrooms and brides will be heard again, along with the joyous songs of people bringing thanksgiving offerings to the LORD. They will sing,

'Give thanks to the LORD Almighty, for the LORD
is good.
His faithful love endures forever!'

For I will restore the prosperity of this land to what it was in the past, says the LORD.

[12]"This is what the LORD Almighty says: This land—though it is now desolate and the people and animals have all disappeared—will once more see shepherds leading sheep and lambs. [13]Once again their flocks will prosper in the towns of the hill country, the foothills of Judah,* the Negev, the land of Benjamin, the vicinity of Jerusalem, and all the towns of Judah. I, the LORD, have spoken!

[14]"The day will come, says the LORD, when I will do for Israel and Judah all the good I have promised them. [15]At that time I will bring to the throne of David a righteous descendant,* and he will do what is just and right throughout the land. [16]In that day Judah will be saved, and Jerusalem will live in safety. And their motto will be 'The LORD is our righteousness!' [17]For this is what the LORD says: David will forever have a descendant sitting on the throne of Israel. [18]And there will always be Levitical priests to offer burnt offerings and grain offerings and sacrifices to me."

**PRIESTS ● ● ● • •**

33:18 **As Christ fulfills the role of King, he also fulfills the role of Priest, maintaining constant fellowship with God and mediating for the people. This verse does not mean that actual priests will perform sacrifices, because sacrifices will no longer be necessary (Hebrews 7:11). Now that Christ is our High Priest, all believers are priests of God and can come before him personally.**

[19]Then this message came to Jeremiah from the LORD: [20]"If you can break my covenant with the day and the night so that they do not come on their usual schedule, [21]only then will my covenant with David, my servant, be broken. Only then will he no longer have a descendant to reign on his throne. The same is true for my covenant with the Levitical priests who minister before me. [22]And as the stars cannot be counted and the sand on the seashores cannot be measured, so I will multiply the descendants of David, my servant, and the Levites who minister before me."

[23]The LORD gave another message to Jeremiah. He said, [24]"Have you heard what people are saying?—'The LORD chose Judah and Israel and then abandoned them!' They are sneering and saying that Israel is not worthy to be counted as a nation. [25]But this is the LORD's reply: I would no more reject my people than I would change my laws of night and day, of earth and sky. [26]I will never abandon the descendants of Jacob or David, my servant, or change the plan that David's descendants will rule the descendants of Abraham, Isaac, and Jacob. Instead, I will restore them to their land and have mercy on them."

33:13 Hebrew *the Shephelah.* 33:15 Hebrew *a righteous Branch.*

## CHAPTER 34 KING ZEDEKIAH WILL BE CAPTURED.

King Nebuchadnezzar of Babylon came with all the armies from the kingdoms he ruled, and he fought against Jerusalem and the towns of Judah. At that time this message came to Jeremiah from the LORD: [2]"Go to King Zedekiah of Judah, and tell him, 'This is what the LORD, the God of Israel, says: I am about to hand this city over to the king of Babylon, and he will burn it. [3]You will not escape his grasp but will be taken into captivity. You will stand before the king of Babylon to be judged and sentenced. Then you will be exiled to Babylon.'

[4]"But listen to this promise from the LORD, O Zedekiah, king of Judah. This is what the LORD says: 'You will not be killed in war [5]but will die peacefully among your people. They will burn incense in your memory, just as they did for your ancestors. They will weep for you and say, "Alas, our king is dead!" This I have decreed, says the LORD.'"

[6]So Jeremiah the prophet delivered the message to King Zedekiah of Judah. [7]At this time the Babylonian army was besieging Jerusalem, Lachish, and Azekah—the only cities of Judah with their walls still standing.

[8]This message came to Jeremiah from the LORD after King Zedekiah made a covenant with the people, proclaiming freedom for the slaves. [9]He had ordered all the people to free their Hebrew slaves—both men and women. No one was to keep a fellow Judean in bondage. [10]The officials and all the people had obeyed the king's command, [11]but later they changed their minds. They took back the people they had freed, making them slaves again.

[12]So the LORD gave them this message through Jeremiah: [13]"This is what the LORD, the God of Israel, says: I made a covenant with your ancestors long ago when I rescued them from their slavery in Egypt. [14]I told them that every Hebrew slave must be freed after serving six years. But this was never done. [15]Recently you repented and did what was right, following my command. You freed your slaves and made a solemn covenant with me in my Temple. [16]But now

**PROMISES ● ● ● • •**

34:15-16 **The people of Israel had a hard time keeping their promises to God. In the Temple, they would solemnly promise to obey God, but back in their homes and at work they wouldn't do it. God expressed his great displeasure. If you want to please God, make sure you keep your promises. God wants promises lived out, not just piously made.**

you have shrugged off your oath and defiled my
name by taking back the men and women you had
freed, making them slaves once again.
17"Therefore, this is what the LORD says: Since you
have not obeyed me by setting your countrymen free,
I will set you free to be destroyed by war, famine, and
disease. You will be considered a disgrace by all the
nations of the earth. 18Because you have refused the
terms of our covenant, I will cut you apart just as you
cut apart the calf when you walked between its
halves to solemnize your vows. 19Yes, I will cut you
apart, whether you are officials of Judah or Jerusalem, court officials, priests, or common people—for
you have broken your oath. 20I will give you to your
enemies, and they will kill you. Your bodies will be
food for the vultures and wild animals. 21I will hand
over King Zedekiah of Judah and his officials to the
army of the king of Babylon. And though Babylon's
king has left this city for a while, 22I will call the
Babylonian armies back again. They will fight
against this city and will capture and burn it. I will
see to it that all the towns of Judah are destroyed and
left completely empty."

## CHAPTER 35 SOME OBEY, SOME DISOBEY.

This is
the message the LORD gave Jeremiah when Jehoiakim son of Josiah was king of Judah: 2"Go to the
settlement where the families of the Recabites live,
and invite them to the LORD's Temple. Take them
into one of the inner rooms, and offer them some
wine."
3So I went to see Jaazaniah son of Jeremiah and
grandson of Habazziniah and all his brothers and
sons—representing all the Recabite families. 4I
took them to the Temple, and we went into the
room assigned to the sons of Hanan son of Igda-
liah, a man of God. This room was located next to
the one used by the palace officials, directly above
the room of Maaseiah son of Shallum, the Temple
gatekeeper.
5I set cups and jugs of wine before them and
invited them to have a drink, 6but they refused.
"No," they said. "We don't drink wine, because
Jehonadab* son of Recab, our ancestor, gave us this
command: 'You and your descendants must never
drink wine. 7And do not build houses or plant crops
or vineyards, but always live in tents. If you follow
these commands, you will live long, good lives in the
land.' 8So we have obeyed him in all these things. We
have never had a drink of wine since then, nor have
our wives, our sons, or our daughters. 9We haven't
built houses or owned vineyards or farms or planted
crops. 10We have lived in tents and have fully obeyed
all the commands of Jehonadab, our ancestor. 11But
when King Nebuchadnezzar* of Babylon arrived in
this country, we were afraid of the Babylonian* and
Aramean armies. So we decided to move to Jerusalem. That is why we are here."
12Then the LORD gave this message to Jeremiah:

### WHY OBEY?

**35:13-17 Consider the contrast between the Recabites and the other Israelites: (1) The Recabites kept their vows to a fallible human leader; Israel broke their covenant with their infallible divine Leader. (2) Johonadab told his family once not to drink and they didn't; God continually commanded Israel to turn from sin and they refused. (3) The Recabites obeyed laws dealing with temporal issues; Israel disobeyed God's laws dealing with eternal issues. (4) The Recabites would be rewarded; Israel would be punished. Often we observe customs because they are tradition. Shouldn't we be even more willing to obey God's Word because it is eternal?**

13"The LORD Almighty, the God of Israel, says: Go
and say to the people in Judah and Jerusalem, 'Come
and learn a lesson about how to obey me. 14The
Recabites do not drink wine because their ancestor
Jehonadab told them not to. But I have spoken to
you again and again, and you refuse to listen or obey.
15I have sent you prophet after prophet to tell you to
turn from your wicked ways and to stop worshiping
other gods, so that you might live in peace here in
the land I gave to you and your ancestors. But you
would not listen to me or obey. 16The families of
Recab have obeyed their ancestor completely, but
you have refused to listen to me.'
17"Therefore, the LORD God Almighty, the God of
Israel, says: Because you refuse to listen or answer
when I call, I will send upon Judah and Jerusalem all
the disasters I have threatened."
18Then Jeremiah turned to the Recabites and said,
"This is what the LORD Almighty, the God of Israel,
says: You have obeyed your ancestor Jehonadab in
every respect, following all his instructions. 19Be-
cause of this, Jehonadab son of Recab will always
have descendants who serve me. I, the LORD Almighty, the God of Israel, have spoken!"

## CHAPTER 36 JEREMIAH'S SCROLL BURNED.

During
the fourth year that Jehoiakim son of Josiah was king
in Judah,* the LORD gave this message to Jeremiah:
2"Get a scroll, and write down all my messages
against Israel, Judah, and the other nations. Begin
with the first message back in the days of Josiah, and
write down every message you have given, right up
to the present time. 3Perhaps the people of Judah will
repent if they see in writing all the terrible things I
have planned for them. Then I will be able to forgive
their sins and wrongdoings."
4So Jeremiah sent for Baruch son of Neriah, and
as Jeremiah dictated, Baruch wrote down all the
prophecies that the LORD had given him. 5Then Jeremiah said to Baruch, "I am a prisoner here and
unable to go to the Temple. 6So you go to the Temple
on the next day of fasting, and read the messages
from the LORD that are on this scroll. On that day
people will be there from all over Judah. 7Perhaps
even yet they will turn from their evil ways and ask

35:6 Hebrew *Jonadab,* a variant name for Jehonadab; also in 35:10, 14, 18, 19. See 2 Kgs 10:15. **35:11a** Hebrew *Nebuchadrezzar,* a variant name for Nebuchadnezzar. **35:11b** Or *Chaldean.* **36:1** The fourth year of Jehoiakim's reign was 605 B.C.

the LORD's forgiveness before it is too late. For the LORD's terrible anger has been pronounced against them."

[8]Baruch did as Jeremiah told him and read these messages from the LORD to the people at the Temple. [9]This happened on the day of sacred fasting held in late autumn,* during the fifth year of the reign of Jehoiakim son of Josiah. People from all over Judah came to attend the services at the Temple on that day. [10]Baruch read Jeremiah's words to all the people from the Temple room of Gemariah son of Shaphan. This room was just off the upper courtyard of the Temple, near the New Gate entrance.

[11]When Micaiah son of Gemariah and grandson of Shaphan heard the messages from the LORD, [12]he went down to the secretary's room in the palace where the administrative officials were meeting. Elishama the secretary was there, along with Delaiah son of Shemaiah, Elnathan son of Acbor, Gemariah son of Shaphan, Zedekiah son of Hananiah, and all the others with official responsibilities. [13]When Micaiah told them about the messages Baruch was reading to the people, [14]the officials sent Jehudi son of Nethaniah, grandson of Shelemiah, and great-grandson of Cushi, to ask Baruch to come and read the messages to them, too. So Baruch took the scroll and went to them. [15]"Sit down and read the scroll to us," the officials said, and Baruch did as they requested.

## CONCENTRATE ● ● • • •

36:9 **Days of fasting often were called at times of national emergency. At such times, the people abstained from eating food and concentrated their energies on showing their humility and repentance. When faced with a spiritual emergency or emotional upheaval, don't let yourself get entangled or caught up in the situation. Instead, try drawing away from distractions and concentrating on God. Seek his guidance and, if necessary, his forgiveness.**

[16]By the time Baruch had finished reading, they were badly frightened. "We must tell the king what we have heard," they said. [17]"But first, tell us how you got these messages. Did they come directly from Jeremiah?"

[18]So Baruch explained, "Jeremiah dictated them to me word by word, and I wrote down his words with ink on this scroll."

[19]"You and Jeremiah should both hide," the officials told Baruch. "Don't tell anyone where you are!" [20]Then the officials left the scroll for safekeeping in the room of Elishama the secretary and went to tell the king.

[21]The king sent Jehudi to get the scroll. Jehudi brought it from Elishama's room and read it to the king as all his officials stood by. [22]It was late autumn, and the king was in a winterized part of the palace,

## GOD'S WORD ● ● • • •

36:27-32 **God told Jeremiah to write his words on a scroll. Because he was not allowed to go to the Temple, Jeremiah asked his scribe, Baruch, to whom he had dictated the message, to read the scroll to the people gathered there. Baruch then read it to the officials, and finally Jehudi read it to the king himself. Although the king burned the scroll, he could not destroy God's Word. Today many people try to put God's Word aside, or say that it contains errors and cannot be trusted. People may reject God's Word, but they cannot destroy it. God's Word will stand forever (Psalm 119:89).**

sitting in front of a fire to keep warm. [23]Whenever Jehudi finished reading three or four columns, the king took his knife and cut off that section of the scroll. He then threw it into the fire, section by section, until the whole scroll was burned up. [24]Neither the king nor his officials showed any signs of fear or repentance at what they heard. [25]Even when Elnathan, Delaiah, and Gemariah begged the king not to burn the scroll, he wouldn't listen.

[26]Then the king commanded his son Jerahmeel, Seraiah son of Azriel, and Shelemiah son of Abdeel to arrest Baruch and Jeremiah. But the LORD had hidden them.

[27]After the king had burned Jeremiah's scroll, the LORD gave Jeremiah another message. He said, [28]"Get another scroll, and write everything again just as you did on the scroll King Jehoiakim burned. [29]Then say to the king, 'This is what the LORD says: You burned the scroll because it said the king of Babylon would destroy this land and everything in it. [30]Now this is what the LORD says about King Jehoiakim of Judah: He will have no heirs to sit on the throne of David. His dead body will be thrown out to lie unburied—exposed to hot days and frosty nights. [31]I will punish him and his family and his officials because of their sins. I will pour out on them and on all the people of Judah and Jerusalem all the disasters I have promised, for they would not listen to my warnings.'"

[32]Then Jeremiah took another scroll and dictated again to his secretary Baruch. He wrote everything that had been on the scroll King Jehoiakim had burned in the fire. Only this time, he added much more!

## CHAPTER 37 EBED-MELECH RESCUES JEREMIAH.

Zedekiah son of Josiah succeeded Jehoiachin* son of Jehoiakim as the king of Judah. He was appointed by King Nebuchadnezzar* of Babylon. [2]But neither King Zedekiah nor his officials nor the people who were left in the land listened to what the LORD said through Jeremiah. [3]Nevertheless, King Zedekiah sent Jehucal son of Shelemiah and Zephaniah the priest, son of Maaseiah, to ask Jeremiah, "Please pray to the LORD our God for us." [4]Jeremiah had not yet been imprisoned, so he could come and go as he pleased.

[5]At this time the army of Pharaoh Hophra* of Egypt appeared at the southern border of Judah.

36:9 Hebrew *in the ninth month,* of the Hebrew calendar (also in 36:22). This month in the fifth year of Jehoiakim's reign occurred in November and December 604 B.C. Also see note on 1:3. 37:1a Hebrew *Coniah,* a variant name for Jehoiachin. 37:1b Hebrew *Nebuchadrezzar,* a variant name for Nebuchadnezzar. 37:5a Hebrew *army of Pharaoh;* see 44:30.

When the Babylonian* army heard about it, they withdrew from their siege of Jerusalem. 6Then the LORD gave this message to Jeremiah: 7"This is what the LORD, the God of Israel, says: Tell the king of Judah, who sent you to ask me what is going to happen, that Pharaoh's army is about to return to Egypt, though he came here to help you. 8Then the Babylonians* will come back and capture this city and burn it to the ground. 9The LORD says: Do not fool yourselves that the Babylonians are gone for good. They aren't! 10Even if you were to destroy the entire Babylonian army, leaving only a handful of wounded survivors, they would still stagger from their tents and burn this city to the ground!"

11When the Babylonian army left Jerusalem because of Pharaoh's approaching army, 12Jeremiah started to leave the city on his way to the land of Benjamin, to see the property he had bought. 13But as he was walking through the Benjamin Gate, a sentry arrested him and said, "You are defecting to the Babylonians!" The sentry making the arrest was Irijah son of Shelemiah and grandson of Hananiah.

14"That's not true!" Jeremiah protested. "I had no intention of doing any such thing." But Irijah wouldn't listen, and he took Jeremiah before the officials. 15They were furious with Jeremiah and had him flogged and imprisoned in the house of Jonathan the secretary. Jonathan's house had been converted into a prison. 16Jeremiah was put into a dungeon cell, where he remained for many days.

17Later King Zedekiah secretly requested that Jeremiah come to the palace, where the king asked him, "Do you have any messages from the LORD?"

"Yes, I do!" said Jeremiah. "You will be defeated by the king of Babylon."

18Then Jeremiah asked the king, "What crime have I committed? What have I done against you, your officials, or the people that I should be imprisoned like this? 19Where are your prophets now who told you the king of Babylon would not attack you? 20Listen, my lord the king, I beg you. Don't send me back to the dungeon in the house of Jonathan the secretary, for I will die there."

21So King Zedekiah commanded that Jeremiah not be returned to the dungeon. Instead, he was imprisoned in the courtyard of the guard in the royal palace. The king also commanded that Jeremiah be given a loaf of fresh bread every day as long as there was any left in the city. So Jeremiah was put in the palace prison.

## CHAPTER 38

Now Shephatiah son of Mattan, Gedaliah son of Pashhur, Jehucal* son of Shelemiah, and Pashhur son of Malkijah heard what Jeremiah had been telling the people. He was saying, 2"This is what the LORD says: Everyone who stays in Jerusalem will die from war, famine, or disease, but those who surrender to the Babylonians* will live. 3The LORD also says: The city of Jerusalem will surely be handed over to the army of the king of Babylon, who will capture it."

4So these officials went to the king and said, "Sir, this man must die! That kind of talk will undermine the morale of the few fighting men we have left, as well as that of all the people, too. This man is a traitor!"

5So King Zedekiah agreed. "All right," he said. "Do as you like. I will do nothing to stop you."

6So the officials took Jeremiah from his cell and lowered him by ropes into an empty cistern in the prison yard. It belonged to Malkijah, a member of the royal family. There was no water in the cistern, but there was a thick layer of mud at the bottom, and Jeremiah sank down into it.

### REWARDS • • • • •

38:6 **Judah's leaders persecuted Jeremiah repeatedly for faithfully proclaiming God's messages. For 40 years of faithful ministry, he received no acclaim, no love, no popular following. He was beaten, jailed, threatened, and even forced to leave his homeland. Only the heathen Babylonians showed him any respect. God does not guarantee that even his faithful servants will escape persecution. But he does promise that he will be with them and will give them strength to endure (2 Corinthians 1:3-7). As you minister to others, recognize that your service is for God and not just for human approval. God's rewards often don't come in this life.**

7But Ebed-melech the Ethiopian,* an important palace official, heard that Jeremiah was in the cistern. At that time the king was holding court at the Benjamin Gate, 8so Ebed-melech rushed from the palace to speak with him. 9"My lord the king," he said, "these men have done a very evil thing in putting Jeremiah the prophet into the cistern. He will soon die of hunger, for almost all the bread in the city is gone."

10So the king told Ebed-melech, "Take along thirty of my men, and pull Jeremiah out of the cistern before he dies."

11So Ebed-melech took the men with him and went to a room in the palace beneath the treasury, where he found some old rags and discarded clothing. He carried these to the cistern and lowered them to Jeremiah on a rope. 12Ebed-melech called down to

### COURAGE • • • • •

38:9-13 **Ebed-melech feared God more than man. He alone among the palace officials stood up against the murder plot. His obedience could have cost him his life. Because he obeyed, however, he was spared when Jerusalem fell (39:15-18). You can either go along with the crowd or speak up for God. When someone is treated unkindly or unjustly, for example, reach out to that person with God's love. You may be the only one who does. And, when you're being treated unkindly yourself, be sure to thank God when he sends an "Ebed-melech" your way.**

**37:5b** Or *Chaldean;* also in 37:10, 11. **37:8** Or *Chaldeans;* also in 37:9, 13. **38:1** Hebrew *Jucal,* a variant name for Jehucal; see 37:3. **38:2** Or *Chaldeans;* also in 38:18, 19, 23. **38:7** Hebrew *the Cushite.*

Jeremiah, "Put these rags under your armpits to protect you from the ropes." Then when Jeremiah was ready, 13they pulled him out. So Jeremiah was returned to the courtyard of the guard—the palace prison—where he remained.

14One day King Zedekiah sent for Jeremiah to meet him at the third entrance of the LORD's Temple. "I want to ask you something," the king said. "And don't try to hide the truth."

15Jeremiah said, "If I tell you the truth, you will kill me. And if I give you advice, you won't listen to me anyway."

16So King Zedekiah secretly promised him, "As surely as the LORD our Creator lives, I will not kill you or hand you over to the men who want you dead."

17Then Jeremiah said to Zedekiah, "The LORD God Almighty, the God of Israel, says: If you surrender to Babylon, you and your family will live, and the city will not be burned. 18But if you refuse to surrender, you will not escape! This city will be handed over to the Babylonians, and they will burn it to the ground."

19"But I am afraid to surrender," the king said, "for the Babylonians will hand me over to the Judeans who have defected to them. And who knows what they will do to me?"

20Jeremiah replied, "You won't be handed over to them if you choose to obey the LORD. Your life will be spared, and all will go well for you. 21But if you refuse to surrender, this is what the LORD has revealed to me: 22All the women left in your palace will be brought out and given to the officers of the Babylonian army. Then the women will taunt you, saying, 'What fine friends you have! They have betrayed and misled you. When your feet sank in the mud, they left you to your fate!' 23All your wives and children will be led out to the Babylonians, and you will not escape. You will be seized by the king of Babylon, and this city will be burned."

24Then Zedekiah said to Jeremiah, "Don't tell anyone you told me this, or you will die! 25My officials may hear that I spoke to you. Then they may say to you, 'Tell us what you and the king were talking about. If you don't tell us, we will kill you.' 26If this happens, just tell them you begged me not to send you back to Jonathan's dungeon, for fear you would die there."

27Sure enough, it wasn't long before the king's officials came to Jeremiah and asked him why the king had called for him. But Jeremiah followed the king's instructions, and they left without finding out the truth. No one had overheard the conversation between Jeremiah and the king. 28And Jeremiah remained a prisoner in the courtyard of the guard until the day Jerusalem was captured.

## CHAPTER 39 **JERUSALEM IS CAPTURED.**

It was in January* during the ninth year of King Zedekiah's reign that King Nebuchadnezzar* and his army returned to besiege Jerusalem. 2Two and a half years later, on July 18,* the Babylonians broke through the wall, and the city fell. 3All the officers of the Babylonian army came in and sat in triumph at the Middle Gate: Nergal-sharezer of Samgar, and Nebo-sarsekim,* a chief officer, and Nergal-sharezer, the king's adviser, and many others.

4King Zedekiah and his royal guard saw the Babylonians in the city gate, so they fled when the darkness of night arrived. They went out through a gate between the two walls behind the king's garden and headed toward the Jordan Valley.* 5But the Babylonians* chased the king and caught him on the plains of Jericho. They took him to King Nebuchadnezzar of Babylon, who was at Riblah in the land of Hamath. There the king of Babylon pronounced judgment upon Zedekiah. 6He made Zedekiah watch as they killed his sons and all the nobles of Judah. 7Then he gouged out Zedekiah's eyes, bound him in chains, and sent him away to exile in Babylon.

8Meanwhile, the Babylonians burned Jerusalem, including the palace, and tore down the walls of the city. 9Then Nebuzaradan, the captain of the guard, sent to Babylon the remnant of the population as well as those who had defected to him. 10But Nebuzaradan left a few of the poorest people in Judah, and he assigned them fields and vineyards to care for.

11King Nebuchadnezzar had told Nebuzaradan to find Jeremiah. 12"See that he isn't hurt," he had said. "Look after him well, and give him anything he wants." 13So Nebuzaradan, the captain of the guard, and Nebushazban, a chief officer, and Nergal-sharezer, the king's adviser, and the other officers of Babylon's king 14sent messengers to bring Jeremiah out of the prison. They put him under the care of Gedaliah son of Ahikam and grandson of Shaphan, who was to take him back to his home. So Jeremiah stayed in Judah among his own people.

15The LORD had given the following message to Jeremiah while he was still in prison: 16"Say to Ebed-melech the Ethiopian,* 'The LORD Almighty, the God of Israel, says: I will do to this city everything I have threatened. I will send disaster, not prosperity. You will see its destruction, 17but I will rescue you from those you fear so much. 18Because you trusted me, I will preserve your life and keep you safe. I, the LORD, have spoken!'"

### A GOOD TURN ● ● • • •

39:17-18 **Ebed-melech risked his life to save God's prophet, Jeremiah. When Babylon conquered Jerusalem, God protected Ebed-melech from the Babylonians. God has special rewards for his faithful people.**

**39:1a** Hebrew *in the tenth month,* of the Hebrew calendar. A number of events in Jeremiah can be cross-checked with dates in surviving Babylonian records and related accurately to our modern calendar. This event occurred on January 15, 588 B.C.; see 52:4 and the note there. **39:1b** Hebrew *Nebuchadrezzar,* a variant name for Nebuchadnezzar; also in 39:11. **39:2** Hebrew *On the ninth day of the fourth month of the eleventh year of Zedekiah.* This event occurred on July 18, 586 B.C.; also see note on 39:1. **39:3** Or *Nergal-sharezer, Samgar-nebo, Sarsekim.* **39:4** Hebrew *the Arabah.* **39:5** Or *Chaldeans;* also in 39:8. **39:16** Hebrew *the Cushite.*

CHAPTER **40** **JEREMIAH IS SET FREE.** The LORD gave a message to Jeremiah after Nebuzaradan, captain of the guard, had released him at Ramah. He had found Jeremiah bound in chains among the captives of Jerusalem and Judah who were being sent to exile in Babylon.

2The captain of the guard called for Jeremiah and said, "The LORD your God has brought this disaster on this land, 3just as he said he would. For these people have sinned against the LORD and disobeyed him. That is why it happened. 4Now I am going to take off your chains and let you go. If you want to come with me to Babylon, you are welcome. I will see that you are well cared for. But if you don't want to come, you may stay here. The whole land is before you—go wherever you like. 5If you decide to stay, then return to Gedaliah son of Ahikam and grandson of Shaphan. He has been appointed governor of Judah by the king of Babylon. Stay there with the people he rules. But it's up to you; go wherever you like."

Then Nebuzaradan gave Jeremiah some food and money and let him go. 6So Jeremiah returned to Gedaliah son of Ahikam at Mizpah and lived in Judah with the few who were still left in the land.

7The leaders of the Judean guerrilla bands in the countryside heard that the king of Babylon had appointed Gedaliah son of Ahikam as governor over the poor people who were left behind in Judah, and that he hadn't exiled everyone to Babylon. 8So they came to see Gedaliah at Mizpah. These are the names of the leaders who came: Ishmael son of Nethaniah, Johanan and Jonathan, sons of Kareah, Seraiah son of Tanhumeth, the sons of Ephai the Netophathite, Jaazaniah* son of the Maacathite, and all their men.

9Gedaliah assured them that it would be safe for them to surrender to the Babylonians.* "Stay here, and serve the king of Babylon," he said, "and all will go well for you. 10As for me, I will stay at Mizpah to represent you before the Babylonians who come to meet with us. Settle in any town you wish, and live off the land. Harvest the grapes and summer fruits and olives, and store them away."

11When the Judeans in Moab, Ammon, Edom, and the other nearby countries heard that the king of Babylon had left a few people in Judah and that Gedaliah was the governor, 12they began to return to Judah from the places to which they had fled. They stopped at Mizpah to discuss their plans with Gedaliah and then went out into the Judean countryside to gather a great harvest of grapes and other crops.

13Soon after this, Johanan son of Kareah and the other guerrilla leaders came to Gedaliah at Mizpah. 14They said to him, "Did you know that Baalis, king of Ammon, has sent Ishmael son of Nethaniah to assassinate you?" But Gedaliah refused to believe them.

15Later Johanan had a private conference with Gedaliah and volunteered to kill Ishmael secretly. "Why should we let him come and murder you?" Johanan asked. "What will happen then to the Judeans who have returned? Why should the few of us who are still left be scattered and lost?"

16But Gedaliah said to Johanan, "I forbid you to do any such thing, for you are lying about Ishmael."

### KNOW HIM ● ● • • •

**40:2-3 The Babylonian captain, who did not know God, acknowledged that God had given the Babylonians victory. It is strange when people recognize that God exists and does miracles, but still they do not personally accept him. Knowing God is more than knowing about him. Be sure you know him personally.**

CHAPTER **41** **THE GOVERNOR DIES.** But in midautumn,* Ishmael son of Nethaniah and grandson of Elishama, who was a member of the royal family, arrived in Mizpah accompanied by ten men. Gedaliah invited them to dinner. While they were eating, 2Ishmael and his ten men suddenly drew their swords and killed Gedaliah, whom the king of Babylon had appointed governor. 3Then they went out and slaughtered all the Judean officials and Babylonian* soldiers who were with Gedaliah at Mizpah.

4The next day, before anyone had heard about Gedaliah's murder, 5eighty men arrived from Shechem, Shiloh, and Samaria. They had come to worship at the Temple of the LORD. They had shaved off their beards, torn their clothes, and cut themselves, and had brought along grain offerings and incense. 6Ishmael left Mizpah to meet them, weeping as he went. When he reached them, he said, "Oh, come and see what has happened to Gedaliah!"

### LAWLESSNESS ● ● • • •

**41:4-9 The 80 men came from three cities of the northern kingdom to worship in Jerusalem. Ishmael probably killed them for the money and food they were carrying. Without a king, with no law, and no loyalty to God, Judah was subjected to complete anarchy, or lawlessness. We need God's law to keep us from destroying each other.**

7But as soon as they were all inside the town, Ishmael and his men killed all but ten of them and threw their bodies into a cistern. 8The other ten had talked Ishmael into letting them go by promising to bring him their stores of wheat, barley, oil, and honey that they had hidden away. 9The cistern where Ishmael dumped the bodies of the men he murdered was the large one made by King Asa when he fortified Mizpah to protect himself against King Baasha of Israel. Ishmael son of Nethaniah filled it with corpses.

10Ishmael made captives of the king's daughters and the other people who had been left under Gedaliah's care in Mizpah by Nebuzaradan, captain of the guard. Taking them with him, he started back toward the land of Ammon.

**40:8** As in parallel text at 2 Kgs 25:23; Hebrew reads *Jezaniah,* a variant name for Jaazaniah. **40:9** Or *Chaldeans;* also in 40:10. **41:1** Hebrew *in the seventh month,* of the Hebrew calendar. This month occurred in October and November 586 B.C. Also see note on 39:1. **41:3** Or *Chaldean.*

[11]But when Johanan son of Kareah and the rest of the guerrilla leaders heard what Ishmael had done, [12]they took all their men and set out to stop him. They caught up with him at the pool near Gibeon. [13]The people Ishmael had captured shouted for joy when they saw Johanan and his men. [14]And all the captives from Mizpah escaped and began to help Johanan. [15]Meanwhile, Ishmael and eight of his men escaped from Johanan into the land of Ammon.

[16]Then Johanan son of Kareah and his officers led away all the people they had rescued—warriors, women, children, and palace officials.* [17]They took them all to the village of Geruth-kimham near Bethlehem, where they prepared to leave for Egypt. [18]They were afraid of what the Babylonians* would do when they heard that Ishmael had killed Gedaliah, the governor appointed by the Babylonian king.

## CHAPTER 42 DON'T GO TO EGYPT!

Then all the army officers, including Johanan son of Kareah and Jezaniah* son of Hoshaiah, and all the people, from the least to the greatest, approached [2]Jeremiah the prophet. They said, "Please pray to the LORD your God for us. As you know, we are only a tiny remnant compared to what we were before. [3]Beg the LORD your God to show us what to do and where to go."

[4]"All right," Jeremiah replied. "I will pray to the LORD your God, and I will tell you everything he says. I will hide nothing from you."

[5]Then they said to Jeremiah, "May the LORD your God be a faithful witness against us if we refuse to obey whatever he tells us to do! [6]Whether we like it or not, we will obey the LORD our God to whom we send you with our plea. For if we obey him, everything will turn out well for us."

### DON'T PRAY ● ● • • •

**42:5-6 Johanan and his associates spoke their own curse; Jeremiah merely elaborated on it. It was a tragic mistake to ask for God's guidance with no intention of following it. Be sure never to ask God for something if you know in your heart that you do not want it. It is better not to pray than to pray deceptively. God cannot be deceived.**

[7]Ten days later, the LORD gave his reply to Jeremiah. [8]So he called for Johanan son of Kareah and the army officers, and for all the people, from the least to the greatest. [9]He said to them, "You sent me to the LORD, the God of Israel, with your request, and this is his reply: [10]'Stay here in this land. If you do, I will build you up and not tear you down; I will plant you and not uproot you. For I am sorry for all the punishment I have had to bring upon you. [11]Do not fear the king of Babylon anymore, says the LORD. For I am with you and will save you and rescue you from his power. [12]I will be merciful to you by making him kind, so he will let you stay here in your land.'

[13]"But if you refuse to obey the LORD your God and say, 'We will not stay here,' [14]and if you insist on going to live in Egypt where you think you will be free from war, famine, and alarms, [15]then this is what the LORD says to the remnant of Judah. The LORD Almighty, the God of Israel, says: 'If you insist on going to Egypt, [16]the war and famine you fear will follow close behind you, and you will die there. [17]That is the fate awaiting every one of you who insists on going to live in Egypt. Yes, you will die from war, famine, and disease. None of you will escape from the disaster I will bring upon you there.'

[18]"For the LORD Almighty, the God of Israel, says: 'Just as my anger and fury were poured out on the people of Jerusalem, so they will be poured out on you when you enter Egypt. You will become an object of damnation, horror, cursing, and mockery. And you will never see your homeland again.'

[19]"Listen, you remnant of Judah. The LORD has told you: 'Do not go to Egypt!' Don't forget this warning I have given you today. [20]For you were deceitful when you sent me to pray to the LORD your God for you, saying, 'Just tell us what the LORD our God says, and we will do it!' [21]And today I have told you exactly what he said, but you will not obey the LORD your God any better now than you have in the past. [22]So you can be sure that you will die from war, famine, and disease in Egypt, where you insist on going."

## CHAPTER 43 THE PEOPLE WON'T BELIEVE.

When Jeremiah had finished giving this message from the LORD their God to all the people, [2]Azariah son of Hoshaiah and Johanan son of Kareah and all the other proud men said to Jeremiah, "You lie! The LORD our God hasn't forbidden us to go to Egypt! [3]Baruch son of Neriah has convinced you to say this, so we will stay here and be killed by the Babylonians* or be carried off into exile."

[4]So Johanan and all the army officers and all the people refused to obey the LORD's command to stay in Judah. [5]Johanan and his officers took with them all the people who had returned from the nearby countries to which they had fled. [6]In the crowd were men, women, and children, the king's daughters, and all those whom Nebuzaradan, the captain of the guard, had left with Gedaliah. Also included were the prophet Jeremiah and Baruch. [7]The people refused to obey the LORD and went to Egypt, going as far as the city of Tahpanhes.

[8]Then at Tahpanhes, the LORD gave another message to Jeremiah. He said, [9]"While the people of Judah are watching, bury large rocks between the pavement stones at the entrance of Pharaoh's palace here in Tahpanhes. [10]Then say to the people of Judah, 'The LORD Almighty, the God of Israel, says: I will surely bring my servant Nebuchadnezzar,* king of Babylon, here to Egypt. I will set his throne on these stones that I have hidden. He will spread his royal canopy over them. [11]And when he comes, he

41:16 Or *eunuchs.* 41:18 Or *Chaldeans.* 42:1 Greek version reads *Azariah;* compare 43:2. 43:3 Or *Chaldeans.* 43:10 Hebrew *Nebuchadrezzar,* a variant name for Nebuchadnezzar.

will destroy the land of Egypt. He will bring death to those destined for death; he will bring captivity to those destined for captivity; he will bring the sword against those destined for the sword. [12]He will set fire to the temples of Egypt's gods, burning all their idols and carrying away the people as captives. He will pick clean the land of Egypt as a shepherd picks fleas from his cloak. And he himself will leave unharmed. [13]He will break down the sacred pillars standing in the temple of the sun* in Egypt, and he will burn down the temples of Egypt's gods.'"

## CHAPTER 44

**GOD GETS ANGRY.** This is the message Jeremiah received concerning the Judeans living in northern Egypt in the cities of Migdol, Tahpanhes, and Memphis,* and throughout southern Egypt as well: [2]"This is what the LORD Almighty, the God of Israel, says: You saw what I did to Jerusalem and to all the towns of Judah. They now lie in ruins, and no one lives in them. [3]Because of all their wickedness, my anger rose high against them. They burned incense and worshiped other gods—gods that neither they nor you nor any of your ancestors have ever known.

[4]"Again and again I sent my servants, the prophets, to plead with them, 'Don't do these horrible things that I hate so much.' [5]But my people would not listen or turn back from their wicked ways. They kept right on burning incense to these gods. [6]And so my fury boiled over and fell like fire on the towns of Judah and into the streets of Jerusalem, and now they are a desolate ruin.

[7]"And now the LORD God Almighty, the God of Israel, asks you: Why are you destroying yourselves? For not one of you will survive—not a man, woman, or child among you who has come here from Judah, not even the babies in your arms. [8]Why arouse my anger by burning incense to the idols you have made here in Egypt? You will only destroy yourselves and make yourselves an object of cursing and mockery for all the nations of the earth. [9]Have you forgotten the sins of your ancestors, the sins of the kings and queens of Judah, and the sins you and your wives committed in Judah and Jerusalem? [10]To this very hour you have shown no remorse or reverence. No one has chosen to follow my law and the decrees I gave to you and your ancestors before you.

[11]"Therefore, the LORD Almighty, the God of Israel, says: I have made up my mind to destroy every one of you! [12]I will take this remnant of Judah that insisted on coming here to Egypt, and I will consume them. They will fall here in Egypt, killed by war and famine. All will die, from the least to the greatest. They will be an object of damnation, horror, cursing, and mockery. [13]I will punish them in Egypt just as I punished them in Jerusalem, by war, famine, and disease. [14]Of those who fled to Egypt with dreams of returning home to Judah, only a handful will escape."

**43:13** Or *in Heliopolis.* **44:1** Hebrew *Noph.*

### REPEATING ● ● • • •

44:9-10 **When we forget a lesson or refuse to learn it, we risk repeating our mistakes. The people of Judah struggled with this same matter; to forget their former sins was to repeat them. To fail to learn from failure is to assure future failure. Your past is your school of experience. Let your past mistakes point you to God's way.**

[15]Then all the women present and all the men who knew that their wives had burned incense to idols—a great crowd of all the Judeans living in Pathros, the southern region of Egypt—answered Jeremiah, [16]"We will not listen to your messages from the LORD! [17]We will do whatever we want. We will burn incense to the Queen of Heaven and sacrifice to her just as much as we like—just as we and our ancestors did before us, and as our kings and princes have always done in the towns of Judah and in the streets of Jerusalem. For in those days we had plenty to eat, and we were well off and had no troubles! [18]But ever since we quit burning incense to the Queen of Heaven and stopped worshiping her, we have been in great trouble and have suffered the effects of war and famine."

[19]"And," the women added, "do you suppose that we were worshiping the Queen of Heaven, pouring out drink offerings to her, and making cakes marked with her image, without our husbands knowing it and helping us? Of course not!"

[20]Then Jeremiah said to all of them, men and women alike, who had given him that answer, [21]"Do you think the LORD did not know that you and your ancestors, your kings and officials, and all the people were burning incense to idols in the towns of Judah and in the streets of Jerusalem? [22]It was because the LORD could no longer bear all the evil things you were doing that he made your land an object of cursing—a desolate ruin without a single inhabitant—as it is today. [23]The very reason all these terrible things have happened to you is because you have burned incense to idols and sinned against the LORD, refusing to obey him and follow his instructions, laws, and stipulations."

[24]Then Jeremiah said to them all, including the women, "Listen to this message from the LORD, all you citizens of Judah who live in Egypt. [25]The LORD Almighty, the God of Israel, says: You and your wives have said that you will never give up your devotion and sacrifices to the Queen of Heaven, and you have

### ESCAPE ● ● • • •

44:14 **Only those who repented of going to Egypt and returned to their own land would escape judgment. God wanted both a change of attitude and some action. God always offers a way of escape—even when we get in so deep it doesn't look like there is any way out. And the steps always are the same: (1) admitting we have rebelled against God, (2) forsaking our sinful direction, and (3) seeking to live as God instructs in his Word.**

# Ultimate Issues

## SEXUAL ABUSE

Seventeen-year-old Shelly sat on the couch in her youth pastor's office, sobbing quietly. "I've never told anyone this," she choked out. **"I feel so dirty.** . . . When I was younger, my father made me have sex with him . . . lots of times . . . over several years. He said if I ever told anyone, I'd regret it. He said it was 'our little secret.' Besides, he's an elder in the church—who would believe me?" Unfortunately, this is not an isolated incident. Sexual abuse is happening more and more. It is the secret, unspoken pain of countless hearts. Sexual abuse may be defined as any contact or interaction (visual, verbal, psychological, or physical) between a child or adolescent and an adult when the younger person is being used for the sexual gratification of the older person (or anyone else).* A recent survey indicates that 38 percent of the women in this country have been sexually abused by age 18. The actual percentage may be even higher. The percentage of sexually abused males, though lower, is still shockingly high. Sexual abuse is like some huge, ***silent tidal wave*** that has reached unbelievable proportions, threatening to destroy countless lives. Surprisingly enough, victims of sexual abuse don't always know they've been abused. Some victims believe it wasn't abuse because the perpetrator was a family member or a friend, not a total stranger. Others believe they must somehow have invited the offense. Regardless of the relationship or the form the abuse takes, it still is abuse and it is wrong. Common results of sexual abuse include feelings of betrayal, fear, anger, powerlessness, shame, depression, and, later on, difficulty in having healthy relationships, especially with the opposite sex. Having been betrayed so devastatingly, many victims have an overwhelming fear of letting anyone get close enough to hurt them again. Often they keep others AT ARM'S LENGTH emotionally, or they just shut down their emotions altogether. They become little more than EMPTY SHELLS who spend their time trying to keep anyone from breaking through their protective front. It is a miserable way to live. So what should a person do who has been, or is now being, sexually abused? First, remember you are not alone. A staggering number of people, male and female, have been sexually abused. There are people who understand and can help you. Second, talk to someone about what has happened or about what you are going through. **THE ABUSER'S GREATEST WEAPON** over you is your silence. Regardless of what you've been told, you must share your pain with someone else. If possible, talk with your youth pastor, Campus Life or Young Life director, school counselor, or a psychologist or psychiatrist you trust. If that person is unable or unwilling to help, don't give up. Find someone who will listen and understand. There may be a "hotline" or agency in your area designed specifically to help victims of sexual abuse. Third, remember that if you have been sexually abused in any way, ***it is not your fault.*** You are not responsible for what happened to you. You are a victim. Do not give in to feelings that you somehow "asked for it" or brought the abuse on yourself. Seek counsel from someone who can help you understand this and can help you work through your pain. Finally, remember that you are made in the image of God. Sexual abuse is a serious crime against that image, and God will deal with those who inflict such damage on others. But there is great comfort in knowing that the same God who judges sin was once a victim of sin himself. Christ knows, he cares, and he understands.

*This definition is based on one given by Dr. Dan Allender in his excellent book *The Wounded Heart* (NavPress, 1990), p. 30.

proved it by your actions. Then go ahead and carry out your promises and vows to her!

26"But listen to this message from the LORD, all you Judeans now living in Egypt: I have sworn by my great name, says the LORD, that my name will no longer be spoken by any of the Judeans in the land of Egypt. None of you may invoke my name or use this oath: 'As surely as the Sovereign LORD lives!' 27For I will watch over you to bring you disaster and not good. You will suffer war and famine until all of you are dead.

28"Only a small number will escape death and return to Judah from Egypt. Then all those who came to Egypt will find out whose words are true, mine or theirs! 29And this is the proof I give you, says the LORD, that all I have threatened will happen to you and that I will punish you here: 30I will turn Pharaoh Hophra, king of Egypt, over to his enemies who want to kill him, just as I turned King Zedekiah of Judah over to King Nebuchadnezzar* of Babylon. I, the LORD, have spoken!"

CHAPTER **45** The prophet Jeremiah gave a message to Baruch son of Neriah in the fourth year of the reign of Jehoiakim son of Josiah,* after Baruch had written down everything Jeremiah had dictated to him. He said, 2"This is what the LORD, the God of Israel, says to you, Baruch: 3You have said, 'I am overwhelmed with trouble! Haven't I had enough pain already? And now the LORD has added more! I am weary of my own sighing and can find no rest.'

4"Baruch, this is what the LORD says: I will destroy this nation that I built. I will uproot what I planted. 5Are you seeking great things for yourself? Don't do it! But don't be discouraged. I will bring great disaster upon all these people, but I will protect you wherever you go. I, the LORD, have spoken!"

CHAPTER **46** **A MESSAGE TO THE EGYPTIANS.** The following messages were given to Jeremiah the prophet from the LORD concerning foreign nations.

2This message concerning Egypt was given in the fourth year of the reign of Jehoiakim son of Josiah,* the king of Judah, on the occasion of the battle of Carchemish when Pharaoh Neco, king of Egypt, and his army were defeated beside the Euphrates River by King Nebuchadnezzar* of Babylon.

3"Buckle on your armor and advance into battle! 4Harness the horses, and prepare to mount them. Put on your helmets, sharpen your spears, and prepare your armor. 5But look! The Egyptian army flees in terror. The bravest of its fighting men run without a backward glance. They are terrorized at every turn, says the LORD. 6The swiftest cannot flee; the mightiest warriors cannot escape. By the Euphrates River to the north they stumble and fall.

7"Who is this, rising like the Nile River at floodtime, overflowing all the land? 8It is the Egyptian army,

**INSIGHTS ● ● • • •**

46:1 **In this chapter, we gain several insights about God and his plan for this world. (1) Although God chose Israel for a special purpose, he loves all people and wants them to come to him. (2) God is holy and will not tolerate sin. (3) God's judgments are not based on prejudice and a desire for revenge, but on fairness and justice. (4) God does not delight in judgment, but in salvation. (5) God is impartial—he judges everyone by the same standard.**

boasting that it will cover the earth like a flood, destroying every foe. 9Then come, you horses and chariots and mighty warriors of Egypt! Come, all you allies from Ethiopia, Libya, and Lydia* who are skilled with the shield and bow! 10For this is the day of the Lord, the LORD Almighty, a day of vengeance on his enemies. The sword will devour until it is satisfied, yes, drunk with your blood! The Lord, the LORD Almighty, will receive a sacrifice today in the north country beside the Euphrates River. 11Go up to Gilead to get ointment, O virgin daughter of Egypt! But your many medicines will bring you no healing. 12The nations have heard of your shame. The earth is filled with your cries of despair. Your mightiest warriors will stumble across each other and fall together."

13Then the LORD gave the prophet Jeremiah this message about King Nebuchadnezzar's plans to attack Egypt.

14"Shout it out in Egypt! Publish it in the cities of Migdol, Memphis,* and Tahpanhes! Mobilize for battle, for the sword of destruction will devour everyone around you. 15Why have your warriors fled in terror? They cannot stand because the LORD has driven them away. 16They stumble and fall over each other and say among themselves, 'Come, let's go back to our homeland where we were born. Let's get away from the sword of the enemy!' 17There they will say, 'Pharaoh, the king of Egypt, is a loudmouth who missed his opportunity!'

18"As surely as I live," says the King, whose name is the LORD Almighty, "one is coming against Egypt who is as tall as Mount Tabor or Mount Carmel by the sea! 19Pack up! Get ready to leave for exile, you citizens of Egypt! The city of Memphis will be destroyed, without a single person living there. 20Egypt is as sleek as a young cow, but a gadfly from the north is on its way! 21Egypt's famed mercenaries have become like fattened calves. They turn and run, for it is a day of great disaster for Egypt, a time of great punishment. 22Silent as a serpent gliding away, Egypt flees. The invading army marches in; they come against her with axes like woodsmen. 23They will cut down her people like trees," says the LORD, "for they are more numerous than grasshoppers. 24Egypt will be humiliated; she will be handed over to men from the north."

25The LORD Almighty, the God of Israel, says: "I will punish Amon, the god of Thebes,* and all the

44:30 Hebrew *Nebuchadrezzar,* a variant name for Nebuchadnezzar. **45:1** The fourth year of Jehoiakim's reign was 605 B.C. **46:2a** The fourth year of Jehoiakim's reign was 605 B.C. **46:2b** Hebrew *Nebuchadrezzar,* a variant name for Nebuchadnezzar; also in 46:13, 26. **46:9** Hebrew *Cush, Put, and Lud.* **46:14** Hebrew *Noph;* also in 46:19. **46:25** Hebrew *No.*

other gods of Egypt. I will punish its rulers and Pharaoh, too, and all who trust in him. [26]I will hand them over to those who want them killed—to King Nebuchadnezzar of Babylon and his army. But afterward the land will recover from the ravages of war. I, the LORD, have spoken!

[27]"But do not be afraid, Jacob, my servant; do not be dismayed, Israel. For I will bring you home again from distant lands, and your children will return from their exile. Israel* will return and will have peace and quiet, and nothing will make them afraid. [28]Fear not, Jacob, my servant," says the LORD, "for I am with you. I will destroy the nations to which I have exiled you, but I will not destroy you. But I must discipline you; I cannot let you go unpunished."

## CHAPTER 47

**A MESSAGE TO THE PHILISTINES.** This is the LORD's message to the prophet Jeremiah concerning the Philistines of Gaza, before it was captured by the Egyptian army.

[2]This is what the LORD says: "A flood is coming from the north to overflow the land. It will destroy the land and everything in it—cities and people alike. People will scream in terror, and everyone in the land will weep. [3]Hear the clatter of hooves and the rumble of wheels as the chariots rush by. Terrified fathers run madly, without a backward glance at their helpless children.

[4]"The time has come for the Philistines to be destroyed, along with their allies from Tyre and Sidon. Yes, the LORD is destroying the Philistines, those colonists from Crete.* [5]The city of Gaza will be demolished; Ashkelon will lie in ruins. You remnant of the Mediterranean plain,* how long will you lament and mourn?

[6]"Now, O sword of the LORD, when will you be at rest again? Go back into your sheath; rest and be still! [7]But how can it be still when the LORD has sent it on an errand? For the city of Ashkelon and the people living along the sea must be destroyed."

## CHAPTER 48

**THE PROUD MOABITES ARE DOOMED.** This message was given concerning Moab.

This is what the LORD Almighty, the God of Israel, says: "Destruction is certain for the city of Nebo; it will soon lie in ruins. The city of Kiriathaim will be humiliated and captured; the fortress will be humiliated and broken down. [2]No one will ever brag about Moab again, for there is a plot against her life. In Heshbon plans have been completed to destroy her. 'Come,' they say, 'we will cut her off from being a nation.' The city of Madmen,* too, will be silenced; the sword will follow you there. [3]And then the roar of battle will surge against Horonaim, [4]for all Moab is being destroyed. Her little ones will cry out.* [5]Her refugees will climb the hills of Luhith, weeping bitterly, while cries of terror rise from Horonaim below. [6]Flee for your lives! Hide in the wilderness!* [7]Because you have trusted in your wealth and skill, you will be taken captive. Your god Chemosh, with his priests and princes, will be exiled to distant lands!

### DON'T PUSH IT ● ● • • •

49:4, 7 **God is loving, merciful, and kind. But he is also just. Eventually he will judge and punish those who do wrong. Listen to God's words in the prophecies of Jeremiah as he speaks to the Moabites who trusted in their military might (48:14), the Ammonites who trusted in their wealth (49:4), the Edomites who trusted in their wisdom (49:7) and secure location (49:16), and others. For a while it may seem as though we can get away with disobeying and defying God. But that's because he is giving us time to repent, to change our ways. What are you doing that you know is wrong? Is there a habit, a hatred, a hassle? Don't push your luck–turn to God and live his way now!**

[8]"All the towns will be destroyed, both on the plateaus and in the valleys, for the LORD has spoken. [9]Oh, that Moab had wings so she could fly away, for her cities will be left empty, with no one living in them. [10]Cursed be those who refuse to do the work the LORD has given them, who hold back their swords from shedding blood!

[11]"From her earliest history, Moab has lived in peace. She is like wine that has been allowed to settle. She has not been poured from flask to flask, and she is now fragrant and smooth. [12]But the time is coming soon," says the LORD, "when I will send troublemakers to pour her from her jar. They will pour her out, then shatter the jar! [13]At last Moab will be ashamed of her idol Chemosh, as Israel was ashamed of her gold calf at Bethel.*

[14]"You used to boast, 'We are heroes, mighty men of war.' [15]But now Moab and her towns will be destroyed. Her most promising youth are doomed to slaughter," says the King, whose name is the LORD Almighty. [16]"Calamity is coming fast to Moab; it threatens ominously.

[17]"You friends of Moab, weep for her and cry! See how the strong scepter is broken, how the beautiful staff is shattered! [18]Come down from your glory and sit in the dust, you people of Dibon, for those who destroy Moab will shatter Dibon, too. They will tear down all your towers. [19]The people of Aroer stand anxiously beside the road to watch. They shout to those who flee from Moab, 'What has happened there?'

[20]"And the reply comes back, 'Moab lies in ruins; weep and wail! Tell it by the banks of the Arnon River: Moab has been destroyed!' [21]All the cities of the plateau lie in ruins, too. Judgment has been poured out on them all—on Holon and Jahaz* and Mephaath, [22]and on Dibon and Nebo and Beth-diblathaim, [23]and on Kiriathaim and Beth-gamul and Beth-meon, [24]and on Kerioth and Bozrah—all the cities of Moab, far and near.

[25]"The strength of Moab has ended. Her horns have been cut off, and her arms have been broken," says the LORD. [26]"Let her stagger and fall like a drunk-

**46:27** Hebrew *Jacob.* **47:4** Hebrew *from Caphtor.* **47:5** Hebrew *the plain.* **48:2** *Madmen* sounds like the Hebrew word for "silence"; it should not be confused with the English word *madmen.* **48:4** Greek version reads *Her cries are heard as far away as Zoar.* **48:6** Or *Be like* [the town of] *Aroer in the wilderness.* **48:13** Hebrew *ashamed when they trusted in Bethel.* **48:21** Hebrew *Jahzah,* a variant name for Jahaz.

ard, for she has rebelled against the LORD. Moab will wallow in her own vomit, ridiculed by all. [27]Did you not make Israel the object of your ridicule? Was she caught in the company of thieves that you should despise her as you do?

[28]"You people of Moab, flee from your cities and towns! Live in the caves like doves that nest in the clefts of the rocks. [29]We have heard of the pride of Moab, for it is very great. We know of her loftiness, her arrogance, and her haughty heart. [30]I know about her insolence," says the LORD, "but her boasts are false; they accomplish nothing. [31]Yes, I wail for Moab; my heart is broken for the men of Kir-hareseth.*

[32]"You people of Sibmah, rich in vineyards, I will weep for you even more than I did for Jazer. Your spreading vines once reached as far as the Dead Sea,* but the destroyer has stripped you bare! He has harvested your grapes and summer fruits. [33]Joy and gladness are gone from fruitful Moab. The presses yield no wine. No one treads the grapes with shouts of joy. There is shouting, yes, but not of joy. [34]Instead, their awful cries of terror can be heard from Heshbon clear across to Elealeh and Jahaz; from Zoar all the way to Horonaim and Eglath-shelishiyah. Even the waters of Nimrim are dried up now.

[35]"I will put an end to Moab," says the LORD, "for they offer sacrifices at the pagan shrines and burn incense to their false gods. [36]My heart moans like a flute for Moab and Kir-hareseth, for all their wealth has disappeared. [37]They shave their heads and beards in mourning. They slash their hands and put on clothes made of sackcloth. [38]Crying and sorrow will be in every Moabite home and on every street. For I have smashed Moab like an old, unwanted bottle. [39]How it is broken! Hear the wailing! See the shame of Moab! She has become an object of ridicule, an example of ruin to all her neighbors.

[40]"An eagle swoops down on the land of Moab," says the LORD. [41]"Her cities will fall; her strongholds will be seized. Even the mightiest warriors will be as frightened as a woman about to give birth. [42]Moab will no longer be a nation, for she has boasted against the LORD.

[43]"Terror and traps and snares will be your lot, O Moab," says the LORD. [44]"Those who flee in terror will fall into a trap, and those who escape the trap will step into a snare. I will see to it that you do not get away, for the time of your judgment has come," says the LORD. [45]"The people flee as far as Heshbon but are unable to go on. For a fire comes from Heshbon, King Sihon's ancestral home, to devour the entire land with all its rebellious people.

[46]"O Moab, your destruction is sure! The people of the god Chemosh are destroyed! Your sons and daughters have been taken away as captives. [47]But in the latter days I will restore the fortunes of Moab," says the LORD.

This is the end of Jeremiah's prophecy concerning Moab.

CHAPTER **49** **A MESSAGE TO THE AMMONITES.** This message was given concerning the Ammonites.

This is what the LORD says: "What are you doing? Are there no descendants of Israel to inherit the land of Gad? Why are you, who worship Molech,* living in its towns? [2]I will punish you for this," says the LORD, "by destroying your city of Rabbah. It will become a desolate heap, and the neighboring towns will be burned. Then Israel will come and take back the land you took from her," says the LORD.

[3]"Cry out, O Heshbon, for the town of Ai is destroyed. Weep, O people of Rabbah! Put on your clothes of mourning. Weep and wail, hiding in the hedges, for your god Molech will be exiled along with his princes and priests. [4]You are proud of your fertile valleys, but they will soon be ruined. You rebellious daughter, you trusted in your wealth and thought no one could ever harm you. [5]But look! I will bring terror upon you," says the Lord, the LORD Almighty. "Your neighbors will chase you from your land, and no one will help your exiles as they flee. [6]But afterward I will restore the fortunes of the Ammonites," says the LORD.

[7]This message was given concerning Edom.

This is what the LORD Almighty says: "Where are all the wise men of Teman? Is there no one left to give wise counsel? [8]Turn and flee! Hide in deep caves, you people of Dedan! For when I bring disaster on Edom,* I will punish you, too! [9]Those who harvest grapes always leave a few for the poor. If thieves came at night, even they would not take everything. [10]But I will strip bare the land of Edom, and there will be no place left to hide. Its children, its brothers, and its neighbors—all will be destroyed—and Edom itself will be no more. [11]But I will preserve the orphans who remain among you. Your widows, too, will be able to depend on me for help."

[12]And this is what the LORD says: "If the innocent must suffer, how much more must you! You will not go unpunished! You must drink this cup of judgment! [13]For I have sworn by my own name," says the LORD, "that Bozrah will become an object of horror and a heap of rubble; it will be mocked and cursed. All its towns and villages will be desolate forever."

[14]I have heard a message from the LORD that an ambassador was sent to the nations to say, "Form a coalition against Edom, and prepare for battle!"

[15]This is what the LORD says: "I will cut you down to size among the nations, Edom. You will be despised by all. [16]You are proud that you inspire fear in others. And you are proud because you live in a rock

## SELF-CENTERED ● ● • • •

49:16 **Edom was destroyed because of its pride. Pride destroys individuals as well as nations. It makes us think we can take care of ourself without God's help. Even serving God and others can lead us into pride. Take inventory of your life and service for God, asking God to point out and remove any self-centeredness.**

**48:31** Hebrew *Kir-heres,* a variant name for Kir-hareseth; also in 48:36. **48:32** Hebrew *the sea of Jazer.* **49:1** Hebrew *Milcom,* a variant name for Molech; also in 49:3. **49:8** Hebrew *Esau;* also in 49:10.

fortress and hide high in the mountains. But don't fool yourselves! Though you live among the peaks with the eagles, I will bring you crashing down," says the LORD.

17"Edom will be an object of horror. All who pass by will be appalled and will gasp at the destruction they see there. 18It will be like the destruction of Sodom and Gomorrah and their neighboring towns," says the LORD. "No one will live there anymore. 19I will come like a lion from the thickets of the Jordan, leaping on the sheep in the pasture. I will chase Edom from its land, and I will appoint the leader of my choice. For who is like me, and who can challenge me? What ruler can oppose my will?"

20Listen to the LORD's plans for Edom and the people of Teman. Even the little children will be dragged off, and their homes will be empty. 21The earth will shake with the noise of Edom's fall, and its cry of despair will be heard all the way to the Red Sea.* 22The enemy will come as swiftly as an eagle, and he will spread his wings against Bozrah. Even the mightiest warriors will be as frightened as a woman about to give birth.

23This message was given concerning Damascus.

This is what the LORD says: "The towns of Hamath and Arpad are struck with fear, for they have heard the news of their destruction. Their hearts are troubled like a wild sea in a raging storm. 24Damascus has become feeble, and all her people turn to flee. Fear, anguish, and pain have gripped her as they do a woman giving birth. 25That famous city, a city of joy, will be forsaken! 26Her young men will fall in the streets and die. Her warriors will all be killed," says the LORD Almighty. 27"And I will start a fire at the edge of Damascus that will burn up the palaces of Ben-hadad."

28This message was given concerning Kedar and the kingdoms of Hazor, which were attacked by King Nebuchadnezzar* of Babylon.

This is what the LORD says: "Advance against Kedar! Blot out the warriors from the East! 29Their flocks and tents will be captured, and their household goods and camels will be taken away. Everywhere shouts of panic will be heard: 'We are terrorized at every turn!' 30Flee for your lives," says the LORD. "Hide yourselves in deep caves, you people of Hazor, for King Nebuchadnezzar of Babylon has plotted against you and is preparing to destroy you.

31"Go up and attack those self-sufficient nomadic tribes," says the LORD. "They live alone in the desert without walls or gates. 32Their camels and cattle will all be yours. I will scatter to the winds these people who live in distant places.* I will bring calamity upon them from every direction," says the LORD. 33"Hazor will be inhabited by jackals, and it will be desolate forever. No one will live there anymore."

34This message concerning Elam came to the prophet Jeremiah from the LORD at the beginning of the reign of King Zedekiah of Judah.

35This is what the LORD Almighty says: "I will destroy the archers of Elam—the best of their marksmen. 36I will bring enemies from all directions, and I will scatter the people of Elam to the four winds. They will be exiled to countries around the world. 37I myself will go with Elam's enemies to shatter it. My fierce anger will bring great disaster upon the people of Elam," says the LORD. "Their enemies will chase them with the sword until I have destroyed them completely. 38I will set my throne in Elam," says the LORD, "and I will destroy its king and princes. 39But in the latter days I will restore the fortunes of Elam," says the LORD.

## CHAPTER 50

**A MESSAGE TO BABYLON.** The LORD gave Jeremiah the prophet this message concerning Babylon and the land of the Babylonians.*

2This is what the LORD says: "Tell the whole world, and keep nothing back! Raise a signal flag so everyone will know that Babylon will fall! Her images and idols will be shattered. Her gods Bel and Marduk will be utterly disgraced. 3For a nation will attack her from the north and bring such destruction that no one will live in her again. Everything will be gone; both people and animals will flee.

### WIPED OUT ● ● • • •

50:1-3 **Babylon is another name for the nation of the Chaldeans. At the height of its power, this empire seemed immovable. But when Babylon had finished serving God's purpose of punishing Judah for her sins, it would be punished and crushed for its own. Babylon was destroyed in 539 B.C. by the Medo-Persians (Daniel 5:30-31). Babylon is also used in Scripture as a symbol of all evil. This message can thus apply to the end times when God wipes out all evil, once and for all.**

4"Then the people of Israel and Judah will join together," says the LORD, "weeping and seeking the LORD their God. 5They will ask the way to Jerusalem* and will start back home again. They will bind themselves to the LORD with an eternal covenant that will never again be broken.

6"My people have been lost sheep. Their shepherds have led them astray and turned them loose in the mountains. They have lost their way and cannot remember how to get back to the fold. 7All who found them devoured them. Their enemies said, 'We are allowed to attack them freely, for they have sinned against the LORD, their place of rest, the hope of their ancestors.'

8"But now, flee from Babylon! Leave the land of the Babylonians. Lead my people home again. 9For look, I am raising up an army of great nations from the north. I will bring them against Babylon to attack her, and she will be captured. The enemies' arrows

**49:21** Hebrew *sea of reeds.* **49:28** Hebrew *Nebuchadrezzar,* a variant name for Nebuchadnezzar; also in 49:30. **49:32** Or *who clip the corners of their hair.* **50:1** Or *Chaldeans;* also in 50:8, 25, 35, 45. **50:5** Hebrew *Zion;* also in 50:28.

will go straight to the mark; they will not miss! [10]Babylonia* will be plundered until the attackers are glutted with plunder," says the LORD.

[11]"You rejoice and are glad, you plunderers of my chosen people. You frisk about like a calf in a meadow and neigh like a stallion. [12]But your homeland* will be overwhelmed with shame and disgrace. You will become the least of nations—a wilderness, a dry and desolate land. [13]Because of the LORD's anger, Babylon will become a deserted wasteland. All who pass by will be horrified and will gasp at the destruction they see there.

[14]"Yes, prepare to attack Babylon, all you nations round about. Let your archers shoot at her. Spare no arrows, for she has sinned against the LORD. [15]Shout against her from every side. Look! She surrenders! Her walls have fallen. The LORD has taken vengeance, so do not spare her. Do to her as she has done to others! [16]Lead from Babylon all those who plant crops; send all the harvesters away. Let the captives escape the sword of the enemy and rush back to their own lands.

[17]"The Israelites are like sheep that have been scattered by lions. First the king of Assyria ate them up. Then King Nebuchadnezzar* of Babylon cracked their bones." [18]Therefore, the LORD Almighty, the God of Israel, says: "Now I will punish the king of Babylon and his land, just as I punished the king of Assyria. [19]And I will bring Israel home again to her own land, to feed in the fields of Carmel and Bashan, and to be satisfied once more on the hill country of Ephraim and Gilead. [20]In those days," says the LORD, "no sin will be found in Israel or in Judah, for I will forgive the remnant I preserve.

[21]"Go up, my warriors, against the land of Merathaim and against the people of Pekod. Yes, march against Babylon, the land of rebels, a land that I will judge! Pursue, kill, and completely destroy* them, as I have commanded you," says the LORD. [22]"Let the battle cry be heard in the land, a shout of great destruction. [23]Babylon, the mightiest hammer in all the earth, lies broken and shattered. Babylon is desolate among the nations! [24]Listen, Babylon, for I have set a trap for you. You are caught, for you have fought against the LORD.

[25]"The LORD has opened his armory and brought out weapons to vent his fury against his enemies. The terror that falls upon the Babylonians will be the work of the Sovereign LORD Almighty. [26]Yes, come against her from distant lands. Break open her granaries. Crush her walls and houses into heaps of rubble. Destroy her completely, and leave nothing! [27]Even destroy her cattle—it will be terrible for them, too! Slaughter them all! For the time has come for Babylon to be devastated. [28]Listen to the people who have escaped from Babylon, as they declare in Jerusalem how the LORD our God has taken vengeance against those who destroyed his Temple.

[29]"Send out a call for archers to come to Babylon. Surround the city so none can escape. Do to her as she has done to others, for she has defied the LORD, the Holy One of Israel. [30]Her young men will fall in the streets and die. Her warriors will all be killed," says the LORD.

[31]"See, I am your enemy, O proud people," says the Lord, the LORD Almighty. "Your day of reckoning has arrived. [32]O land of pride, you will stumble and fall, and no one will raise you up. For I will light a fire in the cities of Babylon that will burn everything around them."

[33]And now the LORD Almighty says this: "The people of Israel and Judah have been wronged. Their captors hold them and refuse to let them go. [34]But the one who redeems them is strong. His name is the LORD Almighty. He will defend them and give them rest again in Israel. But the people of Babylon—there will be no rest for them!

[35]"The sword of destruction will strike the Babylonians," says the LORD. "It will strike the people of Babylon—her princes and wise men, too. [36]And when it strikes her wise counselors, they will become fools! When it strikes her mightiest warriors, panic will seize them! [37]When it strikes her horses and chariots, her allies from other lands will become as weak as women. When it strikes her treasures, they all will be plundered. [38]It will even strike her water supply, causing it to dry up. And why? Because the whole land is filled with idols, and the people are madly in love with them.

[39]"Soon this city of Babylon will be inhabited by ostriches and jackals. It will be a home for the wild animals of the desert. Never again will people live there; it will lie desolate forever. [40]I will destroy it just as I* destroyed Sodom and Gomorrah and their neighboring towns," says the LORD. "No one will live there anymore.

[41]"Look! A great army is marching from the north! A great nation and many kings are rising against you from far-off lands. [42]They are fully armed for slaughter. They are cruel and show no mercy. As they ride forward, the noise of their army is like a roaring sea. They are marching in battle formation to destroy you, Babylon. [43]The king of Babylon has received reports about the enemy, and he is weak with fright. Fear and pain have gripped him, like that of a woman about to give birth.

[44]"I will come like a lion from the thickets of the Jordan, leaping on the sheep in the pasture. I will chase Babylon from its land, and I will appoint the leader of my choice. For who is like me, and who can challenge me? What ruler can oppose my will?"

[45]Listen to the LORD's plans against Babylon and the land of the Babylonians. Even little children will be dragged off, and their homes will be empty. [46]The earth will shake with the noise of Babylon's fall, and her cry of despair will be heard around the world.

**50:10** Or *Chaldea.* **50:12** Hebrew *your mother.* **50:17** Hebrew *Nebuchadrezzar,* a variant name for Nebuchadnezzar. **50:21** The Hebrew term used here refers to the complete consecration of things or people to the LORD, either by destroying them or by giving them as an offering. **50:40** Hebrew *just as God.*

CHAPTER **51** **OUR GREAT AND MIGHTY GOD.** This is
what the LORD says: "I will stir up a destroyer against
Babylon and the people of Babylonia.* 2Foreigners
will come and winnow her, blowing her away as
chaff. They will come from every side to rise against
her in her day of trouble. 3Don't let the archers put
on their armor or draw their bows. No one will be
spared! Young and old alike will be completely destroyed.* 4They will fall dead in the land of the
Babylonians,* slashed to death in her streets. 5For
the LORD Almighty has not forsaken Israel and
Judah. He is still their God, even though their land
was filled with sin against the Holy One of Israel."

## BLOWN AWAY ● ● • • •

**51:2 Winnowers worked to separate the wheat from the chaff. When they threw the mixture into the air, the wind blew away the worthless chaff while the wheat settled to the ground. Babylon would be blown away like chaff in the wind. (See also Matthew 3:12 where John the Baptist says Jesus will separate the wheat from the chaff.) Is there chaff in your life?**

6Flee from Babylon! Save yourselves! Don't get
trapped in her punishment! It is the LORD's time for
vengeance; he will fully repay her. 7Babylon has been
like a golden cup in the LORD's hands, a cup from
which he made the whole earth drink and go mad.
8But now suddenly, Babylon, too, has fallen. Weep
for her, and give her medicine. Perhaps she can yet
be healed. 9We would have helped her if we could,
but nothing can save her now. Let her go; abandon
her. Return now to your own land, for her judgment
will be so great it cannot be measured. 10The LORD
has vindicated us. Come, let us announce in Jerusalem* everything the LORD our God has done.

11Sharpen the arrows! Lift up the shields! For the
LORD has stirred up the spirit of the kings of the
Medes to march against Babylon and destroy her.
This is his vengeance against those who desecrated
his Temple. 12Raise the battle flag against Babylon!
Reinforce the guard and station the watchmen. Pre-
pare an ambush, for the LORD will fulfill all his plans
against Babylon.

13You are a city rich with water, a great center of
commerce, but your end has come. The thread of
your life is cut. 14The LORD Almighty has taken this
vow and has sworn to it by his own name: "Your
cities will be filled with enemies, like fields filled
with locusts, and they will lift their shouts of triumph over you."

15 He made the earth by his power,
    and he preserves it by his wisdom.
He has stretched out the heavens
    by his understanding.
16 When he speaks, there is thunder in the heavens.
    He causes the clouds to rise over the earth.

## SECURITY ● ● • • •

**51:17-19 It is foolish to trust in man-made images rather than God. It is easy to think that the things we see and touch will bring us more security than God. But things rust, rot, and decay. God is eternal. Why put your trust in something that will disappear within a few years?**

He sends the lightning with the rain
    and releases the wind from his storehouses.
17 Compared to him, all people are foolish
    and have no knowledge at all!
They make idols, but the idols will disgrace their
        makers,
    for they are frauds.
    They have no life or power in them.
18 Idols are worthless; they are lies!
    The time is coming when they will all be
        destroyed.
19 But the God of Israel* is no idol!
    He is the Creator of everything that exists,
    including his people, his own special
        possession.
The LORD Almighty is his name!

20"You* are my battle-ax and sword," says the
LORD. "With you I will shatter nations and destroy
many kingdoms. 21With you I will shatter armies,
destroying the horse and rider, the chariot and char-
ioteer. 22With you I will shatter men and women, old
people and children, young men and maidens.
23With you I will shatter shepherds and flocks, farmers and oxen, captains and rulers.

24"As you watch, I will repay Babylon and the
people of Babylonia* for all the wrong they have
done to my people in Jerusalem," says the LORD.

25"Look, O mighty mountain, destroyer of the
earth! I am your enemy," says the LORD. "I will raise
my fist against you, to roll you down from the
heights. When I am finished, you will be nothing but
a heap of rubble. 26You will be desolate forever. Even
your stones will never again be used for building.
You will be completely wiped out," says the LORD.

27Signal many nations to mobilize for war against
Babylon. Sound the battle cry! Bring out the armies
of Ararat, Minni, and Ashkenaz. Appoint a leader,
and bring a multitude of horses! 28Bring against her
the armies of the kings of the Medes and their generals, and the armies of all the countries they rule.

29Babylon trembles and writhes in pain, for everything the LORD has planned against her stands unchanged. Babylon will be left desolate without a
single inhabitant. 30Her mightiest warriors no longer
fight. They stay in their barracks. Their courage is
gone. They have become as fearful as women. The
invaders have burned the houses and broken down
the city gates. 31Messengers from every side come
running to the king to tell him all is lost! 32All the
escape routes are blocked. The fortifications are
burning, and the army is in panic.

51:1 Hebrew *of Leb-kamai,* a code name for Babylonia. 51:3 The Hebrew term used here refers to the complete consecration of things or people to the LORD, either by destroying them or by giving them as an offering. 51:4 Or *Chaldeans;* also in 51:54. 51:10 Hebrew *Zion;* also in 51:24, 35a. 51:19 Hebrew *the Portion of Jacob.* 51:20 Possibly Cyrus, who was used of God to conquer Babylon. Compare Isa 44:28; 45:1. 51:24 Or *Chaldea;* also in 51:35.

33 For the LORD Almighty, the God of Israel, says: "Babylon is like wheat on a threshing floor, about to be trampled. In just a little while her harvest will begin."

34 "King Nebuchadnezzar* of Babylon has eaten and crushed us and emptied out our strength. He has swallowed us like a great monster and filled his belly with our riches. He has thrown us out of our own country. 35 May Babylon be repaid for all the violence she did to us," say the people of Jerusalem. "May the people of Babylonia be paid in full for all the blood they spilled," says Jerusalem.

36 The LORD says to Jerusalem, "I will be your lawyer to plead your case, and I will avenge you. I will dry up her river, her water supply, 37 and Babylon will become a heap of rubble, haunted by jackals. It will be an object of horror and contempt, without a single person living there.

38 "In their drunken feasts, the people of Babylon roar like lions. 39 And while they lie inflamed with all their wine, I will prepare a different kind of feast for them. I will make them drink until they fall asleep, never again to waken," says the LORD. 40 "I will bring them like lambs to the slaughter, like rams and goats to be sacrificed.

41 "How Babylon* is fallen—great Babylon, praised throughout the earth! The world can scarcely believe its eyes at her fall! 42 The sea has risen over Babylon; she is covered by its waves. 43 Her cities now lie in ruins; she is a dry wilderness where no one lives or even passes by. 44 And I will punish Bel, the god of Babylon, and pull from his mouth what he has taken. The nations will no longer come and worship him. The wall of Babylon has fallen.

45 "Listen, my people, flee from Babylon. Save yourselves! Run from the LORD's fierce anger. 46 But do not panic when you hear the first rumor of approaching forces. For rumors will keep coming year by year. Then there will be a time of violence as the leaders fight against each other. 47 For the time is surely coming when I will punish this great city and all her idols. Her whole land will be disgraced, and her dead will lie in the streets. 48 The heavens and earth will rejoice, for out of the north will come destroying armies against Babylon," says the LORD. 49 "Just as Babylon killed the people of Israel and others throughout the world, so must her people be killed. 50 Go, you who escaped the sword! Do not stand and watch—flee while you can! Remember the LORD, even though you are in a far-off land, and think about your home in Jerusalem."

51 "We are ashamed," the people say. "We are insulted and disgraced because the LORD's Temple has been defiled by foreigners."

52 "Yes," says the LORD, "but the time is coming when Babylon's idols will be destroyed. The groans of her wounded people will be heard throughout the land. 53 Though Babylon reaches as high as the heavens, and though she increases her strength immeasurably, I will send enemies to plunder her," says the LORD.

54 Listen! Hear the cry of Babylon, the sound of great destruction from the land of the Babylonians. 55 For the LORD is destroying Babylon. He will silence her. Waves of enemies pound against her; the noise of battle rings through the city. 56 Destroying armies come against Babylon. Her mighty men are captured, and their weapons break in their hands. For the LORD is a God who gives just punishment, and he is giving Babylon all she deserves.

57 "I will make drunk her officials, wise men, rulers, captains, and warriors," says the King, whose name is the LORD Almighty. "They will fall asleep and never wake up again!"

58 This is what the LORD Almighty says: "The wide walls of Babylon will be leveled to the ground, and her high gates will be burned. The builders from many lands have worked in vain, for their work will be destroyed by fire!"

59 The prophet Jeremiah gave this message to Zedekiah's staff officer, Seraiah son of Neriah and grandson of Mahseiah, when he went to Babylon with King Zedekiah of Judah. This was during the fourth year of Zedekiah's reign.* 60 Jeremiah had recorded on a scroll all the terrible disasters that would soon come upon Babylon. 61 He said to Seraiah, "When you get to Babylon, read aloud everything on this scroll. 62 Then say, 'LORD, you have said that you will destroy Babylon so that neither people nor animals will remain here. She will lie empty and abandoned forever.' 63 Then, when you have finished reading the scroll, tie it to a stone, and throw it into the Euphrates River. 64 Then say, 'In this same way Babylon and her people will sink, never again to rise, because of the disasters I will bring upon her.'"

This is the end of Jeremiah's messages.

**JUDGMENT ● ● • • •**

51:60-64 **In this the last of Jeremiah's messages, we find again the twin themes of God's sovereignty and his judgment. Babylon had been allowed to oppress the people of Israel, but here Babylon itself will be judged. Although God brings good out of evil, he does not allow evil to remain unpunished. The wicked may succeed for a while, but they will not last. Resist the temptation to follow them or you may share in their judgment.**

## CHAPTER 52

Zedekiah was twenty-one years old when he became king, and he reigned in Jerusalem eleven years. His mother's name was Hamutal, the daughter of Jeremiah from Libnah. 2 But Zedekiah did what was evil in the LORD's sight, just as Jehoiakim had done. 3 So the LORD, in his anger, finally banished the people of Jerusalem and Judah from his presence and sent them into exile.

Then Zedekiah rebelled against the king of

**51:34** Hebrew *Nebuchadrezzar,* a variant name for Nebuchadnezzar. **51:41** Hebrew *Sheshach,* a code name for Babylon. **51:59** The fourth year of Zedekiah's reign was 593 B.C.

## IN GOD'S EYES ● ● • • •

**52:34 In the world's eyes, Jeremiah looked totally unsuccessful. He had no money, family, or friends. He prophesied the destruction of the nation, the capital city, and the Temple, but the political and religious leaders would not accept or follow his advice. No one liked him or listened to him. Yet we can see that he successfully completed the work God gave him to do. Success must never be measured by prosperity, fame, or fortune—they don't last. King Zedekiah lost everything. God measures our success with the yardsticks of obedience, faithfulness, and righteousness. If you are faithfully doing the work God gives you, you are successful in his eyes.**

Babylon. [4]So on January 15,* during the ninth year of Zedekiah's reign, King Nebuchadnezzar* of Babylon led his entire army against Jerusalem. They surrounded the city and built siege ramps against its walls. [5]Jerusalem was kept under siege until the eleventh year of King Zedekiah's reign.

[6]By July 18 of Zedekiah's eleventh year,* the famine in the city had become very severe, with the last of the food entirely gone. [7]Then a section of the city wall was broken down, and all the soldiers made plans to escape from the city. But since the city was surrounded by the Babylonians,* they waited for nightfall and fled through the gate between the two walls behind the king's gardens. They made a dash across the fields, in the direction of the Jordan Valley.*

[8]But the Babylonians chased after them and caught King Zedekiah on the plains of Jericho, for by then his men had all abandoned him. [9]They brought him to the king of Babylon at Riblah, in the land of Hamath, where sentence was passed against him. [10]There at Riblah, the king of Babylon made Zedekiah watch as all his sons were killed; they also killed all the other leaders of Judah. [11]Then they gouged out Zedekiah's eyes, bound him in bronze chains, and led him away to Babylon. Zedekiah remained there in prison for the rest of his life.

[12]On August 17 of that year,* which was the nineteenth year of Nebuchadnezzar's reign, Nebuzaradan, captain of the guard, an official of the Babylonian king, arrived in Jerusalem. [13]He burned down the Temple of the LORD, the royal palace, and all the houses of Jerusalem. He destroyed all the important buildings in the city. [14]Then the captain of the guard supervised the entire Babylonian* army as they tore down the walls of Jerusalem. [15]Nebuzaradan, captain of the guard, then took as exiles some of the poorest of the people and those who remained in the city, along with the rest of the craftsmen and the troops who had declared their allegiance to the king of Babylon. [16]But Nebuzaradan allowed some of the poorest people to stay behind in Judah to care for the vineyards and fields.

[17]The Babylonians broke up the bronze pillars, the bronze water carts, and the bronze Sea that were at the LORD's Temple, and they carried all the bronze away to Babylon. [18]They also took all the pots, shovels, lamp snuffers, basins, dishes, and all the other bronze utensils used for making sacrifices at the Temple. [19]Nebuzaradan, captain of the guard, also took the small bowls, firepans, basins, pots, lampstands, dishes, bowls used for drink offerings, and all the other utensils made of pure gold or silver.

[20]The bronze from the two pillars, the water carts, and the Sea with the twelve bulls beneath it was too great to be measured. These things had been made for the LORD's Temple in the days of King Solomon. [21]Each of the pillars was 27 feet tall and 18 feet in circumference.* They were hollow, with walls 3 inches thick.* [22]The bronze capital on top of each pillar was 7½ feet* high and was decorated with a network of bronze pomegranates all the way around. [23]There were ninety-six pomegranates on the sides, and a total of one hundred on the network around the top.

[24]The captain of the guard took with him as prisoners Seraiah the chief priest, his assistant Zephaniah, and the three chief gatekeepers. [25]And of the people still hiding in the city, he took an officer of the Judean army, seven of the king's personal advisers, the army commander's chief secretary, who was in charge of recruitment, and sixty other citizens. [26]Nebuzaradan the commander took them all to the king of Babylon at Riblah. [27]And there at Riblah in the land of Hamath, the king of Babylon had them all put to death. So the people of Judah were sent into exile from their land.

[28]The number of captives taken to Babylon in the seventh year of Nebuchadnezzar's reign* was 3,023. [29]Then in Nebuchadnezzar's eighteenth year* he took 832 more. [30]In his twenty-third year* he sent Nebuzaradan, his captain of the guard, who took 745 more—a total of 4,600 captives in all.

[31]In the thirty-seventh year of King Jehoiachin's exile in Babylon, Evil-merodach ascended to the Babylonian throne. He was kind to Jehoiachin and released him from prison on March 31 of that year.* [32]He spoke pleasantly to Jehoiachin and gave him preferential treatment over all the other exiled kings in Babylon. [33]He supplied Jehoiachin with new clothes to replace his prison garb and allowed him to dine at the king's table for the rest of his life. [34]The Babylonian king also gave him a regular allowance to cover his living expenses until the day of his death.

**52:4a** Hebrew *on the tenth day of the tenth month,* of the Hebrew calendar. A number of events in Jeremiah can be cross-checked with dates in surviving Babylonian records and related accurately to our modern calendar. This event occurred on January 15, 588 B.C. **52:4b** Hebrew *Nebuchadrezzar,* a variant name for Nebuchadnezzar; also in 52:12, 28, 29, 30. **52:6** Hebrew *By the ninth day of the fourth month* [of Zedekiah's eleventh year]. This event of the Hebrew lunar calendar occurred on July 18, 586 B.C.; also see note on 52:4a. **52:7a** Or *Chaldeans;* also in 52:8, 17. **52:7b** Hebrew *the Arabah.* **52:12** Hebrew *On the tenth day of the fifth month,* of the Hebrew calendar. This day was August 17, 586 B.C.; also see note on 52:4a. **52:14** Or *Chaldean.* **52:21a** Hebrew *18 cubits* [8.1 meters] *tall and 12 cubits* [5.4 meters] *in circumference.* **52:21b** Hebrew *4 fingers thick* [8 centimeters]. **52:22** Hebrew *5 cubits* [2.3 meters]. **52:28** This exile in the seventh year of Nebuchadnezzar's reign occurred in 597 B.C. **52:29** This exile in the eighteenth year of Nebuchadnezzar's reign occurred in 586 B.C. **52:30** This exile in the twenty-third year of Nebuchadnezzar's reign occurred in 581 B.C. **52:31** Hebrew *on the twenty-fifth day of the twelfth month,* of the Hebrew calendar. This day was March 31, 561 B.C.; also see note on 52:4a.

# MEGA themes

**SIN** King Josiah's reformation failed because the people's repentance was shallow. They continued in their sin. All the leaders rejected God's law and will for the people. Jeremiah lists all their sins, predicts God's judgment, and begs for repentance.

Judah's deterioration and disaster came from the nation's callous disregard and disobedience of God. When we ignore our sin and refuse to listen to God's warnings, we invite disaster. Our heart must remain "tuned in" to his will for us.

1. Describe the people's sins during the reign of King Josiah (3:6-25). You may want to read 2 Kings 22:1–23:30 in order to review Josiah's reign.
2. How does God expect you to respond when you discover a sin in your life?
3. What difference does it make in your life whether or not you respond by dealing with your sin?
4. In what areas of your life do you think God wants you to make changes to avoid sin or to stop sinning? Based on this study, what will you do to respond to his will in these areas?

**PUNISHMENT** Because of sin, Jerusalem was destroyed, the Temple was ruined, and the people were carried off to Babylon. The people were responsible for their destruction and captivity because they refused to listen to God's message.

Unconfessed sin brings God's full punishment. It is useless to blame anyone else for our sin. We must answer to God for how we live.

1. How did God punish Israel and Judah?
2. Describe how you feel about these punishments. Do they seem harsh or lenient to you? Explain.
3. What provision does God supply so that you can be forgiven of your sins?
4. Based on Jeremiah, list principles from Jeremiah that you can use as reasons for why you should not sin against God.

**LORD OF ALL** God is the righteous Creator. He is accountable to no one. He wisely and lovingly directs all creation to fulfill his plans, and he brings events to pass according to his timetable. He is Lord over all the world.

Because of God's majestic power and love, our only duty is to submit to his authority. By following his plans, we can enjoy a loving relationship with God and serve him with our whole heart.

1. What evidence do you see in chapters 46–52 that God is indeed the Lord of all?
2. What type of attitudes and actions in your life currently reflect God's lordship over you? What attitudes and actions do you need to change or adjust to comply with his lordship?
3. Write two ways you will respond to his lordship in the next two weeks. Be specific and hold yourself accountable for doing it.

**NEW HEARTS** Jeremiah predicted that after the destruction of the nation, God would send a new Shepherd, the Messiah. The Messiah would lead them into a new future, a new covenant, and a new day of hope. He would accomplish this by changing their sinful hearts into hearts that loved God.

God still restores his people by renewing their hearts. His love can transform the problems created by sin. We can have hope for a new heart by loving God, trusting Christ to save us, and repenting. Rejoice in the new heart that is God's gift in Christ.

1. What do you think the text means when it speaks of providing a new heart?
2. How does a person receive a new heart when he or she becomes a disciple of Christ?
3. How does becoming a Christian involve a change of behavior? In the motivation for behavior? In one's view of God?
4. In what ways are you living out your new heart? In what ways can this be improved?

**FAITHFUL SERVICE** Jeremiah served God faithfully for 40 years. During that time the people ignored, rejected, and persecuted him. Jeremiah's preaching was unsuccessful by human standards, yet he did not fail. He remained faithful to God.

People's acceptance or rejection of us is not the measure of our success. God's approval alone should be our standard for service. We must bring God's message to others even when we are rejected. We must do God's work even if it means suffering. As Jeremiah shows, being faithful is not always easy.

1. Describe some of the feelings Jeremiah must have experienced as he brought these judgments to the people. (Begin with how he felt about God's calling him in chapter 1.)
2. What do you think kept Jeremiah going through all of his difficult experiences and encounters with people who opposed him?
3. When does it seem difficult for you to continue to serve God faithfully (i.e., when others reject you, when it feels like God is distant, etc.)?
4. How could 1:4-8 provide you with confidence that God can use you even when you feel useless? When you face rejection? When it seems too difficult to keep going?
5. What can you do to be sure that you will not let go of this confidence? How can you help young Christian friends develop this same confidence?

**A**fter Susan broke up with Brad, depression filled his sad eyes for weeks. ■ Tears streamed down Pam's face as she gave a last hug to her best friend. She stood waving good-bye as the moving van pulled out of the drive. ■ The night Chris lost the election, he cried himself to sleep. ■ As the final seconds of the state tournament ticked away, the cheerleaders wept uncontrollably. ■ What breaks your heart? Losing? Saying good-bye? Being dumped or ignored? These are emotional experiences, and worthy of tears. But there are other situations that should tug at our feelings, too: injustice, poverty, war, and famine, to name just a few. And what about the fact that people who don't know Christ are lost and bound for destruction? ■ The things that make a person cry say a lot about that person. They show whether he or she is self-centered or God-centered. The book of Lamentations shows us what made Jeremiah sorrowful. As a prophet and one of God's choice servants, he stands alone in the depths of his emotions, his care for the people, his love for the nation, and his devotion to God. ■ Read Lamentations and discover what it was that broke Jeremiah's—and God's—heart. As you do so, begin to see your world in a new light, through tears. Then determine to do something about it—for God.

## STATS

PURPOSE: To teach people that to disobey God is to invite disaster and to show that God suffers when his people suffer

AUTHOR: Jeremiah

TO WHOM WRITTEN: The nation of Judah and believers everywhere

DATE WRITTEN: Soon after the fall of Jerusalem in 586 B.C.

SETTING: Jerusalem had been destroyed by Babylon and its people killed, tortured, or taken captive

KEY PEOPLE: Jeremiah, the people of Jerusalem

KEY PLACE: Jerusalem

SPECIAL FEATURES: Three strands of Hebrew thought meet in Lamentations—prophecy, ritual, and wisdom. Lamentations is written in the rhythm and style of ancient Jewish funeral songs or chants. It contains five poems corresponding to the five chapters.

# Lamentations

CHAPTER **1** **JEREMIAH'S GREAT SADNESS.** Jerusalem's streets, once bustling with people, are now silent. Like a widow broken with grief, she sits alone in her mourning. Once the queen of nations, she is now a slave.

[2]She sobs through the night; tears stream down her cheeks. Among all her lovers, there is no one left to help her. All her friends have betrayed her; they are now her enemies.

[3]Judah has been led away into captivity, afflicted and enslaved. She lives among foreign nations and has no place of rest. Her enemies have chased her down, and she has nowhere to turn.

[4]The roads to Jerusalem* are in mourning, no longer filled with crowds on their way to celebrate the Temple festivals. The city gates are silent, her priests groan, her young women are crying—how bitterly Jerusalem weeps!

[5]Her oppressors have become her masters, and her enemies prosper, for the LORD has punished Jerusalem for her many sins. Her children have been captured and taken away to distant lands.

[6]All the beauty and majesty of Jerusalem* are gone. Her princes are like starving deer searching for pasture, too weak to run from the pursuing enemy.

[7]And now in the midst of her sadness and wandering, Jerusalem remembers her ancient splendor. But then she fell to her enemy, and there was no one to help her. Her enemy struck her down and laughed as she fell.

[8]Jerusalem has sinned greatly, so she has been tossed away like a filthy rag. All who once honored her now despise her, for they have seen her stripped naked and humiliated. All she can do is groan and hide her face.

[9]She defiled herself with immorality with no thought of the punishment that would follow. Now she lies in the gutter with no one to lift her out. "LORD, see my deep misery," she cries. "The enemy has triumphed."

## FALSE FREEDOM ● • • •

1:1-14 **At first, sin seems to offer freedom. But the liberty to do anything we want gradually becomes a desire to do everything. Then we become captive to sin. Freedom from sin's captivity comes only from God. He gives us the freedom, not to do anything we want, but to do what he knows is best for us. Strange as it may seem, true freedom comes in obeying God—following his guidance so that we can receive his best.**

1:1 Each of the first four chapters of this book is an acrostic, laid out in the order of the Hebrew alphabet. The first word of each verse begins with a successive Hebrew letter. Chapters 1, 2, and 4 have one verse for each of the 22 Hebrew letters. Chapter 3 contains 22 stanzas of three verses each. Though chapter 5 is not an acrostic, it also has 22 verses. 1:4 Hebrew *Zion;* also in 1:17. 1:6 Hebrew *the daughter of Zion.*

10 The enemy has plundered her completely, taking everything precious that she owns. She has seen foreigners violate her sacred Temple, the place the LORD had forbidden them to enter.

11 Her people groan as they search for bread. They have sold their treasures for food to stay alive. "O LORD, look," she mourns, "and see how I am despised.

12 "Is it nothing to you, all you who pass by? Look around and see if there is any suffering like mine, which the LORD brought on me in the day of his fierce anger.

13 "He has sent fire from heaven that burns in my bones. He has placed a trap in my path and turned me back. He has made me desolate, racked with sickness all day long.

14 "He wove my sins into ropes to hitch me to a yoke of captivity. The Lord sapped my strength and gave me to my enemies; I am helpless in their hands.

## DOWNHILL

Sitting on an uncomfortable bench in the visitor's area at a large juvenile correctional facility, Dwight is somber and subdued. He claws unconsciously at the handcuffs that bite into his bony wrists.

Who would imagine that this tiny 14-year-old is a convicted felon—with a rap sheet that includes car theft and armed robbery? How could a young life go so wrong?

"I knew better," Dwight mutters. "My grandmother was always on me to straighten up and do right. I did for a while. I even sang in the church choir. But when it came down to it, I picked my homeboys over church. I chose the wrong thing, and from there it was all downhill. I kept making bad decisions. I let my friends tell me what to do. And, well, here I am.

"I ask the Lord to forgive me every day, but I don't know if it does any good. I just don't know. . . ."

The conversation continues for another twenty minutes. At last the guards come in and usher Dwight away. *Clang!*—just like that, the steel doors slam shut and the little guy disappears from view.

Jeremiah's diary—the book of Lamentations—is a similarly sad account of what happens when people neglect and/or reject the Lord. Yet, despite the book's generally depressing tone, there is a wonderful note of hope in 3:19-26.

The message? Sin always has horrible consequences, but God's love is greater than any sin!

15 "The Lord has treated my mighty men with contempt. At his command a great army has come to crush my young warriors. The Lord has trampled his beloved city* as grapes are trampled in a winepress.

16 "For all these things I weep; tears flow down my cheeks. No one is here to comfort me; any who might encourage me are far away. My children have no future, for the enemy has conquered us."

17 Jerusalem pleads for help, but no one comforts

## WEAK ALLIES ● ● ● • •

**1:19 Jerusalem's allies could not come to its aid because, like Jerusalem, they failed to seek God. Though these allies appeared strong, they were actually weak because God was not with them. Dependable assistance can come only from an ally whose power is from God. When you seek wise counsel, go to Christians who get their wisdom from the all-knowing God.**

her. Regarding his people,* the LORD has said, "Let their neighbors be their enemies! Let them be thrown away like a filthy rag!"

18 "And the LORD is right," she groans, "for I rebelled against him. Listen, people everywhere; look upon my anguish and despair, for my sons and daughters have been taken captive to distant lands.

19 "I begged my allies for help, but they betrayed me. My priests and leaders starved to death in the city, even as they searched for food to save their lives.

20 "LORD, see my anguish! My heart is broken and my soul despairs, for I have rebelled against you. In the streets the sword kills, and at home there is only death.

21 "Others heard my groans, but no one turned to comfort me. When my enemies heard of my troubles, they were happy to see what you had done. Oh, bring the day you promised, when you will destroy them as you have destroyed me.

22 "Look at all their evil deeds, LORD. Punish them, as you have punished me for all my sins. My groans are many, and my heart is faint."

CHAPTER **2** **GOD HATES SIN.** The Lord in his anger has cast a dark shadow over Jerusalem.* The fairest of Israel's cities lies in the dust, thrown down from the heights of heaven. In his day of awesome fury, the Lord has shown no mercy even to his Temple.*

2 Without mercy the Lord has destroyed every home in Israel.* In his anger he has broken down the fortress walls of Jerusalem.* He has brought to dust the kingdom and all its rulers.

3 All the strength of Israel vanishes beneath his fury. The Lord has withdrawn his protection as the enemy attacks. He consumes the whole land of Israel like a raging fire.

4 He bends his bow against his people as though he were their enemy. His strength is used against them to kill their finest youth. His fury is poured out like fire on beautiful Jerusalem.*

5 Yes, the Lord has vanquished Israel like an enemy. He has destroyed her forts and palaces. He has brought unending sorrow and tears to Jerusalem.

6 He has broken down his Temple as though it were merely a garden shelter. The LORD has blotted out all memory of the holy festivals and Sabbath days. Kings and priests fall together before his anger.

7 The Lord has rejected his own altar; he despises

1:15 Hebrew *the virgin daughter of Judah.* 1:17 Hebrew *Jacob.* 2:1a Hebrew *the daughter of Zion;* also in 2:8, 10, 18. 2:1b Hebrew *footstool.* 2:2a Hebrew *Jacob;* also in 2:3. 2:2b Hebrew *the daughter of Judah;* also in 2:5. 2:4 Hebrew *on the tent of the daughter of Zion.*

his own sanctuary. He has given Jerusalem's palaces to her enemies. They shout in the LORD's Temple as though it were a day of celebration.

8The LORD was determined to destroy the walls of Jerusalem. He made careful plans for their destruction, then he went ahead and did it. Therefore, the ramparts and walls have fallen down before him.

9Jerusalem's gates have sunk into the ground. All their locks and bars are destroyed, for he has smashed them. Her kings and princes have been exiled to distant lands; the law is no more. Her prophets receive no more visions from the LORD.

10The leaders of Jerusalem sit on the ground in silence, clothed in sackcloth. They throw dust on their heads in sorrow and despair. The young women of Jerusalem hang their heads in shame.

11I have cried until the tears no longer come. My heart is broken, my spirit poured out, as I see what has happened to my people. Little children and tiny babies are fainting and dying in the streets.

12"Mama, we want food," they cry, and then collapse in their mothers' arms. Their lives ebb away like the life of a warrior wounded in battle.

13In all the world has there ever been such sorrow? O daughter of Jerusalem, to what can I compare your anguish? O virgin daughter of Zion, how can I comfort you? For your wound is as deep as the sea. Who can heal you?

14Your "prophets" have said so many foolish things, false to the core. They did not try to hold you back from exile by pointing out your sins. Instead, they painted false pictures, filling you with false hope.

15All who pass by jeer at you. They scoff and insult Jerusalem,* saying, "Is this the city called 'Most Beautiful in All the World' and 'Joy of All the Earth'?"

16All your enemies deride you. They scoff and grind their teeth and say, "We have destroyed her at last! Long have we awaited this day, and it is finally here!"

17But it is the LORD who did it just as he warned. He has fulfilled the promises of disaster he made long ago. He has destroyed Jerusalem without mercy and caused her enemies to rejoice over her and boast of their power.

18Cry aloud* before the Lord, O walls of Jerusalem! Let your tears flow like a river. Give yourselves no rest from weeping day or night.

19Rise during the night and cry out. Pour out your hearts like water to the Lord. Lift up your hands to him in prayer. Plead for your children as they faint with hunger in the streets.

20"O LORD, think about this!" Jerusalem cries. "You are doing this to your own people! Should mothers eat their little children, those they once

## CATCH THE VISION ● ● • • .

2:7 ***Where* we worship is not so important to God as *how* we worship. A church may be beautiful, but if its people don't sincerely follow God, it decays from within. The people of Judah had a beautiful Temple, but had rejected in their lives what they proclaimed in their worship, thus making their worship a mocking lie. When you worship, do you mean the words you say? Do you believe the help you pray for will come? Do you really have the love you express for God? Seek God and catch a fresh vision of his love and care. Then worship him wholeheartedly.**

## "Here's what I did..."

I had blown it again—my parents and I had another major disagreement. I ran to my room, slammed the door, and threw myself on the bed. Then I burst into tears. It wasn't fair! They weren't being fair! And there seemed to be nothing I could do about it.

After I had cried for a while, I thought about our fight. I still thought my parents were wrong, but I also had to admit that I'd said some pretty ugly things. The more I thought about it, the more I realized I would have to apologize.

It took me a couple of hours. Finally I came out and apologized for some of the hurtful things I had said. My mother's response was, "You think it's that easy? Just say you're sorry, and everything's OK? Well, it doesn't work that way."

I just turned and went back to my room. I cried some more. I had said I was sorry, and I was. Couldn't they forgive me? It seemed like they didn't really know much about forgiveness.

The next morning, still feeling bad, I picked up my Bible. I remembered reading a verse one time that I wanted to look up. Something about God's mercies being new. Something from a strange book in the Old Testament . . . Lamentations. Chapter 3, verses 21-23. "Yet I still dare to hope when I remember this: The unfailing love of the LORD never ends! . . . Great is his faithfulness; his mercies begin afresh each day."

His love for me is being replenished every day. This was a new day; God has forgiven me, his love and mercy are fresh for this day. I don't have to carry my burdens by myself. Even if my parents didn't forgive me, God did. He knew I was sincere, and would help me do better today. And even if I didn't, he'd love me. His compassion would be there for me tomorrow, just like the sun coming up to warm me.

Kara

AGE 19

2:15 Hebrew *the daughter of Jerusalem.* 2:18 Hebrew *Their heart cried.*

## NEVER ENDING ● ● • • •

3:21 **Jeremiah saw one ray of hope in all the sin and sorrow surrounding him: *The unfailing love of the Lord never ends!* God willingly responds with help when we ask. Perhaps there is some sin in your life that you thought God would not forgive. God's unfailing love is greater than any sin, and he promises forgiveness.**

bounced on their knees? Should priests and prophets die within the Lord's Temple?

21 "See them lying in the streets—young and old, boys and girls, killed by the swords of the enemy. You have killed them in your anger, slaughtering them without mercy.

22 "You have invited terrors from all around as though you were calling them to a day of feasting. In the day of the LORD's anger, no one has escaped or survived. The enemy has killed all the children I bore and raised."

CHAPTER **3** **ONE RAY OF HOPE.** I am the one who has seen the afflictions that come from the rod of the LORD's anger. 2 He has brought me into deep darkness, shutting out all light. 3 He has turned against me. Day and night his hand is heavy upon me.

4 He has made my skin and flesh grow old. He has broken my bones. 5 He has attacked me and surrounded me with anguish and distress. 6 He has buried me in a dark place, like a person long dead.

7 He has walled me in, and I cannot escape. He has bound me in heavy chains. 8 And though I cry and shout, he shuts out my prayers. 9 He has blocked my path with a high stone wall. He has twisted the road before me with many detours.

10 He hid like a bear or a lion, waiting to attack me. 11 He dragged me off the path and tore me with his claws, leaving me helpless and desolate. 12 He bent his bow and aimed it squarely at me.

13 He shot his arrows deep into my heart. 14 My own people laugh at me. All day long they sing their mocking songs. 15 He has filled me with bitterness. He has given me a cup of deep sorrow to drink.

16 He has made me grind my teeth on gravel. He has rolled me in the dust. 17 Peace has been stripped away, and I have forgotten what prosperity is. 18 I cry out, "My splendor is gone! Everything I had hoped for from the LORD is lost!"

19 The thought of my suffering and homelessness is bitter beyond words.* 20 I will never forget this awful time, as I grieve over my loss. 21 Yet I still dare to hope when I remember this:

22 The unfailing love of the LORD never ends! By his mercies we have been kept from complete destruction. 23 Great is his faithfulness; his mercies begin afresh each day. 24 I say to myself, "The LORD is my inheritance; therefore, I will hope in him!"

25 The LORD is wonderfully good to those who wait for him and seek him. 26 So it is good to wait quietly for salvation from the LORD. 27 And it is good for the young to submit to the yoke of his discipline.

28 Let them sit alone in silence beneath the LORD's demands. 29 Let them lie face down in the dust; then at last there is hope for them. 30 Let them turn the other cheek to those who strike them. Let them accept the insults of their enemies.

31 For the Lord does not abandon anyone forever. 32 Though he brings grief, he also shows compassion according to the greatness of his unfailing love. 33 For he does not enjoy hurting people or causing them sorrow.

34 But the leaders of his people trampled prisoners underfoot. 35 They deprived people of their God-given rights in defiance of the Most High. 36 They perverted justice in the courts. Do they think the Lord didn't see it?

37 Can anything happen without the Lord's permission? 38 Is it not the Most High who helps one and harms another? 39 Then why should we, mere humans, complain when we are punished for our sins?

40 Instead, let us test and examine our ways. Let us turn again in repentance to the LORD. 41 Let us lift our hearts and hands to God in heaven and say, 42 "We have sinned and rebelled, and you have not forgiven us.

43 "You have engulfed us with your anger, chased us down, and slaughtered us without mercy. 44 You have hidden yourself in a cloud so our prayers cannot reach you. 45 You have discarded us as refuse and garbage among the nations.

46 "All our enemies have spoken out against us. 47 We are filled with fear, for we are trapped, desolate, and ruined." 48 Streams of tears flow from my eyes because of the destruction of my people!

49 My tears flow down endlessly. They will not stop 50 until the LORD looks down from heaven and sees. 51 My heart is breaking over the fate of all the women of Jerusalem.

52 My enemies, whom I have never harmed, chased me like a bird. 53 They threw me into a pit and dropped stones on me. 54 The water flowed above my head, and I cried out, "This is the end!"

55 But I called on your name, LORD, from deep within the well, 56 and you heard me! You listened to my pleading; you heard my weeping! 57 Yes, you came at my despairing cry and told me, "Do not fear."

58 Lord, you are my lawyer! Plead my case! For you have redeemed my life. 59 You have seen the wrong they have done to me, LORD. Be my judge, and prove me right. 60 You have seen the plots my enemies have laid against me.

## HOMEWORK ● ● • • •

3:27-33 **To "submit to the yoke" means to willingly come under God's discipline and learn what he wants to teach. True learning involves several important factors: (1) reflective silence on what God wants, (2) repentant humility, (3) self-control in the face of adversity, and (4) confident patience, depending on the Teacher to bring about the loving lesson in our life. God has several long-term and short-term lessons for you right now. Are you doing your homework?**

3:19 Hebrew *is wormwood and gall.*

GREAT IS
HIS
faithfulness
HIS
mercies
begin
afresh
each
day.
LAMENTATIONS 3:23

[61]LORD, you have heard the vile names they call me. You know all about the plans they have made—[62]the plots my enemies whisper and mutter against me all day long. [63]Look at them! In all their activities, they constantly mock me with their songs.

[64]Pay them back, LORD, for all the evil they have done. [65]Give them hard and stubborn hearts, and then let your curse fall upon them! [66]Chase them down in your anger, destroying them from beneath the LORD's heavens.

CHAPTER **4** **GOD IS NO LONGER ANGRY.** How the gold has lost its luster! Even the finest gold has become dull. The sacred gemstones lie scattered in the streets!

[2]See how the precious children of Jerusalem,* worth their weight in gold, are now treated like pots of clay.

[3]Even the jackals feed their young, but not my people Israel. They ignore their children's cries, like the ostriches of the desert.

[4]The parched tongues of their little ones stick with thirst to the roofs of their mouths. The children cry for bread, but no one has any to give them.

[5]The people who once ate only the richest foods now beg in the streets for anything they can get. Those who once lived in palaces now search the garbage pits for food.

[6]The guilt* of my people is greater than that of Sodom, where utter disaster struck in a moment with no one to help them.

[7]Our princes were once glowing with health; they were as clean as snow and as elegant as jewels.

[8]But now their faces are blacker than soot. No one even recognizes them. Their skin sticks to their bones; it is as dry and hard as wood.

[9]Those killed by the sword are far better off than those who die of hunger, wasting away for want of food.

[10]Tenderhearted women have cooked their own children and eaten them in order to survive the siege.

[11]But now the anger of the LORD is satisfied. His fiercest anger has now been poured out. He started a fire in Jerusalem* that burned the city to its foundations.

[12]Not a king in all the earth—no one in all the world—would have believed an enemy could march through the gates of Jerusalem.

[13]Yet it happened because of the sins of her prophets and priests, who defiled the city by shedding innocent blood.

[14]They wandered blindly through the streets, so defiled by blood that no one dared to touch them.

[15]"Get away!" the people shouted at them. "You are defiled! Don't touch us!" So they fled to distant lands and wandered there among foreign nations, but none would let them stay.

[16]The LORD himself has scattered them, and he no longer helps them. The priests and leaders are no longer honored and respected.

[17]We looked in vain for our allies to come and save us, but we were looking to nations that could offer no help at all.

[18]We couldn't go into the streets without danger to our lives. Our end was near; our days were numbered. We were doomed!

[19]Our enemies were swifter than the eagles. If we fled to the mountains, they found us. If we hid in the wilderness, they were waiting for us there.

[20]Our king, the LORD's anointed, the very life of our nation, was caught in their snares. We had foolishly boasted that under his protection we could hold our own against any nation on earth!

[21]Are you rejoicing in the land of Uz, O people of Edom? But you, too, must drink from the cup of the

**BANKRUPT ● ● • • •**

4:1-22 **This chapter contrasts the situation before the siege of Jerusalem with the situation after the siege. The sights and sounds of prosperity were gone because of the people's sin. This chapter warns us not to assume that when life is going well, it will always stay that way. We must be careful not to glory in our prosperity and fall into spiritual bankruptcy.**

4:2 Hebrew *sons of Zion.* 4:6 Or *punishment.* 4:11 Hebrew *in Zion.*

**TURN ABOUT ● ● • • •**

5:22 **A high calling flouted by low living results in deep suffering. Lamentations gives us a portrait of the bitter suffering the people of Jerusalem experienced when sin caught up with them and God turned his back on them. Every material goal they had lived for disappeared. Even though God turned away from them because of their sin, he did not abandon them—that was their great hope. Despite their sinful past, God would restore them if they returned to him. There is no hope except in the Lord. Thus, our grief should turn us toward him, not away from him.**

LORD's anger. You, too, will be stripped naked in your drunkenness.

[22]O Jerusalem,* your punishment will end; you will soon return from exile. But Edom, your punishment is just beginning; soon your many sins will be revealed.

CHAPTER **5** **JEREMIAH PRAYS.** LORD, remember everything that has happened to us. See all the sorrows we bear! [2]Our inheritance has been turned over to strangers, our homes to foreigners. [3]We are orphaned and fatherless. Our mothers are widowed. [4]We have to pay for water to drink, and even firewood is expensive. [5]Those who pursue us are at our heels; we are exhausted but are given no rest. [6]We submitted to Egypt and Assyria to get enough food to survive. [7]It was our ancestors who sinned, but they died before the hand of judgment fell. We have suffered the punishment they deserved!

[8]Slaves have now become our masters; there is no one left to rescue us. [9]We must hunt for food in the wilderness at the risk of our lives. [10]Because of the famine, our skin has been blackened as though baked in an oven. [11]Our enemies rape the women and young girls in Jerusalem* and throughout the towns of Judah. [12]Our princes are being hanged by their thumbs, and the old men are treated with contempt. [13]The young men are led away to work at millstones, and the children stagger under heavy loads of wood. [14]The old men no longer sit in the city gates; the young men no longer dance and sing.

[15]The joy of our hearts has ended; our dancing has turned to mourning. [16]The garlands have* fallen from our heads. Disaster has fallen upon us because we have sinned. [17]Our hearts are sick and weary, and our eyes grow dim with tears. [18]For Jerusalem* is empty and desolate, a place haunted by jackals.

[19]But LORD, you remain the same forever! Your throne continues from generation to generation. [20]Why do you continue to forget us? Why have you forsaken us for so long? [21]Restore us, O LORD, and bring us back to you again! Give us back the joys we once had! [22]Or have you utterly rejected us? Are you angry with us still?

4:22 Hebrew *daughter of Zion.* 5:11 Hebrew *Zion.* 5:16 Or *The crown has.* 5:18 Hebrew *Mount Zion.*

# MEGA themes

**DESTRUCTION OF JERUSALEM** Lamentations is a sad funeral song for Jerusalem, the great capital city of the Jews. The Temple had been destroyed, the king was gone, and the people were in exile. God had warned the nation that he would destroy them if they abandoned him. Afterward, the people realized their condition and confessed their sin.

God's warnings will be fulfilled. He will do what he promises. His punishment for sin is certain. Only if we confess and renounce our sin will he deliver us. How much better to do so before his warnings are fulfilled.

1. What feelings does Jeremiah express over the devastation of Jerusalem and the Jews?
2. Jeremiah had predicted this destruction and the exile. So why would seeing his prophecy fulfilled be especially painful?
3. What results of sin in your world cause you to feel sad?
4. What can you do in your world to help others see the destruction that comes from sin? How can you help them avoid these results?

**SIN'S CONSEQUENCES** God was angry at the prolonged rebellion of his people. Sin was the cause of their misery, and destruction was the result of their sin. The destruction of the nation shows the emptiness of human glory and pride.

To continue to rebel against God invites disaster. We should never trust our own leadership, resources, intelligence, or power more than God. If we do, we will suffer painful consequences.

1. What were the specific sins of the people that led to their exile? What had they put in place of God as most important in their lives?
2. Are there things or relationships that might possibly replace God as most important in your life?
3. Have you ever placed something or someone before the Lord? What were the consequences? What did you learn from that experience?
4. What are you doing right now to make sure that God remains first in your life?

**GOD'S MERCY** God's loving compassion was at work even when the Israelites were suffering under their Babylonian conquerors. Although the people had been unfaithful, God was faithful to them. He used their suffering to bring them back to him.

God will always be faithful to his people. His mercy is evident even during suffering. At those times, we must pray for forgiveness and then turn to God for deliverance. He always hears our cries of repentance.

1. What evidence do you find that God had not abandoned the Jews, even in their slavery?
2. Describe the attitude you should have toward God when you find yourself suffering the consequences of a sinful choice.
3. How have you needed God's mercy in your life? In what ways has he proven faithful?
4. How does God want you to respond to his mercy?

**HOPE** God's mercy in sparing some of the people offers hope for better days. Eventually they will be restored to a close relationship with God.

Only God can deliver us from sin. Without him there is no comfort or hope for the future. Christ's death for us and his promise to return give us bright hope for tomorrow.

1. God provided hope during punishment. What do you learn about God's character from his sparing the faithful group?
2. How would you encourage a suffering friend to find hope in God?
3. What could you tell a non-Christian friend about the need to place ultimate hope in Christ? What would it mean for him or her to do so?
4. What difference does it make in your life that you can place your hope in God? How will that affect your future choices? The choices you make this week?

627 B.C.
**Jeremiah becomes a prophet to Judah**

605
**Daniel taken captive to Babylon**

597
**Ezekiel taken captive to Babylon**

593
**Ezekiel becomes a prophet to exiles**

586
**Judah falls; Jerusalem destroyed**

571
**Ezekiel's ministry ends**

539
**Babylon overthrown by Cyrus**

537
**First exiles return to Judah**

"Don't worry," Danny chided his friends. "I can get away with anything. I'm my father's favorite." Danny's dad had gone out of town, leaving his new sports car in the garage. Danny was allowed to drive the family station wagon, but not the sports car. "Come on, you guys," he continued, "Dad will never even know." ■The drive to the movie was great. Girls honked and guys stared. "See," Danny said. "No problem. It sure beats the old wagon!" His friends had to agree. ■After the movie, they headed to the car. It was late, and the parking lot was no longer full. "Danny! Danny!" one of his friends suddenly yelled when he reached the car. "It's gone!" Wires dangled where the stereo used to be. ■"What are we going to do?" another friend asked. "Your father will kill us!" ■Danny smiled weakly. "Hey, I'm my dad's favorite. No sweat!" ■Israel reacted like Danny. They thought they could get away with anything. The book of Ezekiel was written to Jews who were captives in Babylon. They were "God's favorites." Surely Jerusalem (their capital) would not be harmed, and they would return home very soon. Ezekiel corrected their thinking: they were captives in Babylon because they had disobeyed God. Though they were his chosen people, God could not overlook sin. ■Ezekiel reminds us that no one can sin without punishment. Just as God loves us, he also loves justice. ■As you read Ezekiel, stand in awe of the God who judges all sin. Then thank him for providing a way (through Jesus) to escape the judgment that we all deserve for our sins.

## STATS

PURPOSE: To announce God's judgment; to foretell the salvation of God's people

AUTHOR: Ezekiel—the son of Buzi, a Zadokite priest

TO WHOM WRITTEN: The Jews in captivity in Babylon and God's people everywhere

DATE WRITTEN: Approximately 571 B.C.

SETTING: While Jeremiah ministered to the people still in Judah, Ezekiel prophesied to those already exiled in Babylon after the defeat of Jehoiachin. He was among the captives taken there in 597 B.C.

KEY PEOPLE: Ezekiel, Israel's leaders, Ezekiel's wife, Nebuchadnezzar, the "prince"

KEY PLACES: Jerusalem, Babylon, and Egypt

CHAPTER **1** **A FIERY CLOUD.** On July 31* of my
thirtieth year,* while I was with the Judean exiles
beside the Kebar River in Babylon, the heavens were
opened to me, and I saw visions of God. [2]This happened during the fifth year of King Jehoiachin's captivity. [3]The LORD gave a message to me, Ezekiel son
of Buzi, a priest, there beside the Kebar River in the
land of the Babylonians,* and I felt the hand of the
LORD take hold of me.

[4]As I looked, I saw a great storm coming toward
me from the north, driving before it a huge cloud
that flashed with lightning and shone with brilliant
light. The fire inside the cloud glowed like gleaming
amber. [5]From the center of the cloud came four
living beings that looked human, [6]except that each
had four faces and two pairs of wings. [7]Their legs
were straight like human legs, but their feet were split
like calves' feet and shone like burnished bronze.
[8]Beneath each of their wings I could see human
hands. [9]The wings of each living being touched the
wings of the two beings beside it. The living beings
were able to fly in any direction without turning
around. [10]Each had a human face in the front, the
face of a lion on the right side, the face of an ox on
the left side, and the face of an eagle at the back.
[11]Each had two pairs of outstretched wings—one
pair stretched out to touch the wings of the living
beings on either side of it, and the other pair covered
its body. [12]They went in whatever direction the spirit
chose, and they moved straight forward in all directions without having to turn around.

[13]The living beings looked like bright coals of fire
or brilliant torches, and it looked as though lightning was flashing back and forth among them. [14]And
the living beings darted to and fro like flashes of
lightning.

[15]As I looked at these beings, I saw four wheels on
the ground beneath them, one wheel belonging to
each. [16]The wheels sparkled as if made of chrysolite.
All four wheels looked the same; each wheel had a
second wheel turning crosswise within it. [17]The

**BLAZING GLORY ● ● • • •**

1:13-28 **A bright light, a dazzling fire—that is what the glory of the Lord looked like to Ezekiel. He fell to the ground, overwhelmed by the holiness of God and his own sinfulness and insignificance. Eventually every person will kneel before God, either out of reverence and awe for his mercy or out of fear of his judgment. Based on the way you are living today, how will you respond?**

**1:1a** Hebrew *On the fifth day of the fourth month,* of the Hebrew calendar. A number of dates in Ezekiel can be cross-checked with dates in surviving Babylonian records and related accurately to our modern calendar. This event occurred on July 31, 593 B.C. **1:1b** Or *in the thirtieth year.* **1:3** Or *Chaldeans.*

beings could move forward in any of the four directions they faced, without turning as they moved.
18The rims of the four wheels were awesomely tall,
and they were covered with eyes all around the
edges. 19When the four living beings moved, the
wheels moved with them. When they flew upward,
the wheels went up, too. 20The spirit of the four
living beings was in the wheels. So wherever the
spirit went, the wheels and the living beings went,
too. 21When the living beings moved, the wheels
moved. When the living beings stopped, the wheels
stopped. When the living beings flew into the air, the
wheels rose up. For the spirit of the living beings was
in the wheels.

22There was a surface spread out above them like
the sky. It sparkled like crystal. 23Beneath this surface
the wings of each living being stretched out to touch
the others' wings, and each had two wings covering
its body. 24As they flew their wings roared like waves
crashing against the shore, or like the voice of the
Almighty,* or like the shouting of a mighty army.
When they stopped, they let down their wings. 25As
they stood with their wings lowered, a voice spoke
from beyond the crystal surface above them.

### CONFRONT

Chad's been hearing little rumors about his friend Eric for a couple of weeks now. Rumors like:

"Did you hear about Eric's and Brandon's latest drinking binge?"

"You should have seen Eric at Rebecca's party last weekend!"

"Man, Eric sure has changed!"

Tonight Chad's worst fears were confirmed. Driving through the school parking lot after a game, Chad happened to see Eric and Brandon sitting in the back of a pick-up truck, drinking tequila. Chad didn't stop, so Eric doesn't know his friend saw him.

Chad is concerned, but also confused. Here's his childhood friend starting to run with a pretty wild crowd. It seems Eric is headed for major-league trouble. Chad ponders what to do: "Should I talk to Eric or just keep my mouth shut? Should I tell my parents what's going on and get their advice? I mean, I want to do what's right, but I'm afraid if I speak up, Eric will just laugh at me. Besides, who am I to tell him how to live?"

When friends start heading for trouble, we have a God-given responsibility to pull them aside and help them get back on track. The question isn't how they may or may not respond—that's irrelevant. The real question is whether or not we love them enough to do what's right and confront them. See Ezekiel 2:3-7.

26Above the surface over their heads was what
looked like a throne made of blue sapphire. And
high above this throne was a figure whose appearance was like that of a man. 27From his waist up, he
looked like gleaming amber, flickering like a fire.
And from his waist down, he looked like a burning
flame, shining with splendor. 28All around him was

1:24 Hebrew *Shaddai.*



### TOUGH TALK ● ● ● • •

**2:6-8 Ezekiel was given the difficult responsibility of presenting God's message to the ungrateful and abusive. Sometimes we too are called to be an example or share our faith with people who may be unkind to us. Just as the Lord told Ezekiel not to give up, he tells us not give up and join the rebels, but rather to tell the Good News whether it's convenient or not (2 Timothy 4:2).**

a glowing halo, like a rainbow shining through the
clouds. This was the way the glory of the LORD appeared to me. When I saw it, I fell face down in the
dust, and I heard someone's voice speaking to me.

CHAPTER **2** **GOD CALLS EZEKIEL.** "Stand up, son of
man," said the voice. "I want to speak with you."
2The Spirit came into me as he spoke and set me on
my feet. I listened carefully to his words. 3"Son of
man," he said, "I am sending you to the nation of
Israel, a nation that is rebelling against me. Their
ancestors have rebelled against me from the beginning, and they are still in revolt to this very day.
4They are a hard-hearted and stubborn people. But I
am sending you to say to them, 'This is what the
Sovereign LORD says!' 5And whether they listen or
not—for remember, they are rebels—at least they
will know they have had a prophet among them.

6"Son of man, do not fear them. Don't be afraid
even though their threats are sharp as thorns and
barbed like briers, and they sting like scorpions. Do
not be dismayed by their dark scowls. For remember,
they are rebels! 7You must give them my messages
whether they listen or not. But they won't listen, for
they are completely rebellious! 8Son of man, listen
to what I say to you. Do not join them in being a
rebel. Open your mouth, and eat what I give you."

9Then I looked and saw a hand reaching out to
me, and it held a scroll. 10He unrolled it, and I saw
that both sides were covered with funeral songs,
other words of sorrow, and pronouncements of
doom.

CHAPTER **3** The voice said to me, "Son of man,
eat what I am giving you—eat this scroll! Then go
and give its message to the people of Israel." 2So I
opened my mouth, and he fed me the scroll. 3"Eat it
all," he said. And when I ate it, it tasted as sweet as
honey.

4Then he said, "Son of man, go to the people of
Israel with my messages. 5I am not sending you to
some foreign people whose language you cannot
understand. 6No, I am not sending you to people
with strange and difficult speech. If I did, they would
listen! 7I am sending you to the people of Israel, but
they won't listen to you any more than they listen to
me! For the whole lot of them are hard-hearted and
stubborn. 8But look, I have made you as hard and
stubborn as they are. 9I have made you as hard as
rock! So don't be afraid of them or fear their angry
looks, even though they are such rebels."

10Then he added, "Son of man, let all my words
sink deep into your own heart first. Listen to them

carefully for yourself. [11]Then go to your people in exile and say to them, 'This is what the Sovereign LORD says!' Do this whether they listen to you or not."

[12]Then the Spirit lifted me up, and I heard a loud rumbling sound behind me. (May the glory of the LORD be praised in his place!)* [13]It was the sound of the wings of the living beings as they brushed against each other and the rumbling of their wheels beneath them.

[14]The Spirit lifted me up and took me away. I went in bitterness and turmoil, but the LORD's hold on me was strong. [15]Then I came to the colony of Judean exiles in Tel-abib, beside the Kebar River. I sat there among them for seven days, overwhelmed.

[16]At the end of the seven days, the LORD gave me a message. He said, [17]"Son of man, I have appointed you as a watchman for Israel. Whenever you receive a message from me, pass it on to the people immediately. [18]If I warn the wicked, saying, 'You are under the penalty of death,' but you fail to deliver the warning, they will die in their sins. And I will hold you responsible, demanding your blood for theirs. [19]If you warn them and they keep on sinning and refuse to repent, they will die in their sins. But you will have saved your life because you did what you were told to do. [20]If good people turn bad and don't listen to my warning, they will die. If you did not warn them of the consequences, then they will die in their sins. Their previous good deeds won't help them, and I will hold you responsible, demanding your blood for theirs. [21]But if you warn them and they repent, they will live, and you will have saved your own life, too."

[22]Then the LORD took hold of me, and he said to me, "Go out into the valley, and I will talk to you there." [23]So I got up and went, and there I saw the glory of the LORD, just as I had seen it in my first vision by the Kebar River. And I fell face down in the dust.

[24]Then the Spirit came into me and set me on my feet. He talked to me and said, "Go, shut yourself up in your house. [25]There you will be bound with ropes so you cannot go out among the people. [26]And I will make your tongue stick to the roof of your mouth so you won't be able to pray for them, for they are rebellious. [27]But whenever I give you a message, I will loosen your tongue and let you speak. Then you will say to them, 'This is what the Sovereign LORD says!' Some of them will listen, but some will ignore you, for they are rebels.

CHAPTER **4** **EZEKIEL DRAWS A PICTURE.** "And now, son of man, take a large brick and set it down in front of you. Then draw a map of the city of Jerusalem on it. [2]Build siege ramps against the city walls. Surround it with enemy camps and battering rams. [3]Then take an iron griddle and place it between you and the city. Turn toward it and demonstrate how the enemy will attack Jerusalem. This will be a warning to the people of Israel.

[4]"Now lie on your left side and place the sins of Israel on yourself. You are to bear their sins for the number of days you lie there on your side. [5]You will bear Israel's sins for 390 days—one day for each year of their sin. [6]After that, turn over and lie on your right side for 40 days—one day for each year of Judah's sin.

[7]"Meanwhile, continue your demonstration of the siege of Jerusalem. Lie there with your arm bared and prophesy her destruction. [8]I will tie you up with ropes so you won't be able to turn from side to side until the days of your siege have been completed.

[9]"Now go and get some wheat, barley, beans, lentils, millet, and spelt, and mix them together in a storage jar. Use this food to make bread for yourself during the 390 days you will be lying on your side. [10]Ration this out to yourself, eight ounces* of food for each day, and eat it at set times. [11]Then measure out a jar* of water for each day, and drink it at set times. [12]Each day prepare your bread as you would barley cakes. While all the people are watching, bake it over a fire using dried human dung as fuel and then eat the bread. [13]For this is what the LORD says: Israel will eat defiled bread in the Gentile lands, where I will banish them!"

[14]Then I said, "O Sovereign LORD, must I be defiled by using human dung? For I have never been defiled before. From the time I was a child until now I have never eaten any animal that died of sickness or that I found dead. And I have never eaten any of the animals that our laws forbid."

[15]"All right," the LORD said. "You may bake your bread with cow dung instead of human dung." [16]Then he told me, "Son of man, I will cause food to be very scarce in Jerusalem. It will be weighed out with great care and eaten fearfully. The water will be portioned out drop by drop, and the people will drink it with dismay. [17]Food and water will be so scarce that the people will look at one another in terror, and they will waste away under their punishment.

CHAPTER **5** **A CRAZY HAIRCUT.** "Son of man, take a sharp sword and use it as a razor to shave your head and beard. Use a scale to weigh the hair into three equal parts. [2]Place a third of it at the center of your map of Jerusalem. After acting out the siege, burn it there. Scatter another third across your map and slash at it with a sword. Scatter the last third to the

**DETAILS ● ● • • •**

**4:1-17 Ezekiel enacted the siege and fall of Jerusalem before it actually happened. God gave Ezekiel specific instructions about what to say and how to say it. Each detail had a special meaning. Often we ignore or disregard the smaller details of God's Word, thinking they probably don't really matter. Like Ezekiel, we should want to obey God completely, even in the details.**

3:12 A likely reading for this verse is *Then the Spirit lifted me up, and as the glory of the LORD rose from its place, I heard behind me a loud rumbling sound.* 4:10 Hebrew *20 shekels* [228 grams]. 4:11 Hebrew *1/6 of a hin,* about 1.3 pints or 0.6 liters.

wind, for I will scatter my people with the sword. [3]Keep just a bit of the hair and tie it up in your robe. [4]Then take a few of these hairs out and throw them into the fire, burning them up. A fire will then spread from this remnant and destroy all of Israel.

[5]"This is what the Sovereign LORD says: This is an illustration of what will happen to Jerusalem. I placed her at the center of the nations, [6]but she has rebelled against my regulations and has been even more wicked than the surrounding nations. She has refused to obey the laws I gave her to follow. [7]So this is what the Sovereign LORD says: Since you have refused to obey my laws and regulations and have behaved even worse than your neighbors, [8]I myself, the Sovereign LORD, am now your enemy. I will punish you publicly while all the nations watch. [9]Because of your detestable idols, I will punish you more severely than I have punished anyone before or ever will again. [10]Parents will eat their own children, and children will eat their parents. And I will punish you by scattering the few who survive to the far reaches of the earth.

[11]"As surely as I live, says the Sovereign LORD, I will cut you off completely. I will show you no pity at all because you have defiled my Temple with idols and vile practices. [12]A third of your people will die in the city from famine and disease. A third of them will be slaughtered by the enemy outside the city walls. And I will scatter a third to the winds and chase them with my sword. [13]Then at last my anger will be spent, and I will be satisfied. And when my fury against them has subsided, all Israel will know that I, the LORD, have spoken to them in my jealous anger.

## THREATS ● ● • • •

**5:13 Have you ever seen a parent try to discipline a child by saying, "If you do that one more time . . ."? If the parent doesn't follow through, the child learns not to listen. Empty threats backfire. God was going to punish the Israelites for their blatant sins, and he wanted them to know that he would do what he said. The people learned the hard way that God always follows through on his word. Too many people ignore God's warnings that he will punish sin. But what God threatens, he does. Don't make the mistake of thinking that God doesn't really mean what he says.**

[14]"So I will turn you into a ruin, a mockery in the eyes of the surrounding nations and to everyone who travels by. [15]You will become an object of mockery and taunting and horror. You will be a warning to all the nations around you. They will see what happens when the LORD turns against a nation in furious rebuke. I, the LORD, have spoken!

[16]"I will shower you with the deadly arrows of famine to destroy you. The famine will become more and more severe until every crumb of food is gone. [17]And along with the famine, wild animals will attack you, robbing you of your children. Disease and war will stalk your land, and I will bring the sword of the enemy against you. I, the LORD, have spoken!"

## CHAPTER 6

**EZEKIEL TALKS TO THE MOUNTAINS.** Again a message came to me from the LORD: [2]"Son of man, look over toward the mountains of Israel and prophesy against them. [3]Give the mountains of Israel this message from the Sovereign LORD. This is what the Sovereign LORD says to the mountains and hills and to the ravines and valleys: I am about to bring war upon you, and I will destroy your pagan shrines. [4]All your altars will be demolished, and your incense altars will be smashed. I will kill your people in front of your idols. [5]I will lay your corpses in front of your idols and scatter your bones around your altars. [6]Wherever you live there will be desolation. I will destroy your pagan shrines, your altars, your idols, your incense altars, and all the other religious objects you have made. [7]Then when the place is littered with corpses, you will know that I am the LORD.

[8]"But I will let a few of my people escape destruction, and they will be scattered among the nations of the world. [9]Then when they are exiled among the nations, they will remember me. They will recognize how grieved I am by their unfaithful hearts and lustful eyes that long for other gods. Then at last they will hate themselves for all their wickedness. [10]They will know that I alone am the LORD and that I was serious when I predicted that all this would happen to them.

[11]"This is what the Sovereign LORD says: Clap your hands in horror, and stamp your feet. Cry out, 'Alas!' because of all the evil that the people of Israel have done. Now they are going to die from war and famine and disease. [12]Disease will strike down those who are far away in exile. War will destroy those who are nearby. And anyone who survives will be killed by famine. So at last I will spend my fury on them. [13]When their dead lie scattered among their idols and altars, on every hill and mountain and under every green tree and great oak where they offered incense to their gods, then they will know that I alone am the LORD. [14]I will crush them and make their cities desolate from the wilderness in the south to Riblah* in the north. Then they will know that I am the LORD."

## CHAPTER 7

**JERUSALEM WILL BE PUNISHED.** Then this message came to me from the LORD: [2]"Son of man, this is what the Sovereign LORD says to Israel: The end is

## ONE AND ONLY ● ● • • •

**6:14 The phrase "then they will know that I am the LORD" (or a variation on this phrase) occurs 70 times in the book of Ezekiel. The purpose of God's punishment was not revenge, but to impress upon the people the truth that the Lord is the only true and living God. Many people in Ezekiel's day were worshiping man-made idols and calling them gods. Today money, sex, and power have become idols for many. Punishment will come upon all who put other things ahead of God. It is easy in our secular world to forget that the Lord alone is God, the supreme authority and the only source of eternal love and life. Remember that God may be using the difficulties of your life to remind you that he alone is God.**

6:14 As in some Hebrew manuscripts; most Hebrew manuscripts read *Diblah*.

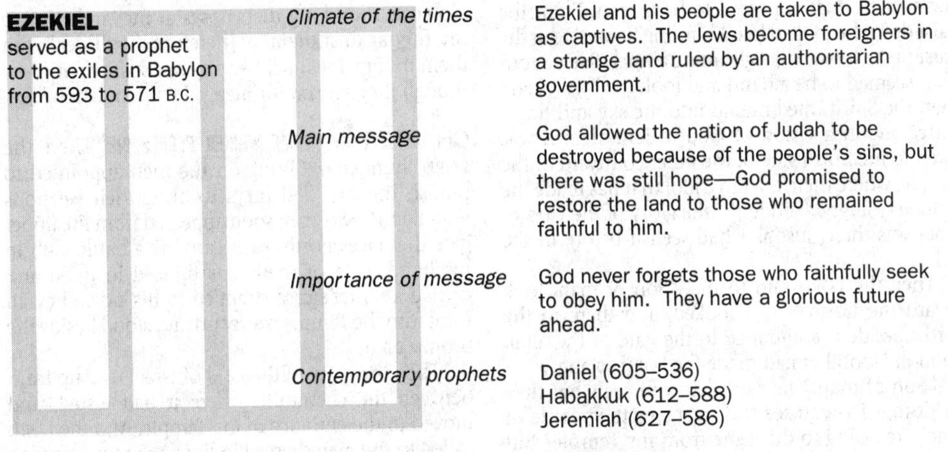

**EZEKIEL**
served as a prophet
to the exiles in Babylon
from 593 to 571 B.C.

| | |
|---|---|
| *Climate of the times* | Ezekiel and his people are taken to Babylon as captives. The Jews become foreigners in a strange land ruled by an authoritarian government. |
| *Main message* | God allowed the nation of Judah to be destroyed because of the people's sins, but there was still hope—God promised to restore the land to those who remained faithful to him. |
| *Importance of message* | God never forgets those who faithfully seek to obey him. They have a glorious future ahead. |
| *Contemporary prophets* | Daniel (605–536)<br>Habakkuk (612–588)<br>Jeremiah (627–586) |

here! Wherever you look—east, west, north, or
south—your land is finished. 3No hope remains, for I
will unleash my anger against you. I will call you to
account for all your disgusting behavior. 4I will turn my
eyes away and show no pity, repaying you in full for all
your evil. Then you will know that I am the LORD!
5"This is what the Sovereign LORD says: With one
blow after another I will bring total disaster! 6The end
has come! It has finally arrived! Your final doom is
waiting! 7O people of Israel, the day of your destruction is dawning. The time has come; the day of trouble
is near. It will ring with shouts of anguish, not shouts
of joy. 8Soon I will pour out my fury to complete your
punishment for all your disgusting behavior. 9I will
neither spare nor pity you. I will repay you for all your
detestable practices. Then you will know that it is I, the
LORD, who is striking the blow.
10"The day of judgment is here; your destruction
awaits! The people's wickedness and pride have
reached a climax. 11Their violence will fall back on
them as punishment for their wickedness. None of
these proud and wicked people will survive. All their
wealth will be swept away. 12Yes, the time has come; the
day is here! There is no reason for buyers to rejoice over
the bargains they find or for sellers to grieve over their
losses, for all of them will fall under my terrible anger.
13And if any merchants should survive, they will never
return to their business. For what God has said applies
to everyone—it will not be changed! Not one person
whose life is twisted by sin will recover.
14"The trumpets call Israel's army to mobilize, but
no one listens, for my fury is against them all. 15Any
who leave the city walls will be killed by enemy
swords. Those who stay inside will die of famine and
disease. 16The few who survive and escape to the
mountains will moan like doves, weeping for their
sins. 17Everyone's hands will be feeble; their knees will
be as weak as water. 18They will dress themselves in
sackcloth; horror and shame will cover them. They will
shave their heads in sorrow and remorse.
19"They will throw away their money, tossing it
out like worthless trash. It won't buy their deliverance in that day of the LORD's anger. It will neither
satisfy nor feed them, for their love of money made
them stumble into sin. 20They were proud of their
gold jewelry and used it to make vile and detestable
idols. That is why I will make all their wealth disgusting to them. 21I will give it as plunder to foreigners
from the most wicked of nations, and they will defile
it. 22I will hide my eyes as these robbers invade my
treasured land and corrupt it.
23"Prepare chains for my people, for the land is
bloodied by terrible crimes. Jerusalem is filled with
violence. 24I will bring the most ruthless of nations
to occupy their homes. I will break down their proud
fortresses and defile their sanctuaries. 25Terror and
trembling will overcome my people. They will look
for peace but will not find it. 26Calamity will follow
calamity; rumor will follow rumor. They will look in
vain for a vision from the prophets. They will receive
no teaching from the priests and no counsel from
the leaders. 27The king and the prince will stand
helpless, weeping in despair, and the people's hands
will tremble with fear. I will bring against them the
evil they have done to others, and they will receive
the punishment they so richly deserve. Then they
will know that I am the LORD!"

CHAPTER **8** **THE SINS OF THE PEOPLE.** Then on September 17,* during the sixth year of King Jehoiachin's captivity, while the leaders of Judah were in
my home, the Sovereign LORD took hold of me. 2I

## MONEY ●●●••

**7:19 Money too often seems to lead people into sin. Paul said the love of money is the first step to sin (1Timothy 6:10). How ironic that we use wealth–a gift of God–to buy things that separate us from him. How tragic it is that we spend so much time looking for ways to satisfy ourselves with money and so little time looking for God, the true source of satisfaction.**

8:1 Hebrew *on the fifth day of the sixth month,* of the Hebrew calendar. This event occurred on September 17, 592 B.C.; also see note on 1:1.

saw a figure that appeared to be a man. From the waist down he looked like a burning flame. From the waist up he looked like gleaming amber. [3]He put out what seemed to be a hand and took me by the hair. Then the Spirit lifted me up into the sky and transported me in a vision of God to Jerusalem. I was taken to the north gate of the inner courtyard of the Temple, where there is a large idol that has made the LORD very angry. [4]Suddenly, the glory of the God of Israel was there, just as I had seen it before in the valley.

[5]Then the LORD said to me, "Son of man, look toward the north." So I looked, and there to the north, beside the entrance to the gate of the altar, stood the idol that had made the LORD so angry.

[6]"Son of man," he said, "do you see what they are doing? Do you see the great sins the people of Israel are doing to drive me from my Temple? But come, and you will see even greater sins than these!" [7]Then he brought me to the door of the Temple courtyard, where I could see an opening in the wall. [8]He said to me, "Now, son of man, dig into the wall." So I dug into the wall and uncovered a door to a hidden room.

## OPEN HOUSE ● ● • • •

8:6 **In scene after scene, God revealed to Ezekiel the extent to which the people had embraced idolatry and wickedness. God's Spirit works with us in a similar way, revealing sin that lurks in our life. How comfortable would you feel if God held an open house in your life today?**

[9]"Go in," he said, "and see the unspeakable wickedness going on in there!" [10]So I went in and saw the walls engraved with all kinds of snakes, lizards, and hideous creatures. I also saw the various idols worshiped by the people of Israel. [11]Seventy leaders of Israel were standing there with Jaazaniah son of Shaphan in the middle. Each of them held an incense burner, so there was a thick cloud of incense above their heads.

[12]Then the LORD said to me, "Son of man, have you seen what the leaders of Israel are doing with their idols in dark rooms? They are saying, 'The LORD doesn't see us; he has deserted our land!'" [13]Then he added, "Come, and I will show you greater sins than these!"

[14]He brought me to the north gate of the LORD's Temple, and some women were sitting there, weeping for the god Tammuz. [15]"Have you seen this?" he asked. "But I will show you even greater sins than these!"

[16]Then he brought me into the inner courtyard of the LORD's Temple. At the entrance, between the foyer and the bronze altar, about twenty-five men were standing with their backs to the LORD's Temple. They were facing eastward, worshiping the sun!

[17]"Have you seen this, son of man?" he asked. "Is it nothing to the people of Judah that they commit these terrible sins, leading the whole nation into violence, thumbing their noses at me, and rousing my fury against them? [18]Therefore, I will deal with them in fury. I will neither pity nor spare them. And though they scream for mercy, I will not listen."

CHAPTER **9** **SOME WICKED PEOPLE DIE.** Then the LORD thundered, "Bring on the men appointed to punish the city! Tell them to bring their weapons with them!" [2]Six men soon appeared from the upper gate that faces north, each carrying a battle club in his hand. One of them was dressed in linen and carried a writer's case strapped to his side. They all went into the Temple courtyard and stood beside the bronze altar.

[3]Then the glory of the God of Israel rose up from between the cherubim, where it had rested, and moved to the entrance of the Temple. And the LORD called to the man dressed in linen who was carrying the writer's case. [4]He said to him, "Walk through the streets of Jerusalem and put a mark on the foreheads of all those who weep and sigh because of the sins they see around them."

[5]Then I heard the LORD say to the other men, "Follow him through the city and kill everyone whose forehead is not marked. Show no mercy; have no pity! [6]Kill them all—old and young, girls and women and little children. But do not touch anyone with the mark. Begin your task right here at the Temple." So they began by killing the seventy leaders. [7]"Defile the Temple!" the LORD commanded. "Fill its courtyards with the bodies of those you kill! Go!" So they went throughout the city and did as they were told.

[8]While they were carrying out their orders, I was all alone. I fell face down in the dust and cried out, "O Sovereign LORD! Will your fury against Jerusalem wipe out everyone left in Israel?"

[9]Then he said to me, "The sins of the people of Israel and Judah are very great. The entire land is full of murder; the city is filled with injustice. They are saying, 'The LORD doesn't see it! The LORD has forsaken the land!' [10]So I will not spare them or have any pity on them. I will fully repay them for all they have done."

[11]Then the man in linen clothing, who carried the writer's case, reported back and said, "I have finished the work you gave me to do."

CHAPTER **10** **BURNING COALS.** As I looked, I saw what appeared to be a throne of blue sapphire above the crystal surface over the heads of the cherubim. [2]Then the LORD spoke to the man in linen clothing

## NO EXCUSE ● ● • • •

9:9-10 **The people said that God had gone away and wouldn't see their sin. People have many convenient explanations to make it easier to sin: "It doesn't matter." "Everybody's doing it." Or, "Nobody will ever know." Do you find yourself making excuses for sin? Rationalizing makes it easier to commit sin, but it does not influence God's promise to punish sin.**

and said, "Go in between the whirling wheels beneath the cherubim, and take a handful of glowing
coals and scatter them over the city." He did this as I
watched. 3The cherubim were standing at the south
end of the Temple when the man went in, and the
cloud of glory filled the inner courtyard. 4Then the
glory of the LORD rose up from above the cherubim
and went over to the door of the Temple. The Temple
was filled with this cloud of glory, and the Temple
courtyard glowed brightly with the glory of the LORD.
5The moving wings of the cherubim sounded like
the voice of God Almighty and could be heard
clearly in the outer courtyard.

6The LORD said to the man in linen clothing, "Go
between the cherubim and take some burning coals
from between the wheels." So the man went in and
stood beside one of the wheels. 7Then one of the
cherubim reached out his hand and took some live
coals from the fire burning among them. He put the
coals into the hands of the man in linen clothing,
and the man took them and went out. 8(All the
cherubim had what looked like human hands hidden beneath their wings.)

9Each of the four cherubim had a wheel beside
him, and the wheels sparkled like chrysolite. 10All
four wheels looked the same; each wheel had a
second wheel turning crosswise within it. 11The cherubim could move forward in any of the four directions they faced, without turning as they moved.
They went straight in the direction in which their
heads were turned, never turning aside. 12Both the
cherubim and the wheels were covered with eyes.
The cherubim had eyes all over their bodies, including their hands, their backs, and their wings. 13I
heard someone refer to the wheels as "the whirling
wheels." 14Each of the four cherubim had four faces—the first was the face of an ox,* the second was
a human face, the third was the face of a lion, and
the fourth was the face of an eagle.

15Then the cherubim rose upward. These were the
same living beings I had seen beside the Kebar River.
16When the cherubim moved, the wheels moved
with them. When they rose into the air, the wheels
stayed beside them, going with them as they flew.
17When the cherubim stood still, the wheels also
stopped, for the spirit of the living beings was in the
wheels.

18Then the glory of the LORD moved from the door
of the Temple and hovered above the cherubim.
19And as I watched, the cherubim flew with their
wheels to the east gate of the LORD's Temple. And the
glory of the God of Israel hovered above them.

20These were the same living beings I had seen
beneath the God of Israel when I was by the Kebar
River. I knew they were cherubim, 21for each had four
faces and four wings and what looked like human
hands under their wings. 22Their faces, too, were just
like the faces of the beings I had seen at the Kebar,
and they traveled straight ahead, just as the others
had.

**STANDARDS ● ● • • •**

11:12 **From the time they entered the Promised Land, the Israelites were warned not to copy the customs and religious practices of other nations. Disobeying this command and following heathen customs instead of God's laws always got them into trouble. Today, believers are still tempted to copy the ways of the world. But we must get our standards of right and wrong from God, not from the popular trends of society.**

## CHAPTER 11 GOD WILL BRING HIS PEOPLE BACK.

Then the Spirit lifted me and brought me over to the
east gateway of the LORD's Temple, where I saw
twenty-five prominent men of the city. Among them
were Jaazaniah son of Azzur and Pelatiah son of
Benaiah, who were leaders among the people.

2Then the Spirit said to me, "Son of man, these are
the men who are responsible for the wicked counsel
being given in this city. 3They say to the people, 'Is it
not a good time to build houses? Our city is like an
iron pot. Inside it we will be like meat—safe from all
harm.*' 4Therefore, son of man, prophesy against
them loudly and clearly."

5Then the Spirit of the LORD came upon me, and
he told me to say, "This is what the LORD says to the
people of Israel: Is that what you are saying? Yes, I
know it is, for I know every thought that comes into
your minds. 6You have murdered endlessly and filled
your streets with the dead.

7"Therefore, this is what the Sovereign LORD says:
This city is an iron pot, but the victims of your
injustice are the pieces of meat. And you are not safe,
for I will soon drag you from the city. 8I will expose
you to the war you so greatly fear, says the Sovereign
LORD. 9I will drive you out of Jerusalem and hand
you over to foreigners who will carry out my judgments against you. 10You will be slaughtered all the
way to the borders of Israel, and then you will know
that I am the LORD. 11No, this city will not be an iron
pot for you, and you will not be the meat, safe inside.
I will judge you even to the borders of Israel, 12and
you will know that I am the LORD. For you have
refused to obey me; instead, you have copied the sins
of the nations around you."

13While I was still speaking, Pelatiah son of Benaiah suddenly died. Then I fell face down in the dust
and cried out, "O Sovereign LORD, are you going to
kill everyone in Israel?"

14Then this message came to me from the LORD:
15"Son of man, the people still left in Jerusalem are
talking about their relatives in exile, saying, 'They are
far away from the LORD, so now he has given their
land to us!' 16Therefore, give the exiles this message
from the Sovereign LORD: Although I have scattered
you in the countries of the world, I will be a sanctuary to you during your time in exile. 17I, the Sovereign
LORD, will gather you back from the nations where
you are scattered, and I will give you the land of
Israel once again.

**10:14** Hebrew *the face of a cherub;* compare 1:10. **11:3** Hebrew *This city is the pot, and we are the meat.*

18"When the people return to their homeland,
they will remove every trace of their detestable idol
worship. 19And I will give them singleness of heart
and put a new spirit within them. I will take away
their hearts of stone and give them tender hearts*
instead, 20so they will obey my laws and regulations.
Then they will truly be my people, and I will be their
God. 21But as for those who long for idols, I will
repay them fully for their sins, says the Sovereign
LORD."

22Then the cherubim lifted their wings and rose
into the air with their wheels beside them, and the
glory of the God of Israel hovered above them.
23Then the glory of the LORD went up from the city
and stopped above the mountain to the east.

24Afterward the Spirit of God carried me back
again to Babylonia,* to the Judeans in exile there.
And so ended the vision of my visit to Jerusalem.
25And I told the exiles everything the LORD had
shown me.

## CHAPTER 12

**EZEKIEL DIGS A TUNNEL.** Again a message came to me from the LORD: 2"Son of man, you
live among rebels who could see the truth if they
wanted to, but they don't want to. They could hear
me if they would listen, but they won't listen because
they are rebellious. 3So now put on a demonstration
to show them what it will be like to go off into exile.
Pack whatever you can carry on your back and leave
your home to go on a journey. Make your preparations in broad daylight so the people can see you, for
perhaps they will even yet consider what this means,
even though they are such rebels. 4Bring your baggage outside during the day so they can watch you.
Then as they are watching, leave your house in the
evening, just as captives do when they begin a long
march to distant lands. 5Dig a hole through the wall
while they are watching and carry your possessions
out through it. 6As they watch, lift your pack to your
shoulders and walk away into the night. Cover your
face and don't look around. All of these actions will
be a sign for the people of Israel."

### OUT OF TIME ● • • • •

12:21-28 **These two short messages were warnings that God's words would come true—*soon!* Less than six years later, Jerusalem was destroyed. Judgment comes swiftly. No one—not you or anyone you know—should dare to assume there is plenty of time to get right with God.**

7So I did as I was told. In broad daylight I brought
my pack outside, filled with the things I might carry
into exile. Then in the evening while the people
looked on, I dug through the wall with my hands
and went out into the darkness with my pack on my
shoulder.

8The next morning this message came to me from
the LORD: 9"Son of man, these rebels, the people of
Israel, have asked you what all this means. 10Say to
them, 'This is what the Sovereign LORD says: These

### LIES ● • • • •

13:2-3 **The false prophets had a large following because they comforted the people and approved of their actions even while they were sinning. Lies often are attractive, and liars may have large followings. Today, for example, some leaders assure us that God wants everyone to have health and material success. This is comforting, but is it true? God's own Son did not have an easy life on earth—he didn't even have a place to lay his head (Matthew 8:20). Make sure the messages you believe are consistent with what God teaches in his Word.**

actions contain a message for Zedekiah in Jerusalem* and for all the people of Israel.' 11Then explain
that your actions are a demonstration of what will
soon happen to them, for they will be driven from
their homes and sent away into exile.

12"Even Zedekiah will leave Jerusalem at night
through a hole in the wall, taking only what he can
carry with him. He will cover his face, and his eyes
will never see his homeland again. 13Then I will
spread out my net and capture him in my snare. I
will bring him to Babylon, the land of the Babylonians,* though he will never see it, and he will die
there. 14I will scatter his servants and guards to the
four winds and send the sword after them. 15And
when I scatter them among the nations, they will
know that I am the LORD. 16But I will spare a few of
them from death by war, famine, or disease, so they
can confess to their captors about how wicked they
have been. Then they will know that I am the LORD!"

17Then this message came to me from the LORD:
18"Son of man, tremble as you eat your food. Drink
your water with fear, as if it were your last. 19Give the
people this message from the Sovereign LORD concerning those living in Israel and Jerusalem: They
will eat their food with trembling and sip their tiny
portions of water in utter despair, because their land
will be stripped bare on account of their violence.
20The cities will be destroyed and the farmland deserted. Then you will know that I am the LORD."

21Again a message came to me from the LORD:
22"Son of man, what is that proverb they quote in
Israel: 'Time passes, making a liar of every prophet'?
23Give the people this message from the Sovereign
LORD: I will put an end to this proverb, and you will
soon stop quoting it. Now give them this new proverb to replace the old one: 'The time has come for
every prophecy to be fulfilled!'

24"Then you will see what becomes of all the false
visions and misleading predictions about peace in
Israel. 25For I am the LORD! What I threaten always
happens. There will be no more delays, you rebels of
Israel! I will fulfill my threat of destruction in your
own lifetime, says the Sovereign LORD."

26Then this message came to me from the LORD:
27"Son of man, the people of Israel are saying, 'His
visions won't come true for a long, long time.'
28Therefore, give them this message from the Sovereign LORD: No more delay! I will now do everything
I have threatened! I, the Sovereign LORD, have spoken!"

11:19 Hebrew *hearts of flesh.* 11:24 Or *Chaldea.* 12:10 Hebrew *the prince in Jerusalem;* also in 12:12. 12:13 Or *Chaldeans.*

CHAPTER **13** **FALSE TEACHERS GET IN TROUBLE.** Then this message came to me from the LORD: 2"Son of man, speak against the false prophets of Israel who are inventing their own prophecies. Tell them to listen to the word of the LORD. 3This is what the Sovereign LORD says: Destruction is certain for the false prophets who are following their own imaginations and have seen nothing at all!

4"O people of Israel, these prophets of yours are like jackals digging around in the ruins. 5They have done nothing to strengthen the breaks in the walls around the nation. They have not helped it to stand firm in battle on the day of the LORD. 6Instead, they have lied and said, 'My message is from the LORD,' even though the LORD never sent them. And yet they expect him to fulfill their prophecies! 7Can your visions be anything but false if you claim, 'This message is from the LORD,' when I have not even spoken to you?

8"Therefore, this is what the Sovereign LORD says: Because what you say is false and your visions are a lie, I will stand against you, says the Sovereign LORD. 9I will raise my fist against all the lying prophets, and they will be banished from the community of Israel. I will blot their names from Israel's record books, and they will never again see their own land. Then you will know that I am the Sovereign LORD!

10"These evil prophets deceive my people by saying, 'All is peaceful!' when there is no peace at all! It's as if the people have built a flimsy wall, and these prophets are trying to hold it together by covering it with whitewash! 11Tell these whitewashers that their wall will soon fall down. A heavy rainstorm will undermine it; great hailstones and mighty winds will knock it down. 12And when the wall falls, the people will cry out, 'Where is the whitewash you applied?'

13"Therefore, this is what the Sovereign LORD says: I will sweep away your whitewashed wall with a storm of indignation, with a great flood of anger, and with hailstones of fury. 14I will break down your wall right to the foundation, and when it falls, it will crush you. Then you will know that I am the LORD! 15At last my anger against the wall and those who covered it with whitewash will be satisfied. Then I will say to you: 'The wall and those who whitewashed it are both gone. 16They were lying prophets who claimed peace would come to Jerusalem when there was no peace. I, the Sovereign LORD, have spoken!'

17"Now, son of man, also speak out against the women who prophesy from their own imaginations. 18This is what the Sovereign LORD says: Destruction is certain for you women who are ensnaring the souls of my people, both young and old alike. You tie magic charms on their wrists and furnish them with magic veils. Do you think you can trap others without bringing destruction on yourselves? 19You turn my people away from me for a few handfuls of barley or a piece of bread. By lying to my people who love to listen to lies, you kill those who should not die, and you promise life to those who should not live.

20"And so the Sovereign LORD says: I am against all your magic charms, which you use to ensnare my people like birds. I will tear them from your arms, setting my people free like birds set free from a cage. 21I will tear off the magic veils and save my people from your grasp. They will no longer be your victims. Then you will know that I am the LORD. 22You have discouraged the righteous with your lies, when I didn't want them to suffer grief. And you have encouraged the wicked by promising them life, even though they continue in their sins. 23But you will no longer talk of seeing visions that you never saw, nor will you practice your magic. For I will rescue my people from your grasp. Then you will know that I am the LORD."

CHAPTER **14** **GOD HATES IDOLS.** Then some of the leaders of Israel visited me, and while they were there, 2this message came to me from the LORD: 3"Son of man, these leaders have set up idols in their hearts. They have embraced things that lead them into sin. Why should I let them ask me anything? 4Give them this message from the Sovereign LORD: I, the LORD, will punish the people of Israel who set up idols in their hearts so they fall into sin and then come to a prophet asking for help. 5I will do this to capture the minds and hearts of all my people who have turned from me to worship their detestable idols.

6"Therefore, give the people of Israel this message from the Sovereign LORD: Repent and turn away from your idols, and stop all your loathsome practices. 7I, the LORD, will punish all those, both Israelites and foreigners, who reject me and set up idols in their hearts so they fall into sin, and who then come to a prophet asking for my advice. 8I will turn against such people and make a terrible example of them, destroying them. Then you will know that I am the LORD. 9And if a prophet is deceived and gives a message anyway, it is because I, the LORD, have deceived that prophet. I will stand against such prophets and cut them off from the community of Israel. 10False prophets and hypocrites—evil people who claim to want my advice—will all be punished for their sins. 11In this way, the people of Israel will learn not to stray from me, polluting themselves with sin. They will be my people, and I will be their God, says the Sovereign LORD."

12Then this message came to me from the LORD:

## INSURANCE POLICY ● ● ● • •

**14:6-11 The nation of Judah, though eager to accept the messages of false prophets, considered the presence of a few godly men in the nation an insurance policy against disaster. But merely having godly people around doesn't help. We must remember that the godliness of our pastor or friends will not protect us from the consequences of our own sins. Each person is responsible for his or her own relationship with God. How are *you* living?**

[13]"Son of man, suppose the people of a country were to sin against me, and I lifted my fist to crush them, cutting off their food supply and sending a famine to destroy both people and animals alike. [14]Even if Noah, Daniel, and Job were there, their righteousness would save no one but themselves, declares the Sovereign LORD.

[15]"Or suppose I were to send an invasion of dangerous wild animals to devastate the land and kill the people. [16]Even if these three men were there, the Sovereign LORD swears that it would do no good—it wouldn't save the people from destruction. Those three alone would be saved, but the land would be devastated.

[17]"Or suppose I were to bring war against the land, and I told enemy armies to come and destroy everything. [18]Even if these three men were in the land, the Sovereign LORD swears that they could not save the people. They alone would be saved.

[19]"Or suppose I were to pour out my fury by sending an epidemic of disease into the land, and the plague killed people and animals alike. [20]Even if Noah, Daniel, and Job were living there, the Sovereign LORD swears that they could not save the people. They alone would be saved by their righteousness.

[21]"Now this is what the Sovereign LORD says: How terrible it will be when all four of these fearsome punishments fall upon Jerusalem—war, famine, beasts, and plague—destroying all her people and animals. [22]Yet there will be survivors, and they will come here to join you as exiles in Babylon. You will see with your own eyes how wicked they are, and then you will feel better about what I have done to Jerusalem. [23]When you meet them and see their behavior, you will agree that these things are not being done to Israel without cause, says the Sovereign LORD."

## USELESS ● ● • • •

15:1-8 **The messages given to Ezekiel in chapters 15 through 17 provided further evidence that God was going to destroy Jerusalem. The first message was about a grapevine, useless at first and even more useless after being burned. The people of Jerusalem were useless to God because of their idol worship, and so they would be destroyed and their cities burned. Be careful you don't become "useless" to God. Each of us needs to take a spiritual inventory, keeping check on how well we are following the guidelines and instructions God has given us.**

CHAPTER **15** **A USELESS VINE.** Then this message came to me from the LORD: [2]"Son of man, how does a grapevine compare to a tree? Is a vine's wood as useful as the wood of a tree? [3]Can its wood be used for making things, like pegs to hang up pots and pans? [4]No, it can only be used for fuel, and even as fuel, it burns too quickly. [5]Vine branches are useless both before and after being put into the fire!

[6]"And this is what the Sovereign LORD says: The

## SPECIAL PRIVILEGES ● ● • • •

16:8-14 **God chose Israel to be the channel through whom he would communicate his message of salvation to the entire world. God gave Israel special privileges and trained Israel to do his work. But these resources and advantages became Israel's source of pride and vanity. We must remember that God made us what we are. To use our gifts and opportunities only for our own selfish pursuits is both dangerous and foolish.**

people of Jerusalem are like grapevines growing among the trees of the forest. Since they are useless, I have set them aside to be burned! [7]And I will see to it that if they escape from one fire, they will fall into another. When this happens, you will know that I am the LORD. [8]And I will make the land desolate because my people have been unfaithful to me, says the Sovereign LORD."

CHAPTER **16** **TERRIBLE SINS.** Then another message came to me from the LORD: [2]"Son of man, confront Jerusalem with her loathsome sins. [3]Give her this message from the Sovereign LORD: You are nothing but a Canaanite! Your father was an Amorite and your mother a Hittite! [4]When you were born, no one cared about you. Your umbilical cord was left uncut, and you were never washed, rubbed with salt, and dressed in warm clothing. [5]No one had the slightest interest in you; no one pitied you or cared for you. On the day you were born, you were dumped in a field and left to die, unwanted.

[6]"But I came by and saw you there, helplessly kicking about in your own blood. As you lay there, I said, 'Live!' [7]And I helped you to thrive like a plant in the field. You grew up and became a beautiful jewel. Your breasts became full, and your hair grew, though you were still naked. [8]And when I passed by and saw you again, you were old enough to be married. So I wrapped my cloak around you to cover your nakedness and declared my marriage vows. I made a covenant with you, says the Sovereign LORD, and you became mine.

[9]"Then I bathed you and washed off your blood, and I rubbed fragrant oils into your skin. [10]I gave you expensive clothing of linen and silk, beautifully embroidered, and sandals made of fine leather. [11]I gave you lovely jewelry, bracelets, and beautiful necklaces, [12]a ring for your nose and earrings for your ears, and a lovely crown for your head. [13]And so you were made beautiful with gold and silver. Your clothes were made of fine linen and were beautifully embroidered. You ate the finest foods—fine flour, honey, and olive oil—and became more beautiful than ever. You looked like a queen, and so you were! [14]Your fame soon spread throughout the world on account of your beauty, because the splendor I bestowed on you perfected your beauty, says the Sovereign LORD.

[15]"But you thought you could get along without me, so you trusted instead in your fame and beauty. You gave yourself as a prostitute to every man who came along. Your beauty was theirs for the asking! [16]You used the lovely things I gave you to make

shrines for idols, where you carried out your acts of
prostitution. Unbelievable! How could such a thing
ever happen? 17 You took the very jewels and gold
and silver ornaments I had given you and made
statues of men and worshiped them, which is adultery against me. 18 You used the beautifully embroidered clothes I gave you to cover your idols. Then
you used my oil and incense to worship them.
19 Imagine it! You set before them as a lovely sacrifice
the fine flour and oil and honey I had given you, says
the Sovereign LORD.

20 "Then you took your sons and daughters—the
children you had borne to me—and sacrificed
them to your gods. Was it not enough that you
should be a prostitute? 21 Must you also slaughter
my children by sacrificing them to idols? 22 In all
your years of adultery and loathsome sin, you have
not once thought of the days long ago when you
lay naked in a field, kicking about in your own
blood.

23 "Your destruction is certain, says the Sovereign
LORD. In addition to all your other wickedness,
24 you built a pagan shrine and put altars to idols in
every town square. 25 On every street corner you
defiled your beauty, offering your body to every
passerby in an endless stream of prostitution.
26 Then you added lustful Egypt to your lovers, fan-
ning the flames of my anger with your increasing
promiscuity. 27 That is why I struck you with my fist
and reduced your boundaries. I handed you over to
your enemies, the Philistines, and even they were
shocked by your lewd conduct! 28 You have prostituted yourselves with the Assyrians, too. It seems
you can never find enough new lovers! And after
your prostitution there, you still were not satisfied.
29 You added to your lovers by embracing that great
merchant land of Babylonia*—but you still
weren't satisfied!

30 "What a sick heart you have, says the Sovereign
LORD, to do such things as these, acting like a
shameless prostitute. 31 You build your pagan
shrines on every street corner and your altars to
idols in every square. You have been worse than a
prostitute, so eager for sin that you have not even
demanded payment for your love! 32 Yes, you are an
adulterous wife who takes in strangers instead of
her own husband. 33 Prostitutes charge for their
services—but not you! You give gifts to your lovers,
bribing them to come to you. 34 So you are the
opposite of other prostitutes. No one pays you;
instead, you pay them!

35 "Therefore, you prostitute, listen to this message from the LORD! 36 This is what the Sovereign
LORD says: Because you have exposed yourself in
prostitution to all your lovers, and because you
have worshiped detestable idols, and because you
have slaughtered your children as sacrifices to your
gods, 37 this is what I am going to do. I will gather
together all your allies—these lovers of yours with
whom you have sinned, both those you loved and
those you hated—and I will strip you naked in
front of them so they can stare at you. 38 I will
punish you for your murder and adultery. I will
cover you with blood in my jealous fury. 39 Then I
will give you to your lovers—these many nations—and they will destroy you. They will knock
down your pagan shrines and the altars to your
idols. They will strip you and take your beautiful
jewels, leaving you completely naked and
ashamed. 40 They will band together in a mob to
stone you and run you through with swords.
41 They will burn your homes and punish you in
front of many women. I will see to it that you stop

16:29 Or *Chaldea.*

---

**It doesn't seem like I'm making too much progress as a Christian. It even seems like I'm going backward. What can I do to reverse my reversal?**

Until about age 25, we grow physically. After that, we start to die. Fortunately, it usually takes another 50 to 60 years to complete the dying process!

Our spiritual life often goes through a living and dying process, too. It's either living and growing, or it's in the process of dying. There is no such thing as leveling out or "plateauing."

You've hit the first stage of beginning to grow spiritually again: You recognize that you've been dying.

The second stage is discovering what caused the dying process. God confronted his people continually about this. Speaking through Ezekiel, he showed them that idols had replaced God in their hearts (see Ezekiel 14:1-5).

Has something been pushing God out of your life—television, a friendship, sports, a boyfriend or girlfriend, music, fun? Any of these can become idols. If they do, they must be removed from the center of your life. When you recognize that something has drawn your heart away from God, turn around! Confess the problem to God and turn it over to him (see 1 John 1:9).

The third stage is the one that many Christians forget—finding someone to hold us accountable. You need someone to encourage you, to ask tough questions, to kick you in the pants when you need it, and to pray for you.

This could be a friend your own age who has a real desire to grow spiritually. It could be a Christian adult whom you like and respect—or anyone who is genuinely concerned for you, who won't get down on you, who will always pull for you.

Ask God to send you such a person. This may be scary, but Christians who are growing have learned the secret of asking others to help them stay on track. Always seek out someone who will walk with you. It will help keep you from falling and provide you with close, lifelong friends.

## FINGER POINTING ● ● • • •

16:49 **It is easy to point a finger at Sodom, especially for its terrible sexual sins. If we do not commit such horrible sins as adultery, homosexuality, stealing, and murder, we may think that we are doing all right. But what about sins like pride, laziness, gluttony, and ignoring the needy (see Revelation 3:14-22)? These sins may not be as openly shocking as the others, but they are just as deserving of punishment.**

your prostitution and end your payments to your many lovers.

42 "Then at last my fury against you will be spent, and my jealous anger will subside. I will be calm and will not be angry with you anymore. 43 But first, because you have not remembered your youth but have angered me by doing all these evil things, I will fully repay you for all of your sins, says the Sovereign LORD. For to all your disgusting sins, you have added these lewd acts. 44 Everyone who makes up proverbs will say of you, 'Like mother, like daughter.' 45 For your mother loathed her husband and her children, and so do you. And you are exactly like your sisters, for they despised their husbands and their children. Truly your mother must have been a Hittite and your father an Amorite.

46 "Your older sister was Samaria, who lived with her daughters in the north. Your younger sister was Sodom, who lived with her daughters in the south. 47 But you have not merely sinned as they did—no, that was nothing to you. In a very short time you far surpassed them! 48 As surely as I live, says the Sovereign LORD, Sodom and her daughters were never as wicked as you and your daughters. 49 Sodom's sins were pride, laziness, and gluttony, while the poor and needy suffered outside her door. 50 She was proud and did loathsome things, so I wiped her out, as you have seen.

51 "Even Samaria did not commit half your sins. You have done far more loathsome things than your sisters ever did. They seem righteous compared to you! 52 You should be deeply ashamed because your sins are so terrible. In comparison, you make your sisters seem innocent!

53 "But someday I will restore the fortunes of Sodom and Samaria, and I will restore you, too. 54 Then you will be truly ashamed of everything you have done, for your sins make them feel good in comparison. 55 Yes, your sisters, Sodom and Samaria, and all their people will be restored, and at that time you also will be restored. 56 In your proud days you held Sodom in contempt. 57 But now your greater wickedness has been exposed to all the world, and you are the one who is scorned—by Edom* and all her neighbors and by Philistia. 58 This is your punishment for all your disgusting sins, says the LORD.

59 "Now this is what the Sovereign LORD says: I will give you what you deserve, for you have taken your solemn vows lightly by breaking your covenant. 60 Yet I will keep the covenant I made with you when you were young, and I will establish an everlasting covenant with you. 61 Then you will remember with shame all the evil you have done. I will make your sisters, Samaria and Sodom, to be your daughters, even though they are not part of our covenant. 62 And I will reaffirm my covenant with you, and you will know that I am the LORD. 63 You will remember your sins and cover your mouth in silence and shame when I forgive you of all that you have done, says the Sovereign LORD."

## CHAPTER 17

**THE GREAT EAGLE.** Then this message came to me from the LORD: 2 "Son of man, tell this story to the people of Israel. 3 Give them this message from the Sovereign LORD: A great eagle with broad wings full of many-colored feathers came to Lebanon. He took hold of the highest branch of a cedar tree 4 and plucked off its topmost shoot. Then he carried it away to a city filled with merchants, where he planted it.

5 "Then he planted one of its seedlings in fertile ground beside a broad river, where it would grow as quickly as a willow tree. 6 It took root there and grew into a low, spreading vine. Its branches turned up toward the eagle, and its roots grew down beneath it. It soon produced strong branches and luxuriant leaves. 7 But then another great eagle with broad wings and full plumage came along. So the vine sent its roots and branches out toward him for water. 8 The vine did this even though it was already planted in good soil and had plenty of water so it could grow into a splendid vine and produce rich leaves and luscious fruit.

9 "So now the Sovereign LORD asks: Should I let this vine grow and prosper? No! I will pull it out, roots and all! I will cut off its fruit and let its leaves wither and die. I will pull it out easily enough—it won't take a strong arm or a large army to do it. 10 Then when the vine is transplanted, will it thrive? No, it will wither away completely when the east wind blows against it. It will die in the same good soil where it had grown so well."

11 Then this message came to me from the LORD: 12 "Say to these rebels of Israel: Don't you understand the meaning of this riddle of the eagles? I will tell you, says the Sovereign LORD. The king of Babylon came to Jerusalem, took away her king and princes, and brought them to Babylon. 13 He made a treaty with a member of the royal family and made him

## EAGLES ● ● • • •

17:1-8 **The first eagle in this chapter represents King Nebuchadnezzar of Babylon (see 17:12), who appointed, or "planted," Zedekiah as king in Jerusalem. Zedekiah rebelled against this arrangement and tried to join with Egypt, the second eagle, to battle Babylon. In Babylon, Ezekiel was describing these events. Jeremiah, a prophet in Judah, also was warning Zedekiah not to form this alliance (Jeremiah 2:36-37). Though miles apart, the prophets had the same message because both spoke for God. God still directs his chosen spokespeople to speak his truth all around the world.**

**16:57** Many ancient manuscripts read *Aram.*

take an oath of loyalty. He also exiled Israel's most influential leaders, 14so Israel would not become strong again and revolt. Only by keeping her treaty with Babylon could Israel maintain her national identity.

15"Nevertheless, this man of Israel's royal family rebelled against Babylon, sending ambassadors to Egypt to request a great army and many horses. Can Israel break her sworn treaties like that and get away with it? 16No! For as surely as I live, says the Sovereign LORD, the king of Israel will die in Babylon, the land of the king who put him in power and whose treaty he despised and broke. 17Pharaoh and all his mighty army will fail to help Israel when the king of Babylon lays siege to Jerusalem again and destroys the lives of many. 18For the king of Israel broke his treaty after swearing to obey; therefore, he will not escape.

19"So this is what the Sovereign LORD says: As surely as I live, I will punish him for breaking my covenant and despising the solemn oath he made in my name. 20I will throw my net over him and capture him in my snare. I will bring him to Babylon and deal with him there for this treason against me. 21And all the best warriors of Israel will be killed in battle, and those remaining in the city will be scattered to the four winds. Then you will know that I, the LORD, have spoken these words.

22"And the Sovereign LORD says: I will take a tender shoot from the top of a tall cedar, and I will plant it on the top of Israel's highest mountain. 23It will become a noble cedar, sending forth its branches and producing seed. Birds of every sort will nest in it, finding shelter beneath its branches. 24And all the trees will know that it is I, the LORD, who cuts down the tall tree and helps the short tree to grow tall. It is I who makes the green tree wither and gives new life to the dead tree. I, the LORD, have spoken! I will do what I have said."

## CHAPTER 18 TURN AND LIVE.

Then another message came to me from the LORD: 2"Why do you quote this proverb in the land of Israel: 'The parents have eaten sour grapes, but their children's mouths pucker at the taste'? 3As surely as I live, says the Sovereign LORD, you will not say this proverb anymore in Israel. 4For all people are mine to judge—both parents and children alike. And this is my rule: The person who sins will be the one who dies.

5"Suppose a certain man is just and does what is lawful and right, 6and he has not feasted in the mountains before Israel's idols or worshiped them. And suppose he does not commit adultery or have intercourse with a woman during her menstrual period. 7Suppose he is a merciful creditor, not keeping the items given in pledge by poor debtors, and does not rob the poor but instead gives food to the hungry and provides clothes for people in need. 8And suppose he grants loans without interest, stays away from injustice, is honest

### FAMILY TRADITION ● ● • • •

**18:14-18 Family traditions were very important to the Jews, but God made it clear that people should not follow a tradition of sin. Although your family is a powerful influence in your life, your actions are not determined by them. You can choose not to follow a pattern of sin. Even if you come from a sinful family, you can follow God. It is far better to begin a new spiritual heritage than to hold on to traditions of sin.**

and fair when judging others, 9and faithfully obeys my laws and regulations. Anyone who does these things is just and will surely live, says the Sovereign LORD.

10"But suppose that man has a son who grows up to be a robber or murderer and refuses to do what is right. 11And suppose that son does all the evil things his father would never do—worships idols on the mountains, commits adultery, 12oppresses the poor and helpless, steals from debtors by refusing to let them redeem what they have given in pledge, worships idols and takes part in loathsome practices, 13and lends money at interest. Should such a sinful person live? No! He must die and must take full blame.

14"But suppose that sinful son, in turn, has a son who sees his father's wickedness but decides against that kind of life. 15Suppose this son refuses to worship idols on the mountains, does not commit adultery, 16and does not exploit the poor, but instead is fair to debtors and does not rob them. And suppose this son feeds the hungry, provides clothes for the needy, 17helps the poor, does not lend money at interest, and obeys all my regulations and laws. Such a person will not die because of his father's sins; he will surely live. 18But the father will die for the many sins he committed—for being cruel and robbing close relatives, doing what was clearly wrong among his people.

19"'What?' you ask. 'Doesn't the child pay for the parent's sins?' No! For if the child does what is right and keeps my laws, that child will surely live. 20The one who sins is the one who dies. The child will not be punished for the parent's sins, and the parent will not be punished for the child's sins. Righteous people will be rewarded for their own goodness, and wicked people will be punished for their own wickedness. 21But if wicked people turn away from all their sins and begin to obey my laws and do what is just and right, they will surely live and not die. 22All their past sins will be forgotten, and they will live because of the righteous things they have done.

23"Do you think, asks the Sovereign LORD, that I like to see wicked people die? Of course not! I only want them to turn from their wicked ways and live. 24However, if righteous people turn to sinful ways and start acting like other sinners, should they be allowed to live? No, of course not! All their previous goodness will be forgotten, and they will die for their sins.

## NO FAIR ● • • • •

**18:25 A typical childish response to punishment is to say, "That's not fair!" In reality, God is fair, but *we* have broken the rules. It is not God who must live up to our ideas of fairness; instead, we must live up to his. Don't spend your time looking for the loopholes in God's law; decide instead to work toward living up to God's standards.**

25 "Yet you say, 'The Lord isn't being just!' Listen to
me, O people of Israel. Am I the one who is unjust,
or is it you? 26 When righteous people turn from
being good and start doing sinful things, they will
die for it. Yes, they will die because of their sinful
deeds. 27 And if wicked people turn away from their
wickedness, obey the law, and do what is just and
right, they will save their lives. 28 They will live, because after thinking it over, they decided to turn from
their sins. Such people will not die. 29 And yet the
people of Israel keep saying, 'The Lord is unjust!'
O people of Israel, it is you who are unjust, not I.

30 "Therefore, I will judge each of you, O people of
Israel, according to your actions, says the Sovereign
LORD. Turn from your sins! Don't let them destroy
you! 31 Put all your rebellion behind you, and get for
yourselves a new heart and a new spirit. For why
should you die, O people of Israel? 32 I don't want you
to die, says the Sovereign LORD. Turn back and live!

CHAPTER **19** **A DEATH SONG.** "Sing this funeral song for the princes of Israel:

2 'What is your mother?
A lioness among lions!
She lay down among the young lions
and reared her cubs.
3 She raised one of her cubs
to become a strong young lion.
He learned to catch and devour prey,
and he became a man-eater.
4 Then the nations heard about him,
and he was trapped in their pit.
They led him away in chains
to the land of Egypt.

5 'When the mother lion saw
that all her hopes for him were gone,
she took another of her cubs
and taught him to be a strong lion.
6 He prowled among the other lions
and became a leader among them.
He learned to catch and devour prey,
and he, too, became a man-eater.
7 He demolished fortresses in nearby nations*
and destroyed their towns and cities.
Their farms were desolated,
and their crops were destroyed.
Everyone in the land trembled in fear
when they heard him roar.
8 Then the armies of the nations attacked him,
surrounding him from every direction.
They spread out their nets for him
and captured him in their pit.
9 With hooks, they dragged him into a cage
and brought him before the king of Babylon.
They held him in captivity,
so his voice could never again be heard
on the mountains of Israel.

10 'Your mother was like a vine
planted by the water's edge.
It had lush, green foliage
because of the abundant water.
11 Its branches became very strong,
strong enough to be a ruler's scepter.
It soon became very tall,
towering above all the others.
It stood out because of its height
and because of its many lush branches.
12 But the vine was uprooted in fury
and thrown down to the ground.
The desert wind dried up its fruit
and tore off its branches.
Its stem was destroyed by fire.
13 Now the vine is growing in the wilderness,
where the ground is hard and dry.
14 A fire has come from its branches
and devoured its fruit.

19:7 As in Greek version; Hebrew reads *He consorted with widows.*

**DO YOU THINK,**
*asks the Sovereign LORD,*
**THAT I LIKE TO SEE WICKED PEOPLE DIE?**
**OF COURSE NOT!**
*I only want them to turn from their wicked ways and* LIVE.

EZEKIEL 18:23

None of the remaining limbs
is strong enough to be a ruler's scepter.'

This is a funeral song, and it is now time for the funeral."

**CHAPTER 20** **GOD SAYS REMEMBER!** On August 14,* during the seventh year of King Jehoiachin's captivity, some of the leaders of Israel came to request a message from the LORD. They sat down in front of me to wait for his reply. [2]Then this message came to me from the LORD: [3]"Son of man, give the leaders of Israel this message from the Sovereign LORD: How dare you come to ask for my help? As surely as I live, I will tell you nothing. This is the word of the Sovereign LORD!

[4]"Son of man, bring judgment against them and condemn them. Make them realize how loathsome the actions of their ancestors really were. [5]Give them this message from the Sovereign LORD: When I chose Israel and revealed myself to her in Egypt, I swore that I, the LORD, would be her God. [6]I promised that I would bring her and her descendants out of Egypt to a land I had discovered and explored for them—a good land, a land flowing with milk and honey, the best of all lands anywhere. [7]Then I said to them, 'Each of you, get rid of your idols. Do not defile yourselves with the Egyptian gods, for I am the LORD your God.'

[8]"But they rebelled against me and would not listen. They did not get rid of their idols or forsake the gods of Egypt. Then I threatened to pour out my fury on them to satisfy my anger while they were still in Egypt. [9]But I didn't do it, for I acted to protect the honor of my name. That way the surrounding nations wouldn't be able to laugh at Israel's God, who had promised to deliver his people. [10]So I brought my people out of Egypt and led them into the wilderness. [11]There I gave them my laws so they could live by keeping them. Yes, all those who keep them will live! [12]And I gave them my Sabbath days of rest as a sign between them and me. It was to remind them that I, the LORD, had set them apart to be holy, making them my special people.

[13]"But the people of Israel rebelled against me, and they refused to obey my laws there in the wilderness. They wouldn't obey my instructions even though obedience would have given them life. And they also violated my Sabbath days. So I threatened to pour out my fury on them, and I made plans to utterly consume them in the desert. [14]But again I held back in order to protect the honor of my name. That way the nations who saw me lead my people out of Egypt wouldn't be able to claim I destroyed them because I couldn't take care of them. [15]But I swore to them in the wilderness that I would not bring them into the land I had given them, a land flowing with milk and honey, the most beautiful place on earth. [16]I told them this because they had rejected my laws, ignored my will for them, and violated my Sabbath days. Their hearts were given to their idols. [17]Nevertheless, I pitied them and held back from destroying them in the wilderness.

**POWER ● • • • •**

19:11-12 **Not even the political and military might of Judah's kings could save the nation. Like branches of a vine, they would be cut off and uprooted by "the desert wind"–the Babylonian army. Don't ever make the mistake of thinking your strength, whether physical or spiritual, can stand against the true power–or judgment–of almighty God.**

[18]"Then I warned their children and told them not to follow in their parents' footsteps, defiling themselves with their idols. [19]'I am the LORD your God,' I told them. 'Follow my laws, pay attention to my instructions, [20]and keep my Sabbath days holy, for they are a sign to remind you that I am the LORD your God.'

[21]"But their children, too, rebelled against me. They refused to keep my laws and follow my instructions, even though obeying them would have given them life. And they also violated my Sabbath days. So again I threatened to pour out my fury on them in the wilderness. [22]Nevertheless, I withdrew my judgment against them to protect the honor of my name among the nations who had seen my power in bringing them out of Egypt. [23]But I took a solemn oath against them while they were in the wilderness. I vowed I would scatter them among all the nations [24]because they did not obey my laws. They scorned my instructions by violating my Sabbath days and longing for the idols of their ancestors. [25]I gave them over to worthless customs and laws that would not lead to life. [26]I let them pollute themselves with the very gifts I had given them, and I allowed them to give their firstborn children as offerings to their gods—so I might devastate them and show them that I alone am the LORD.

[27]"Therefore, son of man, give the people of Israel this message from the Sovereign LORD: Your ancestors continued to blaspheme and betray me, [28]for when I brought them into the land I had promised them, they offered sacrifices and incense on every high hill and under every green tree they saw! They roused my fury as they offered up sacrifices to their gods. They brought their perfumes and incense and poured out their drink offerings to them! [29]I said to them, 'What is this high place where you are going?' (This idol shrine has been called Bamah—'high place'—ever since.)

[30]"Therefore, give the people of Israel this message from the Sovereign LORD: Do you plan to pollute

**POLLUTION ● • • • •**

20:30 **Water containing contaminants is polluted. Likewise, our life is polluted when we accept the contaminants–immoral values–of this world. If we love money, we become greedy. If we lust, we become sexually immoral. Remaining pure in a polluted world is difficult, to say the least. But a heart filled with God's Holy Spirit leaves little room for pollution (see Titus 1:15-16).**

20:1 Hebrew *In the fifth month, on the tenth day,* of the Hebrew calendar. This event occurred on August 14, 591 B.C.; also see note on 1:1.

yourselves just as your ancestors did? Do you intend to keep prostituting yourselves by worshiping detestable idols? 31For when you offer gifts to them and give your little children to be burned as sacrifices,* you continue to pollute yourselves to this day. Should I listen to you or help you, O people of Israel? As surely as I live, says the Sovereign LORD, I will not give you a message even though you have come to me requesting one.

32"You say, 'We want to be like the nations all around us, who serve idols of wood and stone.' But what you have in mind will never happen. 33As surely as I live, says the Sovereign LORD, I will rule you with an iron fist in great anger and with awesome power. 34With might and fury I will bring you out from the lands where you are scattered. 35I will bring you into the wilderness of the nations, and there I will judge you face to face. 36I will judge you there just as I did your ancestors in the wilderness after bringing them out of Egypt, says the Sovereign LORD. 37I will count you carefully and hold you to the terms of the covenant. 38I will purge you of all those who rebel and sin against me. I will bring them out of the countries where they are in exile, but they will never enter the land of Israel. And when that happens, you will know that I am the LORD.

39"As for you, O people of Israel, this is what the

## ALL OF ME ● ● • • ·

**20:39 The Israelites were worshiping idols and sacrificing to God at the same time! Often we think that some religion is better than none at all. While persisting in a life of sin, we may think, *Well, at least I go to church. God will be pleased with this effort.* But God wants all of our life, not just part of it. No amount of religious ritual or personal sacrifice can make up for continuing sinful practices.**

Sovereign LORD says: If you insist, go right ahead and worship your idols, but then don't turn around and bring gifts to me. Such desecration of my holy name must stop! 40For on my holy mountain, says the Sovereign LORD, the people of Israel will someday worship me, and I will accept them. There I will require that you bring me all your offerings and choice gifts and sacrifices. 41When I bring you home from exile, you will be as pleasing to me as an offering of perfumed incense. And I will display my holiness in you as all the nations watch. 42Then when I have brought you home to the land I promised your ancestors, you will know that I am the LORD. 43You will look back at all your sins and hate yourselves because of the evil you have done. 44You will know that I am the LORD, O people of Israel, when I have honored my name by treating you mercifully in spite of your wickedness, says the Sovereign LORD."

45Then this message came to me from the LORD: 46"Son of man, look toward the south* and speak out against it; prophesy against the fields of the Negev. 47Give the southern wilderness this message

## IN THE FIRE ● ● • • ·

**21:1-23 The short message in 20:45-48 introduces the four messages in chapter 21 about the judgments that would come upon Jerusalem. The city would be destroyed because it was defiled. According to Jewish law, defiled objects were to be passed through fire in order to purify them (see Numbers 31:22-23; Psalm 66:10-12; Proverbs 17:3). God's judgment is designed to purify; destruction often is a necessary part of that process.**

from the Sovereign LORD: Hear the word of the LORD! I will set you on fire, O forest, and every tree will be burned—green and dry trees alike. The terrible flames will not be quenched; they will scorch everything from south to north. 48And all the world will see that I, the LORD, have set this fire. It will not be put out."

49Then I said, "O Sovereign LORD, they are saying of me, 'He only talks in riddles!'"

## CHAPTER 21

**EZEKIEL'S GLITTERING SWORD.** Then this message came to me from the LORD: 2"Son of man, look toward Jerusalem and prophesy against Israel and her sanctuaries. 3Give her this message from the LORD: I am your enemy, O Israel, and I am about to unsheath my sword to destroy your people—the righteous and the wicked alike. 4Yes, I will not spare even the righteous! I will make a clean sweep throughout the land from south to north. 5All the world will know that I am the LORD. My sword is in my hand, and it will not return to its sheath until its work is finished.

6"Son of man, groan before the people! Groan before them with bitter anguish and a broken heart. 7When they ask you why, tell them, 'I groan because of the terrifying news I have heard. When it comes true, the boldest heart will melt with fear; all strength will disappear. Every spirit will faint; strong knees will tremble and become as weak as water. And the Sovereign LORD says: It is coming! It's on its way!'"

8Then the LORD said to me, 9"Son of man, give the people this message from the LORD: A sword is being sharpened and polished. 10It is being prepared for terrible slaughter; it will flash like lightning! Now will you laugh? Those far stronger than you have fallen beneath its power!* 11Yes, the sword is now being sharpened and polished; it is being prepared for the executioner!

12"Son of man, cry out and wail; pound your thighs in anguish, for that sword will slaughter my people and their leaders—everyone will die! 13It will put them all to the test! So now the Sovereign LORD asks: What chance do they have?*

14"Son of man, prophesy to them and clap your hands vigorously. Then take the sword and brandish it twice, even three times, to symbolize the great massacre they will face! 15Let their hearts melt with terror, for the sword glitters at every gate. It flashes like lightning; it is polished for slaughter! 16O sword, slash to the right, and slash to the left, wherever you will, wherever you want. 17I, too, will

**20:31** Or *and make your little children pass through the fire.* **20:46** Hebrew *Teman.* **21:10** The meaning of the Hebrew is uncertain. **21:13** The meaning of the Hebrew is uncertain.

clap my hands, and I will satisfy my fury. I, the LORD, have spoken!"

18Then this message came to me from the LORD: 19"Son of man, make a map and trace two routes on it for the sword of Babylon's king to follow. Put a signpost on the road that comes out of Babylon where the road forks into two—20one road going to Ammon and its capital, Rabbah, and the other to Judah and fortified Jerusalem. 21The king of Babylon now stands at the fork, uncertain whether to attack Jerusalem or Rabbah. He will call his magicians to use divination. They will cast lots by shaking arrows from the quiver. They will inspect the livers of their animal sacrifices. 22Then they will decide to turn toward Jerusalem! With battering rams they will go against the gates, shouting for the kill. They will put up siege towers and build ramps against the walls to reach the top. 23The people of Jerusalem will think it is a mistake, because of their treaty with the Babylonians. But the king of Babylon will remind the people of their rebellion. Then he will attack and capture them.

24"Therefore, this is what the Sovereign LORD says: Again and again your guilt cries out against you, for you are not ashamed of your sin. You don't even try to hide it! Wherever you go, whatever you do, all your actions are filled with sin. So now the time of your punishment has come!

25"O you corrupt and wicked prince of Israel, your final day of reckoning is here! 26Take off your jeweled crown, says the Sovereign LORD. The old order changes—now the lowly are exalted, and the mighty are brought low. 27Destruction! Destruction! I will surely destroy the kingdom. And it will not be restored until the one appears who has the right to judge it. Then I will hand it over to him.

28"And now, son of man, prophesy concerning the Ammonites and their mockery. Give them this message from the Sovereign LORD: My sword is drawn for your slaughter; it is sharpened to destroy, flashing like lightning! 29Your magicians and false prophets have given false visions and told lies about the sword. And now it will fall with even greater force on the wicked for whom the day of final reckoning has come. 30Should I return my sword to its sheath before I deal with you? No, I will destroy you in your own country, the land of your birth. 31I will pour out my fury on you and blow on you with the fire of my anger. I will hand you over to cruel men who are skilled in destruction. 32You are fuel for the fire, and your blood will be spilled in your own land. You will be utterly wiped out, your memory lost to history. I, the LORD, have spoken!"

CHAPTER **22** **GOD LISTS THE PEOPLE'S SINS.** Now this message came to me from the LORD: 2"Son of man, are you ready to judge Jerusalem? Are you ready to judge this city of murderers? Denounce her terrible deeds in public, 3and give her this message from the Sovereign LORD: O city of murderers, doomed and damned—city of idols, filthy and foul—4you are guilty of both murder and idolatry. Your day of destruction has come! You have reached the end of your years. I will make you an object of mockery throughout the world. 5O infamous city, filled with confusion, you will be mocked by people both far and near.

6"Every leader in Israel who lives within your walls is bent on murder. 7Fathers and mothers are contemptuously ignored. Resident foreigners are forced to pay for protection. Orphans and widows are wronged and oppressed. 8Inside your walls you despise my holy things and violate my Sabbath days of rest. 9People accuse others falsely and send them to their death. You are filled with idol worshipers and people who take part in lewd activities. 10Men sleep with their fathers' wives and have intercourse with women who are menstruating. 11Within your walls live men who commit adultery with their neighbors' wives, who defile their daughters-in-law or who rape their own sisters. 12There are hired murderers, loan racketeers, and extortioners everywhere! They never even think of me and my commands, says the Sovereign LORD.

13"But now I clap my hands in indignation over your dishonest gain and bloodshed. 14How strong and courageous will you be in my day of reckoning? I, the LORD, have spoken! I will do what I have said. 15I will scatter you among the nations and purge you of your wickedness. 16And when you have been dishonored among the nations, you will know that I am the LORD."

**LEADERS ● ● • • •**

22:6-13 **The leaders were especially responsible for the moral climate of the nation because they had been chosen by God to lead. The same is true today (see James 3:1-2). Unfortunately, many of the sins mentioned here have been committed in recent years by Christian leaders. We are living in a time of unprecedented attacks by Satan. It is vital that we uphold our leaders in prayer, and it is vital for leaders to seek accountability and help in their walk with God.**

17Then this message came to me from the LORD: 18"Son of man, the people of Israel are the worthless slag that remains after silver is smelted. They are the dross that is left over—a useless mixture of copper, tin, iron, and lead. 19So give them this message from the Sovereign LORD: Because you are all worthless slag, I will bring you to my crucible in Jerusalem. 20I will melt you down in the heat of my fury, just as copper, tin, iron, and lead are melted down in a furnace. 21I will gather you together and blow the fire of my anger upon you, 22and you will melt like silver in fierce heat. Then you will know that I, the LORD, have poured out my fury on you."

23Again a message came to me from the LORD: 24"Son of man, give the people of Israel this message: In the day of my indignation, you will become like an uncleared wilderness or a desert without rain. 25Your princes* plot conspiracies just as lions stalk

## NO WAY! ● ● • • •

23:39 **The Israelites went so far as to sacrifice their own children to idols and then sacrifice to the Lord the same day. This made a mockery of worship. We cannot praise God and willfully sin at the same time! That would be like agreeing to go steady with one person, then going on a date with someone else. You have to do more than just say the words; you must show what you really believe and value by your actions.**

their prey. They devour innocent people, seizing treasures and extorting wealth. They increase the number of widows in the land. [26]Your priests have violated my laws and defiled my holy things. To them there is no difference between what is holy and what is not. And they do not teach my people the difference between what is ceremonially clean and unclean. They disregard my Sabbath days so that my holy name is greatly dishonored among them. [27]Your leaders are like wolves, who tear apart their victims. They actually destroy people's lives for profit! [28]And your prophets announce false visions and speak false messages. They say, 'My message is from the Sovereign LORD,' when the LORD hasn't spoken a single word to them. They repair cracked walls with whitewash! [29]Even common people oppress the poor, rob the needy, and deprive foreigners of justice.

[30]"I looked for someone who might rebuild the wall of righteousness that guards the land. I searched for someone to stand in the gap in the wall so I wouldn't have to destroy the land, but I found no one. [31]So now I will pour out my fury on them, consuming them in the fire of my anger. I will heap on them the full penalty for all their sins, says the Sovereign LORD."

CHAPTER **23** **TWO SISTERS.** This message came to me from the LORD: [2]"Son of man, once there were two sisters who were daughters of the same mother. [3]They became prostitutes in Egypt. Even as young girls, they allowed themselves to be fondled and caressed. [4]The older girl was named Oholah, and her sister was Oholibah. I married them, and they bore me sons and daughters. I am speaking of Samaria and Jerusalem, for Oholah is Samaria and Oholibah is Jerusalem.

[5]"Then Oholah lusted after other lovers instead of me, and she gave her love to the Assyrians, her neighbors. [6]They were all attractive young men, captains and commanders dressed in handsome blue, dashing about on their horses. [7]And so she prostituted herself with the most desirable men of Assyria, worshiping their idols and defiling herself. [8]For when she left Egypt, she did not leave her spirit of prostitution behind. She was still as lewd as in her youth, when the Egyptians satisfied their lusts with her and robbed her of her virginity. [9]And so I handed her over to her Assyrian lovers, whom she desired so much. [10]They stripped her and killed her and took away her children as their slaves. Her name was known to every woman in the land as a sinner who had received what she deserved.

[11]"Yet even though Oholibah saw what had happened to Oholah, her sister, she followed right in her footsteps. And she was even more depraved, abandoning herself to her lust and prostitution. [12]She fawned over her Assyrian neighbors, those handsome young men on fine horses, those captains and commanders in handsome uniforms—all of them desirable. [13]I saw the way she was going, defiling herself just like her older sister.

[14]"Then she carried her prostitution even further. She fell in love with pictures that were painted on a wall—pictures of Babylonian* military officers, outfitted in striking red uniforms. [15]Handsome belts encircled their waists, and flowing turbans crowned their heads. They were dressed like chariot officers from the land of Babylonia.* [16]When she saw these paintings, she longed to give herself to them, so she sent messengers to Babylonia to invite them to come to her. [17]So they came and committed adultery with her, defiling her in the bed of love. But later, she became disgusted with them and broke off their relationship.

[18]"So I became disgusted with Oholibah, just as I was with her sister, because she flaunted herself before them and gave herself to satisfy their lusts. [19]But that didn't bother her. She turned to even greater prostitution, remembering her youth when she was a prostitute in Egypt. [20]She lusted after lovers whose attentions were gross and bestial. [21]And so, Oholibah, you celebrated your former days as a young girl in Egypt, when you first allowed yourself to be fondled and caressed.

[22]"Therefore, Oholibah, this is what the Sovereign LORD says: I will send your lovers against you—those very nations from which you turned away in disgust. [23]For the Babylonians will come with all the Chaldeans from Pekod and Shoa and Koa. And all the Assyrians will come with them—handsome young captains, commanders, chariot officers, and other high-ranking officers, riding their horses. [24]They will all come against you from the north with chariots, wagons, and a great army fully prepared for attack. They will take up positions on every side, surrounding you with men armed for battle. And I will hand you over to them so they can do with you as they please. [25]I will turn my jealous anger against you, and they will deal furiously with you. They will cut off your nose and ears, and any survivors will then be slaughtered by the sword. Your children will be taken away as captives, and everything that is left will be burned. [26]They will strip you of your beautiful clothes and jewels. [27]In this way, I will put a stop to the lewdness and prostitution you brought from Egypt. You will never again cast longing eyes on those things or fondly remember your time in Egypt.

[28]"For this is what the Sovereign LORD says: I will surely hand you over to your enemies, to those you loathe. [29]They will deal with you in hatred and rob

**22:25** As in Greek version; Hebrew reads *prophets.* **23:14** Or *Chaldean.* **23:15** Or *Chaldea;* also in 23:16.

you of all you own, leaving you naked and bare. The shame of your prostitution will be exposed to all the world. 30You brought all this on yourself by prostituting yourself to other nations, defiling yourself with all their idols. 31Because you have followed in your sister's footsteps, I will punish you with the same terrors that destroyed her.

32"Yes, this is what the Sovereign LORD says: You will drink from the same cup of terror as your sister—a cup that is large and deep. And all the world will mock and scorn you in your desolation. 33You will reel like a drunkard beneath the awful blows of sorrow and distress, just as your sister Samaria did. 34In deep anguish you will drain that cup of terror to the very bottom. Then you will smash it to pieces and beat your breast in anguish. For I, the Sovereign LORD, have spoken! 35And because you have forgotten me and turned your back on me, says the Sovereign LORD, you must bear the consequences of all your lewdness and prostitution."

36The LORD said to me, "Son of man, you must accuse Oholah and Oholibah of all their awful deeds. 37They have committed both adultery and murder—adultery by worshiping idols and murder by burning their children as sacrifices on their altars. 38Then after doing these terrible things, they defiled my Temple and violated my Sabbath day! 39On the very day that they murdered their children in front of their idols, they boldly came into my Temple to worship! They came in and defiled my house!

40"You sisters sent messengers to distant lands to get men. Then when they arrived, you bathed yourselves, painted your eyelids, and put on your finest jewels for them. 41You sat with them on a beautifully embroidered couch and put my incense and my oil on a table that was spread before you. 42From your room came the sound of many men carousing. They were lustful men and drunkards from the wilderness, who put bracelets on your wrists and beautiful crowns on your heads. 43Then I said, 'If they really want to sleep with worn-out, old prostitutes like these, let them!' 44And that is what they did. They slept with Oholah and Oholibah, these shameless prostitutes, with all the zest of lustful young men. 45But righteous people will judge these sister cities for what they really are—adulteresses and murderers. They will sentence them to all the punishment they deserve.

46"Now this is what the Sovereign LORD says: Bring an army against them and hand them over to be terrorized and plundered. 47For their enemies will stone them and kill them with swords. They will butcher their sons and daughters and burn their homes. 48In this way, I will put an end to lewdness and idolatry in the land, and my judgment will be a warning to others not to follow their wicked example. 49You will be fully repaid for all your prostitution—your worship of idols. Yes, you will suffer the full penalty! Then you will know that I am the Sovereign LORD."

CHAPTER **24** **A COOKING POT.** On January 15,* during the ninth year of King Jehoiachin's captivity, this message came to me from the LORD: 2"Son of man, write down today's date, because on this very day the king of Babylon is beginning his attack against Jerusalem. 3Then show these rebels an illustration; give them a message from the Sovereign LORD. Put a pot of water on the fire to boil. 4Fill it with choice meat—the rump and the shoulder and all the most tender cuts. 5Use only the best sheep from the flock and heap fuel on the fire beneath the pot. Bring the pot to a boil, and cook the bones along with the meat.

6"Now this is what the Sovereign LORD says: Destruction is certain for Jerusalem, the city of murderers! She is a pot filled with corruption. So take the meat out chunk by chunk in whatever order it comes, 7for her wickedness is evident to all. She murders boldly, leaving blood on the rocks for all to see. She doesn't even try to cover it! 8So I will splash her blood on a rock as an open expression of my anger and vengeance against her.

9"This is what the Sovereign LORD says: Destruction is certain for Jerusalem, the city of murderers! I myself will pile up the fuel beneath her. 10Yes, heap on the wood! Let the fire roar to make the pot boil. Cook the meat well with many spices. Then empty the pot and burn the bones. 11Now set the empty pot on the coals to scorch away the filth and corruption. 12But it's hopeless; the corruption remains. So throw it into the fire! 13It is the filth and corruption of your lewdness and idolatry. And now, because I tried to cleanse you but you refused, you will remain filthy until my fury against you has been satisfied. 14I, the LORD, have spoken! The time has come and I won't hold back; I will not change my mind. You will be judged on the basis of all your wicked actions, says the Sovereign LORD."

15Then this message came to me from the LORD: 16"Son of man, I am going to take away your dearest treasure. Suddenly she will die. Yet you must not show any sorrow. Do not weep; let there be no tears. 17You may sigh but only quietly. Let there be no wailing at her grave. Do not uncover your head or take off your sandals. Do not perform the rituals of mourning or accept any food brought to you by consoling friends."

18So I proclaimed this to the people the next morning, and in the evening my wife died. The next

## BURNED ● ● • • •

24:6-13 **The city of Jerusalem was like a pot that was so encrusted with the filth of sin that it would not come clean, even in the hottest fire. God wanted to cleanse those who lived in Jerusalem, and he wants to cleanse people today. Sometimes he tries to purify us through difficulties and troublesome circumstances. When you face tough times, let sin be burned from your life. Look at your problems as an opportunity for your faith to grow. Above all, do not allow sin to dominate your life (see 1 Corinthians 11:29-30).**

24:1 Hebrew *On the tenth day of the tenth month,* of the Hebrew calendar. This event occurred on January 15, 588 B.C.; also see note on 1:1.

morning I did everything I had been told to do. [19]Then the people asked, "What does all this mean? What are you trying to tell us?"

[20]So I said to them, "A message came to me from the LORD, [21]and I was told to give this message to the people of Israel. This is what the Sovereign LORD says: I will desecrate my Temple, the source of your security and pride. Your sons and daughters in Judea will be slaughtered by the sword. [22]Then you will do as Ezekiel has done. You will not mourn in public or console yourselves by eating the food brought to you by sympathetic friends. [23]Your heads must remain covered, and your sandals must not be taken off. You will not mourn or weep, but you will waste away because of your sins. You will mourn privately for all the evil you have done. [24]Ezekiel is an example for you to follow; you will do as he has done. And when that time comes, you will know that I am the LORD."

[25]Then the LORD said to me, "Son of man, on the day I take away their stronghold—their joy and glory, their heart's desire, their dearest treasure—I will also take away their sons and daughters. [26]And on that day a refugee from Jerusalem will come to you in Babylon and tell you what has happened. [27]And when he arrives, your voice will suddenly return so you can talk to him, and you will be a symbol for these people. Then they will know that I am the LORD."

## CHAPTER 25 **THIEVES IN THE DESERT.**

Then this message came to me from the LORD: [2]"Son of man, look toward the land of Ammon and prophesy against its people. [3]Give the Ammonites this message from the Sovereign LORD: Hear the word of the Sovereign LORD! Because you scoffed when my Temple was desecrated, mocked Israel in her desolation, and laughed at Judah as she went away into exile, [4]I will allow nomads from the eastern deserts to overrun your country. They will set up their camps among you and pitch their tents on your land. They will harvest all your fruit and steal your livestock. [5]And I will turn the city of Rabbah into a pasture for camels, and all the land of the Ammonites into an enclosure for sheep. Then you will know that I am the LORD.

[6]"And the Sovereign LORD says: Because you clapped and stamped and cheered with glee at the destruction of my people, [7]I will lift up my fist against you. I will give you as plunder to many nations. I will cut you off from being a nation and destroy you completely. Then you will know that I am the LORD.

[8]"And the Sovereign LORD says: Because the people of Moab have said that Judah is just like all the other nations, [9]I will open up their eastern flank and wipe out their glorious frontier cities—Beth-jeshimoth, Baal-meon, and Kiriathaim. [10]And I will hand Moab over to nomads from the eastern deserts, just as I handed over Ammon. Yes, the Ammonites will no longer be counted among the nations. [11]And in the same way, I will bring my judgment down on the Moabites. Then they will know that I am the LORD.

[12]"And the Sovereign LORD says: The people of Edom have sinned greatly by avenging themselves against the people of Judah. [13]Therefore, says the Sovereign LORD, I will raise my fist of judgment against Edom. I will wipe out their people, cattle, and flocks with the sword. I will make a wasteland of everything from Teman to Dedan. [14]By the hand of my people of Israel, I will accomplish this. They will carry out my furious vengeance, and Edom will know it is from me. I, the Sovereign LORD, have spoken!

[15]"And the Sovereign LORD says: The people of Philistia have acted against Judah out of revenge and long-standing contempt. [16]Therefore, says the Sovereign LORD, I will raise my fist of judgment against the land of the Philistines. I will wipe out the Kerethites and utterly destroy the people who live by the sea. [17]I will execute terrible vengeance against them to rebuke them for what they have done. And when I have inflicted my revenge, then they will know that I am the LORD."

## CHAPTER 26 **A CITY WILL BE RUINED.**

On February 3, during the twelfth year of King Jehoiachin's captivity,* this message came to me from the LORD: [2]"Son of man, Tyre has rejoiced over the fall of Jerusalem, saying, 'Ha! She who controlled the rich trade routes to the east has been broken, and I am the heir! Because she has been destroyed, I will become wealthy!'

[3]"Therefore, this is what the Sovereign LORD says: I am your enemy, O Tyre, and I will bring many nations against you, like the waves of the sea crashing against your shoreline. [4]They will destroy the walls of Tyre and tear down its towers. I will scrape away its soil and make it a bare rock! [5]The island of Tyre will become uninhabited. It will be a place for fishermen to spread their nets, for I have spoken, says the Sovereign LORD. Tyre will become the prey of many nations, [6]and its mainland villages will be destroyed by the sword. Then they will know that I am the LORD.

[7]"For the Sovereign LORD says: I will bring King Nebuchadnezzar* of Babylon—the king of kings

### ROCK PILE ● ● • • •

**26:14 After a 15-year siege, Nebuchadnezzar could not conquer the part of Tyre located on the island; thus certain aspects of the description in 26:12-14 actually go beyond the damage done to Tyre by Nebuchadnezzar and predict what would happen to the island settlement later during the conquests of Alexander the Great. Alexander threw the rubble of the mainland city into the sea until it made a bridge to the island. Today, the island city is still a pile of rubble, a testimony to God's judgment.**

26:1 Hebrew *In the eleventh year, on the first day of the month,* of the Hebrew calendar year. Since an element is missing in the date formula here, scholars have reconstructed this probable reading: *In the eleventh [month of the twelfth] year, on the first day of the month.* This reading would put this message on February 3, 585 B.C.; also see note on 1:1. 26:7 Hebrew *Nebuchadrezzar,* a variant name for Nebuchadnezzar.

from the north—against Tyre with his cavalry, chariots, and great army. 8First he will destroy your mainland villages. Then he will attack you by building a siege wall, constructing a ramp, and raising a roof of shields against you. 9He will pound your walls with battering rams and demolish your towers with sledgehammers. 10The hooves of his cavalry will choke the city with dust, and your walls will shake as the horses gallop through your broken gates, pulling chariots behind them. 11His horsemen will trample every street in the city. They will butcher your people, and your famous pillars will topple.

12"They will plunder all your riches and merchandise and break down your walls. They will destroy your lovely homes and dump your stones and timbers and even your dust into the sea. 13I will stop the music of your songs. No more will the sound of harps be heard among your people. 14I will make your island a bare rock, a place for fishermen to spread their nets. You will never be rebuilt, for I, the LORD, have spoken! This is the word of the Sovereign LORD.

15"This is what the Sovereign LORD says to Tyre: The whole coastline will tremble at the sound of your fall, as the screams of the wounded echo in the continuing slaughter. 16All the seaport rulers will step down from their thrones and take off their royal robes and beautiful clothing. They will sit on the ground trembling with horror at what they have seen. 17Then they will wail for you, singing this funeral song:

'O famous island city,
    once ruler of the sea,
    how you have been destroyed!
Your people, with their naval power,
    once spread fear around the world.
18 Now the coastlands tremble at your fall.
    The islands are dismayed as you pass away.'

19"For the Sovereign LORD says: I will make Tyre an uninhabited ruin. You will sink beneath the terrible waves of enemy attack. Great seas will swallow you. 20I will send you to the pit to lie there with those who descended there long ago. Your city will lie in ruins, buried beneath the earth, like those in the pit who have entered the world of the dead. Never again will you be given a position of respect here in the land of the living. 21I will bring you to a terrible end, and you will be no more. You will be looked for, but you will never be found. I, the Sovereign LORD, have spoken!"

## CHAPTER 27

**A GREAT SEAPORT CITY.** Then this message came to me from the LORD: 2"Son of man, sing a funeral song for Tyre, 3that mighty gateway to the sea, the trading center of the world. Give Tyre this message from the Sovereign LORD: You claimed, O Tyre, to be perfect in beauty. 4You extended your boundaries into the sea. Your builders made you

### DANGER SIGNAL ● ● ● • •

27:3-4 **The beauty of Tyre was the source of its pride, and Tyre's pride guaranteed its judgment. Pride in our own accomplishments should be a danger signal to us (see James 4:13-17). We must maintain a humble dependence upon God.**

glorious! 5You were like a great ship built of the finest cypress from Senir.* They took a cedar from Lebanon to make a mast for you. 6They carved oars for you from the oaks of Bashan. They made your deck of pine wood, brought from the southern coasts of Cyprus.* Then they inlaid it with ivory. 7Your sails were made of Egypt's finest linen, and they flew as a banner above you. You stood beneath blue and purple awnings made bright with dyes from the coasts of Elishah.

8"Your oarsmen came from Sidon and Arvad; your helmsmen were skilled men from Tyre itself. 9Wise old craftsmen from Gebal did all the caulking. Ships came with goods from every land to barter for your trade. 10Men from distant Persia, Lydia, and Libya* served in your great army. They hung their shields and helmets on your walls, giving you great honor. 11Men from Arvad and from Helech stood on your walls as sentinels. Your towers were manned by men from Gammad. Their shields hung on your walls, perfecting your splendor.

12"Tarshish was your agent, trading your wares in exchange for silver, iron, tin, and lead. 13Merchants from Greece,* Tubal, and Meshech brought slaves and bronze dishes. 14From Togarmah came riding horses, chariot horses, and mules. All these things were exchanged for your manufactured goods. 15Merchants came to you from Dedan.* Numerous coastlands were your captive markets; they brought payment in ivory tusks and ebony wood.

16"Aram* sent merchants to buy your wares. They traded turquoise, purple dyes, embroidery, fine linen, and jewelry of coral and rubies. 17Judah and Israel traded for your wares, offering wheat from Minnith, early figs,* honey, oil, and balm. 18Damascus traded for your rich variety of goods, bringing wine from Helbon and white wool from Zahar. 19Greeks from Uzal* came to trade for your merchandise. Wrought iron, cassia, and calamus were bartered for your wares. 20Dedan traded their expensive saddle blankets with you.

21"The Arabians and the princes of Kedar brought lambs and rams and goats in trade for your goods. 22The merchants of Sheba and Raamah came with all kinds of spices, jewels, and gold in exchange for your wares. 23Haran, Canneh, Eden, Sheba, Asshur, and Kilmad came with their merchandise, too. 24They brought choice fabrics to trade—blue cloth, embroidery, and many-colored carpets bound with cords and made secure. 25The ships of Tarshish were your ocean caravans. Your island warehouse was filled to the brim!

27:5 Or *Hermon.* 27:6 Hebrew *Kittim.* 27:10 Hebrew *Paras, Lud, and Put.* 27:13 Hebrew *Javan.* 27:15 Greek version reads *Rhodes.* 27:16 Some manuscripts read *Edom.* 27:17 The meaning of the Hebrew is uncertain. 27:19 Hebrew *Vedan and Javan from Uzal.* The meaning of the Hebrew is uncertain.

## NO DOUBT ● • • • •

**28:24-26 The promise that God's people will live in complete safety has yet to be fulfilled. Although many Jews were allowed to return from exile under Zerubbabel, Ezra, and Nehemiah, and the political nation is restored today, the inhabitants do not yet "live safely in Israel" (28:26). Therefore, this promise will have its ultimate fulfillment when Christ sets up his eternal kingdom. Then all people who have been faithful to God will dwell together in harmony and safety. Never doubt God's promises. They will come true—if not now, then in eternity!**

26 "But look! Your oarsmen are rowing your ship of state into a hurricane! Your mighty vessel flounders in the heavy eastern gale. You are shipwrecked in the heart of the sea! 27 Everything is lost—your riches and wares, your sailors and helmsmen, your ship builders, merchants, and warriors. On that day of vast ruin, everyone on board sinks into the depths of the sea.

28 "Your cities by the sea tremble as your helmsmen cry out in terror. 29 All the oarsmen abandon their ships; the sailors and helmsmen come to stand on the shore. 30 They weep bitterly as they throw dust on their heads and roll in ashes. 31 They shave their heads in grief because of you and dress themselves in sackcloth. They weep for you with bitter anguish and deep mourning. 32 As they wail and mourn, they sing this sad funeral song:

'Was there ever such a city as Tyre,
now silent at the bottom of the sea?
33 The merchandise you traded
satisfied the needs of many nations.
Kings at the ends of the earth
were enriched by your trade.
34 Now you are a wrecked ship,
broken at the bottom of the sea.
All your merchandise and your crew
have passed away with you.
35 All who live along the coastlands
are appalled at your terrible fate.
Their kings are filled with horror
and look on with twisted faces.
36 The merchants of the nations
shake their heads at the sight of you,*
for you have come to a horrible end
and will be no more.'"

## CHAPTER 28

**A PROUD KING WILL FALL.** Then this message came to me from the LORD: 2 "Son of man, give the prince of Tyre this message from the Sovereign LORD: In your great pride you claim, 'I am a god! I sit on a divine throne in the heart of the sea.' But you are only a man and not a god, though you boast that you are like a god. 3 You regard yourself as wiser than Daniel and think no secret is hidden from you. 4 With your wisdom and understanding you have amassed great wealth—gold and silver for your treasuries. 5 Yes, your wisdom has made you very rich, and your riches have made you very proud.

6 "Therefore, this is what the Sovereign LORD says: Because you think you are as wise as a god, 7 I will bring against you an enemy army, the terror of the nations. They will suddenly draw their swords against your marvelous wisdom and defile your splendor! 8 They will bring you down to the pit, and you will die there on your island home in the heart of the sea, pierced with many wounds. 9 Will you then boast, 'I am a god!' to those who kill you? To them you will be no god but merely a man! 10 You will die like an outcast at the hands of foreigners. I, the Sovereign LORD, have spoken!"

11 Then this further message came to me from the LORD: 12 "Son of man, weep for the king of Tyre. Give him this message from the Sovereign LORD: You were the perfection of wisdom and beauty. 13 You were in Eden, the garden of God. Your clothing was adorned with every precious stone*—red carnelian, chrysolite, white moonstone, beryl, onyx, jasper, sapphire, turquoise, and emerald—all beautifully crafted for you and set in the finest gold. They were given to you on the day you were created. 14 I ordained and anointed you as the mighty angelic guardian.* You had access to the holy mountain of God and walked among the stones of fire.

15 "You were blameless in all you did from the day you were created until the day evil was found in you. 16 Your great wealth filled you with violence, and you sinned. So I banished you from the mountain of God. I expelled you, O mighty guardian, from your place among the stones of fire. 17 Your heart was filled with pride because of all your beauty. You corrupted your wisdom for the sake of your splendor. So I threw you to the earth and exposed you to the curious gaze of kings. 18 You defiled your sanctuaries with your many sins and your dishonest trade. So I brought fire from within you, and it consumed you. I let it burn you to ashes on the ground in the sight of all who were watching. 19 All who knew you are appalled at your fate. You have come to a terrible end, and you are no more."

20 Then another message came to me from the LORD: 21 "Son of man, look toward the city of Sidon and prophesy against it. 22 Give the people of Sidon this message from the Sovereign LORD: I am your enemy, O Sidon, and I will reveal my glory by what happens to you. When I bring judgment against you and reveal my holiness among you, everyone watching will know that I am the LORD. 23 I will send a plague against you, and blood will be spilled in your streets. The attack will come from every direction, and your people will lie slaughtered within your walls. Then everyone will know that I am the LORD. 24 No longer will Israel's scornful neighbors prick and tear at her like thorns and briers. For then they will know that I am the Sovereign LORD.

25 "This is what the Sovereign LORD says: The people of Israel will again live in their own land, the land I gave my servant Jacob. For I will gather them from the distant lands where I have scattered them. I will reveal to the nations of the world my holiness

27:36 Hebrew *hiss at you.* 28:13 The identification of some of these gemstones is uncertain. 28:14 Hebrew *guardian cherub;* also in 28:16.

among my people. 26They will live safely in Israel
and build their homes and plant their vineyards.
And when I punish the neighboring nations that
treated them with contempt, they will know that I
am the LORD their God."

## CHAPTER 29 A KING LIKE A DRAGON.

On January 7,* during the tenth year of King Jehoiachin's
captivity, this message came to me from the LORD:
2"Son of man, turn toward Egypt and prophesy
against Pharaoh the king and all the people of Egypt.
3Give them this message from the Sovereign LORD: I
am your enemy, O Pharaoh, king of Egypt—you
great monster, lurking in the streams of the Nile. For
you have said, 'The Nile River is mine; I made it for
myself!' 4I will put hooks in your jaws and drag you
out on the land with fish sticking to your scales. 5I
will leave you and all your fish stranded in the desert
to die. You will lie unburied on the open ground, for
I have given you as food to the wild animals and
birds.

6"All the people of Egypt will discover that I am
the LORD, for you collapsed like a reed when Israel
looked to you for help. 7Israel leaned on you, but like
a cracked staff, you splintered and stabbed her in the
armpit. When she put her weight on you, you gave
way, and her back was thrown out of joint. 8So now
the Sovereign LORD says: I will bring an army against
you, O Egypt, and destroy both people and animals.
9The land of Egypt will become a desolate wasteland, and the Egyptians will know that I am the
LORD.

"Because you said, 'The Nile River is mine; I made
it,' 10I am now the enemy of both you and your river.
I will utterly destroy the land of Egypt, from Migdol
to Aswan, as far south as the border of Ethiopia.*
11For forty years not a soul will pass that way, neither
people nor animals. It will be completely uninhabited. 12I will make Egypt desolate, and it will be
surrounded by other desolate nations. Its cities will
be empty and desolate for forty years, surrounded by
other desolate cities. I will scatter the Egyptians to
distant lands.

13"But the Sovereign LORD also says: At the end of
the forty years I will bring the Egyptians home again
from the nations to which they have been scattered.
14I will restore the prosperity of Egypt and bring its
people back to the land of Pathros in southern Egypt
from which they came. But Egypt will remain an
unimportant, minor kingdom. 15It will be the lowliest of all the nations, never again great enough to rise
above its neighbors.

16"Then Israel will no longer be tempted to trust
in Egypt for help. Egypt's shattered condition will
remind Israel of how sinful she was to trust Egypt in
earlier days. Then Israel will know that I alone am
the Sovereign LORD."

17On April 26,* during the twenty-seventh year of
King Jehoiachin's captivity, this message came to me
from the LORD: 18"Son of man, the army of King
Nebuchadnezzar* of Babylon fought so hard against
Tyre that the warriors' heads were rubbed bare and
their shoulders were raw and blistered. Yet Nebuchadnezzar and his army won no plunder to compensate them for all their work. 19Therefore, this is
what the Sovereign LORD says: I will give the land of
Egypt to Nebuchadnezzar, king of Babylon. He will
carry off their wealth, plundering everything they
have to pay his army. 20Yes, I have given him the land
of Egypt as a reward for his work, says the Sovereign
LORD, because he was working for me when he destroyed Tyre.

21"And the day will come when I will cause the
ancient glory of Israel to revive, and then at last your
words will be respected. Then they will know that I
am the LORD."

### GREATNESS ● ● • • •

**29:9 The Nile River was Egypt's pride and joy, a life-giving river cutting through the middle of the desert. Rather than thanking God, however, Egypt declared, "The Nile is mine!" We do the same when we say, "This house is mine." Or, "I have brought myself to where I am today." Or, "I did it by myself." These statements reveal our pride. We sometimes take for granted what God has given us, thinking we have made it ourselves. Of course, we have put forth a lot of hard effort, but God supplied us with the resources, abilities, and opportunities to make it happen. Don't claim your own greatness, as the Egyptians did—proclaim God's greatness and give him the credit.**

## CHAPTER 30 A DAY OF CLOUDS AND GLOOM.

This is
another message that came to me from the LORD:
2"Son of man, prophesy and give this message from
the Sovereign LORD: Weep, 3for the terrible day is
almost here—the day of the LORD! It is a day of
clouds and gloom, a day of despair for the nations!
4A sword will come against Egypt, and those who are
slaughtered will cover the ground. Their wealth will
be carried away and their foundations destroyed. The
land of Ethiopia* will be ravished. 5Ethiopia, Libya,*
Lydia,* and Arabia, with all their other allies, will be
destroyed in that war.

6"For this is what the LORD says: All of Egypt's
allies will fall, and the pride of their power will end.
From Migdol to Aswan they will be slaughtered by
the sword, says the Sovereign LORD. 7Egypt will be
desolate, surrounded by desolate nations, and its
cities will be in ruins, surrounded by other ruined
cities. 8And the people of Egypt will know that I am
the LORD when I have set Egypt on fire and destroyed
all their allies. 9At that time I will send swift messengers in ships to terrify the complacent Ethiopians.

29:1 Hebrew *On the twelfth day of the tenth month,* of the Hebrew calendar. A number of dates in Ezekiel can be cross-checked with dates in surviving Babylonian records and related accurately to our modern calendar. This event occurred on January 7, 587 B.C. 29:10 Hebrew *Cush.* 29:17 Hebrew *On the first day of the first month,* of the Hebrew calendar. This event occurred on April 26, 571 B.C.; also see note on 29:1. 29:18 Hebrew *Nebuchadrezzar,* a variant name for Nebuchadnezzar; also in 29:19. 30:4 Hebrew *Cush;* also in 30:5, 9. 30:5a Hebrew *Put . . . Kub.* Both *Put* and *Kub* are associated with Libya. 30:5b Hebrew *Lud.*

Great panic will come upon them on that day of Egypt's certain destruction.

10"For this is what the Sovereign LORD says: Through King Nebuchadnezzar* of Babylon, I will destroy the hordes of Egypt. 11He and his armies—ruthless among the nations—have been sent to demolish the land. They will make war against Egypt until slaughtered Egyptians cover the ground. 12I will dry up the Nile River and hand the land over to wicked men. I will destroy the land of Egypt and everything in it, using foreigners to do it. I, the LORD, have spoken!

13"This is what the Sovereign LORD says: I will smash the idols of Egypt and the images at Memphis.* There will be no rulers left in Egypt; anarchy will prevail throughout the land! 14I will destroy Pathros, Zoan, and Thebes,* and they will lie in ruins, burned up by my anger. 15I will pour out my fury on Pelusium,* the strongest fortress of Egypt, and I will stamp out the people of Thebes. 16Yes, I will set fire to all Egypt! Pelusium will be racked with pain; Thebes will be torn apart; Memphis will live in constant terror. 17The young men of Heliopolis and Bubastis* will die in battle, and the women* will be taken away as slaves. 18When I come to break the proud strength of Egypt, it will be a dark day for Tahpanhes, too. A dark cloud will cover Tahpanhes, and its daughters will be led away as captives. 19And so I will greatly punish Egypt, and they will know that I am the LORD."

### ARMIES ● ● • • •

**30:21-26 This prophecy was given to Ezekiel in 587 B.C. God destroyed Egypt's military superiority and gave it to Babylon. God allows nations to rise to power to accomplish a particular purpose, often beyond our immediate understanding. When you read about armies and wars, don't despair. Remember that God is sovereign and in charge of everything, even military might. Besides praying for your military and government leaders, pray that God's greater purposes will be carried out and that his will will be done "on earth just as it is in heaven" (see Matthew 6:10).**

20On April 29,* during the eleventh year of King Jehoiachin's captivity, this message came to me from the LORD: 21"Son of man, I have broken the arm of Pharaoh, the king of Egypt. His arm has not been put in a cast so that it may heal. Neither has it been bound up with a splint to make it strong enough to hold a sword. 22Therefore, this is what the Sovereign LORD says: I am the enemy of Pharaoh, the king of Egypt! I will break both of his arms—the good arm along with the broken one—and I will make his sword clatter to the ground. 23I will scatter the Egyptians to many lands throughout the world. 24I will strengthen the arms of Babylon's king and put my sword in his hand. But I will break the arms of Pharaoh, king of Egypt, and he will lie there mortally wounded, groaning in pain. 25I will strengthen the arms of the king of Babylon, while the arms of Pharaoh fall useless to his sides. And when I put my sword in the hand of Babylon's king and he brings it against the land of Egypt, Egypt will know that I am the LORD. 26I will scatter the Egyptians among the nations. Then they will know that I am the LORD."

## CHAPTER 31

**A MAGNIFICENT TREE CUT DOWN.** On June 21,* during the eleventh year of King Jehoiachin's captivity, this message came to me from the LORD: 2"Son of man, give this message to Pharaoh, king of Egypt, and all his people: To whom would you compare your greatness? 3You are as Assyria was—a great and mighty nation. Assyria, too, was once like a cedar of Lebanon, full of thick branches that cast deep forest shade with its top high among the clouds. 4Deep springs watered it and helped it to grow tall and luxuriant. The water was so abundant that there was enough for all the trees nearby. 5This great tree towered above all the other trees around it. It prospered and grew long thick branches because of all the water at its roots. 6The birds nested in its branches, and in its shade all the wild animals gave birth to their young. All the great nations of the world lived in its shadow. 7It was strong and beautiful, for its roots went deep into abundant water. 8This tree became taller than any of the other cedars in the garden of God. No cypress had branches equal to it; no plane tree had boughs to compare. No tree in the garden of God came close to it in beauty. 9Because of the magnificence I gave this tree, it was the envy of all the other trees of Eden, the garden of God.

10"Therefore, this is what the Sovereign LORD says: Because it became proud and arrogant, and because it set itself so high above the others, reaching to the clouds, 11I handed it over to a mighty nation that destroyed it as its wickedness deserved. I myself discarded it. 12A foreign army—the terror of the nations—cut it down and left it fallen on the ground. Its branches were scattered across the mountains and valleys and ravines of the land. All those who lived beneath its shadow went away and left it lying there. 13The birds roosted on its fallen trunk, and the wild animals lay among its branches. 14Let no other na-

### THE CRASH ● ● • • •

**31:1-4 This message was given in 587 B.C. Ezekiel compared Egypt to Assyria, calling Assyria a great cedar tree that had crashed to the ground. The fall of the mighty nation of Assyria was to be an example to the Egyptians of what would happen to them. Just like Assyria, Egypt took pride in her strength and beauty; just like Assyria, Egypt would come crashing down. Nothing can last apart from God—not even a great society with magnificent culture and military power. Always remember where your strength and survival lie: in the hands of the almighty, all-loving God.**



**30:10** Hebrew *Nebuchadrezzar,* a variant name for Nebuchadnezzar. **30:13** Hebrew *Noph;* also in 30:16. **30:14** Hebrew *No;* also in 30:15, 16. **30:15** Hebrew *Sin;* also in 30:16. **30:17a** Hebrew *of Awen and Pi-beseth.* **30:17b** Or *her cities.* **30:20** Hebrew *On the seventh day of the first month,* of the Hebrew calendar. This event occurred on April 29, 587 B.C.; also see note on 29:1. **31:1** Hebrew *On the first day of the third month,* of the Hebrew calendar. This event occurred on June 21, 587 B.C.; also see note on 29:1.

tion proudly exult in its own prosperity, though it be higher than the clouds, for all are doomed. They will land in the pit along with all the proud people of the world.

15"This is what the Sovereign LORD says: When Assyria went down into the grave,* I made the deep places mourn, and I restrained the mighty waters. I clothed Lebanon in black and caused the trees of the field to wilt. 16I made the nations shake with fear at the sound of its fall, for I sent it down to the grave with all the others like it. And all the other proud trees of Eden, the most beautiful and the best of Lebanon, the ones whose roots went deep into the water, were relieved to find it there with them in the pit. 17Its allies, too, were all destroyed and had passed away. They had gone down to the grave—all those nations that had lived in its shade.

18"O Egypt, to which of the trees of Eden will you compare your strength and glory? You, too, will be brought down to the pit with all these other nations. You will lie there among the outcasts who have died by the sword. This will be the fate of Pharaoh and all his teeming hordes. I, the Sovereign LORD, have spoken!"

## CHAPTER 32

**LION OR CROCODILE?** On March 3,* during the twelfth year of King Jehoiachin's captivity, this message came to me from the LORD: 2"Son of man, mourn for Pharaoh, king of Egypt, and give him this message: You think of yourself as a strong young lion among the nations, but you are really just a sea monster, heaving around in your own rivers, stirring up mud with your feet.

3"Therefore, this is what the Sovereign LORD says: I will send many people to catch you in my net and haul you out of the water. 4I will leave you stranded on the land to die. All the birds of the heavens will land on you, and the wild animals of the whole earth will gorge themselves on you. 5I will cover the hills with your flesh and fill the valleys with your bones. 6I will drench the earth with your gushing blood all the way to the mountains, filling the ravines to the brim. 7When I blot you out, I will veil the heavens and darken the stars. I will cover the sun with a cloud, and the moon will not give you its light. 8Yes, I will bring darkness everywhere across your land. Even the brightest stars will become dark above you. I, the Sovereign LORD, have spoken!

9"And when I bring your shattered remains to distant nations that you have never seen, I will disturb many hearts. 10Yes, I will bring terror to many lands, and their kings will be terrified because of all I do to you. They will shudder in fear for their lives as I brandish my sword before them on the day of your fall.

11"For this is what the Sovereign LORD says: The sword of the king of Babylon will come against

**FUTURE ● ● ● • •**

32:18 **The Hebrews believed in an existence beyond the grave for all people, good and bad, in "the world below." Ezekiel's message assumed that the evil nations had already been sent there and that Egypt would soon follow. The Egyptians had a preoccupation with the afterlife (the pyramids were built solely to ensure the pharaohs' comfort in the next life). This message should remind us that such human attempts are foolish. God alone controls the future and life after death.**

you. 12I will destroy you with the swords of mighty warriors—the terror of the nations. They will shatter the pride of Egypt, and all its hordes will be destroyed. 13I will destroy all your flocks and herds that graze beside the streams. Never again will people or animals disturb those waters with their feet. 14Then I will let the waters of Egypt become calm again, and they will flow as smoothly as olive oil, says the Sovereign LORD. 15And when I destroy Egypt and wipe out everything you have and strike down all your people, then you will know that I am the LORD. 16Yes, this is the funeral song they will sing for Egypt. Let all the nations mourn for Egypt and its hordes. I, the Sovereign LORD, have spoken!"

17On March 17,* during the twelfth year, another message came to me from the LORD: 18"Son of man, weep for the hordes of Egypt and for the other mighty nations. For I will send them down to the world below in company with those who descend to the pit. 19Say to them, 'O Egypt, are you lovelier than the other nations? No! So go down to the pit and lie there among the outcasts.' 20The Egyptians will fall with the many who have died by the sword, for the sword is drawn against them. Egypt will be dragged away to its judgment. 21Down in the grave* mighty leaders will mockingly welcome Egypt and its allies, saying, 'They have come down; they lie among the outcasts, all victims of the sword.'

22"Assyria lies there surrounded by the graves of all its people, those who were slaughtered by the sword. 23Their graves are in the depths of the pit, and they are surrounded by their allies. These mighty men who once struck terror in the hearts of people everywhere are now dead at the hands of their enemies.

24"Elam lies there buried with its hordes who descended as outcasts to the world below. They terrorized the nations while they lived, but now they lie in the pit and share the humiliation of those who have gone to the world of the dead. 25They have a resting place among the slaughtered, surrounded by the graves of all their people. Yes, they terrorized the nations while they lived, but now they lie in shame

**31:15** Hebrew *to Sheol;* also in 31:16, 17. **32:1** Hebrew *On the first day of the twelfth month,* of the Hebrew calendar. This event occurred on March 3, 585 B.C.; also see note on 29:1. **32:17** Hebrew *On the fifteenth day of the month,* presumably in the twelfth month of the Hebrew calendar (see 32:1). This would put this message at the end of King Jehoiachin's twelfth year of captivity, on March 17, 585 B.C.; also see note on 29:1. Greek version reads *On the fifteenth day of the first month,* which would put this message on April 27, 586 B.C., at the beginning of Jehoiachin's twelfth year. **32:21** Hebrew *in Sheol.*

# Ultimate Issues

## WHO'S IN CHARGE?

"I do not believe in predestination. In fact, if I ever became convinced that God predestines some people to go to heaven and some to hell, I'd quit serving him."—Actual comment from a teenage male. **H**ave you ever felt the way that young man did? The idea that God decides our ETERNAL DESTINY goes against our American notions of fairness and individual choice. And yet, we draw strength and comfort from the belief that God is running the universe. (That's what "sovereignty" means.) Which is right? Is God truly sovereign—is he **CALLING THE SHOTS**—or are people free and ultimately responsible for making their own decisions, even those that have eternal consequences? **T**his question has perplexed people for thousands of years. It raises itself here, in the account of Pharaoh in Ezekiel 32. It raised itself about another Pharaoh, too, in the Exodus account of the pharaoh who held the Israelites captive. Did God know even before he put Pharaoh in charge that he would sin? Did God allow it—or cause it? Or did God simply ***roll the dice***, placing this man in authority without knowing whether or not he would obey his command to let his people go? If so, does that mean that since Creation, God has been a spectator in human events, allowing us total freedom and responsibility? Either conclusion leads to some awesome implications. If God is truly and completely sovereign, then I have no real freedom, and I'm just a puppet. But if I'm truly free to do whatever I want, then God isn't really in control of the universe. ***Help!*** **T**he greatest minds of history have wrestled with this issue, and quite frankly, it remains as impenetrable today as ever. So if you were hoping this article would resolve it, you're going to be disappointed. But it is possible to consider it from **a slightly different angle.** **C**ontemporary theologian J. I. Packer, one of the greatest minds of our time, was once asked, "If God is truly sovereign, in what sense is man responsible? And if man is truly responsible, in what sense is God sovereign?" Packer replied, "I think that it is a 'MYSTERY,' and that there's not much getting behind that. . . . The really surprising thing would be if we really could understand God. Then he wouldn't be any bigger than we are." **S**overeignty, responsibility, predestination, free will . . . and *mystery.* The Bible teaches them all. The modern American mind balks at accepting two truths that seem to be contradictory. But when you think about it, it makes sense that God is bigger than our minds—big enough to encompass what seems to us to be paradoxical. One thinker said that he thought of the twin truths of *predestination* and *free will* as parallel lines—he didn't know how to bring them together, but no one could make them cross, either. **I**f someone asks you whether you believe in God's sovereignty or human freedom, the best answer is yes.

---

in the pit, all of them outcasts, slaughtered by the sword.
[26]"Meshech and Tubal are there, surrounded by the graves of all their hordes. They once struck terror into the hearts of all people. But now they are outcasts, all victims of the sword. [27]They are not buried in honor like the fallen heroes of the outcasts, who went down to the grave* with their weapons—their shields covering their bodies,* and their swords beneath their heads. They brought terror to everyone while they were still alive.

[28]"You too, Egypt, will lie crushed and broken among the outcasts, all victims of the sword.
[29]"Edom is there with its kings and princes. Mighty as they were, they also lie among those killed by the sword, with the outcasts who have gone down to the pit. [30]All the princes of the north and the Sidonians are there, all victims of the sword. Once a terror, they now lie there in shame. They lie there as outcasts with all the other dead who have descended to the pit.
[31]"When Pharaoh arrives, he will be relieved to

32:27a Hebrew *to Sheol.* 32:27b The meaning of the Hebrew phrase here is uncertain.

find that he is not alone in having his entire army killed, says the Sovereign LORD. [32]For I have caused my terror to fall upon all the living. And Pharaoh and his hordes will lie there among the outcasts who have died by the sword. I, the Sovereign LORD, have spoken!"

## CHAPTER 33

**GOD WILL BE THE JUDGE.** Once again a message came to me from the LORD: [2]"Son of man, give your people this message: When I bring an army against a country, the people of that land choose a watchman. [3]When the watchman sees the enemy coming, he blows the alarm to warn the people. [4]Then if those who hear the alarm refuse to take action—well, it is their own fault if they die. [5]They heard the warning but wouldn't listen, so the responsibility is theirs. If they had listened to the warning, they could have saved their lives. [6]But if the watchman sees the enemy coming and doesn't sound the alarm to warn the people, he is responsible for their deaths. They will die in their sins, but I will hold the watchman accountable.

[7]"Now, son of man, I am making you a watchman for the people of Israel. Therefore, listen to what I say and warn them for me. [8]If I announce that some wicked people are sure to die and you fail to warn them about changing their ways, then they will die in their sins, but I will hold you responsible for their deaths. [9]But if you warn them to repent and they don't repent, they will die in their sins, but you will not be held responsible.

[10]"Son of man, give the people of Israel this message: You are saying, 'Our sins are heavy upon us; we are wasting away! How can we survive?' [11]As surely as I live, says the Sovereign LORD, I take no pleasure in the death of wicked people. I only want them to turn from their wicked ways so they can live. Turn! Turn from your wickedness, O people of Israel! Why should you die?

[12]"Son of man, give your people this message: The good works of righteous people will not save them if they turn to sin, nor will the sins of evil people destroy them if they repent and turn from their sins. [13]When I tell righteous people that they will live, but then they sin, expecting their past righteousness to save them, then none of their good deeds will be remembered. I will destroy them for their sins. [14]And suppose I tell some wicked people that they will surely die, but then they turn from their sins and do what is just and right. [15]For instance, they might give back a borrower's pledge, return what they have stolen, and obey my life-giving laws, no longer doing what is evil. If they do this, then they will surely live and not die. [16]None of their past sins will be brought up again, for they have done what is just and right, and they will surely live.

[17]"Your people are saying, 'The Lord is not just,' but it is they who are not just. [18]For again I say, when righteous people turn to evil, they will die. [19]But if wicked people turn from their wickedness

### FAITHFUL ● ● ● • •

**33:1-6 This chapter shows a new direction for Ezekiel's prophecies. Up to this point, he had pronounced judgment on Judah (chapters 1–24) and the surrounding evil nations (25–32). After Jerusalem fell, his messages of doom turned to messages of comfort, hope, and restoration for God's people (33–48). Previously God appointed Ezekiel to be a watchman, warning the nation of coming judgment (see 3:17-21). Here God appointed him to be a watchman again, to preach a message of hope. There are still warnings (33:23–34:10; 36:1-7), but these are part of the larger picture of hope. God would not forsake his promise to restore his blessings to the faithful. We must pay attention to both aspects of Ezekiel's message: warning and promise. The hope is given only to the righteous "remnant" in our churches who remain true to God.**

and do what is just and right, they will live. [20]O people of Israel, you are saying, 'The Lord is not just.' But I will judge each of you according to your deeds."

[21]On January 8,* during the twelfth year of our captivity, a man who had escaped from Jerusalem came to me and said, "The city has fallen!" [22]The previous evening the LORD had taken hold of me and opened my mouth, so I would be able to speak when this man arrived the next morning.

[23]Then this message came to me from the LORD: [24]"Son of man, the scattered remnants of Judah living among the ruined cities keep saying, 'Abraham was only one man, and yet he gained possession of the entire land! We are many; surely the land should be given to us as a possession.' [25]Now give these people this message from the Sovereign LORD: You eat meat with blood in it, you worship idols, and you murder the innocent. Do you really think the land should be yours? [26]Murderers! Idolaters! Adulterers! Should the land belong to you?

[27]"Give them this message from the Sovereign LORD: As surely as I live, those living in the ruins will die by the sword. Those living in the open fields will be eaten by wild animals. Those hiding in the forts and caves will die of disease. [28]I will destroy the land and demolish her pride. Her arrogant power will come to an end. The mountains of Israel will be so ruined that no one will even travel through them. [29]When I have ruined the land because of their disgusting sins, then they will know that I am the LORD.

### FACE IT ● ● ● • •

**33:10-12 The exiles were discouraged by their past sins. They felt heavy guilt for living in rebellion against God for so many years. This was an important turning point—elsewhere in Ezekiel the people had refused to face their sins. But God assured them of forgiveness if they repented. God *wants* everyone to turn to him. He looks at what we are and will become, not what we have been. God gives every person the opportunity to turn to him, so take it. Sincerely try to follow him, and ask him to forgive you when you fail.**

**33:21** Hebrew *On the fifth day of the tenth month,* of the Hebrew calendar. This event occurred on January 8, 585 B.C.; also see note on 29:1.

## IGNORED ● ● ● • •

**33:30-32 The people ignored Ezekiel's message. When people mock your witness for Christ or fail to take your advice, don't give up. You are not witnessing for their sakes alone, but out of faithfulness to God. You cannot make others accept your message; you can only be faithful in delivering it.**

30“Son of man, your people are whispering behind your back. They talk about you in their houses and whisper about you at the doors, saying, ‘Come on, let's have some fun! Let's go hear the prophet tell us what the LORD is saying!’ 31So they come pretending to be sincere and sit before you listening. But they have no intention of doing what I tell them. They express love with their mouths, but their hearts seek only after money. 32You are very entertaining to them, like someone who sings love songs with a beautiful voice or plays fine music on an instrument. They hear what you say, but they don't do it! 33But when all these terrible things happen to them—as they certainly will—then they will know a prophet has been among them.”

## PLAY CHURCH ● ● ● • •

**33:32 Many people think of church as entertainment. They enjoy the music, the people, and the activities, but they don't take the messages to heart. Have you reduced church services to the level of entertainment, or does your worship truly have an impact on your life?**

CHAPTER **34** **GOD'S FLOCK.** Then this message came to me from the LORD: 2“Son of man, prophesy against the shepherds, the leaders of Israel. Give them this message from the Sovereign LORD: Destruction is certain for you shepherds who feed yourselves instead of your flocks. Shouldn't shepherds feed their sheep? 3You drink the milk, wear the wool, and butcher the best animals, but you let your flocks starve. 4You have not taken care of the weak. You have not tended the sick or bound up the broken bones. You have not gone looking for those who have wandered away and are lost. Instead, you have ruled them with force and cruelty. 5So my sheep have been scattered without a shepherd. They are easy prey for any wild animal. 6They have wandered through the mountains and hills, across the face of the earth, yet no one has gone to search for them.

7“Therefore, you shepherds, hear the word of the LORD: 8As surely as I live, says the Sovereign LORD, you abandoned my flock and left them to be attacked by every wild animal. Though you were my shepherds, you didn't search for my sheep when they were lost. You took care of yourselves and left the sheep to starve. 9Therefore, you shepherds, hear the word of the LORD. 10This is what the Sovereign LORD says: I now consider these shepherds my enemies, and I will hold them responsible for what has happened to my flock. I will take away their right to feed the flock, along with their right to feed themselves. I will rescue my flock from their mouths; the sheep will no longer be their prey.

11“For this is what the Sovereign LORD says: I myself will search and find my sheep. 12I will be like a shepherd looking for his scattered flock. I will find my sheep and rescue them from all the places to which they were scattered on that dark and cloudy day. 13I will bring them back home to their own land of Israel from among the peoples and nations. I will feed them on the mountains of Israel and by the rivers in all the places where people live. 14Yes, I will give them good pastureland on the high hills of Israel. There they will lie down in pleasant places and feed in lush mountain pastures. 15I myself will tend my sheep and cause them to lie down in peace, says the Sovereign LORD. 16I will search for my lost ones who strayed away, and I will bring them safely home again. I will bind up the injured and strengthen the weak. But I will destroy those who are fat and powerful. I will feed them, yes—feed them justice!

17“And as for you, my flock, my people, this is what the Sovereign LORD says: I will judge between one sheep and another, separating the sheep from the goats. 18Is it not enough for you to keep the best of the pastures for yourselves? Must you also trample down the rest? Is it not enough for you to take the best water for yourselves? Must you also muddy the rest with your feet? 19All that is left for my flock to eat is what you have trampled down. All they have to drink is water that you have fouled.

20“Therefore, this is what the Sovereign LORD says: I will surely judge between the fat sheep and the scrawny sheep. 21For you fat sheep push and butt and crowd my sick and hungry flock until they are scattered to distant lands. 22So I will rescue my flock, and they will no longer be abused and destroyed. And I will judge between one sheep and another. 23And I will set one shepherd over them, even my servant David. He will feed them and be a shepherd to them. 24And I, the LORD, will be their God, and my servant David will be a prince among my people. I, the LORD, have spoken!

25“I will make a covenant of peace with them and drive away the dangerous animals from the land. Then my people will be able to camp safely in the wildest places and sleep in the woods without fear. 26I will cause my people and their homes around my holy hill to be a blessing. And I will send showers, showers of blessings, which will come just when they are needed. 27The orchards and fields of my people will yield bumper crops, and everyone will live in safety. When I have broken their chains of slavery and rescued them from those who enslaved them, then they will know that I am the LORD. 28They will no longer be prey for other nations, and wild

## SHEPHERD ● ● ● • •

**34:18-20 A bad shepherd is not only selfish, but also destructive. A minister who confuses people by raising unnecessary doubts, teaching false ideas, and acting sinfully is destroying his flock's spiritual nourishment.**

animals will no longer attack them. They will live in safety, and no one will make them afraid.

29"And I will give them a land famous for its crops, so my people will never again go hungry or be shamed by the scorn of foreign nations. 30In this way, they will know that I, the LORD their God, am with them. And they will know that they, the people of Israel, are my people, says the Sovereign LORD. 31You are my flock, the sheep of my pasture. You are my people, and I am your God, says the Sovereign LORD."

CHAPTER **35** **EDOM WILL BE RUINED.** Again a message came to me from the LORD: 2"Son of man, turn toward Mount Seir, and prophesy against its people. 3Give them this message from the Sovereign LORD: I am your enemy, O Mount Seir, and I will raise my fist against you to destroy you completely. 4I will demolish your cities and make you desolate, and then you will know that I am the LORD. 5Your continual hatred for the people of Israel led you to butcher them when they were helpless, when I had already punished them for all their sins. 6As surely as I live, says the Sovereign LORD, since you show no distaste for blood, I will give you a bloodbath of your own. Your turn has come! 7I will make Mount Seir utterly desolate, killing off all who try to escape and any who return. 8I will fill your mountains with the dead. Your hills, your valleys, and your streams will be filled with people slaughtered by the sword. 9I will make you desolate forever. Your cities will never be rebuilt. Then you will know that I am the LORD.

10"For you said, 'The lands of Israel and Judah will be ours. We will take possession of them. What do we care that the LORD is there!' 11Therefore, as surely as I live, says the Sovereign LORD, I will pay back your angry deeds with mine. I will punish you for all your acts of anger, envy, and hatred. And I will bring honor to my name by what I do to you. 12Then you will know that I, the LORD, have heard every contemptuous word you spoke against the mountains of Israel. For you said, 'They have been destroyed; they have been given to us as food to eat!' 13In saying that, you boasted proudly against me, and I have heard it all!

**WRATH ● ● • • •**

**35:8 Ezekiel prophesied not only against the people of Edom, but also against their mountains and land. Mountains, symbols of strength and power, represent the pride of these people who thought they could get away with evil. Does such worldly pride typify the nation in which you live? If so, it is in danger of divine wrath similar to that experienced by Edom.**

14"This is what the Sovereign LORD says: The whole world will rejoice when I make you desolate. 15You rejoiced at the desolation of Israel's inheritance. Now I will rejoice at yours! You will be wiped out, you people of Mount Seir and all who live in Edom! Then you will know that I am the LORD!

CHAPTER **36** **A PROMISE OF GOOD TIMES.** "Son of man, prophesy to Israel's mountains. Give them this message: O mountains of Israel, hear the word of the LORD! 2This is what the Sovereign LORD says: Your enemies have taunted you, saying, 'Aha! Now the ancient heights belong to us!' 3Therefore, son of man, give the mountains of Israel this message from the Sovereign LORD: Your enemies have attacked you from all directions, and now you are possessed by many nations. You are the object of much mocking and slander. 4Therefore, O mountains of Israel, hear the word of the Sovereign LORD. He speaks to the hills and mountains, ravines and valleys, and to ruined wastes and long-deserted cities that have been destroyed and mocked by foreign nations everywhere. 5This is what the Sovereign LORD says: My jealous anger is on fire against these nations, especially Edom, because they have shown utter contempt for me by gleefully taking my land for themselves as plunder.

6"Therefore, prophesy to the hills and mountains, the ravines and valleys of Israel. Give them this message from the Sovereign LORD: I am full of fury because you have suffered shame before the surrounding nations. 7Therefore, says the Sovereign LORD, I have raised my hand and sworn an oath that those nations will soon have their turn at suffering

**OLD AND NEW COVENANTS**

| OLD COVENANT | NEW COVENANT |
|---|---|
| Placed upon stone | Placed upon people's hearts |
| Based on the law | Based on desire to love and serve God |
| Must be taught | Known by all |
| Legal relationship with God | Personal relationship with God |

I WILL GIVE YOU *a new heart* *with new and right desires,* AND I WILL PUT *a new spirit* *in you.*

EZEKIEL 36:26

shame. [8]But the mountains of Israel will produce heavy crops of fruit to prepare for my people's return—and they will be coming home again soon! [9]See, I am concerned for you, and I will come to help you. Your ground will be tilled and your crops planted. [10]I will greatly increase the population of Israel, and the ruined cities will be rebuilt and filled with people. [11]Not only the people, but your flocks and herds will also greatly multiply. O mountains of Israel, I will bring people to live on you once again. I will make you even more prosperous than you were before. Then you will know that I am the LORD. [12]I will cause my people to walk on you once again, and you will be their inheritance. You will never again devour their children.

[13]"This is what the Sovereign LORD says: Now the other nations taunt you, saying, 'Israel is a land that devours her own people!' [14]But you will never again devour your people or bereave your nation, says the Sovereign LORD. [15]I will not allow those foreign nations to sneer at you, and you will no longer be shamed by them or cause your nation to fall, says the Sovereign LORD."

[16]Then this further message came to me from the LORD: [17]"Son of man, when the people of Israel were living in their own land, they defiled it by their evil deeds. To me their conduct was as filthy as a bloody rag. [18]They polluted the land with murder and by worshiping idols, so I poured out my fury on them. [19]I scattered them to many lands to punish them for the evil way they had lived. [20]But when they were scattered among the nations, they brought dishonor to my holy name. For the nations said, 'These are the people of the LORD, and he couldn't keep them safe in his own land!' [21]Then I was concerned for my holy name, which had been dishonored by my people throughout the world.

[22]"Therefore, give the people of Israel this message from the Sovereign LORD: I am bringing you back again but not because you deserve it. I am doing it to protect my holy name, which you dishonored while you were scattered among the nations. [23]I will show how holy my great name is—the name you dishonored among the nations. And when I reveal my holiness through you before their very eyes, says the Sovereign LORD, then the nations will know that I am the LORD. [24]For I will gather you up from all the nations and bring you home again to your land.

[25]"Then I will sprinkle clean water on you, and you will be clean. Your filth will be washed away, and you will no longer worship idols. [26]And I will give you a new heart with new and right desires, and I will put a new spirit in you. I will take out your stony heart of sin and give you a new, obedient heart.* [27]And I will put my Spirit in you so you will obey my laws and do whatever I command.

[28]"And you will live in Israel, the land I gave your ancestors long ago. You will be my people, and I will be your God. [29]I will cleanse you of your filthy behavior. I will give you good crops, and I will abolish famine in the land. [30]I will give you great harvests from your fruit trees and fields, and never again will the surrounding nations be able to scoff at your land for its famines. [31]Then you will remember your past sins and hate yourselves for all the evil things you did. [32]But remember, says the Sovereign LORD, I am not doing this because you deserve it. O my people of Israel, you should be utterly ashamed of all you have done!

[33]"This is what the Sovereign LORD says: When I cleanse you from your sins, I will bring people to live in your cities, and the ruins will be rebuilt. [34]The fields that used to lie empty and desolate—a shock to all who passed by—will again be farmed. [35]And when I bring you back, people will say, 'This

**WATCHING ● ● • • •**

36:21 **Why did God want to protect his holy name—his reputation? God was concerned about the salvation not only of his people, but also of the whole world. To allow his people to remain in sin and be destroyed by their enemies would lead other nations to believe their heathen gods were victorious (Isaiah 48:11). God will not share his glory with false gods—he alone is true. The people had the responsibility to represent God properly to the rest of the world. Believers today have that same responsibility. What do people think about God from watching you?**

**36:26** Hebrew *a heart of flesh.*

godforsaken land is now like Eden's garden! The ruined cities now have strong walls, and they are filled with people!' [36]Then the nations all around—all those still left—will know that I, the LORD, rebuilt the ruins and planted lush crops in the wilderness. For I, the LORD, have promised this, and I will do it.

[37]"This is what the Sovereign LORD says: I am ready to hear Israel's prayers for these blessings, and I am ready to grant them their requests. [38]I will multiply them like the sacred flocks that fill Jerusalem's streets at the time of her festivals. The ruined cities will be crowded with people once more, and everyone will know that I am the LORD."

## CHAPTER 37

**DRIED BONES.** The LORD took hold of me, and I was carried away by the Spirit of the LORD to a valley filled with bones. [2]He led me around among the old, dry bones that covered the valley floor. They were scattered everywhere across the ground. [3]Then he asked me, "Son of man, can these bones become living people again?"

"O Sovereign LORD," I replied, "you alone know the answer to that."

[4]Then he said to me, "Speak to these bones and say, 'Dry bones, listen to the word of the LORD! [5]This is what the Sovereign LORD says: Look! I am going to breathe into you and make you live again! [6]I will put flesh and muscles on you and cover you with skin. I will put breath into you, and you will come to life. Then you will know that I am the LORD.'"

[7]So I spoke these words, just as he told me. Suddenly as I spoke, there was a rattling noise all across the valley. The bones of each body came together and attached themselves as they had been before. [8]Then as I watched, muscles and flesh formed over the bones. Then skin formed to cover their bodies, but they still had no breath in them.

[9]Then he said to me, "Speak to the winds and say: 'This is what the Sovereign LORD says: Come, O breath, from the four winds! Breathe into these dead bodies so that they may live again.'"

[10]So I spoke as he commanded me, and the wind entered the bodies, and they began to breathe. They all came to life and stood up on their feet—a great army of them.

[11]Then he said to me, "Son of man, these bones represent the people of Israel. They are saying, 'We have become old, dry bones—all hope is gone.' [12]Now give them this message from the Sovereign LORD: O my people, I will open your graves of exile and cause you to rise again. Then I will bring you back to the land of Israel. [13]When this happens, O my people, you will know that I am the LORD. [14]I will put my Spirit in you, and you will live and return home to your own land. Then you will know that I am the LORD. You will see that I have done everything just as I promised. I, the LORD, have spoken!"

[15]Again a message came to me from the LORD: [16]"Son of man, take a stick and carve on it these words: 'This stick represents Judah and its allied tribes.' Then take another stick and carve these words on it: 'This stick represents the northern tribes of Israel.'* [17]Now hold them together in your hand as one stick. [18]When your people ask you what your actions mean, [19]say to them, 'This is what the Sovereign LORD says: I will take the northern tribes and join them to Judah. I will make them one stick in my hand.' [20]Then hold out the sticks you have inscribed, so the people can see them. [21]And give them this message from the Sovereign LORD: I will gather the people of Israel from among the nations. I will bring them home to their own land from the places where they have been scattered. [22]I will unify them into one nation in the land. One king will rule them all; no longer will they be divided into two nations. [23]They will stop polluting themselves with their detestable idols and other sins, for I will save them from their sinful backsliding. I will cleanse them. Then they will truly be my people, and I will be their God.

[24]"My servant David will be their king, and they will have only one shepherd. They will obey my regulations and keep my laws. [25]They will live in the land of Israel where their ancestors lived, the land I gave my servant Jacob. They and their children and their grandchildren after them will live there forever, generation after generation. And my servant David will be their prince forever. [26]And I will make a covenant of peace with them, an everlasting covenant. I will give them their land and multiply them, and I will put my Temple among them forever. [27]I will make my home among them. I will be their God, and they will be my people. [28]And since my Temple will remain among them forever, the nations will know that I, the LORD, have set Israel apart for myself to be holy."

### DRIED UP ● ● • • •

**37:5 The dry bones represented the people's spiritually dead condition. Your church may seem like a heap of dried-up bones to you, spiritually dead with no hope of vitality. But just as God promised to restore his nation, he can restore any church, no matter how dry or dead it may be. Rather than give up, pray for renewal, for God can restore it to life. The hope and prayer of every church should be that God will put his Spirit into it (37:14). In fact, God is at work calling his people back to himself, bringing new life into dead churches.**

## CHAPTER 38

**EZEKIEL'S MESSAGE TO GOG.** This is another message that came to me from the LORD: [2]"Son of man, prophesy against Gog of the land of Magog, the prince who rules over the nations of Meshech and Tubal. [3]Give him this message from the Sovereign LORD: Gog, I am your enemy! [4]I will turn you around and put hooks into your jaws to lead you out to your destruction. I will mobilize your troops and cavalry and make you a vast and mighty horde, all fully armed. [5]Persia, Ethiopia, and Libya* will join you, too, with all their weapons. [6]Gomer and all its hordes will also join you, along with the

37:16 Hebrew *Ephraim's stick, representing Joseph and all the house of Israel.* 38:5 Hebrew *Paras, Cush, and Put.*

armies of Beth-togarmah from the distant north and many others.

7“Get ready; be prepared! Keep all the armies around you mobilized, and take command of them. 8A long time from now you will be called into action. In the distant future you will swoop down on the land of Israel, which will be lying in peace after her recovery from war and after the return of her people from many lands. 9You and all your allies—a vast and awesome horde—will roll down on them like a storm and cover the land like a cloud.

10“This is what the Sovereign LORD says: At that time evil thoughts will come to your mind, and you will devise a wicked scheme. 11You will say, ‘Israel is an unprotected land filled with unwalled villages! I will march against her and destroy these people who live in such confidence! 12I will go to those once-desolate cities that are again filled with people who have returned from exile in many nations. I will capture vast amounts of plunder and take many slaves, for the people are rich with cattle now, and they think the whole world revolves around them!’ 13But Sheba and Dedan and the merchants of Tarshish will ask, ‘Who are you to rob them of silver and gold? Who are you to drive away their cattle and seize their goods and make them poor?’

14“Therefore, son of man, prophesy against Gog. Give him this message from the Sovereign LORD: When my people are living in peace in their land, then you will rouse yourself.* 15You will come from your homeland in the distant north with your vast cavalry and your mighty army, 16and you will cover the land like a cloud. This will happen in the distant future. I will bring you against my land as everyone watches, and my holiness will be displayed by what happens to you. Then all the nations will know that I am the LORD.

## A SURE WIN ● ● • • •

39:12-16 **Two themes are intertwined: God’s total victory over his enemies and the need to purify the land to make it holy. After the final battle, teams will give proper burial to the bodies of the dead enemies so that the land may be cleansed. Yet there will be so many bodies that the scavenger birds will be called to help dispose of the corpses (39:17-20). The message for us is an exciting one: with God on our side, we are assured of ultimate victory over any foe, for God will fight on our behalf (see also Zephaniah 3:14-17; Romans 8:38-39).**

17“This is what the Sovereign LORD says: You are the one I was talking about long ago, when I announced through Israel’s prophets that in future days I would bring you against my people. 18But when Gog invades the land of Israel, says the Sovereign LORD, my fury will rise! 19For in my jealousy and blazing anger, I promise a mighty shaking in the land of Israel on that day. 20All living things—all the fish, birds, animals, and people—will quake in terror at my presence. Mountains will be thrown down; cliffs will crumble; walls will fall to the earth. 21I will summon the sword against you throughout Israel, says the Sovereign LORD. Your men will turn against each other in mortal combat. 22I will punish you and your hordes with disease and bloodshed; I will send torrential rain, hailstones, fire, and burning sulfur! 23Thus will I show my greatness and holiness, and I will make myself known to all the nations of the world. Then they will know that I am the LORD!

CHAPTER **39** **GOD’S HOLINESS.** “Son of man, prophesy against Gog. Give him this message from the Sovereign LORD: I am your enemy, O Gog, ruler of the nations of Meshech and Tubal. 2I will turn you and drive you toward the mountains of Israel, bringing you from the distant north. 3I will knock your weapons from your hands and leave you helpless. 4You and all your vast hordes will die on the mountains. I will give you as food to the vultures and wild animals. 5You will fall in the open fields, for I have spoken, says the Sovereign LORD. 6And I will rain down fire on Magog and on all your allies who live safely on the coasts. Then they will know that I am the LORD.

7“Thus, I will make known my holy name among my people of Israel. I will not let it be desecrated anymore. And the nations, too, will know that I am the LORD, the Holy One of Israel. 8That day of judgment will come, says the Sovereign LORD. Everything will happen just as I have declared it.

9“Then the people in the towns of Israel will go out and pick up your small and large shields, bows and arrows, javelins and spears, and they will use them for fuel. There will be enough to last them seven years! 10They will need nothing else for their fires. They won’t need to cut wood from the fields or forests, for these weapons will give them all they need. They will take plunder from those who planned to plunder them, says the Sovereign LORD.

11“And I will make a vast graveyard for Gog and his hordes in the Valley of the Travelers, east of the Dead Sea.* The path of those who travel there will be blocked by this burial ground, and they will change the name of the place to the Valley of Gog’s Hordes. 12It will take seven months for the people of Israel to cleanse the land by burying the bodies. 13Everyone in Israel will help, for it will be a glorious victory for Israel when I demonstrate my glory on that day, says the Sovereign LORD. 14At the end of the seven months, special crews will be appointed to search the land for any skeletons and to bury them, so the land will be made clean again. 15Whenever some bones are found, a marker will be set up beside them so the burial crews will see them and take them to be buried in the Valley of Gog’s Hordes. 16(There will be a town there named Hamonah—which means ‘horde.’) And so the land will finally be cleansed.

17“And now, son of man, call all the birds and wild animals, says the Sovereign LORD. Say to them: Gather together for my great sacrificial feast. Come

**38:14** As in Greek version; Hebrew reads *then you will know.* **39:11** Hebrew *the sea.*

from far and near to the mountains of Israel, and there eat the flesh and drink the blood! 18 Eat the flesh of mighty men and drink the blood of princes as though they were rams, lambs, goats, and fat young bulls of Bashan! 19 Gorge yourselves with flesh until you are glutted; drink blood until you are drunk. This is the sacrificial feast I have prepared for you. 20 Feast at my banquet table—feast on horses, riders, and valiant warriors, says the Sovereign LORD.

21 "Thus, I will demonstrate my glory among the nations. Everyone will see the punishment I have inflicted on them and the power I have demonstrated. 22 And from that time on the people of Israel will know that I am the LORD their God. 23 The nations will then know why Israel was sent away to exile—it was punishment for sin, for they acted in treachery against their God. Therefore, I turned my back on them and let their enemies destroy them. 24 I turned my face away and punished them in proportion to the vileness of their sins.

25 "So now the Sovereign LORD says: I will end the captivity of my people*; I will have mercy on Israel, for I am jealous for my holy reputation! 26 They will accept responsibility for their past shame and treachery against me after they come home to live in peace and safety in their own land. And then no one will bother them or make them afraid. 27 When I bring them home from the lands of their enemies, my holiness will be displayed to the nations. 28 Then my people will know that I am the LORD their God—responsible for sending them away to exile and responsible for bringing them home. I will leave none of my people behind. 29 And I will never again turn my back on them, for I will pour out my Spirit upon them, says the Sovereign LORD."

## CHAPTER 40

**THE NEW TEMPLE.** On April 28,* during the twenty-fifth year of our captivity—fourteen years after the fall of Jerusalem—the LORD took hold of me. 2 In a vision of God he took me to the land of Israel and set me down on a very high mountain. From there I could see what appeared to be a city across from me toward the south. 3 As he brought me nearer, I saw a man whose face shone like bronze standing beside a gateway entrance. He was holding in his hand a measuring tape and a measuring rod.

4 He said to me, "Son of man, watch and listen. Pay close attention to everything I show you. You have been brought here so I can show you many things. Then you will return to the people of Israel and tell them everything you have seen."

5 I could see a wall completely surrounding the Temple area. The man took a measuring rod that was 10½ feet* long and measured the wall, and the wall was 10½ feet thick and 10½ feet high.

6 Then he went over to the gateway that goes through the eastern wall. He climbed the steps and measured the threshold of the gateway; it was 10½ feet deep.* 7 There were guard alcoves on each side built into the gateway passage. Each of these alcoves was 10½ feet square, with a distance between them of 8¾ feet along the passage wall. The gateway's inner threshold, which led to the foyer at the inner end of the gateway passage, was 10½ feet deep. 8 He also measured the foyer of the gateway* 9 and found it to be 14 feet deep, with supporting columns 3½ feet thick. This foyer was at the inner end of the gateway structure, facing toward the Temple.

**PLANS ● ● ● ● ●**

**40:1-42:20 Ezekiel explained God's dwelling place in words and images that the people could understand. God wanted them to see the great splendor he has planned for those who are faithful and will live with him forever. Don't let the details obscure the point of this vision—one day all those who have been faithful to God will enjoy eternal life with him. Let the majesty of this vision lift you and teach you about the God you worship and serve.**

10 There were three guard alcoves on each side of the gateway passage. Each had the same measurements, and the dividing walls separating them were also identical. 11 The man measured the gateway entrance, which was 17½ feet wide at the opening and 22¾ feet wide in the gateway passage. 12 In front of each of the guard alcoves was a 21-inch curb. The alcoves themselves were 10½ feet square.

13 Then he measured the entire width of the gateway, measuring the distance between the back walls of facing guard alcoves; this distance was 43¾ feet. 14 He measured the dividing walls all along the inside of the gateway up to the gateway's foyer; this distance was 105 feet.* 15 The full length of the gateway passage was 87½ feet from one end to the other. 16 There were recessed windows that narrowed inward through the walls of the guard alcoves and their dividing walls. There were also windows in the foyer structure. The surfaces of the dividing walls were decorated with carved palm trees.

17 Then the man brought me through the gateway into the outer courtyard of the Temple. A stone pavement ran along the walls of the courtyard, and thirty rooms were built against the walls, opening onto the pavement. 18 This pavement flanked the gates and extended out from the walls into the courtyard the same distance as the gateway entrance. This was the lower pavement. 19 Then the man measured across the Temple's outer courtyard between the outer and inner gateways; the distance was 175 feet.

**39:25** Hebrew *of Jacob.* **40:1** Hebrew *At the beginning of the year, on the tenth day of the month,* of the Hebrew calendar. A number of dates in Ezekiel can be cross-checked with dates in surviving Babylonian records and related accurately to our modern calendar. This event occurred on April 28, 573 B.C. **40:5** Hebrew *6 long cubits* [3.2 meters], *each being a cubit* [18 inches or 45 centimeters] *and a handbreadth* [3 inches or 8 centimeters] *in length.* In this chapter, the distance measures are calculated using the Hebrew long cubit, which equals 21 inches or 53 centimeters. **40:6** Greek version; Hebrew reads *one rod* [10.5 feet or 3.2 meters] *deep, and one threshold, one rod deep.* **40:8** Many Hebrew manuscripts add *which faced inward toward the Temple; it was one rod* [10.5 feet or 3.2 meters] *deep. 9Then he measured the foyer of the gateway, . . .* **40:14** The meaning of the Hebrew in this verse is uncertain.

## CLEANED UP ● ● • • •

40:38-39 **The washing of the sacrifices was done according to the standards of preparation established in Leviticus 1:6-9. This washing was part of the process of presenting an acceptable sacrifice to God. What is there in your life that you would like to present as a sacrifice to God?**

20There was a gateway on the north just like the one on the east, and the man measured it. 21Here, too, there were three guard alcoves on each side, with dividing walls and a foyer. All the measurements matched those of the east gateway. The gateway passage was 87½ feet long and 43¾ feet wide between the back walls of facing guard alcoves. 22The windows, the foyer, and the palm tree decorations were identical to those in the east gateway. There were seven steps leading up to the gateway entrance, and the foyer was at the inner end of the gateway passage. 23Here on the north side, just as on the east, there was another gateway leading to the Temple's inner courtyard directly opposite this outer gateway. The distance between the two gateways was 175 feet.

24Then the man took me around to the south gateway and measured its various parts, and he found they were exactly the same as in the others. 25It had windows along the walls as the others did, and there was a foyer where the gateway passage opened into the outer courtyard. And like the others, the gateway passage was 87½ feet long and 43¾ feet wide between the back walls of facing guard alcoves. 26This gateway also had a stairway of seven steps leading up to it, and there were palm tree decorations along the dividing walls. 27And here again, directly opposite the outer gateway, was another gateway that led into the inner courtyard. The distance between the two gateways was 175 feet.

28Then the man took me to the south gateway leading into the inner courtyard. He measured it and found that it had the same measurements as the other gateways. 29Its guard alcoves, dividing walls, and foyer were the same size as those in the others. It also had windows along its walls and in the foyer structure. And like the others, the gateway passage was 87½ feet long and 43¾ feet wide. 30(The foyers of the gateways leading into the inner courtyard were 8¾ feet deep and 43¾ feet wide.) 31The foyer of the south gateway faced into the outer courtyard. It had palm tree decorations on its columns, and there were eight steps leading to its entrance.

32Then he took me to the east gateway leading to the inner courtyard. He measured it and found that it had the same measurements as the other gateways. 33Its guard alcoves, dividing walls, and foyer were the same size as those of the others, and there were windows along the walls and in the foyer structure. The gateway passage measured 87½ feet long and 43¾ feet wide. 34Its foyer faced into the outer courtyard. It had palm tree decorations on its columns, and there were eight steps leading to its entrance.

35Then he took me around to the north gateway leading to the inner courtyard. He measured it and found that it had the same measurements as the other gateways. 36The guard alcoves, dividing walls, and foyer of this gateway had the same measurements as in the others and the same window arrangements. The gateway passage measured 87½ feet long and 43¾ feet wide. 37Its foyer faced into the outer courtyard, and it had palm tree decorations on the columns. There were eight steps leading to its entrance.

38A door led from the foyer of the inner gateway on the north side into a side room where the meat for sacrifices was washed before being taken to the altar. 39On each side of this foyer were two tables, where the sacrificial animals were slaughtered for the burnt offerings, sin offerings, and guilt offerings. 40Outside the foyer, on each side of the stairs going up to the north entrance, there were two more tables. 41So there were eight tables in all, four inside and four outside, where the sacrifices were cut up and prepared. 42There were also four tables of hewn stone for preparation of the burnt offerings, each 31½ inches square and 21 inches high. On these tables were placed the butchering knives and other implements and the sacrificial animals. 43There were hooks, each three inches* long, fastened to the foyer walls and set on the tables where the sacrificial meat was to be laid.

44Inside the inner courtyard there were two one-room buildings for the singers, one beside the north gateway, facing south, and the other beside the south* gateway, facing north. 45And the man said to me, "The building beside the north inner gate is for the priests who supervise the Temple maintenance. 46The building beside the south inner gate is for the priests in charge of the altar—the descendants of Zadok—for they alone of all the Levites may approach the LORD to minister to him."

47Then the man measured the inner courtyard and found it to be 175 feet square. The altar stood there in the courtyard in front of the Temple. 48Then he brought me to the foyer of the Temple. He measured its supporting columns and found them to be 8¾ feet square. The entrance was 24½ feet wide with walls 5¼ feet thick. 49The depth of the foyer was 35 feet and the width was 19¼ feet. There were ten steps leading up to it, with a column on each side.

## CHAPTER 41

**THE MOST HOLY PLACE.** After that, the man brought me into the Holy Place, the large main room of the Temple, and he measured the columns that framed its doorway. They were 10½ feet* square. 2The entrance was 17½ feet wide, and the walls on each side were 8¾ feet wide. The Holy Place itself was 70 feet long and 35 feet wide.

3Then he went into the inner room at the end of the Holy Place. He measured the columns at the entrance and found them to be 3½ feet thick. The entrance was 10½ feet wide, and the walls on each side of the entrance extended 12¼ feet to the corners

40:43 Hebrew *a handbreadth* [8 centimeters]. 40:44 As in Greek version; Hebrew reads *east.* 41:1 Hebrew *6 cubits* [3.2 meters]. In this chapter, the distance measures are calculated using the Hebrew long cubit, which equals 21 inches or 53 centimeters.

of the inner room. [4]The inner room was 35 feet square. "This," he told me, "is the Most Holy Place."

[5]Then he measured the wall of the Temple and found that it was 10½ feet thick. There was a row of rooms along the outside wall; each room was 7 feet wide. [6]These rooms were built in three levels, one above the other, with thirty rooms on each level. The supports for these rooms rested on ledges in the Temple wall, but the supports did not extend into the wall. [7]Each level was wider than the one below it, corresponding to the narrowing of the Temple wall as it rose higher. A stairway led up from the bottom level through the middle level to the top level.

[8]I noticed that the Temple was built on a terrace, which provided a foundation for the side rooms. This terrace was 10½ feet high. [9]The outer wall of the Temple's side rooms was 8¾ feet thick. This left an open area between these side rooms [10]and the row of rooms along the outer wall of the inner courtyard. This open area measured 35 feet in width, and it went all the way around the Temple. [11]Two doors opened from the side rooms into the terrace yard, which was 8¾ feet wide. One door faced north and the other south.

[12]A large building stood on the west, facing the Temple courtyard. It was 122½ feet wide and 157½ feet long, and its walls were 8¾ feet thick. [13]Then the man measured the Temple, and he found it to be 175 feet long. The courtyard around the building, including its walls, was an additional 175 feet in length. [14]The inner courtyard to the east of the Temple was also 175 feet wide. [15]The building to the west, including its two walls, was also 175 feet wide.

The Holy Place, the Most Holy Place, and the foyer of the Temple were all paneled with wood, [16]as were the frames of the recessed windows. The inner walls of the Temple were paneled with wood above and below the windows. [17]The space above the door leading into the Most Holy Place was also paneled. [18]All the walls were decorated with carvings of cherubim, each with two faces, and there was a palm tree carving between each of the cherubim. [19]One face—that of a man—looked toward the palm tree on one side. The other face—that of a young lion—looked toward the palm tree on the other side. The figures were carved all along the inside of the Temple, [20]from the floor to the top of the walls, including the outer wall of the Holy Place.

[21]There were square columns at the entrance to the Holy Place, and the ones at the entrance of the Most Holy Place were similar. [22]There was an altar made of wood, 3½ feet square and 5¼ feet high. Its corners, base, and sides were all made of wood. "This," the man told me, "is the table that stands in the LORD's presence."

[23]Both the Holy Place and the Most Holy Place had double doorways, [24]each with two swinging doors. [25]The doors leading into the Holy Place were decorated with carved cherubim and palm trees just as on the walls. And there was a wooden canopy over the front of the Temple's foyer. [26]On both sides of the foyer there were recessed windows decorated with carved palm trees.

## CHAPTER 42 THE PRIESTS' ROOMS.

Then the man led me out of the Temple courtyard by way of the north gateway. We entered the outer courtyard and came to a group of rooms against the north wall of the inner courtyard. [2]This group of structures, whose entrance opened toward the north, was 175 feet long and 87½ feet wide.* [3]One block of rooms overlooked the 35-foot width of the inner courtyard. Another block of rooms looked out onto the pavement of the outer courtyard. The two blocks were built three levels high and stood across from each other. [4]Between the two blocks of rooms ran a walkway 17½ feet wide. It extended the entire 175 feet of the complex, and all the doors faced toward the north. [5]Each of the two upper levels of rooms was narrower than the one beneath it because the upper levels had to allow space for walkways in front of them. [6]Since there were three levels and they did not have supporting columns as in the courtyards, each of the upper levels was set back from the level beneath it. [7]There was an outer wall that separated the rooms from the outer courtyard; it was 87½ feet long. [8]This wall added length to the outer block of rooms, which extended for only 87½ feet, while the inner block—the rooms toward the Temple—extended for 175 feet. [9]There was an entrance from the outer courtyard to these rooms from the east.

[10]On the south* side of the Temple there were two blocks of rooms just south of the inner courtyard between the Temple and the outer courtyard. These rooms were arranged just like the rooms on the north. [11]There was a walkway between the two blocks of rooms just like the complex on the north side of the Temple. This complex of rooms was the same length and width as the other one, and it had the same entrances and doors. The dimensions of each were identical. [12]So there was an entrance in the wall facing the doors of the inner block of rooms, and another on the east at the end of the interior walkway.

[13]Then the man told me, "These rooms that overlook the Temple from the north and south are holy. It is there that the priests who offer sacrifices to the LORD will eat the most holy offerings. And they will use these rooms to store the grain offerings, sin offerings, and guilt offerings because these rooms

### INNER SANCTUM ● ● • • •

41:4 **The Most Holy Place was the innermost room in the Temple (Exodus 26:33-34). This was where the Ark of the Covenant was kept and where God's glory was said to dwell. It was entered only once a year by the high priest, who performed a ceremony to atone for the nation's sins. God's holiness is a central theme throughout both the Old and New Testaments.**

42:2 Hebrew *100 cubits* [53 meters] *long and 50 cubits* [26.5 meters] *wide.* In this chapter, the distance measures are calculated using the Hebrew long cubit, which equals 21 inches or 53 centimeters. 42:10 As in Greek version; Hebrew reads *east.*

are holy. [14]When the priests leave the Holy Place, they must not go directly to the outer courtyard. They must first take off the clothes they wore while ministering because these clothes are holy. They must put on other clothes before entering the parts of the building complex open to the public."

[15]When the man had finished taking these measurements, he led me out through the east gateway to measure the entire Temple area. [16]He measured the east side; it was 875 feet long. [17]He also measured the north side and got the same measurement. [18]The south side was the same length, [19]and so was the west side. [20]So the area was 875 feet on each side with a wall all around it to separate the holy places from the common.

## BIG FINISH ● ● ● • •

**43:1-9 This is the culmination of chapters 40 through 42, for God's glory returns to the Temple. It reverses the negative cast of the book and concludes all the passages dealing with the blessings reserved for the restored remnant. All true believers should long for that moment when God's name will finally be glorified once and for all.**

## CHAPTER 43 EZEKIEL RECORDS SOME RULES.

After this, the man brought me back around to the east gateway. [2]Suddenly, the glory of the God of Israel appeared from the east. The sound of his coming was like the roar of rushing waters, and the whole landscape shone with his glory. [3]This vision was just like the others I had seen, first by the Kebar River and then when he came to destroy Jerusalem. And I fell down before him with my face in the dust. [4]And the glory of the LORD came into the Temple through the east gateway.

[5]Then the Spirit took me up and brought me into the inner courtyard, and the glory of the LORD filled the Temple. [6]And I heard someone speaking to me from within the Temple. (The man who had been measuring was still standing beside me.) [7]And the LORD said to me, "Son of man, this is the place of my throne and the place where I will rest my feet. I will remain here forever, living among the people of Israel. They and their kings will not defile my holy name any longer by their adulterous worship of other gods or by raising monuments in honor of their dead kings.* [8]They put their idol altars right next to mine with only a wall between them and me. They defiled my holy name by such wickedness, so I consumed them in my anger. [9]Now let them put away their idols and the sacred pillars erected to honor their kings, and I will live among them forever.

[10]"Son of man, describe to the people of Israel the Temple I have shown you. Tell them its appearance and its plan so they will be ashamed of all their sins. [11]And if they are ashamed of what they have done, describe to them all the specifications of its construction—including its entrances and doors—and everything else about it. Write down all these specifications and directions as they watch so they will be sure to remember them. [12]And this is the basic law of the Temple: absolute holiness! The entire top of the hill where the Temple is built is holy. Yes, this is the primary law of the Temple.

[13]"These are the measurements of the altar*: There is a gutter all around the altar 21 inches wide and 21 inches deep, with a curb 9 inches* wide around its edge. And this is the height of the altar: [14]From the gutter the altar rises 3½ feet to a ledge that surrounds the altar; this lower ledge is 21 inches wide. From the lower ledge the altar rises 7 feet to the upper ledge; this upper ledge is also 21 inches wide. [15]The top of the altar, the hearth, rises still 7 feet higher, with a horn rising up from each of the four corners. [16]The top of the altar is square, measuring 21 feet by 21 feet. [17]The upper ledge also forms a square, measuring 24½ feet on each side, with a 21-inch gutter and a 10½-inch curb all around the edge. There are steps going up the east side of the altar."

[18]Then he said to me, "Son of man, this is what the Sovereign LORD says: These will be the regulations for the burning of offerings and the sprinkling of blood when the altar is built. [19]At that time, the Levitical priests of the family of Zadok, who minister before me, are to be given a young bull for a sin offering, says the Sovereign LORD. [20]You will take some of its blood and smear it on the four horns of the altar, the four corners of the upper ledge, and the curb that runs around that ledge. This will cleanse and make atonement for the altar. [21]Then take the young bull for the sin offering and burn it at the appointed place outside the Temple area.

[22]"On the second day, sacrifice as a sin offering a young male goat that has no physical defects. Then cleanse and make atonement for the altar again, just as you did with the young bull. [23]When you have finished the cleansing ceremony, offer another young bull that has no defects and a perfect ram from the flock. [24]You are to present them to the LORD, and the priests are to sprinkle salt on them and offer them as a burnt offering to the LORD.

[25]"Every day for seven days a male goat, a young bull, and a ram from the flock will be sacrificed as a sin offering. None of these animals may have physical defects of any kind. [26]Do this each day for seven days to cleanse and make atonement for the altar, thus setting it apart for holy use. [27]On the eighth day, and on each day afterward, the priests will sacrifice on the altar the burnt offerings and peace offerings of the people. Then I will accept you, says the Sovereign LORD."

## CHAPTER 44 WHAT THE PRIESTS SHOULD DO.

Then the man brought me back to the east gateway in the outer wall, but it was closed. [2]And the LORD said to me, "This gate must remain closed; it will never again be opened. No man will ever pass through it, for the LORD, the God of Israel, entered here. Thus, it

43:7 Or *by raising pillars on their high places.* 43:13a Hebrew *measurements of the altar in long cubits, each being a cubit* [18 inches or 45 centimeters] *and a handbreadth* [3 inches or 8 centimeters] *in length.* In this chapter, the distance measures are calculated using the Hebrew long cubit, which equals 21 inches or 53 centimeters. 43:13b Hebrew *1 span* [23 centimeters].

must always remain shut. 3Only the prince himself
may sit inside this gateway to feast in the LORD's
presence. But he may come and go only through the
gateway's foyer."

4Then the man brought me through the north gateway to the front of the Temple. I looked and saw that
the glory of the LORD filled the Temple of the LORD,
and I fell to the ground with my face in the dust.

5And the LORD said to me, "Son of man, take
careful notice; use your eyes and ears. Listen to everything I tell you about the regulations concerning the
LORD's Temple. Take careful note of who may be
admitted to the Temple and who is to be excluded
from it. 6And give these rebels, the people of Israel,
this message from the Sovereign LORD: O people of
Israel, enough of your disgusting sins! 7You have
brought uncircumcised foreigners into my sanctuary—people who have no heart for God. In this way,
you profaned my Temple even as you offered me my
food, the fat and blood of sacrifices. Thus, in addition to all your other disgusting sins, you have broken my covenant. 8You have not kept the laws I gave
you concerning these sacred rituals, for you have
hired foreigners to take charge of my sanctuary.

9"So this is what the Sovereign LORD says: No
foreigners, including those who live among the
people of Israel, will enter my sanctuary if they have
not been circumcised and do not love the LORD.
10And the men of the tribe of Levi who abandoned
me when Israel strayed away from me to worship
idols must bear the consequences of their unfaithfulness. 11They may still be Temple guards and gatemen,
and they may still slaughter the animals brought for
burnt offerings and be present to help the people.
12But they encouraged my people to worship other
gods, causing Israel to fall into deep sin. So I have
raised my hand and taken an oath that they must
bear the consequences for their sins, says the Sovereign LORD. 13They may not approach me to minister
as priests. They may not touch any of my holy things
or the holy offerings, for they must bear the shame
of all the sins they have committed. 14They are to
serve as the Temple caretakers and are relegated to
doing maintenance work and helping the people in
a general way.

15"However, the Levitical priests of the family of
Zadok continued to minister faithfully in the Temple
when Israel abandoned me for idols. These men will
serve as my ministers. They will stand in my presence
and offer the fat and blood of the sacrifices, says the
Sovereign LORD. 16They are the ones who will enter
my sanctuary and approach my table to serve me.
They are the ones who will fulfill all my requirements. 17When they enter the gateway to the inner
courtyard, they must wear only linen clothing. They
must wear no wool while on duty in the inner courtyard or in the Temple itself. 18They must wear linen
turbans and linen undergarments. They must not
wear anything that would cause them to perspire.
19When they return to the outer courtyard where the
people are, they must take off the clothes they wear
while ministering to me. They must leave them in
the sacred rooms and put on other clothes so they do
not harm the people by transmitting holiness to
them through this clothing.

20"They must neither let their hair grow too long
nor shave it off completely. Instead, they must trim
it regularly. 21The priests must never drink wine before entering the inner courtyard. 22They may choose
their wives only from among the virgins of Israel or
the widows of the priests. They may not marry other
widows or divorced women. 23They will teach my
people the difference between what is holy and what
is common, what is ceremonially clean and unclean.

24"They will serve as judges to resolve any disagreements among my people. Their decisions must be
based on my regulations. And the priests themselves
must obey my instructions and laws at all the sacred
festivals, and they will see to it that the Sabbath is set
apart as a holy day. 25A priest must never defile himself
by being in the presence of a dead person unless it is
his father, mother, child, brother, or unmarried sister.
In such cases it is permitted. 26But such a priest can
only return to his Temple duties after being ritually
cleansed and then waiting for seven days. 27The first
day he returns to work and enters the inner courtyard
and the sanctuary, he must offer a sin offering for
himself, says the Sovereign LORD.

28"As to property, the priests will not have any, for
I alone am their inheritance. 29Their food will come
from the gifts and sacrifices brought to the Temple
by the people—the grain offerings, the sin offerings,
and the guilt offerings. Whatever anyone sets apart*
for the LORD will belong to the priests. 30The first of
the ripe fruits and all the gifts brought to the LORD
will go to the priests. The first samples of each grain
harvest and the first of your flour must also be given
to the priests so the LORD will bless your homes.
31The priests may never eat meat from any bird or
animal that dies a natural death or that dies after
being attacked by another animal.

CHAPTER **45** **SOME LAND FOR THE LORD.** "When
you divide the land among the tribes of Israel, you
must set aside a section of it for the LORD as his holy
portion. This piece of land will be 8⅓ miles long and
6⅔ miles wide.* The entire area will be holy ground.
2A section of this land, measuring 875 feet by 875
feet, will be set aside for the Temple. An additional
strip of land 87½ feet wide is to be left empty all
around it. 3Within the larger sacred area, measure
out a portion of land 8⅓ miles long and 3⅓ miles
wide. Within it the sanctuary of the Most Holy Place
will be located. 4This area will be a holy land, set

**44:29** The Hebrew term used here refers to the complete consecration of things or people to the LORD, either by destroying them or by giving them as an offering. **45:1** Reflecting the Greek reading *25,000 cubits* [13.3 kilometers] *long and 20,000 cubits* [10.6 kilometers] *wide;* Hebrew reads *25,000 cubits long and 10,000 cubits wide.* Compare 45:3, 5; 48:9. In this chapter, the distance measures are calculated using the Hebrew long cubit, which equals 21 inches or 53 centimeters.

aside for the priests who minister to the LORD in the sanctuary. They will use it for their homes, and my Temple will be located within it. [5]The strip of sacred land next to it, also 8⅓ miles long and 3⅓ miles wide, will be a living area for the Levites who work at the Temple. It will be their possession and a place for their towns.*

[6]"Adjacent to the larger sacred area will be a section of land 8⅓ miles long and 1⅔ miles wide. This will be set aside to be a city where anyone in Israel can come and live.

[7]"Two special sections of land will be set apart for the prince. One section will share a border with the east side of the sacred lands and city, and the second section will share a border on the west side. Then the far eastern and western borders of the prince's lands will line up with the eastern and western boundaries of the tribal areas. [8]These sections of land will be the prince's allotment.

"My princes will no longer oppress and rob my people; they will assign the rest of the land to the people, giving an allotment to each tribe. [9]For this is what the Sovereign LORD says: Enough, you princes of Israel! Stop all your violence and oppression and do what is just and right. Quit robbing and cheating my people out of their land! Stop expelling them from their homes! [10]You must use only honest weights and scales, honest dry volume measures, and honest liquid volume measures.* [11]The homer* will be your standard unit for measuring volume. The ephah and the bath* will each measure one-tenth of a homer. [12]The standard unit for weight will be the silver shekel.* One shekel consists of twenty gerahs, and sixty shekels are equal to one mina.*

**HONESTY ● ● • • •**

**45:9-12 Greed and extortion were two of the major social sins of the nation during this time (see Amos 5:7-13). In the new economy there would be plenty of land for the "princes" (45:7-8) and no longer any basis for greed. Therefore, the princes and the people were commanded to be fair and honest, especially when they did business. Consider the ways you measure goods, money, or services. If you are paid for an hour of work, be sure you work for a full hour. If you sell a bushel of apples, make sure it is a full bushel. God is completely trustworthy, and his followers should be too.**

[13]"This is the tax you must give to the prince: one bushel of wheat or barley for every sixty* you harvest, [14]one percent of your olive oil,* [15]and one sheep for every two hundred in your flocks in Israel. These will be the grain offerings, burnt offerings, and peace offerings that will make atonement for the people who bring them, says the Sovereign LORD. [16]All the people of Israel must join the prince in bringing their offerings. [17]The prince will be required to provide offerings that are given at the religious festivals, the new moon celebrations, the Sabbath days, and all other similar occasions. He will provide the sin offerings, burnt offerings, grain offerings, drink offerings, and peace offerings to make reconciliation for the people of Israel.

[18]"This is what the Sovereign LORD says: In early spring, on the first day of each new year,* sacrifice a young bull with no physical defects to purify the Temple. [19]The priest will take some of the blood of this sin offering and put it on the doorposts of the Temple, the four corners of the upper ledge on the altar, and the gateposts at the entrance to the inner courtyard. [20]Do this also on the seventh day of the new year for anyone who has sinned through error or ignorance. In that way, you will make atonement for the Temple.

[21]"On the fourteenth day of the new year, you must celebrate the Passover. This festival will last for seven days. Only bread without yeast may be eaten during that time. [22]On the day of Passover the prince will provide a young bull as a sin offering for himself and the people of Israel. [23]On each of the seven days of the feast he will prepare a burnt offering to the LORD. This daily offering will consist of seven young bulls and seven rams without any defects. A male goat will also be given each day for a sin offering. [24]The prince will provide a half bushel of flour as a grain offering and a gallon of olive oil* with each young bull and ram.

[25]"During the seven days of the Festival of Shelters, which occurs every year in early autumn,* the prince will provide these same sacrifices for the sin offering, the burnt offering, and the grain offering, along with the required olive oil.

## CHAPTER 46

**SPECIAL OFFERINGS.** "This is what the Sovereign LORD says: The east gateway of the inner wall will be closed during the six workdays each week, but it will be open on Sabbath days and the days of new moon celebrations. [2]The prince will enter the foyer of the gateway from the outside. Then he will stand by the gatepost while the priest offers his burnt offering and peace offering. He will worship inside the gateway passage and then go back out the way he came. The gateway will not be closed until evening. [3]The common people will worship the LORD in front of this gateway on Sabbath days and the days of new moon celebrations.

**RHYTHM ● ● • • •**

**46:1-15 Ezekiel continues to describe various aspects of daily worship. While allowing for diversity in worship, God has prescribed order and continuity. This gave a healthy rhythm to the spiritual life of his people.**

**45:5** As in Greek version; Hebrew reads *They will have as their possession 20 rooms.* **45:10** Hebrew *use honest scales, an honest ephah, and an honest bath.* **45:11a** The *homer* measures about 40 gallons or 182 liters. **45:11b** The *ephah* is a dry measure; the *bath* is a liquid measure. **45:12a** The shekel weighs about 0.4 ounces or 11 grams. **45:12b** Elsewhere the mina is equated to 50 shekels. **45:13** Hebrew *1/6 of an ephah from each homer of wheat . . . and of barley.* **45:14** Hebrew *the portion of oil, measured by the bath, is 1/10 of a bath from each cor, which consists of 10 baths or 1 homer, for 10 baths are equivalent to a homer.* **45:18** Hebrew *On the first day of the first month,* of the Hebrew calendar. This day of the Hebrew lunar calendar occurs in late March or early April. **45:24** Hebrew *an ephah* [18 liters] *of flour . . . a hin* [3.8 liters] *of olive oil.* **45:25** Hebrew *the festival which begins on the fifteenth day of the seventh month* (see Lev 23:33). This day of the Hebrew lunar calendar occurs in late September or October.

4"Each Sabbath day the prince will present to the LORD a burnt offering of six lambs and one ram, all with no physical defects. 5He will present a grain offering of a half bushel of flour to go with the ram and whatever amount of flour he chooses to go with each lamb. He is to offer one gallon of olive oil* for each half bushel of flour. 6At the new moon celebrations, he will bring one young bull, six lambs, and one ram, all with no physical defects. 7With the young bull he must bring a half bushel of flour for a grain offering. With the ram he must bring another half bushel of flour. And with each lamb he is to bring whatever amount of flour that he decides to give. With each half bushel of flour he must offer one gallon of olive oil.

8"The prince must enter the gateway through the foyer, and he must leave the same way he came. 9But when the people come in through the north gateway to worship the LORD during the religious festivals, they must leave by the south gateway. And those who entered through the south gateway must leave by the north gateway. They must never leave by the same gateway they came in; they must always use the opposite gateway. 10The prince will enter and leave with the people on these occasions.

11"So at the special feasts and sacred festivals, the grain offering will be a half bushel of flour with each young bull, another half bushel of flour with each ram, and as much flour as the prince chooses to give with each lamb. One gallon of oil is to be given with each half bushel of flour. 12Whenever the prince offers a voluntary burnt offering or peace offering to the LORD, the east gateway to the inner courtyard will be opened for him to enter, and he will offer his sacrifices just as he does on Sabbath days. Then he will turn and leave the way he entered, and the gateway will be shut behind him.

13"Each morning a year-old lamb with no physical defects must be sacrificed as a burnt offering to the LORD. 14With the lamb, a grain offering must also be given to the LORD—about two and a half quarts of flour with a third of a gallon of olive oil* to moisten the flour. This will be a permanent law for you. 15The lamb, the grain offering, and the olive oil must be given as a daily sacrifice every morning without fail.

16"This is what the Sovereign LORD says: If the prince gives a gift of land to one of his sons, it will belong to him and his descendants forever. 17But if he gives a gift of land to one of his servants, the servant may keep it only until the Year of Jubilee, which comes every fiftieth year.* At that time the servant will be set free, and the land will return to the prince. Only the gifts given to the prince's sons will be permanent. 18And the prince may never take anyone's property by force. If he gives property to his sons, it must be from his own land, for I do not want any of my people unjustly evicted from their property."

19Then the man brought me through the entrance beside the gateway and led me to the sacred rooms assigned to the priests, which faced toward the north. He showed me a place at the extreme west end of these rooms. 20He explained, "This is where the priests will cook the meat from the guilt offerings and sin offerings and bake the flour from the grain offerings into bread. They will do it here to avoid carrying the sacrifices through the outer courtyard and harming the people by transmitting holiness to them."

21Then he brought me back to the outer courtyard and led me to each of its four corners. In each corner I saw an enclosure. 22Each of these enclosures was 70 feet long and 52½ feet wide,* surrounded by walls. 23Along the inside of these walls was a ledge of stone with fireplaces under the ledge all the way around. 24The man said to me, "These are the kitchens to be used by the Temple assistants to boil the sacrifices offered by the people."

CHAPTER **47** **THE RIVER OF HEALING.** Then the man brought me back to the entrance of the Temple. There I saw a stream flowing eastward from beneath the Temple threshold. This stream then passed to the right of the altar on its south side. 2The man brought me outside the wall through the north gateway and led me around to the eastern entrance. There I could see the stream flowing out through the south side of the east gateway. 3Measuring as he went, he led me along the stream for 1,750 feet* and told me to go across. At that point the water was up to my ankles. 4He measured off another 1,750 feet and told me to go across again. This time the water was up to my knees. After another 1,750 feet, it was up to my waist. 5Then he measured another 1,750 feet, and the river was too deep to cross without swimming.

6He told me to keep in mind what I had seen; then he led me back along the riverbank. 7Suddenly, to my surprise, many trees were now growing on both sides of the river! 8Then he said to me, "This river flows east through the desert into the Jordan Valley,* where it enters the Dead Sea.* The waters of this

**SAFE RIVER ● ● • • •**

47:1-12 **This river (or stream) is similar to the river mentioned in Revelation 22:1-2, both of which are associated with the river in the Garden of Eden (see Genesis 2:10). It is a gentle, safe, deep river that expands as it flows and brings life to all it touches. This is one of the images the Bible gives us of heaven: health and well-being for all who love God. When you or someone you know faces illness or other undeserved suffering, remember this wonderful picture of God's healing power.**

46:5 Hebrew *an ephah* [18 liters] *of flour . . . a hin* [3.8 liters] *of olive oil;* also in 46:7, 11. **46:14** Hebrew *1/6 of an ephah* [2.9 liters] *of flour with 1/3 of a hin* [1.3 liters] *of olive oil.* **46:17** Hebrew *until the Year of Release;* see Lev 25:8-17. **46:22** Hebrew *40 cubits* [21.2 meters] *long and 30 cubits* [15.9 meters] *wide.* The distances are calculated using the Hebrew long cubit, which equals 21 inches or 53 centimeters. **47:3** Hebrew *1,000 cubits* [530 meters]; also in 47:4, 5. The distances are calculated using the Hebrew long cubit, which equals 21 inches or 53 centimeters. **47:8a** Hebrew *the Arabah.* **47:8b** Hebrew *the sea;* also in 47:10.

## THE PRESENCE ● ● ● • •

48:1-35 **The book of Ezekiel begins by describing the holiness of God, which Israel had despised and ignored. As a result, God's presence had departed from the Temple, the city, and the people. The book ends with a detailed vision of the new Temple, the new city, and the new people—all demonstrating God's holiness. The pressures of everyday life can persuade us to focus on the here and now and thus forget God. That is why worship is so important; it takes our eyes off our current worries, gives us a glimpse of God's holiness, and allows us to look toward his future kingdom. God's presence makes everything glorious, and worship brings us into his presence.**

stream will heal the salty waters of the Dead Sea and make them fresh and pure. 9Everything that touches the water of this river will live. Fish will abound in the Dead Sea, for its waters will be healed. Wherever this water flows, everything will live. 10Fishermen will stand along the shores of the Dead Sea, fishing all the way from En-gedi to En-eglaim. The shores will be covered with nets drying in the sun. Fish of every kind will fill the Dead Sea, just as they fill the Mediterranean*! 11But the marshes and swamps will not be purified; they will be sources of salt. 12All kinds of fruit trees will grow along both sides of the river. The leaves of these trees will never turn brown and fall, and there will always be fruit on their branches. There will be a new crop every month, without fail! For they are watered by the river flowing from the Temple. The fruit will be for food and the leaves for healing."

13This is what the Sovereign LORD says: "Follow these instructions for dividing the land for the twelve tribes of Israel: The tribe of Joseph will be given two shares of land.* 14Otherwise each tribe will receive an equal share. I swore that I would give this land to your ancestors, and it will now come to you as your inheritance.

15"The northern border will run from the Mediterranean toward Hethlon, then on through Lebo-hamath to Zedad; 16then it will run to Berothah and Sibraim, which are on the border between Damascus and Hamath, and finally to Hazer-hatticon, on the border of Hauran. 17So the northern border will run from the Mediterranean to Hazar-enan, on the border between Hamath to the north and Damascus to the south.

18"The eastern border starts at a point between Hauran and Damascus and runs southward along the Jordan River between Israel and Gilead, past the Dead Sea* and as far south as Tamar.* This will be the eastern border.

19"The southern border will go west from Tamar to the waters of Meribah at Kadesh* and then follow the course of the brook of Egypt to the Mediterranean. This will be the southern border.

20"On the west side the Mediterranean itself will be your border from the southern border to the point where the northern border begins, opposite Lebo-hamath.

21"Divide the land within these boundaries among the tribes of Israel. 22Distribute the land as an inheritance for yourselves and for the foreigners who have joined you and are raising their families among you. They will be just like native-born Israelites to you, and they will receive an inheritance among the tribes. 23All these immigrants are to be given land within the territory of the tribe with whom they now live. I, the Sovereign LORD, have spoken!

## CHAPTER 48

**THE LAND IS DIVIDED.** "Here is the list of the tribes of Israel and the territory each is to receive. The territory of Dan is in the extreme north. Its boundary line follows the Hethlon road to Lebo-hamath and then runs on to Hazar-enan on the border of Damascus, with Hamath to the north. Dan's territory extends all the way across the land of Israel from east to west. 2Asher's territory lies south of Dan's and also extends from east to west. 3Naphtali's land lies south of Asher's, also extending from east to west. 4Then comes Manasseh south of Naphtali, and its territory also extends from east to west. 5South of Manasseh is Ephraim, 6and then Reuben, 7and then Judah, all of whose boundaries extend from east to west.

8"South of Judah is the land set aside for a special purpose. It will be 8⅓ miles wide and will extend as far east and west as the tribal territories, with the Temple at the center.

9"The area set aside for the LORD's Temple will be 8⅓ miles long and 6⅔ miles wide.* 10For the priests there will be a strip of land measuring 8⅓ miles long by 3⅓ miles wide, with the LORD's Temple at the center. 11This area is set aside for the ordained priests, the descendants of Zadok who obeyed me and did not go astray when the people of Israel and the rest of the Levites did. 12It will be their special portion when the land is distributed, the most sacred land of all. Next to the priests' territory will lie the land where the other Levites will live. 13The land allotted to the Levites will be the same size and shape as that belonging to the priests—8⅓ miles long and 3⅓ miles wide. Together these portions of land will measure 8⅓ miles long by 6⅔ miles wide.* 14None of this special land will ever be sold or traded or used by others, for it belongs to the LORD; it is set apart as holy.

15"An additional strip of land 8⅓ miles long by 1⅔ miles wide, south of the sacred Temple area, will be allotted for public use—homes, pasturelands, and common lands, with a city at the center. 16The city will measure 1½ miles* on each side. 17Open

**47:10** Hebrew *the great sea;* also in 47:15, 17, 19, 20. **47:13** A share of land for each of Joseph's two oldest sons, Ephraim and Manasseh. **47:18a** Hebrew *the eastern sea.* **47:18b** As in Greek version; Hebrew reads *you will measure.* **47:19** Hebrew *waters of Meribah-kadesh.* **48:9** Reflecting the Greek reading in 45:1: *25,000 cubits* [13.3 kilometers] *long and 20,000 cubits* [10.6 kilometers] *wide;* Hebrew reads *25,000 cubits long and 10,000 cubits wide.* Compare 45:1-5; 48:10-13. In this chapter, the distance measures are calculated using the Hebrew long cubit, which equals 21 inches or 53 centimeters. **48:13** See note on 48:9. **48:16** Hebrew *4,500 cubits* [2.4 kilometers]; also in 48:30, 32, 33, 34.

lands will surround the city for 150 yards* in every direction. 18 Outside the city there will be a farming area that stretches 3⅓ miles to the east and 3⅓ miles to the west along the border of the sacred area. This farmland will produce food for the people working in the city. 19 Those who come from the various tribes to work in the city may farm it. 20 This entire area—including the sacred lands and the city—is a square that measures 8⅓ miles on each side.

21 "The areas that remain, to the east and to the west of the sacred lands and the city, will belong to the prince. Each of these areas will be 8⅓ miles wide, extending in opposite directions to the eastern and western borders of Israel. 22 So the prince's land will include everything between the territories allotted to Judah and Benjamin, except for the areas set aside for the sacred lands and the city.

23 "These are the territories allotted to the rest of the tribes. Benjamin's territory lies just south of the prince's lands, and it extends across the entire land of Israel from east to west. 24 South of Benjamin's territory lies that of Simeon, also extending across the land from east to west. 25 Next is the territory of Issachar with the same eastern and western boundaries. 26 Then comes the territory of Zebulun, which also extends across the land from east to west. 27 The territory of Gad is just south of Zebulun with the same borders to the east and west. 28 The southern border of Gad runs from Tamar to the waters of Meribah at Kadesh* and then follows the brook of Egypt to the Mediterranean.* 29 These are the allotments that will be set aside for each tribe's inheritance, says the Sovereign LORD.

30 "These will be the exits to the city: On the north wall, which is 1½ miles long, 31 there will be three gates, each one named after a tribe of Israel. The first will be named for Reuben, the second for Judah, and the third for Levi. 32 On the east wall, also 1½ miles long, the gates will be named for Joseph, Benjamin, and Dan. 33 The south wall, also 1½ miles long, will have gates named for Simeon, Issachar, and Zebulun. 34 And on the west wall, also 1½ miles long, the gates will be named for Gad, Asher, and Naphtali.

35 "The distance around the entire city will be six miles.* And from that day the name of the city will be 'The LORD Is There.'* "

**48:17** Hebrew *250 cubits* [133 meters]. **48:28a** Hebrew *waters of Meribath-kadesh.* **48:28b** Hebrew *the great sea.* **48:35a** Hebrew *18,000 cubits* [9.6 kilometers]. **48:35b** Hebrew *Yahweh Shammah.*

# MEGA themes

**GOD'S HOLINESS** Ezekiel wrote of his vision revealing God's moral perfection. God was spiritually and morally superior to Israel's corrupt and compromising society. Ezekiel also wrote to let the people know that God was present with them in Babylon, not just in Jerusalem.

Because God is morally perfect, he can help us live above our tendency to compromise. He can give us the power to overcome sin and to reflect his holiness. Moral purity is an important part of Christian discipleship.

1. List some of the key visions God gave to Ezekiel. How did Ezekiel respond to these visions?
2. What did these visions have to say about God?
3. Why were the messages of these visions so important for the people during their captivity?
4. Why is moral purity important for any person who wants to glorify God?

**SIN** Israel sinned, so God punished them. The fall of Jerusalem and the Babylonian exile were used by God to correct the rebels and draw them back from their sinful way of life. Ezekiel warned them that not only was the nation responsible for sin, but each individual was also accountable to God.

We cannot excuse ourselves from our responsibilities before God. We are accountable to him. Rather than avoid God, we must recognize sin for what it is—rebellion against God—and choose to follow him instead.

1. What sins had the people committed?
2. What do you think was God's purpose for punishing the people like he did?
3. How did God want individuals to respond to his warnings and punishments? How did he want the nation to respond?
4. How has God specifically dealt with sin in your life? How have you responded?

**RESTORATION** Ezekiel consoled the people by telling them that the day would come when God would restore those who turn away from sin. God would be their King and Shepherd. He would give his people a new heart to worship him and establish a new government and a new Temple.

Knowing that they will eventually be rescued and restored should encourage believers during difficult times. But we must be faithful to God because we love him, not for what he can do for us. Our faith must be in *him,* not in possible future benefits.

1. What qualities of God do you see revealed in his promise of restoration?
2. Suppose you had a friend who was a Christian yet had chosen to be deeply involved in a continuous habit of sin. What would you tell this friend about God's restoration as an encouragement to turn from sin and to God?
3. In what ways can you continue to seek and experience God's restoration on a daily basis?

**LEADERS** Ezekiel condemned the unfaithful priests and leaders ("shepherds") who led the people astray. By contrast, Ezekiel was a caring shepherd and a watchful sentry as he warned the people about their sin.

Jesus is our perfect leader. If we truly want him to lead us, our devotion must be more than talk. If we are given the responsibility of leading others, we must take care of them even if it means sacrificing personal pleasure, happiness, time, or money. We are responsible to God for witnessing to and teaching those we lead.

1. Contrast Ezekiel as a man of God and leader of the people with the Hebrews' priests and leaders who led them away from God.
2. What qualities does Jesus have that make him the greatest of all leaders? Which of these qualities did Ezekiel have?

3. Based on this study, what are the most important qualities of a godly leader? Why?
4. Like Ezekiel, we are to reflect godly qualities. We have Jesus' perfect example as well as the example of people like Ezekiel. If someone were to examine your life, what would that person see that reflects the qualities of Jesus?
5. Complete this sentence: "In order to be the most effective I can be in leading others to God, I want to grow more like Jesus in the area of ________." Commit to God the choice you intend to make in order to develop in this area.

**WORSHIP** An angel gave Ezekiel a detailed vision of the Temple. God's holy presence had left Israel and the Temple because of sin. This ideal Temple pictures the return of God's presence when God will cleanse his people and restore true worship.

All of God's promises will be fulfilled under the rule of the Messiah. The faithful followers will be brought back to perfect fellowship with God and with one another. To prepare for this, we must focus on God through regular worship, learning about God's holiness, and making needed changes in our life.

1. What was the role of the Temple in the Hebrew worship during Ezekiel's lifetime?
2. Describe your worship of God in the past week (where, how, attitudes, thoughts, feelings, individual or with others, etc.).
3. Evaluate your worship of God in the past week (value, importance, strengths and weaknesses, things you would change).

**612 B.C.**
**Habakkuk becomes a prophet to Judah**

**609**
**Jehoiakim becomes king of Judah**

**605**
**Daniel taken captive to Babylon**

**600?**
**Daniel becomes a Babylonian official; fiery furnace**

**597**
**Nebuchadnezzar takes more captives**

**593**
**Ezekiel becomes a prophet to exiles**

**586**
**Judah falls; Jerusalem is destroyed; Jeremiah's ministry ends**

**562**
**Nebuchadnezzar dies**

**553**
**Daniel's first vision**

**539**
**Babylon overthrown; Daniel thrown to lions**

**538**
**First exiles return to Judah**

**536**
**Daniel's ministry ends**

Courage is . . . risking injury to help a friend . . . doing what is right against all odds . . . standing for the truth despite the consequences . . . living for God, no matter what. ■ Daniel had courage. Living in a foreign land, he stood for what he believed and did what was right, in spite of incredible pressure from society, from peers, and from the government. And courage was Daniel's trademark throughout his life and through the reigns of four kings. He boldly interpreted dreams, rejected royal food and drink, and publicly lived his faith. Daniel was a man of great courage and faith in God. ■ God still needs men and women of courage and faith. What kinds of risks do you face? What kinds of pressures do you feel to conform or to turn away from God? ■ As you read the book of Daniel, marvel at the man who refused to give in or give up. Ask God to give you the courage to live out your faith, like Daniel did, as you develop a stronger relationship with "the God of gods" (2:47).

## STATS

PURPOSE: To give a historical account of the faithful Jews who lived in captivity and to show how God is in control of heaven and earth, directing the forces of nature, the destiny of nations, and the care of his people

AUTHOR: Daniel

TO WHOM WRITTEN: The other captives in Babylon and God's people everywhere

DATE WRITTEN: Approximately 535 B.C., recording events that occurred from about 605 to 535 B.C.

SETTING: Daniel had been taken captive and deported to Babylon by Nebuchadnezzar in 605 B.C. There he served in the government for about 60 years during the reigns of Nebuchadnezzar, Belshazzar, Darius, and Cyrus.

KEY PEOPLE: Daniel, Nebuchadnezzar, Shadrach, Meshach, Abednego, Belshazzar, Darius

KEY PLACES: Nebuchadnezzar's palace, the fiery furnace, Belshazzar's banquet, the den of lions

SPECIAL FEATURES: Daniel's apocalyptic visions (chapters 8–12) give a glimpse of God's plan for the ages, including a direct prediction of the Messiah

CHAPTER **1** **DANIEL WON'T EAT THE KING'S FOOD.** During the third year of King Jehoiakim's reign in
Judah,* King Nebuchadnezzar of Babylon came to
Jerusalem and besieged it with his armies. 2The Lord
gave him victory over King Jehoiakim of Judah.
When Nebuchadnezzar returned to Babylon, he
took with him some of the sacred objects from the
Temple of God and placed them in the treasure-
house of his god in the land of Babylonia.*

3Then the king ordered Ashpenaz, who was in
charge of the palace officials, to bring to the palace
some of the young men of Judah's royal family and
other noble families, who had been brought to Babylon as captives. 4"Select only strong, healthy, and
good-looking young men," he said. "Make sure they
are well versed in every branch of learning, are gifted
with knowledge and good sense, and have the poise
needed to serve in the royal palace. Teach these
young men the language and literature of the Babylonians.*" 5The king assigned them a daily ration
of the best food and wine from his own kitchens.
They were to be trained for a three-year period, and
then some of them would be made his advisers in
the royal court.

6Daniel, Hananiah, Mishael, and Azariah were
four of the young men chosen, all from the tribe of
Judah. 7The chief official renamed them with these
Babylonian names:

Daniel was called Belteshazzar.
Hananiah was called Shadrach.
Mishael was called Meshach.
Azariah was called Abednego.

8But Daniel made up his mind not to defile himself by eating the food and wine given to them by the
king. He asked the chief official for permission to eat
other things instead. 9Now God had given the chief
official great respect for Daniel. 10But he was alarmed
by Daniel's suggestion. "My lord the king has ordered that you eat this food and wine," he said. "If

**TEMPTATION ● ● • • •**

1:8 **It is easier to resist temptation if you have thought through your convictions well before the temptation arises. Daniel and his friends made their decision to be faithful to the laws of their religion before they were faced with the king's delicacies, so they did not hesitate to stick with their convictions. Sometimes we get into trouble because we have not previously decided where to draw the line. Before such situations arise, decide on your commitments. Then, when temptation comes, you will be ready.**

1:1 The third year of Jehoiakim's reign, according to the Hebrew system of reckoning, was 605 B.C. 1:2 Hebrew *the land of Shinar.* 1:4 Or *of the Chaldeans.*

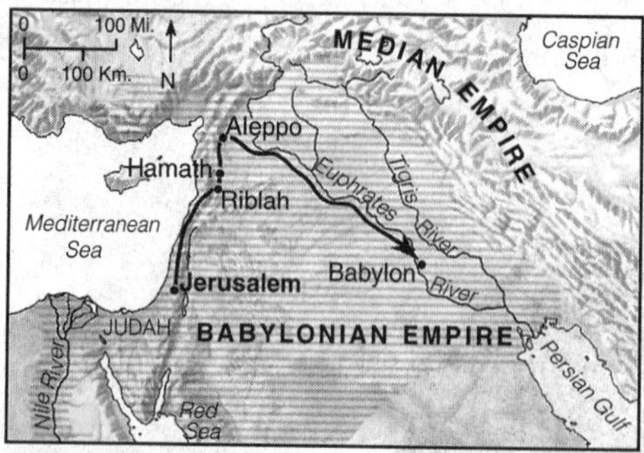


**TAKEN TO BABYLON**
Daniel, as a captive of Babylonian soldiers, faced a long and difficult march to a new land. The five-hundred-mile trek, mostly under harsh conditions, certainly tested Daniel's faith in God.

you become pale and thin compared to the other youths your age, I am afraid the king will have me beheaded for neglecting my duties."

[11]Daniel talked it over with the attendant who had been appointed by the chief official to look after Daniel, Hananiah, Mishael, and Azariah. [12]"Test us for ten days on a diet of vegetables and water," Daniel said. [13]"At the end of the ten days, see how we look compared to the other young men who are eating the king's rich food. Then you can decide whether or not to let us continue eating our diet." [14]So the attendant agreed to Daniel's suggestion and tested them for ten days.

## ALLEGIANCE ● ● • • •

1:17 **Daniel and his friends learned all they could about their new culture so they could do their work with excellence. But while they learned, they maintained steadfast allegiance to God. Culture need not be God's enemy. If it does not violate his commands, it can aid in accomplishing his purpose. We who follow God are free to be leaders in our culture, but we must put our allegiance to God first.**

[15]At the end of the ten days, Daniel and his three friends looked healthier and better nourished than the young men who had been eating the food assigned by the king. [16]So after that, the attendant fed them only vegetables instead of the rich foods and wines. [17]God gave these four young men an unusual aptitude for learning the literature and science of the time. And God gave Daniel special ability in understanding the meanings of visions and dreams.

[18]When the three-year training period ordered by the king was completed, the chief official brought all the young men to King Nebuchadnezzar. [19]The king talked with each of them, and none of them impressed him as much as Daniel, Hananiah, Mishael, and Azariah. So they were appointed to his regular staff of advisers. [20]In all matters requiring wisdom and balanced judgment, the king found the advice of these young men to be ten times better than that of all the magicians and enchanters in his entire kingdom.

[21]Daniel remained there until the first year of King Cyrus's reign.*

## CHAPTER 2 DANIEL DESCRIBES THE KING'S DREAM.

One night during the second year of his reign,* Nebuchadnezzar had a dream that disturbed him so much that he couldn't sleep. [2]He called in his magicians, enchanters, sorcerers, and astrologers,* and he demanded that they tell him what he had dreamed. As they stood before the king, [3]he said, "I have had a dream that troubles me. Tell me what I dreamed, for I must know what it means."

[4]Then the astrologers answered the king in Aramaic,* "Long live the king! Tell us the dream, and we will tell you what it means."

[5]But the king said to the astrologers, "I am serious about this. If you don't tell me what my dream was and what it means, you will be torn limb from limb, and your houses will be demolished into heaps of rubble! [6]But if you tell me what I dreamed and what the dream means, I will give you many wonderful gifts and honors. Just tell me the dream and what it means!"

[7]They said again, "Please, Your Majesty. Tell us the dream, and we will tell you what it means."

[8]The king replied, "I can see through your trick! You are trying to stall for time because you know I am serious about what I said. [9]If you don't tell me the dream, you will be condemned. You have conspired to tell me lies in hopes that something will change. But tell me the dream, and then I will know that you can tell me what it means."

[10]The astrologers replied to the king, "There isn't a man alive who can tell Your Majesty his dream! And no king, however great and powerful, has ever asked such a thing of any magician, enchanter, or astrologer! [11]This is an impossible thing the king requires. No one except the gods can tell you your dream, and they do not live among people."

[12]The king was furious when he heard this, and he sent out orders to execute all the wise men of Babylon. [13]And because of the king's decree, men were sent to find and kill Daniel and his friends. [14]When Arioch, the commander of the king's guard, came to kill them, Daniel handled the situation with wisdom and discretion. [15]He asked Arioch, "Why has the king issued such a harsh decree?" So Arioch told him all that had happened. [16]Daniel went at once to see

## IMPOSSIBLE ● ● • • •

2:11 **The Chaldeans told the king that no one could know the dreams of another person. But Daniel was able to give the answer because God was working through him. In daily life, we face many apparently impossible situations that would be hopeless if we had to handle them with limited human strength alone. But God specializes in the impossible.**

1:21 The first year of Cyrus's reign was 538 B.C. 2:1 The second year of Nebuchadnezzar's reign was 603 B.C. 2:2 Or *Chaldeans;* also in 2:4, 5, 10. 2:4 The original text from this point through chapter 7 is in Aramaic.

the king and requested more time so he could tell
the king what the dream meant.
[17]Then Daniel went home and told his friends
Hananiah, Mishael, and Azariah what had happened. [18]He urged them to ask the God of heaven to
show them his mercy by telling them the secret, so
they would not be executed along with the other
wise men of Babylon. [19]That night the secret was
revealed to Daniel in a vision. Then Daniel praised
the God of heaven, [20]saying,

"Praise the name of God forever and ever,
for he alone has all wisdom and power.
[21] He determines the course of world events;
he removes kings and sets others on the
throne.
He gives wisdom to the wise
and knowledge to the
scholars.
[22] He reveals deep and
mysterious things
and knows what lies
hidden in darkness,
though he himself is
surrounded by light.
[23] I thank and praise you,
God of my
ancestors,
for you have given
me wisdom and
strength.
You have told me what
we asked of you
and revealed to us
what the king
demanded."

[24]Then Daniel went in to
see Arioch, who had been
ordered to execute the wise
men of Babylon. Daniel said
to him, "Don't kill the wise
men. Take me to the king,
and I will tell him the meaning of his dream."
[25]Then Arioch quickly
took Daniel to the king and
said, "I have found one of
the captives from Judah who
will tell Your Majesty the
meaning of your dream!"
[26]The king said to Daniel
(also known as Belteshaz-
zar), "Is this true? Can you
tell me what my dream was
and what it means?"
[27]Daniel replied, "There
are no wise men, enchanters,
magicians, or fortune-tellers
who can tell the king such
things. [28]But there is a God in
heaven who reveals secrets,
and he has shown King Nebuchadnezzar what will
happen in the future. Now I will tell you your dream
and the visions you saw as you lay on your bed.
[29]"While Your Majesty was sleeping, you dreamed
about coming events. The revealer of mysteries has
shown you what is going to happen. [30]And it is not
because I am wiser than any living person that I know
the secret of your dream, but because God wanted you
to understand what you were thinking about.

### ROBBING GOD ● ● • • •

2:27-30 **Before Daniel told the king anything else, he gave credit to God, explaining that he did not know the dream through his own wisdom but only because God revealed it. How easily we take credit for what God does through us! This robs God of the honor that is due him.**

## DANIEL

Daniel's early life shows us there is more to being young than making mistakes. Adults can't help being impressed whenever a young person speaks and acts wisely. Those were Daniel's strongest personal traits—wise words and actions. He spoke the truth and did the right thing, even when it looked like he was the only one doing it. Have you ever noticed how often life's biggest mistakes begin with this thought: *I can do this because everybody else is doing it?*

One example of Daniel's wisdom is the way he held on to his convictions. He didn't give in to pressure. His habits and convictions came from God's Word, and pleasing God was more important to Daniel than pleasing anyone else. Where do your habits come from? What happens to your convictions when the pressure is on?

Daniel's convictions weren't just beliefs; they created positive actions in his life. For instance, he ate carefully and lived prayerfully. His position gave him all-you-can-eat privileges at the king's table, but Daniel chose a simpler menu and proved it was a healthy choice. Our eating habits are a good measure of how well we are doing at controlling all our appetites.

While Daniel cut back on food, he cut loose on prayer. He felt comfortable talking to God because he did it all the time. Even lions couldn't come between him and his habit of prayer. Notice, though, that prayer doesn't necessarily keep us from "lions' dens." Rather, prayer keeps us in touch with God even in the middle of "lions' dens"! Make prayer a daily action in your life.

LESSONS: Wise words and actions often earn long-term respect

Don't wait until you are in a tough situation to learn about prayer

God can use people wherever they are

KEY VERSE: "This man Daniel, whom the king named Belteshazzar, has a sharp mind and is filled with divine knowledge and understanding. He can interpret dreams, explain riddles, and solve difficult problems. Call for Daniel, and he will tell you what the writing means" (5:12).

Daniel's story is told in the book of Daniel. He is also mentioned in Matthew 24:15.

**UPS**
- Although taken from his home at an early age, he remained true to his faith
- Served as a counselor to two Babylonian kings and two Medo-Persian kings
- Was a man of prayer and a statesman with the gift of prophecy
- Survived the lions' den

**STATS**
- Where: Judah and the courts of Babylon and Persia
- Occupation: A captive of Israel who became a counselor of kings
- Contemporaries: Hananiah, Mishael, Azariah, Nebuchadnezzar, Belshazzar, Darius, Cyrus

31 "Your Majesty, in your vision you saw in front of
you a huge and powerful statue of a man, shining
brilliantly, frightening and awesome. 32 The head of
the statue was made of fine gold, its chest and arms
were of silver, its belly and thighs were of bronze, 33 its
legs were of iron, and its feet were a combination of
iron and clay. 34 But as you watched, a rock was cut
from a mountain by supernatural means.* It struck
the feet of iron and clay, smashing them to bits.
35 The whole statue collapsed into a heap of iron,
clay, bronze, silver, and gold. The pieces were
crushed as small as chaff on a threshing floor, and
the wind blew them all away without a trace. But the
rock that knocked the statue down became a great
mountain that covered the whole earth.

## FRIENDSHIP

Sarah, Rebecca, and Melanie are inseparable. Find one and you'll find the other two.

Besides a lot of laughs and six years' worth of great memories, the three-way friendship has helped keep the girls on track with God all through high school. Whenever one of the girls has faltered in her faith, the other two have been there to pick her up. For instance:

- When Rebecca began dating a non-Christian, the other two girls confronted her and convinced her that she was making a mistake.
- When Melanie's parents split up one winter and Melanie was wondering if God really cared, Sarah and Rebecca showered their hurting friend with love and concern.
- When Sarah got so involved in extracurricular school activities one semester that she quit coming to Bible study, the other girls practically dragged her back into the fold!
- When the girls didn't get asked to the prom because of their stand against alcohol, they all dressed up and went to dinner instead.

Without such a strong Christ-centered friendship, the girls might have wandered away from God when the pressure got too intense. However, because they had a friendship like this to lean on, they all were able to have a huge impact for Christ!

Do you have close Christian friends who constantly challenge you to grow in Christ? Read in Daniel 3 about three godly guys who braved some serious heat together.

36 "That was the dream; now I will tell Your Majesty what it means. 37 Your Majesty, you are a king
over many kings. The God of heaven has given you
sovereignty, power, strength, and honor. 38 He has
made you the ruler over all the inhabited world and
has put even the animals and birds under your control. You are the head of gold.
39 "But after your kingdom comes to an end, another great kingdom, inferior to yours, will rise to
take your place. After that kingdom has fallen, yet a
third great kingdom, represented by the bronze belly
and thighs, will rise to rule the world. 40 Following
that kingdom, there will be a fourth great kingdom,
as strong as iron. That kingdom will smash and

## STAND OUT ● ● • • •

3:12 **Why didn't the three men just bow to the image and tell God that they didn't mean it? They had determined never to worship another god, and they courageously took their stand. As a result, they were condemned to be executed. They did not know whether they would be delivered from the fire; all they knew was that they would not bow to an idol. Are you ready to take a stand for God no matter what? When you stand for God, you will stand out. It may be painful, and it may not always have a happy ending. Be prepared to say, "If he delivers me, or if he doesn't, I will serve only God."**

crush all previous empires, just as iron smashes and
crushes everything it strikes. 41 The feet and toes you
saw that were a combination of iron and clay show
that this kingdom will be divided. 42 Some parts of it
will be as strong as iron, and others as weak as clay.
43 This mixture of iron and clay also shows that these
kingdoms will try to strengthen themselves by forming alliances with each other through intermarriage.
But this will not succeed, just as iron and clay do not
mix.
44 "During the reigns of those kings, the God of
heaven will set up a kingdom that will never be
destroyed; no one will ever conquer it. It will shatter
all these kingdoms into nothingness, but it will
stand forever. 45 That is the meaning of the rock cut
from the mountain by supernatural means, crushing
to dust the statue of iron, bronze, clay, silver, and
gold.
"The great God has shown Your Majesty what will
happen in the future. The dream is true, and its
meaning is certain."
46 Then King Nebuchadnezzar bowed to the
ground before Daniel and worshiped him, and he
commanded his people to offer sacrifices and burn
sweet incense before him. 47 The king said to Daniel,
"Truly, your God is the God of gods, the Lord over
kings, a revealer of mysteries, for you have been able
to reveal this secret."
48 Then the king appointed Daniel to a high position and gave him many valuable gifts. He made
Daniel ruler over the whole province of Babylon, as
well as chief over all his wise men. 49 At Daniel's
request, the king appointed Shadrach, Meshach, and
Abednego to be in charge of all the affairs of the
province of Babylon, while Daniel remained in the
king's court.

CHAPTER **3** **THE FIERY FURNACE.** King Nebuchadnezzar made a gold statue ninety feet tall and nine
feet wide* and set it up on the plain of Dura in the
province of Babylon. 2 Then he sent messages to the
princes, prefects, governors, advisers, counselors,
judges, magistrates, and all the provincial officials to
come to the dedication of the statue he had set up.
3 When all these officials* had arrived and were
standing before the image King Nebuchadnezzar
had set up, 4 a herald shouted out, "People of all races
and nations and languages, listen to the king's command! 5 When you hear the sound of the horn, flute,

2:34 Aramaic *not by human hands;* also in 2:45. 3:1 Aramaic *60 cubits* [27 meters] *tall and 6 cubits* [2.7 meters] *wide.* 3:3 Aramaic *the princes, prefects, governors, advisers, counselors, judges, magistrates, and all the provincial officials.*

zither, lyre, harp, pipes, and other instruments,* bow to the ground to worship King Nebuchadnezzar's gold statue. 6Anyone who refuses to obey will immediately be thrown into a blazing furnace."

7So at the sound of the musical instruments,* all the people, whatever their race or nation or language, bowed to the ground and worshiped the statue that King Nebuchadnezzar had set up.

8But some of the astrologers* went to the king and informed on the Jews. 9They said to King Nebuchadnezzar, "Long live the king! 10You issued a decree requiring all the people to bow down and worship the gold statue when they hear the sound of the musical instruments.* 11That decree also states that those who refuse to obey must be thrown into a blazing furnace. 12But there are some Jews—Shadrach, Meshach, and Abednego—whom you have put in charge of the province of Babylon. They have defied Your Majesty by refusing to serve your gods or to worship the gold statue you have set up."

13Then Nebuchadnezzar flew into a rage and ordered Shadrach, Meshach, and Abednego to be brought before him. When they were brought in, 14Nebuchadnezzar said to them, "Is it true, Shadrach, Meshach, and Abednego, that you refuse to serve my gods or to worship the gold statue I have set up? 15I will give you one more chance. If you bow down and worship the statue I have made when you hear the sound of the musical instruments, all will be well. But if you refuse, you will be thrown immediately into the blazing furnace. What god will be able to rescue you from my power then?"

16Shadrach, Meshach, and Abednego replied, "O Nebuchadnezzar, we do not need to defend ourselves before you. 17If we are thrown into the blazing furnace, the God whom we serve is able to save us. He will rescue us from your power, Your Majesty. 18But even if he doesn't, Your Majesty can be sure that we will never serve your gods or worship the gold statue you have set up."

## SHADRACH, MESHACH, & ABEDNEGO

**UPS:**
- Stood with Daniel against eating food from the king's table
- Shared a friendship that stood the tests of hardship, success, wealth, and possible death
- Would not compromise their convictions even in the face of death
- Survived the fiery furnace

**STATS:**
- Where: Babylon
- Occupations: King's servants and counselors
- Contemporaries: Daniel, Nebuchadnezzar

Have you ever gotten too close to a fire that suddenly sent out flames, catching you off guard and sending you hurrying away? If so, you know how powerful and frightening fire can be. Now, imagine willingly walking into a blast furnace rather than denying God . . . and you begin to understand the courageous, tenacious faith of Daniel's friends Shadrach, Meshach, and Abednego.

Along with Daniel and the other people of Jerusalem, these three young Jewish men were taken into captivity by the Babylonians in 605 B.C. Their way of life was totally uprooted, and they were forced to serve in the court of the heathen King Nebuchadnezzar. Although the king obviously respected and admired his young Hebrew servants, he just as clearly did not understand the depth of their relationship with the One True God.

Nebuchadnezzar built a huge golden idol and ordered all his officials to worship it. Whoever refused would be burned alive. Of course, with a choice like that, almost everyone obeyed . . . but not Shadrach, Meshach, and Abednego. Angrily, the king ordered them to worship the idol or be thrown into the fire. Shadrach, Meshach, and Abednego refused, preferring instead to face the fire. That's putting your faith on the line!

Furious, Nebuchadnezzar ordered the fire stoked up seven times hotter than usual. It was so hot, the soldiers assigned to carry out the execution died as they threw the three men in! The men fell in, no doubt expecting to be incinerated. Instead, the ropes which held them fell away, and they miraculously walked around in the midst of the flames unharmed . . . escorted by a fourth person who looked "like a divine being!" (3:25). You never know how God will meet you when you put your faith on the line. But you can be sure he will.

LESSONS: There is great strength in real friendship

It is important to stand with others with whom we share convictions

God can be trusted even when we can't predict the outcome

KEY VERSES: "Shadrach, Meshach, and Abednego replied, 'O Nebuchadnezzar, we do not need to defend ourselves before you. If we are thrown into the blazing furnace, the God whom we serve is able to save us. He will rescue us from your power, Your Majesty. But even if he doesn't, Your Majesty can be sure that we will never serve your gods or worship the gold statue you have set up'" (3:16-18).

The story of Shadrach (Hananiah), Meshach (Mishael), and Abednego (Azariah) is told in the book of Daniel.

3:5 The identification of some of these musical instruments is uncertain. 3:7 Aramaic *the horn, flute, zither, lyre, harp, and other instruments of the musical ensemble.* 3:8 Aramaic *Chaldeans.* 3:10 Aramaic *the horn, flute, zither, lyre, harp, pipes, and other instruments of the musical ensemble;* also in 3:15.

**DANIEL** served as a prophet to the exiles in Babylon from 605 to 536 B.C.

| | |
|---|---|
| *Climate of the times* | The people of Judah were captives in a strange land, feeling hopeless. |
| *Main message* | God is sovereign over all of human history, past, present, and future. |
| *Importance of message* | We should spend less time wondering when future events will happen and more time learning how we should live now. |
| *Contemporary prophets* | Jeremiah (627–586)<br>Habakkuk (612–588) |

19 Nebuchadnezzar was so furious with Shadrach, Meshach, and Abednego that his face became distorted with rage. He commanded that the furnace be heated seven times hotter than usual. 20 Then he ordered some of the strongest men of his army to bind Shadrach, Meshach, and Abednego and throw them into the blazing furnace. 21 So they tied them up and threw them into the furnace, fully clothed. 22 And because the king, in his anger, had demanded such a hot fire in the furnace, the flames leaped out and killed the soldiers as they threw the three men in! 23 So Shadrach, Meshach, and Abednego, securely tied, fell down into the roaring flames.

24 But suddenly, as he was watching, Nebuchadnezzar jumped up in amazement and exclaimed to his advisers, "Didn't we tie up three men and throw them into the furnace?"

"Yes," they said, "we did indeed, Your Majesty."

25 "Look!" Nebuchadnezzar shouted. "I see four men, unbound, walking around in the fire. They aren't even hurt by the flames! And the fourth looks like a divine being*!"

26 Then Nebuchadnezzar came as close as he could to the door of the flaming furnace and shouted: "Shadrach, Meshach, and Abednego, servants of the Most High God, come out! Come here!" So Shadrach, Meshach, and Abednego stepped out of the fire. 27 Then the princes, prefects, governors, and advisers crowded around them and saw that the fire had not touched them. Not a hair on their heads was singed, and their clothing was not scorched. They didn't even smell of smoke!

28 Then Nebuchadnezzar said, "Praise to the God of Shadrach, Meshach, and Abednego! He sent his angel to rescue his servants who trusted in him. They defied the king's command and were willing to die rather than serve or worship any god except their own God. 29 Therefore, I make this decree: If any people, whatever their race or nation or language, speak a word against the God of Shadrach, Meshach, and Abednego, they will be torn limb from limb, and their houses will be crushed into heaps of rubble. There is no other god who can rescue like this!" 30 Then the king promoted Shadrach, Meshach, and Abednego to even higher positions in the province of Babylon.

CHAPTER **4** **THE KING DREAMS ABOUT A TREE.** King Nebuchadnezzar sent this message to the people of every race and nation and language throughout the world:

"Peace and prosperity to you!

2 "I want you all to know about the miraculous signs and wonders the Most High God has performed for me.

3 How great are his signs,
how powerful his wonders!
His kingdom will last forever,
his rule through all generations.

4 "I, Nebuchadnezzar, was living in my palace in comfort and prosperity. 5 But one night I had a dream that greatly frightened me; I saw visions that terrified me as I lay in my bed. 6 So I issued an order calling in all the wise men of Babylon, so they could tell me what my dream meant. 7 When all the magicians, enchanters, astrologers,* and fortune-tellers came in, I told them the dream, but they could not tell me what it meant. 8 At last Daniel came in before me, and I told him the dream. (He was named Belte-

## HARD TO FORGIVE ● ● ● • •

4:19 **When Daniel understood Nebuchadnezzar's dream, he was stunned. How could he be so deeply grieved at the fate of Nebuchadnezzar—the king who was responsible for the destruction of his home and nation? Daniel had forgiven the king, and so God was able to use Daniel. Often when we have been wronged by someone, we find it difficult to forget the past. We may even be glad if that person suffers. Forgiving people means putting the past behind us. Can you love someone who has hurt you? Ask God to help you forgive, forget, and love. God may use you in an extraordinary way in that person's life!**

3:25 Aramaic *like a son of the gods.* 4:7 Or *Chaldeans.*

shazzar after my god, and the spirit of the holy
gods is in him.)
9 "I said to him, 'O Belteshazzar, master
magician, I know that the spirit of the holy gods
is in you and that no mystery is too great for
you to solve. Now tell me what my dream
means.
10 "'While I was lying in my bed, this is what
I dreamed. I saw a large tree in the middle of
the earth. 11 The tree grew very tall and strong,
reaching high into the heavens for all the world
to see. 12 It had fresh green leaves, and it was
loaded with fruit for all to eat. Wild animals lived
in its shade, and birds nested in its branches.
All the world was fed from this tree.
13 "'Then as I lay there dreaming, I saw a messenger,* a holy one, coming down from heaven.
14 The messenger shouted, "Cut down the tree; lop
off its branches! Shake off its leaves, and scatter its
fruit! Chase the animals from its shade and the
birds from its branches. 15 But leave the stump and
the roots in the ground, bound with a band of
iron and bronze and surrounded by tender grass.
Now let him be drenched with the dew of heaven,
and let him live like an animal among the plants
of the fields. 16 For seven periods of time, let him
have the mind of an animal instead of a human.
17 For this has been decreed by the messengers*; it
is commanded by the holy ones. The purpose of
this decree is that the whole world may understand that the Most High rules over the kingdoms
of the world and gives them to anyone he chooses
—even to the lowliest of humans."
18 "'O Belteshazzar, that was the dream that I,
King Nebuchadnezzar, had. Now tell me what
it means, for no one else can help me. All the
wisest men of my kingdom have failed me. But
you can tell me because the spirit of the holy
gods is in you.'
19 "Upon hearing this, Daniel (also known as
Belteshazzar) was overcome for a time, aghast at
the meaning of the dream. Finally, the king said
to him, 'Belteshazzar, don't be alarmed by the
dream and what it means.'
"Belteshazzar replied, 'Oh, how I wish the
events foreshadowed in this dream would happen
to your enemies, my lord, and not to you! 20 You
saw a tree growing very tall and strong, reaching
high into the heavens for all the world to see. 21 It
had fresh green leaves, and it was loaded with
fruit for all to eat. Wild animals lived in its shade,
and birds nested in its branches. 22 That tree, Your
Majesty, is you. For you have grown strong and
great; your greatness reaches up to heaven, and
your rule to the ends of the earth.
23 "'Then you saw a messenger, a holy one,
coming down from heaven and saying, "Cut
down the tree and destroy it. But leave the
stump and the roots in the ground, bound with
a band of iron and bronze and surrounded by
tender grass. Let him be drenched with the dew
of heaven. Let him eat grass with the animals of
the field for seven periods of time."
24 "'This is what the dream means, Your Majesty,
and what the Most High has declared will happen
to you. 25 You will be driven from human society,
and you will live in the fields with the wild
animals. You will eat grass like a cow, and you
will be drenched with the dew of heaven. Seven
periods of time will pass while you live this way,
until you learn that the Most High rules over the
kingdoms of the world and gives them to anyone
he chooses. 26 But the stump and the roots were
left in the ground. This means that you will
receive your kingdom back again when you have
learned that heaven rules.
27 "'O King Nebuchadnezzar, please listen to
me. Stop sinning and do what is right. Break
from your wicked past by being merciful to the
poor. Perhaps then you will continue to prosper.'
28 "But all these things did happen to King
Nebuchadnezzar. 29 Twelve months later, he was
taking a walk on the flat roof of the royal palace
in Babylon. 30 As he looked out across the city, he
said, 'Just look at this great city of Babylon! I, by
my own mighty power, have built this beautiful
city as my royal residence and as an expression
of my royal splendor.'
31 "While he was still speaking these words, a
voice called down from heaven, 'O King Nebuchadnezzar, this message is for you! You are
no longer ruler of this kingdom. 32 You will be
driven from human society. You will live in the
fields with the wild animals, and you will eat
grass like a cow. Seven periods of time will pass
while you live this way, until you learn that the
Most High rules over the kingdoms of the world
and gives them to anyone he chooses.'
33 "That very same hour the prophecy was
fulfilled, and Nebuchadnezzar was driven from
human society. He ate grass like a cow, and he
was drenched with the dew of heaven. He lived
this way until his hair was as long as eagles'
feathers and his nails were like birds' claws.
34 "After this time had passed, I, Nebuchadnezzar, looked up to heaven. My sanity

**4:13** Aramaic *a watcher;* also in 4:23. **4:17** Aramaic *the watchers.*

## ACKNOWLEDGE ● ● • • •

4:34 **Nebuchadnezzar's pilgrimage with God is one of the themes of this book. In 2:47, he acknowledged that God revealed dreams to Daniel. In 3:28-29, he praised the God who delivered the three Hebrews. Despite Nebuchadnezzar's recognition that God exists and works great miracles, in 4:30 we see that he still did not acknowledge God as his own ruler. We may recognize that God exists and does wonderful miracles, but God is not going to shape our life until we acknowledge him as Lord.**

## UNBIASED ● ● • • •

**5:17 The king offered Daniel beautiful gifts and great power if he would explain the writing, but Daniel turned them down. He knew they would be short-lived, and he wanted to show that he was giving an unbiased interpretation to the king. Like Daniel, we need to avoid letting others influence our response to God's call or urgings in our life.**

returned, and I praised and worshiped the Most High and honored the one who lives forever.

His rule is everlasting,
and his kingdom is eternal.
35 All the people of the earth
are nothing compared to him.
He has the power to do as he pleases
among the angels of heaven
and with those who live on earth.
No one can stop him or challenge him,
saying, 'What do you mean by doing
these things?'

36"When my sanity returned to me, so did my honor and glory and kingdom. My advisers and officers sought me out, and I was reestablished as head of my kingdom, with even greater honor than before.

37"Now I, Nebuchadnezzar, praise and glorify and honor the King of heaven. All his acts are just and true, and he is able to humble those who are proud."

CHAPTER **5** **STRANGE WRITING ON THE WALL.** A number
of years later, King Belshazzar gave a great feast for a
thousand of his nobles and drank wine with them.
2While Belshazzar was drinking, he gave orders to
bring in the gold and silver cups that his predecessor,*
Nebuchadnezzar, had taken from the Temple in Jerusalem, so that he and his nobles, his wives, and his
concubines might drink from them. 3So they brought
these gold cups taken from the Temple of God in Jerusalem, and the king and his nobles, his wives, and his
concubines drank from them. 4They drank toasts from them to honor their idols made of gold, silver, bronze, iron, wood, and stone.

5At that very moment they saw the fingers of a human hand writing on the plaster wall of the king's palace, near the lampstand. The king himself saw the hand as it wrote, 6and his face turned pale with fear.
Such terror gripped him that his knees knocked together and his legs gave way beneath him.

7The king shouted for the enchanters, astrologers,* and fortune-tellers to be brought before him. He said to these wise men of Babylon, "Whoever can read this writing and tell me what it means will be dressed in purple robes of royal honor and will wear a gold chain around his neck. He will become the third highest ruler in the kingdom!"
8But when all the king's wise men came in, none of them could read the writing or tell him what it meant. 9So the king grew even more alarmed, and
his face turned ashen white. His nobles, too, were shaken.

10But when the queen mother heard what was happening, she hurried to the banquet hall. She said to Belshazzar, "Long live the king! Don't be so pale and afraid about this. 11There is a man in your kingdom who has within him the spirit of the holy gods. During Nebuchadnezzar's reign, this man was found to have insight, understanding, and wisdom as though he himself were a god. Your predecessor, King Nebuchadnezzar, made him chief over all the magicians, enchanters, astrologers, and fortune-tellers of Babylon. 12This man Daniel, whom the king named Belteshazzar, has a sharp mind and is filled with divine knowledge and understanding. He can interpret dreams, explain riddles, and solve difficult problems. Call for Daniel, and he will tell you what the writing means."

## DO IT NOW ● ● • • •

**5:27 The handwriting on the wall was for Belshazzar. Although he had power and wealth, his kingdom was totally corrupt and he could not withstand the judgment of God. God's time of judgment comes for all people. If there is sin in your life, turn away from it now. Ask God to forgive you, and begin to live by his standards of justice.**

13So Daniel was brought in before the king. The king asked him, "Are you Daniel, who was exiled from Judah by my predecessor, King Nebuchadnezzar? 14I have heard that you have the spirit of the gods within you and that you are filled with insight, understanding, and wisdom. 15My wise men and enchanters have tried to read this writing on the wall, but they cannot. 16I am told that you can give interpretations and solve difficult problems. If you can read these words and tell me their meaning, you will be clothed in purple robes of royal honor, and you will wear a gold chain around your neck. You will become the third highest ruler in the kingdom."

17Daniel answered the king, "Keep your gifts or give them to someone else, but I will tell you what the writing means. 18Your Majesty, the Most High God gave sovereignty, majesty, glory, and honor to your predecessor, Nebuchadnezzar. 19He made him so great that people of all races and nations and languages trembled before him in fear. He killed those he wanted to kill and spared those he wanted to spare. He honored those he wanted to honor and disgraced those he wanted to disgrace. 20But when

## RESPECT ● ● • • •

**6:1-3 At this time, Daniel was in his eighties and was one of Darius's top three administrators. He was working with those who did not believe in his God, but he worked more efficiently and capably than all the rest. Thus, Daniel attracted the attention of the heathen king and earned a place of respect. One of the best ways to influence non-Christian employers is to work hard. How do you represent God to your employer?**

5:2 Aramaic *father;* also in 5:11, 13, 18. 5:7 Or *Chaldeans;* also in 5:11.

his heart and mind were hardened with pride, he was
brought down from his royal throne and stripped of
his glory. [21]He was driven from human society. He
was given the mind of an animal, and he lived
among the wild donkeys. He ate grass like a cow, and
he was drenched with the dew of heaven, until he
learned that the Most High God rules the kingdoms
of the world and appoints anyone he desires to rule
over them.
[22]"You are his successor,* O Belshazzar, and you
knew all this, yet you have not humbled yourself.
[23]For you have defied the Lord of heaven and have
had these cups from his Temple brought before you.
You and your nobles and your wives and concubines
have been drinking wine from them while praising
gods of silver, gold, bronze, iron, wood, and stone—
gods that neither see nor hear nor know anything at
all. But you have not honored the God who gives you
the breath of life and controls your destiny! [24]So God
has sent this hand to write a message.
[25]"This is the message that was written: MENE,
MENE, TEKEL, PARSIN. [26]This is what these words
mean:

*Mene* means 'numbered'—God has numbered
the days of your reign and has brought it to
an end.
[27] *Tekel* means 'weighed'—you have been weighed
on the balances and have failed the test.
[28] *Parsin** means 'divided'—your kingdom has
been divided and given to the Medes and
Persians."

[29]Then at Belshazzar's command, Daniel was
dressed in purple robes, a gold chain was hung
around his neck, and he was proclaimed the third
highest ruler in the kingdom.
[30]That very night Belshazzar, the Babylonian*
king, was killed.* [31]And Darius the Mede took over
the kingdom at the age of sixty-two.

CHAPTER **6** **DANIEL IN THE LIONS' DEN.** Darius the
Mede decided to divide the kingdom into 120 provinces, and he appointed a prince to rule over each
province. [2]The king also chose Daniel and two
others as administrators to supervise the princes and
to watch out for the king's interests. [3]Daniel soon
proved himself more capable than all the other administrators and princes. Because of his great ability,
the king made plans to place him over the entire
empire. [4]Then the other administrators and princes
began searching for some fault in the way Daniel was
handling his affairs, but they couldn't find anything
to criticize. He was faithful and honest and always
responsible. [5]So they concluded, "Our only chance
of finding grounds for accusing Daniel will be in
connection with the requirements of his religion."
[6]So the administrators and princes went to the
king and said, "Long live King Darius! [7]We administrators, prefects, princes, advisers, and other officials
have unanimously agreed that Your Majesty should
make a law that will be strictly enforced. Give orders
that for the next thirty days anyone who prays to
anyone, divine or human—except to Your Majesty—will be thrown to the lions. [8]And let Your
Majesty issue and sign this law so it cannot be
changed, a law of the Medes and Persians, which
cannot be revoked." [9]So King Darius signed the law.
[10]But when Daniel learned that the law had been
signed, he went home and knelt down as usual in his
upstairs room, with its windows open toward Jerusalem. He prayed three times a day, just as he had
always done, giving thanks to his God. [11]The officials

## CRITICS ● ● • • •

**6:4-5 The jealous officials couldn't find anything about Daniel's life to criticize, so they attacked his religion. If you face jealous critics because of your faith, be glad they're criticizing that part of your life—perhaps they had to focus on your religion as a last resort! Respond by continuing to believe and live as you should. Then remember that God is in control, fighting this battle for you.**

**I'm involved in so many activities at school and church lately that I haven't had any time to spend with God. How do I keep from getting too busy for him?**

God knows you live in a busy world, but being busy is no excuse for ignoring him. The pressures and demands on you will increase as you grow older, so you must decide now to do what's important and make your relationship with God your number-one priority.

Busyness is a hard habit to break. People have a tendency to think God wants them rushing from one thing to the next. But busyness, even with "Christian" things, can be unhealthy. It can end up pulling us away from God and spiritual nourishment.

Daniel understood that. He risked death to spend time with God! (Check out Daniel 6:10-15.) It's tough for many Christians to risk missing TV shows, friends, phone calls, and magazines to spend time with him! Our priorities are mixed up, and unless they're brought back in line with what's really best for us—spending time alone with Christ—we'll always be running around, confused about what's really important.

Learn this lesson early in your Christian life: The joy you can have just spending time with Christ is far greater than any positive strokes you may get from being busy. Listen to this plea from Jesus.

"You shouldn't be so concerned about perishable things like food. Spend your energy seeking the eternal life that I, the Son of Man, can give you. For God the Father has sent me for that very purpose" (John 6:27).

**5:22** Aramaic *son.* **5:28** Aramaic *Peres,* the singular of *Parsin.* **5:30a** Or *Chaldean.* **5:30b** The Persians and Medes conquered Babylon in October 539 B.C.

went together to Daniel's house and found him praying and asking for God's help. [12]So they went back to the king and reminded him about his law. "Did you not sign a law that for the next thirty days anyone who prays to anyone, divine or human—except to Your Majesty—will be thrown to the lions?"

"Yes," the king replied, "that decision stands; it is a law of the Medes and Persians, which cannot be revoked."

[13]Then they told the king, "That man Daniel, one of the captives from Judah, is paying no attention to you or your law. He still prays to his God three times a day."

[14]Hearing this, the king was very angry with himself for signing the law, and he tried to find a way to save Daniel. He spent the rest of the day looking for a way to get Daniel out of this predicament. [15]In the evening the men went together to the king and said, "Your Majesty knows that according to the law of the Medes and the Persians, no law that the king signs can be changed."

[16]So at last the king gave orders for Daniel to be arrested and thrown into the den of lions. The king said to him, "May your God, whom you worship continually, rescue you." [17]A stone was brought and placed over the mouth of the den. The king sealed the stone with his own royal seal and the seals of his nobles, so that no one could rescue Daniel from the lions. [18]Then the king returned to his palace and spent the night fasting. He refused his usual entertainment and couldn't sleep at all that night.

[19]Very early the next morning, the king hurried out to the lions' den. [20]When he got there, he called out in anguish, "Daniel, servant of the living God! Was your God, whom you worship continually, able to rescue you from the lions?"

## STRANGE LAND ● ● • • •

**6:25-27 Nebuchadnezzar had believed in God because of the faithfulness of Daniel and his friends. Here Darius was also convinced of God's power because Daniel was faithful and God delivered him. Although Daniel was captive in a strange land, his devotion to God was a testimony to powerful rulers. If you find yourself in new surroundings, take the opportunity to testify about God's power in your life. Be faithful to God so he can use you to reach others.**

[21]Daniel answered, "Long live the king! [22]My God sent his angel to shut the lions' mouths so that they would not hurt me, for I have been found innocent in his sight. And I have not wronged you, Your Majesty."

[23]The king was overjoyed and ordered that Daniel be lifted from the den. Not a scratch was found on him because he had trusted in his God. [24]Then the king gave orders to arrest the men who had maliciously accused Daniel. He had them thrown into the lions' den, along with their wives and children. The lions leaped on them and tore them apart before they even hit the floor of the den.

[25]Then King Darius sent this message to the people of every race and nation and language throughout the world:

"Peace and prosperity to you!

[26]"I decree that everyone throughout my kingdom should tremble with fear before the God of Daniel.

For he is the living God,
and he will endure forever.
His kingdom will never be destroyed,
and his rule will never end.
[27]He rescues and saves his people;
he performs miraculous signs and wonders
in the heavens and on earth.
He has rescued Daniel
from the power of the lions."

[28]So Daniel prospered during the reign of Darius and the reign of Cyrus the Persian.*

## CHAPTER 7

**DANIEL DREAMS ABOUT FOUR BEASTS.** Earlier, during the first year of King Belshazzar's reign in Babylon, Daniel had a dream and saw visions as he lay in his bed. He wrote the dream down, and this is what he saw.

[2]In my vision that night, I, Daniel, saw a great storm churning the surface of a great sea, with strong winds blowing from every direction. [3]Then four huge beasts came up out of the water, each different from the others.

[4]The first beast was like a lion with eagles' wings. As I watched, its wings were pulled off, and it was left standing with its two hind feet on the ground, like a human being. And a human mind was given to it.

[5]Then I saw a second beast, and it looked like a bear. It was rearing up on one side, and it had three ribs in its mouth between its teeth. And I heard a voice saying to it, "Get up! Devour many people!"

[6]Then the third of these strange beasts appeared, and it looked like a leopard. It had four wings like birds' wings on its back, and it had four heads. Great authority was given to this beast.

[7]Then in my vision that night, I saw a fourth beast, terrifying, dreadful, and very strong. It devoured and crushed its victims with huge iron teeth and trampled what was left beneath its feet. It was different from any of the other beasts, and it had ten horns. [8]As I was looking at the horns, suddenly another small horn appeared among them. Three of the first horns were wrenched out, roots and all, to make

## JUDGMENT ● ● • • •

**7:9-10 Daniel saw God judging millions of people as they stood before him. We all must stand before almighty God and give an account of our life. If your life were to be judged by God today, what would he say about it? How would he measure it against his Word? As we look toward God's judgment, we should ask what we would like him to see at that time. Then we should live that way today!**

6:28 Or *of Darius, that is, the reign of Cyrus the Persian.*

room for it. This little horn had eyes like human eyes and a mouth that was boasting arrogantly.

[9]I watched as thrones were put in place and the Ancient One* sat down to judge. His clothing was as white as snow, his hair like whitest wool. He sat on a fiery throne with wheels of blazing fire, [10]and a river of fire flowed from his presence. Millions of angels ministered to him, and a hundred million stood to attend him. Then the court began its session, and the books were opened.

[11]I continued to watch because I could hear the little horn's boastful speech. I kept watching until the fourth beast was killed and its body was destroyed by fire. [12]As for the other three beasts, their authority was taken from them, but they were allowed to live for a while longer.*

[13]As my vision continued that night, I saw someone who looked like a man* coming with the clouds of heaven. He approached the Ancient One and was led into his presence. [14]He was given authority, honor, and royal power over all the nations of the world, so that people of every race and nation and language would obey him. His rule is eternal—it will never end. His kingdom will never be destroyed.

[15]I, Daniel, was troubled by all I had seen, and my visions terrified me. [16]So I approached one of those standing beside the throne and asked him what it all meant. He explained it to me like this: [17]"These four huge beasts represent four kingdoms that will arise from the earth. [18]But in the end, the holy people of the Most High will be given the kingdom, and they will rule forever and ever."

[19]Then I wanted to know the true meaning of the fourth beast, the one so different from the others and so terrifying. It devoured and crushed its victims with iron teeth and bronze claws, and it trampled what was left beneath its feet. [20]I also asked about the ten horns on the fourth beast's head and the little horn that came up afterward and destroyed three of the other horns. This was the horn that seemed greater than the others and had human eyes and a mouth that was boasting arrogantly. [21]As I watched, this horn was waging war against the holy people and was defeating them, [22]until the Ancient One came and judged in favor of the holy people of the Most High. Then the time arrived for the holy people to take over the kingdom.

[23]Then he said to me, "This fourth beast is the fourth world power that will rule the earth. It will be different from all the others. It will devour the whole world, trampling everything in its path. [24]Its ten horns are ten kings that will rule that empire. Then another king will arise, different from the other ten, who will subdue three of them. [25]He will defy the Most High and wear down the holy people of the Most High. He will try to change their sacred festivals and laws, and they will be placed under his control for a time, times, and half a time.

[26]"But then the court will pass judgment, and all

**CONFUSED ● ● ● • •**

7:15 **If you feel as Daniel did about these prophecies—disturbed and confused—recognize with him that their full meaning has not been revealed. The full implications of these prophecies will not be known until God reveals them to his people.**

his power will be taken away and completely destroyed. [27]Then the sovereignty, power, and greatness of all the kingdoms under heaven will be given to the holy people of the Most High. They will rule forever, and all rulers will serve and obey them."

[28]That was the end of the vision. I, Daniel, was terrified by my thoughts and my face was pale with fear, but I kept these things to myself.

CHAPTER **8** **A RAM AND A GOAT.** During the third year of King Belshazzar's reign, I, Daniel, saw another vision, following the one that had already appeared to me. [2]This time I was at the fortress of Susa, in the province of Elam, standing beside the Ulai River.*

[3]As I looked up, I saw in front of me a ram with two long horns standing beside the river.* One of the horns was longer than the other, even though it had begun to grow later than the shorter one. [4]The ram butted everything out of its way to the west, to the north, and to the south, and no one could stand against it or help its victims. It did as it pleased and became very great.

**HORNS ● ● • • •**

8:3 **The two horns were the kings of Media and Persia (8:20). The longer horn represented the growing dominance of Persia in the Medo-Persian empire.**

[5]While I was watching, suddenly a male goat appeared from the west, crossing the land so swiftly that it didn't even touch the ground. This goat, which had one very large horn between its eyes, [6]headed toward the two-horned ram that I had seen standing beside the river. [7]The goat charged furiously at the ram and struck it, breaking off both its horns. Now the ram was helpless, and the goat knocked it down and trampled it. There was no one who could rescue the ram from the goat's power.

[8]The goat became very powerful. But at the height of its power, its large horn was broken off. In the large horn's place grew four prominent horns pointing in the four directions of the earth. [9]From one of the prominent horns came a small horn whose power grew very great. It extended toward the south and the east and toward the glorious land of Israel. [10]His power reached to the heavens where it attacked the heavenly armies, throwing some of the heavenly beings and stars to the ground and trampling them. [11]He even challenged the Commander of heaven's armies by canceling the daily sacrifices offered to him and by

**7:9** Aramaic *an Ancient of Days;* also in 7:13, 22. **7:12** Aramaic *for a season and a time.* **7:13** Or *like a Son of Man;* Aramaic reads *like a son of man.*
**8:2** Or *the Ulai Gate;* also in 8:16. **8:3** Or *the gate;* also in 8:6.

destroying his Temple. 12But the army of heaven was restrained from destroying him for this sin. As a result, sacrilege was committed against the Temple ceremonies, and truth was overthrown. The horn succeeded in everything it did.*

13Then I heard two of the holy ones talking to each other. One of them said, "How long will the events of this vision last? How long will the rebellion that causes desecration stop the daily sacrifices? How long will the Temple and heaven's armies be trampled on?"

14The other replied, "It will take twenty-three hundred evenings and mornings; then the Temple will be restored."

15As I, Daniel, was trying to understand the meaning of this vision, someone who looked like a man suddenly stood in front of me. 16And I heard a human voice calling out from the Ulai River, "Gabriel, tell this man the meaning of his vision."

17As Gabriel approached the place where I was standing, I became so terrified that I fell to the ground. "Son of man," he said, "you must understand that the events you have seen in your vision relate to the time of the end."

18While he was speaking, I fainted and lay there with my face to the ground. But Gabriel roused me with a touch and helped me to my feet. 19Then he said, "I am here to tell you what will happen later in the time of wrath. What you have seen pertains to the very end of time. 20The two-horned ram represents the kings of Media and Persia. 21The shaggy male goat represents the king of Greece,* and the large horn between its eyes represents the first king of the Greek Empire. 22The four prominent horns that replaced the one large horn show that the Greek Empire will break into four sections with four kings, none of them as great as the first.

## INVINCIBLE ● ● • • •

**8:25 This Prince of princes is God himself. No human power could defeat the king whom Daniel saw in his vision, but God would bring him down. There is only one king who will never be defeated—God almighty.**

23"At the end of their rule, when their sin is at its height, a fierce king, a master of intrigue, will rise to power. 24He will become very strong, but not by his own power. He will cause a shocking amount of destruction and succeed in everything he does. He will destroy powerful leaders and devastate the holy people. 25He will be a master of deception, defeating many by catching them off guard. Without warning he will destroy them. He will even take on the Prince of princes in battle, but he will be broken, though not by human power.

26"This vision about the twenty-three hundred evenings and mornings* is true. But none of these things will happen for a long time, so do not tell anyone about them yet."

27Then I, Daniel, was overcome and lay sick for several days. Afterward I got up and performed my duties for the king, but I was greatly troubled by the vision and could not understand it.

## VULNERABLE ● ● • • •

**9:3-19 Daniel knew how to pray. He had read God's words and believed them. As he prayed, he fasted, confessed his sins, and pleaded that God would reveal his will. He prayed with complete surrender to God and with complete openness to what God was saying to him. When you pray, do you speak openly to God? Examine your attitude. Talk to God with openness, vulnerability, and honesty.**

CHAPTER **9** **DANIEL PRAYS FOR HIS PEOPLE.** It was the first year of the reign of Darius the Mede, the son of Ahasuerus, who became king of the Babylonians.* 2During the first year of his reign, I, Daniel, was studying the writings of the prophets. I learned from the word of the LORD, as recorded by Jeremiah the prophet, that Jerusalem must lie desolate for seventy years.* 3So I turned to the Lord God and pleaded with him in prayer and fasting. I wore rough sackcloth and sprinkled myself with ashes.

4I prayed to the LORD my God and confessed: "O Lord, you are a great and awesome God! You always fulfill your promises of unfailing love to those who love you and keep your commands. 5But we have sinned and done wrong. We have rebelled against you and scorned your commands and regulations. 6We have refused to listen to your servants the prophets, who spoke your messages to our kings and princes and ancestors and to all the people of the land.

7"Lord, you are in the right; but our faces are covered with shame, just as you see us now. This is true of us all, including the people of Judah and Jerusalem and all Israel, scattered near and far, wherever you have driven us because of our disloyalty to you. 8O LORD, we and our kings, princes, and ancestors are covered with shame because we have sinned against you. 9But the Lord our God is merciful and forgiving, even though we have rebelled against him. 10We have not obeyed the LORD our God, for we have not followed the laws he gave us through his servants the prophets. 11All Israel has disobeyed your law and turned away, refusing to listen to your voice.

"So now the solemn curses and judgments written in the law of Moses, the servant of God, have been poured out against us because of our sin. 12You have done exactly what you warned you would do against us and our rulers. Never in all history has there been a disaster like the one that happened in Jerusalem. 13Every curse written against us in the law of Moses has come true. All the troubles he predicted have taken place. But we have refused to seek mercy from the LORD our God by turning from our sins and recognizing his truth. 14The LORD has brought against us the disaster he prepared, for we did not obey him, and the LORD our God is just in everything he does.

15"O Lord our God, you brought lasting honor to your name by rescuing your people from Egypt in a great display of power. But we have sinned and are full

**8:11-12** The meaning of the Hebrew for these verses is uncertain. **8:21** Hebrew *of Javan.* **8:26** Hebrew *about the evenings and mornings;* compare 8:14. **9:1** Or *the Chaldeans.* **9:2** See Jer 25:11-12; 29:10.

of wickedness. 16In view of all your faithful mercies,
Lord, please turn your furious anger away from your
city of Jerusalem, your holy mountain. All the neighboring nations mock Jerusalem and your people because of our sins and the sins of our ancestors.
17"O our God, hear your servant's prayer! Listen as
I plead. For your own sake, Lord, smile again on your
desolate sanctuary.
18"O my God, listen to me and hear my request.
Open your eyes and see our wretchedness. See how
your city lies in ruins—for everyone knows that it is
yours. We do not ask because we deserve help, but
because you are so merciful.
19"O Lord, hear. O Lord, forgive. O Lord, listen
and act! For your own sake, O my God, do not delay,
for your people and your city bear your name."
20I went on praying and confessing my sin and the
sins of my people, pleading with the LORD my God for
Jerusalem, his holy mountain. 21As I was praying, Gabriel, whom I had seen in the earlier vision, came
swiftly to me at the time of the evening sacrifice. 22He
explained to me, "Daniel, I have come here to give you
insight and understanding. 23The moment you began
praying, a command was given. I am here to tell you
what it was, for God loves you very much. Now listen,
so you can understand the meaning of your vision.
24"A period of seventy sets of seven* has been
decreed for your people and your holy city to put
down rebellion, to bring an end to sin, to atone for
guilt, to bring in everlasting righteousness, to confirm the prophetic vision, and to anoint the Most
Holy Place.* 25Now listen and understand! Seven
sets of seven plus sixty-two sets of seven* will pass
from the time the command is given to rebuild
Jerusalem until the Anointed One* comes. Jerusalem will be rebuilt with streets and strong defenses,*
despite the perilous times.
26"After this period of sixty-two sets of seven,* the
Anointed One will be killed, appearing to have accomplished nothing, and a ruler will arise whose
armies will destroy the city and the Temple. The end
will come with a flood, and war and its miseries are
decreed from that time to the very end. 27He will
make a treaty with the people for a period of one set
of seven,* but after half this time, he will put an end
to the sacrifices and offerings. Then as a climax to all
his terrible deeds,* he will set up a sacrilegious object that causes desecration,* until the end that has
been decreed is poured out on this defiler."

CHAPTER **10** **A HEAVENLY MESSENGER.** In the third
year of the reign of King Cyrus of Persia, Daniel (also
known as Belteshazzar) had another vision. It concerned events certain to happen in the future—times
of war and great hardship—and Daniel understood
what the vision meant.

## TRUTH HURTS ● ● • • •

**9:6 God had sent many prophets to speak to his people through the years, but their messages had been ignored. The truth was too painful to hear. God still speaks infallibly and authoritatively through the Bible, and he also speaks through preachers, teachers, and concerned friends. Sometimes the truth hurts, and we would rather accept soothing falsehoods. Don't settle for a soothing lie that will bring harsh judgment. Accept and obey God's truth.**

2When this vision came to me, I, Daniel, had been
in mourning for three weeks. 3All that time I had
eaten no rich food or meat, had drunk no wine, and
had used no fragrant oils. 4On April 23,* as I was
standing beside the great Tigris River, 5I looked up
and saw a man dressed in linen clothing, with a belt
of pure gold around his waist. 6His body looked like
a dazzling gem. From his face came flashes like
lightning, and his eyes were like flaming torches. His
arms and feet shone like polished bronze, and his
voice was like the roaring of a vast multitude of
people.
7I, Daniel, am the only one who saw this vision.
The men with me saw nothing, but they were suddenly terrified and ran away to hide. 8So I was left
there all alone to watch this amazing vision. My
strength left me, my face grew deathly pale, and I felt
very weak. 9When I heard him speak, I fainted and
lay there with my face to the ground.
10Just then a hand touched me and lifted me, still
trembling, to my hands and knees. 11And the man
said to me, "O Daniel, greatly loved of God, listen
carefully to what I have to say to you. Stand up, for I
have been sent to you." When he said this to me, I
stood up, still trembling with fear.

## THE TOUCH ● ● • • •

**10:10-18 Daniel was frightened by this vision, but the messenger's hand calmed his fears; Daniel felt weak, but the messenger's words strengthened him. God can bring us healing when we are hurt, peace when we are troubled, and strength when we are weak. Ask God to minister to you as he did to Daniel.**

12Then he said, "Don't be afraid, Daniel. Since the
first day you began to pray for understanding and to
humble yourself before your God, your request has
been heard in heaven. I have come in answer to your
prayer. 13But for twenty-one days the spirit prince* of
the kingdom of Persia blocked my way. Then Michael, one of the archangels,* came to help me, and
I left him there with the spirit prince of the kingdom
of Persia.* 14Now I am here to explain what will
happen to your people in the future, for this vision
concerns a time yet to come."
15While he was speaking to me, I looked down at the
ground, unable to say a word. 16Then the one who

**9:24a** Hebrew *70 sevens.* **9:24b** Or *the Most Holy One.* **9:25a** Hebrew *Seven sevens plus 62 sevens.* **9:25b** Or *an anointed one.* **9:25c** Or *and a moat,* or *and trenches.* **9:26** Hebrew *After 62 sevens.* **9:27a** Hebrew *for one seven.* **9:27b** Hebrew *on the wing of abominations;* the meaning of the Hebrew is uncertain. **9:27c** Hebrew *an abomination of desolation.* **10:4** Hebrew *On the twenty-fourth day of the first month.* This date in the book of Daniel can be cross-checked with dates in surviving Persian records and can be related accurately to our modern calendar. This day of the Hebrew lunar calendar occurred on April 23, 536 B.C. **10:13a** Hebrew *the prince;* also in 10:13c, 20. **10:13b** Hebrew *the chief princes.* **10:13c** As in one Greek version; Hebrew reads *and I was left there with the kings of Persia.* The meaning of the Hebrew is uncertain.

Those who are *WISE*

*will* **SHINE** *as*

BRIGHT *as the* SKY

and those who turn many to

*RIGHTEOUSNESS*

*will* **SHINE** *like*

STARS
FOREVER.

DANIEL 12:3

looked like a man* touched my lips, and I opened my
mouth and began to speak. I said to the one standing
in front of me, "I am terrified by the vision I have seen,
my lord, and I am very weak. 17How can someone like
me, your servant, talk to you, my lord? My strength is
gone, and I can hardly breathe."
18Then the one who looked like a man touched
me again, and I felt my strength returning. 19"Don't
be afraid," he said, "for you are deeply loved by God.
Be at peace; take heart and be strong!"
As he spoke these words, I suddenly felt stronger
and said to him, "Now you may speak, my lord, for
you have strengthened me."
20He replied, "Do you know why I have come?
Soon I must return to fight against the spirit prince
of the kingdom of Persia, and then against the spirit
prince of the kingdom of Greece.* 21But before I do
that, I will tell you what is written in the Book of
Truth. (There is no one to help me against these
spirit princes except Michael, your spirit prince.* 1I
have been standing beside Michael* as his support
and defense since the first year of the reign of Darius
the Mede.)

## CHAPTER 11 THE MESSENGER PREDICTS THE FUTURE.

2"Now then, I will reveal the truth to you. Three
more Persian kings will reign, to be succeeded by a
fourth, far richer than the others. Using his wealth
for political advantage, he will stir up everyone to
war against the kingdom of Greece.*
3"Then a mighty king will rise to power who will
rule a vast kingdom and accomplish everything he
sets out to do. 4But at the height of his power, his
kingdom will be broken apart and divided into four
parts. It will not be ruled by the king's descendants,
nor will the kingdom hold the authority it once had.
For his empire will be uprooted and given to others.
5"The king of the south will increase in power, but
one of this king's own officials will become more
powerful than he and will rule his kingdom with
great strength.
6"Some years later, an alliance will be formed
between the king of the north and the king of the
south. The daughter of the king of the south will be
given in marriage to the king of the north to secure
the alliance, but she will lose her influence over him,
and so will her father. She will be given up along
with her supporters. 7But when one of her relatives*
becomes king of the south, he will raise an army and
enter the fortress of the king of the north and defeat
him. 8When he returns again to Egypt, he will carry
back their idols with him, along with priceless gold
and silver dishes. For some years afterward he will
leave the king of the north alone.
9"Later the king of the north will invade the realm
of the king of the south but will soon return to his
own land. 10However, the sons of the king of the
north will assemble a mighty army that will advance
like a flood and carry the battle as far as the enemy's
fortress. 11Then the king of the south, in great anger,
will rally against the vast forces assembled by the
king of the north and will defeat them. 12After the
enemy army is swept away, the king of the south will
be filled with pride and will have many thousands of
his enemies killed. But his success will be short lived.
13"A few years later, the king of the north will return
with a fully equipped army far greater than the one he
lost. 14At that time there will be a general uprising
against the king of the south. Lawless ones among
your own people will join them in order to fulfill the
vision, but they will not succeed. 15Then the king of the
north will come and lay siege to a fortified city and
capture it. The best troops of the south will not be able
to stand in the face of the onslaught.
16"The king of the north will march onward unop-

**UNSHAKABLE ● ● ● • •**

11:2 **The angelic messenger was revealing Israel's future (see 10:20-21). Only God can reveal future events so clearly. God's work not only deals with the sweeping panorama of history, but also focuses on the intricate details of people's lives. And his plans—whether for nations or for individuals—are unshakable.**

10:16 As in most manuscripts of the Masoretic Text; one manuscript of the Masoretic Text and one Greek version read *Then something that looked like a human hand.* 10:20 Hebrew *of Javan.* 10:21 Hebrew *against these except Michael, your prince.* 11:1 Hebrew *him.* 11:2 Hebrew *of Javan.* 11:7 Hebrew *a branch from her roots.*

posed; none will be able to stop him. He will pause in the glorious land of Israel, intent on destroying it. [17]He will make plans to come with the might of his entire kingdom and will form an alliance with the king of the south. He will give him a daughter in marriage in order to overthrow the kingdom from within, but his plan will fail.

[18]"After this, he will turn his attention to the coastal cities and conquer many. But a commander from another land will put an end to his insolence and will cause him to retreat in shame. [19]He will take refuge in his own fortresses but will stumble and fall, and he will be seen no more.

[20]"His successor will be remembered as the king who sent a tax collector to maintain the royal splendor, but after a very brief reign, he will die, though neither in battle nor open conflict.

[21]"The next to come to power will be a despicable man who is not directly in line for royal succession. But he will slip in when least expected and take over the kingdom by flattery and intrigue. [22]Before him great armies will be swept away, including a covenant prince. [23]By making deceitful promises, he will make various alliances. With a mere handful of followers, he will become strong. [24]Without warning he will enter the richest areas of the land and do something that none of his predecessors ever did—distribute among his followers the plunder and wealth of the rich. He will plot the overthrow of strongholds, but this will last for only a short while.

[25]"Then he will stir up his courage and raise a great army against the king of the south. The king of the south will go to battle with a mighty army, but to no avail, for plots against him will succeed. [26]Those of his own household will bring his downfall. His army will be swept away, and many will be killed. [27]Seeking nothing but each other's harm, these kings will plot against each other at the conference table, attempting to deceive each other. But it will make no difference, for an end will still come at the appointed time.

[28]"The king of the north will then return home with great riches. On the way he will set himself against the people of the holy covenant, doing much damage before continuing his journey.

[29]"Then at the appointed time he will once again invade the south, but this time the result will be different. [30]For warships from western coastlands* will scare him off, and he will withdraw and return home. But he will vent his anger against the people of the holy covenant and reward those who forsake the covenant. [31]His army will take over the Temple fortress, polluting the sanctuary, putting a stop to the daily sacrifices, and setting up the sacrilegious object that causes desecration.* [32]He will flatter those who have violated the covenant and win them over to his side. But the people who know their God will be strong and will resist him.

[33]"Those who are wise will give instruction to many. But for a time many of these teachers will die by fire and sword, or they will be jailed and robbed.

**GET READY ● ● • • •**

11:33 **Trying times remind us of our weaknesses and inability to cope. We reach out for answers, for leadership, for clear direction. God's Word begins to interest even those who, in better times, would never look at it. We who are believers should prepare ourselves to meet opportunities to share God's Word in needy times. We must also prepare ourselves for persecution and rejection as we teach God's Word.**

[34]While all these persecutions are going on, a little help will arrive, though many who join them will not be sincere. [35]And some who are wise will fall victim to persecution. In this way, they will be refined and cleansed and made pure until the time of the end, for the appointed time is still to come.

[36]"The king will do as he pleases, exalting himself and claiming to be greater than every god there is, even blaspheming the God of gods. He will succeed—until the time of wrath is completed. For what has been determined will surely take place. [37]He will have no regard for the gods of his ancestors, or for the god beloved of women, or for any other god, for he will boast that he is greater than them all. [38]Instead of these, he will worship the god of fortresses—a god his ancestors never knew—and lavish on him gold, silver, precious stones, and costly gifts. [39]Claiming this foreign god's help, he will attack the strongest fortresses. He will honor those who submit to him, appointing them to positions of authority and dividing the land among them as their reward.*

[40]"Then at the time of the end, the king of the south will attack him, and the king of the north will storm out against him with chariots, cavalry, and a vast navy. He will invade various lands and sweep through them like a flood. [41]He will enter the glorious land of Israel, and many nations will fall, but Moab, Edom, and the best part of Ammon will escape. [42]He will conquer many countries, and Egypt will not escape. [43]He will gain control over the gold, silver, and treasures of Egypt, and the Libyans and Ethiopians* will be his servants.

[44]"But then news from the east and the north will alarm him, and he will set out in great anger to destroy many as he goes. [45]He will halt between the glorious holy mountain and the sea and will pitch his royal tents there, but while he is there, his time will suddenly run out, and there will be no one to help him.

## CHAPTER 12

**A MESSAGE ABOUT THE END OF TIME.** "At that time Michael, the archangel* who stands guard over your nation, will arise. Then there will be a time of anguish greater than any since nations first came into existence. But at that time every one of your people whose name is written in the book will be rescued. [2]Many of those whose bodies lie dead and buried will rise up, some to everlasting life and some to shame and everlasting contempt. [3]Those who are wise will shine as bright as the sky, and those who

11:30 Hebrew *from Kittim.* 11:31 Hebrew *the abomination of desolation.* 11:39 Or *at a price.* 11:43 Hebrew *Cushites.* 12:1 Hebrew *the great prince.*

## BE OPEN ● ● • • •

12:10 **Daniel was told that to understand what is happening, people have to be open to instruction. Trials and persecutions, when we are in the middle of them, make very little sense. But they can purify us if we are willing to learn from them. After you survive a difficult time, seek to learn from it so that it can help you in the future.**

turn many to righteousness will shine like stars forever. [4]But you, Daniel, keep this prophecy a secret; seal up the book until the time of the end. Many will rush here and there, and knowledge will increase."

[5]Then I, Daniel, looked and saw two others standing on opposite banks of the river. [6]One of them asked the man dressed in linen, who was now standing above the river, "How long will it be until these shocking events happen?"

[7]The man dressed in linen, who was standing above the river, raised both his hands toward heaven and took this solemn oath by the one who lives forever: "It will go on for a time, times, and half a time. When the shattering of the holy people has finally come to an end, all these things will have happened."

[8]I heard what he said, but I did not understand what he meant. So I asked, "How will all this finally end, my lord?"

[9]But he said, "Go now, Daniel, for what I have said is for the time of the end. [10]Many will be purified, cleansed, and refined by these trials. But the wicked will continue in their wickedness, and none of them will understand. Only those who are wise will know what it means.

[11]"From the time the daily sacrifice is taken away and the sacrilegious object that causes desecration* is set up to be worshiped, there will be 1,290 days. [12]And blessed are those who wait and remain until the end of the 1,335 days!

[13]"As for you, go your way until the end. You will rest, and then at the end of the days, you will rise again to receive the inheritance set aside for you."

12:11 Hebrew *the abomination of desolation.*

## REWARD ● ● • • •

12:13 **Daniel stands tall in the gallery of God's remarkable servants. Born of royal heritage, yet taken into captivity when young, Daniel remained faithful to God in the land of his captivity and advised his captors with unusual wisdom. God chose Daniel to record events of the captivity and significant events concerning the future. As an old man, having always been faithful to God, Daniel was assured by God that he would be resurrected from the dead and receive his portion in God's eternal kingdom. Faithfulness to God has a rich reward, not necessarily in this life, but most certainly in the life to come.**

# MEGA themes

**GOD'S CONTROL** God is all-knowing, and he is in charge of world events. God overrules and removes rebellious leaders who defy him. God will overcome evil; no one will escape. He will, however, deliver the faithful who follow him.

Although nations compete for world control now, one day Christ will rule. Our faith is sure because our future is secure in him. We must have courage and put our faith in God, who controls everything. Our role is to be faithful to Christ.

1. Compare the way Nebuchadnezzar responded to God's sovereign control and the way Daniel, Shadrach, Meshach, and Abednego responded.
2. Contrast the difference in the lives of kids who submit to God's control and of those who refuse to acknowledge him.
3. What will be the final results in the lives of those who refuse to submit to God's control?
4. Why do you think so many people choose not to submit to God?
5. Identify one specific area that you need to submit to God's control. Develop a plan for submitting this area to him daily.

**PURPOSE IN LIFE** Daniel and his three friends are examples of dedication and commitment. These three young men, still in their teens at the time of captivity, determined to serve God regardless of the consequences. They did not give in to pressures from an ungodly society because they had a clear purpose in life: to glorify God.

Trusting and obeying God should be our true purpose in life. This will give us direction and peace in any situation. And we should disobey anyone who asks us to disobey God. Young people who make this type of commitment can have a tremendous impact on their world.

1. If you could interview Daniel, how do you think he would respond to this question: "What is your purpose in life?"
2. How do you think most of the kids in your school would answer that same question?
3. If someone were to spend a week with you, following you around, listening to your conversations, and observing your behavior, what would that person identify as your priorities in life? your purpose?
4. Considering your response to question 3, what adjustments should you make based on the purpose you want to have for your life?
5. Write a short statement of your life's purpose. Keep this in a place where it will remind you as you make your daily choices.

**PERSEVERANCE** Daniel served for 70 years in a foreign land that was hostile to God, yet he did not compromise his faith in God. He was truthful, persistent in prayer, and humble.

In order to fulfill your life's purpose, you need staying power. Don't let your Christian values and commitments slip away just because you are surrounded by kids who are not Christ's followers. Be relentless in your prayers, stay firm in your integrity, and be content to serve God wherever he puts you.

1. What do you think Daniel might have been feeling in each of these situations: when he chose not to eat the king's food; when he interpreted the king's dreams; when he was thrown into the lions' den?
2. What kept Daniel from giving in or giving up?
3. When do you find it most difficult to obey and to keep your commitment to Christ strong?
4. What keeps you from giving up?

**GOD'S FAITHFULNESS** God was faithful in Daniel's life, delivering him from prison, from a den of lions, and from enemies. God cares for his people and deals patiently with them.

We can trust God to take us through any trial because he promises to be with us. Because he has been faithful to us, we should remain faithful to him.

1. Identify a time in your life when you experienced God's faithfulness. How did this affect your relationship with God?
2. In what ways can thinking about God's faithfulness to you strengthen your faith?
3. Complete this sentence with as many statements as you can from your understanding of God in Scripture, especially in Daniel: "I can be confident of God's faithfulness in my life because _________."

793 B.C.
**Jeroboam II becomes king of Israel**

760
**Amos becomes a prophet**

753
**Hosea becomes a prophet; King Zechariah of Israel is killed**

752
**King Shallum of Israel is killed**

743
**Tiglath-Pileser III invades Israel**

742
**Micah becomes a prophet to Judah**

740
**Isaiah becomes a prophet to Judah**

722
**Israel (northern kingdom) falls**

715
**Hosea's ministry ends**

**O**h," she whispered. "I love you, too!" Together the reunited lovers rode off into the sunset. ■ Isn't love wonderful? We've grown up believing love is a cure-all; someday we'll meet "Mr. Right" or "Miss Perfect." He will be gorgeous (big muscles and beautiful eyes), or she will be lovely (long hair and a stunning smile). The rest of the world will then lose its meaning as the two of you enter your own private paradise, a totally honest relationship where neither of you ever hurts the other. Now, *that* would be wonderful. ■ Hosea is a book about love, but with an unusual twist. Hosea was a prophet, and he married Gomer (believe it or not, that was her name). But far from being "Miss Perfect," Gomer was a prostitute. In fact, after they were married, she remained a prostitute. But God told Hosea to marry her anyway. ■ The book of Hosea is a love story—but it's not just about Hosea and Gomer—it's about God's love for his people, who, incidentally, acted a lot like Gomer. ■ As you read this story, you'll learn a lot about God and what he expects of his followers. But look for yourself in the story, too. Are you like Hosea? Gomer? Israel? Then decide to have a true love relationship with God.

## STATS

PURPOSE: To illustrate God's love for his sinful people

AUTHOR: Hosea, son of Beeri ("Hosea" means "salvation")

TO WHOM WRITTEN: Israel (the northern kingdom) and God's people everywhere

DATE WRITTEN: Approximately 715 B.C., recording events from about 753 to 715 B.C.

SETTING: Hosea began his ministry during the end of the prosperous but morally declining reign of Jeroboam II of Israel (the upper classes were doing well, but they were oppressing the poor). He prophesied until shortly after the fall of Samaria in 722 B.C.

KEY PEOPLE: Hosea, Gomer, their children

KEY PLACES: The northern kingdom (Israel), Samaria, Ephraim

SPECIAL FEATURES: Hosea employs many images from daily life—God is depicted as husband, father, lion, leopard, she-bear, dew, rain, moth, and others; Israel is pictured as wife, sick person, grapevine, grapes, early fig, olive tree, woman in labor, oven, morning mist, chaff, and smoke, to name a few

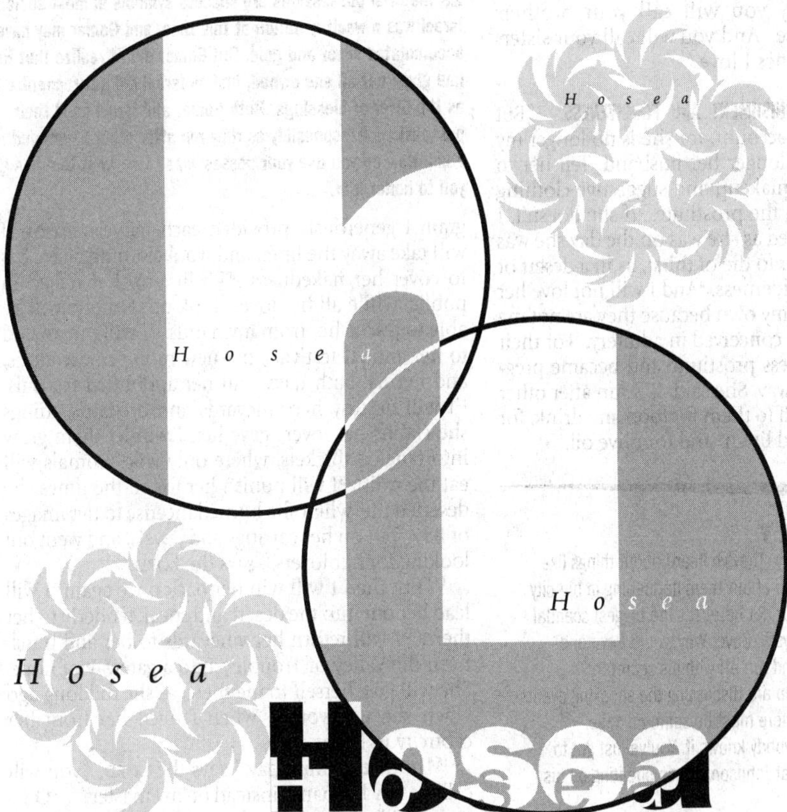


CHAPTER **1** **HOSEA'S WIFE AND CHILDREN.** The LORD
gave these messages to Hosea son of Beeri during the years when Uzziah, Jotham, Ahaz, and Hezekiah were kings of Judah, and Jeroboam son of Jehoash* was king of Israel.

[2]When the LORD first began speaking to Israel through Hosea, he said to him, "Go and marry a prostitute,* so some of her children will be born to you from other men. This will illustrate the way my people have been untrue to me, openly committing adultery against the LORD by worshiping other gods."

[3]So Hosea married Gomer, the daughter of Diblaim, and she became pregnant and gave Hosea a
son. [4]And the LORD said, "Name the child Jezreel, for I am about to punish King Jehu's dynasty to avenge
the murders he committed at Jezreel. [5]In fact, I will put an end to Israel's independence by breaking its military power in the Jezreel Valley."

[6]Soon Gomer became pregnant again and gave birth to a daughter. And the LORD said to Hosea, "Name your daughter Lo-ruhamah—'Not loved'—for I will no longer show love to the people of Israel
or forgive them. [7]But I, the LORD their God, will show love to the people of Judah. I will personally free them from their enemies without any help from weapons or armies."

[8]After Gomer had weaned Lo-ruhamah, she again became pregnant and gave birth to a second
son. [9]And the LORD said, "Name him Lo-ammi—'Not my people'—for Israel is not my people, and
I am not their God. [10]Yet the time will come when Israel will prosper and become a great nation. In that day its people will be like the sands of the seashore—too many to count! Then, at the place where they were told, 'You are not my people,' it will be said, 'You are children of the living God.'
[11]Then the people of Judah and Israel will unite under one leader, and they will return from exile together. What a day that will be—the day of Jezreel*—when God will again plant his people in his

**EXTRAORDINARY ● ● • • .**

1:2 **It is hard to imagine Hosea's feelings when God told him to marry a woman who would be unfaithful to him. He may not have wanted to do this, but he obeyed. God often asked extraordinary obedience from his prophets who were facing extraordinary times. He may ask you to do something difficult and extraordinary, too. If he does, how will you respond? Will you obey him, trusting that he who knows everything has a special purpose for his request? Will you be satisfied with the knowledge that the pain involved in obedience may benefit those you serve, and not you personally?**

1:1 Hebrew *Joash,* a variant name for Jehoash. 1:2 Or *a promiscuous woman.* 1:11 *Jezreel* means "God plants."

land. [1]In that day you will call your brothers Ammi—'My people.' And you will call your sisters Ruhamah—'The ones I love.'

CHAPTER **2** **PUNISHMENT AND FORGIVENESS.** [2]"But now, call Israel* to account, for she is no longer my wife, and I am no longer her husband. Tell her to take off her garish makeup and suggestive clothing and to stop playing the prostitute. [3]If she doesn't, I will strip her as naked as she was on the day she was born. I will leave her to die of thirst, as in a desert or a dry and barren wilderness. [4]And I will not love her children as I would my own because they are not my children! They were conceived in adultery. [5]For their mother is a shameless prostitute and became pregnant in a shameful way. She said, 'I'll run after other lovers and sell myself to them for food and drink, for clothing of wool and linen, and for olive oil.'

## ADULTERY

People are numb. They've heard about things like this; they've read about them happening in big-city churches . . . but not here! It's the biggest scandal ever in the sleepy little town of Crystal Cove: Why would Reverend Johnson leave his wife and kids and run off with his secretary?

Two members of the youth group are discussing the shocking events.

"I still don't believe it. I think there must be some mistake."

"Aw, c'mon, Jan! It's true. Everybody knows it. You've just got to face up to it. My dad found out that Johnson's been cheating on his wife for years!"

"Well, it's just awful. And imagine how Mrs. Johnson must feel. I mean, wouldn't you just die if you married someone and then found out he was messing around with other people behind your back?"

"Oh, I know. That would be like getting a knife right through your heart."

Jan is right–adultery is awful. But how many Christians are guilty of spiritual adultery? We claim to belong to God while we flirt with the world and spend most of our time in other pursuits. Imagine how rejected God must feel!

Don't just imagine it. Read the startling book of Hosea for an intimate look at how our unfaithfulness hurts God's heart. Chapter 2 is especially expressive as it depicts God as a wounded lover who wants desperately for his people to come back.

[6]"But I will fence her in with thornbushes. I will block the road to make her lose her way. [7]When she runs after her lovers, she won't be able to catch up with them. She will search for them but not find them. Then she will think, 'I might as well return to my husband because I was better off with him than I am now.' [8]She doesn't realize that it was I who gave her everything she has—the grain, the wine, the olive oil. Even the gold and silver she used in worshiping the god Baal were gifts from me!

[9]"But now I will take back the wine and ripened

## POSSESSIONS • • • • •

**2:8 Material possessions are success symbols in most societies. Israel was a wealthy nation at this time, and Gomer may have accumulated silver and gold. But Gomer didn't realize that Hosea had given her all she owned, just as Israel did not recognize God as the Giver of blessings. Both Gomer and Israel used their possessions irresponsibly as they ran after other lovers and other gods. How do you use your possessions? Use what God has given you to honor him.**

grain I generously provided each harvest season. I will take away the linen and wool clothing I gave her to cover her nakedness. [10]I will strip her naked in public, while all her lovers look on. No one will be able to rescue her from my hands. [11]I will put an end to her annual festivals, her new moon celebrations, and her Sabbath days—all her appointed festivals. [12]I will destroy her vineyards and orchards, things she claims her lovers gave her. I will let them grow into tangled thickets, where only wild animals will eat the fruit. [13]I will punish her for all the times she deserted me, when she burned incense to her images of Baal, put on her earrings and jewels, and went out looking for her lovers," says the LORD.

[14]"But then I will win her back once again. I will lead her out into the desert and speak tenderly to her there. [15]I will return her vineyards to her and transform the Valley of Trouble* into a gateway of hope. She will give herself to me there, as she did long ago when she was young, when I freed her from her captivity in Egypt.

[16]"In that coming day," says the LORD, "you will call me 'my husband' instead of 'my master.'* [17]O Israel, I will cause you to forget your images of Baal; even their names will no longer be spoken. [18]At that time I will make a covenant with all the wild animals and the birds and the animals that scurry along the ground so that they will not harm you. I will remove all weapons of war from the land, all swords and bows, so you can live unafraid in peace and safety. [19]I will make you my wife forever, showing you righteousness and justice, unfailing love and compassion. [20]I will be faithful to you and make you mine, and you will finally know me as LORD.

[21]"In that day," says the LORD, "I will answer the pleading of the sky for clouds, which will pour down water on the earth in answer to its cries for rain. [22]Then the earth will answer the thirsty cries of the grain, the grapes, and the olive trees for moisture. And the whole grand chorus will sing together, 'Jezreel'—'God plants!'

[23]"At that time I will plant a crop of Israelites and raise them for myself! I will show love to those I called 'Not loved.'* And to those I called 'Not my people,'* I will say, 'Now you are my people.' Then they will reply, 'You are our God!'"

CHAPTER **3** **HOSEA BRINGS GOMER BACK HOME.** Then the LORD said to me, "Go and get your wife again. Bring her back to you and love her, even though she

2:2 Hebrew *call your mother.* 2:15 Hebrew *valley of Achor.* 2:16 Hebrew *'my baal.'* 2:23a Hebrew *Lo-ruhamah;* see 1:6. 2:23b Hebrew *Lo-ammi;* see 1:9.

**HOSEA** served as a prophet to Israel (the northern kingdom) from 753 to 715 B.C.

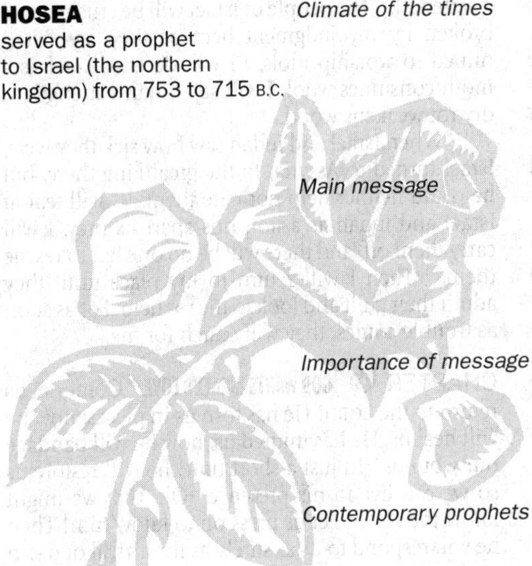

*Climate of the times* — Israel's last six kings were especially wicked; they promoted heavy taxes, oppression of the poor, idol worship, and total disregard for God. Israel was subjected to Assyria and was forced to pay tribute, which robbed its few remaining resources.

*Main message* — The people of Israel had sinned against God as an adulterous woman sins against her husband. They were sure to be judged for living in total disregard for God and fellow humans. Hosea saw the nation fall to Assyria in 722 B.C.

*Importance of message* — When we sin, we sever our relationship with God, which breaks our commitment to him. While all must answer to God for their sins, those who seek God's forgiveness are spared eternal judgment.

*Contemporary prophets* — Jonah (793–753), Amos (760–750), Micah (742–687), Isaiah (740–681)

---

loves adultery. For the LORD still loves Israel even though the people have turned to other gods, offering them choice gifts.*"

2So I bought her back for fifteen pieces of silver* and about five bushels of barley and a measure of wine.* 3Then I said to her, "You must live in my house for many days and stop your prostitution. During this time, you will not have sexual intercourse with anyone, not even with me.*"

4This illustrates that Israel will be a long time without a king or prince, and without sacrifices, temple, priests, or even idols! 5But afterward the people will return to the LORD their God and to David's descendant, their king.* They will come trembling in awe to the LORD, and they will receive his good gifts in the last days.

CHAPTER **4** **GOD'S CASE AGAINST ISRAEL.** Hear the word of the LORD, O people of Israel! The LORD has filed a lawsuit against you, saying: "There is no faithfulness, no kindness, no knowledge of God in your land. 2You curse and lie and kill and steal and commit adultery. There is violence everywhere, with one murder after another. 3That is why your land is not producing. It is filled with sadness, and all living things are becoming sick and dying. Even the animals, birds, and fish have begun to disappear.

4"Don't point your finger at someone else and try to pass the blame! Look, you priests, my complaint is with you!* 5As a sentence for your crimes, you will stumble in broad daylight, just as you might at night, and so will your false prophets. And I will destroy your mother, Israel. 6My people are being destroyed because they don't know me. It is all your fault, you priests, for you yourselves refuse to know me. Now I refuse to recognize you as my priests. Since you have forgotten the laws of your God, I will forget to bless your children. 7The more priests there are, the more they sin against me. They have exchanged* the glory of God for the disgrace of idols.

8"The priests get fed when the people sin and bring their sin offerings to them. So the priests are glad when the people sin! 9'Like priests, like people'—since the priests are wicked, the people are wicked, too. So now I will punish both priests and people for all their wicked deeds. 10They will eat and still be hungry. Though they do a big business as prostitutes, they will have no children, for they have deserted the LORD to worship other gods.

11"Alcohol and prostitution have robbed my people of their brains. 12They are asking a piece of wood to tell them what to do! They think a stick can tell them the future! Longing after idols has made them foolish. They have played the prostitute, serving other gods and deserting their God. 13They offer sacrifices to idols on the tops of mountains. They go up into the hills to burn incense in the pleasant shade of oaks, poplars, and other trees.

## NO HOPE ● ● ● • •

3:3 **After this, Gomer is no longer mentioned by Hosea. This is explained in 3:4. Gomer's absence and isolation show how God will deal with the constantly rebellious northern kingdom (5:6, 15). It is dangerous to rebel against God. If he were ever to withdraw his love and mercy, we would be without hope.**

3:1 Hebrew *raisin cakes.* 3:2a Hebrew *15 shekels of silver,* about 6 ounces or 171 grams in weight. 3:2b As in Greek version, which reads *a homer [182 liters] of barley and a measure of wine;* Hebrew reads *a homer of barley and a lethech* [2.5 bushels or 91 liters] *of barley.* 3:3 Or *and I will live with you.* 3:5 Hebrew *to David their king.* 4:4 Hebrew *Your people are like those with a complaint against the priests.* 4:7 As in Syriac version and an ancient Hebrew tradition; Masoretic Text reads *I will exchange.*

"That is why your daughters turn to prostitution, and your daughters-in-law commit adultery. [14]Why should I punish them? For you men are doing the same thing, sinning with whores and shrine prostitutes. O foolish people! You will be destroyed, for you refuse to understand.

[15]"Though Israel is a prostitute, may Judah avoid such guilt. O Judah, do not join with those who worship me insincerely at Gilgal and at Beth-aven.* Their worship is mere pretense as they take oaths in the LORD's name. [16]Israel is as stubborn as a heifer, so the LORD will put her out to pasture. She will stand alone and unprotected, like a helpless lamb in an open field. [17]Leave her alone because she is married to idolatry. [18]The men of Israel finish up their drinking bouts and off they go to find some prostitutes. Their love for shame is greater than their love for honor.* [19]So a mighty wind will sweep them away. They will die in shame because they offer sacrifices to idols.

CHAPTER **5** **THE VERDICT IS IN: GUILTY.** "Hear this, you priests and all of Israel's leaders! Listen, all you men of the royal family! These words of judgment are for you: You are doomed! For you have led the people into a snare by worshiping the idols at Mizpah and Tabor. [2]You have dug a deep pit to trap them at Acacia.* But never forget—I will settle with all of you for what you have done. [3]I know what you are like, O Israel! You have left me as a prostitute leaves her husband; you are utterly defiled. [4]Your deeds won't let you return to your God. You are a prostitute through and through, and you cannot know the LORD.

## STEER AWAY ● ● • • •

**5:4 Persistent sin hardens a person's heart and makes it difficult to repent. Deliberately choosing to disobey God can sear the conscience; each sin makes the next one easier to commit. Don't allow sin to wear you down, building a hard path deep within you. Steer as far away from sinful practices as possible.**

[5]"The arrogance of Israel* testifies against her; she will stumble under her load of guilt. Judah, too, will fall with her. [6]Then at last, they will come with their flocks and herds to offer sacrifices to the LORD. But it will be too late! They will not find him, because he has withdrawn from them, and they are now alone. [7]For they have betrayed the honor of the LORD, bearing children that aren't his. Now their false religion will devour them, along with their wealth.

[8]"Blow the ram's horn in Gibeah! Sound the alarm in Ramah! Raise the battle cry in Beth-aven*! Lead on into battle, O warriors of Benjamin! [9]One thing is certain, Israel*: When your day of punishment comes, you will become a heap of rubble.

[10]"The leaders of Judah have become as bad as thieves.* So I will pour my anger down on them like a waterfall. [11]The people of Israel will be crushed and broken by my judgment because they are determined to worship idols. [12]I will destroy Israel as a moth consumes wool. I will sap Judah's strength as dry rot weakens wood.

[13]"When Israel and Judah saw how sick they were, Israel turned to Assyria, to the great king there, but he could neither help nor cure them. [14]I will tear at Israel and Judah as a lion rips apart its prey. I will carry them off, and there will be no one left to rescue them. [15]Then I will return to my place until they admit their guilt and look to me for help. For as soon as trouble comes, they will search for me."

CHAPTER **6** **GOD WANTS ISRAEL'S LOVE.** "Come, let us return to the LORD! He has torn us in pieces; now he will heal us. He has injured us; now he will bandage our wounds. [2]In just a short time, he will restore us so we can live in his presence. [3]Oh, that we might know the LORD! Let us press on to know him! Then he will respond to us as surely as the arrival of dawn or the coming of rains in early spring."

[4]"O Israel* and Judah, what should I do with you?" asks the LORD. "For your love vanishes like the morning mist and disappears like dew in the sunlight. [5]I sent my prophets to cut you to pieces. I have slaughtered you with my words, threatening you with death. My judgment will strike you as surely as day follows night. [6]I want you to be merciful; I don't want your sacrifices. I want you to know God; that's more important than burnt offerings.

[7]"But like Adam, you broke my covenant and rebelled against me. [8]Gilead is a city of sinners, tracked with footprints of blood. [9]Its citizens are bands of robbers, lying in ambush for their victims. Gangs of priests murder travelers along the road to Shechem and practice every kind of sin. [10]Yes, I have seen a horrible thing in Israel: My people have defiled themselves by chasing after other gods!

[11]"O Judah, a harvest of punishment is also waiting for you, though I wanted so much to restore the fortunes of my people!

## CHANGES ● ● • • •

**6:1-3 This is far from genuine repentance. The people did not understand the depth of their sins. They did not turn from idols, pledge to change, or regret their sins. They thought God's wrath would last only a few days; little did they know that their nation would soon be taken into exile. Israel was interested in God only for the material benefits he provided; they did not value the eternal benefits of worshiping him. Before judging these people, however, consider *your* attitude. What do you hope to gain from your religion? Do you "repent" easily, without seriously considering what you need to change? Don't treat your relationship with God carelessly.**

4:15 *Beth-aven* means "house of wickedness"; it is being used as another name for Bethel, which means "house of God." 4:18 As in Greek version; the meaning of the Hebrew is uncertain. 5:2 Hebrew *at Shittim.* The meaning of the Hebrew for this sentence is uncertain. 5:5 Hebrew *Israel and Ephraim.* 5:8 *Beth-aven* means "house of wickedness"; it is being used as another name for Bethel, which means "house of God." 5:9 Hebrew *Ephraim,* referring to the northern kingdom of Israel; also in 5:11, 12, 13, 14. 5:10 Hebrew *have become as those who move a boundary marker.* 6:4 Hebrew *Ephraim,* referring to the northern kingdom of Israel.

CHAPTER 7 **ISRAEL: ALWAYS MISSING THE TARGET.** "I
wanted to heal Israel, but its sins were far too great.
Samaria is filled with liars, thieves, and bandits! 2Its
people don't realize I am watching them. Their sinful deeds are all around them; I see them all! 3The
people make the king glad with their wickedness.
The princes laugh about the people's many lies.
4They are all adulterers, always aflame with lust.
They are like an oven that is kept hot even while the
baker is still kneading the dough.
5"On royal holidays, the princes get drunk. The
king makes a fool of himself and drinks with those
who are making fun of him. 6Their hearts blaze like
a furnace with intrigue. Their plot smolders through
the night, and in the morning it flames forth like a
raging fire. 7They kill their kings one after another,
and no one cries out to me for help.
8"My people of Israel* mingle with godless foreigners, picking up their evil ways. Now they have
become as worthless as a half-baked cake! 9Worship-
ing foreign gods has sapped their strength, but they
don't even know it. Israel is like an old man with
graying hair, unaware of how weak and old he has
become. 10His arrogance testifies against him, yet he
doesn't return to the LORD his God or even try to find
him.
11"The people of Israel have become like silly,
witless doves, first calling to Egypt, then flying to
Assyria. 12But as they fly about, I will throw my
net over them and bring them down like a bird
from the sky. I will punish them for all their evil
ways.*
13"How terrible it will be for my people who have
deserted me! Let them die, for they have rebelled
against me. I wanted to redeem them, but they have
only spoken lies about me. 14They do not cry out to
me with sincere hearts. Instead, they sit on their
couches and wail. They cut themselves, begging foreign gods for crops and prosperity.
15"I trained them and made them strong, yet now
they plot evil against me. 16They look everywhere
except to heaven, to the Most High. They are like a
crooked bow that always misses its target. Their leaders will be killed by their enemies because of their
insolence toward me. Then the people of Egypt will
laugh at them.

CHAPTER 8 **A PREDICTION OF CAPTIVITY.** "Sound the
alarm! The enemy descends like an eagle on the
people of the LORD, for they have broken my covenant and revolted against my law. 2Now Israel pleads
with me, 'Help us, for you are our God!' 3But it is too
late! The people of Israel have rejected what is good,
and now their enemies will chase after them. 4The
people have appointed kings and princes, but not
with my consent. By making idols for themselves
from their silver and gold, they have brought about
their own destruction.
5"O Samaria, I reject this calf—this idol you have

Oh, that we might KNOW the LORD! **Let us press on** to KNOW him! Then **he will respond to us** as surely as the arrival of dawn or the coming of rains in early spring.

HOSEA 6:3

made. My fury burns against you. How long will you
be incapable of innocence? 6This calf you worship
was crafted by your own hands! It is not God! Therefore, it must be smashed to bits.
7"They have planted the wind and will harvest the
whirlwind. The stalks of wheat wither, producing no
grain. And if there is any grain, foreigners will eat it.
8The people of Israel have been swallowed up; they
lie among the nations like an old pot that no one
wants. 9Like a wild donkey looking for a mate, they
have gone up to Assyria. The people of Israel* have
sold themselves to many lovers. 10But though they
have sold themselves to many lands, I will now
gather them together. Then they will writhe under
the burden of the great king!
11"Israel has built many altars to take away sin,
but these very altars became places for sinning!

7:8 Hebrew *Ephraim,* referring to the northern kingdom of Israel; also in 7:11. 7:12 Hebrew *I will punish them because of what was reported against them in the assembly.* 8:9 Hebrew *Ephraim,* referring to the northern kingdom of Israel; also in 8:11.

12Even though I gave them all my laws, they act as if those laws don't apply to them. 13The people of Israel love their rituals of sacrifice, but to me their sacrifices are all meaningless! I will call my people to account for their sins, and I will punish them. They will go back down to Egypt.

14"Israel has built great palaces, and Judah has fortified its cities. But they have both forgotten their Maker. Therefore, I will send down fire on their palaces and burn their fortresses."

## GUESS WHO? ● ● • • •

8:12 **It is easy to listen to a sermon and think of all the people we know who should be listening, or to read the Bible and think of those who should do what the passage teaches. The Israelites did this constantly, applying God's laws to others but not to themselves. This is just another way to deflect God's Word and avoid making needed changes. As you think of others who need to apply what you are hearing or reading, check to see if the same application could fit you. And keep in mind that often our own faults are the very ones we see in others.**

CHAPTER **9** **WANDERING WITHOUT GOD.** O people of Israel, do not rejoice as others do. For you have been unfaithful to your God, hiring yourselves out like prostitutes, offering sacrifices to other gods on every threshing floor. 2So now your harvests will be too small to feed you. The grapes you gather will not quench your thirst. 3You may no longer stay here in this land of the LORD. You will be carried off to Egypt and Assyria, where you will live on food that is ceremonially unclean.

4There, far from home, you will not be allowed to pour out wine as a sacrifice to the LORD. None of the sacrifices you offer there will please him. Such sacrifices will be unclean, just as food touched by a person in mourning is unclean. All who present such sacrifices will be defiled. They may eat this food to feed themselves, but they may not offer it to the LORD.

5What then will you do on festival days? What will you do on days of feasting in the LORD's presence? 6Even if you escape destruction from Assyria, you will be conquered by Egypt. Memphis* will bury you. Briers will take over your treasures of silver; brambles will fill your homes.

7The time of Israel's punishment has come; the day of payment is almost here. Soon Israel will know this all too well. "The prophets are crazy!" the people shout. "The inspired men are mad!" So they taunt, for the nation is burdened with sin and shows only hatred for those who love God.

8The prophet is a watchman for my God over Israel,* yet traps are laid in front of him wherever he goes. He faces hostility even in the house of God. 9The things my people do are as depraved as what they did in Gibeah long ago. God will not forget. He will surely punish them for their sins.

## LOOK-ALIKES ● ● • • •

9:10 **Baal-peor was the god of Peor, a mountain in Moab. In Numbers 23, Balaam, a prophet, was hired by King Balak of Moab to curse the Israelites. The Moabites enticed the Israelites into sexual sin and Baal worship. Before long, they became as corrupt as the gods they worshiped. People can take on the characteristics of what or whom they love or worship. What do you worship? Are you becoming more like God, or are you becoming more like someone or something else?**

10The LORD says, "O Israel, when I first found you, it was like finding fresh grapes in the desert! When I saw your ancestors, it was like seeing the first ripe figs of the season! But then they deserted me for Baal-peor, giving themselves to that shameful idol. Soon they became as vile as the god they worshiped. 11The glory of Israel will fly away like a bird, for your children will die at birth or perish in the womb or never even be conceived. 12Even if your children do survive to grow up, I will take them from you. It will be a terrible day when I turn away and leave you alone. 13I have watched Israel become as beautiful and pleasant as Tyre. But now Israel will bring out her children to be slaughtered."

14O LORD, what should I request for your people? I will ask for wombs that don't give birth and breasts that give no milk.

15The LORD says, "All their wickedness began at Gilgal; there I began to hate them. I will drive them from my land because of their evil actions. I will love them no more because all their leaders are rebels. 16The people of Israel are stricken. Their roots are dried up; they will bear no more fruit. And if they give birth, I will slaughter their beloved children."

17My God will reject the people of Israel because they will not listen or obey. They will be wanderers, homeless among the nations.

CHAPTER **10** **A VINE FULL OF SIN.** How prosperous Israel is—a luxuriant vine loaded with fruit! But the more wealth the people got, the more they poured it on the altars of their foreign gods. The richer the harvests they brought in, the more beautiful the statues and idols they built. 2The hearts of the people are fickle; they are guilty and must be punished. The LORD will break down their foreign altars and smash their many idols.

3Then they will say, "We have no king because

## SPENDING ● ● • • •

10:1 **Israel prospered under Jeroboam II, gaining military and economic strength. But the more prosperous the nation became, the more it spent on idols. It seems as if the more God gives, the more we spend. We want bigger houses, better cars, finer clothes, and more expensive educations. But the finest things the world offers may line the pathway to destruction. As you prosper, consider where your money is going. Is it being used for God's purposes, or are you spending it all on yourself?**

9:6 Memphis was the capital of northern Egypt. 9:8 Hebrew *Ephraim,* referring to the northern kingdom of Israel; also in 9:11, 13, 16.

we didn't fear the LORD. But what's the difference? What could a king do for us anyway?" [4]They
spout empty words and make promises they don't
intend to keep. So perverted justice springs up
among them like poisonous weeds in a farmer's
field.
[5]The people of Samaria tremble for their calf idol
at Beth-aven.* The people mourn over it, and the
priests wail for it, because its glory will be stripped
away. [6]This idol they love so much will be carted
away with them when they go as captives to Assyria,
a gift to the great king there. Israel will be laughed at
and shamed because its people have trusted in this
idol. [7]Samaria will be cut off, and its king will disappear like a chip of wood on an ocean wave. [8]And the
pagan shrines of Aven,* the place of Israel's sin, will
crumble. Thorns and thistles will grow up around
them. They will beg the mountains to bury them and
the hills to fall on them.
[9]The LORD says, "O Israel, ever since that awful
night in Gibeah, there has been only sin and more
sin! You have made no progress whatsoever. Was it
not right that the wicked men of Gibeah were
attacked? [10]Now I will attack you, too, for your
rebellion and disobedience. I will call out the armies of the nations to punish you for your multiplied sins.
[11]"Israel* is like a trained heifer accustomed to
treading out the grain—an easy job that she loves.
Now I will put a heavy yoke on her tender neck. I will
drive her in front of the plow. Israel* and Judah must
now break up the hard ground; their days of ease are
gone. [12]I said, 'Plant the good seeds of righteousness,
and you will harvest a crop of my love. Plow up the
hard ground of your hearts, for now is the time to
seek the LORD, that he may come and shower righteousness upon you.'
[13]"But you have cultivated wickedness and
raised a thriving crop of sins. You have eaten the
fruit of lies—trusting in your military might, believing that great armies could make your nation
safe! [14]Now the terrors of war will rise among your
people. All your fortifications will fall, just as they
did when Shalman destroyed Beth-arbel. Even
mothers and children were dashed to death there.
[15]You will share that fate, Bethel, because of your
great wickedness. When the day of judgment
dawns, the king of Israel will be completely destroyed.

CHAPTER **11** **GOD STILL LOVES ISRAEL.** "When Israel was a child, I loved him as a son, and I called
my son out of Egypt. [2]But the more I* called to
him, the more he rebelled, offering sacrifices to the
images of Baal and burning incense to idols. [3]It
was I who taught Israel* how to walk, leading him
along by the hand. But he doesn't know or even
care that it was I who took care of him. [4]I led Israel
along with my ropes of kindness and love. I lifted
the yoke from his neck, and I myself stooped to
feed him.
[5]"But since my people refuse to return to me,
they will go back to Egypt and will be forced to
serve Assyria. [6]War will swirl through their cities;
their enemies will crash through their gates and
destroy them, trapping them in their own evil
plans. [7]For my people are determined to desert me.

**People around me don't act like they need God. How can I share my faith in Christ with them if they don't feel a need to know him?**

Rarely will people want a relationship with someone whom they feel they don't need. The Bible is filled with stories of people who have actively rejected God, who felt no need for him because their lives were going so well. In Hosea 13:6, he confronted the people of Israel—his chosen people—for doing that very thing.

It's funny, though, that when things are rough, people quickly pin the blame on God. This makes as much sense as a six-year-old child hitting himself on the thumb with a hammer and then blaming his dad.

"I saw you use your hammer once, Dad. I know you told me not to use it, but I did it anyway. You should have made sure I never hurt myself with it! So it's your fault I hurt myself!"

People do the same with God: "I'm going to take my life and run it the way I want to, God—but if things go wrong, it's your fault!"

You can't make someone need God, but here are some things you can do:

First, be ready to help your friends when they do have needs. Keep the friendship bridges strong so they will come to you for help. Then you can point them to Christ. Seek the help of a mature Christian friend for advice on how to do this best.

Second, look for people who are hurt already and share the Good News with them. Be sensitive when you do this. Don't make it sound as though you have all the answers, or as if having a relationship with God means you'll never go through bad times. Simply share how God has helped you, and what he means in your life.

Third, watch out for your own heart. The Bible warns us that some things can distract us from God: "Trust in your money and down you go! But the godly flourish like leaves in spring" (Proverbs 11:28), and "There is a path before each person that seems right, but it ends in death" (Proverbs 14:12).

Satan wants us to live the "easy" life, apart from (and even numb to) God. Hey, the stakes are high. Being separated from God now affects where we spend eternity.

**10:5** *Beth-aven* means "house of wickedness"; it is being used as another name for Bethel, which means "house of God." **10:8** *Aven* is a reference to Beth-aven; see 10:5 and the note there. **10:11a** Hebrew *Ephraim*, referring to the northern kingdom of Israel. **10:11b** Hebrew *Jacob*. **11:2** As in Greek version; Hebrew reads *they*. **11:3** Hebrew *Ephraim*, referring to the northern kingdom of Israel; also in 11:8, 9, 12.

**REMEMBER ● ● • • •**

12:8 **Rich people and nations often claim that their material success is due to their own hard work, initiative, and intelligence. Because they have all they want, they don't feel the need for God. They believe their riches are their own, and they feel they have the right to use them any way they please. If you find yourself feeling proud of your accomplishments, remember that all your opportunities, abilities, and resources come from God—and that you hold them in sacred trust for him.**

They call me the Most High, but they don't truly honor me.

[8]"Oh, how can I give you up, Israel? How can I let you go? How can I destroy you like Admah and Zeboiim? My heart is torn within me, and my compassion overflows. [9]No, I will not punish you as much as my burning anger tells me to. I will not completely destroy Israel, for I am God and not a mere mortal. I am the Holy One living among you, and I will not come to destroy.

[10]"For someday the people will follow the LORD. I will roar like a lion, and my people will return trembling from the west. [11]Like a flock of birds, they will come from Egypt. Flying like doves, they will return from Assyria. And I will bring them home again," says the LORD.

[12]Israel surrounds me with lies and deceit, but Judah still walks with God and is faithful to the Holy One.*

CHAPTER **12** **GOD WANTS HIS PEOPLE BACK.** The people of Israel* feed on the wind; they chase after the east wind all day long. They multiply lies and violence; they make alliances with Assyria and cut deals with the Egyptians.

[2]Now the LORD is bringing a lawsuit against Judah. He is about to punish Jacob* for all his deceitful ways. [3]Before Jacob was born, he struggled with his brother; when he became a man, he even fought with God. [4]Yes, he wrestled with the angel and won. He wept and pleaded for a blessing from him. There at Bethel he met God face to face, and God spoke to him*—[5]the LORD God Almighty, the LORD is his name! [6]So now, come back to your God! Act on the principles of love and justice, and always live in confident dependence on your God.

[7]But no, the people are like crafty merchants selling from dishonest scales—they love to cheat. [8]Israel boasts, "I am rich, and I've gotten it all by myself! No one can say I got it by cheating! My record is spotless!"

[9]"I am the LORD your God, who rescued you from your slavery in Egypt. And I will make you live in tents again, as you do each year when you celebrate the Festival of Shelters.* [10]I sent my prophets to warn you with many visions and parables."

[11]But Gilead is filled with sinners who worship idols. And in Gilgal, too, they sacrifice bulls; their altars are lined up like the heaps of stone along the edges of a plowed field. [12]Jacob fled to the land of Aram and earned a wife by tending sheep. [13]Then the LORD led Jacob's descendants, the Israelites, out of Egypt by a prophet, who guided and protected them. [14]But the people of Israel have bitterly provoked the LORD, so their Lord will now sentence them to death in payment for their sins.

CHAPTER **13** **GOD IS ANGRY.** In the past when the tribe of Ephraim spoke, the people shook with fear because the other Israelite tribes looked up to them. But the people of Ephraim sinned by worshiping Baal and thus sealed their destruction. [2]Now they keep on sinning by making silver idols to worship—images shaped skillfully with human hands. "Sacrifice to these," they cry, "and kiss the calf idols!" [3]Therefore, they will disappear like the morning mist, like dew in the morning sun, like chaff blown by the wind, like smoke from a chimney.

[4]"I am the LORD your God, who rescued you from your slavery in Egypt. You have no God but me, for there is no other savior. [5]I took care of you in the wilderness, in that dry and thirsty land. [6]But when you had eaten and were satisfied, then you became proud and forgot me. [7]So now I will attack you like a lion, or like a leopard that lurks along the road. [8]I will rip you to pieces like a bear whose cubs have been taken away. I will tear you apart and devour you like a hungry lion.

[9]"You are about to be destroyed, O Israel, though I am your helper. [10]Where now is* your king? Why don't you call on him for help? Where are all the leaders of the land? You asked for them, now let them save you! [11]In my anger I gave you kings, and in my fury I took them away.

[12]"The sins of Ephraim have been collected and stored away for punishment. [13]The people have been offered new birth, but they are like a child who resists being born. How stubborn they are! How foolish! [14]Should I ransom them from the

**RESTORED ● ● • • •**

14:1-2 **The people could return to God by asking him to take away their sins. The same is true for us: we can pray Hosea's prayer and know our sins are forgiven because Christ paid the penalty for them on the cross (John 3:16).**

**Forgiveness begins when we see the destructiveness of sin and the futility of life without God. Then we admit we cannot save ourself; our only hope is in God's mercy. Though you do not deserve forgiveness and therefore cannot demand it, you can—and must—appeal for God's love and mercy. And you can be confident you will receive God's forgiveness because he is gracious and loving and wants to restore you to himself, just as he wanted to restore Israel.**

11:12 Or *and Judah is unruly against God, the faithful Holy One.* 12:1 Hebrew *Ephraim,* referring to the northern kingdom of Israel; also in 12:8, 14. 12:2 *Jacob* means "he grasps at the heel"; this can also figuratively mean "he deceives." 12:4 As in Greek and Syriac versions; Hebrew reads *to us.* 12:9 Hebrew *as in the days of your appointed feast.* 13:10 As in Greek and Syriac versions and Latin Vulgate; Hebrew reads *I will be.*

**While the prophet Hosea lived out his message regarding Israel's relationship with God, other prophets also used the symbol of marriage to describe God's love for his people.**

## HOSEA AND GOMER

*God said to Hosea:* "Go and marry a prostitute, so some of her children will be born to you from other men. This will illustrate the way my people have been untrue to me, openly committing adultery against the LORD by worshiping other gods." So Hosea married Gomer, the daughter of Diblaim, and she became pregnant and gave Hosea a son. *Hosea 1:2-3*

*Then [Hosea] said to [Gomer, his wife],* "You must live in my house for many days and stop your prostitution. During this time, you will not have sexual intercourse with anyone, not even with me." This illustrates that Israel will be a long time without a king or prince, and without sacrifices, temple, priests, or even idols! *Hosea 3:3-4*

*God said to Hosea:* "Go and get your wife again. Bring her back to you and love her, even though she loves adultery. For the LORD still loves Israel even though the people have turned to other gods, offering them choice gifts." *Hosea 3:1*

*God said to Hosea:* "Afterward the people will return to the LORD their God and to David's descendant, their king. They will come trembling in awe to the LORD, and they will receive his good gifts in the last days." *Hosea 3:5*

## GOD AND ISRAEL

*God said to Israel through Ezekiel:* I wrapped my cloak around you . . . and declared my marriage vows. I made a covenant with you, says the Sovereign LORD, and you became mine. *Ezekiel 16:8*

*God said to Israel through Jeremiah:* I remember how eager you were to please me as a young bride long ago, how you loved me and followed me even through the barren wilderness. *Jeremiah 2:2*

*God said to Israel through Jeremiah:* How can I pardon you? For even your children have turned from me. They have sworn by gods that are not gods at all! I fed my people until they were fully satisfied. But they thanked me by committing adultery and lining up at the city's brothels. *Jeremiah 5:7*

*God said to Israel through Ezekiel:* You thought you could get along without me, so you trusted instead in your fame and beauty. You gave yourself as a prostitute to every man who came along. Your beauty was theirs for the asking! *Ezekiel 16:15*

*God said to Israel through Jeremiah:* O Israel, my faithless people, come home to me again, for I am merciful. I will not be angry with you forever. Only acknowledge your guilt. Admit that you rebelled against the LORD your God and committed adultery against him by worshiping idols under every green tree. . . . Return home . . . for I am your husband. *Jeremiah 3:12-14*

*God said to Israel through Ezekiel:* I will keep the covenant I made with you when you were young, and I will establish an everlasting covenant with you. *Ezekiel 16:60*

---

grave? Should I redeem them from death? O death,
bring forth your terrors! O grave, bring forth your
plagues! For I will not relent! [15]Ephraim was the
most fruitful of all his brothers, but the east
wind—a blast from the LORD—will arise in the
desert. It will blow hard against the people of
Ephraim, drying up their land. All their flowing
springs and wells will disappear. Every precious
thing they have will be plundered and carried
away. [16]The people of Samaria must bear the consequences of their guilt because they rebelled
against their God. They will be killed by an invading army, their little ones dashed to death against
the ground, their pregnant women ripped open by
swords."

CHAPTER **14** **GOD OFFERS FORGIVENESS.** Return,
O Israel, to the LORD your God, for your sins have
brought you down. [2]Bring your petitions, and return
to the LORD. Say to him, "Forgive all our sins and
graciously receive us, so that we may offer you the
sacrifice of praise. [3]Assyria cannot save us, nor can

**NEVER-FAILING ● ● • • •**

14:4 **When our will is weak, when our reason is confused, when our conscience is burdened with a load of guilt, we must remember that God promises forgiveness and boundless love. When friends and family desert us or don't understand us, when we are tired of being good, God's love knows no bounds. When we can't see the way or hear God's voice, when we lack courage to go on, when our shortcomings or an awareness of our sins overwhelms us, God's love knows no bounds. Regardless of how things seem or even how you feel, rely on this truth: God's love knows *no bounds*.**

our strength in battle. Never again will we call the
idols we have made 'our gods.' No, in you alone do
the orphans find mercy."
[4]The LORD says, "Then I will heal you of your
idolatry and faithlessness, and my love will know
no bounds, for my anger will be gone forever! [5]I
will be to Israel like a refreshing dew from heaven.
It will blossom like the lily; it will send roots deep
into the soil like the cedars in Lebanon. [6]Its
branches will spread out like those of beautiful
olive trees, as fragrant as the cedar forests of Lebanon. [7]My people will return again to the safety of
their land. They will flourish like grain and blossom like grapevines. They will be as fragrant as the
wines of Lebanon.
[8]"O Israel,* stay away from idols! I am the one
who looks after you and cares for you. I am like a tree
that is always green, giving my fruit to you all
through the year."
[9]Let those who are wise understand these things.
Let those who are discerning listen carefully. The
paths of the LORD are true and right, and righteous
people live by walking in them. But sinners stumble
and fall along the way.

14:8 Hebrew *Ephraim,* referring to the northern kingdom of Israel.

# MEGA themes

**NATION'S SIN** Just as Hosea's wife, Gomer, was unfaithful to him, so the nation of Israel had been unfaithful to God. Israel's idolatry was like adultery. They sought "illicit" relationships with Assyria and Egypt to give Israel military might, and they mixed Baal worship with the worship of God.

Like Gomer, we can chase after other loves—power, popularity, pleasure, or money. The temptations in this world can be very seductive. Are you loyal to God, remaining completely faithful, or have other loves taken his rightful place?

1. In what ways did Gomer represent the nation of Israel?
2. In today's world, what sins tempt God's people to stray from him?
3. How can you, as a Christian young person, live close to God in a world filled with opportunities to be unfaithful to him?

**GOD'S JUDGMENT** Hosea was solemnly warning Judah not to follow Israel's example. Because Judah broke the covenant, turned away from God, and forgot her maker, she experienced a devastating invasion and exile. Sin has terrible consequences.

Disaster follows rebellion and ingratitude toward God. The Lord is our only true refuge. We will find no safety or security anywhere else. No one who rebels against God will escape his judgment.

1. What happened to Israel as a result of her disobedience?
2. Describe the qualities of God you see revealed both in his promise to judge and his warning to not fall into judgment.
3. When you consider the reality of God's judgment, how do you feel about him? How does that affect the way you relate to God? The way you live your life daily?

**GOD'S LOVE** Just as Hosea went after his unfaithful wife to bring her back, so the Lord pursues us with his love. His love is tender, loyal, unchanging, and undying. No matter what, God still loves us.

Have you forgotten God and become disloyal to him? Don't let prosperity diminish your love for him or success blind you to your need for his love.

1. God used Hosea's relationship with Gomer to illustrate God's relationship with his people. What do you learn about God from this illustration?
2. In what ways could Gomer's failure to remain faithful to Hosea lead her to miss out on love?
3. Gomer's life was sad and empty. How is this like people who know God but fail to respond to his love?
4. What in your life threatens to keep you from fully experiencing God's love for you? Remove this obstacle before it robs you of the best love you will ever know.

**RESTORATION** God said he would discipline his people for sin, but he encouraged and restored those who repented. True repentance opens the way to a new beginning. God forgives and restores those who return to his love.

There is hope for all who turn back to God. Nothing compares to loving him. Turn to the Lord while the offer is still good. No matter how far you have strayed, God is willing to bring you back because his love never fails.

1. After surveying chapters 11 and 14, describe what you discover about God.
2. Through Hosea we see that God wants to rebuild the relationship with the person who has sinned. What does he expect from the sinner for this to happen?
3. Think of an area in your life that has been or is being affected by sin. How did God bring you back to himself?
4. What about this study of restoration can be used to bring hope to those who feel guilty and think God could never love them? What about your experience with God could you share with a person who was feeling and thinking that way?

853 B.C.
**King Ahab dies in battle**

848
**Elisha becomes a prophet**

841
**Jehu becomes king of Israel; Athaliah seizes Judah's throne**

835
**Joel becomes a prophet; Joash becomes king of Judah**

814
**Jehoahaz becomes king of Israel**

798
**Jehoash becomes king of Israel**

796?
**Joel's ministry ends**

793
**Jonah becomes a prophet; Jeroboam II becomes king of Israel**

"OK, students, your final papers are due. Students who do not hand in a paper will receive a zero for 25 percent of this quarter's grade. Don't look startled—we discussed the penalty for late papers when I gave you this assignment." Mr. Donley was a good teacher, but he was tough. Tina expected to get an A or a B in his class, but her paper wasn't ready. She'd meant to write it last weekend but didn't get around to it. Maybe if she talked to him. . . . ■ Tina walked up to Mr. Donley's desk. "Mr. Donley," she began, "I know what you said about the paper being due, but I've been really busy. Can I hand it in next week?" ■ Mr. Donley frowned and answered, "Tina, you're one of my better students, but two months ago I told the class there would be only a few acceptable reasons for a late paper. Not having time isn't good enough. I can't extend the deadline for you. I'm sorry." Sadly, Tina left the room. ■ Deadlines and penalties are a part of life. The book of Joel also is about a deadline . . . for Judah to turn back to God. Joel called this deadline "the day of the LORD," when God would judge people for their actions. The people of Judah had forgotten about God and were living evil, rebellious lives. Joel reminded them that those who ignored God would one day face God's wrath. ■ Joel forces us to remember that God judges sin. As you read this book, ask God to make you aware of the areas in your life where you need to repent. Remember, there is a deadline.

## STATS

PURPOSE: To warn Judah of God's impending judgment because of their sins and to urge them to turn back to God

AUTHOR: Joel son of Pethuel

TO WHOM WRITTEN: The people of Judah, the southern kingdom, and God's people everywhere

DATE WRITTEN: Probably during the time Joel prophesied, from about 835 to 796 B.C.

SETTING: The people of Judah had become prosperous and complacent. Taking God for granted, they had turned to self-centeredness, idolatry, and sin. Joel warned them that this kind of lifestyle would inevitably bring down God's judgment.

KEY PEOPLE: Joel, the people of Judah

KEY PLACE: Jerusalem

# Joel

**CHAPTER 1** **A PLAGUE OF LOCUSTS.** The LORD gave this message to Joel son of Pethuel.

[2]Hear this, you leaders of the people! Everyone listen! In all your history, has anything like this ever happened before? [3]Tell your children about it in the years to come. Pass the awful story down from generation to generation. [4]After the cutting locusts finished eating the crops, the swarming locusts took what was left! After them came the hopping locusts, and then the stripping locusts,* too!

[5]Wake up, you drunkards, and weep! All the grapes are ruined, and all your new wine is gone! [6]A vast army of locusts* has invaded my land. It is a terrible army, too numerous to count! Its teeth are as sharp as the teeth of lions! [7]They have destroyed my grapevines and fig trees, stripping their bark and leaving the branches white and bare.

[8]Weep with sorrow, as a virgin weeps when her fiancé has died. [9]There is no grain or wine to offer at the Temple of the LORD. The priests are mourning because there are no offerings. Listen to the weeping of these ministers of the LORD! [10]The fields are ruined and empty of crops. The grain, the wine, and the olive oil are gone.

[11]Despair, all you farmers! Wail, all you vine growers! Weep, because the wheat and barley—yes, all the field crops—are ruined. [12]The grapevines and the fig trees have all withered. The pomegranate trees, palm trees, and apple trees—yes, all the fruit trees—have dried up. All joy has dried up with them.

[13]Dress yourselves in sackcloth, you priests! Wail, you who serve before the altar! Come, spend the night in sackcloth, you ministers of my God! There is no grain or wine to offer at the Temple of your God. [14]Announce a time of fasting; call the people together for a solemn meeting. Bring the leaders and all the people into the Temple of the LORD your God, and cry out to him there. [15]The day of the LORD is on the way, the day when destruction comes from the Almighty. How terrible that day will be!

## LULLED ASLEEP ● ● • • •

1:5 **The people's moral senses were dulled, making them oblivious to sin. Joel called them to awaken from their complacency and admit their sins before it was too late. Otherwise, everything would be destroyed, even the grapes and wine that caused their drunkenness. Our times of peace and prosperity can lull us to sleep. We must never let material abundance be a substitute for spiritual readiness.**

1:4 The precise identification of the four kinds of locusts mentioned here is uncertain. 1:6 Hebrew *A nation.*

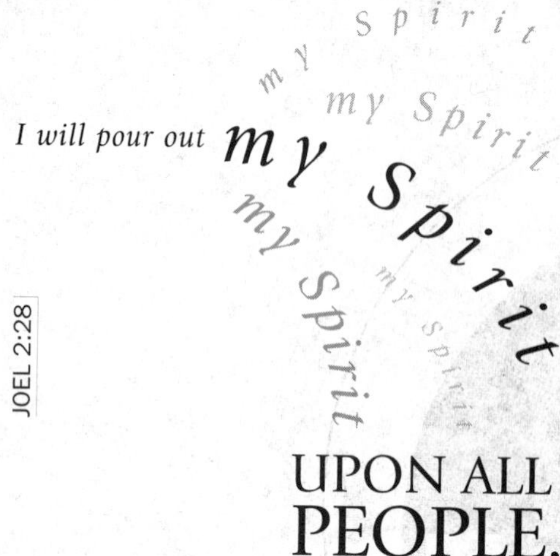


Your sons and daughters
*will prophesy.*
Your old men
*will dream dreams.*
Your young men
*will see visions.*

16 We watch as our food disappears before our very eyes. There are no joyful celebrations in the house of our God. 17 The seeds die in the parched ground, and the grain crops fail. The barns and granaries stand empty and abandoned. 18 How the animals moan with hunger! The cattle wander about confused because there is no pasture for them. The sheep bleat in misery.

19 LORD, help us! The fire has consumed the pastures and burned up all the trees. 20 Even the wild animals cry out to you because they have no water to drink. The streams have dried up, and fire has consumed the pastures.

CHAPTER **2** **JUDGMENT WILL COME.** Blow the trumpet in Jerusalem*! Sound the alarm on my holy mountain! Let everyone tremble in fear because the day of the LORD is upon us. 2 It is a day of darkness and gloom, a day of thick clouds and deep blackness. Suddenly, like dawn spreading across the mountains, a mighty army appears! How great and powerful they are! The likes of them have not been seen before and never will be seen again.

3 Fire burns in front of them and follows them in every direction! Ahead of them the land lies as fair as the Garden of Eden in all its beauty. Behind them is nothing but desolation; not one thing escapes. 4 They look like tiny horses, and they run as fast. 5 Look at them as they leap along the mountaintops! Listen to the noise they make—like the rumbling of chariots, like the roar of a fire sweeping across a field, or like a mighty army moving into battle.

6 Fear grips all the people; every face grows pale with fright. 7 The attackers march like warriors and scale city walls like trained soldiers. Straight forward they march, never breaking rank. 8 They never jostle each other; each moves in exactly the right place. They lunge through the gaps, and no weapon can stop them. 9 They swarm over the city and run along its walls. They enter all the houses, climbing like thieves through the windows.

10 The earth quakes as they advance, and the heavens tremble. The sun and moon grow dark, and the stars no longer shine. 11 The LORD leads them with a shout! This is his mighty army, and they follow his orders. The day of the LORD is an awesome, terrible thing. Who can endure it?

12 That is why the LORD says, "Turn to me now, while there is time! Give me your hearts. Come with fasting, weeping, and mourning. 13 Don't tear your clothing in your grief; instead, tear your hearts." Return to the LORD your God, for he is gracious and merciful. He is not easily angered. He is filled with kindness and is eager not to punish you. 14 Who knows? Perhaps even yet he will give you a reprieve, sending you a blessing instead of this terrible curse. Perhaps he will give you so much that you will be able to offer grain and wine to the LORD your God as before!

15 Blow the trumpet in Jerusalem! Announce a time of fasting; call the people together for a solemn meeting. 16 Bring everyone—the elders, the children, and even the babies. Call the bridegroom from his quarters and the bride from her private room. 17 The priests, who minister in the LORD's presence, will stand between the people and the altar, weeping. Let them pray, "Spare your people, LORD! They belong to you, so don't let them become an object of mockery. Don't let their name become a proverb of unbelieving foreigners who say, 'Where is the God of Israel? He must be helpless!'"

18 Then the LORD will pity his people and be indignant for the honor of his land! 19 He will reply, "Look! I am sending you grain and wine and olive oil, enough to satisfy your needs. You will no longer be an object of mockery among the surrounding nations. 20 I will remove these armies from the north and send them far away. I will drive them back into the parched wastelands, where they will die. Those in the rear will go into the Dead Sea; those at the front will go into the Mediterranean.* The stench of their rotting bodies will rise over the land."

Surely the LORD has done great things! 21 Don't be afraid, my people! Be glad now and rejoice because the LORD has done great things. 22 Don't be afraid, you animals of the field! The pastures will soon be green. The trees will again be filled with

2:1 Hebrew *Zion;* also in 2:15, 23. 2:20 Hebrew *the eastern sea; . . . the western sea.*

luscious fruit; fig trees and grapevines will flourish
once more. 23Rejoice, you people of Jerusalem! Rejoice in the LORD your God! For the rains he sends
are an expression of his grace. Once more the
autumn rains will come, as well as the rains of
spring. 24The threshing floors will again be piled
high with grain, and the presses will overflow with
wine and olive oil.
25The LORD says, "I will give you back what you
lost to the stripping locusts, the cutting locusts, the
swarming locusts, and the hopping locusts.* It was I
who sent this great destroying army against you.
26Once again you will have all the food you want,
and you will praise the LORD your God, who does
these miracles for you. Never again will my people
be disgraced like this. 27Then you will know that I am
here among my people of Israel and that I alone am
the LORD your God. My people will never again be
disgraced like this.
28"Then after I have poured out my rains again, I
will pour out my Spirit upon all people. Your sons
and daughters will prophesy. Your old men will
dream dreams. Your young men will see visions. 29In
those days, I will pour out my Spirit even on servants,
men and women alike.
30"I will cause wonders in the heavens and on the
earth—blood and fire and pillars of smoke. 31The
sun will be turned into darkness, and the moon will
turn bloodred before that great and terrible day of
the LORD arrives. 32And anyone who calls on the
name of the LORD will be saved. There will be people
on Mount Zion in Jerusalem who escape, just as the
LORD has said. These will be among the survivors
whom the LORD has called.

CHAPTER **3** **BAD NEWS FOR ISRAEL'S ENEMIES.** "At that
time, when I restore the prosperity of Judah and
Jerusalem," says the LORD, 2"I will gather the armies
of the world into the valley of Jehoshaphat.* There I
will judge them for harming my people, for scattering my inheritance among the nations, and for dividing up my land. 3They cast lots to decide which of
my people would be their slaves. They traded young
boys for prostitutes and little girls for enough wine
to get drunk.
4"What do you have against me, Tyre and Sidon
and you cities of Philistia? Are you trying to take
revenge on me? If you are, then watch out! I will
strike swiftly and pay you back for everything you
have done. 5You have taken my silver and gold and
all my precious treasures, and you have carried
them off to your pagan temples. 6You have sold the
people of Judah and Jerusalem to the Greeks,*
who took them far from their homeland. 7But I
will bring them back again from all these places to
which you sold them, and I will pay you back for
all you have done. 8I will sell your sons and daughters to the people of Judah, and they will sell them
to the peoples of Arabia,* a nation far away. I, the
LORD, have spoken!"
9Say to the nations far and wide: "Get ready for
war! Call out your best warriors! Let all your fighting
men advance for the attack! 10Beat your plowshares
into swords and your pruning hooks into spears.
Train even your weaklings to be warriors. 11Come
quickly, all you nations everywhere! Gather together
in the valley."
And now, O LORD, call out your warriors!
12"Let the nations be called to arms. Let them
march to the valley of Jehoshaphat. There I, the
LORD, will sit to pronounce judgment on them all.
13Now let the sickle do its work, for the harvest is
ripe. Come, tread the winepress because it is full. The
storage vats are overflowing with the wickedness of
these people."

**I wish God would do more "miracle" type of things in my life. Why don't amazing things happen more often?**

Miracles and "amazing things" are great, but the best miracle God could ever perform is the miracle of salvation.

The fact that God actually chose to forgive our sin and live inside us is an incredible miracle. We should thank him for that every day. But often we forget.

Some teachers of the law once came to Jesus and said, "We want to see a sign" (Matthew 12:38). He answered that they wouldn't see any greater miracle than him being dead, buried in the ground three days, and then coming back to life! But they weren't satisfied.

The real question is, What kind of miracles do you want God to do in your life?

Do you want him to give you *A*'s in subjects you haven't studied for? Let you score the winning touchdown? Perform some healing to "prove" he's there? If so, you'll be disappointed. He doesn't do anything just to prove he exists—beyond, of course, what he's already done through Christ.

But if you want to see him do miracles in your life and in the lives of those around you, stand back. That's the kind he specializes in.

God promised his followers that he would perform wonderful things through them (see Joel 2:28-32). And you'll find that the most exciting miracles are when God uses you to lead someone else to him. Those miracles are better; they lead to something eternal!

The longer you follow Christ, the more you'll see things happen. When someone's eternal destiny is changed, and God used *you* to make it happen, you'll experience a "high" like you've never known.

So ask God to use you to perform the greatest miracle of all—to lead someone to Christ.

**2:25** The precise identification of the four kinds of locusts mentioned here is uncertain. **3:2** *Jehoshaphat* means "the LORD judges." **3:6** Hebrew *to the peoples of Javan.* **3:8** Hebrew *to the Sabeans.*

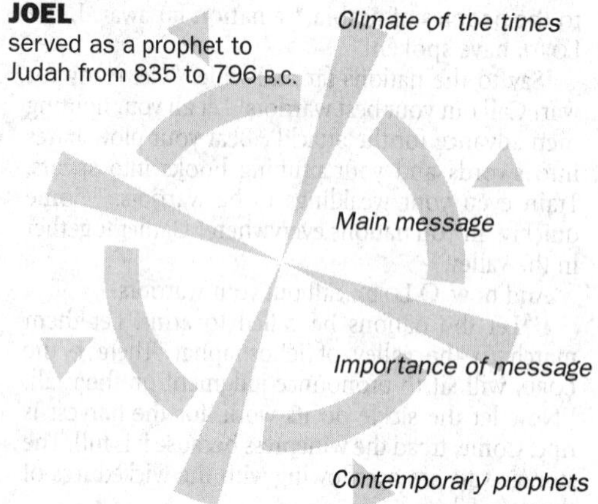

**JOEL**
served as a prophet to Judah from 835 to 796 B.C.

| | |
|---|---|
| *Climate of the times* | Wicked Queen Athaliah seized power in a bloody coup but was overthrown after a few years. Joash was crowned king, but he was only seven years old and in great need of spiritual guidance. Joash followed God in his early years, then turned away from him. |
| *Main message* | A plague of locusts had come to discipline the nation. Joel called the people to turn back to God before an even greater judgment occurred. |
| *Importance of message* | God judges all people for their sins but is merciful and offers eternal salvation to those who turn to him in repentance. |
| *Contemporary prophets* | Elisha (848–797)<br>Jonah (793–753) |

14 Thousands upon thousands are waiting in the
valley of decision. It is there that the day of the
LORD will soon arrive. 15 The sun and moon will
grow dark, and the stars will no longer shine. 16 The
LORD's voice will roar from Zion and thunder from
Jerusalem, and the earth and heavens will begin to
shake. But to his people of Israel, the LORD will be
a welcoming refuge and a strong fortress.
17 "Then you will know that I, the LORD your
God, live in Zion, my holy mountain. Jerusalem
will be holy forever, and foreign armies will never
conquer her again. 18 In that day the mountains will
drip with sweet wine, and the hills will flow with
milk. Water will fill the dry streambeds of Judah,
and a fountain will burst forth from the LORD's
Temple, watering the arid valley of acacias.*
19 Egypt will become a wasteland and Edom a wilderness, because they attacked Judah and killed
her innocent people.
20 "But Judah will remain forever, and Jerusalem
will endure through all future generations. 21 I will
pardon my people's crimes, which I have not yet
pardoned; and I, the LORD, will make my home in
Jerusalem* with my people."

3:18 Hebrew *valley of Shittim.* 3:21 Hebrew *Zion.*

**FOR REAL ● ● • • •**

3:14 **Joel described multitudes waiting in the "valley of decision" (the valley of Jehoshaphat of verses 2 and 12). Billions of people have lived on earth, and every one of them—dead, living, and yet to be born—will face judgment. Look around you. See your friends, those with whom you work and live. Have they received God's forgiveness? Have they been warned about sin's consequences? If we understand the severity of God's final judgment, we will want to take God's offer of hope to them.**

# MEGA themes

**PUNISHMENT** Like a destroying army of locusts, God's punishment for sin is overwhelming, dreadful, and unavoidable. When it comes, there will be no food, no water, no protection, and no escape. The day for settling accounts with God for how we have lived is fast approaching.

All of us must be accountable to God—not to nature, the economy, rulers of nations, or an invading army. We can't ignore or offend God forever. We must pay attention to his message now or face the consequences of his anger later.

1. In what ways were the locusts an accurate illustration of God's judgment and punishment?
2. God's holiness leads him to punish sin severely. What does this teach you about the holiness of God? The danger of sin?
3. Our need for salvation is often illustrated by a large gap between us and God. This gap is caused by our sin. Why does sin cause such a gap?
4. Based on this study of sin and punishment, what do you learn about the importance of the sinless Christ bridging that gap?

**FORGIVENESS** God was ready to forgive and restore all those who would come to him and turn away from sin. God wanted to shower his people with his love and restore them to a proper relationship with him.

We receive forgiveness when we turn from sin and turn toward God. As long as we are alive, it is never too late to receive God's forgiveness. God's greatest desire is for you to enjoy his love and forgiveness.

1. What promise is found in 2:32? How is that promise available to sinners today?
2. The sinless Christ bridged the gap caused by our sin. What specifically has Christ done for you in relationship to God's holiness?
3. What specific ways could you and your Christian friends communicate this message of forgiveness and restoration to non-Christians in your school and community?
4. Develop a plan for sharing this hope of forgiveness with a non-Christian.

**PROMISE OF THE HOLY SPIRIT** Joel predicted the time when God would pour out his Holy Spirit on all people. It would be the beginning of new and fresh worship of God by those who believe in him, but also the beginning of judgment on those who reject him.

God is in control. Justice and restoration are in his hands. The Holy Spirit confirms God's love for us just as he did for the first Christians (Acts 2). We must be faithful to God and place our life under the guidance and power of his Holy Spirit.

1. What does Joel teach you about the work of the Holy Spirit?
2. Why is the Holy Spirit a significant part of God's provision for his people?
3. John 14, Acts 2, and Ephesians 1 are New Testament passages that give more insight on the role of the Holy Spirit. Look at these passages with the following question in mind: As a Christian, how should I respond to the presence of the Holy Spirit in my life?

793 B.C.
**Jeroboam II becomes king of Israel**

760
**Amos becomes a prophet to Israel**

753
**Hosea becomes a prophet to Israel**

752
**King Shallum of Israel is assassinated**

750
**Amos's ministry ends**

740
**Isaiah becomes a prophet to Judah**

**S**it down, right here!" Mr. Evans, the principal, demanded of the four boys he marched into his office. On the couch were Bobby Thomas, Eric Hardin, and Sheldon Milroy: the most feared trio in school. Near Mr. Evans' desk sat Robert Bledsoe—the bullies' skinny, smart, pimply-faced target. ■ "You boys," began Mr. Evans, pointing at the terrible trio, "had better quit. I won't stand for you harassing Robert. Such behavior is totally unacceptable." ■ Mr. Evans wanted to be calm, but his face was turning red and his volume was increasing. "If I ever, *ever* catch you three bothering *anyone* in the schoolyard again, I will make sure you are expelled. Understand?" All three nodded. ■ Robert listened and smiled smugly. The bullies deserved what they were getting. ■ "And you, Mr. Bledsoe." Mr. Evans turned to a startled Robert. "You are not without blame. These boys were wrong, but . . . I might have done the same thing if you had treated me like you treated them. You teased these boys, saying they are stupid and probably headed for lives as bums." Mr. Evans was yelling again. "Mr. Bledsoe, you have been the victim here, but you are just as guilty. Now, all of you, get out." ■ Amos wasn't a professional prophet, but as God's spokesman he gave a similar message to the "bullying" nations and to Israel, the victim. And Amos has lessons for us today. He reminds us to be careful in pointing judgmental fingers at others, since they could end up pointed back at us. If God asked to have a talk with you, in what areas would he find you lacking?

## STATS

PURPOSE: To show God's judgment on Israel, the northern kingdom, for their idolatry and oppression of the poor

AUTHOR: Amos

TO WHOM WRITTEN: Israel, the northern kingdom, and God's people everywhere

DATE WRITTEN: Probably during the reigns of Jeroboam II of Israel and Uzziah of Judah (about 760 to 750 B.C)

SETTING: The wealthy people of Israel were happy, but at the cost of the poor! Soon, however, Israel would be conquered by Assyria, and the rich would themselves be made slaves.

KEY PEOPLE: Amos, Amaziah, Jeroboam II

KEY PLACES: Bethel, Samaria

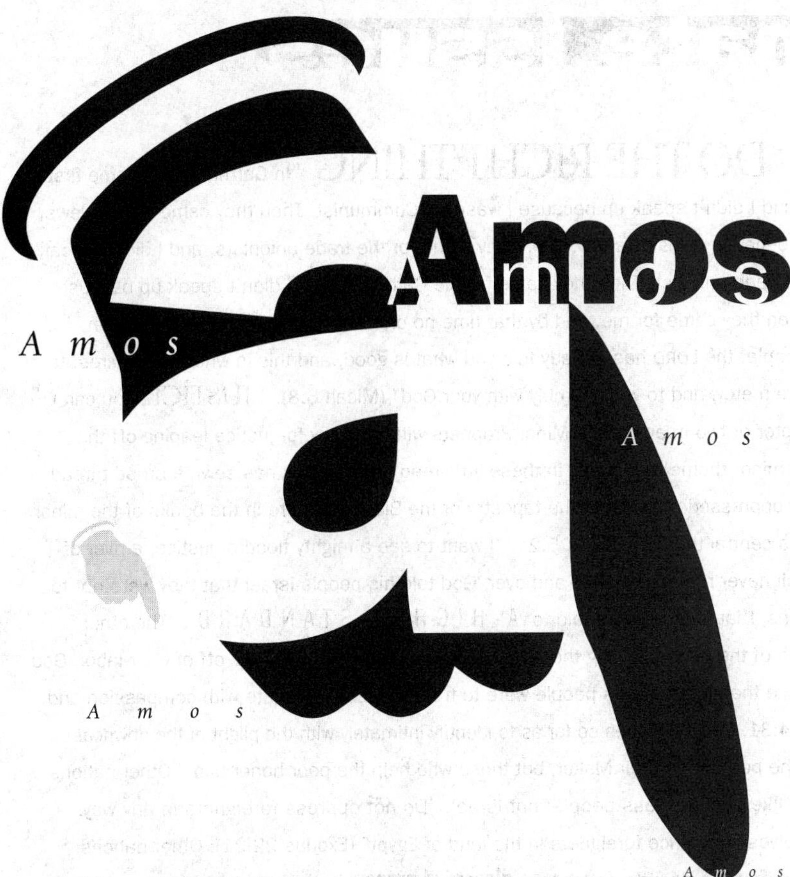


CHAPTER **1** **GOD PUNISHES ISRAEL'S NEIGHBORS.** This message was given to Amos, a shepherd from the town of Tekoa in Judah. He received this message in visions two years before the earthquake, when Uzziah was king of Judah and Jeroboam II, the son of Jehoash,* was king of Israel.

[2]This is his report of what he saw and heard: "The LORD's voice roars from his Temple on Mount Zion; he thunders from Jerusalem! Suddenly, the lush pastures of the shepherds dry up. All the grass on Mount Carmel withers and dies."

[3]This is what the LORD says: "The people of Damascus have sinned again and again, and I will not forget it. I will not let them go unpunished any longer! They beat down my people in Gilead as grain is threshed with threshing sledges of iron. [4]So I will send down fire on King Hazael's palace, and the fortresses of King Ben-hadad will be destroyed. [5]I will break down the gates of Damascus and slaughter its people all the way to the valley of Aven.* I will destroy the ruler in Beth-eden, and the people of Aram will return to Kir as slaves. I, the LORD, have spoken!"

[6]This is what the LORD says: "The people of Gaza have sinned again and again, and I will not forget it. I will not let them go unpunished any longer! They sent my people into exile, selling them as slaves in Edom. [7]So I will send down fire on the walls of Gaza, and all its fortresses will be destroyed. [8]I will slaughter the people of Ashdod and destroy the king of Ashkelon. Then I will turn to attack Ekron, and the few Philistines still left will be killed. I, the Sovereign LORD, have spoken!"

[9]This is what the LORD says: "The people of Tyre have sinned again and again, and I will not forget it. I will not let them go unpunished any longer! They broke their treaty of brotherhood with Israel, selling whole villages as slaves to Edom. [10]So I will send down fire on the walls of Tyre, and all its fortresses will be destroyed."

[11]This is what the LORD says: "The people of Edom have sinned again and again, and I will not forget it. I

1:1 Hebrew *Joash,* a variant name for Jehoash. 1:5 *Aven* means "wickedness."

**WORK ● ● • • •**

1:1 **All day long Amos took care of sheep—not a particularly "spiritual" job—yet he became a channel of God's message to others. Your job may not cause you to feel spiritual or successful, but it is a vital work if you are in the place God wants you to be. God can work through you to do extraordinary things, no matter how ordinary your occupation.**

# Ultimate Issues

## DO THE RIGHT THING

**"I**n Germany they came first for the Communists, and I didn't speak up because I wasn't a Communist. Then they came for the Jews, and I didn't speak up because I wasn't a Jew. Then they came for the trade unionists, and I didn't speak up because I wasn't a trade unionist. Then they came for the Catholics, and I didn't speak up because I was a Protestant. Then they came for me, and by that time no one was left to speak up."—Martin Niemoller. **"N**o, O people, the LORD has already told you what is good, and this is what he requires: to do what is right, to love mercy, and to walk humbly with your God" (Micah 6:8). JUSTICE. You can't read more than a chapter or two in any of the Minor Prophets without a cry for justice leaping off the pages. Not that it is a minor theme found only in these little-read books—God has sewn a broad thread of compassion for the oppressed throughout the tapestry of the Bible. But here in the books of the minor prophets, it becomes a central theme. **A**mos 5:24: "I want to see a mighty flood of justice, a river of righteous living that will never run dry." **O**ver and over, God told his people Israel that they were not to be like the other nations, that they were to hold to A HIGHER STANDARD. The other nations took advantage of the poor, allowing the wealthy and powerful to grow **FAT** off of their labor. God said it was not to be like that in Israel: His people were to treat the less fortunate with compassion and fairness. In Proverbs 14:31, God even goes so far as to identify intimately with the plight of the downcast: "Those who oppress the poor insult their Maker, but those who help the poor honor him." Other nations could treat foreigners like second-class people: not Israel. "Do not oppress foreigners in any way. Remember, you yourselves were once foreigners in the land of Egypt" (Exodus 22:21). Other nations considered widows and orphans as little better than **discarded property**: God said that in Israel, such people had rights and were to be treated with dignity. "'I will put you on trial. . . . I will speak against those who . . . oppress widows and orphans . . .' says the LORD Almighty" (Malachi 3:5). **"T**his is what the LORD Almighty says: Judge fairly and honestly, and show mercy and kindness to one another. Do not oppress widows, orphans, foreigners, and poor people. And do not make evil plans to harm each other" (Zechariah 7:9-10). **W**e are confronted today with ***a great many opportunities*** to minister justice in the name of God. The plight of the homeless, the distress of our inner cities, the suffering of the hungry, questions of racial and economic fairness, the struggle for peace—these and countless other issues cry out for men and women of courage, compassion, and conviction to stand strong for justice in Jesus' name. God is vitally concerned for the widow, the orphan, the Cambodian refugee, the Ethiopian child, the baby addicted to crack, the Cuban political prisoner, and everyone who suffers and needs help. ARE YOU? **"I** assure you, when you did it to one of the least of these my brothers and sisters, you were doing it to me! . . . I assure you, when you refused to help the least of these my brothers and sisters, you were refusing to help me" (Matthew 25:40, 45).

---

will not let them go unpunished any longer! They
chased down their relatives, the Israelites, with swords.
They showed them no mercy and were unrelenting in
their anger. 12So I will send down fire on Teman, and
the fortresses of Bozrah will be destroyed."
13This is what the LORD says: "The people of Ammon have sinned again and again, and I will not
forget it. I will not let them go unpunished any
longer! When they attacked Gilead to extend their
borders, they committed cruel crimes, ripping open
pregnant women with their swords. 14So I will send
down fire on the walls of Rabbah, and all its
fortresses will be destroyed. There will be wild shouts
during the battle, swirling like a whirlwind in a

mighty storm. 15And their king* and his princes will go into exile together. I, the LORD, have spoken!"

CHAPTER **2** **GOD PUNISHES ISRAEL, TOO.** This is what the LORD says: "The people of Moab have sinned again and again, and I will not forget it. I will not let them go unpunished any longer! They desecrated the tomb of Edom's king and burned his bones to ashes. 2So I will send down fire on the land of Moab, and all the fortresses in Kerioth will be destroyed. The people will fall in the noise of battle, as the warriors shout and the trumpets blare. 3And I will destroy their king and slaughter all their princes. I, the LORD, have spoken!"

4This is what the LORD says: "The people of Judah have sinned again and again, and I will not forget it. I will not let them go unpunished any longer! They have rejected the laws of the LORD, refusing to obey him. They have been led astray by the same lies that deceived their ancestors. 5So I will send down fire on Judah, and all the fortresses of Jerusalem will be destroyed."

6This is what the LORD says: "The people of Israel have sinned again and again, and I will not forget it. I will not let them go unpunished any longer! They have perverted justice by selling honest people for silver and poor people for a pair of sandals. 7They trample helpless people in the dust and deny justice to those who are oppressed. Both father and son sleep with the same woman, corrupting my holy name. 8At their religious festivals, they lounge around in clothing stolen from their debtors. In the house of their god, they present offerings of wine purchased with stolen money.

9"Yet think of all I did for my people! I destroyed the Amorites before my people arrived in the land. The Amorites were as tall as cedar trees and strong as oaks, but I destroyed their fruit and dug out their roots. 10It was I who rescued you from Egypt and led you through the desert for forty years so you could possess the land of the Amorites. 11I chose some of your sons to be prophets and others to be Nazirites. Can you deny this, my people of Israel?" asks the LORD. 12"But you caused the Nazirites to sin by making them drink your wine, and you said to my prophets, 'Shut up!'

13"So I will make you groan as a wagon groans when it is loaded down with grain. 14Your fastest runners will not get away. The strongest among you will become weak. Even the mightiest warriors will be unable to save themselves. 15The archers will fail to stand their ground. The swiftest soldiers won't be fast enough to escape. Even warriors on horses won't be able to outrun the danger. 16On that day, the most courageous of your fighting men will drop their weapons and run for their lives. I, the LORD, have spoken!"

CHAPTER **3** **THEY CANNOT WALK WITH GOD.** Listen to this message that the LORD has spoken against you, O people of Israel and Judah—the entire family I rescued from Egypt: 2"From among all the families on the earth, I chose you alone. That is why I must punish you for all your sins."

3Can two people walk together without agreeing on the direction? 4Does a lion ever roar in a thicket without first finding a victim? Does a young lion growl in its den without first catching its prey? 5Does a bird ever get caught in a trap that has no bait? Does a trap ever spring shut when there's nothing there to catch? 6When the war trumpet blares, shouldn't the people be alarmed? When disaster comes to a city, isn't it because the LORD planned it?

7"But always, first of all, I warn you through my servants the prophets. I, the Sovereign LORD, have now done this."

1:15 Hebrew *malcam,* possibly referring to their god Molech.

**My friends do things that my conscience won't let me get away with—yet they never seem to get caught. Why do a lot of people who do wrong never seem to get punished?**

At the dentist, Novocain deadens the nerves in our mouth so we won't feel the drill. Repeated sin deadens the conscience, so the person no longer feels guilty about wrong behavior. But whether a person feels guilty or not, sin *does* have consequences. Some are immediate, like when the teacher catches you cheating on a test and gives you an *F.* Other consequences are short-term and delayed, such as with people who cheat on their income-tax return and seem to get away with it. Then they are audited and receive a hefty fine or even a prison sentence from the IRS.

Without a doubt, the Bible is clear about what will eventually happen to those who act contrary to God's plan: "Don't be misled. Remember that you can't ignore God and get away with it. You will always reap what you sow! Those who live only to satisfy their own sinful desires will harvest the consequences of decay and death. But those who live to please the Spirit will harvest everlasting life from the Spirit" (Galatians 6:7-8).

If we "sow" bad actions, we'll reap that kind of fruit. If we sow good things and genuinely try to follow God's instructions, God will use us, and we'll reap a wonderful harvest.

It can get tiring, however, always trying to be good. Especially when there's so much bad around us. That's when we have to remember God's promise of the eventual harvest: "Don't get tired of doing what is good. Don't get discouraged and give up, for we will reap a harvest of blessing at the appropriate time" (Galatians 6:9).

The prophet Amos told the people of Israel what would happen if they didn't shape up (see Amos 2:6-16). Though his predictions didn't immediately come to pass, they did prove to be right after many years. The Israelites were conquered by the Assyrians and were made slaves, receiving exactly what they had given out.

[8]The lion has roared—tremble in fear! The Sovereign LORD has spoken—I dare not refuse to proclaim his message!

[9]Announce this to the leaders of Philistia* and Egypt: "Take your seats now on the hills around Samaria, and witness the scandalous spectacle of all Israel's crimes."

[10]"My people have forgotten what it means to do right," says the LORD. "Their fortresses are filled with wealth taken by theft and violence. [11]Therefore," says the Sovereign LORD, "an enemy is coming! He will surround them and shatter their defenses. Then he will plunder all their fortresses."

## COMPLACENCY

When Missy got involved in youth activities about three years ago, exciting things were always taking place. One semester, they reached out to a local retirement home. Her sophomore year, the group developed an ongoing outreach to homeless people. Each summer at least 30 or 40 teens went on some sort of mission project.

Nowadays things are different. Most of the older crowd has gone on to college. And for whatever reason, the younger kids in the group only seem to come to "fun" activities—parties, cookouts, etc. Missy is concerned that youth group is becoming more of a social club than a place of ministry.

During sharing time at youth group, she expresses her concerns, telling the group that she misses the commitment to ministry, and sharing stories of the real joy and fun the group had experienced in the past through serving other people.

The group's reaction ranges from glares, to whispers, to yawns. One girl approaches Missy after the meeting and says, "How dare you lecture us! You act like you're the only one in the group who is a good Christian. Just because we like to have fun doesn't make us any less spiritual than you!"

Like Missy, the prophet Amos had the unpleasant task of lighting a spiritual fire under complacent people. Read Amos 5:21-6:8 and ask yourself: Am I more like Amos . . . or the people he was addressing?

[12]This is what the LORD says: "A shepherd who tries to rescue a sheep from a lion's mouth will recover only two legs and a piece of ear. So it will be when the Israelites in Samaria are rescued with only a broken chair and a tattered pillow. [13]Now listen to this, and announce it throughout all Israel,*" says the Lord, the LORD God Almighty. [14]"On the very day I punish Israel for its sins, I will destroy the pagan altars at Bethel. The horns of the altar will be cut off and fall to the ground. [15]And I will destroy the beautiful homes of the wealthy—their winter mansions and their summer houses, too—all their palaces filled with ivory. I, the LORD, have spoken!"

CHAPTER **4** **ISRAEL FAILS TO LEARN.** Listen to me, you "fat cows" of Samaria, you women who oppress the poor and crush the needy and who are always asking

### COW GIRLS ● ● ● • •

**4:1 Israel's wealthy women were compared to the cows of Bashan—pampered, sleek, and well fed (see Psalm 22:12). These women selfishly pushed their husbands to oppress the helpless in order to supply their lavish lifestyle. Be careful not to desire material possessions so much that you are willing to oppress others and displease God to get them.**

your husbands for another drink! [2]The Sovereign LORD has sworn this by his holiness: "The time will come when you will be led away with hooks in your noses. Every last one of you will be dragged away like a fish on a hook! [3]You will leave by going straight through the breaks in the wall; you will be thrown from your fortresses.* I, the LORD, have spoken!

[4]"Go ahead and offer your sacrifices to the idols at Bethel and Gilgal. Keep on disobeying—your sins are mounting up! Offer sacrifices each morning and bring your tithes every three days! [5]Present your bread made with yeast as an offering of thanksgiving. Then give your extra voluntary offerings so you can brag about it everywhere! This is the kind of thing you Israelites love to do," says the Sovereign LORD.

[6]"I brought hunger to every city and famine to every town. But still you wouldn't return to me," says the LORD.

[7]"I kept the rain from falling when you needed it the most, ruining all your crops. I sent rain on one town but withheld it from another. Rain fell on one field, while another field withered away. [8]People staggered from one town to another for a drink of water, but there was never enough. But still you wouldn't return to me," says the LORD.

[9]"I struck your farms and vineyards with blight and mildew. Locusts devoured all your fig and olive trees. But still you wouldn't return to me," says the LORD.

[10]"I sent plagues against you like the plagues I sent against Egypt long ago. I killed your young men in war and slaughtered all your horses. The stench of death filled the air! But still you wouldn't return to me," says the LORD.

[11]"I destroyed some of your cities, as I destroyed* Sodom and Gomorrah. Those of you who survived were like half-burned sticks snatched from a fire. But still you wouldn't return to me," says the LORD.

[12]"Therefore, I will bring upon you all these further disasters I have announced. Prepare to meet your God as he comes in judgment, you people of Israel!"

[13]For the LORD is the one who shaped the mountains, stirs up the winds, and reveals his every thought. He turns the light of dawn into darkness and treads the mountains under his feet. The LORD God Almighty is his name!

CHAPTER **5** **A SAD SONG OF GRIEF.** Listen, you people of Israel! Listen to this funeral song I am singing:

[2]"The virgin Israel has fallen,
never to rise again!

3:9 Hebrew *Ashdod.* 3:13 Hebrew *the house of Jacob.* 4:3 Hebrew *thrown out toward Harmon,* possibly a reference to Mount Hermon. 4:11 Hebrew *as when God destroyed.*

I want to see a
MIGHTY FLOOD OF
JUSTICE,
a river of righteous living
that will NEVER run dry.
AMOS 5:24

She lies forsaken on the ground,
with none to raise her up."

3The Sovereign LORD says: "When one of your cities sends a thousand men to battle, only a hundred will return. When a town sends a hundred, only ten will come back alive."

4Now this is what the LORD says to the family of Israel: "Come back to me and live! 5Don't go to worship the idols of Bethel, Gilgal, or Beersheba. For the people of Gilgal will be dragged off into exile, and the people of Bethel will come to nothing."

6Come back to the LORD and live! If you don't, he will roar through Israel* like a fire, devouring you completely. Your gods in Bethel certainly won't be able to quench the flames! 7You wicked people! You twist justice, making it a bitter pill for the poor and oppressed. Righteousness and fair play are meaningless fictions to you.

8It is the LORD who created the stars, the Pleiades and Orion. It is he who turns darkness into morning and day into night. It is he who draws up water from the oceans and pours it down as rain on the land. The LORD is his name! 9With blinding speed and power he destroys the strong, crushing all their defenses.

10How you hate honest judges! How you despise people who tell the truth! 11You trample the poor and steal what little they have through taxes and unfair rent. Therefore, you will never live in the beautiful stone houses you are building. You will never drink wine from the lush vineyards you are planting. 12For I know the vast number of your sins and rebellions. You oppress good people by taking bribes and deprive the poor of justice in the courts. 13So those who are wise will keep quiet, for it is an evil time.

14Do what is good and run from evil—that you may live! Then the LORD God Almighty will truly be your helper, just as you have claimed he is. 15Hate evil and love what is good; remodel your courts into true halls of justice. Perhaps even yet the LORD God Almighty will have mercy on his people who remain.*

16Therefore, this is what the Lord, the LORD God Almighty, says: "There will be crying in all the public squares and in every street. Call for the farmers to weep with you, and summon professional mourners to wail and lament. 17There will be wailing in every vineyard, for I will pass through and destroy them all. I, the LORD, have spoken!"

18How terrible it will be for you who say, "If only the day of the LORD were here! For then the LORD would rescue us from all our enemies." But you have no idea what you are wishing for. That day will not bring light and prosperity, but darkness and disaster. 19In that day you will be like a man who runs from a lion—only to meet a bear. After escaping the bear, he leans his hand against a wall in his house—and is bitten by a snake. 20Yes, the day of the LORD will be a dark and hopeless day, without a ray of joy or hope.

21"I hate all your show and pretense—the hypocrisy of your religious festivals and solemn assemblies. 22I will not accept your burnt offerings and grain offerings. I won't even notice all your choice peace offerings. 23Away with your hymns of praise! They are only noise to my ears. I will not listen to your music, no matter how lovely it is. 24Instead, I want to see a mighty flood of justice, a river of righteous living that will never run dry.

25"Was it to me you were bringing sacrifices and offerings during the forty years in the wilderness, Israel? 26No, your real interest was in your pagan gods—Sakkuth your king god and Kaiwan your star god—the images you yourselves made.* 27So I will send you into exile, to a land east of Damascus," says the LORD, whose name is God Almighty.

CHAPTER **6** **GOD HATES ISRAEL'S PRIDE.** How terrible it will be for you who lounge in luxury and think you are secure in Jerusalem* and Samaria! You are

## NO GAIN ● ● • • •

**5:12 Why does God put so much emphasis on the way we treat the poor? How we treat the rich or those of equal station too often reflects what we hope to get from them. But since the poor can give us nothing, how we treat them reflects our true character. Do we, like Christ, give without thought of gain? We should treat the poor as we would like God to treat us.**

5:6 Hebrew *the house of Joseph.* 5:15 Hebrew *on the remnant of Joseph.* 5:26 Greek version reads *You took up the shrine of Molech, and the star of your god Rephan, and the images you made for yourselves.* 6:1 Hebrew *Zion.*

**AMOS** served as a prophet to Israel (the northern kingdom) from 760 to 750 B.C.

*Climate of the times* — Israel was enjoying prosperity and peace. But this had caused it to become a selfish, materialistic society. Those who were well off ignored the needs of those less fortunate. The people were self-centered and indifferent toward God.

*Main message* — Amos spoke against those who exploited or ignored the needy.

*Importance of message* — Believing in God is more than a personal matter. God calls all believers to work against injustices in society and to aid those less fortunate.

*Contemporary prophets* — Jonah (793–753)
Hosea (753–715)

---

famous and popular in Israel, you to whom the
people go for help. [2]Go over to Calneh and see what
happened there. Then go to the great city of Hamath
and on down to the Philistine city of Gath. You are
no better than they were, and look at how they were
destroyed. [3]You push away every thought of coming
disaster, but your actions only bring the day of judgment closer.

[4]How terrible it will be for you who sprawl on
ivory beds surrounded with luxury, eating the meat
of tender lambs and choice calves. [5]You sing idle
songs to the sound of the harp, and you fancy yourselves to be great musicians, as King David was. [6]You
drink wine by the bowlful, and you perfume yourselves with exotic fragrances, caring nothing at all
that your nation* is going to ruin. [7]Therefore, you
will be the first to be led away as captives. Suddenly,
all your revelry will end.

[8]The Sovereign LORD has sworn by his own name,
and this is what he, the LORD God Almighty, says: "I
despise the pride and false glory of Israel,* and I hate
their beautiful homes. I will give this city and everything in it to their enemies."

[9]If there are ten men left in one house, they will
all die. [10]And when a close relative—one who is
responsible for burning the dead—goes into the
house to carry away a dead body, he will ask the
last survivor, "Is there anyone else with you?" And
the person will answer, "No!" Then he will say,
"Hush! Don't even whisper the name of the LORD.
He might hear you!"

[11]When the LORD gives the command, homes both
great and small will be smashed to pieces. [12]Can
horses gallop over rocks? Can oxen be used to plow
rocks? Stupid even to ask—but that's how stupid you
are when you turn justice into poison and make
bitter the sweet fruit of righteousness. [13]And just as
stupid is this bragging about your conquest of Lo-
debar.* You boast, "Didn't we take Karnaim* by our
own strength and power?"

[14]"O people of Israel, I am about to bring an
enemy nation against you," says the LORD God Almighty. "It will oppress you bitterly throughout your
land—from Lebo-hamath in the north to the Arabah Valley in the south."

CHAPTER **7** **LOCUSTS, FIRE, AND A PLUMB LINE.** The
Sovereign LORD showed me a vision. I saw him preparing to send a vast swarm of locusts over the land.
This was after the king's share had been harvested
from the fields and as the main crop was coming up.
[2]In my vision the locusts ate everything in sight that
was green. Then I said, "O Sovereign LORD, please
forgive your people! Unless you relent, Israel* will
not survive, for we are only a small nation."

[3]So the LORD relented and did not fulfill the vision. "I won't do it," he said.

[4]Then the Sovereign LORD showed me another
vision. I saw him preparing to punish his people
with a great fire. The fire had burned up the depths
of the sea and was devouring the entire land. [5]Then
I said, "O Sovereign LORD, please don't do it. Unless
you relent, Israel will not survive, for we are only a
small nation."

[6]Then the LORD turned from this plan, too. "I
won't do that either," said the Sovereign LORD.

[7]Then he showed me another vision. I saw the
Lord standing beside a wall that had been built using
a plumb line. He was checking it with a plumb line
to see if it was straight. [8]And the LORD said to me,
"Amos, what do you see?"

I answered, "A plumb line."

And the Lord replied, "I will test my people with
this plumb line. I will no longer ignore all their sins.
[9]The pagan shrines of your ancestors* and the

## PRAYER POWER ● ● ● • •

**7:1-9 Twice Amos was shown a vision of Israel's impending punishment, and his immediate response was to pray that God would spare Israel. Prayer is a powerful privilege. Amos's prayers should remind us to pray for our nation.**

6:6 Hebrew *Joseph.* 6:8 Hebrew *Jacob.* 6:13a *Lo-debar* means "nothing." 6:13b *Karnaim* means "horns," a term that symbolizes strength. 7:2 Hebrew *Jacob;* also in 7:5. 7:9 Hebrew *of Isaac.*

temples of Israel will be destroyed, and I will bring the dynasty of King Jeroboam to a sudden end."

10But when Amaziah, the priest of Bethel, heard what Amos was saying, he rushed a message to King Jeroboam: "Amos is hatching a plot against you right here on your very doorstep! What he is saying is intolerable. It will lead to rebellion all across the land. 11He is saying, 'Jeroboam will soon be killed and the people of Israel will be sent away into exile.'"

12Then Amaziah sent orders to Amos: "Get out of here, you seer! Go on back to the land of Judah and do your preaching there! 13Don't bother us here in Bethel with your prophecies, especially not here where the royal sanctuary is!"

14But Amos replied, "I'm not one of your professional prophets. I certainly never trained to be one. I'm just a shepherd, and I take care of fig trees. 15But the LORD called me away from my flock and told me, 'Go and prophesy to my people in Israel.'

16"Now then, listen to this message from the LORD! You say, 'Don't prophesy against Israel. Stop preaching against my people.*' 17But this is what the LORD says: Because you have refused to listen, your wife will become a prostitute in this city, and your sons and daughters will be killed. Your land will be divided up, and you yourself will die in a foreign land. And the people of Israel will certainly become captives in exile, far from their homeland."

## CHAPTER 8 AMOS SEES A BASKET OF FRUIT.

Then the Sovereign LORD showed me another vision. In it I saw a basket filled with ripe fruit. 2"What do you see, Amos?" he asked.

I replied, "A basket full of ripe fruit."

Then the LORD said, "This fruit represents my people of Israel—ripe for punishment! I will not delay their punishment again. 3In that day the riotous sounds of singing in the Temple will turn to wailing. Dead bodies will be scattered everywhere. They will be carried out of the city in silence. I, the Sovereign LORD, have spoken!"

4Listen to this, you who rob the poor and trample the needy! 5You can't wait for the Sabbath day to be over and the religious festivals to end so you can get back to cheating the helpless. You measure out your grain in false measures and weigh it out on dishonest scales. 6And you mix the wheat you sell with chaff swept from the floor! Then you enslave poor people for a debt of one piece of silver or a pair of sandals.

7Now the LORD has sworn this oath by his own name, the Pride of Israel*: "I will never forget the wicked things you have done! 8The earth will tremble for your deeds, and everyone will mourn. The land will rise up like the Nile River at floodtime, toss about, and sink again. 9At that time," says the Sovereign LORD, "I will make the sun go down at noon and darken the earth while it is still day. 10I will turn your celebrations into times of mourning, and your songs of joy will be turned to weeping. You will wear funeral clothes and shave your heads as signs of sorrow, as if your only son had died. How very bitter that day will be!

11"The time is surely coming," says the Sovereign LORD, "when I will send a famine on the land—not a famine of bread or water but of hearing the words of the LORD. 12People will stagger everywhere from sea to sea, searching for the word of the LORD, running here and going there, but they will not find it. 13Beautiful girls and fine young men will grow faint and weary, thirsting for the LORD's word. 14And those who worship and swear by the idols of Samaria, Dan, and Beersheba will fall down, never to rise again."

### THE ANSWER ● • • • •

**8:11-13 The people had no appetite for God's word when prophets like Amos brought it. Because of their apathy, God said he would take away even the opportunity to hear his word. We have God's Word, the Bible, but many people still look everywhere for answers to life's problems *except* in Scripture. You can help them by directing them to the Bible, showing them the parts that speak to their special needs and questions. God's Word is available to us. Let us help people know it before a time comes when they cannot find it.**

## CHAPTER 9 ISRAEL WILL BE DESTROYED.

Then I saw a vision of the Lord standing beside the altar. He said, "Strike the tops of the Temple columns so hard that the foundation will shake. Smash the columns so the roof will crash down on the people below. Then those who survive will be slaughtered in battle. No one will escape!

2"Even if they dig down to the place of the dead,* I will reach down and pull them up. Even if they climb up into the heavens, I will bring them down. 3Even if they hide at the very top of Mount Carmel, I will search them out and capture them. Even if they hide at the bottom of the ocean, I will send the great sea serpent after them to bite and destroy them. 4Even if they are driven into exile, I will command the sword to kill them there. I am determined to bring disaster upon them and not to help them."

5The Lord, the LORD Almighty, touches the land and it melts, and all its people mourn. The ground rises like the Nile River at floodtime, and then it sinks again. 6The upper stories of the LORD's home are in the heavens, while its foundation is on the earth. He draws up water from the oceans and pours it down as rain on the land. The LORD is his name!

7"Do you Israelites think you are more important to me than the Ethiopians*?" asks the LORD. "I brought you out of Egypt, but have I not done as much for other nations, too? I brought the Philistines from Crete* and led the Arameans out of Kir.

8"I, the Sovereign LORD, am watching this sinful nation of Israel, and I will uproot it and scatter its people across the earth. Yet I have promised that I

7:16 Hebrew *against the house of Isaac.* 8:7 Hebrew *the pride of Jacob.* 9:2 Hebrew *to Sheol.* 9:7a Hebrew *the Cushites.* 9:7b Hebrew *Caphtor.*

## SIGN OF LOVE ● ● • • •

**9:8 Amos assured the Israelites that God would not "completely destroy" Israel—in other words, the punishment would not be permanent or total. God wants to redeem, not punish. But when punishment is necessary, he doesn't withhold it. Like a loving father, God disciplines those he loves in order to correct them. If he disciplines you, accept it as a sign of his love.**

will never completely destroy the family of Israel,*"
says the LORD. [9]"For I have commanded that Israel be
persecuted by the other nations as grain is sifted in a
sieve, yet not one true kernel will be lost. [10]But all the
sinners will die by the sword—all those who say,
'Nothing bad will happen to us.'
[11]"In that day I will restore the fallen kingdom of
David. It is now like a house in ruins, but I will
rebuild its walls and restore its former glory. [12]And
Israel will possess what is left of Edom and all the
nations I have called to be mine. I, the LORD, have
spoken, and I will do these things.
[13]"The time will come," says the LORD, "when the
grain and grapes will grow faster than they can be
harvested. Then the terraced vineyards on the hills of
Israel will drip with sweet wine! [14]I will bring my
exiled people of Israel back from distant lands, and
they will rebuild their ruined cities and live in them
again. They will plant vineyards and gardens; they
will eat their crops and drink their wine. [15]I will
firmly plant them there in the land I have given
them," says the LORD your God. "Then they will
never be uprooted again."

9:8 Hebrew *the house of Jacob.*

# MEGA themes

**EVERYONE ANSWERS TO GOD** Amos pronounced judgment from God on all the surrounding nations. Then he included Judah and Israel. God is in supreme control of the nations. Everyone is accountable to him.

All people will have to account for their sin. When those who reject God seem to be living the good life, don't be jealous of their prosperity or feel sorry for yourself. Remember that we all must answer to God.

1. At times it seems that terrorists and evil leaders are able to avoid punishment for their violent, terrible actions. What does Amos say that contradicts this apparent injustice?
2. How does this truth apply in general to men and women who feel they don't have to be responsible for the way they behave?
3. How would you respond to the following statement from a non-Christian: "Everybody has to decide what is right for himself or herself as an individual. Nobody can say what is and is not a sin."
4. How does the fact that you must answer to God affect your relationship with Christ? how you live?

**COMPLACENCY** Everyone was optimistic, business was booming, people were happy (except for the poor and oppressed). With all the comfort and luxury came self-sufficiency and a false sense of security. But prosperity brought corruption and destruction.

A complacent present can lead to a disastrous future. Don't congratulate yourself for the blessings and benefits you enjoy. They are from God. If you are more satisfied with yourself than with God, remember that everything is meaningless without him. A self-sufficient attitude may be your downfall.

1. What are some things that cause Christians to become complacent about God or to take God for granted?
2. Describe a time in your life when you took God's relationship with you for granted. How did you feel about God during this time? about yourself? What shook you out of it?
3. What have you learned about being complacent in your relationship with God from the book of Amos?
4. What can you do to avoid becoming complacent in your relationship with Christ?

**OPPRESSION** The wealthy and powerful people of Samaria, the capital of Israel, had become prosperous, greedy, and unfair. Illegal and immoral slavery had come as the result of overtaxation and land grabbing. There also was cruelty and indifference toward the poor. God grows weary and angry with greed and will not tolerate injustice.

God made everyone, so ignoring the poor is ignoring those whom God loves and whom Christ came to save. We must go beyond feeling bad for the poor and oppressed. We must act compassionately to stop injustice and to help care for those in need.

1. In what ways were the wealthy taking advantage of the poor? What seems to have been their attitude about the poor?
2. How does God view the poor? the rich who oppress the poor?
3. Who are the poor in your community? In what ways could they be described as oppressed?
4. Who are the outcasts in your school? In what ways could they be described as oppressed?
5. Give specific examples of how you could stand against oppression in your school and community.

**SUPERFICIAL RELIGION** Although many people had abandoned real faith in God, they still pretended to be religious. They "performed" as religious people, just going through the motions instead of having spiritual integrity and practicing heartfelt obedience toward God.

Merely participating in ceremony or ritual falls short of true faith. This leads to religion without relationship. God wants trust in him, not a show. Don't settle for impressing others when God wants sincere obedience and commitment.

1. Give examples of what you think would qualify as superficial religion.
2. Describe a time in your own life when you were just "going through the motions." How do you feel about this type of living?
3. Many people identify a "good Christian" as a person who goes to church and behaves morally. Based on Scripture, what does it mean to be a true disciple of Christ? How is this different from going through the motions?
4. What will you do in the coming week to deepen your relationship with God? What will you do to avoid getting caught in superficial religion?

"Let me tell you a joke!" Five-year-old Alice bubbled with excitement as she spoke. "Which do you want first, the bad news or the bad news?" ■ "You dummy," her brother Al retorted, "don't you know anything? Those jokes are supposed to have *good* news and bad news, not just bad news." ■ "Not this one," answered Alice. ■ Like those jokes, most of life includes both good news and bad news. Positive things almost always seem to have a downside. More important, negative things often have some "silver lining" to give us hope. ■ The books in the Bible written by the prophets (Isaiah—Malachi) are like that. The bad news was that Israel was going to be punished for their sins by becoming prisoners to their enemies. The good news is that God would someday bring his people back from captivity and restore Israel's glory. ■ But one prophetical book is unique: It has no good news. That book is Obadiah. Written about Edom (a nearby nation), the prophet graphically describes the utter ruin that was about to come. Why? Because Edom had rejoiced when Israel was taken captive and had taken advantage of Israel's plight. ■ God loves his children. He will protect his children and will deal harshly with those who attempt to hurt them. ■ If you are God's child, God loves you just as he loved Israel. He will guard and protect you and react angrily against any who might attempt to harm you. ■ As you read Obadiah ask God to help you be more aware that he indeed is watching over you.

## STATS

PURPOSE: To show that God judges those who have harmed his people

AUTHOR: Obadiah. Little is known about him. His name means "servant of the Lord" or "worshiper of Jehovah."

TO WHOM WRITTEN: The Edomites, the Jews in Judah, and God's people everywhere

DATE WRITTEN: Possibly during the reign of Jehoram in Judah, 853–841 B.C.

SETTING: Historically, Edom had constantly harassed the Jews. Prior to the time this book was written, they had participated in attacks against Judah. Given the dates above, this prophecy comes after the division of Israel into the northern and southern kingdoms and before the conquering of Judah by Nebuchadnezzar in 586 B.C.

KEY PEOPLE: The Edomites

KEY PLACES: Edom, Jerusalem

# Obadiah

**EDOM WILL BE DESTROYED.** This is the vision that the
Sovereign LORD revealed to Obadiah concerning the
land of Edom.

We have heard a message from the LORD that an
ambassador was sent to the nations to say, "Get
ready, everyone! Let's assemble our armies and attack Edom!"

2The LORD says, "I will cut you down to size
among the nations, Edom; you will be small and
despised. 3You are proud because you live in a rock
fortress and make your home high in the mountains.
'Who can ever reach us way up here?' you ask boastfully. Don't fool yourselves! 4Though you soar as
high as eagles and build your nest among the stars, I
will bring you crashing down. I, the LORD, have
spoken!

5"If thieves came at night and robbed you, they
would not take everything. Those who harvest grapes
always leave a few for the poor. But your enemies will
wipe you out completely! 6Every nook and cranny of
Edom* will be searched and looted. Every treasure
will be found and taken.

7"All your allies will turn against you. They will
help to chase you from your land. They will promise
you peace, while plotting your destruction. Your
trusted friends will set traps for you, and you won't
even know about it. 8At that time not a single wise
person will be left in the whole land of Edom!" says
the LORD. "For on the mountains of Edom I will
destroy everyone who has wisdom and understanding. 9The mightiest warriors of Teman will be
terrified, and everyone on the mountains of Edom
will be cut down in the slaughter.

10"And why? Because of the violence you did to
your close relatives in Israel.* Now you will be
destroyed completely and filled with shame forever. 11For you deserted your relatives in Israel during their time of greatest need. You stood aloof,

6 Hebrew *Esau;* also in 8b, 9, 18, 19, 21. 10 Hebrew *your brother Jacob.*

## VANISHING ACT ● ● • • •

**3 The Edomites felt secure, and they were proud of their self-sufficiency. But they were fooling themselves because there is no lasting security apart from God. Is your security in objects or people? Ask yourself how much lasting security they really offer. Possessions and people can disappear in a moment, but God does not change. Only he can supply true security.**

refusing to lift a finger to help when foreign invaders carried off their wealth and cast lots to divide up Jerusalem. You acted as though you were one of Israel's enemies.

12 "You shouldn't have done this! You shouldn't have gloated when they exiled your relatives to distant lands. You shouldn't have rejoiced because they were suffering such misfortune. You shouldn't have crowed over them as they suffered these disasters. 13 You shouldn't have plundered the land of Israel when they were suffering such calamity. You shouldn't have gloated over the destruction of your relatives, looting their homes and making yourselves rich at their expense. 14 You shouldn't have stood at the crossroads, killing those who tried to escape. You shouldn't have captured the survivors, handing them over to their enemies in that terrible time of trouble.

15 "The day is near when I, the LORD, will judge the godless nations! As you have done to Israel, so it will be done to you. All your evil deeds will fall back on your own heads. 16 Just as you swallowed up my people on my holy mountain, so you and the surrounding nations will swallow the punishment I pour out on you. Yes, you nations will drink and stagger and disappear from history, as though you had never even existed.

17 "But Jerusalem* will become a refuge for those who escape; it will be a holy place. And the people of Israel* will come back to reclaim their inheritance. 18 At that time Israel will be a raging fire, and Edom, a field of dry stubble. The fire will roar across the field, devouring everything and leaving no survivors in Edom. I, the LORD, have spoken!

19 "Then my people living in the Negev will occupy the mountains of Edom. Those living in the foothills of Judah* will possess the Philistine plains and take over the fields of Ephraim and Samaria. And the people of Benjamin will occupy the land of Gilead. 20 The exiles of Israel will return to their land and occupy the Phoenician coast as far north as Zarephath. The captives from Jerusalem exiled in the north* will return to their homeland and resettle the villages of the Negev. 21 Deliverers will go up to* Mount Zion in Jerusalem to rule over the mountains of Edom. And the LORD himself will be king!"

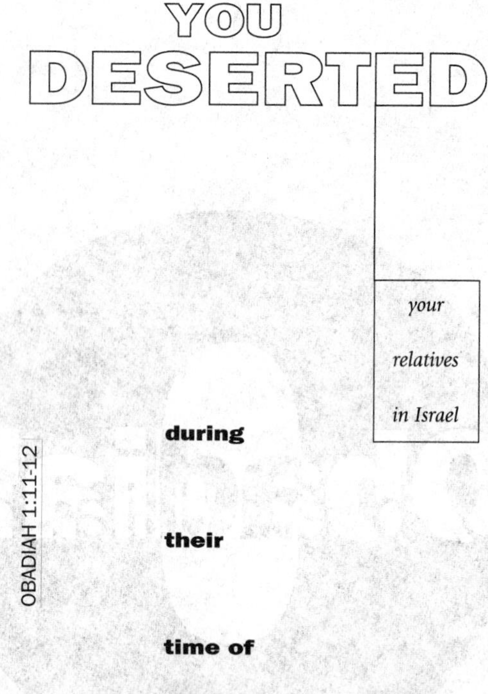
YOU
DESERTED
your
relatives
in Israel
during
their
time of
greatest
OBADIAH 1:11-12

need.

**YOU shouldn't have done this!**

## COCKINESS

Henderson Heights is a basketball community. Between the two high schools there are at least a dozen good basketball players. Then there is Kyle. Kyle is something special. He'll be able to play collegiate ball just about wherever he wants. Some people think that if he works hard enough, Kyle has the skills to play in the NBA.

Kyle's 21 points-per-game scoring average is the good news. The bad news is his hot-dog personality. Kyle talks a steady stream of trash out on the court. Not only does he like to run up the score on his opponents, but he often goes out of his way to humiliate whoever happens to be guarding him. Even his own teammates sometimes get embarrassed by Kyle's showboat antics.

Last night Kyle came crashing back to reality. His team lost a game they were supposed to win easily. Kyle was ejected late in the game for questioning a referee's call. He scored a grand total of seven points. And there were three college scouts in the stands.

See what happened when a whole nation (Edom) had an arrogant, cocky attitude. Read Obadiah 2-10.

17a Hebrew *Mount Zion*. 17b Hebrew *house of Jacob;* also in 18. 19 Hebrew *the Shephelah.* 20 Hebrew *in Sepharad.* 21 Or *from.*

**OBADIAH** served as a prophet to Judah about 853 B.C.

| | |
|---|---|
| *Climate of the times* | Edom was a constant thorn in Judah's side. It often participated in attacks initiated by other enemies. |
| *Main message* | God will judge Edom for its evil actions toward God's people. |
| *Importance of message* | Just as Edom was destroyed and disappeared as a nation, so God will destroy proud and wicked people. |
| *Contemporary prophets* | Elijah (875–848)<br>Micaiah (865–853)<br>Jehu (855–840?) |

# MEGA themes

**JUSTICE** Obadiah predicted that God would destroy Edom as punishment for helping Babylon invade Judah. Because of their treachery, Edom's land would be given to Judah in the day when God rights the wrongs against his people.

God will judge and fiercely punish all who harm his people. We can be confident in God's final victory. He is our champion, and we can trust him to bring about true justice.

1. What sin of the Edomites violated God's holy will?
2. What have you learned about God's qualities as a father to his people?
3. What is meant by the statement "God is a just God"?
4. What hope does this provide for the person who is being persecuted for being a believer?

**PRIDE** Because of their seemingly invincible rock fortress, the Edomites were proud and self-confident. But God humbled them, and their nation disappeared from the face of the earth.

All those who defy God will meet their doom, as Edom did. Any nation that trusts in power, wealth, technology, or wisdom more than in God will be brought down. All who are proud will one day be shocked to discover that no one can escape God's justice.

1. Edom had an attitude of self-reliance and pride. How did their pride lead to their destruction?
2. How does knowing, experiencing, and responding to God as Lord eliminate the roots of pride?
3. In what situations do you tend to be self-reliant and prideful?
4. What knowledge and experience of God leads you to depend on him? What can you do to depend more on God?

793 B.C.
**Jeroboam II becomes king; Jonah becomes a prophet**

792
**Uzziah becomes king of Judah**

783
**Shalmaneser IV becomes king of Assyria**

772
**Ashur-dan III becomes king of Assyria**

760
**Amos becomes a prophet**

759?
**Jonah preaches to Nineveh**

754
**Ashur-Nirari V becomes king of Assyria**

753
**Jonah's ministry ends**

722
**Israel falls to Assyria**

"Don't get mad, get even." We've all heard or said that. Movies reflect the "get even" idea. We watch, cheering and yelling as the victim evens the score and the bad guys get what they deserve. We often live that way, too, sometimes without even knowing it. We do or say things to get back at those whom we think have offended us. ■ Jonah was like that. He's famous for being swallowed by a "great fish," but he ended up in that fish because of his "get even" attitude. ■ God told Jonah to go to Assyria (Israel's greatest enemy) and warn the people of Nineveh (the capital) to repent from their evil lifestyle or God would destroy them. But Jonah thought Assyria should be destroyed (and he was afraid to go there), so he ran the other direction—straight into the fish. Finally, when Jonah cried out to God and was rescued, he obeyed and preached in Nineveh. ■ "Don't get mad, get even." Fortunately, God doesn't work that way. Instead, God is "a gracious and compassionate God, slow to get angry and filled with unfailing love" (4:2). That's what our attitude should be, too. As you read Jonah, give your attitude to God, and ask him to replace it with his attitude.

## STATS

PURPOSE: To show the extent of God's grace—the message of salvation is for *all* people

AUTHOR: Jonah, son of Amittai

TO WHOM WRITTEN: Israel and God's people everywhere

DATE WRITTEN: Approximately 785 to 760 B.C.

SETTING: Jonah preceded Amos and ministered under Jeroboam II, Israel's most powerful king (793–753 B.C., see 2 Kings 14:23-25). Assyria was Israel's greatest enemy; Israel was conquered by them in 722 B.C. Nineveh's repentance must have been short-lived.

KEY PEOPLE: Jonah, the ship's captain and crew

KEY PLACES: Joppa, Nineveh

SPECIAL FEATURES: This book is different from the other prophetic books because it centers on the prophet, not his prophecies. Only one verse summarizes Jonah's message to Nineveh (3:4). Jonah is a historical narrative. It also is mentioned by Jesus as a picture of his death and resurrection (Matthew 12:38-42).

CHAPTER **1** **A BIG FISH SWALLOWS JONAH.** The LORD gave this message to Jonah son of Amittai: [2]"Get up and go to the great city of Nineveh! Announce my judgment against it because I have seen how wicked its people are."

[3]But Jonah got up and went in the opposite direction in order to get away from the LORD. He went down to the seacoast, to the port of Joppa, where he found a ship leaving for Tarshish. He bought a ticket and went on board, hoping that by going away to the west he could escape from the LORD.

[4]But as the ship was sailing along, suddenly the LORD flung a powerful wind over the sea, causing a violent storm that threatened to send them to the bottom. [5]Fearing for their lives, the desperate sailors shouted to their gods for help and threw the cargo overboard to lighten the ship. And all this time Jonah was sound asleep down in the hold. [6]So the captain went down after him. "How can you sleep at a time like this?" he shouted. "Get up and pray to your god! Maybe he will have mercy on us and spare our lives."

[7]Then the crew cast lots to see which of them had offended the gods and caused the terrible storm. When they did this, Jonah lost the toss. [8]"What have you done to bring this awful storm down on us?" they demanded. "Who are you? What is your line of work? What country are you from? What is your nationality?"

[9]And Jonah answered, "I am a Hebrew, and I worship the LORD, the God of heaven, who made the sea and the land." [10]Then he told them that he was running away from the LORD.

The sailors were terrified when they heard this. "Oh, why did you do it?" they groaned. [11]And since the storm was getting worse all the time, they asked him, "What should we do to you to stop this storm?"

## RUNNING AWAY ● ● • • •

1:3 **Jonah was afraid. He knew that God had a specific job for him, but he didn't want to do it. When God gives us directions through his Word, sometimes we run in fear, claiming that God is asking too much. Fear made Jonah run. But running got him into worse trouble. In the end, Jonah knew that it was best to do what God had asked in the first place. But by then he had paid a costly price for running. It is far better to obey from the start.**

## ATTITUDES

Sharon's favorite TV show is a hot new drama, "Manhattan Nights." It's really not new—just a shameless rip-off of the afternoon soaps and programs like "Beverly Hills 90210," "Melrose Place," and "E.R." The only difference is that this show is set in New York, and all the characters work on Wall Street.

Tonight Sharon is dying to find out if Heather is pregnant with Dade's child. But just as the show gets underway, the local TV station breaks in with a special report about a natural gas explosion in a nearby community.

"At least 12 people are known dead, another 17 are en route to area hospitals, at least 9 are still missing," the shaken reporter explains as fires rage out of control behind him.

"Great!" Sharon yells. "Because of this *stupid* fire, I'm gonna miss my show! Why can't they wait until the regular newscast to report all this junk? How stupid can you get?"

Sharon picks up the phone and dials her friend Ashley. "Can you *believe* they're doing this?" she says.

Sharon has a major attitude problem. She's more concerned about some fictional characters on TV than she is about her real-life neighbors. As a child of God, she should know better.

Read about a prophet of God who also had some misplaced priorities—Jonah 3–4.

---

[12]"Throw me into the sea," Jonah said, "and it will
become calm again. For I know that this terrible
storm is all my fault."
[13]Instead, the sailors tried even harder to row the
boat ashore. But the stormy sea was too violent for
them, and they couldn't make it. [14]Then they cried
out to the LORD, Jonah's God. "O LORD," they
pleaded, "don't make us die for this man's sin. And
don't hold us responsible for his death, because it
isn't our fault. O LORD, you have sent this storm
upon him for your own good reasons."
[15]Then the sailors picked Jonah up and threw him
into the raging sea, and the storm stopped at once!
[16]The sailors were awestruck by the LORD's great
power, and they offered him a sacrifice and vowed to
serve him.
[17]Now the LORD had arranged for a great fish to
swallow Jonah. And Jonah was inside the fish for
three days and three nights.

CHAPTER **2** **JONAH PRAYS.** Then Jonah prayed to
the LORD his God from inside the fish. [2]He said, "I
cried out to the LORD in my great trouble, and he
answered me. I called to you from the world of the
dead,* and LORD, you heard me! [3]You threw me into
the ocean depths, and I sank down to the heart of the
sea. I was buried beneath your wild and stormy
waves. [4]Then I said, 'O LORD, you have driven me
from your presence. How will I ever again see your
holy Temple?'

2:2 Hebrew *from Sheol.*

[5]"I sank beneath the waves, and death was very
near. The waters closed in around me, and seaweed
wrapped itself around my head. [6]I sank down to the
very roots of the mountains. I was locked out of life
and imprisoned in the land of the dead. But you,
O LORD my God, have snatched me from the yawning jaws of death!
[7]"When I had lost all hope, I turned my thoughts
once more to the LORD. And my earnest prayer went
out to you in your holy Temple. [8]Those who worship
false gods turn their backs on all God's mercies. [9]But
I will offer sacrifices to you with songs of praise, and
I will fulfill all my vows. For my salvation comes
from the LORD alone."
[10]Then the LORD ordered the fish to spit up Jonah
on the beach, and it did.

CHAPTER **3** **JONAH GOES TO NINEVEH.** Then the LORD
spoke to Jonah a second time: [2]"Get up and go to the
great city of Nineveh, and deliver the message of
judgment I have given you."
[3]This time Jonah obeyed the LORD's command
and went to Nineveh, a city so large that it took

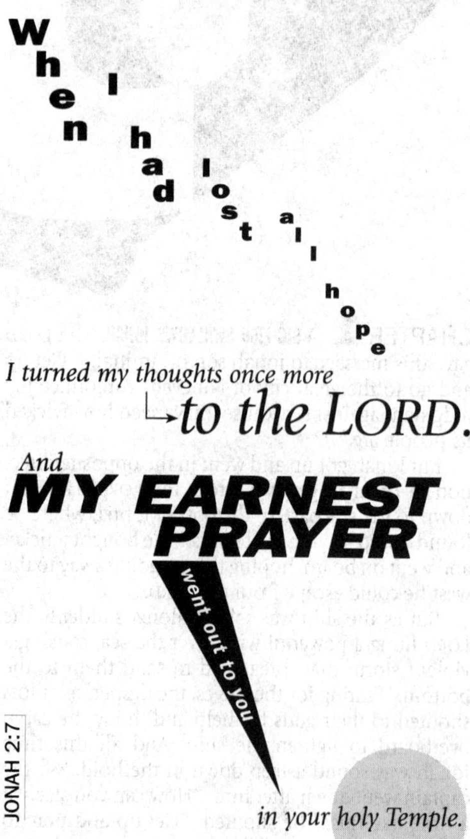
When I had lost all hope
I turned my thoughts once more
to the LORD.
And
MY EARNEST PRAYER
went out to you
in your holy Temple.
JONAH 2:7

three days to see it all. 4 On the day Jonah entered the city, he shouted to the crowds: "Forty days from now Nineveh will be destroyed!" 5 The people of Nineveh believed God's message, and from the greatest to the least, they decided to go without food and wear sackcloth to show their sorrow.

6 When the king of Nineveh heard what Jonah was saying, he stepped down from his throne and took off his royal robes. He dressed himself in sackcloth and sat on a heap of ashes. 7 Then the king and his nobles sent this decree throughout the city: "No one, not even the animals, may eat or drink anything at all. 8 Everyone is required to wear sackcloth and pray earnestly to God. Everyone must turn from their evil ways and stop all their violence. 9 Who can tell? Perhaps even yet God will have pity on us and hold back his fierce anger from destroying us."

10 When God saw that they had put a stop to their evil ways, he had mercy on them and didn't carry out the destruction he had threatened.

CHAPTER **4** This change of plans upset Jonah, and he became very angry. 2 So he complained to the LORD about it: "Didn't I say before I left home that you would do this, LORD? That is why I ran away to Tarshish! I knew that you were a gracious and compassionate God, slow to get angry and filled with unfailing love. I knew how easily you could cancel your plans for destroying these people. 3 Just kill me now, LORD! I'd rather be dead than alive because nothing I predicted is going to happen."

4 The LORD replied, "Is it right for you to be angry about this?"

5 Then Jonah went out to the east side of the city and made a shelter to sit under as he waited to see if anything would happen to the city. 6 And the LORD God arranged for a leafy plant to grow there, and soon it spread its broad leaves over Jonah's head, shading him from the sun. This eased some of his discomfort, and Jonah was very grateful for the plant.

7 But God also prepared a worm! The next morning at dawn the worm ate through the stem of the plant, so that it soon died and withered away. 8 And as the sun grew hot, God sent a scorching east wind to blow on Jonah. The sun beat down on his head until he grew faint and wished to die. "Death is certainly better than this!" he exclaimed.

9 Then God said to Jonah, "Is it right for you to be angry because the plant died?"

"Yes," Jonah retorted, "even angry enough to die!"

10 Then the LORD said, "You feel sorry about the plant, though you did nothing to put it there. And a plant is only, at best, short lived. 11 But Nineveh has more than 120,000 people living in spiritual darkness,* not to mention all the animals. Shouldn't I feel sorry for such a great city?"

4:11 Hebrew *people who don't know their right hands from their left.*

## BROAD VIEW ● ● • • •

4:1-2 **Jonah revealed the reason for his reluctance to go to Nineveh (1:3): He wanted the Ninevites destroyed, not forgiven. Jonah didn't understand that the God of Israel is also the God of the world. Are you surprised when some unexpected person turns to God? Maybe your view is as narrow as Jonah's. Don't forget that, in reality, none of us deserve to be forgiven by God.**

## SENSITIVE ● ● • • •

4:9 **Jonah was angry at the death of the plant, but not over what could have happened to Nineveh. Most of us have cried at the death of a pet or when an object with sentimental value is broken—but have we cried over a friend who does not know God? It is easy to be more sensitive to our own interests than to the spiritual needs of people around us. What are you sensitive to?**

## MIRACLES IN THE BOOK OF JONAH

God caused a great storm 1:4

God arranged for a great fish to swallow Jonah 1:17

God ordered the fish to spit up Jonah 2:10

God made a plant to shade Jonah 4:6

God prepared a worm to eat the plant 4:7

God ordered a scorching wind to blow on Jonah 4:8

**JONAH** served as a prophet to Israel and Assyria from 793 to 753 B.C.

| | |
|---|---|
| *Climate of the times* | While Nineveh was the most important city in Assyria and would soon become the capital of the huge Assyrian empire, it also was a very wicked city. |
| *Main message* | Jonah, who hated the powerful and wicked Assyrians, was called by God to warn the Assyrians that they would receive judgment if they did not repent. |
| *Importance of message* | Jonah didn't want to go to Nineveh, so he tried to run from God. But God has ways of teaching us to obey and follow him. When Jonah finally did preach, the people repented and God withheld his judgment. Even the most wicked will be saved if they truly repent of their sins and turn to God. |
| *Contemporary prophets* | Joel (853–796?)<br>Amos (760–750) |

# MEGA themes

**GOD'S SOVEREIGNTY** Although the prophet Jonah tried to run away from God, God was in control. By controlling the stormy seas and a great fish, God displayed his absolute, yet loving guidance.

Rather than running from God, trust him with your past, present, and future. Saying no to God quickly leads to disaster. Saying yes brings new understanding of God and his purpose in the world. Just say *yes* to God and his will for you.

1. What do you think Jonah was thinking and feeling in these situations: when he ran from God's command to go to Nineveh; when he was on the ship in the storm; when he was in the belly of the great fish?
2. What did Jonah learn about God's sovereignty through these experiences?
3. Have you felt the way Jonah did when he ran from God? What made it difficult for you to obey God at that time?
4. In what ways has God revealed his control in your life even when you were not aware of it or were in rebellion against his will? What does this teach you about God's sovereignty?

**MISSIONARY MESSAGE** God had given Jonah a purpose—to preach to the great Assyrian city of Nineveh. Jonah hated Nineveh, and so he responded with anger and indifference. Jonah had yet to learn that God loves all people. Through Jonah, God reminded Israel of their missionary purpose.

God wants his people to proclaim his love in words and actions to the whole world. He wants us to be his missionaries wherever we are and wherever he sends us.

1. Why was Jonah so opposed to preaching to Nineveh?
2. Jonah seemed to understand and accept part of God's message, yet he missed a key ingredient. What was it that he failed to understand or accept? Why do you think this happened?
3. Put God's message for the Ninevites into your own words.
4. What message do you think God might want to send to your school? How do you think most of the kids would respond to that message?
5. What opportunities do you have to communicate God's message through your own life?

**REPENTANCE** When the reluctant preacher went to Nineveh, there was a great response. People turned from their sins and turned to God. This was a powerful rebuke to Israel who thought they were better than nations like Nineveh, and yet refused to respond to God's message of forgiveness for repentance of sin.

God doesn't honor those who fake it. He wants the sincere devotion of each person. It is not enough to share the privileges of Christianity; we must ask God to forgive us and to remove our sin. Refusing to repent is the same as loving our sin—it keeps us from God.

1. What were the people of Nineveh like before Jonah's message? afterward?
2. Why was repentance (turning away from sin) so necessary for the Ninevites?
3. Why is repentance necessary for those who do not know God today? for those who already are Christians?
4. List any areas in your life where you need to repent in order to be living fully in God's will.

**GOD'S COMPASSION** God's message of love and forgiveness was not just for the Jews. God loves all the people of the world. The Assyrians didn't deserve it, but God spared them when they repented. In his mercy, God did not reject Jonah for aborting his mission. God had great love, patience, and forgiveness.

God loves each of us even when we fail him. He also loves all other people, including those outside our social group, cultural background, race, or denomination. When we accept his love, we must also learn to accept all those he loves. We will find it much easier to love others when we receive and return God's love.

1. Contrast God's view of the Ninevites with Jonah's view.
2. What does it mean to have a godly attitude toward people who are not Christians? Toward those who are racially or culturally different?
3. Who are the people in your world who need to experience God's love through you? How will you demonstrate love and compassion?

753 B.C
Hosea becomes a prophet

750
Jotham becomes king of Judah

743
Tiglath-Pileser III invades Israel

742
Micah becomes a prophet;
Pekahiah becomes king

740
Isaiah becomes a prophet

735
Ahaz becomes king of Judah

722
Israel (the northern kingdom) falls

715
Hosea's ministry ends;
Hezekiah becomes king of Judah

701
Sennacherib surrounds Jerusalem

687
Micah's ministry ends

Yesterday, at 2 A.M., our country officially surrendered. Realizing our situation was hopeless, generals from both sides agreed to end the bloodshed provided we hand over all guns and ammunition. Morale is low. The most perplexing question yet unanswered is, "How could we have been overrun?" ■ Imagine reading that in your newspaper. What a terrible thought! Yet history proves it's possible. It happened to both Israel (the northern 10 tribes) and Judah (the southern 2 tribes). They couldn't understand how they could have been defeated: They were God's chosen people; God had a special love for them; he'd rescued them out of slavery in Egypt; he'd destroyed mighty forces to give them their homeland; and he'd protected them. ■ God had been faithful—but neither Israel nor Judah had. Micah wrote, "Why is this happening? Because of the sins and rebellion of Israel and Judah" (1:5). Israel and Judah were being judged for their sins. Instead of worshiping the true God, the people were worshiping idols they had made. Many were using the religious ceremonies God had prescribed to make money. Those who were rich and influential were harassing the poor. God was going to punish them all because none of them were without guilt. ■ There are lessons in Micah we need to learn. God punishes sin—even in those to whom he has shown special favor—by sometimes humbling whole nations. ■ As you read Micah, remember that we as individuals and as a nation are responsible before God to serve him. Ask God to give you the strength to be faithful to him.

## STATS

PURPOSE: To warn God's people that judgment is coming and to offer pardon to all who repent

AUTHOR: Micah, a native of Moresheth, near Gath, about 20 miles southwest of Jerusalem

TO WHOM WRITTEN: The people of Israel (the northern kingdom) and of Judah (the southern kingdom)

DATE WRITTEN: Possibly during the reigns of Jotham, Ahaz, and Hezekiah (742–687 B.C.)

SETTING: The political situation is described in 2 Kings 15–20 and 2 Chronicles 26–30. Micah was a contemporary of Isaiah and Hosea.

KEY PLACES: Samaria, Jerusalem, Bethlehem

CHAPTER **1** **DARK DAYS FOR ISRAEL AND JUDAH.** The
LORD gave these messages to Micah of Moresheth
during the years when Jotham, Ahaz, and Hezekiah
were kings of Judah. The messages concerned both
Samaria and Jerusalem, and they came to Micah in
the form of visions.
[2]Attention! Let all the people of the world listen!
The Sovereign LORD has made accusations against
you; the Lord speaks from his holy Temple.
[3]Look! The LORD is coming! He leaves his throne in
heaven and comes to earth, walking on the high
places. [4]They melt beneath his feet and flow into the
valleys like wax in a fire, like water pouring down a hill.
[5]And why is this happening? Because of the sins and
rebellion of Israel and Judah.* Who is to blame for
Israel's rebellion? Samaria, its capital city! Where is the
center of idolatry in Judah? In Jerusalem, its capital!
[6]"So I, the LORD, will make the city of Samaria a
heap of rubble. Her streets will be plowed up for
planting vineyards. I will roll the stones of her walls
down into the valley below, exposing all her foundations. [7]All her carved images will be smashed to pieces.
All her sacred treasures will be burned up. These things
were bought with the money earned by her prostitution, and they will now be carried away to pay prostitutes elsewhere."
[8]Because of all this, I will mourn and lament. I will
walk around naked and barefoot in sorrow and
shame. I will howl like a jackal and wail like an ostrich.
[9]For my people's wound is far too deep to heal. It has
reached into Judah, even to the gates of Jerusalem.
[10]Don't tell our enemies in the city of Gath*;
don't weep at all.* You people in Beth-leaphrah,*
roll in the dust to show your anguish and despair.
[11]You people of Shaphir,* go as captives into exile—naked and ashamed. The people of Zaanan*
dare not come outside their walls. The people of
Beth-ezel* mourn because the very foundations of
their city have been swept away. [12]The people of
Maroth* anxiously wait for relief, but only bitterness awaits them as the LORD's judgment reaches
even to the gates of Jerusalem.
[13]Quick! Use your swiftest chariots and flee, you
people of Lachish.* You were the first city in Judah
to follow Israel in the sin of idol worship, and so you

**FOLLOW ME ● ● • • ·**

1:13 **The people of Lachish influenced many to follow their evil example. We often do the same when we sin. Regardless of whether or not you consider yourself a leader, your actions and words are observed by others more than you suspect—and they may choose to follow your example, whether you know it or not.**

1:5 Hebrew *and Jacob.* **1:10a** *Gath* sounds like the Hebrew term for "tell." **1:10b** Greek version reads *weep not in Acco.* **1:10c** *Beth-leaphrah* means "house of dust." **1:11a** *Shaphir* means "pleasant." **1:11b** *Zaanan* sounds like the Hebrew term for "come out." **1:11c** *Beth-ezel* means "adjoining house." **1:12** *Maroth* sounds like the Hebrew term for "bitter." **1:13a** *Lachish* sounds like the Hebrew term for "team of horses."

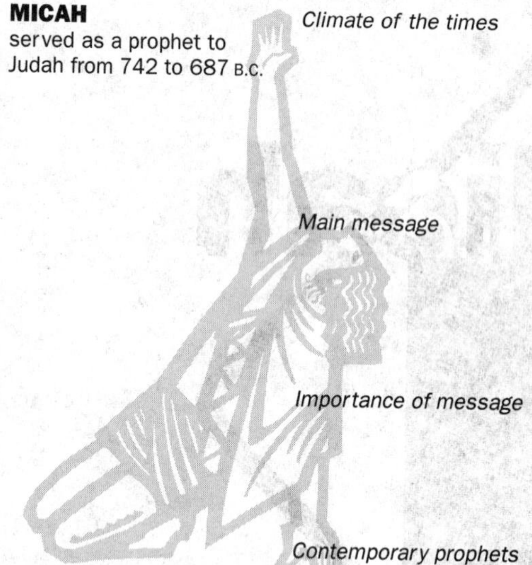

**MICAH**
served as a prophet to Judah from 742 to 687 B.C.

| | |
|---|---|
| *Climate of the times* | King Ahaz set up heathen idols in the Temple and finally nailed the Temple door shut. Four different nations harassed Judah. When Hezekiah became king, the nation began a slow road to recovery and economic strength. Hezekiah probably heeded much of Micah's advice. |
| *Main message* | Predicted the fall of both the northern kingdom of Israel and the southern kingdom of Judah. Through his disciplining the people, God was actually showing how much he cared for them. Hezekiah's good reign helped postpone Judah's punishment. |
| *Importance of message* | Choosing to live a life apart from God is making a commitment to sin. Sin leads to judgment and death. God alone shows us the way to eternal peace. His discipline often keeps us on the right path. |
| *Contemporary prophets* | Hosea (753–715)<br>Isaiah (740–681) |

led Jerusalem* into sin. 14Send a farewell gift to Moresheth-gath; there is no hope of saving it. The town of Aczib* has deceived the kings of Israel, for it promised help it could not give. 15You people of Mareshah,* I will bring a conqueror to capture your town. And the leaders* of Israel will go to Adullam.

16Weep, you people of Judah! Shave your heads in sorrow, for the children you love will be snatched away, and you will never see them again. Make yourselves as bald as an eagle, for your little ones will be exiled to distant lands.

CHAPTER **2** **GOD PUNISHES INJUSTICE.** How terrible it will be for you who lie awake at night, thinking up evil plans. You rise at dawn and hurry to carry out any of the wicked schemes you have power to accomplish. 2When you want a certain piece of land, you find a way to seize it. When you want someone's house, you take it by fraud and violence. No one's family or inheritance is safe with you around!

3But this is what the LORD says: "I will reward your evil with evil; you won't be able to escape! After I am through with you, none of you will ever again walk proudly in the streets."

4In that day your enemies will make fun of you by singing this song of despair about your experience:

"We are finished,
 completely ruined!
God has confiscated our land,
 taking it from us.
He has given our fields
 to those who betrayed us.*"

5Others will set your boundaries then, and the LORD's people will have no say in how the land is divided.

6"Don't say such things," the people say. "Don't prophesy like that. Such disasters will never come our way!"

7Should you talk that way, O family of Israel*? Will the LORD have patience with such behavior? If you would do what is right, you would find my words to be good. 8Yet to this very hour my people rise against me! You steal the shirts right off the backs of those who trusted you, making them as ragged as men who have just come home from battle. 9You have evicted women from their homes and stripped their children of all their God-given rights. 10Up! Begone! This is no longer your land and home, for you have filled it with sin and ruined it completely.

11Suppose a prophet full of lies were to say to you, "I'll preach to you the joys of wine and drink!" That's just the kind of prophet you would like!

12"Someday, O Israel, I will gather the few of you who are left. I will bring you together again like sheep in a fold, like a flock in its pasture. Yes, your land will again be filled with noisy crowds! 13Your leader will break out and lead you out of exile. He will bring you through the gates of your cities of captivity, back to your own land. Your king will lead you; the LORD himself will guide you."

## IN YOUR DREAMS • • • • •

**2:1-2 Micah spoke out against those who planned evil deeds at night and rose at dawn to carry them out. A person's thoughts reflect his character. What do you think about as you lie down to sleep? Do your desires involve greed or stepping on others to achieve your goals? Evil thoughts lead to evil deeds as surely as morning follows night.**

1:13b Hebrew *the daughter of Zion.* 1:14 *Aczib* means "deception." 1:15a *Mareshah* sounds like the Hebrew term for "conqueror." 1:15b Hebrew *the glory.* 2:4 Or *to those who took us captive.* 2:7 Hebrew *house of Jacob.*

CHAPTER **3** **GOD PUNISHES THE LEADERS.** Listen, you leaders of Israel! You are supposed to know right from wrong, [2]but you are the very ones who hate good and love evil. You skin my people alive and tear the flesh off their bones. [3]You eat my people's flesh, cut away their skin, and break their bones. You chop them up like meat for the cooking pot. [4]Then you beg the LORD for help in times of trouble! Do you really expect him to listen? After all the evil you have done, he won't even look at you!

[5]This is what the LORD says to you false prophets: "You are leading my people astray! You promise peace for those who give you food, but you declare war on anyone who refuses to pay you. [6]Now the night will close around you, cutting off all your visions. Darkness will cover you, making it impossible for you to predict the future. The sun will set for you prophets, and your day will come to an end. [7]Then you seers will cover your faces in shame, and you diviners will be disgraced. And you will admit that your messages were not from God."

[8]But as for me, I am filled with power and the Spirit of the LORD. I am filled with justice and might, fearlessly pointing out Israel's sin and rebellion. [9]Listen to me, you leaders of Israel! You hate justice and twist all that is right. [10]You are building Jerusalem on a foundation of murder and corruption. [11]You rulers govern for the bribes you can get; you priests teach God's laws only for a price; you prophets won't prophesy unless you are paid. Yet all of you claim you are depending on the LORD. "No harm can come to us," you say, "for the LORD is here among us."

[12]So because of you, Mount Zion will be plowed like an open field; Jerusalem will be reduced to rubble! A great forest will grow on the hilltop, where the Temple now stands.

CHAPTER **4** **SOMEDAY THE LORD WILL BE KING.** In the last days, the Temple of the LORD in Jerusalem will become the most important place on earth. People from all over the world will go there to worship. [2]Many nations will come and say, "Come, let us go up to the mountain of the LORD, to the Temple of the God of Israel.* There he will teach us his ways, so that we may obey him." For in those days the LORD's teaching and his word will go out from Jerusalem.

[3]The LORD will settle international disputes. All the nations will beat their swords into plowshares and their spears into pruning hooks. All wars will stop, and military training will come to an end. [4]Everyone will live quietly in their own homes in peace and prosperity, for there will be nothing to fear. The LORD Almighty has promised this! [5]Even though the nations around us worship idols, we will follow the LORD our God forever and ever.

[6]"In that coming day," says the LORD, "I will gather together my people who are lame, who have been exiles, filled with grief. [7]They are weak and far from home, but I will make them strong again, a mighty nation. Then I, the LORD, will rule from Jerusalem* as their king forever."

[8]As for you, O Jerusalem, the citadel of God's people, your royal might and power will come back to you again. The kingship will be restored to my precious Jerusalem. [9]But why are you now screaming in terror? Have you no king to lead you? He is dead! Have you no wise people to counsel you? All are gone! Pain

4:2 Hebrew *of Jacob.* 4:7 Hebrew *Mount Zion.*

## SPIRIT POWER ● ● • • •

**3:8 Micah attributed the power of his ministry to the Spirit of the Lord. Our power comes from the same source. Jesus told his followers they would receive power to witness about him when the Holy Spirit came to them (Acts 1:8). You can't witness effectively by relying on your own strength because fear will keep you from speaking out for God. Only by relying on the power of the Holy Spirit can you live and witness for Jesus.**

## "Here's what I did..."

It wasn't easy being a Christian in my junior high and high schools. One time, several of the more popular girls were putting down another girl, Nicole, for being a Christian. I didn't think it was right to remain silent, so I said, "So what if she's a Christian? I am, too. Why does that bother you?"

"Because it's weird," one of them said. "I mean, you don't party, you don't fool around with guys, you don't drink—you must lead a pretty boring life." They all laughed.

"Why don't you try it yourself and see how boring it is," I said. They just laughed and made fun of me.

A few days later, I was walking down the hall and one of the girls from that group called out, "What are you going to do for fun today, Christine? Gonna pray on your knees for a couple of hours?" They all laughed. Other people heard and looked at me curiously. I was beginning to feel like a social outcast.

One day, Nicole told me to read Micah 4:6-13. I did, and it helped me a lot. It reminded me that even though these kids who rejected me were considered "cool" by the school, they weren't cool in God's eyes. In the end, God will punish those who disobey him and reward those who seek to obey him. This passage helped take away the pain of being rejected because I stood up for someone else and for my beliefs.

Christine

AGE 15

has gripped you like it does a woman in labor. 10Writhe
and groan in terrible pain, you people of Jerusalem,*
for you must leave this city to live in the open fields.
You will soon be sent into exile in distant Babylon. But
the LORD will rescue you there; he will redeem you
from the grip of your enemies.
11True, many nations have gathered together
against you, calling for your blood, eager to gloat
over your destruction. 12But they do not know the
LORD's thoughts or understand his plan. These nations don't know that he is gathering them together
to be beaten and trampled like bundles of grain on
a threshing floor.

## HONESTY

Terrance needs some new basketball shoes. He's got the perfect pair all picked out—an air-cushioned, super-grip, lightweight model with reinforced ankle supports. The exact shoe all the best dunkers in the NBA wear. Problem is, the shoe costs well over $100.

A few other guys in the neighborhood already have the shoes. One guy who deals drugs has three pairs. Another kid stole some from a locker at school. A third teenager shoplifted his pair. Terrance really wants these new basketball shoes, but he would never do something illegal or dishonest to get them . . . or would he?

This afternoon, a young guy from the neighborhood, who is the assistant manager of a downtown shoe store, came up with a foolproof plan. By marking certain shoes defective, he can cut the price, then cover it all up by juggling some figures.

"It's cool," a friend tells Terrance. "The store makes money, you get your shoes cheap, and you're not stealing."

Terrance thinks long and hard, then decides it's wrong. "It's hard to walk away from such a good deal," Terrance says, "but those shoes aren't worth doing something dishonest."

Meanwhile all his friends are taking advantage of the store's "defective" merchandise.

Read Micah 7:1-4. Do you think Terrance might be feeling the way the prophet Micah felt? How would you have handled his situation?

13"Rise up and destroy the nations, O Jerusalem!"*
says the LORD. "For I will give you iron horns and
bronze hooves, so you can trample many nations to
pieces. Then you will give all the wealth they acquired
as offerings to me, the Lord of all the earth."

## CHAPTER 5 A RULER WILL COME FROM BETHLEHEM.

Mobilize! Marshal your troops! The enemy is laying
siege to Jerusalem. With a rod they will strike the
leader of Israel in the face.
2But you, O Bethlehem Ephrathah, are only a
small village in Judah. Yet a ruler of Israel will come
from you, one whose origins are from the distant
past. 3The people of Israel will be abandoned to their
enemies until the time when the woman in labor
gives birth to her son. Then at last his fellow coun-

## CHRISTMAS • • • • •

5:2 **This Ruler is Jesus, the Messiah. Micah accurately predicted Christ's birthplace hundreds of years before Jesus was born. The promised eternal King in David's line, who would come to live as a man, had been alive forever—his "origins are from the distant past." Although eternal, he entered human history as the man Jesus of Nazareth.**

trymen will return from exile to their own land. 4And
he will stand to lead his flock with the LORD's
strength, in the majesty of the name of the LORD his
God. Then his people will live there undisturbed, for
he will be highly honored all around the world. 5And
he will be the source of our peace.
When the Assyrians invade our land and break
through our defenses, we will appoint seven rulers
to watch over us, eight princes to lead us. 6They
will rule Assyria with drawn swords and enter the
gates of the land of Nimrod. They* will rescue us
from the Assyrians when they pour over the borders to invade our land.
7Then the few left in Israel* will go out among the
nations. They will be like dew sent by the LORD or
like rain falling on the grass, which no one can hold
back. 8The remnant of Israel will go out among the
nations and be as strong as a lion. And the other
nations will be like helpless sheep, with no one to
rescue them. 9The people of Israel will stand up to
their foes, and all their enemies will be wiped out.
10"At that same time," says the LORD, "I will destroy all your weapons—your horses and chariots. 11I
will tear down your walls and demolish the defenses
of your cities. 12I will put an end to all witchcraft;
there will be no more fortune-tellers to consult. 13I
will destroy all your idols and sacred pillars, so you
will never again worship the work of your own
hands. 14I will abolish your pagan shrines with their
Asherah poles and destroy the cities where your idol
temples stand. 15I will pour out my vengeance on all
the nations that refuse to obey me."

## CHAPTER 6 GOD'S CASE AGAINST HIS PEOPLE.

Listen to
what the LORD is saying: "Stand up and state your
case against me. Let the mountains and hills be
called to witness your complaints.
2"And now, O mountains, listen to the LORD's
complaint! He has a case against his people Israel!
He will prosecute them to the full extent of the law.
3O my people, what have I done to make you turn
from me? Tell me why your patience is exhausted!
Answer me! 4For I brought you out of Egypt and
redeemed you from your slavery. I sent Moses,
Aaron, and Miriam to help you.
5"Don't you remember, my people, how King Balak of Moab tried to have you cursed and how Balaam son of Beor blessed you instead? And
remember your journey from Acacia* to Gilgal,
when I, the LORD, did everything I could to teach you
about my faithfulness."
6What can we bring to the LORD to make up for

4:10 Hebrew *O daughter of Zion.* 4:13 Hebrew *"Rise up and thresh, O daughter of Zion."* 5:6 Hebrew *He.* 5:7 Hebrew *Jacob;* also in 5:8. 6:5 Hebrew *Shittim.*

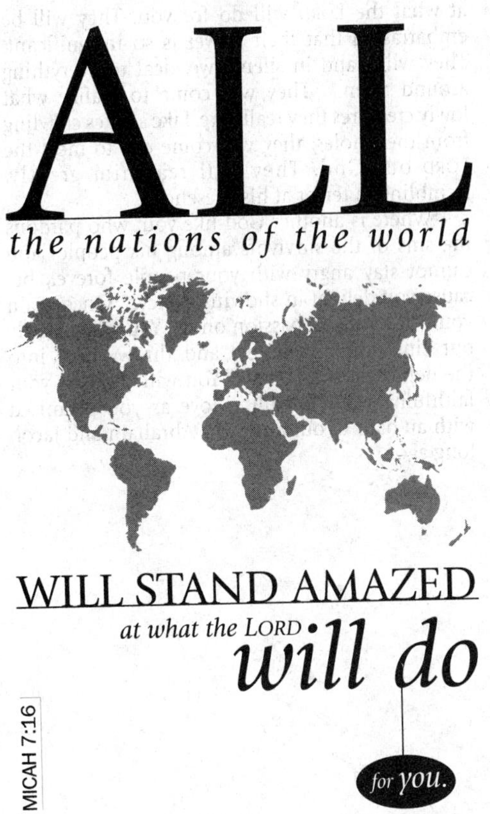
ALL
the nations of the world
WILL STAND AMAZED
at what the LORD
will do
for you.
MICAH 7:16

what we've done? Should we bow before God with
offerings of yearling calves? 7Should we offer him
thousands of rams and tens of thousands of rivers of
olive oil? Would that please the LORD? Should we
sacrifice our firstborn children to pay for the sins of
our souls? Would that make him glad?
8No, O people, the LORD has already told you
what is good, and this is what he requires: to do
what is right, to love mercy, and to walk humbly
with your God.
9Listen! Fear the LORD if you are wise! His voice
is calling out to everyone in Jerusalem: "The armies of destruction are coming; the LORD is sending them.* 10Will there be no end of your getting
rich by cheating? The homes of the wicked are
filled with treasures gained by dishonestly measuring out grain in short measures.* 11And how can I
tolerate all your merchants who use dishonest
scales and weights? 12The rich among you have
become wealthy through extortion and violence.
Your citizens are so used to lying that their tongues
can no longer tell the truth.
13"Therefore, I will wound you! I will bring you to
ruin for all your sins. 14You will eat but never have
enough. Your hunger pangs and emptiness will still
remain. And though you try to save your money, it
will come to nothing in the end. You will save a little,
but I will give it to those who conquer you. 15You will
plant crops but not harvest them. You will press your
olives but not get enough oil to anoint yourselves.
You will trample the grapes but get no juice to make
your wine.
16"The only laws you keep are those of evil King
Omri; the only example you follow is that of wicked
King Ahab! Therefore, I will make an example of
you, bringing you to complete ruin. You will be
treated with contempt, mocked by all who see you."

CHAPTER **7** **HARD TIMES FOR EVERYONE.** What misery
is mine! I feel like the fruit picker after the harvest
who can find nothing to eat. Not a cluster of grapes
or a single fig can be found to satisfy my hunger.
2The godly people have all disappeared; not one
fair-minded person is left on the earth. They are all
murderers, even setting traps for their own brothers.
3They go about their evil deeds with both hands.
How skilled they are at using them! Officials and
judges alike demand bribes. The people with money
and influence pay them off, and together they
scheme to twist justice. 4Even the best of them is like
a brier; the straightest is more crooked than a hedge
of thorns. But your judgment day is coming swiftly
now. Your time of punishment is here.
5Don't trust anyone—not your best friend or even
your wife! 6For the son despises his father. The
daughter defies her mother. The daughter-in-law defies her mother-in-law. Your enemies will be right in
your own household.
7As for me, I look to the LORD for his help. I wait
confidently for God to save me, and my God will
certainly hear me. 8Do not gloat over me, my enemies! For though I fall, I will rise again. Though I sit
in darkness, the LORD himself will be my light. 9I will
be patient as the LORD punishes me, for I have sinned
against him. But after that, he will take up my case
and punish my enemies for all the evil they have
done to me. The LORD will bring me out of my
darkness into the light, and I will see his righteousness. 10Then my enemies will see that the LORD is on
my side. They will be ashamed that they taunted me,
saying, "Where is the LORD—that God of yours?"
With my own eyes I will see them trampled down
like mud in the streets.
11In that day, Israel, your cities will be rebuilt, and
your borders will be extended. 12People from many
lands will come and honor you—from Assyria all

**NOT OK ● ● • • •**

**7:1-4 Micah could not find a godly or fair-minded person anywhere. Godliness is hard to find. Society rationalizes sin; Christians sometimes compromise what is right in order to do what they want. Too often we convince ourselves it's OK, especially when "everyone else is doing it." But our standards for behavior come from God, not society. God is truth, and we are to be like him.**

6:9 Hebrew *"Listen to the rod. Who appointed it?"* 6:10 Hebrew *by using the short ephah;* the ephah was a unit for measuring grain.

## MERCY ● ● ● • •

7:18 **God delights in showing mercy! He does not forgive grudgingly but is glad when we repent. He offers forgiveness to all who come back to him. Today you can confess your sins and receive his loving forgiveness. Don't be too proud to accept God's mercy.**

the way to the towns of Egypt, and from Egypt all the way to the Euphrates River,* and from many distant seas and mountains. [13]But the land* will become empty and desolate because of the wickedness of those who live there.

[14]O LORD, come and rule your people; lead your flock in green pastures. Help them to live in peace and prosperity. Let them enjoy the fertile pastures of Bashan and Gilead as they did long ago.

[15]"Yes," says the LORD, "I will do mighty miracles for you, like those I did when I rescued you from slavery in Egypt."

[16]All the nations of the world will stand amazed at what the LORD will do for you. They will be embarrassed that their power is so insignificant. They will stand in silent awe, deaf to everything around them. [17]They will come to realize what lowly creatures they really are. Like snakes crawling from their holes, they will come out to meet the LORD our God. They will fear him greatly, trembling in terror at his presence.

[18]Where is another God like you, who pardons the sins of the survivors among his people? You cannot stay angry with your people forever, because you delight in showing mercy. [19]Once again you will have compassion on us. You will trample our sins under your feet and throw them into the depths of the ocean! [20]You will show us your faithfulness and unfailing love as you promised with an oath to our ancestors Abraham and Jacob long ago.

7:12 Hebrew *the river.* 7:13 Or *earth.*

# MEGA themes

**PERVERTING FAITH** God said that he would judge the false prophets, dishonest leaders, and selfish priests in Israel and Judah. While they publicly carried out religious ceremonies, they privately were seeking to gain money and influence. Mixing selfish motives with an empty display of religion perverts faith.

Don't mix your selfish desires with true faith in God. One day God will reveal how foolish it is to substitute anything for loyalty to him. Coming up with your own private blend of religion will pervert your faith.

1. What were the specific sins of the religious leaders? Why were they so offensive to God?
2. What does it mean for someone to pervert the faith today?
3. What can you do to keep your faith pure rather than having it be ruined by self-centered choices?

**OPPRESSION** Micah predicted ruin for all nations and leaders who were oppressing others. The upper classes oppressed and exploited the poor. Yet no one was speaking against them or doing anything to stop them. God will not put up with such injustice.

We dare not ask God to help us while we ignore those who are needy and oppressed, or silently condone the actions of those who oppress them. Sharing God's love includes meeting the needs of those who are rejected and neglected by society.

1. What types of oppression were present in Micah's day?
2. What types of oppression are found in today's world?
3. What are Christians doing to bring about God's justice for the poor and oppressed people in your community?
4. What could you do to help people become more aware of the poor in your community and God's concern for them?
5. What can you do to help those who are poor and/or oppressed?

**PLEASING GOD** Micah preached that God's greatest desire was not the offering of sacrifices at the Temple. God delights in faith that produces fairness, love to others, and obedience to him.

True faith in God generates kindness, compassion, justice, mercy, and humility. We can please God by seeking these results in our school, family, church, and neighborhood.

1. In Micah, what false ideas did the people have about pleasing God?
2. What false ideas do you see in the world about what it means to please God?
3. List a few examples of individuals you have seen who are truly pleasing God.
4. What ways in your own life do you find to please God?
5. Commit yourself to specific ways that you can be pleasing to God in the next week at school, home, church, and/or work.

697 B.C.
**Manasseh becomes king of Judah**

669
**Ashurbanipal becomes king of Assyria**

663
**The fall of Thebes; Nahum becomes a prophet**

640
**Josiah becomes king of Judah; Zephaniah becomes a prophet**

627
**Jeremiah becomes a prophet**

612
**Nineveh falls**

609
**Assyria completely conquered**

605
**Babylonians win battle of Carchemish**

586
**Judah falls to Babylon**

**O***h no,* thought Bobby, *we're going to lose again. "Supe" is on their side.* "Supe" was Robert Owens, the best athlete in the school. Whichever team got "Supe" always won. Bobby's phys ed class was beginning to play football, and he loved it—except when "Supe" was on the other team. Bobby was good, but "Supe" was great. He could outrun, outthrow, outcatch, out*everything* anyone. ■ Nineveh, the Assyrian capital, was like "Supe." No one had been able to stand against the Assyrians. They had overthrown Israel, and now their sights were on Judah. The people of Judah were afraid; how could they withstand such a terrible enemy? ■ Through Nahum God brought words of comfort to Judah and words of doom to Assyria. He said, "The LORD is a jealous God. . . . He takes revenge on all who oppose him and furiously destroys his enemies!" (1:2). To Judah God declared, "Now I will break your chains and release you from Assyrian oppression" (1:13). To Assyria God announced, "I am your enemy! . . . Your chariots will soon go up in smoke. . . . Never again will the voices of your proud messengers be heard" (2:13). ■ Such is the end of those who oppose the Lord and hurt his people. God loves his children and will protect them, at all costs. ■ Let Nahum remind you of the futility of fighting against God; let his words encourage you. God protects those whom he loves.

## STATS

PURPOSE: To pronounce God's judgment on Assyria and to comfort Judah with this truth

AUTHOR: Nahum

TO WHOM WRITTEN: The people of Nineveh and Judah

DATE WRITTEN: Sometime during Nahum's prophetic ministry (probably between 663 and 612 B.C.)

SETTING: This particular prophecy takes place after the fall of Thebes in 663 B.C. (see 3:8-10)

KEY PLACE: Nineveh, the capital of Assyria

CHAPTER **1** **GOD IS PATIENT AND POWERFUL.** This message concerning Nineveh came as a vision to Nahum, who lived in Elkosh.
[2]The LORD is a jealous God, filled with vengeance
and wrath. He takes revenge on all who oppose him
and furiously destroys his enemies! [3]The LORD is
slow to get angry, but his power is great, and he never
lets the guilty go unpunished. He displays his power
in the whirlwind and the storm. The billowing
clouds are the dust beneath his feet. [4]At his command the oceans and rivers dry up, the lush pastures
of Bashan and Carmel fade, and the green forests of
Lebanon wilt. [5]In his presence the mountains quake,
and the hills melt away; the earth trembles, and its
people are destroyed. [6]Who can stand before his
fierce anger? Who can survive his burning fury? His
rage blazes forth like fire, and the mountains crumble to dust in his presence.
[7]The LORD is good. When trouble comes, he is a
strong refuge. And he knows everyone who trusts in
him. [8]But he sweeps away his enemies in an overwhelming flood. He pursues his foes into the darkness of night.
[9]Why are you scheming against the LORD? He will
destroy you with one blow; he won't need to strike
twice! [10]His enemies, tangled up like thorns, staggering like drunks, will be burned like dry straw in a
field. [11]Who is this king of yours who dares to plot
evil against the LORD?
[12]This is what the LORD says: "Even though the
Assyrians have many allies, they will be destroyed and
disappear. O my people, I have already punished you
once, and I will not do it again. [13]Now I will break your
chains and release you from Assyrian oppression."
[14]And this is what the LORD says concerning the
Assyrians in Nineveh: "You will have no more children
to carry on your name. I will destroy all the idols in the
temples of your gods. I am preparing a grave for you
because you are despicable and don't deserve to live!"
[15]Look! A messenger is coming over the mountains with good news! He is bringing a message of
peace. Celebrate your festivals, O people of Judah,
and fulfill all your vows, for your enemies from

### TIME'S UP ●●●••

**1:3 God is slow to get angry, but when he is ready to punish, even the earth trembles. Often people avoid God because they see evildoers in the world and hypocrites in the church. They don't realize that because God is slow to anger, he gives his true followers time to share his love and truth with evildoers. But judgment *will* come; God will not allow sin to go unchecked forever. When people wonder why God doesn't punish evil immediately, remind them that if he did, none of us would be here. We can all be thankful that God gives people time to turn to him.**

Nineveh will never invade your land again. They have been completely destroyed!

CHAPTER **2** **NINEVEH WILL FALL.** Nineveh, you are already surrounded by enemy armies! Sound the alarm! Man the ramparts! Muster your defenses, and keep a sharp watch for the enemy attack to begin!
[2]For the land of Israel lies empty and broken after your attacks, but the LORD will restore its honor and power again.

[3]Shields flash red in the sunlight! The attack begins! See their scarlet uniforms! Watch as their glittering chariots move into position, with a forest of spears waving above them. [4]The chariots race recklessly along the streets and through the squares, swift as lightning, flickering like torches. [5]The king shouts to his officers; they stumble in their haste, rushing to the walls to set up their defenses. [6]But too late! The river gates are open! The enemy has entered! The palace is about to collapse!

## VENGEANCE

Whit is one angry guy. And rightly so.

Yesterday before practice he confided in teammates Don and David about his secret attraction to Carolyn, and how he wished he could get up the nerve to ask her to the winter formal.

Not only did Whit's confidants take that information, twist it, and spread embarrassing rumors all over the locker room, but Don went home last night, called Carolyn himself, and asked her to the dance!

All day Whit has wanted to punch Don out, or at the very least, knock his head off in practice this afternoon. He's been daydreaming of ways to get even. Mixed in with his rage is also a measure of hurt. "I thought those guys were my friends."

But at football practice, Whit doesn't react at all. He doesn't yell or scream, he doesn't throw any punches, he even passes up several prime opportunities to hit Don and David with cheap shots and blindsides.

"Just because they were jerks doesn't mean I have to be one, too," he tells a surprised friend later.

When people wrong us, it's natural to want to take revenge. But, like Whit, we need to resist that powerful urge to get even!

The fact is, it's best to leave vengeance in God's hands. He's the One who knows how to handle it the best. See Nahum 1:2-8.

[7]Nineveh's exile has been decreed, and all the servant girls mourn its capture. Listen to them moan like doves; watch them beat their breasts in sorrow.
[8]Nineveh is like a leaking water reservoir! The people are slipping away. "Stop, stop!" someone shouts, but the people just keep on running.

[9]Loot the silver! Plunder the gold! There seems no end to Nineveh's many treasures—its vast, uncounted wealth. [10]Soon the city is an empty shambles, stripped of its wealth. Hearts melt in horror, and knees shake. The people stand aghast, their faces pale and trembling.

## ANGRY GOD ● ● • • •

**2:12-3:1 The major source of the Assyrians' wealth was what they stole from other nations. The Assyrians took the food of people they conquered to maintain their own luxurious standard of living. They deprived others to supply their excesses. Depriving poor people to support the luxury of a few is a sin that angers God. Do you ever find yourself willing to take from someone so that you can benefit or have more? As Christians, we must stand firm against this common but evil practice.**

[11]"Where now is that great Nineveh, lion of the nations, full of fight and boldness, where the old and feeble and the young and tender lived with nothing
to fear? [12]O Nineveh, you were once a mighty lion! You crushed your enemies to feed your cubs and your mate. You filled your city and your homes with captives and plunder.

[13]"I am your enemy!" says the LORD Almighty. "Your chariots will soon go up in smoke. The finest of your youth will be killed in battle. Never again will you bring back plunder from conquered nations. Never again will the voices of your proud messengers be heard."

CHAPTER **3** **DESTRUCTION.** How terrible it will be for Nineveh, the city of murder and lies! She is
crammed with wealth to be plundered. [2]Listen! Hear the crack of the whips as the chariots rush forward against her. Wheels rumble, horses' hooves pound, and chariots clatter as they bump wildly through the
streets. [3]See the flashing swords and glittering spears in the upraised arms of the cavalry! The dead are lying in the streets—dead bodies, heaps of bodies, everywhere. People stumble over them, scramble to
their feet, and fall again. [4]All this because Nineveh, the beautiful and faithless city, mistress of deadly charms, enticed the nations with her beauty. She taught them all to worship her false gods, enchanting people everywhere.

[5]"No wonder I am your enemy!" declares the LORD Almighty. "And now I will lift your skirts so all the earth will see your nakedness and shame. [6]I will
cover you with filth and show the world how vile you
really are. [7]All who see you will shrink back in horror and say, 'Nineveh lies in utter ruin.' Yet no one anywhere will regret your destruction."

[8]Are you any better than Thebes,* surrounded by
rivers, protected by water on all sides? [9]Ethiopia* and the land of Egypt were the source of her strength, which seemed without limit. The nations of Put and Libya also helped and supported her. [10]Yet Thebes
fell, and her people were led away as captives. Her babies were dashed to death against the stones of the streets. Soldiers cast lots to see who would get the Egyptian officers as servants. All their leaders were bound in chains.

[11]And you, Nineveh, will also stagger like a drunkard. You will hide for fear of the attacking enemy. [12]All
your fortresses will fall. They will be devoured like the ripe figs that fall into the mouths of those who shake
the trees. [13]Your troops will be as weak and helpless as

3:8 Hebrew *No-amon;* also in 3:10. 3:9 Hebrew *Cush.*

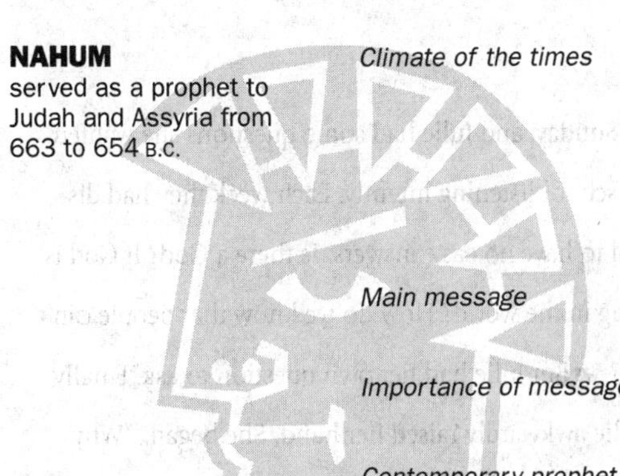

**NAHUM** served as a prophet to Judah and Assyria from 663 to 654 B.C.

*Climate of the times* Manasseh, one of Judah's most wicked kings, ruled the land. He openly defied God and persecuted God's people. Assyria, the world power at that time, made Judah one of its vassal states. The people of Judah wanted to be like the Assyrians, who seemed to have all the power and possessions they wanted.

*Main message* The mighty empire of Assyria, the oppressors of God's people, would tumble soon.

*Importance of message* Those who do evil and oppress others will one day meet a bitter end.

*Contemporary prophet* Zephaniah (640–621)

---

women. The gates of your land will be opened wide to the enemy and set on fire and burned.
[14]Get ready for the siege! Store up water! Strengthen the defenses! Make bricks to repair the walls! Go into the pits to trample clay, and pack it into molds! [15]But in the middle of your preparations, the fire will devour you; the sword will cut you down. The enemy will consume you like locusts, devouring everything they see. There will be no escape, even if you multiply like grasshoppers.
[16]Merchants, as numerous as the stars, have filled your city with vast wealth. But like a swarm of locusts, they strip the land and then fly away.
[17]Your princes and officials are also like locusts, crowding together in the hedges to survive the cold. But like locusts that fly away when the sun comes up to warm the earth, all of them will fly away and disappear.
[18]O Assyrian king, your princes lie dead in the dust. Your people are scattered across the mountains. There is no longer a shepherd to gather them together. [19]There is no healing for your wound; your injury is fatal. All who hear of your destruction will clap their hands for joy. Where can anyone be found who has not suffered from your cruelty?

# MEGA themes

**GOD JUDGES** God would judge the city of Nineveh for its idolatry, arrogance, and oppression. Although Assyria was the leading military power in the world, God would completely destroy this "invincible" nation. God allows no person or power to assume or scoff at his authority.

Anyone who remains arrogant and resists God's authority will face his anger. No ruler or nation will get away with rejecting him. No individual will be able to hide from his judgment. But those who keep trusting God will be kept safe forever.

1. What sins were leading to Nineveh's punishment?
2. In your world, what things do you see that God will certainly judge in the future?
3. What would you say to a person who lived an ungodly lifestyle with the attitude, "I can do what I please"?
4. Describe your hope in light of the holiness of God's judgment.

**GOD RULES** God rules over all the earth, even over those who don't acknowledge him. God is all-powerful, and no one can thwart his plans. God will overcome any who attempt to defy him. Human power is futile against God.

If you are impressed by or afraid of any weapons, armies, or powerful people, remember that God alone can truly rescue you from fear or oppression. We must place our confidence in God because he alone is all-powerful.

1. List the most powerful forces that exist in the world today.
2. Which of the forces do you think are the most feared? Why?
3. What does Nahum teach you about God's ability and power to control the awesome forces that so many people fear?
4. How does knowing about God's power make you feel? What difference does it make in how you live?

627 B.C.
**Jeremiah becomes a prophet**

612
**Habakkuk becomes a prophet**

609
**King Josiah dies in battle**

605
**Daniel taken captive to Babylon**

597
**Ezekiel a captive in Babylon; Zedekiah becomes king**

588
**Habakkuk's ministry ends**

586
**Fall of Judah; Jerusalem destroyed**

It was Sunday, and Julie had some questions she wanted answered. She sat in Sunday school listening intently. Each week they had discussed questions that seemed to have no easy answers: Is there a God? If God is so good, why is there suffering in the world? How do we know that people can't get to heaven except by Jesus? ■ But Julie had her own question to ask. Finally, as the room settled down, Julie awkwardly raised her hand. She began, "Why does it seem like those who are trying to live the way Jesus would want them to are so often abused by those who don't care how they live? Doesn't God care? It doesn't seem fair!" ■ Many centuries ago, Habakkuk posed a similar question. He looked over his own country, Judah, and saw that wherever he looked there was "destruction and violence . . . the wicked far outnumber the righteous" (1:3-4). He questioned God's care for those trying to live righteous lives; it seemed the wicked always got the upper hand. ■ God answered Habakkuk. He answered him well enough that Habakkuk replied, "I have heard all about you, LORD, and I am filled with awe by the amazing things you have done. In this time of our deep need, begin again to help us, as you did in years gone by. Show us your power to save us. And in your anger, remember your mercy" (3:2). ■ As you read this book, take note of God's answer. It may surprise you. And then, like Habakkuk, resolve to trust God to care for you.

## STATS

PURPOSE: To show that God is still in control of the world despite the apparent triumph of evil

AUTHOR: Habakkuk

TO WHOM WRITTEN: Judah (the southern kingdom) and God's people everywhere

DATE WRITTEN: Between 612 and 588 B.C.

SETTING: Babylon was becoming the dominant world power and Judah would soon feel Babylon's destructive force

KEY PEOPLE: Habakkuk, the Chaldeans (Babylonians)

KEY PLACE: Judah

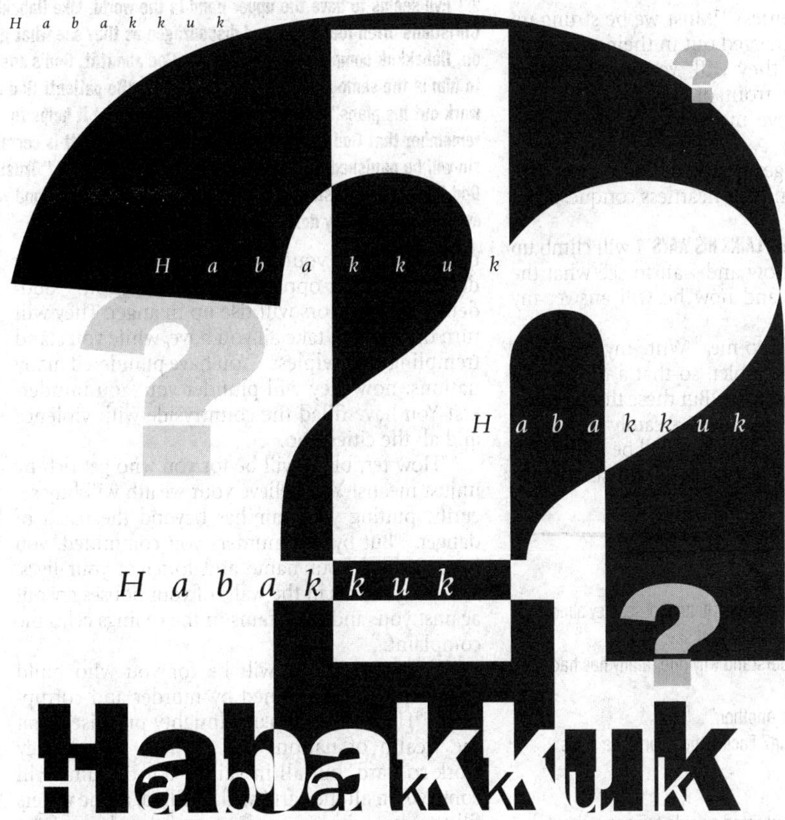


CHAPTER **1** **HABAKKUK HAS QUESTIONS FOR GOD.** This is the message that the prophet Habakkuk received from the LORD in a vision.

[2]How long, O LORD, must I call for help? But you do not listen! "Violence!" I cry, but you do not come to save. [3]Must I forever see this sin and misery all around me? Wherever I look, I see destruction and violence. I am surrounded by people who love to argue and fight. [4]The law has become paralyzed and useless, and there is no justice given in the courts. The wicked far outnumber the righteous, and justice is perverted with bribes and trickery.

[5]The LORD replied, "Look at the nations and be amazed! Watch and be astounded at what I will do! For I am doing something in your own day, something you wouldn't believe even if someone told you about it. [6]I am raising up the Babylonians* to be a new power on the world scene. They are a cruel and violent nation who will march across the world and conquer it. [7]They are notorious for their cruelty. They do as they like, and no one can stop them. [8]Their horses are swifter than leopards. They are a fierce people, more fierce than wolves at dusk. Their horsemen race forward from distant places. Like eagles they swoop down to pounce on their prey.

[9]"On they come, all of them bent on violence. Their hordes advance like a wind from the desert, sweeping captives ahead of them like sand. [10]They scoff at kings and princes and scorn all their defenses. They simply pile ramps of earth against their walls and capture them! [11]They sweep past like the wind and are gone. But they are deeply guilty, for their own strength is their god."

[12]O LORD my God, my Holy One, you who are eternal—is your plan in all of this to wipe us out? Surely not! O LORD our Rock, you have decreed the rise of these Babylonians to punish and correct us for our terrible sins. [13]You are perfectly just in this. But will you, who cannot allow sin in any form, stand idly by while they swallow us up? Should you be silent while the wicked destroy people who are more righteous than they?

[14]Are we but fish to be caught and killed? Are we but creeping things that have no leader to defend

1:6 Or *Chaldeans.*

## FORGOTTEN ● ● • • •

1:2-4 **When circumstances around us become almost unbearable, we wonder if God has forgotten us. But remember, he is in control. God has a plan and will judge evildoers in *his* time. If we are truly humble, we will be willing to accept God's answers and await his timing.**

them from their enemies? [15]Must we be strung up on their hooks and dragged out in their nets while they rejoice? [16]Then they will worship their nets and burn incense in front of them. "These nets are the gods who have made us rich!" they will claim.

[17]Will you let them get away with this forever? Will they succeed forever in their heartless conquests?

CHAPTER **2** **GOD EXPLAINS HIS WAYS.** I will climb up into my watchtower now and wait to see what the LORD will say to me and how he will answer my complaint.

[2]Then the LORD said to me, "Write my answer in large, clear letters on a tablet, so that a runner can read it and tell everyone else. [3]But these things I plan won't happen right away. Slowly, steadily, surely, the time approaches when the vision will be fulfilled. If it seems slow, wait patiently, for it will surely take place. It will not be delayed.

## HARD TIMES

When people drive past the Hunter house, they almost always shake their heads and say:

"I just don't understand why one family has had to undergo so much grief."

"I know—it's been one crisis after another."

"How does Mrs. Hunter keep going? Facing the heartache she's encountered would kill me."

Exaggerations? Not at all.

- Randy, the youngest son, committed suicide two years ago.
- Mr. Hunter had hepatitis, strokes, serious back problems—and finally died last spring.
- The family has faced serious financial problems.
- Nancy, the 18-year-old daughter, has been rebellious and promiscuous. She just moved in with an older, married man.

How *does* Mrs. Hunter keep going? She relies on her faith in God. She keeps clinging to the promise that somehow, some way, God is in control. And in the dark and lonely nights of her ordeals, she keeps hoping that God will one day bring some restoration to her shattered family.

Habakkuk tackles the tough issue of "Where is God when my world is falling apart?" The situation facing the ancient Hebrew prophet was very different from Mrs. Hunter's problems—and probably from yours—but the words of 3:17-19 give hope to all who hurt.

[4]"Look at the proud! They trust in themselves, and their lives are crooked;* but the righteous will live by their faith.* [5]Wealth* is treacherous, and the arrogant are never at rest. They range far and wide, with their mouths opened as wide as death,* but they are never satisfied. In their greed they have gathered up many nations and peoples. [6]But the time is coming when all their captives will taunt them, saying, 'You thieves! At last justice has

## WAIT FOR IT ● ● ● • •

**2:3 Evil seems to have the upper hand in the world. Like Habakkuk, Christians often feel angry and discouraged as they see what goes on. Habakkuk complained vigorously to God about it. God's answer to him is the same answer he would give us, "Be patient! God will work out his plans." It isn't easy to be patient, but it helps to remember that God hates sin even more than we do. It is certain—sin will be punished. As God told Habakkuk, "Wait for it." Trusting God fully means trusting him even when we don't understand why events occur as they do.**

caught up with you! Now you will get what you deserve for your oppression and extortion!' [7]Suddenly, your debtors will rise up in anger. They will turn on you and take all you have, while you stand trembling and helpless. [8]You have plundered many nations; now they will plunder you. You murderers! You have filled the countryside with violence and all the cities, too.

[9]"How terrible it will be for you who get rich by unjust means! You believe your wealth will buy security, putting your families beyond the reach of danger. [10]But by the murders you committed, you have shamed your name and forfeited your lives. [11]The very stones in the walls of your houses cry out against you, and the beams in the ceilings echo the complaint.

[12]"How terrible it will be for you who build cities with money gained by murder and corruption! [13]Has not the LORD Almighty promised that the wealth of nations will turn to ashes? They work so hard, but all in vain! [14]For the time will come when all the earth will be filled, as the waters fill the sea, with an awareness of the glory of the LORD.

[15]"How terrible it will be for you who make your neighbors drunk! You force your cup on them so that you can gloat over their nakedness and shame. [16]But soon it will be your turn! Come, drink and be exposed! Drink from the cup of the LORD's judgment, and all your glory will be turned to shame. [17]You cut down the forests of Lebanon. Now you will be cut down! You terrified the wild animals you caught in your traps. Now terror will strike you because of your murder and violence in cities everywhere!

[18]"What have you gained by worshiping all your man-made idols? How foolish to trust in something made by your own hands! What fools you are to believe such lies! [19]How terrible it will be for you who beg lifeless wooden idols to save you. You

## FAMOUS FAITH ● ● ● • •

**2:4 The just (righteous) live by their faith and trust in God. This verse has inspired countless Christians. Paul refers to it in Romans 1:17 and quotes it in Galatians 3:11. The writer of Hebrews quotes it in 10:38, just before the famous chapter on faith. And it is helpful to all Christians who must live through difficult times without seeing the outcome. Christians can trust that God is directing all things according to his purposes.**

2:4a Greek version reads *I will have no pleasure in anyone who turns away.* 2:4b Or *the just will live by their faithfulness.* 2:5a As in Dead Sea Scroll 1QpHab; other Hebrew manuscripts read *Wine.* 2:5b Hebrew *as Sheol.*

ask speechless stone images to tell you what to do. Can an idol speak for God? They may be overlaid with gold and silver, but they are lifeless inside. [20]But the LORD is in his holy Temple. Let all the earth be silent before him."

CHAPTER **3** **HABAKKUK'S PRAYER.** This prayer was sung by the prophet Habakkuk:*

[2]I have heard all about you, LORD, and I am filled with awe by the amazing things you have done. In this time of our deep need, begin again to help us, as you did in years gone by. Show us your power to save us. And in your anger, remember your mercy.

[3]I see God, the Holy One, moving across the deserts from Edom* and Mount Paran.* His brilliant splendor fills the heavens, and the earth is filled with his praise! What a wonderful God he is! [4]Rays of brilliant light flash from his hands. He rejoices in his awesome power.* [5]Pestilence marches before him; plague follows close behind. [6]When he stops, the earth shakes. When he looks, the nations tremble. He shatters the everlasting mountains and levels the eternal hills. But his power is not diminished in the least! [7]I see the peoples of Cushan and Midian trembling in terror.

[8]Was it in anger, LORD, that you struck the rivers and parted the sea? Were you displeased with them? No, you were sending your chariots of salvation! [9]You were commanding your weapons of power! You split open the earth with flowing rivers! [10]The mountains watched and trembled. Onward swept the raging waters. The mighty deep cried out, lifting its hands to the LORD. [11]The lofty sun and moon began to fade, obscured by brilliance from your arrows and the flashing of your glittering spear.

[12]You marched across the land in awesome anger and trampled the nations in your fury. [13]You went out to rescue your chosen people, to save your anointed ones. You crushed the heads of the wicked and laid bare their bones from head to toe. [14]With their own weapons, you destroyed those who rushed out like a whirlwind, thinking Israel would be easy prey. [15]You trampled the sea with your horses, and the mighty waters piled high.

[16]I trembled inside when I heard all this; my lips quivered with fear. My legs gave way beneath me,* and I shook in terror. I will wait quietly for the coming day when disaster will strike the people who invade us. [17]Even though the fig trees have no blossoms, and there are no grapes on the vine; even though the olive crop fails, and the fields lie empty and barren; even though the flocks die in the fields, and the cattle barns are empty, [18]yet I will rejoice in the LORD! I will be joyful in the God of my salvation. [19]The Sovereign LORD is my strength! He will make me as surefooted as a deer* and bring me safely over the mountains.

(For the choir director: This prayer is to be accompanied by stringed instruments.)

The time will come
when all the earth will be filled
as the waters fill the sea,
with an awareness of
THE GLORY
OF THE LORD.
HABAKKUK 2:14

## AMAZING STRENGTH ● ● • • •

3:17-19 **Crop failure and the death of animals would devastate Judah. But Habakkuk affirmed that even in the midst of starvation, he would still rejoice in the Lord. Habakkuk's feelings were not controlled by the events around him, but by faith in God's ability to give him strength. When nothing seems to make sense, and when troubles seem more than you can handle, remember that God gives strength. Take your eyes off of your difficulties and look to God.**

## CONFIDENCE ● ● • • •

3:19 **Habakkuk had asked God why evil people prosper while the righteous suffer. God's answer: They don't, not in the long run. Habakkuk saw his own limitations in contrast to God's unlimited control of all the world's events. God is alive and in control of the world and its events. We cannot see all that God is doing, and we cannot see all that God will do. But we can be assured that he is God and will do what is right. Knowing this brings us confidence and hope in the midst of a confusing world.**

3:1 Hebrew adds *according to shigionoth,* probably indicating the musical setting for the prayer. 3:3a Hebrew *Teman.* 3:3b Hebrew adds *selah;* also in 3:9, 13. The meaning of this Hebrew term is uncertain; it is probably a musical or literary term. 3:4 Or *He veils his awesome power.* 3:16 Hebrew *Decay entered my bones.* 3:19 Or *will give me the speed of a deer.*

**HABAKKUK** served as a prophet to Judah from 612 to 588 B.C.

*Climate of the times*

Judah's last four kings were wicked men who rejected God and oppressed their own people. Babylon invaded Judah twice before finally destroying it in 586. It was a time of fear, oppression, persecution, lawlessness, and immorality.

*Main message*

Habakkuk couldn't understand why God seemed to do nothing about the wickedness in society. Then he realized that faith in God alone would supply the answers to his questions.

*Importance of message*

Instead of questioning the ways of God, we should realize that he is totally just, and we should have faith that he is in control and that one day evil will be utterly destroyed.

*Contemporary prophets*

Jeremiah (627–586)
Daniel (605–536)
Ezekiel (593–571)

---

# MEGA themes

**STRUGGLE AND DOUBT** Habakkuk asked God why the people of Judah were not being punished for their sin. He couldn't understand why a just God would allow such evil to exist. God promised to use the Babylonians to punish Judah. When Habakkuk cried out for answers in his time of struggle, God answered him with words of hope.

God wants us to come to him with our struggles and doubts. But his answers may not be what we expect. God sustains us by revealing himself to us. Trusting in him leads to quiet hope, not bitterness, because we do not see the immediate results we want.

1. In chapter 1, how did Habakkuk feel about God?
2. When have you felt that way? How did you deal with your emotions and thoughts during that time?
3. What did Habakkuk do with his emotions and thoughts? How did God respond?
4. Describe Habakkuk's feelings toward God in chapter 3. What had made the difference?
5. When in doubt, a Christian must rely on God's revealed truth, even though it temporarily does not feel as though it is true. How can you build your confidence for those times of doubt and struggle?

**GOD'S SOVEREIGNTY** Habakkuk asked God why he would use the wicked Babylonians to punish his people. God said that he would also punish the Babylonians after they had fulfilled his purpose.

God is still in control of this world, despite the apparent triumph of evil; God doesn't overlook sin. One day he will rule the whole earth with perfect justice.

1. How did God use Babylon? What made this so difficult for Habakkuk to accept?
2. When is it most difficult for you to understand God's sovereignty?
3. What confuses you about God and his control? What questions would you ask if you could have a direct conversation with him?
4. For now, how does knowing that God is sovereign help you deal with your questions?

**HOPE** God, the Creator, is all-powerful. God has a plan that he will carry out. God will punish sin. He is our strength and our place of safety. We can have confidence that he will love us and guard our relationship with him forever.

Hope means going beyond our unpleasant daily experiences to the job of knowing God. We live by trusting in him, not in the benefits, happiness, or success we may experience in this life.

1. What can you learn from Habakkuk about hope?
2. How can you build your confidence in God and his love and control in your life?
3. How can you get to really know God?
4. What things do you base your hope on? Do you need to redirect the focus of your hope to God? How can you do that?

**640 B.C.**
**Zephaniah becomes a prophet; Josiah becomes king of Judah**

**627**
**Jeremiah becomes a prophet**

**622**
**Book of the Law found in the Temple**

**621**
**Zephaniah's ministry ends**

**609**
**Josiah dies in battle**

**605**
**First captives taken to Babylon**

**597**
**Babylon's second attack on Judah**

**586**
**Judah (the southern kingdom) falls**

It was the day for report cards and parent/teacher meetings—probably the most dreaded day on the school calendar. No classes were held, but appointments were set between student, parents, homeroom teacher, and the most recent report card. What a deadly mix! ■ Most students hated the idea of such a grand gathering, especially those who were not doing well in school. It was one thing to get bad grades, but quite another to sit in a room with three adults and talk about those grades. Parents were known to scream or cry or both. One never knew. At times, the teachers would get emotional, too. Even students who were doing well in school sometimes got reprimanded— they could be doing better. Not many students slept too well the night before meeting day. ■ When the school paper wrote an article about this day (affectionately termed "death day"), the reactions were varied—but most of the student body agreed with one student who was quoted as saying, "I don't think Judgment Day could be any worse!" ■ Well, that student was wrong. Judgment Day will be much worse! God's prophet, Zephaniah, tells us about it in his book. Like "death day," it will be a day of reckoning. Judgment Day will be a time of terrible wrath and punishment—and it will be a time of mercy. ■ As you read Zephaniah, tremble at the awesomeness of God on the day of judgment—and be thankful that he is merciful to those who are faithful to him.

## STATS

PURPOSE: To shake the people of Judah out of their complacency and urge them to return to God

AUTHOR: Zephaniah

TO WHOM WRITTEN: Judah and all nations

DATE WRITTEN: Probably near the end of Zephaniah's ministry (640–621 B.C.), when King Josiah's great reforms began

SETTING: King Josiah of Judah was attempting to reverse the evil trends set by the two previous kings—Manasseh and Amon. Josiah extended his influence because there wasn't a strong superpower dominating the world at that time (Assyria was declining rapidly). Zephaniah's prophecy may have been the motivating factor in Josiah's reform. Zephaniah was a contemporary of Jeremiah.

KEY PLACE: Jerusalem

# Zephaniah

CHAPTER **1** **A GRIM PREDICTION FOR JUDAH.** The LORD
gave these messages to Zephaniah when Josiah son
of Amon was king of Judah. Zephaniah was the son
of Cushi, son of Gedaliah, son of Amariah, son of
Hezekiah.
[2]"I will sweep away everything in all your land,"
says the LORD. [3]"I will sweep away both people and
animals alike. Even the birds of the air and the fish
in the sea will die. I will reduce the wicked to heaps
of rubble,* along with the rest of humanity," says
the LORD. [4]"I will crush Judah and Jerusalem with
my fist and destroy every last trace of their Baal
worship. I will put an end to all the idolatrous
priests, so that even the memory of them will disappear. [5]For they go up to their roofs and bow to
the sun, moon, and stars. They claim to follow the
LORD, but then they worship Molech,* too. So now
I will destroy them! [6]And I will destroy those who
used to worship me but now no longer do. They no
longer ask for the LORD's guidance or seek my
blessings."
[7]Stand in silence in the presence of the Sovereign
LORD, for the awesome day of the LORD's judgment
has come. The LORD has prepared his people for a
great slaughter and has chosen their executioners.*
[8]"On that day of judgment," says the LORD, "I will
punish the leaders and princes of Judah and all those
following pagan customs. [9]Yes, I will punish those
who participate in pagan worship ceremonies, and
those who steal and kill to fill their masters' homes
with loot.
[10]"On that day," says the LORD, "a cry of alarm
will come from the Fish Gate and echo throughout the newer Mishneh section* of the city. And a
great crashing sound will come from the surrounding hills. [11]Wail in sorrow, all you who live in
the market area, for all who buy and sell there will
die.

## SHORTSIGHTED ● ● • • •

1:2-18 **The people of Judah were clearly warned by the highest authority of all—God. But they refused to listen, either because they doubted God's prophet and thus did not believe the message was from God, or because they doubted God himself and thus did not believe he would do what he said. If we refuse to listen to God's Word, the Bible, we are as shortsighted as the people of Judah.**

1:3 The meaning of the Hebrew is uncertain. 1:5 Hebrew *Malcam,* another name for Molech; or it could possibly mean *their king.* 1:7 Hebrew *has prepared a sacrifice and sanctified his guests.* 1:10 Or *the Second Quarter,* a newer section of Jerusalem.

12"I will search with lanterns in Jerusalem's darkest corners to find and punish those who sit contented in their sins, indifferent to the LORD, thinking he will do nothing at all to them. 13They are the very ones whose property will be plundered by the enemy, whose homes will be ransacked. They will never have a chance to live in the new homes they have built. They will never drink wine from the vineyards they have planted.

14"That terrible day of the LORD is near. Swiftly it comes—a day when strong men will cry bitterly. 15It is a day when the LORD's anger will be poured out. It is a day of terrible distress and anguish, a day of ruin and desolation, a day of darkness and gloom, of clouds, blackness, 16trumpet calls, and battle cries. Down go the walled cities and strongest battlements!

## JUDGMENT

The people of First Church sit in shocked silence as the guest preacher delivers his thundering message of moral decay and imminent judgment.

Point by point, he describes in gripping detail how "our nation has turned its back on God." He cites court decisions, humanistic trends, disturbing statistics, and alarming examples of Christians in this country who are being persecuted by the government.

Afterwards Joey, Skip, and Traci are discussing the evening service over a large pepperoni pizza.

"Do you think that what that preacher said is true?"

"Pretty much."

"So you think this nation is going to be judged by God?"

"Probably so."

"But can't we do anything?"

"I guess if there was a nationwide revival or something like that, maybe God would hold back."

"What are the odds of a revival?"

"I don't know. Who knows what might happen if all the Christians in this town would really get right with God? Just think, if we all started praying and living right and loving people, maybe it would spread. Maybe then things would turn around."

Around 635 B.C. Zephaniah prophesied judgment on the nation of Judah. Read about the only alternative to national (as well as personal) disaster in 1:14–2:3.

17"Because you have sinned against the LORD, I will make you as helpless as a blind man searching for a path. Your blood will be poured out into the dust, and your bodies will lie there rotting on the ground."

18Your silver and gold will be of no use to you on that day of the LORD's anger. For the whole land will be devoured by the fire of his jealousy. He will make a terrifying end of all the people on earth.*

1:18 Or *the people living in the land.* 2:5 Hebrew *Kerethites.*



## DAD KNOWS ● ● • • •

2:7 **Though God said he would destroy Judah, he also promised to save a remnant, thus keeping his original covenant to preserve Abraham's descendants (Genesis 17:4-8). God is holy and can't allow sin to continue, but he also is faithful to his promises. He cannot stay angry with Israel, or with you if you are his child. Like a good parent, he loves his children and always seeks their good.**

CHAPTER **2** **CHANGE, AND GOD MAY SAVE YOU.** Gather together and pray, you shameless nation. 2Gather while there is still time, before judgment begins and your opportunity is blown away like chaff. Act now, before the fierce fury of the LORD falls and the terrible day of the LORD's anger begins. 3Beg the LORD to save you—all you who are humble, all you who uphold justice. Walk humbly and do what is right. Perhaps even yet the LORD will protect you from his anger on that day of destruction.

4Gaza, Ashkelon, Ashdod, Ekron—these Philistine cities, too, will be rooted out and left in desolation. 5And how terrible it will be for you Philistines* who live along the coast and in the land of Canaan, for this judgment is against you, too! The LORD will destroy you until not one of you is left. 6The coastal area will become a pasture, a place of shepherd camps and enclosures for sheep.

7The few survivors of the tribe of Judah will pasture there. They will lie down to rest in the abandoned houses in Ashkelon. For the LORD their God will visit his people in kindness and restore their prosperity again.

8"I have heard the taunts of the people of Moab and Ammon, mocking my people and invading their borders. 9Now, as surely as I live," says the LORD Almighty, the God of Israel, "Moab and Ammon will be destroyed as completely as Sodom and Gomorrah. Their land will become a place of stinging nettles, salt pits, and eternal desolation. Those of my people who are left will plunder them and take their land."

10They will receive the wages of their pride, for they have scoffed at the people of the LORD Almighty. 11The LORD will terrify them as he destroys all the gods in the land. Then people from nations around the world will worship the LORD, each in their own land.

## CLOSED EARS ● ● • • •

3:2 **Do you know people who refuse to listen when someone disagrees with their opinions? Those who are proud often refuse to listen to anything that contradicts their inflated self-esteem, and God's people had become so proud that they would not hear or accept God's correction. Do you find it difficult to listen to the spiritual counsel of others or God's words from the Bible? You will be more willing to listen when you consider how weak and sinful you really are.**

Beg the LORD
to save you—
all you who are
humble,
humble,
all you who
uphold
justice.
Walk humbly and
do what is
right.
ZEPHANIAH 2:3

12“You Ethiopians* will also be slaughtered by my
sword,” says the LORD.
13And the LORD will strike the lands of the north
with his fist. He will destroy Assyria and make its
great capital, Nineveh, a desolate wasteland, parched
like a desert. 14The city that once was so proud will
become a pasture for sheep and cattle. All sorts of
wild animals will settle there. Owls of many kinds
will live among the ruins of its palaces, hooting from
the gaping windows. Rubble will block all the doorways, and the cedar paneling will lie open to the
wind and weather.
15This is the fate of that boisterous city, once so
secure. “In all the world there is no city as great as
I,” it boasted. But now, look how it has become an
utter ruin, a place where animals live! Everyone
passing that way will laugh in derision or shake a
defiant fist.

CHAPTER **3** **JUDGMENT FOR JERUSALEM.** How terrible it will be for rebellious, polluted Jerusalem, the
city of violence and crime. 2It proudly refuses to
listen even to the voice of the LORD. No one can tell
it anything; it refuses all correction. It does not
trust in the LORD or draw near to its God.
3Its leaders are like roaring lions hunting for
their victims—out for everything they can get. Its
judges are like ravenous wolves at evening time,
who by dawn have left no trace of their prey. 4Its
prophets are arrogant liars seeking their own gain.
Its priests defile the Temple by disobeying God's
laws. 5But the LORD is still there in the city, and he
does no wrong. Day by day his justice is more
evident, but no one takes notice—the wicked
know no shame.
6“I have wiped out many nations, devastating
their fortress walls and towers. Their cities are now
deserted; their streets are in silent ruin. There are
no survivors to even tell what happened. 7I
thought, ‘Surely they will have reverence for me
now! Surely they will listen to my warnings, so I
won't need to strike again.’ But no; however much
I punish them, they continue their evil practices
from dawn till dusk and dusk till dawn.” 8So now
the LORD says: “Be patient; the time is coming soon
when I will stand up and accuse these evil nations.
For it is my decision to gather together the kingdoms of the earth and pour out my fiercest anger
and fury on them. All the earth will be devoured by
the fire of my jealousy.
9“On that day I will purify the lips of all people,
so that everyone will be able to worship the LORD
together. 10My scattered people who live beyond
the rivers of Ethiopia* will come to present their
offerings. 11And then you will no longer need to
be ashamed of yourselves, for you will no longer
be rebels against me. I will remove all the proud
and arrogant people from among you. There will
be no pride on my holy mountain. 12Those who
are left will be the lowly and the humble, for it is
they who trust in the name of the LORD. 13The
people of Israel who survive will do no wrong to
each other, never telling lies or deceiving one another. They will live peaceful lives, lying down to
sleep in safety; there will be no one to make them
afraid.”
14Sing, O daughter of Zion; shout aloud, O Israel! Be glad and rejoice with all your heart,
O daughter of Jerusalem! 15For the LORD will remove his hand of judgment and will disperse the
armies of your enemy. And the LORD himself, the
King of Israel, will live among you! At last your
troubles will be over, and you will fear disaster no
more.
16On that day the announcement to Jerusalem
will be, “Cheer up, Zion! Don't be afraid! 17For the

**BE BLESSED ● ● • • ·**

3:12 **God is opposed to the proud and haughty of every generation. But the lowly and humble, both physically and spiritually, will be blessed because they trust in God. Self-reliance and arrogance have no place among God's people or in his kingdom.**

2:12 Hebrew *Cushites.* 3:10 Hebrew *Cush.*

**ZEPHANIAH**
served as a prophet to Judah from 640 to 621 B.C.

| | |
|---|---|
| *Climate of the times* | Josiah was the last good king in Judah. His bold attempts to reform the nation and turn it back to God were probably influenced by Zephaniah. |
| *Main message* | A day will come when God, as Judge, will severely punish all nations. But after judgment, he will show mercy to all who have been faithful to him. |
| *Importance of message* | We will all be judged for our disobedience to God—but if we remain faithful to him, he will show us mercy. |
| *Contemporary prophet* | Jeremiah (627–586) |

---

LORD your God has arrived to live among you. He is a mighty savior. He will rejoice over you with great gladness. With his love, he will calm all your fears. He will exult over you by singing a happy song."

[18]"I will gather you who mourn for the appointed festivals; you will be disgraced no more.*
[19]And I will deal severely with all who have oppressed you. I will save the weak and helpless ones; I will bring together those who were chased away. I will give glory and renown to my former exiles, who have been mocked and shamed.
[20]On that day I will gather you together and bring you home again. I will give you a good name, a name of distinction among all the nations of the earth. They will praise you as I restore your fortunes before their very eyes. I, the LORD, have spoken!"

3:18 The meaning of the Hebrew for this verse is uncertain.

# MEGA themes

**DAY OF JUDGMENT** Destruction was coming because Judah had forsaken the Lord. The people worshiped Baal, Molech, and nature. Even the priests mixed heathen practices with faith in God. God's punishment for sin was on the way.

To escape God's judgment we must listen to him, accept his correction, trust him, and seek his guidance. If we accept God as our Lord, we will escape his condemnation.

1. What is God's attitude toward worshiping idols? Why do you think he has such an intense response to this false worship?
2. In what ways do people worship false idols in today's world?
3. Based upon this study, how can worshipers of false idols expect God to respond?
4. What are the consequences for Christians who replace God with contemporary idols? What can you do to prevent this from happening in your life?

**INDIFFERENCE TO GOD** Although there had been occasional attempts at renewal, Judah had no sorrow for her sins. The people were prosperous and no longer cared about God. God's demands for righteous living seemed irrelevant to the people of Judah, whose security and wealth made them complacent.

Don't let material comfort be a barrier to your commitment to God. Prosperity can produce an attitude of proud self-sufficiency. The only answer is to admit that money won't save us and that we cannot save ourselves. Only God can save us and cure our indifference to spiritual matters.

1. How did prosperity hinder the people's repentance?
2. Do you agree or disagree with this statement: "Prosperity is a false sense of security"? Explain.
3. What tempts you to become indifferent to God?
4. Do you need to sell all your possessions and give up everything you enjoy in order to avoid becoming indifferent to God? Explain.

**DAY OF JOY** The day of judgment will also be a day of joy. God will judge all those who mistreat his people. He will purify his people, purging all sin and evil. God will restore his people and give them hope.

When people are purged of sin, there is great relief and hope. No matter how difficult our experience now, we can look forward to the day of celebration when God will completely restore us.

1. Condemnation is not inevitable because of God's gift of Jesus. How does Jesus provide hope for a day of great joy?
2. When you think about the hope you have in Jesus and the destiny that would be yours without Jesus, how do you feel about God?
3. What difference does this hope make in your daily life as a Christian?

605 B.C.
**Daniel taken to Babylon**

597
**Ezekiel taken to Babylon**

586
**Jerusalem falls**

539
**Babylon overthrown by Cyrus**

538
**Cyrus's decree allowing the exiles to return**

537
**Exiles return to Jerusalem**

536
**Temple construction begins**

530
**Temple work halted**

520
**Haggai, Zechariah become prophets; Temple work resumed**

516
**Temple completed**

458
**Ezra comes to Jerusalem**

445
**Nehemiah comes to Jerusalem**

Hal and Jimmy were camping. Actually, they were in Jimmy's backyard, but it was a big backyard. You could barely see the lights in the house from their tent. On "camping nights" Hal and Jimmy would talk. Their conversations sometimes went on and on. Of course, the topic often was girls, but sometimes they discussed other things. ■ "Jimmy," Hal asked, "if you had to give up everything but one thing in your life, what would you keep?" Hal was not very serious most of the time, but he was that night. ■ "I'd have to give up everything?" Jimmy responded. ■ "All but one thing. What's the most important thing to you?" Hal really was being serious. ■ Jimmy thought and answered, "I can narrow it down to three. I would keep my family, Becky (the girl he just started liking), and my TV." ■ "What about God?" Hal questioned. "You would give him up for Becky?" ■ "Oh," laughed Jimmy, "I didn't even think about God." ■ The Jews, who had returned from captivity, were like Jimmy—they'd forgotten about God. They had let him slip from their life. So God sent Haggai, a prophet, to remind them of what is really important in life. ■ God refuses to be forgotten. He demanded priority in the Jews' life, and he demands priority in our life. As you read the book of Haggai, notice how God blesses those who make him number one. Then ask God to help you live with him in first place.

## STATS

PURPOSE: To call the people to complete the rebuilding of the Temple

AUTHOR: Haggai

TO WHOM WRITTEN: The people living in Jerusalem and those who had returned from exile

DATE WRITTEN: 520 B.C.

SETTING: The Temple in Jerusalem had been destroyed in 586 B.C. Cyrus allowed the Jews to return to their homeland and rebuild their Temple in 538 B.C. They began the work but were unable to complete it. During the ministry of Haggai and Zechariah, the Temple was completed (520–515 B.C.).

KEY PEOPLE: Haggai, Zerubbabel, Joshua

KEY PLACE: Jerusalem

SPECIAL FEATURES: Haggai was the first of the postexilic prophets. The other two were Zechariah and Malachi. The literary style of this book is simple and direct.

CHAPTER **1** **LET'S REBUILD THE TEMPLE.** On August 29* of the second year of King Darius's reign, the LORD gave a message through the prophet Haggai to Zerubbabel son of Shealtiel, governor of Judah, and to Jeshua* son of Jehozadak, the high priest.
2"This is what the LORD Almighty says: The people are saying, 'The time has not yet come to rebuild the LORD's house—the Temple.'"
3So the LORD sent this message through the prophet Haggai: 4"Why are you living in luxurious houses while my house lies in ruins? 5This is what the LORD Almighty says: Consider how things are going for you! 6You have planted much but harvested little. You have food to eat, but not enough to fill you up. You have wine to drink, but not enough to satisfy your thirst. You have clothing to wear, but not enough to keep you warm. Your wages disappear as though you were putting them in pockets filled with holes!
7"This is what the LORD Almighty says: Consider how things are going for you! 8Now go up into the hills, bring down timber, and rebuild my house. Then I will take pleasure in it and be honored, says the LORD. 9You hoped for rich harvests, but they were poor. And when you brought your harvest home, I blew it away. Why? Because my house lies in ruins, says the LORD Almighty, while you are all busy building your own fine houses. 10That is why the heavens have withheld the dew and the earth has withheld its crops. 11I have called for a drought on your fields and hills—a drought to wither the grain and grapes and olives and all your other crops, a drought to starve both you and your cattle and to ruin everything you have worked so hard to get."
12Then Zerubbabel son of Shealtiel, Jeshua son of Jehozadak, the high priest, and the whole remnant of God's people obeyed the message from the LORD their God. It had been delivered by the prophet

**PRIORITIES ● ● ● • •**

**1:9 Judah's problem was confused priorities. Like Judah, our priorities relating to work, family, and God's work often are mixed up. Friends, possessions, and fun may rank higher on our list of importance than God. What is most important to you? Where does God rank?**

1:1a Hebrew *On the first day of the sixth month,* of the Hebrew calendar. A number of dates in Haggai can be cross-checked with dates in surviving Persian records and related accurately to our modern calendar. This event occurred on August 29, 520 B.C. 1:1b Hebrew *Joshua,* a variant name for Jeshua; also in 1:12, 14.

Haggai, whom the LORD their God had sent, and the
people worshiped the LORD in earnest. [13]Then Haggai, the LORD's messenger, gave the people this message from the LORD: "I am with you, says the LORD!"
[14]So the LORD sparked the enthusiasm of Zerubbabel
son of Shealtiel, governor of Judah, Jeshua son of
Jehozadak, the high priest, and the whole remnant
of God's people. They came and began their work on
the house of the LORD Almighty, their God. [15]This
was on September 21* of the second year of King
Darius's reign.

**ATISFACTION**

With nothing more demanding to do than catch rays at the Fairfield Swim Club in early August, 15-year-old Melissa is bored silly. She'd been looking forward to summer ever since the first winter storm (and since her first day in algebra). She'd had big plans to relax and sleep late and have fun—to enjoy three months of doing whatever she wanted.

Now here she sits, frustrated and unsatisfied. She's done a ton of things in the last two months, but summer hasn't been nearly as exciting as she'd imagined it would be. *Something's missing*, she thinks as she sips her diet cola and watches the clouds form shapes against the crystal blue sky.

Two thousand miles away, 14-year-old Greg is drenched in sweat. Along with 19 other teens from his youth group, he's helping to build a church in a poor village near the Texas-Mexico border. It's backbreaking work, the living conditions are brutal, the food is . . . well, not exactly gourmet fare.

Yet Greg and his friends are having the time of their life serving God and serving the Mexican people.

What a paradox! When we chase after satisfaction, we inevitably find frustration. When we stop trying to find personal fulfillment and give our life away in service to God, we find indescribable joy. See Haggai 1 for another example of this truth.

CHAPTER **2** **GOD PROMISES TO BLESS HIS PEOPLE.**
Then on October 17* of that same year, the LORD
sent another message through the prophet Haggai.
[2]"Say this to Zerubbabel son of Shealtiel, governor
of Judah, and to Jeshua* son of Jehozadak, the
high priest, and to the remnant of God's people
there in the land: [3]Is there anyone who can remember this house—the Temple—as it was before? In
comparison, how does it look to you now? It must
seem like nothing at all! [4]But now take courage,
Zerubbabel, says the LORD. Take courage, Jeshua
son of Jehozadak, the high priest. Take courage, all
you people still left in the land, says the LORD. Take
courage and work, for I am with you, says the LORD
Almighty. [5]My Spirit remains among you, just as I

**TOXIC ● ● ● • •**

2:10-19 **The example given in this message (delivered in December, 520 B.C.) makes it clear that holiness will not rub off on others, but contamination will. Now that the people were beginning to obey God, he promised to bless them. But they needed to understand that activities in the Temple would not clean up their sin; only repentance and obedience could do that. If we insist on harboring wrong or "toxic" attitudes and sins, or on maintaining close relationships with sinful people, we will be contaminated. Holy living will come only when we are empowered by God's Holy Spirit. How toxic are you?**

promised when you came out of Egypt. So do not
be afraid.
[6]"For this is what the LORD Almighty says: In just
a little while I will again shake the heavens and the
earth. I will shake the oceans and the dry land, too.
[7]I will shake all the nations, and the treasures of all
the nations will come to this Temple. I will fill this
place with glory, says the LORD Almighty. [8]The silver
is mine, and the gold is mine, says the LORD Almighty. [9]The future glory of this Temple will be
greater than its past glory, says the LORD Almighty.
And in this place I will bring peace. I, the LORD
Almighty, have spoken!"
[10]On December 18* of the second year of King
Darius's reign, the LORD sent this message to the
prophet Haggai: [11]"This is what the LORD Almighty
says! Ask the priests this question about the law: [12]If
one of you is carrying a holy sacrifice in his robes and
happens to brush against some bread or stew, wine
or oil, or any other kind of food, will it also become
holy?"

1:15 Hebrew *on the twenty-fourth day of the sixth month*, of the Hebrew calendar. This event occurred on September 21, 520 B.C.; also see note on 1:1a.
2:1 Hebrew *on the twenty-first day of the seventh month*, of the Hebrew calendar. This event occurred on October 17, 520 B.C.; also see note on 1:1a.
2:2 Hebrew *Joshua*, a variant name for Jeshua; also in 2:4. 2:10 Hebrew *On the twenty-fourth day of the ninth month*, of the Hebrew calendar (also in 2:18). This event occurred on December 18, 520 B.C.; also see note on 1:1a.

The priests replied, "No."
[13]Then Haggai asked, "But if someone becomes
ceremonially unclean by touching a dead person
and then brushes against any of the things mentioned, will it be defiled?"
And the priests answered, "Yes."
[14]Then Haggai said, "That is how it is with this
people and this nation, says the LORD. Everything
they do and everything they offer is defiled. [15]So
think about this from now on—consider how things
were going for you before you began to lay the
foundation of the LORD's Temple. [16]When you hoped
for a twenty-bushel crop, you harvested only ten.
When you expected to draw fifty gallons from the
winepress, you found only twenty. [17]I sent blight and
mildew and hail to destroy all the produce of your
labor. Yet, even so, you refused to return to me, says
the LORD.
[18]"On this eighteenth day of December—the day
when the foundation of the LORD's Temple was
laid—carefully consider this: [19]I am giving you a
promise now while the seed is still in the barn,
before you have harvested your grain and before the
grapevine, the fig tree, the pomegranate, and the
olive tree have produced their crops. From this day
onward I will bless you."
[20]The LORD sent this second message to Haggai on
December 18*: [21]"Tell Zerubbabel, the governor of
Judah, that I am about to shake the heavens and the
earth. [22]I will overthrow royal thrones, destroying the
power of foreign kingdoms. I will overturn their
chariots and charioteers. The horses will fall, and
their riders will kill each other. [23]But when this happens, says the LORD Almighty, I will honor you,
Zerubbabel son of Shealtiel, my servant. I will treat
you like a signet ring on my finger, says the LORD, for
I have specially chosen you. I, the LORD Almighty,
have spoken!"

2:20 Hebrew *on the twenty-fourth day of the month;* see note on 2:10.

**CHOSEN**

2:23 **God closes his message to Zerubbabel with this tremendous affirmation: "I have specially chosen you." Such a proclamation is ours as well—each of us has been chosen by God (Ephesians 1:4). This truth should make us see our value in God's eyes and motivate us to work for him. When you feel down, remind yourself, "God has chosen me!"**

# MEGA themes

**RIGHT PRIORITIES** God had given the Jews the assignment to finish the Temple in Jerusalem when they returned from captivity. But after 15 years, they still had not completed it. They were more concerned about building their own homes than about finishing God's work. Haggai told them to get their priorities straight.

It is easy to make other activities more important than doing God's work. But God wants us to build his kingdom. Don't stop and don't make excuses. Set your heart on what is right and do it. Get your priorities straight by centering them on Christ.

1. How had the people begun to live in Jerusalem (their lifestyle)? Contrast this lifestyle with the way they lived when they first returned from captivity.
2. What had happened in the past 15 years that changed their priorities?
3. What are your priorities?
4. How have your priorities changed in the past five years? the past year?
5. As you think about the next five years, what do you think will be God's challenge to you about right priorities?

**GOD'S ENCOURAGEMENT** Haggai encouraged the people as they worked, assuring them of the presence of the Holy Spirit, of final victory, and the future reign of the Messiah.

If God gives you a task, don't be afraid to get started. His resources are infinite. God will help you complete it by giving you encouragement from others along the way.

1. What do you find in 2:14-19 that served as an encouragement to the people?
2. How would you expect such encouragement to affect them?
3. Think of two instances in which someone's encouragement made a real difference in your life. What did he or she do or say? Why was this so important to you at the time?
4. Think of two people who could use encouragement, especially in their relationship with God. Develop a plan for being God's encourager to them.

**538 B.C.**
**Cyrus's decree allowing the exiles to return**

**537**
**Exiles return to Jerusalem**

**536**
**Temple construction begins**

**530**
**Temple work halted**

**520**
**Haggai, Zechariah become prophets; Temple work resumed**

**516**
**Temple completed**

**458**
**Ezra comes to Jerusalem**

**445**
**Nehemiah comes to Jerusalem**

"Look into my eyes. I see a shadow . . . the future doesn't look good. But now the shadow is passing. Ah yes, now it looks much better. . . ." ■ Almost everyone wants to know the future. Some people fear the future, wondering what evils lurk around the corner; others consult fortune-tellers, astrologers, and other future-telling charlatans who make a living providing personal prophecies. ■ But tomorrow's story is known only by God and by those special messengers, the prophets, to whom he has revealed a chapter or two. A prophet's job was to proclaim the word of the Lord, point out sin, explain its consequences, and point men and women to God. ■ Nestled here, among what are known as the Minor Prophets, is the book of Zechariah. As one of God's spokesmen, Zechariah ministered to the small group of Jews who had returned to Judah to rebuild the Temple and the nation. Zechariah encouraged them, but his message went far beyond. Zechariah gave a spectacular and graphic telling of the Messiah, the one whom God would send to rescue his people and reign over the earth. ■ Zechariah is an important prophetic book because it gives detailed messianic references that were clearly fulfilled in Jesus. Jesus *is* the Messiah, the promised great deliverer of Israel, and the only hope for humankind. ■ God knows and controls the future. We may never see a moment ahead, but we can be secure if we trust in him. Read Zechariah and strengthen your faith in God—he alone is your hope and security.

## STATS

PURPOSE: To give hope to God's people by revealing God's future deliverance through the Messiah

AUTHOR: Zechariah

TO WHOM WRITTEN: The Jews in Jerusalem who had returned from their captivity in Babylon and to God's people everywhere

DATE WRITTEN: Chapters 1–8 were written about 520 to 518 B.C. Chapters 9–14 were written around 480 B.C.

KEY PEOPLE: Zerubbabel, Joshua

KEY PLACE: Jerusalem

SPECIAL FEATURES: This book is the most apocalyptic and messianic of all the Minor Prophets.

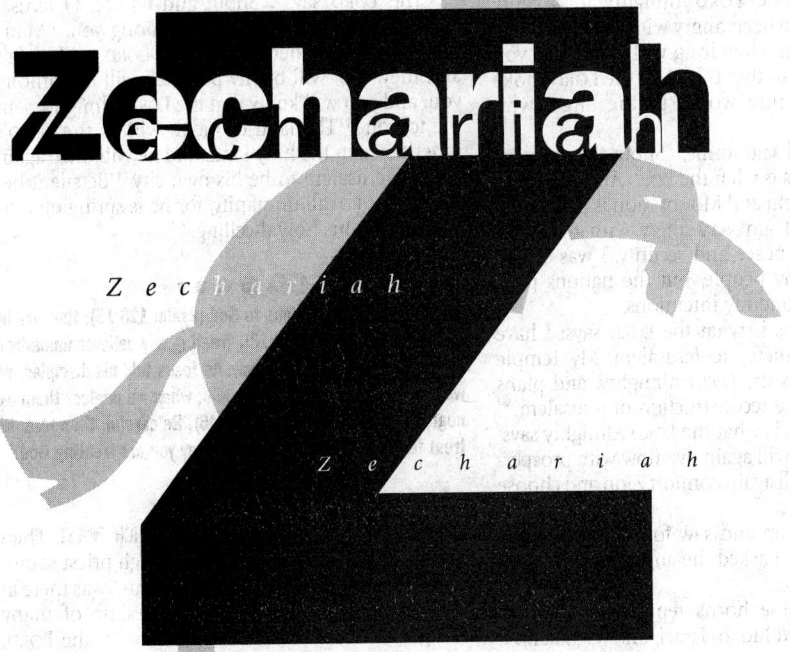


CHAPTER 1 **RETURN TO THE LORD.** In midautumn*
of the second year of King Darius's reign, the LORD
gave this message to the prophet Zechariah son of
Berekiah and grandson of Iddo.
[2]"I, the LORD, was very angry with your ancestors.
[3]Therefore, say to the people, 'This is what the LORD
Almighty says: Return to me, and I will return to you,
says the LORD Almighty.' [4]Do not be like your ancestors who would not listen when the earlier prophets
said to them, 'This is what the LORD Almighty says:
Turn from your evil ways and stop all your evil
practices.'
[5]"Your ancestors and their prophets are now
long dead. [6]But all the things I said through my
servants the prophets happened to your ancestors,
just as I said they would. As a result, they repented
and said, 'We have received what we deserved from
the LORD Almighty. He has done what he said he
would do.' "
[7]Then on February 15* of the second year of King
Darius's reign, the LORD sent another message to the
prophet Zechariah son of Berekiah and grandson of
Iddo. Zechariah said:
[8]In a vision during the night, I saw a man sitting
on a red horse that was standing among some myrtle
trees in a small valley. Behind him were red, brown,
and white horses, each with its own rider. [9]I asked
the angel who was talking with me, "My lord, what
are all those horses for?"
"I will show you," the angel replied.
[10]So the man standing among the myrtle trees
explained, "They are the ones the LORD has sent out
to patrol the earth."
[11]Then the other riders reported to the angel of the
LORD, who was standing among the myrtle trees,
"We have patrolled the earth, and the whole earth is
at peace."

**HEREDITY ● ● ● ● ●**

1:2-3 **The familiar phrase "Like father, like son" implies that children turn out like their parents. But God warned Israel *not* to be like their fathers who disobeyed him and reaped the consequences—his judgment. We are responsible before God for our actions. We aren't trapped by our heredity or environment, and we can't use these as excuses for our sins. We can choose, and we must individually return to God and follow him.**

1:1 Hebrew *In the eighth month.* A number of dates in Zechariah can be cross-checked with dates in surviving Persian records and related accurately to our modern calendar. This month of the Hebrew lunar calendar occurred in October and November 520 B.C. 1:7 Hebrew *on the twenty-fourth day of the eleventh month, the month of Shebat,* of the Hebrew calendar. This event occurred on February 15, 519 B.C.; also see note on 1:1.

## COMEBACK ● ● • • •

**1:13 God's people had lived under his judgment for 70 years during their captivity in Babylon. But here God spoke words of comfort and kindness. God promises that when we return to him, he will heal us (Hosea 6:1). If you feel wounded and torn by the events of your life, turn to God so he can heal and comfort you.**

[12]Upon hearing this, the angel of the LORD prayed this prayer: "O LORD Almighty, for seventy years now you have been angry with Jerusalem and the towns of Judah. How long will it be until you again show mercy to them?" [13]And the LORD spoke kind and comforting words to the angel who talked with me.

[14]Then the angel said to me, "Shout this message for all to hear: 'This is what the LORD Almighty says: My love for Jerusalem and Mount Zion is passionate and strong. [15]But I am very angry with the other nations that enjoy peace and security. I was only a little angry with my people, but the nations punished them far beyond my intentions.

[16]"'Therefore, this is what the LORD says: I have returned to show mercy to Jerusalem. My Temple will be rebuilt, says the LORD Almighty, and plans will be made for the reconstruction of Jerusalem.*' [17]Say this also: 'This is what the LORD Almighty says: The towns of Israel will again overflow with prosperity, and the LORD will again comfort Zion and choose Jerusalem as his own.'"

[18]Then I looked up and saw four animal horns. [19]"What are these?" I asked the angel who was talking with me.

He replied, "These horns represent the world powers that scattered Judah, Israel, and Jerusalem."

[20]Then the LORD showed me four blacksmiths. [21]"What are these men coming to do?" I asked.

The angel replied, "The blacksmiths have come to terrify the four horns that scattered and humbled Judah. They will throw them down and destroy them."

## CHAPTER 2 A MAN WITH A YARDSTICK.

When I looked around me again, I saw a man with a measuring line in his hand. [2]"Where are you going?" I asked.

He replied, "I am going to measure Jerusalem, to see how wide and how long it is."

[3]Then the angel who was with me went to meet a second angel who was coming toward him. [4]The other angel said, "Hurry, and say to that young man, 'Jerusalem will someday be so full of people that it won't have room enough for everyone! Many will live outside the city walls, with all their livestock—and yet they will be safe. [5]For I, myself, will be a wall of fire around Jerusalem, says the LORD. And I will be the glory inside the city!'"

[6]The LORD says, "Come away! Flee from the north, for I have scattered you to the four winds. [7]Come away! Escape to Jerusalem,* you who are exiled in Babylon!"

[8]"After a period of glory, the LORD Almighty sent me against the nations who oppressed you. For he said, 'Anyone who harms you harms my most precious possession.* [9]I will raise my fist to crush them, and their own slaves will plunder them.' Then you will know that the LORD Almighty has sent me."

[10]The LORD says, "Shout and rejoice, O Jerusalem,* for I am coming to live among you. [11]Many nations will join themselves to the LORD on that day, and they, too, will be my people. I will live among you, and you will know that the LORD Almighty sent me to you. [12]The land of Judah will be the LORD's inheritance in the holy land, and he will once again choose Jerusalem to be his own city. [13]Be silent before the LORD, all humanity, for he is springing into action from his holy dwelling."

## HELPING GOD ● ● • • •

**2:8 Believers are precious to God (Psalm 116:15); they are his very own children (Psalm 103:13). Treating any believer unkindly is the same as treating God that way. As Jesus told his disciples, when we help others we are helping him; when we neglect them we are neglecting him (Matthew 25:34-46). Be careful, therefore, how you treat fellow believers—that is the way you are treating God.**

## CHAPTER 3 ZECHARIAH SEES THE HIGH PRIEST.

Then the angel showed me Jeshua* the high priest standing before the angel of the LORD. Satan* was there at the angel's right hand, accusing Jeshua of many things. [2]And the LORD said to Satan, "I, the LORD, reject your accusations, Satan. Yes, the LORD, who has chosen Jerusalem, rebukes you. This man is like a burning stick that has been snatched from a fire."

[3]Jeshua's clothing was filthy as he stood there before the angel. [4]So the angel said to the others standing there, "Take off his filthy clothes." And turning to Jeshua he said, "See, I have taken away your sins, and now I am giving you these fine new clothes."

[5]Then I said, "Please, could he also have a clean turban on his head?" So they put a clean priestly turban on his head and dressed him in new clothes while the angel of the LORD stood by.

[6]Then the angel of the LORD spoke very solemnly to Jeshua and said, [7]"This is what the LORD Almighty says: If you follow my ways and obey my requirements, then you will be given authority over my Temple and its courtyards. I will let you walk in and out of my presence along with these others standing here. [8]Listen to me, O Jeshua the high priest, and all you other priests. You are symbols of the good things to come. Soon I am going to bring my servant, the Branch. [9]Now look at the jewel I have set before Jeshua, a single stone with seven facets.* I will engrave an inscription on it, says the LORD Almighty, and I will remove the sins of this land in a single day.

1:16 Hebrew *and the measuring line will be stretched out over Jerusalem.* 2:7 Hebrew *to Zion.* 2:8 Hebrew *harms the apple of my eye.* 2:10 Hebrew *O daughter of Zion.* 3:1a Hebrew *Joshua,* a variant name for Jeshua; also in 3:3, 4, 6, 8, 9. 3:1b Or *The Accuser;* Hebrew reads *The Adversary;* also in 3:2. 3:9 Hebrew *7 eyes.*

[10]And on that day, says the LORD Almighty, each of you will invite your neighbor into your home to share your peace and prosperity."

CHAPTER **4** **THE GOLDEN LAMPSTAND.** Then the angel who had been talking with me returned and woke me, as though I had been asleep. [2]"What do you see now?" he asked.

I answered, "I see a solid gold lampstand with a bowl of oil on top of it. Around the bowl are seven lamps, each one having seven spouts with wicks. [3]And I see two olive trees, one on each side of the bowl."

[4]Then I asked the angel, "What are these, my lord? What do they mean?"

[5]"Don't you know?" the angel asked.

"No, my lord," I replied.

[6]Then he said to me, "This is what the LORD says to Zerubbabel: It is not by force nor by strength, but by my Spirit, says the LORD Almighty. [7]Nothing, not even a mighty mountain, will stand in Zerubbabel's way; it will flatten out before him! Then Zerubbabel will set the final stone of the Temple in place, and the people will shout: 'May God bless it! May God bless it!'"

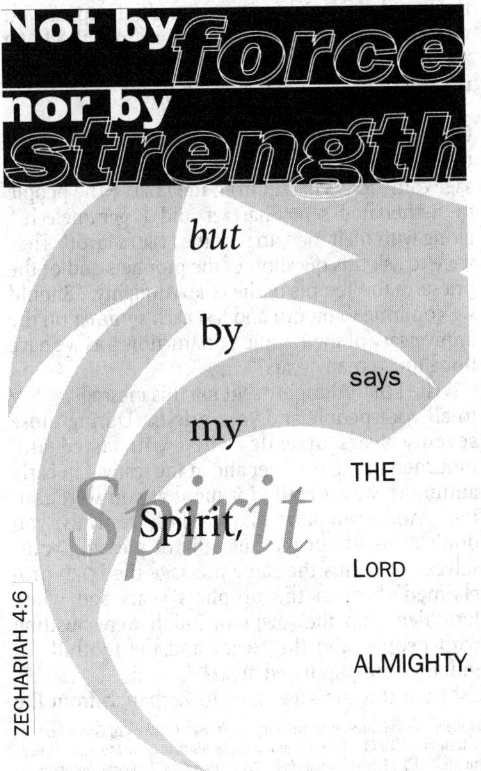
Not by force
nor by strength
but
by
my
Spirit,
says
THE
LORD
ALMIGHTY.
Spirit
ZECHARIAH 4:6

**THE KEY ● ● • • •**

**4:6 Many people believe that to survive in this world a person must be tough, strong, unbending, and harsh. But God says, "It is not by force nor by strength, but by my Spirit." The key words are "by my Spirit." It is *only* through God's Spirit that anything of lasting value is accomplished. The returned exiles were indeed weak—harassed by their enemies, tired, discouraged, and poor. But they had God on their side! As you live for God, determine not to trust in your own strength or abilities. Instead, depend on God and work in the power of his Spirit!**

[8]Then another message came to me from the LORD: [9]"Zerubbabel is the one who laid the foundation of this Temple, and he will complete it. Then you will know that the LORD Almighty has sent me. [10]Do not despise these small beginnings, for the LORD rejoices to see the work begin, to see the plumb line in Zerubbabel's hand. For these seven lamps represent the eyes of the LORD that search all around the world."

[11]Then I asked the angel, "What are these two olive trees on each side of the lampstand, [12]and what are the two olive branches that pour out golden oil through two gold tubes?"

[13]"Don't you know?" he asked.

"No, my lord," I replied.

[14]Then he said to me, "They represent the two anointed ones who assist the Lord of all the earth."

CHAPTER **5** **ZECHARIAH SEES A FLYING SCROLL.** I looked up again and saw a scroll flying through the air.

[2]"What do you see?" the angel asked.

"I see a flying scroll," I replied. "It appears to be about thirty feet long and fifteen feet wide.*"

[3]Then he said to me, "This scroll contains the curse that is going out over the entire land. One side says that those who steal will be banished from the land; the other side says that those who swear falsely will be banished from the land. [4]And this is what the LORD Almighty says: I am sending this curse into the house of every thief and into the house of everyone who swears falsely by my name. And my curse will remain in that house until it is completely destroyed—even its timbers and stones."

[5]Then the angel who was talking with me came forward and said, "Look up! Something is appearing in the sky."

[6]"What is it?" I asked.

He replied, "It is a basket for measuring grain,* and it is filled with the sins* of everyone throughout the land."

[7]When the heavy lead cover was lifted off the basket, there was a woman sitting inside it. [8]The angel said, "The woman's name is Wickedness," and he pushed her back into the basket and closed the heavy lid again.

[9]Then I looked up and saw two women flying

**5:2** Hebrew *20 cubits* [9 meters] *long and 10 cubits* [4.5 meters] *wide.* **5:6a** Hebrew *an ephah,* about half a bushel or 18 liters; also in 5:7, 8, 9, 10, 11. **5:6b** As in Greek version; Hebrew reads *the appearance.*

toward us, with wings gliding on the wind. Their wings were like those of a stork, and they picked up the basket and flew with it into the sky.

10 "Where are they taking the basket?" I asked the angel.

11 He replied, "To the land of Babylonia,* where they will build a temple for the basket. And when the temple is ready, they will set the basket there on its pedestal."

## CHAPTER 6 **ZECHARIAH SEES FOUR CHARIOTS.**

Then I looked up again and saw four chariots coming from between two bronze mountains. 2 The first chariot was pulled by red horses, the second by black horses, 3 the third by white horses, and the fourth by dappled-gray horses. 4 "And what are these, my lord?" I asked the angel who was talking with me.

5 He replied, "These are the four spirits* of heaven who stand before the Lord of all the earth. They are going out to do his work. 6 The chariot with black horses is going north, the chariot with white horses is going west,* and the chariot with dappled-gray horses is going south."

### JUSTICE

Christopher has a twisted sense of humor:

When a convenience store clerk gave him change for $20 instead of $10 (it was her first day on the job and she was nervous), he never said a word. He eagerly pocketed the extra bucks. "She shouldn't have been so stupid," he laughed.

- When he baby-sat his little brother last weekend, he locked the kid in a closet for about an hour.
- While keeping score for an intramural basketball game, Christopher gave his favorite team three extra points.

But you can bet Chris was not amused today when he was treated wrongly. He was docked an hour's pay just for being a measly five minutes late for work because of a wreck on the expressway!

"That's not fair!" he whined.

Like Christopher, we're quick to complain whenever we feel as though we've been treated unfairly. But Zechariah 7:8-14 tells us to watch out for others as well. It insists that we not mistreat and take advantage of those who are weak.

Are you a just and fair person?

7 The powerful horses were eager to be off, to patrol back and forth across the earth. And the LORD said, "Go and patrol the earth!" So they left at once on their patrol.

8 Then the LORD summoned me and said, "Those who went north have vented the anger of my Spirit* there."

### WIPED OUT ● ● ● • • •

**5:9-11 Wickedness and sin (as represented by the woman) were taken away from Israel. One day, when Christ reigns, all sin will be eliminated and people will live in safety and security. When Christ died, he removed sin's power and penalty. When we trust him to forgive us, he removes sin's penalty and gives us the power to overcome sin in our life. When he returns, he will remove sin's presence from the earth.**

9 Then I received another message from the LORD: 10 "Heldai, Tobijah, and Jedaiah will bring gifts of silver and gold from the Jews exiled in Babylon. As soon as they arrive, meet them at the home of Josiah son of Zephaniah. 11 Accept their gifts and make a crown* from the silver and gold. Then put the crown on the head of Jeshua* son of Jehozadak, the high priest. 12 Tell him that the LORD Almighty says: Here is the man called the Branch. He will branch out where he is and build the Temple of the LORD. 13 He will build the LORD's Temple, and he will receive royal honor and will rule as king from his throne. He will also serve as priest from his throne,* and there will be perfect harmony between the two.

14 "The crown will be a memorial in the Temple of the LORD to honor those who gave it—Heldai,* Tobijah, Jedaiah, and Josiah* son of Zephaniah."

15 Many will come from distant lands to rebuild the Temple of the LORD. And when this happens, you will know my messages have been from the LORD Almighty. All this will happen if you carefully obey the commands of the LORD your God.

## CHAPTER 7 **BE JUST AND KIND.**

On December 7* of the fourth year of King Darius's reign, another message came to Zechariah from the LORD. 2 The people of Bethel had sent Sharezer and Regemmelech,* along with their men, to seek the LORD's favor. 3 They were to ask this question of the prophets and of the priests at the Temple of the LORD Almighty: "Should we continue to mourn and fast each summer on the anniversary of the Temple's destruction,* as we have done for so many years?"

4 The LORD Almighty sent me this message: 5 "Say to all your people and your priests, 'During those seventy years of exile, when you fasted and mourned in the summer and at the festival in early autumn,* was it really for me that you were fasting? 6 And even now in your holy festivals, you don't think about me but only of pleasing yourselves. 7 Isn't this the same message the LORD proclaimed through the prophets years ago when Jerusalem and the towns of Judah were bustling with people, and the Negev and the foothills of Judah* were populated areas?'"

8 Then this message came to Zechariah from the

**5:11** Hebrew *the land of Shinar.* **6:5** Or *the four winds.* **6:6** Hebrew *is going after them.* **6:8** Hebrew *have given my Spirit rest.* **6:11a** As in Greek and Syriac versions; Hebrew reads *crowns.* **6:11b** Hebrew *Joshua,* a variant name for Jeshua. **6:13** Or *There will be a priest by his throne.* **6:14a** As in Syriac version (compare 6:10); Hebrew reads *Helem.* **6:14b** As in Syriac version (compare 6:10); Hebrew reads *Hen.* **7:1** Hebrew *On the fourth day of the ninth month, the month of Kislev,* of the Hebrew calendar. This event occurred on December 7, 518 B.C.; also see note on 1:1. **7:2** Or *Bethel-sharezer had sent Regemmelech.* **7:3** Hebrew *mourn and fast in the fifth month.* This month of the Hebrew lunar calendar usually occurs in July and August. **7:5** Hebrew *fasted and mourned in the fifth and seventh months.* The fifth month of the Hebrew lunar calendar usually occurs in July and August. The seventh month usually occurs in September and October; both the Day of Atonement and the Festival of Shelters were celebrated in the seventh month. **7:7** Hebrew *the Shephelah.*

**ZECHARIAH** served as a prophet to Judah about 520 B.C., after the return from exile.

*Climate of the times* — The exiles had returned from captivity to rebuild their Temple. But work on the Temple had stalled, and the people were neglecting their service to God.

*Main message* — Zechariah, like Haggai, encouraged the people to finish rebuilding the Temple. His visions gave the people hope. He told the people of a future King who one day would establish an eternal kingdom.

*Importance of message* — Even in times of discouragement and despair, God is working out his plan. God protects and guides us; we must trust and follow him.

*Contemporary prophet* — Haggai (about 520 B.C.)

---

LORD: 9"This is what the LORD Almighty says: Judge
fairly and honestly, and show mercy and kindness to
one another. 10Do not oppress widows, orphans,
foreigners, and poor people. And do not make evil
plans to harm each other.
11"Your ancestors would not listen to this message. They turned stubbornly away and put their
fingers in their ears to keep from hearing. 12They
made their hearts as hard as stone, so they could
not hear the law or the messages that the LORD
Almighty had sent them by his Spirit through the
earlier prophets. That is why the LORD Almighty
was so angry with them.
13"Since they refused to listen when I called to
them, I would not listen when they called to me, says
the LORD Almighty. 14I scattered them as with a whirlwind among the distant nations, where they lived as
strangers. Their land became so desolate that no one
even traveled through it. The land that had been so
pleasant became a desert."

CHAPTER **8** **JUDAH WILL BE BLESSED.** Then another
message came to me from the LORD Almighty: 2"This
is what the LORD Almighty says: My love for Mount
Zion is passionate and strong; I am consumed with
passion for Jerusalem! 3And now the LORD says: I am
returning to Mount Zion, and I will live in Jerusalem.
Then Jerusalem will be called the Faithful City; the
mountain of the LORD Almighty will be called the
Holy Mountain. 4This is what the LORD Almighty
says: Once again old men and women will walk
Jerusalem's streets with a cane and sit together in the
city squares. 5And the streets of the city will be filled
with boys and girls at play.
6"This is what the LORD Almighty says: All this
may seem impossible to you now, a small and discouraged remnant of God's people. But do you think
this is impossible for me, the LORD Almighty? 7This
is what the LORD Almighty says: You can be sure that
I will rescue my people from the east and from the
west. 8I will bring them home again to live safely in
Jerusalem. They will be my people, and I will be
faithful and just toward them as their God.
9"This is what the LORD Almighty says: Take heart
and finish the task! You have heard what the prophets have been saying about building the Temple of
the LORD Almighty ever since the foundation was
laid. 10Before the work on the Temple began, there
were no jobs and no wages for either people or
animals. No traveler was safe from the enemy, for
there were enemies on all sides. I had turned everyone against each other. 11But now I will not treat the
remnant of my people as I treated them before, says
the LORD Almighty. 12For I am planting seeds of
peace and prosperity among you. The grapevines
will be heavy with fruit. The earth will produce its
crops, and the sky will release the dew. Once more I
will make the remnant in Judah and Israel the heirs
of these blessings. 13Among the nations, Judah and
Israel had become symbols of what it means to be
cursed. But no longer! Now I will rescue you and
make you both a symbol and a source of blessing! So
don't be afraid or discouraged, but instead get on
with rebuilding the Temple!
14"For this is what the LORD Almighty says: I did
not change my mind when your ancestors angered
me and I promised to punish them, says the LORD
Almighty. 15Neither will I change my decision to
bless Jerusalem and the people of Judah. So don't be
afraid. 16But this is what you must do: Tell the truth
to each other. Render verdicts in your courts that are
just and that lead to peace. 17Do not make evil plots
to harm each other. And stop this habit of swearing
to things that are false. I hate all these things, says the
LORD."
18Here is another message that came to me from
the LORD Almighty. 19"This is what the LORD Almighty
says: The traditional fasts and times of mourning you have kept in early summer, midsummer,

**GET GOING! ● ● ● • •**

**8:9 God had to give the Temple workers a push. He as much as said, "Get going and finish the job! You've listened long enough!" Listen to what God says, but once he has shown you a course of action, get going and finish the job.**

## PREDICTIONS ● ● • • •

9:9 **The triumphal entry of Jesus riding into Jerusalem (Matthew 21:1-11) is predicted here, more than 500 years before it happened. Just as this prophecy was fulfilled when Jesus came to earth, so the prophecies of his second coming are certain to come true. We should be ready for his return because he is coming!**

autumn, and winter* are now ended. They will become festivals of joy and celebration for the people of Judah. So love truth and peace.

20"This is what the LORD Almighty says: People from nations and cities around the world will travel to Jerusalem. 21The people of one city will say to the people in another, 'Let us go to Jerusalem to ask the LORD to bless us and to seek the LORD Almighty. We are planning to go ourselves.' 22People from many nations, even powerful nations, will come to Jerusalem to seek the LORD Almighty and to ask the LORD to bless them.

23"This is what the LORD Almighty says: In those days ten people from nations and languages around the world will clutch at the hem of one Jew's robe. And they will say, 'Please let us walk with you, for we have heard that God is with you.'"

## CHAPTER 9 **ISRAEL'S ENEMIES WILL BE PUNISHED.**

This is the message* from the LORD against the land of Aram* and the city of Damascus, for the eyes of all humanity, including the people of Israel, are on the LORD. 2Doom is certain for Hamath, near Damascus, and for the cities of Tyre and Sidon, too, though they are so clever. 3Tyre has built a strong fortress and has piled up so much silver and gold that it is as common as dust in the streets! 4But now the Lord will strip away Tyre's possessions and hurl its fortifications into the Mediterranean Sea.* Tyre will be set on fire and burned to the ground.

5The city of Ashkelon will see Tyre fall and will be filled with fear. Gaza will shake with terror, and so will Ekron, for their hopes will be dashed. Gaza will be conquered and its king killed, and Ashkelon will be completely deserted. 6Foreigners will occupy the city of Ashdod. Thus, I will destroy the pride of the Philistines. 7They will no longer eat meat with blood in it or feed on other forbidden foods. All the surviving Philistines will worship our God and be adopted as a new clan in Judah.* And the Philistines of Ekron will join my people, just as the Jebusites once did. 8I will guard my Temple and protect it from invading armies. I am closely watching their movements. No foreign oppressor will ever again overrun my people's land.

9Rejoice greatly, O people* of Zion! Shout in triumph, O people of Jerusalem! Look, your king is coming to you. He is righteous and victorious, yet he is humble, riding on a donkey—even on a donkey's colt. 10I will remove the battle chariots from Israel* and the warhorses from Jerusalem, and I will destroy all the weapons used in battle. Your king will bring peace to the nations. His realm will stretch from sea to sea and from the Euphrates River* to the ends of the earth.*

11Because of the covenant I made with you, sealed with blood, I will free your prisoners from death in a waterless dungeon. 12Come back to the place of safety, all you prisoners, for there is yet hope! I promise this very day that I will repay you two mercies for each of your woes! 13Judah is my bow, and Israel is my arrow! Jerusalem* is my sword, and like a warrior, I will brandish it against the Greeks.*

14The LORD will appear above his people; his arrows will fly like lightning! The Sovereign LORD will sound the trumpet; he will go out against his enemies like a whirlwind from the southern desert. 15The LORD Almighty will protect his people, and they will subdue their enemies with sling stones. They will shout in battle as though drunk with wine, shedding the blood of their enemies. They will be filled with blood like a bowl, drenched with blood like the corners of the altar.

16When that day arrives, the LORD their God will rescue his people, just as a shepherd rescues his sheep. They will sparkle in his land like jewels in a crown. 17How wonderful and beautiful they will be! The young men and women will thrive on the abundance of grain and new wine.

## CHAPTER 10 **PROMISES FOR ISRAEL AND JUDAH.**

Ask the LORD for rain in the spring, and he will give it. It is the LORD who makes storm clouds that drop showers of rain so that every field becomes a lush pasture.

2Household gods give false advice, fortune-tellers predict only lies, and interpreters of dreams pronounce comfortless falsehoods. So my people are wandering like lost sheep, without a shepherd to protect and guide them.

## FOOLISH TRUST ● ● • • •

10:2 **How often we create idols of popularity, power, fame, or money, and then expect them to give us happiness and security. But these idols can't supply what we need any more than a stone image can make it rain. How foolish it is to trust in idols. Instead, trust God's promises for your future.**

3"My anger burns against your shepherds, and I will punish these leaders.* For the LORD Almighty has arrived to look after his flock of Judah; he will make them strong and glorious, like a proud warhorse in battle. 4From Judah will come the cornerstone, the tent peg, the battle bow, and all the rulers. 5They will be like mighty warriors in battle, trampling their enemies in the mud under their feet. Since the LORD is with them as they fight, they will overthrow even the horsemen of the enemy.

6"I will strengthen Judah and save Israel*; I will reestablish them because I love them. It will be as though I had never rejected them, for I am the LORD

**8:19** Hebrew *in the fourth, fifth, seventh, and tenth months.* The fourth month of the Hebrew lunar calendar usually occurs in June and July. The fifth month usually occurs in July and August. The seventh month usually occurs in September and October. The tenth month usually occurs in December and January. **9:1a** Hebrew *An Oracle: The message.* **9:1b** Hebrew *land of Hadrach.* **9:4** Hebrew *the sea.* **9:7** Hebrew *and will become a leader in Judah.* **9:9** Hebrew *daughter.* **9:10a** Hebrew *from Ephraim;* also in 9:13. **9:10b** Hebrew *the river.* **9:10c** Or *the end of the land.* **9:13a** Hebrew *Zion.* **9:13b** Hebrew *the sons of Javan.* **10:3** Or *these male goats.* **10:6** Hebrew *save the house of Joseph.*

their God, who will hear their cries. 7The people of Israel* will become like mighty warriors, and their hearts will be happy as if by wine. Their children, too, will see it all and be glad; their hearts will rejoice in the LORD. 8When I whistle to them, they will come running, for I have redeemed them. From the few that are left, their population will grow again to its former size. 9Though I have scattered them like seeds among the nations, still they will remember me in distant lands. With their children, they will survive and come home again to Israel. 10I will bring them back from Egypt and Assyria and resettle them in Gilead and Lebanon. There won't be enough room for them all! 11They will pass safely through the sea of distress,* for the waves of the sea will be held back. And the waters of the Nile will become dry. The pride of Assyria will be crushed, and the rule of Egypt will end. 12I will make my people strong in my power, and they will go wherever they wish by my authority. I, the LORD, have spoken!"

## CHAPTER 11 THE TWO SHEPHERDS.

Open your doors, Lebanon, so that fire may sweep through your cedar forests. 2Weep, you cypress trees, for all the ruined cedars; the tallest and most beautiful of them are fallen. Weep, you oaks of Bashan, as you watch the thickest forests being felled. 3Listen to the wailing of the shepherds, for their wealth is gone. Hear the young lions roaring, for their thickets in the Jordan Valley have been destroyed.

4This is what the LORD my God says: "Go and care for a flock that is intended for slaughter. 5The buyers will slaughter their sheep without remorse. The sellers will say, 'Praise the LORD, I am now rich!' Even the shepherds have no compassion for them. 6And likewise, I will no longer have pity on the inhabitants of the land," says the LORD. "I will let them fall into each other's clutches, as well as into the clutches of their king. They will turn the land into a wilderness, and I will not protect them."

7So I cared for the flock intended for slaughter—the flock that was oppressed. Then I took two shepherd's staffs and named one Favor and the other Union. 8I got rid of their three evil shepherds in a single month. But I became impatient with these sheep—this nation—and they hated me, too. 9So I told them, "I won't be your shepherd any longer. If you die, you die. If you are killed, you are killed. And those who remain will devour each other!"

10Then I took my staff called Favor and snapped it in two, showing that I had revoked the covenant I had made with all the nations. 11That was the end of my covenant with them. Those who bought and sold sheep were watching me, and they knew that the LORD was speaking to them through my actions. 12And I said to them, "If you like, give me my wages, whatever I am worth; but only if you want to." So they counted out for my wages thirty pieces* of silver.

13And the LORD said to me, "Throw it to the pot-

### TOUGH JOB

**11:17** **It is a great tragedy for God's people when their leaders fail to care for them adequately. God holds leaders particularly accountable for the condition of his people. The New Testament tells beleivers, "Not many of you should become teachers in the church, for we who teach will be judged by God with greater strictness" (James 3:1). If God puts you in a position of leadership, remember that it is also a place of great responsibility.**

ters*"—this magnificent sum at which they valued me! So I took the thirty coins and threw them to the potters in the Temple of the LORD. 14Then I broke my other staff, Union, to show that the bond of unity between Judah and Israel was broken.

15Then the LORD said to me, "Go again and play the part of a worthless shepherd. 16This will illustrate how I will give this nation a shepherd who will not care for the sheep that are threatened by death, nor look after the young, nor heal the injured, nor feed the healthy. Instead, this shepherd will eat the meat of the fattest sheep and tear off their hooves. 17Doom is certain for this worthless shepherd who abandons the flock! The sword will cut his arm and pierce his right eye! His arm will become useless, and his right eye completely blind!"

## CHAPTER 12 GOD DEFENDS HIS PEOPLE.

This* message concerning the fate of Israel came from the LORD: "This message is from the LORD, who stretched out the heavens, laid the foundations of the earth, and formed the spirit within humans. 2I will make Jerusalem and Judah like an intoxicating drink to all the nearby nations that send their armies to besiege Jerusalem. 3On that day I will make Jerusalem a heavy stone, a burden for the world. None of the nations who try to lift it will escape unscathed.

4"On that day, says the LORD, I will cause every horse to panic and every rider to lose his nerve. I will watch over the people of Judah, but I will blind the horses of her enemies. 5And the clans of Judah will say to themselves, 'The people of Jerusalem have found strength in the LORD Almighty, their God.'

6"On that day I will make the clans of Judah like a brazier that sets a woodpile ablaze or like a burning torch among sheaves of grain. They will burn up all the neighboring nations right and left, while the people living in Jerusalem remain secure. 7The LORD will give victory to the rest of Judah first, before Jerusalem, so that the people of Jerusalem and the royal line of David will not have greater honor than the rest of Judah. 8On that day the LORD will defend

### A GREAT DAY!

**12:3-4** **This speaks of a great future battle against Jerusalem. Some say it is Armageddon, the last great battle on earth. Those who go against God's people will not prevail forever. Evil, pain, and oppression one day will be abolished once and for all. What a great day that will be for God's people!**

**10:7** Hebrew *of Ephraim.* **10:11** Or *the sea of Egypt,* referring to the Red Sea. **11:12** Hebrew *30 shekels,* about 12 ounces or 342 grams in weight. **11:13** Syriac version reads *into the treasury;* also in 11:13b. **12:1** Hebrew *An Oracle: This.*

the people of Jerusalem; the weakest among them will be as mighty as King David! And the royal descendants will be like God, like the angel of the LORD who goes before them! 9For my plan is to destroy all the nations that come against Jerusalem.

10"Then I will pour out a spirit of grace and prayer on the family of David and on all the people of Jerusalem. They will look on me whom they have pierced and mourn for him as for an only son. They will grieve bitterly for him as for a firstborn son who has died. 11The sorrow and mourning in Jerusalem on that day will be like the grievous mourning of Hadad-rimmon in the valley of Megiddo.

12"All Israel will weep in profound sorrow, each family by itself, with the husbands and wives in separate groups. The family of David will mourn, along with the family of Nathan, 13the family of Levi, and the family of Shimei. 14Each of the surviving families from Judah will mourn separately, husbands and wives apart.

## CHAPTER 13 GOD'S FOUNTAIN OF FORGIVENESS.

"On that day a fountain will be opened for the dynasty of David and for the people of Jerusalem, a fountain to cleanse them from all their sins and defilement.

2"And on that day, says the LORD Almighty, I will get rid of every trace of idol worship throughout the land, so that even the names of the idols will be forgotten. I will remove from the land all false prophets and the unclean spirits that inspire them. 3If anyone begins prophesying again, his own father and mother will tell him, 'You must die, for you have prophesied lies in the name of the LORD.' Then his own father and mother will stab him.

4"No one will be boasting then of a prophetic gift! No one will wear prophet's clothes to try to fool the people. 5'No,' he will say. 'I'm not a prophet; I'm a farmer. The soil has been my means of livelihood from my earliest youth.' 6And if someone asks, 'Then what are those scars on your chest*?' he will say, 'I was wounded at the home of friends!'

7"Awake, O sword, against my shepherd, the man who is my partner, says the LORD Almighty. Strike down the shepherd, and the sheep will be scattered, and I will turn against the lambs. 8Two-thirds of the people in the land will be cut off and die, says the LORD. But a third will be left in the land. 9I will bring that group through the fire and make them pure, just as gold and silver are refined and purified by fire. They will call on my name, and I will answer them. I will say, 'These are my people,' and they will say, 'The LORD is our God.'"

## CHAPTER 14 GOD'S RULE OVER ALL THE EARTH.

Watch, for the day of the LORD is coming when your possessions will be plundered right in front of you! 2On that day I will gather all the nations to fight against Jerusalem. The city will be taken, the houses plundered, and the women raped. Half the population will be taken away into captivity, and half will be left among the ruins of the city.

### ANY MOMENT • • • • •

14:1-2 **The Bible speaks of the day of the Lord. What if you knew exactly when this would happen? Would you live differently? Christ could come at any moment. Study the Scriptures carefully and be sure you live as God intends for you to live—in obedience and spiritual readiness.**

3Then the LORD will go out to fight against those nations, as he has fought in times past. 4On that day his feet will stand on the Mount of Olives, which faces Jerusalem on the east. And the Mount of Olives will split apart, making a wide valley running from east to west, for half the mountain will move toward the north and half toward the south. 5You will flee through this valley, for it will reach across to Azal.* Yes, you will flee as you did from the earthquake in the days of King Uzziah of Judah. Then the LORD my God will come, and all his holy ones with him.*

6On that day the sources of light will no longer shine,* 7yet there will be continuous day! Only the LORD knows how this could happen! There will be no normal day and night, for at evening time it will still be light. 8On that day life-giving waters will flow out from Jerusalem, half toward the Dead Sea and half toward the Mediterranean,* flowing continuously both in summer and in winter.

9And the LORD will be king over all the earth. On that day there will be one LORD—his name alone will be worshiped. 10All the land from Geba, north of Judah, to Rimmon, south of Jerusalem, will become one vast plain. But Jerusalem will be raised up in its original place and will be inhabited all the way from the Benjamin Gate over to the site of the old gate, then to the Corner Gate, and from the Tower of Hananel to the king's winepresses. 11And Jerusalem will be filled, safe at last, never again to be cursed and destroyed.

12And the LORD will send a plague on all the nations that fought against Jerusalem. Their people will become like walking corpses, their flesh rotting away. Their eyes will shrivel in their sockets, and their tongues will decay in their mouths. 13On that day they will be terrified, stricken by the LORD with great panic. They will fight against each other in hand-to-hand combat; 14Judah, too, will be fighting at Jerusalem. The wealth of all the neighboring nations will be captured—great quantities of gold and silver and fine clothing. 15This same plague will strike the horses, mules, camels, donkeys, and all the other animals in the enemy camps.

16In the end, the enemies of Jerusalem who survive the plague will go up to Jerusalem each year to worship the King, the LORD Almighty, and to celebrate the Festival of Shelters. 17And any nation anywhere in the world that refuses to come to Jerusalem to worship the King, the LORD Almighty, will have no rain. 18And if the people of Egypt refuse to attend the festival, the LORD will punish them with the same plague that he sends on the other nations who refuse

13:6 Or *scars between your hands.* 14:5a The meaning of the Hebrew is uncertain. 14:5b As in Greek version; Hebrew reads *with you.* 14:6 Hebrew *there will be no light, no cold or frost.* The meaning of the Hebrew is uncertain. 14:8 Hebrew *half toward the eastern sea and half toward the western sea.*

to go. [19]Egypt and the other nations will all be punished if they don't go to celebrate the festival.

[20]On that day even the harness bells of the horses will be inscribed with these words: SET APART AS HOLY TO THE LORD. And the cooking pots in the Temple of the LORD will be as sacred as the basins used beside the altar. [21]In fact, every cooking pot in Jerusalem and Judah will be set apart as holy to the LORD Almighty. All who come to worship will be free to use any of these pots to boil their sacrifices. And on that day there will no longer be traders* in the Temple of the LORD Almighty.

14:21 Hebrew *Canaanites.*

# MEGA themes

**GOD'S JEALOUSY** God was angry at his people for neglecting his prophets through the years, and he was concerned that they not follow the careless and false leaders who exploited them. Disobedience was the root of their problems and the cause of their misery. God was jealous ("zealous") for his people's devotion.

God wants our devotion. To avoid Israel's ruin, don't walk in their steps. Don't reject God, follow false teachers, or lead others astray. Turn to God, faithfully obey his Word, and make sure you are leading others correctly. God calls you to complete loyalty to his Lordship.

1. Jealousy is usually considered a negative quality. How is God's jealousy a positive characteristic of his love?
2. What is it that God seems to desire so jealously from his people? Why do you think this is so important?
3. Describe how you are remaining faithful to God's perfect love. Also describe any areas of your life where you may be lacking in faithfulness.
4. What is your motivation for remaining faithful to God?
5. How do you plan to maintain that faithfulness throughout your life?

**REBUILDING THE TEMPLE** The Jews were discouraged. They were free from exile, but the Temple was not completed. Zechariah encouraged them to rebuild it. God would both protect his workmen and also empower them by his Holy Spirit to carry out and complete his work.

More than the rebuilding of the Temple was at stake—the people were staging the first act in God's wonderful drama of the end times. Those of us who believe in God must complete his work. To do so we must have the Holy Spirit's help. God will empower us to carry out his will in our relationships and daily tasks.

1. What did the men of Israel supply for the rebuilding of the Temple? What did God supply?
2. How were the people responding to God's partnership with them in their task?
3. How does God want you to live for him? What is he supplying? What must you supply?
4. How are you responding to God's partnership in your life? List ways you could increase your productivity in the tasks God has called you to accomplish.

**THE COMING KING** The Messiah will come both to rescue people from sin and to reign as King. He will establish his kingdom, conquer all his enemies, and rule over all the earth. Everything will one day be under his loving and powerful control.

The Messiah came as a servant to die for us. He will return to earth as a victorious King. At that time, he will usher in peace throughout the world. Submit to his leadership now to be ready for the King's triumphant return.

1. Describe the King based on Zechariah.
2. In what ways is Christ's rule evident in lives today? Compare that evidence with how things will be when he returns in glory.
3. What evidence could someone find that Christ is King of your life?

**GOD'S PROTECTION** There was opposition to God's plan in Zechariah's day, and he prophesied future times of trouble. But God's word endures. God remembers his agreements with his people. God cares for his people and will deliver them from all who oppress them.

Although evil is still present, God's infinite love and personal care have been demonstrated through the centuries. God keeps his promises. Although our body may be destroyed, we need never fear our future and final destiny if we love and obey him.

1. What evidence is there in Zechariah that God's protection was present during times of trouble?
2. What potential trouble do you face in living a godly life in your world?
3. How would you describe the protection God has promised to you? How do you feel about this protection?
4. Complete this statement with appropriate phrases: "I need you, Lord, to provide me with your loving care and protection in the areas of: __________ __________."

**586 B.C.**
**Jerusalem is destroyed**

**537**
**First exiles return to Jerusalem**

**536**
**Temple construction begins**

**520**
**Haggai, Zechariah become prophets**

**516**
**Temple completed**

**479**
**Esther becomes queen of Persia**

**465**
**Artaxerxes I becomes king of Persia**

**458**
**Ezra comes to Jerusalem**

**445**
**Nehemiah comes to Jerusalem**

**430**
**Malachi becomes a prophet**

**M**om, she did it again!" Tina's angry voice echoed throughout the house. "Mom!" ■Tina had a little sister, Mary. She was really cute. Except she never learned. Mary was four, old enough to know better. She did know better, but she kept doing it. Because their house was small, Tina and Mary shared a room . . . and a closet. Mary had been told to keep out of Tina's clothes—but as often as she was told, Tina or her mother often found Mary in the bedroom, sitting on the floor, surrounded by Tina's clothes. Lectures hadn't helped; neither had spankings. Nothing seemed to deter Mary from playing in Tina's clothes. Tina wondered if Mary ever would learn. ■God must have thought the same thing about his people. God had warned them repeatedly that he would punish them if they did not stop sinning—but they didn't repent, so God punished them. Israel was taken into captivity, and some years later so was Judah. All because they hadn't learned. ■Then God brought his people back, forgiving them of their sin and offering them a fresh start. Certainly, they must have learned. ■But they hadn't. God's people, rather than learn from the mistakes of their ancestors, chose to repeat their actions. Because they hadn't learned, Malachi came to warn them that God was watching—and he cared. ■As you read, ask God to help you be aware of areas where you need to learn.

## STATS

PURPOSE: To confront the people with their sins and to restore their relationship with God

AUTHOR: Malachi

TO WHOM WRITTEN: The Jews in Jerusalem and God's people everywhere

DATE WRITTEN: About 430 B.C.

SETTING: Malachi, Haggai, and Zechariah were postexilic prophets to Judah (the southern kingdom). Haggai and Zechariah rebuked the people for their failure to rebuild the Temple. Malachi confronted them with their neglect of the Temple and their false and profane worship.

KEY PEOPLE: Malachi, the priests

KEY PLACE: Jerusalem, the Temple

SPECIAL FEATURES: Malachi's literary style displays a continual use of questions asked by God and his people (for example, see 3:7-8)

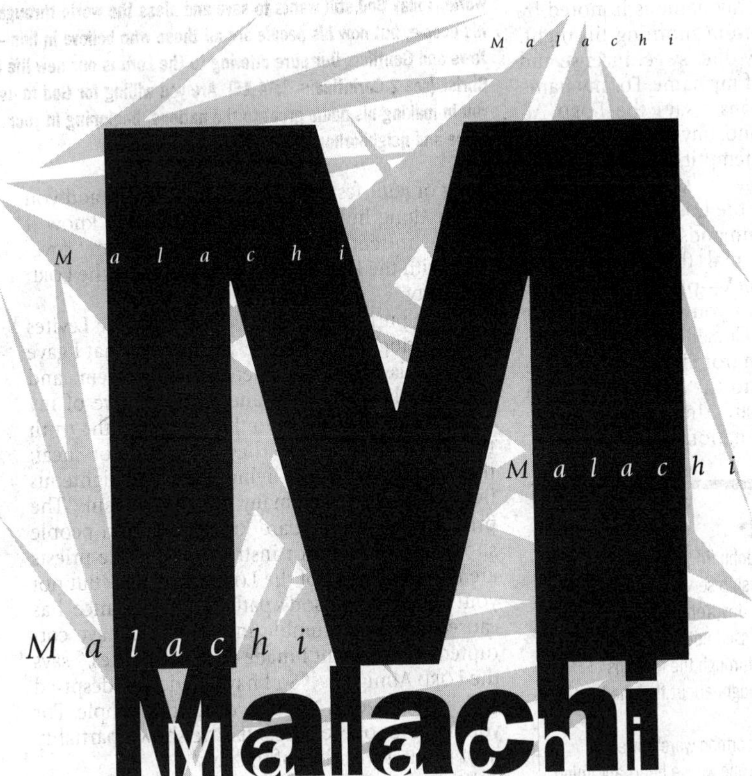

# Malachi

CHAPTER **1** **GOD LOVES HIS PEOPLE.** This is the message* that the LORD gave to Israel through the prophet Malachi.*

2"I have loved you deeply," says the LORD.

But you retort, "Really? How have you loved us?"

And the LORD replies, "I showed my love for you by loving your ancestor Jacob. Yet Esau was Jacob's brother, 3and I rejected Esau and devastated his hill country. I turned Esau's inheritance into a desert for jackals."

4And Esau's descendants in Edom may say, "We have been shattered, but we will rebuild the ruins."

But this is what the LORD Almighty says: "They may try to rebuild, but I will demolish them again! Their country will be known as 'The Land of Wickedness,' and their people will be called 'The People with Whom the LORD Is Forever Angry.' 5When you see the destruction for yourselves, you will say, 'Truly, the LORD's great power reaches far beyond our borders!'"

6The LORD Almighty says to the priests: "A son honors his father, and a servant respects his master. I am your father and master, but where are the honor and respect I deserve? You have despised my name!

"But you ask, 'How have we ever despised your name?'

7"You have despised my name by offering defiled sacrifices on my altar.

"Then you ask, 'How have we defiled the sacrifices*?'

"You defile them by saying the altar of the LORD deserves no respect. 8When you give blind animals as sacrifices, isn't that wrong? And isn't it wrong to offer animals that are crippled and diseased? Try giving gifts like that to your governor, and see how pleased he is!" says the LORD Almighty.

9"Go ahead, beg God to be merciful to you! But when you bring that kind of offering, why should he show you any favor at all?" asks the LORD Almighty.

## LEFTOVERS ● ● ● • •

1:2-8 **God accused Israel of dishonoring him by offering imperfect sacrifices. Our life should be a living sacrifice to God (Romans 12:1). If we give God only our leftover time, money, and energy, we repeat the same sin as these worshipers who didn't want to bring anything valuable to God. What we give God reflects our true attitude toward him.**

1:1a Hebrew *An Oracle: The message.* 1:1b *Malachi* means "my messenger." 1:7 As in Greek version; Hebrew reads *defiled you.*

10 "I wish that someone among you would shut
the Temple doors so that these worthless sacrifices
could not be offered! I am not at all pleased with
you," says the LORD Almighty, "and I will not accept your offerings. 11 But my name is honored by
people of other nations from morning till night.
All around the world they offer sweet incense and
pure offerings in honor of my name. For my name
is great among the nations," says the LORD Almighty. 12 "But you dishonor my name with your
actions. By bringing contemptible food, you are
saying it's all right to defile the Lord's table. 13 You
say, 'It's too hard to serve the LORD,' and you turn
up your noses at his commands," says the LORD
Almighty. "Think of it! Animals that are stolen and
mutilated, crippled and sick—presented as offerings! Should I accept from you such offerings as
these?" asks the LORD. 14 "Cursed is the cheat who
promises to give a fine ram from his flock but then
sacrifices a defective one to the Lord. For I am a
great king," says the LORD Almighty, "and my
name is feared among the nations!

## MESMERIZED

Last Sunday, Byron and John fidgeted their way through the morning worship service, mumbled their way through the songs, daydreamed their way through the prayers, and whispered and passed notes as the minister delivered his message. In short, they went through the motions of worshiping God, but they never actually thought about the one they were in church to honor.

What a shame, because the hymns and sermon were powerful reminders of the greatness of God—to everyone whose heart and mind was attentive.

That same Sunday afternoon, Byron and John rode their bikes over to the cinema at the mall to catch a new sci-fi flick. For two hours they were mesmerized, and they emerged into the bright sunlight enthusiastically buzzing about what they had just witnessed on the screen.

Bored with God in the morning . . . enthralled with Hollywood in the afternoon. That's how Byron and John spent last Sunday.

Why do we take worship so lightly? How can we be so moved by the things of this world and so unimpressed by the majesty of our God?

Read Malachi 1:6-14 to find out what God thinks about our worthless worship and half-hearted devotion.

CHAPTER **2** **GOD WARNS HIS PRIESTS.** "Listen, you
priests; this command is for you! 2 Listen to me and
take it to heart. Honor my name," says the LORD
Almighty, "or I will bring a terrible curse against
you. I will curse even the blessings you receive.
Indeed, I have already cursed them, because you
have not taken my warning seriously. 3 I will rebuke
your descendants and splatter your faces with the

2:12 Hebrew *from the tents of Jacob.*

### CHOSEN ● ● ● • •

**1:11 A theme that runs through the Old Testament is affirmed in this book—"My name is honored by people of other nations. . . . My name is great among the nations." God had a chosen people, the Jews, through whom he planned to save and bless the entire world. Today God still wants to save and bless the world through his people, but now his people are all those who believe in him—Jews and Gentiles. Our pure offering to the Lord is our new life in Christ (see 2 Corinthians 2:14-15). Are you willing for God to use you in making his name great to the nations, beginning in your home and neighborhood?**

dung of your festival sacrifices, and I will add you
to the dung heap. 4 Then at last you will know it
was I who sent you this warning so that my covenant with the Levites may continue," says the LORD
Almighty.
5 "The purpose of my covenant with the Levites
was to bring life and peace, and this is what I gave
them. This called for reverence from them, and
they greatly revered me and stood in awe of my
name. 6 They passed on to the people all the truth
they received from me. They did not lie or cheat;
they walked with me, living good and righteous
lives, and they turned many from lives of sin. 7 The
priests' lips should guard knowledge, and people
should go to them for instruction, for the priests
are the messengers of the LORD Almighty. 8 But not
you! You have left God's paths. Your 'guidance' has
caused many to stumble into sin. You have corrupted the covenant I made with the Levites," says
the LORD Almighty. 9 "So I have made you despised
and humiliated in the eyes of all the people. For
you have not obeyed me but have shown partiality
in your interpretation of the law."
10 Are we not all children of the same Father? Are
we not all created by the same God? Then why are we
faithless to each other, violating the covenant of our
ancestors? 11 In Judah, in Israel, and in Jerusalem
there is treachery, for the men of Judah have defiled
the LORD's beloved sanctuary by marrying women
who worship idols. 12 May the LORD cut off from the
nation of Israel* every last man who has done this
and yet brings an offering to the LORD Almighty.
13 Here is another thing you do. You cover the LORD's
altar with tears, weeping and groaning because he pays
no attention to your offerings, and he doesn't accept
them with pleasure. 14 You cry out, "Why has the LORD

### HOLDING BACK ● ● ● • •

**3:6-12 Malachi urged the people not to hold back their gifts to the priests, their "tithes." Tithing began during Moses' time (Leviticus 27:30-34; Deuteronomy 14:22). The Levites received some of the tithe because they couldn't have land (Numbers 18:20-21). During Malachi's day, the tithes were not used to support God's workers, so the Levites had to go to work. God has given us everything. When we refuse to return to him a part of what he has given, we rob him. Do you selfishly want to keep all you've been given, or are you willing to return the first part for advancing God's kingdom?**

abandoned us?" I'll tell you why! Because the LORD
witnessed the vows you and your wife made to each
other on your wedding day when you were young. But
you have been disloyal to her, though she remained
your faithful companion, the wife of your marriage
vows. 15 Didn't the LORD make you one with your wife?
In body and spirit you are his.* And what does he
want? Godly children from your union. So guard yourself; remain loyal to the wife of your youth. 16 "For I
hate divorce!" says the LORD, the God of Israel. "It is as
cruel as putting on a victim's bloodstained coat," says
the LORD Almighty. "So guard yourself; always remain
loyal to your wife."
17 You have wearied the LORD with your words.
"Wearied him?" you ask. "How have we wearied
him?"
You have wearied him by suggesting that the LORD
favors evildoers since he does not punish them. You
have wearied him by asking, "Where is the God of
justice?"

CHAPTER **3** **THE COMING OF THE MESSIAH.** "Look! I
am sending my messenger, and he will prepare the
way before me. Then the Lord you are seeking will
suddenly come to his Temple. The messenger of
the covenant, whom you look for so eagerly, is
surely coming," says the LORD Almighty. 2 "But who
will be able to endure it when he comes? Who will
be able to stand and face him when he appears?
For he will be like a blazing fire that refines metal
or like a strong soap that whitens clothes. 3 He will
sit and judge like a refiner of silver, watching
closely as the dross is burned away. He will purify
the Levites, refining them like gold or silver, so that
they may once again offer acceptable sacrifices to
the LORD. 4 Then once more the LORD will accept
the offerings brought to him by the people of
Judah and Jerusalem, as he did in former times. 5 At
that time I will put you on trial. I will be a ready
witness against all sorcerers and adulterers and
liars. I will speak against those who cheat employees of their wages, who oppress widows and orphans, or who deprive the foreigners living among
you of justice, for these people do not fear me,"
says the LORD Almighty.
6 "I am the LORD, and I do not change. That is
why you descendants of Jacob are not already completely destroyed. 7 Ever since the days of your
ancestors, you have scorned my laws and failed to
obey them. Now return to me, and I will return to
you," says the LORD Almighty.
"But you ask, 'How can we return when we have
never gone away?'
8 "Should people cheat God? Yet you have cheated
me!
"But you ask, 'What do you mean? When did we
ever cheat you?'
"You have cheated me of the tithes and offerings
due to me. 9 You are under a curse, for your whole

**I see the offering plate passed every Sunday. I'm only a kid. Am I supposed to be giving my money to the church?**

Jesus talked about money more than he talked about anything else. That's because money, unlike any other possession, can take a strong foothold in our life. It can even control us.

Money itself is not evil. But the love of money leads to all sorts of problems (see 1 Timothy 6:10). In Malachi 3:8-10, God warned that refusing to give him tithes and offerings is actually stealing from him!

God doesn't want anything to take his place in our life. For many, money often becomes their god (especially those who don't know Christ).

The best way to keep from making money our god is to learn the joy of giving it away. Building this habit must begin when we're young.

Though not loaded with money, young people almost always have cash (from part-time jobs, gifts, and allowances) to spend. You probably spend your money on clothes, music, junk food, gas for the car (if you drive), and gifts for others. Mostly, though, you probably spend it on yourself.

God doesn't need our money. He owns everything! But we need to give it away. It's an incredible feeling to see our money go for something besides ourselves.

Here is a way to start giving your money back to God. Each time you get some, take 10 percent out and put it in an envelope that says "JESUS" on it. It doesn't matter if it's 50 cents from a $5 allowance or $10 from a $100 paycheck. Collect it for a month.

Next, decide where you want to give it away. Most churches support missionaries (people who have given their lives to spread the Good News of Jesus Christ). Maybe you could select a missionary and ask to receive his or her monthly prayer letter. By giving to a missionary (even if it's $7.23 a month!), you're furthering the cause of Christ here on earth—and you're making a wise investment in others' eternity!

Or you might want to support a child overseas. There are several good organizations who will give you the name of a needy child you can help support, usually for about $20.00 per month. This may be a larger investment than you want to make, but the fun of knowing you're helping a "real person" is worth it!

Of course, you can also give it directly to your church in the offering plate and let them decide how to use it.

At first, it may hurt to give money to something besides yourself. Eventually, however, you'll have such a good time giving that you will want to give more!

Remember, it doesn't matter how much you give. It only matters that you give what you can. See Luke 21:1-4 for a good illustration of this point.

2:15 Or *Did not one God make us and preserve our life and breath?* or *Did not one God make her, both flesh and spirit?* The meaning of the Hebrew is uncertain.

# DIVORCE

We all know how prevalent divorce is in our society today. Sadly, practically every other student who reads this has seen his or her parents divorce. Once divorce was considered a social stigma—sort of a "Scarlet Letter" for our time. Now it's so commonplace that we barely even react to the news that another couple is **calling it quits.**

Before we discuss divorce, let's consider a couple of basic truths about marriage. First, marriage was God's idea. At the beginning of human history, God declared, "It is not good for the man to be alone. I will make a companion who will help him" (Genesis 2:18). God made Adam and Eve to be husband and wife—one man for one woman—setting the parameters for marriage. Jesus added his stamp of approval by performing his first miracle at a wedding (John 2). Marriage is God's institution; it is "HOLY GROUND." No one should enter into it lightly, and no one should walk out of it lightly, either.

Divorce, however, is man's invention. When asked why Moses allowed divorce, Jesus replied: "Moses permitted divorce as a concession to your hard-hearted wickedness, but it was not what God had originally intended" (Matthew 19:8). God allows divorce. He controls, regulates, and contains it—but he does so as a concession, because of our sinfulness. Divorce was never "PLAN A."

We are sinful, fallen people; God does know we will make mistakes—we will fail and "fall short of God's glorious ideal" (Romans 3:23). Our fallen nature affects every area of our lives, including marriage. So God has allowed for divorce in some situations. (For more on the specifics of "biblical divorce," see Matthew 19 and 1 Corinthians 7.) Some marriage relationships become so badly damaged (through sexual immorality, desertion, abuse, or betrayal) that it's impossible to heal them. At those times, God has allowed for divorce. Even so, divorce is always painful, destructive, and damaging. That's why, in Malachi 2:16, God says he "hates divorce": even when it is permissible it is terribly destructive to persons made in God's image—an image that takes a real beating from divorce.

If all this makes you slightly hesitant about marriage—*good.* That is a healthy hesitation to have. Not because you should be terrified to the point of being paralyzed, but because you shouldn't rush into marriage. If a fuller understanding of the awesome implications of *"two becoming one"* causes you to approach the altar with prayer, respect for the holiness of marriage, and a godly perspective on the marriage covenant—great! Marriage is a high calling and should be treated as such. Never approach marriage with the attitude, "Oh well, if it doesn't work out, there's always divorce." Such a mind-set is a formula for **marital meltdown.**

In 1519 the Spanish conquistadors, headed by Hernán Cortés, landed at Veracruz, Mexico. His army, consisting of 500 men and 16 horses, seemed no match for the thousands of Aztec warriors standing between them and their goal of conquering the Aztec empire. Upon landing, Cortés sent a few of his men to do what seemed like a very stupid thing: burn all 10 of the ships they had sailed over on. In so doing, the Spaniards got their leader's message: Conquer or die. There was **NO TURNING BACK.**

When a man and woman say "I do," they are in effect burning their boats. The two become one, and the only way to fully make that transition is by focusing on the goal ahead: a godly marriage. If either one is constantly looking for a way out, the relationship is in serious trouble. Divorce may provide a sometimes necessary escape hatch, but it is never **GOD'S FIRST CHOICE** for his children.

nation has been cheating me. [10]Bring all the tithes into the storehouse so there will be enough food in my Temple. If you do," says the LORD Almighty, "I will open the windows of heaven for you. I will pour out a blessing so great you won't have enough room to take it in! Try it! Let me prove it to you! [11]Your crops will be abundant, for I will guard them from insects and disease.* Your grapes will not shrivel before they are ripe," says the LORD Almighty. [12]"Then all nations will call you blessed, for your land will be such a delight," says the LORD Almighty.

[13]"You have said terrible things about me," says the LORD.

"But you say, 'What do you mean? How have we spoken against you?'

[14]"You have said, 'What's the use of serving God? What have we gained by obeying his commands or by trying to show the LORD Almighty that we are sorry for our sins? [15]From now on we will say, "Blessed are the arrogant." For those who do evil get rich, and those who dare God to punish them go free of harm.'"

[16]Then those who feared the LORD spoke with each other, and the LORD listened to what they said. In his presence, a scroll of remembrance was written to record the names of those who feared him and loved to think about him. [17]"They will be my people," says the LORD Almighty. "On the day when I act, they will be my own special treasure. I will spare them as a father spares an obedient and dutiful child. [18]Then you will again see the difference between the righteous and the wicked, between those who serve God and those who do not."

CHAPTER **4** **THE GREAT JUDGMENT DAY.** The LORD Almighty says, "The day of judgment is coming, burning like a furnace. The arrogant and the wicked will be burned up like straw on that day. They will be consumed like a tree—roots and all.

[2]"But for you who fear my name, the Sun of

3:11 Hebrew *from the devourer.*

## WHY SERVE GOD? ● ● • • •

**3:13-15 These verses deal with the people's arrogant attitude toward God. When we say "What good does it do to serve God?" we really are saying "What good does it do for *me?*" Our focus is selfish. Our real question should be, "What good does it do for God?" We must serve God just because he is God and deserves it.**

**MALACHI** served as a prophet to Judah about 430 B.C. He was the last of the Old Testament prophets.

| | |
|---|---|
| *Climate of the times* | The city of Jerusalem and the Temple had been rebuilt for almost a century, but the people had become complacent in their worship of God. |
| *Main message* | The people's relationship with God was broken because of their sin, and they would soon be punished. But the few who repented would receive God's blessing, illustrated in his promise to send a Messiah. |
| *Importance of message* | Hypocrisy, neglecting God, and careless living have devastating consequences. Service and worship of God must be the primary focus of our life, both now and in eternity. |
| *Contemporary prophets* | None |

**JOY ● ● ● • •**

4:6 **Malachi gives us practical guidelines about commitment to God. God deserves the best we have to offer (1:7-10). We must be willing to change our wrong ways of living (2:1-2), to make family a priority (2:13-16), to be ready for God's refining process (3:3), to tithe (3:8-12), and to forget pride (3:13-15).**

**Malachi closes his message by pointing to the day of judgment. For those committed to God, it will be a day of joy, of ushering in eternity in God's presence. Those who have ignored God will be "straw" to be burned up (4:1). To help people prepare for that day, God was to send a prophet (John the Baptist). The New Testament begins with this prophet calling the people to turn from their sins and turn toward God. Such a commitment to God demands great sacrifice on our part, but we can be sure it will be worth it all in the end.**

Righteousness will rise with healing in his wings.*
And you will go free, leaping with joy like calves let
out to pasture. [3]On the day when I act, you will
tread upon the wicked as if they were dust under
your feet," says the LORD Almighty.
[4]"Remember to obey the instructions of my servant Moses, all the laws and regulations that I gave
him on Mount Sinai* for all Israel.
[5]"Look, I am sending you the prophet Elijah before the great and dreadful day of the LORD arrives.
[6]His preaching will turn the hearts of parents* to
their children, and the hearts of children to their
parents. Otherwise I will come and strike the land
with a curse."

4:2 Or *the sun of righteousness will rise with healing in its wings.* 4:4 Hebrew *Horeb,* another name for Sinai. 4:6 Hebrew *fathers;* also in 4:6b.

# MEGA themes

**GOD'S LOVE** God loves his people even when they neglect or disobey him. He has great blessings to bestow on those who are faithful to him. God's love never ends.

Because God loves us so much, he hates hypocrisy and careless living. This kind of living denies him the relationship he wants to have with us. What we give and how we live reflects the sincerity of our love for God. Live a life of love for God!

1. What do you learn about God's love in the book of Malachi?
2. Contrast the love of God experienced by those who are obedient with the love of God experienced by those who are disobedient.
3. What areas of your life are hindering you from completely enjoying God's love for you?
4. What is it about God's love that you want to know and experience more deeply? Commit yourself to remove hindrances and to actively seek more of God's love.

**THE PRIESTS' SINS** Malachi singled out the priests for condemnation. They knew what God required, yet their sacrifices were unworthy, their service was insincere, and they were lazy, arrogant, and insensitive. They had a casual attitude toward worshiping God and meeting his standards.

If religious leaders go wrong, how will the people be led? We all are leaders in some capacity. Don't neglect your responsibilities or be ruled by what is convenient. Neglect and insensitivity are acts of disobedience. God wants leaders who are faithful and sincere. You can make a difference in how others understand and respond to God.

1. What were the specific sins of the priests? (See 1:1–2:9)
2. What attitudes toward God are apparent in these sinful choices?
3. Why were the priests' sins especially harmful to the people?
4. What attitudes and actions enable leaders to have a positive impact on the church and community?
5. Which of these attitudes are areas of strength for you? Which ones are weak? How can you strengthen the weak areas?

**THE PEOPLE'S SINS** The people had not learned from their exile, nor had they listened to the prophets. Men were callously divorcing their faithful wives to marry younger, heathen women. This disobeyed God's commands about marriage and threatened the religious training of the children—but pride had hardened the people's hearts.

God deserves our total honor, respect, and faithfulness—but sin hardens us to our true condition. Don't let pride keep you from giving God your devotion, money, marriage, and family.

1. How do you feel toward people when you hear about their sins?
2. How does God see their sins?
3. Based on this study, how do you feel about the sins you have committed?
4. Explain your response to the statement: "Little sins are not that big of a deal."
5. What can you do to prepare yourself to live a life that brings God pleasure rather than grief?

**THE LORD'S COMING** God's love for his faithful people is demonstrated by the Messiah's coming to earth. The Messiah's purpose was, and is, to lead the people to the realization of all their fondest hopes. The day of his final coming will be a day of comfort and healing for a faithful few, and a day of judgment for those who reject him.

Christ's first coming brought purification to all those who believe in him. His second coming will expose and condemn those who are proud, insensitive, or unprepared. Yet God can heal and mend. Forgiveness is available now to all who come to Christ.

1. What did God accomplish through Jesus' first coming?
2. What differences has Jesus' coming made in the last 2,000 years?
3. What changes will take place in humanity when Christ returns?
4. As Christians, we know that Jesus will return. How should this knowledge affect our life in the present?

**37** B.C.
**Herod the Great begins to rule**

**6/5** B.C.
**Jesus is born**

**5/4** B.C.
**Escape to Egypt**

**4** B.C.
**Herod the Great dies**

**4/3** B.C.
**Return to Nazareth**

A.D. **6**
**Judea becomes a Roman province**

**6/7**
**Jesus visits Temple as a boy**

**14**
**Tiberius Caesar becomes emperor**

**26**
**Pontius Pilate appointed governor**

**26/27**
**Jesus begins his ministry**

**28**
**Jesus chooses 12 disciples**

**29**
**Jesus feeds 5,000**

**30**
**Jesus is crucified, rises again, and ascends**

**W**ho would you put on a list of the most influential people of all time? Think beyond singers, stars, or athletes. We're talking the real "heavyweights of history." People who took civilization by the scruff of the neck and shook it. Folks about whom we say, "Because of his/her presence, the world will never be the same." ■ Using that criteria, your list might feature Julius Caesar, Karl Marx, Martin Luther King, Jr., William Shakespeare, Adolf Hitler, Napoleon, Abraham Lincoln, Genghis Khan, Elvis Presley, Mohammed, Buddha, Alexander the Great, Mohandas Gandhi, or Henry Ford. ■ Those people—and many others—deserve to be on such a list. But if you're looking for one person who changed the world more than anyone, look at Jesus Christ. Of course, naming a first-century carpenter and itinerant preacher "the most influential person of all time" probably won't sit well with some people. They may prefer to put Jesus on a list of influential "religious" figures. But here's why the founder of Christianity cannot be ignored: ■ Two thousand years ago, Jesus of Nazareth launched a spiritual revolution that is still going strong. He has been the motivation behind more songs and sermons, the inspiration underlying more works of charity, and the object of more affection than all the other great figures of history combined. And don't forget the millions of lives that have been transformed by his timeless touch. ■ Dive into the Gospel of Matthew. See for yourself how Jesus succeeded in turning ancient Israel on its ear. In the process, you'll also begin to see why he still rocks the planet.

## STATS

PURPOSE: To prove that Jesus is the Messiah, the eternal King

AUTHOR: Matthew (Levi)

TO WHOM WRITTEN: Especially for the Jews

DATE WRITTEN: Probably between A.D. 60 and 65

SETTING: Matthew was a Jewish tax collector who became one of Jesus' disciples. This Gospel forms the connecting link between the Old and New Testaments because of its emphasis on the fulfillment of prophecy.

KEY PEOPLE: Jesus, Mary, Joseph, John the Baptist, disciples, religious leaders, Caiaphas, Pilate, Mary Magdalene

KEY PLACES: Bethlehem, Jerusalem, Capernaum, Galilee, Judea

# The NEW Testament

# Matthew

CHAPTER **1** **JESUS' FAMILY TREE.** This is a record of the ancestors of Jesus the Messiah, a descendant of King David and of Abraham:

2 Abraham was the father of Isaac.
Isaac was the father of Jacob.
Jacob was the father of Judah and his brothers.
3 Judah was the father of Perez and Zerah (their mother was Tamar).
Perez was the father of Hezron.
Hezron was the father of Ram.*
4 Ram was the father of Amminadab.
Amminadab was the father of Nahshon.
Nahshon was the father of Salmon.
5 Salmon was the father of Boaz (his mother was Rahab).
Boaz was the father of Obed (his mother was Ruth).
Obed was the father of Jesse.
6 Jesse was the father of King David.
David was the father of Solomon (his mother was Bathsheba, the widow of Uriah).
7 Solomon was the father of Rehoboam.
Rehoboam was the father of Abijah.
Abijah was the father of Asaph.*
8 Asaph was the father of Jehoshaphat.
Jehoshaphat was the father of Jehoram.*
Jehoram was the father* of Uzziah.
9 Uzziah was the father of Jotham.
Jotham was the father of Ahaz.
Ahaz was the father of Hezekiah.
10 Hezekiah was the father of Manasseh.
Manasseh was the father of Amos.*
Amos was the father of Josiah.
11 Josiah was the father of Jehoiachin* and his brothers (born at the time of the exile to Babylon).

## NO LIMITS ● ● ● • • •

1:1-17 **In the first 17 verses of Matthew we meet 46 people spanning 2,000 years. All were ancestors of Jesus, but they varied considerably in personality, spirituality, and experience. Some were heroes (and heroines) of faith—like Abraham, Isaac, Ruth, and David. Some had shady reputations—like Rahab and Tamar. Many were ordinary—like Hezron, Ram, and Akim. Others were evil—like Manasseh and Abijah. God's work has never been limited by human failures or sins; he works through ordinary people. God used all kinds of people to bring his Son into the world; he uses all kinds today to accomplish his will. And he wants to use you.**

**1:3** Greek *Aram;* also in 1:4. See 1 Chr 2:9-10. **1:7** *Asaph* is the same person as Asa; also in 1:8. See 1 Chr 3:10. **1:8a** Greek *Joram.* See 1 Kgs 22:50 and note at 1 Chr 3:11. **1:8b** Or *ancestor;* also in 1:11. **1:10** *Amos* is the same person as Amon. See 1 Chr 3:14. **1:11** Greek *Jeconiah;* also in 1:12. See 2 Kgs 24:6 and note at 1 Chr 3:16.

The broken lines (—·—·) indicate modern boundaries.

Jesus' earthly story begins in the town of Bethlehem in the Roman province of Judea (2:1). A threat to kill the infant King led Joseph to take his family to Egypt (2:14). When they returned, God led them to settle in Nazareth in Galilee (2:22-23). At about age 30, Jesus was baptized in the Jordan River (3:13) and was tempted by Satan in the Judean wilderness (4:1). He set up his base of operations in Capernaum (4:12-13) and from there ministered throughout Israel, telling parables, teaching about the kingdom, and healing the sick. He traveled to the country of the Gergesenes and healed two demon-possessed men (8:28-34); fed over 5,000 people with five small loaves of bread and two fish on the shores of Galilee near Bethsaida (14:13-21); healed the sick in Gennesaret (14:34-36); ministered to the Gentiles in Tyre and Sidon (15:21-28); visited Caesarea Philippi, where Peter declared him to be the Messiah (16:13-20); and taught in Perea, across the Jordan (19:1). As he set out on his last visit to Jerusalem, he told the disciples what would happen to him there (20:17-19). He spent some time in Jericho (20:29), then stayed in Bethany at night as he went back and forth into Jerusalem during his last week (21:17). In Jerusalem he would be crucified, but he would rise again.

12 After the Babylonian exile:
Jehoiachin was the father of Shealtiel.
Shealtiel was the father of Zerubbabel.
13 Zerubbabel was the father of Abiud.
Abiud was the father of Eliakim.
Eliakim was the father of Azor.
14 Azor was the father of Zadok.
Zadok was the father of Akim.
Akim was the father of Eliud.
15 Eliud was the father of Eleazar.
Eleazar was the father of Matthan.
Matthan was the father of Jacob.
16 Jacob was the father of Joseph, the husband of Mary.
Mary was the mother of Jesus, who is called the Messiah.

17All those listed above include fourteen generations
from Abraham to King David, and fourteen from
David's time to the Babylonian exile, and fourteen
from the Babylonian exile to the Messiah.

18Now this is how Jesus the Messiah was born.
His mother, Mary, was engaged to be married to
Joseph. But while she was still a virgin, she became
pregnant by the Holy Spirit. 19Joseph, her fiancé,
being a just man, decided to break the engagement
quietly, so as not to disgrace her publicly.

20As he considered this, he fell asleep, and an
angel of the Lord appeared to him in a dream.
"Joseph, son of David," the angel said, "do not be
afraid to go ahead with your marriage to Mary. For
the child within her has been conceived by the
Holy Spirit. 21And she will have a son, and you are
to name him Jesus,* for he will save his people
from their sins." 22All of this happened to fulfill
the Lord's message through his prophet:

1:21 *Jesus* means "The LORD saves."

[23] "Look! The virgin will conceive a child!
She will give birth to a son,
and he will be called Immanuel*
(meaning, God is with us)."

[24]When Joseph woke up, he did what the angel of the
Lord commanded. He brought Mary home to be his
wife, [25]but she remained a virgin until her son was
born. And Joseph named him Jesus.

CHAPTER **2** **WISE MEN VISIT BABY JESUS.** Jesus was
born in the town of Bethlehem in Judea, during the
reign of King Herod. About that time some wise
men* from eastern lands arrived in Jerusalem, asking, [2]"Where is the newborn king of the Jews? We
have seen his star as it arose,* and we have come to
worship him."

[3]Herod was deeply disturbed by their question, as
was all of Jerusalem. [4]He called a meeting of the
leading priests and teachers of religious law. "Where
did the prophets say the Messiah would be born?" he
asked them.

[5]"In Bethlehem," they said, "for this is what the
prophet wrote:

[6] 'O Bethlehem of Judah,
you are not just a lowly village in Judah,
for a ruler will come from you
who will be the shepherd for my people
Israel.'*"

[7]Then Herod sent a private message to the wise
men, asking them to come see him. At this meeting
he learned the exact time when they first saw the star.
[8]Then he told them, "Go to Bethlehem and search
carefully for the child. And when you find him,
come back and tell me so that I can go and worship
him, too!"

[9]After this interview the wise men went their way.
Once again the star appeared to them, guiding them
to Bethlehem. It went ahead of them and stopped
over the place where the child was. [10]When they saw
the star, they were filled with joy! [11]They entered the
house where the child and his mother, Mary, were,
and they fell down before him and worshiped him.
Then they opened their treasure chests and gave him
gifts of gold, frankincense, and myrrh. [12]But when it
was time to leave, they went home another way,
because God had warned them in a dream not to
return to Herod.

[13]After the wise men were gone, an angel of the
Lord appeared to Joseph in a dream. "Get up and
flee to Egypt with the child and his mother," the
angel said. "Stay there until I tell you to return,
because Herod is going to try to kill the child."
[14]That night Joseph left for Egypt with the child and
Mary, his mother, [15]and they stayed there until Herod's death. This fulfilled what the Lord had spoken
through the prophet: "I called my Son out of
Egypt."*

[16]Herod was furious when he learned that the wise
men had outwitted him. He sent soldiers to kill all
the boys in and around Bethlehem who were two
years old and under, because the wise men had told
him the star first appeared to them about two years
earlier.* [17]Herod's brutal action fulfilled the prophecy of Jeremiah:

[18] "A cry of anguish is heard in Ramah—
weeping and mourning unrestrained.
Rachel weeps for her children,
refusing to be comforted—for they are dead."*

[19]When Herod died, an angel of the Lord appeared in a dream to Joseph in Egypt and told him,
[20]"Get up and take the child and his mother back to
the land of Israel, because those who were trying to
kill the child are dead." [21]So Joseph returned immediately to Israel with Jesus and his mother. [22]But
when he learned that the new ruler was Herod's son
Archelaus, he was afraid. Then, in another dream, he
was warned to go to Galilee. [23]So they went and lived
in a town called Nazareth. This fulfilled what was
spoken by the prophets concerning the Messiah:
"He will be called a Nazarene."

**AFRAID** ● ● • • • ·

2:16-18 **Herod was afraid that this newborn King would one day take his throne. But Jesus wanted to be King of Herod's life. Jesus wanted to give Herod eternal life, not take away his present life. Today people often are afraid that Christ wants to take things away when, in reality, he wants to give them real freedom, peace, and joy.**

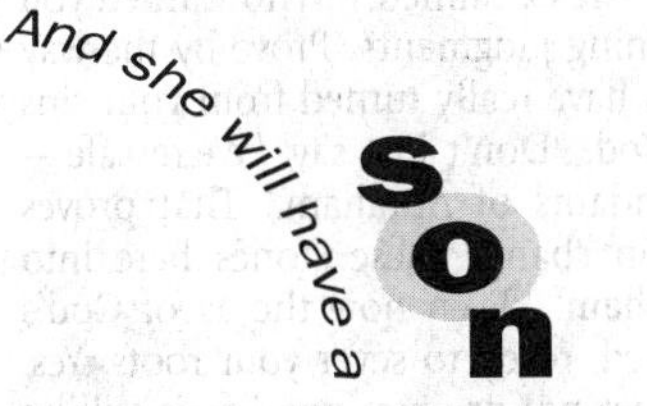
And she will have a
son

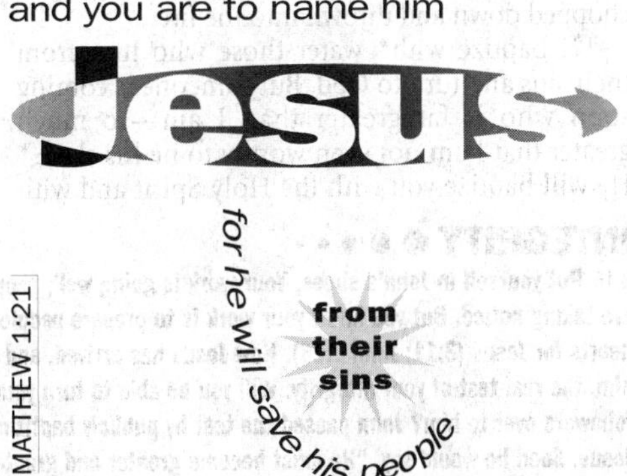
and you are to name him
Jesus
for he will save his people
from their sins
MATTHEW 1:21

**1:23** Isa 7:14; 8:8, 10. **2:1** Or *royal astrologers;* Greek reads *magi;* also in 2:7, 16. **2:2** Or *in the east.* **2:6** Mic 5:2; 2 Sam 5:2. **2:15** Hos 11:1. **2:16** Or *according to the time he calculated from the wise men.* **2:18** Jer 31:15.

## THE PHARISEES AND SADDUCEES

The Pharisees and Sadducees were the two major religious groups in Israel at the time of Christ. The Pharisees were more religiously minded, while the Sadducees were more politically minded. Although the groups disliked and distrusted each other, they became allies in their common hatred for Jesus.

### PHARISEES

*Positive Characteristics*

- Were committed to obeying all of God's Word
- Were admired by the common people for their apparent piety
- Believed in a bodily resurrection and eternal life
- Believed in angels and demons

*Negative Characteristics*

- Behaved as though their own religious rules were just as important as God's rules for living
- Were often hypocritical, forcing others to try to live up to standards they themselves could not live up to
- Believed that salvation came from perfect obedience to the law and was not based on forgiveness of sins
- Became so obsessed with obeying their legal interpretations in every detail that they completely ignored God's message of mercy and grace
- Were more concerned with appearing to be good than with obeying God

### SADDUCEES

*Positive Characteristics*

- Believed God's Word was limited to the first five books of the Bible: Genesis through Deuteronomy
- Were more practically minded than the Pharisees

*Negative Characteristics*

- Relied on logic while placing little importance on faith
- Did not believe all the Old Testament was God's Word
- Did not believe in a bodily resurrection or eternal life
- Did not believe in angels or demons
- Were often willing to compromise their values with the Romans and others in order to maintain their status and influential positions

CHAPTER **3** **JOHN THE BAPTIST PREACHES.** In those
days John the Baptist began preaching in the Judean wilderness. His message was, 2"Turn from
your sins and turn to God, because the Kingdom of
Heaven is near.*" 3Isaiah had spoken of John when
he said,

"He is a voice shouting in the wilderness:
'Prepare a pathway for the Lord's coming!
Make a straight road for him!'"*

4John's clothes were woven from camel hair, and he
wore a leather belt; his food was locusts and wild
honey. 5People from Jerusalem and from every section of Judea and from all over the Jordan Valley
went out to the wilderness to hear him preach. 6And
when they confessed their sins, he baptized them in
the Jordan River.
7But when he saw many Pharisees and Sadducees
coming to be baptized, he denounced them. "You
brood of snakes!" he exclaimed. "Who warned you
to flee God's coming judgment? 8Prove by the way
you live that you have really turned from your sins
and turned to God. 9Don't just say, 'We're safe—
we're the descendants of Abraham.' That proves
nothing. God can change these stones here into
children of Abraham. 10Even now the ax of God's
judgment is poised, ready to sever your roots. Yes,
every tree that does not produce good fruit will be
chopped down and thrown into the fire.
11"I baptize with* water those who turn from
their sins and turn to God. But someone is coming
soon who is far greater than I am—so much
greater that I am not even worthy to be his slave.*
He will baptize you with the Holy Spirit and with

### ACTIONS ● ● • • •

**3:8 John the Baptist called people to more than words or ritual; he told them to change their lives. God looks beyond our words and religious activities to see if our life backs up our words, and he judges our words by the actions that accompany them. Do your actions agree with your words?**

### INTEGRITY ● ● • • •

**3:15 Put yourself in John's shoes. Your work is going well; people are taking notice. But you know your work is to prepare people's hearts for Jesus (3:11; John 1:36). Now Jesus has arrived, and with him, the real test of your integrity. Will you be able to turn your followers over to him? John passed the test by publicly baptizing Jesus. Soon he would say, "He must become greater and greater, and I must become less and less" (John 3:30). Can we put our egos and profitable work aside to point others to Jesus? Will we give up status so that everyone will benefit?**

3:2 Or *has come* or *is coming soon.* 3:3 Isa 40:3. 3:11a Or *in.* 3:11b Greek *to carry his sandals.*

fire.* 12He is ready to separate the chaff from the
grain with his winnowing fork. Then he will
clean up the threshing area, storing the grain in
his barn but burning the chaff with never-ending
fire."
13Then Jesus went from Galilee to the Jordan River
to be baptized by John. 14But John didn't want to
baptize him. "I am the one who needs to be baptized by you," he said, "so why are you coming to
me?"
15But Jesus said, "It must
be done, because we must do
everything that is right.*" So
then John baptized him.
16After his baptism, as
Jesus came up out of the water, the heavens were opened
and he saw the Spirit of God
descending like a dove and
settling on him. 17And a
voice from heaven said,
"This is my beloved Son, and
I am fully pleased with him."

CHAPTER **4** **JESUS IS TEMPTED.** Then Jesus was led
out into the wilderness by
the Holy Spirit to be tempted
there by the Devil. 2For forty
days and forty nights he ate
nothing and became very
hungry. 3Then the Devil*
came and said to him, "If
you are the Son of God,
change these stones into
loaves of bread."
4But Jesus told him, "No!
The Scriptures say,

'People need more than
bread for their life;
they must feed on
every word of
God.'*"

5Then the Devil took him
to Jerusalem, to the highest
point of the Temple, 6and
said, "If you are the Son of
God, jump off! For the
Scriptures say,

'He orders his angels to
protect you.
And they will hold you
with their hands
to keep you from
striking your foot
on a stone.'*"

7Jesus responded, "The
Scriptures also say, 'Do not test the Lord your
God.'*"
8Next the Devil took him to the peak of a very
high mountain and showed him the nations of the
world and all their glory. 9"I will give it all to you,"
he said, "if you will only kneel down and worship
me."
10"Get out of here, Satan," Jesus told him. "For the
Scriptures say,

## MATTHEW

More than any other disciple, Matthew (also called Levi) had a clear idea of how much it would cost to follow Jesus, yet he did not hesitate a moment. When he left his tax-collecting booth, he guaranteed himself unemployment. For several of the other disciples, there was always fishing to return to, but for Matthew, there was no turning back.

Two changes happened to Matthew when he decided to follow Jesus. First, Jesus gave him a new life. He not only belonged to a new group; he belonged to the Son of God. He was not just accepting a different way of life; he was now an accepted person. For a despised tax collector, that change must have been wonderful! Second, Jesus gave Matthew a new purpose for his skills. When he followed Jesus, the only tool from his past job that he carried with him was his pen. From the beginning, God had made him a record keeper. Jesus' call eventually allowed him to put his skills to their finest work. Matthew was a keen observer, and he must have mentally recorded what he saw going on around him. The Gospel that bears his name came as a result.

Matthew's experience points out that each of us, from the beginning, is one of God's works in progress. Much of what God has for us he gives long before we are able to consciously respond to him. He trusts us with skills and abilities ahead of schedule. He has made us each capable of being his servant. When we trust him with what he has given us, we begin a life of real adventure. Matthew couldn't have known that God would use the very skills he had sharpened as a tax collector to record the greatest story ever lived. And God has no less meaningful a purpose for each of us. Have you recognized Jesus saying to you, "Follow me"? What has been your response?

**UPS:**
- Was one of Jesus' 12 disciples
- Responded immediately to Jesus' call
- Invited many friends to his home to meet Jesus
- Compiled the Gospel of Matthew
- Clarified for his Jewish audience Jesus' fulfillment of Old Testament prophecies

**STATS:**
- Where: Capernaum
- Occupation: Tax collector, disciple of Jesus
- Relatives: Father: Alphaeus
- Contemporaries: Jesus, Pilate, Herod, other disciples

LESSONS: Jesus consistently accepted people from every level of society

Matthew was given a new life, and his God-given skills of record keeping and attention to detail were given new purpose

Having been accepted by Jesus, Matthew immediately tried to bring others into contact with Jesus

KEY VERSE: "As he walked along, he saw Levi son of Alphaeus sitting at his tax-collection booth. 'Come, be my disciple,' Jesus said to him. So Levi got up and followed him" (Mark 2:14).

Matthew's story is told in the Gospels. He is also mentioned in Acts 1:13.

**3:11c** Or *in the Holy Spirit and in fire.* **3:15** Or *we must fulfill all righteousness.* **4:3** Greek *the tempter.* **4:4** Deut 8:3. **4:6** Ps 91:11-12. **4:7** Deut 6:16.

## STRANGE ● ● ● • •

**5:3-12 Jesus began his sermon with words that seem to contradict each other. But God's way of living usually contradicts the world's. If you want to live for God, you must be ready to say and do what seems strange to the world. You must be willing to give when others take, to love when others hate, to help when others abuse. In doing this, you will one day receive everything, while the others will end up with nothing.**

'You must worship the Lord your God;
serve only him.'*"

11 Then the Devil went away, and angels came and
cared for Jesus.
12 When Jesus heard that John had been arrested,
he left Judea and returned to Galilee. 13 But instead of
going to Nazareth, he went to Capernaum, beside
the Sea of Galilee, in the region of Zebulun and
Naphtali. 14 This fulfilled Isaiah's prophecy:

15 "In the land of Zebulun and of Naphtali,
beside the sea, beyond the Jordan River—
in Galilee where so many Gentiles live—
16 the people who sat in darkness
have seen a great light.
And for those who lived in the land where death
casts its shadow,
a light has shined."*

17 From then on, Jesus began to preach, "Turn
from your sins and turn to God, because the Kingdom of Heaven is near.*"
18 One day as Jesus was walking along the shore
beside the Sea of Galilee, he saw two brothers—Simon, also called Peter, and Andrew—fishing with a
net, for they were commercial fishermen. 19 Jesus
called out to them, "Come, be my disciples, and I
will show you how to fish for people!" 20 And they
left their nets at once and went with him.
21 A little farther up the shore he saw two other
brothers, James and John, sitting in a boat with their
father, Zebedee, mending their nets. And he called
them to come, too. 22 They immediately followed
him, leaving the boat and their father behind.
23 Jesus traveled throughout Galilee teaching in
the synagogues, preaching everywhere the Good
News about the Kingdom. And he healed people
who had every kind of sickness and disease. 24 News
about him spread far beyond the borders of Galilee
so that the sick were soon coming to be healed
from as far away as Syria. And whatever their illness and pain, or if they were possessed by demons, or were epileptics, or were paralyzed—he
healed them all. 25 Large crowds followed him
wherever he went—people from Galilee, the Ten
Towns,* Jerusalem, from all over Judea, and from
east of the Jordan River.

CHAPTER **5** **THE SERMON ON THE MOUNT.** One day as
the crowds were gathering, Jesus went up the mountainside with his disciples and sat down to teach
them.

2 This is what he taught them:

3 "God blesses those who realize their need for
him,*
for the Kingdom of Heaven is given to them.
4 God blesses those who mourn,
for they will be comforted.
5 God blesses those who are gentle and lowly,
for the whole earth will belong to them.
6 God blesses those who are hungry and thirsty
for justice,
for they will receive it in full.
7 God blesses those who are merciful,
for they will be shown mercy.
8 God blesses those whose hearts are pure,
for they will see God.
9 God blesses those who work for peace,
for they will be called the children of God.
10 God blesses those who are persecuted because
they live for God,
for the Kingdom of Heaven is theirs.

11 "God blesses you when you are mocked and
persecuted and lied about because you are my followers. 12 Be happy about it! Be very glad! For a great
reward awaits you in heaven. And remember, the
ancient prophets were persecuted, too.
13 "You are the salt of the earth. But what good is
salt if it has lost its flavor? Can you make it useful
again? It will be thrown out and trampled underfoot
as worthless. 14 You are the light of the world—like a
city on a mountain, glowing in the night for all to
see. 15 Don't hide your light under a basket! Instead,
put it on a stand and let it shine for all. 16 In the same
way, let your good deeds shine out for all to see, so
that everyone will praise your heavenly Father.
17 "Don't misunderstand why I have come. I did
not come to abolish the law of Moses or the writings
of the prophets. No, I came to fulfill them. 18 I assure
you, until heaven and earth disappear, even the
smallest detail of God's law will remain until its
purpose is achieved. 19 So if you break the smallest
commandment and teach others to do the same, you
will be the least in the Kingdom of Heaven. But
anyone who obeys God's laws and teaches them will
be great in the Kingdom of Heaven.

## OUT OF CONTROL ● ● ● • •

**5:21-22 Killing is a terrible sin, but *anger* is a great sin too because it also violates God's command to love. Anger in this case refers to a seething, brooding bitterness against someone. It is a dangerous emotion that always threatens to leap out of control and lead to violence, emotional hurt, increased mental stress, and other destructive results. There is spiritual damage as well. Anger keeps us from developing a spirit pleasing to God. Have you ever been proud that you didn't strike out and say what was really on your mind? Self-control is good, but Christ wants us to practice thought-control as well. Jesus said we will be held accountable even for our attitudes.**

4:10 Deut 6:13. 4:15-16 Isa 9:1-2. 4:17 Or *has come* or *is coming soon.* 4:25 Greek *Decapolis.* 5:3 Greek *the poor in spirit.*

20 "But I warn you—unless you obey God better
than the teachers of religious law and the Pharisees
do, you can't enter the Kingdom of Heaven at all!
21 "You have heard that the law of Moses says, 'Do
not murder. If you commit murder, you are subject
to judgment.'* 22 But I say, if you are angry with
someone,* you are subject to judgment! If you call
someone an idiot,* you are in danger of being
brought before the high council. And if you curse
someone,* you are in danger of the fires of hell.
23 "So if you are standing before the altar in the
Temple, offering a sacrifice to God, and you suddenly
remember that someone has something against you,
24 leave your sacrifice there beside the altar. Go and be
reconciled to that person. Then come and offer your
sacrifice to God. 25 Come to terms quickly with your
enemy before it is too late and you are dragged into
court, handed over to an officer, and thrown in jail. 26 I
assure you that you won't be free again until you have
paid the last penny.
27 "You have heard that the law of Moses says, 'Do
not commit adultery.'* 28 But I say, anyone who even
looks at a woman with lust in his eye has already
committed adultery with her in his heart. 29 So if your
eye—even if it is your good eye*—causes you to lust,
gouge it out and throw it away. It is better for you to
lose one part of your body than for your whole body
to be thrown into hell. 30 And if your hand—even if
it is your stronger hand*—causes you to sin, cut it
off and throw it away. It is better for you to lose one
part of your body than for your whole body to be
thrown into hell.
31 "You have heard that the law of Moses says, 'A
man can divorce his wife by merely giving her a letter
of divorce.'* 32 But I say that a man who divorces his
wife, unless she has been unfaithful, causes her to
commit adultery. And anyone who marries a divorced woman commits adultery.
33 "Again, you have heard that the law of Moses
says, 'Do not break your vows; you must carry out the
vows you have made to the Lord.'* 34 But I say, don't
make any vows! If you say, 'By heaven!' it is a sacred
vow because heaven is God's throne. 35 And if you say,
'By the earth!' it is a sacred vow because the earth is
his footstool. And don't swear, 'By Jerusalem!' for
Jerusalem is the city of the great King. 36 Don't even
swear, 'By my head!' for you can't turn one hair
white or black. 37 Just say a simple, 'Yes, I will,' or 'No,
I won't.' Your word is enough. To strengthen your
promise with a vow shows that something is
wrong.*
38 "You have heard that the law of Moses says, 'If
an eye is injured, injure the eye of the person who
did it. If a tooth gets knocked out, knock out the
tooth of the person who did it.'* 39 But I say, don't
resist an evil person! If you are slapped on the right
cheek, turn the other, too. 40 If you are ordered to
court and your shirt is taken from you, give your
coat, too. 41 If a soldier demands that you carry his
gear for a mile,* carry it two miles. 42 Give to those
who ask, and don't turn away from those who want
to borrow.
43 "You have heard that the law of Moses says,
'Love your neighbor'* and hate your enemy. 44 But I
say, love your enemies!* Pray for those who persecute you! 45 In that way, you will be acting as true
children of your Father in heaven. For he gives his
sunlight to both the evil and the good, and he sends

**I'm trying to understand how the Old and New Testaments relate to each other. Which one is more important?**

It's not that one is more important than the other. Instead, it's a question of timing.

Imagine being seven years old and your parents sitting you down and telling you all of the rules about driving a car. Not only would you have tuned them out after about two minutes, but ten years later, when it came time to drive, you wouldn't have remembered anything they said.

Timing is everything. Wise parents have figured this out; that's why they didn't give you all their rules as soon as you could talk. They waited until you were ready so that you would want to listen, the rules would make sense to you, and you would remember what they said.

The Old Testament was given to us for several reasons. After explaining Creation, its main purpose was to point the way to God's solution for the problem of mankind's sin. In Matthew 5:21-48, we see Jesus contrasting the Old and New Testaments. Romans 7:7 tells us that the Old Testament Law was good because it showed us what sin was, and thus, showed us our need for a Savior.

The Old Testament points directly to Christ as the Savior that we needed. There are dozens of verses that tell the exact place of Jesus' birth, his sinless life, his death on a cross, his resurrection, and his return. Though the Old Testament was written from about 1450 to 430 B.C., it predicted minute details about the life of Jesus! This also serves to prove the authority of the Scriptures.

Also, the Old Testament is what helps the New Testament make sense. In Matthew 5, Jesus said he came to fulfill the law, not to abolish it. The Old Testament helps us understand why Jesus did what he did.

The Old Testament speaks of sacrifices (picturing Jesus as the ultimate sacrifice) and having faith in God's promise. This was how God prepared the way for Christ.

**5:21** Exod 20:13; Deut 5:17. **5:22a** Greek *your brother;* also in 5:23. Some manuscripts add *without cause.* **5:22b** Greek uses an Aramaic term of contempt: *If you say to your brother, 'Raca.'* **5:22c** Greek *if you say, 'You fool.'* **5:27** Exod 20:14; Deut 5:18. **5:29** Greek *your right eye.* **5:30** Greek *your right hand.* **5:31** Deut 24:1. **5:33** Num 30:2. **5:37** Or *Anything beyond this is from the evil one.* **5:38** Greek *'An eye for an eye and a tooth for a tooth.'* Exod 21:24; Lev 24:20; Deut 19:21. **5:41** Greek *milion* [4,854 feet or 1,478 meters]. **5:43** Lev 19:18. **5:44** Some manuscripts add *Bless those who curse you, do good to those who hate you.*

## SEVEN REASONS NOT TO WORRY

**1** The same God who created life in you can be trusted with the details of your life. 6:25

**2** Worrying about the future hampers your efforts for today. 6:26

**3** Worrying is more harmful than helpful. 6:27

**4** God does not ignore those who depend on him. 6:28-30

**5** Worry shows a lack of faith and understanding of God. 6:31-32

**6** There are real challenges God wants us to pursue, and worrying keeps us from them. 6:33

**7** Living one day at a time keeps us from being consumed with worry. 6:34

---

rain on the just and on the unjust, too. [46]If you love
only those who love you, what good is that? Even
corrupt tax collectors do that much. [47]If you are kind
only to your friends,* how are you different from
anyone else? Even pagans do that. [48]But you are to be
perfect, even as your Father in heaven is perfect.

CHAPTER **6** **HELP OTHERS WITHOUT BRAGGING.** "Take
care! Don't do your good deeds publicly, to be admired, because then you will lose the reward from
your Father in heaven. [2]When you give a gift to
someone in need, don't shout about it as the hypocrites do—blowing trumpets in the synagogues and streets to call attention to their acts of charity! I assure you, they have received all the reward they
will ever get. [3]But when you give to someone, don't
tell your left hand what your right hand is doing.
[4]Give your gifts in secret, and your Father, who
knows all secrets, will reward you.

[5]"And now about prayer. When you pray, don't be like the hypocrites who love to pray publicly on street corners and in the synagogues where everyone can see them. I assure you, that is all the reward they
will ever get. [6]But when you pray, go away by yourself, shut the door behind you, and pray to your Father secretly. Then your Father, who knows all secrets, will reward you.

[7]"When you pray, don't babble on and on as people of other religions do. They think their prayers are answered only by repeating their words again
and again. [8]Don't be like them, because your Father knows exactly what you need even before you ask
him! [9]Pray like this:

Our Father in heaven,
may your name be honored.
[10]May your Kingdom come soon.
May your will be done here on earth,
just as it is in heaven.
[11]Give us our food for today,*
[12]and forgive us our sins,
just as we have forgiven those who have sinned against us.
[13]And don't let us yield to temptation,
but deliver us from the evil one.*

[14]"If you forgive those who sin against you, your heavenly Father will forgive you. [15]But if you refuse
to forgive others, your Father will not forgive your sins.

[16]"And when you fast, don't make it obvious, as the hypocrites do, who try to look pale and disheveled so people will admire them for their fasting. I assure you, that is the only reward they will ever get.
[17]But when you fast, comb your hair and wash your
face. [18]Then no one will suspect you are fasting, except your Father, who knows what you do in secret. And your Father, who knows all secrets, will reward you.

[19]"Don't store up treasures here on earth, where they can be eaten by moths and get rusty, and where thieves break in and steal. [20]Store your treasures in

### INCANTATION ● ● ● • •

6:7-8 **Some people think that repeating the same words over and over—like a magic incantation—will ensure that God will hear them. It's not wrong to come to God with the same requests—Jesus encourages *persistent* prayer. But he condemns the shallow repetition of words that are not offered with a sincere heart. We can never pray too much if our prayers are honest and sincere. Before you start to pray, make sure you mean what you say.**

5:47 Greek *your brothers.* 6:11 Or *for tomorrow.* 6:13 Or *from evil.* Some manuscripts add *For yours is the kingdom and the power and the glory forever. Amen.*

heaven, where they will never become moth-eaten or
rusty and where they will be safe from thieves.
21Wherever your treasure is, there your heart and
thoughts will also be.
22"Your eye is a lamp for your body. A pure eye lets
sunshine into your soul. 23But an evil eye shuts out
the light and plunges you into darkness. If the light
you think you have is really darkness, how deep that
darkness will be!
24"No one can serve two masters. For you will hate
one and love the other, or be devoted to one and
despise the other. You cannot serve both God and
money.
25"So I tell you, don't worry about everyday life—
whether you have enough food, drink, and clothes.
Doesn't life consist of more than food and clothing?
26Look at the birds. They don't need to plant or
harvest or put food in barns because your heavenly
Father feeds them. And you are far more valuable to
him than they are. 27Can all your worries add a single
moment to your life? Of course not.
28"And why worry about your clothes? Look at the
lilies and how they grow. They don't work or make
their clothing, 29yet Solomon in all his glory was not
dressed as beautifully as they are. 30And if God cares
so wonderfully for flowers that are here today and
gone tomorrow, won't he more
surely care for you? You have so
little faith!
31"So don't worry about having
enough food or drink or clothing.
32Why be like the pagans who are
so deeply concerned about these
things? Your heavenly Father already knows all your needs, 33and
he will give you all you need from
day to day if you live for him and
make the Kingdom of God your
primary concern.
34"So don't worry about tomorrow, for tomorrow will bring its
own worries. Today's trouble is
enough for today.

CHAPTER 7 **DON'T CRITICIZE OTHERS.** "Stop judging others, and
you will not be judged. 2For others
will treat you as you treat them.*
Whatever measure you use in
judging others, it will be used to
measure how you are judged. 3And
why worry about a speck in your
friend's eye* when you have a log
in your own? 4How can you think
of saying, 'Let me help you get rid
of that speck in your eye,' when
you can't see past the log in your
own eye? 5Hypocrite! First get rid
of the log from your own eye; then
perhaps you will see well enough to deal with the
speck in your friend's eye.
6"Don't give what is holy to unholy people.*
Don't give pearls to swine! They will trample the
pearls, then turn and attack you.
7"Keep on asking, and you will be given what
you ask for. Keep on looking, and you will find.
Keep on knocking, and the door will be opened.
8For everyone who asks, receives. Everyone who
seeks, finds. And the door is opened to everyone
who knocks. 9You parents—if your children ask for
a loaf of bread, do you give them a stone instead?
10Or if they ask for a fish, do you give them a snake?
Of course not! 11If you sinful people know how to
give good gifts to your children, how much more

**SUBTLE ● ● • • •**

6:13 **Jesus is not implying that God leads us into temptation. He is simply asking for deliverance from Satan and his deceit. All Christians struggle with temptation. Sometimes it is so subtle that we don't even realize what is happening to us. God has promised that he won't allow us to be tempted beyond our endurance (1 Corinthians 10:13). Ask God to help you recognize temptation and to be strong enough to overcome it and choose God's way.**

## "Here's what I did..."

It was during a soccer game that I got to apply Matthew 5:39, about "turning the other cheek," in a very real way.

I was captain of our soccer team. The other team was out for blood—they took cheap shots every chance they got. The refs never saw any of it; I guess people don't realize how dirty girls can play. My team started taking matters into their own hands.

One time I was passed the ball and managed to have a clear break—only one person standing in my way. But she took a cheap shot, and instead of scoring, I was injured and taken out of the game. I was angry, but I started praying about it.

By halftime the other girls on my team were really down. But I told them not to seek revenge—not to take the attitude of "an eye for an eye," but to turn the other cheek, to play fair. I told them that's what I planned to do.

I went back into the game and made sure I played clean. My team followed my example. I scored two goals late in the game and our team tied, 2–2.

The most important thing to me wasn't the score of that game, though. It was the fact that playing clean really was better. Neither resisting nor returning violence was the better way—it really is best to play clean and fair so you can hold your head high. I think the whole team learned something that day. I know I did.

*Susan*
AGE 16

7:2 Or *For God will treat you as you treat others;* Greek reads *For with the judgment you judge you will be judged.* 7:3 Greek *your brother's eye;* also in 7:5.
7:6 Greek *Don't give the sacred to dogs.*

will your heavenly Father give good gifts to those
who ask him.
12 "Do for others what you would like them to do
for you. This is a summary of all that is taught in the
law and the prophets.
13 "You can enter God's Kingdom only through the
narrow gate. The highway to hell* is broad, and its
gate is wide for the many who choose the easy way.
14 But the gateway to life is small, and the road is
narrow, and only a few ever find it.
15 "Beware of false prophets who come disguised
as harmless sheep, but are really wolves that will tear
you apart. 16 You can detect them by the way they act,
just as you can identify a tree by its fruit. You don't
pick grapes from thornbushes, or figs from thistles.
17 A healthy tree produces good fruit, and an unhealthy tree produces bad fruit. 18 A good tree can't
produce bad fruit, and a bad tree can't produce good
fruit. 19 So every tree that does not produce good fruit
is chopped down and thrown into the fire. 20 Yes, the
way to identify a tree or a person is by the kind of
fruit that is produced.
21 "Not all people who sound religious are really
godly. They may refer to me as 'Lord,' but they still
won't enter the Kingdom of Heaven. The decisive
issue is whether they obey my Father in heaven.
22 On judgment day many will tell me, 'Lord,
Lord, we prophesied in your name and cast out
demons in your name and performed many
miracles in your name.' 23 But I will reply, 'I never
knew you. Go away; the things you did were unauthorized.*'

**HABITS ● ● ● • •**

**8:10-12 Jesus told the crowd that many religious Jews who should be in the kingdom would be excluded because of their lack of faith. They were so entrenched in their religious traditions that they could not accept Christ and his new message. We must be careful not to become so set in our religious habits that we expect God to work only in specified ways.**

24 "Anyone who listens to my teaching and obeys
me is wise, like a person who builds a house on solid
rock. 25 Though the rain comes in torrents and the
floodwaters rise and the winds beat against that
house, it won't collapse, because it is built on rock.
26 But anyone who hears my teaching and ignores it
is foolish, like a person who builds a house on sand.
27 When the rains and floods come and the winds
beat against that house, it will fall with a mighty
crash."
28 After Jesus finished speaking, the crowds were
amazed at his teaching, 29 for he taught as one who
had real authority—quite unlike the teachers of religious law.

CHAPTER **8** **TWO MEN BELIEVE AND ARE HEALED.** Large
crowds followed Jesus as he came down the mountainside. 2 Suddenly, a man with leprosy approached

**ANYONE** *who* **listens** *to* **my teaching** *and* **obeys me** *is* **WISE** *like a* **person** *who* **builds** *a* **house** *on* **solid rock.**

MATTHEW 7:24

Jesus. He knelt before him, worshiping. "Lord," the
man said, "if you want to, you can make me well
again."
3 Jesus touched him. "I want to," he said. "Be
healed!" And instantly the leprosy disappeared.
4 Then Jesus said to him, "Go right over to the priest
and let him examine you. Don't talk to anyone along
the way. Take along the offering required in the law
of Moses for those who have been healed of leprosy,
so everyone will have proof of your healing."
5 When Jesus arrived in Capernaum, a Roman officer came and pleaded with him, 6 "Lord, my young
servant lies in bed, paralyzed and racked with pain."
7 Jesus said, "I will come and heal him."
8 Then the officer said, "Lord, I am not worthy to
have you come into my home. Just say the word from
where you are, and my servant will be healed! 9 I
know, because I am under the authority of my superior officers and I have authority over my soldiers. I
only need to say, 'Go,' and they go, or 'Come,' and
they come. And if I say to my slaves, 'Do this or that,'
they do it."
10 When Jesus heard this, he was amazed. Turning
to the crowd, he said, "I tell you the truth, I haven't
seen faith like this in all the land of Israel! 11 And I tell
you this, that many Gentiles will come from all over
the world and sit down with Abraham, Isaac, and
Jacob at the feast in the Kingdom of Heaven. 12 But
many Israelites—those for whom the Kingdom was
prepared—will be cast into outer darkness, where
there will be weeping and gnashing of teeth."
13 Then Jesus said to the Roman officer, "Go on
home. What you have believed has happened." And
the young servant was healed that same hour.

7:13 Greek *The way that leads to destruction.* 7:23 Or *unlawful.*

14When Jesus arrived at Peter's house, Peter's
mother-in-law was in bed with a high fever. 15But
when Jesus touched her hand, the fever left her. Then
she got up and prepared a meal for him.
16That evening many demon-possessed people
were brought to Jesus. All the spirits fled when he
commanded them to leave; and he healed all the
sick. 17This fulfilled the word of the Lord through
Isaiah, who said, "He took our sicknesses and removed our diseases."*
18When Jesus noticed how large the crowd was
growing, he instructed his disciples to cross to the
other side of the lake.
19Then one of the teachers of religious law said
to him, "Teacher, I will follow you no matter where
you go!"
20But Jesus said, "Foxes have dens to live in, and
birds have nests, but I, the Son of Man, have no
home of my own, not even a place to lay my head."
21Another of his disciples said, "Lord, first let me
return home and bury my father."
22But Jesus told him, "Follow me now! Let those
who are spiritually dead care for their own dead."*
23Then Jesus got into the boat and started across
the lake with his disciples. 24Suddenly, a terrible
storm came up, with waves breaking into the boat.
But Jesus was sleeping. 25The disciples went to him
and woke him up, shouting, "Lord, save us! We're
going to drown!"
26And Jesus answered, "Why are you afraid? You
have so little faith!" Then he stood up and rebuked
the wind and waves, and suddenly all was calm.
27The disciples just sat there in awe. "Who is this?"
they asked themselves. "Even the wind and waves
obey him!"
28When Jesus arrived on the other side of the lake
in the land of the Gadarenes,* two men who were
possessed by demons met him. They lived in a cemetery and were so dangerous that no one could go
through that area. 29They began screaming at him,
"Why are you bothering us, Son of God? You have
no right to torture us before God's appointed time!"
30A large herd of pigs was feeding in the distance, 31so
the demons begged, "If you cast us out, send us into
that herd of pigs."
32"All right, go!" Jesus commanded them. So the
demons came out of the men and entered the pigs,
and the whole herd plunged down the steep hillside
into the lake and drowned in the water. 33The herdsmen fled to the nearby city, telling everyone what
happened to the demon-possessed men. 34The entire
town came out to meet Jesus, but they begged him
to go away and leave them alone.

## CHAPTER 9

**JESUS HEALS A PARALYZED MAN.** Jesus
climbed into a boat and went back across the lake to
his own town. 2Some people brought to him a paralyzed man on a mat. Seeing their faith, Jesus said to

### ROUGH ROAD ● ● ● • •

**8:19-20 Following Jesus is not always an easy or comfortable road. Often it means great cost and sacrifice, with no earthly rewards or security. Jesus didn't have a place to call home. You may find that following Christ costs you popularity, friendships, leisure time, or treasured habits. But while the costs of following Christ may be high, the value of being Christ's disciple is an investment that lasts for eternity and yields incredible rewards.**

the paralyzed man, "Take heart, son! Your sins are
forgiven."
3"Blasphemy! This man talks like he is God!"
some of the teachers of religious law said among
themselves.
4Jesus knew what they were thinking, so he asked
them, "Why are you thinking such evil thoughts? 5Is it
easier to say, 'Your sins are forgiven' or 'Get up and
walk'? 6I will prove that I, the Son of Man, have the
authority on earth to forgive sins." Then Jesus turned
to the paralyzed man and said, "Stand up, take your
mat, and go on home, because you are healed!"

**For over six months I've been praying that my dad would become a Christian. Why hasn't God answered my prayer?**

You have certainly been persistent. And you're doing exactly what Matthew 7:7-11 is talking about. You're "asking, seeking, and knocking."

God answers our prayers in three different ways: "Yes," "No," or "Wait." In our instant society, where everything happens when we want it, "Wait" answers are not the ones we're accustomed to hearing. Especially when it seems like the prayer is not being answered. Or is it?

God, in his perfect wisdom, knows the perfect time for people to respond to his call, turn from their sin, and come into a right relationship with him. If we try to manipulate circumstances apart from God's will, perhaps these people will say no instead of yes.

Perhaps there's no one in your dad's life right now who could help him grow. Maybe there are important questions still unanswered that would cause him to respond out of emotion, rather than with his will. Perhaps there are hurts or misconceptions about God and the church that still need to be worked through before he can begin to examine God's love for him.

Whatever the reason, the best thing you can do is to keep praying for him. Also, ask a Christian friend if his or her father would be able to start a friendship with your dad.

Even persistence in prayer will not always change the heart that is hard toward God. People have a will that can say no to any openings God's love may try to penetrate. Just continue your persistent prayer. Never give up.

8:17 Isa 53:4. 8:22 Greek *Let the dead bury their own dead.* 8:28 Some manuscripts read *Gerasenes;* other manuscripts read *Gergesenes.* See Mark 5:1; Luke 8:26.

## LOW LIFE ● ● • • •

**9:11-12 The Pharisees constantly tried to trap Jesus, and they thought his association with these "low lifes" was the perfect opportunity. They were more concerned with criticism than encouragement, with their own appearance of holiness than in helping people, with outward respectability than practical help. But God is concerned for all people, including the sinful and hurting ones. The Christian life is not a popularity contest! We need to follow Jesus' example and share the Good News with the poor, lonely, and outcast—not just the good, talented, and popular.**

7And the man jumped up and went home! 8Fear swept through the crowd as they saw this happen right before their eyes. They praised God for sending a man with such great authority.

9As Jesus was going down the road, he saw Matthew sitting at his tax-collection booth. "Come, be my disciple," Jesus said to him. So Matthew got up and followed him.

10That night Matthew invited Jesus and his disciples to be his dinner guests, along with his fellow tax collectors and many other notorious sinners. 11The Pharisees were indignant. "Why does your teacher eat with such scum*?" they asked his disciples.

12When he heard this, Jesus replied, "Healthy people don't need a doctor—sick people do." 13Then he added, "Now go and learn the meaning of this Scripture: 'I want you to be merciful; I don't want your sacrifices.'* For I have come to call sinners, not those who think they are already good enough."

14One day the disciples of John the Baptist came to Jesus and asked him, "Why do we and the Pharisees fast, but your disciples don't fast?"

15Jesus responded, "Should the wedding guests mourn while celebrating with the groom? Someday he will be taken from them, and then they will fast. 16And who would patch an old garment with unshrunk cloth? For the patch shrinks and pulls away from the old cloth, leaving an even bigger hole than before. 17And no one puts new wine into old wineskins. The old skins would burst from the pressure, spilling the wine and ruining the skins. New wine must be stored in new wineskins. That way both the wine and the wineskins are preserved."

18As Jesus was saying this, the leader of a synagogue came and knelt down before him. "My daughter has just died," he said, "but you can bring her back to life again if you just come and lay your hand upon her."

19As Jesus and the disciples were going to the official's home, 20a woman who had had a hemorrhage for twelve years came up behind him. She touched the fringe of his robe, 21for she thought, "If I can just touch his robe, I will be healed."

22Jesus turned around and said to her, "Daughter, be encouraged! Your faith has made you well." And the woman was healed at that moment.

23When Jesus arrived at the official's home, he noticed the noisy crowds and heard the funeral music. 24He said, "Go away, for the girl isn't dead; she's only asleep." But the crowd laughed at him. 25When the crowd was finally outside, Jesus went in and took the girl by the hand, and she stood up! 26The report of this miracle swept through the entire countryside.

27After Jesus left the girl's home, two blind men followed along behind him, shouting, "Son of David, have mercy on us!"

28They went right into the house where he was staying, and Jesus asked them, "Do you believe I can make you see?"

"Yes, Lord," they told him, "we do."

29Then he touched their eyes and said, "Because of your faith, it will happen." 30And suddenly they could see! Jesus sternly warned them, "Don't tell anyone about this." 31But instead, they spread his fame all over the region.

32When they left, some people brought to him a man who couldn't speak because he was possessed by a demon. 33So Jesus cast out the demon, and instantly the man could talk. The crowds marveled. "Nothing like this has ever happened in Israel!" they exclaimed.

## TESTING ● ● • • •

**9:27-30 Jesus didn't respond immediately to the blind men's pleas. He waited to see how earnest they were. Not everyone who says he or she wants help really wants it badly enough to do something about it. Jesus may have waited and questioned these men to make their desire and faith stronger. If, in your prayers, it seems as if God is too slow in giving his answer, maybe he is testing you as he did the blind men. Do you believe God can help you? Do you *really* want his help?**

34But the Pharisees said, "He can cast out demons because he is empowered by the prince of demons."

35Jesus traveled through all the cities and villages of that area, teaching in the synagogues and announcing the Good News about the Kingdom. And wherever he went, he healed people of every sort of disease and illness. 36He felt great pity for the crowds that came, because their problems were so great and they didn't know where to go for help. They were like sheep without a shepherd. 37He said to his disciples, "The harvest is so great, but the workers are so few. 38So pray to the Lord who is in charge of the harvest; ask him to send out more workers for his fields."

CHAPTER **10** **JESUS SENDS OUT THE DISCIPLES.** Jesus called his twelve disciples to him and gave them authority to cast out evil spirits and to heal every kind of disease and illness. 2Here are the names of the twelve apostles:

first Simon (also called Peter),
then Andrew (Peter's brother),
James (son of Zebedee),
John (James's brother),
3 Philip,

**9:11** Greek *with tax collectors and sinners.* **9:13** Hos 6:6.

Bartholomew,
Thomas,
Matthew (the tax collector),
James (son of Alphaeus),
Thaddaeus,
4 Simon (the Zealot*),
Judas Iscariot (who later betrayed him).

[5]Jesus sent the twelve disciples out with these
instructions: "Don't go to the Gentiles or the Samaritans, [6]but only to the people of Israel—God's lost
sheep. [7]Go and announce to them that the Kingdom
of Heaven is near.* [8]Heal the sick, raise the dead,
cure those with leprosy, and cast out demons. Give
as freely as you have received!

[9]"Don't take any money with you. [10]Don't carry a
traveler's bag with an extra coat and sandals or even
a walking stick. Don't hesitate to accept hospitality,
because those who work deserve to be fed.* [11]When-
ever you enter a city or village, search for a worthy
man and stay in his home until you leave for the next
town. [12]When you are invited into someone's home,
give it your blessing. [13]If it turns out to be a worthy
home, let your blessing stand; if it is not, take back
the blessing. [14]If a village doesn't welcome you or
listen to you, shake off the dust of that place from
your feet as you leave. [15]I assure you, the wicked cities
of Sodom and Gomorrah will be better off on the
judgment day than that place will be.

[16]"Look, I am sending you out as sheep among
wolves. Be as wary as snakes and harmless as doves.
[17]But beware! For you will be handed over to the
courts and beaten in the synagogues. [18]And you must
stand trial before governors and kings because you
are my followers. This will be your opportunity to
tell them about me—yes, to witness to the world.
[19]When you are arrested, don't worry about what to
say in your defense, because you
will be given the right words at the
right time. [20]For it won't be you
doing the talking—it will be the
Spirit of your Father speaking
through you.

[21]"Brother will betray brother to
death, fathers will betray their own
children, and children will rise
against their parents and cause
them to be killed. [22]And everyone
will hate you because of your allegiance to me. But those who endure to the end will be saved.
[23]When you are persecuted in one
town, flee to the next. I assure you
that I, the Son of Man, will return
before you have reached all the
towns of Israel.

[24]"A student is not greater than
the teacher. A servant is not greater
than the master. [25]The student
shares the teacher's fate. The ser-
vant shares the master's fate. And since I, the master
of the household, have been called the prince of
demons,* how much more will it happen to you, the
members of the household! [26]But don't be afraid of
those who threaten you. For the time is coming
when everything will be revealed; all that is secret
will be made public. [27]What I tell you now in the
darkness, shout abroad when daybreak comes. What
I whisper in your ears, shout from the housetops for
all to hear!

[28]"Don't be afraid of those who want to kill you.
They can only kill your body; they cannot touch your
soul. Fear only God, who can destroy both soul and
body in hell. [29]Not even a sparrow, worth only half a
penny, can fall to the ground without your Father
knowing it. [30]And the very hairs on your head are all
numbered. [31]So don't be afraid; you are more valuable to him than a whole flock of sparrows.

[32]"If anyone acknowledges me publicly here on
earth, I will openly acknowledge that person before
my Father in heaven. [33]But if anyone denies me here
on earth, I will deny that person before my Father in
heaven.

[34]"Don't imagine that I came to bring peace to

## VALUE ● ● ● • • ·

10:29-31 **Jesus said that God cares for the sparrows' every need. We are far more valuable to God than these little birds, so valuable that God sent his only Son to die for us (John 3:16). You are of great worth to God. Because he places such value on you, you need never fear personal threats or difficult trials. But don't think that because you are valuable to God he will take away all your troubles (see 10:16). The real test of value is how well something holds up under the wear, tear, and abuse of everyday life. Those who stand up for Christ in spite of their troubles truly have lasting value and will receive great rewards (see 5:11-12).**

## "Here's what I did..."

I used to struggle a lot with doubt. Was God real? Did he really care about what happens to me? Is the Bible relevant? Then someone challenged me to actively try to apply a passage from the Bible every day for two weeks and see if that made any difference. I did. I read some of the psalms and found that they were wonderfully relevant. When I felt lonely and had no one to turn to, I found that David's words perfectly expressed my feelings. Another passage I came across reminded me that God has promised never to leave us. Then when I came across Jesus' words in Matthew 7:24-27, I realized that it's only through obeying and applying God's Word that we know he's real. His Word is the only solid thing we have to build our lives on. The Matthew passage, and my two-week experiment, motivated me to try to live out what I read more and more every day.

Laura
AGE 17

10:4 Greek *the Cananean.* 10:7 Or *has come* or *is coming soon.* 10:10 Or *the worker is worthy of support.* 10:25 Greek *Beelzeboul.*

the earth! No, I came to bring a sword. 35I have come to set a man against his father, and a daughter against her mother, and a daughter-in-law against her mother-in-law. 36Your enemies will be right in your own household! 37If you love your father or mother more than you love me, you are not worthy of being mine; or if you love your son or daughter more than me, you are not worthy of being mine. 38If you refuse to take up your cross and follow me, you are not worthy of being mine. 39If you cling to your life, you will lose it; but if you give it up for me, you will find it.

40"Anyone who welcomes you is welcoming me, and anyone who welcomes me is welcoming the Father who sent me. 41If you welcome a prophet as one who speaks for God,* you will receive the same reward a prophet gets. And if you welcome good and godly people because of their godliness, you will be given a reward like theirs. 42And if you give even a cup of cold water to one of the least of my followers, you will surely be rewarded."

## MOUTH

**Mrs. Rogers puts the groceries in the trunk, buckles four-year-old Richie in his seat, and heads for home.**

**Soon Richie is holding his plastic airplane out the open window, watching its propeller spin. Mrs. Rogers notices what Richie is up to. "Don't do that. Keep your hands–and your toys–inside the car!" Richie smiles and slowly obeys.**

**But soon the hand-held plane banks to the right–back out the window.**

**"Richie!" Mrs. Rogers screams. "I told you, 'No!'"**

**Startled, the little boy drops the plane and lets fly with a word that four-year-old boys have no business knowing.**

**Mrs. Rogers is shocked. "Richie! Where did you learn that word?"**

**"From Christi."**

**"What other words have you heard her say?"**

**Richie rolls off words that would make a sailor blush.**

**When Mrs. Rogers gets home, she marches into her 16-year-old daughter's bedroom. "Christie, Richie used some horrible language in the car today . . . and he said he learned it from you. You want to explain?"**

**"Gee, Mom," Christi responds nervously. "No way. Not me. I don't know why he would say something like that."**

**Obviously Christi is caught up in lying as well as profanity. She needs to read Matthew 12:33-37.**

## CHAPTER 11 JOHN'S QUESTIONS ABOUT JESUS.

When Jesus had finished giving these instructions to his twelve disciples, he went off teaching and preaching in towns throughout the country.

2John the Baptist, who was now in prison, heard about all the things the Messiah was doing. So he sent his disciples to ask Jesus, 3"Are you really the

## DOUBTS

**11:4-6 As John sat in prison, he felt some doubts about whether Jesus really was the Messiah. If John's purpose was to prepare people for the coming Messiah (3:3), and if Jesus really was that Messiah, then why was John in prison instead of preaching to the crowds, preparing their hearts?**

**Jesus answered John's doubts by pointing to his acts of healing, his curing the lepers, raising the dead, and preaching the gospel to the poor. With so much evidence, Jesus' identity was obvious. If you sometimes doubt your salvation, the forgiveness of your sins, or God's work in your life, look at the evidence in Scripture and in your life. When you doubt, don't turn away from Christ, turn *to* him.**

Messiah we've been waiting for, or should we keep looking for someone else?"

4Jesus told them, "Go back to John and tell him about what you have heard and seen—5the blind see, the lame walk, the lepers are cured, the deaf hear, the dead are raised to life, and the Good News is being preached to the poor. 6And tell him: 'God blesses those who are not offended by me.*'"

7When John's disciples had gone, Jesus began talking about him to the crowds. "Who is this man in the wilderness that you went out to see? Did you find him weak as a reed, moved by every breath of wind? 8Or were you expecting to see a man dressed in expensive clothes? Those who dress like that live in palaces, not out in the wilderness. 9Were you looking for a prophet? Yes, and he is more than a prophet. 10John is the man to whom the Scriptures refer when they say,

'Look, I am sending my messenger before you,
and he will prepare your way before you.'*

11"I assure you, of all who have ever lived, none is greater than John the Baptist. Yet even the most insignificant person in the Kingdom of Heaven is greater than he is! 12And from the time John the Baptist began preaching and baptizing until now, the Kingdom of Heaven has been forcefully advancing, and violent people attack it.* 13For before John came, all the teachings of the Scriptures looked forward to this present time. 14And if you are willing to accept what I say, he is Elijah, the one the prophets said would come.* 15Anyone who is willing to hear should listen and understand!

16"How shall I describe this generation? These people are like a group of children playing a game in the public square. They complain to their friends, 17'We played wedding songs, and you weren't happy, so we played funeral songs, but you weren't sad.' 18For John the Baptist didn't drink wine and he often fasted, and you say, 'He's demon possessed.' 19And I, the Son of Man, feast and drink, and you say, 'He's a glutton and a drunkard, and a friend of the worst sort of sinners!' But wisdom is shown to be right by what results from it."

20Then Jesus began to denounce the cities where he had done most of his miracles, because they hadn't turned from their sins and turned to God.

10:41 Greek *welcome a prophet in the name of a prophet.* 11:6 Or *who don't fall away because of me.* 11:10 Mal 3:1. 11:12 Or *until now, eager multitudes have been pressing into the Kingdom of Heaven.* 11:14 See Mal 4:5.

21“What horrors await you, Korazin and Bethsaida!
For if the miracles I did in you had been done in
wicked Tyre and Sidon, their people would have sat
in deep repentance long ago, clothed in sackcloth
and throwing ashes on their heads to show their
remorse. 22I assure you, Tyre and Sidon will be better
off on the judgment day than you! 23And you people
of Capernaum, will you be exalted to heaven? No,
you will be brought down to the place of the dead.*
For if the miracles I did for you had been done in
Sodom, it would still be here today. 24I assure you,
Sodom will be better off on the judgment day than
you.”

25Then Jesus prayed this prayer: “O Father, Lord of
heaven and earth, thank you for hiding the truth
from those who think themselves so wise and clever,
and for revealing it to the childlike. 26Yes, Father, it
pleased you to do it this way!

27“My Father has given me authority over everything. No one really knows the Son except the Father,
and no one really knows the Father except the Son
and those to whom the Son chooses to reveal him.”

28Then Jesus said, “Come to me, all of you who
are weary and carry heavy burdens, and I will give
you rest. 29Take my yoke upon you. Let me teach you,
because I am humble and gentle, and you will find
rest for your souls. 30For my yoke fits perfectly, and
the burden I give you is light.”

CHAPTER **12** **JESUS TALKS ABOUT THE SABBATH.** At
about that time Jesus was walking through some
grainfields on the Sabbath. His disciples were hungry, so they began breaking off heads of wheat and
eating the grain. 2Some Pharisees saw them do it and
protested, “Your disciples shouldn’t be doing that!
It’s against the law to work by harvesting grain on the
Sabbath.”

3But Jesus said to them, “Haven’t you ever read in
the Scriptures what King David did when he and his
companions were hungry? 4He went into the house
of God, and they ate the special bread reserved for
the priests alone. That was breaking the law, too.
5And haven’t you ever read in the law of Moses that
the priests on duty in the Temple may work on the
Sabbath? 6I tell you, there is one here who is even
greater than the Temple! 7But you would not have
condemned those who aren’t guilty if you knew the
meaning of this Scripture: ‘I want you to be merciful;
I don’t want your sacrifices.’* 8For I, the Son of Man,
am master even of the Sabbath.”

9Then he went over to the synagogue, 10where he
noticed a man with a deformed hand. The Pharisees
asked Jesus, “Is it legal to work by healing on the
Sabbath day?” (They were, of course, hoping he
would say yes, so they could bring charges against
him.)

11And he answered, “If you had one sheep, and it
fell into a well on the Sabbath, wouldn’t you get to
work and pull it out? Of course you would. 12And
how much more valuable is a person than a sheep!
Yes, it is right to do good on the Sabbath.” 13Then he
said to the man, “Reach out your hand.” The man
reached out his hand, and it became normal, just
like the other one. 14Then the Pharisees called a
meeting and discussed plans for killing Jesus.

15But Jesus knew what they were planning. He left

11:23 Greek *to Hades.* 12:7 Hos 6:6.

**My parents are quietly putting up with my new faith. Mom thinks it’s “nice” and Dad won’t talk to me about it. How do I make them see Jesus is a real person?**

There are many difficult sayings of Jesus in the New Testament. Matthew 10:34-39 is one of the toughest. What does Jesus mean when he says “Your enemies will be right in your own household”?

If you have faced pressure and opposition from friends because of your new faith, you realize that your decision for Christ causes people to make decisions about you. Some will stay with you and support your decision because they are your true friends. Others will leave because they don’t understand or because your values no longer encourage their lifestyle.

We also may find opposition at home. In these verses, Jesus is not telling us to be disobedient to our parents or to try to cause problems at home. He is just stating the fact that a person with different goals, values, purposes, perhaps even morals, may cause division. This is more than a fact, it is a promise! Rarely will the only Christian in a household go unchallenged.

Though it is uncommon for parents to be openly hostile toward someone in their home, it does happen. Put-downs can really hurt, especially if they come from someone you love.

The best course of action is to not try to make your parents see anything. Instead, just live your life in obedience to them as the Bible commands: “Children, obey your parents because you belong to the Lord, for this is the right thing to do. ‘Honor your father and mother.’ This is the first of the Ten Commandments that ends with a promise. And this is the promise: If you honor your father and mother, ‘you will live a long life, full of blessing’” (Ephesians 6:1-3).

It is not your role or responsibility to make them change. That is the job of the Holy Spirit: “When he comes, he will convince the world of its sin, and of God’s righteousness, and of the coming judgment” (John 16:8). You are to be God’s representative in your home, hopefully to be a part of bringing your family to Christ.

Don’t neglect your family because it does not yet accept your faith. But don’t neglect the higher mission of keeping God as your number-one priority either.

Find some Christian friends who will pray for you and pray with you about your situation. Go to them for encouragement and when you need advice on how to respond as each difficult situation arises.

**EVIDENCE ● ● ● • •**

12:38-40 **The Pharisees were asking for another miracle, but they were not sincerely seeking to know Jesus. Jesus knew that they had already seen enough miracles to prove he was the Messiah. They just had to open their hearts. But the Pharisees had already decided not to believe in Jesus; more miracles would not change that. Many people have thought, *If I could just see a real miracle, then I could really believe in God.* But Jesus' response to the Pharisees applies to us also. We have plenty of evidence—Jesus' death, resurrection, and ascension, plus centuries of his work in the lives of believers around the world. Instead of looking for additional evidence or miracles, accept what God has already given and move forward. He may use your life as evidence to reach another person.**

that area, and many people followed him. He healed all the sick among them, 16but he warned them not to say who he was. 17This fulfilled the prophecy of Isaiah concerning him:

18 "Look at my Servant,
whom I have chosen.
He is my Beloved,
and I am very pleased with him.
I will put my Spirit upon him,
and he will proclaim justice to the nations.
19 He will not fight or shout;
he will not raise his voice in public.
20 He will not crush those who are weak,
or quench the smallest hope,
until he brings full justice with his final victory.
21 And his name will be the hope
of all the world."*

22Then a demon-possessed man, who was both blind and unable to talk, was brought to Jesus. He healed the man so that he could both speak and see. 23The crowd was amazed. "Could it be that Jesus is the Son of David, the Messiah?" they wondered out loud.

24But when the Pharisees heard about the miracle, they said, "No wonder he can cast out demons. He gets his power from Satan,* the prince of demons."

25Jesus knew their thoughts and replied, "Any kingdom at war with itself is doomed. A city or home divided against itself is doomed. 26And if Satan is casting out Satan, he is fighting against himself. His own kingdom will not survive. 27And if I am empowered by the prince of demons,* what about your own followers? They cast out demons, too, so they will judge you for what you have said. 28But if I am casting out demons by the Spirit of God, then the Kingdom of God has arrived among you. 29Let me illustrate this. You can't enter a strong man's house and rob him without first tying him up. Only then can his house be robbed!* 30Anyone who isn't helping me opposes me, and anyone who isn't working with me is actually working against me.

31"Every sin or blasphemy can be forgiven—except blasphemy against the Holy Spirit, which can never be forgiven. 32Anyone who blasphemes against me, the Son of Man, can be forgiven, but blasphemy against the Holy Spirit will never be forgiven, either in this world or in the world to come.

33"A tree is identified by its fruit. Make a tree good, and its fruit will be good. Make a tree bad, and its fruit will be bad. 34You brood of snakes! How could evil men like you speak what is good and right? For whatever is in your heart determines what you say. 35A good person produces good words from a good heart, and an evil person produces evil words from an evil heart. 36And I tell you this, that you must give an account on judgment day of every idle word you speak. 37The words you say now reflect your fate then; either you will be justified by them or you will be condemned."

38One day some teachers of religious law and Pharisees came to Jesus and said, "Teacher, we want you to show us a miraculous sign to prove that you are from God."

39But Jesus replied, "Only an evil, faithless generation would ask for a miraculous sign; but the only sign I will give them is the sign of the prophet Jonah. 40For as Jonah was in the belly of the great fish for three days and three nights, so I, the Son of Man, will be in the heart of the earth for three days and three nights. 41The people of Nineveh will rise up against this generation on judgment day and condemn it, because they repented at the preaching of Jonah. And now someone greater than Jonah is here—and you refuse to repent. 42The queen of Sheba* will also rise up against this generation on judgment day and condemn it, because she came from a distant land to hear the wisdom of Solomon. And now someone greater than Solomon is here—and you refuse to listen to him.

43"When an evil spirit leaves a person, it goes into the desert, seeking rest but finding none. 44Then it says, 'I will return to the person I came from.' So it returns and finds its former home empty, swept, and clean. 45Then the spirit finds seven other spirits more evil than itself, and they all enter the person and live there. And so that person is worse off than before. That will be the experience of this evil generation."

46As Jesus was speaking to the crowd, his mother and brothers were outside, wanting to talk with him. 47Someone told Jesus, "Your mother and your brothers are outside, and they want to speak to you."

48Jesus asked, "Who is my mother? Who are my

**FARMING ● ● ● • •**

13:8 **This parable should encourage spiritual "farmers"—those who teach, preach, and lead others. The farmer sowed good seed, but not all of his sowing brought high yield. Some seed did not sprout, and even the plants that grew had varying yields. Don't be discouraged if no one seems to be listening to you as you faithfully teach the Word. Belief cannot be forced to follow a mathematical formula. Rather, it is a miracle of God's Holy Spirit as he uses your words to move others to come to him.**

12:18-21 Isa 42:1-4. 12:24 Greek *Beelzeboul.* 12:27 Greek *by Beelzeboul.* 12:29 Or *One cannot rob Satan's kingdom without first tying him up. Only then can his demons be cast out.* 12:42 Greek *The queen of the south.*

brothers?" 49Then he pointed to his disciples and said, "These are my mother and brothers. 50Anyone who does the will of my Father in heaven is my brother and sister and mother!"

## CHAPTER 13 A STORY ABOUT A FARMER.

Later that same day, Jesus left the house and went down to the shore, 2where an immense crowd soon gathered. He got into a boat, where he sat and taught as the people listened on the shore. 3He told many stories such as this one:

"A farmer went out to plant some seed. 4As he scattered it across his field, some seeds fell on a footpath, and the birds came and ate them. 5Other seeds fell on shallow soil with underlying rock. The plants sprang up quickly, 6but they soon wilted beneath the hot sun and died because the roots had no nourishment in the shallow soil. 7Other seeds fell among thorns that shot up and choked out the tender blades. 8But some seeds fell on fertile soil and produced a crop that was thirty, sixty, and even a hundred times as much as had been planted. 9Anyone who is willing to hear should listen and understand!"

10His disciples came and asked him, "Why do you always tell stories when you talk to the people?"

11Then he explained to them, "You have been permitted to understand the secrets of the Kingdom of Heaven, but others have not. 12To those who are open to my teaching, more understanding will be given, and they will have an abundance of knowledge. But to those who are not listening, even what they have will be taken away from them. 13That is why I tell these stories, because people see what I do, but they don't really see. They hear what I say, but they don't really hear, and they don't understand. 14This fulfills the prophecy of Isaiah, which says:

'You will hear my words,
but you will not understand;
you will see what I do,
but you will not perceive its meaning.
15For the hearts of these people are hardened,
and their ears cannot hear,
and they have closed their eyes—
so their eyes cannot see,
and their ears cannot hear,
and their hearts cannot understand,
and they cannot turn to me
and let me heal them.'*

16"But blessed are your eyes, because they see; and your ears, because they hear. 17I assure you, many prophets and godly people have longed to see and hear what you have seen and heard, but they could not.

18"Now here is the explanation of the story I told about the farmer sowing grain: 19The seed that fell on the hard path represents those who hear the Good News about the Kingdom and don't understand it. Then the evil one comes and snatches the seed away from their hearts. 20The rocky soil represents those who hear the message and receive it with joy. 21But like young plants in such soil, their roots don't go very deep. At first they get along fine, but they wilt as soon as they have problems or are persecuted because they believe the word. 22The thorny ground represents those who hear and accept the Good News, but all too quickly the message is crowded out by the cares of this life and the lure of wealth, so no crop is produced. 23The good soil represents the hearts of those who truly accept God's message and produce a huge harvest—thirty, sixty, or even a hundred times as much as had been planted."

### DIRT ● ● • • •

13:23 **The four types of soil represent the different responses we can have to God's message. We respond differently because we are in different states of readiness. Some people are hardened, others are shallow, others are contaminated by distracting cares, and some are receptive. How has God's Word taken root in your life? What kind of soil are you?**

24Here is another story Jesus told: "The Kingdom of Heaven is like a farmer who planted good seed in his field. 25But that night as everyone slept, his enemy came and planted weeds among the wheat. 26When the crop began to grow and produce grain, the weeds also grew. 27The farmer's servants came and told him, 'Sir, the field where you planted that good seed is full of weeds!'

28"'An enemy has done it!' the farmer exclaimed.

"'Shall we pull out the weeds?' they asked.

29"He replied, 'No, you'll hurt the wheat if you do. 30Let both grow together until the harvest. Then I will tell the harvesters to sort out the weeds and burn them and to put the wheat in the barn.'"

31Here is another illustration Jesus used: "The Kingdom of Heaven is like a mustard seed planted in a field. 32It is the smallest of all seeds, but it becomes the largest of garden plants and grows into a tree where birds can come and find shelter in its branches."

33Jesus also used this illustration: "The Kingdom of Heaven is like yeast used by a woman making bread. Even though she used a large amount* of flour, the yeast permeated every part of the dough."

34Jesus always used stories and illustrations like these when speaking to the crowds. In fact, he never spoke to them without using such parables. 35This fulfilled the prophecy that said,

"I will speak to you in parables.
I will explain mysteries hidden since the
creation of the world."*

36Then, leaving the crowds outside, Jesus went into the house. His disciples said, "Please explain the story of the weeds in the field."

37"All right," he said. "I, the Son of Man, am the

13:14-15 Isa 6:9-10. 13:33 Greek 3 *measures.* 13:35 Ps 78:2.

farmer who plants the good seed. 38The field is the
world, and the good seed represents the people of
the Kingdom. The weeds are the people who belong
to the evil one. 39The enemy who planted the weeds
among the wheat is the Devil. The harvest is the end
of the world, and the harvesters are the angels.
40"Just as the weeds are separated out and burned,
so it will be at the end of the world. 41I, the Son of
Man, will send my angels, and they will remove from
my Kingdom everything that causes sin and all who
do evil, 42and they will throw them into the furnace
and burn them. There will be weeping and gnashing
of teeth. 43Then the godly will shine like the sun in
their Father's Kingdom. Anyone who is willing to
hear should listen and understand!
44"The Kingdom of Heaven is like a treasure that
a man discovered hidden in a field. In his excitement, he hid it again and sold everything he owned
to get enough money to buy the field—and to get
the treasure, too!
45"Again, the Kingdom of Heaven is like a pearl
merchant on the lookout for choice pearls. 46When
he discovered a pearl of great value, he sold everything he owned and bought it!
47"Again, the Kingdom of Heaven is like a fishing
net that is thrown into the water and gathers fish of
every kind. 48When the net is full, they drag it up
onto the shore, sit down, sort the good fish into
crates, and throw the bad ones away. 49That is the
way it will be at the end of the world. The angels will
come and separate the wicked people from the
godly, 50throwing the wicked into the fire. There will
be weeping and gnashing of teeth. 51Do you understand?"

"Yes," they said, "we do."
52Then he added, "Every teacher of religious law
who has become a disciple in the Kingdom of
Heaven is like a person who brings out of the storehouse the new teachings as well as the old."
53When Jesus had finished telling these stories, he
left that part of the country. 54He returned to Nazareth, his hometown. When he taught there in the
synagogue, everyone was astonished and said,
"Where does he get his wisdom and his miracles?
55He's just a carpenter's son, and we know Mary, his
mother, and his brothers—James, Joseph, Simon,
and Judas. 56All his sisters live right here among us.
What makes him so great?" 57And they were deeply
offended and refused to believe in him.

Then Jesus told them, "A prophet is honored everywhere except in his own hometown and among
his own family." 58And so he did only a few miracles
there because of their unbelief.

## CHAPTER 14 **HEROD KILLS JOHN THE BAPTIST.**
When
Herod Antipas* heard about Jesus, 2he said to his
advisers, "This must be John the Baptist come back
to life again! That is why he can do such miracles."
3For Herod had arrested and imprisoned John as a
favor to his wife Herodias (the former wife of Herod's brother Philip). 4John kept telling Herod, "It is
illegal for you to marry her." 5Herod would have
executed John, but he was afraid of a riot, because all
the people believed John was a prophet.
6But at a birthday party for Herod, Herodias's
daughter performed a dance that greatly pleased
him, 7so he promised with an oath to give her anything she wanted. 8At her mother's urging, the girl
asked, "I want the head of John the Baptist on a
tray!" 9The king was sorry, but because of his oath
and because he didn't want to back down in front of
his guests, he issued the necessary orders. 10So John
was beheaded in the prison, 11and his head was
brought on a tray and given to the girl, who took it
to her mother. 12John's disciples came for his body
and buried it. Then they told Jesus what had happened.

### GIVING IN ● ● • • •

**14:9 Herod did not want to kill John the Baptist, but he gave the order so he wouldn't be embarrassed in front of his guests. How easy it is to give in to crowd pressure, to let ourself be coerced into doing wrong. Don't place yourself in a position where it is too embarrassing to do what is right. Do what is right no matter how embarrassing or painful it may be.**

13As soon as Jesus heard the news, he went off by
himself in a boat to a remote area to be alone. But
the crowds heard where he was headed and followed
by land from many villages. 14A vast crowd was there
as he stepped from the boat, and he had compassion
on them and healed their sick.
15That evening the disciples came to him and said,
"This is a desolate place, and it is getting late. Send
the crowds away so they can go to the villages and
buy food for themselves."
16But Jesus replied, "That isn't necessary—you
feed them."
17"Impossible!" they exclaimed. "We have only
five loaves of bread and two fish!"
18"Bring them here," he said. 19Then he told the
people to sit down on the grass. And he took the
five loaves and two fish, looked up toward heaven,
and asked God's blessing on the food. Breaking the
loaves into pieces, he gave some of the bread and
fish to each disciple, and the disciples gave them to
the people. 20They all ate as much as they wanted,
and they picked up twelve baskets of leftovers.
21About five thousand men had eaten from those
five loaves, in addition to all the women and children!
22Immediately after this, Jesus made his disciples get back into the boat and cross to the other
side of the lake while he sent the people home.
23Afterward he went up into the hills by himself to
pray. Night fell while he was there alone. 24Mean-
while, the disciples were in trouble far away from
land, for a strong wind had risen, and they were
fighting heavy waves.

14:1 Greek *Herod the tetrarch.* He was a son of King Herod and was ruler over one of the four districts in Palestine.

[25]About three o'clock in the morning* Jesus came
to them, walking on the water. [26]When the disciples
saw him, they screamed in terror, thinking he was a
ghost. [27]But Jesus spoke to them at once. "It's all
right," he said. "I am here! Don't be afraid."
[28]Then Peter called to him, "Lord, if it's really you,
tell me to come to you by walking on water."
[29]"All right, come," Jesus said.
So Peter went over the side of the boat and walked
on the water toward Jesus. [30]But when he looked
around at the high waves, he was terrified and began
to sink. "Save me, Lord!" he shouted.
[31]Instantly Jesus reached out his hand and
grabbed him. "You don't have much faith," Jesus
said. "Why did you doubt me?" [32]And when they
climbed back into the boat, the wind stopped.
[33]Then the disciples worshiped him. "You really
are the Son of God!" they exclaimed.
[34]After they had crossed the lake, they landed at
Gennesaret. [35]The news of their arrival spread
quickly throughout the whole surrounding area, and
soon people were bringing all their sick to be healed.
[36]The sick begged him to let them touch even the
fringe of his robe, and all who touched it were
healed.

## CHAPTER 15 **THE RULES THAT COUNT.** Some Phari-
sees and teachers of religious law now arrived from
Jerusalem to interview Jesus. [2]"Why do your disciples disobey our age-old traditions?" they demanded. "They ignore our tradition of ceremonial
hand washing before they eat."
[3]Jesus replied, "And why do you, by your traditions, violate the direct commandments of God?
[4]For instance, God says, 'Honor your father and
mother,' and 'Anyone who speaks evil of father or
mother must be put to death.'* [5]But you say, 'You
don't need to honor your parents by caring for their
needs if you give the money to God instead.' [6]And
so, by your own tradition, you nullify the direct
commandment of God. [7]You hypocrites! Isaiah was
prophesying about you when he said,

[8]'These people honor me with their lips,
but their hearts are far away.
[9]Their worship is a farce,
for they replace God's commands with their
own man-made teachings.'*"

[10]Then Jesus called to the crowds and said, "Listen
to what I say and try to understand. [11]You are not
defiled by what you eat; you are defiled by what you
say and do.*"
[12]Then the disciples came to him and asked, "Do
you realize you offended the Pharisees by what you
just said?"
[13]Jesus replied, "Every plant not planted by my
heavenly Father will be rooted up, [14]so ignore them.
They are blind guides leading the blind, and if one
blind person guides another, they will both fall into
a ditch."
[15]Then Peter asked Jesus, "Explain what you
meant when you said people aren't defiled by what
they eat."
[16]"Don't you understand?" Jesus asked him.
[17]"Anything you eat passes through the stomach and
then goes out of the body. [18]But evil words come
from an evil heart and defile the person who says
them. [19]For from the heart come evil thoughts, murder, adultery, all other sexual immorality, theft, lying,
and slander. [20]These are what defile you. Eating with
unwashed hands could never defile you and make
you unacceptable to God!"
[21]Jesus then left Galilee and went north to the
region of Tyre and Sidon. [22]A Gentile* woman who
lived there came to him, pleading, "Have mercy on
me, O Lord, Son of David! For my daughter has a
demon in her, and it is severely tormenting her."
[23]But Jesus gave her no reply—not even a word.
Then his disciples urged him to send her away. "Tell
her to leave," they said. "She is bothering us with all
her begging."
[24]Then he said to the woman, "I was sent only to
help the people of Israel—God's lost sheep—not
the Gentiles."
[25]But she came and worshiped him and pleaded
again, "Lord, help me!"
[26]"It isn't right to take food from the children and
throw it to the dogs," he said.
[27]"Yes, Lord," she replied, "but even dogs are permitted to eat crumbs that fall beneath their master's
table."

### EYES ● ● • • •

**14:28 Peter was not testing Jesus, something we are told not to do (4:7). Instead he was the only one in the boat to react in faith. His impulsive request led him to experience a rather unusual demonstration of God's power. Peter started to sink because he took his eyes off Jesus and focused on the high waves around him. His faith wavered when he realized what he was doing. We may not walk on water, but we do walk through tough situations. If we focus on the waves of difficult circumstances around us without looking to Christ for help, we too may despair and sink. To maintain your faith in the midst of difficult situations, keep your eyes on Christ's power rather than on your inadequacies.**

### ALL AROUND US ● ● • • •

**15:23 The disciples asked Jesus to get rid of the woman because she was bothering them with her begging. They showed no compassion for her or sensitivity to her needs. It is possible to become so occupied with spiritual matters that we miss real spiritual needs right around us, whether out of prejudice or simply because of the inconvenience they cause. Instead of being bothered, be aware of the opportunities that surround you. Be open to the beauty of God's message for all people, and make an effort not to shut out those who are different from you.**

14:25 Greek *In the fourth watch of the night.* 15:4 Exod 20:12; 21:17; Lev 20:9; Deut 5:16. 15:8-9 Isa 29:13. 15:11 Or *what comes out of the mouth defiles a person.* 15:22 Greek *Canaanite.*

# THE CHURCH

Please check the appropriate box: The church is: ☐ a building where religious people go on Sunday. ☐ a place where you're told all the things you should not do. ☐ where a nice, respectable person tells a bunch of nice, respectable people to be nicer and more respectable (with apologies to Mark Twain). ☐ the people of God all over the world; those who follow Jesus and proclaim him as Lord. **O**K, you probably figured out that the last response is the best. But most of us probably feel there is some truth to the other statements as well. Here in Matthew 16:18 we have the first biblical use of the term *church*. There are a lot of misconceptions about what the church is; here is an attempt to clear up at least a few. MISCONCEPTION #1: ***The church is a building.*** While most local churches in America *own* buildings, they should not be confused as one and the same. The church is people—God's covenant people called to follow him in faith and action—not the structures where they meet. When we say, "I'm going to church," we're not simply talking about driving to, entering, and sitting down in a building. We mean we are meeting together as God's people, gathered in one place for the purposes of worship, fellowship, instruction, etc. **I**n many parts of the world, congregations often do not own property. They meet in homes, stores, schools, prisons, and other creative locations. The earliest Christians met in secret, in caves and other hidden places, for fear of persecution and death. (Even today in some places it's dangerous to be a follower of Jesus.) But it's not *where* the meeting is held, it's *who* holds it. Wherever Christians gather, there is the church. MISCONCEPTION #2: ***The church is where good people go to do religious things.*** Let's make it very plain: There are no "good" people. (If you're unclear on this concept, read Romans, particularly chapter 3.) There are simply sinners who are forgiven and sinners who are not forgiven. The church isn't for "good" people; it's for sinners who know they've been forgiven and who come together regularly to celebrate God and the unbelievable love he has for us. Someone has put it this way: The church is not a showcase for saints; it's a hospital for sinners. **W**hen we come together, it isn't just because that's what religious people do on Sunday mornings and Wednesday nights. We come together to praise and worship our God, to thank him for all he has done for us. We thank and honor him for who he is—God and Creator of all, the One who loved us enough to let his Son die for our sins. We praise God with our attendance, our prayers, our music, the preaching of the Word, our money, our fellowship, and countless other ways. MISCONCEPTION #3: ***The church is a human institution.*** The way many Christians behave, it sometimes is difficult to see any difference between the church and other organizations. But the church is God's own institution, called into being as his instrument on this planet. It is the church that proclaims the Good News (gospel) of Jesus Christ; seeks justice for the poor and rejected and suffering; tries to influence society for the good of all people and the glory of God; and lifts up the name of God the Father, God the Son, and God the Holy Spirit before an unbelieving world. In other words, we exist for God's pleasure and purposes before our own. As Psalm 100:3 says, "Acknowledge that the LORD is God! He made us, and we are his. We are his people, the sheep of his pasture." No, there are no perfect churches. Made up of sinful humans, how could any church be perfect? But the church *is* made up of God's people, called into existence by Jesus himself, and built on the **ROCK-SOLID** foundation of his promise that "all the powers of hell will not conquer it."

28"Woman," Jesus said to her, "your faith is great.
Your request is granted." And her daughter was instantly healed.
29Jesus returned to the Sea of Galilee and climbed
a hill and sat down. 30A vast crowd brought him the
lame, blind, crippled, mute, and many others with
physical difficulties, and they laid them before Jesus.
And he healed them all. 31The crowd was amazed!
Those who hadn't been able to speak were talking,
the crippled were made well, the lame were walking
around, and those who had been blind could see
again! And they praised the God of Israel.
32Then Jesus called his disciples to him and said,
"I feel sorry for these people. They have been here
with me for three days, and they have nothing left to
eat. I don't want to send them away hungry, or they
will faint along the road."
33The disciples replied, "And where would we get
enough food out here in the wilderness for all of
them to eat?"
34Jesus asked, "How many loaves of bread do you
have?"
They replied, "Seven, and a few small fish." 35So
Jesus told all the people to sit down on the ground.
36Then he took the seven loaves and the fish,
thanked God for them, broke them into pieces, and
gave them to the disciples, who distributed the food
to the crowd.
37They all ate until they were full, and when the
scraps were picked up, there were seven large baskets
of food left over! 38There were four thousand men
who were fed that day, in addition to all the women
and children. 39Then Jesus sent the people home,
and he got into a boat and crossed over to the region
of Magadan.

CHAPTER **16** **THE LEADERS WANT A MIRACLE.** One
day the Pharisees and Sadducees came to test Jesus'
claims by asking him to show them a miraculous
sign from heaven.
2He replied, "You know the saying, 'Red sky at
night means fair weather tomorrow, 3red sky in the
morning means foul weather all day.' You are good
at reading the weather signs in the sky, but you can't
read the obvious signs of the times!* 4Only an evil,
faithless generation would ask for a miraculous sign,
but the only sign I will give them is the sign of the
prophet Jonah." Then Jesus left them and went away.
5Later, after they crossed to the other side of the
lake, the disciples discovered they had forgotten to
bring any food. 6"Watch out!" Jesus warned them.
"Beware of the yeast of the Pharisees and Sadducees."
7They decided he was saying this because they
hadn't brought any bread. 8Jesus knew what they
were thinking, so he said, "You have so little faith!
Why are you worried about having no food? 9Won't
you ever understand? Don't you remember the five
thousand I fed with five loaves, and the baskets of
food that were left over? 10Don't you remember the
four thousand I fed with seven loaves, with baskets
of food left over? 11How could you even think I was
talking about food? So again I say, 'Beware of the
yeast of the Pharisees and Sadducees.'"
12Then at last they understood that he wasn't
speaking about yeast or bread but about the false
teaching of the Pharisees and Sadducees.
13When Jesus came to the region of Caesarea Philippi, he asked his disciples, "Who do people say that
the Son of Man is?"
14"Well," they replied, "some say John the Baptist,
some say Elijah, and others say Jeremiah or one of
the other prophets."
15Then he asked them, "Who do you say I am?"
16Simon Peter answered, "You are the Messiah, the
Son of the living God."
17Jesus replied, "You are blessed, Simon son of
John,* because my Father in heaven has revealed this
to you. You did not learn this from any human
being. 18Now I say to you that you are Peter,* and
upon this rock I will build my church, and all the
powers of hell* will not conquer it. 19And I will give
you the keys of the Kingdom of Heaven. Whatever
you lock on earth will be locked in heaven, and
whatever you open on earth will be opened in
heaven." 20Then he sternly warned them not to tell
anyone that he was the Messiah.
21From then on Jesus began to tell his disciples
plainly that he had to go to Jerusalem, and he told
them what would happen to him there. He would
suffer at the hands of the leaders and the leading
priests and the teachers of religious law. He would be
killed, and he would be raised on the third day.
22But Peter took him aside and corrected him.
"Heaven forbid, Lord," he said. "This will never
happen to you!"

**PROTECT ● ● • • •**

**16:21-22 Peter, Jesus' friend and devoted follower who had just eloquently proclaimed his Lord's true identity as the Christ, sought to protect him from the suffering he prophesied. Great temptations can come from those who love us and seek to protect us from something we must experience. Be cautious of advice from a friend who says, "Surely God doesn't want you to face this."**

23Jesus turned to Peter and said, "Get away from
me, Satan! You are a dangerous trap to me. You are
seeing things merely from a human point of view,
and not from God's."
24Then Jesus said to the disciples, "If any of you
wants to be my follower, you must put aside your
selfish ambition, shoulder your cross, and follow
me. 25If you try to keep your life for yourself, you will
lose it. But if you give up your life for me, you will
find true life. 26And how do you benefit if you gain
the whole world but lose your own soul* in the
process? Is anything worth more than your soul?

**16:2-3** Several manuscripts do not include any of the words in 16:2-3 after *He replied.* **16:17** Greek *Simon son of Jonah;* see John 1:42; 21:15-17. **16:18a** *Peter* means "stone" or "rock." **16:18b** Greek *and the gates of Hades.* **16:26** Or *your life.*

27For I, the Son of Man, will come in the glory of my Father with his angels and will judge all people according to their deeds. 28And I assure you that some of you standing here right now will not die before you see me, the Son of Man, coming in my Kingdom."

## CHAPTER 17 **JESUS SHINES LIKE THE SUN.**

Six days later Jesus took Peter and the two brothers, James and John, and led them up a high mountain. 2As the men watched, Jesus' appearance changed so that his face shone like the sun, and his clothing became dazzling white. 3Suddenly, Moses and Elijah appeared and began talking with Jesus. 4Peter blurted out, "Lord, this is wonderful! If you want me to, I'll make three shrines,* one for you, one for Moses, and one for Elijah."

### BELIEVE ● ● • • •

**17:22-23 Again Jesus predicted his death; but more important, he told of his resurrection. Unfortunately, the disciples heard only the first part and became discouraged. They couldn't understand why Jesus wanted to go back to Jerusalem and the trouble he'd find there. The disciples didn't fully comprehend the purpose of Jesus' death and resurrection until Pentecost (Acts 2). Don't get upset at yourself if you are slow to understand everything about Jesus. After all, the disciples were with him, saw his miracles, and heard his words—and they still had difficulty understanding. Despite their questions and doubts, however, they believed. We can do no less.**

5But even as he said it, a bright cloud came over them, and a voice from the cloud said, "This is my beloved Son, and I am fully pleased with him. Listen to him." 6The disciples were terrified and fell face down on the ground.

7Jesus came over and touched them. "Get up," he said, "don't be afraid." 8And when they looked, they saw only Jesus with them. 9As they descended the mountain, Jesus commanded them, "Don't tell anyone what you have seen until I, the Son of Man, have been raised from the dead."

10His disciples asked, "Why do the teachers of religious law insist that Elijah must return before the Messiah comes*?"

11Jesus replied, "Elijah is indeed coming first to set everything in order. 12But I tell you, he has already come, but he wasn't recognized, and he was badly mistreated. And soon the Son of Man will also suffer at their hands." 13Then the disciples realized he had been speaking of John the Baptist.

14When they arrived at the foot of the mountain, a huge crowd was waiting for them. A man came and knelt before Jesus and said, 15"Lord, have mercy on my son, because he has seizures and suffers terribly. He often falls into the fire or into the water. 16So I brought him to your disciples, but they couldn't heal him."

17Jesus replied, "You stubborn, faithless people!

### LITTLE KIDS ● ● • • •

**18:6 Children are trusting by nature. They trust adults, which helps them learn about trusting God. Parents and others who influence young children are held accountable by God for how they affect these little ones' ability to trust. Jesus warned that anyone who turns little children away from faith will receive severe punishment.**

How long must I be with you until you believe? How long must I put up with you? Bring the boy to me." 18Then Jesus rebuked the demon in the boy, and it left him. From that moment the boy was well.

19Afterward the disciples asked Jesus privately, "Why couldn't we cast out that demon?"

20"You didn't have enough faith," Jesus told them. "I assure you, even if you had faith as small as a mustard seed you could say to this mountain, 'Move from here to there,' and it would move. Nothing would be impossible."*

22One day after they had returned to Galilee, Jesus told them, "The Son of Man is going to be betrayed. 23He will be killed, but three days later he will be raised from the dead." And the disciples' hearts were filled with grief.

24On their arrival in Capernaum, the tax collectors for the Temple tax came to Peter and asked him, "Doesn't your teacher pay the Temple tax?"

25"Of course he does," Peter replied. Then he went into the house to talk to Jesus about it.

But before he had a chance to speak, Jesus asked him, "What do you think, Peter*? Do kings tax their own people or the foreigners they have conquered?"

26"They tax the foreigners," Peter replied.

"Well, then," Jesus said, "the citizens are free! 27However, we don't want to offend them, so go down to the lake and throw in a line. Open the mouth of the first fish you catch, and you will find a coin. Take the coin and pay the tax for both of us."

## CHAPTER 18 **WHO IS THE GREATEST?**

About that time the disciples came to Jesus and asked, "Which of us is greatest in the Kingdom of Heaven?"

2Jesus called a small child over to him and put the child among them. 3Then he said, "I assure you, unless you turn from your sins and become as little children, you will never get into the Kingdom of Heaven. 4Therefore, anyone who becomes as humble as this little child is the greatest in the Kingdom of Heaven. 5And anyone who welcomes a little child like this on my behalf is welcoming me. 6But if anyone causes one of these little ones

### KEEP TRACK ● ● • • •

**18:22 The rabbis taught that Jews should forgive three times those who offend them. Peter, in trying to be especially generous, asked Jesus if seven (the "perfect" number) was enough times to forgive someone. But Jesus answered, "Seventy times seven," meaning that we shouldn't even keep track of how many times we forgive someone. We should always forgive those who are truly repentant, no matter how many times they ask.**

17:4 Or *shelters;* Greek reads *tabernacles.* 17:10 Greek *that Elijah must come first.* 17:20 Some manuscripts add verse 21, *But this kind of demon won't leave unless you have prayed and fasted.* 17:25 Greek *Simon.*

who trusts in me to lose faith, it would be better for
that person to be thrown into the sea with a large
millstone tied around the neck.
7 "How terrible it will be for anyone who causes
others to sin. Temptation to do wrong is inevitable,
but how terrible it will be for the person who does
the tempting. 8 So if your hand or foot causes you
to sin, cut it off and throw it away. It is better to
enter heaven* crippled or lame than to be thrown
into the unquenchable fire with both of your
hands and feet. 9 And if your eye causes you to sin,
gouge it out and throw it away. It is better to enter
heaven half blind than to have two eyes and be
thrown into hell.
10 "Beware that you don't despise a single one of
these little ones. For I tell you that in heaven their
angels are always in the presence of my heavenly
Father.*
12 "If a shepherd has one hundred sheep, and one
wanders away and is lost, what will he do? Won't he
leave the ninety-nine others and go out into the hills
to search for the lost one? 13 And if he finds it, he will
surely rejoice over it more than over the ninety-nine
that didn't wander away! 14 In the same way, it is not
my heavenly Father's will that even one of these little
ones should perish.
15 "If another believer* sins against you, go privately and point out the fault. If the other person
listens and confesses it, you have won that person
back. 16 But if you are unsuccessful, take one or two
others with you and go back again, so that everything you say may be confirmed by two or three
witnesses. 17 If that person still refuses to listen, take
your case to the church. If the church decides you are
right, but the other person won't accept it, treat that
person as a pagan or a corrupt tax collector. 18 I tell
you this: Whatever you prohibit on earth is prohibited in heaven, and whatever you allow on earth is
allowed in heaven.
19 "I also tell you this: If two of you agree down
here on earth concerning anything you ask, my
Father in heaven will do it for you. 20 For where two
or three gather together because they are mine,* I am
there among them."
21 Then Peter came to him and asked, "Lord, how
often should I forgive someone* who sins against
me? Seven times?"
22 "No!" Jesus replied, "seventy times seven!*
23 "For this reason, the Kingdom of Heaven can
be compared to a king who decided to bring his
accounts up to date with servants who had borrowed money from him. 24 In the process, one of
his debtors was brought in who owed him millions
of dollars.* 25 He couldn't pay, so the king ordered
that he, his wife, his children, and everything he
had be sold to pay the debt. 26 But the man fell
down before the king and begged him, 'Oh, sir, be
patient with me, and I will pay it all.' 27 Then the
king was filled with pity for him, and he released
him and forgave his debt.
28 "But when the man left the king, he went to a

**Is temptation a sin? If it is, I'm sinning all the time. It seems like thoughts are always coming into my mind to do things that are wrong.**

If temptation were a sin, then Jesus was a sinner (see Matthew 4:1-11 for the story of when Satan tempted Jesus in the wilderness). Temptation is not a sin. According to Matthew 18:7-9, it's the natural consequence of living in this world.

What leads to sin is following the path temptation wants us to take. If taken far enough, the path will cause us to think and do what is wrong.

Though temptation always will be present, we do not have to wave the white flag and admit defeat. We have the power to resist, because the Holy Spirit lives in us.

God's Word also reminds us how to overcome temptation. First Corinthians 10:13 says, "Remember that the temptations that come into your life are no different from what others experience. And God is faithful. He will keep the temptation from becoming so strong that you can't stand up against it. When you are tempted, he will show you a way out so that you will not give in to it."

Find the "way out" in this story:

At school a friend asks if you want to spend the night with some friends and watch videos. You check with your folks, assuring them there will be no R-rated videos. They give the OK. Everything is cool, so far.

Once you arrive, you look at the stack of videos and notice that half of them are R-rated. You get your friend alone and ask him what the deal is. He says the other guys picked out the videos. Besides, everyone (but you) has seen them before, so he didn't think you'd mind.

Do you stay and go against what your parents want, or do you go along with the group?

Let's say you stay. The next day Dad asks what movies you watched. Now you have to lie to stay out of trouble. So you lie. Unfortunately, your mom spoke with the mom of one of your friends on the phone and found out there were R-rated movies at the sleep-over. Now you're grounded until age 27!

Where were the escape hatches to the temptation to disobey your parents? When you found out that R-rated movies would be shown, you had two choices. You could have apologized to your friends, called your dad, and had him pick you up. Or you could have gone to a different part of the house and done something else.

God always provides a way out of every temptation. We choose whether to take his way out or to do things we know are wrong.

If we stay close to God, we'll be more likely to resist and do what is right. We don't have to give in.

18:8 Greek *enter life;* also in 18:9. 18:10 Some manuscripts add verse 11, *And I, the Son of Man, have come to save the lost.* 18:15 Greek *your brother.* 18:20 Greek *gather together in my name.* 18:21 Greek *my brother.* 18:22 Or *77 times.* 18:24 Greek *10,000 talents.*

fellow servant who owed him a few thousand dollars.* He grabbed him by the throat and demanded instant payment. 29His fellow servant fell
down before him and begged for a little more time.
'Be patient and I will pay it,' he pleaded. 30But his
creditor wouldn't wait. He had the man arrested
and jailed until the debt could be paid in full.
31"When some of the other servants saw this, they
were very upset. They went to the king and told him
what had happened. 32Then the king called in the
man he had forgiven and said, 'You evil servant! I
forgave you that tremendous debt because you
pleaded with me. 33Shouldn't you have mercy on
your fellow servant, just as I had mercy on you?'
34Then the angry king sent the man to prison until
he had paid every penny.
35"That's what my heavenly Father will do to you
if you refuse to forgive your brothers and sisters* in
your heart."

## DIVORCE

Annette and Mary are watching the evening soap opera "California Millionaires."

In this particular episode, police are investigating a possible murder at the Stanwick estate, Lance and Natasha are having an affair, and Sutherland is still thinking about having a sex-change operation. But as wild as those events are, they still are not the main plot of this week's show. No, the most disturbing revelation is that Gabrielle and Welborne Stanwick are divorcing.

"I can't believe it!" Annette laments as she clicks off the TV in disgust. "They were so perfect together. Now it's over."

"Yeah, I never thought we'd ever see them call it quits. I guess it just goes to show you that even the best marriages sometimes come to an end."

"Just like my aunt and uncle. They were married for 25 years and . . ."

"Ooh, don't tell me one of them had an affair?" Mary asks, an eager tone in her voice.

"No, they just grew apart over the years. . . ."

"That is so sad!" Mary says.

Mary is right. Divorce is sad. But what about her statement that some marriages have to end? Does God sanction divorce for reasons of incompatibility or "Well, we just don't love each other anymore"?

Read Matthew 19:1-12 to see what Jesus thinks about marriage, commitment, and divorce.

CHAPTER **19** **DIVORCE AND MARRIAGE.** After Jesus
had finished saying these things, he left Galilee and
went southward to the region of Judea and into the
area east of the Jordan River. 2Vast crowds followed
him there, and he healed their sick.
3Some Pharisees came and tried to trap him with
this question: "Should a man be allowed to divorce
his wife for any reason?"
4"Haven't you read the Scriptures?" Jesus replied.
"They record that from the beginning 'God made

## GOD'S GENEROSITY ● ● ● • •

20:15 **This parable is a strong teaching about *grace*, God's generosity. We shouldn't begrudge those who turn to God in the last moments of life, because, in reality, *no one* deserves eternal life. Many people we don't expect to see in the kingdom may be there. The criminal who repented as he was dying (Luke 23:40-43) will be there, as well as the person who has believed and served God for many years. Do you resent God's gracious acceptance of the despised, the outcast, and the sinners who have turned to him for forgiveness? Are you ever jealous of what God has given to another person? Instead, focus on God's gracious benefits to you, and be thankful for what you have.**

them male and female.'* 5And he said, 'This explains
why a man leaves his father and mother and is joined
to his wife, and the two are united into one.'* 6Since
they are no longer two but one, let no one separate
them, for God has joined them together."
7"Then why did Moses say a man could merely
write an official letter of divorce and send her
away?"* they asked.
8Jesus replied, "Moses permitted divorce as a concession to your hard-hearted wickedness, but it was
not what God had originally intended. 9And I tell
you this, a man who divorces his wife and marries
another commits adultery—unless his wife has been
unfaithful.*"
10Jesus' disciples then said to him, "Then it is
better not to marry!"
11"Not everyone can accept this statement," Jesus
said. "Only those whom God helps. 12Some are born
as eunuchs, some have been made that way by
others, and some choose not to marry for the sake of
the Kingdom of Heaven. Let anyone who can, accept
this statement."
13Some children were brought to Jesus so he could
lay his hands on them and pray for them. The disciples told them not to bother him. 14But Jesus said,
"Let the children come to me. Don't stop them! For
the Kingdom of Heaven belongs to such as these."
15And he put his hands on their heads and blessed
them before he left.
16Someone came to Jesus with this question:
"Teacher,* what good things must I do to have eternal life?"
17"Why ask me about what is good?" Jesus replied. "Only God is good. But to answer your question, you can receive eternal life if you keep the
commandments."
18"Which ones?" the man asked.
And Jesus replied: "'Do not murder. Do not commit adultery. Do not steal. Do not testify falsely.
19Honor your father and mother. Love your neighbor
as yourself.'*"
20"I've obeyed all these commandments," the
young man replied. "What else must I do?"
21Jesus told him, "If you want to be perfect, go and
sell all you have and give the money to the poor, and
you will have treasure in heaven. Then come, follow

18:28 Greek *100 denarii.* A denarius was the equivalent of a full day's wage. 18:35 Greek *your brother.* 19:4 Gen 1:27; 5:2. 19:5 Gen 2:24. 19:7 Deut 24:1. 19:9 Some manuscripts add *And the man who marries a divorced woman commits adultery.* 19:16 Some manuscripts read *Good Teacher.* 19:18-19 Exod 20:12-16; Lev 19:18; Deut 5:16-20.

me." 22But when the young man heard this, he went
sadly away because he had many possessions.
23Then Jesus said to his disciples, "I tell you the
truth, it is very hard for a rich person to get into the
Kingdom of Heaven. 24I say it again—it is easier for
a camel to go through the eye of a needle than for a
rich person to enter the Kingdom of God!"
25The disciples were astounded. "Then who in the
world can be saved?" they asked.
26Jesus looked at them intently and said, "Humanly speaking, it is impossible. But with God
everything is possible."
27Then Peter said to him, "We've given up everything to follow you. What will we get out of it?"
28And Jesus replied, "I assure you that when I, the
Son of Man, sit upon my glorious throne in the
Kingdom,* you who have been my followers will
also sit on twelve thrones, judging the twelve tribes
of Israel. 29And everyone who has given up houses or
brothers or sisters or father or mother or children or
property, for my sake, will receive a hundred times as
much in return and will have eternal life. 30But many
who seem to be important now will be the least
important then, and those who are considered least
here will be the greatest then.*

CHAPTER **20** **A STORY ABOUT A VINEYARD.** "For the
Kingdom of Heaven is like the owner of an estate
who went out early one morning to hire workers for
his vineyard. 2He agreed to pay the normal daily
wage* and sent them out to work.
3"At nine o'clock in the morning he was passing
through the marketplace and saw some people
standing around doing nothing. 4So he hired them,
telling them he would pay them whatever was right
at the end of the day. 5At noon and again around
three o'clock he did the same thing. 6At five o'clock
that evening he was in town again and saw some
more people standing around. He asked them, 'Why
haven't you been working today?'
7"They replied, 'Because no one hired us.'
"The owner of the estate told them, 'Then go on
out and join the others in my vineyard.'
8"That evening he told the foreman to call the
workers in and pay them, beginning with the last
workers first. 9When those hired at five o'clock were
paid, each received a full day's wage. 10When those
hired earlier came to get their pay, they assumed they
would receive more. But they, too, were paid a day's
wage. 11When they received their pay, they protested,
12'Those people worked only one hour, and yet
you've paid them just as much as you paid us who
worked all day in the scorching heat.'
13"He answered one of them, 'Friend, I haven't
been unfair! Didn't you agree to work all day for the
usual wage? 14Take it and go. I wanted to pay this last
worker the same as you. 15Is it against the law for me
to do what I want with my money? Should you be
angry because I am kind?'
16"And so it is, that many who are first now will be
last then; and those who are last now will be first
then."
17As Jesus was on the way to Jerusalem, he took the
twelve disciples aside privately and told them what
was going to happen to him. 18"When we get to
Jerusalem," he said, "the Son of Man will be
betrayed to the leading priests and the teachers of
religious law. They will sentence him to die. 19Then
they will hand him over to the Romans to be
mocked, whipped, and crucified. But on the third
day he will be raised from the dead."
20Then the mother of James and John, the sons of
Zebedee, came to Jesus with her sons. She knelt
respectfully to ask a favor. 21"What is your request?"
he asked.
She replied, "In your Kingdom, will you let my
two sons sit in places of honor next to you, one at
your right and the other at your left?"
22But Jesus told them, "You don't know what you
are asking! Are you able to drink from the bitter cup
of sorrow I am about to drink?"
"Oh yes," they replied, "we are able!"
23"You will indeed drink from it," he told them.
"But I have no right to say who will sit on the thrones
next to mine. My Father has prepared those places
for the ones he has chosen."
24When the ten other disciples heard what James
and John had asked, they were indignant. 25But Jesus
called them together and said, "You know that in this
world kings are tyrants, and officials lord it over the
people beneath them. 26But among you it should be
quite different. Whoever wants to be a leader among
you must be your servant, 27and whoever wants to be
first must become your slave. 28For even I, the Son of
Man, came here not to be served but to serve others,
and to give my life as a ransom for many."
29As Jesus and the disciples left the city of Jericho,
a huge crowd followed behind. 30Two blind men
were sitting beside the road. When they heard that
Jesus was coming that way, they began shouting,
"Lord, Son of David, have mercy on us!" 31The
crowd told them to be quiet, but they only shouted
louder, "Lord, Son of David, have mercy on us!"
32Jesus stopped in the road and called, "What do
you want me to do for you?"
33"Lord," they said, "we want to see!" 34Jesus felt
sorry for them and touched their eyes. Instantly they
could see! Then they followed him.

CHAPTER **21** **JESUS RIDES INTO JERUSALEM.** As Jesus
and the disciples approached Jerusalem, they came to
the town of Bethphage on the Mount of Olives. Jesus

**LEADERS ● ● ● • •**

20:27 **Jesus' description of leadership: serve people, don't use them. Jesus served others and gave his life away. A real leader appreciates others and realizes he's not above any job. Does something need to be done? Take the initiative and do it like a faithful servant.**

**19:28** Greek *in the regeneration.* **19:30** Greek *But many who are first will be last; and the last, first.* **20:2** Greek *a denarius,* the payment for a full day's labor; also in 20:9, 10, 13.

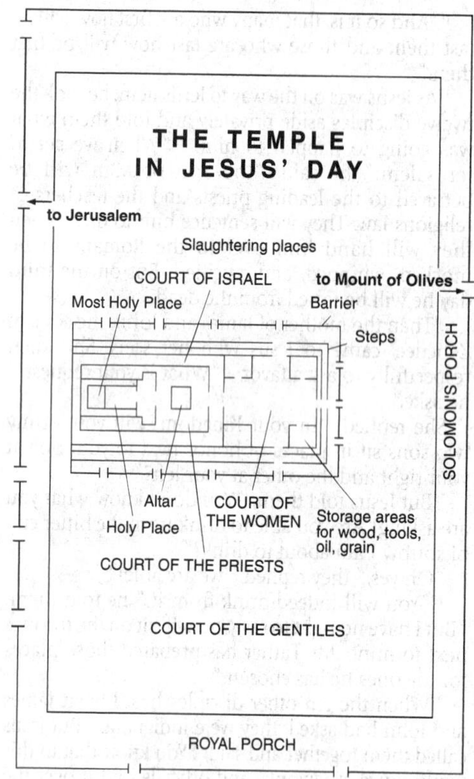


sent two of them on ahead. [2]"Go into the village over
there," he said, "and you will see a donkey tied there,
with its colt beside it. Untie them and bring them here.
[3]If anyone asks what you are doing, just say, 'The Lord
needs them,' and he will immediately send them."
[4]This was done to fulfill the prophecy,

[5] "Tell the people of Israel,*
'Look, your King is coming to you.
He is humble, riding on a donkey—
even on a donkey's colt.'"*

[6]The two disciples did as Jesus said. [7]They brought
the animals to him and threw their garments over
the colt, and he sat on it.*
[8]Most of the crowd spread their coats on the road
ahead of Jesus, and others cut branches from the
trees and spread them on the road. [9]He was in the
center of the procession, and the crowds all around
him were shouting,

"Praise God* for the Son of David!
Bless the one who comes in the name of the Lord!
Praise God in highest heaven!"*

[10]The entire city of Jerusalem was stirred as he
entered. "Who is this?" they asked.
[11]And the crowds replied, "It's Jesus, the prophet
from Nazareth in Galilee."
[12]Jesus entered the Temple and began to drive out
the merchants and their customers. He knocked over
the tables of the money changers and the stalls of
those selling doves. [13]He said, "The Scriptures declare, 'My Temple will be called a place of prayer,' but
you have turned it into a den of thieves!"*
[14]The blind and the lame came to him, and he
healed them there in the Temple. [15]The leading
priests and the teachers of religious law saw these
wonderful miracles and heard even the little children in the Temple shouting, "Praise God for the
Son of David." But they were indignant [16]and asked
Jesus, "Do you hear what these children are saying?"
"Yes," Jesus replied. "Haven't you ever read the
Scriptures? For they say, 'You have taught children
and infants to give you praise.'*" [17]Then he returned
to Bethany, where he stayed overnight.
[18]In the morning, as Jesus was returning to Jerusalem, he was hungry, [19]and he noticed a fig tree beside
the road. He went over to see if there were any figs
on it, but there were only leaves. Then he said to it,
"May you never bear fruit again!" And immediately
the fig tree withered up.
[20]The disciples were amazed when they saw this
and asked, "How did the fig tree wither so quickly?"
[21]Then Jesus told them, "I assure you, if you have
faith and don't doubt, you can do things like this
and much more. You can even say to this mountain,
'May God lift you up and throw you into the sea,'
and it will happen. [22]If you believe, you will receive
whatever you ask for in prayer."
[23]When Jesus returned to the Temple and began
teaching, the leading priests and other leaders came
up to him. They demanded, "By whose authority did
you drive out the merchants from the Temple?* Who
gave you such authority?"
[24]"I'll tell you who gave me the authority to do
these things if you answer one question," Jesus replied. [25]"Did John's baptism come from heaven or
was it merely human?"
They talked it over among themselves. "If we say
it was from heaven, he will ask why we didn't
believe him. [26]But if we say it was merely human,
we'll be mobbed, because the people think he was
a prophet." [27]So they finally replied, "We don't
know."

## BLANK CHECK ● ● • • •

21:22 **This is not a guarantee that we can get anything we want simply by asking Jesus. God does not grant requests that would hurt us or others, or that violate his own nature or will. Jesus' statement is not a blank check—our prayers must focus on the work of God's kingdom. Then we may go to him in peace and confidence, knowing he will respond to us in his love and wisdom.**

21:5a Greek *Tell the daughter of Zion.* Isa 62:11. **21:5b** Zech 9:9. **21:7** Greek *over them, and he sat on them.* 21:9a Greek *Hosanna,* an exclamation of praise that literally means "save now"; also in 21:9b, 15. **21:9b** Pss 118:25-26; 148:1. **21:13** Isa 56:7; Jer 7:11. **21:16** Ps 8:2. **21:23** Or *By whose authority do you do these things?*

And Jesus responded, "Then I won't answer your question either.

[28]"But what do you think about this? A man with two sons told the older boy, 'Son, go out and work in the vineyard today.' [29]The son answered, 'No, I won't go,' but later he changed his mind and went anyway. [30]Then the father told the other son, 'You go,' and he said, 'Yes, sir, I will.' But he didn't go. [31]Which of the two was obeying his father?"

They replied, "The first, of course."

Then Jesus explained his meaning: "I assure you, corrupt tax collectors and prostitutes will get into the Kingdom of God before you do. [32]For John the Baptist came and showed you the way to life, and you didn't believe him, while tax collectors and prostitutes did. And even when you saw this happening, you refused to turn from your sins and believe him.

[33]"Now listen to this story. A certain landowner planted a vineyard, built a wall around it, dug a pit for pressing out the grape juice, and built a lookout tower. Then he leased the vineyard to tenant farmers and moved to another country. [34]At the time of the grape harvest he sent his servants to collect his share of the crop. [35]But the farmers grabbed his servants, beat one, killed one, and stoned another. [36]So the landowner sent a larger group of his servants to collect for him, but the results were the same.

[37]"Finally, the owner sent his son, thinking, 'Surely they will respect my son.'

[38]"But when the farmers saw his son coming, they said to one another, 'Here comes the heir to this estate. Come on, let's kill him and get the estate for ourselves!' [39]So they grabbed him, took him out of the vineyard, and murdered him.

[40]"When the owner of the vineyard returns," Jesus asked, "what do you think he will do to those farmers?"

[41]The religious leaders replied, "He will put the wicked men to a horrible death and lease the vineyard to others who will give him his share of the crop after each harvest."

[42]Then Jesus asked them, "Didn't you ever read this in the Scriptures?

'The stone rejected by the builders
has now become the cornerstone.
This is the Lord's doing,
and it is marvelous to see.'*

[43]What I mean is that the Kingdom of God will be taken away from you and given to a nation that will produce the proper fruit. [44]Anyone who stumbles over that stone will be broken to pieces, and it will crush anyone on whom it falls.*"

[45]When the leading priests and Pharisees heard Jesus, they realized he was pointing at them—that they were the farmers in his story. [46]They wanted to arrest him, but they were afraid to try because the crowds considered Jesus to be a prophet.

**21:42** Ps 118:22-23. **21:44** This verse is omitted in some early manuscripts.

## FAKING IT ● ● • • •

21:30 **The son who said he would obey and then didn't represented the nation of Israel in Jesus' day. They said they wanted to do God's will, but they constantly disobeyed. It is dangerous to pretend to obey God when our heart is far from him, because God knows the intentions of our heart. God isn't fooled. He knows when our actions don't match our words.**

## CHAPTER 22

**A STORY ABOUT A WEDDING.** Jesus told them several other stories to illustrate the Kingdom. He said, [2]"The Kingdom of Heaven can be illustrated by the story of a king who prepared a great wedding feast for his son. [3]Many guests were invited, and when the banquet was ready, he sent his servants to notify everyone that it was time to come. But they all refused! [4]So he sent other servants to tell them, 'The feast has been prepared, and choice meats have been cooked. Everything is ready. Hurry!' [5]But the guests he had invited ignored them and went about their business, one to his farm, another to his store. [6]Others seized his messengers and treated them shamefully, even killing some of them.

[7]"Then the king became furious. He sent out his army to destroy the murderers and burn their city. [8]And he said to his servants, 'The wedding feast is ready, and the guests I invited aren't worthy of the honor. [9]Now go out to the street corners and invite everyone you see.'

## INVITED ● ● • • •

22:1-14 **In this culture, two invitations were expected when wedding dinners were given. The first invitation asked the guests to attend; the second announced that all was ready. Here the king, God, invited his guests three times—and each time they refused to come. God wants us to join him at his banquet, which will last for eternity. That's why he sends us invitations again and again. Have you accepted his invitation?**

[10]"So the servants brought in everyone they could find, good and bad alike, and the banquet hall was filled with guests. [11]But when the king came in to meet the guests, he noticed a man who wasn't wearing the proper clothes for a wedding. [12]'Friend,' he asked, 'how is it that you are here without wedding clothes?' And the man had no reply. [13]Then the king said to his aides, 'Bind him hand and foot and throw him out into the outer darkness, where there is weeping and gnashing of teeth.' [14]For many are called, but few are chosen."

[15]Then the Pharisees met together to think of a way to trap Jesus into saying something for which they could accuse him. [16]They decided to send some of their disciples, along with the supporters of Herod, to ask him this question: "Teacher, we know how honest you are. You teach about the way of God regardless of the consequences. You are impartial and don't play favorites. [17]Now tell us what you

## HEAVEN ● ● • • •

22:29 **The Sadducees asked Jesus what marriage would be like in eternity. Jesus said it was more important to understand God's power than know what heaven will be like. In every generation and culture, views about heaven or eternal life tend to be based upon images and experiences of present life. Jesus said these faulty views are caused by ignorance of God's Word. We must not make up our own ideas about eternity by trying to put it and God into human terms. We should concentrate more on our relationship with God than about what heaven will look like. Eventually we will find out, and it will be far beyond our greatest expectations.**

think about this: Is it right to pay taxes to the Roman government or not?"

18But Jesus knew their evil motives. "You hypocrites!" he said. "Whom are you trying to fool with your trick questions? 19Here, show me the Roman coin used for the tax." When they handed him the coin,* 20he asked, "Whose picture and title are stamped on it?"

21"Caesar's," they replied.

"Well, then," he said, "give to Caesar what belongs to him. But everything that belongs to God must be given to God." 22His reply amazed them, and they went away.

23That same day some Sadducees stepped forward—a group of Jews who say there is no resurrection after death. They posed this question: 24"Teacher, Moses said, 'If a man dies without children, his brother should marry the widow and have a child who will be the brother's heir.'* 25Well, there were seven brothers. The oldest married and then died without children, so the second brother married the widow. 26This brother also died without children, and the wife was married to the next brother, and so on until she had been the wife of each of them. 27And then she also died. 28So tell us, whose wife will she be in the resurrection? For she was the wife of all seven of them!"

29Jesus replied, "Your problem is that you don't know the Scriptures, and you don't know the power of God. 30For when the dead rise, they won't be married. They will be like the angels in heaven. 31But now, as to whether there will be a resurrection of the dead—haven't you ever read about this in the Scriptures? Long after Abraham, Isaac, and Jacob had died, God said,* 32'I am the God of Abraham, the God of Isaac, and the God of Jacob.'* So he is the God of the living, not the dead."

33When the crowds heard him, they were impressed with his teaching.

34But when the Pharisees heard that he had silenced the Sadducees with his reply, they thought up a fresh question of their own to ask him. 35One of them, an expert in religious law, tried to trap him with this question: 36"Teacher, which is the most important commandment in the law of Moses?"

37Jesus replied, "'You must love the Lord your God with all your heart, all your soul, and all your mind.'* 38This is the first and greatest commandment. 39A second is equally important: 'Love your neighbor as yourself.'* 40All the other commandments and all the demands of the prophets are based on these two commandments."

41Then, surrounded by the Pharisees, Jesus asked them a question: 42"What do you think about the Messiah? Whose son is he?"

They replied, "He is the son of David."

43Jesus responded, "Then why does David, speaking under the inspiration of the Holy Spirit, call him Lord? For David said,

44'The LORD said to my Lord,
Sit in honor at my right hand
until I humble your enemies beneath your feet.'*

45Since David called him Lord, how can he be his son at the same time?"

46No one could answer him. And after that, no one dared to ask him any more questions.

## CHAPTER 23

**JESUS WARNS THE PEOPLE.** Then Jesus said to the crowds and to his disciples, 2"The teachers of religious law and the Pharisees are the official interpreters of the Scriptures. 3So practice and obey whatever they say to you, but don't follow their example. For they don't practice what they teach. 4They crush you with impossible religious demands and never lift a finger to help ease the burden.

5"Everything they do is for show. On their arms they wear extra wide prayer boxes with Scripture verses inside,* and they wear extra long tassels on their robes. 6And how they love to sit at the head table at banquets and in the most prominent seats in the synagogue! 7They enjoy the attention they get on the streets, and they enjoy being called 'Rabbi.'* 8Don't ever let anyone call you 'Rabbi,' for you have only one teacher, and all of you are on the same level as brothers and sisters.* 9And don't address anyone here on earth as 'Father,' for only God in heaven is your spiritual Father. 10And don't let anyone call you 'Master,' for there is only one master, the Messiah. 11The greatest among you must be a servant. 12But those who exalt themselves will be humbled, and those who humble themselves will be exalted.

13"How terrible it will be for you teachers of religious law and you Pharisees. Hypocrites! For you won't let others enter the Kingdom of Heaven, and

## INSIDE ● ● • • •

23:25-28 **Jesus condemned the Pharisees and religious leaders for appearing saintly and holy but remaining full of corruption and greed on the inside. Living our Christianity merely as a show for others is like washing a cup on the outside only. When we are clean on the inside, our cleanliness on the outside won't be phony.**

22:19 Greek *a denarius.* 22:24 Deut 25:5-6. 22:31 Greek *in the Scriptures? God said.* 22:32 Exod 3:6. 22:37 Deut 6:5. 22:39 Lev 19:18. 22:44 Ps 110:1. 23:5 Greek *They enlarge their phylacteries.* 23:7 *Rabbi,* from Aramaic, means "master" or "teacher." 23:8 Greek *brothers.*

you won't go in yourselves.* [15]Yes, how terrible it will be for you teachers of religious law and you Pharisees. For you cross land and sea to make one convert, and then you turn him into twice the son of hell as you yourselves are.

[16]"Blind guides! How terrible it will be for you! For you say that it means nothing to swear 'by God's Temple'—you can break that oath. But then you say that it is binding to swear 'by the gold in the Temple.' [17]Blind fools! Which is greater, the gold, or the Temple that makes the gold sacred? [18]And you say that to take an oath 'by the altar' can be broken, but to swear 'by the gifts on the altar' is binding! [19]How blind! For which is greater, the gift on the altar, or the altar that makes the gift sacred? [20]When you swear 'by the altar,' you are swearing by it and by everything on it. [21]And when you swear 'by the Temple,' you are swearing by it and by God, who lives in it. [22]And when you swear 'by heaven,' you are swearing by the throne of God and by God, who sits on the throne.

[23]"How terrible it will be for you teachers of religious law and you Pharisees. Hypocrites! For you are careful to tithe even the tiniest part of your income,* but you ignore the important things of the law—justice, mercy, and faith. You should tithe, yes, but you should not leave undone the more important things. [24]Blind guides! You strain your water so you won't accidentally swallow a gnat; then you swallow a camel!

[25]"How terrible it will be for you teachers of religious law and you Pharisees. Hypocrites! You are so careful to clean the outside of the cup and the dish, but inside you are filthy—full of greed and self-indulgence! [26]Blind Pharisees! First wash the inside of the cup, and then the outside will become clean, too.

[27]"How terrible it will be for you teachers of religious law and you Pharisees. Hypocrites! You are like whitewashed tombs—beautiful on the outside but filled on the inside with dead people's bones and all sorts of impurity. [28]You try to look like upright people outwardly, but inside your hearts are filled with hypocrisy and lawlessness.

[29]"How terrible it will be for you teachers of religious law and you Pharisees. Hypocrites! For you build tombs for the prophets your ancestors killed and decorate the graves of the godly people your ancestors destroyed. [30]Then you say, 'We never would have joined them in killing the prophets.'

[31]"In saying that, you are accusing yourselves of being the descendants of those who murdered the prophets. [32]Go ahead. Finish what they started. [33]Snakes! Sons of vipers! How will you escape the judgment of hell? [34]I will send you prophets and wise men and teachers of religious law. You will kill some by crucifixion and whip others in your synagogues, chasing them from city to city. [35]As a result, you will become guilty of murdering all the godly people from righteous Abel to Zechariah son of Barachiah, whom you murdered in the Temple between the altar and the sanctuary. [36]I assure you, all the accumulated judgment of the centuries will break upon the heads of this very generation.

[37]"O Jerusalem, Jerusalem, the city that kills the prophets and stones God's messengers! How often I have wanted to gather your children together as a hen protects her chicks beneath her wings, but you wouldn't let me. [38]And now look, your house is left to you, empty and desolate. [39]For I tell you this, you will never see me again until you say, 'Bless the one who comes in the name of the Lord!'*"

## CHAPTER 24 **JESUS TELLS ABOUT THE FUTURE.**

As Jesus was leaving the Temple grounds, his disciples pointed out to him the various Temple buildings. [2]But he told them, "Do you see all these buildings? I assure you, they will be so completely demolished that not one stone will be left on top of another!"

[3]Later, Jesus sat on the slopes of the Mount of Olives. His disciples came to him privately and asked, "When will all this take place? And will there be any sign ahead of time to signal your return and the end of the world*?"

[4]Jesus told them, "Don't let anyone mislead you. [5]For many will come in my name, saying, 'I am the Messiah.' They will lead many astray. [6]And wars will break out near and far, but don't panic. Yes, these things must come, but the end won't follow immediately. [7]The nations and kingdoms will proclaim war against each other, and there will be famines and earthquakes in many parts of the world. [8]But all this will be only the beginning of the horrors to come.

### FRAUDS ● ● ● • •

**24:11 The Old Testament frequently mentions false prophets (see 2 Kings 3:13; Isaiah 44:25; Jeremiah 23:16; Ezekiel 13:2-3; Micah 3:5; Zechariah 13:2). False prophets were people who claimed to receive messages from God but preached a "health and wealth" message. They told the people what they wanted to hear, even when the nation was not following God as it should. We have false prophets today, too—popular leaders who spout a false gospel, telling people what they want to hear: "God wants you to be rich." "Do whatever your desires tell you." Or, "There is no such thing as sin or hell." Jesus said false teachers would come, and he warned his disciples—as he warns us—not to listen to their dangerous words.**

[9]"Then you will be arrested, persecuted, and killed. You will be hated all over the world because of your allegiance to me. [10]And many will turn away from me and betray and hate each other. [11]And many false prophets will appear and will lead many people astray. [12]Sin will be rampant everywhere, and the love of many will grow cold. [13]But those who endure to the end will be saved. [14]And the Good News about the Kingdom will be preached throughout the whole

**23:13** Some manuscripts add verse 14, *How terrible it will be for you teachers of religious law and you Pharisees. Hypocrites! You shamelessly cheat widows out of their property, and then, to cover up the kind of people you really are, you make long prayers in public. Because of this, your punishment will be the greater.* **23:23** Greek *to tithe the mint, the dill, and the cumin.* **23:39** Ps 118:26. **24:3** Or *the age.*

world, so that all nations will hear it; and then, finally, the end will come.

15 "The time will come when you will see what Daniel the prophet spoke about: the sacrilegious object that causes desecration* standing in the Holy Place"—reader, pay attention! 16 "Then those in Judea must flee to the hills. 17 A person outside the house* must not go inside to pack. 18 A person in the field must not return even to get a coat. 19 How terrible it will be for pregnant women and for mothers nursing their babies in those days. 20 And pray that your flight will not be in winter or on the Sabbath. 21 For that will be a time of greater horror than anything the world has ever seen or will ever see again. 22 In fact, unless that time of calamity is shortened, the entire human race will be destroyed. But it will be shortened for the sake of God's chosen ones.

23 "Then if anyone tells you, 'Look, here is the Messiah,' or 'There he is,' don't pay any attention. 24 For false messiahs and false prophets will rise up and perform great miraculous signs and wonders so as to deceive, if possible, even God's chosen ones. 25 See, I have warned you.

26 "So if someone tells you, 'Look, the Messiah is out in the desert,' don't bother to go and look. Or, 'Look, he is hiding here,' don't believe it! 27 For as the lightning lights up the entire sky, so it will be when the Son of Man comes. 28 Just as the gathering of vultures shows there is a carcass nearby, so these signs indicate that the end is near.*

29 "Immediately after those horrible days end,

the sun will be darkened,
    the moon will not give light,
the stars will fall from the sky,
    and the powers of heaven will be shaken.*

30 And then at last, the sign of the coming of the Son of Man will appear in the heavens, and there will be deep mourning among all the nations of the earth. And they will see the Son of Man arrive on the clouds of heaven with power and great glory.* 31 And he will send forth his angels with the sound of a mighty trumpet blast, and they will gather together his chosen ones from the farthest ends of the earth and heaven.

32 "Now learn a lesson from the fig tree. When its buds become tender and its leaves begin to sprout, you know without being told that summer is near. 33 Just so, when you see the events I've described beginning to happen, you can know his return is very near, right at the door. 34 I assure you, this generation* will not pass from the scene before all these things take place. 35 Heaven and earth will disappear, but my words will remain forever.

36 "However, no one knows the day or the hour when these things will happen, not even the angels in heaven or the Son himself.* Only the Father knows.

## INVESTING ● ● ● • •

25:15 **The master divided the money (called "talents" in some Bible versions) among his servants according to their abilities—no one received more or less money than he could handle. If he failed in his master's assignment, his excuse could not be that he was overwhelmed. Failure could come only from laziness or hatred for the master. The money in this story represents any kind of resource we are given. God gives us time, abilities, and other resources that he expects us to invest wisely until he returns. We are responsible to use well what God has given us. The issue is not how much we have, but what we do with what we have.**

37 "When the Son of Man returns, it will be like it was in Noah's day. 38 In those days before the Flood, the people were enjoying banquets and parties and weddings right up to the time Noah entered his boat. 39 People didn't realize what was going to happen until the Flood came and swept them all away. That is the way it will be when the Son of Man comes.

40 "Two men will be working together in the field; one will be taken, the other left. 41 Two women will be grinding flour at the mill; one will be taken, the other left. 42 So be prepared, because you don't know what day your Lord is coming.

43 "Know this: A homeowner who knew exactly when a burglar was coming would stay alert and not permit the house to be broken into. 44 You also must be ready all the time. For the Son of Man will come when least expected.

45 "Who is a faithful, sensible servant, to whom the master can give the responsibility of managing his household and feeding his family? 46 If the master returns and finds that the servant has done a good job, there will be a reward. 47 I assure you, the master will put that servant in charge of all he owns. 48 But if the servant is evil and thinks, 'My master won't be back for a while,' 49 and begins oppressing the other servants, partying, and getting drunk—50 well, the master will return unannounced and unexpected. 51 He will tear the servant apart and banish him with the hypocrites. In that place there will be weeping and gnashing of teeth.

## CHAPTER 25 A STORY ABOUT TEN BRIDESMAIDS.

"The Kingdom of Heaven can be illustrated by the story of ten bridesmaids* who took their lamps and went to meet the bridegroom. 2 Five of them were foolish, and five were wise. 3 The five who were foolish took no oil for their lamps, 4 but the other five were wise enough to take along extra oil. 5 When the bridegroom was delayed, they all lay down and slept. 6 At midnight they were roused by the shout, 'Look, the bridegroom is coming! Come out and welcome him!'

7 "All the bridesmaids got up and prepared their lamps. 8 Then the five foolish ones asked the others, 'Please give us some of your oil because our lamps are going out.' 9 But the others replied, 'We don't

24:15 Greek *the abomination of desolation.* See Dan 9:27; 11:31; 12:11. 24:17 Greek *on the roof.* 24:28 Greek *Wherever the carcass is, the vultures gather.* 24:29 See Isa 13:10; 34:4; Joel 2:10. 24:30 See Dan 7:13. 24:34 Or *this age,* or *this nation.* 24:36 Some manuscripts omit the phrase *or the Son himself.* 25:1 Or *virgins;* also in 25:7, 11.

have enough for all of us. Go to a shop and buy some for yourselves.'

10"But while they were gone to buy oil, the bridegroom came, and those who were ready went in with him to the marriage feast, and the door was locked. 11Later, when the other five bridesmaids returned, they stood outside, calling, 'Sir, open the door for us!' 12But he called back, 'I don't know you!'

13"So stay awake and be prepared, because you do not know the day or hour of my return.

14"Again, the Kingdom of Heaven can be illustrated by the story of a man going on a trip. He called together his servants and gave them money to invest for him while he was gone. 15He gave five bags of gold* to one, two bags of gold to another, and one bag of gold to the last—dividing it in proportion to their abilities—and then left on his trip. 16The servant who received the five bags of gold began immediately to invest the money and soon doubled it. 17The servant with two bags of gold also went right to work and doubled the money. 18But the servant who received the one bag of gold dug a hole in the ground and hid the master's money for safekeeping.

19"After a long time their master returned from his trip and called them to give an account of how they had used his money. 20The servant to whom he had entrusted the five bags of gold said, 'Sir, you gave me five bags of gold to invest, and I have doubled the amount.' 21The master was full of praise. 'Well done, my good and faithful servant. You have been faithful in handling this small amount, so now I will give you many more responsibilities. Let's celebrate together!'

22"Next came the servant who had received the two bags of gold, with the report, 'Sir, you gave me two bags of gold to invest, and I have doubled the amount.' 23The master said, 'Well done, my good and faithful servant. You have been faithful in handling this small amount, so now I will give you many more responsibilities. Let's celebrate together!'

24"Then the servant with the one bag of gold came and said, 'Sir, I know you are a hard man, harvesting crops you didn't plant and gathering crops you didn't cultivate. 25I was afraid I would lose your money, so I hid it in the earth and here it is.'

26"But the master replied, 'You wicked and lazy servant! You think I'm a hard man, do you, harvesting crops I didn't plant and gathering crops I didn't cultivate? 27Well, you should at least have put my money into the bank so I could have some interest. 28Take the money from this servant and give it to the one with the ten bags of gold. 29To those who use well what they are given, even more will be given, and they will have an abundance. But from those who are unfaithful,* even what little they have will be taken away. 30Now throw this useless servant into outer darkness, where there will be weeping and gnashing of teeth.'

31"But when the Son of Man comes in his glory, and all the angels with him, then he will sit upon his glorious throne. 32All the nations will be gathered in his presence, and he will separate them as a shepherd separates the sheep from the goats. 33He will place the sheep at his right hand and the goats at his left. 34Then the King will say to those on the right, 'Come, you who are blessed by my Father, inherit the Kingdom prepared for you from the foundation of the world. 35For I was hungry, and you fed me. I was thirsty, and you gave me a drink. I was a stranger, and you invited me into your home. 36I was naked, and you gave me clothing. I was sick, and you cared for me. I was in prison, and you visited me.'

## TOUGH TASK ● ● • • •

**25:31-46 God will separate his obedient followers from pretenders and unbelievers. The real evidence of our belief is the way we act. To treat all persons we encounter as if they are Jesus is no easy task. What we do for others demonstrates what we really think about Jesus' words to us–feed the hungry, give the homeless a place to stay, visit the sick. How well do your actions separate you from pretenders and unbelievers?**

37"Then these righteous ones will reply, 'Lord, when did we ever see you hungry and feed you? Or thirsty and give you something to drink? 38Or a stranger and show you hospitality? Or naked and give you clothing? 39When did we ever see you sick or in prison, and visit you?' 40And the King will tell them, 'I assure you, when you did it to one of the least of these my brothers and sisters,* you were doing it to me!'

41"Then the King will turn to those on the left and say, 'Away with you, you cursed ones, into the eternal fire prepared for the Devil and his demons! 42For I was hungry, and you didn't feed me. I was thirsty, and you didn't give me anything to drink. 43I was a stranger, and you didn't invite me into your home. I was naked, and you gave me no clothing. I was sick and in prison, and you didn't visit me.'

44"Then they will reply, 'Lord, when did we ever see you hungry or thirsty or a stranger or naked or sick or in prison, and not help you?' 45And he will answer, 'I assure you, when you refused to help the least of these my brothers and sisters, you were refusing to help me.' 46And they will go away into eternal punishment, but the righteous will go into eternal life."

## CHAPTER 26

**THE LAST SUPPER.** When Jesus had finished saying these things, he said to his disciples, 2"As you know, the Passover celebration begins in two days, and I, the Son of Man, will be betrayed and crucified."

3At that same time the leading priests and other leaders were meeting at the residence of Caiaphas, the high priest, 4to discuss how to capture Jesus secretly and put him to death. 5"But not during the Passover," they agreed, "or there will be a riot."

**25:15** Greek *talents;* also throughout the story. A talent is equal to 75 pounds or 34 kilograms. **25:29** Or *who have nothing.* **25:40** Greek *my brothers.*

6Meanwhile, Jesus was in Bethany at the home of Simon, a man who had leprosy. 7During supper, a woman came in with a beautiful jar* of expensive perfume and poured it over his head. 8The disciples were indignant when they saw this. "What a waste of money," they said. 9"She could have sold it for a fortune and given the money to the poor."

10But Jesus replied, "Why berate her for doing such a good thing to me? 11You will always have the poor among you, but I will not be here with you much longer. 12She has poured this perfume on me to prepare my body for burial. 13I assure you, wherever the Good News is preached throughout the world, this woman's deed will be talked about in her memory."

14Then Judas Iscariot, one of the twelve disciples, went to the leading priests 15and asked, "How much will you pay me to betray Jesus to you?" And they gave him thirty pieces of silver. 16From that time on, Judas began looking for the right time and place to betray Jesus.

17On the first day of the Festival of Unleavened Bread, the disciples came to Jesus and asked, "Where do you want us to prepare the Passover supper?"

18"As you go into the city," he told them, "you will see a certain man. Tell him, 'The Teacher says, My time has come, and I will eat the Passover meal with my disciples at your house.'" 19So the disciples did as Jesus told them and prepared the Passover supper there.

20When it was evening, Jesus sat down at the table with the twelve disciples. 21While they were eating, he said, "The truth is, one of you will betray me."

22Greatly distressed, one by one they began to ask him, "I'm not the one, am I, Lord?"

23He replied, "One of you who is eating with me now* will betray me. 24For I, the Son of Man, must die, as the Scriptures declared long ago. But how terrible it will be for my betrayer. Far better for him if he had never been born!"

25Judas, the one who would betray him, also asked, "Teacher, I'm not the one, am I?"

And Jesus told him, "You have said it yourself."

26As they were eating, Jesus took a loaf of bread and asked God's blessing on it. Then he broke it in pieces and gave it to the disciples, saying, "Take it and eat it, for this is my body." 27And he took a cup of wine and gave thanks to God for it. He gave it to them and said, "Each of you drink from it, 28for this is my blood, which seals the covenant* between God and his people. It is poured out to forgive the sins of many. 29Mark my words—I will not drink wine again until the day I drink it new with you in my Father's Kingdom." 30Then they sang a hymn and went out to the Mount of Olives.

31"Tonight all of you will desert me," Jesus told them. "For the Scriptures say,

'God* will strike the Shepherd,
  and the sheep of the flock will be scattered.'*

32But after I have been raised from the dead, I will go ahead of you to Galilee and meet you there."

33Peter declared, "Even if everyone else deserts you, I never will."

34"Peter," Jesus replied, "the truth is, this very night, before the rooster crows, you will deny me three times."

35"No!" Peter insisted. "Not even if I have to die with you! I will never deny you!" And all the other disciples vowed the same.

36Then Jesus brought them to an olive grove called Gethsemane, and he said, "Sit here while I go on ahead to pray." 37He took Peter and Zebedee's two sons, James and John, and he began to be filled with anguish and deep distress. 38He told them, "My soul is crushed with grief to the point of death. Stay here and watch with me."

39He went on a little farther and fell face down on the ground, praying, "My Father! If it is possible, let this cup of suffering be taken away from me. Yet I want your will, not mine." 40Then he returned to the disciples and found them asleep. He said to Peter, "Couldn't you stay awake and watch with me even one hour? 41Keep alert and pray. Otherwise temptation will overpower you. For though the spirit is willing enough, the body is weak!"

## ALERT ● ● ● ● ●

26:40 **Jesus used Peter's drowsiness to warn him about the kinds of temptation he would soon face. The way to overcome temptation is to be alert to it and pray. Being alert involves being aware of the possibilities of temptation, sensitive to the subtleties, and spiritually equipped to fight it. Because temptation strikes where we are most vulnerable, we can't resist it alone. Prayer is essential because God's strength can shore up our defenses and defeat Satan's power.**

42Again he left them and prayed, "My Father! If this cup cannot be taken away until I drink it, your will be done." 43He returned to them again and found them sleeping, for they just couldn't keep their eyes open.

44So he went back to pray a third time, saying the same things again. 45Then he came to the disciples and said, "Still sleeping? Still resting?* Look, the time has come. I, the Son of Man, am betrayed into the hands of sinners. 46Up, let's be going. See, my betrayer is here!"

47And even as he said this, Judas, one of the twelve disciples, arrived with a mob that was armed with swords and clubs. They had been sent out by the leading priests and other leaders of the people. 48Judas had given them a prearranged signal: "You will know which one to arrest when I go over and give him the kiss of greeting." 49So Judas came straight to Jesus. "Greetings, Teacher!" he exclaimed and gave him the kiss.

50Jesus said, "My friend, go ahead and do what

26:7 Greek *an alabaster jar.* 26:23 Or *The one who has dipped his hand in the bowl with me.* 26:28 Some manuscripts read *the new covenant.* 26:31a Greek *I.* 26:31b Zech 13:7. 26:45 Or *Sleep on, take your rest.*

you have come for." Then the others grabbed Jesus
and arrested him. 51One of the men with Jesus pulled
out a sword and slashed off an ear of the high priest's
servant.

52"Put away your sword," Jesus told him. "Those
who use the sword will be killed by the sword.
53Don't you realize that I could ask my Father for
thousands* of angels to protect us, and he would
send them instantly? 54But if I did, how would the
Scriptures be fulfilled that describe what must happen now?"

55Then Jesus said to the crowd, "Am I some dangerous criminal, that you have come armed with
swords and clubs to arrest me? Why didn't you arrest
me in the Temple? I was there teaching every day.
56But this is all happening to fulfill the words of the
prophets as recorded in the Scriptures." At that
point, all the disciples deserted him and fled.

57Then the people who had arrested Jesus led him
to the home of Caiaphas, the high priest, where the
teachers of religious law and other leaders had gathered. 58Meanwhile, Peter was following far behind
and eventually came to the courtyard of the high
priest's house. He went in, sat with the guards, and
waited to see what was going to happen to Jesus.

59Inside, the leading priests and the entire high
council* were trying to find witnesses who would lie
about Jesus, so they could put him to death. 60But
even though they found many who agreed to give
false witness, there was no testimony they could use.
Finally, two men were found 61who declared, "This
man said, 'I am able to destroy the Temple of God
and rebuild it in three days.'"

62Then the high priest stood up and said to Jesus,
"Well, aren't you going to answer these charges?
What do you have to say for yourself?" 63But Jesus
remained silent. Then the high priest said to him, "I
demand in the name of the living God that you tell
us whether you are the Messiah, the Son of God."

64Jesus replied, "Yes, it is as you say. And in the
future you will see me, the Son of Man, sitting at
God's right hand in the place of power and coming
back on the clouds of heaven."*

65Then the high priest tore his clothing to show
his horror, shouting, "Blasphemy! Why do we need
other witnesses? You have all heard his blasphemy.
66What is your verdict?"

"Guilty!" they shouted. "He must die!"

67Then they spit in Jesus' face and hit him with
their fists. And some slapped him, 68saying, "Prophesy to us, you Messiah! Who hit you that time?"

69Meanwhile, as Peter was sitting outside in the
courtyard, a servant girl came over and said to him,
"You were one of those with Jesus the Galilean."

70But Peter denied it in front of everyone. "I don't
know what you are talking about," he said.

71Later, out by the gate, another servant girl noticed him and said to those standing around, "This
man was with Jesus of Nazareth."

## DENIAL ● ● ● • •

**26:69-75 There were three stages to Peter's denial. First, he acted confused and said he didn't know what the girl was talking about. Second, using an oath he denied that he knew Jesus. Third, he began to curse and swear. Believers who deny Christ often begin doing so subtly by pretending not to know him. When opportunities to discuss religious issues come up, they walk away or pretend they don't know the answers. With only a little more pressure, they can be induced to flatly deny their relationship with Christ. If you find yourself subtly avoiding occasions to talk about Christ, watch out. You may be on the road to denying him.**

72Again Peter denied it, this time with an oath. "I
don't even know the man," he said.

73A little later some other bystanders came over to
him and said, "You must be one of them; we can tell
by your Galilean accent."

74Peter said, "I swear by God, I don't know the
man." And immediately the rooster crowed. 75Suddenly, Jesus' words flashed through Peter's mind:
"Before the rooster crows, you will deny me three
times." And he went away, crying bitterly.

## CHAPTER 27 **JUDAS HANGS HIMSELF.**

Very early in
the morning, the leading priests and other leaders
met again to discuss how to persuade the Roman
government to sentence Jesus to death. 2Then they
bound him and took him to Pilate, the Roman governor.

3When Judas, who had betrayed him, realized that
Jesus had been condemned to die, he was filled with
remorse. So he took the thirty pieces of silver back to
the leading priests and other leaders. 4"I have
sinned," he declared, "for I have betrayed an innocent man."

"What do we care?" they retorted. "That's your
problem." 5Then Judas threw the money onto the
floor of the Temple and went out and hanged himself. 6The leading priests picked up the money. "We
can't put it in the Temple treasury," they said, "since
it's against the law to accept money paid for murder." 7After some discussion they finally decided to
buy the potter's field, and they made it into a cemetery for foreigners. 8That is why the field is still called
the Field of Blood. 9This fulfilled the prophecy of
Jeremiah that says,

"They took* the thirty pieces of silver—
the price at which he was valued by the
people of Israel—
10 and purchased the potter's field,
as the Lord directed.*"

11Now Jesus was standing before Pilate, the Roman
governor. "Are you the King of the Jews?" the governor asked him.

Jesus replied, "Yes, it is as you say."

12But when the leading priests and other leaders
made their accusations against him, Jesus remained

**26:53** Greek *12 legions.* **26:59** Greek *the Sanhedrin.* **26:64** See Ps 110:1; Dan 7:13. **27:9** Or *I took.* **27:9-10** Greek *as the Lord directed me.* Zech 11:12-13; Jer 32:6-9.

# Ultimate Issues

## THE RESURRECTION

August 2, 1492, was a dark day for the Jewish people in Spain. For political and social reasons, they were expelled from the country. Setting sail from Cadiz, they were scattered all over the area of Europe known as the Levant. The Jews, or part of them, were once again in exile. However, something was to happen the day after they set sail that would change the course of the Jewish nation and, for that matter, the course of history. **On** AUGUST 3, 1492, Christopher Columbus and his men set sail for the West, not knowing what they would find. They hoped to establish a new trade route to the Far East; instead, they discovered the New World! This New World would give birth to dozens of new nations. One of them, the United States of America, would become the promised land for persecuted and oppressed people from all over the planet—including millions of Jews. **Often**, when life seems bleak and hopeless, something happens that puts things in a new perspective. It happened with the Jews, and it happened at the death of Jesus of Nazareth. **Imagine** what must have been going through the disciples' minds as they witnessed (or heard about) the crucifixion of their Master. All their hopes and expectations — LIFELESS AS THE CORPSE that Joseph of Arimathea took away and laid in his tomb. Dead! Broken and crushed . . . along with the dreams of the Twelve and many others who had truly believed that Jesus was the Messiah who would lead Israel to freedom. And now he lay rotting in a tomb. **If** that were the end of the story, you would never have heard of Jesus or Christianity. Jesus' followers would have disappeared like the followers of dozens of other **would-be Messiahs.** If that were the end, you wouldn't be holding this book in your hands, reading it as countless millions of others have, basing your life on its principles. There would be no churches; no trace of what has been the founding faith of the New World that Columbus discovered. But Jesus' death was not the end. It was only the beginning. **You** probably are familiar with the story of the resurrection. The bare facts are that Jesus was put to death by crucifixion; that his body was placed in a borrowed tomb; that Jesus' followers were scattered and dejected. But, as Matthew 28 tells us, Jesus didn't stay dead. On the Sunday morning following his death, some strange events took place around his grave. **THE STRANGEST OF ALL** is that Jesus rose from the dead! **We** have a tendency to take the resurrection story for granted—after all, we may have heard it dozens or even hundreds of times. But we need to remember that people didn't vacate their graveyards 2,000 years ago in Palestine any more than they do today. Dead people stayed dead back then, just like they do now. With one major exception. **And** that exception, the resurrection of Jesus, has made all the difference in eternity for countless Christians. When the early Christians, including the disciples, were called upon to defend their faith in Jesus as Messiah, they didn't point to his great moral teachings and ethical principles. They didn't even refer to his miracles. They pointed to one rock-solid proof: his death and resurrection. If anyone had ever shown that it was science fiction—perhaps by getting one of the disciples to confess that it was a lie, or going to the tomb and showing that Jesus' body was still there—Christianity would have fizzled out on the spot. It hasn't fizzled out yet, and it never will, for the same reason: ***Jesus Christ rose from the dead.*** **Because** Jesus really came back from death, it stands to reason that the rest of what he told us is true: that he is the way to the Father, that anyone who puts his or her faith in Christ can live forever with him in heaven; and that no matter how dark it looks right now, he will conduct us safely to the Promised Land.

silent. 13"Don't you hear their many charges against
you?" Pilate demanded. 14But Jesus said nothing,
much to the governor's great surprise.
15Now it was the governor's custom to release one
prisoner to the crowd each year during the Passover
celebration—anyone they wanted. 16This year there
was a notorious criminal in prison, a man named
Barabbas.* 17As the crowds gathered before Pilate's
house that morning, he asked them, "Which one do
you want me to release to you—Barabbas, or Jesus
who is called the Messiah?" 18(He knew very well
that the Jewish leaders had arrested Jesus out of
envy.)
19Just then, as Pilate was sitting on the judgment
seat, his wife sent him this message: "Leave that
innocent man alone, because I had a terrible nightmare about him last night."
20Meanwhile, the leading priests and other leaders
persuaded the crowds to ask for Barabbas to be
released and for Jesus to be put to death. 21So when
the governor asked again, "Which of these two do
you want me to release to you?" the crowd shouted
back their reply: "Barabbas!"
22"But if I release Barabbas," Pilate asked them,
"what should I do with Jesus who is called the
Messiah?"
And they all shouted, "Crucify him!"
23"Why?" Pilate demanded. "What crime has he
committed?"
But the crowd only roared the louder, "Crucify
him!"
24Pilate saw that he wasn't getting anywhere and
that a riot was developing. So he sent for a bowl of
water and washed his hands before the crowd, saying, "I am innocent of the blood of this man. The
responsibility is yours!"
25And all the people yelled back, "We will take
responsibility for his death—we and our children!"*
26So Pilate released Barabbas to them. He ordered
Jesus flogged with a lead-tipped whip, then turned
him over to the Roman soldiers to crucify him.
27Some of the governor's soldiers took Jesus into
their headquarters and called out the entire battalion. 28They stripped him and put a scarlet robe on
him. 29They made a crown of long, sharp thorns and
put it on his head, and they placed a stick in his right
hand as a scepter. Then they knelt before him in
mockery, yelling, "Hail! King of the Jews!" 30And
they spit on him and grabbed the stick and beat him
on the head with it. 31When they were finally tired of
mocking him, they took off the robe and put his own
clothes on him again. Then they led him away to be
crucified.
32As they were on the way, they came across a man
named Simon, who was from Cyrene,* and they
forced him to carry Jesus' cross. 33Then they went out

**HASSLE ● ● ● • •**

27:29 **People still hassle Christians for their faith, but believers can take courage that Jesus himself was mocked terribly. Taunting may hurt our feelings, but we should never let it change our faith (see 5:11-12).**

to a place called Golgotha (which means Skull Hill).
34The soldiers gave him wine mixed with bitter gall,
but when he had tasted it, he refused to drink it.
35After they had nailed him to the cross, the soldiers gambled for his clothes by throwing dice.*
36Then they sat around and kept guard as he hung
there. 37A signboard was fastened to the cross above
Jesus' head, announcing the charge against him. It
read: "This is Jesus, the King of the Jews."
38Two criminals were crucified with him, their
crosses on either side of his. 39And the people passing
by shouted abuse, shaking their heads in mockery.
40"So! You can destroy the Temple and build it again
in three days, can you? Well then, if you are the Son
of God, save yourself and come down from the
cross!"
41The leading priests, the teachers of religious law,
and the other leaders also mocked Jesus. 42"He saved
others," they scoffed, "but he can't save himself! So
he is the king of Israel, is he? Let him come down
from the cross, and we will believe in him! 43He
trusted God—let God show his approval by delivering him! For he said, 'I am the Son of God.'" 44And
the criminals who were crucified with him also
shouted the same insults at him.
45At noon, darkness fell across the whole land
until three o'clock. 46At about three o'clock, Jesus
called out with a loud voice, *"Eli, Eli, lema sabachthani?"* which means, "My God, my God, why have
you forsaken me?"*
47Some of the bystanders misunderstood and
thought he was calling for the prophet Elijah. 48One
of them ran and filled a sponge with sour wine,
holding it up to him on a stick so he could drink.
49But the rest said, "Leave him alone. Let's see
whether Elijah will come and save him."*
50Then Jesus shouted out again, and he gave up
his spirit. 51At that moment the curtain in the Temple
was torn in two, from top to bottom. The earth
shook, rocks split apart, 52and tombs opened. The
bodies of many godly men and women who had

**DREAD ● ● ● • •**

27:46 **Jesus was not questioning God; he was quoting the first line of Psalm 22—a deep expression of the anguish he felt when he took on the sins of the world and thus was separated from his Father. *This* was what Jesus dreaded as he prayed to God in the garden to take the cup from him (26:39). The physical agony was horrible, but even worse was the period of spiritual separation from God. Jesus suffered this double death so that we would never have to experience eternal separation from God.**

27:16 Some manuscripts read *Jesus Barabbas;* also in 27:17. 27:25 Greek *"His blood be on us and on our children."* 27:32 *Cyrene* was a city in northern Africa. 27:35 Greek *by casting lots.* A few late manuscripts add *This fulfilled the word of the prophet: "They divided my clothes among themselves and cast lots for my robe."* See Ps 22:18. 27:46 Ps 22:1. 27:49 Some manuscripts add *And another took a spear and pierced his side, and out came water and blood.*

## CHOICES ● ● • • •

28:11-15 **Jesus' resurrection was already causing a great stir in Jerusalem. A group of women was moving quickly through the streets, looking for the disciples to tell them the amazing news that Jesus was alive. At the same time, a group of religious leaders was plotting how to cover up the Resurrection. Today there is still a great stir over the Resurrection, and there are still only two choices—to believe that Jesus rose from the dead, or to be closed to the truth, denying it, ignoring it, or trying to explain it away.**

died were raised from the dead 53after Jesus' resurrection. They left the cemetery, went into the holy city of Jerusalem, and appeared to many people.*

54The Roman officer and the other soldiers at the crucifixion were terrified by the earthquake and all that had happened. They said, "Truly, this was the Son of God!"

55And many women who had come from Galilee with Jesus to care for him were watching from a distance. 56Among them were Mary Magdalene, Mary (the mother of James and Joseph), and Zebedee's wife, the mother of James and John.

57As evening approached, Joseph, a rich man from Arimathea who was one of Jesus' followers, 58went to Pilate and asked for Jesus' body. And Pilate issued an order to release it to him. 59Joseph took the body and wrapped it in a long linen cloth. 60He placed it in his own new tomb, which had been carved out of the rock. Then he rolled a great stone across the entrance as he left. 61Both Mary Magdalene and the other Mary were sitting nearby watching.

62The next day—on the first day of the Passover ceremonies*—the leading priests and Pharisees went to see Pilate. 63They told him, "Sir, we remember what that deceiver once said while he was still alive: 'After three days I will be raised from the dead.' 64So we request that you seal the tomb until the third day. This will prevent his disciples from coming and stealing his body and then telling everyone he came back to life! If that happens, we'll be worse off than we were at first."

65Pilate replied, "Take guards and secure it the best you can." 66So they sealed the tomb and posted guards to protect it.

CHAPTER **28** **JESUS COMES BACK TO LIFE!** Early on Sunday morning,* as the new day was dawning, Mary Magdalene and the other Mary went out to see the tomb. 2Suddenly there was a great earthquake, because an angel of the Lord came down from heaven and rolled aside the stone and sat on it. 3His face shone like lightning, and his clothing was as white as snow. 4The guards shook with fear when they saw him, and they fell into a dead faint.

5Then the angel spoke to the women. "Don't be afraid!" he said. "I know you are looking for Jesus, who was crucified. 6He isn't here! He has been raised from the dead, just as he said would happen. Come, see where his body was lying. 7And now, go quickly and tell his disciples he has been raised from the dead, and he is going ahead of you to Galilee. You will see him there. Remember, I have told you."

8The women ran quickly from the tomb. They were very frightened but also filled with great joy, and they rushed to find the disciples to give them the angel's message. 9And as they went, Jesus met them. "Greetings!" he said. And they ran to him, held his feet, and worshiped him. 10Then Jesus said to them, "Don't be afraid! Go tell my brothers to leave for Galilee, and they will see me there."

11As the women were on their way into the city, some of the men who had been guarding the tomb went to the leading priests and told them what had happened. 12A meeting of all the religious leaders was called, and they decided to bribe the soldiers. 13They told the soldiers, "You must say, 'Jesus' disciples came during the night while we were sleeping, and they stole his body.' 14If the governor hears about it, we'll stand up for you and everything will be all right." 15So the guards accepted the bribe and said what they were told to say. Their story spread widely among the Jews, and they still tell it today.

16Then the eleven disciples left for Galilee, going to the mountain where Jesus had told them to go. 17When they saw him, they worshiped him—but some of them still doubted!

18Jesus came and told his disciples, "I have been given complete authority in heaven and on earth. 19Therefore, go and make disciples of all the nations, baptizing them in the name of the Father and the Son and the Holy Spirit. 20Teach these new disciples to obey all the commands I have given you. And be sure of this: I am with you always, even to the end of the age."

## COMMISSIONED ● ● • • •

28:18-20 **When someone is dying or leaving us, his last words are very important. Jesus left the disciples with these last words of instruction: they were under his authority; they were to make more disciples; they were to baptize and teach them to obey him; he would be with them always. Whereas in previous missions Jesus had sent his disciples only to the Jews (10:5-6), their mission from now on would be worldwide. Jesus is Lord of the earth, and he died for the sins of all those who trust him, everywhere.**

**We are to go—whether it is next door or to another country—and make disciples. It is not an option, but a command to all who call Jesus Lord. All of us are not evangelists, but we have all received gifts that we can use in helping to fulfill the great commission. As we obey, we have comfort in the knowledge that Jesus is always with us.**

27:51-53 Or *The earth shook, rocks split apart, tombs opened, and the bodies of many godly men and women who had died were raised from the dead. After Jesus' resurrection, they left the cemetery, went into the holy city of Jerusalem, and appeared to many people.* 27:62 Or *On the next day, which is after the Preparation.* 28:1 Greek *After the Sabbath, on the first day of the week.*

# MEGA themes

**JESUS CHRIST, THE KING** Jesus is revealed as the King of kings. His miraculous birth, his life and teaching, his miracles, and his triumph over death show us who he really is.

Jesus cannot be compared with any other person or power. He is the supreme ruler of time and eternity, heaven and earth, people and angels. We should give him his rightful place as King and Lord in our life.

1. In what ways is Jesus revealed as King in the book of Matthew?
2. In what ways did Jesus, though the King of kings, display humility in the book of Matthew?
3. What do you learn about the personal qualities of Jesus from these two lists? Why did so many people reject Jesus as King?
4. How does Jesus reign in the world today? What does it mean in terms of daily living for Jesus to be "the Lord" of your life?

**THE MESSIAH** Jesus was the Messiah, the One for whom the Jews had waited, who was to deliver them from Roman oppression. Yet, tragically, they didn't recognize him when he came. They were not ready to accept his kingship because it was not what they expected. They didn't understand that the true purpose of God's anointed deliverer was to die for all people, to free them from sin.

Because Jesus was sent by God, we can trust him with our life. It is worth everything we have to accept Christ and give ourself to him because he came to be our Messiah, our Savior.

1. In what ways did Jesus fulfill the prophecy of a coming Savior who would rescue the people?
2. How was Jesus' plan of deliverance different from what the people had anticipated? How was Jesus' deliverance actually greater than they could have imagined?
3. In what ways has Jesus delivered you?
4. Based on the fact that Jesus, the Messiah, has rescued you, what will you do to live for him?

**KINGDOM OF GOD** Jesus came to earth to begin his kingdom. His full kingdom will be realized at his return and will be made up of all those who have faithfully followed him.

The way to enter God's kingdom is by faith—by believing in Christ to save us from sin and change our life. Then we must do the work of his kingdom, helping prepare it for his return.

1. Matthew 5–7, known as the "Sermon on the Mount," introduces the values of Christ's kingdom. In accordance with these chapters, make a list of at least ten guidelines Jesus gave showing how he wants those who belong to the kingdom to live.
2. What would it mean for a person in your school to live by these kingdom guidelines?
3. Chapter 13 is filled with parables that Jesus used when teaching to help describe his kingdom. What do you learn about the kingdom of God from these parables? What is the importance of the kingdom of God?
4. In what ways are you living out the kingdom guidelines or values? In what areas do you need to become more obedient to Christ's call to kingdom values?

**TEACHINGS** Jesus taught the people using sermons, illustrations, and parables. He showed the true ingredients of faith and how to guard against an ineffective and hypocritical life.

Jesus' teachings show us how to prepare for life in his kingdom by living properly right now. His life was an example of his teachings, as our life should be.

1. What were the main purposes of Jesus' teachings?
2. How did different individuals and groups of people react to his teachings?
3. What seems to have caused some people to accept Jesus' teachings and others to reject them?
4. Describe the ways, both positive and negative, that people today respond to Jesus' teachings.
5. How are Jesus' teachings to be your authority in life? In what ways does this authority influence your decisions in your present lifestyle?

**RESURRECTION** When Jesus rose from the dead, he rose in power as the true King. In his victory over death, he established his credentials as King and his power and authority over evil.

The Resurrection shows that Jesus is all-powerful—that not even death could stop his plan of offering eternal life. People who believe in Jesus can hope for a resurrection like his. Our role is to live in that victory and share the message of his victory with those who do not yet know that "Jesus is alive!"

1. What difference does it make whether or not Jesus was resurrected?
2. What impact did Jesus' resurrection have on his disciples?
3. What impact has Jesus' resurrection made on mankind as a whole? On you specifically?

37 B.C.
**Herod the Great begins to rule**

6/5 B.C.
**Jesus is born**

5/4 B.C.
**Escape to Egypt**

4 B.C.
**Herod the Great dies**

4/3 B.C.
**Return to Nazareth**

A.D. 6/7
**Jesus visits Temple as a boy**

14
**Tiberius Caesar becomes emperor**

26
**John's ministry begins**

26/27
**Jesus begins his ministry**

28
**Jesus chooses 12 disciples**

29
**Jesus feeds 5,000**

30
**Jesus is crucified, rises again, and ascends**

**H**as this ever happened to you? ■ Friends invite you to a just-released, critically acclaimed movie. ■ "It's supposed to be great," they insist. "You'll like it. Trust us." ■ So you go—with high expectations. Only the movie isn't great. It drags on and on. As far as excitement goes, this particular film ranks right up there with reading the phone book. ■ You keep thinking, *This has got to get better. Surely there's a car chase or a joke or some sort of surprise plot twist in the next scene.* But nothing happens—nothing at all. The most adventurous moment of the film comes at the end when two of the actors go to a fancy French restaurant and eat snails. It's gross, but at least they're finally doing something. ■ When the final credits roll, you leave the theater, vowing, "Never again!" ■ Guess what? You don't have to spend your time with stale stories, boring characters, or tedious plots! Instead, you can read one of the most exciting books in existence! And it's right here, on the next few pages. ■ You name it, and the Gospel of Mark has it—demons, death, and outrageous special effects (also called miracles), all served up in a swirling atmosphere of intrigue, jealousy, controversy, and murder. In short, this book is an action-packed biography of the most influential person in the history of the world. ■ Go for it! And when you're done, you will vow, "Never again . . . never again will I think of the Bible as a boring book!"

## STATS

PURPOSE: To present Jesus' person, work, and teachings

AUTHOR: John Mark. He accompanied Paul on his first missionary journey (Acts 13:13).

TO WHOM WRITTEN: The Christians in Rome, where Mark wrote the Gospel, and believers everywhere

DATE WRITTEN: Between A.D. 55 and 65

SETTING: The Roman Empire. The empire, with its common language and excellent transportation and communication systems, was ripe to hear Jesus' message.

KEY PEOPLE: Jesus, the twelve disciples, Pilate, the Jewish religious leaders

KEY PLACES: Capernaum, Nazareth, Caesarea Philippi, Jericho, Bethany, Mount of Olives, Jerusalem, Golgotha

SPECIAL FEATURES: Mark was the first Gospel written. The other Gospels quote all but 31 verses of Mark. Mark records more miracles than does any other Gospel.

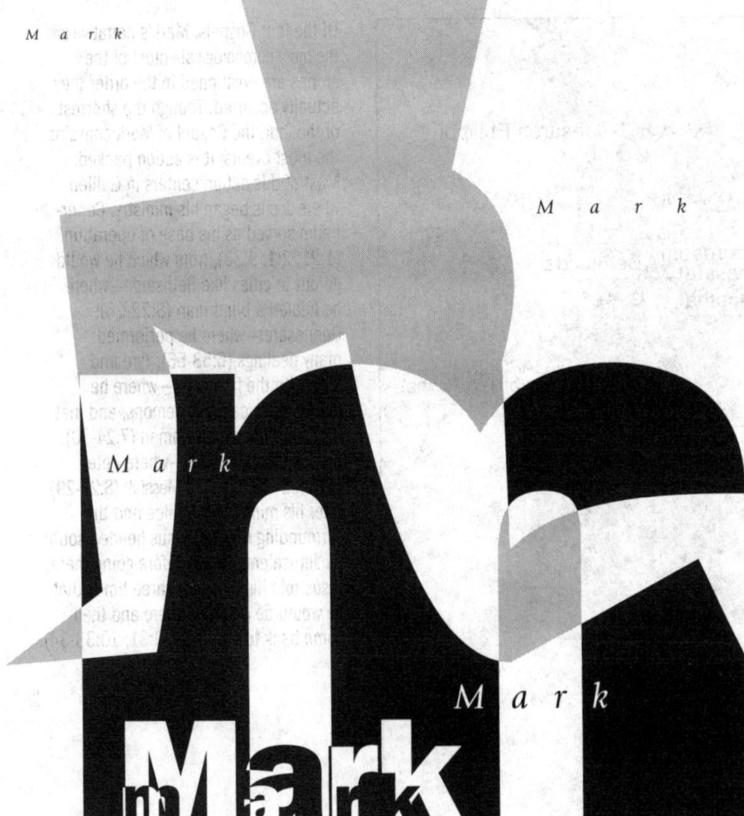


CHAPTER **1** **PREPARING THE WAY FOR JESUS.** Here begins the Good News about Jesus the Messiah, the Son of God.*

[2]In the book of the prophet Isaiah, God said,

"Look, I am sending my messenger before you,
and he will prepare your way.*
[3] He is a voice shouting in the wilderness:
'Prepare a pathway for the Lord's coming!
Make a straight road for him!'*"

[4]This messenger was John the Baptist. He lived in the wilderness and was preaching that people should be baptized to show that they had turned from their sins and turned to God to be forgiven.* [5]People from Jerusalem and from all over Judea traveled out into the wilderness to see and hear John. And when they confessed their sins, he baptized them in the Jordan River. [6]His clothes were woven from camel hair, and he wore a leather belt; his food was locusts and wild honey. [7]He announced: "Someone is coming soon who is far greater than I am—so much greater that I am not even worthy to be his slave.* [8]I baptize you with* water, but he will baptize you with the Holy Spirit!"

[9]One day Jesus came from Nazareth in Galilee, and he was baptized by John in the Jordan River. [10]And when Jesus came up out of the water, he saw the heavens split open and the Holy Spirit descending like a dove on him. [11]And a voice came from heaven saying, "You are my beloved Son, and I am fully pleased with you."

[12]Immediately the Holy Spirit compelled Jesus to go into the wilderness. [13]He was there for forty days, being tempted by Satan. He was out among the wild animals, and angels took care of him.

[14]Later on, after John was arrested by Herod Antipas, Jesus went to Galilee to preach God's Good News. [15]"At last the time has come!" he announced. "The Kingdom of God is near! Turn from your sins and believe this Good News!"

[16]One day as Jesus was walking along the shores of the Sea of Galilee, he saw Simon* and his brother,

**THRILLS ● ● • • ·**

1:1 **When you experience the excitement of a big event, you naturally want to tell someone. Telling the story can bring back that original thrill as you relive the experience. As you read Mark's first words, you can sense his excitement. Picture yourself in the crowd as Jesus heals and teaches. Imagine yourself as one of the disciples. Respond to Jesus' words of love and encouragement—and remember that he came for us who live today as well as for those who lived two thousand years ago.**

1:1 Some manuscripts do not include *the Son of God.* 1:2 Mal 3:1. 1:3 Isa 40:3. 1:4 Greek *preaching a baptism of repentance for the forgiveness of sins.* 1:7 Greek *to stoop down and untie his sandals.* 1:8 Or *in.* 1:16 *Simon* is called *Peter* in 3:16 and thereafter.

# KEY PLACES IN MARK

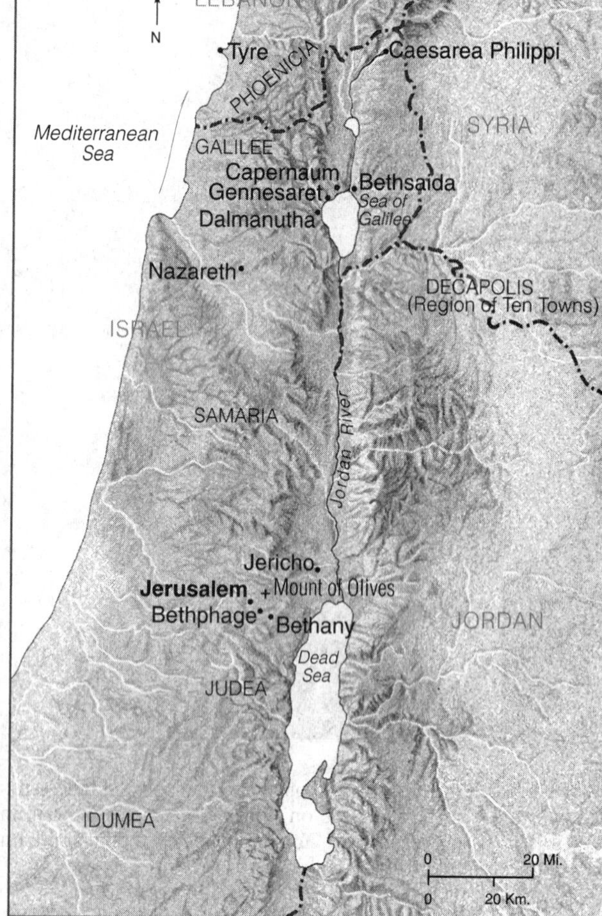

The broken lines (–·–·) indicate modern boundaries.

Of the four Gospels, Mark's narrative is the most chronological—most of the stories are positioned in the order they actually occurred. Though the shortest of the four, the Gospel of Mark contains the most events; it is action packed. Most of this action centers in Galilee, where Jesus began his ministry. Capernaum served as his base of operation (1:21; 2:1; 9:33), from which he would go out to cities like Bethsaida—where he healed a blind man (8:22-26); Gennesaret—where he performed many healings (6:53-56); Tyre and Sidon (to the far north)—where he cured many, cast out demons, and met the Syro-Phoenician woman (7:24-30); and Caesarea Philippi—where Peter declared him to be the Messiah (8:27-29). After his ministry in Galilee and the surrounding regions, Jesus headed south for Jerusalem (10:1). Before going there, Jesus told his disciples three times that he would be crucified there and then come back to life (8:31; 9:31; 10:33-34).

Andrew, fishing with a net, for they were commercial
fishermen. 17Jesus called out to them, "Come, be my
disciples, and I will show you how to fish for people!"
18And they left their nets at once and went with him.
19A little farther up the shore Jesus saw Zebedee's
sons, James and John, in a boat mending their nets.
20He called them, too, and immediately they left
their father, Zebedee, in the boat with the hired men
and went with him.
21Jesus and his companions went to the town of
Capernaum, and every Sabbath day he went into the
synagogue and taught the people. 22They were amazed
at his teaching, for he taught as one who had real
authority—quite unlike the teachers of religious law.
23A man possessed by an evil spirit was in the
synagogue, 24and he began shouting, "Why are you
bothering us, Jesus of Nazareth? Have you come to
destroy us? I know who you are—the Holy One sent
from God!"
25Jesus cut him short. "Be silent! Come out of the
man." 26At that, the evil spirit screamed and threw
the man into a convulsion, but then he left him.
27Amazement gripped the audience, and they began to discuss what had happened. "What sort of
new teaching is this?" they asked excitedly. "It has
such authority! Even evil spirits obey his orders!"
28The news of what he had done spread quickly
through that entire area of Galilee.
29After Jesus and his disciples left the synagogue,
they went over to Simon and Andrew's home, and
James and John were with them. 30Simon's mother-in-law was sick in bed with a high fever. They told
Jesus about her right away. 31He went to her bedside,

## FIND TIME! ● ● ● • •

1:35 **Jesus took time to pray. Finding time to pray is not easy, but prayer is the vital link between us and God. Like Jesus, we must find time away from others to talk with God, even if we have to get up very early in the morning to do it!**

and as he took her by the hand and helped her to sit
up, the fever suddenly left, and she got up and
prepared a meal for them.
32That evening at sunset, many sick and demon-
possessed people were brought to Jesus. 33And a huge
crowd of people from all over Capernaum gathered
outside the door to watch. 34So Jesus healed great
numbers of sick people who had many different kinds
of diseases, and he ordered many demons to come out
of their victims. But because they knew who he was, he
refused to allow the demons to speak.
35The next morning Jesus awoke long before daybreak and went out alone into the wilderness to pray.
36Later Simon and the others went out to find him.
37They said, "Everyone is asking for you."
38But he replied, "We must go on to other towns
as well, and I will preach to them, too, because that
is why I came." 39So he traveled throughout the
region of Galilee, preaching in the synagogues and
expelling demons from many people.
40A man with leprosy came and knelt in front of
Jesus, begging to be healed. "If you want to, you can
make me well again," he said.
41Moved with pity,* Jesus touched him. "I want to,"
he said. "Be healed!" 42Instantly the leprosy disappeared—the man was healed. 43Then Jesus sent him
on his way and told him sternly, 44"Go right over to the
priest and let him examine you. Don't talk to anyone
along the way. Take along the offering required in the
law of Moses for those who have been healed of
leprosy, so everyone will have proof of your healing."
45But as the man went on his way, he spread the
news, telling everyone what had happened to him.
As a result, such crowds soon surrounded Jesus that
he couldn't enter a town anywhere publicly. He had
to stay out in the secluded places, and people from
everywhere came to him there.

CHAPTER **2** **A HOLE IN THE ROOF.** Several days later
Jesus returned to Capernaum, and the news of his
arrival spread quickly through the town. 2Soon the
house where he was staying was so packed with visitors that there wasn't room for one more person, not
even outside the door. And he preached the word to
them. 3Four men arrived carrying a paralyzed man on
a mat. 4They couldn't get to Jesus through the crowd,
so they dug through the clay roof above his head. Then
they lowered the sick man on his mat, right down in
front of Jesus. 5Seeing their faith, Jesus said to the
paralyzed man, "My son, your sins are forgiven."
6But some of the teachers of religious law who
were sitting there said to themselves, 7"What? This is
blasphemy! Who but God can forgive sins!"
8Jesus knew what they were discussing among
themselves, so he said to them, "Why do you think
this is blasphemy? 9Is it easier to say to the paralyzed
man, 'Your sins are forgiven' or 'Get up, pick up your
mat, and walk'? 10I will prove that I, the Son of Man,
have the authority on earth to forgive sins." Then Jesus
turned to the paralyzed man and said, 11"Stand up,

1:41 Some manuscripts read *Moved with anger.*

**I used to like to go to parties a lot before I became a Christian. Are parties bad?**

In answering this type of question, it's tough not to sound heavy handed. After all, teenage parties do not exactly have a great reputation.

The key word to remember is not *yes* or *no*, but *why*—your motive is the key.

If you were honest, you'd have to agree that many of the reasons people party are pretty selfish. Most parties cater to the notion that it's a person's right to have a good time, especially if it's not hurting anyone else.

If someone is living apart from God, why would he or she think anything different? The Bible agrees that if this life doesn't matter, then "Let's feast and get drunk, for tomorrow we die!" (1 Corinthians 15:32).

The motive behind going to parties is what God is most concerned about. If it's to get drunk, take drugs, pick up the opposite sex, then God wouldn't want you at parties.

The motive might be to be seen with the "cool" people. Being with certain people sometimes may help you feel accepted and even popular, but God accepts you as you are—and his acceptance is more important than anyone else's.

Jesus isn't against parties. He went to parties, and was, in fact, the life of the party! But his motives were entirely different from the selfish ones described above. He went to show people that he accepted them, to communicate truth about the character of God, and to celebrate life (see Mark 2:13-17).

Should you do the same? Perhaps, but here are a few questions to consider:

- Have you grown sufficiently in your faith that you will not be tempted if there is pressure to drink (or whatever)?
- Do you know someone who will go with you, so you can encourage each other to stay clean?
- Are you going as a light or as a hammer? That is, do you genuinely want to help those in darkness, or do you want to pound on them to feel good about your "moral" lifestyle?
- Is there a chance that you could be found "guilty by association"? When others hear you were at the party, how will they know you didn't drink? Is it worth the hassle it may cause in making sure your reputation stays intact?
- What do your parents think about you attending that party? Would you have to not tell them in order to go?

Remember, motive is the key. But even with good motives, be cautious. The results of such activities, even with the best of motives, may be more than you can handle.

## DON'T WAIT ● ● • • •

**2:14-15 The day that Levi met Jesus, he held a meeting at his house to introduce others to Jesus. Levi didn't waste any time starting to witness! Some people feel that new believers should wait for time, maturity, or training before they start telling others about Christ. But, like Levi, new believers can tell others about their faith right away with whatever knowledge, skill, or experience they already have.**

take your mat, and go on home, because you are healed!"

12 The man jumped up, took the mat, and pushed his way through the stunned onlookers. Then they all praised God. "We've never seen anything like this before!" they exclaimed.

13 Then Jesus went out to the lakeshore again and taught the crowds that gathered around him. 14 As he walked along, he saw Levi son of Alphaeus sitting at his tax-collection booth. "Come, be my disciple," Jesus said to him. So Levi got up and followed him.

15 That night Levi invited Jesus and his disciples to be his dinner guests, along with his fellow tax collectors and many other notorious sinners. (There were many people of this kind among the crowds that followed Jesus.) 16 But when some of the teachers of religious law who were Pharisees* saw him eating with people like that, they said to his disciples, "Why does he eat with such scum*?"

17 When Jesus heard this, he told them, "Healthy people don't need a doctor—sick people do. I have come to call sinners, not those who think they are already good enough."

18 John's disciples and the Pharisees sometimes fasted. One day some people came to Jesus and asked, "Why do John's disciples and the Pharisees fast, but your disciples don't fast?"

19 Jesus replied, "Do wedding guests fast while celebrating with the groom? Of course not. They can't fast while they are with the groom. 20 But someday he will be taken away from them, and then they will fast. 21 And who would patch an old garment with unshrunk cloth? For the new patch shrinks and pulls away from the old cloth, leaving an even bigger hole than before. 22 And no one puts new wine into old wineskins. The wine would burst the wineskins, spilling the wine and ruining the skins. New wine needs new wineskins."

23 One Sabbath day as Jesus was walking through some grainfields, his disciples began breaking off heads of wheat. 24 But the Pharisees said to Jesus, "They shouldn't be doing that! It's against the law to work by harvesting grain on the Sabbath."

25 But Jesus replied, "Haven't you ever read in the Scriptures what King David did when he and his companions were hungry? 26 He went into the house of God (during the days when Abiathar was high priest), ate the special bread reserved for the priests alone, and then gave some to his companions. That was breaking the law, too." 27 Then he said to them, "The Sabbath was made to benefit people, and not people to benefit the Sabbath. 28 And I, the Son of Man, am master even of the Sabbath!"

# CHAPTER 3

**JESUS HEALS A CRIPPLED HAND.** Jesus went into the synagogue again and noticed a man with a deformed hand. 2 Since it was the Sabbath, Jesus' enemies watched him closely. Would he heal the man's hand on the Sabbath? If he did, they planned to condemn him. 3 Jesus said to the man, "Come and stand in front of everyone." 4 Then he turned to his critics and asked, "Is it legal to do good deeds on the Sabbath, or is it a day for doing harm? Is this a day to save life or to destroy it?" But they wouldn't answer him. 5 He looked around at them angrily, because he was deeply disturbed by their hard hearts. Then he said to the man, "Reach out your hand." The man reached out his hand, and it became normal again! 6 At once the Pharisees went away and met with the supporters of Herod to discuss plans for killing Jesus.

## ANGER ● ● • • •

**3:5 Jesus was angry about the Pharisees' uncaring attitudes. Anger itself is not wrong. It depends on what makes us angry and what we do with our anger. Too often we express our anger in selfish and harmful ways. By contrast, Jesus expressed his anger by correcting a problem—healing the man's hand. Use your anger to find constructive solutions rather than to add to the problem by tearing people down.**

7 Jesus and his disciples went out to the lake, followed by a huge crowd from all over Galilee, Judea, 8 Jerusalem, Idumea, from east of the Jordan River, and even from as far away as Tyre and Sidon. The news about his miracles had spread far and wide, and vast numbers of people came to see him for themselves.

9 Jesus instructed his disciples to bring around a boat and to have it ready in case he was crowded off the beach. 10 There had been many healings that day. As a result, many sick people were crowding around him, trying to touch him. 11 And whenever those possessed by evil spirits caught sight of him, they would fall down in front of him shrieking, "You are the Son of God!" 12 But Jesus strictly warned them not to say who he was.

13 Afterward Jesus went up on a mountain and called the ones he wanted to go with him. And they came to him. 14 Then he selected twelve of them to be his regular companions, calling them apostles.* He sent them out to preach, 15 and he gave them authority to cast out demons. 16 These are the names of the twelve he chose:

Simon (he renamed him Peter),
17 James and John (the sons of Zebedee, but Jesus nicknamed them "Sons of Thunder"*),
18 Andrew,
Philip,
Bartholomew,
Matthew,
Thomas,
James (son of Alphaeus),

2:16a Greek *the scribes of the Pharisees.* 2:16b Greek *with tax collectors and sinners.* 3:14 Some manuscripts do not include *calling them apostles.*
3:17 Greek *whom he named Boanerges, which means Sons of Thunder.*

Thaddaeus,
Simon (the Zealot*),
19 Judas Iscariot (who later betrayed him).

[20]When Jesus returned to the house where he was
staying, the crowds began to gather again, and soon
he and his disciples couldn't even find time to eat.
[21]When his family heard what was happening,
they tried to take him home
with them. "He's out of his
mind," they said.

[22]But the teachers of religious law who had arrived
from Jerusalem said, "He's
possessed by Satan,* the
prince of demons. That's
where he gets the power to
cast out demons."

[23]Jesus called them over
and said to them by way of
illustration, "How can Satan
cast out Satan? [24]A kingdom at
war with itself will collapse.
[25]A home divided against itself is doomed. [26]And if Satan
is fighting against himself,
how can he stand? He would
never survive. [27]Let me illustrate this. You can't enter a
strong man's house and rob
him without first tying him
up. Only then can his house
be robbed!*

[28]"I assure you that any sin
can be forgiven, including
blasphemy; [29]but anyone who
blasphemes against the Holy
Spirit will never be forgiven. It
is an eternal sin." [30]He told
them this because they were
saying he had an evil spirit.

[31]Jesus' mother and brothers arrived at the house where
he was teaching. They stood
outside and sent word for him
to come out and talk with
them. [32]There was a crowd
around Jesus, and someone
said, "Your mother and your
brothers and sisters* are outside, asking for you."

[33]Jesus replied, "Who is my
mother? Who are my broth-
ers?" [34]Then he looked at
those around him and said,
"These are my mother and
brothers. [35]Anyone who does
God's will is my brother and
sister and mother."

CHAPTER 4 **A STORY ABOUT FOUR KINDS OF SOIL.** Once
again Jesus began teaching by the lakeshore. There
was such a large crowd along the shore that he got
into a boat and sat down and spoke from there. [2]He
began to teach the people by telling many stories
such as this one:
[3]"Listen! A farmer went out to plant some seed.

## JUDAS ISCARIOT

**UPS:**
- He was chosen as one of the 12 disciples; the only non-Galilean
- He kept the money bag for the expenses of the group
- He was able to recognize the evil in his betrayal of Jesus

**DOWNS:**
- He was greedy (John 12:6)
- He betrayed Jesus
- He committed suicide instead of seeking forgiveness

**STATS:**
- Where: probably from the town of Kerioth
- Occupation: disciple of Jesus
- Relatives: Father: Simon
- Contemporaries: Jesus, Pilate, Herod, the other 11 disciples

It is easy to forget that Jesus chose Judas to be his disciple. We may also miss the point that while Judas betrayed Jesus, all the disciples abandoned him. The disciples, including Judas, all had the wrong idea of Jesus' mission on earth. They expected Jesus to become a political leader. But when he kept talking about dying, they all felt a mixture of anger, fear, and disappointment. They couldn't understand why Jesus had asked them to follow him if his mission was going to fail.

We don't know exactly why Judas betrayed Jesus. But we can see that Judas let his own desires become so important that Satan was able to control him. He got paid to set up Jesus for the religious leaders.

He tried to undo the evil he had done by returning the money to the priests, but it was too late. How sad that Judas ended his life in despair without ever experiencing the gift of forgiveness God could give to even him through Jesus Christ.

In betraying Jesus, Judas made the greatest mistake in history. But just the fact that Jesus knew Judas would betray him doesn't mean that Judas was a puppet of God's will. Judas made the choice. God knew what that choice would be and made it part of the plan. Judas didn't lose his relationship with Jesus; rather, he had never found Jesus. He is called "the one headed for destruction" (John 17:12) because he was never saved.

Judas's life can help us if he makes us think again about our commitment to God. Is God's Spirit in us? Are we true disciples and followers, or uncommitted pretenders? We can choose disobedience and death, or we can choose repentance, forgiveness, hope, and eternal life. Judas's betrayal sent Jesus to the cross to guarantee that second choice, our only chance. Will we accept Christ's free gift, or—like Judas—betray him?

LESSONS: Evil plans and motives leave us open to being used by Satan for even greater evil

The consequences of evil are so devastating that even small lies and little wrongdoings have serious results

God's plan and purposes are worked out even in the worst possible events

KEY VERSES: "Then Satan entered into Judas Iscariot, who was one of the twelve disciples, and he went over to the leading priests and captains of the Temple guard to discuss the best way to betray Jesus to them" (Luke 22:3-4).

Judas's story is told in the Gospels. He is also mentioned in Acts 1:17-19.

3:18 Greek *the Cananean.* 3:22 Greek *Beelzeboul.* 3:27 Or *One cannot rob Satan's kingdom without first tying him up. Only then can his demons be cast out.* 3:32 Some manuscripts do not include *and sisters.*

4As he scattered it across his field, some seed fell on a footpath, and the birds came and ate it. 5Other seed fell on shallow soil with underlying rock. The plant sprang up quickly, 6but it soon wilted beneath the hot sun and died because the roots had no nourishment in the shallow soil. 7Other seed fell among thorns that shot up and choked out the tender blades so that it produced no grain. 8Still other seed fell on fertile soil and produced a crop that was thirty, sixty, and even a hundred times as much as had been planted." Then he said, 9"Anyone who is willing to hear should listen and understand!"

10Later, when Jesus was alone with the twelve disciples and with the others who were gathered around, they asked him, "What do your stories mean?"

## READY ● ● • • .

4:11-12 **Some people do not understand God's truth because they are not ready for it. God reveals truth to people who will do something about it. When you talk with people about God, be aware that they will not understand if they are not yet ready. Be patient, taking every chance to tell them more of the truth about God and praying that the Holy Spirit will open their minds and hearts, making them ready to receive the truth and act on it.**

11He replied, "You are permitted to understand the secret about the Kingdom of God. But I am using these stories to conceal everything about it from outsiders, 12so that the Scriptures might be fulfilled:

'They see what I do,
    but they don't perceive its meaning.
They hear my words,
    but they don't understand.
So they will not turn from their sins
    and be forgiven.'*

13"But if you can't understand this story, how will you understand all the others I am going to tell? 14The farmer I talked about is the one who brings God's message to others. 15The seed that fell on the hard path represents those who hear the message, but then Satan comes at once and takes it away from them. 16The rocky soil represents those who hear the message and receive it with joy. 17But like young plants in such soil, their roots don't go very deep. At first they get along fine, but they wilt as soon as they have problems or are persecuted because they believe the word. 18The thorny ground represents those who hear and accept the Good News, 19but all too quickly the message is crowded out by the cares of this life, the lure of wealth, and the desire for nice things, so no crop is produced. 20But the good soil represents those who hear and accept God's message and produce a huge harvest—thirty, sixty, or even a hundred times as much as had been planted."

21Then Jesus asked them, "Would anyone light a lamp and then put it under a basket or under a bed to shut out the light? Of course not! A lamp is placed on a stand, where its light will shine.

4:12 Isa 6:9-10.

## RESPONSES ● ● • • .

4:14-20 **The four soils represent four different ways people respond to God's Word. Usually we think Jesus was talking about four different kinds of people, but he may also have been talking about (1) different times or phases in a person's life, or (2) how we willingly receive God's message in some areas of our life and resist it in others. For example, you may be open to God where your future is concerned, but closed concerning how you spend your money. You may respond like good soil to God's demand for worship, but like rocky soil to his demand to give to those in need. Strive to be like good soil in every area of your life.**

22"Everything that is now hidden or secret will eventually be brought to light. 23Anyone who is willing to hear should listen and understand! 24And be sure to pay attention to what you hear. The more you do this, the more you will understand—and even more, besides. 25To those who are open to my teaching, more understanding will be given. But to those who are not listening, even what they have will be taken away from them."

26Jesus also said, "Here is another illustration of what the Kingdom of God is like: A farmer planted seeds in a field, 27and then he went on with his other activities. As the days went by, the seeds sprouted and grew without the farmer's help, 28because the earth produces crops on its own. First a leaf blade pushes through, then the heads of wheat are formed, and finally the grain ripens. 29And as soon as the grain is ready, the farmer comes and harvests it with a sickle."

30Jesus asked, "How can I describe the Kingdom of God? What story should I use to illustrate it? 31It is like a tiny mustard seed. Though this is one of the smallest of seeds, 32it grows to become one of the largest of plants, with long branches where birds can come and find shelter."

Go
home
to your friends,
and tell them
what
wonderful
things
the LORD
has done
for you
and
how
merciful
he has been.
MARK 5:19

[33]He used many such stories and illustrations to teach the people as much as they were able to understand. [34]In fact, in his public teaching he taught only with parables, but afterward when he was alone with his disciples, he explained the meaning to them.

[35]As evening came, Jesus said to his disciples, "Let's cross to the other side of the lake." [36]He was already in the boat, so they started out, leaving the crowds behind (although other boats followed). [37]But soon a fierce storm arose. High waves began to break into the boat until it was nearly full of water.

[38]Jesus was sleeping at the back of the boat with his head on a cushion. Frantically they woke him up, shouting, "Teacher, don't you even care that we are going to drown?"

[39]When he woke up, he rebuked the wind and said to the water, "Quiet down!" Suddenly the wind stopped, and there was a great calm. [40]And he asked them, "Why are you so afraid? Do you still not have faith in me?"

[41]And they were filled with awe and said among themselves, "Who is this man, that even the wind and waves obey him?"

CHAPTER **5** **JESUS HEALS A DEMON-POSSESSED MAN.** So they arrived at the other side of the lake, in the land of the Gerasenes.* [2]Just as Jesus was climbing from the boat, a man possessed by an evil spirit ran out from a cemetery to meet him. [3]This man lived among the tombs and could not be restrained, even with a chain. [4]Whenever he was put into chains and shackles—as he often was—he snapped the chains from his wrists and smashed the shackles. No one was strong enough to control him. [5]All day long and throughout the night, he would wander among the tombs and in the hills, screaming and hitting himself with stones.

[6]When Jesus was still some distance away, the man saw him. He ran to meet Jesus and fell down before him. [7]He gave a terrible scream, shrieking, "Why are you bothering me, Jesus, Son of the Most High God? For God's sake, don't torture me!" [8]For Jesus had already said to the spirit, "Come out of the man, you evil spirit."

[9]Then Jesus asked, "What is your name?"

And the spirit replied, "Legion, because there are many of us here inside this man." [10]Then the spirits begged him again and again not to send them to some distant place. [11]There happened to be a large herd of pigs feeding on the hillside nearby. [12]"Send us into those pigs," the evil spirits begged. [13]Jesus gave them permission. So the evil spirits came out of the man and entered the pigs, and the entire herd of two thousand pigs plunged down the steep hillside into the lake, where they drowned.

[14]The herdsmen fled to the nearby city and the surrounding countryside, spreading the news as they ran. Everyone rushed out to see for themselves. [15]A crowd soon gathered around Jesus, but they were frightened when they saw the man who had been demon possessed, for he was sitting there fully clothed and perfectly sane. [16]Those who had seen what happened to the man and to the pigs told everyone about it, [17]and the crowd began pleading with Jesus to go away and leave them alone.

[18]When Jesus got back into the boat, the man who had been demon possessed begged to go, too. [19]But Jesus said, "No, go home to your friends, and tell

5:1 Some manuscripts read *Gadarenes;* others read *Gergesenes.* See Matt 8:28; Luke 8:26.

**ENTHUSIASTIC ● ● ● • •**

5:19-20 **This man who had been demon-possessed became a living example of Jesus' power. He wanted to go with Jesus, but Jesus told him to go home and share his story there. If you have experienced Jesus' power, you, too, are a living example. Are you, like this man, enthusiastic about sharing the Good News with those around you? Just as we would tell others about a doctor who cured a physical disease, we should tell about Christ, who cures our sin.**

**Now that I am a Christian, how should I act around my friends and family who are not believers?**

The most important thing you have going for you in both sets of relationships is that you already have a "relational bridge." Your friends and family knew what your life was like before you met Christ. Now they will have the chance to see you afterward.

In Mark 5:1-20, Jesus recognized that this was the case with the man he had just cleansed from demon possession. So he sent him back to his home instead of asking him to leave those who knew him best.

Another passage calls us Christ's ambassadors to our world (2 Corinthians 5:17-20). This means we are his hand-picked representatives! If people want to know what God is like, all they have to do is look at us.

God does not expect you to be perfect, but he does expect your faith to grow (Romans 10:17), and he expects you to try to live more like Jesus Christ would (Romans 12:1-2).

The people around you will be able to relate to your progress, not to perfection. Progress may be slow at first, but eventually, as you give areas of your life to Christ's control, changes will become noticeable. When this happens, you may find others starting to ask questions about your new faith.

When this happens, don't worry—although you may "feel" inadequate answering some of their questions, your responsibility is only to share what God has done for you and what you have learned, not to be the Bible expert. Sharing and living your faith as a new Christian is just as important (and biblical!) as being more mature in the faith or being a Bible scholar. God is not limited by our lack of knowledge.

Though new Christians sometimes face unique hardships, Jesus knows that, as with the Gadarene demoniac, your changed life may have a much greater impact on those with whom you have relational bridges already built than a stranger who may speak more eloquently!

them what wonderful things the Lord has done for you and how merciful he has been." [20]So the man started off to visit the Ten Towns* of that region and began to tell everyone about the great things Jesus had done for him; and everyone was amazed at what he told them.

[21]When Jesus went back across to the other side of the lake, a large crowd gathered around him on the shore. [22]A leader of the local synagogue, whose name was Jairus, came and fell down before him, [23]pleading with him to heal his little daughter. "She is about to die," he said in desperation. "Please come and place your hands on her; heal her so she can live."

[24]Jesus went with him, and the crowd thronged behind. [25]And there was a woman in the crowd who had had a hemorrhage for twelve years. [26]She had suffered a great deal from many doctors through the years and had spent everything she had to pay them, but she had gotten no better. In fact, she was worse. [27]She had heard about Jesus, so she came up behind him through the crowd and touched the fringe of his robe. [28]For she thought to herself, "If I can just touch his clothing, I will be healed." [29]Immediately the bleeding stopped, and she could feel that she had been healed!

[30]Jesus realized at once that healing power had gone out from him, so he turned around in the crowd and asked, "Who touched my clothes?"

[31]His disciples said to him, "All this crowd is pressing around you. How can you ask, 'Who touched me?'"

[32]But he kept on looking around to see who had done it. [33]Then the frightened woman, trembling at the realization of what had happened to her, came and fell at his feet and told him what she had done. [34]And he said to her, "Daughter, your faith has made you well. Go in peace. You have been healed."

[35]While he was still speaking to her, messengers arrived from Jairus's home with the message, "Your daughter is dead. There's no use troubling the Teacher now."

[36]But Jesus ignored their comments and said to Jairus, "Don't be afraid. Just trust me." [37]Then Jesus stopped the crowd and wouldn't let anyone go with him except Peter and James and John. [38]When they came to the home of the synagogue leader, Jesus saw the commotion and the weeping and wailing. [39]He went inside and spoke to the people. "Why all this weeping and commotion?" he asked. "The child isn't dead; she is only asleep."

[40]The crowd laughed at him, but he told them all to go outside. Then he took the girl's father and mother and his three disciples into the room where the girl was lying. [41]Holding her hand, he said to her, "Get up, little girl!"* [42]And the girl, who was twelve years old, immediately stood up and walked around! Her parents were absolutely overwhelmed. [43]Jesus commanded them not to tell anyone what had happened, and he told them to give her something to eat.

CHAPTER **6** **JESUS IS REJECTED AT NAZARETH.** Jesus left that part of the country and returned with his disciples to Nazareth, his hometown. [2]The next Sabbath he began teaching in the synagogue, and many who heard him were astonished. They asked, "Where did he get all his wisdom and the power to perform such miracles? [3]He's just the carpenter, the son of Mary and brother of James, Joseph,* Judas, and Simon. And his sisters live right here among us." They were deeply offended and refused to believe in him.

## PREJUDICE ●●●••

**6:2-3 Jesus was teaching effectively and wisely, but the people of his hometown saw him as only a carpenter. "He's no better than we are—he's just a common laborer," they said. They were offended that others could be impressed by him and follow him. They rejected his authority because he was one of their peers. They thought they knew him, but their preconceived notions about who he was made it impossible for them to accept his message. Don't let prejudice blind you to truth. As you learn more about Jesus, try to see him for who he really is.**

[4]Then Jesus told them, "A prophet is honored everywhere except in his own hometown and among his relatives and his own family." [5]And because of their unbelief, he couldn't do any mighty miracles among them except to place his hands on a few sick people and heal them. [6]And he was amazed at their unbelief.

Then Jesus went out from village to village, teaching. [7]And he called his twelve disciples together and sent them out two by two, with authority to cast out evil spirits. [8]He told them to take nothing with them except a walking stick—no food, no traveler's bag, no money. [9]He told them to wear sandals but not to take even an extra coat. [10]"When you enter each village, be a guest in only one home," he said. [11]"And if a village won't welcome you or listen to you, shake off its dust from your feet as you leave. It is a sign that you have abandoned that village to its fate."

[12]So the disciples went out, telling all they met to turn from their sins. [13]And they cast out many demons and healed many sick people, anointing them with olive oil.

[14]Herod Antipas, the king, soon heard about Jesus, because people everywhere were talking about him. Some were saying,* "This must be John the Baptist come back to life again. That is why he can do such miracles." [15]Others thought Jesus was the ancient prophet Elijah. Still others thought he was a prophet like the other great prophets of the past. [16]When Herod heard about Jesus, he said, "John, the man I

5:20 Greek *Decapolis.* 5:41 Greek text uses Aramaic *"Talitha cumi"* and then translates it as "Get up, little girl." 6:3 Greek *Joses;* see Matt 13:55. 6:14 Some manuscripts read *He was saying.*

beheaded, has come back from the dead." 17For
Herod had sent soldiers to arrest and imprison John
as a favor to Herodias. She had been his brother
Philip's wife, but Herod had married her. 18John kept
telling Herod, "It is illegal for you to marry your
brother's wife." 19Herodias was enraged and wanted
John killed in revenge, but without Herod's approval
she was powerless. 20And Herod respected John,
knowing that he was a good and holy man, so he
kept him under his protection. Herod was disturbed
whenever he talked with John, but even so, he liked
to listen to him.
21Herodias's chance finally came. It was Herod's
birthday, and he gave a party for his palace aides,
army officers, and the leading citizens of Galilee.
22Then his daughter, also named Herodias,* came in
and performed a dance that greatly pleased them all.
"Ask me for anything you like," the king said to the
girl, "and I will give it to you." 23Then he promised,
"I will give you whatever you ask, up to half of my
kingdom!"
24She went out and asked her mother, "What
should I ask for?"
Her mother told her, "Ask for John the Baptist's
head!"
25So the girl hurried back to the king and told him,
"I want the head of John the Baptist, right now, on a
tray!"
26Then the king was very sorry, but he was embarrassed to break his oath in front of his guests.
27So he sent an executioner to the prison to cut off
John's head and bring it to him. The soldier
beheaded John in the prison, 28brought his head
on a tray, and gave it to the girl, who took it to her
mother. 29When John's disciples heard what had
happened, they came for his body and buried it in
a tomb.
30The apostles returned to Jesus from their ministry tour and told him all they had done and what
they had taught. 31Then Jesus said, "Let's get away
from the crowds for a while and rest." There were so
many people coming and going that Jesus and his
apostles didn't even have time to eat. 32They left by
boat for a quieter spot. 33But many people saw them
leaving, and people from many towns ran ahead
along the shore and met them as they landed. 34A
vast crowd was there as he stepped from the boat,
and he had compassion on them because they were
like sheep without a shepherd. So he taught them
many things.
35Late in the afternoon his disciples came to him
and said, "This is a desolate place, and it is getting
late. 36Send the crowds away so they can go to the
nearby farms and villages and buy themselves some
food."
37But Jesus said, "You feed them."
"With what?" they asked. "It would take a small
fortune* to buy food for all this crowd!"

**TEAMWORK ● ● ● • •**

6:7 **The disciples were sent out in pairs. Individually they could have reached more areas of the country, but this was not Christ's plan. One advantage in going out by twos was that they could strengthen and encourage each other, especially when they faced rejection. Our strength comes from God, but he meets many of our needs through others. As you serve Christ, don't try to go it alone.**

38"How much food do you have?" he asked. "Go
and find out."
They came back and reported, "We have five
loaves of bread and two fish." 39Then Jesus told the
crowd to sit down in groups on the green grass. 40So
they sat in groups of fifty or a hundred.
41Jesus took the five loaves and two fish, looked up
toward heaven, and asked God's blessing on the
food. Breaking the loaves into pieces, he kept giving
the bread and fish to the disciples to give to the
people. 42They all ate as much as they wanted, 43and
they picked up twelve baskets of leftover bread and
fish. 44Five thousand men had eaten from those five
loaves!
45Immediately after this, Jesus made his disciples
get back into the boat and head out across the lake
to Bethsaida, while he sent the people home. 46After-
ward he went up into the hills by himself to pray.
47During the night, the disciples were in their boat
out in the middle of the lake, and Jesus was alone on
land. 48He saw that they were in serious trouble,
rowing hard and struggling against the wind and
waves. About three o'clock in the morning* he came
to them, walking on the water. He started to go past
them, 49but when they saw him walking on the
water, they screamed in terror, thinking he was a
ghost. 50They were all terrified when they saw him.
But Jesus spoke to them at once. "It's all right," he
said. "I am here! Don't be afraid." 51Then he
climbed into the boat, and the wind stopped. They
were astonished at what they saw. 52They still didn't
understand the significance of the miracle of the
multiplied loaves, for their hearts were hard and they
did not believe.
53When they arrived at Gennesaret on the other
side of the lake, they anchored the boat 54and
climbed out. The people standing there recognized
him at once, 55and they ran throughout the whole
area and began carrying sick people to him on mats.
56Wherever he went—in villages and cities and out
on the farms—they laid the sick in the market plazas
and streets. The sick begged him to let them at least
touch the fringe of his robe, and all who touched it
were healed.

## CHAPTER 7

**A BUNCH OF HYPOCRITES.** One day some
Pharisees and teachers of religious law arrived from
Jerusalem to confront Jesus. 2They noticed that some
of Jesus' disciples failed to follow the usual Jewish
ritual of hand washing before eating. 3(The Jews,

6:22 Some manuscripts read *the daughter of Herodias herself.* 6:37 Greek *200 denarii.* A denarius was the equivalent of a full day's wage. 6:48 Greek *About the fourth watch of the night.*

especially the Pharisees, do not eat until they have poured water over their cupped hands,* as required by their ancient traditions. [4]Similarly, they eat nothing bought from the market unless they have immersed their hands in water. This is but one of many traditions they have clung to—such as their ceremony of washing cups, pitchers, and kettles.*) [5]So the Pharisees and teachers of religious law asked him, "Why don't your disciples follow our age-old customs? For they eat without first performing the hand-washing ceremony."

## LEGALISM

Perhaps you know someone like 17-year-old Neal. A very opinionated churchgoer, he's got the Christian life all figured out (so he thinks). For Neal, there are no "gray areas." Everything is black and white, cut and dry. Certain deeds are expected, and most other activities simply are not acceptable for believers. And if you don't see things his way, Neal treats you like your relationship with the Lord is defective. Just look at some of his recent pronouncements:

- "Anybody who goes dancing is not walking with God."
- "How a girl who wears an outfit like that could call herself a Christian is beyond me!"
- "Going to a movie theater is no different than going into a bar. Both places are evil."
- "If you guys are serious about God, you'll be at youth group Wednesday night."

Is it any wonder that this outspoken junior has been nicknamed "Negative Neal"?

Legalism is the crazy idea that we can earn God's acceptance by strenuously following a lot of dos and don'ts. Legalistic people almost always feel either prideful ("I'm better than the people who do these things") or frustrated ("I can never measure up").

Is that what the Christian life is all about? A long list of rules and regulations? Not at all! Even if you don't know anyone as extreme as Neal, and even if you don't think you struggle with legalism, see what Jesus said in Mark 7:1-23.

[6]Jesus replied, "You hypocrites! Isaiah was prophesying about you when he said,

[7]'These people honor me with their lips,
but their hearts are far away.
Their worship is a farce,
for they replace God's commands with their
own man-made teachings.'*

[8]For you ignore God's specific laws and substitute your own traditions."

[9]Then he said, "You reject God's laws in order to hold on to your own traditions. [10]For instance, Moses gave you this law from God: 'Honor your father and mother,' and 'Anyone who speaks evil of father or mother must be put to death.'* [11]But you say it is all

## EXCUSES

**7:10-11 The Pharisees used God as an excuse to avoid helping their families, especially their parents. They thought it was more important to put money in the Temple treasury than to help their needy parents, although God's law specifically says to honor fathers and mothers (Exodus 20:12) and to care for those in need (Leviticus 25:35-43). We should give money and time to God, but we must never use God as an excuse to neglect our responsibilities. Helping those in need is one of the most important ways to honor God.**

right for people to say to their parents, 'Sorry, I can't help you. For I have vowed to give to God what I could have given to you.'* [12]You let them disregard their needy parents. [13]As such, you break the law of God in order to protect your own tradition. And this is only one example. There are many, many others."

[14]Then Jesus called to the crowd to come and hear. "All of you listen," he said, "and try to understand. [15]You are not defiled by what you eat; you are defiled by what you say and do!*"

[17]Then Jesus went into a house to get away from the crowds, and his disciples asked him what he meant by the statement he had made. [18]"Don't you understand either?" he asked. "Can't you see that what you eat won't defile you? [19]Food doesn't come in contact with your heart, but only passes through the stomach and then comes out again." (By saying this, he showed that every kind of food is acceptable.)

[20]And then he added, "It is the thought-life that defiles you. [21]For from within, out of a person's heart, come evil thoughts, sexual immorality, theft, murder, [22]adultery, greed, wickedness, deceit, eagerness for lustful pleasure, envy, slander, pride, and foolishness. [23]All these vile things come from within; they are what defile you and make you unacceptable to God."

[24]Then Jesus left Galilee and went north to the region of Tyre.* He tried to keep it secret that he was there, but he couldn't. As usual, the news of his arrival spread fast. [25]Right away a woman came to him whose little girl was possessed by an evil spirit. She had heard about Jesus, and now she came and fell at his feet. [26]She begged him to release her child from the demon's control.

Since she was a Gentile, born in Syrian Phoenicia, [27]Jesus told her, "First I should help my own family, the Jews.* It isn't right to take food from the children and throw it to the dogs."

[28]She replied, "That's true, Lord, but even the dogs under the table are given some crumbs from the children's plates."

[29]"Good answer!" he said. "And because you have answered so well, I have healed your daughter." [30]And when she arrived home, her little girl was lying quietly in bed, and the demon was gone.

[31]Jesus left Tyre and went to Sidon, then back to the Sea of Galilee and the region of the Ten Towns.*

7:3 Greek *washed with the fist.* 7:4 Some Greek manuscripts add *and dining couches.* 7:7 Isa 29:13. 7:10 Exod 20:12; 21:17; Lev 20:9; Deut 5:16. 7:11 Greek *'What I could have given to you is Corban' (that is, a gift).* 7:15 Some manuscripts add verse 16, *Anyone who is willing to hear should listen and understand.* 7:24 Some Greek manuscripts add *and Sidon.* 7:27 Greek *Let the children eat first.* 7:31 Greek *Decapolis.*

32A deaf man with a speech impediment was brought to him, and the people begged Jesus to lay his hands on the man to heal him. 33Jesus led him to a private place away from the crowd. He put his fingers into the man's ears. Then, spitting onto his own fingers, he touched the man's tongue with the spittle. 34And looking up to heaven, he sighed and commanded, "Be opened!"* 35Instantly the man could hear perfectly and speak plainly!

36Jesus told the crowd not to tell anyone, but the more he told them not to, the more they spread the news, 37for they were completely amazed. Again and again they said, "Everything he does is wonderful. He even heals those who are deaf and mute."

## CHAPTER 8

**ANOTHER MEALTIME MIRACLE.** About this time another great crowd had gathered, and the people ran out of food again. Jesus called his disciples and told them, 2"I feel sorry for these people. They have been here with me for three days, and they have nothing left to eat. 3And if I send them home without feeding them, they will faint along the road. For some of them have come a long distance."

4"How are we supposed to find enough food for them here in the wilderness?" his disciples asked.

5"How many loaves of bread do you have?" he asked.

"Seven," they replied. 6So Jesus told all the people to sit down on the ground. Then he took the seven loaves, thanked God for them, broke them into pieces, and gave them to his disciples, who distributed the bread to the crowd. 7A few small fish were found, too, so Jesus also blessed these and told the disciples to pass them out.

8They ate until they were full, and when the scraps were picked up, there were seven large baskets of food left over! 9There were about four thousand people in the crowd that day, and he sent them home after they had eaten. 10Immediately after this, he got into a boat with his disciples and crossed over to the region of Dalmanutha.

11When the Pharisees heard that Jesus had arrived, they came to argue with him. Testing him to see if he was from God, they demanded, "Give us a miraculous sign from heaven to prove yourself."

12When he heard this, he sighed deeply and said, "Why do you people keep demanding a miraculous sign? I assure you, I will not give this generation any such sign." 13So he got back into the boat and left them, and he crossed to the other side of the lake.

14But the disciples discovered they had forgotten to bring any food, so there was only one loaf of bread with them in the boat. 15As they were crossing the lake, Jesus warned them, "Beware of the yeast of the Pharisees and of Herod."

16They decided he was saying this because they hadn't brought any bread. 17Jesus knew what they were thinking, so he said, "Why are you so worried about having no food? Won't you ever learn or understand? Are your hearts too hard to take it in?

### HE KNOWS ● ● ● • •

**8:1-3 Do you ever feel that God is so busy with important concerns that he can't possibly be aware of your needs? Just as Jesus was concerned about those people's need for food, he is concerned about our daily needs. At another time Jesus said, "Don't worry about having enough food or drink or clothing. . . . Your heavenly Father already knows all your needs" (Matthew 6:31-32). Do you have concerns that you think would not interest God? There is no concern too large for him to handle, and no need too small to escape his interest.**

18'You have eyes—can't you see? You have ears—can't you hear?'* Don't you remember anything at all? 19What about the five thousand men I fed with five loaves of bread? How many baskets of leftovers did you pick up afterward?"

"Twelve," they said.

20"And when I fed the four thousand with seven loaves, how many large baskets of leftovers did you pick up?"

"Seven," they said.

21"Don't you understand even yet?" he asked them.

22When they arrived at Bethsaida, some people brought a blind man to Jesus, and they begged him to touch and heal the man. 23Jesus took the blind man by the hand and led him out of the village. Then, spitting on the man's eyes, he laid his hands on him and asked, "Can you see anything now?"

24The man looked around. "Yes," he said, "I see people, but I can't see them very clearly. They look like trees walking around."

25Then Jesus placed his hands over the man's eyes again. As the man stared intently, his sight was completely restored, and he could see everything clearly. 26Jesus sent him home, saying, "Don't go back into the village on your way home."

27Jesus and his disciples left Galilee and went up to the villages of Caesarea Philippi. As they were walking along, he asked them, "Who do people say I am?"

28"Well," they replied, "some say John the Baptist, some say Elijah, and others say you are one of the other prophets."

29Then Jesus asked, "Who do you say I am?"

Peter replied, "You are the Messiah." 30But Jesus warned them not to tell anyone about him.

31Then Jesus began to tell them that he, the Son of Man, would suffer many terrible things and be rejected by the leaders, the leading priests, and the teachers of religious law. He would be killed, and

### YOU ● ● ● • •

**8:29 Jesus asked the disciples who others thought he was; then he focused on them: "Who do you say I am?" It is not enough to know what others say about Jesus: you must know, understand, and accept for yourself that he is the Messiah. You must move from curiosity to commitment and from admiration to adoration.**

7:34 Greek text uses Aramaic *"Ephphatha"* and then translates it as "Be opened." **8:18** Jer 5:21.

three days later he would rise again. 32 As he talked about this openly with his disciples, Peter took him aside and told him he shouldn't say things like that.*

33 Jesus turned and looked at his disciples and then said to Peter very sternly, "Get away from me, Satan! You are seeing things merely from a human point of view, not from God's."

**UCCESS**

You've heard of *A Tale of Two Cities?* Call this "A Tale of Two Sisters."

Karen, a senior, has a 4.0 grade-point average and is practically guaranteed a scholarship. She is president of her class and is both captain and number one seed on the girl's tennis team. Tan and very pretty, Karen dates Mitchell. Together they were voted by their class as "most likely to succeed." Karen's ambition? To marry Mitchell and be a stockbroker on Wall Street in New York City.

If Karen represents "the best of times," then to many, Alice, a sophomore, probably embodies "the worst of times." She struggles in school, making mostly *C*s. She is not especially popular, nor is she very athletic. No, the truth is that Alice is painfully shy and average-looking. She has not been blessed with a boyfriend, voted into office, or had predictions of greatness bestowed upon her. Most of her free time goes to serving as a Big Sister to two youngsters at a local orphanage. Her goal in life? To be a social worker.

Do you know anyone like Karen? Like Alice? Which girl do you think is the most successful? By what standards does our society judge success and failure? What does Jesus say in Mark 9:33-37?

34 Then he called his disciples and the crowds to come over and listen. "If any of you wants to be my follower," he told them, "you must put aside your selfish ambition, shoulder your cross, and follow me. 35 If you try to keep your life for yourself, you will lose it. But if you give up your life for my sake and for the sake of the Good News, you will find true life. 36 And how do you benefit if you gain the whole world but lose your own soul* in the process? 37 Is anything worth more than your soul? 38 If a person is ashamed of me and my message in these adulterous and sinful days, I, the Son of Man, will be ashamed of that person when I return in the glory of my Father with the holy angels."

## CHAPTER 9 **THE TRANSFIGURATION.**

Jesus went on to say, "I assure you that some of you standing here right now will not die before you see the Kingdom of God arrive in great power!"

2 Six days later Jesus took Peter, James, and John to the top of a mountain. No one else was there. As the men watched, Jesus' appearance changed, 3 and his clothing became dazzling white, far whiter than any earthly process could ever make it. 4 Then Elijah and Moses appeared and began talking with Jesus.

5 "Teacher, this is wonderful!" Peter exclaimed. "We will make three shrines*—one for you, one for Moses, and one for Elijah." 6 He didn't really know what to say, for they were all terribly afraid.

7 Then a cloud came over them, and a voice from the cloud said, "This is my beloved Son. Listen to him." 8 Suddenly they looked around, and Moses and Elijah were gone, and only Jesus was with them. 9 As they descended the mountainside, he told them not to tell anyone what they had seen until he, the Son of Man, had risen from the dead. 10 So they kept it to themselves, but they often asked each other what he meant by "rising from the dead."

11 Now they began asking him, "Why do the teachers of religious law insist that Elijah must return before the Messiah comes?"

12 Jesus responded, "Elijah is indeed coming first to set everything in order. Why then is it written in the Scriptures that the Son of Man must suffer and be treated with utter contempt? 13 But I tell you, Elijah has already come, and he was badly mistreated, just as the Scriptures predicted."

14 At the foot of the mountain they found a great crowd surrounding the other disciples, as some teachers of religious law were arguing with them. 15 The crowd watched Jesus in awe as he came toward them, and then they ran to greet him. 16 "What is all this arguing about?" he asked.

17 One of the men in the crowd spoke up and said, "Teacher, I brought my son for you to heal him. He can't speak because he is possessed by an evil spirit that won't let him talk. 18 And whenever this evil spirit seizes him, it throws him violently to the ground and makes him foam at the mouth and grind his teeth and become rigid.* So I asked your disciples to cast out the evil spirit, but they couldn't do it."

19 Jesus said to them, "You faithless people! How long must I be with you until you believe? How long must I put up with you? Bring the boy to me." 20 So they brought the boy. But when the evil spirit saw Jesus, it threw the child into a violent convulsion, and he fell to the ground, writhing and foaming at the mouth. 21 "How long has this been happening?" Jesus asked the boy's father.

He replied, "Since he was very small. 22 The evil spirit often makes him fall into the fire or into water, trying to kill him. Have mercy on us and help us. Do something if you can."

23 "What do you mean, 'If I can'?" Jesus asked. "Anything is possible if a person believes."

**POWER ● ● • • •**

9:23 **Jesus' words do not mean that we can automatically obtain anything we want if we just think positively. Jesus meant that anything is *possible* with faith because nothing is too difficult for God. This is not a teaching on how to pray as much as a statement about God's power to overcome obstacles to his work. We cannot have everything we pray for as if by magic, but, with faith, we can have everything we need to serve God.**

8:32 Or *and began to correct him.* 8:36 Or *your life;* also in 8:37. 9:5 Or *shelters;* Greek reads *tabernacles.* 9:18 Or *become weak.*

24The father instantly replied, "I do believe, but help me not to doubt!"

25When Jesus saw that the crowd of onlookers was growing, he rebuked the evil spirit. "Spirit of deafness and muteness," he said, "I command you to come out of this child and never enter him again!" 26Then the spirit screamed and threw the boy into another violent convulsion and left him. The boy lay there motionless, and he appeared to be dead. A murmur ran through the crowd, "He's dead." 27But Jesus took him by the hand and helped him to his feet, and he stood up.

28Afterward, when Jesus was alone in the house with his disciples, they asked him, "Why couldn't we cast out that evil spirit?"

29Jesus replied, "This kind can be cast out only by prayer.*"

30Leaving that region, they traveled through Galilee. Jesus tried to avoid all publicity 31in order to spend more time with his disciples and teach them. He said to them, "The Son of Man is going to be betrayed. He will be killed, but three days later he will rise from the dead." 32But they didn't understand what he was saying, and they were afraid to ask him what he meant.

33After they arrived at Capernaum, Jesus and his disciples settled in the house where they would be staying. Jesus asked them, "What were you discussing out on the road?" 34But they didn't answer, because they had been arguing about which of them was the greatest. 35He sat down and called the twelve disciples over to him. Then he said, "Anyone who wants to be the first must take last place and be the servant of everyone else."

36Then he put a little child among them. Taking the child in his arms, he said to them, 37"Anyone who welcomes a little child like this on my behalf welcomes me, and anyone who welcomes me welcomes my Father who sent me."

38John said to Jesus, "Teacher, we saw a man using your name to cast out demons, but we told him to stop because he isn't one of our group."

39"Don't stop him!" Jesus said. "No one who performs miracles in my name will soon be able to speak evil of me. 40Anyone who is not against us is for us. 41If anyone gives you even a cup of water because you belong to the Messiah, I assure you, that person will be rewarded.

42"But if anyone causes one of these little ones who trusts in me to lose faith, it would be better for that person to be thrown into the sea with a large millstone tied around the neck. 43If your hand causes you to sin, cut it off. It is better to enter heaven* with only one hand than to go into the unquenchable fires of hell with two hands.* 45If your foot causes you to sin, cut it off. It is better to enter heaven with only one foot than to be thrown into hell with two feet.* 47And if your eye causes you to sin, gouge it out. It is better to enter the Kingdom of God half blind than to have two eyes and be thrown into hell, 48'where the worm never dies and the fire never goes out.'*

## RUTHLESS ● ● • • •

9:43-48 **Jesus used startling language to stress the importance of cutting sin out of our life. Painful discipline is required of his true followers. Giving up a relationship, job, or habit that is against God's will may seem just as painful as cutting off a hand. Our high goal, however, is worth any sacrifice; Christ is worth any possible loss. Nothing should stand in the way of faith. We must be ruthless in removing sins from our life now, in order to avoid being stuck with them for eternity. Make your choices from an eternal perspective.**

## "Here's what I did..."

In my school, people are popular only if they have the right looks, the right clothes, live in a certain neighborhood, play on the football team or are a cheerleader, or date a football player or cheerleader. The lines are pretty clearly drawn. And I'm on the other side of every one of those lines.

For a while it really bothered me. But when I tried to break into one of the cliques I found myself acting phony, and I couldn't stand it. I couldn't seem to help it, though; I wanted people to like me. I wanted to be popular.

Then, slowly, my viewpoint changed. The change started when my youth group studied the book of Mark. I really related to the disciples in chapters 9 and 10. They were trying to see who was more popular with Jesus, who would be considered the greatest. And Jesus said, "Many who seem to be important now will be the least important then, and those who are considered least here will be the greatest then" (Mark 10:31).

I realized it didn't really matter whether kids in my school thought I was great; what matters is what God thinks of me. If I want him to think I'm great, I have to forget about the phoniness and just try to be friends with all kinds of people.

I've started doing that, and now I have lots of friends. I still wouldn't be considered one of the "popular" people, but that's OK now. I'm in touch with God, and because of that, I know I'm popular with one Person whose opinion really matters.

*Marita*

AGE 16

9:29 Some manuscripts add *and fasting.* 9:43a Greek *enter life;* also in 9:45. 9:43b Some manuscripts add verse 44 (which is identical with 9:48). 9:45 Some manuscripts add verse 46 (which is identical with 9:48). 9:48 Isa 66:24.

49"For everyone will be purified with fire.* 50Salt is
good for seasoning. But if it loses its flavor, how do
you make it salty again? You must have the qualities
of salt among yourselves and live in peace with each
other."

CHAPTER **10** **DIVORCE AND MARRIAGE.** Then Jesus
left Capernaum and went southward to the region of
Judea and into the area east of the Jordan River. As
always there were the crowds, and as usual he taught
them.

2Some Pharisees came and tried to trap him with
this question: "Should a man be allowed to divorce
his wife?"

3"What did Moses say about divorce?" Jesus asked
them.

4"Well, he permitted it," they replied. "He said a
man merely has to write his wife an official letter of
divorce and send her away."*

5But Jesus responded, "He wrote those instructions only as a concession to your hard-hearted
wickedness. 6But God's plan was seen from the beginning of creation, for 'He made them male and
female.'* 7'This explains why a man leaves his father
and mother and is joined to his wife,* 8and the two
are united into one.'* Since they are no longer two
but one, 9let no one separate them, for God has
joined them together."

**BARRIERS ● ● ● • •**

10:17-23 **This young man wanted to be sure he would get eternal life, so he asked what he could *do*. Jesus lovingly addressed him with a challenge that brought out his true motives: "Sell all you have and give the money to the poor." Here was the barrier that could keep this young man out of the kingdom: his love of money. Money represented his pride of accomplishment and self-effort. Ironically, the young man's attitude kept him from keeping the first commandment, to let nothing be more important than God (Exodus 20:3). He could not meet the one requirement Jesus gave—to turn his whole heart and life over to God. The man came to Jesus wondering what he could do; he left seeing what he was unable to do. What barriers are keeping you from turning your life over to Christ?**

10Later, when he was alone with his disciples in the
house, they brought up the subject again. 11He told
them, "Whoever divorces his wife and marries
someone else commits adultery against her. 12And if
a woman divorces her husband and remarries, she
commits adultery."

13One day some parents brought their children to
Jesus so he could touch them and bless them, but the
disciples told them not to bother him. 14But when
Jesus saw what was happening, he was very displeased with his disciples. He said to them, "Let the
children come to me. Don't stop them! For the
Kingdom of God belongs to such as these. 15I assure
you, anyone who doesn't have their kind of faith will
never get into the Kingdom of God." 16Then he took
the children into his arms and placed his hands on
their heads and blessed them.

17As he was starting out on a trip, a man came
running up to Jesus, knelt down, and asked, "Good
Teacher, what should I do to get eternal life?"

18"Why do you call me good?" Jesus asked. "Only
God is truly good. 19But as for your question, you
know the commandments: 'Do not murder. Do not
commit adultery. Do not steal. Do not testify falsely.
Do not cheat. Honor your father and mother.'*"

20"Teacher," the man replied, "I've obeyed all
these commandments since I was a child."

21Jesus felt genuine love for this man as he looked
at him. "You lack only one thing," he told him. "Go
and sell all you have and give the money to the poor,
and you will have treasure in heaven. Then come,
follow me." 22At this, the man's face fell, and he went
sadly away because he had many possessions.

23Jesus looked around and said to his disciples,
"How hard it is for rich people to get into the Kingdom of God!" 24This amazed them. But Jesus said
again, "Dear children, it is very hard* to get into the
Kingdom of God. 25It is easier for a camel to go
through the eye of a needle than for a rich person to
enter the Kingdom of God!"

26The disciples were astounded. "Then who in the
world can be saved?" they asked.

27Jesus looked at them intently and said, "Humanly speaking, it is impossible. But not with God.
Everything is possible with God."

28Then Peter began to mention all that he and the
other disciples had left behind. "We've given up
everything to follow you," he said.

29And Jesus replied, "I assure you that everyone
who has given up house or brothers or sisters or
mother or father or children or property, for my sake
and for the Good News, 30will receive now in return,
a hundred times over, houses, brothers, sisters,
mothers, children, and property—with persecutions. And in the world to come they will have
eternal life. 31But many who seem to be important
now will be the least important then, and those who
are considered least here will be the greatest then.*"

32They were now on the way to Jerusalem, and
Jesus was walking ahead of them. The disciples were
filled with dread and the people following behind
were overwhelmed with fear. Taking the twelve disciples aside, Jesus once more began to describe everything that was about to happen to him in Jerusalem.
33"When we get to Jerusalem," he told them, "the
Son of Man will be betrayed to the leading priests
and the teachers of religious law. They will sentence
him to die and hand him over to the Romans. 34They
will mock him, spit on him, beat him with their
whips, and kill him, but after three days he will rise
again."

35Then James and John, the sons of Zebedee, came

9:49 Greek *salted with fire.* Some manuscripts add *and every sacrifice will be salted with salt.* 10:4 Deut 24:1. 10:6 Gen 1:27; 5:2. 10:7 Some manuscripts do not include *and is joined to his wife.* 10:7-8 Gen 2:24. 10:19 Exod 20:12-16; Deut 5:16-20. 10:24 Some manuscripts add *for those who trust in riches.* 10:31 Greek *But many who are first will be last; and the last, first.*

over and spoke to him. "Teacher," they said, "we
want you to do us a favor."
36"What is it?" he asked.
37"In your glorious Kingdom, we want to sit in
places of honor next to you," they said, "one at your
right and the other at your left."
38But Jesus answered, "You don't know what you
are asking! Are you able to drink from the bitter cup
of sorrow I am about to drink? Are you able to be
baptized with the baptism of suffering I must be
baptized with?"
39"Oh yes," they said, "we are able!"
And Jesus said, "You will indeed drink from my
cup and be baptized with my baptism, 40but I have
no right to say who will sit on the thrones next to
mine. God has prepared those places for the ones he
has chosen."
41When the ten other disciples discovered what
James and John had asked, they were indignant. 42So
Jesus called them together and said, "You know that
in this world kings are tyrants, and officials lord it
over the people beneath them. 43But among you it
should be quite different. Whoever wants to be a
leader among you must be your servant, 44and whoever wants to be first must be the slave of all. 45For
even I, the Son of Man, came here not to be served
but to serve others, and to give my life as a ransom
for many."
46And so they reached Jericho. Later, as Jesus and
his disciples left town, a great crowd was following.
A blind beggar named Bartimaeus (son of Timaeus)
was sitting beside the road as Jesus was going by.
47When Bartimaeus heard that Jesus from Nazareth
was nearby, he began to shout out, "Jesus, Son of
David, have mercy on me!"
48"Be quiet!" some of the people yelled at him.
But he only shouted louder, "Son of David, have
mercy on me!"
49When Jesus heard him, he stopped and said,
"Tell him to come here."
So they called the blind man. "Cheer up," they
said. "Come on, he's calling you!" 50Bartimaeus
threw aside his coat, jumped up, and came to Jesus.
51"What do you want me to do for you?" Jesus
asked.
"Teacher," the blind man said, "I want to see!"
52And Jesus said to him, "Go your way. Your faith
has healed you." And instantly the blind man could
see! Then he followed Jesus down the road.*

## CHAPTER 11

**CROWDS WELCOME JESUS.** As Jesus
and his disciples approached Jerusalem, they came
to the towns of Bethphage and Bethany, on the
Mount of Olives. Jesus sent two of them on ahead.
2"Go into that village over there," he told them, "and
as soon as you enter it, you will see a colt tied there
that has never been ridden. Untie it and bring it here.
3If anyone asks what you are doing, just say, 'The
Lord needs it and will return it soon.'"
4The two disciples left and found the colt standing
in the street, tied outside a house. 5As they were
untying it, some bystanders demanded, "What are
you doing, untying that colt?" 6They said what Jesus
had told them to say, and they were permitted to take
it. 7Then they brought the colt to Jesus and threw
their garments over it, and he sat on it.
8Many in the crowd spread their coats on the road
ahead of Jesus, and others cut leafy branches in the
fields and spread them along the way. 9He was in the
center of the procession, and the crowds all around
him were shouting,

"Praise God!*
Bless the one who comes in the name of the
Lord!
10 Bless the coming kingdom of our ancestor David!
Praise God in highest heaven!"*

11So Jesus came to Jerusalem and went into the
Temple. He looked around carefully at everything,
and then he left because it was late in the afternoon.
Then he went out to Bethany with the twelve disciples.
12The next morning as they were leaving Bethany,
Jesus felt hungry. 13He noticed a fig tree a little way
off that was in full leaf, so he went over to see if he
could find any figs on it. But there were only leaves
because it was too early in the season for fruit.
14Then Jesus said to the tree, "May no one ever eat
your fruit again!" And the disciples heard him say it.
15When they arrived back in Jerusalem, Jesus entered the Temple and began to drive out the merchants and their customers. He knocked over the
tables of the money changers and the stalls of those
selling doves, 16and he stopped everyone from bringing in merchandise. 17He taught them, "The
Scriptures declare, 'My Temple will be called a place
of prayer for all nations,' but you have turned it into
a den of thieves."*
18When the leading priests and teachers of religious law heard what Jesus had done, they began
planning how to kill him. But they were afraid of
him because the people were so enthusiastic about
Jesus' teaching. 19That evening Jesus and the disciples* left the city.
20The next morning as they passed by the fig tree
he had cursed, the disciples noticed it was withered
from the roots. 21Peter remembered what Jesus had
said to the tree on the previous day and exclaimed,
"Look, Teacher! The fig tree you cursed has withered!"

### UPSET ● ● • • •

11:14-15 **Jesus became angry, but he did not sin in his anger. There is a place for righteous indignation. Christians should be upset about sin and injustice and should take a stand against them. Unfortunately, believers often are passive about these important issues and get angry over personal insults and petty irritations. Direct your anger toward the right issues.**

10:52 Or *on the way.* 11:9 Greek *Hosanna,* an exclamation of praise that literally means "save now"; also in 11:10. 11:9-10 Pss 118:25-26; 148:1. 11:17 Isa 56:7; Jer 7:11. 11:19 Greek *they;* some manuscripts read *he.*

## MOTIVATIONS ● • • • •

**11:24** **Jesus, our example for prayer, once prayed, "Everything is possible for you. . . . Yet I want your will, not mine" (Mark 14:36). Often when we pray, we are motivated by our own interests and desires. We like to hear that we can have anything. But Jesus prayed with God's interests in mind. When we pray, we are to express our desires, but we should want God's will above ours. Check yourself to see if your prayers are focusing on your interests or on God's.**

[22]Then Jesus said to the disciples, "Have faith in God. [23]I assure you that you can say to this mountain, 'May God lift you up and throw you into the sea,' and your command will be obeyed. All that's required is that you really believe and do not doubt in your heart. [24]Listen to me! You can pray for anything, and if you believe, you will have it. [25]But when you are praying, first forgive anyone you are holding a grudge against, so that your Father in heaven will forgive your sins, too.*"

[27]By this time they had arrived in Jerusalem again. As Jesus was walking through the Temple area, the leading priests, the teachers of religious law, and the other leaders came up to him. They demanded, [28]"By whose authority did you drive out the merchants from the Temple?* Who gave you such authority?"

[29]"I'll tell who gave me authority to do these things if you answer one question," Jesus replied. [30]"Did John's baptism come from heaven or was it merely human? Answer me!"

[31]They talked it over among themselves. "If we say it was from heaven, he will ask why we didn't believe him. [32]But do we dare say it was merely human?" For they were afraid that the people would start a riot, since everyone thought that John was a prophet. [33]So they finally replied, "We don't know."

And Jesus responded, "Then I won't answer your question either."

## CHAPTER 12

**A STORY ABOUT A FARM.** Then Jesus began telling them stories: "A man planted a vineyard, built a wall around it, dug a pit for pressing out the grape juice, and built a lookout tower. Then he leased the vineyard to tenant farmers and moved to another country. [2]At grape-picking time he sent one of his servants to collect his share of the crop. [3]But the farmers grabbed the servant, beat him up, and sent him back empty-handed.

[4]"The owner then sent another servant, but they beat him over the head and treated him shamefully. [5]The next servant he sent was killed. Others who were sent were either beaten or killed, [6]until there was only one left—his son whom he loved dearly. The owner finally sent him, thinking, 'Surely they will respect my son.'

[7]"But the farmers said to one another, 'Here comes the heir to this estate. Let's kill him and get the estate for ourselves!' [8]So they grabbed him and murdered him and threw his body out of the vineyard.

[9]"What do you suppose the owner of the vineyard will do?" Jesus asked. "I'll tell you—he will come and kill them all and lease the vineyard to others. [10]Didn't you ever read this in the Scriptures?

'The stone rejected by the builders
has now become the cornerstone.
[11]This is the Lord's doing,
and it is marvelous to see.'*"

[12]The Jewish leaders wanted to arrest him for using this illustration because they realized he was pointing at them—they were the wicked farmers in his story. But they were afraid to touch him because of the crowds. So they left him and went away.

[13]The leaders sent some Pharisees and supporters of Herod to try to trap Jesus into saying something for which he could be arrested. [14]"Teacher," these men said, "we know how honest you are. You are impartial and don't play favorites. You sincerely teach the ways of God. Now tell us—is it right to pay taxes to the Roman government or not? [15]Should we pay them, or should we not?"

Jesus saw through their hypocrisy and said, "Whom are you trying to fool with your trick questions? Show me a Roman coin,* and I'll tell you." [16]When they handed it to him, he asked, "Whose picture and title are stamped on it?"

"Caesar's," they replied.

[17]"Well, then," Jesus said, "give to Caesar what belongs to him. But everything that belongs to God must be given to God." This reply completely amazed them.

[18]Then the Sadducees stepped forward—a group of Jews who say there is no resurrection after death. They posed this question: [19]"Teacher, Moses gave us a law that if a man dies, leaving a wife without children, his brother should marry the widow and have a child who will be the brother's heir.* [20]Well, there were seven brothers. The oldest of them married and then died without children. [21]So the second brother married the widow, but soon he too died and left no children. Then the next brother married her and died without children. [22]This continued until all the brothers had married her and died, and still there were no children. Last of all, the woman died, too. [23]So tell us, whose wife will she be in the resurrection? For all seven were married to her."

[24]Jesus replied, "Your problem is that you don't know the Scriptures, and you don't know the power of God. [25]For when the dead rise, they won't be married. They will be like the angels in heaven. [26]But

## IMAGE ● • • • •

**12:17** **The Pharisees and Herodians thought they had the perfect question to trap Jesus. But Jesus answered wisely, once again exposing their self-interest and wrong motives. Jesus said that the coin bearing the emperor's image should be given to the emperor. But whatever bears God's image—our life—belongs to God. Are you giving God all that is rightfully his? Make sure your life is given to God—you bear his image.**

**11:25** Some manuscripts add verse 26, *But if you do not forgive, neither will your Father who is in heaven forgive your sins.* **11:28** Or *By whose authority do you do these things?* **12:10-11** Ps 118:22-23. **12:15** Greek *a denarius.* **12:19** Deut 25:5-6.

## WHAT JESUS SAID ABOUT LOVE

In Mark 12:28, a religious teacher asked Jesus which one of all the commandments was the most important to follow. Jesus mentioned two commandments, one from Deuteronomy 6:5, the other from Leviticus 19:18. Both had to do with love. Why is love so important? Jesus said that all of the commandments were given for two simple reasons—to help us love God and love others as we should.

*What Else Did Jesus Say about Love?*

God loves us. . . . John 3:16

We are to love God. . . . Matthew 22:37

Because God loves us, he cares for us. . . . Matthew 6:25-34

God wants everyone to know how much he loves them. . . . John 17:23

God loves even those who hate him; we are to do the same. . . . Matthew 5:43-47; Luke 6:35

God seeks out even those most alienated from him. . . . Luke 15

God must be your first love. . . . Matthew 6:24; 10:37

You love God when you obey him. . . . John 14:21; 15:10

God loves Jesus, his Son. . . . John 5:20; 10:17

Jesus loves God. . . . John 14:31

Those who refuse Jesus don't have God's love. . . . John 5:41-44

Jesus loves us just as God loves Jesus. . . . John 15:9

Jesus proved his love for us by dying on the cross so that we could live eternally with him. . . . John 3:14-15; 15:13-14

The love between God and Jesus is the perfect example of how we are to love others. . . . John 17:21-26

We are to love one another (John 13:34-35) and demonstrate that love. . . . Matthew 5:40-42; 10:42

We are not to love the praise of men (John 12:43), selfish recognition (Matthew 23:6), earthly belongings (Luke 16:19-31), or anything more than God. . . . Luke 16:13

Jesus' love extends to each individual. . . . John 10:11-15; Mark 10:21

Jesus wants us to love him through both the good and difficult times. . . . Matthew 26:31-35

Jesus wants our love to be genuine. . . . John 21:15-17

---

now, as to whether the dead will be raised—haven't
you ever read about this in the writings of Moses, in
the story of the burning bush? Long after Abraham,
Isaac, and Jacob had died, God said to Moses,* 'I am
the God of Abraham, the God of Isaac, and the God
of Jacob.'* 27So he is the God of the living, not the
dead. You have made a serious error."
28One of the teachers of religious law was standing
there listening to the discussion. He realized that
Jesus had answered well, so he asked, "Of all the
commandments, which is the most important?"
29Jesus replied, "The most important commandment is this: 'Hear, O Israel! The Lord our God is the
one and only Lord. 30And you must love the Lord
your God with all your heart, all your soul, all your
mind, and all your strength.'* 31The second is
equally important: 'Love your neighbor as yourself.'* No other commandment is greater than
these."
32The teacher of religious law replied, "Well said,
Teacher. You have spoken the truth by saying that
there is only one God and no other. 33And I know it
is important to love him with all my heart and all my
understanding and all my strength, and to love my
neighbors as myself. This is more important than to
offer all of the burnt offerings and sacrifices required
in the law."
34Realizing this man's understanding, Jesus said to
him, "You are not far from the Kingdom of God."
And after that, no one dared to ask him any more
questions.
35Later, as Jesus was teaching the people in the
Temple, he asked, "Why do the teachers of religious
law claim that the Messiah will be the son of David?

### SIMPLE ● • • • ·

12:29-31 **God's laws are not burdensome in number or detail. They can be reduced to two simple rules for life: love God and love others. These commands are from the Old Testament (Deuteronomy 6:5; Leviticus 19:18). When you love God completely and care for others as you care for yourself, then you have fulfilled the intent of the Ten Commandments and the other Old Testament laws. According to Jesus, these two rules summarize all God's laws. Let them rule your thoughts, decisions, and actions. When you are uncertain about what to do, ask yourself which course of action best demonstrates love for God and love for others.**

**12:26a** Greek *in the story of the bush? God said to him.* **12:26b** Exod 3:6. **12:29-30** Deut 6:4-5. **12:31** Lev 19:18.

36 For David himself, speaking under the inspiration of the Holy Spirit, said,

'The LORD said to my Lord,
Sit in honor at my right hand
until I humble your enemies beneath your feet.'*

37 Since David himself called him Lord, how can he be his son at the same time?" And the crowd listened to him with great interest.

38 Here are some of the other things he taught them at this time: "Beware of these teachers of religious law! For they love to parade in flowing robes and to have everyone bow to them as they walk in the marketplaces. 39 And how they love the seats of honor in the synagogues and at banquets. 40 But they shamelessly cheat widows out of their property, and then, to cover up the kind of people they really are, they make long prayers in public. Because of this, their punishment will be the greater."

41 Jesus went over to the collection box in the Temple and sat and watched as the crowds dropped in their money. Many rich people put in large amounts. 42 Then a poor widow came and dropped in two pennies.* 43 He called his disciples to him and said, "I assure you, this poor widow has given more than all the others have given. 44 For they gave a tiny part of their surplus, but she, poor as she is, has given everything she has."

## CHAPTER 13

**JESUS TELLS ABOUT THE FUTURE.** As Jesus was leaving the Temple that day, one of his disciples said, "Teacher, look at these tremendous buildings! Look at the massive stones in the walls!"

2 Jesus replied, "These magnificent buildings will be so completely demolished that not one stone will be left on top of another."

### OPPONENTS • • • • •

13:9-10 **As the early church began to grow, most of the disciples experienced the kind of persecution Jesus was talking about. Since the time of Christ, Christians have been persecuted in their own lands and in foreign mission fields. Though you may be safe from persecution now, your vision of God's kingdom must not be limited by what happens only to you. A quick look at a newspaper will show you that many Christians in other parts of the world daily face hardships. Persecutions are an opportunity for Christians to witness for Christ to those opposed to him. They serve God's desire that the Good News be made available to everyone.**

3 Later, Jesus sat on the slopes of the Mount of Olives across the valley from the Temple. Peter, James, John, and Andrew came to him privately and asked him, 4 "When will all this take place? And will there be any sign ahead of time to show us when all this will be fulfilled?"

5 Jesus replied, "Don't let anyone mislead you, 6 because many will come in my name, claiming to be the Messiah.* They will lead many astray. 7 And wars will break out near and far, but don't panic. Yes, these things must come, but the end won't follow immediately. 8 Nations and kingdoms will proclaim war against each other, and there will be earthquakes in many parts of the world, and famines. But all this will be only the beginning of the horrors to come. 9 But when these things begin to happen, watch out! You will be handed over to the courts and beaten in the synagogues. You will be accused before governors and kings of being my followers. This will be your opportunity to tell them about me.* 10 And the Good News must first be preached to every nation. 11 But when you are arrested and stand trial, don't worry about what to say in your defense. Just say what God tells you to. Then it is not you who will be speaking, but the Holy Spirit.

12 "Brother will betray brother to death, fathers will betray their own children, and children will rise against their parents and cause them to be killed. 13 And everyone will hate you because of your allegiance to me. But those who endure to the end will be saved.

14 "The time will come when you will see the sacrilegious object that causes desecration* standing where it should not be"—reader, pay attention! "Then those in Judea must flee to the hills. 15 A person outside the house* must not go back into the house to pack. 16 A person in the field must not return even to get a coat. 17 How terrible it will be for pregnant women and for mothers nursing their babies in those days. 18 And pray that your flight will not be in winter. 19 For those will be days of greater horror than at any time since God created the world. And it will never happen again. 20 In fact, unless the Lord shortens that time of calamity, the entire human race will be destroyed. But for the sake of his chosen ones he has shortened those days.

21 "And then if anyone tells you, 'Look, here is the Messiah,' or, 'There he is,' don't pay any attention. 22 For false messiahs and false prophets will rise up and perform miraculous signs and wonders so as to deceive, if possible, even God's chosen ones. 23 Watch out! I have warned you!

24 "At that time, after those horrible days end,

the sun will be darkened,
the moon will not give light,
25 the stars will fall from the sky,
and the powers of heaven will be shaken.*

26 Then everyone will see the Son of Man arrive on the clouds with great power and glory.* 27 And he will

### HIGHEST LOVE • • • • •

14:6-7 **Jesus was not saying that we should neglect the poor, nor was he justifying indifference to them. He was praising Mary for her unselfish act of worship. The essence of worshiping Christ is to regard him with utmost love, respect, and devotion and to be willing to sacrifice to him what is most precious.**

12:36 Ps 110:1. 12:42 Greek *2 lepta, which is a kodrantes.* 13:6 Greek *name, saying, 'I am.'* 13:9 Or *This will be your testimony against them.* 13:14 Greek *the abomination of desolation.* See Dan 9:27; 11:31; 12:11. 13:15 Greek *on the roof.* 13:24-25 See Isa 13:10; 34:4; Joel 2:10. 13:26 See Dan 7:13.

send forth his angels to gather together his chosen
ones from all over the world—from the farthest ends
of the earth and heaven.
28 "Now, learn a lesson from the fig tree. When its
buds become tender and its leaves begin to sprout,
you know without being told that summer is near.
29 Just so, when you see the events I've described
beginning to happen, you can be sure that his return
is very near, right at the door. 30 I assure you, this
generation* will not pass from the scene until all
these events have taken place. 31 Heaven and earth
will disappear, but my words will remain forever.
32 "However, no one knows the day or hour when
these things will happen, not even the angels in
heaven or the Son himself. Only the Father knows.
33 And since you don't know when they will happen,
stay alert and keep watch.*
34 "The coming of the Son of Man can be compared with that of a man who left home to go on a
trip. He gave each of his employees instructions
about the work they were to do, and he told the
gatekeeper to watch for his return. 35 So keep a sharp
lookout! For you do not know when the homeowner
will return—at evening, midnight, early dawn, or
late daybreak. 36 Don't let him find you sleeping
when he arrives without warning. 37 What I say to you
I say to everyone: Watch for his return!"

## CHAPTER 14

**A PLOT TO KILL JESUS.** It was now
two days before the Passover celebration and the
Festival of Unleavened Bread. The leading priests
and the teachers of religious law were still looking
for an opportunity to capture Jesus secretly and put
him to death. 2 "But not during the Passover," they
agreed, "or there will be a riot."
3 Meanwhile, Jesus was in Bethany at the home of
Simon, a man who had leprosy. During supper, a
woman came in with a beautiful jar of expensive
perfume.* She broke the seal and poured the perfume over his head. 4 Some of those at the table were
indignant. "Why was this expensive perfume
wasted?" they asked. 5 "She could have sold it for a
small fortune* and given the money to the poor!"
And they scolded her harshly.
6 But Jesus replied, "Leave her alone. Why berate
her for doing such a good thing to me? 7 You will
always have the poor among you, and you can help
them whenever you want to. But I will not be here
with you much longer. 8 She has done what she could
and has anointed my body for burial ahead of time.
9 I assure you, wherever the Good News is preached
throughout the world, this woman's deed will be
talked about in her memory."
10 Then Judas Iscariot, one of the twelve disciples,
went to the leading priests to arrange to betray Jesus
to them. 11 The leading priests were delighted when
they heard why he had come, and they promised
him a reward. So he began looking for the right time
and place to betray Jesus.

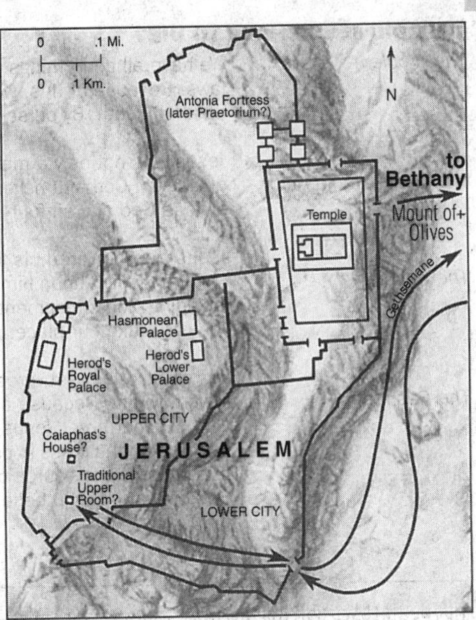


**UPPER ROOM AND GETHSEMANE**
Jesus and the disciples ate the traditional Passover meal in an upper room in the city and then went to the Mount of Olives into a garden called Gethsemane. In the cool of the evening, Jesus prayed for strength to face the trial and suffering ahead.

12 On the first day of the Festival of Unleavened
Bread (the day the Passover lambs were sacrificed),
Jesus' disciples asked him, "Where do you want us
to go to prepare the Passover supper?"
13 So Jesus sent two of them into Jerusalem to
make the arrangements. "As you go into the city," he
told them, "a man carrying a pitcher of water will
meet you. Follow him. 14 At the house he enters, say
to the owner, 'The Teacher asks, Where is the guest
room where I can eat the Passover meal with my
disciples?' 15 He will take you upstairs to a large room
that is already set up. That is the place; go ahead and
prepare our supper there." 16 So the two disciples
went on ahead into the city and found everything
just as Jesus had said, and they prepared the Passover
supper there.
17 In the evening Jesus arrived with the twelve disciples. 18 As they were sitting around the table eating,
Jesus said, "The truth is, one of you will betray me,
one of you who is here eating with me."
19 Greatly distressed, one by one they began to ask
him, "I'm not the one, am I?"
20 He replied, "It is one of you twelve, one who is
eating with me now.* 21 For I, the Son of Man, must
die, as the Scriptures declared long ago. But how
terrible it will be for my betrayer. Far better for him
if he had never been born!"
22 As they were eating, Jesus took a loaf of bread
and asked God's blessing on it. Then he broke it in

13:30 Or *this age,* or *this nation.* 13:33 Some manuscripts add *and pray.* 14:3 Greek *an alabaster jar of expensive ointment, pure nard.* 14:5 Greek *300 denarii.* A denarius was the equivalent of a full day's wage. 14:20 Or *one who is dipping bread into the bowl with me.*

## WHY DID JESUS HAVE TO DIE?

| | |
|---|---|
| *The Problem* | We have all done things that are wrong, and we have failed to obey God's laws. Because of this, we have been separated from God our Creator and deserve death. By ourselves we can do nothing to become reunited with God. |
| *Why Jesus Could Help* | Jesus was not only a man, he was God's unique Son. Because Jesus never disobeyed God and never sinned, only he can bridge the gap between the sinless God and sinful humanity. |
| *The Solution* | Jesus freely offered his life for us, dying on the cross in our place, taking all our wrongdoing upon himself, and saving us from the consequences of sin—including God's judgment and death. God in his love and his justice sent Jesus to take our place. |
| *The Results* | Jesus took our past, present, and future sins upon himself so that we could have new life. Because all our wrongdoing is forgiven, we are reconciled to God. Furthermore, Jesus' resurrection from the dead is the proof that his sacrifice on the cross in our place was acceptable to God, and his resurrection has become the source of new life for those who believe that Jesus is the Son of God. All who believe in him may have new life and live it in union with him. |

pieces and gave it to the disciples, saying, "Take it, for this is my body."
[23]And he took a cup of wine and gave thanks to God for it. He gave it to them, and they all drank from it.
[24]And he said to them, "This is my blood, poured out for many, sealing the covenant* between God and his people.
[25]I solemnly declare that I will not drink wine again until that day when I drink it new in the Kingdom of God."
[26]Then they sang a hymn and went out to the Mount of Olives.
[27]"All of you will desert me," Jesus told them. "For the Scriptures say,

'God* will strike the Shepherd,
and the sheep will be scattered.'*

[28]But after I am raised from the dead, I will go ahead of you to Galilee and meet you there."
[29]Peter said to him, "Even if everyone else deserts you, I never will."
[30]"Peter," Jesus replied, "the truth is, this very night, before the rooster crows twice, you will deny me three times."
[31]"No!" Peter insisted. "Not even if I have to die with you! I will never deny you!" And all the others vowed the same.
[32]And they came to an olive grove called Gethsemane, and Jesus said, "Sit here while I go and pray."
[33]He took Peter, James, and John with him, and he began to be filled with horror and deep distress.
[34]He told them, "My soul is crushed with grief to the point of death. Stay here and watch with me."
[35]He went on a little farther and fell face down on the ground. He prayed that, if it were possible, the awful hour awaiting him might pass him by.
[36]"Abba,* Father," he said, "everything is possible for you. Please take this cup of suffering away from me. Yet I want your will, not mine."
[37]Then he returned and found the disciples asleep. "Simon!" he said to Peter. "Are you asleep? Couldn't you stay awake and watch with me even one hour?
[38]Keep alert and pray. Otherwise temptation will overpower you. For though the spirit is willing enough, the body is weak."
[39]Then Jesus left them again and prayed, repeating his pleadings.
[40]Again he returned to them and found them sleeping, for they just couldn't keep their eyes open. And they didn't know what to say.
[41]When he returned to them the third time, he said, "Still sleeping? Still resting?* Enough! The time has come. I, the Son of Man, am betrayed into the hands of sinners.
[42]Up, let's be going. See, my betrayer is here!"
[43]And immediately, as he said this, Judas, one of the twelve disciples, arrived with a mob that was armed with swords and clubs. They had been sent out by the leading priests, the teachers of religious law, and the other leaders.
[44]Judas had given them a prearranged signal: "You will know which one to arrest when I go over and give him the kiss of greeting. Then you can take him away under guard."

## NO EXCUSES • • • • •

14:71 **It is easy to get angry at the Jewish Sanhedrin for their injustice in condemning Jesus, but Peter and the rest of the disciples also contributed to Jesus' pain by deserting him (14:50). While most of us are not like the Jewish leaders, we are all like the disciples, for all of us have been guilty of denying Christ as Lord in vital areas of our life. We may pride ourself that we have not committed certain sins, but we are all guilty of sin. Don't excuse yourself by pointing the finger at others whose sins seem worse than yours.**

14:24 Some manuscripts read *the new covenant.* 14:27a Greek *I.* 14:27b Zech 13:7. 14:36 *Abba* is an Aramaic term for "father." 14:41 Or *Sleep on, take your rest.*

[45]As soon as they arrived, Judas walked up to Jesus. "Teacher!" he exclaimed, and gave him the kiss. [46]Then the others grabbed Jesus and arrested him. [47]But someone pulled out a sword and slashed off an ear of the high priest's servant.

[48]Jesus asked them, "Am I some dangerous criminal, that you come armed with swords and clubs to arrest me? [49]Why didn't you arrest me in the Temple? I was there teaching every day. But these things are happening to fulfill what the Scriptures say about me."

[50]Meanwhile, all his disciples deserted him and ran away. [51]There was a young man following along behind, clothed only in a linen nightshirt. When the mob tried to grab him, [52]they tore off his clothes, but he escaped and ran away naked.

[53]Jesus was led to the high priest's home where the leading priests, other leaders, and teachers of religious law had gathered. [54]Meanwhile, Peter followed far behind and then slipped inside the gates of the high priest's courtyard. For a while he sat with the guards, warming himself by the fire.

[55]Inside, the leading priests and the entire high council* were trying to find witnesses who would testify against Jesus, so they could put him to death. But their efforts were in vain. [56]Many false witnesses spoke against him, but they contradicted each other. [57]Finally, some men stood up to testify against him with this lie: [58]"We heard him say, 'I will destroy this Temple made with human hands, and in three days I will build another, made without human hands.'" [59]But even then they didn't get their stories straight!

[60]Then the high priest stood up before the others and asked Jesus, "Well, aren't you going to answer these charges? What do you have to say for yourself?" [61]Jesus made no reply. Then the high priest asked him, "Are you the Messiah, the Son of the blessed God?"

[62]Jesus said, "I am, and you will see me, the Son of Man, sitting at God's right hand in the place of power and coming back on the clouds of heaven."*

[63]Then the high priest tore his clothing to show his horror and said, "Why do we need other witnesses? [64]You have all heard his blasphemy. What is your verdict?" And they all condemned him to death.

[65]Then some of them began to spit at him, and they blindfolded him and hit his face with their fists. "Who hit you that time, you prophet?" they jeered. And even the guards were hitting him as they led him away.

[66]Meanwhile, Peter was below in the courtyard. One of the servant girls who worked for the high priest [67]noticed Peter warming himself at the fire. She looked at him closely and then said, "You were one of those with Jesus, the Nazarene."

[68]Peter denied it. "I don't know what you're talking about," he said, and he went out into the entryway. Just then, a rooster crowed.*

[69]The servant girl saw him standing there and began telling the others, "That man is definitely one of them!" [70]Peter denied it again.

A little later some other bystanders began saying to Peter, "You must be one of them because you are from Galilee."

[71]Peter said, "I swear by God, I don't know this man you're talking about." [72]And immediately the rooster crowed the second time. Suddenly, Jesus' words flashed through Peter's mind: "Before the rooster crows twice, you will deny me three times." And he broke down and cried.

## CHAPTER 15 PILATE QUESTIONS JESUS.

Very early in the morning the leading priests, other leaders, and teachers of religious law—the entire high council*—met to discuss their next step. They bound Jesus and took him to Pilate, the Roman governor.

[2]Pilate asked Jesus, "Are you the King of the Jews?"

Jesus replied, "Yes, it is as you say."

[3]Then the leading priests accused him of many crimes, [4]and Pilate asked him, "Aren't you going to say something? What about all these charges against you?" [5]But Jesus said nothing, much to Pilate's surprise.

[6]Now it was the governor's custom to release one

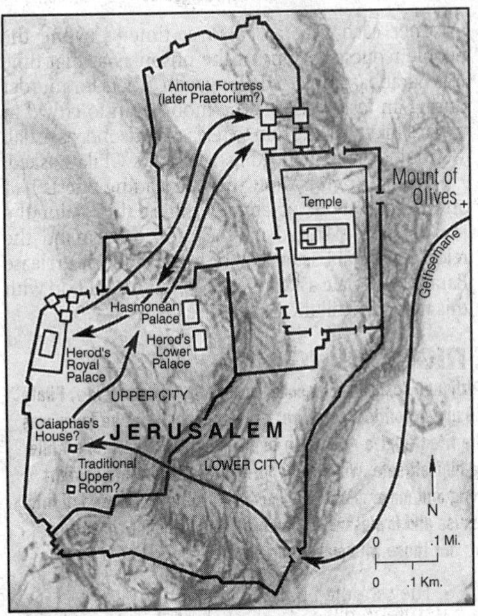


**JESUS' TRIAL**

From Gethsemane, Jesus' trial began at the home of Caiaphas, the high priest. He was then taken to Pilate, the Roman governor. Luke records that Pilate sent him to Herod, who was in Jerusalem—presumably in one of his two palaces (Luke 23:5-12). Herod sent him back to Pilate, who sentenced him to be crucified.

14:55 Greek *the Sanhedrin.* 14:62 See Ps 110:1; Dan 7:13. 14:68 Some manuscripts do not include *Just then, a rooster crowed.* 15:1 Greek *the Sanhedrin;* also in 15:43.

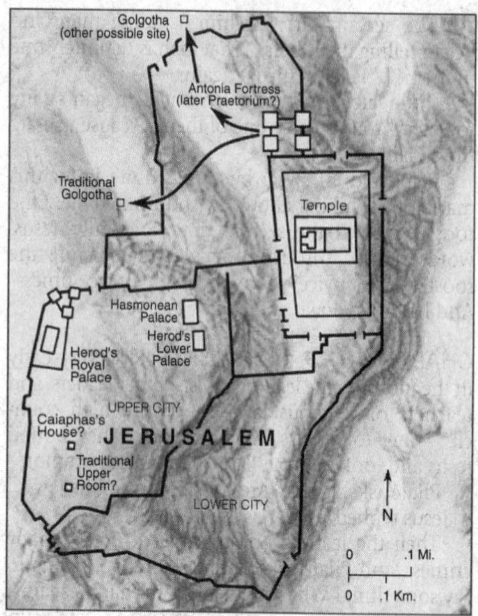


**JESUS' ROUTE TO GOLGOTHA**
After being sentenced by Pilate, Jesus was taken from the Praetorium to a place outside the city, Golgotha, for crucifixion.

prisoner each year at Passover time—anyone the people requested. [7]One of the prisoners at that time was Barabbas, convicted along with others for murder during an insurrection. [8]The mob began to crowd in toward Pilate, asking him to release a prisoner as usual. [9]"Should I give you the King of the Jews?" Pilate asked. [10](For he realized by now that the leading priests had arrested Jesus out of envy.) [11]But at this point the leading priests stirred up the mob to demand the release of Barabbas instead of Jesus. [12]"But if I release Barabbas," Pilate asked them, "what should I do with this man you call the King of the Jews?"

## THE RIGHT THING ● ● • • •

15:15 **Although Jesus was innocent according to Roman law, Pilate caved in under political pressure. He abandoned what he knew was right. He tried to give a decision that would please everyone while keeping himself safe. When we ignore God's statements of right and wrong and make decisions based on our audience, we fall into compromise and lawlessness. God promises to honor those who do right; not those who make everyone happy.**

[13]They shouted back, "Crucify him!"

[14]"Why?" Pilate demanded. "What crime has he committed?"

But the crowd only roared the louder, "Crucify him!"

[15]So Pilate, anxious to please the crowd, released Barabbas to them. He ordered Jesus flogged with a lead-tipped whip, then turned him over to the Roman soldiers to crucify him.

[16]The soldiers took him into their headquarters* and called out the entire battalion. [17]They dressed him in a purple robe and made a crown of long, sharp thorns and put it on his head. [18]Then they saluted, yelling, "Hail! King of the Jews!" [19]And they beat him on the head with a stick, spit on him, and dropped to their knees in mock worship. [20]When they were finally tired of mocking him, they took off the purple robe and put his own clothes on him again. Then they led him away to be crucified.

[21]A man named Simon, who was from Cyrene,* was coming in from the country just then, and they forced him to carry Jesus' cross. (Simon is the father of Alexander and Rufus.) [22]And they brought Jesus to a place called Golgotha (which means Skull Hill). [23]They offered him wine drugged with myrrh, but he refused it. [24]Then they nailed him to the cross. They gambled for his clothes, throwing dice* to decide who would get them.

[25]It was nine o'clock in the morning when the crucifixion took place. [26]A signboard was fastened to the cross above Jesus' head, announcing the charge against him. It read: "The King of the Jews." [27]Two criminals were crucified with him, their crosses on either side of his.* [29]And the people passing by shouted abuse, shaking their heads in mockery. "Ha! Look at you now!" they yelled at him. "You can destroy the Temple and rebuild it in three days, can you? [30]Well then, save yourself and come down from the cross!"

[31]The leading priests and teachers of religious law also mocked Jesus. "He saved others," they scoffed, "but he can't save himself! [32]Let this Messiah, this king of Israel, come down from the cross so we can see it and believe him!" Even the two criminals who were being crucified with Jesus ridiculed him.

[33]At noon, darkness fell across the whole land until three o'clock. [34]Then, at that time Jesus called out with a loud voice, *"Eloi, Eloi, lema sabachthani?"* which means, "My God, my God, why have you forsaken me?"*

[35]Some of the bystanders misunderstood and thought he was calling for the prophet Elijah. [36]One of them ran and filled a sponge with sour wine, holding it up to him on a stick so he could drink. "Leave him alone. Let's see whether Elijah will come and take him down!" he said.

## REMEMBERED ● ● • • •

15:42-43 **After Jesus died on the cross, Joseph of Arimathea asked for his body and then sealed it in a new tomb. Although an honored member of the Jewish Sanhedrin, Joseph was a secret disciple of Jesus. Not all the religious leaders hated Jesus. Joseph risked his reputation as a religious leader to give a proper burial to the One he followed. It is frightening to risk one's reputation even for what is right. If your Christian witness endangers your reputation, consider Joseph. Today he is well known in the Christian church. How many of the other members of the Jewish Supreme Court can you name?**

15:16 Greek *the courtyard, which is the praetorium.* 15:21 *Cyrene* was a city in northern Africa. 15:24 Greek *casting lots.* See Ps 22:18. 15:27 Some manuscripts add verse 28, *And the Scripture was fulfilled that said, "He was counted among those who were rebels."* See Isa 53:12. 15:34 Ps 22:1.

## EVIDENCE THAT JESUS ACTUALLY DIED AND AROSE

This evidence demonstrates Jesus' uniqueness in history and proves that he is God's Son. No one else was able to predict his own resurrection and then accomplish it.

| *Proposed Explanations for Empty Tomb* | *Evidence against These Explanations* | *References* |
|---|---|---|
| Jesus was only unconscious and later revived. | A Roman soldier told Pilate Jesus was dead. | Mark 15:44-45 |
| | The Roman soldiers did not break Jesus' legs because he had already died, and one of them pierced Jesus' side with a spear. | John 19:32-34 |
| | Joseph of Arimathea and Nicodemus wrapped Jesus' body and placed it in the tomb. | John 19:38-40 |
| The women made a mistake and went to the wrong tomb. | Mary Magdalene and Mary the mother of Jesus saw Jesus placed in the tomb. | Matthew 27:59-61<br>Mark 15:47<br>Luke 23:55 |
| | On Sunday morning, Peter and John also went to the same tomb. | John 20:3-9 |
| Unknown thieves stole Jesus' body. | The tomb was sealed and guarded by Roman soldiers. | Matthew 27:65-66 |
| The disciples stole Jesus' body | The disciples were ready to die for their faith. Stealing Jesus' body would have been admitting their faith was meaningless. | Acts 12:2 |
| | The tomb was guarded and sealed. | Matthew 27:65-66 |
| The religious leaders stole Jesus' body to secure it. | If the religious leaders had taken Jesus' body, they would have produced it to stop the rumors of his resurrection. | None |

[37]Then Jesus uttered another loud cry and
breathed his last. [38]And the curtain in the Temple was
torn in two, from top to bottom. [39]When the Roman
officer who stood facing him saw how he had died,
he exclaimed, "Truly, this was the Son of God!"

[40]Some women were there, watching from a distance, including Mary Magdalene, Mary (the mother
of James the younger and of Joseph*), and Salome.
[41]They had been followers of Jesus and had cared for
him while he was in Galilee. Then they and many
other women had come with him to Jerusalem.

[42]This all happened on Friday, the day of preparation,* the day before the Sabbath. As evening approached, [43]an honored member of the high council,
Joseph from Arimathea (who was waiting for the
Kingdom of God to come), gathered his courage and
went to Pilate to ask for Jesus' body. [44]Pilate couldn't
believe that Jesus was already dead, so he called for
the Roman military officer in charge and asked him.
[45]The officer confirmed the fact, and Pilate told
Joseph he could have the body. [46]Joseph bought a
long sheet of linen cloth, and taking Jesus' body

**15:40** Greek *Joses;* also in 15:47. See Matt 27:56. **15:42** Greek *on the day of preparation.*

## OPPORTUNITIES ● ● • • •

15:47 **These women could do very little—they couldn't speak before the Sanhedrin in Jesus' defense; they couldn't appeal to Pilate; they couldn't stand against the crowds; they couldn't overpower the Roman guards. But they did what they could. They stayed at the cross when the disciples had fled; they followed Jesus' body to its tomb; and they prepared spices for his body. Because they used the opportunities they had, they were the first to witness the Resurrection. God blessed their devotion and diligence. As believers, we should take advantage of the opportunities we have and do what we *can* for Christ, instead of worrying about what we *cannot* do.**

down from the cross, he wrapped it in the cloth and laid it in a tomb that had been carved out of the rock. Then he rolled a stone in front of the entrance.
47Mary Magdalene and Mary the mother of Joseph saw where Jesus' body was laid.

CHAPTER **16** **WOMEN VISIT JESUS' TOMB.** The next evening, when the Sabbath ended, Mary Magdalene and Salome and Mary the mother of James went out and purchased burial spices to put on
Jesus' body. 2Very early on Sunday morning,* just
at sunrise, they came to the tomb. 3On the way they
were discussing who would roll the stone away
from the entrance to the tomb. 4But when they
arrived, they looked up and saw that the stone—a
very large one—had already been rolled aside. 5So
they entered the tomb, and there on the right sat a young man clothed in a white robe. The women
were startled, 6but the angel said, "Do not be so surprised. You are looking for Jesus, the Nazarene, who was crucified. He isn't here! He has been raised from the dead! Look, this is where they laid
his body. 7Now go and give this message to his disciples, including Peter: Jesus is going ahead of you to Galilee. You will see him there, just as he
told you before he died!" 8The women fled from the tomb, trembling and bewildered, saying nothing to anyone because they were too frightened to talk.*

[*Shorter Ending of Mark*]

Then they reported all these instructions briefly to Peter and his companions. Afterward Jesus himself sent them out from east to west with the sacred and unfailing message of salvation that gives eternal life. Amen.

[*Longer Ending of Mark*]

9It was early on Sunday morning when Jesus rose from the dead, and the first person who saw him was Mary Magdalene, the woman from whom he had
cast out seven demons. 10She went and found the
disciples, who were grieving and weeping. 11But when she told them that Jesus was alive and she had seen him, they didn't believe her.
12Afterward he appeared to two who were walking from Jerusalem into the country, but they didn't recognize him at first because he had changed his appearance. 13When they realized who he was, they rushed back to tell the others, but no one believed them.
14Still later he appeared to the eleven disciples as they were eating together. He rebuked them for their unbelief—their stubborn refusal to believe those who had seen him after he had risen.
15And then he told them, "Go into all the world and preach the Good News to everyone, everywhere.
16Anyone who believes and is baptized will be saved. But anyone who refuses to believe will be condemned. 17These signs will accompany those who believe: They will cast out demons in my name, and
they will speak new languages.* 18They will be able to handle snakes with safety, and if they drink anything poisonous, it won't hurt them. They will be able to place their hands on the sick and heal them."
19When the Lord Jesus had finished talking with them, he was taken up into heaven and sat down in
the place of honor at God's right hand. 20And the disciples went everywhere and preached, and the Lord worked with them, confirming what they said by many miraculous signs.

## DRIVING POWER ● ● • • •

16:15 **Jesus told his disciples to go into all the world telling everyone he paid the penalty for sin and that those who believe in him can be forgiven and live eternally with God. Christian disciples today are living in all parts of the world, telling this good news to people who haven't heard it. The driving power that carries missionaries around the world and sets Christ's church in motion is the faith that comes from the Resurrection. Do you ever feel that you don't have the skill or determination to be a witness for Christ? You must personally realize that Jesus rose from the dead and lives for you today. As you grow in your relationship with him, he will provide you with both the opportunities and the inner strength to tell his message.**

**16:2** Greek *on the first day of the week;* also in 16:9. **16:8** The most reliable early manuscripts conclude the Gospel of Mark at verse 8. Other manuscripts include various endings to the Gospel. Two of the more noteworthy endings are printed here. **16:17** Or *new tongues.* Some manuscripts omit *new.*

# MEGA themes

**JESUS CHRIST** Jesus Christ alone is the Son of God. In Mark, Jesus demonstrates his divinity by overcoming disease, demons, and death. Although he had the power to be king of the earth, Jesus chose to obey the Father and die for us. Thus we see him in Mark as both Son of God and servant to man.

When Jesus rose from the dead, he proved that he was God, that he could forgive sin, and that he has the power to change our life. By trusting in Christ for forgiveness, we can begin a new life with him. As our guide, Jesus calls us to follow his example of obedience and service.

1. Which of Jesus' qualities do you see demonstrated in the Gospel of Mark?
2. Which of these qualities have you seen demonstrated in your church? Your youth group?
3. Which of these qualities have you experienced personally?
4. Which of Jesus' qualities do your non-Christian friends find it difficult to understand?
5. What could you do to be a living testimony of the gospel so that your friends could "read" your life to know Jesus?

**SERVANT** As the "Messiah," Jesus fulfilled the prophecies of the Old Testament by coming to earth. He did not come as a conquering king; he came as a servant. Jesus helped humankind by telling about God, showing compassion, and healing. But his ultimate act of service was giving his life as the sacrifice for sin.

Because of Jesus' example, we should be willing to serve God and others.

1. Read 10:45. How do you feel toward Jesus when you read this verse?
2. In what ways did Jesus display his servanthood in Mark? What do you learn about being a servant from the life of Jesus?
3. How do you feel about being a servant to others? What can you do to deal with any negative feelings you may have about being a servant?
4. What specific actions could you perform that would serve your family members? Your friends at school? Your friends at church? Someone in your community who is needy? A non-Christian who has not known Jesus' love?
5. From your list above, identify two specific actions you will choose to do in order to be a servant for Jesus' love.

**MIRACLES** Mark records more of Jesus' miracles than his sermons. Jesus was clearly a man of power and action, not just words. Jesus did miracles to confirm his message to the people and to teach the disciples his true identity as God. His miracles of forgiveness bring healing, wholeness, and changed lives to those who trust him.

1. Why were miracles such an important part of Jesus' ministry?
2. What do you learn about Jesus from Mark's record of his miracles?
3. What displays of Jesus' power do you see today?
4. What testimony could you give to Jesus' ability to change lives through his miraculous power?
5. Are there situations in your life, or in the lives of your friends or family, that need Jesus' healing touch? Choose one or two, and ask God to bring his power into those situations.

**SPREADING THE GOSPEL** Jesus directed his public ministry to the Jews first. When the Jewish leaders opposed him, Jesus also went to the non-Jewish world, healing and preaching.

Jesus' message of faith and forgiveness is for the whole world and not just for our church, neighborhood, or nation. We must reach out beyond our own people and needs to fulfill the worldwide vision of Jesus Christ so that people everywhere might hear this great message and be saved from sin and death.

1. How did Jesus show that God's love and grace are available to all types of people?
2. The book of Mark literally pivots on 8:29. Read 8:27-30 and consider these questions:
   a. What would people today say if they were asked about Jesus?
   b. How would you answer Jesus' question, "Who do you say I am?"
   c. What does your life say about who Jesus is?
3. What key truth do people need to know about Jesus?
4. Which of your friends need to know this truth? What could you do and say to give them the Good News?
5. Choose one friend and identify two specific ways you will share the Good News with him or her.

37 B.C.
**Herod the Great begins to rule**

6/5 B.C.
**Jesus is born**

5/4 B.C.
**Escape to Egypt**

4 B.C.
**Herod the Great dies**

4/3 B.C.
**Return to Nazareth**

A.D. 6/7
**Jesus visits Temple as a boy**

14
**Tiberius Caesar becomes emperor**

26
**John's ministry begins**

26/27
**Jesus begins his ministry**

28
**Jesus chooses 12 disciples**

29
**Jesus feeds 5,000**

30
**Jesus is crucified, rises again, and ascends**

They were two kids in love. In fact, they were *engaged*. As in "headed for the altar," "marital bliss." And M. & J. had big plans, and even bigger dreams. Then the roof caved in. M. found out she was pregnant. J. was hurt, confused, and ticked—he knew he wasn't the father. There was only one thing to do: call off the wedding. ■ But weird things started happening. M. claimed she'd been visited by a real-life angel, and that she'd been made pregnant by the Spirit of God! J. had heard some wild stories before, but *angels? Divine fertilization?* Come on! ■ Then J. started seeing angels! Surely it was all a dream . . . until the angel said (in a serious tone and with a straight face), "Hey, J., don't break off the engagement! The child inside M. really *is* the Savior of the world." J. gulped and mumbled, "Um, yeah . . . whatever you say." Soon M. could no longer hide her pregnancy. People stared. Rumors flew. M. and J. purposely kept a low profile. Together they wondered what it would be like to be parents—especially of such a special child. ■ Did M. realize that her little baby would incite a king to slaughter thousands of newborn infants? Did J. know that the child would one day speak such profound words or perform astounding miracles? Did these two realize their precious boy would die in a brutal manner? ■ Even if they *were* able to grasp any of that, did they truly believe that their murdered son would come back to life? ■ Read about M. & J. and their son—mainly about their son—in the following pages. The story is the Gospel of Luke. It's one you won't forget.

## STATS

PURPOSE: To present an accurate account of the life of Christ and to present Christ as the perfect man and Savior

AUTHOR: Luke—a doctor (Colossians 4:14), a Greek and Gentile Christian. He is the only known Gentile author in the New Testament. He was a close friend and companion of Paul. He also wrote Acts, and the two books go together.

TO WHOM WRITTEN: Theophilus ("lover of God"), Gentiles, and people everywhere

DATE WRITTEN: About A.D. 60

SETTING: Luke wrote from Caesarea or from Rome

KEY PEOPLE: Jesus, Elizabeth, Zechariah, John the Baptist, Mary, the disciples, Herod the Great, Pilate, Mary Magdalene

KEY PLACES: Bethlehem, Galilee, Judea, Jerusalem

CHAPTER **1** **AN ANGEL VISITS ZECHARIAH.** Most honorable Theophilus:

Many people have written accounts about the events that took place* among us. [2]They used as their source material the reports circulating among us from the early disciples and other eyewitnesses of what God has done in fulfillment of his promises. [3]Having carefully investigated all of these accounts from the beginning, I have decided to write a careful summary for you, [4]to reassure you of the truth of all you were taught.

[5]It all begins with a Jewish priest, Zechariah, who lived when Herod was king of Judea. Zechariah was a member of the priestly order of Abijah. His wife, Elizabeth, was also from the priestly line of Aaron. [6]Zechariah and Elizabeth were righteous in God's eyes, careful to obey all of the Lord's commandments and regulations. [7]They had no children because Elizabeth was barren, and now they were both very old.

[8]One day Zechariah was serving God in the Temple, for his order was on duty that week. [9]As was the custom of the priests, he was chosen by lot to enter the sanctuary and burn incense in the Lord's presence. [10]While the incense was being burned, a great crowd stood outside, praying.

[11]Zechariah was in the sanctuary when an angel of the Lord appeared, standing to the right of the incense altar. [12]Zechariah was overwhelmed with fear. [13]But the angel said, "Don't be afraid, Zechariah! For God has heard your prayer, and your wife, Elizabeth, will bear you a son! And you are to name him John. [14]You will have great joy and gladness, and many will rejoice with you at his birth, [15]for he will be great in the eyes of the Lord. He must never touch wine or hard liquor, and he will be filled with the Holy Spirit, even before his birth.* [16]And he will persuade many Israelites to turn to the Lord their God. [17]He will be a man with the spirit and power of Elijah, the prophet of old. He will precede the coming of the Lord, preparing the people for his arrival. He will turn the hearts of the fathers to their children, and he will change disobedient minds to accept godly wisdom."*

[18]Zechariah said to the angel, "How can I know

## CHECKED OUT ● ● • • •

1:3 **As a medical doctor, Luke knew the importance of a thorough checkup. He used his skills in observation and analysis to do a complete investigation of the stories about Jesus. His diagnosis? The gospel of Jesus Christ is true! You can read Luke's account of Jesus' life with confidence that it was written by a clear thinker and a thoughtful researcher. Because the gospel is founded on historical truth, our spiritual growth must involve careful, disciplined, thorough investigation of God's Word. If this kind of study is not part of your life, find a pastor, teacher, or book to help you get started and to guide you in this important part of Christian growth.**

1:1 Or *have been fulfilled.* 1:15 Or *even from birth.* 1:17 See Mal 4:5-6.

# KEY PLACES IN **LUKE**

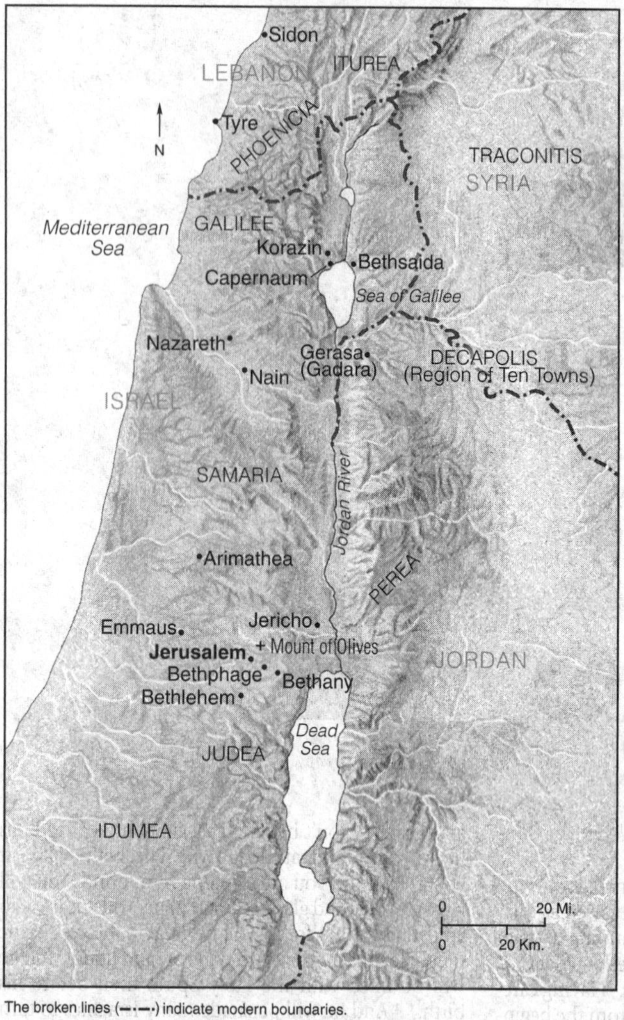

The broken lines (—·—·) indicate modern boundaries.

Luke begins his account in the Temple in Jerusalem, giving us the background for the birth of John the Baptist, and then moves on to the city of Nazareth and the story of Mary, chosen to be Jesus' mother (1:26-38). As a result of Caesar's call for a census, Mary and Joseph had to travel to Bethlehem, where Jesus was born in fulfillment of prophecy (2:1-20). Jesus grew up in Nazareth and began his earthly ministry by being baptized by John (3:21-22) and tempted by Satan (4:1-13). Much of his ministry focused on Galilee—he set up his "home" in Capernaum (4:31), and from there he taught throughout the region (8:1-3). Later he visited the Gadarene country, where he healed a demon-possessed man from Gadara (8:36-39). He fed more than 5,000 people with one lunch on the shores of the Sea of Galilee near Bethsaida (9:10-17). Jesus always traveled to Jerusalem for the major feasts and enjoyed visiting friends in nearby Bethany (10:38-42). He healed 10 men with leprosy on the border between Galilee and Samaria (17:11) and helped a dishonest tax collector in Jericho turn his life around (19:1-10). The little villages of Bethphage and Bethany on the Mount of Olives were Jesus' resting places during his last days on earth. He was crucified outside Jerusalem's walls, but he would rise again. Two people on the road leading to Emmaus were among the first to see the resurrected Christ (24:13-34).

this will happen? I'm an old man now, and my wife
is also well along in years."
[19]Then the angel said, "I am Gabriel! I stand in
the very presence of God. It was he who sent me to
bring you this good news! [20]And now, since you
didn't believe what I said, you won't be able to speak
until the child is born. For my words will certainly
come true at the proper time."
[21]Meanwhile, the people were waiting for Zechariah to come out, wondering why he was taking so
long. [22]When he finally did come out, he couldn't
speak to them. Then they realized from his gestures
that he must have seen a vision in the Temple sanctuary.
[23]He stayed at the Temple until his term of service
was over, and then he returned home. [24]Soon afterward his wife, Elizabeth, became pregnant and went
into seclusion for five months. [25]"How kind the Lord
is!" she exclaimed. "He has taken away my disgrace
of having no children!"
[26]In the sixth month of Elizabeth's pregnancy,
God sent the angel Gabriel to Nazareth, a village in
Galilee, [27]to a virgin named Mary. She was engaged
to be married to a man named Joseph, a descendant of King David. [28]Gabriel appeared to her and
said, "Greetings, favored woman! The Lord is with
you!*"
[29]Confused and disturbed, Mary tried to think

**UNLIKELY ● ● ● • •**

1:46-55 **Mary was young, poor, and female—all characteristics that, to the people of her day, would make her seem useless to God for any major task. But God chose Mary for one of the most important acts of obedience he has ever demanded of anyone. You may feel that your situation in life makes you an unlikely candidate for God's service. Don't limit God's choices. He can use you if you trust him.**

**1:28** Some manuscripts add *Blessed are you among women.*

what the angel could mean. 30"Don't be frightened, Mary," the angel told her, "for God has decided to bless you! 31You will become pregnant and have a son, and you are to name him Jesus. 32He will be very great and will be called the Son of the Most High. And the Lord God will give him the throne of his ancestor David. 33And he will reign over Israel* forever; his Kingdom will never end!"

34Mary asked the angel, "But how can I have a baby? I am a virgin."

35The angel replied, "The Holy Spirit will come upon you, and the power of the Most High will overshadow you. So the baby born to you will be holy, and he will be called the Son of God. 36What's more, your relative Elizabeth has become pregnant in her old age! People used to say she was barren, but she's already in her sixth month. 37For nothing is impossible with God."

38Mary responded, "I am the Lord's servant, and I am willing to accept whatever he wants. May everything you have said come true." And then the angel left.

39A few days later Mary hurried to the hill country of Judea, to the town 40where Zechariah lived. She entered the house and greeted Elizabeth. 41At the sound of Mary's greeting, Elizabeth's child leaped within her, and Elizabeth was filled with the Holy Spirit.

42Elizabeth gave a glad cry and exclaimed to Mary, "You are blessed by God above all other women, and your child is blessed. 43What an honor this is, that the mother of my Lord should visit me! 44When you came in and greeted me, my baby jumped for joy the instant I heard your voice! 45You are blessed, because you believed that the Lord would do what he said."

46Mary responded,

"Oh, how I praise the Lord.
47 How I rejoice in God my Savior!
48 For he took notice of his lowly servant girl,
and now generation after generation
will call me blessed.
49 For he, the Mighty One, is holy,
and he has done great things for me.

1:33 Greek *over the house of Jacob.*

# MARY

**UPS:**
- The mother of Jesus, the Messiah
- The one human who was with Jesus from birth to death
- Willing to be available to God
- Knew and applied God's Word

**STATS:**
- Where: Nazareth, Bethlehem
- Occupation: Homemaker
- Relatives: Husband: Joseph. Uncle and Aunt: Zechariah and Elizabeth. Children: Jesus, James, Joseph, Judas, and Simon, plus daughters.

Motherhood is a painful privilege. Young Mary of Nazareth had the unique role of being mother to the Son of God. Yet the pains and pleasures of her motherhood are understood by mothers everywhere. Mary was the only human present at Jesus' birth who also witnessed his death. She saw Jesus arrive as her baby son, and she watched him die as her Savior.

Until Gabriel's surprise visit, Mary's life was going well. She had recently become engaged to a local carpenter, Joseph, and was anticipating married life. But God had other plans for her.

Angels don't usually make appointments before visiting. The angel greeted Mary as if she were the winner of a contest she had never entered; she found the angel's greeting puzzling and his presence frightening. What she heard next was the news almost every woman in Israel hoped to hear—that her child would be the Messiah, God's promised Savior. Mary did not doubt the message, but she wondered how she could be pregnant. Gabriel told her that the baby would be God's Son.

Mary's answer was one that God waits to hear from every person: "I am the Lord's servant, and I am willing to accept whatever he wants. May everything you have said come true" (Luke 1:38). Later, her song of joy to Elizabeth shows us how well Mary knew God—her thoughts were filled with his words from the Old Testament.

Just days after his birth, Jesus was taken to the Temple to be dedicated to God. There Joseph and Mary were met by two prophets, Simeon and Anna, who recognized the child as the Messiah and praised God. Simeon added some words for Mary that she must have remembered many times in the years that followed: "And a sword will pierce your very soul" (Luke 2:35).

We can imagine that even if she had known all she would suffer as Jesus' mother, Mary would have given the same response. Is your life as available to be used by God as Mary's was?

LESSONS: God's best servants are often plain people available to him

God's plans involve extraordinary events in the lives of ordinary people

A person's character is revealed by his or her response to the unexpected

KEY VERSE: "Mary responded, 'I am the Lord's servant, and I am willing to accept whatever he wants. May everything you have said come true.' And then the angel left" (Luke 1:38).

Mary's story is told throughout the Gospels. She is also mentioned in Acts 1:14.

## GROW UP ● ● • • •

**2:7 Although our first impression of Jesus is as a baby in a manger, it must not be our last. The Christ child in the manger makes a beautiful Christmas scene, but we cannot leave him there. This tiny, helpless baby lived an amazing life, died for us, ascended to heaven, and will return to earth as King of kings. He will rule the world and judge all people according to their decisions about him. Do you still picture Jesus as a baby in a manger—or is he your Lord? Make sure you don't underestimate Jesus. Let him grow up in your life.**

50 His mercy goes on from generation to generation,
to all who fear him.
51 His mighty arm does tremendous things!
How he scatters the proud and haughty ones!
52 He has taken princes from their thrones
and exalted the lowly.
53 He has satisfied the hungry with good things
and sent the rich away with empty hands.
54 And how he has helped his servant Israel!
He has not forgotten his promise to be
merciful.
55 For he promised our ancestors—Abraham and
his children—
to be merciful to them forever."

56 Mary stayed with Elizabeth about three months
and then went back to her own home.
57 Now it was time for Elizabeth's baby to be born,
and it was a boy. 58 The word spread quickly to her
neighbors and relatives that the Lord had been very
kind to her, and everyone rejoiced with her.
59 When the baby was eight days old, all the relatives and friends came for the circumcision ceremony. They wanted to name him Zechariah, after his
father. 60 But Elizabeth said, "No! His name is John!"
61 "What?" they exclaimed. "There is no one in all
your family by that name." 62 So they asked the baby's
father, communicating to him by making gestures.
63 He motioned for a writing tablet, and to everyone's
surprise he wrote, "His name is John!" 64 Instantly
Zechariah could speak again, and he began praising
God.
65 Wonder fell upon the whole neighborhood, and
the news of what had happened spread throughout
the Judean hills. 66 Everyone who heard about it reflected on these events and asked, "I wonder what
this child will turn out to be? For the hand of the
Lord is surely upon him in a special way."
67 Then his father, Zechariah, was filled with the
Holy Spirit and gave this prophecy:

68 "Praise the Lord, the God of Israel,
because he has visited his people and
redeemed them.
69 He has sent us a mighty Savior
from the royal line of his servant David,
70 just as he promised
through his holy prophets long ago.
71 Now we will be saved from our enemies
and from all who hate us.
72 He has been merciful to our ancestors
by remembering his sacred covenant with
them,
73 the covenant he gave to our ancestor Abraham.
74 We have been rescued from our enemies,
so we can serve God without fear,
75 in holiness and righteousness forever.
76 "And you, my little son,
will be called the prophet of the Most High,
because you will prepare the way for the Lord.
77 You will tell his people how to find salvation
through forgiveness of their sins.
78 Because of God's tender mercy,
the light from heaven is about to break upon
us,
79 to give light to those who sit in darkness and in
the shadow of death,
and to guide us to the path of peace."

80 John grew up and became strong in spirit. Then
he lived out in the wilderness until he began his
public ministry to Israel.

CHAPTER **2** **JESUS IS BORN.** At that time the Roman emperor, Augustus, decreed that a census
should be taken throughout the Roman Empire.
2 (This was the first census taken when Quirinius was
governor of Syria.) 3 All returned to their own towns
to register for this census. 4 And because Joseph was a
descendant of King David, he had to go to Bethlehem in Judea, David's ancient home. He traveled
there from the village of Nazareth in Galilee. 5 He
took with him Mary, his fiancée, who was obviously
pregnant by this time.
6 And while they were there, the time came for her
baby to be born. 7 She gave birth to her first child, a
son. She wrapped him snugly in strips of cloth and
laid him in a manger, because there was no room for
them in the village inn.
8 That night some shepherds were in the fields
outside the village, guarding their flocks of sheep.
9 Suddenly, an angel of the Lord appeared among
them, and the radiance of the Lord's glory surrounded them. They were terribly frightened, 10 but
the angel reassured them. "Don't be afraid!" he said.
"I bring you good news of great joy for everyone!
11 The Savior—yes, the Messiah, the Lord—has been
born tonight in Bethlehem, the city of David! 12 And
this is how you will recognize him: You will find a
baby lying in a manger, wrapped snugly in strips of
cloth!"

## OLDER PEOPLE ● ● • • •

**2:36 Although Simeon and Anna were very old, they still hoped to see the Messiah. Led by the Holy Spirit, they were among the first to bear witness to Jesus. In the Jewish culture, elders were respected, so Simeon's and Anna's prophecies carried extra weight. Our society, however, values youthfulness over wisdom, and potential contributions by the elderly often are ignored. As Christians, we should reverse those values wherever we can. Encourage older people to share their wisdom and experience. Listen carefully when they speak. Offer them your friendship and help them find ways to continue to serve God.**

13 Suddenly, the angel was joined by a vast host of others—the armies of heaven—praising God:

14 "Glory to God in the highest heaven,
 and peace on earth to all whom God favors.*"

15 When the angels had returned to heaven, the shepherds said to each other, "Come on, let's go to Bethlehem! Let's see this wonderful thing that has happened, which the Lord has told us about."

16 They ran to the village and found Mary and Joseph. And there was the baby, lying in the manger. 17 Then the shepherds told everyone what had happened and what the angel had said to them about this child. 18 All who heard the shepherds' story were astonished, 19 but Mary quietly treasured these things in her heart and thought about them often. 20 The shepherds went back to their fields and flocks, glorifying and praising God for what the angels had told them, and because they had seen the child, just as the angel had said.

21 Eight days later, when the baby was circumcised, he was named Jesus, the name given him by the angel even before he was conceived.

22 Then it was time for the purification offering, as required by the law of Moses after the birth of a child; so his parents took him to Jerusalem to present him to the Lord. 23 The law of the Lord says, "If a woman's first child is a boy, he must be dedicated to the Lord."* 24 So they offered a sacrifice according to what was required in the law of the Lord—"either a pair of turtledoves or two young pigeons."*

25 Now there was a man named Simeon who lived in Jerusalem. He was a righteous man and very devout. He was filled with the Holy Spirit, and he eagerly expected the Messiah to come and rescue Israel. 26 The Holy Spirit had revealed to him that he would not die until he had seen the Lord's Messiah. 27 That day the Spirit led him to the Temple. So when Mary and Joseph came to present the baby Jesus to the Lord as the law required, 28 Simeon was there. He took the child in his arms and praised God, saying,

29 "Lord, now I can die in peace!
 As you promised me,
30 I have seen the Savior
31  you have given to all people.
32 He is a light to reveal God to the nations,
 and he is the glory of your people Israel!"

33 Joseph and Mary were amazed at what was being said about Jesus. 34 Then Simeon blessed them, and he said to Mary, "This child will be rejected by many in Israel, and it will be their undoing. But he will be the greatest joy to many others. 35 Thus, the deepest thoughts of many hearts will be revealed. And a sword will pierce your very soul."

36 Anna, a prophet, was also there in the Temple. She was the daughter of Phanuel, of the tribe of Asher, and was very old. She was a widow, for her husband had died when they had been married only seven years. 37 She was now eighty-four years old. She never left the Temple but stayed there day and night, worshiping God with fasting and prayer. 38 She came along just as Simeon was talking with Mary and Joseph, and she began praising God. She talked about Jesus to everyone who had been waiting for the promised King to come and deliver Jerusalem.

39 When Jesus' parents had fulfilled all the requirements of the law of the Lord, they returned home to Nazareth in Galilee. 40 There the child grew up healthy and strong. He was filled with wisdom beyond his years, and God placed his special favor upon him.

41 Every year Jesus' parents went to Jerusalem for the Passover festival. 42 When Jesus was twelve years old, they attended the festival as usual. 43 After the celebration was over, they started home to Nazareth, but Jesus stayed behind in Jerusalem. His parents didn't miss him at first, 44 because they assumed he was with friends among the other travelers. But when he didn't show up that evening, they started to look for him among their relatives and friends. 45 When they couldn't find him, they went back to Jerusalem to search for him there. 46 Three days later they finally discovered him. He was in the Temple, sitting among the religious teachers, discussing deep questions with them. 47 And all who heard him were amazed at his understanding and his answers.

**PARENTS ● ● • • •**

2:46-52 **This is the first hint that Jesus realized he was God's Son. Even though Jesus knew his real Father, he did not reject his earthly parents. Jesus went back to Nazareth with them and lived under their authority for another 18 years. God's people do not despise human relationships or family responsibilities. If the Son of God obeyed his human parents, how much more should we honor our family members!**

48 His parents didn't know what to think. "Son!" his mother said to him. "Why have you done this to us? Your father and I have been frantic, searching for you everywhere."

49 "But why did you need to search?" he asked. "You should have known that I would be in my Father's house."* 50 But they didn't understand what he meant.

51 Then he returned to Nazareth with them and was obedient to them; and his mother stored all these things in her heart. 52 So Jesus grew both in height and in wisdom, and he was loved by God and by all who knew him.

CHAPTER **3** **JOHN THE BAPTIST PREACHES.** It was now the fifteenth year of the reign of Tiberius, the Roman emperor. Pilate was governor over

2:14 Or *and peace on earth for all those pleasing God.* Some manuscripts read *and peace on earth, goodwill among people.* 2:23 Exod 13:2. 2:24 Lev 12:8. 2:49 Or *"Didn't you realize that I should be involved with my Father's affairs?"*

Judea; Herod Antipas was ruler* over Galilee; his
brother Philip was ruler* over Iturea and Traconitis;
Lysanias was ruler over Abilene. 2Annas and Caiaphas were the high priests. At this time a message
from God came to John son of Zechariah, who was
living out in the wilderness. 3Then John went from
place to place on both sides of the Jordan River,
preaching that people should be baptized to show
that they had turned from their sins and turned to
God to be forgiven.* 4Isaiah had spoken of John
when he said,

"He is a voice shouting in the wilderness:
'Prepare a pathway for the Lord's coming!
Make a straight road for him!
5 Fill in the valleys,
and level the mountains and hills!
Straighten the curves,
and smooth out the rough places!
6 And then all people will see
the salvation sent from God.'"*

7Here is a sample of John's preaching to the
crowds that came for baptism: "You brood of
snakes! Who warned you to flee God's coming
judgment? 8Prove by the way you live that you have
really turned from your sins and turned to God.
Don't just say, 'We're safe—we're the descendants
of Abraham.' That proves nothing. God can change
these stones here into children of Abraham. 9Even
now the ax of God's judgment is poised, ready to
sever your roots. Yes, every tree that does not produce good fruit will be chopped down and thrown
into the fire."

## ON YOUR OWN ● ● • • ·

3:8 **Many of John's hearers were shocked when he said that being Abraham's descendants was not enough. The religious leaders relied more on their family line than on their faith for their standing with God. For them, religion was inherited. But a relationship with God is not handed down from parents to children. Everyone has to find it on his or her own. Don't rely on someone else for your salvation. Put your faith in Jesus, and then exercise your faith by acting on it every day.**

10The crowd asked, "What should we do?"
11John replied, "If you have two coats, give one to
the poor. If you have food, share it with those who
are hungry."
12Even corrupt tax collectors came to be baptized
and asked, "Teacher, what should we do?"
13"Show your honesty," he replied. "Make sure
you collect no more taxes than the Roman government requires you to."
14"What should we do?" asked some soldiers.
John replied, "Don't extort money, and don't accuse people of things you know they didn't do. And
be content with your pay."
15Everyone was expecting the Messiah to come

## TIMING ● ● • • ·

3:23 **Imagine the Savior of the world driving nails in some small-town carpenter's shop until he was 30 years old! Jesus patiently trusted the Father's timing for his life and ministry. Are you waiting and wondering what your next step should be? Don't jump ahead. Instead, like Jesus, trust God's timing and guidance.**

soon, and they were eager to know whether John
might be the Messiah. 16John answered their questions by saying, "I baptize with* water; but someone
is coming soon who is greater than I am—so much
greater that I am not even worthy to be his slave.* He
will baptize you with the Holy Spirit and with fire.*
17He is ready to separate the chaff from the grain with
his winnowing fork. Then he will clean up the
threshing area, storing the grain in his barn but
burning the chaff with never-ending fire." 18John
used many such warnings as he announced the
Good News to the people.
19John also publicly criticized Herod Antipas,
ruler of Galilee, for marrying Herodias, his brother's
wife, and for many other wrongs he had done. 20So
Herod put John in prison, adding this sin to his
many others.
21One day when the crowds were being baptized,
Jesus himself was baptized. As he was praying, the
heavens opened, 22and the Holy Spirit descended on
him in the form of a dove. And a voice from heaven
said, "You are my beloved Son, and I am fully
pleased with you.*"
23Jesus was about thirty years old when he began
his public ministry.

Jesus was known as the son of Joseph.
Joseph was the son of Heli.
24 Heli was the son of Matthat.
Matthat was the son of Levi.
Levi was the son of Melki.
Melki was the son of Jannai.
Jannai was the son of Joseph.
25 Joseph was the son of Mattathias.
Mattathias was the son of Amos.
Amos was the son of Nahum.
Nahum was the son of Esli.
Esli was the son of Naggai.
26 Naggai was the son of Maath.
Maath was the son of Mattathias.
Mattathias was the son of Semein.
Semein was the son of Josech.
Josech was the son of Joda.
27 Joda was the son of Joanan.
Joanan was the son of Rhesa.
Rhesa was the son of Zerubbabel.
Zerubbabel was the son of Shealtiel.
Shealtiel was the son of Neri.
28 Neri was the son of Melki.
Melki was the son of Addi.
Addi was the son of Cosam.
Cosam was the son of Elmadam.
Elmadam was the son of Er.

3:1a Greek *Herod was tetrarch.* Herod Antipas was a son of King Herod. **3:1b** Greek *tetrarch;* also in 3:19. **3:3** Greek *preaching a baptism of repentance for the forgiveness of sins.* **3:4-6** Isa 40:3-5. **3:16a** Or *in.* **3:16b** Greek *to untie his sandals.* **3:16c** Or *in the Holy Spirit and in fire.* **3:22** Some manuscripts read *and today I have become your Father.*

29 Er was the son of Joshua.
Joshua was the son of Eliezer.
Eliezer was the son of Jorim.
Jorim was the son of Matthat.
Matthat was the son of Levi.
30 Levi was the son of Simeon.
Simeon was the son of Judah.
Judah was the son of Joseph.
Joseph was the son of Jonam.
Jonam was the son of Eliakim.
31 Eliakim was the son of Melea.
Melea was the son of Menna.
Menna was the son of Mattatha.
Mattatha was the son of Nathan.
Nathan was the son of David.
32 David was the son of Jesse.
Jesse was the son of Obed.
Obed was the son of Boaz.
Boaz was the son of Salmon.*
Salmon was the son of Nahshon.
33 Nahshon was the son of Amminadab.
Amminadab was the son of Admin.
Admin was the son of Arni.*
Arni was the son of Hezron.
Hezron was the son of Perez.
Perez was the son of Judah.
34 Judah was the son of Jacob.
Jacob was the son of Isaac.
Isaac was the son of Abraham.
Abraham was the son of Terah.
Terah was the son of Nahor.
35 Nahor was the son of Serug.
Serug was the son of Reu.
Reu was the son of Peleg.
Peleg was the son of Eber.
Eber was the son of Shelah.
36 Shelah was the son of Cainan.
Cainan was the son of Arphaxad.
Arphaxad was the son of Shem.
Shem was the son of Noah.
Noah was the son of Lamech.
37 Lamech was the son of Methuselah.
Methuselah was the son of Enoch.
Enoch was the son of Jared.
Jared was the son of Mahalalel.
Mahalalel was the son of Kenan.
38 Kenan was the son of Enosh.*
Enosh was the son of Seth.
Seth was the son of Adam.
Adam was the son of God.

CHAPTER **4** **JESUS RESISTS TEMPTATION.** Then Jesus,
full of the Holy Spirit, left the Jordan River. He was
led by the Spirit to go out into the wilderness,
2where the Devil tempted him for forty days. He
ate nothing all that time and was very hungry.
3Then the Devil said to him, "If you are the Son
of God, change this stone into a loaf of bread."

## VULNERABLE ● ● • • •

**4:13 Christ's defeat of Satan was decisive but not final. Throughout his ministry, Jesus would confront Satan in many forms. Too often we see temptation as a once-and-for-all proposition. In reality, we need to be constantly on guard against the devil's ongoing attacks. Where are you most susceptible to temptation right now? How are you preparing to withstand it?**

4But Jesus told him, "No! The Scriptures say,
'People need more than bread for their life.'*"
5Then the Devil took him up and revealed to
him all the kingdoms of the world in a moment of
time. 6The Devil told him, "I will give you the glory
of these kingdoms and authority over them—because they are mine to give to anyone I please. 7I
will give it all to you if you will bow down and
worship me."
8Jesus replied, "The Scriptures say,

'You must worship the Lord your God;
serve only him.'*"

9Then the Devil took him to Jerusalem, to the
highest point of the Temple, and said, "If you
are the Son of God, jump off! 10For the Scriptures
say,

'He orders his angels to protect and guard you.
11 And they will hold you with their hands
to keep you from striking your foot on a
stone.'*"

12Jesus responded, "The Scriptures also say, 'Do
not test the Lord your God.'*"
13When the Devil had finished tempting Jesus, he
left him until the next opportunity came.
14Then Jesus returned to Galilee, filled with
the Holy Spirit's power. Soon he became well
known throughout the surrounding country. 15He
taught in their synagogues and was praised by
everyone.

## JESUS' EXAMPLE ● ● • • •

**4:16 Jesus went to the synagogue "as usual." Even though he was the perfect Son of God, and his local synagogue left much to be desired, he attended services every week. Jesus' example makes most excuses for not attending church sound weak and self-serving. Make regular worship a part of your life.**

16When he came to the village of Nazareth, his
boyhood home, he went as usual to the synagogue
on the Sabbath and stood up to read the Scriptures.
17The scroll containing the messages of Isaiah the
prophet was handed to him, and he unrolled the
scroll to the place where it says:

18 "The Spirit of the Lord is upon me,
for he has appointed me to preach Good
News to the poor.
He has sent me to proclaim
that captives will be released,

3:32 Greek *Sala;* see Ruth 4:22. 3:33 *Arni* is the same person as Ram; see 1 Chr 2:9-10. 3:38 Greek *Enos;* see Gen 5:6. 4:4 Deut 8:3. 4:8 Deut 6:13. 4:10-11 Ps 91:11-12. 4:12 Deut 6:16.

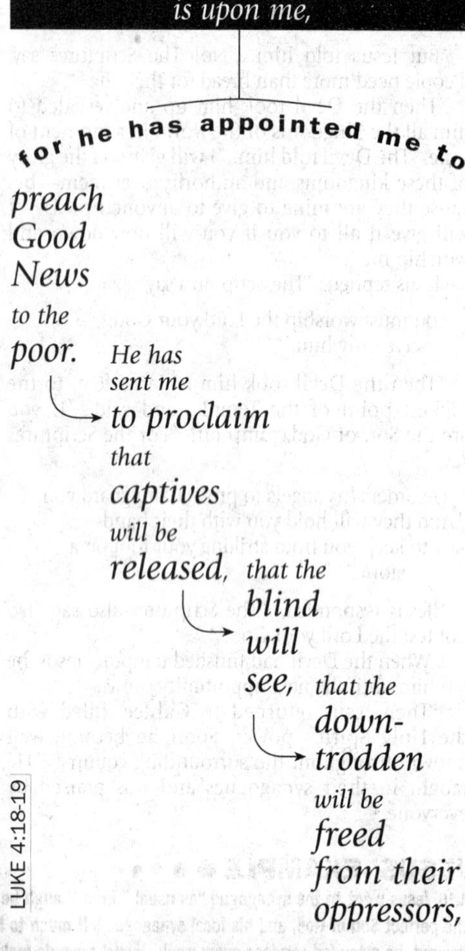
THE SPIRIT
OF THE LORD
is upon me,
for he has appointed me to
preach
Good
News
to the
poor.
He has
sent me
to proclaim
that
captives
will be
released,
that the
blind
will
see,
that the
down-
trodden
will be
freed
from their
oppressors,
and that the time
of the Lord's favor
has come
LUKE 4:18-19

that the blind will see,
that the downtrodden will be freed from their
oppressors,
19 and that the time of the Lord's favor has
come.*"

20He rolled up the scroll, handed it back to the
attendant, and sat down. Everyone in the synagogue stared at him intently. 21Then he said, "This
Scripture has come true today before your very
eyes!"

22All who were there spoke well of him and were
amazed by the gracious words that fell from his lips.
"How can this be?" they asked. "Isn't this Joseph's
son?"

23Then he said, "Probably you will quote me
that proverb, 'Physician, heal yourself'—meaning,
'Why don't you do miracles here in your hometown like those you did in Capernaum?' 24But the
truth is, no prophet is accepted in his own hometown.

25"Certainly there were many widows in Israel
who needed help in Elijah's time, when there was
no rain for three and a half years and hunger
stalked the land. 26Yet Elijah was not sent to any of
them. He was sent instead to a widow of Zarephath—a foreigner in the land of Sidon. 27Or think
of the prophet Elisha, who healed Naaman, a Syrian, rather than the many lepers in Israel who
needed help."

28When they heard this, the people in the synagogue were furious. 29Jumping up, they mobbed him
and took him to the edge of the hill on which the city
was built. They intended to push him over the cliff,
30but he slipped away through the crowd and left
them.

31Then Jesus went to Capernaum, a town in Galilee, and taught there in the synagogue every Sabbath day. 32There, too, the people were amazed at
the things he said, because he spoke with authority.

33Once when he was in the synagogue, a man
possessed by a demon began shouting at Jesus, 34"Go
away! Why are you bothering us, Jesus of Nazareth?
Have you come to destroy us? I know who you
are—the Holy One sent from God."

35Jesus cut him short. "Be silent!" he told the
demon. "Come out of the man!" The demon threw
the man to the floor as the crowd watched; then it
left him without hurting him further.

36Amazed, the people exclaimed, "What authority
and power this man's words possess! Even evil spirits
obey him and flee at his command!" 37The story of
what he had done spread like wildfire throughout
the whole region.

38After leaving the synagogue that day, Jesus
went to Simon's home, where he found Simon's
mother-in-law very sick with a high fever. "Please
heal her," everyone begged. 39Standing at her bedside, he spoke to the fever, rebuking it, and immediately her temperature returned to normal. She
got up at once and prepared a meal for them.

40As the sun went down that evening, people
throughout the village brought sick family members to Jesus. No matter what their diseases were,
the touch of his hand healed every one. 41Some
were possessed by demons; and the demons came
out at his command, shouting, "You are the Son of
God." But because they knew he was the Messiah,
he stopped them and told them to be silent.

42Early the next morning Jesus went out into the

**4:18-19** Or *and to proclaim the acceptable year of the Lord.* Isa 61:1-2.

wilderness. The crowds searched everywhere for
him, and when they finally found him, they begged
him not to leave them. [43]But he replied, "I must
preach the Good News of the Kingdom of God in
other places, too, because that is why I was sent."
[44]So he continued to travel around, preaching in
synagogues throughout Judea.*

CHAPTER **5** **FISHING WITH JESUS.** One day as Jesus
was preaching on the shore of the Sea of Galilee,*
great crowds pressed in on him to listen to the word
of God. [2]He noticed two empty boats at the water's
edge, for the fishermen had left them and were washing their nets. [3]Stepping into one of the boats, Jesus
asked Simon,* its owner, to
push it out into the water. So
he sat in the boat and taught
the crowds from there.
[4]When he had finished
speaking, he said to Simon,
"Now go out where it is
deeper and let down your
nets, and you will catch
many fish."
[5]"Master," Simon replied,
"we worked hard all last
night and didn't catch a
thing. But if you say so, we'll
try again." [6]And this time
their nets were so full they
began to tear! [7]A shout for
help brought their partners
in the other boat, and soon
both boats were filled with
fish and on the verge of sinking.
[8]When Simon Peter real-
ized what had happened, he
fell to his knees before Jesus
and said, "Oh, Lord, please
leave me—I'm too much of
a sinner to be around you."
[9]For he was awestruck by the
size of their catch, as were
the others with him. [10]His
partners, James and John,
the sons of Zebedee, were
also amazed.
Jesus replied to Simon,
"Don't be afraid! From now
on you'll be fishing for
people!" [11]And as soon as
they landed, they left everything and followed Jesus.
[12]In one of the villages,
Jesus met a man with an advanced case of leprosy. When
the man saw Jesus, he fell to
the ground, face down in the
dust, begging to be healed. "Lord," he said, "if you
want to, you can make me well again."
[13]Jesus reached out and touched the man. "I want
to," he said. "Be healed!" And instantly the leprosy
disappeared. [14]Then Jesus instructed him not to tell
anyone what had happened. He said, "Go right to
the priest and let him examine you. Take along the
offering required in the law of Moses for those who
have been healed of leprosy, so everyone will have
proof of your healing." [15]Yet despite Jesus' instructions, the report of his power spread even faster, and
vast crowds came to hear him preach and to be
healed of their diseases. [16]But Jesus often withdrew
to the wilderness for prayer.

## JAMES

**UPS:**
- One of the 12 disciples
- One of a special inner circle of three with Peter and John
- First of the 12 disciples to be killed for his faith

**DOWN:**
- There are two outbursts from James that indicate struggles with temper (Luke 9:54) and selfishness (Mark 10:37). Both times, he and his brother, John, spoke as one.

**STATS:**
- Where: Galilee
- Occupation: Fisherman, disciple
- Relatives: Father: Zebedee. Mother: Salome. Brother: John.
- Contemporaries: Jesus, Pilate, Herod, other disciples

Jesus chose 3 of his 12 disciples for special training. James, his brother John, and Peter made up this inner circle. Later, each played a key role among the first Christians. Peter became a great speaker; John became a great writer; James became the first of the 12 disciples to die for the faith.

James was older than his brother, John. Zebedee, their father, owned a fishing business where they worked along with Peter and Andrew, who also became disciples of Jesus. While Peter, Andrew, and John spent some time with John the Baptist, James stayed with the boats and nets. Later, when Jesus called them all, James was as eager as his partners to follow.

James liked the idea of being chosen as one of Jesus' disciples, but he misunderstood Jesus' purpose. He and his brother even tried asking Jesus for special positions in the kingdom they expected him to set up. Like all the disciples, James had a limited view of what Jesus was doing on earth. He hoped Jesus would start an earthly kingdom that would overthrow Rome and restore the nation of Israel. More than anything, James wanted to be with Jesus. He didn't understand his leader, but he understood that Jesus was worth following. But when Jesus died and rose from the grave, James finally understood.

James was the first of many to die for the gospel. He was willing to die because he knew Jesus had conquered death. And he realized that death was only the doorway to eternal life. Our lives will be affected by what we think about death. Jesus promised eternal life to those willing to trust him. If we believe this promise, he will give us the courage to stand for him even during dangerous times.

LESSON: Many of Jesus' followers do not consider the loss of life too heavy a price to pay for following him

KEY VERSES: "Then James and John, the sons of Zebedee, came over and spoke to him. 'Teacher,' they said, 'we want you to do us a favor.' 'What is it?' he asked. 'In your glorious Kingdom, we want to sit in places of honor next to you,' they said, 'one at your right and the other at your left'" (Mark 10:35-37).

James's story is told in the Gospels. He is also mentioned in Acts 1:13 and 12:2.

4:44 Some manuscripts read *Galilee.* 5:1 Greek *Lake Gennesaret,* another name for the Sea of Galilee. 5:3 *Simon* is called *Peter* in 6:14 and thereafter.

## JESUS AND FORGIVENESS

Jesus not only taught frequently about forgiveness, he also demonstrated his own willingness to forgive. Here are several examples that should help us recognize his willingness to forgive us also.

*Jesus forgave . . .*

the paralyzed man lowered on a mat through the roof . . . Luke 5:17-26
the woman caught in adultery . . . John 8:3-11
the woman who anointed his feet with oil . . . Luke 7:47-50
Peter, for denying he knew Jesus . . . John 18:15-18, 25-27; 21:15-19
the criminal on the cross . . . Luke 23:39-43
the people who crucified him . . . Luke 23:34

---

17One day while Jesus was teaching, some Pharisees and teachers of religious law were sitting nearby. (It seemed that these men showed up from every village in all Galilee and Judea, as well as from Jerusalem.) And the Lord's healing power was strongly with Jesus. 18Some men came carrying a paralyzed man on a sleeping mat. They tried to push through the crowd to Jesus, 19but they couldn't reach him. So they went up to the roof, took off some tiles, and lowered the sick man down into the crowd, still on his mat, right in front of Jesus. 20Seeing their faith, Jesus said to the man, "Son, your sins are forgiven."

21"Who does this man think he is?" the Pharisees and teachers of religious law said to each other. "This is blasphemy! Who but God can forgive sins?"

22Jesus knew what they were thinking, so he asked them, "Why do you think this is blasphemy? 23Is it easier to say, 'Your sins are forgiven' or 'Get up and walk'? 24I will prove that I, the Son of Man, have the authority on earth to forgive sins." Then Jesus turned to the paralyzed man and said, "Stand up, take your mat, and go on home, because you are healed!"

### TRY IT! ● ● ● • •

**5:18-20 It wasn't the sick man's faith that impressed Jesus, but the faith of his friends. Jesus responded to their faith and healed the man. For better or worse, our faith affects others. We cannot make another person a Christian, but we can do much through our words, actions, and love to give him or her a chance to respond. Look for opportunities to bring your friends to the living Christ.**

25And immediately, as everyone watched, the man jumped to his feet, picked up his mat, and went home praising God. 26Everyone was gripped with great wonder and awe. And they praised God, saying over and over again, "We have seen amazing things today."

27Later, as Jesus left the town, he saw a tax collector named Levi sitting at his tax-collection booth. "Come, be my disciple!" Jesus said to him. 28So Levi got up, left everything, and followed him.

29Soon Levi held a banquet in his home with Jesus as the guest of honor. Many of Levi's fellow tax collectors and other guests were there. 30But the Pharisees and their teachers of religious law complained bitterly to Jesus' disciples, "Why do you eat and drink with such scum*?"

31Jesus answered them, "Healthy people don't need a doctor—sick people do. 32I have come to call sinners to turn from their sins, not to spend my time with those who think they are already good enough."

33The religious leaders complained that Jesus' disciples were feasting instead of fasting. "John the Baptist's disciples always fast and pray," they declared, "and so do the disciples of the Pharisees. Why are yours always feasting?"

34Jesus asked, "Do wedding guests fast while celebrating with the groom? 35Someday he will be taken away from them, and then they will fast."

36Then Jesus gave them this illustration: "No one tears a piece of cloth from a new garment and uses it to patch an old garment. For then the new garment would be torn, and the patch wouldn't even match the old garment. 37And no one puts new wine into old wineskins. The new wine would burst the old skins, spilling the wine and ruining the skins. 38New wine must be put into new wineskins. 39But no one who drinks the old wine seems to want the fresh and the new. 'The old is better,' they say."

## CHAPTER 6 **PICKING WHEAT ON THE SABBATH.**

One Sabbath day as Jesus was walking through some grainfields, his disciples broke off heads of wheat, rubbed off the husks in their hands, and ate the grains. 2But some Pharisees said, "You shouldn't be doing that! It's against the law to work by harvesting grain on the Sabbath."

3Jesus replied, "Haven't you ever read in the Scriptures what King David did when he and his companions were hungry? 4He went into the house of God, ate the special bread reserved for the priests alone, and then gave some to his friends. That was

5:30 Greek *with tax collectors and sinners.*

breaking the law, too." 5And Jesus added, "I, the Son
of Man, am master even of the Sabbath."
6On another Sabbath day, a man with a deformed
right hand was in the synagogue while Jesus was
teaching. 7The teachers of religious law and the Pharisees watched closely to see whether Jesus would
heal the man on the Sabbath, because they were
eager to find some legal charge to bring against him.
8But Jesus knew their thoughts. He said to the man
with the deformed hand, "Come and stand here
where everyone can see." So the man came forward.
9Then Jesus said to his critics, "I have a question for
you. Is it legal to do good deeds on the Sabbath, or
is it a day for doing harm? Is this a day to save life or
to destroy it?" 10He looked around at them one by
one and then said to the man, "Reach out your
hand." The man reached out his hand, and it became normal again! 11At this, the enemies of Jesus
were wild with rage and began to discuss what to do
with him.
12One day soon afterward Jesus went to a mountain to pray, and he prayed to God all night. 13At
daybreak he called together all of his disciples and
chose twelve of them to be apostles. Here are their
names:

14 Simon (he also called him Peter),
Andrew (Peter's brother),
James,
John,
Philip,
Bartholomew,
15 Matthew,
Thomas,
James (son of Alphaeus),
Simon (the Zealot),
16 Judas (son of James),
Judas Iscariot (who later betrayed him).

17When they came down the slopes of the mountain, the disciples stood with Jesus on a large, level
area, surrounded by many of his followers and by
the crowds. There were people from all over Judea
and from Jerusalem and from as far north as the
seacoasts of Tyre and Sidon. 18They had come to hear
him and to be healed, and Jesus cast out many evil
spirits. 19Everyone was trying to touch him, because
healing power went out from him, and they were all
cured.
20Then Jesus turned to his disciples and said,

"God blesses you who are poor,
for the Kingdom of God is given to you.
21 God blesses you who are hungry now,
for you will be satisfied.
God blesses you who weep now,
for the time will come when you will laugh
with joy.
22 God blesses you who are hated and excluded and
mocked and cursed
because you are identified with me, the Son of
Man.

## QUALIFIED ● ● • • •

6:13-16 **Jesus picked ordinary men as his disciples. Today, God calls "ordinary" people to build his church, teach salvation, and serve others. Alone we may feel unqualified to serve Christ well. Together we are strong enough to serve God in any way. Ask for patience to accept differences and to build on the variety of strengths in your group.**

23"When that happens, rejoice! Yes, leap for joy!
For a great reward awaits you in heaven. And remember, the ancient prophets were also treated that way
by your ancestors.

24 "What sorrows await you who are rich,
for you have your only happiness now.
25 What sorrows await you who are satisfied and
prosperous now,
for a time of awful hunger is before you.
What sorrows await you who laugh carelessly,
for your laughing will turn to mourning and
sorrow.
26 What sorrows await you who are praised by the
crowds,
for their ancestors also praised false prophets.

27"But if you are willing to listen, I say, love your
enemies. Do good to those who hate you. 28Pray for
the happiness of those who curse you. Pray for those
who hurt you. 29If someone slaps you on one cheek,
turn the other cheek. If someone demands your coat,
offer your shirt also. 30Give what you have to anyone
who asks you for it; and when things are taken away
from you, don't try to get them back. 31Do for others
as you would like them to do for you.
32"Do you think you deserve credit merely for
loving those who love you? Even the sinners do that!
33And if you do good only to those who do good to
you, is that so wonderful? Even sinners do that
much! 34And if you lend money only to those who
can repay you, what good is that? Even sinners will
lend to their own kind for a full return.
35"Love your enemies! Do good to them! Lend to
them! And don't be concerned that they might not
repay. Then your reward from heaven will be very
great, and you will truly be acting as children of the
Most High, for he is kind to the unthankful and to
those who are wicked. 36You must be compassionate,
just as your Father is compassionate.
37"Stop judging others, and you will not be judged.
Stop criticizing others, or it will all come back on you.

## TOUGH LOVE ● ● • • •

6:27 **The Jews despised the Romans because they oppressed God's people, but Jesus told them to love these enemies. Such words turned many away from Christ. But Jesus wasn't talking about having affection for enemies; he was talking about an act of the will. You can't "fall into" this kind of love—it takes conscious effort. Loving our enemies means acting in their best interests. We can pray for them and we can think of ways to help them. Jesus loved the whole world, even though the world was in rebellion against God. He asks us to follow his example by loving our enemies.**

## NO POINTING ● ● • • •

**6:41 Jesus doesn't mean we should ignore wrongdoing, but we are not to be so worried about others' sins that we overlook our own. We often rationalize our sins by pointing out the same mistakes in others. What kinds of specks in others' eyes are the easiest for you to criticize? Remember your own planks when you feel like criticizing, and you may find you have less to say.**

If you forgive others, you will be forgiven. [38]If you give, you will receive. Your gift will return to you in full measure, pressed down, shaken together to make room for more, and running over. Whatever measure you use in giving—large or small—it will be used to measure what is given back to you."

[39]Then Jesus gave the following illustration: "What good is it for one blind person to lead another? The first one will fall into a ditch and pull the other down also. [40]A student is not greater than the teacher. But the student who works hard will become like the teacher.

[41]"And why worry about a speck in your friend's eye* when you have a log in your own? [42]How can you think of saying, 'Friend,* let me help you get rid of that speck in your eye,' when you can't see past the log in your own eye? Hypocrite! First get rid of the log from your own eye; then perhaps you will see well enough to deal with the speck in your friend's eye.

[43]"A good tree can't produce bad fruit, and a bad tree can't produce good fruit. [44]A tree is identified by the kind of fruit it produces. Figs never grow on thornbushes or grapes on bramble bushes. [45]A good person produces good deeds from a good heart, and an evil person produces evil deeds from an evil heart. Whatever is in your heart determines what you say.

[46]"So why do you call me 'Lord,' when you won't obey me? [47]I will show you what it's like when someone comes to me, listens to my teaching, and then obeys me. [48]It is like a person who builds a house on a strong foundation laid upon the underlying rock. When the floodwaters rise and break against the house, it stands firm because it is well built. [49]But anyone who listens and doesn't obey is like a person who builds a house without a foundation. When the floods sweep down against that house, it will crumble into a heap of ruins."

CHAPTER **7** **A MAN IS HEALED FAR AWAY.** When Jesus had finished saying all this, he went back to Capernaum. [2]Now the highly valued slave of a Roman officer was sick and near death. [3]When the officer heard about Jesus, he sent some respected Jewish leaders to ask him to come and heal his slave. [4]They earnestly begged Jesus to come with them and help the man. "If anyone deserves your help, it is he," they said, [5]"for he loves the Jews and even built a synagogue for us."

[6]So Jesus went with them. But just before they arrived at the house, the officer sent some friends to say, "Lord, don't trouble yourself by coming to my home, for I am not worthy of such an honor. [7]I am not even worthy to come and meet you. Just say the word from where you are, and my servant will be healed. [8]I know because I am under the authority of my superior officers, and I have authority over my soldiers. I only need to say, 'Go,' and they go, or 'Come,' and they come. And if I say to my slaves, 'Do this or that,' they do it."

[9]When Jesus heard this, he was amazed. Turning to the crowd, he said, "I tell you, I haven't seen faith like this in all the land of Israel!" [10]And when the officer's friends returned to his house, they found the slave completely healed.

[11]Soon afterward Jesus went with his disciples to the village of Nain, with a great crowd following him. [12]A funeral procession was coming out as he approached the village gate. The boy who had died was the only son of a widow, and many mourners from the village were with her. [13]When the Lord saw her, his heart overflowed with compassion. "Don't cry!" he said. [14]Then he walked over to the coffin and touched it, and the bearers stopped. "Young man," he said, "get up." [15]Then the dead boy sat up and began to talk to those around him! And Jesus gave him back to his mother.

## QUESTIONS ● ● • • •

**7:18-28 John was confused because the reports he received about Jesus were unexpected and incomplete. John's doubts were natural, and Jesus didn't rebuke him for them. Instead, Jesus responded in a way that John would understand by explaining that he had in fact accomplished the things the Messiah was supposed to accomplish. God also can handle our doubts, and he welcomes our questions. Do you have questions about Jesus—about who he is or what he expects of you? Admit them to yourself and to God, and begin looking for answers. Only as you admit your doubts can you begin to resolve them.**

[16]Great fear swept the crowd, and they praised God, saying, "A mighty prophet has risen among us," and "We have seen the hand of God at work today." [17]The report of what Jesus had done that day spread all over Judea and even out across its borders.

[18]The disciples of John the Baptist told John about everything Jesus was doing. So John called for two of his disciples, [19]and he sent them to the Lord to ask him, "Are you the Messiah we've been expecting, or should we keep looking for someone else?"

[20]John's two disciples found Jesus and said to him, "John the Baptist sent us to ask, 'Are you the Messiah we've been expecting, or should we keep looking for someone else?'"

## DISCOVER ● ● • • •

**7:29-30 The wicked people heard John's message and repented. In contrast, the religious leaders rejected his words. Wanting to live their own way, they refused to listen to other ideas. Rather than trying to force your plans on God, try to discover his plan for you.**

6:41 Greek *your brother's eye;* also in 6:42. 6:42 Greek *Brother.*

[21]At that very time, he cured many
people of their various diseases, and
he cast out evil spirits and restored
sight to the blind. [22]Then he told
John's disciples, "Go back to John
and tell him what you have seen and
heard—the blind see, the lame
walk, the lepers are cured, the deaf
hear, the dead are raised to life, and
the Good News is being preached to
the poor. [23]And tell him, 'God
blesses those who are not offended
by me.*'"
[24]After they left, Jesus talked to
the crowd about John. "Who is
this man in the wilderness that you
went out to see? Did you find him
weak as a reed, moved by every
breath of wind? [25]Or were you expecting to see a man dressed in
expensive clothes? No, people who
wear beautiful clothes and live in
luxury are found in palaces, not in
the wilderness. [26]Were you looking
for a prophet? Yes, and he is more
than a prophet. [27]John is the man
to whom the Scriptures refer when
they say,

'Look, I am sending my
messenger before you,
and he will prepare your way
before you.'*

[28]I tell you, of all who have ever
lived, none is greater than John. Yet
even the most insignificant person
in the Kingdom of God is greater
than he is!"
[29]When they heard this, all the
people, including the unjust tax
collectors, agreed that God's plan
was right,* for they had been baptized by John. [30]But the Pharisees
and experts in religious law had
rejected God's plan for them, for
they had refused John's baptism.
[31]"How shall I describe this generation?" Jesus asked. "With what will
I compare them? [32]They are like a
group of children playing a game in
the public square. They complain to
their friends, 'We played wedding
songs, and you weren't happy, so we
played funeral songs, but you
weren't sad.' [33]For John the Baptist
didn't drink wine and he often
fasted, and you say, 'He's demon
possessed.' [34]And I, the Son of Man,
feast and drink, and you say, 'He's a
glutton and a drunkard, and a friend

## "Here's what I did..."

Even before I became a Christian, the Bible amazed me. I remember being floored the first time I read Luke 6:27-38. That's the passage about loving and doing good to your enemies. *How could anyone act like that?*

A year later, just before my freshman year in high school, I became a Christian. And that year I had the chance to find out firsthand how someone can follow Jesus' words.

I did well in shop class, so I decided to make a small bookcase for my mother for Christmas. I designed it myself. I worked on it a lot in my spare time, finally getting to the point where I put final touches on it and left it in the finishing room, which was always locked.

After school, when I went back to get the bookcase, it was gone. The shop teacher did some investigating and finally discovered that a student named Andy had stolen it. "We've had problems with Andy before," Mr. Petrako said. "Andy needs to learn a lesson. I've arranged to have him meet you after school to return your bookshelf." That's all he said, but I knew what he meant.

I didn't need any encouragement to "teach Andy a lesson." I was furious. And since I was a football player, big for my age, I wouldn't have any trouble beating someone up.

I waited for Andy, psyching myself up to face my enemy. Finally he walked in.

Something happened to me when I saw him. I had expected a hoodlum, but what I saw was just a boy, smaller and younger than me, who was obviously afraid to face the person he had hurt. When I saw Andy's scared face, all the hate just leaked out of me. Andy said, "Here's your bookshelf. I'm sorry." I had no words for him. I growled something, took the bookcase, and fled.

That night I felt very confused. *What happened? What took away my hate?* As I thought about these things, I remembered the passage in Luke. I read it again: "Love your enemies. . . . When things are taken away from you, don't try to get them back."

*Father God*, I thought, *am I supposed to give the bookcase back to him? I can't! I made it for my mom!* I felt like God was asking me to respond to what I was reading. But how? Suddenly I knew. The next morning I went to school early and started work on an identical bookcase. For four days straight I stayed as long as shop was open.

When the bookcase was finished, I had Andy meet me after school in an empty shop class. I said, "Andy, I want to give you this. It's a gift from me to you, and from me to Jesus. I'd never be able to do this if it weren't for Jesus."

That's all I could say then. I didn't know how to share my faith. All I knew was that Jesus had touched my life and I wanted to share it.

Well, after that I got to know Andy. Seeing his family situation, I understood him better. I invited him to youth group on Thursday afternoons. When there was a retreat and Andy couldn't afford to go, my friends and I scraped up enough money for him. And at that retreat, Andy became a Christian.

It's hard to know who was more excited about God right then, me or Andy.

David

AGE 17

7:23 Or *who don't fall away because of me.* 7:27 Mal 3:1. 7:29 Or *praised God.*

## PIGS ● ● • • •

**8:33 The demons destroyed the pigs and hurt the herdsmen's finances. But can pigs and money compare with a human life? A man had been freed from the devil's power, but the villagers thought only about their pocketbooks. People have always tended to value personal gain over other people. Throughout history many wars have been fought to protect economic interests. Much injustice and oppression, both at home and abroad, is the direct result of some individual's or company's urge to get rich. People continually are being sacrificed to money. Don't think more highly of "pigs" than of people. Think carefully about how your decisions will affect other human beings, and be willing to choose a simpler lifestyle if it would keep other people from being harmed.**

of the worst sort of sinners!' 35But wisdom is shown to be right by the lives of those who follow it.*"

36One of the Pharisees asked Jesus to come to his home for a meal, so Jesus accepted the invitation and sat down to eat. 37A certain immoral woman heard he was there and brought a beautiful jar* filled with expensive perfume. 38Then she knelt behind him at his feet, weeping. Her tears fell on his feet, and she wiped them off with her hair. Then she kept kissing his feet and putting perfume on them.

39When the Pharisee who was the host saw what was happening and who the woman was, he said to himself, "This proves that Jesus is no prophet. If God had really sent him, he would know what kind of woman is touching him. She's a sinner!"

40Then Jesus spoke up and answered his thoughts. "Simon," he said to the Pharisee, "I have something to say to you."

"All right, Teacher," Simon replied, "go ahead."

41Then Jesus told him this story: "A man loaned money to two people—five hundred pieces of silver* to one and fifty pieces to the other. 42But neither of them could repay him, so he kindly forgave them both, canceling their debts. Who do you suppose loved him more after that?"

43Simon answered, "I suppose the one for whom he canceled the larger debt."

"That's right," Jesus said. 44Then he turned to the woman and said to Simon, "Look at this woman kneeling here. When I entered your home, you didn't offer me water to wash the dust from my feet, but she has washed them with her tears and wiped them with her hair. 45You didn't give me a kiss of greeting, but she has kissed my feet again and again from the time I first came in. 46You neglected the courtesy of olive oil to anoint my head, but she has anointed my feet with rare perfume. 47I tell you, her sins—and they are many—have been forgiven, so she has shown me much love. But a person who is forgiven little shows only little love." 48Then Jesus said to the woman, "Your sins are forgiven."

49The men at the table said among themselves, "Who does this man think he is, going around forgiving sins?"

50And Jesus said to the woman, "Your faith has saved you; go in peace."

## CHAPTER 8

**WOMEN GO WITH JESUS.** Not long afterward Jesus began a tour of the nearby cities and villages to announce the Good News concerning the Kingdom of God. He took his twelve disciples with him, 2along with some women he had healed and from whom he had cast out evil spirits. Among them were Mary Magdalene, from whom he had cast out seven demons; 3Joanna, the wife of Chuza, Herod's business manager; Susanna; and many others who were contributing from their own resources to support Jesus and his disciples.

4One day Jesus told this story to a large crowd that had gathered from many towns to hear him: 5"A farmer went out to plant some seed. As he scattered it across his field, some seed fell on a footpath, where it was stepped on, and the birds came and ate it. 6Other seed fell on shallow soil with underlying rock. This seed began to grow, but soon it withered and died for lack of moisture. 7Other seed fell among thorns that shot up and choked out the tender blades. 8Still other seed fell on fertile soil. This seed grew and produced a crop one hundred times as much as had been planted." When he had said this, he called out, "Anyone who is willing to hear should listen and understand!"

9His disciples asked him what the story meant. 10He replied, "You have been permitted to understand the secrets of the Kingdom of God. But I am using these stories to conceal everything about it from outsiders, so that the Scriptures might be fulfilled:

'They see what I do,
  but they don't really see;
they hear what I say,
  but they don't understand.'*

11"This is the meaning of the story: The seed is God's message. 12The seed that fell on the hard path represents those who hear the message, but then the Devil comes and steals it away and prevents them from believing and being saved. 13The rocky soil represents those who hear the message with joy. But like young plants in such soil, their roots don't go very deep. They believe for a while, but they wilt when the hot winds of testing blow. 14The thorny ground represents those who hear and accept the message, but all too quickly the message is crowded out by the cares and riches and pleasures of this life. And so they never grow into maturity. 15But the good soil represents honest, good-hearted people who hear God's message, cling to it, and steadily produce a huge harvest.

16"No one would light a lamp and then cover it up or put it under a bed. No, lamps are mounted in the open, where they can be seen by those entering the house. 17For everything that is hidden or secret will eventually be brought to light and made plain to all. 18So be sure to pay attention to what you hear. To those who are open to my teaching, more understanding will be given. But to those who are not

7:35 Or *But wisdom is justified by all her children.* 7:37 Greek *an alabaster jar.* 7:41 Greek *500 denarii.* A denarius was the equivalent of a full day's wage. 8:10 Isa 6:9.

listening, even what they think they have will be
taken away from them."
19 Once when Jesus' mother and brothers came to
see him, they couldn't get to him because of the
crowds. 20 Someone told Jesus, "Your mother and
your brothers are outside, and they want to see you."
21 Jesus replied, "My mother and my brothers are
all those who hear the message of God and obey it."
22 One day Jesus said to his disciples, "Let's cross
over to the other side of the lake." So they got into a
boat and started out. 23 On the way across, Jesus lay
down for a nap, and while he was sleeping the wind
began to rise. A fierce storm developed that threatened to swamp them, and they were in real danger.
24 The disciples woke him up, shouting, "Master,
Master, we're going to drown!"
So Jesus rebuked the wind and the raging waves.
The storm stopped and all was calm! 25 Then he
asked them, "Where is your faith?"
And they were filled with awe and amazement.
They said to one another, "Who is this man, that
even the winds and waves obey him?"
26 So they arrived in the land of the Gerasenes,*
across the lake from Galilee. 27 As Jesus was climbing
out of the boat, a man who was possessed by demons came out to meet him. Homeless and naked,
he had lived in a cemetery for a long time. 28 As soon
as he saw Jesus, he shrieked and fell to the ground
before him, screaming, "Why are you bothering me,
Jesus, Son of the Most High God? Please, I beg you,
don't torture me!" 29 For Jesus had already commanded the evil spirit to come out of him. This spirit
had often taken control of the man. Even when he
was shackled with chains, he simply broke them and
rushed out into the wilderness, completely under the
demon's power.
30 "What is your name?" Jesus asked.
"Legion," he replied—for the man was filled with
many demons. 31 The demons kept begging Jesus not
to send them into the Bottomless Pit. 32 A large herd
of pigs was feeding on the hillside nearby, and the
demons pleaded with him to let them enter into the
pigs. Jesus gave them permission. 33 So the demons
came out of the man and entered the pigs, and the
whole herd plunged down the steep hillside into the
lake, where they drowned.
34 When the herdsmen saw it, they fled to the
nearby city and the surrounding countryside, spreading the news as they ran. 35 A crowd soon gathered
around Jesus, for they wanted to see for themselves
what had happened. And they saw the man who had
been possessed by demons sitting quietly at Jesus'
feet, clothed and sane. And the whole crowd was
afraid. 36 Then those who had seen what happened
told the others how the demon-possessed man had
been healed. 37 And all the people in that region
begged Jesus to go away and leave them alone, for a
great wave of fear swept over them.
So Jesus returned to the boat and left, crossing
back to the other side of the lake. 38 The man who
had been demon possessed begged to go, too, but
Jesus said, 39 "No, go back to your family and tell
them all the wonderful things God has done for
you." So he went all through the city telling about
the great thing Jesus had done for him.
40 On the other side of the lake the crowds received
Jesus with open arms because they had been waiting
for him. 41 And now a man named Jairus, a leader of
the local synagogue, came and fell down at Jesus'
feet, begging him to come home with him. 42 His
only child was dying, a little girl twelve years old.
As Jesus went with him, he was surrounded by the
crowds. 43 And there was a woman in the crowd who
had had a hemorrhage for twelve years. She had
spent everything she had on doctors* and still could

**There are so many things in my life that could pull me away from God. How can I make sure I will always be "good soil"?**

Skyscrapers must be carefully planned in order for them not to topple when a stiff wind hits. First, a huge hole is dug deep in the ground. Thousands of tons of concrete are poured, steel girders are welded into place, and everything is made to fit according to exact specifications. If the foundation is strong and straight, a strong building can be built on it.

The rest of the structure, however, must also be built strong, with the right materials fitted together in the right way, at the right time.

In Luke 8:9-18, Jesus tells a parable about the Word of God. He compares it to a seed being planted. Like the skyscraper, seeds need to be planted in the right kind of soil, at the right time. So it is with the Word of God. Only God knows when and how to plant his Spirit and life within each of us.

The first phase in your new life began when you accepted Christ's forgiveness and became a Christian: "For no one can lay any other foundation than the one we already have—Jesus Christ" (1 Corinthians 3:11).

The second phase starts with the Word of God. If you study the Bible and have other Christians help you understand and apply it, your life in Christ will be strong. "Now anyone who builds on that foundation may use gold, silver, jewels, wood, hay, or straw" (1 Corinthians 3:12-13). If you are exposed to teaching that downplays God's Word, it is like building your life with wood, hay, and straw. It will collapse when problems or persecution from friends and family arise (see Matthew 7:21-28).

To build a solid Christian life, you should make sure that all you're hearing is lining up with what the Bible really says. You can do this by praying for direction, asking questions, and finding people who believe as you do that the Bible is God's blueprint for building a strong life.

8:26 Some manuscripts read *Gadarenes;* other manuscripts read *Gergesenes.* See Matt 8:28; Mark 5:1. 8:43 Some manuscripts omit *She had spent everything she had on doctors.*

# Ultimate Issues

## WHO IS JESUS?

**G**orillas are amazingly bright animals. Researchers have even been able to teach some gorillas to communicate by using sign language. Koko, one of the best ape "students" ever trained, has an impressive sign vocabulary through which she is able to communicate a number of surprisingly complicated concepts. But she was unprepared for the day an **EARTHQUAKE** shook the ground underneath her. **A**fter it was over, one of her trainers asked Koko to describe what she had just experienced. Having no word in her vocabulary for "earthquake," Koko described it as best she could. Using sign language, she said, "Darn floor—big bite." **I**t's not entirely clear what she was TRYING TO COMMUNICATE with those words; perhaps the fear that the floor might open up and swallow her. She was trying to express something beyond her limited ability the only way she knew how. **P**eople have struggled throughout history in a similar way with a different—and much more significant—problem: how to describe who God is and what he's like. (See the Ultimate Issue "Who Is God?" in Isaiah 4.) God communicated with humans in many ways in the past: talking freely with Adam and Eve, through the covenant sign of the rainbow, through a burning bush and columns of fire and smoke, through his Law, and through miracles and visions. Still, powerful and meaningful as all those were, they were only a hint of the reality behind them. The people who witnessed those signs must have felt like Koko—overwhelmed by what they'd experienced but with no adequate way to express their feelings. But God had one more ultimate revelation to make: ***he came to our planet and became one of us.*** We refer to this revelation as "Jesus of Nazareth." **U**nderstandably, the coming of Jesus was an explosive event. Nothing like it had ever happened before, nor has it happened since. God—in human form—**walking** the same ground with us! **Breathing** our air, sharing our pain, **laughing** and **bleeding** just like we do, entering into all the exhilaration—and the anguish—of being human. Before this revelation, God had given us hints, glimpses, and whispers of who he was. Then he came in all his fullness. **B**ut Jesus was not what people expected. Even the Jewish authorities—the people who knew more about God than anyone—were totally unprepared for the way God came. They expected a strong political and military Messiah, one who would free his people from Rome. Instead, the Messiah came as a "suffering servant," proclaiming a kingdom that was not of this world. Like so many others, the Jews were very confused as to who Jesus really was. Jesus himself knew that even his closest followers felt that uncertainty. He asked them POINT-BLANK: "Who do you say I am?" Peter's response to this question, given here in Luke, was simple, direct, and tremendously powerful: "The Messiah sent from God." **P**eter's answer, simple though it was, set off shock waves that have rippled down through history. If Jesus was—and is—indeed the Messiah, the Son of the living God, then God had entered into human history in a way he had never done before, and life on this planet could never be the same again. Countless millions of lives since then give testimony that that is exactly what has happened. Jesus of Nazareth was, and is, the unique Son of God: fully God, fully human, Lord of lords and King of kings. **T**hat same question Jesus asked his disciples confronts each of us today: ***Who do you say Jesus is?*** Be careful how you answer. It makes all the difference in eternity.

find no cure. 44She came up behind Jesus and touched the fringe of his robe. Immediately, the bleeding stopped.

45"Who touched me?" Jesus asked.

Everyone denied it, and Peter said, "Master, this whole crowd is pressing up against you."

46But Jesus told him, "No, someone deliberately touched me, for I felt healing power go out from me." 47When the woman realized that Jesus knew, she began to tremble and fell to her knees before him. The whole crowd heard her explain why she had touched him and that she had been immediately healed. 48"Daughter," he said to her, "your faith has made you well. Go in peace."

49While he was still speaking to her, a messenger arrived from Jairus's home with the message, "Your little girl is dead. There's no use troubling the Teacher now."

50But when Jesus heard what had happened, he said to Jairus, "Don't be afraid. Just trust me, and she will be all right."

51When they arrived at the house, Jesus wouldn't let anyone go in with him except Peter, James, John, and the little girl's father and mother. 52The house was filled with people weeping and wailing, but he said, "Stop the weeping! She isn't dead; she is only asleep."

53But the crowd laughed at him because they all knew she had died. 54Then Jesus took her by the hand and said in a loud voice, "Get up, my child!" 55And at that moment her life returned, and she immediately stood up! Then Jesus told them to give her something to eat. 56Her parents were overwhelmed, but Jesus insisted that they not tell anyone what had happened.

## CHAPTER 9

**AN ASSIGNMENT FOR THE DISCIPLES.** One day Jesus called together his twelve apostles and gave them power and authority to cast out demons and to heal all diseases. 2Then he sent them out to tell everyone about the coming of the Kingdom of God and to heal the sick. 3"Don't even take along a walking stick," he instructed them, "nor a traveler's bag, nor food, nor money. Not even an extra coat. 4When you enter each village, be a guest in only one home. 5If the people of the village won't receive your message when you enter it, shake off its dust from your feet as you leave. It is a sign that you have abandoned that village to its fate."

6So they began their circuit of the villages, preaching the Good News and healing the sick.

7When reports of Jesus' miracles reached Herod Antipas,* he was worried and puzzled because some were saying, "This is John the Baptist come back to life again." 8Others were saying, "It is Elijah or some other ancient prophet risen from the dead."

9"I beheaded John," Herod said, "so who is this man about whom I hear such strange stories?" And he tried to see him.

### RABBLE-ROUSER ● ● • • ·

9:7 **People couldn't accept Jesus for who he was, so they tried to come up with other solutions. Many thought he was John the Baptist or another prophet come back to life. Some suggested he was Elijah, the great prophet who did not die but was taken to heaven in a whirlwind (2 Kings 2:1-11). Few found the correct answer, as Peter did (9:20). Many today find it no easier to accept Jesus as the fully human yet fully divine Son of God—they still are trying to find alternate explanations: he was a great prophet, a radical political leader, a self-deceived rabble-rouser. None of these explanations can account for Jesus' miracles or, especially, his glorious resurrection. In the end, the attempts to explain Jesus away are far more difficult to believe than the truth.**

10When the apostles returned, they told Jesus everything they had done. Then he slipped quietly away with them toward the town of Bethsaida. 11But the crowds found out where he was going, and they followed him. And he welcomed them, teaching them about the Kingdom of God and curing those who were ill. 12Late in the afternoon the twelve disciples came to him and said, "Send the crowds away to the nearby villages and farms, so they can find food and lodging for the night. There is nothing to eat here in this deserted place."

13But Jesus said, "You feed them."

"Impossible!" they protested. "We have only five loaves of bread and two fish. Or are you expecting us to go and buy enough food for this whole crowd?" 14For there were about five thousand men there.

"Just tell them to sit down on the ground in groups of about fifty each," Jesus replied. 15So the people all sat down. 16Jesus took the five loaves and two fish, looked up toward heaven, and asked God's blessing on the food. Breaking the loaves into pieces, he kept giving the bread and fish to the disciples to give to the people. 17They all ate as much as they wanted, and they picked up twelve baskets of leftovers!

18One day as Jesus was alone, praying, he came over to his disciples and asked them, "Who do people say I am?"

19"Well," they replied, "some say John the Baptist, some say Elijah, and others say you are one of the other ancient prophets risen from the dead."

20Then he asked them, "Who do you say I am?"

Peter replied, "You are the Messiah sent from God!"

21Jesus warned them not to tell anyone about this. 22"For I, the Son of Man, must suffer many terrible things," he said. "I will be rejected by the leaders, the leading priests, and the teachers of religious law. I will be killed, but three days later I will be raised from the dead."

23Then he said to the crowd, "If any of you wants to be my follower, you must put aside your selfish ambition, shoulder your cross daily, and follow me. 24If you try to keep your life for yourself, you will lose

9:7 Greek *Herod the tetrarch.* He was a son of King Herod and was ruler over one of the four districts in Palestine.

it. But if you give up your life for me, you will find
true life. 25And how do you benefit if you gain the
whole world but lose or forfeit your own soul in the
process? 26If a person is ashamed of me and my
message, I, the Son of Man, will be ashamed of that
person when I return in my glory and in the glory of
the Father and the holy angels. 27And I assure you
that some of you standing here right now will not die
before you see the Kingdom of God."
28About eight days later Jesus took Peter, James,
and John to a mountain to pray. 29And as he was
praying, the appearance of his face changed, and his
clothing became dazzling white. 30Then two men,
Moses and Elijah, appeared and began talking with
Jesus. 31They were glorious to see. And they were
speaking of how he was about to fulfill God's plan
by dying in Jerusalem.

## ENEMIES

The situation: Shannon is driving home from youth group on a stormy night. As she rounds a curve in the road, she sees someone walking along in the mud. It's Jenny. A hundred yards up the road, Shannon sees Jenny's car in the ditch.

Should she stop and help?

Maybe that seems like a stupid question, but consider . . .

The background:

Jenny's life is like a fairy tale . . . no exaggeration:

- —Her family has some major bucks.
- —She drives a brand new BMW convertible.
- —She always looks like she just stepped off the cover of a fashion magazine.
- —She dates a really handsome college sophomore.
- —She makes straight *A*'s.
- —She has traveled all over the world.

As you might imagine, many people are jealous of Jenny's good fortune. Shannon is right there among them. But Shannon's feelings go beyond envy to include, shall we say, extreme dislike.

See, last year, Jenny made some really rude remarks about Shannon—behind her back. Then, two weeks later, she absolutely humiliated her at a big party—right in front of everyone! The two haven't spoken since, and when they're in the same room, everyone can feel the tension.

The solution:

Read Luke 10:25-37.

32Peter and the others were very drowsy and had
fallen asleep. Now they woke up and saw Jesus' glory
and the two men standing with him. 33As Moses and
Elijah were starting to leave, Peter, not even knowing
what he was saying, blurted out, "Master, this is
wonderful! We will make three shrines*—one for
you, one for Moses, and one for Elijah." 34But even
as he was saying this, a cloud came over them; and
terror gripped them as it covered them.
35Then a voice from the cloud said, "This is my
Son, my Chosen One.* Listen to him." 36When the
voice died away, Jesus was there alone. They didn't

## ENDANGERED

9:24-25 **If this life is most important to you, you will do everything you can to protect it. You will not want to do anything that might endanger your safety, health, or comfort. By contrast, if following Jesus is most important, you may find yourself in some very unsafe, unhealthy, and uncomfortable places. You will risk death, but you will not fear it because you know Jesus will raise you to eternal life. The person who is concerned only with this life has no such assurance. His earthly life may be longer, but it will most likely be marred by feelings of boredom and worthlessness.**

tell anyone what they had seen until long after this
happened.
37The next day, after they had come down the
mountain, a huge crowd met Jesus. 38A man in the
crowd called out to him, "Teacher, look at my boy,
who is my only son. 39An evil spirit keeps seizing
him, making him scream. It throws him into convul-
sions so that he foams at the mouth. It is always
hitting and injuring him. It hardly ever leaves him
alone. 40I begged your disciples to cast the spirit out,
but they couldn't do it."
41"You stubborn, faithless people," Jesus said,
"how long must I be with you and put up with you?
Bring him here." 42As the boy came forward, the
demon knocked him to the ground and threw him
into a violent convulsion. But Jesus rebuked the evil
spirit and healed the boy. Then he gave him back to
his father. 43Awe gripped the people as they saw this
display of God's power.
While everyone was marveling over all the wonderful things he was doing, Jesus said to his disciples,
44"Listen to me and remember what I say. The Son of
Man is going to be betrayed." 45But they didn't know
what he meant. Its significance was hidden from
them, so they could not understand it, and they were
afraid to ask him about it.
46Then there was an argument among them as to
which of them would be the greatest. 47But Jesus
knew their thoughts, so he brought a little child to
his side. 48Then he said to them, "Anyone who
welcomes a little child like this on my behalf welcomes me, and anyone who welcomes me welcomes
my Father who sent me. Whoever is the least among
you is the greatest."
49John said to Jesus, "Master, we saw someone
using your name to cast out demons. We tried to stop
him because he isn't in our group."
50But Jesus said, "Don't stop him! Anyone who is
not against you is for you."
51As the time drew near for his return to heaven,
Jesus resolutely set out for Jerusalem. 52He sent messengers ahead to a Samaritan village to prepare for
his arrival. 53But they were turned away. The people
of the village refused to have anything to do with
Jesus because he had resolved to go to Jerusalem.
54When James and John heard about it, they said to
Jesus, "Lord, should we order down fire from heaven
to burn them up*?" 55But Jesus turned and rebuked
them.* 56So they went on to another village.

9:33 Or *shelters;* Greek reads *tabernacles.* 9:35 Some manuscripts read *This is my beloved Son.* 9:54 Some manuscripts add *as Elijah did.* 9:55 Some manuscripts add *And he said, "You don't realize what your hearts are like.* 56*For the Son of Man has not come to destroy men's lives, but to save them."*

[57]As they were walking along someone said to Jesus, "I will follow you no matter where you go."

[58]But Jesus replied, "Foxes have dens to live in, and birds have nests, but I, the Son of Man, have no home of my own, not even a place to lay my head."

[59]He said to another person, "Come, be my disciple."

The man agreed, but he said, "Lord, first let me return home and bury my father."

[60]Jesus replied, "Let those who are spiritually dead care for their own dead.* Your duty is to go and preach the coming of the Kingdom of God."

[61]Another said, "Yes, Lord, I will follow you, but first let me say good-bye to my family."

[62]But Jesus told him, "Anyone who puts a hand to the plow and then looks back is not fit for the Kingdom of God."

CHAPTER **10** **JESUS SENDS OUT 70 MESSENGERS.** The Lord now chose seventy-two* other disciples and sent them on ahead in pairs to all the towns and villages he planned to visit. [2]These were his instructions to them: "The harvest is so great, but the workers are so few. Pray to the Lord who is in charge of the harvest, and ask him to send out more workers for his fields. [3]Go now, and remember that I am sending you out as lambs among wolves. [4]Don't take along any money, or a traveler's bag, or even an extra pair of sandals. And don't stop to greet anyone on the road.

[5]"Whenever you enter a home, give it your blessing. [6]If those who live there are worthy, the blessing will stand; if they are not, the blessing will return to you. [7]When you enter a town, don't move around from home to home. Stay in one place, eating and drinking what they provide you. Don't hesitate to accept hospitality, because those who work deserve their pay.

[8]"If a town welcomes you, eat whatever is set before you [9]and heal the sick. As you heal them, say, 'The Kingdom of God is near you now.' [10]But if a town refuses to welcome you, go out into its streets and say, [11]'We wipe the dust of your town from our feet as a public announcement of your doom. And don't forget the Kingdom of God is near!' [12]The truth is, even wicked Sodom will be better off than such a town on the judgment day.

[13]"What horrors await you, Korazin and Bethsaida! For if the miracles I did in you had been done in wicked Tyre and Sidon, their people would have sat in deep repentance long ago, clothed in sackcloth and throwing ashes on their heads to show their remorse. [14]Yes, Tyre and Sidon will be better off on the judgment day than you. [15]And you people of Capernaum, will you be exalted to heaven? No, you will be brought down to the place of the dead.*"

[16]Then he said to the disciples, "Anyone who accepts your message is also accepting me. And anyone who rejects you is rejecting me. And anyone who rejects me is rejecting God who sent me."

## MOUNTAINS ● ● • • •

9:33 **Peter, James, and John experienced a wonderful moment on the mountain, and they didn't want to leave. Sometimes we, too, have such an exciting experience we want to stay where we are—away from the reality and problems of our daily life. Knowing that struggles await us encourages us to retreat from reality. Yet staying on top of a mountain does not allow us to minister to others. Instead of becoming spiritual giants, we would soon become giants of self-centeredness. We need times of retreat and renewal, but only so we can return to minister to the world. Our faith must make sense off the mountain as well as on it.**

[17]When the seventy-two disciples returned, they joyfully reported to him, "Lord, even the demons obey us when we use your name!"

[18]"Yes," he told them, "I saw Satan falling from heaven as a flash of lightning! [19]And I have given you authority over all the power of the enemy, and you can walk among snakes and scorpions and crush them. Nothing will injure you. [20]But don't rejoice just because evil spirits obey you; rejoice because your names are registered as citizens of heaven."

[21]Then Jesus was filled with the joy of the Holy Spirit and said, "O Father, Lord of heaven and earth, thank you for hiding the truth from those who think themselves so wise and clever, and for revealing it to the childlike. Yes, Father, it pleased you to do it this way.

[22]"My Father has given me authority over everything. No one really knows the Son except the Father, and no one really knows the Father except the Son and those to whom the Son chooses to reveal him."

[23]Then when they were alone, he turned to the disciples and said, "How privileged you are to see what you have seen. [24]I tell you, many prophets and kings have longed to see and hear what you have seen and heard, but they could not."

[25]One day an expert in religious law stood up to test Jesus by asking him this question: "Teacher, what must I do to receive eternal life?"

[26]Jesus replied, "What does the law of Moses say? How do you read it?"

[27]The man answered, "'You must love the Lord your God with all your heart, all your soul, all your strength, and all your mind.' And, 'Love your neighbor as yourself.'"*

[28]"Right!" Jesus told him. "Do this and you will live!"

[29]The man wanted to justify his actions, so he asked Jesus, "And who is my neighbor?"

## NEIGHBORS ● ● • • •

10:27-37 **From the parable we learn three principles about loving our neighbors: (1) lack of love is often easy to justify; (2) our neighbor is anyone of any race or creed or social background who is in need; and (3) love means acting to meet the need. Wherever you live, there are needy people close by. There are no good reasons for refusing to help.**

9:60 Greek *Let the dead bury their own dead.* 10:1 Some manuscripts read *70;* also in 10:17. 10:15 Greek *to Hades.* 10:27 Deut 6:5; Lev 19:18.

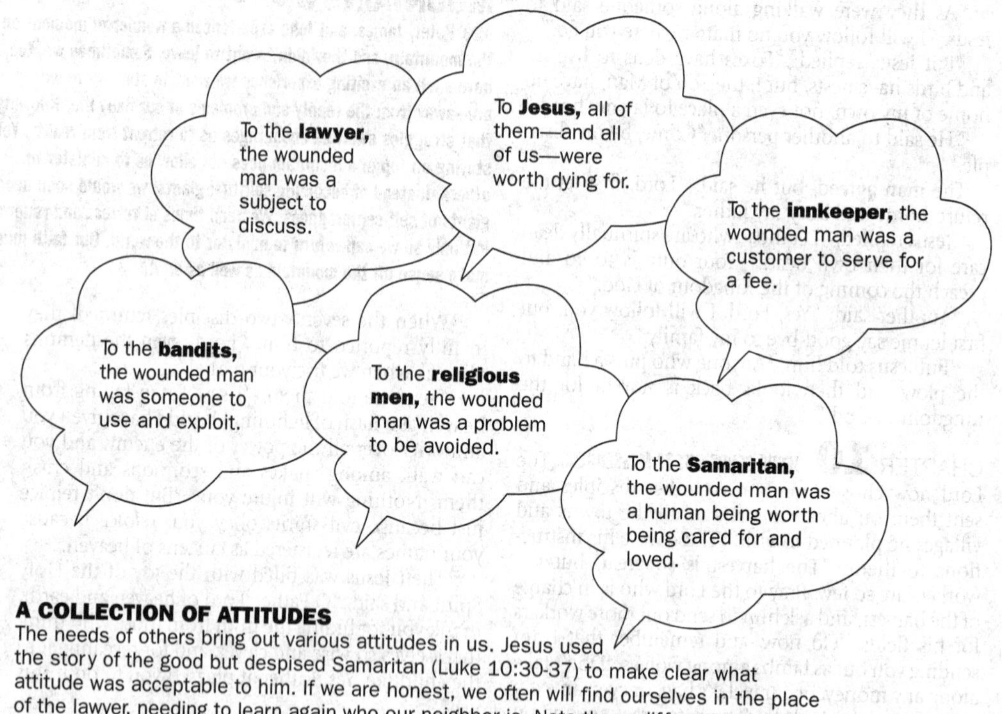

To the **lawyer,** the wounded man was a subject to discuss.
To **Jesus,** all of them—and all of us—were worth dying for.
To the **innkeeper,** the wounded man was a customer to serve for a fee.
To the **bandits,** the wounded man was someone to use and exploit.
To the **religious men,** the wounded man was a problem to be avoided.
To the **Samaritan,** the wounded man was a human being worth being cared for and loved.


**A COLLECTION OF ATTITUDES**
The needs of others bring out various attitudes in us. Jesus used the story of the good but despised Samaritan (Luke 10:30-37) to make clear what attitude was acceptable to him. If we are honest, we often will find ourselves in the place of the lawyer, needing to learn again who our neighbor is. Note these different attitudes toward the wounded man.

---

30Jesus replied with an illustration: "A Jewish man was traveling on a trip from Jerusalem to Jericho, and he was attacked by bandits. They stripped him of his clothes and money, beat him up, and left him half dead beside the road.

31"By chance a Jewish priest came along; but when he saw the man lying there, he crossed to the other side of the road and passed him by. 32A Temple assistant* walked over and looked at him lying there, but he also passed by on the other side.

33"Then a despised Samaritan came along, and when he saw the man, he felt deep pity. 34Kneeling beside him, the Samaritan soothed his wounds with medicine and bandaged them. Then he put the man on his own donkey and took him to an inn, where he took care of him. 35The next day he handed the innkeeper two pieces of silver* and told him to take care of the man. 'If his bill runs higher than that,' he said, 'I'll pay the difference the next time I am here.'

36"Now which of these three would you say was a neighbor to the man who was attacked by bandits?" Jesus asked.

37The man replied, "The one who showed him mercy."

Then Jesus said, "Yes, now go and do the same."

38As Jesus and the disciples continued on their way to Jerusalem, they came to a village where a woman named Martha welcomed them into her home. 39Her sister, Mary, sat at the Lord's feet, listening to what he taught. 40But Martha was worrying over the big dinner she was preparing. She came to Jesus and said, "Lord, doesn't it seem unfair to you that my sister just sits here while I do all the work? Tell her to come and help me."

41But the Lord said to her, "My dear Martha, you are so upset over all these details! 42There is really only one thing worth being concerned about. Mary has discovered it—and I won't take it away from her."

## CHAPTER 11

**JESUS TEACHES ABOUT PRAYER.** Once when Jesus had been out praying, one of his disciples came to him as he finished and said, "Lord, teach us to pray, just as John taught his disciples."

2He said, "This is how you should pray:

"Father, may your name be honored.
May your Kingdom come soon.
3Give us our food day by day.

**SHOPPING LISTS • • • . .**
11:1-4 **Notice the order in this prayer. First Jesus praised God; then he made his requests. Praising God first puts us in the right frame of mind to tell him about our needs. Too often our prayers are more like shopping lists than conversations.**

10:32 Greek *A Levite.* 10:35 Greek *2 denarii.* A denarius was the equivalent of a full day's wage.

[4]And forgive us our sins—
just as we forgive those who have sinned
against us.
And don't let us yield to temptation.*"

[5]Then, teaching them more about prayer, he used
this illustration: "Suppose you went to a friend's
house at midnight, wanting to borrow three loaves
of bread. You would say to him, [6]'A friend of mine
has just arrived for a visit, and I have nothing for him
to eat.' [7]He would call out from his bedroom, 'Don't
bother me. The door is locked for the night, and we
are all in bed. I can't help you this time.' [8]But I tell
you this—though he won't do it as a friend, if you
keep knocking long enough, he will get up and give
you what you want so his reputation won't be damaged.*

[9]"And so I tell you, keep on asking, and you will
be given what you ask for. Keep on looking, and you
will find. Keep on knocking, and the door will be
opened. [10]For everyone who asks, receives. Everyone
who seeks, finds. And the door is opened to everyone
who knocks.

[11]"You fathers—if your children ask* for a fish, do
you give them a snake instead? [12]Or if they ask for an
egg, do you give them a scorpion? Of course not! [13]If
you sinful people know how to give good gifts to
your children, how much more will your heavenly
Father give the Holy Spirit to those who ask him."

[14]One day Jesus cast a demon out of a man who
couldn't speak, and the man's voice returned to him.
The crowd was amazed, [15]but some said, "No wonder he can cast out demons. He gets his power from
Satan,* the prince of demons!" [16]Trying to test Jesus,
others asked for a miraculous sign from heaven to
see if he was from God.

[17]He knew their thoughts, so he said, "Any kingdom at war with itself is doomed. A divided home is
also doomed. [18]You say I am empowered by the
prince of demons.* But if Satan is fighting against
himself by empowering me to cast out his demons,
how can his kingdom survive? [19]And if I am empowered by the prince of demons, what about your own
followers? They cast out demons, too, so they will
judge you for what you have said. [20]But if I am
casting out demons by the power of God, then the
Kingdom of God has arrived among you. [21]For when
Satan,* who is completely armed, guards his palace,
it is safe—[22]until someone who is stronger attacks
and overpowers him, strips him of his weapons, and
carries off his belongings.

[23]"Anyone who isn't helping me opposes me, and
anyone who isn't working with me is actually working against me.

[24]"When an evil spirit leaves a person, it goes into
the desert, searching for rest. But when it finds none,
it says, 'I will return to the person I came from.' [25]So
it returns and finds that its former home is all swept
and clean. [26]Then the spirit finds seven other spirits
more evil than itself, and they all enter the person
and live there. And so that person is worse off than
before."

[27]As he was speaking, a woman in the crowd called
out, "God bless your mother—the womb from
which you came, and the breasts that nursed you!"

[28]He replied, "But even more blessed are all who
hear the word of God and put it into practice."

[29]As the crowd pressed in on Jesus, he said, "These
are evil times, and this evil generation keeps asking
me to show them a miraculous sign. But the only
sign I will give them is the sign of the prophet Jonah.
[30]What happened to him was a sign to the people of
Nineveh that God had sent him. What happens to
me will be a sign that God has sent me, the Son of
Man, to these people.

## PRO JESUS ● ● • • •

**11:23 Jesus says, "Anyone who isn't working with me is actually working against me," while earlier he stated, "Anyone who is not against you is for you" (9:50). People who are neutral toward Christians are actually helping them more than hurting them because they are not setting up barriers. But while people can be neutral toward Christians, they cannot be neutral in their relationship with Jesus, or in the battle between Jesus and Satan. You can't be aloof or noncommittal, because there are only two sides. Since God has already won the battle, why be on the losing side? If you aren't actively for Christ, you are against him.**

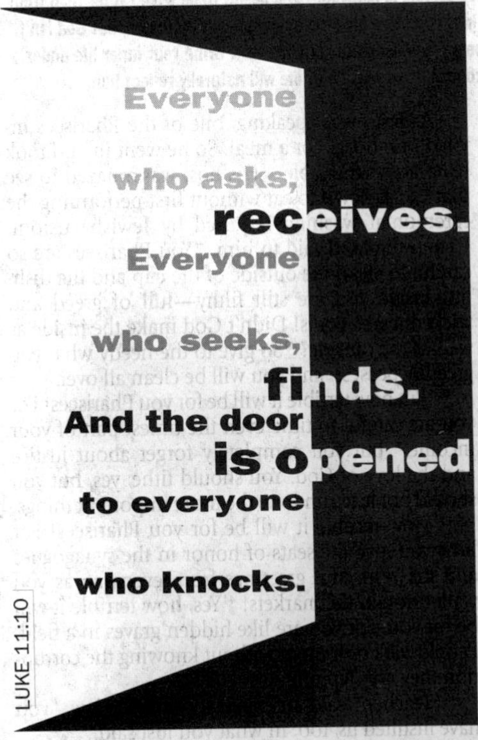
Everyone
who asks,
receives.
Everyone
who seeks,
finds.
And the door
is opened
to everyone
who knocks.
LUKE 11:10

11:2-4 Some manuscripts add additional portions of the Lord's Prayer as it reads in Matt 6:9-13. 11:8 Greek *in order to avoid shame,* or *because of [your] persistence.* 11:11 Some manuscripts add *for bread, do you give them a stone? Or if they ask.* 11:15 Greek *Beelzeboul.* 11:18 Greek *by Beelzeboul;* also in 11:19. 11:21 Greek *the strong one.*

31 “The queen of Sheba* will rise up against this
generation on judgment day and condemn it, because she came from a distant land to hear the
wisdom of Solomon. And now someone greater
than Solomon is here—and you refuse to listen to
him. 32 The people of Nineveh, too, will rise up
against this generation on judgment day and condemn it, because they repented at the preaching of
Jonah. And now someone greater than Jonah is
here—and you refuse to repent.
33 “No one lights a lamp and then hides it or puts
it under a basket. Instead, it is put on a lampstand to
give light to all who enter the room. 34 Your eye is a
lamp for your body. A pure eye lets sunshine into
your soul. But an evil eye shuts out the light and
plunges you into darkness. 35 Make sure that the light
you think you have is not really darkness. 36 If you are
filled with light, with no dark corners, then your
whole life will be radiant, as though a floodlight is
shining on you.”

## MOTIVES ● ● • • •

11:52 **Jesus criticized the Pharisees harshly because they (1) washed their hands but not their hearts, (2) remembered to tithe but forgot justice, (3) loved people's praise, (4) made impossible religious demands, and (5) didn't accept the truth about Jesus and prevented others from believing it. They wrongly focused on outward appearances and ignored the condition of their hearts. We do the same when our service is motivated by a desire to be seen rather than from a pure heart and love for others. Others may be fooled, but God isn't. Don't be a Christian on the outside only. Bring your inner life under God's control; then your outer life will naturally reflect him.**

37 As Jesus was speaking, one of the Pharisees invited him home for a meal. So he went in and took
his place at the table. 38 His host was amazed to see
that he sat down to eat without first performing the
ceremonial washing required by Jewish custom.
39 Then the Lord said to him, “You Pharisees are so
careful to clean the outside of the cup and the dish,
but inside you are still filthy—full of greed and
wickedness! 40 Fools! Didn't God make the inside as
well as the outside? 41 So give to the needy what you
greedily possess, and you will be clean all over.
42 “But how terrible it will be for you Pharisees! For
you are careful to tithe even the tiniest part of your
income,* but you completely forget about justice
and the love of God. You should tithe, yes, but you
should not leave undone the more important things.
43 “How terrible it will be for you Pharisees! For
how you love the seats of honor in the synagogues
and the respectful greetings from everyone as you
walk through the markets! 44 Yes, how terrible it will
be for you. For you are like hidden graves in a field.
People walk over them without knowing the corruption they are stepping on.”
45 “Teacher,” said an expert in religious law, “you
have insulted us, too, in what you just said.”
46 “Yes,” said Jesus, “how terrible it will be for you

## REAL VALUE ● ● • • •

12:7 **Our true value is God's estimate of our worth, not our peers'. Other people evaluate and categorize us according to how we perform, what we achieve, and how we look. But God's love gives us the real basis for our worth—we belong to him.**

experts in religious law! For you crush people beneath impossible religious demands, and you never
lift a finger to help ease the burden. 47 How terrible it
will be for you! For you build tombs for the very
prophets your ancestors killed long ago. 48 Murderers! You agree with your ancestors that what they did
was right. You would have done the same yourselves.
49 This is what God in his wisdom said about you:* ‘I
will send prophets and apostles to them, and they
will kill some and persecute the others.’
50 “And you of this generation will be held responsible for the murder of all God's prophets from the
creation of the world—51 from the murder of Abel to
the murder of Zechariah, who was killed between
the altar and the sanctuary. Yes, it will surely be
charged against you.
52 “How terrible it will be for you experts in religious law! For you hide the key to knowledge from
the people. You don't enter the Kingdom yourselves,
and you prevent others from entering.”
53 As Jesus finished speaking, the Pharisees and
teachers of religious law were furious. From that time
on they grilled him with many hostile questions,
54 trying to trap him into saying something they
could use against him.

## CHAPTER 12 JESUS WARNS AGAINST HYPOCRISY.

Meanwhile, the crowds grew until thousands were
milling about and crushing each other. Jesus turned
first to his disciples and warned them, “Beware of
the yeast of the Pharisees—beware of their hypocrisy. 2 The time is coming when everything will be
revealed; all that is secret will be made public.
3 Whatever you have said in the dark will be heard in
the light, and what you have whispered behind
closed doors will be shouted from the housetops for
all to hear!
4 “Dear friends, don't be afraid of those who want
to kill you. They can only kill the body; they cannot
do any more to you. 5 But I'll tell you whom to fear.
Fear God, who has the power to kill people and then
throw them into hell.
6 “What is the price of five sparrows? A couple of
pennies? Yet God does not forget a single one of
them. 7 And the very hairs on your head are all numbered. So don't be afraid; you are more valuable to
him than a whole flock of sparrows.
8 “And I assure you of this: If anyone acknowledges
me publicly here on earth, I, the Son of Man, will
openly acknowledge that person in the presence of
God's angels. 9 But if anyone denies me here on earth,
I will deny that person before God's angels. 10 Yet
those who speak against the Son of Man may be
forgiven, but anyone who speaks blasphemies
against the Holy Spirit will never be forgiven.

11:31 Greek *the queen of the south.* 11:42 Greek *to tithe the mint and the rue and every herb.* 11:49 Greek *Therefore, the wisdom of God said.*

11"And when you are brought to trial in the synagogues and before rulers and authorities, don't
worry about what to say in your defense, 12for the
Holy Spirit will teach you what needs to be said even
as you are standing there."
13Then someone called from the crowd, "Teacher,
please tell my brother to divide our father's estate
with me."
14Jesus replied, "Friend, who made me a judge
over you to decide such things as that?" 15Then he
said, "Beware! Don't be greedy for what you don't
have. Real life is not measured by how much we
own."
16And he gave an illustration: "A rich man had a
fertile farm that produced fine crops. 17In fact, his
barns were full to overflowing. 18So he said, 'I know!
I'll tear down my barns and build bigger ones. Then
I'll have room enough to store everything. 19And I'll
sit back and say to myself, My friend, you have
enough stored away for years to come. Now take it
easy! Eat, drink, and be merry!'
20"But God said to him, 'You fool! You will die
this very night. Then who will get it all?'
21"Yes, a person is a fool to store up earthly wealth
but not have a rich relationship with God."
22Then turning to his disciples, Jesus said, "So I
tell you, don't worry about everyday life—whether
you have enough food to eat or clothes to wear. 23For
life consists of far more than food and clothing.
24Look at the ravens. They don't need to plant or
harvest or put food in barns because God feeds
them. And you are far more valuable to him than any
birds! 25Can all your worries add a single moment to
your life? Of course not! 26And if worry can't do little
things like that, what's the use of worrying over
bigger things?
27"Look at the lilies and how they grow. They
don't work or make their clothing, yet Solomon in
all his glory was not dressed as beautifully as they
are. 28And if God cares so wonderfully for flowers
that are here today and gone tomorrow, won't he
more surely care for you? You have so little faith!
29And don't worry about food—what to eat and
drink. Don't worry whether God will provide it for
you. 30These things dominate the thoughts of most
people, but your Father already knows your needs.
31He will give you all you need from day to day if you
make the Kingdom of God your primary concern.
32"So don't be afraid, little flock. For it gives your
Father great happiness to give you the Kingdom.
33"Sell what you have and give to those in need.
This will store up treasure for you in heaven! And the
purses of heaven have no holes in them. Your treasure will be safe—no thief can steal it and no moth
can destroy it. 34Wherever your treasure is, there your
heart and thoughts will also be.
35"Be dressed for service and well prepared, 36as
though you were waiting for your master to return
from the wedding feast. Then you will be ready to
open the door and let him in the moment he arrives
and knocks. 37There will be special favor for those
who are ready and waiting for his return. I tell you,
he himself will seat them, put on an apron, and serve
them as they sit and eat! 38He may come in the
middle of the night or just before dawn.* But whenever he comes, there will be special favor for his
servants who are ready!
39"Know this: A homeowner who knew exactly
when a burglar was coming would not permit the
house to be broken into. 40You must be ready all the
time, for the Son of Man will come when least
expected."
41Peter asked, "Lord, is this illustration just for us
or for everyone?"
42And the Lord replied, "I'm talking to any faithful, sensible servant to whom the master gives the
responsibility of managing his household and feeding his family. 43If the master returns and finds that
the servant has done a good job, there will be a
reward. 44I assure you, the master will put that servant in charge of all he owns. 45But if the servant
thinks, 'My master won't be back for a while,' and
begins oppressing the other servants, partying, and
getting drunk—46well, the master will return unannounced and unexpected. He will tear the servant
apart and banish him with the unfaithful. 47The
servant will be severely punished, for though he
knew his duty, he refused to do it.
48"But people who are not aware that they are
doing wrong will be punished only lightly. Much is
required from those to whom much is given, and
much more is required from those to whom much
more is given.
49"I have come to bring fire to the earth, and I wish
that my task were already completed! 50There is a
terrible baptism ahead of me, and I am under a
heavy burden until it is accomplished. 51Do you
think I have come to bring peace to the earth? No, I
have come to bring strife and division! 52From now
on families will be split apart, three in favor of me,
and two against—or the other way around. 53There
will be a division between father and son, mother
and daughter, mother-in-law and daughter-in-law."
54Then Jesus turned to the crowd and said, "When
you see clouds beginning to form in the west, you
say, 'Here comes a shower.' And you are right.
55When the south wind blows, you say, 'Today will
be a scorcher.' And it is. 56You hypocrites! You know

**LOYALTIES ● ● ● • •**

12:51-53 **In these strange and unsettling words, Jesus revealed that his coming often results in conflict. He demands a response, and close groups can be torn apart when some choose to follow him and others refuse to do so. There is no middle ground with Jesus. Loyalties must be declared and commitments made, sometimes to the severing of other relationships. Life is easiest when a family believes together in Christ, but this often does not happen. Are you willing to risk your family's disapproval to gain eternal life?**

12:38 Greek *in the second or third watch.*

**SAVED ● ● • • •**

13:27 **The people were eager to know who would be saved. Jesus explained that although many people know something about God, only a few have accepted his forgiveness. Just listening to his words or admiring his miracles is not enough—it is vital to turn from sin and trust in God to save us.**

how to interpret the appearance of the earth and the sky, but you can't interpret these present times.

57 "Why can't you decide for yourselves what is right? 58 If you are on the way to court and you meet your accuser, try to settle the matter before it reaches the judge, or you may be sentenced and handed over to an officer and thrown in jail. 59 And if that happens, you won't be free again until you have paid the last penny."

## CHAPTER 13 JESUS TELLS THE PEOPLE TO REPENT.

About this time Jesus was informed that Pilate had murdered some people from Galilee as they were sacrificing at the Temple in Jerusalem. 2 "Do you think those Galileans were worse sinners than other people from Galilee?" he asked. "Is that why they suffered? 3 Not at all! And you will also perish unless you turn from your evil ways and turn to God. 4 And what about the eighteen men who died when the Tower of Siloam fell on them? Were they the worst sinners in Jerusalem? 5 No, and I tell you again that unless you repent, you will also perish."

6 Then Jesus used this illustration: "A man planted a fig tree in his garden and came again and again to see if there was any fruit on it, but he was always disappointed. 7 Finally, he said to his gardener, 'I've waited three years, and there hasn't been a single fig! Cut it down. It's taking up space we can use for something else.'

8 "The gardener answered, 'Give it one more chance. Leave it another year, and I'll give it special attention and plenty of fertilizer. 9 If we get figs next year, fine. If not, you can cut it down.'"

10 One Sabbath day as Jesus was teaching in a synagogue, 11 he saw a woman who had been crippled by an evil spirit. She had been bent double for eighteen years and was unable to stand up straight. 12 When Jesus saw her, he called her over and said, "Woman, you are healed of your sickness!" 13 Then he touched her, and instantly she could stand straight. How she praised and thanked God!

14 But the leader in charge of the synagogue was indignant that Jesus had healed her on the Sabbath day. "There are six days of the week for working," he said to the crowd. "Come on those days to be healed, not on the Sabbath."

15 But the Lord replied, "You hypocrite! You work on the Sabbath day! Don't you untie your ox or your donkey from their stalls on the Sabbath and lead them out for water? 16 Wasn't it necessary for me, even on the Sabbath day, to free this dear woman* from the bondage in which Satan has held her for eighteen years?" 17 This shamed his enemies. And all the people rejoiced at the wonderful things he did.

18 Then Jesus said, "What is the Kingdom of God like? How can I illustrate it? 19 It is like a tiny mustard seed planted in a garden; it grows and becomes a tree, and the birds come and find shelter among its branches."

20 He also asked, "What else is the Kingdom of God like? 21 It is like yeast used by a woman making bread. Even though she used a large amount* of flour, the yeast permeated every part of the dough."

22 Jesus went through the towns and villages, teaching as he went, always pressing on toward Jerusalem. 23 Someone asked him, "Lord, will only a few be saved?"

He replied, 24 "The door to heaven is narrow. Work hard to get in, because many will try to enter, 25 but when the head of the house has locked the door, it will be too late. Then you will stand outside knocking and pleading, 'Lord, open the door for us!' But he will reply, 'I do not know you.' 26 You will say, 'But we ate and drank with you, and you taught in our streets.' 27 And he will reply, 'I tell you, I don't know you. Go away, all you who do evil.'

28 "And there will be great weeping and gnashing of teeth, for you will see Abraham, Isaac, Jacob, and all the prophets within the Kingdom of God, but you will be thrown out. 29 Then people will come from all over the world to take their places in the Kingdom of God. 30 And note this: Some who are despised now will be greatly honored then; and some who are greatly honored now will be despised then.*"

31 A few minutes later some Pharisees said to him, "Get out of here if you want to live, because Herod Antipas wants to kill you!"

32 Jesus replied, "Go tell that fox that I will keep on casting out demons and doing miracles of healing today and tomorrow; and the third day I will accomplish my purpose. 33 Yes, today, tomorrow, and the next day I must proceed on my way. For it wouldn't do for a prophet of God to be killed except in Jerusalem!

34 "O Jerusalem, Jerusalem, the city that kills the prophets and stones God's messengers! How often I have wanted to gather your children together as a hen protects her chicks beneath her wings, but you wouldn't let me. 35 And now look, your house is left to you empty. And you will never see me again

**ON TOP ● ● • • •**

14:7-11 **Jesus advised people not to rush for the best seats at a feast. People today are just as eager to raise their social status, whether by being with the right people, dressing for success, or driving the right car. Wanting a nice car or hoping to be successful in your career is not wrong in itself—it is wrong only when you want these things just to impress others. Whom do you try to impress? Don't aim for prestige; look for a place to serve. If God wants you to serve on a wider scale, he will invite you to take a higher place.**

13:16 Greek *this woman, a daughter of Abraham.* 13:21 Greek *3 measures.* 13:30 Greek *Some are last who will be first, and some are first who will be last.*

until you say, 'Bless the one who comes in the name of the Lord!'*"

## CHAPTER 14 JESUS HEALS ON THE SABBATH.

One Sabbath day Jesus was in the home of a leader of the Pharisees. The people were watching him closely, 2because there was a man there whose arms and legs were swollen.* 3Jesus asked the Pharisees and experts in religious law, "Well, is it permitted in the law to heal people on the Sabbath day, or not?" 4When they refused to answer, Jesus touched the sick man and healed him and sent him away. 5Then he turned to them and asked, "Which of you doesn't work on the Sabbath? If your son* or your cow falls into a pit, don't you proceed at once to get him out?" 6Again they had no answer.

7When Jesus noticed that all who had come to the dinner were trying to sit near the head of the table, he gave them this advice: 8"If you are invited to a wedding feast, don't always head for the best seat. What if someone more respected than you has also been invited? 9The host will say, 'Let this person sit here instead.' Then you will be embarrassed and will have to take whatever seat is left at the foot of the table!

10"Do this instead—sit at the foot of the table. Then when your host sees you, he will come and say, 'Friend, we have a better place than this for you!' Then you will be honored in front of all the other guests. 11For the proud will be humbled, but the humble will be honored."

12Then he turned to his host. "When you put on a luncheon or a dinner," he said, "don't invite your friends, brothers, relatives, and rich neighbors. For they will repay you by inviting you back. 13Instead, invite the poor, the crippled, the lame, and the blind. 14Then at the resurrection of the godly, God will reward you for inviting those who could not repay you."

15Hearing this, a man sitting at the table with Jesus exclaimed, "What a privilege it would be to have a share in the Kingdom of God!"

16Jesus replied with this illustration: "A man prepared a great feast and sent out many invitations. 17When all was ready, he sent his servant around to notify the guests that it was time for them to come. 18But they all began making excuses. One said he had just bought a field and wanted to inspect it, so he asked to be excused. 19Another said he had just bought five pair of oxen and wanted to try them out. 20Another had just been married, so he said he couldn't come.

21"The servant returned and told his master what they had said. His master was angry and said, 'Go quickly into the streets and alleys of the city and invite the poor, the crippled, the lame, and the blind.' 22After the servant had done this, he reported, 'There is still room for more.' 23So his master said, 'Go out into the country lanes and behind the hedges and urge anyone you find to come, so that the house will be full. 24For none of those I invited first will get even the smallest taste of what I had prepared for them.'"

25Great crowds were following Jesus. He turned around and said to them, 26"If you want to be my follower you must love me more than* your own father and mother, wife and children, brothers and sisters—yes, more than your own life. Otherwise, you cannot be my disciple. 27And you cannot be my disciple if you do not carry your own cross and follow me.

28"But don't begin until you count the cost. For who would begin construction of a building without first getting estimates and then checking to see if there is enough money to pay the bills? 29Otherwise, you might complete only the foundation before running out of funds. And then how everyone would laugh at you! 30They would say, 'There's the person who started that building and ran out of money before it was finished!'

31"Or what king would ever dream of going to war without first sitting down with his counselors and discussing whether his army of ten thousand is strong enough to defeat the twenty thousand soldiers who are marching against him? 32If he is not able, then while the enemy is still far away, he will send a delegation to discuss terms of peace. 33So no one can become my disciple without giving up everything for me.

34"Salt is good for seasoning. But if it loses its flavor, how do you make it salty again? 35Flavorless salt is good neither for the soil nor for fertilizer. It is thrown away. Anyone who is willing to hear should listen and understand!"

### SALTY ● ● • • •

14:34 **Salt can lose its flavor. When it gets wet and then dries, nothing is left but a tasteless residue. Many Christians blend into the world to avoid the cost of standing for Christ. Jesus says if Christians lose their distinctive saltiness, they become worthless. Just as salt flavors and preserves food, we are to preserve the good in the world, keep it from spoiling, and bring new flavor to life. This requires planning, willing sacrifice, and unswerving commitment to Christ's kingdom. Being "salty" is not easy, but if a Christian fails in this function, he or she fails to represent Christ in the world. How salty are you?**

## CHAPTER 15 A STORY ABOUT A LOST SHEEP.

Tax collectors and other notorious sinners often came to listen to Jesus teach. 2This made the Pharisees and teachers of religious law complain that he was associating with such despicable people—even eating with them!

3So Jesus used this illustration: 4"If you had one hundred sheep, and one of them strayed away and was lost in the wilderness, wouldn't you leave the ninety-nine others to go and search for the lost one until you found it? 5And then you would joyfully

13:35 Ps 118:26. 14:2 Traditionally translated *who had dropsy.* 14:5 Some manuscripts read *donkey.* 14:26 Greek *you must hate.*

carry it home on your shoulders. [6]When you arrived, you would call together your friends and neighbors to rejoice with you because your lost sheep was found. [7]In the same way, heaven will be happier over one lost sinner who returns to God than over ninety-nine others who are righteous and haven't strayed away!

[8]"Or suppose a woman has ten valuable silver coins* and loses one. Won't she light a lamp and look in every corner of the house and sweep every nook and cranny until she finds it? [9]And when she finds it, she will call in her friends and neighbors to rejoice with her because she has found her lost coin. [10]In the same way, there is joy in the presence of God's angels when even one sinner repents."

[11]To illustrate the point further, Jesus told them this story: "A man had two sons. [12]The younger son told his father, 'I want my share of your estate now, instead of waiting until you die.' So his father agreed to divide his wealth between his sons.

[13]"A few days later this younger son packed all his belongings and took a trip to a distant land, and there he wasted all his money on wild living. [14]About the time his money ran out, a great famine swept over the land, and he began to starve. [15]He persuaded a local farmer to hire him to feed his pigs. [16]The boy became so hungry that even the pods he was feeding the pigs looked good to him. But no one gave him anything.

[17]"When he finally came to his senses, he said to himself, 'At home even the hired men have food enough to spare, and here I am, dying of hunger! [18]I will go home to my father and say, "Father, I have sinned against both heaven and you, [19]and I am no longer worthy of being called your son. Please take me on as a hired man."'

[20]"So he returned home to his father. And while he was still a long distance away, his father saw him coming. Filled with love and compassion, he ran to his son, embraced him, and kissed him. [21]His son said to him, 'Father, I have sinned against both heaven and you, and I am no longer worthy of being called your son.*'

[22]"But his father said to the servants, 'Quick! Bring the finest robe in the house and put it on him. Get a ring for his finger, and sandals for his feet. [23]And kill the calf we have been fattening in the pen. We must celebrate with a feast, [24]for this son of mine was dead and has now returned to life. He was lost, but now he is found.' So the party began.

[25]"Meanwhile, the older son was in the fields working. When he returned home, he heard music and dancing in the house, [26]and he asked one of the servants what was going on. [27]'Your brother is back,' he was told, 'and your father has killed the calf we were fattening and has prepared a great feast. We are celebrating because of his safe return.'

[28]"The older brother was angry and wouldn't go in. His father came out and begged him, [29]but he replied, 'All these years I've worked hard for you and never once refused to do a single thing you told me to. And in all that time you never gave me even one young goat for a feast with my friends. [30]Yet when this son of yours comes back after squandering your money on prostitutes, you celebrate by killing the finest calf we have.'

[31]"His father said to him, 'Look, dear son, you and I are very close, and everything I have is yours. [32]We had to celebrate this happy day. For your brother was dead and has come back to life! He was lost, but now he is found!'"

## OPPORTUNITY ● ● • • •

15:30 **In the story of the lost son, there is a contrast between the father's response and the older brother's reaction. The father was forgiving and overjoyed. The brother was unforgiving and bitter. The father forgave because he was joyful, and the son refused to forgive because he was bitter. The difference between bitterness and joy is our capacity to forgive. If you are refusing to forgive people, you are missing a wonderful opportunity of experiencing joy and sharing it with them.**

CHAPTER **16** **A SHREWD MANAGER.** Jesus told this story to his disciples: "A rich man hired a manager to handle his affairs, but soon a rumor went around that the manager was thoroughly dishonest. [2]So his employer called him in and said, 'What's this I hear about your stealing from me? Get your report in order, because you are going to be dismissed.'

[3]"The manager thought to himself, 'Now what? I'm through here, and I don't have the strength to go out and dig ditches, and I'm too proud to beg. [4]I know just the thing! And then I'll have plenty of friends to take care of me when I leave!'

[5]"So he invited each person who owed money to his employer to come and discuss the situation. He asked the first one, 'How much do you owe him?' [6]The man replied, 'I owe him eight hundred gallons of olive oil.' So the manager told him, 'Tear up that bill and write another one for four hundred gallons.*'

[7]"'And how much do you owe my employer?' he asked the next man. 'A thousand bushels of wheat,' was the reply. 'Here,' the manager said, 'take your bill and replace it with one for only eight hundred bushels.*'

[8]"The rich man had to admire the dishonest rascal for being so shrewd. And it is true that the citizens of this world are more shrewd than the godly are. [9]I tell you, use your worldly resources to benefit others and make friends. In this way, your generosity stores up a reward for you in heaven.*

[10]"Unless you are faithful in small matters, you won't be faithful in large ones. If you cheat even a little, you won't be honest with greater responsibili-

15:8 Greek *10 drachmas.* A drachma was the equivalent of a full day's wage. 15:21 Some manuscripts add *Please take me on as a hired man.* 16:6 Greek *100 baths . . . 50 [baths].* 16:7 Greek *100 korous . . . 80 [korous].* 16:9 Or *Then when you run out at the end of this life, your friends will welcome you into eternal homes.*

ties. [11]And if you are untrustworthy about worldly wealth, who will trust you with the true riches of heaven? [12]And if you are not faithful with other people's money, why should you be trusted with money of your own?

[13]"No one can serve two masters. For you will hate one and love the other, or be devoted to one and despise the other. You cannot serve both God and money."

[14]The Pharisees, who dearly loved their money, naturally scoffed at all this. [15]Then he said to them, "You like to look good in public, but God knows your evil hearts. What this world honors is an abomination in the sight of God.

[16]"Until John the Baptist began to preach, the laws of Moses and the messages of the prophets were your guides. But now the Good News of the Kingdom of God is preached, and eager multitudes are forcing their way in. [17]But that doesn't mean that the law has lost its force in even the smallest point. It is stronger and more permanent than heaven and earth.

[18]"Anyone who divorces his wife and marries someone else commits adultery, and anyone who marries a divorced woman commits adultery."

[19]Jesus said, "There was a certain rich man who was splendidly clothed and who lived each day in luxury. [20]At his door lay a diseased beggar named Lazarus. [21]As Lazarus lay there longing for scraps from the rich man's table, the dogs would come and lick his open sores. [22]Finally, the beggar died and was carried by the angels to be with Abraham.* The rich man also died and was buried, [23]and his soul went to the place of the dead.* There, in torment, he saw Lazarus in the far distance with Abraham.

[24]"The rich man shouted, 'Father Abraham, have some pity! Send Lazarus over here to dip the tip of his finger in water and cool my tongue, because I am in anguish in these flames.'

[25]"But Abraham said to him, 'Son, remember that during your lifetime you had everything you wanted, and Lazarus had nothing. So now he is here being comforted, and you are in anguish. [26]And besides, there is a great chasm separating us. Anyone who wanted to cross over to you from here is stopped at its edge, and no one there can cross over to us.'

[27]"Then the rich man said, 'Please, Father Abraham, send him to my father's home. [28]For I have five brothers, and I want him to warn them about this place of torment so they won't have to come here when they die.'

[29]"But Abraham said, 'Moses and the prophets have warned them. Your brothers can read their writings anytime they want to.'

[30]"The rich man replied, 'No, Father Abraham! But if someone is sent to them from the dead, then they will turn from their sins.'

[31]"But Abraham said, 'If they won't listen to Moses and the prophets, they won't listen even if someone rises from the dead.'"

CHAPTER **17** **A STORY ABOUT A SERVANT.** One day Jesus said to his disciples, "There will always be temptations to sin, but how terrible it will be for the

## DIVORCE ● ● ● • •

16:18 **Most religious leaders of Jesus' day permitted a man to divorce his wife for nearly any reason. Jesus' words about divorce went beyond Moses' (Deuteronomy 24:1-4). Stricter than any of the then-current schools of thought, they shocked his hearers (see Matthew 19:10) just as they shake today's readers. Jesus says in unmistakable terms that marriage is a lifetime commitment. As you think about marriage, remember that God intends it to be a permanent commitment.**

## "Here's what I did..."

My mother and I had difficulty getting along. Often we would argue, sometimes over the stupidest things. After our fights, I'd feel real bad, but I didn't know what to do about it. I felt it was all her fault; she just didn't understand me; she was being totally unreasonable; etc.

Then I read in Luke 15:11-32 the parable about the lost son. And I began to realize that the younger son felt he had every right to take his inheritance and go off on his own. But it didn't get him anywhere, and finally he decided to go back home. His father gave him a big welcome and didn't say "I told you so" or anything like that.

I got to thinking about my own attitude with my mom. And I had to admit that I probably was at fault at least some of the time. Hard as it was, I had to apologize when I was wrong and ask forgiveness. (It was probably really hard for the lost son, too.)

I sat down and went over the past several arguments that weren't really resolved and wrote down the specifics on where I was wrong. Then I prayed hard that I could swallow my pride and go and ask my mom to forgive me.

I finally did. And my mom reacted very much like the father in the story; she was very forgiving. Since then, I've tried to concentrate more on my own attitude than on my mom's. And, amazingly, we're arguing less. But even when we do argue, and I fall into the old patterns, I know that God will forgive me when I ask for it. (So does Mom—usually.)

Tracy AGE 16

16:22 Greek *into Abraham's bosom.* 16:23 Greek *to Hades.*

## FACE IT ● ● • • ·

**17:3-4 To rebuke does not mean to point out every sin we see; it means to bring sin to a person's attention with the purpose of restoring him or her to God and to fellow humans. When you feel you must rebuke another Christian for a sin, check your attitudes before opening your mouth. Do you love the person? Are you willing to forgive? Unless rebuke is tied to forgiveness, it will not help the sinning person.**

person who does the tempting. [2]It would be better to
be thrown into the sea with a large millstone tied
around the neck than to face the punishment in
store for harming one of these little ones. [3]I am
warning you! If another believer* sins, rebuke him;
then if he repents, forgive him. [4]Even if he wrongs
you seven times a day and each time turns again and
asks forgiveness, forgive him."

[5]One day the apostles said to the Lord, "We need
more faith; tell us how to get it."

[6]"Even if you had faith as small as a mustard
seed," the Lord answered, "you could say to this
mulberry tree, 'May God uproot you and throw you
into the sea,' and it would obey you!

[7]"When a servant comes in from plowing or taking care of sheep, he doesn't just sit down and eat.
[8]He must first prepare his master's meal and serve
him his supper before eating his own. [9]And the
servant is not even thanked, because he is merely
doing what he is supposed to do. [10]In the same way,
when you obey me you should say, 'We are not
worthy of praise. We are servants who have simply
done our duty.'"

[11]As Jesus continued on toward Jerusalem, he
reached the border between Galilee and Samaria.
[12]As he entered a village there, ten lepers stood at a
distance, [13]crying out, "Jesus, Master, have mercy on
us!"

[14]He looked at them and said, "Go show yourselves to the priests." And as they went, their leprosy
disappeared.

[15]One of them, when he saw that he was healed,
came back to Jesus, shouting, "Praise God, I'm
healed!" [16]He fell face down on the ground at Jesus'
feet, thanking him for what he had done. This man
was a Samaritan.

[17]Jesus asked, "Didn't I heal ten men? Where are
the other nine? [18]Does only this foreigner return to
give glory to God?" [19]And Jesus said to the man,
"Stand up and go. Your faith has made you well."

[20]One day the Pharisees asked Jesus, "When will
the Kingdom of God come?"

Jesus replied, "The Kingdom of God isn't ushered
in with visible signs.* [21]You won't be able to say,
'Here it is!' or 'It's over there!' For the Kingdom of
God is among you.*"

[22]Later he talked again about this with his disciples. "The time is coming when you will long to
share in the days of the Son of Man, but you won't
be able to," he said. [23]"Reports will reach you that
the Son of Man has returned and that he is in this
place or that. Don't believe such reports or go out to
look for him. [24]For when the Son of Man returns, you
will know it beyond all doubt. It will be as evident as
the lightning that flashes across the sky. [25]But first the
Son of Man must suffer terribly* and be rejected by
this generation.

[26]"When the Son of Man returns, the world will
be like the people were in Noah's day. [27]In those
days before the flood, the people enjoyed banquets
and parties and weddings right up to the time
Noah entered his boat and the flood came to destroy them all.

[28]"And the world will be as it was in the days of
Lot. People went about their daily business—eating
and drinking, buying and selling, farming and building—[29]until the morning Lot left Sodom. Then fire
and burning sulfur rained down from heaven and
destroyed them all. [30]Yes, it will be 'business as usual'
right up to the hour when the Son of Man returns.*
[31]On that day a person outside the house* must not
go into the house to pack. A person in the field must
not return to town. [32]Remember what happened to
Lot's wife! [33]Whoever clings to this life will lose it,
and whoever loses this life will save it. [34]That night
two people will be asleep in one bed; one will be
taken away, and the other will be left. [35]Two women
will be grinding flour together at the mill; one will
be taken, the other left.*"

[37]"Lord, where will this happen?" the disciples
asked.

Jesus replied, "Just as the gathering of vultures
shows there is a carcass nearby, so these signs indicate that the end is near."*

## CHAPTER 18 A STORY ABOUT A PERSISTENT WIDOW.

One day Jesus told his disciples a story to illustrate
their need for constant prayer and to show them that
they must never give up. [2]"There was a judge in a
certain city," he said, "who was a godless man with
great contempt for everyone. [3]A widow of that city
came to him repeatedly, appealing for justice against
someone who had harmed her. [4]The judge ignored
her for a while, but eventually she wore him out. 'I
fear neither God nor man,' he said to himself, [5]'but
this woman is driving me crazy. I'm going to see that

## CHILDREN ● ● • • ·

**18:15-17 It was customary for a mother to bring her children to a rabbi for a blessing, and that is why these mothers gathered about Jesus. The disciples, however, thought the children were unworthy of the Master's time—less important than whatever else he was doing. But Jesus welcomed them because little children have the kind of faith and trust needed to enter God's kingdom. It is important to approach God with childlike attitudes of acceptance, faith, and trust.**

17:3 Greek *your brother.* 17:20 Or *by your speculations.* 17:21 Or *within you.* 17:25 Or *suffer many things.* 17:30 Or *on the day the Son of Man is revealed.* 17:31 Greek *on the roof.* 17:35 Some manuscripts add verse 36, *Two men will be working in the field; one will be taken, the other left.* 17:37 Greek *Wherever the carcass is, the vultures gather.*

she gets justice, because she is wearing me out with
her constant requests!'"
6Then the Lord said, "Learn a lesson from this evil
judge. 7Even he rendered a just decision in the end,
so don't you think God will surely give justice to his
chosen people who plead with him day and night?
Will he keep putting them off? 8I tell you, he will
grant justice to them quickly! But when I, the Son of
Man, return, how many will I find who have faith?"
9Then Jesus told this story to some who had great
self-confidence and scorned everyone else: 10"Two
men went to the Temple to pray. One was a Pharisee,
and the other was a dishonest tax collector. 11The
proud Pharisee stood by himself and prayed this
prayer: 'I thank you, God, that I am not a sinner like
everyone else, especially like that tax collector over
there! For I never cheat, I don't sin, I don't commit
adultery, 12I fast twice a week, and I give you a tenth
of my income.'
13"But the tax collector stood at a distance and
dared not even lift his eyes to heaven as he prayed.
Instead, he beat his chest in sorrow, saying, 'O God,
be merciful to me, for I am a sinner.' 14I tell you, this
sinner, not the Pharisee, returned home justified
before God. For the proud will be humbled, but the
humble will be honored."
15One day some parents brought their little children to Jesus so he could touch them and bless them,
but the disciples told them not to bother him.
16Then Jesus called for the children and said to the
disciples, "Let the children come to me. Don't stop
them! For the Kingdom of God belongs to such as
these. 17I assure you, anyone who doesn't have their
kind of faith will never get into the Kingdom of
God."
18Once a religious leader asked Jesus this question:
"Good teacher, what should I do to get eternal life?"
19"Why do you call me good?" Jesus asked him.
"Only God is truly good. 20But as for your question,
you know the commandments: 'Do not commit
adultery. Do not murder. Do not steal. Do not testify
falsely. Honor your father and mother.'*"
21The man replied, "I've obeyed all these commandments since I was a child."
22"There is still one thing you lack," Jesus said.
"Sell all you have and give the money to the poor,
and you will have treasure in heaven. Then come,
follow me." 23But when the man heard this, he became sad because he was very rich.
24Jesus watched him go and then said to his disciples, "How hard it is for rich people to get into the
Kingdom of God! 25It is easier for a camel to go
through the eye of a needle than for a rich person to
enter the Kingdom of God!"
26Those who heard this said, "Then who in the
world can be saved?"
27He replied, "What is impossible from a human
perspective is possible with God."

## GIVE UP ● ● ● • •

18:26-30 **Peter and the other disciples had paid a high price—leaving their homes and jobs—to follow Jesus. But Jesus reminded Peter that following him has its benefits as well as its sacrifices. Any believer who has had to give up something to follow Christ will be paid back in this life as well as in the next. If you give up friends, you will find that God offers a secure relationship with himself now and forever. If you give up your family's approval, you will gain the love of the family of God. Don't dwell on what you have given up; think about what you have gained and give thanks for it. You can never outgive God.**

28Peter said, "We have left our homes and followed you."
29"Yes," Jesus replied, "and I assure you, everyone
who has given up house or wife or brothers or
parents or children, for the sake of the Kingdom of

**I've always been taught to be independent and self-sufficient. My youth leader says this isn't right. What's wrong about being proud about doing your best?**

Have you ever known someone who thought he was so good in sports that he rarely listened to the coach? Although all coaches love to have players with great natural ability, most would settle for those with a few skills who are teachable. An athlete is much easier to mold than to motivate.

Being totally self-reliant is sort of like an athlete allowing the coach to give him advice only when he wants it. Before too long the athlete will start to deteriorate in talent and in the eyes of the coach. In the same way, we need to depend on God to lead us. And we should do what he says.

God wants us always to try to do our best. We should never do anything halfway. But there's a difference between doing our best and allowing God to do his best through us.

Taking the credit for everything we do is called pride—it's a dangerous thing. There is a good type of pride that comes from doing something well. Perhaps we've worked hard at something and everything has come out great. We feel good about ourselves, and that's OK. The problem comes when we take all the credit. That's the wrong kind of pride.

God wants us to recognize that he gave us our life and our talents. This shows humility and a deep respect for God.

The Pharisee in Luke 18:9-14 is a perfect example of someone with "bad pride." He was proud of his "holy" life. Although he acted like he was talking to God, he was really just talking to himself.

On the flip side is the tax collector. He had nothing to be proud of, especially as it related to his relationship with God. In humility, he asked God for mercy.

If we go through life with an I-can-make-it-OK-by-myself attitude, we're really saying to God, "I don't really need you after all." But God wants us to depend on him.

**18:20** Exod 20:12-16; Deut 5:16-20.

## UNPOPULAR ● ● ● • •

19:1-10 **Tax collectors were among the most unpopular people in Israel. Jews by birth who chose to work for Rome were considered traitors. Besides, it was common knowledge that tax collectors made themselves rich by gouging their fellow Jews. No wonder the crowds were displeased when Jesus went home with the tax collector Zacchaeus. But despite the fact that Zacchaeus was both dishonest and a turncoat, Jesus loved him—and in response, the little tax collector was converted. In every society, certain groups of people are considered "untouchable" because of their politics, immoral behavior, or lifestyle. We should not avoid these people. Jesus loves them, and they need to hear his Good News.**

God, [30]will be repaid many times over in this life, as well as receiving eternal life in the world to come."

[31]Gathering the twelve disciples around him, Jesus told them, "As you know, we are going to Jerusalem. And when we get there, all the predictions of the ancient prophets concerning the Son of Man will come true. [32]He will be handed over to the Romans to be mocked, treated shamefully, and spit upon. [33]They will whip him and kill him, but on the third day he will rise again."

[34]But they didn't understand a thing he said. Its significance was hidden from them, and they failed to grasp what he was talking about.

[35]As they approached Jericho, a blind beggar was sitting beside the road. [36]When he heard the noise of a crowd going past, he asked what was happening. [37]They told him that Jesus of Nazareth was going by. [38]So he began shouting, "Jesus, Son of David, have mercy on me!" [39]The crowds ahead of Jesus tried to hush the man, but he only shouted louder, "Son of David, have mercy on me!"

[40]When Jesus heard him, he stopped and ordered that the man be brought to him. [41]Then Jesus asked the man, "What do you want me to do for you?"

"Lord," he pleaded, "I want to see!"

[42]And Jesus said, "All right, you can see! Your faith has healed you." [43]Instantly the man could see, and he followed Jesus, praising God. And all who saw it praised God, too.

## CHAPTER **19** JESUS GIVES ZACCHAEUS A NEW LIFE.

Jesus entered Jericho and made his way through the town. [2]There was a man there named Zacchaeus. He was one of the most influential Jews in the Roman tax-collecting business, and he had become very rich. [3]He tried to get a look at Jesus, but he was too short to see over the crowds. [4]So he ran ahead and climbed a sycamore tree beside the road, so he could watch from there.

[5]When Jesus came by, he looked up at Zacchaeus and called him by name. "Zacchaeus!" he said. "Quick, come down! For I must be a guest in your home today."

[6]Zacchaeus quickly climbed down and took Jesus to his house in great excitement and joy. [7]But the crowds were displeased. "He has gone to be the guest of a notorious sinner," they grumbled.

[8]Meanwhile, Zacchaeus stood there and said to the Lord, "I will give half my wealth to the poor, Lord, and if I have overcharged people on their taxes, I will give them back four times as much!"

[9]Jesus responded, "Salvation has come to this home today, for this man has shown himself to be a son of Abraham. [10]And I, the Son of Man, have come to seek and save those like him who are lost."

[11]The crowd was listening to everything Jesus said. And because he was nearing Jerusalem, he told a story to correct the impression that the Kingdom of God would begin right away. [12]He said, "A nobleman was called away to a distant empire to be crowned king and then return. [13]Before he left, he called together ten servants and gave them ten pounds of silver* to invest for him while he was gone. [14]But his people hated him and sent a delegation after him to say they did not want him to be their king.

[15]"When he returned, the king called in the servants to whom he had given the money. He wanted to find out what they had done with the money and what their profits were. [16]The first servant reported a tremendous gain—ten times as much as the original amount! [17]'Well done!' the king exclaimed. 'You are a trustworthy servant. You have been faithful with the little I entrusted to you, so you will be governor of ten cities as your reward.'

[18]"The next servant also reported a good gain—five times the original amount. [19]'Well done!' the king said. 'You can be governor over five cities.'

[20]"But the third servant brought back only the original amount of money and said, 'I hid it and kept it safe. [21]I was afraid because you are a hard man to deal with, taking what isn't yours and harvesting crops you didn't plant.'

[22]"'You wicked servant!' the king roared. 'Hard, am I? If you knew so much about me and how tough I am, [23]why didn't you deposit the money in the bank so I could at least get some interest on it?' [24]Then turning to the others standing nearby, the king ordered, 'Take the money from this servant, and give it to the one who earned the most.'

[25]"'But, master,' they said, 'that servant has enough already!'

[26]"'Yes,' the king replied, 'but to those who use well what they are given, even more will be given. But from those who are unfaithful,* even what little they have will be taken away. [27]And now about these enemies of mine who didn't want me to be their king—bring them in and execute them right here in my presence.'"

[28]After telling this story, Jesus went on toward Jerusalem, walking ahead of his disciples. [29]As they came to the towns of Bethphage and Bethany, on the Mount of Olives, he sent two disciples ahead. [30]"Go into that village over there," he told them, "and as you enter it, you will see a colt tied there that has never been ridden. Untie it and bring it here. [31]If anyone asks what you are doing, just say, 'The Lord needs it.'"

[32]So they went and found the colt, just as Jesus

19:13 Greek *10 minas;* 1 mina was worth about 3 months' wages. 19:26 Or *who have nothing.*

had said. 33And sure enough, as they were untying it, the owners asked them, "Why are you untying our colt?"

34And the disciples simply replied, "The Lord needs it." 35So they brought the colt to Jesus and threw their garments over it for him to ride on.

36Then the crowds spread out their coats on the road ahead of Jesus. 37As they reached the place where the road started down from the Mount of Olives, all of his followers began to shout and sing as they walked along, praising God for all the wonderful miracles they had seen.

38 "Bless the King who comes in the name of the
Lord!
Peace in heaven
and glory in highest heaven!"*

39But some of the Pharisees among the crowd said, "Teacher, rebuke your followers for saying things like that!"

40He replied, "If they kept quiet, the stones along the road would burst into cheers!"

41But as they came closer to Jerusalem and Jesus saw the city ahead, he began to cry. 42"I wish that even today you would find the way of peace. But now it is too late, and peace is hidden from you. 43Before long your enemies will build ramparts against your walls and encircle you and close in on you. 44They will crush you to the ground, and your children with you. Your enemies will not leave a single stone in place, because you have rejected the opportunity God offered you."

45Then Jesus entered the Temple and began to drive out the merchants from their stalls. 46He told them, "The Scriptures declare, 'My Temple will be a place of prayer,' but you have turned it into a den of thieves."*

47After that, he taught daily in the Temple, but the leading priests, the teachers of religious law, and the other leaders of the people began planning how to kill him. 48But they could think of nothing, because all the people hung on every word he said.

## CHAPTER 20 LEADERS CHALLENGE JESUS' AUTHORITY.

One day as Jesus was teaching and preaching the Good News in the Temple, the leading priests and teachers of religious law and other leaders came up to him. 2They demanded, "By whose authority did you drive out the merchants from the Temple?* Who gave you such authority?"

3"Let me ask you a question first," he replied. 4"Did John's baptism come from heaven, or was it merely human?"

5They talked it over among themselves. "If we say it was from heaven, he will ask why we didn't believe him. 6But if we say it was merely human, the people will stone us, because they are convinced he was a prophet." 7Finally they replied, "We don't know."

8And Jesus responded, "Then I won't answer your question either."

9Now Jesus turned to the people again and told them this story: "A man planted a vineyard, leased it out to tenant farmers, and moved to another country to live for several years. 10At grape-picking time, he sent one of his servants to collect his share of the crop. But the farmers attacked the servant, beat him up, and sent him back empty-handed. 11So the owner sent another servant, but the same thing happened; he was beaten up and treated shamefully, and he went away empty-handed. 12A third man was sent and the same thing happened. He, too, was wounded and chased away.

13"'What will I do?' the owner asked himself. 'I know! I'll send my cherished son. Surely they will respect him.'

14"But when the farmers saw his son, they said to each other, 'Here comes the heir to this estate. Let's kill him and get the estate for ourselves!' 15So they dragged him out of the vineyard and murdered him.

"What do you suppose the owner of the vineyard will do to those farmers?" Jesus asked. 16"I'll tell you—he will come and kill them all and lease the vineyard to others."

"But God forbid that such a thing should ever happen," his listeners protested.

17Jesus looked at them and said, "Then what do the Scriptures mean?

'The stone rejected by the builders
has now become the cornerstone.'*

18All who stumble over that stone will be broken to pieces, and it will crush anyone on whom it falls."

19When the teachers of religious law and the leading priests heard this story, they wanted to arrest Jesus immediately because they realized he was pointing at them—that they were the farmers in the story. But they were afraid there would be a riot if they arrested him.

20Watching for their opportunity, the leaders sent secret agents pretending to be honest men. They tried to get Jesus to say something that could be reported to the Roman governor so he would arrest Jesus. 21They said, "Teacher, we know that you speak and teach what is right and are not influenced by what others think. You sincerely teach the ways of God. 22Now tell us—is it right to pay taxes to the Roman government or not?"

23He saw through their trickery and said, 24"Show me a Roman coin.* Whose picture and title are stamped on it?"

"Caesar's," they replied.

25"Well then," he said, "give to Caesar what belongs

**DUTY ●●●••**

**20:20-26 Jesus turned his enemies' attempt to trap him into a powerful lesson: God's followers have legitimate obligations to both God and the government. But what is important is to keep our priorities straight. When the two authorities conflict, our duty to God always comes before our duty to the government.**

**19:38** Pss 118:26; 148:1. **19:46** Isa 56:7; Jer 7:11. **20:2** Or *By whose authority do you do these things?* **20:17** Ps 118:22. **20:24** Greek *a denarius.*

to him. But everything that belongs to God must be
given to God." [26]So they failed to trap him in the
presence of the people. Instead, they were amazed by
his answer, and they were silenced.
[27]Then some Sadducees stepped forward—a
group of Jews who say there is no resurrection after
death. [28]They posed this question: "Teacher, Moses
gave us a law that if a man dies, leaving a wife but no
children, his brother should marry the widow and
have a child who will be the brother's heir.* [29]Well,
there were seven brothers. The oldest married and
then died without children. [30]His brother married
the widow, but he also died. Still no children. [31]And
so it went, one after the other, until each of the seven
had married her and died, leaving no children. [32]Finally, the woman died, too. [33]So tell us, whose wife
will she be in the resurrection? For all seven were
married to her!"

**IVING**

The hot topic at school is what Kyla Whitfield will do with the huge inheritance she's getting as a result of her grandfather's death last week.

"How much do you think she'll end up getting?"

"Well, everyone says old man Whitfield was worth at least nine million dollars."

"Kyla gets it all?"

"No, I think they have to split it four ways."

"Oh my gosh! That's over two million dollars!"

"Well, she'll have to pay inheritance taxes on it first."

"But she'll still be a millionaire!"

"That's right."

"Oh, man! What I would do if I had a million dollars!"

"What would you do?"

"Spend most of it."

"On what?"

"I don't know . . . cars, a ski boat, whatever I wanted."

"What about giving?"

"What about it?"

"Would you give any of it away? You know, to other people, to your church, to charity?"

"Are you serious?"

That's a common response to the suggestion of giving. Unfortunately, even many Christians are that way.

What about you? Do you regularly give part of your money back to God? If not, why not? (By the way: "I will when I'm rich like Kyla" is a lousy excuse! See Luke 21:1-4.)

[34]Jesus replied, "Marriage is for people here on
earth. [35]But that is not the way it will be in the age to
come. For those worthy of being raised from the dead
won't be married then. [36]And they will never die again.
In these respects they are like angels. They are children
of God raised up to new life. [37]But now, as to whether
the dead will be raised—even Moses proved this when

## THE TEMPLE ● ● • • •

**21:5 The Temple the disciples were admiring was not Solomon's Temple. That was destroyed by the Babylonians in the sixth century B.C. This Temple was built by Zerubbabel after the return from exile in the sixth century B.C. It was a beautiful, imposing structure with a significant history, but Jesus said it would be completely destroyed. This happened in A.D. 70, when a Roman army burned Jerusalem. Now, as then, we can be sure of this: if God says something will happen, it will indeed take place!**

he wrote about the burning bush. Long after Abraham,
Isaac, and Jacob had died, he referred to the Lord* as
'the God of Abraham, the God of Isaac, and the God
of Jacob.'* [38]So he is the God of the living, not the
dead. They are all alive to him."
[39]"Well said, Teacher!" remarked some of the
teachers of religious law who were standing there.
[40]And that ended their questions; no one dared to
ask any more.
[41]Then Jesus presented them with a question.
"Why is it," he asked, "that the Messiah is said to be
the son of David? [42]For David himself wrote in the
book of Psalms:

'The LORD said to my Lord,
Sit in honor at my right hand
43 until I humble your enemies,
making them a footstool under your feet.'*

[44]Since David called him Lord, how can he be his son
at the same time?"
[45]Then, with the crowds listening, he turned to his
disciples and said, [46]"Beware of these teachers of
religious law! For they love to parade in flowing
robes and to have everyone bow to them as they walk
in the marketplaces. And how they love the seats of
honor in the synagogues and at banquets. [47]But they
shamelessly cheat widows out of their property, and
then, to cover up the kind of people they really are,
they make long prayers in public. Because of this,
their punishment will be the greater."

CHAPTER **21** **THE WIDOW'S TWO PENNIES.** While
Jesus was in the Temple, he watched the rich people
putting their gifts into the collection box. [2]Then a
poor widow came by and dropped in two pennies.*
[3]"I assure you," he said, "this poor widow has given
more than all the rest of them. [4]For they have given
a tiny part of their surplus, but she, poor as she is, has
given everything she has."
[5]Some of his disciples began talking about the
beautiful stonework of the Temple and the memorial decorations on the walls. But Jesus said, [6]"The
time is coming when all these things will be so
completely demolished that not one stone will be
left on top of another."
[7]"Teacher," they asked, "when will all this take
place? And will there be any sign ahead of time?"
[8]He replied, "Don't let anyone mislead you. For
many will come in my name, claiming to be the
Messiah* and saying, 'The time has come!' But don't

20:28 Deut 25:5-6. 20:37a Greek *when he wrote about the bush. He referred to the Lord.* 20:37b Exod 3:6. 20:42-43 Ps 110:1. 21:2 Greek *2 lepta.* 21:8 Greek *name, saying, 'I am.'*

believe them. 9And when you hear of wars and insurrections, don't panic. Yes, these things must come, but the end won't follow immediately." 10Then he added, "Nations and kingdoms will proclaim war against each other. 11There will be great earthquakes, and there will be famines and epidemics in many lands, and there will be terrifying things and great miraculous signs in the heavens.

12"But before all this occurs, there will be a time of great persecution. You will be dragged into synagogues and prisons, and you will be accused before kings and governors of being my followers. 13This will be your opportunity to tell them about me. 14So don't worry about how to answer the charges against you, 15for I will give you the right words and such wisdom that none of your opponents will be able to reply! 16Even those closest to you—your parents, brothers, relatives, and friends—will betray you. And some of you will be killed. 17And everyone will hate you because of your allegiance to me. 18But not a hair of your head will perish! 19By standing firm, you will win your souls.

20"And when you see Jerusalem surrounded by armies, then you will know that the time of its destruction has arrived. 21Then those in Judea must flee to the hills. Let those in Jerusalem escape, and those outside the city should not enter it for shelter. 22For those will be days of God's vengeance, and the prophetic words of the Scriptures will be fulfilled. 23How terrible it will be for pregnant women and for mothers nursing their babies. For there will be great distress in the land and wrath upon this people. 24They will be brutally killed by the sword or sent away as captives to all the nations of the world. And Jerusalem will be conquered and trampled down by the Gentiles until the age of the Gentiles comes to an end.

25"And there will be strange events in the skies—signs in the sun, moon, and stars. And down here on earth the nations will be in turmoil, perplexed by the roaring seas and strange tides. 26The courage of many people will falter because of the fearful fate they see coming upon the earth, because the stability of the very heavens will be broken up. 27Then everyone will see the Son of Man arrive on the clouds with power and great glory.* 28So when all these things begin to happen, stand straight and look up, for your salvation is near!"

29Then he gave them this illustration: "Notice the fig tree, or any other tree. 30When the leaves come out, you know without being told that summer is near. 31Just so, when you see the events I've described taking place, you can be sure that the Kingdom of God is near. 32I assure you, this generation* will not pass from the scene until all these events have taken place. 33Heaven and earth will disappear, but my words will remain forever.

34"Watch out! Don't let me find you living in careless ease and drunkenness, and filled with the worries of this life. Don't let that day catch you unaware, 35as in a trap. For that day will come upon everyone living on the earth. 36Keep a constant watch. And pray that, if possible, you may escape these horrors and stand before the Son of Man."

37Every day Jesus went to the Temple to teach, and each evening he returned to spend the night on the Mount of Olives. 38The crowds gathered early each morning to hear him.

## CHAPTER 22

**A PLAN TO KILL JESUS.** The Festival of Unleavened Bread, which begins with the Passover celebration, was drawing near. 2The leading priests and teachers of religious law were actively plotting Jesus' murder. But they wanted to kill him without starting a riot, a possibility they greatly feared.

3Then Satan entered into Judas Iscariot, who was one of the twelve disciples, 4and he went over to the leading priests and captains of the Temple guard to discuss the best way to betray Jesus to them. 5They were delighted that he was ready to help them, and they promised him a reward. 6So he began looking for an opportunity to betray Jesus so they could arrest him quietly when the crowds weren't around.

7Now the Festival of Unleavened Bread arrived, when the Passover lambs were sacrificed. 8Jesus sent Peter and John ahead and said, "Go and prepare the Passover meal, so we can eat it together."

9"Where do you want us to go?" they asked him.

10He replied, "As soon as you enter Jerusalem, a man carrying a pitcher of water will meet you. Follow him. At the house he enters, 11say to the owner, 'The Teacher asks, Where is the guest room where I can eat the Passover meal with my disciples?' 12He will take you upstairs to a large room that is already set up. That is the place. Go ahead and prepare our supper there." 13They went off to the city and found everything just as Jesus had said, and they prepared the Passover supper there.

14Then at the proper time Jesus and the twelve apostles sat down together at the table. 15Jesus said, "I have looked forward to this hour with deep longing, anxious to eat this Passover meal with you before my suffering begins. 16For I tell you now that I won't eat it again until it comes to fulfillment in the Kingdom of God."

### BETRAYED ● ● ● • •

**21:14-19 Jesus warned that in the coming persecutions his followers would be betrayed by their family members and friends. Christians of every age have had to face this possibility. It is reassuring to know that even when we feel completely abandoned, the Holy Spirit stays with us. He will comfort us, protect us, and give us the words we need. This assurance can give us the courage and hope to stand firm for Christ through all the difficult situations we face.**

**21:27** See Dan 7:13. **21:32** Or *this age,* or *this nation.*

# WHY THE CROSS?

A youth pastor was talking to a group of junior highers about the cross of Christ, explaining how Jesus' death had provided for their individual forgiveness and salvation. "It's personal," he said. "Jesus didn't just die for people in general. He died for you." He paused to let the impact of the statement sink in. Suddenly one seventh-grade girl blurted out: "So?" **"So?"** As irreverent and inappropriate as that question seems, that seventh grader's response is sadly representative of how people think today. We know Jesus died on a cross for us; we just don't see the connection between that event 2,000 years ago and our lives today. **W**hat is the cross about? Why did Jesus have to die such a horrible death? **T**he cross has inspired endless debates, wars, books, songs, and lives through the centuries. I hope this short note may help you gain some insight into why Jesus had to die and why he died in such a ***gruesome*** way. **F**irst, there's humanity's problem. All humans are sinners. We've broken God's laws, so we stand guilty before God and deserving of punishment. Sin has **WARPED** every aspect of human life; it has had such a radical effect on us that we stand in open rebellion and defiance of the God who made us and loves us. Think this is overstating the case? Consider this: God made himself vulnerable to human beings one time, and we murdered him. **B**ecause of our sinful nature, we are incapable of pleasing God or doing anything on our own to change the situation. We are, as Paul writes in Ephesians 2:5 and Colossians 2:13, dead in our sins—and DEAD PEOPLE can't exactly help themselves. We desperately need help from someone who can please God, who can do something about the desperate state of human souls. Jesus, by virtue of his sinless life, is that Someone. But helping us is a terribly expensive process. **A**gain, we are guilty before God—we deserve his anger and punishment. But God took the wrath we deserve and poured it out on Jesus, on the cross. In some ways, it is beyond human understanding. Jesus took upon himself our sins—every mean, dishonest, disgusting thought or action—and was transformed from the perfect, holy, righteous Person he was into utter sin itself. Second Corinthians 5:21 tells us, "For God made Christ, who never sinned, to be the offering for our sin, so that we could be made right with God through Christ." On the cross Jesus received the punishment our sins deserve. As the perfect God-man, he alone was in a position to do that. JESUS STOOD IN THE CHASM between God and man, which was created by our sins, and brought us back together by his blood. As horrible as the physical agony must have been, the spiritual agony of this transformation and punishment was worse. No wonder he screamed out, "My God, My God, why have you forsaken me?" Jesus was DESERTED BY GOD so that you and I never have to be. **T**hat's the second fact you need to know. Jesus took your place on the cross and bore the terrible brunt of the sentence God could have imposed on you. He died for you.

***Take it personally.*** **I**t's still a mystery how the death of one righteous Man—the only righteous Man—pays for the sins of the world. Still, though we may not understand it, we can depend upon it for our salvation. It is the only way to peace with God and eternal life. It's fitting that God took the cross of Christ—**the single darkest hour in the history of humanity**—and turned it into the way of redemption for all people everywhere. That's the kind of God the Bible talks about. A God who loves you so much he would even die on a cross for you.

[17]Then he took a cup of wine, and when he had
given thanks for it, he said, "Take this and share it
among yourselves. [18]For I will not drink wine again
until the Kingdom of God has come."
[19]Then he took a loaf of bread; and when he had
thanked God for it, he broke it in pieces and gave
it to the disciples, saying, "This is my body, given
for you. Do this in remembrance of me." [20]After
supper he took another cup of wine and said,
"This wine is the token of God's new covenant to
save you—an agreement sealed with the blood I
will pour out for you.*
[21]"But here at this table, sitting among us as a
friend, is the man who will betray me. [22]For I, the
Son of Man, must die since it is part of God's plan.
But how terrible it will be for my betrayer!" [23]Then
the disciples began to ask each other which of
them would ever do such a thing.
[24]And they began to argue among themselves as
to who would be the greatest in the coming Kingdom. [25]Jesus told them, "In this world the kings
and great men order their people around, and yet
they are called 'friends of the people.' [26]But among
you, those who are the greatest should take the
lowest rank, and the leader should be like a servant. [27]Normally the master sits at the table and is
served by his servants. But not here! For I am your
servant. [28]You have remained true to me in my time
of trial. [29]And just as my Father has granted me a
Kingdom, I now grant you the right [30]to eat and
drink at my table in that Kingdom. And you will sit
on thrones, judging the twelve tribes of Israel.
[31]"Simon, Simon, Satan has asked to have all of
you, to sift you like wheat. [32]But I have pleaded in
prayer for you, Simon, that your faith should not
fail. So when you have repented and turned to me
again, strengthen and build up your brothers."
[33]Peter said, "Lord, I am ready to go to prison with
you, and even to die with you."
[34]But Jesus said, "Peter, let me tell you something. The rooster will not crow tomorrow morning until you have denied three times that you even
know me."
[35]Then Jesus asked them, "When I sent you out to
preach the Good News and you did not have money,
a traveler's bag, or extra clothing, did you lack anything?"
"No," they replied.
[36]"But now," he said, "take your money and a
traveler's bag. And if you don't have a sword, sell
your clothes and buy one! [37]For the time has come
for this prophecy about me to be fulfilled: 'He was
counted among those who were rebels.'* Yes,
everything written about me by the prophets will
come true."
[38]"Lord," they replied, "we have two swords
among us."
"That's enough," he said.
[39]Then, accompanied by the disciples, Jesus left
the upstairs room and went as usual to the Mount of

## WRAPPED UP ●●●●●

**22:24 The most important event in human history was about to take place, but the disciples were still arguing about their prestige in the kingdom! Looking back, we say, "This was no time to worry about status." But the disciples, wrapped up in their own concerns, did not perceive what Jesus had been trying to tell them about his approaching death and resurrection. What are your major concerns today? Twenty years from now will these worries look petty and inappropriate? Get your eyes off yourself and look for signs of the kingdom of God that is about to break into human history for the second time.**

**There aren't very many Christians at my school, and I'm kind of embarrassed about admitting I am one. Do I have to come out and let the whole world know I've become a Christian?**

High school guys and girls wear letter jackets that tell the world they're athletes. Most people wear such jackets with pride. They have accomplished something, and they want other people to know it.

Identifying yourself as a Christian, however, is not always real popular. Peter found that out when he was confronted by the people who were trying to get warm around the fire (see Luke 22:54-62). Although he had been with Jesus for three years and was one of his best friends, Peter denied even knowing who Jesus was! He was afraid and embarrassed. But something happened during the next two months that convinced him he would never be ashamed of Jesus again (read about Peter in the first four chapters of the book of Acts).

As a new Christian, it is hard to identify yourself with Christ because you don't know him very well. It's like striking up a friendship with the new kid at school. You want to be his friend, but you hold back because you aren't sure how popular he's going to be.

Jesus understands our fears. It can be tough to admit we're his followers. He will patiently wait until we are confident in our relationship with him before we begin to speak out for him. But I can imagine he is kind of disappointed, too.

It takes most new Christians some time before they aren't embarrassed about admitting they're Christians. But at some point, something clicks that convinces them that Jesus Christ *is* alive. It could be the feeling of being forgiven, a miraculous answer to prayer, or a quiet realization that the Bible is accurate and everything Jesus said about himself is true!

However it happens, God doesn't expect you to get on the P.A. at school and make the "big announcement." He just expects you to be prepared in case anyone asks you about your faith: "If you are asked about your Christian hope, always be ready to explain it" (1 Peter 3:15).

22:19-20 Some manuscripts omit 22:19b-20, *given for you . . . I will pour out for you.* 22:37 Isa 53:12.

## BITTER TEARS ● ● • • •

**22:62 Peter wept bitterly because he realized he had denied his Lord and because he had turned away from a dear friend who had loved and taught him for three years. Peter had said he would *never* deny Christ, but he went against all he had boldly promised. Unable to stand up for his Lord for even 12 hours, he had failed as a disciple and as a friend. We need to be aware of our own breaking points and not become overconfident or self-sufficient. When we fail, we must remember that Christ can use those who recognize their failure. From this humiliating experience Peter learned much that would help him in the leadership responsibilities he soon would assume.**

Olives. [40]There he told them, "Pray that you will not be overcome by temptation."

[41]He walked away, about a stone's throw, and knelt down and prayed, [42]"Father, if you are willing, please take this cup of suffering away from me. Yet I want your will, not mine." [43]Then an angel from heaven appeared and strengthened him. [44]He prayed more fervently, and he was in such agony of spirit that his sweat fell to the ground like great drops of blood.* [45]At last he stood up again and returned to the disciples, only to find them asleep, exhausted from grief. [46]"Why are you sleeping?" he asked. "Get up and pray. Otherwise temptation will overpower you."

[47]But even as he said this, a mob approached, led by Judas, one of his twelve disciples. Judas walked over to Jesus and greeted him with a kiss. [48]But Jesus said, "Judas, how can you betray me, the Son of Man, with a kiss?"

[49]When the other disciples saw what was about to happen, they exclaimed, "Lord, should we fight? We brought the swords!" [50]And one of them slashed at the high priest's servant and cut off his right ear.

[51]But Jesus said, "Don't resist anymore." And he touched the place where the man's ear had been and healed him. [52]Then Jesus spoke to the leading priests and captains of the Temple guard and the other leaders who headed the mob. "Am I some dangerous criminal," he asked, "that you have come armed with swords and clubs to arrest me? [53]Why didn't you arrest me in the Temple? I was there every day. But this is your moment, the time when the power of darkness reigns."

[54]So they arrested him and led him to the high priest's residence, and Peter was following far behind. [55]The guards lit a fire in the courtyard and sat around it, and Peter joined them there. [56]A servant girl noticed him in the firelight and began staring at him. Finally she said, "This man was one of Jesus' followers!"

[57]Peter denied it. "Woman," he said, "I don't even know the man!"

[58]After a while someone else looked at him and said, "You must be one of them!"

"No, man, I'm not!" Peter replied.

[59]About an hour later someone else insisted, "This must be one of Jesus' disciples because he is a Galilean, too."

[60]But Peter said, "Man, I don't know what you are talking about." And as soon as he said these words, the rooster crowed. [61]At that moment the Lord turned and looked at Peter. Then Peter remembered that the Lord had said, "Before the rooster crows tomorrow morning, you will deny me three times." [62]And Peter left the courtyard, crying bitterly.

[63]Now the guards in charge of Jesus began mocking and beating him. [64]They blindfolded him; then they hit him and asked, "Who hit you that time, you prophet?" [65]And they threw all sorts of terrible insults at him.

[66]At daybreak all the leaders of the people assembled, including the leading priests and the teachers of religious law. Jesus was led before this high council,* [67]and they said, "Tell us if you are the Messiah."

But he replied, "If I tell you, you won't believe me. [68]And if I ask you a question, you won't answer. [69]But the time is soon coming when I, the Son of Man, will be sitting at God's right hand in the place of power."*

[70]They all shouted, "Then you claim you are the Son of God?"

And he replied, "You are right in saying that I am."

[71]"What need do we have for other witnesses?" they shouted. "We ourselves heard him say it."

CHAPTER **23** **JESUS STANDS BEFORE PILATE.** Then the entire council took Jesus over to Pilate, the Roman governor. [2]They began at once to state their case: "This man has been leading our people to ruin by telling them not to pay their taxes to the Roman government and by claiming he is the Messiah, a king."

[3]So Pilate asked him, "Are you the King of the Jews?"

Jesus replied, "Yes, it is as you say."

[4]Pilate turned to the leading priests and to the crowd and said, "I find nothing wrong with this man!"

[5]Then they became desperate. "But he is causing riots everywhere he goes, all over Judea, from Galilee to Jerusalem!"

## NEW LIFE ● ● • • •

**23:34 Jesus asked God to forgive the people who were putting him to death– Jewish leaders, Roman politicians and soldiers, bystanders– and God answered that prayer by opening up the way of salvation even to Jesus' murderers. The Roman officer and soldiers who witnessed the crucifixion said, "Truly, this was the Son of God!" (Matthew 27:54). Soon many priests were converted to the Christian faith (Acts 6:7). Since we are all sinners, we all played a part in putting Jesus to death. The Good News is that God is gracious. He will forgive us and give us new life through his Son.**

22:43-44 These verses are not included in many ancient manuscripts. 22:66 Greek *before their Sanhedrin.* 22:69 See Ps 110:1.

6"Oh, is he a Galilean?" Pilate asked. 7When
they answered that he was, Pilate sent him to
Herod Antipas, because Galilee was under Herod's
jurisdiction, and Herod happened to be in Jerusalem at the time.
8Herod was delighted at the opportunity to see
Jesus, because he had heard about him and had
been hoping for a long time to see him perform a
miracle. 9He asked Jesus question after question,
but Jesus refused to answer. 10Meanwhile, the leading priests and the teachers of religious law stood
there shouting their accusations. 11Now Herod and
his soldiers began mocking and ridiculing Jesus.
Then they put a royal robe on him and sent him
back to Pilate. 12Herod and Pilate, who had been
enemies before, became friends that day.
13Then Pilate called together the leading priests
and other religious leaders, along with the
people, 14and he announced his verdict. "You
brought this man to me, accusing him of leading a
revolt. I have examined him thoroughly on this
point in your presence and find him innocent.
15Herod came to the same conclusion and sent him
back to us. Nothing this man has done calls for the
death penalty. 16So I will have him flogged, but
then I will release him."*
18Then a mighty roar rose from the crowd, and
with one voice they shouted, "Kill him, and release
Barabbas to us!" 19(Barabbas was in prison for
murder and for taking part in an insurrection in
Jerusalem against the government.) 20Pilate argued
with them, because he wanted to release Jesus.
21But they shouted, "Crucify him! Crucify him!"
22For the third time he demanded, "Why? What
crime has he committed? I have found no reason to
sentence him to death. I will therefore flog him and
let him go."
23But the crowd shouted louder and louder for
Jesus' death, and their voices prevailed. 24So Pilate
sentenced Jesus to die as they demanded. 25As they
had requested, he released Barabbas, the man in
prison for insurrection and murder. But he delivered Jesus over to them to do as they wished.
26As they led Jesus away, Simon of Cyrene,* who
was coming in from the country just then, was
forced to follow Jesus and carry his cross. 27Great
crowds trailed along behind, including many
grief-stricken women. 28But Jesus turned and said
to them, "Daughters of Jerusalem, don't weep for
me, but weep for yourselves and for your children. 29For the days are coming when they will say,
'Fortunate indeed are the women who are childless, the wombs that have not borne a child and
the breasts that have never nursed.' 30People will
beg the mountains to fall on them and the hills
to bury them. 31For if these things are done when
the tree is green, what will happen when it is
dry?*"

**MERCY ● ● • • •**

**23:39-43 As this man was about to die, he turned to Christ for forgiveness, and Christ accepted him. This shows that our works don't save us—our faith in Christ does. It is never too late to turn to God. Even in his misery, Jesus had mercy on this criminal who decided to believe in him. Our life is much more useful and fulfilling if we turn to God early, but even those who repent at the very last moment will be with God in his kingdom.**

32Two others, both criminals, were led out to be
executed with him. 33Finally, they came to a place
called The Skull.* All three were crucified there—
Jesus on the center cross, and the two criminals on
either side.
34Jesus said, "Father, forgive these people, because they don't know what they are doing."* And
the soldiers gambled for his clothes by throwing
dice.*

**My church regularly does something called "Communion." What is it supposed to do for me?**

Have you ever saved something from a special event because you wanted to remember how great that moment was? Odds are you have. And if you ask your parents to take you through their "nostalgia boxes" sometime, they'll probably say things like: "This is the varsity letter I won my senior year for swimming." Or, "Here is the ring box from the ring your father gave me the day he proposed."

Certain items help us remember special moments in our life.

When Jesus was about to die, be resurrected, and return to heaven, he wanted to leave his followers something tangible to remember him by. He could have left a physical item like a robe or a cup. But people probably would begin to worship the object instead of God, and the object would be seen by just a few. So instead, he left an "act," something we could do.

Communion (the Lord's Supper, Eucharist) is that act—a word picture of what Jesus did on the cross. There, his body was broken and his blood was shed . . . for us. Luke 24:13-35 says that Jesus was recognized "as he was breaking the bread" (verse 35). Communion helps us recognize who Jesus is and that he is with us as we worship.

Because Communion is celebrated by believers throughout the world, it is a unifying act. And because we retell the message of Christ's death, we are reminded that he is going to return someday to take us to heaven. (See also 1 Corinthians 11:23-26.)

Christians will always need those reminders. There are too many distractions that cause us to lose our focus on what really matters in this life. Communion briefly reminds us that real *life* revolves not around us, but around one incredible act of love at a certain time in history.

23:16 Some manuscripts add verse 17, *For it was necessary for him to release one [prisoner] for them during the feast.* 23:26 *Cyrene* was a city in northern Africa. 23:31 Or *If these things are done to me, the living tree, what will happen to you, the dry tree?* 23:33 Sometimes rendered *Calvary,* which comes from the Latin word for "skull." 23:34a This sentence is not included in many ancient manuscripts. 23:34b Greek *by casting lots.* See Ps 22:18.

## SCRIPTURE ● ● • • •

24:25-27 **After the two disciples told Jesus they were puzzled, he answered them by going to Scripture and applying it to his ministry. When we are puzzled by questions or problems, we, too, can go to Scripture and find authoritative help. If we, like these two disciples, do not understand what the Bible means, we can turn to other believers who know the Bible and have the wisdom to apply it to our situation.**

35The crowd watched, and the leaders laughed and scoffed. "He saved others," they said, "let him save himself if he is really God's Chosen One, the Messiah." 36The soldiers mocked him, too, by offering him a drink of sour wine. 37They called out to him, "If you are the King of the Jews, save yourself!" 38A signboard was nailed to the cross above him with these words: "This is the King of the Jews."

39One of the criminals hanging beside him scoffed, "So you're the Messiah, are you? Prove it by saving yourself—and us, too, while you're at it!"

40But the other criminal protested, "Don't you fear God even when you are dying? 41We deserve to die for our evil deeds, but this man hasn't done anything wrong." 42Then he said, "Jesus, remember me when you come into your Kingdom."

43And Jesus replied, "I assure you, today you will be with me in paradise."

44By this time it was noon, and darkness fell across the whole land until three o'clock. 45The light from the sun was gone. And suddenly, the thick veil hanging in the Temple was torn apart. 46Then Jesus shouted, "Father, I entrust my spirit into your hands!"* And with those words he breathed his last.

47When the captain of the Roman soldiers handling the executions saw what had happened, he praised God and said, "Surely this man was innocent.*" 48And when the crowd that came to see the crucifixion saw all that had happened, they went home in deep sorrow.* 49But Jesus' friends, including the women who had followed him from Galilee, stood at a distance watching.

50Now there was a good and righteous man named Joseph. He was a member of the Jewish high council, 51but he had not agreed with the decision and actions of the other religious leaders. He was from the town of Arimathea in Judea, and he had been waiting for the Kingdom of God to come. 52He went to Pilate and asked for Jesus' body. 53Then he took the body down from the cross and wrapped it in a long linen cloth and laid it in a new tomb that had been carved out of rock. 54This was done late on Friday afternoon, the day of preparation* for the Sabbath.

55As his body was taken away, the women from Galilee followed and saw the tomb where they placed his body. 56Then they went home and prepared spices and ointments to embalm him. But by the time they were finished it was the Sabbath, so they rested all that day as required by the law.

CHAPTER **24** **JESUS IS ALIVE!** But very early on Sunday morning* the women came to the tomb, taking the spices they had prepared. 2They found that the stone covering the entrance had been rolled aside. 3So they went in, but they couldn't find the body of the Lord Jesus. 4They were puzzled, trying to think what could have happened to it. Suddenly, two men appeared to them, clothed in dazzling robes. 5The women were terrified and bowed low before them. Then the men asked, "Why are you looking in a tomb for someone who is alive? 6He isn't here! He has risen from the dead! Don't you remember what he told you back in Galilee, 7that the Son of Man must be betrayed into the hands of sinful men and be crucified, and that he would rise again the third day?"

## INSIGHT ● ● • • •

24:45 **Jesus opened these people's minds to understand the Scriptures. The Holy Spirit does this in our life today when we study the Bible. Have you ever wondered how to understand a difficult Bible passage? Besides reading surrounding passages, asking other people, and consulting reference works, pray that the Holy Spirit will open your mind to understand, giving you the needed insight to put God's Word into action in your life.**

8Then they remembered that he had said this. 9So they rushed back to tell his eleven disciples—and everyone else—what had happened. 10The women who went to the tomb were Mary Magdalene, Joanna, Mary the mother of James, and several others. They told the apostles what had happened, 11but the story sounded like nonsense, so they didn't believe it. 12However, Peter ran to the tomb to look. Stooping, he peered in and saw the empty linen wrappings; then he went home again, wondering what had happened.*

13That same day two of Jesus' followers were walking to the village of Emmaus, seven miles* out of Jerusalem. 14As they walked along they were talking about everything that had happened. 15Suddenly, Jesus himself came along and joined them and began walking beside them. 16But they didn't know who he was, because God kept them from recognizing him.

17"You seem to be in a deep discussion about something," he said. "What are you so concerned about?"

They stopped short, sadness written across their faces. 18Then one of them, Cleopas, replied, "You must be the only person in Jerusalem who hasn't heard about all the things that have happened there the last few days."

23:46 Ps 31:5. 23:47 Or *righteous.* 23:48 Greek *beating their breasts.* 23:54 Greek *on the day of preparation.* 24:1 Greek *But on the first day of the week, very early in the morning.* 24:12 Some manuscripts do not include this verse. 24:13 Greek *60 stadia* [11.1 kilometers].

## JESUS AND THE TEN COMMANDMENTS

| *The Ten Commandments said . . .* | *Jesus said . . .* |
|---|---|
| Do not worship any other gods besides me. *Exodus 20:3* | You must worship the Lord your God; serve only him. *Matthew 4:10* |
| Do not make idols of any kind, whether in the shape of birds or animals or fish. *Exodus 20:4* | No one can serve two masters. *Luke 16:13* |
| Do not misuse the name of the LORD your God. The LORD will not let you go unpunished if you misuse his name. *Exodus 20:7* | Don't make any vows! If you say, "By heaven!" it is a sacred vow because heaven is God's throne. *Matthew 5:34* |
| Remember to observe the Sabbath day by keeping it holy. *Exodus 20:8* | The Sabbath was made to benefit people, and not people to benefit the Sabbath. And I, the Son of Man, am master even of the Sabbath! *Mark 2:27-28* |
| Honor your father and mother. Then you will live a long, full life in the land the LORD your God will give you. *Exodus 20:12* | If you love your father or mother more than you love me, you are not worthy of being mine; or if you love your son or daughter more than me, you are not worthy of being mine. *Matthew 10:37* |
| Do not murder. *Exodus 20:13* | If you are angry with someone, you are subject to judgment! If you say to your friend, "You idiot," you are in danger of being brought before the court. And if you curse someone, you are in danger of the fires of hell. *Matthew 5:22* |
| Do not commit adultery. *Exodus 20:14* | Anyone who even looks at a woman with lust in his eye has already committed adultery with her in his heart. *Matthew 5:28* |
| Do not steal. *Exodus 20:15* | If you are ordered to court and your shirt is taken from you, give your coat, too. *Matthew 5:40* |
| Do not testify falsely against your neighbor. *Exodus 20:16* | You must give an account on judgment day of every idle word you speak. The words you say now reflect your fate then; either you will be justified by them or you will be condemned. *Matthew 12:36* |
| Do not covet your neighbor's house. Do not covet your neighbor's wife, male or female servant, ox or donkey, or anything else your neighbor owns. *Exodus 20:17* | Don't be greedy for what you don't have. Real life is not measured by how much we own. *Luke 12:15* |

19 "What things?" Jesus asked.
"The things that happened to Jesus, the man
from Nazareth," they said. "He was a prophet who
did wonderful miracles. He was a mighty teacher,
highly regarded by both God and all the people.
20 But our leading priests and other religious leaders
arrested him and handed him over to be condemned to death, and they crucified him. 21 We had
thought he was the Messiah who had come to
rescue Israel. That all happened three days ago.
22 Then some women from our group of his followers were at his tomb early this morning, and they
came back with an amazing report. 23 They said his
body was missing, and they had seen angels who
told them Jesus is alive! 24 Some of our men ran out
to see, and sure enough, Jesus' body was gone, just
as the women had said."
25 Then Jesus said to them, "You are such foolish
people! You find it so hard to believe all that the
prophets wrote in the Scriptures. 26 Wasn't it
clearly predicted by the prophets that the Messiah
would have to suffer all these things before entering his time of glory?" 27 Then Jesus quoted passages from the writings of Moses and all the
prophets, explaining what all the Scriptures said
about himself.

28By this time they were nearing Emmaus and
the end of their journey. Jesus would have gone on,
29but they begged him to stay the night with them,
since it was getting late. So he went home with
them. 30As they sat down to eat, he took a small
loaf of bread, asked God's blessing on it, broke it,
then gave it to them. 31Suddenly, their eyes were
opened, and they recognized him. And at that
moment he disappeared!

32They said to each other, "Didn't our hearts feel
strangely warm as he talked with us on the road
and explained the Scriptures to us?" 33And within
the hour they were on their way back to Jerusalem,
where the eleven disciples and the other followers
of Jesus were gathered. When they arrived, they
were greeted with the report, 34"The Lord has really
risen! He appeared to Peter*!"

35Then the two from Emmaus told their story of
how Jesus had appeared to them as they were
walking along the road and how they had recognized him as he was breaking the bread. 36And just
as they were telling about it, Jesus himself was
suddenly standing there among them. He said,
"Peace be with you."* 37But the whole group
was terribly frightened, thinking they were seeing a ghost! 38"Why are you frightened?" he asked.
"Why do you doubt who I am? 39Look at my
hands. Look at my feet. You can see that it's
really me. Touch me and make sure that I am not
a ghost, because ghosts don't have bodies, as you
see that I do!" 40As he spoke, he held out his
hands for them to see, and he showed them his
feet.*

41Still they stood there doubting, filled with joy
and wonder. Then he asked them, "Do you have
anything here to eat?" 42They gave him a piece of
broiled fish, 43and he ate it as they watched.

44Then he said, "When I was with you before, I
told you that everything written about me by
Moses and the prophets and in the Psalms must
all come true." 45Then he opened their minds to
understand these many Scriptures. 46And he
said, "Yes, it was written long ago that the Messiah
must suffer and die and rise again from the dead
on the third day. 47With my authority, take this
message of repentance to all the nations, beginning in Jerusalem: 'There is forgiveness of sins for
all who turn to me.' 48You are witnesses of all these
things.

49"And now I will send the Holy Spirit, just as my
Father promised. But stay here in the city until the
Holy Spirit comes and fills you with power from
heaven."

50Then Jesus led them to Bethany, and lifting his
hands to heaven, he blessed them. 51While he was
blessing them, he left them and was taken up to
heaven.* 52They worshiped him and* then returned to Jerusalem filled with great joy. 53And
they spent all of their time in the Temple, praising
God.

**24:34** Greek *Simon.* **24:36** Some manuscripts do not include *He said, "Peace be with you."* **24:40** Some manuscripts do not include this verse. **24:51** Some manuscripts do not include *and was taken up to heaven.* **24:52** Some manuscripts do not include *worshiped him and.*

# MEGA themes

**JESUS CHRIST, THE SAVIOR** Luke describes how God's Son entered human history. Jesus lived as the perfect man. After a perfect ministry, he provided a perfect sacrifice for our sin so we could be saved.

Jesus is our perfect leader and Savior. He offers forgiveness to all who believe that what he says is true and accept him as Lord of their life.

1. How do you think Luke would answer this question: "What was Jesus like?"
2. What do you learn about Jesus in Luke 2:41-52?
3. Why is it so important that Jesus shared our human experiences, including all types of temptations?
4. Based on your responses to these questions, how would you describe Jesus to someone who had never heard of him?
5. What impact does this have on the person you are today? This is your testimony of who Jesus is in your life. Who do you know that needs to hear and understand your testimony?

**HISTORY** Luke was a medical doctor and historian. He put great emphasis on dates and details, connecting Jesus to events and people in history.

Luke's devotion to accuracy gives us confidence

in the reliability of the history of Jesus' life. Even more important, we can believe with certainty that Jesus is God.

1. What difference does it make whether or not Luke is historically accurate?
2. Why is it so important that Jesus actually lived, died, and rose again as opposed to this just being an allegory (symbolic story) that someone used to describe how much God loves us?
3. What historical facts clearly reveal that Jesus was both man and God?
4. How does the fact that Jesus was both man and God affect your relationship with him? How does it affect your life?

**CARING FOR PEOPLE** Jesus was deeply interested in people and relationships. He showed warm concern for his followers and friends—men, women, and children.

Jesus' love for people is good news for everyone. His message is for all people in every nation. Each of us has an opportunity to respond to him in faith.

1. Jesus built his earthly ministry through personal relationships. What does this imply for how he wants you to minister to others?
2. What does it take for you to feel loved by someone? To trust that the person truly cares for you?
3. How would a person have to act to touch the people in your school with Christ's love?
4. What can you do to show Christ's love to the kids at your school?

**HOLY SPIRIT** The Holy Spirit was present at Jesus' birth, baptism, ministry, and resurrection. As a perfect example for us, Jesus lived in dependence on the Holy Spirit.

The Holy Spirit was sent by God as confirmation of Jesus' authority. The Holy Spirit is given to enable people to live for Christ. By faith we can have the Holy Spirit's presence and power to witness and to serve.

1. In 4:1-20, what role did the Holy Spirit play in Jesus' life?
2. In what ways does the Spirit work in you during times of temptation or weariness, and during opportunities to do his ministry?
3. What do you think it means to be "full of the Spirit"?
4. How can you keep yourself daily filled with his Spirit?
5. What do you want to see the Holy Spirit do in your life? What will you do to keep yourself reliant on God's Spirit so that this will be accomplished?

**37 B.C.**
**Herod the Great begins to rule**

**6/5 B.C.**
**Jesus is born**

**5/4 B.C.**
**Escape to Egypt**

**4 B.C.**
**Herod the Great dies**

**4/3 B.C.**
**Return to Nazareth**

**A.D. 6**
**Judea becomes a Roman province**

**14**
**Tiberius Caesar becomes emperor**

**26**
**Pontius Pilate appointed governor**

**26/27**
**Jesus begins his ministry**

**27**
**Jesus and Nicodemus**

**28**
**Jesus chooses 12 disciples**

**29**
**Jesus feeds 5,000**

**30**
**Jesus is crucified, rises again, and ascends**

**Q**uestions. Life is jam-packed with them. ■ *Dumb* questions: ■ "If the plural of goose is geese, shouldn't the plural of moose be meese?" ■ "Um, if God can do anything, can he make a rock so big that even he couldn't lift it?" ■ *Mysterious* questions: ■ "Gentlemen, we know that buttered bread usually falls butter-side-down and cats generally land feet-first. Now we will discover what happens when a piece of buttered bread is strapped to the back of a cat and both are tossed off a two-story building." ■ *Serious* questions: ■ "What will bring me long-lasting fulfillment?" ■ "How can I have a rich and satisfying life?" ■ Even people who don't (or won't) openly discuss serious issues have ideas about where to find happiness. Ray's formula for fulfillment includes partying and an active sex life. Anne thinks she'll find it in a 4.0 grade point average and a college scholarship. Kevin is banking on his athletic ability to do the trick. Sherry's relying on beauty and bucks. ■ *Nagging* questions: ■ "If happiness really *is* found in the things mentioned above, why are there people with awesome sex lives, staggering IQs, truckloads of trophies, drop-dead good looks, or bulging bank accounts who are unhappy?" ■ "Why don't more people consider what Jesus had to say about happiness and fulfillment?" ■ *Personal* questions: ■ "Have *you* ever really looked at and pondered Jesus' teachings in the Gospel of John?" ■ "What are you waiting for?"

## STATS

PURPOSE: To prove conclusively that Jesus is the Son of God and that all who believe in him will have eternal life

AUTHOR: John, the apostle, son of Zebedee, brother of James, called a "Son of Thunder"

TO WHOM WRITTEN: New Christians and searching non-Christians

DATE WRITTEN: Probably between A.D. 85 and 90

SETTING: Written after the destruction of Jerusalem in A.D. 70 and before John's exile to the island of Patmos

KEY PEOPLE: Jesus, John the Baptist, the disciples, Mary, Martha, Lazarus, Jesus' mother, Pilate, Mary Magdalene

KEY PLACES: Judean countryside, Samaria, Galilee, Bethany, Jerusalem

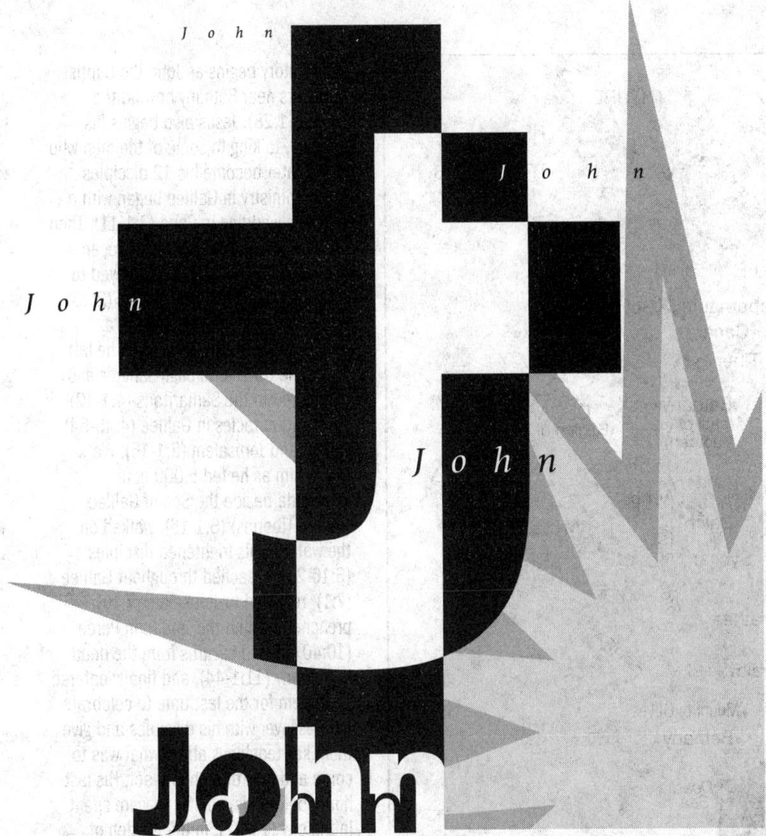


CHAPTER 1 **GOD BECOMES A HUMAN.** In the beginning the Word already existed. He was with God, and
he was God. [2]He was in the beginning with God. [3]He
created everything there is. Nothing exists that he
didn't make. [4]Life itself was in him, and this life gives
light to everyone. [5]The light shines through the darkness, and the darkness can never extinguish it.

[6]God sent John the Baptist [7]to tell everyone about
the light so that everyone might believe because of
his testimony. [8]John himself was not the light; he
was only a witness to the light. [9]The one who is the
true light, who gives light to everyone, was going to
come into the world.

[10]But although the world was made through him,
the world didn't recognize him when he came.
[11]Even in his own land and among his own people,
he was not accepted. [12]But to all who believed him
and accepted him, he gave the right to become children of God. [13]They are reborn! This is not a physical
birth resulting from human passion or plan—this
rebirth comes from God.

[14]So the Word became human and lived here on
earth among us. He was full of unfailing love and
faithfulness.* And we have seen his glory, the glory
of the only Son of the Father.

[15]John pointed him out to the people. He shouted
to the crowds, "This is the one I was talking about
when I said, 'Someone is coming who is far greater
than I am, for he existed long before I did.'"

[16]We have all benefited from the rich blessings he
brought to us—one gracious blessing after another.*
[17]For the law was given through Moses; God's unfailing love and faithfulness came through Jesus Christ.
[18]No one has ever seen God. But his only Son, who
is himself God,* is near to the Father's heart; he has
told us about him.

[19]This was the testimony of John when the Jewish
leaders sent priests and Temple assistants* from Jerusalem to ask John whether he claimed to be the
Messiah. [20]He flatly denied it. "I am not the Messiah," he said.

[21]"Well then, who are you?" they asked. "Are you
Elijah?"

"No," he replied.

"Are you the Prophet?"*

"No."

[22]"Then who are you? Tell us, so we can give an

**SO COMPLEX ● ● ● • •**

1:3-5 **Do you ever feel as though your life is so complex that God would never understand? Remember, God created the entire universe—nothing is too complex for him to understand. He created you, he is alive today, and his love is bigger than any problem you may face.**

1:14 Greek *grace and truth;* also in 1:17. 1:16 Greek *grace upon grace.* 1:18 Some manuscripts read *his one and only Son.* 1:19 Greek *and Levites.* 1:21 See Deut 18:15, 18; Mal 4:5-6.

## KEY PLACES IN JOHN

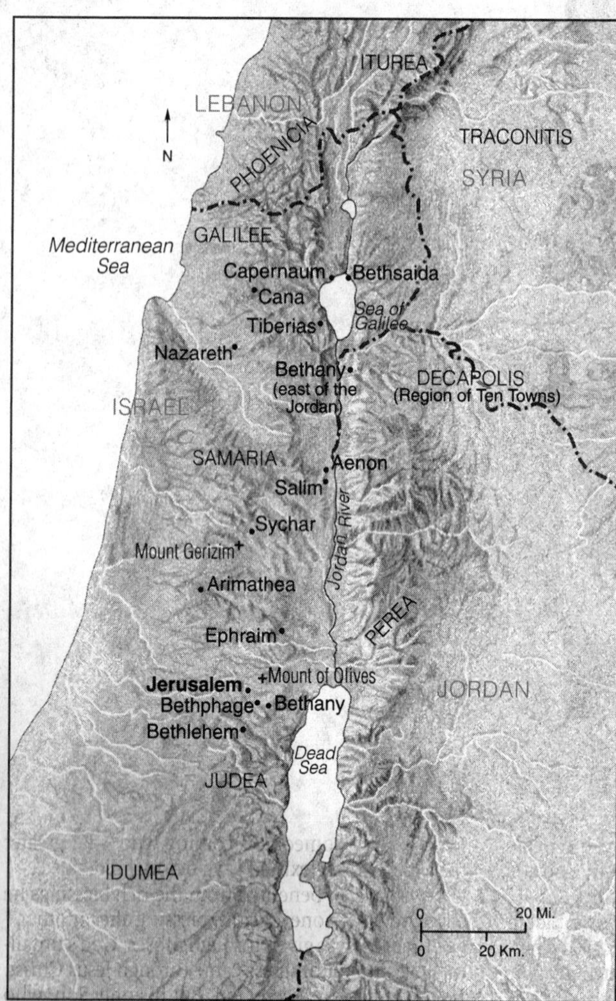


The broken lines (—·—·) indicate modern boundaries.

John's story begins as John the Baptist ministers near Bethany beyond the Jordan (1:28). Jesus also begins his ministry, talking to some of the men who would later become his 12 disciples. Jesus' ministry in Galilee began with a visit to a wedding in Cana (2:1-11). Then he went to Capernaum, which became his new home (2:12). He journeyed to Jerusalem for the special feasts (2:13) and there met with Nicodemus, a religious leader (3:1-21). When he left Judea, he traveled through Samaria and ministered to the Samaritans (4:1-42). Jesus did miracles in Galilee (4:46-54), Judea, and Jerusalem (5:1-15). We follow him as he fed 5,000 near Bethsaida beside the Sea of Galilee (Sea of Tiberias) (6:1-15), walked on the water to his frightened disciples (6:16-21), preached throughout Galilee (7:1), returned to Jerusalem (7:10), preached beyond the Jordan in Perea (10:40), raised Lazarus from the dead in Bethany (11:1-44), and finally entered Jerusalem for the last time to celebrate the Passover with his disciples and give them key teachings about what was to come and how they should act. His last hours before his crucifixion were spent in the city (13–17), in the Garden of Gethsemane (18:1-11), and finally in various buildings in Jerusalem during his trial (18:12-16). He would be crucified, but he would rise again as he had promised.

answer to those who sent us. What do you have to
say about yourself?"
23John replied in the words of Isaiah:

"I am a voice shouting in the wilderness,
'Prepare a straight pathway for the Lord's
coming!'"*

24Then those who were sent by the Pharisees
25asked him, "If you aren't the Messiah or Elijah or
the Prophet, what right do you have to baptize?"
26John told them, "I baptize with* water, but right
here in the crowd is someone you do not know,
27who will soon begin his ministry. I am not even
worthy to be his slave.*" 28This incident took place
at Bethany, a village east of the Jordan River, where
John was baptizing.
29The next day John saw Jesus coming toward him
and said, "Look! There is the Lamb of God who
takes away the sin of the world! 30He is the one I was
talking about when I said, 'Soon a man is coming
who is far greater than I am, for he existed long
before I did.' 31I didn't know he was the one, but I
have been baptizing with water in order to point him
out to Israel."
32Then John said, "I saw the Holy Spirit descending
like a dove from heaven and resting upon him. 33I
didn't know he was the one, but when God sent me to
baptize with water, he told me, 'When you see the

1:23 Isa 40:3. 1:26 Or *in;* also in 1:31, 33. 1:27 Greek *to untie his sandals.*

### HUMILITY

**1:30 Although John the Baptist was a well-known preacher and attracted large crowds, he was content for Jesus to take the higher place. This is true humility, the basis for greatness in preaching, teaching, or any other work we do for Christ. When you are content to do what God wants you to do and let Jesus Christ be honored for it, God will do great things through you.**

Holy Spirit descending and resting upon someone, he
is the one you are looking for. He is the one who
baptizes with the Holy Spirit.' 34 I saw this happen to
Jesus, so I testify that he is the Son of God.*"
35 The following day, John was again standing with
two of his disciples. 36 As Jesus walked by, John
looked at him and then declared, "Look! There is the
Lamb of God!" 37 Then John's two disciples turned
and followed Jesus.
38 Jesus looked around and saw them following.
"What do you want?" he asked them.
They replied, "Rabbi" (which means Teacher),
"where are you staying?"
39 "Come and see," he said. It was about four
o'clock in the afternoon when they went with him to
the place, and they stayed there the rest of the day.
40 Andrew, Simon Peter's brother, was one of these
men who had heard what John said and then followed Jesus. 41 The first thing Andrew did was to find
his brother, Simon, and tell him, "We have found
the Messiah" (which means the Christ).
42 Then Andrew brought Simon to meet Jesus.
Looking intently at Simon, Jesus said, "You are Simon, the son of John—but you will be called Cephas" (which means Peter*).
43 The next day Jesus decided to go to Galilee. He
found Philip and said to him, "Come, be my disciple." 44 Philip was from Bethsaida, Andrew and Peter's hometown.
45 Philip went off to look for Nathanael and told him, "We have
found the very person Moses and
the prophets wrote about! His
name is Jesus, the son of Joseph
from Nazareth."
46 "Nazareth!" exclaimed Nathanael. "Can anything good
come from there?"
"Just come and see for yourself," Philip said.
47 As they approached, Jesus
said, "Here comes an honest
man—a true son of Israel."
48 "How do you know about
me?" Nathanael asked.
And Jesus replied, "I could see
you under the fig tree before Philip
found you."
49 Nathanael replied, "Teacher,
you are the Son of God—the King
of Israel!"
50 Jesus asked him, "Do you believe all this just because I told you I
had seen you under the fig tree? You
will see greater things than this."
51 Then he said, "The truth is, you
will all see heaven open and the
angels of God going up and down
upon the Son of Man."*

## CHAPTER 2

**JESUS TURNS WATER INTO WINE.** The next
day* Jesus' mother was a guest at a wedding celebration in the village of Cana in Galilee. 2 Jesus and his
disciples were also invited to the celebration. 3 The
wine supply ran out during the festivities, so Jesus'
mother spoke to him about the problem. "They
have no more wine," she told him.
4 "How does that concern you and me?" Jesus
asked. "My time has not yet come."
5 But his mother told the servants, "Do whatever
he tells you."
6 Six stone waterpots were standing there; they
were used for Jewish ceremonial purposes and held
twenty to thirty gallons* each. 7 Jesus told the servants, "Fill the jars with water." When the jars had
been filled to the brim, 8 he said, "Dip some out and
take it to the master of ceremonies." So they followed his instructions.
9 When the master of ceremonies tasted the water
that was now wine, not knowing where it had come
from (though, of course, the servants knew), he
called the bridegroom over. 10 "Usually a host serves
the best wine first," he said. "Then, when everyone
is full and doesn't care, he brings out the less expensive wines. But you have kept the best until now!"
11 This miraculous sign at Cana in Galilee was
Jesus' first display of his glory. And his disciples
believed in him.

## "Here's what I did..."

It was an incredible weekend. A twister hit my town, and suddenly our house was ruined, my wrist was broken, and I lost my best friend.

I didn't know what to do, where to turn. It was too much to take in all at once. I felt depressed. Then I was angry; I felt ripped off. In all the confusion of adjusting to these disasters, I finally decided to open the Bible.

I started reading the Gospel of John. And as I thought about Jesus and all he gave up to come down to earth and live among us, my attitude started to change. I thought about verses 10-12 in the first chapter, how Jesus wasn't respected by the very people he came to help. If anybody had the right to feel self-pity, he did! But Jesus did it all for love, all for us.

The first 27 verses of chapter one opened my eyes to God's faithfulness and love. They made me realize that God would stand by me through everything, even this terrible time. I turned everything over to God and discovered a joy that was as incredible as everything that had happened to me in that one terrible weekend. I began to live the kind of Christian life I'd been missing so long when I was just going my own way. The following weeks were the happiest I'd ever felt, even though I still had to deal with the sorrow over losing my friend and our home. I found that the love of God was so much more real, and it gave me strength.

Barbara



1:34 Some manuscripts read *the chosen One of God.* 1:42 The names *Cephas* and *Peter* both mean "rock." 1:51 See Gen 28:10-17, the account of Jacob's ladder. 2:1 Greek *On the third day;* see 1:35, 43. 2:6 Greek *2 or 3 measures* [75 to 113 liters].

12After the wedding he went to Capernaum for a few days with his mother, his brothers, and his disciples.

13It was time for the annual Passover celebration, and Jesus went to Jerusalem. 14In the Temple area he saw merchants selling cattle, sheep, and doves for sacrifices; and he saw money changers behind their counters. 15Jesus made a whip from some ropes and chased them all out of the Temple. He drove out the sheep and oxen, scattered the money changers' coins over the floor, and turned over their tables. 16Then, going over to the people who sold doves, he told them, "Get these things out of here. Don't turn my Father's house into a marketplace!"

17Then his disciples remembered this prophecy from the Scriptures: "Passion for God's house burns within me."*

18"What right do you have to do these things?" the Jewish leaders demanded. "If you have this authority from God, show us a miraculous sign to prove it."

19"All right," Jesus replied. "Destroy this temple, and in three days I will raise it up."

20"What!" they exclaimed. "It took forty-six years to build this Temple, and you can do it in three days?" 21But by "this temple," Jesus meant his body. 22After he was raised from the dead, the disciples remembered that he had said this. And they believed both Jesus and the Scriptures.

For GOD SO LOVED the world

**THAT HE GAVE HIS ONLY SON**

so that **EVERYONE** who believes in him will not perish but have **ETERNAL LIFE.**

JOHN 3:16

## ANGER ●●•••

2:15-16 **Jesus was obviously angry at the merchants who exploited those who had come to God's house to worship. There is a difference between uncontrolled rage and righteous indignation—yet both are called anger. We must be very careful how we use the powerful emotion of anger. It is right to be angry about injustice and sin; it is wrong to be angry over small, personal offenses.**

23Because of the miraculous signs he did in Jerusalem at the Passover celebration, many people were convinced that he was indeed the Messiah. 24But Jesus didn't trust them, because he knew what people were really like. 25No one needed to tell him about human nature.

CHAPTER **3** **JESUS TALKS WITH NICODEMUS.** After dark one evening, a Jewish religious leader named Nicodemus, a Pharisee, 2came to speak with Jesus. "Teacher," he said, "we all know that God has sent you to teach us. Your miraculous signs are proof enough that God is with you."

3Jesus replied, "I assure you, unless you are born again,* you can never see the Kingdom of God."

4"What do you mean?" exclaimed Nicodemus. "How can an old man go back into his mother's womb and be born again?"

5Jesus replied, "The truth is, no one can enter the Kingdom of God without being born of water and the Spirit.* 6Humans can reproduce only human life, but the Holy Spirit gives new life from heaven. 7So don't be surprised at my statement that you* must be born again. 8Just as you can hear the wind but can't tell where it comes from or where it is going, so you can't explain how people are born of the Spirit."

9"What do you mean?" Nicodemus asked.

10Jesus replied, "You are a respected Jewish teacher, and yet you don't understand these things? 11I assure you, I am telling you what we know and have seen, and yet you won't believe us. 12But if you don't even believe me when I tell you about things that happen here on earth, how can you possibly believe if I tell you what is going on in heaven? 13For

## NEW LIFE ●●•••

3:6 **Jesus says that the Holy Spirit gives new life from heaven. Who is the Holy Spirit? God is three persons in one—the Father, the Son, and the Holy Spirit. God became a man in Jesus so that Jesus could die for our sins. Jesus rose from the dead to offer salvation to all people through spiritual renewal and rebirth. When Jesus ascended into heaven, his physical presence left the earth, but he promised to send the Holy Spirit so that his spiritual presence would still be among us (see Luke 24:49). In Old Testament days, the Holy Spirit empowered specific individuals for specific purposes. Then came Pentecost (Acts 2), and now all believers have the power of the Holy Spirit available to them. For more on the Holy Spirit, read 14:16-28; Romans 8:9; 1 Corinthians 12:13; and 2 Corinthians 1:22.**

2:17 Or *"Concern for God's house will be my undoing."* Ps 69:9. 3:3 Or *born from above;* also in 3:7. 3:5 Or *spirit.* The Greek word for *Spirit* can also be translated *wind;* see 3:8. 3:7 The Greek word for *you* is plural; also in 3:12.

only I, the Son of Man,* have come to earth and will return to heaven again. 14And as Moses lifted up the bronze snake on a pole in the wilderness, so I, the Son of Man, must be lifted up on a pole,* 15so that everyone who believes in me will have eternal life.

16"For God so loved the world that he gave his only Son, so that everyone who believes in him will not perish but have eternal life. 17God did not send his Son into the world to condemn it, but to save it.

18"There is no judgment awaiting those who trust him. But those who do not trust him have already been judged for not believing in the only Son of God. 19Their judgment is based on this fact: The light from heaven came into the world, but they loved the darkness more than the light, for their actions were evil. 20They hate the light because they want to sin in the darkness. They stay away from the light for fear their sins will be exposed and they will be punished. 21But those who do what is right come to the light gladly, so everyone can see that they are doing what God wants."

22Afterward Jesus and his disciples left Jerusalem, but they stayed in Judea for a while and baptized there.

23At this time John the Baptist was baptizing at Aenon, near Salim, because there was plenty of water there and people kept coming to him for baptism. 24This was before John was put into prison. 25At that time a certain Jew began an argument with John's disciples over ceremonial cleansing. 26John's disciples came to him and said, "Teacher, the man you met on the other side of the Jordan River, the one you said was the Messiah, is also baptizing people. And everybody is going over there instead of coming here to us."

27John replied, "God in heaven appoints each person's work. 28You yourselves know how plainly I told you that I am not the Messiah. I am here to prepare the way for him—that is all. 29The bride will go where the bridegroom is. A bridegroom's friend rejoices with him. I am the bridegroom's friend, and I am filled with joy at his success. 30He must become greater and greater, and I must become less and less.

31"He has come from above and is greater than anyone else. I am of the earth, and my understanding is limited to the things of earth, but he has come from heaven.* 32He tells what he has seen and heard, but how few believe what he tells them! 33Those who believe him discover that God is true. 34For he is sent by God. He speaks God's words, for God's Spirit is upon him without measure or limit. 35The Father loves his Son, and he has given him authority over everything. 36And all who believe in

## JOHN THE BAPTIST

In almost any crowd, John the Baptist would be called unique. He wore odd clothes, ate strange food, and preached an unusual message. He would not have agreed with our habit of evaluating people by how they dress—or by how they act. He would have insisted that we listen to what he had to say.

John really wasn't interested in being unique. What he wanted to do more than anything was to obey God. And he wasn't afraid to ask others to do the same. John realized that he had a special role to play in the world. His job was to tell the world that the Savior was about to arrive. John was totally committed to his purpose.

This wild-looking man stood face-to-face with people and told them to repent. He told them the best way to get ready for the Savior was to be deeply sorry for their sins. Although John was preparing people to receive Jesus when he physically came to the world, John's message still applies today when we realize that Jesus wants to come into our life, too. We can't receive the Savior until we know we need him. We won't know we need him until we realize we are sinners.

Today, we still need to hear John's favorite word—*repent!* If you don't know what it means, you may not have done it. Repenting means that you are not only deeply sorry for your sinfulness but are also serious in wanting God's help to live his way. Until you have repented, you won't experience God's forgiveness or the strength he offers to live a life of obedience. Repentance may be the most important thing you think about today.

**UPS:**
- The God-appointed messenger to announce the arrival of Jesus
- A preacher whose theme was repentance
- A fearless confronter
- Known for his remarkable lifestyle
- Uncompromising

**STATS:**
- Where: Judea
- Occupation: Prophet
- Relatives: Father: Zechariah. Mother: Elizabeth. Distant cousin: Jesus.
- Contemporaries: Herod, Herodias

LESSONS: God does not guarantee an easy or safe life to those who serve him

Doing what God desires is the greatest possible life investment

Standing for the truth is more important than life itself

KEY VERSE: "I assure you, of all who have ever lived, none is greater than John the Baptist. Yet even the most insignificant person in the Kingdom of Heaven is greater than he is!" (Matthew 11:11).

John's story is told in all four Gospels. His coming was predicted in Isaiah 40:3 and Malachi 4:5-6; and he is mentioned in Acts 1:5, 22; 10:37; 11:16; 13:24-25; 18:25; 19:3-4.

3:13 Some manuscripts add *who lives in heaven.* 3:14 Greek *must be lifted up.* 3:31 Some manuscripts omit *but he has come from heaven.*

God's Son have eternal life. Those who don't obey the Son will never experience eternal life, but the wrath of God remains upon them."

## CHAPTER 4 JESUS AND A WOMAN AT A WELL.

Jesus* learned that the Pharisees had heard, "Jesus is baptizing and making more disciples than John"
[2](though Jesus himself didn't baptize them—his disciples did). [3]So he left Judea to return to Galilee.
[4]He had to go through Samaria on the way. [5]Eventually he came to the Samaritan village of Sychar, near the parcel of ground that Jacob gave to his son Joseph. [6]Jacob's well was there; and Jesus, tired from the long walk, sat wearily beside the well about noontime. [7]Soon a Samaritan woman came to draw water, and Jesus said to her, "Please give me a drink."
[8]He was alone at the time because his disciples had gone into the village to buy some food.
[9]The woman was surprised, for Jews refuse to have

### PREJUDICE

It may be the dawn of the twenty-first century, but some people's attitudes show they are still living in the past.

Here's the story: Randy C. and Darnell T. are close friends. Randy is white; Darnell is black. When Darnell's parents went cross-country to a funeral, Darnell stayed for the week with Randy. No big deal, right?

Wrong. The first afternoon, Randy took Darnell to the neighborhood pool. Everyone glared at them, most started whispering, and some actually got out of the pool and left.

The second night of Darnell's stay, someone shattered the rear window in Mr. C.'s car. The third night, someone (or some ones) scrawled racial slurs on the C.'s garage door.

When school started, Randy's white friends avoided him. Randy finally confronted Keith, asked what his problem was, and got this reply: "Hey, look, Randy–you changed, not us. You're the one who's trying to be Mr. Civil Rights, OK?"

Randy was (and is) shocked.

Even at church, people are treating him weirdly. Says Randy, "What is going on?! I invited a friend to stay with me while his parents were gone. Would someone please tell me what in the world is wrong with that? So what if his skin is a different color? I don't understand why so many people are so full of hate."

Which person are you most like? Randy, Darnell, or Keith? Consider how Jesus treated people who were different from himself. (See John 4:1-42.)

anything to do with Samaritans. She said to Jesus, "You are a Jew, and I am a Samaritan woman. Why are you asking me for a drink?"
[10]Jesus replied, "If you only knew the gift God has for you and who I am, you would ask me, and I would give you living water."
[11]"But sir, you don't have a rope or a bucket," she said, "and this is a very deep well. Where would you get this living water? [12]And besides, are you greater

### NO LESS ● • • • •

4:7-9 **This woman (1) was a Samaritan, a member of the hated mixed race; (2) had a bad reputation; and (3) was in a public place. No respectable Jewish man would talk to a woman under such circumstances. But Jesus did. The gospel is for every person, no matter what his or her race, social position, or past sins. We must be prepared to share this gospel at any time in any place. Jesus crossed all barriers to share the Good News; we who follow him must do no less.**

than our ancestor Jacob who gave us this well? How can you offer better water than he and his sons and his cattle enjoyed?"
[13]Jesus replied, "People soon become thirsty again after drinking this water. [14]But the water I give them takes away thirst altogether. It becomes a perpetual spring within them, giving them eternal life."
[15]"Please, sir," the woman said, "give me some of that water! Then I'll never be thirsty again, and I won't have to come here to haul water."
[16]"Go and get your husband," Jesus told her.
[17]"I don't have a husband," the woman replied.
Jesus said, "You're right! You don't have a husband—[18]for you have had five husbands, and you aren't even married to the man you're living with now."
[19]"Sir," the woman said, "you must be a prophet.
[20]So tell me, why is it that you Jews insist that Jerusalem is the only place of worship, while we Samaritans claim it is here at Mount Gerizim,* where our ancestors worshiped?"
[21]Jesus replied, "Believe me, the time is coming when it will no longer matter whether you worship the Father here or in Jerusalem. [22]You Samaritans know so little about the one you worship, while we Jews know all about him, for salvation comes through the Jews. [23]But the time is coming and is already here when true worshipers will worship the Father in spirit and in truth. The Father is looking for anyone who will worship him that way. [24]For God is Spirit, so those who worship him must worship in spirit and in truth."
[25]The woman said, "I know the Messiah will come—the one who is called Christ. When he comes, he will explain everything to us."
[26]Then Jesus told her, "I am the Messiah!"*
[27]Just then his disciples arrived. They were astonished to find him talking to a woman, but none of them asked him why he was doing it or what they had been discussing. [28]The woman left her water jar beside the well and went back to the village and told everyone, [29]"Come and meet a man who told me everything I ever did! Can this be the Mes-

### READY ● • • • •

4:35 **Sometimes Christians excuse themselves from witnessing by saying their family or friends aren't ready to believe. Jesus, however, makes it clear that around us a continual harvest waits to be reaped. Don't let Jesus find you making excuses. Look around. You will find people ready to hear God's Word.**

4:1 Some manuscripts read *The Lord.* 4:20 Greek *on this mountain.* 4:26 Greek *"I am, the one speaking to you."*

siah?" 30So the people came streaming from the
village to see him.
31Meanwhile, the disciples were urging Jesus to
eat. 32"No," he said, "I have food you don't know
about."
33"Who brought it to him?" the disciples asked
each other.
34Then Jesus explained: "My nourishment comes
from doing the will of God, who sent me, and from
finishing his work. 35Do you think the work of harvesting will not begin until the summer ends four
months from now? Look around you! Vast fields are
ripening all around us and are ready now for the
harvest. 36The harvesters are paid good wages, and
the fruit they harvest is people brought to eternal life.
What joy awaits both the planter and the harvester
alike! 37You know the saying, 'One person plants
and someone else harvests.' And it's true. 38I sent you
to harvest where you didn't plant; others had already
done the work, and you will gather the harvest."
39Many Samaritans from the village believed in
Jesus because the woman had said, "He told me
everything I ever did!" 40When they came out to see
him, they begged him to stay at their village. So he
stayed for two days, 41long enough for many of them
to hear his message and believe. 42Then they said to
the woman, "Now we believe because we have heard
him ourselves, not just because of what you told us.
He is indeed the Savior of the world."
43At the end of the two days' stay, Jesus went on
into Galilee. 44He had previously said, "A prophet is
honored everywhere except in his own country."
45The Galileans welcomed him, for they had been in
Jerusalem at the Passover celebration and had seen
all his miraculous signs.
46In the course of his journey through Galilee, he
arrived at the town of Cana, where he had turned the
water into wine. There was a government official in
the city of Capernaum whose son was very sick.
47When he heard that Jesus had come from Judea
and was traveling in Galilee, he went over to Cana.
He found Jesus and begged him to come to Capernaum with him to heal his son, who was about to
die.
48Jesus asked, "Must I do miraculous signs and
wonders before you people will believe in me?"
49The official pleaded, "Lord, please come now
before my little boy dies."
50Then Jesus told him, "Go back home. Your son
will live!" And the man believed Jesus' word and
started home.
51While he was on his way, some of his servants
met him with the news that his son was alive and
well. 52He asked them when the boy had begun to
feel better, and they replied, "Yesterday afternoon at
one o'clock his fever suddenly disappeared!" 53Then
the father realized it was the same time that Jesus
had told him, "Your son will live." And the officer
and his entire household believed in Jesus. 54This

**BELIEVE IT! ● ● • • •**

4:50 **This nobleman not only believed that Jesus could heal, he also obeyed Jesus by returning home and thus demonstrating his faith. It isn't enough for us to say we believe that Jesus can take care of our problems. We need to act as if he can. When you pray about a need or problem, live as though you believe Jesus can do what he says.**

was Jesus' second miraculous sign in Galilee after
coming from Judea.

CHAPTER **5** **JESUS HEALS A LAME MAN.** Afterward
Jesus returned to Jerusalem for one of the Jewish
holy days. 2Inside the city, near the Sheep Gate, was
the pool of Bethesda,* with five covered porches.
3Crowds of sick people—blind, lame, or paralyzed—lay on the porches.* 5One of the men lying
there had been sick for thirty-eight years. 6When
Jesus saw him and knew how long he had been ill,
he asked him, "Would you like to get well?"
7"I can't, sir," the sick man said, "for I have no one
to help me into the pool when the water is stirred up.
While I am trying to get there, someone else always
gets in ahead of me."
8Jesus told him, "Stand up, pick up your sleeping
mat, and walk!"
9Instantly, the man was healed! He rolled up the
mat and began walking! But this miracle happened
on the Sabbath day. 10So the Jewish leaders objected.
They said to the man who was cured, "You can't
work on the Sabbath! It's illegal to carry that sleeping mat!"
11He replied, "The man who healed me said to me,
'Pick up your sleeping mat and walk.'"
12"Who said such a thing as that?" they demanded.
13The man didn't know, for Jesus had disappeared
into the crowd. 14But afterward Jesus found him in
the Temple and told him, "Now you are well; so stop
sinning, or something even worse may happen to
you." 15Then the man went to find the Jewish leaders
and told them it was Jesus who had healed him.
16So the Jewish leaders began harassing Jesus for
breaking the Sabbath rules. 17But Jesus replied, "My
Father never stops working, so why should I?" 18So
the Jewish leaders tried all the more to kill him. In
addition to disobeying the Sabbath rules, he had

**TRAPPED ● • • • •**

5:6 **Jesus appropriately asked, "Would you like to get well?" After 38 years, this man's problem had become a way of life. No one had ever helped him. He had no hope of ever being healed and no desire to help himself. No matter how trapped you feel in your infirmities, God can minister to your deepest needs. Don't let a problem or hardship cause you to lose hope. God may have special work for you to do in spite of your condition, or even because of it. Many have ministered effectively to hurting people because they have triumphed, with God's help, over their own hurts.**

5:2 Some manuscripts read *Beth-zatha;* other manuscripts read *Bethsaida.* 5:3 Some manuscripts add *waiting for a certain movement of the water,* 4*for an angel of the Lord came from time to time and stirred up the water. And the first person to step down into it afterward was healed.*

## CHOICES ● ● • • •

5:19-23 **Because of his unity with God, Jesus lived as God wanted him to live. Because of our identification with Jesus, we must live as he wants us to live. The questions "What would Jesus do?" and "What would Jesus have me do?" can help us make the right choices.**

spoken of God as his Father, thereby making himself equal with God.

[19]Jesus replied, "I assure you, the Son can do nothing by himself. He does only what he sees the Father doing. Whatever the Father does, the Son also does. [20]For the Father loves the Son and tells him everything he is doing, and the Son will do far greater things than healing this man. You will be astonished at what he does. [21]He will even raise from the dead anyone he wants to, just as the Father does. [22]And the Father leaves all judgment to his Son, [23]so that everyone will honor the Son, just as they honor the Father. But if you refuse to honor the Son, then you are certainly not honoring the Father who sent him.

[24]"I assure you, those who listen to my message and believe in God who sent me have eternal life. They will never be condemned for their sins, but they have already passed from death into life.

[25]"And I assure you that the time is coming, in fact it is here, when the dead will hear my voice—the voice of the Son of God. And those who listen will live. [26]The Father has life in himself, and he has granted his Son to have life in himself. [27]And he has given him authority to judge all mankind because he is the Son of Man. [28]Don't be so surprised! Indeed, the time is coming when all the dead in their graves will hear the voice of God's Son, [29]and they will rise again. Those who have done good will rise to eternal life, and those who have continued in evil will rise to judgment. [30]But I do nothing without consulting the Father. I judge as I am told. And my judgment is absolutely just, because it is according to the will of God who sent me; it is not merely my own.

[31]"If I were to testify on my own behalf, my testimony would not be valid. [32]But someone else is also testifying about me, and I can assure you that everything he says about me is true. [33]In fact, you sent messengers to listen to John the Baptist, and he preached the truth. [34]But the best testimony about me is not from a man, though I have reminded you about John's testimony so you might be saved. [35]John shone brightly for a while, and you benefited and rejoiced. [36]But I have a greater witness than John—my teachings and my miracles. They have been assigned to me by the Father, and they testify that the Father has sent me. [37]And the Father himself has also testified about me. You have never heard his voice or seen him face to face, [38]and you do not have his message in your hearts, because you do not believe me—the one he sent to you.

[39]"You search the Scriptures because you believe they give you eternal life. But the Scriptures point to me! [40]Yet you refuse to come to me so that I can give you this eternal life.

[41]"Your approval or disapproval means nothing to me, [42]because I know you don't have God's love within you. [43]For I have come to you representing my Father, and you refuse to welcome me, even though you readily accept others who represent only themselves. [44]No wonder you can't believe! For you gladly honor each other, but you don't care about the honor that comes from God alone.

[45]"Yet it is not I who will accuse you of this before the Father. Moses will accuse you! Yes, Moses, on whom you set your hopes. [46]But if you had believed Moses, you would have believed me because he wrote about me. [47]And since you don't believe what he wrote, how will you believe what I say?"

CHAPTER **6** **JESUS FEEDS 5,000 PEOPLE.** After this, Jesus crossed over the Sea of Galilee, also known as the Sea of Tiberias. [2]And a huge crowd kept following him wherever he went, because they saw his miracles as he healed the sick. [3]Then Jesus went up into the hills and sat down with his disciples around him. [4](It was nearly time for the annual Passover celebration.) [5]Jesus soon saw a great crowd of people climbing the hill, looking for him. Turning to Philip, he asked, "Philip, where can we buy bread to feed all these people?" [6]He was testing Philip, for he already knew what he was going to do.

[7]Philip replied, "It would take a small fortune* to feed them!"

[8]Then Andrew, Simon Peter's brother, spoke up. [9]"There's a young boy here with five barley loaves and two fish. But what good is that with this huge crowd?"

## RESOURCES ● ● • • •

6:8-9 **The disciples are contrasted with the youngster who brought what he had. They certainly had more resources than he did, but they knew they didn't have enough, so they didn't give anything at all. The youngster gave what little he had and it made all the difference. If we offer nothing to God, he will have nothing to use. But he can take what little we have and turn it into something great.**

[10]"Tell everyone to sit down," Jesus ordered. So all of them—the men alone numbered five thousand—sat down on the grassy slopes. [11]Then Jesus took the loaves, gave thanks to God, and passed them out to the people. Afterward he did the same with the fish. And they all ate until they were full. [12]"Now gather the leftovers," Jesus told his disciples, "so that nothing is wasted." [13]There were only five barley loaves to start with, but twelve baskets were filled with the pieces of bread the people did not eat!

[14]When the people saw this miraculous sign, they exclaimed, "Surely, he is the Prophet* we have been expecting!" [15]Jesus saw that they were ready to take him by force and make him king, so he went higher into the hills alone.

[16]That evening his disciples went down to the

6:7 Greek *200 denarii*. A denarius was the equivalent of a full day's wage. 6:14 See Deut 18:15, 18.

shore to wait for him. 17But as darkness fell and Jesus still hadn't come back, they got into the boat and headed out across the lake toward Capernaum. 18Soon a gale swept down upon them as they rowed, and the sea grew very rough. 19They were three or four miles* out when suddenly they saw Jesus walking on the water toward the boat. They were terrified, 20but he called out to them, "I am here! Don't be afraid." 21Then they were eager to let him in, and immediately the boat arrived at their destination!

22The next morning, back across the lake, crowds began gathering on the shore, waiting to see Jesus. For they knew that he and his disciples had come over together and that the disciples had gone off in their boat, leaving him behind. 23Several boats from Tiberias landed near the place where the Lord had blessed the bread and the people had eaten. 24When the crowd saw that Jesus wasn't there, nor his disciples, they got into the boats and went across to Capernaum to look for him. 25When they arrived and found him, they asked, "Teacher, how did you get here?"

26Jesus replied, "The truth is, you want to be with me because I fed you, not because you saw the miraculous sign. 27But you shouldn't be so concerned about perishable things like food. Spend your energy seeking the eternal life that I, the Son of Man, can give you. For God the Father has sent me for that very purpose."

28They replied, "What does God want us to do?"

29Jesus told them, "This is what God wants you to do: Believe in the one he has sent."

30They replied, "You must show us a miraculous sign if you want us to believe in you. What will you do for us? 31After all, our ancestors ate manna while they journeyed through the wilderness! As the Scriptures say, 'Moses gave them bread from heaven to eat.'*"

32Jesus said, "I assure you, Moses didn't give them bread from heaven. My Father did. And now he offers you the true bread from heaven. 33The true bread of God is the one who comes down from heaven and gives life to the world."

34"Sir," they said, "give us that bread every day of our lives."

35Jesus replied, "I am the bread of life. No one who comes to me will ever be hungry again. Those who believe in me will never thirst. 36But you haven't believed in me even though you have seen me. 37However, those the Father has given me will come to me, and I will never reject them. 38For I have come down from heaven to do the will of God who sent me, not to do what I want. 39And this is the will of God, that I should not lose even one of all those he has given me, but that I should raise them to eternal life at the last day. 40For it is my Father's will that all who see his Son and believe in him should have eternal life—that I should raise them at the last day."

41Then the people* began to murmur in disagreement because he had said, "I am the bread from heaven." 42They said, "This is Jesus, the son of Joseph. We know his father and mother. How can he say, 'I came down from heaven'?"

43But Jesus replied, "Don't complain about what I said. 44For people can't come to me unless the Father who sent me draws them to me, and at the last day I will raise them from the dead. 45As it is written in the Scriptures, 'They will all be taught by God.'* Everyone who hears and learns from the Father comes to me. 46(Not that anyone has ever seen the Father; only I, who was sent from God, have seen him.)

47"I assure you, anyone who believes in me already has eternal life. 48Yes, I am the bread of life! 49Your ancestors ate manna in the wilderness, but they all died. 50However, the bread from heaven gives eternal life to everyone who eats it. 51I am the living bread that came down out of heaven. Anyone who eats this bread will live forever; this bread is my flesh, offered so the world may live."

## THE WAY ● ● ● • •

6:26 **Jesus criticized the people who followed him only for the physical and temporal benefits, not because they were spiritually hungry. We should follow Christ because we need the truth. Many people use religion to gain prestige, comfort, friends, or votes. But those are self-centered motives. True believers follow Jesus simply because they know his way is the way to live.**

52Then the people began arguing with each other about what he meant. "How can this man give us his flesh to eat?" they asked.

53So Jesus said again, "I assure you, unless you eat the flesh of the Son of Man and drink his blood, you cannot have eternal life within you. 54But those who eat my flesh and drink my blood have eternal life, and I will raise them at the last day. 55For my flesh is the true food, and my blood is the true drink. 56All who eat my flesh and drink my blood remain in me, and I in them. 57I live by the power of the living Father who sent me; in the same way, those who partake of me will live because of me. 58I am the true bread from heaven. Anyone who eats this bread will live forever and not die as your ancestors did, even though they ate the manna."

59He said these things while he was teaching in the synagogue in Capernaum.

60Even his disciples said, "This is very hard to understand. How can anyone accept it?"

61Jesus knew within himself that his disciples were complaining, so he said to them, "Does this offend

## THE SOURCE ● ● ● • •

6:67-68 **After many of Jesus' followers had deserted him, he asked the 12 disciples if they were also going to leave. Peter responded, "To whom will we go?" In his straightforward way, Peter answered for all of us—there is no other way. Jesus alone gives life. People look everywhere for eternal life and miss Christ, the only source. Stay with him, especially when you are confused or feel alone.**

6:19 Greek *25 or 30 stadia* [4.6 or 5.5 kilometers]. 6:31 Exod 16:4; Ps 78:24. 6:41 Greek *Jewish people;* also in 6:52. 6:45 Isa 54:13.

you? 62Then what will you think if you see me, the Son of Man, return to heaven again? 63It is the Spirit who gives eternal life. Human effort accomplishes nothing. And the very words I have spoken to you are spirit and life. 64But some of you don't believe me." (For Jesus knew from the beginning who didn't believe, and he knew who would betray him.) 65Then he said, "That is what I meant when I said that people can't come to me unless the Father brings them to me."

66At this point many of his disciples turned away and deserted him. 67Then Jesus turned to the Twelve and asked, "Are you going to leave, too?"

68Simon Peter replied, "Lord, to whom would we go? You alone have the words that give eternal life. 69We believe them, and we know you are the Holy One of God."

70Then Jesus said, "I chose the twelve of you, but one is a devil." 71He was speaking of Judas, son of Simon Iscariot, one of the Twelve, who would betray him.

## CHAPTER 7

**JESUS' BROTHERS MAKE FUN OF HIM.** After this, Jesus stayed in Galilee, going from village to village. He wanted to stay out of Judea where the Jewish leaders were plotting his death. 2But soon it was time for the Festival of Shelters, 3and Jesus' brothers urged him to go to Judea for the celebration. "Go where your followers can see your miracles!" they scoffed. 4"You can't become a public figure if you hide like this! If you can do such wonderful things, prove it to the world!" 5For even his brothers didn't believe in him.

6Jesus replied, "Now is not the right time for me to go. But you can go anytime, and it will make no difference. 7The world can't hate you, but it does hate me because I accuse it of sin and evil. 8You go on. I am not yet* ready to go to this festival, because my time has not yet come." 9So Jesus remained in Galilee.

### TEST ● ● ● ● ●

7:16-18 **Have you ever listened to religious speakers and wondered if they were telling the truth? Test them—(1) ask if their words agree with or contradict the Bible; and (2) ask if their words point to Christ or to themselves.**

10But after his brothers had left for the festival, Jesus also went, though secretly, staying out of public view. 11The Jewish leaders tried to find him at the festival and kept asking if anyone had seen him. 12There was a lot of discussion about him among the crowds. Some said, "He's a wonderful man," while others said, "He's nothing but a fraud, deceiving the people." 13But no one had the courage to speak favorably about him in public, for they were afraid of getting in trouble with the Jewish leaders.

14Then, midway through the festival, Jesus went up to the Temple and began to teach. 15The Jewish leaders were surprised when they heard him. "How

### DON'T JUMP ● ● ● ● ●

7:40-43 **The crowd was asking questions about Jesus. As a result, some believed, others were hostile, and others disqualified Jesus as the Messiah because he was from Nazareth, not Bethlehem (Micah 5:2). But he *was* born in Bethlehem (Luke 2:1-7), although he grew up in Nazareth. If they had looked more carefully, they would not have jumped to the wrong conclusions. When you search for God's truth, make sure you look carefully and thoughtfully at the Bible with an open heart and mind. Don't jump to conclusions before knowing more of what the Bible says.**

does he know so much when he hasn't studied everything we've studied?" they asked.

16So Jesus told them, "I'm not teaching my own ideas, but those of God who sent me. 17Anyone who wants to do the will of God will know whether my teaching is from God or is merely my own. 18Those who present their own ideas are looking for praise for themselves, but those who seek to honor the one who sent them are good and genuine. 19None of you obeys the law of Moses! In fact, you are trying to kill me."

20The crowd replied, "You're demon possessed! Who's trying to kill you?"

21Jesus replied, "I worked on the Sabbath by healing a man, and you were offended. 22But you work on the Sabbath, too, when you obey Moses' law of circumcision. (Actually, this tradition of circumcision is older than the law of Moses; it goes back to Abraham.) 23For if the correct time for circumcising your son falls on the Sabbath, you go ahead and do it, so as not to break the law of Moses. So why should I be condemned for making a man completely well on the Sabbath? 24Think this through and you will see that I am right."

25Some of the people who lived there in Jerusalem said among themselves, "Isn't this the man they are trying to kill? 26But here he is, speaking in public, and they say nothing to him. Can it be that our leaders know that he really is the Messiah? 27But how could he be? For we know where this man comes from. When the Messiah comes, he will simply appear; no one will know where he comes from."

28While Jesus was teaching in the Temple, he called out, "Yes, you know me, and you know where I come from. But I represent one you don't know, and he is true. 29I know him because I have come from him, and he sent me to you." 30Then the leaders tried to arrest him; but no one laid a hand on him, because his time had not yet come.

31Many among the crowds at the Temple believed in him. "After all," they said, "would you expect the Messiah to do more miraculous signs than this man has done?"

32When the Pharisees heard that the crowds were murmuring such things, they and the leading priests sent Temple guards to arrest Jesus. 33But Jesus told them, "I will be here a little longer. Then I will return to the one who sent me. 34You will search for me but not find me. And you won't be able to come where I am."

7:8 Some manuscripts omit *yet*.

35The Jewish leaders were puzzled by this statement. "Where is he planning to go?" they asked.
"Maybe he is thinking of leaving the country and
going to the Jews in other lands, or maybe even to
the Gentiles! 36What does he mean when he says,
'You will search for me but not find me,' and 'You
won't be able to come where I am'?"

37On the last day, the climax of the festival, Jesus
stood and shouted to the crowds, "If you are thirsty,
come to me! 38If you believe in me, come and drink!
For the Scriptures declare that rivers of living water
will flow out from within."* 39(When he said "living
water," he was speaking of the Spirit, who would be
given to everyone believing in him. But the Spirit
had not yet been given, because Jesus had not yet
entered into his glory.)

40When the crowds heard him say this, some of
them declared, "This man surely is the Prophet."*
41Others said, "He is the Messiah." Still others said,
"But he can't be! Will the Messiah come from Galilee? 42For the Scriptures clearly state that the Messiah
will be born of the royal line of David, in Bethlehem,
the village where King David was born."* 43So the
crowd was divided in their opinion about him. 44And
some wanted him arrested, but no one touched him.

45The Temple guards who had been sent to arrest
him returned to the leading priests and Pharisees.
"Why didn't you bring him in?" they demanded.

46"We have never heard anyone talk like this!" the
guards responded.

47"Have you been led astray, too?" the Pharisees
mocked. 48"Is there a single one of us rulers or
Pharisees who believes in him? 49These ignorant
crowds do, but what do they know about it? A curse
on them anyway!"

50Nicodemus, the leader who had met with Jesus
earlier, then spoke up. 51"Is it legal to convict a man
before he is given a hearing?" he asked.

52They replied, "Are you from Galilee, too? Search
the Scriptures and see for yourself—no prophet ever
comes from Galilee!"

[*The most ancient Greek manuscripts do not include John 7:53–8:11.*]

53Then the meeting broke up and everybody went
home.

## CHAPTER 8 **JESUS FORGIVES A GUILTY WOMAN.** Jesus
returned to the Mount of Olives, 2but early the next
morning he was back again at the Temple. A crowd
soon gathered, and he sat down and taught them.
3As he was speaking, the teachers of religious law and
Pharisees brought a woman they had caught in the
act of adultery. They put her in front of the crowd.

4"Teacher," they said to Jesus, "this woman was
caught in the very act of adultery. 5The law of Moses
says to stone her. What do you say?"

6They were trying to trap him into saying something they could use against him, but Jesus stooped
down and wrote in the dust with his finger. 7They
kept demanding an answer, so he stood up again
and said, "All right, stone her. But let those who have
never sinned throw the first stones!" 8Then he
stooped down again and wrote in the dust.

9When the accusers heard this, they slipped away
one by one, beginning with the oldest, until only
Jesus was left in the middle of the crowd with the
woman. 10Then Jesus stood up again and said to her,
"Where are your accusers? Didn't even one of them
condemn you?"

11"No, Lord," she said.

And Jesus said, "Neither do I. Go and sin no
more."

12Jesus said to the people, "I am the light of the
world. If you follow me, you won't be stumbling
through the darkness, because you will have the light
that leads to life."

### STONED ● ● • • •

**8:9 When Jesus said that only those who had not sinned should throw the first stone, the leaders slipped away, the eldest to the youngest. Evidently the older men were more aware of their sins than the younger. Age and experience temper youthful idealism and self-righteousness. Whatever your age, take an honest look at your life, recognize your sinful nature, and spend more time looking for ways to help others rather than hurt them.**

13The Pharisees replied, "You are making false
claims about yourself!"

14Jesus told them, "These claims are valid even
though I make them about myself. For I know where
I came from and where I am going, but you don't
know this about me. 15You judge me with all your
human limitations,* but I am not judging anyone.
16And if I did, my judgment would be correct in every
respect because I am not alone—I have with me the
Father who sent me. 17Your own law says that if two
people agree about something, their witness is accepted as fact.* 18I am one witness, and my Father
who sent me is the other."

19"Where is your father?" they asked.

Jesus answered, "Since you don't know who I am,
you don't know who my Father is. If you knew me,
then you would know my Father, too." 20Jesus made
these statements while he was teaching in the section
of the Temple known as the Treasury. But he was not
arrested, because his time had not yet come.

21Later Jesus said to them again, "I am going away.
You will search for me and die in your sin. You
cannot come where I am going."

22The Jewish leaders asked, "Is he planning to
commit suicide? What does he mean, 'You cannot
come where I am going'?"

23Then he said to them, "You are from below; I am
from above. You are of this world; I am not. 24That is
why I said that you will die in your sins; for unless
you believe that I am who I say I am, you will die in
your sins."

7:37-38 Or *"Let anyone who is thirsty come to me and drink. 38For the Scriptures declare that rivers of living water will flow from the heart of those who believe in me."* 7:40 See Deut 18:15, 18. 7:42 See Mic 5:2. 8:15 Or *judge me by human standards.* 8:17 See Deut 19:15.

## FREE ● ● • • •

**8:34-35 Sin has a way of enslaving us, controlling us, dominating us, and dictating our actions. Jesus can free you from this slavery that keeps you from becoming the person that God created you to be. If sin is restraining, mastering, or enslaving you, Jesus can break its power over your life.**

25 "Tell us who you are," they demanded.

Jesus replied, "I am the one I have always claimed to be.* 26 I have much to say about you and much to condemn, but I won't. For I say only what I have heard from the one who sent me, and he is true." 27 But they still didn't understand that he was talking to them about his Father.

28 So Jesus said, "When you have lifted up the Son of Man on the cross, then you will realize that I am he and that I do nothing on my own, but I speak what the Father taught me. 29 And the one who sent me is with me—he has not deserted me. For I always do those things that are pleasing to him." 30 Then many who heard him say these things believed in him.

31 Jesus said to the people* who believed in him, "You are truly my disciples if you keep obeying my teachings. 32 And you will know the truth, and the truth will set you free."

33 "But we are descendants of Abraham," they said. "We have never been slaves to anyone on earth. What do you mean, 'set free'?"

34 Jesus replied, "I assure you that everyone who sins is a slave of sin. 35 A slave is not a permanent member of the family, but a son is part of the family forever. 36 So if the Son sets you free, you will indeed be free. 37 Yes, I realize that you are descendants of Abraham. And yet some of you are trying to kill me because my message does not find a place in your hearts. 38 I am telling you what I saw when I was with my Father. But you are following the advice of your father."

39 "Our father is Abraham," they declared.

"No," Jesus replied, "for if you were children of Abraham, you would follow his good example.* 40 I told you the truth I heard from God, but you are trying to kill me. Abraham wouldn't do a thing like that. 41 No, you are obeying your real father when you act that way."

They replied, "We were not born out of wedlock! Our true Father is God himself."

42 Jesus told them, "If God were your Father, you would love me, because I have come to you from God. I am not here on my own, but he sent me. 43 Why can't you understand what I am saying? It is because you are unable to do so! 44 For you are the children of your father the Devil, and you love to do the evil things he does. He was a murderer from the beginning and has always hated the truth. There is no truth in him. When he lies, it is consistent with his character; for he is a liar and the father of lies. 45 So when I tell the truth, you just naturally don't believe me! 46 Which of you can truthfully accuse me of sin? And since I am telling you the truth, why don't you believe me? 47 Anyone whose Father is God listens gladly to the words of God. Since you don't, it proves you aren't God's children."

48 The people retorted, "You Samaritan devil! Didn't we say all along that you were possessed by a demon?"

49 "No," Jesus said, "I have no demon in me. For I honor my Father—and you dishonor me. 50 And though I have no wish to glorify myself, God wants to glorify me. Let him be the judge. 51 I assure you, anyone who obeys my teaching will never die!"

52 The people said, "Now we know you are possessed by a demon. Even Abraham and the prophets died, but you say that those who obey your teaching will never die! 53 Are you greater than our father Abraham, who died? Are you greater than the prophets, who died? Who do you think you are?"

54 Jesus answered, "If I am merely boasting about myself, it doesn't count. But it is my Father who says these glorious things about me. You say, 'He is our God,' 55 but you do not even know him. I know him. If I said otherwise, I would be as great a liar as you! But it is true—I know him and obey him. 56 Your ancestor Abraham rejoiced as he looked forward to my coming. He saw it and was glad."

57 The people said, "You aren't even fifty years old. How can you say you have seen Abraham?*"

58 Jesus answered, "The truth is, I existed before Abraham was even born!"* 59 At that point they picked up stones to kill him. But Jesus hid himself from them and left the Temple.

## CHAPTER 9 JESUS HEALS A BLIND MAN.

As Jesus was walking along, he saw a man who had been blind from birth. 2 "Teacher," his disciples asked him, "why was this man born blind? Was it a result of his own sins or those of his parents?"

3 "It was not because of his sins or his parents' sins," Jesus answered. "He was born blind so the power of God could be seen in him. 4 All of us must quickly carry out the tasks assigned us by the one who sent me, because there is little time left before

## WHAT'S HAPPENING? ● ● • • •

**9:2-3 A common belief in Jewish culture was that calamity or suffering was the result of some great sin. But Christ used this man's suffering to teach about faith and to glorify God. We live in a sinful world where good behavior is not always rewarded and bad behavior is not always punished. Therefore, innocent people sometimes suffer. If God took suffering away whenever we asked, we would follow him for comfort and convenience, not out of love and devotion. Regardless of the reasons for our suffering, Jesus has the power to help us deal with it. When you suffer from a disease, tragedy, or handicap, try not to ask, "Why did this happen to me?" or "What did I do wrong?" Instead, ask God to give you strength through the trial and offer you a deeper perspective on what is happening.**

8:25 Or *"Why do I speak to you at all?"* 8:31 Greek *Jewish people;* also in 8:48, 52, 57. 8:39 Some manuscripts read *if you are children of Abraham, follow his example.* 8:57 Some manuscripts read *How can you say Abraham has seen you?* 8:58 Or *"Truly, truly, before Abraham was, I am."*

the night falls and all work comes to an end. [5]But while I am still here in the world, I am the light of the world."

[6]Then he spit on the ground, made mud with the saliva, and smoothed the mud over the blind man's eyes. [7]He told him, "Go and wash in the pool of Siloam" (Siloam means Sent). So the man went and washed, and came back seeing!

[8]His neighbors and others who knew him as a blind beggar asked each other, "Is this the same man—that beggar?" [9]Some said he was, and others said, "No, but he surely looks like him!"

And the beggar kept saying, "I am the same man!"

[10]They asked, "Who healed you? What happened?"

[11]He told them, "The man they call Jesus made mud and smoothed it over my eyes and told me, 'Go to the pool of Siloam and wash off the mud.' I went and washed, and now I can see!"

[12]"Where is he now?" they asked.

"I don't know," he replied.

[13]Then they took the man to the Pharisees. [14]Now as it happened, Jesus had healed the man on a Sabbath. [15]The Pharisees asked the man all about it. So he told them, "He smoothed the mud over my eyes, and when it was washed away, I could see!"

[16]Some of the Pharisees said, "This man Jesus is not from God, for he is working on the Sabbath." Others said, "But how could an ordinary sinner do such miraculous signs?" So there was a deep division of opinion among them.

[17]Then the Pharisees once again questioned the man who had been blind and demanded, "This man who opened your eyes—who do you say he is?"

The man replied, "I think he must be a prophet."

[18]The Jewish leaders wouldn't believe he had been blind, so they called in his parents. [19]They asked them, "Is this your son? Was he born blind? If so, how can he see?"

[20]His parents replied, "We know this is our son and that he was born blind, [21]but we don't know how he can see or who healed him. He is old enough to speak for himself. Ask him." [22]They said this because they were afraid of the Jewish leaders, who had announced that anyone saying Jesus was the Messiah would be expelled from the synagogue. [23]That's why they said, "He is old enough to speak for himself. Ask him."

[24]So for the second time they called in the man who had been blind and told him, "Give glory to God by telling the truth,* because we know Jesus is a sinner."

[25]"I don't know whether he is a sinner," the man replied. "But I know this: I was blind, and now I can see!"

[26]"But what did he do?" they asked. "How did he heal you?"

[27]"Look!" the man exclaimed. "I told you once. Didn't you listen? Why do you want to hear it again? Do you want to become his disciples, too?"

## NEW FAITH ● ● ● • •

9:28, 34 **The man's new faith was severely tested by some of the authorities. He was cursed and evicted from the Temple. You also may expect persecution when you follow Jesus. You may lose friends; you may even lose your life. But no one can ever take away the eternal life you have been given by Jesus.**

[28]Then they cursed him and said, "You are his disciple, but we are disciples of Moses. [29]We know God spoke to Moses, but as for this man, we don't know anything about him."

[30]"Why, that's very strange!" the man replied. "He healed my eyes, and yet you don't know anything about him! [31]Well, God doesn't listen to sinners, but he is ready to hear those who worship him and do his will. [32]Never since the world began has anyone been able to open the eyes of someone born blind. [33]If this man were not from God, he couldn't do it."

[34]"You were born in sin!" they answered. "Are you trying to teach us?" And they threw him out of the synagogue.

[35]When Jesus heard what had happened, he found the man and said, "Do you believe in the Son of Man*?"

[36]The man answered, "Who is he, sir, because I would like to."

[37]"You have seen him," Jesus said, "and he is speaking to you!"

[38]"Yes, Lord," the man said, "I believe!" And he worshiped Jesus.

[39]Then Jesus told him, "I have come to judge the world. I have come to give sight to the blind and to show those who think they see that they are blind."

[40]The Pharisees who were standing there heard him and asked, "Are you saying we are blind?"

[41]"If you were blind, you wouldn't be guilty," Jesus replied. "But you remain guilty because you claim you can see.

CHAPTER **10** **JESUS: THE GOOD SHEPHERD.** "I assure you, anyone who sneaks over the wall of a sheepfold, rather than going through the gate, must surely be a thief and a robber! [2]For a shepherd enters through the gate. [3]The gatekeeper opens the gate for him, and the sheep hear his voice and come to him. He calls his own sheep by name and leads them out. [4]After he has gathered his own flock, he walks ahead of them, and they follow him because they recognize his voice. [5]They won't follow a stranger; they will run from him because they don't recognize his voice."

[6]Those who heard Jesus use this illustration didn't understand what he meant, [7]so he explained it to them. "I assure you, I am the gate for the sheep," he said. [8]"All others who came before me were thieves and robbers. But the true sheep did not listen to them. [9]Yes, I am the gate. Those who come in through me will be saved. Wherever they go, they will find green pastures. [10]The thief's purpose is to

9:24 Or *Give glory to God, not to Jesus;* Greek reads *Give glory to God.* 9:35 Some manuscripts read *the Son of God.*

steal and kill and destroy. My purpose is to give life in all its fullness.

11"I am the good shepherd. The good shepherd lays down his life for the sheep. 12A hired hand will run when he sees a wolf coming. He will leave the sheep because they aren't his and he isn't their shepherd. And so the wolf attacks them and scatters the flock. 13The hired hand runs away because he is merely hired and has no real concern for the sheep.

14"I am the good shepherd; I know my own sheep, and they know me, 15just as my Father knows me and I know the Father. And I lay down my life for the sheep. 16I have other sheep, too, that are not in this sheepfold. I must bring them also, and they will listen to my voice; and there will be one flock with one shepherd.

17"The Father loves me because I lay down my life that I may have it back again. 18No one can take my life from me. I lay down my life voluntarily. For I have the right to lay it down when I want to and also the power to take it again. For my Father has given me this command."

19When he said these things, the people* were again divided in their opinions about him. 20Some of them said, "He has a demon, or he's crazy. Why listen to a man like that?" 21Others said, "This doesn't sound like a man possessed by a demon! Can a demon open the eyes of the blind?"

22It was now winter, and Jesus was in Jerusalem at the time of Hanukkah.* 23He was at the Temple, walking through the section known as Solomon's Colonnade. 24The Jewish leaders surrounded him and asked, "How long are you going to keep us in suspense? If you are the Messiah, tell us plainly."

**BLIND ● ● • • •**

**10:24 These leaders were waiting for the signs and answers *they* thought would convince them of Jesus' identity. Thus they couldn't hear the truth Jesus was giving them. Jesus tried to correct their mistaken ideas, but they clung to the wrong idea of what kind of Messiah God would send. Such blindness still keeps people away from Jesus. They want him on their own terms; they do not want him if it means changing their whole life.**

25Jesus replied, "I have already told you, and you don't believe me. The proof is what I do in the name of my Father. 26But you don't believe me because you are not part of my flock. 27My sheep recognize my voice; I know them, and they follow me. 28I give them eternal life, and they will never perish. No one will snatch them away from me, 29for my Father has given them to me, and he is more powerful than anyone else. So no one can take them from me. 30The Father and I are one."

31Once again the Jewish leaders picked up stones to kill him. 32Jesus said, "At my Father's direction I have done many things to help the people. For which one of these good deeds are you killing me?"

33They replied, "Not for any good work, but for blasphemy, because you, a mere man, have made yourself God."

34Jesus replied, "It is written in your own law that God said to certain leaders of the people, 'I say, you are gods!'* 35And you know that the Scriptures cannot be altered. So if those people, who received God's message, were called 'gods,' 36why do you call it blasphemy when the Holy One who was sent into the world by the Father says, 'I am the Son of God'? 37Don't believe me unless I carry out my Father's work. 38But if I do his work, believe in what I have done, even if you don't believe me. Then you will realize that the Father is in me, and I am in the Father."

39Once again they tried to arrest him, but he got away and left them. 40He went beyond the Jordan River to stay near the place where John was first baptizing. 41And many followed him. "John didn't do miracles," they remarked to one another, "but all his predictions about this man have come true." 42And many believed in him there.

## CHAPTER 11 JESUS BRINGS LAZARUS TO LIFE.

A man named Lazarus was sick. He lived in Bethany with his sisters, Mary and Martha. 2This is the Mary who poured the expensive perfume on the Lord's feet and wiped them with her hair.* Her brother, Lazarus, was sick. 3So the two sisters sent a message to Jesus telling him, "Lord, the one you love is very sick."

4But when Jesus heard about it he said, "Lazarus's sickness will not end in death. No, it is for the glory of God. I, the Son of God, will receive glory from this." 5Although Jesus loved Martha, Mary, and Lazarus, 6he stayed where he was for the next two days and did not go to them. 7Finally after two days, he said to his disciples, "Let's go to Judea again."

8But his disciples objected. "Teacher," they said, "only a few days ago the Jewish leaders in Judea were trying to kill you. Are you going there again?"

9Jesus replied, "There are twelve hours of daylight every day. As long as it is light, people can walk safely. They can see because they have the light of this world. 10Only at night is there danger of stumbling because there is no light." 11Then he said, "Our friend Lazarus has fallen asleep, but now I will go and wake him up."

12The disciples said, "Lord, if he is sleeping, that means he is getting better!" 13They thought Jesus meant Lazarus was having a good night's rest, but Jesus meant Lazarus had died.

14Then he told them plainly, "Lazarus is dead.

**TIMING ● ● • • •**

**11:5-7 Jesus loved this family and often stayed with them. He knew their pain but did not respond immediately. His delay had a specific purpose. God's timing, especially his delays, may make us think he is not answering or is not answering the way we want. But he will meet all our needs according to his perfect schedule and purpose. Patiently await his timing.**

10:19 Greek *Jewish people.* 10:22 Or *the Festival of Dedication.* 10:34 Ps 82:6. 11:2 This incident is recorded in chapter 12.

15And for your sake, I am glad I wasn't there, because
this will give you another opportunity to believe in
me. Come, let's go see him."
16Thomas, nicknamed the Twin,* said to his fellow disciples, "Let's go, too—and die with Jesus."
17When Jesus arrived at Bethany, he was told that
Lazarus had already been in his grave for four days.
18Bethany was only a few miles* down the road from
Jerusalem, 19and many of the people* had come to pay
their respects and console Martha and Mary on their
loss. 20When Martha got word that Jesus was coming,
she went to meet him. But Mary stayed at home.
21Martha said to Jesus, "Lord, if you had been here, my
brother would not have died. 22But even now I know
that God will give you whatever you ask."
23Jesus told her, "Your
brother will rise again."
24"Yes," Martha said,
"when everyone else rises, on
resurrection day."
25Jesus told her, "I am the
resurrection and the life.*
Those who believe in me,
even though they die like
everyone else, will live again.
26They are given eternal life
for believing in me and will
never perish. Do you believe
this, Martha?"
27"Yes, Lord," she told
him. "I have always believed
you are the Messiah, the Son
of God, the one who has
come into the world from
God." 28Then she left him
and returned to Mary. She
called Mary aside from the
mourners and told her, "The
Teacher is here and wants to
see you." 29So Mary immediately went to him.
30Now Jesus had stayed
outside the village, at the
place where Martha met
him. 31When the people who
were at the house trying to
console Mary saw her leave
so hastily, they assumed she
was going to Lazarus's grave
to weep. So they followed
her there. 32When Mary arrived and saw Jesus, she fell
down at his feet and said,
"Lord, if you had been here,
my brother would not have
died."
33When Jesus saw her
weeping and saw the other
people wailing with her, he
was moved with indignation and was deeply troubled. 34"Where have you put him?" he asked them.
They told him, "Lord, come and see." 35Then
Jesus wept. 36The people who were standing nearby
said, "See how much he loved him." 37But some

## HE CARES ● ● ● • •

11:33-38 **John stresses that we have a God who cares. This contrasts with the Greek concept of God that was popular in his day—a God with no emotions and no messy involvement with humans. Here we see many of Jesus' emotions—compassion, indignation, sorrow, even frustration. Jesus often expressed deep emotion, and we must never be afraid to reveal our true feelings to him. He understands what we feel because he experienced emotions, too. Be honest, and don't try to hide anything from your Savior. He cares.**

## MARY & MARTHA

Hospitality is an art. Making sure a guest is welcomed, warmed, and well fed requires creativity, organization, and teamwork. Mary and Martha's ability to accomplish these makes them the best sister hospitality team in the Bible. Jesus often stayed in their home.

For Mary, hospitality meant giving more attention to the guest himself than to his needs. She was more interested in her guest's words than in the cleanliness of her home or the timeliness of her meals. She let her sister Martha take care of those details. Mary was mainly a "responder." She did little preparation and lots of participation. She needed to learn that action often is appropriate and necessary.

Unlike her sister, Martha worried about details. She wished to please, to serve, to do the right thing—but she often succeeded in making everyone around her feel uncomfortable. Perhaps she was the oldest and felt specially responsible. So she tried too hard to have everything perfect. Mary's lack of cooperation bothered Martha so much that she finally asked Jesus to tell Mary to help. Jesus gently pointed out that Mary was actually doing her part.

Each sister had her own lesson to learn. Mary learned that worship sometimes involves service. Do people in your life know you care about them? Martha learned that obedient service often goes unnoticed. The last time she appears in the Gospels she is again serving a meal to Jesus and the disciples—this time without complaint. When was the last time you gladly served someone without being noticed?

**UPS:**
- Known as hospitable homeowners
- Friends of Jesus, they believed in him with growing faith
- Martha had a strong desire to do everything exactly right
- Mary had a deep concern for people's feelings

**DOWNS:**
- Martha expected others to agree with her priorities and was overly concerned with details
- Martha tended to feel sorry for herself when her efforts were not recognized
- Mary would let others do the work
- Mary tended to respond, not prepare

**STATS:**
- Where: Bethany
- Relative: Brother: Lazarus

LESSONS: Getting caught up in details can make us forget the main reasons for our actions

There is a proper time to listen to Jesus and a proper time to work for him

KEY VERSE: "Martha was worrying over the big dinner she was preparing. She came to Jesus and said, 'Lord, doesn't it seem unfair to you that my sister just sits here while I do all the work? Tell her to come and help me'" (Luke 10:40).

Mary and Martha's story is told in Luke 10:38-42 and John 11:17-45.

11:16 Greek *the one who was called Didymus.* 11:18 Greek *was about 15 stadia* [about 2.8 kilometers]. 11:19 Greek *Jewish people;* also 11:31, 33, 36, 45, 54. 11:25 Some manuscripts do not include *and the life.*

## LOOK BACK ● ● • • •

12:16 **After Jesus' resurrection, the disciples understood many of the prophecies they had missed along the way. Jesus' words and actions took on new meaning and made more sense. In retrospect, they saw how Jesus had led them into a deeper and better understanding of his truth. Stop now and think about the events in your life leading up to where you are now. How has God led you to this point? As you grow older, you will look back and see God's involvement more clearly than you do now. Let this truth encourage you to live a life of faith today.**

said, "This man healed a blind man. Why couldn't he keep Lazarus from dying?"

38And again Jesus was deeply troubled. Then they came to the grave. It was a cave with a stone rolled across its entrance. 39"Roll the stone aside," Jesus told them.

But Martha, the dead man's sister, said, "Lord, by now the smell will be terrible because he has been dead for four days."

40Jesus responded, "Didn't I tell you that you will see God's glory if you believe?" 41So they rolled the stone aside. Then Jesus looked up to heaven and said, "Father, thank you for hearing me. 42You always hear me, but I said it out loud for the sake of all these people standing here, so they will believe you sent me." 43Then Jesus shouted, "Lazarus, come out!" 44And Lazarus came out, bound in graveclothes, his face wrapped in a headcloth. Jesus told them, "Unwrap him and let him go!"

45Many of the people who were with Mary believed in Jesus when they saw this happen. 46But some went to the Pharisees and told them what Jesus had done. 47Then the leading priests and Pharisees called the high council* together to discuss the situation. "What are we going to do?" they asked each other. "This man certainly performs many miraculous signs. 48If we leave him alone, the whole nation will follow him, and then the Roman army will come and destroy both our Temple and our nation."

49And one of them, Caiaphas, who was high priest that year, said, "How can you be so stupid? 50Why should the whole nation be destroyed? Let this one man die for the people."

51This prophecy that Jesus should die for the entire nation came from Caiaphas in his position as high priest. He didn't think of it himself; he was inspired to say it. 52It was a prediction that Jesus' death would be not for Israel only, but for the gathering together of all the children of God scattered around the world.

53So from that time on the Jewish leaders began to plot Jesus' death. 54As a result, Jesus stopped his public ministry among the people and left Jerusalem. He went to a place near the wilderness, to the village of Ephraim, and stayed there with his disciples.

55It was now almost time for the celebration of Passover, and many people from the country arrived in Jerusalem several days early so they could go through the cleansing ceremony before the Passover began. 56They wanted to see Jesus, and as they talked in the Temple, they asked each other, "What do you think? Will he come for the Passover?" 57Meanwhile, the leading priests and Pharisees had publicly announced that anyone seeing Jesus must report him immediately so they could arrest him.

CHAPTER **12** **MARY ANOINTS JESUS' FEET.** Six days before the Passover ceremonies began, Jesus arrived in Bethany, the home of Lazarus—the man he had raised from the dead. 2A dinner was prepared in Jesus' honor. Martha served, and Lazarus sat at the table with him. 3Then Mary took a twelve-ounce jar* of expensive perfume made from essence of nard, and she anointed Jesus' feet with it and wiped his feet with her hair. And the house was filled with fragrance.

4But Judas Iscariot, one of his disciples—the one who would betray him—said, 5"That perfume was worth a small fortune.* It should have been sold and the money given to the poor." 6Not that he cared for the poor—he was a thief who was in charge of the disciples' funds, and he often took some for his own use.

7Jesus replied, "Leave her alone. She did it in preparation for my burial. 8You will always have the poor among you, but I will not be here with you much longer."

9When all the people* heard of Jesus' arrival, they flocked to see him and also to see Lazarus, the man Jesus had raised from the dead. 10Then the leading priests decided to kill Lazarus, too, 11for it was because of him that many of the people had deserted them and believed in Jesus.

12The next day, the news that Jesus was on the way to Jerusalem swept through the city. A huge crowd of Passover visitors 13took palm branches and went down the road to meet him. They shouted,

"Praise God!*
Bless the one who comes in the name of the
Lord!
Hail to the King of Israel!"*

14Jesus found a young donkey and sat on it, fulfilling the prophecy that said:

15"Don't be afraid, people of Israel.*
Look, your King is coming,
sitting on a donkey's colt."*

16His disciples didn't realize at the time that this was a fulfillment of prophecy. But after Jesus entered into

## REACH OUT ● ● • • •

12:37-38 **Jesus had performed many miracles, but most people still didn't believe in him. Likewise, many today won't believe despite all God does. Don't be discouraged if your witness for Christ doesn't turn as many to him as you'd like. Your job is to continue as a faithful witness. You are not responsible for the decisions of others, but simply to reach out to others.**

11:47 Greek *the Sanhedrin.* 12:3 Greek *took 1 litra* [327 grams]. 12:5 Greek *300 denarii.* A denarius was equivalent to a full day's wage. 12:9 Greek *Jewish people;* also in 12:11. 12:13a Greek *Hosanna,* an exclamation of praise that literally means "save now." 12:13b Ps 118:25-26; Zeph 3:15. 12:15a Greek *daughter of Zion.* 12:15b Zech 9:9.

his glory, they remembered that these Scriptures had
come true before their eyes.
[17]Those in the crowd who had seen Jesus call Lazarus back to life were telling others all about it. [18]That
was the main reason so many went out to meet him—
because they had heard about this mighty miracle.
[19]Then the Pharisees said to each other, "We've lost.
Look, the whole world has gone after him!"
[20]Some Greeks who had come to Jerusalem to
attend the Passover [21]paid a visit to Philip, who was
from Bethsaida in Galilee. They said, "Sir, we want to
meet Jesus." [22]Philip told Andrew about it, and they
went together to ask Jesus.
[23]Jesus replied, "The time has come for the Son of
Man to enter into his glory. [24]The truth is, a kernel of
wheat must be planted in the soil. Unless it dies it will
be alone—a single seed. But its death will produce
many new kernels—a plentiful harvest of new lives.
[25]Those who love their life in this world will lose it.
Those who despise their life in this world will keep it
for eternal life. [26]All those who want to be my disciples
must come and follow me, because my servants must
be where I am. And if they follow me, the Father will
honor them. [27]Now my soul is deeply troubled.
Should I pray, 'Father, save me from what lies ahead'?
But that is the very reason why I came! [28]Father, bring
glory to your name."
Then a voice spoke from heaven, saying, "I have
already brought it glory, and I will do it again."
[29]When the crowd heard the voice, some thought it
was thunder, while others declared an angel had
spoken to him.
[30]Then Jesus told them, "The voice was for your
benefit, not mine. [31]The time of judgment for the
world has come, when the prince of this world* will
be cast out. [32]And when I am lifted up on the cross,*
I will draw everyone to myself." [33]He said this to
indicate how he was going to die.
[34]"Die?" asked the crowd. "We understood from
Scripture that the Messiah would live forever. Why
are you saying the Son of Man will die? Who is this
Son of Man you are talking about?"
[35]Jesus replied, "My light will shine out for you
just a little while longer. Walk in it while you can, so
you will not stumble when the darkness falls. If you
walk in the darkness, you cannot see where you are
going. [36]Believe in the light while there is still time;
then you will become children of the light." After
saying these things, Jesus went away and was hidden
from them.
[37]But despite all the miraculous signs he had done,
most of the people did not believe in him. [38]This is
exactly what Isaiah the prophet had predicted:

"Lord, who has believed our message?
To whom will the Lord reveal his saving
power?"*

[39]But the people couldn't believe, for as Isaiah also
said,

**Bad things seem to happen all the time. Does God care about what is happening in the world?**

There are bad things that happen, and then there are tragedies. At some time in life everyone will experience both of these. Let's cover them one at a time.

The person who flunks a math test had something bad happen to him. Did he learn that it is important to keep up with assignments and study before a test? Hopefully.

A 10-year-old boy races out from behind a parked car and is almost hit by a car. He is scared to death, realizing that he could have been killed! Did he learn a lesson about not darting into the street? He better have; he may not get another chance!

In each case the person probably was not happy about what happened. But each situation in life, good or bad, is a learning experience.

Does God care that we learn important lessons about studying and safety? He cares very much!

Ask your folks about the five worst things that have happened to them. Then ask what they learned from these bad experiences. Finally, ask them if they were thankful that these occurred.

Going through tough times is bad only when you don't learn something when it's over.

Now let's discuss tragedy.

Unfortunately, no one is immune from what we believe is the ultimate tragedy—death. Even Jesus went through the loss of someone he loved (see John 11). It is the timing of death (especially when someone dies young), and how it occurs (like an innocent victim killed by a drunk driver), that makes us wonder if God really cares.

When Adam and Eve disobeyed God in the Garden of Eden, their punishment was separation from God. This incident also set in motion the life cycle, ending in death. But the good news is that Jesus Christ's death on the cross killed death—not physical death, but spiritual death—for all those who receive his gift of forgiveness!

The curse brought on the human race by Adam was physical death. Since that time people have discovered ways to make death happen in some pretty ugly ways (nuclear bombs, lung cancer, AIDS, and many others).

Still, as terrible as those may be, God knows that spiritual death is far worse than physical death. That's why he focused his attention on taking care of the real penalty for our sin—spiritual death! (See Romans 6:23.) God also knows how tragedy can point us to him and his purposes: "We know that God causes everything to work together for the good of those who love God and are called according to his purpose for them" (Romans 8:28).

Although God is not in heaven pushing buttons to make people die young, he can use any situation for good. And remember, whatever happens to you, God cares. He loves you and wants to work out his purposes in your life.

12:31 *The prince of this world* is a name for Satan. 12:32 Greek *lifted up from the earth.* 12:38 Isa 53:1.

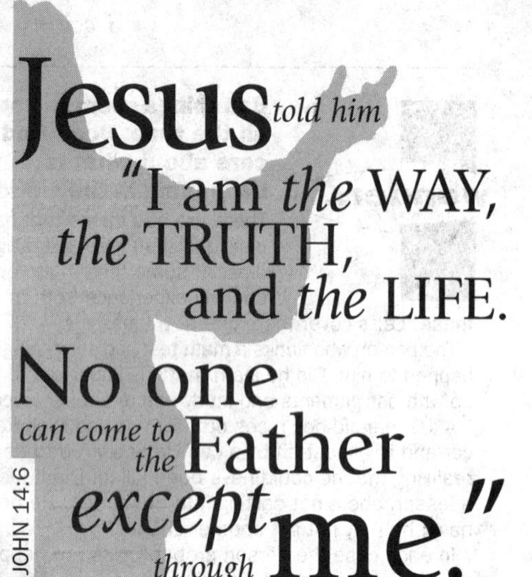
Jesus told him
"I am the WAY,
the TRUTH,
and the LIFE.
No one
can come to the Father
except through me."
JOHN 14:6

40 "The Lord has blinded their eyes
and hardened their hearts—
so their eyes cannot see,
and their hearts cannot understand,
and they cannot turn to me
and let me heal them."*

41 Isaiah was referring to Jesus when he made this prediction, because he was given a vision of the Messiah's glory. 42 Many people, including some of the Jewish leaders, believed in him. But they wouldn't admit it to anyone because of their fear that the Pharisees would expel them from the synagogue. 43 For they loved human praise more than the praise of God.

44 Jesus shouted to the crowds, "If you trust me, you are really trusting God who sent me. 45 For when you see me, you are seeing the one who sent me. 46 I have come as a light to shine in this dark world, so that all who put their trust in me will no longer remain in the darkness. 47 If anyone hears me and doesn't obey me, I am not his judge—for I have come to save the world and not to judge it. 48 But all who reject me and my message will be judged at the day of judgment by the truth I have spoken. 49 I don't speak on my own authority. The Father who sent me gave me his own instructions as to what I should say. 50 And I know his instructions lead to eternal life; so I say whatever the Father tells me to say!"

CHAPTER **13** **JESUS WASHES HIS DISCIPLES' FEET.** Before the Passover celebration, Jesus knew that his hour had come to leave this world and return to his Father. He now showed the disciples the full extent of his love.* 2 It was time for supper, and the Devil had already enticed Judas, son of Simon Iscariot, to carry out his plan to betray Jesus. 3 Jesus knew that the Father had given him authority over everything and that he had come from God and would return to God. 4 So he got up from the table, took off his robe, wrapped a towel around his waist, 5 and poured water into a basin. Then he began to wash the disciples' feet and to wipe them with the towel he had around him.

6 When he came to Simon Peter, Peter said to him, "Lord, why are you going to wash my feet?"

7 Jesus replied, "You don't understand now why I am doing it; someday you will."

8 "No," Peter protested, "you will never wash my feet!"

Jesus replied, "But if I don't wash you, you won't belong to me."

9 Simon Peter exclaimed, "Then wash my hands and head as well, Lord, not just my feet!"

10 Jesus replied, "A person who has bathed all over does not need to wash, except for the feet,* to be entirely clean. And you are clean, but that isn't true of everyone here." 11 For Jesus knew who would betray him. That is what he meant when he said, "Not all of you are clean."

12 After washing their feet, he put on his robe again and sat down and asked, "Do you understand what I was doing? 13 You call me 'Teacher' and 'Lord,' and you are right, because it is true. 14 And since I, the Lord and Teacher, have washed your feet, you ought to wash each other's feet. 15 I have given you an example to follow. Do as I have done to you. 16 How true it is that a servant is not greater than the master. Nor are messengers more important than the one who sends them. 17 You know these things—now do them! That is the path of blessing.

18 "I am not saying these things to all of you; I know so well each one of you I chose. The Scriptures declare, 'The one who shares my food has turned against me,'* and this will soon come true. 19 I tell you this now, so that when it happens you will believe I am the Messiah. 20 Truly, anyone who welcomes my messenger is welcoming me, and anyone who welcomes me is welcoming the Father who sent me."

21 Now Jesus was in great anguish of spirit, and he exclaimed, "The truth is, one of you will betray me!"

22 The disciples looked at each other, wondering whom he could mean. 23 One of Jesus' disciples, the one Jesus loved, was sitting next to Jesus at the table.* 24 Simon Peter motioned to him to ask who would do this terrible thing. 25 Leaning toward Jesus, he asked, "Lord, who is it?"

26 Jesus said, "It is the one to whom I give the bread dipped in the sauce." And when he had dipped it, he gave it to Judas, son of Simon Iscariot. 27 As soon as

## ACTIVE LOVE ● ● • • •

13:35 **Love is not simply warm feelings; instead it is an attitude that reveals itself in action. How can we love others as Christ loves us? By helping when it's not convenient, by giving when it hurts, by devoting energy to others' welfare rather than our own, by absorbing hurts from others without complaining or fighting back. This kind of loving is hard to do. That is why people will notice when you do it and will know you are empowered by a supernatural source. The Bible has another beautiful description of love in 1 Corinthians 13.**

12:40 Isa 6:10. 13:1 Or *He loved his disciples to the very end.* 13:10 Some manuscripts do not include *except for the feet.* 13:18 Ps 41:9. 13:23 Greek *was reclining on Jesus' bosom.* The "disciple whom Jesus loved" was probably John.

Judas had eaten the bread, Satan entered into him. Then Jesus told him, "Hurry. Do it now." [28]None of the others at the table knew what Jesus meant. [29]Since Judas was their treasurer, some thought Jesus was telling him to go and pay for the food or to give some money to the poor. [30]So Judas left at once, going out into the night.

[31]As soon as Judas left the room, Jesus said, "The time has come for me, the Son of Man, to enter into my glory, and God will receive glory because of all that happens to me. [32]And God will bring* me into my glory very soon. [33]Dear children, how brief are these moments before I must go away and leave you! Then, though you search for me, you cannot come to me—just as I told the Jewish leaders. [34]So now I am giving you a new commandment: Love each other. Just as I have loved you, you should love each other. [35]Your love for one another will prove to the world that you are my disciples."

[36]Simon Peter said, "Lord, where are you going?"

And Jesus replied, "You can't go with me now, but you will follow me later."

[37]"But why can't I come now, Lord?" he asked. "I am ready to die for you."

[38]Jesus answered, "Die for me? No, before the rooster crows tomorrow morning, you will deny three times that you even know me.

## CHAPTER 14 JESUS, THE WAY TO THE FATHER.

"Don't be troubled. You trust God, now trust in me. [2]There are many rooms in my Father's home, and I am going to prepare a place for you. If this were not so, I would tell you plainly. [3]When everything is ready, I will come and get you, so that you will always be with me where I am. [4]And you know where I am going and how to get there."

[5]"No, we don't know, Lord," Thomas said. "We haven't any idea where you are going, so how can we know the way?"

[6]Jesus told him, "I am the way, the truth, and the life. No one can come to the Father except through me. [7]If you had known who I am, then you would have known who my Father is.* From now on you know him and have seen him!"

[8]Philip said, "Lord, show us the Father and we will be satisfied."

[9]Jesus replied, "Philip, don't you even yet know who I am, even after all the time I have been with you? Anyone who has seen me has seen the Father! So why are you asking to see him? [10]Don't you believe that I am in the Father and the Father is in me? The words I say are not my own, but my Father who lives in me does his work through me. [11]Just believe that I am in the Father and the Father is in me. Or at least believe because of what you have seen me do.

[12]"The truth is, anyone who believes in me will do the same works I have done, and even greater works, because I am going to be with the Father. [13]You can ask for anything in my name, and I will

**ACCURATE ● ● • • •**

**14:26 Jesus promised the disciples that the Holy Spirit would help them remember what he had been teaching them. This promise underscores the validity of the New Testament. The disciples were eyewitnesses of Jesus' life and teachings, and the Holy Spirit helped them remember without taking away their individual perspective. We can be confident that the Gospels are accurate records of what Jesus taught and did (see 1 Corinthians 2:10-14).**

do it, because the work of the Son brings glory to the Father. [14]Yes, ask anything in my name, and I will do it!

[15]"If you love me, obey my commandments. [16]And I will ask the Father, and he will give you another Counselor,* who will never leave you. [17]He is the Holy Spirit, who leads into all truth. The world at large cannot receive him, because it isn't looking for him and doesn't recognize him. But you do, because he lives with you now and later will be in you. [18]No, I will not abandon you as orphans—I will come to you. [19]In just a little while the world will not see me again, but you will. For I will live again, and you will, too. [20]When I am raised to life again, you will know that I am in my Father, and you are in me, and I am in you. [21]Those who obey my commandments are the ones who love me. And because they love me, my Father will love them, and I will love them. And I will reveal myself to each one of them."

[22]Judas (not Judas Iscariot, but the other disciple with that name) said to him, "Lord, why are you going to reveal yourself only to us and not to the world at large?"

[23]Jesus replied, "All those who love me will do what I say. My Father will love them, and we will come to them and live with them. [24]Anyone who doesn't love me will not do what I say. And remember, my words are not my own. This message is from the Father who sent me. [25]I am telling you these things now while I am still with you. [26]But when the Father sends the Counselor as my representative—and by the Counselor I mean the Holy Spirit—he will teach you everything and will remind you of everything I myself have told you.

[27]"I am leaving you with a gift—peace of mind and heart. And the peace I give isn't like the peace the world gives. So don't be troubled or afraid. [28]Remember what I told you: I am going away, but I will come back to you again. If you really love me, you will be very happy for me, because now I can go to the Father, who is greater than I am. [29]I have told you these things before they happen so that you will believe when they do happen.

[30]"I don't have much more time to talk to you, because the prince of this world approaches. He has no power over me, [31]but I will do what the Father requires of me, so that the world will know that I love the Father. Come, let's be going.

13:32 Some manuscripts read *And if God is glorified in him [the Son of Man], God will bring.* 14:7 Some manuscripts read *If you really have known me, you will know who my Father is.* 14:16 Or *Comforter,* or *Encourager,* or *Advocate.* Greek *Paraclete;* also in 14:26.

## CHAPTER 15 **JESUS, THE TRUE VINE.**

"I am the true vine, and my Father is the gardener. [2]He cuts off every branch that doesn't produce fruit, and he prunes the branches that do bear fruit so they will produce even more. [3]You have already been pruned for greater fruitfulness by the message I have given you. [4]Remain in me, and I will remain in you. For a branch cannot produce fruit if it is severed from the vine, and you cannot be fruitful apart from me.

[5]"Yes, I am the vine; you are the branches. Those who remain in me, and I in them, will produce much fruit. For apart from me you can do nothing. [6]Anyone who parts from me is thrown away like a useless branch and withers. Such branches are gathered into a pile to be burned. [7]But if you stay joined to me and my words remain in you, you may ask any request you like, and it will be granted! [8]My true disciples produce much fruit. This brings great glory to my Father.

[9]"I have loved you even as the Father has loved me. Remain in my love. [10]When you obey me, you remain in my love, just as I obey my Father and remain in his love. [11]I have told you this so that you will be filled with my joy. Yes, your joy will overflow! [12]I command you to love each other in the same way that I love you. [13]And here is how to measure it—the greatest love is shown when people lay down their lives for their friends. [14]You are my friends if you obey me. [15]I no longer call you servants, because a master doesn't confide in his servants. Now you are my friends, since I have told you everything the Father told me. [16]You didn't choose me. I chose you. I appointed you to go and produce fruit that will last, so that the Father will give you whatever you ask for, using my name. [17]I command you to love each other.

### WARNINGS ● ● • • •

16:1-16 **In his last moments with his disciples, Jesus (1) warned them about further persecution, (2) told them where he was going, when he was leaving, and why, and (3) assured them they would not be left alone, but that the Spirit would come. He knew what lay ahead, and he did not want their faith shaken or destroyed. God wants you to know that you are not alone in the world. You have the Holy Spirit to comfort you, teach you truth, and help you.**

[18]"When the world hates you, remember it hated me before it hated you. [19]The world would love you if you belonged to it, but you don't. I chose you to come out of the world, and so it hates you. [20]Do you remember what I told you? 'A servant is not greater than the master.' Since they persecuted me, naturally they will persecute you. And if they had listened to me, they would listen to you! [21]The people of the world will hate you because you belong to me, for they don't know God who sent me. [22]They would not be guilty if I had not come and spoken to them. But now they have no excuse for their sin. [23]Anyone who hates me hates my Father, too. [24]If I hadn't done such miraculous signs among them that no one else could do, they would not be counted guilty. But as it is, they saw all that I did and yet hated both of us—me and my Father. [25]This has fulfilled what the Scriptures said: 'They hated me without cause.'*

[26]"But I will send you the Counselor*—the Spirit of truth. He will come to you from the Father and will tell you all about me. [27]And you must also tell others about me because you have been with me from the beginning.

## CHAPTER 16 **THE HOLY SPIRIT.**

"I have told you these things so that you won't fall away. [2]For you will be expelled from the synagogues, and the time is coming when those who kill you will think they are doing God a service. [3]This is because they have never known the Father or me. [4]Yes, I'm telling you these things now, so that when they happen, you will remember I warned you. I didn't tell you earlier because I was going to be with you for a while longer.

[5]"But now I am going away to the one who sent me, and none of you has asked me where I am going. [6]Instead, you are very sad. [7]But it is actually best for you that I go away, because if I don't, the Counselor* won't come. If I do go away, he will come because I will send him to you. [8]And when he comes, he will convince the world of its sin, and of God's righteousness, and of the coming judgment. [9]The world's sin is unbelief in me. [10]Righteousness is available because I go to the Father, and you will see me no more. [11]Judgment will come because the prince of this world has already been judged.

[12]"Oh, there is so much more I want to tell you, but you can't bear it now. [13]When the Spirit of truth comes, he will guide you into all truth. He will not be presenting his own ideas; he will be telling you what he has heard. He will tell you about the future. [14]He will bring me glory by revealing to you whatever he receives from me. [15]All that the Father has is mine; this is what I mean when I say that the Spirit will reveal to you whatever he receives from me.

[16]"In just a little while I will be gone, and you won't see me anymore. Then, just a little while after that, you will see me again."

[17]The disciples asked each other, "What does he mean when he says, 'You won't see me, and then you will see me'? And what does he mean when he says, 'I am going to the Father'? [18]And what does he mean by 'a little while'? We don't understand."

[19]Jesus realized they wanted to ask him, so he said, "Are you asking yourselves what I meant? I said in just a little while I will be gone, and you won't see me anymore. Then, just a little while after that, you will see me again. [20]Truly, you will weep and mourn over what is going to happen to me, but the world will rejoice. You will grieve, but your grief will suddenly turn to wonderful joy when you see me again. [21]It will be like a woman experiencing the pains of labor. When her child is born, her anguish gives place to joy because she has brought a new person into the world. [22]You have sorrow now, but I will see you again; then you will rejoice, and no one can rob you of that joy. [23]At that time you won't need to ask me for anything. The truth

15:25 Pss 35:19; 69:4. 15:26 Or *Comforter,* or *Encourager,* or *Advocate.* Greek *Paraclete.* 16:7 Or *Comforter,* or *Encourager,* or *Advocate.* Greek *Paraclete.*

is, you can go directly to the Father and ask him, and
he will grant your request because you use my name.
24You haven't done this before. Ask, using my name,
and you will receive, and you will have abundant joy.
25"I have spoken of these matters in parables,
but the time will come when this will not be necessary, and I will tell you plainly all about the
Father. 26Then you will ask in my name. I'm not
saying I will ask the Father on your behalf, 27for the
Father himself loves you dearly because you love
me and believe that I came from God. 28Yes, I came
from the Father into the world, and I will leave the
world and return to the Father."
29Then his disciples said, "At last you are speaking
plainly and not in parables. 30Now we understand
that you know everything and don't need anyone to
tell you anything.* From this we believe that you
came from God."
31Jesus asked, "Do you finally believe? 32But the
time is coming—in fact, it is already here—when
you will be scattered, each one going his own way,
leaving me alone. Yet I am not alone because the
Father is with me. 33I have told you all this so that
you may have peace in me. Here on earth you will
have many trials and sorrows. But take heart, because
I have overcome the world."

CHAPTER **17** **JESUS PRAYS FOR HIMSELF.** When Jesus
had finished saying all these things, he looked up to
heaven and said, "Father, the time has come. Glorify
your Son so he can give glory back to you. 2For you
have given him authority over everyone in all the earth.
He gives eternal life to each one you
have given him. 3And this is the way
to have eternal life—to know you,
the only true God, and Jesus Christ,
the one you sent to earth. 4I brought
glory to you here on earth by doing
everything you told me to do. 5And
now, Father, bring me into the glory
we shared before the world began.
6"I have told these men about you.
They were in the world, but then
you gave them to me. Actually, they
were always yours, and you gave
them to me; and they have kept your
word. 7Now they know that everything I have is a gift from you, 8for I
have passed on to them the words
you gave me; and they accepted
them and know that I came from
you, and they believe you sent me.
9"My prayer is not for the world,
but for those you have given me,
because they belong to you. 10And
all of them, since they are mine,
belong to you; and you have given
them back to me, so they are my
glory! 11Now I am departing the
world; I am leaving them behind and coming to you.
Holy Father, keep them and care for them—all those
you have given me—so that they will be united just as
we are. 12During my time here, I have kept them safe.*
I guarded them so that not one was lost, except the one
headed for destruction, as the Scriptures foretold.
13"And now I am coming to you. I have told them
many things while I was with them so they would be
filled with my joy. 14I have given them your word.
And the world hates them because they do not belong to the world, just as I do not. 15I'm not asking
you to take them out of the world, but to keep them
safe from the evil one. 16They are not part of this
world any more than I am. 17Make them pure and
holy by teaching them your words of truth. 18As you
sent me into the world, I am sending them into the
world. 19And I give myself entirely to you so they also
might be entirely yours.
20"I am praying not only for these disciples but
also for all who will ever believe in me because of
their testimony. 21My prayer for all of them is that
they will be one, just as you and I are one, Father—
that just as you are in me and I am in you, so they
will be in us, and the world will believe you sent me.

## IN THE WORLD ● ● ● • •

17:18 **Jesus didn't ask God to take believers *out* of the world, but instead to use them *in* the world. Because Jesus sends us into the world, we should not try to escape from the world or avoid all relationships with non-Christians. We are called to be salt and light (Matthew 5:13-16), and we are to do the work God sent us to do.**

## "Here's what I did..."

One day I came home from school only to find a note saying that my mother had been rushed to the hospital! I called the hospital and discovered that she had a blood clot in her upper leg and would have to be hospitalized for a while.

Suddenly our household was thrown into chaos. Nothing seemed normal without Mom. Plus I was worried that this could be something serious, or lead to something serious.

Through this time, I read the Bible a lot. I memorized John 14:27: "I am leaving you with a gift—peace of mind and heart. And the peace I give isn't like the peace the world gives. So don't be troubled or afraid." These words of Jesus' helped me not to freak out. Instead I gave the situation to God and trusted him to see me through it. Every time I started to worry, I repeated this verse to myself and felt calmer. Jesus understood what I was going through—and he was in control! The more I concentrated on this, the more peace I felt. It was strange to feel so peaceful even when there was plenty I could worry about. But I just kept reminding myself of this verse, and it helped me get through that difficult time.

Kris

AGE 15

16:30 Or *don't need that anyone should ask you anything.* 17:12 Greek *I have kept in your name those whom you have given me.*

**COME!** ● ● • • •

18:22-27 **We can easily get angry at the Jewish council for their injustice in condemning Jesus, but Peter and the rest of the disciples also contributed to Jesus' pain by deserting and denying him (Matthew 26:56). While most of us are not like the religious leaders, we all are like the disciples, for all of us have been guilty of denying Christ as Lord in vital areas of our life. Don't excuse yourself by pointing at others whose sins seem worse than yours. Instead, come to Jesus for forgiveness and healing.**

22"I have given them the glory you gave me, so that they may be one, as we are—23I in them and you in me, all being perfected into one. Then the world will know that you sent me and will understand that you love them as much as you love me. 24Father, I want these whom you've given me to be with me, so they can see my glory. You gave me the glory because you loved me even before the world began!

25"O righteous Father, the world doesn't know you, but I do; and these disciples know you sent me. 26And I have revealed you to them and will keep on revealing you. I will do this so that your love for me may be in them and I in them."

CHAPTER **18** **JESUS IS BETRAYED AND ARRESTED.** After saying these things, Jesus crossed the Kidron Valley with his disciples and entered a grove of olive trees. 2Judas, the betrayer, knew this place, because Jesus had gone there many times with his disciples. 3The leading priests and Pharisees had given Judas a battalion of Roman soldiers and Temple guards to accompany him. Now with blazing torches, lanterns, and weapons, they arrived at the olive grove.

4Jesus fully realized all that was going to happen to him. Stepping forward to meet them, he asked, "Whom are you looking for?"

5"Jesus of Nazareth," they replied.

"I am he,"* Jesus said. Judas was standing there with them when Jesus identified himself. 6And as he said, "I am he," they all fell backward to the ground! 7Once more he asked them, "Whom are you searching for?"

And again they replied, "Jesus of Nazareth."

8"I told you that I am he," Jesus said. "And since I am the one you want, let these others go." 9He did this to fulfill his own statement: "I have not lost a single one of those you gave me."*

10Then Simon Peter drew a sword and slashed off the right ear of Malchus, the high priest's servant. 11But Jesus said to Peter, "Put your sword back into its sheath. Shall I not drink from the cup the Father has given me?"

12So the soldiers, their commanding officer, and the Temple guards arrested Jesus and tied him up. 13First they took him to Annas, the father-in-law of Caiaphas, the high priest that year. 14Caiaphas was the one who had told the other Jewish leaders, "Better that one should die for all."

15Simon Peter followed along behind, as did another of the disciples. That other disciple was acquainted with the high priest, so he was allowed to enter the courtyard with Jesus. 16Peter stood outside the gate. Then the other disciple spoke to the woman watching at the gate, and she let Peter in. 17The woman asked Peter, "Aren't you one of Jesus' disciples?"

"No," he said, "I am not."

18The guards and the household servants were standing around a charcoal fire they had made because it was cold. And Peter stood there with them, warming himself.

19Inside, the high priest began asking Jesus about his followers and what he had been teaching them. 20Jesus replied, "What I teach is widely known, because I have preached regularly in the synagogues and the Temple. I have been heard by people* everywhere, and I teach nothing in private that I have not said in public. 21Why are you asking me this question? Ask those who heard me. They know what I said."

22One of the Temple guards standing there struck Jesus on the face. "Is that the way to answer the high priest?" he demanded.

23Jesus replied, "If I said anything wrong, you must give evidence for it. Should you hit a man for telling the truth?"

24Then Annas bound Jesus and sent him to Caiaphas, the high priest.

25Meanwhile, as Simon Peter was standing by the fire, they asked him again, "Aren't you one of his disciples?"

"I am not," he said.

26But one of the household servants of the high priest, a relative of the man whose ear Peter had cut off, asked, "Didn't I see you out there in the olive grove with Jesus?" 27Again Peter denied it. And immediately a rooster crowed.

28Jesus' trial before Caiaphas ended in the early hours of the morning. Then he was taken to the headquarters of the Roman governor. His accusers didn't go in themselves because it would defile them, and they wouldn't be allowed to celebrate the Passover feast. 29So Pilate, the governor, went out to them and asked, "What is your charge against this man?"

30"We wouldn't have handed him over to you if he weren't a criminal!" they retorted.

31"Then take him away and judge him by your own laws," Pilate told them.

"Only the Romans are permitted to execute someone," the Jewish leaders replied. 32This fulfilled Jesus' prediction about the way he would die.*

33Then Pilate went back inside and called for Jesus to be brought to him. "Are you the King of the Jews?" he asked him.

34Jesus replied, "Is this your own question, or did others tell you about me?"

35"Am I a Jew?" Pilate asked. "Your own people and their leading priests brought you here. Why? What have you done?"

36Then Jesus answered, "I am not an earthly king. If I were, my followers would have fought when I was arrested by the Jewish leaders. But my Kingdom is not of this world."

37Pilate replied, "You are a king then?"

18:5 Greek *I am;* also in 18:6, 8. 18:9 See John 6:39 and 17:12. 18:20 Greek *Jewish people;* also in 18:38. 18:32 See John 12:32-33.

"You say that I am a king, and you are right," Jesus said. "I was born for that purpose. And I came to bring truth to the world. All who love the truth recognize that what I say is true."

38"What is truth?" Pilate asked. Then he went out again to the people and told them, "He is not guilty of any crime. 39But you have a custom of asking me to release someone from prison each year at Passover. So if you want me to, I'll release the King of the Jews."

40But they shouted back, "No! Not this man, but Barabbas!" (Barabbas was a criminal.)

CHAPTER **19** **PILATE JUDGES JESUS.** Then Pilate had Jesus flogged with a lead-tipped whip. 2The soldiers made a crown of long, sharp thorns and put it on his head, and they put a royal purple robe on him. 3"Hail! King of the Jews!" they mocked, and they hit him with their fists.

4Pilate went outside again and said to the people, "I am going to bring him out to you now, but understand clearly that I find him not guilty." 5Then Jesus came out wearing the crown of thorns and the purple robe. And Pilate said, "Here is the man!"

6When they saw him, the leading priests and Temple guards began shouting, "Crucify! Crucify!"

"You crucify him," Pilate said. "I find him not guilty."

7The Jewish leaders replied, "By our laws he ought to die because he called himself the Son of God."

8When Pilate heard this, he was more frightened than ever. 9He took Jesus back into the headquarters again and asked him, "Where are you from?" But Jesus gave no answer. 10"You won't talk to me?" Pilate demanded. "Don't you realize that I have the power to release you or to crucify you?"

11Then Jesus said, "You would have no power over me at all unless it were given to you from above. So the one who brought me to you has the greater sin."

12Then Pilate tried to release him, but the Jewish leaders told him, "If you release this man, you are not a friend of Caesar. Anyone who declares himself a king is a rebel against Caesar."

13When they said this, Pilate brought Jesus out to them again. Then Pilate sat down on the judgment seat on the platform that is called the Stone Pavement (in Hebrew, *Gabbatha*). 14It was now about noon of the day of preparation for the Passover. And Pilate said to the people,* "Here is your king!"

## THOMAS

Even though some of Thomas's attitudes earned him the nickname "Doubter," we also need to respect his faith. Thomas expressed his doubts because he wanted to know the truth. He didn't hang on to his doubts but humbly believed when they were answered. Expressing doubts is a good way to clarify the truth.

The Bible doesn't tell us a lot about Thomas, but the brief glimpses are consistent. He tried hard to be faithful to what he knew, even though he didn't always feel like it. At one point, when it was clear to everyone that Jesus' life was in danger, only Thomas put into words what most were feeling: "Let's go, too—and die with Jesus" (John 11:16). He didn't hesitate to follow Jesus. Sometimes we have to go against our feelings in order to obey Christ.

We don't know why Thomas was missing the first time Jesus appeared to the disciples after the Resurrection. Whatever the reason, Thomas was reluctant to believe their story that Jesus was alive. Not even 10 friends could change his mind! But, because Thomas's doubt was honest, God didn't leave him in doubt.

We can doubt without having to live a doubting way of life. Doubt helps us clarify what we believe. Doubt works better at sharpening our mind than changing it. Doubts can help us ask good questions, seek for answers, push for decisions. But doubt was never meant to be a permanent condition. Doubt is one foot lifted, poised to step forward or back. There is no motion until the foot comes down.

When you experience doubt, take encouragement from Thomas. He didn't stay in his doubt but allowed Jesus to bring him to belief. Take encouragement also from the fact that countless other followers of Christ have struggled with doubts. The answers God gave them may be of great help. Don't settle into doubt, but move beyond it to decision and belief. Find another Christian with whom you can share your doubts. Silent doubts rarely find answers.

**UPS:**
- One of Jesus' 12 disciples
- Had a great capacity for intensity, both in doubt and belief
- Was a loyal and honest man

**DOWNS:**
- Along with the others, abandoned Jesus at his arrest
- Refused to believe the others' claims to have seen Christ and demanded proof
- Struggled with a pessimistic outlook

**STATS:**
- Where: Galilee, Judea, Samaria
- Occupation: Disciple of Jesus
- Contemporaries: Jesus, other disciples, Herod, Pilate

LESSONS: Jesus does not reject doubts that are honest and directed toward belief

Better to doubt out loud than to disbelieve in silence

KEY VERSES: "Then [Jesus] said to Thomas, 'Put your finger here and see my hands. Put your hand into the wound in my side. Don't be faithless any longer. Believe!' 'My Lord and my God!' Thomas exclaimed" (John 20:27-28).

Thomas's story is told in the Gospels. He also is mentioned in Acts 1:13.

19:14 Greek *Jewish people;* also in 19:20.

## JESUS' APPEARANCES AFTER HIS RESURRECTION

The truth of Christianity rests heavily on the Resurrection. If Jesus rose from the grave, who saw him? How trustworthy were the witnesses? Those who claimed to have seen the risen Jesus went on to turn the world upside down. Most of them also died for being followers of Christ. People rarely die for halfhearted belief. These are people who saw Jesus risen from the grave:

| | |
|---|---|
| Mary Magdalene | Mark 16:9-11; John 20:10-18 |
| The other women at the tomb | Matthew 28:8-10 |
| Peter in Jerusalem | Luke 24:34; 1 Corinthians 15:5 |
| The two travelers on the road | Mark 16:12-13; Luke 24:13-35 |
| Ten disciples behind closed doors | Mark 16:14; Luke 24:36-43; John 20:19-25 |
| All the disciples, with Thomas (excluding Judas Iscariot) | John 20:26-31; 1 Corinthians 15:5 |
| Seven disciples while fishing | John 21:1-14 |
| Eleven disciples on the mountain | Matthew 28:16-20 |
| A crowd of more than five hundred | 1 Corinthians 15:6 |
| Jesus' brother James | 1 Corinthians 15:7 |
| Those who watched Jesus ascend into heaven | Luke 24:44-49; Acts 1:3-8 |

---

15"Away with him," they yelled. "Away with
him—crucify him!"

"What? Crucify your king?" Pilate asked.

"We have no king but Caesar," the leading priests
shouted back.

16Then Pilate gave Jesus to them to be crucified.

So they took Jesus and led him away. 17Carrying
the cross by himself, Jesus went to the place called
Skull Hill (in Hebrew, *Golgotha*). 18There they crucified him. There were two others crucified with him,
one on either side, with Jesus between them. 19And
Pilate posted a sign over him that read, "Jesus of
Nazareth, the King of the Jews." 20The place where
Jesus was crucified was near the city; and the sign was
written in Hebrew, Latin, and Greek, so that many
people could read it.

21Then the leading priests said to Pilate, "Change
it from 'The King of the Jews' to 'He said, I am King
of the Jews.'"

22Pilate replied, "What I have written, I have written. It stays exactly as it is."

23When the soldiers had crucified Jesus, they divided his clothes among the four of them. They also
took his robe, but it was seamless, woven in one
piece from the top. 24So they said, "Let's not tear it
but throw dice* to see who gets it." This fulfilled the
Scripture that says, "They divided my clothes among
themselves and threw dice for my robe."* So that is
what they did.

25Standing near the cross were Jesus' mother, and
his mother's sister, Mary (the wife of Clopas), and
Mary Magdalene. 26When Jesus saw his mother
standing there beside the disciple he loved, he said
to her, "Woman, he is your son." 27And he said to
this disciple, "She is your mother." And from then
on this disciple took her into his home.

28Jesus knew that everything was now finished, and
to fulfill the Scriptures he said, "I am thirsty."* 29A jar
of sour wine was sitting there, so they soaked a sponge
in it, put it on a hyssop branch, and held it up to his
lips. 30When Jesus had tasted it, he said, "It is finished!" Then he bowed his head and gave up his spirit.

31The Jewish leaders didn't want the victims hanging there the next day, which was the Sabbath (and a
very special Sabbath at that, because it was the Pass-

### FAMILY ● ● • • •

19:25-27 **Even while dying on the cross, Jesus was concerned about his family. He instructed John to care for Mary, his mother. Our families are precious gifts from God, and we should value and care for them under all circumstances. What can you do today to show your love to your family?**

19:24a Greek *cast lots.* 19:24b Ps 22:18. 19:28 See Pss 22:15; 69:21.

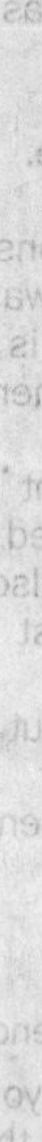

over), so they asked Pilate to hasten their deaths by ordering that their legs be broken. Then their bodies could be taken down. [32]So the soldiers came and broke the legs of the two men crucified with Jesus. [33]But when they came to Jesus, they saw that he was dead already, so they didn't break his legs. [34]One of the soldiers, however, pierced his side with a spear, and blood and water flowed out. [35]This report is from an eyewitness giving an accurate account; it is presented so that you also can believe. [36]These things happened in fulfillment of the Scriptures that say, "Not one of his bones will be broken,"* [37]and "They will look on him whom they pierced."*

[38]Afterward Joseph of Arimathea, who had been a secret disciple of Jesus (because he feared the Jewish leaders), asked Pilate for permission to take Jesus' body down. When Pilate gave him permission, he came and took the body away. [39]Nicodemus, the man who had come to Jesus at night, also came, bringing about seventy-five pounds* of embalming ointment made from myrrh and aloes. [40]Together they wrapped Jesus' body in a long linen cloth with the spices, as is the Jewish custom of burial. [41]The place of crucifixion was near a garden, where there was a new tomb, never used before. [42]And so, because it was the day of preparation before the Passover and since the tomb was close at hand, they laid Jesus there.

CHAPTER **20** **PETER AND JOHN AT JESUS' TOMB.** Early Sunday morning,* while it was still dark, Mary Magdalene came to the tomb and found that the stone had been rolled away from the entrance. [2]She ran and found Simon Peter and the other disciple, the one whom Jesus loved. She said, "They have taken the Lord's body out of the tomb, and I don't know where they have put him!"

[3]Peter and the other disciple ran to the tomb to see. [4]The other disciple outran Peter and got there first. [5]He stooped and looked in and saw the linen cloth lying there, but he didn't go in. [6]Then Simon Peter arrived and went inside. He also noticed the linen wrappings lying there, [7]while the cloth that had covered Jesus' head was folded up and lying to the side. [8]Then the other disciple also went in, and he saw and believed—[9]for until then they hadn't realized that the Scriptures said he would rise from the dead. [10]Then they went home.

[11]Mary was standing outside the tomb crying, and as she wept, she stooped and looked in. [12]She saw two white-robed angels sitting at the head and foot of the place where the body of Jesus had been lying. [13]"Why are you crying?" the angels asked her.

"Because they have taken away my Lord," she replied, "and I don't know where they have put him."

[14]She glanced over her shoulder and saw someone standing behind her. It was Jesus, but she didn't recognize him. [15]"Why are you crying?" Jesus asked her. "Who are you looking for?"

She thought he was the gardener. "Sir," she said, "if you have taken him away, tell me where you have put him, and I will go and get him."

[16]"Mary!" Jesus said.

She turned toward him and exclaimed, "Teacher!"*

[17]"Don't cling to me," Jesus said, "for I haven't yet ascended to the Father. But go find my brothers and tell them that I am ascending to my Father and your Father, my God and your God."

**After I became a Christian I was told to start reading the Bible. But it is hard to understand and is bigger than any book I ever even attempted to read. Where do I start?**

Unfortunately, at no place in the Bible does it say, "Start here," and then, "Read this next." Consequently, we need help.

When two people in love have to be separated for a while, they usually send streams of letters to each other. Webbed inside the boring facts about daily life is a story of love and devotion to the other person.

To find the "good stuff" you would have to wade through the details. If you wanted to find out how the relationship developed, you would need to go through those details.

Sometimes that's how it is with the Bible. The events that occurred so long ago don't seem to have any relevance to us today. But if your goal was to understand the relationship between God and his people, from Adam to Jesus, those details would become essential information.

New Christians usually want the "good stuff." Later, as they grow in their faith, they will be more interested in the details that will help them put God's whole plan together.

So for now, consider these suggestions:

- Get to know Jesus the Christ. Listen to his words. Try to understand what each story is saying and watch how Christ treats others. John tells us that he wrote his book "so that you may believe that Jesus is the Messiah, the Son of God, and that by believing in him you will have life" (John 20:31). The first four books of the New Testament give four different perspectives on Jesus' life. Getting to know him should be your first priority.
- Next, start reading through some of the smaller letters that Paul, Peter, and John wrote (Paul's letters are everything between Romans and Philemon).
- Try Proverbs next. You can read one chapter a day and finish the book in a month.
- After this, read Genesis, Exodus, Daniel, and Jonah. They offer stories of real people whose problems were not all that different from yours. Learn from their lives so that you don't make the same mistakes they did.

There is no short-cut to the Christian life. We must be disciplined enough to dig in the Bible to find all the buried treasure that God wants to give those who will dig deep enough. Have fun.

19:36 Exod 12:46; Num 9:12; Ps 34:20. 19:37 Zech 12:10. 19:39 Greek *100 litras* [32.7 kilograms]. 20:1 Greek *On the first day of the week.* 20:16 Greek *and said in Hebrew, "Rabboni," which means "Teacher."*

## PROOF ● ● • • •

20:29 **Some people think they would believe in Jesus if they could see a definite sign or miracle. But Jesus says we are blessed if we can believe without seeing. We have all the proof we need in the words of the Bible and the testimony of believers. A physical appearance would not make Jesus any more real to us than he is while living within us.**

[18]Mary Magdalene found the disciples and told them, "I have seen the Lord!" Then she gave them his message.

[19]That evening, on the first day of the week, the disciples were meeting behind locked doors because they were afraid of the Jewish leaders. Suddenly, Jesus was standing there among them! "Peace be with you," he said. [20]As he spoke, he held out his hands for them to see, and he showed them his side. They were filled with joy when they saw their Lord! [21]He spoke to them again and said, "Peace be with you. As the Father has sent me, so I send you." [22]Then he breathed on them and said to them, "Receive the Holy Spirit. [23]If you forgive anyone's sins, they are forgiven. If you refuse to forgive them, they are unforgiven."

[24]One of the disciples, Thomas (nicknamed the Twin*), was not with the others when Jesus came. [25]They told him, "We have seen the Lord!" But he replied, "I won't believe it unless I see the nail wounds in his hands, put my fingers into them, and place my hand into the wound in his side."

[26]Eight days later the disciples were together again, and this time Thomas was with them. The doors were locked; but suddenly, as before, Jesus was standing among them. He said, "Peace be with you." [27]Then he said to Thomas, "Put your finger here and see my hands. Put your hand into the wound in my side. Don't be faithless any longer. Believe!"

[28]"My Lord and my God!" Thomas exclaimed.

[29]Then Jesus told him, "You believe because you have seen me. Blessed are those who haven't seen me and believe anyway."

[30]Jesus' disciples saw him do many other miraculous signs besides the ones recorded in this book. [31]But these are written so that you may believe* that Jesus is the Messiah, the Son of God, and that by believing in him you will have life.

## CHAPTER 21

**JESUS HELPS CATCH FISH.** Later Jesus appeared again to the disciples beside the Sea of Galilee.* This is how it happened. [2]Several of the disciples were there—Simon Peter, Thomas (nicknamed the Twin*), Nathanael from Cana in Galilee, the sons of Zebedee, and two other disciples.

[3]Simon Peter said, "I'm going fishing."

"We'll come, too," they all said. So they went out in the boat, but they caught nothing all night.

[4]At dawn the disciples saw Jesus standing on the beach, but they couldn't see who he was. [5]He called out, "Friends, have you caught any fish?"

"No," they replied.

[6]Then he said, "Throw out your net on the right-hand side of the boat, and you'll get plenty of fish!" So they did, and they couldn't draw in the net because there were so many fish in it.

[7]Then the disciple whom Jesus loved said to Peter, "It is the Lord!" When Simon Peter heard that it was the Lord, he put on his tunic (for he had stripped for work), jumped into the water, and swam ashore. [8]The others stayed with the boat and pulled the loaded net to the shore, for they were only out about three hundred feet.* [9]When they got there, they saw that a charcoal fire was burning and fish were frying over it, and there was bread.

[10]"Bring some of the fish you've just caught," Jesus said. [11]So Simon Peter went aboard and dragged the net to the shore. There were 153 large fish, and yet the net hadn't torn.

[12]"Now come and have some breakfast!" Jesus said. And no one dared ask him if he really was the Lord because they were sure of it. [13]Then Jesus served them the bread and the fish. [14]This was the third time Jesus had appeared to his disciples since he had been raised from the dead.

[15]After breakfast Jesus said to Simon Peter, "Simon son of John, do you love me more than these?"

"Yes, Lord," Peter replied, "you know I love you."

"Then feed my lambs," Jesus told him.

[16]Jesus repeated the question: "Simon son of John, do you love me?"

"Yes, Lord," Peter said, "you know I love you."

"Then take care of my sheep," Jesus said.

[17]Once more he asked him, "Simon son of John, do you love me?"

Peter was grieved that Jesus asked the question a third time. He said, "Lord, you know everything. You know I love you."

Jesus said, "Then feed my sheep. [18]The truth is, when you were young, you were able to do as you liked and go wherever you wanted to. But when you are old, you will stretch out your hands, and others will direct you and take you where you don't want to go." [19]Jesus said this to let him know what kind of death he would die to glorify God. Then Jesus told him, "Follow me."

[20]Peter turned around and saw the disciple Jesus loved following them—the one who had leaned over to Jesus during supper and asked, "Lord, who among us will betray you?" [21]Peter asked Jesus, "What about him, Lord?"

[22]Jesus replied, "If I want him to remain alive until I return, what is that to you? You follow me." [23]So the rumor spread among the community of believers* that that disciple wouldn't die. But that isn't what Jesus said at all. He only said, "If I want him to remain alive until I return, what is that to you?"

[24]This is that disciple who saw these events and recorded them here. And we all know that his account of these things is accurate.

[25]And I suppose that if all the other things Jesus did were written down, the whole world could not contain the books.

20:24 Greek *the one who was called Didymus.* 20:31 Some manuscripts read *may continue to believe.* 21:1 Greek *Sea of Tiberias,* another name for the Sea of Galilee. 21:2 Greek *the one who was called Didymus.* 21:8 Greek *200 cubits* [90 meters]. 21:23 Greek *the brothers.*

# MEGA themes

**JESUS CHRIST, SON OF GOD** John shows us that Jesus is unique as God's special Son, yet he is fully God. Because Jesus is fully God, he is able to reveal God to us clearly and accurately.

Because Jesus is God's Son, we can perfectly trust what he says. By trusting him, we can gain an open mind to understand God's message and fulfill his purpose in our life.

1. What are the key points that John emphasizes in John 1:1-18?
2. What do you learn about God by looking at Jesus?
3. In what ways has knowing Christ made a difference in your life?
4. Based on John's Gospel and your life, what would you say this statement means: "Jesus Christ is God's perfect revelation of himself"?

**ETERNAL LIFE** Because Jesus is God, he lives forever. Before the world began, Jesus lived with God, and he will reign forever with God. In John, we see Jesus revealed in power and magnificence even before his resurrection.

Jesus offers eternal life to us. We are invited to live in a personal, eternal relationship with him that begins now. Although we must eventually age and die, by trusting Christ we can have a new life that lasts forever.

1. How does the idea of eternal life affect the way you view your earthly life?
2. What effect should the promise of eternal life in Jesus Christ have on the way you relate to non-Christians?
3. How can you be more faithful to the reality of eternal life in how you live your life now on earth?

**BELIEVE** John records eight specific signs or miracles that reveal the nature of Jesus' power and love. We see Christ's power over everything created, and we see his love for all people. These signs encourage us to believe in him.

Believing is active, living, and continuous trust in Jesus as God. When we believe in Jesus' life, words, death, and resurrection, and when we commit our life to him, he cleanses us from sin and empowers us to follow him. Jesus provides the cleansing and empowering; it is our role to respond in true belief.

1. What did John want to communicate about Jesus through the eight miracles he included in his book?
2. What did John want to communicate through the names or descriptions of Jesus?
3. What is the difference between knowing about Jesus and believing in him?
4. How did you come to believe in Jesus? What does it mean to you to be a "believer"?
5. What would you want to communicate about Jesus to your non-Christian friends? What could you do to begin to clearly communicate that message?

**HOLY SPIRIT** Jesus taught his disciples that after he went back to heaven, the Holy Spirit would come. Then the Holy Spirit would indwell, guide, counsel, and comfort all those who follow Jesus. Through the Holy Spirit, Christ's presence and power are multiplied in all who believe.

Through God's Holy Spirit we are drawn to him in faith. We must know the Holy Spirit to understand all that Jesus taught. We can experience Jesus' love and guidance as we allow the Holy Spirit to do his work in us.

1. In 14:15-31 and 16:5-16 Jesus teaches specifically about the Holy Spirit. List the key points of his teaching.
2. What resources are provided by the Holy Spirit?
3. Why do you think God gives his Holy Spirit to believers?
4. What can you do to develop a daily reliance on the Spirit so that you are able to enjoy his presence and blessings?

**RESURRECTION** On the third day after Jesus died, he rose from the dead. This was verified by his disciples and many eyewitnesses. This reality changed the disciples from frightened deserters to dynamic leaders in the new church. This fact is the foundation of the Christian faith.

We can be changed, as the disciples were, and have confidence that our bodies will one day be raised to live with Christ forever. The same power that raised Christ to life can give you the ability to follow Christ each day. God wants us to live in victory, not in fear or despair.

1. What makes the Resurrection so essential to Christian faith?
2. Describe how you might have felt if you had been one of the disciples who thought Jesus was dead and then saw him alive. What impact would this experience have had on your life?
3. What does it mean to live as a Christian who takes the Resurrection seriously?

A.D. **30**
**Jesus crucified; Pentecost; church begun**

**35**
**Stephen martyred; Paul's conversion**

**38**
**Paul returns to Tarsus**

**43**
**Barnabas goes to find Paul**

**44**
**James martyred; Peter in prison**

**46–48**
**Paul's first missionary journey**

**50**
**Jerusalem council**

**50–52**
**Paul's second missionary journey**

**53–57**
**Paul's third missionary journey**

**54**
**Nero becomes emperor**

**57–59**
**Paul imprisoned in Caesarea**

**59**
**Paul's voyage to Rome**

**62**
**Paul released from prison**

**67?**
**Paul martyred**

**70**
**Rome destroys Jerusalem**

Assemble nine very different people: ■ The class cut-up who makes everything funny ■ The preppie rich kid with her very own BMW ■ The minority student from the not-so-nice part of town ■ The human computer who would rather do calculus problems than anything else ■ The mammoth football jock who loves to bash things—especially quarterbacks ■ The student whose recent "achievements" read like a sleazy novel ■ The school airhead who is not exactly headed for a career as a genetic scientist ■ The campus philosopher/political activist who *loves* to argue and *hates* shallow people ■ The quiet classmate who, for whatever reasons, never fits in ■ Now, give this diverse crowd a simple task to do . . . together. ■ Even if you could get them all in the same room, they'd *never* complete the assignment. What they'd most likely produce is nonstop arguing, bickering, and chaos! If they functioned as a team at all, it would be bumpy and very brief. ■ So, how do we explain the first-century church? How did *several hundred* radically different people accomplish the *complicated and time-consuming project* of taking Jesus' story all over the world? ■ How did they handle conflicts? What kept them going when hard times hit? What is it that those first Christians had that is lacking among believers today? ■ If you'd like the answers to those questions (and you'd like to see how you can help improve your own church), dive into the book of Acts.

## STATS

PURPOSE: To give an accurate account of the birth and growth of the Christian church

AUTHOR: Luke

TO WHOM WRITTEN: Theophilus ("lover of God") and people everywhere

DATE WRITTEN: Between A.D. 63 and 70

SETTING: Acts is the link between Christ's life and the life of the church, between the Gospels and the Epistles

KEY PEOPLE: Peter, John, James, Stephen, Philip, Paul, Barnabas, Cornelius, James (Jesus' brother), Timothy, Lydia, Silas, Titus, Apollos, Agabus, Ananias, Felix, Festus, Agrippa, Luke

KEY PLACES: Jerusalem, Samaria, Lydda, Joppa, Antioch in Syria, Cyprus, Antioch in Pisidia, Iconium, Lystra, Derbe, Philippi, Thessalonica, Berea, Athens, Corinth, Ephesus, Caesarea, Malta, Rome

CHAPTER **1** **JESUS GOES UP TO HEAVEN.** Dear Theophilus:

In my first book* I told you about everything
Jesus began to do and teach [2]until the day he ascended to heaven after giving his chosen apostles
further instructions from the Holy Spirit. [3]During
the forty days after his crucifixion, he appeared to the apostles from time to time and proved to them in many ways that he was actually alive. On these occasions he talked to them about the Kingdom of God.
[4]In one of these meetings as he was eating a meal with them, he told them, "Do not leave Jerusalem until the Father sends you what he promised. Remember, I have told you about this before. [5]John
baptized with* water, but in just a few days you will be baptized with the Holy Spirit."
[6]When the apostles were with Jesus, they kept asking him, "Lord, are you going to free Israel now and restore our kingdom?"
[7]"The Father sets those dates," he replied, "and they are not for you to know. [8]But when the Holy
Spirit has come upon you, you will receive power and will tell people about me everywhere—in Jerusalem, throughout Judea, in Samaria, and to the ends of the earth."
[9]It was not long after he said this that he was taken up into the sky while they were watching, and he disappeared into a cloud. [10]As they were straining
their eyes to see him, two white-robed men suddenly stood there among them. [11]They said, "Men of Galilee, why are you standing here staring at the sky? Jesus has been taken away from you into heaven. And someday, just as you saw him go, he will return!"
[12]The apostles were at the Mount of Olives when this happened, so they walked the half mile* back to
Jerusalem. [13]Then they went to the upstairs room of the house where they were staying. Here is the list of those who were present:

**CHANGED ● ● ● ● •**

**1:3 Today there are still people who doubt Jesus' resurrection. But Jesus appeared to the apostles on many occasions after his resurrection, proving that he was alive. Look at the change the Resurrection made in the disciples' lives. At Jesus' death, they scattered. They were disillusioned and they feared for their lives. Then, after seeing the resurrected Christ, they grew fearless and risked everything to spread the Good News about him around the world. They faced imprisonment, beatings, rejection, and martyrdom, yet they never compromised their mission. These men would not have risked their lives for something they knew was a fraud. They knew Jesus was raised from the dead, and the early church was fired with their enthusiasm to tell others.**

1:1 The reference is to the book of Luke. 1:5 Or *in;* also in 1:5b. 1:12 Greek *a Sabbath day's journey.*

# KEY PLACES IN **ACTS**

Modern names and boundaries are shown in gray.

The apostle Paul, whose missionary journeys fill much of this book, traveled tremendous distances as he tirelessly spread the gospel across much of the Roman Empire. His combined trips, by land and ship, total more than 13,000 airline miles, to say nothing of the circuitous land routes he walked and climbed.

**Judea** Jesus ascended to heaven from the Mount of Olives outside Jerusalem, and his followers returned to the city to await the infilling of the Holy Spirit, which occurred at Pentecost. Peter gave a powerful sermon that was heard by Jews from across the empire. The Jerusalem church grew, but Stephen was martyred for his faith by Jewish leaders who did not believe in Jesus (1:1-7:59).

**Samaria** After Stephen's death, persecution of Christians intensified, but it caused the believers to leave Jerusalem and spread the gospel to other cities in the empire. Philip took the gospel into Samaria and even to a man from Ethiopia (8:1-40).

**Syria** Paul began his story as a persecutor of Christians, only to be met by Jesus himself on the road to Damascus. He became a believer, but his new faith caused opposition, so he returned to Tarsus, his home, for safety. Barnabas sought out Paul in Tarsus and brought him to the church in Antioch in Syria, where they worked together. Meanwhile, Peter had received a vision that led him to Caesarea, where he presented the gospel to a Gentile family, who became believers (9:1-12:25).

**Cyprus and Galatia** Paul and Barnabas were dedicated by the church in Antioch in Syria for God's work of spreading the gospel to other cities. They set off on their first missionary journey through Cyprus and Galatia (13:1-14:28).

**Jerusalem** Controversy between Jewish Christians and Gentile Christians over the matter of keeping the law led to a special council, with delegates from the churches in Antioch and Jerusalem meeting in Jerusalem. Together they resolved the conflict, and the news was taken back to Antioch (15:1-35).

**Macedonia** Barnabas traveled to Cyprus while Paul took a second missionary journey. He revisited the churches in Galatia and headed toward Ephesus, but the Holy Spirit said no. He then turned north toward Bithynia and Pontus, but again was told not to go. He then received the "Macedonian call" and followed the Spirit's direction to the cities in Macedonia (15:36-17:14).

**Achaia** Paul traveled from Macedonia to Athens and Corinth in Achaia, then traveled by ship to Ephesus before returning to Caesarea, Jerusalem, and finally back to Antioch (17:15-18:22).

**Ephesus** Paul's third missionary journey took him back through Cilicia and Galatia, this time straight to Ephesus in Asia. He visited other cities in Asia before going back to Macedonia and Achaia. He returned to Jerusalem by ship, despite knowing that arrest awaited him there (18:23-23:30).

**Caesarea** Paul was arrested in Jerusalem and taken to Antipatris, then on to Caesarea under Roman guard. Paul always took advantage of any opportunity to share the gospel, and he did so before many Gentile leaders. But because Paul appealed to Caesar, he began the long journey to Rome (23:31-26:32).

**Rome** After storms, layovers in Crete, and a shipwreck on the island of Malta, Paul arrived in Sicily, and finally Italy, where he traveled by land, under guard, to his long-awaited destination, Rome, the capital of the empire (27:1-28:31).

Peter,
John,
James,
Andrew,
Philip,
Thomas,
Bartholomew,
Matthew,
James (son of Alphaeus),
Simon (the Zealot),
and Judas (son of James).

14 They all met together continually for prayer, along
with Mary the mother of Jesus, several other women,
and the brothers of Jesus.

15 During this time, on a day when about 120
believers* were present, Peter stood up and addressed them as follows:

16 "Brothers, it was necessary for the Scriptures to
be fulfilled concerning Judas, who guided the
Temple police to arrest Jesus. This was predicted long
ago by the Holy Spirit, speaking through King David.
17 Judas was one of us, chosen to share in the ministry
with us."

18 (Judas bought a field with the money he received for his treachery, and falling there, he burst
open, spilling out his intestines. 19 The news of his
death spread rapidly among all the people of Jerusalem, and they gave the place the Aramaic name
*Akeldama*, which means "Field of Blood.")

20 Peter continued, "This was predicted in the
book of Psalms, where it says, 'Let his home become
desolate, with no one living in it.' And again, 'Let his
position be given to someone else.'*

21 "So now we must choose another man to take
Judas's place. It must be someone who has been with

But when the
Holy Spirit
has
come upon
YOU
YOU WILL RECEIVE
POWER
and will tell people about me.
ACTS 1:8


## CHOOSE WELL

1:21-22 **The apostles had to choose a replacement for Judas Iscariot. They outlined specific criteria for making the choice. When the "finalists" had been chosen, the apostles prayed, asking God to guide the selection process. This gives us a good example of how to proceed when we are making important decisions. Set up criteria consistent with the Bible, examine the alternatives, and pray for wisdom and guidance to reach a wise decision.**

us all the time that we were with the Lord Jesus—
22 from the time he was baptized by John until the
day he was taken from us into heaven. Whoever is
chosen will join us as a witness of Jesus' resurrection."

23 So they nominated two men: Joseph called
Barsabbas (also known as Justus) and Matthias.
24 Then they all prayed for the right man to be chosen. "O Lord," they said, "you know every heart.
Show us which of these men you have chosen 25 as an
apostle to replace Judas the traitor in this ministry,
for he has deserted us and gone where he belongs."
26 Then they cast lots, and in this way Matthias was
chosen and became an apostle with the other eleven.

CHAPTER **2** **THE HOLY SPIRIT COMES.** On the day of
Pentecost, seven weeks after Jesus' resurrection,* the
believers were meeting together in one place. 2 Suddenly, there was a sound from heaven like the roaring of a mighty windstorm in the skies above them,
and it filled the house where they were meeting.
3 Then, what looked like flames or tongues of fire
appeared and settled on each of them. 4 And everyone present was filled with the Holy Spirit and began
speaking in other languages,* as the Holy Spirit gave
them this ability.

5 Godly Jews from many nations were living in
Jerusalem at that time. 6 When they heard this sound,
they came running to see what it was all about, and
they were bewildered to hear their own languages
being spoken by the believers.

7 They were beside themselves with wonder. "How
can this be?" they exclaimed. "These people are all
from Galilee, 8 and yet we hear them speaking the
languages of the lands where we were born! 9 Here
we are—Parthians, Medes, Elamites, people from
Mesopotamia, Judea, Cappadocia, Pontus, the province of Asia, 10 Phrygia, Pamphylia, Egypt, and the
areas of Libya toward Cyrene, visitors from Rome
(both Jews and converts to Judaism), 11 Cretans, and
Arabians. And we all hear these people speaking in
our own languages about the wonderful things God
has done!" 12 They stood there amazed and perplexed. "What can this mean?" they asked each
other. 13 But others in the crowd were mocking.
"They're drunk, that's all!" they said.

14 Then Peter stepped forward with the eleven
other apostles and shouted to the crowd, "Listen

1:15 Greek *brothers*. 1:20 Pss 69:25; 109:8. 2:1 Greek *When the day of Pentecost arrived.* This annual celebration came 50 days after the Passover ceremonies. See Lev 23:16. 2:4 Or *in other tongues.*

# THE HOLY SPIRIT

**A**uthor Sheldon Vanauken has described a scene in which the characters in a drama sit around and discuss their play. The playwright's name is Smith. Some of the characters believe Smith exists; some don't. One of them recalls an earlier scene where a character named Smithson claimed that *he* was Smith, and that he had written himself into the play. After considerable debate over the likelihood of that happening, another character speaks: **"L**ook, do you know what's so impressive about all this? It's the idea of a sort of a TRINITY: Smith outside writing the play; and inside as a character; and inside each of us, too. I don't know whether it's true, but it's exactly the way it would be if it were. . . . This thing has the feel of something true. A sort of rightness." **N**o one can truly understand—much less explain—the Trinity, **God in three persons.** But Vanauken's analogy is a good attempt: an Author who writes characters into existence, then writes himself in as one of the players, and also is somehow *in* each of his characters. **H**istorically, Christians have believed that God exists in three persons: the Father, Son, and Holy Spirit. The least understood of these three, though, is the Holy Spirit. So just who is the Holy Spirit and what does he do? • ***"He," not "it."*** The New Testament always refers to the Holy Spirit as "he," not "it." The Spirit is personal, not merely a "force" or instrument. Just as God the Father and God the Son represent distinct personalities within the Trinity, so does the Spirit. We don't have any real point of reference to help us understand this since we don't know anyone else who is pure spirit. Still, it is true: the Holy Spirit is a person with intellect, feelings, will, and other personal characteristics. • ***Truly God.*** The Holy Spirit is not in any way less than or inferior to the Father or the Son. One of the clearest statements of this reality is found in Matthew 28:19, where Jesus tells the disciples: "Therefore, go and make disciples of all the nations, baptizing them in the name of the Father and the Son and the Holy Spirit." (Also check out John 14:16-26 and 15:26-27; 2 Corinthians 3:17 and 13:14.) The classic description of the Trinity is "one in essence, three in persons." The Holy Spirit is the third person described here, and he is just as much God as are the Father and the Son. • ***The Spirit's functions.*** We can do little more here than simply list the roles that the Holy Spirit fulfills: he anoints and serves alongside the Messiah (Isaiah 48:16; 61:1; Luke 4:18-19); he ushers in the "last days" (Joel 2:28-32; Acts 2:14-36); he unifies the body of Christ (1 Corinthians 12:4-11; Ephesians 4:1-16); he gives new life (John 3:5-8); he convicts us of sin and enables us to repent and come to faith in Christ (John 16:8); he testifies to Jesus as the Messiah (John 14:26 and 16:14); he guides us into truth (John 16:13); he bears fruit in our life (Galatians 5:22-25); he gives us supernatural gifts (1 Corinthians 12–14); he prays for us (Romans 8:26); he is present in *all* Christians (Romans 8:9-11; 1 Corinthians 6:19). Even from this very brief list you can begin to see how crucial the Spirit's role is in our life. Knowing this, it is understandable that Jesus calls the Holy Spirit the "Counselor" or "Encourager" (John 15:26). As characters in a DIVINE DRAMA, it is comforting for us to know that there is indeed an Author who knows and loves the people he created so much that he "wrote himself into the play." And that now, having left the visible stage, he remains behind in an unseen—but no less real—way, guiding and strengthening his people.

carefully, all of you, fellow Jews and residents of
Jerusalem! Make no mistake about this. 15Some of
you are saying these people are drunk. It isn't true!
It's much too early for that. People don't get drunk
by nine o'clock in the morning. 16No, what you see
this morning was predicted centuries ago by the
prophet Joel:

17 'In the last days, God said,
I will pour out my Spirit upon all people.
Your sons and daughters will prophesy,
your young men will see visions,
and your old men will dream dreams.
18 In those days I will pour out my Spirit
upon all my servants, men and women alike,
and they will prophesy.
19 And I will cause wonders in the heavens above
and signs on the earth below—
blood and fire and clouds of smoke.
20 The sun will be turned into darkness,
and the moon will turn bloodred,
before that great and glorious day of the Lord
arrives.
21 And anyone who calls on the name of the Lord
will be saved.'*

22 "People of Israel, listen! God publicly endorsed
Jesus of Nazareth by doing wonderful miracles, wonders, and signs through him, as you well know. 23But
you followed God's prearranged plan. With the help
of lawless Gentiles, you nailed him to the cross and
murdered him. 24However, God released him from
the horrors of death and raised him back to life
again, for death could not keep him in its grip. 25King
David said this about him:

'I know the Lord is always with me.
I will not be shaken, for he is right beside me.
26 No wonder my heart is filled with joy,
and my mouth shouts his praises!
My body rests in hope.
27 For you will not leave my soul among the dead*
or allow your Holy One to rot in the grave.
28 You have shown me the way of life,
and you will give me wonderful joy in your
presence.'*

29 "Dear brothers, think about this! David wasn't
referring to himself when he spoke these words I
have quoted, for he died and was buried, and his
tomb is still here among us. 30But he was a prophet,
and he knew God had promised with an oath that
one of David's own descendants would sit on
David's throne as the Messiah. 31David was looking
into the future and predicting the Messiah's resurrection. He was saying that the Messiah would not be
left among the dead and that his body would not rot
in the grave.
32 "This prophecy was speaking of Jesus, whom
God raised from the dead, and we all are witnesses
of this. 33Now he sits on the throne of highest honor
in heaven, at God's right hand. And the Father, as he
had promised, gave him the Holy Spirit to pour out
upon us, just as you see and hear today. 34For David
himself never ascended into heaven, yet he said,

**My mom has said some pretty bad things to me over the years. Now that I'm a Christian, I know I should forgive her, but I can't. What should I do?**

The gap between knowing you need to forgive someone and actually being able to do it often seems like a vast canyon. You can see the other side, but getting there seems impossible.

Ever seen a shower drain plugged up with a two-month accumulation of hair? The water slowly seeps through the molding mass of greasy, soapy yuk. No amount of plunging can bring the glob up because it's too deep.

The next solution usually is to burn away the clog by applying something like Drano. Sometimes this works if the buildup is not too severe. The last resort, of course, is to call a plumber. He'll come in with a narrow, hard, yet flexible piece of metal called a snake and drill through the clog until the water is flowing freely.

Unforgiveness is like a clogged drain. Sometimes it is fairly easy to unclog. Someone hurts us, we let them know they hurt us, they say they're sorry, we forgive them, and the whole episode is forgotten. But when unforgiveness collects from years of hurt it becomes similar to what a drain would look like after years of bathing your cat in the sink without cleaning out the drain! You might as well buy a new sink.

Likewise, our sin can collect and become a gross, yucky mass that eventually clogs our relationship with God. Until it is removed, we can't really receive anything meaningful from him. Jesus came to "unclog our pipes" so God's love and forgiveness could flow to us freely. He did nothing wrong—we were the transgressors—yet he died to open the way for that flow of love.

From what you wrote, your mom's sin against you has clogged your relationship. You may have every right not to forgive your mom, but you must put aside that right for a greater goal—you must "die" and open yourself to learning how you and your mom can love each other. Otherwise the clog will only get worse.

God took the initiative with us by humbling himself and forgiving all of our sin (to see the comparison of how much God has forgiven us and how much we must forgive others, see Matthew 18:21-34). You must do the same with the person who has wronged you.

The forgiveness must be from your heart and must not be dependent upon whether she feels sorry for what she has done. Forgiving someone is a gift only you can offer. You can't make someone take a free gift, they must reach out and receive it. Though the canyon looks deep and treacherous, the reward on the other side is a clear conscience, times of wonderful refreshment (see Acts 3:19), and—hopefully—a renewed relationship.

2:17-21 Joel 2:28-32. 2:27 Greek *in Hades;* also in 2:31. 2:25-28 Ps 16:8-11.

'The LORD said to my Lord,
Sit in honor at my right hand
35 until I humble your enemies,
making them a footstool under your feet.'*

[36]So let it be clearly known by everyone in Israel that
God has made this Jesus whom you crucified to be
both Lord and Messiah!"
[37]Peter's words convicted them deeply, and they
said to him and to the other apostles, "Brothers,
what should we do?"
[38]Peter replied, "Each of you must turn from your
sins and turn to God, and be baptized in the name
of Jesus Christ for the forgiveness of your sins. Then
you will receive the gift of the Holy Spirit. [39]This
promise is to you and to your children, and even to
the Gentiles*—all who have been called by the Lord
our God." [40]Then Peter continued preaching for a
long time, strongly urging all his listeners, "Save
yourselves from this generation that has gone
astray!"

**TOGETHER ● ● • • •**

2:44 **Recognizing the other believers as brothers and sisters in the family of God, the Christians in Jerusalem shared all they had so that all could benefit from God's blessings. It is tempting—especially if we have material wealth—to cut ourselves off from one another, each taking care of, providing for, and enjoying his own little piece of the world. But as part of God's spiritual family, we have a responsibility to help one another in every way possible. God's family works best when its members work together.**

[41]Those who believed what Peter said were baptized and added to the church—about three thousand in all. [42]They joined with the other believers
and devoted themselves to the apostles' teaching
and fellowship, sharing in the Lord's Supper and in
prayer.
[43]A deep sense of awe came over them all, and the
apostles performed many miraculous signs and
wonders. [44]And all the believers met together constantly and shared everything they had. [45]They sold
their possessions and shared the proceeds with those
in need. [46]They worshiped together at the Temple
each day, met in homes for the Lord's Supper, and
shared their meals with great joy and generosity—
[47]all the while praising God and enjoying the goodwill of all the people. And each day the Lord added
to their group those who were being saved.

## CHAPTER 3 PETER AND JOHN HEAL A MAN.

Peter and
John went to the Temple one afternoon to take part
in the three o'clock prayer service. [2]As they approached the Temple, a man lame from birth was
being carried in. Each day he was put beside the
Temple gate, the one called the Beautiful Gate, so he
could beg from the people going into the Temple.
[3]When he saw Peter and John about to enter, he
asked them for some money.
[4]Peter and John looked at him intently, and Peter
said, "Look at us!" [5]The lame man looked at them
eagerly, expecting a gift. [6]But Peter said, "I don't have
any money for you. But I'll give you what I have. In
the name of Jesus Christ of Nazareth, get up and
walk!"
[7]Then Peter took the lame man by the right hand
and helped him up. And as he did, the man's feet
and anklebones were healed and strengthened. [8]He
jumped up, stood on his feet, and began to walk!
Then, walking, leaping, and praising God, he went
into the Temple with them.
[9]All the people saw him walking and heard him
praising God. [10]When they realized he was the
lame beggar they had seen so often at the Beautiful
Gate, they were absolutely astounded! [11]They all
rushed out to Solomon's Colonnade, where he was
holding tightly to Peter and John. Everyone stood
there in awe of the wonderful thing that had happened.
[12]Peter saw his opportunity and addressed the
crowd. "People of Israel," he said, "what is so astounding about this? And why look at us as though
we had made this man walk by our own power and
godliness? [13]For it is the God of Abraham, the God
of Isaac, the God of Jacob, the God of all our ancestors who has brought glory to his servant Jesus by
doing this. This is the same Jesus whom you handed
over and rejected before Pilate, despite Pilate's decision to release him. [14]You rejected this holy, righteous one and instead demanded the release of a
murderer. [15]You killed the author of life, but God
raised him to life. And we are witnesses of this fact!
[16]"The name of Jesus has healed this man—and
you know how lame he was before. Faith in Jesus'
name has caused this healing before your very eyes.
[17]"Friends,* I realize that what you did to Jesus
was done in ignorance; and the same can be said of
your leaders. [18]But God was fulfilling what all the
prophets had declared about the Messiah beforehand—that he must suffer all these things. [19]Now
turn from your sins and turn to God, so you can be
cleansed of your sins. [20]Then wonderful times of
refreshment will come from the presence of the
Lord, and he will send Jesus your Messiah to you
again. [21]For he must remain in heaven until the time
for the final restoration of all things, as God promised long ago through his prophets. [22]Moses said,
'The Lord your God will raise up a Prophet like me
from among your own people. Listen carefully to
everything he tells you.'* [23]Then Moses said, 'Any-

**BETTER ● ● • • •**

3:6 **The lame beggar asked for money, but Peter gave him something much better—the use of his legs. We often ask God to solve a small problem, but he wants to give us a new life and help for *all* our problems. When we ask God for help, he may say, "I've got something even better for you." Ask God for what you want, but don't be surprised when he gives you what you really need.**

2:34-35 Ps 110:1. 2:39 Greek *to those far away.* 3:17 Greek *Brothers.* 3:22 Deut 18:15.

one who will not listen to that Prophet will be cut off from God's people and utterly destroyed.'*

[24]"Starting with Samuel, every prophet spoke about what is happening today. [25]You are the children of those prophets, and you are included in the covenant God promised to your ancestors. For God said to Abraham, 'Through your descendants all the families on earth will be blessed.'* [26]When God raised up his servant, he sent him first to you people of Israel, to bless you by turning each of you back from your sinful ways."

## CHAPTER 4

**PETER AND JOHN'S COURAGE.** While Peter and John were speaking to the people, the leading priests, the captain of the Temple guard, and some of the Sadducees came over to them. [2]They were very disturbed that Peter and John were claiming, on the authority of Jesus, that there is a resurrection of the dead. [3]They arrested them and, since it was already evening, jailed them until morning. [4]But many of the people who heard their message believed it, so that the number of believers totaled about five thousand men, not counting women and children.*

[5]The next day the council of all the rulers and elders and teachers of religious law met in Jerusalem. [6]Annas the high priest was there, along with Caiaphas, John, Alexander, and other relatives of the high priest. [7]They brought in the two disciples and demanded, "By what power, or in whose name, have you done this?"

[8]Then Peter, filled with the Holy Spirit, said to them, "Leaders and elders of our nation, [9]are we being questioned because we've done a good deed for a crippled man? Do you want to know how he was healed? [10]Let me clearly state to you and to all the people of Israel that he was healed in the name and power of Jesus Christ from Nazareth, the man you crucified, but whom God raised from the dead. [11]For Jesus is the one referred to in the Scriptures, where it says,

'The stone that you builders
rejected
has now become the
cornerstone.'*

[12]There is salvation in no one else! There is no other name in all of heaven for people to call on to save them."

[13]The members of the council were amazed when they saw the boldness of Peter and John, for they could see that they were ordinary men who had had no special training. They also recognized them as men who had been with Jesus. [14]But since the man who had been healed was standing right there among them, the council had nothing to say. [15]So they sent Peter and John out of the council chamber* and conferred among themselves.

[16]"What should we do with these men?" they asked each other. "We can't deny they have done a miraculous sign, and everybody in Jerusalem knows about it. [17]But perhaps we can stop them from spreading their propaganda. We'll warn them not to speak to anyone in Jesus' name again." [18]So they called the apostles back in and told them never again to speak or teach about Jesus.

[19]But Peter and John replied, "Do you think God wants us to obey you rather than him? [20]We cannot stop telling about the wonderful things we have seen and heard."

[21]The council then threatened them further, but they finally let them go because they didn't know how to punish them without starting a riot. For everyone was praising God [22]for this miraculous sign—the healing of a man who had been lame for more than forty years.

[23]As soon as they were freed, Peter and John found the other believers and told them what the leading priests and elders had said. [24]Then all the believers were united as they lifted their voices in prayer: "O Sovereign Lord, Creator of heaven and earth, the sea, and everything in them—[25]you spoke long ago by the Holy Spirit through our ancestor King David, your servant, saying,

### REFRESHED ● ● • • •

3:19 **When we repent, God promises not only to wipe away our sin, but also to bring spiritual refreshment. Repentance may seem painful at first because it is hard to give up certain sins. But God will give you a better way. As Hosea promised, "Let us press on to know him! Then he will respond to us as surely as the arrival of dawn or the coming of rains in early spring" (Hosea 6:3). Do you feel a need to be refreshed?**

### "Here's what I did..."

I don't find it easy to witness. I haven't memorized a lot of verses, and I'm still working my way through the Bible. It's easy to tell myself that I can wait until I know more.

But when I read Acts 4:13, I realized I was kidding myself. The verse talks about the boldness of Peter and John, and says that the Jewish council noticed that they were uneducated and nonprofessionals. But they knew Jesus. In other words, you don't have to know the whole Bible or go to seminary to be able to share your faith. The main thing is to know Jesus and share what you know with other people. I'm finding that he gives me the boldness to open my mouth, if I ask him.

Kenneth

3:23 Deut 18:19; Lev 23:29. 3:25 Gen 22:18. 4:4 Greek *5,000 adult males.* 4:11 Ps 118:22. 4:15 Greek *the Sanhedrin.*

'Why did the nations rage?
Why did the people waste their time with
futile plans?
[26]The kings of the earth prepared for battle;
the rulers gathered together
against the Lord
and against his Messiah.'*

[27]"That is what has happened here in this city! For
Herod Antipas, Pontius Pilate the governor, the Gentiles, and the people of Israel were all united against
Jesus, your holy servant, whom you anointed. [28]In
fact, everything they did occurred according to your
eternal will and plan. [29]And now, O Lord, hear their
threats, and give your servants great boldness in their
preaching. [30]Send your healing power; may miraculous signs and wonders be done through the name
of your holy servant Jesus."

## STRENGTH ● ● • • •

4:24-30 **Notice how the believers prayed. First they praised God, then they told God their specific problem and asked for his help. They did not ask God to remove the problem, but to help them deal with it. This is a model for us to follow when we pray. We may ask God to remove our problems, and he may choose to do so, but we must recognize that often God will leave the problem in place and give us the strength to deal with it.**

[31]After this prayer, the building where they were
meeting shook, and they were all filled with the Holy
Spirit. And they preached God's message with boldness.

[32]All the believers were of one heart and mind,
and they felt that what they owned was not their
own; they shared everything they had. [33]And the
apostles gave powerful witness to the resurrection of
the Lord Jesus, and God's great favor was upon them
all. [34]There was no poverty among them, because
people who owned land or houses sold them [35]and
brought the money to the apostles to give to others
in need.

[36]For instance, there was Joseph, the one the apostles nicknamed Barnabas (which means "Son of
Encouragement"). He was from the tribe of Levi and
came from the island of Cyprus. [37]He sold a field he
owned and brought the money to the apostles for
those in need.

## CHAPTER 5 ANANIAS AND SAPPHIRA LIE TO GOD.

There was also a man named Ananias who, with
his wife, Sapphira, sold some property. [2]He
brought part of the money to the apostles, but he
claimed it was the full amount. His wife had agreed
to this deception.

[3]Then Peter said, "Ananias, why has Satan filled
your heart? You lied to the Holy Spirit, and you kept
some of the money for yourself. [4]The property was
yours to sell or not sell, as you wished. And after
selling it, the money was yours to give away. How

4:25-26 Ps 2:1-2.

## ATTRACTIONS ● ● • • •

5:14 **What makes Christianity attractive? It is easy to be drawn to churches because of exciting programs, good speakers, beautiful facilities, or friendly people. Believers were attracted to the early church by God's power and miracles; the generosity, sincerity, honesty, and unity of the members; and the character of the leaders. We must be careful that our standards don't slip. God wants to add to his *church*, not just to programs or congregations.**

could you do a thing like this? You weren't lying to
us but to God."

[5]As soon as Ananias heard these words, he fell to
the floor and died. Everyone who heard about it was
terrified. [6]Then some young men wrapped him in a
sheet and took him out and buried him.

[7]About three hours later his wife came in, not
knowing what had happened. [8]Peter asked her, "Was
this the price you and your husband received for
your land?"

"Yes," she replied, "that was the price."

[9]And Peter said, "How could the two of you even
think of doing a thing like this—conspiring together
to test the Spirit of the Lord? Just outside that door
are the young men who buried your husband, and
they will carry you out, too."

[10]Instantly, she fell to the floor and died. When the
young men came in and saw that she was dead, they
carried her out and buried her beside her husband.
[11]Great fear gripped the entire church and all others
who heard what had happened.

[12]Meanwhile, the apostles were performing many
miraculous signs and wonders among the people.
And the believers were meeting regularly at the
Temple in the area known as Solomon's Colonnade.
[13]No one else dared to join them, though everyone
had high regard for them. [14]And more and more
people believed and were brought to the Lord—
crowds of both men and women. [15]As a result of the
apostles' work, sick people were brought out into the
streets on beds and mats so that Peter's shadow
might fall across some of them as he went by.
[16]Crowds came in from the villages around Jerusalem, bringing their sick and those possessed by evil
spirits, and they were all healed.

[17]The high priest and his friends, who were Sadducees, reacted with violent jealousy. [18]They ar-

## REACTIONS ● ● • • •

5:17-18 **The apostles had power to do miracles, great boldness in preaching, and God's presence in their lives—yet they were not free from hatred and persecution. They were arrested and put in jail, beaten with rods and whips, and slandered by community leaders. Faith in God does not make troubles disappear; it makes troubles appear less fearsome because it puts them in the right perspective. You cannot expect everyone to react favorably when you share something as dynamic as your faith in Christ. Some will be jealous of you, frightened, or threatened. Expect some negative reactions. But remember that you must be more concerned about God's reactions than people's reactions.**

rested the apostles and put them in the jail. [19]But an angel of the Lord came at night, opened the gates of the jail, and brought them out. Then he told them, [20]"Go to the Temple and give the people this message of life!" [21]So the apostles entered the Temple about daybreak and immediately began teaching.

When the high priest and his officials arrived, they convened the high council,* along with all the elders of Israel. Then they sent for the apostles to be brought for trial. [22]But when the Temple guards went to the jail, the men were gone. So they returned to the council and reported, [23]"The jail was locked, with the guards standing outside, but when we opened the gates, no one was there!"

[24]When the captain of the Temple guard and the leading priests heard this, they were perplexed, wondering where it would all end. [25]Then someone arrived with the news that the men they had jailed were out in the Temple, teaching the people.

[26]The captain went with his Temple guards and arrested them, but without violence, for they were afraid the people would kill them if they treated the apostles roughly. [27]Then they brought the apostles in before the council. [28]"Didn't we tell you never again to teach in this man's name?" the high priest demanded. "Instead, you have filled all Jerusalem with your teaching about Jesus, and you intend to blame us for his death!"

[29]But Peter and the apostles replied, "We must obey God rather than human authority. [30]The God of our ancestors raised Jesus from the dead after you killed him by crucifying him. [31]Then God put him in the place of honor at his right hand as Prince and Savior. He did this to give the people of Israel an opportunity to turn from their sins and turn to God so their sins would be forgiven. [32]We are witnesses of these things and so is the Holy Spirit, who is given by God to those who obey him."

[33]At this, the high council was furious and decided to kill them. [34]But one member had a different perspective. He was a Pharisee named Gamaliel, who was an expert on religious law and was very popular with the people. He stood up and ordered that the apostles be sent outside the council chamber for a while. [35]Then he addressed his colleagues as follows: "Men of Israel, take care what you are planning to do to these men! [36]Some time ago there was that fellow Theudas, who pretended to be someone great. About

## STEPHEN

**UPS:**

- One of seven leaders chosen to supervise food distribution to the needy in the early church
- Known for his spiritual qualities of faith, wisdom, grace, and power, and for the Spirit's presence in his life
- Outstanding leader, teacher, and debater
- First to give his life for the gospel

**STATS:**

- Church responsibilities: Deacon—distributing food to the needy
- Contemporaries: Paul, Caiaphas, Gamaliel, the apostles

The book you hold in your hand is there today because thousands of Christians thoughout history have given their lives to carry the gospel around the world. They died for the Good News. It is important for us to remember, though, that a person cannot *give* his life for the gospel until he has learned to *live* his life for the gospel. Stephen was just that kind of person.

One way God trains his servants is to have them do jobs that don't seem very important or glamorous. We meet Stephen in the New Testament when he is appointed with others to manage the distribution of food among Christians in Jerusalem. Because many people lost jobs and belongings when they became Christians, it became necessary for all Christians to share what they had with each other. Stephen and others were asked to make sure that the available food was handed out fairly. It was probably a job with more headaches than thank-yous.

Stephen also proved himself as a powerful speaker. When he was harassed in the Temple by several troublemakers about his faith, he responded calmly and clearly. His logic devastated their arguments. Stephen was hauled before the official religious court, where he used a summary of the Jews' own history to show that Jesus was the Savior. The court was unable to answer him, so they decided to silence him. They stoned him to death while he prayed for their forgiveness. Stephen's final words show how much he had become like Jesus in a short time. His death had a lasting effect on a young Paul, who would later change from fiercely destroying the faith to radically defending it.

Stephen's life is a continual challenge to Christians. Because he was the first to die for the faith, his sacrifice raises questions: How many risks do we take in being Jesus' followers? Would we be willing to die for him? Are we really willing to live for him?

LESSONS: Striving for excellence in small assignments prepares a person for greater responsibilities

Real understanding of God always leads to practical and compassionate actions

KEY VERSES: "And as they stoned him, Stephen prayed, 'Lord Jesus, receive my spirit.' And he fell to his knees, shouting, 'Lord, don't charge them with this sin!' And with that, he died" (Acts 7:59-60).

Stephen's story is told in Acts 6:3–8:2. He also is mentioned in Acts 11:19; 22:20.

5:21 Greek *Sanhedrin;* also in 5:27, 41.

four hundred others joined him, but he was killed, and his followers went their various ways. The whole movement came to nothing. [37]After him, at the time of the census, there was Judas of Galilee. He got some people to follow him, but he was killed, too, and all his followers were scattered.

[38]"So my advice is, leave these men alone. If they are teaching and doing these things merely on their own, it will soon be overthrown. [39]But if it is of God, you will not be able to stop them. You may even find yourselves fighting against God."

[40]The council accepted his advice. They called in the apostles and had them flogged. Then they ordered them never again to speak in the name of Jesus, and they let them go. [41]The apostles left the high council rejoicing that God had counted them worthy to suffer dishonor for the name of Jesus. [42]And every day, in the Temple and in their homes,* they continued to teach and preach this message: "The Messiah you are looking for is Jesus."

## CHAPTER 6 **SEVEN MEN WITH SPECIAL WORK.**

But as the believers* rapidly multiplied, there were rumblings of discontent. Those who spoke Greek complained against those who spoke Hebrew, saying that their widows were being discriminated against in the daily distribution of food. [2]So the Twelve called a meeting of all the believers.

"We apostles should spend our time preaching and teaching the word of God, not administering a food program," they said. [3]"Now look around among yourselves, brothers, and select seven men who are well respected and are full of the Holy Spirit and wisdom. We will put them in charge of this business. [4]Then we can spend our time in prayer and preaching and teaching the word."

### THE WAVE ● ● • • ·

**6:7 The gospel spread like ripples on a pond where, from a single center, each wave touches the next, spreading wider and farther. The gospel still spreads this way today. You don't have to change the world single-handedly—it is enough just to be part of the wave, touching those around you, who in turn will touch others until all have felt the movement. Don't ever feel that your part is insignificant or unimportant.**

[5]This idea pleased the whole group, and they chose the following: Stephen (a man full of faith and the Holy Spirit), Philip, Procorus, Nicanor, Timon, Parmenas, and Nicolas of Antioch (a Gentile convert to the Jewish faith, who had now become a Christian). [6]These seven were presented to the apostles, who prayed for them as they laid their hands on them.

[7]God's message was preached in ever-widening circles. The number of believers greatly increased in Jerusalem, and many of the Jewish priests were converted, too.

[8]Stephen, a man full of God's grace and power, performed amazing miracles and signs among the people. [9]But one day some men from the Synagogue of Freed Slaves, as it was called, started to debate with him. They were Jews from Cyrene, Alexandria, Cilicia, and the province of Asia. [10]None of them was able to stand against the wisdom and Spirit by which Stephen spoke.

[11]So they persuaded some men to lie about Stephen, saying, "We heard him blaspheme Moses, and even God." [12]Naturally, this roused the crowds, the elders, and the teachers of religious law. So they arrested Stephen and brought him before the high council.* [13]The lying witnesses said, "This man is always speaking against the Temple and against the law of Moses. [14]We have heard him say that this Jesus of Nazareth will destroy the Temple and change the customs Moses handed down to us." [15]At this point everyone in the council stared at Stephen because his face became as bright as an angel's.

## CHAPTER 7 **STEPHEN IS EXECUTED.**

Then the high priest asked Stephen, "Are these accusations true?"

[2]This was Stephen's reply: "Brothers and honorable fathers, listen to me. Our glorious God appeared to our ancestor Abraham in Mesopotamia before he moved to Haran.* [3]God told him, 'Leave your native land and your relatives, and come to the land that I will show you.'* [4]So Abraham left the land of the Chaldeans and lived in Haran until his father died. Then God brought him here to the land where you now live. [5]But God gave him no inheritance here, not even one square foot of land. God did promise, however, that eventually the whole country would belong to Abraham and his descendants—though he had no children yet. [6]But God also told him that his descendants would live in a foreign country where they would be mistreated as slaves for four hundred years. [7]'But I will punish the nation that enslaves them,' God told him, 'and in the end they will come out and worship me in this place.'* [8]God also gave Abraham the covenant of circumcision at that time. And so Isaac, Abraham's son, was circumcised when he was eight days old. Isaac became the father of Jacob, and Jacob was the father of the twelve patriarchs of the Jewish nation.

[9]"These sons of Jacob were very jealous of their brother Joseph, and they sold him to be a slave in Egypt. But God was with him [10]and delivered him

### ACCUSED ● ● • • ·

**7:2-53 Stephen wasn't really defending himself. Instead he took the offensive, seizing the opportunity to summarize his teaching about Jesus. Stephen was accusing these religious leaders of failing to obey God's laws—the laws they prided themselves in following so meticulously. This was the same accusation that Jesus had leveled against them. When we witness for Jesus, we don't need to be on the defensive. Instead we should simply share our faith.**

5:42 Greek *from house to house.* 6:1 Greek *disciples;* also in 6:2, 7. 6:12 Greek *Sanhedrin;* also in 6:15. 7:2 *Mesopotamia* was the region now called Iraq. *Haran* was a city in what is now called Syria. 7:3 Gen 12:1. 7:5-7 Gen 12:7; 15:13-14; Exod 3:12.

from his anguish. And God gave him favor before
Pharaoh, king of Egypt. God also gave Joseph unusual wisdom, so that Pharaoh appointed him
governor over all of Egypt and put him in charge of
all the affairs of the palace.
11 "But a famine came upon Egypt and Canaan.
There was great misery for our ancestors, as they ran
out of food. 12 Jacob heard that there was still grain in
Egypt, so he sent his sons* to buy some. 13 The
second time they went, Joseph revealed his identity
to his brothers, and they were introduced to Pharaoh. 14 Then Joseph sent for his father, Jacob, and all
his relatives to come to Egypt, seventy-five persons in
all. 15 So Jacob went to Egypt. He died there, as did all
his sons. 16 All of them were taken to Shechem and
buried in the tomb Abraham had bought from the
sons of Hamor in Shechem.
17 "As the time drew near when God would fulfill
his promise to Abraham, the number of our people
in Egypt greatly increased. 18 But then a new king
came to the throne of Egypt who knew nothing
about Joseph. 19 This king plotted against our
people and forced parents to abandon their newborn babies so they would die.
20 "At that time Moses was born—a beautiful child
in God's eyes. His parents cared for him at home for
three months. 21 When at last they had to abandon
him, Pharaoh's daughter found him and raised him
as her own son. 22 Moses was taught all the wisdom
of the Egyptians, and he became mighty in both
speech and action.
23 "One day when he was forty years old, he decided to visit his relatives, the people of Israel. 24 During this visit, he saw an Egyptian mistreating a man
of Israel. So Moses came to his defense and avenged
him, killing the Egyptian. 25 Moses assumed his
brothers would realize that God had sent him to
rescue them, but they didn't.
26 "The next day he visited them again and saw two
men of Israel fighting. He tried to be a peacemaker.
'Men,' he said, 'you are brothers. Why are you hurting each other?'
27 "But the man in the wrong pushed Moses aside
and told him to mind his own business. 'Who made
you a ruler and judge over us?' he asked. 28 'Are you
going to kill me as you killed that Egyptian yesterday?' 29 When Moses heard that, he fled the country
and lived as a foreigner in the land of Midian, where
his two sons were born.
30 "Forty years later, in the desert near Mount Sinai,
an angel appeared to Moses in the flame of a burning bush. 31 Moses saw it and wondered what it was.
As he went to see, the voice of the Lord called out to
him, 32 'I am the God of your ancestors—the God of
Abraham, Isaac, and Jacob.' Moses shook with terror
and dared not look.
33 "And the Lord said to him, 'Take off your
sandals, for you are standing on holy ground.
34 You can be sure that I have seen the misery of my
people in Egypt. I have heard their cries. So I have
come to rescue them. Now go, for I will send you
to Egypt.'* 35 And so God sent back the same man
his people had previously rejected by demanding,
'Who made you a ruler and judge over us?'
Through the angel who appeared to him in the
burning bush, Moses was sent to be their ruler and
savior. 36 And by means of many miraculous signs
and wonders, he led them out of Egypt, through
the Red Sea, and back and forth through the wilderness for forty years.
37 "Moses himself told the people of Israel, 'God
will raise up a Prophet like me from among your
own people.'* 38 Moses was with the assembly of
God's people in the wilderness. He was the mediator between the people of Israel and the angel who
gave him life-giving words on Mount Sinai to pass
on to us.

**Some kids at school (and even some teachers) give Christians a pretty tough time. This makes me not want to let anyone know I'm a believer. What should I do?**

Rejection comes with being a Christian, because our life and beliefs go against the flow of the rest of the world. Growing closer to God will naturally make you grow further away from the world.

Read Acts 7:54-60. Stephen took a stand for Christ that cost him much more than rejection from a few friends. It cost him his life. Read further, and in Acts 8 and 9 you will see what the results of a fearless faith can be.

Imagine being able to see all of history from beginning to end. You would understand so much more because you could see the whole picture. But only God can do that—so we have to trust him. We have to live on this earth without being able to see the future.

If Stephen had known what his death would accomplish, he would have died smiling. A man named Paul was one of the foremost persecutors of Christians. But Paul's life was turned around, and he became a follower of Christ. Paul had heard Stephen speak—and he had watched him die.

Paul didn't just become a church-only, pew-sitter type of follower. He traveled throughout the world, sharing the Good News about Christ. He also wrote nearly half of the books of the New Testament! Stephen's rejection helped bring Paul to Christ.

People are watching you and other Christians at school. They are seeing how you respond to rejection and verbal abuse. Within those crowded halls are people who want to believe in something true, something worth living for no matter what the cost. And when they find it, they may make an incredible impact in their world for Christ.

What do they learn from watching you?

7:12 Greek *our fathers;* also in 7:15. 7:31-34 Exod 3:5-10. 7:37 Deut 18:15.

## PREPARING ● ● • • •

8:4 **Persecution forced the believers out of their homes in Jerusalem, but with them went the gospel. Often we have to become uncomfortable before we'll move. Discomfort may be unwanted, but it is not unproductive, for out of our hurting God works his purposes. The next time you are tempted to complain about uncomfortable or painful circumstances, stop and ask if God may be preparing you for a special task.**

39 "But our ancestors rejected Moses and wanted
to return to Egypt. 40 They told Aaron, 'Make us
some gods who can lead us, for we don't know
what has become of this Moses, who brought us
out of Egypt.' 41 So they made an idol shaped like a
calf, and they sacrificed to it and rejoiced in this
thing they had made. 42 Then God turned away
from them and gave them up to serve the sun,
moon, and stars as their gods! In the book of the
prophets it is written,

'Was it to me you were bringing sacrifices
during those forty years in the wilderness,
Israel?
43 No, your real interest was in your pagan gods—
the shrine of Molech,
the star god Rephan,
and the images you made to worship them.
So I will send you into captivity
far away in Babylon.'*

44 "Our ancestors carried the Tabernacle* with
them through the wilderness. It was constructed in
exact accordance with the plan shown to Moses by
God. 45 Years later, when Joshua led the battles
against the Gentile nations that God drove out of
this land, the Tabernacle was taken with them into
their new territory. And it was used there until the
time of King David.
46 "David found favor with God and asked for
the privilege of building a permanent Temple for
the God of Jacob.* 47 But it was Solomon who
actually built it. 48 However, the Most High doesn't
live in temples made by human hands. As the
prophet says,

49 'Heaven is my throne,
and the earth is my footstool.
Could you ever build me a temple as good
as that?'
asks the Lord.
'Could you build a dwelling place for me?
50 Didn't I make everything in heaven and
earth?'*

51 "You stubborn people! You are heathen at heart
and deaf to the truth. Must you forever resist the
Holy Spirit? But your ancestors did, and so do you!
52 Name one prophet your ancestors didn't persecute! They even killed the ones who predicted the
coming of the Righteous One—the Messiah whom
you betrayed and murdered. 53 You deliberately disobeyed God's law, though you received it from the
hands of angels.*"
54 The Jewish leaders were infuriated by Stephen's
accusation, and they shook their fists in rage.* 55 But
Stephen, full of the Holy Spirit, gazed steadily upward into heaven and saw the glory of God, and he
saw Jesus standing in the place of honor at God's
right hand. 56 And he told them, "Look, I see the
heavens opened and the Son of Man standing in the
place of honor at God's right hand!"
57 Then they put their hands over their ears, and
drowning out his voice with their shouts, they
rushed at him. 58 They dragged him out of the city
and began to stone him. The official witnesses took
off their coats and laid them at the feet of a young
man named Saul.*
59 And as they stoned him, Stephen prayed, "Lord
Jesus, receive my spirit." 60 And he fell to his knees,
shouting, "Lord, don't charge them with this sin!"
And with that, he died.

## CHAPTER 8

**PHILIP AND AN ETHIOPIAN.** Saul was one
of the official witnesses at the killing of Stephen.
A great wave of persecution began that day,
sweeping over the church in Jerusalem, and all the
believers except the apostles fled into Judea and
Samaria. 2 (Some godly men came and buried Stephen with loud weeping.) 3 Saul was going everywhere to devastate the church. He went from house
to house, dragging out both men and women to
throw them into jail.
4 But the believers who had fled Jerusalem went
everywhere preaching the Good News about Jesus.
5 Philip, for example, went to the city of Samaria
and told the people there about the Messiah.
6 Crowds listened intently to what he had to say
because of the miracles he did. 7 Many evil spirits
were cast out, screaming as they left their victims.
And many who had been paralyzed or lame were
healed. 8 So there was great joy in that city.
9 A man named Simon had been a sorcerer there
for many years, claiming to be someone great.
10 The Samaritan people, from the least to the greatest, often spoke of him as "the Great One—the
Power of God." 11 He was very influential because of
the magic he performed. 12 But now the people
believed Philip's message of Good News concerning the Kingdom of God and the name of Jesus
Christ. As a result, many men and women were
baptized. 13 Then Simon himself believed and was
baptized. He began following Philip wherever he

## CRITICISM ● ● • • •

8:24 **Do you remember the last time a parent or friend strongly criticized you? Were you hurt? Angry? Defensive? Learn a lesson from Simon and his reaction to Peter's words. Simon exclaimed, "Pray to the Lord for me." When you are rebuked for a serious mistake, it is for your good. Admit your error and ask for prayer.**

7:42-43 Amos 5:25-27. 7:44 Greek *the tent of witness.* 7:46 Some manuscripts read *the house of Jacob.* 7:49-50 Isa 66:1-2. 7:53 Greek *received the Law as it was ordained by angels.* 7:54 Greek *they were grinding their teeth against him.* 7:58 *Saul* is later called Paul; see 13:9.

went, and he was amazed by the great miracles and
signs Philip performed.
14When the apostles back in Jerusalem heard that
the people of Samaria had accepted God's message,
they sent Peter and John there. 15As soon as they
arrived, they prayed for these new Christians to receive the Holy Spirit. 16The Holy Spirit had not yet
come upon any of them, for they had only been
baptized in the name of the
Lord Jesus. 17Then Peter and
John laid their hands upon
these believers, and they received the Holy Spirit.
18When Simon saw that
the Holy Spirit was given
when the apostles placed
their hands upon people's
heads, he offered money to
buy this power. 19"Let me
have this power, too," he
exclaimed, "so that when I
lay my hands on people,
they will receive the Holy
Spirit!"
20But Peter replied, "May
your money perish with you
for thinking God's gift can
be bought! 21You can have
no part in this, for your heart
is not right before God.
22Turn from your wicked-
ness and pray to the Lord.
Perhaps he will forgive your
evil thoughts, 23for I can see
that you are full of bitterness
and held captive by sin."
24"Pray to the Lord for
me," Simon exclaimed,
"that these terrible things
won't happen to me!"
25After testifying and
preaching the word of the
Lord in Samaria, Peter and
John returned to Jerusalem.
And they stopped in many
Samaritan villages along
the way to preach the Good
News to them, too.
26As for Philip, an angel
of the Lord said to him,
"Go south* down the des-
ert road that runs from Jerusalem to Gaza." 27So he
did, and he met the trea-
surer of Ethiopia, a eunuch
of great authority under the
queen of Ethiopia.* The eunuch had gone to Jerusa-
lem to worship, 28and he
was now returning. Seated
in his carriage, he was reading aloud from the book
of the prophet Isaiah.
29The Holy Spirit said to Philip, "Go over and
walk along beside the carriage."
30Philip ran over and heard the man reading from
the prophet Isaiah; so he asked, "Do you understand
what you are reading?"
31The man replied, "How can I, when there is no

## PAUL

No person, apart from Jesus himself, shaped the history of Christianity as much as the apostle Paul. Paul was a leader in the frenzied persecution of Christians following Stephen's death. Eventually, Paul met Christ personally and his life was changed. However, Paul never lost his energy or intensity—it was redirected so that it was dedicated to Christ.

Paul was brought up in a very religious home. He was an expert in the Jewish Bible, the Old Testament. Convinced Christianity was dangerous to Judaism, Paul hated the Christian faith and persecuted Christians without mercy. At one point, Paul got permission to travel to Damascus to arrest Christians and bring them back to Jerusalem. His plans would have resulted in the death of many believers—but God had other plans. Paul was met on the road to Damascus by Jesus Christ . . . and Paul's life was never the same.

Paul became God's key tool in taking the gospel to non-Jewish people. Until Paul was converted, little had been done to carry Christ's message to the Gentiles. Paul and his missionary teams eventually carried the gospel across the entire Roman Empire.

Paul worked hard to convince the Jews that Gentiles were acceptable to God, but he spent even more time convincing Gentiles themselves that they were acceptable to God. People's lives were changed and challenged by meeting Christ through Paul.

God did not waste any part of Paul—his background, his training, his citizenship, his mind, or even his weaknesses. He used them all. Are you willing to let God do the same for you? You will never know what he can do with you until you allow him to have all that you are!

**UPS:**
- Transformed by God from a persecutor of Christians to a preacher for Christ
- Preached for Christ throughout the Roman Empire on three missionary journeys
- Wrote letters, which became part of the New Testament, to various churches
- Was never afraid to face an issue head-on and deal with it
- Was sensitive to God's leading and, despite his strong personality, always did as God directed
- Often is called the apostle to the Gentiles

**DOWNS:**
- Witnessed and approved of Stephen's stoning
- Set out to destroy Christianity by persecuting Christians

**STATS:**
- Where: Born in Tarsus but became a world traveler for Christ
- Occupations: Trained as a Pharisee, learned the tentmaking trade, served as a missionary
- Contemporaries: Gamaliel, Stephen, the apostles, Luke, Barnabas, Timothy

LESSONS: The Good News is that forgiveness and eternal life are a gift of God's grace received by faith in Christ and available to all people

Obedience results from a relationship with God, but obedience will never create or earn that relationship

God will use our past and present so that we may serve him with our future

KEY VERSES: "For to me, living is for Christ, and dying is even better. Yet if I live, that means fruitful service for Christ. I really don't know which is better. I'm torn between two desires: Sometimes I want to live, and sometimes I long to go and be with Christ. That would be far better for me, but it is better for you that I live" (Philippians 1:21-24).

Paul's story is told in Acts 7:58–28:31 and throughout his New Testament letters.

8:26 Or *Go at noon.* 8:27 Greek *under the Candace, the queen of Ethiopia.*

one to instruct me?" And he begged Philip to come
up into the carriage and sit with him. [32]The passage
of Scripture he had been reading was this:

"He was led as a sheep to the slaughter.
And as a lamb is silent before the shearers,
he did not open his mouth.
[33]He was humiliated and received no justice.
Who can speak of his descendants?
For his life was taken from the earth."*

[34]The eunuch asked Philip, "Was Isaiah talking
about himself or someone else?" [35]So Philip began
with this same Scripture and then used many others
to tell him the Good News about Jesus.
[36]As they rode along, they came to some water,
and the eunuch said, "Look! There's some water!
Why can't I be baptized?"* [38]He ordered the carriage
to stop, and they went down into the water, and
Philip baptized him.
[39]When they came up out of the water, the Spirit
of the Lord caught Philip away. The eunuch never
saw him again but went on his way rejoicing.
[40]Meanwhile, Philip found himself farther north at
the city of Azotus! He preached the Good News there
and in every city along the way until he came to
Caesarea.

CHAPTER **9** **PAUL MEETS JESUS.** Meanwhile, Saul
was uttering threats with every breath. He was eager
to destroy the Lord's followers,* so he went to the
high priest. [2]He requested letters addressed to the
synagogues in Damascus, asking their cooperation
in the arrest of any followers of the Way he found
there. He wanted to bring them—both men and
women—back to Jerusalem in chains.

**DON'T WAIT ● ● • • •**

**9:20 Immediately after receiving his sight, Paul went to the synagogue to tell the Jews about Jesus Christ. Some Christians counsel new believers to wait until they are thoroughly grounded in their faith before attempting to share the gospel. Paul took time alone to learn about Jesus before beginning his worldwide ministry, but he did not wait to witness. Although we should not rush into a ministry unprepared, we do not need to wait before telling others what has happened to us.**

[3]As he was nearing Damascus on this mission, a
brilliant light from heaven suddenly beamed down
upon him! [4]He fell to the ground and heard a voice
saying to him, "Saul! Saul! Why are you persecuting
me?"
[5]"Who are you, sir?" Saul asked.
And the voice replied, "I am Jesus, the one you are
persecuting! [6]Now get up and go into the city, and
you will be told what you are to do."
[7]The men with Saul stood speechless with surprise, for they heard the sound of someone's voice,
but they saw no one! [8]As Saul picked himself up off
the ground, he found that he was blind. [9]So his
companions led him by the hand to Damascus. He
remained there blind for three days. And all that
time he went without food and water.
[10]Now there was a believer* in Damascus named
Ananias. The Lord spoke to him in a vision, calling,
"Ananias!"
"Yes, Lord!" he replied.
[11]The Lord said, "Go over to Straight Street, to the
house of Judas. When you arrive, ask for Saul of
Tarsus. He is praying to me right now. [12]I have shown
him a vision of a man named Ananias coming in
and laying his hands on him so that he can see
again."
[13]"But Lord," exclaimed Ananias, "I've heard
about the terrible things this man has done to the
believers in Jerusalem! [14]And we hear that he is
authorized by the leading priests to arrest every believer in Damascus."
[15]But the Lord said, "Go and do what I say. For
Saul is my chosen instrument to take my message to
the Gentiles and to kings, as well as to the people of
Israel. [16]And I will show him how much he must
suffer for me."
[17]So Ananias went and found Saul. He laid his
hands on him and said, "Brother Saul, the Lord
Jesus, who appeared to you on the road, has sent me
so that you may get your sight back and be filled with
the Holy Spirit." [18]Instantly something like scales fell
from Saul's eyes, and he regained his sight. Then he
got up and was baptized. [19]Afterward he ate some
food and was strengthened.
Saul stayed with the believers* in Damascus for a
few days. [20]And immediately he began preaching
about Jesus in the synagogues, saying, "He is indeed
the Son of God!"
[21]All who heard him were amazed. "Isn't this the
same man who persecuted Jesus' followers with such
devastation in Jerusalem?" they asked. "And we understand that he came here to arrest them and take
them in chains to the leading priests."
[22]Saul's preaching became more and more powerful, and the Jews in Damascus couldn't refute his
proofs that Jesus was indeed the Messiah. [23]After a
while the Jewish leaders decided to kill him. [24]But
Saul was told about their plot, and that they were
watching for him day and night at the city gate so
they could murder him. [25]So during the night, some
of the other believers* let him down in a large basket
through an opening in the city wall.
[26]When Saul arrived in Jerusalem, he tried to meet
with the believers, but they were all afraid of him.
They thought he was only pretending to be a believer! [27]Then Barnabas brought him to the apostles
and told them how Saul had seen the Lord on the
way to Damascus. Barnabas also told them what the
Lord had said to Saul and how he boldly preached
in the name of Jesus in Damascus. [28]Then the apos-

8:32-33 Isa 53:7-8. 8:36 Some manuscripts add verse 37, *"You can," Philip answered, "if you believe with all your heart." And the eunuch replied, "I believe that Jesus Christ is the Son of God."* 9:1 Greek *disciples.* 9:10 Greek *disciple;* also in 9:36. 9:19 Greek *disciples;* also in 9:26. 9:25 Greek *his disciples.*

## UNSUNG HEROES IN ACTS

When we think of the success of the early church, we often think of the work of the apostles. But the church could have died if it hadn't been for the "unsung" heroes, the men and women who through some small but committed act moved the church forward.

| *Hero* | *Reference* | *Heroic Action* |
|---|---|---|
| LAME BEGGAR | 3:9-12 | After his healing, he praised God. With the crowds gathering to see what happened, Peter used the opportunity to tell many about Jesus. |
| FIVE DEACONS | 6:2-5 | Everyone knows Stephen, and many people know Philip, but there were five other men chosen to be deacons. They not only laid the foundation for service in the church, but their hard work gave the apostles more time to preach the gospel. |
| ANANIAS | 9:10-19 | He had the responsibility of being the first to demonstrate Christ's love to Saul (Paul) after his conversion. |
| CORNELIUS | 10:30-35 | His example showed Peter that the gospel was for all people, Jews and Gentiles. |
| RHODA | 12:13-15 | Her persistence brought Peter inside Mary's home, where he would be safe. |
| JAMES | 15:13-21 | He took command of the Jerusalem council and had the courage and discernment to make a decision that would affect literally millions of Christians over many generations. |
| LYDIA | 16:13-15 | She opened her home to Paul, from which he led many to Christ and founded a church in Philippi. |
| JASON | 17:5-9 | He risked his life for the gospel by allowing Paul to stay in his home. He stood up for what was true and right, even though he faced persecution for it. |
| PAUL'S NEPHEW | 23:16-24 | He saved Paul's life by telling officials of a plot to murder Paul. |
| JULIUS | 27:1, 43 | He spared Paul's life when the other soldiers wanted to kill him. |

tles accepted Saul, and after that he was constantly
with them in Jerusalem, preaching boldly in the
name of the Lord. 29He debated with some Greek-
speaking Jews, but they plotted to murder him.
30When the believers* heard about it, however, they
took him to Caesarea and sent him on to his hometown of Tarsus.

31The church then had peace throughout Judea,
Galilee, and Samaria, and it grew in strength and
numbers. The believers were walking in the fear of
the Lord and in the comfort of the Holy Spirit.

32Peter traveled from place to place to visit the
believers, and in his travels he came to the Lord's
people in the town of Lydda. 33There he met a man
named Aeneas, who had been paralyzed and bedrid-
den for eight years. 34Peter said to him, "Aeneas, Jesus
Christ heals you! Get up and make your bed!" And
he was healed instantly. 35Then the whole population of Lydda and Sharon turned to the Lord when
they saw Aeneas walking around.

36There was a believer in Joppa named Tabitha
(which in Greek is Dorcas*). She was always doing
kind things for others and helping the poor.
37About this time she became ill and died. Her

### IMPACT ● ● • • •

**9:36-42** **Dorcas had an enormous impact on her community by "doing kind things for others and helping the poor." When she died, the room was filled with mourners, people she had helped. When she was brought back to life, the news raced through the town. God uses great preachers like Peter and Paul, but he also uses those who have other gifts, like kindness. Make good use of the gifts God has given you.**

9:30 Greek *brothers.* 9:36 The names *Tabitha* in Aramaic and *Dorcas* in Greek both mean "gazelle."

friends prepared her for burial and laid her in an upstairs room. 38But they had heard that Peter was nearby at Lydda, so they sent two men to beg him, "Please come as soon as possible!"

39So Peter returned with them; and as soon as he arrived, they took him to the upstairs room. The room was filled with widows who were weeping and showing him the coats and other garments Dorcas had made for them. 40But Peter asked them all to leave the room; then he knelt and prayed. Turning to the body he said, "Get up, Tabitha." And she opened her eyes! When she saw Peter, she sat up! 41He gave her his hand and helped her up. Then he called in the widows and all the believers, and he showed them that she was alive.

42The news raced through the whole town, and many believed in the Lord. 43And Peter stayed a long time in Joppa, living with Simon, a leatherworker.

## CHAPTER 10

**A ROMAN CAPTAIN CALLS FOR PETER.** In Caesarea there lived a Roman army officer named Cornelius, who was a captain of the Italian Regiment. 2He was a devout man who feared the God of Israel, as did his entire household. He gave generously to charity and was a man who regularly prayed to God. 3One afternoon about three o'clock, he had a vision in which he saw an angel of God coming toward him. "Cornelius!" the angel said.

4Cornelius stared at him in terror. "What is it, sir?" he asked the angel.

And the angel replied, "Your prayers and gifts to the poor have not gone unnoticed by God! 5Now send some men down to Joppa to find a man named Simon Peter. 6He is staying with Simon, a leatherworker who lives near the shore. Ask him to come and visit you."

7As soon as the angel was gone, Cornelius called two of his household servants and a devout soldier, one of his personal attendants. 8He told them what had happened and sent them off to Joppa.

9The next day as Cornelius's messengers were nearing the city, Peter went up to the flat roof to pray. It was about noon, 10and he was hungry. But while lunch was being prepared, he fell into a trance. 11He saw the sky open, and something like a large sheet was let down by its four corners. 12In the sheet were all sorts of animals, reptiles, and birds. 13Then a voice said to him, "Get up, Peter; kill and eat them."

14"Never, Lord," Peter declared. "I have never in all my life eaten anything forbidden by our Jewish laws.*"

15The voice spoke again, "If God says something is acceptable, don't say it isn't."* 16The same vision was repeated three times. Then the sheet was pulled up again to heaven.

17Peter was very perplexed. What could the vision mean? Just then the men sent by Cornelius found the house and stood outside at the gate. 18They asked if this was the place where Simon Peter was staying. 19Meanwhile, as Peter was puzzling over the vision, the Holy Spirit said to him, "Three men have come looking for you. 20Go down and go with them without hesitation. All is well, for I have sent them."

21So Peter went down and said, "I'm the man you are looking for. Why have you come?"

22They said, "We were sent by Cornelius, a Roman officer. He is a devout man who fears the God of Israel and is well respected by all the Jews. A holy angel instructed him to send for you so you can go to his house and give him a message." 23So Peter invited the men to be his guests for the night. The next day he went with them, accompanied by some other believers* from Joppa.

24They arrived in Caesarea the following day. Cornelius was waiting for him and had called together his relatives and close friends to meet Peter. 25As Peter entered his home, Cornelius fell to the floor before him in worship. 26But Peter pulled him up and said, "Stand up! I'm a human being like you!" 27So Cornelius got up, and they talked together and went inside where the others were assembled.

28Peter told them, "You know it is against the Jewish laws for me to come into a Gentile home like this. But God has shown me that I should never think of anyone as impure. 29So I came as soon as I was sent for. Now tell me why you sent for me."

30Cornelius replied, "Four days ago I was praying in my house at three o'clock in the afternoon. Suddenly, a man in dazzling clothes was standing in front of me. 31He told me, 'Cornelius, your prayers have been heard, and your gifts to the poor have been noticed by God! 32Now send some men to Joppa and summon Simon Peter. He is staying in the home of Simon, a leatherworker who lives near the shore.' 33So I sent for you at once, and it was good of you to come. Now here we are, waiting before God to hear the message the Lord has given you."

34Then Peter replied, "I see very clearly that God doesn't show partiality. 35In every nation he accepts those who fear him and do what is right. 36I'm sure you have heard about the Good News for the people of Israel—that there is peace with God through Jesus Christ, who is Lord of all. 37You know what happened all through Judea, beginning in Galilee after John the Baptist began preaching. 38And no doubt you know that God anointed Jesus of Nazareth with the Holy Spirit and with power. Then Jesus went around doing good and healing all who were oppressed by the Devil, for God was with him.

39"And we apostles are witnesses of all he did throughout Israel and in Jerusalem. They put him to death by crucifying him, 40but God raised him to life

**EAGER ● ● • • .**

**10:48 Cornelius wanted Peter to stay with him for several days. As a new believer, Cornelius realized his need for teaching and fellowship. Are you that eager to learn more about Christ? Recognize your need to be with more mature Christians, and then learn from them.**

10:14 Greek *anything common and unclean.* 10:15 Greek *"What God calls clean you must not call unclean."* 10:23 Greek *brothers.*

**SHOCKED ● ● • • •**

11:2-18 **When Peter brought the news of Cornelius's conversion back to Jerusalem, the believers were shocked that he had eaten with Gentiles. After they heard the whole story, however, they began praising God (11:18). Their reactions teach us how to handle disagreements with other Christians. Before judging the behavior of fellow believers, it is important to hear them out. The Holy Spirit may be using them to teach us something important.**

three days later. Then God allowed him to appear,
41not to the general public,* but to us whom God
had chosen beforehand to be his witnesses. We were
those who ate and drank with him after he rose from
the dead. 42And he ordered us to preach everywhere
and to testify that Jesus is ordained of God to be the
judge of all—the living and the dead. 43He is the one
all the prophets testified about, saying that everyone
who believes in him will have their sins forgiven
through his name."

44Even as Peter was saying these things, the Holy
Spirit fell upon all who had heard the message. 45The
Jewish believers who came with Peter were amazed
that the gift of the Holy Spirit had been poured out
upon the Gentiles, too. 46And there could be no
doubt about it, for they heard them speaking in
tongues and praising God.

Then Peter asked, 47"Can anyone object to their
being baptized, now that they have received the Holy
Spirit just as we did?" 48So he gave orders for them to
be baptized in the name of Jesus Christ. Afterward
Cornelius asked him to stay with them for several days.

## CHAPTER 11 WHY PETER PREACHES TO GENTILES.

Soon the news reached the apostles and other believers* in Judea that the Gentiles had received the word
of God. 2But when Peter arrived back in Jerusalem,
some of the Jewish believers* criticized him. 3"You
entered the home of Gentiles* and even ate with
them!" they said.

4Then Peter told them exactly what had happened. 5"One day in Joppa," he said, "while I was
praying, I went into a trance and saw a vision. Something like a large sheet was let down by its four
corners from the sky. And it came right down to me.
6When I looked inside the sheet, I saw all sorts of
small animals, wild animals, reptiles, and birds that
we are not allowed to eat. 7And I heard a voice say,
'Get up, Peter; kill and eat them.'

8"'Never, Lord,' I replied. 'I have never eaten anything forbidden by our Jewish laws.*'

9"But the voice from heaven came again, 'If God
says something is acceptable, don't say it isn't.'*

10"This happened three times before the sheet and
all it contained was pulled back up to heaven. 11Just
then three men who had been sent from Caesarea
arrived at the house where I was staying. 12The Holy
Spirit told me to go with them and not to worry
about their being Gentiles. These six brothers here
accompanied me, and we soon arrived at the home
of the man who had sent for us. 13He told us how an
angel had appeared to him in his home and had told
him, 'Send messengers to Joppa to find Simon Peter.
14He will tell you how you and all your household
will be saved!'

15"Well, I began telling them the Good News, but
just as I was getting started, the Holy Spirit fell on
them, just as he fell on us at the beginning. 16Then I
thought of the Lord's words when he said, 'John
baptized with* water, but you will be baptized with
the Holy Spirit.' 17And since God gave these Gentiles
the same gift he gave us when we believed in the
Lord Jesus Christ, who was I to argue?"

18When the others heard this, all their objections
were answered and they began praising God. They
said, "God has also given the Gentiles the privilege
of turning from sin and receiving eternal life."

19Meanwhile, the believers who had fled from
Jerusalem during the persecution after Stephen's
death traveled as far as Phoenicia, Cyprus, and
Antioch of Syria. They preached the Good News,
but only to Jews. 20However, some of the believers
who went to Antioch from Cyprus and Cyrene
began preaching to Gentiles* about the Lord Jesus.
21The power of the Lord was upon them, and large
numbers of these Gentiles believed and turned to
the Lord.

22When the church at Jerusalem heard what had
happened, they sent Barnabas to Antioch. 23When
he arrived and saw this proof of God's favor, he was
filled with joy, and he encouraged the believers to
stay true to the Lord. 24Barnabas was a good man, full
of the Holy Spirit and strong in faith. And large
numbers of people were brought to the Lord.

25Then Barnabas went on to Tarsus to find Saul.
26When he found him, he brought him back to
Antioch. Both of them stayed there with the church
for a full year, teaching great numbers of people. (It
was there at Antioch that the believers* were first
called Christians.)

27During this time, some prophets traveled from
Jerusalem to Antioch. 28One of them named Agabus
stood up in one of the meetings to predict by the
Spirit that a great famine was coming upon the entire
Roman world. (This was fulfilled during the reign of
Claudius.) 29So the believers in Antioch decided to
send relief to the brothers and sisters* in Judea,
everyone giving as much as they could. 30This they
did, entrusting their gifts to Barnabas and Saul to
take to the elders of the church in Jerusalem.

## CHAPTER 12 AN ANGEL LETS PETER OUT OF PRISON.

About that time King Herod Agrippa* began to persecute some believers in the church. 2He had the

10:41 Greek *the people.* 11:1 Greek *brothers.* 11:2 Greek *those of the circumcision.* 11:3 Greek *of uncircumcised men.* 11:8 Greek *anything common or unclean.* 11:9 Greek *'What God calls clean you must not call unclean.'* 11:16 Or *in;* also in 11:16b. 11:20 Greek *the Greeks;* other manuscripts read *the Hellenists.* 11:26 Greek *disciples;* also in 11:29. 11:29 Greek *the brothers.* 12:1 Greek *Herod the king.* He was the nephew of Herod Antipas and a grandson of Herod the Great.

apostle James (John's brother) killed with a sword.
[3]When Herod saw how much this pleased the Jewish
leaders, he arrested Peter during the Passover celebration* [4]and imprisoned him, placing him under
the guard of four squads of four soldiers each. Herod's intention was to bring Peter out for public trial
after the Passover. [5]But while Peter was in prison, the
church prayed very earnestly for him.
[6]The night before Peter was to be placed on trial,
he was asleep, chained between two soldiers, with
others standing guard at the prison gate. [7]Suddenly,
there was a bright light in the cell, and an angel of
the Lord stood before Peter. The angel tapped him
on the side to awaken him and said, "Quick! Get
up!" And the chains fell off his wrists. [8]Then the
angel told him, "Get dressed and put on your sandals." And he did. "Now put on your coat and follow
me," the angel ordered.

## PRIDE

Seventeen-year-old Leslie loves music and has always wanted to be a singer. Not just a member of the youth choir. No, Leslie wants to be big-time, performing in front of a packed auditorium of cheering fans.

Leslie is talented, she practices a lot, and every now and then she gets to do solos at church. But last night, she finally got the big break she's been hoping for. She sang three songs at a huge youth rally in a city 250 miles away. Over 2,000 young people. A big stage. Lights. Professional sound equipment. Top-notch technicians. A $300 honorarium. We're talking "big time"!

Well, it went great. The audience loved her. Afterward, a handful of youth pastors asked her, "How can I book you to sing for my group?" People complimented her like crazy, tossing around words and phrases like "wonderful," "beautiful," and "going places." Some even asked when her first album would be out. The killer was the group of younger kids who asked Leslie to autograph their Bibles!

The day after, Leslie is still basking in her sudden success.

The day after, Leslie is a victim of pride.

Why is success and/or adulation so difficult to handle? Where do our talents come from? What happens if we forget God and get a big head? See Acts 12:19-23.

[9]So Peter left the cell, following the angel. But all
the time he thought it was a vision. He didn't realize
it was really happening. [10]They passed the first and
second guard posts and came to the iron gate to the
street, and this opened to them all by itself. So they
passed through and started walking down the street,
and then the angel suddenly left him.
[11]Peter finally realized what had happened. "It's
really true!" he said to himself. "The Lord has sent
his angel and saved me from Herod and from what
the Jews were hoping to do to me!"
[12]After a little thought, he went to the home of
Mary, the mother of John Mark, where many were
gathered for prayer. [13]He knocked at the door in the

### ANSWERS ● ● ● • •

12:13-15 **The prayers of the little group of believers were answered, even as they prayed. But when the answer arrived at the door, they didn't believe it. We should be people of faith who believe that God answers the prayers of those who seek his will. When you pray, believe you'll get an answer—and when the answer comes, don't be surprised!**

gate, and a servant girl named Rhoda came to open
it. [14]When she recognized Peter's voice, she was so
overjoyed that, instead of opening the door, she ran
back inside and told everyone, "Peter is standing at
the door!"
[15]"You're out of your mind," they said. When she
insisted, they decided, "It must be his angel."
[16]Meanwhile, Peter continued knocking. When
they finally went out and opened the door, they were
amazed. [17]He motioned for them to quiet down and
told them what had happened and how the Lord
had led him out of jail. "Tell James and the other
brothers what happened," he said. And then he went
to another place.
[18]At dawn, there was a great commotion among
the soldiers about what had happened to Peter.
[19]Herod Agrippa ordered a thorough search for him.
When he couldn't be found, Herod interrogated the
guards and sentenced them to death. Afterward
Herod left Judea to stay in Caesarea for a while.
[20]Now Herod was very angry with the people of
Tyre and Sidon. So they sent a delegation to make
peace with him because their cities were dependent
upon Herod's country for their food. They made
friends with Blastus, Herod's personal assistant,
[21]and an appointment with Herod was granted.
When the day arrived, Herod put on his royal robes,
sat on his throne, and made a speech to them. [22]The
people gave him a great ovation, shouting, "It is the
voice of a god, not of a man!"
[23]Instantly, an angel of the Lord struck Herod with
a sickness, because he accepted the people's worship
instead of giving the glory to God. So he was consumed with worms and died.
[24]But God's Good News was spreading rapidly,
and there were many new believers.
[25]When Barnabas and Saul had finished their mission in Jerusalem, they returned to Antioch, taking
John Mark with them.

## CHAPTER 13 PAUL'S FIRST MISSIONARY JOURNEY.

Among the prophets and teachers of the church at
Antioch of Syria were Barnabas, Simeon (called "the
black man"*), Lucius (from Cyrene), Manaen (the
childhood companion of King Herod Antipas*),
and Saul. [2]One day as these men were worshiping

### THREAD ● ● ● • •

13:1 **What variety there is in the church! The only common thread among these five men was their deep faith in Christ. We must never exclude anyone whom Christ has called to follow him.**

12:3 Greek *the days of unleavened bread.* 13:1a Greek *who was called Niger.* 13:1b Greek *Herod the tetrarch.*

the Lord and fasting, the Holy Spirit said, "Dedicate
Barnabas and Saul for the special work I have for
them." [3]So after more fasting and prayer, the men
laid their hands on them and sent them on their way.
[4]Sent out by the Holy Spirit, Saul and Barnabas
went down to the seaport of Seleucia and then sailed
for the island of Cyprus. [5]There, in the town of
Salamis, they went to the Jewish synagogues and
preached the word of God. (John Mark went with
them as their assistant.)
[6]Afterward they preached
from town to town across
the entire island until finally they reached Paphos,
where they met a Jewish
sorcerer, a false prophet
named Bar-Jesus. [7]He had
attached himself to the governor, Sergius Paulus, a
man of considerable in-
sight and understanding.
The governor invited Bar-
nabas and Saul to visit him,
for he wanted to hear the
word of God. [8]But Elymas,
the sorcerer (as his name
means in Greek), interfered
and urged the governor to
pay no attention to what
Saul and Barnabas said. He
was trying to turn the governor away from the Chris-
tian faith.
[9]Then Saul, also known
as Paul, filled with the Holy
Spirit, looked the sorcerer
in the eye and said, [10]"You
son of the Devil, full of
every sort of trickery and
villainy, enemy of all that is
good, will you never stop
perverting the true ways of
the Lord? [11]And now the
Lord has laid his hand of
punishment upon you, and
you will be stricken awhile
with blindness." Instantly
mist and darkness fell upon
him, and he began wander-
ing around begging for
someone to take his hand
and lead him. [12]When the
governor saw what had
happened, he believed and
was astonished at what he
learned about the Lord.
[13]Now Paul and those
with him left Paphos by ship
for Pamphylia,* landing at
the port town of Perga. There John Mark left them
and returned to Jerusalem. [14]But Barnabas and Paul
traveled inland to Antioch of Pisidia.*
On the Sabbath they went to the synagogue for
the services. [15]After the usual readings from the
books of Moses and from the Prophets, those in
charge of the service sent them this message: "Brothers, if you have any word of encouragement for us,
come and give it!"
[16]So Paul stood, lifted his hand to quiet them,

## JOHN MARK

What did you learn from your last mistake? Mistakes can be effective teachers because the consequences have a way of making lessons painfully clear. But those who learn from their mistakes gain wisdom. John Mark, with the help of some time and encouragement, became a wise learner.

Mark was eager to do the right thing, but he had trouble staying with a task. In his Gospel, Mark mentions a young man (probably referring to himself) who fled in such fear during Jesus' arrest that he left his clothes behind. A tendency to run showed up later in Mark's life when Paul and Barnabas took him as their assistant on their first missionary journey. Early in the trip, Mark left them and returned to Jerusalem. Paul didn't appreciate Mark's quitting. Two years later, Paul would not consider letting Mark try again. As a result, the team split up. Barnabas took Mark with him, and Paul chose Silas. Barnabas was patient with Mark, and the young man turned out to be a good investment. In fact, Paul and Mark were later reunited and the older apostle became a close friend of the young disciple.

Mark was able to watch closely the lives of three Christian leaders—Barnabas, Paul, and Peter. The material in Mark's Gospel seems to have come mostly from Peter. As his helper, Mark had a chance to hear Peter's stories of the years with Jesus over and over. Mark became one of the first to put Jesus' life into writing. He had someone who encouraged him to learn from his mistakes.

Barnabas played a key role in Mark's life. He stood beside the young man in his failure, giving him patient encouragement. Mark's experience can remind us to learn from our mistakes and to appreciate the patience of others. Is there a Barnabas in your life whom you need to thank for his or her encouragement to you?

LESSONS: Personal maturity usually comes from a combination of time and mistakes

Effective living is not measured by what we accomplish so much as by what we overcome in order to accomplish

Encouragement can change a person's life

KEY VERSE: "Only Luke is with me. Bring Mark with you when you come, for he will be helpful to me" (Paul writing to Timothy, 2 Timothy 4:11).

John Mark's story is told in Acts 12:23–13:13 and 15:36-39. He is also mentioned in Colossians 4:10; 2 Timothy 4:11; Philemon 24; 1 Peter 5:13.

**UPS:**
- Wrote the Gospel of Mark
- He and his mother provided their home as one of the main meeting places for the Christians in Jerusalem
- Persistent beyond his youthful mistakes
- Was an assistant and traveling companion to three of the greatest early missionaries

**DOWNS:**
- Probably the nameless young man described in the Gospel of Mark who fled in panic when Jesus was arrested
- Left Paul and Barnabas during the first missionary journey

**STATS:**
- Where: Jerusalem
- Occupation: Missionary-in-training, Gospel writer, traveling companion
- Relatives: Mother: Mary. Cousin: Barnabas.
- Contemporaries: Paul, Peter, Timothy, Luke, Silas

13:13-14 *Pamphylia* and *Pisidia* were districts in the land now called Turkey.

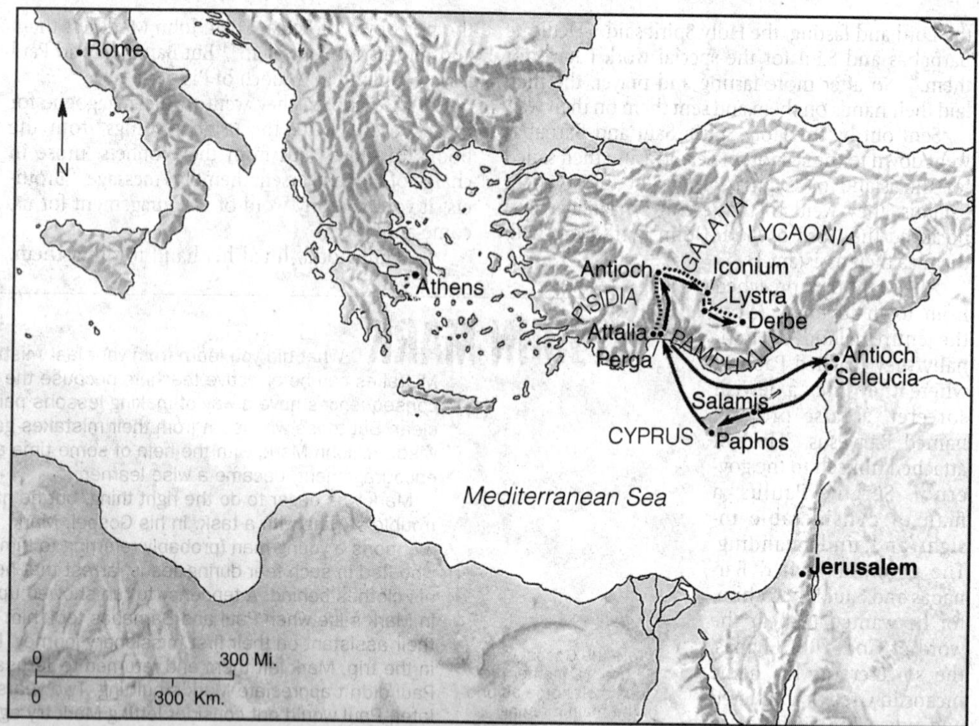


**PAUL'S FIRST MISSIONARY JOURNEY** (ACTS 13:1—14:28)

and started speaking. "People of Israel," he said, "and you devout Gentiles who fear the God of Israel, listen to me.

17 "The God of this nation of Israel chose our ancestors and made them prosper in Egypt. Then he powerfully led them out of their slavery. 18 He put up with them* through forty years of wandering around in the wilderness. 19 Then he destroyed seven nations in Canaan and gave their land to Israel as an inheritance. 20 All this took about 450 years. After that, judges ruled until the time of Samuel the prophet. 21 Then the people begged for a king, and God gave them Saul son of Kish, a man of the tribe of Benjamin, who reigned for forty years. 22 But God removed him from the kingship and replaced him with David, a man about whom God said, 'David son of Jesse is a man after my own heart, for he will do everything I want him to.'*

23 "And it is one of King David's descendants, Jesus, who is God's promised Savior of Israel! 24 But before he came, John the Baptist preached the need for everyone in Israel to turn from sin and turn to God and be baptized. 25 As John was finishing his ministry he asked, 'Do you think I am the Messiah? No! But he is coming soon—and I am not even worthy to be his slave.*'

26 "Brothers—you sons of Abraham, and also all of you devout Gentiles who fear the God of Israel—this salvation is for us! 27 The people in Jerusalem and their leaders fulfilled prophecy by condemning Jesus to death. They didn't recognize him or realize that he is the one the prophets had written about, though they hear the prophets' words read every Sabbath. 28 They found no just cause to execute him, but they asked Pilate to have him killed anyway.

29 "When they had fulfilled all the prophecies concerning his death, they took him down from the cross and placed him in a tomb. 30 But God raised him from the dead! 31 And he appeared over a period of many days to those who had gone with him from Galilee to Jerusalem—these are his witnesses to the people of Israel.

32 "And now Barnabas and I are here to bring you this Good News. God's promise to our ancestors has come true in our own time, 33 in that God raised Jesus. This is what the second psalm is talking about when it says concerning Jesus,

## BE HAPPY ● ● ● • .

**13:42-45 The Jewish leaders brought theological arguments against Paul and Barnabas, but the Bible tells us that the real reason for their denunciation was that they were jealous. When we see others succeeding where we haven't or receiving the glory that we want, it is hard to be happy for them. Jealousy is our natural reaction. But it is tragic when our own jealous feelings make us try to stop God's work. If a work is God's work, rejoice in it—no matter who is doing it.**

13:18 Other manuscripts read *He cared for them;* compare Deut 1:31. 13:22 1 Sam 13:14. 13:25 Greek *to untie his sandals.*

'You are my Son.
Today I have become your Father.*'

[34]For God had promised to raise him from the dead,
never again to die. This is stated in the Scripture that
says, 'I will give you the sacred blessings I promised
to David.'* [35]Another psalm explains more fully,
saying, 'You will not allow your Holy One to rot in
the grave.'* [36]Now this is not a reference to David, for
after David had served his generation according to
the will of God, he died and was buried, and his
body decayed. [37]No, it was a reference to someone
else—someone whom God raised and whose body
did not decay.

[38]"Brothers, listen! In this man Jesus there is forgiveness for your sins. [39]Everyone who believes in
him is freed from all guilt and declared right with
God—something the Jewish law could never do.
[40]Be careful! Don't let the
prophets' words apply to
you. For they said,

[41]'Look you mockers,
be amazed and die!
For I am doing
something in your
own day,
something you
wouldn't believe
even if someone told
you about it.'*"

[42]As Paul and Barnabas
left the synagogue that day,
the people asked them to return again and speak about
these things the next week.
[43]Many Jews and godly converts to Judaism who wor-
shiped at the synagogue
followed Paul and Barnabas,
and the two men urged
them, "By God's grace, remain faithful."

[44]The following week almost the entire city turned
out to hear them preach
the word of the Lord. [45]But
when the Jewish leaders
saw the crowds, they were
jealous; so they slandered
Paul and argued against
whatever he said.

[46]Then Paul and Barna-
bas spoke out boldly and
declared, "It was necessary
that this Good News from
God be given first to you
Jews. But since you have rejected it and judged yourselves unworthy of eternal
life—well, we will offer it to Gentiles. [47]For this is as
the Lord commanded us when he said,

'I have made you a light to the Gentiles,
to bring salvation to the farthest corners of the
earth.'*"

[48]When the Gentiles heard this, they were very
glad and thanked the Lord for his message; and all
who were appointed to eternal life became believers.
[49]So the Lord's message spread throughout that region.

[50]Then the Jewish leaders stirred up both the influential religious women and the leaders of the city,
and they incited a mob against Paul and Barnabas
and ran them out of town. [51]But they shook off the
dust of their feet against them and went to the city of
Iconium. [52]And the believers* were filled with joy
and with the Holy Spirit.

---

## BARNABAS

Think about the people who really matter in your life. Odds are that many of them are encouragers who have found ways to help you keep going. Good friends can tell when you are doing well and when you need to try harder. Mostly, they never give up on you! Everyone needs that kind of encouragement.

Among the first Christians, a man named Joseph was such an encourager that other believers nicknamed him "Son of Encouragement," or "Barnabas." Barnabas had an unusual ability to find people he could help. Whenever Barnabas encouraged Christians, the result was that others became believers!

Barnabas's actions were crucial to the early church. In a way, we can thank him for most of the New Testament. God used Barnabas's relationship with Paul at one point and with Mark at another to help these two men when either might have failed. Barnabas did wonders with encouragement.

We are surrounded by people we can encourage. Instead, we usually criticize. It may be important at times to show people where they are wrong, but we will be of greater help in the long run if we encourage people. They will accept our honest criticism if they know we want the best for them. Be prepared to encourage people today.

LESSONS: Encouragement is one of the most effective ways to help others

Sooner or later, true obedience to God will involve risk

There always is someone who needs encouragement

KEY VERSES: "When he arrived and saw this proof of God's favor, he was filled with joy, and he encouraged the believers to stay true to the Lord. Barnabas was a good man, full of the Holy Spirit and strong in faith. And large numbers of people were brought to the Lord" (Acts 11:23-24).

Barnabas's story is told in Acts 4:36-37; 9:27–15:39. He also is mentioned in 1 Corinthians 9:6; Galatians 2:1, 9, 13; Colossians 4:10.

**UPS:**
- One of the first to sell possessions to help the Christians in Jerusalem
- First to travel with Paul as a missionary team
- Was an encourager, as his nickname shows, and thus one of the most quietly influential people in the early days of Christianity
- Called an apostle, although not one of the original Twelve

**DOWN:**
- Temporarily stayed aloof from Gentile believers until Paul corrected him

**STATS:**
- Where: Cyprus, Jerusalem, Antioch
- Occupation: Missionary, teacher
- Relatives: Sister: Mary. Cousin: John Mark.
- Contemporaries: Peter, Silas, Paul, Herod Agrippa I

---

13:33 Or *Today I reveal you as my Son.* Ps 2:7. 13:34 Isa 55:3. 13:35 Ps 16:10. 13:41 Hab 1:5. 13:47 Isa 49:6. 13:52 Greek *the disciples.*

## EVIDENCE ● ● • • •

14:15-18 **Responding to the people of Lystra, Paul and Barnabas reminded them that God never leaves himself "without a witness." Rain and crops, for example, demonstrate God's goodness, as did the health and gladness people enjoyed because they had the food they needed. Later, Paul wrote that this evidence in nature and in people's lives leaves people without an excuse for unbelief (Romans 1:20). When in doubt about God, look around and you will see plenty of evidence that he is at work in our world.**

CHAPTER **14** **PAUL AND BARNABAS SEEN AS GODS.** In Iconium,* Paul and Barnabas went together to the synagogue and preached with such power that a great number of both Jews and Gentiles believed. 2But the Jews who spurned God's message stirred up distrust among the Gentiles against Paul and Barnabas, saying all sorts of evil things about them. 3The apostles stayed there a long time, preaching boldly about the grace of the Lord. The Lord proved their message was true by giving them power to do miraculous signs and wonders. 4But the people of the city were divided in their opinion about them. Some sided with the Jews, and some with the apostles.

5A mob of Gentiles and Jews, along with their leaders, decided to attack and stone them. 6When the apostles learned of it, they fled for their lives. They went to the region of Lycaonia, to the cities of Lystra and Derbe and the surrounding area, 7and they preached the Good News there.

8While they were at Lystra, Paul and Barnabas came upon a man with crippled feet. He had been that way from birth, so he had never walked. 9He was listening as Paul preached, and Paul noticed him and realized he had faith to be healed. 10So Paul called to him in a loud voice, "Stand up!" And the man jumped to his feet and started walking.

11When the listening crowd saw what Paul had done, they shouted in their local dialect, "These men are gods in human bodies!" 12They decided that Barnabas was the Greek god Zeus and that Paul, because he was the chief speaker, was Hermes. 13The temple of Zeus was located on the outskirts of the city. The priest of the temple and the crowd brought oxen and wreaths of flowers, and they prepared to sacrifice to the apostles at the city gates.

14But when Barnabas and Paul heard what was happening, they tore their clothing in dismay and ran out among the people, shouting, 15"Friends,* why are you doing this? We are merely human beings like yourselves! We have come to bring you the Good News that you should turn from these worthless things to the living God, who made heaven and earth, the sea, and everything in them. 16In earlier days he permitted all the nations to go their own ways, 17but he never left himself without a witness. There were always his reminders, such as sending you rain and good crops and giving you food and joyful hearts." 18But even so, Paul and Barnabas could scarcely restrain the people from sacrificing to them.

19Now some Jews arrived from Antioch and Iconium and turned the crowds into a murderous mob. They stoned Paul and dragged him out of the city, apparently dead. 20But as the believers* stood around him, he got up and went back into the city. The next day he left with Barnabas for Derbe.

21After preaching the Good News in Derbe and making many disciples, Paul and Barnabas returned again to Lystra, Iconium, and Antioch of Pisidia, 22where they strengthened the believers. They encouraged them to continue in the faith, reminding them that they must enter into the Kingdom of God through many tribulations. 23Paul and Barnabas also appointed elders in every church and prayed for them with fasting, turning them over to the care of the Lord, in whom they had come to trust. 24Then they traveled back through Pisidia to Pamphylia. 25They preached again in Perga, then went on to Attalia.

26Finally, they returned by ship to Antioch of Syria, where their journey had begun and where they had been committed to the grace of God for the work they had now completed. 27Upon arriving in Antioch, they called the church together and reported about their trip, telling all that God had done and how he had opened the door of faith to the Gentiles, too. 28And they stayed there with the believers in Antioch for a long time.

CHAPTER **15** **A CHURCH CONFLICT.** While Paul and Barnabas were at Antioch of Syria, some men from Judea arrived and began to teach the Christians*: "Unless you keep the ancient Jewish custom of circumcision taught by Moses, you cannot be saved." 2Paul and Barnabas, disagreeing with them, argued forcefully and at length. Finally, Paul and Barnabas were sent to Jerusalem, accompanied by some local believers, to talk to the apostles and elders about this question. 3The church sent the delegates to Jerusalem, and they stopped along the way in Phoenicia and Samaria to visit the believers.* They told them—much to everyone's joy—that the Gentiles, too, were being converted.

4When they arrived in Jerusalem, Paul and Barnabas were welcomed by the whole church, including the apostles and elders. They reported on what God had been doing through their ministry. 5But then some of the men who had been Pharisees before their conversion stood up and declared that all Gen-

## YOUR ATTITUDE ● ● • • •

15:23-29 **This letter answered their questions and brought great joy to the Gentile Christians in Antioch (15:31). Beautifully written, it appeals to the Holy Spirit's guidance and explains what should be done as though the readers already knew it. It is helpful when people learn to be careful not only in what they say, but also in how they say it. We may be correct in our content, but we can lose our audience by our tone of voice or attitude.**

14:1 *Iconium,* as well as *Lystra* and *Derbe* (14:6), were cities in the land now called Turkey. 14:15 Greek *Men.* 14:20 Greek *disciples;* also in 14:22, 28. 15:1 Greek *brothers;* also in 15:32, 33. 15:3 Greek *brothers;* also in 15:23, 36, 40.

tile converts must be circumcised and be required to follow the law of Moses.

6So the apostles and church elders got together to decide this question. 7At the meeting, after a long discussion, Peter stood and addressed them as follows: "Brothers, you all know that God chose me from among you some time ago to preach to the Gentiles so that they could hear the Good News and believe. 8God, who knows people's hearts, confirmed that he accepts Gentiles by giving them the Holy Spirit, just as he gave him to us. 9He made no distinction between us and them, for he also cleansed their hearts through faith. 10Why are you now questioning God's way by burdening the Gentile believers* with a yoke that neither we nor our ancestors were able to bear? 11We believe that we are all saved the same way, by the special favor of the Lord Jesus."

12There was no further discussion, and everyone listened as Barnabas and Paul told about the miraculous signs and wonders God had done through them among the Gentiles.

13When they had finished, James stood and said, "Brothers, listen to me. 14Peter* has told you about the time God first visited the Gentiles to take from them a people for himself. 15And this conversion of Gentiles agrees with what the prophets predicted. For instance, it is written:

16 'Afterward I will return,
and I will restore the fallen kingdom of David.
From the ruins I will rebuild it,
and I will restore it,
17 so that the rest of humanity might find the Lord,
including the Gentiles—
all those I have called to be mine.
This is what the Lord says,
18 he who made these things known long ago.'*

19And so my judgment is that we should stop troubling the Gentiles who turn to God, 20except that we should write to them and tell them to abstain from eating meat sacrificed to idols, from sexual immorality, and from consuming blood or eating the meat of strangled animals. 21For these laws of Moses have been preached in Jewish synagogues in every city on every Sabbath for many generations."

22Then the apostles and elders and the whole church in Jerusalem chose delegates, and they sent

## SILAS

One word that doesn't fit in the lives of the first Christians is *boring*. There were just too many exciting things happening. Hundreds of people who had never heard of Jesus before were trusting him with their lives. Christian missionaries were taking hazardous journeys over land and sea. Even preaching the gospel was sometimes dangerous, since there was often resistance and hatred of the message. Right in the middle of all the excitement was a young man named Silas.

We first meet Silas when he is sent as a representative from Jerusalem, with Paul and Barnabas, to spread the official news that people did not have to become Jews before they became Christians. It was an important mission. Later, Silas joined Paul and Timothy as an effective traveling ministry team. Life continued to be exciting. Paul and Silas spent a night singing in a Philippian prison after being severely beaten. Another time, they were almost beaten in Thessalonica but were able to pull off a daring escape in the night. Then Paul left Silas and Timothy in Berea while he traveled on to Athens. Their job was to encourage the young believers in that new church. The team was reunited in Corinth. In each place they visited, they left behind a small group of Christians.

We don't know what eventually happened to Silas. He spent some time with Peter and is mentioned as the coauthor of 1 Peter. He continued to live the same faithful life that had made him a good choice to represent the church in Jerusalem. He was a helpful and encouraging member of Paul's team. Though he was never in the spotlight, his consistent life is a good model for us.

LESSONS: Partnership is a significant part of effective ministry

God never guarantees that his servants will not suffer

Obedience to God may mean giving up what makes us feel secure

KEY VERSES: "So it seemed good to us, having unanimously agreed on our decision, to send you these official representatives . . . who have risked their lives for the sake of our Lord Jesus Christ. So we are sending Judas and Silas" (Acts 15:25-27).

Silas's story is told in Acts 15:22–19:10. He is also mentioned in 2 Corinthians 1:19; 1 Thessalonians 1:1; 2 Thessalonians 1:1; 1 Peter 5:12.

**UPS:**

- A leader in the Jerusalem church
- Represented the church in carrying the "acceptance letter" prepared by the Jerusalem council to the Gentile believers in Antioch
- Was closely associated with Paul from the second missionary journey on
- When imprisoned with Paul in Philippi, sang songs of praise to God
- Worked as a secretary for both Paul and Peter, using "Silvanus" as his pen name

**STATS:**

- Where: Roman citizen living in Jerusalem
- Occupation: One of the first career missionaries
- Contemporaries: Paul, Timothy, Peter, Mark, Barnabas

15:10 Greek *disciples*. 15:14 Greek *Simon*. 15:16-18 Amos 9:11-12; Isa 45:21.

## BARRIERS ● ● ● ● ●

**16:2-3 Timothy and his mother, Eunice, were from Lystra. Eunice had probably heard Paul's preaching during his first missionary journey (Acts 14:6-18). Timothy was the son of a Jewish mother and a Greek father—to the Jews, he was a half-breed, like a Samaritan. So Paul asked Timothy to be circumcised to erase some of the stigma he had with Jewish believers. Timothy was not required to be circumcised (the Jerusalem council had decided that—chapter 15), but he voluntarily did so to overcome barriers to his witness for Christ. Sometimes we must go beyond minimum requirements to help our audience receive our testimony.**

them to Antioch of Syria with Paul and Barnabas to report on this decision. The men chosen were two of the church leaders*—Judas (also called Barsabbas) and Silas. 23This is the letter they took along with them:

"This letter is from the apostles and elders, your brothers in Jerusalem. It is written to the Gentile believers in Antioch, Syria, and Cilicia. Greetings!

24"We understand that some men from here have troubled you and upset you with their teaching, but they had no such instructions from us. 25So it seemed good to us, having unanimously agreed on our decision, to send you these official representatives, along with our beloved Barnabas and Paul, 26who have risked their lives for the sake of our Lord Jesus Christ. 27So we are sending Judas and Silas to tell you what we have decided concerning your question.

28"For it seemed good to the Holy Spirit and to us to lay no greater burden on you than these requirements: 29You must abstain from eating food offered to idols, from consuming blood or eating the meat of strangled animals, and from sexual immorality. If you do this, you will do well. Farewell."

30The four messengers went at once to Antioch, where they called a general meeting of the Christians and delivered the letter. 31And there was great joy throughout the church that day as they read this encouraging message.

32Then Judas and Silas, both being prophets, spoke extensively to the Christians, encouraging and strengthening their faith. 33They stayed for a while, and then Judas and Silas were sent back to Jerusalem, with the blessings of the Christians, to those who had sent them.* 35Paul and Barnabas stayed in Antioch to assist many others who were teaching and preaching the word of the Lord there.

36After some time Paul said to Barnabas, "Let's return to each city where we previously preached the word of the Lord, to see how the new believers are getting along." 37Barnabas agreed and

15:22 Greek *were leaders among the brothers.* 15:33 Some manuscripts add verse 34, *But Silas decided to stay there.*

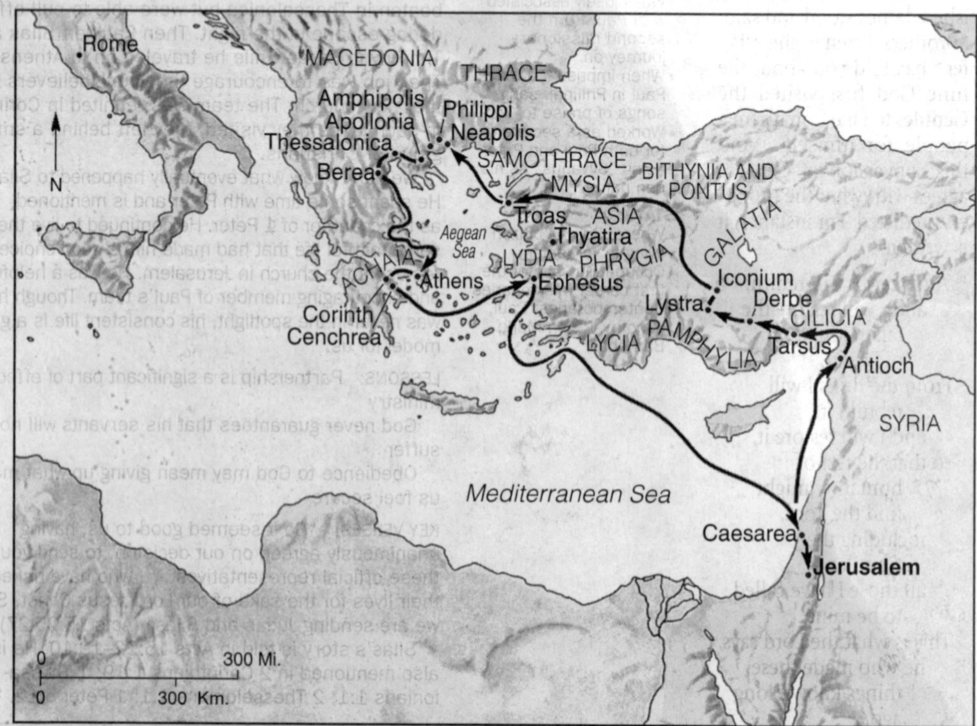


**PAUL'S SECOND MISSIONARY JOURNEY** (ACTS 15:36—18:22)

wanted to take along John Mark. [38]But Paul disagreed strongly, since John Mark had deserted
them in Pamphylia and had not shared in their
work. [39]Their disagreement over this was so
sharp that they separated. Barnabas took John
Mark with him and sailed for Cyprus. [40]Paul chose
Silas, and the believers sent them off, entrusting
them to the Lord's grace. [41]So they traveled
throughout Syria and Cilicia to strengthen the
churches there.

CHAPTER **16** **TIMOTHY IS PAUL'S HELPER.** Paul and
Silas went first to Derbe and then on to Lystra.
There they met Timothy, a young disciple whose
mother was a Jewish believer, but whose father was
a Greek. [2]Timothy was well thought of by the
believers* in Lystra and Iconium, [3]so Paul wanted
him to join them on their journey. In deference to
the Jews of the area, he arranged for Timothy to be
circumcised before they left, for everyone knew
that his father was a Greek. [4]Then they went from
town to town, explaining the decision regarding
the commandments that were to be obeyed, as
decided by the apostles and elders in Jerusalem.
[5]So the churches were strengthened in their faith
and grew daily in numbers.

[6]Next Paul and Silas traveled through the area
of Phrygia and Galatia, because the Holy Spirit
had told them not to go into the province of Asia
at that time. [7]Then coming to the borders of Mysia,
they headed for the province of Bithynia,* but
again the Spirit of Jesus did not let them go. [8]So
instead, they went on through Mysia to the city of
Troas.

[9]That night Paul had a vision. He saw a man from
Macedonia in northern Greece, pleading with him,
"Come over here and help us." [10]So we* decided to
leave for Macedonia at once, for we could only con-
clude that God was calling us to preach the Good
News there.

[11]We boarded a boat at Troas and sailed straight
across to the island of Samothrace, and the next
day we landed at Neapolis. [12]From there we
reached Philippi, a major city of the district of
Macedonia and a Roman colony; we stayed there
several days.

[13]On the Sabbath we went a little way outside the
city to a riverbank, where we supposed that some
people met for prayer, and we sat down to speak with
some women who had come together. [14]One of
them was Lydia from Thyatira, a merchant of expensive purple cloth. She was a worshiper of God. As she
listened to us, the Lord opened her heart, and she
accepted what Paul was saying. [15]She was baptized
along with other members of her household, and
she asked us to be her guests. "If you agree that I am
faithful to the Lord," she said, "come and stay at my
home." And she urged us until we did.

[16]One day as we were going down to the place of

## GOD'S WILL ● ● ● • •

16:6 **We don't know how the Holy Spirit told Paul that he and his men were not to go into Asia. It may have been through a prophet, a vision, an inner conviction, or some other circumstance. To know God's will does not mean we must hear his voice. He leads in many ways. When seeking God's will: (1) make sure your plan is in harmony with God's Word; (2) ask mature Christians for their advice; (3) check your own motives (are you doing what you want or what you think God wants?); and (4) ask God to open and close doors of circumstances.**

prayer, we met a demon-possessed slave girl. She
was a fortune-teller who earned a lot of money for
her masters. [17]She followed along behind us shouting, "These men are servants of the Most High
God, and they have come to tell you how to be
saved."

[18]This went on day after day until Paul got so
exasperated that he turned and spoke to the demon
within her. "I command you in the name of Jesus
Christ to come out of her," he said. And instantly it
left her.

[19]Her masters' hopes of wealth were now shattered, so they grabbed Paul and Silas and dragged
them before the authorities at the marketplace.
[20]"The whole city is in an uproar because of these
Jews!" they shouted. [21]"They are teaching the
people to do things that are against Roman customs."

[22]A mob quickly formed against Paul and Silas,
and the city officials ordered them stripped and
beaten with wooden rods. [23]They were severely
beaten, and then they were thrown into prison.
The jailer was ordered to make sure they didn't
escape. [24]So he took no chances but put them into
the inner dungeon and clamped their feet in the
stocks.

[25]Around midnight, Paul and Silas were praying
and singing hymns to God, and the other prisoners
were listening. [26]Suddenly, there was a great earthquake, and the prison was shaken to its foundations.
All the doors flew open, and the chains of every
prisoner fell off! [27]The jailer woke up to see the
prison doors wide open. He assumed the prisoners
had escaped, so he drew his sword to kill himself.
[28]But Paul shouted to him, "Don't do it! We are all
here!"

[29]Trembling with fear, the jailer called for lights
and ran to the dungeon and fell down before Paul
and Silas. [30]He brought them out and asked, "Sirs,
what must I do to be saved?"

## IN THE DUNGEON ● ● ● • •

16:22-25 **Paul and Silas were stripped, beaten, whipped, and placed in stocks in the inner dungeon. Despite this dismal situation, they praised God, praying and singing as the other prisoners listened. No matter what our circumstances, we should praise God. Others may come to Christ because of our example.**

16:2 Greek *brothers;* also in 16:40. 16:6-7 *Phrygia, Galatia, Asia, Mysia,* and *Bithynia* were all districts in the land now called Turkey. 16:10 Luke, the writer of this book, here joined Paul and accompanied him on his journey.

31 They replied, "Believe on the Lord Jesus and you will be saved, along with your entire household." 32 Then they shared the word of the Lord with him and all who lived in his household. 33 That same hour the jailer washed their wounds, and he and everyone in his household were immediately baptized. 34 Then he brought them into his house and set a meal before them. He and his entire household rejoiced because they all believed in God.

35 The next morning the city officials sent the police to tell the jailer, "Let those men go!" 36 So the jailer told Paul, "You and Silas are free to leave. Go in peace."

## COMPARE ● ● • • •

**17:11 How do you evaluate sermons and teachings? The people in Berea opened the Scriptures for themselves and searched for truths to verify or disprove the message they heard. Always compare what you hear with what the Bible says. A preacher or teacher who gives God's true message will never contradict or explain away anything in God's Word.**

37 But Paul replied, "They have publicly beaten us without trial and jailed us—and we are Roman citizens. So now they want us to leave secretly? Certainly not! Let them come themselves to release us!"

38 When the police made their report, the city officials were alarmed to learn that Paul and Silas were Roman citizens. 39 They came to the jail and apologized to them. Then they brought them out and begged them to leave the city. 40 Paul and Silas then returned to the home of Lydia, where they met with the believers and encouraged them once more before leaving town.

CHAPTER **17** **PAUL VISITS TWO TOWNS.** Now Paul and Silas traveled through the towns of Amphipolis and Apollonia and came to Thessalonica, where there was a Jewish synagogue. 2 As was Paul's custom, he went to the synagogue service, and for three Sabbaths in a row he interpreted the Scriptures to the people. 3 He was explaining and proving the prophecies about the sufferings of the Messiah and his rising from the dead. He said, "This Jesus I'm telling you about is the Messiah." 4 Some who listened were persuaded and became converts, including a large number of godly Greek men and also many important women of the city.*

5 But the Jewish leaders were jealous, so they gathered some worthless fellows from the streets to form a mob and start a riot. They attacked the home of Jason, searching for Paul and Silas so they could drag them out to the crowd.* 6 Not finding them there, they dragged out Jason and some of the other believers* instead and took them before the city council. "Paul and Silas have turned the rest of the world upside down, and now they are here disturbing our city," they shouted. 7 "And Jason has let them into his home. They are all guilty of treason against Caesar, for they profess allegiance to another king, Jesus."

8 The people of the city, as well as the city officials, were thrown into turmoil by these reports. 9 But the officials released Jason and the other believers after they had posted bail.

10 That very night the believers sent Paul and Silas to Berea. When they arrived there, they went to the synagogue. 11 And the people of Berea were more open-minded than those in Thessalonica, and they listened eagerly to Paul's message. They searched the Scriptures day after day to check up on Paul and Silas, to see if they were really teaching the truth. 12 As a result, many Jews believed, as did some of the prominent Greek women and many men.

13 But when some Jews in Thessalonica learned that Paul was preaching the word of God in Berea, they went there and stirred up trouble. 14 The believers acted at once, sending Paul on to the coast, while Silas and Timothy remained behind. 15 Those escorting Paul went with him to Athens; then they returned to Berea with a message for Silas and Timothy to hurry and join him.

16 While Paul was waiting for them in Athens, he was deeply troubled by all the idols he saw everywhere in the city. 17 He went to the synagogue to debate with the Jews and the God-fearing Gentiles, and he spoke daily in the public square to all who happened to be there.

18 He also had a debate with some of the Epicurean and Stoic philosophers. When he told them about Jesus and his resurrection, they said, "This babbler has picked up some strange ideas." Others said, "He's pushing some foreign religion."

19 Then they took him to the Council of Philosophers.* "Come and tell us more about this new religion," they said. 20 "You are saying some rather startling things, and we want to know what it's all about." 21 (It should be explained that all the Athenians as well as the foreigners in Athens seemed to spend all their time discussing the latest ideas.)

22 So Paul, standing before the Council,* addressed them as follows: "Men of Athens, I notice that you are very religious, 23 for as I was walking along I saw your many altars. And one of them had this inscription on it—'To an Unknown God.' You have been worshiping

## WORTH IT ● ● • • •

**17:32-34 Paul's speech received a mixed reaction: some laughed, some kept searching for more information, and a few believed. Don't hesitate to tell others about Christ because you fear that some will not believe you. And don't expect a unanimously positive response to your witnessing. Even if only a few believe, it's worth the effort.**

17:4 Some manuscripts read *many of the wives of the leading men.* 17:5 Or *the city council.* 17:6 Greek *brothers;* also in 17:10, 14. 17:19 Greek *the Areopagus.* 17:22 Or *in the middle of Mars Hill;* Greek reads *in the middle of the Areopagus.*

him without knowing who he is, and now I wish to tell
you about him.
24 "He is the God who made the world and everything in it. Since he is Lord of heaven and earth, he
doesn't live in man-made temples, 25 and human
hands can't serve his needs—for he has no
needs. He himself gives life and breath to everything, and he satisfies every need there is. 26 From
one man he created all the nations throughout
the whole earth. He decided beforehand which
should rise and fall, and he determined their
boundaries.
27 "His purpose in all of this was that the nations
should seek after God and perhaps feel their way
toward him and find him—though he is not far
from any one of us. 28 For in him we live and move
and exist. As one of your own poets says, 'We are his
offspring.' 29 And since this is true, we shouldn't think
of God as an idol designed by craftsmen from gold
or silver or stone. 30 God overlooked people's former
ignorance about these things, but now he commands everyone everywhere to turn away from idols
and turn to him.* 31 For he has set a day for judging
the world with justice by the man he has appointed,
and he proved to everyone who this is by raising him
from the dead."
32 When they heard Paul speak of the resurrection
of a person who had been dead, some laughed, but
others said, "We want to hear more about this later."
33 That ended Paul's discussion with them, 34 but
some joined him and became believers. Among
them were Dionysius, a member of the Council,* a
woman named Damaris, and others.

## CHAPTER 18 PAUL MEETS PRISCILLA AND AQUILA.

1 Then Paul left Athens and went to Corinth.*
2 There he became acquainted with a Jew named
Aquila, born in Pontus, who had recently arrived
from Italy with his wife, Priscilla. They had been
expelled from Italy as a result of Claudius Caesar's
order to deport all Jews from Rome. 3 Paul lived and
worked with them, for they were tentmakers* just
as he was.
4 Each Sabbath found Paul at the synagogue, trying to convince the Jews and Greeks alike. 5 And
after Silas and Timothy came down from Macedonia, Paul spent his full time preaching and testifying to the Jews, telling them, "The Messiah you are
looking for is Jesus." 6 But when the Jews opposed
him and insulted him, Paul shook the dust from
his robe and said, "Your blood be upon your own
heads—I am innocent. From now on I will go to
the Gentiles."
7 After that he stayed with Titius Justus, a Gentile
who worshiped God and lived next door to the
synagogue. 8 Crispus, the leader of the synagogue,
and all his household believed in the Lord. Many
others in Corinth also became believers and were
baptized.
9 One night the Lord spoke to Paul in a vision and
told him, "Don't be afraid! Speak out! Don't be
silent! 10 For I am with you, and no one will harm you
because many people here in this city belong to me."
11 So Paul stayed there for the next year and a half,
teaching the word of God.
12 But when Gallio became governor of Achaia,
some Jews rose in concerted action against Paul and
brought him before the governor for judgment.
13 They accused Paul of "persuading people to worship God in ways that are contrary to the law." 14 But
just as Paul started to make his defense, Gallio
turned to Paul's accusers and said, "Listen, you Jews,
if this were a case involving some wrongdoing or a
serious crime, I would be obliged to listen to you.
15 But since it is merely a question of words and
names and your Jewish laws, you take care of it. I
refuse to judge such matters." 16 And he drove them
out of the courtroom. 17 The mob had grabbed Sosthenes, the leader of the synagogue, and had beaten
him right there in the courtroom. But Gallio paid no
attention.
18 Paul stayed in Corinth for some time after that
and then said good-bye to the brothers and sisters*
and sailed for the coast of Syria, taking Priscilla and
Aquila with him. (Earlier, at Cenchrea, Paul had
shaved his head according to Jewish custom, for he
had taken a vow.) 19 When they arrived at the port of

**I'm not the kind of person that can take everything at face value. I have to have more proof. Is it wrong to want to know the answers to questions I have about the Bible?**

The Christians in Berea were complimented by Luke, the writer of Acts, because "they searched the Scriptures day after day to check up on Paul and Silas, to see if they were really teaching the truth" (Acts 17:11).

Because being a Christian means accepting Christ's forgiveness by faith, some think we must believe everything just because another Christian said it. But getting your questions answered by studying the Bible is an important part of being a Christian. Although not every question can be answered, most of them can.

Some people are natural skeptics. They challenge everything in the Bible. But often they aren't looking for answers—just an argument. If, however, you have the prayerful heart of a seeker, God will help you unlock the secrets of his word. "Keep on asking, and you will be given what you ask for. Keep on looking, and you will find. Keep on knocking, and the door will be opened. For everyone who asks, receives. Everyone who seeks, finds. And the door is opened to everyone who knocks" (Matthew 7:7-8).

Keep asking your questions and looking for answers.

17:30 Greek *everywhere to repent.* 17:34 Greek *an Areopagite.* 18:1 *Athens* and *Corinth* were major cities in Achaia, the region on the southern end of the Greek peninsula. 18:3 Or *leatherworkers.* 18:18 Greek *brothers;* also in 18:27.

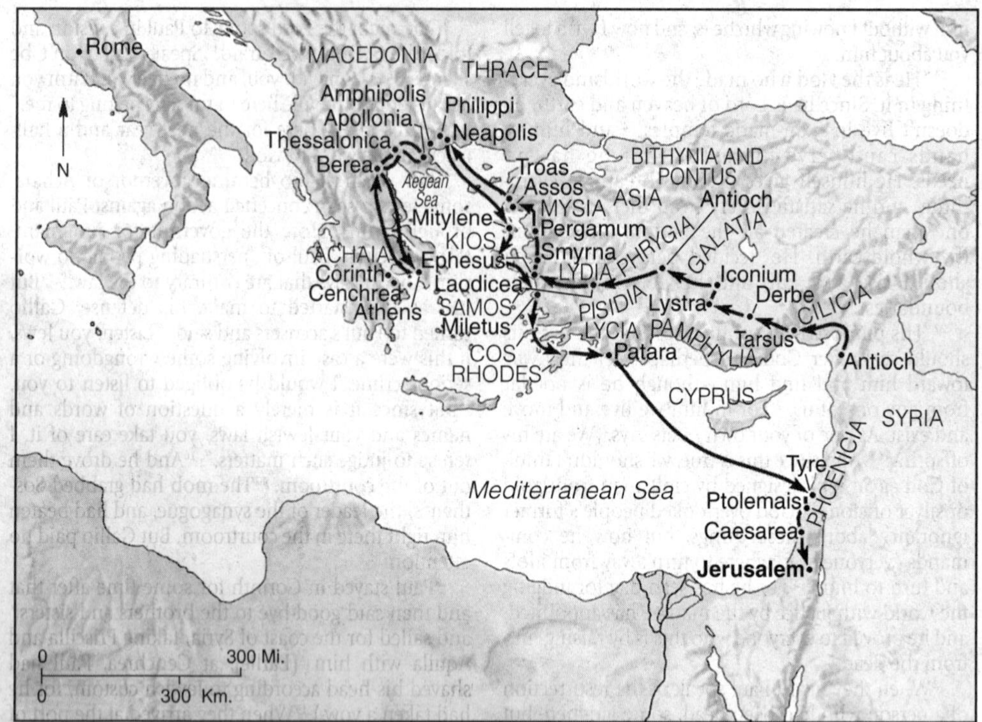


**PAUL'S THIRD MISSIONARY JOURNEY** (ACTS 18:23—21:16)

Ephesus, Paul left the others behind. But while he was there, he went to the synagogue to debate with the Jews. [20]They asked him to stay longer, but he declined. [21]So he left, saying, "I will come back later,* God willing." Then he set sail from Ephesus. [22]The next stop was at the port of Caesarea. From there he went up and visited the church at Jerusalem* and then went back to Antioch.

[23]After spending some time in Antioch, Paul went back to Galatia and Phrygia, visiting all the believers,* encouraging them and helping them to grow in the Lord.

[24]Meanwhile, a Jew named Apollos, an eloquent speaker who knew the Scriptures well, had just arrived in Ephesus from Alexandria in Egypt. [25]He had been taught the way of the Lord and talked to others with great enthusiasm and accuracy about Jesus. However, he knew only about John's baptism. [26]When Priscilla and Aquila heard him preaching boldly in the synagogue, they took him aside and explained the way of God more accurately.

[27]Apollos had been thinking about going to Achaia, and the brothers and sisters in Ephesus encouraged him in this. They wrote to the believers in Achaia, asking them to welcome him. When he arrived there, he proved to be of great benefit to those who, by God's grace, had believed. [28]He refuted all the Jews with powerful arguments in public debate. Using the Scriptures, he explained to them, "The Messiah you are looking for is Jesus."

CHAPTER **19** **GOD SENDS THE HOLY SPIRIT.** While Apollos was in Corinth, Paul traveled through the interior provinces. Finally, he came to Ephesus, where he found several believers.* [2]"Did you receive the Holy Spirit when you believed?" he asked them.

"No," they replied, "we don't know what you mean. We haven't even heard that there is a Holy Spirit."

[3]"Then what baptism did you experience?" he asked.

And they replied, "The baptism of John."

[4]Paul said, "John's baptism was to demonstrate a desire to turn from sin and turn to God. John him-

## DEBATABLE ● ● ● • •

18:27-28 **Apollos was from Alexandria in Egypt, the second largest city in the Roman Empire, home of a great university. He was a scholar, orator, and debater. After his knowledge about Christ was more complete, God greatly used his gifts to strengthen and encourage the church. Reason is a powerful tool in the right hands and the right situation. Apollos used his reasoning ability to convince many in Greece of the truth of the gospel. You don't have to turn off your mind when you turn to Christ. You can use logic or debate to bring others to God.**

18:21 Some manuscripts read *"I must by all means be at Jerusalem for the upcoming festival, but I will come back later."* 18:22 Greek *the church.* 18:23 Greek *disciples;* also in 18:27. 19:1 Greek *disciples;* also in 19:9, 30.

self told the people to believe in Jesus, the one John
said would come later."
5As soon as they heard this, they were baptized
in the name of the Lord Jesus. 6Then when Paul
laid his hands on them, the Holy Spirit came on
them, and they spoke in other tongues and prophesied. 7There were about twelve men in all.
8Then Paul went to the synagogue and preached
boldly for the next three months, arguing persuasively about the Kingdom of God. 9But some rejected his message and publicly spoke against the
Way, so Paul left the synagogue and took the believers with him. Then he began preaching daily at
the lecture hall of Tyrannus. 10This went on for the
next two years, so that people throughout the province of Asia—both Jews
and Greeks—heard the
Lord's message.
11God gave Paul the
power to do unusual mir-
acles, 12so that even when
handkerchiefs or cloths
that had touched his skin
were placed on sick people,
they were healed of their
diseases, and any evil spirits within them came out.
13A team of Jews who
were traveling from town
to town casting out evil
spirits tried to use the
name of the Lord Jesus. The
incantation they used was
this: "I command you by
Jesus, whom Paul preaches,
to come out!" 14Seven sons
of Sceva, a leading priest,
were doing this. 15But
when they tried it on a man
possessed by an evil spirit,
the spirit replied, "I know
Jesus, and I know Paul. But
who are you?" 16And he
leaped on them and at-
tacked them with such violence that they fled from
the house, naked and
badly injured.
17The story of what hap-
pened spread quickly all
through Ephesus, to Jews
and Greeks alike. A solemn
fear descended on the
city, and the name of the
Lord Jesus was greatly
honored. 18Many who be-
came believers confessed
their sinful practices. 19A
number of them who had
been practicing magic
brought their incantation books and burned
them at a public bonfire. The value of the books
was several million dollars.* 20So the message

## MAGIC CHARMS ● ● ● • •

**19:13 Many Ephesians engaged in exorcism and occult practices for profit (see 19:18-19). The sons of Sceva were impressed by Paul's work, whose power to cast out demons came from God's Holy Spirit, not from witchcraft, and was obviously more powerful than theirs. They discovered, however, that no person can control or duplicate God's power. These men were calling upon the name without knowing the person. It is knowing Jesus, not reciting his name like a magic charm, that gives us the power to change people. Christ works his power only through those he chooses.**

# AQUILA & PRISCILLA

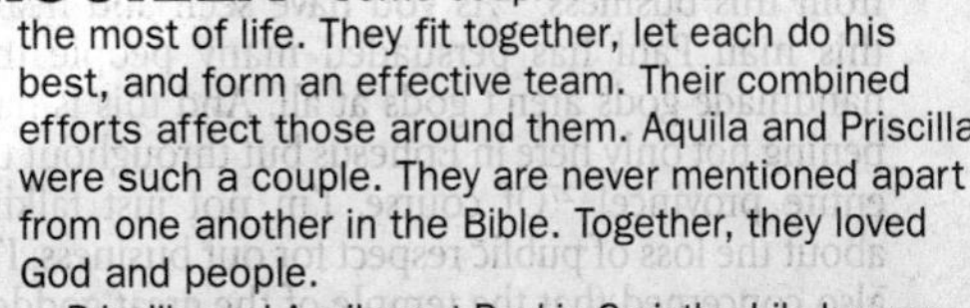

Some couples know how to make the most of life. They fit together, let each do his best, and form an effective team. Their combined efforts affect those around them. Aquila and Priscilla were such a couple. They are never mentioned apart from one another in the Bible. Together, they loved God and people.

Priscilla and Aquila met Paul in Corinth while he was on his second missionary journey. They had just left Rome. Their home was as movable as the tents they made in their business. They invited Paul to stay with them, and he joined them in making tents. He helped them by sharing his wisdom about God.

Priscilla and Aquila made good use of what they learned from Paul. They listened and evaluated what they heard. For instance, when another preacher, Apollos, came to town, they listened to what he had to say. They realized he was a good speaker, but that there were important things he needed to learn. Instead of correcting Apollos in public, they quietly took him home with them and shared with him what he needed to know. Apollos had been preaching John the Baptist's message of repentance. Priscilla and Aquila told Apollos about Jesus' life, death, and resurrection, and how God's Spirit wanted to live in us. Apollos then used his great ability to tell the whole story!

This couple continued to use their home as a place for training and worship. Later, back in Rome, one of the churches met in their house. (The first Christians did not meet in church buildings, but in the homes of believers.) It is easy to imagine that anywhere Aquila and Priscilla lived would be a place of fellowship.

**UPS:**
- Outstanding husband-wife team who ministered in the early church
- Supported themselves by making tents while serving Christ
- Close friends of Paul
- Explained the full message of Christ to Apollos

**STATS:**
- Where: Originally from Rome; moved to Corinth, then Ephesus
- Occupation: Tentmakers
- Contemporaries: Emperor Claudius, Paul, Timothy, Apollos

LESSONS: Couples can have an effective ministry together

The home is a valuable tool for evangelism

KEY VERSES: "Greet Priscilla and Aquila. They have been co-workers in my ministry for Christ Jesus. In fact, they risked their lives for me. I am not the only one who is thankful to them; so are all the Gentile churches" (Romans 16:3-4).

Their story is told in Acts 18. They are also mentioned in Romans 16:3-5; 1 Corinthians 16:19; 2 Timothy 4:19.

19:19 Greek *50,000 pieces of silver,* each of which was the equivalent of a day's wage.

about the Lord spread widely and had a powerful effect.

[21]Afterward Paul felt impelled by the Holy Spirit* to go over to Macedonia and Achaia before returning to Jerusalem. "And after that," he said, "I must go on to Rome!" [22]He sent his two assistants, Timothy and Erastus, on ahead to Macedonia while he stayed awhile longer in the province of Asia.

[23]But about that time, serious trouble developed in Ephesus concerning the Way. [24]It began with Demetrius, a silversmith who had a large business manufacturing silver shrines of the Greek goddess Artemis.* He kept many craftsmen busy. [25]He called the craftsmen together, along with others employed in related trades, and addressed them as follows:

"Gentlemen, you know that our wealth comes from this business. [26]As you have seen and heard, this man Paul has persuaded many people that handmade gods aren't gods at all. And this is happening not only here in Ephesus but throughout the entire province! [27]Of course, I'm not just talking about the loss of public respect for our business. I'm also concerned that the temple of the great goddess Artemis will lose its influence and that Artemis—this magnificent goddess worshiped throughout the province of Asia and all around the world—will be robbed of her prestige!"

**SUCCESS ● ● • • •**

**20:24 We often feel that life is a failure unless we're getting a lot out of it: glory, fun, money, popularity. But Paul thought life was worth *nothing* unless he used it for God's work. What he put *into* life was far more important than what he got out. Which is more important to you–what you get out of life, or what you put into it?**

[28]At this their anger boiled, and they began shouting, "Great is Artemis of the Ephesians!" [29]A crowd began to gather, and soon the city was filled with confusion. Everyone rushed to the amphitheater, dragging along Gaius and Aristarchus, who were Paul's traveling companions from Macedonia. [30]Paul wanted to go in, but the believers wouldn't let him. [31]Some of the officials of the province, friends of Paul, also sent a message to him, begging him not to risk his life by entering the amphitheater.

[32]Inside, the people were all shouting, some one thing and some another. Everything was in confusion. In fact, most of them didn't even know why they were there. [33]Alexander was thrust forward by some of the Jews, who encouraged him to explain the situation. He motioned for silence and tried to speak in defense. [34]But when the crowd realized he was a Jew, they started shouting again and kept it up for two hours: "Great is Artemis of the Ephesians! Great is Artemis of the Ephesians!"

[35]At last the mayor was able to quiet them down enough to speak. "Citizens of Ephesus," he said. "Everyone knows that Ephesus is the official guardian of the temple of the great Artemis, whose image fell down to us from heaven. [36]Since this is an indisputable fact, you shouldn't be disturbed, no matter what is said. Don't do anything rash. [37]You have brought these men here, but they have stolen nothing from the temple and have not spoken against our goddess. [38]If Demetrius and the craftsmen have a case against them, the courts are in session and the judges can take the case at once. Let them go through legal channels. [39]And if there are complaints about other matters, they can be settled in a legal assembly. [40]I am afraid we are in danger of being charged with rioting by the Roman government, since there is no cause for all this commotion. And if Rome demands an explanation, we won't know what to say." [41]Then he dismissed them, and they dispersed.

CHAPTER **20** **ON TO MACEDONIA AND GREECE.** When it was all over, Paul sent for the believers* and encouraged them. Then he said good-bye and left for Macedonia. [2]Along the way, he encouraged the believers in all the towns he passed through. Then he traveled down to Greece, [3]where he stayed for three months. He was preparing to sail back to Syria when he discovered a plot by some Jews against his life, so he decided to return through Macedonia.

[4]Several men were traveling with him. They were Sopater of Berea, the son of Pyrrhus; Aristarchus and Secundus, from Thessalonica; Gaius, from Derbe; Timothy; and Tychicus and Trophimus, who were from the province of Asia. [5]They went ahead and waited for us at Troas. [6]As soon as the Passover season* ended, we boarded a ship at Philippi in Macedonia and five days later arrived in Troas, where we stayed a week.

[7]On the first day of the week, we gathered to observe the Lord's Supper.* Paul was preaching; and since he was leaving the next day, he talked until midnight. [8]The upstairs room where we met was lighted with many flickering lamps. [9]As Paul spoke on and on, a young man named Eutychus, sitting on the windowsill, became very drowsy. Finally, he sank into a deep sleep and fell three stories to his death below. [10]Paul went down, bent over him, and took him into his arms. "Don't worry," he said, "he's alive!" [11]Then they all went back upstairs and ate the Lord's Supper together.* And Paul continued talking to them until dawn; then he left. [12]Meanwhile, the young man was taken home unhurt, and everyone was greatly relieved.

[13]Paul went by land to Assos, where he had arranged for us to join him, and we went on ahead by ship. [14]He joined us there and we sailed together to Mitylene. [15]The next day we passed the island of Kios. The following day, we crossed to the island of Samos. And a day later we arrived at Miletus.

[16]Paul had decided against stopping at Ephesus

19:21 Or *purposed in his spirit.* 19:24 *Artemis* is otherwise known as Diana. 20:1 Greek *disciples.* 20:6 Greek *the days of unleavened bread.* 20:7 Greek *to break bread.* 20:11 Greek *broke the bread.*

this time because he didn't want to spend further
time in the province of Asia. He was hurrying to get
to Jerusalem, if possible, for the Festival of Pentecost.
[17]But when we landed at Miletus, he sent a message
to the elders of the church at Ephesus, asking them
to come down to meet him.

[18]When they arrived he declared, "You know that
from the day I set foot in the province of Asia until
now [19]I have done the Lord's work humbly—yes,
and with tears. I have endured the trials that came to
me from the plots of the Jews. [20]Yet I never shrank
from telling you the truth, either publicly or in your
homes. [21]I have had one message for Jews and Gentiles alike—the necessity of turning from sin and
turning to God, and of faith in our Lord Jesus.

[22]"And now I am going to Jerusalem, drawn there
irresistibly by the Holy Spirit,* not knowing what
awaits me, [23]except that the Holy Spirit has told me
in city after city that jail and suffering lie ahead. [24]But
my life is worth nothing unless I use it for doing the
work assigned me by the Lord Jesus—the work of
telling others the Good News about God's wonderful kindness and love.

[25]"And now I know that none of you to whom I
have preached the Kingdom will ever see me again.
[26]Let me say plainly that I have been faithful. No one's
damnation can be blamed on me,* [27]for I didn't shrink
from declaring all that God wants for you.

[28]"And now beware! Be sure that you feed and
shepherd God's flock—his church, purchased with
his blood—over whom the Holy Spirit has appointed you as elders.* [29]I know full well that false
teachers, like vicious wolves, will come in among
you after I leave, not sparing the
flock. [30]Even some of you will distort the truth in order to draw a
following. [31]Watch out! Remember
the three years I was with you—my
constant watch and care over you
night and day, and my many tears
for you.

[32]"And now I entrust you to God
and the word of his grace—his
message that is able to build you
up and give you an inheritance
with all those he has set apart for
himself.

[33]"I have never coveted anyone's
money or fine clothing. [34]You
know that these hands of mine
have worked to pay my own way,
and I have even supplied the needs
of those who were with me. [35]And
I have been a constant example of
how you can help the poor by
working hard. You should remember the words of the Lord Jesus: 'It
is more blessed to give than to receive.'"

**FOCUS ● ● • • •**

20:33 **Paul was satisfied with whatever he had, wherever he was, as long as he could do God's work. Examine your attitudes toward wealth and comfort. If you focus more on what you don't have than on what you do have, it's time to reexamine your priorities and put God's work back in first place.**

[36]When he had finished speaking, he knelt and
prayed with them. [37]They wept aloud as they embraced him in farewell, [38]sad most of all because he
had said that they would never see him again. Then
they accompanied him down to the ship.

CHAPTER **21** **PAUL JOURNEYS TO JERUSALEM.** After
saying farewell to the Ephesian elders, we sailed
straight to the island of Cos. The next day we reached
Rhodes and then went to Patara. [2]There we boarded a
ship sailing for the Syrian province of Phoenicia. [3]We
sighted the island of Cyprus, passed it on our left, and
landed at the harbor of Tyre, in Syria, where the ship
was to unload. [4]We went ashore, found the local believers,* and stayed with them a week. These disciples
prophesied through the Holy Spirit that Paul should
not go on to Jerusalem. [5]When we returned to the ship
at the end of the week, the entire congregation, including wives and children, came down to the shore with
us. There we knelt, prayed, [6]and said our farewells.
Then we went aboard, and they returned home.

[7]The next stop after leaving Tyre was Ptolemais,
where we greeted the brothers and sisters* but stayed
only one day. [8]Then we went on to Caesarea and
stayed at the home of Philip the Evangelist, one of the

## "Here's what I did..."

At my high school we have a Christian Bible study group called Saints' Battalion. A few months ago, Satanists on our campus formed a group they call Young Satanists of America. Before their own group meetings, held on the same day we have ours, they come into our meetings and bother us in every way they can. I know that in their meetings they put down Christianity and exalt Satan as a "philosophy."

We cannot ban them from coming to our meetings because our group has to be open to all. They still remain a problem. Our group and my church continue to pray about this problem. A passage that has really encouraged us is Acts 19:13-20. It talks about the power in the name of Jesus to cast out evil spirits, and about how lots of people who heard about Christ burned their witchcraft books and turned to God. We use this passage to claim the power of Jesus, and we pray that many of the Young Satanists who come to our meetings will hear God's Word and turn to Christ.

Rick AGE 16

20:22 Or *by my spirit,* or *by an inner compulsion.* Greek reads *by the spirit.* 20:26 Greek *I am innocent of the blood of all.* 20:28 Greek *overseers.* 21:4 Greek *disciples;* also in 21:16. 21:7 Greek *brothers;* also in 21:17.

## HE HAD TO ● ● ● • •

21:13-14 **Paul knew that he would be imprisoned in Jerusalem. His friends pleaded with him not to go there, but Paul knew God wanted him to. No one wants to face hardship or suffering, but a faithful disciple wants above all else to please God. When we really want to do God's will, we must accept all that comes with it—even the pain. Then we can say with Paul's friends, "The will of the Lord be done."**

seven men who had been chosen to distribute food. [9]He had four unmarried daughters who had the gift of prophecy.

[10]During our stay of several days, a man named Agabus, who also had the gift of prophecy, arrived from Judea. [11]When he visited us, he took Paul's belt and bound his own feet and hands with it. Then he said, "The Holy Spirit declares, 'So shall the owner of this belt be bound by the Jewish leaders in Jerusalem and turned over to the Romans.'" [12]When we heard this, we who were traveling with him, as well as the local believers, begged Paul not to go on to Jerusalem.

[13]But he said, "Why all this weeping? You are breaking my heart! For I am ready not only to be jailed at Jerusalem but also to die for the sake of the Lord Jesus." [14]When it was clear that we couldn't persuade him, we gave up and said, "The will of the Lord be done."

[15]Shortly afterward we packed our things and left for Jerusalem. [16]Some believers from Caesarea accompanied us, and they took us to the home of Mnason, a man originally from Cyprus and one of the early disciples. [17]All the brothers and sisters in Jerusalem welcomed us cordially.

[18]The next day Paul went in with us to meet with James, and all the elders of the Jerusalem church were present. [19]After greetings were exchanged, Paul gave a detailed account of the things God had accomplished among the Gentiles through his ministry.

[20]After hearing this, they praised God. But then they said, "You know, dear brother, how many thousands of Jews have also believed, and they all take the law of Moses very seriously. [21]Our Jewish Christians here at Jerusalem have been told that you are teaching all the Jews living in the Gentile world to turn their backs on the laws of Moses. They say that you teach people not to circumcise their children or follow other Jewish customs. [22]Now what can be done? For they will certainly hear that you have come.

[23]"Here's our suggestion. We have four men here who have taken a vow and are preparing to shave their heads. [24]Go with them to the Temple and join them in the purification ceremony, and pay for them to have their heads shaved. Then everyone will know that the rumors are all false and that you yourself observe the Jewish laws.

[25]"As for the Gentile Christians, all we ask of them is what we already told them in a letter: They should not eat food offered to idols, nor consume blood, nor eat meat from strangled animals, and they should stay away from all sexual immorality."

[26]So Paul agreed to their request, and the next day he went through the purification ritual with the men and went to the Temple. Then he publicly announced the date when their vows would end and sacrifices would be offered for each of them.

[27]The seven days were almost ended when some Jews from the province of Asia saw Paul in the Temple and roused a mob against him. They grabbed him, [28]yelling, "Men of Israel! Help! This is the man who teaches against our people and tells everybody to disobey the Jewish laws. He speaks against the Temple—and he even defiles it by bringing Gentiles in!" [29](For earlier that day they had seen him in the city with Trophimus, a Gentile from Ephesus,* and they assumed Paul had taken him into the Temple.)

[30]The whole population of the city was rocked by these accusations, and a great riot followed. Paul was dragged out of the Temple, and immediately the gates were closed behind him. [31]As they were trying to kill him, word reached the commander of the Roman regiment that all Jerusalem was in an uproar. [32]He immediately called out his soldiers and officers and ran down among the crowd. When the mob saw the commander and the troops coming, they stopped beating Paul. [33]The commander arrested him and ordered him bound with two chains. Then he asked the crowd who he was and what he had done. [34]Some shouted one thing and some another. He couldn't find out the truth in all the uproar and confusion, so he ordered Paul to be taken to the fortress. [35]As they reached the stairs, the mob grew so violent the soldiers had to lift Paul to their shoulders to protect him. [36]And the crowd followed behind shouting, "Kill him, kill him!"

## IN COMMON ● ● ● • •

22:3 **By saying that at one time he was as zealous for God as any of his listeners, Paul was acknowledging their sincere motives in trying to kill him and recognizing that he would have done the same to Christian leaders a few years earlier. Paul always tried to find something he and his audience had in common before he launched into a full-scale defense of Christianity. When you witness for Christ, first identify yourself with your audience. They are much more likely to listen to you if they feel they have something in common with you.**

[37]As Paul was about to be taken inside, he said to the commander, "May I have a word with you?"

"Do you know Greek?" the commander asked, surprised. [38]"Aren't you the Egyptian who led a rebellion some time ago and took four thousand members of the Assassins out into the desert?"

[39]"No," Paul replied, "I am a Jew from Tarsus in Cilicia, which is an important city. Please, let me talk to these people." [40]The commander agreed, so Paul stood on the stairs and motioned to the people to be quiet. Soon a deep silence enveloped the crowd, and he addressed them in their own language, Aramaic.*

21:29 Greek *Trophimus, the Ephesian.* 21:40 Or *Hebrew.*

CHAPTER **22** **PAUL IS ARRESTED.** "Brothers and esteemed fathers," Paul said, "listen to me as I offer my defense." [2]When they heard him speaking in their own language,* the silence was even greater. [3]"I am a Jew, born in Tarsus, a city in Cilicia, and I was brought up and educated here in Jerusalem under Gamaliel. At his feet I learned to follow our Jewish laws and customs very carefully. I became very zealous to honor God in everything I did, just as all of you are today. [4]And I persecuted the followers of the Way, hounding some to death, binding and delivering both men and women to prison. [5]The high priest and the whole council of leaders can testify that this is so. For I received letters from them to our Jewish brothers in Damascus, authorizing me to bring the Christians from there to Jerusalem, in chains, to be punished.

[6]"As I was on the road, nearing Damascus, about noon a very bright light from heaven suddenly shone around me. [7]I fell to the ground and heard a voice saying to me, 'Saul, Saul, why are you persecuting me?'

[8]"'Who are you, sir?' I asked. And he replied, 'I am Jesus of Nazareth, the one you are persecuting.' [9]The people with me saw the light but didn't hear the voice.

[10]"I said, 'What shall I do, Lord?' And the Lord told me, 'Get up and go into Damascus, and there you will be told all that you are to do.'

[11]"I was blinded by the intense light and had to be led into Damascus by my companions. [12]A man named Ananias lived there. He was a godly man in his devotion to the law, and he was well thought of by all the Jews of Damascus. [13]He came to me and stood beside me and said, 'Brother Saul, receive your sight.' And that very hour I could see him!

[14]"Then he told me, 'The God of our ancestors has chosen you to know his will and to see the Righteous One and hear him speak. [15]You are to take his message everywhere, telling the whole world what you have seen and heard. [16]And now, why delay? Get up and be baptized, and have your sins washed away, calling on the name of the Lord.'

[17]"One day after I returned to Jerusalem, I was praying in the Temple, and I fell into a trance. [18]I saw a vision of Jesus saying to me, 'Hurry! Leave Jerusalem, for the people here won't believe you when you give them your testimony about me.'

[19]"'But Lord,' I argued, 'they certainly know that I imprisoned and beat those in every synagogue who believed on you. [20]And when your witness Stephen was killed, I was standing there agreeing. I kept the coats they laid aside as they stoned him.'

[21]"But the Lord said to me, 'Leave Jerusalem, for I will send you far away to the Gentiles!'"

[22]The crowd listened until Paul came to that word; then with one voice they shouted, "Away with such a fellow! Kill him! He isn't fit to live!" [23]They yelled, threw off their coats, and tossed handfuls of dust into the air.

[24]The commander brought Paul inside and ordered him lashed with whips to make him confess his crime. He wanted to find out why the crowd had become so furious. [25]As they tied Paul down to lash him, Paul said to the officer standing there, "Is it legal for you to whip a Roman citizen who hasn't even been tried?"

[26]The officer went to the commander and asked, "What are you doing? This man is a Roman citizen!"

[27]So the commander went over and asked Paul, "Tell me, are you a Roman citizen?"

"Yes, I certainly am," Paul replied.

[28]"I am, too," the commander muttered, "and it cost me plenty!"

## IN THE HEAT ● ● • • •

**22:30 God used Paul's persecution as an opportunity for him to witness. Here even his enemies were creating a platform for him to address the entire Jewish council. If we are sensitive to the Holy Spirit's leading, we will notice increased opportunities to share our faith, even in the heat of opposition.**

"But I am a citizen by birth!"

[29]The soldiers who were about to interrogate Paul quickly withdrew when they heard he was a Roman citizen, and the commander was frightened because he had ordered him bound and whipped.

[30]The next day the commander freed Paul from his chains and ordered the leading priests into session with the Jewish high council.* He had Paul brought in before them to try to find out what the trouble was all about.

CHAPTER **23** Gazing intently at the high council,* Paul began: "Brothers, I have always lived before God in all good conscience!"

[2]Instantly Ananias the high priest commanded those close to Paul to slap him on the mouth. [3]But Paul said to him, "God will slap you, you whitewashed wall! What kind of judge are you to break the law yourself by ordering me struck like that?"

[4]Those standing near Paul said to him, "Is that the way to talk to God's high priest?"

[5]"I'm sorry, brothers. I didn't realize he was the high priest," Paul replied, "for the Scriptures say, 'Do not speak evil of anyone who rules over you.'*"

[6]Paul realized that some members of the high council were Sadducees and some were Pharisees, so he shouted, "Brothers, I am a Pharisee, as were all my ancestors! And I am on trial because my hope is in the resurrection of the dead!"

[7]This divided the council—the Pharisees against the Sadducees—[8]for the Sadducees say there is no resurrection or angels or spirits, but the Pharisees believe in all of these. [9]So a great clamor arose. Some of the teachers of religious law who were Pharisees jumped up to argue that Paul was all right. "We see nothing wrong with him," they shouted. "Perhaps a spirit or an angel spoke to him." [10]The shouting grew

22:2 Greek *in Aramaic.* 22:30 Greek *Sanhedrin.* 23:1 Greek *Sanhedrin;* also in 23:6, 15, 20, 28. 23:5 Exod 22:28.

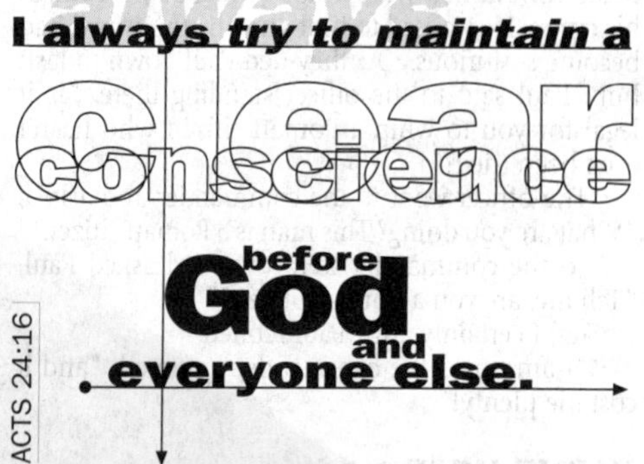


louder and louder, and the men were tugging at Paul from both sides, pulling him this way and that. Finally, the commander, fearing they would tear him apart, ordered his soldiers to take him away from them and bring him back to the fortress.

11That night the Lord appeared to Paul and said, "Be encouraged, Paul. Just as you have told the people about me here in Jerusalem, you must preach the Good News in Rome."

12The next morning a group of Jews got together and bound themselves with an oath to neither eat nor drink until they had killed Paul. 13There were more than forty of them. 14They went to the leading priests and other leaders and told them what they had done. "We have bound ourselves under oath to neither eat nor drink until we have killed Paul. 15You and the high council should tell the commander to bring Paul back to the council again," they requested. "Pretend you want to examine his case more fully. We will kill him on the way."

16But Paul's nephew heard of their plan and went to the fortress and told Paul. 17Paul called one of the officers and said, "Take this young man to the commander. He has something important to tell him."

18So the officer did, explaining, "Paul, the prisoner, called me over and asked me to bring this young man to you because he has something to tell you."

19The commander took him by the arm, led him aside, and asked, "What is it you want to tell me?"

20Paul's nephew told him, "Some Jews are going to ask you to bring Paul before the Jewish high council tomorrow, pretending they want to get some more information. 21But don't do it! There are more than forty men hiding along the way ready to jump him and kill him. They have vowed not to eat or drink until they kill him. They are ready, expecting you to agree to their request."

22"Don't let a soul know you told me this," the commander warned the young man as he sent him away.

23Then the commander called two of his officers and ordered, "Get two hundred soldiers ready to leave for Caesarea at nine o'clock tonight. Also take two hundred spearmen and seventy horsemen. 24Provide horses for Paul to ride, and get him safely to Governor Felix." 25Then he wrote this letter to the governor:

> 26"From Claudius Lysias, to his Excellency, Governor Felix. Greetings! 27This man was seized by some Jews, and they were about to kill him when I arrived with the troops. When I learned that he was a Roman citizen, I removed him to safety. 28Then I took him to their high council to try to find out what he had done. 29I soon discovered it was something regarding their religious law—certainly nothing worthy of imprisonment or death. 30But when I was informed of a plot to kill him, I immediately sent him on to you. I have told his accusers to bring their charges before you."

31So that night, as ordered, the soldiers took Paul as far as Antipatris. 32They returned to the fortress the next morning, while the horsemen took him on to Caesarea. 33When they arrived in Caesarea, they presented Paul and the letter to Governor Felix. 34He read it and then asked Paul what province he was from. "Cilicia," Paul answered.

35"I will hear your case myself when your accusers arrive," the governor told him. Then the governor ordered him kept in the prison at Herod's headquarters.

CHAPTER **24** **PAUL APPEARS BEFORE FELIX.** Five days later Ananias, the high priest, arrived with some of the Jewish leaders and the lawyer* Tertullus, to press charges against Paul. 2When Paul was called in, Tertullus laid charges against Paul in the following address to the governor:

"Your Excellency, you have given peace to us Jews and have enacted reforms for us. 3And for all of this we are very grateful to you. 4But lest I bore you, kindly give me your attention for only a moment as I briefly outline our case against this man. 5For we have found him to be a troublemaker, a man who is constantly inciting the Jews throughout the world to riots and rebellions against the Roman government. He is a ringleader of the sect known as the Nazarenes. 6Moreover he was trying to defile the Temple

## AMAZING! ● ● ● • •

23:23-24 **The Roman commander ordered Paul to be sent to Caesarea. Jerusalem was the seat of Jewish government, but Caesarea was the area's Roman headquarters. God works in amazing and amusing ways. He could have gotten Paul to Caesarea in many ways, but he chose to use the Roman army to deliver Paul from his enemies. God's ways are not ours—we are limited, he is not. Don't ask him to respond your way. When God intervenes, anything can happen—often much more and much better than you could ever anticipate.**

24:1 Greek *some elders and an orator.*

when we arrested him.* 8You can find out the truth of our accusations by examining him yourself." 9Then the other Jews chimed in, declaring that everything Tertullus said was true.

10Now it was Paul's turn. The governor motioned for him to rise and speak. Paul said, "I know, sir, that you have been a judge of Jewish affairs for many years, and this gives me confidence as I make my defense. 11You can quickly discover that it was no more than twelve days ago that I arrived in Jerusalem to worship at the Temple. 12I didn't argue with anyone in the Temple, nor did I incite a riot in any synagogue or on the streets of the city. 13These men certainly cannot prove the things they accuse me of doing.

14"But I admit that I follow the Way, which they call a sect. I worship the God of our ancestors, and I firmly believe the Jewish law and everything written in the books of prophecy. 15I have hope in God, just as these men do, that he will raise both the righteous and the ungodly. 16Because of this, I always try to maintain a clear conscience before God and everyone else.

17"After several years away, I returned to Jerusalem with money to aid my people and to offer sacrifices to God. 18My accusers saw me in the Temple as I was completing a purification ritual. There was no crowd around me and no rioting. 19But some Jews from the province of Asia were there—and they ought to be here to bring charges if they have anything against me! 20Ask these men here what wrongdoing the Jewish high council* found in me, 21except for one thing I said when I shouted out, 'I am on trial before you today because I believe in the resurrection of the dead!'"

22Felix, who was quite familiar with the Way, adjourned the hearing and said, "Wait until Lysias, the garrison commander, arrives. Then I will decide the case." 23He ordered an officer to keep Paul in custody but to give him some freedom and allow his friends to visit him and take care of his needs.

24A few days later Felix came with his wife, Drusilla, who was Jewish. Sending for Paul, they listened as he told them about faith in Christ Jesus. 25As he reasoned with them about righteousness and self-control and the judgment to come, Felix was terrified. "Go away for now," he replied. "When it is more convenient, I'll call for you again." 26He also hoped that Paul would bribe him, so he sent for him quite often and talked with him.

27Two years went by in this way; then Felix was succeeded by Porcius Festus. And because Felix wanted to gain favor with the Jewish leaders, he left Paul in prison.

## CHAPTER 25

**PAUL APPEARS BEFORE FESTUS.** Three days after Festus arrived in Caesarea to take over his new responsibilities, he left for Jerusalem, 2where the leading priests and other Jewish leaders met with him and made their accusations against Paul. 3They asked Festus as a favor to transfer Paul to Jerusalem. (Their plan was to waylay and kill him.) 4But Festus replied that Paul was at Caesarea and he himself would be returning there soon. 5So he said, "Those of you in authority can return with me. If Paul has done anything wrong, you can make your accusations."

6Eight or ten days later he returned to Caesarea, and on the following day Paul's trial began. 7On Paul's arrival in court, the Jewish leaders from Jerusalem gathered around and made many serious accusations they couldn't prove. 8Paul denied the charges. "I am not guilty," he said. "I have committed no crime against the Jewish laws or the Temple or the Roman government."

9Then Festus, wanting to please the Jews, asked him, "Are you willing to go to Jerusalem and stand trial before me there?"

10But Paul replied, "No! This is the official Roman court, so I ought to be tried right here. You know very well I am not guilty. 11If I have done something worthy of death, I don't refuse to die. But if I am innocent, neither you nor anyone else has a right to turn me over to these men to kill me. I appeal to Caesar!"

12Festus conferred with his advisers and then replied, "Very well! You have appealed to Caesar, and to Caesar you shall go!"

13A few days later King Agrippa arrived with his sister, Bernice,* to pay their respects to Festus. 14During their stay of several days, Festus discussed Paul's case with the king. "There is a prisoner here," he told him, "whose case was left for me by Felix. 15When I was in Jerusalem, the leading priests and other Jewish leaders pressed charges against him and asked me to sentence him. 16Of course, I quickly pointed out to them that Roman law does not convict people without a trial. They are given an opportunity to defend themselves face to face with their accusers.

17"When they came here for the trial, I called the case the very next day and ordered Paul brought in. 18But the accusations made against him weren't at all what I expected. 19It was something about their religion and about someone called Jesus who died, but whom Paul insists is alive. 20I was perplexed as to how to conduct an investigation of this kind, and I

### PERSONAL ● ● ● • •

**24:25 Paul's talk with Felix became so personal that Felix felt convicted. Felix, like Herod Antipas (Mark 6:17-18), had taken another man's wife. Paul's words were interesting until they focused on "righteousness and self-control and the judgment to come." Many people are glad to discuss the gospel as long as it doesn't touch their lives too personally. When it does, some will resist or run away. But this is what the gospel is all about—God's power to change lives. The gospel must move from principles and doctrine into a life-changing dynamic.**

24:6 Some manuscripts add *We would have judged him by our law, 7but Lysias, the commander of the garrison, came and took him violently away from us, 8commanding his accusers to come before you.* 24:20 Greek *Sanhedrin.* 25:13 Greek *Agrippa the king and Bernice arrived.*

## OPPORTUNITIES ● ● ● • •

25:23 **Paul was in prison, but that didn't stop him from making the most of his situation. Military officers and prominent city leaders met in the palace room with Agrippa to hear this case. Paul saw this new audience as yet another opportunity to present the gospel. Rather than complain about your present situation, look for opportunities to serve God and share him with others. Problems may be opportunities in disguise.**

asked him whether he would be willing to stand trial on these charges in Jerusalem. 21But Paul appealed to the emperor. So I ordered him back to jail until I could arrange to send him to Caesar."

22"I'd like to hear the man myself," Agrippa said.

And Festus replied, "You shall—tomorrow!"

23So the next day Agrippa and Bernice arrived at the auditorium with great pomp, accompanied by military officers and prominent men of the city. Festus ordered that Paul be brought in. 24Then Festus said, "King Agrippa and all present, this is the man whose death is demanded both by the local Jews and by those in Jerusalem. 25But in my opinion he has done nothing worthy of death. However, he appealed his case to the emperor, and I decided to send him. 26But what shall I write the emperor? For there is no real charge against him. So I have brought him before all of you, and especially you, King Agrippa, so that after we examine him, I might have something to write. 27For it doesn't seem reasonable to send a prisoner to the emperor without specifying the charges against him!"

CHAPTER **26** **AGRIPPA WANTS TO HEAR PAUL.** Then Agrippa said to Paul, "You may speak in your defense."

So Paul, with a gesture of his hand, started his defense: 2"I am fortunate, King Agrippa, that you are the one hearing my defense against all these accusations made by the Jewish leaders, 3for I know you are an expert on Jewish customs and controversies. Now please listen to me patiently!

4"As the Jewish leaders are well aware, I was given a thorough Jewish training from my earliest childhood among my own people and in Jerusalem. 5If they would admit it, they know that I have been a member of the Pharisees, the strictest sect of our religion. 6Now I am on trial because I am looking forward to the fulfillment of God's promise made to our ancestors. 7In fact, that is why the twelve tribes of Israel worship God night and day, and they share the same hope I have. Yet, O king, they say it is wrong for me to have this hope! 8Why does it seem incredible to any of you that God can raise the dead?

9"I used to believe that I ought to do everything I could to oppose the followers of Jesus of Nazareth.* 10Authorized by the leading priests, I caused many of the believers in Jerusalem to be sent to prison. And I cast my vote against them when they were condemned to death. 11Many times I had them whipped in the synagogues to try to get them to curse Christ. I was so violently opposed to them that I even hounded them in distant cities of foreign lands.

12"One day I was on such a mission to Damascus, armed with the authority and commission of the leading priests. 13About noon, Your Majesty, a light from heaven brighter than the sun shone down on me and my companions. 14We all fell down, and I heard a voice saying to me in Aramaic,* 'Saul, Saul, why are you persecuting me? It is hard for you to fight against my will.*'

15"'Who are you, sir?' I asked.

"And the Lord replied, 'I am Jesus, the one you are persecuting. 16Now stand up! For I have appeared to you to appoint you as my servant and my witness. You are to tell the world about this experience and about other times I will appear to you. 17And I will protect you from both your own people and the Gentiles. Yes, I am going to send you to the Gentiles, 18to open their eyes so they may turn from darkness to light, and from the power of Satan to God. Then they will receive forgiveness for their sins and be given a place among God's people, who are set apart by faith in me.'

19"And so, O King Agrippa, I was not disobedient to that vision from heaven. 20I preached first to those in Damascus, then in Jerusalem and throughout all Judea, and also to the Gentiles, that all must turn from their sins and turn to God—and prove they have changed by the good things they do. 21Some Jews arrested me in the Temple for preaching this, and they tried to kill me. 22But God protected me so that I am still alive today to tell these facts to everyone, from the least to the greatest. I teach nothing except what the prophets and Moses said would happen—23that the Messiah would suffer and be the first to rise from the dead as a light to Jews and Gentiles alike."

24Suddenly, Festus shouted, "Paul, you are insane. Too much study has made you crazy!"

25But Paul replied, "I am not insane, Most Excellent Festus. I am speaking the sober truth. 26And King Agrippa knows about these things. I speak frankly, for I am sure these events are all familiar to him, for they were not done in a corner! 27King Agrippa, do you believe the prophets? I know you do—"

28Agrippa interrupted him. "Do you think you can make me a Christian so quickly?"*

## FACTS ● ● ● • •

26:26 **Paul was appealing to the *facts*—people were still alive who had heard Jesus and seen his miracles; the empty tomb could still be seen; and the Christian message was turning the world upside down (17:6). The history of Jesus' life and the early church are facts that are still open for us to examine. We can study eyewitness accounts of Jesus' life in the Bible as well as historical and archaeological records of the early church. Examine the events and facts as verified by many witnesses. Reconfirm your faith with the truth of these accounts.**

26:9 Greek *oppose the name of Jesus the Nazarene.* 26:14a Or *Hebrew.* 26:14b Greek *It is hard for you to kick against the oxgoads.* 26:28 Or *"A little more, and your arguments would make me a Christian."*

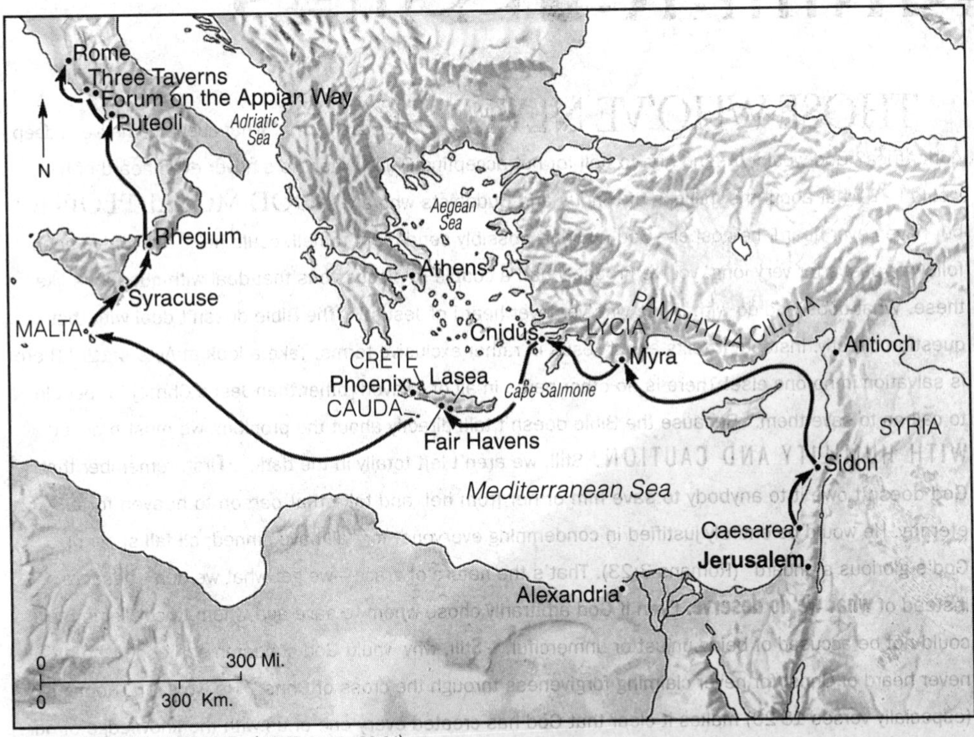


PAUL'S JOURNEY TO ROME (ACTS 21:17—28:31)

29Paul replied, "Whether quickly or not, I pray to
God that both you and everyone here in this audience might become the same as I am, except for
these chains."
30Then the king, the governor, Bernice, and all the
others stood and left. 31As they talked it over they
agreed, "This man hasn't done anything worthy of
death or imprisonment." 32And Agrippa said to Festus, "He could be set free if he hadn't appealed to
Caesar!"

## CHAPTER 27 **PAUL'S SHIP IS WRECKED.**

When the
time came, we set sail for Italy. Paul and several other
prisoners were placed in the custody of an army
officer named Julius, a captain of the Imperial Regiment. 2And Aristarchus, a Macedonian from Thessalonica, was also with us. We left on a boat whose
home port was Adramyttium; it was scheduled to
make several stops at ports along the coast of the
province of Asia.
3The next day when we docked at Sidon, Julius
was very kind to Paul and let him go ashore to visit
with friends so they could provide for his needs.
4Putting out to sea from there, we encountered head-
winds that made it difficult to keep the ship on
course, so we sailed north of Cyprus between the
island and the mainland. 5We passed along the coast
of the provinces of Cilicia and Pamphylia, landing at
Myra, in the province of Lycia. 6There the officer
found an Egyptian ship from Alexandria that was
bound for Italy, and he put us on board.
7We had several days of rough sailing, and after
great difficulty we finally neared Cnidus. But the
wind was against us, so we sailed down to the lee-
ward side of Crete, past the cape of Salmone. 8We
struggled along the coast with great difficulty and
finally arrived at Fair Havens, near the city of Lasea.
9We had lost a lot of time. The weather was becoming dangerous for long voyages by then because it
was so late in the fall,* and Paul spoke to the ship's
officers about it.
10"Sirs," he said, "I believe there is trouble ahead
if we go on—shipwreck, loss of cargo, injuries, and

### EVEN BETTER ● ● • • .

**27:1-28:24 One of Paul's most important journeys was to Rome, but he didn't get there in quite the way he had expected. It turned out to be more of a legal journey than a missionary journey, thanks to a series of legal trials and transactions. These events resulted in Paul being delivered to Rome, where he told his story of the gospel in the most amazing places, including the palace of the emperor! Sometimes we feel frustrated because our plans don't work out the way we wanted them to. But God is never out of control! He knows how to work things out so that the results are even better than we expected. Trusting God with your plans is a surefire plan for success!**

27:9 Greek *because the fast was now already gone by.* This fast happened on the Day of Atonement (*Yom Kippur*), which occurred in late September or early October.

## Ultimate Issues

### THOSE WHO'VE NEVER HEARD

"What about the native in deep dark Africa? God wouldn't send him to hell for not accepting Christ when he's never even heard of him, would he? What about the millions of Hindus and Buddhists who are GOOD MORAL PEOPLE, but have never heard the gospel—God couldn't possibly send them to hell, could he?" If you've been following Jesus for very long, you've probably had a couple of discussions that deal with questions like these. What does God do with those who've never heard of Jesus? The Bible doesn't deal with that question directly. Instead, it talks about Jesus in rather exclusive terms. Take a look at Acts 4:12: "There is salvation in no one else! There is no other name in all of heaven [other than Jesus Christ] for people to call on to save them." Because the Bible doesn't talk directly about the problem, we must proceed WITH HUMILITY AND CAUTION. Still, we aren't left totally in the dark. First, remember that God doesn't owe it to anybody to save him or her from hell and take that person to heaven for all eternity. He would be entirely justified in condemning everyone, for "all have sinned; all fall short of God's glorious standard" (Romans 3:23). That's the nature of grace—we get what we don't deserve, instead of **what we do deserve.** Even if God arbitrarily chose whom to save and whom to condemn, he could not be accused of being unjust or unmerciful. Still, why would God condemn someone who has never heard of Christ for never claiming forgiveness through the cross of Christ? He wouldn't. Romans 1 (especially verses 18-20) makes it clear that God has created every one of us with the knowledge of our Creator. We have to try to suppress it. Psalm 19 begins, "The heavens tell of the glory of God. The skies display his marvelous craftsmanship. Day after day they continue to speak; night after night they make him known." Every person ever born has an **INNATE KNOWLEDGE** that there is a Creator, someone bigger, smarter, and more powerful than we are, who put us here in this universe. Those who do not hear the message about Jesus are responsible for how they respond to the knowledge they *do* have about God. So, for anyone who has heard the Good News of Jesus—that God came to earth as a man named Jesus of Nazareth, and that he lived, died, and rose again so that through him we could have forgiveness of sins and eternal life—salvation comes through faith in Jesus. For the person who's never heard of Jesus and his love for us, salvation comes based on the knowledge of our loving Creator, and responding to that knowledge with love, obedience, and worship. For all people, Christ is the only one who has opened the way for us to be restored to God. It is his act on the cross and his resurrection that enables any of us to approach our holy and all-righteous God. **We don't have all the answers** to all the questions that confuse us about life and death, heaven and hell, and so on. But we can know the one who not only knows the truth, but is the Truth—and we know that he is loving, kind, and merciful. ***He will do what is right.***

---

danger to our lives." [11]But the officer in charge of the prisoners listened more to the ship's captain and the owner than to Paul. [12]And since Fair Havens was an exposed harbor—a poor place to spend the winter—most of the crew wanted to go to Phoenix, farther up the coast of Crete, and spend the winter there. Phoenix was a good harbor with only a southwest and northwest exposure.

[13]When a light wind began blowing from the south, the sailors thought they could make it. So they pulled up anchor and sailed along close to shore. [14]But the weather changed abruptly, and a wind of typhoon strength (a "northeaster," they called it) caught the ship and blew it out to sea. [15]They couldn't turn the ship into the wind, so they gave up and let it run before the gale.

16 We sailed behind a small island named Cauda,* where with great difficulty we hoisted aboard the lifeboat that was being towed behind us. 17 Then we banded the ship with ropes to strengthen the hull. The sailors were afraid of being driven across to the sandbars of Syrtis off the African coast, so they lowered the sea anchor and were thus driven before the wind.

18 The next day, as gale-force winds continued to batter the ship, the crew began throwing the cargo overboard. 19 The following day they even threw out the ship's equipment and anything else they could lay their hands on. 20 The terrible storm raged unabated for many days, blotting out the sun and the stars, until at last all hope was gone.

21 No one had eaten for a long time. Finally, Paul called the crew together and said, "Men, you should have listened to me in the first place and not left Fair Havens. You would have avoided all this injury and loss. 22 But take courage! None of you will lose your lives, even though the ship will go down. 23 For last night an angel of the God to whom I belong and whom I serve stood beside me, 24 and he said, 'Don't be afraid, Paul, for you will surely stand trial before Caesar! What's more, God in his goodness has granted safety to everyone sailing with you.' 25 So take courage! For I believe God. It will be just as he said. 26 But we will be shipwrecked on an island."

27 About midnight on the fourteenth night of the storm, as we were being driven across the Sea of Adria,* the sailors sensed land was near. 28 They took soundings and found the water was only 120 feet deep. A little later they sounded again and found only 90 feet.* 29 At this rate they were afraid we would soon be driven against the rocks along the shore, so they threw out four anchors from the stern and prayed for daylight. 30 Then the sailors tried to abandon the ship; they lowered the lifeboat as though they were going to put out anchors from the prow. 31 But Paul said to the commanding officer and the soldiers, "You will all die unless the sailors stay aboard." 32 So the soldiers cut the ropes and let the boat fall off.

33 As the darkness gave way to the early morning light, Paul begged everyone to eat. "You haven't touched food for two weeks," he said. 34 "Please eat something now for your own good. For not a hair of your heads will perish." 35 Then he took some bread, gave thanks to God before them all, and broke off a piece and ate it. 36 Then everyone was encouraged, 37 and all 276 of us began eating—for that is the number we had aboard. 38 After eating, the crew lightened the ship further by throwing the cargo of wheat overboard.

39 When morning dawned, they didn't recognize the coastline, but they saw a bay with a beach and wondered if they could get between the rocks and get the ship safely to shore. 40 So they cut off the anchors and left them in the sea. Then they lowered the rudders, raised the foresail, and headed toward shore. 41 But the ship hit a shoal and ran aground. The bow of the ship stuck fast, while the stern was repeatedly smashed by the force of the waves and began to break apart.

42 The soldiers wanted to kill the prisoners to make sure they didn't swim ashore and escape. 43 But the commanding officer wanted to spare Paul, so he didn't let them carry out their plan. Then he ordered all who could swim to jump overboard first and make for land, 44 and he told the others to try for it on planks and debris from the broken ship. So everyone escaped safely ashore!

## CHAPTER 28

**PAUL IS SHIPWRECKED ON MALTA.** Once we were safe on shore, we learned that we were on the island of Malta. 2 The people of the island were very kind to us. It was cold and rainy, so they built a fire on the shore to welcome us and warm us.

3 As Paul gathered an armful of sticks and was laying them on the fire, a poisonous snake, driven out by the heat, fastened itself onto his hand. 4 The people of the island saw it hanging there and said to each other, "A murderer, no doubt! Though he escaped the sea, justice will not permit him to live." 5 But Paul shook off the snake into the fire and was unharmed. 6 The people waited for him to swell up or suddenly drop dead. But when they had waited a long time and saw no harm come to him, they changed their minds and decided he was a god.

7 Near the shore where we landed was an estate belonging to Publius, the chief official of the island. He welcomed us courteously and fed us for three days. 8 As it happened, Publius's father was ill with fever and dysentery. Paul went in and prayed for him, and laying his hands on him, he healed him. 9 Then all the other sick people on the island came and were cured. 10 As a result we were showered with honors, and when the time came to sail, people put on board all sorts of things we would need for the trip.

11 It was three months after the shipwreck that we set sail on another ship that had wintered at the island—an Alexandrian ship with the twin gods* as its figurehead. 12 Our first stop was Syracuse,* where we stayed three days. 13 From there we sailed across to Rhegium.* A day later a south wind began blowing, so the following day we sailed up the coast to Puteoli. 14 There we found some believers,* who invited us to stay with them seven days. And so we came to Rome.

15 The brothers and sisters* in Rome had heard we were coming, and they came to meet us at the Forum* on the Appian Way. Others joined us at The

27:16 Some manuscripts read *Clauda.* 27:27 The *Sea of Adria* is in the central Mediterranean; it is not to be confused with the Adriatic Sea. 27:28 Greek *20 fathoms . . . 15 fathoms* [37 meters . . . 27 meters]. 28:11 The *twin gods* were the Roman gods Castor and Pollux. 28:12 *Syracuse* was on the island of Sicily. 28:13 *Rhegium* was on the southern tip of Italy. 28:14 Greek *brothers.* 28:15a Greek *brothers.* 28:15b *The Forum* was about 43 miles (70 kilometers) from Rome.

## HEROES ● ● • • •

28:31 **The book of Acts shows the history of the Christian church and its expansion in ever-widening circles to Jerusalem, Antioch, Ephesus, and Rome—the most influential cities in the western world. Acts also shows the mighty miracles and testimonies of the heroes and martyrs of the early church—Peter, Stephen, James, Paul. All the ministry was prompted and held together by the Holy Spirit working in the lives of ordinary people—merchants, slaves, jailers, church leaders, men, women, Gentiles, Jews. Many unsung heroes of the faith continued the acts of the Holy Spirit, changing the world with a changeless message: Jesus Christ is Savior and Lord for all who call upon him. Today we can take part in the continuing story of the spread of the gospel, bringing that same message to our world so that others may hear and believe.**

Three Taverns.* When Paul saw them, he thanked
God and took courage.
[16]When we arrived in Rome, Paul was permitted to
have his own private lodging, though he was
guarded by a soldier.
[17]Three days after Paul's arrival, he called together
the local Jewish leaders. He said to them, "Brothers,
I was arrested in Jerusalem and handed over to the
Roman government, even though I had done nothing against our people or the customs of our ancestors. [18]The Romans tried me and wanted to release
me, for they found no cause for the death sentence.
[19]But when the Jewish leaders protested the decision,
I felt it necessary to appeal to Caesar, even though I
had no desire to press charges against my own
people. [20]I asked you to come here today so we could
get acquainted and so I could tell you that I am
bound with this chain because I believe that the
hope of Israel—the Messiah—has already come."
[21]They replied, "We have heard nothing against
you. We have had no letters from Judea or reports
from anyone who has arrived here. [22]But we want to
hear what you believe, for the only thing we know
about these Christians* is that they are denounced
everywhere."
[23]So a time was set, and on that day a large number of people came to Paul's house. He told them
about the Kingdom of God and taught them about
Jesus from the Scriptures—from the five books of
Moses and the books of the prophets. He began
lecturing in the morning and went on into the evening. [24]Some believed and some didn't. [25]But after
they had argued back and forth among themselves,
they left with this final word from Paul: "The Holy
Spirit was right when he said to our ancestors
through Isaiah the prophet,

[26]'Go and say to my people,
You will hear my words,
but you will not understand;
you will see what I do,
but you will not perceive its meaning.
[27]For the hearts of these people are hardened,
and their ears cannot hear,
and they have closed their eyes—
so their eyes cannot see,
and their ears cannot hear,
and their hearts cannot understand,
and they cannot turn to me
and let me heal them.'*

[28]So I want you to realize that this salvation from
God is also available to the Gentiles, and they will
accept it."*
[30]For the next two years, Paul lived in his own
rented house.* He welcomed all who visited him,
[31]proclaiming the Kingdom of God with all boldness
and teaching about the Lord Jesus Christ. And no
one tried to stop him.

28:15c *The Three Taverns* was about 35 miles (57 kilometers) from Rome. 28:22 Greek *this sect.* 28:26-27 Isa 6:9-10. 28:28 Some manuscripts add verse 29, *And when he had said these words, the Jews departed, greatly disagreeing with each other.* 28:30 Or *at his own expense.*

# MEGA themes

**CHURCH BEGINNINGS** Acts is the history of how Christianity was founded and organized and solved its problems. The community of believers began by faith in the risen Christ and in the power of the Holy Spirit, who enabled them to witness, love, and serve, and so reach their world for Christ.

New churches are continually being founded. By faith in Jesus Christ and in the power of the Holy Spirit, the church can be a vibrant agent for change. Acts gives important remedies for solving new problems we may face. God wants us to work together to bring his Good News to the world.

1. Read 2:42-47 and 4:32-37. Describe the relationships in these first gatherings.

2. What is similar and what is different about your church and these early gatherings?
3. What do you learn from 6:1-7 about how to deal with conflict in the church? What do you learn about the importance of servants in the church?
4. What can you do to help resolve a conflict or to serve in your church?

**HOLY SPIRIT** The church did not start or grow by its own power or enthusiasm. The disciples were empowered by God's Holy Spirit, the promised Counselor sent by Jesus when he went to heaven.

The Holy Spirit's work demonstrated that Christianity is supernatural. Thus the church became more Holy Spirit–conscious than problem-conscious. By faith, any believer can experience the Holy Spirit's power to do Christ's work.

1. Summarize the various acts God performed through his Holy Spirit in chapters 1–5. What was God's purpose in acting so dramatically?
2. What were the key results of the Holy Spirit's work in the early church?
3. In what ways do you need to rely upon the Holy Spirit?

**CHURCH GROWTH** Acts presents the history of a dynamic, growing community of believers from Jerusalem to Syria, Africa, Asia, and Europe. In the first century, it spread from believing Jews to non-Jews in 39 cities and 30 countries or provinces.

When the Holy Spirit works, there is movement, excitement, and growth. He gives us the motivation and ability to get the gospel to the whole world. You can be an important part of this great world movement. Begin in your neighborhood and school to live for Christ and share the gospel with others.

1. How did the growth of the church in Acts accomplish Jesus' words in 1:8?
2. Look again at 1:8. What would be your Jerusalem? Judea? Samaria?
3. In what specific ways can you be used by God in each of the areas you listed above?

**WITNESSING** Peter, John, Philip, Paul, Barnabas, and thousands more told others about their new faith in Christ. By personal testimony, preaching, or defense before authorities, they shared the story with boldness and courage.

We are God's people, chosen to be part of his plan to reach the world. In love and by faith, we can have the Holy Spirit's help as we share the gospel. Witnessing also strengthens our faith.

1. In what ways did the early witnesses for Jesus share their message?
2. Looking back at your responses under church growth, what are some of the opportunities you have for being a witness for Christ?
3. What are you doing now to be a witness for Christ? What could you do to be more effective?

**OPPOSITION** Through imprisonment, beatings, plots, and riots, Christians were persecuted by both Jews and Gentiles. But the opposition became a catalyst, an energizer for the spread of Christianity. In the face of opposition it became evident that Christianity was not the work of humans, but of God.

God can work through any opposition. When you are treated harshly through ridicule, lies, or physical abuse from hostile unbelievers, realize that it is happening because of your faithful witness. Take every opportunity, even those that opposition brings, for communicating the Good News of Jesus Christ.

1. Describe how the various followers of Jesus responded to opposition and persecution.
2. How do you think these individuals felt when they were being threatened, ridiculed, beaten, even stoned? What motivated them to continue?
3. What potential opposition awaits you in your efforts to be a witness for Christ?
4. What are some possible responses that you might have when faced with this opposition?
5. How might God use the opposition you face to bring glory to himself and further his kingdom?

**I**magine you're out on an evening run when you happen upon your dream car. As you admire its beauty, you notice a key in the ignition . . . and unlocked doors. The car seems to say, "Take me out for a quick spin." You glance around. The street is deserted. ■ "But that would be stealing!" your conscience protests. "No way!" another voice blurts in. "You're not going to *keep* it." For an agonizingly long moment the inner voices battle—then adventure wins out. Your heart pounds as you slide into the driver's seat and the engine hums to life. ■ "This is awesome!" you say, slipping the car into gear. You intend to make one slow trip around the block—but the speedometer goes up to 160 mph, and when will you *ever* get another chance like this? You head for the open road. ■ What happens next is a blur. You remember the exhilaration of 143 mph, then flashing blue lights, cold steel handcuffs, being in court, and the judge's gavel pounding out a guilty verdict. The sentence: $10,000 and six months incarceration. You deserve punishment, but that's a severe penalty! ■ Then the judge does something curious. He removes his robe, whips out his checkbook, and pays your fine! Next he announces he will serve your jail sentence. Then he looks you in the eyes and says, "I love you." ■ This analogy isn't perfect, but it *does* help explain how God deals with sinful humanity. The very penalty he demands (death for sin), he provided (the death of Christ on the cross). If you'd like an even better explanation of God's perfect justice and his intense love for you, read the book of Romans.

## STATS

PURPOSE: To introduce Paul to the Romans and to give a sample of his message before he arrives in Rome

AUTHOR: Paul

TO WHOM WRITTEN: The Christians in Rome and believers everywhere

DATE WRITTEN: About A.D. 57, from Corinth, as Paul was preparing for his visit to Jerusalem

SETTING: Apparently Paul had finished his work in the east, and he planned to visit Rome on his way to Spain after first bringing a collection to Jerusalem for the poor Christians there (15:22-28). The Roman church was mostly Jewish but also contained many Gentiles.

KEY PEOPLE: Paul, Phoebe

KEY PLACE: Rome

# Ultimate Issues

## HOMOSEXUALITY

If you're like most American teenagers, the day you get your driver's license and can take the car out for a drive—alone—is a day you dream (or dreamed) of. Before that, Mom, Dad, or the driving teacher rode "shotgun" to make sure you drove safely. But now, with your license, **you're on your own.** The thrill of freedom and the increased sense of responsibility make you feel more like an adult. No one will tell you when to stop or remind you to use your turn signal. It's up to you. **S**uppose you decide that, contrary to everything you've been told up to now, you want to drive on the left-hand side of the road. (Remember, we're talking about the U.S., not England or Hong Kong.) You will quickly encounter serious opposition to your choice of driving style (like a head-on collision). You can either learn from your observations and experiences, or you can insist that you have the right to drive however you wish, and whatever happens, happens. **W**hen it comes to driving, it's pretty obvious what the wisest choice is. Here in Romans 1, Paul addresses an issue that seems equally clear-cut, and yet men and women have struggled with it since Adam and Eve were ***evicted from Eden.*** The issue is homosexuality. **P**aul argues that all people everywhere are without excuse in knowing that there is a God. Proclaiming that nature itself reveals its Creator, Paul then begins a scathing rebuke against people who deny God and HIS PLAN FOR CREATION. Paul has particularly harsh words for those who engage in the sins of idolatry and homosexuality. These people, he writes, go against God's design for human sexuality, and in so doing will experience drastic consequences for their behavior. Like our fictional teenage driver, men and women who practice homosexuality experience tremendous opposition—socially, emotionally, physically, and spiritually. Yet they ignore all these warning signs. Sooner or later, though, they will **CRASH AND BURN.** **T**wo important messages need to be given on the subject of homosexuality. One is for our society, which has lost any meaningful idea of sin, righteousness, holiness, and truth. That message is that all lifestyles are *not* acceptable. Some lifestyles—such as alcoholism, or materialism . . . or homosexuality—are wrong; they are sinful. Those who engage in such behaviors should come to God in confession and repentance and ask for his forgiveness and healing. **T**he second message is for the church (meaning all Christians). What they need to understand is that while homosexuality is sin, it is not the unforgivable sin. God loves homosexuals just as much as he loves other sinners. Jesus' death on the cross paid for the sin of homosexuality, just as it paid for the sins of lying, greed, lust, hate, and pride. It has been said—and it is true—that the church is a HOSPITAL FOR SINNERS, not a showcase for saints. It is a place where those caught in the sin of homosexuality can come to be freed and forgiven. It is a place where believers who have committed the sins of hatred, prejudice, and self-righteousness toward homosexuals need to go to ask the Lord for forgiveness and healing. **H**omosexuals, like all sinners, stand guilty before God. If that were the whole story, there would be no hope. The great message of Romans—and of the entire Bible—is that there is hope for sinners of all kinds through the life, death, and resurrection of Jesus Christ. He is the one who will set us free, regardless of our sin.

CHAPTER **1** **PAUL WRITES WITH GOOD NEWS.** This letter
is from Paul, Jesus Christ's slave, chosen by God to be
an apostle and sent out to preach his Good News.
2This Good News was promised long ago by God
through his prophets in the holy Scriptures. 3It is the
Good News about his Son, Jesus, who came as a man,
born into King David's royal family line. 4And Jesus
Christ our Lord was shown to be the Son of God when
God powerfully raised him from the dead by means of
the Holy Spirit.* 5Through Christ, God has given us
the privilege and authority to tell Gentiles everywhere
what God has done for them, so that they will believe
and obey him, bringing glory to his name.

6You are among those who have been called to
belong to Jesus Christ, 7dear friends in Rome. God
loves you dearly, and he has called you to be his very
own people.

May grace and peace be yours from God our
Father and the Lord Jesus Christ.

8Let me say first of all that your faith in God is
becoming known throughout the world. How I
thank God through Jesus Christ for each one of you.
9God knows how often I pray for you. Day and night
I bring you and your needs in prayer to God, whom
I serve with all my heart* by telling others the Good
News about his Son.
10One of the things I always pray for is the opportunity, God willing, to come at last to see you. 11For I
long to visit you so I can share a spiritual blessing
with you that will help you grow strong in the Lord.
12I'm eager to encourage you in your faith, but I also
want to be encouraged by yours. In this way, each of
us will be a blessing to the other.

13I want you to know, dear brothers and sisters,*
that I planned many times to visit you, but I was prevented until now. I want to work among you and see
good results, just as I have done among other Gentiles.
14For I have a great sense of obligation to people in our
culture and to people in other cultures,* to the educated and uneducated alike. 15So I am eager to come to
you in Rome, too, to preach God's Good News.

16For I am not ashamed of this Good News about
Christ. It is the power of God at work, saving everyone who believes—Jews first and also Gentiles.

**GOOD NEWS ● ● ● ●**

1:2-17 **Paul was not ashamed because his message was *Good News.* It was powerful, it was for everyone, and it was part of God's revealed plan. When you are tempted to be ashamed, remember what the Good News is all about. If you focus on God and on what he is doing in the world rather than on your own inadequacy, your embarrassment will soon disappear.**

1:4 Or *the Spirit of holiness.* 1:9 Or *in my spirit.* 1:13 Greek *brothers.* 1:14 Greek *to Greeks and to barbarians.*

17 This Good News tells us how God makes us right
in his sight. This is accomplished from start to finish
by faith. As the Scriptures say, "It is through faith that
a righteous person has life."*
18 But God shows his anger from heaven against all
sinful, wicked people who push the truth away from
themselves.* 19 For the truth about God is known to
them instinctively.* God has put this knowledge in
their hearts. 20 From the time the world was created,
people have seen the earth and sky and all that God
made. They can clearly see his invisible qualities—
his eternal power and divine nature. So they have no
excuse whatsoever for not knowing God.
21 Yes, they knew God, but they wouldn't worship
him as God or even give him thanks. And they began
to think up foolish ideas of what God was like. The
result was that their minds became dark and confused. 22 Claiming to be wise, they became utter fools
instead. 23 And instead of worshiping the glorious,
ever-living God, they worshiped idols made to look
like mere people, or birds and animals and snakes.
24 So God let them go ahead and
do whatever shameful things their
hearts desired. As a result, they did
vile and degrading things with
each other's bodies. 25 Instead of
believing what they knew was the
truth about God, they deliberately
chose to believe lies. So they worshiped the things God made but
not the Creator himself, who is to
be praised forever. Amen.
26 That is why God abandoned
them to their shameful desires.
Even the women turned against
the natural way to have sex and
instead indulged in sex with each
other. 27 And the men, instead of
having normal sexual relationships with women, burned with
lust for each other. Men did
shameful things with other men
and, as a result, suffered within
themselves the penalty they so
richly deserved.
28 When they refused to acknowledge God, he abandoned
them to their evil minds and let
them do things that should
never be done. 29 Their lives became
full of every kind of wickedness,
sin, greed, hate, envy, murder,
fighting, deception, malicious
behavior, and gossip. 30 They are
backstabbers, haters of God, insolent, proud, and boastful. They
are forever inventing new ways of
sinning and are disobedient to
their parents. 31 They refuse to understand, break their promises, and are heartless
and unforgiving. 32 They are fully aware of God's
death penalty for those who do these things, yet
they go right ahead and do them anyway. And,
worse yet, they encourage others to do them, too.

### NO EXCUSE ●●●••

1:18-20 **Paul answers a common objection: How could a loving God send anyone to hell, especially someone who has never heard the Good News of Jesus? In fact, says Paul, God has revealed himself to *all* people. Everyone knows what God requires, but no one lives up to it. If people suppress God's truth in order to live their own way, they have no excuse. They know the truth, and they will have to endure the consequences of ignoring it.**

CHAPTER **2** **GOD WILL JUDGE US ALL.** You may be
saying, "What terrible people you have been talking
about!" But you are just as bad, and you have no
excuse! When you say they are wicked and should be
punished, you are condemning yourself, for you do

## "Here's what I did..."

During my freshman and sophomore years in high school, I led something of a double life. At home and at church, I was a "good Christian kid." I read my Bible, helped with Sunday school, and went to youth group. I really wanted to live a committed Christian life, but at school I was embarrassed to make it known that I was a Christian. I guess I was afraid of what people would think of me if they knew. When people said, "Come on, let's party," I'd feel torn. I loved God and knew he didn't approve of their idea of "party," but too often I just couldn't stand up to these people. I'd give in, then feel bad about myself for compromising what I knew was right.

The summer before my junior year, I knew things would have to change. That's when I read Romans 2:6-8. Verse 6 says God will judge all people according to what they have done. I got to thinking about what I've done, and it scared me. I realized how self-seeking I was. I really did want to please God, not hurt him or get him mad at me. I decided right then to make my goal eternal life that God promises "to those who persist in doing what is good, seeking after the glory and honor and immortality that God offers."

So I memorized that verse and decided to let people at school know I'm a Christian. It's made a big difference. For one thing, I met other Christians who were there all the time, but whom I hadn't bothered to get to know before. The last two years have been much better than the first two. I found that taking a stand against certain things didn't really cost me friends. In fact, because I've found other friends who know what friendship is about, I actually have more and better friends than before. But most of all I have a clear conscience; I know I'm trying to do God's will every day, at school as well as at church.

*Lisa*



1:17 Hab 2:4. 1:18 Or *who prevent the truth from being known.* 1:19 Greek *is manifest in them.*

these very same things. 2And we know that God, in
his justice, will punish anyone who does such things.
3Do you think that God will judge and condemn
others for doing them and not judge you when you
do them, too? 4Don't you realize how kind, tolerant,
and patient God is with you? Or don't you care?
Can't you see how kind he has been in giving you
time to turn from your sin?
5But no, you won't listen. So you are storing up
terrible punishment for yourself because of your
stubbornness in refusing to turn from your sin. For
there is going to come a day of judgment when God,
the just judge of all the world, 6will judge all people
according to what they have done. 7He will give
eternal life to those who persist in doing what is
good, seeking after the glory and honor and immortality that God offers. 8But he will pour out his anger
and wrath on those who live for themselves, who
refuse to obey the truth and practice evil deeds.
9There will be trouble and calamity for everyone
who keeps on sinning—for the Jew first and also for
the Gentile. 10But there will be glory and honor and
peace from God for all who do good—for the Jew
first and also for the Gentile. 11For God does not
show favoritism.

## ALTERNATIVES

James and Kristy are watching a popular afternoon talk show. Today's topic is "Should homosexual marriage be legalized?" Most of the guests, as well as members of the studio audience, are gay and lesbian activists who are "tired of being treated like second-class citizens."

Says the most outspoken member of the panel: "Why can't people just accept us as we are? We didn't choose to be homosexual. We were born this way. We don't condemn straight people for acting on their natural desires. Why condemn us for being the way God made us?"

With each statement like this, the talk show host nods approvingly and the audience cheers loudly.

All except the one guy on the panel who is a minister. He is trying patiently (and lovingly) to point out why homosexuality is not acceptable behavior, but the others keep interrupting him and describing him as "backwards," "narrow-minded," and a "religious extremist."

By the end of the show, James and Kristy feel a little bit differently. They aren't ready to accept everything about the homosexual lifestyle, but they do wonder if maybe they haven't been a bit intolerant in their views.

What do you think? Is homosexuality just "an alternative lifestyle"? Is it really OK? See what God says about it in Romans 1:24-28.

12God will punish the Gentiles when they sin,
even though they never had God's written law. And
he will punish the Jews when they sin, for they do
have the law. 13For it is not merely knowing the law
that brings God's approval. Those who obey the law
will be declared right in God's sight. 14Even when
Gentiles, who do not have God's written law, instinctively follow what the law says, they show that
in their hearts they know right from wrong. 15They
demonstrate that God's law is written within them,
for their own consciences either accuse them or tell
them they are doing what is right. 16The day will
surely come when God, by Jesus Christ, will judge
everyone's secret life. This is my message.
17If you are a Jew, you are relying on God's law for
your special relationship with him. You boast that all
is well between yourself and God. 18Yes, you know
what he wants; you know right from wrong because
you have been taught his law. 19You are convinced
that you are a guide for the blind and a beacon light
for people who are lost in darkness without God.
20You think you can instruct the ignorant and teach
children the ways of God. For you are certain that in
God's law you have complete knowledge and truth.
21Well then, if you teach others, why don't you
teach yourself? You tell others not to steal, but do
you steal? 22You say it is wrong to commit adultery,
but do you do it? You condemn idolatry, but do you
steal from pagan temples? 23You are so proud of
knowing the law, but you dishonor God by breaking
it. 24No wonder the Scriptures say, "The world blasphemes the name of God because of you."*
25The Jewish ceremony of circumcision is worth
something only if you obey God's law. But if you
don't obey God's law, you are no better off than an
uncircumcised Gentile. 26And if the Gentiles obey
God's law, won't God give them all the rights and
honors of being his own people? 27In fact, uncircumcised Gentiles who keep God's law will be much
better off than you Jews who are circumcised and
know so much about God's law but don't obey it.
28For you are not a true Jew just because you were
born of Jewish parents or because you have gone
through the Jewish ceremony of circumcision. 29No,
a true Jew is one whose heart is right with God. And
true circumcision is not a cutting of the body but a
change of heart produced by God's Spirit. Whoever
has that kind of change seeks praise from God, not
from people.

CHAPTER **3** **GOD REMAINS FAITHFUL.** Then what's the
advantage of being a Jew? Is there any value in the
Jewish ceremony of circumcision? 2Yes, being a Jew
has many advantages. First of all, the Jews were
entrusted with the whole revelation of God.*
3True, some of them were unfaithful; but just
because they broke their promises, does that mean
God will break his promises? 4Of course not!
Though everyone else in the world is a liar, God
is true. As the Scriptures say, "He will be proved
right in what he says, and he will win his case in
court."*
5"But," some say, "our sins serve a good purpose,
for people will see God's goodness when he declares
us sinners to be innocent. Isn't it unfair, then, for
God to punish us?" (That is actually the way some

2:24 Isa 52:5. 3:2 Greek *the oracles of God.* 3:4 Ps 51:4.

## SALVATION'S FREEWAY

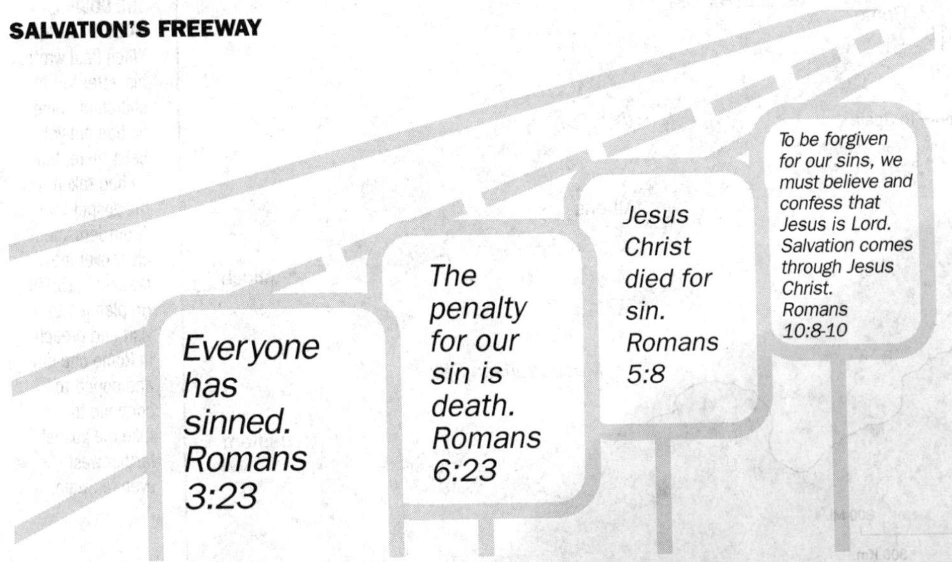


people talk.) [6]Of course not! If God is not just, how is he qualified to judge the world? [7]"But," some might still argue, "how can God judge and condemn me as a sinner if my dishonesty highlights his truthfulness and brings him more glory?" [8]If you follow that kind of thinking, however, you might as well say that the more we sin the better it is! Those who say such things deserve to be condemned, yet some slander me by saying this is what I preach!

Everyone has sinned. Romans 3:23
The penalty for our sin is death. Romans 6:23
Jesus Christ died for sin. Romans 5:8
To be forgiven for our sins, we must believe and confess that Jesus is Lord. Salvation comes through Jesus Christ. Romans 10:8-10

[9]Well then, are we Jews better than others?* No, not at all, for we have already shown that all people, whether Jews or Gentiles, are under the power of sin. [10]As the Scriptures say,

"No one is good—
not even one.
[11] No one has real understanding;
no one is seeking God.
[12] All have turned away from God;
all have gone wrong.
No one does good,
not even one."*
[13] "Their talk is foul, like the stench from an open grave.
Their speech is filled with lies."
"The poison of a deadly snake drips from their lips."*
[14] "Their mouths are full of cursing and bitterness."*
[15] "They are quick to commit murder.
[16] Wherever they go, destruction and misery follow them.
[17] They do not know what true peace is."*
[18] "They have no fear of God to restrain them."*

[19]Obviously, the law applies to those to whom it was given, for its purpose is to keep people from having excuses and to bring the entire world into judgment before God. [20]For no one can ever be made right in God's sight by doing what his law commands. For the more we know God's law, the clearer it becomes that we aren't obeying it.

[21]But now God has shown us a different way of being right in his sight—not by obeying the law but by the way promised in the Scriptures long ago. [22]We are made right in God's sight when we trust in Jesus Christ to take away our sins. And we all can be saved in this same way, no matter who we are or what we have done.

[23]For all have sinned; all fall short of God's glorious standard. [24]Yet now God in his gracious kindness declares us not guilty. He has done this through Christ Jesus, who has freed us by taking away our sins. [25]For God sent Jesus to take the punishment for our sins and to satisfy God's anger against us. We are made right with God when we believe that Jesus shed his blood, sacrificing his life for us. God was being entirely fair

### CUT OFF ● ● • • •

3:23 **Some sins seem bigger than others because their obvious consequences are much more serious. Murder, for example, seems much worse than hatred; adultery seems worse than lust. But this does not mean we can get away with some sins and not with others. All sin makes us sinners, and all sin cuts us off from our holy God. All sin, therefore, leads to death (because it disqualifies us from living with God), regardless of how great or small it seems. Don't minimize "little" sins or overrate "big" sins. All sins separate us from God—but they all can be forgiven.**

3:9 Greek *Are we better?* 3:10-12 Pss 14:1-3; 53:1-3. 3:13 Pss 5:9; 140:3. 3:14 Ps 10:7. 3:15-17 Isa 59:7-8. 3:18 Ps 36:1.

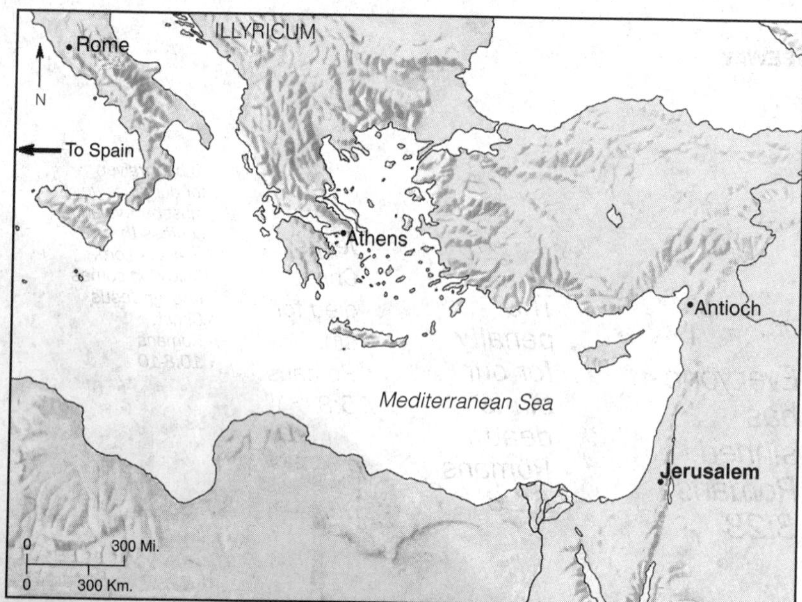


**THE GOSPEL GOES TO ROME**
When Paul wrote his letter to the church in Rome he had not yet been there, but he had taken the gospel "from Jerusalem clear over into Illyricum" (15:19). He planned to visit and preach in Rome one day, and hoped to continue to take the gospel farther west—even to Spain.

and just when he did not punish those who sinned in
former times. [26]And he is entirely fair and just in this
present time when he declares sinners to be right in his
sight because they believe in Jesus.
[27]Can we boast, then, that we have done anything
to be accepted by God? No, because our acquittal is
not based on our good deeds. It is based on our faith.
[28]So we are made right with God through faith and
not by obeying the law.
[29]After all, God is not the God of the Jews only, is
he? Isn't he also the God of the Gentiles? Of course
he is. [30]There is only one God, and there is only one
way of being accepted by him. He makes people
right with himself only by faith, whether they are
Jews or Gentiles. [31]Well then, if we emphasize faith,
does this mean that we can forget about the law? Of
course not! In fact, only when we have faith do we
truly fulfill the law.

## CHAPTER 4 **ABRAHAM BELIEVED GOD.** Abraham was,
humanly speaking, the founder of our Jewish nation.
What were his experiences concerning this question of
being saved by faith? [2]Was it because of his good deeds
that God accepted him? If so, he would have had
something to boast about. But from God's point of
view Abraham had no basis at all for pride. [3]For the
Scriptures tell us, "Abraham believed God, so God
declared him to be righteous."*
[4]When people work, their wages are not a gift.
Workers earn what they receive. [5]But people are declared righteous because of their faith, not because
of their work.
[6]King David spoke of this, describing the happiness of an undeserving sinner who is declared to be
righteous:

[7]"Oh, what joy for those whose disobedience is
forgiven,
whose sins are put out of sight.
[8]Yes, what joy for those
whose sin is no longer counted against them
by the Lord."*

[9]Now then, is this blessing only for the Jews, or is
it for Gentiles, too? Well, what about Abraham? We
have been saying he was declared righteous by God
because of his faith. [10]But how did his faith help
him? Was he declared righteous only after he had
been circumcised, or was it before he was circumcised? The answer is that God accepted him first, and
then he was circumcised later!
[11]The circumcision ceremony was a sign that Abraham already had faith and that God had already
accepted him and declared him to be righteous—
even before he was circumcised. So Abraham is the
spiritual father of those who have faith but have not
been circumcised. They are made right with God by
faith. [12]And Abraham is also the spiritual father of
those who have been circumcised, but only if they

### A GIFT ● ● ● • •
4:4-5 **When some people learn we are saved through faith, they start to worry: "Do I have enough faith?" "Is my faith strong enough to save me?" These people miss the point. It is Jesus Christ who saves us, not *our* feelings or actions. He is strong enough to save us no matter how weak our faith is. Jesus offers us salvation as a gift because he loves us, not because we have earned it through our powerful faith. What, then, is the role of faith? Faith is believing and trusting in Jesus Christ, reaching out to accept his wonderful gift of salvation. Faith is effective whether it is great or small, timid or bold—because God loves us.**

4:3 Gen 15:6. 4:7-8 Ps 32:1-2.

have the same kind of faith Abraham had before he was circumcised.

[13]It is clear, then, that God's promise to give the whole earth to Abraham and his descendants was not based on obedience to God's law, but on the new relationship with God that comes by faith. [14]So if you claim that God's promise is for those who obey God's law and think they are "good enough" in God's sight, then you are saying that faith is useless. And in that case, the promise is also meaningless. [15]But the law brings punishment on those who try to obey it. (The only way to avoid breaking the law is to have no law to break!)

[16]So that's why faith is the key! God's promise is given to us as a free gift. And we are certain to receive it, whether or not we follow Jewish customs, if we have faith like Abraham's. For Abraham is the father of all who believe. [17]That is what the Scriptures mean when God told him, "I have made you the father of many nations."* This happened because Abraham believed in the God who brings the dead back to life and who brings into existence what didn't exist before.

[18]When God promised Abraham that he would become the father of many nations, Abraham believed him. God had also said, "Your descendants will be as numerous as the stars,"* even though such a promise seemed utterly impossible! [19]And Abraham's faith did not weaken, even though he knew that he was too old to be a father at the age of one hundred and that Sarah, his wife, had never been able to have children.

[20]Abraham never wavered in believing God's promise. In fact, his faith grew stronger, and in this he brought glory to God. [21]He was absolutely convinced that God was able to do anything he promised. [22]And because of Abraham's faith, God declared him to be righteous.

[23]Now this wonderful truth—that God declared him to be righteous—wasn't just for Abraham's benefit. [24]It was for us, too, assuring us that God will also declare us to be righteous if we believe in God, who brought Jesus our Lord back from the dead. [25]He was handed over to die because of our sins, and he was raised from the dead to make us right with God.

## CHAPTER 5

**FINDING PEACE AND JOY.** Therefore, since we have been made right in God's sight by faith, we have peace with God because of what Jesus Christ our Lord has done for us. [2]Because of our faith, Christ has brought us into this place of highest privilege where we now stand, and we confidently and joyfully look forward to sharing God's glory.

[3]We can rejoice, too, when we run into problems and trials, for we know that they are good for us—they help us learn to endure. [4]And endurance develops strength of character in us, and character strengthens our confident expectation of salvation. [5]And this expectation will not disappoint us. For we know how dearly God loves us, because he has given us the Holy Spirit to fill our hearts with his love.

### OVERCOME • • • • •

5:2-4 **Paul tells us that in the future we will *become*, but until then we must *overcome*. This means we will experience difficulties that will help us grow. Problems we face will help develop our patience—which in turn will strengthen our character, deepen our trust in God, and give us greater confidence about the future. You probably find your patience tested in some way every day. Thank God for these opportunities to grow and deal with them in his strength (see also James 1:2-4; 1 Peter 1:6-7).**

[6]When we were utterly helpless, Christ came at just the right time and died for us sinners. [7]Now, no one is likely to die for a good person, though someone might be willing to die for a person who is especially good. [8]But God showed his great love

**Since becoming a Christian, it seems like I am always fighting against certain thoughts and habits that I used to never give a second thought about. Why is this happening?**

Picture your life as a door. Before you became a Christian, your sins were like nails being pounded into the door and left there. When you asked Christ to forgive you, all of the nails you had collected were removed! Unfortunately, what was left was a door full of holes, not very pleasant to look at and not very useful.

But God began patching up the holes! More accurately, he began to heal the scars left by sin, making your life into a door that will look unscarred after years of constant pounding. We truly can become a new creation (see 2 Corinthians 5:17).

That is why it is so important for people to come to know Christ's forgiveness early in life. Because we inherited a sinful nature from Adam (Romans 5:12), time and wrong choices can pound some pretty large nails into our life. And those scars may take longer to heal. Paul knew this all too well, as you can see if you read his words in Romans 7:15–8:2. Like him, we all experience the tug to give in again to our sin nature, but our new nature moves us to resist.

So what you are experiencing is a new sensitivity to sin. Since sin wants to "drive a hole" in you and Christ wants to keep you unscarred by the effects of sin, it is no longer comfortable to ignore the constant pounding. Confessing your sin will always remove the nail.

This new sensitivity to sin means two things. First, it is a definite sign that the Spirit of God has truly entered your life (Romans 8:9). It is likely you would still be numb to the nails (sin) if you had rejected Christ's forgiveness. Second, it means that God is reminding you of his great love for you (Romans 8:38-39). Now your conscience advises you where you could stray off course. He does not want you to be left scarred by the consequences of your sin, so he begins at the source of it—your thoughts.

4:17 Gen 17:5. 4:18 Gen 15:5.

**BEFORE ● ● • • •**

5:8 ***While we were still sinners*—these are amazing words. God sent Jesus to die for us not because we were good enough, but because he loved us so much. Whenever you feel uncertain about God's love for you, remember that God loved you even before you turned to him.**

for us by sending Christ to die for us while we were
still sinners. 9And since we have been made right in
God's sight by the blood of Christ, he will certainly
save us from God's judgment. 10For since we were
restored to friendship with God by the death of his
Son while we were still his enemies, we will certainly be delivered from eternal punishment by his
life. 11So now we can rejoice in our wonderful new
relationship with God—all because of what our Lord Jesus Christ has done for us in making us friends of God.

12When Adam sinned, sin entered the entire human race. Adam's sin brought death, so death
spread to everyone, for everyone sinned. 13Yes,
people sinned even before the law was given. And though there was no law to break, since it had not
yet been given, 14they all died anyway—even though they did not disobey an explicit commandment of God, as Adam did. What a contrast between Adam and Christ, who was yet to come!
15And what a difference between our sin and God's generous gift of forgiveness. For this one man, Adam, brought death to many through his sin. But this other man, Jesus Christ, brought forgiveness to
many through God's bountiful gift. 16And the result of God's gracious gift is very different from the result of that one man's sin. For Adam's sin led to condemnation, but we have the free gift of being accepted by God, even though we are guilty of
many sins. 17The sin of this one man, Adam, caused death to rule over us, but all who receive God's wonderful, gracious gift of righteousness will live in triumph over sin and death through this one man, Jesus Christ.

18Yes, Adam's one sin brought condemnation upon everyone, but Christ's one act of righteousness makes all people right in God's sight and gives them
life. 19Because one person disobeyed God, many people became sinners. But because one other person obeyed God, many people will be made right in God's sight.

20God's law was given so that all people could see how sinful they were. But as people sinned more and more, God's wonderful kindness became more
abundant. 21So just as sin ruled over all people and brought them to death, now God's wonderful kindness rules instead, giving us right standing with God and resulting in eternal life through Jesus Christ our Lord.

CHAPTER **6** **CHRIST BROKE SIN'S POWER.** Well then, should we keep on sinning so that God can show us
more and more kindness and forgiveness? 2Of
course not! Since we have died to sin, how can we
continue to live in it? 3Or have you forgotten that
when we became Christians and were baptized to become one with Christ Jesus, we died with him?
4For we died and were buried with Christ by baptism. And just as Christ was raised from the dead by the glorious power of the Father, now we also may live new lives.

5Since we have been united with him in his death,
we will also be raised as he was. 6Our old sinful selves

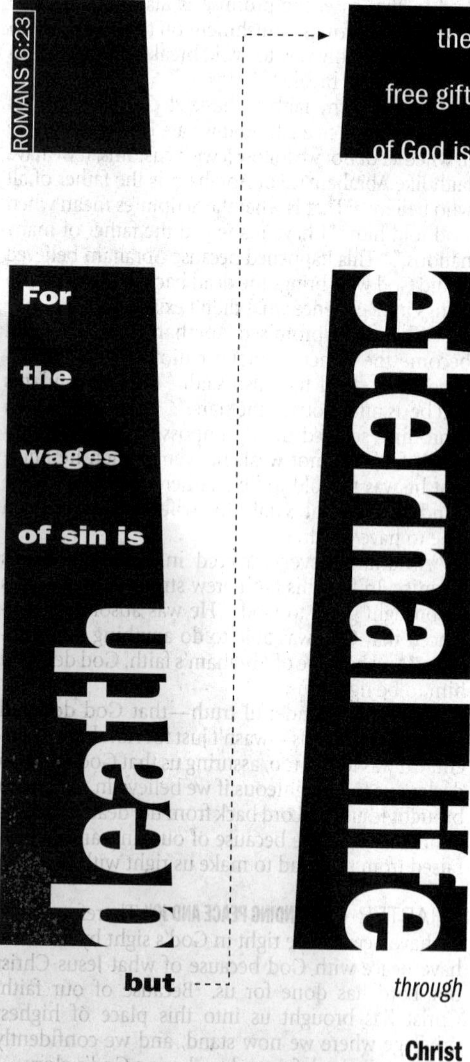
ROMANS 6:23
For the wages of sin is
death
but
the free gift of God is
eternal life
through Christ Jesus our Lord.

were crucified with Christ so that sin might lose its power in our lives. We are no longer slaves to sin. 7For when we died with Christ we were set free from the power of sin. 8And since we died with Christ, we know we will also share his new life. 9We are sure of this because Christ rose from the dead, and he will never die again. Death no longer has any power over him. 10He died once to defeat sin, and now he lives for the glory of God. 11So you should consider yourselves dead to sin and able to live for the glory of God through Christ Jesus.

12Do not let sin control the way you live;* do not give in to its lustful desires. 13Do not let any part of your body become a tool of wickedness, to be used for sinning. Instead, give yourselves completely to God since you have been given new life. And use your whole body as a tool to do what is right for the glory of God. 14Sin is no longer your master, for you are no longer subject to the law, which enslaves you to sin. Instead, you are free by God's grace.

15So since God's grace has set us free from the law, does this mean we can go on sinning? Of course not! 16Don't you realize that whatever you choose to obey becomes your master? You can choose sin, which leads to death, or you can choose to obey God and receive his approval. 17Thank God! Once you were slaves of sin, but now you have obeyed with all your heart the new teaching God has given you. 18Now you are free from sin, your old master, and you have become slaves to your new master, righteousness.

19I speak this way, using the illustration of slaves and masters, because it is easy to understand. Before, you let yourselves be slaves of impurity and lawlessness. Now you must choose to be slaves of righteousness so that you will become holy.

20In those days, when you were slaves of sin, you weren't concerned with doing what was right. 21And what was the result? It was not good, since now you are ashamed of the things you used to do, things that end in eternal doom. 22But now you are free from the power of sin and have become slaves of God. Now you do those things that lead to holiness and result in eternal life. 23For the wages of sin is death, but the free gift of God is eternal life through Christ Jesus our Lord.

CHAPTER **7** **YOU CAN SERVE GOD.** Now, dear brothers and sisters*—you who are familiar with the law—don't you know that the law applies only to a person who is still living? 2Let me illustrate. When a woman marries, the law binds her to her husband as long as he is alive. But if he dies, the laws of marriage no longer apply to her. 3So while her husband is alive, she would be committing adultery if she married another man. But if her husband dies, she is free from that law and does not commit adultery when she remarries.

4So this is the point: The law no longer holds you in its power, because you died to its power when you died with Christ on the cross. And now you are united with the one who was raised from the dead. As a result, you can produce good fruit, that is, good deeds for God. 5When we were controlled by our old nature, sinful desires were at work within us, and the law aroused these evil desires that produced sinful deeds, resulting in death. 6But now we have been released from the law, for we died with Christ, and we are no longer captive to its power. Now we can really serve God, not in the old way by obeying the letter of the law, but in the new way, by the Spirit.

7Well then, am I suggesting that the law of God is evil? Of course not! The law is not sinful, but it was the law that showed me my sin. I would never have known that coveting is wrong if the law had not said, "Do not covet."* 8But sin took advantage of this law and aroused all kinds of forbidden desires within me! If there were no law, sin would not have that power.

9I felt fine when I did not understand what the law demanded. But when I learned the truth, I realized I had broken the law and was a sinner, doomed to die. 10So the good law, which was supposed to show me the way of life, instead gave me the death penalty. 11Sin took advantage of the law and fooled me; it took the good law and used it to make me guilty of death. 12But still, the law itself is holy and right and good.

13But how can that be? Did the law, which is good, cause my doom? Of course not! Sin used what was good to bring about my condemnation. So we can see how terrible sin really is. It uses God's good commandment for its own evil purposes.

14The law is good, then. The trouble is not with the law but with me, because I am sold into slavery, with sin as my master. 15I don't understand myself at all, for I really want to do what is right, but I don't

### SHARKS

**7:9-11 If people feel fine without the law, why did God give it? Because sin is real and dangerous. Imagine a sunny day at the beach. You have just plunged into the surf and you've never felt better. Suddenly you notice a sign on the pier: "No swimming: Sharks in water." Your day is ruined. Is it the sign's fault? Are you angry with the people who put it up? Of course not. The law is like the sign. It is essential, and we are grateful for it–but it doesn't get rid of the sharks.**

### STRUGGLE

**7:15 This is more than the cry of one desperate man–it describes the experience of any Christian struggling against sin. We must never underestimate the power of sin. Satan is a crafty tempter, and we have a great ability to make excuses. Instead of trying to overcome sin with human willpower, we must take hold of the tremendous power of Christ that is available to us. This is God's provision for victory over sin; he sends the Holy Spirit to live in us and give us power. And when we fall, he lovingly reaches out to us and helps us get up again.**

6:12 Or *Do not let sin reign in your body, which is subject to death.* 7:1 Greek *brothers.* 7:7 Exod 20:17; Deut 5:21.

do it. Instead, I do the very thing I hate. 16I know perfectly well that what I am doing is wrong, and my bad conscience shows that I agree that the law is good. 17But I can't help myself, because it is sin inside me that makes me do these evil things.

18I know I am rotten through and through so far as my old sinful nature is concerned. No matter which way I turn, I can't make myself do right. I want to, but I can't. 19When I want to do good, I don't. And when I try not to do wrong, I do it anyway. 20But if I am doing what I don't want to do, I am not really the one doing it; the sin within me is doing it.

21It seems to be a fact of life that when I want to do what is right, I inevitably do what is wrong. 22I love God's law with all my heart. 23But there is another law at work within me that is at war with my mind. This law wins the fight and makes me a slave to the sin that is still within me. 24Oh, what a miserable person I am! Who will free me from this life that is dominated by sin?* 25Thank God! The answer is in Jesus Christ our Lord. So you see how it is: In my mind I really want to obey God's law, but because of my sinful nature I am a slave to sin.

CHAPTER **8** **THE HOLY SPIRIT FREES US FROM SIN.** So now there is no condemnation for those who belong to Christ Jesus. 2For the power* of the life-giving Spirit has freed you* through Christ Jesus from the power of sin that leads to death. 3The law of Moses could not save us, because of our sinful nature. But God put into effect a different plan to save us. He sent his own Son in a human body like ours, except that ours are sinful. God destroyed sin's control over us by giving his Son as a sacrifice for our sins. 4He did this so that the requirement of the law would be fully accomplished for us* who no longer follow our sinful nature but instead follow the Spirit.

5Those who are dominated by the sinful nature think about sinful things, but those who are controlled by the Holy Spirit think about things that please the Spirit. 6If your sinful nature controls your mind, there is death. But if the Holy Spirit controls your mind, there is life and peace. 7For the sinful nature is always hostile to God. It never did obey God's laws, and it never will. 8That's why those who are still under the control of their sinful nature can never please God.

9But you are not controlled by your sinful nature. You are controlled by the Spirit if you have the Spirit of God living in you. (And remember that those who do not have the Spirit of Christ living in them are not Christians at all.) 10Since Christ lives within you, even though your body will die because of sin, your spirit is alive* because you have been made right with God. 11The Spirit of God, who raised Jesus from the dead, lives in you. And just as he raised Christ from the dead, he will give life to your mortal body by this same Spirit living within you.

12So, dear brothers and sisters,* you have no obligation whatsoever to do what your sinful nature urges you to do. 13For if you keep on following it, you will perish. But if through the power of the Holy Spirit you turn from it* and its evil deeds, you will live. 14For all who are led by the Spirit of God are children* of God.

15So you should not be like cowering, fearful slaves. You should behave instead like God's very own children, adopted into his family*—calling him "Father, dear Father."* 16For his Holy Spirit speaks to us deep in our hearts and tells us that we are God's children. 17And since we are his children, we will share his treasures—for everything God gives to his Son, Christ, is ours, too. But if we are to share his glory, we must also share his suffering.

18Yet what we suffer now is nothing compared to the glory he will give us later. 19For all creation is waiting eagerly for that future day when God will reveal who his children really are. 20Against its will, everything on earth was subjected to God's curse. 21All creation anticipates the day when it will join God's children in glorious freedom from death and decay. 22For we know that all creation has been groaning as in the pains of childbirth right up to the present time. 23And even we Christians, although we have the Holy Spirit within us as a foretaste of future glory, also groan to be released from pain and suffering. We, too, wait anxiously for that day when God will give us our full rights as his children,* including the new bodies he has promised us. 24Now that we are saved, we eagerly look forward to this freedom. For if you already have something, you don't need to hope for it. 25But if we look forward to something we don't have yet, we must wait patiently and confidently.

26And the Holy Spirit helps us in our distress. For we don't even know what we should pray for, nor how we should pray. But the Holy Spirit prays for us with groanings that cannot be expressed in words. 27And the Father who knows all hearts knows what the Spirit is saying, for the Spirit pleads for us believers in harmony with God's own will. 28And we know that God causes everything to work together* for the

**LONG-RANGE ● ● • • •**

8:28 **God works out all things—not just isolated incidents—for our good. This does not mean that all that happens to us is good. Evil is prevalent in our fallen world, but God is able to turn it around for our long-range good. Note that God is not working to make us happy, but to fulfill his purpose. Note also that this promise is not for everybody. It can be claimed only by those who love God and are fitting into his plans. Such people have a new perspective, a new mind-set. They trust in God, not life's treasures; they look to their security in heaven, not on earth; they learn to accept pain and persecution rather than resent it, because it brings them closer to God.**

7:24 Greek *from this body of death?* 8:2a Greek *the law;* also in 8:2b. 8:2b Some manuscripts read *me.* 8:4 Or *accomplished by us.* 8:10 Or *the Spirit will bring you eternal life.* 8:12 Greek *brothers;* also in 8:29. 8:13 Greek *put it to death.* 8:14 Greek *sons;* also in 8:19. 8:15a Greek *You received a spirit of sonship.* 8:15b Greek *"Abba, Father." Abba* is an Aramaic term for "father." 8:23 Greek *wait anxiously for sonship.* 8:28 Some manuscripts read *And we know that everything works together.*

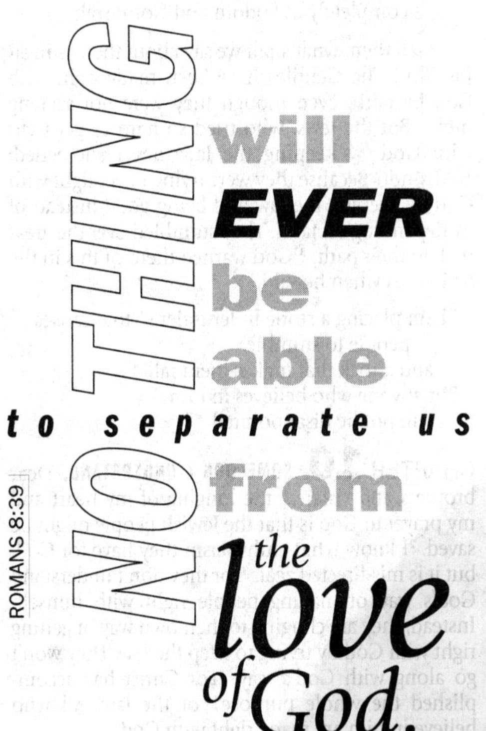
NOTHING
will
EVER
be
able
to separate us
from
the
love
of God.
ROMANS 8:39

good of those who love God and are called according to his purpose for them. 29For God knew his people in advance, and he chose them to become like his Son, so that his Son would be the firstborn, with many brothers and sisters. 30And having chosen them, he called them to come to him. And he gave them right standing with himself, and he promised them his glory.

31What can we say about such wonderful things as these? If God is for us, who can ever be against us? 32Since God did not spare even his own Son but gave him up for us all, won't God, who gave us Christ, also give us everything else?

33Who dares accuse us whom God has chosen for his own? Will God? No! He is the one who has given us right standing with himself. 34Who then will condemn us? Will Christ Jesus? No, for he is the one who died for us and was raised to life for us and is sitting at the place of highest honor next to God, pleading for us.

35Can anything ever separate us from Christ's love? Does it mean he no longer loves us if we have trouble or calamity, or are persecuted, or are hungry or cold or in danger or threatened with death? 36(Even the Scriptures say, "For your sake we are killed every day; we are being slaughtered like sheep."*) 37No, despite all these things, overwhelming victory is ours through Christ, who loved us.

38And I am convinced that nothing can ever separate us from his love. Death can't, and life can't. The angels can't, and the demons can't. Our fears for today, our worries about tomorrow, and even the powers of hell can't keep God's love away. 39Whether we are high above the sky or in the deepest ocean, nothing in all creation will ever be able to separate us from the love of God that is revealed in Christ Jesus our Lord.

CHAPTER **9** **GOD IS SOVEREIGN.** In the presence of Christ, I speak with utter truthfulness—I do not lie—and my conscience and the Holy Spirit confirm that what I am saying is true. 2My heart is filled with bitter sorrow and unending grief 3for my people, my Jewish brothers and sisters.* I would be willing to be forever cursed—cut off from Christ!—if that would save them. 4They are the people of Israel, chosen to be God's special children.* God revealed his glory to them. He made covenants with them and gave his law to them. They have the privilege of worshiping him and receiving his wonderful promises. 5Their ancestors were great people of God, and Christ himself was a Jew as far as his human nature is concerned. And he is God, who rules over everything and is worthy of eternal praise! Amen.*

6Well then, has God failed to fulfill his promise to the Jews? No, for not everyone born into a Jewish family is truly a Jew! 7Just the fact that they are descendants of Abraham doesn't make them truly Abraham's children. For the Scriptures say, "Isaac is the son through whom your descendants will be counted,"* though Abraham had other children, too. 8This means that Abraham's physical descendants are not necessarily children of God. It is the children of the promise who are considered to be Abraham's children. 9For God had promised, "Next year I will return, and Sarah will have a son."*

10This son was our ancestor Isaac. When he grew up, he married Rebekah, who gave birth to twins. 11But before they were born, before they had done anything good or bad, she received a message from God. (This message proves that God chooses according to his own plan, 12not according to our good or bad works.) She was told, "The descendants of your older son will serve the descendants of your younger son."* 13In the words of the Scriptures, "I loved Jacob, but I rejected Esau."*

14What can we say? Was God being unfair? Of course not! 15For God said to Moses,

"I will show mercy to anyone I choose,
and I will show compassion to anyone I
choose."*

16So receiving God's promise is not up to us. We can't get it by choosing it or working hard for it. God will show mercy to anyone he chooses.

8:36 Ps 44:22. 9:3 Greek *my brothers.* 9:4 Greek *chosen for sonship.* 9:5 Or *May God, who rules over everything, be praised forever. Amen.* 9:7 Gen 21:12. 9:9 Gen 18:10, 14. 9:12 Gen 25:23. 9:13 Mal 1:2-3. 9:15 Exod 33:19.

## FOREVER TRYING ● ● • • •

9:31-33 **Sometimes we are like these people, trying to get right with God by keeping his laws. We may think church attendance, church work, giving offerings, and being nice will be enough. After all, we've played by the rules, haven't we? But Paul's words sting—this approach never succeeds. Paul explains that God's plan is not for those who try to earn his favor by being good; it is for those who realize they can never be good enough and so must depend on Christ. Only by putting our faith in what Jesus Christ has done will we be saved. If we do that, we will never be "put to shame" or be disappointed.**

17For the Scriptures say that God told Pharaoh, "I have appointed you for the very purpose of displaying my power in you, and so that my fame might spread throughout the earth."* 18So you see, God shows mercy to some just because he wants to, and he chooses to make some people refuse to listen.

19Well then, you might say, "Why does God blame people for not listening? Haven't they simply done what he made them do?"

20No, don't say that. Who are you, a mere human being, to criticize God? Should the thing that was created say to the one who made it, "Why have you made me like this?" 21When a potter makes jars out of clay, doesn't he have a right to use the same lump of clay to make one jar for decoration and another to throw garbage into? 22God has every right to exercise his judgment and his power, but he also has the right to be very patient with those who are the objects of his judgment and are fit only for destruction. 23He also has the right to pour out the riches of his glory upon those he prepared to be the objects of his mercy—24even upon us, whom he selected, both from the Jews and from the Gentiles.

25Concerning the Gentiles, God says in the prophecy of Hosea,

"Those who were not my people,
I will now call my people.
And I will love those
whom I did not love before."*

26And,

"Once they were told,
'You are not my people.'
But now he will say,
'You are children of the living God.'*"

27Concerning Israel, Isaiah the prophet cried out,

"Though the people of Israel are as numerous as
the sand on the seashore,
only a small number will be saved.
28For the Lord will carry out his sentence upon the
earth
quickly and with finality."*

29And Isaiah said in another place,

"If the Lord Almighty
had not spared a few of us,
we would have been wiped out
as completely as Sodom and Gomorrah."*

30Well then, what shall we say about these things? Just this: The Gentiles have been made right with God by faith, even though they were not seeking him. 31But the Jews, who tried so hard to get right with God by keeping the law, never succeeded. 32Why not? Because they were trying to get right with God by keeping the law and being good instead of by depending on faith. They stumbled over the great rock in their path. 33God warned them of this in the Scriptures when he said,

"I am placing a stone in Jerusalem* that causes
people to stumble,
and a rock that makes them fall.*
But anyone who believes in him
will not be disappointed.*"

CHAPTER **10** **SOME DON'T UNDERSTAND.** Dear brothers and sisters,* the longing of my heart and my prayer to God is that the Jewish people might be saved. 2I know what enthusiasm they have for God, but it is misdirected zeal. 3For they don't understand God's way of making people right with himself. Instead, they are clinging to their own way of getting right with God by trying to keep the law. They won't go along with God's way. 4For Christ has accomplished the whole purpose* of the law. All who believe in him are made right with God.

5For Moses wrote that the law's way of making a person right with God requires obedience to all of its commands.* 6But the way of getting right with God through faith says, "You don't need to go to heaven" (to find Christ and bring him down to help you). 7And it says, "You don't need to go to the place of the dead" (to bring Christ back to life again). 8Salvation that comes from trusting Christ—which is the message we preach—is already within easy reach. In fact, the Scriptures say, "The message is close at hand; it is on your lips and in your heart."*

9For if you confess with your mouth that Jesus is Lord and believe in your heart that God raised him from the dead, you will be saved. 10For it is by believing in your heart that you are made right with God, and it is by confessing with your mouth that you are saved. 11As the Scriptures tell us, "Anyone who believes in him will not be disappointed.*" 12Jew and Gentile are the same in this respect. They all have the same Lord, who gener-

## SO CLOSE ● ● • • •

10:8-12 **Have you ever been asked, "How do I become a Christian?" These verses give you the beautiful answer—salvation is as close as your own heart and mouth. People think it must be a complicated process, but it isn't. If they believe in their hearts and say with their mouths that Christ is the risen Lord, they will be saved.**

9:17 Exod 9:16. 9:25 Hos 2:23. 9:26 Greek *You are sons of the living God.* Hos 1:10. 9:27-28 Isa 10:22-23. 9:29 Isa 1:9. 9:33a Greek *in Zion.* 9:33b Isa 8:14. 9:33c Or *will not be put to shame.* Isa 28:16. 10:1 Greek *Brothers.* 10:4 Or *the end.* 10:5 Lev 18:5. 10:6-8 Deut 30:12-14. 10:11 Or *will not be put to shame.* Isa 28:16.

ously gives his riches to all who ask for them. 13For
"Anyone who calls on the name of the Lord will be
saved."*
14But how can they call on him to save them
unless they believe in him? And how can they believe in him if they have never heard about him? And
how can they hear about him unless someone tells
them? 15And how will anyone go and tell them without being sent? That is what the Scriptures mean
when they say, "How beautiful are the feet of those
who bring good news!"*
16But not everyone welcomes the Good News, for
Isaiah the prophet said, "Lord, who has believed our
message?"* 17Yet faith comes from listening to this
message of good news—the Good News about
Christ.
18But what about the Jews? Have they actually
heard the message? Yes, they have:

"The message of God's creation has gone out
to everyone,
and its words to all the world."*

19But did the people of Israel really understand? Yes,
they did, for even in the time of Moses, God had
said,

"I will rouse your jealousy by blessing other
nations.
I will make you angry by blessing the foolish
Gentiles."*

20And later Isaiah spoke boldly for God:

"I was found by people
who were not looking for me.
I showed myself to those
who were not asking for me."*

21But regarding Israel, God said,

"All day long I opened my arms to them,
but they kept disobeying me and arguing
with me."*

## CHAPTER 11

**GOD'S MERCY ON ISRAEL.** I ask, then,
has God rejected his people, the Jews? Of course not!
Remember that I myself am a Jew, a descendant of
Abraham and a member of the tribe of Benjamin.
2No, God has not rejected his own people, whom
he chose from the very beginning. Do you remember
what the Scriptures say about this? Elijah the
prophet complained to God about the people of
Israel and said, 3"Lord, they have killed your prophets and torn down your altars. I alone am left, and
now they are trying to kill me, too."*
4And do you remember God's reply? He said,
"You are not the only one left. I have seven thousand
others who have never bowed down to Baal!"*
5It is the same today, for not all the Jews have
turned away from God. A few* are being saved as a
result of God's kindness in choosing them. 6And if
they are saved by God's kindness, then it is not by
their good works. For in that case, God's wonderful
kindness would not be what it really is—free and
undeserved.
7So this is the situation: Most of the Jews have not
found the favor of God they are looking for so
earnestly. A few have—the ones God has chosen—
but the rest were made unresponsive. 8As the
Scriptures say,

"God has put them into a deep sleep.
To this very day he has shut their eyes so they do
not see,
and closed their ears so they do not hear."*

9David spoke of this same thing when he said,

"Let their bountiful table become a snare,
a trap that makes them think all is well.
Let their blessings cause them to stumble.
10Let their eyes go blind so they cannot see,
and let their backs grow weaker and weaker."*

11Did God's people stumble and fall beyond recovery? Of course not! His purpose was to make his
salvation available to the Gentiles, and then the Jews
would be jealous and want it for themselves. 12Now
if the Gentiles were enriched because the Jews turned
down God's offer of salvation, think how much
greater a blessing the world will share when the Jews
finally accept it.

**FREE ● ● ● • •**

**11:6 This great truth can be hard to grasp. Do you think it's easier for God to love you when you're good? Do you secretly suspect God chose you because you deserved to be chosen? Do you think some people's behavior is so bad that God couldn't possibly save them? If you ever think this way, you don't entirely understand the Good News that salvation is a free gift. It cannot be earned, in whole or in part; it can only be accepted with thankfulness and praise.**

13I am saying all of this especially for you Gentiles. God has appointed me as the apostle to the
Gentiles. I lay great stress on this, 14for I want to
find a way to make the Jews want what you Gentiles have, and in that way I might save some of
them. 15For since the Jews' rejection meant that
God offered salvation to the rest of the world, how
much more wonderful their acceptance will be. It
will be life for those who were dead! 16And since
Abraham and the other patriarchs were holy, their
children will also be holy.* For if the roots of the
tree are holy, the branches will be, too.
17But some of these branches from Abraham's
tree, some of the Jews, have been broken off. And
you Gentiles, who were branches from a wild olive
tree, were grafted in. So now you also receive the
blessing God has promised Abraham and his children, sharing in God's rich nourishment of his special olive tree. 18But you must be careful not to brag

10:13 Joel 2:32. 10:15 Isa 52:7. 10:16 Isa 53:1. 10:18 Ps 19:4. 10:19 Deut 32:21. 10:20 Isa 65:1. 10:21 Isa 65:2. 11:3 1 Kgs 19:10, 14. 11:4 1 Kgs 19:18. 11:5 Greek *A remnant.* 11:8 Deut 29:4; Isa 29:10. 11:9-10 Ps 69:22-23. 11:16 Greek *If the dough offered as firstfruits is holy, so is the whole lump.*

about being grafted in to replace the branches that were broken off. Remember, you are just a branch, not the root.

19“Well,” you may say, “those branches were broken off to make room for me.” 20Yes, but remember—those branches, the Jews, were broken off because they didn't believe God, and you are there because you do believe. Don't think highly of yourself, but fear what could happen. 21For if God did not spare the branches he put there in the first place, he won't spare you either.

22Notice how God is both kind and severe. He is severe to those who disobeyed, but kind to you as you continue to trust in his kindness. But if you stop trusting, you also will be cut off. 23And if the Jews turn from their unbelief, God will graft them back into the tree again. He has the power to do it.

## AUTHORITY

“What a stupid law!” Chris complains. “How can they–”

“I know,” Eric interrupts. “Can you believe it? An 11 o'clock curfew!”

“And,” chimes in Julie, “all because some redneck bozos from across town crashed a party and trashed a house. It's not fair!”

“Well,” Chris concludes, “I don't know about you guys, but I am not gonna let a bunch of 80-year-olds at city hall tell me what to do.”

“Huh?”

“I mean, I'm gonna pretend like the dumb curfew doesn't exist. I'll be 18 in less than two months anyway.”

“What about your parents?”

“Aw, they're cool. They know I'm not gonna go out and make a big scene. The secret is to keep on doing what we're doing; we just have to be quiet about it. If we're good, the cops will never even know.”

Julie is nodding her head. “I can understand the law for those people who really get out of hand. But we're not like that.”

“Right,” Eric agrees. “What's wrong with some Christian friends having a low-key party on the weekend, watching a few videos?”

“Nothing!” Chris yells.

“Then, we're all agreed?” Julie asks.

“Yep,” Eric responds. “We basically ignore the curfew.”

Everyone smiles.

For an eye-opening look at how we should respond to our civil authorities, read Romans 13:1-7.

24For if God was willing to take you who were, by nature, branches from a wild olive tree and graft you into his own good tree—a very unusual thing to do—he will be far more eager to graft the Jews back into the tree where they belong.

25I want you to understand this mystery, dear brothers and sisters,* so that you will not feel proud and start bragging. Some of the Jews have hard hearts, but this will last only until the complete number of Gentiles comes to Christ. 26And so all Israel will be saved. Do you remember what the prophets said about this?

“A Deliverer will come from Jerusalem,*
and he will turn Israel* from all ungodliness.
27And then I will keep my covenant with them
and take away their sins.”*

28Many of the Jews are now enemies of the Good News. But this has been to your benefit, for God has given his gifts to you Gentiles. Yet the Jews are still his chosen people because of his promises to Abraham, Isaac, and Jacob. 29For God's gifts and his call can never be withdrawn. 30Once, you Gentiles were rebels against God, but when the Jews refused his mercy, God was merciful to you instead. 31And now, in the same way, the Jews are the rebels, and God's mercy has come to you. But someday they,* too, will share in God's mercy. 32For God has imprisoned all people in their own disobedience so he could have mercy on everyone.

33Oh, what a wonderful God we have! How great are his riches and wisdom and knowledge! How impossible it is for us to understand his decisions and his methods! 34For who can know what the Lord is thinking? Who knows enough to be his counselor?* 35And who could ever give him so much that he would have to pay it back? 36For everything comes from him; everything exists by his power and is intended for his glory. To him be glory evermore. Amen.

CHAPTER **12** **GIVE YOUR LIFE TO GOD.** And so, dear brothers and sisters,* I plead with you to give your bodies to God. Let them be a living and holy sacrifice—the kind he will accept. When you think of what he has done for you, is this too much to ask? 2Don't copy the behavior and customs of this world, but let God transform you into a new person by changing the way you think. Then you will know what God wants you to do, and you will know how good and pleasing and perfect his will really is.

3As God's messenger, I give each of you this warning: Be honest in your estimate of yourselves, measuring your value by how much faith God has given

## BRAND-NEW ● ● • • •

**12:2 “The behavior and customs of this world” are usually selfish and often corrupting, and many Christians wisely decide that much worldly behavior is off-limits for them. Our refusal to conform to the world, however, must go even deeper than the level of behavior and customs–it must be firmly founded in our mind. This verse is also translated, “Do not be conformed to this world, but be transformed by the renewing of your mind.” It is possible to avoid most worldly customs and still be proud, covetous, selfish, stubborn, and arrogant. Only when our mind is renewed by the new attitude Christ gives us are we truly transformed. If our character is like Christ's, we can be sure our behavior will honor God.**

11:25 Greek *brothers.* 11:26a Greek *from Zion.* 11:26b Greek *Jacob.* 11:26-27 Isa 59:20-21. 11:31 Some manuscripts read *But now they;* other manuscripts read *But they.* 11:34 See Isa 40:13. 12:1 Greek *brothers.*

you. 4Just as our bodies have many parts and each part has a special function, 5so it is with Christ's body. We are all parts of his one body, and each of us has different work to do. And since we are all one body in Christ, we belong to each other, and each of us needs all the others.

6God has given each of us the ability to do certain things well. So if God has given you the ability to prophesy, speak out when you have faith that God is speaking through you. 7If your gift is that of serving others, serve them well. If you are a teacher, do a good job of teaching. 8If your gift is to encourage others, do it! If you have money, share it generously. If God has given you leadership ability, take the responsibility seriously. And if you have a gift for showing kindness to others, do it gladly.

9Don't just pretend that you love others. Really love them. Hate what is wrong. Stand on the side of the good. 10Love each other with genuine affection,* and take delight in honoring each other. 11Never be lazy in your work, but serve the Lord enthusiastically.

12Be glad for all God is planning for you. Be patient in trouble, and always be prayerful. 13When God's children are in need, be the one to help them out. And get into the habit of inviting guests home for dinner or, if they need lodging, for the night.

14If people persecute you because you are a Christian, don't curse them; pray that God will bless them. 15When others are happy, be happy with them. If they are sad, share their sorrow. 16Live in harmony with each other. Don't try to act important, but enjoy the company of ordinary people. And don't think you know it all!

17Never pay back evil for evil to anyone. Do things in such a way that everyone can see you are honorable. 18Do your part to live in peace with everyone, as much as possible.

19Dear friends, never avenge yourselves. Leave that to God. For it is written,

"I will take vengeance;
I will repay those who
deserve it,"*
says the Lord.

20Instead, do what the Scriptures say:

"If your enemies are hungry,
feed them.
If they are thirsty, give them
something to drink,
and they will be ashamed
of what they have done
to you."*

21Don't let evil get the best of you, but conquer evil by doing good.

**GIFTS ● ● ● ● •**

12:4-8 **God gives us gifts so we can build up his church. To use them effectively, we must (1) realize that all gifts and abilities come from God; (2) understand that not everyone has the same gifts; (3) know who we are and what we do best; (4) dedicate our gifts to God's service and not to our personal success; (5) be willing to spend our gifts generously, not holding back anything from God's service.**

## CHAPTER 13 OBEY THE GOVERNMENT.

Obey the government, for God is the one who put it there. All governments have been placed in power by God. 2So those who refuse to obey the laws of the land are refusing to obey God, and punishment will follow. 3For the authorities do not frighten people who are doing right, but they frighten those who do wrong. So do what they say, and you will get along well. 4The authorities are sent by God to help you. But if you are doing something wrong, of course you should be afraid, for you will be punished. The authorities are established by God for that very purpose, to punish those who do wrong. 5So you must obey the government for two reasons: to keep from being punished and to keep a clear conscience.

6Pay your taxes, too, for these same reasons. For government workers need to be paid so they can keep on doing the work God intended them to do. 7Give to everyone what you owe them: Pay your taxes and import duties, and give respect and honor to all to whom it is due.

## "Here's what I did..."

My boyfriend and I didn't have a very good relationship; we couldn't communicate much. I decided that it was time to break up. I tried to be as tactful as I could; I didn't want to hurt his feelings. His reaction was to call me a couple of names that were hurtful, demeaning, and completely untrue. Not only did he say these things to me, he said them to other people.

That enraged me. I thought of different ways to respond, to get even. But then I recalled a verse that tells us not to take revenge. I looked up Romans 12:19; it says, "Dear friends, never avenge yourselves. Leave that to God. For it is written, 'I will take vengeance; I will repay those who deserve it,' says the Lord." This helped me to remove any thoughts of revenge from my mind and to concentrate instead on forgiving him and praying for him. As I do this, concern for his spiritual life overshadows my feelings of anger and hurt.

*Lavonne*

AGE 16

12:10 Greek *with brotherly love.* 12:19 Deut 32:35. 12:20 Greek *and you will heap burning coals on their heads.* Prov 25:21-22.

## IN DEBT ● ● • • •

13:8 **Why is love for others called a debt? We are permanently in debt to Christ for the lavish love he has poured out on us. The only way we can even begin to repay this debt is by loving others in turn. Because Christ's love will always be infinitely greater than ours, we will always have the obligation to love our neighbors.**

[8]Pay all your debts, except the debt of love for others. You can never finish paying that! If you love your neighbor, you will fulfill all the requirements of God's law. [9]For the commandments against adultery and murder and stealing and coveting—and any other commandment—are all summed up in this one commandment: "Love your neighbor as yourself."* [10]Love does no wrong to anyone, so love satisfies all of God's requirements.

[11]Another reason for right living is that you know how late it is; time is running out. Wake up, for the coming of our salvation is nearer now than when we first believed. [12]The night is almost gone; the day of salvation will soon be here. So don't live in darkness. Get rid of your evil deeds. Shed them like dirty clothes. Clothe yourselves with the armor of right living, as those who live in the light. [13]We should be decent and true in everything we do, so that everyone can approve of our behavior. Don't participate in wild parties and getting drunk, or in adultery and immoral living, or in fighting and jealousy. [14]But let the Lord Jesus Christ take control of you, and don't think of ways to indulge your evil desires.

## SELF-INVENTORY ● ● • • •

14:1 **Who is weak in faith and who is strong? We are all weak in some areas and strong in others. Our faith is strong in an area if we can survive contact with sin without falling into it. It is weak if we must avoid certain activities or places in order to protect our spiritual life. We need to take a self-inventory to find our weaknesses and strengths.**

**In areas of strength, we should not fear that we will be defiled by the world. Rather, from our position of strength we should lead the world. In areas of weakness, however, we need to play it safe. If we have a strong faith but shelter it, we are not doing Christ's work in the world. If we have a weak faith but expose it, we are being extremely foolish.**

CHAPTER **14** **DON'T CRITICIZE OTHER CHRISTIANS.** Accept Christians who are weak in faith, and don't argue with them about what they think is right or wrong. [2]For instance, one person believes it is all right to eat anything. But another believer who has a sensitive conscience will eat only vegetables. [3]Those who think it is all right to eat anything must not look down on those who won't. And those who won't eat certain foods must not condemn those who do, for God has accepted them. [4]Who are you to condemn God's servants? They are responsible to the Lord, so let him tell them whether they are right or wrong. The Lord's power will help them do as they should.

[5]In the same way, some think one day is more holy than another day, while others think every day is alike. Each person should have a personal conviction about this matter. [6]Those who have a special day for worshiping the Lord are trying to honor him. Those who eat all kinds of food do so to honor the Lord, since they give thanks to God before eating. And those who won't eat everything also want to please the Lord and give thanks to God. [7]For we are not our own masters when we live or when we die. [8]While we live, we live to please the Lord. And when we die, we go to be with the Lord. So in life and in death, we belong to the Lord. [9]Christ died and rose again for this very purpose, so that he might be Lord of those who are alive and of those who have died.

[10]So why do you condemn another Christian*? Why do you look down on another Christian? Remember, each of us will stand personally before the judgment seat of God. [11]For the Scriptures say,

"'As surely as I live,' says the Lord,  
'every knee will bow to me  
and every tongue will confess allegiance  
to God.'"*

[12]Yes, each of us will have to give a personal account to God. [13]So don't condemn each other anymore. Decide instead to live in such a way that you will not put an obstacle in another Christian's path.

[14]I know and am perfectly sure on the authority of the Lord Jesus that no food, in and of itself, is wrong to eat. But if someone believes it is wrong, then for that person it is wrong. [15]And if another Christian is distressed by what you eat, you are not acting in love if you eat it. Don't let your eating ruin someone for whom Christ died. [16]Then you will not be condemned for doing something you know is all right.

[17]For the Kingdom of God is not a matter of what we eat or drink, but of living a life of goodness and peace and joy in the Holy Spirit. [18]If you serve Christ with this attitude, you will please God. And other people will approve of you, too. [19]So then, let us aim for harmony in the church and try to build each other up.

[20]Don't tear apart the work of God over what you eat. Remember, there is nothing wrong with these things in themselves. But it is wrong to eat anything if it makes another person stumble. [21]Don't eat meat or drink wine or do anything else if it might cause another Christian to stumble. [22]You may have the faith to believe that there is nothing wrong with what you are doing, but keep it between yourself and God. Blessed are those who do not condemn themselves by doing something they know is all right. [23]But if people have doubts about whether they should eat something, they shouldn't eat it. They

## SILENCE ● ● • • •

14:23-15:6 **We try to steer clear of actions forbidden by Scripture, of course. But when Scripture is silent, we should follow our conscience. When God shows us something is wrong for us, we should avoid it—but we should not look down on other Christians who exercise their freedom in those areas.**

13:9 Lev 19:18. 14:10 Greek *your brother;* also in 14:10b, 13, 15, 21. 14:11 Isa 45:23.

would be condemned for not acting in faith before God. If you do anything you believe is not right, you are sinning.

CHAPTER **15** **THINK OF OTHERS FIRST.** We may know that these things make no difference, but we cannot just go ahead and do them to please ourselves. We must be considerate of the doubts and fears of those who think these things are wrong. 2We should please others. If we do what helps them, we will build them up in the Lord. 3For even Christ didn't please himself. As the Scriptures say, "Those who insult you are also insulting me."* 4Such things were written in the Scriptures long ago to teach us. They give us hope and encouragement as we wait patiently for God's promises.

5May God, who gives this patience and encouragement, help you live in complete harmony with each other—each with the attitude of Christ Jesus toward the other. 6Then all of you can join together with one voice, giving praise and glory to God, the Father of our Lord Jesus Christ.

7So accept each other just as Christ has accepted you; then God will be glorified. 8Remember that Christ came as a servant to the Jews to show that God is true to the promises he made to their ancestors. 9And he came so the Gentiles might also give glory to God for his mercies to them. That is what the psalmist meant when he wrote:

"I will praise you among the Gentiles;
I will sing praises to your name."*

10And in another place it is written,

"Rejoice, O you Gentiles,
along with his people, the Jews."*

11And yet again,

"Praise the Lord, all you Gentiles;
praise him, all you people of the earth."*

12And the prophet Isaiah said,

"The heir to David's throne* will come,
and he will rule over the Gentiles.
They will place their hopes on him."*

13So I pray that God, who gives you hope, will keep you happy and full of peace as you believe in him. May you overflow with hope through the power of the Holy Spirit.

14I am fully convinced, dear brothers and sisters,* that you are full of goodness. You know these things so well that you are able to teach others all about them. 15Even so, I have been bold enough to emphasize some of these points, knowing that all you need is this reminder from me. For I am, by God's grace, 16a special messenger from Christ Jesus to you Gentiles. I bring you the Good News and offer you up as a fragrant sacrifice to God so that you might be pure and pleasing to him by the Holy Spirit. 17So it is right for me to be enthusiastic about all Christ Jesus has done through me in my service to God. 18I dare not boast of anything else. I have brought the Gentiles to God by my message and by the way I lived before them. 19I have won them over by the miracles done through me as signs from God—all by the power of God's Spirit. In this way, I have fully presented the Good News of Christ all the way from Jerusalem clear over into Illyricum.*

20My ambition has always been to preach the Good News where the name of Christ has never been heard, rather than where a church has already been started by someone else. 21I have been following the plan spoken of in the Scriptures, where it says,

"Those who have never been told about him
will see,
and those who have never heard of him will
understand."*

22In fact, my visit to you has been delayed so long because I have been preaching in these places.

23But now I have finished my work in these regions, and after all these long years of waiting, I am eager to visit you. 24I am planning to go to Spain, and when I do, I will stop off in Rome. And after I have enjoyed your fellowship for a little while, you can send me on my way again.

25But before I come, I must go down to Jerusalem to take a gift to the Christians there. 26For you see, the believers in Greece* have eagerly taken up an offering for the Christians in Jerusalem, who are going through such hard times. 27They were very glad to do this because they feel they owe a real

## GOD'S WORK ● ● • • •

**15:17 Paul was not proud of what he had done, but of what God had done through him. Being proud of God's work is not a sin—it is worship. If you are not sure whether your pride is selfish or holy, ask yourself this question: Are you just as proud of what God is doing through other people as of what he is doing through you?**

## GOOD ADVICE ● ● • • •

**15:25-27 In Paul's day, Rome was the world's political, religious, social, and economic center. The major governmental decisions were made in Rome, and it was from Rome that the gospel spread to the ends of the earth. The church in Rome was a mixture of Jews, Gentiles, slaves, free people, men, women, Roman citizens, and world travelers. Because of this, it had potential for both great influence and great conflict.**

**Paul had not yet been to Rome to meet all the Christians there, and, of course, he has not yet met us. But he knew what it would take for the Roman Christians, and for us today, to live in peace and unity. We, too, live in a mixed world, full of different kinds of people. We have the potential for both widespread influence and terrible conflict. We should listen carefully to Paul's teaching about unity, service, and love. It is some of the best advice we will ever receive.**

15:3 Ps 69:9. 15:9 Ps 18:49. 15:10 Deut 32:43. 15:11 Ps 117:1. 15:12a Greek *The root of Jesse.* 15:12b Isa 11:10. 15:14 Greek *brothers;* also in 15:30. 15:19 *Illyricum* was a region northeast of Italy. 15:21 Isa 52:15. 15:26 Greek *Macedonia and Achaia,* the northern and southern regions of Greece.

## CHECK ● ● • • •

16:17-20 **When we read books or listen to sermons, we should check the content of what is written or said and not be fooled by smooth style. Christians who study God's Word do not need to be fooled, even if superficial listeners are easily taken in. For an example of believers who carefully checked God's Word, see Acts 17:10-12.**

debt to them. Since the Gentiles received the wonderful spiritual blessings of the Good News from the Jewish Christians, they feel the least they can do in return is help them financially. [28]As soon as I have delivered this money and completed this good deed of theirs, I will come to see you on my way to Spain. [29]And I am sure that when I come, Christ will give me a great blessing for you.

[30]Dear brothers and sisters, I urge you in the name of our Lord Jesus Christ to join me in my struggle by praying to God for me. Do this because of your love for me, given to you by the Holy Spirit. [31]Pray that I will be rescued from those in Judea who refuse to obey God. Pray also that the Christians there will be willing to accept the donation I am bringing them. [32]Then, by the will of God, I will be able to come to you with a happy heart, and we will be an encouragement to each other.

[33]And now may God, who gives us his peace, be with you all. Amen.

CHAPTER **16** **PAUL GREETS HIS FRIENDS.** Our sister Phoebe, a deacon in the church in Cenchrea, will be coming to see you soon. [2]Receive her in the Lord, as one who is worthy of high honor. Help her in every way you can, for she has helped many in their needs, including me.

[3]Greet Priscilla and Aquila. They have been co-workers in my ministry for Christ Jesus. [4]In fact, they risked their lives for me. I am not the only one who is thankful to them; so are all the Gentile churches. [5]Please give my greetings to the church that meets in their home.

Greet my dear friend Epenetus. He was the very first person to become a Christian in the province of Asia. [6]Give my greetings to Mary, who has worked so hard for your benefit. [7]Then there are Andronicus and Junia,* my relatives,* who were in prison with me. They are respected among the apostles and became Christians before I did. Please give them my greetings. [8]Say hello to Ampliatus, whom I love as one of the Lord's own children, [9]and Urbanus, our co-worker in Christ, and beloved Stachys.

[10]Give my greetings to Apelles, a good man whom Christ approves. And give my best regards to the members of the household of Aristobulus. [11]Greet Herodion, my relative.* Greet the Christians in the household of Narcissus. [12]Say hello to Tryphena and Tryphosa, the Lord's workers, and to dear Persis, who has worked so hard for the Lord. [13]Greet Rufus, whom the Lord picked out to be his very own; and also his dear mother, who has been a mother to me.

[14]And please give my greetings to Asyncritus, Phlegon, Hermes, Patrobas, Hermas, and the brothers and sisters* who are with them. [15]Give my greetings to Philologus, Julia, Nereus and his sister, and to Olympas and all the other believers who are with them. [16]Greet each other in Christian love.* All the churches of Christ send you their greetings.

[17]And now I make one more appeal, my dear brothers and sisters. Watch out for people who cause divisions and upset people's faith by teaching things that are contrary to what you have been taught. Stay away from them. [18]Such people are not serving Christ our Lord; they are serving their own personal interests. By smooth talk and glowing words they deceive innocent people. [19]But everyone knows that you are obedient to the Lord. This makes me very happy. I want you to see clearly what is right and to stay innocent of any wrong. [20]The God of peace will soon crush Satan under your feet. May the grace of our Lord Jesus Christ be with you.

[21]Timothy, my fellow worker, and Lucius, Jason, and Sosipater, my relatives, send you their good wishes.

[22]I, Tertius, the one who is writing this letter for Paul, send my greetings, too, as a Christian brother.

[23]Gaius says hello to you. I am his guest, and the church meets here in his home. Erastus, the city treasurer, sends you his greetings, and so does Quartus, a Christian brother.*

[25]God is able to make you strong, just as the Good News says. It is the message about Jesus Christ and his plan for you Gentiles, a plan kept secret from the beginning of time. [26]But now as the prophets* foretold and as the eternal God has commanded, this message is made known to all Gentiles everywhere, so that they might believe and obey Christ. [27]To God, who alone is wise, be the glory forever through Jesus Christ. Amen.

16:7a Or *Junias;* some manuscripts read *Julia.* 16:7b Or *compatriots;* also in 16:21. 16:11 Or *compatriot.* 16:14 Greek *brothers;* also in 16:17. 16:16 Greek *with a sacred kiss.* 16:23 Some manuscripts add verse 24, *May the grace of our Lord Jesus Christ be with you all. Amen.* 16:26 Greek *the prophetic writings.*

# MEGA themes

**SIN** Sin means refusing to do God's will and failing to do all that God wants. Since Adam rebelled against God, it has become our nature to disobey God. Our sin cuts us off from God; sin causes us to want to live our own way rather than God's way. Because God is morally perfect, just, and fair, he is right to condemn sin.

Each person has sinned, either by rebelling against God or by ignoring his will. No matter what our background or how hard we try to live a good and moral life, we cannot earn salvation or remove our sin. Only Christ can save us.

1. Through Paul's writings to Rome, God reveals to us how destructive sin is in our world, how widespread it is in mankind, how fatal it is to individuals. Survey chapters 1, 3, and 5 and list the key teachings you find on the topic of sin.
2. What are some of the consequences of mankind's choices to rebel against God's will?
3. How does sin enslave a person?
4. Now read 7:14-25 to catch a glimpse of Paul's personal battle with sin. How does Paul overcome his weaknesses?
5. Check out your life in light of this study. What are the consequences of your sinful choices? At what points has sin enslaved you? Where can you identify with the feelings and thoughts of Paul?
6. How does an awareness of your sin lead you to a deeper reliance upon Jesus Christ?

**SALVATION** Our sin points out our need to be forgiven and cleansed. Although we don't deserve it, God in his kindness reaches out to love and forgive us. He provides the way for us to be saved. Christ's death paid the penalty for our sin.

It is good news that God saves us from our sin. But we must believe in Jesus Christ, that he forgave our sin, to enter into a wonderful new relationship with God.

1. Read Romans 3:23; 5:8; 6:23; and 10:9-10. How would you use these verses to explain what it means to receive salvation through Jesus Christ?
2. Describe your own personal response to the message of salvation. When did you first hear it? When did you first believe?
3. What difference has Christ's salvation made in your daily life?
4. How does knowing that God has forgiven your sins affect the way you live?

**GROWTH** By God's power, believers are made holy. This is known as "sanctification." It means we are set apart from sin, enabled to obey and to become more like Christ. When we are growing in our relationship with Christ, the Holy Spirit frees us from the demands of the law and from the fear of God's judgment.

Because we are free from sin's control, the law's demands, and fear of God's punishment, we can grow in our relationship with Christ. By trusting in the Holy Spirit and allowing him to help us, we can overcome sin and temptation. Without the Holy Spirit, we will be unable to conquer sin's power.

1. Rewrite 12:1-2 in your own words.
2. How has God transformed you?
3. In what areas of your life have you struggled—or are now struggling—with conformity to the world?
4. What should you do to submit more fully to God?

**SOVEREIGNTY** God oversees and cares about his people—past, present, and future. God's ways of dealing with people are always fair. Because God is in charge of all creation, he can save whomever he wills.

Because of God's mercy, both Jews and Gentiles can be saved—we all need to respond to God's mercy and accept his gracious offer of forgiveness. God is sovereign, so let him reign in your heart.

1. Contrast the life of the person who seeks to accept and live under God's rule with the person who ignores or rejects him as Lord.
2. Describe Jesus' lordship in your life. What does it mean to let him be Lord over your life?
3. What confidence do you have because of the sovereignty of God?

**SERVICE** When our purpose is to give credit to God for his love, power, and perfection in all we do, we can serve him properly. Serving God unifies all believers and enables them to be loving and sensitive to others.

None of us can be fully Christlike by himself or herself—it takes the entire body of Christ to fully express Christ. By actively and vigorously building up other believers, Christians can be a symphony of service to God.

1. Chapters 12–15 include various teachings on how to live with fellow believers as members of Christ's body. List a number of the ways we are to relate to each other to show that we are unified.
2. Who are the Christians with whom you are the closest? Why do you feel close to these people?
3. What Christians are hard for you to love? What could you do to get along better with them?
4. What acts of service could you do for those you listed in questions 2 and 3?

**F**ifteen-year-old Dicky just recently accepted Christ. Yesterday, he watched in total disbelief as two of the "leaders" of his church got into a shouting (and shoving!) match after Sunday services. Dicky quietly asks *you* why supposedly "mature" Christians act that way. What do you say? ■ Kim has discovered that a man and woman who are active in the church aren't really married, but are living together. "How can they do that? Why doesn't the preacher talk to them? Isn't that a sin?" Kim says, puzzled. What would you tell her? ■ Twelve-year-old Abby knows, as a Christian, that certain activities are wrong—drunkenness, premarital sex, lying, stealing, etc. But what about all those "gray areas" that God's Word *doesn't* address? Is it OK to dance, go to certain parties, or buy expensive clothes? What about her favorite videos on MTV and songs on the radio? And how does God feel about the movies she's watched recently? "I want to do what's right," she tells you, "but sometimes it's hard to know. Aren't there some guidelines from the Bible that can help?" How do you answer? ■ These questions are far from new. Christians (and churches) have struggled with immaturity, division, and immorality since the first hymn was sung. Fortunately, the apostle Paul's first letter to the Corinthians has some real and practical answers. If you're looking to live a godly life in a godless culture, or if you want to help someone else do so, keep reading.

## STATS

PURPOSE: To identify problems in the Corinthian church, to offer solutions, and to teach the believers how to live for Christ in a corrupt society

AUTHOR: Paul

TO WHOM WRITTEN: The church in Corinth, and Christians everywhere

DATE WRITTEN: About A.D. 55, near the end of Paul's three-year ministry in Ephesus during his third missionary journey

SETTING: Corinth was a major cosmopolitan city, a seaport and major trade center—the most important city in Achaia. It was also filled with idolatry and immorality. The church was largely made up of Gentiles. Paul had established this church on his second missionary journey.

KEY PEOPLE: Paul, Timothy, members of Chloe's household

KEY PLACES: Worship meetings in Corinth

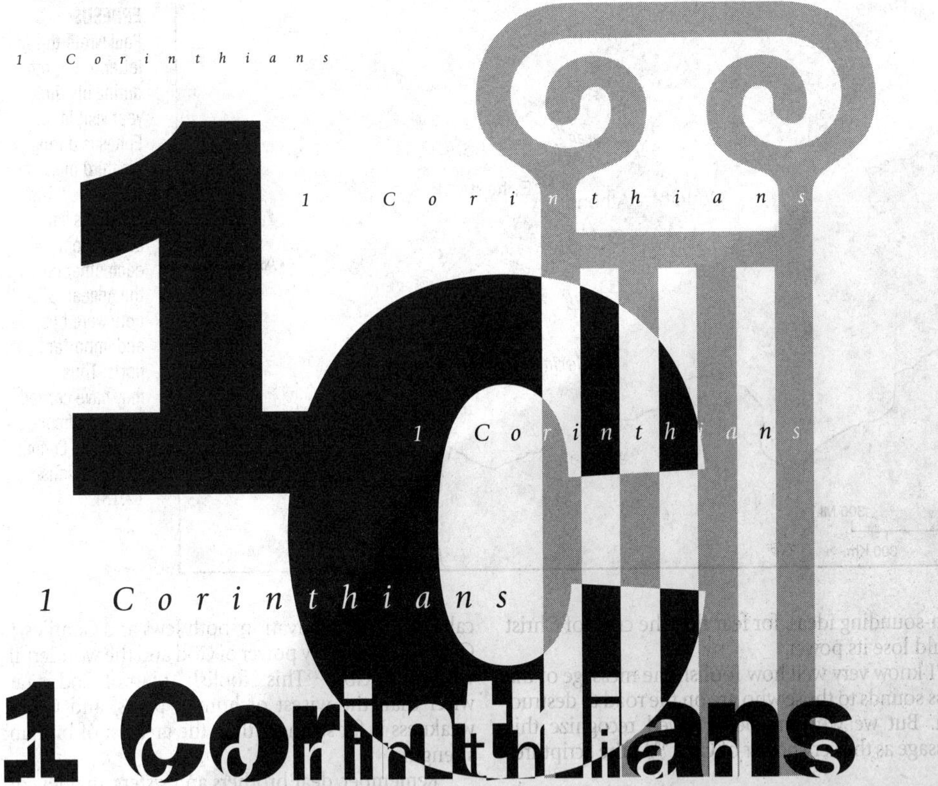

# 1 Corinthians

CHAPTER **1** **PAUL: CHOSEN TO BE A MISSIONARY.** This
letter is from Paul, chosen by the will of God to be
an apostle of Christ Jesus, and from our brother
Sosthenes.
[2]We are writing to the church of God in Corinth,
you who have been called by God to be his own holy
people. He made you holy by means of Christ Jesus,
just as he did all Christians everywhere—whoever
calls upon the name of Jesus Christ, our Lord and
theirs.
[3]May God our Father and the Lord Jesus Christ
give you his grace and peace.

[4]I can never stop thanking God for all the generous gifts he has given you, now that you belong to
Christ Jesus. [5]He has enriched your church with the
gifts of eloquence and every kind of knowledge.
[6]This shows that what I told you about Christ is true.
[7]Now you have every spiritual gift you need as you
eagerly wait for the return of our Lord Jesus Christ.
[8]He will keep you strong right up to the end, and he
will keep you free from all blame on the great day
when our Lord Jesus Christ returns. [9]God will surely
do this for you, for he always does just what he says,
and he is the one who invited you into this wonderful friendship with his Son, Jesus Christ our Lord.
[10]Now, dear brothers and sisters,* I appeal to you
by the authority of the Lord Jesus Christ to stop
arguing among yourselves. Let there be real harmony
so there won't be divisions in the church. I plead
with you to be of one mind, united in thought and
purpose. [11]For some members of Chloe's household
have told me about your arguments, dear brothers
and sisters. [12]Some of you are saying, "I am a follower of Paul." Others are saying, "I follow Apollos,"
or "I follow Peter,*" or "I follow only Christ." [13]Can
Christ be divided into pieces?
Was I, Paul, crucified for you? Were any of you
baptized in the name of Paul? [14]I thank God that I
did not baptize any of you except Crispus and Gaius,
[15]for now no one can say they were baptized in my
name. [16](Oh yes, I also baptized the household of
Stephanas. I don't remember baptizing anyone else.)
[17]For Christ didn't send me to baptize, but to preach
the Good News—and not with clever speeches and

**USEFUL ● ● • • •**

**1:1 Paul was specially selected by God to preach about Jesus Christ. Each Christian has a task to do. One task may seem more spectacular than another, but all are necessary to carry out God's greater plans for the world (12:12-27). Be useful to God by using your gifts in his service. As you discover what he wants, be ready to serve.**

1:10 Greek *brothers;* also in 1:11, 26. 1:12 Greek *Cephas.*

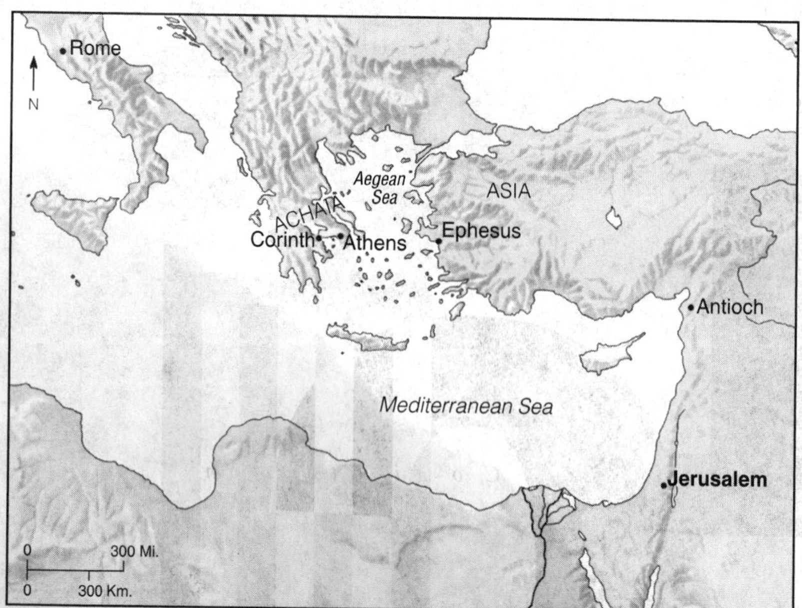


**CORINTH AND EPHESUS**
Paul wrote this letter to Corinth during his three-year visit in Ephesus during his third missionary journey. The two cities sat across from each other on the Aegean Sea—both were busy and important ports. Titus may have carried this letter from Ephesus to Corinth (2 Corinthians 12:18).

high-sounding ideas, for fear that the cross of Christ would lose its power.

[18]I know very well how foolish the message of the cross sounds to those who are on the road to destruction. But we who are being saved recognize this message as the very power of God. [19]As the Scriptures say,

"I will destroy human wisdom
and discard their most brilliant ideas."*

## SIMPLE FAITH ● ● • • •

1:28-31 **Paul continues to emphasize that the way to receive salvation is so ordinary and simple that *any* person who wants to can understand it. Skill does not get you into God's kingdom—simple faith does. God planned it this way so no one could boast that his achievements helped him secure eternal life. Salvation is totally from God through Jesus' death, which allowed us to become perfect in God's eyes. There is *nothing* we can do to become acceptable to God; we need only accept what Jesus has already done for us. He has done the work.**

[20]So where does this leave the philosophers, the scholars, and the world's brilliant debaters? God has made them all look foolish and has shown their wisdom to be useless nonsense. [21]Since God in his wisdom saw to it that the world would never find him through human wisdom, he has used our foolish preaching to save all who believe. [22]God's way seems foolish to the Jews because they want a sign from heaven to prove it is true. And it is foolish to the Greeks because they believe only what agrees with their own wisdom. [23]So when we preach that Christ was crucified, the Jews are offended, and the Gentiles say it's all nonsense. [24]But to those called by God to salvation, both Jews and Gentiles,* Christ is the mighty power of God and the wonderful wisdom of God. [25]This "foolish" plan of God is far wiser than the wisest of human plans, and God's weakness is far stronger than the greatest of human strength.

[26]Remember, dear brothers and sisters, that few of you were wise in the world's eyes, or powerful, or wealthy when God called you. [27]Instead, God deliberately chose things the world considers foolish in order to shame those who think they are wise. And he chose those who are powerless to shame those who are powerful. [28]God chose things despised by the world, things counted as nothing at all, and used them to bring to nothing what the world considers important, [29]so that no one can ever boast in the presence of God.

[30]God alone made it possible for you to be in Christ Jesus. For our benefit God made Christ to be wisdom itself. He is the one who made us acceptable to God. He made us pure and holy, and he gave himself to purchase our freedom. [31]As the Scriptures say,

"The person who wishes to boast
should boast only of what the Lord has
done."*

## WHAT'S IN STORE? ● ● • • •

2:9 **We cannot imagine all that God has in store for us both in this life and for eternity. He will create a new heaven and a new earth (Isaiah 65:17; Revelation 21:1), and we will live with him forever. Until then, his Holy Spirit comforts and guides us. Knowing the future that awaits us should give us hope and courage to press on in this life, to endure hardship, and to avoid giving in to temptation. This world is not all there is.**

1:19 Isa 29:14. 1:24 Greek *Greeks.* 1:31 Jer 9:24.

CHAPTER **2** **THE HOLY SPIRIT GIVES US WISDOM.** Dear
brothers and sisters,* when I first came to you I
didn't use lofty words and brilliant ideas to tell you
God's message.* 2For I decided to concentrate only
on Jesus Christ and his death on the cross. 3I came
to you in weakness—timid and trembling. 4And
my message and my preaching were very plain. I
did not use wise and persuasive speeches, but the
Holy Spirit was powerful among you. 5I did this so
that you might trust the power of God rather than
human wisdom.

6Yet when I am among mature Christians, I do
speak with words of wisdom, but not the kind of
wisdom that belongs to this world, and not the
kind that appeals to the rulers of this world, who
are being brought to nothing. 7No, the wisdom we
speak of is the secret wisdom of God,* which was
hidden in former times, though he made it for
our benefit before the world began. 8But the rulers of this world have not understood it; if they
had, they would never have crucified our glorious
Lord. 9That is what the Scriptures mean when they
say,

"No eye has seen, no ear has heard,
and no mind has imagined
what God has prepared
for those who love him."*

10But we know these things because God has revealed them to us by his Spirit, and his Spirit
searches out everything and shows us even God's
deep secrets. 11No one can know what anyone else
is really thinking except that person alone, and no
one can know God's thoughts except God's own
Spirit. 12And God has actually given us his Spirit
(not the world's spirit) so we can know the wonderful things God has freely given us. 13When we
tell you this, we do not use words of human wisdom. We speak words given to us by the Spirit,
using the Spirit's words to explain spiritual truths.*
14But people who aren't Christians can't understand these truths from God's Spirit. It all sounds
foolish to them because only those who have the
Spirit can understand what the Spirit means. 15We
who have the Spirit understand these things, but
others can't understand us at all. 16How could
they? For,

"Who can know what the Lord is thinking?
Who can give him counsel?"*

But we can understand these things, for we have the mind of Christ.

CHAPTER **3** Dear brothers and sisters,* when
I was with you I couldn't talk to you as I would
to mature Christians. I had to talk as though
you belonged to this world or as though you
were infants in the Christian life.* 2I had to feed
you with milk and not with solid food, because

**I hear a lot about the New Age movement. Some of my friends say they are in it. How is this different from what I believe as a Christian?**

The most convenient religion is one you create yourself, and that is what the New Age movement does for people. It allows them to create their own rules concerning God, their behavior, and how to make it to the next life.

Because of this, *New Age* is impossible to define! But, generally, here is what most New-Agers believe:

- They believe that God is everywhere and in everybody. Because we are humans, we all have a unity of spirit that allows us to be brothers no matter what. God is not good or bad. In fact, each person is a god. He or she is the center of the universe. Morality, therefore, isn't important (since God is not seen as either good or bad). But the mind and intellect are very important, because, supposedly, a person has to think deep thoughts to understand these concepts.
- They believe that "salvation" comes through reincarnation. This means coming back to life again in the form of someone or something else, again and again, until you get it right. (Reincarnation is a lie; the Bible is very clear on this point. See Hebrews 9:27.)

There are so many strains within the New Age movement that it's impossible to outline them all. But the key is believing that there is no personal God, that humans are not sinful, and that the next life is assured in some form, no matter what you have done. This is a very convenient religion if you just want to do your own thing.

But listen to God: "Cursed are those who put their trust in mere humans and turn their hearts away from the LORD" (Jeremiah 17:5). When people set their own beliefs and thoughts up as more important than what God thinks, they are actually being cursed by him!

Nearly every belief within the New Age movement allows you to become your own god. Eve was told by Satan that she would become like God if she ate of the fruit of the tree (Genesis 3:1-6). People are being told they can be god of their life if they would just look away from the one, true God.

The Bible must be our authority on what we are to believe about God, ourself, and what it takes to be saved from our sin. If it isn't, everyone can create a religion to suit his or her own desires. And that is a religion that will lead to destruction. Don't believe that? Just take a look at 1 Corinthians 1:19: "I will destroy human wisdom and discard their most brilliant ideas."

There's only one place to find the real answers to who God is and what he's about: his holy Word, the Bible.

2:1a Greek *Brothers.* 2:1b Greek *mystery;* other manuscripts read *testimony.* 2:7 Greek *we speak God's wisdom in a mystery.* 2:9 Isa 64:4. 2:13 Or *explaining spiritual truths in spiritual language,* or *explaining spiritual truths to spiritual people.* 2:16 Isa 40:13. 3:1a Greek *Brothers.* 3:1b Greek *in Christ.*

**Ultimate Issues**

## AIDS: WHAT WOULD JESUS DO?

There are few more explosive topics in America than that of AIDS. Conservatives believe AIDS is God's judgment on certain sinners. Gay rights groups and others scream just as loudly that this is a medical issue, not a moral one. Who's right? And how should Christians respond to this overwhelming problem? In one sense, AIDS (Acquired Immune Deficiency Syndrome) *is* primarily a medical issue. The AIDS virus attacks the body's immune system, making the body defenseless against the diseases a healthy person's immune system would destroy. AIDS is an "equal opportunity" **NIGHTMARE**—it affects everyone: young, old, male, female, gay, or straight. If AIDS isn't a punishment from God, why has it hit the male gay community and IV drug abusers so hard? The answer is that gay men and IV drug abusers participate in activities that pass the virus from person to person very effectively. God hasn't singled out particular groups for special judgment; rather, those people engage in activities that are particularly risky in regard to the transmission of AIDS. God created the universe to run in accordance with NATURAL LAWS, like gravity, inertia, etc. When you try to defy those laws, you lose. You may not like the law of gravity, but jump off a building and you will—like it or not—encounter it. There are natural laws governing human behavior, too. One such law is that your body is not made for sexual promiscuity. Violate that law and you **RISK** contracting AIDS or other diseases (syphilis, gonorrhea, herpes, etc.). Likewise, your body was not made to handle large amounts of drugs. Continually inject them into your veins and you probably will experience a lot of physical problems— one of which may be AIDS. So it's not that God is using AIDS to "get" certain kinds of people. AIDS simply is a natural—though terrifying—result of human behavior that goes against God's design for our lives. Those who believe AIDS is a special divine judgment simply don't understand the reality of their own sin. As the psalmist wrote in Psalm 143:1-2, "Hear my prayer, O LORD; listen to my plea! Answer me because you are faithful and righteous. Don't bring your servant to trial! Compared to you, no one is perfect." A cure for AIDS is still years away; but even if it weren't, the only reasonable, Christian response is to follow God's standards for sexual morality. Sex is made for marriage only—to be kept in the context of a faithful, monogamous relationship between husband and wife. Anything else is unbiblical, sinful, and potentially fatal. Likewise, we must reaffirm ***God's ownership of our body*** by not abusing it with drugs. Paul writes in 1 Corinthians 6:19-20, "Don't you know that your body is the temple of the Holy Spirit, who lives in you? . . . God bought you with a high price. So you must honor God with your body." Where we have failed to live up to this, we need to confess our sins, repent, and ask God's forgiveness. Many Christians also need to confess their judgmental attitudes toward persons with AIDS. There is no room in Christianity for feelings of superiority or self-righteousness. Jesus had strong words for those who were guilty of spiritual pride, of thinking they were better than others. Our response toward anyone with this terrible disease should be concern, compassion, and a hand reaching out to ease his or her pain and distress. Isn't that how Jesus deals with people, regardless of their sins?

---

you couldn't handle anything stronger. And you
still aren't ready, [3]for you are still controlled by
your own sinful desires. You are jealous of one
another and quarrel with each other. Doesn't
that prove you are controlled by your own
desires? You are acting like people who don't belong to the Lord. [4]When one of you says, "I am a
follower of Paul," and another says, "I prefer

**DESIRES ● ● • • •**

**3:1-3 Paul called the Corinthians infants in the Christian life because they were not yet spiritually healthy and mature. The proof was that they quarreled like children. Baby Christians are controlled by their own desires; mature believers, by God's desires. How much influence do your own desires have on your life? Make it your goal to let God's desires be your own.**

Apollos," aren't you acting like those who are not
Christians?*
5Who is Apollos, and who is Paul, that we should
be the cause of such quarrels? Why, we're only servants. Through us God caused you to believe. Each
of us did the work the Lord gave us. 6My job was
to plant the seed in your hearts, and Apollos watered it, but it was God, not we, who made it grow.
7The ones who do the planting or watering aren't
important, but God is important because he is the
one who makes the seed grow. 8The one who plants
and the one who waters work as a team with the
same purpose. Yet they will be rewarded individually, according to their own hard work. 9We work
together as partners who belong to God. You are
God's field, God's building—not ours.
10Because of God's special favor to me, I have
laid the foundation like an expert builder. Now
others are building on it. But whoever is building
on this foundation must be very careful. 11For no
one can lay any other foundation than the one we
already have—Jesus Christ. 12Now anyone who
builds on that foundation may use gold, silver,
jewels, wood, hay, or straw. 13But there is going to
come a time of testing at the judgment day to see
what kind of work each builder has done. Everyone's work will be put through the fire to see
whether or not it keeps its value. 14If the work
survives the fire, that builder will receive a reward.
15But if the work is burned up, the builder will
suffer great loss. The builders themselves will be
saved, but like someone escaping through a wall of
flames.
16Don't you realize that all of you together are the
temple of God and that the Spirit of God lives in*
you? 17God will bring ruin upon anyone who ruins
this temple. For God's temple is holy, and you Christians are that temple.
18Stop fooling yourselves. If you think you are wise
by this world's standards, you will have to become a
fool so you can become wise by God's standards.
19For the wisdom of this world is foolishness to God.
As the Scriptures say,

"God catches those who think they are wise
in their own cleverness."*

20And again,

"The Lord knows the thoughts of the wise,
that they are worthless."*

21So don't take pride in following a particular leader.
Everything belongs to you: 22Paul and Apollos and
Peter*; the whole world and life and death; the
present and the future. Everything belongs to you,
23and you belong to Christ, and Christ belongs to
God.

CHAPTER **4** **CLIQUES IN THE CHURCH.** So look at
Apollos and me as mere servants of Christ who have
been put in charge of explaining God's secrets. 2Now,
a person who is put in charge as a manager must be
faithful. 3What about me? Have I been faithful? Well,
it matters very little what you or anyone else thinks.
I don't even trust my own judgment on this point.

**My Christian friends are dragging me down. How am I supposed to grow as a Christian if these friends aren't really trying to do anything with their faith?**

Because God is the one "who invited you into this wonderful friendship with his Son" (1 Corinthians 1:9), it's his responsibility, not yours, to make sure you grow in your faith. He has no intention of abandoning you.

Many people have been touched by divorce in one way or another. Kids of divorced parents are often determined to make sure that their own marriage is a success. They seek out positive role models to observe, and they pore over numerous resources about having a quality marriage. But the opposite also can be true. Kids who grow up without a good model of what a family is supposed to look like can easily repeat their parents' mistakes.

Because your friends are acting like they have "divorced God," you are faced with a choice. Will you learn from their mistakes and search out people and other resources to help you succeed in your relationship with Christ? Or will you follow their lead and turn your back on God as well? If you're serious about giving God every chance to make himself real in your life, consider these suggestions:

First, pray for your friends and for an opportunity to talk to them about the situation. Don't worry about how much you've blown it by participating in whatever they've done. It's more important to think about your future than to dwell on the past. Next, go to one of your Christian friends, perhaps the leader of the group, and say something like: "I really want to give God a shot, but you're not helping much. I need your help. Can I count on you?" If this person says yes, it worked! If not, go to another friend and tell him the same thing. If no one responds, wait a week or two and start the process again, trusting that God has been working in their hearts. Or find some new friends you can count on. Maybe that's the answer God has for you.

Remember, God is faithful. He knows that you need friends and a group to hang around with. The last thing you need are people who are heading in the wrong direction.

3:4 Greek *aren't you merely human?* 3:16 Or *among.* 3:19 Job 5:13. 3:20 Ps 94:11. 3:22 Greek *Cephas.*

**HIGHLIGHTS OF 1 CORINTHIANS**

*The Meaning of the Cross, 1:18–2:16.* Be considerate of one another because of what Christ has done for us. There is no place for pride or a know-it-all attitude. We are to have the mind of Christ.

*The Story of the Lord's Supper, 11:23-29.* The Lord's Supper is a time of reflection on Christ's final words to his disciples before he died on the cross; we must celebrate this in an orderly and correct manner.

*The Poem of Love, 13:1-13.* Love is to guide all we do. We have different gifts, abilities, likes, dislikes—but we are called, without exception, to love.

*The Christian's Destiny, 15:42-58.* We are promised by Christ, who died for us, that, just as he came back to life after death, our perishable bodies will be exchanged for heavenly bodies. Then we will live and reign with Christ.

[4]My conscience is clear, but that isn't what matters. It
is the Lord himself who will examine me and decide.
[5]So be careful not to jump to conclusions before
the Lord returns as to whether or not someone is
faithful. When the Lord comes, he will bring our
deepest secrets to light and will reveal our private
motives. And then God will give to everyone whatever praise is due.
[6]Dear brothers and sisters,* I have used Apollos
and myself to illustrate what I've been saying. If you
pay attention to the Scriptures,* you won't brag
about one of your leaders at the expense of another.
[7]What makes you better than anyone else? What do
you have that God hasn't given you? And if all you
have is from God, why boast as though you have
accomplished something on your own?
[8]You think you already have everything you need!
You are already rich! Without us you have become
kings! I wish you really were on your thrones already, for then we would be reigning with you! [9]But
sometimes I think God has put us apostles on display, like prisoners of war at the end of a victor's
parade, condemned to die. We have become a spectacle to the entire world—to people and angels alike.
[10]Our dedication to Christ makes us look like
fools, but you are so wise! We are weak, but you are
so powerful! You are well thought of, but we are
laughed at. [11]To this very hour we go hungry and
thirsty, without enough clothes to keep us warm. We
have endured many beatings, and we have no homes
of our own. [12]We have worked wearily with our own
hands to earn our living. We bless those who curse
us. We are patient with those who abuse us. [13]We
respond gently when evil things are said about us.
Yet we are treated like the world's garbage, like everybody's trash—right up to the present moment.
[14]I am not writing these things to shame you, but
to warn you as my beloved children. [15]For even if you
had ten thousand others to teach you about Christ,
you have only one spiritual father. For I became your
father in Christ Jesus when I preached the Good
News to you. [16]So I ask you to follow my example
and do as I do.
[17]That is the very reason I am sending Timothy—
to help you do this. For he is my beloved and trustworthy child in the Lord. He will remind you of what
I teach about Christ Jesus in all the churches wherever I go.
[18]I know that some of you have become arrogant,
thinking I will never visit you again. [19]But I will
come—and soon—if the Lord will let me, and then
I'll find out whether these arrogant people are just

4:6a Greek *Brothers.* 4:6b Or *You must learn not to go beyond "what is written," so that.*

big talkers or whether they really have God's power.
20For the Kingdom of God is not just fancy talk; it is
living by God's power. 21Which do you choose?
Should I come with punishment and scolding, or
should I come with quiet love and gentleness?

## CHAPTER 5 **SIN IN THE CHURCH.**
I can hardly believe
the report about the sexual immorality going on
among you, something so evil that even the pagans
don't do it. I am told that you have a man in your
church who is living in sin with his father's wife.
2And you are so proud of yourselves! Why aren't you
mourning in sorrow and shame? And why haven't
you removed this man from your fellowship?
3Even though I am not there with you in person, I
am with you in the Spirit.* Concerning the one who
has done this, I have already passed judgment 4in the
name of the Lord Jesus. You are to call a meeting of
the church,* and I will be there in spirit, and the
power of the Lord Jesus will be with you as you meet.
5Then you must cast this man out of the church and
into Satan's hands, so that his sinful nature will be
destroyed* and he himself* will be saved when the
Lord returns.
6How terrible that you should boast about your
spirituality, and yet you let this sort of thing go on.
Don't you realize that if even one person is allowed
to go on sinning, soon all will be affected? 7Remove
this wicked person from among you so that you can
stay pure.* Christ, our Passover Lamb, has been sacrificed for us. 8So let us celebrate the festival, not by
eating the old bread* of wickedness and evil, but by
eating the new bread* of purity and truth.
9When I wrote to you before, I told you not to
associate with people who indulge in sexual sin.
10But I wasn't talking about unbelievers who indulge
in sexual sin, or who are greedy or are swindlers or
idol worshipers. You would have to leave this world
to avoid people like that. 11What I meant was that
you are not to associate with anyone who claims to
be a Christian* yet indulges in sexual sin, or is
greedy, or worships idols, or is abusive, or a drunkard, or a swindler. Don't even eat with such people.
12It isn't my responsibility to judge outsiders, but
it certainly is your job to judge those inside the
church who are sinning in these ways. 13God will
judge those on the outside; but as the Scriptures say,
"You must remove the evil person from among
you."*

## CHAPTER 6 **LAWSUITS.**
When you have some-
thing against another Christian, why do you file a
lawsuit and ask a secular court to decide the matter,
instead of taking it to other Christians to decide
who is right? 2Don't you know that someday we
Christians are going to judge the world? And since
you are going to judge the world, can't you decide

### JUDGING ● ● • • •

**4:5 It is tempting to judge fellow Christians, evaluating whether or not they are good followers of Christ. But only God knows a person's heart, and he is the only one with the right to judge. Paul's warning to the Corinthians should also warn us. We should help those who are sinning (see 5:12-13), but we must not judge who is a better servant for Christ. When you judge someone, you automatically consider yourself better, and that is pride.**

these little things among yourselves? 3Don't you
realize that we Christians will judge angels? So you
should surely be able to resolve ordinary disagreements here on earth. 4If you have legal disputes
about such matters, why do you go to outside
judges who are not respected by the church? 5I am
saying this to shame you. Isn't there anyone in all
the church who is wise enough to decide these
arguments? 6But instead, one Christian* sues another—right in front of unbelievers!
7To have such lawsuits at all is a real defeat for you.
Why not just accept the injustice and leave it at that?
Why not let yourselves be cheated? 8But instead, you
yourselves are the ones who do wrong and cheat
even your own Christian brothers and sisters.*
9Don't you know that those who do wrong will
have no share in the Kingdom of God? Don't fool
yourselves. Those who indulge in sexual sin, who are
idol worshipers, adulterers, male prostitutes, homosexuals, 10thieves, greedy people, drunkards, abusers,
and swindlers—none of these will have a share in
the Kingdom of God. 11There was a time when some
of you were just like that, but now your sins have
been washed away,* and you have been set apart for
God. You have been made right with God because of
what the Lord Jesus Christ and the Spirit of our God
have done for you.
12You may say, "I am allowed to do anything." But
I reply, "Not everything is good for you." And even
though "I am allowed to do anything," I must not
become a slave to anything. 13You say, "Food is for
the stomach, and the stomach is for food." This is
true, though someday God will do away with both of
them. But our bodies were not made for sexual

### SEX ● ● • • •

**6:13 Sexual sin is a temptation we cannot escape. In movies and on television, sex outside of marriage is treated as a normal—even desirable—part of life, while marriage is often shown as confining and joyless. We can even be looked down upon by others if suspected of being pure. But God does not forbid sexual sin just to be difficult. He knows its power to destroy us physically and spiritually. No one should underestimate the power of sexual sin. It has devastated countless lives and destroyed families, communities, and even nations. God wants to protect us from damaging ourself and others, so he offers to fill us—our loneliness, our desires—with himself.**

5:3 Or *in spirit.* 5:4 Or *In the name of the Lord Jesus, you are to call a meeting of the church.* 5:5a Or *so that he will die;* Greek reads *for the destruction of the flesh.* 5:5b Greek *and the spirit.* 5:6-7 Greek *Don't you realize that even a little leaven spreads quickly through the whole batch of dough? 7Purge out the old leaven so that you can be a new batch of dough, just as you are already unleavened.* 5:8a Greek *not with old leaven.* 5:8b Greek *but with unleavened [bread].* 5:11 Greek *a brother.* 5:13 Deut 17:7. 6:6 Greek *one brother.* 6:8 Greek *brothers.* 6:11 Or *you have been cleansed.*

immorality. They were made for the Lord, and the Lord cares about our bodies. [14]And God will raise our bodies from the dead by his marvelous power, just as he raised our Lord from the dead. [15]Don't you realize that your bodies are actually parts of Christ? Should a man take his body, which belongs to Christ, and join it to a prostitute? Never! [16]And don't you know that if a man joins himself to a prostitute, he becomes one body with her? For the Scriptures say, "The two are united into one."* [17]But the person who is joined to the Lord becomes one spirit with him.

**RUGS**

*Scene 1:* Lyle is having a massive argument with his parents. (They've just discovered a small amount of marijuana in his coat pocket.)

"Lighten up, OK? It's no big deal! It's just a little grass."

"'No big deal'? Listen here, that grass is illegal! You could go to jail for that grass!"

"Lyle, how could you do this to your father and me?"

"What? I'm not doing anything to you! It's my life!"

"That's right. It's your life. But you're gonna cut it short if you fill your body with drugs."

"Aw, come off of it! I don't 'fill my body with drugs.' I smoke a little harmless grass."

*Scene 2:* Gary looks nervously over his shoulder. No one is watching, so he pulls a pill bottle—containing anabolic steroids—out of his locker.

Quickly he turns and heads for the gym. Time to pump some serious iron.

*Scene 3:* With her parents out for the evening, Staci and her friend Kimberly search the workshop and garage for gas, paint thinner, or anything else with the right kind of fumes to get them high.

Drugs (no matter what kind) damage the human body. If you're a Christian, your body doesn't belong to you. God owns it, and he tells you to take care of it.

For that reason alone, you must resist the temporary thrill of a chemical high. See 1 Corinthians 6:19-20.

[18]Run away from sexual sin! No other sin so clearly affects the body as this one does. For sexual immorality is a sin against your own body. [19]Or don't you know that your body is the temple of the Holy Spirit, who lives in you and was given to you by God? You do not belong to yourself, [20]for God bought you with a high price. So you must honor God with your body.

## CHAPTER 7 QUESTIONS ABOUT MARRIAGE.

Now about the questions you asked in your letter. Yes, it is good to live a celibate life. [2]But because there is so much sexual immorality, each man should have his own wife, and each woman should have her own husband.

[3]The husband should not deprive his wife of sexual intimacy, which is her right as a married woman, nor should the wife deprive her husband. [4]The wife gives authority over her body to her husband, and the husband also gives authority over his body to his wife. [5]So do not deprive each other of sexual relations. The only exception to this rule would be the agreement of both husband and wife to refrain from sexual intimacy for a limited time, so they can give themselves more completely to prayer. Afterward they should come together again so that Satan won't be able to tempt them because of their lack of self-control. [6]This is only my suggestion. It's not meant to be an absolute rule. [7]I wish everyone could get along without marrying, just as I do. But we are not all the same. God gives some the gift of marriage, and to others he gives the gift of singleness.

[8]Now I say to those who aren't married and to widows—it's better to stay unmarried, just as I am. [9]But if they can't control themselves, they should go ahead and marry. It's better to marry than to burn with lust.

[10]Now, for those who are married I have a command that comes not from me, but from the Lord.* A wife must not leave her husband. [11]But if she does leave him, let her remain single or else go back to him. And the husband must not leave his wife.

[12]Now, I will speak to the rest of you, though I do not have a direct command from the Lord. If a Christian man* has a wife who is an unbeliever and she is willing to continue living with him, he must not leave her. [13]And if a Christian woman has a husband who is an unbeliever, and he is willing to continue living with her, she must not leave him. [14]For the Christian wife brings holiness to her marriage, and the Christian husband brings holiness to his marriage. Otherwise, your children would not have a godly influence, but now they are set apart for him. [15](But if the husband or wife who isn't a Christian insists on leaving, let them go. In such cases the Christian husband or wife is not required to stay with them, for God wants his children to live in peace.) [16]You wives must remember that your husbands might be converted because of you. And you husbands must remember that your wives might be converted because of you.

[17]You must accept whatever situation the Lord has put you in, and continue on as you were when God first called you. This is my rule for all the churches. [18]For instance, a man who was circumcised before he

**COUPLES ● ● • • •**

7:9 **Sexual pressure is not the best motive for getting married, but it is better to marry the right person than to burn with lust. Many new believers in Corinth thought that all sex was wrong, so engaged couples were deciding not to get married. In this passage, Paul is telling couples who wanted to marry that they should not deny their normal sexual drives by avoiding marriage. This does not mean, however, that people who have trouble controlling their thoughts should marry the first person who comes along. It is better to deal with the pressure of desire than to deal with an unhappy marriage.**

6:16 Gen 2:24. 7:10 See Matt 5:32; 19:9; Mark 10:11-12; Luke 16:18. 7:12 Greek *a brother.*

became a believer should not try to reverse it. And
the man who was uncircumcised when he became a
believer should not be circumcised now. 19For it
makes no difference whether or not a man has been
circumcised. The important thing is to keep God's
commandments.
20You should continue on as you were when God
called you. 21Are you a slave? Don't let that worry
you—but if you get a chance to be free, take it. 22And
remember, if you were a slave when the Lord called
you, the Lord has now set you free from the awful
power of sin. And if you were free when the Lord
called you, you are now a slave of Christ. 23God
purchased you at a high price. Don't be enslaved by
the world.* 24So, dear brothers and sisters,* whatever situation you were in when you became a believer, stay there in your new relationship with God.
25Now, about the young women who are not yet
married. I do not have a command from the Lord for
them. But the Lord in his kindness has given me
wisdom that can be trusted, and I will share it with
you. 26Because of the present crisis,* I think it is best
to remain just as you are. 27If you have a wife, do not
end the marriage. If you do not have a wife, do not
get married. 28But if you do get married, it is not a sin.
And if a young woman gets married, it is not a sin.
However, I am trying to spare you the extra problems
that come with marriage.
29Now let me say this, dear brothers and sisters: The
time that remains is very short, so husbands should
not let marriage be their major concern. 30Happiness
or sadness or wealth should not keep anyone from
doing God's work. 31Those in frequent contact with the
things of the world should make good use of them
without becoming attached to them, for this world
and all it contains will pass away. 32In everything you
do, I want you to be free from the concerns of this life.
An unmarried man can spend his time doing the
Lord's work and thinking how to please him. 33But a
married man can't do that so well. He has to think
about his earthly responsibilities and how to please his
wife. 34His interests are divided. In the same way, a
woman who is no longer married or has never been
married can be more devoted to the Lord in body and
in spirit, while the married woman must be concerned
about her earthly responsibilities and how to please
her husband.
35I am saying this for your benefit, not to place
restrictions on you. I want you to do whatever will
help you serve the Lord best, with as few distractions
as possible. 36But if a man thinks he ought to marry
his fiancée because he has trouble controlling his
passions and time is passing, it is all right; it is not a
sin. Let them marry. 37But if he has decided firmly
not to marry and there is no urgency and he can
control his passion, he does well not to marry. 38So
the person who marries does well, and the person
who doesn't marry does even better.
39A wife is married to her husband as long as he

## RIGHT HERE ● ● • • •

7:20 **Often we are so concerned about what we *could* be doing for God somewhere else that we miss great opportunities right where we are. Paul says that when someone becomes a Christian, he should usually continue with the work he previously has been doing—provided it isn't immoral or unethical. Every job can become Christian work when you realize that the purpose of your life is to honor, serve, and speak out for Christ. Because God has placed you where you are, look carefully for opportunities to serve him there.**

lives. If her husband dies, she is free to marry whomever she wishes, but this must be a marriage acceptable
to the Lord.* 40But in my opinion it will be better for
her if she doesn't marry again, and I think I am giving
you counsel from God's Spirit when I say this.

CHAPTER **8** **FOOD OFFERED TO IDOLS.** Now let's talk
about food that has been sacrificed to idols. You
think that everyone should agree with your perfect
knowledge. While knowledge may make us feel important, it is love that really builds up the church.
2Anyone who claims to know all the answers doesn't
really know very much. 3But the person who loves
God is the one God knows and cares for.
4So now, what about it? Should we eat meat that
has been sacrificed to idols? Well, we all know that
an idol is not really a god and that there is only one
God and no other. 5According to some people, there
are many so-called gods and many lords, both in
heaven and on earth. 6But we know that there is only
one God, the Father, who created everything, and we
exist for him. And there is only one Lord, Jesus
Christ, through whom God made everything and
through whom we have been given life.
7However, not all Christians realize this. Some are
accustomed to thinking of idols as being real, so
when they eat food that has been offered to idols,
they think of it as the worship of real gods, and their
weak consciences are violated. 8It's true that we can't
win God's approval by what we eat. We don't miss
out on anything if we don't eat it, and we don't gain

## NO PROBLEMS? ● ● • • •

7:28 **Many people think that finding the right boyfriend or girlfriend, and especially getting married, will solve all their problems. It does feel good to have someone special, someone who cares for you and whom you care for. But no relationship, even marriage, is a "cure for whatever ails you"! For example, here are a few of the problems even marriage won't solve: (1) loneliness, (2) sexual temptation, (3) satisfaction of one's deepest emotional needs, (4) elimination of life's difficulties. Marriage alone does not hold two people together, but commitment does—commitment to Christ and to each other despite conflicts and problems. Marriage can be great, but it isn't the solution to problems. There is only one reliable solution for anyone: trusting in Christ! Focus on Christ, not humans, to solve your problems.**

7:23 Greek *don't become slaves of people.* 7:24 Greek *brothers;* also in 7:29. 7:26 Or *pressures of life.* 7:39 Or *but only to a Christian;* Greek reads *but only in the Lord.*

. . . will it help my witness for Christ? (9:19-22)

. . . am I motivated by a desire to help others to know Christ? (9:23; 10:33)

. . . will it help me do my best? (9:25)

**MAKING CHOICES IN SENSITIVE ISSUES**

All of us make hundreds of choices every day. Most choices have no right or wrong attached to them—like what to wear or what to eat. But we always face decisions that carry a little more weight. We don't want to do wrong, and we don't want to cause others to do wrong. So how can we make right decisions?

*If I choose one course of action . . .*

. . . will it encourage someone else to sin? (10:32)

. . . is it against a specific command in Scripture and thus will cause me to sin? (10:12)

. . . will it glorify God? (10:31)

. . . will it be best and helpful? (10:23,33)

. . . will I be acting lovingly or selfishly? (10:28-31)

. . . will I be thinking only of myself, or do I truly care about the other person? (10:24)

anything if we do. [9]But you must be careful with this
freedom of yours. Do not cause a brother or sister
with a weaker conscience to stumble.
[10]You see, this is what can happen: Weak Christians who think it is wrong to eat this food will see
you eating in the temple of an idol. You know there's
nothing wrong with it, but they will be encouraged
to violate their conscience by eating food that has
been dedicated to the idol. [11]So because of your
superior knowledge, a weak Christian,* for whom
Christ died, will be destroyed. [12]And you are sinning
against Christ when you sin against other Christians* by encouraging them to do something they
believe is wrong. [13]If what I eat is going to make
another Christian sin, I will never eat meat again as
long as I live—for I don't want to make another
Christian stumble.

CHAPTER **9** **THE RIGHT OF AN APOSTLE.** Do I not have
as much freedom as anyone else?* Am I not an
apostle? Haven't I seen Jesus our Lord with my own
eyes? Isn't it because of my hard work that you are in
the Lord? [2]Even if others think I am not an apostle, I
certainly am to you, for you are living proof that I am
the Lord's apostle.
[3]This is my answer to those who question my
authority as an apostle.* [4]Don't we have the right to
live in your homes and share your meals? [5]Don't we
have the right to bring a Christian wife* along with
us as the other disciples and the Lord's brothers and
Peter* do? [6]Or is it only Barnabas and I who have to
work to support ourselves? [7]What soldier has to pay
his own expenses? And have you ever heard of a
farmer who harvests his crop and doesn't have the
right to eat some of it? What shepherd takes care of
a flock of sheep and isn't allowed to drink some of
the milk? [8]And this isn't merely human opinion.
Doesn't God's law say the same thing? [9]For the law
of Moses says, "Do not keep an ox from eating as it
treads out the grain."* Do you suppose God was
thinking only about oxen when he said this?
[10]Wasn't he also speaking to us? Of course he was.
Just as farm workers who plow fields and thresh the

**FREEDOM ● ● • • •**

**8:10-13 Christian freedom does not mean "anything goes." It means that our salvation is not determined by legalism, good works, or rules, but by the free gift of God (Ephesians 2:8-9). Christian freedom is tied to Christian responsibility. New believers are sensitive to what is right or wrong. Some actions may be perfectly all right for us to do, but may harm a Christian brother or sister who is still young in the faith. We must be careful not to offend a sensitive or younger Christian or, by our example, to cause him or her to sin.**

8:11 Greek *brother;* also in 8:13. 8:12 Greek *brothers.* 9:1 Greek *Am I not free?* 9:3 Greek *those who examine me.* 9:5a Greek *a sister, a wife.*
9:5b Greek *Cephas.* 9:9 Deut 25:4.

grain expect a share of the harvest, Christian workers
should be paid by those they serve.
11We have planted good spiritual seed among you.
Is it too much to ask, in return, for mere food and
clothing? 12If you support others who preach to you,
shouldn't we have an even greater right to be supported? Yet we have never used this right. We would
rather put up with anything than put an obstacle in
the way of the Good News about Christ.
13Don't you know that those who work in the
Temple get their meals from the food brought to the
Temple as offerings? And those who serve at the altar
get a share of the sacrificial offerings. 14In the same
way, the Lord gave orders that those who preach the
Good News should be supported by those who benefit from it. 15Yet I have never used any of these rights.
And I am not writing this to suggest that I would like
to start now. In fact, I would rather die than lose my
distinction of preaching without charge. 16For
preaching the Good News is not something I can
boast about. I am compelled by God to do it. How
terrible for me if I didn't do it!
17If I were doing this of my own free will, then I
would deserve payment. But God has chosen me and
given me this sacred trust, and I have no choice.
18What then is my pay? It is the satisfaction I get from
preaching the Good News without expense to anyone, never demanding my rights as a preacher.
19This means I am not bound to obey people just
because they pay me, yet I have become a servant of
everyone so that I can bring them to Christ. 20When
I am with the Jews, I become one of them so that I
can bring them to Christ. When I am with those who
follow the Jewish laws, I do the same, even though I
am not subject to the law, so that I can bring them to
Christ. 21When I am with the Gentiles who do not
have the Jewish law,* I fit in with them as much as I
can. In this way, I gain their confidence and bring
them to Christ. But I do not discard the law of God;
I obey the law of Christ.
22When I am with those who are oppressed, I
share their oppression so that I might bring them to
Christ. Yes, I try to find common ground with everyone so that I might bring them to Christ. 23I do all
this to spread the Good News, and in doing so I
enjoy its blessings.
24Remember that in a race everyone runs, but only
one person gets the prize. You also must run in such
a way that you will win. 25All athletes practice strict
self-control. They do it to win a prize that will fade
away, but we do it for an eternal prize. 26So I run
straight to the goal with purpose in every step. I am
not like a boxer who misses his punches.* 27I discipline my body like an athlete, training it to do what
it should. Otherwise, I fear that after preaching to
others I myself might be disqualified.

## CHAPTER 10 LESSONS ABOUT IDOL WORSHIP.

1I
don't want you to forget, dear brothers and sisters,*
what happened to our ancestors in the wilderness
long ago. God guided all of them by sending a
cloud that moved along ahead of them, and he
brought them all safely through the waters of the
sea on dry ground. 2As followers of Moses, they
were all baptized in the cloud and the sea. 3And all
of them ate the same miraculous* food, 4and all of
them drank the same miraculous water. For they all
drank from the miraculous rock that traveled with
them, and that rock was Christ. 5Yet after all this,
God was not pleased with most of them, and he
destroyed them in the wilderness.
6These events happened as a warning to us, so
that we would not crave evil things as they did 7or
worship idols as some of them did. For the
Scriptures say, "The people celebrated with feasting and drinking, and they indulged themselves in
pagan revelry."* 8And we must not engage in sexual immorality as some of them did, causing
23,000 of them to die in one day. 9Nor should we

The temptations that come into your life ***are no different*** **from what others experience.**

**And God *is* faithful.**

***He will keep the temptation*** **from becoming so strong that** you can't stand up against it.

**When you are tempted, *he will show you a way out*** so that you will not give in to it.

1 CORINTHIANS 10:13

9:21 Greek *those without the law.* 9:26 Or *I am not just shadowboxing.* 10:1 Greek *brothers.* 10:3 Greek *spiritual;* also in 10:4. 10:7 Exod 32:6.

## TEMPTATION • • • • •

**10:13 In a culture filled with moral depravity and pressures, Paul gave strong encouragement to the Corinthians about temptation. He said: (1) wrong desires and temptations happen to everyone, so don't feel you've been singled out; (2) others have resisted temptation, and so can you; (3) any temptation can be resisted because God will help you resist it. God helps you resist temptation by helping you recognize people and situations that give you trouble. Run from anything you know is wrong, choose to do only what is right, pray for God's help, and seek friends who love God and can offer help in times of temptation. Running from a tempting situation is the first step to victory (see 2 Timothy 2:22).**

put Christ* to the test, as some of them did and then died from snakebites. 10 And don't grumble as some of them did, for that is why God sent his angel of death to destroy them. 11 All these events happened to them as examples for us. They were written down to warn us, who live at the time when this age is drawing to a close.

12 If you think you are standing strong, be careful, for you, too, may fall into the same sin. 13 But remember that the temptations that come into your life are no different from what others experience. And God is faithful. He will keep the temptation from becoming so strong that you can't stand up against it. When you are tempted, he will show you a way out so that you will not give in to it.

14 So, my dear friends, flee from the worship of idols. 15 You are reasonable people. Decide for yourselves if what I am about to say is true. 16 When we bless the cup at the Lord's Table, aren't we sharing in the benefits of the blood of Christ? And when we break the loaf of bread, aren't we sharing in the benefits of the body of Christ? 17 And we all eat from one loaf, showing that we are one body. 18 And think about the nation of Israel; all who eat the sacrifices are united by that act.

19 What am I trying to say? Am I saying that the idols to whom the pagans bring sacrifices are real gods and that these sacrifices are of some value? 20 No, not at all. What I am saying is that these sacrifices are offered to demons, not to God. And I don't want any of you to be partners with demons. 21 You cannot drink from the cup of the Lord and from the cup of demons, too. You cannot eat at the Lord's Table and at the table of demons, too. 22 What? Do you dare to rouse the Lord's jealousy as Israel did? Do you think we are stronger than he is?

23 You say, "I am allowed to do anything"—but not everything is helpful. You say, "I am allowed to do anything"—but not everything is beneficial. 24 Don't think only of your own good. Think of other Christians and what is best for them.

25 Here's what you should do. You may eat any meat that is sold in the marketplace. Don't ask whether or not it was offered to idols, and then your conscience won't be bothered. 26 For "the earth is the Lord's, and everything in it."*

27 If someone who isn't a Christian asks you home for dinner, go ahead; accept the invitation if you want to. Eat whatever is offered to you and don't ask any questions about it. Your conscience should not be bothered by this. 28 But suppose someone warns you that this meat has been offered to an idol. Don't eat it, out of consideration for the conscience of the one who told you. 29 It might not be a matter of conscience for you, but it is for the other person.

Now, why should my freedom be limited by what someone else thinks? 30 If I can thank God for the food and enjoy it, why should I be condemned for eating it? 31 Whatever you eat or drink or whatever you do, you must do all for the glory of God. 32 Don't give offense to Jews or Gentiles or the church of God. 33 That is the plan I follow, too. I try to please everyone in everything I do. I don't just do what I like or what is best for me, but what is best for them so they may be saved.

## CHAPTER 11

**HONOR AND RESPECT IN WORSHIP.** And you should follow my example, just as I follow Christ's.

2 I am so glad, dear friends, that you always keep me in your thoughts and you are following the Christian teaching I passed on to you. 3 But there is one thing I want you to know: A man is responsible to Christ, a woman is responsible to her husband, and Christ is responsible to God. 4 A man dishonors Christ* if he covers his head while praying or prophesying. 5 But a woman dishonors her husband* if she prays or prophesies without a covering on her head, for this is the same as shaving her head. 6 Yes, if she refuses to wear a head covering, she should cut off all her hair. And since it is shameful for a woman to have her hair cut or her head shaved, then she should wear a covering.* 7 A man should not wear anything on his head when worshiping, for man is God's glory, made in God's own image, but woman is the glory of man. 8 For the first man didn't come from woman, but the first woman came from man. 9 And man was not made for woman's benefit, but woman was made for man. 10 So a woman should wear a covering on her head as a sign of authority because the angels are watching.

## THE BEST • • • • •

**10:33 Paul's criterion was not what he liked best, but what was best for those around him. There are several hurtful attitudes toward others: (1) being insensitive and doing what we want, no matter who is hurt by our actions; (2) being oversensitive and doing nothing, for fear that someone may be displeased; (3) being a "yes person" by going along with everything, trying to gain approval from people rather than from God. In this age of "me first" and "looking out for number one," Paul's startling statement is a good standard. When we make the good of others one of our primary goals, we develop a servant's heart.**

10:9 Some manuscripts read *the Lord.* 10:26 Ps 24:1. 11:4 Greek *his head.* 11:5 Greek *her head.* 11:6 Or *then she should have long hair.*

11But in relationships among the Lord's people,
women are not independent of men, and men are not
independent of women. 12For although the first
woman came from man, all men have been born from
women ever since, and everything comes from God.
13What do you think about this? Is it right for a
woman to pray to God in public without covering
her head? 14Isn't it obvious that it's disgraceful for a
man to have long hair? 15And isn't it obvious that
long hair is a woman's pride and joy? For it has been
given to her as a covering. 16But if anyone wants to
argue about this, all I can say is that we have no other
custom than this, and all the churches of God feel
the same way about it.

17But now when I mention this next issue, I
cannot praise you. For it sounds as if more harm
than good is done when you meet together. 18First
of all, I hear that there are divisions among you
when you meet as a church, and to some extent I
believe it. 19But, of course, there must be divisions
among you so that those of you who are right will
be recognized!

20It's not the Lord's Supper you are concerned
about when you come together. 21For I am told that
some of you hurry to eat your own meal without
sharing with others. As a result, some go hungry
while others get drunk. 22What? Is this really true?
Don't you have your own homes for eating and
drinking? Or do you really want to disgrace the
church of God and shame the poor? What am I
supposed to say about these things? Do you want
me to praise you? Well, I certainly do not!

23For this is what the Lord himself said, and I pass it on to you just
as I received it. On the night when
he was betrayed, the Lord Jesus
took a loaf of bread, 24and when he
had given thanks, he broke it and
said, "This is my body, which is
given* for you. Do this in remembrance of me." 25In the same way,
he took the cup of wine after supper, saying, "This cup is the new
covenant between God and you,
sealed by the shedding of my
blood. Do this in remembrance of
me as often as you drink it." 26For
every time you eat this bread and
drink this cup, you are announcing
the Lord's death until he comes
again.

27So if anyone eats this bread or
drinks this cup of the Lord unworthily, that person is guilty of sinning against the body and the
blood of the Lord. 28That is why
you should examine yourself before eating the bread and drinking
from the cup. 29For if you eat the
bread or drink the cup unworthily,
not honoring the body of Christ,* you are eating and
drinking God's judgment upon yourself. 30That is
why many of you are weak and sick and some have
even died.

31But if we examine ourselves, we will not be examined by God and judged in this way. 32But when
we are judged and disciplined by the Lord, we will
not be condemned with the world. 33So, dear brothers and sisters,* when you gather for the Lord's
Supper, wait for each other. 34If you are really hungry,
eat at home so you won't bring judgment upon
yourselves when you meet together.

I'll give you instructions about the other matters
after I arrive.

## EQUALS ● ● • • •

**11:3 Submission is a key element in the smooth functioning of any business, government, or family. God ordained submission in certain relationships to prevent chaos. We must understand, however, that submission is not surrender, withdrawal, or apathy. Nor does it mean inferiority. God created all people in his image; all have equal value. Submission is mutual commitment and cooperation.**

**Thus God calls for submission among *equals*. He did not make the man superior; he made a way for the man and woman to work together. Jesus Christ, although equal with God the Father, submitted to him to carry out the plan for salvation. Likewise, although equal to man under God, the wife should submit to her husband for the sake of their marriage and family. Submission between equals is submission by choice, not force. We serve God in these relationships through willing submission to others in our church, to our spouse, and to our government leaders.**

## "Here's what I did..."

For many years I had a problem with gossiping. I knew it was wrong, but I kept giving in to temptation. I prayed about it a lot. Then the Lord gave me two Scriptures that have helped me begin to conquer it.

The first is 1 Corinthians 10:13. That verse says that God will always provide a way to escape temptation's power. So I reminded myself of this whenever the temptation to pass on some juicy bit of news came my way. It helped some, but I still gave in more often than I wanted to.

Then God gave me something that's helped me even more. It's Psalm 141:3: "Take control of what I say, O LORD, and keep my lips sealed." That's exactly the prayer I started praying whenever I was tempted to gossip. This prayer-verse became my way to escape the temptation; whenever I take the time to pray it, I find I can keep my mouth shut. But I have to take a moment to refocus my thoughts on the prayer rather than on the temptation to say something, or I find myself giving in to temptation.

This experience has shown me just how practical the Bible can be. With God's power I can conquer anything!

Brooke

AGE 18

11:24 Some manuscripts read *broken*. 11:29 Greek *the body;* some manuscripts read *the Lord's body*. 11:33 Greek *brothers*.

## CHAPTER 12

**EVERYONE HAS SPECIAL ABILITIES.** And now, dear brothers and sisters,* I will write about the special abilities the Holy Spirit gives to each of us, for I must correct your misunderstandings about them. [2]You know that when you were still pagans you were led astray and swept along in worshiping speechless idols. [3]So I want you to know how to discern what is truly from God: No one speaking by the Spirit of God can curse Jesus, and no one is able to say, "Jesus is Lord," except by the Holy Spirit.

### TEST THEM ● • • •

**12:3 Anyone can claim to speak for God, and the world is full of false teachers. Paul gives us a test to help us discern whether or not a messenger is really from God: does he or she confess Christ as Lord? Don't naively accept the words of all who claim to speak for God. Test their credentials by finding what they teach about Christ.**

[4]Now there are different kinds of spiritual gifts, but it is the same Holy Spirit who is the source of them all. [5]There are different kinds of service in the church, but it is the same Lord we are serving. [6]There are different ways God works in our lives, but it is the same God who does the work through all of us. [7]A spiritual gift is given to each of us as a means of helping the entire church.

[8]To one person the Spirit gives the ability to give wise advice; to another he gives the gift of special knowledge. [9]The Spirit gives special faith to another, and to someone else he gives the power to heal the sick. [10]He gives one person the power to perform miracles, and to another the ability to prophesy. He gives someone else the ability to know whether it is really the Spirit of God or another spirit that is speaking. Still another person is given the ability to speak in unknown languages,* and another is given the ability to interpret what is being said. [11]It is the one and only Holy Spirit who distributes these gifts. He alone decides which gift each person should have.

[12]The human body has many parts, but the many parts make up only one body. So it is with the body of Christ. [13]Some of us are Jews, some are Gentiles, some are slaves, and some are free. But we have all been baptized into Christ's body by one Spirit, and we have all received the same Spirit.*

[14]Yes, the body has many different parts, not just one part. [15]If the foot says, "I am not a part of the body because I am not a hand," that does not make it any less a part of the body. [16]And if the ear says, "I am not part of the body because I am only an ear and not an eye," would that make it any less a part of the body? [17]Suppose the whole body were an eye—then how would you hear? Or if your whole body were just one big ear, how could you smell anything?

[18]But God made our bodies with many parts, and he has put each part just where he wants it. [19]What a strange thing a body would be if it had only one part! [20]Yes, there are many parts, but only one body.

### BODY LIFE ● • • •

**12:14-17 Using the analogy of the body, Paul emphasizes the importance of each church member. If a seemingly insignificant part is taken away, the whole body becomes less effective (12:22). Thinking that your gift is more important than someone else's is spiritual pride. We should not look down on those who seem unimportant, and we should not be jealous of others who have impressive gifts. Instead, we must use the gifts we have been given and encourage others to use theirs. If we don't, the body of believers will be less effective.**

[21]The eye can never say to the hand, "I don't need you." The head can't say to the feet, "I don't need you."

[22]In fact, some of the parts that seem weakest and least important are really the most necessary. [23]And the parts we regard as less honorable are those we clothe with the greatest care. So we carefully protect from the eyes of others those parts that should not be seen, [24]while other parts do not require this special care. So God has put the body together in such a way that extra honor and care are given to those parts that have less dignity. [25]This makes for harmony among the members, so that all the members care for each other equally. [26]If one part suffers, all the parts suffer with it, and if one part is honored, all the parts are glad.

[27]Now all of you together are Christ's body, and each one of you is a separate and necessary part of it. [28]Here is a list of some of the members that God has placed in the body of Christ:

first are apostles,
second are prophets,
third are teachers,
then those who do miracles,
those who have the gift of healing,
those who can help others,
those who can get others to work together,
those who speak in unknown languages.

[29]Is everyone an apostle? Of course not. Is everyone a prophet? No. Are all teachers? Does everyone have the power to do miracles? [30]Does everyone have the gift of healing? Of course not. Does God give all of us the ability to speak in unknown languages? Can everyone interpret unknown languages? No! [31]And in any event, you should desire the most helpful gifts.

First, however, let me tell you about something else that is better than any of them!

## CHAPTER 13

**WHAT IS LOVE?** If I could speak in any language in heaven or on earth* but didn't love others, I would only be making meaningless noise like a loud gong or a clanging cymbal. [2]If I had the gift of prophecy, and if I knew all the mysteries of the future and knew everything about everything, but didn't love others, what good would I be? And if I had the gift of faith so that I could speak to a

12:1 Greek *brothers.* 12:10 Or *in tongues;* also in 12:28, 30. 12:13 Greek *we were all given one Spirit to drink.* 13:1 Greek *in tongues of people and angels.*

mountain and make it move, without love I would
be no good to anybody. 3If I gave everything I have
to the poor and even sacrificed my body, I could
boast about it;* but if I didn't love others, I would be
of no value whatsoever.

4Love is patient and kind. Love is not jealous or
boastful or proud 5or rude. Love does not demand its
own way. Love is not irritable, and it keeps no record
of when it has been wronged. 6It is never glad about
injustice but rejoices whenever the truth wins out.
7Love never gives up, never loses faith, is always
hopeful, and endures through every circumstance.

8Love will last forever, but prophecy and speaking
in unknown languages* and special knowledge will
all disappear. 9Now we know only a little, and even
the gift of prophecy reveals little! 10But when the end
comes, these special gifts will all disappear.

11It's like this: When I was a child, I spoke and
thought and reasoned as a child does. But when I grew
up, I put away childish things. 12Now we see things
imperfectly as in a poor mirror, but then we will see
everything with perfect clarity.* All that I know now is
partial and incomplete, but then I will know everything completely, just as God knows me now.

13There are three things that will endure—faith,
hope, and love—and the greatest of these is love.

CHAPTER **14** **TONGUES AND PROPHECY.** Let love be
your highest goal, but also desire the special abilities
the Spirit gives, especially the gift of prophecy. 2For if
your gift is the ability to speak in tongues,* you will
be talking to God but not to people, since they won't
be able to understand you. You will be speaking by
the power of the Spirit, but it will all be mysterious.
3But one who prophesies is helping others grow in
the Lord, encouraging and com-
forting them. 4A person who
speaks in tongues is strengthened
personally in the Lord, but one
who speaks a word of prophecy
strengthens the entire church.

5I wish you all had the gift of
speaking in tongues, but even
more I wish you were all able to
prophesy. For prophecy is a greater
and more useful gift than speaking
in tongues, unless someone inter-
prets what you are saying so that
the whole church can get some
good out of it.

6Dear brothers and sisters,* if I
should come to you talking in an
unknown language,* how would
that help you? But if I bring you
some revelation or some special
knowledge or some prophecy or
some teaching—that is what will
help you. 7Even musical instru-

**LOVE ● ● • • •**

13:4-7 **Our society confuses love and lust. Unlike lust, God's kind of love is directed outward toward others, not inward toward ourself. It is utterly unselfish.**

ments like the flute or the harp, though they are
lifeless, are examples of the need for speaking in plain
language. For no one will recognize the melody unless
the notes are played clearly. 8And if the bugler doesn't
sound a clear call, how will the soldiers know they are
being called to battle? 9And it's the same for you. If you
talk to people in a language they don't understand,
how will they know what you mean? You might as well
be talking to an empty room.

10There are so many different languages in the
world, and all are excellent for those who understand them, 11but to me they mean nothing. I will
not understand people who speak those languages,
and they will not understand me. 12Since you are so
eager to have spiritual gifts, ask God for those that
will be of real help to the whole church.

13So anyone who has the gift of speaking in
tongues should pray also for the gift of interpretation
in order to tell people plainly what has been said.
14For if I pray in tongues, my spirit is praying, but I
don't understand what I am saying.

15Well then, what shall I do? I will do both. I will
pray in the spirit,* and I will pray in words I understand. I will sing in the spirit, and I will sing in words
I understand. 16For if you praise God only in the
spirit, how can those who don't understand you
praise God along with you? How can they join you
in giving thanks when they don't understand what
you are saying? 17You will be giving thanks very

**"Here's what I did..."**

After a bad dating experience, I decided to find out what God wanted a dating relationship to be. I talked to my youth pastor and studied Scripture. This time, when I felt ready to date again, I made sure I went out with a Christian.

Jenny and I talked about God's will right from the beginning and adopted 1 Corinthians 13 as the basis for our relationship. Even though the romance didn't last forever, it was a very positive experience. We both tried to let verses 4-7 guide all our thoughts and actions toward each other, even when we broke up. I learned a lot from that. God's way really is so much better than any other way of running your life—or of having a relationship.

Sam

AGE 16

13:3 Some manuscripts read *and even gave my body to be burned.* 13:8 Or *in tongues.* 13:12 Greek *see face to face.* 14:2 Or *in unknown languages;* also in 14:4, 5, 13, 14, 18, 22, 28, 39. 14:6a Greek *brothers;* also in 14:20, 26, 39. 14:6b Or *in tongues;* also in 14:19, 23, 26, 27. 14:15 Or *in the Spirit;* also in 14:15b, 16.

nicely, no doubt, but it doesn't help the other people
present.
18 I thank God that I speak in tongues more than
all of you. 19 But in a church meeting I would much
rather speak five understandable words that will
help others than ten thousand words in an unknown
language.
20 Dear brothers and sisters, don't be childish in
your understanding of these things. Be innocent as
babies when it comes to evil, but be mature and wise
in understanding matters of this kind. 21 It is written
in the Scriptures,*

"I will speak to my own people
through unknown languages
and through the lips of foreigners.
But even then, they will not listen to me,"*
says the Lord.

22 So you see that speaking in tongues is a sign, not
for believers, but for unbelievers; prophecy, however,
is for the benefit of believers, not unbelievers. 23 Even
so, if unbelievers or people who don't understand
these things come into your meeting and hear everyone talking in an unknown language, they will think
you are crazy. 24 But if all of you are prophesying, and
unbelievers or people who don't understand these
things come into your meeting, they will be convicted of sin, and they will be condemned by what
you say. 25 As they listen, their secret thoughts will be
laid bare, and they will fall down on their knees and
worship God, declaring, "God is really here among
you."

**REAL WORSHIP ● ● • • •**

14:26 **Everything done in worship services must be beneficial to the worshipers. This principle touches every aspect–singing, preaching, and the exercise of spiritual gifts. Those contributing to the service (singers, speakers, readers) must have love as their chief motivation, giving useful words or help that will strengthen the faith of other believers.**

26 Well, my brothers and sisters, let's summarize
what I am saying. When you meet, one will sing,
another will teach, another will tell some special
revelation God has given, one will speak in an unknown language, while another will interpret what is
said. But everything that is done must be useful to all
and build them up in the Lord. 27 No more than two
or three should speak in an unknown language. They
must speak one at a time, and someone must be
ready to interpret what they are saying. 28 But if no
one is present who can interpret, they must be silent
in your church meeting and speak in tongues to God
privately.
29 Let two or three prophesy, and let the others
evaluate what is said. 30 But if someone is prophesying and another person receives a revelation from
the Lord, the one who is speaking must stop. 31 In this
way, all who prophesy will have a turn to speak, one
after the other, so that everyone will learn and be
encouraged. 32 Remember that people who prophesy
are in control of their spirit and can wait their turn.
33 For God is not a God of disorder but of peace, as in
all the other churches.*
34 Women should be silent during the church
meetings. It is not proper for them to speak. They
should be submissive, just as the law says. 35 If they
have any questions to ask, let them ask their husbands at home, for it is improper for women to
speak in church meetings.*
36 Do you think that the knowledge of God's word
begins and ends with you Corinthians? Well, you are
mistaken! 37 If you claim to be a prophet or think you
are very spiritual, you should recognize that what I
am saying is a command from the Lord himself.
38 But if you do not recognize this, you will not be
recognized.*
39 So, dear brothers and sisters, be eager to prophesy, and don't forbid speaking in tongues. 40 But be
sure that everything is done properly and in order.

## CHAPTER 15 **CHRIST ROSE FROM THE DEAD.** Now let
me remind you, dear brothers and sisters,* of the
Good News I preached to you before. You welcomed
it then and still do now, for your faith is built on this
wonderful message. 2 And it is this Good News that
saves you if you firmly believe it—unless, of course,
you believed something that was never true in the
first place.
3 I passed on to you what was most important and
what had also been passed on to me—that Christ
died for our sins, just as the Scriptures said. 4 He was
buried, and he was raised from the dead on the third
day, as the Scriptures said. 5 He was seen by Peter*
and then by the twelve apostles. 6 After that, he was
seen by more than five hundred of his followers* at
one time, most of whom are still alive, though some
have died by now. 7 Then he was seen by James and
later by all the apostles. 8 Last of all, I saw him, too,
long after the others, as though I had been born at
the wrong time. 9 For I am the least of all the apostles,
and I am not worthy to be called an apostle after the
way I persecuted the church of God.
10 But whatever I am now, it is all because God
poured out his special favor on me—and not without results. For I have worked harder than all the
other apostles, yet it was not I but God who was
working through me by his grace. 11 So it makes no
difference whether I preach or they preach. The important thing is that you believed what we preached
to you.
12 But tell me this—since we preach that Christ
rose from the dead, why are some of you saying there
will be no resurrection of the dead? 13 For if there is
no resurrection of the dead, then Christ has not been
raised either. 14 And if Christ was not raised, then all

**14:21a** Greek *in the law.* **14:21b** Isa 28:11-12. **14:33** The phrase *as in all the other churches* could be joined to the beginning of 14:34. **14:35** Some manuscripts place verses 34-35 after 14:40. **14:38** Some manuscripts read *If you are ignorant of this, stay in your ignorance.* **15:1** Greek *brothers;* also in 15:31, 50, 58. **15:5** Greek *Cephas.* **15:6** Greek *the brothers.*

our preaching is useless, and your trust in God is
useless. 15And we apostles would all be lying about
God, for we have said that God raised Christ from
the grave, but that can't be true if there is no resurrection of the dead. 16If there is no resurrection of the
dead, then Christ has not been raised. 17And if Christ
has not been raised, then your faith is useless, and
you are still under condemnation for your sins. 18In
that case, all who have died believing in Christ have
perished! 19And if we have hope in Christ only for
this life, we are the most miserable people in the
world.

20But the fact is that Christ has been raised from
the dead. He has become the first of a great harvest
of those who will be raised to life again.

21So you see, just as death came into the world
through a man, Adam, now the resurrection from
the dead has begun through another man, Christ.
22Everyone dies because all of us are related to Adam,
the first man. But all who are related to Christ, the
other man, will be given new life. 23But there is an
order to this resurrection: Christ was raised first; then
when Christ comes back, all his people will be
raised.

24After that the end will come, when he will turn
the Kingdom over to God the Father, having put
down all enemies of every kind.* 25For Christ must
reign until he humbles all his enemies beneath his
feet. 26And the last enemy to be destroyed is death.
27For the Scriptures say, "God has given him authority over all things."* (Of course, when it says "authority over all things," it does not include God
himself, who gave Christ his authority.) 28Then,
when he has conquered all things, the Son will
present himself to God, so that God, who gave his
Son authority over all things, will be utterly supreme
over everything everywhere.

29If the dead will not be raised, then what point is
there in people being baptized for those who are
dead? Why do it unless the dead will someday rise
again?

30And why should we ourselves be continually
risking our lives, facing death hour by hour? 31For I
swear, dear brothers and sisters, I face death daily.
This is as certain as my pride in what the Lord Jesus
Christ has done in you. 32And what value was there
in fighting wild beasts—those men of Ephesus*—if
there will be no resurrection from the dead? If there
is no resurrection,

"Let's feast and get drunk,
for tomorrow we die!"*

33Don't be fooled by those who say such things, for
"bad company corrupts good character." 34Come to
your senses and stop sinning. For to your shame I say
that some of you don't even know God.

35But someone may ask, "How will the dead be
raised? What kind of bodies will they have?" 36What
a foolish question! When you put a seed into the
ground, it doesn't grow into a plant unless it dies
first. 37And what you put in the ground is not the
plant that will grow, but only a dry little seed of
wheat or whatever it is you are planting. 38Then God
gives it a new body—just the kind he wants it to
have. A different kind of plant grows from each kind
of seed. 39And just as there are different kinds of
seeds and plants, so also there are different kinds of
flesh—whether of humans, animals, birds, or fish.

40There are bodies in the heavens, and there are
bodies on earth. The glory of the heavenly bodies is
different from the beauty of the earthly bodies. 41The
sun has one kind of glory, while the moon and stars
each have another kind. And even the stars differ
from each other in their beauty and brightness.

42It is the same way for the resurrection of the
dead. Our earthly bodies, which die and decay, will
be different when they are resurrected, for they will
never die. 43Our bodies now disappoint us, but when
they are raised, they will be full of glory. They are
weak now, but when they are raised, they will be full
of power. 44They are natural human bodies now, but
when they are raised, they will be spiritual bodies.
For just as there are natural bodies, so also there are
spiritual bodies.

45The Scriptures tell us, "The first man, Adam,
became a living person."* But the last Adam—that
is, Christ—is a life-giving Spirit. 46What came first
was the natural body, then the spiritual body comes
later. 47Adam, the first man, was made from the dust
of the earth, while Christ, the second man, came
from heaven. 48Every human being has an earthly
body just like Adam's, but our heavenly bodies will
be just like Christ's. 49Just as we are now like Adam,
the man of the earth, so we will someday be like
Christ, the man from heaven.

50What I am saying, dear brothers and sisters, is
that flesh and blood cannot inherit the Kingdom of
God. These perishable bodies of ours are not able to
live forever.

51But let me tell you a wonderful secret God has
revealed to us. Not all of us will die, but we will all
be transformed. 52It will happen in a moment, in the
blinking of an eye, when the last trumpet is blown.
For when the trumpet sounds, the Christians who
have died* will be raised with transformed bodies.
And then we who are living will be transformed so
that we will never die. 53For our perishable earthly

**PROOF ● • • • •**

15:5-8 **There will always be people who will say that Jesus didn't rise from the dead. Paul assures us that many people saw Jesus after his resurrection, including more than 500 Christian believers. The Resurrection is a historical fact. Don't be discouraged by doubters who deny the Resurrection. Be filled with hope by the knowledge that one day you, and they, will stand before the living proof when Christ returns.**

15:24 Greek *every ruler and every authority and power.* 15:27 Ps 8:6. 15:32a Greek *fighting wild beasts in Ephesus.* 15:32b Isa 22:13. 15:45 Gen 2:7. 15:52 Greek *the dead.*

## RESULTS ● ● ● ● •

15:58 **Paul said that because of the Resurrection, nothing we do is useless. Sometimes we hesitate to do good because we don't see any results. But if we can maintain a heavenly perspective, we will understand that we don't often see the good that results from our efforts. Truly believing that Christ has won the ultimate victory will affect the way we live right now. Don't let discouragement over an apparent lack of results keep you from working. Do the good that you have opportunity to do, knowing that your work will have eternal results.**

bodies must be transformed into heavenly bodies
that will never die.
54When this happens—when our perishable
earthly bodies have been transformed into heavenly
bodies that will never die—then at last the Scriptures
will come true:

"Death is swallowed up in victory.*
55O death, where is your victory?
O death, where is your sting?"*

56For sin is the sting that results in death, and the law
gives sin its power. 57How we thank God, who gives
us victory over sin and death through Jesus Christ
our Lord!
58So, my dear brothers and sisters, be strong and
steady, always enthusiastic about the Lord's work, for
you know that nothing you do for the Lord is ever
useless.

## CHAPTER 16

**GIVING AN OFFERING.** Now about the
money being collected for the Christians in Jerusalem: You should follow the same procedures I gave
to the churches in Galatia. 2On every Lord's Day,*
each of you should put aside some amount of
money in relation to what you have earned and save
it for this offering. Don't wait until I get there and
then try to collect it all at once. 3When I come I will
write letters of recommendation for the messengers
you choose to deliver your gift to Jerusalem. 4And if
it seems appropriate for me also to go along, then we
can travel together.
5I am coming to visit you after I have been to
Macedonia, for I am planning to travel through
Macedonia. 6It could be that I will stay awhile with
you, perhaps all winter, and then you can send me
on my way to the next destination. 7This time I
don't want to make just a short visit and then go
right on. I want to come and stay awhile, if the
Lord will let me. 8In the meantime, I will be staying
here at Ephesus until the Festival of Pentecost, 9for
there is a wide-open door for a great work here,
and many people are responding. But there are
many who oppose me.
10When Timothy comes, treat him with respect.
He is doing the Lord's work, just as I am. 11Don't
let anyone despise him. Send him on his way with
your blessings when he returns to me. I am looking
forward to seeing him soon, along with the other
brothers.
12Now about our brother Apollos—I urged him to
join the other brothers when they visit you, but he
was not willing to come right now. He will be seeing
you later, when the time is right.
13Be on guard. Stand true to what you believe. Be
courageous. Be strong. 14And everything you do must
be done with love.
15You know that Stephanas and his household
were the first to become Christians in Greece,* and
they are spending their lives in service to other
Christians. I urge you, dear brothers and sisters,*
16to respect them fully and others like them who
serve with such real devotion. 17I am so glad that
Stephanas, Fortunatus, and Achaicus have come
here. They have been making up for the help you
weren't here to give me. 18They have been a wonderful encouragement to me, as they have been to
you, too. You must give proper honor to all who
serve so well.
19The churches here in the province of Asia* greet
you heartily in the Lord, along with Aquila and
Priscilla and all the others who gather in their home
for church meetings. 20All the brothers and sisters
here have asked me to greet you for them. Greet each
other in Christian love.*
21Here is my greeting, which I write with my own
hand—PAUL.
22If anyone does not love the Lord, that person is
cursed. Our Lord, come!*
23May the grace of the Lord Jesus be with you.
24My love to all of you in Christ Jesus.*

## GRAND FINALE ● ● ● ● •

16:22 **The Lord Jesus Christ is coming back to earth again. To Paul, this was a glad hope, the best he could look forward to. He was not afraid of seeing Christ—he could hardly wait! Do you share Paul's eager anticipation? Those who love Christ are looking forward to that wonderful time of his return (Titus 2:13).**

15:54 Isa 25:8. 15:55 Hos 13:14. 16:2 Greek *every first day of the week.* 16:15a Greek *were the firstfruits in Achaia,* the southern region of the Greek peninsula. 16:15b Greek *brothers;* also in 16:20. 16:19 *Asia* was a Roman province in what is now western Turkey. 16:20 Greek *with a sacred kiss.* 16:22 From Aramaic, *Marana tha.* 16:24 Some manuscripts add *Amen.*

# MEGA themes

**LOYALTIES** The Corinthians were rallying around various church leaders and teachers—Peter, Paul, and Apollos. These loyalties led to intellectual pride and divided the church.

Our loyalty to human leaders or human wisdom must never divide us into various groups. We must care for our fellow Christians, not fight with them. Your allegiance must be to Christ. Let him lead you.

1. How did Paul feel about the various groups who were giving their allegiance to him or Peter or Apollos?
2. What did Paul want to change about their attitude? Why?
3. Based on this passage, at what point does loyalty become a problem in the church?
4. Who are the key Christian leaders you respect? Describe the attitude you should have toward them.

**IMMORALITY** Paul received a report of uncorrected sexual sin in the church at Corinth. The people had grown indifferent to immorality. Others had misconceptions about marriage. We are to live morally because our body should be ready to serve God.

Christians must never compromise with sinful ideas and practices. You should not become just like those around you, even if everyone seems to disagree with your moral beliefs. You must live up to God's standard of morality and not go along with immoral behavior.

1. What specific immorality does Paul condemn in chapter 5?
2. Why is this type of immorality such an offense to God?
3. Why do you think the Corinthians were tolerating this behavior? How did Paul indicate that they should deal with this ongoing sin? How is this different than the way they should respond to someone who was sinning but was not claiming to be a Christian? (See 5:9-11.)
4. How can you make an impact on your world without allowing the world to influence you?

**FREEDOM** Paul taught freedom of choice on practices not expressly forbidden in Scripture. Some believers thought that certain actions—like buying the meat of animals used in heathen rituals—were wrong. Others believed they could do such things without sinning because they were free from the law.

We are free in Christ, yet we must not abuse our Christian freedom by being inconsiderate and insensitive to others. We must never encourage others to do wrong by anything we do. Love should guide our behavior.

1. In chapter 8, Paul instructs the Corinthians on their freedom in Christ. What key principles do you find in this passage for dealing with areas of conduct that are "grays," not black or white?
2. What are some of the "gray areas" that Christians have different opinions about?
3. How could you as a Christian misuse your freedom in Christ and hurt someone else in these "gray" areas?
4. Identify specific ways that you could apply the principles of chapter 8 to your freedom in Christ.

**WORSHIP** Paul addressed disorder in worship. People were taking the Lord's Supper without first confessing sin. There was misuse of spiritual gifts and confusion over the role of women in the church.

Worship must be carried out properly and orderly. Everything we do to worship God should be done in a manner worthy of his high honor.

1. What concerns did Paul have concerning worship in the Corinthian church? What does this teach you about Paul's view of worship?
2. What actions or attitudes sometimes disrupt true worship in your church?
3. What actions and attitudes encourage true worship in your church?
4. What can you do in your church to help people's worship remain true?

**RESURRECTION** Some people denied that Christ rose from the dead. Others believed that people would not be physically resurrected. Christ's resurrection assures us that we will have a new, living body after we die. The fact of the Resurrection is the secret of Christian hope.

Because we will be raised again to life after we die, our life is not in vain. We must stay faithful to God in how we live and serve. And we should live today knowing that we will spend eternity with Christ. Eternal life has already begun!

1. Read chapter 15. According to Paul, what is the importance of the Resurrection?
2. What misconceptions did some of the Corinthians have regarding the resurrection of the dead? How did Paul correct those wrong ideas?
3. What would be different about life if Jesus had not risen from the dead?
4. How would you respond if asked to describe the difference Christ's resurrection has made in your own life?

**M**inistry . . . or Madness?: A Quiz Just for You.

■ 1. At Bible club, it rains, a kid throws up on you, and one obnoxious six-year-old complains for *90 minutes* about watery punch. Do you: (a) Dump the watery punch on the obnoxious kid? (b) Wipe throw up *and* dump the punch on the obnoxious kid? (c) Retire from your Bible club career? (d) Pray (really hard!) for patience and kindness? ■ 2. Your youth group gives 400 hard-earned dollars to a family whose house just burned down. The family never even acknowledges the gift! Do you: (a) Break out your lecture on the importance of gratitude? (b) Think of all the ways *you* could have used the cash? (c) Ask for the money back? (d) Trust that God is in control? ■ 3. During a church mission trip, some older teens surround you and call you names, shove you, and make fun of the Christian message on your T-shirt. Do you: (a) "Do a Samson" (i.e., beat them up in the name of Jesus)? (b) Change your shirt? (c) Vow never to stand up for Christ again? (d) Consider it an honor to suffer for Christ? ■ 4. Second Corinthians discusses: (a) Living for the Lord when nothing seems to go right. (b) Why it *is* worth it (no matter what happens) to serve God and others. (c) The amazing truth that we can't outgive God. (d) The importance of telling others about Jesus Christ. (e) All of the above. ■ Being Christ's ambassador isn't crazy—it's the only way to find deep-down satisfaction! Tempted to give up? Second Corinthians is just what you need.

## STATS

PURPOSE: To affirm Paul's own ministry, defend his authority as an apostle, and refute the false teachers in Corinth

AUTHOR: Paul

TO WHOM WRITTEN: The church in Corinth, and Christians everywhere

DATE WRITTEN: About A.D. 55 through 57, from Macedonia

SETTING: Paul had already written three letters to the Corinthians (two are now lost). In 1 Corinthians (the second of these letters), he used strong words to correct and teach. Most of the church had responded in the right spirit. There were, however, those who were denying Paul's authority and questioning his motives.

KEY PEOPLE: Paul, Timothy, Titus, false teachers

KEY PLACES: Corinth, Jerusalem

CHAPTER 1 **PAUL: A MESSENGER OF GOD.** This letter is from Paul, appointed by God to be an apostle of Christ Jesus, and from our dear brother Timothy.

We are writing to God's church in Corinth and to all the Christians throughout Greece.*

[2]May God our Father and the Lord Jesus Christ give you his grace and peace.

[3]All praise to the God and Father of our Lord Jesus Christ. He is the source* of every mercy and the God who comforts us. [4]He comforts us in all our troubles so that we can comfort others. When others are troubled, we will be able to give them the same comfort God has given us. [5]You can be sure that the more we suffer for Christ, the more God will shower us with his comfort through Christ. [6]So when we are weighed down with troubles, it is for your benefit and salvation! For when God comforts us, it is so that we, in turn, can be an encouragement to you. Then you can patiently endure the same things we suffer. [7]We are confident that as you share in suffering, you will also share God's comfort.

[8]I think you ought to know, dear brothers and sisters,* about the trouble we went through in the province of Asia. We were crushed and completely overwhelmed, and we thought we would never live through it. [9]In fact, we expected to die. But as a result, we learned not to rely on ourselves, but on God who can raise the dead. [10]And he did deliver us from mortal danger. And we are confident that he will continue to deliver us. [11]He will rescue us because you are helping by praying for us. As a result, many will give thanks to God because so many people's prayers for our safety have been answered.

[12]We can say with confidence and a clear conscience that we have been honest* and sincere in all our dealings. We have depended on God's grace, not on our own earthly wisdom. That is how we have acted toward everyone, and especially toward you. [13]My letters have been straightforward, and there is nothing written between the lines and nothing you can't understand. I hope someday you will fully understand us, [14]even if you don't fully understand

**COMFORT ● ● • • •**

1:3-4 **Many think that when God comforts us, our hardships go away. If that were so, people would turn to God only to be relieved of pain and not out of love for him. Real comfort can also mean receiving strength, encouragement, and hope to deal with our hardships. The more we suffer, the more comfort God gives us (1:5). If you are feeling overwhelmed, allow God to comfort you. Remember, every trial you endure will later become an opportunity to minister to others suffering similar hardships.**

1:1 Greek *Achaia,* the southern region of the Greek peninsula. 1:3 Greek *the Father.* 1:8 Greek *brothers.* 1:12 Some manuscripts read *holy.*

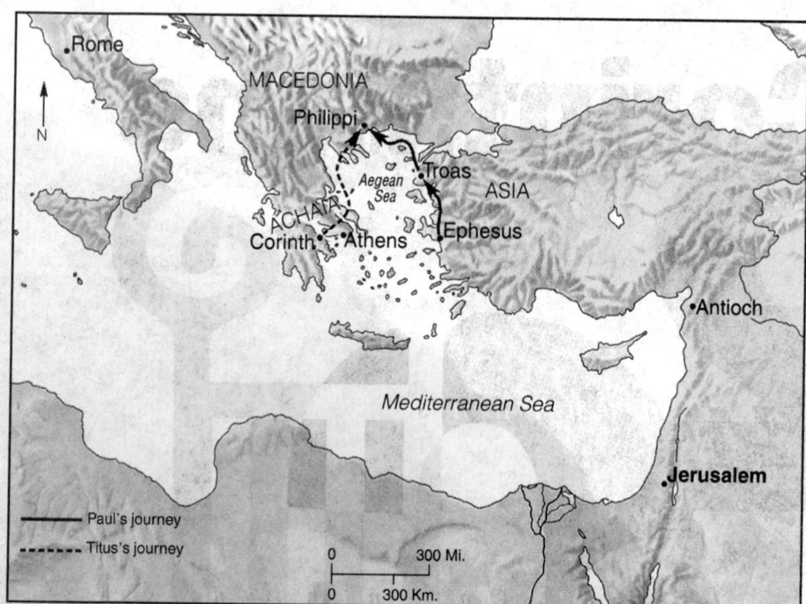


**PAUL SEARCHES FOR TITUS**
Paul had searched for Titus, hoping to meet him in Troas and receive news about the Corinthian church. When he did not find Titus in Troas, Paul went on to Macedonia (2:13), most likely to Philippi, where he found Titus.

us now. Then on the day when our Lord Jesus comes back again, you will be proud of us in the same way we are proud of you.
15Since I was so sure of your understanding and
trust, I wanted to give you a double blessing. 16I
wanted to stop and see you on my way to Macedonia and again on my return trip. Then you could send me on my way to Judea.

## SEAL OF APPROVAL ● ● ● • •

**1:21-22 Paul mentions two gifts God gives us when we become believers: (1) a seal of ownership to show who our master is, and (2) the Holy Spirit as a guarantee that we belong to him (Ephesians 1:13-14). With the privilege of belonging to God comes the responsibility of identifying ourself as a faithful representative and servant of our master. Don't be ashamed to let others know you are his.**

17You may be asking why I changed my plan.
Hadn't I made up my mind yet? Or am I like people
of the world who say yes when they really mean no?
18As surely as God is true, I am not that sort of
person. My yes means yes 19because Jesus Christ, the
Son of God, never wavers between yes and no. He is the one whom Timothy, Silas,* and I preached to you, and he is the divine Yes—God's affirmation.
20For all of God's promises have been fulfilled in
him. That is why we say "Amen" when we give glory
to God through Christ. 21It is God who gives us,
along with you, the ability to stand firm for Christ.*
He has commissioned us, 22and he has identified us
as his own by placing the Holy Spirit in our hearts as the first installment of everything he will give us.
23Now I call upon God as my witness that I am
telling the truth. The reason I didn't return to Corinth was to spare you from a severe rebuke. 24But that
does not mean we want to tell you exactly how to put your faith into practice.* We want to work together with you so you will be full of joy as you stand firm in your faith.

CHAPTER **2** **FORGIVENESS AND ACCEPTANCE.** So I said to myself, "No, I won't do it. I won't make them unhappy with another painful visit." 2For if I cause
you pain and make you sad, who is going to make
me glad? 3That is why I wrote as I did in my last
letter, so that when I do come, I will not be made sad by the very ones who ought to give me the greatest joy. Surely you know that my happiness depends on
your happiness. 4How painful it was to write that
letter! Heartbroken, I cried over it. I didn't want to hurt you, but I wanted you to know how very much I love you.
5I am not overstating it when I say that the man
who caused all the trouble hurt your entire church
more than he hurt me. 6He was punished enough
when most of you were united in your judgment
against him. 7Now it is time to forgive him and
comfort him. Otherwise he may become so discouraged that he won't be able to recover. 8Now show
him that you still love him.
9I wrote to you as I did to find out how far you
would go in obeying me. 10When you forgive this
man, I forgive him, too. And when I forgive him (for whatever is to be forgiven), I do so with Christ's
authority for your benefit, 11so that Satan will not
outsmart us. For we are very familiar with his evil schemes.
12Well, when I came to the city of Troas to preach
the Good News of Christ, the Lord gave me tremendous opportunities. 13But I couldn't rest because my

1:19 Greek *Silvanus.* 1:21 Or *who has identified us and you as genuine Christians.* 1:24 Greek *want to lord it over your faith.*

dear brother Titus hadn't yet arrived with a report from you. So I said good-bye and went on to Macedonia to find him.

[14]But thanks be to God, who made us his captives and leads us along in Christ's triumphal procession. Now wherever we go he uses us to tell others about the Lord and to spread the Good News like a sweet perfume. [15]Our lives are a fragrance presented by Christ to God. But this fragrance is perceived differently by those being saved and by those perishing. [16]To those who are perishing we are a fearful smell of death and doom. But to those who are being saved we are a life-giving perfume. And who is adequate for such a task as this? [17]You see, we are not like those hucksters—and there are many of them—who preach just to make money. We preach God's message with sincerity and with Christ's authority. And we know that the God who sent us is watching us.

CHAPTER **3** **OUR SUCCESS COMES FROM GOD.** Are we beginning again to tell you how good we are? Some people need to bring letters of recommendation with them or ask you to write letters of recommendation for them. [2]But the only letter of recommendation we need is you yourselves! Your lives are a letter written in our* hearts, and everyone can read it and recognize our good work among you. [3]Clearly, you are a letter from Christ prepared by us. It is written not with pen and ink, but with the Spirit of the living God. It is carved not on stone, but on human hearts.

[4]We are confident of all this because of our great trust in God through Christ. [5]It is not that we think we can do anything of lasting value by ourselves. Our only power and success come from God. [6]He is the one who has enabled us to represent his new covenant. This is a covenant, not of written laws, but of the Spirit. The old way ends in death; in the new way, the Holy Spirit gives life.

[7]That old system of law etched in stone led to death, yet it began with such glory that the people of Israel could not bear to look at Moses' face. For his face shone with the glory of God, even though the brightness was already fading away. [8]Shouldn't we expect far greater glory when the Holy Spirit is giving life? [9]If the old covenant, which brings condemnation, was glorious, how much more glorious is the new covenant, which makes us right with God! [10]In fact, that first glory was not glorious at all compared with the overwhelming glory of the new covenant. [11]So if the old covenant, which has been set aside, was full of glory, then the new covenant, which remains forever, has far greater glory.

[12]Since this new covenant gives us such confidence, we can be very bold. [13]We are not like Moses, who put a veil over his face so the people of Israel would not see the glory fading away. [14]But the people's minds were hardened, and even to this day whenever the old covenant is being read, a veil covers their minds so they cannot understand the truth. And this veil can be removed only by believing in Christ. [15]Yes, even today when they read Moses' writings, their hearts are covered with that veil, and they do not understand.

[16]But whenever anyone turns to the Lord, then the veil is taken away. [17]Now, the Lord is the Spirit, and wherever the Spirit of the Lord is, he gives freedom. [18]And all of us have had that veil removed so that we can be mirrors that brightly reflect* the glory of the Lord. And as the Spirit of the Lord works within us, we become more and more like him and reflect his glory even more.

**LIKE HIM ● ● ● • •**

3:17-18 **The glory that the Spirit imparts to the believer is greater both in quality and longevity than that which Moses experienced. The glory gradually transforms the believer into Christlikeness. Becoming Christlike is a progressive experience (see Romans 8:29; Galatians 4:19; Philippians 3:21; 1 John 3:2). The more closely we relate to him, the more we will be like him.**

**"Here's what I did..."**

Last year I went through a very difficult time for a whole month. It was one thing after another; I wasn't sure I could take it. God saw me through it, but I still had lots of unresolved questions about why those things had to happen to me.

Not long afterward my friend's sister had a leukemia relapse. When I found out, I prayed and cried for a while. Then I decided to write her a note of encouragement. Later that night, I read 2 Corinthians 1:3-7 and it felt like God was speaking tender words of comfort right to me. I realized that there *was* a reason for the pain I had gone through not long before; it was so that I could relate to the pain of other people and offer true encouragement.

I was not only able to offer my friend's sister some sincere encouragement, but also my nagging questions over why God let me go through my pain were answered. Since then, whenever something painful happens to me I find it much easier to believe that there's a good reason for it.

Linda, AGE 17

3:2 Some manuscripts read *your.* 3:18 Or *so that we can see in a mirror.*

CHAPTER **4** **SATAN BLINDS, BUT GOD GIVES LIGHT.** And
so, since God in his mercy has given us this wonderful ministry, we never give up. [2]We reject all shameful
and underhanded methods. We do not try to trick
anyone, and we do not distort the word of God. We
tell the truth before God, and all who are honest
know that.
[3]If the Good News we preach is veiled from
anyone, it is a sign that they are perishing. [4]Satan,
the god of this evil world, has blinded the minds
of those who don't believe, so they are unable to
see the glorious light of the Good News that is
shining upon them. They don't understand the
message we preach about the glory of Christ, who
is the exact likeness of God.

## SERVING GOD

"Tom, maybe you've got the dates mixed up," Jeff says.

"No way—the prison outreach is the same weekend."

"But what about Ben's ski party?"

"I guess I'll have to miss it."

"But, Tom, you can't! Everybody will be at Ben's—including every babe in the whole sophomore class! It's the party of the year!"

"Look, I wish I could go. But I promised to sing with the group at this prison thing."

"Can't you get out of it?"

Tom shakes his head. "Jeff, you just don't understand."

"Well, I say you're making a huge mistake. You'll regret it if you miss Ben's party."

Two weeks later "the" weekend has come and gone. Ben's party was every bit as fun as advertised. Great weather, great skiing—it was a certified blast!

And the prison outreach? Not quite so successful. Not only did the prisoners shower Tom's group with verbal abuse during the concert, but afterwards, during a meal stop on the way home, someone broke into the church van and stole the group's sound equipment!

Does it really pay to serve the Lord? Is the hardship encountered worth all the effort? Take it from the apostle Paul, a guy who should know. He endured unbelievable difficulties (2 Corinthians 4:8-10; 6:4-10; 11:23-28), and yet he was faithful to the end of his life.

Ask God to make you like that.

[5]We don't go around preaching about ourselves;
we preach Christ Jesus, the Lord. All we say about
ourselves is that we are your servants because of what
Jesus has done for us. [6]For God, who said, "Let there
be light in the darkness," has made us understand
that this light is the brightness of the glory of God
that is seen in the face of Jesus Christ.
[7]But this precious treasure—this light and power
that now shine within us—is held in perishable
containers, that is, in our weak bodies.* So everyone
can see that our glorious power is from God and is
not our own.
[8]We are pressed on every side by troubles, but we
are not crushed and broken. We are perplexed, but
we don't give up and quit. [9]We are hunted down, but
God never abandons us. We get knocked down,
but we get up again and keep going. [10]Through suffering, these bodies of ours constantly share in the
death of Jesus so that the life of Jesus may also be
seen in our bodies.
[11]Yes, we live under constant danger of death because we serve Jesus, so that the life of Jesus will be
obvious in our dying bodies. [12]So we live in the face
of death, but it has resulted in eternal life for you.
[13]But we continue to preach because we have the
same kind of faith the psalmist had when he said, "I
believed in God, and so I speak."* [14]We know that
the same God who raised our Lord Jesus will also
raise us with Jesus and present us to himself along
with you. [15]All of these things are for your benefit.
And as God's grace brings more and more people to
Christ, there will be great thanksgiving, and God will
receive more and more glory.
[16]That is why we never give up. Though our bodies
are dying, our spirits are* being renewed every day.
[17]For our present troubles are quite small and won't
last very long. Yet they produce for us an immeasurably great glory that will last forever! [18]So we don't
look at the troubles we can see right now; rather, we
look forward to what we have not yet seen. For the
troubles we see will soon be over, but the joys to
come will last forever.

CHAPTER **5** **WE WILL HAVE NEW BODIES.** For we know
that when this earthly tent we live in is taken
down—when we die and leave these bodies—we
will have a home in heaven, an eternal body made
for us by God himself and not by human hands. [2]We
grow weary in our present bodies, and we long for
the day when we will put on our heavenly bodies like
new clothing. [3]For we will not be spirits without
bodies, but we will put on new heavenly bodies.
[4]Our dying bodies make us groan and sigh, but it's
not that we want to die and have no bodies at all. We
want to slip into our new bodies so that these dying
bodies will be swallowed up by everlasting life. [5]God

## FOCUS ● ● • • ·

4:5 **The focus of Paul's preaching was Christ, not himself. When you witness, tell people about what Christ has done rather than about your abilities and accomplishments. People must be introduced to Christ, not to you. If you hear someone preaching about himself or his own ideas rather than Christ, beware—he is a false teacher.**

## TROUBLES ● ● • • ·

4:18 **Our troubles should not diminish our faith or disillusion us. Instead, we should realize that there is a purpose in our suffering. Problems and human limitations have several benefits: (1) they help us remember Christ's suffering for us; (2) they help keep us from pride; (3) they help us look beyond this brief life; (4) they prove our faith to others; and (5) they give God the opportunity to demonstrate his great power. Don't resent your troubles—see them as opportunities!**

4:7 Greek *But we have this treasure in earthen vessels.* 4:13 Ps 116:10. 4:16 Greek *our inner being is.*

himself has prepared us for this, and as a guarantee
he has given us his Holy Spirit.
6So we are always confident, even though we
know that as long as we live in these bodies we are
not at home with the Lord. 7That is why we live by
believing and not by seeing. 8Yes, we are fully confident, and we would rather be away from these bodies, for then we will be at home with the Lord. 9So
our aim is to please him always, whether we are here
in this body or away from this body. 10For we must
all stand before Christ to be judged. We will each

Those WHO BECOME CHRISTIANS become new persons. They are NOT the same anymore, for the old life is gone. A new life has begun!

2 CORINTHIANS 5:17

**MADE NEW**

5:16-17 **Christians are brand-new people on the *inside.* The Holy Spirit gives them new life, and they are not the same any more. We are not reformed, rehabilitated, or reeducated—we are new creations, living in vital union with Christ (Colossians 2:6-7). We are not merely turning over a new leaf; we are beginning a new life under a new Master.**

receive whatever we deserve for the good or evil we
have done in our bodies.
11It is because we know this solemn fear of the
Lord that we work so hard to persuade others. God
knows we are sincere, and I hope you know this, too.
12Are we trying to pat ourselves on the back again?
No, we are giving you a reason to be proud of us, so
you can answer those who brag about having a
spectacular ministry rather than having a sincere
heart before God. 13If it seems that we are crazy, it is
to bring glory to God. And if we are in our right
minds, it is for your benefit. 14Whatever we do, it is
because Christ's love controls us.* Since we believe
that Christ died for everyone, we also believe that we
have all died to the old life we used to live.* 15He
died for everyone so that those who receive his new
life will no longer live to please themselves. Instead,
they will live to please Christ, who died and was
raised for them.
16So we have stopped evaluating others by what the
world thinks about them. Once I mistakenly thought
of Christ that way, as though he were merely a human
being. How differently I think about him now! 17What
this means is that those who become Christians become new persons. They are not the same anymore,
for the old life is gone. A new life has begun!
18All this newness of life is from God, who
brought us back to himself through what Christ did.
And God has given us the task of reconciling people
to him. 19For God was in Christ, reconciling the
world to himself, no longer counting people's sins
against them. This is the wonderful message he has
given us to tell others. 20We are Christ's ambassadors,
and God is using us to speak to you. We urge you, as
though Christ himself were here pleading with you,
"Be reconciled to God!" 21For God made Christ, who
never sinned, to be the offering for our sin, so that
we could be made right with God through Christ.

CHAPTER **6** **WHEN LIFE IS HARD, LEAN ON GOD.** As God's
partners,* we beg you not to reject this marvelous
message of God's great kindness. 2For God says,

"At just the right time, I heard you.
On the day of salvation, I helped you."*

Indeed, God is ready to help you right now. Today is
the day of salvation.
3We try to live in such a way that no one will be
hindered from finding the Lord by the way we act,
and so no one can find fault with our ministry. 4In
everything we do we try to show that we are true

**5:14a** Or *urges us on.* **5:14b** Greek *Since one died on behalf of all, then all died.* **6:1** Or *As we work together.* **6:2** Isa 49:8.

**PRINCIPLES OF CONFRONTATION IN 2 CORINTHIANS**

Sometimes rebuke is necessary, but it must be used with caution. The purpose of any rebuke, confrontation, or discipline is to help people, not hurt them.

Affirm all you see that is good. (7:4)

Be accurate and honest. (7:14; 8:21)

Know the facts. (11:22-27)

Follow up after the confrontation. (7:13; 12:14)

Be gentle after being firm. (7:15; 13:11-13)

Speak words that reflect Christ's message, not your own ideas. (10:3,12-13; 12:19)

Use discipline only when all else fails. (13:2)

Be firm. (7:9; 10:2)

ministers of God. We patiently endure troubles and
hardships and calamities of every kind. 5 We have
been beaten, been put in jail, faced angry mobs,
worked to exhaustion, endured sleepless nights, and
gone without food. 6 We have proved ourselves by
our purity, our understanding, our patience, our
kindness, our sincere love, and the power of the Holy
Spirit.* 7 We have faithfully preached the truth. God's
power has been working in us. We have righteousness as our weapon, both to attack and to defend
ourselves. 8 We serve God whether people honor us
or despise us, whether they slander us or praise us.
We are honest, but they call us impostors. 9 We are
well known, but we are treated as unknown. We live
close to death, but here we are, still alive. We have
been beaten within an inch of our lives. 10 Our hearts
ache, but we always have joy. We are poor, but we
give spiritual riches to others. We own nothing, and
yet we have everything.
11 Oh, dear Corinthian friends! We have spoken
honestly with you. Our hearts are open to you. 12 If
there is a problem between us, it is not because of a
lack of love on our part, but because you have withheld your love from us. 13 I am talking now as I would
to my own children. Open your hearts to us!
14 Don't team up with those who are unbelievers.
How can goodness be a partner with wickedness?
How can light live with darkness? 15 What harmony
can there be between Christ and the Devil*? How
can a believer be a partner with an unbeliever? 16 And
what union can there be between God's temple and
idols? For we are the temple of the living God. As
God said:

"I will live in them
and walk among them.
I will be their God,
and they will be my people.*
17 Therefore, come out from them
and separate yourselves from them, says
the Lord.
Don't touch their filthy things,
and I will welcome you.*
18 And I will be your Father,
and you will be my sons and daughters,
says the Lord Almighty.*"

## ADMIT IT ● ● ● • •

7:11 **It is difficult to hear that we have sinned, and even more difficult to get rid of sin. Paul praised the Corinthians for clearing up an especially troublesome situation. Do you tend to be defensive when confronted? Don't let pride keep you from admitting your sins. Accept confrontation as a tool for growth, and do all you can to correct problems that are pointed out to you.**

6:6 Or *the holiness of spirit.* 6:15 Greek *and Beliar.* 6:16 Lev 26:12; Ezek 37:27. 6:17 Isa 52:11; Ezek 20:34. 6:18 2 Sam 7:14.

**THE POINT ● ● • • •**

8:2 **While on his third missionary journey, Paul was collecting money for the impoverished believers in Jerusalem. The churches in Macedonia—Philippi, Thessalonica, and Berea—gave money even though they were poor, and they gave more than Paul expected. This was sacrificial giving; they were poor themselves, but they wanted to help. The point of giving is not the amount we give, but why and how we give. God wants us to give as these churches did—out of dedication to him, love for fellow believers, the joy of helping those in need, and because it is right to do so. How does your giving measure up?**

CHAPTER **7** **PAUL IS PROUD OF THE CHRISTIANS.** Because we have these promises, dear friends, let us cleanse ourselves from everything that can defile our body or spirit. And let us work toward complete purity because we fear God.

[2]Please open your hearts to us. We have not done wrong to anyone. We have not led anyone astray. We have not taken advantage of anyone. [3]I'm not saying this to condemn you, for I said before that you are in our hearts forever. We live or die together with you. [4]I have the highest confidence in you, and my pride in you is great. You have greatly encouraged me; you have made me happy despite all our troubles.

[5]When we arrived in Macedonia there was no rest for us. Outside there was conflict from every direction, and inside there was fear. [6]But God, who encourages those who are discouraged, encouraged us by the arrival of Titus. [7]His presence was a joy, but so was the news he brought of the encouragement he received from you. When he told me how much you were looking forward to my visit, and how sorry you were about what had happened, and how loyal your love is for me, I was filled with joy!

[8]I am no longer sorry that I sent that letter to you, though I was sorry for a time, for I know that it was painful to you for a little while. [9]Now I am glad I sent it, not because it hurt you, but because the pain caused you to have remorse and change your ways. It was the kind of sorrow God wants his people to have, so you were not harmed by us in any way. [10]For God can use sorrow in our lives to help us turn away from sin and seek salvation. We will never regret that kind of sorrow. But sorrow without repentance is the kind that results in death.

[11]Just see what this godly sorrow produced in you! Such earnestness, such concern to clear yourselves, such indignation, such alarm, such longing to see me, such zeal, and such a readiness to punish the wrongdoer. You showed that you have done everything you could to make things right. [12]My purpose was not to write about who did the wrong or who was wronged. I wrote to you so that in the sight of God you could show how much you really do care for us. [13]We have been encouraged by this.

In addition to our own encouragement, we were especially delighted to see how happy Titus was at the way you welcomed him and set his mind at ease. [14]I had told him how proud I was of you—and you didn't disappoint me. I have always told you the truth, and now my boasting to Titus has also proved true! [15]Now he cares for you more than ever when he remembers the way you listened to him and welcomed him with such respect and deep concern. [16]I am very happy now because I have complete confidence in you.

CHAPTER **8** **GENEROUS GIVING PLEASES GOD.** Now I want to tell you, dear brothers and sisters,* what God in his kindness has done for the churches in Macedonia. [2]Though they have been going through much trouble and hard times, their wonderful joy

**I've been a Christian about nine months. Although I have made a lot of friends who are Christians, I still have quite a few who aren't. Should I still be hanging out with friends who aren't Christians?**

Find a quarter and two pennies. Place the quarter on a table. Put the two pennies about five inches below the quarter, one inch apart.

Now, pretend God is the quarter, you are the penny on the left, and your friend is the penny on the right. As you grow closer to God (move your penny up an inch or two), what happens to the distance between you and your friend? It gets wider! When only one person in a friendship moves closer to God, that's what happens to the relationship automatically!

There are degrees in friendships and stages we go through to make them stronger. But all friendships take time. And our closest friends affect us. Think about the friends you used to hang around with. You probably did the same things, used the same slang, laughed at the same type of jokes, etc.

Hanging around with old friends who aren't Christians will probably not help you become a stronger Christian. That's what 2 Corinthians 6:14 is about. If you spend all of your deeper friendship time with unbelievers, you'll tend to become like them and not move closer to God.

However, God doesn't want you to be totally isolated from those who aren't Christians. In fact, if you get to the point where you don't have any non-Christian friends, you're probably doing something wrong. If you're going to be Christ's representative to those who don't know him (see 2 Corinthians 5:18-20), you have to be around them! Just be careful, and remember that your goal is to point them to Christ.

"Whoever walks with the wise will become wise; whoever walks with fools will suffer harm" (Proverbs 13:20).

Especially in the early stages of your Christian life, you need to be around people who will be your friends and help you grow spiritually at the same time.

8:1 Greek *brothers*.

and deep poverty have overflowed in rich generosity. [3]For I can testify that they gave not only what they could afford but far more. And they did it of their own free will. [4]They begged us again and again for the gracious privilege of sharing in the gift for the Christians in Jerusalem. [5]Best of all, they went beyond our highest hopes, for their first action was to dedicate themselves to the Lord and to us for whatever directions God might give them.

[6]So we have urged Titus, who encouraged your giving in the first place, to return to you and encourage you to complete your share in this ministry of giving. [7]Since you excel in so many ways—you have so much faith, such gifted speakers, such knowledge, such enthusiasm, and such love for us*—now I want you to excel also in this gracious ministry of giving. [8]I am not saying you must do it, even though the other churches are eager to do it. This is one way to prove your love is real.

[9]You know how full of love and kindness our Lord Jesus Christ was. Though he was very rich, yet for your sakes he became poor, so that by his poverty he could make you rich.

[10]I suggest that you finish what you started a year ago, for you were the first to propose this idea, and you were the first to begin doing something about it. [11]Now you should carry this project through to completion just as enthusiastically as you began it. Give whatever you can according to what you have. [12]If you are really eager to give, it isn't important how much you are able to give. God wants you to give what you have, not what you don't have. [13]Of course, I don't mean you should give so much that you suffer from having too little. I only mean that there should be some equality. [14]Right now you have plenty and can help them. Then at some other time they can share with you when you need it. In this way, everyone's needs will be met. [15]Do you remember what the Scriptures say about this? "Those who gathered a lot had nothing left over, and those who gathered only a little had enough."*

## MORE TO GIVE ● ● • • •

**9:10 God gives us resources to use and invest for him. Paul used the illustration of seeds to explain that the resources God gives us are not to be hidden, foolishly devoured, or thrown away. Instead, they should be cultivated to produce more crops. When we invest what God has given us in his work, he will provide us with even more to give.**

[16]I am thankful to God that he has given Titus the same enthusiasm for you that I have. [17]He welcomed our request that he visit you again. In fact, he himself was eager to go and see you. [18]We are also sending another brother with Titus. He is highly praised in all the churches as a preacher of the Good News. [19]He was appointed by the churches to accompany us as we take the offering to Jerusalem*—a service that glorifies the Lord and shows our eagerness to help. [20]By traveling together we will guard against any suspicion, for we are anxious that no one should find fault with the way we are handling this generous gift. [21]We are careful to be honorable before the Lord, but we also want everyone else to know we are honorable.

[22]And we are also sending with them another brother who has been thoroughly tested and has shown how earnest he is on many occasions. He is now even more enthusiastic because of his increased confidence in you. [23]If anyone asks about Titus, say that he is my partner who works with me to help you. And these brothers are representatives* of the churches. They are splendid examples of those who bring glory to Christ. [24]So show them your love, and prove to all the churches that our boasting about you is justified.

CHAPTER **9** **GOD LIKES PEOPLE TO GIVE HAPPILY.** I really don't need to write to you about this gift for the Christians in Jerusalem.* [2]For I know how eager you are to help, and I have been boasting to our friends in Macedonia that you Christians in Greece* were ready to send an offering a year ago. In fact, it was your enthusiasm that stirred up many of them to begin helping. [3]But I am sending these brothers just to be sure that you really are ready, as I told them you would be, with your money all collected. I don't want it to turn out that I was wrong in my boasting about you. [4]I would be humiliated—and so would you—if some Macedonian Christians came with me, only to find that you still weren't ready after all I had told them! [5]So I thought I should send these brothers ahead of me to make sure the gift you promised is ready. But I want it to be a willing gift, not one given under pressure.

[6]Remember this—a farmer who plants only a few seeds will get a small crop. But the one who plants generously will get a generous crop. [7]You must each make up your own mind as to how much you should give. Don't give reluctantly or in response to pressure. For God loves the person who gives cheerfully. [8]And God will generously provide all you need. Then you will always have everything you need and plenty left over to share with others. [9]As the Scriptures say,

"Godly people give generously to the poor.
Their good deeds will never be forgotten."*

[10]For God is the one who gives seed to the farmer and then bread to eat. In the same way, he will give you many opportunities to do good, and he will produce a great harvest of generosity* in you.

[11]Yes, you will be enriched so that you can give even more generously. And when we take your gifts to those who need them, they will break out in thanksgiving to God. [12]So two good things will happen—the needs of the Christians in Jerusalem will be met, and they will joyfully express their thanksgiving to God. [13]You will be glorifying God through your generous gifts. For your generosity to them will

8:7 Some manuscripts read *love from us to you.* 8:15 Exod 16:18. 8:19 See 1 Cor 16:3-4. 8:23 Greek *apostles.* 9:1 Greek *about the offering for the saints.* 9:2 Greek *Achaia,* the southern region of the Greek peninsula. 9:9 Ps 112:9. 9:10 Greek *righteousness.*

prove that you are obedient to the Good News of Christ. 14And they will pray for you with deep affection because of the wonderful grace of God shown through you.

15Thank God for his Son—a gift too wonderful for words!*

## CHAPTER 10 PAUL'S AUTHORITY.

Now I, Paul, plead with you. I plead with the gentleness and kindness that Christ himself would use, even though some of you say I am bold in my letters but timid in person. 2I hope it won't be necessary, but when I come I may have to be very bold with those who think we act from purely human motives. 3We are human, but we don't wage war with human plans and methods. 4We use God's mighty weapons, not mere worldly weapons, to knock down the Devil's strongholds. 5With these weapons we break down every proud argument that keeps people from knowing God. With these weapons we conquer their rebellious ideas, and we teach them to obey Christ. 6And we will punish those who remained disobedient after the rest of you became loyal and obedient.

7The trouble with you is that you make your decisions on the basis of appearance.* You must recognize that we belong to Christ just as much as those who proudly declare that they belong to Christ. 8I may seem to be boasting too much about the authority given to us by the Lord. But this authority is to build you up, not to tear you down. And I will not be put to shame by having my work among you destroyed.

9Now this is not just an attempt to frighten you by my letters. 10For some say, "Don't worry about Paul. His letters are demanding and forceful, but in person he is weak, and his speeches are really bad!" 11The ones who say this must realize that we will be just as demanding and forceful in person as we are in our letters.

12Oh, don't worry; I wouldn't dare say that I am as wonderful as these other men who tell you how important they are! But they are only comparing themselves with each other, and measuring themselves by themselves. What foolishness!

13But we will not boast of authority we do not have. Our goal is to stay within the boundaries of God's plan for us, and this plan includes our working there with you. 14We are not going too far when we claim authority over you, for we were the first to travel all the way to you with the Good News of Christ. 15Nor do we claim credit for the work someone else has done. Instead, we hope that your faith will grow and that our work among you will be greatly enlarged. 16Then we will be able to go and preach the Good News in other places that are far beyond you, where no one else is working. Then there will be no question about being in someone else's territory. 17As the Scriptures say,

"The person who wishes to boast
should boast only of what the Lord has
done."*

18When people boast about themselves, it doesn't count for much. But when the Lord commends someone, that's different!

### WEAPONS ● ● ● • •

**10:3-6 Christians must choose whose methods to use, God's or man's. Paul assures us that God's mighty weapons—prayer, faith, hope, love, God's Word, the Holy Spirit—are powerful and effective (see Ephesians 6:13-18)! When dealing with the pride that keeps people from a relationship with Christ, we may be tempted to use our own methods. But nothing can break down Satan's barriers like God's weapons.**

## CHAPTER 11 SMOOTH TALKERS & PHONY TEACHERS.

I hope you will be patient with me as I keep on talking like a fool. Please bear with me. 2I am jealous for you with the jealousy of God himself. For I promised you as a pure bride* to one husband, Christ. 3But I fear that somehow you will be led away from your pure and simple devotion to Christ, just as Eve was deceived by the serpent. 4You seem to believe whatever anyone tells you, even if they preach about a different Jesus than the one we preach, or a different Spirit than the one you received, or a different kind of gospel than the one you believed. 5But I don't think I am inferior to these "super apostles." 6I may not be a trained speaker, but I know what I am talking about. I think you realize this by now, for we have proved it again and again.

7Did I do wrong when I humbled myself and honored you by preaching God's Good News to you without expecting anything in return? 8I "robbed" other churches by accepting their contributions so I could serve you at no cost. 9And when I was with you and didn't have enough to live on, I did not ask you to help me. For the brothers who came from Macedonia brought me another gift. I have never yet asked you for any support, and I never will. 10As surely as the truth of Christ is in me, I will never stop boasting about this all over Greece.* 11Why? Because I don't love you? God knows I do.

12But I will continue doing this to cut the ground out from under the feet of those who boast that their work is just like ours. 13These people are false apostles. They have fooled you by disguising themselves as apostles of Christ. 14But I am not

### SMOOTH TALK ● ● ● • •

**11:3-4 The Corinthian believers fell for smooth talk and messages that sounded good and seemed to make sense. Today there are many false teachings that seem to make sense. Don't believe anyone simply because he or she sounds like an authority or says things you like to hear. Search the Bible and check people's words against God's Word. The Bible should be your authoritative guide to all teaching.**

9:15 Greek *Thank God for his indescribable gift.* 10:7 Or *Look at the obvious facts.* 10:17 Jer 9:24. 11:2 Greek *a virgin.* 11:10 Greek *Achaia.*

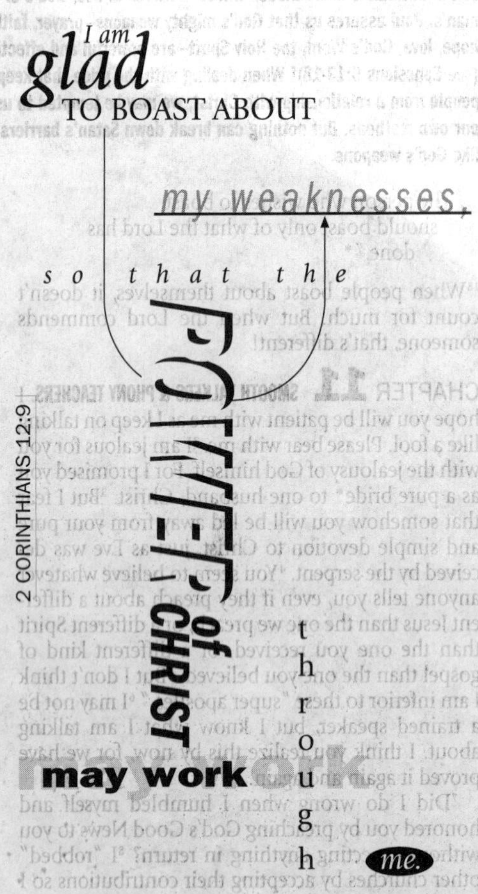

I am glad
TO BOAST ABOUT
my weaknesses,
so that the
POWER
of CHRIST
may work
through
me.
2 CORINTHIANS 12:9

surprised! Even Satan can disguise himself as an angel of light. [15]So it is no wonder his servants can also do it by pretending to be godly ministers. In the end they will get every bit of punishment their wicked deeds deserve.

[16]Once again, don't think that I have lost my wits to talk like this. But even if you do, listen to me, as you would to a foolish person, while I also boast a little. [17]Such bragging is not something the Lord wants, but I am acting like a fool. [18]And since others boast about their human achievements, I will, too. [19]After all, you, who think you are so wise, enjoy listening to fools! [20]You put up with it when they make you their slaves, take everything you have, take advantage of you, put on airs, and slap you in the face. [21]I'm ashamed to say that we were not strong enough to do that!

But whatever they dare to boast about—I'm talking like a fool again—I can boast about it, too. [22]They say they are Hebrews, do they? So am I. And they say they are Israelites? So am I. And they are descendants of Abraham? So am I. [23]They say they serve Christ? I know I sound like a madman, but I have served him far more! I have worked harder, been put in jail more often, been whipped times without number, and faced death again and again. [24]Five different times the Jews gave me thirty-nine lashes. [25]Three times I was beaten with rods. Once I was stoned. Three times I was shipwrecked. Once I spent a whole night and a day adrift at sea. [26]I have traveled many weary miles. I have faced danger from flooded rivers and from robbers. I have faced danger from my own people, the Jews, as well as from the Gentiles. I have faced danger in the cities, in the deserts, and on the stormy seas. And I have faced danger from men who claim to be Christians but are not.* [27]I have lived with weariness and pain and sleepless nights. Often I have been hungry and thirsty and have gone without food. Often I have shivered with cold, without enough clothing to keep me warm.

[28]Then, besides all this, I have the daily burden of how the churches are getting along. [29]Who is weak without my feeling that weakness? Who is led astray, and I do not burn with anger?

[30]If I must boast, I would rather boast about the things that show how weak I am. [31]God, the Father of our Lord Jesus, who is to be praised forever, knows I tell the truth. [32]When I was in Damascus, the governor under King Aretas kept guards at the city gates to catch me. [33]But I was lowered in a basket through a window in the city wall, and that's how I got away!

## CHAPTER 12 PAUL'S PHYSICAL PROBLEMS.

This boasting is all so foolish, but let me go on. Let me tell about the visions and revelations I received from the Lord. [2]I* was caught up into the third heaven fourteen years ago. [3]Whether my body was there or just my spirit, I don't know; only God knows. [4]But I do know that I* was caught up into paradise and heard things so astounding that they cannot be told. [5]That experience is something worth boasting about, but I am not going to do it. I am going to boast only about my weaknesses. [6]I have plenty to boast about and would be no fool in doing it, because I would be telling the truth. But I won't do it. I don't want anyone to think more highly of me than what they can actually see in my life and my message, [7]even though I have received wonderful revelations from God. But to

### PUT ON TRIAL • • • • •

12:11-15 **Paul is not merely revealing his feelings but defending his authority as an apostle of Jesus Christ. He was hurt that the church in Corinth was doubting and questioning him—but he was defending himself for the cause of the gospel, not to satisfy his ego. When you are "put on trial," do you think only about saving your reputation or are you more concerned about what people will think about Christ?**

11:26 Greek *from false brothers.* 12:2 Greek *I know a man in Christ who.* 12:4 Greek *he.*

keep me from getting puffed up, I was given a
thorn in my flesh, a messenger from Satan to torment me and keep me from getting proud.
[8]Three different times I begged the Lord to take it
away. [9]Each time he said, "My gracious favor is all
you need. My power works best in your weakness."
So now I am glad to boast about my weaknesses, so
that the power of Christ may work through me.
[10]Since I know it is all for Christ's good, I am quite
content with my weaknesses and with insults, hardships, persecutions, and calamities. For when I am
weak, then I am strong.
[11]You have made me act like a fool—boasting
like this. You ought to be writing commendations
for me, for I am not at all inferior to these "super
apostles," even though I am nothing at all. [12]When
I was with you, I certainly gave you every proof that
I am truly an apostle, sent to you by God himself.
For I patiently did many signs and wonders and
miracles among you. [13]The only thing I didn't do,
which I do in the other churches, was to become a
burden to you. Please forgive me for this wrong!
[14]Now I am coming to you for the third time, and
I will not be a burden to you. I don't want what you
have; I want you. And anyway, little children don't
pay for their parents' food. It's the other way around;
parents supply food for their children. [15]I will gladly
spend myself and all I have for your spiritual good,
even though it seems that the more I love you, the
less you love me.
[16]Some of you admit I was not a burden to you.
But they still think I was sneaky and took advantage of you by trickery. [17]But how? Did any of the
men I sent to you take advantage of you? [18]When I
urged Titus to visit you and sent our other brother
with him, did Titus take advantage of you? No, of
course not! For we both have the same Spirit and
walk in each other's steps, doing things the same
way.
[19]Perhaps you think we are saying all this just to
defend ourselves. That isn't it at all. We tell you this
as Christ's servants, and we know that God is listening. Everything we do, dear friends, is for your
benefit. [20]For I am afraid that when I come to visit
you I won't like what I find, and then you won't
like my response. I am afraid that I will find quarreling, jealousy, outbursts of anger, selfishness,
backstabbing, gossip, conceit, and disorderly behavior. [21]Yes, I am afraid that when I come, God
will humble me again because of you. And I will
have to grieve because many of you who sinned
earlier have not repented of your impurity, sexual
immorality, and eagerness for lustful pleasure.

CHAPTER **13** **CHECK UP ON YOURSELVES.** This is
the third time I am coming to visit you. As the
Scriptures say, "The facts of every case must be
established by the testimony of two or three
witnesses."* [2]I have already warned those who had
been sinning when I was there on my second visit.
Now I again warn them and all others, just as I did
before, that this next time I will not spare them.
[3]I will give you all the proof you want that Christ
speaks through me. Christ is not weak in his dealings
with you; he is a mighty power among you. [4]Al-
though he died on the cross in weakness, he now
lives by the mighty power of God. We, too, are weak,
but we live in him and have God's power—the
power we use in dealing with you.

13:1 Deut 19:15.

**My grandma has been a Christian for 40 years. She has faced so much trouble during those years I can't believe it. Why would God allow so much trouble to come into one person's life?**

No doubt you've seen weight lifters on TV or have friends who work out with weights.

The goal of lifting weights is to develop the muscles and make them stronger. But this muscle-building process involves the muscles being constantly broken down!

At first, the strain of lifting causes the person to feel weak. In the long run, however, it makes him or her strong.

Like a muscle, faith grows stronger when it is exercised. That's why James 1:2-4 says to be happy when facing difficult trials and temptations. The entire book of Hebrews is about faith—how to strengthen it, how it can help you endure. In Hebrews 11, you will find the "Hall of Faith," a list of those who suffered for their faith . . . and who will one day receive wonderful rewards for standing firm!

One of God's goals for us is to learn to trust him more. When a Christian asks God for more faith, he or she is really asking for more trials. God knows that only through exercise can our faith be strengthened.

Eventually, James says, we will be "strong in character and ready for anything" (1:4).

Another reason for trials and problems is found in 2 Corinthians 1:3-5: helping others.

"All praise to the God and Father of our Lord Jesus Christ. He is the source of every mercy and the God who comforts us. He comforts us in all our troubles so that we can comfort others. When others are troubled, we will be able to give them the same comfort God has given us. You can be sure that the more we suffer for Christ, the more God will shower us with his comfort through Christ."

Helping someone else is probably the last thing we are thinking about when we are going through problems. But our success at coming through trials is very important to God. Then he can use us to pass along comfort and encouragement to others.

Some Christians are glad that they have few problems. Unfortunately, they won't have the opportunity to see their character grow stronger. And they won't receive the joy that comes when they help others.

## EXAMS ● ● ● • •

13:5 **Just as we get physical examinations, Paul urges us to give ourselves spiritual examinations. We should look for a growing awareness of Christ's presence and power in our life. Only then will we know if we are true Christians or impostors. If we're not taking active steps to grow closer to God, we are moving away from him.**

[5]Examine yourselves to see if your faith is really genuine. Test yourselves. If you cannot tell that Jesus Christ is among you,* it means you have failed the test. [6]I hope you recognize that we have passed the test and are approved by God.

[7]We pray to God that you will not do anything wrong. We pray this, not to show that our ministry to you has been successful, but because we want you to do right even if we ourselves seem to have failed. [8]Our responsibility is never to oppose the truth, but to stand for the truth at all times. [9]We are glad to be weak, if you are really strong. What we pray for is your restoration to maturity.

[10]I am writing this to you before I come, hoping that I won't need to deal harshly with you when I do come. For I want to use the authority the Lord has given me to build you up, not to tear you down.

[11]Dear brothers and sisters,* I close my letter with these last words: Rejoice. Change your ways. Encourage each other. Live in harmony and peace. Then the God of love and peace will be with you.

[12]Greet each other in Christian love.* All the Christians here send you their greetings.

[13]May the grace of our Lord Jesus Christ, the love of God, and the fellowship of the Holy Spirit be with you all.*

13:5 Or *in you.* 13:11 Greek *Brothers.* 13:12 Greek *with a sacred kiss.* 13:12-13 Some English versions divide verse 12 into verse 12 and 13, and then verse 13 becomes verse 14.

# MEGA themes

**TRIALS** Paul experienced great suffering, persecution, and opposition in his ministry. He even struggled with a personal weakness—a "thorn in the flesh." Through it all, Paul affirmed God's faithfulness.

God is faithful. His strength is sufficient for any trial—and trials can keep us from becoming prideful and teach us dependence on God. We must look to God for comfort during trials. As he comforts us, we can learn to comfort others.

1. What are some of the feelings Paul expressed regarding his personal trial?
2. What truth had Paul learned from his suffering and persecution?
3. Based on Paul's example, what feelings can you expect when you encounter trials?
4. What attitude does God want you to have during trials? Why?
5. Describe a time when you encountered personal difficulty. How did you feel then? How do you feel about the experience now? What did you learn about God from that experience?

**CHURCH DISCIPLINE** Paul defends his role in church discipline. Neither immorality nor false teaching could be ignored. The church was to be neither too lax nor too severe in administering discipline. The church was to restore the corrected person when he or she repented.

The goal of discipline in the church should be correction, not vengeance. For churches to be effective, they must confront and solve problems, not ignore them. But in everything we must act in and on behalf of God's love.

1. In 2:5-11, we are given a glimpse into what church discipline should be about. What does this passage teach you about Paul?
2. What was Paul's motive for seeing the person disciplined?
3. What should the church's role be when dealing with members who refuse to repent of sin?
4. What does this teach you about how God wants you to deal with your personal sins?

**HOPE** Paul tried to encourage the Corinthians as they faced trials by reminding them that they would receive new bodies in heaven. This would be a great victory in contrast to their present suffering.

Knowing we will receive new bodies gives us hope. No matter what we face, we can keep going, for our faithful service will result in triumph.

1. Summarize the hope Paul gives to the Corinthians in 5:1-11.

2. Why did Paul use this part of his letter to communicate this hope to the Corinthians? (See 4:13-18.)
3. Under what circumstances would you most need to be reminded of your heavenly hope?
4. How should being reminded of that promise bring hope to you in your present circumstances?

**GIVING** Paul organized a collection of funds for the poor in the Jerusalem church. Many of the Asian churches gave money. Paul explains and defends his beliefs about giving, and he urges the Corinthians to follow through on their previous commitment.

We, too, should honor our financial commitments. Our giving must be generous, sacrificial, according to a plan, and based on need. Generosity helps the needy, enabling them to thank God. Giving is a part of our godliness.

1. What benefit had Paul received from the believers' giving? What benefit had the believers themselves received as a result of their giving?
2. What should Christians understand about giving money for God's work in the church? How could this be applied to giving other personal resources, such as time and service?
3. In what ways would God want you to continue what you are doing in your giving? How should you change what you are doing?

**SOUND DOCTRINE** False teachers were challenging Paul's ministry and authority as an apostle. Paul asserted his authority to preserve correct Christian doctrine. His sincerity, love for Christ, and concern for the people were his defense.

We should share Paul's concern for correct teaching in our churches. In so doing, we must also share his motivation—love for Christ and people—and we should be sincere.

1. Describe the common characteristics of those who were opposing Paul (chapters 10–11).
2. How was Paul responding to their opposition? Why do you think he was so concerned about their influence?
3. Contrast Paul's ministry with the actions of those who opposed him. What were the key differences?
4. How can you avoid being deceived by teachers of false doctrine?
5. We must not only know sound doctrine, but also live according to its truth. What areas of your daily life reflect sound doctrine?

**E**ver known a church like Matt's? Words like *different* and *strict* don't even begin to tell the story. Maybe Matt's best friend Randy gave the best description. He attended Matt's church for several months—then quit. Matt wanted to know why. ■ "I just don't like it, OK?" Randy finally said. "It's the 'don't church.' You guys have about fifty million rules—Don't date. Don't wear certain clothes. Don't go to the movies. Don't dance. Don't go to parties. Don't wear jewelry. Don't be friends with non-Christians. And the list just keeps going. I can't even *remember* all the rules, much less *follow* them! Besides, some people there act like they're *better* than people who go to other churches." ■ "But you said you *liked* our preacher—and the services." ■ "I guess I did—at first. But I came home feeling more and more guilty, and further away from God than ever. Sorry, Matt, but if following all those rules is how I'm supposed to get close to God, I might as well forget it . . . . Hey, I want to be a good Christian—but I'll never be *that* good." ■ Almost 2,000 years ago there was another "don't church" of Christians trying to follow rules. In fact, a whole book of the Bible addresses trying to *earn* God's acceptance by doing "right" things. ■ Read Galatians. You'll find that anyone who thinks the Bible doesn't relate to modern times has never read it!

## STATS

PURPOSE: To refute the Judaizers (who taught that Gentile believers must obey the Jewish law to be saved), and to call Christians to faith and freedom in Christ

AUTHOR: Paul

TO WHOM WRITTEN: The churches in southern Galatia founded on Paul's first missionary journey (including Iconium, Lystra, Derbe), and Christians everywhere

DATE WRITTEN: About A.D. 49, from Antioch, prior to the Jerusalem council (A.D. 50)

SETTING: The most pressing controversy of the early church was the relationship of new believers, especially Gentiles, to the Jewish laws. When this problem hit the converts and young churches Paul founded on his first missionary journey, Paul wrote to correct it. Later, at the council in Jerusalem, the conflict was officially resolved by the church leaders.

KEY PEOPLE: Paul, Peter, Barnabas, Titus, Abraham, false teachers

KEY PLACES: Galatia, Jerusalem

# Galatians

CHAPTER 1 **PAUL: CHRIST'S MISSIONARY.** This letter is
from Paul, an apostle. I was not appointed by any
group or by human authority. My call is from Jesus
Christ himself and from God the Father, who raised
Jesus from the dead.

2All the brothers and sisters* here join me in
sending greetings to the churches of Galatia.

3May grace and peace be yours from God our
Father and from the Lord Jesus Christ. 4He died for
our sins, just as God our Father planned, in order to
rescue us from this evil world in which we live. 5That
is why all glory belongs to God through all the ages
of eternity. Amen.

6I am shocked that you are turning away so soon
from God, who in his love and mercy called you to
share the eternal life he gives through Christ. You are
already following a different way 7that pretends to be
the Good News but is not the Good News at all. You
are being fooled by those who twist and change the
truth concerning Christ.

8Let God's curse fall on anyone, including myself,
who preaches any other message than the one we
told you about. Even if an angel comes from heaven
and preaches any other message, let him be forever
cursed. 9I will say it again: If anyone preaches any
other gospel than the one you welcomed, let God's
curse fall upon that person.

10Obviously, I'm not trying to be a people pleaser!
No, I am trying to please God. If I were still trying to
please people, I would not be Christ's servant.

11Dear brothers and sisters, I solemnly assure you
that the Good News of salvation which I preach is
not based on mere human reasoning or logic. 12For
my message came by a direct revelation from Jesus
Christ himself. No one else taught me.

13You know what I was like when I followed the
Jewish religion—how I violently persecuted the
Christians.* I did my best to get rid of them. 14I was

**TWISTED ● ● • • •**

1:7 **Twisted truth is sometimes more difficult to spot than outright lies. The Judaizers were twisting and changing the truth about Christ because they believed that all believers had to follow the Jewish laws in order to be saved. They claimed to follow him, but they denied that Jesus' work on the cross was sufficient for salvation. There will always be people who twist the Good News. Either they do not understand what the Bible teaches, or they are uncomfortable with the truth as it stands. How can we tell when people are twisting the truth? Find out what they teach about Jesus Christ. If their teaching does not match the truth in God's Word, then it is wrong.**

1:2 Greek *brothers;* also in 1:11. 1:13 Greek *the church of God.*

one of the most religious Jews of my own age, and I
tried as hard as possible to follow all the old traditions of my religion.
15But then something happened! For it pleased
God in his kindness to choose me and call me,
even before I was born! What undeserved mercy!
16Then he revealed his Son to me* so that I could
proclaim the Good News about Jesus to the Gentiles. When all this happened to me, I did not rush
out to consult with anyone else; 17nor did I go up
to Jerusalem to consult with those who were apostles before I was. No, I went away into Arabia and
later returned to the city of Damascus. 18It was not
until three years later that I finally went to Jerusalem for a visit with Peter* and stayed there with
him for fifteen days. 19And the only other apostle I
met at that time was James, our Lord's brother.
20You must believe what I am saying, for I declare
before God that I am not lying. 21Then after this
visit, I went north into the provinces of Syria and
Cilicia. 22And still the Christians in the churches in
Judea didn't know me personally. 23All they knew
was that people were saying, "The one who used to
persecute us now preaches the very faith he tried to
destroy!" 24And they gave glory to God because
of me.

CHAPTER **2** **CHURCH LEADERS ACCEPT PAUL.** Then
fourteen years later I went back to Jerusalem again,
this time with Barnabas; and Titus came along,
too. 2I went there because God revealed to me that
I should go. While I was there I talked privately
with the leaders of the church. I wanted them to
understand what I had been preaching to the Gen-

## BIG CHANGE ● ● ● • •

1:24 **Paul's changed life brought many comments from people who saw or heard of him. His new life astonished them, and they glorified God because only God could have turned this zealous persecutor of Christians into a Christian himself. We may not have had as dramatic a change as Paul had, but our new life should glorify our Savior. When people look at us, do they recognize that God has made changes in us? If not, perhaps we are not living as we should.**

tiles. I wanted to make sure they did not disagree,
or my ministry would have been useless. 3And they
did agree. They did not even demand that my
companion Titus be circumcised, though he was a
Gentile.*
4Even that question wouldn't have come up except for some so-called Christians there—false
ones, really*—who came to spy on us and see our
freedom in Christ Jesus. They wanted to force us,
like slaves, to follow their Jewish regulations. 5But
we refused to listen to them for a single moment.
We wanted to preserve the truth of the Good News
for you.
6And the leaders of the church who were there
had nothing to add to what I was preaching. (By
the way, their reputation as great leaders made no
difference to me, for God has no favorites.) 7They
saw that God had given me the responsibility of
preaching the Good News to the Gentiles, just as
he had given Peter the responsibility of preaching
to the Jews. 8For the same God who worked
through Peter for the benefit of the Jews worked
through me for the benefit of the Gentiles. 9In fact,
James, Peter,* and John, who were known as pillars of the church, recognized the gift God had

1:16 Or *in me.* 1:18 Greek *Cephas.* 2:3 Greek *a Greek.* 2:4 Greek *some false brothers.* 2:9 Greek *Cephas;* also in 2:11, 14.

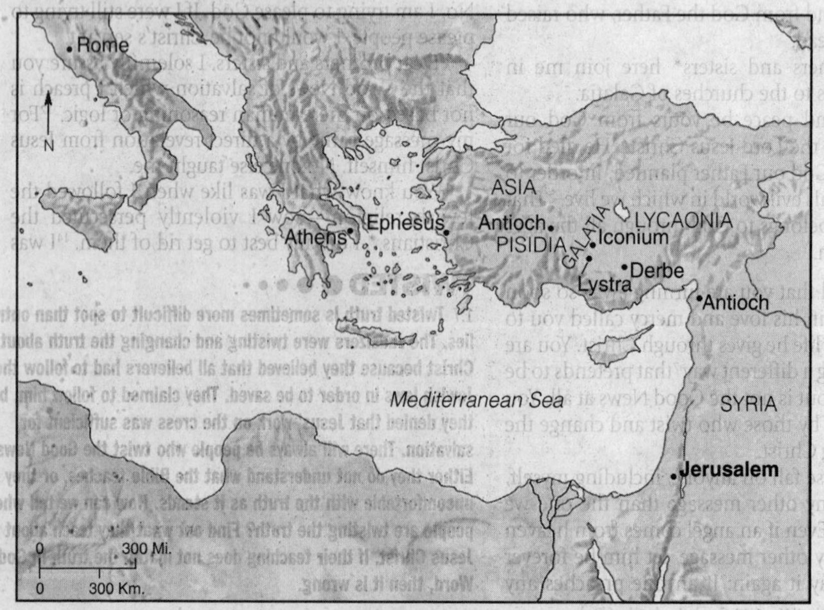


**CITIES IN GALATIA**
Paul visited several cities in Galatia on each of his three missionary journeys. On his first journey he went through Antioch in Pisidia, Iconium, Lystra, and Derbe, then retraced his steps. On his second journey he went by land from Antioch in Syria through the four cities in Galatia. On his third journey he also went through those cities on the main route to Ephesus.

## WHAT IS THE LAW?

Part of the Jewish law included those laws found in the Old Testament. In the Old Testament there were three categories of law: ceremonial laws, civil laws, and moral laws. When Paul says that non-Jews (Gentiles) are no longer bound by these laws, he is not saying that the Old Testament laws do not apply to us today. He is saying certain types of laws may not apply to us.

*Ceremonial Law*
This kind of law relates specifically to Israel's worship (for example, see Leviticus 1:1-13). Its primary purpose was to point forward to Jesus Christ. Therefore, these laws were no longer necessary after Jesus' death and resurrection. While we are no longer bound by ceremonial laws, the principles behind them—to worship and love a holy God—still apply. The Jewish Christians often accused the Gentile Christians of violating the ceremonial law.

*Civil Law*
This type of law dictated Israel's daily living (for example, see Deuteronomy 24:10-11). Because modern society and culture are so radically different, some of these guidelines cannot be followed specifically. But the principles behind the commands should guide our conduct. At times, Paul asked Gentile Christians to follow some of these laws, not because they had to, but to promote unity.

*Moral Law*
This sort of law is the direct command of God—for example, the Ten Commandments (Exodus 20:1-17). It requires strict obedience. It reveals the nature and will of God, and it still applies to us today. We are to obey this moral law, not to obtain salvation, but to live in ways pleasing to God.

---

given me, and they accepted Barnabas and me as
their co-workers. They encouraged us to keep
preaching to the Gentiles, while they continued
their work with the Jews. 10The only thing they
suggested was that we remember to help the poor,
and I have certainly been eager to do that.
11But when Peter came to Antioch, I had to oppose him publicly, speaking strongly against what
he was doing, for it was very wrong. 12When he first
arrived, he ate with the Gentile Christians, who
don't bother with circumcision. But afterward,
when some Jewish friends of James came, Peter
wouldn't eat with the Gentiles anymore because he
was afraid of what these legalists would say. 13Then
the other Jewish Christians followed Peter's hypocrisy, and even Barnabas was influenced to join
them in their hypocrisy.
14When I saw that they were not following the
truth of the Good News, I said to Peter in front of
all the others, "Since you, a Jew by birth, have
discarded the Jewish laws and are living like a
Gentile, why are you trying to make these Gentiles
obey the Jewish laws you abandoned? 15You and I
are Jews by birth, not 'sinners' like the Gentiles.
16And yet we Jewish Christians know that we become right with God, not by doing what the law
commands, but by faith in Jesus Christ. So we have
believed in Christ Jesus, that we might be accepted
by God because of our faith in Christ—and not
because we have obeyed the law. For no one will
ever be saved by obeying the law."*
17But what if we seek to be made right with God
through faith in Christ and then find out that we
are still sinners? Has Christ led us into sin? Of
course not! 18Rather, I make myself guilty if I rebuild the old system I already tore down. 19For
when I tried to keep the law, I realized I could never
earn God's approval. So I died to the law so that I
might live for God. I have been crucified with
Christ. 20I myself no longer live, but Christ lives in
me. So I live my life in this earthly body by trusting
in the Son of God, who loved me and gave himself
for me. 21I am not one of those who treats the grace
of God as meaningless. For if we could be saved by
keeping the law, then there was no need for Christ
to die.

## POOR PEOPLE ● ● • • •

**2:10 Here the apostles were referring to the poor people of Jerusalem. While many Gentile converts were financially comfortable, the Jerusalem church was suffering from a severe famine in Palestine (see Acts 11:28-30). Much of Paul's time was spent gathering funds for the Jewish Christians (Acts 24:17; Romans 15:25-29; 1 Corinthians 16:1-4; 2 Corinthians 8). Believers caring for the poor is a constant theme of Scripture, but often we do nothing about it. Both in your own city and across the oceans, there are people who need help. What can you do to show them God's love?**

2:16 Some translators hold that the quotation extends through verse 14; others through verse 16; and still others through verse 21.

CHAPTER **3** **JEWISH LAW AND FAITH IN CHRIST.** Oh, foolish Galatians! What magician has cast an evil spell on you? For you used to see the meaning of Jesus Christ's death as clearly as though I had shown you a signboard with a picture of Christ dying on the cross. 2Let me ask you this one question: Did you receive the Holy Spirit by keeping the law? Of course not, for the Holy Spirit came upon you only after you believed the message you heard about Christ. 3Have you lost your senses? After starting your Christian lives in the Spirit, why are you now trying to become perfect by your own human effort? 4You have suffered so much for the Good News. Surely it was not in vain, was it? Are you now going to just throw it all away?

## FREEDOM

Cindi storms up upstairs, slams her bedroom door, and flings herself onto the bed. Burying her face in a pillow, she lets out a yell of disgust.

Rolling over, she stares at the ceiling and begins thinking:

*Ooooh. I can't believe them! They're like the Gestapo! Why don't they just go ahead and put bars around my room? They don't let me do anything. They ask me six million questions about everything. They hate all my friends. They make me dress like a street person.*

Cindi glances at the calendar above her desk.

*Nine more months—then I can go to college and do whatever I want. I'll be totally free. If I don't want to go to church, I won't have to. If I want to trash my room and leave it that way the whole semester, I can. I'll be able to go out when I want and see who I want without them totally humiliating me.*

*Oh, gosh, that is gonna be so great! No more missing out on life. There'll be parties, tons of awesome guys, and . . .*

Cindi's daydream is shattered by a voice yelling:

"Cindi! Come pick up your shoes from out of the middle of the living room floor—now!"

Cindi groans and heads downstairs, mumbling, "Enjoy it now, Mom. Because in nine months, I'm out of here."

Is that freedom? Being able to do whatever you want? Or does real freedom have certain limits? See Galatians 5:16-25 to find out.

5I ask you again, does God give you the Holy Spirit and work miracles among you because you obey the law of Moses? Of course not! It is because you believe the message you heard about Christ.

6In the same way, "Abraham believed God, so God declared him righteous because of his faith."* 7The real children of Abraham, then, are all those who put their faith in God.

8What's more, the Scriptures looked forward to this time when God would accept the Gentiles, too, on the basis of their faith. God promised this good news to Abraham long ago when he said, "All nations will be blessed through you."* 9And so it

## DIFFERENCES

3:28 **Our natural inclination is to feel uncomfortable around those who are different from us and to spend time with those who resemble us. But when we allow our differences to separate us from our fellow believers, we disregard clear biblical teaching. Make a point of seeking out and appreciating people who are different from you and your friends. You may find that you and they have a lot in common.**

is: All who put their faith in Christ share the same blessing Abraham received because of his faith.

10But those who depend on the law to make them right with God are under his curse, for the Scriptures say, "Cursed is everyone who does not observe and obey all these commands that are written in God's Book of the Law."* 11Consequently, it is clear that no one can ever be right with God by trying to keep the law. For the Scriptures say, "It is through faith that a righteous person has life."* 12How different from this way of faith is the way of law, which says, "If you wish to find life by obeying the law, you must obey all of its commands."* 13But Christ has rescued us from the curse pronounced by the law. When he was hung on the cross, he took upon himself the curse for our wrongdoing. For it is written in the Scriptures, "Cursed is everyone who is hung on a tree."* 14Through the work of Christ Jesus, God has blessed the Gentiles with the same blessing he promised to Abraham, and we Christians receive the promised Holy Spirit through faith.

15Dear brothers and sisters,* here's an example from everyday life. Just as no one can set aside or amend an irrevocable agreement, so it is in this case. 16God gave the promise to Abraham and his child.* And notice that it doesn't say the promise was to his children,* as if it meant many descendants. But the promise was to his child—and that, of course, means Christ. 17This is what I am trying to say: The agreement God made with Abraham could not be canceled 430 years later when God gave the law to Moses. God would be breaking his promise. 18For if the inheritance could be received only by keeping the law, then it would not be the result of accepting God's promise. But God gave it to Abraham as a promise.

19Well then, why was the law given? It was given to show people how guilty they are. But this system of law was to last only until the coming of the child to whom God's promise was made. And there is this further difference. God gave his laws to angels to give to Moses, who was the mediator between God and the people. 20Now a mediator is needed if two people enter into an agreement, but God acted on his own when he made his promise to Abraham.

21Well then, is there a conflict between God's law and God's promises? Absolutely not! If the law could have given us new life, we could have been made right with God by obeying it. 22But the

3:6 Gen 15:6. 3:8 Gen 12:3; 18:18; 22:18. 3:10 Deut 27:26. 3:11 Hab 2:4. 3:12 Lev 18:5. 3:13 Deut 21:23. 3:15 Greek *Brothers.* 3:16a Greek *seed;* also in 3:16c, 19. See Gen 12:7. 3:16b Greek *seeds.*

Scriptures have declared that we are all prisoners of
sin, so the only way to receive God's promise is to
believe in Jesus Christ.
23Until faith in Christ was shown to us as the
way of becoming right with God, we were guarded
by the law. We were kept in protective custody, so
to speak, until we could put our faith in the coming Savior.
24Let me put it another way. The law was our
guardian and teacher to lead us until Christ came.
So now, through faith in Christ, we are made right
with God. 25But now that faith in Christ has come,
we no longer need the law as our guardian. 26So
you are all children* of God through faith in Christ
Jesus. 27And all who have been united with Christ
in baptism have been made like him. 28There is no
longer Jew or Gentile,* slave or free, male or
female. For you are all Christians—you are one in
Christ Jesus. 29And now that you belong to Christ,
you are the true children of Abraham. You are his
heirs, and now all the promises God gave to him
belong to you.

## CHAPTER 4 PAUL'S CONCERN FOR THE GALATIANS.

Think of it this way. If a father dies and leaves great
wealth for his young children, those children are not
much better off than slaves until they grow up, even
though they actually own everything their father
had. 2They have to obey their guardians until they
reach whatever age their father set.
3And that's the way it was with us before Christ
came. We were slaves to the spiritual powers of this
world. 4But when the right time came, God sent his
Son, born of a woman, subject to the law. 5God sent
him to buy freedom for us who were slaves to the
law, so that he could adopt us as his very own
children.* 6And because you Gentiles have become
his children, God has sent the Spirit of his Son into
your hearts, and now you can call God your dear
Father.* 7Now you are no longer a slave but God's
own child.* And since you are his child, everything
he has belongs to you.
8Before you Gentiles knew God, you were slaves
to so-called gods that do not even exist. 9And now
that you have found God (or should I say, now that
God has found you), why do you want to go back
again and become slaves once more to the weak
and useless spiritual powers of this world? 10You
are trying to find favor with God by what you do or
don't do on certain days or months or seasons or
years. 11I fear for you. I am afraid that all my hard
work for you was worth nothing. 12Dear brothers
and sisters,* I plead with you to live as I do in
freedom from these things, for I have become like
you Gentiles were—free from the law.
You did not mistreat me when I first preached to
you. 13Surely you remember that I was sick when I
first brought you the Good News of Christ. 14But
even though my sickness was revolting to you, you
did not reject me and turn me away. No, you took me
in and cared for me as though I were an angel from
God or even Christ Jesus himself. 15Where is that
joyful spirit we felt together then? In those days, I
know you would gladly have taken out your own
eyes and given them to me if it had been possible.
16Have I now become your enemy because I am
telling you the truth?
17Those false teachers who are so anxious to win
your favor are not doing it for your good. They are
trying to shut you off from me so that you will pay
more attention to them. 18Now it's wonderful if
you are eager to do good, and especially when I am
not with you. 19But oh, my dear children! I feel as
if I am going through labor pains for you again,
and they will continue until Christ is fully developed in your lives. 20How I wish I were there with
you right now, so that I could be more gentle with
you. But at this distance I frankly don't know what
else to do.
21Listen to me, you who want to live under the
law. Do you know what the law really says? 22The
Scriptures say that Abraham had two sons, one
from his slave-wife and one from his freeborn
wife.* 23The son of the slave-wife was born in a
human attempt to bring about the fulfillment of
God's promise. But the son of the freeborn wife
was born as God's own fulfillment of his promise.
24Now these two women serve as an illustration
of God's two covenants. Hagar, the slave-wife, represents Mount Sinai where people first became
enslaved to the law. 25And now Jerusalem is just
like Mount Sinai in Arabia, because she and her
children live in slavery. 26But Sarah, the free
woman, represents the heavenly Jerusalem. And
she is our mother. 27That is what Isaiah meant
when he prophesied,

> "Rejoice, O childless woman!
> Break forth into loud and joyful song,
> even though you never gave birth to a child.
> For the woman who could bear no children
> now has more than all the other women!"*

28And you, dear brothers and sisters, are children
of the promise, just like Isaac. 29And we who are
born of the Holy Spirit are persecuted by those
who want us to keep the law, just as Isaac, the child
of promise, was persecuted by Ishmael, the son of
the slave-wife.

**BE OPEN • • • • •**

4:16 **Paul did not gain great popularity when he criticized the Galatians for turning away from their first faith in Christ. Human nature hasn't changed much—we still get angry when we're scolded. But don't write off someone who challenges you. There may be truth in what he or she says. Receive the challenge with humility; carefully think it over. If you discover you need to change an attitude or action, take steps to do it.**

3:26 Greek *sons.* 3:28 Greek *Jew or Greek.* 4:5 Greek *sons;* also in 4:6. 4:6 Greek *into your hearts, crying, "Abba, Father." Abba* is an Aramaic term for "father." 4:7 Greek *son;* also in 4:7b. 4:12 Greek *brothers;* also in 4:28, 31. 4:22 See Gen 16:15; 21:2-3. 4:27 Isa 54:1.

**LOVE ● ● ● • •**

5:14-15 **When we are not motivated by love, we become critical of others. We stop looking for good in them and see only their faults. Soon the unity of believers becomes broken. Have you talked behind someone's back? Have you focused on others' shortcomings instead of their strengths? Remind yourself of Jesus' command to love others as we love ourselves (Matthew 22:39). When you begin to feel critical of someone, make a list of that person's positive qualities. And don't say anything behind his back that you wouldn't say to his face.**

30 But what do the Scriptures say about that? "Get rid of the slave and her son, for the son of the slave woman will not share the family inheritance with the free woman's son."* 31 So, dear brothers and sisters, we are not children of the slave woman, obligated to the law. We are children of the free woman, acceptable to God because of our faith.

CHAPTER **5** **FREEDOM: CHRIST'S SPECIAL GIFT.** So Christ has really set us free. Now make sure that you stay free, and don't get tied up again in slavery to the law.

2 Listen! I, Paul, tell you this: If you are counting on circumcision to make you right with God, then Christ cannot help you. 3 I'll say it again. If you are trying to find favor with God by being circumcised, you must obey all of the regulations in the whole law of Moses. 4 For if you are trying to make yourselves right with God by keeping the law, you have been cut off from Christ! You have fallen away from God's grace.

5 But we who live by the Spirit eagerly wait to receive everything promised to us who are right with God through faith. 6 For when we place our faith in Christ Jesus, it makes no difference to God whether we are circumcised or not circumcised. What is important is faith expressing itself in love.

**FRUIT ● ● ● • •**

5:22-23 **The Holy Spirit produces character traits, not specific actions. We can't go out and *do* these things, and we can't obtain them by trying to get them. If we want the fruit of the Holy Spirit to develop in our life, we must recognize that all of these characteristics are found in Christ. The way to grow them is to know Christ, love him, remember him, imitate him (see John 15:4-5). The result will be that we will fulfill the intended purpose of the law—loving God and people. Which of these qualities most needs further development in your life?**

7 You were getting along so well. Who has interfered with you to hold you back from following the truth? 8 It certainly isn't God, for he is the one who called you to freedom. 9 But it takes only one wrong person among you to infect all the others—a little yeast spreads quickly through the whole batch of dough! 10 I am trusting the Lord to bring you back to believing as I do about these things. God will judge that person, whoever it is, who has been troubling and confusing you.

*But when the Holy Spirit controls our lives, he will produce this kind of fruit in us:*

**love joy peace patience kindness goodness faithfulness gentleness and self-control.**

GALATIANS 5:22-23

11 Dear brothers and sisters,* if I were still preaching that you must be circumcised—as some say I do—why would the Jews persecute me? The fact that I am still being persecuted proves that I

4:30 Gen 21:10. 5:11 Greek *Brothers.*

am still preaching salvation through the cross of
Christ alone. 12I only wish that those troublemakers who want to mutilate you by circumcision
would mutilate themselves.*
13For you have been called to live in freedom—
not freedom to satisfy your sinful nature, but freedom to serve one another in love. 14For the whole
law can be summed up in this one command:
"Love your neighbor as yourself."* 15But if instead
of showing love among yourselves you are always
biting and devouring one another, watch out! Beware of destroying one another.
16So I advise you to live according to your new
life in the Holy Spirit. Then you won't be doing
what your sinful nature craves. 17The old sinful
nature loves to do evil, which is just opposite from
what the Holy Spirit wants. And the Spirit gives us
desires that are opposite from what the sinful nature desires. These two forces are constantly fighting each other, and your choices are never free
from this conflict. 18But when you are directed by
the Holy Spirit, you are no longer subject to the
law.
19When you follow the desires of your sinful
nature, your lives will produce these evil results:
sexual immorality, impure thoughts, eagerness for
lustful pleasure, 20idolatry, participation in demonic activities, hostility, quarreling, jealousy,
outbursts of anger, selfish ambition, divisions, the
feeling that everyone is wrong except those in your
own little group, 21envy, drunkenness, wild parties,
and other kinds of sin. Let me tell you again, as I
have before, that anyone living that sort of life will
not inherit the Kingdom of God.
22But when the Holy Spirit controls our lives, he
will produce this kind of fruit in us: love, joy, peace,
patience, kindness, goodness, faithfulness, 23gen-
tleness, and self-control. Here there is no conflict
with the law.
24Those who belong to Christ Jesus have nailed
the passions and desires of their sinful nature to
his cross and crucified them there. 25If we are living
now by the Holy Spirit, let us follow the Holy
Spirit's leading in every part of our lives. 26Let us
not become conceited, or irritate one another, or
be jealous of one another.

CHAPTER **6** **WE REAP WHAT WE SOW.** Dear brothers
and sisters, if another Christian* is overcome by
some sin, you who are godly should gently and
humbly help that person back onto the right path.
And be careful not to fall into the same temptation
yourself. 2Share each other's troubles and problems,
and in this way obey the law of Christ. 3If you think
you are too important to help someone in need, you
are only fooling yourself. You are really a nobody.
4Be sure to do what you should, for then you
will enjoy the personal satisfaction of having
done your work well, and you won't need to

5:12 Or *castrate themselves;* Greek reads *cut themselves off.* 5:14 Lev 19:18. 6:1 Greek *Brothers, if a man.*

## EVERY PART ● ● ● • •

5:25 **God is interested in every part of our life, not just the spiritual part. As we live by the Holy Spirit's power, we need to submit every aspect of our life to God—emotional, physical, social, intellectual, and vocational. Paul says, in effect, "You're saved, so live like it!" The Holy Spirit is the source of your new life, so walk with him. Don't let anything or anyone else determine your values and standards in any area of your life.**

### I know that taking drugs is wrong, but the Bible doesn't talk about them. What should I say to someone who asks me about drugs?

There are some areas where the Bible is silent. A good example is R-rated movies. The Bible doesn't specifically forbid attending movies that contain vulgar language, violence, or sex. In such cases, it is essential to seek the wisdom of those who know God's Word well. By looking at a number of passages, it is obvious we should avoid those kind of movies.

Of course, there are many areas where the Bible is specific in its warnings. Homosexuality is a good example (see 1 Corinthians 6:9-10). Then there are areas that are "hidden" to a degree. Taking drugs falls into this category.

Originally the New Testament was written in Greek, a much more complicated language than English. Trying to translate a word from Greek to English often can only be done by a phrase.

In Galatians 5:20, Christians are warned against becoming involved in demonic activities. The term translated "demonic activities" actually comes from the Greek noun *pharmakeia*, from which we get the word *pharmacy* (better known as a drug store!). When most of the Bible was translated, drug problems were not common, but there was "demonic activity."

The connection is frightening. Demonic activity actually takes place when drugs are taken! These aren't the aspirin type of drugs, but the kinds that alter a person's emotions, reflexes, and brain waves.

To get even more specific, taking drugs is like opening your subconscious to demons! The connection between drugs and witchcraft is easily seen by going to the original Greek word.

Unknowingly, a person who takes drugs opens himself or herself to demonic influence. It's like an invitation to the spirit world to start influencing that person's life. That's why it's so dangerous.

Although many may laugh at this explanation, it's a message that must be given to those who are taking drugs.

Drugs also should be avoided because they harm our body. The Bible is very clear about our responsibility to take care of ourself. See 1 Corinthians 6:19-20; Romans 12:1-2; and 3 John 1:2-3.

## LOOK AT JESUS ● ● • • •

6:4 **When you do your very best, you feel good about the results, and there is no need to compare yourself with others. People make comparisons for many reasons. Some point out others' flaws in order to feel better about themselves. Others simply want reassurance that they are doing well. When you are tempted to compare, look at Jesus Christ. His example will inspire you to do your very best, and his loving acceptance will comfort you when you fall short of your goals.**

compare yourself to anyone else. [5]For we are each responsible for our own conduct.

[6]Those who are taught the word of God should help their teachers by paying them.

[7]Don't be misled. Remember that you can't ignore God and get away with it. You will always reap what you sow! [8]Those who live only to satisfy their own sinful desires will harvest the consequences of decay and death. But those who live to please the Spirit will harvest everlasting life from the Spirit. [9]So don't get tired of doing what is good. Don't get discouraged and give up, for we will reap a harvest of blessing at the appropriate time. [10]Whenever we have the opportunity, we should do good to everyone, especially to our Christian brothers and sisters.

[11]Notice what large letters I use as I write these closing words in my own handwriting. [12]Those who are trying to force you to be circumcised are doing it for just one reason. They don't want to be persecuted for teaching that the cross of Christ alone can save. [13]And even those who advocate circumcision don't really keep the whole law. They only want you to be circumcised so they can brag about it and claim you as their disciples.

[14]As for me, God forbid that I should boast about anything except the cross of our Lord Jesus Christ. Because of that cross,* my interest in this world died long ago, and the world's interest in me is also long dead. [15]It doesn't make any difference now whether we have been circumcised or not. What counts is whether we really have been changed into new and different people. [16]May God's mercy and peace be upon all those who live by this principle. They are the new people of God.*

[17]From now on, don't let anyone trouble me with these things. For I bear on my body the scars that show I belong to Jesus.

[18]My dear brothers and sisters,* may the grace of our Lord Jesus Christ be with you all. Amen.

6:14 Or *Because of him.* 6:16 Greek *the Israel of God.* 6:18 Greek *Brothers.*

# MEGA themes

**LAW** A group of Jewish teachers were insisting that non-Jewish believers obey Jewish laws and traditions. These teachers believed that a person was saved by following the law of Moses (with emphasis on circumcision, the sign of the covenant) in addition to faith in Christ. Paul opposed them, showing that the law can't save anyone.

The law can't save us. It wasn't ever meant to be our salvation. It was intended to be a guide, to point out our need to be forgiven. Christ fulfilled the obligations of the law for us. We must turn to him to be saved. Christ alone can make us right with God. Then we should obey God in response to what he has done for us.

1. What error had the Jewish believers made concerning the role of the law?
2. What truth did Paul use to correct their error?
3. Based on Galatians, why are good works not enough to bring a person salvation?
4. How does the law point out our need for salvation?
5. How should you respond to the law now that you have been saved through Jesus Christ?

**FAITH** God's gracious gift to us saves us from God's judgment and the penalty for sin. We receive salvation by faith—trusting in Christ, not in anything else. Becoming a Christian is in no way based on our work, wise choices, or good character. We can only be right with God by believing in Christ.

Eternal life comes only through faith in Christ. You must never add to this truth or twist it. We are saved by faith and faith alone. Have you placed your whole trust and confidence in Christ? He alone can forgive you and bring you into relationship with God.

1. What does it mean to be saved by faith?
2. How would you answer a person who said:

"I have been good, so I know God will let me into heaven"?

3. In spite of your sin, God gave you faith. What does this reveal to you about God?
4. How have you responded to God's offer of salvation?
5. During this past week, how have you lived your life by faith?

**FREEDOM** Galatians sets forth our freedom in Christ. We are not under the jurisdiction of Jewish laws and traditions, nor under the authority of Jerusalem. Faith in Christ brings true freedom from sin and from the futile attempt to be right with God by keeping the law.

We are free in Christ, free to serve him—but freedom is a privilege. Let us use our freedom to love and to serve, not to do wrong.

1. Finish these sentences:
   a) Christian freedom means ________
   b) Christian freedom does not mean ________
2. In what ways could your freedom in Christ be misused?
3. For what purpose has God given you freedom? How are you fulfilling that purpose in your life?

**HOLY SPIRIT** We become Christians through the work of the Holy Spirit. The Spirit brings new life, and even our faith is a gift from him. The Holy Spirit instructs us, guides us, leads us, and gives us power. He ends our bondage to evil desires; brings us love, joy, and peace; and changes us into the image of Christ.

When the Holy Spirit controls us, he produces his fruit in us. Through faith, we can have the Holy Spirit within us, strengthening and guarding us and helping us grow spiritually.

1. According to chapter 3, how does a person receive the Holy Spirit?
2. According to 5:16-26, what difference does the Holy Spirit bring to a person's life? What difference has the Holy Spirit made in your life?
3. Why do you need the Holy Spirit to be at work in your life?
4. What can you do to continue to "walk in the Spirit"?

**A**n argument with a friend ■ A hug from Mom ■ A drive with Dad ■ A note in your locker ■ A prayer before bedtime ■ Every event of every day underlines this fundamental fact: *Life is made up of relationships.* We relate in a "horizontal" way to other people; we relate in a "vertical" manner to our Creator. Pretty basic stuff, right? ■ But here's where things get profound: Our problems, individual and national, are due to *broken-down relationships.* It's because we fail to relate properly to God and to each other that we lie, cheat, steal, murder, drink and drive, divorce, engage in illicit sex, abort our babies, fight wars, pollute, buy and sell drugs, ignore the needy, commit suicide, and all the other wrong things we do. ■ So what is the remedy for ruptured relationships? In a nutshell: *Jesus Christ can repair our broken-down relationships!* ■ First, Jesus pardons our sins, bringing us into a right relationship with God. (Get this—by faith in Christ we are adopted into God's family! We become his children . . . eternally!) Then Christ gives us the wisdom and the power to build stronger horizontal ties—with parents, friends, bosses . . . even enemies! ■ Can your relationships stand a little improving? Check out Ephesians. The first three chapters explain how Jesus has made it possible for us to know God in a personal way. The rest of the book provides practical tips for getting along with people. ■ Hey, it just might change your life!

## STATS

PURPOSE: To strengthen the Christian faith of the believers in Ephesus by explaining the nature and purpose of the church, the body of Christ

AUTHOR: Paul

TO WHOM WRITTEN: The church at Ephesus, and all believers everywhere

DATE WRITTEN: About A.D. 60, from Rome, during Paul's imprisonment there

SETTING: The letter was not written to confront any heresy or problem. It was sent with Tychicus to strengthen and encourage area churches. Paul spent over three years with the Ephesian church; he was very close to them. His last meeting with the Ephesian elders was at Miletus (Acts 20:17-38)—a meeting filled with great sadness because Paul was leaving them forever. There are no specific references to people or problems in the Ephesian church, so Paul may have intended this letter to be read to all the area churches.

KEY PEOPLE: Paul, Tychicus

CHAPTER 1 **PAUL: A LOYAL FOLLOWER OF CHRIST.** This letter is from Paul, chosen by God to be an apostle of Christ Jesus.

It is written to God's holy people in Ephesus,* who are faithful followers of Christ Jesus.

2May grace and peace be yours, sent to you from God our Father and Jesus Christ our Lord.

3How we praise God, the Father of our Lord Jesus
Christ, who has blessed us with every spiritual blessing in the heavenly realms because we belong to
Christ. 4Long ago, even before he made the world,
God loved us and chose us in Christ to be holy and
without fault in his eyes. 5His unchanging plan has
always been to adopt us into his own family by bringing us to himself through Jesus Christ. And this gave him great pleasure.

6So we praise God for the wonderful kindness he
has poured out on us because we belong to his
dearly loved Son. 7He is so rich in kindness that he
purchased our freedom through the blood of his
Son, and our sins are forgiven. 8He has showered his
kindness on us, along with all wisdom and understanding.

9God's secret plan has now been revealed to us;
it is a plan centered on Christ, designed long ago
according to his good pleasure. 10And this is his
plan: At the right time he will bring everything together under the authority of Christ—everything
in heaven and on earth. 11Furthermore, because of
Christ, we have received an inheritance from God,* for he chose us from the beginning, and all
things happen just as he decided long ago. 12God's
purpose was that we who were the first to trust in
Christ should praise our glorious God. 13And now
you also have heard the truth, the Good News that God saves you. And when you believed in Christ, he identified you as his own by giving you the Holy
Spirit, whom he promised long ago. 14The Spirit is
God's guarantee that he will give us everything he

## THE MYSTERY

**1:4 Paul says that God "chose us in Christ" to emphasize that salvation depends totally on God. We are not saved because we deserve it, but because God is gracious and freely gives salvation. We did not influence God's decision to save us; he did it according to his plan. Thus there is no way to take credit for your salvation or to find room for pride. The mystery of salvation originated in the timeless mind of God long before we existed. It is hard to understand how God could accept us, but because of Christ, we are holy and blameless in his eyes. God chose you, and when you belong to him through Jesus Christ, he looks at you as if you had never sinned.**

1:1 Some manuscripts do not include *in Ephesus.* 1:11 Or *we have become God's inheritance.*

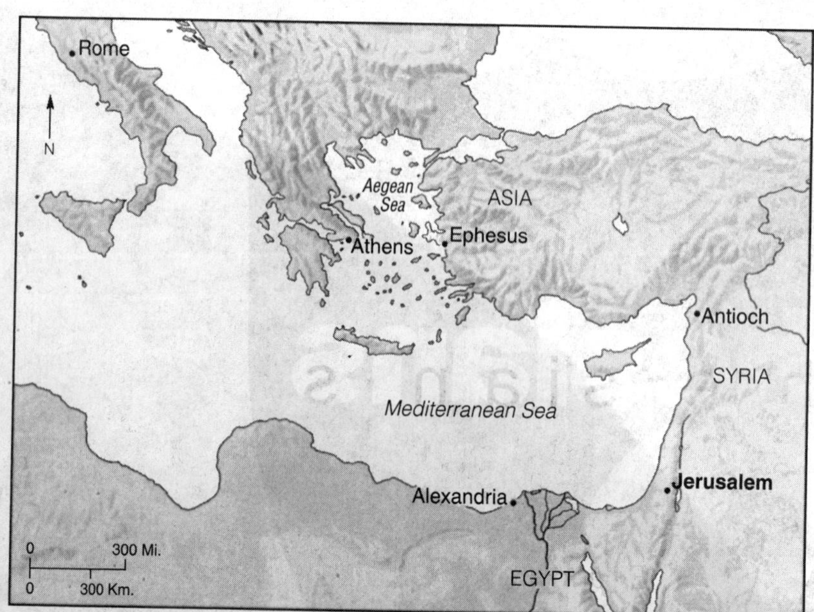


**LOCATION OF EPHESUS**
Ephesus was a strategic city, ranking in importance with Alexandria in Egypt and Antioch in Syria as a port. It lay on the western-most edge of Asia Minor (modern-day Turkey), the most important port on the Aegean Sea on the main route from Rome to the east.

promised and that he has purchased us to be his own people. This is just one more reason for us to praise our glorious God.

15Ever since I first heard of your strong faith in the Lord Jesus and your love for Christians everywhere, 16I have never stopped thanking God for you. I pray for you constantly, 17asking God, the glorious Father of our Lord Jesus Christ, to give you spiritual wisdom and understanding, so that you might grow in your knowledge of God. 18I pray that your hearts will be flooded with light so that you can understand the wonderful future he has promised to those he called. I want you to realize what a rich and glorious inheritance he has given to his people.*

19I pray that you will begin to understand the incredible greatness of his power for us who believe him. This is the same mighty power 20that raised Christ from the dead and seated him in the place of honor at God's right hand in the heavenly realms. 21Now he is far above any ruler or authority or power or leader or anything else in this world or in the world to come. 22And God has put all things under the authority of Christ, and he gave him this authority for the benefit of the church. 23And the church is his body; it is filled by Christ, who fills everything everywhere with his presence.

CHAPTER **2** **OUR LIFE BEFORE AND AFTER CHRIST.** Once you were dead, doomed forever because of your many sins. 2You used to live just like the rest of the world, full of sin, obeying Satan, the mighty prince of the power of the air. He is the spirit at work in the hearts of those who refuse to obey God. 3All of us used to live that way, following the passions and desires of our evil nature. We were born with an evil nature, and we were under God's anger just like everyone else.

4But God is so rich in mercy, and he loved us so very much, 5that even while we were dead because of our sins, he gave us life when he raised Christ from the dead. (It is only by God's special favor that you have been saved!) 6For he raised us from the dead along with Christ, and we are seated with him in the heavenly realms—all because we are one with Christ Jesus. 7And so God can always point to us as examples of the incredible wealth of his favor and kindness toward us, as shown in all he has done for us through Christ Jesus.

8God saved you by his special favor when you believed. And you can't take credit for this; it is a gift from God. 9Salvation is not a reward for the good things we have done, so none of us can boast about it. 10For we are God's masterpiece. He has created us anew in Christ Jesus, so that we can do the good things he planned for us long ago.

11Don't forget that you Gentiles used to be outsiders by birth. You were called "the uncircumcised ones" by the Jews, who were proud of their circum-

## GOD'S SCALE ● ● • • •

2:3 **The fact that all people, without exception, commit sin proves that they share in the sinful nature. Does this mean there are no good people who are not Christians? Of course not—many people do good to others. On a relative scale, many are moral, kind, keep the laws, and so on. Comparing these people to criminals, we would say they are very good indeed. But on God's absolute scale, *no one* is good. Only through uniting our life to Christ's perfect life can we become good in God's sight.**

1:18 Or *realize how much God has been honored by acquiring his people.*

cision, even though it affected only their bodies and not their hearts. [12]In those days you were living apart from Christ. You were excluded from God's people, Israel, and you did not know the promises God had made to them. You lived in this world without God and without hope. [13]But now you belong to Christ Jesus. Though you once were far away from God, now you have been brought near to him because of the blood of Christ.

[14]For Christ himself has made peace between us Jews and you Gentiles by making us all one people. He has broken down the wall of hostility that used to separate us. [15]By his death he ended the whole system of Jewish law that excluded the Gentiles. His purpose was to make peace between Jews and Gentiles by creating in himself one new person from the two groups. [16]Together as one body, Christ reconciled both groups to God by means of his death, and our hostility toward each other was put to death. [17]He has brought this Good News of peace to you Gentiles who were far away from him, and to us Jews who were near. [18]Now all of us, both Jews and Gentiles, may come to the Father through the same Holy Spirit because of what Christ has done for us.

[19]So now you Gentiles are no longer strangers and foreigners. You are citizens along with all of God's holy people. You are members of God's family. [20]We are his house, built on the foundation of the apostles and the prophets. And the cornerstone is Christ Jesus himself. [21]We who believe are carefully joined together, becoming a holy temple for the Lord. [22]Through him you Gentiles are also joined together as part of this dwelling where God lives by his Spirit.

## CHAPTER 3

**SALVATION IS FOR EVERYONE.** I, Paul, am a prisoner of Christ Jesus because of my preaching to you Gentiles. [2]As you already know, God has given me this special ministry of announcing his favor to you Gentiles. [3]As I briefly mentioned earlier in this letter, God himself revealed his secret plan to me. [4]As you read what I have written, you will understand what I know about this plan regarding Christ. [5]God did not reveal it to previous generations, but now he has revealed it by the Holy Spirit to his holy apostles and prophets.

[6]And this is the secret plan: The Gentiles have an equal share with the Jews in all the riches inherited by God's children. Both groups have believed the Good News, and both are part of the same body and enjoy together the promise of blessings through Christ Jesus. [7]By God's special favor and mighty power, I have been given the wonderful privilege of serving him by spreading this Good News.

[8]Just think! Though I did nothing to deserve it, and though I am the least deserving Christian there is, I was chosen for this special joy of telling the Gentiles about the endless treasures available to them in Christ. [9]I was chosen to explain to everyone this plan that God, the Creator of all things, had kept secret from the beginning.

[10]God's purpose was to show his wisdom in all its rich variety to all the rulers and authorities in the heavenly realms. They will see this when Jews and Gentiles are joined together in his church. [11]This was his plan from all eternity, and it has now been carried out through Christ Jesus our Lord.

[12]Because of Christ and our faith in him, we can now come fearlessly into God's presence, assured

### PROUD ● • • • •

2:11-13 **Jews and Gentiles alike could be guilty of spiritual pride—Jews for thinking their ceremonies elevated them above everyone else, Gentiles for forgetting the hopelessness of their condition apart from Christ. Spiritual pride blinds us to our own faults and magnifies the faults of others. Be careful not to become proud of your salvation. Instead, humbly thank God for what he has done and encourage others who might be struggling in their faith.**

### OUR LIFE BEFORE AND AFTER CHRIST

| *Before* | *After* |
|---|---|
| Under God's curse | Loved by God |
| Doomed because of our sins | Shown God's mercy and given salvation |
| Went along with the crowd | Stand for Christ and truth |
| God's enemies | God's children |
| Enslaved to Satan | Free to love and serve Christ |
| Followed our evil thoughts and passions | Seated with Christ in glory |
| Under God's anger | Given undeserved favor |
| Spiritually dead | Given new spiritual life in Christ |

of his glad welcome. [13]So please don't despair because of what they are doing to me here. It is for you that I am suffering, so you should feel honored and encouraged.

[14]When I think of the wisdom and scope of God's plan, I fall to my knees and pray to the Father,* [15]the Creator of everything in heaven and on earth. [16]I pray that from his glorious, unlimited resources he will give you mighty inner strength through his Holy Spirit. [17]And I pray that Christ will be more and more at home in your hearts as you trust in him. May your roots go down deep into the soil of God's marvelous love. [18]And may you have the power to understand, as all God's people should, how wide, how long, how high, and how deep his love really is. [19]May you experience the love of Christ, though it is so great you will never fully understand it. Then you will be filled with the fullness of life and power that comes from God.

## DATING

Michelle met Greg at a party during the holidays, and they've been going out ever since. She fell in love with his quick wit, and he fell right into her baby blue eyes.

In some ways, theirs is a really positive relationship. They both have trusted Christ as their Savior. They share a lot of the same interests and goals. They even attend a campus Bible study together.

But there are also some negative aspects to the "Michelle-n-Greg" romance. For instance, on the weekends the two have gradually gotten into the habit of watching whatever movies happen to be on cable TV (that usually means a large dose of skin, sex, and raw language). At the same time, Michelle has noticed that four-letter words are slipping out of her mouth with increasing frequency (she never used to say such things)! And, as if that weren't enough to deal with, Michelle and Greg suddenly seem powerless to resist the constant sexual pressures they feel (they haven't gone all the way, but they've come awfully close).

"What's happened to us?" Michelle asks. "It's like we've thrown our standards out the window!"

What would you do in Michelle's situation? Find help in Ephesians 5:3-11.

[20]Now glory be to God! By his mighty power at work within us, he is able to accomplish infinitely more than we would ever dare to ask or hope. [21]May he be given glory in the church and in Christ Jesus forever and ever through endless ages. Amen.

CHAPTER **4** **SPECIAL ABILITIES.** Therefore I, a prisoner for serving the Lord, beg you to lead a life worthy of your calling, for you have been called by God. [2]Be humble and gentle. Be patient with each other, making allowance for each other's faults because of your love. [3]Always keep yourselves united in the Holy Spirit, and bind yourselves together with peace.

## LITTLE BY LITTLE ● ● ● • •

4:17-24 **People should be able to see a difference between Christians and non-Christians because of the way Christians live. Paul tells the Ephesians to leave behind the old life of sin now that they are followers of Christ. The Christian life is a process. Despite our new nature in Christ, we don't automatically have all good thoughts and attitudes. But if we keep listening to God, we will be changing all the time. As you look over the last year, do you see a process of change for the better in your thoughts, attitudes, and actions? Although change may be slow, it comes about if you trust God to change you. For more about our new nature as believers see Romans 6:6; 8:9; Galatians 5:16-26; and Colossians 3:3-8.**

[4]We are all one body, we have the same Spirit, and we have all been called to the same glorious future. [5]There is only one Lord, one faith, one baptism, [6]and there is only one God and Father, who is over us all and in us all and living through us all. [7]However, he has given each one of us a special gift according to the generosity of Christ. [8]That is why the Scriptures say,

"When he ascended to the heights,
he led a crowd of captives
and gave gifts to his people."*

[9]Notice that it says "he ascended." This means that Christ first came down to the lowly world in which we live.* [10]The same one who came down is the one who ascended higher than all the heavens, so that his rule might fill the entire universe.

[11]He is the one who gave these gifts to the church: the apostles, the prophets, the evangelists, and the pastors and teachers. [12]Their responsibility is to equip God's people to do his work and build up the church, the body of Christ, [13]until we come to such unity in our faith and knowledge of God's Son that we will be mature and full grown in the Lord, measuring up to the full stature of Christ.

[14]Then we will no longer be like children, forever changing our minds about what we believe because someone has told us something different or because someone has cleverly lied to us and made the lie sound like the truth. [15]Instead, we will hold to the truth in love, becoming more and more in every way like Christ, who is the head of his body, the church. [16]Under his direction, the whole body is fitted together perfectly. As each part does its own special work, it helps the other parts grow, so that the whole body is healthy and growing and full of love.

[17]With the Lord's authority let me say this: Live no longer as the ungodly* do, for they are hopelessly confused. [18]Their closed minds are full of darkness; they are far away from the life of God because they have shut their minds and hardened their hearts against him. [19]They don't care anymore about right and wrong, and they have given themselves over to immoral ways. Their lives are filled with all kinds of impurity and greed.

[20]But that isn't what you were taught when you

3:14 Some manuscripts read *the Father of our Lord Jesus Christ.* 4:8 Ps 68:18. 4:9 Or *to the lowest parts of the earth.* 4:17 Greek *Gentiles.*

learned about Christ. 21Since you have heard all
about him and have learned the truth that is in Jesus,
22throw off your old evil nature and your former way
of life, which is rotten through and through, full of
lust and deception. 23Instead, there must be a spiritual renewal of your thoughts and attitudes. 24You
must display a new nature because you are a new
person, created in God's likeness—righteous, holy,
and true.
25So put away all falsehood and "tell your neighbor the truth"* because we belong to each other.
26And "don't sin by letting anger gain control over
you."* Don't let the sun go down while you are still
angry, 27for anger gives a mighty foothold to the
Devil.
28If you are a thief, stop stealing. Begin using your
hands for honest work, and then give generously to
others in need. 29Don't use foul or abusive language.
Let everything you say be good and helpful, so that
your words will be an encouragement to those who
hear them.
30And do not bring sorrow to God's Holy Spirit by
the way you live. Remember, he is the one who has
identified you as his own, guaranteeing that you will
be saved on the day of redemption.
31Get rid of all bitterness, rage, anger, harsh words,
and slander, as well as all types of malicious behavior. 32Instead, be kind to each other, tenderhearted,
forgiving one another, just as God through Christ
has forgiven you.

CHAPTER **5** **LEARN WHAT PLEASES GOD.** Follow God's
example in everything you do, because you are his
dear children. 2Live a life filled with love for others,
following the example of Christ, who loved you and
gave himself as a sacrifice to take away your sins. And
God was pleased, because that sacrifice was like
sweet perfume to him.
3Let there be no sexual immorality, impurity, or
greed among you. Such sins have no place among
God's people. 4Obscene stories, foolish talk, and
coarse jokes—these are not for you. Instead, let
there be thankfulness to God. 5You can be sure that
no immoral, impure, or greedy person will inherit
the Kingdom of Christ and of God. For a greedy
person is really an idolater who worships the
things of this world. 6Don't be fooled by those who
try to excuse these sins, for the terrible anger of
God comes upon all those who disobey him.
7Don't participate in the things these people do.
8For though your hearts were once full of darkness, now you are full of light from the Lord, and
your behavior should show it! 9For this light
within you produces only what is good and right
and true.
10Try to find out what is pleasing to the Lord.
11Take no part in the worthless deeds of evil and
darkness; instead, rebuke and expose them. 12It is
shameful even to talk about the things that ungodly
people do in secret. 13But when the light shines on
them, it becomes clear how evil these things are.
14And where your light shines, it will expose their evil
deeds. This is why it is said,

"Awake, O sleeper,
rise up from the dead,
and Christ will give you light."

15So be careful how you live, not as fools but as
those who are wise. 16Make the most of every opportunity for doing good in these evil days. 17Don't
act thoughtlessly, but try to understand what the
Lord wants you to do. 18Don't be drunk with wine,
because that will ruin your life. Instead, let the
Holy Spirit fill and control you. 19Then you will
sing psalms and hymns and spiritual songs among

4:25 Zech 8:16. 4:26 Ps 4:4.

## SPEAK OUT

5:10-14 **It is important to avoid evil pleasures, but we must go even further. Paul instructs us to rebuke and expose them, for often our silence is interpreted as approval. God needs people who will take a stand for what is right. Wherever you are, lovingly speak out for what is true and right.**

### What does it mean to "grow as a Christian"?

Spiritual growth is a lot like physical growth. To stay healthy and grow physically, we must eat the right foods, exercise, and get plenty of rest. You've heard that since you were a child. According to Scripture, especially in verses such as Ephesians 4:14-15, growing spiritually involves the same formula.

Christians must eat the right "spiritual food": God's Word. Many Christians are trying to survive on spiritual "fast food." That is, they watch Christian TV, read Christian magazines, and listen to Christian music, but they rarely give attention to God's Word. There is only one food that will nourish our soul—reading the Bible. Everything else is only meant to be supplementary.

Christians exercise through resisting temptation, enduring trials, serving others, and telling others about our faith. We need to be pushed to stay strong. This means exercise. Temptation and problems test our character; serving others stretches our faith; telling people about Christ strengthens our devotion.

Christians rest through worship. Our world has a tendency to tighten us, like a rubber band pulled to the limit. Unless we take time weekly (and daily!) to recognize and worship God, he won't have the opportunity to minister to our needs.

We need sleep, rest, and times of vacation to get our physical batteries recharged. In the same way, we need worship to keep us spiritually renewed.

Spiritual growth takes time—a lifetime! This means growing in a relationship, not just changing our behavior. Growing a strong Christian life means learning how to love the person of Jesus Christ more each day, staying close to him and getting to know him better.

# Ultimate Issues

## MARRIAGE

Maria was 23 years old, bright, attractive—and headed for divorce. She and Danny had been married two years. Now she sat in her former youth pastor's office and dissolved into tears. "It's not working out," she choked out between sobs. "I don't know what happened. We were really in love, but we've lost something. I don't think we're going to make it. . . ." Tragically, this scene is repeated over and over. Why is it that two people who are *"made for each other"* so often end up looking for the escape hatch labeled "divorce"? Maybe a better question is: What does it take to keep a marriage from becoming a casualty? If marriage were just another human institution—like a corporation or a university—then getting out of it would be no more significant or painful than changing jobs or switching schools. Indeed, many people have tried to treat marriage that way, as something to enjoy when it's good or helpful and to terminate when it isn't. But those who have experienced a divorce will explain that a failed marriage is infinitely more painful. There's more to marriage than the human dimension. Marriage was God's holy and sacred idea. He performed "THE FIRST WEDDING" in the Garden of Eden (Genesis 2:18-25), thus setting up guidelines for all people to follow: marriage is for one man and one woman for life. There *are* valid reasons for sometimes breaking this pattern (for example, death or adultery). But the intended pattern is **one man, one woman, for life.** Unfortunately, in a fallen world it often is difficult to submit to God's standards, especially since his standards do not change. Marriage is a covenant between a husband and wife. A covenant is an agreement between two people (or groups) that has benefits for keeping the arrangement and penalties for breaking it. Our relationship to God is described in covenant language throughout Scripture. The marriage relationship is described as a covenant (Malachi 2:14-15), and is used as an illustration of our relationship with God (Hosea 1:2; Ephesians 5:22-33). Just as our relationship with God is built on his steadfast, unchanging love and commitment toward us, so a marriage relationship is designed to be solid, faithful, and committed. Therein lies another extremely important—but often overlooked—principle for a successful marriage: commitment. Marriage is based on commitment, not emotions. The **EMOTIONAL RUSH** two people experience when they "fall in love" and when they decide to marry is wonderful. It also is a terribly inadequate basis for marriage. That "rush," as powerful and enjoyable as it may be, will undoubtedly wear off at some point. If that's what the relationship is based on—physical attraction, romantic ideals, passion—the flame may burn brightly, but it will not burn for long. Romance, sexual attraction, and passion are tremendous God-given elements of a love relationship. But do not mistake them for the foundation of a lifelong commitment. They are like ***icing on a cake.*** Icing makes the cake much sweeter, but a diet of 100 percent refined sugar doesn't make for good health. To survive the pressure and temptations that attack a marriage, both husband and wife have to be totally committed to making it work. Even when the romance is gone (as it sometimes will be in any marriage), when the money is tight, or the urge to run out is overwhelming, Christians must stand strong on the commitment they have made. Instead of allowing the stresses to divide them, they must cling that much more tightly together. "What God has joined together, let no one"—and no thing—"separate." Marriage, when seen from God's perspective, can be one of his greatest gifts to his children. It can also, as Maria and millions of others have unfortunately discovered, be a source of deepest pain. Whether or not to marry—and what happens if you do marry—is up to you.

yourselves, making music to the Lord in your hearts. [20]And you will always give thanks for everything to God the Father in the name of our Lord Jesus Christ.

[21]And further, you will submit to one another out of reverence for Christ. [22]You wives will submit to your husbands as you do to the Lord. [23]For a husband is the head of his wife as Christ is the head of his body, the church; he gave his life to be her Savior. [24]As the church submits to Christ, so you wives must submit to your husbands in everything.

[25]And you husbands must love your wives with the same love Christ showed the church. He gave up his life for her [26]to make her holy and clean, washed by baptism and God's word.* [27]He did this to present her to himself as a glorious church without a spot or wrinkle or any other blemish. Instead, she will be holy and without fault. [28]In the same way, husbands ought to love their wives as they love their own bodies. For a man is actually loving himself when he loves his wife. [29]No one hates his own body but lovingly cares for it, just as Christ cares for his body, which is the church. [30]And we are his body.

[31]As the Scriptures say, "A man leaves his father and mother and is joined to his wife, and the two are united into one."* [32]This is a great mystery, but it is an illustration of the way Christ and the church are one. [33]So again I say, each man must love his wife as he loves himself, and the wife must respect her husband.

CHAPTER **6** **FAMILY ADVICE.** Children, obey your parents because you belong to the Lord, for this is the right thing to do. [2]"Honor your father and mother." This is the first of the Ten Commandments that ends with a promise. [3]And this is the promise: If you honor your father and mother, "you will live a long life, full of blessing."*

[4]And now a word to you fathers. Don't make your children angry by the way you treat them. Rather, bring them up with the discipline and instruction approved by the Lord.

[5]Slaves, obey your earthly masters with deep respect and fear. Serve them sincerely as you would serve Christ. [6]Work hard, but not just to please your masters when they are watching. As slaves of Christ, do the will of God with all your heart. [7]Work with enthusiasm, as though you were working for the Lord rather than for people. [8]Remember that the Lord will reward each one of us for the good we do, whether we are slaves or free.

[9]And in the same way, you masters must treat your slaves right. Don't threaten them; remember, you both have the same Master in heaven, and he has no favorites.

[10]A final word: Be strong with the Lord's mighty power. [11]Put on all of God's armor so that you will be able to stand firm against all strategies and tricks of the Devil. [12]For we are not fighting against people made of flesh and blood, but against the evil rulers and authorities of the unseen world, against those mighty powers of darkness who rule this world, and against wicked spirits in the heavenly realms.

[13]Use every piece of God's armor to resist the enemy in the time of evil, so that after the battle you will still be standing firm. [14]Stand your ground, putting on the sturdy belt of truth and the body armor of God's righteousness. [15]For shoes, put on the peace that comes from the Good News, so that you will be fully prepared.* [16]In every battle

## "Here's what I did..."

"Greg, what have you decided about going to the college we talked about? The deadline is coming up, isn't it?" Though my dad was trying to be casual, I could tell he wanted an answer.

"Yeah, I've decided. I don't want to go to that school, but you won't take that for an answer," I said.

"Greg," Dad began, but I could tell by his tone what he was going to say. We'd been through this too many times before. I didn't want to go; he wanted me to—and his pressuring me just made me angry.

I talked to my youth pastor about it the next day. "What do you think the Bible says about your situation?" Les asked me.

"Well, I know I'm not supposed to be angry at my dad, but I can't stand him pressuring me."

"Read Ephesians and let me know what you discover," Les suggested. So I read the book of Ephesians—and I saw that I can't always do what I want. Loving God means wanting to do *his* will, not mine. When I read Ephesians 6:1-3, I realized that God often chooses to work through my earthly parents. I tried to think through all the reasons Dad wanted me to go to that particular college and why I didn't want to go. Finally I decided it would be best to trust God and believe that he was leading me there.

God did bless my decision to attend this college. I am really growing in my faith here.

Greg

AGE 19

5:26 Greek *having cleansed her by the washing of water with the word.* 5:31 Gen 2:24. 6:2-3 Exod 20:12; Deut 5:16. 6:15 Or *For shoes, put on the readiness to preach the Good News of peace with God.*

## GOD'S ARMOR FOR US

We are engaged in a spiritual battle—all believers find themselves subject to Satan's attacks because they are no longer on Satan's side. Thus, Paul tells us in Ephesians 6:10-17 to use every piece of God's armor to resist Satan's attacks and to stand true to God in the midst of them.

| *Piece of Armor* | *Use* | *Application* |
|---|---|---|
| BELT | Truth | Satan fights with lies, and sometimes his lies sound like truth; but believers have God's truth, which can defeat Satan's lies. |
| BODY ARMOR | God's righteousness | Satan often attacks our heart—the seat of our emotions, self-worth, and trust. God's righteousness is the breastplate that protects our heart and ensures his approval. He approves of us because we have trusted Christ to save us and cleanse our hearts from sin. |
| SHOES | The peace that comes from the Good News | Satan wants us to think that telling others the Good News is a worthless and hopeless task—the size of the task is too big, and the negative responses are too much to handle. But the "shoes" God gives us are the true peace that is available in God, which prepares us to share the news with others. |
| SHIELD | Faith | The shield of faith protects us from Satan's fiery darts in the form of insults, setbacks, and temptations. With God's perspective, we can see beyond our circumstances and know that ultimate victory is ours. |
| HELMET | Salvation | Satan wants to make us doubt God, Jesus, and our salvation. The helmet protects our mind from doubting God's saving work for us. |
| SWORD | The Word of God | The sword is the only weapon of offense in this list of armor. There are times when we need to take the offensive against Satan. When we are tempted, we need to trust in the truth of God's Word. |

you will need faith as your shield to stop the fiery
arrows aimed at you by Satan.* [17]Put on salvation
as your helmet, and take the sword of the Spirit,
which is the word of God. [18]Pray at all times and
on every occasion in the power of the Holy Spirit.
Stay alert and be persistent in your prayers for all
Christians everywhere.

[19]And pray for me, too. Ask God to give me the
right words as I boldly explain God's secret plan that
the Good News is for the Gentiles, too.* [20]I am in
chains now for preaching this message as God's
ambassador. But pray that I will keep on speaking
boldly for him, as I should.

[21]Tychicus, a much loved brother and faithful
helper in the Lord's work, will tell you all about how
I am getting along. [22]I am sending him to you for just
this purpose. He will let you know how we are, and
he will encourage you.

[23]May God give you peace, dear brothers and sisters,* and love with faith, from God the Father and
the Lord Jesus Christ. [24]May God's grace be upon all
who love our Lord Jesus Christ with an undying love.

6:16 Greek *by the evil one.* 6:19 Greek *explain the mystery of the gospel.* 6:23 Greek *brothers.*

**GOD'S PURPOSE FOR A LIVING CHURCH**
According to God's eternal, loving plan, he directs, carries out, and sustains our salvation.

When we respond to Christ's love by trusting in him, his purpose becomes our mission. Have you committed yourself to fulfilling God's purpose? We should always be seeking to understand more of who God created us to be and what he wants us to do with our life.

1. What does God want to accomplish through his children (the body of Christ) working together?
2. What attitudes and actions are necessary for the body to function as it should? (Check Romans 12 and 1 Corinthians 12 for similar teaching on "Body Life.")
3. In what ways can these attitudes be displayed and these actions lived out in your church and among your Christian friends?
4. What do you think God wants to accomplish through you for other believers?

**CHRIST, THE CENTER** Christ is exalted as the central meaning of the universe and the focus of history. He is the Head of his body, the church.

Because Christ is central to everything, his power must be central in us. Begin by placing all your priorities under his control. Your life decisions should be based on who you are as his disciple.

1. According to 1:3-15, what do we have in Christ?
2. According to 2:11-21, how does Christ change human relationships?
3. According to 4:11-16, what role does Christ play in the body?
4. Review your responses to questions 1–3. Why is it so important to make Jesus, in our heart and mind, the central focus of our life?
5. Where is your focus today? (At home, by yourself, with your best friends, at school, at church.) In what sense are you "on center" in your commitment to Christ? In what sense are you "off center"?

**NEW FAMILY** Because God through Christ paid our penalty for sin and forgave us, we have been reconciled and brought near to him. We are a new society, a new family. Being united with Christ means that we are to treat each other as family members.

We are one family in Christ; so there should be no barriers, no divisions, and no discrimination. Because we all belong to him, we should live in harmony with one another. We have a responsibility toward each other as brothers and sisters in Christ.

1. Check out 2:11–3:13. What does God desire concerning relationships between Jews and Gentiles?
2. Who are the people in your community who do not relate well to each other because of difference in color, race, culture, social status, or other personal barriers?
3. From what people are you most separated or alienated in your personal life? What does this study teach you about those relationships?
4. What can you do to change those relationships because of your faith in Christ?

**CHRISTIAN CONDUCT** Paul encourages all Christians to make wise, dynamic Christian living a goal.

God provides his Holy Spirit to enable us to live his way. To utilize his power, we must lay aside our evil desires and draw upon the power of his new life. Submit your will to Christ and seek to love with *his* love by the power of the Spirit.

1. Ephesians gives several specific commands to obey in following Christ (for instance 4:25—tell the truth!). Make a quick list of these commands.
2. Now consider each item on your list in light of this question: "How does doing this action relate to my loving God?"
3. Read 5:1-2. How does God's love become the motivation for Christian conduct?
4. As you look at your list from question one, which actions are areas of strength in your life? Which ones are weaknesses? How can you strengthen your areas of weaknesses so that your life is a greater "walk in the light"?

**T**ime for a little daydreaming: ■ Scenario #1—A high-powered attorney calls to inform you that a distant relative has left you her entire estate worth *several million bucks!* ■ Scenario #2—You ace all of your midterm exams! ■ Scenario #3—In the biggest game of the year, you score with one second left to give your school an upset victory. ■ Scenario #4—You learn that the most attractive member of the opposite sex (in your whole school!) likes you. ■ Some dreams, huh? So, do you think you could get *excited* about those situations? OK, let's daydream some more: ■ Scenario #5—Your dad accidentally throws away your term paper—the one you worked on for over a month—the one that is due *today.* ■ Scenario #6—You develop a huge pimple on the end of your nose the night before the most important date of your life. ■ Scenario #7—You've trained for months for track team tryouts. On the way to school, you get in a wreck and break your ankle. ■ Scenario #8—Your boyfriend/girlfriend dumps you—for your best friend! ■ OK, so these are more like nightmares. Is it possible to be *joyful* in bad situations like these? ■ Believe it or not, it *is* possible to be content—even in the midst of horrible, terrible circumstances. ■ Facing problems or trials? Get a fresh perspective. Read Philippians, Paul's letter to a group of Christians. The message is clear: Joy and contentment really *can* be ours . . . as long as we keep trusting God through life's hard times.

## STATS

PURPOSE: To thank the Philippians and to strengthen them by showing that true joy comes from Jesus Christ

AUTHOR: Paul

TO WHOM WRITTEN: Christians at Philippi and all believers

DATE WRITTEN: About A.D. 61, from Rome, during Paul's imprisonment there

SETTING: Paul and his companions founded the church at Philippi on the second missionary journey (Acts 16:11-40). This was the first church established on the European continent. The Philippian church had sent a gift with Epaphroditus (one of their members) to be delivered to Paul (4:18).

KEY PEOPLE: Paul, Timothy, Epaphroditus, Euodias, Syntyche

KEY PLACE: Philippi

# Philippians

CHAPTER **1** **PAUL'S PRAYER: KEEP GROWING.** This letter
is from Paul and Timothy, slaves of Christ Jesus.

It is written to all of God's people in Philippi, who believe in Christ Jesus, and to the elders* and deacons.

[2]May God our Father and the Lord Jesus Christ give you grace and peace.

[3]Every time I think of you, I give thanks to my
God. [4]I always pray for you, and I make my requests with a heart full of joy [5]because you have
been my partners in spreading the Good News
about Christ from the time you first heard it until
now. [6]And I am sure that God, who began the good
work within you, will continue his work until it is
finally finished on that day when Christ Jesus
comes back again.

[7]It is right that I should feel as I do about all of you,
for you have a very special place in my heart. We have
shared together the blessings of God, both when I was
in prison and when I was out, defending the truth and
telling others the Good News. [8]God knows how much
I love you and long for you with the tender compassion of Christ Jesus. [9]I pray that your love for each other
will overflow more and more, and that you will keep
on growing in your knowledge and understanding.

[10]For I want you to understand what really matters, so
that you may live pure and blameless lives until Christ
returns. [11]May you always be filled with the fruit of your
salvation*—those good things that are produced in
your life by Jesus Christ—for this will bring much
glory and praise to God.

[12]And I want you to know, dear brothers and
sisters,* that everything that has happened to me
here has helped to spread the Good News. [13]For
everyone here, including all the soldiers in the palace
guard, knows that I am in chains because of Christ.
[14]And because of my imprisonment, many of the
Christians* here have gained confidence and become more bold in telling others about Christ.

[15]Some are preaching out of jealousy and rivalry. But
others preach about Christ with pure motives. [16]They
preach because they love me, for they know the Lord
brought me here to defend the Good News. [17]Those

**JOY SOURCE ● ● • • ·**

**1:4 This is the first of many times Paul uses the word *joy* in his letter. Here he says that the Philippians were a source of joy when he prayed. By helping Paul, they were helping Christ's cause. The Philippians were willing to be used by God for whatever task he had in store for them. When others think about you, are you a source of joy for them?**

1:1 Greek *overseers.* 1:11 Greek *the fruit of righteousness.* 1:12 Greek *brothers.* 1:14 Greek *brothers in the Lord.*

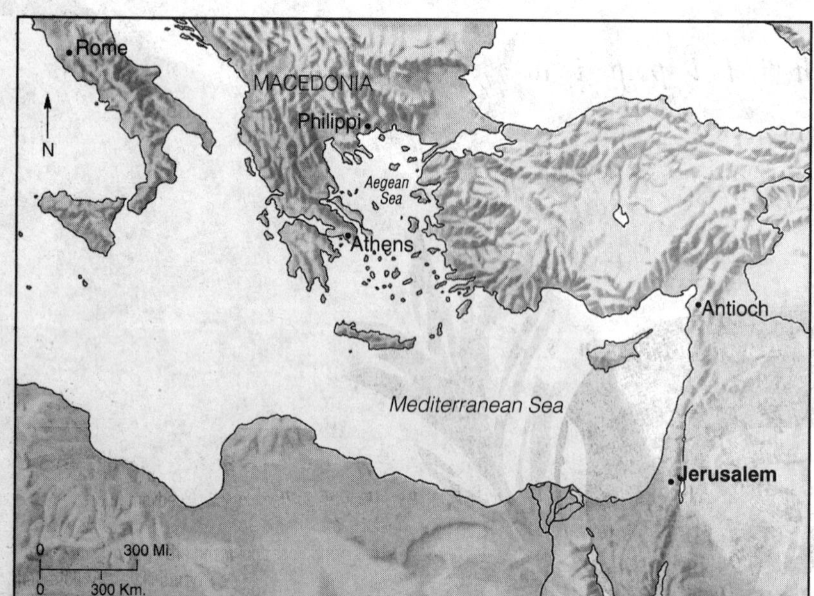


**LOCATION OF PHILIPPI**
Philippi sat on the Egnatian Way, the main transportation route in Macedonia, an extension of the Appian Way, which joined the eastern empire with Italy.

others do not have pure motives as they preach about Christ. They preach with selfish ambition, not sincerely, intending to make my chains more painful to me. [18]But whether or not their motives are pure, the fact remains that the message about Christ is being preached, so I rejoice. And I will continue to rejoice. [19]For I know that as you pray for me and as the Spirit of Jesus Christ helps me, this will all turn out for my deliverance.

[20]For I live in eager expectation and hope that I will never do anything that causes me shame, but that I will always be bold for Christ, as I have been in the past, and that my life will always honor Christ, whether I live or I die. [21]For to me, living is for Christ, and dying is even better. [22]Yet if I live, that means fruitful service for Christ. I really don't know which is better. [23]I'm torn between two desires: Sometimes I want to live, and sometimes I long to go and be with Christ. That would be far better for me, [24]but it is better for you that I live.

[25]I am convinced of this, so I will continue with you so that you will grow and experience the joy of your faith. [26]Then when I return to you, you will have even more reason to boast about what Christ Jesus has done for me.

[27]But whatever happens to me, you must live in a manner worthy of the Good News about Christ, as citizens of heaven. Then, whether I come and see you again or only hear about you, I will know that you are standing side by side, fighting together for the Good News. [28]Don't be intimidated by your enemies. This will be a sign to them that they are going to be destroyed, but that you are going to be saved, even by God himself. [29]For you have been given not only the privilege of trusting in Christ but also the privilege of suffering for him. [30]We are in this fight together. You have seen me suffer for him in the past, and you know that I am still in the midst of this great struggle.

## CHAPTER 2

**A CHRISTLIKE ATTITUDE.** Is there any encouragement from belonging to Christ? Any comfort from his love? Any fellowship together in the Spirit? Are your hearts tender and sympathetic? [2]Then make me truly happy by agreeing wholeheartedly with each other, loving one another, and working together with one heart and purpose.

[3]Don't be selfish; don't live to make a good impression on others. Be humble, thinking of others as better than yourself. [4]Don't think only about your own affairs, but be interested in others, too, and what they are doing.

[5]Your attitude should be the same that Christ Jesus had. [6]Though he was God, he did not demand and cling to his rights as God. [7]He made himself nothing;* he took the humble position of a slave and appeared in human form.* [8]And in human form he obediently humbled himself even further by dying a criminal's

### SUFFERING

1:29 **Suffering, in and of itself, is not a privilege. But when we suffer because we faithfully represent Christ, we know that our message and example are having an effect and that God considers us worthy to represent him (see Acts 5:41). Suffering has these additional benefits: (1) it takes our eyes off of earthly comforts; (2) it weeds out superficial believers; (3) it strengthens the faith of those who endure; (4) it serves as an example to others who may follow us. Suffering for our faith doesn't mean we have done something wrong. In fact, the opposite is often true—it may verify that we have been faithful.**

2:7a Or *He laid aside his mighty power and glory.* 2:7b Greek *and was born in the likeness of men and was found in appearance as a man.*

death on a cross. 9Because of this, God raised him up to the heights of heaven and gave him a name that is above every other name, 10so that at the name of Jesus every knee will bow, in heaven and on earth and under the earth, 11and every tongue will confess that Jesus Christ is Lord, to the glory of God the Father.

12Dearest friends, you were always so careful to follow my instructions when I was with you. And now that I am away you must be even more careful to put into action God's saving work in your lives, obeying God with deep reverence and fear. 13For God is working in you, giving you the desire to obey him and the power to do what pleases him.

14In everything you do, stay away from complaining and arguing, 15so that no one can speak a word of blame against you. You are to live clean, innocent lives as children of God in a dark world full of crooked and perverse people. Let your lives shine brightly before them. 16Hold tightly to the word of life, so that when Christ returns, I will be proud that I did not lose the race and that my work was not useless. 17But even if my life is to be poured out like a drink offering to complete the sacrifice of your faithful service (that is, if I am to die for you), I will rejoice, and I want to share my joy with all of you. 18And you should be happy about this and rejoice with me.

19If the Lord Jesus is willing, I hope to send Timothy to you soon. Then when he comes back, he can cheer me up by telling me how you are getting along. 20I have no one else like Timothy, who genuinely cares about your welfare. 21All the others care only for themselves and not for what matters to Jesus Christ. 22But you know how Timothy has proved himself. Like a son with his father, he has helped me in preaching the Good News. 23I hope to send him to you just as soon as I find out what is going to happen to me here. 24And I have confidence from the Lord that I myself will come to see you soon.

25Meanwhile, I thought I should send Epaphroditus back to you. He is a true brother, a faithful worker, and a courageous soldier. And he was your messenger to help me in my need. 26Now I am sending him home again, for he has been longing to see you, and he was very distressed that you heard he was ill. 27And he surely was ill; in fact, he almost died. But God had mercy on him—and also on me, so that I would not have such unbearable sorrow.

28So I am all the more anxious to send him back to you, for I know you will be glad to see him, and that will lighten all my cares. 29Welcome him with Christian love* and with great joy, and be sure to honor people like him. 30For he risked his life for the work of Christ, and he was at the point of death while trying to do for me the things you couldn't do because you were far away.

CHAPTER **3** **KNOW HIM.** Whatever happens, dear brothers and sisters,* may the Lord give you joy. I never get tired of telling you this. I am doing this for your own good.

2Watch out for those dogs, those wicked men and their evil deeds, those mutilators who say you must be circumcised to be saved. 3For we who worship God in the Spirit* are the only ones who are truly circumcised. We put no confidence in human effort. Instead, we boast about what Christ Jesus has done for us.

4Yet I could have confidence in myself if anyone could. If others have reason for confidence in their own efforts, I have even more! 5For I was circumcised when I was eight days old, having been born into a pure-blooded Jewish family that is a branch of the tribe of Benjamin. So I am a real Jew if there ever was one! What's more, I was a member of the Pharisees, who demand the strictest obedience to the Jewish law. 6And zealous? Yes, in fact, I harshly persecuted the church. And I obeyed the Jewish law so carefully that I was never accused of any fault.

7I once thought all these things were so very important, but now I consider them worthless because of

## "Here's what I did..."

My grandmother was in the hospital. I heard my mom say over the phone to someone that the doctors weren't sure whether Grandma would make it; things looked pretty serious.

I went to my room feeling agitated. As far as I knew, Grandma didn't know that Jesus died for her sins. I had always wanted to tell her, but how would I do it? I felt so unsure of myself. What would I say? Would she even listen to me?

I prayed about this for quite a while. I knew God would want my grandmother to hear that God loves her and wants to save her for eternity. I tried to think through what I could say to her. Then I started reading my Bible. I read in Philippians, and the 13th verse in chapter 4 leaped out at me: "I can do everything with the help of Christ who gives me the strength I need." It seemed like God was giving me direct encouragement that I would know what to say to my grandmother.

I went to the hospital and I told my grandmother about Jesus. And she listened and accepted Christ as her Lord and Savior!

One week later, she died. But I know she is now with the Lord.

Jeff

2:29 Greek *in the Lord.* 3:1 Greek *brothers;* also in 3:13, 17. 3:3 Or *in spirit;* some manuscripts read *worship by the Spirit of God.*

what Christ has done. [8]Yes, everything else is worthless when compared with the priceless gain of knowing Christ Jesus my Lord. I have discarded everything else, counting it all as garbage, so that I may have Christ [9]and become one with him. I no longer count on my own goodness or my ability to obey God's law, but I trust Christ to save me. For God's way of making us right with himself depends on faith. [10]As a result, I can really know Christ and experience the mighty power that raised him from the dead. I can learn what it means to suffer with him, sharing in his death, [11]so that, somehow, I can experience the resurrection from the dead!

**ELF**

Marie's favorite topic for discussion, her major concern, the number one thing on her mind is . . . Marie. Seriously, when we say she's stuck on herself, we're talking really stuck—super-glue style.

Just look:

- When Beth was extremely upset at not being asked to Homecoming, Marie responded by going on and on about her date.
- When anyone asks, "How was your weekend?" Marie gives a twenty-minute discourse. (Funny how she never asks anyone else that question.)
- When her favorite daytime TV show was interrupted last summer by a live news report about a four-alarm apartment fire, Marie got emotional. Not at the fact that people were dying and losing their homes, but at the fact that she had to miss her program.
- When Marie's neighbor called, desperately needing a baby-sitter at the last minute, Marie wouldn't go, even though she had no other plans. She ended up going to work out at the health club.
- When Marie receives money (allowance, pay, or cash from an unexpected source), she immediately goes to the mall and buys something for herself.

Do you know anyone like Marie? Are you like Marie? See Philippians 2:3-11 for a better way.

[12]I don't mean to say that I have already achieved these things or that I have already reached perfection! But I keep working toward that day when I will finally be all that Christ Jesus saved me for and wants me to be. [13]No, dear brothers and sisters, I am still not all I should be,* but I am focusing all my energies on this one thing: Forgetting the past and looking forward to what lies ahead, [14]I strain to reach the end of the race and receive the prize for which God, through Christ Jesus, is calling us up to heaven.*

[15]I hope all of you who are mature Christians will agree on these things. If you disagree on some point, I believe God will make it plain to you. [16]But we must be sure to obey the truth we have learned already.

[17]Dear brothers and sisters, pattern your lives after mine, and learn from those who follow our example. [18]For I have told you often before, and I

## NO WORRIES ● ● • • •

4:6-18 **Imagine never being worried about anything! It seems like an impossibility—we all have worries on the job, in our home, at school. But Paul's advice is to turn our worries into prayers. Do you want to worry less? Then pray more! Whenever you start to worry, stop and pray.**

say it again with tears in my eyes, that there are many whose conduct shows they are really enemies of the cross of Christ. [19]Their future is eternal destruction. Their god is their appetite, they brag about shameful things, and all they think about is this life here on earth. [20]But we are citizens of heaven, where the Lord Jesus Christ lives. And we are eagerly waiting for him to return as our Savior. [21]He will take these weak mortal bodies of ours and change them into glorious bodies like his own, using the same mighty power that he will use to conquer everything, everywhere.

CHAPTER **4** **THINK ABOUT THE GOOD.** Dear brothers and sisters,* I love you and long to see you, for you are my joy and the reward for my work. So please stay true to the Lord, my dear friends.

[2]And now I want to plead with those two women, Euodia and Syntyche. Please, because you belong to the Lord, settle your disagreement. [3]And I ask you, my true teammate,* to help these women, for they worked hard with me in telling others the Good News. And they worked with Clement and the rest of my co-workers, whose names are written in the Book of Life.

[4]Always be full of joy in the Lord. I say it again—rejoice! [5]Let everyone see that you are considerate in all you do. Remember, the Lord is coming soon.

[6]Don't worry about anything; instead, pray about everything. Tell God what you need, and thank him for all he has done. [7]If you do this, you will experience God's peace, which is far more wonderful than the human mind can understand. His peace will guard your hearts and minds as you live in Christ Jesus.

[8]And now, dear brothers and sisters, let me say one more thing as I close this letter. Fix your thoughts on what is true and honorable and right. Think about things that are pure and lovely and admirable. Think about things that are excellent and worthy of praise. [9]Keep putting into practice all you learned from me and heard from me and saw me doing, and the God of peace will be with you.

## SECRET ● ● • • •

4:23 **In many ways the Philippian church was a model congregation. It was made up of different kinds of people who were learning to work together. But Paul knew problems could arise, so he prepared the Philippians for possible difficulties. Though a prisoner in Rome, Paul had learned the true secret of joy and peace—imitating Christ and serving others. By focusing on Christ we learn unity, humility, joy, and peace.**

3:13 Some manuscripts read *I am not all I should be.* 3:14 Or *from heaven.* 4:1 Greek *brothers;* also in 4:8. 4:3 Greek *true yokefellow,* or *loyal Syzygus.*

PHILIPPIANS 4:13
everything
everything
I
CAN
DO
everything
everything
WITH THE HELP OF CHRIST
who
gives
me the
STRENGTH

I need.

10How grateful I am, and how I praise the Lord
that you are concerned about me again. I know you
have always been concerned for me, but for a while
you didn't have the chance to help me. 11Not that I
was ever in need, for I have learned how to get
along happily whether I have much or little. 12I
know how to live on almost nothing or with everything. I have learned the secret of living in every
situation, whether it is with a full stomach or
empty, with plenty or little. 13For I can do everything with the help of Christ who gives me the
strength I need. 14But even so, you have done well
to share with me in my present difficulty.
15As you know, you Philippians were the only
ones who gave me financial help when I brought
you the Good News and then traveled on from
Macedonia. No other church did this. 16Even when
I was in Thessalonica you sent help more than
once. 17I don't say this because I want a gift from
you. What I want is for you to receive a well-earned
reward because of your kindness.
18At the moment I have all I need—more than I
need! I am generously supplied with the gifts
you sent me with Epaphroditus. They are a sweet-
smelling sacrifice that is acceptable to God and
pleases him. 19And this same God who takes care
of me will supply all your needs from his glorious
riches, which have been given to us in Christ Jesus.
20Now glory be to God our Father forever and ever.
Amen.
21Give my greetings to all the Christians there. The
brothers who are with me here send you their greetings. 22And all the other Christians send their greetings,
too, especially those who work in Caesar's palace.
23May the grace of the Lord Jesus Christ be with
your spirit.

---

i
wonder...

**Before I became a Christian, I put some real garbage through my mind. How do I clean up my thought life?**

Almost every school in America is equipped with computers. Most businesses remain competitive because they're able to access and store large amounts of information. Computers are serving nearly every segment of society. But they have one flaw—they are dependent on the programs and information put in them.

Your mind works like a computer. If it's programmed to think about crud, that's what will happen. If it's programmed to think about things that are healthy, you will think healthy thoughts. It's as simple as that.

The hard part comes in trying to keep out the unhealthy thoughts. It doesn't take much to pollute a mind.

So what's God's solution? Reprogram the mind! For this job, there are no shortcuts. The more exposure to things that have polluted us, whether from bad movies, magazines, TV, music, concerts, or just the everyday conversation of friends who don't care what they say, the longer it will take to clear our mind and reprogram it.

The reprograming process begins when we realize that destructive thoughts and images are trying to get a foothold in our mind, and then kick them out. The next step, as we see from Philippians 4:8, is choosing to dwell on "what is true and honorable and right . . . pure and lovely and admirable . . . excellent and worthy of praise."

# MEGA themes

**HUMILITY** Christ showed true humility when he laid aside his rights and privileges as God to become human. He poured out his life to pay the penalty we deserve. Laying aside self-interest is essential to all our relationships.

We are to take Christ's attitude in serving others. We must not be concerned about personal recognition. When we give up the need to receive credit and praise, we will be able to serve with joy, love, and kindness.

1. If a person was described to you as "humble," what would be your impression of that person? Positive or negative? Weak or strong? Unique or average?
2. How did Jesus display his attitude of humility?
3. If Jesus were to attend your school, how do you think people would respond to him as he humbly served others?
4. What would it mean for you to display humility toward kids at school?

**SELF-SACRIFICE** Christ suffered and died so that we might have eternal life. With courage and faithfulness, Paul sacrificed himself for the ministry, preaching the gospel even while he was in prison.

Christ gives us power to lay aside our personal needs and concerns. To utilize his power, we must imitate those leaders who deny themselves and serve others. We dare not be self-centered in view of such a self-sacrificing Savior.

1. What are the differences between a self-sacrificing person and a self-centered one?
2. What makes it difficult for a person to be self-sacrificing?
3. What was the connection between the self-sacrifice of Jesus and the self-sacrifice of Paul?
4. How could you overcome areas of self-centeredness through the help of Jesus and the work of his Spirit? What will you do to begin this work?

**UNITY** In every church, in every generation, there are problems that divide people (issues, loyalties, and conflicts). It is easy to turn against each other. Paul encouraged the Philippians to agree with one another, stop complaining, and work together.

As believers, we should fight against a common enemy, not each other. United in love, we become aware of Christ's strength. Always remember teamwork, consideration, and unselfishness. Keep your focus on the model of Jesus Christ.

1. What are some of the things that cause anger, hurt, and division among God's people?
2. What specific principles do you find in Philippians that could prevent or help resolve such conflict?
3. As you examine these principles, what truth is the key to maintaining unity in the body of believers?
4. What can you do to apply these principles in relationships with your Christian friends—specifically those in your church?

**CHRISTIAN LIVING** Paul shows us how to live a successful Christian life. We can become mature by being so identified with Christ that his attitude of humility and sacrifice rules us. Christ is both our source of power and our guide.

Developing our character begins with God's work in us, but it also requires discipline, obedience, and continual concentration on our part.

1. Read 3:1-16. If you had never heard of Paul before, what would be your impression of him

after reading these verses? Do you agree or disagree with this statement: "Paul thought the Christian life was basically easy"? Explain your response based on Philippians.
2. Summarize the key points you find in Paul's testimony of himself and his life in Christ. What can you do to develop godly character?
3. Describe your life as a Christian. In what ways is your experience similar to Paul's? In what ways is it different?

**JOY** Believers can have profound contentment, serenity, and peace no matter what happens. This joy comes from knowing Christ personally and from depending on his strength rather than on our own.

Joy does not come from outward circumstances but from inner strength. As Christians, we must not rely on what we have or what we experience to give us joy, but on Christ within us. His joy is greater than life's trials.

1. Based on Paul's circumstances and the content of his letter to the Philippians, how do you think Paul would have described being "joyful"?
2. How can a Christian find joy in apparently unhappy circumstances?
3. If a Christian friend were to say to you, "How can I possibly find joy in the Lord when life seems so unfair?" what would you say?
4. How will you find joy in Jesus this week?

**W**ill the Real Jesus Please Stand Up? ■ Sometimes it's hard to know what to think about Jesus Christ. ■ Christians say he is God with skin on—the second person of the Trinity and the carpenter from Nazareth all rolled into one. Others insist he never even existed. Still others regard Jesus as a troublesome politician with a messiah complex, who ended up being executed. Then there is the Hollywood Jesus—weak, wishy-washy, misguided, filled with contradictions, and surrounded by controversy. ■ How about the increasingly popular "New Age" Jesus who is but one of many ways to God? And don't forget some cults who claim that Christ is *now living on the earth* in the person of their leader! ■ So, was Jesus just a good man and great moral teacher? Or was he, as Islam teaches, a prophet like Moses, Buddha, and Mohammed? Was he just one of many gods? Was he truly divine, or was he just more than human, or was he simply one manifestation of a divine, universal force? ■ There are hundreds of conflicting ideas floating around about who Jesus is. But only one of the views can be true—which makes the others wrong . . . and extremely dangerous! ■ Don't fall for lies about Christ. Meet him as he really is. See for yourself how superior he is to everything and everyone else in the universe. See what it means to know him in a personal way. See all of this and more in the book of Colossians.

## STATS

PURPOSE: To combat errors in the church and to show that believers have everything they need in Christ

AUTHOR: Paul

TO WHOM WRITTEN: The church at Colosse, a city in Asia Minor, and all believers everywhere

DATE WRITTEN: About A.D. 60, during Paul's imprisonment in Rome

SETTING: Paul had never visited Colosse—evidently the church had been founded by Epaphras and other converts from Paul's missionary travels. The church, however, had been infiltrated by religious relativism with some believers attempting to combine elements of heathenism and secular philosophy with Christian doctrine. Paul confronts these false teachings and affirms the sufficiency of Christ.

KEY PEOPLE: Paul, Timothy, Tychicus, Onesimus, Aristarchus, Mark, Epaphras

KEY PLACES: Colosse, Laodicea (4:15-16)

# Colossians

CHAPTER **1** **PAUL: CHOSEN BY GOD.** This letter is
from Paul, chosen by God to be an apostle of Christ
Jesus, and from our brother Timothy.
[2]It is written to God's holy people in the city of
Colosse, who are faithful brothers and sisters* in
Christ.

May God our Father give you grace and peace.

[3]We always pray for you, and we give thanks to
God the Father of our Lord Jesus Christ, [4]for we have
heard that you trust in Christ Jesus and that you love
all of God's people. [5]You do this because you are
looking forward to the joys of heaven—as you have
been ever since you first heard the truth of the Good
News. [6]This same Good News that came to you is
going out all over the world. It is changing lives
everywhere, just as it changed yours that very first
day you heard and understood the truth about God's
great kindness to sinners.
[7]Epaphras, our much loved co-worker, was the
one who brought you the Good News. He is Christ's
faithful servant, and he is helping us in your place.*
[8]He is the one who told us about the great love for
others that the Holy Spirit has given you.
[9]So we have continued praying for you ever since
we first heard about you. We ask God to give you a
complete understanding of what he wants to do in
your lives, and we ask him to make you wise with
spiritual wisdom. [10]Then the way you live will always
honor and please the Lord, and you will continually
do good, kind things for others. All the while, you
will learn to know God better and better.
[11]We also pray that you will be strengthened with
his glorious power so that you will have all the
patience and endurance you need. May you be filled
with joy, [12]always thanking the Father, who has enabled you to share the inheritance that belongs to
God's holy people, who live in the light. [13]For he has
rescued us from the one who rules in the kingdom

**CHANGED ● ● ● • •**

**1:6 Wherever Paul went, he preached the gospel—to Gentile audiences, to hostile Jewish leaders, and even to his Roman guards. Whenever people believed in the message he spoke, they were changed. God's Word is not just for our information, it is for our transformation! Becoming a Christian means beginning a whole new relationship with God, not just turning over a new leaf or determining to do right. New believers have a changed purpose, direction, attitude, and behavior. They no longer seek to serve themselves but to serve God. In what areas has hearing God's Word changed your life? Where should it do so?**

1:2 Greek *faithful brothers.* 1:7 Greek *he is ministering on your behalf;* other manuscripts read *he is ministering on our behalf.*

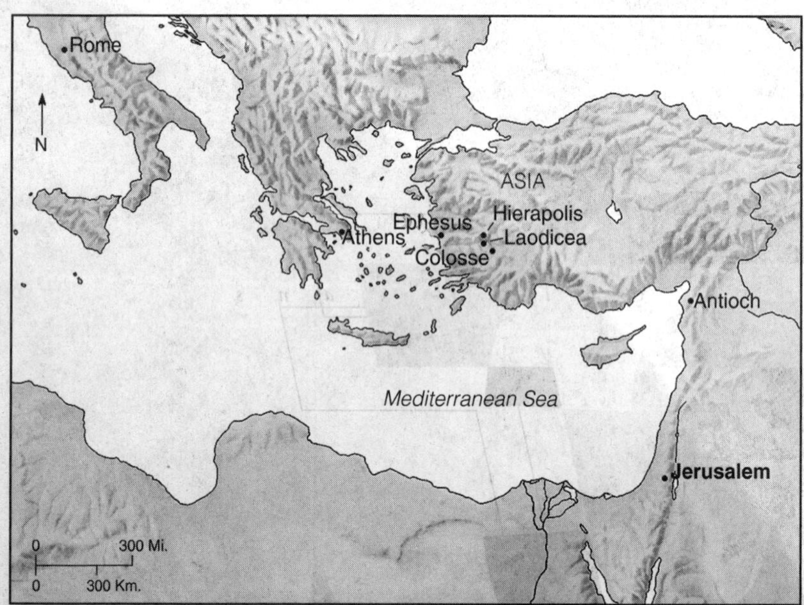


**LOCATION OF COLOSSE**
Paul had undoubtedly been through Laodicea on his third missionary journey because it lay on the main route to Ephesus, but he had never been to Colosse. Though a large city with a significant population, Colosse was smaller and less important than the nearby cities of Laodicea and Hieropolis.

of darkness, and he has brought us into the Kingdom of his dear Son. [14]God has purchased our freedom with his blood* and has forgiven all our sins.

[15]Christ is the visible image of the invisible God. He existed before God made anything at all and is supreme over all creation.* [16]Christ is the one through whom God created everything in heaven and earth. He made the things we can see and the things we can't see—kings, kingdoms, rulers, and authorities. Everything has been created through him and for him. [17]He existed before everything else began, and he holds all creation together.

## HOW TO PRAY ● ● • • .

1:9-14 **Sometimes we wonder how to pray for missionaries and other leaders we have never met. Paul had never met the Colossians, but he faithfully prayed for them. His prayers teach us how to pray for others, whether we know them or not. We can request that they (1) understand God's will, (2) gain wisdom and spiritual understanding, (3) please and honor God, (4) bear good fruit, (5) know God better and better, (6) be filled with God's strength, (7) have great patience, (8) stay full of Christ's joy, and (9) always be thankful. All believers have these same basic needs. When you don't know how to pray for someone, remember Paul's prayer pattern for the Colossians.**

[18]Christ is the head of the church, which is his body. He is the first of all who will rise from the dead,* so he is first in everything. [19]For God in all his fullness was pleased to live in Christ, [20]and by him God reconciled everything to himself. He made peace with everything in heaven and on earth by means of his blood on the cross. [21]This includes you who were once so far away from God. You were his enemies, separated from him by your evil thoughts and actions, [22]yet now he has brought you back as his friends. He has done this through his death on the cross in his own human body. As a result, he has brought you into the very presence of God, and you are holy and blameless as you stand before him without a single fault. [23]But you must continue to believe this truth and stand in it firmly. Don't drift away from the assurance you received when you heard the Good News. The Good News has been preached all over the world, and I, Paul, have been appointed by God to proclaim it.

[24]I am glad when I suffer for you in my body, for I am completing what remains of Christ's sufferings for his body, the church. [25]God has given me the responsibility of serving his church by proclaiming his message in all its fullness to you Gentiles. [26]This message was kept secret for centuries and generations past, but now it has been revealed to his own holy people. [27]For it has pleased God to tell his people that the riches and glory of Christ are for you Gentiles, too. For this is the secret: Christ lives in you, and this is your assurance that you will share in his glory.

## FOR THE BETTER ● ● • • .

2:20-23 **People should be able to see a difference between the way Christians and non-Christians live. Still, we should not expect instant maturity of new Christians. The Christian life is a process. Although we have a new nature, we don't automatically have all good thoughts and attitudes when we become new people in Christ. But if we keep listening to God, we will be changing all the time. As you look over the last year, what changes for the better have you seen in your thoughts and attitudes? Change may be slow, but your life will change significantly if you trust God to change you.**

1:14 Some manuscripts do not include *with his blood.* 1:15 Greek *He is the firstborn of all creation.* 1:18 Greek *He is the beginning, the firstborn from the dead.*

28So everywhere we go, we tell everyone about
Christ. We warn them and teach them with all the
wisdom God has given us, for we want to present
them to God, perfect* in their relationship to Christ.
29I work very hard at this, as I depend on Christ's
mighty power that works within me.

CHAPTER **2** **A NEW LIFE IN CHRIST.** I want you to
know how much I have agonized for you and for
the church at Laodicea, and for many other friends
who have never known me personally. 2My goal is
that they will be encouraged and knit together by
strong ties of love. I want them to have full confidence because they have complete understanding
of God's secret plan, which is Christ himself. 3In
him lie hidden all the treasures of wisdom and
knowledge.
4I am telling you this so that no one will be able
to deceive you with persuasive arguments. 5For
though I am far away from you, my heart is with
you. And I am very happy because you are living as
you should and because of your strong faith in
Christ.
6And now, just as you accepted Christ Jesus as your
Lord, you must continue to live in obedience to him.
7Let your roots grow down into him and draw up
nourishment from him, so you will grow in faith,
strong and vigorous in the truth you were taught. Let
your lives overflow with thanksgiving for all he has
done.
8Don't let anyone lead you astray with empty
philosophy and high-sounding nonsense that come
from human thinking and from the evil powers of
this world,* and not from Christ. 9For in Christ the
fullness of God lives in a human body,* 10and you
are complete through your union with Christ. He is
the Lord over every ruler and authority in the universe.
11When you came to Christ, you were "circumcised," but not by a physical procedure. It was a
spiritual procedure—the cutting away of your sinful
nature. 12For you were buried with Christ when you
were baptized. And with him you were raised to a
new life because you trusted the mighty power of
God, who raised Christ from the dead.
13You were dead because of your sins and because your sinful nature was not yet cut away. Then
God made you alive with Christ. He forgave all our
sins. 14He canceled the record that contained the
charges against us. He took it and destroyed it by
nailing it to Christ's cross. 15In this way, God dis-
armed the evil rulers and authorities. He shamed
them publicly by his victory over them on the cross
of Christ.
16So don't let anyone condemn you for what you
eat or drink, or for not celebrating certain holy days
or new-moon ceremonies or Sabbaths. 17For these
rules were only shadows of the real thing, Christ
himself. 18Don't let anyone condemn you by insisting on self-denial. And don't let anyone say you
must worship angels, even though they say they have
had visions about this. These people claim to be so
humble, but their sinful minds have made them
proud. 19But they are not connected to Christ, the
head of the body. For we are joined together in his
body by his strong sinews, and we grow only as we
get our nourishment and strength from God.
20You have died with Christ, and he has set you

**I have been a Christian for about two months and I feel so far behind spiritually, compared to friends who have been Christians for a lot longer. Sometimes it gets pretty discouraging. How do I catch up?**

We live in a world that makes it nearly impossible not to compare ourselves with others.

Sometimes we even compare our life as a Christian to others. However, you must fight this urge and recognize two essential facts.

First, receiving forgiveness for our sin and asking Christ to come into our life is like a seed being planted in our heart (see 1 Corinthians 3:6). Any seed planted must first take root before it grows and blossoms.

Do you remember in first grade when you planted a seed in a clear plastic cup? If the seed was planted close enough to the edge, you would see that the roots would grow downward first; then a few days later a plant would appear above the dirt. It was miraculous!

The only difference between you and your friends is that they have had more time to spread their roots down deep. They have let their "roots grow down into him and draw up nourishment from him" for a longer period of time.

When you took the first step of faith to trust Christ with your life, that was like the seed being planted. From this point it is up to you and God to nourish the seed and let the roots grow deep (see Colossians 2:6-7).

Your faith is nourished by rooting your new relationship with Christ. This means getting to know God better through reading and obeying his Word in the Bible (Romans 10:17). As with any relationship, time together helps you to appreciate God's character and will lead to a greater love for him (2 Peter 3:18).

Second, God doesn't compare one Christian to another. So you shouldn't, either. That would be like a father wanting his two-year-old son to throw a baseball as well as his nine-year-old. He can't!

As Christians, we never get to a point where we have arrived and are totally mature. Our love and appreciation for God can always grow deeper as he shows us new areas in our life to trust him with.

Enjoy these beginning stages of your faith by taking in all of the spiritual nourishment you can handle. Remember, the stronger and deeper your roots grow below the surface, the more beautiful and fruitful you will be as a Christian (see John 15:4-5).

1:28 Or *mature.* 2:8 Or *from the basic principles of this world;* also in 2:20. 2:9 Greek *in him dwells all the fullness of the Godhead bodily.*

free from the evil powers of this world. So why do
you keep on following rules of the world, such as,
21“Don’t handle, don’t eat, don’t touch.” 22Such
rules are mere human teaching about things that
are gone as soon as we use them. 23These rules may
seem wise because they require strong devotion,
humility, and severe bodily discipline. But they
have no effect when it comes to conquering a
person’s evil thoughts and desires.

## LUST

Last year, thirteen-year-old Danny found a secret stash of pornographic magazines in his older brother’s bedroom. Since then, he’s developed a system. Each time his brother goes out for the evening, Danny sneaks one of the magazines into his own bedroom. There he’ll stay for long hours fantasizing about being with each of the beautiful models. After a few days, he smuggles the much-studied magazine back into its place, whereupon he takes another one and repeats the process.

Each time he yields to these lustful temptations, Danny is overcome by a wave of guilt. After the short-term pleasure, Danny experiences only feelings of emptiness and loneliness. Even so, he rationalizes it this way:

“It’s better to do what I’m doing than to be like my friends and actually go out and have sex! At least this way, I don’t get myself or anybody else in trouble. Besides, I can’t help it if I have a healthy sex drive. And anyway, I’m not sure I can stop.”

What about Danny’s ideas on lust? Are they sound arguments? Is it OK to stare at pictures (or real people) and imagine having sex with them? Take a look at Colossians 3:5 for God’s thoughts on the issue.

CHAPTER **3** **SOME RULES TO OBEY.** Since you have
been raised to new life with Christ, set your sights
on the realities of heaven, where Christ sits at
God’s right hand in the place of honor and power.
2Let heaven fill your thoughts. Do not think only
about things down here on earth. 3For you died
when Christ died, and your real life is hidden with
Christ in God. 4And when Christ, who is your* real
life, is revealed to the whole world, you will share
in all his glory.
5So put to death the sinful, earthly things lurking within you. Have nothing to do with sexual sin,
impurity, lust, and shameful desires. Don’t be
greedy for the good things of this life, for that is
idolatry. 6God’s terrible anger will come upon
those who do such things. 7You used to do them
when your life was still part of this world. 8But now
is the time to get rid of anger, rage, malicious
behavior, slander, and dirty language. 9Don’t lie to
each other, for you have stripped off your old evil
nature and all its wicked deeds. 10In its place you
have clothed yourselves with a brand-new nature
that is continually being renewed as you learn
more and more about Christ, who created this new
nature within you. 11In this new life, it doesn’t
matter if you are a Jew or a Gentile,* circumcised
or uncircumcised, barbaric, uncivilized,* slave, or
free. Christ is all that matters, and he lives in all
of us.
12Since God chose you to be the holy people
whom he loves, you must clothe yourselves with
tenderhearted mercy, kindness, humility, gentleness,
and patience. 13You must make allowance for each
other’s faults and forgive the person who offends
you. Remember, the Lord forgave you, so you must
forgive others. 14And the most important piece of
clothing you must wear is love. Love is what binds us
all together in perfect harmony. 15And let the peace
that comes from Christ rule in your hearts. For as
members of one body you are all called to live in
peace. And always be thankful.

## PEACE RULES ● ● • • •

**3:15 The word *rule* comes from athletics: Paul tells us to let God’s peace be “umpire” in our heart. Our heart is the center of conflict because that is where our feelings and desires clash—our fears and hopes, distrust and trust, jealousy and love. How can we deal with these constant conflicts and live as God wants? Paul explains that we must decide between conflicting elements on the basis of peace. Ask yourself which choice will promote peace in your soul, your family, and your church.**

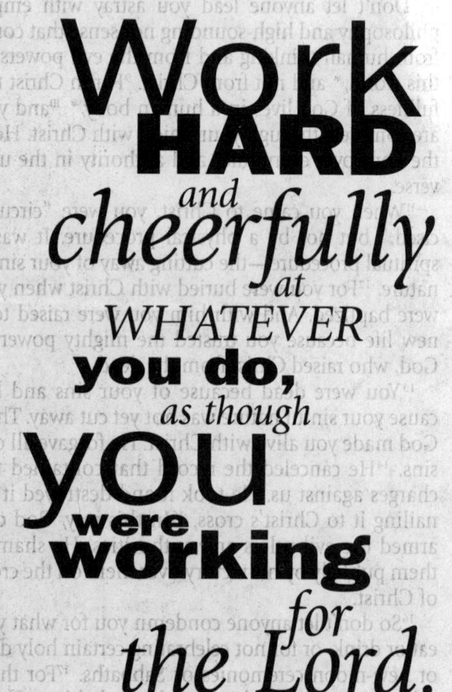
Work
HARD
and
cheerfully
at
WHATEVER
you do,
as though
YOU
were
working
for
the Lord.
COLOSSIANS 3:23

3:4 Some manuscripts read *our.* 3:11a Greek *Greek.* 3:11b Greek *Barbarian, Scythian.*

16 Let the words of Christ, in all their richness, live
in your hearts and make you wise. Use his words to
teach and counsel each other. Sing psalms and
hymns and spiritual songs to God with thankful
hearts. 17 And whatever you do or say, let it be as a
representative of the Lord Jesus, all the while giving
thanks through him to God the Father.

18 You wives must submit to your husbands, as is
fitting for those who belong to the Lord. 19 And you
husbands must love your wives and never treat them
harshly.

20 You children must always obey your parents, for
this is what pleases the Lord. 21 Fathers, don't aggra-
vate your children. If you do, they will become discouraged and quit trying.

22 You slaves must obey your earthly masters in
everything you do. Try to please them all the time,
not just when they are watching you. Obey them
willingly because of your reverent fear of the Lord.
23 Work hard and cheerfully at whatever you do, as
though you were working for the Lord rather than
for people. 24 Remember that the Lord will give
you an inheritance as your reward, and the Master
you are serving is Christ. 25 But if you do what is
wrong, you will be paid back for the wrong you
have done. For God has no favorites who can get
away with evil.

CHAPTER **4** **PAUL SAYS GOOD-
BYE.** You slave owners must be just
and fair to your slaves. Remember
that you also have a Master—in
heaven.

2 Devote yourselves to prayer
with an alert mind and a thankful
heart. 3 Don't forget to pray for us,
too, that God will give us many
opportunities to preach about his
secret plan—that Christ is also for
you Gentiles. That is why I am here
in chains. 4 Pray that I will proclaim this message as clearly as I
should.

5 Live wisely among those who
are not Christians, and make the
most of every opportunity. 6 Let
your conversation be gracious
and effective so that you will have
the right answer for everyone.

7 Tychicus, a much loved brother,
will tell you how I am getting along.
He is a faithful helper who serves
the Lord with me. 8 I have sent him
on this special trip to let you know
how we are doing and to encourage
you. 9 I am also sending Onesimus,
a faithful and much loved brother,
one of your own people. He and
Tychicus will give you all the latest
news.

10 Aristarchus, who is in prison with me, sends
you his greetings, and so does Mark, Barnabas's
cousin. And as you were instructed before, make
Mark welcome if he comes your way. 11 Jesus (the
one we call Justus) also sends his greetings.
These are the only Jewish Christians among my
co-workers; they are working with me here for the
Kingdom of God. And what a comfort they have
been!

12 Epaphras, from your city, a servant of Christ
Jesus, sends you his greetings. He always prays
earnestly for you, asking God to make you strong
and perfect, fully confident of the whole will of
God. 13 I can assure you that he has agonized for
you and also for the Christians in Laodicea and
Hierapolis.

14 Dear Doctor Luke sends his greetings, and so

## PERSIST

4:2 **Have you ever grown tired of praying for something or someone? Paul says, "Devote yourselves to prayer." Vigilance demonstrates our faith that God answers our prayers. Faith shouldn't die if the answers don't come immediately, for the delay may be God's way of working his will in your life. When you feel weary in your prayers, know that God is present, always listening, always acting—maybe not in ways you had hoped, but in ways that he knows are best.**

## "Here's what I did..."

For a couple of years in high school, I didn't get along very well with my dad. I'm not sure why, now. It just seemed like everything he said irritated me. Dad seemed old-fashioned, too restrictive. I began to rebel, not openly, but more in my heart and on the sly. For instance, I would tell him that I'd do something he had asked me to, but then I never would get around to doing it. Then when he'd get angry, I'd tune him out. Or I would tell Dad I was going somewhere that I knew he'd approve, when I really was with friends he didn't like very much.

I knew things weren't great between us, but I didn't think much about it until our youth group was doing a study on relationships. When we talked about parents, we studied Colossians 3:20 and Ephesians 6:1-3. We talked about why we should obey our parents, and what it means to obey.

I felt cut to the heart. I realized that Dad was a good dad, and suddenly I understood that his restrictions were because he loved me. If I was honest with myself, a lot of them (not all, but a lot) made sense. I was being disobedient and rebellious. I cried some, knowing that I had been hurting my dad for a long time.

That evening I asked Dad to forgive me for all the ways I'd gone against him. It was hard to apologize, but it cleared the air. Dad took my apology well—he even admitted to some areas where he might have been too hard on me. That was the start of a much better father-son relationship, which has continued.

*Brad*, AGE 18

does Demas. [15]Please give my greetings to our Christian brothers and sisters* at Laodicea, and to Nympha and those who meet in her house.

[16]After you have read this letter, pass it on to the church at Laodicea so they can read it, too. And you should read the letter I wrote to them. [17]And say to Archippus, "Be sure to carry out the work the Lord gave you."

[18]Here is my greeting in my own handwriting—PAUL.

Remember my chains.

May the grace of God be with you.

4:15 Greek *brothers*.

# MEGA themes

**CHRIST IS GOD** Jesus Christ is God in the flesh, Lord of all creation, and Lord of the new creation. He is the exact reflection of the invisible God. He is eternal, preexistent, all-powerful, and equal with the Father. Christ is supreme and complete.

Because Christ is supreme, our life must be Christ centered. To recognize Jesus as God means to regard our relationship with him as most vital and to make his interests our top priority. He must become the navigator of our life's voyage.

1. List the words and phrases that are used to describe Jesus Christ in chapters 1 and 2. What do you learn about Christ as God in these descriptions?
2. Why is it important to understand that Christ is both God and man?
3. Based on the fact that Christ is truly God, how should you respond to his lordship (control and leadership)?
4. How are you responding to his lordship in your life at the present? What can you do to be more submissive to Christ's role as your Lord?

**CHRIST IS THE HEAD OF THE CHURCH** Because Christ is God, he is the head of the church, his true believers. Christ is the founder and leader of the church and the highest authority on earth. He requires first place in all our thoughts and activities.

To acknowledge Christ as our leader, we must welcome his leadership in all we do or think. No person, group, or church should have more loyalty from us than Christ.

1. What does this phrase mean: "Christ is the head of the church"?
2. If you were starting a local church, what kinds of things would you insist on in order to keep Christ as the central leader of that church?
3. Write a statement for yourself and other young people that challenges them to respond to Christ's headship of your local church.

**UNION WITH CHRIST** Because our sin has been forgiven and we have been reconciled to God, we have a union with Christ that can never be broken. In our faith connection with Christ, we identify with his death, burial, and resurrection.

We should live in constant contact and communication with God. When we do, we will be unified with Christ and with our fellow believers. We are a part of each other's "spiritual life-support system."

1. Read 2:6-15. What does it mean to have new life in Christ?
2. From what things were you set free when you were united with Christ?
3. Read 3:1-17. What things were you called to be and do when you were united to Christ?
4. In what specific ways has your union with Christ made a difference in your past? In your present? In your future?

**MAN-MADE RELIGION** False teachers were promoting a heresy that stressed man-made rules (legalism). They also sought spiritual growth by denying themselves personal contacts and by mysterious rules. This search created pride in their self-centered efforts.

We must not hold on to our own ideas and try to blend them into Christianity. Nor should we let our hunger for a more fulfilling Christian experience cause us to trust in a teacher, group, or system of thought more than in Christ himself. Christ is our hope and our true source of wisdom. We must reject any teacher whose message is not based absolutely on the truth of Christ.

1. What lie was behind the legalism that the false teachers taught to the Colossians?
2. What is the danger of promoting a religion that is based on people's responsibility to save themselves with good works?
3. What are some current examples of the false teachings of legalism? Why are these harmful? How does this hinder non-Christians from understanding and accepting the gospel?

**P**hobias are "phascinating" phenomena. Psychiatrists and psychologists have catalogued hundreds of them. Check out this list: ■ Anthophobia—the fear of flowers ■ Belonophobia—the fear of pins and needles ■ Decidophobia—the fear of making decisions ■ Mysophobia—the fear of dirt ■ Trichophobia—the fear of hair ■ Would you believe that some people are even terrified about *peanut butter sticking to the roof of their mouth?* That's called arachidutyrophobia. ■ You may not struggle with such odd fears, but you probably *do* worry about more common stuff. Every day, the media spotlights a different concern: ■ Is the environment damaged beyond repair? Will researchers ever find a cure for AIDS? How many people are infected without knowing it? ■ Are we on the brink of a worldwide economic collapse? How are we going to deal with a generation of drug-addicted babies? Can we confront and correct our country's epidemic of violent crimes? How has war affected our lives? ■ These are scary issues, but the Christian has real hope and genuine peace—even in uncertain times. ■ That's the message of this book: Be comforted, for no matter what happens, God is with us. Rest in the reassuring truth that Jesus Christ is coming back soon to . . . . ■ Aw, that's enough blabbering. Read it yourself. You won't believe your eyes.

## STATS

PURPOSE: To strengthen the Thessalonian Christians in their faith and give them assurance of Christ's return

AUTHOR: Paul

TO WHOM WRITTEN: The church at Thessalonica and all believers everywhere

DATE WRITTEN: About A.D. 51 from Corinth; one of Paul's earliest letters

SETTING: The church at Thessalonica had been established only two or three years before this letter was written. The Christians needed to mature in their faith. Also, there was a misunderstanding about Christ's second coming—some thought he would return immediately, others wondered if the dead would experience a bodily resurrection at his return.

KEY PEOPLE: Paul, Timothy, Silas

KEY PLACE: Thessalonica

# 1 Thessalonians

CHAPTER 1 **CHOSEN BY GOD.** This letter is from Paul, Silas,* and Timothy.

It is written to the church in Thessalonica, you who belong to God the Father and the Lord Jesus Christ.

May his grace and peace be yours.

2We always thank God for all of you and pray for
you constantly. 3As we talk to our God and Father
about you, we think of your faithful work, your
loving deeds, and your continual anticipation of the
return of our Lord Jesus Christ.
4We know that God loves you, dear brothers
and sisters,* and that he chose you to be his own
people. 5For when we brought you the Good News,
it was not only with words but also with power, for
the Holy Spirit gave you full assurance that what we
said was true. And you know that the way we lived
among you was further proof of the truth of our
message. 6So you received the message with joy from
the Holy Spirit in spite of the severe suffering it
brought you. In this way, you imitated both us and
the Lord. 7As a result, you yourselves became an
example to all the Christians in Greece.* 8And now
the word of the Lord is ringing out from you to
people everywhere, even beyond Greece, for wherever we go we find people telling us about your faith
in God. We don't need to tell them about it, 9for they
themselves keep talking about the wonderful welcome you gave us and how you turned away from
idols to serve the true and living God. 10And they
speak of how you are looking forward to the coming
of God's Son from heaven—Jesus, whom God raised
from the dead. He is the one who has rescued us
from the terrors of the coming judgment.

CHAPTER 2 **PAUL'S FRIENDS.** You yourselves know,
dear brothers and sisters,* that our visit to you was
not a failure. 2You know how badly we had been
treated at Philippi just before we came to you and
how much we suffered there. Yet our God gave us the
courage to declare his Good News to you boldly,
even though we were surrounded by many who
opposed us. 3So you can see that we were not preaching with any deceit or impure purposes or trickery.
4For we speak as messengers who have been approved by God to be entrusted with the Good News.
Our purpose is to please God, not people. He is the
one who examines the motives of our hearts. 5Never
once did we try to win you with flattery, as you very
well know. And God is our witness that we were not
just pretending to be your friends so you would give
us money! 6As for praise, we have never asked for it

1:1 Greek *Silvanus.* 1:4 Greek *brothers.* 1:7 Greek *Macedonia and Achaia,* the northern and southern regions of Greece; also in 1:8. 2:1 Greek *brothers;* also in 2:9, 14, 17.

from you or anyone else. [7]As apostles of Christ we certainly had a right to make some demands of you, but we were as gentle among you as a mother* feeding and caring for her own children. [8]We loved you so much that we gave you not only God's Good News but our own lives, too.

[9]Don't you remember, dear brothers and sisters, how hard we worked among you? Night and day we toiled to earn a living so that our expenses would not be a burden to anyone there as we preached God's Good News among you. [10]You yourselves are our witnesses—and so is God—that we were pure and honest and faultless toward all of you believers. [11]And you know that we treated each of you as a father treats his own children. [12]We pleaded with you, encouraged you, and urged you to live your lives in a way that God would consider worthy. For he called you into his Kingdom to share his glory.

## SEX

Melanie is confused about sex—not how (she learned that a long time ago), but when. Her mom tells her to wait. Her youth director gives her the same advice. But everywhere else the message is clearly, "Go for it!" Or, "If you're still a virgin, you're a total loser!"

- Friends at school tell her how great it is and how experienced they are.
- All the glamorous stars in TV shows and movies seem to be hopping from bed to bed—both on- and off-screen.
- In a health class lecture on birth control two weeks ago, the teacher stated, "Now, most normal young people are sexually active. I'm assuming you all are normal, so . . ."
- Melanie's boyfriend keeps telling her how much sex will strengthen their relationship.
- Almost every ad and billboard Melanie sees has a sexual twist or theme.
- A talk show featured live-in lovers talking about their "great" lifestyle.

"What am I supposed to think?" Melanie asks. "I feel like everybody else in the world is enjoying this really fantastic experience . . . and I'm like a nun or something. I want to wait, at least I think I do. Tell me, is it really worth saving yourself till marriage?"

The Bible says it's definitely wiser to wait until marriage for sex. Think hard about the message in 1 Thessalonians 4:1-8.

[13]And we will never stop thanking God that when we preached his message to you, you didn't think of the words we spoke as being just our own. You accepted what we said as the very word of God—which, of course, it was. And this word continues to work in you who believe.

[14]And then, dear brothers and sisters, you suffered persecution from your own countrymen. In this way, you imitated the believers in God's churches in Judea who, because of their belief in Christ Jesus, suffered from their own people, the Jews.

## OPPOSED ● ● • • •

2:14 **Just as the Jewish Christians in Jerusalem were persecuted by their own people, so the Gentile Christians in Thessalonica were persecuted by their fellow Gentiles. It is discouraging to face persecution, especially when it comes from your own people. But when we take a stand for Christ, we will face opposition, disapproval, ridicule, and even persecution from our neighbors, friends, and even family members.**

[15]For some of the Jews had killed their own prophets, and some even killed the Lord Jesus. Now they have persecuted us and driven us out. They displease God and oppose everyone [16]by trying to keep us from preaching the Good News to the Gentiles, for fear some might be saved. By doing this, they continue to pile up their sins. But the anger of God has caught up with them at last.

[17]Dear brothers and sisters, after we were separated from you for a little while (though our hearts never left you), we tried very hard to come back because of our intense longing to see you again. [18]We wanted very much to come, and I, Paul, tried again and again, but Satan prevented us. [19]After all, what gives us hope and joy, and what is our proud reward and crown? It is you! Yes, you will bring us much joy as we stand together before our Lord Jesus when he comes back again. [20]For you are our pride and joy.

CHAPTER **3** **A JOB WELL DONE.** Finally, when we could stand it no longer, we decided that I should stay alone in Athens, [2]and we sent Timothy to visit you. He is our co-worker for God and our brother in proclaiming the Good News of Christ. We sent him to strengthen you, to encourage you in your faith, [3]and to keep you from becoming disturbed by the troubles you were going through. But, of course, you know that such troubles are going to happen to us Christians. [4]Even while we were with you, we warned you that troubles would soon come—and they did, as you well know.

[5]That is why, when I could bear it no longer, I sent Timothy to find out whether your faith was still strong. I was afraid that the Tempter had gotten the best of you and that all our work had been useless. [6]Now Timothy has just returned, bringing the good news that your faith and love are as strong as ever. He reports that you remember our visit with joy and that you want to see us just as much as we want to see you. [7]So we have been greatly comforted, dear brothers and sisters,* in all of our own crushing troubles and suffering, because you have remained strong in your faith. [8]It gives us new life, knowing you remain strong in the Lord.

[9]How we thank God for you! Because of you we have great joy in the presence of God. [10]Night and day we pray earnestly for you, asking God to let us see you again to fill up anything that may still be missing in your faith.

[11]May God himself, our Father, and our Lord Jesus make it possible for us to come to you very soon.

2:7 Some manuscripts read *we were as infants among you; we were as a mother.* 3:7 Greek *brothers.*

[12]And may the Lord make your love grow and overflow to each other and to everyone else, just as our
love overflows toward you. [13]As a result, Christ will
make your hearts strong, blameless, and holy when
you stand before God our Father on that day when
our Lord Jesus comes with all those who belong to
him.

## CHAPTER 4 HOW CAN I PLEASE GOD?

Finally, dear
brothers and sisters,* we urge you in the name of
the Lord Jesus to live in a way that pleases God,
as we have taught you. You are doing this already,
and we encourage you to do so more and more.
[2]For you remember what we taught you in the
name of the Lord Jesus. [3]God wants you to be
holy, so you should keep clear of all sexual sin.
[4]Then each of you will control your body* and live
in holiness and honor—[5]not in lustful passion
as the pagans do, in their ignorance of God and
his ways.

[6]Never cheat a Christian brother in this matter
by taking his wife, for the Lord avenges all such
sins, as we have solemnly warned you before. [7]God
has called us to be holy, not to live impure lives.
[8]Anyone who refuses to live by these rules is not
disobeying human rules but is rejecting God, who
gives his Holy Spirit to you.

[9]But I don't need to write to you about the
Christian love* that should be shown among
God's people. For God himself has taught you to
love one another. [10]Indeed, your love is already
strong toward all the Christians* in all of Macedonia. Even so, dear brothers and sisters, we beg you
to love them more and more. [11]This should be your
ambition: to live a quiet life, minding your own
business and working with your hands, just as we
commanded you before. [12]As a result, people who
are not Christians will respect the way you live, and
you will not need to depend on others to meet
your financial needs.

[13]And now, brothers and sisters, I want you to
know what will happen to the Christians who have
died so you will not be full of sorrow like people
who have no hope. [14]For since we believe that Jesus
died and was raised to life again, we also believe that
when Jesus comes, God will bring back with Jesus all
the Christians who have died.

[15]I can tell you this directly from the Lord: We who
are still living when the Lord returns will not rise to
meet him ahead of those who are in their graves.
[16]For the Lord himself will come down from heaven
with a commanding shout, with the call of the archangel, and with the trumpet call of God. First, all the
Christians who have died will rise from their graves.
[17]Then, together with them, we who are still alive
and remain on the earth will be caught up in the
clouds to meet the Lord in the air and remain with
him forever. [18]So comfort and encourage each other
with these words.

## CHAPTER 5 ARE YOU READY FOR CHRIST'S RETURN?

I
really don't need to write to you about how and when
all this will happen, dear brothers and sisters.* [2]For
you know quite well that the day of the Lord will come
unexpectedly, like a thief in the night. [3]When people
are saying, "All is well; everything is peaceful and
secure," then disaster will fall upon them as suddenly
as a woman's birth pains begin when her child is about
to be born. And there will be no escape.

[4]But you aren't in the dark about these things,
dear brothers and sisters, and you won't be surprised
when the day of the Lord comes like a thief. [5]For you
are all children of the light and of the day; we don't
belong to darkness and night. [6]So be on your guard,
not asleep like the others. Stay alert and be sober.
[7]Night is the time for sleep and the time when

**Even though I know I'm going to heaven, I'm still afraid of dying. How can I quit being so afraid of death?**

Extreme fear of the unknown can cripple a person. Unfortunately, death is an unknown for everyone, even for Christians.

What will we find on the other side? How is God going to take me? Will the people left behind be able to adjust? What if I die before I have a chance to get married or experience what I want to experience?

There are a lot of questions that don't have concrete answers. That can be frustrating. Someone once said that trying to explain to another person what God and heaven are like is similar to one dog telling another dog what it's like to be a human. It's impossible!

But death is not something that Christians have to fear, because—for them—death is not the end of the story. It is the gateway to a place of indescribable joy and beauty. It's the beginning of a new life!

Fear is a learned emotion. Through the years we are conditioned to fear certain things. Little kids aren't afraid of death because they don't understand it. Yet as they grow and see the response of adults and the media to death, they learn that it's something awful and to be avoided at all costs.

After we become Christians, we need to go through a relearning process about death. Paul, the author of half the books in the New Testament, said this about death, "For to me, living is for Christ, and dying is even better" (Philippians 1:21).

Paul had learned that death would actually put an end to the struggles he faced on earth. He looked forward to the day when he could see Christ face-to-face. In the meantime, though, he had work to do: winning people to Christ. Life wasn't a chore—it was a privilege!

Fear of dying doesn't disappear instantly. But as you spend time in the Bible and with other Christians who have the same hope you do, you will grow to realize that death is only a door to an eternity far better than your wildest dreams (see 1 Thessalonians 4:13-14).

4:1 Greek *brothers;* also in 4:10, 13. 4:4 Or *will know how to take a wife for himself;* Greek reads *will know how to possess his own vessel.* 4:9 Greek *brotherly love.* 4:10 Greek *the brothers.* 5:1 Greek *brothers;* also in 5:4, 12, 14, 25, 26, 27.

**LOCATION OF THESSALONICA**
Paul visited Thessalonica on his second and third missionary journeys. It was a seaport and trade center located on the Egnatian Way, a busy international highway. Paul probably wrote his two letters to the Thessalonians from Corinth.

people get drunk. [8]But let us who live in the light
think clearly, protected by the body armor of faith
and love, and wearing as our helmet the confidence
of our salvation. [9]For God decided to save us through
our Lord Jesus Christ, not to pour out his anger on
us. [10]He died for us so that we can live with him
forever, whether we are dead or alive at the time of
his return. [11]So encourage each other and build each
other up, just as you are already doing.

## THE FINISH LINE ● ● • • •

**5:9-11 As you near the end of a foot race, your legs ache, your throat burns, and your whole body cries out for you to stop. This is when friends and fans are most valuable. Their encouragement helps you push through the pain to the finish. In the same way, Christians are to encourage one another. A word of encouragement offered at the right moment can be the difference between finishing well and collapsing along the way. Look around you. Be sensitive to others' need for encouragement and offer supportive words or actions.**

[12]Dear brothers and sisters, honor those who are
your leaders in the Lord's work. They work hard
among you and warn you against all that is wrong.
[13]Think highly of them and give them your wholehearted love because of their work. And remember to
live peaceably with each other.
[14]Brothers and sisters, we urge you to warn those
who are lazy. Encourage those who are timid. Take
tender care of those who are weak. Be patient with
everyone.
[15]See that no one pays back evil for evil, but always
try to do good to each other and to everyone else.
[16]Always be joyful. [17]Keep on praying. [18]No matter
what happens, always be thankful, for this is God's
will for you who belong to Christ Jesus.
[19]Do not stifle the Holy Spirit. [20]Do not scoff at
prophecies, [21]but test everything that is said. Hold
on to what is good. [22]Keep away from every kind of
evil.
[23]Now may the God of peace make you holy in
every way, and may your whole spirit and soul and
body be kept blameless until that day when our Lord
Jesus Christ comes again. [24]God, who calls you, is
faithful; he will do this.
[25]Dear brothers and sisters, pray for us.
[26]Greet all the brothers and sisters in Christian
love.*
[27]I command you in the name of the Lord to read
this letter to all the brothers and sisters.
[28]And may the grace of our Lord Jesus Christ be
with all of you.

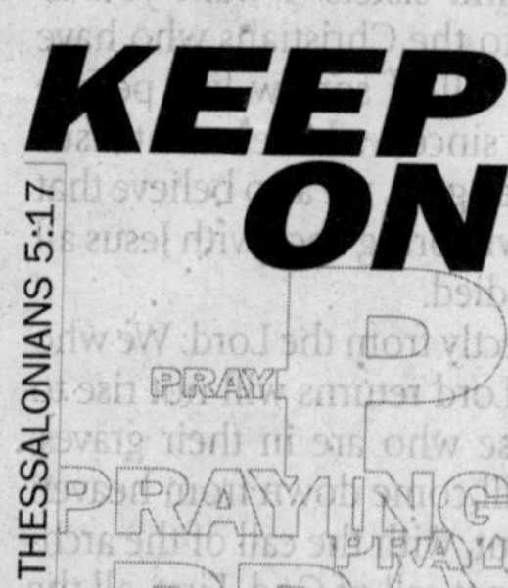
1 THESSALONIANS 5:17
KEEP
ON
PRAYING.

5:26 Greek *with a holy kiss.*

# MEGA themes

**PERSECUTION** Paul and the new Christians at Thessalonica experienced persecution because of their faith in Christ. We can expect trials and troubles as well. We need to stand firm in our faith during our trials, being strengthened by the Holy Spirit.

The Holy Spirit helps us to remain strong in faith; he enables us to show genuine love to others and to maintain our moral character even when we are being persecuted, slandered, or oppressed.

1. How did the Thessalonians respond to pressure and opposition that came because of their faith in Christ?
2. During this persecution, where did they get their strength?
3. What pressures and/or opposition have you faced as a Christian? How did you feel when that happened? How have you responded to such situations?
4. What does it mean to "stand firm" when you are persecuted?
5. What can you do to prepare yourself so that you will stand firm throughout your life, even during intense persecution?

**PAUL'S MINISTRY** Paul expressed his concern for this church even while he was being slandered. Paul's commitment to share the gospel in spite of difficult circumstances is an example that we should follow.

Paul not only gave his message, he also gave himself. In our ministries, we must become like Paul—faithful and bold, yet sensitive and self-sacrificing. Achieving such maturity results from years of commitment to God's will—the younger you begin, the deeper your growth will be.

1. What qualities do you see in Paul's wonderful example of godly ministry that enabled his message to be so powerful?
2. If you were Paul's companion in ministry, what would you most want to learn from him?
3. Who are the people closest to you who need to hear God's message? How will you follow Paul's example and do this?
4. What thoughts, attitudes, or actions do you have as a result of the hope that is within you in Christ? What can you do to comfort and encourage others with this truth?

**BEING PREPARED** No one knows when Christ will return. In the meantime, we are to live a moral and holy life, ever watching for his coming. Believers must not neglect their daily responsibilities, but always work and live as unto the Lord.

The gospel tells us not only what we should believe, but also how we must live. The Holy Spirit leads us in faithfulness, so we can avoid lust and fraud. Live as though you expect Christ's return at any time. Don't be caught unprepared.

1. Summarize the events of Christ's return as revealed in 1 Thessalonians.
2. What does it mean to be prepared for these events? Why is this so important? (Check Matthew 25 for Jesus' teaching.)
3. What are you doing to be ready for Christ's return?

**A** prominent author's best-selling new book has predicted that Christ is coming back in a few days. ■ Anne: "It's supposed to happen *this* weekend." ■ Sandra: "I guess I'm ready, but if it *does* happen, I'll never get my license—and I'll never get to . . . well, you know." ■ (Everyone but Pam giggles.) ■ Karen: "I think it's *great.* I've got a *huge* algebra test on Monday that I can't possibly pass. *Now* I can just relax and forget about it." ■ Sandra: "Right, and no more abuse from Steve Hampton and his atheist friends!" ■ Anne: "Omigosh, I never even thought about that. *That* will be the best!" ■ Pam: "You guys *cannot* be serious! You talk like you actually *believe* that stuff!" ■ Anne: "Of course we do! It all fits together, and it's in the Bible, Pam. It's going to be this weekend—you better get ready." ■ Jesus *is* coming back. And his return *will* radically change things. It *will* be great, just as the girls imagine. ■ But that doesn't mean we should start picking dates and sitting around waiting. The prospect of Christ's return should motivate us to action, not laziness. He is coming back, so let's live for him—and encourage others to do the same. ■ That's the message of 2 Thessalonians. Yes, the world is gross. Yes, the Christian life is hard. But Jesus is coming back soon to make everything right. So keep watching, waiting—and working. ■ (And by all means, study for your algebra exam!)

## STATS

PURPOSE: To clear up the confusion about the second coming of Christ

AUTHOR: Paul

TO WHOM WRITTEN: The church at Thessalonica and all believers everywhere

DATE WRITTEN: About A.D. 51 or 52, a few months after 1 Thessalonians, from Corinth

SETTING: Many in the church were confused about the timing of Christ's return. Because of increasing persecution, they thought the Lord must return soon, so they interpreted Paul's first letter to say that the Second Coming would be at any moment. In light of this misunderstanding, some became lazy and disorderly.

KEY PEOPLE: Paul, Silas, Timothy

KEY PLACE: Thessalonica

SPECIAL FEATURES: This is a follow-up letter to 1 Thessalonians. In this epistle, Paul tells of various events that must precede the second coming of Christ.

CHAPTER **1** **PATIENCE IN SUFFERING.** This letter is from Paul, Silas,* and Timothy.

It is written to the church in Thessalonica, you who belong to God our Father and the Lord Jesus Christ.

[2]May God our Father and the Lord Jesus Christ give you grace and peace.

[3]Dear brothers and sisters,* we always thank God for you, as is right, for we are thankful that your faith is flourishing and you are all growing in love for each other. [4]We proudly tell God's other churches about your endurance and faithfulness in all the persecutions and hardships you are suffering. [5]But God will use this persecution to show his justice. For he will make you worthy of his Kingdom, for which you are suffering, [6]and in his justice he will punish those who persecute you. [7]And God will provide rest for you who are being persecuted and also for us when the Lord Jesus appears from heaven. He will come with his mighty angels, [8]in flaming fire, bringing judgment on those who don't know God and on those who refuse to obey the Good News of our Lord Jesus. [9]They will be punished with everlasting destruction, forever separated from the Lord and from his glorious power [10]when he comes to receive glory and praise from his holy people. And you will be among those praising him on that day, for you believed what we testified about him.

[11]And so we keep on praying for you, that our God will make you worthy of the life to which he called you. And we pray that God, by his power, will fulfill all your good intentions and faithful deeds. [12]Then everyone will give honor to the name of our Lord Jesus because of you, and you will be honored along with him. This is all made possible because of the undeserved favor of our God and Lord, Jesus Christ.*

CHAPTER **2** **THE ANTICHRIST.** And now, brothers and sisters,* let us tell you about the coming again of our Lord Jesus Christ and how we will be gathered together to meet him. [2]Please don't be so easily shaken and troubled by those who say that the day of the Lord has already begun. Even if they claim to have had a vision, a revelation, or a letter supposedly from us, don't believe them. [3]Don't be fooled by what they say.

For that day will not come until there is a great rebellion against God and the man of lawlessness is

**TROUBLES ● ● • • ·**
1:5 **As we live for Christ, we will experience troubles and hardships. Some say that troubles are a result of sin or lack of faith; Paul teaches that they may be a part of God's plan for believers. Our problems help us look upward and forward, not inward (Mark 13:35-36); help build strong character (Romans 5:3-4); and help us to be sensitive to others (2 Corinthians 1:3-5).**

1:1 Greek *Silvanus.* 1:3 Greek *Brothers.* 1:12 Or *of our God and the Lord Jesus Christ.* 2:1 Greek *brothers;* also in 2:13, 15.

revealed—the one who brings destruction.* [4]He will exalt himself and defy every god there is and tear down every object of adoration and worship. He will position himself in the temple of God, claiming that he himself is God. [5]Don't you remember that I told you this when I was with you? [6]And you know what is holding him back, for he can be revealed only when his time comes.

## LAZINESS

Trip walks in the door, drops his books on the couch, and heads straight for the kitchen. Opening the pantry, he scans the shelves and scowls. "How come there's never anything to eat in this stupid house?" he mutters to no one in particular.

Grabbing a banana, he settles back in the recliner, remote control in hand. *Click . . . Click . . . Click.*

The phone rings. Trip doesn't budge.

A voice from the hallway: "Trip, can you get the phone? I've got shaving cream all over my hands."

Trip sits impassively, staring at the TV.

The phone continues to ring. The voice from the rear of the house gets louder. "Trip! Answer the phone!"

Just as the mystery caller gives up, Trip's mom staggers through the door, her arms loaded with grocery sacks.

Trip watches her struggle from his easy chair and greets her by saying, "I hope you bought something decent to eat."

"Go get the other sacks and I'll get supper started."

"Sheesh!" Trip complains as he grudgingly leaves his comfortable throne. "Why do I always have to do everything around here? You and Dad treat me like a slave!"

Are you a lazy person? See what the Bible says about individuals who are unwilling to pull their share of the load—2 Thessalonians 3:6-13.

[7]For this lawlessness is already at work secretly, and it will remain secret until the one who is holding it back steps out of the way. [8]Then the man of lawlessness will be revealed, whom the Lord Jesus will consume with the breath of his mouth and destroy by the splendor of his coming. [9]This evil man will come to do the work of Satan with counterfeit power and signs and miracles. [10]He will use every kind of wicked deception to fool those who are on their way to destruction because they refuse to believe the truth that would save them. [11]So God will send great deception upon them, and they will believe all these lies. [12]Then they will be condemned for not believing the truth and for enjoying the evil they do.

[13]As for us, we always thank God for you, dear brothers and sisters loved by the Lord. We are thankful that God chose you to be among the first* to experience salvation, a salvation that came through the Spirit who makes you holy and by your belief in the truth. [14]He called you to salvation when we told you the Good News; now you can share in the glory of our Lord Jesus Christ.

## ATTACKS

**3:2-3 Beneath the surface of the routine of daily life, a fierce struggle among invisible spiritual powers is being waged. Like the wind, the force of evil powers can be devastating. Our main defense is prayer that God will protect us from evil and that he will make us strong. (See also comments on Ephesians 6:10-19 concerning our armor for spiritual warfare.) The following guidelines can help you prepare for and survive satanic attacks: (1) take the threat of spiritual attack seriously; (2) pray for strength and help from God; (3) study the Bible to recognize Satan's style and tactics; (4) memorize Scripture; (5) associate with those who speak the truth; and (6) practice what you are taught by spiritual leaders.**

[15]With all these things in mind, dear brothers and sisters, stand firm and keep a strong grip on everything we taught you both in person and by letter.

[16]May our Lord Jesus Christ and God our Father, who loved us and in his special favor gave us everlasting comfort and good hope, [17]comfort your hearts and give you strength in every good thing you do and say.

CHAPTER **3** **GOD MAKES US STRONG.** Finally, dear brothers and sisters,* I ask you to pray for us. Pray first that the Lord's message will spread rapidly and be honored wherever it goes, just as when it came to you. [2]Pray, too, that we will be saved from wicked and evil people, for not everyone believes in the Lord. [3]But the Lord is faithful; he will make you strong and guard you from the evil one.* [4]And we are confident in the Lord that you are practicing the things we commanded you, and that you always will. [5]May the Lord bring you into an ever deeper understanding of the love of God and the endurance that comes from Christ.

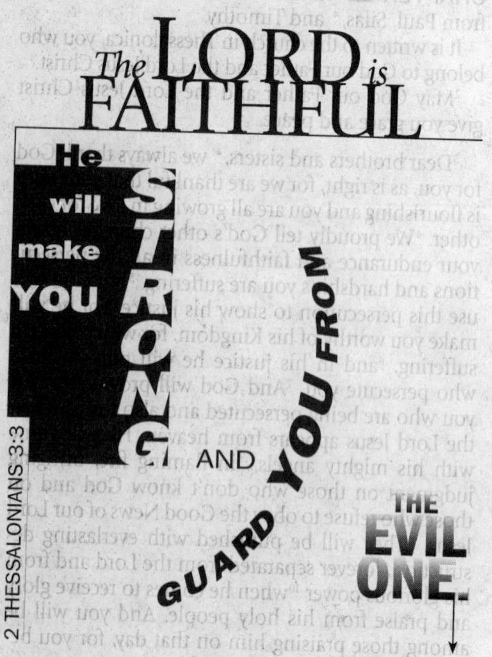
The LORD is FAITHFUL
He will make YOU STRONG AND GUARD YOU FROM THE EVIL ONE.
2 THESSALONIANS 3:3

2:3 Greek *the son of destruction.* 2:13 Some manuscripts read *God chose you from the very beginning.* 3:1 Greek *brothers;* also in 3:6, 13. 3:3 Or *from evil.*

6And now, dear brothers and sisters, we give you
this command with the authority of our Lord Jesus
Christ: Stay away from any Christian* who lives in
idleness and doesn't follow the tradition of hard
work we gave you. 7For you know that you ought to
follow our example. We were never lazy when we
were with you. 8We never accepted food from anyone without paying for it. We worked hard day and
night so that we would not be a burden to any of
you. 9It wasn't that we didn't have the right to ask
you to feed us, but we wanted to give you an
example to follow. 10Even while we were with you,
we gave you this rule: "Whoever does not work
should not eat."
11Yet we hear that some of you are living idle lives,
refusing to work and wasting time meddling in other
people's business. 12In the name of the Lord Jesus
Christ, we appeal to such people—no, we command
them: Settle down and get to work. Earn your own
living. 13And I say to the rest of you, dear brothers
and sisters, never get tired of doing good.
14Take note of those who refuse to obey what we say
in this letter. Stay away from them so they will be
ashamed. 15Don't think of them as enemies, but speak
to them as you would to a Christian who needs to be
warned.
16May the Lord of peace himself always give you
his peace no matter what happens. The Lord be with
you all.
17Now here is my greeting, which I write with my
own hand—PAUL. I do this at the end of all my letters
to prove that they really are from me.
18May the grace of our Lord Jesus Christ be with
you all.

3:6 Greek *brother;* also in 3:15.

# MEGA themes

**PERSECUTION** Paul encouraged the church to have patience in spite of troubles and hardships. God will bring victory to his faithful followers, and he will judge those who persecute them.

God promises to reward our faith with his power and to help us bear persecution. Suffering for our faith will strengthen us to serve Christ. God never will allow us to experience suffering apart from his power and presence.

1. How did the Thessalonians respond to persecution?
2. What did Paul say to encourage them?
3. What was the basis of Paul's belief that the Thessalonians could stand firm in their faith in spite of these painful experiences?
4. In what ways can Paul's words help you?

**CHRIST'S RETURN** Paul had said that Christ would come back at any moment, so some of the Thessalonian believers had stopped work to wait.

Christ will return and bring total victory to all who trust in him. If we stand firm and keep working, we will be ready. If we are ready, we don't have to be concerned about *when* he will return. Our life is already eternally secure in Christ.

1. What concerns did Paul express in chapter 3? What false ideas had developed about what it means to prepare for Christ's coming?
2. How did the promise of Christ's ultimate reign affect Paul's attitude toward life? How did he challenge the Thessalonians to live in light of Christ's coming?
3. How does thinking about the promise of Christ's ultimate reign affect your feelings? Thoughts? Actions?
4. What is your plan of preparation? How does this relate to Paul's prayer request in 3:5?

**GREAT REBELLION** Before Christ's return, there will be a great rebellion against God led by the man of lawlessness (the Antichrist). God will remove all the restraints on evil before he brings judgment on the rebels. The Antichrist will attempt to deceive many.

We should not be afraid when we see evil increase. God is in control, no matter how evil the world becomes. God guards us from satanic attack. We can have victory over evil by remaining faithful to God. Satan and all evil are subject to God.

1. What is the danger of the Antichrist?
2. In light of the fact that the Antichrist will impact the world and that evil is already present, how should we live?
3. How should you live in an evil world? How can this give you the confidence to endure even the dangers of the Antichrist?

**PERSISTENCE** Because church members had quit working and become disorderly and disobedient, Paul criticized them for their laziness. He told them to show courage and to live as Christians should.

We must never get so tired of doing right that we quit. We can be persistent by making the most of our time and talent. Our endurance will be rewarded.

**W**hat does it take to be a leader? Brains? Good looks? A magnetic personality? The ability to speak persuasively? A ruthless obsession for power? That's what the world says. ■ The world is wrong. Leadership is not about being tall, tan, and telegenic. Leadership has nothing to do with impressive résumés or rousing speeches. Leadership is far more than being wellborn or highly educated or multitalented. Jesus defined leadership as servanthood. It involves compassion, courage, and conviction. ■ So here's the shocker: *Anyone who takes the time to develop those qualities can be a leader.* ■ Even you. ■ "Who? Me?! You must be kidding. I don't have any special talents. Besides, I'm young and kind of shy. I could never lead anyone." ■ Funny you should say that. A young man by the name of Timothy once felt the exact same way. He found himself facing big responsibilities and even bigger challenges. He wondered what to do and whether he had what leadership requires. ■ Then he got the following letter from his friend and mentor, Paul. More than a mere letter, the Epistle of 1 Timothy is also an essay on leadership. ■ Hey, you may never be a major politician or the president of a big company, but you'll always have friends, relatives, neighbors, and acquaintances who need to be influenced. People you can (and should) influence for Christ. ■ So read about the character, compassion, courage, and conviction that leadership involves. ■ Then give it a try. Be a leader.

## STATS

PURPOSE: To encourage and instruct Timothy

AUTHOR: Paul

TO WHOM WRITTEN: Timothy, young church leaders, and all believers everywhere

DATE WRITTEN: About A.D. 64, from Rome or Macedonia (possibly Philippi), probably just prior to Paul's final imprisonment in Rome

SETTING: Timothy was one of Paul's closest companions. Paul had sent him to the church at Ephesus to counter the false teaching that had arisen there (1 Timothy 1:3-4). Timothy probably served for a time as a leader in the church at Ephesus. Paul hoped to visit Timothy (3:14-15; 4:13), but in the meantime, he wrote this letter to give Timothy practical advice for the ministry.

KEY PEOPLE: Paul, Timothy

KEY PLACE: Ephesus

CHAPTER **1** **PAUL'S SON IN THE LORD.** This letter is
from Paul, an apostle of Christ Jesus, appointed by
the command of God our Savior and by Christ Jesus
our hope.
²It is written to Timothy, my true child in the faith.
May God our Father and Christ Jesus our Lord give
you grace, mercy, and peace.

³When I left for Macedonia, I urged you to stay
there in Ephesus and stop those who are teaching
wrong doctrine. ⁴Don't let people waste time in
endless speculation over myths and spiritual pedigrees.* For these things only cause arguments;
they don't help people live a life of faith in God.*
⁵The purpose of my instruction is that all the
Christians there would be filled with love that
comes from a pure heart, a clear conscience, and
sincere faith.

⁶But some teachers have missed this whole
point. They have turned away from these things
and spend their time arguing and talking foolishness. ⁷They want to be known as teachers of the
law of Moses, but they don't know what they are
talking about, even though they seem so confident. ⁸We know these laws are good when they are
used as God intended. ⁹But they were not made for
people who do what is right. They are for people
who are disobedient and rebellious, who are ungodly and sinful, who consider nothing sacred and
defile what is holy, who murder their father or
mother or other people. ¹⁰These laws are for people
who are sexually immoral, for homosexuals and
slave traders, for liars and oath breakers, and for
those who do anything else that contradicts the
right teaching ¹¹that comes from the glorious Good
News entrusted to me by our blessed God.

¹²How thankful I am to Christ Jesus our Lord for
considering me trustworthy and appointing me to
serve him, ¹³even though I used to scoff at the

**ALLEGIANCE ●●●••**

**1:3-11 The world is filled with people demanding our allegiance. Many would have us turn from Christ to follow them. Often their influence is subtle. How can you recognize false teaching before it does irreparable damage? (1) It stirs up questions and arguments instead of helping people come to Jesus (1:4). (2) It is often promoted by teachers whose motivation is to make a name for themselves (1:7). (3) It is contrary to the true teaching of the Scriptures (1:6-7; 4:1-3). Instead of listening to false teachers, we should learn what the Bible teaches and remain strong in our faith in Christ alone.**

1:4a Greek *in myths and endless genealogies, which cause speculation.* 1:4b Greek *a stewardship of God in faith.*

name of Christ. I hunted down his people, harming them in every way I could. But God had mercy on me because I did it in ignorance and unbelief.
[14]Oh, how kind and gracious the Lord was! He filled me completely with faith and the love of Christ Jesus.

[15]This is a true saying, and everyone should believe it: Christ Jesus came into the world to save sinners—and I was the worst of them all.
[16]But that is why God had mercy on me, so that Christ Jesus could use me as a prime example of his great patience with even the worst sinners. Then others will realize that they, too, can believe in him and receive eternal life. [17]Glory and honor to God forever and ever. He is the eternal King, the unseen one who never dies; he alone is God. Amen.

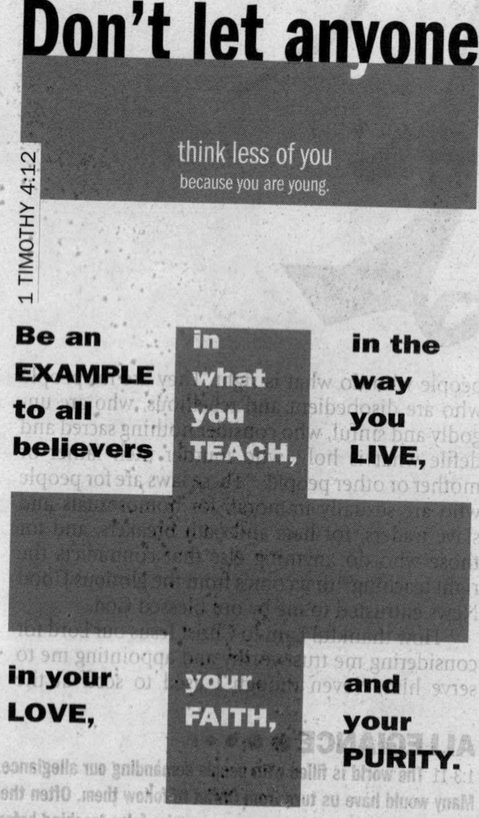

Don't let anyone
think less of you
because you are young.
1 TIMOTHY 4:12
Be an EXAMPLE to all believers
in what you TEACH,
in the way you LIVE,
in your LOVE,
your FAITH,
and your PURITY.


[18]Timothy, my son, here are my instructions for you, based on the prophetic words spoken about you earlier. May they give you the confidence to fight well in the Lord's battles. [19]Cling tightly to your faith in Christ, and always keep your conscience clear. For some people have deliberately violated their consciences; as a result, their faith has been shipwrecked. [20]Hymenaeus and Alexander are two examples of this. I turned them over to Satan so they would learn not to blaspheme God.

### INNER TUGS ● ● ● • •

**1:19 How can you keep a good conscience? Treasure your faith in Christ more than anything else and do what you know is right. Each time you deliberately ignore your conscience, you are hardening your heart. Soon your capacity to tell right from wrong will disappear. But when you walk with God, he is able to speak to you through your conscience, letting you know the difference between right and wrong. Be sure to act on those inner tugs to do what is right—then your conscience will remain clear.**

## CHAPTER 2 GUIDELINES FOR WORSHIP.

I urge you, first of all, to pray for all people. As you make your requests, plead for God's mercy upon them, and give thanks. [2]Pray this way for kings and all others who are in authority, so that we can live in peace and quietness, in godliness and dignity. [3]This is good and pleases God our Savior, [4]for he wants everyone to be saved and to understand the truth. [5]For there is only one God and one Mediator who can reconcile God and people. He is the man Christ Jesus. [6]He gave his life to purchase freedom for everyone. This is the message that God gave to the world at the proper time. [7]And I have been chosen—this is the absolute truth—as a preacher and apostle to teach the Gentiles about faith and truth.

[8]So wherever you assemble, I want men to pray with holy hands lifted up to God, free from anger and controversy. [9]And I want women to be modest in their appearance. They should wear decent and appropriate clothing and not draw attention to themselves by the way they fix their hair or by wearing gold or pearls or expensive clothes. [10]For women who claim to be devoted to God should make themselves attractive by the good things they do.

[11]Women should listen and learn quietly and submissively. [12]I do not let women teach men or have authority over them. Let them listen quietly. [13]For God made Adam first, and afterward he made Eve. [14]And it was the woman, not Adam, who was deceived by Satan, and sin was the result. [15]But women will be saved through childbearing* and by continuing to live in faith, love, holiness, and modesty.

## CHAPTER 3 GUIDELINES FOR CHURCH LEADERS.

It is a true saying that if someone wants to be an elder,* he desires an honorable responsibility. [2]For an elder

### GREAT EXPECTATIONS ● ● ● • •

**3:1-13 The word *elder* can refer to a pastor, church leader, or presiding elder. It is good to want to be a spiritual leader, but the standards are high. Paul lists some of the qualifications here. Do you hold a position of spiritual leadership, or would you like to be a leader some day? Check yourself against Paul's standard of excellence. Those with great responsibility must meet high expectations.**

2:15 Or *will be saved by accepting their role as mothers,* or *will be saved by the birth of the Child.* 3:1 Greek *overseer;* also in 3:2.

must be a man whose life cannot be spoken against.
He must be faithful to his wife.* He must exhibit
self-control, live wisely, and have a good reputation.
He must enjoy having guests in his home and must
be able to teach. 3He must not be a heavy drinker or
be violent. He must be gentle, peace loving, and not
one who loves money. 4He must manage his own
family well, with children who respect and obey
him. 5For if a man cannot manage his own household, how can he take care of
God's church?
6An elder must not be a
new Christian, because he
might be proud of being chosen so soon, and the Devil
will use that pride to make
him fall.* 7Also, people outside the church must speak
well of him so that he will not
fall into the Devil's trap and
be disgraced.
8In the same way, deacons
must be people who are respected and have integrity.
They must not be heavy
drinkers and must not be
greedy for money. 9They must
be committed to the revealed
truths of the Christian faith
and must live with a clear
conscience. 10Before they are
appointed as deacons, they
should be given other responsibilities in the church as a test
of their character and ability.
If they do well, then they may
serve as deacons.
11In the same way, their
wives* must be respected
and must not speak evil of
others. They must exercise
self-control and be faithful
in everything they do.
12A deacon must be faith-
ful to his wife, and he must
manage his children and
household well. 13Those
who do well as deacons will
be rewarded with respect
from others and will have
increased confidence in
their faith in Christ Jesus.
14I am writing these things
to you now, even though I
hope to be with you soon,
15so that if I can't come for a
while, you will know how
people must conduct them-
selves in the household of
God. This is the church of the living God, which is
the pillar and support of the truth.
16Without question, this is the great mystery of
our faith:

Christ* appeared in the flesh
and was shown to be righteous by the Spirit.*
He was seen by angels
and was announced to the nations.

---

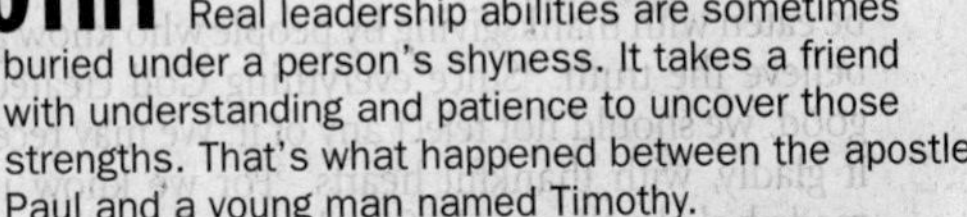

# TIMOTHY

Real leadership abilities are sometimes buried under a person's shyness. It takes a friend with understanding and patience to uncover those strengths. That's what happened between the apostle Paul and a young man named Timothy.

Timothy probably became a Christian when Paul visited his hometown of Lystra during his first missionary journey (Acts 14:8-20). Timothy's Jewish mother and grandmother had prepared him by teaching him from the Old Testament. By the time Paul visited Lystra again, Timothy was known as a growing Christian. When invited, Timothy jumped at the chance to travel with Paul and Silas.

Away from home, Timothy struggled with his shyness. Unfortunately, shy people are often written off as being unable to carry much responsibility. But Paul chose to give Timothy important responsibilities in the ministry. Paul even made Timothy his personal representative on several occasions. Sometimes Timothy failed on his missions, but Paul never gave up on him. Timothy became a "son" to Paul.

Our last pictures of Timothy come from the most personal letters in the New Testament: 1 and 2 Timothy. They were written by Paul in such a way that his deep friendship with Timothy is obvious; they had traveled, suffered, cried, and laughed together. The letters were intended to encourage and direct Timothy in Ephesus, where Paul had left him in charge of a young church (1 Timothy 1:3-4). These same letters have helped and encouraged countless other "Timothys" through the years. When you face a challenge that is beyond your abilities, read 1 and 2 Timothy. Remember, others have shared your experience.

**UPS:**
- Became a believer after Paul's first missionary journey and joined him for his other two journeys
- Was a respected Christian in his hometown
- Was Paul's special representative on several occasions
- Received two personal letters from Paul
- Probably knew Paul better than any other person, becoming like a son to him

**DOWNS:**
- Struggled with a timid and reserved nature
- Allowed others to look down on his youthfulness
- Was apparently unable to correct some of the problems in the church at Corinth when Paul sent him there

**STATS:**
- Where: Lystra
- Occupations: Missionary, church leader
- Relatives: Mother: Eunice; Grandmother: Lois; Greek father.
- Contemporaries: Paul, Silas, Luke, Mark, Peter, Barnabas

LESSONS: Youthfulness should not be an excuse for ineffectiveness

Our inadequacies and inabilities should not keep us from being available to God

KEY VERSES: "I have no one else like Timothy, who genuinely cares about your welfare. All the others care only for themselves and not for what matters to Jesus Christ. But you know how Timothy has proved himself. Like a son with his father, he has helped me in preaching the Good News" (Philippians 2:20-22).

Timothy's story is told in Acts, starting in chapter 16. He is also mentioned in Romans 16:21; 1 Corinthians 4:17; 16:10-11; 2 Corinthians 1:1, 19; Philippians 1:1; 2:19-23; Colossians 1:1; 1 Thessalonians 1:1-10; 2:3-4; 3:2-6; 1 and 2 Timothy; Philemon 1; Hebrews 13:23.

---

3:2 Greek *be the husband of one wife;* also in 3:12. 3:6 Or *he might fall into the same judgment as the Devil.* 3:11 Or *the women deacons.* The Greek word can be translated *women* or *wives.* 3:16a Greek *Who;* some manuscripts read *God.* 3:16b Or *in his spirit.*

He was believed on in the world
and was taken up into heaven.*

**CHAPTER 4** **IGNORE FALSE TEACHERS: THEY LIE.** Now the Holy Spirit tells us clearly that in the last times some will turn away from what we believe; they will follow lying spirits and teachings that come from demons. [2]These teachers are hypocrites and liars. They pretend to be religious, but their consciences are dead.*

[3]They will say it is wrong to be married and wrong to eat certain foods. But God created those foods to be eaten with thanksgiving by people who know and believe the truth. [4]Since everything God created is good, we should not reject any of it. We may receive it gladly, with thankful hearts. [5]For we know it is made holy by the word of God and prayer.

## MATERIALISM

Jeremy and his girlfriend Blair can hardly wait until next Tuesday. That's the day when the winning numbers in the state lottery will be announced. Everybody is buzzing about the jackpot—now more than 100 million dollars!

"Just think if we won," Jeremy dreams out loud. "We'd be able—"

"I'm not even going to think about it," Blair interrupts. "I'll just get my hopes up; and then I'll be all disappointed."

"C'mon, Blair, why do you always have to be so negative?! We've got as much of a chance as anyone else. In fact, we've got 10 chances to win. It's got to happen to someone—it might as well be us. And if we do win, just think of all the stuff we could do, of all the things we could buy!"

"It would be great to be rich. You wouldn't have a care in the world. Imagine going into the mall and picking up whatever you want and not even having to look at the price tag."

"Yeah, or going to any car dealership, walking over to the car you want, and saying, 'I'll take it.' Imagine that!"

"That'd be awesome!" Blair exclaims.

The two dreamers sit thinking quietly for a few minutes. Finally Blair breaks the silence. "Jeremy, I still can't help feeling like we just poured 10 dollars down the drain!"

"Blair!"

See what God's Word says about the desire to get rich quick—1 Timothy 6:9-10.

[6]If you explain this to the brothers and sisters,* you will be doing your duty as a worthy servant of Christ Jesus, one who is fed by the message of faith and the true teaching you have followed. [7]Do not waste time arguing over godless ideas and old wives' tales. Spend your time and energy in training yourself for spiritual fitness. [8]Physical exercise has some value, but spiritual exercise is much more important, for it promises a reward in both this life and the next. [9]This is true, and everyone should

## YOUR FAMILY ● ● • • •

5:8 **Almost everyone has relatives, family of some kind. Family relationships are so important in God's eyes, Paul says, that a person who neglects his or her family responsibilities has denied the faith. Are you doing your part to meet the needs of those included in your family circle? Even your little brothers and sisters?**

accept it. [10]We work hard and suffer much* in order that people will believe the truth, for our hope is in the living God, who is the Savior of all people, and particularly of those who believe.

[11]Teach these things and insist that everyone learn them. [12]Don't let anyone think less of you because you are young. Be an example to all believers in what you teach, in the way you live, in your love, your faith, and your purity. [13]Until I get there, focus on reading the Scriptures to the church, encouraging the believers, and teaching them.

[14]Do not neglect the spiritual gift you received through the prophecies spoken to you when the elders of the church laid their hands on you. [15]Give your complete attention to these matters. Throw yourself into your tasks so that everyone will see your progress. [16]Keep a close watch on yourself and on your teaching. Stay true to what is right, and God will save you and those who hear you.

**CHAPTER 5** **YOUR PART.** Never speak harshly to an older man,* but appeal to him respectfully as though he were your own father. Talk to the younger men as you would to your own brothers. [2]Treat the older women as you would your mother, and treat the younger women with all purity as your own sisters.

[3]The church should care for any widow who has no one else to care for her. [4]But if she has children or grandchildren, their first responsibility is to show godliness at home and repay their parents by taking care of them. This is something that pleases God very much.

[5]But a woman who is a true widow, one who is truly alone in this world, has placed her hope in God. Night and day she asks God for help and spends much time in prayer. [6]But the widow who lives only for pleasure is spiritually dead. [7]Give these instructions to the church so that the widows you support* will not be criticized.

[8]But those who won't care for their own relatives, especially those living in the same household, have denied what we believe. Such people are worse than unbelievers.

[9]A widow who is put on the list for support must be a woman who is at least sixty years old and was faithful to her husband.* [10]She must be well respected by everyone because of the good she has done. Has she brought up her children well? Has she been kind to strangers? Has she served other Christians humbly?* Has she helped those who are in trouble? Has she always been ready to do good?

3:16c Greek *in glory.* 4:2 Greek *are seared.* 4:6 Greek *brothers.* 4:10 Some manuscripts read *and strive.* 5:1 Or *an elder.* 5:7 Or *so the church;* Greek reads *so they.* 5:9 Greek *was the wife of one man.* 5:10 Greek *Has she washed the feet of saints?*

[11]The younger widows should not be on the list,
because their physical desires will overpower their
devotion to Christ and they will want to remarry.
[12]Then they would be guilty of breaking their previous pledge. [13]Besides, they are likely to become
lazy and spend their time gossiping from house to
house, getting into other people's business and
saying things they shouldn't. [14]So I advise these
younger widows to marry again, have children, and
take care of their own homes. Then the enemy will
not be able to say anything against them. [15]For I am
afraid that some of them have already gone astray
and now follow Satan.

[16]If a Christian woman has relatives who are widows, she must take care of them and not put the
responsibility on the church. Then the church can
care for widows who are truly alone.

[17]Elders who do their work well should be paid
well,* especially those who work hard at both
preaching and teaching. [18]For the Scripture says, "Do
not keep an ox from eating as it treads out the grain."
And in another place, "Those who work deserve
their pay!"*

[19]Do not listen to complaints against an elder
unless there are two or three witnesses to accuse him.
[20]Anyone who sins should be rebuked in front of the
whole church so that others will have a proper fear
of God.

[21]I solemnly command you in the presence of God
and Christ Jesus and the holy angels to obey these
instructions without taking sides or showing special
favor to anyone. [22]Never be in a hurry about appointing an elder. Do not participate in the sins of others.
Keep yourself pure.

[23]Don't drink only water. You ought to drink a
little wine for the sake of your stomach because you
are sick so often.

[24]Remember that some people lead sinful lives,
and everyone knows they will be judged. But there
are others whose sin will not be revealed until later.
[25]In the same way, everyone knows how much good
some people do, but there are others whose good
deeds won't be known until later.

CHAPTER **6** **MONEY ISN'T EVERYTHING.** Christians
who are slaves should give their masters full respect
so that the name of God and his teaching will not be
shamed. [2]If your master is a Christian, that is no
excuse for being disrespectful. You should work all
the harder because you are helping another believer*
by your efforts.

Teach these truths, Timothy, and encourage everyone to obey them. [3]Some false teachers may deny
these things, but these are the sound, wholesome
teachings of the Lord Jesus Christ, and they are the
foundation for a godly life. [4]Anyone who teaches
anything different is both conceited and ignorant.
Such a person has an unhealthy desire to quibble
over the meaning of words. This stirs up arguments
ending in jealousy, fighting, slander, and evil suspicions. [5]These people always cause trouble. Their
minds are corrupt, and they don't tell the truth. To
them religion is just a way to get rich.

[6]Yet true religion with contentment is great
wealth. [7]After all, we didn't bring anything with us

## MONEY CYCLE ● ● ● • •

6:6-10 **Despite almost overwhelming evidence to the contrary, some people still believe money brings happiness. Rich people craving greater riches can be caught in an endless cycle that only ends in ruin and desperation. How can you avoid the love of money? Paul gives us some principles: (1) realize that one day riches will all be gone (6:7, 17); (2) be content with what you have (6:8); (3) watch what you are willing to do to get more money (6:9-10); (4) love people and God's work more than money (6:11); (5) freely share what you have with others (6:18). (See also Proverbs 30:7-9.)**

**Trying to stay pure and not sin seems like a full-time job. How can anyone stay pure? Why would anyone want to?**

Jesus talked a lot about the Pharisees. These men had created long lists of dos and don'ts about behavior of every kind. They wanted to be pure! Many of them were very, very good.

But in Matthew 5:20, Jesus made an incredible statement! "But I warn you—unless you obey God better than the teachers of religious law and the Pharisees do, you can't enter the Kingdom of Heaven at all!"

Wow! If the Pharisees couldn't make it, who can?

Those who make it into the kingdom of heaven are not just pure on the outside, like the Pharisees. Anyone can make sure their behavior is correct (at least for a while).

Jesus was talking about being pure on the inside. This begins by accepting Christ's death on the cross as punishment for our sins. When we do this, we take on Christ's goodness, and, in God's eyes, we are pure and worthy of eternity in heaven! Now that's a pretty good deal!

It doesn't stop there, of course. God wants us to be like Jesus. This is a lifelong process of allowing God to mold us and change us (see 1 Timothy 6:11-12). It happens by staying close to Christ and living like he wants us to. It's what keeps the Christian life fun, interesting, and challenging.

A Christian who's really alive realizes that his eternity is settled. But he also genuinely wants to be more like the one who paid such a high price for his soul—Jesus. His motivation is not to parade his goodness in front of others, but rather to please God.

Staying pure and growing as a Christian are "full-time jobs." But they are also natural by-products of staying close to Christ.

5:17 Greek *should be worthy of double honor.* 5:18 Deut 25:4; Luke 10:7. 6:2 Greek *a brother.*

## YOU'RE RICH ● ● • • •

**6:17-19 Ephesus was a wealthy city, and the Ephesian church probably had many wealthy members. Paul advised Timothy to deal with a potential problem by teaching that the possession of riches carries great responsibility. Those who have money must be generous, not arrogant. They must be careful not to put their trust in money instead of in the living God. Even if we don't have material wealth, we can be rich in good works toward others. No matter how poor we are, we have something to share with someone.**

when we came into the world, and we certainly cannot carry anything with us when we die. [8]So if we have enough food and clothing, let us be content. [9]But people who long to be rich fall into temptation and are trapped by many foolish and harmful desires that plunge them into ruin and destruction. [10]For the love of money is at the root of all kinds of evil. And some people, craving money, have wandered from the faith and pierced themselves with many sorrows.

[11]But you, Timothy, belong to God; so run from all these evil things, and follow what is right and good. Pursue a godly life, along with faith, love, perseverance, and gentleness. [12]Fight the good fight for what we believe. Hold tightly to the eternal life that God has given you, which you have confessed so well before many witnesses. [13]And I command you before God, who gives life to all, and before Christ Jesus, who gave a good testimony before Pontius Pilate, [14]that you obey his commands with all purity. Then no one can find fault with you from now until our Lord Jesus Christ returns. [15]For at the right time Christ will be revealed from heaven by the blessed and only almighty God, the King of kings and Lord of lords. [16]He alone can never die, and he lives in light so brilliant that no human can approach him. No one has ever seen him, nor ever will. To him be honor and power forever. Amen.

[17]Tell those who are rich in this world not to be proud and not to trust in their money, which will soon be gone. But their trust should be in the living God, who richly gives us all we need for our enjoyment. [18]Tell them to use their money to do good. They should be rich in good works and should give generously to those in need, always being ready to share with others whatever God has given them. [19]By doing this they will be storing up their treasure as a good foundation for the future so that they may take hold of real life.

[20]Timothy, guard what God has entrusted to you. Avoid godless, foolish discussions with those who oppose you with their so-called knowledge. [21]Some people have wandered from the faith by following such foolishness.

May God's grace be with you all.

# MEGA themes

**SOUND DOCTRINE** Paul instructed Timothy to preserve the Christian faith by teaching sound doctrine and modeling right living. Timothy had to oppose false teachers who were leading church members away from belief in salvation by faith in Jesus Christ alone.

We must know the truth to defend it. And the truth is that Christ came to save us. We should stay away from those who twist the words of the Bible for their own purposes. Therefore, we must study and know the Bible ourselves.

1. What do you consider to be the main points in the Bible concerning God and people, sin and salvation, life and death?
2. Why are these truths so important to the Bible's message?
3. Paul greatly opposed those who taught against the truth of the gospel. What did Paul tell Timothy to do about false teachers?
4. Based on this study, how should you respond to the message of a false teacher? What can you do to be able to discern the truth from error?

**PUBLIC WORSHIP** In public worship, prayer must be done with a proper attitude toward God and fellow believers.

Christian character must be evident in every aspect of worship. We must rid ourselves of any anger, resentment, or offensive attire that might disrupt worship or damage church unity. Christian unity begins with your own attitude and actions toward others.

1. What were Paul's instructions to Timothy about worship?
2. What aspects of public, congregational worship do you most enjoy? Least enjoy? How do you feel about worship overall?
3. What should be a Christian's attitude in worship? What actions should be a part of worship services?
4. What steps can you take to deepen your worship as well as to encourage others in your church to do the same?

**CHURCH LEADERSHIP** Paul gives specific instructions concerning the qualifications for church leaders so that the church might honor God and run smoothly.

Church leaders must be wholly committed to Christ. If you are a new or young Christian, don't be anxious to become a leader in your church. Develop your Christian character first. Be sure to consider God, not your own ambition.

1. Describe the overall character of the persons who are qualified to serve in church leadership according to 3:1-16.
2. In what specific ways does Paul challenge Timothy to mature and develop personally?
3. How can a young person who is a Christian prepare now to be a man or woman of God later, as he or she matures?
4. Praise God for your areas of personal strength. Design a plan to work on your personal weaknesses so that, by his grace, you will be a godly leader throughout your life.

**PERSONAL DISCIPLINE** It takes discipline to be a leader in the church. Timothy, like all church leaders, had to guard his motives, minister faithfully, and live right. Any pastor must keep morally and spiritually fit.

To stay in good spiritual shape, you must discipline yourself to study God's Word and to live a godly life. Put your spiritual abilities to work!

1. What areas of personal discipline would Timothy have to develop as a result of what Paul told him?
2. How do you think Timothy felt as he read this letter? Read chapters 4 and 6 and describe how you would have felt if this letter had been written to you.
3. What beginning steps can you take to deepen your faith?
4. How will the Holy Spirit of God help you to deal with the personal difficulties you may face as you attempt to step out?

**CARING CHURCH** The church has a responsibility to care for the needs of all its members, especially the sick, the poor, and the widowed.

Caring for the family of believers demonstrates our Christlike attitude and genuine love. We are Christ's touch of love in one another's lives.

1. What did Paul think about the church's responsibility for reaching out to others?
2. Why is this so important for the church as Christ's body?
3. On a scale of A-B-C-D-F, give your church a grade in terms of Paul's descriptions of what it means to serve those in need.
4. Grade yourself on the above scale. What can you do to improve your grade? What can you do to get involved with your church to improve its grade?

Trivia is "unimportant matters." It's all that information that's often interesting but doesn't really matter much. For instance, did you know that: ■ Grasshoppers are approximately three times more nutritious than rib-eye steak? ■ Kangaroos can't jump when their tails are lifted off the ground? ■ France's King Louis XIV feared water so much that he never took a bath and rarely washed more than the tip of his nose? ■ It's impossible to sneeze with your eyes open? ■ Benjamin Franklin invented swim fins and the rocking chair? ■ Mozart wrote the tune "Twinkle, Twinkle, Little Star" when he was five? ■ Eating too many carrots can make your skin turn yellow? ■ Nine-hundred-and-twenty-eight average size fleas will fit inside a Ping-Pong ball? ■ Though amusing—and helpful for filling the silence in an awkward conversation—the facts just cited are worthless. They won't change your life. They're trivia. *Trivial* trivia. ■ Not so the book of 2 Timothy. ■ The apostle Paul's second letter to Timothy is serious stuff. History says that these were Paul's last words; he died shortly after penning them. ■ Perhaps the aged saint recognized that his time was running out. If so, it's not surprising that he talked about important matters. Consider carefully Paul's final thoughts. He is, after all, one of the most influential individuals in history. ■ And Paul's challenge to Timothy is just as appropriate 2,000 years later. ■ The bottom line? Second Timothy is no trivial pursuit!

## STATS

PURPOSE: To give final instructions and encouragement to Timothy, a leader of the church at Ephesus

AUTHOR: Paul

TO WHOM WRITTEN: Timothy

DATE WRITTEN: About A.D. 66 or 67 from prison in Rome. After a year or two of freedom, Paul was arrested again and executed under Emperor Nero.

SETTING: Paul was virtually alone in prison; only Luke was with him. He wrote this letter to pass the torch to the new generation of church leaders. He also asked for visits from his friends, for his books, and especially the parchments—possibly parts of the Old Testament, the Gospels, and other biblical manuscripts.

KEY PEOPLE: Paul, Timothy, Luke, Mark, and others

KEY PLACES: Rome, Ephesus

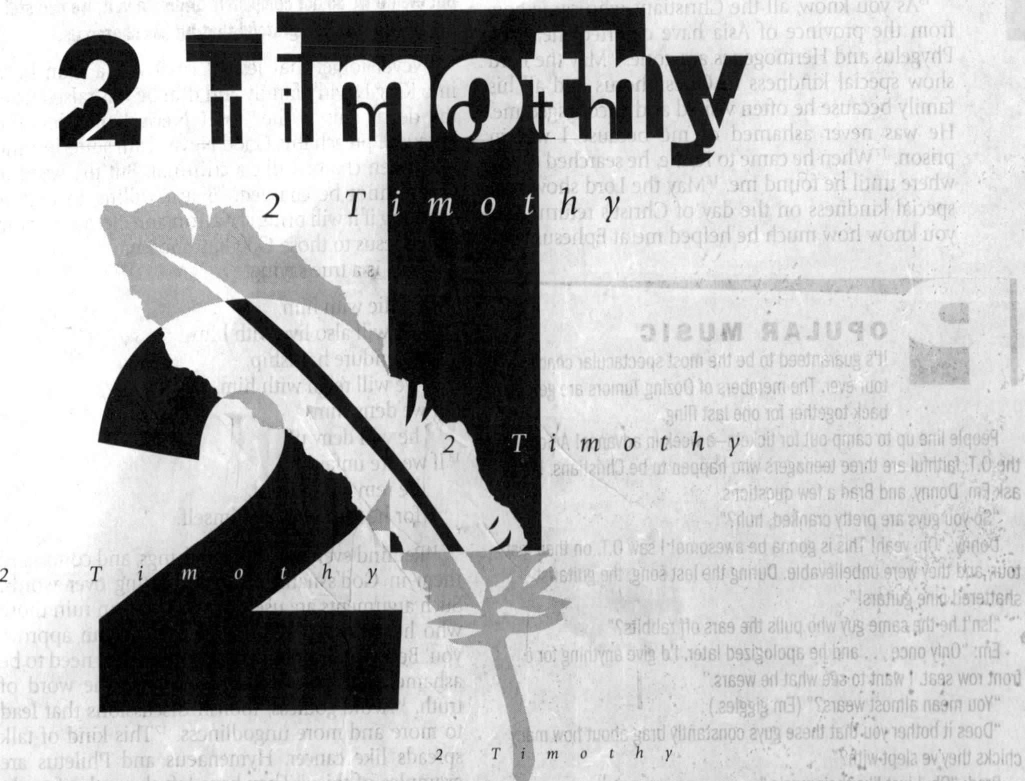


CHAPTER **1** **A LETTER TO ENCOURAGE TIMOTHY.** This
letter is from Paul, an apostle of Christ Jesus by
God's will, sent out to tell others about the life he has
promised through faith in Christ Jesus.
²It is written to Timothy, my dear son.

May God our Father and Christ Jesus our Lord give
you grace, mercy, and peace.

³Timothy, I thank God for you. He is the God I
serve with a clear conscience, just as my ancestors
did. Night and day I constantly remember you in my
prayers. ⁴I long to see you again, for I remember your
tears as we parted. And I will be filled with joy when
we are together again.

⁵I know that you sincerely trust the Lord, for you
have the faith of your mother, Eunice, and your
grandmother, Lois. ⁶This is why I remind you to fan
into flames the spiritual gift God gave you when I
laid my hands on you. ⁷For God has not given us a
spirit of fear and timidity, but of power, love, and
self-discipline. ⁸So you must never be ashamed to tell
others about our Lord. And don't be ashamed of me,
either, even though I'm in prison for Christ. With the
strength God gives you, be ready to suffer with me
for the proclamation of the Good News.

⁹It is God who saved us and chose us to live a holy
life. He did this not because we deserved it, but
because that was his plan long before the world
began—to show his love and kindness to us through
Christ Jesus. ¹⁰And now he has made all of this plain
to us by the coming of Christ Jesus, our Savior, who
broke the power of death and showed us the way to
everlasting life through the Good News. ¹¹And God
chose me to be a preacher, an apostle, and a teacher
of this Good News.

¹²And that is why I am suffering here in prison. But
I am not ashamed of it, for I know the one in whom
I trust, and I am sure that he is able to guard what I
have entrusted to him* until the day of his return.

¹³Hold on to the pattern of right teaching you
learned from me. And remember to live in the faith
and love that you have in Christ Jesus. ¹⁴With the

## BE BOLD ● ● • • •

**1:6-7 Timothy was experiencing great opposition to his message and to himself as a leader. Timothy's youth, his association with Paul, and his leadership had come under fire. Paul urged Timothy to be bold. When we allow people to intimidate us, we neutralize our effectiveness for God. The power of the Holy Spirit can help us overcome our fear of what some might say or do to us so we can continue to do God's work.**

1:12 Or *what has been entrusted to me.*

help of the Holy Spirit who lives within us, carefully
guard what has been entrusted to you.
15As you know, all the Christians who came here
from the province of Asia have deserted me; even
Phygelus and Hermogenes are gone. 16May the Lord
show special kindness to Onesiphorus and all his
family because he often visited and encouraged me.
He was never ashamed of me because I was in
prison. 17When he came to Rome, he searched everywhere until he found me. 18May the Lord show him
special kindness on the day of Christ's return. And
you know how much he helped me at Ephesus.

## OPULAR MUSIC

It's guaranteed to be the most spectacular concert tour ever. The members of Oozing Tumors are getting back together for one last fling.

People line up to camp out for tickets—a week in advance! Among the O.T. faithful are three teenagers who happen to be Christians. Let's ask Em, Donny, and Brad a few questions.

"So you guys are pretty cranked, huh?"

Donny: "Oh, yeah! This is gonna be awesome! I saw O.T. on their last tour, and they were unbelievable. During the last song, the guitarist shattered nine guitars!"

"Isn't he the same guy who pulls the ears off rabbits?"

Em: "Only once . . . and he apologized later. I'd give anything for a front row seat. I want to see what he wears."

"You mean almost wears?" (Em giggles.)

"Does it bother you that these guys constantly brag about how many chicks they've slept with?"

Brad: "Oh, I just like their music."

"But should Christians support people who laugh at our beliefs and values?"

Em: "Whoa, dude! It's just a concert!"

What about popular music? Whether it's rock, metal, rap, country & western, or whatever? Read 2 Timothy 3:1-5, noting especially the end of verse 5.

CHAPTER **2** **BE A GOOD SOLDIER.** Timothy, my dear
son, be strong with the special favor God gives you
in Christ Jesus. 2You have heard me teach many
things that have been confirmed by many reliable
witnesses. Teach these great truths to trustworthy
people who are able to pass them on to others.
3Endure suffering along with me, as a good soldier
of Christ Jesus. 4And as Christ's soldier, do not let
yourself become tied up in the affairs of this life, for
then you cannot satisfy the one who has enlisted you
in his army. 5Follow the Lord's rules for doing his
work, just as an athlete either follows the rules or is
disqualified and wins no prize. 6Hardworking farmers are the first to enjoy the fruit of their labor.
7Think about what I am saying. The Lord will give
you understanding in all these things.

## CHOSEN ● ● ● • •

**2:10 We are free to choose between life and death, yet God has chosen us. This is a mystery our finite minds cannot easily grasp. But even if we do not completely understand it, we can still choose Jesus and be grateful that he has chosen us.**

8Never forget that Jesus Christ was a man born
into King David's family and that he was raised from
the dead. This is the Good News I preach. 9And
because I preach this Good News, I am suffering and
have been chained like a criminal. But the word of
God cannot be chained. 10I am willing to endure
anything if it will bring salvation and eternal glory in
Christ Jesus to those God has chosen.
11This is a true saying:

If we die with him,
  we will also live with him.
12If we endure hardship,
  we will reign with him.
If we deny him,
  he will deny us.
13If we are unfaithful,
  he remains faithful,
  for he cannot deny himself.

14Remind everyone of these things, and command
them in God's name to stop fighting over words.
Such arguments are useless, and they can ruin those
who hear them. 15Work hard so God can approve
you. Be a good worker, one who does not need to be
ashamed and who correctly explains the word of
truth. 16Avoid godless, foolish discussions that lead
to more and more ungodliness. 17This kind of talk
spreads like cancer. Hymenaeus and Philetus are
examples of this. 18They have left the path of truth,
preaching the lie that the resurrection of the dead
has already occurred; and they have undermined the
faith of some.
19But God's truth stands firm like a foundation
stone with this inscription: "The Lord knows those
who are his,"* and "Those who claim they belong to
the Lord must turn away from all wickedness."*
20In a wealthy home some utensils are made of
gold and silver, and some are made of wood and
clay. The expensive utensils are used for special occasions, and the cheap ones are for everyday use. 21If
you keep yourself pure, you will be a utensil God can
use for his purpose. Your life will be clean, and you
will be ready for the Master to use you for every good
work.
22Run from anything that stimulates youthful lust.

## RUN! ● ● ● • •

**2:22 Running away is sometimes considered cowardly. But wise people realize that removing themselves physically from temptation is often very wise. Timothy, a young man, was warned to run from anything that produced evil thoughts. Perhaps you experience a recurring temptation that is difficult to resist. Remove yourself physically from the situation. Knowing when to run is as important in a spiritual battle as knowing when and how to fight. (See also 1 Timothy 6:11.)**

2:19a Num 16:5. 2:19b See Isa 52:11.

Follow anything that makes you want to do right. Pursue faith and love and peace, and enjoy the companionship of those who call on the Lord with pure hearts.

[23]Again I say, don't get involved in foolish, ignorant arguments that only start fights. [24]The Lord's servants must not quarrel but must be kind to everyone. They must be able to teach effectively and be patient with difficult people. [25]They should gently teach those who oppose the truth. Perhaps God will change those people's hearts, and they will believe the truth. [26]Then they will come to their senses and escape from the Devil's trap. For they have been held captive by him to do whatever he wants.

CHAPTER **3** **BEING A CHRISTIAN CAN BE TOUGH.** You should also know this, Timothy, that in the last days there will be very difficult times. [2]For people will love only themselves and their money. They will be boastful and proud, scoffing at God, disobedient to their parents, and ungrateful. They will consider nothing sacred. [3]They will be unloving and unforgiving; they will slander others and have no self-control; they will be cruel and have no interest in what is good. [4]They will betray their friends, be reckless, be puffed up with pride, and love pleasure rather than God. [5]They will act as if they are religious, but they will reject the power that could make them godly. You must stay away from people like that.

[6]They are the kind who work their way into people's homes and win the confidence of* vulnerable women who are burdened with the guilt of sin and controlled by many desires. [7]Such women are forever following new teachings, but they never understand the truth. [8]And these teachers fight the truth just as Jannes and Jambres fought against Moses. Their minds are depraved, and their faith is counterfeit. [9]But they won't get away with this for long. Someday everyone will recognize what fools they are, just as happened with Jannes and Jambres.

[10]But you know what I teach, Timothy, and how I live, and what my purpose in life is. You know my faith and how long I have suffered. You know my love and my patient endurance. [11]You know how much persecution and suffering I have endured. You know all about how I was persecuted in Antioch, Iconium, and Lystra—but the Lord delivered me from all of it. [12]Yes, and everyone who wants to live a godly life in Christ Jesus will suffer persecution. [13]But evil people and impostors will flourish. They will go on deceiving others, and they themselves will be deceived.

✓ [14]But you must remain faithful to the things you have been taught. You know they are true, for you know you can trust those who taught you. [15]You have been taught the holy Scriptures from childhood, and they have given you the wisdom to receive the salvation that comes by trusting in Christ Jesus. [16]All Scripture is inspired by God and is useful to teach us what is true and to make us realize what is wrong in our lives. It straightens us out and teaches us to do what is right. [17]It is God's way of preparing us in every way, fully equipped for every good thing God wants us to do.

3:6 Greek *and take captive.*

## SUPERNATURAL ● ● ● • •

**3:16 The Bible is not a collection of stories, fables, myths, or merely human ideas about God. It is not a human book. Through the Holy Spirit, God revealed his person and plan to godly men, who wrote down God's message for his people (2 Peter 1:20-21). This process is known as *inspiration*. The writers wrote from their own personal, historical, and cultural contexts. Yet, though they used their own minds, talents, languages, and styles, they wrote what God wanted them to write. Scripture is completely trustworthy because God was in control of its writing. Its words are authoritative for our faith and life.**

CHAPTER **4** **SHARE YOUR FAITH.** And so I solemnly urge you before God and before Christ Jesus—who will someday judge the living and the dead when he appears to set up his Kingdom: [2]Preach the word of God. Be persistent, whether the time is favorable or not. Patiently correct, rebuke, and encourage your people with good teaching.

[3]For a time is coming when people will no longer listen to right teaching. They will follow their own desires and will look for teachers who will tell them

**A friend of mine stopped coming to church because he said that God had stopped answering his prayers. How do I answer him?**

Like Demas, who deserted Paul (see 2 Timothy 4:10), many Christians have a what-have-you-done-for-me-lately type of faith in God. They are willing to trust him in the good times, but when trouble hits they figure God has "checked out on them"—so they "check out on God."

Because we live in a society where we often can get what we want, when we want it, we may begin to think that God's only purpose is to meet our needs. Then when something doesn't work out—when we think that God hasn't come through for us—we turn away from him.

God is in the business of molding our character. One way he does this is by allowing us to go through tough times. When Paul wrote this letter, the church was going through intense persecution. Demas got tired of it and left. He wanted his comforts more than he wanted God's will.

Encourage your friend to change the what-have-you-done-for-me-lately attitude. Help him realize that God wants to build his character. His goal is not to make us feel good, but to develop us into the kind of people he wants.

whatever they want to hear. 4They will reject the
truth and follow strange myths.
5But you should keep a clear mind in every situation. Don't be afraid of suffering for the Lord. Work
at bringing others to Christ. Complete the ministry
God has given you.
6As for me, my life has already been poured out as
an offering to God. The time of my death is near. 7I
have fought a good fight, I have finished the race,

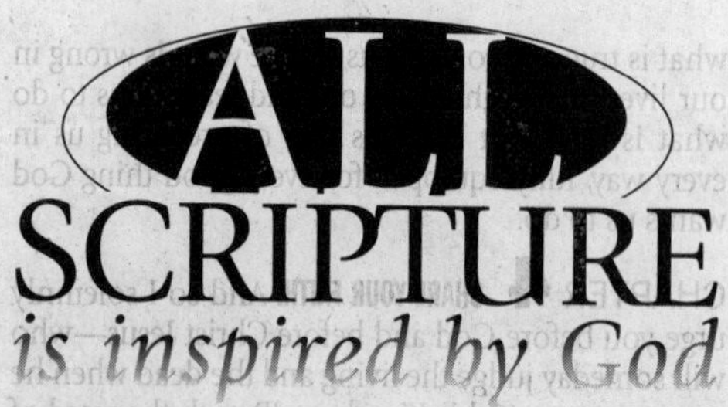

ALL
SCRIPTURE
is inspired by God

*and is useful to teach us*
what is TRUE
AND
*to make us realize*
what is wrong
in our lives.
It straightens us out
AND
*teaches us to do*
what is RIGHT.

2 TIMOTHY 3:16

## THIS LIFE

4:10 **Demas had been one of Paul's co-workers (Colossians 4:14; Philemon 24), but he deserted Paul because he loved "the things of this life." Do you love what the world has to offer—wealth, power, pleasure—even if gaining it means hurting people and neglecting the work God has given you to do?**

and I have remained faithful. 8And now the prize
awaits me—the crown of righteousness that the
Lord, the righteous Judge, will give me on that great
day of his return. And the prize is not just for me but
for all who eagerly look forward to his glorious
return.
9Please come as soon as you can. 10Demas has
deserted me because he loves the things of this life
and has gone to Thessalonica. Crescens has gone to
Galatia, and Titus has gone to Dalmatia. 11Only Luke
is with me. Bring Mark with you when you come, for
he will be helpful to me. 12I sent Tychicus to Ephesus.
13When you come, be sure to bring the coat I left with
Carpus at Troas. Also bring my books, and especially
my papers.*
14Alexander the coppersmith has done me much
harm, but the Lord will judge him for what he has
done. 15Be careful of him, for he fought against
everything we said.
16The first time I was brought before the judge, no
one was with me. Everyone had abandoned me. I
hope it will not be counted against them. 17But the
Lord stood with me and gave me strength, that I
might preach the Good News in all its fullness for all
the Gentiles to hear. And he saved me from certain
death.* 18Yes, and the Lord will deliver me from
every evil attack and will bring me safely to his
heavenly Kingdom. To God be the glory forever and
ever. Amen.
19Give my greetings to Priscilla and Aquila and
those living at the household of Onesiphorus. 20Eras-
tus stayed at Corinth, and I left Trophimus sick at
Miletus.
21Hurry so you can get here before winter. Eubulus
sends you greetings, and so do Pudens, Linus, Clau-
dia, and all the brothers and sisters.*
22May the Lord be with your spirit. Grace be with
you all.

4:13 Greek *especially the parchments.* 4:17 Greek *from the mouth of a lion.* 4:21 Greek *brothers.*

# MEGA themes

**BOLDNESS** In the face of opposition and persecution, Timothy was told to carry out his ministry unashamed and unafraid of the earthly consequences. Paul urged Timothy to use the gifts of preaching and teaching that the Holy Spirit had given him.

God honors our confident testimony even when we suffer. To get over our fear of what people might say or do, we must take our eyes off people and look only to God. People will disappoint us; God will always be faithful.

1. Why was boldness important in Timothy's ministry? How did Paul challenge Timothy to find this boldness?
2. Describe a time in your life when you felt bold in your faith. Describe a time in your life when you felt timid about your faith.
3. What caused the difference between the time of boldness and the time of timidity?
4. What is your level of boldness for Christ at church? In your neighborhood? At home? In school? At social activities? In which areas is it most difficult for you to be boldly honest about your faith and lifestyle?

**FAITHFULNESS** Jesus was faithful to all of us when he died for our sins. Paul was a faithful minister even when he was in prison. Paul urged Timothy to maintain not only sound doctrine, but also loyalty, diligence, and endurance.

We can count on opposition, suffering, and hardship as we serve Christ. But that will show that our faithfulness is having an effect on others. As we trust Christ, he counts us worthy to suffer and will give us the strength we need to be steadfast.

1. How did Paul challenge Timothy to live out his faithfulness to God?
2. What reasons do you have for being faithful to God? What struggles do you face in trying to be faithful?
3. When you find yourself drifting away from God, what can you do to remember your commitment of faithfulness to God?
4. How are you being faithful today?

**PREACHING AND TEACHING** Paul and Timothy were active in preaching and teaching the Good News about Jesus Christ. Paul encouraged Timothy not only to carry the torch of truth but also to train others, passing on to them sound doctrine and enthusiasm for Christ's mission.

We must prepare people to pass on God's Word to others. Does your church carefully train others to teach? Each of us should look for ways to become better equipped to serve, as well as for ways to teach others what we have learned.

1. Why do you think Paul stressed to Timothy the importance of training others to carry out preaching and teaching?
2. How was Paul a good example of this?
3. Who are the preachers and teachers in your church? How are they training others? (Are they training others?)
4. What type of ministry training would you want to receive? Who could provide this training?

**ERROR** In the final days before Christ returns, there will be false teachers, spiritual dropouts, and heresy. The remedy for error is to have a solid program for teaching Christians.

Because of deception and false teaching, we must be disciplined and ready to reject error by knowing God's Word. Knowing the Bible is your sure defense against error and confusion.

1. What are the dangers of deceptive teachers?
2. According to 3:14-17, how does God use his Word to prevent his people from being deceived?
3. Based on this study, how should you respond to Bible teaching?
4. What can you do to improve yourself as a student of God's Word?

In many of life's situations—whether from natural instinct, repeated instruction, or unpleasant experience—you know precisely what to do. ■ For instance: ■ If your clothing catches fire, drop to the ground and roll. ■ In case of emergency, call 9-1-1. ■ Never stare at the sun during an eclipse. ■ Always wash your hands after using the restroom and before eating. ■ On a romantic first date, never order pizza with extra garlic and onions. ■ Don't run while carrying sharp objects. ■ Never swim right after eating. ■ When attacked by a bear, fall face down and play dead. ■ Look both ways before crossing a street. ■ Make certain you know the price of an object before you agree to buy it. ■ Never sign *anything* until you read the fine print. ■ You've probably heard these rules before; no doubt you could handle each situation with ease. But what about the millions of other life circumstances where it's really *hard* to know what to do? ■ That's why the next book of the Bible is so important. The apostle Paul's epistle to Titus gives us plenty of practical advice for living a pure life in an impure world. Commitment, discipline, self-control, moral purity, solid relationships, civic duties—you'll learn about all those important topics and more. By the way—as you prepare to dive into this dynamite little letter, here's a reminder of one more famous rule of life (it's one our mom pounded into our head!): Never cross your eyes while reading; they might get stuck that way.

## STATS

PURPOSE: To advise Titus in his responsibility of supervising the churches on the island of Crete

AUTHOR: Paul

TO WHOM WRITTEN: Titus, a Greek convert, who had become Paul's special representative to the island of Crete

DATE WRITTEN: About A.D. 64, around the same time 1 Timothy was written; probably from Macedonia when Paul traveled in between his Roman imprisonments

SETTING: Paul had sent Titus to organize and oversee the churches on Crete. This letter tells him how to do this job.

KEY PEOPLE: Paul, Titus

KEY PLACES: Crete, Nicopolis

SPECIAL FEATURE: Titus is very similar to 1 Timothy with its instructions to church leaders

CHAPTER **1** **PAUL IS SENT TO BRING FAITH.** This letter
is from Paul, a slave of God and an apostle of
Jesus Christ. I have been sent to bring faith to those
God has chosen and to teach them to know the
truth that shows them how to live godly lives. 2 This
truth gives them the confidence of eternal life,
which God promised them before the world began—and he cannot lie. 3 And now at the right time
he has revealed this Good News, and we announce
it to everyone. It is by the command of God our
Savior that I have been trusted to do this work for
him.

4 This letter is written to Titus, my true child in the
faith that we share.

May God the Father and Christ Jesus our Savior
give you grace and peace.

5 I left you on the island of Crete so you could
complete our work there and appoint elders in
each town as I instructed you. 6 An elder must be
well thought of for his good life. He must be faithful to his wife,* and his children must be believers
who are not wild or rebellious. 7 An elder* must
live a blameless life because he is God's minister.
He must not be arrogant or quick-tempered; he
must not be a heavy drinker, violent, or greedy for
money. 8 He must enjoy having guests in his home
and must love all that is good. He must live wisely
and be fair. He must live a devout and disciplined
life. 9 He must have a strong and steadfast belief in
the trustworthy message he was taught; then he
will be able to encourage others with right teaching
and show those who oppose it where they are
wrong.

10 For there are many who rebel against right
teaching; they engage in useless talk and deceive
people. This is especially true of those who insist
on circumcision for salvation. 11 They must be silenced. By their wrong teaching, they have already
turned whole families away from the truth. Such
teachers only want your money. 12 One of their own

**NO LIE ● ● • • •**

1:1-2 **The foundation of our faith is trust in God's character. Because he is truth, he is the source of all truth and cannot lie. The eternal life he has promised will be ours because he keeps his promises. Build your faith on the foundation of a trustworthy God who will not lie.**

1:6 Or *have only one wife,* or *be married only once;* Greek reads *be the husband of one wife.* 1:7 Greek *overseer.*

men, a prophet from Crete, has said about them,
"The people of Crete are all liars; they are cruel
animals and lazy gluttons." 13This is true. So rebuke them as sternly as necessary to make them
strong in the faith. 14They must stop listening to
Jewish myths and the commands of people who
have turned their backs on the truth.
15Everything is pure to those whose hearts are
pure. But nothing is pure to those who are corrupt
and unbelieving, because their minds and consciences are defiled. 16Such people claim they know
God, but they deny him by the way they live. They
are despicable and disobedient, worthless for doing
anything good.

**NTEGRITY**

When Dawn sticks her head into her youth pastor's office, it's plain to see she is troubled.

"Mike, can I talk to you?"

"Sure, Dawn. Come in."

"It's this whole youth group leadership team thing."

"What do you mean?"

"Well, you know Kelly, the girl who's been coming with me to church the last few weeks?"

"Yeah."

"Well, she told me that she wants to be on the team. She wants to be in charge of publicity for the youth group."

"That's great. We've been looking for someone to fill that–"

"No, that's not great! You don't know Kelly. She's pretty wild . . . I mean, she's not exactly living like a Christian."

"I see."

"Don't get me wrong. I really love Kelly, and I'm trying to be a good influence on her and everything. I just don't think it's a very good idea to have her out there in charge of publicizing our group. At least not while she's living like she is. People might get the wrong idea, you know?"

"I agree. So, are you going to talk to her?"

"Oh, I guess so. Any advice?"

"Sure. If I were you, I'd . . ."

Christians in leadership positions are expected to adhere to the highest standards of godly character. Read Titus 1:5-8; 2:11-3:8 for a quick glimpse at the integrity Christian leaders must possess.

CHAPTER **2** **SPECIAL GUIDELINES.** But as for you,
promote the kind of living that reflects right teaching. 2Teach the older men to exercise self-control, to
be worthy of respect, and to live wisely. They must
have strong faith and be filled with love and patience.
3Similarly, teach the older women to live in a way
that is appropriate for someone serving the Lord.
They must not go around speaking evil of others and
must not be heavy drinkers. Instead, they should
teach others what is good. 4These older women must
train the younger women to love their husbands and

## SEE AND DO ● ● • • •

2:6-8 **Paul urged Titus to be a good example to those around him so that others might see his good works and imitate him. Titus's life would give his words greater impact. If you want someone to act a certain way, be sure to live that way yourself. Then you will earn the right to be heard.**

their children, 5to live wisely and be pure, to take
care of their homes, to do good, and to be submissive to their husbands. Then they will not bring
shame on the word of God.
6In the same way, encourage the young men to live
wisely in all they do. 7And you yourself must be an
example to them by doing good deeds of every kind.
Let everything you do reflect the integrity and seriousness of your teaching. 8Let your teaching be so
correct that it can't be criticized. Then those who
want to argue will be ashamed because they won't
have anything bad to say about us.
9Slaves must obey their masters and do their best
to please them. They must not talk back 10or steal,
but they must show themselves to be entirely trustworthy and good. Then they will make the teaching about God our Savior attractive in every way.
11For the grace of God has been revealed, bringing salvation to all people. 12And we are instructed
to turn from godless living and sinful pleasures.
We should live in this evil world with self-control,
right conduct, and devotion to God, 13while we
look forward to that wonderful event when the
glory of our great God and Savior, Jesus Christ, will
be revealed. 14He gave his life to free us from every
kind of sin, to cleanse us, and to make us his very
own people, totally committed to doing what is
right. 15You must teach these things and encourage
your people to do them, correcting them when
necessary. You have the authority to do this, so
don't let anyone ignore you or disregard what
you say.

CHAPTER **3** **OBEY THE GOVERNMENT.** Remind your
people to submit to the government and its officers.
They should be obedient, always ready to do what is
good. 2They must not speak evil of anyone, and they
must avoid quarreling. Instead, they should be gentle and show true humility to everyone.
3Once we, too, were foolish and disobedient. We
were misled by others and became slaves to many
wicked desires and evil pleasures. Our lives were
full of evil and envy. We hated others, and they
hated us.
4But then God our Savior showed us his kindness and love. 5He saved us, not because of the
good things we did, but because of his mercy. He

## SLAVE TO SIN ● ● • • •

3:3 **Following a life of pleasure and giving in to every sensual desire leads to slavery. Many think freedom consists in doing anything they want. But this path leads to a slavish addiction to sensual gratification. A person is no longer free, but is a slave to what his or her body dictates (2 Peter 2:19). Christ frees us from the desires and control of sin. Have you been released?**

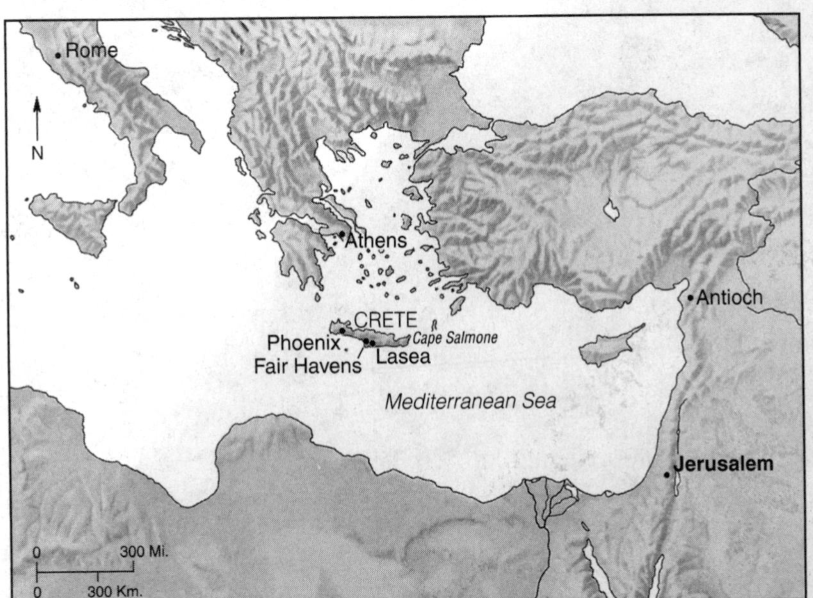


**TITUS GOES TO CRETE**
Tradition says that after Paul was released from prison in Rome, he and Titus traveled together for a while. They stopped in Crete. When it was time for Paul to go, he left Titus behind to help the churches there.

washed away our sins and gave us a new life
through the Holy Spirit.* [6]He generously poured
out the Spirit upon us because of what Jesus Christ
our Savior did. [7]He declared us not guilty because
of his great kindness. And now we know that we
will inherit eternal life. [8]These things I have told
you are all true. I want you to insist on them so that
everyone who trusts in God will be careful to do
good deeds all the time. These things are good and
beneficial for everyone.

[9]Do not get involved in foolish discussions about
spiritual pedigrees* or in quarrels and fights about
obedience to Jewish laws. These kinds of things are
useless and a waste of time. [10]If anyone is causing
divisions among you, give a first and second warning. After that, have nothing more to do with that
person. [11]For people like that have turned away from
the truth. They are sinning, and they condemn
themselves.

[12]I am planning to send either Artemas or Tychicus to you. As soon as one of them arrives, do your
best to meet me at Nicopolis as quickly as you can,
for I have decided to stay there for the winter. [13]Do
everything you can to help Zenas the lawyer and
Apollos with their trip. See that they are given everything they need. [14]For our people should not have
unproductive lives. They must learn to do good by
helping others who have urgent needs.

[15]Everybody here sends greetings. Please give my
greetings to all of the believers who love us.

May God's grace be with you all.

## ARGUMENTS ● ● • • •

3:9-11 **Paul warns Titus, as he warned Timothy, not to get involved in foolish and unprofitable disputes (2 Timothy 2:14). This does not mean that we should refuse to study, discuss, and examine different interpretations of difficult Bible passages. Paul is warning against petty quarrels, not honest discussion that leads to wisdom. When foolish arguments develop, it is best to either turn the discussion back to a track that is going somewhere or to politely excuse yourself.**

3:5 Greek *He saved us through the washing of regeneration and renewing of the Holy Spirit.* 3:9 Greek *discussions and genealogies.*

# MEGA themes

**A GOOD LIFE** The Good News of salvation is that we can't be saved by living a good life; we are saved only by faith in Jesus Christ. But the gospel transforms people's lives, so that they eventually perform good works. Our service won't save us, but we are saved to serve.

A good life is a witness to the gospel's power. As Christians, we must have commitment and discipline to serve. Each of us is to be a living servant; none of us is to consider himself or herself inactive.

1. Why do you think it is important for a Christian to live a good and pure life even though this is not the basis of salvation?
2. Describe a life that would be pleasing to God.
3. What areas of your life do you think are pleasing to God? In what areas of your life do you need to make changes in order to be more like the life you described in question 2?
4. Outline your personal plan for improving these areas for God's glory.

**CHARACTER** Titus's responsibility on Crete was to appoint church leaders (elders) to maintain proper organization and discipline, so Paul listed the qualities that elders should have. Their conduct in their homes revealed their fitness for service in the church.

It's not enough to be educated or have a following to be Christ's kind of leader. You must have self-control, spiritual and moral fitness, and Christian character. Who you are is just as important as what you can do.

1. Summarize Paul's description of those who are qualified to serve as church leaders.
2. Describe the person you want to be when you are older. What will be your personal qualities? What will be your priorities? What will be the impact of your life? How will you be serving God?
3. What choices are you making now that will help you fulfill the above description one day?

**CHURCH RELATIONSHIPS** Church teaching was supposed to relate to various groups. Older Christians were to teach and to be examples to younger men and women. Every age and group has a lesson to learn and a role to play.

Right living and right relationships go along with right doctrine. Treat relationships with other believers as important parts of your relationship with God.

1. Summarize Paul's teaching on church relationships in 2:1-15.
2. What groups in your church seem to be the most "distant" in their personal relationships (young-old, wealthy-average-poor, liberal ideas–conservative ideas, traditional worshipers–nontraditional worshipers, etc.)?
3. What would Paul say to those groups if he were to write a letter to your church leaders about

this distance? From your perspective, how could this gap be bridged?

4. What might you do to be a "bridge builder" in your church?

**CITIZENSHIP** Christians must be good citizens in society, not just in church. Believers must obey the government and work honestly.

How you fulfill your civic duties is a witness to the watching world. Your community life should reflect Christ's love as much as your church life does. You must guard against trying to separate your walk with God from the way you live each day.

1. Why is it important for Christians to obey the government?
2. Do you agree or disagree with this statement: "Being a good citizen involves more than just not breaking the law"? Explain your response.
3. What are the biggest issues facing your community? How would you apply this study to your role as a member of the community?
4. How can a Christian have an impact for Christ by simply being a citizen who contributes positively? How can you provide this impact in your community?

I could *never* forgive her!" ■ "He'll *never* get serious about God!" ■ "I wish things would work out, but they won't. My situation is *impossible!*" ■ Ever heard—or made—statements like those? If so, take this hint! Never say *never.* Many of the hard-to-believe things we declare "impossible!" eventually do come to pass . . . right before our embarrassed eyes. ■ Consider the Munich elementary school teacher who told ten-year-old Albert Einstein, "You will never amount to very much." ■ Or the misguided executive with the Decca Recording Company in the early '60s who decided *not* to offer a contract to an obscure musical group called The Beatles. ■ And you can be sure Simon Newcomb is red-faced in his grave. He's the guy who asserted in the 1800s that "flight by machines heavier than air is . . . utterly impossible." ■ Never say *never.* Don't end that friendship or relationship just because you've been wronged. Don't give up on that friend who claims to be an atheist. Don't throw in the towel on your dream. Don't write off your future just because you've made some bad choices in the past. ■ Never say *never.* The Gospel of Matthew states that same principle ("With God everything is possible," Matthew 19:26), and the book of Philemon illustrates it—describing how a poor slave and his rich master ended up as Christian brothers. You are about to read a story of betrayal and forgiveness, and of how Jesus Christ breaks down all barriers. ■ So before you say, "That's *impossible!*" Or, "That could *never* happen!" take five minutes to read Paul's postcard to Philemon.

## STATS

PURPOSE: To convince Philemon to forgive—and accept as a brother in the faith—his runaway slave, Onesimus

AUTHOR: Paul

TO WHOM WRITTEN: Philemon, who probably was a wealthy member of the Colossian church

DATE WRITTEN: About A.D. 60, during Paul's first imprisonment in Rome, at about the same time the books of Ephesians and Colossians were written

SETTING: Slavery was very common in the Roman Empire. Evidently some Christians had slaves. Paul makes a radical statement by calling this slave Philemon's brother in Christ.

KEY PEOPLE: Paul, Philemon, Onesimus

KEY PLACES: Colosse, Rome

# Philemon

**ONESIMUS COMES HOME.** This letter is from Paul, in prison for preaching the Good News about Christ Jesus, and from our brother Timothy.

It is written to Philemon, our much loved co-worker, 2and to our sister Apphia and to Archippus, a fellow soldier of the cross. I am also writing to the church that meets in your house.

3May God our Father and the Lord Jesus Christ give you grace and peace.

4I always thank God when I pray for you, Philemon, 5because I keep hearing of your trust in the Lord Jesus and your love for all of God's people. 6You are generous because of your faith. And I am praying that you will really put your generosity to work, for in so doing you will come to an understanding of all the good things we can do for Christ. 7I myself have gained much joy and comfort from your love, my brother, because your kindness has so often refreshed the hearts of God's people.

8That is why I am boldly asking a favor of you. I could demand it in the name of Christ because it is the right thing for you to do, 9but because of our love, I prefer just to ask you. So take this as a request from your friend Paul, an old man, now in prison for the sake of Christ Jesus.

10My plea is that you show kindness to Onesimus. I think of him as my own son because he became a believer as a result of my ministry here in prison. 11Onesimus* hasn't been of much use to you in the past, but now he is very useful to both of us. 12I am sending him back to you, and with him comes my own heart.

13I really wanted to keep him here with me while I am in these chains for preaching the Good News,

11 *Onesimus* means "useful."

## GOOD DEAL ● ● • • •

**8-9 Because Paul was an elder and an apostle, he could have used his authority with Philemon, commanding him to deal kindly with his runaway slave. But Paul based his request not on his own authority, but on Philemon's Christian commitment. Paul wanted Philemon's heartfelt obedience. When you know something is right and you have the power to demand it, do you appeal to your authority or the other person's commitment? Here Paul provides a good example of how to deal with a possible conflict between Christian friends.**

and he would have helped me on your behalf.
[14]But I didn't want to do anything without your consent. And I didn't want you to help because you were forced to do it but because you wanted to.
[15]Perhaps you could think of it this way: Onesimus ran away for a little while so you could have him back forever. [16]He is no longer just a slave; he is a beloved brother, especially to me. Now he will mean much more to you, both as a slave and as a brother in the Lord.

## RECONCILIATION

As roommates (and total opposites), college freshmen Melanie and Laura had a very awkward relationship:

- Laura was short and stout; Melanie was tall and thin.
- Laura was refined and reserved; Melanie was loud and obnoxious.
- Laura was upper-class prep; Melanie was a middle-class freak.
- Laura was a conservative; Melanie was a liberal.
- Laura was a morning person; Melanie was a night owl.
- Laura was a Christian; Melanie clearly was not.

At the end of the fall semester, Melanie moved out of the dorm into an apartment. Right about that same time, Laura couldn't find her diamond pendant. She suspected Melanie, but she never said a word.

The following summer, Laura got a letter from Melanie. The first part of the letter told how she had come to Christ during a beach outreach. The second half was a confession. Melanie had indeed taken the pendant and pawned it for some needed cash. She was pleading for forgiveness.

Laura immediately wrote back—welcoming Melanie to the family of God, granting the requested forgiveness, and asking if the girls could get together first thing in the fall.

Could you have responded to Melanie as Laura did? Their story isn't a fairy tale. Read Philemon to see for yourself the amazing reconciliation that is possible in Jesus Christ.

[17]So if you consider me your partner, give him the same welcome you would give me if I were coming. [18]If he has harmed you in any way or stolen anything from you, charge me for it. [19]I, Paul, write this in my own handwriting: "I will repay it." And I won't mention that you owe me your very soul!
[20]Yes, dear brother, please do me this favor for the Lord's sake. Give me this encouragement in Christ.

**He is no longer just a slave;** *he is a beloved brother.*

PHILEMON 1:16

[21]I am confident as I write this letter that you will do what I ask and even more!
[22]Please keep a guest room ready for me, for I am hoping that God will answer your prayers and let me return to you soon.
[23]Epaphras, my fellow prisoner in Christ Jesus, sends you his greetings. [24]So do Mark, Aristarchus, Demas, and Luke, my co-workers.
[25]The grace of the Lord Jesus Christ be with your spirit.

## FORGIVEN • • • • •

10, 16 **Paul asked Philemon not only to forgive his runaway slave who had become a Christian, but to accept him as a brother. As Christians, we should forgive as we have been forgiven (Matthew 6:12; Ephesians 4:31-32). True forgiveness means that we treat the person we've forgiven as we would want to be treated. Is there someone you say you have forgiven, but who still needs your kindness?**

# MEGA themes

**FORGIVENESS** Philemon was Paul's friend and Onesimus's owner. Paul asked Philemon not to punish Onesimus, but to forgive and restore him as a new Christian brother.

Christian relationships must be full of forgiveness and acceptance. Forgiving those who have wronged you is the appropriate response to Christ's forgiveness of you.

1. If you were Philemon, how would you have felt before you received the letter? How would Paul's letter have changed your attitude? What verses in the letter would have had the most impact on your thinking?
2. How is Paul's request for Onesimus in verses 18-20 a reflection of what Christ has done for all of us?
3. As you reflect on this study and the people involved, what do you learn about the importance of forgiveness in Christian relationships? What is the basis of this forgiveness? How is this forgiveness lived out when someone has been wronged?
4. What difference does it make whether or not you forgive a Christian friend who wrongs you? If there is such a wrong that you have not forgiven, how can you go to that friend and make things right?

**BARRIERS** Slavery was widespread in the Roman Empire. Slavery was a barrier between people, but Christian love and fellowship can overcome such barriers.

In Christ we are one family. No walls of race, economic status, or political differences should separate believers. Let Christ work through you to remove barriers between Christian brothers and sisters. Take steps to act out the love of Christ in you.

1. What are some of the differences and prejudices that separate and alienate people from one another?
2. Why are such conflicts offensive to God?
3. In your community, what groups of people do not relate to each other simply because of external differences?
4. What can you do to demonstrate to your school or church that God is greater than all barriers?

**RESPECT** Paul was a friend of both Philemon and Onesimus. He had the authority as an apostle to tell Philemon what to do. Yet Paul chose to appeal to his friend in Christian love rather than to order him to do what he wished.

When dealing with people, tactful persuasion accomplishes a great deal more than commands. Remember to exhibit courtesy and respect in dealing with people.

1. What do you think it means to respect a person?
2. Who are the people you most respect? What are the qualities that lead you to respect them?
3. Which of these qualities do you most want to develop as you grow into an adult who can be respected by others?
4. What about now? What leads others to respect you as a young person?

**F**our Very Uncool Activities You Can Do: ■ 1. Wear a diaper to school and suck on a pacifier during all your classes. ■ 2. Treat yourself to a lunch of jars of baby food: strained carrots, creamed spinach, and milk (out of a baby bottle, of course). ■ 3. Drool all over yourself. ■ 4. Crawl from class to class. Anytime anything doesn't go your way, kick your legs, flail your arms, and cry uncontrollably. ■ Such behavior is uncool for a teenager—it's immature, the kind of things we expect *babies* to do. We would never tolerate such immaturity in an older person. ■ So why do we tolerate such infantile behavior in the spiritual realm? ■ The church has far too many "baby Christians." Some have only been believers in Christ a short time, so it's understandable that *they* might do silly or immature things. But for those Christians who have been in God's family for years and who still act like infants—well, there's just no excuse. ■ In the same way that little kids grow up physically, "baby" Christians need to grow up in their relationship with Christ. That's what Hebrews is all about—growing up spiritually. You should know up front that Hebrews contains some tough statements and some sobering challenges. It's a risky book to read—especially if you apply it. ■ Neglect its powerful message, and you face an even greater risk—remaining a spiritual infant. You can't get more uncool than that.

## STATS

PURPOSE: To present Christ's sufficiency and superiority

AUTHOR: Unknown. Paul, Luke, Barnabas, Apollos, Silas, Philip, Priscilla, and others have been suggested. Whoever the author was speaks of Timothy as "brother" (13:23).

TO WHOM WRITTEN: Hebrew Christians who may have been considering a return to Judaism, perhaps because of immaturity due to their lack of understanding of biblical truths. They seem to be "second-generation" Christians (2:3). And to all believers everywhere.

DATE WRITTEN: Probably before the destruction of the Temple in Jerusalem in A.D. 70; the religious sacrifices and ceremonies are referred to, but not the Temple's destruction

SETTING: These Jewish Christians were probably undergoing fierce persecution, socially and physically, from both Jews and from Romans. The people needed to be reassured that Christianity was true and that Jesus was the Messiah.

KEY PEOPLE: Old Testament men and women of faith (chapter 11)

CHAPTER **1** **JESUS CHRIST IS GOD'S SON.** Long ago
God spoke many times and in many ways to our
ancestors through the prophets. [2]But now in these
final days, he has spoken to us through his Son. God
promised everything to the Son as an inheritance,
and through the Son he made the universe and
everything in it. [3]The Son reflects God's own glory,
and everything about him represents God exactly. He
sustains the universe by the mighty power of his
command. After he died to cleanse us from the stain
of sin, he sat down in the place of honor at the right
hand of the majestic God of heaven.
[4]This shows that God's Son is far greater than the
angels, just as the name God gave him is far greater
than their names. [5]For God never said to any angel
what he said to Jesus:

"You are my Son.
Today I have become your Father.*"

And again God said,

"I will be his Father,
and he will be my Son."*

[6]And then, when he presented his honored* Son to
the world, God said, "Let all the angels of God
worship him."* [7]God calls his angels

"messengers swift as the wind,
and servants made of flaming fire."*

[8]But to his Son he says,

"Your throne, O God, endures forever and ever.
Your royal power is expressed in righteousness.
[9]You love what is right and hate what is wrong.
Therefore God, your God, has anointed you,
pouring out the oil of joy on you more than
on anyone else."*

[10]And,

"Lord, in the beginning you laid the foundation
of the earth,
and the heavens are the work of your hands.
[11]Even they will perish, but you remain forever.
They will wear out like old clothing.

**JESUS ● ● ● • •**

1:2-3 **Not only is Jesus God's exact representation; he is God himself—the very God who spoke in Old Testament times. Christ is eternal; he worked with the Father in creating the world (John 1:3; Colossians 1:16). He is the full revelation of God. You can have no clearer view of God than by looking at him. Jesus Christ is the complete expression of God in a human body.**

1:5a Or *Today I reveal you as my Son.* Ps 2:7. 1:5b 2 Sam 7:14. 1:6a Greek *firstborn.* 1:6b Deut 32:43. 1:7 Ps 104:4. 1:8-9 Ps 45:6-7.

> 12 You will roll them up like an old coat.
> They will fade away like old clothing.
> But you are always the same;
> you will never grow old."*

13 And God never said to an angel, as he did to his Son,

> "Sit in honor at my right hand
> until I humble your enemies,
> making them a footstool under your feet."*

14 But angels are only servants. They are spirits sent from God to care for those who will receive salvation.

## CHAPTER 2

**LISTEN CAREFULLY AND OBEY GOD.** So we must listen very carefully to the truth we have heard, or we may drift away from it. 2 The message God delivered through angels has always proved true, and the people were punished for every violation of the law and every act of disobedience. 3 What makes us think that we can escape if we are indifferent to this great salvation that was announced by the Lord Jesus himself? It was passed on* to us by those who heard him speak, 4 and God verified the message by signs and wonders and various miracles and by giving gifts of the Holy Spirit whenever he chose to do so.

5 And furthermore, the future world we are talking about will not be controlled by angels. 6 For somewhere in the Scriptures it says,

> "What is man that you should think of him,
> and the son of man* that you should care for him?
> 7 For a little while you made him lower than the angels,
> and you crowned him with glory and honor.*
> 8 You gave him authority over all things."*

**STABILITY ● ● ● • •**

**2:9 God has put Jesus in charge of everything, and Jesus has revealed himself to us. We do not yet see Jesus reigning on earth, but we can picture him in his heavenly glory. When confused by tomorrow and anxious about the future, keep a clear view of Jesus Christ—who he is, what he has done, and what he is doing for you right now. This will give stability to your decisions day by day.**

Now when it says "all things," it means nothing is left out. But we have not yet seen all of this happen. 9 What we do see is Jesus, who "for a little while was made lower than the angels" and now is "crowned with glory and honor" because he suffered death for us. Yes, by God's grace, Jesus tasted death for everyone in all the world. 10 And it was only right that God—who made everything and for whom everything was made—should bring his many children into glory. Through the suffering of Jesus, God made him a perfect leader, one fit to bring them into their salvation.

Since he himself
*has gone through*
**suffering**
and
**temptation**
he is **ABLE**
*to help us*
when
we are
being
**tempted.**

HEBREWS 2:18

11 So now Jesus and the ones he makes holy have the same Father. That is why Jesus is not ashamed to call them his brothers and sisters.* 12 For he said to God,

> "I will declare the wonder of your name to my brothers and sisters.*
> I will praise you among all your people."

13 He also said, "I will put my trust in him." And in the same context he said, "Here I am—together with the children God has given me."*

14 Because God's children are human beings—made of flesh and blood—Jesus also became flesh and blood by being born in human form. For only as a human being could he die, and only by dying could he break the power of the Devil, who had the power of death. 15 Only in this way could he deliver those who have lived all their lives as slaves to the fear of dying.

16 We all know that Jesus came to help the descendants of Abraham, not to help the angels. 17 Therefore, it was necessary for Jesus to be in every respect like us, his brothers and sisters, so that he could be our merciful and faithful High Priest before God. He then could offer a sacrifice that would take away the sins of the people. 18 Since he himself has gone through suffering and temptation, he is able to help us when we are being tempted.

## CHAPTER 3

**JESUS: GREATER THAN MOSES.** And so, dear brothers and sisters who belong to God* and are bound for heaven, think about this Jesus whom we declare to be God's Messenger and High Priest. 2 For he

1:10-12 Ps 102:25-27. 1:13 Ps 110:1. 2:3 Or *and confirmed.* 2:6 Or *Son of Man.* 2:7 Some manuscripts add *You put him in charge of everything you made.* 2:6-8 Ps 8:4-6. 2:11 Greek *his brothers;* also in 2:17. 2:12 Greek *my brothers.* Ps 22:22. 2:13 Isa 8:17-18. 3:1 Greek *And so, holy brothers.*

was faithful to God, who appointed him, just as Moses
served faithfully and was entrusted with God's entire
house. 3But Jesus deserves far more glory than Moses,
just as a person who builds a fine house deserves more
praise than the house itself. 4For every house has a
builder, but God is the one who made everything.
5Moses was certainly faithful in God's house, but
only as a servant. His work was an illustration of the
truths God would reveal later. 6But Christ, the faithful Son, was in charge of the entire household. And
we are God's household, if we keep up our courage
and remain confident in our hope in Christ. 7That is
why the Holy Spirit says,

"Today you must listen to his voice.
8 Don't harden your hearts against him
as Israel did when they rebelled,
when they tested God's patience in the
wilderness.
9 There your ancestors tried my patience,
even though they saw my miracles for forty
years.
10 So I was angry with them, and I said,
'Their hearts always turn away from me.
They refuse to do what I tell them.'
11 So in my anger I made a vow:
'They will never enter my place of rest.'"*

12Be careful then, dear brothers and sisters.* Make
sure that your own hearts are not evil and unbelieving, turning you away from the living God. 13You
must warn each other every day, as long as it is called
"today," so that none of you will be deceived by sin
and hardened against God. 14For if we are faithful to
the end, trusting God just as firmly as when we first
believed, we will share in all that belongs to Christ.
15But never forget the warning:

"Today you must listen to his voice.
Don't harden your hearts against him
as Israel did when they rebelled."*

16And who were those people who rebelled
against God, even though they heard his voice?
Weren't they the ones Moses led out of Egypt? 17And
who made God angry for forty years? Wasn't it the
people who sinned, whose bodies fell in the wilderness? 18And to whom was God speaking when he
vowed that they would never enter his place of rest?
He was speaking to those who disobeyed him. 19So
we see that they were not allowed to enter his rest
because of their unbelief.

CHAPTER **4** **GOD'S PROMISE OF REST.** God's promise
of entering his place of rest still stands, so we ought
to tremble with fear that some of you might fail to
get there. 2For this Good News—that God has prepared a place of rest—has been announced to us just
as it was to them. But it did them no good because
they didn't believe what God told them.* 3For only
we who believe can enter his place of rest. As for
those who didn't believe, God said,

"In my anger I made a vow:
'They will never enter my place of rest,'"*

even though his place of rest has been ready since he
made the world. 4We know it is ready because the

## TURN BACK ● ● ● ● ●

**4:1-3 Some of the Jewish Christians who received this letter may have been on the verge of turning back from their promised rest in Christ, just as the people in Moses' day turned back from the Promised Land. In both cases, the difficulties of the present moment overshadowed the reality of God's promise, and people stopped believing that God was able to fulfill his promises. When we trust our own efforts instead of Christ, we too are in danger of turning back. Our own efforts are never adequate; only Christ can see us through.**

**I have heard so many different opinions on what God is really like that I'm beginning to wonder if someone can ever know. Is there any way to know for sure?**

Have you ever assembled a complicated jigsaw puzzle? If so, you know how important the picture on the box is. As you put the puzzle together, you use the picture as a reference, your guide.

But what if you had the wrong box top, and the picture didn't match the puzzle? The puzzle would be nearly impossible to assemble (at least until you realized the mistake).

People throughout the world are trying to put the "God puzzle" together. But often they are trying to match the pieces to the wrong picture!

God is not trying to hide. As Hebrews 1:1-3 tells us, God has clearly shown the world what he is like, through nature, through the Bible, and especially through Christ.

Jesus said it plainly, "The Father and I are one" (John 10:30).

Even when he was asked point-blank by Philip, he was straightforward in his reply. "Philip, don't you even yet know who I am, even after all the time I have been with you? Anyone who has seen me has seen the Father!" (John 14:9).

It doesn't get more obvious than that! To know what God is like, all you have to do is look at Jesus.

People get their God-pictures from TV preachers; friends who say they believe in God, but never act like it; religious relatives; coaches who pray before games and then swear the paint off of the walls at halftime; and so forth. These are pictures of God that aren't anything like what he's really like. No wonder they can't put the puzzle together.

That's why it's so important not to settle for hearsay when it comes to finding out what God is like. Instead, look at the right picture—look at Christ.

3:7-11 Ps 95:7-11. 3:12 Greek *brothers.* 3:15 Ps 95:7-8. 4:2 Some manuscripts read *they didn't share the faith of those who listened [to God].*
4:3 Ps 95:11.

# Ultimate Issues

**PRAYER** Imagine that you were about to meet someone famous—maybe the queen of England or the president of the United States. Chances are you'd be nervous, wondering what to say and how to act. You wouldn't want to make a fool of yourself by doing or saying something inappropriate. Now imagine you're just sitting around gabbing with your best friend. You don't worry about what to say or do. ***You can just be yourself;*** the talk flows freely and naturally. These two situations illustrate something about the nature of prayer. On the one hand, prayer brings you into the presence of the King of the universe, the Lord and Creator of everything. That's fairly intimidating! No wonder people feel **awkward and tongue-tied** when they pray. On the other hand, prayer is simply talking with your heavenly Father, the person who knows you better and loves you more than anyone else does. He is, in a very real way, your best friend; you can talk with him openly and honestly—about anything. Prayer has inspired countless books, debates, songs, poems, and lives. Though there is little that is new to be said about prayer, consider the following perspectives: Prayer is simply communication with God. Christianity talks about a personal God, not a "force," "concept," or "abstract idea." God is a person—we can know him. Imagine that! Small, limited, finite human beings are invited to know God in a personal way. When you want to get to know a person, there really is only one way to do it: spend time together. The same is true of God. What happens when we spend time with God? Basically, three things: First, we can tell God WHAT IS ON OUR MIND: our worries, joys, pains, fears, hopes—everything. Nothing is too big or too trivial to tell God. He is a loving Father, and good fathers want to hear what is on the heart of their children. We can be ourselves with God; we don't need to change how we talk when we talk with him, or say "thee," "thou," "beseecheth," etc. We can speak to God the way we would to **OUR MOST TRUSTED FRIEND.** Second, in prayer we can hear what God has to say to us. Listening to God requires more patience and more practice than talking to him. That shouldn't be surprising—most of us are better talkers than listeners—but listening to God can be a very rewarding experience. It is one more way God can give us guidance as we seek his will (other ways include the Bible, the counsel of other Christians, and knowing our own particular gifts and limitations). One caution: if you ever feel God is telling you to do something that runs contrary to Scripture, you have misunderstood. God never contradicts himself or his inspired Word. Seek counsel from your parents, your pastor, your youth minister, or other Christians when this happens. Third, when we pray we are in the presence of God. Prayer brings us into THE THRONE ROOM OF GOD (Hebrews 4:16), where we may present our requests, praise, confessions, etc. This time spent in the presence of God will begin to have an effect on us: we will begin to become more like him. Have you ever noticed that when two people spend a lot of time together, they begin to talk, act, and even think alike? The same principle applies to our relationship with God. The more we're with him, the more we become like him. It's easy to get discouraged when we pray, to feel our prayers are having no effect. Remember, though, that prayer is more than simply asking God to give us what we want. It is living, active, and powerful communication with the Lord of all. That's much more significant than meeting with the queen or the president. And, through prayer, we always have access to the One who knows us, loves us, hears us, and is molding us into his image.

Scriptures mention the seventh day, saying, "On the seventh day God rested from all his work."* 5But in the other passage God said, "They will never enter my place of rest."* 6So God's rest is there for people to enter. But those who formerly heard the Good News failed to enter because they disobeyed God. 7So God set another time for entering his place of rest, and that time is today. God announced this through David a long time later in the words already quoted:

"Today you must listen to his voice.
Don't harden your hearts against him."*

8This new place of rest was not the land of Canaan, where Joshua led them. If it had been, God would not have spoken later about another day of rest. 9So there is a special rest* still waiting for the people of God. 10For all who enter into God's rest will find rest from their labors, just as God rested after creating the world. 11Let us do our best to enter that place of rest. For anyone who disobeys God, as the people of Israel did, will fall.

12For the word of God is full of living power. It is sharper than the sharpest knife, cutting deep into our innermost thoughts and desires. It exposes us for what we really are. 13Nothing in all creation can hide from him. Everything is naked and exposed before his eyes. This is the God to whom we must explain all that we have done.

14That is why we have a great High Priest who has gone to heaven, Jesus the Son of God. Let us cling to him and never stop trusting him. 15This High Priest of ours understands our weaknesses, for he faced all of the same temptations we do, yet he did not sin. 16So let us come boldly to the throne of our gracious God. There we will receive his mercy, and we will find grace to help us when we need it.

CHAPTER **5** **JESUS CHRIST IS OUR HIGH PRIEST.** Now a high priest is a man chosen to represent other human beings in their dealings with God. He presents their gifts to God and offers their sacrifices for sins. 2And because he is human, he is able to deal gently with the people, though they are ignorant and wayward. For he is subject to the same weaknesses they have. 3That is why he has to offer sacrifices, both for their sins and for his own sins. 4And no one can become a high priest simply because he wants such an honor. He has to be called by God for this work, just as Aaron was.

5That is why Christ did not exalt himself to become High Priest. No, he was chosen by God, who said to him,

"You are my Son.
Today I have become your Father."*

6And in another passage God said to him,

"You are a priest forever
in the line of Melchizedek."*

7While Jesus was here on earth, he offered prayers and pleadings, with a loud cry and tears, to the one who could deliver him out of death. And God heard his prayers because of his reverence for God. 8So even though Jesus was God's Son, he learned obedience from the things he suffered. 9In this way, God qualified him as a perfect High Priest, and he became the source of eternal salvation for all those who obey him. 10And God designated him to be a High Priest in the line of Melchizedek.

11There is so much more we would like to say about this. But you don't seem to listen, so it's hard to make you understand. 12You have been Christians a long time now, and you ought to be teaching others. Instead, you need someone to teach you again the basic things a beginner must learn about the Scriptures.* You are like babies who drink only milk and cannot eat solid food. 13And a person who is living on milk isn't very far along in the Christian life and doesn't know much about doing what is right. 14Solid food is for those who are mature, who have trained themselves to recognize the difference between right and wrong and then do what is right.

CHAPTER **6** **COUNT ON GOD'S PROMISES.** So let us stop going over the basics of Christianity* again and again. Let us go on instead and become mature in our understanding. Surely we don't need to start all over again with the importance of turning away from evil deeds and placing our faith in God. 2You don't

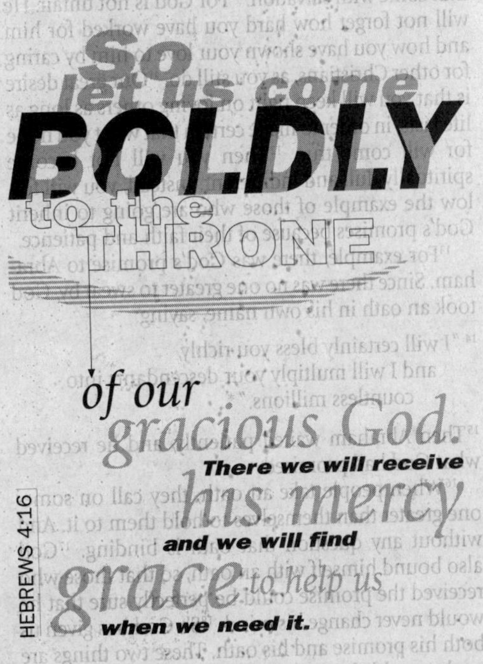
So let us come
BOLDLY
to the THRONE
of our
gracious God.
There we will receive
his mercy
and we will find
grace to help us
when we need it.
HEBREWS 4:16

4:4 Gen 2:2. 4:5 Ps 95:11. 4:7 Ps 95:7-8. 4:9 Or *Sabbath rest.* 5:5 Or *Today I reveal you as my Son.* Ps 2:7. 5:6 Ps 110:4. 5:12 Or *about the oracles of God.* 6:1 Or *the basics about Christ.*

need further instruction about baptisms, the laying on of hands, the resurrection of the dead, and eternal judgment. [3]And so, God willing, we will move forward to further understanding.

[4]For it is impossible to restore to repentance those who were once enlightened—those who have experienced the good things of heaven and shared in the Holy Spirit, [5]who have tasted the goodness of the word of God and the power of the age to come—[6]and who then turn away from God. It is impossible to bring such people to repentance again because they are nailing the Son of God to the cross again by rejecting him, holding him up to public shame.

**EVIDENCE ● ● • • •**

6:7-8 **Land that produces a good crop receives loving care, but land that produces thorns and briers has to be burned off so that the farmer can start over. God condemns an unproductive Christian life. We are not saved by works or conduct, but what we do is the evidence of our faith. Being productive for Christ is serious business.**

[7]When the ground soaks up the rain that falls on it and bears a good crop for the farmer, it has the blessing of God. [8]But if a field bears thistles and thorns, it is useless. The farmer will condemn that field and burn it.

[9]Dear friends, even though we are talking like this, we really don't believe that it applies to you. We are confident that you are meant for better things, things that come with salvation. [10]For God is not unfair. He will not forget how hard you have worked for him and how you have shown your love to him by caring for other Christians, as you still do. [11]Our great desire is that you will keep right on loving others as long as life lasts, in order to make certain that what you hope for will come true. [12]Then you will not become spiritually dull and indifferent. Instead, you will follow the example of those who are going to inherit God's promises because of their faith and patience.

[13]For example, there was God's promise to Abraham. Since there was no one greater to swear by, God took an oath in his own name, saying:

[14] "I will certainly bless you richly,
and I will multiply your descendants into
countless millions."*

[15]Then Abraham waited patiently, and he received what God had promised.

[16]When people take an oath, they call on someone greater than themselves to hold them to it. And without any question that oath is binding. [17]God also bound himself with an oath, so that those who received the promise could be perfectly sure that he would never change his mind. [18]So God has given us both his promise and his oath. These two things are unchangeable because it is impossible for God to lie. Therefore, we who have fled to him for refuge can take new courage, for we can hold on to his promise with confidence.

[19]This confidence is like a strong and trustworthy anchor for our souls. It leads us through the curtain of heaven into God's inner sanctuary. [20]Jesus has already gone in there for us. He has become our eternal High Priest in the line of Melchizedek.

## CHAPTER 7

**MELCHIZEDEK: JUSTICE AND PEACE.** This Melchizedek was king of the city of Salem and also a priest of God Most High. When Abraham was returning home after winning a great battle against many kings, Melchizedek met him and blessed him. [2]Then Abraham took a tenth of all he had won in the battle and gave it to Melchizedek. His name means "king of justice." He is also "king of peace" because *Salem* means "peace." [3]There is no record of his father or mother or any of his ancestors—no beginning or end to his life. He remains a priest forever, resembling the Son of God.

[4]Consider then how great this Melchizedek was. Even Abraham, the great patriarch of Israel, recognized how great Melchizedek was by giving him a tenth of what he had taken in battle. [5]Now the priests, who are descendants of Levi, are commanded in the law of Moses to collect a tithe from all the people, even though they are their own relatives.* [6]But Melchizedek, who was not even related to Levi, collected a tenth from Abraham. And Melchizedek placed a blessing upon Abraham, the one who had already received the promises of God. [7]And without question, the person who has the power to bless is always greater than the person who is blessed.

[8]In the case of Jewish priests, tithes are paid to men who will die. But Melchizedek is greater than they are, because we are told that he lives on. [9]In addition, we might even say that Levi's descendants, the ones who collect the tithe, paid a tithe to Melchizedek through their ancestor Abraham. [10]For although Levi wasn't born yet, the seed from which he came was in Abraham's loins when Melchizedek collected the tithe from him.

[11]And finally, if the priesthood of Levi could have achieved God's purposes—and it was that priesthood on which the law was based—why did God need to send a different priest from the line of Melchizedek, instead of from the line of Levi and Aaron?*

[12]And when the priesthood is changed, the law must also be changed to permit it. [13]For the one we are talking about belongs to a different tribe, whose members do not serve at the altar. [14]What I mean is, our Lord came from the tribe of Judah, and Moses never mentioned Judah in connection with the priesthood.

[15]The change in God's law is even more evident from the fact that a different priest, who is like Melchizedek, has now come. [16]He became a priest,

6:14 Gen 22:17. 7:5 Greek *their brothers, who are descendants of Abraham.* 7:11 Greek *according to the order of Aaron.*

not by meeting the old requirement of belonging to the tribe of Levi, but by the power of a life that cannot be destroyed. 17 And the psalmist pointed this out when he said of Christ,

"You are a priest forever
in the line of Melchizedek."*

18 Yes, the old requirement about the priesthood was set aside because it was weak and useless. 19 For the law made nothing perfect, and now a better hope has taken its place. And that is how we draw near to God.

20 God took an oath that Christ would always be a priest, but he never did this for any other priest. 21 Only to Jesus did he say,

"The Lord has taken an oath
and will not break his vow:
'You are a priest forever.'"*

22 Because of God's oath, it is Jesus who guarantees the effectiveness of this better covenant.

23 Another difference is that there were many priests under the old system. When one priest died, another had to take his place. 24 But Jesus remains a priest forever; his priesthood will never end. 25 Therefore he is able, once and forever, to save* everyone who comes to God through him. He lives forever to plead with God on their behalf.

26 He is the kind of high priest we need because he is holy and blameless, unstained by sin. He has now been set apart from sinners, and he has been given the highest place of honor in heaven. 27 He does not need to offer sacrifices every day like the other high priests. They did this for their own sins first and then for the sins of the people. But Jesus did this once for all when he sacrificed himself on the cross. 28 Those who were high priests under the law of Moses were limited by human weakness. But after the law was given, God appointed his Son with an oath, and his Son has been made perfect forever.

## CHAPTER 8 OUR NEW HIGH PRIEST.

Here is the main point: Our High Priest sat down in the place of highest honor in heaven, at God's right hand. 2 There he ministers in the sacred tent, the true place of worship that was built by the Lord and not by human hands.

3 And since every high priest is required to offer gifts and sacrifices, our High Priest must make an offering, too. 4 If he were here on earth, he would not even be a priest, since there already are priests who offer the gifts required by the law of Moses. 5 They serve in a place of worship that is only a copy, a shadow of the real one in heaven. For when Moses was getting ready to build the Tabernacle, God gave him this warning: "Be sure that you make everything according to the design I have shown you here on the mountain."* 6 But our High Priest has been given a ministry that is far superior to the ministry of those who serve under the old laws, for he is the one who

### PAID THE PRICE ● ● • • •

**7:25 What does it mean that Jesus is able to save "once and forever" (or "to save completely")? No one else can add to what Jesus did to save us; our past, present, and future sins are all forgiven. Jesus is with the Father as a sign that our sins are forgiven. If you are a Christian, remember that Christ has paid the price for your sins once and for all. (See also 9:24-28.)**

guarantees for us a better covenant with God, based on better promises.

7 If the first covenant had been faultless, there would have been no need for a second covenant to replace it. 8 But God himself found fault with the old one when he said:

"The day will come, says the Lord,
when I will make a new covenant
with the people of Israel and Judah.
9 This covenant will not be like the one
I made with their ancestors
when I took them by the hand
and led them out of the land of Egypt.
They did not remain faithful to my covenant,
so I turned my back on them, says the Lord.
10 But this is the new covenant I will make
with the people of Israel on that day, says the Lord:
I will put my laws in their minds
so they will understand them,
and I will write them on their hearts
so they will obey them.
I will be their God,
and they will be my people.
11 And they will not need to teach their neighbors,
nor will they need to teach their family,
saying, 'You should know the Lord.'
For everyone, from the least to the greatest,
will already know me.
12 And I will forgive their wrongdoings,
and I will never again remember their sins."*

13 When God speaks of a new covenant, it means he has made the first one obsolete. It is now out of date and ready to be put aside.

## CHAPTER 9 OLD RULES ABOUT WORSHIP.

Now in that first covenant between God and Israel, there were regulations for worship and a sacred tent here on earth. 2 There were two rooms in this tent. In the first room were a lampstand, a table, and loaves of holy bread on the table. This was called the Holy Place. 3 Then there was a curtain, and behind the curtain was the second room called the Most Holy Place. 4 In that room were a gold incense altar and a wooden chest called the Ark of the Covenant, which was covered with gold on all sides. Inside the Ark were a gold jar containing some manna, Aaron's staff that sprouted leaves, and the stone tablets of the covenant with the Ten Commandments written on them. 5 The glorious cherubim were above the Ark. Their

7:17 Ps 110:4. 7:21 Ps 110:4. 7:25 Or *able to save completely.* 8:5 Exod 25:40; 26:30. 8:8-12 Jer 31:31-34.

## UNLOAD ● ● ● • •

**9:9-14 Though you know Christ, you may still be trying to make yourself good enough for God. But rules and rituals have never cleansed people's hearts. By Jesus' blood alone: (1) our conscience is cleared, (2) we are freed from death and can live to serve God, and (3) we are freed from sin's power. If you are carrying a load of guilt because you can't be good enough for God, take another look at Jesus' death and what it means for you.**

wings were stretched out over the Ark's cover, the place of atonement. But we cannot explain all of these things now.

6 When these things were all in place, the priests went in and out of the first room* regularly as they performed their religious duties. 7 But only the high priest goes into the Most Holy Place, and only once a year, and always with blood, which he offers to God to cover his own sins and the sins the people have committed in ignorance. 8 By these regulations the Holy Spirit revealed that the Most Holy Place was not open to the people as long as the first room and the entire system it represents were still in use.

9 This is an illustration pointing to the present time. For the gifts and sacrifices that the priests offer are not able to cleanse the consciences of the people who bring them. 10 For that old system deals only with food and drink and ritual washing—external regulations that are in effect only until their limitations can be corrected.

11 So Christ has now become the High Priest over all the good things that have come. He has entered that great, perfect sanctuary in heaven, not made by human hands and not part of this created world. 12 Once for all time he took blood into that Most Holy Place, but not the blood of goats and calves. He took his own blood, and with it he secured our salvation forever.

13 Under the old system, the blood of goats and bulls and the ashes of a young cow could cleanse people's bodies from ritual defilement. 14 Just think how much more the blood of Christ will purify our hearts from deeds that lead to death so that we can worship the living God. For by the power of the eternal Spirit, Christ offered himself to God as a perfect sacrifice for our sins. 15 That is why he is the one who mediates the new covenant between God and people, so that all who are invited can receive the eternal inheritance God has promised them. For Christ died to set them free from the penalty of the sins they had committed under that first covenant.

16 Now when someone dies and leaves a will, no one gets anything until it is proved that the person who wrote the will* is dead.* 17 The will goes into effect only after the death of the person who wrote it. While the person is still alive, no one can use the will to get any of the things promised to them.

18 That is why blood was required under the first covenant as a proof of death. 19 For after Moses had given the people all of God's laws, he took the blood of calves and goats, along with water, and sprinkled both the book of God's laws and all the people, using branches of hyssop bushes and scarlet wool. 20 Then he said, "This blood confirms the covenant God has made with you."* 21 And in the same way, he sprinkled blood on the sacred tent and on everything used for worship. 22 In fact, we can say that according to the law of Moses, nearly everything was purified by sprinkling with blood. Without the shedding of blood, there is no forgiveness of sins.

23 That is why the earthly tent and everything in it—which were copies of things in heaven—had to be purified by the blood of animals. But the real things in heaven had to be purified with far better sacrifices than the blood of animals.

24 For Christ has entered into heaven itself to appear now before God as our Advocate.* He did not go into the earthly place of worship, for that was merely a copy of the real Temple in heaven. 25 Nor did he enter heaven to offer himself again and again, like the earthly high priest who enters the Most Holy Place year after year to offer the blood of an animal. 26 If that had been necessary, he would have had to die again and again, ever since the world began. But no! He came once for all time, at the end of the age, to remove the power of sin forever by his sacrificial death for us.

27 And just as it is destined that each person dies only once and after that comes judgment, 28 so also Christ died only once as a sacrifice to take away the sins of many people. He will come again but not to deal with our sins again. This time he will bring salvation to all those who are eagerly waiting for him.

## CHAPTER 10 **FORGIVENESS ONCE AND FOR ALL.**

The old system in the law of Moses was only a shadow of the things to come, not the reality of the good things Christ has done for us. The sacrifices under the old system were repeated again and again, year after year, but they were never able to provide perfect cleansing for those who came to worship. 2 If they could have provided perfect cleansing, the sacrifices would have stopped, for the worshipers would have been purified once for all time, and their feelings of guilt would have disappeared.

3 But just the opposite happened. Those yearly sacrifices reminded them of their sins year after year. 4 For it is not possible for the blood of bulls and goats

## VALUE ● ● ● • •

**9:15 Value, in our human way of thinking, is not measured by how *many* people can have something good, but by how *few*. "Limited edition" means "valuable" because only a few can have it. God's great plan of redemption, however, is dramatically different. It is the most valuable of all treasures, yet it is available to all. The more who have it, and the more they use it, the greater its value! Exercise your faith by sharing it and using it to serve God, and so increase its value.**

9:6 Greek *first tent;* also in 9:8. 9:16a Or *covenant.* 9:16b Or *Now when someone makes a covenant, it is necessary to ratify it with the death of a sacrifice.* 9:20 Exod 24:8. 9:24 Greek *on our behalf.*

to take away sins. 5That is why Christ, when he came
into the world, said,

"You did not want animal sacrifices and grain
offerings.
But you have given me a body so that I may
obey you.
6 No, you were not pleased with animals burned
on the altar
or with other offerings for sin.
7 Then I said, 'Look, I have come to do your will,
O God—
just as it is written about me in the
Scriptures.'"*

8Christ said, "You did not want animal sacrifices or
grain offerings or animals burned on the altar or
other offerings for sin, nor were you pleased with
them" (though they are required by the law of
Moses). 9Then he added, "Look, I have come to do
your will." He cancels the first covenant in order to
establish the second. 10And what God wants is for us
to be made holy by the sacrifice of the body of Jesus
Christ once for all time.

11Under the old covenant, the priest stands before
the altar day after day, offering sacrifices that can
never take away sins. 12But our High Priest offered
himself to God as one sacrifice for sins, good for all
time. Then he sat down at the place of highest honor
at God's right hand. 13There he waits until his enemies are humbled as a footstool under his feet. 14For
by that one offering he perfected forever all those
whom he is making holy.

15And the Holy Spirit also testifies that this is so.
First he says,

16 "This is the new covenant I will make
with my people on that day, says the Lord:
I will put my laws in their hearts
so they will understand them,
and I will write them on their minds
so they will obey them."

17Then he adds,

"I will never again remember
their sins and lawless deeds."*

18Now when sins have been forgiven, there is no
need to offer any more sacrifices.

19And so, dear brothers and sisters,* we can boldly
enter heaven's Most Holy Place because of the blood
of Jesus. 20This is the new, life-giving way that Christ
has opened up for us through the sacred curtain, by
means of his death for us.*

21And since we have a great High Priest who rules
over God's people, 22let us go right into the presence
of God, with true hearts fully trusting him. For our
evil consciences have been sprinkled with Christ's
blood to make us clean, and our bodies have been
washed with pure water.

23Without wavering, let us hold tightly to the hope
we say we have, for God can be trusted to keep his
promise. 24Think of ways to encourage one another
to outbursts of love and good deeds. 25And let us not
neglect our meeting together, as some people do, but
encourage and warn each other, especially now that
the day of his coming back again is drawing near.

26Dear friends, if we deliberately continue sinning
after we have received a full knowledge of the truth,
there is no other sacrifice that will cover these sins.
27There will be nothing to look forward to but the
terrible expectation of God's judgment and the raging fire that will consume his enemies. 28Anyone
who refused to obey the law of Moses was put to
death without mercy on the testimony of two or

## BE THERE! ●●●••

**10:25 To neglect Christian meetings is to give up the encouragement and help of other Christians. We gather together to share our faith and strengthen each other in the Lord. As we get closer to the time of Christ's return, we may face many spiritual struggles, tribulations, and even persecution. Anti-Christian forces will grow in strength. Difficulties should never be excuses for missing church services. Rather, as difficulties arise, we should make an even greater effort to be faithful in attendance.**

**I like the idea about having a personal faith in God. What I don't like is having to go to church. It seems boring and a waste of time. I have been to other churches and it all seems the same. Why can't there be a church with just kids my own age?**

Imagine growing up without a family. It's tough to think of life without at least one parent who really cares.

Now imagine growing up with just brothers and sisters in the house and no parents at all! For a day or two it may seem like heaven, but very soon you would see that it is chaos! Eventually you would miss not having someone take care of your basic needs.

Families are designed to take care of your daily needs and to give you the continual love and guidance you need as you are growing up. Because Mom and Dad have been around longer, they often know what to do when a tough circumstance comes up (as much as you may hate to admit it!).

In Hebrews 10:24-25, we are warned against neglecting our church meetings. Church is our spiritual family. If we stay away, we are left to try to survive by ourselves. If all we had around were other kids, church would be like a house with no adults. Pretty soon we would recognize that many of our needs were not being met.

The church, like the family, can often be underappreciated for the role it plays in our spiritual growth. Some Christians do not recognize its influence until years later, then they realize they would still be spiritual babies without the church's influence and love.

10:5-7 Ps 40:6-8. 10:16-17 Jer 31:33-34. 10:19 Greek *brothers*. 10:20 Greek *his flesh*.

three witnesses. 29 Think how much more terrible the punishment will be for those who have trampled on the Son of God and have treated the blood of the covenant as if it were common and unholy. Such people have insulted and enraged the Holy Spirit who brings God's mercy to his people.
30 For we know the one who said,

"I will take vengeance.
I will repay those who deserve it."

He also said,

"The Lord will judge his own people."*

31 It is a terrible thing to fall into the hands of the living God.

**ONSISTENCY**

Follow for six months the paths of Ramsey and Tyrone, two guys who made commitments to Christ in August at youth camp:

September: Both guys begin attending a midweek Bible study sponsored by a local church.

October: Both guys are taught how to have a morning devotional time and start digging into God's Word.

November: Ramsey shares his newfound faith in Christ with two friends on the football team. Tyrone, claiming a busy schedule, begins skipping Bible study.

December: Ramsey decides to nix his habit of weekend carousing with the boys. Tyrone is no longer reading his Bible.

January: Ramsey has signed up to go to a Christian discipleship conference over spring break. Tyrone doesn't want to go to the conference, and he acts weird whenever Ramsey tries to talk to him about spiritual matters.

February: Ramsey leads his girlfriend to Christ. Tyrone's girlfriend is pregnant and planning to get an abortion.

Why the difference in the two guys? Why was Ramsey able to be so consistent and why did Tyrone fall away? For a possible answer, read Hebrews 12:1-4.

32 Don't ever forget those early days when you first learned about Christ. Remember how you remained faithful even though it meant terrible suffering. 33 Sometimes you were exposed to public ridicule and were beaten, and sometimes you helped others who were suffering the same things. 34 You suffered along with those who were thrown into jail. When all you owned was taken from you, you accepted it with joy. You knew you had better things waiting for you in eternity.

35 Do not throw away this confident trust in the Lord, no matter what happens. Remember the great reward it brings you! 36 Patient endurance is what you need now, so you will continue to do God's will. Then you will receive all that he has promised.

## VISION ● ● ● ● ●

11:13-16 **The people of faith listed here died without receiving all that God had promised, but they never lost their vision of heaven. Many Christians become frustrated and defeated because their needs, wants, expectations, and demands were not immediately met when they believed in Christ. They become impatient and want to quit. Are you discouraged because your goal seems far away? Take courage from these heroes of faith who lived and died without seeing the fruit of their faith on earth, yet continued to believe.**

37 "For in just a little while,
the Coming One will come and not delay.
38 And a righteous person will live by faith.
But I will have no pleasure in anyone who turns away."*

39 But we are not like those who turn their backs on God and seal their fate. We have faith that assures our salvation.

# CHAPTER 11

**GREAT HEROES OF THE FAITH.** What is faith? It is the confident assurance that what we hope for is going to happen. It is the evidence of things we cannot yet see. 2 God gave his approval to people in days of old because of their faith.

3 By faith we understand that the entire universe was formed at God's command, that what we now see did not come from anything that can be seen.

4 It was by faith that Abel brought a more acceptable offering to God than Cain did. God accepted Abel's offering to show that he was a righteous man. And although Abel is long dead, he still speaks to us because of his faith.

5 It was by faith that Enoch was taken up to heaven without dying—"suddenly he disappeared because God took him."* But before he was taken up, he was approved as pleasing to God. 6 So, you see, it is impossible to please God without faith. Anyone who wants to come to him must believe that there is a God and that he rewards those who sincerely seek him.

7 It was by faith that Noah built an ark to save his family from the flood. He obeyed God, who warned him about something that had never happened before. By his faith he condemned the rest of the world and was made right in God's sight.

8 It was by faith that Abraham obeyed when God called him to leave home and go to another land that God would give him as his inheritance. He went without knowing where he was going. 9 And even when he reached the land God promised him, he lived there by faith—for he was like a foreigner, living in a tent. And so did Isaac and Jacob, to whom God gave the same promise. 10 Abraham did this because he was confidently looking forward to a city with eternal foundations, a city designed and built by God.

11 It was by faith that Sarah together with Abraham was able to have a child, even though they were too old and Sarah was barren. Abraham believed that God would keep his promise.* 12 And so a whole

10:30 Deut 32:35-36. 10:37-38 Hab 2:3-4. 11:5 Gen 5:24. 11:11 Some manuscripts read *It was by faith that Sarah was able to have a child, even though she was too old and barren. Sarah believed that God would keep his promise.*

nation came from this one man, Abraham, who was
too old to have any children—a nation with so
many people that, like the stars of the sky and the
sand on the seashore, there is no way to count them.
13All these faithful ones died without receiving
what God had promised them, but they saw it all
from a distance and welcomed the promises of
God. They agreed that they were no more than
foreigners and nomads here on earth. 14And obviously people who talk like that are looking forward
to a country they can call their own. 15If they had
meant the country they came from, they would
have found a way to go back. 16But they were
looking for a better place, a heavenly homeland.
That is why God is not ashamed to be called their
God, for he has prepared a heavenly city for them.
17It was by faith that Abraham
offered Isaac as a sacrifice when
God was testing him. Abraham,
who had received God's promises,
was ready to sacrifice his only son,
Isaac, 18though God had promised
him, "Isaac is the son through
whom your descendants will be
counted."* 19Abraham assumed
that if Isaac died, God was able to
bring him back to life again. And
in a sense, Abraham did receive his
son back from the dead.
20It was by faith that Isaac
blessed his two sons, Jacob and
Esau. He had confidence in what
God was going to do in the future.
21It was by faith that Jacob,
when he was old and dying,
blessed each of Joseph's sons and
bowed in worship as he leaned on
his staff.
22And it was by faith that Joseph, when he was about to die,
confidently spoke of God's bringing the people of Israel out of
Egypt. He was so sure of it that he
commanded them to carry his
bones with them when they left!
23It was by faith that Moses' parents hid him for three months.
They saw that God had given
them an unusual child, and they
were not afraid of what the king
might do.
24It was by faith that Moses,
when he grew up, refused to be
treated as the son of Pharaoh's
daughter. 25He chose to share the
oppression of God's people instead of enjoying the fleeting pleasures of sin. 26He thought it was
better to suffer for the sake of the
Messiah than to own the treasures of Egypt, for he
was looking ahead to the great reward that God
would give him. 27It was by faith that Moses left the
land of Egypt. He was not afraid of the king. Moses
kept right on going because he kept his eyes on the
one who is invisible. 28It was by faith that Moses
commanded the people of Israel to keep the Passover and to sprinkle blood on the doorposts so that
the angel of death would not kill their firstborn sons.
29It was by faith that the people of Israel went right
through the Red Sea as though they were on dry
ground. But when the Egyptians followed, they were
all drowned.
30It was by faith that the people of Israel marched
around Jericho seven days, and the walls came crashing down.

## "Here's what I did..."

Money and material things used to be very important to me. I cared a lot about the clothes I wore. I liked it that my parents had a nice home and nice cars—and I wasn't very interested in people who didn't have nice clothes or nice things. I just didn't think I had much in common with people who didn't have as much money as I did.

Then I met Cathy. She attended my school, but I didn't know her because we hung around different groups. I got to know Cathy at a Christian camp. She and I were worlds apart in lots of ways. Her parents didn't have much money and she didn't care about fashion at all, but Cathy was the most caring person I had ever met. She knew how to listen, and that summer she turned out to be a good friend to me as I went through a rough time. Some other kids at the camp spread some untrue rumors about me, and it hurt me a lot. But Cathy was always there, to listen and encourage.

That fall when we returned to school, I began to see how shallow some of my other friendships were compared to what I'd experienced with Cathy. I began to do more things with her and her friends, and I found that I liked her friends, even though they weren't "cool." My old friends started making fun of me for hanging around Cathy, but that only showed me more that those people weren't true friends.

I asked Cathy once why she didn't seem to care about money. She said, "Sometimes I do care that I don't have nice clothes like you. But I found a Bible verse that says we're not to love money, but to be satisfied with what we have. I try to do that." She showed me the verse: Hebrews 13:5. What struck me was that she seemed to be more satisfied with what she had than I was, even though she owned much less. I knew she had something that I was just beginning to appreciate: the sense that God really was with her.

My attitude toward money and toward people started to change as I prayed that God would help me to be satisfied with what I had and not to care so much about externals. I saw that God—and true friends—look on the heart, not on whether you wear the latest fashions.

Katie
AGE 16

11:18 Gen 21:12.

31 It was by faith that Rahab the prostitute did not die with all the others in her city who refused to obey God. For she had given a friendly welcome to the spies.

32 Well, how much more do I need to say? It would take too long to recount the stories of the faith of Gideon, Barak, Samson, Jephthah, David, Samuel, and all the prophets. 33 By faith these people overthrew kingdoms, ruled with justice, and received what God had promised them. They shut the mouths of lions, 34 quenched the flames of fire, and escaped death by the edge of the sword. Their weakness was turned to strength. They became strong in battle and put whole armies to flight. 35 Women received their loved ones back again from death.

## REPUTATION

There's a time-out on the floor, and the varsity cheerleaders are building a pyramid at midcourt. Their complicated stunt, however, is not the most fascinating thing taking place in Butler Gymnasium.

Far more interesting are the thoughts that fill the minds of those in the student section. What if you could crawl through each set of watching eyes into each churning brain? What would you discover?

Well, you'd find that most of the students, when they glance at Tammy (the girl at the apex of the pyramid), are thinking words like *conceited, snotty, snob, fake,* and *back-stabber*. Her reputation is, frankly, not the best.

Meanwhile the girl doing the splits out in front of the others, Amy, is regarded by almost everyone in the stands as "sweet," "nice," "friendly," "fun-to-be-with," and "likable."

Three quick questions:

1. Why would you suppose there is such a sharp contrast in reputations?
2. Do you know any people like Tammy and Amy?
3. How do other people regard you?

Read Hebrews 13 for a fast lesson in reputation making.

But others trusted God and were tortured, preferring to die rather than turn from God and be free. They placed their hope in the resurrection to a better life. 36 Some were mocked, and their backs were cut open with whips. Others were chained in dungeons. 37 Some died by stoning, and some were sawed in half; others were killed with the sword. Some went about in skins of sheep and goats, hungry and oppressed and mistreated. 38 They were too good for this world. They wandered over deserts and mountains, hiding in caves and holes in the ground.

39 All of these people we have mentioned received God's approval because of their faith, yet none of them received all that God had promised. 40 For God had far better things in mind for us that would also benefit them, for they can't receive the prize at the end of the race until we finish the race.*

# CHAPTER 12

**LET GOD TRAIN YOU.** Therefore, since we are surrounded by such a huge crowd of witnesses to the life of faith, let us strip off every weight that slows us down, especially the sin that so easily hinders our progress. And let us run with endurance the race that God has set before us. 2 We do this by keeping our eyes on Jesus, on whom our faith depends from start to finish.* He was willing to die a shameful death on the cross because of the joy he knew would be his afterward. Now he is seated in the place of highest honor beside God's throne in heaven. 3 Think about all he endured when sinful people did such terrible things to him, so that you don't become weary and give up. 4 After all, you have not yet given your lives in your struggle against sin.

5 And have you entirely forgotten the encouraging words God spoke to you, his children? He said,

"My child, don't ignore it when the Lord
disciplines you,
and don't be discouraged when he corrects
you.
6 For the Lord disciplines those he loves,
and he punishes those he accepts as his
children."*

7 As you endure this divine discipline, remember that God is treating you as his own children. Whoever heard of a child who was never disciplined? 8 If God doesn't discipline you as he does all of his children, it means that you are illegitimate and are not really his children after all. 9 Since we respect our earthly fathers who disciplined us, should we not all the more cheerfully submit to the discipline of our heavenly Father and live forever*?

10 For our earthly fathers disciplined us for a few years, doing the best they knew how. But God's discipline is always right and good for us because it means we will share in his holiness. 11 No discipline is enjoyable while it is happening—it is painful! But afterward there will be a quiet harvest of right living for those who are trained in this way.

12 So take a new grip with your tired hands and stand firm on your shaky legs. 13 Mark out a straight path for your feet. Then those who follow you, though they are weak and lame, will not stumble and fall but will become strong.

## OUR COACH

12:12-13 **God is not only a disciplining parent, he is also a demanding coach who pushes us to our limit and requires of us a disciplined life. Although we may not feel strong enough to push on to victory, we will be able to continue as we follow Christ and draw upon his strength. Then we can use our growing strength to help those around us who are weak and struggling.**

11:40 Greek *for us, for they apart from us can't finish.* 12:2 Or *Jesus, the Originator and Perfecter of our faith.* 12:5-6 Prov 3:11-12. 12:9 Or *really live.*

14 Try to live in peace with everyone, and seek to live a clean and holy life, for those who are not holy will not see the Lord. 15 Look after each other so that none of you will miss out on the special favor of God. Watch out that no bitter root of unbelief rises up among you, for whenever it springs up, many are corrupted by its poison. 16 Make sure that no one is immoral or godless like Esau. He traded his birthright as the oldest son for a single meal. 17 And afterward, when he wanted his father's blessing, he was rejected. It was too late for repentance, even though he wept bitter tears.

18 You have not come to a physical mountain, to a place of flaming fire, darkness, gloom, and whirlwind, as the Israelites did at Mount Sinai when God gave them his laws. 19 For they heard an awesome trumpet blast and a voice with a message so terrible that they begged God to stop speaking. 20 They staggered back under God's command: "If even an animal touches the mountain, it must be stoned to death."* 21 Moses himself was so frightened at the sight that he said, "I am terrified and trembling."*

22 No, you have come to Mount Zion, to the city of the living God, the heavenly Jerusalem, and to thousands of angels in joyful assembly. 23 You have come to the assembly of God's firstborn children, whose names are written in heaven. You have come to God himself, who is the judge of all people. And you have come to the spirits of the redeemed in heaven who have now been made perfect. 24 You have come to Jesus, the one who mediates the new covenant between God and people, and to the sprinkled blood, which graciously forgives instead of crying out for vengeance as the blood of Abel did.

25 See to it that you obey God, the one who is speaking to you. For if the people of Israel did not escape when they refused to listen to Moses, the earthly messenger, how terrible our danger if we reject the One who speaks to us from heaven! 26 When God spoke from Mount Sinai his voice shook the earth, but now he makes another promise: "Once again I will shake not only the earth but the heavens also."* 27 This means that the things on earth will be shaken, so that only eternal things will be left.

28 Since we are receiving a kingdom that cannot be destroyed, let us be thankful and please God by worshiping him with holy fear and awe. 29 For our God is a consuming fire.

## CHAPTER 13 LIVE GOOD AND OBEDIENT LIVES.

Continue to love each other with true Christian love.* 2 Don't forget to show hospitality to strangers, for some who have done this have entertained angels without realizing it! 3 Don't forget about those in prison. Suffer with them as though you were there yourself. Share the sorrow of those being mistreated, as though you feel their pain in your own bodies.

**UNCHANGING ● ● • • •**

13:1-21 **We must keep our eyes on Christ, our ultimate leader, who, unlike human leaders, will never change. He has been and will be the same forever. In a changing world we can trust our unchanging Lord.**

4 Give honor to marriage, and remain faithful to one another in marriage. God will surely judge people who are immoral and those who commit adultery.

5 Stay away from the love of money; be satisfied with what you have. For God has said,

"I will never fail you.
I will never forsake you."*

6 That is why we can say with confidence,

"The Lord is my helper,
so I will not be afraid.
What can mere mortals do to me?"*

7 Remember your leaders who first taught you the word of God. Think of all the good that has come from their lives, and trust the Lord as they do.

8 Jesus Christ is the same yesterday, today, and forever. 9 So do not be attracted by strange, new ideas. Your spiritual strength comes from God's special favor, not from ceremonial rules about food, which don't help those who follow them.

10 We have an altar from which the priests in the Temple on earth have no right to eat. 11 Under the system of Jewish laws, the high priest brought the blood of animals into the Holy Place as a sacrifice for sin, but the bodies of the animals were burned outside the camp. 12 So also Jesus suffered and died outside the city gates in order to make his people holy by shedding his own blood. 13 So let us go out to him outside the camp and bear the disgrace he bore. 14 For this world is not our home; we are looking forward to our city in heaven, which is yet to come.

15 With Jesus' help, let us continually offer our sacrifice of praise to God by proclaiming the glory of his name. 16 Don't forget to do good and to share what you have with those in need, for such sacrifices are very pleasing to God.

17 Obey your spiritual leaders and do what they say. Their work is to watch over your souls, and they know they are accountable to God. Give them reason to do this joyfully and not with sorrow. That would certainly not be for your benefit.

18 Pray for us, for our conscience is clear and we want to live honorably in everything we do. 19 I especially need your prayers right now so that I can come back to you soon.

20-21 And now, may the God of peace, who brought again from the dead our Lord Jesus, equip you with all you need for doing his will. May he

12:20 Exod 19:13. 12:21 Deut 9:19. 12:26 Hag 2:6. 13:1 Greek *with brotherly love.* 13:5 Deut 31:6, 8. 13:6 Ps 118:6.

## MATURITY ● ● ● • • •

13:24-25 **Hebrews is a call to Christian maturity. This book was addressed to first-century Jewish Christians, but it applies to Christians of any age or background. Christian maturity means making Christ the beginning and end of our faith. To mature, we must center our life on him, not depending on religious ritual, not falling back into sin, not trusting in ourselves, and not letting anything come between us and Christ.**

produce in you, through the power of Jesus Christ, all that is pleasing to him. Jesus is the great Shepherd of the sheep by an everlasting covenant, signed with his blood. To him be glory forever and ever. Amen.

[22]I urge you, dear brothers and sisters,* please listen carefully to what I have said in this brief letter.

[23]I want you to know that our brother Timothy is now out of jail. If he comes here soon, I will bring him with me to see you.

[24]Give my greetings to all your leaders and to the other believers there. The Christians from Italy send you their greetings.

[25]May God's grace be with you all.

13:22 Greek *brothers.*

# MEGA themes

**CHRIST IS SUPERIOR** Hebrews reveals Jesus' true identity as God. Christ is the ultimate authority. He is greater than any religion or any angel, and superior to any Jewish leader (such as Abraham, Moses, or Joshua) or priest. Christ is the complete revelation of God.

Jesus alone can forgive your sin. He has secured your forgiveness and salvation by his death on the cross. With Christ you can find peace with God and real meaning for life. Without him, there is no hope for true life.

1. What was unique about Jesus Christ?
2. Why did the first-century Jews have difficulty accepting these truths about Jesus?
3. How do the majority of people in your school feel about being a Christian? What are their misconceptions about Jesus?
4. If you could explain one thing about Christ to those who do not understand him, what would you tell them?

**HIGH PRIEST** In the Old Testament, the high priest represented the Jews before God. Jesus Christ links us with God. There is no other way to reach God. Because Jesus Christ lived a sinless life, he is the perfect substitute to die for our sin. Christ is our perfect representative with God.

Jesus guarantees our access to God the Father. He intercedes for us so that we can boldly come to the Father with our needs. When we are weak we can come confidently to God for forgiveness and help. He never shuts us out or refuses to respond to our needs.

1. In Hebrews, what do you learn about the role of a high priest?
2. Based on 4:14-16 and 7:19-28, what are the ways that Jesus is the perfect High Priest?
3. What benefits do you have because Jesus is your High Priest?
4. What hurts, needs, or wants do you want to bring to God, your Father? How does Jesus, your High Priest, provide the way for you to present these to God? Express your needs to God and share with him your feelings about the perfect High Priest he has provided in Jesus.

**SACRIFICE** Christ's sacrifice was the ultimate fulfillment of all that the Old Testament sacrifices represented—God's forgiveness for sin. Because Christ was the perfect sacrifice, our sins have been completely forgiven—past, present, and future.

Christ removed sin that kept us from God's presence and fellowship. But we must accept Christ's sacrifice for us. By believing in him we are declared "not guilty," cleansed, and made whole. Christ's sacrifice provided the way for us to have eternal life.

1. What qualified Jesus to be the perfect, once-and-for-all fulfillment of the Old Testament sacrificial requirements?
2. What blessings do you have as a result of Jesus' sacrifice?
3. Contrast the difference for those who reject Christ's sacrifice and those who accept it (check 10:26-39).
4. What have you personally received from the one who sacrificed himself for your sins? What difference has Jesus' sacrifice made in your life?

**FAITH** Faith is confident trust in God. God's salvation is in his Son, Jesus, who is the only one who can save us from sin.

If you trust in Jesus Christ for your salvation, he will transform you completely. Then you should live a life of faith.

1. Rewrite 11:3 in your own words.
2. Explain what you think is meant by this statement: "Faith is not just knowing, it is doing."
3. Read chapter 11. What do you learn about the life of faith from the great men and women listed there?
4. If someone were to write a couple of verses describing your life of faith, what would they include?
5. In what ways would you like to see your faith grow? How do you develop this growth in faith?

**MATURITY THROUGH ENDURANCE** Faith enables Christians to face trials. Genuine faith includes the commitment to stay true to God when we are under fire. Endurance builds character and leads to victory.

You can have victory in your trials if you don't give up or turn your back on Christ. Stay true to Christ and pray for endurance. He will never grow tired of supporting you.

1. Hebrews 12 describes what it means to grow through endurance and discipline. Why is discipline necessary for growth?
2. Based on 12:1-5, what are the keys to endurance? How can you apply these principles to where you are in "the race" at this point in your life?
3. What are the main points of Hebrews' teaching concerning God's discipline?
4. If someone were to ask you, "Why should I take obedience to God so seriously?" how would you respond?

**Y**ou've been feeling strange all week. At first you had trouble sleeping. Then came the headaches. Yesterday your teeth began hurting and your fingernails turned blue for several hours. This morning you realized it was time to consult your family doctor when, after a morning jog, your mom asked if you'd been sprayed by a skunk. ■The doctor tries to hold her breath as she asks you questions. She nods knowingly as you tick off your symptoms. After looking in your eyes and noting your swollen eardrums, she orders some lab work. ■A few hours later she returns to tell you, "Just what I suspected—you have an extremely high number of antibiomolecularsucrothyamin microbes in your liver." ■"Huh?" you gulp. ■"Oh, don't worry. You have a common ailment we call odoramonia. We'll put you on an antibiotic and get you eating a balanced diet, and you'll be fine." ■Aren't doctors amazing? By examining us and noting our symptoms, they're usually able to diagnose our physical ailments and prescribe the proper treatment. ■God does the same thing in our spiritual realm. ■By looking at our actions (or lack of action) God can tell us exactly what attitudes and desires need healing. His Word gives detailed prescriptions for curing wrong behavior patterns. ■Is your spiritual life on the sick side? Are you fighting worldly infections or possibly even the disease of disobedience? ■Follow the advice of the Great Physician. No matter what your ailment, the Epistle of James has the cure.

## STATS

PURPOSE: To expose unethical practices and to teach right Christian behavior

AUTHOR: James, Jesus' brother, a leader in the Jerusalem church

TO WHOM WRITTEN: First-century Jewish Christians residing in Gentile communities outside Palestine; all Christians everywhere

DATE WRITTEN: Probably A.D. 49, prior to the Jerusalem council held in A.D. 50

SETTING: This letter expresses James's concern for persecuted Christians who were once part of the Jerusalem church

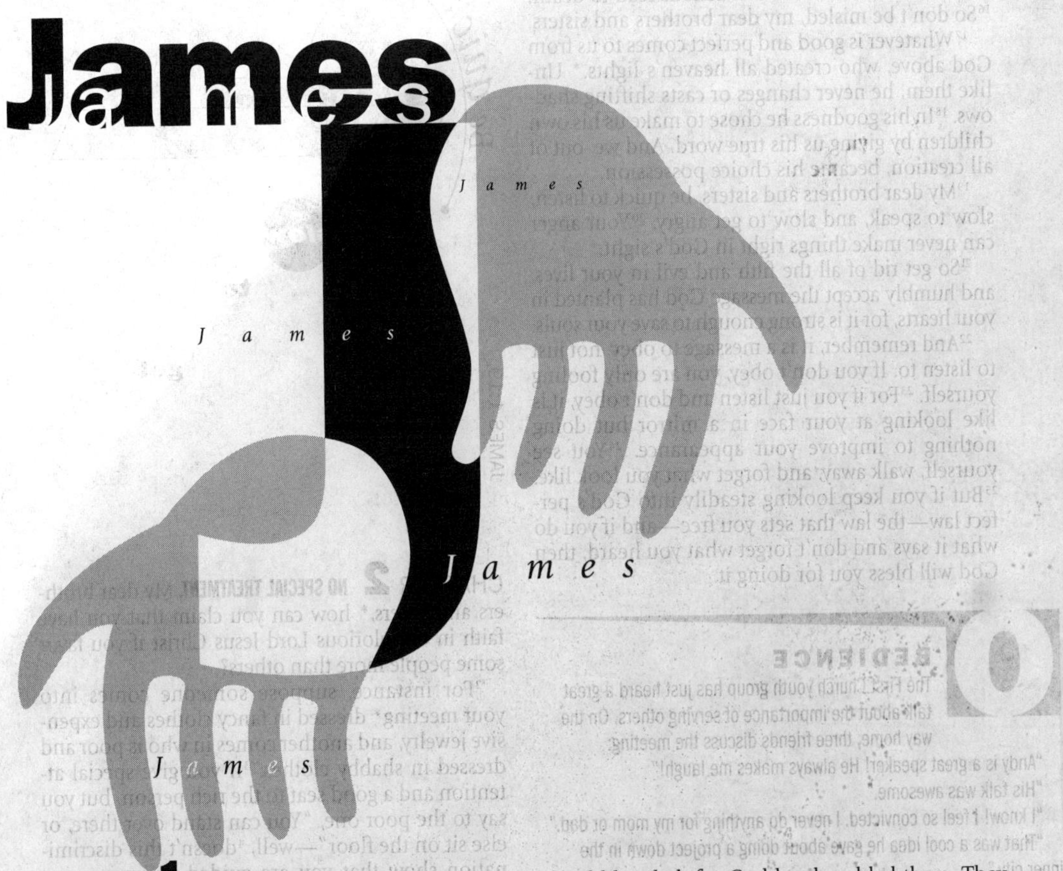


CHAPTER **1** **JAMES: A SERVANT OF GOD.** This letter is
from James, a slave of God and of the Lord Jesus
Christ.

It is written to Jewish Christians scattered among
the nations.*

Greetings!

2 Dear brothers and sisters,* whenever trouble
comes your way, let it be an opportunity for joy. 3 For
when your faith is tested, your endurance has a
chance to grow. 4 So let it grow, for when your endurance is fully developed, you will be strong in character and ready for anything.

5 If you need wisdom—if you want to know what
God wants you to do—ask him, and he will gladly
tell you. He will not resent your asking. 6 But when
you ask him, be sure that you really expect him to
answer, for a doubtful mind is as unsettled as a
wave of the sea that is driven and tossed by the
wind. 7 People like that should not expect to receive
anything from the Lord. 8 They can't make up their
minds. They waver back and forth in everything
they do.

9 Christians who are* poor should be glad, for
God has honored them. 10 And those who are rich
should be glad, for God has humbled them. They
will fade away like a flower in the field. 11 The hot
sun rises and dries up the grass; the flower withers, and its beauty fades away. So also, wealthy
people will fade away with all of their achievements.

12 God blesses the people who patiently endure
testing. Afterward they will receive the crown of life
that God has promised to those who love him.
13 And remember, no one who wants to do wrong
should ever say, "God is tempting me." God is
never tempted to do wrong, and he never tempts
anyone else either. 14 Temptation comes from the
lure of our own evil desires. 15 These evil desires

**SNOWBALL ● ● • • •**

**1:12-15 Temptation comes from evil desires inside us, not from God. It begins with an evil thought and becomes sin when we dwell on the thought and allow it to become an action. Like a snowball rolling downhill, sin's destruction grows the more we let sin have its way. The best time to stop a snowball is at the top of the hill, before it is too big or moving too fast to control. See Matthew 4:1-11; 1 Corinthians 10:13; and 2 Timothy 2:22 for more about escaping temptation.**

1:1 Greek *To the twelve tribes in the dispersion.* 1:2 Greek *brothers;* also in 1:16, 19. 1:9 Greek *The brother who is.*

lead to evil actions, and evil actions lead to death.
16So don't be misled, my dear brothers and sisters.
17Whatever is good and perfect comes to us from
God above, who created all heaven's lights.* Unlike them, he never changes or casts shifting shadows. 18In his goodness he chose to make us his own
children by giving us his true word. And we, out of
all creation, became his choice possession.
19My dear brothers and sisters, be quick to listen,
slow to speak, and slow to get angry. 20Your anger
can never make things right in God's sight.
21So get rid of all the filth and evil in your lives,
and humbly accept the message God has planted in
your hearts, for it is strong enough to save your souls.
22And remember, it is a message to obey, not just
to listen to. If you don't obey, you are only fooling
yourself. 23For if you just listen and don't obey, it is
like looking at your face in a mirror but doing
nothing to improve your appearance. 24You see
yourself, walk away, and forget what you look like.
25But if you keep looking steadily into God's perfect law—the law that sets you free—and if you do
what it says and don't forget what you heard, then
God will bless you for doing it.

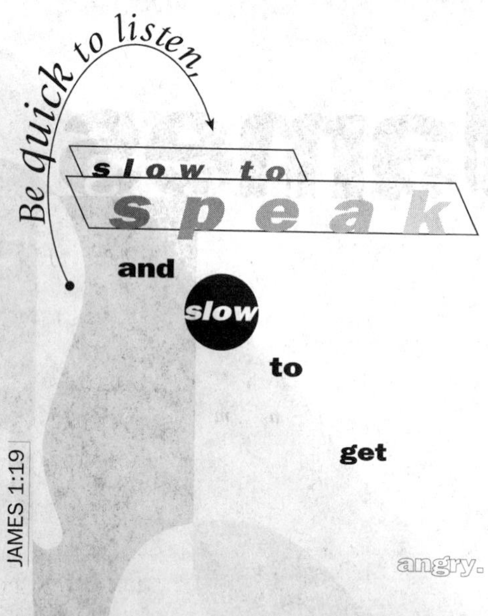

Be quick to listen,
slow to
speak
and
slow
to
get
angry.
JAMES 1:19

## OBEDIENCE

The First Church youth group has just heard a great talk about the importance of serving others. On the way home, three friends discuss the meeting:

"Andy is a great speaker! He always makes me laugh!"

"His talk was awesome."

"I know! I feel so convicted. I never do anything for my mom or dad."

"That was a cool idea he gave about doing a project down in the inner city."

"Yeah, wouldn't that be great? We should do that sometime."

Now, let's listen in on the conversation a few minutes later:

"So, what are you guys going to do this weekend?"

"Probably the same old stuff–go to a movie, sit around and be bored."

"That drives me nuts! How come there is nothing for kids our age to do? If I have to go to the mall one more time, I'm going to puke!"

"I agree!"

What's wrong with that conversation? Anything? Read over it again.

Less than 30 minutes after being challenged to serve others, these teens are complaining they don't have anything to do.

The point? Christians should never be bored! We always have opportunities to serve others. In fact, if we're not putting our faith into practice on a regular basis, the Bible says our religion isn't worth very much. See James 1:21-27.

26If you claim to be religious but don't control
your tongue, you are just fooling yourself, and your
religion is worthless. 27Pure and lasting religion in
the sight of God our Father means that we must care
for orphans and widows in their troubles, and refuse
to let the world corrupt us.

CHAPTER **2** **NO SPECIAL TREATMENT.** My dear brothers and sisters,* how can you claim that you have
faith in our glorious Lord Jesus Christ if you favor
some people more than others?
2For instance, suppose someone comes into
your meeting* dressed in fancy clothes and expensive jewelry, and another comes in who is poor and
dressed in shabby clothes. 3If you give special attention and a good seat to the rich person, but you
say to the poor one, "You can stand over there, or
else sit on the floor"—well, 4doesn't this discrimination show that you are guided by wrong motives?
5Listen to me, dear brothers and sisters. Hasn't
God chosen the poor in this world to be rich in faith?
Aren't they the ones who will inherit the kingdom
God promised to those who love him? 6And yet, you
insult the poor man! Isn't it the rich who oppress
you and drag you into court? 7Aren't they the ones
who slander Jesus Christ, whose noble name you
bear?
8Yes indeed, it is good when you truly obey our
Lord's royal command found in the Scriptures:
"Love your neighbor as yourself."* 9But if you pay
special attention to the rich, you are committing a
sin, for you are guilty of breaking that law.
10And the person who keeps all of the laws ex-

## SAY WHAT? ● ● ● • ·

3:2-3 **What you say and what you *don't* say are both important. Proper speech is not only saying the right words at the right time, but also controlling your desire to say what you shouldn't. Examples of wrongly using the tongue include gossiping, putting others down, bragging, manipulating, false teaching, exaggerating, complaining, flattering, and lying. Before you speak, ask, "Is it true, is it necessary, and is it kind?"**

1:17 Greek *from above, from the Father of lights.* 2:1 Greek *brothers;* also in 2:5, 14. 2:2 Greek *synagogue.* 2:8 Lev 19:18.

cept one is as guilty as the person who has broken
all of God's laws. [11]For the same God who said,
"Do not commit adultery," also said, "Do not
murder."* So if you murder someone, you have
broken the entire law, even if you do not commit
adultery.

[12]So whenever you speak, or whatever you do,
remember that you will be judged by the law of
love, the law that set you free. [13]For there will be no
mercy for you if you have not been merciful to
others. But if you have been merciful, then God's
mercy toward you will win out over his judgment
against you.

[14]Dear brothers and sisters, what's the use of saying you have faith if you don't prove it by your
actions? That kind of faith can't save anyone. [15]Sup-
pose you see a brother or sister who needs food or
clothing, [16]and you say, "Well, good-bye and God
bless you; stay warm and eat well"—but then you
don't give that person any food or clothing. What
good does that do?

[17]So you see, it isn't enough just to have faith.
Faith that doesn't show itself by good deeds is no
faith at all—it is dead and useless.

[18]Now someone may argue, "Some people have
faith; others have good deeds." I say, "I can't see your
faith if you don't have good deeds,
but I will show you my faith
through my good deeds."

[19]Do you still think it's enough
just to believe that there is one
God? Well, even the demons believe this, and they tremble in terror! [20]Fool! When will you ever
learn that faith that does not result
in good deeds is useless?

[21]Don't you remember that our
ancestor Abraham was declared
right with God because of what he
did when he offered his son Isaac
on the altar? [22]You see, he was
trusting God so much that he was
willing to do whatever God told
him to do. His faith was made
complete by what he did—by his
actions. [23]And so it happened just
as the Scriptures say: "Abraham believed God, so God declared him
to be righteous."* He was even
called "the friend of God."* [24]So
you see, we are made right with
God by what we do, not by faith
alone.

[25]Rahab the prostitute is another example of this. She was
made right with God by her actions—when she hid those messengers and sent them safely away
by a different road. [26]Just as the
body is dead without a spirit, so also faith is dead
without good deeds.

CHAPTER **3** **CONTROL WHAT YOU SAY.** Dear brothers
and sisters,* not many of you should become teachers in the church, for we who teach will be judged by
God with greater strictness.

[2]We all make many mistakes, but those who control their tongues can also control themselves in
every other way. [3]We can make a large horse turn
around and go wherever we want by means of a
small bit in its mouth. [4]And a tiny rudder makes a
huge ship turn wherever the pilot wants it to go, even
though the winds are strong. [5]So also, the tongue is
a small thing, but what enormous damage it can do.
A tiny spark can set a great forest on fire. [6]And the
tongue is a flame of fire. It is full of wickedness that
can ruin your whole life. It can turn the entire course
of your life into a blazing flame of destruction, for it
is set on fire by hell itself.

[7]People can tame all kinds of animals and birds
and reptiles and fish, [8]but no one can tame the
tongue. It is an uncontrollable evil, full of deadly
poison. [9]Sometimes it praises our Lord and Father,
and sometimes it breaks out into curses against
those who have been made in the image of God.

## "Here's what I did..."

I went to a special school where several classes were held in a zoo two days a week. Because of this, I didn't always feel a part of the high school student body. Even worse, I didn't know any other Christians at the high school or in my classes at the zoo. Then I started studying the book of James. My Bible notes said that the book was written to Christians who were scattered everywhere. That's how I felt: scattered among a couple thousand students who didn't know or care about God.

One day I was working with a friend on an assignment at the zoo. As he and I talked about life, I found out he was a Christian. But he said his faith was weak. He was going through all these trials—his mom was sick, he was feeling pressured about taking the SAT and choosing a school, and other things were going wrong in his life.

I had a Bible in my book bag, so I opened it to James 1 and showed him the verses I had been studying. The look on his face when he finished reading it clearly said, "Wow, this fits!" Later he thanked me and told me that the Scripture I'd shared had helped him a lot.

I knew what he meant. James 1 always encourages me, too. But it encouraged me even more to be able to share it with him, and to see God speaking so clearly to him through his Word. Plus, I now had a Christian friend at school!

Shea

AGE 15

2:11 Exod 20:13-14; Deut 5:17-18. 2:23a Gen 15:6. 2:23b See Isa 41:8. 3:1 Greek *brothers;* also in 3:10.

**BUILD UP ● ● • • •**

4:11-12 **Jesus summarized the law as loving God and your neighbor (Matthew 22:37-40), and Paul said that love demonstrated toward a neighbor fully satisfies the law (Romans 13:6-10). When we fail to love, we break God's law. Examine your attitude and actions. Do you build people up or tear them down? Instead of criticizing someone, remember God's law of love and say something good instead. If you make this a habit, your tendency to find fault with others will decrease and your ability to obey God will increase.**

10 And so blessing and cursing come pouring out of
the same mouth. Surely, my brothers and sisters,
this is not right! 11 Does a spring of water bubble
out with both fresh water and bitter water? 12 Can
you pick olives from a fig tree or figs from a grapevine? No, and you can't draw fresh water from a
salty pool.

13 If you are wise and understand God's ways, live
a life of steady goodness so that only good deeds
will pour forth. And if you don't brag about the
good you do, then you will be truly wise! 14 But if
you are bitterly jealous and there is selfish ambition in your hearts, don't brag about being wise.
That is the worst kind of lie. 15 For jealousy and
selfishness are not God's kind of wisdom. Such
things are earthly, unspiritual, and motivated by
the Devil. 16 For wherever there is jealousy and selfish ambition, there you will find disorder and
every kind of evil.

17 But the wisdom that comes from heaven is first
of all pure. It is also peace loving, gentle at all
times, and willing to yield to others. It is full of
mercy and good deeds. It shows no partiality and
is always sincere. 18 And those who are peacemakers
will plant seeds of peace and reap a harvest of
goodness.

**REARRANGED ● ● • • •**

4:13-16 **It is good to have goals, but goals can disappoint us if we leave God out of them. There is no point in making plans as though God does not exist because the future is in his hands. What would you like to be doing ten years from now? One year from now? Tomorrow? How will you react if God steps in and rearranges your plans? Plan ahead, but hang on to your plans lightly. If you put God's desires at the center of your planning, you will not be disappointed.**

CHAPTER **4** **HOW CAN YOU GET CLOSE TO GOD?** What is
causing the quarrels and fights among you? Isn't it
the whole army of evil desires at war within you?
2 You want what you don't have, so you scheme and
kill to get it. You are jealous for what others have, and
you can't possess it, so you fight and quarrel to take
it away from them. And yet the reason you don't
have what you want is that you don't ask God for it.
3 And even when you do ask, you don't get it because
your whole motive is wrong—you want only what
will give you pleasure.

4 You adulterers! Don't you realize that friendship
with this world makes you an enemy of God? I say it
again, that if your aim is to enjoy this world, you can't
be a friend of God. 5 What do you think the Scriptures
mean when they say that the Holy Spirit, whom God
has placed within us, jealously longs for us to be
faithful*? 6 He gives us more and more strength to
stand against such evil desires. As the Scriptures say,

"God sets himself against the proud,
but he shows favor to the humble."*

7 So humble yourselves before God. Resist the
Devil, and he will flee from you. 8 Draw close to God,
and God will draw close to you. Wash your hands,
you sinners; purify your hearts, you hypocrites. 9 Let
there be tears for the wrong things you have done.
Let there be sorrow and deep grief. Let there be
sadness instead of laughter, and gloom instead of
joy. 10 When you bow down before the Lord and
admit your dependence on him, he will lift you up
and give you honor.

**TODAY! ● ● • • •**

4:14 **Life is short no matter how long we live. Don't be deceived into thinking that you have lots of time to live for Christ, to enjoy your loved ones, or to do what you know you should. Live for God today! Then, no matter when your life ends, you will have fulfilled God's plan for you.**

11 Don't speak evil against each other, my dear
brothers and sisters.* If you criticize each other and
condemn each other, then you are criticizing and
condemning God's law. But you are not a judge who
can decide whether the law is right or wrong. Your
job is to obey it. 12 God alone, who made the law, can
rightly judge among us. He alone has the power to
save or to destroy. So what right do you have to
condemn your neighbor?

13 Look here, you people who say, "Today or tomorrow we are going to a certain town and will stay
there a year. We will do business there and make a
profit." 14 How do you know what will happen tomorrow? For your life is like the morning fog—it's
here a little while, then it's gone. 15 What you ought
to say is, "If the Lord wants us to, we will live and do
this or that." 16 Otherwise you will be boasting about
your own plans, and all such boasting is evil.

17 Remember, it is sin to know what you ought to
do and then not do it.

**GREAT RESULTS ● ● • • •**

5:16-18 **The Christian's most powerful resource is communion with God through prayer. The results are often greater than we thought were possible. Some people see prayer as a last resort to be tried when all else fails. This is backward. Prayer should come first. Because God's power is infinitely greater than our own, it only makes sense to rely on it—especially because God encourages us to do so.**

4:5 Or *the spirit that God placed within us tends to envy,* or *the Holy Spirit, whom God has placed within us, opposes our envy.* 4:6 Prov 3:34. 4:11 Greek *brothers.*

CHAPTER **5** **A WARNING TO THE RICH.** Look here,
you rich people, weep and groan with anguish
because of all the terrible troubles ahead of you.
[2]Your wealth is rotting away, and your fine clothes
are moth-eaten rags. [3]Your gold and silver have
become worthless. The very wealth you were
counting on will eat away your flesh in hell.* This
treasure you have accumulated will stand as evidence against you on the day of judgment. [4]For
listen! Hear the cries of the field workers whom
you have cheated of their pay. The wages you held
back cry out against you. The cries of the reapers
have reached the ears of the Lord Almighty.

[5]You have spent your years on earth in luxury,
satisfying your every whim. Now your hearts are nice
and fat, ready for the slaughter. [6]You have condemned and killed good people who had no power
to defend themselves against you.

[7]Dear brothers and sisters,* you must be patient
as you wait for the Lord's return. Consider the farmers who eagerly look for the rains in the fall and in
the spring. They patiently wait for the precious harvest to ripen. [8]You, too, must be patient. And take
courage, for the coming of the Lord is near.

[9]Don't grumble about each other, my brothers
and sisters, or God will judge you. For look! The
great Judge is coming. He is standing at the door!

[10]For examples of patience in suffering, dear
brothers and sisters, look at the prophets who spoke
in the name of the Lord. [11]We give great honor to
those who endure under suffering. Job is an example
of a man who endured patiently. From his experience we see how the Lord's plan finally ended in
good, for he is full of tenderness and mercy.

[12]But most of all, my brothers and sisters, never
take an oath, by heaven or earth or anything else. Just
say a simple yes or no, so that you will not sin and
be condemned for it.

[13]Are any among you suffering? They should keep
on praying about it. And those who have reason to
be thankful should continually sing praises to the
Lord.

[14]Are any among you sick? They should call
for the elders of the church and have them pray
over them, anointing them with oil in the name of
the Lord. [15]And their prayer offered in faith will
heal the sick, and the Lord will make them well.
And anyone who has committed sins will be forgiven.

[16]Confess your sins to each other and pray for
each other so that you may be healed. The earnest
prayer of a righteous person has great power and
wonderful results. [17]Elijah was as human as we are,
and yet when he prayed earnestly that no rain
would fall, none fell for the next three and a half
years! [18]Then he prayed for rain, and down it
poured. The grass turned green, and the crops began to grow again.

[19]My dear brothers and sisters, if anyone among
you wanders away from the truth and is brought
back again, [20]you can be sure that the one who brings
that person back will save that sinner from death and
bring about the forgiveness of many sins.

5:3 Or *will eat your flesh like fire.* 5:7 Greek *brothers;* also in 5:9, 10, 12, 19.

---

**I feel guilty more often now that I'm a Christian. Sometimes the guilt comes on for just little stuff that I used to never give a second thought about. When do I need to ask God for forgiveness?**

God's goal is not to overwhelm us with our sin so that we become discouraged. He knows when to point out sin in our life.

Some people are basically pretty "good" people when they come to faith in Christ. They don't have many destructive habits to overcome, and their parents have tried to teach them right from wrong. Others come with a lot of sin "baggage."

Although each person is unique, we're the same when it comes to our nature—we're sinners. In fact, we were born with a sinful nature. This is called "original sin." And throughout our life, we do all sorts of things that are wrong.

When we accept Christ as Savior, God declares us "not guilty." But this doesn't mean that we're perfect and don't sin anymore. We must daily deal with sin while we're still alive on earth. It's part of being human. Christians, like everyone, have two types of sin to deal with. Past sins and present sins.

As I said, when we become Christians, all of our past sins are wiped away. "He has removed our rebellious acts as far away from us as the east is from the west" (Psalm 103:12). That's a distance that can't be measured!

Ideally, having past sins removed should also take away our guilt feelings. We can put the past behind us. We're forgiven!

But what about present sin? One of the roles of the Holy Spirit is to remind us when we sin. He doesn't do this to condemn us, but to prompt us to confess it, forsake it, and move on. God has forgiven us for these present sins, too. We confess them to him to keep the communication channels open and to keep the relationship close. So we should talk to God about our life, and confess, whenever we need to. And remember, sins aren't limited to doing what is wrong. They also include not doing what is right.

The passage in James 4:17 is plain. "It is sin to know what you ought to do and then not do it."

If we know we should help someone stop gossiping; give our parents the whole truth, instead of only part of it; turn off the TV and spend time with God . . . and don't do it—we sin!

Let God, not others, do the convicting in your life and you'll be glad to confess your sins to him. He's eager to clear away the barriers between you and himself and start fresh.

# MEGA themes

**LIVING FAITH** James wants believers to hear the truth *and* to do it. He contrasts empty faith ("claims without conduct") with faith that works. Commitment to love and to serve is evidence of true faith.

Living faith makes a difference. Make sure your faith results in action. Be alert to ways of putting your faith to work. Be certain that you not only "talk" the gospel, but that you "walk" the gospel as well.

1. Contrast "living faith" with "dead faith."
2. What would it mean to have a dead faith in your school? What would it mean to have a living faith in your school?
3. How are your vital signs? Identify evidence of life in your faith.
4. In what ways can you become more alive as a doer of God's Word in your school? With your friends? In your relationships at church? In response to the needy in your community?

**TRIALS** In the Christian life there are trials and temptations. Successfully overcoming these adversities produces maturity and strong character.

Don't resent troubles when they come. Pray for wisdom; God will supply all you need to face persecution or adversity. He will give you patience and keep you strong.

1. What attitude does James teach you to have concerning trials?
2. What trials and problems have you recently experienced?
3. How did you feel when you were facing these trials and problems? How did you feel toward God?
4. Describe how you can choose to respond with an appropriate attitude the next time you face a trial or problem. Why is developing such responses important for a Christian? (Check the results of enduring trials in chapter 1.)

**LAW OF LOVE** We are saved by God's gracious mercy, not by keeping the law. But Christ gave us a special command, "Love your neighbor as yourself" (Matthew 19:19). We are to love and serve those around us.

Keeping the law of love shows that our faith is vital and real. To show love to others, we must root out our own selfishness. This begins by acting on what we know to be true about God's will in our life.

1. What does James teach in chapter 2 about the life of faith?
2. What would happen if every Christian in your community lived with the attitude and actions described in 2:2-16?
3. Why are the acts of giving to those in need and not showing favoritism important expressions of living faith?
4. What does it mean in your life (home, school, church) not to show favoritism? Who are the needy who can benefit from your resources (time, love, food, money, work)?

**WISE SPEECH** Wisdom shows itself in speech. We are responsible for the destructive results of our talk. The wisdom of God that helps control the tongue can help control all our actions.

Accepting God's wisdom will affect your speech because your words will reveal their godly source. Think of God and others before you speak, and allow God to strengthen your self-control.

1. Why does James devote so much of this book to the issue of controlling the tongue?
2. When did someone's words hurt you or a person you really care about? How did you feel? What were the results?
3. When did your words hurt another person? How did you feel? What were the results?
4. Taking the principles from James, what could have been done differently in those situations that would have led to positive communication?

**WEALTH** James teaches Christians not to compromise with worldly attitudes about wealth. Because the glory of wealth fades, Christians should store up God's treasures through sincere service. Christians must not show partiality to the wealthy or be prejudiced against the poor.

We all are accountable for how we use what we have. We should be generous toward others. We are to see one another as God sees us—created as equals in his image.

1. What does James think about rich people? What is it about these wealthy men in chapter 5 that causes James to react so strongly?
2. After studying James 2 and 5, what should be the Christian lifestyle of a person who is blessed with great wealth?
3. How can you make your possessions a part of your life of faith? Why is it important that you not separate what you have from your responsibility to God?

**E**ach year a few individuals compete in what may be the most grueling athletic competition of all: a bicycle race across the U.S. Consider the obstacles: blazing deserts, towering mountain ranges, inclement weather, 18- to 20-hour stretches of pedaling, flat tires, potholes, skin-scraping spills, inconsiderate motorists, and sheer fatigue. It's *amazing* anyone ever finishes. The fact that some complete the 2,000-plus mile trip in *just over a week* is downright unbelievable! ■ How do they do it? ■ With the help of carefully trained support teams. These support teams follow the cyclists in specially equipped recreational vehicles, providing whatever the rider needs—food, drink, a repair job, a replacement bike, medical attention, a rubdown, a short nap, coaching, or a few shouts of encouragement. These support teams make an otherwise impossible trip very possible. ■ The Christian life is similar to that grueling bicycle marathon. The occasional joys of gliding downhill are obscured by the more frequent times of having to churn our way up steep mountain peaks. We get weary. We feel like quitting. The finish line seems far, far away. ■ Fortunately God has given us a first-rate support team to help us go the distance. With the Holy Spirit, the Word of God, and other believers to encourage us, we can not only finish the race, we can *win!* ■ Find out more about your spiritual support team in the book that follows, the book called 1 Peter. ■ (But don't wait too long. The race has already started!)

## STATS

PURPOSE: To offer encouragement to suffering Christians

AUTHOR: Peter

TO WHOM WRITTEN: Jewish Christians who had been driven out of Jerusalem and scattered throughout Asia Minor; all believers everywhere

DATE WRITTEN: About A.D. 62 to 64 from Rome

SETTING: Peter was probably in Rome when the great persecution under Emperor Nero began (Peter was eventually executed during the persecution). Throughout the Roman Empire, Christians were being tortured and killed for their faith, and the church in Jerusalem was being scattered throughout the Mediterranean world.

KEY PEOPLE: Peter, Silas (Silvanus), Mark

KEY PLACES: Jerusalem, Rome, and the regions of Pontus, Galatia, Cappadocia, Asia Minor, and Bithynia

CHAPTER **1** **GREETINGS FROM PETER.** This letter is from Peter, an apostle of Jesus Christ.

I am writing to God's chosen people who are living as foreigners in the lands of Pontus, Galatia, Cappadocia, the province of Asia, and Bithynia. [2]God the Father chose you long ago, and the Spirit has made you holy. As a result, you have obeyed Jesus Christ and are cleansed by his blood.

May you have more and more of God's special favor and wonderful peace.

[3]All honor to the God and Father of our Lord Jesus Christ, for it is by his boundless mercy that God has given us the privilege of being born again. Now we live with a wonderful expectation because Jesus Christ rose again from the dead. [4]For God has reserved a priceless inheritance for his children. It is kept in heaven for you, pure and undefiled, beyond the reach of change and decay. [5]And God, in his mighty power, will protect you until you receive this salvation, because you are trusting him. It will be revealed on the last day for all to see. [6]So be truly glad!* There is wonderful joy ahead, even though it is necessary for you to endure many trials for a while.

[7]These trials are only to test your faith, to show that it is strong and pure. It is being tested as fire tests and purifies gold—and your faith is far more precious to God than mere gold. So if your faith remains strong after being tried by fiery trials, it will bring you much praise and glory and honor on the day when Jesus Christ is revealed to the whole world.

[8]You love him even though you have never seen him. Though you do not see him, you trust him; and even now you are happy with a glorious, inexpressible joy. [9]Your reward for trusting him will be the salvation of your souls.

[10]This salvation was something the prophets wanted to know more about. They prophesied about this gracious salvation prepared for you, even though they had many questions as to what it all

**LIVE IN HOPE ● ● • • •**

1:3-6 **Do you need encouragement? Peter's words offer joy and hope in times of trouble, and he bases his confidence on what God has done for us in Christ Jesus. We're called into a *living* hope of eternal life (1:3). Our hope is not only for the future; eternal life begins when we believe in God and join his family. The eternal life we now have gives us hope and enables us to live with confidence in God.**

1:6 Or *So you are truly glad.*

## SET APART ● ● • • •

**1:15-16 Peter tells us to be like our heavenly Father—holy in everything we do. Holiness means being totally devoted or dedicated to God, set aside for his special use, and set apart from sin and its influence. We're not to blend in with the crowd, yet we shouldn't be different just to be different. What makes us different are God's qualities in our life. Our focus and priorities must be his. All this is in direct contrast to our old ways (1:14). We cannot become holy on our own, but God gives us his Holy Spirit to help us obey and to give us power to overcome sin. Don't use the excuse that you can't help slipping into sin. Ask all-powerful God to free you from sin's grip.**

could mean. 11 They wondered what the Spirit of
Christ within them was talking about when he told
them in advance about Christ's suffering and his
great glory afterward. They wondered when and to
whom all this would happen.
12 They were told that these things would not happen during their lifetime, but many years later, during yours. And now this Good News has been
announced by those who preached to you in the
power of the Holy Spirit sent from heaven. It is all so
wonderful that even the angels are eagerly watching
these things happen.
13 So think clearly and exercise self-control. Look
forward to the special blessings that will come to you
at the return of Jesus Christ. 14 Obey God because you
are his children. Don't slip back into your old ways
of doing evil; you didn't know any better then. 15 But
now you must be holy in everything you do, just as
God—who chose you to be his children—is holy.
16 For he himself has said, "You must be holy because
I am holy."*
17 And remember that the heavenly Father to
whom you pray has no favorites when he judges.
He will judge or reward you according to what you
do. So you must live in reverent fear of him during
your time as foreigners here on earth. 18 For you
know that God paid a ransom to save you from the
empty life you inherited from your ancestors. And
the ransom he paid was not mere gold or silver.
19 He paid for you with the precious lifeblood of
Christ, the sinless, spotless Lamb of God. 20 God
chose him for this purpose long before the world
began, but now in these final days, he was sent to
the earth for all to see. And he did this for you.
21 Through Christ you have come to trust in God.
And because God raised Christ from the dead and
gave him great glory, your faith and hope can be
placed confidently in God. 22 Now you can have sincere love for each other as brothers and sisters*
because you were cleansed from your sins when you
accepted the truth of the Good News. So see to it that
you really do love each other intensely with all your
hearts.*
23 For you have been born again. Your new life did
not come from your earthly parents because the life
they gave you will end in death. But this new life will
last forever because it comes from the eternal, living
word of God. 24 As the prophet says,

"People are like grass that dies away;
their beauty fades as quickly as the beauty
of wildflowers.
The grass withers,
and the flowers fall away.
25 But the word of the Lord will last forever."*

And that word is the Good News that was preached
to you.

1:16 Lev 11:44-45; 19:2; 20:7. 1:22a Greek *can have brotherly love.* 1:22b Some manuscripts read *with a pure heart.* 1:24-25 Isa 40:6-8.

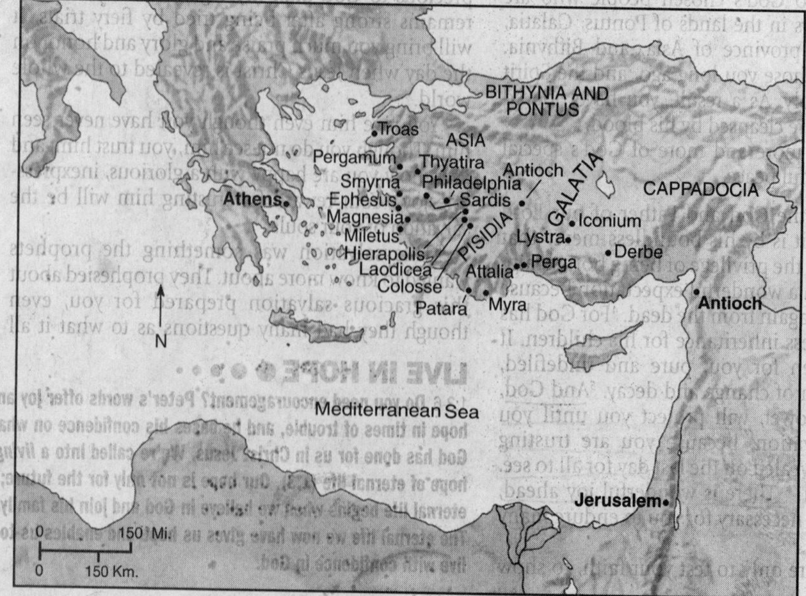


**THE CHURCHES OF PETER'S LETTER**
Peter addressed his letter to the churches located throughout Bithynia, Pontus, Asia, Galatia, and Cappadocia. Paul had evangelized many of these areas; others had churches that were begun by the Jews who were in Jerusalem on the day of Pentecost and had heard Peter's powerful sermon (see Acts 2:9-11).

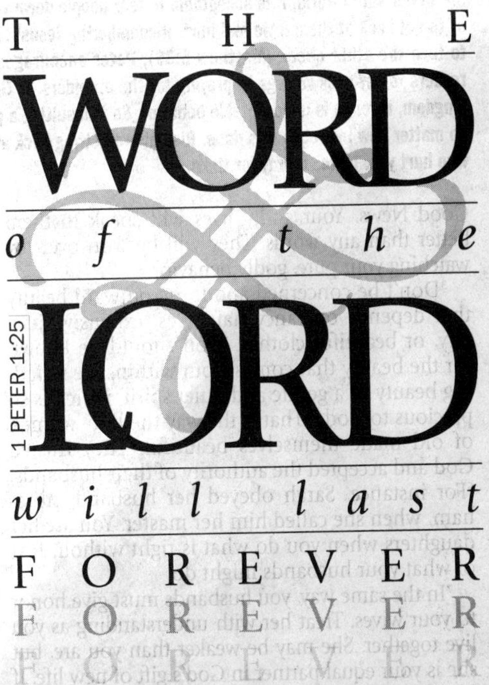

THE
WORD
of the
LORD
will last
FOREVER
1 PETER 1:25

CHAPTER **2** **A LIVING STONE FOR GOD'S HOUSE.** So get
rid of all malicious behavior and deceit. Don't just
pretend to be good! Be done with hypocrisy and
jealousy and backstabbing. [2]You must crave pure
spiritual milk so that you can grow into the fullness
of your salvation. Cry out for this nourishment as a
baby cries for milk, [3]now that you have had a taste of
the Lord's kindness.

[4]Come to Christ, who is the living cornerstone of
God's temple. He was rejected by the people, but he
is precious to God who chose him.

[5]And now God is building you, as living stones,
into his spiritual temple. What's more, you are God's
holy priests, who offer the spiritual sacrifices that
please him because of Jesus Christ. [6]As the Scriptures
express it,

"I am placing a stone in Jerusalem,*
a chosen cornerstone,
and anyone who believes in him
will never be disappointed.*"

[7]Yes, he is very precious to you who believe. But for
those who reject him,

"The stone that was rejected by the builders
has now become the cornerstone."*

[8]And the Scriptures also say,

"He is the stone that makes people stumble,
the rock that will make them fall."*

They stumble because they do not listen to God's
word or obey it, and so they meet the fate that has
been planned for them.

[9]But you are not like that, for you are a chosen
people. You are a kingdom of priests, God's holy
nation, his very own possession. This is so you can
show others the goodness of God, for he called you
out of the darkness into his wonderful light.

[10]"Once you were not a people;
now you are the people of God.
Once you received none of God's mercy;
now you have received his mercy."*

[11]Dear brothers and sisters, you are foreigners and
aliens here. So I warn you to keep away from evil
desires because they fight against your very souls.
[12]Be careful how you live among your unbelieving
neighbors. Even if they accuse you of doing wrong,
they will see your honorable behavior, and they will
believe and give honor to God when he comes to
judge the world.*

[13]For the Lord's sake, accept all authority—the
king as head of state, [14]and the officials he has appointed. For the king has sent them to punish all
who do wrong and to honor those who do right.

[15]It is God's will that your good lives should silence those who make foolish accusations against
you. [16]You are not slaves; you are free. But your
freedom is not an excuse to do evil. You are free to

i
wonder...

**It's hard to believe in anything you can't see. Why has God made it so difficult for people who would believe in him if they could only see him?**

God is big, strong, powerful, and able to appear to anyone he wants. But if he did that, most people would feel forced or intimidated into following him, rather than loved into it. God wants us to respond out of love for him, not fear!

The truth is that people *can* see God . . . through the eyes of faith. This means taking God at his word—opening ourselves up to him. Some people say "seeing is believing." The truth is that "believing is seeing."

All of us believe in things we have never seen. A person in history. Gravity. The wind. Everyone has the capacity to believe things that aren't seen. The bottom line for most who say, "I can't believe in something I haven't seen," is "I won't believe in God, because I want to run my own life." God doesn't work that way. Each person must trust in Christ, acknowledging him as Savior.

Peter said that loving God, even though we have never seen him, will bring us "a glorious, inexpressible joy" (1 Peter 1:8). Jesus said, "Blessed are those who haven't seen me and believe anyway" (John 20:29). We live by faith, then we meet God.

2:6a Greek *in Zion.* 2:6b Or *will never be put to shame.* Isa 28:16. 2:7 Ps 118:22. 2:8 Isa 8:14. 2:10 Hos 1:6, 9; 2:23. 2:12 Or *on the day of visitation.*

live as God's slaves. [17]Show respect for everyone. Love your Christian brothers and sisters.* Fear God. Show respect for the king.

[18]You who are slaves must accept the authority of your masters. Do whatever they tell you—not only if they are kind and reasonable, but even if they are harsh. [19]For God is pleased with you when, for the sake of your conscience, you patiently endure unfair treatment. [20]Of course, you get no credit for being patient if you are beaten for doing wrong. But if you suffer for doing right and are patient beneath the blows, God is pleased with you.

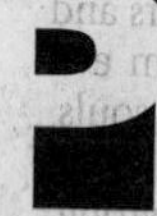

**ARTIES**

It's prom time, and Courtney and Shelby are getting nervous.

Their problem?

Getting their dates, Terry and Peter, to forget the idea of an unchaperoned party in a hotel suite after the prom.

Maybe that situation seems simple to solve, but consider the facts:

The girls are freshmen. Their dates are seniors and so are expected at the hotel.

The party will feature an open bar and several available beds.

Terry and Peter each have already kicked in $75 to pay for this private affair.

A similar party last year featured some unbelievably wild activities.

"What are we gonna do?" Courtney pleads.

"Well, we could just tell our parents and let them get us out of this."

"Oh, right, Shelby! And get laughed out of school? We can't do that!"

"OK, what if we fake like we're sick or something?"

"Shelby!! And miss the whole prom? It's our first one—and I don't want it to be our last. Look, this whole mess isn't our fault. Let's just pray about it. Maybe God wants us to go and be good examples or something."

"OK," Shelby agrees.

The girls bow their heads.

Do Courtney and Shelby need to pray about such a decision? Especially when God's Word is pretty clear about Christians avoiding wild parties? See 1 Peter 4:3-6.

[21]This suffering is all part of what God has called you to. Christ, who suffered for you, is your example. Follow in his steps. [22]He never sinned, and he never deceived anyone. [23]He did not retaliate when he was insulted. When he suffered, he did not threaten to get even. He left his case in the hands of God, who always judges fairly. [24]He personally carried away our sins in his own body on the cross so we can be dead to sin and live for what is right. You have been healed by his wounds! [25]Once you were wandering like lost sheep. But now you have turned to your Shepherd, the Guardian of your souls.

CHAPTER **3** **ADVICE FOR HUSBANDS AND WIVES.** In the same way, you wives must accept the authority of your husbands, even those who refuse to accept the

## CUT DOWN ● ● ● • •

3:9 **In our sinful world, it is acceptable to tear people down verbally or to get back at them if we feel hurt. Remembering Jesus' teaching to turn the other cheek (Matthew 5:39), Peter encourages his readers to pay back wrongs by praying for the offenders. In God's kingdom, revenge is unacceptable behavior. So is insulting a person, no matter how indirectly it is done. Rise above getting back at those who hurt you. Instead, pray for them.**

Good News. Your godly lives will speak to them better than any words. They will be won over [2]by watching your pure, godly behavior.

[3]Don't be concerned about the outward beauty that depends on fancy hairstyles, expensive jewelry, or beautiful clothes. [4]You should be known for the beauty that comes from within, the unfading beauty of a gentle and quiet spirit, which is so precious to God. [5]That is the way the holy women of old made themselves beautiful. They trusted God and accepted the authority of their husbands. [6]For instance, Sarah obeyed her husband, Abraham, when she called him her master. You are her daughters when you do what is right without fear of what your husbands might do.

[7]In the same way, you husbands must give honor to your wives. Treat her with understanding as you live together. She may be weaker than you are, but she is your equal partner in God's gift of new life. If you don't treat her as you should, your prayers will not be heard.

[8]Finally, all of you should be of one mind, full of sympathy toward each other, loving one another with tender hearts and humble minds. [9]Don't repay evil for evil. Don't retaliate when people say unkind things about you. Instead, pay them back with a blessing. That is what God wants you to do, and he will bless you for it. [10]For the Scriptures say,

"If you want a happy life and good days,
keep your tongue from speaking evil,
and keep your lips from telling lies.
[11]Turn away from evil and do good.
Work hard at living in peace with others.
[12]The eyes of the Lord watch over those who do right,
and his ears are open to their prayers.
But the Lord turns his face
against those who do evil."*

[13]Now, who will want to harm you if you are eager to do good? [14]But even if you suffer for doing what is right, God will reward you for it. So don't be afraid and don't worry. [15]Instead, you must worship Christ as Lord of your life. And if you are asked about your Christian hope, always be ready to explain it. [16]But you must do this in a gentle and respectful way. Keep your conscience clear. Then if people speak evil against you, they will be ashamed when they see what a good life you live because you belong to Christ. [17]Remember, it is better to suffer for doing good, if that is what God wants, than to suffer for doing wrong!

2:17 Greek *Love the brotherhood.* 3:10-12 Ps 34:12-16.

[18]Christ also suffered when he died for our sins
once for all time. He never sinned, but he died for
sinners that he might bring us safely home to God.
He suffered physical death, but he was raised to life
in the Spirit.*
[19]So he went and preached to the spirits in
prison—[20]those who disobeyed God long ago when
God waited patiently while Noah was building his
boat. Only eight people were saved from drowning
in that terrible flood.* [21]And this is a picture of
baptism, which now saves you by the power of Jesus
Christ's resurrection. Baptism is not a removal of dirt
from your body; it is an appeal to God from* a clean
conscience.
[22]Now Christ has gone to heaven. He is seated in
the place of honor next to God, and all the angels
and authorities and powers are bowing before him.

CHAPTER **4** **CONTINUE TO LOVE ONE ANOTHER.** So then,
since Christ suffered physical pain, you must arm
yourselves with the same attitude he had, and be
ready to suffer, too. For if you are willing to suffer for
Christ, you have decided to stop sinning. [2]And you
won't spend the rest of your life
chasing after evil desires, but you
will be anxious to do the will of
God. [3]You have had enough in the
past of the evil things that godless
people enjoy—their immorality
and lust, their feasting and drunkenness and wild parties, and their
terrible worship of idols.
[4]Of course, your former friends
are very surprised when you no
longer join them in the wicked
things they do, and they say evil
things about you. [5]But just remember that they will have to
face God, who will judge everyone, both the living and the dead.
[6]That is why the Good News was
preached even to those who have
died—so that although their
bodies were punished with death,
they could still live in the spirit as
God does.
[7]The end of the world is coming soon. Therefore, be earnest
and disciplined in your prayers.
[8]Most important of all, continue to show deep love for each
other, for love covers a multitude of sins. [9]Cheerfully share your
home with those who need a
meal or a place to stay.
[10]God has given gifts to each of
you from his great variety of spiritual gifts. Manage them well so
that God's generosity can flow
through you. [11]Are you called to be a speaker? Then
speak as though God himself were speaking
through you. Are you called to help others? Do it
with all the strength and energy that God supplies.
Then God will be given glory in everything through
Jesus Christ. All glory and power belong to him
forever and ever. Amen.
[12]Dear friends, don't be surprised at the fiery trials
you are going through, as if something strange were
happening to you. [13]Instead, be very glad—because
these trials will make you partners with Christ in his
suffering, and afterward you will have the wonderful
joy of sharing his glory when it is displayed to all the
world.
[14]Be happy if you are insulted for being a

## SPEAK UP ● ● • • •

3:15 **Some Christians believe that faith is a personal matter and should be kept to oneself. It is true that we shouldn't be boisterous or obnoxious in sharing our faith, but we should always be ready to answer, gently and respectfully, when asked about our beliefs, our lifestyle, or our Christian perspective. Will you tell others what Christ has done in your life?**

## "Here's what I did..."

I attended a Christian school during junior high and the first year of high school. But after three years at Christian schools, I felt led to go back to a public school. I talked it over in depth with my parents. They supported me, but reminded me of how difficult it could be because of all the pressures to live for yourself, not for God.

They were right—the pressures and temptations were greater. I didn't know quite how to be a Christian in that atmosphere. I was afraid people would make fun of me once they found out I was a Christian, yet I was determined not to hide my faith. After all, I knew Jesus, the one person in this life who will never let me down. I wanted to share my faith with the new friends I was making.

I decided to adopt 1 Peter 3:15 as my key verse to get me through public school. It shows me how to live my life in that setting, among people who really need to hear some Good News.

This verse helps me keep in line in difficult situations. For instance, if I'm at a party and drinking only Coke, often someone will ask me why I'm not drinking any alcohol. I tell them that I don't need alcohol to help me have a good time, and that Jesus helps me to enjoy life and people just as they are. Most people respect me when I say that. (Even when they don't, as it says in 1 Peter 3:16-17, it's better that they mock me for doing something right than for making a fool of myself for getting drunk.)

First Peter 3:15 helps me overcome temptations like this and reminds me of my purpose for being in a public school: to be ready to tell people of the hope I have in Jesus.

*Jenny*

AGE 16

3:18 Or *spirit.* 3:20 Greek *saved through water.* 3:21 Or *for.*

## GOOD MARKS ● ● • • •

**4:16 It is not shameful to suffer for being a Christian. When Peter and John were persecuted for preaching the Good News, they rejoiced because such persecution was a mark of God's approval of their work (Acts 5:41). Don't seek out suffering, and don't try to avoid it. Instead, keep on doing what is right regardless of the suffering it might bring.**

Christian, for then the glorious Spirit of God will come upon you. [15]If you suffer, however, it must not be for murder, stealing, making trouble, or prying into other people's affairs. [16]But it is no shame to suffer for being a Christian. Praise God for the privilege of being called by his wonderful name! [17]For the time has come for judgment, and it must begin first among God's own children. And if even we Christians must be judged, what terrible fate awaits those who have never believed God's Good News? [18]And

"If the righteous are barely saved,
what chance will the godless and sinners have?"*

[19]So if you are suffering according to God's will, keep on doing what is right, and trust yourself to the God who made you, for he will never fail you.

## CHAPTER 5 ADVICE FOR TEACHERS AND STUDENTS.

And now, a word to you who are elders in the churches. I, too, am an elder and a witness to the sufferings of Christ. And I, too, will share his glory and his honor when he returns. As a fellow elder, this is my appeal to you: [2]Care for the flock of God entrusted to you. Watch over it willingly, not grudgingly—not for what you will get out of it, but because you are eager to serve God. [3]Don't lord it over the people assigned to your care, but lead them by your good example. [4]And when the head Shepherd comes, your reward will be a never-ending share in his glory and honor.

[5]You younger men, accept the authority of the elders. And all of you, serve each other in humility, for

"God sets himself against the proud,
but he shows favor to the humble."*

[6]So humble yourselves under the mighty power of God, and in his good time he will honor you. [7]Give all your worries and cares to God, for he cares about what happens to you.

[8]Be careful! Watch out for attacks from the Devil, your great enemy. He prowls around like a roaring lion, looking for some victim to devour. [9]Take a firm stand against him, and be strong in your faith. Remember that your Christian brothers and sisters* all over the world are going through the same kind of suffering you are.

[10]In his kindness God called you to his eternal glory by means of Jesus Christ. After you have suffered a little while, he will restore, support, and strengthen you, and he will place you on a firm foundation. [11]All power is his forever and ever. Amen.

[12]I have written this short letter to you with the help of Silas,* whom I consider a faithful brother. My purpose in writing is to encourage you and assure you that the grace of God is with you no matter what happens.

[13]Your sister church here in Rome* sends you greetings, and so does my son Mark. [14]Greet each other in Christian love.*

Peace be to all of you who are in Christ.

## BOTH WAYS ● ● • • •

**5:5 Both young and old can benefit from Peter's instructions. Pride often keeps elders from trying to understand young people and young people from listening to their elders. Peter's instructions go both ways: he told both young and old to be humble, to serve each other. Young men should follow the leadership of older men, who should lead by example. Respect your elders, listen to those younger than you, and be humble enough to admit that you can learn from each other.**

4:18 Prov 11:31. 5:5 Prov 3:34. 5:9 Greek *your brothers.* 5:12 Greek *Silvanus.* 5:13 Greek *The elect one in Babylon.* Babylon was probably a code name for Rome. 5:14 Greek *with a kiss of love.*

# MEGA themes

**SALVATION** Salvation is a gracious gift from God. God chose us out of his love for us, Jesus died to pay the penalty for our sin, and the Holy Spirit cleansed us from sin when we believed. Eternal life is a wonderful privilege for those who trust in Christ.

Our safety and security are in God. If we experience joy in our relationship with Christ now, how much greater will our joy be when he returns and we see him face-to-face! Such a hope should motivate us to serve Christ even more.

1. What are the blessings of our salvation that have been revealed to us through Jesus?
2. Why would this be such an important message

for Jewish Christians who had been suffering for their faith?
3. What does it mean to you to be saved? Include your feelings, the present benefits, and your hope for the future.
4. How can you communicate this through your life to someone who is without Christ? Why is it important that others come to know Christ?

**PERSECUTION** Peter offers faithful believers comfort and hope. We should expect ridicule, rejection, and suffering because we are Christians. Persecution makes us stronger because it refines our faith. We can face persecution victoriously as Christ did, if we rely on him.

We don't have to be terrified by persecution. The fact that we will live eternally with Christ should give us the confidence, patience, and hope to stand firm even when we are persecuted. Suffering can glorify God.

1. Read 2:21-25. Describe Jesus' response to suffering.
2. How does Jesus' example provide encouragement and inspiration during suffering?
3. How do fellow believers provide encouragement and inspiration during suffering?
4. When you face ridicule or oppression for your faith, what are the specific ways that you can cope with this suffering?

**GOD'S FAMILY** We are privileged to belong to God's family, a community with Christ as the Founder and Foundation. Everyone in this community is related—we are all brothers and sisters, loved equally by God.

We must be devoted, loyal, and faithful to Christ, the foundation of our family. Through obedience, we show that we are his children. We must live differently from the society around us. Our relationships are to be patterned by what we see in Christ, not by what we see in the world.

1. List the specific teachings concerning Christian fellowship in 4:7-11.
2. Who are the people who have ministered Christ's love and grace to you? In what ways have they provided this love and grace?
3. Why is it necessary for you and other believers to be providers of his love to one another?
4. In what two ways will you become a part of God's love and grace in the life of fellow believers this week?

**FAMILY LIFE** Peter encouraged the wives of unbelievers to submit to the authority of their husband as a means of winning them to Christ. He urged all family members to treat others with sympathy, love, tenderness, and humility.

We must treat our families lovingly. Though it's never easy, willing service is the best way to influence our loved ones. To gain the needed strength, we must pray for God's help. Relationships with parents, brothers and sisters, and spouses are important aspects of Christian discipleship.

1. In 1 Peter, what principles do you find for a godly marriage?
2. How could 3:6 be misused by a domineering husband? What corrective does God's Word provide against misusing this husband-wife relationship? (Also check Ephesians 5.)
3. What qualities do you want in a marriage partner someday?
4. What qualities do you think your mate will desire in you? How can you develop those qualities so that you bring godliness and maturity to your marriage?

**JUDGMENT** God will judge everyone with perfect justice. He will punish evildoers and those who persecute his people; those who love God will be rewarded with life forever in his presence.

Because all are accountable to God, we can leave judgment of others to him. We must not hate or resent those who persecute us. We should realize that we will be held responsible for how we live each day.

1. What will happen to those without Christ when they face God's judgment?
2. What difference will having Jesus as your Lord make when you face God's judgment?
3. Review 1:14-25. If you will not be condemned because of Jesus, why should God's holiness continue to be your motivation for living a holy life?
4. What are the specific areas of your life that still need to become holy through obedience to Christ? How can this be accomplished?

**W**e've all come face-to-face with life's ironies: ■ One man, noting the regularity (and certainty) of these quirks, decided to make a list. The result? The famous "Murphy's Laws." ■ Some of Murphy's more interesting observations: ■ If anything *can* go wrong it *will*. ■ "Broken" gadgets will operate perfectly in the presence of a repairman. ■ Saying "Watch this!" guarantees that the behavior you want others to witness will not happen. ■ A poorly thrown Frisbee will always come to rest under the exact center of a parked car. ■ Stored objects are never needed . . . until immediately after they are discarded. ■ The bowl that breaks is never the one that was already chipped. ■ The other line always moves faster. ■ If you put a napkin in your lap you will not spill; failure to use a napkin ensures spillage. ■ You will only be forced to wait when you do not have time to wait. ■ We nod and smile at those "laws" because we've lived them. They're amazingly true to life. How about some other laws of life? Perhaps not as humorous, but just as true—and much more life-changing: ■ Spiritual growth only happens when we get to know God and make the effort to serve him. ■ The world is full of people who will try to lead you astray. ■ Jesus Christ is coming back. ■ Would you like to know more about these critical principles? They're all contained in the book that follows, the Bible book we call 2 Peter.

## STATS

PURPOSE: To warn Christians about false teachers and to exhort them to grow in their faith and knowledge of Christ

AUTHOR: Peter

TO WHOM WRITTEN: The church at large

DATE WRITTEN: About A.D. 67, three years after 1 Peter was written, possibly from Rome

SETTING: Peter knew that his time on earth was limited (1:13-14), so he was writing about what was on his heart, warning believers of what would happen when he was gone—especially about false teachers. He reminded believers of the unchanging truth of the gospel.

KEY PEOPLE: Peter, Paul

SPECIAL FEATURES: The date and destination are uncertain, and the authorship has been disputed. Because of this, 2 Peter was the last epistle admitted to the canon of the New Testament Scripture. Also, there are similarities between 2 Peter and Jude.

CHAPTER **1** **STEPS TO SPIRITUAL GROWTH.** This letter is from Simon* Peter, a slave and apostle of Jesus Christ.

I am writing to all of you who share the same precious faith we have, faith given to us by Jesus Christ, our God and Savior, who makes us right with God.

[2]May God bless you with his special favor and wonderful peace as you come to know Jesus, our God and Lord,* better and better.

[3]As we know Jesus better, his divine power gives us everything we need for living a godly life. He has called us to receive his own glory and goodness! [4]And by that same mighty power, he has given us all of his rich and wonderful promises. He has promised that you will escape the decadence all around you caused by evil desires and that you will share in his divine nature.

[5]So make every effort to apply the benefits of these promises to your life. Then your faith will produce a life of moral excellence. A life of moral excellence leads to knowing God better. [6]Knowing God leads to self-control. Self-control leads to patient endurance, and patient endurance leads to godliness. [7]Godliness leads to love for other Christians,* and finally you will grow to have genuine love for everyone. [8]The more you grow like this, the more you will become productive and useful in your knowledge of our Lord Jesus Christ. [9]But those who fail to develop these virtues are blind or, at least, very shortsighted. They have already forgotten that God has cleansed them from their old life of sin.

[10]So, dear brothers and sisters,* work hard to prove that you really are among those God has called and chosen. Doing this, you will never stumble or fall away. [11]And God will open wide the gates of heaven for you to enter into the eternal Kingdom of our Lord and Savior Jesus Christ.

[12]I plan to keep on reminding you of these things—even though you already know them and are standing firm in the truth. [13]Yes, I believe I should

**PERSEVERE!** ● ● • • •

1:5-9 **Faith must be more than belief in certain facts; it must result in action, growth in Christian character, and the practice of moral discipline, or it will die (James 2:14-17). Peter lists several of faith's actions: learning to know God better, developing endurance and godliness, loving others. These actions do not come automatically; they require hard work. They are not optional; all must be a continual part of the Christian life. We need to work on them all together, not one at a time. If it sounds tough, don't worry; God will help us to become what he wants us to be.**

1:1 Greek *Simeon.* 1:2 Or *come to know God and Jesus our Lord.* 1:7 Greek *brotherly love.* 1:10 Greek *brothers.*

keep on reminding you of these things as long as I
live. [14]But the Lord Jesus Christ has shown me that
my days here on earth are numbered and I am soon
to die.* [15]So I will work hard to make these things
clear to you. I want you to remember them long after
I am gone.
[16]For we were not making up clever stories when
we told you about the power of our Lord Jesus Christ
and his coming again. We have seen his majestic
splendor with our own eyes. [17]And he received honor
and glory from God the Father when God's glorious,
majestic voice called down from heaven, "This is my
beloved Son; I am fully pleased with him." [18]We
ourselves heard the voice when we were there with
him on the holy mountain.

The day of the Lord
will come as unexpectedly
AS A THIEF.
2 PETER 3:10

## ULTS

A month ago, while on a city bus, Patricia picked up a discarded leaflet advertising a free music festival and complimentary vegetarian meal. She called her friend Elaine, and the two of them went to see what it was all about.

The whole afternoon Elaine was whispering, "Let's get out of here. This is weird!" But Patricia kept replying, "Lighten up, Elaine! You're too intense."

On the way home, Elaine made it clear what she thought. "Look, I don't care what you say. That group is some kind of cult or something."

"Why? Name one thing they did or said that was bad."

"Well, I don't know—they gave me the creeps."

"Aw, I think you're paranoid. Who knows? I just might go to one of their classes."

Patricia did go back. And now she's a full-fledged member of the "church," The Society of Enlightened Minds. The people there accept her and make her feel special.

Elaine's parents did some checking. Patricia's "church" doesn't accept the Bible; nor does it believe that Christ is God. It teaches that each of us is a god and that together, we can recreate the world.

With their popular, feel-good philosophies, dangerous cult groups are capturing millions of hungry hearts and uncritical minds. No wonder we are told in 2 Peter 2:17-22 to carefully consider the ideas that we hear every day. Read it and heed it!

[19]Because of that, we have even greater confidence
in the message proclaimed by the prophets. Pay close
attention to what they wrote, for their words are like
a light shining in a dark place—until the day Christ
appears and his brilliant light shines in your hearts.*
[20]Above all, you must understand that no prophecy
in Scripture ever came from the prophets themselves* [21]or because they wanted to prophesy. It was
the Holy Spirit who moved the prophets to speak
from God.

CHAPTER **2** **BEWARE OF FALSE TEACHERS.** But there
were also false prophets in Israel, just as there will
be false teachers among you. They will cleverly
teach their destructive heresies about God and
even turn against their Master who bought them.
Theirs will be a swift and terrible end. [2]Many will
follow their evil teaching and shameful immorality. And because of them, Christ and his true way
will be slandered. [3]In their greed they will make up
clever lies to get hold of your money. But God
condemned them long ago, and their destruction
is on the way.
[4]For God did not spare even the angels when they
sinned; he threw them into hell,* in gloomy caves*
and darkness until the judgment day. [5]And God did
not spare the ancient world—except for Noah and
his family of seven. Noah warned the world of God's
righteous judgment. Then God destroyed the whole
world of ungodly people with a vast flood. [6]Later, he
turned the cities of Sodom and Gomorrah into
heaps of ashes and swept them off the face of the
earth. He made them an example of what will happen to ungodly people. [7]But at the same time, God
rescued Lot out of Sodom because he was a good
man who was sick of all the immorality and wickedness around him. [8]Yes, he was a righteous man who
was distressed by the wickedness he saw and heard
day after day.
[9]So you see, the Lord knows how to rescue godly
people from their trials, even while punishing the
wicked right up until the day of judgment. [10]He is
especially hard on those who follow their own evil,
lustful desires and who despise authority. These
people are proud and arrogant, daring even to
scoff at the glorious ones* without so much as
trembling. [11]But the angels, even though they are
far greater in power and strength than these false
teachers, never speak out disrespectfully against*
the glorious ones.
[12]These false teachers are like unthinking animals, creatures of instinct, who are born to be
caught and killed. They laugh at the terrifying powers they know so little about, and they will be
destroyed along with them. [13]Their destruction is

1:14 Greek *I must soon put off this earthly tent.* 1:19 Or *until the day dawns and the morning star rises in your hearts.* 1:20 Or *is a matter of one's own interpretation.* 2:4a Greek *Tartaros.* 2:4b Some manuscripts read *chains of gloom.* 2:10 *The glorious ones* are probably evil angels; also in 2:11. 2:11 Greek *never bring blasphemous judgment from the Lord against.*

their reward for the harm they have done. They love to indulge in evil pleasures in broad daylight. They are a disgrace and a stain among you. They revel in deceitfulness while they feast with you.
14They commit adultery with their eyes, and their lust is never satisfied. They make a game of luring unstable people into sin. They train themselves to be greedy; they are doomed and cursed. 15They
have wandered off the right road and followed the way of Balaam son of Beor,* who loved to earn money by doing wrong. 16But Balaam was stopped
from his mad course when his donkey rebuked him with a human voice.
17These people are as useless as dried-up springs
of water or as clouds blown away by the wind—promising much and delivering nothing. They are doomed to blackest darkness. 18They brag about
themselves with empty, foolish boasting. With lustful desire as their bait, they lure back into sin those who have just escaped from such wicked living.
19They promise freedom, but they themselves are slaves to sin and corruption. For you are a slave to whatever controls you. 20And when people escape
from the wicked ways of the world by learning about our Lord and Savior Jesus Christ and then get tangled up with sin and become its slave again, they are worse off than before. 21It
would be better if they had never known the right way to live than to know it and then reject the holy commandments that were given to them. 22They make these proverbs come true: "A dog returns to its vomit,"* and "A washed pig returns to the mud."

CHAPTER **3** **HOPE FOR GROWING CHRISTIANS.** This is my second letter to you, dear friends, and in both of them I have tried to stimulate your wholesome thinking and refresh your memory. 2I want you to
remember and understand what the holy prophets said long ago and what our Lord and Savior commanded through your apostles.
3First, I want to remind you that
in the last days there will be scoffers who will laugh at the truth and do every evil thing they desire.
4This will be their argument:
"Jesus promised to come back, did he? Then where is he? Why, as far back as anyone can remember, everything has remained exactly the same since the world was first created."

5They deliberately forget that God made the
heavens by the word of his command, and he brought the earth up from the water and surrounded it with water. 6Then he used the water to
destroy the world with a mighty flood. 7And God
has also commanded that the heavens and the earth will be consumed by fire on the day of judgment, when ungodly people will perish.
8But you must not forget, dear friends, that a day
is like a thousand years to the Lord, and a thousand years is like a day. 9The Lord isn't really being slow
about his promise to return, as some people think. No, he is being patient for your sake. He does not want anyone to perish, so he is giving more time for everyone to repent. 10But the day of the Lord will
come as unexpectedly as a thief. Then the heavens

**FREEDOM ● ● ● ● ●**

**2:19 Many people believe that freedom means doing anything you want. But no one is ever completely free in that way. If we refuse to follow God, we will follow our own sinful desires and become enslaved to what our body wants. If we submit our life to Christ, he will free us from slavery to sin. Christ frees us to serve him, and that will always result in our ultimate good.**

## "Here's what I did..."

I didn't want to break up with my girlfriend, but the more I prayed about the relationship, the more I saw that it was interfering with my relationship with God. My girlfriend wasn't a Christian; her values were completely different from mine. I cared about her, but it came down to a choice: either her or God.

The clincher came when I read 2 Peter 1:5-8. It says: "Make every effort to apply the benefits of these promises to your life. Then your faith will produce a life of moral excellence. A life of moral excellence leads to knowing God better. Knowing God leads to self-control. Self-control leads to patient endurance, and patient endurance leads to godliness. Godliness leads to love for other Christians, and finally you will grow to have genuine love for everyone. The more you grow like this, the more you will become productive and useful in your knowledge of our Lord Jesus Christ."

I didn't need any more guidance; I knew I had to break up and concentrate on strengthening my relationship with the Lord. Though I felt bad after breaking up, I was confident that I had done the right thing and that the Lord still cared about me and my decisions.

I also was encouraged. God was showing me that I was slowly but surely becoming stronger spiritually. Every verse of that passage fit a part of my life. As I put God first and determined to obey him, I could see times when I put aside my own desires and how I was becoming more patient, etc. Yes, breaking up was hard, but knowing that I did it to obey God made all the difference.

*Joel*

AGE 16

2:15 Other manuscripts read *Bosor.* 2:22 Prov 26:11.

## ANY DAY ● ● • • •

**3:14 We should not become lazy and complacent because Christ has not yet returned. Instead, our life should express our eager expectation of his coming. What would you like to be doing when Christ returns? Is that the way you are living each day?**

will pass away with a terrible noise, and everything
in them will disappear in fire, and the earth and
everything on it will be exposed to judgment.*
[11]Since everything around us is going to melt
away, what holy, godly lives you should be living!
[12]You should look forward to that day and hurry it
along—the day when God will set the heavens on
fire and the elements will melt away in the flames.
[13]But we are looking forward to the new heavens
and new earth he has promised, a world where
everyone is right with God.
[14]And so, dear friends, while you are waiting
for these things to happen, make every effort to live
a pure and blameless life. And be at peace with God.

3:10 Some manuscripts read *will be burned up.*

[15]And remember, the Lord is waiting so that
people have time to be saved. This is just as our
beloved brother Paul wrote to you with the wisdom God gave him—[16]speaking of these things in
all of his letters. Some of his comments are hard to
understand, and those who are ignorant and unstable have twisted his letters around to mean
something quite different from what he meant,
just as they do the other parts of Scripture—and
the result is disaster for them.
[17]I am warning you ahead of time, dear friends,
so that you can watch out and not be carried away
by the errors of these wicked people. I don't want
you to lose your own secure footing. [18]But grow in
the special favor and knowledge of our Lord and
Savior Jesus Christ.

To him be all glory and honor, both now and forevermore. Amen.

# MEGA themes

**DILIGENCE** If our faith is real, it will be evident in our faithful behavior. If people are diligent in Christian growth, they won't backslide or be deceived by false teachers.

Growth is essential. It begins with faith and culminates in love for others. To keep growing, we need to know God, keep on following him, and remember what he taught us. It may not always be easy, but it will always be worthwhile.

1. According to chapter 1, what are the attitudes and actions that lead to maturity?
2. If a Christian friend were to ask you, "How are you growing?" what would be your response?
3. Based on this study, identify five practical steps to personal spiritual growth.
4. How and when will you apply these five steps to your relationship with God?

**FALSE TEACHERS** Peter warns the church to beware of false teachers. These teachers were proud of their position, promoted sexual sin, and advised against keeping the Ten Commandments. Peter countered them by pointing to the Spirit-inspired Scriptures as our authority.

Christians need discernment to resist false teachers. God can rescue us from their lies if we stay true to his Word, the Bible, and reject those who twist the truth. The truth is our best defense because it exposes the lies of those who try to deceive us.

1. Contrast the lives of the false teachers with the lives of those who follow God's truth.
2. Why can God's Word be trusted more than all teachers?
3. What false teaching have you heard about God and Jesus?
4. What would you say to someone who wanted to be certain not to fall into the deception of a false teacher?

**CHRIST'S RETURN** One day Christ will create a new heaven and earth where we will live forever. As Christians, our hope is in this promise. But with Christ's return comes his judgment on all who refuse to believe.

The cure for complacency, lawlessness, and heresy is found in the confident assurance that Christ will return. God is still giving unbelievers time to repent. To be ready, Christians must keep on trusting Christ and resist the pressure to give up waiting for his return.

1. What reason does Peter give for Christ's patience in waiting to return?
2. How does Peter say we should live in light of Christ's expected return?
3. How do most Christians view Christ's eventual return?
4. What difference does Christ's expected return make in your life?

Love. ■ We can't touch it, count it, bottle it, or even see it. But who among us would argue that love isn't real? ■ Love. ■ It makes sane people do and say crazy things. It prompts snobby, selfish people to do noble things. It turns boring people into exciting, unpredictable creatures. What else on earth has that kind of power? ■ Love. ■ It can hurt like nothing else in the world. And yet, paradoxically, *not* loving is much more painful. ■ Love. ■ The most talked-about and sung-about and thought-about theme in all the world. And also the most misunderstood. ■ Love. ■ Would you like to know more about it and see it in a brand new light? Then read *1 John,* the most eloquent description of love ever penned. ■ Love. ■ It's not everything you think it is. It's more . . . much, much more.

## STATS

PURPOSE: To reassure Christians in their faith and to counter false teachings

AUTHOR: The apostle John

TO WHOM WRITTEN: The letter is untitled and was written to no particular church. It was sent as a pastoral letter to several Gentile congregations. It was also written to all believers everywhere.

DATE WRITTEN: Probably between A.D. 85 and 90 from Ephesus

SETTING: John was an older man and perhaps the only surviving apostle at this time. He had not yet been banished to the island of Patmos, where he would live in exile. As an eyewitness of Christ, he wrote authoritatively to give this new generation of believers assurance and confidence in God and in their faith.

KEY PEOPLE: John, Jesus

SPECIAL FEATURES: John is the apostle of love, and love is mentioned throughout this letter. There are a number of similarities in vocabulary, style, and main ideas between this letter and John's Gospel. John uses brief statements and simple words, and he features sharp contrasts—light and darkness, truth and error, God and Satan, life and death, love and hate.

CHAPTER **1** **JESUS CHRIST IS ETERNAL LIFE.** The one who existed from the beginning* is the one we have heard and seen. We saw him with our own eyes and touched him with our own hands. He is Jesus Christ, the Word of life. [2]This one who is life from God was shown to us, and we have seen him. And now we testify and announce to you that he is the one who is eternal life. He was with the Father, and then he was shown to us. [3]We are telling you about what we ourselves have actually seen and heard, so that you may have fellowship with us. And our fellowship is with the Father and with his Son, Jesus Christ.

[4]We are writing these things so that our* joy will be complete.

[5]This is the message he has given us to announce to you: God is light and there is no darkness in him at all. [6]So we are lying if we say we have fellowship with God but go on living in spiritual darkness. We are not living in the truth. [7]But if we are living in the light of God's presence, just as Christ is, then we have fellowship with each other, and the blood of Jesus, his Son, cleanses us from every sin.

[8]If we say we have no sin, we are only fooling ourselves and refusing to accept the truth. [9]But if we confess our sins to him, he is faithful and just to forgive us and to cleanse us from every wrong. [10]If we claim we have not sinned, we are calling God a liar and showing that his word has no place in our hearts.

CHAPTER **2** **LOVE GOD, NOT THIS WORLD.** My dear children, I am writing this to you so that you will not sin. But if you do sin, there is someone to plead for

1:1 Greek *What was from the beginning.* 1:4 Some manuscripts read *your.*

**OVER & OVER • • • • •**

**1:9 Confession frees us to enjoy fellowship with Christ. But some Christians do not understand confession. They feel guilty that they confess the same sins over and over, and then they wonder if they have forgotten something. Others believe that if they died with unconfessed sins, they would be lost forever. But *God wants to forgive us.* He allowed his beloved Son to die so he could pardon us. We don't need to confess the same sins all over again, and we don't need to be afraid that God will reject us if we don't keep our slate perfectly clear. Since our hope in Christ is secure, we should confess so that we can enjoy maximum fellowship and joy with Christ. And we must pray for strength to defeat the temptation the next time it appears.**

you before the Father. He is Jesus Christ, the one who pleases God completely.* [2]He is the sacrifice for our sins. He takes away not only our sins but the sins of all the world.

[3]And how can we be sure that we belong to him? By obeying his commandments. [4]If someone says, "I belong to God," but doesn't obey God's commandments, that person is a liar and does not live in the truth. [5]But those who obey God's word really do love him. That is the way to know whether or not we live in him. [6]Those who say they live in God should live their lives as Christ did.

[7]Dear friends, I am not writing a new commandment, for it is an old one you have always had, right from the beginning. This commandment—to love one another—is the same message you heard before. [8]Yet it is also new. This commandment is true in Christ and is true among you, because the darkness is disappearing and the true light is already shining.

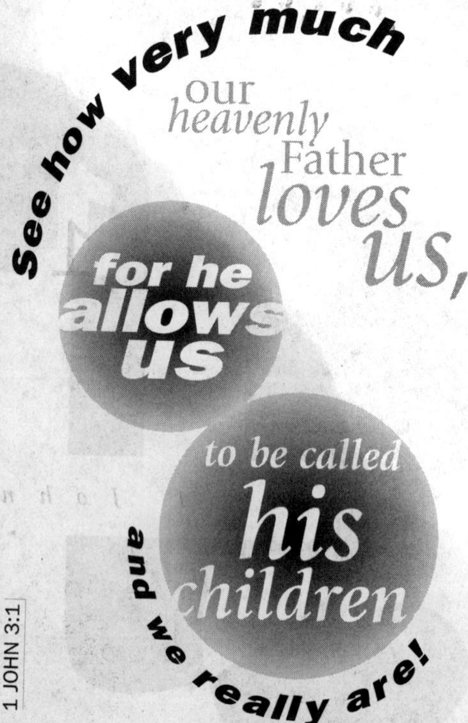


## LOVE

At a slumber party, Wendy makes the terrible mistake of being the first to fall asleep. A few hours later she is awakened by a funny smell and a damp feeling on her head. Staggering into the bathroom, she discovers her hair is filled with petroleum jelly, shaving cream, eggs, honey, and flour . . . all great products, but not exactly the sort of things you want to wear in your hair.

As she tries (in vain) to wash all the glop out, Wendy hears giggles and whispers coming from the living room.

Guess how Wendy feels?

(a) angry
(b) sad
(c) hurt
(d) rejected
(e) all of the above

You guessed it: (e) describes *exactly* how she feels.

Guess what Wendy wants to do?

(a) leave
(b) tell her friends off
(c) get back at them
(d) cry
(e) all of the above

That's right: (e) again. You are *so* smart!

So what does Wendy *actually* do? Here's the shocker: She prays and asks the Lord to give her the strength to love her friends in spite of what they have done. Later, when she has the chance to get back at them, she refuses.

Why is Wendy being so kind when her friends are being so mean? Because 1 John 4:7-21 is real to her. Check it out.

[9]If anyone says, "I am living in the light," but hates a Christian brother or sister,* that person is still living in darkness. [10]Anyone who loves other Christians* is living in the light and does not cause anyone to stumble. [11]Anyone who hates a Christian brother or sister is living and walking in darkness. Such a person is lost, having been blinded by the darkness.

[12]I am writing to you, my dear children, because your sins have been forgiven because of Jesus.

[13]I am writing to you who are mature because you know Christ, the one who is from the beginning.

I am writing to you who are young because you have won your battle with Satan.

[14]I have written to you, children, because you have known the Father.

I have written to you who are mature because you know Christ, the one who is from the beginning.

I have written to you who are young because you are strong with God's word living in your hearts, and you have won your battle with Satan.

### A CHOICE ● ● ● • •

2:9-11 **Does this mean if you dislike anyone you aren't a Christian? These verses are not talking about disliking a disagreeable Christian brother or sister. There will always be people we will not like as well as others. John's words focus on the attitude that causes us to ignore or despise others, to treat them as irritants, competitors, or enemies. Fortunately, Christian love is not a feeling but a choice. We can choose to be concerned with people's well-being and to treat them with respect, whether or not we feel affection toward them. If we choose to love others, God will give us the necessary strength and will show us how to express our love.**

2:1 Greek *Jesus Christ, the righteous.* 2:9 Greek *his brother;* also in 2:11. 2:10 Greek *his brother.*

[15]Stop loving this evil world and all that it offers you, for when you love the world, you show that you do not have the love of the Father in you. [16]For the world offers only the lust for physical pleasure, the lust for everything we see, and pride in our possessions. These are not from the Father. They are from this evil world. [17]And this world is fading away, along with everything it craves. But if you do the will of God, you will live forever.

[18]Dear children, the last hour is here. You have heard that the Antichrist is coming, and already many such antichrists have appeared. From this we know that the end of the world has come. [19]These people left our churches because they never really belonged with us; otherwise they would have stayed with us. When they left us, it proved that they do not belong with us. [20]But you are not like that, for the Holy Spirit has come upon you,* and all of you know the truth. [21]So I am writing to you not because you don't know the truth but because you know the difference between truth and falsehood. [22]And who is the great liar? The one who says that Jesus is not the Christ. Such people are antichrists, for they have denied the Father and the Son. [23]Anyone who denies the Son doesn't have the Father either. But anyone who confesses the Son has the Father also.

[24]So you must remain faithful to what you have been taught from the beginning. If you do, you will continue to live in fellowship with the Son and with the Father. [25]And in this fellowship we enjoy the eternal life he promised us.

[26]I have written these things to you because you need to be aware of those who want to lead you astray. [27]But you have received the Holy Spirit,* and he lives within you, so you don't need anyone to teach you what is true. For the Spirit teaches you all things, and what he teaches is true—it is not a lie. So continue in what he has taught you, and continue to live in Christ.

[28]And now, dear children, continue to live in fellowship with Christ so that when he returns, you will be full of courage and not shrink back from him in shame. [29]Since we know that God is always right, we also know that all who do what is right are his children.

CHAPTER **3** **WE ARE GOD'S CHILDREN.** See how very much our heavenly Father loves us, for he allows us to be called his children, and we really are! But the people who belong to this world don't know God, so they don't understand that we are his children. [2]Yes, dear friends, we are already God's children, and we can't even imagine what we will be like when Christ returns. But we do know that when he comes we will be like him, for we will see him as he really is. [3]And all who believe this will keep themselves pure, just as Christ is pure.

[4]Those who sin are opposed to the law of God, for all sin opposes the law of God. [5]And you know that Jesus came to take away our sins, for there is no sin in him. [6]So if we continue to live in him, we won't sin either. But those who keep on sinning have never known him or understood who he is.

[7]Dear children, don't let anyone deceive you about this: When people do what is right, it is because they are righteous, even as Christ is righteous. [8]But when people keep on sinning, it shows they belong to the Devil, who has been sinning since the beginning. But the Son of God came to destroy these works of the Devil. [9]Those who have been born into God's family do not sin, because God's life is in them. So they can't

## "Here's what I did..."

I was the master of rationalization—at least in some areas of my life. When I got into an argument with my parents, I always knew they were totally wrong. If I talked about someone behind her back, I told myself that it wasn't gossip, it was information the person really needed to know. When my boyfriend and I started having sex, I rationalized that it was OK because we loved each other, and didn't the Bible say that love was what it was all about?

Then I heard my pastor preach on 1 John 1:8-10, and suddenly I knew I was just fooling myself. God called these things—rebelliousness toward my parents, gossip, premarital sex—*sins*. I was kidding myself, but not God. The preacher said we are calling God a liar when we don't acknowledge our sins! That shook me up pretty bad.

I reread the passage after church, when I was alone in my room, and I cried. Not only because I'd been lying to myself and to God, but because this passage also talks about how willing God is to forgive us and cleanse us.

Before God that day, I owned up to the sins I had been rationalizing away. It was hard to do because I knew I had to be willing to change, not just to say "I'm sorry." Change would be hard, particularly in my relationship with my boyfriend. But verse 9 encouraged me that God would not only forgive, but also give me the strength to make a clean new start.

I did end up breaking up with my boyfriend; it proved impossible to start over in our physical relationship. The breakup hurt a lot. But underneath the pain, something felt very good, very right: I knew I was no longer lying to myself or to God. A new, clear conscience is helping me through the pain of change.

Tricia
AGE 16

2:20 Greek *But you have an anointing from the Holy One.* 2:27 Greek *the anointing.*

**FOOTHOLD ● ● • • •**

3:8-9 **We all have areas where temptation is strong and habits are hard to break. However, John is not talking about people who are working to overcome a particular sin; he is talking about people who make a practice of sinning and look for ways to justify it. Use these three steps to overcome prevailing sin: (1) seek the power of the Holy Spirit and God's Word; (2) stay away from tempting situations; and (3) seek the help of other Christians.**

keep on sinning, because they have been born of God.
[10]So now we can tell who are children of God and who
are children of the Devil. Anyone who does not obey
God's commands and does not love other Christians*
does not belong to God.

[11]This is the message we have heard from the beginning: We should love one another. [12]We must not be
like Cain, who belonged to the evil one and killed his
brother. And why did he kill him? Because Cain had
been doing what was evil, and his brother had been
doing what was right. [13]So don't be surprised, dear
brothers and sisters,* if the world hates you.

[14]If we love our Christian brothers and sisters, it
proves that we have passed from death to eternal life.
But a person who has no love is still dead. [15]Anyone
who hates another Christian* is really a murderer at
heart. And you know that murderers don't have
eternal life within them. [16]We know what real love is
because Christ gave up his life for us. And so we also
ought to give up our lives for our Christian brothers
and sisters. [17]But if anyone has enough money to live
well and sees a brother or sister in need and refuses
to help—how can God's love be in that person?

[18]Dear children, let us stop just saying we love
each other; let us really show it by our actions. [19]It is
by our actions that we know we are living in the
truth, so we will be confident when we stand before
the Lord, [20]even if our hearts condemn us. For God
is greater than our hearts, and he knows everything.

[21]Dear friends, if our conscience is clear, we can
come to God with bold confidence. [22]And we will
receive whatever we request because we obey him
and do the things that please him. [23]And this is his
commandment: We must believe in the name of his
Son, Jesus Christ, and love one another, just as he
commanded us. [24]Those who obey God's commandments live in fellowship with him, and he with
them. And we know he lives in us because the Holy
Spirit lives in us.

CHAPTER **4** **WHAT'S TRUE AND WHAT'S NOT?** Dear
friends, do not believe everyone who claims to speak
by the Spirit. You must test them to see if the spirit
they have comes from God. For there are many false
prophets in the world. [2]This is the way to find out if
they have the Spirit of God: If a prophet acknowledges that Jesus Christ became a human being, that
person has the Spirit of God. [3]If a prophet does not
acknowledge Jesus, that person is not from God.
Such a person has the spirit of the Antichrist. You
have heard that he is going to come into the world,
and he is already here.

[4]But you belong to God, my dear children. You
have already won your fight with these false prophets, because the Spirit who lives in you is greater than
the spirit who lives in the world. [5]These people
belong to this world, so they speak from the world's
viewpoint, and the world listens to them. [6]But we
belong to God; that is why those who know God
listen to us. If they do not belong to God, they do not
listen to us. That is how we know if someone has the
Spirit of truth or the spirit of deception.

[7]Dear friends, let us continue to love one another,

**I became a Christian at a big youth rally last fall. Afterwards, I felt great for a few days—I knew that having a relationship with God was something I wanted—but soon my good feelings went away. Did I lose God? Why didn't the good feelings stay around?**

Picture yourself meeting your favorite TV or music superstar face-to-face. It would be an experience that you would likely never forget. Yet over time you would forget the intensity of the emotion you once felt. Would it mean that you did not actually meet this person? Of course not, but it does illustrate that our feelings often come and go based on current experience.

Asking Jesus Christ into your life is far better than meeting another human, famous or not! What you have begun is a lifelong relationship with God, who created everything! He actually wants to live in you so that you will live forever *and* so others can see that he really loves them, too.

In John 14:23 Jesus says, "All those who love me will do what I say. My Father will love them, and we will come to them and live with them." The phrase *live with them* actually means "build a mansion" in them. God wants to come into your life and make something extraordinary out of it. God has begun a process of molding your character to become more like that of Jesus Christ. Within this lifelong process will be some good feelings, but more often we will not have, or want, continual, intense excitement.

The wonder of getting to know someone as loving and forgiving as Jesus Christ has similarities to other relationships you enjoy. There is the initial experience of meeting a person, followed by months and years of growing to appreciate his or her friendship and influence. Anything worthwhile takes time.

First John 5:10-12 assures us that "whoever has God's Son has life." Once you have genuinely chosen to follow Jesus Christ you can never lose him. He will always be there in your life to guide and love you, even in the midst of all our world may throw your way. This should outweigh your tendency to base your relationship with God on your up-and-down feelings.

3:10 Greek *his brother.* 3:13 Greek *brothers;* also in 3:14, 16. 3:15 Greek *his brother.*

for love comes from God. Anyone who loves is born of God and knows God. [8]But anyone who does not love does not know God—for God is love.

[9]God showed how much he loved us by sending his only Son into the world so that we might have eternal life through him. [10]This is real love. It is not that we loved God, but that he loved us and sent his Son as a sacrifice to take away our sins.

[11]Dear friends, since God loved us that much, we surely ought to love each other. [12]No one has ever seen God. But if we love each other, God lives in us, and his love has been brought to full expression through us.

[13]And God has given us his Spirit as proof that we live in him and he in us. [14]Furthermore, we have seen with our own eyes and now testify that the Father sent his Son to be the Savior of the world. [15]All who proclaim that Jesus is the Son of God have God living in them, and they live in God. [16]We know how much God loves us, and we have put our trust in him.

God is love, and all who live in love live in God, and God lives in them. [17]And as we live in God, our love grows more perfect. So we will not be afraid on the day of judgment, but we can face him with confidence because we are like Christ here in this world.

[18]Such love has no fear because perfect love expels all fear. If we are afraid, it is for fear of judgment, and this shows that his love has not been perfected in us. [19]We love each other* as a result of his loving us first.

[20]If someone says, "I love God," but hates a Christian brother or sister,* that person is a liar; for if we don't love people we can see, how can we love God, whom we have not seen? [21]And God himself has commanded that we must love not only him but our Christian brothers and sisters, too.

## CHAPTER 5 LOVE GOD AND OBEY HIM.

Everyone who believes that Jesus is the Christ is a child of God. And everyone who loves the Father loves his children, too. [2]We know we love God's children if we love God and obey his commandments. [3]Loving God means keeping his commandments, and really, that isn't difficult. [4]For every child of God defeats this evil world by trusting Christ to give the victory. [5]And the ones who win this battle against the world are the ones who believe that Jesus is the Son of God.

[6]And Jesus Christ was revealed as God's Son by his baptism in water and by shedding his blood on the cross*—not by water only, but by water and blood. And the Spirit also gives us the testimony that this is true. [7]So we have these three witnesses*—[8]the Spirit, the water, and the blood—and all three agree. [9]Since we believe human testimony, surely we can believe the testimony that comes from God. And God has testified about his Son. [10]All who believe in the Son

### A TEST

**4:20-21** **It is easy to say we love God when it doesn't cost us anything more than weekly attendance at a religious service. But the real test of our love for God is how we treat the people right in front of us—our family members and fellow believers. We cannot truly love God while neglecting to love those who are created in his image.**

**UPS:**
- First human child
- First to follow in father's profession: farming

**DOWNS:**
- When disappointed, reacted out of anger and discouragement
- Took the negative choice even when a positive possibility was offered
- Was the first murderer

**STATS:**
- Where: Near Eden, which probably was located in the present-day countries of Iraq or Iran
- Occupations: Farmer at first, later a nomad
- Relatives: Parents: Adam and Eve. Brothers and sisters: Abel, Seth, and others not mentioned by name.

**CAIN** and his brother Abel worshiped God. In some way, God let them know that Abel's worship was right and Cain's was wrong. God told Cain to start over. Cain got angry. God saw his anger and warned him to be careful. Though Cain was angry at God, he took it out on his brother. Then, instead of making things right with God by changing his attitude, he chose to kill his brother.

Anger is a powerful reaction. When something happens to us that we didn't expect, we get angry! It starts like a small hot flame and, unless it is put out, the flame can destroy a great deal. Cain's anger got out of control, but he wasn't in trouble until he acted out his anger in a wrong way. His attitude could have been corrected, but his actions couldn't. When we get angry, we're in the same danger.

Our anger may not result in murder, but we still act like Cain. We get angry. We see that we have a choice to make between right and wrong. And we often choose wrong. Being angry should remind us that we need God's help. Asking for his help to do the right thing may keep us from making mistakes we can't correct.

LESSONS: Anger is not sin. What causes our anger or what we do with our anger can be sinful.

What we offer to God must be from the heart, the best we are and have

The consequences of sin are sometimes for life

KEY VERSE: "We must not be like Cain, who belonged to the evil one and killed his brother. And why did he kill him? Because Cain had been doing what was evil, and his brother had been doing what was right" (1 John 3:12).

Cain's story is told in Genesis 4:1-17. He is also mentioned in Hebrews 11:4; Jude 1:11.

4:19 Or *We love him;* Greek reads *We love.* 4:20 Greek *brother;* also in 4:21. 5:6 Greek *This is he who came by water and blood.* 5:7 Some very late manuscripts add *in heaven—the Father, the Word, and the Holy Spirit, and these three are one. And we have three witnesses on earth.*

## YOU KNOW IT! ● ● • • •

**5:13 Some people *hope* they will be given eternal life. John says that we can *know* we have it. Our certainty is based on God's promise that he has given us eternal life through his Son. This is true whether you feel close to God or distant from him. Eternal life is not based on feelings, but on facts. You can know you have eternal life if you believe God's truth. If you lack assurance as to whether you are a Christian, ask yourself if you have honestly committed your life to Christ as your Savior and Lord. If so, you know by faith that you are indeed a child of God.**

of God know that this is true. Those who don't believe this are actually calling God a liar because they don't believe what God has testified about his Son.

[11]And this is what God has testified: He has given us eternal life, and this life is in his Son. [12]So whoever has God's Son has life; whoever does not have his Son does not have life.

[13]I write this to you who believe in the Son of God, so that you may know you have eternal life. [14]And we can be confident that he will listen to us whenever we ask him for anything in line with his will. [15]And if we know he is listening when we make our requests, we can be sure that he will give us what we ask for.

[16]If you see a Christian brother or sister* sinning in a way that does not lead to death, you should pray, and God will give that person life. But there is a sin that leads to death, and I am not saying you should pray for those who commit it. [17]Every wrong is sin, but not all sin leads to death.

[18]We know that those who have become part of God's family do not make a practice of sinning, for God's Son holds them securely, and the evil one cannot get his hands on them. [19]We know that we are children of God and that the world around us is under the power and control of the evil one. [20]And we know that the Son of God has come, and he has given us understanding so that we can know the true God. And now we are in God because we are in his Son, Jesus Christ. He is the only true God, and he is eternal life.

[21]Dear children, keep away from anything that might take God's place in your hearts.*

5:16 Greek *your brother.* 5:21 Greek *keep yourselves from idols.*

# MEGA themes

**SIN** Even Christians sin. Sin requires God's forgiveness, which Christ's death provides. Determining to live according to God's biblical standards shows we are forgiven and that our life is being transformed.

We cannot deny our sinful nature or minimize the consequences of sin in our relationship with God. We must resist the attraction of sin, yet we must confess when we do sin. Sin is our fault—Christ is our redeemer.

1. What happened when the sinless Christ entered the sinful world?
2. What happens when the sinless Christ enters the life of a sinful person?
3. What does John say we should do about our sins?
4. What is happening in your life in terms of dealing with sin? Are you dealing with your sin with the action and attitude of 1:9? Explain.

**LOVE** Christ commands us to love others as he did. This love is evidence that we are truly saved. God is the creator of love; and he wants his children to love each other.

Love means putting others first. Love is action—showing others we care, not just saying it. To show love, we must give our time and money to meet the needs of others.

1. Describe God's love for you as described in 1 John.
2. Why is knowing and experiencing God's love essential to living a full life?
3. Who are the people you love most? How does your "love life" compare to your description of God's love? What are your strengths and weaknesses?
4. Whom do you have difficulty loving? How can you apply God's love to those relationships? Why should you do this?

**FAMILY OF GOD** We become God's children by believing in Christ. God's life in us enables us to love our fellow family members.

How we treat others shows who our Father is. Live as a faithful, loving family member. Remember whose child you are!

1. Who are the children of God according to 1 John?
2. What privileges do these children have? What responsibilities?
3. Complete this statement with specific responses from your own life: "Being a child of God enables me to ________."
4. How would those who know you describe your Father based on their knowledge of you as his child?

**TRUTH AND ERROR** False teachers encouraged believers to throw off moral restraints, teaching that the body does not matter. They also taught that Christ wasn't really a man and that we must be saved by having some special mystical knowledge. The result was that people became indifferent to sin.

God is truth and light, so the more we get to know him, the better we can keep focused on the truth. Don't be led astray by any teaching that denies Christ's deity or humanity. Check the message; test the claims.

1. Identify several false teachings that John was correcting in his letter.
2. What are our resources for discerning and dealing with false teachings?
3. How can you live so that others can see the difference between God's truth and the false messages in the world?
4. How would you describe your commitment to God's truth? What will you do this week? *Do* what you answered for question number 3.

**ASSURANCE** God is in control of heaven and earth. Because God's Word is true, we can have assurance of eternal life and victory over sin. By faith we can be certain of our eternal destiny with him.

Assurance of our relationship with God is a promise, but it is also a way of life. We build our confidence by trusting in God's Word and in Christ's provision for our sin.

1. If a young Christian were to ask you, "How can I be sure I am saved?" what would be your response?
2. How could you use 3:12-16 in your answer?
3. How do you know that *you* are saved? What impact does this assurance have in the way you are currently living?

Practical jokes have been around a long time. Just read through the Old Testament; it's full of sneaky characters. There's Abraham, trying to pass off his wife Sarah as his sister—*twice.* There's Jacob donning a goatskin disguise to snatch his big brother's inheritance and blessing. (And that's just in the first half of the first book—Genesis!) ■ Most people have tried shocking or embarrassing someone with a joy buzzer or a whoopee cushion. Others have short-sheeted beds or done various phone pranks. Perhaps you have attempted a more complicated stunt—turning a friend's dresser drawers upside down, freezing your brother's underwear, toilet papering a house. (It's reported that some university pals lined a dorm mate's room with plastic and turned it into a giant aquarium—complete with a shark!) ■ As long as no one gets hurt, no laws are broken, and there's no property damage, pranks are no big deal. It's fun to fool people—or even be fooled. ■ Except in the spiritual dimension. There we can't afford to be deceived because our enemy, the devil, packs his pranks with disaster! ■ One of Satan's favorite methods of suckering us is to get us to listen to *false teaching.* This can come in many different forms, some very pleasing—but no matter how pleasant it may seem, false teaching is always deadly. ■ The book of 2 John warns us against false teaching. That's a warning we need to heed because the enemy's tricks aren't just for amusement—they're meant for destruction!

## STATS

PURPOSE: To emphasize the basics of following Christ—truth and love—and to warn against false teachers

AUTHOR: The apostle John

TO WHOM WRITTEN: To "the chosen lady" and her children (some think that the greeting refers instead to a local church) and to Christians everywhere

DATE WRITTEN: About the same time as 1 John, around A.D. 90, from Ephesus

SETTING: Evidently this woman and her family were involved in one of the churches that John was overseeing—they had developed a strong friendship. John was warning her of the false teachers that were becoming prevalent in some of the churches.

KEY PEOPLE: John, the chosen lady, and her children

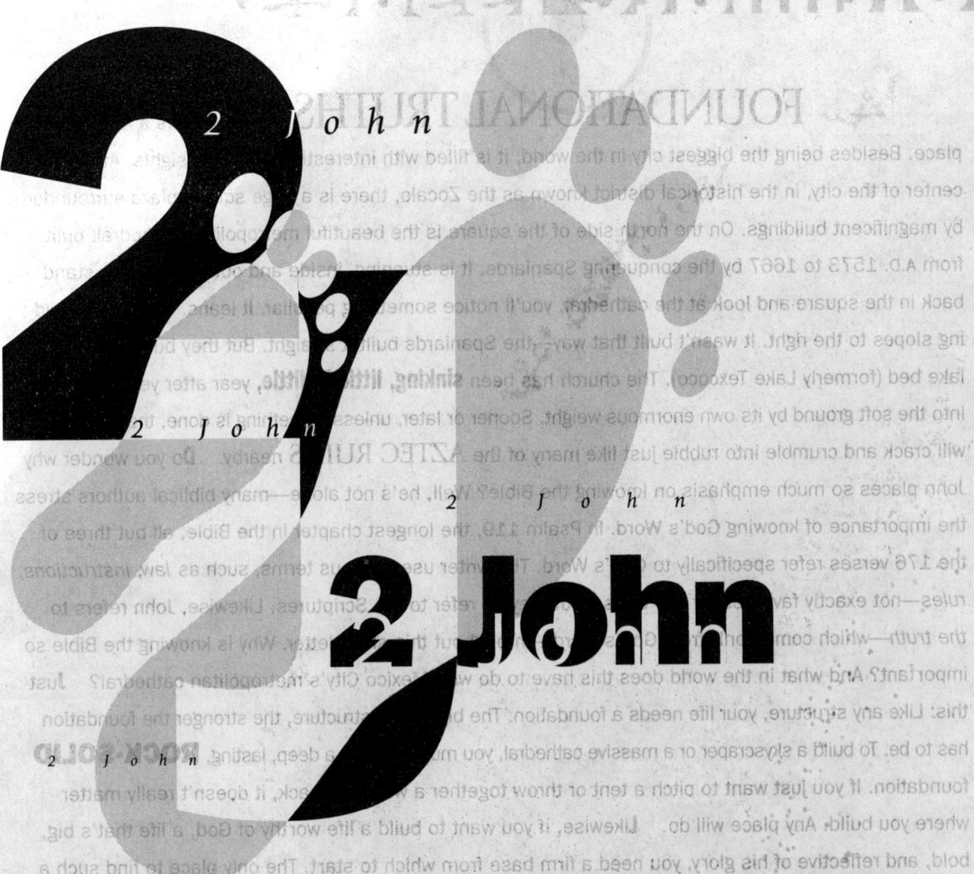

# 2 John

**BEWARE OF FALSE TEACHERS.** This letter is from John the
Elder.*
It is written to the chosen lady and to her children,* whom I love in the truth, as does everyone
else who knows God's truth—[2]the truth that lives in
us and will be in our hearts forever.
[3]May grace, mercy, and peace, which come from
God our Father and from Jesus Christ his Son, be
with us who live in truth and love.

[4]How happy I was to meet some of your children
and find them living in the truth, just as we have
been commanded by the Father.
[5]And now I want to urge you, dear lady, that we
should love one another. This is not a new commandment, but one we had from the beginning.
[6]Love means doing what God has commanded us,
and he has commanded us to love one another, just
as you heard from the beginning.
[7]Many deceivers have gone out into the world.
They do not believe that Jesus Christ came to earth
in a real body. Such a person is a deceiver and an
antichrist. [8]Watch out, so that you do not lose the
prize for which we* have been working so hard. Be
diligent so that you will receive your full reward. [9]For
if you wander beyond the teaching of Christ, you will
not have fellowship with God. But if you continue in
the teaching of Christ, you will have fellowship with
both the Father and the Son.
[10]If someone comes to your meeting and does not
teach the truth about Christ, don't invite him into your
house or encourage him in any way. [11]Anyone who
encourages him becomes a partner in his evil work.
[12]Well, I have much more to say to you, but I don't
want to say it in a letter. For I hope to visit you soon
and to talk with you face to face. Then our joy will be
complete.
[13]Greetings from the children of your sister,* chosen by God.

**DANGER! ● ● • • •**

10 **False teaching is serious business, and we dare not overlook it. It is so serious that John wrote this letter especially to warn against it. There are so many false teachings in our world today that we might be tempted to take them lightly. Instead, we should realize the dangers they pose and actively refuse to give heresies any foothold.**

**1a** Greek *From the elder.* **1b** Or *the church God has chosen and her members,* or *the chosen Kyria and her children.* **8** Some manuscripts read *you.*
**13** Or *from the members of your sister church.*

# Ultimate Issues

## FOUNDATIONAL TRUTHS

**M**exico City is a fascinating place. Besides being the biggest city in the world, it is filled with interesting historical sights. At the very center of the city, in the historical district known as the Zocalo, there is a huge square plaza surrounded by magnificent buildings. On the north side of the square is the beautiful metropolitan cathedral, built from A.D. 1573 to 1667 by the conquering Spaniards. It is stunning, inside and out. **B**ut if you stand back in the square and look at the cathedral, you'll notice something peculiar. It leans. The entire building slopes to the right. It wasn't built that way—the Spaniards built it straight. But they built it on a dry lake bed (formerly Lake Texcoco). The church has been **sinking, little by little,** year after year, pushed into the soft ground by its own enormous weight. Sooner or later, unless something is done, the cathedral will crack and crumble into rubble just like many of the AZTEC RUINS nearby. **D**o you wonder why John places so much emphasis on knowing the Bible? Well, he's not alone—many biblical authors stress the importance of knowing God's Word. In Psalm 119, the longest chapter in the Bible, all but three of the 176 verses refer specifically to God's Word. The writer uses various terms, such as *law, instructions, rules*—not exactly favorites for any of us—but they all refer to the Scriptures. Likewise, John refers to *the truth*—which comes only from God's Word—throughout this short letter. Why is knowing the Bible so important? And what in the world does this have to do with Mexico City's metropolitan cathedral? **J**ust this: Like any structure, your life needs a foundation. The bigger the structure, the stronger the foundation has to be. To build a skyscraper or a massive cathedral, you must build on a deep, lasting, **ROCK-SOLID** foundation. If you just want to pitch a tent or throw together a wooden shack, it doesn't really matter where you build. Any place will do. **L**ikewise, if you want to build a life worthy of God, a life that's big, bold, and reflective of his glory, you need a firm base from which to start. The only place to find such a support structure is in the Word of God. It is the only platform that will NEVER BUCKLE UNDER the pressure of living for Christ in a very non-Christian world. When you spend time reading the Bible—even when you don't feel like it—you're working on laying your solid foundation. **I**f you don't care what kind of life you're offering up to the Lord, sleep in or watch soap operas all day. But don't be surprised when your life's structure begins to sink and tilt. If you want to have a life worthy of the high calling of following Jesus, ***start digging.*** You're already in the right place.

# MEGA themes

**TRUTH** Following God's Word, the Bible, is essential to Christian living because God is truth. Christ's true followers consistently obey his truth.

To be loyal to Christ's teaching we must know the Bible, but we must never twist the Bible's message to our own needs or purposes, nor encourage others who misuse it. We should be servants to the truth of the Word.

1. According to John, why is truth important?
2. How do we know truth?
3. Who are the enemies of the truth? What should be our response to these enemies?
4. How does your life compare with the enemies of the truth in your world?

**LOVE** Christ's command is for Christians to love one another. This is the basic ingredient of true Christianity.

To obey Christ fully, we must believe his command to love others. Helping, giving, and meeting needs puts love into practice. Love in deed is love indeed.

1. How does John connect love for one another with love for God?
2. What seems to be the connection between love and truth?
3. Identify the people in your life who do not know Christ and his love. What can you do for them that will be a witness concerning the reality of the truth and love of God?

**FALSE LEADERS** We must be wary of religious leaders who are not true to Christ's teachings. We should not give them a platform to spread false teachings.

Don't encourage those who are contrary to Christ. Politely remove yourself from association with false leaders. Be aware of what's being taught in the church.

1. How can you tell who is a false teacher?
2. What do you see as the main dangers of false teachings?
3. What passages of Scripture would you use to correct the error of these false teachers?
4. Why is it important, based on this study, to be a student of God's Word?
5. What steps are you taking to be led by the truth and to avoid error?

"It was over before it got started!" "Blink and you'll miss it." "Short, sweet, and to the point." ■Those are just some of the expressions you might use to describe: ■The 1896 war between the United Kingdom and Zanzibar. (It lasted a mere 38 minutes!) ■Boxer Al Couture's 1946 knockout of opponent Ralph Walton in only 10½ seconds (and that included a 10-second count by the referee)! ■The 20-minute reign of King Dom Luis III of Portugal in 1908. ■Montana's Roe River. (Its length? A measley 201 feet!) ■The 10-yard-long (or should we say "10-yard-*short*") McKinley Street in Bellefontaine, Ohio. ■But just because things are brief or small or short doesn't mean they're unimportant. ■Take 3 John for instance. With only 15 verses, it is one of the shortest books of the Bible—a quick contrast between godly living and worldly behavior. ■In fact, this introduction is about as long as the book itself! So go ahead and read this warm, personal note from the apostle John to his friend Gaius. ■When you do, another familiar expression may come to mind: ■"Good things come in small packages."

## STATS

PURPOSE: To commend Gaius for his hospitality and to encourage him in his Christian life

AUTHOR: The apostle John

TO WHOM WRITTEN: Gaius, a prominent Christian in one of the churches known to John, and all Christians everywhere

DATE WRITTEN: About A.D. 90, from Ephesus

SETTING: Church leaders traveled from town to town helping to establish new congregations. They depended on the hospitality of fellow believers. Gaius was one who welcomed them into his home.

KEY PEOPLE: John, Gaius, Diotrephes, Demetrius

**HOSPITALITY PLEASES GOD.** This letter is from John the Elder.*

It is written to Gaius, my dear friend, whom I love in the truth.

[2]Dear friend, I am praying that all is well with you
and that your body is as healthy as I know your soul
is. [3]Some of the brothers recently returned and made
me very happy by telling me about your faithfulness
and that you are living in the truth. [4]I could have no
greater joy than to hear that my children live in the truth.

[5]Dear friend, you are doing a good work for God when you take care of the traveling teachers* who are passing through, even though they are strangers to you. [6]They have told the church here of your
friendship and your loving deeds. You do well to send them on their way in a manner that pleases
God. [7]For they are traveling for the Lord* and accept nothing from those who are not Christians.* [8]So we ourselves should support them so that we may become partners with them for the truth.

[9]I sent a brief letter to the church about this, but Diotrephes, who loves to be the leader, does not
acknowledge our authority. [10]When I come, I will report some of the things he is doing and the wicked things he is saying about us. He not only refuses to welcome the traveling teachers, he also tells others not to help them. And when they do help, he puts them out of the church.

[11]Dear friend, don't let this bad example

## OPEN HOUSE ● ● • • •

**5 In the church's early days, traveling prophets, evangelists, and teachers were helped on their way by people like Gaius who housed and fed them. Hospitality is a lost art in many churches today. We would do well to invite more people into our home for meals—fellow church members, young people, traveling missionaries, those in need, visitors. This is an active and much appreciated way to show your love. In fact, it probably is more important today than ever because of our individualistic, self-centered society. There are many lonely people who wonder if anyone cares whether they live or die. If you find such a lonely person, show him or her that *you* care!**

1 Greek *From the elder.* 5 Greek *the brothers;* also in verse 10. 7a Greek *the Name.* 7b Greek *from Gentiles.*

# THE NEW AGE MOVEMENT

Following Christ isn't easy. Consider John's words: "Dear friend, don't let this bad example influence you. Follow only what is good. Remember that those who do good prove that they are God's children, and those who do evil prove that they do not know God." Now take a look at Luke 9:23-24, where Jesus tells us, "If any of you wants to be my follower, you must put aside your selfish ambition, shoulder your cross daily, and follow me. . . . If you give up your life for me, you will find true life." That's quite a **PRICE TAG** for following Jesus! Isn't there an easier path to God—one that doesn't make such tough demands on us? Yes! At least, that's what those in the "New Age movement" say. And lots of people are listening. New religions researchers Bob and Gretchen Passantino describe the New Age movement as "the fastest growing alternative belief system" in the U.S. Alternative to what? To the Jewish-Christian tradition that most Americans have been raised in. J. Gordon Melton, another new religions expert, defines New Age as "a vision of a world transformed, A HEAVEN ON EARTH, a society in which the problems of today are overcome and a new existence emerges." New Agers believe that we stand on the threshold of a new era, a "new age," a major transitional shift into humanity's next evolutionary stage. The overriding philosophy of the New Age movement is the belief that "all is one." There is **no distinction between right or wrong,** male or female, good or bad. There isn't even a division between God and man. Everything is divine. This philosophy isn't new. It's been around for thousands of years and is called "pantheism." Pantheism is the basis for all Eastern mystical religions (Hinduism, Buddhism, Confucianism, etc.). But New Agers differ from these religions in that they see this unity from a positive and optimistic view. The New Age is kind of an "Eastern-religion-meets-American-positive-thinking." This blend of exotic religious thought and popular psychology attracts many people to New Age teachings. But there's a catch. A big one. If all is one, then there's no difference between right and wrong—or God and man. If there's no difference between God and man, the next logical step is that man *is* god. No one can tell me "no"; I can do whatever I want. After all, I'm god. (Sound *farfetched?* That's exactly what Shirley MacLaine, the "high priestess" of the New Age movement, claims in her autobiography, *Out On a Limb*. And she is not alone.) The New Age movement is growing rapidly. The belief in the oneness of all things (along with things like ecological harmony, reincarnation, unlimited human potential) appeals to modern, "ENLIGHTENED" people. The idea that I can be my own god is very seductive. However, history is littered with the atrocities committed by people who thought they answered to no one—Hitler, Pol Pot, Idi Amin, Saddam Hussein. In fact, this was Lucifer's sin, which resulted in his expulsion from heaven. Don't be deceived. There is only one true God—the God of Abraham, Moses, David, Peter, James, and John. He will not share his throne with anyone, and he has certain demands for his followers, like carrying your cross and losing your life for his sake. It's a high price, but Jesus promises us it is worth it. And he is worthy of our sacrificial commitment. The god of the New Age—the god that looks like us—doesn't ask anything of us. But that kind of god can't deliver us from our sins, show us how to love, or die on a cross for us. That god isn't real—he's a lie. Someone has said, "History is filled with men who **would be gods;** but only one God who would be man." His name is Jesus. Take up your cross and follow him.

influence you. Follow only what is good. Remember that those who do good prove that they are God's children, and those who do evil prove that they do not know God.
12But everyone speaks highly of Demetrius, even truth itself. We ourselves can say the same for him, and you know we speak the truth.
13I have much to tell you, but I don't want to do it in a letter.
14For I hope to see you soon, and then we will talk face to face.
15May God's peace be with you.
Your friends here send you their greetings. Please give my personal greetings to each of our friends there.

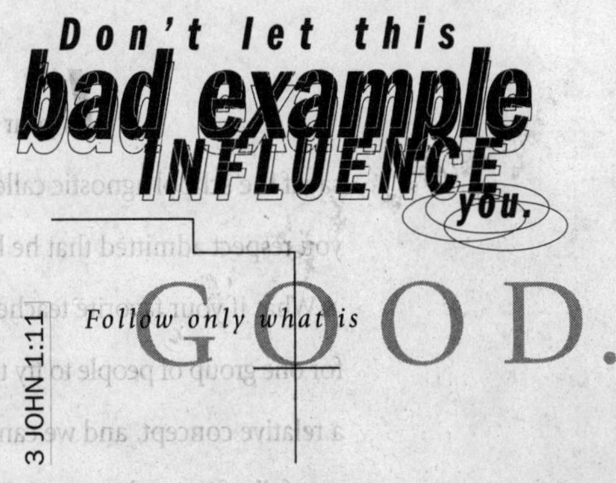
Don't let this
bad example
INFLUENCE
you.
3 JOHN 1:11
Follow only what is
GOOD.

# MEGA themes

**HOSPITALITY** John wrote to encourage those who were kind to others. Genuine hospitality for traveling Christian workers was needed then and is still important.

Faithful Christian teachers and missionaries need our support. Whenever you can extend hospitality to others, it will make you a partner in their ministry.

1. Why is Christian hospitality important?
2. In what specific ways can you and your friends at church extend Christian hospitality?
3. How might your actions of hospitality enable you to become partners in God's work in and through others?
4. What attitudes are required in order to be truly hospitable? How are you doing in terms of these attitudes?
5. Develop a hospitality plan of action based on this study.

**PRIDE** Diotrephes not only refused to offer hospitality, but he set himself up as a church boss. Pride disqualified him as a real leader.

Christian leaders must shun pride and its effects on them. Be careful not to misuse your position of leadership. The best leaders are always the best servants.

1. What were Diotrephes' sinful actions?
2. Why does John label Diotrephes as prideful?
3. How can a person who is prideful learn to be more humble?
4. Do you struggle with sinful pride? If so, how can you apply your responses in number 3 to your pride?

**FAITHFULNESS** Gaius and Demetrius were commended for their faithful work in the church. They were held up as examples of faithful, selfless servants.

Don't take for granted Christian workers who serve faithfully. Be sure to encourage these workers so they won't grow weary of serving.

1. What do you learn about Gaius in 3 John?
2. What Christians do you know who live faithfully in their relationship with God? What qualities do you see in them that reflect faithfulness to God? How could you encourage them in their ministry and leadership?
3. Why is faithfulness such an essential quality in the Christian life?
4. What is currently reflecting faithfulness in your life? Identify the ways that your faithfulness, like that of Gaius and those you listed in number 2, makes a difference to others.

Is your faith fit for a (spiritual) fight? ■ What would you say if the school agnostic called the resurrection of Christ a myth? Or if a minister you respect admitted that he believes the Bible contains errors and contradictions? ■ What if your favorite teacher announced, "It is insensitive and downright *wrong* for one group of people to try to force its views on another group! Right and wrong is a relative concept, and we cannot legislate morality"? ■ Imagine meeting someone full of joy and peace, a person *seemingly* very much in touch with God. As you converse, this person tells you that she is content and fulfilled because of daily yoga exercises, meditation, and also because of an experience she recently had in which she journeyed back through her previous incarnations. She nods when you mention Jesus Christ and says, "If that works for you, great! But I found the truth another way." ■ If you haven't already had encounters like the ones just described, then just wait. Your time is definitely coming! ■ The fact of the matter is that our world is *full* of confused people who are eagerly spreading their confusing ideas. ■ Don't get caught off-guard! Get your Christian beliefs and behavior ready for spiritual battle by understanding what you believe and why. There's no better place to start your Bible Bootcamp Training than in Jude, the brief book that follows.

## STATS

PURPOSE: To remind the church of the need for constant vigilance—to keep strong in the faith and defend it against heresy

AUTHOR: Jude, James's brother and Jesus' half brother

TO WHOM WRITTEN: Jewish Christians and all believers everywhere

DATE WRITTEN: About A.D. 65

SETTING: From the first century on, the church has been threatened by heresy and false teaching—we must always be on our guard

KEY PEOPLE: Jude, James, Jesus

**TO CHRISTIANS EVERYWHERE.** This letter is from Jude, a slave of Jesus Christ and a brother of James.

I am writing to all who are called to live in the love of God the Father and the care of Jesus Christ.

2May you receive more and more of God's mercy, peace, and love.

3Dearly loved friends, I had been eagerly planning to write to you about the salvation we all share. But now I find that I must write about something else, urging you to defend the truth of the Good News.* God gave this unchanging truth once for all time to his holy people. 4I say this because some godless people have wormed their way in among you, saying that God's forgiveness allows us to live immoral lives. The fate of such people was determined long ago, for they have turned against our only Master and Lord, Jesus Christ.

5I must remind you—and you know it well—that even though the Lord* rescued the whole nation of Israel from Egypt, he later destroyed every one of those who did not remain faithful. 6And I remind you of the angels who did not stay within the limits of authority God gave them but left the place where they belonged. God has kept them chained in prisons of darkness, waiting for the day of judgment. 7And don't forget the cities of Sodom and Gomorrah and their neighboring towns, which were filled with sexual immorality and every kind of sexual perversion. Those cities were destroyed by fire and are a warning of the eternal fire that will punish all who are evil.

8Yet these false teachers, who claim authority from their dreams, live immoral lives, defy authority, and scoff at the power of the glorious ones.* 9But even Michael, one of the mightiest of the angels, did not dare accuse Satan of blasphemy, but simply said, "The Lord rebuke you." (This took place when

**DOCTRINE ● ● • • •**

**4 Because people think theology is dry, they avoid studying the Bible. Those who refuse to learn correct doctrine, however, are susceptible to false teaching because they are not fully grounded in God's truth. We must understand the basic doctrines of our faith so that we can recognize false doctrines and prevent them from hurting us and others.**

3 Greek *to contend for the faith.* 5 Some manuscripts read *Jesus.* 8 *The glorious ones* are probably evil angels.

Michael was arguing with Satan about Moses' body.)
[10]But these people mock and curse the things they do
not understand. Like animals, they do whatever their
instincts tell them, and they bring about their own
destruction. [11]How terrible it will be for them! For
they follow the evil example of Cain, who killed his
brother. Like Balaam, they will do anything for
money. And like Korah, they will perish because of
their rebellion.

## PERSEVERANCE

Cindy and Kate met way back in 8th grade. Not only did the girls become fast friends, but by the end of that school year Cindy had helped Kate find a personal relationship with Jesus Christ.

Throughout high school Cindy always did her best to help Kate grow in the Christian faith. It was sometimes comical—Cindy practically dragging Kate to retreats and youth functions. Had you known the girls in those years, you would have predicted that Cindy was destined to do great things for God. And you would have seriously doubted the long-term stability of Kate's faith.

Boy, would you have been wrong!

During their first year of college, Cindy got too physically involved with her boyfriend, a non-Christian. When she got pregnant, she married the guy and dropped out of sight. Meanwhile, Kate has continued to mature in her walk with God. She's the one with the dynamic ministry on campus.

Yogi Berra said, "It ain't over till it's over." Another sports figure quipped, "The opera isn't over until the fat lady sings." The point? The Christian life is a long, long race.

Read about perseverance in the Epistle of Jude, and ask God to give you the grace and strength to hang in there for God all the days of your life.

[12]When these people join you in fellowship meals
celebrating the love of the Lord, they are like dangerous reefs that can shipwreck you.* They are shameless in the way they care only about themselves. They
are like clouds blowing over dry land without giving
rain, promising much but producing nothing. They
are like trees without fruit at harvesttime. They are
not only dead but doubly dead, for they have been
pulled out by the roots. [13]They are like wild waves of
the sea, churning up the dirty foam of their shameful
deeds. They are wandering stars, heading for everlasting gloom and darkness.
[14]Now Enoch, who lived seven generations after
Adam, prophesied about these people. He said,

"Look, the Lord is coming
with thousands of his holy ones.
[15]He will bring the people of the world
to judgment.
He will convict the ungodly of all the evil things
they have done in rebellion
and of all the insults that godless sinners
have spoken against him."*

12 Or *they are contaminants among you,* or *they are stains.* 14-15 The quotation comes from the Apocrypha: Enoch 1:9.

## WATCH OUT!

**10 False teachers were claiming that they possessed secret knowledge that gave them authority. Their "knowledge" of God was mystical and beyond human understanding. In reality, the nature of God *is* beyond our understanding. But God in his grace has chosen to reveal himself to us—in his Word, and supremely in Jesus Christ. Therefore, we must seek to know all we can about what God has revealed, even though we cannot fully comprehend God with our finite human mind. Beware of those who claim to have all the answers and who belittle what they do not understand.**

[16]These people are grumblers and complainers, doing whatever evil they feel like. They are loud-
mouthed braggarts, and they flatter others to get
favors in return.
[17]But you, my dear friends, must remember what
the apostles of our Lord Jesus Christ told you, [18]that
in the last times there would be scoffers whose purpose in life is to enjoy themselves in every evil way
imaginable. [19]Now they are here, and they are the
ones who are creating divisions among you. They
live by natural instinct because they do not have
God's Spirit living in them.
[20]But you, dear friends, must continue to build
your lives on the foundation of your holy faith. And

All glory
to God
WHO
IS
ABLE
to keep you from stumbling
and
who
will
bring
you
INTO HIS
GLORIOUS
PRESENCE
innocent of sin
and with great joy.
JUDE 1:24

continue to pray as you are directed by the Holy
Spirit.* [21]Live in such a way that God's love can bless
you as you wait for the eternal life that our Lord Jesus
Christ in his mercy is going to give you. [22]Show
mercy to those whose faith is wavering. [23]Rescue
others by snatching them from the flames of judgment. There are still others to whom you need to
show mercy, but be careful that you aren't contaminated by their sins.*

[24]And now, all glory to God, who is able to keep
you from stumbling, and who will bring you into his
glorious presence innocent of sin and with great joy.
[25]All glory to him, who alone is God our Savior,
through Jesus Christ our Lord. Yes, glory, majesty,
power, and authority belong to him, in the beginning, now, and forevermore. Amen.

20 Greek *Pray in the Holy Spirit.* 23 Greek *mercy, hating even the clothing stained by the flesh.*

## QUICKSAND ● ● ● • •

**23 In trying to find common ground with those to whom we witness, we must be careful not to fall into the quicksand of compromise. When reaching out to others, we must be sure that our own footing is safe and secure. Be careful not to become so much like non-Christians that no one can tell who you are or what you believe. Influence them for Christ—don't allow them to influence you to sin!**

# MEGA themes

**FALSE TEACHERS** Jude warns against false teachers and leaders who reject the lordship of Christ, undermine the faith of others, and lead people astray. These leaders and any who follow them will be punished.

We must stoutly defend Christian truth. Make sure that you avoid leaders and teachers who change the Bible to suit their own purposes. Genuine servants of God will faithfully portray Christ in their words and conduct.

1. How does Jude describe the false teachers?
2. What were the negative results of their teachings?
3. How were the Christians supposed to respond to teachings of error?
4. What safeguards can you build into your life to insure that you are not deceived by false teachings?
5. What are you doing to serve as a living testimony of the truth of God?

**APOSTASY** Jude warns against apostasy—turning away from Christ. We are to remember that God punishes rebellion against him. We must be careful not to drift away from a firm commitment to Christ.

Those who do not study God's Word are susceptible to apostasy. Christians must guard against any false teachings that would distract them from the truth preached by the apostles and written in God's Word.

1. Contrast those who are led by God with those who are living in rebellion.
2. What are the principles found in verses 20 through 23 for dealing with the rebellious?
3. How would you apply those principles to your life at school? In church? In your social life?
4. What confidence do you find in verses 24 and 25 that tells you God will remain faithful to you as you follow him? Take time to praise God for who he is and for how he keeps you in his love.

**F**airy tales always end perfectly. The frog turns into a prince, the unloved stepsister becomes a beloved bride, and mean and greedy people get paid back for the rotten things they've done. ■ Unfortunately, fairy tales aren't true. "Happily ever after"? No way! The real world doesn't work that way. ■ Or does it? ■ We are near the end of the Bible. One book left to read: Revelation. This strange vision of the apostle John's is one of the most discussed, mysterious, and controversial books ever written. It's labeled "prophecy" and "theology." And it's like a fairy tale. ■ *"A fairy tale"?!* ■ That's right. According to Revelation, those who have become God's children by faith in Christ will have the happiest of all endings: being in the very presence of God, enjoying an existence untouched by sorrow or death. ■ And every bad and wicked creature (including the devil himself) will "face the music." All injustices will be righted; all unforgiven sin will be judged. That, in a nutshell, is the message of Revelation: happiness and reward for the good, punishment and justice for all the guilty. A picture-perfect ending. ■ You must admit it *does* sound like a fairy tale. There is, however, one important difference: this too-good-to-be-true story is truer than anything that ever existed. It *is* going to happen. ■ You can count on it.

## STATS

PURPOSE: To reveal the full identity of Christ and to give warning and hope to believers

AUTHOR: The apostle John

TO WHOM WRITTEN: Seven Asian churches, and all believers everywhere

DATE WRITTEN: About A.D. 95, from the island of Patmos

SETTING: Most scholars believe that the seven churches of Asia to whom John wrote were experiencing the persecution that took place under Emperor Domitian (A.D. 90–95). Apparently the Roman authorities had exiled John to the island of Patmos (off the coast of Asia). John, an eyewitness of the incarnate Christ, had a vision of the glorified Christ. God also revealed to him what is to take place in the future—judgment and the ultimate triumph of God over evil.

KEY PEOPLE: John, Jesus

KEY PLACES: Island of Patmos, the seven churches, the New Jerusalem

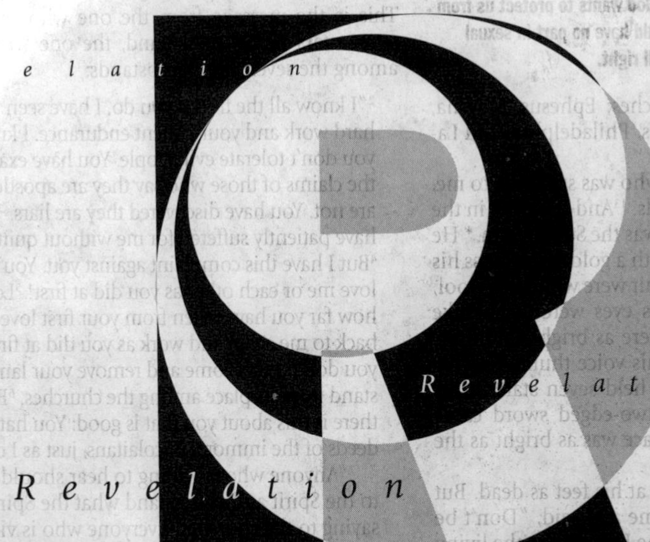

# Revelation

CHAPTER **1** **A REVELATION ABOUT THE FUTURE.** This is a revelation from* Jesus Christ, which God gave him concerning the events that will happen soon. An angel was sent to God's servant John so that John could share the revelation with God's other servants. [2]John faithfully reported the word of God and the testimony of Jesus Christ—everything he saw.

[3]God blesses the one who reads this prophecy to the church, and he blesses all who listen to it and obey what it says. For the time is near when these things will happen.

[4]This letter is from John to the seven churches in the province of Asia. Grace and peace from the one who is, who always was, and who is still to come; from the sevenfold Spirit* before his throne; [5]and from Jesus Christ, who is the faithful witness to these things, the first to rise from the dead, and the commander of all the rulers of the world.

All praise to him who loves us and has freed us from our sins by shedding his blood for us. [6]He has made us his kingdom and his priests who serve before God his Father. Give to him everlasting glory! He rules forever and ever! Amen!

[7]Look! He comes with the clouds of heaven. And everyone will see him—even those who pierced him. And all the nations of the earth will weep because of him. Yes! Amen!

[8]"I am the Alpha and the Omega—the beginning and the end," says the Lord God. "I am the one who is, who always was, and who is still to come, the Almighty One."

[9]I am John, your brother. In Jesus we are partners in suffering and in the Kingdom and in patient endurance. I was exiled to the island of Patmos for preaching the word of God and speaking about Jesus. [10]It was the Lord's Day, and I was worshiping in the Spirit.* Suddenly, I heard a loud voice behind me, a voice that sounded like a trumpet blast. [11]It said, "Write down what you see, and

1:1 Or *of*. 1:4 Greek *the seven spirits*. 1:10 Or *in spirit*.

**GREAT VISION ● ● • • •**

1:1 **Jesus gave his message to John in a vision, allowing John to see and record certain future events as an encouragement to all believers. The vision includes many signs and symbols to effectively show what will happen. What John saw, in most cases, was indescribable, so he used illustrations to show what it was *like*. When reading this symbolic language, don't try to understand every detail—John didn't. Instead, let the imagery show you that Christ is the glorious, victorious Lord of all.**

## SEXUAL SIN ● ● • • •

**2:20 Why is sexual immorality serious? Sex outside marriage always hurts someone. It hurts God because it shows that we prefer to follow our own desires instead of God's Word. It hurts others because it violates the commitment so necessary to a marriage relationship. It hurts us because it often brings disease to our body and harms our personality. Sexual sin has tremendous power to destroy families, communities, and even nations because it destroys the relationships upon which these institutions are built. God wants to protect us from hurting ourselves and others, so we should have no part in sexual immorality, even if our society says it's all right.**

send it to the seven churches: Ephesus, Smyrna,
Pergamum, Thyatira, Sardis, Philadelphia, and Laodicea."
12 When I turned to see who was speaking to me,
I saw seven gold lampstands. 13 And standing in the
middle of the lampstands was the Son of Man.* He
was wearing a long robe with a gold sash across his
chest. 14 His head and his hair were white like wool,
as white as snow. And his eyes were bright like
flames of fire. 15 His feet were as bright as bronze
refined in a furnace, and his voice thundered like
mighty ocean waves. 16 He held seven stars in his
right hand, and a sharp two-edged sword came
from his mouth. And his face was as bright as the
sun in all its brilliance.
17 When I saw him, I fell at his feet as dead. But
he laid his right hand on me and said, "Don't be
afraid! I am the First and the Last. 18 I am the living
one who died. Look, I am alive forever and ever!
And I hold the keys of death and the grave.*
19 Write down what you have seen—both the things
that are now happening and the things that will
happen later. 20 This is the meaning of the seven
stars you saw in my right hand and the seven gold
lampstands: The seven stars are the angels of* the
seven churches, and the seven lampstands are the
seven churches.

CHAPTER **2** **JOHN WRITES TO SEVEN CHURCHES.** "Write
this letter to the angel of* the church in Ephesus.
This is the message from the one who holds the
seven stars in his right hand, the one who walks
among the seven gold lampstands:
2 "I know all the things you do. I have seen your
hard work and your patient endurance. I know
you don't tolerate evil people. You have examined
the claims of those who say they are apostles but
are not. You have discovered they are liars. 3 You
have patiently suffered for me without quitting.
4 But I have this complaint against you. You don't
love me or each other as you did at first! 5 Look
how far you have fallen from your first love! Turn
back to me again and work as you did at first. If
you don't, I will come and remove your lampstand from its place among the churches. 6 But
there is this about you that is good: You hate the
deeds of the immoral Nicolaitans, just as I do.
7 "Anyone who is willing to hear should listen
to the Spirit and understand what the Spirit is
saying to the churches. Everyone who is victorious will eat from the tree of life in the paradise
of God.
8 "Write this letter to the angel of the church in
Smyrna. This is the message from the one who is the
First and the Last, who died and is alive:

1:13 Or *one who looked like a man;* Greek reads *one like a son of man.* See Dan 7:13. 1:18 Greek *and Hades.* 1:20 Or *the messengers for.* 2:1 Or *the messenger for;* also in 2:8, 12, 18.

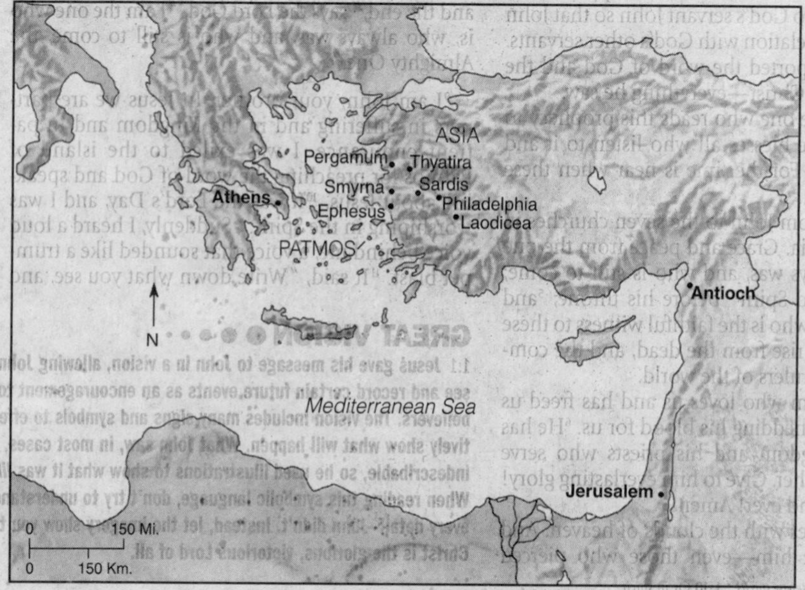


**THE SEVEN CHURCHES**
The seven churches were located on a major Roman road. A letter carrier would leave the island of Patmos (where John was exiled), arriving first at Ephesus. He would travel north to Smyrna and Pergamum (Pergamos), turn southeast to Thyatira, and continue on to Sardis, Philadelphia, and Laodicea—in the exact order in which the letters were dictated.

[9]"I know about your suffering and your poverty—but you are rich! I know the slander of those opposing you. They say they are Jews, but they really aren't because theirs is a synagogue of Satan. [10]Don't be afraid of what you are about to suffer. The Devil will throw some of you into prison and put you to the test. You will be persecuted for 'ten days.' Remain faithful even when facing death, and I will give you the crown of life.

[11]"Anyone who is willing to hear should listen to the Spirit and understand what the Spirit is saying to the churches. Whoever is victorious will not be hurt by the second death.

[12]"Write this letter to the angel of the church in Pergamum. This is the message from the one who has a sharp two-edged sword:

[13]"I know that you live in the city where that great throne of Satan is located, and yet you have remained loyal to me. And you refused to deny me even when Antipas, my faithful witness, was martyred among you by Satan's followers. [14]And yet I have a few complaints against you. You tolerate some among you who are like Balaam, who showed Balak how to trip up the people of Israel. He taught them to worship idols by eating food offered to idols and by committing sexual sin. [15]In the same way, you have some Nicolaitans among you—people who follow the same teaching and commit the same sins. [16]Repent, or I will come to you suddenly and fight against them with the sword of my mouth.

[17]"Anyone who is willing to hear should listen to the Spirit and understand what the Spirit is saying to the churches. Everyone who is victorious will eat of the manna that has been hidden away in heaven. And I will give to each one a white stone, and on the stone will be engraved a new name that no one knows except the one who receives it.

[18]"Write this letter to the angel of the church in Thyatira. This is the message from the Son of God, whose eyes are bright like flames of fire, whose feet are like polished bronze:

[19]"I know all the things you do—your love, your faith, your service, and your patient endurance. And I can see your constant improvement in all these things. [20]But I have this complaint against you. You are permitting that woman—that Jezebel who calls herself a prophet—to lead my servants astray. She is encouraging them to worship idols, eat food offered to idols, and commit sexual sin. [21]I gave her time to repent, but she would not turn away from her immorality. [22]Therefore, I will throw her upon a sickbed, and she will suffer greatly with all who commit adultery with her, unless they turn away from all their evil deeds. [23]I will strike her children dead. And all the churches will know that I am the one who searches out the thoughts and intentions of every person. And I will give to each of you whatever you deserve. [24]But I also have a message for the rest of you in Thyatira who have not followed this false teaching ('deeper truths,' as they call them—depths of Satan, really). I will ask nothing more of you [25]except that you hold tightly to what you have until I come.

[26]"To all who are victorious, who obey me to the very end, I will give authority over all the nations. [27]They will rule the nations with an iron rod and smash them like clay pots. [28]They will have the same authority I received from my Father, and I will also give them the morning star! [29]Anyone who is willing to hear should listen to the Spirit and understand what the Spirit is saying to the churches.

**Because of my shyness and my family situation, I find it difficult to let people get close to me. As a Christian, I hear all the time how much God loves me. How close does God want to get with me?**

As close as you'll let him.

God knows everything about us, and yet he still wants to be a Father to us. Isn't that amazing? King David wrote about how close God wants to be.

"How precious are your thoughts about me, O God! They are innumerable! I can't even count them; they outnumber the grains of sand! And when I wake up in the morning, you are still with me!" (Psalm 139:17-18).

Knowing how much God thinks about us (especially in light of how little we think of him) should give us an incredible feeling of worth. Our response to God's constant attentiveness, however, should never be out of obligation. God does not want us to come close to him only because we feel we have to.

Revelation 2:4 warns us not to allow our love for God to grow weaker. God wants us to progress and grow beyond our initial commitment to him, just like in a marriage where love should continue to grow. Unfortunately, this doesn't always happen. Many people who become Christians are really excited about their new relationship with God. But as problems come up, the excitement often wears off (just like what happens in some marriages!).

To maintain a growing relationship with God, the key word is time: daily time with him, time with others who know him, and time (in years) to grow to appreciate his love for you.

Though God is anxious for an intimate relationship with us, he will wait for the day when we'll experience for ourselves what loving him really means. And what a wonderful day that will be!

CHAPTER **3** 1"Write this letter to the angel of*
the church in Sardis. This is the message from the
one who has the sevenfold Spirit* of God and the
seven stars:

"I know all the things you do, and that you have
a reputation for being alive—but you are dead.
2Now wake up! Strengthen what little remains,
for even what is left is at the point of death. Your
deeds are far from right in the sight of God. 3Go
back to what you heard and believed at first; hold
to it firmly and turn to me again. Unless you do,
I will come upon you suddenly, as unexpected as
a thief.

4"Yet even in Sardis there are some who have
not soiled their garments with evil deeds. They
will walk with me in white, for they are worthy.
5All who are victorious will be clothed in white.
I will never erase their names from the Book of
Life, but I will announce before my Father and his
angels that they are mine. 6Anyone who is willing
to hear should listen to the Spirit and understand
what the Spirit is saying to the churches.

## SEEK THE TRUTH

"Dana, are you still planning to talk to Rhonda?"

"I've got to. Those people she's been hanging around are weird. My mom even thinks they're a cult!"

"So why don't her parents say something? I mean, my folks would kill me if I came home spouting all that junk!"

"Oh, Mr. and Mrs. Jordan don't care what she does. He's all wrapped up in his business, and she's got some pretty strange religious ideas herself. Their basic attitude is, 'Whatever makes you happy, Rhonda.'"

"What do you think she'll say?"

"I don't know."

"What are you going to say?"

"I'm going to tell her that what she's been hearing from those people isn't true. I'll show her what the Bible says about false teachers. And I'll challenge her to quit seeking some kind of ooey-gooey feeling and start seeking the truth."

We need more people like Dana—people who cling doggedly to the truth and who encourage others to do the same. Would you have the courage to confront a friend who was caught up in a false religion? Would you know what to say?

As you read Revelation, notice the constant emphasis on seeking the truth.

7"Write this letter to the angel of the church in
Philadelphia. This is the message from the one who
is holy and true. He is the one who has the key of
David. He opens doors, and no one can shut them;
he shuts doors, and no one can open them.

8"I know all the things you do, and I have opened
a door for you that no one can shut. You have
little strength, yet you obeyed my word and did
not deny me. 9Look! I will force those who belong

## YOUR CHOICE ● ● • • •

**3:20 Jesus is knocking on the door of our heart every time we sense that we should turn to him. He wants to have fellowship with us, and he wants us to open up to him. Jesus is patient and persistent in trying to get through to us—not breaking and entering, but knocking. He allows us to decide whether or not to open our life to him. Do you intentionally keep Christ's life-changing presence and power on the other side of the door?**

to Satan—those liars who say they are Jews but
are not—to come and bow down at your feet.
They will acknowledge that you are the ones I love.

10"Because you have obeyed my command to
persevere, I will protect you from the great time
of testing that will come upon the whole world
to test those who belong to this world. 11Look, I
am coming quickly. Hold on to what you have,
so that no one will take away your crown. 12All
who are victorious will become pillars in the Temple
of my God, and they will never have to leave it.
And I will write my God's name on them, and
they will be citizens in the city of my God—the
new Jerusalem that comes down from heaven
from my God. And they will have my new name
inscribed upon them. 13Anyone who is willing to
hear should listen to the Spirit and understand
what the Spirit is saying to the churches.

14"Write this letter to the angel of the church in
Laodicea. This is the message from the one who is
the Amen—the faithful and true witness, the ruler*
of God's creation:

15"I know all the things you do, that you are
neither hot nor cold. I wish you were one or the
other! 16But since you are like lukewarm water,
I will spit you out of my mouth! 17You say, 'I am
rich. I have everything I want. I don't need a
thing!' And you don't realize that you are wretched
and miserable and poor and blind and naked.
18I advise you to buy gold from me—gold that
has been purified by fire. Then you will be rich.
And also buy white garments so you will not be
shamed by your nakedness. And buy ointment
for your eyes so you will be able to see. 19I am the
one who corrects and disciplines everyone I love.
Be diligent and turn from your indifference.

20"Look! Here I stand at the door and knock.
If you hear me calling and open the door, I will
come in, and we will share a meal as friends.
21I will invite everyone who is victorious to sit
with me on my throne, just as I was victorious
and sat with my Father on his throne. 22Anyone

## NO FEAR ● ● • • •

**4:1 Chapters 4 and 5 are a glimpse into Christ's glory. Here we see into the throne room of heaven. God is orchestrating all the events that John will record. The world is not spinning out of control; the God of creation will carry out his plans as Christ initiates the final battle with the forces of evil. John shows us heaven before showing us earth so we will not be frightened by future events.**

3:1a Or *the messenger for;* also in 3:7, 14. 3:1b Greek *the seven spirits.* 3:14 Or *the source.*

I stand at the door and knock.
If you hear me calling and open the door,
I will come in,
and we will share a meal
as friends.
REVELATION 3:20

who is willing to hear should listen to the Spirit
and understand what the Spirit is saying to the
churches."

CHAPTER **4** **THE GLORIOUS THRONE.** Then as I
looked, I saw a door standing open in heaven, and
the same voice I had heard before spoke to me with
the sound of a mighty trumpet blast. The voice said,
"Come up here, and I will show you what must
happen after these things." 2And instantly I was in
the Spirit,* and I saw a throne in heaven and someone sitting on it! 3The one sitting on the throne was
as brilliant as gemstones—jasper and carnelian. And
the glow of an emerald circled his throne like a
rainbow. 4Twenty-four thrones surrounded him, and
twenty-four elders sat on them. They were all clothed
in white and had gold crowns on their heads. 5And
from the throne came flashes of lightning and the
rumble of thunder. And in front of the throne were
seven lampstands with burning flames. They are the
seven spirits* of God. 6In front of the throne was a
shiny sea of glass, sparkling like crystal.

In the center and around the throne were four
living beings, each covered with eyes, front and back.
7The first of these living beings had the form of a
lion; the second looked like an ox; the third had a
human face; and the fourth had the form of an eagle
with wings spread out as though in flight. 8Each of
these living beings had six wings, and their wings
were covered with eyes, inside and out. Day after day
and night after night they keep on saying,

"Holy, holy, holy is the Lord God Almighty—
the one who always was, who is, and who is
still to come."

9Whenever the living beings give glory and honor
and thanks to the one sitting on the throne, the one
who lives forever and ever, 10the twenty-four elders
fall down and worship the one who lives forever and
ever. And they lay their crowns before the throne and
say,

11"You are worthy, O Lord our God,
to receive glory and honor and power.
For you created everything,
and it is for your pleasure that they exist and
were created."

CHAPTER **5** **THE LAMB OPENS THE SCROLL.** And I saw
a scroll in the right hand of the one who was sitting
on the throne. There was writing on the inside and
the outside of the scroll, and it was sealed with seven
seals. 2And I saw a strong angel, who shouted with a
loud voice: "Who is worthy to break the seals on this
scroll and unroll it?" 3But no one in heaven or on
earth or under the earth was able to open the scroll
and read it.

4Then I wept because no one could be found who
was worthy to open the scroll and read it. 5But one
of the twenty-four elders said to me, "Stop weeping!
Look, the Lion of the tribe of Judah, the heir to
David's throne,* has conquered. He is worthy to
open the scroll and break its seven seals."

6I looked and I saw a Lamb that had been killed
but was now standing between the throne and the
four living beings and among the twenty-four elders.
He had seven horns and seven eyes, which are the
seven spirits* of God that are sent out into every part
of the earth. 7He stepped forward and took the scroll
from the right hand of the one sitting on the throne.
8And as he took the scroll, the four living beings and
the twenty-four elders fell down before the Lamb.
Each one had a harp, and they held gold bowls filled
with incense—the prayers of God's people!

9And they sang a new song with these words:

"You are worthy to take the scroll
and break its seals and open it.

**ALL TYPES ● ● ● • •**

5:9-10 **People from every nation are praising God before his throne. The gospel is not limited to a specific culture, race, or country. Anyone who comes in repentance and faith is accepted by God and will be part of his kingdom. Don't allow prejudice or bias to stop you from sharing Christ with others. Christ welcomes all types of people into his kingdom.**

4:2 Or *in spirit.* 4:5 See 1:4 and 3:1, where the same expression is translated *the sevenfold Spirit.* 5:5 Greek *the root of David.* 5:6 See note on 4:5.

## GOD'S TIME ● ● • • •

6:9-11 **The martyrs are eager for God to bring justice to the earth, but they are told to wait. Those who suffer and die for their faith will not be forgotten, nor do they die in vain. Rather, they will be singled out by God for special honor. We may wish for justice immediately, as these martyrs did, but we must be patient. God works on his own timetable, and he promises justice. No suffering for the sake of God's kingdom is wasted effort.**

For you were killed, and your blood has ransomed
  people for God
 from every tribe and language and people
  and nation.
10 And you have caused them to become God's
  kingdom and his priests.
 And they will reign* on the earth."

11 Then I looked again, and I heard the singing of thousands and millions of angels around the throne and the living beings and the elders. 12 And they sang in a mighty chorus:

"The Lamb is worthy—the Lamb who was killed.
 He is worthy to receive power and riches
 and wisdom and strength
 and honor and glory and blessing."

13 And then I heard every creature in heaven and on earth and under the earth and in the sea. They also sang:

"Blessing and honor and glory and power
 belong to the one sitting on the throne
 and to the Lamb forever and ever."

14 And the four living beings said, "Amen!" And the twenty-four elders fell down and worshiped God and the Lamb.

CHAPTER **6** **THE LAMB BREAKS THE FIRST SIX SEALS.** As I watched, the Lamb broke the first of the seven seals on the scroll. Then one of the four living beings called out with a voice that sounded like thunder, "Come!" 2 I looked up and saw a white horse. Its rider carried a bow, and a crown was placed on his head. He rode out to win many battles and gain the victory.

3 When the Lamb broke the second seal, I heard the second living being say, "Come!" 4 And another horse appeared, a red one. Its rider was given a mighty sword and the authority to remove peace from the earth. And there was war and slaughter everywhere.

5 When the Lamb broke the third seal, I heard the third living being say, "Come!" And I looked up and saw a black horse, and its rider was holding a pair of scales in his hand. 6 And a voice from among the four living beings said, "A loaf of wheat bread or three loaves of barley for a day's pay.* And don't waste* the olive oil and wine."

7 And when the Lamb broke the fourth seal, I heard the fourth living being say, "Come!" 8 And I looked up and saw a horse whose color was pale green like a corpse. And Death was the name of its rider, who was followed around by the Grave.* They were given authority over one-fourth of the earth, to kill with the sword and famine and disease* and wild animals.

9 And when the Lamb broke the fifth seal, I saw under the altar the souls of all who had been martyred for the word of God and for being faithful in their witness. 10 They called loudly to the Lord and said, "O Sovereign Lord, holy and true, how long will it be before you judge the people who belong to this world for what they have done to us? When will you avenge our blood against these people?" 11 Then a white robe was given to each of them. And they were told to rest a little longer until the full number of their brothers and sisters*—their fellow servants of Jesus—had been martyred.

12 I watched as the Lamb broke the sixth seal, and there was a great earthquake. The sun became as dark as black cloth, and the moon became as red as blood. 13 Then the stars of the sky fell to the earth like green figs falling from trees shaken by mighty winds. 14 And the sky was rolled up like a scroll and taken away. And all of the mountains and all of the islands disappeared. 15 Then the kings of the earth, the rulers, the generals, the wealthy people, the people with great power, and every slave and every free person—all hid themselves in the caves and among the rocks of the mountains. 16 And they cried to the mountains and the rocks, "Fall on us and hide us from the face of the one who sits on the throne and from the wrath of the Lamb. 17 For the great day of their wrath has come, and who will be able to survive?"

## THE ONLY WAY ● ● • • •

7:10 **People try many methods to remove the guilt of sin—good works, intellectual pursuits, and even placing blame on others. The crowd in heaven, however, praises God, saying that salvation comes from him and from the Lamb. Salvation from sin's penalty can come only through Jesus Christ. Have you had the guilt of sin removed in the only way possible?**

CHAPTER **7** **THE 144,000 CHOSEN BY GOD.** Then I saw four angels standing at the four corners of the earth, holding back the four winds from blowing upon the earth. Not a leaf rustled in the trees, and the sea became as smooth as glass. 2 And I saw another angel coming from the east, carrying the seal of the living God. And he shouted out to those four angels who had been given power to injure land and sea, 3 "Wait! Don't hurt the land or the sea or the trees until we have placed the seal of God on the foreheads of his servants."

4 And I heard how many were marked with the seal of God. There were 144,000 who were sealed from all the tribes of Israel:

5 from Judah . . . . . . . . . . . . . . . . . . . . . 12,000
 from Reuben . . . . . . . . . . . . . . . . . . . . 12,000
 from Gad . . . . . . . . . . . . . . . . . . . . . . 12,000

5:10 Some manuscripts read *they are reigning.* 6:6a Greek *A choinix of wheat for a denarius, and 3 choinix of barley for a denarius.* 6:6b Or *hurt*
6:8a Greek *by Hades.* 6:8b Greek *death.* 6:11 Greek *their brothers.*

**THE NAMES OF JESUS**

| JESUS' NAME | REFERENCE |
|---|---|
| A AND THE Ω THE BEGINNING AND THE END | 1:8 |
| LORD | 1:8 |
| THE ALMIGHTY ONE | 1:8 |
| Son of Man | 1:13 |
| THE FIRST AND THE LAST | 1:17 |
| Son of GOD | 2:18 |
| WITNESS | 3:14 |
| CREATOR | 4:11 |
| *Lion of the tribe of Judah* | 5:5 |
| HEIR TO DAVID'S THRONE | 5:5 |
| Lamb | 5:6 |
| Shepherd | 7:17 |
| CHRIST | 12:10 |
| FAITHFUL FAITHFUL FAITHFUL FAITHFUL AND TRUE | 19:11 |
| THE WORD OF GOD | 19:13 |
| KING of KINGS | 19:16 |
| LORD of LORDS | 19:16 |
| THE BRIGHT MORNING STAR | 22:16 |

Scattered among the vivid images of the book of Revelation is a large collection of names for Jesus. Each one tells something of his character and highlights a particular aspect of his role within God's plan of redemption.

6 from Asher. . . . . . . . . . . . . . . . . . . . . . . . 12,000
from Naphtali . . . . . . . . . . . . . . . . . . . . . . 12,000
from Manasseh . . . . . . . . . . . . . . . . . . . . . 12,000
7 from Simeon . . . . . . . . . . . . . . . . . . . . . . . 12,000
from Levi . . . . . . . . . . . . . . . . . . . . . . . . . . 12,000
from Issachar. . . . . . . . . . . . . . . . . . . . . . . 12,000
8 from Zebulun . . . . . . . . . . . . . . . . . . . . . . 12,000
from Joseph. . . . . . . . . . . . . . . . . . . . . . . . 12,000
from Benjamin . . . . . . . . . . . . . . . . . . . . . . 12,000

9 After this I saw a vast crowd, too great to count,
from every nation and tribe and people and language, standing in front of the throne and before the
Lamb. They were clothed in white and held palm
branches in their hands. 10 And they were shouting
with a mighty shout, "Salvation comes from our
God on the throne and from the Lamb!"

11 And all the angels were standing around the
throne and around the elders and the four living
beings. And they fell face down before the throne
and worshiped God. 12 They said,

"Amen! Blessing and glory and wisdom
and thanksgiving and honor and power and strength
belong to our God forever and forever. Amen!"

13 Then one of the twenty-four elders asked me,
"Who are these who are clothed in white? Where do
they come from?"

14 And I said to him, "Sir, you are the one who
knows."

Then he said to me, "These are the ones coming
out of the great tribulation. They washed their robes
in the blood of the Lamb and made them white.
15 That is why they are standing in front of the throne
of God, serving him day and night in his Temple.
And he who sits on the throne will live among them
and shelter them. 16 They will never again be hungry
or thirsty, and they will be fully protected from the
scorching noontime heat. 17 For the Lamb who
stands in front of the throne will be their Shepherd.
He will lead them to the springs of life-giving water.
And God will wipe away all their tears."

## CHAPTER 8 THE LAMB BREAKS THE SEVENTH SEAL.

When the Lamb broke the seventh seal, there was
silence throughout heaven for about half an hour.
2 And I saw the seven angels who stand before God,
and they were given seven trumpets.

3 Then another angel with a gold incense burner
came and stood at the altar. And a great quantity of
incense was given to him to mix with the prayers of
God's people, to be offered on the gold altar before
the throne. 4 The smoke of the incense, mixed with
the prayers of the saints, ascended up to God from
the altar where the angel had poured them out.
5 Then the angel filled the incense burner with fire
from the altar and threw it down upon the earth; and
thunder crashed, lightning flashed, and there was a
terrible earthquake.

## MAKE SURE ● ● • • •

**8:6 The trumpet blasts have three purposes: (1) to warn that judgment is certain, (2) to call the forces of good and evil to battle, and (3) to announce the return of the King, the Messiah. These warnings urge us to make sure our faith is firmly fixed on Christ.**

[6]Then the seven angels with the seven trumpets prepared to blow their mighty blasts.

[7]The first angel blew his trumpet, and hail and fire mixed with blood were thrown down upon the earth, and one-third of the earth was set on fire. One-third of the trees were burned, and all the grass was burned.

[8]Then the second angel blew his trumpet, and a great mountain of fire was thrown into the sea. And one-third of the water in the sea became blood. [9]And one-third of all things living in the sea died. And one-third of all the ships on the sea were destroyed.

[10]Then the third angel blew his trumpet, and a great flaming star fell out of the sky, burning like a torch. It fell upon one-third of the rivers and on the springs of water. [11]The name of the star was Bitterness.* It made one-third of the water bitter, and many people died because the water was so bitter.

[12]Then the fourth angel blew his trumpet, and one-third of the sun was struck, and one-third of the moon, and one-third of the stars, and they became dark. And one-third of the day was dark and one-third of the night also.

[13]Then I looked up. And I heard a single eagle crying loudly as it flew through the air, "Terror, terror, terror to all who belong to this world because of what will happen when the last three angels blow their trumpets."

CHAPTER **9** Then the fifth angel blew his trumpet, and I saw a star that had fallen to earth from the sky, and he was given the key to the shaft of the bottomless pit. [2]When he opened it, smoke poured out as though from a huge furnace, and the sunlight and air were darkened by the smoke.

[3]Then locusts came from the smoke and descended on the earth, and they were given power to sting like scorpions. [4]They were told not to hurt the grass or plants or trees but to attack all the people who did not have the seal of God on their foreheads. [5]They were told not to kill them but to torture them for five months with agony like the pain of scorpion stings. [6]In those days people will seek death but will not find it. They will long to die, but death will flee away!

[7]The locusts looked like horses armed for battle. They had gold crowns on their heads, and they had human faces. [8]Their hair was long like the hair of a woman, and their teeth were like the teeth of a lion. [9]They wore armor made of iron, and their wings roared like an army of chariots rushing into battle. [10]They had tails that stung like scorpions, with power to torture people. This power was given to them for five months. [11]Their king is the angel from the bottomless pit; his name in Hebrew is *Abaddon,* and in Greek, *Apollyon*—the Destroyer.

[12]The first terror is past, but look, two more terrors are coming!

[13]Then the sixth angel blew his trumpet, and I heard a voice speaking from the four horns of the gold altar that stands in the presence of God. [14]And the voice spoke to the sixth angel who held the trumpet: "Release the four angels who are bound at the great Euphrates River." [15]And the four angels who had been prepared for this hour and day and month and year were turned loose to kill one-third of all the people on earth. [16]They led an army of 200 million mounted troops—I heard an announcement of how many there were.

[17]And in my vision, I saw the horses and the riders sitting on them. The riders wore armor that was fiery red and sky blue and yellow. The horses' heads were like the heads of lions, and fire and smoke and burning sulfur billowed from their mouths. [18]One-third of all the people on earth were killed by these three plagues—by the fire and the smoke and burning sulfur that came from the mouths of the horses. [19]Their power was in their mouths, but also in their tails. For their tails had heads like snakes, with the power to injure people.

[20]But the people who did not die in these plagues still refused to turn from their evil deeds. They continued to worship demons and idols made of gold, silver, bronze, stone, and wood—idols that neither see nor hear nor walk! [21]And they did not repent of their murders or their witchcraft or their immorality or their thefts.

## SLIPPING ● ● • • •

**9:20-21 These people were so hardhearted that even plagues did not drive them to God. People don't usually fall into immorality and evil suddenly—they slip into it a little at a time until they are entangled in their wicked ways. Any person who allows sin to take root in his life can find himself in this predicament. Temptation entertained today becomes sin tomorrow, a habit the next day, then death and separation from God forever (see James 1:15). To think you could never become this evil is the first step toward a hard heart. Acknowledge your need to confess your sin to God.**

CHAPTER **10** **AN ANGEL WITH A SCROLL TO EAT.** Then I saw another mighty angel coming down from heaven, surrounded by a cloud, with a rainbow over his head. His face shone like the sun, and his feet were like pillars of fire. [2]And in his hand was a small scroll, which he had unrolled. He stood with his right foot on the sea and his left foot on the land. [3]And he gave a great shout, like the roar of a lion. And when he shouted, the seven thunders answered.

[4]When the seven thunders spoke, I was about to write. But a voice from heaven called to me: "Keep secret what the seven thunders said. Do not write it down."

8:11 Greek *Wormwood.*

[5]Then the mighty angel standing on the sea and
on the land lifted his right hand to heaven. [6]And he
swore an oath in the name of the one who lives
forever and ever, who created heaven and everything
in it, the earth and everything in it, and the sea and
everything in it. He said, "God will wait no longer.
[7]But when the seventh angel blows his trumpet,
God's mysterious plan will be fulfilled. It will happen just as he announced it to his servants the
prophets."

[8]Then the voice from heaven called to me again:
"Go and take the unrolled scroll from the angel who
is standing on the sea and on the land."

[9]So I approached him and asked him to give me
the little scroll. "Yes, take it and eat it," he said. "At
first it will taste like honey, but when you swallow it,
it will make your stomach sour!" [10]So I took the little
scroll from the hands of the angel, and I ate it! It was
sweet in my mouth, but it made my stomach sour.
[11]Then he said to me, "You must prophesy again
about many peoples, nations, languages, and kings."

CHAPTER **11** **TWO PROPHETS.** Then I was given a
measuring stick, and I was told, "Go and measure
the Temple of God and the altar, and count the
number of worshipers. [2]But do not measure the outer
courtyard, for it has been turned over to the nations.
They will trample the holy city for 42 months. [3]And
I will give power to my two witnesses, and they will
be clothed in sackcloth and will prophesy during
those 1,260 days."

[4]These two prophets are the two olive trees and
the two lampstands that stand before the Lord of all
the earth. [5]If anyone tries to harm them, fire flashes
from the mouths of the prophets and consumes
their enemies. This is how anyone who tries to harm
them must die. [6]They have power to shut the skies so
that no rain will fall for as long as they prophesy.
And they have the power to turn the rivers and
oceans into blood, and to send every kind of plague
upon the earth as often as they wish.

[7]When they complete their testimony, the beast
that comes up out of the bottomless pit will declare war against them. He will conquer them and
kill them. [8]And their bodies will lie in the main
street of Jerusalem,* the city which is called
"Sodom" and "Egypt," the city where their Lord
was crucified. [9]And for three and a half days, all
peoples, tribes, languages, and nations will come
to stare at their bodies. No one will be allowed to
bury them. [10]All the people who belong to this
world will give presents to each other to celebrate
the death of the two prophets who had tormented
them.

[11]But after three and a half days, the spirit of life
from God entered them, and they stood up! And
terror struck all who were staring at them. [12]Then a
loud voice shouted from heaven, "Come up here!"
And they rose to heaven in a cloud as their enemies
watched.

11:8 Greek *the great city.*

**CARPE DIEM ● ● • • •**

10:4 **Throughout history people have wanted to know what would happen in the future, and God reveals some of it in this book. But John was stopped from revealing certain parts of his vision. An angel also told the prophet Daniel that some things he saw were not to be revealed yet to everyone (Daniel 12:9), and Jesus told his disciples that the time of the end is known by no one but God (Mark 13:32-33). God has revealed all we need to know to live for him now. In our desire to be ready for the end, we must not place more emphasis on speculation about the last days than on living for God while we wait.**

[13]And in the same hour there was a terrible earthquake that destroyed a tenth of the city. Seven thousand people died in that earthquake. And everyone
who did not die was terrified and gave glory to the
God of heaven.

[14]The second terror is past, but look, now the third
terror is coming quickly.

[15]Then the seventh angel blew his trumpet, and
there were loud voices shouting in heaven: "The
whole world has now become the kingdom of our
Lord and of his Christ, and he will reign forever and
ever."

[16]And the twenty-four elders sitting on their
thrones before God fell on their faces and worshiped
him. [17]And they said,

"We give thanks to you, Lord God Almighty,
the one who is and who always was,
for now you have assumed your great power
and have begun to reign.
[18]The nations were angry with you,
but now the time of your wrath has come.
It is time to judge the dead and reward your
servants.
You will reward your prophets and your holy
people,
all who fear your name, from the least to the
greatest.
And you will destroy all who have caused
destruction on the earth."

[19]Then, in heaven, the Temple of God was opened
and the Ark of his covenant could be seen inside the
Temple. Lightning flashed, thunder crashed and
roared; there was a great hailstorm, and the world
was shaken by a mighty earthquake.

CHAPTER **12** **THE WOMAN AND THE DRAGON.** Then I
witnessed in heaven an event of great significance. I
saw a woman clothed with the sun, with the moon
beneath her feet, and a crown of twelve stars on her
head. [2]She was pregnant, and she cried out in the
pain of labor as she awaited her delivery.

[3]Suddenly, I witnessed in heaven another significant event. I saw a large red dragon with seven
heads and ten horns, with seven crowns on his
heads. [4]His tail dragged down one-third of the
stars, which he threw to the earth. He stood before

# Ultimate Issues

## SATAN

April, 1989—Matamoros, Mexico: Police unearth thirteen bodies, all showing signs of torture and mutilation. The cause? The murders were part of satanic sacrificial rites. **S**atan, the deceiver, the evil one, the tempter. The Bible has many names for the devil. And today, interest in Satan and satanism—and activities performed in Satan's name—are on the rise. What does the Bible teach about this dark creature? **I**n the Old Testament, the Hebrew word from which we get "Satan" primarily means **"ADVERSARY."** Passages such as 1 Chronicles 21:1, Job 1–2, and Zechariah 3 portray him as an accuser of God's people. It is historically believed that Satan was behind the serpent that deceived Eve in Genesis 3. Many interpret Isaiah 14 (a prophecy about the "king of Babylon") as a veiled reference to Satan: "How you are FALLEN FROM HEAVEN, O shining star, son of the morning! You have been thrown down to the earth, you who destroyed the nations of the world." **T**he New Testament is filled with references to Satan. Matthew 4:1-11 and Mark 1:12-13 tell of Jesus' being tempted by Satan. In Matthew 12 Jesus describes Satan as a powerful ruler over a demonic kingdom. John quotes Jesus as referring to Satan as "the prince of this world" (John 12:31, 14:30, and 16:11). Passages such as Matthew 13:19; 2 Corinthians 4:4; and Ephesians 6:16 show that Satan's goal is to keep people from hearing, understanding, and believing God's Word and the good news of salvation through Christ. Ultimately, Satan wants to destroy us: "Watch out for attacks from the Devil, your great enemy. He prowls around like a roaring lion, looking for some victim to devour" (1 Peter 5:8; see also 2 Thessalonians 2:1-12 and Revelation 13). **S**atan is a powerful enemy, but the universe is not a **cosmic tug-of-war contest** between God and Satan. For all Satan's power and cunning, he is not God's equal; he is one of God's creatures, given some freedom to cause evil for a period of time. We can't really understand why God allows Satan this freedom, but we can be certain that God is still in control. Satan is like ***a mean dog on a leash.*** If you get close to him he can hurt you; but his Master can always rein him in. (This book of the Bible, Revelation, shows how the battle turns out.) **S**ome find it difficult to believe in Satan. Others, like many heavy metal bands, display an obsessive preoccupation with the satanic world and the occult. Over 50 years ago, in *The Screwtape Letters*, C. S. Lewis wrote: "There are two equal and opposite errors into which our race can fall about the devils. One is to disbelieve in their existence. The other is to believe, and to feel an excessive and unhealthy interest in them. They themselves are equally pleased by both errors." **T**he Bible clearly teaches that there is a literal, personal evil being called Satan. He is not to be taken lightly, but neither does the Christian need to be afraid. We know THE ONE WHO HOLDS SATAN'S LEASH securely in his nail-scarred hands.

---

the woman as she was about to give birth to her child, ready to devour the baby as soon as it was born.
[5]She gave birth to a boy who was to rule all nations with an iron rod. And the child was snatched away from the dragon and was caught up to God and to his throne. [6]And the woman fled into the wilderness, where God had prepared a place to give her care for 1,260 days.

[7]Then there was war in heaven. Michael and the angels under his command fought the dragon and his angels. [8]And the dragon lost the battle and was forced out of heaven. [9]This great dragon—the ancient serpent called the Devil, or Satan, the one deceiving the whole world—was thrown down to the earth with all his angels.
[10]Then I heard a loud voice shouting across the heavens,

"It has happened at last—the salvation and power
and kingdom of our God, and the authority of
his Christ! For the Accuser has been thrown down
to earth—the one who accused our brothers and
sisters* before our God day and night. 11 And they
have defeated him because of the blood of the
Lamb and because of their testimony. And they
were not afraid to die. 12 Rejoice, O heavens! And
you who live in the heavens, rejoice! But terror
will come on the earth and the sea. For the Devil
has come down to you in great anger, and he
knows that he has little time."

13 And when the dragon realized that he had been
thrown down to the earth, he pursued the woman
who had given birth to the child. 14 But she was given
two wings like those of a great eagle. This allowed her
to fly to a place prepared for her in the wilderness,
where she would be cared for and protected from the
dragon* for a time, times, and half a time.
15 Then the dragon tried to drown the woman with
a flood of water that flowed from its mouth. 16 But the
earth helped her by opening its mouth and swallow-
ing the river that gushed out from the mouth of
the dragon. 17 Then the dragon became angry at the
woman, and he declared war against the rest of her
children—all who keep God's commandments and
confess that they belong to Jesus.
18 Then he stood* waiting on the shore of the sea.

CHAPTER **13** **THE TWO STRANGE CREATURES.** And
now in my vision I saw a beast rising up out of the sea.
It had seven heads and ten horns, with ten crowns on
its horns. And written on each head were names that
blasphemed God. 2 This beast looked like a leopard,
but it had bear's feet and a lion's mouth! And the
dragon gave him his own power and
throne and great authority.
3 I saw that one of the heads of the
beast seemed wounded beyond recovery—but the fatal wound was
healed! All the world marveled at
this miracle and followed the beast
in awe. 4 They worshiped the dragon
for giving the beast such power, and
they worshiped the beast. "Is there
anyone as great as the beast?" they
exclaimed. "Who is able to fight
against him?"
5 Then the beast was allowed to
speak great blasphemies against
God. And he was given authority to
do what he wanted for forty-two
months. 6 And he spoke terrible
words of blasphemy against God,
slandering his name and all who
live in heaven, who are his temple.
7 And the beast was allowed to wage
war against God's holy people and
to overcome them. And he was given authority to rule
over every tribe and people and language and nation.
8 And all the people who belong to this world worshiped the beast. They are the ones whose names were
not written in the Book of Life, which belongs to the
Lamb who was killed before the world was made.
9 Anyone who is willing to hear should listen and
understand. 10 The people who are destined for
prison will be arrested and taken away. Those who
are destined for death will be killed. But do not be
dismayed, for here is your opportunity to have endurance and faith.
11 Then I saw another beast come up out of the earth.
He had two horns like those of a lamb, and he spoke
with the voice of a dragon. 12 He exercised all the
authority of the first beast. And he required all the
earth and those who belong to this world to worship
the first beast, whose death-wound had been healed.
13 He did astounding miracles, such as making fire flash
down to earth from heaven while everyone was watching. 14 And with all the miracles he was allowed to

## CREATURES ● ● ● • •

**13:1-18 Satan (the dragon) has two evil accomplices: (1) the beast out of the sea (13:1-10) and (2) the beast out of the earth (13:11-18). Together, the three form an unholy trinity in direct opposition to the holy Trinity of God, Christ, and the Holy Spirit.**

**When Satan tempted Jesus in the wilderness, he wanted Jesus to show his power (see Matthew 4:1-11). Satan wanted to rule the world through Jesus, but Jesus refused to do what Satan asked. Thus Satan turns to the fearsome beasts of Revelation, giving them special powers. This unholy trinity—the dragon, the beast out of the sea, and the false prophet (see 16:13)—unite in a desperate attempt to overthrow God. To find out what becomes of them, read Revelation 19:19-21 and 20:10.**

## "Here's what I did..."

I struggle with apathy. I guess you can say I'm not very self-disciplined. This affects both my schoolwork and my Christian life: I have trouble applying myself to what I need to do if I don't feel like doing it at the moment.

In my youth group we studied 2 Timothy and one verse has really challenged me directly: verse 15 of chapter 2. It says, "Work hard so God can approve you. Be a good worker, one who does not need to be ashamed and who correctly explains the word of truth." These words remind me that my actions and attitudes are significant, and someday I'll have to answer to God for them. Revelation tells about when that will happen (14:7). That helps me make an extra effort to do the right thing, whether it's reading my Bible regularly or turning off the TV and opening a textbook.

Sue

AGE 15

12:10 Greek *brothers.* 12:14 Greek *the serpent;* also in 12:15. See 12:9. 12:18 Some manuscripts read *Then I stood,* and some translations put this entire sentence into 13:1.

## PASSED OUT ● ● • • •

**14:14-17 This is an image of judgment: Christ is separating the faithful from the unfaithful like a farmer harvesting his crops. This will be a time of joy for the Christians who have been persecuted and martyred—they will receive their long awaited reward. Christians should not fear the last judgment. Jesus said, "I assure you, those who listen to my message and believe in God who sent me have eternal life. They will never be condemned for their sins, but they have already passed from death into life" (John 5:24).**

perform on behalf of the first beast, he deceived all the people who belong to this world. He ordered the people of the world to make a great statue of the first beast, who was fatally wounded and then came back to life. [15]He was permitted to give life to this statue so that it could speak. Then the statue commanded that anyone refusing to worship it must die.

[16]He required everyone—great and small, rich and poor, slave and free—to be given a mark on the right hand or on the forehead. [17]And no one could buy or sell anything without that mark, which was either the name of the beast or the number representing his name. [18]Wisdom is needed to understand this. Let the one who has understanding solve the number of the beast, for it is the number of a man.* His number is 666.*

CHAPTER **14** **THE LAMB AND A GREAT CHOIR.** Then I saw the Lamb standing on Mount Zion, and with him were 144,000 who had his name and his Father's name written on their foreheads. [2]And I heard a sound from heaven like the roaring of a great waterfall or the rolling of mighty thunder. It was like the sound of many harpists playing together.

[3]This great choir sang a wonderful new song in front of the throne of God and before the four living beings and the twenty-four elders. And no one could learn this song except those 144,000 who had been redeemed from the earth. [4]For they are spiritually undefiled, pure as virgins,* following the Lamb wherever he goes. They have been purchased from among the people on the earth as a special offering* to God and to the Lamb. [5]No falsehood can be charged against them; they are blameless.

[6]And I saw another angel flying through the heavens, carrying the everlasting Good News to preach to the people who belong to this world—to every nation, tribe, language, and people. [7]"Fear God," he shouted. "Give glory to him. For the time has come when he will sit as judge. Worship him who made heaven and earth, the sea, and all the springs of water."

[8]Then another angel followed him through the skies, shouting, "Babylon is fallen—that great city is fallen—because she seduced the nations of the world and made them drink the wine of her passionate immorality."

[9]Then a third angel followed them, shouting, "Anyone who worships the beast and his statue or who accepts his mark on the forehead or the hand [10]must drink the wine of God's wrath. It is poured out undiluted into God's cup of wrath. And they will be tormented with fire and burning sulfur in the presence of the holy angels and the Lamb. [11]The smoke of their torment rises forever and ever, and they will have no relief day or night, for they have worshiped the beast and his statue and have accepted the mark of his name. [12]Let this encourage God's holy people to endure persecution patiently and remain firm to the end, obeying his commands and trusting in Jesus."

[13]And I heard a voice from heaven saying, "Write this down: Blessed are those who die in the Lord from now on. Yes, says the Spirit, they are blessed indeed, for they will rest from all their toils and trials; for their good deeds follow them!"

[14]Then I saw the Son of Man* sitting on a white cloud. He had a gold crown on his head and a sharp sickle in his hand.

[15]Then an angel came from the Temple and called out in a loud voice to the one sitting on the cloud, "Use the sickle, for the time has come for you to harvest; the crop is ripe on the earth." [16]So the one sitting on the cloud swung his sickle over the earth, and the whole earth was harvested.

[17]After that, another angel came from the Temple in heaven, and he also had a sharp sickle. [18]Then another angel, who has power to destroy the world with fire, shouted to the angel with the sickle, "Use your sickle now to gather the clusters of grapes from the vines of the earth, for they are fully ripe for judgment." [19]So the angel swung his sickle on the earth and loaded the grapes into the great winepress of God's wrath. [20]And the grapes were trodden in the winepress outside the city, and blood flowed from the winepress in a stream about 180 miles* long and as high as a horse's bridle.

CHAPTER **15** Then I saw in heaven another significant event, and it was great and marvelous. Seven angels were holding the seven last plagues, which would bring God's wrath to completion. [2]I saw before me what seemed to be a crystal sea mixed with fire. And on it stood all the people who had been victorious over the beast and his statue and the number representing his name. They were all holding harps that God had given them. [3]And they were singing the song of Moses, the servant of God, and the song of the Lamb:

"Great and marvelous are your actions,
  Lord God Almighty.
Just and true are your ways,
  O King of the nations.*
[4]Who will not fear, O Lord, and glorify your name?

## READY OR NOT ● ● • • •

**16:15 Christ will return unexpectedly (1 Thessalonians 5:1-6), so we must be ready when he returns. We can prepare ourselves by resisting temptation and by being committed to God's moral standards. In what ways does your life show your readiness for Christ's return?**

13:18a Or *of humanity.* 13:18b Some manuscripts read *616.* 14:4a Greek *they are virgins who have not defiled themselves with women.* 14:4b Greek *as firstfruits.* 14:14 Or *one who looked like a man;* Greek reads *one like a son of man.* 14:20 Greek *1,600 stadia* [296 kilometers]. 15:3 Some manuscripts read *King of the ages;* other manuscripts read *King of the saints.*

## THE BEGINNING AND THE END

The Bible records for us the beginning of the world and the end of the world. The story of humanity, from beginning to end—from the fall into sin to the redemption of Christ and God's ultimate victory over evil—is found in the pages of the Bible.

GENESIS
The sun is created
Satan is victorious
Sin enters the human race
People run and hide from God
People are cursed
Tears are shed, with sorrow for sin
The garden and earth are cursed
The fruit from the tree of life is not to be eaten
Paradise is lost
People are doomed to death

REVELATION
The sun is not needed
Satan is defeated
Sin is banished
People are invited to live with God forever
The curse is removed
No more sin, no more tears or sorrow
God's city is glorified, the earth is made new
God's people may eat from the tree of life
Paradise is regained
Death is defeated, believers live forever with God

For you alone are holy.
All nations will come and worship before you,
for your righteous deeds have been revealed."

[5]Then I looked and saw that the Temple in heaven,
God's Tabernacle, was thrown wide open! [6]The seven
angels who were holding the bowls of the seven
plagues came from the Temple, clothed in spotless
white linen* with gold belts across their chests. [7]And
one of the four living beings handed each of the seven
angels a gold bowl filled with the terrible wrath of
God, who lives forever and forever. [8]The Temple was
filled with smoke from God's glory and power. No one
could enter the Temple until the seven angels had
completed pouring out the seven plagues.

CHAPTER **16** **SEVEN FLASKS OF WRATH.** Then I
heard a mighty voice shouting from the Temple to
the seven angels, "Now go your ways and empty out
the seven bowls of God's wrath on the earth."

[2]So the first angel left the Temple and poured out
his bowl over the earth, and horrible, malignant
sores broke out on everyone who had the mark of
the beast and who worshiped his statue.

[3]Then the second angel poured out his bowl on
the sea, and it became like the blood of a corpse. And
everything in the sea died.

[4]Then the third angel poured out his bowl on the
rivers and springs, and they became blood. [5]And I
heard the angel who had authority over all water
saying, "You are just in sending this judgment, O Holy
One, who is and who always was. [6]For your holy
people and your prophets have been killed, and their
blood was poured out on the earth. So you have given
their murderers blood to drink. It is their just reward."
[7]And I heard a voice from the altar saying, "Yes, Lord
God Almighty, your punishments are true and just."

[8]Then the fourth angel poured out his bowl on
the sun, causing it to scorch everyone with its fire.
[9]Everyone was burned by this blast of heat, and they
cursed the name of God, who sent all of these
plagues. They did not repent and give him glory.

[10]Then the fifth angel poured out his bowl on the
throne of the beast, and his kingdom was plunged
into darkness. And his subjects ground their teeth in
anguish, [11]and they cursed the God of heaven for
their pains and sores. But they refused to repent of
all their evil deeds.

[12]Then the sixth angel poured out his bowl on the
great Euphrates River, and it dried up so that the
kings from the east could march their armies westward without hindrance. [13]And I saw three evil spirits
that looked like frogs leap from the mouth of the
dragon, the beast, and the false prophet. [14]These
miracle-working demons caused all the rulers of the
world to gather for battle against the Lord on that
great judgment day of God Almighty.

[15]"Take note: I will come as unexpectedly as a
thief! Blessed are all who are watching for me,

15:6 Some manuscripts read *in bright and sparkling stone.*

who keep their robes ready so they will not need to walk naked and ashamed."

[16]And they gathered all the rulers and their armies to a place called *Armageddon* in Hebrew.

[17]Then the seventh angel poured out his bowl into the air. And a mighty shout came from the throne of the Temple in heaven, saying, "It is finished!" [18]Then the thunder crashed and rolled, and lightning flashed. And there was an earthquake greater than ever before in human history. [19]The great city of Babylon split into three pieces, and cities around the world fell into heaps of rubble. And so God remembered all of Babylon's sins, and he made her drink the cup that was filled with the wine of his fierce wrath. [20]And every island disappeared, and all the mountains were leveled. [21]There was a terrible hailstorm, and hailstones weighing seventy-five pounds* fell from the sky onto the people below. They cursed God because of the hailstorm, which was a very terrible plague.

## CHAPTER 17 A DRUNKEN WOMAN.

One of the seven angels who had poured out the seven bowls came over and spoke to me. "Come with me," he said, "and I will show you the judgment that is going to come on the great prostitute, who sits on many waters. [2]The rulers of the world have had immoral relations with her, and the people who belong to this world have been made drunk by the wine of her immorality."

[3]So the angel took me in spirit* into the wilderness. There I saw a woman sitting on a scarlet beast that had seven heads and ten horns, written all over with blasphemies against God. [4]The woman wore purple and scarlet clothing and beautiful jewelry made of gold and precious gems and pearls. She held in her hand a gold goblet full of obscenities and the impurities of her immorality. [5]A mysterious name was written on her forehead: "Babylon the Great, Mother of All Prostitutes and Obscenities in the World." [6]I could see that she was drunk—drunk with the blood of God's holy people who were witnesses for Jesus. I stared at her completely amazed.

[7]"Why are you so amazed?" the angel asked. "I will tell you the mystery of this woman and of the beast with seven heads and ten horns. [8]The beast you saw was alive but isn't now. And yet he will soon come up out of the bottomless pit and go to eternal destruction. And the people who belong to this world, whose names were not written in the Book of Life from before the world began, will be amazed at the reappearance of this beast who had died.

[9]"And now understand this: The seven heads of the beast represent the seven hills of the city where this woman rules. They also represent seven kings. [10]Five kings have already fallen, the sixth now reigns, and the seventh is yet to come, but his reign will be brief. [11]The scarlet beast that was alive and then died is the eighth king. He is like the other seven, and he, too, will go to his doom. [12]His ten horns are ten kings who have not yet risen to power; they will be appointed to their kingdoms for one brief moment to reign with the beast. [13]They will all agree to give their power and authority to him. [14]Together they will wage war against the Lamb, but the Lamb will defeat them because he is Lord over all lords and King over all kings, and his people are the called and chosen and faithful ones."

[15]And the angel said to me, "The waters where the prostitute is sitting represent masses of people of every nation and language. [16]The scarlet beast and his ten horns—which represent ten kings who will reign with him—all hate the prostitute. They will strip her naked, eat her flesh, and burn her remains with fire. [17]For God has put a plan into their minds, a plan that will carry out his purposes. They will mutually agree to give their authority to the scarlet beast, and so the words of God will be fulfilled. [18]And this woman you saw in your vision represents the great city that rules over the kings of the earth."

### IN CHARGE ● ● ● • •

17:17 **No matter what happens, we must trust that God is still in charge, that his plans will happen just as he says. He even uses people opposed to him to execute his will. Although he allows evil to permeate this present world, the new earth will never know sin.**

## CHAPTER 18 THE FALL OF BABYLON.

After all this I saw another angel come down from heaven with great authority, and the earth grew bright with his splendor. [2]He gave a mighty shout, "Babylon is fallen—that great city is fallen! She has become the hideout of demons and evil spirits, a nest for filthy buzzards, and a den for dreadful beasts. [3]For all the nations have drunk the wine of her passionate immorality. The rulers of the world have committed adultery with her, and merchants throughout the world have grown rich as a result of her luxurious living."

[4]Then I heard another voice calling from heaven, "Come away from her, my people. Do not take part in her sins, or you will be punished with her. [5]For her sins are piled as high as heaven, and God is ready to judge her for her evil deeds. [6]Do to her as she has done to your people. Give her a double penalty for all her evil deeds. She brewed a cup of terror for others, so give her twice as much as she gave out. [7]She has lived in luxury and pleasure, so match it now with torments and sorrows. She boasts, 'I am queen on my throne. I am no helpless widow. I will not experience sorrow.' [8]Therefore, the sorrows of death and mourning and famine will overtake her in a single day. She will be utterly consumed by fire, for the Lord God who judges her is mighty."

[9]And the rulers of the world who took part in her immoral acts and enjoyed her great luxury will mourn for her as they see the smoke rising from her charred remains. [10]They will stand at a distance, terrified by her

16:21 Greek *1 talent* [34 kilograms]. 17:3 Or *in the Spirit.*

great torment. They will cry out, "How terrible, how
terrible for Babylon, that great city! In one single
moment God's judgment came on her."
[11]The merchants of the world will weep and
mourn for her, for there is no one left to buy their
goods. [12]She bought great quantities of gold, silver,
jewels, pearls, fine linen, purple dye, silk, scarlet
cloth, every kind of perfumed wood, ivory goods,
objects made of expensive wood, bronze, iron, and
marble. [13]She also bought cinnamon, spice, incense, myrrh, frankincense, wine, olive oil, fine
flour, wheat, cattle, sheep, horses, chariots, and
slaves—yes, she even traded in human lives.
[14]"All the fancy things you loved so much are
gone," they cry. "The luxuries and splendor that you
prized so much will never be yours again. They are
gone forever."
[15]The merchants who became wealthy by selling
her these things will stand at a distance, terrified by
her great torment. They will weep and cry. [16]"How
terrible, how terrible for that great city! She was so
beautiful—like a woman clothed in finest purple
and scarlet linens, decked out with gold and precious stones and pearls! [17]And in one single moment
all the wealth of the city is gone!"
And all the shipowners and captains of the merchant ships and their crews will stand at a distance.
[18]They will weep as they watch the smoke ascend,
and they will say, "Where in all the world is there
another city like this?" [19]And they will throw dust on
their heads to show their great sorrow. And they will
say, "How terrible, how terrible for the great city! She
made us all rich from her great wealth. And now in
a single hour it is all gone."
[20]But you, O heaven, rejoice over her fate. And you
also rejoice, O holy people of God and apostles and
prophets! For at last God has judged her on your
behalf.
[21]Then a mighty angel picked up a boulder as
large as a great millstone. He threw it into the
ocean and shouted, "Babylon, the great city, will
be thrown down as violently as I have thrown away
this stone, and she will disappear forever. [22]Never
again will the sound of music be heard there—no
more harps, songs, flutes, or trumpets. There will
be no industry of any kind, and no more milling of
grain. [23]Her nights will be dark, without a single
lamp. There will be no happy voices of brides and
grooms. This will happen because her merchants,
who were the greatest in the world, deceived the
nations with her sorceries. [24]In her streets the
blood of the prophets was spilled. She was the one
who slaughtered God's people all over the world."

CHAPTER **19** **A HALLELUJAH CHORUS.** After this, I
heard the sound of a vast crowd in heaven shouting,
"Hallelujah! Salvation is from our God. Glory and
power belong to him alone. [2]His judgments are just
and true. He has punished the great prostitute who
corrupted the earth with her immorality, and he has
avenged the murder of his servants." [3]Again and
again their voices rang, "Hallelujah! The smoke
from that city ascends forever and forever!"
[4]Then the twenty-four elders and the four living
beings fell down and worshiped God, who was sitting
on the throne. They cried out, "Amen! Hallelujah!"
[5]And from the throne came a voice that said,
"Praise our God, all his servants, from the least to the
greatest, all who fear him."
[6]Then I heard again what sounded like the shout
of a huge crowd, or the roar of mighty ocean waves,
or the crash of loud thunder: "Hallelujah! For the
Lord our God, the Almighty, reigns. [7]Let us be glad
and rejoice and honor him. For the time has come
for the wedding feast of the Lamb, and his bride
has prepared herself. [8]She is permitted to wear the
finest white linen." (Fine linen represents the good
deeds done by the people of God.)
[9]And the angel said, "Write this: Blessed are
those who are invited to the wedding feast of the
Lamb." And he added, "These are true words that
come from God."
[10]Then I fell down at his feet to worship him, but he
said, "No, don't worship me. For I am a servant of God,
just like you and other brothers and sisters* who
testify of their faith in Jesus. Worship God. For the
essence of prophecy is to give a clear witness for
Jesus.*"
[11]Then I saw heaven opened, and a white horse
was standing there. And the one sitting on the horse
was named Faithful and True. For he judges fairly
and then goes to war. [12]His eyes were bright like
flames of fire, and on his head were many crowns. A
name was written on him, and only he knew what it
meant. [13]He was clothed with a robe dipped in
blood, and his title was the Word of God. [14]The
armies of heaven, dressed in pure white linen, followed him on white horses. [15]From his mouth came
a sharp sword, and with it he struck down the nations. He ruled them with an iron rod, and he trod
the winepress of the fierce wrath of almighty God.
[16]On his robe and thigh was written this title: King of
kings and Lord of lords.
[17]Then I saw an angel standing in the sun, shouting
to the vultures flying high in the sky: "Come! Gather
together for the great banquet God has prepared.

19:10a Greek *brothers*. 19:10b Or *is the message confirmed by Jesus*.

## GREED GUARD ● ● • • •

18:11-19 **God's people should not live for money. Instead, they should keep on guard constantly against greed, which is always ready to take over their life. Money will be worthless in eternity, and God calls greed sinful.**

## TRUE WORSHIP ● ● • • •

19:1-10 **Praise is the heartfelt response to God by those who love him. The more you get to know God and realize what he has done, the more you will respond with praise. Praise is at the heart of true worship. Let your praise of God flow out of your realization of who he is and how much he loves you.**

18Come and eat the flesh of kings, captains, and strong
warriors; of horses and their riders; and of all humanity, both free and slave, small and great."
19Then I saw the beast gathering the kings of
the earth and their armies in order to fight against
the one sitting on the horse and his army. 20And the
beast was captured, and with him the false prophet
who did mighty miracles on behalf of the beast—
miracles that deceived all who had accepted the
mark of the beast and who worshiped his statue.
Both the beast and his false prophet were thrown
alive into the lake of fire that burns with sulfur.
21Their entire army was killed by the sharp sword
that came out of the mouth of the one riding the
white horse. And all the vultures of the sky gorged
themselves on the dead bodies.

**ESPAIR**

Blood, violence, murder, mayhem, images of doom and gloom.

What have we got here? Some kind of horror movie? No, just another edition of the nightly news.

With smiling faces and playful banter, the channel 2 news anchors recite one horror story after another: the ongoing drug war, tensions in the Middle East, 18 killed in a school bus tragedy, a psychotic killer on the loose, alarming new predictions about AIDS, a devastating flood in India, the growing nightmare of pollution, the possible consequences of the greenhouse effect.

As Wes turns off the TV, he sighs.

"I'm telling you," he mutters to himself, "this world is totally messed up. What's the point? I mean, what do I have to live for? The way things are going, I won't even make it to age 30."

Is it any wonder the guy's depressed? The human race does seem bent on self-destruction. Is there any hope in a world that seems to be spinning out of control?

Yes! One of the greatest, most encouraging passages in the whole Bible is found right at the end. Read Revelation 21 and 22 for a fascinating and faith-building look at what the future holds for those who know Christ. (If you don't know Christ as your Savior, now is a perfect time to ask him to forgive your sins and to give you eternal life.)

## CHAPTER 20 THE THOUSAND YEARS.

Then I saw
an angel come down from heaven with the key to
the bottomless pit and a heavy chain in his hand.
2He seized the dragon—that old serpent, the Devil,
Satan—and bound him in chains for a thousand
years. 3The angel threw him into the bottomless
pit, which he then shut and locked so Satan could
not deceive the nations anymore until the thousand years were finished. Afterward he would be
released again for a little while.
4Then I saw thrones, and the people sitting on
them had been given the authority to judge. And I
saw the souls of those who had been beheaded for

### NO CONTEST

20:9 **This is not a typical battle where the outcome is in doubt during the heat of the conflict. Here there is no contest. Two mighty forces of evil—those of the beast (19:19) and of Satan (20:8)—unite to do battle against God. The Bible uses just two verses to describe each battle—the evil beast and his forces are captured and thrown into the lake of fire (19:20-21), and fire from heaven consumes Satan and his attacking armies (20:9-10). There will be no doubt, no worry, and no second thoughts for believers about whether they have chosen the right side. If you choose God, you will experience this tremendous victory with Christ.**

their testimony about Jesus, for proclaiming the
word of God. And I saw the souls of those who had
not worshiped the beast or his statue, nor accepted
his mark on their forehead or their hands. They
came to life again, and they reigned with Christ
for a thousand years. 5This is the first resurrection.
(The rest of the dead did not come back to life until
the thousand years had ended.) 6Blessed and holy are
those who share in the first resurrection. For them
the second death holds no power, but they will be
priests of God and of Christ and will reign with him
a thousand years.
7When the thousand years end, Satan will be let
out of his prison. 8He will go out to deceive the
nations from every corner of the earth, which are
called Gog and Magog. He will gather them together for battle—a mighty host, as numberless as
sand along the shore. 9And I saw them as they went
up on the broad plain of the earth and surrounded
God's people and the beloved city. But fire from
heaven came down on the attacking armies and
consumed them.
10Then the Devil, who betrayed them, was thrown
into the lake of fire that burns with sulfur, joining
the beast and the false prophet. There they will be
tormented day and night forever and ever.
11And I saw a great white throne, and I saw the
one who was sitting on it. The earth and sky fled
from his presence, but they found no place to hide.
12I saw the dead, both great and small, standing
before God's throne. And the books were opened,
including the Book of Life. And the dead were
judged according to the things written in the
books, according to what they had done. 13The sea
gave up the dead in it, and death and the grave*
gave up the dead in them. They were all judged
according to their deeds. 14And death and the grave
were thrown into the lake of fire. This is the second
death—the lake of fire. 15And anyone whose name
was not found recorded in the Book of Life was
thrown into the lake of fire.

## CHAPTER 21 A NEW HEAVEN AND NEW EARTH.

Then
I saw a new heaven and a new earth, for the old
heaven and the old earth had disappeared. And the
sea was also gone. 2And I saw the holy city, the new
Jerusalem, coming down from God out of heaven
like a beautiful bride prepared for her husband.
3I heard a loud shout from the throne, saying,

20:13 Greek *and Hades;* also in 20:14.

"Look, the home of God is now among his people!
He will live with them, and they will be his people.
God himself will be with them.* 4He will remove all
of their sorrows, and there will be no more death or
sorrow or crying or pain. For the old world and its
evils are gone forever."
5And the one sitting on the throne said, "Look,
I am making all things new!" And then he said to
me, "Write this down, for what I tell you is trustworthy and true." 6And he also said, "It is finished!
I am the Alpha and the Omega—the Beginning
and the End. To all who are thirsty I will give the
springs of the water of life without charge! 7All
who are victorious will inherit all these blessings,
and I will be their God, and they will be my children. 8But cowards who turn away from me, and
unbelievers, and the corrupt, and murderers, and
the immoral, and those who practice witchcraft,
and idol worshipers, and all liars—their doom is
in the lake that burns with fire and sulfur. This is
the second death."
9Then one of the seven angels who held the seven
bowls containing the seven last plagues came and
said to me, "Come with me! I will show you the
bride, the wife of the Lamb."
10So he took me in spirit* to a great, high mountain, and he showed me the holy city, Jerusalem,
descending out of heaven from God. 11It was filled
with the glory of God and sparkled like a precious
gem, crystal clear like jasper. 12Its walls were broad
and high, with twelve gates guarded by twelve angels. And the names of the twelve tribes of Israel
were written on the gates. 13There were three gates
on each side—east, north, south, and west. 14The
wall of the city had twelve foundation stones, and
on them were written the names of the twelve
apostles of the Lamb.
15The angel who talked to me held in his hand a
gold measuring stick to measure the city, its gates,
and its wall. 16When he measured it, he found it was
a square, as wide as it was long. In fact, it was in the
form of a cube, for its length and width and height
were each 1,400 miles.* 17Then he measured the
walls and found them to be 216 feet thick* (the
angel used a standard human measure).
18The wall was made of jasper, and the city was
pure gold, as clear as glass. 19The wall of the city was
built on foundation stones inlaid with twelve gems:
the first was jasper, the second sapphire, the third
agate, the fourth emerald, 20the fifth onyx, the sixth
carnelian, the seventh chrysolite, the eighth beryl,
the ninth topaz, the tenth chrysoprase, the eleventh
jacinth, the twelfth amethyst.
21The twelve gates were made of pearls—each gate
from a single pearl! And the main street was pure
gold, as clear as glass.
22No temple could be seen in the city, for the
Lord God Almighty and the Lamb are its temple.
23And the city has no need of sun or moon, for the
glory of God illuminates the city, and the Lamb is
its light. 24The nations of the earth will walk in its
light, and the rulers of the world will come and
bring their glory to it. 25Its gates never close at the
end of day because there is no night. 26And all the
nations will bring their glory and honor into
the city. 27Nothing evil will be allowed to enter—
no one who practices shameful idolatry and dishonesty—but only those whose names are written
in the Lamb's Book of Life.

CHAPTER **22** **THE RIVER OF LIFE.** And the angel
showed me a pure river with the water of life, clear as
crystal, flowing from the throne of God and of the
Lamb, 2coursing down the center of the main street.
On each side of the river grew a tree of life, bearing
twelve crops of fruit,* with a fresh crop each month.
The leaves were used for medicine to heal the nations.
3No longer will anything be cursed. For the throne
of God and of the Lamb will be there, and his
servants will worship him. 4And they will see his face,
and his name will be written on their foreheads.
5And there will be no night there—no need for

He *will remove all of their sorrows*

**and there will be**

**NO MORE**

**death**

**or sorrow**

**or crying**

**or pain.**

REVELATION 21:4

21:3 Some manuscripts read *God himself will be with them, their God.* 21:10 Or *in the Spirit.* 21:16 Greek *12,000 stadia* [2,220 kilometers]. 21:17 Greek *144 cubits* [65 meters]. 22:2 Or *12 kinds of fruit.*

## EYEWITNESS ● ● ● • •

**22:8-9 Hearing or reading an eyewitness account is the next best thing to seeing the event yourself. John witnessed the events reported in Revelation and wrote them down so we could "see" and believe as he did. If you have read this far, you have "seen." Have you also believed?**

lamps or sun—for the Lord God will shine on them.
And they will reign forever and ever.
6Then the angel said to me, "These words are
trustworthy and true: 'The Lord God, who tells his
prophets what the future holds, has sent his angel to
tell you what will happen soon.'"

7"Look, I am coming soon! Blessed are those
who obey the prophecy written in this scroll."

8I, John, am the one who saw and heard all these
things. And when I saw and heard these things, I fell
down to worship the angel who showed them to me.
9But again he said, "No, don't worship me. I am a
servant of God, just like you and your brothers the
prophets, as well as all who obey what is written in
this scroll. Worship God!"
10Then he instructed me, "Do not seal up the
prophetic words you have written, for the time is
near. 11Let the one who is doing wrong continue to
do wrong; the one who is vile, continue to be vile;
the one who is good, continue to do good; and the
one who is holy, continue in holiness."

12"See, I am coming soon, and my reward is with
me, to repay all according to their deeds. 13I am
the Alpha and the Omega, the First and the Last,
the Beginning and the End."

14Blessed are those who wash their robes so they can
enter through the gates of the city and eat the fruit
from the tree of life. 15Outside the city are the dogs—
the sorcerers, the sexually immoral, the murderers, the
idol worshipers, and all who love to live a lie.

16"I, Jesus, have sent my angel to give you this
message for the churches. I am both the source
of David and the heir to his throne.* I am the
bright morning star."

17The Spirit and the bride say, "Come." Let each
one who hears them say, "Come." Let the thirsty
ones come—anyone who wants to. Let them come
and drink the water of life without charge. 18And I
solemnly declare to everyone who hears the prophetic words of this book: If anyone adds anything
to what is written here, God will add to that person
the plagues described in this book. 19And if anyone
removes any of the words of this prophetic book,
God will remove that person's share in the tree of
life and in the holy city that are described in this
book.
20He who is the faithful witness to all these things
says, "Yes, I am coming soon!"
Amen! Come, Lord Jesus!
21The grace of the Lord Jesus be with you all.

22:16 Greek *I am the root and offspring of David.*

## YOU ARE INVITED ● ● ● • •

**22:17 When Jesus met the Samaritan woman at the well, he told her of the living water that he could supply (John 4:10-15). This image is used again as Christ invites anyone to come and drink of the water of life. The gospel is unlimited in scope—all people, everywhere, may come. Salvation cannot be earned, but God gives it freely. We live in a world desperately thirsty for living water, and many are dying of thirst. But it's still not too late. Let us invite everyone to come and drink.**

# MEGA themes

**GOD'S SOVEREIGNTY** God is sovereign. He is greater than any power in the universe, and not to be compared with any leader, government, or religion. He controls history for the purpose of uniting true believers in loving fellowship with him.

Though Satan's power may temporarily increase, we are not to be led astray. God is all-powerful. Satan is not equivalent to God. God is supreme, in control, and will safely bring his family into eternal life. God cares for us; we can trust him with our life.

1. In what ways is God revealed as sovereign in Revelation?
2. How does God's sovereignty offer security to you?
3. Based on your security in God, what plans, dreams, worries, and/or problems can you

bring to him today? How does trusting God with both hopes and fears enable you to experience his sovereignty?

**CHRIST'S RETURN** Christ came to earth as a "Lamb," the symbol of his perfect sacrifice for our sin. He will return as the triumphant "Lion," the rightful ruler and conqueror. Christ will defeat Satan, settle accounts with all those who rejected him, and bring his faithful people into eternity.

Assurance of Christ's return gives suffering Christians the strength to endure. We can look forward to Christ's return as King and Judge. Because no one knows the time when Christ will appear, we must be ready at all times by keeping our faith strong.

1. Contrast the nature of Christ's first coming with his second coming.
2. What impact did Christ's first coming have on the world? On you?
3. What impact will Christ's second coming have on the world? On you?
4. How can the reality of Christ's second coming have a positive impact on you now?

**GOD'S FAITHFUL PEOPLE** John wrote to encourage the church not to worship the Roman emperor. He warns all God's faithful people to be devoted only to Christ. Revelation identifies the faithful people and what they should be doing until Christ returns.

Take your place in the ranks of God's faithful people: believe in Christ. Victory is sure for those who resist temptation and make loyalty to Christ their top priority.

1. What were some of the problems facing the churches in chapters 2 and 3? How were they to correct those problems?
2. Which of these churches can you identify with? How would you apply the command for correction?
3. What is the reward of those who endure faithfully?
4. Why is the cost of being a Christian worth it? Explain how this motivates you to grow in Christ rather than just surrendering to your weaknesses.

**JUDGMENT** One day God's anger toward sin will be fully and completely unleashed. Satan will be defeated; false religion will be destroyed. God will reward the faithful with eternal life, but all who refuse to believe in him will face eternal punishment.

God's final judgment will put an end to evil and injustice. We must be certain of our commitment to Christ if we want to escape this great final judgment. No one who is uncommitted to Christ will escape God's punishment. All who belong to Christ will receive their full reward based on what Christ has done.

1. What will happen in the final judgment? (chapter 20)
2. Whose names are written in the Book of Life?
3. How does knowledge of this final judgment affect the way you live your life? The way you view death?
4. What would you like to communicate to your friends about the final judgment? How can you do this?

**HOPE** One day God will create a new heaven and a new earth. All believers will live with God forever in perfect peace and security. Those who have already died will be raised to life. These promises for the future bring us hope.

Our greatest hope is that what Christ promises will be true. When we have confidence in our final destination, we will be able to follow Christ with unwavering dedication no matter what we must face. Because we belong to him, there is no room for despair.

1. What will God do after the final judgment?
2. What is your ultimate hope in Christ?
3. When do you find yourself most needing to rely on this ultimate hope? How does "final hope" provide hope in the present?
4. What would you like to communicate to your friends about the final hope? How can you do this?

## BIBLE READING PLAN

### INTRODUCTION

We usually think of the Bible as one book. That's logical because it looks like one book and claims to come from one Author. We also speak of it as God's Word. But when we read and study the Bible, we discover that it is actually an entire library between two covers. Not one book, but 66 (39 in the Old Testament; 27 in the New Testament)! Each book has its own style and uniqueness—yet each book contributes to the message God wants to get across with the whole Bible. What's more, though we use the word *book*, some parts of the Bible are letters (like Paul's letter to the Romans) or collections (like the Psalms). Still, the overall message of the Bible is one message because it has one main Author—God. The reason the styles throughout the Bible vary is because God teamed up with dozens of people to write his Word.

### HOW THIS PLAN IS DIFFERENT

There are many plans to help you read through the Bible library. You can even start at page one and read straight through. The approach taken here, however, is designed to help you get a flavor of the whole Bible by reading selections from it throughout a year. You will be reading the best-known stories and many important lessons. Some parts of the Bible offer so much help that they can be read every day. Among these are the Gospels, Psalms, and Proverbs. One way or another, you need to read God's Word!

### BEFORE YOU BEGIN

Notice that each day's reading has a title and a question. These are important application questions that will help you as you read. Always pray before you read and ask God to help you understand, apply, and obey his Word. And remember, this is only the start of the great adventure of reading God's Word and getting to know him.

## OLD TESTAMENT

**Genesis 1:1–2:3** How It All Started
*Why do human beings have value and worth?*
**Genesis 2:15–3:24** Adam and Eve
*In what ways are you like those first humans?*
**Genesis 4:1-16** Cain and Abel
*How do you handle anger?*
**Genesis 6:9-22** Noah Gets to Build a Boat
*What is the most difficult act that God has asked you to do?*
**Genesis 7:1-24** All Aboard!
*If you were alive at this time, would you have been invited to get on the boat? Would you have accepted?*
**Genesis 8:1-22** A Long Wait
*How would you have spent your time on the boat?*
**Genesis 9:1-17** Rules and Rainbows
*What could you do the next time you see a rainbow?*
**Genesis 11:1-9** The Tower of Babel
*Whom do you trust more than God?*
**Genesis 12:1-9; 17:1-8** God's Promises to Abraham
*How does God affect the way you make decisions?*
**Genesis 18:1-15** Unusual Visitors
*What is your basic attitude toward strangers?*
**Genesis 19:15-29** Destruction of Sodom and Gomorrah
*How does God feel about sin?*
**Genesis 21:8-21** Hagar and Ishmael
*How does God deal with the messes in your life?*
**Genesis 22:1-19** Abraham's Painful Decision
*What do you have trouble giving up to God?*
**Genesis 24:1-27** A Man Named Eliezar
*How do you approach difficult tasks?*
**Genesis 24:28-67** Isaac and Rebekah
*What unexpected good thing has God done for you recently?*
**Genesis 25:19-34** Jacob and Esau
*How do you treat your brothers or sisters?*
**Genesis 27:1-40** Jacob Tricks His Father
*How honestly have you treated your parents?*
**Genesis 28:10-22** Jacob Meets God
*In what places in your life has God been the most real?*
**Genesis 29:14-30** Jacob's Marriages
*What are the qualities that make up the way you love others?*
**Genesis 32:1–33:16** Jacob Returns Home
*What happens inside you when you try to avoid a problem?*
**Genesis 37:1-36** Jacob's Children
*How are disagreements settled in your family?*
**Genesis 39:1-23** Joseph in Trouble
*How do you feel about getting in trouble for doing right?*
**Genesis 40:1-23** Dreams in Prison
*When have you helped someone even though you had your own problems?*
**Genesis 41:1-36** Dreams in the Palace
*Whom has God used to give you guidance?*
**Genesis 41:37-57** Joseph in Charge
*How well do you handle big responsibilities?*
**Genesis 42:1-38** Joseph Sees His Brothers Again
*What would you do with a chance for revenge?*
**Genesis 43:1-34** Back to Joseph
*How well do you know how to forgive?*
**Genesis 44:1-34** Crisis in the Palace
*How do you react when someone points out a mistake you've made?*
**Genesis 45:1-28** Finding a Lost Son
*When did you last let your parents know you appreciate them?*
**Genesis 49:1-33** Jacob's Final Words
*What's the strongest impression you've made on your parents?*
**Exodus 1:8–2:10** Moses Is Born
*How have you appreciated the gift of birth?*
**Exodus 2:11-25** Moses on the Run
*When was the last time you found yourself running from God?*
**Exodus 3:1-22** God's Burning Bush
*In what ways has God made himself known to you?*
**Exodus 4:1-17** Moses Isn't Sure
*How willing are you to do what you feel God wants you to do?*
**Exodus 5:1-23** Resistance
*What have people said when you've tried to obey God?*
**Exodus 6:1-13** Rejection
*What would it cost you to do what God wants?*
**Exodus 7:1-14** A Stubborn Ruler
*How does stubbornness affect your relationship with God?*
**Exodus 7:15–9:7** Five out of Ten Plagues
*When do you try to bargain with God?*
**Exodus 9:8–10:29** Four More Plagues
*How does God get your attention?*
**Exodus 11:1-10; 12:29-36** The Ultimate Plague
*What does it mean to fear God in your life?*
**Exodus 13:17–14:31** A Narrow Escape
*When have you experienced God's protection?*
**Exodus 15:22-27; 17:1-7** God Provides Water
*What do you complain to God about?*
**Exodus 16:1-36** God's Unusual Food Supply
*For what specific gift did you last say thanks to God?*
**Exodus 18:1-27** Helpful Advice
*Who are the dependable advisers in your life?*
**Exodus 19:1-25** An Appointment with God
*How would you prepare to meet with God?*
**Exodus 20:1-22** The Ten Commandments
*How often do you think about God's standards?*
**Exodus 32:1-29** The Gold Calf
*What distracts you from obeying God?*
**Exodus 40** Instructions about God's Tent
*When are you most aware of God's presence in your life?*
**Numbers 12:1-16** Moses under Fire
*What do you do when you find yourself feeling jealous of someone?*
**Numbers 13:1–14:4** Spying on the Promised Land
*How does God affect the word* impossible *in your mind?*
**Numbers 14:5-45** A Majority That Was Wrong
*How often are your decisions based on peer pressure?*
**Numbers 21:4-9** Another Hard Lesson
*What can you do to avoid repeating mistakes?*
**Numbers 22:5-38** Balaam and His Donkey
*What happens when you do what you know you shouldn't do?*
**Deuteronomy 29:1-29** Moses Reviews God's Actions
*How do you keep track of what God has done for you?*
**Deuteronomy 30:1-20** Moses Challenges the People
*How do you show that you love God?*
**Deuteronomy 31:1-8** Moses Appoints New Leaders
*If you were Joshua, who would be "Moses" in your life?*
**Deuteronomy 34:1-12** The Death of Moses
*How would you most like to be remembered?*

**Joshua 1:1-18** God Takes Over
*Which of these qualities would you most need to be like Joshua?*
**Joshua 2:1-24** Spies Visit Jericho
*What persons has God used in your life unexpectedly?*
**Joshua 3:1-17** The Invasion of Canaan
*How would you illustrate God's guidance in your life?*
**Joshua 5:13–6:27** The Battle of Jericho
*How serious are you about having God use you?*
**Joshua 7:1-26** Ultimate Consequences
*What strongly negative or positive consequences have you experienced?*
**Joshua 10:1-15** The Longest Day
*How do you know God is powerful?*
**Joshua 23:1-16** Joshua Warns the Leaders
*Which of Joshua's warnings do you most need to obey?*
**Joshua 24:1-31** Joshua's Last Words
*How can you get hope from history?*
**Judges 4:4-24** Judge Deborah
*How do people know that you care about them?*
**Judges 6:1-40** Gideon Becomes a Judge
*What examples of obedience can be found in your life?*
**Judges 7:1-25** Gideon and the Midianites
*In what area of your life do you need to trust God more?*
**Judges 13:1-25** The Birth of Samson
*In which part of your life do you need more discipline?*
**Judges 14:1-20** Samson's Riddle
*How carefully do you consider the wisdom of your parents?*
**Judges 15:1-20** Samson and the Jawbone
*What proof do you have that mistakes usually don't correct themselves?*
**Judges 16:1-21** Samson and Delilah
*In what situations do you find yourself flirting with disaster?*
**Judges 16:22-31** Samson's Death
*How well do you understand God's patience?*
**Ruth 1:1-22** Ruth and Naomi—A Friendship
*How do difficulties affect your friendships?*
**Ruth 2:1-23** Ruth Meets Boaz
*When have you found your reputation to be an advantage?*
**Ruth 3:1-18** Ruth Finds a Husband
*What unexpected methods has God used in your life?*
**Ruth 4:1-22** A Happy Ending
*What future reasons could there be for obeying God today?*
**1 Samuel 1:1-28** A Serious Prayer
*What promises have you made to God lately that you have kept?*
**1 Samuel 3:1-21** God Calls Samuel
*When you read God's Word, what do you expect him to say to you?*
**1 Samuel 8** The People Want a King
*What has God taught you about being responsible for your own choices?*
**1 Samuel 8:1-22** Samuel's Disappointing Sons
*What positive lessons have you learned from your parents' mistakes?*
**1 Samuel 9:1-21** Saul and the Lost Donkeys
*What is God's part in your daily decisions?*
**1 Samuel 10:1-27** Saul Becomes King
*How do you evaluate people?*
**1 Samuel 14:1-23** A Son to Make a Father Proud
*What would it mean to have a friend like Jonathan?*
**1 Samuel 16:1-13** Samuel Appoints David
*What people do you appreciate for something other than how they look?*
**1 Samuel 17:1-31** David and Goliath's Challenge
*How does your confidence in God affect your decision to accept challenges?*
**1 Samuel 17:32-58** David Kills Goliath
*What "giants" need to be defeated in your life?*
**1 Samuel 18:1-30** Trouble between Saul and David
*How do you treat your friends who succeed?*
**1 Samuel 20:1-42** David and Jonathan
*How much can your friends trust you?*
**1 Samuel 24:1-22** David Spares Saul's Life
*Do you treat others the way you want to be treated?*
**1 Samuel 25:1-42** David and Abigail
*How does God keep you from making big mistakes?*
**1 Samuel 28:1-25** Saul and the Occult
*What kinds of things could be considered "occult practices"? How would God feel about your involvement in such things?*
**2 Samuel 5:1-12** David Becomes King over All Israel
*How could you become a person who is more pleasing to God, as David was?*
**2 Samuel 9:1-13** The King's Kindness
*What promises need to be kept in your life?*
**2 Samuel 11:1-27** David and Bathsheba
*How often are you tempted to correct one sin by committing another?*
**2 Samuel 12:1-25** David and Nathan
*Which of your friends love you enough to correct you?*
**2 Samuel 13:1-19** Family Consequences of Sin
*What actions do you take to avoid temptation?*
**2 Samuel 13:20-39** Family Revenge
*Are you more likely to have committed David's sin or Absalom's?*
**2 Samuel 15:1-37** Family Betrayal
*Who helps you keep your motives clear?*
**2 Samuel 18:1-18** The Death of Absalom
*In what situations are you most likely to lose control?*
**1 Kings 1:5-27** Conflict over the Throne
*What happens when you don't make good decisions?*
**1 Kings 1:28-53** David Gives Solomon the Crown
*When things in your world get confusing, how do you know God is still in control?*
**1 Kings 3:1-15** Solomon's Wisdom
*Which of Solomon's choices would you have made?*
**1 Kings 3:16-28** Solomon Solves a Problem
*In what situation in your life do you presently need God's wisdom?*
**1 Kings 6:1-38** Solomon Builds the Temple
*What can you learn from Solomon about making and carrying out plans?*
**1 Kings 10:1-13** Solomon and the Queen of Sheba
*When are you tempted to try to impress people?*
**1 Kings 12:1-24** Solomon's Unwise Son
*Who are the people you know will give you good advice?*
**1 Kings 17:1-24** God Takes Care of Elijah
*How do obeying and trusting God go together in your life?*
**1 Kings 18:16-46** Elijah versus the Priests of Baal
*How would you describe your attitude toward God's power today?*
**1 Kings 19:1-21** Spiritual Burnout
*When was the last time you felt sorry for yourself?*
**1 Kings 21:1-29** The Stolen Vineyard
*How important is justice in your life?*
**1 Kings 22:29-40** The Death of King Ahab
*When are you tempted to think that you can hide from God?*

2 Kings 2:1-12 Elijah's Chariot
*When you make a commitment, how far will you go to carry it out?*

2 Kings 2:13-25 Elisha's Miracles
*How would someone else know that you have a deep respect for God?*

2 Kings 5:1-27 The Healing of Naaman
*What "small" things have you refused to do for God?*

2 Kings 11:1-21 The King Who Was Seven Years Old
*Who were your best examples in childhood?*

2 Kings 22:1–23:3 Discovery of the Lost Book
*What happens in your life when the Bible is a "lost book"?*

Ezra 3:7-13 Rebuilding the Temple
*How do you feel when you're working on a large, important project?*

Nehemiah 2:1-20 Nehemiah Returns to Jerusalem
*What relationships in your past need to be rebuilt?*

Nehemiah 5:1-19 Nehemiah's Concern for the Poor
*How do you express your concern for the poor?*

Nehemiah 8:1-18 Reading God's Word
*What are your expectations when you open God's Word?*

Esther 1:1-22 The Fall of a Queen
*How often do you take the important people in your life for granted?*

Esther 2:1-23 A Strange Way to Become Queen
*When have difficult or confusing events in your life actually been a preparation for something you would later experience?*

Esther 3:1-15 The Jews in Danger
*In what situations are you tempted to compromise your faith?*

Esther 4:1-17 The Queen Decides to Help
*In what ways has your faith cost you?*

Esther 5:1-14 Esther Risks Her Life
*When was the last time you did something scary to obey God?*

Esther 6:1–7:10 God Protects His People
*When is it helpful to remember that God is still in control of the world?*

Job 1:1-22 The Testing of Job
*In what situations do you most quickly question God's care?*

Job 2:1-13 Job and His Friends
*How do you normally respond to someone else's pain? How should you respond?*

Job 38:1-41 God Speaks to Job
*What things around you remind you of God's greatness?*

Job 42:1-17 The Rest of Job's Story
*What difference does it make to know and remember that God always has the last word?*

Psalm 1:1-6 Two Kinds of Lives
*What kind of person do you really want to be?*

Psalm 8:1-9 The Value of Humans
*How do you know you have worth?*

Psalm 23:1-6 A Sheep's Song
*What is the most comforting phrase to you in this psalm?*

Psalm 51:1-19 A Confession
*What examples of repentance have been part of your life?*

Psalm 103:1-22 What God Is Like
*Which picture in this psalm helps you understand God better?*

Psalm 139:1-24 How Well God Knows Us
*What do you feel when you read this psalm?*

Psalm 145:1-21 God for All People and Time
*Which of God's qualities do you most need today?*

Proverbs 4:1-27 Wise Words about Life
*What priority have you given finding wisdom?*

Proverbs 5:1-23 Wise Words about Sex
*How do these words match what you hear around you every day?*

Ecclesiastes 12:1-14 A Summary of Life
*In what way can you remember your Creator today?*

Isaiah 6:1-13 God Chooses Isaiah
*When did you last realize your continuing need for God's forgiveness?*

Isaiah 53 The Suffering Servant
*How would you describe what Jesus did for you?*

Jeremiah 1:1-9 God Calls a Prophet
*What is your reaction to the possibility of God using your life?*

Jeremiah 36 The Book Burning
*How much risk is involved in your relationship with God?*

Jeremiah 38:1-13 Jeremiah in the Well
*What part of your life compares in any way with Jeremiah's time in the well?*

Ezekiel 37:1-14 A Valley of Dry Bones
*What can you do to help you understand God's plan for the world?*

Daniel 1:1-21 Coping with Pressure to Conform
*How might Daniel react to the pressure situations in your life?*

Daniel 2:1-24 A King's Dream
*What do you do in seemingly hopeless situations?*

Daniel 2:25-49 The Meaning of the Dream
*Who gets the credit when things go right in your life?*

Daniel 3:1-30 Three Friends in a Furnace
*What examples can you give of God's protection in your life?*

Daniel 5:1-30 The Writing on the Wall
*What reasons would God have for passing judgment on the society in which you live?*

Daniel 6:1-28 Daniel and the Lions
*When do you pray regularly?*

Jonah 1:1–2:10 Bending God's Directions
*When did you last try to avoid doing what you knew God wanted you to do?*

Jonah 3:1–4:11 Wrong Motives
*About what things do you complain to God?*

## NEW TESTAMENT

You will be reading various parts of the four Gospels in order to have a fairly chronological biography of Jesus' life.

Luke 1:1-4; John 1:1-18 Beginnings
*Have you personally received Jesus as your Savior and become a child of God?*

Luke 1:5-25 The Angel and Zacharias
*How would you react to an angel's visit?*

Luke 1:26-56 Mary and Elizabeth
*What gives you joy in your life?*

Luke 1:57-80 John the Baptist Is Born
*When did you last say thank you to your parents?*

Matthew 1:1-25 A Family Tree
*Which of these people have you read about in the Old Testament?*

Luke 2:1-20 Jesus Is Born!
*What does Christmas mean to you?*

**Luke 2:21-39** Jesus' First Trip to Church
*How would you react to holding Jesus when he was a baby?*
**Matthew 2:1-12** Foreign Visitors
*What gifts have you ever given Christ?*
**Matthew 2:13-23** Escape and Return
*How has knowing God brought excitement into your life?*
**Luke 2:41-52** Jesus in the Temple Again
*What four words would summarize your teenage years?*
**Mark 1:1-13** Baptism and Temptation
*What are your most difficult temptations? Compare them to Jesus' temptations.*
**John 1:19-34** John the Baptist and Jesus
*To whom did you last talk about Christ?*
**John 1:35-51** Jesus' First Disciples
*How would someone know that you're a disciple of Jesus?*
**John 2:1-25** Jesus and Surprises
*How has Christ been unpredictable in your life?*
**John 3:1-21** Jesus and Nicodemus
*When did you first meet Jesus? How?*
**John 3:22-36; Luke 3:19-20** John Gets into Trouble
*When has knowing Christ ever gotten you into trouble?*
**John 4:1-42** Jesus Changes a Town
*In what ways has Jesus affected your town?*
**John 4:43-54** Jesus Preaching and Healing
*Why do you believe in Christ?*
**Luke 4:16-30** Jesus Rejected
*How would Jesus be received in your church next Sunday?*
**Mark 1:16-39** Jesus Calls People to Follow
*What specific things have you left behind to follow Christ?*
**Luke 5:1-39** Miracles and Questions
*How do Jesus' miracles affect you today?*
**John 5:1-47** Jesus Demonstrates He Is God's Son
*What do you find most attractive about Jesus?*
**Mark 2:23–3:19** Jesus and Disciples
*How would Jesus treat your personal traditions?*
**Matthew 5:1-16** Jesus Gives the Beatitudes
*Which of these attitudes most needs to be in your life today?*
**Matthew 5:17-30** Jesus on Law, Anger, and Lust
*How do Jesus' views compare with yours?*
**Matthew 5:31-48** Jesus on Relationships
*What part of your life could be most radically changed by these words?*
**Matthew 6:1-18** Jesus on Doing Good Things
*How do your public and private lives compare?*
**Matthew 6:19-34** Jesus on Money and Worry
*In what ways are money and worry related in your life?*
**Matthew 7:1-12** Jesus on Criticizing and Praying
*Which one are you most persistent in doing? Why?*
**Matthew 7:13-29** How Jesus Looks at Us
*What is your foundation in life?*
**Luke 7:1-17** Jesus and Foreigners
*What is your attitude toward foreigners? How can you show them God's love?*
**Matthew 11:1-30** Jesus Describes John
*How would you want Jesus to summarize your life?*
**Luke 7:36–8:3** Jesus and Women
*How would you have fit into the group that followed Jesus?*
**Matthew 12:22-50** Troubles for Jesus
*When are you tempted to have Jesus prove himself to you?*
**Mark 4:1-29** Jesus Seeks, Seeds, and Weeds
*What kind of soil is your life right now?*
**Matthew 13:24-43** More of Jesus' Parables
*How concerned are you about the eternal fates of the people you know?*
**Matthew 13:44-52** Even More Parables
*How and where did you find the hidden treasure?*
**Luke 8:22-56** Jesus in Control
*Which of these examples gives you greatest comfort?*
**Matthew 9:27-38** The Concerns of Jesus
*How do you picture Jesus caring for you?*
**Mark 6:1-13** Some Don't Listen; Some Need to Hear
*How clear an idea do you have of what God wants you to do?*
**Matthew 10:16-42** Jesus Prepares His Disciples
*In what ways do Jesus' words speak to the fears you have?*
**Mark 6:14-29** Herod Kills John the Baptist
*How do you most want to be like John the Baptist?*
**Matthew 14:13-36** Jesus: Cook, Water Walker, Healer
*Would you have been more likely to step out with Peter or to stay in the boat? Why?*
**John 6:22-40** Jesus Is the Bread from Heaven
*How is Jesus "bread" to you?*
**John 6:41-71** Jesus Criticized and Deserted
*How do you react when you hear critical or derogatory comments about Jesus?*
**Mark 7:1-37** Jesus Teaches and Creates Purity
*What would God have to do to improve the purity of your life?*
**Matthew 15:32–16:12** Jesus Feeds and Warns
*How do you evaluate what you hear?*
**Mark 8:22–9:1** Peter Identifies Jesus
*In what specific ways have you come to understand Jesus better in the last few weeks?*
**Luke 9:28-45** Jesus Is Transfigured
*Would you rather leave the world and be with Christ or be with Christ in the world?*
**Matthew 17:24–18:6** Who's the Greatest?
*When do you worry about status?*
**Mark 9:38-50** Who's on Our Side?
*How do you respond to the beliefs of others?*
**Matthew 18:10-22** Jesus as He Teaches
*How do you react to the failures of others?*
**John 7:1-31** Jesus Out in the Open
*Which of Jesus' teachings are difficult for you to accept?*
**John 7:32-53** A Warrant for Jesus' Arrest
*What does it mean to have "rivers of living water" flowing from within you?*
**John 8:1-20** Jesus: Forgiveness and Light
*Who is the last person you had to forgive?*
**John 8:21-59** Jesus: Giver of Freedom
*How has Christ made you free?*
**Luke 10:1-24** Jesus Sends Seventy Messengers
*What would have been most exciting about this trip for you?*
**Luke 10:25-42** Jesus Tells a Story and Visits Friends
*Who has been a good Samaritan to you?*
**Luke 11:1-13** Jesus Teaches about Prayer
*How could your prayer habits be improved?*
**Luke 11:14-32** Accusations and Unbelief
*What are your strongest reasons for being a faithful follower of Christ?*
**Luke 11:33-54** Real Spirituality versus Unreal Spirituality
*Who has noticed light in your life recently?*
**Luke 12:1-21** Religious and Rich Fools
*In what situations do you get too caught up in the goals of this world?*
**Luke 12:22-48** Jesus Warns about Worry
*Do you feel worried or hopeful when you think about the future? Why?*

**Luke 12:49-59** Jesus Warns about Troubles
*What examples have you seen of the problems Jesus mentions?*
**Luke 13:1-21** Jesus and the Kingdom of God
*When in your life would Jesus have to call for your repentance?*
**John 9:1-41** Jesus and a Blind Man
*What different stages of "seeing" have been part of your life?*
**John 10:1-18** Jesus Is the Good Shepherd
*How have you experienced God's guidance in your life?*
**Luke:13:22-35** Jesus: The King Who Grieves
*How do you feel about those around you who don't know Christ?*
**Luke 14:1-14** Jesus on Seeking Honor
*When would others say that you look out for yourself too much?*
**Luke 14:15-35** Jesus on Being His Disciple
*What is it going to cost you to be a follower of Jesus? Are you willing to pay the price?*
**Luke 15:1-10** Two Parables of Losing and Finding
*How do these stories help you understand God's love for you?*
**Luke 15:11-32** A Son Who Was Found
*In what ways is this story like your life?*
**Luke 16:1-18** The Parable of the Shrewd Accountant
*What does it mean to be an honest person?*
**Luke 16:19-31** The Rich Man and the Beggar
*Where are the poor people in your community? Whom do you know who is poor? How can you help the poor?*
**John 11:1-36** Lazarus Dies
*In what situations have you been disappointed with God?*
**John 11:37-57** Jesus Raises Lazarus
*How would you have felt watching Lazarus walk out of the tomb?*
**Luke 17:1-19** Jesus and Ten Lepers
*For what are you thankful to God?*
**Luke 17:20-37** Jesus and the Kingdom of God
*What difference would it make in your life if Jesus returned today?*
**Luke 18:1-14** Jesus Teaches about Prayer
*What is the attitude of your prayers?*
**Mark 10:1-16** Jesus on Family Matters
*How far will you go to keep your word?*
**Mark 10:17-31** Jesus and the Rich Man
*What is the most difficult thing Jesus could ask you to give up?*
**Matthew 20:1-19** A Parable about Equal Pay
*How often are you jealous of what God has given to someone else?*
**Mark 10:35-52** Jesus on Serving Others
*In what ways are you learning to be a servant?*
**Luke 19:1-27** Jesus and Zacchaeus
*What personal physical characteristic has most affected how you feel about yourself?*
**John 12:1-11** A Woman Anoints Jesus
*What have you ever "wasted" as an expression of love for Christ?*
**Matthew 21:1-17** Jesus Rides into Jerusalem
*If you had been part of the crowd that day, what would have been your most lasting memory?*
**John 12:20-36** Jesus Explains Why He Must Die
*How would you explain to someone why Jesus had to die on the cross?*

**John 12:37-50** Jesus and His Message
*What kinds of pressures make you hesitant to tell others about your belief in Christ?*
**Mark 11:20-33** Permission to Pray for Anything
*How bold is your prayer life?*
**Matthew 21:28-46** Two Parables
*Which son do you resemble most?*
**Matthew 22:1-14** Jesus Tells about the Wedding Feasts
*At what point in your life did you realize that you were invited? How did you respond?*
**Luke 20:20-40** Jesus Answers Questions
*How do you really feel about living forever?*
**Mark 12:28-37** Questions Given and Taken
*Whom do you know who is not far from the Kingdom of God?*
**Matthew 23:1-39** Jesus: Warnings and Grieving
*Which of these seven warnings most directly relate to your life?*
**Luke 21:1-24** Jesus Talks about the Future
*What do your giving habits say about your level of trust in God?*
**Luke 21:25-38** Jesus on Being Prepared
*What does your schedule today say about your watchfulness?*
**Matthew 25:1-30** Parables about Being Prepared
*With which of the people in these two stories do you identify most?*
**Matthew 25:31-46** Jesus on the Final Judgment
*What people in your life are you treating in ways you would want to treat Christ?*
**Luke 22:1-13** Preparing the Last Supper
*How do you prepare yourself for Communion?*
**John 13:1-20** Jesus Washes His Disciples' Feet
*What is the greatest service someone has done for you? How do you serve others?*
**John 13:21-38** A Sad Prediction
*How well do you feel Christ knows you?*
**John 14:1-14** Jesus Is the Way
*How would you rate your present level of understanding of Christ and his teachings?*
**John 14:15-31** Jesus Promises the Comforter
*How have you experienced the Comforter?*
**John 15:1-16** Jesus on the Vine and the Branches
*What kind of fruit has the Gardener produced in you?*
**John 15:17–16:4** Jesus Warns about Troubles
*What have you learned recently about loving others?*
**John 16:5-33** Jesus on the Holy Spirit and Prayers
*Where in these verses do you find peace of heart and mind?*
**John 17:1-26** Jesus Prays
*Where do you find yourself in this prayer?*
**Mark 14:26-52** A Repeated Prediction
*What practical prayer problems do you need to work on?*
**John 18:1-24** Jesus Betrayed and Abandoned
*How close have you come to Peter's denial of Christ?*
**Matthew 26:57-75** Trial and Denial
*In what ways has being a follower of Jesus complicated your life?*
**Matthew 27:1-10** The Religious Trial and Judas's Death
*When you think of sin's consequences, what personal examples come to mind?*
**Luke 23:1-12** Two Political Trials
*In what ways did your childhood and background prepare you to respond to Jesus?*

**Mark 15:6-24** Sentencing and Torture
*Was there a time you chose to do the wrong thing on purpose? Why? What happened?*
**Luke 23:32-49** Jesus Crucified
*What do you feel when you read the description of the Crucifixion?*
**Matthew 27:57-66** Jesus' Body Laid in a Guarded Tomb
*What have you seen people do in their resistance to Christ?*
**John 20:1-18** Jesus Is Alive!
*What makes Easter an important celebration in your life?*
**Matthew 28:8-15** Reactions to the Resurrection
*What would be your first words to Jesus if he appeared to you?*
**Luke 24:13-43** Appearances of Jesus
*Would you recognize Jesus if you saw him today? How?*
**John 20:24–21:14** More Appearances of Jesus
*How has Christ answered your doubts?*
**John 21:15-25** Jesus Talks with Peter
*What difference would it make to you to read these verses with your name in the place of Simon Peter's?*
**Matthew 28:16-20** Jesus Gives the Great Commission
*What are you doing specifically to obey Christ's words?*
**Luke 24:44-53** Jesus Says Farewell
*How do you find Christ opening your mind as you read the Bible?*
**Acts 1:1-11** The Departure of Jesus
*What one thing would you be sure to do if you knew Jesus was coming back today?*
**Acts 1:12-26** First Things First
*What is your idea of the right amount of time for prayer?*
**Acts 2:1-13** An Amazing Gift
*What is the main purpose of any gift God might have given you?*
**Acts 2:14-40** Peter's First Sermon
*How would you put this sermon into your own words?*
**Acts 2:41–3:11** Daily Life in the Early Church
*What part of these early days would you have enjoyed the most?*
**Acts 3:12–4:4** Peter's Second Sermon
*If you were given three minutes to tell the story of your spiritual life, what would you say?*
**Acts 4:5-22** Hostile Reactions
*What excuses are you most likely to use to keep from sharing your faith?*
**Acts 4:23-37** Praying and Sharing
*When was the last time you shared something with someone else?*
**Acts 5:1-16** Strange Events
*How often are you tempted to take God lightly?*
**Acts 5:17-42** Arrested!
*How do you react when you are treated unfairly?*
**Acts 6:1-15** Stephen: Special Servant
*What specific responsibilities do you have in your local church?*
**Acts 7:1-29** History Review I
*How familiar are you becoming with "his story" in history?*
**Acts 7:30-60** History Review II
*In what ways would you want to be more like Stephen?*
**Acts 8:1-25** Benefits of Persecution
*Which difficulties in your life has God used to help you grow spiritually?*
**Acts 8:26-40** Unexpected Appointment
*What have you done about baptism?*
**Acts 9:1-19** Paul Meets Jesus
*What unusual events has God used to catch your attention?*
**Acts 9:20-31** Paul's New Life
*What are three ways that Christ has changed your life?*
**Acts 9:32-42** God Uses Peter
*This past week, what special ability did you use to meet someone's need?*
**Acts 10:1-23** Peter Sees a Lesson
*What lessons has God had to repeat in your life?*
**Acts 10:24-48** Peter Learns a Lesson
*How has God helped you change your mind about some attitudes?*
**Acts 11:1-18** Gentiles Get a Chance
*On which of your prejudices is God still working?*
**Acts 11:19-29** Christians Helping One Another
*What do you do when you hear stories of extreme poverty or hardship among Christians in other parts of the world?*
**Acts 12:1-25** A Great Escape and Capital Punishment
*How do you react when God answers your prayers?*
**Acts 13:1-12** Paul and Barnabas: Travel Preaching
*What Christians do you know who might help you discover more clearly how God wants you to invest your time and abilities?*
**Acts 14:1-28** Response and Reaction
*How does the gospel act like Good News in your life?*
**Acts 15:1-21** A Church Conference
*How important is it for you to talk problems over with other Christians?*
**Acts 15:22-41** The Gentiles Are Accepted
*In what ways is God affecting the way you live and plan?*
**Acts 16:1-15** Paul, Silas, and Timothy
*How would you describe the spiritual team of which you are part?*
**Acts 16:16-40** Adventures in Jail
*How would you react to God using a difficult situation of yours to help another person discover him?*
**Acts 17:1-15** Different Responses from Two Cities
*What part does the Bible play in your evaluation of what you hear and read?*
**Acts 17:16-34** Paul in Athens
*What unconscious symbols of God's presence do you see around you in society?*
**Acts 19:1-20** Paul in Ephesus
*In what situations are you most likely to become discouraged?*
**Acts 19:21-41** The Riot
*When are you most likely to forget that God is in control?*
**Acts 20:1-12** Sleeping in Church
*How does God respond to your human weaknesses?*
**Acts 20:13-38** Saying Good-bye to Ephesus
*When have painful good-byes worked for the best in your life?*
**Acts 21:1-17** Difficult Decision
*What hard decisions do you have to make?*
**Acts 21:18-36** Paul in Jerusalem
*How important is it to respect the consciences of others?*
**Acts 21:37–22:29** Paul Speaks
*How can you relate what Paul is saying to what God has done in your life?*
**Acts 22:30–23:22** A Plan to Kill Paul
*How well do you know your rights and fulfill your responsibilities as a citizen of your country?*
**Acts 23:23–24:27** Paul in Prison
*What would be harder for you, the pressure or the prison?*

Acts 25:1-27 Paul Speaks to Festus
*If Christianity were outlawed, what evidence could be brought against you to prove you are a Christian?*
Acts 26:1-32 Paul Speaks to Agrippa
*How comfortable are you in explaining your faith?*
Acts 27:1-26 The Storm at Sea
*What is your attitude when you are going through difficulties as part of a group?*
Acts 27:27-44 The Shipwreck
*What disasters in your life has God used to teach you?*
Acts 28:1-14 The Winter on Malta
*How often are you aware of God in everyday occurrences?*
Acts 28:15-31 Paul in Rome
*What would you most like to be doing when your time on this earth is over?*
Romans 5:1-11 Faith Brings Joy
*When was the last time you thanked God for all he's done for you?*
Romans 8:1-18 Truly Free from Sin
*In what areas are you still struggling with your sinful nature?*
Romans 8:19-39 How God Loves
*What things do you sometimes feel might be able to separate you from the love of Christ?*
Romans 12:1-21 Living Sacrifice
*What act of a living sacrifice might God allow you to do today?*
1 Corinthians 13:1-13 Real Love
*Which quality of real love do you most need to ask God to increase in your life?*
1 Corinthians 15:1-20 The Basic Gospel
*What parts of the gospel are especially helpful to you in times of doubt or stress?*
1 Corinthians 15:42-58 Destiny!
*How much are you looking forward to all Christ has planned for you?*
2 Corinthians 4:1-18 Weak Containers; Strong Contents
*With which of the four difficult situations Paul mentions do you identify most clearly?*
Galatians 5:13-26 Two Radically Different Lives
*Who comes to mind as someone who you need to love as you love yourself?*
Ephesians 1:3-23 God's Action
*In what ways has God marked your life?*
Ephesians 2:1-22 God's Plan
*When have you recently reminded yourself and God that you want your life to be used for his purposes?*
Ephesians 4:1-16 Picture of the Church
*What is your role in Christ's body?*
Ephesians 6:10-20 Armor of God
*Which of these weapons do you need to learn to use better?*
Philippians 2:1-18 The Mind of Jesus
*In what ways would having Christ's attitude make you face this day differently?*
Philippians 3:1-21 Learning Joy
*What areas of your life could God be using to teach you joy?*
Colossians 2:1-15 What We Have in Christ
*What dangerous philosophy is present in your environment that could affect your relationship with Christ?*
Colossians 3:1-17 Christian Relationships
*What do you envision when you think about heaven?*
1 Thessalonians 1:1-10 Spiritual Reputation
*How do you think others would evaluate your spiritual life?*

1 Thessalonians 4:1-18 Living for God
*What specific action could you take today simply out of obedience to God?*
2 Thessalonians 1:1-12 Encouragement
*What other Christians could you encourage today?*
2 Thessalonians 3:1-18 Final Requests
*How aware and involved are you in the worldwide spread of the gospel?*
1 Timothy 4:1-16 Always Going Forward
*Which of these positive commands need to be given a higher priority in your life?*
1 Timothy 6:3-21 A Friend's Final Words
*How does your attitude toward money match Paul's advice?*
2 Timothy 1:1-18 The Importance of Examples
*Who has been a good spiritual example for you? How can you thank him or her?*
2 Timothy 3:1-17 Last Days
*How many of these characteristics are part of your world today?*
Titus 3:1-11; Philemon 1:4-7 Good Counsel
*Which of these commands apply directly to your life?*
Hebrews 10:19-39 The New Life
*What do your prayer habits and church habits say about the real importance of faith in your life?*
Hebrews 11:1-40 A Review of Faith
*How deep is your commitment to Christ?*
Hebrews 12:1-13 Our Turn
*Which of these directions would have a significant impact on your faith?*
James 1:2-27 Tough Times, Happy People
*In what difficulty could you use the "James plan" right now?*
James 2:1-13 Valuing Other People
*Which tendencies do you have to watch out for in how you treat others?*
James 3:1-12 Words as Weapons
*How sharp would others consider your tongue?*
1 Peter 2:1-25 Living Stones
*Which would you choose as the biggest personal challenge in these verses?*
1 Peter 3:1-22 Relationships and Pain
*How willing are you to carry out your relationships God's way, even when there are difficulties?*
2 Peter 1:2-21 Knowing God
*How would you answer someone who asked you what it means to know God?*
1 John 1:1-10 The Way of Forgiveness
*What part does confession have in your life?*
1 John 3:1-24 God Is Love
*How can you tell if your love is growing?*
1 John 5:1-21 The Life God Gives
*How do you know that you have eternal life?*
2 John 1:4-6; 3 John 1:5-8; Jude 1:17-25 Family Matters
*How often do you go out of your way to meet the needs of other Christians?*
Revelation 1:1-20 Jesus the King
*How would you describe your mental picture of Jesus?*
Revelation 21:1-27 Everything Made New
*What difference do you think you will most notice between the new world and the old?*
Revelation 22:1-21 Life in the New City
*When was the last time you were excited about heaven?*

## FOLLOW-UP FOR NEW CHRISTIANS

"So now we can rejoice in our wonderful new relationship with God—all because of what our Lord Jesus Christ has done for us in making us friends of God" (Romans 5:11).

*You have just helped someone become a new Christian, or you have been given the responsibility to do the follow-up of a new Christian . . . so now what do you do?*

First of all, you can be excited about this opportunity. Second, you need to be serious about this responsibility. Read Romans 5:11 again. You have the privilege of helping someone grow in his or her new relationship with your friend Jesus Christ. Here are some ways you can help a new Christian and Jesus grow closer. Remember, we all need FRIENDS:

***Follow up with your new Christian friend by getting together regularly.*** Get together within 48 hours after your friend receives Christ, and at least once a week during the next six weeks (Matthew 28:20).

***Reinforce what Christ has done in your friend's life.*** Do this by looking at Scriptures that affirm God's commitment to Christians (John 14:20; Hebrews 13:5; Colossians 2:13-14; 1 John 5:13; Galatians 5:25).

***Involve your friend in a Bible-teaching church.*** Take your friend with you and help answer any of his or her questions (Hebrews 10:24-25).

***Exhibit Christ in your life through your actions and words.*** You don't have to be perfect, just someone who wants to obey and please God (Colossians 3:17).

***Nurture your friend's spiritual growth.*** A new Christian is like a newborn baby who needs spiritual food and care. Try using the 14 appointments with God included in this section (1 Peter 2:2-3).

***Do things together.*** Spending time together will give you opportunities to encourage your friend and put your faith into practice (Acts 14:21-22).

***Stand by your friend in both the good and bad times.*** Your friend will fall down spiritually. Get ready to help him or her to get up and go again (Ephesians 4:11-16).

*You have recently trusted Jesus Christ to be your Savior . . . so now what do you do?*

First of all, you must know that through Christ you have become friends with God. Read Romans 5:11. Remember:

- You realized that your sin was keeping you from a relationship with God;
- You understood that Jesus Christ died on the cross to pay the penalty for your sin and that he rose again from the dead;
- You prayed, asking Jesus to forgive your sins and be your Savior.

Next, please understand that you have begun an exciting and lasting friendship. As in any relationship, getting to know someone takes time—it doesn't just happen by itself. (Make sure you have a friend who has been a Christian for a while who can help you grow in your new faith. If no one has contacted you, you should go back to the person who helped you become a Christian and ask for help.)

You can grow closer to God just like you grow closer to people. God created you to have a relationship with him, to be his very own son or daughter. Now that you're his child and friend, he will patiently help you get to know him better and better.

Here are some ideas you can use to help you and God become close friends. Remember, all it takes is TIME:

***Talk to God through prayer.*** To help you learn how to talk to God, the 14 appointments with God include ideas for prayer. Give them a try. God will listen when you talk to him.

***Investigate God's Word.*** Decide on a time and place to read the Bible each day. The schedule for 14 appointments with God will help you know what to read. This will help you grow.

***Make it practical.*** One of the best ways to learn is by doing. The 14-appointment schedule includes action steps to help you make your friendship with God active and practical.

***Express your thoughts.*** You know how important it is to show appreciation to a friend. As you finish your daily time with God, tell him thank you. During the next 14 appointments with God, try to keep a personal journal. Simply write down your thoughts, your questions, and, most important of all, why you're thankful to God!

Finally, to get to know God better, try using the following "14 Appointments with God." These appointments are great ways to spend some time with God and find out more about who he is and who he wants you to be.

## ••••● 14 APPOINTMENTS WITH GOD

**APPOINTMENT**

# 1

*It's Guaranteed*

■ ASSURANCE

You recently became a Christian. Have you had any doubts about whether or not Jesus really came into your life? Do you wonder if you'll really go to heaven someday?

***Talk to God:*** "Father, thank you for giving me a relationship with you. Jesus, thank you for giving me life. Please teach me and help me learn more about you. Amen."

***Investigate God's Word:*** Read 1 John 5:11-13. Memorize verse 13.

***Make it practical:*** Check out "I Wonder"—1 John 5:10-12, page 1246, or "Here's What I Did"—Matthew 7:24-27, page 917. How can you put the ideas presented here into action in your own life?

***Express your thoughts:*** In your journal, write a description of when, where, and how you became a Christian. Say thanks to God!

**APPOINTMENT**

# 2

*Part of the Family*

■ GOD, OUR FATHER

Everyone knows what it's like to not feel totally accepted by others. Did you know that when you became a Christian, God adopted you into his family and accepted you unconditionally?

***Talk to God:*** "Dear God, thanks for making me part of your family. You accept me. That's awesome! Amen."

***Investigate God's Word:*** Ephesians 1:3-8. Memorize verse 5.

***Make it practical:*** "I Wonder"—Hebrews 1:1-3, page 1207, or "Here's What I Did"—Mark 9–10, page 955.

***Express your thoughts:*** In your journal, make a list of what you like about being part of God's family. Don't forget to thank him.

**APPOINTMENT**

# 3

*New Life in Christ*

■ GROWTH

OK, now that you're a new Christian, what's next? Well, the best relationships are those that grow and deepen. It's the same way in your relationship with Jesus Christ. It's time for growth.

***Talk to God:*** "Lord, help me to let my roots sink down into you. Thanks for helping me grow. Amen."

***Investigate God's Word:*** Colossians 2:6-7. Memorize the first part of verse 7.

***Make it practical:*** "I Wonder"—Colossians 2:6-7, page 1165, or "Here's What I Did"—2 Peter 1:5-8, page 1239.

***Express your thoughts:*** Think of one way that you'd like to grow spiritually, share it with one friend, and write it in your journal. Then ask God to help you do what you've decided to do.

**APPOINTMENT**

# 4

*Time to Talk*

■ PRAYER

You know how good friends love to talk with each other. God, our heavenly Father, is ready for a heart-to-heart talk all the time. Conversation with God is a must!

**Talk to God:** "God, I'm so glad we can talk anytime. Thank you that you'll listen to my needs. Help me learn to listen to you. Amen."

**Investigate God's Word:** Philippians 4:6-7. Memorize verse 6.

**Make it practical:** "I Wonder"—1 Kings 3:3-14, page 335, or "Here's What I Did"—Ecclesiastes 5:1-7, page 637.

**Express your thoughts:** Commit yourself to spending at least three minutes in prayer every day. In your journal, keep a record of your prayer requests and answers. Tell God thanks for those answers.

**APPOINTMENT**

# 5

*Dig In*

■ BIBLE

When you get something new, you often receive an instruction manual. With your new life in Christ, you need God's instruction manual, the Bible. God communicates to us through his Word.

**Talk to God:** "Dear God, thank you for showing me what you're like through your Word. Help me to read it, study it, and obey it. Amen."

**Investigate God's Word:** 2 Timothy 3:14-17. Memorize verse 16.

**Make it practical:** "I Wonder"—John 20:31, page 1035, or "Here's What I Did"—Isaiah 41:10, page 681.

**Express your thoughts:** Commit yourself to spending five minutes a day reading the Bible. As a result of something you read, write down in your journal something you will do. Ask God to help you.

**APPOINTMENT**

# 6

*Jesus Did It All*

■ JESUS, OUR SAVIOR

Friendships get stronger when you really get to know the other person. You have trusted Christ to be your Savior and to give you new life. Really get to know who he is and what he has done! It's incredible!

**Talk to God:** "Jesus, you are so powerful! I'm thankful that you hold everything together, including me! Amen."

**Investigate God's Word:** Colossians 1:15-23. Memorize verse 17.

**Make it practical:** "I Wonder"—Judges 17:6, page 241.

**Express your thoughts:** Ask a friend to tell you what he or she really likes about Jesus. In your journal, write a note to Jesus about what you really appreciate about him.

**APPOINTMENT**

# 7

*Solid Rock*

■ OBEDIENCE

A good foundation is essential for a house to stand strong. Jesus wants you to realize that obeying God will give your life a solid foundation.

**Talk to God:** "Dear God, you know what's best for me. Help me to be strong and obey you in each area of my life. Amen."

**Investigate God's Word:** Luke 6:46-49. Memorize the first part of verse 47.

**Make it practical:** "I Wonder"—Joshua 24:14-15, page 227, or "Here's What I Did"—Ephesians 6:1-3, page 1151.

**Express your thoughts:** In your journal, list one area of your life where you are obeying God and one where you are not. Say thanks to God for helping you to want to obey.

## APPOINTMENT 8

*You Have Insight*

■ HOLY SPIRIT

Nobody in this world knows you better than you know yourself. Nobody knows God like God's Spirit knows God. As a new Christian, you have been given God's Holy Spirit. He will give you insight into what God is like and what he wants you to do.

***Talk to God:*** "Thank you, God, for giving me your Spirit. You know me so well, and I will trust your Spirit to help me know more about you. Amen."

***Investigate God's Word:*** 1 Corinthians 2:9-16. Memorize verse 12.

***Make it practical:*** "I Wonder"—Romans 7:15–8:2, page 1087, or "Here's What I Did"—Isaiah 7:9, page 659.

***Express your thoughts:*** In your journal, write down one question that you'd like the Holy Spirit to help you with. Now take a couple of minutes and just listen to God. Tell him thanks.

## APPOINTMENT 9

*Don't Give In*

■ TEMPTATION

The Bible says in 1 Peter 5:8 that our enemy Satan is like a lion that wants to rip us apart. Satan will tempt us to disobey God, but God will show us a way out!

***Talk to God:*** "Dear God, you know the temptations I struggle with. Thank you that you have promised me a way to escape. Amen."

***Investigate God's Word:*** 1 Corinthians 10:13. Memorize verse 13.

***Make it practical:*** "I Wonder"—Matthew 18:7-9, page 927, or "Here's What I Did"—1 Peter 3:15, page 1233.

***Express your thoughts:*** List the three temptations that Satan really uses on you. Now thank God ahead of time that he will show you how to not give in next time.

## APPOINTMENT 10

*I'm Sorry*

■ FORGIVENESS

As a child in God's family, you'll still mess up. But God's love for you is so great that he will forgive you! He can do that because he loves you!

***Talk to God:*** "Dear God, I confess to you my sin of _____. I admit that it was wrong. Thank you that Jesus died on the cross to forgive me for this sin. Amen."

***Investigate God's Word:*** 1 John 1:8-10. Memorize verse 9.

***Make it practical:*** "I Wonder"—James 4:17, page 1225, or "Here's What I Did"—Lamentations 3:22-23, page 751.

***Express your thoughts:*** Write down ways that you have disobeyed God recently. Look at each one and confess it through prayer. Cross out each sin. Let this remind you of God's loving forgiveness. Be sure to thank him!

## APPOINTMENT 11

*Worship Him*

■ CHURCH

Christians are part of the body of Christ, which is called his church. Be sure you get together with other believers, members of the "body." It's an opportunity to love God and each other.

***Talk to God:*** "Dear God, thank you for your body of believers, the church. Teach me how to get involved with other Christians and really worship you. Amen."

***Investigate God's Word:*** Hebrews 10:22-25. Memorize verse 25.

***Make it practical:*** "I Wonder"—Hebrews 10:24-25, page 1213, or "Here's What I Did"—James 1, page 1223.

***Express your thoughts:*** Go with some friends or family to church this week. List two ways you worshiped God.

**APPOINTMENT**

# 12

*I Gotta Tell You Something*

■ WITNESSING

If you have a close friend, you can't keep from talking about that person. When you love someone, you can hardly contain yourself! Let your love for Christ motivate you to tell others about him.

***Talk to God:*** "Lord, you have changed my life. Give me the courage and opportunities to tell others about you. Amen."

***Investigate God's Word:*** Romans 1:16-17. Memorize verse 16.

***Make it practical:*** "I Wonder"—Luke 22:54-62, page 1003, or "Here's What I Did"—Acts 4:13, page 1045.

***Express your thoughts:*** Write down the name of one person who needs to know Jesus Christ. Start praying for that person to become a Christian. Ask a Christian friend to pray with you for the person and to help you learn how to share your faith with him or her.

**APPOINTMENT**

# 13

*Do You Remember*

■ BIBLE MEMORY

To fight a battle you need powerful equipment. The Holy Spirit will use the power of God's Word like a sword to defeat Satan. So a great strategy is to memorize Scripture! What verses have you already learned?

***Talk to God:*** "Lord, I need your power! Help me to memorize Scripture verses. I know this will help me live for you. Amen."

***Investigate God's Word:*** Ephesians 6:10-17. Memorize verse 17.

***Make it practical:*** "I Wonder"—Philippians 4:8, page 1159, or "Here's What I Did"—Isaiah 46:4, page 685.

***Express your thoughts:*** Review your memory verses from the past 12 days. In your journal, write down your favorite verse.

**APPOINTMENT**

# 14

*Be like Christ*

■ SPIRITUAL GOAL

You've been a Christian for a short time now, and you're learning that you have a lifelong relationship with Christ. So what's your long-range plan? Becoming like Christ is the ultimate goal.

***Talk to God:*** "Dear Jesus, more than anything else I want to become more like you. Thanks that you'll be patient and help me. Amen."

***Investigate God's Word:*** Colossians 3:10-11. Memorize verse 10.

***Make it practical:*** "I Wonder"—Jeremiah 29:11-13, page 725, or "Here's What I Did"—Micah 4:6-13, page 859.

***Express your thoughts:*** Make a list of at least five ways you want to become more like Jesus. Spend time asking God to help you. Remind yourself to read this part of your journal in one month to check on your spiritual growth.

## LIFE-CHANGER INDEX

(Look up notes by referring to Scripture location or page number.)

## INDEX TO THE MORAL DILEMMAS

(Look up notes by referring to Scripture location or page number.)

## INDEX TO "I WONDER"

(Look up notes by referring to Scripture location or page number.)

# INDEX TO THE ULTIMATE ISSUES

(Look up notes by referring to Scripture location or page number.)

## INDEX TO THE CHARTS

(Look up charts by referring to Scripture location or page number.)

## INDEX TO THE PERSONALITY PROFILES

(Look up profiles by referring to Scripture location or page number.)

## INDEX TO THE MAPS

(Look up maps by referring to Scripture location or page number.)

## INDEX TO "HERE'S WHAT I DID"

(Look up notes by referring to Scripture location or page number.)

# •••●● "WHERE TO FIND IT" INDEX

Apostles names · Matthew 10: